2001

ALMANAC *Plus*

107TH CONGRESS
1ST SESSION

VOLUME LVII

Congressional Quarterly Inc.
1414 22nd Street N.W.
Washington, D.C. 20037

President & Publisher   Robert W. Merry
Executive Editor, Sr. V.P.   David Rapp

CQ WEEKLY
Managing Editor   Susan Benkelman

Assistant Managing Editors
Jan Austin, David Hawkings, Scott Montgomery

News Editors
Donna Cassata, Mike Christensen, John Cochran

Associate Editors
Brian Nutting, Amy Stern, Andrew Taylor

Copy Desk Chief   Pat Joy

Senior Writers
Mary Agnes Carey, David Nather, Pat Towell

Senior Correspondent
Alan K. Ota

Reporters
Rebecca Adams, Jill Barshay, James C. Benton,
Adriel Bettelheim, Karen Foerstel, Julie Hirschfeld Davis,
Gebe Martinez, Chuck McCutcheon, Anjetta McQueen,
Elizabeth A. Palmer, Daniel J. Parks, Keith Perine,
Miles A. Pomper, Bob Williams

Contributing Reporters
Wendy Boudreau, Peter W. Cohn, Chuck Conlon,
Mary Dalrymple, Jennifer A. Dlouhy, Loren Duggan, Su-
san Ferrechio, John Godfrey, Samuel Goldreich,
Noella Kertes, Ted Monoson, Joe Nyitray,
Adam Pallotto, Steven Patrick, Emily Pierce, B. J. Rudell,
Joseph J. Schatz, Niels C. Sorrells, Bill Swindell,
Nathaniel Teti, Robert Tomkin,
Matthew Tully, Derek Willis

CQ
2001
ALMANAC
Plus

Editor
Jan Austin

Production Editor
Melinda W. Nahmias

Copy Editors
Arwen Bicknell, Melinda W. Nahmias,
Charles Southwell, Lisa Weintraub,
Yolie Dawson (design editor/production)

Contributing Editor   Jonathan Broder

Systems Editor   Ron Brodmann

Staff Photographer   Scott J. Ferrell

Graphic Artist   Marilyn Gates-Davis

News Research
Nell Benton (supervisor)
Alecia Marzullo, Jay Millikan, Ragan Naresh,
Amol Sharma, Michael Slevin (indexer)

Editorial Assistant   Alexandra C. Moller

HOUSE ACTION REPORTS
Managing Editor   Kerry Jones

CQ DAILY MONITOR
Editor of Daily News   Mike Mills
Managing Editor   Randy Wynn

CQ.COM ON CONGRESS
Managing Editor   Jackie Frank

NEW MEDIA
Director   Susan Dillingham Shipp

POLITICS
Politics Editor   Bob Benenson

BUSINESS OFFICES
General Manager, Sr. V.P.   Keith A. White

Circulation Marketing Director   Bob Shew

Circulation Sales Director   Jim Gale

Ad Sales, V.P.   Joan Daly

Chief Financial Officer   Diane Atwell

Product Development, V.P.   Michael K. Connelly

Customer Support Services Director   Brack Boehler

CQ Press
General Manager, Sr. V.P.   John A. Jenkins

Published by
CONGRESSIONAL QUARTERLY INC.
Chairman   Andrew Barnes
Vice Chairman   Andrew P. Corty
Founder   Nelson Poynter
(1903-1978)

Congressional Quarterly Inc.

Congressional Quarterly Inc. is a publishing and information services company and the recognized national leader in political journalism. For more than half a century, CQ has served clients in the fields of business, government, news and education with complete, timely and nonpartisan information on Congress, politics and national issues.

The flagship publication is the CQ Weekly, a news magazine on Congress and its legislative activities. The award-winning reporters and editors of CQ Weekly are top experts in their subject specialties. They track legislation as it is created in subcommittee, committee, floor, House-Senate conferences and leadership offices, providing detail and analysis unavailable anywhere else.

The CQ Daily Monitor is a morning news report on Congress and the scheduled hearings and markups of congressional committees. It provides a comprehensive breaking news report of everything that just happened or is about to happen on Capitol Hill.

CQ now offers the most comprehensive, detailed and up-to-the-minute legislative tracking information on the World Wide Web. CQ.com On Congress is an Internet service with immediate access to exclusive CQ coverage of bill action, votes, schedules and member profiles, with direct links to relevant texts of bills, committee reports, testimony and verbatim transcripts.

CQ serves the academic and education markets with a special weekly publication — The CQ Researcher — which focuses each week on a single topic of current interest.

Also CQ Press publishes a variety of books, including political science textbooks, to keep journalists, scholars and the public abreast of developing issues and events. This includes a line of print and Web-based directories, such as the Congressional Staff Directory, plus reference books on the federal government, national elections and politics.

The Congressional Quarterly Almanac®, published annually, provides a legislative history for each session of Congress. Congress and the Nation, published every four years, provides a record of government for a presidential term.

Copyright 2002, Congressional Quarterly Inc. (CQ)

Library of Congress Catalog Number 47-41081
ISBN: 1-56802-637-4   ISSN: 0095-6007

**CONGRESSIONAL QUARTERLY OFFERS A COMPLETE LINE
OF PUBLICATIONS AND RESEARCH SERVICES.**

The CQ Almanac 'Plus'

Congressional Quarterly has added a "Plus" to the name of its oldest publication to highlight something very important about the 2001 volume: This is a compilation of CQ "legislative histories" that chronicle and explain a tumultuous year in Congress from a unique vantage point.

It has been called a session of Congress without historical precedent, one that unfolded in three parts. For five months, Republicans controlled both chambers of Congress, as well as the White House, while President Bush tested out his tentative mandate in the early months of his presidency. In June, the defection of a single Republican senator, Vermont's James M. Jeffords, abruptly turned the Senate over to Democratic control, creating a new dynamic in Congress. The final phase began Sept. 11, when the terrorist attacks in New York and at the Pentagon transformed the nation's agenda and put issues of foreign policy and anti-terrorism on the front burner.

The CQ Almanac "Plus" looks closely at each of these chapters of the first session of the 107th Congress. Edited by Jan Austin, a 15-year veteran of the CQ newsroom, the book contains complete retellings of more than 75 bills. Each legislative story describes what was in the bill, how it was shaped as it moved through Congress, what mattered and why. It is based on reporting and analysis conducted throughout the year by the staff of the CQ Weekly, the CQ Daily Monitor, CQ.com On Congress, and CQ House Action Reports. Each of those publications covers bills as they move through Congress. The Almanac adds to that running portrait with a postmortem perspective of an entire year.

The bills covered in this edition — selected by Congressional Quarterly's editors as the most significant of the year — include the reauthorization of the Elementary and Secondary Education Act, the main federal law affecting education; the overhaul of the 1996 "Freedom to Farm" law; and the renewal of the president's "fast track" authority to negotiate trade agreements.

This edition also covers the extraordinary legislation enacted after Sept. 11: an anti-terrorism measure that gave sweeping new powers to law enforcement; an airline security bill that federalized airport security operations and baggage screening; a $15 billion aid bill for the airline industry; and a $40 billion emergency spending bill to help respond to the terrorist attacks.

And, of course, it details each of the 13 regular appropriations bills, which funded all federal government programs and operations in fiscal 2002.

In the back of the book, we have included a number of useful appendixes, including:

- Congress and Its Members: An 11-page glossary of terms that arise in discussing Congress and legislation and a list of members of the House and Senate in the first session of the 107th Congress.
- **Vote studies.** CQ's popular study of the roll call votes cast in Congress during the year. Separate studies analyze the level of presidential support, party unity and member participation during the year, providing aggregate scores for each chamber along with individual ratings for every member.
- **Key votes.** An account of the votes chosen by the CQ editors as most critical in determining the outcome of congressional action on major issues during the year.
- **Texts.** Presidential statements, Democratic responses and other key documents from the year.
- **Public laws.** A detailed list of all the bills enacted into law during the year.
- **Roll call votes.** A complete set of roll call vote charts for both chambers, describing every vote and every member's position on each vote.

CQ produces the Almanac for public policy specialists, scholars, journalists and all interested citizens and students of the U.S. legislative system.

This volume is the 57th in a series that began in 1946. We believe it remains true to the mandate laid out more than 50 years ago by CQ founders Henrietta and Nelson Poynter: "Congressional Quarterly presents the facts in as complete, concise and unbiased form as we know how. The editorial comment on the acts and votes of Congress, we leave to our subscribers."

David Rapp
Executive Editor

CQ *"By providing a link between the local newspaper and Capitol Hill we hope Congressional Quarterly can help to make public opinion the only effective pressure group in the country. Since many citizens other than editors are also interested in Congress, we hope that they too will find Congressional Quarterly an aid to a better understanding of their government."*

Foreword, Congressional Quarterly, Vol. I, 1945
Henrietta Poynter, 1901-1968
Nelson Poynter, 1903-1978

SUMMARY TABLE OF CONTENTS

Table of Contents

Chapter 1 – Inside Congress

Chapter 2 – Appropriations

Chapter 3 – Agriculture

Chapter 4 – Banking & Finance

Chapter 5 – Budget

Chapter 6 – Congressional Affairs

Chapter 7 – Defense

Chapter 8 – Education

Chapter 9 – Energy & Environment

Chapter 10 – Executive Branch

Chapter 11 – Foreign Policy

Chapter 12 – Health

Chapter 13 – Industry & Labor

Chapter 14 – Law & Judiciary

Chapter 15 – Politics & Elections

Chapter 16 – Science & Technology

Chapter 17 — Social Policy

Chapter 18 — Taxes

Chapter 19 — Trade

Chapter 20 — Transportation

Appendixes

Congress and Its Members

Vote Studies

Key Votes

Texts

Public Laws

Roll Call Votes

General Index

Chapter 1

INSIDE CONGRESS

A Tumultuous Year in Congress

The 107th Congress opened Jan. 3 with an evenly divided Senate, a House that Republicans controlled by just six votes, and a president put in office by the Supreme Court after an election that was too close to call.

By the time the session ended Dec. 20, nearly a year later, the Senate had shifted to a Democratic majority, and Congress' agenda had been turned upside down by the Sept. 11 terrorist attacks that stunned the nation and left more than 3,000 people dead in New York and Washington.

A massive tax cut and a rewrite of the nation's education programs shared top billing with a broad anti-terrorism law and a federalization of airport security that was on nobody's agenda at the beginning of the year. South Dakota Democrat Tom Daschle had gone from Senate minority leader to majority leader, potential presidential candidate and Republicans' No. 1 political target.

"This is a session of Congress without historical precedent," said congressional scholar Thomas Mann of the Brookings Institution. "Agendas changed as radically as I have seen them change."

It was a year that played out in three parts.

The first was a period of one-party government, with Republicans narrowly controlling Congress and President Bush making the most of his tentative mandate in the early months of his presidency. Under Speaker J. Dennis Hastert, R-Ill., the GOP conservatives running the House were able to set the agenda and pace with few concessions to Democrats. In the 50-50 Senate, however, Republicans had to win over at least some Democrats to get anything done, giving Democrats some input on Bush initiatives.

In June, the defection of moderate Republican James M. Jeffords of Vermont abruptly turned the Senate over to the Democrats, ending the short-lived period, the first since 1954, of unilateral GOP control of Congress and the White House. The switch allowed Senate Democrats to challenge the GOP agenda and press forward on some of their own issues.

The final phase began Sept. 11. After a frantic day of uncertainty and near paralysis, lawmakers regrouped to rewrite their agenda and search for ways to retain their party identities while acting with the unity the nation needed. Domestic issues slid to the back burner, replaced by newly urgent debates over foreign policy and anti-terrorism. The war in Afghanistan and the need to bolster domestic security and safeguard the nation's airports took precedence. Both parties united behind a newly powerful commander in chief, quickly authorized the use of force against those responsible for the attacks, appropriated $40 billion in

Lawmakers sing "God Bless America" in the Capitol Rotunda the day after terrorist attacks.

emergency spending for disaster recovery and the war against terrorism, and provided $15 billion to aid an airline industry reeling from its losses.

Those bills were followed by an extraordinary expansion of police powers to prevent more terrorist attacks, and an aviation security bill that federalized most baggage and passenger screening at airports.

With recovery and war dominating the agenda, most of the debates that typically stalled the appropriations process at year's end melted away and each of the 13 bills cleared separately. The last three cleared Dec. 20, the final day of the session.

While the rewrite of the nation's education law cleared Dec. 18, most of the bills on domestic issues that dominated the pre-Sept. 11 agenda remained unfinished when the session ended. They included a patients' bill of rights, a rewrite of the nation's farm policy, aid to faith-based organizations, an energy bill, a bankruptcy bill and an overhaul of the nation's election laws that became a top priority after the ugly partisan rancor of the 2000 presidential elections.

Part One: One-Party Rule

The session began with Republicans in control of both Congress and the White House for the first time since President Dwight D. Eisenhower. Though their majority was slim, they managed to push through a massive tax cut (PL 107-16), the deepest in 20 years, and take significant steps on Bush's second top priority, a rewrite of the 1965 Elementary and Secondary Education Act.

Getting Organized

In the Senate, the even split of 50 Republicans and 50 Democrats left the tie-breaking vote of Vice President Dick Cheney as the GOP's only edge. Recognizing the potential for deadlock, Daschle and Republican Leader Trent Lott of Mississippi quickly negotiated a power-sharing arrangement, unprecedented in Senate history, which gave the two parties equal representation on committees. If a committee was tied on a bill or nomination, the full Senate could vote to bring the matter to the floor, where Cheney could cast the deciding vote if necessary. The deal was announced Jan. 5 and given voice vote approval by the Senate the same day. One unresolved issue was how to structure the Senate delegation to a House-Senate conference committee. As a result, no bills went through conference before Democrats took control in June. (The budget resolution moved under its own rules.)

Conservative Republicans were furious at the amount of power Lott gave the Democrats, as well as the secretive nature of the negotiations. Lott acknowledged that the concessions "may haunt me," but he argued that they were a practical necessity if the Senate was to avoid a prolonged fight over procedure. "We have work to do, and we need to begin it now, not in a week or two or three or four," he said.

While negotiating the deal, Lott and Daschle were in the middle of a temporary switch in titles that underscored how close the balance of power truly was. Between Jan. 3 and Jan. 20, President Bill Clinton was still in office, so the tie-breaking vote in the Senate belonged to Democratic Vice President Al Gore, the man who had lost the presidency to Bush. For 17 days, Daschle became majority leader while Lott served as minority leader. When Bush and Cheney were sworn in Jan. 20, Lott regained the title of majority leader, which he had held since the 104th Congress, while Daschle went back to his job leading the minority.

Across the Capitol, the party breakdown in the House was close — with 221 Republicans, 211 Democrats and two independents — but the leadership was in control, and lawmakers had the luxury of arguing over more routine changes to committee names and jurisdiction.

A package of new rules, adopted 215-206 on Jan. 3, included a committee realignment that shifted jurisdiction over securities and insurance from the Commerce Committee to a new Financial Services Committee. The Commerce Committee became Energy and Commerce; Financial Services replaced the Banking and Financial Services Committee. (*House vote 4, p. H-4*)

The new rules expanded the Select Committee on Intelligence from 16 to 18 members, giving each party one additional seat. The rules also required that appropriations bills with unauthorized spending include details on when the program was last authorized and for how much.

The jurisdictional change enabled Hastert to defuse a battle between Republicans Billy Tauzin of Louisiana and Michael G. Oxley of Ohio, who were competing for chairmanship of the Commerce panel. Tauzin took over Commerce, while Oxley was given the newly reconstituted Financial Services Committee.

Commerce Committee members complained angrily but continued to support Hastert, who was re-elected as Speaker, 222-207, before the rules vote Jan. 3. (*House vote 2, p. H-4*)

Tauzin and Oxley were among 13 new House committee chairmen, a changing of the guard that resulted largely from term limits Republicans had imposed on their committee chairmen when they gained the House majority in 1995. Members of the GOP Steering Committee nominated the new chairmen after a six-hour meeting Jan. 4, and the entire Republican conference confirmed them several hours later.

The new chairmen, all Republicans, were:
- Armed Services: Bob Stump, Ariz.
- Budget: Jim Nussle, Iowa.
- Education and the Workforce: John A. Boehner, Ohio.
- Energy and Commerce: Tauzin.
- Financial Services: Oxley.
- International Relations: Henry J. Hyde, Ill.
- Judiciary: F. James Sensenbrenner Jr., Wis.
- Resources: James V. Hansen, Utah.
- Science: Sherwood Boehlert, N.Y.
- Small Business: Donald Manzullo, Ill.
- Transportation and Infrastructure: Don Young, Alaska.
- Veterans' Affairs: Christopher H. Smith, N.J.
- Ways and Means: Bill Thomas, Calif.

One casualty of the selection process was the goodwill of moderate Republicans, who had hoped for a more prominent voice to reflect the decisive role the thin party margin was expected to give them in the 107th. Tom Petri, R-Wis., a moderate who lost to Boehner in his bid for the Education and the Workforce chairmanship, sent out a press release calling the selection process a "purge of moderate Republicans." Many moderates also were angry at the rejection of Marge Roukema, R-N.J., who had made a bid for the Banking chairmanship. Had she won, she would have been the first woman ever to head a major committee. Bush offered to name her U.S. Treasurer, but she declined.

Democrats were furious that the new rules package, unlike the agreement in the Senate, did not reflect their gain of two seats in the 2000 elections. Minority Leader Richard A. Gephardt, D-Mo., attacked the Republican rules package on opening day as an effort to "undermine the rights of Democratic members."

Bush's Agenda

It was conventional wisdom in Washington that, given his narrow electoral victory, Bush lacked a mandate for sweeping changes and would have to limit his agenda to proposals that had bipartisan support. From the start, however, Bush made it clear he would ask as much from Congress as he would if he had won a landslide victory.

His top priorities were enactment of the tax cut package he had championed during his campaign and his plan to overhaul education, including annual testing, rewards for the best states and schools and penalties for the worst, and a limited voucher plan to allow poor students to transfer out of underperforming schools.

He asked Congress to approve a "faith-based initiative" to make it easier for religious charities to qualify for federal funds for social services such as after-school programs, rehabilitation for prisoners and counseling for children of prisoners. That proposal was controversial from the start because of its "charitable choice" provisions, which would allow faith-based groups to receive federal funds even if they refused to hire staffers who did not share their religious beliefs.

Bush highlighted his plans in an unofficial State of the Union address to a joint session of Congress on Feb. 27, followed by an outline of his $1.96 trillion budget for fiscal 2002, submitted to Congress the next day. (Bush provided a full-blown budget April 9, though his proposal was not actually complete until June, when he requested an additional $18.4 billion for defense.) (*Text, p. D-14*)

At the time, the White House Office of Management and Budget (OMB) estimated the federal government would run a $5.6 trillion budget surplus over the next 10 years, $2.6 trillion of it in the Social Security trust fund. Bush wanted $1.62 trillion in tax cuts over 10 years, while holding fiscal 2002 discretionary spending to a 4 percent increase over the previous year. He indicated he would seek more for defense once the administration completed a strategic review of the Pentagon. The budget assumed this could be done while also reducing the national debt and

Session Highlights

CONGRESS DID:

- Lower income tax rates, erase the "marriage penalty," phase out the estate tax, increase the child tax credit, expand tax benefits of education and retirement savings.
- Revise the Elementary and Secondary Education Act, with testing requirements to ensure results.
- Authorize the use of force against those responsible for the Sept. 11 terrorist attacks on the United States.
- Give the federal government broad new law enforcement powers to fight terrorism.
- Agree to federalize most airport security.
- Appropriate $40 billion to respond to and recover from the terrorist attacks.
- Provide $15 billion to help airlines after Sept. 11.
- Repeal workplace requirements on ergonomics.
- Authorize payment of U.S. debts to the U.N.
- Facilitate the cleanup of brownfields.
- Renew the moratorium on Internet-specific taxes.
- Open U.S. highways to Mexican trucks.

CONGRESS DID NOT:

- Agree on a year-end plan to stimulate the economy.
- Finish a bill overhauling bankruptcy law.
- Complete a reauthorization of farm subsidies, nutrition and rural development programs.
- Finish an overhaul of campaign finance rules.
- Expand patients' rights in managed-care plans.
- Provide prescription drug coverage under Medicare.
- Renew fast-track procedures for trade bills.
- Open Alaska's Arctic National Wildlife Refuge to drilling.
- Set federal standards for voting procedures.
- Widen faith-based groups' role in providing federally funded social services.
- Overhaul export control law.
- Deregulate broadband Internet service.
- Authorize bio-terrorism programs.
- Backstop the insurance industry in cases of terrorism.

saving for future initiatives. "Some say my tax plan is too big. Others say it's too small. I respectfully disagree. This plan is just right," Bush said in his Feb. 27 speech.

Democrats, argued that a 4 percent increase was not enough to fund vital domestic priorities such as the education overhaul Bush was seeking, and that the tax-cut target was so high it would shortchange efforts to reduce the deficit. That argument resonated with Republican moderates more than their leaders initially realized.

Tenuous GOP Hold in the Senate

While the House plunged immediately into Bush's tax proposals, the Senate had an unexpected added starter that demonstrated the power a single maverick member could wield in such an evenly divided body.

John McCain, R-Ariz., Bush's rival for the 2000 GOP presidential nomination, fulfilled his oft-repeated promise Jan. 22 and wedged campaign finance overhaul legislation (S 27) onto the congressional agenda by threatening to force a vote in the Senate. Neither Bush nor Republican leaders wanted Congress to pass the bill at all, let alone as one of the first actions of the 107th Congress. "I also have a mandate," McCain declared when he introduced his bill together with Russell D. Feingold, D-Wis.

After a debate that stretched over 10 days, the Senate passed the campaign finance bill April 2. Bush signaled he was unlikely to pick a fight with McCain over it. "I look forward to signing a good piece of legislation," he said March 29. Ari Fleischer, his spokesman, was more direct: "The president has sent the signal that he wants to send, that he cannot be counted on to veto it because he wants to reform the system."

Democrats, meanwhile, delivered an early message to the administration that they would be a force in future debates — particularly on judicial nominees. The occasion was the

confirmation of former Sen. John Ashcroft (1995-2001), Bush's pick for attorney general. His selection galvanized opposition from Democrats and liberal groups who feared he would use the office to advance his personal agenda of rigid opposition to gun control and abortion rights. A coalition of more than 200 civil rights, women's rights, labor and environmental groups united to pressure the Senate to reject him. Republicans and conservative groups rallied around Ashcroft, determined not to let liberal opponents defeat him as they had defeated Robert H. Bork's Supreme Court nomination 14 years earlier. (*1987 Almanac, p. 271*)

Ultimately, Ashcroft and Bush prevailed. The Judiciary Committee approved the nomination 10-8, and the full Senate confirmed Ashcroft on Feb. 1 by a vote of 58-42, the closest vote of any successful Cabinet nominee in decades.

Democrats felt they had made their point: "We hope nominees for the courts . . . come from the center, not the far right," Daschle said. Republicans said the confirmation process had run roughshod over the nominee. "They trashed John Ashcroft," said Judiciary Committee Chairman Orrin G. Hatch, R-Utah.

Budget Battles

The first step in the GOP drive to enact Bush's tax proposals was the congressional budget resolution — Congress' annual blueprint for the year's tax and spending decisions — that would establish the size of the tax cut bill and give it special protection against Democratic challenges in the free-wheeling Senate. "It's going to require some discipline on Capitol Hill," Bush said. Republican leaders were eager to oblige: "There hasn't been any fiscal discipline in a great deal of the budget in a long time, and a little discipline wouldn't hurt a thing," said Senate Majority Whip Don Nickles, R-Okla.

In the House, Republicans had little trouble adopting a budget resolution March 28 that was based largely on Bush's plan. Just three conservative Democrats broke ranks to vote for it, and two Republicans bucked Bush to vote against it.

In the evenly divided Senate, however, Democrats were able to make some headway in limiting the tax cut and increasing spending. The Senate adopted a budget April 6 that limited the size of the tax cut to $1.28 trillion and set a discretionary spending target of $688 billion, a 7 percent increase over fiscal 2001. The pivotal vote came April 4, when Tom Harkin, D-Iowa, succeeded in reducing the tax cut by $448 billion, with the money split between education and debt relief. Harkin lost one Democrat — Miller — but picked up three Republicans — Jeffords, Lincoln Chafee of Rhode Island, and Arlen Specter of Pennsylvania. The amendment set aside $100 billion for federal aid to special education, a priority close to the hearts of both Harkin and Jeffords.

The vote effectively ended Bush's hope of getting his full tax cut through the Senate. The final budget (H Con Res 83), adopted May 10, allowed $1.35 trillion in tax cuts from 2001 through 2011 — less than Bush wanted though still a major victory. The increase in fiscal 2002 discretionary spending — $661.3 billion or 4.2 percent — was close to Bush's request. It was a disappointment to Harkin and Jeffords, who had fought hard not only for more education money, but for making special education an entitlement outside the regular appropriations process.

By that time, House leaders already had passed the major pieces of Bush's tax package — individual rate cuts, repeal of the estate tax, benefits for married couples and families — as separate bills. The Senate waited for the budget resolution, which gave the tax bill crucial protection from filibusters and points of order that took 60 votes to overcome. Unlike the House, which stuck with Bush's tax proposal, the Senate on May 23 passed a $1.35 trillion bipartisan tax bill drafted by the leaders of the Senate Finance Committee — Charles E. Grassley, R-Iowa, and Max Baucus, D-Mont.

The final $1.35 trillion tax bill (PL 107-16) was quickly negotiated by a small group comprised of White House officials; top tax writers Grassley, Baucus and Thomas; and Senate moderate, John B. Breaux, D-La. Breaux's role was a testament to the critical part centrist Democrats played in passing the bill in the Senate. The tax bill cleared May 26, ushering in the largest tax cut since President Ronald Reagan. Part of the urgency for both sides was the news that Jeffords was about to switch parties, turning the Senate over to the Democrats.

Part Two: Democratic Senate

In perhaps the ultimate demonstration of the influence one senator could wield in a 50-50 Senate, Jeffords' decision in May to leave the Republican Party shifted the entire balance of power in the Senate. Unknown to all except a few key staffers, Jeffords had made up his mind to leave the Republican Party and become an independent May 14, after a meeting with Daschle and Senate Democratic Whip Harry Reid, D-Nev. Jeffords later said he had been toying with the idea for several weeks.

On May 24, after a week of growing speculation in the press and frantic Republican efforts to dissuade him, Jeffords announced he would become an independent and caucus with the Democrats — putting them in charge of the Senate and throwing the GOP into the minority. "It is only natural to expect that people like myself, who have been honored with positions of leadership, will largely support the president's agenda," Jeffords said as he announced his decision in Burlington, Vt. "And yet, more and more, I find I cannot."

Jeffords said he foresaw many disagreements with Bush over issues such as tax and spending decisions, the direction of the judiciary, abortion, missile defense, energy and the environment. But the biggest, he said, was education — mainly because Bush was not willing to put more funding behind the education overhaul, particularly special education.

Jeffords had helped write the 1975 Individuals with Disabilities Education Act (PL 94-142), which authorized the federal government to pay an estimated 40 percent of the cost of educating children with physical and mental disabilities — a goal that had never been reached. When the White House and other Republicans tried in April to persuade Jeffords not to vote for Harkin's amendment trimming Bush's tax cut, Jeffords pressed in vain for more money for special education, and for a commitment to turn it into an entitlement, not subject to annual appropriations.

By the time Cheney and Bush met with Jeffords on May 22, he had made up his mind. There was little Bush could do but ask Jeffords to hold off until the tax bill was finished so Democrats would not suddenly control the conference committee on a piece of legislation that had traveled so far. Jeffords agreed. He did not officially switch his party identification until the close of business June 5, allowing Democrats to take control of the Senate at 11 a.m. on June 6.

With a 50-49-1 split, they did not control the chamber by much. "We know that we have a divided government — Republicans in the White House and now Democrats leading the Senate," Daschle said after Jeffords' announcement. "The only way we can accomplish our agenda, the only way that this administration will be able to accomplish their agenda, is if we truly work together."

As Republicans met to discuss their next steps, Olympia J. Snowe, R-Maine, one of the remaining Senate GOP moderates, urged them to give moderates a position in the leadership. "This should never have happened," Snowe said. "For the first time in history, we had all three branches of government, and we lost it. Hopefully, we're going to learn something from that." Specter, a moderate, was made an unelected member of the leadership team.

Lott, who became minority leader, made little effort to hide his anger. In a June 2 memorandum to "Republican opinion leaders," he said Jeffords' defection was a "coup of one" that "puts at peril the agenda that Republicans were given a mandate by the American people to deliver." Many of Lott's GOP colleagues thought the memo churlish, and most quickly dropped the confrontational rhetoric.

Reorganizing the Senate

It took the Senate until the end of June to adopt a new organizing resolution to replace the power-sharing agreement Lott and Daschle had worked out for the 50-50 Senate. Burned by the criticism of his handling of the earlier agreement, Lott left the task to a "gang of five" Republican negotiators: Hatch, Domenici, Specter, Phil Gramm of

First Session by the Numbers

The first session of the 107th Congress began, as the Constitution requires, at noon on Jan. 3, 2001. Under the terms of the annual adjournment resolution (H Con Res 295), the House adjourned *sine die* at 5:08 p.m. on Dec. 20; the Senate adjourned *sine die* at 10:06 p.m the same day.

The following are some statistical comparisons of the two chambers over the past decade:

		2001	2000	1999	1998	1997	1996	1995	1994	1993	1992
Days in Session	Senate	173	141	162	143	153	132	211	138	153	129
	House	142	135	137	119	132	122	168	123	142	123
Time in Session	Senate	1,236	1,018	1,184	1,095	1,093	1,037	1,839	1,244	1,270	1,091
(hours)	House	922	1,054	1,125	999	1,004	919	1,525	905	982	857
Avg. Length Daily	Senate	7.1	7.2	7.3	7.7	7.1	7.9	8.7	9.0	8.3	8.5
Session (hours)	House	6.5	7.8	8.2	8.4	7.6	7.5	9.1	7.4	6.9	7.0
Public Laws Enacted		136	410	170	241	153	245	88	255	210	347
Bills/Resolutions	Senate	2,203	1,546	2,352	1,321	1,839	860	1,801	999	2,178	1,544
Introduced	House	4,318	2,701	4,241	2,253	3,662	1,899	3,430	2,104	4,543	2,714
	TOTAL	6,521	4,247	6,593	3,574	5,501	2,759	5,231	3,103	6,721	4,258
Recorded Votes	Senate	380	298	374	314	298	306	613	329	395	270
	House[1]	512	603	611	547	640	455	885	507	615	488
	TOTAL	892	901	985	861	938	761	1,498	836	1,010	758
Vetoes		0	7[2]	5	5	3[3]	6	11	0	0	21[2]

SOURCE: Congressional Record   [1] includes quorum calls   [2] includes pocket vetoes   [3] does not include line-item vetoes

Texas, and Mitch McConnell of Kentucky.

The talks, which involved setting new committee ratios and allocating staff and office space, stalled for weeks over Republicans' demands that they be guaranteed floor debate on any Bush Supreme Court nominee, even if it had been rejected by the Judiciary Committee. When Republicans dropped that demand, the new organizing resolution was adopted easily by voice vote June 29.

The new committee chairmen — all Democrats except Jeffords — were:
- Agriculture, Nutrition and Forestry: Harkin.
- Appropriations: Robert C. Byrd, W.Va.
- Armed Services: Carl Levin, Mich.
- Banking, Housing and Urban Affairs: Paul S. Sarbanes, Md.
- Budget: Kent Conrad, N.D.
- Commerce, Science and Transportation: Ernest F. Hollings, S.C.
- Energy and Natural Resources: Jeff Bingaman, N.M.
- Environment and Public Works: Jeffords.
- Finance: Baucus.
- Foreign Relations: Joseph R. Biden Jr., Del.
- Governmental Affairs: Joseph I. Lieberman, Conn.
- Health, Education, Labor and Pensions: Edward M. Kennedy, Mass.
- Judiciary: Patrick J. Leahy, Vt.
- Rules: Christopher J. Dodd, Conn.

- Small Business: John Kerry, Mass.
- Veterans' Affairs: John D. Rockefeller IV, W.Va.
- Special Committee on Aging: Breaux.
- Select Committee on Ethics: Reid.
- Indian Affairs: Daniel K. Inouye, Hawaii.
- Select Intelligence: Bob Graham, Fla.

New Priorities

The Democrats' first priority in the Senate was one they shared with Bush: finishing the education overhaul bill, which already had consumed substantial floor time. In reality, the Democrats had put their stamp on the bill weeks earlier. With the help of GOP moderates, they had added amendments to authorize significant funding increases in a variety of areas — including $181 billion over 10 years to "fully fund" special education, just as Jeffords had wanted.

The bipartisan compromises — which produced an overwhelming vote for the bill in the Senate on June 14 — were part of a pattern that made the education bill an exception in both chambers to the parties' tendency to try to muscle bills through with a minimum of negotiations.

In the House, Boehner, the chairman of the Education and the Workforce Committee, and ranking Democrat George Miller of California, had steered a similar compromise to passage May 23. By clinging to the center and fighting off controversial amendments from both sides, including attempts to remove the annual testing that was at the heart

of Bush's proposal, Boehner and Miller won passage on an equally lopsided vote.

With the education bill ready for conference, Daschle turned to an issue that he and other Democrats had been pushing for years: an overhaul of managed care. The Senate bill (S 1052), sponsored by McCain, Kennedy, and John Edwards, D-N.C., offered many patient protections that both parties supported. But the centerpiece, giving patients the right to sue managed-care plans over decisions that resulted in injury or death, was broader and potentially more expensive to employers than Bush was prepared to support. Although he had called for a patients' rights bill during his campaign, Bush threatened to veto the McCain-Kennedy-Edwards bill if it reached his desk.

Daschle, in his first big test as majority leader, fought off repeated GOP attempts to change the liability provisions, threatening to keep the Senate in session through the July 4 break if necessary. Eventually, he simply wore the Republicans down. The bill passed June 29, with Daschle holding all 50 Democrats and picking up nine Republicans.

Thanks to the Senate's coalition of Democrats and maverick Republicans, Bush now faced the prospect of a patients' rights bill he did not like and a campaign finance overhaul bill he was lukewarm about, at best.

Tremors in the House

With Democrats in control of the Senate, House Republicans became even more central to advancing the Bush agenda. For a time in early July, however, it seemed that Hastert might be losing control of his moderate wing.

On July 12, the House GOP leadership suffered an embarrassing setback, when 19 Republicans joined 208 Democrats and one independent to defeat a rule for floor debate on the campaign finance bill. Supporters of the bill said the rule was stacked against them.

The bill (HR 2356) — by Christopher Shays, R-Conn., and Martin T. Meehan, D-Mass. — was the House companion to the McCain-Feingold bill that the Senate had passed in April. House leaders opposed it, but Hastert had promised sponsors a full debate and a vote. Shays and Meehan wanted to fine-tune the bill to bring it as close as possible to McCain-Feingold in the hope of avoiding a conference. But the Rules Committee refused to let Shays and Meehan bundle 14 changes to their bill into a single "manager's amendment." Instead, the rule required the House to vote on each of the 14 changes separately, a process the sponsors said could shatter their coalition.

Six days later, on July 18, House leaders had to pull a signature Bush proposal — his faith-based initiative — from the floor to quell another rebellion. At Bush's urging, Hastert had moved the bill (HR 7) quickly without taking much time to make sure Republican moderates were on board. At the last minute, the moderates raised concerns about language in the bill that would pre-empt state and local laws against hiring discrimination.

The uprising was short-lived. After 24 hours of negotiations, moderates accepted an offer from the bill's lead sponsor, House Republican Conference Chairman J.C. Watts Jr. of Oklahoma, to promise on the House floor to "more clearly address" their objections when a House-Senate conference committee negotiated the final bill. The bill passed

easily July 19, but the spat generated embarrassing headlines about "discrimination" in the bill. Daschle made it clear that the faith-based initiative had no future in the Senate without tougher safeguards against discrimination.

Reviving the Republican Agenda

By the end of the summer, both Bush and the House Republicans were regaining their footing, largely through a legislative victory on the managed-care overhaul that had caused Bush so many problems in the Senate.

With just days to go before the vote, Hastert had all but conceded that Bush's preferred bill, sponsored by Ernie Fletcher, R-Ky., and Collin C. Peterson, D-Minn., had no chance of passing. Instead, the House appeared certain to pass a bill (HR 2563) by Greg Ganske, R-Iowa, and John D. Dingell, D-Mich., that had broader right-to-sue language.

On Aug. 1, however, Bush persuaded Charlie Norwood, R-Ga., a longtime ally of Ganske and Dingell and a leading supporter of their bill to cut a deal. Norwood agreed to support an amendment to the Ganske-Dingell bill that would allow lawsuits against managed-care plans, but with much stricter limits on damages than in the Senate bill. On Aug. 2, the amendment was narrowly approved, and the bill passed. Ganske and Dingell were livid. Dingell said the changes would pre-empt stronger patient protection laws that already had been enacted by the states. Norwood, however, said he was being realistic. "We want to change the law," he said. "The last time I looked, that's pretty difficult to do without the presidential signature."

Also on Aug. 1, the House passed an omnibus energy bill (HR 4) that closely followed the recommendations of a task force headed by Cheney that proposed the first comprehensive national energy policy since 1992. Like the White House plan, the bill focused on increasing domestic production of oil and gas. Republicans were able to rebuff Democratic objections to a key Bush proposal to open a swath of coastal plain in Alaska's Arctic National Wildlife Refuge to drilling.

Looking to the Fall

Members began their monthlong recess Aug. 3, looking ahead to a showdown over spending in the fall. Just five of the 13 regular fiscal 2002 spending bills were ready for conference. The two biggest bills — for defense and for the departments of Labor, Health and Human Services and Education — had not started to move. Democrats calling for more social spending and defense hawks looking to increase Pentagon funding were poised for battle over limited resources.

Both parties had declared the portion of the surplus in the Social Security trust funds sacrosanct, off limits for anything but debt reduction. The notion of walling off Social Security funds, and to a lesser extent the Medicare surplus — putting them in a "lockbox" — had become a political test of fiscal responsibility that neither party could afford to flout.

In August, revised surplus projections from OMB and the Congressional Budget Office (CBO) made that test virtually impossible to pass. The tax cut and the flagging economy were expected to produce a dramatically smaller federal surplus than had been projected a few months earlier. The $304

billion surplus for fiscal 2002 that CBO had projected in May, for example, had shrunk to $176 billion. Only $2 billion of that was outside of Social Security. By that point, resistance to counting the Medicare surplus as part of the general budget had largely disappeared, but the new numbers meant it would be difficult not to tap the Social Security surplus as well.

Democrats blamed Bush's tax cut and called for the president to submit a new budget that showed a path to balancing the budget without Social Security revenue. Republicans blamed the economy and urged even more tax cuts. Fiscal conservatives promised to support Bush if he needed to follow through on his threat from early in the year to veto appropriations bills to maintain fiscal discipline.

On Sept. 6, Bush reiterated that only a war, recession or "severe emergency" would justify using Social Security funds for other purposes.

Part Three: The War Congress

Confusion and fear spread rapidly Sept. 11 as news of the attack on the World Trade Center, and then the Pentagon, spread. With uncertainty about the possibility of additional attacks, the Capitol police ordered the Capitol and surrounding legislative office buildings emptied. As next in the line of succession after the vice president, Hastert was whisked away to a military bunker in the Virginia wilderness, where congressional leaders from both chambers and both parties later joined him.

Rank-and-file lawmakers and their staffs flooded into streets filled with running crowds and snarled traffic, and lined with heavily armed police. Most went home as they were told to do. Many later complained that they received no further instructions about where to go or what to do.

By late afternoon, lawmakers were clamoring to get back into their offices, and some wanted to go back into session to show their defiance of the terrorists. About 100 House members gathered at Capitol Police headquarters for a conference call with Hastert and Gephardt. Although the nation's airspace had been shut down for the first time in history, at least two international flights scheduled to arrive in the United States were not yet accounted for. National security officials and Capitol Police could not guarantee that the Capitol was out of danger, and Hastert decided a full-blown session was too big a risk.

Instead, about 200 House and Senate members from both parties gathered on the Capitol's east steps that night for a brief, and heavily guarded, show of unity. With police checkpoints at every intersection in the surrounding streets, and the intermittent clatter of a helicopter flying overhead, Daschle promised that "Congress will convene tomorrow," and the lawmakers broke into applause. They sang "God Bless America," unaccompanied.

Once again, the agenda of the 107th Congress had been rewritten.

The War Agenda

Foreign policy and defense questions that had lingered on the back burner shot to the fore. Military strikes against Afghanistan, the home of Osama bin Laden and the al Qaeda terrorist network believed to be behind the attacks, were

imminent. The top priorities at home were providing legal tools to fight terrorism, overhauling the airport security that had failed so spectacularly and enacting new appropriations to pay for retaliation against the terrorists and the rebuilding in New York and at the Pentagon. Work on the patients' rights bill, energy legislation, the farm bill — even the education overhaul — slowed to a crawl.

There was also a change in the relationship between congressional leaders. In a show of unity, Hastert and Gephardt, who had maintained an icy distance for months, began speaking almost daily as a result of the hours they spent together in the military bunker in Virginia. Daschle and Lott started holding joint press conferences.

When Bush came to the Capitol on Sept. 20 to address a joint session of Congress, both his longtime supporters and his fiercest critics had nothing but praise for his declaration of a war on terrorism. Cheney stayed away that night, the first time a vice president had been absent from a joint session of Congress for security reasons.

"The advance of human freedom — the great achievement of our time, and the great hope of every time — now depends on us," Bush said. "We will not tire, we will not falter, and we will not fail." Democrats cheered him on. "Right now, the president has approval to do almost anything he wants," said Rep. Maxine Waters, D-Calif. "Everyone was sitting there hoping this guy hits a home run," Biden said. "We need a home run." (*Text, p. D-31*)

Daschle and Lott delivered a joint response. "We want President Bush to know, we want the world to know, that he can depend on us," Daschle said. "We will take up the president's initiatives with speed. We may encounter differences of opinion along the way, but there is no difference in our aim. We are resolved to work together."

With 535 voices, however, unqualified support from Congress could not last. For the moment, lawmakers' task was to "lock arms in support of the commander in chief," said Lieberman, the running mate of Bush's rival for the presidency in 2000. But in the long run, he said, "we're going to need to talk about funding and how it's carried out."

Moving Ahead, With Limits

That reality left lawmakers searching for the appropriate role to play. Within three days of the attacks, they began clearing a series of high-priority bills, many of which illustrated their efforts to support the president without abdicating congressional responsibility or party principles.

● **Emergency spending.** On Sept. 14, the Senate cleared a $40 billion emergency supplemental spending bill (PL 107-38) to begin the recovery and launch a war on terrorism. The GOP talked at first of sending Bush a "blank check," without limits or conditions, but Democrats and some Republicans balked. "There has to be consultation, and there has to be reporting," said Byrd, the Senate Appropriations Committee chairman. "We still have a Constitution."

A compromise reached with the White House provided $40 billion, divided into three installments: $10 billion available immediately for emergency rescue and rebuilding efforts, another $10 billion available after Bush told Congress how he planned to spend it, and $20 billion that had to be appropriated separately by Congress.

● **Use of force.** A second measure (PL 107-40) cleared

Sept. 11: A Chronology

The following is a summary of events on Sept. 11 and the immediate aftermath. At the end of the year, revised estimates showed 3,161 dead, including those on the planes: 2,927 at the World Trade Center, 189 at the Pentagon and 45 on the plane that crashed in Pennsylvania.

Sept. 11, 2001

- 8:46 a.m. — American Airlines Flight 11, hijacked after take-off in Boston, crashes into the North Tower of the World Trade Center in New York. The plane was carrying 81 passengers, two pilots and nine flight attendants.
- 9:03 a.m. — United Flight 175, also hijacked after a Boston take-off, crashes into the South Tower of the World Trade Center. Fifty-six passengers, two pilots and seven flight attendants were aboard.
- 9:25 a.m. — Federal Aviation Administration shuts down all U.S. airports.
- 9:45 a.m. — American Flight 77, hijacked from Washington's Dulles International Airport, crashes into the Pentagon. The plane carried 58 passengers, two pilots and four flight attendants.
- 10:05 a.m. — The South Tower of the World Trade Center collapses.
- 10:10 a.m. — One side of the Pentagon collapses.

- 10:10 a.m. — United Flight 93, hijacked after take-off from Newark, N.J., crashes in rural Pennsylvania after passengers confront hijackers. Thirty-eight passengers, two pilots and five flight attendants were aboard.
- 10:28 a.m. — The North Tower of the World Trade Center collapses.
- 8:30 p.m. — President Bush speaks to the nation from the Oval Office after returning to Washington from Florida, via bases in Louisiana and Nebraska.

The Immediate Aftermath

- Bush declares a national emergency and authorizes the military to call up to 50,000 reservists to active duty. He has called the attacks an "act of war." (Sept. 14)
- The New York Stock Exchange reopens. (Sept. 17)
- In an address to a joint session of Congress, Bush says Afghanistan's Taliban government must turn over terrorist leaders or share their fate. He also announces creation of a Homeland Security office. (Sept. 20)
- Bush announces that U.S. airstrikes have begun in Afghanistan. He vows: "We will not waver, we will not tire, we will not falter and we will not fail." (Oct. 7)
- U.S. ground troops are sent to Afghanistan after two weeks of bombing and airstrikes. (Oct. 19)

Sept. 14 authorized the use of force against the terrorists. The White House initially requested a sweeping resolution endorsing not only retaliation for the Sept. 11 attacks, but "all necessary and appropriate force" to "deter and pre-empt any future acts of terrorism or aggression against the United States." That went too far for many lawmakers, particularly Democrats, who compared it with the 1964 Gulf of Tonkin resolution (PL 88-408), cited as congressional authorization for waging the Vietnam War.

Instead, Congress authorized Bush to "use all necessary and appropriate force against those nations, organizations or persons he determines planned, authorized, committed or aided the terrorist attacks that occurred on Sept. 11, 2001, or harbored such organizations or persons."

- **Airline aid.** One week later, Congress cleared a $15 billion bill (PL 107-42) to help airlines recover from the two days when all airports were closed, as well as from the subsequent slump in air travel. Republicans blocked efforts by Democrats and organized labor to include assistance for workers displaced by the attacks.
- **U.N. dues.** With the White House putting maximum priority on building a global coalition to back its fight against terrorism, House GOP leaders dropped their objections to a bill releasing $582 million in back dues to the United Nations. The bill, which had been held up since February, cleared Sept. 24 (PL 107-46). In return, the administration agreed to support legislation, backed by con-

servatives, to prohibit U.S. participation in a proposed International Criminal Court.

- **Anti-terrorism.** One of the most sweeping responses to the attacks cleared with little public debate. Despite misgivings over the possible impact on civil liberties, both chambers overwhelmingly agreed to give Attorney General Ashcroft wide new authority to track, arrest and prosecute suspected terrorists. Lawmakers did insist on taking more time than the administration wanted. Ashcroft submitted his proposal Sept. 19 and asked Congress to clear it by the end of the week. Democrats and a few Republicans said they needed time to consider his request more carefully.

Lawmakers ended up rejecting one major proposal, which would have allowed the Justice Department to detain immigrants indefinitely without charging them with a crime if the attorney general viewed them as national security threats. Otherwise, the legislation that cleared Oct. 25 (PL 107-56) was basically the package Ashcroft had asked for, including provisions that allowed nationwide search warrants, "roving wiretaps" assigned to specific individual under surveillance, rather than to telephone lines, and secret searches that could be conducted before suspects were served with search warrants.

- **Aviation security.** One of the most divisive issues was how to strengthen security at the nation's airports, and whether to have the federal government take over responsibility for screening passengers and baggage. On this issue,

Bush left House Republican leaders twisting in the wind.

Bush came out against federalizing airport security, a step that helped House GOP leaders pass a bill giving the president the option to hire either government employees or private contract workers. House Majority Whip Tom DeLay, R-Texas, and Majority Leader Dick Armey, R-Texas, lashed out against a competing Senate-passed bill that called for a federalized airport security work force, saying it would not make flying safer and would only increase the rolls of labor unions that supported the Democratic Party.

But the Senate had passed the bill unanimously, and public opinion polls showed most Americans supported a federalized airport security work force. When White House Chief of Staff Andrew H. Card Jr. said Bush would reluctantly sign the Senate bill, DeLay and his allies were left without much leverage. The final bill (PL 107-71), cleared Nov. 16, required airports to federalize the baggage screening work force for two years; after that, they could seek permission from the Transportation Department to use contract workers.

Appropriations and Other Old Business

The crowded agenda in the first weeks following the attacks left little time to focus on bills that had dominated debate earlier in the session. Still, the government had to be funded — the new fiscal year began Oct. 1 with only one of the spending bills enacted.

Before Sept. 11, Congress' top priority for the fall was finishing the 13 regular fiscal 2002 appropriations bill, none of which had cleared. The main issue was money: No one had a credible plan to pay for all the programs Congress and the White House were insisting on without breaking into the "lockbox" and spending part of the Social Security surplus.

With Sept. 11, the lockbox vanished. Appropriators and the White House reached an agreement Oct. 2 to add $6 billion to the discretionary spending limit for the 13 regular bills, $4 billion of it for education. When emergency spending was added, CBO calculated total discretionary spending for fiscal 2002 at $712 billion in budget authority and $731 billion in outlays.

Disputes over policy riders that threatened some of the bills — efforts to challenge the administration over Cuba policy, abortion restrictions and the environment, for example — fell by the wayside. The biggest bills — for defense and for the departments of Labor, Health and Human Services and education — took until Dec. 20 to clear. But the delays were related to other disputes — finishing the education overhaul, and agreeing on how to spend the last $20 billion of the emergency spending package, which was attached to the defense bill. A third spending bill, for foreign operations, was held to the end in a familiar dispute over abortion and aid to international family planning groups.

Kept in town by drawn-out debates on emergency spending and a proposed economic stimulus bill, lawmakers found time to act on some other domestic priorities. The House passed its version of the farm bill, voted to give the president so-called fast-track authority to negotiate trade agreements, and passed an election overhaul bill. Congress also cleared Bush's top environmental priority, a bill (PL 107-118) to clean up polluted and abandoned industrial sites known as "brownfields."

House Democrats took time Oct. 10 to elect a new whip, Nancy Pelosi of California, to replace David E. Bonior of Michigan when he stepped down in January 2002 to pursue his gubernatorial campaign. The election set Pelosi up to become the highest-ranking woman in congressional history. She ran a hard-fought campaign against Steny H. Hoyer of Maryland, getting 118 votes in the secret ballot, compared with 95 for Hoyer.

The Return of Partisanship

Gradually, the bipartisan stance all congressional leaders had adopted after the attacks began to break down. With an election that could determine the control of both chambers less than a year away, both parties looked for ways to define themselves. Daschle was the most prominent elected Democratic official in the country — and a potential presidential candidate in 2004, a possibility he was careful never to rule out. Cautiously, he set the tone for his party, supporting Bush on the war while challenging Republicans on domestic issues. "I agree with what the president is doing right now on the international front. I strongly disagree with him on many of the economic questions," he said Dec. 6.

Democrats tried to pass an economic stimulus bill that would extend unemployment benefits and health insurance for laid-off workers, called for $20 billion in extra spending for domestic "infrastructure" projects, and sought Senate passage of a farm bill that Republicans saw as bloated.

Soon, Republicans' gloves came off. They started calling Daschle an "obstructionist" who was blocking Bush's agenda and could not get anything done. The attacks were especially bitter over the stimulus package. Led by Bush, Republicans said the package should be devoted to tax cuts, not new spending. Ways and Means Chairman Thomas began referring to Daschle as "Coalition Leader Daschle" — arguing that 50 Democrats plus Jeffords did not make a true majority. Even Cheney joined in, calling Daschle an obstructionist for his handling of the bill.

The House passed two versions of the stimulus bill, but even with the intervention of Democratic centrists led by Breaux, Senate Democrats could not muster the 60 votes needed to bring it to the floor over GOP objections.

Partisan fireworks also were set off by an attempt by Byrd to attach an extra $20 billion — later reduced to $15 billion — in homeland security spending to the defense appropriations bill. The bill already was carrying the second half of the $40 billion supplemental enacted in September. But Byrd said additional money was needed to protect the public from bio-terrorism, rebuild New York, screen baggage on airlines, and improve security at nuclear power plants and airports. Bush and the Republicans said there was more emergency spending in the pipe than could be absorbed. Bush threatened to veto the entire bill if it exceeded his spending agreement with Congress. After Republicans won three procedural votes showing they were willing to derail the bill to support the president, Byrd settled for reshaping the $20 billion already in the bill to provide more for homeland security spending and less for defense than Bush had wanted.

Republicans also stopped the Democrats' farm bill for the year, defeating three attempts to invoke cloture, thereby ending a filibuster. The White House opposed both the Senate and House versions, and did not want the distraction from the campaign against terrorism.

Anthrax Attacks Disrupt Legislating

A small white envelope hand-addressed to Senate Majority Leader Tom Daschle, D-S.D., brought the threat of bio-terrorism home to Congress on Oct. 15. Inside was a letter, written in clunky, black letters, with a chilling message: "You can not stop us. We have this anthrax. You die now. Are you afraid? Death to America. Death to Israel. Allah is great." As an aide opened the letter, a puff of fine, white dust escaped into the air of Daschle's personal office in the Hart Senate Office Building.

Congress had become the target of an anthrax attack. One man had already died from anthrax exposure in Florida. A similar anthrax-spiked letter with the same postmark had been sent to NBC news anchor Tom Brokaw. In the days that followed, postal workers in New Jersey and at the Brentwood branch in Washington tested positive for anthrax; two Brentwood workers died.

The letter to Daschle, which contained two grams of anthrax, started a chain of events on Capitol Hill that led to the closing of the Hart building, where half of all senators had office space, for 96 days. The other Senate and House office buildings were closed temporarily as authorities searched for more anthrax contamination.

That morning, 22 congressional aides and six Capitol police officers were exposed; many others were scared and uncertain. By the end of the week, more than 3,900 lawmakers, aides, reporters, lobbyists and others had lined up at four testing centers to receive nasal swabs and a few days' supply of the antibiotic Cipro as a precaution until the tests came back. Ultimately, nearly 1,200 people who were treated at the Capitol, including 70 Senate aides, were put on 60-day courses of Cipro to prevent anthrax infections. As an extra precaution, 48 of the aides later received an extra 40 days of Cipro and an experimental anthrax vaccine.

Congress Improvises Way Back to Business

Congress' initial response was confused. House leaders told members and aides to go home Oct. 17, believing that their Senate counterparts were doing likewise. They were not. Facing a rebellion within their ranks at the idea of leaving town, Daschle and Minority Leader Trent Lott, R-Miss., announced with a defiant tone that the Senate would remain at work and that its half of the Capitol would not be shuttered.

That left House Speaker J. Dennis Hastert, R-Ill., and Minority Leader Richard A. Gephardt, D-Mo., to absorb the grumbling derision of House members and senators alike. It was the first time in history that the Houes had posponed its deliberations in teh face of danger.

Lawmakers returned to Washington on Oct. 23 with almost no place to go. All the offices remained off-limits, as agents from an array of federal law enforcement agencies, dressed in white polymer "moon suits" and gas masks, continued to search for additional bacteria.

The leadership scrambled to establish temporary offices where lawmakers could make telephone calls, talk to aides, tap into their computer networks or at least park their briefcases. A flurry of floor action allowed Congress to project an air of cautious normalcy. But behind the scenes — in ways impossible to notice outside the Beltway — it was anything but business as usual. Dozens of committee hearings were canceled for lack of meeting space. An array of legislation, most prominently conference agreements on fiscal 2002 appropriations bills, was stalled because the necessary paperwork could not be retrieved from quarantined offices. Lawmakers worked in coffee shops, colleagues' office, the cloakrooms and sometimes outdoors, with cellphones

Education Bill: Breaking the Mold

The education overhaul bill was the one major exception to the pattern of partisan bickering that ended the year.

The measure had been a model of bipartisanship from the beginning, when the White House met with working groups from both parties in each chamber to write the initial bills. After Sept. 11, the bill dropped from view. But the four men most responsible for getting it to conference — Boehner, Kennedy, Miller and Gregg — pressed on, reaching compromises on issues such as how much annual progress to expect on the tests and how much flexibility to give states and school districts. The last major dispute in conference was over money.

Democrats Kennedy and Miller wanted an even bigger education funding increase than the $4 billion that had been added to the appropriations bills, and they pressed conferees to accept Senate bill language fully funding special education and turning it into an entitlement. They said shifting special education costs from discretionary to mandatory spending would free up money on the discretionary side that could be used for other education costs.

But they were unable to persuade GOP conferees who, like Bush, argued that special education needed to be overhauled before Congress threw any more money at it. With that disputed ended, the final bill cleared Dec. 18 (PL 107-110) with overwhelming support in both chambers.

The Record

Despite the midyear change in the Senate, Bush was able to shape much of what Congress accomplished in 2001. He did not get everything he wanted, but what became law had more to do with his agenda than with Democratic priorities.

Part of the reason for Bush's successes — Congressional Quarterly's annual vote studies showed him with an 87 percent success rate, the highest since 1965 — was his style of dealing with Congress. He typically began by outlining his desires in broad terms or principles, rather than offering detailed legislative language. Then, after achieving what he considered to be the best outcome he could get, he declared victory, even when some of his original principles were scrapped or desires ignored.

and hand-held computers to check e-mail messages. Some used borrowed space at the General Accounting Office, a 20-minute walk from the Capitol.

New Precautions

The Russell Building was the first to reopen, allowing 36 senators back in their suites Oct. 24. The next day, the House re-opened its Cannon and Rayburn buildings, where 310 members work. On Oct. 26, all of the Dirksen Building was re-opened except the mailroom, which had handled the Daschle letter; anthrax spores were found in the mailroom Oct. 17. On Nov. 5, Longworth, where four suites had been contaminated, re-opened. But the Hart Building remained closed through the end of the year. In addition to Daschle's office and that of his neighbor, Russell D. Feingold, D-Wis., spores were found in an elevator lobby, a stairwell and a ventilation duct. (After three applications of chlorine dioxide gas, the building reopened Jan. 22, 2002.)

On Nov. 16, another anthrax-filled letter — this one addressed to Senate Judiciary Committee Chairman Patrick J. Leahy, D-Vt. — was found among the hundreds of thousands of pieces of mail that had been quarantined by the FBI. It bore the same Trenton, N.J., postmark and the same handwriting as the Daschle letter. Leahy later said he was told the amount of anthrax discovered in the letter was enough to kill 100,000 people. The envelope was opened in a sealed and controlled environment to avoid releasing deadly spores into the air. The FBI concluded the letters to Daschle and Leahy, as well as two other anthrax-tainted letters to NBC News and the New York Post, all had come from the same source.

The Daschle and Leahy letters contaminated other pieces of mail, which spread trace amounts of anthrax to other offices. Ultimately, 13 Senate offices and four House offices were found to be contaminated with minimal amounts of anthrax.

To prevent the possibility of another dangerous letter from finding its way into a lawmaker's office, congressional mail was subject to a laborious and time-consuming process. All mail to lawmakers' Washington offices was sent from a Virginia sorting center to be irradiated at facilities in Ohio and New Jersey. The irradiation process made letters look old and slightly burned. From there, the mail was sent back to separate screening centers for the House and Senate, where all non-paper contents were opened and searched for bombs or other hazards before the mail was finally delivered.

No one on Capitol Hill was infected by anthrax. In all, five Americans died of exposure to the bacteria.

Capitol Security

The anthrax scare, coming on top of the Sept. 11 terrorist attacks, also generated new concern about the security of the Capitol. One immediate effect was to spur action on an underground Capitol Visitor Center. Lawmakers added $70 million to the fiscal 2002 legislative branch spending bill (PL 107-68) so that construction on the 588,000-square foot center, set to be built under the East Lawn and completed in 2005, could begin in early 2002.

Congress also decided to include new congressional office space, with the Select Intelligence Committee as the main tenant on the House side. Bush released additional funds for the visitor center under the emergency fiscal 2001 supplemental spending bill (PL 107-38).

As part of the legislative branch bill, conferees ordered up a plan for allowing members and their aides easier access to their office computer networks from remote locations, in case future emergencies forced the evacuation of the Capitol or congressional office buildings. The legislative branch bill and the supplemental also provided additional funds for the Capitol Police.

He asked for a $1.6 trillion tax cut, settled for $290 billion less, and still was able to claim credit for the deepest tax cut in two decades. He asked for an education bill and signaled that everything was negotiable but annual testing in reading and math. By the time the final bill came together, annual testing was about all that remained of his original plan. Bush hailed the outcome as a "great symbol of what is possible in Washington when good people come together to do what's right."

Also, while Democrats controlled the Senate for more than half the session, their window to pursue their priorities was relatively brief. After pushing their managed-care bill through the Senate in June, Democrats spent much of July working on the annual appropriations bills. After returning from the August recess, they had one week before the terrorists attacks set the agenda for the rest of the year. Democrats did have significant influence on two major domestic initiatives: They scaled back the size of the tax cut, added funding to the education bill, and limited the scope of the flexibility given to states and schools. The bills, however, still were unquestionably Bush's priorities rather than theirs.

The most sobering lesson of the first session of the 107th Congress was that a narrowly divided House and Senate was not necessarily a prescription for the bipartisan cooperation the public said it wanted from lawmakers. After the near tie in the 2000 elections, leaders of both parties said the results represented a mandate for cooperation. But the effect was just the opposite. With control of the House and Senate within reach for either side in 2002, the parties spent most of their energy trying to satisfy their political bases.

With the notable exception of the education bill, and much of the legislation that passed in response to the Sept. 11 attacks, the story of 2001 was the insistence of both parties on trying to peel away just enough votes from the other side to squeeze out a victory, not a concerted effort to build solid and unshakable support on both sides of the aisle. Sometimes the gamble paid off; other times it led to failure or to a fleeting victory. Either way, it was a gamble neither side was able to resist. And all signs pointed to even greater partisanship in the second session, as the elections approached and the memories of Sept. 11 receded. ◆

Chapter 2

APPROPRIATIONS

Spending Fights Put on Hold

The fiscal 2002 appropriations season came to a surprisingly calm conclusion after the September terrorist attacks forced all sides to substantially adjust their budget goals. Republican leaders agreed to spend more on domestic programs to help minimize partisan bickering over the 13 regular spending bills. Democrats agreed to the first installment of President Bush's defense buildup without a whimper. Talk of a "lockbox" to protect surpluses in the Social Security and Medicare trust funds evaporated, and a balanced budget became a distant goal.

The outcome left many lawmakers disgruntled: Deficit hawks were in despair, defense hawks charged that the troops were shortchanged, and liberal Democrats said unemployed workers were being left in the lurch.

It was the final twist in a year filled with unpredictable turns. When the appropriators met in May to allocate money among their 13 subcommittees, they were working with a $661.3 billion limit on discretionary spending — the funding under their control — set by the fiscal 2002 budget resolution (H Con Res 83). The budget allowed for a further increase in defense spending once Bush finished his review of the Defense Department and, in June, Bush asked for an additional $18.4 billion.

Although the $661.3 billion limit was a 4.2 percent increase over fiscal 2001, it was $27.1 billion less than the Senate had wanted. Appropriators warned that the cap was unreasonably tight and would leave many congressional priorities under-funded or not funded at all.

The appropriators became more skeptical as they began assembling the bills over the summer, caught between demands for more spending and both parties' pledge to hold the Social Security trusts funds sacrosanct. Meanwhile, the flagging economy and Bush's $1.35 trillion, 10-year tax cut (PL 107-16) were eating away the surplus. When the Congressional Budget Office (CBO) issued its midyear forecast in August, the $313 billion fiscal 2002 surplus projected in January had fallen to $176 billion, just $2 billion of it outside the Social Security trust funds.

September Showdown Expected

By the August recess, a major showdown was looming. None of the fiscal 2002 spending bills had gone to conference. Appropriators said they needed more money, while fiscal conservatives looked to Bush to follow through on a threat made early in the year to veto bills that broke the spending limits. Democrats wanted Bush to revise his own request upward. Otherwise, they said they would stick to the budget resolution, forcing Bush to accept bills with none of the big increases he wanted for defense and education, or veto the bills because they did not spend enough.

Few could see any realistic way to accommodate all the needs within the $661.3 billion total, but no one wanted to be the first to break the budget cap or to suggest fixing the problem with Social Security money. Bush reiterated Sept. 6 that only war, recession or "severe emergency" would justify using Social Security funds for other purposes.

Then came Sept. 11 and the overwhelming need to clean up the carnage, aid the victims and find and punish the attackers. Washington was instantly unshackled from the lockbox. Within three days, Congress had cleared a $40 billion emergency supplemental spending bill (PL 107-38) — $20 billion of it available for Bush to spend and $20 billion to be allocated by the appropriators. A week later, lawmakers completed a $15 billion bill to help airlines recover.

The regular spending bills also began to move, with closed-door deliberations producing near-agreements on as many as seven. On Oct. 2, top appropriators reached agreement with the White House to increase the fiscal 2002 discretionary spending limit by $6 billion, to $686 billion. Of that, $4 billion went to education and $2 billion to emergency firefighting. Appropriators had known the likely total for weeks, but they insisted on getting the White House imprimatur to shield them from attacks later by fiscal conservatives. They settled for a letter from Bush stating that he would sign bills that complied with the new limit.

Problems Melt Away

One-by-one, the bills began to clear. Stubborn disputes over exports to Cuba, mining regulations, the International Space Station, drinking water standards and other issues were sidestepped or resolved. Perhaps the biggest battle — whether to open the U.S. border to Mexican trucks — ended in a victory for Bush, who had threatened to veto the Transportation spending bill if the trucks were barred.

Three bills — for Defense; Labor, Health and Human Services (HHS); and foreign operations — did not clear until Dec. 20. The Labor-HHS bill was held up by efforts to keep education funding in line with the education overhaul bill that cleared Dec. 18.

The defense bill was caught up in a debate over how to spend the second half of the $40 billion appropriated in September and whether to let Senate Democrats add as much as $15 billion in homeland security funding. The bill was the vehicle for the supplemental spending. With the pledge to protect Social Security gone, the main obstacle to more spending was the president. Bush said enough emergency money was already in the pipeline to last until the end of the year, and he vowed to veto the defense bill if it carried more than the $20 billion already agreed to. Democrats backed down, though they managed to redirect some of the emergency money to domestic spending.

House GOP leaders held up the foreign operations bill while they tried to avert a blowup over extra funds for international family planning demanded by the Senate. Though the funds were strongly opposed by GOP conservatives, House leaders largely gave in to the Senate.

With the final spending bill cleared, the session ended.

A series of eight continuing resolutions kept the government operating while the bills were being completed. When the books were closed on fiscal 2002, CBO calculated total discretionary spending at $712 billion in budget authority and $731 billion in outlays. ◆

Appropriations Mileposts
107th Congress — First Session

Bill	House Passed	Senate Passed	House Final*	Senate Final*	Signed	Story
Agriculture (HR 2330 — PL 107-76)	7/11/01	10/25/01	11/13/01	11/15/01	11/28/01	2-5
Commerce-Justice-State (HR 2500 — PL 107-77)	7/18/01	9/13/01	11/14/01	11/15/01	11/28/01	2-9
Defense (HR 3338 — PL 107-117)	11/28/01	12/7/01	12/20/01	12/20/01	1/10/02	2-13
District of Columbia (HR 2944 — PL 107-96)	9/25/01	11/7/01	12/6/01	12/7/01	12/21/01	2-18
Energy-Water Development (HR 2311 — PL 107-66)	6/28/01	7/19/01	11/1/01	11/1/01	11/12/01	2-21
Foreign Operations (HR 2506 — PL 107-115)	7/24/01	10/24/01	12/19/01	12/20/01	1/10/02	2-25
Interior (HR 2217 — PL 107-63)	6/21/01	7/12/01	10/17/01	10/17/01	11/5/01	2-30
Labor-HHS-Education (HR 3061 — PL 107-116)	10/11/01	11/6/01	12/19/01	12/20/01	1/10/02	2-34
Legislative Branch (HR 2647 — PL 107-68)	7/31/01	7/19/01	11/1/01	11/1/01	11/12/01	2-38
Military Construction (HR 2904 — PL 107-64)	9/21/01	9/26/01	10/17/01	10/18/01	11/5/01	2-41
Transportation (HR 2299 — PL 107-87)	6/26/01	8/1/01	11/30/01	12/4/01	12/18/01	2-43
Treasury-Postal Service (HR 2590 — PL 107-67)	7/25/01	9/19/01	10/31/01	11/1/01	11/12/01	2-47
VA-HUD (HR 2620 — PL 107-73)	7/31/01	8/2/01	11/8/01	11/8/01	11/26/01	2-51
Midyear Supplemental (HR 2216 — PL 107-20)	6/20/01	7/10/01	7/20/01	7/20/01	7/24/01	2-55
Anti-Terrorism Supplemental (HR 2888 — PL 107-38)	9/14/01	9/14/01	—	—	9/18/01	2-59

*Adoption of conference report.

Drug Plan Cut From Agriculture Bill

The $75.9 billion fiscal 2002 spending bill for the Agriculture Department and the Food and Drug Administration (FDA) cleared with relative ease, mainly because lawmakers decided to drop contentious provisions so that Congress could focus on war-related issues after the Sept. 11 terrorist attacks. The president signed the bill, which was $1.6 billion above his original request, on Nov. 28 (HR 2330 — PL 107-76).

The bill allocated $16 billion in discretionary spending for animal and crop research, marketing assistance, farmer education, rural development and FDA operations. The other $59.9 billion, nearly four-fifths of the bill, was for mandatory commodity, conservation and nutrition assistance programs outside the control of the appropriators.

In an acknowledgment of the deepening recession, the bill provided a dramatic increase in funding for nutrition programs, especially for food stamps. The food stamp program got $23 billion — $2.9 billion more than in fiscal 2001 and $1 billion more than was requested by Bush or contained in the House-passed bill. Agriculture research programs also got a boost, as did the FDA, the primary federal consumer protection agency.

When work began on the bill in June, several fights from the previous year threatened to return. The House added a plan to help the elderly by allowing the re-importation of U.S.-made prescription drugs that were available abroad for less than they cost in the United States. In the Senate, Byron L. Dorgan, D-N.D., promised to renew his efforts to lift sanctions on food and medicine exports to Cuba. The issue pitted farm-state lawmakers against Republican conservatives and Cuban-American representatives in Congress.

By the time the bill reached the Senate floor in October, however, Democrats had decided Congress did not need the distraction of a debate on Cuba policy while it was considering war-time emergencies. Since the House bill had no Cuba provision, the debate was put off for the year. The drug provisions were not included in the Senate bill, and they were dropped in conference.

The bill's discretionary total was $2.7 billion below the fiscal 2001 appropriation, but the comparison is somewhat misleading because the fiscal 2001 figure included $3.6 billion in emergency discretionary aid to pay for natural disasters and assist farmers hit by weather related crop losses and low prices.

Highlights

Major spending allocations in the bill included:
● **Agriculture programs.** $31.9 billion — more than 40 percent of the bill's total — for programs ranging from com-

BoxScore 2002
Agriculture — Fiscal Year

Bill:
HR 2330 — PL 107-76
Legislative Action:
House passed HR 2330 (H Rept 107-116), 414-16, on July 11.
Senate passed HR 2330, amended (S Rept 107-41), 91-5, on Oct. 25.
House adopted the conference report (H Rept 107-275), 379-33, on Nov. 13.
Senate cleared the bill, 92-7, on Nov. 15.
President signed Nov. 28.

modity price supports and farm lending to soil conservation and environmental development.

The Farm Service Agency — responsible for administering farm income support, disaster assistance, and domestic and international food aid programs — received $1.4 billion. Agricultural Credit Programs, which provide loans for farm operations, farm ownership and emergencies, received $3.9 billion. $1.1 billion went to the Agricultural Research Service, which conducts basic and applied research on soil and water conservation, plant and animal productivity, and genetics and human nutrition. Inspection agencies received $1.3 billion — $628 million for animals and plant health and $716 million for food safety.
● **Conservation programs.** $962 million — $55 million more than the fiscal 2001 level and $34 million more than the president's request — for soil and water conservation, flood-prevention and other programs aimed at promoting environmentally conscious farming techniques.
● **Rural development.** $2.6 billion — an increase of $101 million over fiscal 2001 and $180 million over Bush's request — for loans, loan guarantees, and grant aid for rural infrastructure, housing, businesses and other programs.
● **Food and nutrition programs.** $37.9 billion — half of the bill's spending — for food stamps, the Women, Infants and Children (WIC) program, children's nutrition and other programs. The total was $3.7 billion above the fiscal 2001 level and $1.2 billion more than requested.
● **Foreign assistance.** $1.1 billion — $34 million more than the previous level and $28 million more than requested — for programs to provide international food aid and expand the U.S. agricultural market abroad.
● **FDA.** $1.2 billion — a $123 million increase over fiscal 2001 and virtually the same as Bush's request — for the agency that sets federal standards for food and cosmetics and tests new drugs and medical devices before they are marketed.

Background

Traditionally among the least controversial of the spending measures, the agriculture appropriations bill had spawned enough debate — and unresolved issues — in 2000 to portend several tough fights on the fiscal 2002 measure.

Farm-state lawmakers had successfully added language to the fiscal 2001 bill (PL 106-387) removing sanctions on food and medicine exports to Cuba, a change bitterly opposed by conservative Republicans and Cuban-Americans in Congress. The price for the provision, however, was agreement to bar public or private financing of Cuban agri-

Where the Money Goes

Agriculture Spending Highlights

(figures are in thousands of dollars of new budget authority)

	Fiscal 2001 Appropriation	Fiscal 2002 Bush Request	House Bill	Senate Bill	Conference Report
Agricultural programs	$33,212,900	$31,636,339	$31,759,514	$31,849,392	$31,873,688
Conservation programs	907,056	928,605	909,032	985,416	962,139
Rural development programs	2,481,127	2,401,520	2,488,414	2,793,742	2,581,924
Domestic food programs	34,111,685	36,629,391	36,658,628	37,739,891	37,855,627
Foreign food aid and export assistance	1,090,199	1,096,953	1,106,701	1,128,077	1,124,518
Food and Drug Administration, other agencies	1,165,304	1,281,304	1,288,554	1,288,351	1,288,651
Other provisions	3,691,306*	1,996	149,000	12,596	107,896
Contingent emergency appropriations	($11,463,780)	($12,028,476)	($13,713,692)	($14,067,362)	($13,962,986)
GRAND TOTAL	**$76,659,577***	**$73,976,108**	**$74,359,843**	**$75,797,465**	**$75,794,443**
Total adjusted for scorekeeping	($77,039,941)*	($74,293,492)	($74,553,227)	($76,020,849)	($75,902,827)

Includes "emergency" spending not subject to overall congressional discretionary appropriations limits

Table: House Appropriations Committee

cultural purchases, and to codify travel restrictions, previously implemented by executive order, that prevented most Americans from traveling to Cuba. Much of the compromise language was set to expire after a year, opening the door for a second round of debate for fiscal 2002.

Concern over rising prescription drug prices had led to language in the bill allowing pharmacists and drug wholesalers to re-import U.S. prescription drugs; previously, only drug manufacturers could re-import the products. But the language had been weakened in conference, and the Clinton administration said it could not be implemented. *(2000 Almanac, p. 2-8)*

Legislative Action

House Subcommittee Action

The House Agriculture Appropriations Subcommittee approved a $74.2 billion draft of the bill by voice vote with no dissent June 6. Of the total, $15.5 billion was discretionary spending. Members generally refrained from offering controversial amendments. Only minor changes were made to the draft put forward by Henry Bonilla, R-Texas, in his first year as the subcommittee chairman. Still, the discussion exposed several cracks in an otherwise smooth beginning to the fiscal 2002 appropriations season.

The liveliest debate was about whether to continue the Global Food for Education Initiative for a second year. The program, which made surplus commodities available to school lunchrooms in developing countries, had broad bipartisan support, but top GOP appropriators said it was not affordable in light of overall spending limits. The panel rejected, 7-8, an amendment by Marcy Kaptur of Ohio, the panel's top Democrat, to add $300 million to keep the program alive.

The subcommittee also made several minor changes to the bill; for example, shifting $500,000 from food safety accounts to the National Center for Toxicological Research

for a study on the health effects of irradiating food. The panel rejected, by voice vote, a proposal by George Nethercutt, R-Wash., to increase criminal penalties against terrorists who target agricultural research centers.

House Committee Action

The full Appropriations Committee approved the bill (H Rept 107-116) by voice vote June 13, after adding $150 million in emergency aid for apple growers. The extra money brought the discretionary total to $15.7 billion. Because the aid was designated as an emergency, technically it did not put the bill over its discretionary spending ceiling, but the maneuver angered GOP conservatives. The amendment, designed mainly to help growers in New York and Michigan hurt by freezes and other bad weather, was approved 34-24 with bipartisan support.

Short of votes, James T. Walsh, R-N.Y., withdrew an amendment to reauthorize the Northeast Dairy Compact, which was due to expire on Sept. 30. The amendment would have allowed New York, Delaware, New Jersey, and Pennsylvania to join the system and permitted other regions to create compacts of their own. It was ardently opposed by dairy farmers in the Upper Midwest, who said the regional pricing system hurt them by subsidizing farmers in other regions, encouraging them to produce more milk and shrinking the market for Midwestern products. But farmers in less dairy-rich areas saw compacts as a way to guarantee stable prices for an otherwise volatile commodity.

Republicans spent much of the markup fending off attempts by Democrats to spend additional money on their priorities. The committee rejected, 18-31, an amendment by Kaptur to provide $500 million in emergency funds for research, development and assistance in turning agricultural products into energy. A renewed effort by Kaptur to add $300 million for the international school meals program was rejected, 26-32. The committee defeated, 23-29, a proposal by Rosa DeLauro, D-Conn., to add $213 million in emergency money to increase the number of do-

mestic and international food inspections.

Democrats and Republicans also differed sharply over federal food labeling policies. On a nearly party line vote of 31-25, the panel eliminated a $500,000 earmark for a study on the health effects of irradiation, used to kill microorganisms such as bacteria and fungus.

The panel approved several less controversial amendments. One proposal added by voice vote, by Nita M. Lowey, D-N.Y., ordered the FDA to report by the end of the year on its plans for issuing rules to help prevent contamination of foods by allergens — such as peanut or egg ingredients — not declared on their labels.

House Floor Action

Almost a month after the bill emerged from committee, the House passed the $74.4 billion measure July 11 by a vote of 414-16, after adding language to allow more drug re-importation. (*House vote 221, p. H-80*)

The amendment, sponsored by Republicans Gil Gutknecht of Minnesota and Jo Ann Emerson of Missouri, was adopted by a vote of 324-101. It called for allowing individuals to import U.S.-made, FDA-approved drugs other than narcotics in quantities suitable for personal use. Supporters hoped to use the provision as an opening to pursue stronger language in the Democratic-controlled Senate. A broader amendment by Bernard Sanders, I-Vt., that would have allowed wholesalers and pharmacists to import U.S.-made, FDA-approved drugs in bulk was defeated, 159-267. Sanders said allowing such imports could cut the cost of prescription drugs in the United States by 30 percent to 50 percent. Pharmaceutical companies blitzed Capitol Hill, arguing that the proposals would undermine the FDA's ability to ensure a safe drug supply by allowing medicines with dubious origins into the United States. (*House votes 217, 216, pp. H-80, H-78*)

The committee adopted by voice vote an amendment by Sherrod Brown, D-Ohio, aimed at expediting the development of cheaper generic alternatives. The amendment earmarked $1 million for the FDA to enforce rules against frivolous patent listings by drug manufacturers that could delay the development of cheaper generic medicines.

Lawmakers also sparred over the federal farm support programs. An amendment by Ed Royce, R-Calif., to eliminate the Market Access Program, which provides trade associations and cooperatives with funding to promote their agricultural products overseas, failed overwhelmingly, 85-341. (*House vote 220, p. H-80*)

The controversy over money for apple growers was defused by the rule for floor debate, which eliminated the emergency designation but left the money intact.

Senate Committee Action

The Senate Appropriations Committee approved a $73.9 billion agriculture spending bill (S 1191 — S Rept 107-41) on July 17. With contentious policy debates postponed, the vote was 27-0. However, Dorgan made it clear that, as the bill moved forward, he planned to revisit the divisive issue of loosening restrictions on commerce with Cuba. He said he would not use the Senate debate on the bill as a vehicle to try to relax rules on re-importing pharmaceuticals.

The higher level of discretionary spending in the bill —

the subcommittee had been allocated $16.1 billion for discretionary programs, $468 million more than its House counterpart — allowed the appropriators to provide $2.1 billion for Agriculture Department research ($83 million more than the House and $315 million more than Bush requested); $1 billion for rural infrastructure and business enterprise effort ($233 million more than the House and $308 million more than requested); and $4.2 billion for the WIC nutrition program ($110 million more than both the House bill and Bush's request).

The biggest difference between the two bills was the Senate's recommendation of $100 million for a food stamp contingency reserve. The House had approved $1 billion, as requested by the Bush administration. The two versions also differed on how much would be needed to cover commodity price supports and other mandatory programs.

By voice vote, the committee adopted an amendment making minor changes to the report accompanying the bill, including non-binding language urging the Agriculture Department to continue funding the Global Food for Education Initiative.

Senate Floor Action

The Senate passed HR 2330 by a vote of 91-5 on Oct. 25, after substituting the text of its own $73.9 billion bill. Intent on finishing the spending bills without bipartisan flare-ups in the aftermath of Sept. 11, senators agreed to skip some of the anticipated policy debates. (*Senate vote 315, p. S-66*)

Dorgan announced that he would not seek a debate on lifting Cuba sanctions or on the re-importation of prescription drugs. A number of other senators offered amendments but subsequently withdrew them to assure rapid passage, preferring to address the issues in conference.

Carl Levin, D-Mich., withdrew a proposal to add the House provision of $150 million in market loss payments to apple growers.

Agriculture Committee Chairman Tom Harkin, D-Iowa, offered and then withdrew an amendment aimed at clarifying the Agriculture Department's authority to enforce pathogen reduction standards in meat and poultry plants. A federal judge ruled in May 2000 that the agency lacked authority to remove inspectors from a Texas meat processing plant. Harkin withdrew his amendment after the Senate voted 45-50 not to table (kill) a second-degree amendment by Ben Nelson, D-Neb., that would have prohibited the USDA from stamping meat that was tainted. (*Senate vote 314, p. S-66*)

Conference/Final Action

House and Senate conferees agreed by voice vote Nov. 8 on a $75.9 billion compromise bill that included $16 billion in discretionary spending. The House adopted the conference report (H Rept 107-275) by a vote of 379-33 on Nov. 13. The Senate cleared the bill, 92-7, on Nov. 15. (*House vote 436, p. H-150; Senate vote 339, p. S-70*)

Major issues resolved in conference included:

● **WIC.** The bill provided $4.3 billion for the WIC nutrition program, more than either the House or Senate had approved.

● **Food stamps.** The food stamp program received $23 billion, including $2 billion in reserves, an increase of $2.9 bil-

lion from fiscal 2001. The amount was $1 billion more than requested by Bush or recommended by the House.

● **FDA.** The FDA got $1.2 billion, $120 million above the fiscal 2001 level and $7 million more than the administration's request.

● **Prescription drugs.** Conferees agreed to drop the House-passed language on drug reimportation.

● **Apple growers.** The final bill allowed $75 million in market loss payments, half the amount approved by the House.

● **International school lunch aid.** No funds were included in the bill for the program. ◆

CJS Bill Includes Anti-Terror Funds

For the first time since Republicans won control of Congress in 1994, the annual spending bill for the departments of Commerce, Justice and State and the federal judiciary was enacted free of controversy and comparatively early in the process. The fiscal 2002 bill, signed into law Nov. 28 (HR 2500 — PL 107-77), provided $41.6 billion, a $1.9 billion increase over fiscal 2001 and $828 billion more than President Bush had requested.

The House passed a version of the bill in mid-July that was notably lacking in contentious riders. Senate appropriators quickly injected some disputes into the debate, approving a version that included a permanent change to immigration law opposed by House conservatives, and a reduction in international peacekeeping funds that drew objections from the administration. The Senate took up the bill just two days after the Sept. 11 terrorist attacks, at a time when members were intent on avoiding policy battles, and passed it quickly.

Most provisions likely to provoke fights, such as the change in immigration policy, were dropped in conference. The final bill did retain a provision barring the use of funds to support creation of the International Criminal Court, but the White House had no intention of contributing to the court or its creation.

Though most of the money approved after Sept. 11 to fight terrorism was enacted in a separate supplemental, the Commerce, Justice, State bill included $459 million for the FBI's Terrorism program and another $251 million in grants to state and local governments for anti-terrorism and terrorism prevention efforts. Among the items were $12 million to strengthen the FBI's ability to guard against chemical, biological and nuclear attacks on the United States, and $12 million for security related to the 2002 Winter Olympics in Salt Lake City.

Highlights

Major spending categories in the bill included:
● **State Department.** $7.8 billion for State Department programs, including embassy security and international peacekeeping, as well as for international broadcasting. That was an increase of nearly $800 million over fiscal 2001, making the State Department the biggest winner in the bill, though the total was slightly less ($136 million) than Bush had requested. The bill included $3.6 billion, a $462 million increase, for diplomatic and consular affairs programs, much of it to improve security at U.S. embassies. Funding for International Broadcasting Operations, which

BoxScore 2002
Commerce-Justice-State
Fiscal Year

Bill:
HR 2500 — PL 107-77
Legislative Action:
House passed HR 2500 (H Rept 107-139), 408-19, on July 18.
Senate passed HR 2500, amended (S Rept 107-42), 97-0, on Sept. 13.
House adopted the conference report (H Rept 107-278), 411-15, on Nov. 14.
Senate cleared the bill, 98-1, on Nov. 15.
President signed Nov. 28.

broadcast news and information programs worldwide, increased by $30 million, to $428 million.
● **Justice Department.** $21.7 billion, more than half the bill's total, for Justice Department programs. The total was a $612 million increase over fiscal 2001 and $554 million more than requested. It included $3.5 billion for the FBI, exactly what Bush had requested long before the Sept. 11 attacks; $1.5 billion, as requested, for the Drug Enforcement Agency (DEA); and $5.6 billion for the Immigration and Naturalization Service (INS) — $2.1 billion of which was to come from fees.
● **Commerce Department.** $5.5 billion, $278 million more than the fiscal 2001 level, for Commerce. The increase was not as large as those for Justice and State, but the total was still $341 million more than Bush requested. The National Institute of Standards and Technology got $675 million, 38 percent more than requested and 13 percent above Bush's request — including $184.5 million for the Advanced Technology Program, a science research project that House appropriators had tried to kill for years. Bush also wanted to discontinue it. The National Oceanic and Atmospheric Administration got nearly $3.3 billion, a $215 million increase over fiscal 2001.
● **Federal judiciary.** $4.6 billion for the judiciary, $357 million more than in fiscal 2001 but $261 million less than requested. The total included nearly $1.4 billion for the offices of the 94 U.S. attorneys across the country, many of which were involved in the anti-terrorism investigation. The total was slightly more than the president's request.

Background

The bill funds the departments of Commerce, Justice and State (CJS), the federal judiciary and almost 20 other agencies, including the Equal Employment Opportunity Commission, Federal Trade Commission, Legal Services Corporation and Small Business Administration. In recent years, the bill had been caught up in intense battles over issues ranging from peacekeeping to immigration, making it one of the last measures to be signed into law.

Negotiations on the fiscal 2001 bill (PL 106-553) continued into December of 2000, despite the fact the Senate had cleared the measure in late October. The main stumbling block was a package of unrelated immigration provisions sought by the Clinton administration and congressional Democrats. The bill was sent to the White House only after the immigration provisions were included in a separate omnibus

Where the Money Goes

Commerce-Justice-State Spending

(figures are in thousands of dollars of new budget authority)

	Fiscal 2001 Appropriation	Fiscal 2002 Bush Request	House Bill	Senate Bill	Conference Report
Department of Justice	$21,049,475	$21,107,774	$21,723,303	$21,544,699	$21,661,850
Commerce and related agencies	$5,230,210	$5,171,005	$5,190,191	$5,678,373	$5,511,943
The Judiciary	$4,254,781	$4,872,713	$4,681,132	$4,500,203	$4,611,755
Department of State	$7,041,288	$7,976,536	$7,867,222	$7,631,097	$7,840,565
Related agencies*	$2,246,522	$1,804,192	$2,119,167	$2,300,379	$2,114,165
Rescissions	−130,444	−125,000	−125,000	−126,620	−105,100
GRAND TOTAL	$39,691,832	$40,807,220	$41,456,015	$41,528,131	$41,635,178
Total adjusted for scorekeeping	($38,262,731)	($38,568,458)	($39,160,801)	($39,268,196)	($39,283,452)

*Includes $49,890 for wildlife conservation and restoration planning

TABLE: House and Senate Appropriations committees

spending bill (PL 106-554). Virtually all the spending fights were resolved by adding more money. The final bill totaled $39.9 billion. *(2000 Almanac, p. 2-23)*

President Bill Clinton vetoed the first fiscal 2000 CJS bill, insisting that it did not provide enough for his priorities, particularly community policing, and would jeopardize Washington's ability to lead in the world by failing to meet U.S. financial obligations to the United Nations. Negotiators then drafted a second bill that both sides said split the difference between the GOP and the White House. Congress cleared the $39.6 billion bill as part of an omnibus package (PL 106-113) that included five of the 13 fiscal 2000 appropriations measures. *(1999 Almanac, p. 2-17)*

Legislative Action

House Subcommittee Action

The House CJS Appropriations Subcommittee approved a $38.5 billion draft of the fiscal 2002 bill by voice vote June 27 with less than an hour of discussion and no real debate.

Democrats expressed pleasure that the measure included the full $330 million requested for the Legal Services Corporation, a government-funded private organization that helped provide legal aid to the poor. Republicans had long tried to slash the group's funding.

Although the subcommittee reduced some accounts from fiscal 2001 levels, the cuts were much smaller than Bush had proposed. For example, law enforcement grants to states and localities were trimmed by about $324 million, instead of the roughly $1 billion proposed by Bush. The FBI was slated to get $3.49 billion, close to Bush's request. The Small Business Administration (SBA) got $728 million, compared with $542 million requested by Bush.

The panel agreed to Bush's request for $844 million for U.S. contributions to international peacekeeping efforts, an account that had triggered arguments in previous years. The Clinton-era Community Oriented Policing Services (COPS) program, which paid for more police officers, got $1.01 billion, a $155 million increase over Bush's proposal.

The bill also included a new $3 fee on cruise ship passengers arriving in the United States, and an increase from $6 to $7 in the fee on airline passengers; the fees paid for INS inspection services, including visa verification.

House Full Committee Action

The full Appropriations Committee gave relatively quick voice vote approval July 10 to a somewhat larger, $41.5 billion version of the bill (H Rept 107-139), despite brief flare-ups over gun control and the medical use of marijuana.

The gun debate concerned a decision by Attorney General John Ashcroft to dramatically shorten the time the FBI was permitted to hold records of background checks on gun buyers. To buy a gun through a federally licensed dealer, purchasers had to have their names run through the National Instant Check System to determine whether they had a felony conviction or other records that would prevent the gun purchase. Under Clinton, the FBI had held the records for up to 180 days to do audits of the system. Ashcroft said he wanted to destroy the records within 24 hours of their creation, a position the National Rifle Association had advocated for years. James P. Moran, D-Va., offered an amendment to require that the records be retained for no less than 90 days and no more than 100. CJS Subcommittee Chairman Frank R. Wolf, R-Va., persuaded him to withdraw the proposal, at least temporarily, saying the comment period for collecting public opinions on Ashcroft's proposed change had just begun.

Maurice D. Hinchey, D-N.Y., offered an amendment, defeated by voice vote, that would have prohibited the Justice Department from prosecuting states that had approved the use of marijuana for medical purposes. Eight states allowed medical marijuana; the Supreme Court had ruled earlier in the year that there was no medical necessity exception to the federal drug law barring the use of marijuana, though the court did not throw out the eight state laws.

House Floor Action

The House passed the $41.5 billion bill July 18 by a vote of 408-19, the widest margin of support for a CJS spending measure in the House in more than a decade.

Lawmakers debated issues ranging from gun control to AIDS in Africa but made only a few small changes to the bill. (*House vote 248, p. H-88*)

The Bush administration gave mostly high marks to the bill, criticizing only the number of earmarks — spending specifically designated for one program or organization, typically at the behest of a member of Congress. The administration said the Justice Department section of the bill contained at least $329 million in earmarks for some 220 projects.

The closest the House came to a controversy was over Moran's amendment on background checks. Gun rights supporters decisively defeated his proposal to require that the records be kept for 90 days during fiscal 2002. Moran said an April study of the system showed that more than 5,000 people were able to get around the background check and purchase weapons, something that probably would not have been noticed if the records were not available for review. The amendment was rejected, 161-268. (*House vote 244, p. H-88*)

In other action, the House:

• Rejected, 123-306, an amendment by Maxine Waters, D-Calif., designed to protect developing countries from fights with drug companies over efforts to provide HIV/AIDS medications to infected populations. The amendment would have prohibited the U.S. trade representative from asking the World Trade Organization to enforce U.S. patents in certain foreign countries. (*House vote 247, p. H-88*)

• Adopted, 424-6, an amendment by Majority Whip Tom DeLay, R-Texas, to bar use of money in the bill to pay China for the cost of detaining the crew of a U.S. surveillance plane held for 10 days in April after the aircraft was forced to land in China. (*House vote 241, p. H-86*)

• Adopted by voice vote an amendment by John W. Olver, D-Mass., to strike language in the bill that would have prohibited funds from being used to implement the Kyoto Protocol on global warming.

The House adopted several amendments by voice vote, including a proposal by Donald Manzullo, R-Ill., to increase to $6 billion the amount of guaranteed commitments the SBA could make for fiscal 2002; the bill had capped the level at $4.1 billion. Another, by Nydia M. Velázquez, D-N.Y., increased by $7 million salaries for the SBA and increased by $10 million the Business Loans programs.

Hinchey withdrew his medical marijuana amendment, saying he lacked the votes.

Senate Committee Action

The day after the House floor vote, the Senate Appropriations Committee approved a $41.6 billion version of the bill (S 1215 — S Rept 107-42). The vote, on July 19, was 29-0; the CJS Subcommittee had sent the bill directly to the committee without voting on it.

Several provisions seemed likely to raise objections in the House. For example, the bill included a permanent extension of the 245(i) program, which allowed immigrants to stay in the country while they applied for residency, even if they were here illegally. The program had expired in April, and Bush had asked Congress to renew it for up to one year. The House passed a separate bill (HR 1885) to revive the program for four months, but House conservatives said they would not support a longer extension. (*Immigration, p. 14-13*)

The bill also recommended reducing the U.S. contribution for international peacekeeping to $773 million, $71 million less than the president's request and the House-passed bill.

Senate appropriators denied a request from Supreme Court justices for money to renovate their 65-year-old building. The bill included $7.5 million of the $118 million requested for renovations. The House bill included $63.5 million for the first year's construction costs. The report accompanying the Senate bill said the committee supported replacing the building's faltering systems, but was "very concerned" over the court's plan to create an underground annex as a swing space for displaced staff. The committee said it would be far less costly to move staffers to other buildings or use ceremonial offices in the court as temporary workspace. The committee proposed delaying the project until fiscal 2003 so the court could come up with an alternate plan.

The bill called on the Justice Department to create a new position of deputy attorney general for combating domestic terrorism. A similar provision in the 2001 Senate CJS bill was dropped in conference. There was strong disagreement over which federal agency — Justice, Defense or some other agency — should have supremacy in the fight against terrorism.

The measure included $1.02 billion for the COPS local police-hiring program, an increase of $165 million over the president's request. It also included the $1 fee increase on airline passengers entering the country and the $3 fee on cruise ship passengers. CJS Subcommittee Chairman Ernest F. Hollings, D-S.C., said the changes would increase revenues by more than $200 million.

The bill recommended $3.47 billion for the FBI, a slight reduction from Bush's request and from the House version.

Senate Floor Action

The Senate passed HR 2500 by a vote of 97-0 on Sept. 13, after substituting a slightly altered, $41.5 billion version of its own bill. It was the first substantive legislation considered by the Senate following the Sept. 11 terrorist attacks, and senators went out of their way to avoid policy battles. Republicans said the measure would appropriate about $485.3 million for counterterrorism investigations, foreign counterintelligence and other related national security activities. (*Senate vote 278, p. S-58*)

The only real disagreement came on a last-minute proposal by Judiciary Committee ranking Republican Orrin G. Hatch of Utah to add a series of law enforcement provisions aimed at countering domestic terrorism. Despite significant concerns about the broad authority in the amendment, Democrats allowed it to become part of the bill by voice vote.

Sponsored by Hatch, Jon Kyl, R-Ariz., and Dianne Feinstein, D-Calif., the amendment included provisions to: make it easier for law enforcement officials to track Internet communication; rescind a 1995 CIA regulation barring the recruitment of intelligence sources who had been associated with human rights violations; and study whether to give National Guard troops a primary role in preventing and responding to attacks involving weapons of mass destruction. Other provisions called on the administration to develop a program of research and development in technologies to combat terrorism, and to enhance the physical security of

biological pathogens located at hospitals and research facilities across the country.

The Senate had begun work on the bill Sept. 10, giving voice vote approval to an amendment by Larry E. Craig, R-Idaho, to prohibit U.S. money from going to the creation of the International Criminal Court or to the commission behind it. Craig said countries hostile to the United States could use the court to try U.S. military personnel or U.S. allies, such as Israel, for crimes against humanity.

Tom Harkin, D-Iowa, and Robert C. Smith, R-N.H., teamed up to offer an amendment, strongly opposed by the administration, to prohibit the State and Justice departments from spending taxpayer dollars to file briefs or motions challenging the validity of slave-labor claims against Japanese companies. The amendment, adopted by voice vote Sept. 10, was in response to a 50-year-old policy stating that because the United States signed the 1951 San Francisco Peace Treaty, U.S. citizens who were prisoners of war in Japan during World War II could not win reparations from Japan or private Japanese companies. In recent court cases, the State and Justice departments had filed briefs arguing against allowing the POW reparations cases to proceed on the basis that the claims were moot under the treaty.

Other amendments adopted by voice vote with no debate changed the proposed passenger inspection fees from $3 to $1.50 for cruise ship passengers and from $7 to $6.50 for airline travelers, and incorporated a separate bill (S 1084) aimed at prohibiting the import of diamonds sold by rebel groups in several African countries. The Senate also amended the bill to set aside $2 million for grants to improve the election process, subject to authorization.

Conference/Final Action

A House-Senate conference committee approved the final $41.6 billion bill by voice vote Nov. 8. The House adopted the conference report (H Rept 107-278) on Nov. 14 by a vote of 411-15. The Senate cleared the measure the next day, 98-1. (*House vote 438, p. H-150; Senate vote 340, p. S-70*)

John McCain, R-Ariz., was the one senator to vote against the final bill. He said the measure contained too many special projects. Of the $62.4 million provided for construction at NIST, "$41.5 million is for non-construction related 'pork' projects," he said. Earlier in the year, the Bush administration had proposed eliminating Byrne law enforcement grants because nearly all of the money was earmarked by members of Congress every year. Conferees included $94.5 million for the grants — of which $86.2 million was earmarked for specific programs.

Major issues resolved in conference included:
● **Peacekeeping.** The bill provided $844 million, the amount requested by Bush and passed by the House, for international peace-keeping.
● **Slave labor.** In a major policy victory for State, the final bill dropped the provision that would have prohibited either State or Justice from spending taxpayer dollars to file briefs or motions challenging slave labor claims against Japanese companies from World War II. The provision had passed both chambers by wide margins. The conference report directed the State Department to try to work out some kind of agreement.
● **Immigration.** Conferees dropped the Senate provision that would have permanently extended the 245(i) program. Without the extension, would-be residents in those situations were required to return to their home countries to apply for residency, and since they had been in the United States illegally, other immigration laws could prevent their return for up to 10 years.
● **Passenger fees.** The bill adopted the House provision imposing a new $3 fee on cruise ship passengers and increasing from $6 to $7 the fee on airline passengers.
● **Background checks.** Like the House and Senate versions, the final bill simply required the destruction of gun records and did not require that they be held for a specific period of time.
● **Gun violence.** The bill provided $49.8 million for a new program to fight gun violence, including hiring and training local prosecutors. It also included $50 million for gun-safety locks. Bush had requested $75 million to provide gun locks to gun owners and $29 million for more prosecutors to handle gun-related crimes.
● **COPS.** Conferees agreed on $1.05 billion for the COPS program, $195 million more than Bush requested.
● **Faith-based initiatives.** Although Bush's plan to expand the ability of faith-based social organizations to get federal money for service programs ran into skepticism in Congress, the bill included $5 million to start five faith-based pilot programs in federal prisons to help inmates prepare for release. (*Faith-based initiatives, p. 17-3*)
● **Supreme Court renovation.** Conferees included $37.5 million of the $118 million requested by the court for renovations to its facility.
● **Small Business Administration.** The bill gave a major reprieve to the SBA, providing $739 million for the agency. Bush had called for $542 million, a cut of more than $300 million from fiscal 2001.
● **Anti-terrorism surveillance.** The Senate amendment giving law enforcement greater surveillance authority was dropped; it was no longer needed after Bush signed an anti-terrorism bill Oct. 26 (PL 107-56) that had many of the same provisions. (*Anti-terrorism, p. 14-3*)

In other provisions, the bill granted U.S. citizenship posthumously to people who died in the Sept. 11 attacks while they were in the process of becoming American citizens. It also authorized a pay raise for federal judges and appropriated $8.6 million to pay for it. It increased to $90 the hourly rate paid to federal defenders for work both in and out of the courtroom.

Among the programs targeted for cuts were law enforcement grants for state and local governments. The bill provided $400 million for the block grants, equal to Bush's request but $122 million less than in fiscal 2001. Conferees agreed to Bush's request that they eliminate grants to states for prison construction, which had totaled $685 million in fiscal 2001. However, a program to help reimburse states for the cost of incarcerating illegal immigrants who committed crime was increased to $565 million; Bush had requested $265 million. ◆

Anti-Terror Funds Slow Defense Bill

Congress cleared a $317.5 billion Defense Department spending bill for fiscal 2002 that postponed tough choices about the future shape of the military and funded nearly everything on the Pentagon's wish list — from Cold War-style weapons to equipment for unconventional battles. As was customary, the measure closely followed the outlines of the annual defense authorization bill (PL 107-107).

Still, the spending bill was dogged by controversy and delay, much of it tied to a separate fight between Congress and the Bush administration over emergency funding for counterterrorism and New York's recovery from the Sept. 11 terrorist attacks. The defense bill was not cleared until Dec. 20, the final day of the session, making it the last of the 13 regular appropriations measures sent to the White House. President Bush signed it into law (HR 3338 — PL 107-117) on Jan. 10, 2002.

The final bill was $1.9 billion less than Bush requested, but about the same amount as was approved by both the House and Senate. The total was almost $19 billion more than the fiscal 2001 level, including fiscal 2001 supplemental spending.

The measure had an inauspicious start. Members of the House Defense Appropriations Subcommittee were meeting in the Capitol to begin work on the bill the morning of Sept. 11, when the session was suddenly canceled and the building evacuated shortly after terrorists crashed jetliners into the World Trade Center and the Pentagon.

Nearly a month later, on Oct. 9, the subcommittee tried again, but again the session was canceled — this time to protest Bush's decision to limit the number of lawmakers who would be briefed on secret information about the administration's counterterrorism campaign. Leaks of information and published reports citing congressional sources infuriated Bush, who tried to restrict the closed sessions. The White House eventually relented, allowing key members of defense, foreign policy and intelligence oversight committees to be briefed in closed meetings.

The subcommittee finally met Oct. 10, approving the bill by voice vote. Members of the panel declined to provide any details, a reflection of the secretive atmosphere triggered by the dispute with the White House.

When the full House Appropriations Committee met Oct. 24 to consider the defense measure, the terrorist attacks and the subsequent U.S. and allied war in Afghanistan loomed large. "We have before us a defense bill that is a peacetime defense bill," complained David R. Obey of Wisconsin, the committee's ranking Democrat.

BoxScore 2002 Fiscal Year
Defense

Bill:
HR 3338 — PL 107-117
Legislative Action:
House passed HR 3338 (H Rept 107-298), 406-20, on Nov. 28.
Senate passed HR 3338, amended (S Rept 107-109), by voice vote Dec. 7.
House adopted the conference report (H Rept 107-350), 408-6, on Dec. 20.
Senate cleared the bill, 94-2, on Dec. 20.
President signed Jan. 10, 2002.

"We ain't at peace no more."

The committee included nearly $1.7 billion for anti-terrorism efforts by the Pentagon and CIA, including money to protect against cyberterror attacks on computers and to stockpile vaccines to respond to the potential threat of biological warfare.

Although the panel had completed the bill, Appropriations Committee Chairman C.W. Bill Young, R-Fla., delayed filing the measure with the House until appropriators decided what and how much to include in the fiscal 2001 supplemental spending package that was to be attached to the defense bill. The dispute over funds and how much spending authority to grant the president delayed both measures.

More than a month later, the House overwhelmingly passed a defense bill that only made changes at the margins to Bush's budget request. Paired with the bill was the $20 billion emergency spending package, with $7.3 billion to pay for the war in Afghanistan.

In the Senate, lawmakers added a provision that would allow the Air Force to dispose of 40-year-old refueling tankers and lease modified 767s from Boeing Co., a financial boon for the airline manufacturer hard hit by the downturn in the industry. While the deal had the backing of Boeing benefactors, including members of the Washington state delegation, some lawmakers derided it as a corporate buyout.

The Senate passed its version of the defense bill in early December, and House and Senate negotiators spent the final weeks of the session trying to resolve disagreements with the administration over the leasing deal and differences over shipbuilding.

Controversy remained even after Congress cleared the bill as some opponents of the leasing deal vowed not to let the issue rest.

Highlights

The defense bill included $60.8 billion for weapons procurement, $48.9 billion for research and development, $105 billion for operations and maintenance, $82 billion for personnel and $18.4 billion for military-related health programs.

The following are major components of the measure:
● **Missile defense.** $7.8 billion for development of a missile defense system — about 50 percent above the fiscal 2001 level, but nearly $500 million less than Bush requested for the signature program in his national security plans. Arguing that the Pentagon was rushing development of a missile

Where the Money Goes

Defense Spending

(figures are in thousands of dollars of new budget authority)

	Fiscal 2001 Appropriation	Fiscal 2002 Bush Request	House Bill	Senate Bill	Conference Report
Military personnel	$75,847,740	$82,307,281	$81,617,291	$81,965,391	$82,056,651
Operation and maintenance	96,889,774	106,788,645	105,282,379	106,449,689	105,047,644
Procurement	59,232,846	60,440,297	60,190,124	60,881,434	60,864,948
Research and development	41,359,605	47,429,433	40,090,256	46,006,678	48,921,641
Revolving and management funds	4,157,857	2,458,394	1,937,694	2,234,394	1,745,394
Other Defense Department programs	14,114,424	20,024,928	20,349,862	20,498,963	20,491,353
Counterterrorism	—	—	11,719,889	—	881,000
Miscellaneous and rescissions	–4,227,773	–299,638	–3,953,335	–852,842	–2,832,813
GRAND TOTAL	**$298,515,154**	**$319,547,116**	**$317,624,089**	**$317,623,483**	**$317,623,747**
Total adjusted for scorekeeping	$298,515,154	$319,397,116	$317,474,089	$317,473,483	$317,473,747

TABLE: House Appropriations Committee

detection system designated SBIRS Low, the bill provided $250 million of the $385 million requested and ordered the military to go back to the drawing board.

● **Military pay raise.** A 4.6 percent pay increase for military personnel, which was specified in the fiscal 2002 defense authorization bill, as well as targeted pay raises for a variety of enlisted personnel and officer grades.

● **Active duty personnel.** A ceiling on the number of active duty personnel at 1,387,400, equal to the president's request. The number was 4,983 above the fiscal 2001 level.

● **Tanker leasing.** Authority for the Air Force to lease new, modified 767s from Boeing at a cost of $20 billion over 10 years. The 100 leased planes would replace the fleet of 40-year-old refueling tankers.

● **F-22 Raptor.** $2.6 billion for 13 of the Air Force's next generation fighter plane, designed to replace the F-16, plus $882 million for research and development.

● **Joint Strike Fighter.** $1.5 billion for development of the multi-role aircraft, about the amount sought by the administration. Three versions of the fighter were slated to replace several 1970s-vintage planes used by the Navy, Air Force and Marine Corps. The Pentagon had selected Lockheed Martin to build the plane.

● **F/A-18 E/F.** $3 billion for 48 of the next general Navy fighter jet, the Navy's upgrade of the existing F/A-18 C/D.

● **Destroyers.** $3 billion for three DDG-51 Arleigh Burke-class guided-missile destroyers, as requested.

● **Shipbuilding conversion.** $324 million to allow the Navy to convert four Trident submarines, rather than two, to carry dozens of Tomahawk cruise missiles each.

● **New attack submarine.** $1.6 billion, as requested, to buy the fourth boat in the Virginia class of new attack submarines to replace the retiring Los Angeles-class submarines.

● **Counterterrorism.** $881 million for a new account devoted to activities to counter terrorism and other nonconventional threats.

● **Russian nuclear security.** $403 million to help dismantle nuclear weapons in the former Soviet Union.

Background

The fiscal 2002 budget that Bush submitted to Congress in April included a $310.5 billion placeholder for defense, contingent on a comprehensive review of military needs undertaken by Defense Secretary Donald H. Rumsfeld. During the presidential campaign, candidate Bush had promised to increase defense spending, arguing that the Clinton administration had underfunded the military and stretched the services with too many missions. The fiscal 2002 budget resolution (H Con Res 83), allowed for $325.1 billion. *(Bush budget, p. 5-3; budget resolution, p. 5-7)*

Many in Congress expected a significant boost beyond that, once Rumsfeld finished his assessment. Bush requested an additional $18.4 billion for defense in June, bringing the total to about $343.5 billion. Most of the money was earmarked for pay, medical care, facilities and other routine operating expenses. Defense hawks were disappointed, but the appropriators pushed ahead.

The Sept. 11 attacks, the campaign against terrorism and the sudden war-footing significantly altered the budget dynamic, postponing the hard choices on where to spend money. While the appropriations bill was less than Bush's request, the Pentagon got an additional $7.2 billion in the supplemental spending bill.

Legislative Action

House Subcommittee, Committee Action

The House Appropriations Committee gave voice vote approval to a $317.5 billion defense bill (HR 3338 — H Rept 107-298) on Oct. 24. The Defense Subcommittee had approved a draft by voice vote Oct. 10, but declined to provide information on the measure. The committee met again Nov. 14 to vote on the details of the $20 billion supplemental package, after which the report was finally filed.

During the Oct. 24 markup, subcommittee Chairman Jerry Lewis, R-Calif., and John P. Murtha of Pennsylvania,

the panel's senior Democrat, insisted that the military needed significantly more money than the bill could provide. Under the tight discretionary budget ceiling, part of the funds had been diverted to cover defense needs under the military construction bill (PL 107-64) and the energy and water spending bill (PL 107-66).

Within the bill's total, the appropriators also made room for nearly $1.7 billion for extra anti-terrorism operations by the Pentagon and the CIA. The add-ons included $275 million to improve the Defense Department's ability to protect against cyberterror attacks on computer networks vital to the military and essential public services, and $299 million to develop and stockpile vaccines and antibiotics to cope with biological weapons. The additional funds also included $156 million to train military personnel to deal with nuclear, chemical or biological attacks.

The $1.7 billion increase in anti-terrorism funds was mostly offset by across-the-board cuts of more than $1.5 billion that the committee ordered the Defense Department to absorb by reducing the payroll at headquarters, hiring fewer consultants and cutting back on the use of government credit cards for small purchases.

The bill also added $70 million to Bush's $996 million request for chemical and biological defense programs, and $75 million to accelerate the development of defenses against terrorist attacks using small nuclear weapons.

Among the items in the spending bill was continued development of the 40-ton Crusader mobile cannon at a cost of $23 million each. The legislation provided the $448 million requested to continue developing the Crusader, which was supposed to be operational by 2008. Army officials, who wanted 480 of the cannons at a cost of $11 billion, insisted that the new gun was necessary because the existing one lacked the range of enemy artillery.

The bill included several congressional add-ons that would help the military fight the unconventional battle it was waging in Afghanistan. Some of the money would be used to improve the military's ability to strike distant targets by allowing long-range stealth bombers to drop precision-guided "smart" bombs on more targets during a single mission. The rest would provide commanders with more information about the enemy by modernizing the Air Force's aging fleet of long-range surveillance planes and complementing it with remotely piloted drone aircraft, or unmanned aerial vehicles (UAVs).

The committee made relatively minor changes to the amounts requested for hundreds of procurement and research programs. However, there were a few significant initiatives. The committee:

• Added $340 million to test the feasibility of using modified Boeing 767 jetliners to replace hundreds of aging midair refueling tankers and various types of large electronic eavesdropping and radar planes. The plan was promoted by Air Force Chief of Staff Gen. John Jumper and Defense Appropriations Subcommittee member Norm Dicks, D-Wash., a tireless advocate for Boeing, his state's economic linchpin.

• Trimmed $67 million from the $2.88 billion requested for 15 Boeing-built C-17 long-range cargo jets. But the committee added $180 million to lay the groundwork for buying more C-17s than the 134 being planned.

• Slashed to $150 million the $643 million requested to continue designing a new class of Navy vessel, the first of which was slated for funding in 2005. The ships, designed to bomb distant land targets with long-range guns and missiles, would incorporate new technologies allowing them to operate with a crew of fewer than 100, less than a third of the number being used by similar vessels.

• Added $820 million for a fourth Aegis destroyer, in addition to the $3 billion requested for three vessels.

• Added $463 million to accelerate the conversion of four submarines, built to carry Trident long-range nuclear missiles, to carry 154 Tomahawk land-attack cruise missiles apiece. The administration sought $86 million.

House Floor Action

On Nov. 28, with U.S. forces fighting in Afghanistan, the House passed the $317.5 billion defense bill by a vote of 406-20. With many of the legislative fights having already played out on the defense authorization bill, much of the floor debate focused on the emergency spending package. (*House vote 458, p. H-158*)

Overall, the defense bill's adjustments to Bush's budget request were at the margins. "Sometimes it is very difficult to separate the boys from the toys," Lewis said in an interview Nov. 28.

An amendment by Bob Filner, D-Calif., that would have required the government to pay the difference in salaries for federal employees called to active duty as members of the National Guard or reserves, was ruled out of order for violating the House rule barring legislation on an appropriations bill. Filner appealed the ruling, but it was upheld by a vote of 275-141. (*House vote 456, p. H-156*)

Senate Committee Action

The Senate Appropriations Committee approved a $317 billion version of the defense bill (S Rept 107-109) by voice vote Dec. 4. The measure largely tracked Bush's request, but the panel took at least one step that angered the administration, slashing $600 million from the $2.8 billion requested for operations in Bosnia and Kosovo.

"Without these funds, the department may be unable to meet emerging requirements either in the Balkans or for unforeseen costs in Operation Enduring Freedom" in Afghanistan, the administration said in a Dec. 6 statement. The committee argued that the cut would have no impact on U.S. forces overseas because the Defense Department had hundreds of millions of dollars left in its Balkans operations account and the number of troops involved in the region had declined steadily.

Far more contentious was a decision by Senate appropriators to allow the Air Force to lease 100 Boeing 767s for the crucial mission of refueling aircraft in midair. Under the Senate plan, the Air Force would be able to dispose of 136 smaller Boeing tankers that had become very expensive to maintain after four decades of hard use.

The delegation from Washington state vigorously supported the plan, pushing the Air Force's argument that the 767s would be cheaper to operate than the aging tankers. Proponents of the plan, including Ted Stevens of Alaska, ranking Republican on the Defense Appropriations Subcommittee, argued that the leasing arrangement would reduce the initial cost of the program.

Critics feared that the relatively low short-term cost would mask a higher price tag in the long run. John McCain, R-Ariz., assailed the plan as a "sweet deal . . . that I'm sure is the envy of corporate lobbyists from one end of K St. to the other."

Office of Management and Budget (OMB) Director Mitchell E. Daniels Jr. strongly opposed a proposal to lease the planes for 20 years, arguing that it would cost more than buying the aircraft.

Senate Floor Action

The Senate passed the $317 billion bill by voice vote Dec. 7, following two days of debate. Once again, the focus was on supplemental spending for homeland defense and the cost of helping New York recover from the terrorist attacks. Robert C. Byrd, D-W.Va., was thwarted in an attempt to add $15 billion in emergency spending beyond the $20 billion in the bill, after Bush threatened to veto the entire defense measure.

Like the House version, the Senate defense bill provided the Pentagon with virtually everything it sought, but there were still several contentious issues.

The Senate adopted, 78-21, an amendment by Jesse Helms, R-N.C., to restrict U.S. participation in U.N. peacekeeping operations unless U.S. troops were exempted from prosecution by a proposed International Criminal Court. Helms also proposed to bar U.S. military aid to countries unless they signed agreements to shield U.S. troops from being handed over to the court. (*Senate vote 359, p. S-74*)

The court was supposed to handle war crimes and other human rights violations, but U.S. military leaders and many lawmakers worried that it would expose U.S. troops to politically motivated accusations and trials.

A counter amendment by Christopher J. Dodd, D-Conn., that would have permitted significant U.S. cooperation with the court to try war criminals was rejected, 51-48. (*Senate vote 358, p. S-74*)

By voice vote, the Senate adopted dozens of minor amendments, including 73 that would earmark a total of $438 million for specific projects. Most of them stated only that the specified amount "may" be used for a particular program, but three were mandatory. They were:

• By Richard G. Lugar, R-Ind., to restore $46 million that the committee had cut from the administration's $403 million request for the so-called Nunn-Lugar program intended to help former Soviet republics dispose of nuclear, chemical and biological weapons.

• By Robert G. Torricelli, D-N.J., to provide $9.8 million to buy digital recorders for Navy patrol planes.

• By Torricelli to provide $2 million to Green Tree Chemical Technologies which, according to the senator, had lost money because of a failed Pentagon effort to centralize gunpowder production in a consortium that would have shut out the small firm in Sayreville, N.J.

Of the 73 amendments, only two involved more than $10 million. More than two-thirds of them involved $5 million or less.

One of those amendments, by Christopher S. Bond, R-Mo., and Jean Carnahan, D-Mo., provided up to $1.5 million for a study of the risks of having too few companies competing to build combat jets for the Pentagon. Their concern was that the St. Louis-based division of Boeing, which built fighter planes, would be forced out of business after losing the competition to build the Joint Strike Fighter to Lockheed Martin in October.

Conference/Final Action

An agreement to allow the Air Force to lease new, modified Boeing 767s to replace its 40-year-old refueling tankers cleared the way for House and Senate conferees to sign off on a final defense bill Dec. 18. The House agreed to the conference report (H Rept 107-350) by a vote of 408-6 on Dec. 20, and the Senate cleared the bill hours later, 94-2. (*House vote 510, p. H-174; Senate vote 380, p. S-77*)

Boeing's decision months earlier to move its corporate headquarters from Seattle to Chicago had gained the aircraft builder a powerful patron — House Speaker J. Dennis Hastert, R-Ill. Washington's congressional delegation had remained loyal to Boeing, which maintained jet plants in Puget Sound, and they lobbied hard to get the $20 billion deal in the defense bill that would allow the Air Force to lease the tankers for the next 10 years. The idea faced hurdles, including resistance from OMB. But several meetings, and the support of Hastert, sealed the deal.

In other major decisions, conferees:

• **Missile defense.** Agreed to provide $7.8 billion of $8.3 billion request by Bush to develop and field anti-missile defenses. The Pentagon was required to overhaul development of the SBIRS-Low program, a fleet of satellites carrying infrared telescopes to detect attacking missiles and help steer intercepting rockets. Arguing that the program was plagued with delays, technical shortcomings and cost overruns, the conferees provided $250 million of the $385 million requested.

It also provided $100 million to pay the contract termination costs for a Navy anti-missile program that the Pentagon canceled Dec. 14.

The bill met the president's request for $3.2 billion for ground-based midcourse defense programs, $1.4 billion above the fiscal 2001 level. The total included $786 million in advanced funding for the Pacific missile defense test bed, including upgrades and construction at Fort Greely, Alaska.

• **B-2.** Provided $155 million, as requested, to improve the capability of the B-2 stealth bomber, plus an additional $63 million for a data link to allow the planes to exchange targeting data with other U.S. aircraft, ships and ground units. The House had proposed cutting the funds by $80 million.

• **Shipbuilding.** Met the Navy's requests for its major shipbuilding programs, including $3 billion for three Aegis destroyers, $267 million to continue work on a helicopter carrier and $371 million for a supply ship.

• **UAVs.** Provided $250 million more than requested for UAVs, reflecting widespread consensus among House and Senate negotiators over the development of remotely piloted vehicles for reconnaissance. In Afghanistan, the drones were being equipped successfully with laser-guided missiles for combat.

• **C-17s.** Trimmed $36 million from the $2.9 billion requested for 15 additional C-17 wide-body, long-range cargo jets, but added $143 million as a first installment toward buying more of the Boeing-built planes than the 134 already purchased or included in budget plans.

• **Osprey.** Provided $1 billion for procurement of nine V-22 Ospreys for the Marine Corps and two of the aircraft for the Special Operations Forces. Despite two crashes involving the tilt-rotor aircraft that killed 23 people in 2000, the Pentagon and Congress continued to buy more of the controversial tilt-rotor aircraft.

• **Aegis destroyers.** Agreed to Bush's request for $3 billion for three Aegis-class destroyers, and added $125 million in advanced funding for a fourth ship. The House bill had included $820 million for the fourth ship, with lawmakers arguing that a new boat was needed to keep the two shipbuilding yards in Mississippi and Maine busy because of delays in designing a new class of destroyers.

• **Crusader cannon.** $448 million, as the president requested, to continue developing the 40-ton Crusader mobile cannon. ◆

D.C. Bill Allows Partners' Benefits

The $408 million fiscal 2002 District of Columbia appropriations bill, the smallest of the 13 annual spending bills, cleared Dec. 7 with little of the rancorous debate that typically accompanies the measure. President Bush signed the bill, which also approved the city's $7.15 billion annual budget, on Dec. 21 (HR 2944 — PL 107-96).

Early signs were that the bill would once again be caught up in contentious efforts to direct District policies on various social issues. But appropriators did not begin work until early September, and the Sept. 11 terrorist attacks quickly cooled partisan debate in Congress, facilitating passage of the D.C. bill in both chambers.

The total appropriation equaled that approved by the Senate. It was $10 million more than the House had recommended and $49 million more than Bush's request, but $56 million below the fiscal 2001 level.

In a victory for home-rule advocates, the bill permitted the city for the first time to use local, though not federal, money to implement a 1992 D.C. law that allowed city employee health plans to provide benefits to unmarried and same-sex domestic partners. The measure was not entirely friendly to local interests, however. It prohibited the use of either local or federal money for the District's needle-exchange program for drug addicts. It also barred the city from using local or federal money to lobby for statehood.

Despite White House objections, conferees dropped a Senate provision that would have continued a cap on the fees that plaintiffs' attorneys could collect in cases brought against the District's public school system for violations of the Individuals with Disabilities Education Act.

Highlights

The following were the main spending components of the bill:

• **D.C. courts.** $112 million — just over $7 million more than fiscal 2001, but less than $1 million more than Bush's request. The total included $66 million for the Superior Court, $32 million for the District of Columbia Court System, $6.5 million for capital improvements to courthouse facilities and $8 million for the Court of Appeals. The bill provided an additional $24 million for carrying out the District of Columbia Family Court Act

• **Corrections Trustee operations.** $30 million — significantly less than the $134 million appropriated in fiscal 2001, and $2.5 million below Bush's request. The reduction was due to the closure of the Lorton prison, which closed Nov. 19,

---

BoxScore 2002
District of Columbia — Fiscal Year

Bill:
HR 2944 — PL 107-96

Legislative Action:

House passed HR 2944 (H Rept 107-216), 327-88, on Sept. 25.

Senate passed HR 2944, amended (S Rept 107-85), 75-24, on Nov. 7.

House adopted the conference report (H Rept 107-321), 302-84, on Dec. 6.

Senate cleared HR 2944, 79-20, on Dec. 7.

President signed Dec. 21.

2001. Congress established the corrections trustee in 1997 to exercise financial oversight over all aspects of the District's Department of Corrections.

• **Court Defender Services.** $34 million — matching Bush's request and nearly the same as in fiscal 2001. The bill increased the hourly pay rate for court-appointed attorneys for indigents from $50 to $65 and for investigators from $10 to $25.

• **Court Services and Offender Supervision.** $147 million — consistent with Bush's request and $35 million more than in fiscal 2001. The Court Services and Offender Agency was established in 1997 to prevent crime and reduce recidivism by reorganizing and running pretrial services, parole, and adult probation and offender supervision.

• **Tuition support.** $17 million — equal to fiscal 2001 appropriations and Bush's request. The college resident tuition program allowed D.C. residents to pay in-state tuition rates at colleges and universities outside the District.

• **Emergency response planning.** $16.1 million — $12.7 million of it to fund the design and implementation of an emergency response plan for the District. The remaining $3.4 million was to reimburse the city for what it had already spent on preparing for the World Bank and International Monetary Fund (IMF) meetings that were scheduled for September in Washington but canceled due to security concerns after the Sept. 11 terrorist attacks.

Background

For many years, the District received a federal payment as compensation for the costs of hosting the federal government, whose properties are not subject to local taxes. In 1997, the payment was replaced by an arrangement in which the federal government assumed responsibilities comparable to those of a state government. The change was enacted under the 1997 reconciliation spending bill (PL 105-33) and the companion tax bill (PL 105-34). (*1997 Almanac, p. 3-10*)

The District's bill often was among the last to move through Congress because of the riders it attracted on controversial social issues such as medical marijuana, the city's needle-exchange program for drug addicts and funding for abortion. When the fiscal 2001 D.C. bill cleared as a stand-alone measure (PL 106-522) in November 2000, it was the first time that had happened since 1997. The $445 million measure ($464 million was ultimately appropriated for fiscal 2001) had been combined with the bill for the departments of Commerce, Justice and State (CJS) but was split off at the last

Where the Money Goes

District of Columbia Spending

(figures are in thousands of dollars of new budget authority)

	Fiscal 2001 Appropriation	Fiscal 2002 Bush Request	House Bill	Senate Bill	Conference Report
D.C. courts	$105,000	$111,378	$111,238	$140,181	$112,180
Corrections Trustee operations	134,200	32,700	32,700	32,700	30,200
Court Defender Services	34,387	34,311	34,311	39,311	34,311
Court Services and Offender Supervision	112,527	147,300	147,300	147,300	147,300
Tuition support	17,000	17,000	17,000	17,000	17,000
Total federal funds	464,125	358,607	398,058	408,000	408,000
TOTAL D.C. Budget	$6,774,159	$7,144,312	$7,146,437	$7,154,201	$7,150,716

TABLE: House, Senate Appropriation committees

minute because the CJS add-on brought with it a veto threat of the whole bill. One of the last issues resolved concerned needle exchanges. Rep. Todd Tiahrt, R-Kan., tried to block the program from operating within 1,000 feet of any area where children gather; conferees eventually agreed to ban it within 1,000 feet of city schools. (*2000 Almanac, p. 2-54*)

Legislative Action

House Subcommittee Action

The House D.C. Appropriations Subcommittee approved a $398 million draft of the fiscal 2002 bill by voice vote Sept. 6. The funding was $66.1 million below the fiscal 2001 level. Still, it exceeded the subcommittee's spending allocation by $16 million to fund a last-minute request by Bush to pay for security for the IMF and World Bank meetings in Washington. Subcommittee Chairman Joe Knollenberg, R-Mich., said the bill met the District's requests dollar for dollar; it also approved the city's own $7.1 billion budget.

Knollenberg asked members to hold their controversial amendments for the full committee markup, and none were offered. But ranking Democrat Chaka Fattah of Pennsylvania made it clear the bill would not advance further without more rigorous debate, particularly over provisions barring local or federal funding for abortion services and the city's needle-exchange program.

House Committee Action

The full Appropriations Committee approved the bill (H Rept 107-216) by voice vote Sept. 20, nine days after the terrorist attacks.

The full committee's version included $16.1 million for emergency security planning. Ranking Democrat David R. Obey of Wisconsin introduced the amendment, saying the Sept. 11 attacks had illustrated how unprepared D.C. was for such an event. He proposed that D.C. get $4.6 million immediately to develop an emergency plan and $3.4 million as reimbursement for money already spent preparing for the World Bank-IMF meetings. The remaining $8 million would be withheld until the city submitted an emergency security plan to the federal government. Half the money for a

tuition reimbursement program and other small programs would be withheld pending receipt of the plan. The amendment was adopted by voice vote.

In the spirit of unity that prevailed in Congress after the attacks, appropriators generally avoided controversial social policy amendments. Nearly half the legislative riders long opposed by local leaders were dropped in the committee. Many of them dealt with the city's financial management; their removal was due to the Districts' improved financial situation, which also resulted in the dissolution of the financial control board that had overseen the city's finances since 1995.

However, the panel did give voice vote approval to an amendment by Jim Kolbe, R-Ariz., to allow the city to use local money to allow D.C. employee health plans to provide benefits to unmarried domestic partners.

House Floor Action

The House passed the bill, 327-88, on Sept. 25, after rejecting an amendment to reverse the committee language on domestic partner benefits. The amendment, by Dave Weldon, R-Fla., was defeated 194-226. As passed, the bill allowed the District to spend local, but not federal, money on the benefits. (*House votes 352, 355, p. H-122*)

The House adopted, 262-152, an amendment to bar use of funds in the bill to enforce a ruling by the D.C. Commission on Human Rights that the Boy Scouts of America should reinstate and compensate two adult Boy Scouts who were dismissed because they were gay. (*House vote 354, p. H-122*)

Del. Eleanor Holmes Norton, D-D.C., wrote an amendment to remove the bill's 34 general provisions, including the prohibitions on spending money for needle-exchange programs and abortions. But she withdrew it, saying she had gotten assurances from Knollenberg that he would try to eliminate most of the riders before the bill went to conference.

Senate Committee Action

The Senate Appropriations Committee approved a $408 million version of the bill (S 1543 — S Rept 107-85) on Oct. 1. The vote was 16-13, with only one Republican, Arlen Specter of Pennsylvania, supporting the measure. Like the House bill, the Senate version called for allowing D.C. to use local funds to pay health benefits to

unmarried domestic partners.

The bill also allowed the District to use local, though not federal, money for federal and state lobbying and for needle-exchange programs. Neither use was allowed under the House bill. Like the House, the Senate retained an existing ban on local and federal funding of abortion services.

The bill included $16.1 million for the District to establish an emergency response plan, but it did not seek to withhold any funding until the city submitted its proposal. It approved a $7.2 billion budget for the District, itself, almost $8 million more than in the House bill.

Senate Floor Action

The Senate passed HR 2944 by a vote of 75-24 on Nov. 7, after substituting the text of the Senate bill. By a 53-47 vote, the Senate tabled, or killed, an attempt by George Allen, R-Va., to restore the bill's provision banning the use of local money for needle-exchange programs. The White House supported its inclusion. *(Senate votes 328, 331, pp. S-68, S-69)*

Republicans did win one victory for the White House when the Senate voted, 51-49, to adopt a proposal by Kay Bailey Hutchison, R-Texas, to continue the cap on plaintiffs' attorney's fees. Richard J. Durbin, D-Ill., quickly followed up with a proposal to lift the cap if the lawsuit was brought by a child who had been judged neglected or abused, had a parent who was a disabled veteran, or was from a family with an annual income of less than $17,600. His amendment was adopted, 73-26. *(Senate votes 329, 330, p. S-69)*

Conference/Final Action

It was nearly a month before conferees finished work on the bill, but once they did, it moved rapidly. The conference report (H Rept 107-321) was filed the evening of Dec. 5; the House adopted it, 302-84, on Dec. 6; and the Senate cleared the bill, 79-20, the next day. *(House vote 482, p. H-164; Senate vote 356, p. S-74)*

The resolution of social policy issues generally favored the House. Conferees adopted the House language continuing the ban on local and federal money for needle-exchange programs. They dropped the Senate provision allowing the use of local money to lobby Congress for statehood. And, despite White House objections, they removed the Senate provision that would have continued the cap on plaintiffs' attorney's fees.

House language withholding portions of the $16.1 million for emergency planning was not included. All funding was made available immediately, with quarterly reports on progress expected.

The House amendment on the D.C. Human Rights Commission ruling on the Boy Scouts was retained, as was the language allowing the use of local money for domestic partner health benefits. As in past years, the agreement continued the prohibition on the use of local or federal funds for abortions, except to save the life of the woman or in cases of rape or incest. It also continued language blocking a District initiative on the legalization of marijuana for medical treatment from taking effect. ◆

Cuts Restored in Energy-Water Bill

The fiscal 2002 energy and water development appropriations bill provided $24.6 billion, a $2.1 billion increase over the president's request. A last-minute attempt to add money for non-proliferation programs to keep nuclear materials out of the hands of terrorists was blocked, though appropriators promised to find another way to provide the money. President Bush signed the bill into law (HR 2311 — PL 107-66) on Nov. 12.

The bill funds the Energy Department's defense and non-defense programs, the Army Corps of Engineers, the Interior Department's water programs in Western states and programs of several related agencies. Of the money Congress added, $1.2 billion was for Energy Department nuclear weapons programs, a priority for several influential senators. Another $680 million was added for water projects, which are a favorite of House members.

Controversy over a Corps of Engineers plan to release water from upstream dams on the Missouri River in spring to help endangered wildlife was settled in the Senate, with lawmakers agreeing on language requiring the corps to explore alternatives. The compromise was subsequently adopted in conference.

Before conference, another potential fight loomed over funding for technical work at Nevada's Yucca Mountain, 100 miles northwest of Las Vegas, which the Energy Department was studying as the burial site for high-level waste from the nation's nuclear power plants.

Harry Reid, D-Nev., chairman of the Senate Energy and Water Appropriations Subcommittee and a fierce opponent of the Yucca Mountain project, wanted to cut funding to $275 million, but he and other conferees agreed to provide $375 million, still $70 million below what Bush sought.

The main issue in conference became whether to increase spending for Energy Department counterproliferation programs. The final bill included $804 million, $30 million more than Bush requested but less than either the House or Senate had approved and $69 million less than enacted for fiscal 2001. Democrats tried unsuccessfully to get the conference to add more money.

The bill's $24.6 billion total, which included scorekeeping adjustments, was $573 million above the fiscal 2001 level. Bush, by contrast, had sought $1.2 billion less than the previous level, arguing that many of the water projects in the fiscal 2001 bill were wasteful. Congress brushed off such concerns, as it had in previous years.

BoxScore **2002** Fiscal Year

Energy-Water Projects

Bill:
HR 2311 — PL 107-66
Legislative Action:
House passed HR 2311
(H Rept 107-112), 405-15, on
June 28.
Senate passed HR 2311,
amended (S Rept 107-39), 97-
2, on July 19.
House adopted the conference
report (H Rept 107-258), 399-
29, on Nov 1.
Senate cleared the bill, 96-2,
on Nov. 1.
President signed Nov. 12.

Highlights

Major spending components in the bill included:

• **Corps of Engineers.** $4.5 billion for the corps, which builds and maintains civil works projects for flood control, navigation, storm damage reduction and environmental restoration. States and local governments share the costs of federal water control projects. The bill exceeded Bush's request by $586 million, though it was $200 million below the fiscal 2001 level.

• **Interior Department.** $914 million for water projects, much of it ($815 million) for the Bureau of Reclamation, which is charged with managing water and related resources in the Western states. Projects include irrigation, water supply, hydroelectric power generation, flood control, recreation and wildlife habitat protection. The total was nearly $100 more than Bush's request and the fiscal 2001 level.

• **Energy Department.** $19.5 billion, $1.4 billion more than Bush sought and an $877 million increase over fiscal 2001. The total included funding for regulating domestic energy industries, managing nuclear waste and researching and developing energy technologies. But nearly 75 percent of the department's funding ($14.5 billion) was for nuclear weapons programs. The bill included $396 million for renewable energy programs — $120 million more than requested and $20 million more than the fiscal 2001 level.

Background

The energy and water bill typically is one of the least controversial of the regular appropriations bills, though disagreements sometimes arise between the House — where members want the bill to focus on water projects, including earmarked provisions for their districts — and the Senate — where members often view such projects as "pork" and would rather focus on nuclear weapons programs.

The fiscal 2001 bill, however, was caught up in an unusually contentious debate over language added in the Senate that would have prevented the administration from adopting a new Missouri River management plan that emphasized wildlife over navigation. The Fish and Wildlife Service recommended in 2000 that more water be released from upstream dams in the spring and less in the summer, providing additional habitat for endangered species. Lawmakers from downstream states argued that changing the springtime flow could cause flooding and impede barge traffic.

President Bill Clinton cited the provision in vetoing the

Where the Money Goes

Energy and Water Spending

(figures are in thousands of dollars of new budget authority)

	Fiscal 2001 Appropriation	Fiscal 2002 Bush Request	House Bill	Senate Bill	Conference Report
Corps of Engineers (Defense Department)	$4,686,565	$3,900,000	$4,468,233	$4,305,474	$4,486,096
Interior Department	816,637	819,727	842,890	884,226	914,261
Energy Department	18,623,901	18,106,554	18,747,360	20,061,975	19,501,126
Atomic Energy Defense Activities	(13,745,329)	(13,355,167)	(13,875,363)	(15,088,547)	(14,538,500)
Independent Agencies	171,474	181,721	136,517	197,162	184,517
Contingent Emergency Supplemental	213,988	—	—	—	—
Rescissions	– 172,000	—	—	—	—
GRAND TOTAL	$24,512,565	$23,008,002	$24,195,000	$25,448,837	$25,086,000
Total adjusted for scorekeeping	($24,022,583)	($22,518,002)	($23,705,000)	($24,958,837)	($24,596,000)

TABLE: House Appropriations Committee

first version of the bill; the language ultimately was dropped and the revised bill was enacted as part of the year-end omnibus spending bill (PL 106-377). (*2000 Almanac, p. 2-59*)

Republicans tried to use the issue in the 2000 elections against Democratic candidate and then-Vice President Al Gore in key downstream states such as Missouri.

Legislative Action

House Subcommittee Action

The fiscal 2002 bill began in the House Energy and Water Development Appropriations Subcommittee, which approved a $23.7 billion draft in a closed markup June 19. The subcommittee first adopted an amendment by Tom Latham, R-Iowa, to block the corps from implementing the Missouri River plan. The draft and the amendment were both approved by voice vote.

The draft added $1.2 billion to Bush's request, substantially increasing money for renewable energy programs and corps water projects. Subcommittee Chairman Sonny Callahan, R-Ala., said he particularly wanted to increase funding for beach repair, erosion control and other corps projects. The bill provided $4.5 billion for the corps, a 15 percent increase over Bush's request.

The subcommittee approved $843 million, $23 million more than requested, for the Interior Department. However, it did not include funding for unauthorized projects, including the California Bay-Delta Restoration Program (CALFED), a massive water program whose authorization expired in 2000.

Reviving a decades-old debate over flood control on California's American River, the subcommittee included a provision requiring a reassessment of the the Auburn Dam, a project authorized by Congress in 1965 but halted a decade later after an earthquake raised safety concerns. Under the bill, a corps study on improving the 45-year-old Folsom Dam on the American River would be delayed pending the reassessment of Auburn.

The subcommittee approved $18.7 billion for the Energy Department, compared with $18.6 appropriated in fiscal 2001 and $18.1 requested by Bush. The panel rejected cuts that Bush proposed in renewable energy programs, approving $377 million, $100 million more than requested and roughly equal to the fiscal 2001 level. The panel also added $72 million to the administration's request for programs to reduce the spread of nuclear weapons, bringing the total to $845 million.

House Full Committee Action

The full Appropriations Committee approved the bill (HR 2311 — H Rept 107-112) by voice vote June 25. The measure was virtually unchanged from subcommittee.

Callahan won voice vote approval for an amendment to bar the Federal Energy Regulatory Commission from financing construction of the Gulfstream Natural Gas Project, a 735-mile pipeline that would take natural gas from Callahan's district on the Alabama coast to the Tampa Bay area. Callahan was angry over an amendment to the House Interior spending bill (HR 2217) that would block oil and gas exploration in the Gulf of Mexico in waters that lay within Alabama's boundaries but were less then 30 miles from Pensacola, Fla. Florida Gov. Jeb Bush and the Florida congressional delegation argued that the drilling would be too near the tourist-friendly beaches of Florida's panhandle. (*Interior, p. 2-30*)

House Floor Action

The House easily passed the $23.7 billion bill, 405-15, on June 28, after adding language to ban any new drilling beneath the Great Lakes. (*House vote 206, p. H-76*)

The drilling ban, proposed by Minority Whip David E. Bonior, D-Mich., was adopted, 265-157, with 70 Republicans, many from the Midwest, breaking ranks to support it. The proposal barred the use of funds in the bill to issue permits for directional or "slant" drilling of wells on land near the lakes to tap potential reservoirs of oil and gas. Majority Whip Tom DeLay, R-Texas, called the amend-

ment "environmental extremism," decrying what he said were Democratic efforts "to systematically choke off every promising source of domestic energy." Bonior said drilling risked contaminating the drinking water and despoiling the shoreline. (*House vote 203, p. H-74*)

The vote followed by the House's overwhelming rejection one week earlier of Bush's proposals for increased oil and gas exploration on federal lands in the fiscal 2001 Interior spending bill.

Defying Bush on another issue, the House defeated, 84-333, an amendment by Tom Tancredo, R-Colo., that would have required local governments to pay 65 percent of the cost of beach restoration projects by the Corps of Engineers. Bush had asked for a similar change in the existing formula, which required the federal government to pay for 65 percent of beach repairs. (*House vote 200, p. H-74*)

The House rejected, 210-213, an attempt by Jim Davis, D-Fla., to remove Callahan's Gulf Stream amendment from the bill. (*House vote 205, p. H-76*)

The House also rejected amendments by:

• Dennis J. Kucinich, D-Ohio, to increase funding for nuclear nonproliferation activities by $66 million, and cut funding for the Energy Department's National Ignition Facility, a giant laser under construction at California's Lawrence Livermore National Laboratory, by $122.5 million. Rejected 91-331. (*House vote 202, p. H-74*)

• Maurice D. Hinchey, D-N.Y., to increase spending on renewable energy programs by $50 million and cut $60 million from nuclear weapons programs. Rejected 163-258. (*House vote 201, p. H-74*)

• Tancredo, to increase funding for renewable energy by $8.9 million and cut the Corps' budget. Rejected 39-372. (*House vote 199, p. H-74*)

• Shelley Berkeley, D-Nev., to transfer $500,000 within the Energy Department to study transportation routes to Yucca Mountain. Rejected 102-321. (*House vote 204, p. H-74*)

In hopes of reducing controversy on the bill, House leaders had removed the Auburn Dam provision before bringing the measure to the floor.

Senate Committee Action

The $25 billion Senate version of the bill (S 1171 — S Rept 107-39) moved quickly through the Energy and Water Development Subcommittee and the full Appropriations Committee on July 12. Both panels approved the measure by voice vote. Hoping to pre-empt a floor fight over the Missouri River, appropriators included a provision to prohibit the Corps of Engineers from changing the existing management plan before fiscal 2003.

The draft, written by Reid's Energy and Water Subcommittee, included significantly less money for the Yucca Mountain nuclear waste disposal program — $275 million, $160 million less than Bush requested or the House approved, and $125 million less than Congress had appropriated for fiscal 2001. Most of the money was for scientific analysis of Yucca Mountain as a permanent storage site for civilian nuclear waste, an idea that had been opposed by Nevada politicians for years.

As in previous years, the Senate bill included significantly more for Energy Department nuclear weapons programs — $15.1 billion, compared with $13.9 billion in the House

bill and $13.4 billion requested by Bush. Overall, the Senate included $20.1 billion for the Energy Department, $2 billion more than the administration requested and $1.4 billion more than in the House bill.

Although the House had taken the lead in adding money for Corps water projects, the Senate was not far behind with $4.3 billion, compared with $4.5 billion in the House bill and $3.9 billion requested by Bush.

Reflecting Reid's interest in more funding for solar and renewable energy, the bill included $435 million for those programs, $59 million more than the House version and $159 million above the administration's request.

Senate Floor Action

The Senate passed HR 2311 on July 19 by a vote of 97-2, after substituting the text of S 1171. (*Senate vote 240, p. S-50*)

Senators agreed, 100-0, to adopt compromise language offered by Christopher S. Bond, R-Mo., to require the Corps to explore alternatives to the proposed Missouri River management plan. (*Senate vote 237, p. S-49*)

Republicans considered offering an amendment to increase spending for the Yucca Mountain project but settled for non-binding language stating that the funding should be increased to "an amount closer to that included in the House-passed version."

In other action, the Senate voted 56-44, to table (kill) an amendment by Frank H. Murkowski, R-Alaska, that would have earmarked $10 million for enhanced job training in energy-related fields and reduced funding related to the CALFED water project by the same amount. The Senate bill included $40 million for the project under other accounts. (*Senate vote 238, p. S-49*)

Senators adopted by voice vote an amendment by Debbie Stabenow, D-Mich., and Peter G. Fitzgerald, R-Ill., to ban oil and gas drilling beneath the Great Lakes for two years.

Conference/Final Action

House and Senate conferees completed work on the final, $24.6 billion bill Oct. 30. The House adopted the conference report (H Rept 107-258) by a vote of 399-29 on Nov. 1; the Senate cleared the bill, 96-2, later the same day. (*House vote 416, p. H-142; Senate vote 320, p. S-67*)

The following are the major issues resolved in conference.

• **Nonproliferation.** The chief dispute was over Democrats' demands for more money for programs to detect, prevent and counter the spread of nuclear materials worldwide. The $804 million in the bill was $30 million more than requested, but it was less than in either the House version ($845 million) or the Senate bill ($881 million). House conferees rejected a proposal by Chet Edwards, D-Texas, to shift $131 million from weapons programs to nonproliferation efforts in the former Soviet Union. Edwards and others cited concerns that Osama bin Laden and other terrorists might try to acquire nuclear weapons from Russia or elsewhere.

Several House Democrats voted against the conference report specifically because of the failure to increase nonproliferation funding. "Is there a person who thinks we should be doing less this year than last year to keep nuclear materials out of the hands of terrorists?" asked Rush D. Holt, D-N.J.

"We're going to find those funds," said Callahan. "There were just no [available] funds in this bill." Several Democrats, however, argued that the need to safeguard nuclear materials was so urgent that an increase should be provided immediately.

An additional $226 million was subsequently appropriated as part of the fiscal 2002 defense spending bill (PL 107-117). (*Anti-terrorism supplemental, p. 2-59*)

● **Missouri River.** The other issue that dominated the conference was the differing language in the House- and Senate-passed versions regarding plans for the Missouri River. House conferees tried to include language to prohibit the Corps from altering the Missouri's flow to benefit endangered species upriver, but they eventually accepted the less restrictive Senate compromise postponing any change until 2003 and directing the Corps to study other ways of protecting those species.

● **Yucca Mountain.** Reid agreed to the House's demand to increase funding for ongoing scientific work at Yucca Mountain to $375 million, $100 million more than Reid's subcommittee had approved.

● **Great Lakes drilling.** The bill barred oil and natural gas drilling in the Great Lakes for two years. Both chambers had endorsed a ban, though some Republicans argued that new domestic sources of oil and gas should be explored.

● **Gulfstream pipeline.** The House provisions barring the pipeline were not included in the Senate bill and were dropped in conference. ◆

Foreign Aid Bill Sticks to Tradition

Lawmakers cleared a $15.4 billion fiscal 2001 foreign operations spending bill on Dec. 20, the final day of the session. The measure, written well before the Sept. 11 terrorist attacks, emphasized long-standing foreign policy priorities, from anti-drug aid to South America to combating AIDS overseas. The need to assist partners in the post-Sept. 11 global coalition against terrorism was addressed in separate supplemental spending bills (PL 107-38, PL 107-117) or deferred to the second session. President Bush signed the foreign aid bill (HR 2506 — PL 107-115) on Jan. 10, 2002.

Debate on the bill focused largely on perennial controversies, especially the anti-drug aid and the link between international family planning assistance and abortion. Final action was delayed until the end of the session by the abortion dispute, the same conflict that had held up the bill many times in the past.

This time, the flash point was a decision Bush made shortly after taking office to reinstate Reagan-era abortion restrictions. Known as the "Mexico City policy," they prohibited aid to international family planning organizations that performed or promoted abortions, even if they used their own funds to do so. The policy had been revoked by President Bill Clinton in 1993.

The Republican-controlled House backed Bush's decision, but the Democratic-controlled Senate voted to overturn it, drawing a veto threat from the White House. Senate Democrats subsequently agreed to drop the provision, but insisted on increasing by 50 percent the aid for international family planning efforts. That angered conservative Republicans, led by Rep. Christopher H. Smith of New Jersey, causing Republican leaders to hold off clearing the bill until the last moment.

The final bill largely tracked Bush's budget request, with a few notable exceptions. The total was only $178 million more than Bush sought and $403 million more than had been provided for fiscal 2001.

However, appropriators reduced aid for U.S. anti-drug programs in Colombia, with lawmakers expressing growing skepticism that the aid was doing much to help save that country from guerrilla warfare and drug trafficking. The House bill had come close to Bush's request for $731 million, with the strong backing of Speaker J. Dennis Hastert, R-Ill. But the Senate, where Vermont Democrat Patrick J. Leahy, a critic of such assistance, became chairman of the Foreign Operations Appropriations Subcommittee in June, proposed a substantial reduction. The final bill included $625 million for the Andean Counterdrug Initiative.

Lawmakers also rebuffed a proposal by Bush to cut fund-

BoxScore 2002
Foreign Operations — Fiscal Year

Bill:
HR 2506 — PL 107-115

Legislative Action:
House passed HR 2506 (H Rept 107-142), 381-46, on July 24.

Senate passed HR 2506, amended (S Rept 107-58), 96-2, on Oct. 24.

House adopted the conference report (H Rept 107-345), 357-66, on Dec. 19.

Senate cleared the bill by voice vote Dec. 20.

President signed Jan. 10, 2002.

ing for the Export-Import (Ex-Im) Bank by 25 percent, and voted to restore much of the money.

Highlights

Major spending components of the bill included:

• **Export assistance.** $578 million in net funding, $163 million less than provided for fiscal 2001, but $92 million more than Bush's request. Virtually all of the money was for the Export-Import Bank, which finances overseas purchases of U.S. good through low-interest direct loans, loan guarantees and export credit insurance.

• **Bilateral economic aid.** $9.6 billion — $388 million more than in fiscal 2001 and $118 million more than Bush requested. The aid made up almost two-thirds of the bill; much of it was administered by the U.S. Agency for International Development (AID) and went to humanitarian assistance, direct development aid, anti-drug programs and specific accounts for aid to the countries of the former Soviet Union and the nations of Central Europe.

AID funds included $1.4 billion for child health programs aimed at reducing child mortality and preventing infectious disease — $380 million more than fiscal 2001 and $462 million above the president's request.

AID also got $2.9 billion for assistance to reduce poverty and promote long-term development — $189 million above fiscal 2001 and $351 million more than requested.

The bill included $2.2 billion — $86 million less than in fiscal 2001 and $50 million less Bush requested — for economic support to specific countries in the Middle East, the Balkans, South America and the former Soviet Union.

• **Bilateral military assistance.** $3.9 billion for military aid — $94 million more than in fiscal 2001 but $19 million short of the administration's request. Most of the funding — $3.6 billion — went to Israel and Egypt, with the Baltic region and international military training receiving smaller amounts. It also included funding for land mine removal and peacekeeping.

• **Multilateral aid.** $1.4 billion — $50 million more than in fiscal 2001 but $12 million less than requested — primarily to pay U.S. contributions to international financial institutions, including $898 million for the World Bank.

Background

The foreign aid bill provided about two-thirds of total U.S. international affairs spending, including most foreign aid expenditures. Most of the increase in international af-

fairs spending for fiscal 2002, however, was appropriated under the separate bill for the Commerce, Justice and State departments. (*CJS, p. 2-9*)

The foreign aid measure had become an annual battleground over abortion and other issues such as debt relief for developing countries and, more recently, anti-drug efforts in Colombia.

In 2000, congressional Republicans ultimately yielded to Clinton on key issues, clearing a fiscal 2001 bill (PL 106-429) that gave him the $435 million he wanted for Third World debt relief, as well as increased funds for Russia and other former Soviet republics. But the primary concession was on family planning aid. The final bill provided $425 million for international family planning programs, although it specified that the funds could not be spent until Feb. 15, 2001, a month after Clinton left office. (*2000 Almanac, p. 2-70*)

The issue of abortion-related restrictions on family planning aid had been debated line by line since 1984, when the Reagan administration announced it would deny assistance to any foreign, non-governmental organization "which performs or actively promotes abortion as a method of family planning," even if it was done with the group's private funds. The directive, announced at the second U.N. International Conference on Population in Mexico City, became known as the Mexico City policy. (*History, p. 2-28*)

Democratic efforts to overturn the Reagan directive were unsuccessful until 1993, when Clinton took office and rescinded it. Clinton used his veto power to hold off repeated GOP efforts to restore the restrictions, but abortion opponents were able to reduce funding for family planning programs. Republicans finally succeeded in including Mexico City language in the fiscal 2000 bill (PL 106-113) as their price for allowing U.S. payment of back U.N. dues. Clinton was able to waive the restriction, but under the law the decision meant reduced funding. Bush reinstated the Mexico City policy by directive on Jan. 22, 2001, in time to govern the fiscal 2001 funds.

Legislative History

House Subcommittee Action

The House Foreign Operations Appropriations Subcommittee approved a $15.2 billion draft of the bill by voice vote June 27, after cutting back the amount for anti-drug efforts in South America and adding more for the the Ex-Im Bank and international HIV/AIDS efforts.

The subcommittee rejected, by voice vote, an amendment by Nita M. Lowey, D-N.Y., to reverse Bush's Mexico City policy.

The panel reduced the aid for drug interdiction in Colombia and six neighboring countries from the $731 million requested by Bush to $676 million.

It restored about half Bush's proposed cut to the Ex-Im Bank, a priority of Subcommittee Chairman Jim Kolbe, R-Ariz. Administration officials argued that businesses, particularly large exporters, should shoulder more of the burden when selling products overseas. Lawmakers from both parties protested; 30 Republicans senators had written Bush in February arguing that the funds should be restored. Bush re-

quested $687 million, a cut of $223 million from fiscal 2001. The subcommittee recommended $805 million.

The subcommittee also recommended $474 million in bilateral assistance for HIV/AIDS programs abroad, $45 million more than Bush had requested. Beyond that, the bill included $100 million toward Bush's pledge of $200 million for a multilateral U.N. AIDS fund.

The bill generally followed the administration's request for aid to the Middle East but omitted $800 million in extra help for Israel that Clinton had requested in November 2000. Kolbe said he would not act without a request from Bush. Administration officials told pro-Israel groups they did not want to provide the extra money at a time of high tensions in the region.

Pro-Israeli lawmakers did succeed in winning new language requiring that the Palestinian Authority demonstrate "substantial compliance" with its commitments to renounce terrorism, or face possible U.S. sanctions or withdrawal of $75 million of U.S. aid.

The bill also included a provision that conditioned all U.S. assistance to Serbia on a presidential assurance that Belgrade was cooperating with the International Court. Bush only opted to make a certification at the last moment in March after former president Slobodan Milosevic was arrested by Serbian authorities.

It also provided the president with the greater flexibility on imposing sanctions on Pakistan and India, first used in response to nuclear tests in those countries in 1998.

House Committee Action

The full House Appropriations Committee approved the bill (H Rept 107-142) by voice vote July 10, leaving the subcommittee draft virtually unchanged, including the $676 million allotted for Bush's Andean program.

Most of the debate centered on the anti-drug funds. The committee rejected, 22-39, a proposal by Nancy Pelosi, D-Calif., to shift $100 million to combat infectious disease. An attempt by David R. Obey of Wisconsin, ranking Democrat on the committee, to eliminate funding for the Andean program was rejected, 18-43.

House Floor Action

The House passed the $15.2 billion bill, 381-46, on July 24, avoiding much of the contentious debate of previous years. The House voted to increase congressional oversight of drug-fighting programs in South America, while stopping short of making substantial cuts in funding. (*House vote 266, p. H-94*)

Hastert had made a personal crusade out of saving Colombia, South America's oldest democracy, from drug trafficking and guerrilla war, and he urged Kolbe to hold the line and helped rally Republicans behind the scenes. The Andean Counterdrug Initiative had begun as a joint effort between Hastert and Clinton, with an initial $1.3 billion in economic and military aid provided as part of a fiscal 2000 supplemental appropriations law (PL 106-246) enacted in July 2000. (*2000 Almanac, p. 2-162*)

However, the standing of the Colombian government was deteriorating both in public opinion polls and on the battleground, and the poorly run drug-interdiction program was drawing criticism from both sides of the aisle. Lawmakers worried that new weapons could intensify the

Where the Money Goes

Foreign Operations Spending

(figures are in thousands of dollars of new budget authority)

	Fiscal 2001 Appropriation	Fiscal 2002 Bush Request	House Bill	Senate Bill	Conference Report
Export and investment assistance	$741,000	$485,955	$585,955	$578,955	$577,955
Bilateral economic assistance	9,186,414	9,456,880	9,453,422	9,714,529	9,574,529
Military assistance	3,760,875	3,874,000	3,827,000	3,889,000	3,855,000
Multilateral assistance	1,332,879	1,395,796	1,345,796	1,386,396	1,383,296
GRAND TOTAL	$15,021,168	$15,212,631	$15,212,173	$15,568,880	$15,390,780
Total adjusted for scorekeeping	($14,988,168)	($15,212,631)	($15,212,173)	($15,568,880)	$15,390,780

TABLE: House Appropriations Committee

Colombia conflict on both sides, while others warned that U.S. pilots could be killed or taken hostage, drawing the United States more deeply into the fighting that had sometimes been perceived as more a guerrilla war than a drug war.

Two Democratic attempts to reduce the Andean funding and shift money to global health programs were rejected. The amendments, by Barbara Lee of California and Jim McGovern of Massachusetts, were defeated by votes of 188-240 and 179-249, respectively. *(House votes 262, 263, p. H-94)*

John Conyers Jr., D-Mich., won voice vote adoption of an amendment to extend an existing law that limited to 800 the number of U.S. military personnel or civilian contractors allowed to participate in anti-drug efforts in Colombia. The committee had dropped the requirement at the administration's request.

The House adopted by voice vote an amendment by Peter Hoekstra, R-Mich., to withhold $65 million in aid to Peru until the administration had safeguards to prevent a repeat of an April 20 incident in which Peruvian jets accidentally shot down a light plane carrying U.S. missionaries.

The House reallocated some money in the bill. Ex-Im Bank funding was cut to $787 million, for example, and money for HIV/AIDs programs increased to $487 million.

Senate Committee Action

The Senate Appropriations Committee approved a $15.5 billion version of the bill (S Rept 107-58) by voice vote on July 26. The bottom line was $340 million above the House bill, reflecting the larger allocation given to the subcommittee by Senate appropriators.

Drafted by Leahy, the measure cut Bush's request for anti-drug programs in Colombia and other Andean nations by nearly one-fourth — from $731 million to $567 million. It also inserted several human rights conditions and required the administration to determine the safety of an herbicide sprayed on Colombia's coca crop.

During the markup, the committee gave voice vote approval to an amendment by Leahy to overturn Bush's reinstatement of the Mexico City policy.

Like the House, the Senate bill proposed to extend the cap on U.S. military personnel and civilian contractors in anti-drug efforts in Colombia. The Senate also included $50 million for the U.N. fund devoted to combating the spread of HIV/AIDS in Africa in addition to $400 million in bilateral funding for AIDS programs.

The amount for the Ex-Im Bank was $806 million, about $19 million more than the House had agreed to.

Senate Floor Action

The Senate passed the $15.5 billion bill, 96-2, on Oct. 24. Leahy successfully argued that debate should be limited, arguing that the ongoing war on terrorism — as well overall limits on spending — did not allow for extended deliberation on typically litigious concerns. Floor debate had already been delayed by Republicans protesting what they said was the Democrats' slow pace in confirming Bush's judicial nominees. *(Senate vote 312, p. S-66)*

The Senate moved some money around, reducing funding for the Ex-Im Bank to $780 million, and for the drug-interdiction effort to $547 million, while increasing spending for global health and population control programs.

Leahy held off on discussing his committee's effort to reverse Bush's abortion restrictions on family planning aid. And he managed to beat back an attempt by Bob Graham, D-Fla., to increase the Andean anti-drug money to the level requested by Bush. Graham argued that failure to fully fund the program would lead to more cocaine on U.S. streets and put an unstable region at risk only a year after Congress had approved $1.3 billion in emergency funding for the region. But Leahy argued that budget rules capped the bill's funding, and any additions would have to be offset by cuts in other programs. Graham's attempt to waive the budget rules failed, 27-72. *(Senate vote 311, p. S-65)*

Sam Brownback, R-Kan., won voice vote adoption of an amendment to allow the president to waive restrictions on aid to Azerbaijan until Dec. 31, 2002, if he determined it was in the national interest. The administration said Azerbaijan was cooperating in the war against terrorism.

Conference/Final Action

House and Senate conferees completed work on the bill Dec. 18. The House adopted the conference report (H Rept 107-345) the following day by a vote of 357-66, and

'Mexico City' Policy

The following is a brief history of the "Mexico City" policy:

• **1984** — At the second U.N. International Conference on Population in Mexico City, the Reagan administration announced a new policy of denying assistance to any foreign, non-governmental organization "which performs or actively promotes abortion as a method of family planning," even if it was done with the group's private funds. The directive became known as the Mexico City policy.

• **1991** — The House passed a foreign aid authorization bill that proposed to drop the Mexico City restrictions. The provision drew a veto threat from President George Bush and was ultimately dropped. (*1991 Almanac, p. 470*)

• **1993** — In a memorandum to the director of the Agency for International Development, President Bill Clinton rescinded the Mexico City restrictions. "These excessively broad anti-abortion conditions are unwarranted," Clinton wrote. "Moreover, they have undermined efforts to promote safe and efficacious family planning programs in foreign nations." (*1993 Almanac, p. 603*)

• **1995** — Blocked in attempts to reinstate the Mexico City policy through legislation, anti-abortion forces in the House tried to cut appropriations for international family planning programs by 35 percent and block payments until July 1996. (*1995 Almanac, p. 11-40*)

• **1996** — Anti-abortion lawmakers succeeded in delaying payment of fiscal 1997 family planning funds until July 1, unless Congress voted separately to release them in March. Congress subsequently approved the early release. (*1996 Almanac, p. 10-48*)

• **1997** — Negotiators on the fiscal 1998 foreign aid spending bill (PL 105-118) deadlocked over a House provision to essentially reinstate the Mexico City policy. GOP leaders dropped the language but limited spending to the fiscal 1997 level, released at 8 percent a month. (*1997 Almanac, p. 9-37*)

• **1998** — House leaders kept anti-abortion restrictions off the fiscal 1999 foreign operations spending bill (PL 105-277), but the Mexico City policy was added to a State Department authorization bill, which failed. (*1998 Almanac, pp. 2-45, 16-3*)

• **1999** — After months of negotiations, Clinton agreed to a one-year deal on the fiscal 2000 foreign aid bill (PL 106-113) that barred aid to family planning groups that performed abortions — except in cases of rape or incest, or to save the life of the woman — or that lobbied to change abortion laws or government policies in other countries. Clinton waived the restriction, but under the law that triggered a shift of $12.5 million in family planning aid to an account for child survival and disease prevention programs. (*1999 Almanac, p. 2-62*)

• **2000** — Republicans agreed to increase aid for family planning programs, but the fiscal 2001 foreign aid spending bill (PL 106-429) prevented spending the money until Feb. 15, 2001, after the inauguration of a new president. Republicans gambled that it would be George W. Bush (*2000 Almanac, p. 2-70*)

• **2001** — President Bush reinstated the Mexico City prohibition by directive. "It is my conviction that taxpayer funds should not be used to pay for abortions or advocate or actively promote abortion, either here or abroad," Bush wrote.

the Senate cleared the bill by voice vote Dec. 20. (*House vote 505, p. H-172*)

The bill's $15.4 billion total roughly split the difference between the earlier House and Senate versions. Having used a number of other measures to aid Bush's anti-terrorism agenda, lawmakers largely stuck to the pre-Sept. 11 spending allotments. Compromise came relatively quickly on all but the family planning provisions.

Although Senate conferees were ready to relent on the Mexico City policy, they insisted on getting a 50 percent increase in funds — a total of $37.5 million — for the United Nations Fund for Population Activities (UNFPA), which aids international family planning efforts. Angry GOP conservatives, led by Smith, threatened to block the conference report on the House floor. Conservatives were especially critical of UNFPA for undertaking family planning programs in China, where the government was accused of forcing women to undergo abortions as part of its population control programs.

Hoping to appease Smith and his allies and prevent their anger from affecting other bills, House GOP leaders kept postponing final consideration of the bill. In the end, they largely gave in to Senate demands. The final bill increased the U.S. contribution to UNFPA and dropped an annual provision that cut the U.S. contribution in direct proportion to the agency's activities in China.

The following are other highlights of the conference report:

• **Middle East.** The Middle East got the lion's share of the bilateral aid, with $5.1 billion going to Israel, Egypt, Lebanon and the Palestinian Authority. Conferees included language urging Bush to impose sanctions on the Palestinian Authority if it did not crack down on terrorists, but they opted not to mandate such a step as called for by the House.

Mirroring both bills, the final measure provided $2.8 billion in aid for Israel and $2 billion for Egypt, about $100

million less than each got in fiscal 2001. The decrease was part of a 10-year phase-out of economic aid. The total for Israel included $2 billion for military grants and $720 million in economic assistance. Aid to Egypt consisted of $1.3 billion in military grants and $655 million in economic assistance. The measure also provides $225 million for Jordan.

● **Andean counterdrug initiative.** The agreement provided $625 million for the next stage of the anti-drug campaign, a compromise between the $675 million agreed to by the House and the $547 million ultimately passed by the Senate.

● **Former Soviet Republics/Eastern Europe.** The bill included $784 million for the republics of the former Soviet Union and $621 million for Eastern Europe and the Baltic states.

● **Azerbaijan.** The conference report included the Senate language temporarily setting aside the longstanding ban on U.S. aid to Azerbaijan.

● **HIV/AIDS.** Conferees agreed on $475 million to fight AIDS worldwide, less than either chamber had proposed but an increase of $175 million over fiscal 2001 and $46 million above Bush's request. In addition, they agreed on $100 million, as requested, as a contribution to the Global Trust Fund to Combat HIV/AIDS, Malaria and Tuberculosis, $40 million of it to come from the $475 million. The global fund also received funding under the fiscal 2001 Labor HHS bill (PL 107-116) and the fiscal 2001 supplemental (PL 107-20).

● **Family planning funds.** At the insistence of Senate Democrats, conferees agreed to $447 million for family planning programs, close to the $450 million Senate number and well above the $425 million passed by the House. They also provided $34 million to the UNFPA, specifying that it could not be used for programs in China.

● **Ex-Im Bank.** The final bill provided $779 million for the Ex-Im Bank, close to the Senate figure. The funding was $131 million below fiscal 2001 but $94 million more than Bush wanted.

● **Debt relief.** The bill provided $229 million for international debt relief for poor countries, close to the $224 million requested by Bush and approved by both chambers. ◆

Interior Tops Request by $1 Billion

Putting aside most of their disputes over energy and public lands, lawmakers cleared the fiscal 2002 Interior Department appropriations bill with relative ease Oct. 17. The $19.1 billion measure provided $1 billion more than the president had requested, with increases going to a variety of accounts, including land conservation, energy research and firefighting. President Bush had only minor objections and signed the bill (HR 2217 — PL 107-63) on Nov. 5.

The bill initially was put together when the nation was experiencing a serious energy crisis, marked by power outages on the West Coast and exceptionally high prices for gasoline and natural gas nationwide. Democrats called for increased conservation and an emphasis on alternative fuels, while Republicans pushed for increased energy production.

Debate in both chambers revolved around Democratic attempts to challenge administration environmental policies, including drilling for oil and gas on national monument lands and in coastal waters, easing restrictions on hard-rock mining and making it more difficult to add to the endangered species list. Both bills exceeded Bush's request — the House by $791 million, the Senate by $592 million.

By the time conferees met to negotiate a final bill in October, however, the environment had changed dramatically. Following the Sept. 11 terrorist attacks, energy worries took a back seat to national defense concerns, and lawmakers were putting aside partisan issues to complete the appropriations process. As a result, what could have been a contentious conference turned out to be relatively smooth and expeditious.

House and Senate negotiators dropped earlier provisions that would have barred funds from being used to revise hard-rock mining regulations, implement the Kyoto Protocol on global warming and allow oil and gas drilling in certain areas of the Gulf of Mexico. The final bill did include provisions barring new oil exploration in national monuments, and it rejected proposals to make it more difficult for citizens to add to the endangered species list. Strong Democratic opposition from the outset assured the death of administration proposals to allow drilling for oil and gas in the Arctic National Wildlife Refuge (ANWR).

Highlights

The Interior Department accounted for nearly half the money in the bill — $9.4 billion, an increase of $269 mil-

BoxScore **2002** Fiscal Year
Interior

Bill:
HR 2217 — PL 107-63
Legislative Action:
House passed HR 2217 (H Rept 107-103), 376-32, on June 21.
Senate passed HR 2217, amended (S Rept 107-36), by voice vote July 12.
House adopted the conference report (H Rept 107-234), 380-28, on Oct. 17.
Senate cleared the bill, 95-3, on Oct. 17
President signed Nov. 5.

lion over Bush's request and $48 million over fiscal 2001. The money went mainly for land management — the Bureau of Land Management, the National Parks Service, and the Fish and Wildlife Services — and to the department's Bureau of Indian Affairs. The bill also funded the Agriculture Department's Forest Service, Energy Department research and conservation programs, and the Indian Health Service, run by the Department of Health and Human Services. Several cultural programs also received funding.

Major spending components of the fiscal 2002 bill included:

● **Bureau of Land Management.** $1.9 billion — a $275 million cut from fiscal 2001 but $100 million more than Bush requested — to manage more than 200 million of acres of federal land, especially in Western states. The lands are used for grazing, logging, mining and recreational purposes.

● **National Park Service.** $2.3 billion — $188 million above the previous year but $195 million less than requested. The bill increased funding over Bush's request for some accounts, particularly for congressionally designated national heritage areas, but significantly cut his proposal for state conservation grants. The Park Services manages about 83 million acres of public lands and has nearly 300 million visitors a year.

● **U.S. Fish and Wildlife Service.** $1.3 billion — a $49 million increase over fiscal 2001 and $185 million more than requested. The agency runs the National Wildlife Refuge System and manages 93 million acres of land with 35 million visitors a year.

● **Forest Service.** $4.1 billion for the Forest Service — $305 million less than in fiscal 2001 but $398 million more than Bush requested and more than either the House or Senate had voted to provide. The Forest Service manages 192 million acres of federal land and attracts 220 million visitors a year.

● **Indian programs.** $2.2 billion to the Bureau of Indian Affairs — $35 million over fiscal 2001 and $19 million more than requested — and $2.8 billion for the Indian Health Service — $130 million more than the previous year and $52 million more than requested.

● **Energy Department.** $1.8 billion for energy research and conservation programs, including research into clean and alternative fuel technologies — $310 million above fiscal 2001 and $264 million more than Bush requested.

● **Cultural programs.** $125 million for the National Endowment for the Humanities (NEH), $5 million above fiscal 2001 and $4 million more than requested. The National

Where the Money Goes

Interior Spending

(figures are in thousands of dollars of new budget authority)

	Fiscal 2001 Appropriation	Fiscal 2002 Bush Request	House Bill	Senate Bill	Conference Report
Interior Department	$9,386,982	$9,167,124	$9,411,563	$9,373,683	$9,435,792
(Bureau of Land Management)	(2,147,182)	(1,771,538)	(1,872,422)	(1,859,084)	(1,871,192)
(U.S. Fish and Wildlife Service)	(1,227,010)	(1,091,265)	(1,335,516)	(1,271,265)	(1,276,424)
(National Park Service)	(2,135,219)	(2,517,691)	(2,284,685)	(2,295,142)	(2,323,057)
(U.S. Geological Survey)	(882,800)	(813,376)	(900,489)	(892,474)	(914,002)
Forest Service	4,435,391	3,732,125	3,914,063	3,815,574	4,130,416
Department of Energy	1,453,644	1,502,680	1,796,680	1,739,070	1,766,470
Other Related Agencies	3,558,431	3,670,706	3,741,549	3,735,708	3,745,542
GRAND TOTAL	**$18,892,320**	**$18,072,635**	**$18,863,855**	**$18,664,035**	**$19,078,220**

TABLE: House, Senate Appropriations committees

Endowment for the Arts (NEA) received $98 million, slightly more than in the previous year and equal to the administration's request.

Background

The annual spending bill for the Department of the Interior and related agencies frequently got caught up in controversies over policy riders on the environment, land use and related issues such as grazing fees, disposal of mining waste, and oil exploration on public lands. Though the cultural and arts programs funded under the bill got relatively little money, they sometimes generated intense disputes — for example, over restrictions on the types of art that should receive taxpayer funding under the NEA.

The fiscal 2001 bill (PL 106-291) was enacted after lengthy negotiations over spending on public lands. Weeks of bargaining between appropriators and the White House led to the creation of a protected six-year, $12 billion discretionary fund devoted to land conservation, preservation and maintenance. The fund was an alternative to a bipartisan proposal, the Conservation and Reinvestment Act (CARA), that would have created a mandatory 15-year fund for land conservation fed by federal gas and oil royalties. Though CARA had broad bipartisan support, it was opposed by a determined group of appropriators, who regarded it as an end run around their committees, and by Western lawmakers opposed to more federal land purchases. (*2000 Almanac, pp. 2-83, 10-6*)

Legislative Action

House Subcommittee Action

Ignoring Bush's call for reduced spending, the House Interior Appropriations Subcommittee approved an $18.9 billion draft bill by voice vote June 7 after less than an hour of debate. The administration had requested a total of $18.1 billion, $700 million less than the fiscal 2001 level. The subcommittee added $800 million to Bush's request and made several significant changes, including denying a request for $2 million to study energy exploration in ANWR.

The subcommittee approved a total of $1.8 billion for energy research and conservation, $294 million more than the administration wanted. The draft also restored cuts proposed by Bush for the U.S. Geological Survey, the Abandoned Mine Reclamation Fund and the Payment in Lieu of Taxes program. The draft included $1.32 billion for the conservation fund enacted as part of the fiscal 2001 Interior bill; Bush had requested $1.26 billion.

Democrats praised the bipartisan draft for restoring Bush's proposed cuts. David R. Obey of Wisconsin, ranking Democrat on the Appropriations Committee, called it "a very reasonable bill."

The subcommittee agreed to Bush's request for $60 million to fund two new programs that would give landowners incentives to help protect endangered species, but proposed giving oversight of the programs to the U.S. Fish and Wildlife Service rather than the National Park Service, as Bush had requested.

The appropriators also rejected an administration request to include language that would have made it more difficult for citizens to sue the government in disputes over the addition of plants and animals to the endangered species list.

House Committee Action

The full Appropriations Committee approved the $18.9 billion bill (H Rept 107-103) by voice vote June 13. Obey tried but failed to add language explicitly forbidding the use of funds anywhere in the bill to study drilling in ANWR. The amendment was rejected, 21-38.

Republicans also turned back amendments by:

• Norm Dicks of Washington, ranking Democrat on the Interior Subcommittee, to add $25 million for arts funding by deferring funds for a "clean coal" program aimed at lowering greenhouse gas emissions from power plants. It was rejected, 27-37.

• Maurice D. Hinchey, D-N.Y., to add $200 million for research and development of energy efficiency programs, defeated 27-33.

Appropriations

House Floor Action

The House passed the $18.9 billion spending bill on June 21 by a lopsided vote of 376-32, after rejecting by wide margins Bush's proposals for increased oil and gas exploration on federal lands. (*House vote 185, p. H-68*)

The House adopted, 247-164, an amendment by Jim Davis, D-Fla., to delay oil and gas drilling in an area of the Gulf of Mexico known as Lease Sale 181 until April 1, 2002. Most Democrats and 70 GOP lawmakers, some of whom feared that attempts to drill in their coastal waters could be next, supported the amendment. The amendment was aimed at delaying administration plans to proceed on oil and gas drilling in waters that lay within Alabama's boundaries but were less than 30 miles from Florida. Opponents, led by the president's brother, Florida Gov. Jeb Bush, said the drilling would be too near the tourist-friendly beaches of Florida's panhandle. (*House vote 181, p. H-68*)

The House adopted, 242-173, an amendment by Nick J. Rahall II of West Virginia, ranking Democrat on the Resources Committee, to bar the approval of new energy leases within existing national monuments. Limited drilling and mining already were permitted on some monument lands, but the administration was interested in expanding development. Interior Secretary Gale A. Norton had asked local officials in March to point out any monument lands with untapped natural resources. (*House vote 180, p. H-68*)

Members also adopted, 216-194, an amendment by Jay Inslee, D-Wash., to retain Clinton administration regulations on hard-rock mining. The regulations, issued in November 2000, required mining companies to post cleanup bonds and meet environmental standards for protecting water from pollutants such as cyanide and sulfuric acid. The Interior Department had announced June 15 that it would retain the cleanup bond requirement but drop the other main provisions. (*House vote 182, p. H-68*)

On other amendments, the House:

• Adopted, 221-193, a proposal by Louise M. Slaughter, D-N.Y., to increase NEH funding by $3 million and NEA funding by $10 million, offset by cuts in Interior Department and Forest Service administrative budgets. (*House vote 177, p. H-66*)

• Rejected, 145-264, an amendment by Cliff Stearns, R-Fla., that would have removed the arts increases. (*House vote 184, p. H-68*)

• Adopted, by voice vote, an amendment by Carolyn B. Maloney, D-N.Y., to require oil companies to pay fees to the federal government in dollars rather than through so-called royalties in kind, which involve the transfer of petroleum.

Senate Committee Action

The Senate Appropriations Committee gave quick approval to its $18.7 billion version of the bill (S Rept 107-36) on June 28, following approval the same day by the Interior Subcommittee. Both were voice votes. Appropriations Chairman Robert C. Byrd, D-W.Va., insisted that any policy riders be put off at least until floor debate.

The Senate bill was less generous than the $18.9 billion House version in most categories, including the Bureau of Land Management, the Forest Service and the Department of Energy, but the total was still hundreds of millions of dollars above Bush's $18.1 billion request. For example, the bill increased funding for energy research and conservation — exceeding Bush's request by $236 million, instead of $294 million as in the House bill.

Like the House bill, the Senate version rejected Bush's request for funding to prepare for ANWR drilling, but did not contain an outright ban on drilling in the refuge.

Senate Floor Action

The Senate passed the bill by voice vote July 12, making it the first fiscal 2002 spending bill to move to conference.

The biggest Democratic victory was the overwhelming adoption of an amendment by Richard J. Durbin, D-Ill., to ban new oil and gas drilling on national monument lands. Durbin's amendment, which was adopted by voice vote after a move to table (or kill) it was rejected, 42-57. It mirrored language included in the House bill, essentially ensuring that the provision would remain in the conference report. (*Senate vote 229, p. S-48*)

But in a victory for proponents of increased energy drilling, the Senate adopted, 67-33, a motion to table, or kill, an amendment by Bill Nelson, D-Fla., that would have temporarily blocked all new oil and gas leases off Florida's Gulf Coast. Eighteen Democrats voted with Republicans to kill the amendment. To avoid a defeat in the Senate, the Interior Department had announced July 2 that it would scale back the drilling area from 6 million acres to about 1.5 million acres, one-fourth the size it had originally sought. (*Senate vote 231, p. S-48*)

Before passing the bill, the House agreed to a manager's amendment that included a number of Democratic resolutions opposing more energy drilling. However, Sen. Mary L. Landrieu, D-La., succeeded in adding a sense-of-Congress provision stating that a "significant portion of federal offshore mineral revenues" should go to states that allowed oil and gas drilling near their coasts. The manager's amendment also included a provision by John Kerry, D-Mass., to strengthen a moratorium on new drilling off the West Coast and Eastern seaboard by banning any pre-leasing activities to explore for oil or gas that could lead to drilling later.

The amendment also included a rider by Byrd, which survived in the final bill, making the federal steel loan guarantee program more generous. Ted Stevens of Alaska, ranking Republican on the Appropriations Committee, angered environmentalists by including a provision to allow the same number of cruise ships to enter Glacier Bay National Park as had arrived the previous year.

Conference/Final Action

House and Senate conferees finished work on the bill in little more than an hour Oct. 10, resolving the most controversial riders quickly and with little contention. Total funding was $19.1 billion, more than either the House or Senate version. However, it included the $400 million in emergency funds for wildfires. The House adopted the conference report (H Rept 107-234), 380-28, on Oct. 17. The Senate cleared the bill, 95-3, later the same day. (*House vote 393, p. H-134; Senate vote 304, p. S-64*)

Only a few thorny policy riders divided the House and Senate versions, and they were resolved or set aside in the wake of Sept. 11.

● **National monuments.** In a victory for environmentalists, the bill barred the administration from expanding the territory available for oil or gas drilling on national monument lands. Both chambers had approved the ban.

● **Gulf of Mexico.** With the administration having drastically reduced the size of the lease area, conferees dropped the House's six-month ban on oil and gas drilling in the Gulf of Mexico.

● **Hard-rock mining.** In the face of sharp criticism by Senate Majority Whip Harry Reid, D-Nev., and a number of Republicans, conferees dropped the House proposal to retain Clinton administration regulations on hard-rock mining operations.

● **Endangered species.** Conferees denied the administration's request to remove deadlines for the department to respond to citizens' requests to make additions to the list of endangered species. However, the final bill funded two new Fish and Wildlife Service programs sought by the administration to provide incentives for private action to protect endangered species.

● **Alaska cruise ships.** Stevens won approval in conference for language allowing the same number of cruise ships to enter Glacier Bay National Park as had the previous year, despite a federal court decision announced Aug. 3 ordering

a reduction for environmental reason.

● **Wildfire management.** The final bill provided $1.6 billion for wildland fire management, including $346 million designated as emergency spending. An additional $54 million under the Bureau of Land Management brought the total emergency funding for fire management to $400 billion. The House bill had included no emergency spending for fire fighting; the Senate bill included $235 million.

● **Conservation initiative.** As recommended by both chambers, the final bill included $1.3 billion, spread across numerous accounts, for the conservation initiative begun under the fiscal 2001 bill. The total was 10 percent more than the amount provided in fiscal 2001 and $64 million more than Bush requested.

● **Energy programs.** In providing $264 million more than Bush requested for fossil fuel research and energy conservation, conferees roughly split the difference between the increases recommended by the House and Senate.

● **Recreation fees.** Conferees decided to extend for two years, until fiscal 2004, a demonstration program that allowed national parks to keep part of their entry and service fees. The Senate bill did not include an extension; the House bill would have extended the program through 2006 and allowed fees at additional sites. ◆

HHS, Education Get Big Increases

Substantial increases for medical research and low-income school children paved the way for Congress to clear the Labor, Health and Human Services (HHS), and Education appropriations bill by wide margins the week of Dec. 17. Both chambers started unusually late on the biggest and most contentious of all the spending bills; the fiscal 2002 measure did not even begin moving through the Appropriations committees until October. But an agreement to provide generous funding increases for social programs helped the bill clear after some of the easiest negotiations in years. President Bush signed it into law (HR 3061 — PL 107-116) on Jan. 10, 2002.

The Education Department and HHS were the big winners. Total spending for HHS increased by nearly 14 percent over fiscal 2001. Education spending grew by 15 percent. Overall, the bill appropriated $407.7 billion, most of it mandatory spending for programs such as Medicaid and unemployment benefits.

Total discretionary spending, the portion under the control of the appropriators, was $123.4 billion, making the bill the biggest single source of domestic discretionary spending in the budget. It was a substantial increase over the $109.4 billion provided in fiscal 2001 but less than the $135.1 billion requested by Bush. The bill funded more than 300 social programs and initiatives, ranging from the popular Head Start for preschoolers and the National Institutes of Health (NIH) to special education and workplace safety.

The Labor-HHS bill was expected all along to move late in the session. Appropriators were having trouble figuring out how to fit their domestic and defense priorities within limits set in the budget resolution (H Con Res 83); they also wanted to wait until they found out how much would be required for education under the separate overhaul of the 1965 Elementary and Secondary Education Act (ESEA) that was also moving through Congress. Both sides, however, wanted to avoid the extended debates over labor, standoffs over education priorities and fights over abortion that had led to lengthy end-of-year negotiations in the past.

House Appropriations Committee Chairman C.W. Bill Young, R-Fla.; Labor-HHS Subcommittee Chairman Ralph Regula, R-Ohio; and ranking committee Democrat David R. Obey of Wisconsin agreed in June to push the White House for an extra $4 billion for education. They got the increase as part of an agreement with the administration finalized Oct. 2. Senate Democrats, led by Health, Education, Labor and Pensions Committee Chairman Edward M.

BoxScore **2002** Fiscal Year

Labor-HHS-Education

Bill:
HR 3061 — PL 107-116
Legislative Action:
House passed HR 3061 (H Rept 107-229), 373-43, on Oct. 11.
Senate passed HR 3061, amended (S Rept 107-84), 89-10, on Nov. 6.
House adopted the conference report (H Rept 107-342), 393-30, on Dec. 19.
Senate cleared the bill, 90-7, on Dec. 20.
President signed on Jan. 10, 2002.

Kennedy, D-Mass., wanted substantially more, arguing that it was needed to help low-income schools comply with new testing requirements in the education overhaul bill (HR 1), but they were unsuccessful. (*ESEA, p. 8-3*)

The House and Senate versions of the bill both provided $123.4 billion in discretionary spending. Both focused spending increases on ailing schools and bio-terror-related research at the NIH. The Senate measure, however, was skewed slightly more toward health care spending, while the House bill leaned more toward education.

Highlights

Major spending allocations in the final bill included:

● **Education.** $51.4 billion — $6.8 billion, or 15 percent, above fiscal 2001 spending, and $3.9 billion, or 8 percent, more than Bush requested. The total included $10.4 billion for Title I grants to local schools to educate low-income students, an 18 percent increase over fiscal 2001. Funding for special education programs under the 1975 Individuals with Disabilities Education Act (IDEA) (PL 94-142) increased by 17 percent, to $8.7 billion; of the total, $7.5 billion was for basic state grants, a 19 percent increase.

● **Health and Human Services.** $302.6 billion, a $36.3 billion increase over fiscal 2001. More than 80 percent of the agency's budget was mandatory spending, with criteria set in law outside the hands of the appropriators. The biggest slice was $134.3 billion in grants to states under Medicaid, the federal-state health program for the poor. Another $82 billion in mandatory spending went to payments to Medicare trust funds. Of the discretionary spending, the NIH received $23.3 billion and the Centers for Disease Control and Prevention got $4.3 billion.

● **Labor.** $14.2 billion, an increase of just $468 million over fiscal 2001 and $655 million more than requested. In response to fears of recession, however, the total included about $1.5 billion for aid to dislocated workers, a $111 million increase over fiscal 2001.

Background

Because of its sheer size and the number of controversial issues it covers, the Labor-HHS-Education measure was usually one of the last of the 13 appropriations bills to be debated. Since 1995, when Republicans took control of the House, a freestanding Labor-HHS bill had been enacted just once, in 1997.

Where the Money Goes

Labor-HHS-Education Spending

(figures are in thousands of dollars of new budget authority)

	Fiscal 2001 Appropriation	Fiscal 2002 Bush Request	House Bill	Senate Bill	Conference Report
Department of Labor	$13,697,779	$13,510,866	$14,099,407	$14,107,003	$14,166,160
Department of Health and Human Services	266,255,183	300,091,185	301,508,579	302,731,086	302,559,804
Department of Education	44,637,611	47,481,546	52,528,765	52,885,825	51,413,596
Related Agencies	40,383,281	39,084,845	39,460,800	39,504,266	39,523,242
GRAND TOTAL	$364,973,854	$400,168,442	$407,597,551	$409,228,180	$407,662,802
Total adjusted for scorekeeping	($357,928,480)	($407,607,256)	($395,865,315)	($395,941,915)	($395,927,315)
Trust Funds	($10,397,554)	($10,729,825)	($10,739,425)	($10,845,863)	($10,820,534)

TABLE: House Appropriations Committee

A deal on funding for the fiscal 2001 Labor-HHS bill had eluded lawmakers until the bitter end, pushing the measure to the center of end-of-session battles with the administration in late 2000. Although Republicans managed to resist some of President Bill Clinton's growing spending demands, the final measure (PL 106-554) still included a record $6.5 billion increase for education, $2 billion more than Clinton had originally sought. The bill did not clear until Dec. 15. *(2000 Almanac, p. 2-97)*

The fiscal 2000 version cleared Nov. 19, 1999, and served as the vehicle for that year's omnibus appropriations package (PL 106-113). The $318.5 billion Labor-HHS measure cleared only after lawmakers had agreed to a one-year extension of Clinton's plan to hire 100,000 new teachers at a cost of $1.62 billion. *(1999 Almanac, p. 2-94)*

Legislative Action

House Subcommittee Action

Aided by the additional $4 billion, as well as the bipartisan advance work that had been going on for months, the House Labor-HHS Appropriations Subcommittee approved a draft of the bill Oct. 3, after less than an hour of debate and without a single amendment. The draft, approved by voice vote, provided $407.6 billion, including $123.4 billion in discretionary spending.

The bill included $22.3 billion for ESEA programs, a $3.6 billion increase over fiscal 2001. The total was close to the $5 billion increase authorized in the House version of the education overhaul bill, but well short of the $14.4 billion increase called for in the Senate version and the $10 billion compromise being advocated by Kennedy. Still, education groups were pleased: Counting money for special education and higher education, the department stood to receive $49.3 billion in fiscal 2002 — an increase of $7 billion, or nearly 17 percent, over fiscal 2001 spending. Title I spending was slated to increase by $1.7 billion to $10.5 billion. The bill set aside $7.7 billion in discretionary spending for special education grants to states, a $1.4 billion increase. "The reality," said Obey, "is this is a pretty doggone good budget."

The appropriators went to great lengths to defuse controversies. To head off a potential clash over a Bush proposal to fund research on stem cells already extracted from human embryos, the appropriators reaffirmed a 1995 ban on using federal money for research involving embryos outside the womb, but declared that Bush's plan did not violate the policy. Overall, the bill included enough spending increases to keep lawmakers from both parties happy. Among the highlights:

● **Bio-terrorism.** $393 million for measures to defend against biological or chemical attacks, a $102 million increase above fiscal 2001. This was the bill's most direct response to the terrorist attacks.

● **Testing.** $400 million for the states to cover the costs of developing the annual reading and math tests that would be required by the education overhaul bill.

● **Biomedical research.** $22.9 billion for the NIH, a $2.6 billion increase.

● **Faith-based initiatives.** $30 million to be set aside for a Compassion Capital Fund to help start new charities. Bush had asked for $89 million.

● **Dislocated workers.** $1.5 billion for the Labor Department to provide aid to unemployed workers, a $100 million increase.

House Committee Action

The full Appropriations Committee approved the bill (H Rept 107-229) by voice vote after a quick markup Oct. 9. Young, Regula and Obey teamed up to discourage the normal slew of amendments. Chet Edwards, D-Texas, withdrew an amendment that would have prohibited charitable and religious organizations that used federal funds to provide social services from employment discrimination based on religion.

House Floor Action

The $407.6 billion bill sailed through the House on Oct. 11 by a vote of 373-43, after members sidestepped several potential controversies. The only successful amendment was a rider by Bernard Sanders, I-Vt., approved by voice vote, to require that pharmaceutical companies benefiting from NIH research sell their drugs for "reasonable" prices. *(House vote 381, p. H-130)*

A proposal by Ernest Istook, R-Okla., to add $33 million for programs to discourage young people from engaging in sex before marriage was defeated, 106-311. The bill already included $102 million for that purpose. (*House vote 379, p. H-130*)

Another Istook amendment, defeated, 156-262, would have blocked an executive order issued by Clinton requiring federally funded services to translate for people with limited English skills. Istook said the requirement could impose a "huge unfunded mandate" on businesses and cities. (*House vote 380, p. H-130*)

The House also rejected, 76-349, an amendment by Bob Schaffer, R-Colo., to boost special-education funding by $1.1 billion, taking the money from other education programs, including higher education, bilingual education and education research. (*House vote 377, p. H-130*)

Senate Committee Action

The Senate Appropriations Committee approved its version of the bill (S 1536 — S Rept 107-84) on Oct. 11 by a vote of 29-0. The bill was virtually unchanged from a draft that the Labor-HHS Appropriations Subcommittee had approved by voice vote the previous day. The $123.4 billion in discretionary spending matched the total in the House bill, but the Senate was somewhat more generous to health-care spending, with slightly less for education.

The bill included $23.7 billion for the NIH, a $3.4 billion increase over fiscal 2001. Labor-HHS Appropriations Subcommittee Chairman Tom Harkin, D-Iowa, and Arlen Specter of Pennsylvania, the ranking subcommittee Republican, shared a goal of doubling the fiscal 1998 NIH budget over five years. They said the $2.6 billion increase recommended by the House would fall $800 million short.

For the Department of Education, the Senate bill recommended $48.5 billion in discretionary spending, an increase of $6.3 billion, compared to the $7 billion increase in the House bill. Harkin, together with Chuck Hagel, R-Neb., was trying, under the separate education overhaul bill, to turn special education into a mandatory spending program with automatic increases of $2.5 billion a year over the next six years. The Bush administration opposed the move, saying it wanted to wait for an overhaul of the program due in 2002 before committing to substantial increases. With the issue undecided, Harkin included a $1 billion increase over fiscal 2001 in discretionary spending for special education in the Labor-HHS bill. For Title I aid, the Senate bill included $10.2 billion, about $200 million less than the House bill.

Senate Floor Action

Policy disputes that had been kept in abeyance finally erupted when the bill reached the Senate floor Oct. 30, delaying final action and adding several controversial amendments. The Senate passed HR 3061, 89-10, on Nov. 6, after substituting the text of its own $409.2 billion bill. (*Senate vote 324, p. S-68*)

Senate action bogged down over an attempt by Majority Leader Tom Daschle, D-S.D., to attach an amendment granting firefighters, police officers and rescue workers the right to unionize in the 18 states that barred collective bargaining for those workers. Daschle framed it as a tribute to those who responded to the Sept. 11 attacks; Republicans saw it as a way to enlarge the Democrats' labor union base.

The fight dragged on until Nov. 6, when Democrats pulled the amendment after losing a cloture vote, 56-44 (60 votes were required to prevail). (*Senate vote 323, p. S-68*)

An even bigger fight was averted when Specter removed a provision that would have allowed the president to fund research on stem cells extracted from embryos that would otherwise be discarded. (The House bill, by contrast, did not seek to change the law, but merely declared that Bush's proposals did not conflict with it.) The provision was the only part of the Senate bill that drew an outright veto threat from the White House.

A "mental health parity" amendment, easily adopted by voice vote Oct. 30, drew opposition from business and health insurance groups and from House GOP leaders, and promised to be a stumbling block in conference. Under the amendment, by Paul Wellstone, D-Minn., Pete V. Domenici, R-N.M., and Kennedy, employers who offered mental health coverage would be barred from putting tighter restrictions on it than on coverage they provided for physical illnesses — for example, by allowing fewer doctors' visits or charging higher co-payments.

That was a significant expansion of a more limited 1996 mental health parity law (PL 104-204) that required health plans to treat annual and lifetime payment limits equally for mental and physical health coverage. Domenici and Wellstone said the amendment was needed to end discrimination against mental health patients. Critics said it would increase health costs and force businesses to cut or drop worker benefits. "It's going to be a fierce battle," Wellstone predicted of the conference.

In other action, the Senate on Nov. 1 rejected, 46-54, an amendment by Judd Gregg, R-N.H., to shift $925 million set aside for school repair grants under the bill, to Title I aid to disadvantaged schools. Harkin said the grants were needed to repair aging schools, but Republicans argued that school construction should remain a state and local responsibility. The Bush administration warned that it strongly objected to the provision. (*Senate vote 316, p. S-67*)

The Senate adopted, 81-19, an amendment by Mary L. Landrieu, D-La., to require that new Title I funds be funneled more directly to poor schools. Though that was supposed to happen under existing law, in practice Congress had allowed money to be steered to districts that were no longer poor but still wanted the funds. (*Senate vote 317, p. S-67*)

Byron L. Dorgan, D-N.D., won voice vote approval for a proposal to refuse landing rights to any international airline that did not provide passenger lists in advance. Dorgan said most countries provided the lists voluntarily, but some such as Pakistan, Saudi Arabia and Egypt did not participate. Dorgan initially had attached the provision to the Senate anti-terrorism bill, but it was left out of the final bill (PL 107-56).

Conference/Final Action

It took House and Senate conferees until Nov. 18 to agree on a final bill. The main stumbling block — the Senate proposal to ease restrictions on insurance coverage for mental health — was ultimately dropped from the bill at the insistence of House GOP conferees. The House adopted the conference report (H Rept 107-342) by a vote of 393-30 on Dec. 19. The Senate cleared the bill, 90-7, on Dec. 20. (*House vote 504, p. H-172; Senate vote 378, p. S-77*)

In an attempt to find a compromise, Nancy L. Johnson, R-Conn., who chaired the House Ways and Means Health Subcommittee, proposed adding the mental-health parity provision to the economic stimulus bill (HR 3090), which ultimately stalled, with the proviso that insurers could opt out of the rule if they could prove it would force them to raise their premiums by at least 1 percent. But Wellstone and Domenici were not enthusiastic about the plan, and it did not go forward. Conferees included a one-year extension of the existing mental health parity law in the Labor-HHS bill.

Other major issues resolved in conference included:

● **Education funding.** The Education Department got $51.4 billion for programs serving students from preschool to college. While it was a 15 percent increase over fiscal 2001, it was $1.1 billion less than the House level and $1.5 billion less than the Senate bill. The $10.4 billion in funding for Title I grants in the final bill was $929 million below the House number and $1.5 billion below the Senate. Still, it was $1.6 billion above the fiscal 2001 level and about $830 million more than Bush had requested.

The $22 billion provided for elementary and secondary education programs covered under ESEA was a $3.5 billion increase over fiscal 2001, but it was considerably less than the $26.5 billion increase authorized by the education overhaul bill. Kennedy called it an "impressive achievement," noting that many of the allocations were higher than originally proposed. But he made it clear that the drive for more funding would be back the following year.

The $925 million in the Senate bill to continue the Clinton-era school renovation program fell by the wayside. Another Clinton initiative to help pay for thousands of new teachers in an effort to reduce class sizes was folded into a broader teacher-quality grant program.

● **Special education.** Conferees split the difference between the House and Senate on special education, providing $7.5 billion for state grants to schools, compared to $7.7 billion in the House bill and $7.3 billion in the Senate version. The total for special education programs was $8.7 billion. None of the funding was mandatory.

● **Bio-terrorism.** The conferees agreed to provide $393 million, the same as in the House bill, to stockpile vaccines and drugs to limit damage from biological or chemical attacks. The Senate bill would have provided $338 million.

● **Stem cell research.** Conferees adopted the House language continuing the 1995 ban on funding for research on embryos, but declaring in the conference report that Bush's proposal to fund research on stem cells already extracted from embryos did not violate this policy.

● **Biomedical research.** The final deal gave the NIH a $3 billion increase, $400 million more than in the House bill and $400 million less than in the Senate version.

● **LIHEAP.** Lawmakers agreed to appropriate $1.7 billion for the Low-Income Home Energy Assistance Program (LIHEAP) and to provide $300 million in emergency spending to be distributed after the winter's big heating bills came in. But they asked the administration to release left-over LIHEAP money from the previous year; the administration was holding the money for future crises.

● **Earmarks.** The bill also lived up to its reputation as a magnet for members' local projects. The conference report contained hundreds of "earmarks," many of them under a grants program for education innovation that was set to grow from $339 million in fiscal 2001 to $833 million in fiscal 2002. ◆

A Little for All in Legislative Branch

The fiscal 2002 legislative branch appropriations bill was cleared Nov. 1 after a last-minute decision to add $70 million for the Capitol Visitor Center, set to be built under the East Lawn and completed in 2005. The $3 billion measure was a 9 percent increase over the amount appropriated in fiscal 2001 — essentially what Congress had asked President Bush to request. Bush signed the bill (HR 2647 — PL 107-68) on Nov. 12.

The bill funds congressional overhead — staff and committee salaries and expenses, mail, security and the maintenance of the Capitol complex — as well as the agencies and offices that exist primarily to serve Congress, such as the Library of Congress and the General Accounting Office.

The only spending in the bill that was mandatory, and therefore out of the appropriators' control, was $99 million to cover the payroll for members of Congress. The bill assumed a 4.6 percent salary increase for all congressional aides — the same cost of living raise appropriated for executive branch workers — although on Capitol Hill most raises were at the discretion of the workers' bosses.

Although both chambers settled for slightly less than they wanted, the Senate's overhead budget grew by 16 percent and the House's by 6 percent. The Senate's budget included big boosts for committee investigations and for the Sergeant at Arms.

The House and Senate passed initial versions of the bill in July, putting it nearly in final form by fall, when new attention was focused on congressional security by the Sept. 11 terrorist attacks and the arrival of anthrax-tainted mail on Capitol Hill. Most of the ensuing safety measures were paid for under the supplemental appropriations laws (PL 107-38 and PL 107-117) enacted Sept. 18, 2001, and Jan. 10, 2002. Still, the Capitol Police received an 18 percent increase under the legislative branch bill, to $126 million, mainly to cover an expansion of the payroll envisioned before the terrorist attacks.

The extra money for the Capitol Visitor Center was provided so that the facility could include new congressional office space; the Select Intelligence Committee was to be the main tenant on the House side. Conferees also ordered up a plan for allowing members and their aides easier access to their office computer networks from remote locations, in case future emergencies forced the evacuation of the Capitol or congressional office buildings.

Highlights

Major spending components in the bill included:
• **House of Representatives.** $878 million, a 6 percent in-

---

BoxScore 2002
Fiscal Year
Legislative Branch

Bill:
HR 2647 — PL 107-68
Legislative Action:
Senate passed S 1172 (S Rept 107-37), 88-9, on July 19.
House passed HR 2647 (H Rept 107-169), 380-38, on July 31.
House adopted the conference report on HR 2647 (H Rept 107-259), 374-52, on Nov. 1.
Senate cleared HR 2647 by voice vote Nov. 1.
President signed Nov. 12.

---

crease over fiscal 2001. The total covered expenses of leadership offices, members' representational allowances, committees, officers' and employees' salaries, and allowances and expenses.
• **Senate.** $607 million, 16 percent more than the fiscal 2001 level.
• **Capitol Police.** $126 million for the Capitol Police, more than either the House or Senate originally approved. The 18 percent increase over fiscal 2001 paid for 79 more officers and gave the force a salary increase so its pay scale was akin to those of other federal law enforcement agencies.
• **Architect of the Capitol.** $314 million for the various operational and maintenance activities related to the operations of Congress, including the Capitol Visitor Center and the Library of Congress. Excluding the visitor center, the total was 16 percent more than the fiscal 2001 level.

Background

The legislative branch bill is typically one of the least controversial of the 13 regular appropriations measures. The president simply passes along the requests of Congress and its related agencies, and the White House does not take a position on the bill. By custom, the House and Senate accept each other's operating budgets, and differences are usually minor disputes over joint items or related agencies.

The fiscal 2002 bill was a return to that pattern after a tumultuous year in which the fiscal 2001 bill became part of a package that was pulled twice from the House floor, rejected once by the Senate, and vetoed by President Bill Clinton before the legislative branch portion was enacted as part of an omnibus appropriations bill (PL 106-554). The chief problem was the fact that GOP leaders decided to use the bill as a vehicle for a repeal of the telephone excise tax, as well as the Treasury-Postal appropriations bill, which faced strong Democratic opposition. Negotiators eventually struck a deal on the Treasury-Postal spending without touching the legislative branch funding levels. (*2000 Almanac, p. 2-115*)

Legislative Action

House Subcommittee Action

In a markup that lasted only about five minutes, the House Legislative Branch Appropriations Subcommittee approved the fiscal 2002 bill by voice vote July 20. The draft provided $2.2 million, a 4.4 percent increase over the fiscal 2001 level.

Where the Money Goes

Legislative Branch Spending

(figures are in thousands of dollars of new budget authority)

	Fiscal 2001 Appropriation	Fiscal 2002 Bush Request	House Bill	Senate Bill	Conference Report
House of Representatives	$830,449	$882,100	$882,100	$882,100	$878,195
Senate	522,023	612,675	—	606,735	606,885
Capitol Police	106,897	122,316	123,673	125,316	126,190
Other joint items	14,963	14,464	14,564	14,464	14,564
Architect of the Capitol	194,813	271,426	175,095	203,909	221,289
Library of Congress	438,297	363,147	368,594	362,059	370,594
General Accounting Office	384,020	427,794	421,844	417,843	421,844
Other	238,065	267,948	253,130	251,688	323,581
GRAND TOTAL	$2,729,527	$2,961,870	$2,239,000	$2,874,114	$2,971,142
Total adjusted for scorekeeping	($2,826,409)	($3,060,870)	($2,321,000)	($2,974,114)	($3,073,142)

TABLE: House Appropriations Committee

The bill contained several benefits for House staff members, including a 4.6 percent cost of living pay increase and a $65 per month public transit subsidy, eventually rising to $100 per month. The bill also called for a study on the feasibility of constructing a gym for House staff members.

Based on a deal worked out earlier in the year by House Administration Committee Chairman Bob Ney, R-Ohio, and the panel's ranking Democrat, Steny H. Hoyer of Maryland, the draft set a committee staff ratio of two-thirds for the majority party to one-third for the minority.

The bill recommended $124 million for Capitol Police, including a $17 million increase in salaries to provide for pay raises and the hiring of an additional 79 officers. It included $197 million for the Architect of the Capitol, not counting funds for Senate-related work.

House Committee Action

The full Appropriations Committee gave voice vote approval to the bill (H Rept 107-169) on July 26, with little debate on the dollar figures.

However, Marcy Kaptur, D-Ohio, raised hackles with an amendment she said was designed to call attention to a decision by Speaker J. Dennis Hastert, R-Ill., to make H-208, the former Ways and Means Committee room just off the House floor, available as a Capitol Hill office for Vice President Dick Cheney. Kaptur subsequently withdrew the amendment.

Inspired by the requirement for a study of a staff gym, Anne M. Northup, R-Ky., offered an amendment calling for a study within 60 days of the bill's enactment on the differences in access to the House gym for female and male members, and for the elimination of those differences. Northup said that while the gym, located in the Rayburn House Office Building, was technically open to female lawmakers, women were strongly discouraged from using it and were relegated to a smaller facility with less equipment. She said male lawmakers frequently walked nude through the main gym creating an unwelcome atmosphere for women. After drawing what Northup described as a "backlash" from male lawmakers on both sides

of the aisle, the amendment was eventually adopted by voice vote.

House Floor Action

The $2.2 billion package won overwhelming House support, passing 380-38, on July 31. *(House vote 298, p. H-104)*

An amendment by Steven R. Rothman, D-N.J., adopted by voice vote, provided $75,000 to purchase energy-efficient light bulbs for House offices.

Senate Committee Action

Senate appropriators actually started before their House counterparts. The Legislative Branch Appropriations Subcommittee sent its draft of the bill straight to the full Appropriations Committee, which approved the measure (S 1172 — S Rept 107-37) by voice vote July 12. The $1.9 billion bill included $607 million for Senate operations; it did not include money for the House.

Senate appropriators approved $1 million for the Capitol Visitor Center in response to flagging private donations. Congress had appropriated $100 million for the project in 1998, with the rest of the $266 million cost to be covered by private sector fundraising. So far, just $35 million in private money had been raised.

The committee report accompanying the bill was particularly critical of the Architect of the Capitol, noting "persistent management shortcomings" and an "unacceptably high level of worker injuries." The committee provided $178 million for the Architect, excluding House-related costs, but the report insisted that the Architect submit quarterly reports on worker safety improvements.

The bill included $125 million for the Capitol Police to cover pay increases, 79 additional officers and the purchase of 24 Harley-Davidson motorcycles to replace the last of the the force's foreign-made bikes being used in operational missions.

Senate Floor Action

The Senate passed the $1.9 billion bill July 19 by a vote of 88-9. No amendments were added, and debate was mini-

mal. On July 31, the Senate took up the House-passed bill and passed it by voice vote, after inserting portions of S 1172. The step was necessary before the two chambers could go to conference. (*Senate vote 241, p. S-50*)

Conference/Final Action

Negotiators reached agreement on a $3 billion final bill Oct. 30. The House adopted the conference report (H Rept 107-259) by a vote of 374-52 on Nov. 1. The Senate cleared the bill by voice vote several hours later. (*House vote 417, p. H-142*)

● **Capitol Police.** The $126 million for the police was more than recommended in either bill. The total included $55 million for salaries for police attached to the House, $57 million for those attached to the Senate, and $13 million for police general expenses, including $1.5 million to purchase 40 vehicles to transport police dogs. The bill also authorized the Capitol Police to accept donations of meals and refreshments during emergency situations — one of several policy changes written into the bill after Sept. 11.

● **Architect of the Capitol.** The bill provided a total of $314 million for the Architect including money earmarked for the demolition of the O'Neill House Office Building, a decaying former hotel near the Cannon Building. It also included the $70 million for the Capitol Visitor Center. Of the total, $51 million was for salaries and expenses, $15 million for the Capitol building, $42 million for Senate office buildings, $54 million for House office buildings and $52.5 million for the Capitol power plant. The agency's rules were to be changed to allow more laborers to receive benefits.

● **Library of Congress.** Conferees provided $452 million, more than the $450 million passed by the House or the $443 million recommended by the Senate. The total was 12 percent more than the fiscal 2001 level, not counting a $100 million supplemental fiscal 2001 appropriation for digitization.

● **Congressional Budget Office.** The bill provided $30.8 million for CBO, a 9 percent increase over fiscal 2001 and virtually the same amount recommended by both chambers.

● **General Accounting Office.** The GAO got $422 million, a 10 percent increase over the previous year, the same as the House approved and slightly more than the Senate figure.

● **Government Printing Office.** The GPO got $81 million for the printing and binding of congressional documents, $205,000 less than in fiscal 2001 and $10 million less than the request. ◆

Easy Pass for Military Construction

Congress on Oct. 18 cleared a $10.5 billion fiscal 2002 military construction appropriations bill that exceeded President Bush's request by a little more than $500 million. The smallest and least controversial of the 13 appropriations bills, the annual measure pays the costs of building military bases around the world, housing military personnel and their families, closing unneeded military bases and providing the U.S. share of NATO's infrastructure fund. President Bush signed the bill into law (HR 2904 — PL 107-64) on Nov. 5.

The bill provided $1.6 billion, or 18 percent, more than Congress appropriated in fiscal 2001, and $529 million more than Bush's request. It did not include funds for reconstructing the part of the Pentagon damaged in the Sept. 11 terrorist attacks; money for those repairs was included in the emergency supplemental spending bill (PL 107-38) enacted Sept. 18.

The bill added about $100 million to Bush's $532 million request to complete the shutdown of military bases already designated for closure. Senators argued that the extra money was necessary to ensure that environmental cleanup at the shuttered bases would be adequately funded.

Funding for family housing totaled $4.1 billion — $10 million more than the House level and $438 million more than the fiscal 2001 level, but about $33 million less than initially passed by the Senate. Clearing up the backlog of dilapidated military housing at home and abroad was a top objective for appropriators on the Military Construction subcommittee, who said housing conditions were making it more difficult for the armed forces to retain skilled personnel. Bush toured bases early in 2001, promising to devote an additional $400 million to military housing in fiscal 2002.

Highlights

Following are the major spending components of the bill:
● **Military construction.** $5.8 billion, a $1.5 billion increase over fiscal 2001 and $572 million more than Bush requested for projects such as barracks, weapons and training facilities. Most of the funds were destined for local companies that contracted to build structures on military bases.
● **Family housing.** $4.1 billion, about $438 million above fiscal 2001 levels and $29 million more than the administration's request, to operate and maintain existing housing units and for new construction and improvements.
● **Base closings.** $633 million, $101 million more than Bush requested and $389 million less than fiscal 2001 levels, including funding for environmental restoration and the

BoxScore **2002** Fiscal Year

Military Construction

Bill:
HR 2904 — PL 107-64
Legislative Action:
House passed HR 2904
(H Rept 107-207), 401-0, on
Sept. 21.
Senate passed HR 2904,
amended (S Rept 107-68),
97-0, on Sept. 26.
House adopted the conference
report (H Rept 107-246),
409-1, on Oct. 17.
Senate cleared the bill, 96-1,
on Oct. 18.
President signed Nov. 5.

Homeowners Assistance Fund, which helps personnel affected by the closure of military bases.

The bill included no money for new base closings. Bush had asked Congress to authorize a new round in 2003, but lawmakers put that off until 2005 as part of the defense authorization bill (PL 107-107). (*Defense authorization, p. 7-3*)

Background

Typically one of the most popular appropriations measures in Congress, the military construction bill includes money for almost every state and is usually the first measure out of the gate.

The fiscal 2001 bill provided $8.8 billion — $800 million more than President Bill Clinton requested and $459.9 million, or 5.5 percent, more than the fiscal 2000 level. Despite the dismal shape of family housing, the funding level was nearly $6 million less than in fiscal 2000, though it was $125 million more than Clinton requested. The bill was also the vehicle for $11.2 billion in fiscal 2000 supplemental spending, mostly to cover the cost of peacekeeping operations in Kosovo, anti-drug aid to Colombia and disaster assistance at home and abroad. It was signed July 13, making it the first of the fiscal 2001 appropriations bills to become law (PL 106-246) (*2000 Almanac, p. 2-123*)

The fiscal 2000 bill (PL 106-52) differed slightly from Clinton's plan. The bill's $8.4 billion total was $125 million less than Clinton requested and $81 million short of fiscal 1999. The bill allocated $4 billion for military construction, 15 percent more than Clinton's $3.5 billion request, because Congress rejected the president's plan to pay for construction projects incrementally. Congress cut Clinton's request for NATO construction funds by more than one-half, from $191 million to $81 million, and reduced his request for base closing funds by 48 percent, from $1.3 billion to $672 million. (*1999 Almanac, p. 2-112*)

Legislative Action

House Subcommittee/Committee Action
Its work slowed by a Bush administration review of defense policy, the House Military Construction Appropriations Subcommittee gave voice vote approval to a $10.5 billion spending bill Sept. 6. The full Appropriations Committee approved the bill (HR 2904 — H Rept 107-207) by voice vote Sept. 20.

The subcommittee initially was allocated $10 billion,

Where the Money Goes

Military Construction Spending

(figures are in thousands of dollars of new budget authority)

	Fiscal 2001 Appropriation	Fiscal 2002 Bush Request	House Bill	Senate Bill	Conference Report
Military construction	$4,259,143	$5,209,995	$5,526,817	$5,698,850	$5,781,750
NATO infrastructure	171,622	162,600	162,600	162,600	162,600
Family housing	3,657,618	4,066,517	4,128,383	4,085,837	4,095,739
Base closure and realignment	1,031,115	532,200	682,200	552,713	632,713
Rescissions	−2,400	—	−67,163	−120,193	−130,193
GRAND TOTAL	$8,936,498	$9,971,312	$10,500,000	$10,500,000	$10,500,000

SOURCE: House and Senate Appropriations committees.

but the amount was subsequently increased by about $400 million to reflect extra money that became available out of the $18.4 billion added by Bush to his defense request in June. Tracking provisions in the House defense authorization measure, the military construction bill proposed:

• $5.9 billion for military construction projects, including $1.2 billion to build 51 new barracks, an increase of $39 million and five buildings above Bush's request.

• $4.1 billion for family housing, including $1.1 billion to build or improve 6,800 family housing units and privatize another 28,000 units.

• $199 million for hospital and medical centers, equal to Bush's request and $58 million more than in fiscal 2001.

• $43 million for child day-care centers, about $17 million more than Bush sought and roughly equal to the existing level.

• $553 million to complete base closure projects, $21 million more than requested but $478 million less than in fiscal 2001.

The bill proposed making permanent a popular program that allowed the military to turn over the construction, operations and maintenance of military housing programs to private companies. The military, initially skeptical of the privatization program, had embraced the idea as it found it could get superior housing for less money.

House Floor Action

The House took up the bill Sept. 21, the day after the committee acted and passed it, 401-0. *(House vote 344, p. H-120)*

Appropriators stressed that the fiscal 2003 version would have to focus on better defending the Pentagon and other military buildings. Military Construction Appropriations Subcommittee Chairman David L. Hobson, R-Ohio, said the Pentagon should have more of the protective windows and sprinkler systems that had been installed in the section of the building struck by a hijacked plane Sept. 11. Those changes were credited with helping to save lives.

Hobson also said soldiers should be provided with safe, adequate housing as the military prepared for its unconventional war against terrorism. "We have to improve the quality of life for these people," he said. "Even more, now."

Senate Action

The Senate Appropriations Committee approved its version of the $10.5 billion bill (S 1460 — S Rept 107-68) by voice vote Sept. 25 after brief consideration. The Senate passed HR 2904 the next day by a vote of 97-0, after substituting the text of its bill. *(Senate vote 288, p. S-60)*

One main difference with the House was an increase of $129 million for base closings. The Senate bill included:

• $5.5 billion for military construction projects.

• $4.13 billion for family housing.

• $682 million for base closure projects. Supporters argued that base closure programs had been underfunded and questioned whether the $682 million would be sufficient to meet the costs of the accompanying environmental cleanups.

Overall, the amounts for military construction were about the same in the House and Senate bills. The breakdowns for each branch were approximately: Army, $1.7 billion; Navy, $1.13 billion; and Air Force, $1.15 billion.

Conference/Final Action

Conferees reached agreement Oct. 16, and the House adopted the conference report (H Rept 107-246) by a vote of 409-1 the next day. The Senate cleared the bill, 96-1, on Oct. 18. Ron Paul, R-Texas, often the House contrarian, and Sen. John McCain, R-Ariz., a frequent critic of spending on lawmakers' pet projects, cast the dissenting votes. *(House vote 394, p. H-134; Senate vote 305, p. S-64)*

Conferees agreed on $633 million to complete the shutdown of military bases already designated for closure. Senators argued that without the extra money, environmental cleanup at the shuttered bases would be grossly underfunded. "This is certainly something that we should consider before we embark on any future rounds of base closures," said Dianne Feinstein, D-Calif., who chaired the Senate Military Construction Appropriations Subcommittee. ◆

Deal on Mexican Trucks Frees Bill

Congress cleared a $59.6 billion fiscal 2002 Transportation spending bill Dec. 4 that provided a substantial increase in funding for highway, transit and aviation programs. It also allowed Mexican trucks to operate nationwide, giving President Bush a key victory and ending a long-running battle involving free trade, organized labor and highway safety. The bill provided significant spending increases for the Coast Guard and included new funding for a transportation security agency created by a separate aviation security law. President Bush signed the appropriations bill (HR 2299 — PL 107-87) on Dec. 18.

Most of the funding in the bill was beyond the control of the appropriators. More than 70 percent of it was guaranteed under landmark highway and aviation funding laws enacted in 1998 and 2000, respectively. The $15.3 billion in discretionary spending was a $1.3 billion decrease from fiscal 2001. By eliminating new funding for specific highway projects, appropriators were still able to provide modest discretionary increases for core transportation programs.

The bill was held up for nearly four months by the dispute over Mexican trucks, which stemmed from the 1993 North American Free Trade Agreement (NAFTA). Under the pact, the United States and Mexico were to be open to each others' trucks by January 2000. But U.S. unions objected, saying the change would cost jobs and make U.S. highways unsafe. President Bill Clinton decided to restrict Mexican trucks to a 20-mile commercial zone along the border. After a NAFTA commission ruled in February 2001 that the restriction violated the trade agreement, Bush issued rules to allow the trucks into the country starting Jan. 1, 2002. That set off a fight in Congress between lawmakers who argued that an open border would increase international trade, and others who said Mexico's lack of regulations covering hours of service, insurance and licensing for truck drivers would unleash dangerous vehicles on U.S. highways.

House appropriators wrote a $59.1 billion bill that would have opened the border while screening out unsafe trucks, but the House voted June 26 to ban all Mexican trucks. On Aug. 1, after weeks of debate, the Senate approved a $60.1 billion transportation bill that would have opened the border. However, the Senate included more than 20 safety requirements added by Patty Murray, D-Wash., and Richard C. Shelby, R-Ala., the chairman and ranking Republican on the Senate Transportation Appropriations Subcommittee. Bush threatened to veto either version if it reached him, setting up a difficult conference.

Negotiations did not resume until November, when Mur-

BoxScore 2002
Transportation — Fiscal Year

Bill:
HR 2299 — PL 107-87

Legislative Action:

House passed HR 2299 (H Rept 107-108), 426-1, on June 26.

Senate passed HR 2299, amended (S Rept 107-38), by voice vote Aug. 1.

House adopted the conference report (H Rept 107-308), 371-11, on Nov. 30.

Senate cleared HR 2299, 97-2, on Dec. 4.

President signed Dec. 18.

ray and Harold Rogers, R-Ky., chairman of the House Transportation Appropriations Subcommittee, reached a deal to open the border but impose many of the safety standards added by the Senate, including inspecting Mexican trucks traveling to the United States every 90 days and ensuring that trucking firms had insurance from U.S.-licensed companies.

Highlights

The bill increased total transportation funding by $1.5 billion over fiscal 2001 and exceeded Bush's request by $624 million. The following are major spending components of the final bill:

● **Aviation.** $13.3 billion for the Federal Aviation Administration (FAA), which is responsible for operating the nation's air traffic control system. The total was a $584 million increase over fiscal 2001 and virtually the same as Bush's request. It included $6.9 billion for FAA operations, $3.3 billion from the Airport and Airway Trust Fund for airport improvement grants, and $20 million for a new program to expand service at smaller airports to help reduce aviation congestion and flight delays.

● **Aviation security.** $1.3 billion for the new Transportation Security Administration, created under the aviation security law (PL 107-71) to manage security at the nation's airports and protect the transportation system from terrorist attacks. The funding was to come from a charge of up to $5 per one-way trip added to airline tickets.

● **Highways.** $32.9 billion, an increase of $1.2 billion over fiscal 2001, for federal highway programs and other activities administered by the Federal Highway Administration. All of the money was allocated from the Highway Trust Fund, which is fed by the federal tax on gasoline.

● **Highway safety.** $425 million for the National Highway Traffic Safety Administration, which sets and enforces safety performance standards for motor vehicles and carries out motor vehicle-related consumer programs.

● **Mass transit.** $6.7 billion, a $476 million increase over fiscal 2001, for mass transit under the Federal Transit Administration. The total consisted of $1.3 billion in appropriated funds and $5.4 billion to be released from the mass transit account of the Highway Trust Fund.

● **Coast Guard.** $5 billion, a 12 percent increase over fiscal 2001, for the Coast Guard. Funding included an initial $320 million installment to begin a 20-year, $10 billion program to replace outmoded deep-water vessels, the Transportation Department's largest acquisition program.

● **Amtrak.** $521 million for continued capital assistance to

Transportation Spending

(figures are in thousands of dollars of new budget authority)

	Fiscal 2001 Appropriation	Fiscal 2002 Bush Request	House Bill	Senate Bill	Conference Report
Federal Aviation Administration	$9,511,000	$9,987,781	$9,975,481	$10,045,808	$9,995,000
Federal Highway Administration*	—	—	—	—	—
Federal Railroad Administration	745,618	651,258	704,412	755,158	733,633
Federal Transit Administration	1,254,400	1,349,200	1,349,200	1,449,200	1,349,200
Coast Guard	4,632,895	5,055,816	4,996,243	5,110,566	5,030,509
National Highway Traffic Safety Administration	118,876	124,000	124,420	134,000	129,780
Secretary of Transportation	87,285	87,093	99,039	95,341	105,171
General provisions	1,769,996	785	450	20,420	144,225
GRAND TOTAL**	$18,702,897	$17,163,605	$17,159,786	$17,885,293	17,579,970
Total adjusted for scorekeeping	$18,694,141	$17,116,605	$17,117,786	$17,800,293	17,524,970
Limits on obligations and exempt obligations	($39,501,600)	($41,854,801)	($41,962,800)	($42,177,799)	($42,062,800)

* Receives no general funds; all money comes from trust funds. ** Includes rescissions.

TABLE: House and Senate Appropriations committees

the national passenger railway, equal to Bush's request and the amount provided in fiscal 2001. Amtrak was facing a fiscal 2003 deadline to start paying for itself.

Background

Enactment of the 1998 surface transportation law, known as TEA-21 (PL 105-178) and the 2000 FAA reauthorization law, dubbed AIR-21 (PL 106-181), left relatively little to the discretion of the appropriators. The two laws modified the budgetary treatment of federal highway, mass-transit and aviation programs, with the result that the vast majority of spending under the bill was guaranteed. What controversy did arise was usually over legislative riders. (*2000 Almanac, p. 21-3; 1998 Almanac, p. 24-3*)

In 2000, the riders included a House provision to continue a ban on considering changes to federal fuel-efficiency standards for vehicles, known as "corporate average fuel economy" (CAFE) standards. The Senate included language in its bill to delay a proposal by the National Highway Traffic Safety Administration to establish a new rating system to indicate the potential for sport utility vehicles (SUVs) to roll over.

The fiscal 2001 Transportation spending law (PL 106-346) resolved these controversies by continuing the CAFE prohibition but also requiring a study by the National Academy of Sciences to evaluate the effectiveness and impact of CAFE standards. It allowed the safety administration to continue its rule-making on a roll-over rating system for SUVs while the science academy conducted a study on the scientific validity of the proposed standards. (*2000 Almanac, p. 2-128*)

Under the existing standards, car fleets were required to average 27.5 miles per gallon; vehicles in the light truck category — including SUVs and minivans — were required to average 20.7 miles per gallon.

(The National Academy of Sciences issued its report on

July 31, 2001. It made no specific recommendations about increasing CAFE standards, but said higher fuel economy could be achieved "without degradation of safety." The White House supported "increasing automobile fuel economy" but asked Congress to leave the Transportation Department free to determine how best to accomplish that.)

Legislative Action

House Subcommittee Action

The House Transportation Appropriations Subcommittee gave voice vote approval June 12 to a $59.1 billion draft of the bill that included $14.9 billion in discretionary spending, down by 10 percent from fiscal 2001.

The bill called for a 5 percent increase in FAA funding, to $13.3 billion, slightly less than Bush's request. It allowed for the hiring of 300 additional air traffic controllers to reduce flight congestion at the beginning of fiscal 2002, with another 300 to be hired during the year.

It included funding for a "free flight" initiative by the FAA that would allow airline pilots, with help from satellites, to chart their own more direct routes from city to city rather than relying on fixed airways.

The bill recommended $5 billion for the Coast Guard.

For the first time since 1995, the legislation did not include language to prohibit the Transportation Department from considering stricter CAFE standards for cars and light trucks.

House Committee Action

Leaving the spending levels virtually unchanged, the full Appropriations Committee approved the bill (HR 2299 — H Rept 107-108) by voice vote June 20. However, an hour-long debate on access for Mexican trucks pointed to trouble for the bill on the House floor.

Most Democrats supported an amendment by Martin

Olav Sabo of Minnesota, ranking Democrat on the Transportation Subcommittee, that would have blocked the Transportation Department from allowing Mexican motor carriers to travel beyond the 20-mile zone unless they first passed safety reviews similar to those for domestic trucks.

But Republicans and members from districts along the Mexican border succeeded in substituting language that reflected the Bush administration's position. The amendment, offered by Rogers, called for Mexican trucks to operate in the United States for an 18-month provisional period while they were monitored for safety. Operators that failed the safety audits would be prohibited from further entry, while those that met the standards would be able to operate in the United States permanently. Sabo argued that the proposal was "not stringent enough to make sure that these drivers of these trucks are safe enough for travel within our country." The substitute was adopted, 37-27.

The appropriators rejected a request by Bush to redirect $145 million from surplus gas-tax revenue in the Highway Trust Fund to improve transportation options for the disabled. Soaring gasoline sales were expected to result in a $4.5 billion surplus in the fund in fiscal 2002, but the 1998 surface transportation law required that the excess be returned to the states. Congress had rebuffed Clinton the preceding year when he tried to use some of the surplus for high-speed rail projects.

On another issue, the committee adopted by voice vote an amendment by Todd Tiahrt, R-Kan., to require the Washington Metropolitan Area Transit Authority to change the signs for its Metrorail stop at Ronald Reagan Washington National Airport from "National Airport" to reflect the airport's full name.

House Floor Action

The House passed the $59.1 billion spending bill, 426-1, on June 26, after agreeing to ban Mexican trucks from operating nationwide under any conditions. (*House vote 194, p. H-72*)

Blocked by the GOP-controlled Rules Committee from offering his amendment to require full safety reviews for Mexican trucks, Sabo proposed to bar the use of funds in the bill to process applications by Mexico-domiciled motor carriers to operate beyond the border zone. The amendment was adopted, 285-143, with 82 Republicans joining 201 Democrats and two independents to support it. The ban drew strong White House opposition. (*House vote 193, p. H-72*)

"You cannot do that. You are in violation of a treaty, in violation of the law," Rogers said, trying to talk colleagues out of the amendment. David R. Obey of Wisconsin, ranking Democrat on the Appropriations Committee responded: "We are not required to allow unsafe trucks on American highways in order to satisfy some pencil-happy bureaucrat dealing with NAFTA."

Transportation and Infrastructure Committee Chairman Don Young, R-Alaska, also succeeded in striking $88 million that Bush wanted to redirect from the gas-tax surplus to build and staff truck inspection stations on the U.S.-Mexico border.

Democrat James P. Moran of suburban Virginia raised a point of order against the provision requiring a change in signs indicating the metro stop at Ronald Reagan National Airport, saying it was an unfunded mandate. But on a procedural vote the House supported the provision 219-202. (*House vote 190, p. H-70*)

An attempt by Frank A. LoBiondo, R-N.J., to increase Coast Guard spending by $250 million was blocked on a voice vote. The House adopted by voice vote a proposal by Robert E. Andrews, D-N.J., to cut $335,000 from the budget of the Amtrak Reform Council, reducing its allocation to $450,000. The council was an independent oversight board created as part of Amtrak's 1997 reauthorization (PL 105-134).

Senate Committee Action

The Senate Appropriations Committee approved a $60 billion version of the bill (S 1178 — S Rept 107-38) by voice vote July 12. The bill's larger total — discretionary spending was $15.6 billion, compared to $14.9 billion in the House bill — enabled appropriators to include more money for highway projects, air traffic controllers and Coast Guard operations. The Transportation Subcommittee had approved the measure earlier the same day without amendment, also by voice vote.

The bill included a compromise engineered by Murray and Shelby to lift the truck ban but add nearly two dozen safety requirements. Mexican truck drivers would have to adhere to a number of safety regulations, including inspections, weight restrictions and limits on the number of hours a driver could stay behind the wheel.

The proposal included $103 million for truck inspections and 80 inspectors, $15 million more than Bush sought, and required that Mexican trucks cross the border only at facilities where inspectors were present and on duty. The full opening of the border would be delayed until the Transportation Department had published final rules covering safety regulations and confirmed that the new inspectors were fully trained. Mexican firms would be required to provide sufficient information on the safety records of their companies and drivers to permit U.S. monitoring and show that they understood U.S. safety standards. Mexican truck companies would have to have U.S. insurance and complete two safety audits within 18 months before receiving a permanent operating certificate for travel in the United States.

"I believe this is a far better approach than the one taken by the House bill, which has drawn a veto threat by the administration," Murray said.

Senate appropriators sought to placate Bush and state highway officials on the gas-tax surplus issue by increasing the total available for highway construction by $202 million to $32.9 billion — enough to pay for Bush's proposed program for the disabled and for inspection stations at the border.

The Senate bill also included $23.8 million to hire 600 additional air traffic controllers and $12.2 million for 221 additional aviation safety inspectors. The House bill did not provide for additional inspectors.

The bill included $13.3 billion for the FAA, essentially the same as in the House bill; $5.1 billion for the Coast Guard, slightly more than the House or Bush's budget; $521 million for Amtrak, the same as the House bill; and $420,000 for the Amtrak Reform Council, $30,000 below the House level.

Senate Floor Action

The Senate passed the $60.1 billion bill by voice vote Aug. 1, after ending a nine-day filibuster by border-state senators opposed to the restrictions on Mexican trucks.

Republicans John McCain of Arizona and Phil Gramm of Texas finally allowed the vote after Majority Leader Tom Daschle, D-S.D., agreed to put off appointing members to a House-Senate conference on the bill until the Senate returned from its August recess. The Senate then voted, 100-0, to cut off the debate. *(Senate vote 262, p. S-54)*

The protracted floor fight began after Murray won voice vote approval July 27 for the stringent safety guidelines approved in committee. Gramm, McCain and Pete V. Domenici, R-N.M., opposed the amendment, saying it would further delay opening the border. The White House threatened to veto the bill if it was included.

Gramm had lost an attempt July 25 to block any safety requirements on Mexican trucks that did not also extend to trucks from Canada and the United States. His amendment was tabled, or killed, 65-35. *(Senate vote 250, p. S-52)*

On July 26, the Senate voted 70-30, to limit debate on the Murray amendment, with 19 Republicans joining James M. Jeffords, I-Vt., and the entire Democratic caucus to invoke cloture. The vote boosted their hopes that they could override a presidential veto. *(Senate vote 252, p. S-52)*

But Gramm and McCain refused to fold, continuing to file amendments and forcing Daschle to file a cloture motion on the bill. Mexico's President Vicente Fox said Aug. 2 that if there were no agreement, Mexican trucks would not go to the United States. "But neither will there be American trucks here," he added.

Conference/Final Action

House and Senate conferees reached agreement Nov. 29 on a $59.6 billion bill. The House adopted the conference report (H Rept 107-308) the next day by a vote of 371-11. The Senate cleared the bill, 97-2, on Dec. 4. *(House vote 465, p. H-160; Senate vote 346, p. S-72)*

Work had been delayed while Bush transportation officials focused on completing separate airline bailout legislation (PL 107-42) and an aviation security bill (PL 107-71) in the aftermath of Sept. 11. Rogers and Murray finally were able to reach a deal on Mexican trucks with Transportation Department officials the week of Nov. 26. "We took the Murray-Shelby language and brought it within the parameters we could live with," Rogers said. The compromise removed the last obstacle to finishing the bill.

Following are the main compromises reached in conference, with resolution of the trucking dispute topping the list:

● **Mexican Trucks.** In a deal that included assurances for highway safety advocates but was a clear victory for Bush and business interests, the bill allowed Bush to open the Southwest border to long-haul Mexican trucks in accordance with NAFTA. The bill provided $140 million for border inspection stations and staff, and it barred the trucks until the Transportation Department certified that opening the border would not threaten highway safety. Sen. Kay Bailey Hutchison, R-Texas, said the process should take about six months.

Under the deal, Mexican trucking companies that wanted to operate within the United States had to have their equipment, insurance and driving records inspected and certified by the Transportation Department. The trucks could enter the United States only at border crossings with inspectors and adequate capacity to carry out safety checks. At least half of all Mexican truck drivers had to have their licenses checked upon entering the country, including all those carrying hazardous cargo. Each truck had to be physically inspected every 90 days, similar to a border inspection system in place in California.

"I have said all along that we can ensure our safety and promote commerce at the same time," Murray said.

Teamsters President James P. Hoffa, by contrast, was bitter even before the agreement was finished. "They don't care about highway safety. They just care about money," he said. Other union officials said they were satisfied with the safety requirements, but that did not assuage fears that low-wage Mexican drivers would cost U.S. jobs and depress wages.

● **Surplus highway funds.** Congress rejected Bush's request to use $145 million in surplus gas-tax revenue from the Highway Trust Fund for a transportation program for the disabled. However, lawmakers directed $998 million ($423 million in surplus revenue, plus $574 million originally directed to projects under the 1998 surface transportation law) for other purposes, including funding increases for members' projects. The $56 million Bush requested for truck inspection facilities was included as part of the deal on Mexican trucks.

● **FAA.** The amount for FAA operations was $6.89 billion, more than the $6.87 billion in the House bill, but not as generous as the $6.92 billion approved by the Senate. The final amount was $342 million more than that provided in fiscal 2001.

The conference report provided $192 million for the FAA's "free flight" initiative.

● **Reagan airport.** The bill included the House provision directing the Washington transit authority to modify signs, maps, directories and documents to reflect the designation, "Ronald Reagan Washington National Airport Station." The Senate had no similar provision.

● **Amtrak.** While there was no disagreement on the $521 million provided to Amtrak, differences over the Amtrak Reform Council resulted in an appropriation of $225,000, down from $750,000 in fiscal 2001 and less than in either the House or Senate bill.

● **CAFE standards.** The bill did not block efforts to update CAFE standards. ◆

Treasury Bill Skirts Usual Fights

With perennial debates over issues such as abortion and members' pay subdued, Congress on Nov. 1 cleared a $32.8 billion fiscal 2002 spending bill for the Treasury Department and Postal Service. President Bush signed the measure (HR 2590 — PL 107-67), which also funds the Customs Service, Secret Service, the Executive Office of the President, the IRS and an array of other agencies, on Nov. 12.

The bill provided $2 billion, or 6 percent, more than the fiscal 2001 version. More than half the added money was for mandatory programs, which are outside the control of the appropriators. Of the $32.8 billion in the bill, $17.1 billion went to discretionary programs; $15.7 billion was mandatory, virtually all of it for health and pension benefits for retired federal workers.

The biggest winner among discretionary accounts was the U.S. Customs Service, which got an 18 percent increase over fiscal 2001, almost doubling the amount for the agency's automated commercial system and providing funds to hire more agents along the U.S.-Canada border. The IRS got a 6 percent increase, primarily to modernize its outdated computer system and hire more employees. The bill gave federal employees a 4.6 percent pay increase, equal to the raise for military personnel.

The Treasury-Postal bill moved quickly through the House in July, despite the addition of controversial language to bar the use of funds to enforce the U.S. ban on travel to Cuba. In the Senate, Byron L. Dorgan, D-N.D., chairman of the Treasury-Postal Appropriations Subcommittee, took advantage of a period of bipartisanship after Sept. 11 to push the measure through with no substantive amendments.

The bill stalled for a time in conference over the Cuba travel language, which Dorgan championed in the face of a White House veto threat, and an administration push to consolidate several White House offices into a single account to give the president more flexibility. Conferees broke the impasse by dropping both provisions.

Background

Much of the Treasury-Postal bill funds essential programs, including the IRS, which brings in far more than it spends, and the Office of Personnel Management (OPM), the government's personnel office. The narrow focus tends to make the legislation easy to move early on, but it often also makes it a magnet for unrelated controversies.

The fiscal 2001 bill was battered by White House de-

BoxScore | **2002** Fiscal Year

Treasury-Postal Service

Bill:
HR 2590 — PL 107-67
Legislative Action:
House passed HR 2590 (H Rept 107-152), 334-94, on July 25.
Senate passed HR 2590, amended (S Rept 107-57), by voice vote Sept. 19.
House adopted conference report (H Rept 107-253), 339-85, on Oct. 31
Senate cleared HR 2590, 83-15, on Nov. 1.
President signed Nov. 12.

---

mands for more spending, a House provision to loosen sanctions against Cuba, and Democratic threats to add gun-control provisions on the Senate floor.

Hoping to avoid difficult votes, GOP leaders kept the bill from coming to the Senate floor, instead attaching it to the conference report on the legislative branch spending bill. President Bill Clinton vetoed the package, in part because it also included a separate telephone excise tax repeal. The Treasury-Postal measure was not enacted until Dec. 21, 2000, when Clinton signed it as part of a fiscal 2001 omnibus appropriations bill (PL 106-554). (*2000 Almanac, p. 2-138*)

The fiscal 2000 bill (PL 106-58) cleared with relative ease Sept. 16, 1999, thanks to a generous funding allocation, though it had stalled for weeks in the House over Democratic threats to attach gun control amendments and passed that chamber by a margin of one vote. (*1999 Almanac, p. 2-128*)

Highlights

The fiscal 2002 bill included the following major spending components:

● **Treasury Department.** $15 billion, a $1 billion increase over fiscal 2001 and $410 million more than Bush requested. The total included:

  ● **Customs Service.** $2.7 billion, about $409 million above fiscal 2001 appropriations and $303 million more than Bush requested to collect tariffs and duties, and to enforce U.S. border laws governing international traffic and trade.

  ● **IRS.** $9.4 billion, slightly above the president's request and surpassing the fiscal 2001 level by $548 million, mainly to modernize the agency's outdated computer system and complete the hiring of 4,000 additional employees.

  ● **U.S. Secret Service.** $924 million, $90 million more than the fiscal 2001 level and $64 million more than requested, to protect senior government officials and enforce anti-counterfeiting laws.

● **Office of Personnel Management.** $15.6 billion, slightly above Bush's request and about $1 billion more than the fiscal 2001 level. Virtually all the money — $15.4 billion — was mandatory spending on federal employee health and retirement benefits. OPM also helps recruit federal civilian workers, and develops job qualifications policies for pay and leave.

● **Executive Office of the President.** $748 million, about $47 million more than in fiscal 2001 and $16 million more than Bush requested, to staff the White House, various poli-

Where the Money Goes

Treasury-Postal Service Spending

(figures are in thousands of dollars of new budget authority)

	Fiscal 2001 Appropriation	Fiscal 2002 Bush Request	House Bill	Senate Bill	Conference Report
Office of Personnel Management	$14,608,948	$15,633,378	$15,634,078	$15,633,378	$15,634,078
Treasury Department	14,038,200	14,631,710	15,032,170	14,908,859	15,041,918
IRS	(8,888,926)	(9,422,387)	(9,457,439)	(9,450,387)	(9,437,079)
Customs Service	(2,279,294)	(2,385,226)	(2,669,289)	(2,555,922)	(2,688,049)
Secret Service	(833,806)	(860,469)	(923,569)	(902,967)	(924,072)
Executive Office of the President	700,273	731,725	751,967	755,519	747,531
General Services Administration	657,968	474,476	459,021	466,550	472,081
Postal Service	95,888	143,712	143,712	143,712	143,712
Other	473,445	420,350	443,821	455,432	453,749
GRAND TOTAL	$30,574,722	$32,035,351	$32,464,769	$32,363,450	$32,493,069
Total adjusted for scorekeeping	($30,779,357)	($32,371,351)	($32,712,150)	($32,808,450)	($32,759,450)

TABLE: House Appropriations Committee

cy offices — including the Office of Management and Budget and the National Security Council — and the presidential and vice presidential residences.

● **General Services Administration (GSA).** $472 million — $2 million less than requested and $186 million below fiscal 2001 — to support the agency that serves as the government's landlord, purchaser and travel agent. In addition, the bill made available $6.2 billion from the GSA's General Buildings Fund, which derives most of its funding from rents paid by federal agencies. The GSA uses the money for construction, repairs, rents and building operations.

● **U.S. Postal Service.** A $144 million subsidy to the self-financed, quasi-autonomous Postal Service to cover free mailings for blind and overseas voters. The 50 percent increase over the previous year was to compensate for a shortfall in fiscal 2001.

Legislative Action

House Subcommittee Action

A $32.7 billion draft of the bill moved easily through the Treasury, Postal Service and General Government Appropriations Subcommittee on July 11; members refrained from offering amendments and approved the measure by voice vote. The bill's generous increase in discretionary spending won bipartisan support and promise of quick action. Most controversies were put off until the full committee.

The subcommittee proposed $300 million — more than double the administration's $130 million request — to hasten the replacement of 18-year-old Customs Service computers. The new system, due to go online in five years, was designed to ease the processing of commercial shipments at international ports and airports, in part by allowing businesses to fill out the required forms by accessing a Web site. It also was intended to enhance Customs' ability to analyze its database of trade transactions. The funding was a top goal

of several business lobbying groups and an easy way for lawmakers to take a non-controversial position in favor of expanding trade.

The subcommittee included $9.5 billion for the IRS, agreeing with Bush's proposed 6 percent increase to help the agency carry out a 1998 mandate (PL 105-206) to improve customer service. (*1998 Almanac, p. 21-3*)

The bill was silent on the automatic congressional pay raise. Under a 1989 law (PL 101-194), members received an annual pay increase unless they vote to prevent it. Although the Treasury-Postal bill did not fund members' pay, it had become the vehicle for annual efforts to block the increase. Speaker J. Dennis Hastert, R-Ill., and Minority Leader Richard A. Gephardt, D-Mo., had agreed quietly in May not to make a political issue of the increase. (*1989 Almanac, p. 51*)

House Full Committee Action

The full Appropriations Committee approved the bill (H Rept 107-152) by voice vote July 17, after Democrats won several changes.

Democrats' biggest victory was the adoption, by a vote of 40-21, of an amendment by Nita M. Lowey, D-N.Y., to restore language that she had helped write into law three years earlier, requiring federal employee health plans that paid for prescription drugs to cover contraceptives. At the administration's request, the subcommittee draft had dropped the provision. Thirteen Republicans voted with 27 Democrats for the amendment.

In other action, the committee:

● Adopted by voice vote, an amendment by Carrie P. Meek, D-Fla., to take $10 million from the bill's IRS account and spend it to continue the "first accounts" program, created in fiscal 2001 to encourage banks to provide accounts with minimal fees to low-income people. Bush proposed nothing for the program, which critics noted had not yet spent all of its initial $8 million.

● Adopted by voice vote an amendment by ranking sub-

committee Democrat Steny H. Hoyer of Maryland to give all civilian federal workers a 4.6 percent pay raise, starting Oct. 1. The new figure matched Bush's original request for the military, though the president had since raised that request to 5 percent. The Treasury-Postal bill set personnel policies but did not actually fund the payroll, so Hoyer's amendment directed all agencies to absorb their share of the $893 million in added cost. Congress had reaffirmed its commitment to "pay parity" in the fiscal 2002 budget resolution (H Con Res 83).

• Rejected, on a 31-31 tie, the White House proposal to consolidate 18 of its appropriations accounts into one. Republicans said the change was needed to give the executive branch more budgeting flexibility; Democrats said it would hinder congressional oversight.

• Rejected, 26-33, a proposal by Rosa DeLauro, D-Conn., to drop language barring health plans from paying for the abortions of government workers.

The only big partisan fight came over the symbolic issue of who should pay the electricity bills for the vice presidential residence, located on the grounds of the Naval Observatory in Northwest Washington. The Navy and the office of the vice president had shared the cost for the past three years. But the bill had more than doubled, to an estimated $134,000 in fiscal 2001, when Al Gore moved out and Vice President Dick Cheney moved in. The administration wanted the Navy to reassume full responsibility to insulate Cheney from "the fluctuating and unpredictable nature of utility costs." Democrats lambasted the request as hypocritical, citing a widely quoted Cheney comment that energy consumption should be a matter of individual responsibility. They also said the bills were evidence that Cheney, who had taken the lead in shaping Bush's energy policy, was insufficiently attuned to the need for conservation.

The panel rejected, 29-33, an amendment by ranking committee Democrat David R. Obey of Wisconsin to delete the cost-shifting language and to drop a second administration proposal to permit donations of food, drinks, flowers, tents and other supplies for use in Cheney's official entertaining. A similar exception to the government gratuities rule applied to the White House.

House Floor Action

The House passed the $32.7 billion bill by a vote of 334-94 on July 25, after adding controversial language to lift restrictions on travel to Cuba. (*House vote 274, p. H-98*)

The amendment to lift the curbs, offered by Jeff Flake, R-Ariz., was adopted 240-186. Under existing law, U.S. citizens could travel to Cuba only if they obtained a special license from the Treasury Department — which generally limited access to journalists, academics, government officials and people on humanitarian missions. The White House strongly opposed any weakening of the sanctions and subsequently threatened to veto the bill if the language remained. (*House vote 270, p. H-96*)

The House rejected, 201-227, a broader amendment by Charles B. Rangel, D-N.Y., that effectively would have repealed the Cuba trade embargo initiated by President John F. Kennedy in February 1962. (*House vote 271, p. H-96*)

In other action, the House:

• Agreed by voice vote to merge 10 of the 18 accounts

that the White House wanted consolidated.

• Defeated, 141-285, an attempt by Jay Inslee, D-Wash., to bar the Navy from paying the electricity bill at the vice president's mansion. It also also rejected, 151-274, an effort by Maurice D. Hinchey, D-N.Y., to strike the provision on donated food and drinks. (*House votes 268, 269, p. H-96*)

• Blocked an attempt — led by Jim Matheson, D-Utah, and Doug Ose, R-Calif. — to deny members of Congress the cost of living pay increase. A procedural motion that prevented them from offering such an amendment was defeated, 293-129; that was the closest the House got to a direct vote on its own pay. (*House vote 267, p. H-94*)

Senate Full Committee Action

The Senate Appropriations Committee approved its version of the $32.7 billion bill (S 1398 — S Rept 107-57) by a vote of 29-0 on July 26. The bill included $17.1 billion in discretionary spending, only slightly more than the House version. As in the House bill, the biggest boost was for the Customs Service.

The Senate bill was silent on Cuba, but Treasury-Postal subcommittee chairman Dorgan said he would either offer his own amendment on the floor or ask the Senate to adopt the same travel provision added by the House. Dorgan was an ardent advocate of easing U.S.-Cuba economic sanctions in order to expand the world market for U.S. crops and other goods. Dorgan said he also expected the combining of White House accounts to be questioned on the floor.

As in the House, the Senate bill included a 4.6 percent pay raise for federal civilian workers. It maintained coverage for contraceptives in the medical insurance plans of government workers. And it did not seek to deny members of Congress their automatic cost of living increase.

Senate appropriators decided against joining the symbolic House campaign to compel the vice president's office to pay the entire electricity bill for the vice presidential residence.

At Dorgan's behest, the bill earmarked $25 million for nearly 300 more Customs Service agents on the 4,000-mile-long U.S.-Canada border. It also proposed doubling, to $10 million, spending on programs to stop imports of goods manufactured by child labor. The bill allocated $230 million for the new Customs Service computer system.

Dorgan earmarked $1 million for monthly audits on the accuracy of IRS customer service. The Treasury's inspector general recently had found that 73 percent of questions posed at IRS offices were being answered incorrectly.

Senate Floor Action

In the spirit of bipartisanship that swept the Capitol after the Sept. 11 terrorist attacks, the Senate passed the bill Sept. 19 with no dissent and virtually no debate. The $32.8 billion measure passed by voice vote, with none of the controversial amendments that had been anticipated.

The bill came to the floor on a day when no roll call votes were permitted because of the Rosh Hashana holiday. Behind the scenes, Dorgan and top subcommittee Republican Ben Nighthorse Campbell of Colorado worked to limit amendments to those that did not require a vote. Dorgan led by example, holding back his proposal to suspend the ban on travel by U.S. citizens to Cuba. Campbell successfully urged

his colleagues to hold off terrorism-related amendments that would have increased the bill's bottom line.

The most significant amendments — to require Treasury to issue war and "unity" bonds — came from Mitch McConnell, R-Ky., and Timothy V. Johnson, D-S.D., and were adopted by voice vote. The purpose was to raise funds to finance recovery from and response to the terrorist attacks.

Conference/Final Action

House and Senate conferees agreed Oct. 25 on a final, $32.8 billion bill, with $17.1 billion in discretionary spending. The House adopted the conference report (H Rept 107-253), 339-85, on Oct. 31 and the Senate cleared the bill the next day, 83-15. *(House vote 413, p. H-140; Senate vote 321, p. S-67)*

The speedy action came after conferees broke a several-week logjam over the White House demand to consolidate appropriations accounts and the House language to overturn the ban on travel to Cuba. Senate opponents, led by Dorgan, succeeded in dropping the White House plan, despite personal intervention by Cheney. Dorgan, however, was on the losing side of the Cuba travel issue.

The final bill provided $47 million more than the House version and $49 million less than the Senate measure. Issues resolved in conference included:

● **Customs.** The $2.7 billion agreed to for the Customs Service was several million dollars more than either chamber had approved initially. It included $428 million to modernize the agency's information technology, the same as in the House bill but $70 million more than approved by the Senate. Dorgan won $28 million for additional Customs agents to tighten security along the U.S.-Canada border.

● **IRS.** The $9.4 billion included for the IRS was slightly less than either chamber had recommended. It included $392 million to modernize the agency's information technology, close to a 500 percent increase over fiscal 2001. However, the report specified that the IRS could not use any of the funds until it had a spending plan that had been approved by the Appropriations committees.

● **Abortion.** Like the House and Senate bills, the agreement banned use of funds to pay for abortions under federal employee health plans, except in cases of rape, incest or danger to the life of the woman.

● **Contraceptives.** Like both bills, the agreement continued the requirement that federal health plans offering prescription drug coverage include coverage of contraceptives, with exceptions for health plans or physicians who objected to providing contraceptives on religious grounds.

● **Congressional pay raise.** Both chambers had successfully avoided amendments to block members' cost of living pay raise, and the final bill was silent on the subject.

● **Vice president's budget.** Despite House Democrats' opposition, the bill retained the provisions directing the Navy to pick up the tab for utilities at Cheney's Naval Observatory residence, and authorizing the Navy to accept donations of money, food and beverages for official functions at the vice presidential residence. Senate Democrats did not oppose the provisions.

● **Counterterrorism.** The bill provided $46 million to the Treasury's Financial Crimes Enforcement Network to combat money-laundering. Interest in examining such activity had been heightened in the wake of the terrorist attacks. The bill also included $40 million for Treasury's counterterrorism fund, used to investigate terrorism and prevent the importing of weapons of mass destruction.

● **High-intensity drug areas.** The bill allotted $226 million to fund law enforcement efforts in several so-called high intensity drug trafficking areas around the country. The program, which started in 1990 with five designated areas, had expanded to 26 areas, many of them in states and districts of senior members of the Appropriations committees.

The bill also made $386 million available for construction of more than a dozen new federal courthouses, courthouse annexes, border stations, and other federal facilities. It barred the Postal Service from reducing six-day mail delivery or closing rural post offices in fiscal 2002. And it made permanent a provision allowing federal agencies to use funds appropriated for salaries and expenses to pay for child care, particularly for lower-income federal employees. ◆

VA-HUD Funds Grow $4.4 Billion

Lawmakers cleared a $112.7 billion spending bill for the departments of Veterans Affairs (VA) and Housing and Urban Development (HUD) late in the session, after sidestepping lingering disputes over federal drinking water standards and grants to fight drug-related crime in public housing. The bill, which also funded the Environmental Protection Agency (EPA), the National Aeronautics and Space Administration (NASA) and a number of other independent agencies, was signed into law Nov. 26 (HR 2620 — PL 107-73)

The bill's final spending total was $609 million less than the Senate version and roughly equal to the House-passed level. On a programmatic basis, however, lawmakers actually brought spending close to Senate levels by rescinding $1.2 billion of unspent HUD money, mostly from Section 8 rental assistance funds that had not been used by public housing authorities. The bookkeeping changes allowed appropriators to provide an 8 percent increase to the National Science Foundation (NSF), raising its funding to $4.8 billion — its highest level ever. The VA's appropriation rose 6.6 percent, to $51.1 billion, while HUD funding rose 5.9 percent, to $30.1 billion.

Even without the bookkeeping help, the final bill exceeded President Bush's request by $2.1 billion and provided $4.4 billion more than the fiscal 2001 version.

The bill moved quickly through the House and Senate during the summer, with the two chambers passing separate versions before the August recess. At that point, significant differences between the two bills pointed to a contentious conference.

The GOP-controlled House had approved a number of administration-proposed cuts to public housing programs, as well as a White House plan to eliminate 270 EPA environmental enforcement jobs and direct the savings to state enforcement efforts. Democrats in both chambers opposed those moves. The House also included $275 million in extra NASA funding for a Crew Return Vehicle for the International Space Station. And House Democrats succeeded in adding an amendment to bar the EPA from easing standards set by the Clinton administration for arsenic levels in drinking water.

The Senate, under Democratic control when it passed the bill, was more generous to housing programs but inserted strict spending limits on the International Space Station, fearing that $4.8 billion in cost overruns associated with the project would eat into the space agency's other science programs. The Senate reinstated the EPA environmental enforcement provisions, funded the drug elimination grants and included funding for AmeriCorps, which House Republicans,

BoxScore — VA-HUD — 2002 Fiscal Year

Bill:
HR 2620 — PL 107-73
Legislative Action:
House passed HR 2620 (H Rept 107-159), 336-89, on July 31.
Senate passed HR 2620, amended (S Rept 107-43), 94-5, on Aug. 2.
House adopted the conference report (H Rept 107-272), 401-18, on Nov. 8.
Senate cleared HR 2620, 87-7, on Nov. 8.
President signed Nov. 26.

following past practice, had targeted for extinction. The bill also barred the EPA from delaying new, stricter standards for arsenic levels in drinking water.

By the time the conferees met in October, the Sept. 11 terrorist attacks had altered the agenda. The emphasis was on avoiding fights and finishing their work. They set aside some issues, resolved others and looked for ways to allocate spending cuts.

They agreed to Bush's request to delete a $300 million HUD grant program to combat drug-related crime in housing projects, though they made most of the funds available through another program. The bill dropped both the House and Senate drinking water language and instead required the EPA to implement the Clinton standards without delay. Conferees adopted the Senate position on EPA environmental jobs and on AmeriCorps, and agreed to delete funding for the NASA Crew Return Vehicle.

Despite the budget constraints, the bill was still a magnet for lawmakers' projects. The conference report included more than $1 billion for economic development, university research and water and sewer construction projects not requested by the administration. The final version had a record 1,600 earmarks.

Highlights

Major spending categories in the bill included:
- **Veterans.** $51.1 billion for the VA — nearly $3.2 billion more than the fiscal 2001 level and almost $450 million above Bush's request. The total included $27.5 billion for the Veterans Benefits Administration, which provides pensions and benefits, including education, housing and vocational assistance; and $21.8 billion for the Veterans Health Administration, which funds VA hospitals and provides medical care.
- **HUD.** $30.1 billion — $1.7 billion more than fiscal 2001, but $433 million less than the president's request. The total included $15.6 billion for the Housing Certificate Fund, which provides Section 8 rental housing subsidy contracts and vouchers for low-income families, and $2.8 billion for public housing modernization and other capital improvements administered by the Public Housing Capital Fund. The bill also provided $3.5 billion for public housing operating assistance and $5 billion for Community Development Block Grants.
- **EPA.** $7.9 billion — just $74 million above the fiscal 2001 level, but nearly $587 million more than the president's request. The EPA regulates air and water quality, solid and hazardous wastes, pesticides and dangerous materials, and other potential environmental hazards.

VA-HUD Spending

(figures are in thousands of dollars of new budget authority)

	Fiscal 2001 Appropriation	Fiscal 2002 Bush Request	House Bill	Senate Bill	Conference Report
Department of Veterans Affairs	$47,948,336	$50,686,213	$51,354,821	$51,138,976	$51,135,398
Department of Housing and Urban Development	28,476,435	30,580,617	29,979,968	31,014,459	30,147,695
NASA	14,285,300	14,511,400	14,951,400	14,561,400	14,793,200
Environmental Protection Agency	7,828,851	7,316,599	7,545,445	7,751,600	7,903,213
National Science Foundation	4,426,122	4,472,520	4,840,160	4,672,520	4,788,940
Federal Emergency Management Agency	4,439,800	2,212,945	3,557,352	3,277,945	3,057,854
Other independent agencies	938,597	891,356	513,407	934,408	916,237
Contingent emergency appropriations	3,300,000	—	1,300,000	2,000,000	1,500,000
Rescissions	-1,977,300	-6,700	-892,700	-621,700	-1,217,700
GRAND TOTAL*	$108,346,441	$110,671,650	$112,742,553	$113,351,308	$112,742,537
Total adjusted for scorekeeping	$107,976,025	$114,867,650	$112,617,553	$113,347,308	$112,738,537

* Includes emergency spending
Source: House and Senate Appropriations committees

● **NSF.** $4.8 billion — $363 million more than in fiscal 2001, and $316 million more than Bush's request. The NSF supports education and research in science and engineering through grants and contracts.

● **NASA.** $14.8 billion — $508 million more than in fiscal 2001, and $282 million above the president's request. NASA conducts space and aeronautical research and development through space exploration, scientific research, and support of collaborative international programs such as the International Space Station.

● **FEMA.** $3.1 billion — nearly $1.4 billion less than in fiscal 2001 but $845 million more than Bush's request — for the agency that coordinates federal disaster preparation and recovery activities. The total included $1.5 billion in emergency funding for unanticipated disasters.

Background

The fiscal 2001 VA-HUD bill (PL 106-377) had been enacted only after negotiators from the White House and Congress blunted several House Republican policy proposals and agreed to a substantial spending increase that gave President Bill Clinton almost all of what he sought.

Clinton threatened to veto the original House-passed bill, citing what he said was inadequate spending for housing, environment, space and NSF accounts, as well as several GOP policy riders that would have restricted activities of HUD, the EPA and the VA. Senate appropriators declined to mark up their version of the bill until their leadership allowed them to allocate more to discretionary accounts, which did not happen until September. They approved a bill that was more generous than the House version, but GOP leaders feared it would become a magnet for Democratic amendments on election-year issues. Instead, House and Senate appropriators and administration officials negotiated for three weeks, producing a $107.3 billion bill that exceeded the prior year's version by 8 percent. (*2000 Almanac, p 2-148*)

Legislative Action

House Subcommittee Action

The House VA-HUD Appropriations Subcommittee approved a $111.3 billion draft of the bill by voice vote after less than an hour of debate July 10. Members agreed to save most of their fights for the floor.

Democrats complained that Bush's tax cuts had sliced too deeply into budget allocations and eaten into critical spending for VA and HUD programs, but Republicans argued that the breadth of the bill required tough funding decisions to be made, with or without the tax cuts.

In several cases, the subcommittee decided to spend more than Bush had requested for space and science programs. The panel rejected the modest $47 million increase proposed for the NSF, approving $4.8 billion in new budget authority, a $414 million increase over fiscal 2001. The subcommittee also went beyond Bush's request for NASA, approving $14.9 billion for the space agency, $641 million over 2001 levels and $415 million more than Bush proposed. The biggest difference was the decision to provide $275 million for the station's Crew Return Vehicle, a winged lifeboat capable of carrying six or seven astronauts, which the administration had proposed eliminating. Majority Whip Tom DeLay, R-Texas, whose district included the Lyndon B. Johnson Space Center, argued that scrapping the vehicle would permanently restrict the station's capacity and ability to do scientific research.

The subcommittee continued what had become an annual effort to end the AmeriCorps volunteer service program begun by Clinton in 1993; it eliminated new funds in the bill and directed the agency to use remaining fiscal 2001 money to begin closing down. Bush had requested $416 million for the program in fiscal 2002.

The subcommittee approved $30 billion for HUD, including $197 million for 34,000 new Section 8 rental housing assistance vouchers. The panel specified that the vouchers go primarily to public housing authorities that could show they

had used at least 97 percent of their previous vouchers. Appropriators were frustrated that some housing authorities had not used all of the vouchers they had been allotted.

The panel cut HUD's public housing capital fund by $445 million to $2.6 billion, citing HUD estimates that public authorities had more than $6 billion in unspent funds for capital improvements to public housing.

In its $7.5 billion provision for the EPA, the panel included language barring the agency from using any funds to implement provisions of the controversial Kyoto Protocol on global warming. The Bush administration had announced its opposition to the treaty, which was supposed to set binding standards for emissions of greenhouse gases.

DeLay won voice vote approval of an amendment to allow lawmakers to add money for FEMA to deal with damage caused by Tropical Storm Allison, which struck communities along the Gulf of Mexico in June.

House Full Committee Action

The full Appropriations Committee approved a $112.6 billion version of the bill (H Rept 107-159) by voice vote July 17, after adding $1.3 billion for emergency disaster relief at the behest of DeLay. The committee also accepted, by voice vote, a bipartisan managers' amendment that dropped the language blocking funds to implement the Kyoto treaty, reversing the position congressional Republicans had taken for the previous three years.

An attempt by Democrats to increase funding for veterans, housing and environmental programs by $1 billion, offset by reducing the cut in the top income tax bracket enacted in June (PL 107-16), was rejected, 24-29. The amendment, offered by ranking committee Democrat David R. Obey of Wisconsin, also would have restored funding for the AmeriCorps program.

The $1.3 billion placeholder for "emergency" funding for FEMA was adopted by voice vote. DeLay said the emergency relief would address rising claims resulting from Tropical Storm Allison. The funding was contingent on a White House request.

House Floor Action

The House passed the $112.7 billion VA-HUD bill by a vote of 336-89 on July 31, after three days of barbed exchanges over housing, veterans and environmental programs. (House vote 297, p. H-104)

The AmeriCorps program got an early reprieve when the House adopted, by voice vote, an amendment by Sheila Jackson-Lee, D-Texas, to allow the agency to use the leftover fiscal 2001 money to continue operating.

Democrats won approval of a controversial amendment to prohibit the EPA from using taxpayer funds to weaken a Clinton administration standard published Jan. 22, 2001, reducing the amount of arsenic permitted in drinking water from 50 parts per billion to 10 parts per billion by 2006. The Bush administration had suspended the Clinton rule in March, arguing that it had been adopted hastily and without adequate scientific or cost-benefit studies. The amendment, offered by Democratic Whip David E. Bonior of Michigan, was adopted 218-189 on July 27, with 19 Republicans crossing party lines to support it. (House vote 288, p. H-102)

Republicans defeated another Democratic amendment

that would have restored $25 million for the EPA's Office of Compliance and Enforcement. The Bush administration and House Republicans wanted to shift the money to grants for state environmental efforts, eliminating 270 EPA jobs. The amendment, by Robert Menendez, D-N.J., was rejected, 182-214. (House vote 289, p. H-102)

In an attempt to mollify fiscal conservatives angry over the inclusion of $1.3 billion in emergency disaster relief, the rule for floor debate allowed an amendment asking the Bush administration to formally request the release of the funds when it determined how much money was needed. The amendment was not offered.

Democrats tried repeatedly to increase funding for veterans, housing and environmental programs. Obey again sought to roll back the reduction in the top income tax bracket from 38.6 percent to 39.1 percent in order to pay for a $1 billion increase, but he was ruled out of order because appropriators lacked the authority to change tax rates.

The House rejected, 139-284, an amendment by Jerrold Nadler, D-N.Y., that would have doubled, to 68,000, the number of new Section 8 housing assistance vouchers funded under the bill. The cost would have been offset by deleting $200 million in the bill requested by Bush for a new homeowner down payment assistance initiative under HUD's Home Investment Partnerships program. (House vote 282, p. H-100)

Marcy Kaptur, D-Ohio, took aim at another Bush administration initiative, offering an amendment to restore $175 million in funding for a program that awarded grants to public housing authorities to fight drug-related crime. Republicans argued that the program was outside the scope of HUD's core missions. Democrats said it was working in many cities. The amendment was defeated, 197-213. (House vote 287, p. H-102)

The House also rejected, by voice vote, an amendment by Tim Roemer, D-Ind., and Greg Ganske, R-Iowa, to cap future spending on the International Space Station at $4.2 billion.

Senate Committee Action

The Senate Appropriations Committee approved a $113.4 billion version of the bill (S 1216 — S Rept 107-43) on July 19 by a vote of 29-0. The VA-HUD Subcommittee had approved the measure earlier in the day with little discussion.

Democrats used their majority control in the Senate to vigorously resist Bush's call for cuts in public housing programs. The bill allocated $31 billion for HUD, more than $1 billion above the House bill and $434 million more than Bush had requested. The total included $300 million in grants to public housing authorities to fight drug-related crimes.

The bill included nearly $2.9 billion for HUD's public housing capital fund, compared to $2.6 billion in the House version. Democrats contended that any cuts would handcuff efforts by housing authorities to cope with deteriorating buildings and rising energy bills.

The panel approved only half of the Bush administration's request for 34,000 new Section 8 vouchers. The committee's report expressed concern that the vouchers did "not always provide the best opportunities for low-income families to obtain affordable housing."

Several senators voiced deep concern over NASA esti-

mates showing that, as of June, the International Space Station had incurred $4.8 billion in cost overruns over five years. The appropriators cut $150 million from the space station budget, designating $50 million of that for safety upgrades to NASA's aging fleet of shuttles and directing the remainder to agency science programs. They also capped total spending on station development and operations between fiscal 2002 and 2006 at $6.68 billion. The panel agreed with the president and did not include funding for the Crew Return Vehicle.

At the request of Kay Bailey Hutchison, R-Texas, the committee included $2 billion in disaster relief contingency funds for communities hit by Tropical Storm Allison. The money was part of $3.3 billion the panel approved for FEMA.

The committee recommended $7.8 billion for the EPA, including funding to retain the 270 environmental enforcement positions that were to be cut under the White House budget request.

Senate Floor Action

The Senate passed the $113.4 billion measure by a 94-5 vote Aug. 2. (*Senate vote 269, p. S-55*)

An amendment by Barbara Boxer, D-Calif., adopted 97-1, called for the EPA to establish a stricter arsenic standard as soon as the bill was enacted, though it did not recommend a specific level. (*Senate vote 265, p. S-54*)

VA-HUD Appropriations Subcommittee Chairwoman Barbara A. Mikulski, D-Md., won voice vote approval for a proposal to make the $2 billion in emergency disaster relief available on enactment of the bill, rather than on Oct. 1, as the committee had proposed.

In other action over two days of debate, the Senate:

• Rejected, 25-75, a proposal by Paul Wellstone, D-Minn., to add $650 million for veterans' health benefits. (*Senate vote 263, p. S-54*)

• Tabled (killed), 58-41, an amendment by Jon Kyl, R-Ariz., to create a new formula to distribute EPA funding for wastewater projects. (*Senate vote 266, p. S-54*)

• Tabled, 65-33, an amendment by Charles E. Schumer, D-N.Y., to designate $15 million of HUD funding for a Clinton administration initiative to buy back unwanted guns and raise gun safety awareness. (*Senate vote 267, p. S-55*)

• Tabled, 69-30, an amendment by John McCain, R-Ariz., to cut $5 million from local projects funded by HUD's Community Development Fund and apply the money to speed up regional offices' processing of veterans' health claims. (*Senate vote 268, p. S-55*)

• Adopted, by voice vote, an amendment by Bill Nelson, D-Fla., calling on the EPA to study health risks to children who use playground equipment treated with arsenic-containing chemicals.

Conference/Final Action

The conference agreement on the bill was not filed until Nov. 8. The House adopted the report (H Rept 107-272) by a vote of 401-18 that day, and the Senate cleared the bill, 87-7, a few hours later. (*House vote 434, p. H-148; Senate vote 334, p. S-69*)

The conference had been delayed while appropriators tried to decide how to fit all the fiscal 2002 spending bills within the total agreed to under the budget resolution (H Con Res 83). The attacks of Sept. 11 further delayed the bill, creating other more urgent demands on appropriators' time and tighter spending allocations for the VA-HUD bill.

The final bill provided $112.7 billion, including $85.4 billion in discretionary spending. Conferees managed to squeeze in extra funding by rescinding some unused funds in HUD public housing accounts and redistributing it to other programs funded under the bill. The transaction enabled them to provide extra money without adding to the bottom line.

Major issues resolved in conference included:

• **Housing.** As requested by Bush, the bill terminated funding for public housing drug-elimination grants. However, $250 million of the money was shifted to a HUD general fund for public housing operating subsidies, with the stipulation that local housing authorities could use the money for anti-drug activities. The remaining $50 million was applied to Bush's initiative to provide down payment assistance for first-time, low-income homebuyers. The bill funded public housing capital needs at $2.8 billion.

• **Section 8 subsidies.** Conferees agreed to provide HUD with $16.3 billion to renew all Section 8 rental contracts due to expire in fiscal 2002 and to fund 25,900 new vouchers. The funding consisted of $15.6 billion in direct appropriations and $640 million from reserve funds for local public housing authorities. The bill rescinded $1.2 billion in previously appropriated but unused Section 8 funds.

• **Arsenic levels.** Conferees rejected both the House and Senate language, instead requiring the EPA to implement the Clinton standards without delay. But they also required the agency to develop criteria that would allow time extensions for small communities that could not afford to make the change by 2006. The Bush administration had announced in September that it would adopt the Clinton standards after all, following a report by the National Academy of Sciences that concluded that even 10 parts per billion produced an unacceptable cancer risk.

• **EPA enforcement.** The bill fully funded EPA's enforcement activities at fiscal 2001 levels of $465 million.

• **Kyoto Protocol.** Unlike previous years, the bill did not include language limiting EPA activities related to the climate change treaty.

• **Space station.** The bill transferred $283.6 million in space station funding to NASA's biological and physical sciences account in an effort to prevent the space agency from using that funding for space station hardware. Spending on the space station was capped at $1.96 billion, $75 million less than the administration requested. Uncertainty over the future of the program had increased with the resignation of longtime NASA Administrator Daniel S. Goldin on Nov. 17. Conferees eliminated the $275 million for the Crew Return Vehicle, although DeLay persuaded them to add report language requiring NASA to spend no less than $40 million to continue developing the craft.

• **FEMA.** The agency got $3.1 billion, including a contingent emergency appropriation of $1.5 billion.

• **AmeriCorps.** The bill provided $407 million for the AmeriCorps volunteer service program. Bush had endorsed the idea of using AmeriCorps volunteers in homeland defense efforts, including public safety, public health and disaster preparedness. ◆

Lawmakers Clear Midyear Package

Congress cleared a bill July 20 to provide $6.5 billion in additional fiscal 2001 spending, most of it for the Pentagon. Predictions of a dwindling surplus resulting from newly enacted tax cuts and a slowing economy helped foster a bipartisan commitment to fiscal restraint, leading to a package that hewed closely to President Bush's proposal. The bill was signed into law (HR 2216 — PL 107-20) on July 24.

Bush's request for a net $6.5 billion in supplemental spending was the leanest such proposal in the previous two decades. In order to stay within the limit permitted by the congressional budget resolution (H Con Res 83), Bush combined $7.1 billion in new discretionary spending with offsets and rescissions in prior appropriations totaling more than $600 million. The request was a marked shift from the pattern set by the Clinton administration and the Appropriations committees, which had found numerous ways in recent years to exceed the amount set in the budget resolution.

Most of the request, a net $5.8 billion, was for defense-related spending, including replenishing operations and maintenance accounts tapped to finance overseas operations in Kosovo. Non-defense items included $150 million to help low-income families pay heating and air conditioning bills, $35 million to increase safeguards against the spread of foot-and-mouth disease and $116 million to cover the cost of mailings related to the tax rebate mandated by the tax-cut bill (PL 107-16).

House and Senate appropriators stuck with Bush's bottom line, although each emphasized different programs and proposed different types of rescissions. The bill came together relatively quickly. After briefly withholding action to counter a GOP threat to slow progress on the 13 regular fiscal 2002 appropriations bills, Senate Majority Leader Tom Daschle, D-S.D., backed down, allowing the bill to clear on a voice vote July 20 after a personal appeal by Vice President Dick Cheney. Cheney warned that while military leaders had been unusually patient waiting for their midyear funding increase, some training exercises might have to be canceled if the money was delayed further.

The final bill was remarkably similar to Bush's original request. The net total for new discretionary budget authority was the same $6.5 billion that the president requested. The bulk of the spending, a net $5.8 billion, was for defense. However, the overall total for new spending had grown to $8.3 billion — with $1.8 billion in rescissions, including a rescission of $527 million for procurement of the troubled V-22 Osprey aircraft.

The bill also included $937 million in mandatory fiscal

BoxScore 2001
Midyear Supplemental — Fiscal Year

Bill:
HR 2216 — PL 107-20

Legislative Action:
House passed HR 2216 (H Rept 107-102), 341-87, on June 20.
Senate passed HR 2216, amended (S Rept 107-33), 98-1, on July 10.
House adopted the conference report (H Rept 107-148), 375-30, on July 20.
Senate cleared the bill by voice vote July 20.
President signed July 24.

2001 funds to pay for an increase in veterans' benefits mandated in 2000 (PL 106-398). Negotiators dropped a House provision, opposed by the White House, that would have designated $473 million as emergency spending. The House bill would have offset the cost largely by rescinding $389 million previously appropriated for the Federal Emergency Management Agency (FEMA) disaster relief reserve fund.

In most years, supplemental bills were magnets, attracting large numbers of add-ons for items that were unfunded or underfunded in the regular appropriations bills. In 2000, President Bill Clinton proposed a $5.5 billion supplemental, which grew to $13.2 billion in the House. Hoping to hold down the overall cost, then-Majority Leader Trent Lott, R-Miss., forced Senate appropriators to use the unusual tactic of attaching about $8 billion in fiscal 2000 supplemental spending piecemeal to three of the regular spending bills for fiscal 2001. When that strategy stalled, and with the Pentagon pleading for help, $11.2 billion in supplemental spending was added to the first of the year's regular appropriations bills (PL 106-246), for military construction. (*2000 Almanac, p. 2-162*)

Legislative Action

House Committee Action

House Republicans insisted on keeping the fiscal 2001 package focused on the midyear needs of the military — and on restraining spending even there. The Appropriations Committee on June 14 gave voice-vote approval to the bill (H Rept 107-102) without adding to its $6.5 billion net cost. Republicans offered no amendments to raise the cost, and they held together to defeat six Democratic attempts to spend more money to alleviate the nation's energy problems, fight AIDS, and boost animal and plant inspections. Several other proposals were withdrawn. At every turn, Republicans said the spending was unwarranted or could be accommodated under existing law.

The bottom line — $7.5 billion in new spending offset by more than $1.4 billion in rescissions — was close to what Bush requested. The details generally hewed to his proposals, although the House found room for slightly more spending by making deeper midyear cuts. Of the total, $5.8 billion was for defense-related programs, the figure Bush requested, though the bill sought to alter some of his priorities.

In a departure from Bush's request, appropriators designated $473 million of the spending as an emergency not of-

Where the Money Goes

Midyear Spending Highlights

ISSUE	DESCRIPTION
Defense and national security	$6.9 billion, including: $3 billion to replenish general operation and maintenance accounts; $1.6 billion for health programs; $515 million for military personnel; $573 million for procurement; $493 million for research, development, testing and evaluation; $297 million for shipbuilding and conversion programs; $277 million for nuclear weapons programs, including waste management; $44 million for repair of the USS *Cole*; $126 million for housing and other construction programs; $40 million to repair natural disaster damage to defense facilities; and $20 million for the radiation exposure compensation trust fund.
Agriculture	$66 million, including: $20 million for farmers in the Klamath River area; $5 million for inspection services to prevent foot-and-mouth disease; and $36 million for flood prevention.
Coast Guard	$84 million for operating expenses and acquisitions.
Utility bill subsidies	$300 million for the Low Income Heating and Energy Assistance Program, which helps pay heating and air conditioning bills of the poor.
Corps of Engineers	$146 million for flood control and maintenance.
Energy Department (non-defense)	$44 million, including: $30 million for uranium facilities maintenance and $12 million for environmental programs.
International aid	$100 million for international HIV/AIDS assistance.
Education	$161 million for programs for the disadvantaged.
Congress	$62 million for House members' staff salaries and office expenses.
Olympics	$60 million for security at the 2002 Winter Games in Salt Lake City.
Tax rebates	$116 million to process letters and rebate checks.
Rescissions	$1.1 billion from defense, including $200 million in overseas contingency operations funds, $527 million in Navy and Air Force aircraft procurement, and $85 billion in classified equipment procurement. Agriculture rescissions of $85 million, including $45 million from conservation programs and $43 million from the food stamp program. Also, $114 million from a Housing and Urban Development public housing program, $30 million from a Federal Aviation Administration airport grant program, and $18 million from the IRS.

ficially subject to the overall spending limits for fiscal 2001. GOP appropriators said the money was for responses to true emergencies, such as disaster relief. But Mitchell E. Daniels Jr., director of the White House Office of Management and Budget (OMB), disagreed. OMB issued a statement June 19 saying, "Emergency supplemental appropriations should be limited to extremely rare events, which do not include those provided in this bill." While not explicitly threatening a veto, the statement said the president "does not intend to concur" with the House designation of $473 million as emergency spending.

House appropriators, however, were eager to reassert their right to designate emergency funds, a practice the White House had been working to curtail. "We will use the emergency designation as we see fit," Appropriations Committee spokesman John D. Scofield said June 20. "If that makes the OMB uncomfortable, that's not my problem."

The $389 million in the bill for natural disaster relief was entirely offset by rescinding an equal amount in a reserve fund for FEMA. The administration opposed that plan, saying it could leave FEMA unprepared for additional emergencies later in the year.

The bill included $300 million for the Low Income Heating and Energy Assistance Program (LIHEAP), double Bush's request, and $115 million to deliver the rebates called for by the new tax law (PL 107-16).

Republicans turned back Democratic amendments to cap electricity prices in Western states (defeated 27-34), double the amount of funds in the bill for LIHEAP (rejected 29-32), provide federal guarantees for loans to enhance the reliability of the electrical power supply (rejected 24-35), and include money for hydroelectric power plant improvements (defeated 24-31). Republicans said existing federal programs were already sufficient, or that the amendments did not address the true causes of the nation's energy problem.

By far the largest change to Bush's request was the committee's addition of $200 million to the $1.45 billion he sought for the Pentagon's health care system, including Tricare, its medical insurance program for dependents and retirees. In its report, the committee complained that this would mark the 12th time in 16 years that Congress had had to cover a significant budget shortfall for the program late in the fiscal year, a situation it ascribed to a habitual underestimation by the Pentagon of the rising cost of medical care. For example, the panel noted, while prescription drug costs had increased by an average rate of 12 percent annually since 1996, the Pentagon budgeted for annual cost increases of only 4 percent to 5 percent. The committee ordered the Pentagon to explain how it would change its health care budget projections to prevent systematically underfunding the program.

House Floor Action

The House passed the bill, 341-87, on June 20. As they had in committee, Democrats tried unsuccessfully to attach amendments addressing the energy crunch in the West. Republicans thwarted seven such energy-related amendments without a vote by raising points of order against them, saying they were not germane to an appropriations bill. (*House vote 176, p. H-66*)

Another round of testy exchanges occurred over a mass mailing by the Treasury Department announcing the impending arrival of the rebates provided under the tax law. The supplemental included $116 million to mail the letters and then write and deliver the checks over 10 weeks beginning the week of July 23.

Democrats said the letter amounted to a government-funded pat on the back for the president, who made the tax cut the main emphasis of his first months in office. The White House acknowledged that it helped draft the letter but insisted there was nothing improper about it. "This is a government keeping in touch with the taxpayers who pay the bills informing them that they overpaid their bills," presidential spokesman Ari Fleischer said June 19.

The House rejected an effort by David R. Obey of Wisconsin, top Democrat on the Appropriations Committee, to take the $30.5 million needed to process the letter and give it instead to a program to combat drug trafficking. The proposal was defeated, 212-216, but only after Republican leaders persuaded at least six Republicans to switch their initial "yes" votes. In the end, only five Republicans voted for Obey's amendment. (*House vote 173, p. H-66*)

The House rejected, 65-362, an amendment by Patrick J. Toomey, R-Pa., calling for a $1 billion across-the-board cut in fiscal 2001 non-defense discretionary spending to partially offset the non-defense expenditures in the bill. (*House vote 174, p. H-66*)

Three proposals that would have had the effect of undoing the FEMA rescission were put before the House, although none presented members with a straightforward vote on the issue. One was the Toomey amendment. Another, by Ken Bentsen, D-Texas, was struck down on a point of order. The third, a Democratic motion to recommit the bill, was rejected, 209-218. (*House vote 175, p. H-66*)

Senate Committee Action

The Senate Appropriations Committee approved its version of the $6.5 billion bill (S 1077 — S Rept 107-33) by voice vote June 21, after less than an hour of debate and no amendments.

Like the version passed by the House the day before, the bill closely tracked Bush's request. Most of the money would go to the Pentagon for operations and maintenance, repairs, procurement and medical care. Funds for natural disaster aid and to help the poor pay their utility bills were other big-ticket items. The Senate proposed adding about $70 million for Pentagon health care programs.

Unlike the House bill, the measure did not seek to designate any of the supplemental as "emergency" spending, not subject to the overall fiscal 2001 discretionary spending ceiling. The Senate bill also did not include the House plan to rescind $389 million in the FEMA account for disaster response.

Chairman Robert C. Byrd, D-W.Va., and the committee's ranking Republican, Ted Stevens of Alaska, persuaded their colleagues to withhold any amendments, at least until the floor debate, in the interest of keeping the package's cost under control. Byrd vowed the bill would not spend "one thin dime" over Bush's request.

Senate Floor Action

The Senate passed HR 2216, 98-1, on July 10, after substituting the text of its own bill. The bill included $5.9 billion net for defense. A total of $7.9 billion in new spending was offset by about $1.4 billion in rescissions. (*Senate vote 228, p. S-48*)

"Unlike every supplemental for quite a long time, both houses have acted at the level requested without gimmicks, without add-ons and Christmas ornaments," Daniels said the next day. He said the president would sign the bill, assuming there were no surprises in conference.

Leaders used small but important deals on disaster relief to appease key groups of colleagues while adding more offsets to keep the net total unchanged. The Senate adopted by voice vote amendments that added $20 million for farmers in the Klamath River basin — which secured support from California's and Oregon's senators — and dictated spending for storm damage relief in Arkansas and Oklahoma, firefighting efforts in Alaska and emergency housing on an American Indian reservation in North Dakota.

The Senate also voted to block a Pentagon plan to consolidate its B-1 force in South Dakota and Texas as part of an effort to save $165 million by shrinking the number of bombers — a move ardently opposed by lawmakers in the states that would lose planes: Georgia, Kansas and Idaho.

John McCain, R-Ariz., denounced his GOP colleagues for "micromanaging the Department of Defense" and said the amendment was a bad way to get started on restructuring the military. But Larry E. Craig, R-Idaho, said the Senate deserved more consultation about the proposal. The House bill did not mention the B-1. A McCain amendment to add another $848 million for the military and offset it with about a dozen non-defense rescissions was tabled, or killed, 83-16. (*Senate vote 226, p. S-47*)

The Senate also:

• Rejected, 49-50, an amendment by Charles E. Schumer, D-N.Y., to delete $34 million for letters to taxpayers explaining their rebates under the new tax law. (*Senate vote 227, p. S-48*)

• Rejected, 3-94, an amendment by Ernest F. Hollings, D-S.C., to repeal the fiscal 2001 portion of the new tax law, including the rebates. Hollings had pushed the amendment to the budget resolution that laid the groundwork for the rebates, but now he said the government's worsening fiscal condition made rebates irresponsible. (*Senate vote 223, p. S-47*)

• Rejected procedural moves to keep alive two trust fund "lockbox" amendments. One, aimed at shielding the Social Security surplus, was rejected, 43-54. Opponents offered little support for their position, but the amendment's enforcement measures included politically unpopular automatic spending cuts. The other, to create points of order against spending the Medicare trust fund, was rejected, 42-54. (*Senate votes 222, 221, p. S-47*)

Conference/Final Action

The final bill was completed July 19, after a week of negotiations. The House adopted the conference report (H Rept 107-148) by a vote of 375-30 the morning of July 20, and the Senate cleared the measure by voice vote a few hours later. *(House vote 256, p. H-92)*

Daniels praised the measure, saying, "It funds the president's priorities, stays within the spending caps and resists unnecessary spending." He called it "proof that fiscal discipline can be exercised and enacted in a timely manner."

The final bill retained most of the natural disaster assistance originally in the House bill, while dropping the emergency designation.

It included the Senate language barring the use of funds in the bill to retire any B-1 bombers.

The total for Pentagon health-care assistance was $1.6 billion, $81 million more than in the Senate bill but about $52 million less than the House wanted.

The main stumbling block in conference was an effort by Texas Republicans — House Majority Whip Tom DeLay and Sen. Kay Bailey Hutchison — to add $1.3 billion in emergency funds to pay for damage from Tropical Storm Allison, which spawned widespread floods in the Houston area and along the Gulf Coast in June. The White House opposed those efforts, as did Democratic leaders who had pledged not to exceed the spending total in Bush's request. The two Texans were already preparing for the rebuff, however. They eventually won inclusion of $1.5 billion in emergency funds for FEMA in the fiscal 2002 VA-HUD spending bill (PL 107-73). *(VA-HUD, p. 2-51)* ◆

$40 Billion Emergency Bill Clears

Within days of the Sept. 11 terrorist attacks, President Bush and Congress came together to provide $40 billion in emergency appropriations for what was widely described as a down payment on military action, national security and reconstruction. The bill was signed into law (HR 2888 — PL 107-38) on Sept. 18. But it took another three months for Congress and the White House to finally allocate all of the money. In the end, the Defense Department received the largest share, more than $17 billion. New York, Pennsylvania and Virginia laid claim to more than $11 billion, leaving about $11 billion to agencies charged with protecting the home front from future attacks.

The White House distributed half the money on its own; the remaining $20 billion was allocated under the fiscal 2002 defense appropriations bill (HR 3338 — PL 107-117), signed Jan. 10, 2002.

House and Senate leaders initially agreed to appropriate $20 billion to start repairing the damage and hunt down the attackers. A day later, Bush doubled the price tag to $40 billion, giving New York's congressional delegation assurances they would not be slighted at the expense of military action. Despite disagreements over how much discretion to give the White House, both chambers passed the $40 billion supplemental bill Sept. 14. The quick agreement, however, soon gave way to struggles over whether to stay within the $40 billion total or add more funds for domestic security and recovery aid for New York City.

Early GOP talk of sending Bush a "blank check" was rejected by Democrats and some Republicans who balked at surrendering so much authority to the White House. The result was a hybrid bill: The White House got half the $40 billion to distribute as it saw fit — $10 billion to spend immediately and $10 billion to spend subject to congressional notification. The remaining $20 billion was to be appropriated later under normal procedures.

The appropriators soon chafed under their $20 billion limit. Lawmakers called for increased security at the nation's borders, ports and airports. New Yorkers demanded that Congress live up to its pledge to provide $20 billion for their recovery and rebuilding efforts. The arrival of anthrax-tainted mail on Capitol Hill highlighted additional security weaknesses that lawmakers wanted to address.

When the clamor became too loud for Bush to ignore, he called top appropriators to the White House on Nov. 6 to announce that he would veto any bill that spent more than the $20 billion that had already been agreed to. Reassured by

BoxScore
Anti-Terrorism Supplemental

Bills:
HR 2888 — PL 107-38;
HR 3338 — PL 107-117
Legislative Action:
House passed HR 2888, 422-0, on Sept. 14.
Senate cleared HR 2888 by voice vote Sept. 14.
President signed HR 2888 on Sept. 18.
House adopted the conference report on HR 3338 (H Rept 107-350), 408-6, on Dec. 20.
Senate cleared HR 3338, 94-2, on Dec. 20.
President signed HR 3338 on Jan. 10, 2002.

promises of another supplemental spending bill in the spring, most Republicans closed ranks behind the president.

New York Republicans, however, did not. The state's delegation waged a campaign to win $9.7 billion more and fulfill the pledge of at least $20 billion. After losing in the House Appropriations Committee, the New Yorkers threatened to undermine the $317 billion fiscal 2002 defense appropriations bill — the vehicle that was being used to allocate the remaining $20 billion — unless they got a vote on their proposal on the House floor.

The threat brought the White House back to the bargaining table. New York Republicans agreed to back off in exchange for more grants and loans directed to small businesses and unemployed workers.

But Bush's hard line did not deter Senate Democrats. Appropriations Committee Chairman Robert C. Byrd, D-W.Va., added $15 billion more to the Senate's version of the defense appropriations bill for homeland defense and recovery from the attacks. After three procedural votes proved Republicans would derail the entire bill to support the president, Democrats backed down and rewrote the package.

Byrd's move proved shrewd and led to a final bill that devoted $8.3 billion of the remaining $20 billion to homeland defense, almost double Bush's request. New Yorkers also won $8.2 billion. Defense received about $3.5 billion.

Of the total $40 billion in emergency spending, $17.5 billion, or about 44 percent, went to defense. The remaining $22.5 billion went to non-defense accounts, the biggest of which was the Federal Emergency Management Agency (FEMA), which received about $6.6 billion.

Highlights

The emergency spending — split evenly between fiscal 2001 and fiscal 2002 — was allocated in three parts:
• **President's discretion.** $10 billion was available immediately to the president to allocate for emergency rescue and rebuilding efforts; security at airports and other transportation centers and at public buildings; investigating and prosecuting those responsible for the attacks; and supporting national security. The White House allocated $5.9 billion for defense and $4.1 billion to non-defense spending.
• **Presidential notification.** $10 billion became available 15 days after Bush gave to Congress his plan for allocating the money. The White House submitted the plan Oct. 17, with most of the funds — $8.1 billion — going to defense.

• **Congressional appropriation.** $20 billion was available only after it was appropriated separately by Congress. This is the portion that was allocated as emergency supplemental spending under the defense appropriations bill. Most of these funds — $16.5 billion — were devoted to domestic recovery and homeland defense.

$40 Billion Supplemental

On Sept. 14, three days after the terrorist attacks, Congress cleared the $40 billion emergency spending package (HR 2888) without a single dissenting vote. The House passed the bill, 422-0, and the Senate cleared it by voice vote, after passing an identical bill (S 1426) earlier in the day by a vote of 96-0. (*House vote 341, p. H-118; Senate vote 280, p. S-59*)

The votes were an anticlimactic end to two days of behind-the-scenes bickering between senior administration officials and bipartisan congressional leadership over how much latitude Bush should have in allocating the money.

With Washington still stunned by the attacks, lawmakers at first seemed ready to write a blank check. "We think the president needs that flexibility," House Appropriations Committee Chairman C.W. Bill Young, R-Fla., said Sept. 12. The nation is at war, said fiscal conservative Patrick J. Toomey, R-Pa., and "that's going to cost a great deal of money. So spend it." But David R. Obey of Wisconsin, ranking Democrat on the House Appropriations Committee, refused, saying he was willing to give the president every dime requested, but he would not agree to release the money without preserving members' rights to control spending. Byrd took the same position. "There has to be consultation, and there has to be reporting," he said. "We still have a Constitution."

By the end of Sept. 12, leaders and appropriators from both parties were in agreement that some restrictions would be necessary. Aides said White House officials had pressed for such sweeping, unfettered presidential power over the special purse that Republicans and Democrats alike were drawn together to rebuff them.

In a sign of how tense and clearly defined the standoff was between Congress and the White House, after a deal was finally struck, Obey and other Democrats went out of their way to lavish praise on Speaker J. Dennis Hastert, R-Ill., for his leadership in resolving the dispute. In a remark apparently aimed at the White House, Obey said "a respectful relationship between the two branches of government" will be crucial in the months ahead.

By the night of Sept. 13, the leadership and appropriators from both parties believed they had struck a deal, but officials from the White House Office of Management and Budget objected to the proposed restrictions on spending. The situation created a dilemma for congressional leaders. They could send the president their package and dare him to veto it — placing both sides in an uncomfortable and confrontational posture at a time when the nation was demanding unified leadership. Or they could give him what he wanted, which essentially would have removed Congress from involvement in the response to the attacks, at least in the short term.

The standoff was resolved when the White House relented in the early morning hours of Sept. 14 and essentially accepted the deal it had been offered the day before.

Young said the final package "allows the federal government to use every tool in its arsenal to help America recover from this tragedy and to locate and prosecute the cowards who committed this crime."

Appropriating the $20 Billion

As they prepared to allocate the remaining $20 billion, House and Senate appropriators jockeyed to add more money. Byrd rallied Senate Democrats around a plan for an extra $20 billion for homeland defense, which he wanted to attach either to the emergency supplemental or to an economic stimulus bill (HR 3090) moving through Congress. In the House, Young and his subcommittee chairmen also supported more spending and worried that Byrd might try to take the lead. "The fact is we are going to go over the $20 billion," Young said. "The question is, when do you do it?"

But Bush insisted that the $40 billion package provided all the cash the government needed or could spend in the next several months. Additional spending, he said, should wait until Congress returned in 2002. To drive home his point, Bush met with bipartisan congressional leaders Nov. 6, threatening to veto any attempt to exceed the $40 billion limit. "If I need to, I'll veto the bill," he told them.

House Committee Action

The House Appropriations Committee approved by voice vote on Nov. 14 an emergency spending package (HR 3338 — H Rept 107-298) that stayed within the $20 billion limit set by Bush. The supplemental spending was tacked on to the fiscal 2002 defense appropriations bill that the committee had approved Oct. 24. (*Defense, p. 2-13*)

The supplemental largely followed Bush's request. It was composed of:

• $7.3 billion for defense to prosecute the war in Afghanistan, rebuild the section of the Pentagon damaged Sept. 11 and otherwise boost military readiness.

• $6.9 billion in disaster relief, including debris removal and infrastructure repair at the World Trade Center site, community development grants for New York City, funds for workers' compensation for New York state and Small Business Administration disaster loans.

• $5.8 billion for homeland security, including airport security and bio-terrorism response programs.

With the exception of the New Yorkers, Republicans united behind Bush after his veto threat. An attempt by New York Republicans James T. Walsh and John E. Sweeney to add $9.7 billion for New York's recovery efforts failed, 31-33. Rather than continue the battle, Walsh and Sweeney instead recessed behind closed doors Nov. 16 to negotiate with the White House. In the end, they accepted a pledge that $1.5 billion of the $20 billion emergency spending package would be shifted to Community Development Block Grants, with the understanding that New York would be the chief beneficiary.

Other efforts to add to the bill's bottom line were equally unsuccessful. The committee rejected, 31-34, a proposal by Obey to add $7.2 billion for domestic anti-terrorism pro-

grams. It defeated by voice vote an effort by John P. Murtha, D-Pa., to add $6.5 billion more in defense spending.

House Floor Action

The House passed the defense/emergency supplemental appropriations bill Nov. 28 by a vote of 406-20. *(House vote 458, p. H-158)*

Democrats, who complained that the emergency spending provisions were woefully inadequate, were incensed that GOP leaders brought the bill to the floor under a rule that blocked three Democratic amendments to increase spending. Despite their objections, the House agreed, 216-211, to debate the bill on the leadership's terms. *(House vote 454, p. H-156)*

A dispute did arise within Republican ranks over the Appropriations Committee's attempt to use $541.5 million in funds from the aviation and highway trust funds for airplane security and infrastructure repairs. That drew the ire of members of the Transportation Committee, who zealously guard their authority to allocate the trust funds without interference from appropriators. The use of the trust funds was struck on a point of order, but appropriators expected the language to be restored in conference.

Senate Committee Action

The Senate Appropriations Committee approved its version of the supplemental package, along with the rest of the defense spending bill (S Rept 107-109), by voice vote Dec. 4. Essentially daring Bush to carry out his threat, Byrd added $15 billion — split evenly between homeland security and disaster recovery — bringing the package to $35 billion. Responding to administration claims that there was plenty of supplemental spending already in the pipeline, Byrd made the extra $15 billion contingent on a request from Bush.

Overall, the committee-approved package included:

• $7.4 billion for defense, including the war in Afghanistan and repairing the Pentagon.

• $16.4 billion for disaster relief, including $13.3 billion for FEMA, chiefly for New York City.

• $11.2 billion for homeland security.

Senate Floor Action

Bush's veto threat and procedural hardball by Senate Republicans combined to thwart Byrd's bid to add $15 billion to the bill. As passed by the Senate, the defense bill included $20 billion in emergency supplemental spending. The measure passed by voice vote Dec. 7.

When the Senate took up the bill Dec. 6, no one was certain of the outcome. But Byrd and his allies ultimately relented after losing three procedural votes — which required 60 votes to prevail — directed against the additional $15 billion. On the evening of Dec. 6, Russell D. Feingold, D-Wis., who had a history of casting maverick votes, joined Republicans on a pair of 50-48 procedural votes challenging portions of Byrd's $15 billion add-on. The following morning, the Senate failed, 50-50, to muster the votes to protect Byrd's entire bill from a point of order, forcing hasty closed-door talks to produce a new one. *(Senate votes 354, 355, 357, pp. S-73, S-74)*

On each vote the Republicans united, forcing Democrats to face the unpalatable alternative of losing the defense/emergency supplemental bill altogether or surrendering their additional money. Feingold's defection also raised the possibility that the Republicans might even win — with the aid of a tie-breaking vote cast by Vice President Dick Cheney — adoption of an amendment that would delete Byrd's $35 billion emergency spending proposal and replace it with a $20 billion package written by Ted Stevens, R-Alaska.

Such a vote never occurred, however, because the Democrats backed down, announcing that they would replace Byrd's $35 billion measure with a new $20 billion plan of their own. Once taken, that step permitted the entire bill to cruise toward easy passage.

Byrd exacted a stern price, slicing defense funds in the committee's supplemental package to $2 billion, redirecting the rest to provide $9.5 billion for disaster recovery and $8.5 billion for homeland security.

Conference/Final Action

The final compromise, negotiated as part of the defense bill, provided $3.5 billion for defense, compared with $7.3 billion requested by Bush. It provided $8.2 billion for disaster recovery and $8.3 billion for homeland security.

The House adopted the conference report (H Rept 107-350), 408-6, on Dec. 20, the final day of the session. The Senate cleared the bill, 94-2, later that day. *(House vote 510, p. H-174; Senate vote 380, p. S-77)* ◆

Chapter 3

AGRICULTURE

Farm Bill Delayed a Year

An effort by farm-state lawmakers to enact a sweeping overhaul of federal farm law a year early ran into regional and partisan deadlocks late in the year, and was put off until 2002. The House passed an omnibus 10-year farm bill (HR 2646) in October, but Senate Democrats were unable to break a Republican filibuster of their five-year version (S 1731) in the final days of the session.

Although existing farm law, enacted in 1996 (PL 104-127), was not due to expire until 2002, farm groups and their congressional allies were anxious at the start of the 107th Congress to claim a share of the huge projected budget surplus for agriculture. They worried that if they waited, a return to deficits could mean less generous farm programs over the coming decade. They lobbied successfully to secure a set-aside of $73.5 billion over 10 years in the fiscal 2002 budget resolution (H Con Res 83) for new spending on farm programs.

The promise of extra funding paved the way later in the year for both the House and Senate to consider legislation that aimed at turning federal farm policy on its head. After five years of acute problems in the farm economy, the legislation sought a return to the commodity subsidy programs of the previous three decades. While the 1996 law, known as "Freedom to Farm," aimed to wean farmers from price supports, the new bills proposed keeping two existing subsidy programs and adding yet a third.

The legislation called for retaining the fixed payments based on crop production that were created by the 1996 law to help farmers adjust to the free market, as well as a marketing loan program that paid farmers when prices fell below a set level. In addition, it resurrected the "target price" system, first created in 1973 (PL 93-86), under which the government paid farmers the difference, if any, between the price they received on the market and a predetermined price floor set by Congress.

The House bill represented a 10-year, $73.5 billion increase over existing law for agriculture programs — including $48.8 billion more for commodity programs and $15.8 billion more for conservation. The five-year Senate measure, which cost about $40.9 billion, was projected to cost $73.4 billion over 10 years — including $43.2 billion for commodities and $20.5 billion for conservation. Those totals did not include the cost of continuing the existing food stamp program, estimated at $245.5 billion over 10 years.

Rethinking the Government's Role

Among the many obstacles that ultimately prevented the farm bill from being enacted in 2001 was a fundamental disagreement — like many agriculture debates, more along regional and philosophical lines than partisan ones — over the proper shape of federal support for agriculture.

BoxScore

Bills:
HR 2646, S 1731

Legislative Action:

House passed HR 2646 (H Rept 107-191, Parts 1-3), 291-120, on Oct. 5.

Senate Agriculture Committee approved S 1731 (S Rept 107-117) by voice vote Nov. 15.

The House passed its version of the bill after narrowly defeating an amendment that would have led to a dramatic shift in farm programs. The proposal would have moved federal policy away from traditional crop subsidies — which generally had benefited large farms — and toward conservation initiatives that would be available to any farmer. The bitter debate pitted a powerful and close-knit coalition of farm-state lawmakers who wanted to maintain the status quo against a group of urban and suburban members who hoped to bring about broad changes.

In the Senate, Agriculture Committee Chairman Tom Harkin, D-Iowa, initially set out to write a bill that would reduce government subsidies for commodities and increase conservation payments. But in the end, the Senate Agriculture Committee, like its House counterpart, approved a bill that returned to and built on the commodity-based support policies of the past.

The Bush administration called for a greater emphasis on conservation, but after Sept. 11 it pressed Congress to hold off on the bill until 2002 so it could focus on the war against terrorism. The White House attacked the approach taken by both chambers, saying it would encourage overproduction, increase government support in a time of declining revenue, and risk violating the restrictions on agriculture subsidies in global trade agreements.

Looming large over all the negotiations was a recognition by farm-state lawmakers and the Bush administration that they would have to structure federal agriculture programs for the next decade with an eye toward ongoing multilateral trade talks, which were likely to limit the amount of domestic subsidies the federal government could provide to U.S. farmers in the future. Already, the 1994 Uruguay Round agreement on agriculture limited U.S. spending to no more than $19.1 billion per year for domestic farm supports deemed most likely to distort production and trade.

Highlights

Though the House and Senate bills differed in some areas, they were based on the same general principles: fixed federal payments to farmers; new countercyclical aid tied to a guaranteed per-bushel target price; marketing loans for grains, cotton and oilseeds, and planting flexibility with no supply controls. The following are some of the main farm issues covered in the two bills:

● **Fixed payments.** Both bills proposed to expand the main subsidy program created by the 1996 farm law to include soybeans and other oilseeds. Farmers of those and other major row crops could receive fixed annual cash payments through production contracts negotiated with the Agricul-

ture Department based on their eligible acreage and yield in past years.

● **Marketing assistance loans.** Both bills would continue marketing assistance loans for grains, cotton, oilseeds, wool, mohair and honey. The House generally retained existing levels. The Senate bill called for increasing the loan levels and added peas, lentils and chickpeas. Under these programs, if the market price for a crop was less than the price established in the loan program, farmers who obtained loans could forfeit the crop to the government as full payment, and farmers who did not obtain loans could receive a "deficiency payment" equal to the difference between the loan rate and the repayment rate.

● **Countercyclical payments.** Farmers would qualify for an additional subsidy whenever their crop's price — the higher of either the national market average or its national average loan rate, plus the fixed payment rate — fell below a set "target price." The payment rate would make up the difference between the effective and target prices.

● **Payment limits.** Both bills would increase the existing limit on the combined federal payments that one farmer or farm operation could receive each year. The House wanted to increase it to $550,000, the Senate to $500,000.

● **Sugar**. Price support loans for sugar beet and sugarcane producers would continue, but the interest rates would be lowered; marketing assessments would be dropped and marketing allotments on domestically grown sugar would be instituted.

● **Dairy.** Under both bills, the government would continue to buy surplus butter, cheese and nonfat dry milk powder at prices that ensured processors could pay dairy farmers the minimum federal support price for their milk. In addition, the Senate bill included a new direct payment program that would guarantee dairy producers a minimum price for their milk.

● **Peanuts.** Both bills included a new support program for peanuts, replacing the existing marketing quotas, though the Senate version had higher loan and target prices.

● **Trade**. Both bills authorized the Agriculture secretary to keep farm program benefits within the annual World Trade Organization limit of $19.1 billion. The Senate bill required Congress to vote on modifying any programs that might cause the United States to exceed the limit.

Both bills would more than double the annual authorization for the Market Access Program, which helped U.S. producers and exporters finance promotional activities abroad. The House would immediately increase it from $90 million to $200 million; the Senate bill would reach $200 million in 2006.

● **Conservation**. The House agreed to $16 billion in new spending for conservation over 10 years, an 80 percent increase over existing spending. The enrollment ceiling for the Conservation Reserve Program, which paid farmers to idle environmentally sensitive land for 10 years and devote the acreage to conservation uses, would rise from 36.4 million acres to 39.2 million acres. A wetlands test program would be expanded from six states to all states. Funding for the Environmental Quality Incentives Program, which subsidized farmers' nutrient and manure management efforts to improve water quality, would increase from $200 million to $1.5 billion in the 10th year. A program that paid farmers to preserve or restore wetlands would be authorized at $1.5 billion annually. A new program would be created to convert 2

million acres of cropland into grassland.

The Senate bill called for $8.5 billion in new spending over five years, or $20.5 billion over 10 years. The Conservation Reserve Program ceiling would increase to 40 million acres, and new land and water conservation programs would be added. Environmental Quality Incentives Program funding would increase from $500 million to $1.25 billion by the fifth year.

● **Farm savings accounts.** The Senate bill included an $18 million test program to aid farmers who had set up farm-related savings accounts. The House did not have a similar provisions.

● **Energy.** The Senate bill contained a new energy title, authorizing $110 million per year for grants to farmers and ranchers to develop renewable energy projects, including wind, solar, biomass and geothermal sources. The federal government would be required to purchase these products if they were comparable in price, performance and availability to other conventional fuels.

● **Rural development.** The House bill would authorize $3.6 billion in combined mandatory and discretionary spending for rural development over 10 years. The Senate bill called for $3.4 billion over five years.

Background

Direct federal involvement in the farm economy dated to the Great Depression. Hoping to bring temporary relief to suffering farmers, Congress passed and President Franklin D. Roosevelt signed the first-ever farm bill, the Agricultural Adjustment Act of 1933 (PL 73-10).

The stopgap measure, which sought to stabilize the market by propping up prices and holding down production, quickly became permanent. The Agricultural Act of 1949 revised the system by giving the secretary of Agriculture more flexibility in setting price-support levels. The overhaul represented a middle-ground position in the debate that Congress would revisit time and again in the next decades between those who favored government management of farm programs and those who advocated a free market for agricultural products.

The government added yet another layer to its efforts in the 1960s: income support for farmers in the form of direct payments. Since then, federal programs had grown to become an increasingly large part of farmers' incomes.

Key revisions to the farm law included:

● The Agricultural Act of 1970 (PL 91-524), which maintained crop and price controls, but added a "set-aside" program that paid farmers for taking portions of their land out of production. (*1970 Almanac, p. 634*)

● The Agriculture and Consumer Protection Act of 1973 (PL 93-86), which replaced the old support prices for major commodities — cotton, wheat, rice, corn and other feed grains — with "target prices" that reimbursed farmers when the market dropped sharply. (*1973 Almanac, p. 287*)

● The 1981 farm bill (PL 97-98), which maintained price supports and added a new support program for sugar. (*1981 Almanac, p. 535*)

● The 1985 farm bill (PL 99-198), which provided massive income-support payments to farmers struggling in the midst of a devastating farm depression, at a cost of $69.4 billion over five years. (*1985 Almanac, p. 517*)

• The 1990 farm bill (PL 101-624), which sought to reduce the cost of federal farm programs. It froze farm price support and income-support rates at existing levels and began the "triple base acreage" program, which made 15 percent of farmland ineligible for crop subsidy payments but still allowed farmers to cultivate the land and sell its products. *(1990 Almanac, p. 323)*

• The 1993 budget-reconciliation bill (PL 103-66), which contained another round of cuts, totaling $3.2 billion, to agriculture programs. The largest savings — $586 million over five years — came from limiting the Agriculture secretary's ability to threaten increased price-support payments as a bargaining chip in trade negotiations. Other savings came from reducing fraud and abuse in the crop insurance system; decreasing participation in the Conservation Reserve Program; and reducing the size of payments to farmers who agreed not to plant certain subsidized grain crops. *(1993 Almanac, p. 226)*

Freedom to Farm: Breaking the Cycle

The 1996 farm law was a major departure from past farm policy. It aimed to end farmers' dependence on government subsidies and move them to the free market, while at the same time freeing them from government mandates on what they planted. It retained marketing loans, but eliminated other farm subsidies. Instead it provided fixed, declining payments — known as AMTA payments, after the provision that created them, the Agricultural Market Transition Act — to help farmers adapt to the new system. *(1996 Almanac, p. 3-15)*

But the law did not work as intended. When crop prices fell from record highs in the mid-1990s, the fixed payments proved insufficient to protect farmers from the devastating dips. So each year after the 1996 law's enactment, Congress and the White House propped up farmers and the agriculture economy by providing ad hoc "disaster" payments, ultimately totaling $30.5 billion over five years.

Those emergency packages made clear that the system enacted in 1996 had not curbed production enough to keep prices from falling when supply exceeded demand. "We thought the market loan concept was going to provide a competitive, level playing field, or even an advantage, for American producers. It doesn't seem to have worked that way," said Charles W. Stenholm of Texas, the ranking Democrat on the House Agriculture Committee. "No matter how low the prices go, they don't seem to be adjusting production anywhere."

As the 107th Congress prepared to write a new multiyear farm law, farm-state lawmakers were determined to address needs that had been demonstrated since 1996, including a "countercyclical" income support component that would kick in when prices plummeted.

Legislative Action

House Committee Action

The House Agriculture Committee took the first step July 27, approving by voice vote a bill to make $167 billion available over 10 years for farm programs. The measure (HR 2646 — H Rept 107-Parts 1, 2) included increases of $45 billion in subsidies for growers of the nation's principal crops — corn, wheat, soybeans, rice and cotton — $16.3 billion for conservation, and $3.7 billion for food and nutrition assistance.

Committee Chairman Larry Combest, R-Texas, and Stenholm had managed to garner crucial support from committee members, mostly Democrats, who were seeking to bolster spending on conservation and nutrition programs. Revised estimates from the Congressional Budget Office (CBO) of the long-term cost of the commodity programs, which comprised the bulk of the bill, allowed Combest and Stenholm to redirect $3.7 billion that had been set aside for farmer support in an earlier draft, moving $1.3 billion to conservation and $1.4 billion to food stamps and other nutrition aid.

The new estimates allowed bigger allocations to virtually every section of the bill, including a higher fixed-payment rate and higher target prices for soybean farmers. The authors also resurrected subsidy programs for honey, mohair and wool that had been dropped under the 1996 law, and included a new, $350 million-a-year program for peanut farmers similar to the one in place for grain and cotton farmers.

The bill proposed to revive sugar marketing allotments, limiting domestic production for U.S. processors of sugarcane and sugar beets, although the Agriculture Department could lift them if imports grew too high. That provision was an attempt to address the concerns of domestic sugar refiners, who complained that imports of low-cost "stuffed molasses" — a mixture of molasses, sugar and water that was allowed to enter the United States duty-free — constituted unfair competition for their products.

Lawmakers who wanted to steer agriculture funding away from commodity subsidies and toward new conservation and research initiatives held off, recognizing that they did not have the votes in the farm-state-dominated panel. Collin C. Peterson, D-Minn., offered — but then withdrew — an amendment to overhaul and scale-back crop subsidies to make room in the bill for more conservation funding. Ron Kind, D-Wis., offered — but later withdrew — an amendment he said would provide $5 billion a year for conservation, compared with $3.7 billion under the Combest-Stenholm bill. Kind and others were interested in, among other things, increasing the amount of acreage eligible for the Conservation Reserve Program.

After more than three hours of debate July 27, the panel rejected, by voice vote, an amendment by John Thune, R-S.D., that would have required country-of-origin labeling on beef, lamb, pork, farm-raised fish and perishable commodities. Lawmakers representing both ranchers and catfish farmers — who were feeling increasingly threatened by a surge in imported fish from Vietnam — argued that U.S. consumers had a right to know where their food came from. Opponents said the labeling would be burdensome to U.S. producers and would provoke retaliation by foreign governments.

The panel gave voice vote approval to amendments:

• By Marion Berry, D-Ark., to double to $150,000 the limit on payments that farmers could receive under the commodity loan program.

• By Richard W. Pombo, R-Calif., to allow a program that developed overseas markets for commodities, funded at

$67 million under the bill, to focus on value-added products.

• By Bob Etheridge, D-N.C., to make tobacco eligible for the Market Access Program.

• By Saxby Chambliss, R-Ga., to phase-out "last resort" loans to farmers.

• By Ernie Fletcher, R-Ky., to classify horses for the first time as livestock qualifying for benefits under the farm bill.

House Floor Action

The House passed the farm bill by a vote of 291-120 on Oct. 5, agreeing to spend $167 billion on agriculture programs over 10 years — most of it to maintain and expand subsidies for growers of row crops. By that point, however, the federal surplus was vanishing, the White House was urging the House not to pass the bill, and Congress' priorities had been transformed by Sept. 11. *(House vote 371, p. H-128)*

Farm-state lawmakers had scrambled to complete the committee bill before the August recess, hoping to bring it to the floor their first week back in September. By the time they returned, both CBO and the White House Office of Management and Budget (OMB) had revised their fiscal projections to show a sharply reduced budget surplus. The new numbers touched off concerns about whether the huge agriculture increases farm-state lawmakers had envisioned would be possible. Critics of farm spending, as well as Democratic leaders, said the debate should be put off until Bush produced a new budget that provided for more farm spending. GOP leaders worried the bill would give Democrats a vehicle to accuse Republicans of fiscal recklessness.

In the end, they concluded that a delay would make matters worse, not only for the farm bill, but also for Bush's top trade priority: revival of presidential "fast track" trade authority. Combest already had yanked his support from the fast track bill (HR 2149) to signal displeasure over a Bush administration decision on the treatment of U.S. farm subsidies under world trade rules. Other farm-state members indicated that their support for fast track might be contingent upon passing a generous farm bill. *(Fast track, p. 19-3)*

But plans to bring the bill to the floor the week of Sept. 10 were shelved after the Sept. 11 terrorist attacks. Then, on Sept. 19, the administration came out against the approach embodied in the House bill, calling for "fundamental, far-reaching changes" in farm policy and urging a shift in emphasis from commodity supports to conservation programs.

On Oct. 3, as the House was about to open its debate, the White House issued a statement strongly opposing the Combest-Stenholm bill. The OMB statement said the legislation "misses the opportunity to modernize the nation's farm programs through market-oriented tools, innovative environmental programs, including extending benefits to working lands, and aid programs that are consistent with our trade agenda." It advised that "the administration does not support HR 2646 and urges the House of Representatives to defer action." Combest, Stenholm and other bill supporters said they felt sandbagged by the White House, which had offered little guidance on Bush's views until shortly before the vote.

• **Conservation**. The key House vote came the night of Oct. 4, when members rejected, 200-226, an amendment by Kind to shift spending away from crop subsidies and into conservation programs. The proposal was much closer to what administration officials and leaders of the Senate Agriculture Committee said they preferred. *(House vote 366, p. H-126)*

Kind had allied with two leading environmentalists among House Republicans, Sherwood Boehlert of New York and Wayne T. Gilchrest of Maryland, as well as with John D. Dingell, D-Mich. The four proposed reducing the bill's 10-year increase in commodity subsidies by $19 billion and dedicating the money instead to conservation programs, such as paying farmers to idle environmentally sensitive land and protecting wildlife and wetlands.

Combest and other Agriculture Committee members contended that amendment supporters — members from urban and suburban districts, lawmakers interested in preserving wildlife for hunting and fishing and members with constituencies that did not produce the crops that got the lion's share of federal payments — were tinkering with a farm policy they did not understand, and putting farmers at risk. "This amendment, if passed, would totally devastate the bill," Combest said, warning he would pull the measure from the House floor if the amendment were adopted. The amendment drew the support of 25 percent of the Republicans and 69 percent of the Democrats.

• **Dairy**. Lawmakers from the Upper Midwest thwarted attempts from the Northeast and South to resurrect, if not expand, a regional milk pricing system that could benefit those areas. The coalition had been trying all year to preserve the Northeast Dairy Compact, which allowed six New England states to band together to set a higher price for fluid milk than the federal price floor. Created under the 1996 farm law, the program expired Sept. 30.

Opponents, who viewed the compacts as cartels that rewarded overproduction and depressed dairy prices, prevailed on parliamentary grounds. Judiciary Committee Chairman F. James Sensenbrenner Jr., R-Wis., whose state's dairy farmers stood to lose the most from such compacts, argued successfully that because dairy compacts involve interstate commerce and the Constitution, they should be considered by his committee and not be debated as part of the farm bill.

The House rejected, 194-224, an amendment by leading compact proponent Bernard Sanders, I-Vt., to create a national dairy policy that would allow any state to receive a premium above the federally set price floor for its fluid milk. *(House vote 368, p. H-126)*

• **Sugar**. The House rejected, 177-239, an amendment by Democrat George Miller of California and Republican Dan Miller of Florida to phase out the existing sugar program, reduce sugar loan rates and increase the penalty that producers had to pay if they forfeited their sugar to the federal government. The amendment reflected longstanding complaints by urban and suburban lawmakers that sugar price supports drove up the cost of their constituents' cereal, soda and candy purchases. *(House vote 367, p. H-126)*

The House also adopted a number of amendments not related to specific commodities, including proposals to:

• Shift $1 billion from fixed commodity payments into rural development programs. Offered by Eva Clayton, D-N.C., it was adopted 235-183. *(House vote 369, p. H-126)*

• Require country-of-origin information on perishable agricultural products. Offered by Mary Bono, R-Calif., it was adopted 296-121. *(House vote 370, p. H-126)*

• Prevent labeling a type of fish imported from Vietnam

as "catfish." Offered by Charles W. "Chip" Pickering Jr., R-Miss., the amendment was adopted by voice vote.

Senate Committee Action

After promising to produce a five-year bill that would restructure federal farm policy, Harkin ended up producing legislation that differed little from the House bill — except that it was slightly bigger. It combined traditional congressional support for commodity programs with greater incentives for land conservation and energy production and help for economic development in rural areas.

The Senate Agriculture Committee approved the five-year, roughly $90 billion bill (S 1731 — S Rept 107-117) by voice vote on Nov. 15, after a markup that spanned two weeks. Aides projected at the time that if the measure were extended over 10 years, it would cost a total of $174 billion.

Agriculture Secretary Ann M. Veneman telephoned members of the Agriculture Committee the week of Oct. 22 asking that the bill be postponed.

Harkin called the bill a "broad and balanced" approach to farm policy. But he acknowledged having to make numerous concessions, such as moving money from his pet conservation proposal to commodities subsidies, in order to win the votes of committee Democrats.

He retreated from his earlier pledge to cut payments to big grain and cotton farmers, and added money for rice and peanuts to placate Southern Democrats Blanche Lincoln of Arkansas and Zell Miller of Georgia. The inclusion of a national dairy support program favored by Patrick J. Leahy, D-Vt., added $3 billion over 10 years to the bill's cost. The commodities program, initially structured to cost $11 billion less than the House version over a 10-year period, had grown by the end of the markup process to $1.5 billion more than the House measure over five years.

The Senate committee began debating the bill Oct. 31, approving a $50 million agricultural credit section designed to help beginning farmers and ranchers obtain loans.

On Nov. 6-8, members adopted additional provisions dealing with energy, forestry, trade, research and rural development, including provisions to authorize:

• $600 million for energy programs, including grants to farmers and ranchers to develop renewable energy projects.

• $250 million for forestry programs, including grants to develop sustainable forestry cooperatives and teach landowners about sustainable forestry practices.

• $2.1 billion for trade, which included doubling the funding for the Market Access Program to promote U.S. agricultural products abroad.

• $610 million for research, including a program to conduct food security research — a need highlighted after the Sept. 11 attacks.

• $2.3 billion for rural development, including equity capital for businesses that wanted to start or expand in rural areas. Harkin initially proposed $2.8 billion, but scaled that back in a concession to members' concerns that too much was being spent before they got to the commodities debate. "I am embarrassed," he said. "We need more money in rural development, not less."

• **Commodities.** The panel demonstrated its preference for commodity programs Nov. 8, rejecting, 7-13, an amendment by ranking Republican Richard G. Lugar of Indiana that would have increased annual funding for the Agricultural Research and Extension program from $120 million to $360 million over four years. "I think you are finding a new dynamic here," said Pat Roberts, R-Kan., who supported Lugar's amendment. "A majority on the other side, primarily those that represent the Southern crops, are much more interested in the commodities programs" at the expense of research.

On Nov. 15, the panel approved, 12-9, a contentious commodities section that would increase loan rates slightly, continue AMTA payments and create a countercyclical program to reimburse farmers when crop prices fell below government target levels. Soybeans and oilseeds were added to the program for the first time.

Lugar, who had pushed an $82 billion, five-year alternative (S 1571) that would have phased out subsidies and emphasized water and land conservation, withdrew his measure after the committee tabled it, saying he would renew his efforts before the full Senate. He called the Harkin commodities plan "wild" and "totally out of bounds."

That day, the Bush administration, which had earlier spoken favorably of Lugar's plan, issued a statement supporting another alternative sponsored by Roberts and Thad Cochran, R-Miss. The proposal, which the committee rejected, 9-11, would have simplified complex funding formulas, allowed for countercyclical payments, and set up farm "savings accounts" to help eligible farmers save money for lean years with federal matching funds.

• **Competition.** The committee dealt Harkin's bill a major setback Nov. 13, rejecting, 9-12, a proposal intended to curb unfair or deceptive practices by agribusinesses. Harkin said the provision was necessary because of the trend away from competition in agriculture, where he said the top four firms that slaughtered steers and heifers accounted for 81 percent of the market, up from 36 percent in 1980.

• **Nutrition.** The panel agreed by voice vote on nutrition provisions that would authorize increased spending on food stamps and restore benefits to legal immigrants. If stretched out over 10 years, the nutrition programs were projected to cost $6.2 billion. Lugar failed, by a vote of 12-9, to win approval of an alternative plan that would have cost $10 billion over 10 years.

• **Conservation.** The cornerstone of Harkin's bill was the conservation section, approved by voice vote, which increased funds for conservation on land in production while expanding government support for programs that remove crop and grazing land from production. It included a new Conservation Security Program that would give incentive payments to farmers and ranchers who voluntarily adopted conservation measures. It increased funding for the Environmental Quality Incentives Program by $200 million a year, to $1.25 billion.

Senate Floor Action

After a grueling, two-week debate that descended into filibuster and rank partisanship, and saw three failed attempts in seven days to move toward final passage, Senate Majority Leader Tom Daschle, D-S.D., pulled the farm bill Dec. 19. Democrats accused Republicans, who backed the White House view that the bill should be postponed, of stalling. Republicans argued that Democrats had written

sloppy, bad policy.

Eleventh-hour changes to the Agriculture Committee-approved measure had allowed Democratic leaders to cut the cost and bring the bill to the floor in late November. The changes included revising the dairy proposal, which required fluid milk processors and the federal government to contribute to a fund whenever farm milk prices fell below a federal target price. The money would be paid to milk producers in monthly increments. The committee bill had routed the money through new regional boards; under the revised bill, the money would be administered through the existing federal milk marketing orders, thus taking them off-budget and bringing the bill within budget limits. Also, under the revisions, states with their own milk marketing programs, such as California, could opt out.

Democrats survived one key challenge Dec. 11, when the Senate voted 51-47 to table an amendment by Michael D. Crapo, R-Idaho, to delete the dairy provisions. Eliminating the provisions would have cost the bill the crucial votes of senators from the Northeast. (*Senate vote 362, S-74*)

Bill supporters also rejected proposals to:

• Shift $6.3 billion from commodities to nutrition programs. The amendment, by Lugar, was tabled, or killed, by a 70-30 vote. (*Senate vote 363, p. S-74*)

• Cut out the federal sugar program and shift funds to nutrition programs. The amendment, by Judd Gregg, R-N.H., was tabled on a vote of 71-29. (*Senate vote 364, p. S-75*)

• Allow the use of the term "catfish" on imported Vietnamese fish. The Senate tabled the amendment, by John McCain, R-Ariz, 68-27. (*Senate vote 373, p. S-76*)

• Allow the administration to block food and medicine sales to Cuba. The amendment, by Robert C. Smith, R-N.H., was tabled on a vote of 61-33. (*Senate vote 375, p. S-76*)

The Senate also killed two last-minute alternatives. The amendments would have:

• Created IRA-type farm savings accounts to be matched by government funds, instead of using target price-based payments. The proposal, offered by Roberts and Cochran, was tabled Dec. 18 by a 55-40 vote. (*Senate vote 374, p. S-76*)

• Replaced the text of the bill with provisions similar to the House bill. The amendment, by Tim Hutchinson, R-Ark., was tabled, 59-38, on Dec. 19. (*Senate vote 376, p. S-77*)

Democratic attempts to invoke cloture, thereby limiting debate and moving to a vote on the bill, were rejected Dec. 13 (53-45), Dec. 18 (54-43) and Dec. 19 (54-43). Sixty votes were required to prevail. (*Senate votes 368, 372, 377, pp. S-75, S-76, S-77*)

Daschle warned Republicans that they risked cutting the farm funding allotment by "25, 30, 40 billion [dollars.] . . . It is clearly an open question how much in resources will be available for agriculture next year," he said after the Senate failed for the third time to invoke cloture.

Democrats nonetheless vowed to regroup and bring the same bill back at their first opportunity in 2002. ◆

Farmers Get $5.5 Billion in Aid

Congress cleared a farm aid package in August that provided $5.5 billion in additional mandatory agriculture spending for fiscal 2001. It was the fourth time in as many years that lawmakers had agreed to supplement the subsidies already being received by farmers. Bush signed the bill into law (HR 2213 — PL 107-25) on Aug. 13.

The total was equal to the amount requested by the administration and set aside under the fiscal 2002 budget resolution. The bill provided the money by changing the rules for mandatory spending, a move unrelated to the appropriations process; the supplemental payments had to be made by Sept. 30.

The bill provided:

• $4.6 billion to be distributed among farmers eligible for federal payments under the Agricultural Marketing Transition Act (AMTA) — the primary mechanism, created by the 1996 farm law, for distributing annual support payments to producers of the nation's principal crops: wheat, corn, rice and cotton.

• $169 million for producers of specialty crops, mostly fruits and vegetables, distributed through grants to states.

• Additional funding for producers of soybeans and other

BoxScore

Bill:
HR 2213 — PL 107-25
Legislative Action:
House passed HR 2213
(H Rept 107-111) by voice
vote June 26.
Senate cleared HR 2213 by
voice vote Aug. 3
President signed Aug. 13.

oilseeds ($423 million); tobacco ($129 million); cottonseed ($85 million); peanuts ($52 million); and wool and mohair ($17 million).

• Language stating that federal block grants for specialty crops were not gratuitous payments, ensuring that grape-growers received compensation for the impact of Pierce's Disease, and increasing the loan deficiency payment limit to $150,000.

Background

The farm aid bill was viewed as further evidence that the 1996 "Freedom to Farm" law (PL 104-127) had fallen short of its main objective. The 1996 overhaul instituted a system of fixed but declining subsidies intended to wean farmers from payments that surged and subsided based on the weather and crop prices. But the farm economy had sagged soon after the law was enacted, and between 1998 and 2000, Congress had stepped in with a combined $25 billion in aid. The fiscal 2001 farm aid bill was viewed as a precursor to a rewrite of the 1996 law, which was due to expire Sept. 30, 2002. (*1996 Almanac, p. 3-15; farm bill, p. 3-3*)

Anticipating the demand both for short-term aid and for money to pay for a new farm bill, the fiscal 2002 budget resolution (H Con Res 83) set aside $79.1 billion in emergency agricultural assistance for fiscal years 2001 through 2011. Of the total, $5.5 billion was allocated for fiscal 2001, $7.4 billion for fiscal 2002 and the remaining $66.2 billion for fiscal 2003 through 2011. One of the main issues in debating the short-term aid bill was whether to dip into the money intended for future years, thereby reducing the amount that would be available for the farm bill rewrite.

Legislative History

House Committee Action

The House Agriculture Committee approved $5.5 billion in extra help for farmers after narrowly resisting a Republican attempt to increase the total by $1 billion. The panel approved the bill (HR 2213 — H Rept 107-111) on June 20 by a lopsided vote of 31-14, but the vote to stay within the $5.5 billion was a narrow 24-23.

The draft bill brought to the markup by committee Chairman Larry Combest, R-Texas, would have allowed $6.5 billion in spending. The $5.5 billion set aside for fiscal 2001 would have been used to give farmers who received AMTA payments the same amount they got in 1999. The additional $1 billion — taken from the money set aside for fiscal 2002 — would have gone to other producers.

The Bush administration opposed Combest's plan. In a June 14 letter, Office of Management and Budget (OMB) Director Mitchell E. Daniels Jr. said he would recommend that Bush not sign the legislation if it cost more than $5.5 billion.

But it fell to the committee's senior Democrat, Charles W. Stenholm of Texas, and the No. 2 Republican, John A. Boehner of Ohio, to write the key amendment and orchestrate its adoption. Their alternative called for $4.6 billion in AMTA payments — about 85 percent of the 2000 total — and $900 million for other farmers. To keep the package within the $5.5 billion limit, the amendment also required that any additional spending be offset with prorated cuts in the rest of the bill.

Stenholm's majority — seven Republicans and 17 Democrats — included fiscal conservatives from both parties who worried about the precedent of dipping into fiscal 2002 funds set aside for the new farm bill. It also included Democrats who viewed the existing distribution of farm assistance as inequitable, and Republicans whose farm constituents grew crops other than the row crops that had benefited most from recent emergency farm aid packages.

Taking Combest's side were 19 Republicans and four Democrats, generally those whose House districts were home to the grain and cotton farms that had received the lion's share of the recent aid. Combest argued that farmers were counting on receiving AMTA payments at the 1999 level, as they had in 2000, and that the extra $1 billion would be spent soon regardless. Stenholm and Boehner argued that once the committee consented to spending even one cent more than allotted for fiscal 2001, the floodgates would open in both the House and the Senate.

After the committee adopted the substitute, which limited the bill to programs that could be implemented and paid for by Sept. 30, proposals to add more funds quickly disappeared or were pared back. The panel did adopt, by voice vote, an amendment by Marion Berry, D-Ark., to double to $150,000 the limit on Agriculture Department payments triggered when prices fell below a certain level, but only for crops sold in fiscal 2001.

House Floor Action

The House passed the $5.5 billion bill by voice vote June 26. "In my opinion, this amount is not sufficient to meet the needs of our producers," Combest said during the floor debate. "But today, the important point is to move this process along."

Combest and other Republicans said they would focus — as commodity lobbyists and farmer groups already had begun to do — on boosting the total in the Senate bill. "I intend to work with the other body to ensure that the cuts made last week are restored," said Frank D. Lucas, R-Okla., whose district was in the heart of wheat country.

Stenholm said such a move would be irresponsible. "I cannot disagree with those who say that $5.5 billion is inadequate," he said, but "this is all we can afford at the moment."

Senate Committee Action

Picking a multibillion-dollar fight with Bush, the Senate Agriculture Committee approved a $7.4 billion farm aid bill (S 1246) by voice vote July 25. "The truth is that the farm and ranch families across the nation are in need," committee Chairman Tom Harkin, D-Iowa, said at the markup. "Some of these just can't wait another year, and they need this money right now."

Led by Richard G. Lugar of Indiana, the ranking GOP member on the panel, Republicans tried to limit the package to $5.5 billion, arguing that spending the extra money would shrink the amount available for the farm bill rewrite. OMB Director Daniels again warned he would counsel Bush not to sign a bill that exceeded $5.5 billion for 2001. Dipping into next year's money "is premature" because the money provided for this year "is adequate," he said.

"I don't think anybody on this committee wants to taunt the president and see if he will shoot it all down," said Lugar, whose amendment to keep the measure to $5.5 billion was rejected, 9-12, nearly along party lines. "We're on the brink of making that experiment."

The action was a partisan role reversal from the situation in the House, where Democrats had spearheaded the effort to hold down the bill's price tag. Senate Democrats argued that the extra funding would help compensate farmers who had not benefited from the existing subsidy structure. The committee bill included $5.5 billion for those farmers, plus another $1.2 billion for growers of oilseeds and "specialty crops" including tobacco, peanuts and sugar, and $542 million for conservation programs. Harkin viewed conservation spending as a means to equalize federal farm support, because all producers could qualify for the benefits. The House bill had no conservation money.

"This is a mini-farm bill," Pat Roberts, R-Kan., complained. "I don't believe that agriculture policy should be written in the back room."

Senate Floor Action

After a week of wrangling, the Senate on Aug. 3 cleared the House-passed version of the bill by voice vote. The ac-

tion came after the leaders of the Democratic majority — faced with the impending August recess and an explicit veto threat from Bush — found themselves unable to muster sufficient support for the $7.4 billion committee bill.

"Let the record show who is prepared to stand up for farmers and who, in the end, opposed their interests," Budget Committee Chairman Kent Conrad, D-N.D., declared at a news conference following the final vote. "We did the right thing for farmers," countered Minority Leader Trent Lott, R-Miss., and "we did the right thing for the budget."

Democrats abandoned their campaign for Harkin's more generous package Aug. 3 after they lost, 49-48, an attempt to invoke cloture, thereby limiting debate on their bill. Sixty votes were required. (*Senate vote 273, p. S-56*)

With senators ready to head to the airport for the recess, Lugar was able to get a vote on the House bill. His victory reversed a decision made in the first key vote of the debate July 31, when the Senate voted, 52-48, to table (kill) a Lugar amendment that would have reduced the cost of Harkin's bill to $5.5 billion. (*Senate vote 261, p. S-54*)

"There is a tremendous and collective sigh of relief in farm country," Roberts said after the Senate cleared the House bill. "Rather than a train wreck and a partisan battle, we have emergency relief for our farmers and ranchers." ◆

Chapter 4

BANKING & FINANCE

Bankruptcy Revamp Stalls Again

For the third year in a row, legislation to overhaul federal bankruptcy law passed the House and Senate, but failed to make it into law. The effort stalled in conference as time ran out at the end of the session.

The legislation (HR 333) was designed to force more debtors to file under Chapter 13 of the bankruptcy code, which requires a filer to repay debts over five years, instead of Chapter 7, which allows the cancellation of most debts after some of the debtor's assets are liquidated.

At the start of the year, bankruptcy reform seemed an odds-on favorite to be the first major legislative achievement of the 107th Congress. The House and Senate overwhelmingly passed separate bills in March. But efforts to go to conference were stalled by a power-sharing struggle in the 50-50 Senate and by parliamentary delaying tactics by Sen. Paul Wellstone, D-Minn., who opposed the bill. An initial conference scheduled for Sept. 12 was called off in the wake of the Sept. 11 terrorist attacks. Conferees finally met Nov. 14, but the session was devoted to opening statements, not negotiating.

The legislation was a top priority for the credit card industry, which wanted to curb what it said was rampant abuse of the bankruptcy system. It was opposed by consumer advocates and bankruptcy attorneys, who argued that it was a draconian assault on struggling debtors, especially with the economy in recession.

Highlights

The following are key elements of the legislation:
● **Means test.** Both the House and Senate bills required that individuals filing for bankruptcy use Chapter 13, rather than Chapter 7, if they were capable of repaying 25 percent of their remaining debt or $10,000, whichever was less, over five years. Debtors earning less than the state median income would be exempt from the restriction.
● **Homestead exemption.** Both bills would limit the homestead exemption, which protects a debtors' home against seizure. The House version, backed by the White House, had a cap of $100,000, but it applied only to homes purchased within two years before a filing. The Senate limit was $125,000 for all homes.
● **Luxury items.** Both bills required that debtors pay in full for luxury purchases — defined as those that exceeded $250 under the House bill and $750 in the Senate version — made within 90 days of filing for bankruptcy, and for cash advances above $750 acquired within 70 days of filing.
● **Savings accounts.** Tax-exempt retirement savings accounts were to be exempt from creditor claims. So were de-

BoxScore

Bill:

HR 333

Legislative Action:

House passed HR 333 (H Rept 107-3, Part 1), 306-108, on March 1.

Senate passed S 420, 83-15, on March 15.

Senate passed HR 333, amended, 82-16, on July 17.

posits of up to $5,000 per beneficiary in tax-exempt education savings accounts made one year or more before filing for bankruptcy.
● **Consumer disclosure.** Both bills called for increased disclosure by credit card companies, including information related to minimum payments, introductory rates and and late payment deadlines and penalties.
● **Chapter 12.** Both bills included provisions to make permanent Chapter 12, which gives bankruptcy protection to farmers.
● **Abortion protesters.** The Senate bill included a provision, aimed at anti-abortion protesters and strongly opposed by House Republicans, to bar debtors from getting bankruptcy courts to discharge fines and civil judgments incurred for violations of federal, state or local laws.

Background

Both the House and Senate bills were modeled on a measure that had been pocket vetoed by President Bill Clinton in December 2000. Clinton objected on the grounds that the $100,000 homestead exemption in the bill would allow wealthy debtors to shield assets in real estate and that conferees had dropped a provision sponsored by Sen. Charles E. Schumer, D-N.Y., aimed at barring violent anti-abortion protesters from using bankruptcy to avoid penalties.

With the election of President Bush, bankruptcy overhaul supporters had an ally in the White House and were hoping for quick action. Republicans leaders made it clear they did not intend to let opponents topple the measure by loading it down with amendments.

Bankruptcy overhaul bills had been stymied in the 105th and 106th Congresses by delays and an inability to reach agreement with Clinton on a final draft. In 1998, a GOP-fashioned conference report was adopted in the House but died without a vote in the Senate, where Democrats rejected the final bill as anti-consumer. In 2000, the House adopted the conference report on the bill by voice vote, and the bill cleared the Senate, 70-28, before it was pocket-vetoed by Clinton on Dec. 19. (*2000 Almanac, p. 5-3; 1998 Almanac, p. 5-15*)

A broad coalition of retailers, banks and credit card companies had been lobbying for the legislation since 1997, arguing that the federal bankruptcy code needed tightening to prevent rampant abuse by borrowers who could afford to repay some of their debts but instead took advantage of permissive bankruptcy rules. They pointed to a wave of consumer bankruptcies, which increased from 500,000 in 1986 to 1.4 million in 1998, declining to 1.3 million in 1999.

Unions, women's groups and consumer groups portrayed

the measure as an attempt to help big banks at the expense of low-wage workers and single-parent families. They blamed much of the rise in bankruptcy filings on aggressive marketing by credit card issuers.

Legislative Action

House Committee Action

The House Judiciary Committee approved HR 333 (H Rept 107-3, Part 1) by a vote of 19-8 on Feb. 14, after rejecting a series of Democratic amendments aimed mainly at making the measure more lenient toward consumers and small businesses in dire financial straits.

F. James Sensenbrenner Jr., R-Wis., running his first markup as Judiciary Committee chairman, said the GOP leadership's dictate that amendments be kept off the bill — at least until it reached the floor — was akin to the Ten Commandments.

While professing a willingness to negotiate with Democrats, the bill's main sponsor, George W. Gekas, R-Pa., said, "I apologize to no one for the strength of my efforts to protect the integrity of this bill." The tone infuriated committee Democrats, only one of whom voted for the bill.

The session, scheduled for two days, was forced to a close by Sensenbrenner on the evening of the first day. After Democrats sharply criticized his effort to defeat all amendments, the chairman invoked a rarely used procedure to squelch any additional amendments. The committee backed him, 16-5, allowing him to force a vote to approve the bill.

Jerrold Nadler, D-N.Y., said the chairman was "acting like a total tyrant" but acknowledged that the Republicans had the votes to prevail.

Rejected Democratic amendments included:

• A proposal by Bill Delahunt, D-Mass., to increase the cap on home equity that could be sheltered from creditors to $500,000; it was defeated, 6-18. As drafted, the bill capped the exemption at $100,000, but only for homes purchased within two years of a bankruptcy filing.

• A Nadler amendment, defeated 9-20, to bar abortion protesters from discharging debts that resulted from court judgments for violence at abortion clinics.

• An amendment by John Conyers Jr., D-Mich., rejected 6-18, that would have allowed judges to extend deadlines in business bankruptcy cases.

House Floor Action

The House passed the bankruptcy bill March 1 by a vote of 306-108. (*House vote 25, p. H-14*)

Opponents seized on a new study by the Administrative Office of U.S. Courts showing that after quadrupling over the previous two decades and reaching a peak of 1.4 million in 1998, consumer bankruptcy filings had dropped for the second year in a row from 1.3 million in 1999 to 1.2 million in 2000. But efforts to change the bill failed.

An attempt by liberal Democrats to soften many of the proposed restrictions on Chapter 7 filings failed, 160-258. The substitute, offered by Sheila Jackson-Lee of Texas, would have allowed debtors to deduct additional medical and child care expenses before determining their eligibility for Chapter 7, changed the standards for calculating median income and added debtor privacy provisions. Gekas argued that the underlying bill struck the proper balance between creditors and debtors. (*House vote 23, p. H-14*)

A proposal by John Conyers Jr., D-Mich, to bar companies from issuing credit cards to individuals under age 21 without a parent's co-signature was rejected, 165-253. (*House vote 24, p. H-14*)

Jackson-Lee did win voice vote approval for an amendment to allow debtors to deduct up to $1,500 a year for public school expenses before calculating whether they had sufficient means to repay debts. A deduction for private school tuition was covered under existing law.

Senate Committee Action

The Senate Judiciary Committee approved a nearly identical bill (S 420), 10-8, on Feb. 28. Joseph R. Biden Jr. of Delaware was the only Democrat to break ranks and vote for the measure. In an effort to avert potential snags when the bill reached the floor, Republicans cut several deals with committee Democrats.

In a major concession, Judiciary Chairman Orrin G. Hatch, R-Utah, worked out a compromise with Schumer on his provision aimed at abortion protesters. The new, broader language would prevent discharge of debts related to the violation of any federal, state or local laws, including harassing or intimidating anyone who was providing legal goods or services. The compromise did not refer directly to abortion clinics, but it stated that the language would apply to violations of a 1994 law, the Freedom of Access to Clinic Entrances Act (PL 103-259), which made it a federal crime to obstruct access to abortion services. The amendment was adopted by voice vote. (*1994 Almanac, p. 355*)

"I think we have resolved this major problem with Schumer," Hatch said. "Unless somebody on our side goes berserk, it should stand." Schumer said he was pleased but warned that opponents might try to kill the compromise in conference.

Hatch and ranking committee Democrat Patrick J. Leahy of Vermont reached agreement on an amendment, also adopted by voice vote, that would create a consumer privacy ombudsman to prevent bankrupt businesses from selling personal customer information.

Over strong GOP opposition, Russell D. Feingold, D-Wis., won approval on a 10-8 vote for an amendment to make it more difficult to evict a tenant during bankruptcy proceedings. The amendment included language by Dianne Feinstein, D-Calif., that would allow landlords to evict tenants who repeatedly failed to pay rent on time or allowed use of drugs on the property.

The panel defeated, 8-10, an amendment by Feinstein to require that judges be given flexibility to waive restrictions on bankruptcy filings for debtors who could prove "extreme hardship." A Feinstein amendment to place restrictions on issuing credit cards to those under age 21 was rejected, 7-11.

Senate Floor Action

In a striking triumph for GOP leaders, the Senate passed the bill by a vote of 83-15 on March 15, after a two-week floor debate. (*Senate vote 36, p. S-12*)

"We are sending a message that those people who have the ability to pay their debts are not going to get off scot-

free," said Charles E. Grassley, R-Iowa, who had been trying for six years to build a bipartisan coalition behind bankruptcy overhaul.

The lopsided nature of the vote was foreshadowed March 14, when the Senate agreed, 80-19, to invoke cloture, bringing the debate to a close. "There's been a full court press. The big guys are going to win," said Wellstone, referring to the financial services giants that had lobbied hard for the legislation. *(Senate vote 29, p. S-11)*

Liberal Democrats continued to oppose the bill, arguing that it would hurt low- and middle-income consumers threatened with mounting debts because of the economic slow down and a spate of layoffs by big companies. But Republicans and most Democrats embraced the measure, which had been modified by a series of amendments that increase consumer protections and removed some of the tougher restrictions on debtors in the House-passed version.

Schumer won voice vote approval March 13 of an amendment to allow borrowers to sue bankrupt lenders — or investors who acquired their assets — for unfair lending practices under the 1968 Truth in Lending Act (PL 90-321), which requires creditors to notify borrowers of the terms of loans. The provision was aimed at punishing companies that used deceptive marketing practices to lure customers into high-interest loans. It was adopted after a motion to table (kill) it was defeated, 44-55. *(Senate vote 24, p. S-10)*

A manager's amendment, offered by Hatch and adopted by voice vote, added provisions to extend protection for farmers under Chapter 12 to family fishermen, clarify that bankrupt companies must fulfill duties as sponsors of health care and benefit plans, and prevent government contractors from discharging penalties for violations of a 1986 rewrite of the False Claims Act (PL 99-562). *(1986 Almanac, p. 86)*

The Senate adopted by voice vote March 15 a compromise amendment by Leahy to prevent courts from "cramming down," or reducing, debt owed on an automobile if it was purchased within three years of a filing for bankruptcy. The Senate also adopted, 99-0, a Leahy privacy amendment to prohibit disclosing of the names of minor children in bankruptcy filings. *(Senate vote 31, p. S-11)*

Feinstein and Herb Kohl, D-Wis., succeeded in increasing the homestead exemption cap to $125,000 for all homes. The change was adopted by voice vote March 15, after an effort to table their amendment was defeated, 39-60. *(Senate vote 30, p. S-11)*

A number of other Democratic amendments were rejected or sidestepped, including proposals to:

• Give businesses with fewer than 25 full-time employees priority over credit card companies and other firms in making claims on bankrupt debtors. The amendment by Leahy was tabled, 58-41, on March 7. *(Senate vote 17, p. S-9)*

• Exempt from the bill's restrictions anyone who filed for bankruptcy because of medical debts. The proposal by Wellstone was rejected, 34-65, on March 7. *(Senate vote 16, p. S-9)*

• Bar creditors from collecting debts in bankruptcy if they failed to comply with the 1968 Truth in Lending Act. The proposal, by Richard J. Durbin, D-Ill., was tabled March 8, 50-49. *(Senate vote 18, p. S-9)*

• Delete the bill's tough new terms for small-business bankruptcies, including a requirement for periodic financial reports. The amendment by John Kerry, D-Mass., was tabled, 55-41 on March 8. *(Senate vote 19, p. S-9)*

• Put a $2,500 credit cap on credit cards issued to persons under the age of 21 without a parent's signature or proof of independent means. The Feinstein amendment was tabled, 55-42, on March 13. *(Senate vote 20, p. S-10)*

Conference

The overwhelming votes for House and Senate passage in March were the high-water mark for the bill. For the rest of the year, procedural roadblocks and other, more pressing priorities prevented lawmakers from reaching a final compromise.

The first obstacle came in the 50-50 Senate, where party leaders were unable to agree on how a conference committee should be structured. Grassley and other Senate leaders tried to get around the need for a conference by persuading the House to simply accept the Senate version of the bankruptcy bill. But House leaders resisted, saying they would not set a precedent that could put the House at a disadvantage in the long run. Also, sponsors of the House bankruptcy bill strongly objected to three provisions in the Senate version: the provision on filing for bankruptcy to avoid paying civil penalties, the homestead exemption limit and the protections against unscrupulous lenders.

The Senate stalemate over the makeup of conference committees ended in June, when Democrats became the majority party and the chamber returned to its regular procedures. Liberal Democrats opposed to the bill then launched a parliamentary assault to further delay conference. Finally, on July 17, the Senate agreed to go to conference, passing HR 333 by a vote of 82-16, after substituting the text of its own bill. *(Senate vote 236, p. S-49)*

Wellstone, who had led the procedural attack, gave up after his colleagues voted, 88-10, to invoke cloture, thereby limiting debate on whether to insert the Senate text into the bill — a normally routine motion that speeds the start of conference negotiations. *(Senate vote 234, p. S-49)*

The new Democratic majority named a delegation of seven Democrats and six Republicans. Leahy, the new Judiciary chairman, said he hoped negotiations would begin quickly, but that sentiment was not shared by Sensenbrenner, who lamented that the large Senate delegation would complicate the talks. Leahy insisted that the Senate negotiators include three of the Democrats who opposed the bill: Durbin, Feingold and Edward M. Kennedy of Massachusetts. The House appointed its conferees on July 31.

Conferees were scheduled to meet Sept. 12, after their return from the August recess, but the Sept. 11 attacks forced a revision of Congress' schedule and priorities. The conferees ended up meeting only once, on Nov. 14. The meeting was little more than an initial skirmish in what were expected to be contentious negotiations in the second session of the 107th Congress.

Chapter 12 Extension

To hedge against delays in finishing the bankruptcy overhaul, Congress cleared two bills temporarily extending Chapter 12 of the bankruptcy code, which covers family farmers. The first extension (HR 256 — PL 107-8) renewed the provisions retroactively to June 30, 2000, when they had

last expired, and continued them through July 31, 2001. The House passed the bill, 408-2, on Feb. 28; the Senate cleared it by voice vote April 26 and Bush signed it May 11. (*House vote 17, p. H-12*)

When it became clear that the overhaul bill would not be enacted by June 30, Chapter 12 was extended through Sept. 30, 2001 (HR 1914 — PL 107-17). The House passed the bill, 411-1, on June 6; the Senate cleared it by voice vote June 8 and the president signed it June 26. (*House vote 153, p. H-58*) ◆

Terrorism Insurance Measure Stalls

Despite intense lobbying and broad support among lawmakers, Congress ended the year without completing a bill to backstop commercial property and casualty insurers against future acts of terrorism. Differences centered on the extent to which taxpayers should be liable for future losses and whether to ban punitive damages in lawsuits related to terrorist acts.

Following Sept. 11, commercial property and casualty insurers said they could pay claims resulting from the terrorist attacks — expected to reach $50 billion or more — but without federal help, they would not be able to continue providing insurance against acts of terrorism. That raised widespread fears that construction companies and other businesses would lose terrorism coverage, and thus their ability to obtain credit, with effects that could reverberate through the economy. Lawmakers scrambled to draft legislation that would encourage insurance companies to continue issuing terrorism coverage in the short term, while giving the market time to develop mechanisms to provide commercial coverage at reasonable prices in the future.

The Senate Banking and House Financial Services committees unveiled sharply different plans for federal intervention at competing news conferences Nov. 1. The bipartisan Senate plan, negotiated with the White House, called for a direct federal subsidy to insurers in the event of a future terrorist attack that caused more than $10 billion in losses. The House bill, drafted without much Democratic input, took a different tack, calling for federal loans to cover losses above $1 billion, with the assistance paid back by the industry and policyholders. Both bills proposed to consolidate claims arising from any one terrorist act in federal court; both included so-called tort reform provisions to bar punitive damages, except against terrorists or conspirators.

The House passed its bill (HR 3210) on Nov. 29, but the Senate was hamstrung, first by a jurisdictional dispute between the Banking and Commerce committees and then by a controversy over the proposed ban on punitive damage awards. The Senate came close to a compromise in the final week of the session, but the tort reform dispute scuttled it.

Senate Majority Leader Tom Daschle, D-S.D., said the Senate would "absolutely" come back to the issue in the second session. Though no one was sure what would happen on Jan. 1, when most existing policies expired, some of the dire predictions were fading.

BoxScore

Bill:
HR 3210

Legislative Action:
House passed HR 3210 (H Rept 107-300, Parts 1, 2), 227-193, on Nov. 29.

Background

The September terrorist attacks sent shock waves through the property and casualty insurance industry. Instantly, acts of terrorism went from a casually overlooked provision in commercial property and casualty policies to a very real risk that insurers said they had no idea how to price.

The insurance industry testified that it was well-capitalized and would be able to cover all claims from Sept. 11. But, absent federal intervention, insurers said, coverage for future acts of terrorism would be scarce or nonexistent. Reinsurance firms, which insure the insurers, warned that they would not provide coverage in 2002. About 70 percent of existing reinsurance contracts were due to expire at the end of 2001. There was widespread concern that a lack of affordable terrorism insurance could severely disrupt the U.S. economy, further deepening the nation's economic problems. Commercial insurers, real estate investors, retailers and others pressed Congress to act.

Legislative Action

House Financial Services Committee

The House Financial Services Committee agreed by voice vote Nov. 7 to a bill (HR 3210 — H Rept 107-300, Part 1) that would create a temporary federal terrorism insurance loan program. The federal government would provide short-term aid to the insurance industry to cover 90 percent of losses resulting from terrorism, with the assistance to be repaid by the insurance industry and policyholders. Drafted by Chairman Michael G. Oxley, R-Ohio, and Capital Markets subcommittee Chairman Richard H. Baker, R-La., the bill provided for a one-year program, with an option to extend it for two more years.

Under the committee bill:

• The federal program would kick in once industrywide losses exceeded $1 billion in a year. Smaller insurance companies that suffered disproportionately large losses from terrorism could receive federal aid once industrywide losses exceeded $100 million.

• For losses above the threshold, the federal government would pay the property and casualty insurance industry to cover 90 percent of insured losses, up to $100 billion.

• The first $20 billion in federal assistance would be re-

coupled through direct assessments on insurance companies.

• Assistance between $20 billion and $100 billion would be repaid through surcharges on insurance policyholders.

• All lawsuits involving losses or injuries due to acts of terrorism would be considered in federal court, rather than state courts.

• Punitive damage awards would be prohibited, except against terrorists and conspirators, and non-economic damages would be limited.

The committee bill also would have allowed commercial insurers to set aside long-term tax-free reserves to prepare for paying future claims related to terrorism. The provision was the one remnant of an industry proposal circulated soon after the September attacks that would have created a government-backed reinsurance pool for the industry.

The bill was approved after a raucous, day-long markup. Ranking Democrat John J. LaFalce of New York complained that he had not been consulted in drafting the measure, and slowed the session with technical questions and procedural maneuvers. Oxley and Baker briefly held their ground before relenting and heading into a back room with LaFalce and Paul E. Kanjorski, D-Pa., where they agreed to negotiate changes to the bill before it reached the House floor.

House Ways and Means Committee

On Nov. 16, the Ways and Means Committee, gave voice vote approval to an amended version of the bill (H Rept 107-300, Part 2) that eliminated the provision on tax treatment of long-term terrorism loss reserves, replacing it with language calling for a Treasury Department study.

House Floor Action

The House passed the bill, 227-193, on Nov. 29, after the Rules Committee had incorporated changes from the Financial Services, Ways and Means and Judiciary committees. Judiciary had not held a mark up. *(House vote 464, p. H-158)*

At the behest of Judiciary Committee Chairman F. James Sensenbrenner Jr., R-Wis., the bill included broad new language requiring that all lawsuits related to terrorist acts — not just those involving insurers — be tried in federal court. The bill would ban punitive damages against any defendant and sharply limit rewards for other damages, such as pain and suffering. Attorneys' fees would be capped at 20 percent of damages or settlements. Democrats cried foul, and most voted against the bill.

A Democratic substitute by LaFalce that would have increased the threshold for government loans and eliminated restrictions on lawsuits was rejected, 197-222. *(House vote 462, p. H-158)*

Industry lobbyists welcome the legislation as a step forward, but were wary of the repayment provisions, saying that they would not give insurance companies enough incentive to keep covering acts of terrorism. The White House also expressed concern that the assessments could "negatively affect important sectors of the economy."

Senate Bill

The Senate Banking proposal — negotiated with the Treasury Department and announced by Banking Chairman Paul S. Sarbanes, D-Md., on Nov. 1 — proposed a straight subsidy, with no premiums or repayment requirements. Under the two-year plan:

• Insurance companies would pay terrorism-related insurance claims up to an industrywide total of $10 billion in one year.

• The federal government would pay 90 percent of claims after that, up to $100 billion.

• Lawsuits involving losses or injuries resulting from terrorist acts would be considered in federal court. Punitive damages would be barred.

Phil Gramm, R-Texas, who developed the plan with Christopher J. Dodd, D-Conn., called the measure "bipartisanship at its very best." No sooner had the bill been unveiled, however, than it was hastily pulled back, derailed by opposition from Daschle and others to the punitive damages ban. "Unfortunately, the Senate leadership . . . is not letting that bill be marked up," Lawrence Lindsey, chairman of the White House National Economic Council, said Nov. 25.

Further complicating matters, Senate Commerce Chairman Ernest F. Hollings, D-S.C., claimed jurisdiction over the issue, promising to introduce a bill of his own. Seeking to head off a turf war between Hollings and Sarbanes, Daschle took control of the process. He tried to broker a deal among members of the two committees and the administration that he could take straight to the floor.

"My only concern is that we get this bill done," Daschle said Dec. 5. But he also made his own stance clear: "A debate about tort reform . . . well, I wouldn't call it reform . . . undermining the tort laws of this country would elongate the debate well into next year." Daschle had stuck to that position for weeks, despite Republican taunts that he was a captive of trial lawyer lobbyists.

During the week of Dec. 17, Senate negotiators neared agreement on a measure that would require the federal government to pay 90 percent of terrorism-related claims in 2002 after an industrywide threshold of $10 billion had been reached. Insurance companies would be individually responsible for losses under that amount commensurate with their market share. For example, a company with a 2 percent market share would be responsible for paying $200 million. Companies whose insured losses exceeded their individual responsibility before industrywide losses exceeded $10 billion would be eligible for government assistance sooner. The plan also included a ban on the use of federal money to pay punitive damage claims.

In the end, tort reform proved too high a hurdle to overcome. Key senators were unable Dec. 20 to figure out how to set up a unanimous consent agreement permitting a Republican amendment banning punitive damages in terrorism-related lawsuits. Gramm insisted that such an amendment would have succeeded if Daschle had allowed a vote. ◆

SEC Law a Win for Wall Street

Wall Street won one of its top legislative priorities on the last day of the session when lawmakers cleared a bill reducing securities transaction fees charged by the Securities and Exchange Commission (SEC). The legislation, which also increased the pay scale for SEC employees, had languished for six months in a dispute over costs and interchamber jurisdictional battles.

President Bush signed the measure into law (HR 1088 —PL 107-123) on Jan. 16, 2002.

The new law was expected to reduce fees on stock transactions, the registration of securities, and merger and tender offers by $14 billion over the next decade. Supporters of the move noted that the volume of Wall Street trading had pushed revenue in the past several years to about six times what was required to cover the SEC's annual expenses. The leftover money went to Treasury and was treated like general tax revenue.

The SEC salary increase was aimed at creating pay parity between the agency's 3,000 employees and the better-paid employees at three agencies charged with regulating banks: the Federal Reserve, the Comptroller of the Currency and the Office of Thrift Supervision. Critics, including the White House, said the change would fragment the federal personnel system.

The legislation was promoted all year not only by Wall Street, which saw the fee reductions as a boon to institutional investors, but also by the SEC, which hoped the new pay scale would improve employee retention.

The House passed the bill overwhelmingly in June, after resolving a dispute over the pay increase that had held it up for weeks. The measure then languished for the next six months in the Senate, where Democrats suggested it would be preferable to dedicate the revenue that would be lost under the bill to financing patients' rights legislation. That objection was lifted only on the final day of the session.

Highlights

The following are the main provisions of the new law:
- **SEC fee reductions.** Fees on securities transactions were reduced from $33.33 to $15 for each $1 million in securities bought or sold. Registration fees, paid by corporations and investment companies to register securities that they planned to sell, were reduced from $239 to $92 for each $1 million in securities. Fees on merger and tender offers were cut from $200 to $92 per $1 million in securities.
- **SEC pay parity.** The bill provided for a demonstration program under which the SEC could increase the pay and benefits of any of its employees to levels comparable to

BoxScore

Bill:
HR 1088 — PL 107-123
Legislative Action:
Senate passed S 143
(S Rept 107-3) by voice vote
March 22.
House passed HR 1088
(H Rept 107-52, Part 1), 404-22, on June 14.
Senate cleared HR 1088 by
voice vote Dec. 20.
President signed Jan. 16, 2002.

those at other federal bank regulatory agencies. The SEC was directed to consult with the Office of Personnel Management (OPM) in planning the new pay system, and to submit a report to Congress and OPM before implementing the plan.
- **GAO study.** The General Accounting Office (GAO) was directed to prepare a study on the feasibility of allowing the SEC to collect fees to pay for its own operations without requiring the money to be appropriated, as it was under current law, and to set employee pay and benefit levels outside the federal civil service system.

Background

Securities transaction fees, assessed on securities dealers each time a stock is bought or sold, were initiated as a way to provide dedicated funding for the SEC. But the amount collected had skyrocketed in recent years as trading volume soared, far outpacing the agency's operating expenses. The SEC also collected fees for stock registration and for mergers and tender offers.

For fiscal 2001, the SEC was expected to receive $2.47 billion in total fees; the agency's expenses were about $423 million. Lawmakers said the collection amounted to an unfair tax because the costs were passed on to investors. "The bottom line is, we're collecting six times as much in fees as we're spending," said Phil Gramm, R-Texas, sponsor of the Senate bill. "This is imposing a burden on everybody in America who is trying to save and invest."

Some Democrats saw the extra revenue as a possible source of funding for initiatives such as low-cost mortgages for teachers, police and fire employees. Other lawmakers agreed that the fees were too high, but said they should be cut by a smaller amount, with the remaining surplus revenue spent to increase SEC enforcement activity.

An SEC fee cut foundered in the 106th Congress, partly because key Senate Republicans insisted on including the pay parity provisions and partly because key House Republicans resisted, saying the extra money could open the door to overly aggressive securities regulation and enforcement.

The SEC had long complained that it was unable to keep professional personnel, especially lawyers, who often were lured away by Wall Street firms and other companies that needed experts in securities regulation and could pay higher salaries.

Laura S. Unger, the acting SEC chairman, told the Senate Banking Committee on Feb. 14 that the staffing crisis was "threatening our ability to oversee the nation's securities markets." She said the SEC had lost nearly a third of its accountants, attorneys and examiners in the past two years.

The bill would allow the agency to go above normal federal pay grades and offer salaries comparable to those of the Federal Deposit Insurance Corporation and other agencies.

Legislative Action

Senate Action

The Senate Banking, Housing and Urban Affairs Committee approved Gramm's bill (S 143 — S Rept 107-3) by voice vote March 1.

Determined to make good on a promise to Arthur Levitt before he departed as SEC chairman in February, Gramm insisted that the bill include both the fee cuts and the pay increases.

The Senate passed the bill by voice vote March 22.

House Committee Action

The House Financial Services Committee approved its version of the bill (HR 1088 — H Rept 107-52, Part 1) on March 28. The panel's Subcommittee on Capital Markets had approved it by voice vote March 21. The bill's chief sponsor was Vito J. Fossella, R-N.Y.

The main difference was that the House proposed deeper cuts in the fees on stock sales, which were passed on to investors, while the Senate would make deeper reductions in fees on mergers, tender offers and stock registrations.

The committee approved by voice vote an amendment by Ken Bentsen, D-Texas, to require the SEC to determine the extent to which the fee reductions were passed on to investors.

House Floor Action

The House passed the bill, 404-22, on June 14, after a turf battle over the pay parity issue was resolved. The Bush administration opposed the compromise language designed to end that impasse but did not threaten a veto — mainly because of its enthusiasm for the fee reduction. (*House vote 165, p. H-62*)

The dispute pitted Michael G Oxley, R-Ohio, chairman of the Financial Services Committee, against Government Reform Committee Chairman Dan Burton, R-Ind.

Burton, whose panel had jurisdiction over civil service law, said the pay raise proposal would spur other agencies to demand higher pay scales. He portrayed the bill as an attempt to revise the Civil Services Reform Act of 1978 (PL 95-454), which set limits on incentives that agencies could offer to retain key employees. He argued that the SEC's request should not be granted without a broader review of the impact on the civil service system. (*1978 Almanac, p. 818*)

"We have to limit who gets these pay raises. If not, you'll have every agency coming in and saying the same thing. Everybody has got an excuse to get those salaries up," he said May 1. GOP leaders already had rejected a proposal from the Commodities Futures Trading Commission that its employees get a similar pay raise under the SEC bill.

In the weeks before the House vote, Oxley worked behind the scenes to write new pay-parity language. At one point, he and Burton agreed to confine the pay raises to SEC attorneys, securities examiners and accountants — already the better-paid 60 percent of the work force — while requiring the SEC to seek approval for raises for other employees from OPM. But Gramm opposed the deal, and it quickly unraveled.

In the end, Oxley adopted language from the Senate bill describing the new SEC pay scale as a demonstration project to provide a temporary exemption from civil service limits. Burton continued to argue against the bill, saying he doubted the pay raises ever would be rolled back and that they would invite similar salary increase requests by other agencies. But he stopped the procedural and jurisdictional ploys he had used to block it. "It's wired. I can't stop the bill," he said June 14.

The bill that was brought to the floor also had smaller cuts in transaction fees and deeper reductions in registration fees than the committee bill, bringing it closer to the Senate version.

A substitute by Financial Services ranking Democrat John J. LaFalce of New York, to cut the fees by $4.8 billion in the next 10 years, was rejected, 126-299. He and others argued that the existing fees were excessive, but said the proposed cut was too large and that the SEC should be using more of the surplus to boost its enforcement efforts. (*House vote 164, p. H-62*)

Final Action

The bill stalled for another six months in the Senate, where Democrats argued that there was not enough money available under the fiscal 2002 budget resolution (H Con Res 83) to pay for both the SEC fee reductions and a separate patients' rights bill (S 1052). Several senators urged the House to take up the Senate bill and clear it for the president, but House leaders said that would violate the constitutional requirement that revenue bills start in their chamber.

Finally, with pressure building to get the measure finished, the Senate cleared it by voice vote Dec. 20. ◆

Chapter 5

BUDGET

Bush Budget Stresses Tax Cuts

President Bush sent an outline of his $1.96 trillion fiscal 2002 budget to Congress on Feb. 28, following it up with a more detailed, multi-volume request submitted April 9. The vision he laid out was far from the sweeping reductions in federal power and the dramatic cuts in federal spending that his fellow Republicans had proposed when the party took over the Capitol six years before.

Bush proposed holding discretionary spending to $660.6 billion, which he calculated as a 4 percent increase in budget authority. Defense and education were slated to get significant increases, which meant that most other departments would have to settle with less. As promised during his presidential campaign, the central feature of the budget was a huge package of tax cuts that included across-the-board reductions in marginal income tax rates, repeal of the estate tax, an increase in the child tax credit and wider benefits for charitable giving. The cost — $1.6 trillion over 10 years — was revised from the $1.3 trillion estimated during the campaign.

The April 9 budget gave full details of Bush's domestic and foreign aid spending proposals, but the defense request— $310.5 billion — was essentially a place-holder, pending the results of a review of military strategy and resources that was being conducted by Defense Secretary Donald H. Rumsfeld. The targeted completion date for the review was May 15.

The administration said the budget's late release — two months after the usual deadline of early February — was logistically necessary because it took that much time to rework the budget left by the Clinton administration. In a break from his predecessors, President Bill Clinton had not proposed a full fiscal 2002 budget as he left office. The document, released Jan. 16, was what the White House Office of Management and Budget (OMB) described as "an economic outlook, a set of baseline projections and a review . . . of the last eight years" that did not include policy recommendations.

The delay also helped Bush win endorsement for the broad outlines of his plan, including sweeping tax cuts, in the congressional budget resolution (H Con Res 83) before lawmakers were faced with the details of the spending cuts that would be required to make it happen.

Economic Assumptions

Despite some indications of a softening in the economy, at the start of the year fiscal experts were predicting healthy growth and a mounting federal budget surplus. (It was not until November that a recession was declared to have begun in March.) At the time of Bush's February budget, OMB projected that the gross domestic product would grow 2.4 percent in 2001 and average 3.2 percent growth from 2002 through 2011. Inflation was expected to average 2.5 percent over that period.

The projection was in line with other estimates. The Congressional Budget Office (CBO) predicted average growth of 3.1 percent. A widely regarded consensus among economists known as the "Blue Chip" indicators predicted average growth of 3.4 percent a year. OMB Director Mitchell E. Daniels Jr. said at a Feb. 28 briefing that the budget was built upon "exceedingly cautious" assumptions about future revenue and that budget writers were "over-reserved against the unknown." Taking a thinly veiled swipe at President Ronald Reagan's first budget, Daniels remarked, "You may search, but you will not find magic asterisks, unspecified savings or other speculative additions to the surplus, or reductions from spending." Reagan's fiscal 1982 budget was dotted with asterisks representing large savings from unspecified spending cuts. The cuts never materialized, and deficits exploded.

OMB did not change its economic assumptions for the April budget. "Most forecasters, including the administration, anticipate that an economic recovery will begin later this year," the budget stated. "Forward-looking indicators have begun to strengthen recently, pointing to faster growth in the coming months." As a result, the administration predicted that even if Bush's proposed tax cut was fully implemented, federal revenues would grow every year through 2011.

Democrats disagreed. "The president's plan depends far too heavily on a 10-year budget estimate, which is no more reliable than a 10-year weather forecast, and there's no room for error," Senate Minority Leader Tom Daschle of South Dakota said in a nationally televised response to Bush's address to Congress on Feb. 27 outlining his budget.

Federal Surplus

OMB projected a federal surplus of $5.6 trillion over 10 years — $2.6 trillion of it in the Social Security trust fund, which both parties had agreed could not be spent. Bush proposed allocating $2 trillion of the Social Security surplus for debt reduction.

While both parties had previously stressed their shared goal of paying off all of the publicly held debt, Daniels said the administration had concluded that this was neither a financially sound nor technically easy approach. Some Treasury bonds had maturation dates beyond 2011, and coaxing investors to redeem them ahead of time would cost billions of dollars in premium payments. To wipe out all publicly held debt, other securities, such as U.S. savings bonds, that were linked to Treasury debt would also have to be eliminated, which was not considered a viable option. As a result, OMB said Feb. 28 that no more than $2 trillion in publicly held debt could be prudently paid off in the next 10 years, leaving about $1.2 trillion.

Under Bush's plan, the remaining $600 billion of the projected Social Security surplus would eventually be used to enhance the long-term solvency of the retirement income security program, probably by providing seed money to implement Bush's proposal to allow workers to direct a portion of their Social Security payroll taxes into self-directed ac-

(continued on p. 5-6)

Bush's Fiscal 2002 Proposal:

(fiscal years, in millions of dollars; figures may not add due to rounding)

	BUDGET AUTHORITY			OUTLAYS		
	2000*	2001	2002	2000*	2001	2002
NATIONAL DEFENSE						
Military Defense	$290,496	$295,060	$309,357	$281,223	$283,915	$303,449
Atomic energy defense activities	12,437	14,065	14,249	12,161	13,746	14,317
Defense-related activities	1,203	1,498	1,470	1,110	1,475	1,427
Total, National defense	304,136	310,623	325,076	294,494	299,136	319,193
INTERNATIONAL AFFAIRS						
International development and humanitarian assistance	6,741	7,053	7,592	6,518	7,027	7,247
International security assistance	7,763	5,621	6,067	6,387	6,320	6,701
Conduct of foreign affairs	5,615	6,204	7,090	4,709	6,721	7,187
Foreign information and exchange activities	770	733	769	817	860	818
International financial programs	1,756	-971	787	-1,215	-3,467	-953
Total, International affairs	22,645	18,640	22,305	17,216	17,461	21,000
General science, space and technology						
General science and basic research	6,750	7,686	7,744	6,210	6,851	7,440
Space flight, research, and supporting activities	12,541	13,331	13,622	12,427	12,875	13,358
Total, General science, space and technology	19,291	21,017	21,366	18,637	19,726	20,798
ENERGY						
Energy supply	-2,302	-2,010	-1,576	-2,118	-1,744	-1,493
Energy conservation	737	815	795	666	743	798
Emergency energy preparedness	158	149	169	162	162	167
Energy information, policy, and regulation	223	194	210	230	184	206
Total, Energy	-1,184	-852	-402	-1,060	-655	-322
NATURAL RESOURCES AND ENVIRONMENT						
Water resources	4,803	5,242	4,586	5,081	5,431	4,993
Conservation and land management	5,738	7,348	6,277	5,901	6,808	6,796
Recreational resources	3,603	4,105	4,377	3,419	3,808	4,140
Pollution control and abatement	7,490	7,762	7,285	7,402	7,666	7,753
Other natural resources	3,397	4,063	4,078	3,228	3,657	3,812
Total, Natural resources and environment	25,031	28,520	26,603	25,031	27,370	27,494
AGRICULTURE						
Farm income stabilization	30,227	25,259	12,170	33,452	22,096	14,673
Agricultural research and services	3,480	4,026	3,670	3,189	3,826	3,949
Total, Agriculture	33,707	29,285	15,840	36,641	25,922	18,622
COMMERCE AND HOUSING CREDIT						
Mortgage credit	1,000	-6,010	622	-3,335	1,295	-2,965
Postal Service (on-budget)	100	93	144	100	93	144
Postal Service (off-budget)	3,712	4,840	2,519	2,029	2,596	3,061
Deposit insurance	2	1	-96	-3,051	-986	-652
Other advancement of commerce	10,618	-5,393	7,142	7,468	-3,766	7,358
Total, Commerce and housing credit	15,432	-6,469	10,331	3,211	-768	6,946
(On-budget)	(11,720)	(-11,309)	(7,812)	(1,182)	(-3,364)	(3,885)
(Off-budget)	(3,712)	(4,840)	(2,519)	(2,029)	(2,596)	(3,061)
TRANSPORTATION						
Ground transportation	38,609	43,995	43,515	31,697	34,458	37,400
Air transportation	12,006	12,952	13,891	10,571	11,970	13,121
Water transportation	4,527	4,298	4,798	4,394	4,357	4,622
Other transportation	234	244	-101	192	294	-105
Total, Transportation	55,376	61,489	62,103	46,854	51,079	55,038
COMMUNITY AND REGIONAL DEVELOPMENT						
Community development	5,395	5,852	5,453	5,480	5,549	5,681
Area and regional development	2,836	3,248	2,831	2,538	2,757	2,828
Disaster relief and insurance	3,036	1,267	1,811	2,611	2,266	3,234
Total, Community and regional development	11,267	10,367	10,095	10,629	10,572	11,743
EDUCATION, TRAINING, EMPLOYMENT, AND SOCIAL SERVICES						
Elementary, secondary and vocational education	17,136	25,878	44,543	20,578	23,508	26,151
Higher education	11,878	10,980	16,738	10,116	9,605	15,614
Research and general education aids	2,636	3,148	2,667	2,532	3,029	3,043
Training and employment	4,854	7,801	9,795	6,772	8,128	9,044
Other labor services	1,250	1,457	1,484	1,199	1,405	1,461
Social services	17,412	21,060	23,319	18,004	19,576	21,289
Total, Education, training, employment and social services	55,166	70,324	98,546	59,201	65,251	76,602

Budget Authority, Outlays by Function

	BUDGET AUTHORITY			OUTLAYS		
	2000*	2001	2002	2000*	2001	2002
HEALTH						
Health care services	140,566	157,520	178,352	136,231	154,238	177,345
Health research and training	18,563	21,334	23,832	15,979	18,547	21,509
Consumer and occupational health and safety	2,370	2,554	2,669	2,324	2,521	2,647
Total, Health	161,499	181,408	204,853	154,534	175,306	201,501
MEDICARE	200,588	218,960	229,881	197,113	219,258	229,903
INCOME SECURITY						
General retirement and disability insurance	5,914	6,807	6,275	4,975	5,594	4,664
Federal employee retirement and disability	79,010	82,756	86,012	77,152	81,176	84,398
Unemployment compensation	23,023	27,809	30,749	23,012	27,808	30,749
Housing assistance	18,112	25,258	32,247	28,800	30,972	32,465
Food and nutrition assistance	35,925	35,068	37,484	32,483	35,005	36,589
Other income security	81,612	84,161	84,326	81,473	82,062	86,810
Total, Income security	243,596	261,859	277,093	247,895	262,617	275,675
SOCIAL SECURITY	412,047	435,349	456,844	409,436	433,623	455,119
(On-budget)	(13,277)	(11,722)	(14,027)	(13,267)	(11,722)	(14,027)
(Off-budget)	(398,770)	(423,627)	(442,817)	(396,169)	(421,901)	(441,092)
VETERANS BENEFITS AND SERVICES						
Income security	22,642	24,494	26,141	24,872	22,377	26,043
Education, training and rehabilitation	1,312	1,711	1,949	1,342	1,690	1,952
Hospital and medical care	19,584	20,952	21,823	19,516	20,797	21,781
Housing	774	-906	354	342	-987	327
Other benefits and services	1,202	1,416	1,499	1,011	1,486	1,479
Total, Veterans benefits and services	45,514	47,667	51,766	47,083	45,363	51,582
ADMINISTRATION OF JUSTICE						
Federal law enforcement activities	11,656	12,616	13,547	11,617	12,698	13,202
Federal litigative and judicial activities	7,844	8,302	9,187	7,762	8,235	9,042
Federal correctional activities	3,667	4,304	4,664	3,707	4,238	4,280
Criminal justice assistance	3,563	5,157	4,189	4,734	4,259	5,759
Total, Administration of justice	26,730	30,379	31,587	27,820	29,430	32,283
GENERAL GOVERNMENT						
Legislative functions	2,237	2,308	2,669	2,222	2,402	2,685
Executive direction and management	637	715	774	631	682	830
Central fiscal operations	8,523	9,213	9,791	8,345	9,513	9,762
General property and records management	188	718	748	225	902	417
Central personnel management	161	170	178	184	171	174
General purpose fiscal assistance	2,058	2,415	2,312	2,084	2,431	2,320
Other general government	2,151	2,080	1,535	2,241	2,119	1,513
Deductions for offsetting receipts	−2,478	−1,386	−1,393	−2,478	−1,386	−1,393
Total, General government	13,477	16,233	16,614	13,454	16,834	16,308
NET INTEREST						
Interest on the public debt	361,978	357,907	350,951	361,978	357,907	350,951
Interest received by on-budget trust funds	−69,113	−73,662	−76,316	−69,113	−73,662	−76,316
Interest received by off-budget trust funds	−59,796	−68,886	−76,086	−59,796	−68,886	−76,086
Other interest	−9,849	−8,989	−10,417	−9,851	−8,990	−10,418
Total, Net interest	223,220	206,370	188,132	223,218	206,369	188,131
(On-budget)	(283,016)	(275,256)	(264,218)	(283,014)	(275,255)	(264,217)
(Off-budget)	(−59,796)	(−68,886)	(−76,086)	(−59,796)	(−68,886)	(−76,086)
ALLOWANCES	—	—	5,321	—	—	2,351
UNDISTRIBUTED OFFSETTING RECEIPTS	−42,581	−47,656	−49,403	−42,581	−47,656	−49,403
(On-budget)	(−34,944)	(−39,779)	(−40,486)	(−34,944)	(−39,779)	(−40,486)
(Off-budget)	(−7,637)	(−7,877)	(−8,917)	(−7,637)	(−7,877)	(−8,917)
TOTAL	$1,824,957	$1,893,513	$2,004,551	$1,788,826	$1,856,238	$1,960,564
(On-budget)	(1,489,908)	(1,541,809)	(1,644,218)	(1,458,061)	(1,508,504)	(1,601,414)
(Off-budget)	(335,049)	(351,704)	(360,333)	(330,765)	(347,734)	(359,150)

*Includes supplemental spending
SOURCE: President's fiscal 2002 budget

The President's Budget Totals

(fiscal years, in billions of dollars)

	Estimated 2001	2002	2003	Proposed 2004	2005	2006
Budget authority	$1,891.5	$1,981.6	$2,038.7	$2,099.6	$2,187.7	$2,253.5
Outlays	1,856.3	1,959.3	2,011.6	2,071.0	2,163.6	2,220.6
Revenues	2,137.0	2,190.0	2,258.0	2,339.0	2,436.0	2,528.0
Off-budget surplus	157.0	171.0	193.0	211.0	237.0	252.0
On-budget surplus	124.0	60.0	53.0	57.0	36.0	55.0

SOURCE: Office of Management and Budget

(continued from p. 5-3)

counts that could invest in securities, in theory allowing them to make a greater return on the money they would still be required to set aside.

Of the remaining "on-budget" surplus, Bush proposed allocating $1.6 trillion for his tax cuts. He labeled the remaining $1.4 trillion as a "contingency" reserve. Administration officials conceded that about $400 billion of that would be needed to cover additional interest on the debt since the loss of revenue from Bush's tax cut would mean that the debt would have to be paid off more slowly. Out of the final $1 trillion, Bush proposed setting aside $156 billion for Medicare, including funds for a prescription drug benefit for its nearly 40 million elderly beneficiaries. Pentagon officials and their allies in Congress hoped to lay claim to a sizable portion of what was left to modernize the military during the next decade.

Budget Rules

Bush called for maintaining so-called pay-as-you-go budget rules, which required that any time Congress increased the cost of an entitlement program or cut taxes, it provide offsetting spending cuts or tax increases. He also recommended extending the annual discretionary spending caps for an additional five years. The caps, last extended in the 1997 budget-balancing deal between Clinton and the Republican Congress (PL 105-33), had been ignored since the surplus arrived in fiscal 1998. The legal limit for fiscal 2000 was $541 billion, but Congress had waived it with almost no dissent and ended up enacting $637 billion in appropriations, $37 billion more than was specified in its own budget resolution. Both the PAYGO rules and budget caps were set to expire at the end of fiscal 2002. *(1997 Almanac, p. 2-23)*

The president also encouraged Congress to adopt budget process changes that the House had rejected the previous year, including a switch to a two-year cycle with money appropriated every other year.

Bush's Tax Plan

The tax cut package included in Bush's April 9 budget reflected proposals that he had been advocating since the 2000 presidential primary. The total had risen from $1.3 trillion, largely because the timeframe was shifted from 2001-2010 to 2002-2011. The costs of the proposal were back-loaded, so that most would occur in the final years.

Bush's Proposals, by Appropriations Panel

(in billions of dollars)

	FISCAL 2001 ESTIMATE		FISCAL 2002 PROPOSED		PROPOSED CHANGE	
	Budget Authority	Outlays	Budget Authority	Outlays	Budget Authority	Outlays
Agriculture	$ 16.1	$ 16.3	$ 15.4	$ 16.4	– $ 0.7	$ 0.1
Commerce, Justice, State	37.6	37.5	37.9	39.6	0.2	2.1
Defense	287.5	276.2	301.0	296.1	13.4	19.9
District of Columbia	0.5	0.5	0.3	0.3	– 0.1	– 0.1
Energy and water development	23.6	23.3	22.5	23.2	– 1.1	– 0.1
Foreign operations	14.9	15.7	15.2	15.7	0.3	< .5
Interior	19.0	17.9	18.1	18.3	– 0.9	0.4
Labor, HHS, Education	109.4	100.3	116.4	110.3	7.0	10.0
Legislative branch	2.7	2.6	3.0	3.0	0.3	0.3
Military construction	9.0	8.9	9.6	8.6	0.7	– 0.3
Transportation	18.3	48.2	16.2	52.7	– 2.0	4.4
Treasury, Postal Service	15.8	16.1	16.6	16.3	0.8	0.2
VA, HUD	80.7	85.9	83.1	89.0	2.4	3.1
Allowances	—	—	5.3	2.4	5.3	2.4
TOTALS	**$ 634.9**	**$ 649.4**	**$ 660.6**	**$ 691.7**	**$ 25.7**	**$ 42.4**

NOTE: Figures may not add due to rounding.

SOURCE: President's fiscal 2002 budget

Key elements of Bush's proposal and their estimated costs through 2011 included:

● **Income tax rates.** An $811.3 billion reduction in personal income taxes, accomplished by creating a new 10 percent bracket for the first $6,000 of an individual's income and the first $12,000 of a married couple's income, and by reducing the five existing brackets (15 percent, 28 percent, 31 percent, 36 percent and 39.6 percent) to four (10 percent, 15 percent, 25 percent and 33 percent).

● **"Marriage penalty."** A $112.8 billion plan to allow the lower-earning partner in a dual-income married couple to deduct up to $3,000 in an effort to alleviate the so-called marriage penalty, a quirk of the tax code that required some married couples to pay more in taxes than they would if they had remained single.

● **Estate tax.** A $271.5 billion proposal to phase out the taxation of estates, gifts and trust funds by 2009.

● **Child tax credit.** A $200.3 billion plan to double to $1,000 by 2006 the tax credit that could be claimed for each dependent younger than 17. Those subject to the alternative minimum tax could claim the credit. The income threshold for the credit's phase-out would increase to $200,000, up from $110,000 for married couples and $75,000 for single filers.

● **Research credit.** A $49.6 billion proposal to make permanent the research and development tax credit, the only part of the package specifically targeted to benefit large corporations.

● **Charitable contributions.** A plan to allow the 80 million taxpayers who did not itemize to claim the deduction for charitable contributions.

In submitting the full details of Bush's budget to Congress on April 9, OMB also described $134 billion in tax cut proposals not detailed in previous administration documents — contributing to a total cost of $1.64 trillion through 2011. The revenue loss was still estimated at $1.62 trillion, however, because $26 billion in proposed refundable tax credits to filers whose incomes were so low that they did not owe taxes counted as federal spending, or outlays, not as lost revenue. ◆

Economic Forecasts Compared

	2001	2002	2003	2004	2005	2006
Real GDP growth (chain-weighted)						
OMB	2.4%	3.3%	3.2%	3.2%	3.1%	3.1%
CBO	2.4	3.4	3.3	3.0	3.0	3.0
Blue Chip	2.1	3.5	3.2	3.5	3.4	3.4
Inflation (CPI)						
OMB	2.7	2.6	2.6	2.5	2.5	2.5
CBO	2.8	2.8	2.7	2.5	2.5	2.5
Blue Chip	2.6	2.4	2.7	2.6	2.6	2.6
Unemployment						
OMB	4.4	4.6	4.5	4.5	4.5	4.5
CBO	4.4	4.5	4.5	4.7	4.8	4.9
Blue Chip	4.5	4.5	4.5	4.5	4.5	4.5
91-Day Treasury bills						
OMB	5.3	5.6	5.6	5.6	5.3	5.0
CBO	4.9	5.0	5.1	5.0	4.9	4.9
Blue Chip	4.8	5.0	5.6	5.5	5.5	5.4
10-Year Treasury bonds						
OMB	5.4	5.6	5.7	5.7	5.7	5.7
CBO	4.9	5.3	5.5	5.6	5.7	5.8
Blue Chip	5.2	5.5	5.9	5.9	6.0	6.0

This comparison of the forecasts of the White House's Office of Management and Budget (OMB), the Congressional Budget Office (CBO) and the Blue Chip consensus of private economists uses 4th quarter-over-4th quarter changes in inflation-adjusted gross domestic product (GDP) and the Consumer Price Index (CPI). The unemployment rate and the T-bill and T-bond interest rates are annual averages. The OMB forecast assumes enactment of the president's budget and therefore is not strictly comparable with those of CBO and the Blue Chip.

SOURCES: President's fiscal 2002 budget, CBO, Aspen Publishers Inc.

GOP Resolution Squeaks By

The first bellwether test for President Bush's budget agenda was the fiscal 2002 budget resolution, Congress' guide for the year's tax and spending decisions. Although the House was quick to endorse Bush's budget, including his call for $1.62 trillion in tax cuts, the Senate voted to limit the tax cuts to three-fourths of what the president wanted and allow discretionary spending to grow by at least $6.3 billion more than he sought. Bush had asked Congress to limit discretionary spending to $660.6 billion, but $5.6 billion of that was for a reserve fund for unforeseen emergencies.

Final negotiations produced a compromise (H Con Res 83) that called for $1.35 trillion in tax relief from 2001 through 2011, and $661.3 billion, a 4 percent increase, in fiscal 2002 discretionary spending, with the understanding that more

would be added later for defense after the new administration had reviewed Pentagon needs. The resolution allowed for additional tax cuts if the Congressional Budget Office (CBO) increased its estimate of the on-budget surplus.

While the final budget, adopted May 10, did not give Bush all that he had asked for, it was still a major victory, setting the stage for the biggest federal tax cut in a generation while endorsing his pledge to restrain spending.

Background

Though the budget resolution does not become law, it is an important planning tool for Congress, setting parameters for appropriations and effectively limiting the scope of any

tax cut. During the previous six years, the budget resolution had been drafted largely as a political statement underscoring the GOP majority's commitment to tax cuts and spending restraints. President Bill Clinton vetoed a series of ambitious tax measures, and, aided by appropriators from both parties, routinely demanded and won far more spending than the GOP budget resolution allowed. In 2000, for example, Congress simply included language in the foreign operations bill (PL 106-249) raising the caps on discretionary spending.

But with Republicans in control of the Senate, House and White House at the outset of the 107th Congress, the dynamic had changed. Republicans were under pressure to set a spending ceiling they could live with, since they knew they could no longer blame the White House if it was broken. And the minority Democrats, no longer able to rely on a presidential veto, saw the budget resolution as their best hope for limiting tax cuts.

The budget resolution gives procedural protection to a tax bill in the Senate, allowing it to move under special "reconciliation" rules that bar a filibuster, impose a 20-hour limit on debate and restrict amendments. In the Senate, which was split 50-50 in the first months of the 107th Congress, Democrats knew that once a tax bill got such protection, it would be virtually impossible to stop. So limiting the size of the cut in the budget resolution was a key Democratic goal.

The fiscal 2002 budget resolution was drafted without the usual benefit of a full presidential budget from which to work. Although Bush submitted a budget outline Feb. 28, It took the new administration until April 9 to prepare and release a full-blown budget. By then, initial versions of the budget resolution had already been adopted by both chambers. (*Bush's budget, p. 5-3*)

Legislative Action

House Committee Action

The House Budget Committee voted 23-19 along party lines March 21 to approve a budget resolution that called for $1.62 trillion in tax cuts through 2011 and a maximum of $660.6 billion in discretionary budget authority in fiscal 2002 — 3.9 percent more than was appropriated for fiscal 2001, which the resolution pegged at $635.5 billion. The measure (H Rept 107-26) also included a $5.6 billion emergency reserve fund as requested by Bush.

While the document generally echoed Bush's priorities, it gave broad authority for House Budget Committee Chairman Jim Nussle, R-Iowa, to raise the proposed ceilings on discretionary spending later in the year. It singled out agriculture and the military as possible candidates for increases, potentially easing two of the year's most difficult spending debates. It also provided for Nussle to adjust the resolution's spending ceilings to accommodate a refundable tax credit if

BoxScore

Bill:

H Con Res 83

Legislative Action:

House adopted H Con Res 83 (H Rept 107-26), 222-205, on March 28.

Senate adopted H Con Res 83, amended, 65-35, on April 6.

House adopted the conference report (H Rept 107-60), 221-207, on May 9.

Senate adopted the conference report, 53-47, on May 10.

the Ways and Means Committee approved such legislation. And it stated that if CBO issued a 10-year surplus forecast during the summer that exceeded its January projection of $5.6 trillion, the tax cut total could be increased by the difference.

The House resolution instructed the Ways and Means Committee to write four tax-cutting reconciliation bills with deadlines of May 2, May 23, June 20 and Sept. 11. It called for a fifth reconciliation measure — to be reported by the Ways and Means and Energy and Commerce committees by July 24 — to alter Medicare, the federal health insurance program for the elderly and disabled, and to add a limited prescription drug benefit. Bush proposed spending $153 billion to that end in the next decade. CBO Director Dan L. Crippen told the Senate Finance Committee on March 22 that a comprehensive drug benefit could cost nine times as much.

John M. Spratt Jr. of South Carolina, the Budget Committee's top Democrat, said the measure would give Nussle too much control over congressional budget priorities, and Democrats said it gave an unrealistic picture of where spending would wind up by the end of the annual appropriations process — not to mention 10 years down the road.

But Republicans hung together and rejected all but a few of the roughly three dozen Democratic amendments offered during the 12-hour markup. The principal Democratic proposal was not a detailed alternative, but a "framework" calling for a $713 billion tax cut; at least inflationary increases in all categories of spending; and more than that — no amounts were specified — for education, defense, agriculture, health research, transportation, veterans benefits, conservation, law enforcement and other priorities. It was rejected by voice vote.

Indicative of the controversy surrounding the issue, the budget did not include Bush's assumption of new revenues from leases for oil drilling in the Arctic National Wildlife Refuge (ANWR).

House Floor Action

The House adopted the budget resolution March 28 on a party-line vote of 222-205. Three Democrats voted for the plan; only two Republicans voted no. (*House vote 70, p. H-30*)

During the debate, Republicans argued that their budget would allow discretionary spending to grow faster than overall inflation. CBO, however, assumed that the cost of running the government was rising faster than the consumer price index, and that a spending cap of $661 billion would be $4 billion less than what would be needed to continue programs at current service levels. Democrats complained that the budget's tax cut target would shortchange debt reduction and that its spending limits would force cuts in critical social programs.

The House rejected four alternative budgets:
- The group of fiscally conservative Democrats known as

the Blue Dogs offered a five-year budget that called for a $180 billion tax cut through fiscal 2006 and more defense spending. It was defeated, 204-221, but drew the support of a dozen Republicans. (*House vote 67, p. H-28*)

• A version offered by the Republican Study Committee, a group made up of the most fiscally conservative GOP members, called for a $2.3 trillion tax cut and would have limited the growth in spending to 2.9 percent annually over the next 10 years. It was defeated, 81-341. (*House vote 68, p. H-28*)

• The Progressive Caucus budget, which called for a $737 billion tax cut and higher levels of domestic spending, was defeated, 79-343. (*House vote 66, p. H-28*)

• The Democratic leadership's version called for a 7 percent spending increase in fiscal 2001 and $797 billion in tax cuts through 2011, although $60 billion of that would have been earmarked for a retroactive cut in 2001. It was defeated, 183-243. (*House vote 69, p. H-30*)

GOP leaders averted a potential revolt by appropriators from their own party by deleting Budget Committee language that would have given Nussle new power to block emergency spending legislation. Still, Nussle retained the power to sign off on deeper tax cuts protected by reconciliation rules and on increases in the spending ceiling. Armed Services Committee Chairman Bob Stump, R-Ariz., said that "immediate and compelling needs facing the military" would prompt him to appeal for an increase in the defense spending ceiling.

Senate Committee Action

Senate Budget Committee Chairman Pete V. Domenici, R-N.M., concluded that a markup by his panel would end in an 11-11 tie, and thus fail to send the budget to the floor. The committee was evenly divided between the parties under a power sharing agreement worked out in January. So Republicans took advantage of special budget rules that allowed them to put the measure directly before the Senate after April 1. The document Domenici readied for floor debate generally hewed to Bush's Feb. 28 budget outline.

Like the House version, however, it did not count on any revenue from oil exploration in ANWR.

Senate Floor Action

One week after Republicans pushed the president's version of the budget through the House, Bush's aspirations landed hard in the 50-50 Senate. When the horsetrading and compromises were over, the Senate voted 65-35 on April 6 to adopt a budget that limited the size of the tax cut to $1.18 trillion from 2002 through 2011. That was $440 billion less than Bush proposed. The Senate budget called for as much as $85 billion in retroactive tax cuts for 2001, which Bush had not sought, bringing the aggregate total to $1.28 trillion. (*Senate vote 86, p. S-22*)

The target for discretionary spending was at least $688 billion, 7 percent more than the level being spent in fiscal 2001, compared to the 4 percent growth that Bush wanted.

The Senate adopted the revised budget only after White House negotiators and the GOP leadership gave up trying to find enough votes to preserve Bush's full tax cut.

The key vote came April 4, when three GOP moderates — James M. Jeffords of Vermont, Lincoln Chafee of Rhode Island and Arlen Specter of Pennsylvania — broke from the fold to ensure adoption of an amendment reducing the tax

cut by $448 billion, with the difference to be split evenly between education spending and more debt reduction. The amendment, by Tom Harkin, D-Iowa, was adopted 53-47, after Majority Leader Trent Lott, R-Miss., switched from a "no" to a "yes" so that he could move to reconsider the vote later; he never did. (*Senate vote 69, p. S-19*)

Adoption of the amendment — ensuring that Bush would have to accept lower tax cuts to get a bill through the chamber — appeared to stun the Senate.

Democrats savored the moment. Minority Leader Tom Daschle of South Dakota went upstairs to the press gallery, as did several other Democratic senators, to tout the victory. Daschle predicted that more amendments to boost spending and reduce the tax cuts would be adopted. "With each one," he said, "there is a greater realization that we're getting further and further from the president's budget."

Senate Republicans were able to claim one important procedural victory: the inclusion of reconciliation protection for tax cut legislation, without which their chances of writing a tax bill to their liking would have diminished markedly. By a vote of 51-49, the Senate adopted a Domenici amendment to instruct the Finance Committee to report two reconciliation bills to the Senate that would reduce taxes by no more than Bush's goal of $1.6 billion. Zell Miller joined a united GOP bloc to form the majority. Democrats, led by Robert C. Byrd of West Virginia, had argued that reconciliation rules — written to make it easier to pass deficit-reduction bills in the Senate — should not be used to shield major tax cuts. (*Senate vote 75, p. S-20*)

Generally, Republicans were able to best Democratic proposals only by offering slightly less ambitious amendments of their own on the same topics.

On April 3, Vice President Dick Cheney cast his first tie-breaking vote on an amendment by Charles E. Grassley, R-Iowa, to reserve $300 billion over 10 years to create a Medicare prescription drug benefit and overhaul the program — nearly double the amount Bush had proposed. The amendment was a response to a Democratic amendment that would have allocated $311 billion for that purpose but specified that the drug benefit could not be funded by the Medicare hospital trust fund surplus, an idea Republicans opposed. The Republican amendment, which also would have made the writing of prescription drug legislation optional, triumphed, 51-50, while the Democratic proposal failed on a 50-50 tie. The vice president does not vote when the administration's aim is achieved by allowing a proposal to fail on a tie. (*Senate votes 65, 66, p. S-18*)

Senators voted 51-49 the following day to adopt an amendment by Grassley calling for a $64 billion increase in agriculture spending through 2011. The amendment was an alternative to a proposal by Tim Johnson, D-S.D., to boost the figure by $97 billion. Johnson's proposal was defeated, 47-53. (*Senate votes 67, 68, p. S-19*)

Similarly, senators voted 84-16 on April 4 to adopt an amendment by Armed Services Committee Chairman John W. Warner, R-Va., calling for an increase of $8.5 billion in fiscal 2002 defense spending, in addition to the $14 billion added in Bush's budget, with the extra funds coming from the surplus. Warner's proposal trumped a Democratic alternative, by Mary L. Landrieu of Louisiana, to take $100 billion from the 10-year tax cut and dedicate it to the military. Hers was re-

jected, 47-52. (*Senate votes 72, 71, p. S-19*)

Warner only offered his amendment as a way to quiet the Democrats; Republicans were awaiting results of the administration's review of long-term military needs before deciding how much they actually wanted for defense.

On April 5, the day after the vote on the Harkin amendment, senators engaged in a tit-for-tat battle over tax cuts, while leaders tried to work out a broader agreement behind closed doors. The Senate:

• Adopted, by voice vote, an amendment by Robert F. Bennett, R-Utah, to increase the tax cut by $42 billion, all of it in 2002 and 2003.

• Adopted, 51-50, a proposal by Kay Bailey Hutchison, R-Texas, to increase the tax cut by $69 billion to make sure it was large enough to fix the so-called marriage penalty. Cheney cast the deciding vote. (*Senate vote 79, p. S-21*)

• Adopted, 54-46, an amendment by John B. Breaux, D-La., and Jeffords to reduce the tax cut by $70 billion and allocate the money for education, on top of the amount added by Harkin. (*Senate vote 82, p. S-21*)

• Defeated, 39-61, an amendment by Richard J. Durbin, D-Ill., that echoed the Democratic leadership's plan, calling for a $750 billion limit on the tax cut, and $60 billion in rebates. Eleven Democrats defected. (*Senate vote 76, p. S-20*)

• Adopted, 94-6, a proposal by Ernest F. Hollings, D-S.C., calling for an $85 billion fiscal 2001 stimulus package. (*Senate vote 80, p. S-21*)

• Rejected, 49-51, an effort by Susan Collins, R-Maine, to increase the tax cut by $70 billion for health insurance tax credits and deductions. (*Senate vote 83, p. S-21*)

The net result was the restoration of $100 billion of the tax cuts removed by Harkin's amendment.

Bush put the best face on the outcome. "The fact that both houses of Congress have committed to finding significant relief is good for the American people and good for the economy," he said after the Senate's final vote. "I applaud today's action and congratulate the Republicans and Democrats who helped make it happen."

Conference/Final Action

House and Senate conferees met only once. The real negotiations took place in meetings among GOP budget writers, the White House and centrist Democrats. The White House bypassed Democratic leaders to concentrate on a handful of moderate but influential Senate Democrats such as Breaux and Ben Nelson of Nebraska. Budget committee Democrats were shut out. "We don't expect you to sign [the conference report], so we don't expect you to be needed," Domenici told them.

Bush, who had held doggedly to his position during the House and Senate debates — even stumping in members' districts to build support for his $1.6 billion tax cut proposal — became more pragmatic when it was time to negotiate. "The dynamics have shifted in this debate," he said April 25. "We've come from the ideological to the practical, and I'm a practical man. I want to get it done."

The Republican conferees completed their work May 3. The House adopted the conference report (H Rept 107-60) on May 9 by a vote of 221-207. The Senate followed suit the next day, 53-47. While Bush and his spokesman characterized the votes as "bipartisan" endorsements for the new ad-

ministration's fiscal program, only six Democrats in the House and five in the Senate supported the final budget. Republicans lost only three GOP votes in the House and two in the Senate. The measure did not require the president's signature. (*House vote 104, p. H-42; Senate vote 98, p. S-26*)

Highlights

The following are highlights of the conference report:

• **Tax cuts.** The House Ways and Means and Senate Finance committees were each instructed to report a reconciliation bill by May 18 that would reduce taxes by as much as $1.35 trillion through 2011. Of that, $100 billion was intended as an economic stimulus in fiscal 2001 and 2002.

• **Discretionary spending.** The final budget provided for $661.3 billion, 4.2 percent above the $634.9 billion Bush said had been appropriated for fiscal 2001. In terms of regular appropriations, the total was actually $6.3 billion more than Bush had sought; Bush's budget included a $5.6 billion reserve fund for unforeseen emergencies that was not part of the budget resolution. A $5 billion emergency fund initially included in the conference report was dropped when Nussle and House Appropriations Committee Chairman C.W. Bill Young, R-Fla., could not agree on a method for allocating the money. The idea was to set aside money for the inevitable, if unpredictable, annual emergencies, thus restraining supplemental spending and making it more predictable.

• **Non-defense spending.** The overall discretionary spending limit included $336.2 billion for domestic and international programs, a 3.9 percent increase. CBO estimated that an additional $6.8 billion would be needed to continue those programs at current service levels. The total was about $390 million more than the House or the president sought, but $17.4 billion less than the Senate endorsed.

• **Defense spending.** Defense was allocated $325.1 billion, a 4.7 percent increase, as requested, pending completion of the long-term review of defense needs and a supplemental request. The agreement also included $6.5 billion for a fiscal 2001 defense supplemental appropriations, a provision that was not contained in either the House or Senate resolutions.

• **Agriculture.** One of the big winners, agriculture was allocated an extra $79 billion over 10 years, beyond existing programs. The conference agreement set aside $5.5 billion for support payments to farm producers before the end of fiscal 2001, $7.4 billion for a fiscal 2002 farm bailout, and $66.2 billion over 10 years to pay for a new multi-year farm bill.

• **Medicare.** The agreement called for increasing Medicare spending by $313.7 billion over 10 years. The total included a $300 billion reserve fund for a Medicare prescription drug benefit and Medicare reform, should they be enacted. The remaining $13.7 billion was to restore payments to Medicare home health care providers.

• **Education.** The final budget did not include the $294 billion over 10 years that the Senate added for education programs.

• **Surplus.** The budget projected a fiscal 2002 surplus of $218.6 billion, $47.7 billion of it on-budget and the remainder off-budget, almost entirely in the Social Security trust fund. The budget forecast a cumulative surplus of $3.38 trillion through fiscal 2011, $897 billion of it on-budget.

• **Debt reduction.** The publicly held debt was to be reduced by $2.43 trillion by fiscal 2011, leaving $818 billion. ◆

Budget Surplus Dwindles

The hefty on-budget surpluses forecast in January all but vanished between May and the end of the year. The final numbers for fiscal 2001, which ended Sept. 30, showed that the government had to dip into the surplus in the Social Security trust funds to avoid a deficit. The picture for fiscal 2002 did not look much better.

● **Fiscal 2001.** In its January budget outlook, the Congressional Budget Office (CBO) projected a fiscal 2001 surplus of $281 billion — $125 billion of it on-budget. The rest was in the Social Security trust funds, money both parties vowed not to spend. A CBO update in May showed the surplus declining slightly, to $275 billion, with $119 billion on-budget.

But when the books were closed on fiscal 2001, the actual surplus was $127 billion. Excluding the surplus in the Social Security trust funds, the government actually ran a $33 billion on-budget deficit.

● **Fiscal 2002.** CBO's January outlook for fiscal 2002 showed a $313 billion surplus, $142 billion of it on-budget. In May, the numbers slipped to $304 billion, $132 billion of it on-budget. By the time CBO issued its August forecast, the projected surplus had slid to $176 billion — just $2 billion of it outside the Social Security trusts funds. Tentative CBO estimates in Oc-

tober put the total surplus at $52 billion.

● **Fiscal 2002-11.** The cumulative surplus for fiscal years 2002-11 fell as well. In January, CBO forecast a $5.6 trillion cumulative surplus, $3.1 trillion of it on-budget. The numbers showed little change in May. But by August, the total had fallen to $3.4 trillion, $847 billion of it on-budget. The White House Office of Management and Budget had a similar forecast in August, projecting a cumulative surplus for fiscal 2002-11 of $3.1 trillion.

Two factors were credited for the abrupt changes — one planned, the other unforeseen. The first was Bush's tax cut (PL 107-16) enacted in June, which was intended to reduce the nation's surplus to about the level of the Social Security surplus. The administration believed that drawing a line at Social Security funds would act as a brake on spending.

The second was the wobbly economy, teetering in a recession since March, which had the effect of reducing tax revenue and increasing mandatory spending for unemployment assistance.

The Sept. 11 terrorist attacks, which lifted the brake on spending and prompted swift enactment of a $40 billion emergency supplemental spending package (PL 107-38), promised to further swell the on-budget deficit.

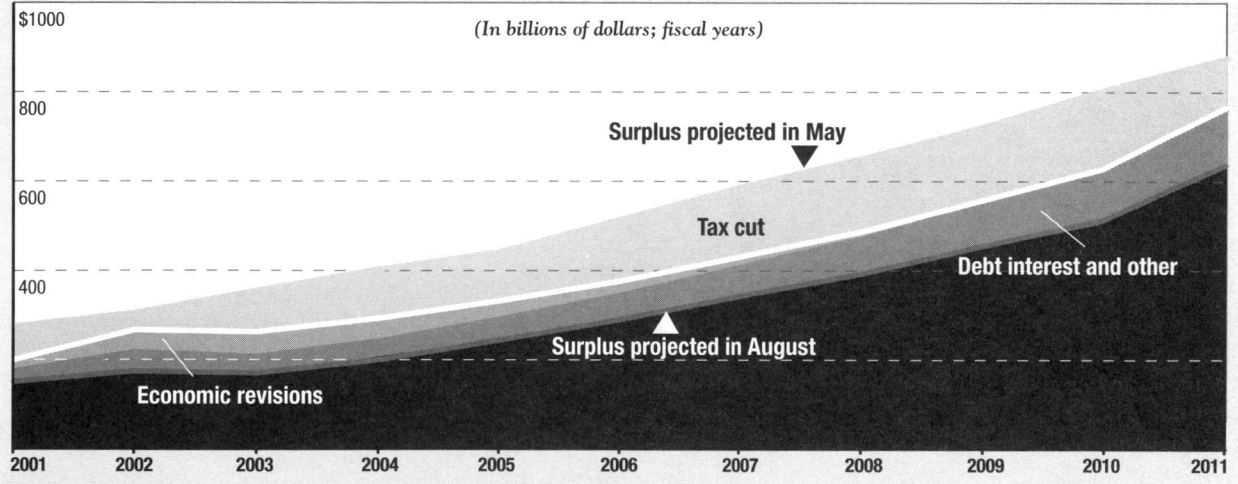

	2001	2002	2003	2004	2005	2006	2007	2008	2009	2010	2011	2002-11
Surplus projected in May	**$275**	$304	$353	$400	$437	$508	$578	$641	$718	$806	$883	**$5,629**
Tax cut	-74	-38	-91	-108	-107	-135	-152	-160	-168	-187	-130	**-1,275**
Economic revisions	-25	-48	-54	-50	-40	-31	-23	-16	-9	-6	-5	**-283**
Debt interest and other*	-23	-41	-37	-41	-46	-52	-62	-77	-90	-106	-120	**-673**
Surplus projected in August	**$153**	$176	$172	$201	$244	$289	$340	$389	$450	$507	$628	**$3,397**

*Interest payments on the federal debt were slated to increase because of slower debt repayment. Other factors included $6.5 billion fiscal 2001 supplemental spending (PL 107-20) and a $5.5 billion boost in fiscal 2001 payment to farmers (PL 107-25).   NOTE: Numbers may not add due to rounding.

Chapter 6

CONGRESSIONAL AFFAIRS

Campaign Finance Comes Close

Supporters of a broad overhaul of the nation's campaign finance laws ended the year in a familiar spot: Their legislation had stalled, short of final passage. This time, however, they were closer to victory than they had ever been.

The year began with a remarkable showdown in the Senate. Republican John McCain of Arizona, riding momentum from his 2000 run for the GOP presidential nomination, managed to build enough support for his campaign finance bill (S 27) to force the Senate's first wide-open debate of the issue in years. Majority Leader Trent Lott, R-Miss., who had long maneuvered to keep the legislation off the floor, agreed to clear the calendar of all other business for two weeks.

McCain's bill, cosponsored by Democrat Russell D. Feingold of Wisconsin, sought to ban unregulated "soft money" contributions to national political parties and restrict "issue-advocacy advertising," the often thinly veiled campaign ads bankrolled by corporate or union money. With several key compromises — and despite new concerns from Democrats that the soft-money ban would put them at a competitive disadvantage — McCain and Feingold managed to maneuver their bill through the Senate, which passed it April 2.

The focus then turned to the House, which had voted for similar bills twice before. In the past, however, members had voted for campaign finance legislation knowing it would die in the Senate.

The sponsors of the House bill (HR 2356) — Democrat Martin T. Meehan of Massachusetts and Republican Christopher Shays of Connecticut — set about rewriting their legislation with two challenges in mind: First, they were trying to hold together an increasingly restless coalition of supporters to get the bill through the House again.

Second, they wanted to keep the legislation close enough to the Senate-passed version to avoid a conference committee, where opponents would get another chance to kill or rewrite it. They hoped the bill would clear the Senate cleanly and go directly to the president to be signed into law.

House Republican leaders, who opposed the bill, introduced an alternative aimed at exploiting new reservations about the soft-money ban, particularly among members of the Congressional Black Caucus. The GOP bill (HR 2360) proposed to restrict soft money, rather than ban it.

Neither bill made it to a House vote. Shays-Meehan supporters went to the floor July 12 ready for a fight, but before the day was over, the bill had collapsed in a dispute over the rule for debate.

Shays and Meehan had wanted to bundle 14 changes, mostly aimed at bringing the bill into line with the Senate version, into one "manager's amendment." The House Rules Committee, controlled by the GOP leadership, decided to

BoxScore

Bills:
S 27, HR 2356

Legislative Action:
Senate passed S 27, 59-41, on April 2.
House defeated the rule (H Res 188) for debating HR 2356 (H Rept 107-131), 203-228, on July 12.

put each of those changes to a separate floor vote, which Shays and Meehan said would make it harder to pass the bill. Efforts at compromise stalled, and when the rule came to a vote, it failed.

Speaker J. Dennis Hastert, R-Ill., refused to bring the bill back to the floor. Within days, bill supporters launched a campaign to get 218 members, a majority of the House, to sign a discharge petition to force Hastert's hand. They got off to a strong start, gathering 209 signatures by early September. They were forced to put the petition on hold after Sept. 11, but in December, just before Congress adjourned for the year, four more members signed. Shays and Meehan ended the year within striking distance of forcing a vote on their bill.

Highlights

The following are key provisions of the Senate-passed campaign finance bill:

● **Soft money.** National party committees could not accept or spend soft money. State and local party committees could spend soft money on voter registration and mobilization in federal elections under certain conditions. For example, they could not mention a federal candidate. No donor could give more than $10,000 a year.

● **Hard money.** Limits on individual contributions to Senate candidates would increase from $1,000 to $2,000 per election and would be indexed to inflation. Aggregate contribution limits for individuals would rise from $25,000 to $37,500 per year. Limits on individual contributions to national parties would rise from $20,000 to $25,000 per year and would be indexed to inflation. Higher limits would be allowed for candidates facing wealthy opponents who financed their own campaigns.

● **Broadcast advertising.** The ability of labor unions, for-profit corporations and nonprofits to fund broadcast advertising directly would be restricted if the ads referred to a federal candidate, reached the candidate's electorate, and ran 60 or fewer days before a general election or 30 days before a primary. Such ads could be paid for only with regulated hard money through political action committees.

● **Independent expenditures.** Independent expenditures of more than $1,000 made in a candidate's behalf within 20 days of an election would have to be reported to the Federal Election Commission (FEC) within 24 hours. Before that, such expenditures of $10,000 or more would have to be reported within 48 hours. When spending to help a candidate, political parties would have to choose whether to work independently or in concert with the candidate.

● **TV ad rates.** Candidates and political parties would be guaranteed an advertising rate not to exceed the lowest rate

offered in the preceding year. Broadcasters could not pre-empt the ads for higher-paying advertisers.

Background

The House and Senate had debated since 1980 whether to overhaul the campaign finance system, which had been in place since the Watergate scandal in 1974 (PL 93-433). Both chambers passed versions of a campaign finance bill in 1993, but the Democratic majority allowed the legislation to languish until the final days of the 103rd Congress, when Senate Republicans used a filibuster to block a conference with the House. (*1994 Almanac, p. 32*)

Leaders of both parties continued to promise an over-haul, but they made little effort to deliver. In 1996, a bipartisan bill including voluntary spending limits and a ban on contributions by political action committees (PACs) was stopped by a Senate filibuster. The House defeated both a GOP bill to impose new limits on contributions and a Democratic alternative. (*1996 Almanac, p. 1-21*)

Soft money — unregulated contributions to political parties by corporations, labor unions and wealthy individuals — became central to the debate after the 1996 elections, when questionable fundraising practices by both parties focused public attention on the widening loophole in existing law. Soft money was supposed to be used for "party-building" activities, such as get-out-the-vote efforts and voter registration drives, but it had come to be used for campaign activities. The U.S. Supreme Court opened the door for broader use of soft money with a June 1996 ruling that parties could spend an unlimited amount to promote their position on issues as long as they did not coordinate the activity directly with candidates. (*1996 Almanac, p. 5-47*)

In 1997, McCain and Feingold introduced a version of their bill, which quickly became the focal point of the debate. The provisions included a ban on soft money, free or discounted television advertising and postage for candidates who adhered to voluntary spending limits, and new restrictions intended to draw a clearer line between spending to promote candidates and spending to promote issues. Shays and Meehan introduced a companion bill in the House. (*1997 Almanac, p. 1-26*)

What followed, however, were years of disappointment for bill supporters. Shays and Meehan managed twice, in 1998 and 1999, to use the threat of a discharge petition to force votes on their version of the bill. In both cases, the Speaker — first Newt Gingrich, R-Ga., (1979-99), then Hastert — agreed to put the legislation on the floor when supporters got close to gathering the signatures they needed. The legislation passed, with 252 votes both times. (*1999 Almanac, p. 8-3; 1998 Almanac, p. 18-3*)

In the Senate, however, Republican leaders, who opposed the legislation, managed to block it each time.

Legislative Action: Senate

Senate Floor Action

McCain and Feingold brought their bill directly to the Senate floor March 19. After rejecting a number of "poison pill" amendments, as well as the leading alternative, spon-sored by Chuck Hagel, R-Neb., the Senate passed the bill, 59-41, on April 2. (*Senate vote 64, p. S-18*)

The breakthrough for McCain-Feingold had come four months earlier, at the Republican caucus retreat Jan. 4, when Thad Cochran of Mississippi announced that he had decided to support the bill. He was the first old-style conservative to sign on, and his support gave McCain and Feingold the 60 votes needed to make their bill filibuster-proof.

Cochran said he had watched his colleagues struggle against a tide of opposition money. "It became obvious to me that the influence of soft money and independent groups was overwhelming the effort of candidates," he said.

The announcement was an embarrassment to Lott, who was struggling to consolidate his power in the evenly divided Senate. The next month, he bowed to pressure and agreed to a two-week debate with an open amendment process.

The McCain-Feingold bill took a twofold approach to overhauling the campaign finance system: It banned soft money to national parties while also regulating the flood of issue-advocacy ads that soft money had financed. Under existing law, there were no restrictions on the money that businesses, unions, special-interest groups and political parties could pump into ads targeting specific candidates, as long as the ads did not expressly advocate a candidate's defeat or election. Groups could spend whatever they liked and did not have to disclose the names of their contributors.

Under McCain-Feingold, "electioneering communication" that ran 60 or fewer days before a general election or 30 days before a primary would have to be paid for with regulated, or "hard," money through PACs. Unions and corporations would be forbidden from directly sponsoring such advertising. The restrictions would apply to any broadcast, satellite or cable ads that mentioned a candidate's name and constituents. Outside groups that ran the ads would be required to disclose the names of contributors of $1,000 or more.

The bill also included regulations on "independent expenditures" made in behalf of candidates. Independent expenditures of more than $1,000 within 20 days of an election would have to be reported to the FEC within 24 hours. Further from elections, independent expenditures of $10,000 or more would have to be reported within 48 hours. When spending to help candidates, parties would have to choose whether to work independently or in concert with the candidate.

After being blocked for so long, the debate itself was seen by many as a victory for McCain and Feingold. There was no guarantee, however, that they would recognize their bill once the fight was over. Under the agreed-upon procedures, a new amendment was to be debated and voted on every three hours, ensuring a wild pace. "The ground is shifting constantly," said Mitch McConnell, R-Ky., the bill's leading opponent. "There is no one smart enough to predict how this thing looks in the end."

McCain and Feingold warned that McConnell and other opponents would seek to weigh the bill down with so many amendments that everyone would have a reason to oppose it. "They'll try and kill it with poison pills," McCain said. "They'll try and kill it with amendments that look good but which under close inspection are troublesome."

Both sides walked into the fight knowing the stakes were

especially high. Political momentum, as well as public sentiment, seemed to be with McCain and Feingold. Moreover, the White House was signaling that President Bush might sign a campaign finance bill. Opponents of the bill could not count on him for a veto if the legislation cleared Congress.

'A Bill Markup on the Floor'

Over the next two weeks, the Senate made a number of significant changes to the legislation. McConnell likened the process to "a bill markup on the Senate floor."

McConnell stayed on the floor for most of the debate, leading the fight against the bill. He argued that it would infringe on free speech rights and undercut the political parties by diverting contributions to outside groups operating independently of the parties and the candidates. McCain-Feingold supporters argued that the bill would end the corrupting influence of big-money contributions on the political system.

● **Soft-money exception**. The bill sought to ban soft money in federal elections in most instances. On the floor, however, the Senate adopted by voice vote an amendment by Carl Levin, D-Mich., to allow local and state party committees to spend soft money on get-out-the vote and voter registration drives in federal elections under certain conditions. Most important, the effort could not mention a federal candidate. Also, no donor could give more than $10,000 per year.

The Levin amendment was a key compromise, particularly for Democrats concerned that the ban on soft money would put them at a disadvantage. It would grow in importance in the House as supporters there worked to shore up Democratic support.

● **Hard-money increase.** In another critical compromise, the Senate voted to increase the limits on hard-money contributions. Republicans, who typically had the edge in raising hard money, demanded the change. Many Democrats balked, and the deal threatened to drive a wedge between the bill's supporters. The Democratic Party had come to rely on soft money to counter the GOP's hard-money advantage, and Democrats were increasingly worried that banning soft money would put them at a financial disadvantage. Raising the limits on hard money at the same time, in their view, would make matters even worse.

"Raising hard money [limits] will split our caucus big time," said Tom Daschle, D-S.D., who was then minority leader. "It's so anti-reform, and secondly, it so greatly advantages Republicans."

Ultimately, Republican Fred Thompson of Tennessee and Democrat Dianne Feinstein of California reached a deal. Under their amendment, the limit on individual hard-money contributions to Senate candidates would increase from $1,000 per election to $2,000 and would be indexed to grow with inflation. Aggregate contribution limits for individuals would increase from $25,000 per year to $37,500. Limits on individual contributions to national parties would increase from $20,000 per year to $25,000 and be indexed to inflation. The amendment was adopted, 84-16, with all the no votes coming from Democrats. (*Senate vote 55, p. S-16*)

● **"Millionaires amendment."** The Senate also adopted an amendment by Republican Pete V. Domenici of New Mexico to raise the hard-money contribution limits for candidates facing wealthy opponents who poured their own mon-

ey into their campaigns. The proposal, dubbed the "millionaires amendment," increased limits on contributions from both individuals and PACs, using a sliding scale based on state voting-age population and how much personal money a wealthy "self-financing" candidate spent. The amendment was adopted 70-30. (*Senate vote 38, p. S-13*)

● **Low-cost airtime.** Democrat Robert G. Torricelli of New Jersey successfully pushed through a provision to require broadcasters to offer cheap airtime to candidates and political parties. Under Torricelli's amendment, candidates and parties would be guaranteed an advertising rate not to exceed the lowest rate offered in the preceding year. Torricelli argued that it would help cut more money out of politics by reducing the cost of campaigning. Broadcasters could not pre-empt the ads for higher-paying advertisers. The Senate adopted the amendment, 69-31. (*Senate vote 41, p. S-13*)

Preparing for Legal Challenges

● **Low broadcast rates.** Charles E. Schumer, D-N.Y., introduced an amendment intended as insurance against a pending Supreme Court case, *Federal Election Commission v. Colorado Republican Federal Campaign Committee*, that many feared would open a new loophole in campaign finance laws. Justices were considering whether to uphold a lower-court decision that eliminated limits on the money that political parties could spend in coordination with candidates to help them pay for television advertising and other expenses. Schumer's provision, written to take effect if the court upheld the lower-court decision, guaranteed the low broadcast ad rates to parties only if they agreed voluntarily to abide by coordinated spending limits. The amendment was adopted, 52-48. (*Senate vote 56, p. S-16*)

In a 5-4 ruling June 25, the Supreme Court struck down the earlier court's ruling, upholding the limits on coordinated spending.

● **Issue ads.** An amendment by Arlen Specter, R-Pa., providing an alternative definition of "electioneering communications," for use if the courts struck down the original provision, was adopted, 82-17. Specter's fallback language said the restrictions on issue ads would apply to any advertising that supported or attacked a candidate, "regardless of whether the communication expressly advocates a vote for or against a candidate and which also is suggestive of no plausible meaning other than an exhortation to vote for or against a specific candidate." (*Senate vote 61, p. S-17*)

A more divisive amendment, by Democrat Paul Wellstone of Minnesota, broadened the bill's restrictions on issue advertising to cover nonprofits, such as the National Rifle Association or the Sierra Club. As originally written, the restrictions applied only to for-profit corporations and labor unions. McCain and Feingold fought Wellstone's amendment, arguing that it appeared unconstitutional.

The courts had long said that the Constitution demands a delicate balance between free speech and the government's need to combat the corrupting influence of campaign cash. In a 1986 case, *Massachusetts Citizens for Life v. FEC*, the Supreme Court said the Constitution protects the ability of outside advocacy groups to run issue-related ads. But with the help of Republicans who hoped the broader language might undercut the bill's support on final passage, the amendment was adopted, 51-46. (*Senate vote 48, p. S-15*)

Among those supporting Wellstone's amendment was McConnell. "I thought a bill that's already unconstitutional ought to be made a little more unconstitutional," he said. "This bill, if it ever becomes law, is going to end up in court, and you're looking at the plaintiff."

● **Union fees.** The Senate also adopted an amendment by Republican Don Nickles of Oklahoma to strike language in McCain-Feingold that would have codified a court decision requiring unions to let non-members opt out of having their fees used for political purposes. The vote on Nickles' amendment was 99-0. (*Senate vote 45, p. S-14*)

Final Passage

All of the amendments deemed poison pills by the bill's backers were rejected.

● **"Severability."** Republican Bill Frist of Tennessee proposed making the legislation "non-severable," meaning that it would stand or fall as a whole in the courts. If courts struck down one provision, the entire bill would be thrown out. The issue took on particular importance with the adoption of Wellstone's amendment broadening the bill's issue-ad restrictions, which many worried had made the bill even more vulnerable to a legal challenge.

As written, McCain-Feingold contained a "severability clause," explicitly stating that the rest of the legislation would stand if courts struck down any of its provisions. Such a clause does not necessarily protect a law; a court still could throw out the entire legislation if it found one part questionable. But supporters argued that Frist's amendment was a "self-destruct mechanism" and said supporting it was "the ultimate anti-reform vote." In the end, the Senate voted 57-43 to table (kill) the amendment. (*Senate vote 59, p. S-17*)

● **Paycheck amendment.** Also tabled was an amendment by Republican Orrin G. Hatch of Utah to require unions and corporations to get the permission of dues-paying members or shareholders before spending money for political purposes. Amendment supporters called it "paycheck protection," and argued that it would give union members a greater voice regarding which candidates their unions support. Bush had supported such a measure in a statement of campaign finance "principles" released not long before the debate. Opponents, however, said Hatch's amendment was a GOP effort to make it difficult for organized labor, which often leaned Democratic, to exert influence over elections. The amendment was tabled, 69-31. (*Senate vote 43, p. S-14*)

● **Hagel alternative.** The Senate also rejected what had been viewed, going into the debate, as one of the main threats to McCain-Feingold: an alternative by Hagel that would have capped soft money, not banned it.

Hagel's plan had three parts: The first would cap soft-money contributions to national parties at $60,000 per year, rather than banning them. The second would raise hard-money contribution limits for individuals and PACs. Individuals would be able to give $3,000 per election to candidates and $60,000 per year to parties. PACs could give $7,500 per election to candidates and $30,000 per year to parties. The third part would require greater disclosure of who was funding political advertising, as well as more frequent disclosure of the contributors to candidates and political parties.

In an unusual move, Hagel presented the three parts of his plan as separate amendments. McCain moved to table each in turn. The amendment to increase hard-money limits was tabled, 52-47. The cap on soft money was tabled, 60-40. (*Senate votes 49, 51, p. S-15*)

However, the Senate rejected, 0-100, McCain's motion to table Hagel's increased disclosure requirements, the least controversial part of his plan. The amendment then was adopted by voice vote. (*Senate vote 50, p. S-15*)

Some Democrats continued to complain about the hard-money increases in the Senate bill. Republicans accused them of seeking an excuse to vote against a soft-money ban now that it seemed likely to become law. "It sounds like people who are looking for the exit sign in the tall grass," Thompson said. The accusation stung, and ultimately helped save the bill in the Senate. Even with elements of their base opposed to the legislation and their own careers perhaps at stake, Democrats found they had painted themselves into a corner. Saying no to McCain-Feingold was no longer an option. "We've taken so strong a position as a party in favor of this bill and against soft money that we've got to stay the course," said Joseph I. Lieberman, D-Conn.

Legislative Action: House

House Committee Action

After twice watching campaign finance bills pass over their objections, Republican leaders made a serious play for the legislation's base of support in the House. The alternative bill they offered was quickly approved by the House Administration Committee on June 28 — the same day it was unveiled by committee Chairman Bob Ney, R-Ohio, and less than two weeks before the debate moved to the floor.

The bill (HR 2360 — H Rept 107-132), similar to Hagel's in the Senate, proposed to cap soft-money contributions to national parties at $75,000 per year, rather than banning them, while keeping existing limits on individual hard-money contributions to candidates. Both provisions were designed to appeal to minority Democrats and others who had supported an overhaul in the past but feared the soft-money ban would put them at a disadvantage against Republicans when combined with the Senate's increase in hard-money limits.

Under Ney's bill, parties could not spend soft money on anything but "generic" party activities, such as get-out-the-vote efforts and voter registration, that did not mention specific federal candidates.

Ney's bill did not restrict the ability of unions, for-profit corporations and nonprofits to directly fund broadcast ads. But groups running television or radio ads that mentioned federal candidates, reached their electorate, and aired within 120 days of a primary or a general election would have to disclose within 24 hours the names of their officers and the amount spent on the ad. The same rule would apply to groups that spent more than $50,000 for "targeted mass communication" in broadcast or print.

The committee approved Ney's bill, 5-3. By the same vote, the panel reported the Shays-Meehan bill (HR 2356 — H Rept 107-131) to the House floor with an unfavorable recommendation. Ney and other Republican leaders said their intention was to see both bills get a vote on the floor.

House Floor Action

Many members, Republicans and Democrats alike, had qualms about Shays-Meehan when it reached the House floor July 12. When the debate collapsed over the rule for debate, each side blamed the other for the failure. In the end, there were no votes for or against the bill in the House, nothing to put members clearly on record. The vote on the rule was open to interpretation.

In the days before the debate, Shays and Meehan were still making adjustments to their bill in an effort to shore up support in the House while avoiding a conference with the Senate. "We have never been this close" to seeing a bill become law, Meehan said. "So the stakes are very, very high."

Ney said the ongoing work on Shays-Meehan was a sign the bill was in trouble — and that he was winning. "They're having to make changes because members from all walks of life have taken a second look at their bill and they are seeing problems with it," he said. "We've provided a good, positive alternative that's not a sham bill, and it's caused a crumbling of the Shays-Meehan base."

The Senate compromise to raise hard-money limits continued to dog Shays and Meehan in the House. Democrats already were having second thoughts about banning soft money as the 2002 midterm elections approached. Raising the limits on hard money gave them one more reason to say no to the bill. The fractures were most visible in the 36-member Congressional Black Caucus, whose members said soft money was crucial to get-out-the-vote activities and voter registration efforts in minority communities. Hispanic members, too, expressed doubts.

With the blessings of McCain and Feingold, Shays and Meehan altered their bill to hold the line on individual hard-money contributions to House candidates while doubling the limits for Senate candidates. But it was a fragile compromise that even Shays did not like.

The reworked Shays-Meehan bill also proposed that aggregate contribution limits for individuals and limits on contributions to parties would increase as they would in the Senate measure, and would be indexed to inflation.

The House version included a provision lifting hard-money caps for candidates facing wealthy opponents who bankrolled their own campaigns, but applied it only to Senate candidates.

Shays and Meehan tinkered with some of the Senate-passed provisions — again, with the blessings of Senate leaders. The restrictions on issue ads would apply only if a broadcast ad reached at least 50,000 people within the targeted candidate's electorate.

Partly to ease the concerns of black and Hispanic members, they retained the Senate provision that allowed state and local parties to spend some soft money on get-out-the-vote and voter registration efforts in federal elections. But the House version included some additional restrictions. The money, for example, could not be used for broadcast advertising.

Also included in the House version was the guarantee of cheap broadcast advertising rates for candidates, though it, too, was slightly reworked. For example, parties would get the lower rate only for spending that was coordinated with candidates, which was limited under federal law.

House Minority Leader Richard A. Gephardt, D-Mo., who had taken flak for not fighting visibly enough for Shays-Meehan, lobbied his caucus to stay behind the bill. He was still working to secure votes when the dispute over the rule came to a head July 12.

The night before the bill was to come up, Shays and Meehan had asked the Rules Committee to bundle 14 proposed changes to the bill, mostly aimed at bringing it into line with the Senate version, into a single manager's amendment. The Rules Committee said no, requiring instead that each of the changes be voted on separately on the floor.

Shays, Meehan and their supporters angrily accused the GOP leadership of trying to bring down the bill with a complicated, obstacle-strewn rule.

At a news conference the morning of the debate, Shays said he was deeply disappointed by the Rules Committee's decision. He had said repeatedly that he was confident Hastert would give his bill a fair shot. Asked if the Speaker had broken that promise, Shays looked down for a few moments. Then he said, "I had a distinguished senator say we're going to get screwed. I said no. But he was right." McCain, standing to his right, broke in with a wry crack: "I would never use such language," he said.

Republicans countered that Democrats were looking for a face-saving way to scuttle the bill because they did not have the votes to pass it. Hastert told reporters he had "bent over backwards" to accommodate Shays. He said he had promised a full, fair debate just after the Fourth of July recess. "I stuck by that commitment," he said.

As the dispute grew, Hastert offered to compromise on the rule, but conservatives in his caucus demanded that the original rule go forward. In the end, the rule was rejected, 203-228. (*House vote 228, p. H-82*)

It was the first time Hastert had lost a vote on a rule, which is typically seen as a matter of party loyalty from which members have little room to deviate. With the defeat, campaign finance dropped from the House agenda; Hastert said he had no intention of bringing it up again.

Discharge Petition

Shays-Meehan supporters quickly began collecting signatures on a discharge petition to force the bill back to the floor under rules more to their liking. By Sept. 11, they were just nine names short of the 218 they needed.

With the terrorist attacks, however, the effort was put on hold. The petition sat in the House, all but forgotten, for more than three months. Then, in December, as Congress headed for adjournment, four more lawmakers stepped up and signed: Alcee L. Hastings, D-Fla., a member of the Black Caucus, followed by Black Caucus Chairwoman Eddie Bernice Johnson, D-Texas; Greg Ganske, R-Iowa; and Peter J. Visclosky, D-Ind.

Suddenly, it appeared to Shays and Meehan that victory was possible, and they began planning for another push to get their bill through the House just after the start of the new year. ◆

Slow Year for Ethics Investigators

The House and Senate ethics committees each had a relatively quiet year, with only a handful of investigations. None rose to the level of the high-profile, lengthy cases that had tied up the panels for months in past years.

The Senate Select Ethics Committee had not recommended disciplinary action against a senator since it recommended expelling Bob Packwood, R-Ore. (1969-95), in 1995. Packwood then resigned. The committee was left to the responsibility that occupies much of its time — questions about gift rules and financial disclosure. *(1995 Almanac, p. 1-47)*

The House panel, formally called the Committee on Standards of Official Conduct, had a few minor cases that were resolved in a matter of weeks, or settled by political or legal developments outside Congress.

Hilliard Rebuked

The House ethics committee formally rebuked Rep. Earl F. Hilliard, D-Ala., on June 20, following a 19-month investigation into misuse of campaign money by the five-term lawmaker. The committee issued a "letter of reproval," the lowest level of punishment that can be issued. It was part of a negotiated settlement in which Hilliard agreed to admit to violating House rules. *(1999 Almanac, p. 8-17)*

The committee found that Hilliard had diverted campaign money to pay for, among other things, campaign aides who were doing work for businesses connected to Hilliard's family. The committee rebuked Hilliard for "serious official misconduct that brought discredit to the House."

The committee voted unanimously to issue the letter, but the report made it clear that more severe punishment had been considered. It said the "imposition of a sanction greater than a letter of reproval could be supported by many factors, including the demonstrated systematic and deliberate conversion of campaign funds by Representative Hilliard to personal use and . . . the lack of complete cooperation and candor by" Hilliard and his attorney.

Panel members, however, concluded that Hilliard's admission under the settlement and the public release of the investigative report provided adequate punishment.

Hilliard denied receiving "monetary gains" but did not dispute the committee's report. "I'm happy at this point to get it over with," he said.

The committee had launched its investigation in September 1991. It was the second time the panel had looked into Hilliard's activities. In 1997, the panel dismissed a complaint that Hilliard traveled to Libya without required State Department permission.

Buyer Complaint Dismissed

The House ethics committee on Aug. 1 dismissed a complaint that Rep. Steve Buyer, R-Ind., had used his office to lend support to Republican operatives during the 2000 ballot recount in Florida following the disputed presidential election between George W. Bush and Al Gore.

Committee Chairman Joel Hefley, R-Colo., and ranking member Howard L. Berman, D-Calif., sent a letter to Buyer informing him that the committee had found the allegations to be baseless.

Peter Deutsch, D-Fla., had asked for an investigation on July 16, the day after The New York Times published a story saying that in November 2000, Buyer had asked the Pentagon for contact information for service men and women whose absentee ballots had been disqualified. The newspaper said the information was used to put the voters in touch with Florida Republicans organizing a public relations campaign to persuade counties to reconsider rejected ballots.

Buyer said he requested the contact information because his Armed Services Military Personnel Subcommittee was investigating reports of problems with military ballots. He said he only sent surveys and knew nothing about information going to the Republican Party in Florida.

Condit Complaint Filed

Rep. Bob Barr, R-Ga., requested a formal ethics investigation July 20 into whether Gary A. Condit, D-Calif., impeded a police investigation into the disappearance of intern Chandra Levy. "I believe U.S. Rep. Gary Condit . . . has clearly obstructed a law enforcement investigation, and otherwise engaged in behavior in violation of the Rules of the House," Barr said in a statement.

Levy, one of Condit's constituents from Modesto, Calif., worked in Washington as an intern with the Bureau of Prisons. She disappeared without a trace in early May and had been the focus of a highly publicized police search. Condit originally said he and Levy, 24, were just friends, but according to published reports, he later told police they had an affair. The congressman's relationship with Levy, her subsequent disappearance and his less than forthcoming responses touched off a media frenzy.

Barr's seven-page formal complaint to the ethics panel accused Condit of obstructing justice and other "improper conduct that brings discredit" to the House.

A spokesman for Condit had no comment.

Traficant Case in Federal Court

Nine-term Rep. James A. Traficant, D-Ohio, pleaded not guilty May 11 to 10 counts of bribery, racketeering, obstruction of justice and other charges in U.S. District Court in Ohio. The 41-page indictment contained 10 criminal counts and detailed activities dating as far back as 1987 in which Traficant allegedly solicited and accepted bribes. Two people pleaded guilty to charges stemming from the Traficant investigation.

Among the counts, federal prosecutors charged that over a period of nine years Traficant handed out political favors to the Asphalt Specialist company in Ohio in exchange for free construction services on his Greenford, Ohio, farm. Prosecutors also charged that Traficant helped Ohio businessman Arthur David Sugar obtain a reduced sentence for his son, who had been convicted of drunken driving. In exchange, Sugar, his son and Sugar's Honey Creek Contracting Company Inc. provided free work on Traficant's farm.

Traficant also was charged with obstructing justice by asking a Youngstown-area attorney hired as an administrative counsel to destroy evidence and provide false testimony

to a federal grand jury.

There are no House rules that require an ethics investigation when a member is indicted. Ethics probes are automatically triggered only when a member is convicted of a felony.

Torricelli Case

Democrat Robert G. Torricelli's fundraising practices in the hard-fought New Jersey Senate race in 1996 was the subject of a lengthy investigation by the U.S. Attorney's Office for the Southern Division of New York.

The federal probe included allegations that Torricelli might have accepted thousands of dollars in unreported gifts. David Chang, a former Torricelli supporter who pleaded guilty in 2000 to making $53,700 in illegal campaign contributions to Torricelli's expensive election campaign, alleged that he gave Torricelli cash, suits, a Rolex watch and an expensive television set, according to news reports.

Federal law and congressional gift rules barred lawmakers from accepting gifts worth $50 or more, though gifts from close personal friends were exempt if they were not given in return for official favors. Chang, a New Jersey businessman, was once among Torricelli's closest political supporters, and Torricelli had called him a "friend" of several years.

The political fallout from the investigation forced Torricelli to defend himself to his Democratic colleagues, telling them he had done nothing wrong and assailing Chang. "It is unbelievable to me that someone awaiting sentencing with an extensive record of perjury would make claims about me and those claims would be taken seriously," Torricelli said April 24.

Torricelli raised and spent $9 million in the 1996 race.

U.S. Attorney Mary Jo White announced Jan. 3, 2002, that no charges would be filed against Torricelli and that the criminal investigation had been closed. She said she had forwarded information uncovered during the probe to the ethics committee. ◆

Chapter 7

DEFENSE

Compromise on Base Closings

For all the talk of reshaping the post-Cold War military to deal with emerging threats such as terrorism, Congress put off the wholesale changes that would be necessary, passing a defense budget that largely tracked President Bush's early proposal and closely resembled previous years' bills.

The $343 billion defense authorization bill for fiscal 2002 (S 1438) was roughly equal to the amount Bush sought, with a significant chunk dedicated to operations and maintenance for the armed services and the purchase of new weapons. The measure, cleared Dec. 13, was $30 billion more than Congress authorized for fiscal 2001.

The president had sought authorization for another round of military base closings in 2003, but the divisive issue delayed final action on the bill. As a compromise, House and Senate negotiators agreed to conduct another round — in 2005. Despite his disappointment over the two-year delay, Bush signed the bill into law (PL 107-107) on Dec. 28.

A comprehensive review of the nation's military by Defense Secretary Donald H. Rumsfeld, in his second tour of duty at the Pentagon helm, delayed Bush's detailed fiscal 2002 budget proposal until late June. Potential changes that emerged early on from the strategic study — base closings, weapons cuts and shifts in spending from conventional tanks and ships to high-tech weapons — drew criticism from the uniformed services and some in Congress.

The House and Senate Armed Services committees began shaping their versions of the defense budget to reflect the political leadership and meet the demands of their rank-and-file. In the GOP-controlled House, the committee ignored Bush's politically explosive request for another round of base closings. Meanwhile the Senate, with Democrat Carl Levin of Michigan chairing the Armed Services Committee, took aim at Bush's request to increase spending to develop a missile defense system and begin construction at an Alaska site that would violate the 1972 Anti-Ballistic Missile (ABM) Treaty with the former Soviet Union. Defense hawks wanted more money for defense but were thwarted by Bush's $1.35 trillion tax cut and the economic slowdown.

The Sept. 11 terrorist attacks and the subsequent war in Afghanistan to root out al Qaeda and Taliban forces quashed the partisan fights over the defense budget. A handful of Democrats in the House and Senate, including Levin and Rep. John M. Spratt Jr., D-S.C., abandoned their plans to press for cuts in missile defense spending, a tacit acknowledgment that they would lose a fight with the Bush administration over a system that the Pentagon could tout as key for a nation under siege.

But the issue of base closings did not go away. Proponents, particularly those in the Senate, argued that closing unnecessary installations would free up dollars for the war on terrorism. Opponents said it was premature to proceed while the military was still figuring out what was needed to combat terrorism.

Even after completing their versions of the defense budget, House and Senate negotiators remained at an impasse for weeks over the issue, finally settling on a 2005 round, after Bush's first term in office.

Highlights

The bill authorized $62 billion for weapons procurement, a 5 percent increase over the fiscal 2001 level, and $125 billion for operations and maintenance, a 29 percent increase. It also authorized $10.5 billion for military construction and family housing and $14.4 billion for defense-related activities of the Energy Department. The following are major components of the bill:

● **Missile defense.** $8.3 billion for development of a missile defense system, the full amount requested by Bush for the cornerstone of his plans for a future military force. The amount was a $3 billion increase over fiscal 2001. An announcement by Bush in December that the United States would abandon the ABM Treaty cleared the way for construction of a site in Alaska.

● **Base closings.** Another round of base closings, but not until 2005, using the same process as in the 1991 and 1996 rounds. An independent commission, chosen by the president and Congress, would review the Pentagon's proposed shutdown and realignment list and pick the bases to close. Congress would have to accept or reject the list in toto.

● **F-22 Raptor.** $2.7 billion, as requested by Bush, for 13 of the Air Force's next generation fighter plane, with an additional $865 million for research and development.

● **Joint Strike Fighter.** $1.5 billion, close to the administration's request, for development of the Joint Strike Fighter, an aircraft to be used by the Air Force, Navy and Marine Corps.

● **F/A-18 E and F.** $3.1 billion for 48 aircraft, the Navy's upgrade of the existing F/A-18 C/D.

● **Assault ships.** $594 million for the Navy's next generation surface combat ship, the DD-21.

● **New attack submarines.** $1.6 billion, as requested, to purchase the fourth boat in the *Virginia* class of attack submarines to replace the *Los Angeles*-class subs, which were being retired.

BoxScore

Bill:
S 1438 — PL 107-107
Legislative Action:
House passed HR 2586 (H Rept 107-194), 398-17, on Sept. 25. (House passed S 1438 by voice vote Oct. 17 after substituting the text of HR 2586.)
Senate passed S 1438 (S Rept 107-62), 99-0, on Oct. 2.
House adopted the conference report (H Rept 107-333), 382-40, on Dec. 13.
Senate cleared the bill, 96-2, on Dec. 13.
President signed Dec. 28.

- **DDG-51.** $3 billion, as requested, for three *Arleigh Burke*-class guided missile destroyers.
- **Anti-terrorism.** $6 billion for Defense Department programs to combat terrorism.
- **Military pay raise.** An average pay increase of 4.6 percent for military personnel, equal to what Bush sought.
- **Vieques.** Cancellation of a controversial local referendum on the future of the Navy bombing range on the Puerto Rican island of Vieques, putting the future of the facility in the hands of the Navy. Before closing the range, the Navy was required to find a qualified replacement site or sites.
- **Drug interdiction.** $820 million for the military's drug interdiction efforts.

Background

During the 2000 presidential campaign, Bush and vice presidential candidate Dick Cheney assailed the Clinton-Gore administration, arguing that the military had been underfunded for years and vowing to boost defense spending if elected. In the later stages of President Bill Clinton's tenure, Congress had routinely added billions of dollars for defense — largely for items that had been requested by the services but dropped by the Clinton White House.

Expectations ran high among conservatives and defense hawks that once in office, Bush would make good on his promises.

However, the new president devoted much of his attention and expended a great deal of early political capital on the centerpiece of his campaign, a $1.35 trillion tax cut enacted in June (PL 107-16), which squeezed the amount left for defense in the fiscal 2002 budget. Meanwhile, Rumsfeld drew the ire of the service chiefs and some in Congress with his plans to transform the military, placing a greater focus on advanced technology and relying less on conventional weapons. *(Tax bill, p. 18-3)*

In April, Bush submitted a $310.5 billion placeholder budget for defense, with the promise of more money following Rumsfeld's review. The fiscal 2002 budget resolution (H Con Res 83), adopted May 10, put the temporary ceiling for defense at $325.1 billion. After months of delay, and with Rumsfeld's study still evolving, Bush on June 27 requested an additional $18.4 billion, bringing the total defense request to about $343.5 billion. Most of the money was earmarked for pay, medical care, facilities and other routine operating expenses.

Conservatives criticized the overall numbers. Robert Kagan and William Kristol of the Weekly Standard magazine urged Rumsfeld to resign, saying Bush had refused to request enough money for defense. Many pro-military lawmakers were particularly unhappy that, with the review under way, little of the money was targeted to replace aging weapons or to modernize U.S. forces with new technology.

Several lawmakers also balked at the administration's call for a new round of base closings in 2003 and Rumsfeld's plans to retire some B-1 bombers at bases in Idaho, Kansas and Georgia. The president's proposed hike in spending on a missile defense system, a 56 percent increase over the fiscal 2001 level to $8.3 billion, was sharply criticized by several Democrats.

Legislative Action

House Subcommittee Action

Three House Armed Services subcommittees approved by voice vote on July 26 their portions of the defense budget, amid complaints that Bush's tax cut and the economic slowdown created a budget squeeze. Specifically, lawmakers said the four services' list of "unfunded priorities" — which added up to more than $32 billion — would remain largely unfunded.

The Readiness Subcommittee squeezed $190 million out of the budget for administrative overhead to compensate for savings that the administration expected to realize by narrowing the application of the Davis-Bacon Act, which links wage rates on federal construction projects to prevailing local wages. Under existing law, projects costing less than $2,000 were exempt from Davis-Bacon; the administration proposed raising that threshold to $1 million. Repealing Davis-Bacon had long been a goal of Republicans, who argued that the law made the government pay union wages that were higher than the prevailing wages in a local area. Organized labor adamantly opposed such a change.

The subcommittee cut $140 million from the budget by targeting administrative accounts to make up for savings that the White House expected to see from shifting some scheduled overhauls of aircraft and other equipment from government-operated depots to private contractors.

The subcommittee on the Merchant Marine recommended adding $100 million to continue a loan guarantee program for commercial shipbuilders, which the administration proposed to terminate. The shipbuilding industry had lobbied vigorously to save the program, arguing that without the commercial work some shipyards would go out of business.

House Full Committee Action

The full Armed Services Committee approved a $343 billion authorization bill (HR 2586 — H Rept 107-194) on Aug. 1. The vote was 58-1, with Cynthia A. McKinney, D-Ga., casting the only "nay." The committee made only relatively minor changes in Bush's proposal for how the money would be spent.

The committee rejected, on a party-line vote of 28-31, an amendment by Spratt that would have shifted $985 million from the missile defense request to other projects, including C-130 cargo and tanker planes ($311 million), Blackhawk helicopters ($138 million), and ship overhauls ($211 million).

Nearly 60 percent of Spratt's proposed cut ($584 million) would have come from the plan to install five test missiles in launch silos with their maintenance and communications equipment at Fort Greely in eastern Alaska. The Pentagon considered the base a test site; critics said it was a back-door effort to deploy weapons in violation of the ABM Treaty. Administration officials acknowledged that the missiles would provide a rudimentary defense against an attack.

The committee bill already trimmed $135 million from Bush's $8.3 billion missile defense request, but Democrats complained that it still overemphasized missile defense at the expense of other programs and could violate the ABM Treaty.

On the issue of Vieques, the committee included a provision to prohibit closing the Puerto Rico range until the Pentagon found a single replacement site. Bush had announced that the Navy would leave after 2003, and Pentagon officials were looking for a combination of sites to replace the facility. Military leaders had argued for years that "integrated" training exercises at a single site are more effective than partial exercises at several sites.

The committee agreed, as proposed by Bush, to repeal a provision in the fiscal 2001 defense authorization bill (PL 106-398) that required a referendum to let the residents of Vieques choose between allowing the Navy to continue using live ammunition at the firing range on the island or requiring it to give up the firing range after 2003.

The committee also added a provision stating that if the Navy vacated the firing range, the land would be managed by the Interior Department as a wilderness area and wildlife refuge, preventing commercial development. An amendment to eliminate that provision by Silvestre Reyes, D-Texas, was rejected, 20-35.

In other action, the committee:

• Adopted, 33-26, an amendment by Saxby Chambliss, R-Ga., to delay the retirement of 33 of the B-1 bombers at bases in Georgia, Kansas and Idaho, pending a military review. The committee bill also added $100 million to the requested B-1 budget for the continued operation of the 33 bombers.

• Adopted by voice vote an amendment by Tom Allen, D-Maine, to repeal part of a fiscal 1998 defense authorization law (PL 105-85) that prohibited the government from retiring all 50 MX intercontinental ballistic missiles as Bush had proposed. (*1997 Almanac, p. 8-3*)

• Adopted, 34-25, an amendment by Neil Abercrombie, D-Hawaii, to make it easier for federal employees to compete successfully with private companies for Defense Department work.

• Rejected, 22-31, an amendment by Allen that would have repealed prohibitions against the retirement of intercontinental missiles and bombers.

• Rejected, 23-35, an amendment by Loretta Sanchez, D-Calif., to allow female service members or military dependents to obtain privately funded abortions at overseas U.S. military hospitals.

House Floor Action

The Sept. 11 terrorist attacks and the subsequent push for bipartisanship overwhelmed several efforts to challenge the president's defense priorities. Members largely went along with Bush's request as the House passed its defense bill by a lopsided, 398-17 vote Sept. 25. (*House vote 359, p. H-122*)

(In preparation for going to conference, the House subsequently took up the Senate-passed bill (S 1438), substituted its own text, and passed the measure by voice vote Oct. 17.)

House Democrats abandoned plans to try to cut $920 million from the anti-missile program, agreeing instead with Republicans on a $265 million reduction and a $135 million cut from the budget for consultants. The $400 million savings that resulted was earmarked to beef up intelligence and anti-terrorism programs. The compromise was adopted on the House floor Sept. 25 by voice vote.

The only real fight came on a perennially divisive issue:

allowing the Pentagon to contract out some of the work performed by federal employees. Abercrombie's committee language to enable federal employees to compete with private companies for Pentagon work was reversed as part of a managers' amendment adopted by voice vote Sept. 25. The new provision gave the Pentagon more leeway to contract out government jobs. A procedural move by Minority Whip David E. Bonior, D-Mich., to reinstate the Abercrombie provision failed, 197-221. (*House vote 358, p. H-122*)

Sanchez again proposed to allow female service members or their dependents overseas to obtain privately funded abortions in military hospitals, but was defeated, 199-217. (*House vote 357, p. H-122*)

The House adopted, 242-173, a proposal by James A. Traficant Jr., D-Ohio, to allow military personnel to be assigned to border patrol and customs duties, at the request of the attorney general and the Treasury secretary. (*House vote 356, p. H-122*)

Senate Committee Action

The Senate Armed Services Committee approved its own $343 billion defense authorization bill (S 1438 — S Rept 107-62) Sept. 7 on a party-line vote of 13-12, after a divisive fight in which the majority Democrats prevailed in limiting Bush's missile defense program. Underscoring the depth of partisan feeling on the issue, the senior Democrat and Republican on the committee for the first time in decades held separate news conferences on the bill.

The bill cut $1.3 billion from Bush's $8.3 billion request for missile defense and prohibited any anti-missile tests that violated the ABM Treaty unless Congress voted to allow the test or the United States and Russia agreed to change the treaty so it would not be violated.

An attempt by John W. Warner of Virginia, ranking Republican on the committee, to restore $1 billion of the missile defense funding was rejected on a party-line vote of 12-13. A second Warner amendment to eliminate the curbs on testing failed on a similar vote.

The bill required Congress to vote within 30 days on whether to allow a particular missile defense, thus ruling out a filibuster. If the United States and Russia reached an agreement that allowed a particular test prohibited by the existing treaty, congressional approval would not be required. However, if Bush unilaterally withdrew from the pact on six months' notice, as provided for in the treaty, any subsequent test during fiscal 2002 that would violate the treaty would require congressional approval. "We have a responsibility to know whether or not a testing activity which we are funding conflicts with an arms control agreement," Levin said.

Rumsfeld warned that if the provisions remained in the bill he would recommend a presidential veto.

The other changes made to Bush's budget request were minor in comparison to the action on missile defense.

The committee:

• Accepted the president's proposal for another round of base closings in 2003.

• Agreed to a pay raise of at least 5 percent for all military personnel.

• Added $232 million to increase the housing allowance for service personnel living off base, and $30 million to al-

low some midlevel personnel to transfer to spouses or children a portion of the education benefits earned under the Montgomery GI bill.

• Added $307 million to accelerate the conversion of submarines designed to carry nuclear-armed ballistic missile launchers to instead carry conventionally armed cruise missiles and Navy SEAL teams.

• Added $103 million to buy 10 Blackhawk troop-carrying helicopters for the National Guard, in addition to the $422 million for 25 Blackhawk-type helicopters that Bush requested and the committee approved.

• Added $125 million to upgrade B-52 and B-2 bombers, plus $100 million to temporarily keep in service 33 B-1 bombers that the administration wanted to retire.

• Cut $593 million from the $1.8 billion requested to continue development and production of the V-22 Osprey tilt-rotor aircraft, the troubled Marine Corps plane that was being redesigned after two fatal crashes in 2000.

• Trimmed $247 million from the $1.5 billion requested to continue development of the Joint Strike Fighter, three versions of which were planned to replace 1970s-era jets.

Senate Floor Action

The Senate passed a $345 billion version of the bill Oct. 2 by a vote of 99-0, after narrowly endorsing Bush's plan to close unneeded military bases, the most contentious issue during nearly two weeks of floor debate, The measure exceeded Bush's request by $1.3 billion. (*Senate vote 290, p. S-61*)

The terrorist attacks and the push for bipartisanship tamped down many potential fights. Like their House counterparts, Senate Democrats abandoned any concerted effort to limit Bush's missile defense program. Days after the attacks, Democrats dropped their efforts to limit tests that would violate the ABM Treaty. On Sept. 21, the Senate adopted by voice vote an amendment by Levin and Warner that restored $1.3 billion to the bill, allowing Bush to use the money either to replace the $1.3 billion Levin's committee cut from the missile defense request or to pay for anti-terrorist efforts.

That left base closings as the most divisive issue. The Senate voted 53-47 to table an amendment by Armed Services Committee member Jim Bunning, R-Ky., to strip the authority for base closings from the bill. (*Senate vote 286, p. S-60*)

"Now more than ever we should hold off further downsizing of our military infrastructure as we analyze how to fight the first war of the 21st century," Bunning said. Byron L. Dorgan, D-N.D., whose state was home to two Air Force bases, cited the weakening economy as an additional argument against confronting localities with the threat of losing a significant source of jobs. But Levin and John McCain, R-Ariz., countered that the terrorist attacks made it imperative that the Pentagon shed unneeded bases to free up money for other installations.

In other floor action, the Senate:

• Rejected an effort by Phil Gramm, R-Texas, to scrap a provision in the bill that would allow private companies to compete with federal prison work programs to sell office furniture and other goods and services to the Pentagon. Under existing law, the Defense Department, like other federal agencies, was required to purchase items and services from federal prison work programs, if available. For years, industry, small businesses and organized labor had tried to break what they said was an unfair monopoly. Gramm had been the prison industries' leading Senate ally, beating back efforts by Levin to eliminate the system's privileged status in selling to the Pentagon.

Gramm's position was swamped in a procedural maneuver, with the Senate voting 74-24 to table a proposal to drop the provision. A week later, the Senate adopted by voice vote an amendment by Gramm and Craig Thomas, R-Wyo., that made minor changes in the provision. (*Senate vote 287, p. S-60*)

• Adopted by voice vote a Warner amendment to clear the way for rebuilding the Pentagon, which was badly damaged on Sept. 11. Warner proposed repealing a cap of $1.1 billion on spending to renovate the Pentagon that had been included in the fiscal 1997 defense authorization bill (PL 104-201) to control the cost of a reconstruction project slated to run through 2012. The first phase of that work was nearly complete when a hijacked airliner crashed into the newly renovated section of the building.

• Adopted by voice vote a proposal by Armed Services Committee members Mary L. Landrieu, D-La., and Susan Collins, R-Maine, to change a provision in the Defense Department's medical insurance program considered particularly onerous for pregnant women. Under existing policy, the wife of a service member could elect health care coverage that allowed her to choose her own physician. But once she was pregnant, she would have to be treated at a military hospital unless the facility certified that it could not accommodate her. The amendment eliminated the certification and allowed a woman to continue seeing her own doctor.

• Adopted by voice vote an amendment by Pete V. Domenici, R-N.M., to provide $655 million through fiscal 2011 to compensate people exposed to radiation as a result of nuclear weapons testing or uranium mining.

• Adopted by voice vote an amendment by Russell D. Feingold, D-Wis., requiring a report to Congress on technical problems with the V-22 tilt-rotor aircraft. In 2000, two crashes involving the aircraft killed 23 people.

• Adopted by voice vote an amendment by Harry Reid, D-Nev., to repeal an existing law under which disabled military retirees' pensions were reduced dollar-for-dollar to offset any monthly disability payments received from the Department of Veterans Affairs.

• Adopted by voice vote an amendment by Wayne Allard, R-Colo., that included several provisions intended to guarantee military personnel the right to vote — for example, prohibiting states from disqualifying absentee ballots from military personnel for such reasons as a lack of a postmark, as occurred in some cases in Florida during the disputed 2000 election.

Conference/Final Action

Breaking a monthlong stalemate over base closings, House and Senate negotiator agreed on a final bill Dec. 11. The House adopted the conference report (H Rept 107-333) by a vote of 382-40 on Dec. 13, and the Senate cleared the bill for the president, 96-2, the same day. (*House vote 496, p, H-170; Senate vote 369, p. S-75*)

In a Nov. 15 letter to Congress, Rumsfeld had raised the specter of a presidential veto if the final bill did not include

a base-closing provision. All the living Defense secretaries, except Vice President Dick Cheney, lent their support to another round of base closings in 2003. What finally spurred the authorizers to compromise on a new round in 2005, however, was the push to complete legislation in the closing weeks of the session — and their fear of being marginalized in the defense debate as the defense appropriations bill (HR 3338) suddenly surged forward.

Issues resolved in conference included the following:

● **Health care.** The bill authorized $17.6 billion for defense health programs, about the same as Bush requested but $6 billion more than the fiscal 2001 amount. The fiscal 2001 authorization bill had expanded the military's health care system, ensuring lifetime care for Medicare-eligible military retirees and their families, beginning in 2002.

● **Commercial shipbuilders.** The final bill provided $104 million in loan guarantees, $100 million more than Bush sought.

● **B-1 bombers.** The Air Force was authorized to proceed with the retirement of the B-1 bombers after providing Congress with a report on the consolidation. The bill fulfilled Bush's request for $96 million for B-1 modifications and $195 million for research and development. It also backed Chambliss' plan, adding $100 million for the Air Guard B-1 fleet until the retirement of the 33 aircraft was completed.

● **MX missiles.** Conferees adopted Senate-passed language repealing restrictions on retiring strategic weapons. The House would have repealed the restrictions only as they affected the MX. As in the Senate bill, the final measure added $12 million for equipment to be used in retiring the MX.

● **V-22 Osprey.** The final bill authorized $1.3 billion for 11 V-22s for the Marine Corps — $70 million and one aircraft less than Bush requested; $447 million for V-22 Navy research and development — $100 million less than requested; and $102 million as Bush sought for special operations command of V-22 component development. The bill also required a report to Congress on technical problems with the aircraft.

● **Davis-Bacon.** As in the House version, the final bill rejected Bush's assumption that the Pentagon would save $190 million by increasing the Davis-Bacon threshold from $2,000 to $1 million. It also rejected an assumption that more depot maintenance would be contracted out. To make up the savings, the bill cut $330 million across the board from Bush's operations and maintenance budget.

● **Pentagon repairs.** The bill included the Senate provision repealing the $1.1 billion cap on Pentagon renovations.

While the bill did not embody the wide-ranging changes Rumsfeld had talked of early in the year, it took some modest steps to transform the military to deal with unconventional threats such as terrorism.

Congress added $63 million to modify B-2 bombers to enable them to strike newly discovered targets with so-called smart bombs. Congress strongly backed the notion of equipping long-range weapons with high-tech sensors that would enable them to locate and attack ground targets. In addition to modifying the B-2, it added $33 million to the $233 million Bush requested to buy or modify various remotely piloted airplanes with target detection equipment.

In the report accompanying the bill, House and Senate conferees ordered the Pentagon to produce a long-range plan to modernize its fleet of reconnaissance planes, many of which were modified versions of aging Boeing jetliners.

The bill added $178 million for the Navy to modify four Trident submarines to carry 154 Tomahawk cruise missiles each; the subs currently carried 24 nuclear-armed ballistic missiles. Bush had sought $116 million to begin modification of just two submarines.

The bill also added $15 million to the $50 million requested for the Tomahawk missile program to accelerate work on a new, less costly version that could hover over a battlefield until a target location was radioed to the missile.

The bill added $30 million to increase the number of Marine Corps Harrier jets equipped with an Israeli-designed pod that carried night-vision television designed to hunt for ground targets and a laser to direct smart bombs. The system was built by Northrop Grumman Corp.

In addition to authorizing funds for traditional warships, the bill included $594 million of the $644 million requested to build a new class of destroyers designed to attack ground targets with precision-guided cannon shells and missiles. The cut reflected the Navy's decision to reorganize the program, which would delay the service's choice between two competing teams of shipbuilders.

The bill also added $11 million to the $20 million requested for the Navy to begin work on a new smaller warship intended to operate close to shore. To protect existing boats, $7.5 million was authorized to equip the ships with night-vision television cameras capable of detecting small, missile-launching boats. Another $5 million was authorized to modify computer-operated anti-aircraft guns designed to shoot down approaching cruise missiles.

The bill authorized the $511 million requested for the Army to develop a futuristic combat vehicle, intended to be as lethal as a 70-ton M-1 tank but less than one-third the weight. A C-130 cargo plane could transport the vehicle. The bill also authorized the $663 million requested to buy off-the-shelf armored cars for combat units. Congress added $35 million to accelerate work on versions of the armored car and a commercial truck with hybrid-electric propulsion. Theoretically, such systems would reduce the amount of fuel required by a combat unit, cutting the amount of supplies that would have to be hauled to the front line and making combat units more agile.

In a nod to Bush's work on a global coalition against terrorism, and as the United States and Russia moved toward reducing their respective nuclear arsenals, the bill repealed a law prohibiting any reduction in the long-range missile and bomber forces until the U.S-Russia START II arms reduction treaty took effect. Russia had attached conditions to its ratification of the treaty that made it uncertain whether or when the pact would go into effect. ◆

Congress OKs Force After Sept. 11

Lawmakers from both parties in both chambers quickly rallied around the president after the Sept. 11 terrorist attacks, endorsing the use of force to track down and punish those responsible.

The Senate passed a joint resolution to that effect, 98-0, on Sept. 14. The House cleared the measure by voice vote late the same evening, after voting, 420-1, for identical House language (H J Res 64). President Bush signed the measure into law (S J Res 23 — PL 107-40) on Sept. 18. (*Senate vote 281, p. S-59; House vote 342, p. H-118*)

The measure authorized the president to "use all necessary and appropriate force against those nations, organizations or persons he determines planned, authorized, committed or aided the terrorist attacks that occurred on September 11, 2001, or harbored such organizations or persons." (*Text, p. D-26*)

Senate Foreign Relations Committee Chairman Joseph R. Biden Jr., D-Del., who helped write the final resolution, said it struck the right balance by giving both branches of government a say over military action. "We gave the president all the authority he needed, without giving up our constitutional right to decide whether force should be used," Biden said on the Senate floor Sept. 14.

The lone "no" vote in the House was cast by Barbara Lee, D-Calif., who said the resolution "authorizes an open-ended action and significantly reduces Congress's authority in this matter."

Even as lawmakers pledged unqualified support for the effort to punish the attackers, however, they also struggled with an old debate over how much power Congress should cede to the president to initiate and conduct war. Earlier moments in history and prior legislative battles seemed an inadequate guide.

More than one lawmaker equated the shock of the attacks to the surprise Japanese bombing of Pearl Harbor. Some, including conservatives such as Senate Republican Policy Committee Chairman Larry E. Craig, R-Idaho, and Rep. Bob Barr, R-Ga., suggested that Congress declare war, as it did on Dec. 8, 1941. But that was also the last time Congress had invoked its constitutional mandate to declare war. As many lawmakers pointed out, it also was not clear how such a declaration would apply when the enemy was a small group of terrorists rather than a foreign nation.

"Who do we declare war against?" asked John W. Warner of Virginia, ranking Republican on the Senate Armed Services Committee.

Others pointed to the more recent example of the joint resolution (PL 102-1) cleared in 1991, authorizing the use of military force to evict Iraqi troops from Kuwait. But Republican critics said that legislation was too narrowly focused to help fight the new danger. It authorized the president to go

BoxScore

Bill:

S J Res 23 — PL 107-40

Legislative Action:

Senate passed S J Res 23, 98-0, on Sept. 14.

House cleared S J Res 23 by voice vote Sept. 14, after passing H J Res 64, 420-1.

President signed Sept. 18.

to war against Iraq to enforce a U.N. Security Council resolution requiring it to end its occupation of Kuwait by Jan. 15. (*1991 Almanac, p. 437*)

"I'm not for putting a lot of strings on it," said Sen. Jon Kyl, R-Ariz., a member of the Intelligence Committee. "Are we going to be able to give the president enough flexibility to act if we put a lot of restrictions in legislation?"

Kyl's view was shared by the Bush administration, which initially proposed that Congress support not only retaliation for the Sept. 11 attacks but also "all necessary and appropriate force" to "deter and pre-empt any future acts of terrorism or aggression against the United States."

That went too far for many lawmakers, particularly Democrats, who feared that such an open-ended commitment could came back to haunt them, much as an earlier generation of lawmakers came to lament their support for the 1964 Gulf of Tonkin resolution (PL 88-408). That resolution was cited by the Johnson and Nixon administrations as congressional authorization for waging the Vietnam War. (*1964 Almanac, p. 331*)

The White House welcomed the resolution though it was careful to cite the Constitution as the basis for the president's authority to act. "The administration is gratified by Congress' show of unity," White House spokesman Ari Fleischer said Sept. 12. "But, also, as previous presidents have maintained — and as President Bush does — under the Constitution, the president of course has the authority as commander in chief to protect our nation." Fleischer went on to say that, "the president knows that the strength of our nation comes from that Constitution, which gives an important role to Congress, and he will continue to consult closely with Congress and its leaders."

Background

Since the Vietnam War, Congress and the White House had engaged in periodic battles over their respective responsibilities in initiating military hostilities. The debate was grounded in the divided powers provided under the Constitution, which gives the president the role of commander in chief, while entrusting to Congress the power to declare war. But war had been declared only five times in the nation's history; every conflict since World War II had been fought without such a declaration.

Congressional efforts to circumscribe the president's war-making powers peaked in the turbulent 1970s with the 1973 War Powers Resolution (PL 93-148). Enacted over President Richard M. Nixon's veto, the resolution stated that the president could commit U.S. armed forces to hostilities or imminent hostilities only if there was a declaration of war,

specific statutory authority, or a national emergency created by an attack on the United States, its territories or its armed forces. *(1973 Almanac, p. 905)*

It required the president to consult with Congress "in every possible instance" before committing U.S. troops, report such a commitment to Congress within 48 hours, and terminate it within 60 to 90 days unless Congress authorized an extension.

The practical effect in constraining the president was limited. No president from either party had acknowledged the constitutionality of the War Powers Resolution. They typically sought subsequent congressional support — but not prior authority — for decisions to use U.S. troops abroad. Congress, for its part, was reluctant to act while U.S.

forces were in harm's way or to do anything to undermine the president during a national crisis.

A report issued Sept. 11 by the Congressional Research Service found that presidents had submitted 90 reports consistent with the resolution. But the "consultation" came after, not before, the decision to deploy had been made. President Gerald R. Ford set the precedent in 1975 when he sent the Marines to free the ship *Mayaguez*, a U.S. merchant marine vessel that was captured by Cambodian forces. Ford did not seek prior congressional approval, relying instead on inherent constitutional powers. He did report to Congress within 48 hours but consulted with selected lawmakers only after the attack order had been issued. *(1975 Almanac, p. 310)* ◆

Chapter 8

EDUCATION

Landmark Education Bill Signed

Congress on Dec. 18 cleared a landmark education bill that for the first time tied federal education aid to improvements in students' test scores. The bill required annual student testing and school improvements aimed at helping disadvantaged children catch up with their peers. It created consequences for schools with chronically low student test scores and offered children in those schools alternatives such as private tutoring and other services partly at public expense.

The new law, the most ambitious overhaul to date of the 1965 Elementary and Secondary Education Act (ESEA), enabled President Bush to deliver on a major campaign promise in the first year of his presidency. Bush signed the bill (HR 1 — PL 107-110) on Jan. 8, 2002. It contained the bulk of his education overhaul proposals, with the exception of his plan for government vouchers that could be used for private school tuition.

The six-year bill authorized $26.3 billion for assistance to elementary and secondary schools in fiscal 2002, an increase of $8 billion over fiscal 2001. The total was $3.5 billion more than the House proposed, but $5.4 billion less than the Senate recommended.

Enactment followed three years of bitter debate over how far the federal government should go in influencing public school policy, which is determined chiefly by the state and local governments that provide most education funding. Democrats wanted to hold on to Clinton-era education budget expansions. Republicans wanted to streamline federal education spending and leave program design to the states.

The landmark 1965 education act, which governs federal aid to public schools for everything from help for disadvantaged and low-income children to arts education and teacher training, had last been rewritten in 1994. That version expired in 2000, but amidst election-year maneuvering, Congress failed for the first time in the law's 35-year history to renew it. As a stopgap solution, lawmakers funded ESEA programs for one year at $18.6 billion under the fiscal 2001 Labor, Health and Human Services, and Education appropriations law (PL 106-554).

Bush made overhauling education the centerpiece of his 2000 presidential campaign and a top legislative priority of his new administration. He called for states to design and administer annual tests to measure student performance as a condition for receiving federal education money. Schools that repeatedly fell short of state-set standards would be subject to sanctions, such as being forced to divert a share of their federal funds to "vouchers" to pay for private schooling or tutoring for needy children.

By mid-June, both chambers had passed versions of the

BoxScore

Bill:
HR 1 — PL 107-110
Legislative Action:
House passed HR 1 (H Rept 107-63), 384-45, on May 23.
Senate passed HR 1, amended (S Rept 107-7), 91-8, June 14.
House adopted the conference report (H Rept 107-334), 381-41, on Dec. 13.
Senate cleared the bill, 87-10, on Dec. 18.
President signed Jan. 8, 2002.

ESEA reauthorization that required annual testing in reading and math in third through eighth grades, with rewards for the best schools and penalties for the worst. Both tied progress to federal aid, and both turned GOP proposals for open-ended block grants into pilot programs. Neither bill allowed for private-school vouchers — a proposal Bush abandoned after it became clear it could not win in either chamber.

There were still significant differences between the two versions, however. The five-year House bill (HR 1), passed May 23, called for $22.8 billion in education spending in fiscal 2002 — a 20 percent increase over what was spent in fiscal 2001. It included a pilot project to allow 100 school districts to spend funds from four major programs however they chose as long as they maintained student progress. GOP leaders argued that years of one-size-fits-all policies from Washington had resulted in lackluster reading and math scores despite $120 billion spent over three decades.

The seven-year Senate bill (S 1), passed June 14 after the chamber had shifted to Democratic control, called for a much larger, $14.4 billion spending increase for fiscal 2002. It focused on sending a greater share of government grants to the poorest schools and making federal aid for special education a mandatory item in federal budgets. It included a pilot program to allow seven states and 25 school districts to consolidate most federal aid into block grants.

House and Senate conferees made scant progress in reconciling the two bills over the summer. With the Sept. 11 terrorist attacks and the need to focus on recovery and protection against terrorism, the urgency of finishing the education overhaul seemed to dim.

However, four lawmakers dismissed party leadership talk of postponing the work. The bill's main shepherds — Reps. John A. Boehner, R-Ohio, and George Miller, D-Calif., and Sens. Edward M. Kennedy, D-Mass., and Judd Gregg, R-N.H. — met regularly in an office tucked away in the Capitol. There the lawmakers, respectively the chairmen and ranking member of each chambers' education committees, hashed out differences over funding, definitions of a failing school and whether the federal government should pay for programs to teach children about hate crimes.

The last major dispute was over a provision in the Senate bill to substantially increase funding for programs under the 1975 Individuals With Disabilities Education Act (IDEA) (PL 94-142) and make the spending mandatory rather than discretionary. The Senate's newly installed Democratic leadership argued that schools would need the extra funding to follow the new ESEA mandates as well as the special education

law. Led by the White House, Republicans opposed the provision on the grounds that IDEA, due to expire in 2002, needed too many revisions to be funded automatically. Gregg, who had once favored the mandatory spending idea, argued that lawmakers must first address reports of too many minority students being steered to special education classes and misbehaving students being shielded from routine classroom discipline.

Negotiations culminated in mid-December. Lawmakers reached a deal to omit the mandatory special education funding provision, delay state implementation of the testing until the 2005-06 school year and give states 12 years to steadily reach the goal of bringing students to a state-defined "proficient" level on their tests.

Highlights

The following are major spending and policy components of the legislation:

● **Annual testing.** By the 2005-06 school year, states were required to begin administering annual, statewide reading and math tests in third through eighth grades. States could select and design their own tests, which had to be in line with state academic standards. By the 2007-08 school year, states had to begin giving annual statewide science tests to one grade within each of the three levels of a K-12 education: elementary, middle and high school. The law authorized $400 million for fiscal 2002 to help states pay for developing and administering their annual tests. The federal government was responsible for paying the cost of giving the tests; $69 million was authorized for fiscal 2002.

● **Academic progress.** States could set their own definition for "academic proficiency," but were required to reach the goal for all students within 12 years. States could not set the minimum bar for proficiency below the performance level of the lowest-achieving student group or schools at the time of enactment. States were supposed to pace themselves by raising the bar for students incrementally. The law provided a "safe harbor" for schools where particular groups of students had not technically made annual progress under the law.

● **Title I.** The law authorized $13.5 billion in fiscal 2002 for Title I, the largest program within ESEA, which focuses federal money on the poorest districts and neediest children, including funds for teachers, lessons and special programs. The law's definition of "disadvantaged children" included American Indian children, those from poor families, those who speak little or no English, are disabled, neglected or abused, or are from migrant-worker families. The bill made minor changes to formulas for computing grants for all school districts. For instance, states that worked to distribute their own funds more equally throughout the state instead of using property tax-based formulas also would be eligible for targeted aid. For the first time, Congress appropriated money for such aid, $1 billion in fiscal 2002 for targeted grants and $793 million for education finance incentive grants.

● **Teacher training and development.** Class-size reduction and Eisenhower professional development programs were combined into a single "teacher quality" program, authorized at $3.6 billion for fiscal 2002. The funds could be used to hire new teachers to limit class sizes, train special-education teachers or principals, and create incentives for schools and districts to improve their teacher work force.

Educators were protected from legal liability for undertaking "reasonable actions" to maintain order and discipline in the classroom.

● **Reading.** The bill authorized $900 million in fiscal 2002 for a new initiative to help states and districts create reading programs for children in kindergarten through third grade. States could use up to 20 percent of the money to train teachers, among other options.

● **School technology.** Several education technology programs were consolidated into a single technology grant, authorized at $1 billion in fiscal 2002. Eligible programs ranged from helping poor and rural students get computer access to training more teachers. Districts had to use at least 25 percent of the money to help teachers become proficient in technology, unless they could show that they already provided such training.

● **Bilingual education.** Several bilingual education programs were consolidated into one, authorized at $750 million in fiscal 2002. Students with limited English skills had to be tested in reading and language arts in English after they had attended school in the United States for three consecutive years. Some children could receive a two-year waiver. The bill ended the requirement that 75 percent of federal bilingual education funds be spent on programs that used a child's native language for instruction.

● **21st Century Community Learning Centers.** The program — which paid for activities before and after school and was authorized at $1.25 billion in fiscal 2002 — was expanded beyond school districts to include faith-based groups and other community groups.

Background

Enacted in 1965 as one of President Lyndon Johnson's Great Society anti-poverty programs, the Elementary and Secondary Education Act (PL 89-10) provided grants for several K-12 programs, most of them aimed at students from poor communities or at risk of failing their lessons or dropping out of school.

Over the years, other social issues became entangled in the debate on the education law. In 1988, the rewrite was almost killed over a bid to outlaw pornographic phone services. In the 1994 reauthorization, President Bill Clinton sought to steer extra money to needy schools and stave off Republican calls to abolish the Education Department, while lawmakers battled over gun control and school prayer. (*1988 Almanac, p. 330; 1994 Almanac, 383*)

The next attempt to reauthorize the law, at the end of 1999, foundered on the upcoming presidential elections. In poll after poll, voters said education was their top concern, but views on how to improve education varied widely. Finding little incentive for compromise, lawmakers used the issue largely to make political points. Republicans and Democrats were already far apart on what defined good education policy — less federal intervention for Republicans, school construction and other new programs for Democrats. In 1999 and 2000, House Republicans passed party-line bills, only to have them stopped in the more evenly divided Senate. (*2000 Almanac, p. 9-3; 1999 Almanac, p. 10-3*)

Having made education a priority in his 2000 White House bid, Bush sent Congress a plan in January 2001

proposing to consolidate dozens of programs into five general grant categories, test students annually to hold schools accountable for how well students were learning, and offer children federal aid to attend private schools. The estimated price tag was $47.6 billion over 10 years. Bush was backed by House conservatives, who unveiled HR 1 and dubbed it the "Leave No Child Behind Act," echoing a Bush campaign refrain.

Some conservatives continued to worry, however, that the testing proposal could lead to a national test and curriculum that was outside the control of the states. Liberal Democrats argued that any testing plan had to be accompanied by a substantial increase in aid to poor schools to ensure that their students were equally prepared for the tests.

Democrats soon countered with a proposal for unprecedented spending on education — $110 billion over five years. They sought to preserve technology discounts for schools and continue bilingual instruction projects not specified in the Bush proposal.

Legislative Action

House Committee Action

The House Education and the Workforce Committee approved its five-year bill (HR 1 — H Rept 107-63) on May 9 by a vote of 41-7. The bill was a delicate compromise worked out by Boehner and Miller. The deal, approved by voice vote as the markup opened May 2, assured Democratic support but left GOP conservatives complaining that their priorities were slipping away and that Bush was not fighting for his principles. All but six Republicans supported the bill, though some said they did so only to give Bush a needed win.

The bill required states to set education standards and test all students in third through eighth grades annually in reading and math to measure progress in meeting the goals. Poor parents of children in failing schools could use federal money for additional tutoring through public or private programs, and local districts would get unprecedented flexibility in spending federal aid.

To get Democrats' support, Boehner agreed to a significant increase in authorized funding for education, including a doubling of Title I aid to poor schools over five years. Total ESEA funding would grow from $18.6 billion to $22.8 billion. Title I funding would rise from $8.6 billion in fiscal 2001 to $17.2 billion in fiscal 2006.

Boehner also toned down a GOP proposal — known as "Straight A's" — that would let states spend federal funds for virtually any education purpose as long as they got better academic results. The compromise was to let school districts use up to 50 percent of federal funds for other educational purposes but otherwise leave the existing programs intact. Boehner also dropped a "charitable choice" provision in the Bush proposal that would have allowed faith-based after-school programs to receive federal funds without abandoning their religious content.

The one major conservative proposal Boehner left in the bill — to give poor parents of students at failing schools the option of using federal funds to help pay for private school tuition — turned out to be the easiest to knock out. Hours

after the markup began, five Republicans joined all 22 Democrats in a 27-2 vote to strip vouchers from the measure.

More than two dozen conservative groups — including the Family Research Council, Focus on the Family, the Eagle Forum and the Traditional Values Coalition — announced they would not support the measure. "We are never going to be able to compensate for the damage done to this bill by this committee," said Bob Schaffer, R-Colo. "Clearly, the majority of this committee is not committed to the president's bill."

Boehner had to put the markup on hold May 3 to talk conservatives out of offering a Straight A's amendment, which Democrats said would blow apart the compromise.

Though the annual testing requirement remained in the bill, committee members on both sides were wary. In a close call, Betty McCollum, D-Minn., offered an amendment to strip out the testing, gaining enough support to indicate she might have a strong chance of winning. To prevent a crippling blow to Bush's education plan, Miller persuaded McCollum not to ask for a roll call vote, and Boehner declared the amendment defeated on a voice vote.

Democrats repeatedly pushed to dedicate and increase funding for individual programs — the opposite of the Straight A's approach — scoring some successes. In one case, the panel voted 35-5 to approve an amendment by Dale E. Kildee, D-Mich., Carolyn McCarthy, D-N.Y., and Mark Souder, R-Ind., to maintain drug-abuse prevention and after-school programs as separate programs rather than consolidating them into a single block grant.

Bush said he would support a House floor amendment to restore vouchers, though his congressional liaisons made it clear he would declare victory even if the House bill remained as it was. "This bill is a manifestation of his proposal," said Bush education adviser Sandy Kress. "I believe 90 to 95 percent of his proposal is in this bill."

House Floor Action

The House overwhelmingly passed the five-year, $22.8 billion ESEA reauthorization May 23 by a vote of 384-45. Though unhappy GOP conservatives and skeptical liberal Democrats were looking for reasons to bolt, in the end, only 34 Republicans, 10 Democrats and one independent voted against the package. Moderate Republicans aligned with most Democrats to rebuff a series of challenges, leaving the bill in the same basic form as when it emerged from committee. That was the key to its success: In each instance, the bipartisan compromise remained intact, losing a few lawmakers from both ends of the political spectrum but keeping everyone else in the fold. (*House vote 145, p. H-54*)

● **Testing.** The biggest challenge was an attempt by Peter Hoekstra, R-Mich., and Barney Frank, D-Mass., to strike the annual testing. Though they drew heavy support from conservative Republicans and liberal Democrats, the amendment was rejected, 173-255. Hoekstra and Frank blamed their defeat on heavy lobbying by White House officials, including Chief of Staff Andrew H. Card Jr. and presidential adviser Karl Rove, to discourage conservative support for the amendment. (*House vote 130, p. H-50*)

Although conservative groups such as the Christian Coalition warned that Bush's state-based testing proposal could lead to national tests, the White House and its allies

in the business community saw it as the centerpiece of Bush's proposal. While only 52 Republicans and two independents voted to strike the testing, the amendment drew the support of 119 Democrats, including Minority Leader Richard A. Gephardt of Missouri, Minority Whip David E. Bonior of Michigan, and David R. Obey of Wisconsin, ranking member on the Appropriations Committee.

• **Local flexibility.** The biggest potential threat to the bill's bipartisan support was defused before it ever came to the floor. Bush persuaded Jim DeMint, R-S.C., not to offer an amendment that would have established a Straight A's demonstration program in seven states and 25 school districts. Although Senate Democrats had accepted similar language, their House colleagues said they would abandon their support for the bill if it was approved. "[Bush] assured me that he is a strong supporter of Straight A's. He is just looking at a different strategy to get this thing done," DeMint said. "I trust him."

Republicans came close to losing Democratic support when they pushed through an amendment to allow two districts in each state to spend funds from four major programs however they chose — a provision many Democrats considered to be Straight A's under another name. The proposal, by Pat Tiberi, R-Ohio, and Michael N. Castle, R-Del., squeaked through, 217-209. The four programs were teacher quality, the Innovative Programs block grant, Safe and Drug Free Schools, and technology grants. (*House vote 132, p. H-50*)

• **Vouchers.** Majority Leader Dick Armey, R-Texas, failed in two attempts to revive school vouchers. The first, to restore Bush's proposal to give vouchers to children in failing schools, was defeated 155-273, losing 68 Republicans and gaining only two Democrats. The second, which called for setting up five voucher demonstration projects, was defeated, 186-241. (*House votes 135, 136, p. H-52*)

• **Other amendments.** Conservative Republicans won some small victories, including a rider by Charlie Norwood, R-Ga., to allow school districts to suspend or expel special education students who brought weapons to school. It was adopted 246-181. Under existing law, schools could suspend or expel a student with disabilities, but the school district had to continue providing education services to the student at home or in an alternative setting. Under the amendment, the services would not have to continue unless the state required such treatment of children without disabilities. (*House vote 138, p. H-52*)

Van Hilleary, R-Tenn., won voice vote approval for a proposal to cut off federal funds to school districts that refused to let the Boy Scouts of America use their school facilities. The amendment was aimed at several school districts that were boycotting the Boy Scouts for excluding homosexuals as members and leaders.

Democrats suffered several defeats, including an attempt by Major Owens, D-N.Y., to send the bill back to committee to add money to renovate schools and to reduce class size by hiring more teachers, which was rejected 207-223. Democrats began looking to the Senate, where their party was about to take over the leadership and shepherd a bill from the Senate's Health, Education Labor and Pensions panel through a House-Senate conference. (*House vote 144, p. H-54*)

Senate Committee Action

The Senate Health, Education, Labor and Pensions Committee had approved a seven-year reauthorization bill (S 1 — S Rept 107-7) by a vote of 20-0 on March 8.

Crafted while Republicans still held the majority in the Senate, the bill included Bush's provisions to test students each year in grades 3 through 8 in reading and math and launch a new reading program. But committee Democrats persuaded Republicans to steer extra federal money to the neediest schools and give states an additional year — four years rather than three — to begin the new tests. The bill included $400 million to help states develop the new exams.

Despite the bipartisan spirit, sharp differences emerged between Democrats and Republicans over how much leeway to give states in spending federal money and how many federal education programs should be consolidated.

Democrats chafed at their inability to add more money to the bill and said their support might not come so easily on the Senate floor if the funding was not increased.

Christopher J. Dodd, D-Conn., lost, 10-10, on an amendment that would have increased Title I funding by $3.8 billion a year, giving it enough money to serve all eligible low-income children by fiscal 2008. Democrats said the $8.6 billion for Title I in fiscal 2001 was only enough to reach about a third of eligible low-income children. The committee's bill already included a major increase, boosting the authorization to $15 billion in fiscal 2002. Dodd's amendment would have increased that to $37.7 billion in fiscal 2008.

Committee Republicans, who had agreed to the $15 billion figure in negotiations with Democrats when the bill was being drafted, refused to go any higher without a commitment to more state and local flexibility. "I will support a dramatic increase in funding, but only if we have real, meaningful, comprehensive reform, as the president has proposed," said Tim Hutchinson of Arkansas.

Democrats also lost party-line votes in the evenly divided committee on proposals to increase funding to hire more teachers and renovate schools. The committee defeated, 10-10, amendments by:

• Patty Murray, D-Wash., to authorize $2.6 billion for schools to reduce class sizes.

• Edward M. Kennedy, D-Mass., to reserve $1.5 billion for teacher training. The bill instead called for $3 billion for class-size reduction and teacher training.

• Tom Harkin, D-Iowa, to authorize $1.6 billion for school renovation.

• Dodd, to require the government to increase Title I spending by $3.8 billion a year to a spending level of $37.7 billion in fiscal 2008.

Conservatives expressed disappointment that the bill contained neither vouchers nor a "charter states" proposal that would let some states use federal education money for any purpose as long as they achieved better results.

Gregg offered, then withdrew, an amendment that mirrored Bush's campaign-trail proposal for private school vouchers. The money would go to children in low-performing public schools, but Democrats said it would only remove aid from schools that needed the most help. "It is the essence of the debate," Gregg said. "What do you do for a parent who has a child in a failing school? The purpose of this amendment is to empower the parents."

Bill Frist, R-Tenn., offered and withdrew an amendment similar to Bush's block grant proposal that would give states greater latitude in spending funds in exchange for improving performance. Both Frist and Gregg promised their amendments would resurface on the Senate floor.

Senate Floor Action

After six weeks of floor debate, the Senate passed HR 1 on June 14 by an overwhelming vote of 91-8, after substituting the amended version of its own bill. "The message is that help is on the way," said Kennedy, who took over as the bill's manager and remained on the Senate floor throughout most of the proceedings to preserve as much of a Democratic stamp as possible. (*Senate vote 192, p. S-41*)

The bill proposed authorizing $33 billion for ESEA programs in fiscal 2002, compared with the $22.8 billion in the House bill. It included a demonstration program — negotiated with the administration and included in the manager's amendment to the bill — to give seven states and 25 school districts broad powers to spend federal funds as long as test scores improved.

● **IDEA.** The Senate added $8.8 billion in mandatory spending for fiscal 2002 — $181 billion over 10 years — for IDEA. The amendment, by Harkin and Chuck Hagel, R-Neb., was adopted by voice vote shortly after Senate debate opened May 3. It required full funding of IDEA within six years. The program, which was being funded at $16.3 billion, would get an additional $2.5 billion a year until it covered 40 percent of state and local special education costs, the goal set by authors of the 1995 law.

● **Title I.** Also on the first day, the Senate agreed to authorize a $132 billion increase over 10 years to make sure Title I aid to poor schools reached all eligible children. The amendment, by Dodd and Susan Collins, R-Maine, was adopted, 79-21, with support from all 50 Democrats and 29 Republicans. (*Senate vote 91, p. S-24*)

An attempt by Larry E. Craig, R-Idaho, to limit the funding increase to schools that were improving their test scores was rejected May 8 by a vote of 27-73. (*Senate vote 93, p. S-25*)

Mary L. Landrieu, D-La., subsequently added a requirement that Congress target any new Title I funds specifically to school districts with the highest concentrations of poor children. The vote, on June 11, was 57-36. Landrieu said she wanted to highlight the fact that Title I money often did not reach the poor schools it was supposed to help. Use of old formulas allowed the funds to continue to flow to districts that were no longer poor. (*Senate vote 178, p. S-39*)

● **Vouchers, school choice.** Bush and his conservative Senate allies were again rebuffed on the issue of private school vouchers. Democrats beat back an attempt by Gregg to create a demonstration program that would allow public school students in three states and 10 school districts to use federal money for transportation to other public schools, such as charters, or tuition at a private school. The amendment drew support from conservative Republicans, but 11 GOP moderates voted with 46 Democrats and one independent to reject it, 41-58. (*Senate vote 179, p. S-39*)

The Senate did adopt, by voice vote, an amendment by Gregg and Thomas R. Carper, D-Del., to authorize $125 million in grants to help communities that allowed children in underperforming schools to attend better public schools.

● **Testing.** Attempts to delay or defer the testing provisions also were defeated. An amendment by Jean Carnahan, D-Mo., to defer testing if the federal government did not provide the full authorized funding was rejected 43-55. Paul Wellstone, D-Minn., lost a similar bid to defer testing until Congress provided a $24.72 billion maximum for the bulk of Title I programs for poor students. The amendment was rejected 23-71. (*Senate votes 174, 176, p. S-38*)

The Senate did adopt a proposal by James M. Jeffords, R-Vt., 93-7, to allow states to suspend testing if Congress did not appropriate at least $370 million in fiscal 2002, rising to $430 million in fiscal 2008, to offset the costs. (*Senate vote 90, p. S-24*)

● **Other amendments.** The Senate rejected two amendments by Dodd that Republicans said were deal-breakers. The first, to require states to even out the financing disparities between rich and poor school districts, was rejected, 42-58. The second, to exempt after-school programs from a block grant demonstration program, was rejected, 47-51. (*Senate votes 180, p. S-39; 184, p. S-40*)

Conservatives logged some victories. On the final day of debate, the Senate adopted an amendment by Jeff Sessions, R-Ala., to allow schools to expel disabled students for bad behavior. The proposal initially failed on a 50-50 tie vote, but a procedural lapse gave it new life. No one tabled the motion to reconsider the vote, a common practice. The Senate then agreed, 51-47, to reconsider the amendment and adopted it by voice vote. (*Senate votes 188, 190, p. S-41*)

Harkin argued that Sessions' amendment, which was similar to language in the House bill, would "turn the clock back and segregate these kids." Harkin's alternative, which would have allowed schools to expel students only if their behavior was not related to their disability, was rejected, 36-64. (*Senate vote 187, p. S-40*)

The Senate also fought over, and ultimately approved, an amendment by Jesse Helms, R-N.C., to cut off federal aid to districts that refused to let the Boy Scouts use school facilities because of the group's refusal to admit gays. It was adopted, 51-49. (*Senate vote 189, p. S-41*)

However, the Senate adopted by voice vote an amendment by Robert C. Byrd, D-W.Va., to specify that the Helms proposal applied to "patriotic societies," including the Boys and Girls Clubs of America and Little League Baseball, Inc. Byrd said the original language was so broad that it could have shielded hate groups as well. Barbara Boxer, D-Calif., then succeeded in adding language that would give the groups equal access to school facilities regardless of their policies toward homosexuals — without threatening the loss of federal funds if school districts violated the policy. Her amendment was adopted, 52-47. (*Senate vote 191, p. S-41*)

Conference/Final Action

Nearly five months after they began work, House and Senate conferees agreed to a final version of the ESEA reauthorization bill Dec. 11. The House adopted the conference report (H Rept 107-334), 381-41, on Dec. 13. The Senate cleared the bill, 87-10, on Dec. 18. (*House vote 497, p. H-170; Senate vote 371, p. S-76*)

The following are the main compromises reached in conference, including the agreement to drop plans to make special education funding a mandatory federal obligation:

● **Special education.** House Republicans kept all plans to make special education funding mandatory out of the final conference report. Democrats struggled to retain the plan, hoping it would free up more discretionary spending for ESEA programs, particularly Title I. Kennedy and Miller were especially eager to carve out the extra money after appropriators agreed to limit the actual increase for education in fiscal 2002 to $3.5 billion, rather than the $10 billion increase they were urging. (*Appropriations, p. 2-34*)

● **Title I funding.** The final bill authorized $13.5 billion in fiscal 2002 for grants for disadvantaged children, more than double the fiscal 2001 appropriation. The bill authorized increasing amounts for each of the succeeding five years, reaching $25 billion in fiscal 2006.

● **Testing and accountability.** Conferees agreed to require that states design and administer annual tests within four years or lose a small portion of federal money. To verify the results, states also were required to give a national independent test to a sample of children. States had to set a standard test score for "proficiency" and get all children to that level in 12 years. Schools that consistently failed to reach state goals would lose some federal money and

much of their autonomy.

● **Local control.** House GOP leaders, long proponents of states' rights and local control, wanted to give school districts the flexibility to shift up to half their federal education money among education programs of their choosing. The Senate, concerned about local governments diluting the intent of federal programs, such as bilingual education, opted for a demonstration project that would limit flexibility to seven states and a handful of school districts. Negotiators agreed to combine elements of both approaches: All states and school districts could shift small portions of their federal grant money from one program to another, though money directed to the poorest children could not be diverted. A pilot program would let seven states and up to 150 local districts shift more of their federal money among programs as long as test scores improved.

● **Hate crimes.** Conferees agreed to allow the Education Department to continue to issue grants for programs designed to prevent hate crimes. Some Republicans had argued to end federal aid to programs that taught children about hate crimes, amid concerns that government money was used to portray some religious groups as bigots. ◆

Provisions of ESEA Reauthorization

The following are the main provisions of the six-year reauthorization of the 1965 Elementary and Secondary Education Act (ESEA), which cleared Dec. 18 and was signed into law Jan. 8, 2002.

Testing, Accountability

The bill made states responsible for administering annual standardized tests, collecting and reporting test scores by school and overseeing the corrective actions required for schools that fail to make annual progress in meeting state standards. Previous law did not require annual testing.

● **Annual reading and math tests.** By the 2005-06 school year, states were required to begin administering annual, statewide reading and math tests for grades 3 through 8. States could select and design their own tests, which had to be in line with state academic standards.

● **Science tests.** By the 2007-08 school year, states were required to begin giving annual statewide science tests to one grade within each of the three levels of a K-12 education: elementary, middle and high school.

● **National Assessment of Educational Progress (NAEP).** States were required to give a sample of fourth- and eighth-graders the NAEP in reading and math every other year. The tests, often called the nation's report card, would be a benchmark for verifying the results on state-administered tests.

● **Funding.** The law authorized $400 million for fiscal 2002 to help states pay for developing and administering their annual tests. The federal government would pay the cost of giving the NAEP tests; $69 million was authorized for fiscal 2002. States could delay or interrupt for one year their annual testing schedules for each year that Congress failed to appropriate the testing funds. No federal rewards or sanctions would be based on test results.

● **Report cards.** Test results would be reported by race, income, disability status and other categories with an aim toward identifying and helping any groups of children who were falling behind.

Beginning with the 2002-03 school year, states and school districts were required to provide annual report cards with a range of information, including scores broken down by subgroups. Existing report cards had to be changed to comply with the law.

● **Academic progress.** States could set their own definition for "academic proficiency," but they had to reach the goal for all students within 12 years. States could not set the minimum bar for proficiency below the performance of the lowest-achieving student group or schools at the time of enactment. States were to pace themselves by raising the bar for students incrementally.

● **Safe harbor.** The law provided a "safe harbor" for schools in which particular groups of students had not technically made annual progress under the law. As long as schools could show that those students were making significant progress toward proficiency, the schools would not be deemed to be failing under the law.

● **Other measures of achievement.** States were also required to find another way of measuring school progress besides the math and reading test scores. For high schools, that measurement had to include graduation rates.

● **Two years of failure.** Schools that failed to make progress for two consecutive years would get technical assistance. The neediest children at those schools would be given the choice of attending another better-performing public school. The school district would have to use up to 5 percent of its administrative funds under the Title I program for disadvantaged students to provide transportation for students who chose schools in other districts.

● **Three years of failure.** Schools that failed to make progress for three straight years would have to expand school choice options by offering parents supplemental educational services, including private tutoring. The district would have to use up to 5 percent of its Title I money to pay for that option. The district could use an additional 10 percent of its Title I money to pay for public school transportation costs or supplemental services.

● **Four years of failure.** Schools that failed to make adequate progress for four consecutive years would be subject to corrective

actions by the district. Such actions could include replacing certain staff members or adopting a new curriculum.

● **Five years of failure.** Schools that failed to make adequate progress for five consecutive years would be "reconstituted." They could be turned over to state control, or closed and reopened as a charter school — a public school that operates with public money but is free of many of the rules for traditional public schools.

● **Already failing schools.** Schools identified as failures under previous law had to begin giving students the option of attending another public school in the fall of 2002.

Disadvantaged Children

The law authorized $13.5 billion in fiscal 2002 for the largest program within ESEA — Title I — which focuses federal money on the poorest districts and neediest children, including funds for teachers, lessons and special programs. Rules and funds for testing and reading programs also fall under this section. The law defined "disadvantaged children" to include those who are American Indian; are from poor families; speak little or no English; are disabled, neglected or abused; or are from migrant-worker families.

● **Targeting funds.** The law made minor changes to formulas used to compute grants for all school districts. For instance, Puerto Rico would receive money to place its schools more on par with states. States with smaller populations received an increase in the minimum amounts they could receive. States that strive to distribute their own funds more equally throughout the state instead of using property tax-based formulas would also receive targeted aid. For the first time, Congress appropriated money for that aid — $1 billion for targeted grants and $793 million for education finance incentive grants.

Teacher Training and Development

The law consolidated the class-size reduction and Eisenhower professional development programs into a single "teacher quality" program, authorized to receive $3.6 billion for fiscal 2002. The funds could be used to hire new teachers to limit class sizes, train special-education teachers or principals, and create incentives to schools and districts that improve their teacher work force.

● **"Highly qualified" teachers.** All states were required to employ only "highly qualified" teachers by the end of the 2005-06 school year. The law defined highly qualified teachers as those who have been certified or licensed by a state and have demonstrated through a test or other means that they are highly competent in the subjects they teach. Highly qualified teachers could take alternative routes to certification, including mid-career training that does not require a graduate degree in education.

● **Teachers' aides.** Within three years, all paraprofessionals, or aides, hired with federal funds had to have completed at least two years of college, have an associate's or higher degree, or have reached a high-quality standard that has been locally established.

● **Liability Protection.** The law protected educators from legal liability for undertaking "reasonable actions" to maintain order and discipline in the classroom. Educators were protected as long as their actions did not include the commission of a crime.

● **Troops to Teachers.** The law continued the Troops to Teachers program, which encouraged retired military personnel to become teachers.

● **National Writing Project.** The law continued the main federal program aimed at improving writing, which trained educators to teach writing more effectively at 164 sites in the 50 states, the District of Columbia and Puerto Rico.

● **Math and science education.** Authorized to receive $450 million in fiscal 2002, the new program aimed to encourage states, colleges, districts and schools to form partnerships to improve student performance in math and science.

● **Teaching of traditional American history.** This new grant program was aimed at teaching American history in a course separate from general social studies curricula. Congress did not authorize a specific amount for the grants program.

Reading

● **Reading First.** This new program, authorized to receive $900 million in fiscal 2002, was intended to help states and districts create reading programs for children in kindergarten through third grade. States could use up to 20 percent of the money to train teachers, among other options.

● **Early Reading First.** This new program, authorized to receive $75 million in fiscal 2002, was aimed at helping children ages 3 to 5 prepare to read. Roughly 30,000 preschoolers nationwide were expected to benefit, including children in impoverished areas.

● **Even Start.** The law authorized $260 million for the program, aimed at helping young children as well as their parents develop better reading skills. The program was named after retired Rep. William F. Goodling, R-Pa. (1975-2000), former chairman of the House Education and the Workforce Committee.

School Technology

Several education technology programs were consolidated into a single technology grant program, authorized to receive $1 billion in fiscal 2002. Programs allowed under the law ranged from helping poor and rural students get computer access to training more teachers. Districts were required to use at least 25 percent of the money to help teachers become proficient in technology unless they could show that they already provided such training.

● **Ready-to-learn television.** The law continued the 1994 public television Ready to Learn program, a daily commercial-free broadcast of educational shows such as "Clifford the Big Red Dog" and "Reading Between the Lions."

Bilingual Education

The law consolidated several bilingual education programs into one, authorized to receive $750 million in fiscal 2002. Students with limited English skills had to be tested in reading and language arts in English after they attended school in the United States for three consecutive years. Some children could receive a two-year waiver, on a case-by-case basis. The new law ended a requirement that 75 percent of federal bilingual education funds be spent on programs that use a child's native language for instruction.

School Safety

The program, authorized to receive $650 million in fiscal 2002, helped states and districts improve safety and reduce drug use in schools. Activities receiving money had to be based on scientific research.

● **Hate Crimes.** The Education Department was to continue to issue grants for programs designed to prevent hate crimes.

● **21st Century Community Learning Centers.** The program, authorized to receive $1.25 billion in fiscal 2002, paid for activities before and after school. Under the new law, in addition to school districts, other community groups, including faith-based groups, could receive the funds.

● **Gun-free schools.** The law included several changes to the existing requirement that students who brought guns to school be expelled for one year. The punishment was made to apply to anyone caught with a gun at school, whether or not he was the one who brought it. It also clarified that the term "school" meant the entire school campus, any setting under the control and supervision of

the local school district. It also required that all modifications of the terms of a student's expulsion be put in writing.

● **Environmental tobacco smoke.** The law banned the use of tobacco in government facilities that house programs for children, including schools, kindergartens and day care facilities.

Flexibility

The law allowed school districts and states to transfer certain federal funds to a variety of programs that paid for their most-pressing needs, such as hiring more teachers or buying new books, in exchange for meeting certain performance goals.

● **Innovative Education Program Strategies.** The program, authorized to receive $450 million for fiscal 2002, provided block grants to states for innovative approaches to helping students learn. However, states had to send at least 85 percent of the money to districts. The law added school repair and other projects to the list of items on which the money could be spent.

● **Transferability.** Districts were allowed to transfer up to 50 percent of the money to several major education programs. However, funds could be transferred into, but not out of, the Title I program for poor and otherwise disadvantaged children. States could transfer up to 50 percent of state-activity funds to several major education programs.

● **Flexibility demonstration.** A new demonstration project would give some school districts and states even more flexibility in spending federal dollars. The law allowed 150 districts to consolidate all of their funding under major education programs in exchange for an annual Education Department review of their student performance. Money for Title I was excluded. Seven states could consolidate all their administration and state-activity funds for major education programs. Title I money was included.

Other Provisions

● **Boy Scouts.** No school or district could deny the Boy Scouts, or any other group listed as a "patriotic society," the same access to schools for after-school meetings as other outside groups.

● **Public Charter Schools.** The program, authorized to receive $300 million in fiscal 2002, helped states and local districts support charter schools. Support included money for buildings and research.

● **Fund for the Improvement of Education.** The law authorized $550 million in fiscal 2002 for projects and programs deemed to be nationally significant by the education secretary. The wide range of programs included those for character education, Reading is Fundamental book distributions to poor children, activities for gifted and talented students, foreign language lessons, physical education, arts education, and economics education. Congress also earmarked dozens of local projects in this program.

● **Rural Education.** The law authorized $300 million in 2002 for two programs. The first gave small, rural districts more latitude in spending federal money; the second provided flexible grants to rural districts with at least 20 percent of students living in poverty.

● **Indian Education.** By 2004, schools funded by the Bureau of Indian Affairs had to be be accredited or be in the process of obtaining accreditation by an approved agency, state or tribal.

● **Impact Aid.** The law made minor changes to how funds were distributed to school districts that lost tax money because they were on federal land, such as military bases and American Indian reservations. The law authorized $150 million in fiscal 2002 for school construction. The entire Impact Aid program was reauthorized in a separate law in 2000.

● **School Prayer.** The Education Department was directed to provide guidance to states, districts and the public on constitutionally protected prayer in public schools. The guide had to be revised every two years. All school districts had to prove that their local policies did not restrict such prayer or lose federal aid.

● **Military Recruitment.** Schools that received federal education funds had to provide military recruiters the same access to students allowed for college and job recruiters. ◆

Chapter 9

ENERGY & ENVIRONMENT

House Passes Bush Energy Plan

House Republicans answered President Bush's call for a new energy policy by passing a comprehensive bill in August over the objections of environmentalists and many Democrats, who complained that the measure tilted too far toward industry. But the legislation stalled in the Senate over the insistence of some Republicans that portions of Alaska's Arctic National Wildlife Refuge (ANWR) be opened to oil and natural gas drilling.

The House package grew out of recommendations for a national energy strategy issued in May by a White House energy task force headed by Vice President Dick Cheney. The recommendations, which centered on increasing production of domestic oil and gas, were incorporated into a package of four bills later combined into HR 4.

The House plan did not address electricity deregulation, which sponsors considered too complex and divisive, or extend liability protection for nuclear power plants, considered too controversial. It did include $33.5 billion in tax incentives for energy producers and consumers. (*Price-Anderson, p. 9-10*)

Aggressive lobbying by the Bush administration, some labor unions, and the oil, gas and coal industries helped get the measure through the House on Aug. 1. Democrats were unsuccessful in removing language that would open ANWR to drilling or in adding a provision to raise fuel economy standards for sport utility vehicles and other light trucks. The fuel standards issue caused alarm among many Democrats from blue-collar Midwestern states, who feared it might lead to job losses in the auto industry.

In the Senate, Alaska Republican Frank Murkowski, chairman of the Energy and Natural Resources Committee, predicted in mid-May that he would have a bill on the floor within a month. Murkowski had introduced a bill (S 388) that emphasized domestic oil and gas production. But GOP plans were thwarted when the Senate shifted to Democratic control in June.

House passage of HR 4 raised hopes among supporters that the Senate would act quickly. Initial efforts by the Energy and Natural Resources Committee were sidetracked by the Sept. 11 terrorist attacks. Then, when it became clear that a majority on the panel supported drilling in ANWR, Majority Leader Tom Daschle, D-S.D., canceled further markups. In December, Senate Democrats introduced their own comprehensive bill (S 1766), which included a ban on drilling in ANWR, and focused on renewable energy and conservation. Daschle promised a floor debate by mid-February of 2002.

Highlights

The following are highlights of the House-passed energy bill. The bill proposed to:
- **ANWR.** Open 1.5 million acres of coastal plain in Alas-

BoxScore

Bills:
HR 4, S 1766
Legislative Action:
House passed HR 4, 240-189, on Aug. 1.

ka's ANWR to oil and gas exploration.
- **Fuel economy.** Require fuel economy standards for sport-utility vehicles (SUVs) and other light trucks between the 2004 and 2010 model years that would save 5 billion gallons of gasoline compared with 2002 standards.
- **Production.** Provide incentives for more offshore oil and gas drilling and authorize increased funding for renewable energy research and clean coal programs.
- **Tax incentives.** Provide $33.5 billion over 10 years in tax credits and deductions to encourage energy production and conservation and encourage other energy-related activities.

Background

Escalating gasoline prices and an electricity shortage that produced rolling blackouts in California pushed energy issues onto the national agenda at the start of the year. For the first time since the 1970s, the public believed the country was facing a serious energy crisis.

In the past, major crises had spawned significant changes in energy policy. The 1975 Energy Policy and Conservation Act (PL 94-163) followed the Arab oil embargo. The 1979 oil shortage caused by the fall of the Shah of Iran helped President Jimmy Carter persuade Congress to enact conservation and emergency rationing programs (PL 96-102, PL 96-126). High oil prices after Iraq invaded Kuwait helped drive the 1992 energy bill (PL 102-486), the last major piece of comprehensive energy legislation to be signed into law. (*1975 Almanac, p. 220; 1979 Almanac, p. 606; 1992 Almanac, p. 231*)

Even before the latest energy crisis captured public attention, Bush had pledged during his presidential campaign to develop a comprehensive national energy policy. Shortly after entering office, he established the National Energy Policy Development Group charged with putting together a national energy strategy. Chaired by Cheney, the group issued over 100 recommendations May 17. Warning of "the most serious energy shortage since the oil embargoes of the 1970s," the task force emphasized increased production, while also offering some proposals to reduce energy demand. On June 28, Bush sent Congress a plan for a comprehensive energy bill that filled in some of the details of the Cheney report.

Republicans hoped to drive that plan, or something close to it, to enactment. But falling gasoline prices and stabilization of electricity supplies on the West Coast reduced the sense of crisis, and old disputes stymied progress on the bill.

Republicans argued that increasing domestic production of oil and gas was a national security issue. With 56 percent of the nation's oil coming from imports, they warned, a future reduction of supplies from the Middle East could trigger another conflict like the Persian Gulf War.

Democrats generally maintained that greater energy independence lay in conservation, not more drilling. They stressed renewable energy sources, and vowed to fight to keep oil companies out of such environmentally sensitive areas such as Alaska's ANWR. Democrats cast their GOP opponents as champions of large oil, gas and coal companies.

The intense rhetoric and emotions buried the fact that the two parties had broad agreement on many of the issues, including tax incentives for energy production and conservation, research on cleaner-burning coal, pipeline safety and fuel assistance for low-income people.

Drilling in ANWR

The Arctic refuge was what Murkowski called the "lightning rod" for the debate between the parties on energy — and a potent fundraising issue for both sides. Bush proposed exploration and drilling on a coastal plain that covered 1.5 million acres of the 19 million acre refuge. The U.S. Geological Survey estimated that the area harbored 5.7 billion to 16 billion barrels of oil.

The issue had divided lawmakers and pitted environmentalists against oil companies and Alaskan officials for more than 40 years. The refuge was set aside in 1960, after years of fighting between oil companies and environmentalists. In 1980, Congress passed a law (PL 96-487) that put most of the refuge off-limits but left it up to future Congresses to decide the fate of the coastal plain. (*1980 Almanac, p. 575*)

The Interior Department sought to open the land for drilling in 1987, during the Reagan administration, provoking an outcry from environmentalists and a rebuff from Congress. In 1991, after the Persian Gulf War, a provision to allow drilling was included in an energy bill, but it was dropped after a filibuster. (*1991 Almanac, p. 195*)

When Republicans took control of Congress in 1995, they tried to open ANWR to exploration as part of a budget reconciliation bill. President Bill Clinton cited that provision when he vetoed the bill. (*1995 Almanac, p. 5-22*)

The stakes were high for all sides. For Alaska residents, drilling in the federal refuge meant money. With neither a sales tax nor an income tax, the state got two-thirds of its revenue from oil royalties. Much of the remaining royalties went into a permanent fund that paid each Alaskan man, woman and child an annual dividend that approached $1,900 in 2001. Under existing law, Alaska stood to receive 90 percent of the royalties and other revenue from development of ANWR — $200 million to $2.5 billion annually, according to the Congressional Research Service.

For Bush and many Republicans, developing the swath of treeless wilderness along the Barents Sea was the linchpin of a strategy they said was essential to wean the United States from its dependence on foreign oil. Proponents of drilling also said new computer-based exploration technologies significantly improved the probability of hitting oil while minimizing environmental disruptions.

Democrats and environmental lobbyists said the coastal plain was tantamount to sacred ground, serving as an important birthing place for caribou, a feeding ground for snow geese and a den site for polar bears. Opening the area permanently would alter it, they argued, no matter how carefully it was done. In the fragile permafrost, a lone tractor passing in winter could damage the landscape for decades. Crit-

ics also said it would take about 10 years to begin piping oil from the refuge.

Environmentalists said they had public opinion on their side. An Associated Press poll released Feb. 1 found that 53 percent of those polled opposed opening the refuge to oil exploration, compared with 33 percent in favor. The rest were undecided.

Fuel Economy Standards

The dispute over fuel standards had a long history, as well. Under existing Corporate Average Fuel Economy (CAFE) standards, each manufacturer's fleet of passenger cars had to average at least 27.5 miles per gallon, while light truck fleets — the popular SUVs, minivans and pickups— had to meet a 20.7 mpg standard. Automakers lobbied aggressively against an increase, saying it would force them to produce fewer of the vehicles American consumers were purchasing and more of those that were in lower demand. Instead, they urged Congress to provide tax incentives for technology that would improve fuel efficiency. The Cheney task force called for about $4 billion in tax credits for buyers of hybrid gas/electric or fuel cell cars.

CAFE standards had been introduced in 1975 and had remained virtually unchanged since 1985. Between 1995 and 1999, House Majority Whip Tom DeLay, R-Texas, led a group of Republicans who inserted language in the annual transportation appropriations bill to block even a study of new standards on the assumption that a study would lead to tougher restrictions. In 2000, under pressure from the Senate, House negotiators accepted provisions in the fiscal 2001 transportation spending law (PL 106-346) that required a study by the National Academy of Sciences to evaluate the effectiveness and impact of CAFE standards. (*2000 Almanac, p. 2-128*)

The National Academy of Sciences issued its report July 31, 2001. While making no specific recommendations about increasing CAFE standards, it said higher fuel economy could be achieved "without degradation of safety." The White House supported "increasing automobile fuel economy" but asked Congress to leave the Transportation Department free to determine how best to accomplish that. The fiscal 2002 transportation law (PL 107-87) did not seek to block new standards. (*Appropriations, p. 2-43*)

Legislative Action

Four House committees approved major pieces of the GOP energy plan the week of July 16. The committees were Energy and Commerce, Ways and Means, Resources and Science. As part of their sales strategy, Cheney and members of Bush's Cabinet joined congressional Republicans in town hall meetings across the country during the week to stress what they said was a balanced approach on energy.

House Energy and Commerce Subcommittee

The main bill in the package began in the Energy and Commerce Subcommittee on Energy and Air Quality, which approved the draft, 29-1, on July 12.

Energy Secretary Spencer Abraham and other administration officials worked closely with the subcommittee's majority and minority staff to write the provisions.

The measure disappointed some Republicans, who said it left out important features, such as deregulating the electric utility industry. "The bill before us is not the heavy lifting we need to do — these are easy, short-term solutions," said Steve Largent, R-Okla.

The bill called for:

• Fuel economy standards for SUVs and other light trucks between the 2004 and 2010 model years that would save a total of 5 billion gallons of gasoline compared with the 2002 standards.

• A National Academy of Sciences study of alternatives to the existing CAFE system. The bill did not propose to change existing CAFE standards..

• A joint study by the EPA and Energy Department of federal, state and local pollution requirements for motor fuels that could lead to regional or national specifications.

• Off-budget protection for the $10 billion Nuclear Waste Fund. Established in 1982 (PL 97-425), the fund collected fees from utilities to finance construction of a storage site for spent nuclear fuel. The fund, fed by a surcharge on consumers of nuclear power, would be reserved for developing a nuclear waste repository. (*1982 Almanac, p. 304*)

• Accelerated programs for producing electric power using "clean coal" methods. The draft also proposed tax credits for emission reductions and efficiency improvements in existing coal-fired electric power plants.

• A requirement for the EPA to develop a rule for switching to reformulated gasoline in summertime to help combat ozone depletion.

• Mandatory efficiency requirements for federal buildings, requiring them to consume 35 percent less energy in 2010 than they did in 1985.

• Expanded grants to states for weatherizing homes to make them more energy-efficient. The grants would total $500 million by 2005.

• Authorization for $3.4 billion a year through fiscal 2005 for home heating aid to low-income residents.

Edward J. Markey, D-Mass., offered an amendment to increase the CAFE standard for all vehicles to 40 mpg by 2016, but withdrew it when it became clear he lacked enough votes. The proposal to have the National Academy of Sciences study possible alternatives to the CAFE system was offered by Joe L. Barton, R-Texas, and adopted by voice vote.

The fuel requirement for SUVs and other light trucks was written by Barton and committee Chairman Billy Tauzin, R-La., after extensive negotiations with John D. Dingell of Michigan, the panel's ranking Democrat and the key congressional supporter of the automobile industry. It was adopted, 29-3.

Supporters said the savings could equal taking all new SUVs and minivans off the road for two years. The auto industry opposed the amendment, however, and Dingell said it was "the limit of what I can support." Democrats and even some Republican supporters of the provision said it would have a negligible effect, increasing fuel efficiency by only around 1 mpg, or less than what several major automakers had already volunteered to attain.

The subcommittee also:

• Rejected, 12-19, a Markey amendment to mandate a higher efficiency standard for air conditioners proposed in a final rule by the Clinton administration in January but rejected by the Bush administration.

• Rejected, 13-17, a Markey amendment to set a 1-watt maximum standard for household appliances and other devices that used electricity while operating in standby mode.

• Approved, 11-4, an amendment by Ed Bryant, R-Tenn., to eliminate a phase-in period for a new rule to clean diesel sulfur from gasoline. The proposal was made at the request of convenience stores, which wanted to avoid having to carry two types of fuel during the phase-in. The amendment was opposed by a diverse coalition that included the Bush administration, environmentalists and the auto industry, which warned that any change could lead to delays in implementing the rule.

House Energy and Commerce Committee

The full Energy and Commerce Committee approved the bill (HR 2587 — H Rept 107-162, Parts 1,2) by a vote of 50-5 on July 19 without substantial changes to the subcommittee draft. More than two dozen amendments were adopted, but most were non-controversial and approved by voice vote.

Barton and Tauzin succeeded in ensuring that the most heavily debated provision in the bill remained intact — the requirement that SUVs and other light trucks save at least 5 billion gallons of gasoline by 2010. The committee rejected, 11-43, a proposal by Markey to increase the fuel-economy standard for passenger cars to 37.5 mpg and light trucks to 29 mpg by 2011. It later rejected, 7-47, an amendment by Henry A. Waxman, D-Calif., that would have reinstated the 40 mpg requirement by 2016.

Tauzin argued that the bill's fuel economy language represented a "historic achievement" on a matter that lawmakers had not addressed in more than a decade. He said Markey's amendment was "much too dramatic an increase, particularly in a CAFE system that's flawed."

The committee also:

• Adopted by voice vote Markey's proposal to set standards for household appliances that operate in standby modes.

• Rejected, 24-31, Markey's proposal to increase air conditioner efficiency ratings.

• Rejected, 23-28, a Markey proposal to set standards for certain appliances and commercial products, such as traffic signals and lights, not covered by efficiency standards.

• Agreed, 31-20, to restore the phase-in period for implementing the diesel sulfur rule. The amendment, by Democrats Diana DeGette of Colorado and Gene Green of Texas, reversed the subcommittee decision.

• Rejected, 22-33, an effort by California lawmakers to allow an exemption from certain clean-air requirements, as long as the states continued to meet federal clean-air standards. The administration in June had denied California a waiver from provisions of the Clean Air Act (PL 101-549) aimed at reducing emissions by requiring more oxygen in gasoline. The most popular additive, methyl tertiary butyl ether (MTBE), was thought to be polluting drinking water supplies. The amendment, by Waxman and Christopher Cox, R-Calif., was intended to ban MTBE without requiring that refiners add ethanol — an oxygenated additive derived from corn — to gasoline. It would have allowed states to petition the EPA to waive oxygenate requirements and given the agency 270 days to rule. The debate followed regional

rather than party lines, with Californians and lawmakers from states with MTBE pollution supporting the amendment and Midwestern lawmakers opposed.

California lawmakers lost several other attempts to rewrite the bill to address their state's electricity problems. The committee rejected, 17-31, a proposal by Democrat Jane Harman and other Californians that would have required the Federal Energy Regulatory Commission (FERC) to take stronger steps to order refunds for consumers who believed they had been overcharged by electricity companies.

House Resources Committee

On July 17, the House Resources Committee approved a bill (HR 2436 — H Rept 107-160, Part 1) to open up more federal lands to oil and gas exploration. The vote was 26-17. The six-hour markup was dominated by debate over ANWR, which Markey labeled "the No. 1 environmental issue of the entire Congress."

The bill contained provisions to:
• Open ANWR's coastal plain to oil and gas leasing.
• Expedite reviews of barriers to additional onshore oil and gas leases.
• Require government officials to explain in detail the reasons for denying oil and gas leases.
• Provide financial incentives for offshore drilling in the central and western Gulf of Mexico.
• Require a study of whether new pipelines could be laid in existing rights-of-way across federal lands.
• Require a federal inventory of the coal, geothermal, wind and solar power potential on all federal lands except parks and wilderness areas.
• Provide greater flexibility for oil companies to pay federal royalties with oil rather than cash.
• Expedite federal action on geothermal energy leases.

The committee defeated, 19-30, an attempt by Markey to strike the ANWR section of the bill. The committee also rejected, 21-30, a Democratic alternative by Nick J. Rahall II of West Virginia that did not include permission to drill in ANWR.

House Ways and Means Committee

On July 18, the Ways and Means Committee approved $33.5 billion in energy tax breaks through 2011. The bill (HR 2511 — H Rept 107-157), approved 24-17, combined tax incentives for energy conservation favored by members of both parties in Congress, with tax benefits for oil and gas producers to encourage exploration and distribution. Of the total, almost $12.6 billion in tax breaks was devoted to conservation, $13 billion to improving the reliability of the nation's energy supply and $8 billion to energy producers. The main elements were:
• $3.3 billion in tax credits for investing in or producing electricity with "clean coal" technology.
• $2.8 billion to extend a tax credit for companies producing fuel from non-traditional sources, including shale, tar sands and biomass.
• $2.1 billion in tax credits for purchasers of fuel cell, hybrid and other low-emission vehicles.
• $1.6 billion to provide a 20 percent credit of up to $2,000 for energy-efficient home improvements.
• $992 million to phase out the 4.3-cents-per-gallon excise tax on diesel fuel used in trains and barges that operate in inland waterways.
• $958 million to allow businesses to deduct oil and gas exploration expenses.
• $292 million in credits for appliance manufacturers for energy-efficient refrigerators and clothes washers.
• $125 million in tax credits to homeowners who purchased solar energy systems and heaters. The credit would not apply to systems for heating swimming pools or hot tubs.

The bill's $33.5 billion price tag raised concerns. "We will have to wait until the endgame to see just how much more in tax cuts we can do," said Jim McCrery, R-La. "We have a long way to go before any energy tax proposals get to the president's desk." Mark Weinberger, assistant Treasury secretary for tax policy, hesitated to endorse the measure and said the administration would wait until the summer's economic review to weigh into the debate.

Committee Democrats, who voted unanimously against the bill, argued that its 10-year cost would force the government to divert some Medicare and Social Security trust fund surpluses from debt reduction to general operations. "I don't think we can afford the proposals before us," said Earl Pomeroy, D-N.D.

The committee rejected, 15-25, a proposal by Charles B. Rangel of New York, the panel's top Democrat, to generate $33.8 billion in revenue by increasing the top income tax rate by eight-tenths of 1 percentage point in 2002-2003 and nine-tenths of 1 percentage point in 2004-2010. The panel also rejected, 17-23, an amendment by Karen L. Thurman, D-Fla., to retract the energy tax cuts if budget projections showed that the surplus outside the trust funds had evaporated.

The votes belied the fact that many Democrats and Republicans found common ground in the tax cuts. The measure dovetailed with Democrats' environmental priorities, for example, by proposing to help individuals buy solar water heaters and hybrid vehicles, and allow homeowners to claim credit for making energy-efficient home improvements.

Lloyd Doggett, D-Texas, however, complained that the bill would give generous tax subsidies to coal, oil, gas and nuclear producers that "have expressed great concern about being left out" of the recently enacted $1.35 trillion tax cut.

Environmental groups echoed that sentiment. "This tax credit is an incredible ripoff of taxpayers and directly subsidizes environmental destruction," said Sean Moulton, spokesman for Friends of the Earth. Republicans pointed out that the committee designed the tax breaks for small, independent energy producers.

House Science Committee

The House Science Committee approved the last piece of the package by voice vote July 18. The bill (HR 2460 — H Rept 107-177) proposed authorizing $6 billion in fiscal 2002 for an array of programs on renewable energy, conservation and nuclear power. The authorizations included:
• $200 million for grants to develop commercial applications for alternative-fuel vehicles.
• $2.1 billion over three years for energy conservation.
• $490 million over three years for global climate change programs.
• $1.7 billion over three years for renewable energy.
• $690 million over three years for nuclear energy.

- $2.5 billion over 10 years for coal technology.
- $742 million over three years for oil and gas research and development.
- $655 million in fiscal 2002-03 for a magnetic fusion burning plasma experiment and a fusion energy sciences program.
- $276.3 million for fiscal 2002 and declining amounts through fiscal 2006 for the Spallation Neutron Source project at Oak Ridge National Laboratory in Tennessee.

The panel rejected, 18-20, an amendment by Lynn Woolsey, D-Calif., to decrease the authorization for Department of Energy nuclear programs, including a report on new reactor technology.

The committee adopted, by voice vote, an amendment by Chairman Sherwood Boehlert, R-N.Y., and ranking Democrat Ralph M. Hall of Texas, to authorize Bush's proposal to spend $2 billion on "clean coal" technology over the next decade while attaching environmental requirements. By 2020, coal-fired power plants would have to remove 99 percent of sulfur dioxide and 95 percent of mercury and allow no more than 0.05 pounds of nitrogen oxides per million BTU generated. The proposed standards did not mention carbon dioxide, a greenhouse gas and major source of power-plant pollution.

"Coal will be and continues to be a part of a national energy policy," said Jerry F. Costello, D-Ill., who sponsored the fossil fuel title of the bill.

The legislation also called for a new research program on oil and natural gas drilling in deep water, including the Gulf of Mexico. Hall said the program "will make it possible to bring extraordinarily large volumes of natural gas on shore for delivery to gas-deprived markets."

House Floor Action

The House passed the GOP energy plan — assembled into a single package (HR 4) by the leadership — by a vote of 240-189 on Aug. 1. Aggressive lobbying by the administration, labor unions, and the oil, gas and coal industries helped keep Bush's plan intact through the acrimonious daylong debate. Lawmakers rejected a significant increase in fuel economy standards for SUVs and other light trucks as well as an attempt to block oil and gas exploration in ANWR. (*House vote 320, p. H-110*)

"I expect there to be an historic conference between the House and Senate," said Markey, a sponsor of both the rejected amendments. "We're going to see one of the most contentious conferences we've seen in a generation."

The administration, however, was pleased. "A lot of the pundits said we'll never get an energy bill out of the Congress, and we had, I thought, a surprisingly strong vote over here last night for a good, sound, solid, comprehensive, long-term energy plan," said Cheney.

In addition to lobbying undecided House members, Cheney and other Republicans turned to the International Brotherhood of Teamsters and other unions to help them argue that increased oil, gas and coal production on public lands would create jobs. Opponents of higher CAFE standards enlisted the United Auto Workers to reinforce their contention that requiring more fuel efficiency from popular SUVs would hurt sales by the auto industry and cost jobs.

Environmental groups also lobbied intensively, particu-

larly to prevent oil exploration in ANWR, a fight they thought they could win in the House.

The House-passed bill contained no substantive changes from the package of legislation that emerged from the Energy and Commerce, Ways and Means, Resources and Science committees in July. As part of the rule for floor debate, however, the House adopted an amendment by Jim Gibbons, R-Nev., to strike language that would have taken the $10 billion Nuclear Waste Fund off budget and made it a dedicated funding source for a future nuclear waste repository. The administration had joined House appropriators in objecting to the provision.

- **Taxes.** Lawmakers made no changes to the $33.5 billion in proposed energy tax incentives, despite a statement from the White House Office of Management and Budget that some of the tax language "significantly exceeds the president's budget and sets unrealistic targets for future programmatic funding decisions."

The House rejected, 206-223, a motion by Thurman to recommit the bill to the Ways and Means Committee. Thurman and other Democrats wanted to make the tax provisions contingent on a surplus in the non-Social Security and non-Medicare portions of the federal budget. Charles W. Stenholm of Texas, a leader of the conservative "Blue Dog" Democrats, said the tax language made the bill "fiscally irresponsible." (*House vote 319, p. H-110*)

- **ANWR.** The House rejected, 206-223, an attempt by Markey and Nancy L. Johnson, R-Conn., to drop language in the bill opening portions of ANWR to drilling. (*House vote 317, p. H-108*)

Drilling proponents focused the debate on the potential economic benefits. The Teamsters ran a series of radio advertisements saying that opening the refuge to oil and gas exploration would create as many as 750,000 jobs — a figure environmentalists immediately disputed as overblown. Jack Quinn, R-N.Y., a moderate with close ties to organized labor, said that argument helped persuade him to vote against Markey's amendment.

All of the Texas delegation's 13 Republicans and eight of its 17 Democrats voted against Markey.

Despite lobbying by environmental groups, some lawmakers dismissed arguments about the potential ecological harm to the refuge. "You can't always cave in to the environmental wackos," said moderate Peter T. King, R-N.Y. "I'm not against conservation, but there's no reason why we can't walk and chew gum at the same time."

To win over others who were concerned about the possible environmental effects, GOP leaders encouraged lawmakers to support two amendments by John E. Sununu, R-N.H., and Heather A. Wilson, R-N.M.

The first, adopted 241-186, proposed to split future oil and gas royalties from ANWR evenly between the state of Alaska and the federal government. The federal government's share would be divided between a fund for renewable energy research and another for maintaining and improving the condition of federal lands. (*House vote 315, p. H-108*)

The second amendment, adopted 228-201, specified that the maximum surface area devoted to oil production facilities at the refuge, including airstrips, could not exceed 2,000 acres. Critics said it would be impossible to limit the environmental effects to such a small area and suggested the ac-

tual impact would cover hundreds of thousands of acres. "This is a very clever, well-crafted attempt to give people cover to say they oppose drilling when they do not," said Boehlert. (House vote 316, p. H-108)

● **Fuel-economy standards.** The House rejected, 160-269, the amendment by Boehlert and Markey to increase combined CAFE standards for cars and light trucks, including SUVs, to 26 mpg for model years 2005 and 2006, and 27.5 mpg, the same as for cars, in model year 2007 and beyond. (House vote 311, p. H-108)

Boehlert met strong objections from lawmakers who said stricter fuel economy would result in lighter, more dangerous cars. "We need to ask ourselves, how many new fatalities are we willing to accept in exchange for increased fuel miles?" DeLay asked. In the end, Boehlert failed to make inroads among Democrats from blue-collar Midwestern states. Eighty-six Democrats joined 182 Republicans in voting against his amendment, including Minority Leader Richard A. Gephardt, D-Mo., and Minority Whip David E. Bonior, D-Mich.

● **Other amendments.** In other action, the House:

• Adopted, 281-148, a multipart manager's amendment by Tauzin making technical changes and authorizing studies, including the feasibility of using federal excise taxes on gasoline to promote cleaner-burning fuel. (House vote 309, p. H-106)

• Adopted, 411-15, an amendment by Mary Bono, R-Calif., authorizing $10 million a year for fiscal years 2002 through 2006 for a partnership program between the Department of Energy, the EPA and private industry to promote renewable energy products. (House vote 310, p. H-108)

• Rejected, 154-275, a proposal by Green to authorize FERC to regulate natural-gas pipelines that operated only within California. The pipelines were exempt from federal control under a 1954 provision called the "Hinshaw exemption." (House vote 312, p. H-108)

• Rejected, 125-300, an amendment by Waxman and Cox to give California a waiver from federal requirements to use cleaner-burning gasoline (reformulated fuel with at least 2 percent oxygen) if the state could meet federal clean air standards without it. (House vote 313, p. H-108)

• Rejected, 154-274, a proposal by Waxman that FERC be required to limit wholesale electricity rates in the Western United States to rates based on the cost of service for 18 months. The limits would not apply to power plants coming on line after Jan. 1, 2001. (House vote 314, p. H-108)

Senate Energy Bills

Working with a number of Senate Republicans, Murkowski introduced a comprehensive energy bill (S 388) on Feb. 26 aimed at reducing U.S. dependence on foreign oil to 50 percent by 2010. The bill focused on promoting development of coal, oil and natural gas resources and nuclear power. A companion bill (S 389) called for an array of tax incentives for energy producers. Democrats followed March 22 with their own pair of bills (S 597, S 596) emphasizing energy conservation.

The Energy and Natural Resources Committee held hearings, but before it got to the markup stage, the Senate had changed hands, and Jeff Bingaman, D-N.M., had taken over as committee chairman. Bingaman said repeatedly that

he wanted a bill built on proposals that had broad support. His draft focused on electricity instead of oil, and conservation instead of drilling. On Aug. 2, the committee approved some relatively non-controversial provisions aimed at increasing energy research and development.

During the August recess, Bingaman's aides met with environmentalists, energy industry lobbyists and Republicans to try to develop a consensus bill.

They decided to avoid the two most contentious issues in the House bill: opening ANWR to oil and gas drilling and increasing fuel efficiency standards for SUVs and other light trucks. As an alternative to ANWR, Bingaman included language to make it easier to build a $20 billion, 2,000-mile pipeline from Alaska's North Slope to the lower 48 states. The House-passed energy bill included similar language. The question of fuel economy standards was left to the Commerce Committee.

The main focus of Bingaman's bill was electricity. "We face a crucial turning point," he said, noting that electric utilities would invest billions of dollars in new power lines and transmission facilities in the next few years to upgrade a system operating largely on a century-old design. "Will we put in place a structure to maximize the chances that investments will go to new technologies that will give consumers real choices over their energy use? Or will Congress, by its inaction, perpetuate obsolete frameworks for managing electricity markets with the result that we wind up with little improvement from the status quo?"

Walking a narrow line in an attempt to build a bill with bipartisan support, Bingaman included provisions to:

• Reauthorize the Price-Anderson Act, a top priority for the nuclear utility industry and many Republicans. The act indemnified utilities against costly nuclear accidents, something industry officials said was essential to ensuring that new power plants were built. The House put the reauthorization in a separate bill (HR 2983). (Nuclear liability, p. 9-10)

• Expand FERC's authority to include investor-owned utilities, municipal utilities and rural electric cooperatives that were outside its jurisdiction. Bingaman proposed to strengthen FERC's jurisdiction over utility mergers, and authorize the agency to establish and enforce mandatory power-grid reliability standards in conjunction with the industry's voluntary reliability group and regional transmission organizations that FERC was requiring to come on line in December.

• Allow those regional transmission organizations that could obtain approval for siting a transmission line to seek eminent-domain authority from FERC — a position Bingaman aides said tried to strike a balance between federal and state control. One of the biggest debates over electricity was whether the federal government should have the right to seize private property through the power of eminent domain in order to make room for new power lines. FERC already had such authority in siting natural gas pipelines. Republicans said the matter was best left up to states.

• Give FERC more authority to address "market power," the clout that established utilities could wield to control markets and forestall competition. The bill would enable FERC to order power generators found to be committing market-power abuses to submit mitigation plans.

• Repeal the Public Utility Holding Company Act

(PUHCA), enacted in 1935 to halt abuses by electricity and gas holding companies. Utilities wanted the law repealed so they could diversify and do business outside their franchise areas.

• Set up a "public benefits fund," with fees on electricity sales to support energy efficiency programs, renewable energy development and low-income energy assistance.

• Require electric utilities to increase the amount of renewable sources — such as solar, wind and hydroelectric power — used at plants going into service after 2001.

Although momentum for an energy bill was flagging, Bingaman pressed ahead. Gasoline prices were falling, and the West Coast appeared to have plenty of power. Government budget forecasts in late August showed little money available to pay for energy tax incentives and other initiatives. "We've got two problems: We've got a loss of momentum, and we've got no dollars," said Charles E. Schumer, D-N.Y., a member of the Energy and Natural Resources Committee. "It's going to be much harder to address energy now." Bingaman acknowledged that tax incentives were in trouble unless budget offsets could be found, but he said the bill pending before his committee offered "a great opportunity to be visionary about the future of electricity."

Senate leaders agreed to try to bring the legislation to the floor in October, as sought by the Bush administration. "I urge the Congress to pass an energy package," Bush told reporters Sept. 6. "That's a job-creation package. That's part of economic growth."

Though additional work on the bill was put off after the Sept. 11 attacks, Bingaman had markups scheduled for the week of Oct. 8.

Democrats Cancel Markup

Before the Energy and Natural Resources Committee could mark up the bill, however, Daschle intervened. On Oct. 9, Bingaman announced that committee work on the legislation was suspended and that further action would be left to the Democratic leadership. Lawmakers on both sides said if the markup had taken place, Democrats probably would have lost on a number of sensitive issues, including proposals to allow drilling in ANWR.

Democrats said their first duty was to complete work on measures that were critical to national security or the federal budget. Majority Whip Harry Reid of Nevada said Oct. 10 that Democrats would "do our best," but finding the time to

finish the measure "would be very difficult."

On Nov. 27, Daschle announced he would schedule a full debate on energy legislation by mid-February of 2002. The debate would start with a Democratic bill.

Murkowski, however, refused to give up, insisting that he had enough votes in committee to approve ANWR drilling. "The thing I really object to," he said Dec. 6, "is the way the Democratic leadership high-handedly refuses to let us go through the committee process. It's a flagrant abuse of the system, intended to bypass public opinion." But polls showed that a majority of Americans opposed drilling in the refuge, and Senate Republicans were not united on the issue.

Republicans tried to add the ANWR drilling proposal to an unrelated bill (HR 10), but their amendment also included a six-month moratorium on human cloning. Republican leaders apparently believed it would be politically perilous for Democrats to vote against both sensitive proposals. Rank-and-file Republicans revolted, refusing to support the amendment. By Dec. 3, GOP leaders were advising their members to vote against cutting off debate on their own amendment so that they could label the vote "meaningless." Murkowski continued to insist that he had the support of about 54 senators for ANWR drilling. But he, too, voted against a motion to protect the amendment from a filibuster. The tally was 1-94. (*Senate vote 344, p. S-72*)

On Dec. 5, Senate Democratic leaders introduced their revised energy bill (S 1766), which emphasized alternative energy and conservation. "They've completely ignored harsh realities in favor of their distant dreams," charged House Resources Committee Chairman James V. Hansen, R-Utah.

The bill included a requirement that 10 percent of the nation's electricity come from renewable sources by 2020, compared with 2 percent in 2001. It encouraged drilling on federal lands that were already open to oil and gas development, and it called for up to $10 billion in federal loan guarantees for a natural gas pipeline from Alaska to the lower 48 states. Many provisions were similar to Bingaman's earlier bill, although the new measure had broader provisions on electricity and added protection for energy infrastructure.

The bill left the issue of higher mileage standards to the Commerce, Science and Transportation Committee. The Finance Committee was expected to fashion energy tax incentives. ◆

House OKs Nuclear Liability Limit

The House on Nov. 27 passed a 15-year extension of a law limiting the liability of nuclear power plants. Senate leaders, however, refused to take up the bill. Senate Majority Whip Harry Reid, D-Nev., strongly opposed the measure out of concern that it might lead to more high-level nuclear waste, which the government was planning to store in Nevada's Yucca Mountain.

The bill (HR 2983) sought to extend the 1954 Price-Anderson Act through 2017. The act permanently limited the liability of owners of existing nuclear reactors in case of a catastrophic accident. But the law was set to expire in August 2002, and without an extension, reactors built after that would not be covered.

Congressional debate centered on whether the government should continue to shield the nuclear power industry from liability. The Price-Anderson Act — part of the Atomic Energy Act (PL 83-703) — was designed to protect an industry in its infancy and help it to compete better with coal-fired and hydro power plants. (*1954 Almanac, p. 534*)

Under Price-Anderson protections, last reauthorized in 1988 (PL 100-408), the entire industry's liability was capped at $9.4 billion. If an accident occurred, the federal government would be responsible for damages above the cap. Each operator was required to carry as much commercial insurance as it could get for its own facility — about $200 million for each reactor, per incident, through the Hartford, Conn.-based American Nuclear Insurers — and contribute an additional $88 million to an insurance pool. (*1988 Almanac, p. 169*)

The law had never been tested. Damages from the nuclear power industry's worst accident, at Pennsylvania's Three Mile Island in 1979, did not exceed that year's cap.

Companies such as Exelon Nuclear, General Electric Co., Westinghouse Electric Co. and General Atomics, which were eager to develop new types of nuclear reactors, lobbied hard for a renewal. Utility companies said that without the liability cap, insurers might refuse to provide coverage, jeopardizing the nuclear power industry. Some also expressed concern that if the law lapsed, the congressional climate could shift so that one day the industry might lose its protection.

Environmentalists, on the other hand, argued that Congress should avoid extending legal protection for nuclear producers, especially in light of the increased fear of disasters after the Sept. 11 terrorist attacks. Some public interest groups and environmental lobbyists said the measure was a potential giveaway of federal taxpayer dollars to a dangerous industry. Rep. Edward J. Markey, D-Mass., a leading critic of the nuclear industry, argued that it should have to compete on its own without a federal subsidy.

The Bush administration supported the extension as part of its comprehensive energy plan. (*Energy policy, p. 9-3*)

BoxScore

Bill:

HR 2983

Legislative Action:

House passed HR 2983 (H Rept 107-299, Part 1) by voice vote Nov. 27.

Legislative Action

House Committee Action

The Energy and Commerce Committee approved the bill (H Rept 107-299, Part 1) by voice vote Oct. 31, after ranking Democrat John D. Dingell of Michigan reached a deal with Republicans requiring more accountability from Department of Energy contractors.

The bill had started in the Energy and Air Quality Subcommittee, where Chairman Joe L. Barton, R-Texas, won voice vote approval for it Oct. 4. But full committee consideration was delayed while Chairman Billy Tauzin, R-La., sought a compromise with Dingell. Dingell wanted to require accountability from negligent contractors at Energy Department nuclear facilities, who under Price-Anderson were shielded from liability. Dingell said that without the change, the bill was "an enticement and incentive to misconduct."

The Tauzin-Dingell compromise, adopted by voice vote, stripped liability protection for contractors who engaged in "intentional misconduct" and allowed the attorney general to recover all profits derived from the contract.

The committee also gave voice vote approval to amendments by:

• Ted Strickland, D-Ohio, to require Energy Department contractors to meet health and safety standards similar to those for federal workers.

• Charlie Norwood, R-Ga., to change the definition of a single reactor site from one that produced less than 950 megawatts to one that produced less than 1,300 megawatts. The change benefited next-generation gas turbine or pebble bed nuclear reactors by allowing several small reactors on a single site to count as one, thereby allowing for the purchase of a single insurance policy.

• Henry A. Waxman, D-Calif., to require the Nuclear Regulatory Commission (NRC) to consult with the director of homeland security about whether any proposed nuclear plant could create a health risk if terrorists attacked it.

• Markey, to require the NRC to increase security for the transportation of nuclear waste. The White House also would have to assess and issue regulations to address the threats facing nuclear facilities.

The committee rejected, 5-30, an amendment by Markey that would have denied Price-Anderson coverage to new plants unless the producers could show they had tried and failed to obtain private coverage. Markey also said there should be stronger security requirements for nuclear reactors.

House Floor Action

The House passed the bill by voice vote Nov. 27 under suspension of the rules, a procedure that allows no amendments and is generally reserved for legislation with broad support. ◆

Congress Clears Brownfields Bill

A bill to increase funding for the cleanup and redevelopment of polluted industrial sites known as brownfields cleared shortly before Congress adjourned for the year. The bill, which also extended superfund liability protection for small businesses and landowners, was signed into law Jan. 11, 2002 (HR 2869 — PL 107-118).

Brownfields legislation was one of President Bush's top environmental priorities, and with wide support in both the House and Senate, passage had seemed ensured. But the bill ran into several obstacles, including disagreements over the proper role of the Environmental Protection Agency (EPA), concern about wages for workers at the cleanup sites and the crowded post-Sept. 11 legislative agenda. Through deal making and administration pressure, the bill finally cleared Dec. 20.

The bill combined two measures: S 350, passed by the Senate in April, and HR 1831, passed by the House in May. The Senate bill provided grants to states to study and clean up contaminated urban brownfields sites. The House bill provided protection from liability under the superfund hazardous-waste law to small businesses and others responsible for small amounts of contamination. The final bill also guaranteed that workers on brownfields projects would receive the prevailing wage in the area, usually the union wage.

Highlights

The following are major provisions of the new law:
- **Brownfields grants**. The law provided a total of $1.25 billion for fiscal years 2002 through 2006 — $150 million a year for grants to states to assess sites for cleanup and $50 million a year for grants to clean up the sites. An additional $50 million was targeted for cleaning up sites contaminated with petroleum.
- **EPA limitations**. The law limited the EPA's authority to re-evaluate and reopen a site that had been declared clean. The EPA could take additional actions if a state requested federal help, if contamination had or would migrate across state lines or onto federal property, if a release of toxins posed a danger to public health or the environment, or if new information concerning contamination levels emerged.

The EPA could not designate a moderately polluted waste site as a superfund site as long as the state or another party was actively engaged in cleaning it up. It could do so after one year if the state was not making reasonable progress on the cleanup or a cleanup agreement had not been reached.
- **Jurisdiction**. The president and the EPA were responsible for determining the distribution of the grants, although the

BoxScore

Bill:
HR 2869 — PL 107-118
Legislative Action:
Senate passed S 350 (S Rept 107-2), 99-0, on April 25.
House passed HR 1831 (H Rept 107-70, Parts 1, 2), 419-0, on May 22.
House passed HR 2869 by voice vote Dec. 20.
Senate cleared the bill by voice vote Dec. 20.
President signed Jan. 11, 2002.

law required that funds be available for sites where there was a threat to minority communities or public health. State governments had jurisdiction over projects, unless a site crossed state lines or state-federal property lines. The EPA would have jurisdiction in those cases, and it could take over a brownfields cleanup if there was a significant risk to public health or the environment, particularly when the state was unaware of what led to the contamination. The EPA had to consult with state authorities before taking over a project.
- **State lists.** States were required to maintain and annually update public lists with the name and location of waste sites at which cleanup activities had been completed under state response programs, as well as sites where future response actions were planned.
- **Superfund liability exemptions.** The new law exempted from liability under the superfund hazardous waste law businesses that were responsible for less than 110 pounds of liquid waste or 200 pounds of solid waste. Small business with fewer than 100 employees were protected against lawsuits by companies responsible for a majority of the waste matter. Owners of residential property and small businesses were also exempt for disposing household garbage in a site previously designated to fall under the superfund program.
- **Davis-Bacon compliance.** The bill specified that federal wage laws, including the 1931 Davis-Bacon Act requiring that workers be paid the wages prevailing in the area, apply to workers participating in cleanup programs, including work done by the states.

Background

For years, the restoration of brownfields had been caught up in debates about revising the superfund program itself. Created in 1980, the superfund hazardous-waste cleanup program (PL 96-510) was a response to dangers posed by abandoned toxic waste. A key feature of the act made any and all parties that contributed to the pollution of a site liable for the cost of the cleanup. That meant a single business could be forced to pay for the entire cost, even if others contributed to the pollution.

While approximately half of the identified sites had been successfully decontaminated and redeveloped, the program was plagued by lawsuits as polluters tried to find others to share their liability. Repeated efforts to overhaul the system foundered over issues such as the proper roles for state and federal government, although there were some piecemeal changes. The most recent was language in the fiscal 2000 Omnibus Appropriations Act (PL 106-113) that exempted businesses that recycle paper, glass, plastic, metals, textiles

and rubber from certain superfund liability. *(1997 Almanac, p. 4-11; 1999 Almanac, p. 12-11)*

Cleanup of the more lightly polluted brownfields sites was not specifically authorized under the superfund law, but the EPA created a grant program in 1995. States took the lead, but the problem was huge — there were an estimated 450,000 potential brownfields sites nationwide — and cleanup efforts were slowed by the lack of liability protection for those developing previously contaminated sites. State governments urged Congress to authorize an EPA brownfields program with its own set of liability standards and funding for cleanup efforts. The initiative had broad support in Congress, but some lawmakers feared that breaking it out as separate legislation would undercut any momentum for a broader superfund rewrite.

The Bush administration strongly supported the legislation, helping to break it free in the 107th Congress.

Legislative Action

Senate Brownfields Bill

● **Committee action.** The Senate Energy and Natural Resources Committee approved S 350 (S Rept 107-2) on March 12 by a vote of 15-3. Introduced by Lincoln Chafee, R-R.I., it was similar to a bill that had received the support of 67 senators, the National Governors Association and the Clinton administration in the 106th Congress.

Despite the approval, members expressed concern that the EPA could re-evaluate and reopen a site it had previously declared clean. Some senators, including Mike Castle, D-Del., argued that the measure would give the EPA too much authority, while others, such as Hillary Rodham Clinton, D-N.Y., said it would bind the hands of the EPA too tightly.

The panel rejected, 3-15, two amendments by James Inhofe, R-Okla., to prevent the EPA from using other waste management laws to require cleanup of brownfields sites over and above the level required by the superfund law.

● **Floor action.** The Senate passed the bill, 99-0, on April 25, but only after Environment and Public Works Chairman Robert C. Smith, R-N.H., had worked with colleagues to produce a substitute amendment to assuage the concerns of opponents. Bush issued a statement supporting the bill. *(Senate vote 87, p. S-23)*

As passed, the Senate bill authorized more than $1 billion over five years in federal grants for cleanups, provided some liability protections for landowners and developers, and gave states the lead role in cleanup decisions. Smith's manager's amendment, approved by voice vote, redefined the EPA's role in the cleanup projects to give most jurisdiction to the states. It required that one-fourth of the cleanup funds be used to restore sites, such as gas stations, that were contaminated by petroleum and thus not covered under the superfund law. The substitute limited the EPA's ability to seek additional cleanup once a state certified a site as restored and allowed the agency to step in only when a potential release of contaminants posed an "imminent and substantial danger" to public health or the environment. It also gave preference to cleanup sites where contamination affected minority groups and children.

Smith expressed concern that the delicate compromise could unravel in the House, killing hopes for enactment.

House Superfund Liability Bill

The House took a different tack, concentrating on superfund liability protection rather than on funding specific projects. The Energy and Commerce Committee gave voice vote approval May 17 to a bill (HR 1831 — H Rept 107-70, Part 1) introduced by Paul E. Gillmor, R-Ohio, chairman of the panel's Environment and Hazardous Materials Subcommittee. The subcommittee had approved it a day earlier. The Transportation and Infrastructure committee endorsed the bill by voice vote May 16 (H Rept 107-70, Part 2). Neither committee amended the legislation.

The bill focused on limiting the liability of small businesses. It included an exemption for businesses responsible for dumping less than 110 pounds of liquid waste or 200 pounds of solid waste prior to April 1, 2001. If a company met these requirements, it would not be forced to pay for the cleanup; however, the burden of proof would fall on the company. Small businesses, defined as having fewer than 100 employees, would also receive exemptions. The measure also codified the EPA's practice of reducing fines for companies that could not afford the cost of cleanup.

The House passed the bill, 419-0, under suspension of the rules May 22. *(House vote 134, H-52)*

Final Action

After months of negotiations, the House on Dec. 20 passed a bill (HR 2869) containing the core provisions of S 350 and HR 1831. The Senate cleared the measure later that day; both chambers acted by voice vote.

Haggling over the scope of federal oversight had stalled competing drafts of brownfields legislation in the House, with the GOP holding out for a version that offered the states more authority in the cleanup process. EPA Administrator Christine Todd Whitman warned in June that, without a strong guarantee of federal oversight similar to what was in the Senate bill, the measure was likely to die. Under pressure from the White House and the House GOP leadership, Republicans on the Energy and Commerce Committee agreed to accept the Senate language in return for support for the House liability reform bill. The compromise was introduced by Gillmor on Sept. 10 and scheduled for House floor action the next day. With the Sept. 11 terrorist attacks, the measure was rescheduled for the week of Sept. 24.

By then, however, a new issue emerged, further delaying consideration. In September, House Democrats, along with Sen. James M. Jeffords, I-Vt., requested that the EPA clarify that provisions of the Davis-Bacon law would be used to determine the wages paid to workers involved in cleanups in all states At the time, 19 states would not have met the requirement that workers be paid the prevailing wages in the area. HR 2869 did not address the issue, and the EPA refused to provide the requested clarification.

In December, the House managers agreed to rewrite the language so that the wage requirements would apply to all cleanups. Though conservatives were unhappy, they went along with the revision at the urging of House Speaker J. Dennis Hastert, R-Ill. With this language in place, the bill cleared in the closing hours of the session. In signing the measure on Jan. 11, 2002, Bush said it would "protect innocent small business owners and employees from unfair lawsuits, and focus our efforts instead on actually cleaning up contaminated sites." ◆

Chapter 10

EXECUTIVE BRANCH

Cabinet Controversy Starts Year

The majority of President Bush's nominees for the Cabinet sailed through the congressional confirmation process with little or no opposition. Two of the 14 selections, however, touched off fierce and polarizing debates before eventually winning Senate approval.

John Ashcroft, Bush's choice for attorney general, was the most controversial. Ashcroft's conservative stands on issues such as abortion and civil rights, and the role he played in thwarting President Bill Clinton's judicial nominees, made him a lightning rod for criticism from congressional Democrats, as well as from pro-choice and civil liberties organizations.

Separately, environmental groups worked to defeat the nomination of Gale A. Norton to be Interior secretary. Norton, the former attorney general of Colorado, was a protégé of Reagan administration Interior Secretary James G. Watt. Environmentalists feared she would be a friend of business and open up public lands to drilling, mining and other resource development.

John Ashcroft

The Senate confirmed Ashcroft on Feb. 1, after weeks of acrimonious debate and intense lobbying by outside groups. The vote was 58-42. All 50 Republicans supporting the nominee, as well as eight Democrats who broke ranks to back the former Missouri senator and state attorney general. Ashcroft won with fewer votes than any successful Cabinet nominee in decades in the most contested nomination for attorney general since Edwin Meese III of the Reagan administration. (*Senate vote 8, p. S-5*)

Opposition Democrats said the 40-plus votes — the most ever cast against an attorney general nominee — sent a message to the White House not to pick nominees for the federal bench, especially the Supreme Court, from the GOP's conservative base. "We hope nominees for the courts . . . come from the center, not the far right," said the Senate's top Democrat, Tom Daschle of South Dakota.

Ashcroft was just weeks removed from the Senate when President-elect Bush tapped him to be his attorney general. In one of the oddest turns of the 2000 election, Ashcroft had lost by less than 3 percent on Election Day to a Democratic candidate — Missouri Gov. Mel Carnahan — who had died several weeks earlier in a plane crash. Carnahan's widow, Jean, was appointed to fill the Senate seat until the next regular election in 2002. Ashcroft, who had been elected to the Senate in 1994, did not contest the results.

Bush expressed confidence that Ashcroft would "withstand the scrutiny about his fairness and his heart," but the nomination was divisive from the start.

Opponents focused on Ashcroft's record during his one term in the Senate. Ashcroft had sponsored legislation to outlaw all abortions except to save the life of the woman. He opposed adding new restrictions to gun show purchases and expanding the federal definition of hate crimes to cover acts motivated by the victim's sexual identity. His outspoken

opposition to a number of Clinton nominations, from those for surgeon general to appointments to the federal courts, drew the most scrutiny. Ashcroft's successful fight to defeat the promotion to the federal bench of Missouri's first black Supreme Court justice, Ronnie L. White, was the most controversial.

Clinton nominated White for a U.S. District Court judgeship in Missouri in June 1997. Ashcroft's Missouri colleague, Republican Sen. Christopher S. Bond, spoke enthusiastically of the nominee at his confirmation hearing. The Senate Judiciary Committee reported White's nomination favorably, 13-3, in 1988, but the full Senate did not act.

Clinton renominated White in January 1999, the start of the 106th Congress. The Judiciary Committee again approved White, and the nomination was brought to the Senate floor in October. The day of the vote, Ashcroft sent a letter to his colleagues urging defeat of White, citing dissents he wrote in state Supreme Court cases that upheld death sentences. White lost on a party-line vote of 54-45, the first judicial nominee to be rejected since Supreme Court nominee Robert P. Bork. (*1999 Almanac, p. 18-49*)

The argument against Ashcroft was not that he opposed a judicial nominee, but that he did so in a way that distorted White's record and thus unfairly argued the case before the Senate. During his two days of confirmation hearings before the Senate Judiciary Committee, Ashcroft defended his actions on the White nomination, saying White should not be on the District Court. White told the panel that he believed Ashcroft seriously distorted his record.

The broader question for the committee was whether Ashcroft would defend laws with which he disagreed. Democrats feared he would use his position as attorney general to advance his rigid opposition to gun control and abortion rights. "It's very hard to change your stripes or change your spots. Quite frankly, I don't know what to believe," said Dianne Feinstein, D-Calif. But Ashcroft insisted he would enforce the nation's laws, even those he strongly opposed. "As a man of faith, I take my word and my integrity seriously," he said. "So, when I swear to uphold the law, I will keep my oath, so help me God."

Liberal and conservative groups used advertising and public protests to argue for and against the nomination. People for the American Way spent $280,000 on print ads opposing Ashcroft. The Family Research Council and the Traditional Values Coalition urged conservatives to contact lawmakers and express their support for the nominee. Amid the public fight, Democrats won a one-week postponement of the Judiciary Committee vote, citing the need for answers to written questions, though the delay also gave opponents more time to lobby. But Republicans were united in their support for Ashcroft, and the move simply postponed the inevitable. On Jan. 31, the committee voted for the nominee, 10-8, after nearly three hours of emotional debate.

Russell D. Feingold, D-Wis., the lone Democrat to support Ashcroft, said he was worried it would look like "political payback" to do to Ashcroft what he had so often done to

other nominees. But Feingold assailed Ashcroft's record and said Bush should renominate White to the federal bench.

Within hours of the Senate vote on Feb. 1, Ashcroft was sworn in by Supreme Court Justice Clarence Thomas, who had been the subject of his own bitter confirmation fight in 1991.

Gale A. Norton

The fervent battle over Ashcroft's nomination took some of the steam out of the Norton confirmation fight. Environmental groups spent nearly $1 million on an advertising campaign to defeat the nomination, and Norton faced tough questions from Democrats, but she easily won confirmation. The Senate voted 75-24 on Jan. 30 to make Norton the head of the Interior Department. (*Senate vote 6, p. S-5*)

Some moderate Republicans indicated they might oppose some of Bush's environmental policies, but they said the Norton nomination was the wrong arena in which to challenge the new administration.

Environmental groups spent close to $1 million on an ad campaign to defeat Norton's nomination. The opposition of the Sierra Club, the Natural Resources Defense Council and other groups stemmed from Norton's association with Watt, who hired her out of law school to work at the Mountain States Legal Foundation. In 1985, she joined the Interior Department's solicitor office, where she worked on issues that included opening up the Arctic National Wildlife Refuge (ANWR) to oil exploration.

Norton used her Jan. 18-19 confirmation hearings before the Senate Energy and Natural Resources Committee to try to reassure the panel that she was not anti-environment. "We care about farmers and ranchers, but we also care about endangered species," she told the panel. Democrats acknowledged she had the votes to win confirmation, but they still pursued a number of issues, including oil and gas leases, global warming, property rights and specifics of Norton's record.

Norton said she supported opening up ANWR, citing the power crisis in California as the rationale to explore for oil and gas. Under questioning, she backed away from a 1997 statement that there was no scientific consensus that pollution was slowly causing the earth's climate to warm. "There is beginning to be more of a consensus that global warming is occurring," she said. Norton said a 1989 speech in which she said property owners might have a homesteading "right to pollute" was taken out of context.

Norton also said she would enforce the Endangered Species Act as written, distancing herself from previous skepticism. To counter criticism from environmental groups, Norton called on a bipartisan group of other state attorneys general to attest to her willingness to balance environmental protection with economic concerns. She also used her Denver law firm's Democratic ties to reach out to senators who might oppose her.

The Energy Committee approved her nomination, 18-2, on Jan. 24. Only two of the panel's Democrats — Ron Wyden of Oregon and Charles E. Schumer of New York — said they had too many reservations to support her.

Chavez Nomination

Another Bush nominee was gone before her confirmation process could get into full swing. Linda Chavez, the president-elect's choice for Labor secretary, was forced to withdraw her candidacy on Jan. 9, a week after Bush named her.

Chavez was dogged by reports that she had given shelter in the early 1990s to an illegal Guatemalan immigrant who did household chores for her and received at least $1,500 in spending money. Chavez blamed the failure of her candidacy on "search and destroy politics," but she would have faced a bruising confirmation fight from labor and civil rights groups, which were ready to attack her opposition to the minimum wage and affirmative action.

Two days after Chavez withdrew her nomination, reportedly under pressure from the White House, Bush tapped Elaine L. Chao as his nominee for Labor secretary. Chao was the former president of the United Way of America and the wife of Sen. Mitch McConnell, R-Ky. The Senate confirmed Chao by voice vote Jan. 29. ◆

New Security Office Scrutinized

On Sept. 20, less than two weeks after the attacks on the World Trade Center and the Pentagon, President Bush used his speech to a joint session of Congress to announce the creation of a new Cabinet-level post to centralize and coordinate the counterterrorism efforts of 40 agencies and departments. Bush tapped Pennsylvania Gov. Tom Ridge, a Vietnam veteran and former House member (1983-95) to head the Office of Homeland Security. "He will lead, oversee and coordinate a comprehensive national strategy to safeguard our country against terrorism and respond to any attacks that may come," Bush said in his speech. (*Text, p. D-31*)

Lawmakers who had pushed for the establishment of a homeland defense office welcomed the president's decision, but they were eager to put a congressional imprimatur on the Cabinet post, as well as to ensure that Ridge had the power to carry out his formidable job. "In the strongest terms, we have to explain his authority as well as responsibility," which must be "bestowed by an act of Congress," said John McCain, R-Ariz., a member of the Senate Armed Services Committee.

The White House, however, resisted congressional efforts to make the new office subject to Senate confirmation and to ensure that it had the authority to put together counterterrorism budgets. Lawmakers held back, unwilling to antagonize the administration or appear to be undermining its national security efforts at a time of heightened alert about terrorism. But the dispute over the parameters of the new post

lingered for the rest of the year, hampering Ridge's efforts and further aggravating the relationship between the White House and Congress.

Ridge's Role

The White House envisioned Ridge's job as similar to that of the national security adviser, an Eisenhower-era position that owed its creation to congressional passage of the National Security Act of 1947 but did not require Senate approval. Since the 1950s, the role of national security adviser had evolved based on presidential expectations and the force of the personality in the job, with some advisers eclipsing members of the Cabinet.

Joining Ridge in the new Homeland Security Council were the attorney general, the secretaries of Defense, Treasury, Agriculture, and Health and Human Services (HHS), and the directors of the FBI and the Federal Emergency Management Agency (FEMA).

Bush said on Sept. 27 that Ridge's job would be "to coordinate activities to make sure that anybody who wants to harm America will have a hard time doing so, to make sure that we're as strong at home as we are abroad, to make sure our resources are deployed effectively."

But many lawmakers feared that without legislation giving Ridge statutory authority, the job would be merely advisory and the homeland chief would get caught in the turf wars among agencies. They also wanted Ridge to have authority over the $11 billion the government was set to spend on counterterrorism.

The 56-year-old Ridge, who had received serious consideration for the 2000 Republican vice presidential nomination, resigned as Pennsylvania governor Oct. 5 and assumed his new duties Oct. 8. He worked out of a windowless office in the West Wing with a staff of fewer than 20.

Congressional Concerns

Bush installed Ridge in the Cabinet by executive order, but there was near-unanimous sentiment in Congress that the homeland chief needed specific powers outlined in law to coordinate a multi-agency system for protecting the United States.

At least a half-dozen bills were introduced to codify Ridge's power by giving him budget authority over the more than 40 agencies and departments involved in homeland security. Senate Intelligence Committee Chairman Bob Graham, D-Fla., introduced a bill (S 1449) that would make Ridge's office subject to Senate confirmation and give it control over all counterterrorism spending. A bill (S 1534) by Joseph I. Lieberman, D-Conn., and Arlen Specter, R-Pa., proposed a new Cabinet-level Department of National Homeland Security made up of FEMA, the Customs Service, the Border Patrol and the Coast Guard. Creation of such a department was a key recommendation made earlier in the year by a terrorism panel headed by former Sens. Warren B. Rudman, R-N.H. (1980-93), and Gary Hart, D-Colo. (1975-87).

In the House, Jim Gibbons, R-Nev., and Jane Harman, D-Calif., offered a bill (HR 3026) to give Ridge authority over counterintelligence budgets and require Senate confirmation.

The White House insisted that Ridge had all the authority he needed, but lawmakers predicted that the collaborative effort among the agencies and departments in a time of crisis would give way to turf fights and conflicting priorities.

A muddled administration response to anthrax attacks on the Senate and U.S. postal offices in October, along with contradictory assessments of the gravity of the anthrax threat, raised more questions about the authority of the homeland chief. With conflicting accounts from HHS, the FBI and the Pentagon of the potential risks of the bacteria, members of Congress and their staffs were quickly tested for exposure and given antibiotics, while similar precautions were not taken for postal workers until two in the Washington area died from anthrax exposure and two others fell ill.

The year ended with no resolution and a Homeland Security Office dogged by skepticism. ◆

Chapter 11

FOREIGN POLICY

Hill Meets Intelligence Needs

Congress responded to the failure of U.S. intelligence agencies to anticipate or prevent the Sept. 11 terrorist attacks by increasing the intelligence budget and putting a greater emphasis on human spying and new technologies. Lawmakers rejected proposals to create an outside commission to investigate the intelligence lapses, deciding that Congress, itself, should conduct any inquiry.

The fiscal 2002 intelligence authorization bill provided an increase of about 8 percent over the previous year's appropriations for national intelligence activities. Intelligence spending was classified, but the total in recent years was widely believed to have been in the range of $30 billion. The measure covered the activities of 11 agencies, including the CIA, the National Security Agency (NSA) and intelligence agencies in the State, Energy and Defense departments. President Bush signed it into law (HR 2883 — PL 107-108) on Dec. 28.

Senate Intelligence Committee Chairman Bob Graham, D-Fla., described the increase as significant and said it would inaugurate a five-year plan to accomplish four congressional objectives: improve human spying; upgrade the eavesdropping capabilities of the NSA, which collects intelligence from spy satellites and other sophisticated equipment; foster better analysis of intelligence data; and enhance research and development of new technologies.

Revitalizing the NSA, which had been criticized for failing to keep pace with technological changes in signals intelligence such as fiber-optic communications, was a top priority, as was improving the agency's coordination with the CIA's human spies. "Five years from now, the NSA must have the ability to collect and exploit electronic signals in a vastly different communications environment," said Graham. "Along with a significant investment in technology, this means closer collaboration with clandestine human collectors."

When work on the bill began in early September, Graham and his House counterpart, Porter J. Goss, R-Fla., voiced concern that civilian spy agencies might lose out to the Defense Department in the fierce competition for appropriations. Although intelligence activities were authorized separately, most intelligence agencies were funded in the defense appropriations bill. But the increases that became available after Sept. 11, both for the regular appropriations bills and in supplemental spending, reduced the competition for funds.

Highlights

● **Outside commission.** The House Intelligence Committee's version of the bill originally called for a special com-

BoxScore

Bill:
HR 2883 — PL 107-108

Legislative Action:

House passed HR 2883 (H Rept 107-219) by voice vote Oct. 5.

Senate passed HR 2883, amended (S Rept 107-63), 100-0, on Nov. 8.

House adopted the conference report (H Rept 107-328) by voice vote Dec. 12.

Senate cleared the bill by voice vote Dec. 13.

President signed Dec. 28.

mission to examine why intelligence agencies failed to foresee the Sept. 11 attacks on the World Trade Center and the Pentagon. The language was modified on the floor to focus the study on existing impediments to better intelligence collection, rather than a retroactive probe of what went wrong.

The Senate version of the bill contained no similar language, and conferees eventually decided to let the two committees conduct their own investigations unless Bush and congressional leaders decided otherwise; neither Bush nor the leadership showed any interest in an outside panel.

● **Foreign agents.** The bill rescinded 1995 CIA guidelines that restricted the recruitment of foreign intelligence agents who had human rights violations in their background, and instructed the CIA to establish more flexible guidelines.

● **Wiretaps.** The bill made minor technical changes to the Foreign Intelligence Surveillance Act (PL 95-511), the main law used in obtaining wiretap information about suspected foreign criminals. Attorney General John Ashcroft had asked the intelligence committees to consider broader revisions. More extensive provisions were included in the anti-terrorism bill (PL 107-56) enacted Oct. 26. (*Anti-terrorism, p. 14-3*)

Background

There was widespread agreement in the wake of the Sept. 11 attacks that better coordination was needed among the intelligence agencies, but some rifts — particularly between the CIA and the Pentagon, and between the Intelligence and Armed Services committees — were too deep-seated to be resolved quickly. The spending increase in the fiscal 2002 bill "is probably adequate for now, but money alone is not the answer," said Richard C. Shelby of Alabama, the Senate Intelligence Committee's ranking Republican. "Our intelligence community is still too little of a community and too much of a freewheeling federation that lacks effective centralized control and management."

Under existing law, the director of central intelligence had nominal oversight of all 13 intelligence agencies, but he had direct authority only over the CIA. Many lawmakers and intelligence officials said it made sense to give the CIA director more control, but they conceded that opposition from the military was a formidable barrier. "Is this a good idea? Yes. Should it be explored? Yes," said Goss, a former intelligence agent. "Is it politically feasible? That's the hardest part."

The Intelligence committees had tried in the mid-1990s to push similar changes to expand the CIA director's au-

thority, but were forced to scale back their proposals in the face of opposition from the Pentagon and its congressional allies. Defense Department officials argued that since they were the biggest consumers of intelligence, they ought to oversee the agencies. (*1996 Almanac, p. 9-16*)

An expert panel led by former national security adviser Brent Scowcroft had been meeting since July and was expected to recommend that three Defense Department agencies — the NSA, the National Reconnaissance Office, and the National Imagery and Mapping Agency — be placed under the control of the director of central intelligence.

Legislative Action

House Committee Action

The House Select Committee on Intelligence took up its version of the bill Sept. 24, at a time when the CIA and other spy agencies were coming under sharp criticism for having failed to foresee the terrorist attacks. The committee approved a version of the bill (HR 2883 — H Rept 107-219) that congressional sources said would increase intelligence spending by nearly 9 percent over the existing level and 2 percent over the president's pre-Sept. 11 request. Goss said the House bill would add "a significant amount" over a pre-Sept. 11 version approved by the Senate Intelligence Committee in such critical areas as human intelligence and electronic eavesdropping.

The bill called for a commission to examine why the intelligence agencies had failed to warn of the attacks. In the report accompanying the bill, the committee said it had "been concerned for some time that intelligence agencies were not well-positioned to respond to the national security challenges of the 21st century, including terrorism." The proposed commission — a 10-member bipartisan group of presidential and congressional appointees — would devote six months to examining the failure of intelligence agencies to anticipate the attacks.

The commission was the subject of considerable debate inside the normally cordial and bipartisan committee. Some Republicans thought the the scope was too broad; others argued that no panel was needed because the committee had already created a new Subcommittee on Terrorism and Homeland Security, chaired by Saxby Chambliss, R-Ga.

The committee cautioned against singling out the agencies. "If blame must be assigned, the blame lies with a government, as a whole, that did not fully understand nor wanted to appreciate the significance of the new threats to our national security, despite the warnings offered by the intelligence community," the committee's report said.

The question of blame was a volatile one outside the committee as well. Two days after the committee markup, Shelby publicly criticized Director of Central Intelligence George J. Tenet, a former Democratic committee staff director and a holdover from the Clinton administration." I personally like George Tenet, and he has done some good things, but I believe the job is getting away from him," Shelby said on NBC's "Today" show.

Many other lawmakers, however, said such criticism was premature or unwarranted. In a vote of confidence for Tenet and his CIA employees, Bush made a personal appearance at CIA headquarters in Langley, Va., on Sept. 26. "I've got a lot

of confidence in [Tenet], and I've got a lot of confidence in the CIA," Bush said. "And so should America."

The proposal to scrap the 1995 guidelines on recruiting foreign agents also sparked considerable debate in the closed-door markup. "Nobody wants to be soft on terrorism. But we do have people saying they don't want us to get out of bounds," Goss said afterwards.

During the mid 1990s, then-director of central intelligence John M. Deutch had ordered the CIA to review all its contacts and operations to determine whether any involved links to humans rights abuses. The agency subsequently developed guidelines that required field officers to obtain approval from headquarters before establishing a relationship with an individual who had engaged in disreputable activities. Many lawmakers argued that the guidelines should be dropped to enable the agency to get better intelligence. The CIA and other lawmakers maintained that the restrictions had not been a hindrance to obtaining information.

The Senate had already gone on record, adopting similar language as part of an amendment to its version of the Commerce, Justice, State spending bill.

In its report, the House committee said the 1995 CIA guidelines had the unintended consequence of deterring the effective recruitment of potentially high-value agents. The panel voiced concern that a culture of "risk aversion" had hindered decision-making across the intelligence community, especially within the CIA. The committee called for a new balance that recognized concerns about egregious human rights behavior, but provided the flexibility to seize upon opportunities as they present themselves.

House Floor Action

The House passed the bill by voice vote Oct. 5, after refocusing the proposed intelligence commission on the impediments to current and future intelligence collection.

The amendment, by Goss, was approved by voice vote after considerable debate. It called for an eight-member Commission on National Security Readiness to look at how intelligence agencies were structured to collect, analyze and share information on terrorism and other national security threats. Goss said it was aimed at "avoiding the blame game and getting to the future."

Several Democrats, led by House Minority Whip Nancy Pelosi of California, ranking Democrat on the Intelligence Committee, said that while it was not a bad idea, it was no substitute for an independent review. Democrats promised to continue pushing for a panel that would look retroactively at what went wrong.

Senate Committee Action

The Senate had begun work on the bill before the terrorist attacks. The Intelligence Committee approved its version (S 1428 — S Rept 107-63) in closed session Sept. 6. The bill focused on four areas: more spies, better electronic eavesdropping, more research and development and better analysis of intelligence data.

Before the markup, committee members removed a provision that would have made almost all unauthorized and willful disclosures of classified information a felony, whether or not they jeopardized national security. The bill directed the Justice Department to send new recommendations to

Congress by May 2002. The change was agreed upon after Ashcroft asked for more time to study the issue. President Bill Clinton had cited a similar provision as a cause for vetoing the fiscal 2001 bill, calling the disclosure language "badly flawed" and "overbroad." A second bill without the provision was enacted (PL 106-567). *(2000 Almanac, p. 11-17)*

In putting together the fiscal 2002 bill, Graham focused on the same issues that Republicans dealt with when they were in the majority, including ensuring that the NSA could improve its ability to intercept computer communications and signals transmitted on fiber optics, as well as keep up with other technological changes.

"It's going to be a major challenge of the intelligence community to adapt to that new reality if we're going to maintain the previous levels of signals capability," Graham said. He said the bill also encouraged the CIA's aggressive efforts to hire more spies.

Senate Floor Action

The Senate passed HR 2883 by a vote of 100-0 on Nov. 8, after substituting the text of S 1428. The bill had been reworked in the aftermath of Sept. 11 to bring it in line with the version the House had passed in October. Aides said the measure would fund activities at the CIA and other spy agencies at 7.7 percent above the existing level. *(Senate vote 332, p. S-69)*

The legislation sought to increase funding for the analysis of raw intelligence data while at the same time adding money for research and development of new technologies, an area where Graham said funding often had been used to pay other bills.

To help finance those increases, the bill reduced spending for two defense-related intelligence and reconnaissance programs. Although details were classified, the proposed reductions troubled the Armed Services Committee. In their report on the bill, Armed Services members urged House and Senate conferees "to restore funding for these . . . important programs that will support the war on terrorism and other critical defense intelligence activities."

Most of the floor debate on the Senate bill focused on an amendment by Robert C. Smith, R-N.H., to make it easier for the Justice Department to deport illegal aliens suspected of terrorism by limiting the dissemination of classified information to the judge only.

Democrats complained that the proposal would lead other nations to withhold details on U.S. citizens detained abroad. The Senate adopted an amendment by voice vote calling for the attorney general to study the issue.

Conference/Final Action

House and Senate negotiators reached swift agreement Dec. 5 on a final bill that deleted the House provision for an independent review commission. The House adopted the conference report (H Rept 107-328) by voice vote Dec. 12, and the Senate cleared the bill by voice vote the following day.

The bill's 8 percent increase in funding was a compromise between the 7.7 percent increase in the Senate bill and the 9 percent hike in the House version.

Some House Democrats had hoped to restore the original committee language calling for a commission to look retroactively at intelligence missteps, but Graham said conferees agreed that "if there is going to be a commission, it should be done at the level of the president and leadership of Congress." Opponents of the commission idea warned it would be viewed as an exercise in political finger-pointing and would distract from the war on terrorism.

Graham said he and Goss were ready to have their committees examine the state of the intelligence agencies as well as their performance leading up to the attacks on the World Trade Center and Pentagon. "Whether there is a commission or not, our committees are going to do a review of what happened before Sept. 11, on Sept. 11 and after Sept. 11, and then make recommendations as to what changes are called for," Graham said.

Pelosi said an independent review "would have had the credibility with the American people that a congressional review, no matter how professionally done, would not."

The following were among the issues resolved in the House-Senate conference:

● **International drug interdiction.** The president was required to report annually to Congress on the interdiction of aircraft used in illicit drug trafficking, including certifying the existence of a drug threat in the country at issue and the existence of appropriate procedures to protect against innocent loss of life. The provision was a response to the accidental shooting down by the Peruvian Air Force of a civilian aircraft carrying U.S. missionaries.

● **Liability insurance.** The bill provided full reimbursement for professional liability insurance for counterterrorism employees. Previous law paid only for half.

● **Unauthorized disclosures.** Conferees adopted the Senate provision directing the attorney general to review protections against the unauthorized disclosure of classified information. The bill did not include the provision that would have made most unauthorized and willful disclosures a felony.

● **Alien terrorists.** The attorney general was required to report on the status of proceedings to remove alien terrorists by the Immigration and Naturalization Services.

● **Whistleblower protection.** Protection was strengthened for intelligence community whistleblowers who disclose information to Congress.

● **National Drug Interdiction Center.** The bill authorized $44 million for the National Drug Interdiction Center in Johnstown, Pa. The center, established in 1991, coordinated and consolidated drug intelligence from national security and drug enforcement agencies.

● **Coast Guard.** The bill added the U.S. Coast Guard as an element of the intelligence community, and established Coast Guard as a National Foreign Intelligence Program agency under the National Security Act. ◆

Iran-Libya Sanctions Extended

Congress cleared a five-year extension of sanctions on foreign businesses that invested in the energy industries of Iran or Libya. The sanctions, which also were tightened under the new law, were aimed at punishing Iran and Libya for their alleged support for terrorism and their efforts to acquire nuclear, chemical and biological weapons. Although President Bush had tried to limit the extension to two years, he signed the bill (HR 1954 — PL 107-24) on Aug. 3.

Business groups and European governments successfully blocked the implementation of the original 1996 Iran-Libya sanctions act (PL 104-172), which was set to expire Aug. 5. They hoped that with a new Republican administration in office, the law would not be renewed. Bush and Vice President Dick Cheney had signaled their opposition to the law in the past, and Iran and Libya had taken some steps toward rapprochement with the United States.

But strong lobbying by pro-Israel groups — aided by mixed views within the administration — enabled supporters to pass the five-year extension with relative ease. The final measure also lowered the threshold for investment, triggering sanctions on firms that invested more than $20 million in either country's oil or gas industries.

The new law:

• Extended the 1996 Iran-Libya sanctions act until Aug. 5, 2006.

• Lowered the threshold for investment in Libya from $40 million to $20 million — the same as for companies investing in Iran.

• Closed a loophole that allowed companies with oil contracts in Libya or Iran that existed before the 1996 law went into effect to amend those contracts without being subject to sanctions.

• Required the president to submit a report on the effectiveness of sanctions within 18 months.

• Allowed the president to waive penalties in the national interest, or delay sanctions for 90 days in order to cancel transactions that might violate the law.

Background

U.S. sanctions on Iran dated to the 1979 seizure of the U.S. embassy in Tehran. Economic sanctions were first imposed in 1984 after the Reagan administration determined that Iran had been involved in the bombing of a U.S. marine barracks in Beirut the year before. In 1995, President Bill Clinton issued a series of executive orders that effectively prohibited the export of U.S. goods and services to Iran, banned the re-export of certain U.S. goods and technology to Iran from third countries, and prohibited any U.S. invest-

BoxScore

Bill:
HR 1954 — PL 107-24
Legislative Action:
Senate passed S 1218 (no written report), 96-2, July 25.
House passed HR 1954 (H Rept 107-107, Parts 1,2), 409-6, on July 26.
Senate cleared HR 1954 by voice vote July 27.
President signed Aug. 3.

ment in or financing of Iran-related ventures. Clinton's actions were a response to Iran's growing efforts to get nuclear expertise and its ties to groups accused of carrying out terrorist attacks in Israel.

Sanctions on Libya were initially a response to the 1998 bombing of Pan Am flight 103 over Lockerbie, Scotland, which killed 270 people, including 189 Americans.

The 1996 Iran-Libya sanctions law was passed as a response to Iran's decision to open its petroleum and gas markets to foreign investment in the mid-1990s. It required the president to impose at least two out of a list of six possible sanctions on foreign firms that invested more than $20 million a year in Iran's energy sector, or $40 million a year in Libya's. Sanctioned firms could be denied access to Export-Import Bank credits, U.S. military exports, U.S. bank loans or U.S. government contracts.

However, because of strong opposition from business groups, especially within the European Union (EU), the sanctions were never imposed. The EU argued that the sanctions were an attempt by the United States to apply U.S. law internationally and threatened to take the matter to the World Trade Organization. Clinton waived sanctions several times in return for increased cooperation in fighting terrorism and arms and technology trade with those nations.

With energy prices at historically high levels, and with Cheney, who had opposed sanctions during his years as an oil industry executive, in charge of drafting the administration's energy plan, opponents of an extension hoped to limit, if not end, the sanctions.

Moreover, Iran and Libya had taken some steps since 1996 to improve their relations with the United States. Iran had twice elected a moderate cleric, Mohammad Khatami, as president, and Iranian and U.S. officials had taken some tentative steps toward rapprochement. Libya, meanwhile, turned over two intelligence agents believed to have carried out the Pam Am Flight 103 bombing. One of those suspects was sentenced to life in prison Jan. 31.

The administration, however, did not push to end the sanctions, calling instead for a comprehensive review and a two-year, rather than a five-year, extension.

Legislative Action

House International Relations Committee

The House International Relations Committee approved the Iran-Libya Sanctions Act (HR 1954 — H Rept 107-107, Part 1) by a vote of 41-3 on June 20, a week after

first taking up the bill.

The lopsided vote came after the committee rejected, 41-3, the administration proposal to extend the law for two years, in the hope that the political climate in Iran would moderate. The administration and other supporters of the amendment by Ron Paul, R-Texas, also argued that a five-year extension would further irritate the European allies, whose companies had invested in Iran and Libya.

Dana Rohrabacher, R-Calif., supported Paul, saying the amendment would signal U.S. backing for Khatami, who had been involved in an internal struggle with hard-line Muslim clerics. Khatami overwhelmingly won re-election June 8. "It tells the Iranian people you're standing up to the mullahs and we're on your side," Rohrabacher said.

Former committee chairman Benjamin A. Gilman, R-N.Y., responded that there was no need to shorten the term of the sanctions since the bill allowed them to be dropped if Iran ended its support for terrorism, its opposition to the Middle East peace process, and its efforts to develop missiles capable of carrying nuclear, chemical or biological weapons.

In a small concession to foreign energy companies and the Bush administration, Democrats Eliot L. Engel of New York and Donald M. Payne of New Jersey dropped plans to to try to expand the sanctions to Syria and Sudan.

A day after the committee reported the bill, proponents of a five-year extension got a boost from Attorney General John Ashcroft, who linked the Iranian government to the 1996 bombing of the Khobar Towers barracks in Saudi Arabia, which killed 19 U.S. military personnel.

House Ways and Means Committee

The Ways and Means Committee weighed in July 12, approving by voice vote a revised version of the bill (H Rept 107-107, Part 2) that reduced the extension to two years.

The committee had jurisdiction over only a small sliver of the legislation: a provision allowing the president to use the International Emergency Economic Powers Act (PL 95-223) to further punish foreign nations whose companies invested in Iran and Libya by limiting imports from their countries.

But Chairman Bill Thomas, R-Calif., used the opening to propose significant changes. Along with the shorter extension, Thomas' version required that the president submit a report on the effectiveness of the sanctions 18 months after enactment. Trade Subcommittee Chairman Philip M. Crane, R-Ill., who backed Thomas, said he expected the report to conclude that the sanctions were ineffective. If the report reached such a conclusion, the mea-sure set up a procedure to guarantee expedited consideration of a joint resolution to suspend them.

House Floor Action

The House passed the sanctions bill, 409-6, on July 26 after a week's delay during which the two committees fought over which version would come to the floor. (*House vote 276, p. H-98*)

The final bill largely reflected the International Relations Committee version. It extend the sanctions for five years rather than two, lowered the threshold for investment in Libyan oil companies to $20 million and closed a "grandfather" loophole that allowed companies that had been doing business with Iranian and Libyan energy companies before 1996 to amend their contracts without penalty.

International Relations Committee Chairman Henry J. Hyde, R-Ill., initially agreed to go along with the Ways and Means plan, but two key members of his committee — Gilman and ranking Democrat Tom Lantos of California — objected.

Lantos claimed to have enough votes to deny the Ways and Means bill the two-thirds majority needed for passage under suspension of the rules. "Any deviation [from the International Relations bill] sends a signal to the governments of Iran and Libya that we are not serious about using sanctions," Lantos said. His stance was endorsed by the powerful pro-Israel lobbying group, the American Israel Public Affairs Committee, which had made the bill a top legislative priority.

The vote was originally scheduled for July 17, but Speaker J. Dennis Hastert, R-Ill., pulled the bill from the floor after he, Thomas and White House officials failed to reach a compromise.

In the end, the Ways and Means proposal for a presidential report survived, although the final version did not provide for an expedited vote on removing the sanctions if the report was critical. However, Hastert promised he would ensure a timely floor vote should the report be negative.

Senate/Final Action

The Senate Banking Committee had voted 20-1 on July 18 to approve a bill — subsequently introduced as S 1218 — that was identical to the House International Relations Committee measure. The lone dissenter was Chuck Hagel, R-Neb., who failed on a voice vote to reduce the extension to two years instead of five.

On July 25, the Senate passed its bill by a vote of 96-2. (*Senate vote 251, p. S-52*)

Following House passage of HR 1954, the Senate took up that bill and cleared it by voice vote July 27. ◆

Pakistan Sanctions Waiver Clears

At the urging of an administration eager to reward Pakistan for its cooperation in the war against terrorism, Congress cleared a bill allowing President Bush to waive key sanctions on that country for two years. The bill was signed into law (S 1465 — PL 107-57) on Oct. 27.

Bush moved quickly after the Sept. 11 terrorist attacks to aid Pakistan, including lifting sanctions related to the country's 1998 nuclear weapons test. He also provided $100 million in aid — $50 million each in fiscal 2001 and 2002. To provide additional assistance, however, Bush needed congressional authority.

The new law provided that authority, though it required the president to certify that such aid "would facilitate the transition to democratic rule" before releasing the fiscal 2003 portion. The Senate passed the bill easily Oct. 4. The House followed suit Oct. 16, despite stiff resistance from appropriators who were concerned they would lose control over the aid, and lawmakers who favored close ties with India, Pakistan's arch rival.

BoxScore

Bill:
S 1465 — PL 107-57
Legislative Action:
Senate passed S 1465 by voice vote Oct. 4.
House cleared S 1465 by voice vote Oct. 16.
President signed Oct. 27.

Highlights

The key provisions of the bill:

• Gave Bush the authority to waive all sanctions against Pakistan in fiscal 2002. The president could waive the sanctions in fiscal 2003 if he certified to Congress that doing so would ease Pakistan's transition to democracy and assist U.S. actions against international terrorism. He would have to notify Congress five days in advance of such a waiver.

• Allowed the president in fiscal 2003 to waive additional sanctions imposed on Pakistan for violating the Missile Control Technology Regime by acquiring arms from China.

• Ended prohibitions on loans and economic assistance placed on Pakistani because of its default on loans.

• Eased restrictions on U.S. shipments of excess weaponry to nations able to assist in anti-terrorism efforts.

Background

Pakistan had been subject to a variety of U.S. sanctions dating to the mid-1980s. Under a 1985 amendment to the Foreign Assistance Act, sponsored by Larry Pressler, R-S.D. (House 1975-79; Senate 1979-97), economic and military aid to Pakistan was cut off automatically unless the president certified before the start of each fiscal year that Pakistan "does not possess a nuclear explosive device."

During the 1980s, Presidents Ronald Reagan and George Bush provided the certification despite some serious reservations about Pakistan's emerging nuclear potential. At the time, Pakistan was viewed as a strategic ally in the drive to expel the Soviet Union from neighboring Afghanistan. But

in 1990, with reports that Pakistan had developed the ability to launch a nuclear strike, Bush declined to renew the certification and aid was suspended. By then, the Soviets had withdrawn from Afghanistan. (*1985 Almanac, p. 41; 1990 Almanac, p. 768*)

Pakistan's test of a nuclear weapon in May 1998, following a similar test by India, triggered sanctions against both countries under the 1994 Arms Control Export Act (PL 103-236). However, President Bill Clinton soon lifted most of them, and the fiscal 2000 defense appropriations bill (PL 106-79) gave him further authority to waive the nuclear sanctions. Pakistan's failure to make payments on its debts to the United States, and the 1999 overthrow of Pakistan's democratically elected government by Gen. Pervez Musharraf, who later became president, triggered new layers of sanctions under various provisions of the Foreign Assistance Act (PL 87-195). The act allowed the president to waive sanctions under certain conditions, but limited the amount of aid that could be provided to $50 million a year.

After the Sept. 11 attacks in New York and at the Pentagon, the Bush administration, led by Secretary of State Colin L. Powell, concentrated on assembling an international coalition to combat terrorism. Powell praised Musharraf for facing down strong domestic opposition to provide the United States with military bases, overflight rights and intelligence to counter terrorist leader Osama bin Laden's al Qaeda network and Afghanistan's Taliban government.

On Sept. 22, Bush issued an executive order lifting the nuclear weapons sanctions in return for Pakistan's cooperation as a frontline ally in the campaign in Afghanistan. That allowed him to release $50 million in aid; he released another $50 million Oct. 17, after the start of the new fiscal year.

Legislative Action

At the administration's urging, the Senate Foreign Relations Committee approved the two-year waiver of Pakistan sanctions Oct. 4. The bill, introduced by Sam Brownback, R-Kan., was approved by voice vote. The Senate passed it by voice vote later the same day.

The pace slowed slightly when the bill reached the House, where it ran into opposition from lawmakers who favored warm ties with India and from appropriators concerned about losing jurisdiction over foreign aid. But with Powell in Islamabad seeking to bolster Musharraf, few lawmakers were willing to buck the administration, and the bill cleared Oct. 16, also by voice vote.

Speaker J. Dennis Hastert, R-Ill., initially had slated the bill for floor consideration Oct. 9, but appropriators objected to full House action without their prior approval. They

were particularly concerned with losing control over pro-democracy sanctions in fiscal 2003, when Pakistan was scheduled to hold elections. The language in the Senate-passed measure required the president to certify that aid to Pakistan would "facilitate the transition to democratic rule."

On Oct. 11, just before Powell was scheduled to leave for Pakistan and India, David R. Obey of Wisconsin, ranking Democrat on the House Appropriations Committee, blocked GOP attempts to move on the bill. At that point, Pakistani Finance Minister Shaukut Aziz was in Washington seeking $500 million in additional U.S. aid, debt relief and trade preferences.

Members of the International Relations Committee urged the full House to act. "It's very important that we get this waiver because Pakistan is a country with about 20 nuclear bombs, and it would not be a great situation if these were to fall into the hands of Islamic extremists," said committee Chairman Henry J. Hyde R-Ill.

The floor debate focused on maintaining relations with India. Frank Pallone Jr., D-N.J., the founder of the Congressional Caucus on India and Indian-Americans, objected to the measure, deriding Musharraf's pledge to hold democratic elections as "lip service." Appropriators again expressed concern that Congress would lose its oversight in a key area of foreign policy. Nita M. Lowey of New York, ranking Democrat on the Foreign Operation Appropriations Subcommittee, argued that the estimated $500 million in aid to Pakistan would leave lawmakers with little say.

But Tom Lantos of California, ranking Democrat on International Relations, said Bush planned to provide only non-military aid. Supporting the bill, Lantos said Pakistan was carrying an "unusually heavy burden" because of its support for the United States. ◆

State Department Bill Sidetracked

Efforts to clear a broad State Department reauthorization bill were sidetracked after the Sept. 11 terrorist attacks, which forced more urgent priorities to the top of Congress' agenda. The House passed an authorization bill (HR 1646) in May, and the Senate Foreign Relations Committee approved a companion bill (S 1401) just before the August recess. The legislation went no further in the first session.

Members from both parties expressed enthusiastic support early in the year when Secretary of State Colin L. Powell vowed to restructure the State Department's management and asked lawmakers to reciprocate by providing additional resources. But the legislation soon began to run into problems, starting with the perennial dispute over abortion.

The House International Relations Committee amended the bill to overturn a decision by President Bush to reimpose a Reagan-era ban on federal aid to international family planning organizations that perform or promote abortions. The full House, where conservatives had more influence, reversed the committee decision.

A decision by the committee to release the second and third installments of $926 million that had been appropriated to pay U.S. back dues to the United Nations suddenly became controversial when the United States lost its seat on the U.N. Human Rights Commission. Pressed by the Bush administration, the House held off on immediate retaliation, threatening instead to hold up a 2003 payment if the United States did not regain its seat. The second installment ultimately was authorized in a separate bill (PL 107-46) enacted Oct. 5. (*U.N. dues, p. 11-13*)

On another issue, the Bush administration agreed to support a provision in the House-passed bill that would bar cooperation with a proposed International Criminal Court. The Senate had adopted a version of that provision as an amendment to the fiscal 2002 defense spending bill (PL 107-117).

BoxScore

Bills:
HR 1646, S 1401
Legislative Action:
House passed HR 1646 (H Rept 107-57), 352-73, on May 16.
Senate Foreign Relations Committee approved S 1401 (S Rept 107-60) by voice vote Aug. 1.

House Bill Highlights

Key provisions of the House-passed bill would:

● **International family planning.** Endorse Bush's policy barring aid to groups that perform or lobby for abortion.

● **U.N. dues.** Authorize release of a second installment of $582 million in back dues to the United Nations. The third installment could not be released until the United States regained its seat on the U.N. Human Rights Commission. To permit the release, the bill included language to increase the allowable limit on U.S. contributions to the United Nations to 28 percent for fiscal 2002 and 2003.

● **International court.** Bar funding for the International Criminal Court.

● **Authorization.** Authorize $8.2 billion for fiscal 2002, and such sums as were needed for fiscal 2003, including:

• $3.7 billion in fiscal 2002 for diplomatic and consular programs.

• $944 million in fiscal 2002 for contributions to international organizations.

• $844 million in fiscal 2002 for international peacekeeping activities.

• $817 million each in fiscal 2002 and 2003 for migration and refugee assistance.

• $428 million in fiscal 2002 for international broadcasting operations.

Background

The biannual State Department authorization bill, also known as the foreign relations bill, primarily authorized funding for State Department programs; multilateral aid administered by the department, such as international peacekeeping funds and refugee assistance; and U.S. information programs, such as Radio Free Asia and broadcasting to Cuba. Most bilateral aid was authorized separately.

The programs had to be reauthorized every two years. But foreign affairs spending was not popular, and lawmakers typically avoided passing a separate State Department bill, instead attaching provisions to an appropriations bill. A separate State Department authorization bill had not been enacted since 1994. (*1994 Almanac, p. 454*)

Topping the list of issues that threatened smooth passage of the fiscal 2002-03 bill were abortion restrictions on international family planning aid and repayment of U.S. dues to the United Nations.

The debate over abortion-related restrictions on family planning aid went back to President Ronald Reagan's 1984 "Mexico City policy," which blocked U.S. aid to international family planning organizations that offered abortion counseling or lobbied nations to legalize abortion, even if they used their own money. The policy was rescinded in 1993 by President Bill Clinton, but Bush reinstated it shortly after taking office in January. (*Mexico City, p. 2-28*)

U.N. debt payments became an issue after the 1994-95 State Department Authorization (PL 103-236) capped U.S. contributions to the peacekeeping budget at 25 percent. The United Nations continued to assess the United States at a higher rate, and arrears kept mounting.

The Clinton administration negotiated a compromise in December 2000, agreeing to pay $926 million in three annual installments, in exchange for organizational changes including a reduction in U.S. contributions. The compromise was written into the fiscal 2000 omnibus appropriations bill (PL 106-113), but release of the funds required enactment of a separate authorization bill specifying that the changes had been made. (*1999 Almanac, p. 14-3*)

Another issue concerned the proposed creation of an International Criminal Court to handle war crimes and other human rights violations. Clinton had signed a treaty Dec. 31, 2000, to create the court, though he said the treaty had "significant flaws" and that he would not submit it for Senate ratification, nor would he recommend that Bush do so. The Pentagon and key congressional leaders opposed the pact, warning that it could expose U.S. troops to politically motivated accusations and trials.

Legislative Action

House Committee Action

The House International Relations Committee approved its version of the State Department bill (H Rept 107-57) by voice vote May 2, after members added language to reverse Bush's decision on the Mexico City restrictions and made several other changes opposed by the administration.

The bill, written by Chairman Henry J. Hyde, R-Ill., and ranking Democrat Tom Lantos of California, proposed to authorize $8.2 billion for the State Department in fiscal 2002 and "such sums as may be necessary" for fiscal 2003. It also authorized $584 million for international broadcasting operations. Most of the accounts were close to Bush's request, which called for a 13 percent increase for the State Department over fiscal 2001. However, the committee added $100 million each for international broadcasting and refugee programs.

The bill authorized the release of $582 million — the second installment of the three-year, $926 million schedule of back payment of U.S. dues to the United Nations. It also increased the cap on U.S. contributions to the U.N. peacekeeping budget from 25 percent to 28 percent for two years to match the changes negotiated in 2000.

Republicans Benjamin A. Gilman and Amo Houghton of New York and Jim Leach of Iowa joined with Democrats to adopt the Mexico City amendment, 26-22. Hyde, a longtime opponent of abortion, warned that the change could doom the legislation. "I think we ought to think about whether we want to have this bill vetoed," he said. But the committee was more liberal than the House as a whole, and the amendment was expected to be reversed on the floor.

With some Republicans out of the room, the committee took aim at Bush's environmental policies, voting 23-20 to adopt a sense-of-Congress amendment by Robert Menendez, D-N.J., calling for continued participation in negotiations on the Kyoto Protocol on global warming. Bush had rejected the protocol as harmful to the U.S. economy.

Conservative Republicans also promised to challenge a Leach amendment, adopted 23-14, urging Bush to "take all necessary steps" to have the United States rejoin the United Nations Education, Scientific and Cultural Organization (UNESCO). The United States withdrew from UNESCO in 1984 complaining of financial mismanagement and anti-Western bias. Leach argued that UNESCO had changed substantially. Opponents acknowledged some of the changes, but questioned devoting scarce budget resources to the agency.

House Floor Action

After two days of heated debate, separated by a week, the House passed the State Department bill May 16 by a vote of 352-73. (*House vote 121, p. H-48*)

While abortion rights forces in the House had gained some support over the winter, it was not enough to reverse Bush's policy on family planning, and the House voted, 218-210, on May 16 to support Bush's order reinstating the Mexico City policy. Abortion rights supporters picked up support from three Republican women: Jennifer Dunn of Washington, Kay Granger of Texas and Shelley Moore Capito of West Virginia. On the vote, 32 Democrats crossed party lines to support the restrictions; 33 Republicans opposed them. (*House vote 115, p. H-46*)

In other action, the House:

• Voted, 252-165, to block the third and final installment of back payments to the United Nations, due October 2002, unless the United States regained its seat on the Human Rights Commission. The second installment was not affected. (*House vote 107, p. H-42*)

Loss of the seat in a secret ballot May 3 incensed lawmakers; the United States had been a member of the com-

mission since its creation. Some Republicans, including Majority Leader Dick Armey of Texas, had threatened to strike the entire $582 million. Seeking compromise, Hyde and Lantos agreed to make the third-year payment of $244 million conditional on the United States first regaining its seat.

• Rejected, 193-225, an attempt to remove the $67 million in the bill for the United States to rejoin UNESCO. (*House vote 108, p. H-42*)

• Adopted, 282-137, an amendment by Majority Whip Tom DeLay, R-Texas, to bar any U.S. cooperation with the International Criminal Court. (*House vote 106, p. H-42*)

• Adopted, 216-210, an amendment by Lantos to cut off military education and training funds for Lebanon unless that country used its army to oust Hezbollah guerrillas from Israel's northern border. The amendment also called for the administration to develop a plan for cutting off $35 million in economic assistance if Lebanon did not comply within six months. The amendment was opposed by Powell and many lawmakers, who said it would further destabilize the Middle East. (*House vote 119, p. H-46*)

Senate Committee Action

On Aug. 1, the Senate Foreign Relations Committee gave voice vote approval to an $18.4 billion State Department bill for fiscal 2002-03 (S 1401 — S Rept 107-60).

The bill provided for release of the second installment of U.N. dues payments, and the administration hoped it would be finished before Bush attended the opening of the General Assembly in September. But Chairman Joseph R. Biden Jr., D-Del., said a crowded Senate calendar and significant differences between the House and Senate versions of the bill made that unlikely. The delay was compounded by the shift in control of the Senate to the Democrats in June.

Among the issues that made quick compromise appear difficult were the House restrictions on U.N. payments and a small but important provision added by the Senate to move regular payment of U.N. dues from October to January to coincide with the U.N.'s budget cycle, which was on a calendar-year basis. For the past two decades, the late U.S. payment, timed to place it in a later U.S. fiscal year, had crimped the U.N.'s cash flow. However, advancing the payment would essentially require Congress to double its regular payment to the United Nations in fiscal 2002 in order to cover its 2001 and 2002 obligations.

Also during the Aug. 1 markup, the Foreign Relations Committee adopted, by voice vote, a non-binding amendment by John Kerry, D-Mass., calling for the United States to negotiate a treaty to combat global climate change. ◆

Sudan Sanctions Stall in Senate

Legislation to tighten sanctions on Sudan, where civil war had killed several million people over nearly two decades, passed both chambers, but the Senate was unable to finish appointing conferees. Sudan's inclusion in the anti-terrorism coalition assembled by the United States after the Sept. 11 terrorist attacks also helped stall the legislation.

Both the House and Senate versions of the bill were aimed at pressuring the Sudanese National Islamic Front government to end terrorism, slave raids and human rights violations, particularly against southern rebels. The legislation called on the administration to facilitate peace talks and to circumvent the government if it tried to veto humanitarian aid to rebel-held areas.

There was one major difference, however. While the Senate bill (S 180) relied mainly on diplomatic pressure, the House version (HR 2052) contained a controversial proposal to prevent companies from raising capital in the United States if they played a role in Sudan's expanding oil and gas industries. Several interest groups argued that such a provision was essential, while Wall Street and the Bush administration opposed it.

BoxScore

Bill:

S 180

Legislative Action:

House passed HR 2052 (H Rept 107-92, Part 1), 422-2, on June 13.

Senate passed S 180 by voice vote July 19.

House passed S 180 by voice vote, after substituting the text of HR 2502, and appointed conferees Nov. 15.

Highlights

Both the House and Senate bills contained provisions to:

• Condemn the government of Sudan for its human rights violations.

• Urge the Bush administration to use $10 million in previously appropriated funds (PL 106-429) for non-military aid to Sudan and direct the State Department to focus resources on negotiating a Sudanese peace agreement.

• Direct the U.S. ambassador to the United Nations to seek international support in condemning abuses.

In addition, the House-passed bill proposed to bar any foreign company from raising capital or listing its securities on U.S. markets if the company was engaged in oil and gas development in Sudan. Companies that did any business in Sudan would be required to disclose details to the Securities and Exchange Commission (SEC).

Background

War between Sudan's northern Muslim government and people in the south — most of whom practiced folk religions or Christianity — had raged since the early 1980s, causing

widespread famine, killing an estimated 2 million people and displacing another 4 million. The government had been accused of blocking humanitarian aid and food shipments, bombing villages and allowing slavery. Alleged terrorist mastermind Osama bin Laden had been based in Sudan from 1991 to 1996, and Khartoum was regularly identified as a state sponsor of terrorism.

A coalition of religious conservatives and African-American lawmakers pushed the issue onto the congressional agenda. They nearly reached their goal in 2000, when both chambers passed legislation targeting Sudan's human rights abuses. But Congress ran out of time before it could reconcile the House bill, which called for a significant tightening of sanctions, and the Senate bill, which did not.

The proposed sanctions faced strong opposition from vocal Wall Street groups such as the Securities Industry Association, the New York Stock Exchange and Goldman Sachs Group Inc.

In 2001, the new Bush administration condemned human rights violations in Sudan, though it opposed sanctions. Secretary of State Colin L. Powell told members of the House International Relations Committee in March that he would review U.S. policy toward Sudan, saying there was "perhaps no greater tragedy on the face of the earth today." Responding to requests from members of Congress, Bush in September named former Sen. John Danforth, R-Mo. (1976-95), an Episcopal priest, as an envoy to try to bring peace to Sudan. "For nearly two decades, the government of Sudan has waged a brutal and shameful war against its own people, and this isn't right and this must stop," Bush said.

Legislative History

House Subcommittee/Committee Action

The bill began as HR 931, approved by the House International Relations Subcommittee on Africa by voice vote May 16. The subcommittee version included a provision, added by voice vote, to block businesses that operated in Sudan from trading securities in U.S. capital markets unless they disclosed details of those activities.

After making some adjustments to satisfy committees that might otherwise have claimed jurisdiction, sponsor Tom Tancredo, R-Colo., reintroduced the bill as HR 2052. The full International Relations Committee approved it (H Rept 107-92, Part 1) by voice vote June 6.

The bill relied principally on diplomatic pressure to negotiate an end to the civil war in Sudan, though it required that businesses operating in Sudan that wanted to trade securities in U.S. capital markets file forms with the SEC. The company would have to disclose the nature of its activity in Sudan, the identity of all Sudanese agencies with which it did business and whether the proceeds from capital market transactions would be reinvested in Sudanese commercial activity. The SEC would have to make the reports public.

The White House issued a statement supporting the bill but opposing the disclosure requirement, which it said could "damage U.S. and international capital markets and undermine the independence and prerogative of the Securities and Exchange Commission to determine the nature and definition of information that is material to the investor."

House Floor Action

The House passed the bill by a 422-2 vote June 13, but only after agreeing to add a sanctions provision. (*House vote 160, p. H-60*)

An amendment by Spencer Bachus, R-Ala., adopted by voice vote, would bar foreign companies from raising capital in the United States if they participated in Sudan's oil or gas industry. Bachus called Sudanese oil revenue "blood money, which is resulting in the deaths of millions of people." No one rose to challenge him on the floor.

Senate Action

The Senate passed its version of the Sudan Peace Act (S 180) by voice vote July 19, one week after the Foreign Relations Committee approved the bill, also by voice vote. The measure, sponsored by Bill Frist, R-Tenn., relied primarily on diplomatic pressure. It condemned the violence in Sudan, supported peace efforts and directed the United States to provide humanitarian aid in areas of the country considered too dangerous for normal relief efforts.

Conference

House leaders delayed going to conference on the bill in the wake of the Sept. 11 terrorist attacks. Though the State Department had regularly labeled Khartoum a state sponsor of terrorism, Sudan was cooperating in the effort to build an anti-terrorism coalition. Late in the session, however, the House leadership relented. The House agreed by voice vote Nov. 15 to pass S 180, after inserting the text of its own bill, and to appoint conferees.

But in the Senate, Phil Gramm, R-Texas, blocked appointment of a final conferee, concerned that it could tip the balance in conference toward accepting the House sanctions provision. With adjournment looming and appropriations bills competing for attention, the measure was put on hold for the year. ◆

U.N. Dues Bill Sees Quick Action

A bill to release $582 million in back U.S. dues to the United Nations was signed into law (S 248 — PL 107-46) on Oct. 5, as congressional resistance melted away in the face of efforts to build a global anti-terrorism coalition.

The Senate passed the stand-alone bill in February. Similar provisions were in the House version of the fiscal 2002-03 State Department authorization bill (HR 1646), but that measure was caught up in a number of other disputes. Henry J. Hyde, R-Ill., chairman of the House International Relations Committee resisted pressure to break out the U.N. dues provisions, arguing that they should be paired with a bill (HR 1794) by Majority Whip Tom DeLay, R-Texas, to bar U.S. participation in a proposed International Criminal Court. The State Department bill included DeLay's language. (*State Department, p. 11-9*)

After the Sept. 11 terrorist attacks, Bush administration officials pressed for quick action, arguing that failure to pay the debt was an obstacle to rallying diplomatic support for the war on terrorism. The House quickly relented and cleared the bill.

The new law:

• Authorized the release of $582 million — the second installment of a three-year, $926 million schedule of back payment of U.S. dues to the United Nations.

• Modified conditions for releasing the money set in existing law to bring them in line with an agreement struck with the United Nations in December 2000.

Background

During the previous decade, concern over some U.N. programs, dissatisfaction with U.S. financial contribution levels and partisan politicking had frayed relations between the United States and the United Nations. Arrears had mounted primarily as a result of abortion restrictions on U.S. international family planning aid and concern over the U.S. share of the U.N. regular and peacekeeping budgets.

The fiscal 1994-95 State Department authorization law (PL 103-236) passed in the wake of expensive peacekeeping operations in Somalia and Bosnia, capped contributions to the U.N. budget at one-fourth of the total. Since the United Nations calculated U.S. dues at over 30 percent, the arrears continued to build. (*1994 Almanac, p. 454*)

The fiscal 2000 omnibus appropriations law (PL 106-113) contained what was known as the Helms-Biden agreement, after then-Foreign Relations Chairman Jesse Helms, R-N.C., and ranking Democrat Joseph R. Biden Jr. of Delaware. The agreement authorized $926 million in back payments. The total consisted of $819 million ($100 million in fiscal 1998 funds, $475 million in fiscal 1999, and $244 million in fiscal

BoxScore

Bill:
S 248 — PL 107-46

Legislative Action:
Senate passed S 248, 99-0, on Feb. 7.

House cleared the bill by voice vote Sept. 24.

President signed Oct. 5.

2000), plus $107 million owed by the United Nations for U.S. peacekeeping that would be used instead to reduce U.S. arrears. The first $100 million was released in December 1999. To receive the remaining money, the U.N. had to agree to a number of conditions, including a reduction in the U.S. share of the regular U.N. budget from 25 percent to 22 percent and a cut in the U.S. portion of the peacekeeping budget from 31 percent to 25 percent. Release of the second and third installments required authorizing legislation confirming that the United Nations had met the conditions. (*1999 Almanac, p. 14-3*)

In December 2000, Richard C. Holbrooke, the Clinton administration's representative to the United Nations, negotiated an agreement that came close enough to the Helms-Biden plan to receive endorsement from both senators. The United States agreed to repay $926 million in exchange for permanent reduction in U.S. payments to 22 percent of the regular budget and 28 percent of the peacekeeping budget, declining to about 26 percent by 2004.

Legislative Action

Senate Committee/Floor Action

The Senate Foreign Relations Committee approved S 248, ratifying the Holbrooke agreement, 18-0, on Feb. 7. The full Senate passed the bill, 99-0, later the same day. Helms and Biden had already endorsed the agreement. (*Senate vote 10, p. S-6*)

The bill authorized the release of the second installment of $582 million ($475 million in fiscal 1999 funds and the $107 million in forgiven debt). It also amended the Helms-Biden provision in the fiscal 2000 appropriations law to allow the United States to pay 28 percent of the peacekeeping budget, as negotiated by Holbrooke.

During the markup, members said the conditions set in the fiscal 1994-95 State Department authorization law also should be amended. Lawmakers pointed to a letter from Secretary of State Colin L. Powell, who said the United States would run up $77 million in debts in fiscal 2001 alone unless the cap was revised. But Biden, who had become chairman of the committee, and Helms assured members that the cap would be addressed when the committee took up the State Department authorization bill later in the year.

House Action

The House cleared S 248 by voice vote Sept. 24, a little less than two weeks after the Sept. 11 attacks.

The House had included the U.N. repayment as part of the fiscal 2002-03 State Department authorization bill

(HR 1646), passed in May. That bill initially authorized the release of both the $582 million and the third installment of $244 million. However, two weeks before House passage, the United States was removed from the U.N. Commission on Human Rights by a secret U.N. ballot. The House responded by adopting an amendment conditioning the third installment on the United States regaining its seat. The State Department bill also amended the 1994-95 law to increase permissible U.S. payments to 28 percent for two years.

The administration hoped to have the debt payment in hand by September, when Bush was due to attend the opening of the General Assembly. U.N. General Secretary Kofi Annan warned July 31 that unless the debts were repaid they would soon undermine U.S. effectiveness in the United Nations.

But Biden warned that quick action on a final State Department bill was unlikely. And Hyde said he did not want to move the U.N. payment without DeLay's court provisions.

With the Sept. 11 attacks, however, Washington put a premium on international cooperation against terrorism. After receiving assurance from the administration that it would support legislation barring cooperation with the International Criminal Court, the House cleared S 248 under suspension of the rules with only 20 minutes of debate. "Meeting our financial obligations to the United Nations will help to ensure that our policymakers can keep the focus on broad policies that unite the members of the Security Council in the fight against global terrorism," Hyde said. ◆

House Passes Restrictions On 'Blood Diamond' Trade

The House overwhelmingly passed legislation aimed at restricting trade in illegal diamonds, but the Senate did not act on the measure before the end of the session. The diamonds — known as conflict or blood diamonds — came from regions in Sierra Leone, Liberia and the Congo, where rebel, and sometimes government, militias forced civilians to mine the gems under threat of death or mutilation and used the profits to finance their operations.

For nearly two years, legislation aimed at restricting trade in illegal diamonds met with limited success. That changed following the Sept. 11 attacks, with reports that the al Qaeda terrorist network had used the illegal diamond trade to launder money. One of the main challenges was devising an approach to block the illegal diamonds while not thwarting trade in clean diamonds. House members moved quickly to negotiate with the Bush administration on a bill (HR 2722) that would allow but not require the president to restrict imports of conflict diamonds, with the strictest rules applying to polished, set diamonds.

The United States was the world's largest consumer of diamonds. Existing sanctions barred rough diamonds from Liberia and restricted the importation of rough diamonds from Angola and Sierra Leone unless they were accompanied by a certificate of origin. A conference aimed at setting up a process to keep conflict diamonds off the world market was held in 2001 in Botswana as part of the so-called Kimberly Process to establish an international certification system to identify clean diamonds.

Highlights

The main provisions of the House-passed bill would:

• Authorize the president to bar the importation of rough diamonds from any country that did not have effective controls to stop trade in conflict diamonds.

• Authorize the president to prohibit specific entries of polished diamonds and jewelry containing diamonds if there was credible evidence that they were produced with conflict diamonds.

• Set penalties, including seizure and forfeiture and criminal and civil penalties for anyone convicted of violating the importation restrictions.

• Require annual reports to Congress on the actions taken by countries exporting rough diamonds to the United States to stop trade in conflict diamonds; countries that failed to take such action would be identified.

• Authorize $5 million a year in fiscal 2002 and 2003 for assistance to countries seeking to eliminate the trade in conflict diamonds.

House Floor Action

The House passed the bill by a vote of 408-6 on Nov. 28. The measure was brought directly to the floor and did not see committee action. The bill, which originally had required the president to prohibit imports of all conflict diamonds, was modified to reflect the negotiations with the White House. (*House vote 453, p. H-156*) ◆

Chapter 12

HEALTH

No Score on Managed Care

After years of politicized debate, supporters of legislation to give patients more leverage over their managed-care health insurance plans were hopeful that the issue might be resolved in 2001. But following tough battles on the floor in both chambers, and a surprise victory by Republicans in the House, the measure stalled. House and Senate conferees were not appointed before the session ended.

The biggest dispute, as it had been in the previous Congress, was over the legal rights of patients to sue their health plans. Democrats pushed for broad rights to sue. Republicans generally insisted on more limited safeguards, warning that providing expansive new legal remedies could increase health costs.

About a dozen Democrats and Republicans from both chambers unveiled a proposal Feb. 6 modeled after legislation that had passed the House in October 1999 with the support of 68 Republicans. Senate backers — including John McCain, R-Ariz., Edward M. Kennedy, D-Mass., and John Edwards, D-N.C. — believed they had the votes to pass the proposal. House proponents were confident they would prevail as well.

On Feb. 7, President Bush offered his own outline for managed-care legislation, telling leaders from both parties he did "not believe that any bill currently before the Congress meets all of these principles." The patient protections on Bush's list were similar to those in the Democratic plan — access to specialty care, for example, and the right to a speedy decision if care were denied. The real difference came on liability. Bush wanted employers shielded from lawsuits unless they were responsible for "final medical decisions." He wanted to restrict lawsuits to federal courts and allow patients to sue only after they exhausted appeals processes. Damages would be subject to "reasonable" caps.

Democrats, by contrast, proposed allowing patients to sue managed-care plans over decisions that resulted in injury or death. Those cases would be tried in state court. Cases related to administrative decisions or contract disputes would be decided in federal courts.

When Democrats took control of the Senate in June, Majority Leader Tom Daschle, D-S.D., said his top priority would be the managed-care bill. Bush threatened to veto the McCain-Kennedy-Edwards bill if it reached his desk, and White House spokesman Ari Fleischer warned that sending the bill to the president would be "akin to spinning wheels."

But Daschle stuck to his plan, bringing the bill to the floor without any committee markups and holding his caucus together through a series of Republicans assaults. The bill passed June 29, with every Democrat and nine Republicans supporting it.

The focus then turned to the House, where health insur-

BoxScore

Bills:
HR 2563, S 1052

Legislative Action:
Senate passed S 1052, 59-36, on June 29.

House passed HR 2563, 226-203, on Aug. 2.

ance and business groups joined forces to fight a companion bill introduced by Greg Ganske, R-Iowa, and John D. Dingell, D-Mich. Hoping to build on the momentum in the Senate, Ganske and Dingell announced July 2 that they would incorporate some of the changes made by the Senate into their own bill.

That complicated the task of Speaker J. Dennis Hastert, R-Ill., who hoped to peel away supporters of Ganske-Dingell for a rival measure (HR 2315) favored by GOP leaders and the White House. The bill they preferred, written by Ernie Fletcher, R-Ky., would have allowed patients to sue in state courts only if an insurer ignored the decisions made by an external reviewer, with damages limited to state caps. Patients would have been able to sue insurers in federal courts over contractual disputes, with unlimited economic damages but a limit of $500,000 in non-economic damages and no punitive damages.

As the vote neared, the White House and House leaders were forced to acknowledge that the Fletcher bill did not have the votes to pass. Bush and Charlie Norwood, R-Ga., began meeting privately to try to broker a deal. Norwood said he felt torn between his Democratic allies, who had helped him for years in his drive to enact patients' rights legislation, and the president, who was not only the leader of Norwood's party but also a friend.

On Aug. 1, the day before the House was scheduled to vote, Norwood reached an agreement with Bush. He said he accepted a number of Bush's demands because he wanted to avoid a veto and push all sides toward compromise. The House passed the bill the next day, after narrowly adopting Norwood's amendment. The Bush-Norwood deal is "not going to ensure that you have a level playing field for patients dealing with HMOs," said Kennedy. "I think that's regrettable, and it means we will have a continued battle in the Senate and in the conference."

Immediately after the vote, lawmakers left for their August recess. Few believed that the gap between the House and Senate bills could be bridged in the limited amount of time that remained in the session. "If we can't fix the problems, maybe we will have no bill at all," said House Minority Leader Richard A. Gephardt, D-Mo.

Conferees had not met before terrorist attacks struck New York and Washington on Sept. 11. After that, White House and congressional attention focused on the demands of national security rather than on thorny domestic issues such as patients' rights that would have required deep commitments of time and resources.

Highlights

The House- and Senate-passed bills had many similarities, particularly when it came to patient protections. The

chief differences were on issues such as damage caps, state vs. federal jurisdiction, and employer liability. The following are the key provisions of the two bills:

● **Right to sue.** Both bills would allow lawsuits in federal and state courts, depending on the issue. Patients could sue in federal court over administrative decisions, such as whether a certain treatment was covered by a plan's contract with the patient. They could sue in state courts when the challenge focused on the plan's influence over medical decisions. Cases in state courts would be subject to state law under the Senate bill, but federal law under the House version.

● **Damage caps.** Under the Senate bill, patients could collect civil damages of up to $5 million in federal cases, with unlimited economic and pain-and-suffering awards. In state cases, damage caps would be governed by state law.

The House bill would allow patients to receive unlimited economic damages in either state or federal court, but non-economic damages would be limited to $1.5 million. Patients could sue for punitive damages, which would be capped at $1.5 million, only if the insurance plan failed to comply with an independent medical reviewer's decision that the claim should be granted.

● **Patient protections.** The two bills offered similar safeguards. Patients would have access to any emergency room without prior authorization. The bills would expand access to clinical trials, ban restrictions on communications about treatment options between doctors and patients, and allow women to see obstetrician-gynecologists without prior authorization. Parents could take children for visits to pediatricians without prior authorization. Group plans would be required to offer patients an option to see doctors who did not participate in the plan's network; plans could charge more for the service. Any plan that terminated a doctor from its network or changed plan benefits would have to allow patients in certain serious conditions to continue seeing the doctor during a transition period.

● **Internal and external appeals.** Both bills required that managed health plans offer patients an internal and an independent, external review when the plan denied a certain type of treatment based on questions about whether it was medically appropriate, such as whether the service was an experimental treatment.

● **Utilization review.** Both bills would regulate the way health plans evaluated the use or coverage of health services, such as the appropriateness or efficiency of treatments, including plans for discharging patients from hospitals. Plans could not pay doctors to recommend that they deny health care claims. Each plan would have to offer patients access to administrative officials who would field questions on coverage, through toll-free telephone services during normal business hours.

● **Prompt decisions.** Both bills would require plans to determine whether a service was covered within 28 days of receiving the claim. If prior authorization was required before the service was performed, a plan would have 14 days in which to make a decision after health plan officials received the information needed to make a determination. In life-threatening or serious emergencies, the bill would require plans to issue coverage decisions within 72 hours.

● **Restrictions on new legal remedies.** Both plans would require patients to exhaust a health plan's internal and external appeals processes before filing a lawsuit in state or federal court. Patients could still file a lawsuit if they lost the appeal, and the results of the appeal process could be admissible in court.

● **Liability protections for employers.** Under both bills, employers who appointed a "designated decision-maker" for medical decisions and did not participate in the decision would be shielded from lawsuits. Companies could appoint their health insurer to serve in that role. The Senate bill would shield the small number of employers that both financed and administered health plans for their workers from lawsuits in federal court. The House bill would allow them to be sued in federal court but shield them from state lawsuits.

● **Other limits to new legal rights.** The House bill, but not the Senate measure, would ban patients from using the Racketeer-Influenced and Corrupt Organizations (RICO) law (PL 91-452) against insurers. The House bill also would give health plans a new protective legal argument. If patients lost an appeal to an external review panel, they would then have to overcome a "rebuttable presumption" in favor of the health plans by clear and convincing evidence — the highest civil standard of proof — that the insurer had been correct in denying care. Patients would not get the same advantage if they won a review decision. Patients would have to prove that a denial was "the" proximate cause of an injury. Previous bills had said that the denial would have to be shown to be "a" cause of injury.

● **Medical savings accounts.** The House bill, only, would lift existing restrictions on medical savings accounts. The accounts were fiercely opposed by Democrats, who said they undermined the health system and allowed members of trade associations to pool their funds to buy insurance.

● **Scope of bill.** Under the Senate bill, states would have to comply with the substance of the new federal standards, although they would have some limited flexibility in implementing them. All privately insured Americans would be governed, as would those covered by federal health programs such as Medicare and Medicaid. The House bill would cover all Americans in private insurance plans.

Background

Although the debate on patients' rights sounded much the same as it had for years, the ground beneath it had shifted considerably. Changes in the marketplace, the courts, the states and even in Congress itself had reshaped the discussion. "Things that were tremendously controversial two years ago and basically saw hand-to-hand combat then are now no-brainers," said Sara Rosenbaum, a health policy expert at George Washington University in Washington. "The biggest question left is how you structure liability."

Patient protections for those in managed-care health plans — once a hotly debated issue — had changed significantly. Many major health plans already had responded to patients' calls for broader coverage, in part because of new state laws and a 1998 executive order by President Bill Clinton that gave more access to specialists and expanded appeals rights to about 80 million Americans in Medicare, Medicaid or federal workers' managed-care plans. Most

states had passed laws making it easier for insured patients to get emergency room treatment and direct access to specialists. Most banned gag clauses that limited what a physician could tell patients about treatment options. Most also required an independent medical review of appeals.

Even in the areas of liability and state flexibility, the world was changing. Courts traditionally had interpreted the 1974 Employee Retirement Income Security Act (ERISA) (PL 93-406), which governed employee benefits, to mean that patients could sue health plans only in federal court, with damages limited to the cost of denied care. (*1974 Almanac, p. 244*)

But ERISA limits were being chipped away from several directions. State courts, which traditionally oversee tort law involving medical treatment decisions by doctors, had started to allow lawsuits against insurers if the case involved medical judgment. Appellate courts had held in several cases that only matters involving a patient's contract, benefits or coverage belonged in federal court. And the U.S. Supreme Court signaled in 2000 in *Pegram v. Herdrich* that it considered the states to be the proper venue for personal injury or wrongful death claims, including some cases against health plans.

Patients' Rights Legislation

Managed health care plans grew in prominence in the 1990s, as employers tried to hold down the spiralling costs of health benefits. By monitoring care and channeling patients toward approved doctors, the plans held the steep price hikes in check, reducing the cost of health benefits for businesses and out-of-pocket costs for employees. Premium increases, which had been rising 15 percent to 20 percent per year, were reduced to single digits, and for three consecutive years in the mid-'90s they were lower than the rate of inflation. By 2001, nearly 90 percent of people in private health insurance plans had moved to managed-care plans such as health maintenance organizations (HMOs) or preferred provider organizations (PPOs).

But patients complained about their limited choice of doctors, the need to get approval before going to the emergency room and reports that doctors were paid incentives to withhold information about health care options. Patients demanded a right to appeal when their plan denied care and to sue insurers if they were harmed because of a plan's refusal to pay for medical treatment.

Democrats embraced the issue, pushing for comprehensive legislation to rein in managed-care plans. Their efforts were applauded by the American Medical Association and the nation's trial attorneys.

With public interest growing, House GOP leaders assembled a managed-care task force in 1998. A bill produced by the group passed the House mostly along party lines. but died in the Senate. (*1998 Almanac, p. 14-3*)

Frustrated that his efforts had gone nowhere, Norwood, who had dropped a bill of his own to work on the GOP task force, joined forces with Dingell and other House Democrats in 2000. Their broad managed-care bill, which included the right to sue in state courts, passed 275-151. As punishment, Hastert refused to appoint Norwood to the conference committee with the Senate, which had passed a narrower bill. The legislation ultimately foundered in confer-

ence, in part because of the House provisions that would have expanded patients' rights to sue health insurers. (*1999 Almanac, p. 16-3*)

That stalemate left supporters of patients' rights legislation itching for action in 2001. Norwood saw promise in the election of George W. Bush, because the candidate had promised to pass some type of managed-care legislation. Democrats, on the other hand, were skeptical about what type of bill Bush wanted to enact.

Legislative Action

Senate Floor Action

The Senate passed the McCain-Kennedy-Edwards bill June 29 by a vote of 59-36, with universal backing from Democrats and increased support from Republicans over previous years. Besides McCain, eight Republicans voted for the bill, including three who were up for re-election in 2002 — Susan Collins of Maine, Gordon H. Smith of Oregon and John W. Warner of Virginia. (*Senate vote 220, p. S-46*)

The measure would, for the first time, allow millions of Americans to sue their health plans in federal courts, where patients could collect civil damages of up to $5 million and unlimited economic and non-economic damages. The bill also included new freedom to sue in state courts, with damages set by individual states.

Opponents tried but largely failed to weaken those provisions. The Senate rejected, 36-59, a substitute by Bill Frist, R-Tenn., that was backed by Bush. Frist proposed federal protections similar to those in the underlying bill, such as access to specialists and emergency room care. But the substitute would have capped non-economic damages at $750,000, or three times economic damages, and prohibited punitive damages. A patient would have been required to exhaust the administrative appeals process before filing a lawsuit for denial of benefits. (*Senate vote 219, p. S-46*)

"Sens. Kennedy and Edwards have pushed through a proposal more concerned about protecting the rights of trial lawyers than providing Americans with affordable, high-quality health care," said Frist.

Senators had begun debate on the bill June 19, and Daschle had threatened to keep them in session through the July Fourth recess, if necessary, to finish. By the time it was over, the Senate had taken 28 roll-call votes.

The White House made its opposition clear, issuing a veto threat, but Democrats refused to compromise, determined to enter conference negotiations with a strong position. During the two weeks of debate, Republicans proposed amendment after amendment aimed at changing the bill's liability provisions. Most of them failed.

Early in the debate, Republicans lost a test vote when they tried to send the bill to the committees that had jurisdiction but had not marked up the measure. That motion was rejected, 39-61, the same margin that eventually approved the overall bill. (*Senate vote 196, p. S-43*)

● **Employer liability.** GOP moderates did succeed in attaching amendments aimed at making the bill more acceptable to business, especially large employers.

One of the most important was a proposal by Olympia J. Snowe, R-Maine, to allow employers to appoint a "designat-

ed decision-maker" for medical decisions, thereby shielding themselves from lawsuits. Big business groups and their Republican allies had seized on the issue, painting the bill as one that would make large employers, not just less-popular insurance companies, vulnerable to higher costs. "Employers beware," warned Minority Whip Don Nickles, R-Okla. "There's language in this bill that will bankrupt you." The Snowe amendment, which gave Republicans some cover, was adopted, 96-4, on June 28. (*Senate vote 205, p. S-44*)

An amendment by Fred Thompson, R-Tenn. — approved 98-0, shortly before the bill passed June 29 — required that patients exhaust their health plan's internal and independent review mechanisms before filing a lawsuit in either state or federal court. If an external appeals board did not act within 31 days after a patient filed an appeal, then a lawsuit could be filed. (*Senate vote 213, p. S-45*)

But the Senate rejected a broad amendment by Phil Gramm, R-Texas, that would have protected all employers from liability. It failed, 43-57, with 43 Republicans and six Democrats supporting it. (*Senate vote 197, p. S-43*)

A move by Wayne Allard, R-Colo., to exempt employers with 50 or fewer workers from all liability under the bill failed, 45-53, on June 27. (*Senate vote 199, p. S-43*)

A proposal by Michael B. Enzi, R-Wyo., to provide protection from state lawsuits to the approximately 6 percent of employers who both financed and administered health plans for their workers was tabled (killed) on a 55-45 vote June 28. The underlying bill would protect those groups from federal lawsuits. (*Senate vote 206, p. S-44*)

McCain won unanimous support June 27 for an amendment to block reviewers from requiring a plan to cover benefits specifically excluded under its contracts. It was adopted 100-0 on June 27. (*Senate vote 201, p. S-43*)

McCain had just defeated a broader amendment by Jon Kyl, R-Ariz., that included a requirement for the Department of Health and Human Services (HHS) to define "medically necessary" care that plans could use when determining whether to cover a treatment. Kyl's amendment, tabled 54-45 on June 27, would have prevented reviewers from requiring coverage of benefits that were denied on the basis of those standards as well. (*Senate vote 200, p. S-43*)

● **Scope.** Ben Nelson, D-Neb., and Collins, both former state insurance commissioners, lost an attempt to allow state laws to remain intact as long as they were "consistent with" the bill. The proposal was tabled, 53-44, on June 28, partly because of criticisms that the standard would not adequately protect millions of Americans covered under state-regulated plans. (*Senate vote 202, p. S-44*)

Later that day, the Senate adopted, 64-36, a tougher amendment by John B. Breaux, D-La., to require that state laws "substantially comply" with new federal standards, as determined by HHS. (*Senate vote 203, p. S-44*)

The Senate adopted by voice vote an amendment by Nickles to require that federal health programs comply with the bill's mandates. The proposal covered programs such as Medicare, which serves the elderly and disabled; Medicaid, which serves low-income beneficiaries; and the Federal Employees Health Benefit Program, which covers federal workers.

● **Other liability issues.** Senators approved by voice vote an amendment by Warner to cap attorneys' fees in managed-care lawsuits to one-third of the total award amount.

The Senate had rejected an amendment by Christopher S. Bond, R-Mo., that would have limited the fees to 15 percent of any award over $100,000. The stricter Bond amendment was tabled, 62-38, on June 28. (*Senate vote 204, p. S-44*)

Arlen Specter, R-Pa., lost a bid to require that all lawsuits brought under the bill be heard in federal court, but that the courts abide by state damage caps. It was rejected, 42-58, on June 28. (*Senate vote 207, p. S-44*)

The Senate narrowly rejected an amendment by Rick Santorum, R-Pa., that would have required three-fourths of any punitive damages that a patient won from an insurer in court to be put into a federal trust fund to finance tax credits for uninsured individuals. The amendment was tabled, 50-46, on June 29. (*Senate vote 217, p. S-46*)

John Ensign, R-Nev., lost an attempt to exempt from malpractice liability any health care professionals who provided pro bono medical services to uninsured, indigent individuals. The amendment was tabled, 52-46, on June 29. (*Senate vote 212, p. S-45*)

Ensign won voice vote approval for a proposal to ban genetic discrimination by insurers against patients.

The Senate agreed, 98-0, on June 29 to an amendment by Santorum specifying that the words "person," "human being," "child," and "individual" include infants who are born alive at any stage of development. This definition would be required in determining the meaning of any act of Congress, or any regulation. (*Senate vote 208, p. S-45*)

House Floor Action

The House passed its bill by a vote of 226-203 on Aug. 2. But with debate tightly controlled by the Rules Committee, the floor action was less interesting than the intrigue that preceded it. (*House vote 332, p. H-112*)

Norwood's decision to break with his colleagues and strike a separate deal with Bush — announced on national television in an impromptu news conference — was a surprise to his allies and even his aides.

"We want to change the law," Norwood said as he stood with the president in the White House briefing room late in the afternoon of Aug. 1. "The last time I looked, that's pretty difficult to do without the presidential signature."

But his erstwhile comrades were furious, especially because they thought they had the president over a barrel. Bush made them even angrier by claiming that he had broken "six years of deadlock." Democrats believed that Republicans had been the ones holding up action on the bill for all those years.

The Norwood-Bush deal was adopted Aug. 2 on a near party-line vote of 218-213. Opponents said the changes in liability and damage provisions would gut the bill and undercut stronger state laws. Supporters argued that the changes would provide for court redress without inviting frivolous lawsuits, and that they were necessary to avoid a veto. Three Republicans who had cosponsored the original Norwood-Dingell-Ganske bill in 1999 followed Norwood in his new amendment. They were Bob Barr of Georgia, Benjamin A. Gilman of New York and Steve Horn of California. (*House vote 329, p. H-112*)

Under the amendment,

● Cases against insurers involving medically reviewable decisions would be heard in state courts, but would be sub-

ject to federal law and rules. The underlying bill provided for such cases to be heard in state courts under state laws. Under the amendment, employers being sued in cases involving medically reviewable decisions could have those cases moved to federal courts.

• Non-economic damages in both state and federal courts would be capped at $1.5 million; punitive damages also would be capped at $1.5 million. The underlying bill would have set no limit on economic or non-economic damages in federal court, and limited civil monetary penalties in federal court to $5 million. Cases in state court would have been subject to state caps.

• Punitive damages would be allowed only if the designated decision-maker failed to comply with an independent medical reviewer's decision that a claim should be granted. The underlying bill generally barred punitive damages against a plan that complied with the decisions of the internal and external reviewer, but permitted such damages if the plan acted with willful disregard for the safety and rights of others.

On a small handful of other amendments, the House:

• Rejected, 207-221, an amendment by Ways and Means Committee Chairman Bill Thomas, R-Calif., to put restrictions on medical malpractice claims. The amendment would have required a plaintiff to initiate a lawsuit within two years of discovering an injury; all health care actions would have to be filed within five years of the injury. Those requirements would pre-empt other tort law. The amendment would have limited pain-and-suffering damage awards to $250,000 and divided damages with multiple defendants based on responsibility. It also would have restricted punitive damages, including limiting recovery to the greater of twice the amount of economic damages or $250,000. (*House vote 330, p. H-112*)

• Adopted, 236-194, a Thomas amendment favored by GOP leaders to lift existing restrictions on the use of medical savings accounts. The proposal would allow the creation of so-called association health plans, which businesses could use to pool their resources to negotiate lower cost insurance plans. The amendment was strongly backed by business groups. Eighteen Democrats voted to approve it, while two Republicans opposed it. (*House vote 328, p. H-112*)

Gephardt was impassioned in his closing speech: "This is not a patients' bill of rights. This is an HMO and health insurance companies' bill of rights. In the name of God . . . vote against this bill."

For his part, Norwood insisted the deal he had cut with Bush was not the final word, and suggested changes could be made in conference. "I know this isn't the final bill, and so do you," he told his colleagues. ◆

Medicare Drug Coverage Stalls

Reaching a deal on Medicare prescription drug coverage was seen from the outset as one of the most difficult health care issues facing the 107th Congress. Both chambers agreed as part of the fiscal 2002 budget resolution (H Con Res 83) to set aside $300 billion to cover prescriptions as part of a Medicare overhaul. But while several bills were introduced, none made it to the markup stage. By the fall, the recession and tax cuts had dried up any money that might have been available for such an initiative.

Both parties had much to gain — and lose — as they tried to design a strategy for Medicare prescription drug coverage. Medicare, the federal health insurance program for nearly 40 million elderly and disabled Americans, did not pay for most outpatient drugs. In a post-election poll presented Jan. 25 by the Henry J. Kaiser Family Foundation and the Harvard School of Public Health, 56 percent of voters surveyed said the federal government should expand Medicare to pay directly for part of prescription drug costs, rather than rely on private plans. Two-thirds of Democrats agreed with that statement, while 43 percent of Republicans said the government should help seniors buy private health coverage to help pay for prescription costs.

President Bush endorsed a bipartisan plan (S 358, S 357) sponsored by Sens. John B. Breaux, D-La., and Bill Frist, R-Tenn., to allow private insurers to compete for Medicare enrollees by offering prescription drug coverage as part of their health care plans. The proposal relied heavily on expanding the private Medicare+Choice managed-care program, which limited the unrestricted access to specialists and hospitals enjoyed by senior citizens and others under the traditional Medicare fee-for-service program. Breaux and Frist hoped that holding down costs would allow private insurers to offer enrollees prescription drug coverage and other expanded benefits.

The leading Democratic alternative (S 1135) offered drug coverage as an optional Medicare benefit that beneficiaries could buy. The bill, sponsored by Democratic Sen. Bob Graham of Florida, proposed setting monthly premiums on a sliding scale pegged to enrollees' income. Graham wanted to cover half the price of drugs — up to $3,500 annually — after a $250 deductible. Breaux-Frist would set the bar at $6,000.

Bush Steps Out Early

Democrats had made prescription drugs for seniors one of their top political priorities for years. But Bush indicated shortly after taking office that he would be a player. On Jan. 29, he announced an "Immediate Helping Hand" prescription drug plan for low-income seniors, and signaled a willingness to work with Congress for a broader Medicare overhaul that would include a prescription drug benefit. He called for $48 billion in block grants over four years to states that chose to participate. Key elements of the plan included:

• Full drug coverage without monthly premiums for seniors with incomes of up to $11,600 per individual and $15,700 per couple.

• At least a 50 percent subsidy for seniors with incomes of up to $15,000 per individual and $20,300 per couple.

• Coverage for all out-of-pocket costs above $6,000.

Consumer groups and some lawmakers criticized the

plan, saying millions of seniors just above the income limit would not be helped. According to an analysis by Consumers Union, about 5 percent of seniors without prescription coverage would benefit under Bush's plan. But Senate Finance Committee Chairman Charles E. Grassley, R-Iowa, said it was the right move for Bush to send his plan to Congress. "He's fulfilling a campaign promise. He's also showing Congress that he intends to . . . get prescription drugs for seniors," Grassley said.

CBO Estimates

In March, the Congressional Budget Office (CBO) introduced a new note of caution into the debate, estimating that adding a prescription drug benefit to Medicare could cost more than $1 trillion over the following decade. CBO Director Dan L. Crippen, told the Senate Finance Committee on March 22 that total spending on prescription drugs for Medicare enrollees would reach $1.5 trillion through 2011. That included hospital prescription bills already covered by Medicare and outpatient costs already paid either by private insurers or by seniors themselves.

"It is not possible to provide a generous drug benefit to all Medicare beneficiaries at a low cost," Crippen said. "Either enrollees' premiums or the government's subsidy cost would be high. If most of the costs were paid by enrollees' premiums to keep federal costs low, some Medicare beneficiaries would be unwilling or unable to participate in the program."

Crippen said covering half of seniors' prescription drug costs would require $728 billion over 10 years. If the benefit kicked in after a senior spent $5,000 out of pocket, the cost would be $365 billion. A $1,000 deductible would drive up the federal bill to $1.1 trillion.

"In light of the enormity of the potential costs of prescription drug coverage and Medicare's worsening financial condition, we must be fiscally responsible in adding any new benefits," Grassley commented.

CBO took some of the sting out of its projections in a briefing for Senate Finance Committee aides June 8. CBO said that the three leading proposals to create a seniors drug benefit were in the ballpark of the $300 billion included for a Medicare overhaul in the budget resolution.

Before the briefing, aides had braced for bad news all around because of the agency's warning in March. But CBO said that Graham's bill would cost $318 billion; aides had prepared for a new estimate of more than $400 billion.

The Breaux-Frist bill was scored at $176 billion over 10 years. CBO said a third alternative, which passed the House in 2000, would cost $157 billion over 10 years, up from an earlier estimate of $140 billion. That measure, sponsored by Ways and Means Committee Chairman Bill Thomas, R-

Calif., was structured similarly to Breaux's proposal but included no premium subsidy. (*2000 Almanac, p. 12-16*)

Bush Proposes Discount Card

Bush weighed in again in July, announcing plans for a privately administered discount program to help seniors buy medications at a reduced price. He presented the plan at a Rose Garden ceremony July 12, as part of a broader set of principles for overhauling Medicare. The privately administered prescription drug discount cards would be endorsed and promoted by Medicare. The cards, which Bush lauded as simple and convenient, would cost a maximum of $25. The White House estimated such cards could cut Medicare recipients' drug bills 20 percent or more, with the greatest savings on generic medications and mail-order prescriptions. The administration expected card sponsors to receive discounts from manufacturers for buying the most widely used drugs in bulk.

Officials from Merck-Medco and four other health care companies appeared with Bush at the White House to endorse his drug card proposal. The plan could be implemented without congressional action.

Democrats said the plan offered seniors little beyond what was already in the marketplace. For example, 1.1 million members of AARP (formerly the American Association of Retired Persons) participated in prescription discount programs that saved them 10 percent to 40 percent on prescriptions and were accepted at 48,000 retail pharmacies. Another discount program — a venture between the Reader's Digest Association, Inc. and pharmaceutical benefit manager Merck-Medco — had a prescription plan that offered discounts at more than 40,000 drug stores.

Daschle said Bush's plan "may help on the periphery, [but] it is no substitute for a meaningful prescription drug benefit. We're talking here about the difference between a small discount and the ability to allow those seniors who have prescription drug bills to be able to pay for them at all."

The National Association of Chain Drug Stores and other pharmacy trade groups said in a July 11 letter to Bush that existing discount card programs "do not provide seniors with meaningful access to prescription drugs" and placed price controls on pharmacies. They also complained that Bush's program would "do nothing to reduce the prices we are charged for these medications."

The association subsequently filed a complaint July 17 to halt the program. A federal district court judge agreed Sept. 6, saying the discount card plan was not authorized by Congress and was put forward without following proper regulatory procedures. The administration said it would revise the proposal before moving forward. ◆

Bio-Terrorism Bill Founders

The House and Senate passed similar bills in December designed to fight bioterrorism and prepare the country for an attack that used anthrax or other toxins, but there was not enough time left in the session to reconcile the differences. Congress separately appropriated $2.5 billion to buy more vaccines and antibiotics and to improve public health facilities. That money was provided as part of a supplemental spending package tied to the fiscal 2002 defense appropriations bill (PL 107-117).

Although the appropriation took some of the momentum out of efforts to finish the bio-terrorism bill, lawmakers said authorizing legislation was still necessary to provide clear guidance and legal certainty to federal and state governments — for instance, to efforts by the Health and Human Services Department (HHS) to expedite the development of new drugs. Lobbyists also worried that without an authorization bill, provisions important to their industries could be lost. Both versions, for instance, had incentives for pharmaceutical companies researching new vaccines or drugs to treat toxins.

The bills were introduced out of concern that the nation's public health system was unprepared to handle a major biological attack. Federal and local officials had trouble dealing with a limited spate of anthrax cases in Florida, New York, Connecticut and Washington, D.C., including the temporary closure of a Senate and a House office building after some lawmakers received tainted mail. Five people died of exposure to anthrax, most likely through the mail. *(Anthrax, p. 1-12)*

On Oct. 17, the Bush administration asked Congress for $1.5 billion to better prepare for bio-terrorist attacks. Administration officials made it clear they would be happy to get more — as long as it could be accommodated within the $40 billion in emergency spending enacted Sept. 18 (PL 107-38). Bush opposed additional emergency spending before the end of the year.

Edward M. Kennedy, D-Mass., chairman of the Senate Health, Education, Labor and Pensions Committee, and Bill Frist of Tennessee, ranking Republican on the Public Safety Subcommittee, took the lead, introducing a bill in mid-November, but they were unable to get it to the floor until immediately before adjournment.

Both the House and Senate bills included provisions authorizing funds for the accelerated production of smallpox vaccine, as well as antibiotics and other medicines to combat bio-terrorism. Both called for grants to states, local governments and public health departments to prepare for health emergencies. Both would authorize aid to hospitals, the Centers for Disease Control and Prevention (CDC), public health networks and food safety programs.

While the White House request focused mainly on build-

BoxScore

Bill:

HR 3448

Legislative Action:

House passed HR 3448, 418-2, on Dec. 12.

Senate passed HR 3448 by voice vote Dec. 20, after substituting the text of S 1765.

ing up the federal stockpile of vaccines and antibiotics, with just $175 million for aid to the states, both the House and Senate bills called for more than $1 billion for state and local preparedness.

Legislative Action

Frustrated with the slow pace in the Senate, the House passed a $2.9 billion bio-terrorism bill (HR 3448) under suspension of the rules Dec. 12. The vote was 418-2. No amendments were allowed. The measure was drafted by Billy Tauzin, R-La., chairman of the Energy and Commerce Committee, and John D. Dingell of Michigan, the panel's ranking Democrat. *(House vote 493, p. H-168)*

House members said they thought their vote would pressure the Senate to act. "The fact that the House — as diverse as it is — is pushing this should send a strong message to the Senate," said Jane Harman of California, the ranking Democrat on the House Intelligence Subcommittee on Terrorism and Homeland Security.

Bush indicated he would sign the bill and praised it as "bipartisan legislation that will help meet our immediate bio-terrorism defense needs." He added that the bill "includes many of my priorities."

The House bill was somewhat narrower than the bipartisan Senate bill. One of the biggest difference was that it did not include a number of food import restrictions contained in the Senate bill. The food industry, which was trying to avoid new regulations, preferred the House version. "We're quite pleased with the success that we've seen in limiting the scope of the bill," said Kelly Johnston, vice president for the National Food Producers Association.

The Senate passed the bill by voice vote Dec. 20, the last day of the session, after substituting the text of its own $3.2 billion measure (S 1765). HHS Secretary Tommy G. Thompson said the Senate bill was "very much in line with what the administration wants."

Kennedy and Frist had spent more than a month working out the details. Kennedy originally wanted to invest $10 billion in preparations for bio-terrorism but reduced his request to $3.2 billion in the interest of prompt floor action. Senators continued in the waning days of the session to haggle over provisions.

The bill also got caught up in an argument among Senate leaders over a separate proposal by Appropriations Committee Chairman Robert C. Byrd, D-W.Va., to increase emergency spending on homeland defense, including $4 billion for bio-terrorism programs. Though Byrd failed to get extra money, he was able to direct $8.3 billion out of $20 billion in already appropriated emergency spending to homeland security, including the $2.5 billion for bio-terrorism.

Issues for Conference

Both bio-terrorism bills would authorize about $1 billion to increase the nation's stockpile of vaccines and antidotes as preparation for a biological attack. However, the bills differed in several other areas including:

● **CDC.** The House bill would authorize up to $450 million for the CDC, with $300 million available to modernize labs and other facilities. The Senate bill included just under $120 million, including funds to update the labs.

● **Water.** The House bill included a $135 million authorization to protect drinking water systems against terrorist attacks; the Senate did not set a dollar amount.

● **Food safety.** The Senate bill would authorize almost $525 million for food safety. It would require food processors to register with the Food and Drug Administration (FDA). Im-

porters would have to notify the FDA before a food shipment arrived and provide detailed information on the country of origin and the contents of the shipment. The FDA could inspect the records of processors and manufacturers. The Senate also included incentives for research into vaccines and antidotes for use if livestock or crops were damaged in an attack. The House bill included $100 million for food safety, with a focus on FDA inspectors, and had fewer requirements.

● **Drugs.** The Senate bill included a limited antitrust exemption for drug companies so they could collaborate on drugs to prevent and fight a biological attack. Another Senate provision would provide fast-track approval of drugs by allowing drug companies to use expedited research procedures with animals. Critics worried that such abbreviated research could compromise safety. ◆

Patent Exclusivity Plan Extended

Congress renewed a program giving pharmaceutical companies an extra six months of exclusive rights to name-brand drugs in exchange for agreeing to test the drug for use by children. The program, begun in 1997, was aimed at encouraging companies to provide consumers with information on the appropriate usage of adult drugs for children. The bill, signed into law (S 1789 — PL 107-109) on Jan. 4, 2002, extended the program through fiscal 2007. It had been set to expire at the end of 2001.

Supporters of the five-year extension said the law had worked, encouraging the development of information on proper dosages for children, as well as the side effects of many drugs. Critics, such as Rep. Henry A. Waxman, D-Calif., however, argued that granting the six months of additional patent protection for brand-name drugs gave a windfall to drug companies, while delaying the availability to consumers of cheaper generic drugs. They said drug companies could increase their profits by billions of dollars, while spending no more than a few million dollars on the tests.

The bill was endorsed by the Pharmaceutical Research and Manufacturers of America, as well as by many patient and children's health groups. However, the final bill was a rebuff to Bristol-Myers Squibb Co., which had lobbied vigorously to win three years' protection from competition for Glucophage, a popular diabetes drug.

BoxScore

Bill:
S 1789 — PL 107-109

Legislative Action:
Senate passed S 838 (S Rept 107-79) by voice Oct. 18.
House passed HR 2887 (H Rept 107-277), 338-86 on Nov. 15.
Senate passed S 1789 by voice vote Dec. 12.
House cleared S 1789 by voice vote Dec. 18.
President signed Jan. 4, 2002.

ket exclusivity for a brand-name drug if the company tested the drug for use on children at the request of the Food and Drug Administration (FDA). During the six-month period, the company could market the drug without competition from generic alternatives.

● **Pediatric health.** Established two new offices — the Foundation for Pediatric Research at the National Institutes of Health (NIH) and the Office of Pediatric Therapeutics within the FDA — charged with overseeing activities dealing with pediatric health and medicine for their respective agencies.

● **NIH testing.** Authorized $200 million in fiscal 2002 and such sums as necessary through fiscal 2007 for pediatric testing of medicines that were not protected by patents. If a drug company declined an FDA request to study a patented drug for pediatric use, the NIH was authorized to fund a study.

● **Labeling.** Amended labeling requirements, mandating the inclusion of pediatric testing results. The new law shortened the period for negotiation between companies and the FDA concerning labeling information and established an appeals process for drug companies. If a drug was found to be unsuitable for children, the company was required to label the product accordingly.

● **Studies.** Required the comptroller general to report to Congress by 2006 on the program's effectiveness in ensuring that medicines used by children were tested and properly labeled, and on its economic impact on pharmaceutical companies, medical insurance programs and consumers. The General Accounting Office (GAO) was required to conduct a study on the extent that children of ethnic and racial minorities were included in studies by no later than Jan. 10, 2003.

Highlights

As enacted, the new law:

● **Exclusivity.** Reauthorized through Oct. 1, 2007, provisions that gave drug companies an extra six months of mar-

Background

The six-month extension of patent exclusivity was originally enacted as part of the 1997 Food and Drug Administration Modernization Act (PL 105-115). President Bill Clinton wanted drug companies to be required to test their drugs for use by children. Instead, the bill authorized the six months of extra patent protection as an incentive. During that period, no other company could market a generic alternative to the medicine. (*1997 Almanac, p. 6-18*)

The goal was to provide information on the safety and efficacy of treating children with medicines initially designed for adult use. For many major medications, there was no information on potential side effects, the proper dosage or method of administration for pediatric patients. The law authorized the Department of Health and Human Services (HHS) to develop a list of drugs on which additional research would be beneficial. To receive the extension, drug manufacturers had to submit their product for review by Jan. 1, 2002. The HHS secretary gave good marks to the program in early 2001 in a report required under the 1997 law.

Legislative Action

Senate Action

The Senate Health, Education, Labor and Pensions Committee approved a version of the bill (S 838 — S Rept 107-79) by voice vote Aug. 1. Senators generally agreed to withhold amendments until the measure came to the floor. Hillary Rodham Clinton, D-N.Y., offered an amendment to limit the patent protection to drugs with annual sales below $800 million, but withdrew it following a request from Christopher J. Dodd, D-Mass., who sponsored the bill with Mike DeWine, R-Ohio.

The Senate passed the bill by voice vote without debate Oct. 18.

House Subcommittee Action

A companion bill (HR 2887) introduced in the House by James C. Greenwood, R-Pa., ran into greater opposition. The Energy and Commerce Subcommittee on Health approved the measure, 24-5, on Oct. 4, after five hours of debate. Democrats attacked the bill as a boon to drug manufacturers, offering many amendments to scale it back — all of them unsuccessful. Amendments included proposals by:

• Waxman, to reimburse drug companies for twice the amount of the tests rather than granting the extended exclusivity, rejected 9-20.

• Gene Green, D-Texas, to prohibit protection for drugs that received NIH development funding that exceeded the cost of the proposed study, defeated 9-19.

• Green, to authorize a GAO study on the costs, benefits and profits the bill would provide to drug companies and the public, defeated by voice vote.

• Frank Pallone Jr., D-N.J., to deny the protection if sales of the drug during the excluded period exceeded 100 times the cost of the study, defeated 9-20.

• Waxman, to deny the extra protection to drugs whose average wholesale price exceeded their average market price, rejected 9-19.

• Peter Deutsch, D-Fla., to limit the exclusivity extension for a drug to three months unless the maker requested and the FDA granted a three-month extension, rejected 8-17.

• Deutsch, to provide three-month exclusivity to a drug if its annual gross sales topped $400 million, and six-month protection to those with sales of less than $400 million, defeated 9-20.

House Committee Action

The full Energy and Commerce Committee approved the bill (H Rept 107-277), by a vote of 41-6 on Oct. 11. Democrats again tried to limit the benefits to the drug companies. The committee defeated amendments by:

• Sherrod Brown, D-Ohio, to replace the exclusivity period with federal reimbursement for pediatric testing. Health Subcommittee Chairman Michael Bilirakis, R-Fla., argued that the change would destroy the system. It was defeated, 12-36.

• Brown to reduce the exclusivity period from six months to three, rejected 13-33.

• Bart Stupak, D-Mich., to require labeling changes resulting from drug studies to take effect within 90 days of the conclusion of the study, rejected 17-27.

The committee adopted an amendment by Bilirakis to add a toll-free number operated by the FDA to provide information on drug testing, as well as a GAO study on including children from ethnic and racial minorities in drug studies.

House Floor Action

The House passed the bill, 338-86, on Nov. 15 under suspension of the rules, a procedure that limits debate and bars amendments. Supporters tried to counter Democratic arguments that the bill would line the pockets of drug companies by stressing that most of the medications that had been granted exclusivity were not "top sellers." (*House vote 444, p. H-152*)

Final Action

A compromise measure negotiated by the bills' sponsors was introduced as a clean bill (S 1789) on Dec. 8. The Senate passed it by voice vote Dec. 12, and the House cleared it Dec. 18, also by voice vote.

The final bill closed a loophole that had been used by Bristol-Myers and several other drugmakers to seek extended protection from low-cost competitors. Bristol-Myers said that because it now marketed Glucophage to treat teenagers under new labeling approved by the FDA, it should get three years of patent protection under a law (PL 98-417) that rewarded companies for discovering new uses for drugs. The company argued that without the protection, it would lose $1.7 billion in profits annually. (*1984 Almanac, p. 451*)

But generic drugmakers countered that approving Glucophage for teenagers did not constitute a new use. The FDA had given tentative approval to a low-cost competitor, pending resolution of the patent issue by Congress. Waxman said that Congress never intended to allow drugmakers to delay competition "simply by changing the label." ◆

Chapter 13

INDUSTRY & LABOR

GOP Rejects Ergonomics Rules

Working swiftly and quietly, Republicans used a little-known legislative device to overturn regulations on repetitive motion injuries issued in the final days of the Clinton administration. President Bush signed the bill (S J Res 6 — PL 107-5) on March 20. A subsequent measure calling for narrow, clearly defined regulations stalled in committee.

The ergonomics rules had taken effect Jan. 16, with enforcement scheduled to begin Oct. 14. But, with the help of a united business community, congressional Republicans persuaded a handful of centrist Democrats in both chambers to join them in passing legislation to repeal the rules. They were aided by an untested law known as the Congressional Review Act (CRA). Enacted in 1996 (PL 104-121), the CRA allowed lawmakers to erase major rules by a simple majority in each chamber.

Democrats said they felt ambushed by the GOP maneuver, developed behind the scenes by Republican Sen. Don Nickles of Oklahoma and lobbyists for the business community.

"I'm still trying to figure out what the hell happened," said one Democratic aide after the Senate vote.

The regulations, issued by the Occupational Safety and Health Administration (OSHA), would have required employers to educate workers about ways to prevent injuries from repetitive motion such as typing, sorting or lifting heavy loads. If a worker reported an injury, the employer would have had to reconfigure the workplace to prevent recurrences. Workers who reported injuries lasting seven days or longer would have been eligible for compensation of up to 90 percent of their salary for as long as 90 days if they were unable to work.

The business community was unified to an almost unprecedented degree on the need to overturn the ergonomics rules. Business groups argued that they would cost U.S. companies more than $100 billion annually.

Democrats were particularly upset over the use of the CRA because it barred the administration from writing a substitute regulation in "substantially the same form." Bills (S 598, HR 1241) to order the secretary of Labor to issue narrower, clearly defined ergonomics regulations never got out of committee.

BoxScore

Bill:

S J Res 6 — PL 107-5

Legislative Action:

Senate passed S J Res 6, 56-44, on March 6.

House cleared S J Res 6, 223-206, on March 7.

President signed March 20.

Background

Since the first Bush administration, OSHA had been working on regulations to limit injuries or disabilities from performing repetitive tasks. Earlier attempts by the Clinton administration to finalize the rules were blocked by the GOP majority in Congress.

In 2000, the GOP tried to include language in the fiscal 2001 Labor-HHS-Education appropriations bill to bar OSHA from finalizing the rules. The White House offered to accept language allowing OSHA to publish the final rules but delaying enforcement until June 2001, after a new president was in office, but GOP leaders rejected the deal. When the spending bill stalled for several weeks, OSHA published the final rules, effectively taking the issue off the table but fanning partisan flames. (*2000 Almanac, p. 2-111*)

Republicans and business groups argued that the administration had overstepped its authority, a claim that became the basis for using the CRA to overturn the ergonomics rule.

The CRA required that agencies submit reports on rules to Congress, delayed the implementation of major rules and created special parliamentary procedures to allow Congress to block executive action. If Congress wanted to block a rule, it had 60 legislative days from the time it received the report to pass a joint resolution of disapproval. Key to the fate of President Bill Clinton's ergonomics rules was a provision specifying that, when a rule was submitted near the end of a Congress or after it adjourned, the 60-day clock began ticking again on the 15th day of the new session. Under most circumstances, the president could be expected to veto the resolution, but with a change of administrations, Republicans had a president who was ready to sign.

Legislative Action

The Senate passed S J Res 6 by a vote of 56-44 on March 6 with the help of six centrist Democrats. Careful planning by Nickles, Michael B. Enzi, R-Wyo., and others had given Democrats and their labor allies only four days to mobilize, which proved insufficient to counter the anti-regulation campaign. The House followed suit March 7, clearing the measure, 223-206. Sixteen Democrats supported the resolution, more than making up for the 13 Republicans who sided with organized labor. (*Senate vote 15, p. S-9; House vote 33, p. H-18*) ◆

Rail Workers' Pensions Revamped

In an unusual joint victory for labor and management, Congress cleared a bill restructuring the federal railroad pension system to allow part of the funds to be invested in stocks and bonds. By earning higher returns in the private market, the railroads and the railway workers' unions hoped to cover the shortfall between what was being held in the pension fund and the potential claims of railroad retirees. President Bush signed the measure (HR 10 — PL 107-90) on Dec. 21.

The bill allowed a new board of railroad company and union representatives to invest $15.3 billion from a federal railroad retirement fund in stocks and bonds, rather than in Treasury securities. It also decreased payroll taxes on employers, increased benefits, lowered the retirement age for longtime railroad workers, and increased benefits for survivors.

The House passed the legislation by an overwhelming vote in July. But Sens. Don Nickles, R-Okla., and Phil Gramm, R-Texas, opposed the bill, arguing that it would drain the federal fund and inevitably lead to a taxpayer bailout. With action on the House bill (HR 1140) blocked, Senate Majority Leader Tom Daschle, D-S.D., found another vehicle, a House-passed bill (HR 10) that had been set aside because most of its provisions were enacted as part of Bush's tax bill (PL 107-16). Daschle succeeded in inserting the railroad retirement provisions, passing the revised bill and sending it back to the House, which easily cleared it.

Two significant problems had be over come first. Under budget rules, transferring the trust fund money to the new board counted as $15.3 billion in federal spending — essentially busting the budget for fiscal 2002. Similar concerns prompted Senate GOP leaders to kill a House-passed version of the bill in the 106th Congress. The solution was to include language exempting the bill from the rule.

Also, while the plan originally was portrayed as a test, albeit on a small scale, for Bush's proposal to partially privatize Social Security, the administration was opposed to the government itself investing in the stock market. So the bill put the investment decisions in the hands of a private board.

Background

Enactment of the railroad retirement bill ended a three-year odyssey that began with historical foes — rail management and labor — coming together to negotiate an agreement. For both, there was a major incentive: The existing Railroad Retirement System was $40 billion shy of what was required to meet its obligations to more than 900,000 current and future beneficiaries, a shortfall that fueled the call for a new financing mechanism.

BoxScore

Bill:
HR 10 — PL 107-90
Legislative Action:
House passed HR 1140
(H Rept 107-82), 384-33, on
July 31.
Senate passed HR 10, 90-9,
on Dec. 5.
House cleared HR 10, 369-33,
on Dec. 11.
President signed Dec. 21.

The system was created in 1936 to help an industry that was vital to ending the Depression. Payroll taxes paid by railroads and their workers were held in a federal trust fund that invested in government securities. Benefits were paid in two tiers: The first, financed by a 15.3 percent payroll tax (with half paid by railroads and half by employees), provided benefits similar to those of Social Security, which rail workers did not receive. The second, funded by an additional 21 percent payroll tax (16.1 percent from the railroads and 4.9 percent from workers) was based on an earnings formula.

The federal railroad retirement system was the only private industry pension plan established by statute and administered by the federal government, so any changes required legislative action. The last major overhaul of the system occurred in 1983, with enactment of the Railroad Retirement Solvency Act (PL 98-76). That law raised Tier 2 tax rates for both employers and employees, and for the first time subjected Tier 2 retirement benefits to federal income tax. It also raised from 60 to 62 the age at which workers with 30 years of service could receive a full annuity. (*1983 Almanac, p. 272*)

In 1998, in response to congressional hearings on the railroad retirement system — particularly the need to increase benefits for the widows of railroad workers — rail labor and management initiated discussions on comprehensive restructuring of the system.

In 2000, the House passed a bill that embodied an agreement reached between railroads and a majority of rail labor to reform the Tier 2 program. But the Senate never acted on the measure, and efforts to add it to a year-end appropriations bill stalled because of concerns over the cost. (*2000 Almanac, p. 14-7*)

Highlights

The new railroad retirement law contained provisions to:
● **Investments.** Create a National Railroad Retirement Investment Trust, through which Tier 2 assets, previously invested only in Treasury securities, could be invested in private securities. Enactment required a one-time transfer of $15.3 billion in Tier 2 assets held by the Treasury to the new trust.
● **Board.** Create a seven-member independent board of trustees — three chosen by labor, three by management and one chosen by the other six — to manage and oversee investment of the assets.
● **Employer taxes.** Reduce the Tier 2 payroll tax on railroad employers to 14.2 percent by 2003 and adjust it thereafter to reflect the earnings performance of the investment fund.
● **Surviving spouse.** Double the Tier 2 benefits paid to sur-

viving spouses.

• **Eligibility.** Lower from 62 to 60 the age at which rail workers with 30 years of service were eligible for full Tier 1 benefits.

• **Vesting.** Reduce from 10 years to five years the time that railroad employees had to work before being vested.

Legislative Action

House Action

The House Transportation Committee approved the bill (HR 1140 — H Rept 107-82, Part 1) by voice vote May 16, after the panel's subcommittee on Railroads endorsed it by voice vote May 9. The bill also was referred to the Ways and Means Committee, which did not take it up.

The House passed the bill, 384-33, on July 31, after GOP leaders inserted language that eliminated the main budgetary hurdle. (*House vote 305, p. H-106*)

The new language declared that the transfer was not an outlay, but a budget-neutral "means of financing" government operations, akin to buying Treasury bonds with surplus revenue. Transportation Committee Chairman Don Young, R-Alaska, argued that the existing rules required only a "fictional outlay."

But Sam Johnson, R-Texas, and other opponents maintained that it might be necessary to tap into the Social Security and Medicare trust funds to support the new system if bad investments were made. They argued that a fail-safe in the bill — potential payroll tax increases to cover a shortfall in funds — would be insufficient to cover big losses in the market.

Also, the nature of the board that would make the investment decisions was changed. Originally, members would have been appointed by the Railroad Retirement Board to represent the interests of labor and management. As passed, the bill required a board made up of three members chosen by labor, three chosen by management, and a seventh chosen by the other six. The White House had called for leaving investment decisions in the hands of beneficiaries, not the government.

Senate Action

Although the bill enjoyed broad bipartisan support in the Senate, it became ensnared in procedural and political maneuvering, prompting Daschle to start from scratch with the shell of a House-passed bill (HR 10). Overcoming objections from a handful of conservatives and a bid by GOP leaders to use the bill as a vehicle to debate other high-profile issues, the Senate passed the measure by an overwhelming vote of 90-9 on Dec. 5. (*Senate vote 351, p. S-73*)

When Daschle tried to call up the moribund bill Nov. 29, he was opposed by a small group of Republican conservatives, who described the railroad retirement plan as a boondoggle, and from GOP leaders, who insisted the Senate should concentrate exclusively on the fiscal 2002 appropriations bills and an economic stimulus package (HR 3090). The Senate voted 96-4 to prevent a filibuster. (*Senate vote 343, p. S-71*)

With lobbyists for the railroads and their workers lining the ropes outside the chamber to urge a "yes" vote, several GOP senators said their desire to block the Democrats from setting the agenda was exceeded by their support for the bill. "The Democrats have the votes, they're in charge, so we have to take it as it comes," said Chuck Hagel, R-Neb. Besides, he said, "it's still the same good bill that it was."

Next, Minority Leader Trent Lott, R-Miss., tried to slow the bill by offering an amendment consisting of major energy legislation and a six-month moratorium on human cloning. He gambled that enough senators would support one or the other to hand him an impressive majority, but the strategy backfired. With whip counts coming up short, GOP leaders gave up, losing a vote to limit debate on the amendment, 1-94. Daschle promptly won cloture on the railroad bill on a 81-15 vote. (*Senate votes 344, 345, p. S-72; energy, p. 9-3; human cloning, p. 16-3*)

Senate Republicans conceded that the combination of energy and cloning, along with the broad support enjoyed by the railroad measure and Democrats' unity behind Daschle, ultimately derailed the amendment.

A handful of other GOP amendments were defeated, including a proposal by Pete V. Domenici, R-N.M., to strike the House language specifying that the $15.3 billion transfer from the trust fund should not be considered an outlay under budget rules. The amendment failed, 40-59, despite the support of Budget Chairman Kent Conrad, D-N.D. "Directed scoring is a bad idea," Conrad said. "We ought to report accurately to our colleagues the true cost." (*Senate vote 347, p. S-72*)

Before passing the bill, the Senate agreed by voice vote to substitute the railroad pension provisions.

The House cleared the bill, 369-33, on Dec. 11. (*House vote 485, p. H-166*) ◆

Chapter 14

LAW & JUDICIARY

Anti-Terror Bill Zooms Into Law

Despite concerns about the possible impact on civil liberties, the House and Senate overwhelmingly agreed to give the Bush administration sweeping new authority to track, arrest and prosecute suspected terrorists after the Sept. 11 attacks on the World Trade Center and the Pentagon. President Bush signed the anti-terrorism legislation into law (HR 3162 — PL 107-56) on Oct. 26.

When Attorney General John Ashcroft asked for the new law enforcement powers Sept. 19 — calling on Congress to clear a bill by the end of that week — both Republicans and Democrats balked. Members in both parties urged careful deliberation of Ashcroft's proposal, which included powers that the Justice Department had sought unsuccessfully for years. But the Bush administration pushed hard, telling Congress it needed the new powers immediately to guard against further terrorist attacks. Concern was heightened by several FBI warnings that more attacks could be imminent.

In the end, the bill contained much of what Ashcroft sought, including authority for the government to obtain nationwide search warrants and "roving wiretaps," to conduct secret searches of suspects' property, and to detain immigrants indefinitely if they were viewed as national security threats. It also strengthened money-laundering laws and removed the statute of limitations on some terrorism crimes.

The legislation had several incarnations, in part because of a dispute in the House, where the Judiciary Committee laboriously marked up a consensus bill (HR 2975) that was opposed by the White House. In the Senate, by contrast, Judiciary Committee Chairman Patrick J. Leahy, D-Vt., worked behind closed doors with colleagues and Justice Department officials to write a bill (S 1510) acceptable to the administration.

The House and Senate Judiciary committees held one hearing each on the Ashcroft proposal, but no one who opposed the request testified for the record. The Senate bill, drafted in secret, was never marked up in committee.

After the Senate passed its bill, administration officials pressured House GOP leaders to take up that version. Ultimately, the leadership capitulated, replacing the language negotiated by House Judiciary Committee members with a version closer to the Senate bill.

Rather than hold a formal conference, key lawmakers met with administration officials to resolve about a dozen differences behind closed doors and then introduced a clean bill (HR 3162), which passed both chambers and was signed into law. The final bill included a version of a House-passed "sunset" clause that made most of the surveillance provi-

BoxScore

Bill:
HR 3162 — PL 107-56

Legislative Action:

Senate passed S 1510, 96-1, on Oct. 11.

House passed HR 2975, revised, 337-79, on Oct. 12.

House passed HR 3162, 357-66, on Oct. 24.

Senate cleared HR 3162, 98-1, on Oct. 25.

President signed Oct. 26.

sions expire after four years unless Congress reauthorized them.

Highlights

The new law included provisions to:

● **Search warrants.** Create "one-stop shopping" for court orders for many law enforcement investigations, allowing one judge to issue a search warrant or approve surveillance that is applicable across the country.

● **Electronic surveillance.** Make it easier for investigators to track Internet communications using surveillance tools such as so-called pen register and trap-and-trace devices, which record the numbers of outgoing and incoming calls to a phone.

● **Secret searches.** Allow secret searches before suspects are served with search warrants. Investigators could withhold information about the searches for a "reasonable" time, though the bill did not define what that meant.

● **Grand jury disclosure.** Allow disclosure of information received during grand jury proceedings to law enforcement, intelligence, protective, immigration or national defense or national security personnel.

● **Money laundering.** Expand the list of offenses eligible for prosecution under money laundering statutes, and ban the undeclared movement of more than $10,000 across U.S. borders. U.S. banks were prohibited from offering correspondent accounts, used for wire transfers and currency exchanges to foreign "shell" banks that had no physical location.

● **Automatic expiration.** Sunset, or automatically repeal, some of the most controversial wiretap and other provisions in 2005.

Background

The horror of the terrorist attacks left official Washington desperate to respond. Within days, Congress began to debate new anti-terrorism legislation that just weeks before would not have been seriously considered.

Next to authorizing the use of military force, members argued that some of the most important decisions Congress had to make involved striking a balance between law enforcement powers and civil liberties. Lawmakers had to consider whether existing laws worked in a digital world and whether law enforcement had the resources it needed to keep one step ahead of wrongdoers.

They debated such fundamental questions as whether to give government carte blanche to track e-mail and other electronic communications between individuals, and

whether to make it easier for law enforcement agencies to peek over the shoulders of computer users. "The worst thing that could happen is we damage our Constitution," Leahy said. "If the Constitution is shredded, the terrorists win."

The FBI and other agencies said they needed to use up-to-date technology to help infiltrate terrorist cells and head off future threats. In particular, they urged Congress to expand wiretapping and other surveillance authority to cover information transmitted via the Internet. The prime suspect in the Sept. 11 assault, Saudi dissident Osama bin Laden, and his associates were believed to have communicated via e-mail, messages embedded in computer files, and encryption software that scrambled electronic messages.

Many of the tools Ashcroft sought had been requested previously without success. In 1996, in the wake of the 1995 bombing of the federal building in Oklahoma City, the Clinton administration sought many of the same changes to surveillance law, including the ability to conduct multiple wiretaps that could follow a person rather than a phone. But conservative GOP lawmakers were unwilling to give the government such powerful tools, and House Republicans successfully stripped much of the wiretap language from the bill. The final 1996 anti-terrorism law (PL 104-132) authorized the president to stop certain suspected terrorist groups from raising funds in the United States and gave the administration greater authority to turn people away at the border. (*1996 Almanac, p. 5-18*)

Highlights of Ashcroft's Proposal

Congressional deliberations on the 2001 anti-terrorism package began in earnest Sept. 19, when the Justice Department sent a 21-page draft proposal to Capitol Hill. "We need every tool available to us to curtail the potential of additional terrorist attacks," Ashcroft said after a meeting with congressional leaders.

The attorney general asked for:

• **Roving wiretap authority.** Authority to link wiretaps to an individual, not a phone line, to hear all conversations. Existing law required authorities to get a separate court order for each phone line they wanted to tap.

• **Nationwide search warrants.** The ability to get a single warrant in a nationwide investigation to proceed with searches and some electronic surveillance. Some of this authority would apply only to terrorist investigations. Under existing law, authorities had to get a warrant or other permission from a judge in each jurisdiction where they were conducting an investigation.

• **Wider electronic access.** Authority to use surveillance equipment to track e-mail and Web travel. Ashcroft wanted more access to information from Internet service providers. Under existing law, providers were required to supply only limited information, such as a customer's name and address and how long he or she had used the service. Under Ashcroft's proposals, investigators would be able to use subpoenas to gain access to credit card billing information. Authorities could seize stored voice mail with search warrants, rather than going through the more difficult process of obtaining a court order for a wiretap.

• **Internet disclosure.** Authority for service providers to decide on their own to disclose Internet communication and information about customers if they believed there was

a threat of death or serious injury.

• **Immigrant detention.** Authority for the federal government to hold non-citizens indefinitely.

• **Consolidated appeals.** A requirement that all appeals from non-citizens challenging deportations be handled by the federal district court for the District of Columbia. Under existing law, the cases were heard by the district closest to the plaintiff's home.

• **Foreign wiretap evidence.** The ability to use information obtained by foreign government wiretaps in U.S. criminal investigations, even if the surveillance violated the rights of Americans.

• **Defining "terrorist."** Inclusion in the term "terrorist" of anyone who "affords material support to an organization that the individual knows or should know is a terrorist organization," regardless of whether the support was related to the terrorism.

• **Tougher penalties.** Repeal of the five-year statute of limitations on terrorist crimes, and increases in both the sentences and fines that could be levied on convicted terrorists.

Legislative Action

House Committee Action

After weeks of intense negotiations, Republicans and Democrats on the House Judiciary Committee reached a deal Oct. 2 on a streamlined version of the Ashcroft proposal. The committee approved the bill (HR 2975 — H Rept 107-236, Part 1) the next day by a vote of 36-0. While the panel saw the action as a triumph for the committee system, the Bush administration began pressing the House leadership to ignore the committee's actions and bring something closer to the administration's proposal to the floor instead.

The committee bill included provisions to:

• Sunset many of the expanded surveillance and investigative powers in 2003, unless they were reauthorized by Congress. That compromise, seen as essential to getting the legislation past critics on the right and the left in the House, was opposed by the Bush administration.

• Allow "one-stop shopping" for court orders for many law enforcement investigations, make it easier for investigators to track Internet communications, and allow agencies to get other information, such as an individual's credit card number, with a subpoena.

• Permit Foreign Intelligence Surveillance Act (FISA) searches or surveillance as long as the "significant purpose" was gathering intelligence information, rather than evidence for a criminal case. Existing law required intelligence gathering to be a "primary purpose." The Bush administration wanted the requirement reduced to simply "a purpose."

• Grant permanent legal resident status to immigrants who had already applied but whose sponsors died in the Sept. 11 attacks.

• Create a deputy inspector general within the Justice Department to oversee the FBI and review alleged infringements of civil rights or civil liberties.

• Permit the IRS to disclose tax information to the head of federal law enforcement agencies.

The committee rejected Ashcroft's request to allow information obtained by foreign government wiretaps to be used

against Americans even if the wiretap was unconstitutional. It also declined to give the attorney general the authority to detain non-citizens indefinitely or to conduct more secret searches.

Negotiations on the bill were largely confined to the committee's bipartisan leadership and its staff. Their definition of a consensus bill was one that could get through the Judiciary Committee and the full House, without much concern over whether the Bush administration had signed off first. Of greater importance to Chairman F. James Sensenbrenner Jr., R-Wis., was maintaining his committee's jurisdiction and preventing the House leadership from taking the bill away. Although the leadership did not seem eager to do that at the time, Sensenbrenner said he was "very fearful that if this bill is put on a slow roll, all of a sudden we will lose as a committee our right to make improvements and to attempt to reach a bipartisan process to present to the House of Representatives."

Some panel members had signaled early on that they were unwilling to go as far as Ashcroft wanted. Bob Barr, R-Ga., and four other members of the committee sent a letter Sept. 21 to Sensenbrenner and ranking Democrat John Conyers Jr. of Michigan that divided Ashcroft's requests into four categories — from those they would readily approve to those that were "unacceptable as written." Included in the "unacceptable" category were requests for nationwide authority for e-mail search warrants and authorization for agents to seize terrorist suspects' assets before the suspects had been convicted of a crime.

The committee considered 18 amendments during five and a half hours of deliberation, making mostly minor changes to the bill. The only committee member who did not vote for the bill was Robert Wexler, D-Fla., who was absent during the tally. The normally fractious committee cheered the final, unanimous vote. "This bill represents the essence of compromise," Sensenbrenner said. "The left is not completely happy with the bill, neither is the right. It certainly doesn't represent the Justice Department's wish list. I think it means we've got it just about right."

By voice vote, the committee approved an amendment by Barney Frank, D-Mass., to make it easier for people to sue the government when agencies leaked sensitive personal information about them. The change was meant to balance a provision that would expand how much personal information various government agencies could exchange about suspects. Frank cited examples of abuses, such as the FBI's disclosure of personal information about Martin Luther King Jr. during the civil rights struggle. Frank said he wanted to "increase the negative incentive for this kind of leaking."

Drafting a Senate Bill

Leahy kicked off work on the bill in the Senate with a draft counterproposal to the Ashcroft plan. While Leahy's draft accommodated the Bush administration by authorizing greater surveillance on the Internet, it also proposed raising the legal threshold that authorities would have to meet to conduct such surveillance — something the law enforcement community had opposed.

Leahy left out many of the wiretap provisions requested by Ashcroft, and said he was concerned over a provision that would allow the indefinite detention of aliens.

The Senate had already given voice vote approval to a narrower form of the Ashcroft proposal as an amendment to the fiscal 2002 appropriations bill for the departments of Commerce, Justice and State (HR 2500). The amendment, by Orrin G. Hatch, R-Utah, included an expanded definition of trap-and-trace devices and pen registers to allow their use in cyberspace. It would have greatly expanded the information the government could capture, including which Web sites suspects visited, what files they downloaded and the e-mail addresses of people with whom they communicated. The amendment was dropped after the anti-terrorism bill cleared. (*Appropriations, p. 2-9*)

Negotiations on the Senate bill included Democrats and Republicans, lawmakers and their staffs, and representatives from the White House and Justice Department. Their goal was to write a bill that could pass the Senate with White House support.

Leahy reportedly called Ashcroft on Sept. 26 to ask him to urge his staff to work harder to find compromises on several of the sticking points, including Ashcroft's request for broad authority to share secret grand jury information with law enforcement officials. The Senate's closed-door discussions all but broke down Oct. 2, when Democrats accused the White House of reneging on a deal on how information from wiretaps and other sources could be shared among government agencies. But the talks resumed, and at 3 a.m. on Oct. 4, the Senate and White House reached a deal.

"It's a consensus bill now," said Hatch, that contains "virtually everything that Attorney General Ashcroft and the Bush administration have asked for."

Ashcroft lost on a few points. The bill did not include provisions allowing the IRS to disclose tax information to federal law enforcement and intelligence agents, or allowing information obtained by foreign government wiretaps to be used against Americans even if the wiretap was unconstitutional. The bill restricted the Attorney General's authority to detain non-citizens indefinitely.

But generally, it followed Ashcroft's proposal. The bill did not include a sunset provision, something the Bush administration opposed. It included provisions to allow more secret searches if the government showed "reasonable cause to believe" that notifying the suspect of the search would produce an "adverse result," such as the destruction of evidence. And it included the same provision to broaden FISA surveillance activities as did the House bill.

The bill also included new tools to combat money laundering, such as additional record keeping requirements and restrictions on dealing with suspect foreign financiers.

Senate Floor Action

The Senate passed the bill (S 1510) on Oct. 11, by a vote of 96-1, after less than three hours of actual debate. Russell D. Feingold, D-Wis., cast the only "nay" vote. The bill had never been considered by the Judiciary Committee, and members were not given a report explaining its provisions. (*Senate vote 302, p. S-63*)

Majority Leader Tom Daschle, D-S.D., told colleagues to avoid offering amendments so as to maintain the balance of the deal struck by the bipartisan leadership, top members of the Senate Judiciary Committee and the Bush administration. That angered Feingold. "What have we come to when we

don't have committee or floor deliberation on an issue of this magnitude?" he asked. Feingold offered three amendments, all of which were overwhelmingly defeated after Daschle made his pitch. The amendments would have limited computer trespass provisions, limited roving surveillance to instances when it was ascertained that the surveillance target was present in the house or was using the phone that had been tapped, and ensured that the bill would not supercede certain state and federal privacy protections. (*Senate votes 299, 300, 301, p. S-63*)

Arlen Specter, R-Pa., was one of the few senators to discuss the bill. He expressed concern that the lack of a legislative record could lead the Supreme Court to declare the bill unconstitutional if it became law. He noted the court "has invalidated acts of Congress where there was not a considered judgment" made by Congress.

House Floor Action

The House passed HR 2975 by a vote of 337-79 on Oct. 12, one day after the Senate acted. Though the bill number was the same, the committee's text had been replaced by a leadership measure that was far more to the administration's liking. (*House vote 398, p. H-136*)

The move, which came after days of intense White House pressure, was aimed at heading off a difficult battle with the Senate and clearing the way for quick final negotiations to get a bill to the president's desk. In pushing the measure through, Speaker J. Dennis Hastert, R-Ill., squelched dissent from members on the right and left who warned that Ashcroft's proposals could infringe on civil liberties. He also shattered the strong bipartisan support for the House position.

As late as Oct. 10, the House had appeared likely to rebuff the demands from Ashcroft and others to put aside its more limited legislation and embrace something closer to the Senate bill. Majority Leader Dick Armey and Majority Whip Tom DeLay, both Texas Republicans, said they wanted the Judiciary Committee bill to come to the floor. But Hastert was more open to the administration's concerns. Adding intensity to the debate was a message posted on the FBI's Web site Oct. 11 warning of possible new terrorist attacks within the United States and against U.S. interests overseas.

Hastert closeted himself with Sensenbrenner and White House negotiators and staff for the entire day Oct. 11, trying to move the House bill closer to the administration's position. Democrats, who had helped write the committee bill, no longer were included. After completing their discussions late that day, Hastert and Sensenbrenner introduced a new bill (HR 3108) containing their agreement. It was the text of the bill that was passed under the number HR 2975.

The leadership version of the bill included Ashcroft's request for more secret searches and lengthened the period of time that the wiretap provisions would be law. The 2003 expiration date set by the committee for many of the provisions was extended to 2006.

House leaders left out provisions to toughen laws prohibiting money laundering, a change significant enough to merit a warning from Daschle that a bill without such language would not become law. "We will not support a counterterrorism bill that does not have money-laundering provisions in it," Daschle said. "So whether it's done in conference or whether it's done in the House of Representatives, it must be done, and we will insist that it be done."

The House subsequently passed a separate money laundering bill (HR 3004 on Oct. 17.)

The House bill also dropped a provision included in the Senate version to repeal a law that required federal prosecutors to obey the ethics laws of the state in which they practiced. The statute was known as the McDade law after former House member Joseph M. McDade, R-Pa. (1963-99), who had been investigated by federal prosecutors for eight years before being acquitted at his bribery trial in 1996. (*1996 Almanac, p. 1-35*)

House leaders' decision to drop the Judiciary Committee bill and substitute their own enraged Democrats, who argued that the new measure lacked sufficient safeguards on the authority to be given to law enforcement. "I believe it was done in a sneaky, dishonest fashion that reflects very poorly on this body," John D. Dingell, D-Mich., said of the late-night deal. "The United States is not so threatened that we have to throw away our rights with no consideration."

Sensenbrenner defended the new bill, arguing that there was a "clear and present danger" of more terrorist attacks that required Congress to act quickly. The reworked bill was the best way to do that, he said. Hastert succeeded in pressuring or persuading GOP colleagues to back the bill. The 79 votes against the measure included those of just three Republicans: Ray LaHood of Illinois, C. L. "Butch" Otter of Idaho and Ron Paul of Texas.

Conference/Final Action

Negotiators worked out the differences between the two bills behind closed doors and issued no report. The House leadership decided to put the agreement into yet another new bill (HR 3162), which passed the House and Senate and went to the president with no conference or committee reports. The House passed the bill Oct. 24 by a vote of 357-66. The Senate cleared it Oct. 25, 98-1. (*House vote 398, p. H-136; Senate vote 313, p. S-66*)

On some of the more controversial issues, the final bill:

● **Sunset.** Set an expiration date of 2005 for many but not all intelligence provisions, although the expiration would not apply to investigations already under way at that time.

● **Surveillance.** Allowed the government in certain cases to conduct searches without first notifying the suspects. Also grand jury information could be shared with law enforcement, intelligence, national security and other agencies.

● **Foreign intelligence.** Allowed use of FISA wiretaps for purposes other than foreign intelligence gathering as long as such intelligence remained a "significant purpose" of the operation.

● **Alien detention.** Allowed the attorney general to detain an alien for up to seven days before bringing deportation or criminal charges.

Even as the House had its final debate, members were complaining that they had not had a chance to read the measure, which had been introduced that day.

"This legislation is not perfect," Sensenbrenner said. "However, these are difficult times that require steadfast leadership and an expeditious response. The legislation is desperately needed." ◆

Provisions of the Anti-Terrorism Law

The following are the main provisions of the new anti-terrorism law (PL 107-56), signed Oct. 26.

Surveillance

● **Wiretap predicates.** Terrorism and computer fraud and abuse were added to the list of crimes that are "predicates" for obtaining a wiretap, which means a court can give government agents permission to tap telephones when they are investigating such crimes. (Provision expires Dec. 31, 2005.)

● **Information sharing.** Information received during grand jury proceedings can be disclosed to law enforcement, intelligence, protective, immigration or national defense or national security personnel. Any foreign intelligence information obtained by law enforcement officials during wiretaps, electronic surveillance or a criminal investigation can be made available as well.

"Intelligence information" is defined as any information that would help the United States protect against attacks, sabotage and clandestine intelligence activities or that concerns foreign powers and relates to national defense or foreign affairs.

A federal court must be notified after any grand jury information is disclosed. The attorney general must develop standards for release of this information when the subject is a "U.S. person," generally a citizen, a legal permanent resident or a U.S. company. Grand jury information also may be disclosed at the request of defendants when they argue that it includes information that may be grounds for dismissal of the indictment against them.

Individuals who receive information under this authorization may use it only in the official performance of their duties.

The authority for law enforcement to share foreign intelligence information obtained through wiretaps or electronic surveillance expires Dec. 31, 2005.

● **Intelligence information collection.** The law clarifies that authorities using wiretaps and other kinds of electronic surveillance to collect information for a foreign intelligence investigation are not bound by the procedures and restrictions that apply to authorities conducting the same kinds of surveillance for a criminal investigation.

● **Hiring translators.** The FBI is authorized to hire additional translators. The administration must report to Congress on the number of translators working for the FBI and for the Justice Department overall.

● **"Roving" wiretaps.** Investigators working under the authority of the Federal Intelligence Surveillance Act (FISA) may use "roving" wiretaps when a court finds that the actions of a suspect may thwart traditional wiretaps. In those cases, investigators can obtain a court order allowing them to tap whatever telephones a suspect may use, rather than getting a court order for each telephone. (Provision expires Dec. 31, 2005.) FISA (PL 95-511) is the law authorizing wiretaps of suspected foreign criminals or spies. *(1978 Almanac, p. 186)*

● **Intelligence investigations.** Court orders for FISA investigations against people considered to be agents of a foreign power and who are not U.S. persons are good for 120 days, rather than the 90 days allowed previously. After that period, a court can extend the order anywhere from 90 days to a year. Search warrants in such cases are good for 90 days, rather than the 15 days allowed previously. (Provision expires Dec. 31, 2005.)

● **FISA judges increase.** The law authorizes an increase in the number of district court judges who approve FISA requests from seven to 11 and requires that three of them live within 20 miles of the District of Columbia.

● **Voice mail seizure.** The government is allowed to seize voice mail messages with a warrant. Investigators may get one warrant that is good nationwide, rather than having to obtain a separate warrant for each jurisdiction. (Provision expires Dec. 31, 2005.)

● **Credit card information.** Investigators can get subpoenas to obtain subscriber credit card or bank account numbers and other payment information from electronic communication providers, such as cable companies or Internet services.

● **Cable companies and the Internet.** The government can conduct surveillance on Internet users without notice, even if they obtain their Internet access through a cable company rather than over telephone lines. Previously, to protect the privacy of consumers, if the government sought information about a cable customer, the company had to notify the client of the request. Revealing subscribers' cable viewing habits is expressly forbidden.

● **Emergency information disclosure.** Internet service providers can show the government a subscriber's electronic communications when they believe there is a risk of immediate danger, death or serious bodily injury. With a court order or search warrant, law enforcement agents also can force the providers to disclose such information. (Provision expires Dec. 31, 2005.)

● **"Sneak and peek" searches.** Investigators can search suspects' property without notifying them immediately if the government thinks prior notice of the search would have an "adverse result" on the investigation. The warrant could not be used to seize any property or electronic information, unless the court finds reasonable necessity for the seizure. The individual must be notified within a "reasonable period" after the search has taken place, although the law does not define "reasonable." A court can allow investigators to keep the search secret longer if "good cause" is shown.

● **FISA wiretaps.** The law broadens the authority of the government to get court orders under FISA for using pen registers and trap-and-trace devices, which can be used to track telephone calls and Internet communications. Instead of showing that the person under surveillance is the "agent of a foreign power," investigators must show the information is "relevant" to an ongoing investigation aimed at protecting against international terrorism or clandestine intelligence activities. The government may not use this enhanced surveillance power against U.S. citizens if the investigation was triggered solely by activities protected by the First Amendment. For example, citizens cannot be investigated simply based on what groups they associate with or things they have said. (Provision expires Dec. 31, 2005.)

● **Business records.** A court may issue a FISA order allowing investigators to obtain business records, but only in international terrorism or clandestine intelligence investigations. Investigations of U.S. citizens may not be based solely on activities protected by the First Amendment. The type of business records that may be obtained with the FISA court order is broadened to include any books, records, documents or items. Twice a year, the attorney general must report to Congress how many times such a court order has been requested and the outcome of each request. (Provision expires Dec. 31, 2005.)

● **Internet communications tracking.** Pen registers and trap-and-trace devices, which track incoming and outgoing telephone calls, may be used to track Internet communications. Investigators can get one federal court order good throughout the country allowing them to use such devices, but they may not record the content of the communications. Internet service providers are protected from liability in such cases. If investigators install their own pen registers

and trap-and-trace devices on a packet-switched data network, they must note who installed the device and anyone who had access to it, the date and time of installation and removal, the duration of any access to the information, what data was collected, and how the device was configured, including any modifications. This record must be provided to the court in secret within 30 days after the device is removed.

● **Computer hacking interception.** Law enforcement agents can intercept electronic communication if the owners of a computer system or network believe someone is attacking their system from the outside. The agents' actions must be part of an ongoing investigation and involve only communications to or from the suspects. (The provision expires Dec. 31, 2005.) Intelligence agents working under the authority of FISA also may intercept such communications.

● **Broadening intelligence authority.** The law allows FISA investigations in those cases where obtaining foreign intelligence information is a "significant" purpose of the investigation. Such surveillance previously was permitted only when obtaining foreign intelligence information was "the purpose" of the investigation. (Provision expires Dec. 31, 2005.)

● **Nationwide search warrant.** The law authorizes nationwide federal search warrants good in any U.S. jurisdiction for terrorism investigations, instead of requiring a separate warrant in each jurisdiction.

● **Nationwide electronic search warrant.** Courts with jurisdiction over the crime under investigation may issue a nationwide federal search warrant, good anywhere in the country, for e-mail and other electronic information. (Provision expires Dec. 31, 2005.)

● **Exports to Taliban.** The president may unilaterally restrict exports of agricultural products, food and medicine or medical devices to the Taliban or any part of Afghanistan controlled by the Taliban.

● **Internet service provider protection.** The law states that it does not impose any new technical obligation on Internet service providers in order to comply with its provisions. Compensation is authorized for Internet service providers or anyone else who helps set up pen registers and trap-and-trace devices on computer networks.

● **Civil suits for disclosure of information.** If anyone unlawfully discloses information obtained through the law's wiretap authority, the United States can be sued in civil court. If the court finds the disclosure to have been unlawful, there is a minimum fine of $10,000 plus litigation costs. No jury trials are permitted for these cases. If the court finds a government employee is guilty of unlawfully disclosing the information, the government must investigate whether administrative action against the employee is also warranted. (Provision expires Dec. 31, 2005.)

● **Liability protection.** Providers of wire or electronic communication services, a landlord, custodian or anyone else who assists with investigations cannot be sued for providing information to law enforcement under this law.

● **Continuing investigations.** Investigations into offenses committed before the law's various surveillance provisions expire will be allowed to continue past the expiration date of Dec. 31, 2005.

Money Laundering

● **Special measure for risky institutions.** The law authorizes the Treasury secretary to impose new "special measures" against foreign jurisdictions, foreign banks, transactions involving such jurisdictions or institutions, or one or more types of accounts that the secretary, after consulting with the secretary of State and the attorney general, determines are being used for money-laundering.

The special measures are: (1) requiring additional record-keeping or reporting for particular transactions; (2) requiring the identi-

fication of the real owners of the money in certain accounts at U.S. banks; (3) requiring the identification of customers of a foreign bank who write checks out of the bank's U.S. bank accounts; (4) requiring the identification of customers of a foreign bank who use one of its U.S. bank accounts for currency exchanges and other purposes; and (5) after consulting with the secretary of State, the attorney general and the chairman of the Federal Reserve Board, restricting or prohibiting the the ability of certain foreign banks to open or maintain U.S. bank accounts. The first four measures may not be imposed for longer than 120 days without writing new regulations. Measure five may be imposed only by regulation.

● **Due diligence requirements.** Foreign financial institutions that establish, maintain, administer or manage private bank accounts in the United States for non-U.S. citizens must ensure that the accounts are not being used for money-laundering. U.S. financial institutions doing business with foreign banks at risk of being used for money-laundering also must watch for such transactions. The law sets out minimum standards that institutions must meet in ensuring that transactions are legal.

● **Prohibition on foreign "shell banks."** Depository institutions, credit unions and branches or agencies of foreign banks are prohibited from establishing, maintaining, administering or managing bank accounts in the United States for foreign banks that have no physical property.

● **Information sharing.** Regulators may help banks meet the law's new standards for oversight by giving them information about people engaged in or suspected of terrorist acts or money-laundering. Banks may cooperate with each other in identifying and reporting people and counties suspected of terrorism or money-laundering.

● **Money-laundering predicates.** The list of offenses covered by money-laundering laws is expanded to include foreign corruption offenses, such as export control violations, some customs and firearms offenses, and felony violations of the Foreign Agents Registration Act of 1938, which requires agents of foreign governments to register with the Department of Justice.

● **Property confiscation rights.** Owners of property confiscated under money-laundering laws are permitted to present an "affirmative defense" — meaning they can go on the offensive against the government, rather than simply defending themselves. They can argue, for example, that there were mitigating circumstances that should exempt their property from confiscation.

● **Federal jurisdiction.** The law gives U. S. district courts jurisdiction over foreigners engaged in money-laundering in the United States, over foreign banks opening U.S. bank accounts, and over foreigners who use, sell, or otherwise transfer assets that have been forfeited by order of a U.S. court. Federal courts may issue a pretrial restraining order or take other action to keep forfeited property in the United States. Federal courts also are authorized to appoint a receiver to collect and take custody of assets forfeited because of criminal or civil money-laundering or forfeiture judgments.

● **Money-laundering crime.** The law makes it a crime to use foreign banks for money-laundering.

● **"Payable-through" accounts.** Amounts deposited by foreign banks in an interbank "payable-through" account, a type of account they can hold at a U.S. bank, will be treated as having been deposited in the United States for purposes of forfeiture rules. The attorney general may, in the interest of justice and in keeping with the U.S. national interest, suspend a forfeiture proceeding.

● **Information response time.** U.S. banks must reply within 120 hours to a request for information from a U.S. regulator who is checking on their compliance with money-laundering laws.

● **Foreign bank records.** Foreign banks that maintain their own accounts at U.S. banks must appoint agents to receive legal documents within the United States. The attorney general and the Treasury secretary may issue a summons or subpoena to any foreign

bank for records, wherever located, from "correspondent accounts," another kind of account that foreign banks can maintain in the United States. U.S. banks must sever correspondent arrangements with foreign banks that do not answer or comply with such summons or subpoenas.

● **Foreign forfeiture.** The government may seek a restraining order to keep people from moving or disposing of property outside the United States that has been ordered forfeited or confiscated. U.S. courts may force a convicted criminal to return forfeited property located abroad. Courts can order such property returned even if the owners have challenged the government's right to take it from them and are waiting for a ruling on their case.

● **Broadened definition of financial institution.** Credit unions, futures commission merchants, commodity trading advisors and commodity pool operators are added to the definition of financial institution for purposes of the Bank Secrecy Act, a 1970 law that established transaction reporting requirements for financial institutions. The law also clarifies that the term "federal functional regulator" includes the Commodity Futures Trading Commission for purposes of the Bank Secrecy Act.

● **Corporate fugitive.** Corporations cannot challenge forfeiture orders against them if their majority shareholder is a fugitive. No fugitive may challenge a forfeiture claim on behalf of a corporation.

● **Anonymous funds transfers.** The Treasury secretary is authorized to issue regulations concerning the maintenance of concentrated assets in accounts at U.S. depository institutions in order to prevent an institution's customers from anonymously directing funds into or through concentration accounts, a type of bank account that commingles funds from various sources.

● **Customer identification.** The Treasury secretary must establish minimum standards that financial institutions must meet in verifying the identities of customers. Financial institutions must keep verification records and check the names of customers against lists of known or suspected terrorists.

● **Foreign customer identification.** By April 2002, the Treasury secretary must report to Congress on the most effective way to verify the identities of foreigners opening accounts in U.S. financial institutions and assign them identification numbers that work like the tax identification number now given to U.S. citizens.

● **Money laundering record.** In ruling on bank mergers or similar applications, the Federal Reserve Board and the Federal Deposit Insurance Corporation must look at how effectively banks or bank holding companies have combatted money-laundering in the United States and in overseas branches. This provision applies only to applications submitted after Dec. 31, 2001.

● **Wire transfer origination.** The law requires the Treasury secretary to take all reasonable steps to encourage foreign governments to require that wire transfers sent to the United States include the name of the person requesting the transfer. The secretary must report annually to the House Committee on Financial Services and the Senate Committee on Banking, Housing and Urban Affairs on the progress toward that goal.

● **Anonymous funds transfers.** The law increases civil and criminal penalties for people or institutions who try to move money anonymously in and out of bank accounts in violation of the new monitoring standards.

● **Anti-money-laundering programs.** The law requires financial institutions to establish anti-money-laundering programs. The Treasury secretary may set minimum standards for such programs. This section takes effect April 26, 2002.

● **Safe harbor.** When checking employment references, banks can share information with each other about employees who may have taken part in illegal activities. Banks cannot be sued for releasing such information as long as they do not do it with malicious intent.

● **Suspicious activity reports.** The Treasury secretary is required

to publish proposed regulations requiring broker-dealers to report suspicious transactions. The secretary must publish final regulations by July 1, 2002. The secretary also may require futures commission merchants, commodity trading advisers and certain commodity pool operators to report suspicious transactions.

● **IRS and bank secrecy.** By April 2002, the Treasury secretary must report to Congress whether the responsibility for certain regulatory functions under the Bank Secrecy Act should be taken from the IRS and given to another agency.

● **Information sharing.** The government may use banking and financial information in intelligence activities aimed at fighting international terrorism.

● **Underground banking systems.** The law clarifies that the Bank Secrecy Act treats certain underground banking systems as financial institutions, and that record-keeping rules apply to them. The Treasury secretary must report to Congress by Oct. 26, 2002, on the need for additional legislation or regulatory controls addressing underground banking systems.

● **Loans and fighting terrorism.** The Treasury secretary may instruct the U.S. executive director of the World Bank and other international financial institutions to support loans and other assistance for nations that the president determines are contributing to the fight against terrorism. The Treasury secretary can require audits of those financial institutions to ensure that the money is not paid to people engaged in terrorism or supporting it.

● **Financial crimes enforcement.** The law makes the Financial Crimes Enforcement Network (FinCEN) a bureau within the Treasury Department and describes the duties of the FinCEN's director. The Treasury secretary is required to establish operating procedures for the governmentwide data access service and communications center that FinCEN maintains. The secretary must report by April 2002, and annually thereafter, on ways to improve the system for monitoring foreign bank and brokerage accounts owned by U.S. citizens. By July 2002, the secretary is required to work with FinCEN to establish a security network for financial institutions to file reports on suspicious transactions and provide them with information about transactions that deserve special scrutiny.

● **Increased penalties.** The law increases from $100,000 to $1 million the maximum civil and criminal penalties for a violation of the new investigation and special measures requirements.

● **Law enforcement.** Certain Federal Reserve personnel may act as law enforcement officers and carry firearms to protect and safeguard Federal Reserve employees and premises.

● **Reporting large transactions.** Any person who receives more than $10,000 in one transaction or two or more related transactions in the course of his trade or business must file a report with FinCEN. People who do not report large transactions to FinCEN may have their money confiscated.

Companies offering wire transfers must be licensed under state law or registered under federal law. Funds transmitted illegally may be seized.

● **Reporting exemptions.** The Treasury secretary must report to Congress before Oct. 26, 2002, on the results of a study of the possible expansion of the system for exempting transactions from the currency transaction reporting requirements, and on ways to improve the use of the exemption system by financial institutions to reduce the volume of unneeded currency transaction reports.

● **New smuggling crime.** Smuggling more than $10,000 into or out of the United States is a violation of the Bank Secrecy Act.

● **Counterfeiting sentences increased.** The law increases the maximum sentences for various counterfeiting offenses and expands the definition of counterfeiting to include making or acquiring an analog, digital or electronic image of any "obligation or other security of the United States," such as U.S. currency. It also increases the maximum sentences for various counterfeiting offenses

involving foreign money and expands the definition of counterfeiting to include making or acquiring an analog, digital, or electronic image of the currency of a foreign government.

● **Material support for terrorism.** The law expands the legal definition of money-laundering the proceeds of terrorism to include providing material support or resources to terrorist organizations.

● **Reporting large transactions.** The law applies the financial crimes prohibitions to conduct committed abroad in cases where the tools or proceeds of the offense pass through or are in the United States.

● **Sunset provisions.** The money-laundering provisions are to be terminated Oct. 1, 2005, if Congress enacts a joint resolution saying these provisions no longer have the force of law. Any joint resolution to this effect will receive expedited congressional consideration.

Border Control

● **INS employees.** The law waives caps on the number of full-time employees at the Immigration and Naturalization Service (INS). It also lifts the cap in PL 106-553 on the amount of overtime the INS can pay its employees.

● **Northern border personnel.** The law authorizes money to triple the number of Border Patrol agents, INS inspectors and Customs Service personnel along the border with Canada.

● **Sharing of criminal background information.** To help the INS and the State Department determine whether people applying for admission to the United States have criminal records, the FBI and the attorney general must provide information from the National Crime Information Center's Interstate Identification Index, the Wanted Persons File and other sources. By Oct. 26, 2003, the State Department and the attorney general must report to Congress on how this system has been implemented.

● **Identification technology.** The attorney general, working with the secretary of State and others, must develop a reliable technology standard for checking the identities of those seeking visas or trying to enter the United States. A report is due to Congress on April 26, 2003, and every two years thereafter, on how work on this standard is progressing.

● **Automated fingerprint system.** The law authorizes $2 million for the attorney general, the FBI and the INS to study whether the FBI's Integrated Automated Fingerprint Identification System could be used at U.S. ports of entry and at overseas consular posts.

● **Terrorist activity.** The law broadens the definition of "terrorist activity" for individuals seeking to enter the United States. It bars from the United States anyone who is a representative of a political or social group that publicly endorses terrorist activity in the United States, and anyone who uses a position of prominence within a country to endorse terrorist activities or encourage others to do so. The law also bars the spouses or children of anyone engaging in terrorist activities, unless they could not reasonably have known of the activities.

● **Authorized exclusions.** The attorney general or the secretary of State can forbid entry to anyone they consider to be associated with a terrorist organization and who they determine will engage in activities that could endanger the welfare, safety or security of the United States.

● **Terrorist activities.** The law adds the use of explosives, firearms and other dangerous devices to the definition of "terrorist activities." It broadens the definition of "a terrorist engaging in terrorist activity" to include those who have provided support to a group that they knew or should have known was engaged in terrorism, regardless of whether the support provided was for a terrorist purpose. These are offenses that would keep someone out of the United States or lead to deportation.

● **Terrorist organization.** The law creates a new definition of "ter-

rorist organization" for use when determining whether to admit foreigners to the United States or deport those already here. The term is defined as a group of two or more individuals that the secretary of State determines is involved with terrorist activities. These provisions are retroactive for any group that the secretary of State had previously listed as a terrorist organization.

● **Mandatory detention.** The attorney general or the deputy attorney general can certify a foreigner as a terrorist if they have reasonable grounds to believe that the person is a terrorist or has committed a terrorist activity. Those certified as terrorists must be jailed.

The INS may detain suspected terrorists for seven days before bringing immigration or criminal charges against them. Foreigners not charged within seven days must be released.

The law allows detainees to challenge the government's case against them, something called "habeas review." All habeas decisions are to be based on the legal principles articulated by the U.S. Court of Appeals for the District of Columbia and the Supreme Court. All appeals of habeas decisions will be heard by the U.S. Court of Appeals for the District of Columbia. Aliens who were ordered deported but remain in U.S. detention are entitled to have their cases reviewed by the attorney general every six months. Continued detention is allowed only upon a showing that "the release of the alien will endanger the national security of the United States or the safety of the community or any person."

The attorney general must submit a report to Congress on the use of this section every six months.

● **Visa information sharing.** The secretary of State may give foreign governments information in the State Department's computer database and other records on people seeking to enter the United States — if that disclosure would help prevent, investigate or punish acts of terrorism or trafficking in drugs, weapons or people.

● **Entry-exit system.** The law authorizes "such sums as may be necessary" to implement an automated entry-exit data system for the United States. The law includes a "sense of Congress" resolution saying the attorney general should fully implement the entry-exit system as quickly as practicable, focusing in particular on the use of "biometric technology," such as fingerprint scanning devices, and the development of tamper-resistant documents.

● **Foreign students.** The attorney general must implement a system to track foreign students in the United States. The law makes $36.8 million available through Jan. 1, 2003, for the creation and implementation of the system.

● **Machine-readable passports.** All countries that want to participate in the Visa Waiver Program must issue machine-readable passports by Oct. 1, 2003. The deadline had been 2007. The secretary of State may extend this deadline for a country that is making progress. The Visa Waiver Program allows citizens from a select group of mostly industrial countries to come into the United States for short visits for either business or pleasure without having to get a visa. The secretary of State must perform annual audits of those countries allowed to participate in the program.

Benefits for Aliens

● **Permanent residency status.** The law grants permanent residency status to aliens whose sponsors died in the Sept. 11 attacks. Aliens who were disabled or lost their jobs as a direct result of the attacks also can be declared permanent legal residents. Their children and spouses can become permanent legal residents if they come to the United States no later than Sept. 11, 2003. The spouse or fiancé of a U.S. citizen killed in the Sept. 11 attacks also is eligible for permanent resident status.

● **Disability extension.** Aliens who are legally in the country and were disabled in the Sept. 11 attacks may remain in the United States, along with their spouses and children, and get legal autho-

rization to work for one year after the point when they were disabled. Spouses and children of aliens who died in the terrorist attacks can get the same extension; they must be admitted to the United States, even if they may require government assistance.

● **Extensions of deadlines.** The law generally provides a grace period for aliens who missed any filing deadlines because of the Sept. 11 attacks. For example, it gives an extra 60 days to aliens prevented from filing for an extension of their stay, including those who were abroad at the time. Aliens who overstayed their time in the country because the attacks prevented them from leaving are considered to have left legally if they departed before Nov. 11, 2001.

● **Waiver for some would-be immigrants.** For aliens who were married to a citizen killed in the attacks, the law waives the requirement that they be married for two years before they are eligible for immigrant status. If a permanent resident killed in the attacks had filed papers to allow his or her spouse, child, or unmarried adult son or daughter to become a legal permanent resident, those aliens are eligible for the residency. In addition, if an alien spouse, child, or unmarried adult son or daughter of a permanent resident who died in the attacks was present in the United States on Sept. 11 but had not yet applied for permanent residence, the alien can petition for permanent residence.

● **Broadens definition of child.** The law lengthens the amount of time that aliens will be considered children for the purposes of immigration law if they filed petitions on or before Sept. 11. It is easier for children to qualify for citizenship than adults.

● **Humanitarian relief.** For aliens not covered by the relief in this law, the attorney general may provide temporary administrative relief for humanitarian purposes or to keep families together.

● **Prohibition for terrorists.** None of this relief will be provided to anyone culpable for the terrorist attacks on Sept. 11 or to any family member of such an individual.

Investigating Terrorism

● **Increased rewards.** There is no limit on the size of the rewards that the attorney general can offer to combat terrorism. Rewards of $250,000 or more require the personal approval of the attorney general or president, as well as notice to Congress. Rewards for help in investigating crimes other than terrorism are subject to budgetary caps. The secretary of State can pay rewards for identifying and locating a terrorist organization. The maximum size of such rewards is increased to $10 million. The secretary of State may raise that limit to $25 million if he or she believes it is in the national interest. The law includes a sense of Congress that there should be a $25 million reward for information on Osama bin Laden and other leaders of the Sept. 11 attacks.

● **DNA database.** Those convicted of terrorism must provide DNA for inclusion in the federal DNA database of convicted offenders.

● **Intelligence information sharing.** Federal agents conducting foreign intelligence wiretaps may consult with law enforcement officials to coordinate efforts to investigate or protect against international terrorism, clandestine intelligence activities, or other hostile acts of a foreign power or an agent of a foreign power.

● **Financial information.** The FBI director or a designee no lower than deputy assistant director may request telephone, financial or credit records if he or she certifies that the information is relevant to an ongoing foreign counterintelligence investigation and that there are "specific, articulable" facts showing that the person targeted is the agent of a foreign power. An investigation of a U.S. citizen may not be based solely on activities protected by the First Amendment.

● **Secret Service jurisdiction.** The Secret Service has concurrent jurisdiction with the Justice Department to investigate offenses involving computer fraud and related activity. The law also gives the

Secret Service the authority to investigate fraud at financial institutions.

● **Education records.** A court may release student education records if the attorney general or the Education secretary determines that the records would reasonably assist in investigating or preventing an act of terrorism. The provision also applies to information obtained by the National Center for Educational Statistics.

Victims Compensation

● **Paperwork eased.** The law streamlines the Public Safety Officers Benefits Program application process for family members of law enforcement officers, firefighters and emergency personnel who were killed or suffered serious injury in the terrorist attacks. The law raises the total payment allowed under the Public Safety Officers Benefits Program to $250,000, effective for any death or disability occurring on or after Jan. 1, 2001.

● **Victims of Crime fund.** The Office for Victims of Crime is authorized to replenish the anti-terrorism emergency reserve with as much as $50 million. The law establishes a mechanism for replenishing the fund in future years and replaces the annual cap on the fund with a self-regulating system intended to keep the fund healthy. Private gifts to the fund are now allowed, and the law increases the portion of the fund available for discretionary grants and assistance to victims of federal crimes.

● **State programs.** The law increases the minimum amount authorized for the annual grant to state compensation programs. It clarifies that compensation paid to a victim shall not be used in means tests for federal benefit programs. The law removes the requirement that state crime victim compensation programs include victims of terrorism occurring outside the United States. States may give victims compensation funds to U.S. attorneys offices in jurisdictions where the U.S. attorney is the local prosecutor.

● **Non-discrimination for victims.** Victim assistance programs may not discriminate against victims who disagree with the way the state is prosecuting the case. The law authorizes grants to eligible victim assistance programs for program evaluation and compliance efforts, and it allows money to be used for fellowships, clinical internships and training programs.

● **Governmental cooperation.** The Department of Justice Regional Information Sharing Systems Program is expanded to facilitate information sharing among federal, state and local law enforcement agencies to investigate and prosecute terrorist conspiracies and activities. The law doubles the program's authorized funding for fiscal 2002-2003, authorizing $50 million in fiscal 2002 and $100 million in fiscal 2003.

Changes in Criminal Law

● **Mass transit.** The law makes it a federal crime to attack a mass transit system, punishable by a fine and as much as 20 years in prison. If the vehicle was carrying a passenger at the time of the attack, or if the attack killed someone, the maximum sentence increases to life.

● **Domestic terrorism.** The law defines "domestic terrorism" as activities that involve acts dangerous to human life that are a violation of federal or state laws and that appear intended to intimidate or coerce a civilian population, change government policy or affect the conduct of government by mass destruction, assassination or kidnaping, and that occur primarily within the United States.

● **Harboring terrorists.** The law makes it a federal crime for individuals to harbor a person who they know or should have known was engaged in or would engage in terrorist activities.

● **U.S. criminal jurisdiction.** The law extends U.S. jurisdiction to offenses committed by or against a U.S. national, U.S. diplomatic, consular and military missions, and residences used by U.S. person-

nel assigned to such missions.

● **Material support for terrorism.** Three terrorism-related offenses are added to the list of those considered as providing material support to a terrorist. These violations may be prosecuted in any federal judicial district in which the offense was committed. The law explicitly prohibits providing terrorists with "expert advice or assistance," such as flight training, knowing or intending that it will be used to prepare for or carry out an act of terrorism.

● **U.S. forfeiture authority.** U.S. forfeiture authority is extended to "all assets, foreign or domestic" that are owned or controlled by any person or group planning or carrying out an act of terrorism against the United States, its citizens or residents or their property.

● **Material support for terrorists.** The law clarifies that the provisions of the Trade Sanctions Reform and Export Enhancement Act of 2000 (PL 106-387, Title IX) do not limit or otherwise affect the criminal prohibitions against providing material support to terrorists or designated terrorist organizations.

● **Crime of terrorism defined.** The law adds the following as a list of offenses under the definition of "federal crime of terrorism": destruction of aircraft or aircraft facilities; violence at international airports; arson within special maritime and territorial jurisdiction; offenses involving biological or chemical weapons; kidnapping or assassination of members of Congress, the Cabinet or the Supreme Court; offenses involving nuclear materials or plastic explosives; arson and bombing of government property risking or causing death; arson and bombing of property used in interstate commerce; killing or attempted killing during an attack on a federal facility with a dangerous weapon; conspiracy to murder, kidnap, or maim persons abroad; offenses against the protection of computers; killing or attempted killing of officers and employees of the United States; murder or manslaughter of foreign officials, official guests, or internationally protected persons; hostage taking; destruction of communication lines, stations, or systems; injury to buildings or property within special maritime and territorial jurisdiction of the United States; destruction of an energy facility; presidential and presidential staff assassination and kidnapping; wrecking trains; terrorist attacks and other acts of violence against mass transportation systems; destruction of national defense materials, premises, or utilities; violence against maritime navigation; violence against maritime fixed platforms; certain homicides and other violence against United States nationals occurring outside the United States; use of weapons of mass destruction; acts of terrorism transcending national boundaries; harboring terrorists; providing material support to terrorists or terrorist organizations; torture; sabotage of nuclear facilities or fuel; aircraft piracy; assault on a flight crew with a dangerous weapon, explosive or incendiary devices or endangerment of human life by means of weapons on aircraft.

● **No statute of limitations.** The law eliminates the statute of limitations for certain terrorism-related offenses if they result in or create a foreseeable risk of death or serious bodily injury to another person.

● **Increased prison terms.** The law raises the maximum prison terms to 15 to 20 years — or, if death results, life — for the following crimes: arson within the special maritime and territorial jurisdiction of the United States, destruction of an energy facility, destruction of national-defense materials, provision of material support to terrorists and terrorist organizations, sabotage of nuclear facilities or fuel, killings on aircraft, destruction of interstate gas or hazardous liquid pipeline facility.

● **Conspiracy penalties.** The law adds conspiracy provisions to the following criminal statutes: arson within special maritime and territorial jurisdiction of the United States; killings in federal facilities; destruction of communications lines, stations or systems; destruction of property within special maritime and territorial jurisdiction of the United States; wrecking trains; material support to terrorists; torture; sabotage of nuclear facilities or fuel; interference with flight crews; carrying weapons or explosives on aircraft; and destruction of interstate gas or hazardous liquid pipeline facilities.

● **Supervised release.** The law authorizes an extended period of supervised release for persons who have served their prison sentence for certain terrorism-related offenses that resulted in, or created a foreseeable risk of, death or serious bodily injury to another person.

● **Terrorism as racketeering.** Certain terrorism-related offenses are included within the definition of "racketeering activity." This allows multiple acts of terrorism to be charged as a pattern of racketeering for purposes of the Racketeer Influenced and Corrupt Organizations (RICO) statute, which can triple the damages imposed. The law expands the ability of prosecutors to prosecute members of established, ongoing terrorist organizations.

● **Computer hacking.** The criminal statute prohibiting computer hacking includes computers located outside the United States when used in a manner that affects the interstate commerce or communications of the United States. The law updates the definition of "loss" to ensure that the full costs to victims of hacking offenses are counted.

● **Forensic laboratories.** The attorney general must establish regional computer forensic laboratories and support existing computer forensic laboratories to help combat computer crime.

● **U.S. criminal jurisdiction.** The biological weapons statute's definition of "for use as a weapon" is expanded to include all situations in which it can be proven that the defendant had any purpose not prophylactic, protective, or peaceful. Certain persons, including non-resident foreign nationals of countries that support international terrorism, are forbidden to possess a listed biological agent or toxin.

Intelligence Changes

● **Foreign intelligence management.** The law clarifies the role of the CIA director in managing the collection, analysis and dissemination of foreign intelligence gathered under FISA. The CIA director must assist the attorney general in ensuring that FISA investigations follow constitutional guidelines.

● **Revised definitions.** The definitions section of the National Security Act of 1947 (PL 253) is revised to include international terrorism as a subset of "foreign intelligence," clarifying the CIA director's responsibility for collecting foreign intelligence related to international terrorism.

● **Informant recruitment.** The law expresses the sense of Congress that the CIA should make efforts to recruit informants to fight terrorism.

● **Reports deferred.** The secretary of Defense, the attorney general and the CIA director may defer submitting certain reports on intelligence activities to Congress until Feb. 1, 2002.

● **Information sharing.** Law enforcement agencies must notify intelligence agencies when a criminal investigation reveals information of intelligence value. Constitutional and statutory prohibitions against certain types of information sharing still apply.

● **Intelligence training.** The attorney general, in consultation with the CIA director, must establish a program to train federal, state and local officials in the recognition and appropriate handling of intelligence information discovered in the normal course of their duties.

Miscellaneous

● **Civil rights oversight.** The Justice Department's inspector general must designate one official to review information and receive complaints alleging abuses of civil rights and civil liberties by employees and officials of the Department of Justice.

● **Condemnation of discrimination.** The law condemns discrimi-

nation and acts of violence against Sikh Americans, as well as Arab and Muslim Americans.

● **Denial of admission for money laundering.** Any alien who a consular officer or the attorney general knows, or has reason to believe, is involved in a federal money-laundering offense is barred from the United States.

● **Biometric identifier.** The attorney general must report to Congress on the feasibility of using a "biometric identifier" system, with access to the FBI fingerprint database, at consular offices abroad and at points of entry into the United States. Such devices scan fingerprints or other physical characteristics to check an individual's identity.

● **Suspect lists to airlines.** The FBI must report to Congress on the feasibility of providing airlines with computer access to the names of suspected terrorists.

● **Military installation security.** The Defense Department has temporary authority to enter contracts with a state or local government for the performance of security functions at any military installation or facility in the United States.

● **Charity telemarketing.** Any telemarketer soliciting for charity must disclose to people they call that they are telephoning to solicit charitable contributions, and make other disclosures that the Federal Trade Commission considers appropriate.

● **Hazardous materials background check.** The Department of Transportation may check the background of any individual applying for a license to transport hazardous materials in interstate commerce.

● **State and local bio-terrorism preparedness.** The law expresses the sense of the Senate that the United States should make a substantial new investment this year toward improving state and local preparedness to respond to potential bio-terrorism attacks.

● **Terrorism grants.** The law authorizes a Justice Department program to provide grants to states to prepare for and respond to terrorist acts including, but not limited to, acts involving weapons of mass destruction and biological, nuclear, radiological, incendiary,

chemical and explosive devices.

The law revises this grant program to provide additional flexibility to purchase needed equipment; training and technical assistance to state and local first responders; and a more equitable allocation of funds among the states. It also clarifies that grants under the Crime Identification Technology Act can be used for anti-terrorism, and authorizes grants under that act at $250 million a year through fiscal 2007. The law authorizes another $25 million annually from fiscal 2003 through fiscal 2007 for grants to state and local authorities to respond to and prevent acts of terrorism.

● **Infrastructure protection.** The law establishes a National Infrastructure Simulation and Analysis Center to address critical infrastructure protection and continuity through support for activities related to counterterrorism, threat assessment and risk mitigation.

● **Severability.** Any portion of this law found to be invalid or unenforceable shall be severable from the rest of the law.

● **Counterterrorism fund.** The law creates a separate fund to reimburse the Justice Department and any other federal agency for the costs of rebuilding facilities destroyed by terrorism or conducting counterterrorism investigations.

● **Technical support funding.** The law authorizes $200 million in each of fiscal years 2002, 2003 and 2004 for the FBI's Technical Support Center.

● **Domestic military aid.** The attorney general may call for military help in situations involving chemical weapons.

● **Electronic crimes task forces.** The Secret Service may create a national network of electronic crimes task forces, designed to prevent, detect and investigate electronic crimes, including possible terrorist attacks on the United States.

● **Property confiscation.** The president may confiscate and vest properties of an enemy, defined as a country, person or organization, when the United States is engaged in hostilities or has been the subject of an attack by that enemy. Classified information may be used to defend this determination to a judge and may be kept secret from the property owner. ◆

245(i) Extension Left Unfinished

With the backing of the White House, the Senate passed a compromise bill in September to extend a program that permitted some immigrants to apply for U.S. residency even if they were in the country illegally. The House was poised to clear the bill Sept. 11, but the terrorist attacks put it on hold, leaving the extension in limbo at the end of the year.

The program — known as 245(i) after its section in immigration law — allowed immigrants who were eligible for residency, but who had overstayed their visa or were otherwise in the country illegally, to pay a $1,000 fine and complete their residency application in the United States. The applicant also had to be sponsored by an employer or a family member who was a legal resident or U.S. citizen. Without the program, immigrants had to return to their home countries and apply there to become

BoxScore

Bill:
HR 1885

Legislative Action:
House passed HR 1885, 336-43, on May 21.
Senate passed HR 1885, amended to reflect S 778, by voice vote Sept. 6.

U.S. residents. But because of their illegal status while in the United States, they could be barred from returning for up to 10 years.

The 245(i) program expired April 30, but many applicants missed the deadline because the Immigration and Naturalization Service (INS) was slow to draft rules for the process. All sides agreed the program should be extended, but the House and Senate disagreed over how long.

The House easily passed a four-month extension in May, but the proposal stalled in the Senate, where many wanted to give the program a longer life span. The Senate passed an extension through April 2002 on Sept. 6, and that version was schedule for floor action Sept. 11, when the Capitol was evacuated. The vote was never taken.

The White House supported attaching the extension to

Bill Aims at Tighter Border Security

The House passed a bill (HR 3525) by voice vote Dec. 19 designed to tighten federal control over U.S. borders and prevent terrorists from entering the country.

The bill contained provisions to:

● **Border and Customs inspections.** Require the Immigration and Naturalization Service (INS) to hire additional employees in each of fiscal years 2002 through 2006, including at least 200 additional inspectors and 200 additional investigators. The Customs Service would be required to hire 200 additional customs agents each of those years. The INS would be authorized to increase salaries of border patrol agents and inspection assistants, and INS inspectors and customs agents would be required to receive ongoing training.

● **Upgraded facilities.** Authorize $150 million for the INS and $150 million for the Customs Service for technology upgrade at their inspection facilities, including systems to improve pre-enrollment and pre-clearance programs and facilitate the lawful and efficient cross-border movement of commerce and people, without compromising safety and security.

● **Terrorist database.** Require the establishment of a governmentwide, electronic data-sharing system on persons with terrorist ties that federal officials could use to determine whether to grant visa applications or permit an individual to enter the United States. Federal law enforcement and intelligence agencies would have to share relevant information on potential terrorists through the system. The INS would be required to fully integrate all of its existing alien databases with the system.

U.S. missions in each foreign country would be required to establish a "terrorist lookout committee" to ensure that the names of known and suspected terrorists were entered into the system. The system would then be used by U.S. consular offices in reviewing whether to approve visa applications, and by INS officials responsible for admitting or deporting aliens.

A nine-member federal commission would oversee the operation of the data-sharing system.

● **High-tech visas.** Require the State Department — beginning Oct. 26, 2003 — to issue only machine-readable, tamper-resistant visas that include biometric identifiers. Biometric scanners and identification devices would have to be installed at all U.S. ports of entry by that date, and all nations that participated in the reciprocal visa-waiver program would have to begin issuing passports with the same high-tech features to their citizens.

● **Visa fees.** Authorize the State Department to charge $65, or the cost of the service, whichever was higher to issue machine-readable visas.

● **Consular offices.** Require the State Department to upgrade security in its consular offices for reviewing visa applications, and provide ongoing training for consular officers and diplomatic security agents.

● **Temporary visas.** Prohibit the issuance of temporary visas to citizens of nations considered to be state sponsors of terrorism, unless it was determined that the alien posed no threat to Americans or to U.S. national security.

● **Student visas.** Require the Justice Department to establish a system to electronically track all foreign students in the United States on visas. Colleges and other educational institutions would have to notify the government if a foreign student failed to enroll or attend classes. At least one of the suspected Sept. 11 hijackers entered the country on a student visa but never attended class.

● **Passenger manifests.** Require all commercial airlines and vessels destined for the United States to submit to the INS a passenger and crew manifest listing everyone aboard. A similar manifest would have to be provided when a plane or ship departs the United States. The manifests would have to be submitted electronically, beginning Jan. 1, 2003.

the fiscal 2002 Commerce-Justice-State (CJS) spending bill. The Senate version of the bill contained a permanent extension of 245(i) that was opposed by House conservatives. House Judiciary Chairman F. James Sensenbrenner Jr., R-Wis., said the 245(i) bill should go through regular order and asked his Republican colleagues to drop it from the CJS conference report, which they reluctantly did. (*Appropriations, p. 2-9*)

The bill that was ready to clear Sept. 11 would have:

● Extended the 245(i) program through April 30, 2002, or four months after the Justice Department issued final or interim final regulations to carry out the measure, whichever was earlier.

● Limited the extension to those who were in the United States as of Dec. 15, 2000, and whose immigration petition was based on a family relationship that existed before Aug. 15, or on an application for labor certification that was filed before Aug. 15.

Background

The legislation to extend the 245(i) program was part of a broader debate about revising U.S. immigration laws, particularly toward Mexico. As governor of Texas and then as president, Bush took a particular interest in promoting closer relations with Mexico. He also was at the forefront of Republican efforts to court the increasingly powerful Hispanic electorate, for whom immigration was an important issue.

Bush's first official trip abroad was to Mexico, where he met with President Vicente Fox on Feb. 16. The two announced plans to conduct negotiations on migration policy, with the goal of having a deal by the time Fox came to Washington in early September for the Bush' administration's first state visit. However, the administration's plan remained vague; reports said only that it would likely include some kind of temporary guest-worker program as well as a process that would allow some of the millions of illegal im-

migrants in the United State to become legal residents.

When Fox came to Washington on Sept. 5, he presented a surprise timetable that called for a U.S-Mexico agreement by the end of the year. The White House at first downplayed the idea, but Bush said Sept. 6 that he understood why Fox felt such urgency on immigration and pledged to try to accommodate his schedule. "One thing he'll find is we will put 100 percent effort during the year, and I hope we can come up with a solution," Bush said. Fox addressed a joint meeting of Congress on Sept. 6. Despite significant opposition from within his own party, it looked likely that Bush would push through a major rewrite of immigration laws.

Then came Sept. 11, which abruptly refocused the immigration debate on issues of border security and visas. Any overhaul of immigration policy was put on hold. Some wrote off the liberalization move entirely. Sensenbrenner called it a "casualty" of Sept. 11. Bush was careful, however, to distinguish between "people who come to our country to visit, to study or to work" and those "who come to hurt the American people." And he and congressional leaders of both parties took pains to assure pro-immigrant groups that a larger move toward liberalizing immigration laws would not be abandoned.

The 245(i) Program

The most immediate immigration issue for Congress was the 245(i) extension. The program was created in 1994 as a three-year trial, and expired at the end of 1997. Under a compromise worked out between the Clinton administration — which supported a permanent extension — and congressional Republicans, the provisions were renewed for four months, through April 30, 2001, as part of a fiscal 2001 omnibus appropriations bill (PL 106-554). On the final days of the extension, huge lineups surrounded immigration offices as thousands sought to file their applications before the deadline.

On May 1, Bush sent a letter to congressional leaders seeking a temporary extension of the program. He noted that up to 200,000 of the 500,000 estimated eligible immigrants did not file applications by the April 30 deadline, in part, because INS regulations were not issued until late March. Bush did not say how long an extension he wanted, but a senior administration official said that a six- to 12-month time frame was discussed when Bush met with Fox.

Bush's backing for an extension of the program was difficult for GOP conservatives, who previously opposed any such move. But the opponents of 245(i) agreed to consider a brief extension because the INS had not issued regulations for the previous extension quickly enough.

Legislative Action

House Action

The four-month extension (HR 1885) sailed through the House on May 21 on a vote of 336-43. The bill, sponsored by George W. Gekas, R-Pa., was limited to applicants who had been in the United States by Dec. 21, 2000. The family or employment relationship that qualified them for visa status had to have existed before the law expired April 30. *(House vote 127, p. H-50)*

Sensenbrenner urged the Senate to accept the House bill, saying it was a "compassionate compromise to a very contentious issue." But Judiciary Chairman Orrin G. Hatch of Utah and other Senate Republicans argued that four months would not be enough time to get all the applications processed by INS, an agency that had a reputation for inefficiency. "It would be better to try and do it right" than push the House bill through, Hatch said. Many Democrats wanted to extend the program for a year.

White House spokesman Ari Fleischer said May 22 that Bush was siding with the Senate. "The president supports an extension to help immigrants stay in this country," Fleischer said. "He believes a longer period should be in order." Replied Sensenbrenner: "I am concerned this tack would cause House support for a 245(i) extension to dissipate."

Senate Action

On July 26, the Senate Judiciary Committee gave voice vote approval to a bill (S 778) that would extend the program through April 30, 2002.

The committee adopted, by voice vote, an amendment by Jon Kyl, R-Ariz., to make 245(i) available only to those who had been in the United States since Dec. 21, 2000, and had established family or job ties at the time the bill was enacted. Kyl argued that the way the original bill was worded, anyone who established their eligibility by April 2002 would be able to use it.

The Senate passed HR 1885 by voice vote Sept. 6, after substituting the text of its own bill. ◆

House Passes Fetal Protection Bill

A bill to make it a federal crime to harm or kill a fetus while committing a violent offense against a pregnant woman passed the House on April 26 but stalled in the Senate. If enacted, the bill (HR 503) would have given legal status to a fetus for the first time.

Bill sponsor Lindsey Graham, R-S.C., said the legislation would send a strong signal: "If you attack a pregnant woman, you get prosecuted not once but twice."

Democratic opponents said the bill was a back-door attempt to undermine the landmark 1973 *Roe v. Wade* Supreme Court decision, which legalized abortion after concluding that "the unborn have never been recognized in the law as persons in the whole sense." Democrats tried unsuccessfully to substitute language that would increase penalties for attacking a pregnant woman, but would not recognize the fetus as a separate human being.

The House had passed a similar bill in 1999, but the Senate did not act on it. That version had been presented as a crime-fighting bill, although it was drafted with the help of anti-abortion groups. (*1999 Almanac, p. 18-33*)

With the GOP initially controlling both chambers and the White House, enactment seemed likely. But action in the Senate stalled after it switched to Democratic control in June.

According to the National Right to Life Committee, 24 states had such statutes on the books.

Highlights

The bill, which supporters said was modeled after several existing state laws, contained provisions to:

• Make it a federal crime to harm or kill a fetus while committing any one of 68 existing federal offenses or a crime under military law.

• Make the punishment for harming a fetus the same as if the offense had been committed against the pregnant woman — whether or not the assailant knew the woman was pregnant or intended to harm the fetus.

• Exclude the death penalty as a possible punishment for the new crime.

• Exempt from prosecution doctors who perform consensual abortions and women whose actions harm fetuses they carry.

Legislative History

House Judiciary Committee

After extensive debate, the House Judiciary Committee approved the fetal protection legislation March 28 on a 15-9 party line vote (H Rept 107-42, Part 1). The panel's Constitution subcommittee had given approval by voice vote March 21.

BoxScore

Bill:

HR 503

Legislative Action:

House passed HR 503 (H Rept 107-42, Part 1), 252-172, on April 26.

Subcommittee Chairman Steve Chabot, R-Ohio, said the bill would help close "an unfortunate gap in the law" that allowed offenders who attacked pregnant women to escape punishment for harm done to the fetus. He rejected Democrats' argument that the aim was to erode abortion rights established with Roe v. Wade. "The bill simply does not apply to abortion," Chabot said.

Jerrold Nadler, D-N.Y., disagreed. "We should have no illusions about the purpose of this bill — that it is yet another battle of a war of symbols in the abortion debate, in which opponents of a woman's right to choose attempt to portray fetuses . . . as children," he said. The bill "clearly recognizes the fetus as the victim of violence," a premise that he said was "at odds with the holdings of the Supreme Court and the Constitution."

Chabot countered that the Supreme Court had never determined when life begins. He said the court's decision in *Roe v. Wade* "protects the woman's right to abortion, not some third party's right to destroy the fetus." He said Congress had clear authority to pass such a law because it would only affect conduct already prohibited by federal law.

Democrats offered a substitute amendment, defeated 13-20, to increase penalties for attacking a pregnant woman and causing harm to her pregnancy but without recognizing the fetus as a crime victim.

Adam B. Schiff, D-Calif., said the Democratic substitute was preferable because it would "not [force] the court to determine when life begins."

Republicans also defeated, 11-19, a Democratic amendment to prevent the bill from taking effect until all domestic abuse programs in the Violence Against Women Act were fully funded. Existing funding levels were $207 million short of what Congress authorized, Democrats said.

House Floor Action

The House passed the bill April 26 by a vote of 252-172, with the support of 53 Democrats. The vote in 1999 had been 254-172, with 56 Democrats in favor. The Bush administration issued a statement endorsing the bill and strongly opposing the Democratic substitute. (*House vote 89, p. H-36*)

The highly charged floor debate focused on the question of when life begins. Democrats and abortion rights advocates insisted the bill was an unconstitutional assault on abortion rights. Supporters insisted the measure was aimed at punishing crime. They cited the case of Glendale Black of Wisconsin, who beat his wife when she was nine months pregnant. She survived the attack but lost the pregnancy, and Black was prosecuted only for assaulting his wife.

The Democratic alternative — to create a federal crime for an attack on a pregnant woman that kills or damages the fetus — was rejected, 196-229. (*House vote 88, p. H-36*) ◆

Juvenile Crime Bills Stall in Senate

The House passed a pair of bills on juvenile crime — one focused on penalties, the other on prevention — but the Senate did not act on either of the measures.

The first of the bills (HR 863), passed Oct. 16, would authorize $1.5 billion over three years for juvenile justice grants to state and local governments. The second (HR 1900), passed Sept. 20, would consolidate five juvenile justice and delinquency preventing programs into a single block grant to be used by states for activities designed to prevent and reduce juvenile crime.

BoxScore

Bills:

HR 863, HR 1900

Legislative Action:

House passed HR 1900 (H Rept 107-203) by voice vote Sept. 20.

House passed HR 863 (H Rept 107-46) by voice vote Oct. 16.

Penalties

Supporters of the juvenile justice bill (HR 863) were determined to avoid the kind of controversial amendments that had sunk a nearly identical bill in 1999. Then, the relatively small block grant bill was caught up in an intense reaction following the massacre at Columbine High School in Colorado, where two teenagers killed themselves after gunning down 12 other students and a teacher. After days of floor debate and amendments, the bill included provisions to create a number of mandatory minimum sentences for juvenile crimes and allow some juveniles to be prosecuted as adults in federal court. House members turned back efforts to add gun control language to the bill, but the Senate version contained several gun control provisions, including one requiring background checks for sales of guns at gun shows. That died in conference. (1999 Almanac, p. 18-3)

As passed, the 2001 bill contained provisions to:

● **Authorization.** Authorize $500 million in each of fiscal years 2002 through 2004 for grants to state and local governments for juvenile justice programs — twice the amount appropriated for juvenile justice block grants for fiscal 2001. The grants could be used for a wide range of activities, including developing graduated sanctions, building corrections facilities, hiring additional juvenile court judges, officers and prosecutors, training police officers to prevent and control juvenile crime and establishing juvenile drug and gun courts.

● **Eligibility.** Require states and localities receiving grants to establish a graduated sanctions plan for juvenile offenders. Graduated sanctions punish an offender in some way for each offense he or she commits. Although the punishment usually increases in severity along with the crime, the bill would not require harsher penalties at each stage.

House Action

The House Judiciary Committee Crime Subcommittee approved the bill— sponsored by subcommittee Chairman Lamar Smith, R-Texas — by voice vote March 21.

Smith and ranking Democrat Robert C. Scott of Virginia

worked to keep the $1.5 billion measure free of amendments that could bog it down. "We're trying to avoid what we're calling mutually assured destruction," Smith said The only requirement on states seeking the grant money was that they allow local jurisdictions to develop and implement a program of graduated sanctions for juvenile offenders. Smith said the point of graduated sanctions was to "break the cycle of delinquency," which can allow a young offender to commit a series of ever-more-serious offenses without consequence until he or she commits a crime that results in a jail sentence.

Asa Hutchinson, R-Ark., and Mark Green, R-Wis., won voice vote approval for an amendment to add "restorative justice" programs to the list of approved uses for the money. Restorative justice programs let juveniles work out restitution agreements with their victims.

The full Judiciary Committee approved the bill (H Rept 107-46) by voice vote March 28. Ranking Democrat John Conyers Jr. of Michigan argued that "preventing juvenile crime is about thwarting easy access to guns," but he was blocked by committee rules from offering gun control amendments. The committee approved, by voice vote, a manager's amendment by Smith that broadened the kinds of programs that could be funded under the bill.

The House passed the bill by voice vote Oct. 16. Supporters succeeded in having the measure brought to the floor under suspension of the rules, which barred Conyers and others from offering amendments.

It was not clear, however, that it would be so easy to ward off amendments in the Senate. Dianne Feinstein, D-Calif., a leader in the gun control movement, said she considered the juvenile justice bill a fair target for gun control amendments. She was writing a provision on trigger locks, which she indicated she might offer when the bill was debated in the Senate.

Prevention

The second bill (HR 1900) would reauthorize the 1974 Juvenile Justice and Delinquency Prevention Act through fiscal 2006.

As passed by the House, the bill would:

● **Authorization.** Consolidate five federal juvenile justice programs — dealing with mentoring, state challenge activities, boot camps, victims of child abuse and neglect, and gang prevention — into a single block grant, authorized for fiscal years 2002 through 2006. Grants would go to states based on the size of their juvenile population and their crime statistics. Recipients of the funds could include community-based organizations, law enforcement agencies,

school districts, local governments and social service providers.

● **Eligibility.** Continue existing conditions for states receiving the grants, including requirements that juveniles be held separate from adults in jails and lock-ups. But the bill would double the time — from 24 to 48 hours — that youths in rural areas could be incarcerated with adults before making an initial court appearance.

House Action

The bill, cosponsored by James C. Greenwood, R-Pa., and Robert C. Scott, D-Va., began in the Education and the Workforce Committee. It won voice vote approval in the Select Education Subcommittee on June 21, and the full committee approved the bill (H Rept 107-203) by a vote of 41-2 on Sept. 10.

The House passed the bill by voice vote Sept. 20. ◆

Chapter 15

POLITICS & ELECTIONS

Election Overhaul On Hold

The 2000 presidential elections exposed the nation's voting system as an unreliable hodgepodge of local standards, inconsistent procedures and old equipment. Congress rushed to devise remedies, but the work soon slowed to a crawl. Partisan differences complicated the negotiations, as did resistance from state and local officials to federal mandates.

The delay cost Congress any opportunity it might have had to affect the 2002 elections. However, a flurry of action before lawmakers adjourned for the year brought them close to a final deal, renewing hope that they could institute changes at least in time for the next presidential elections, in 2004. The House passed a bipartisan bill (HR 3295) on Dec. 12, and a hard-won compromise was announced in the Senate just before the end of the session.

The 2000 post-election standoff in Florida between presidential candidates Al Gore and George W. Bush had been accompanied by tales of lost ballots, faulty voting machines, and voters turned away from the polls in large numbers. Local election officials, in many cases operating on meager budgets, struggled to recount thousands of ballots, often without clear standards to guide them. The world watched as election workers argued over the meaning of dimples on punch cards.

The public was outraged, and lawmakers from both parties promised sweeping changes to restore confidence in the system. "The experience of the last election must never, ever be repeated," Sen. Robert G. Torricelli, D-N.J., said in a January news conference with Sen. Mitch McConnell, R-Ky.

But discussions in the House stalled early in the year after Speaker J. Dennis Hastert, R-Ill., and Democratic leader Richard A. Gephardt of Missouri failed to agree on the makeup of a bipartisan commission on election overhaul. Gephardt wanted Democrats to have equal representation on the panel; Hastert insisted that Republicans have a one-seat majority. Talks did not begin again in earnest until May, when House Administration Committee Chairman Bob Ney, R-Ohio, and ranking Democrat Steny H. Hoyer of Maryland agreed to work together to write a bipartisan election overhaul bill.

About the same time, a bipartisan group in the Senate, including Torricelli and McConnell, introduced a bill (S 953) aimed at encouraging states to modernize voting machines and update election procedures.

Old partisan dynamics remained. Democrats focused on confusion at the polls that kept voters from casting ballots. The groups most affected and most angered by the problems were blacks and other minorities who tended to vote Democratic. Republicans, meanwhile, focused on vote fraud. They said lax oversight in state and county election offices, loose rules for mail-in registrations, and sloppy voter rolls were undermining the system's integrity.

BoxScore

Bills:
HR 3295, S 565
Legislative Action:
House passed HR 3295
(H Rept 107-329), 362-63, on
Dec. 12.

But the problems ran deeper than party rivalries. The main point of contention was the proper role of the federal government in a process that had always been within the purview of the states. Many lawmakers, both Democrats and Republicans, were leery of imposing national standards on state-run systems. Others argued for federal mandates, saying that with the integrity of the nation's democratic system and the legitimacy of the federal government at stake, Congress had to be forceful in ordering changes.

Members of the Congressional Black Caucus and other advocates of strong federal election mandates went further. Drawing parallels to the struggles of the 1960s to end segregation and secure equal rights for African-Americans, they called for federal intervention to protect the voting rights of minorities.

After working for months to find a compromise, Ney and Hoyer introduced a bill in November to set broad new minimum standards for elections, with federal grants to help states replace punch-card voting devices and improve the administration of elections. In December, a year after the Supreme Court brought the 2000 presidential election to a controversial conclusion, the House passed the bill.

Across the Capitol, a bipartisan group of senators broke a months-long impasse and reached a compromise on a package of election changes. Majority Leader Tom Daschle, D-S.D., promised quick action when Congress reconvened in January 2002.

Highlights

The House and Senate bills took somewhat different approaches.

- **Federal mandates.** The Senate bill proposed explicit national standards for accuracy and accessibility that the states would have to follow. The House measure set out broad minimum standards and offered states considerable latitude in implementing them.
- **Enforcement.** The Senate bill called for the Justice Department to monitor compliance with the national standards, with authority to sue states that failed to comply. To receive federal funding, states also would have to give the Justice Department a plan for identifying and deterring election fraud. The House bill would authorize the Justice Department to sue states to compel compliance with minimum standards, but it specified no penalties for states that failed to comply.
- **Federal aid.** Both bills proposed federal aid for the first time to help states improve their voting systems. The House bill would authorize $2.65 billion in grants to help states modernize equipment, encourage voting and comply with new standards. States could get extra money if they went be-

yond the minimum standards. An additional $20 million in grants would go to developing new voting equipment. The Senate bill would authorize $3.5 billion in grants over five years to help states meet the new federal mandates.

● **Election commission.** Under the Senate bill, a new election commission would recommend additional regulations or legislation to improve elections and would have power to approve or deny federal aid to states to improve their voting systems. As envisioned in the House bill, the commission would help states meet minimum standards and monitor compliance but would not be able to issue new regulations.

Background

Since the nation's founding, the states have run and paid for all elections, with minimal federal involvement. At the same time, the Constitution gives Congress wide authority to regulate the election of federal candidates. As a practical matter, that means Congress can regulate the conduct of all elections, since states are unlikely to maintain separate voting systems for federal candidates.

Under Article 1, Section 4, it is up to each state to set the "time, place and manner" of House and Senate elections, but Congress may "by law make or alter such regulations" at any time. In 1842, Congress used its authority under this section to require that states elect their congressional delegations from single-member districts. In February 2001, the Supreme Court reaffirmed Congress' power over congressional elections in *Cook v. Gralike,* striking down a Missouri law requiring that ballots specially label those candidates opposed to term limits. The high court stressed that any authority states have over congressional elections is delegated by Congress.

Congress also has the power to force changes in state laws by attaching conditions to federal money, much as it used highway dollars to force states to set speed limits on interstates. That power, upheld by the courts, is rooted in the taxing and spending authority granted Congress by Article 1, Section 8, of the Constitution.

In addition, the 14th Amendment guarantees all citizens equal protection under the law, and the 15th Amendment forbids states to deny anyone the right to vote on the basis of race. If there is evidence that minority voters or others are being treated unfairly, Congress has the power to step in.

Bush v. Gore

It was the 14th Amendment's guarantee of "equal protection" that formed the basis for the Supreme Court's ruling in *Bush v. Gore,* which stopped the recounts of Florida's presidential ballots and effectively handed the presidency to Bush. In a 5-4 decision, the majority said the recounts should be halted because standards for determining voter intent on partially punched ballots varied by county and therefore violated constitutional rights to equal protection.

Proponents of national standards said the logic for a uniform system was inescapable. "I think *Bush v. Gore* opens the door," said Rep. Sheila Jackson-Lee, vice chairman of the Congressional Black Caucus. "The Supreme Court said there must be uniform standards. Now obviously, you would like to think that the 50 states could collaborate together and uniform standards all of a sudden would be there at the

end of the day. Frankly, I don't think that will occur."

Some legal experts said *Bush v. Gore* seemed at least to provide an opening for requiring some internal uniformity in the way states and counties run elections.

But the court took pains to limit its ruling to the standoff in Florida, writing that "the problem of equal protection in election processes generally presents many complexities." That qualifier muddied the waters for many lawmakers, analysts and scholars. Some legal experts said they doubted the ruling gave Congress any more power than the authority it already had to regulate elections.

How Big a Federal Role?

Many lawmakers, along with state and local officials, argued against creating federal election mandates. The tradition of local control is so long, the costs so varied and the bureaucracies so entrenched, some said, that Congress would have trouble making changes even if it wanted to.

Some, like McConnell, preferred to offer federal money with strings attached, making grants contingent on states meeting standards for accuracy, accessibility and accountability while maintaining the long tradition of local control.

In congressional hearings, state and county officials were united in their opposition to edicts from Washington. They called for federal guidance in setting standards and identifying the best practices in election administration. They also wanted federal money to help pay for new equipment and training of election workers. But ultimately, state and local officials said they knew best what kinds of equipment and procedures worked for their constituents.

"I want something that debunks the myth that we have federal elections," Ohio Secretary of State J. Kenneth Blackwell told the House Administration Committee in April. "We don't. We have 50 state elections where the president and other federal officeholders are elected. I want to make sure we don't go down the slippery slope of federalizing elections."

Some states and localities were already working to address the problems on their own. Florida, the epicenter of the previous year's battles, acted the most decisively. On May 9, Republican Gov. Jeb Bush, President Bush's brother, signed a bill banning error-prone punch-card machines and ordering counties to replace them by 2002 with electronic or "optical scan" machines. The new law set aside state money for the new equipment, a computerized statewide voter-registration database and education for poll workers.

Elsewhere, Georgia passed a law requiring a uniform statewide system by 2004. A new Maryland law required that state to work with counties to adopt a uniform voting system. "Some critics have recently suggested that states are dragging their feet on enacting necessary reforms, that we are waiting for federal money to address this problem," Democrat John A. Hurson, majority leader of the Maryland House of Delegates, said at a congressional hearing. "Nothing could be further from the truth."

A number of ad hoc groups outside Congress also warned against edicts from Washington. Two of the most prominent — a study group of state and local election officials and a national task forced led by former presidents Jimmy Carter and Gerald R. Ford — urged states to adopt uniform statewide standards for counting votes. They also said the federal gov-

ernment should get more involved in helping to set standards for elections and in paying for the upgrade of voting equipment, though both groups opposed federal mandates.

Legislative Action

House Committee Action

The House Administration Committee approved the Ney-Hoyer bill (H Rept 107-329) on Nov. 15 by a vote of 8-0. By voice vote the panel adopted an amendment by Mark Steven Kirk, R-Ill., to allow polling places on military installations for people who lived on the bases and were registered locally. The military commander would set the opening and closing times of the polling stations.

The committee rejected, 3-5, an amendment that would have required states to equip polling places so that voters who are blind or disabled could cast secret ballots.

The bill was the result of a lengthy process that started in April, when Ney and Hoyer began a series of hearings. In May, they announced plans to collaborate on a bill, but it took another six months before they were ready to introduce the measure. The bill (HR 3295) proposed creating a new set of national standards, while giving states broad latitude to carry them out. States would have until November 2002 to set a procedure for voters to cast provisional ballots. A total of $2.65 billion would be authorized to help states overhaul their voting systems, including $400 million to replace punch-card machines.

By 2004, states would be required to have statewide registration systems accessible by local jurisdictions, have accurate voter registration records, and adopt a uniform definition of a valid vote on each type of equipment used in the state. To reduce the number of invalidated ballots, states would have to set rules allowing voters to correct errors in the polling place.

The Ney-Hoyer bill included a federal commission that could develop standards, but not issue regulations. The commission also could assist states in counting votes and monitoring error rates and voter turnout, notifying the Justice Department when states failed to comply with the minimum standards.

House Floor Action

The House passed the bill Dec. 12, one year to the day after the Supreme Court's ruling in *Bush v. Gore*. The vote was 362-63. *(House vote 489, p. H-168)*

No amendments were allowed, but the rule for floor consideration included a "manager's amendment" that made several changes to address the concerns of some lawmakers. Among them:

• Jurisdictions receiving money for replacing punch cards would be required to "consider the use of new technology by individuals with disabilities," including blindness.

• States receiving federal aid would have to report to the new election commission how the money was spent.

• Votes cast by military personnel and citizens overseas would have to be reported separately.

The manager's amendment also eliminated a provision that would have allowed official election materials to be mailed for half the cost of first-class mail.

The bill "addresses virtually every major election system flaw that came to light after our elections," Hoyer said. "This is not a perfect bill, but it goes much further than many people would have bet at the beginning of this session."

Senate Action

The bipartisan Senate bill, negotiated by the leaders of the Rules and Administration Committee, was unveiled Dec. 19, just as Congress was preparing to adjourn.

Initially, Rules Chairman Christopher J. Dodd, D-Conn., and McConnell, the ranking Republican on the committee, offered separate bills that illustrated the split in Congress over the question of federal mandates. While the two men agreed that the federal government should, for the first time in history, help pay for voting machines and other improvements to state election systems, they disagreed sharply over how expansive the federal role should be.

Dodd's bill (S 565) called for national standards for voting machines, access to polling places and the upkeep of voter rolls, and offered federal money to help states meet the new standards.

It required that voting systems be designed to notify voters when they made a mistake that would invalidate their ballots, such as voting twice for a single office, and give them a chance to fix their errors. States would have to mail sample ballots and voting instructions 10 days before Election Day and offer "provisional ballots," allowing voters whose registration was in doubt to cast a vote that would be counted later if they were found to be on the rolls.

"In federal elections, national elections, there must be basic, minimum standards," Dodd said.

McConnell's bill (S 953), a synthesis of two competing pieces of legislation, pointedly steered clear of federal mandates. Sponsoring the compromise bill with McConnell were Republican Sam Brownback of Kansas and Democrats Torricelli and Charles E. Schumer of New York.

The bill offered money to states as an incentive to improve their voting systems. The grants — $2.5 billion over five years — would be contingent on states adopting provisional balloting and meeting standards for accuracy, accessibility and accountability. A new Election Administration Commission would set the standards. "A carrot is much better than a stick," Schumer said. "I've talked with many secretaries of state. They'd be on the warpath if we mandated something." State governments know their needs best, McConnell said.

At McConnell's urging, Republicans boycotted a Rules Committee markup of Dodd's bill on Aug. 2, leaving Democrats to approve the legislation, 10-0. McConnell had demanded that the committee agree beforehand to send his bill to the Senate floor for a vote. Dodd refused, though he said McConnell could offer his bill as a substitute in committee.

Meanwhile, the two Democratic cosponsors of McConnell's legislation — Torricelli and Schumer, both also members of the Rules Committee — switched their allegiance and backed Dodd's bill.

The bitter breakdown stalled talks in the Senate for months. It was not until December that Dodd and McConnell, joined by Christopher S. Bond, R-Mo., managed

to strike a deal to rework Dodd's bill and get it moving again. Schumer and Torricelli endorsed the agreement.

The compromise called for creating national standards, to take effect in 2006, that were more explicit than those laid out in the House legislation.

States would have to allow voters to verify their ballots and correct errors before their votes were counted. States also would have to provide voters who are disabled or blind with the same voting accessibility and privacy as others. States with large numbers of non-English speakers would have to provide ballots in other languages.

States also would have to provide provisional ballots, post detailed explanations about voting procedures in all polling places, and ensure that election returns met new standards aimed at limiting mechanical errors in voting equipment.

The legislation would authorize $3.5 billion in grants over five years to help states meet the new federal mandates, including $100 million to make polling places more accessible to voters who are disabled or blind.

A federal commission would be created to administer the new federal requirements, as well as to approve grants to states. The Justice Department would monitor compliance with the national standards and could sue states that failed to comply.

To receive federal funding under the Senate bill, states also would have to provide the Justice Department with a plan to identify, deter and investigate election fraud. Voters who registered by mail would be required to present a valid identification when voting for the first time in their new jurisdiction. Those who voted by mail would be required to submit their ballot with a copy of a photo ID card or other verification of their name and address. ◆

Chapter 16

SCIENCE & TECHNOLOGY

House Passes Cloning Ban

The House voted in July to ban all cloning of human embryos, whether for reproductive purposes or for biomedical research. It was the first time either chamber had gone on record on what was one of the most rapidly growing areas of the life sciences. The Bush administration backed the bill; the biotechnology industry lobbied strongly against it. However, the measure got no further in the first session. The Senate planned to take up the issue in 2002.

Under the House bill (HR 2505), sponsored by Dave Weldon, R-Fla., researchers who cloned human embryos would face up to 10 years in prison and at least $1 million in fines. The bill also would prohibit the importation of a cloned human embryo or any product derived from one. The proposed ban was aimed at a process known as somatic cell nuclear transfer, which involves stripping an egg of its DNA, implanting genetic material from another egg and then inducing the egg to develop.

Human cloning was one of the most passionate science and technology issues facing the 107th Congress, requiring lawmakers to consider whether days-old embryos deserve the same moral status as a person. There was general agreement that cloning a human was morally objectionable. But many Democrats and medical researchers urged lawmakers to distinguish between cloning to produce a complete human being and "therapeutic" cloning that could create healthy replacement cells for sufferers of disease. They argued that Weldon's bill would go too far, banning vital biomedical research and blocking the importation of new disease-fighting drugs.

The questions gained added urgency when Advanced Cell Technology, based in Worcester, Mass., and the Jones Institute for Reproductive Medicine in Norfolk, Va., announced plans to clone human embryos to harvest stem cells for research purposes.

The debate was closely linked to the question of whether to allow federal funding for research on stem cells — primordial cells in embryos capable of evolving into any kind of human tissue. Scientists believed the cells could hold the key to curing juvenile diabetes, Parkinson's disease and a host of other afflictions. But extracting them involved destroying the embryo — an act that abortion foes equated with murder.

Highlights

The House-passed bill would amend the U.S. criminal code to:
- **Human cloning.** Prohibit any person or entity, public or private, from cloning a human embryo for any reason.
- **Imports.** Ban the import of cloned human embryos or any product derived from such embryos.
- **Penalties.** Impose penalties of up to 10 years in prison and up to $1 million dollars in fines for violators.

BoxScore

Bill:
HR 2505
Legislative Action:
House passed HR 2505 (H Rept 107-170), 265-162, on July 31.

Background

In 1996, scientists in Scotland used the somatic cell process to successfully clone the first mammal — a sheep named Dolly. Shortly afterward, President Bill Clinton issued a ban on the use of federal funding to clone humans in this manner and asked the National Bioethics Advisory Commission to address the ethical and legal issues relating to human cloning. In June 1997, the commission recommended that the moratorium on federal funding for human cloning be continued, and that legislation be enacted to prohibit anyone from attempting to create a child using this cloning process. The panel cited the harm such cloning might have on family relationships, identity and religious beliefs. The commission also recommended that any legislation include a sunset clause to ensure that Congress reviewed the issue to determine whether the ban should continue.

In 1997, the House Science Committee approved a bill similar to Weldon's proposal, but it never reached the floor. The next year, the Senate debated a similar bill offered by Bill Frist, R-Tenn., and Christopher S. Bond, R-Mo. In a pattern that would continue, they had some unlikely opponents: abortion foes, such as Strom Thurmond, R-S.C., and former Sen. Connie Mack, R-Fla. (1989-2001), argued that the bill was too broad, citing personal and family experiences with serious diseases. The Frist-Bond proposal died after Dianne Feinstein, D-Calif., objected to bringing it up, and proponents failed to muster the 60 votes needed to overcome her objection. (*1998 Almanac, p. C-3; 1997 Almanac, p. 5-13*)

Legislative Action

House Subcommittee Action

The House Judiciary Crime Subcommittee approved Weldon's bill by voice vote July 19, but the conflicting views on the issue were evident. Chairman Lamar Smith, R-Texas, urged quick action, warning that there were "a growing number of groups that claim they can and will" clone human beings. His strategy was bolstered by White House support of the bill. On the other side, ranking subcommittee member Robert C. Scott, D-Va., cited a letter from the American Society for Reproductive Medicine stating that anti-cloning legislation would outlaw promising scientific techniques "before we could even explore [their] potential good." The group also said a complete ban would cause "the burgeoning biotech industry [to] suffer" because foreign competitors had no such restrictions.

House Committee Action

The full Judiciary Committee approved the bill (H Rept 107-170) on July 24 on an 18-11 party-line vote. Democrats

offered several amendments aimed at weakening the bill, all of which were rejected on party-line votes. Among them were proposals by Scott and Zoe Lofgren of California to allow foreign medicines derived from cloning to be imported. Before approving the bill, the committee rejected, 11-19, an amendment by Adam B. Schiff, D-Calif., to ban reproductive cloning but allow therapeutic cloning. Schiff's amendment was similar to a bill (HR 2608) introduced by James C. Greenwood, R-Pa., on the same day.

Lawmakers on the politically polarized committee weighed in on both sides. Jerrold Nadler, D-N.Y., said early-stage embryos lack the essential characteristics that make them equivalent to people. "[The embryo] has no nerve cells, no feelings, no brain, no heart, no nerve impulses," he said. "I don't give it the same moral worth as a human being." But Henry J. Hyde, R-Ill., argued that embryos, however primitive, represent human life that would be destroyed no matter how worthy the research. "It's tiny, it's microscopic, but what you're doing is creating human life," he said.

House Floor Action

The House passed the bill July 31 by a vote of 265-162. "The House spoke very, very loudly today that this is morally and ethically inappropriate," Weldon said after the vote. "It clearly sends a message that there is a place we don't want to go, and that is the manufacture of scientific embryos for research." (*House vote 304, p. H-106*)

The House rejected, 175-251, a substitute amendment offered by Greenwood that would have outlawed human cloning for the purpose of creating a child but allowed it for medical research. Opponents termed his amendment unworkable, saying it would be impossible to track what became of all cloned embryos. (*House vote 303, p. H-106*)

The four hours of often emotional floor debate again suggested that members' views on human cloning did not break precisely along the same lines as abortion-related issues. Sixty-three Democrats joined with two independents and 200 Republicans to support the bill.

"We ban the hunting of bald eagles. Communities ban open-air burning. We have banned chlorofluorocarbons. Congress voted to ban drilling in the Great Lakes. A ban on human cloning is a transcendent issue which requires no less vigilance," said Dennis J. Kucinich, D-Ohio, who supported the Weldon bill.

But many opponents expressed discomfort with the idea of having to assimilate complicated technical information and impose new regulations on a still-developing field. "I think the Senate will look at this with a lot more deliberation and avoid a rush to judgment," said Henry A. Waxman, D-Calif., who supported Greenwood's substitute. "This came so quickly to the House floor, and is so new and complicated, that many members didn't understand the differences between what the Weldon bill and the Greenwood bill would do," he said.

Senate Action

Majority Leader Tom Daschle, D-S.D. — who supported a ban on cloning for reproductive but not for medical research purposes — promised a floor debate in 2002.

But when Advanced Cell Technology announced Nov. 25 that it had successfully cloned a human embryo, Sam Brownback, R-Kan., who had introduced a companion bill to Weldon's, pressed for a six-month interim moratorium. Senate GOP leaders decided to offer the moratorium as part of a complex ploy to derail a Democratic economic stimulus bill. Minority Leader Trent Lott, R-Miss., paired it with a separate proposal to allow oil drilling in part of Alaska's Arctic National Wildlife Refuge in an amendment that drew so much opposition that Lott himself voted against bringing it up. His motion to cut off debate was rejected, 1-94, on Dec. 3. (*Senate vote 344, p. S-72*) ◆

House Leaders Delay Tauzin-Dingell

House Republican leaders abruptly postponed a floor vote at the end of the year on a bill (HR 1542) to deregulate the market for broadband Internet service over telephone lines, deferring action until at least March 2002 on the most heavily lobbied high-tech issue of the session.

The legislation — sponsored by House Energy and Commerce Committee Chairman Billy Tauzin, R-La., and ranking Democrat John D. Dingell of Michigan — sought to ease certain restrictions in the 1996 Telecommunications Act designed to promote local phone competition. Specifically, Tauzin and Dingell wanted to allow the Bells — Verizon Communications, BellSouth Corp., SBC Communications Inc. and Qwest Communications International Inc. — to offer advanced data services over long distances without first having to meet requirements in the 1996 act that they open their local systems to competition.

The Bells said the bill was necessary to level the playing field with cable television companies, which did not face such requirements, and that it would speed the deployment of broadband services over enhanced telephone lines, known as digital subscriber lines, or DSL.

Opponents — chiefly AT&T Corp., which offered broadband services through its cable TV systems; other long-distance companies; and small Bell competitors known as competitive local exchange carriers, or CLECs — said the bill would remove all incentives for the Bells to open their local systems and would create a new Bell monopoly leading to higher prices for consumers and weaker oversight by the Federal Communications Commission (FCC).

Tauzin's Energy and Commerce Committee approved the bill in May, but Judiciary Committee Chairman F. James Sensenbrenner Jr., R-Wis., was able to slow the measure by asserting jurisdiction over provisions related to the Justice Department. His committee, which was less sympathetic to the Bells, took the unusual step in June of amending the bill and then reporting it unfavorably to the House.

Tauzin tried to reach a compromise with Sensenbrenner and other critics of the bill, but was unable to settle the issue of whether to require Justice Department approval in granting the Bells access to the long-distance market. Reluctance within the House Republican caucus to vote on such a contentious measure late in the session led leaders to postpone the vote.

The bill's prospects in the Senate were clouded by staunch opposition from Ernest F. Hollings, D-S.C., who became chairman of the Commerce, Science and Transportation Committee in June and introduced a bill to break up each of the Bells.

The Tauzin-Dingell bill was the subject of intense lobbying in the media and on Capitol Hill. It generated new interest groups, such as Voices for Choices, and millions of dollars in ad campaigns. The Bells enlisted the support of disparate groups, such as the Communications Workers of America, the National Black Chamber of Commerce and the Grange, representing the interests of underserved urban areas and rural communities that wanted access to broadband services.

Highlights

As reported by the Energy and Commerce Committee, the Tauzin-Dingell bill would:

● **Long-distance service.** Amend the 1996 Telecommunications Act to allow the regional Bells to offer high-speed data services (but not voice services) across long-distance boundaries in their service regions without first having to open up their local systems to competition.

● **Local competition.** Exempt the Bells from requirements that they lease to competitors any parts of their local network that had been upgraded for broadband use. As a result, the Bells would have to share only their all-copper telephone lines, not their new fiber-optic lines. The Bells also could increase the fees they charged competitors for using the all-copper lines for broadband service.

● **Broadband exemption.** Generally exempt broadband Internet services from FCC or state regulation.

● **Broadband deployment.** Require the Bell companies to upgrade their systems so that all their central switching offices could handle high-speed Internet traffic within five years of enactment.

● **Open access.** Require phone companies to allow customers to choose and use their own Internet service provider over the phone company's broadband services, without also having to pay for the phone company's Internet service.

Background

The Tauzin-Dingell bill raised issues that had been the subject of long-running battles within the telecommunications industry.

BoxScore

Bill:
HR 1542
Legislative Action:
House Energy and Commerce Committee approved HR 1542 (H Rept 107-83, Part 1), 32-23, on May 9.
House Judiciary Committee amended the bill (H Rept 107-83, Part 2) and agreed by voice vote June 13 to report it unfavorably.

In an effort to promote competition and expand service to consumers, the 1996 Telecommunications Act (PL 104-104) offered a basic trade-off — if the regional Bell telephone operating companies would open their local telephone systems to competition, they would be allowed to provide long distance services within their service territories. The law also required the local telephone companies to lease out individual parts of their local network to competitors at below-retail prices. (*1996 Almanac, p. 3-43*)

The 1996 act modified a 1982 court order, under which the old AT&T telephone monopoly was broken up into seven regional companies to provide local phone service and a separate AT&T long distance company. The regional Bells — which later consolidated into four companies — were expressly prohibited from entering the long distance market.

From the outset, the Bells resisted the requirement in the 1996 act that they open their networks to telephone competitors. With the growth of high-speed Internet access in the late 1990s, they had new worries. Cable companies were starting to use their cable connections to provide high-speed Internet services. In 1999, the FCC ruled that the 1996 line sharing requirements applied to equipment and lines used for DSL broadband services, which meant that competitors such as the CLECs could use the Bells' local lines to offer limited DSL services.

The Bell's themselves began to offer limited DSL services and to upgrade their lines and facilities to allow expanded services. But the Bells complained that the telephone competition requirements of the 1996 act unduly impeded them, creating economic disincentives to upgrading their lines and equipment to further deploy broadband DSL services. They argued that the regulations were intended for voice traffic and that the 1996 law did not anticipate the swift introduction of high-speed data services.

The issue for Congress was what role, if any, the government should play.

The majority of House members and FCC Chairman Michael K. Powell favored lifting the 1996 restrictions and allowing the Bells to compete head-to-head with cable. Tauzin and Dingell had gotten 224 cosponsors in the 105th Congress for a bill to allow the Bells to provide long-distance data services. The bill did not get out of the Commerce Committee, however, because of objections from then-Chairman Thomas J. Bliley Jr., R-Va.

There was less sympathy for the Bells in the Senate, where veteran senators such as Hollings, Minority Leader Trent Lott, R-Miss., Ted Stevens, R-Alaska, and Daniel K. Inouye, D-Hawaii, were wary of tinkering with the 1996 act, which they had spent long months negotiating. Some remained angry that the Bells mounted court challenges to provisions in the act after participating in negotiations leading to its passage. "They have litigated, they have complained and they have combined," Hollings said. "In other

words, they have done everything except work to ensure competition in local markets." *(1997 Almanac, p. 3-42)*

Legislative Action

House Energy and Commerce Subcommittee

The Tauzin-Dingell bill got off to a somewhat rocky start April 26, winning approval from an Energy and Commerce subcommittee by a slim, 19-14 margin.

The five-hour markup in the Telecommunications and the Internet Subcommittee revealed significant differences over whether the legislation would alter the competitive balance in a telecommunications market being buffeted by an economic slowdown.

Critics warned it could give the Bells the ability to squeeze out small, independent Internet service providers. Many Democrats complained that Tauzin muscled the bill through the subcommittee by taking the unusual step of holding a full committee hearing on the measure the day before the markup, giving lawmakers and their staffs only hours to prepare amendments. "I think it's disrespectful to the issues at stake," said Edward J. Markey, D-Mass., a Bell critic and the subcommittee's ranking Democrat. "What's the rush?"

The measure survived a major challenge when the subcommittee defeated, 14-19, an amendment by Steve Largent, R-Okla., to kill language that critics said would remove safeguards ensuring that competitors had access to the Bells' local networks.

House Energy and Commerce Committee

The full Energy and Commerce Committee approved the Tauzin-Dingell bill (H Rept 107-83, Part 1) by a narrower-than-expected 32-23 vote May 9, after a contentious markup that illustrated some of the trouble the legislation would face.

Before approving the bill, lawmakers deadlocked, 27-27, on a provision that Tauzin and Dingell considered a "killer amendment." It pitted regional Bell companies against smaller competitors over the question of whether the Bells should be forced to share their new high-speed, fiber-optic lines with their rivals. "We always knew line-sharing was a very sensitive issue for the committee," said Tauzin, who pledged to add language at some point to codify an FCC rule mandating limited sharing of the Bells' copper-based lines that still connected many homes.

Looking over his shoulder at Sensenbrenner, Tauzin insisted his committee was the only appropriate venue for the bill because it dealt with telecommunications issues and would not abrogate the Justice Department's power to police competition in telecommunications. "That doesn't say that the other committee can't produce another bill, which it very well may do, in which case we'll duke it out on the floor, which is the way we do things around here," he said.

Tauzin and Dingell offered an amendment in the nature of a substitute to address concerns that were raised during the subcommittee markup. The revised language allowed for small Internet service providers offering high-speed DSL service to connect with the Bells' copper-based phone lines. But those copper lines, built when the Bells were still a monopoly, could carry DSL transmissions only a limited distance, thereby limiting DLSL service to just homes within a

few miles of a central switching office.

The proposal that produced the dramatic tie vote, by Bill Luther, D-Minn., and Heather A. Wilson, R-N.M., would have forced the Bells to share with CLECs and other competitors any new high-speed, fiber-optic lines they built to deploy DSL services to farther sites and additional homes. The Bells argued that such a requirement would give them no incentive to build out systems and provide high-speed Internet service in new markets.

Tauzin tried to persuade wavering lawmakers that the Luther-Wilson amendment ran counter to the deregulatory nature of the underlying bill. Dingell went further, saying the amendment would prevent the Bells from competing with giant cable system owners, such as AT&T, in the broadband arena. Wilson argued that a line-sharing requirement on fiber-optic networks would keep the Bells in check and assure that residential customers would have a choice of high-speed Internet providers.

Tauzin and Dingell succeeded in persuading the committee to kill several other amendments they said would weaken the measure. The committee:

• Rejected, 18-36, an amendment by Thomas M. Davis III, R-Va., to define broadband service as any transmission rate to the subscriber of 1,500 kilobits per second or higher. The Tauzin-Dingell bill would set the lower speed of 384 kilobits per second as the threshold. Davis argued his provision would ensure that the Bells offered the best service available when they built new systems. But opponents such as Eliot L. Engel, D-N.Y., and Dingell said it would force the Bells to deploy more expensive service that would shut out some small businesses and lower-income individuals.

• Rejected, 17-37, an amendment by Largent, Bart Stupak, D-Mich., and Ted Strickland, D-Ohio, to require the Bells to deploy broadband networks to underserved areas 150,000 feet or closer to the companies' central offices within three years of enactment. Instead, the committee adopted, by voice vote, an amendment by Bobby L. Rush, D-Ill., and Tom Sawyer, D-Ohio, that would require the Bells to offer high-speed service to underserved areas within 15,000 feet of their central offices within five years. The Rush-Sawyer amendment also would require the Bells to report to the FCC regularly on their progress in upgrading their central switching facilities.

• Rejected, 18-28, an amendment by Anna G. Eshoo, D-Calif., that would have codified FCC rules requiring the Bells or their affiliates to regularly report the quality of their service. Tauzin said such a requirement was counter to the bill's deregulatory intent and that the FCC had already indicated it would revisit the rules.

• Rejected, by voice vote, two Davis amendments, offered en bloc, that would have allowed the FCC to impose fines of up to $25 million on Bells repeatedly found to have engaged in anti-competitive activities in the broadband market. Davis said the Bells paid $492.6 million in federal and state fines between December 1999 and April 2001 for actions ranging from deceptive marketing practices to failing to meet minimum service standards. Tauzin argued that the amendment singled out the Bells and raised constitutional issues.

The committee adopted several amendments aimed at ensuring fairness in the broadband market, including one by

Cliff Stearns, R-Fla., stipulating that the bill would not affect existing contracts allowing telecommunications companies to connect with each others' systems.

Tauzin said he would ask the House Rules Committee to merge his broadband bill with a related measure by Fred Upton, R-Mich., chairman of the Telecommunications and the Internet Subcommittee. Upton's bill (HR 1765) would significantly increase penalties for violations of the Telecommunications Act, and tracked recent requests by the FCC's Powell that Congress increase the fines the agency could levy on phone companies that violated local competition rules. The bill proposed to increase maximum penalties from $120,000 to $1 million per violation and cap monetary fines at $10 million for repeated offenses. It also would increase the amount of time the FCC had to take action against violators from one to two years.

House Judiciary Committee

After winning a limited referral of the bill from Speaker J. Dennis Hastert, R-Ill., Sensenbrenner held a markup June 13. The Judiciary Committee amended the bill (H Rept 107-83, Part 2), then agreed by voice vote to report it unfavorably. "The Judiciary Committee has sent the message today to the House leadership that the Tauzin-Dingell bill is in deeply troubled waters," said John Conyers Jr. of Michigan, ranking Democrat on the committee and one of the measure's most vocal opponents.

However, supporters of Tauzin-Dingell also declared victory, saying the divided Judiciary Committee had not been able to muster enough votes to scuttle the legislation or have a roll-call vote on the amended bill. They said the committee's refusal to publicly debate a motion to report the bill was evidence of widespread division among lawmakers.

Staff aides and others close to the situation later said that Sensenbrenner had to exert significant pressure on panel members to accept an amendment he wrote that would undo some of the provisions in the bill giving regulatory relief to the Bells.

Sensenbrenner's amendment, adopted by voice vote, would require the Bells to seek antitrust approval from the Department of Justice before they could enter the long-distance market. That would allow new Justice regulation over the Bells, requiring the attorney general to approve any requests to offer long-distance broadband services. The attorney general would determine whether the companies had opened their local facilities to competitors under provisions in the 1996 act.

Under existing law, it was up to the FCC to make the determination. The Justice Department's role was advisory.

Sensenbrenner's amendment also sought to overturn a 2000 decision by the 7th U.S. Court of Appeals. The court ruled in *Goldwasser v. Ameritech* that a Bell's refusal to allow a competitor to connect to its local network would not constitute an antitrust violation. Sensenbrenner's amendment affirmed that antitrust laws could apply to the Bells — a distinction that would subject them to increased fines and possible divestiture.

Tauzin-Dingell supporters on the committee, led by Rick Boucher, D-Va., and Robert W. Goodlatte, R-Va., said the amendment exceeded the scope of the committee's jurisdiction because it would give the Justice Department new regulatory powers. In particular, Boucher said it would give the Justice Department regulatory power to block the Bells' entry into the long-distance market. He contended it would also carve out new functions for the department without ensuring the agency had the necessary expertise or resources.

Sensenbrenner argued that his amendment would help preserve his panel's "future jurisdictional interests."

Lawmakers' ambivalence over the language became more pronounced minutes later, when the committee rejected, 15-19, a stand-alone bill (HR 2120) drafted hours before the markup by Christopher B. Cannon, R-Utah, and Conyers that largely mirrored Sensenbrenner's amendment. Conyers said the bill would have been used as backup if Sensenbrenner's language were ruled out of order.

Adding antitrust provisions to the mix could subject the Bells to treble damages under federal law or force them to divest some of their holdings if they were found to have engaged in monopolistic behavior in the broadband market. The Bells argued that existing laws already allowed the FCC to levy fines or bar a company from offering service in new markets if it impeded competition or broke other rules.

House Floor Action

The bill remained in limbo until early December, when House leaders scheduled a Dec. 14 floor vote. But in a setback for Tauzin, Dingell and the regional Bells, Hastert changed his mind, announcing the day before the bill was scheduled for floor action that the vote would be postponed until early March. Some 50 Republican members, led by bill opponent Jeff Flake, R-Ariz., had circulated a letter requesting a meeting of the Republican conference before any vote was taken. During the 30-minute session in the Capitol basement, lawmakers expressed discomfort about holding what was expected to be a close vote on one of the most heavily lobbied bills of the session. Members also resisted being forced to choose between the Bells and the long-distance companies.

Tauzin spokesman Ken Johnson termed the decision a temporary setback, adding that a whip count earlier in the week showed the measure would have passed by a wide margin. "This was a delay, not a defeat," Johnson insisted. "We have a firm commitment to move to the House floor, we have the votes to pass it, and we have the champagne on order."

Tauzin had been trying to strike deals with House colleagues on at least three issues dealing with competition while trying to firm up support for the measure. Sensenbrenner was pressing for language that would give the Justice Department an advisory role when the FCC considered Bell requests to offer long-distance service. He also wanted language to effectively overturn the 2000 court ruling that a Bell's refusal to allow a competitor to connect to its local network would not constitute an antitrust violation.

Meanwhile, a group of Republican members led by Charles W. "Chip" Pickering Jr. of Mississippi, was pressing Tauzin for provisions requiring the Bells to grant competitors access to individual elements of their networks and to sell them at below-retail prices so the competitors could offer advanced services. Under the FCC interpretation of the 1996 law, such requirements already applied to all Bell equipment and facilities used to provide broadband services. But it would no longer apply under the Tauzin-Dingell bill.

Pickering's proposed change would continue the requirement that the Bells give their rivals access to their new high-speed networks.

Senate Action

In the Senate, the Democrats' takeover in June had put Hollings, a staunch foe of the Bells, in charge of the Committee on Commerce, Science and Transportation. At a hearing that month on the state of local phone competition, he launched a defense of the 1996 Telecommunications Act and criticized the Bells for failing to let competitors interconnect with their networks. "There's a lot of weeping and wailing on the House side . . . about how there's no competition," Hollings said, alluding to claims by Tauzin-Dingell supporters that deregulation would lower prices and speed deployment of high-speed Internet service. "It's the biggest bunch of nonsense I've ever heard of."

Hollings, one of the architects of the 1996 law, not only vowed to block Tauzin-Dingell. He introduced a bill (S 1364) in August that would split each of the Bells into separate retail and wholesale companies in order to spur more local telephone competition. Hollings' bill was considered a long shot for passage, but it complicated efforts to pass the Tauzin-Dingell bill.

The concept behind Hollings' proposal, called "structural separation" in industry parlance, would require a retail Bell company that sold voice, video and data services to consumers to buy network services from its wholesale counterpart. The wholesale company would be required to offer services to competitors on the same terms as the retail Bell. Under Hollings' bill, the FCC could fine the Bells $10 million for each violation and impose triple damages for repeated violations.

The Bells strenuously opposed the bill, saying it would tilt the competitive balance in favor of long-distance and cable companies, such as their arch-rival AT&T Corp., and drive up prices. Small local telecommunications vendors, however, were enthusiastic about the proposal. ◆

Chapter 17

SOCIAL POLICY

Faith-Based Charities Bill Idles

Seeking a quick victory for one of President Bush's signature social policy initiatives, the House passed a bill (HR 7) in July aimed at making federal money available for nine new categories of faith-based social services and creating tax incentives for private charitable donations. But Senate Democrats were hostile to a core provision that would have allowed faith-based groups participating in the program to use religion as a basis for hiring, and the bill languished.

The House bill, drafted by J.C. Watts Jr. of Oklahoma, chairman of the GOP Conference, and Tony P. Hall, D-Ohio, sought to expand the concept of "charitable choice" — allowing faith-based organizations to provide federally funded services without sacrificing their religious character — to virtually the entire range of social programs. To encourage more private donations to charities, the bill proposed expanding the tax deduction for charitable donations by making it available to some 84 million taxpayers who did not itemize on their returns.

While the tax incentives had broad bipartisan support, the charitable choice provisions set off a political firestorm. Constitutional experts argued that the provisions could violate the separation of church and state, but a more painful sticking point was a civil rights problem: Democrats and some GOP moderates worried the bill could put the federal government in the position of subsidizing job discrimination.

By the time the bill reached the House floor, it had been scaled back so much that some lawmakers wondered if there was any point left. It had been rewritten by the House Judiciary Committee to prevent religious charities from proselytizing to recipients during treatment programs. And, with the budget surplus disappearing, the Ways and Means Committee cut back the tax incentives, starting them at $25 for individuals and $50 for married couples in 2002.

Even the modified bill, however, met with problems in the Democratic-controlled Senate. Majority Leader Tom Daschle, D-S.D., said he did not feel in any rush to bring it up, and Joseph I. Lieberman, D-Conn., who had been working on faith-based legislation with Senate Republican Conference Chairman Rick Santorum of Pennsylvania, pushed for greater civil rights protections.

Highlights

The following are the main provisions of HR 7 as passed by the House:
● **Faith-based services.** Religious organizations would be eligible to compete on an equal basis with other groups to provide a greatly expanded list of federally funded social services. Programs would include juvenile delinquency prevention, crime prevention, after-school programs, housing grants, job training, programs for senior citizens under the

BoxScore

Bill:
HR 7
Legislative Action:
House passed HR 7 (H Rept 107-138, Parts 1, 2), 233-198, on July 19.

Older Americans Act, and domestic violence prevention initiatives. Faith-based organizations also could receive federal funds indirectly, through vouchers used by beneficiaries of certain federal programs.
● **Rules for faith-based groups.** Groups participating in the program would not have to alter their religious practices or remove religious art or symbols. They would not lose their exemption under the 1964 Civil Rights Act to hire people who shared their religious beliefs, nor would they have to comply with state and local anti-bias laws that went beyond federal law. The groups could not use federal funds to worship, proselytize or give religious instruction; however, the restriction would not apply to funding received through vouchers.
● **Beneficiary rights.** Recipients could not be discriminated against on the basis of race, color, religion or national origin. Any beneficiary who objected to the religious character of an organization would have the right to receive services from an alternate provider.
● **Charitable giving.** Individual taxpayers who did not itemize deductions could deduct up to $25 ($50 for couples filing jointly) for charitable donations in 2002, increasing to $100 ($200 for couples) by 2010. The corporate deduction would rise from 10 percent of income to 15 percent by 2010.

Background

The idea of allowing faith-based groups to provide federal services was not new. The federal government had a long history of funding groups with religious affiliations, such as Catholic Charities, that provided social services without overt religious content. Until 1996, though, any religious organization that wanted federal funds had to strip out all references to its religious beliefs in its social programs.

That changed with the 1996 welfare overhaul (PL 104-193), which allowed faith-based organizations to deliver some federally funded services without sacrificing their spiritual aspects. The charitable choice provisions, written by then-Sen. John Ashcroft, R-Mo. (1995-2001), allowed the use of federal funds under the Temporary Assistance for Needy Families program for faith-based family assistance services as well as for foster care and adoption assistance. (*1996 Almanac, p. 6-3*)

The faith-based groups did not have to remove religious icons or drop the religious content from their services. More significantly, they could use religious beliefs in their hiring and firing decisions without losing federal funds. Religious groups had always been exempt from the ban on hiring discrimination under the 1964 Civil Rights Act, but until charitable choice came along, they had not been subsidized with federal money. (*1964 Almanac, p. 338*)

Congress subsequently expanded charitable choice to sev-

eral other programs: welfare-to-work grants to the states (PL 105-33); services under the Community Services Block Grant (PL 105-285), which allowed states to help nonprofit community antipoverty groups; and drug treatment programs under the 2000 Community Renewal Tax Relief Act (PL 106-554).

Bush championed charitable choice during his presidential campaign, and shortly after taking office he laid out a plan for a faith-based social safety net. "Government cannot be replaced by charities," he said Feb. 1, "but it can welcome them as partners instead of resenting them as rivals." A new Office of Faith-Based and Community Initiatives was established in the White House to coordinate federal partnerships with religious and community groups. Bush called for involving churches, synagogues, mosques and other religious institutions in more social programs, and urged tax breaks to encourage donations to charitable organizations.

By giving the idea such a high profile, Bush also drew fire from critics across the political spectrum. Liberals were concerned that such an expansion would erode the separation of church and state, and that it would weaken the nation's civil rights laws by allowing more religious groups to practice hiring discrimination in programs that take federal funds. Some religious leaders, meanwhile, worried that federal funding would subject them to ever-increasing levels of bureaucratic scrutiny, restricting their freedom to operate their faith-based social services as they chose.

Legislative Action

House Judiciary Committee

After considerable prodding from the White House, the House Judiciary Committee approved HR 7 by a 20-5 party-line vote June 28 (H Rept 107-138, Part 1). Democrats were adamant that religious overtures should be kept out of federally funded social services.

Committee Chairman F. James Sensenbrenner Jr., R-Wis., had met with House GOP leaders and several top administration officials — including Vice President Dick Cheney and White House Chief of Staff Andrew H. Card Jr. — in the weeks before the markup in search of a compromise that could withstand lawsuits alleging a breech of the constitutional separation of church and state. Sensenbrenner said he worked most closely with Solicitor General Theodore Olson, noting that Olson would be "the one who defends this law in the Supreme Court."

Sensenbrenner rewrote the bill to bar charities from using federal funds to proselytize while delivering services. He said charities could, for instance, hold a Bible study during a lunch break in a social service program, but that participation could not be a condition for staying in the program. The rewritten bill appeared to foreclose funding for some of the very programs that supporters has touted as model beneficiaries of a charitable choice law. One, Teen Challenge, for example, tried to help drug-addicted teenagers in part through Christian worship. "A personal relationship with Jesus Christ permeates everything we do," the group's Web site said.

Jim DeMint, R-S.C., said such groups should be allowed to receive funds without altering their programs because "the faith component is why they have a better success

rate." He and others in the House conservatives' Republican Study Committee nonetheless said they were generally satisfied with the bill. The measure also required that governments provide a secular alternative for needy people who did not want to receive social services from religiously oriented providers — a provision conservatives saw as key to ensuring that church-run programs could maintain their religious tone.

Democrats and some city officials charged that money would not be available for secular alternatives to many programs.

The amendment embodying Sensenbrenner's changes was adopted by voice vote. It also included provisions specifying how social service recipients could opt out of religious programs and a requirement that organizations deposit federal funding in separate bank accounts.

The committee rejected, 7-22, an amendment by Jerrold Nadler, D-N.Y., to bar organizations that provided social services from engaging in religious worship or instruction with recipients, regardless of who paid for the program or whether recipients requested the religious activity.

Democrats, however, said their concerns extended beyond the question of proselytizing. A provision that Sensenbrenner did not alter — an exemption from civil rights laws that allowed faith-based charities to base hiring decisions on an applicant's religion — drew particular fire.

"We are promoting religious discrimination," Barney Frank, D-Mass., charged. But Steve Chabot of Ohio, echoing many other Republicans, said removing the language would deny "the guarantee of institutional autonomy" for religious groups.

The committee defeated, 11-19, an amendment by Robert C. Scott, D-Va., to require that charities providing non-religious services comply fully with civil rights laws.

The committee subsequently adopted by voice vote an amendment by Melvin Watt, D-N.C., intended to limit religious discrimination in hiring for federally financed jobs. Committee aides said its effect was unclear.

The panel rejected amendments:
• By Scott, defeated 10-17, to bar religious groups from receiving funds for after-school activities or other programs under the Elementary and Secondary Education Act.
• By Frank and Tammy Baldwin, D-Wis., defeated 7-15, to require charities to follow state anti-discrimination laws, including those banning discrimination on the basis of sexual orientation.
• By Scott, defeated 7-20, to prohibit discrimination against "minority" religions in the awarding of grants.

House Ways and Means Committee

The Ways and Means Committee took up the bill July 11, approving a drastically reduced set of tax incentives (H Rept 107-138, Part 2) by a party-line vote of 23-16. The tax provisions were estimated to cost $13.3 billion over 10 years — just 15 percent of the $91.7 billion proposed by Bush.

Lower projected surpluses and the high cost of Bush's tax cut package (PL 107-16) had left the committee little choice. By voice vote, members approved an amendment by Chairman Bill Thomas, R-Calif., that cut Bush's proposal to the bone. The amendment:
• Replaced Bush's $84.4 billion plan that would have al-

lowed non-itemizers to deduct 100 percent of their charitable contributions by 2006, with a $6.4 billion plan to allow a maximum deduction of $100 for individuals and $200 for married couples filing jointly by 2010. The limit for 2002 was $25 for individuals and $50 for couples. Because deductions reduce the amount of income that is subject to tax, not the tax itself, the typical single non-itemizer would see only $3.75 in actual tax savings in 2002 under the Thomas plan.

• Dropped a proposed new tax credit for financial institutions that set up accounts for low-income people. Instead, the bill would double, to $50 million, annual spending for a program (PL 105-285) that directed federal funds to tribes, community groups, credit unions and other organizations that set up savings accounts for low-income people. *(1998 Almanac, p. 9-19)*

• Modified a Bush plan to allow older people to give their Individual Retirement Accounts to charities tax-free, setting the age for eligibility at 70½ instead of Bush's proposed 59½.

• Modified the phase-in of Bush's plan to boost from 10 percent to 15 percent the amount of charitable contributions that corporations could deduct.

The panel rejected, by a 16-23 party-line vote, an amendment by ranking Democrat Charles B. Rangel of New York to offset the bill's cost by increasing the top tax rates, which had just been cut under the new tax law. An amendment by Karen L. Thurman, D-Fla., to allow the charity-oriented tax cuts only in years when there was a budget surplus was rejected, 17-23. The committee also rejected a proposal by Benjamin L. Cardin, D-Md., to authorize increased funding for the federal social programs that faith-based charities and other groups could access under the bill.

Attempts by Democrats to raise the issue of hiring discrimination were ruled as being outside the committee's jurisdiction.

House Floor Action

Pressed by the administration to act quickly, the House passed the bill July 19 by a vote of 233-198. But the win for Bush was tempered by the fact that Republican leaders had had to pull the measure from the floor July 18 to cool a rebellion by GOP moderates. Despite the delay, the leadership lost only four Republican votes while gaining the votes of 15 Democrats and one Independent. *(House vote 254, p. H-90)*

The moderates' uprising was short-lived and easily quelled, but it generated a spate of headlines about discrimination that discomfited the White House. Led by Mark Foley of Florida, the GOP moderates threatened to send the bill back to the Judiciary and Ways and Means committees with instructions to drop the pre-emption of state and local bias laws and require federally funded groups to comply with the ban on hiring discrimination in the 1964 Civil Rights Act. In return for abandoning the motion to recommit, they extracted a public pledge from Watts that any House-Senate conference on the bill would "more clearly address" their concerns. In the end, only four Republicans supported the motion, which fell, 195-234. *(House vote 253, p. H-90)*

A Democratic substitute, offered by Rangel, would have banned hiring discrimination, dropped the exemption from state and local laws, barred groups from using indirect aid for religious purposes, and offset the bill's costs by increasing the top tax rates. It was rejected 168-261. *(House vote 252, p. H-90)*

Senate Action

In the Senate, advocates of faith-based programs never managed to get beyond the basic dilemma of how to increase faith-based charities' access to federal funds enough to address unmet social needs, but not so much as to violate the constitutional separation of church and state. The main Senate bill — S 592 introduced by Santorum and Lieberman — included none of the charitable choice provisions backed by the House. It focused instead on the far less controversial goal of creating tax incentives to encourage contributions to faith-based groups.

As the year wore on, Lieberman became increasingly wary, particularly about the issue of hiring discrimination. Daschle and Lieberman both made it clear that no bill would get through the Senate unless the pre-emption of state and local anti-discrimination laws in the House measure were removed. "We can't move backwards on the progress we've made on discrimination in this country," Daschle told reporters July 19.

Such worries were exacerbated by the revelation in early July of a Salvation Army document claiming that the White House — to secure the group's support for the faith-based initiative — had promised to issue a regulation exempting religious groups from state and local laws banning discrimination against gays or requiring domestic-partner benefits. The White House quickly announced it would not pursue the regulation.

Santorum and Lieberman continued to look for a compromise on charitable choice, but they ended the session without success. ◆

Social Security Changes Suggested

A bipartisan commission on Social Security, appointed by President Bush in May, released its recommendations for overhauling the system Dec. 11. The 16-member commission offered three options, all centered on Bush's proposal to allow workers to invest some Social Security contributions in private markets through personal savings accounts, potentially earning greater returns. The panel was co-chaired by former New York Sen. Daniel Patrick Moynihan (1977-2001) and Richard Parsons, chief executive-designate of AOL-Time Warner.

The 141-page report made clear that personal retirement accounts alone would not solve Social Security's financial problems, as more workers retired over the next 50 years and fewer were left to pay into the system. The panel acknowledged that some combination of benefit reductions and tax increases would be needed to keep the program solvent, and that Congress would still have to find approximately $2 trillion over the next 75 years to cover startup costs for the accounts and the program's remaining cash deficits.

But the report said personal savings accounts would allow Americans to "build substantial wealth" in a way they had not been able to do through the 12.4 percent annual payroll tax contributed to Social Security. Even after the startup costs to the government, the options would still be less costly than the $3.4 trillion in deficits Social Security would run if nothing was done, the panel argued. "I think we have given [lawmakers] some options that they will find sensible, as we do," Parsons said.

When Bush announced the commission's creation at a Rose Garden ceremony May 2, he said the threat to Social Security had been apparent for decades. "We can postpone action no longer. Social Security is a challenge now; if we fail to act, it will become a crisis. We must save Social Security and we now have the opportunity to do so."

But the commission's report generated only modest interest, and there were no plans for immediate action. A number of factors contributed to the tepid reception. The White House had not made Social Security a high-profile issue, and top Bush advisers had warned pro-overhaul groups not to expect legislative action until after the 2002 elections. The Sept. 11 attacks focused attention elsewhere. The on-budget surplus that might have taken some of the pain out of a Social Security overhaul had vanished, at least in the short term. And the stock market's dismal performance gave Democrats ammunition to argue that putting Social Security funds into the market was a bad idea.

Democrats and labor groups lambasted the report. Senate Democratic Policy Committee Chairman Byron L. Dorgan, D-N.D., charged that the panel was "handpicked to arrive at a preconceived conclusion" that personal savings accounts must be included in any Social Security overhaul. "The commission's options will not seriously be pursued by Congress or anyone else who reviews them thoroughly," he said.

But the critics did not offer their own solutions — a fact that allowed supporters of private savings accounts to claim the high ground in the debate. "This is a bit like sitting on the Titanic and saying, 'Well, I don't like that lifeboat,' " said Michael D. Tanner, director of the libertarian Cato Institute's Project on Social Security Privatization. "Well, that's fine, but you've got to find a lifeboat you do like."

The Commission's Recommendations

The Commission to Strengthen Social Security recommended three ways to add private savings accounts to Social Security:

- **Option 1.**
- Allow workers to invest 2 percent of their Social Security payroll taxes in personal retirement accounts.
- No other changes to Social Security, meaning this option would not address the financing problems expected as the number of retirees grows.
- Cost: $3.4 trillion over 75 years to make up for Social Security's expected cash shortfall, plus $1 trillion in startup costs for the retirement accounts.
- **Option 2.**
- Allow workers to invest 4 percent of their payroll taxes, up to $1,000 a year, in personal retirement accounts.
- Slow future benefit increases by linking them to inflation rather than growth in personal wages.
- Increase benefits to widows, and guarantee that low-income workers (disproportionately women) retire with an income of at least 120 percent of the federal poverty level.
- Cost: $2 trillion over 75 years to cover startup costs of the retirement accounts and any deficits not eliminated by the benefit changes.
- **Option 3.**
- Allow workers to redirect 2.5 percent of their payroll taxes, up to $1,000 a year, into personal retirement accounts if they also contribute 1 percent of their annual earnings to the accounts.
- Slow future benefit increases by adjusting them to reflect the fact that most people are expected to live longer.
- Dedicate new tax revenues to shoring up Social Security's finances. No specific sources were recommended.
- Increase benefits to widows, and guarantee that low-income workers (disproportionately women) retire with an income of at least 100 percent of the federal poverty level.
- Cost: $2.25 trillion over 75 years to cover startup costs of the retirement accounts and any cash deficits not eliminated by the benefit changes. ◆

Chapter 18

TAXES

Congress Cuts Deal on Taxes

Congress cleared legislation May 26 aimed at cutting taxes by $1.35 trillion through fiscal 2011, handing President Bush the biggest domestic policy victory of his first year in office. To win broad support, the benefits were focused more on low-income taxpayers than Bush had proposed, and the total was somewhat less than he sought. The White House said the president's plan was worth $1.64 trillion, while the congressional Joint Committee on Taxation put the cost at up to $1.78 trillion.

By any measure, however, the package amounted to the deepest tax cut since the one President Ronald Reagan had pushed to enactment 20 years earlier, in his first year as president. And the central features of the 2001 law — a reduction in income tax rates, alleviation of the so-called marriage penalty, a phase-out of the estate tax and expansion of the child tax credit — were the proposals at the heart of Bush's presidential campaign platform. Bush signed the measure into law June 7 (HR 1836 — PL 107-16).

House Republicans began building momentum for Bush's proposal early in the year, passing four major elements of the package in quick succession. The first, a sweeping reduction in income tax rates (HR 3), was passed March 8 with no attempt to bring Democrats on board. Republicans then began courting Democrats, with some success, passing legislation to cut income taxes for married couples and people with children (HR 6) on March 29, followed by the phase-out of the estate tax (HR 8) on April 4 and a package of tax incentives for retirement benefits (HR 10) on May 2.

The dynamic was far different in the 50-50 Senate. Republican Charles E. Grassley of Iowa, who chaired the Finance Committee at the time, and ranking Democrat Max Baucus of Montana were slowed by the need to develop a bill that could win at least some bipartisan support. They also were waiting for Congress to complete the fiscal 2002 budget resolution (H Con Res 83), which was crucial in the Senate because it allowed the tax bill to move under special "reconciliation" rules that barred filibusters and limited amendments. It turned out, however, that it also set a $1.35 trillion ceiling on the tax cuts.

With the budget resolution in place and the Senate ready to act, the House repassed its income tax reduction measure as an official reconciliation bill (HR 1836) on May 16. The Senate then passed its own bill — similar to the comprehensive $1.35 trillion package that became law — on May

BoxScore

Bill:
HR 1836 — PL 107-16

Legislative Action:

House passed HR 3 (H Rept 107-7), 230-198, on March 8.

House passed HR 6 (H Rept 107-29), 282-144, March 29.

House passed HR 8 (H Rept 107-37), 274-154, on April 4.

House passed HR 10 (H Rept 107-51, Parts 1, 2), 407-24, on May 2.

House passed HR 1836, 230-197, on May 16.

Senate passed HR 1836, amended, 62-38, on May 23.

House adopted conference report (H Rept 107-84), 240-154, on May 26.

Senate cleared HR 1836, 58-33, on May 26.

President signed June 7.

23. The House-Senate conference was completed two days later.

Reflecting the need to maintain the crucial support of moderate Democrats, and aware that their party was about to lose control of the Senate with the impending switch by James M. Jeffords of Vermont from Republican to Independent, Republicans saw to it that the final package was negotiated by representatives of the White House and just four lawmakers: Grassley, Baucus, House Ways and Means Committee Chairman Bill Thomas, R-Calif., and John B. Breaux, D-La., a leader of the Senate centrists. The House and Senate stayed in session into the Saturday of Memorial Day weekend in order to clear the bill.

Highlights

The bill included provisions to:

● **Income tax rates.** Replace five existing tax brackets (15 percent, 28 percent, 31 percent, 36 percent and 39.6 percent) with six brackets (10 percent, 15 percent, 25 percent, 28 percent 33 percent and 35 percent) by 2006.

● **Rebate.** Send rebate checks of $300 for individuals, $500 for single parents and $600 for married couples filing jointly to those who paid taxes in 2001. The rebate was added late in the process in hopes of stimulating the economy.

● **Child tax credit.** Gradually double the child tax credit to $1,000 by 2010. Those with incomes above $10,000 could qualify for up to 10 percent of the credit as a tax refund from 2001 to 2004, and 15 percent thereafter.

● **Married couples.** Increase the standard deduction for married couples, and the amount of income subject to the 15 percent bracket, to double that of singles by 2005. Previously, under a quirk of the tax code known as the marriage penalty, many married couples, mostly those in which both people had similar incomes, had incurred more tax liability than they would have as two single filers.

● **Estate tax.** Gradually phase out taxes on estates, with a full repeal set for 2010. The tax on gifts made by a living donor continued but at a lower rate.

● **Education expenses.** Create or expand a host of benefits for education programs, including increasing the limit on annual tax-free deposits in education savings accounts from $500 to $2,000.

● **Retirement savings.** Increase annual limits on contributions to individual retirement accounts — both traditional and Roth IRAs — and on 401(k)s and other retirement accounts starting in 2002. Low-income individuals could re-

ceive a tax credit for up to $2,000 annually for contributions to such plans.

• **AMT.** Increase the income threshold for taxpayers subject to the alternative minimum tax (AMT) — a parallel tax system intended to ensure that filers did not entirely wipe out their liability through deductions, exemptions and credits.

• **Sunset.** End all of the bill's provisions automatically on Dec. 31, 2010. The provision was needed to keep the cost of the bill within the limit set by the budget resolution.

At $875 billion, the cuts in income taxes account for 65 percent of the law's price tag. The increase in the child tax credit was expected to cost $172 billion (13 percent of the total); the estate tax cut, $138 billion (10 percent); the marriage penalty relief, $63 billion (5 percent); the retirement savings breaks, $50 billion (4 percent); and the education breaks, $29 billion (2 percent).

The only major item dropped from the final bill was a Senate provision to make permanent the research and development credit for businesses. It was one of the few provisions that would have benefited corporations, which had to change the quarterly schedules under which they paid taxes in 2001 and 2004 to help fund the measure. The bill did not extend a handful of other popular expiring provisions.

Background

Bush had made a 10-year tax cut package totaling $1.3 trillion through 2010 the centerpiece of his presidential campaign. The federal surplus, he argued, belonged to the taxpayers and they should get part of it back. Even before he took office, however, evidence of a softening economy provided another rationale: Tax cuts were increasingly portrayed as a way to rejuvenate the economy. On Jan. 3, House Minority Leader Dick Gephardt, D-Mo., said that in the interests of strengthening the economy, House Democrats would be amenable to deeper tax cuts than they had supported in the last Congress, when they had fought the GOP at every turn. The outlook for Bush was further bolstered by the fact that, despite signs that the economy was slowing, the federal surplus was expected to show bigger-than-ever increases. (*Surplus, p. 5-11*)

Federal Reserve Board Chairman Alan Greenspan weighed in Jan. 25, telling the Senate Budget Committee that tax cuts enacted "sooner rather than later" could help ease a protracted economic slump. "Should current economic weakness spread beyond what now appears likely, having a tax cut in place may, in fact, do noticeable good," he said. Previously, Greenspan had urged that the surplus be used to reduce the debt and had tried to dampen the push for tax cuts or increased spending, though when pressed he had said tax reduction was the preferable of the two.

Bush pressed to keep the bill focused on his priorities. "Some in Congress view this as an opportunity to load up the tax relief plan with their own visions," he said on the White House lawn Feb. 5. "I want the members of Congress and the American people to hear loud and clear: This is the right-size plan, it is the right approach, and I'm going to defend it mightily." Two days later, Bush delivered an equally clear message to corporate America, which was eager to broaden the package's focus beyond tax relief for individuals and Main Street businesses: Your priorities will have to wait, the president told the

19 executives he had invited to the White House.

Corporations, including the U.S. Chamber of Commerce, the National Association of Manufacturers, the National Association of Wholesaler-Distributors and the National Federation of Independent Business, responded by joining together to push for passage of the tax bill without corporate add-ons.

On Feb. 27, Bush addressed a joint session of Congress, offering a preliminary outline of his budget that put the cost of the tax cut package in fiscal 2002 through 2011 at $1.62 trillion, an amount he said was "just right." The central features, as in his campaign, included an across-the-board reduction in marginal income tax rates; steps to alleviate the marriage penalty; an increase in the child tax credit; a phase-out of the tax on estates, gifts and trust funds; and expansion of the charitable deductions to those who did not itemize their deductions.

When Bush submitted the full details of his budget on April 9, he estimated the cost of the tax cut at $1.64 trillion. (The Joint Committee on Taxation, Congress' official scorekeeper on tax issues, subsequently calculated the cost at $1.78 trillion.) By then, Congress was starting to weigh in. The Senate had approved a version of the budget resolution that set a $1.27 trillion limit on tax cuts — $1.18 trillion in 2002 through 2011, plus $85 billion for a retroactive tax cut for 2001, mostly in the form of refunds. While the House endorsed Bush's total, it had passed three pieces of the package that differed at least slightly — and sometimes substantially — from what the president was proposing.

Phase One: Separate House Bills

House Republicans spent March and early April passing the main pieces of Bush's tax package, albeit with significant modifications. They had the majority required to pass the bills, and they had no need to wait until the budget resolution was finished. Though some members complained about endorsing a huge tax cut before they saw the overall size of the budget, the crucial procedural protection offered by the budget resolution in the Senate was not relevant in the House, where floor debate was controlled by the GOP-run Rules Committee.

INCOME TAX RATE REDUCTIONS

With no pretense of seeking bipartisan support, House Republicans pushed the most expensive and controversial piece of the package — a $559.9 billion, 10-year reduction in income tax rates — through the Ways and Means Committee just two days after Bush's speech to Congress on Feb. 27. House passage came a week later.

The bill, similar to Bush's plan, proposed reducing the five existing income tax brackets to four (33 percent, 25 percent, 15 percent and 10 percent) by 2006. The main difference was that it would phase in the new bottom rate more quickly by creating a 12 percent bracket retroactive to Jan. 1, and reducing it to 10 percent in 2006. Bush proposed starting the new rate at 14 percent in 2002, lowering it gradually to 10 percent in 2006. Making it retroactive was expected to mean a cut in 2001 of $180 for individuals taxpayers, $360 for married couples filing jointly and $300 for single parents. The bill also would repeal the existing limits on claiming the refundable child credit for taxpayers subject to the AMT.

Committee Action

The Ways and Means Committee approved the bill (HR 3 — H Rept 107-7) on March 1 by a vote of 23-15, with no Democratic support.

Republicans argued that focusing tax cuts on individuals would help shore up consumer confidence and the economy. Democrats maintained that the bill would help the rich at the expense of the poor, and would not stimulate the kind of spending the GOP foresaw. Richard E. Neal, D-Mass., warned that by reducing the tax rates, the bill would force more people into the parallel AMT system. Republicans said they were working on changes to the AMT, which Neal wanted to repeal.

Democrats' only success came when Republicans agreed, by voice vote, to an amendment designed to ensure that the bill would not eat into the Social Security and Medicare surpluses. Most taxes that the wealthier elderly paid on their benefits were routed back to the Medicare and Social Security programs. The amendment directed Treasury officials to ignore the tax decrease and direct the usual amount to the Social Security and Medicare trusts, using general government funds to make up the difference.

The committee rejected an attempt by Democrats William J. Jefferson of Louisiana and Karen L. Thurman of Florida to link the tax cuts to debt reduction. The party-line vote was 16-22.

A Democratic substitute offered by ranking member Charles B. Rangel of New York was rejected, 12-26. Estimated to cost $585.5 billion through 2011, the plan would have created a new 12 percent bracket, expanded the earned-income tax credit (EITC) for the working poor and alleviated the marriage penalty.

Floor Action

The House passed the bill, 230-198, on March 8, with 10 Democrats joining a unified Republican bloc to support it. Most Democrats insisted that it was the GOP leadership, not Bush, who had excluded them from any role in writing the bill, but most Republicans said Bush was solidly behind the decision. (*House vote 45, p. H-20*)

In opposing the bill, Democrats tended to focus on warnings that the tax cut would jeopardize efforts to pay down the publicly held debt. Liberals also said the bill was too focused on benefits for the rich. Most conservatives opposed it because it was moving before the budget resolution. Most moderates opposed it for a combination of the two reasons as well as their anger at the process. The 10 who voted for the bill were mostly from politically competitive districts.

Democrats had less success holding together on Rangel's substitute. One-quarter of the caucus voted against the $585.5 billion plan, which was rejected, 155-273. (*House vote 42, p. H-20*)

Though the Republicans successfully papered over their differences — none voted against the bill — factions existed beneath the surface. At a meeting in the Capitol the day before the vote, about 40 GOP conservatives urged Vice President Dick Cheney to support a more ambitious tax cut than Bush's. Some moderates in the party, meanwhile, worried aloud that Bush's bill might cut taxes too much or might not be generous enough to lower-income Americans.

'MARRIAGE PENALTY' TAX BILL

The second piece of the package — a tax reduction for married couples and an increase in the child tax credit — had far broader appeal in Congress. Estimated to cost $399.2 billion through 2011, it also was the most substantial — and expensive — deviation from Bush's plans. Drafted by Ways and Means Chairman Thomas, the bill called for cutting taxes for almost all married couples at a cost of $223.3 billion. It proposed making the standard deduction for married couples filing jointly double that of singles beginning in 2001, and the portion of a couples' income subject to the low, 15 percent tax bracket double that of singles by 2004.

The result would be a break not only for the mostly two-earner couples who suffered the penalty, but also for an almost equal number of couples whose tax liability declined as a result of their marriage. Those couples tended to have only one breadwinner or one spouse who earned much more than the other. The approach appealed to social conservatives, who argued that couples with a stay-at-home spouse should get a tax break, too. By contrast, Bush's proposal, estimated to cost $111.8 billion, focused exclusively on those couples who paid more as a result of being married. It would have revived a provision enacted in Reagan's first year as president (PL 97-34) but repealed five years later, that allowed married couples to deduct up to $3,000 of the lower-earning spouse's income from their return.

Other provisions in the bill proposed changing the EITC to allow more low-income married couples to claim a greater refund even if they earned too little to be liable for income taxes. To answer criticism from both Democrats and Republicans that Bush's package would respond too slowly to the weakening economy, Thomas proposed making the initial $100 increase in the child tax credit retroactive to the start of 2001; Bush proposed making it effective in 2002. In both plans, the full $1,000 credit was to be phased in by 2006. The bill omitted Bush's proposal to raise the income levels of those who could claim the credit, instead retaining the existing phase-out, which began at $110,000 of modified adjusted gross income for married couples and $75,000 for single parents. The estimated cost of Thomas' child care credit expansion was $175.9 billion, compared with $210.7 billion in Bush's plan.

Committee Action

The Ways and Means Committee approved the bill (HR 6 — H Rept 107-29), 23-16, on March 22. In a reversal of the strategy used on the first tax bill, Thomas specifically included provisions aimed at attracting Democrats, designating extra help for the working poor and eschewing Bush's proposal to give wealthier parents and couples more of the package's proposed benefits. Still, Democrats were no more involved in writing the measure than they were in HR 3, and all Democrats present at the markup voted against the bill.

Much of the debate centered on how the marriage and child taxes would fit into the rest of the tax puzzle. Many Democrats who might have been inclined to vote for the measure worried that the cost of the two bills already moving — combined with a third that Ways and Means planned to mark up the following week — would force Congress to cut programs or dip into the surplus in the Medicare trust fund, which pays the hospital bills of the elderly and disabled.

Rangel offered essentially the same Democratic substi-

tute he had proposed for the income tax rate bill; it was defeated 13-26.

Floor Action

The breadth of support for a family tax cut was confirmed March 29, when 30 percent of House Democrats joined a unified Republican bloc to pass the bill by a vote of 282-144. (*House vote 75, p. H-30*)

The 64 Democratic votes constituted a high-water mark for proposals to alleviate the marriage penalty. The previous high point had come in July 2000, when 51 Democrats voted for the final version of a similar bill, which subsequently died when the House fell 16 votes short of overriding President Bill Clinton's veto. (*2000 Almanac, p. 18-3*)

Reiterating Democratic concerns, Robert T. Matsui of California said the bill's $399.2 billion cost over10 years, when added to other tax proposals under consideration, would create a total cut significantly in excess of the $1.62 trillion Bush proposed. As a result, Matsui said, government programs would eventually have to be cut. "We do want a tax cut," Matsui said of Democrats. "We want to make sure it's modest."

Majority Leader Dick Armey, R-Texas, said the bill should be viewed as correcting an immoral part of the IRS code. "We should be embarrassed" when couples are taxed more after they get married, he said.

The House rejected Rangel's Democratic substitute, 196-231. Rangel also lost, 184-240, when he sought to return the bill to committee with instructions that it be rewritten to include a $300 rebate in 2001 for individual taxpayers and a $600 rebate for married couples. (*House votes 73, 74, p. H-30*)

ESTATE TAX REPEAL

The third tax bill passed by the House was a phaseout of taxes on estates, gifts and trust funds at a cost estimated by Joint Tax at $185.6 billion through 2011. The bill called for gradually reducing the combined tax on gifts (assets given during a taxpayer's lifetime) and estates (assets transferred at death) until it disappeared in 2011. The existing top rate of 55 percent was to fall to 39 percent by 2010, and to zero thereafter. As under existing law, the first $675,000 in assets, set to rise to $1 million in 2006, would be exempt from the tax. The measure was less expensive than the president's plan, because the proposed phaseout was slower and heirs who sold inherited property would be required to pay additional capital gains taxes on profits above $1.3 million. An estate tax repeal that would have cost $104 billion in the first 10 years cleared in 2000 but was vetoed by Clinton. (*2000 Almanac, p. 18-18*)

Committee Action

The Ways and Means Committee approved the bill (HR 8 — H Rept 107-37) by a vote of 24-14 on March 29. John Tanner of Tennessee was the only Democrat to vote "yes." Amo Houghton of New York, a scion of one of the nation's wealthiest families, was the only Republican to vote "no." Nine other Republican moderates signaled that they might oppose the bill as well. They and nine moderate Democrats signed a letter to Bush asking him to consider something short of repeal. "We do not believe all estates, particularly the largest, should escape all taxation," they wrote.

Democrats said that by their calculations the three House bills already moving exceeded Bush's target by more than $1 trillion. They included in their calculations the increased interest payments that would be required because the national debt would be paid down at a slower pace.

Matsui offered an amendment — tongue in cheek — to make the repeal immediate. He said he wanted to illustrate his view of the dangers of setting tax law 10 years into the future. Other Democrats predicted the final repeal would never come to fruition because it would be stopped by a future Congress. E. Clay Shaw Jr. of Florida responded that fellow Republicans were phasing in the repeal to "be responsible and know we are going to have enough money left" for other priorities. Matsui's amendment was defeated, 7-31, with all Republicans and seven Democrats voting against it.

The panel also rejected, 14-24 along party lines, an amendment by Rangel that would have exempted estates worth $2 million from the tax beginning in 2002 and increased the threshold to $2.5 million in 2010.

Floor Action

The House passed the measure April 4 by a solid majority of 274-154. The bill drew fewer "yes" votes than the 2000 version, in part because this time the president was ready to sign the bill, making the votes more consequential. The measure still had significant Democratic support — 58 members from across the party's political spectrum voted for it, compared with 65 in 2000. Three Republicans opposed it; none did in 2000. (*House vote 84, p. H-34*)

The House voted 201-227 to reject the Democratic substitute, which would have increased the exemption limits to offer immediate relief to most of those who inherited family-owned farms and small businesses — the people that many members said were most deserving of estate tax relief. (*House vote 82, p. H-34*)

Some Democrats predicted the repeal would be stopped by a future, cash-strapped Congress. "You will have to run five times in order to tell your constituents by the year 2011 that the 'death tax' is finally gone," Tim Roemer, D-Ind., said, using the term coined by repeal supporters. Republican opponents said they could not vote to void taxes for the super-rich. "It is not within the spirit of the Founding Fathers to develop a sort of a leisure class," said Houghton, whose family founded the glass and fiber-optic giant Corning Inc.

Others said the tax was so onerous that any repeal was better than tinkering. It "robs families of their heritage," said Sanford D. Bishop Jr., D-Ga.

RETIREMENT SAVINGS

The fourth tax bill — what sponsor Rob Portman, R-Ohio, called "the last big piece that can fit under the umbrella" — sought to increase the tax benefits of contributing to Individual Retirement Accounts (IRAs), 401(k)s and other retirement accounts, and to make pensions more portable for the many workers who switched jobs.The product of a four-year partnership between Portman and Benjamin L. Cardin, D-Md., the bill was estimated to cost $51.7 billion in lost Treasury revenue through 2011. It proposed to increase annual contribution limits for IRAs from $2,000 to $5,000 by 2004 and index them for inflation after that; increase annual limits on employee contributions to pension plans from $10,500 to $15,000 by 2005; repeal the cap on combined employer and employee contributions to pension

plans and increase the annual limit on benefits from $140,000 to $160,000; and ease "rollover" rules so that workers who switch jobs could move their pensions savings to a different type of plan.

A nearly identical measure had won 401 House votes in 2000, but had become entangled in a larger tax measure that stalled in the face of opposition from Clinton.

Committee Action

The Ways and Means Committee approved the bill (HR 10 — H Rept 107-51, Part 1) on April 25 by a vote of 35-6. The Education and the Workforce Committee approved the pension provisions over which it had jurisdiction by voice vote April 26 (H Rept 107-51, Part 2). While all but half a dozen Democrats on Ways and Means voted for the measure, several more worried aloud that the bill would not do enough for the 70 million workers who did not have pension plans. Richard E. Neal, D-Mass., proposed allowing workers with adjusted gross incomes up to $25,000 to claim a refundable credit on half their annual contributions to IRAs, 401(k)s or other plans; those earning as much as $75,000 would have qualified for part of the credit. The cost was estimated at $35.5 billion over 10 years. The amendment was defeated, 15-24.

Another Neal amendment, defeated 16-24, would have provided a tax credit for half the administrative and education expenses of businesses with 100 or fewer employees that start retirement plans and given those same small businesses a tax credit worth 50 percent of their contributions to the retirement plans of lower-earning workers. Portman indicated he might support the first provision, but not the second.

The Education panel defeated, by voice vote, an amendment on the controversial topic of employers who switch from traditional defined-benefit pension plans to so-called cash balance plans. The switch often hurt older workers who, under seniority-based systems, were entitled to larger pensions. Offered by Dennis J. Kucinich, D-Ohio, the amendment would have allowed employees to stay in the old pension system even if their employer changed plans.

Floor Action

The House passed the bill by an overwhelming vote of 407-24 on May 2. (*House vote 96, p. H-38*)

An amendment by Neal that combined his unsuccessful committee proposals was rejected, 207-223. The House also defeated, 153-276, an attempt to send the bill back to both the Education and the Workforce and the Ways and Means committees and require those panels to attach language that would give workers more options when their companies switched from traditional pension to cash balance plans. (*House votes 94, 95, p. H-38*)

Phase Two: Reconciliation

House Floor Action

With the completion of the budget resolution May 10, Congress had the go-ahead to move an official tax reconciliation bill. The House acted quickly, repassing the income tax rate reduction measure as a new bill (HR 1836) on May 16. The vote was 230-197. (*House vote 118, p. H-46*)

Deputy Majority Whip Roy Blunt, R-Mo., said the bill was repassed to let the Senate know that a deep cut in the top rate was "critically important to the House." The day before, the Senate Finance Committee had approved a top rate of 36 percent, compared with a 33 percent top rate in the House bill.

Though the House reconciliation bill only contained the rate reduction, all of the House-passed tax legislation was subject to discussions in conference, because the Senate's reconciliation bill included versions of each. Critics of the House maneuver said it was a signal of capitulation to the Senate. "This debate is about how fast can we relinquish our responsibilities as House members," Rangel said. "The real bill will come from the Senate." Thomas said he shared Rangel's "outrage that we are told when and how we are to deal with this issue by the other body."

Senate Committee Action

After weeks of negotiations, the Senate Finance Committee on May 15 approved a $1.35 trillion comprehensive tax-reconciliation bill written by Grassley and Baucus with enough tradeoffs to win the support of all 10 of the panel's Republicans and four of its 10 Democrats. The vote was 14-6. The bill had been unveiled on May 11, the day after the Senate adopted the final version of the budget resolution.

Grassley and Baucus followed the outlines of Bush's overall tax plan. But they rewrote the pieces, often in ways designed to keep the package's scope and cost within the confines of the budget resolution. They also crammed in several additional provisions, principally to secure the support of four key fiscal moderates on the panel: Jeffords of Vermont, Olympia J. Snowe, R-Maine, and Democrats Robert G. Torricelli of New Jersey and Blanche Lincoln of Arkansas.

They also wrote in several gimmicks that shaved the bill's official 11-year cost and eased its consideration under the Senate's complex parliamentary rules. The most dramatic of these was a provision to "sunset," or repeal, the entire bill on Sept. 30, 2011, when the revenue protected under the budget resolution would no longer be available. Without that provision, the bill would have been subject to a point of order when it reached the floor, a 60-vote threshold that tax cut proponents concluded they could not reach. Another provision, to delay the due date for certain quarterly corporate income tax payments by 15 days, was added to shift revenue to years in which the surplus might not be sufficient to support that year's tax reductions without tapping the surplus in the Medicare Part A hospital trust fund.

Following are highlights of the bill:

● **Income tax rates.** Shifting the focus more to lower-income taxpayers, the Senate proposed reducing the top rates by less than Bush or the House had proposed and making the new 10 percent rate retroactive to Jan. 1. The House and Bush had proposed phasing it in by 2006, though at different rates. By 2007, the upper rates under the Senate bill would be 36 percent, 33 percent, 28 percent and 25 percent; the 15 percent rate would be unchanged.

● **"Marriage penalty."** The less expensive Senate proposal would increase the standard deduction for married couples and the portion of their income subject to the 15 percent bracket to double that of singles by 2005.

● **Child tax credit.** The credit would be increased to $600 retroactively to Jan 1, as under the House bill, but it would not reach $1,000 until 2011.

• **Estate tax.** Estate taxes would be cut gradually until their repeal in 2011, as in the House bill, but the exemption would increase to $4 million in 2010. The gift tax would remain, but at a lower rate. Like the House, the Senate included the proviso that heirs pay capital gains taxes on the profits that had accrued since the asset was originally purchased.

The biggest challenges came from Democrats. Minority Leader Tom Daschle of South Dakota, who was a member of the panel, joined Conrad and John D. Rockefeller IV of West Virginia in leveling a spate of withering criticism. Conrad called the bill "a monument to fiscal irresponsibility" because so many of its provisions would take effect in the second part of the decade, when the Baby Boomers neared retirement and the surplus projections on which the tax cut depended were the least reliable. Daschle described his vote in the House for Reagan's 1981 tax cut (PL 97-34) as "one of the greatest mistakes of my public career" and lamented that Congress was "faced with almost exactly the same circumstances and once again on the threshold of making that same mistake."

But Democrats were unable to alter the measure. The committee defeated, 7-13, a Daschle amendment to make permanent the corporate credit for research and development and to make smaller reductions in the estate tax. It rejected, 6-14, an amendment by Bob Graham, D-Fla., to replace the bill's cuts with a $693 billion, 10-year plan to establish a new 10 percent bracket retroactive to Jan. 1. It rejected, 6-14, a Conrad amendment to speed up the fixes to the marriage penalty and pay for them by making the cut in the top income tax rate less generous. And it rejected, 8-12, a Graham amendment to allow a tax deduction for the purchase of long-term care insurance and offset the $75 billion cost with less generous cuts to the upper income tax rates.

Despite criticism from their respective caucuses that each side had given too much, Grassley and Baucus had an incentive to compromise. Each knew that if the committee was unable to report a bill, its jurisdiction would be quickly usurped. In recent years, GOP leaders had overruled the Finance chairman when his plans did not coincide with theirs. As recently as mid-April, the leaders had warned that they might bypass the committee and go straight to the floor with their own proposal — an increase in the minimum wage combined with tax cuts for businesses.

Senate Floor Action

The Senate passed an amended version of the Grassley-Baucus bill May 23 that left most of the major compromises in place. The 62-38 vote came in a chamber stunned by news that Jeffords was about to abandon the GOP to become an Independent, turning control of the Senate over to the Democrats. The impending change spurred Daschle to end a Democratic assault that had kept the bill on the floor for four days and two nights as amendment after amendment was offered and defeated. (*Senate vote 165, p S-36*)

The proposed income tax rate cut drew the sharpest attacks. Though Grassley and Baucus defended their compromise as the only one that could move through the Senate, many Democrats — and one prominent Republican, John McCain of Arizona — were skeptical.

Democrats lost an attempt May 21 by Jean Carnahan of Missouri to limit the rate reduction in each of the brackets to 1 percentage point, while creating a new 10 percent bracket, as the bill proposed. The main objective was to cut the 15 percent bracket rather than leaving it unchanged. The proposal was rejected, 48-50, on May 21. (*Senate vote 116, p. S-29*)

Later that night, with McCain's help, Democrats nearly succeeded in cutting taxes further for low-and middle-income taxpayers. McCain called up an amendment to reduce the 39.6 percent rate by 1 percentage point and expand the portion of income taxed at the 15 percent rate. It failed on a 49-49 tie. Four Republicans — Lincoln Chafee of Rhode Island, Susan Collins of Maine, Arlen Specter of Pennsylvania and Jeffords — joined McCain in backing the amendment, as did all but five Democrats: Baucus, Breaux, Georgians Max Cleland and Zell Miller, and Nebraska's Ben Nelson. (*Senate vote 126, p. S-30*)

Democrats tried again the next day, making minor adjustments to the amendment so they could reintroduce it. That time it failed on a 50-50 tie. (*Senate vote 149, p. S-34*)

Democrats made slight changes to many of their other proposals and offered them again and again as part of a campaign to delay the bill's passage. Although the strictures of the reconciliation process limited "debate" on the bill to 20 hours, the time spent in roll calls was not taken off the clock — allowing an almost limitless number of amendments to be offered, debated for a minute or less, and then put to a vote.

The bill would have been subjected to even more votes, but Grassley and Baucus persuaded senators with amendments destined for adoption to work with them behind the scenes. Many of these proposals were assembled into a single amendment to make $65.7 billion worth of changes to the bill. The cost was offset by requiring corporations to pay 170 percent of what they would normally pay in income taxes in July, August and September 2011. The amendment, adopted May 24 by voice vote, included provisions to:

• Increase the credit for adopting a child from $5,000 to the actual cost of the adoption and from $6,000 to $10,000 for a special-needs child, with the amount indexed for inflation beginning in 2003. Similar legislation (HR 622) had passed the House.

• Allow self-employed people to deduct 100 percent of their medical insurance costs as of Dec. 31, 2001, instead of in 2003 as under existing law.

• Make permanent the credit for 20 percent of a business's research and experimentation expenses and provide a credit of up to 30 percent for the costs of developing vaccines for widespread diseases, including malaria, tuberculosis and HIV/AIDS.

• Increase the tax credit for dependent care from $2,400 to $3,000 for one child and from $4,800 to $6,000 for two or more children.

The Senate also adopted, 98-2, an amendment by Collins and John W. Warner, R-Va., to create a deduction for teachers' professional development expenses and an annual tax credit of up to $250 for teachers' out-of-pocket classroom expenses, whether they itemized their deductions or not. Bush has made a similar proposal. (*Senate vote 164, p. S-36*)

Many of the failed Democratic amendments were attempts to limit the reduction in the top tax brackets and divert the funds to Medicare, education or other social programs. Many of the proposals fell on points of order when the Senate failed to muster the 60 votes needed to override rules requiring that amendments be germane to the reconciliation bill.

Among the more significant proposals rejected were amendments by:

• Judd Gregg, R-N.H., to temporarily cut the tax on capital gains held more than one year from 20 percent to 15 percent. The cuts would have expired in 2003. The amendment fell after the Senate voted 47-51 against waiving a point of order. (*Senate vote 115, p. S-29*)

• Evan Bayh, D-Ind., and other moderates in both parties to create an expedited procedure for Congress to delay tax cuts if debt levels rose, or to increase discretionary spending if more debt was paid off than anticipated. Known as the "trigger," it fell when the Senate failed, 49-50, to waive a point of order. (*Senate vote 118, p. S-29*)

• Byron L. Dorgan, D-N.D., to retain the estate tax but allow family-owned businesses and farms to escape it entirely and let couples exclude as much as $4 million from the tax. It was rejected, 43-56. (*Senate vote 124, p. S-30*)

• John Kerry, D-Mass., to exempt individuals with adjusted gross incomes below $100,000 from the alternative minimum tax. It was defeated, 46-53. (*Senate vote 138, p. S-32*)

• Thomas R. Carper, D-Del., to substitute tax cut proposals more tailored to lower-income people. It was defeated, 43-55, on a point of order. (*Senate vote 143, p. S-32*)

In earlier action May 17, the Senate rejected amendments by:

• Charles E. Schumer, D-N.Y., that would have allowed taxpayers to deduct as much as $12,000 a year in college tuition from their taxable income. Grassley and Baucus had included a more modest tuition credit. Schumer proposed to offset the expense of his more generous deduction by limiting the cut in the top estate tax rate. It was rejected, 43-55. (*Senate vote 114, p. S-28*)

• Kent Conrad, D-N.D., to begin implementing the marriage penalty provisions in 2002 instead of 2005, and offset the extra cost by slowing cuts to the top two income tax rates. The amendment was defeated, 44-56. (*Senate vote 112, p. S-28*)

• Kay Bailey Hutchison, R-Texas, tried to make the standard deduction for a married couple twice that of a single taxpayer by 2002, with the cost offset by phasing in education tax incentives more slowly. The amendment was defeated, 27-73. (*Senate vote 113, p. S-28*)

Conference

Although it took time for the political realities of the impending Democratic takeover of the Senate to set in, Republican conservatives ultimately swallowed their pride and agreed to a $1.35 trillion package of tax cuts that favored those of modest means far more than Bush and most Republicans advocated. Prodded by Bush, and cognizant that their unilateral control of the Capitol was about to end, weary Republican leaders in both chambers agreed to a deal with the ever-more-powerful centrist Senate Democrats the evening of May 25.

The House adopted the conference report, 240-154, on Sat., May 26, and the Senate cleared it, 58-33, the same day. (*House vote 149, p. H-56; Senate vote 170, p. S-37*)

"This is loaded towards low-income people," outgoing Senate Majority Whip Don Nickles, R-Okla., said in describing how the package's tone had been transformed. "We've done a whole heck of a lot both in size and composition to accommodate many of the moderate influences that we now have in the Senate."

During the conference negotiations, White House officials abandoned the administration's previous resistance to compromise and urged their Republican allies in Congress to quickly embrace any version of a tax cut deal that could become law. "The sooner the Congress completes its work, the sooner the American people will have their own money in their own pockets to save and invest as they see fit. Our economy cannot afford any further delays," Bush declared May 23. No matter the details, the final package was certain to be the largest tax cut since Reagan.

In the end, the compromise was a slightly altered version of the bill passed by the Senate with a dozen Democrats joining all of the Senate's Republicans in a sign that it had captured the middle ground. Conferees followed the Senate model of postponing some effective dates and lengthening some phase-ins to make room for priorities of both conservatives and moderates. They also included the language repealing the entire bill in 2010, allowing a somewhat deeper rate cut than the earlier Senate version while staying under the overall ceiling set by the budget resolution.

Senate Republicans' dismay over their impending loss of control after the Memorial Day break, combined with anger of GOP conservatives in both chambers at Jeffords' decision, added to the strain of the conference.

During the three days of negotiations, the acerbic Thomas tangled with centrist Democrats such as Baucus and Breaux, as well as with Republican Sen. Phil Gramm of Texas, one of the few lawmakers readily capable of matching Thomas in both venom and fact-filled repartee.

Although House Republicans made an effort in conference to cut tax rates by about $1 trillion — up from the $958 billion the House had supported and the Senate's $824 billion — Thomas had evidence from the outset that such a big increase could not survive in the Senate. He had been a frequent visitor to that chamber during the tax debate, spending more than half an hour talking with Baucus on the floor May 21 and many more hours in cloakroom meetings with the pivotal moderates.

The proposals he and Majority Leader Dick Armey, R-Texas, pressed during much of the conference were designed at least as much to appeal to hesitant House conservatives as to make progress in the negotiations.

Fifteen Senate moderates, led by Breaux and Snowe, signed a letter threatening to oppose any conference report that did not "closely reflect the delicate compromise that was reached in the Senate."

The most expensive of Bush's proposals left out of the final bill — and the only major component directed explicitly at business — was the plan to make permanent the tax credit that companies could claim on as much as 20 percent of their research and experimentation expenses at a cost of $8 billion through 2011. The idea was popular in Congress. But — in part because the credit did not expire until 2004, and in part because its extension could be used as a vehicle or sweetener for some future tax package — the urgency of addressing it faded in the final round of negotiations.

As for the sunset provision, the administration said it was confident it would never be realized because a future Congress and president would agree to extend the tax cuts. "To do anything other than that is to raise taxes on the American people," White House spokesman Ari Fleischer said May 31. ◆

Provisions of the Tax Law

What follows is a summary of the main provisions in the 10-year, $1.35 trillion tax package (PL 107-16) enacted June 7.

Individual Income Tax Rates

Before the bill's enactment, individual income was taxed in five rate brackets: 15 percent, 28 percent, 31 percent, 36 percent and 39.6 percent. The bill created a new 10 percent bracket, redefined the 15 percent bracket and gradually reduced the four remaining marginal rates.

The bill also gradually repealed limits on the itemized deductions and personal exemptions that taxpayers can use to reduce their taxable income. Before enactment, the amount of the deductions and exemptions was limited for taxpayers with income above certain thresholds.

● **10 percent bracket.** The bill created a new 10 percent bracket, retroactive to Jan. 1, 2001, for a portion of the taxable income previously taxed at 15 percent.

In 2001 through 2007, the 10 percent rate applied to the first $6,000 of taxable income for individual taxpayers, $10,000 for single parents and $12,000 for married couples filing joint returns. Beginning in 2008, the 10 percent bracket would apply to the first $7,000 of income for individuals, $10,000 for single parents and $14,000 for married couples. Those amounts were to be indexed for inflation beginning in 2009.

● **Rebate.** In lieu of the 10 percent bracket in 2001, the bill provided a one-time refund of up to $300 for single taxpayers, $500 for single parents and $600 for married couples. The refund was 5 percent of the income that would have been eligible for the 10 percent bracket in 2001. Taxpayers could not receive more than the actual amount of taxes they paid in 2000.

● **15 percent bracket.** The 15 percent tax bracket began where the new 10 percent bracket left off and ended at the same level as under previous law for a single person ($27,050) or a single parent ($36,250). For married couples filing jointly, the level was raised, as explained in the "Marriage Penalty" section.

● **Marginal rate cuts.** The bill gradually reduced the marginal rates of 28 percent, 31 percent, 36 percent and 39.6 percent. Cuts began July 1, 2001, when rates were reduced by 1 percentage point to 27 percent, 30 percent, 35 percent and 38.6 percent; the amount of federal income tax withheld from paychecks was reduced in 2001 in accordance with the cuts. In 2004, the rates were slated to fall by an additional 1 percent, to 26 percent, 29 percent, 34 percent and 37.6 percent. For 2006, the rates were set at 25 percent, 28 percent, 33 percent and 35 percent.

● **Repeal of restrictions on itemized deductions and personal exemptions.** The limits on deductions and personal exemptions available to high-income taxpayers were to be gradually eliminated, beginning in 2006. They were scheduled to fall by one-third in 2006 and 2007 and two-thirds in 2008 and 2009, before being fully eliminated in 2010. Itemized deductions include state and local income and property taxes, unreimbursed medical expenses, charitable contributions and certain other expenses. Taxpayers also were generally allowed to exempt a set amount from their taxes for each dependent, their spouse and themselves. In 2001, the personal exemption was $2,900; after that, it was to be indexed annually for inflation.

Until 2006, itemized deductions would continue to be reduced by 3 percent of a taxpayer's adjusted gross income in excess of $132,950 ($66,475 per person for married couples filing separate returns), though the total could not be reduced by more than 80 percent. The personal exemption would continue to be phased out for individuals with adjusted gross incomes over $132,950 and for married couples filing jointly with incomes above $199,450. The two limits, both enacted as part of the 1990 deficit-reduction bill (PL 101-508), were known as PEP (personal exemption phaseout) and Pease, for former Rep. Don J. Pease, D-Ohio (1977-93), the primary sponsor of the deduction limit.

'Marriage Penalty'

There were more than 60 provisions in the tax code that treated single taxpayers differently than married couples filing jointly. When combined with other provisions in the code, they created a "marriage penalty" for couples who paid more taxes than they would have as two single filers and a "marriage bonus" for others. Those in households where both spouses contributed significantly to the family income tended to have a marriage penalty. One-earner couples or those in which one spouse earned much more than the other tended to have a marriage bonus. The bill addressed the two major components of the marriage penalty, while giving additional tax relief to those who already enjoyed a marriage bonus.

● **Increased standard deduction.** The bill gradually increased the basic standard deduction for a married couple filing jointly to twice the deduction for an unmarried couple. The increase was phased in over a five-year period beginning in 2005, and would be fully effective by 2009. Before enactment, the standard deduction for married couples filing jointly was 167 percent of that for a single individual.

● **Expansion of 15 percent bracket.** Beginning in 2005, the bill phased in, over a four-year period, an increase in the upper boundary of the 15 percent tax bracket for married couples filing jointly, until the upper limit became double that for single taxpayers. Previously, the 15 percent bracket covered taxable income up to $27,050 for individuals and $45,200 for couples. When the increase was fully phased in, up to $54,100 of a married couples' income would be taxed at 15 percent.

● **Expansion of earned-income tax credit.** The bill made more married couples eligible for the earned-income tax credit (EITC) — a program designed to enhance tax refunds for certain low-income workers, including those who did not earn enough to owe income taxes. Before enactment, for example, the full credit was available to a filer with two or more children and an adjusted gross or earned income of $13,090 or less; a partial credit was available for a similar filer with income up to $32,121. Under the bill, those limits were to increase to $16,090 and $35,121, respectively, by 2007. Income limits for individuals and those with one child were similarly increased. All increases were phased in gradually — with limits going up by $1,000 per year in 2002, 2005 and 2007. Starting in 2009, the beginning and ending points would be adjusted annually for inflation. The bill also made several changes aimed at simplifying calculation of the credit.

Child and Family Tax Credits

Before enactment, the child tax credit — part of the 1997 tax reconciliation law (PL 105-34) — provided a $500 tax credit for each child under age 17. The credit was available to individuals with modified adjusted gross incomes of up to $75,000 a year and couples making up to $110,000; it was phased out above these income levels

and was not indexed for inflation. The credit was generally non-refundable for taxpayers with fewer than three children, meaning they could not get the money in a check if they owed no taxes. However, for taxpayers with three or more qualifying children, the credit was refundable up to the amount that their Social Security and Medicare taxes exceeded their earned-income tax credit.

- **Child tax credit increase.** The child tax credit was doubled, to $1,000, over a 10-year period. It was scheduled to increase to $600 in 2001, to $700 in 2005, to $800 in 2009 and to $1,000 in 2010.

- **Refundability.** The child tax credit was made refundable for all families, no matter the number of children, for up to 10 percent of the taxpayer's earned income in excess of $10,000. This meant that those earning too little to be liable for income tax could qualify for the refundable child tax credit. The $10,000 earned-income floor was to be indexed for inflation beginning in 2002. Beginning in 2005, the credit would be available for up to 15 percent of earned income in excess of $10,000. Any refund that low-income taxpayers received because of the credit would not be counted as income when determining their eligibility for federal social programs or state or local programs financed with federal funds.

- **Adoption tax credit and exclusion.** Beginning in 2003, the adoption credit was increased to $10,000 per eligible child, up from $6,000 for special-needs children and $5,000 for all other children. The new law also increased to $10,000, from $5,000 or $6,000, the amount that an employee could exclude from taxable income for expenses reimbursed through an employer adoption assistance program. In both cases, taxpayers adopting special-needs children did not have to actually incur adoption expenses to claim the credit, but those adopting other children did.

The beginning point of the income phaseout range for both the credit and the exclusion was increased from $75,000 to $150,000 of modified adjusted gross income, effective in 2003. In both cases, taxpayers with incomes greater than $190,000 were not eligible for any tax reduction for the adoption.

- **Dependent care tax credit.** Beginning in 2003, the tax credit to help offset the cost of child care or the care of physically or mentally disabled dependents was increased from 30 percent of costs to 35 percent. The amount of expenses that could be claimed increased from $2,400 to $3,000 for one dependent and from $4,800 to $6,000 for two or more. As a result, the maximum credit would be $1,050 for one dependent (up from $720) and $2,100 for two or more (up from $1,440). The income phase-out range began at $15,000 of adjusted gross income. Those with adjusted gross incomes over $43,000 would be eligible for a 20 percent credit.

- **Employer-provided child care.** The bill created a tax credit for companies that provide day care for their workers' children. Employers who construct, operate or contract with a facility to provide child care would be eligible for a credit of up to 25 percent of expenses. Those who provided a child care resource or referral service were eligible for a credit of up to 10 percent of expenses. The total of the credits taken in one year could not exceed $150,000.

Alternative Minimum Tax

Created in 1969 and bolstered over the years, the alternative minimum tax (AMT) was designed to ensure that wealthy individuals and corporations could not wipe out their entire tax liability by claiming a large number of deductions, exemptions and credits. If a taxpayer's tax liability was greater under the AMT than under the regular system, he could not claim most tax breaks and was taxed on a greater portion of his income. Because the system's income thresholds were not adjusted annually for inflation, as the rest of the tax system was, more and more middle-income taxpayers were becoming subject to the AMT.

- **Increasing the income threshold.** The limit on exemptions

from the AMT for single taxpayers was increased by $2,000, to $35,750, and by $4,000 for married couples filing jointly, to $49,000. The provision took effect in 2001 and was set to sunset at the end of 2004.

- **Allowing AMT taxpayers certain tax credits.** Under the bill, the refundable child credit no longer was reduced by the amount of the taxpayer's AMT liability. Those subject to the AMT could claim the child credit, the adoption credit and the new credit available to low- to moderate-income taxpayers for contributing to retirement savings.

Education Incentives

The bill contained provisions to encourage taxpayers to set aside money for their children's education by utilizing tax-favored education savings accounts (ESAs) and state prepaid tuition programs. The measure also instituted a deduction for college tuition.

- **Education savings accounts.** The annual contribution limit to ESAs increased from $500 to $2,000, beginning in 2002. Contributions to ESAs were not tax-deductible, but distributions from these accounts would not be taxed if they were used to meet qualified education expenses.

Under prior law, such distributions could be used only to pay for college expenses. The bill expanded the program to include qualified elementary and secondary school expenses — such as tuition, tutoring, books and computers — for public or private schools.

Eligibility for the accounts was phased out for married couples with modified adjusted gross incomes higher than $190,000, up from $150,000 in prior law. Couples with incomes above $220,000, up from $160,000, were not eligible for the program. The thresholds were increased to make a married couple's limit double that of a single taxpayer.

A prohibition on claiming education tax credits known as HOPE credits and Lifetime Learning credits in the same year a taxpayer took tax-free distributions from an ESA was repealed. The distribution could not be used for the same education expenses for which the credit was claimed, however. Both the HOPE and Lifetime Learning credits were created by the 1997 tax law (PL 105-34). Under the HOPE program, joint filers with adjusted gross incomes below $80,000 and individuals earning $40,000 or less could claim a tax credit of up to $1,500 for the cost of the first two years of college. Under the Lifetime Learning program, such taxpayers could claim a credit of up to $1,000 to cover the cost of tuition and fees for the last two years of college, advanced degrees or professional development classes.

- **Prepaid tuition programs.** Tax-exempt status was extended to prepaid tuition programs at private universities. Under prior law, such benefits were only available for state tuition programs. Under the new law, distributions from prepaid tuition programs could be excluded from a beneficiary's or contributor's gross income, and taxpayers could claim the HOPE or Lifetime Learning credit and take tax-free distributions from the prepaid account in the same year. Most of the provisions were effective beginning in 2002, except the tax exclusion, which would not take effect until 2004.

- **Higher education expenses deduction.** From 2002 through 2005, taxpayers could claim an above-the-line deduction for tuition and other higher education expenses. Above-the-line deductions are available whether or not the taxpayer itemizes. Individuals with an adjusted gross income of up to $65,000 and married couples earning $130,000 could deduct up to $3,000 per year in 2002 and 2003. In 2004 and 2005, the deduction was set to increase to $4,000 per year for taxpayers in those income ranges. Taxpayers who earned between $65,000 and $80,000 could deduct up to $2,000 in education expenses. A taxpayer could not claim the deduction and the HOPE or Lifetime Learning credit for the same

student. In addition, most distributions from ESAs or prepaid tuition plans would not be tax-free in years when the taxpayer claimed the deduction.

- **Employer-provided education assistance.** Beginning in 2002, the income tax exclusion for employer-provided educational assistance was expanded to cover both undergraduate and graduate education and was made permanent. The exclusion allows employees to receive up to $5,250 annually for education expenses without having to include it in their taxable income. Prior to enactment, the exclusion covered undergraduate courses only and was set to expire at the end of 2001.

- **Student loan interest deduction.** Beginning in 2002, a 60-month time limit on deducting interest on student loans were repealed and voluntary payments of interest were deductible. Individuals with modified adjusted gross incomes of $50,000 and married couples with incomes of $100,000 could qualify for the full deduction, which was limited to $2,500 a year. Individuals earning up to $65,000 and married couples earning up to $130,000 could qualify for a reduced deduction. Beginning in 2003, income ranges would be adjusted annually for inflation. Prior to enactment, the deduction was phased out for individuals making between $40,000 and $55,000 and joint filers making between $60,000 and $75,000.

- **School construction bonds.** Private, for-profit corporations could contract with school districts and use government-issued bond proceeds to build or rehabilitate a public school, beginning in 2002. Small governments could issue up to $15 million in such bonds, increased from $10 million, without having to forfeit some of the proceeds if they engaged in arbitrage. Arbitrage occurs when school districts and other governments direct the proceeds of a bond to an investment that earns a rate of interest higher than the borrowing rate. This is used to increase the money available for public facilities, but under the tax code the entities generally must forfeit some of the proceeds to the federal government if they do not use the bond for construction within certain time limits.

- **Taxation of certain medical and military scholarships.** Effective in 2002, recipients of National Health Service Corps or F. Edward Hebert Armed Forces Health Professional scholarships did not have to pay taxes on their awards, even if they did not complete the programs' service requirements.

Estate and Gift Taxes

The bill phased out the estate and generation-skipping taxes over 10 years and reduced the gift tax, but it required that heirs pay more capital gains taxes on inherited assets that are sold.

- **Declining rates.** In 2002, the top estate, gift and generation-skipping tax rates were lowered from 55 percent to 50 percent, and the 5 percent surtax — added to the highest of the marginal tax rates — was repealed. From 2003 through 2007, the top rate was to decline by 1 percentage point each year until it reached 45 percent.

- **Estate, generation-skipping repeal.** All estate and generation-skipping taxes were to be repealed in 2010.

- **Gift tax.** The bill retained the gift tax and set the rate at the highest individual income tax rate (in 2010, that rate would be 35 percent).

- **Unified credit.** The point at which estate and generation-skipping taxes apply, known as the unified credit, was increased to $1 million in 2002, $1.5 million in 2004, $2 million in 2006 and $3.5 million in 2009. Beginning in 2004, the increase in the unified credit would apply only to transfers at death, leaving the unified credit for lifetime transfers (i.e., for gifts) at $1 million. Under prior law, the exemption from taxes under the unified credit was $675,000, with the amount scheduled to increase to $1 million by 2006.

- **State credit.** Taxpayers subject to federal estate taxes could

claim a credit equal to the amount of inheritance taxes they paid to states. The bill reduced the credit by 25 percent in 2002, 50 percent in 2003 and 75 percent in 2004, and repealed it in 2005. However, taxpayers subject to such state levies would be able take the cost as a deduction on their federal taxes.

- **Capital gains basis.** The bill repealed the stepped-up basis, under which the value of a property transferred to an heir was based on its fair-market value at the time of the deceased's death, not at the time the deceased acquired the property. Beginning in 2010 when the estate tax would be repealed, the value of inherited assets would "carry over" from the deceased. Heirs would have to pay capital gains taxes on any increase in the value of the property from the time the asset was acquired by the deceased until it was sold by the heirs, generally resulting in a higher capital gain and higher tax liability for the heirs than under previous law.

The bill provided an exemption of $1.3 million in gain from the carry-over basis, with an additional $3 million exemption for a surviving spouse, for a total of $4.3 million.

- **Conservation easements.** The bill expanded the estate tax rule for conservation easements, which generally allows an executor to exclude from the taxable estate 40 percent of the value (up to $400,000 in 2001) of certain lands set aside for conservation purposes. Prior to enactment, a qualified conservation easement had to be within 10 miles of an urban national forest or within 25 miles of a metropolitan area, national park or wilderness area. The bill repealed — effective 2001 — the 10- and 25-mile limits.

- **Modification to generation-skipping transfer tax rules.** The measure made various modifications, starting in 2001, to simplify the generation-skipping transfer tax prior to repeal in 2010. The tax was levied on transfers to a beneficiary more than one generation away from the individual transferring the benefit.

- **Increased eligibility for installment payments.** Prior to enactment, heirs who inherited the estate of a person who held more than a 35 percent interest in a sole proprietorship or another closely held business could qualify to make those payments over as many as 14 years. Under the bill, heirs of decedents involved in certain lending and financing businesses also would qualify for installment payments, though both the tax and the interest had be paid over five years.

Pension and Retirement Provisions

The bill increased the annual contribution limit for both traditional Individual Retirement Accounts (IRAs) and Roth IRAs. Contributions to a traditional IRA are tax deductible for some taxpayers, but amounts withdrawn are taxable. Contributions to Roth IRAs are not deductible, but withdrawals, including interest, are tax-free.

- **IRA contribution limits.** The limit on IRA contributions was increased to $5,000 per year, from the previous limit of $2,000 per year, phased in over seven years. The new limits: $3,000 in 2002, $4,000 in 2005 and $5,000 in 2008. Beginning in 2009, the amount would be indexed for inflation in $500 increments.

- **IRA catch-up contributions.** Taxpayers age 50 and older could make catch-up contributions to their IRAs, totaling $500 per year in 2002 through 2005 and an additional $1,000 in 2006 and each year thereafter. The catch-up contributions were in addition to the increased limits on all IRAs.

- **401(k) and other plans.** The amount that an individual could contribute annually to a 401(k) plan, a tax-sheltered annuity, known as a 403(b), or a simplified employee pension (SEP) plan increased from $10,500 in 2001 to $11,000 in 2002. In 2003 and thereafter, the limit was scheduled to increase in $1,000 annual increments until it reached $15,000 in 2006, with adjustments for inflation thereafter, in $500 increments.

• **SIMPLE plans.** The amount that an individual could contribute to a small-business (SIMPLE) retirement plan increased from $6,500 in 2001 to $7,000 in 2002, $8,000 in 2003, $9,000 in 2004 and $10,000 in 2005. Beginning in 2006, the $10,000 limit would be adjusted for inflation in $500 increments.

• **Section 457 plans.** The amount that could be contributed on a tax-deferred basis to a Section 457 plan — a type of pension plan offered by a state or local government or tax-exempt organization to its employees — increased from $8,500 in 2001 to $11,000 in 2002. It was then scheduled to increase in $1,000 increments each year until it reached $15,000 in 2006. The limit would be indexed for inflation in $500 increments beginning in 2007.

• **Catch-up contributions.** Individuals 50 and older could make catch-up contributions to a 401(k) plan, a tax-sheltered annuity, a SEP or a Section 457 plan. They would be able to make additional contributions of up to $1,000 in 2002, $2,000 in 2003, $3,000 in 2004, $4,000 in 2005 and $5,000 in 2006. Contribution limits for SIMPLE small-business plans were 50 percent of the applicable catch-up provisions for other plans. Beginning in 2007, the limits would be indexed for inflation in $500 increments.

• **Compensation limitation.** The cap on total annual payments (from both employers and employees) to defined contribution plans, such as 401(k)s, was raised. Previously, the cap was the lesser of $35,000 or 25 percent of an employee's compensation. Beginning in 2002, it was the lesser of $40,000 or 100 percent of compensation. Government and nonprofit workers who participated in 457(b) plans were to have their compensation limit increased from 33.3 percent to 100 percent.

In 2002, the bill increased from $170,000 to $200,000 the annual compensation of each participant that could be taken into account when plan managers determined contributions and benefits. The number would be indexed for inflation in increments of $5,000 beginning in 2003.

• **Defined benefit plans.** The annual benefit limit under a defined benefit plan — a traditional pension plan — was increased from $140,000 to $160,000 in 2002. The bill also lowered the age at which benefits were reduced, from before age 65 to before age 62. Previously, benefits were reduced if the recipient began receiving them before the Social Security retirement age — currently 65 — and increased if they began after the Social Security retirement age.

• **Top-heavy rules.** The definition of a "top-heavy" retirement plan — one that mostly benefits the highest-paid employees — was loosened to ensure that fewer companies faced the stricter vesting and contribution requirements placed on top-heavy plans. The bill redefined a "key" employee as an officer with compensation in excess of $130,000, instead of $70,000 as under prior law, and made several other changes to definitions, all effective in 2002.

• **Deduction limits.** The annual limit on the amount of tax-deductible contributions an employer could make to a profit-sharing or stock bonus plan increased from 15 percent of the taxable compensation of the plan's participants to 25 percent, beginning in 2002.

• **Roth 401(k) plans.** The bill provided for the establishment, beginning in 2006, of a qualified contribution program that allowed an employee to have all or a portion of his or her elective deferrals (i.e., employee contributions to 401(k) and tax-sheltered annuities) treated as qualified contributions. Employee contributions to such a plan would receive the same tax treatment as contributions to a Roth IRA, meaning contributions would be in after-tax dollars, but withdrawals after retirement were tax-free. The annual contribution limit for designated plus contributions would be the regular contribution limit for the plan (for example, $11,500 for 2001) minus contributions not allocated to the qualified plus contribution program. Contributions to such plans would be offi-cially designated "Roth contributions," for former Senate Finance Committee Chairman William V. Roth Jr., R-Del. (1970-2000), who sponsored the bill creating the Roth IRA.

• **Pension for non-resident cruise ship workers.** U.S. cruise companies were allowed to exclude foreigners who worked on their ships in retirement plans. The bill lifted requirements that a company's plan include at least a minimum of its lowest-paid workers in order for the company to qualify for tax benefits. This meant cruise ships could set up plans that offered retirement coverage only to the highest-paid employees, who tended to be U.S. citizens.

• **Retirement contribution tax credit.** Effective in 2002 through 2006, certain middle- and low-income taxpayers were eligible for a temporary, non-refundable tax credit for contributions to eligible retirement plans.

Individuals with incomes up to $25,000 and married couples with incomes up to $50,000 were eligible for a credit of up to 50 percent on a maximum contribution of $2,000 to a 401(k) plan, a tax-sheltered annuity, a section 457 plan for government workers, a SIMPLE plan or a SEP, traditional or Roth IRA. The credit would be phased out for single taxpayers earning more than $15,000 and for married couples earning more than $30,000.

• **Credit for small businesses.** Beginning in 2002, small firms that set up a new defined benefit or defined contribution plan could claim a tax credit for up to 50 percent of the first $1,000 in administrative and retirement-education expenses incurred during the plan's first three years. Businesses that claimed the credit would not be allowed to also deduct the amount. A small business was defined as one that has no more than 100 employees who receive compensation in excess of $5,000. For the company to claim the credit, the retirement plan had to cover at least one employee who was not among the highest paid.

• **Hardship withdrawals from 401(k)s.** Before enactment, employees who withdrew money from their retirement account because of extreme financial hardship were prohibited in some cases from making any contributions to their account for a year after the payment was made. The bill directed the Treasury Department to immediately reduce that time to six months. It also clarified that all such withdrawals were not eligible to be treated as "rollovers," and were thus subject to tax beginning in 2002.

• **Retirement plans for domestic workers.** A 10 percent excise tax on certain retirement plan contributions not classified as a business or trade expense was lifted effective 2002, removing a disincentive to providing retirement plans for maids, nannies, gardeners and other domestic workers.

• **Portability.** Employees moving from a job with one type of retirement plan — for example, a 401(k) — to a job with another kind — for instance, a government 457 — could transfer their retirement savings to the new account, beginning in 2002. Under prior law, savings often could be moved only to the same type of retirement account or to a traditional IRA. In addition, the Treasury secretary was given more leeway to waive rules requiring employees to "roll over" their savings to the new retirement plan within 60 days for the transfer to be tax-free.

• **Vesting.** Rules for pension plans were changed to require that workers be "vested" — or given the right to their employer's contribution to their pension accounts — within three years or in increments of 20 percent for each year beginning with an employee's second year of service. Once a worker is vested, the benefit cannot be taken away if he or she changes jobs. Prior law required vesting within five years or in increments of 20 percent beginning with the employee's third year of service.

• **Pension changes due to a merger.** The Treasury secretary was required to issue regulations no later than Dec. 31, 2003, on how companies could make slight pension changes that could allow the merged plan to function better but that might have a minimal neg-

ative effect on a few employees.

● **Government credit service purchases.** Beginning in 2002, state and local government employees could use funds from their 403(b) or 457(b) retirement plans to purchase service credits, which generally allow them to retire earlier.

● **Limits on defined benefit plan assets.** Employers generally were limited in the amount of contributions to a traditional pension plan that they could deduct if the plan was more than fully funded. In 2001, the level at which contributions could no longer be deducted was 160 percent of current liability. Under the bill, that level was increased to 165 percent in 2002 and 170 percent in 2003; it would be repealed in 2004. Employers still would be unable to claim deductions in excess of the plan's accrued liability minus the value of its assets.

● **Cash balance plans and other pension changes.** Within 90 days of enactment, the Treasury secretary was required to issue regulations on the details that companies switching from a traditional defined benefit pension to another plan were required to include in notices to their employees. The bill required that companies issue such a notice "within a reasonable time," although it permitted Treasury to set a more specific deadline. The notice had to describe the benefit reduction caused by the proposed change in such a way that it could be understood by the average plan participant. Officials who failed to distribute such a notice could be fined $100 per day for each participant entitled to the notice, to a maximum of $500,000 per year. In cases of willful neglect, the switch to a new pension plan could be rejected under the Employee Retirement Income Security Act of 1974 (PL 93-406).

The issue came to the forefront after some companies, including IBM, came under public pressure for switching from a traditional pension to a so-called "cash-balance plan." The change put longtime workers at a disadvantage.

● **Repealing benefit limits for certain laborers.** Prior law limited the annual benefits that retirees could receive from multiemployer plans to no more than 100 percent of their average compensation over the three highest-paid years of their career. Such plans often are set up for construction workers and other laborers who work for many companies during their lifetime. Under the bill, the limit was repealed in 2002. The change was strongly supported by many of the building-trades unions.

● **Employee Stock Ownership Plans (ESOPs).** Beginning in 2002, employers could deduct from their taxes dividends they paid to employees, regardless of whether the employees took the dividend in cash or reinvested it in the company. Prior law allowed deductions only for cash dividends. The Treasury secretary was given the authority to disallow deductions in cases in which the chief purpose of the transaction appeared to be tax evasion.

● **Cashing out.** Under prior law, when a worker with no more than $5,000 in vested retirement savings left a company, the savings were automatically distributed to him in cash, unless he elected to roll them over to another savings account. Under the bill, employers would automatically transfer distributions of $1,000 to $5,000 to IRAs unless the worker requested the distribution in cash. The Labor secretary was required to issue regulations on this provision within three years.

● **Employer-provided retirement advice.** Employer-provided retirement planning advice and information would not be considered a part of income and wages.

● **Non-discrimination tests.** The bill repealed, effective 2002, one of three tests that under prior law limited some highly compensated employees' ability to contribute to their retirement accounts if they were already contributing a much greater percentage than the lower-paid workers.

Miscellaneous Provisions

● **Alaska native settlement trusts.** Alaska natives were allowed to transfer money or property to a trust for the purpose of promoting the health, education and welfare of the beneficiaries and preserving their heritage and culture. Under the bill, the trust would be taxed at the lowest personal income tax rate — 10 percent.

● **Corporate estimated tax payments.** Payment of corporate quarterly estimated taxes, due Sept. 17, 2001, were deferred until Oct. 1, 2001. Corporations were required to pay only 80 percent of the quarterly estimated taxes due Sept. 15, 2004. The rest were due Oct. 1, 2004. The changes were included to shift federal revenue to years in which the budget surplus might not be sufficient to support that year's tax reductions without tapping into money set aside in the Medicare Part A hospital trust fund.

● **Postponing tax deadlines in disaster areas.** The Treasury secretary was allowed to delay certain tax due-dates for residents of presidentially declared disaster areas by 120 days, up from 90 days.

● **Tax treatment of Holocaust funds.** Restitution payments from the governments of former Nazi-controlled countries, returned assets and other funds provided to survivors of the Holocaust, their heirs or their estates were excluded from the calculation of gross income. Eligible individuals included those persecuted because of their religion, their race, their sexual orientation or their physical or mental disabilities.

Sunset Provision

● All provisions of the law were due to expire after Dec. 31, 2010. ◆

Stimulus Bill Dies in Senate

A bill to stimulate the economy through business-oriented tax breaks, unemployment and health insurance assistance for laid-off workers, and tax rebates for the working poor died in the Senate after becoming embroiled in a battle over which party was responsible for the economic recession. The highly partisan debate was one of the first and deepest cracks in the united front Republicans and Democrats had put forth in the immediate wake of the Sept. 11 terrorist attacks.

The collapse of the stimulus bill (HR 3090, HR 3529) followed weeks of futile negotiations, legislative action that often proved symbolic, and an endgame that combined intensified negotiations with efforts by Republicans and Democrats to blame each other for the failure of the effort.

The bitter party differences obscured general accord on a number of proposals that most agreed should be part of a bipartisan stimulus plan. Lawmakers in both parties supported accelerating the rate at which businesses could write off capital purchases, extending the period of time during which firms could carry back losses to offset past tax liability, and renewing a package of narrow, expiring tax provisions. There also was widespread agreement that a stimulus bill should extend unemployment insurance and include checks for those working poor who did not receive rebates earlier in the year as part of President Bush's tax cut (PL 107-16).

But there were considerable partisan differences over the rest of the package. Republicans wanted to speed up at least some of the individual rate cuts enacted in the Bush tax law, and include relief from the corporate alternative minimum tax (AMT), which prevented companies from claiming certain credits and deductions to ensure that they paid at least some tax. Democrats demanded that the package expand eligibility for unemployment insurance, subsidize 75 percent of COBRA continuation health coverage premiums for those who had lost their jobs, and expand Medicaid to cover those ineligible for employer-sponsored COBRA plans. Enacted in 1986, the Consolidated Omnibus Budget Reconciliation Act (PL 99-272), allowed the jobless to maintain coverage through former employers' plans if they paid up to 102 percent of the cost. (*1986 Almanac, p. 252*)

The White House and congressional leaders began trying to write a bipartisan plan shortly after the Sept. 11 terrorist attacks, but House Ways and Means Committee Chairman Bill Thomas, R-Calif., soon left the talks and wrote his own stimulus measure costing $99.5 billion, composed mostly of individual and corporate tax cuts, with about $3 billion in grants for unemployment and health insurance assistance for displaced workers. The bill squeaked through the House.

In the Senate, Majority Leader Tom Daschle, D-S.D., and Finance Committee Chairman Max Baucus, D-Mont., pushed an equally partisan stimulus plan through the Fi-

BoxScore

Bills:
HR 3090, HR 3529

Legislative Action:

House passed HR 3090 (H Rept 107-251), 216-214, on Oct. 24.

Senate Finance Committee approved HR 3090, amended, 11-10, on Nov. 8.

House passed HR 3529, 224-193, on Dec. 20.

nance Committee. The $66.4 billion bill was split between tax cuts and assistance for displaced workers. Republicans blocked the measure on the Senate floor and Democrats withdrew, blaming the GOP for stalling efforts to help the economy recover from a recession that began in March.

Negotiations involving House and Senate leaders, congressional tax-writers and the Bush administration made little substantive progress until a group of Senate moderates led by Democrat John B. Breaux of Louisiana — the same centrists who had ushered the Bush tax cut to enactment earlier in the year — weighed in. They offered a middle ground on health insurance for displaced workers, agreeing with Bush, as well as House and Senate Republicans, on a plan that would subsidize 60 percent of premiums through tax credits. Most House and Senate Democrats objected to the plan, saying it offered no real assurances to the poorest of the uninsured.

As the clock wound down with no bipartisan deal in sight, the House passed a new $89.8 billion stimulus measure (HR 3529) on Dec. 20 that incorporated the centrist health care plan in an effort to pressure Daschle to bring up the measure before the Senate adjourned for the year. But Democrats objected and used procedural maneuvers to block the Senate from considering the bill.

Congress ended the year without an economic stimulus bill, and consequently without two narrower tax measures that had been part of the negotiations. The first would have renewed a number of popular expiring tax provisions, such as employment tax credits and school construction bonds. The second was a package of tax breaks for rebuilding parts of New York City affected by the Sept. 11 terrorist attacks.

The only piece of the original stimulus bill to be enacted was a bill (HR 2884 — PL 107-134) to provide tax relief to families of the victims of the Sept. 11 attacks, the subsequent anthrax mail attacks and the 1995 Oklahoma City bombing.

Throughout the process, the stimulus bill suffered from a nagging sense on the part of Republicans and Democrats alike that, in reality, it would have a minor influence at best on the economy. Many of the provisions would not take effect until the spring of 2002, when experts thought the economy might be well on its way to recovery anyway. Also, the government already had taken several steps that economists said should help, including interest rate cuts by the Federal Reserve, Bush's tax cut, and $40 billion in emergency spending enacted in the immediate wake of the terrorist attacks (PL 107-38).

Highlights

The centrist plan, which seemed in late December to offer the best hope for compromise, was contained in the bill

passed by the House on Dec. 20. The proposal was assembled during negotiations among congressional Republicans, the Bush administration and three Senate Democratic centrists — Breaux, Zell Miller of Georgia and Ben Nelson of Nebraska. The bill proposed to:

- **Stimulus checks.** Send checks of up to $300 for individuals and $600 for couples to the working poor who did not receive rebates under the Bush tax cut law.
- **Rate reduction.** Accelerate the phase-in of a 25 percent individual tax rate, making it effective in 2002, rather than 2006, as provided in the tax cut law.
- **Unemployment extension.** Allow for a 13-week extension of unemployment insurance benefits for those who had exhausted their regular 26 weeks of benefits.
- **Health care tax credits.** Create a new refundable, advanceable health care tax credit for the jobless, providing those eligible for unemployment benefits with a voucher covering 60 percent of their premiums.
- **Accelerated depreciation.** Allow businesses to take an immediate 30 percent deduction for the cost of capital purchases, thereby speeding up the rate at which they could write off equipment investments.
- **Small-business expensing.** Increase, from $24,000 to $35,000, the amount of capital purchases that small businesses could expense.
- **Net operating loss carrybacks.** Extend, from two to five years, the period of time during which companies could carry back losses to offset past tax liability.
- **Tax extenders.** Extend temporarily a popular set of expiring tax provisions that allowed U.S. financial services companies and manufacturers with operations abroad to defer taxes on the income they earned overseas.
- **Victims' tax relief.** Refund victims' income taxes for two years, and provide $10,000 rebates for those who made too little to owe income tax; shield up to $8.5 billion in victims' assets from federal estate taxes; and prevent the taxation of death benefits or debt forgiveness provided to victims, and of charitable contributions to victims' organizations.
- **New York "Liberty Zone" package.** Provide temporary tax incentives, totaling $4.1 billion over five years, for rebuilding the area of Manhattan affected by the attacks.

Background

The Sept. 11 terrorist attacks quickly transformed the mindset on Capitol Hill and in the White House about the state of the economy and the realities of the federal budget. The ensuing military operation in Afghanistan, the drop in the securities markets and the destruction at the nation's financial epicenter jolted all sides into rethinking how the federal government should stimulate an already weak economy.

Bickering over whether more spending would threaten Social Security, the dominant theme before the attacks, evaporated. All sides said the nation could afford a substantial defense buildup, the rebuilding of New York City, a bailout for the airline industry and perhaps more tax cuts without jeopardizing the nation's long-term fiscal health. Asked on Sept. 19 how much he was willing to spend of the surplus revenue once dedicated to the Social Security trust funds — the so-called lockbox — Bush responded, "Enough to get America going again."

The emphasis was on bipartisanship as congressional tax-writers quickly convened a series of discussions about what their role should be in trying to stimulate the economy. They heard from a variety of economists, including Federal Reserve Chairman Alan Greenspan, who counseled Congress to take its time. "It's far more important to be right than quick," he told the Senate Banking Committee on Sept. 20.

A major question was how large the stimulus package should be. Senate Budget and Finance committee members said Greenspan indicated in a closed-door meeting Sept. 25 that $100 billion would be appropriate. But the Fed said that figure was meant to include what Congress already had allocated since Sept. 11 — $40 billion in emergency spending for defense and disaster relief, and $15 billion to stabilize the airline industry (PL 107-42). (*Appropriations, p. 2-59; airline assistance, p. 20-3*)

On Oct. 5, Bush outlined plans for a $75 billion package, saying it should focus exclusively on tax cuts. "In order to stimulate the economy, Congress doesn't need to spend any more money," he said. "What they need to do is to cut taxes." As his priorities, Bush listed accelerating income tax rate cuts, giving low-income workers tax relief, expanding tax breaks for businesses' capital expenses and eliminating the corporate AMT. His plan also included $14 billion in grants to states to help the unemployed and those without medical insurance.

Senate Democrats called for a $55 billion to $60 billion package divided evenly between spending and tax cuts.

Though negotiations continued between the White House and congressional leaders of both parties on the shape of a bill, Thomas pulled out Oct. 10 to write his own measure. Partisanship made a quick return as lawmakers turned to debating the specifics. Senate leaders continued to negotiate, but as time wore on, ideological positions hardened in that chamber as well. The day before Thomas squeezed his bill through the House, Baucus unveiled a $70 billion stimulus package heavy on Democratic priorities. And Appropriations Chairman Robert C. Byrd, D-W.Va., unveiled a $20 billion infrastructure spending plan he said should be included in the stimulus measure.

Legislative Action

House Committee Action

After a bitter markup Oct. 12, the House Ways and Means Committee approved Thomas' bill (HR 3090 — H Rept 107-251). It included $99.5 billion worth of individual and business tax cuts and tax credit extensions in 2002 — projected to cost $151.9 billion over 10 years. The vote was 23-14, with no Democrats supporting the measure.

Major provisions of the GOP bill would:

- Send $300 checks ($600 for joint filers) to the working poor who had not gotten rebates under the Bush tax cut, and make up the difference for those who received partial rebates.
- Make the 25 percent tax rate effective in 2002, rather than in 2006.
- Permanently reduce rates on adjusted net capital gains from 10 percent and 20 percent to 8 percent and 18 percent.
- Repeal the corporate AMT and refund the additional

tax that companies had paid since 1986 because of the alternate tax.

• Accelerate the depreciation schedule for certain items so companies could more quickly recover the costs of new equipment.

• Extend from two years to five the time during which companies could apply a loss to offset their taxable income.

• Provide $3 billion under the existing social services block grant program to states that experienced joblessness spikes in the wake of the Sept. 11 attacks to supplement unemployment and health benefits.

• Provide $9 billion to the states in surplus federal unemployment funds for enhanced benefits and services.

• Extend expiring tax provisions, including credits for employers who hired hard-to-place workers.

Democrats complained angrily about the timing of the markup and the substance of the bill, arguing it would provide little help to the laid-off workers who should be the target of a stimulus package, while being overly generous to wealthy individuals and corporations.

The panel turned back Democratic amendments to:

• Provide a 75 percent federal subsidy of health insurance premiums for the unemployed under the 1985 COBRA law at a cost of $15 billion. The proposal by Pete Stark, D-Calif., was rejected, 16-25.

• Require the federal government to pick up the added cost of a one-year expansion of state unemployment benefits at a cost of $15 billion. The proposal by Benjamin L. Cardin, D-Md., was defeated, 18-22.

• Delete the proposed repeal of the corporate AMT. The amendment, by Gerald D. Kleczka, D-Wis., was rejected, 13-23.

House Floor Action

After another fiercely partisan debate, the House passed the GOP bill by the narrowest of margins, 216-214, on Oct. 24. Enough Republicans, mostly moderates, broke with their party to make the final vote extremely close. Twice in the last minutes, the tally stood deadlocked, first at 213-213, then at 214-214, before Republicans who had held off from voting, such as Michael N. Castle of Delaware, provided the narrow margin of victory. (*House vote 404, p. H-138*)

Republicans defended the bill's emphasis — about 70 percent of the tax relief would go to businesses — saying it would spur companies to invest and consequently to hire more workers. Thomas repeatedly urged his colleagues to stop thinking of his plan as help for corporations and instead view it as support for "job-creating machines."

The only amendment allowed during debate — a $110 billion Democratic alternative — was rejected, 166-261. The proposal, offered by Charles B. Rangel, D. N.Y., included a rebate for low-income individuals, expanded and increased unemployment benefits, and a federal subsidy for unemployed workers to purchase costly health care coverage. Democrats proposed to offset $91 billion of the cost by freezing the top marginal tax rate at 38.6 percent, rather than reducing it to 35 percent over five years, as scheduled under Bush's tax cut. (*House vote 402, p. H-138*)

Democrats left the floor vowing not to be shut out of future negotiations on the stimulus package as they had been

during final talks on Bush's tax bill. "You can run and hide all over this House of Representatives, but Rangel is going to find that conference this time, and . . . be involved in the conference this time," said Rangel, the top Democrat on Ways and Means.

Senate Committee Action

After weeks of fruitless negotiations, Democrats pushed their own $66.4 billion stimulus bill through the Senate Finance Committee on Nov. 8 on a party-line vote of 11-10. The plan, by Daschle and Baucus, was light on pro-business tax cuts and heavy on new spending.

As approved by the committee, the bill, a substitute for HR 3090, included:

• $23 billion in business tax breaks, far smaller than those passed by the House or recommended by Bush. It included provisions to let businesses immediately write off 10 percent of capital purchases; increase from $25,000 to $35,000 the amount that small businesses could expense; and extend from two to five years the period during which companies could apply 2001 losses to offset their tax liability in past years.

• A $1.8 billion package to rebuild New York, championed aggressively by Robert G. Torricelli, D-N.J., who was facing a potentially difficult 2002 re-election campaign.

• $9 billion worth of tax-exempt bonding authority for Amtrak costing about $39 million — also by Torricelli.

• $14 billion in checks for low- and middle-income people who did not receive tax rebates earlier.

• $31 billion in health and unemployment spending, including a federally funded 13-week extension of unemployment benefits and a 75 percent federal subsidy of the premiums that displaced workers had to pay for COBRA continuation health coverage. States could receive federal matching funds to provide health care coverage to jobless who were not eligible for COBRA. The rate at which the federal government matched state Medicaid spending would increase by 1.5 percent.

• $6 billion in agriculture spending, some of it to enable the Agriculture Department to purchase specialty crops — including apples, pumpkins and watermelons — that had experienced low prices during the preceding two years.

Republicans made it clear that they would not stand for anything resembling the Democratic package and would insist on further tax relief. "There is not one cent in this bill that provides any tax incentive to any American who pays income taxes," said Phil Gramm, R-Texas, calling the measure "pitiful" and "insulting."

"This is not a tax bill; this is a stimulus bill," Baucus said.

Daschle defended the decision to move the bill on a party-line basis: "There comes a time when we've got to get the job done," he said.

But even some Democrats complained about a panoply of special-interest items their leaders included to ensure the unanimous Democratic support they needed to get the bill out of committee. Perhaps the most stunning example was a last minute manager's amendment by Baucus that included Torricelli's amendments, a $4 million tax break for crop dusters sought by Blanche Lincoln, D-Ark., and $10 million in tax relief for citrus farmers sought by Bob Graham, D-Fla.

Democrats were under pressure to stick with Daschle, with

the goal of getting to conference talks with the House in the strongest possible position. But the leadership decision also created a dilemma: In the free-wheeling Senate, 60 votes were needed to pass the bill, which meant a Democrats-only strategy would not work. It took 60 votes to stop a filibuster or overcome a point of order. The bill was vulnerable to points of order because it violated the limits on tax cuts in the fiscal 2002 budget resolution (H Con Res 83).

The Finance markup was especially frustrating to centrists such as Breaux and Olympia J. Snowe, R-Maine, who had spent weeks trying to work out a bipartisan deal. "We're certainly not soaring to great legislative heights here today . . . this is not my idea of profiles in courage," said a visibly irritated Snowe. "What does it do to go into a conference so divided?"

One GOP option laid out by senior leadership aides was to quickly kill the Democrats' bill, creating a situation in which centrist Democrats and the White House could broker a deal — a reprise of the center-right coalition that pulled Bush's $1.35 trillion tax cut into law earlier in the year.

Senate Floor Action

It took less than two days Nov. 13-14 for the bill to fall into a procedural trap on the Senate floor and be pulled by Daschle. Democrats brought up the House-passed bill as the underlying vehicle, and Baucus offered an all-Democratic stimulus plan that also included a $15 billion homeland security spending proposal by Byrd, trimmed from his initial $20 billion plan. Republicans raised a point of order against the proposal Nov. 14 , and an attempt by Baucus to waive the objection failed, 51-47, with 60 votes required for victory. (*Senate vote 338, p. S-70*)

Congressional leaders and the White House then signaled they would hold bipartisan, bicameral negotiations after Congress returned from the Thanksgiving recess. Despite scathing partisan rhetoric in dueling news conferences, leaders from both parties still seemed willing to try to work out a compromise.

But the challenges were considerable. Daschle vowed not to compromise on the economic stimulus bill unless Republicans ensured a vote in 2001 on Byrd's $15 billion homeland security plan — a stance he subsequently dropped under a barrage of criticism from congressional Republicans and the White House. Democrats wanted to send $14 billion worth of checks to the working poor — an idea Republicans had accepted only grudgingly — while the GOP preferred to help higher-earning taxpayers by accelerating the marginal rate cuts in the new tax law. Speeding up rate cuts that most of them had voted against earlier in the year was anathema to Democrats.

Sen. Pete V. Domenici of New Mexico, the senior Budget Committee Republican, stirred brief interest with a proposal to solve the dispute over individual tax relief by providing a one-month payroll tax holiday for all taxpayers, at a cost of $38 billion. Negotiations continued in fits and starts. "It's a glacial pace," Breaux commented Nov. 27.

The Final Round

The final round of negotiations began Dec. 11, when Senate Minority Leader Trent Lott, R-Miss., arranged a White House meeting where Bush and Republican and Democratic Senate moderates, including Senate Centrist Coalition co-chairmen Breaux and Snowe, agreed on a $93 billion outline of a stimulus bill. Bipartisan talks continued into the Dec. 15-16 weekend, with the centrists' plan emerging as the likely framework for any final deal. The fatal blow came when negotiators began seriously discussing the highly charged issue of health insurance for the jobless and uninsured. Democrats said that had to be resolved before they would even consider GOP proposals to accelerate income tax cuts or provide corporate tax relief. Democrats wanted a 75 percent federal subsidy of COBRA for laid-off workers and Medicaid assistance for those ineligible for employer-sponsored COBRA plans.

Republicans were loath to set a precedent for a direct federal health care subsidy or a Medicaid expansion, and instead proposed health insurance tax credits for the jobless, as well as grants to states to help them cover the uninsured. The compromise was for the government to provide those eligible for unemployment benefits with a voucher covering 60 percent of their premiums. They could use the credit to stay in COBRA plans or to purchase coverage individually on the private market, where insurers would be required to sell policies to workers who had employer-sponsored coverage for one year. But most Democrats adamantly opposed the idea, saying it would turn loose those least able to support themselves into a health insurance market would will deny them affordable coverage.

In the end, the two parties were unable and unwilling to reconcile their dueling approaches in the short time that remained. Both were "holding everything hostage to a philosophical concept," said Snowe.

In the absence of a consensus package, House leaders introduced the centrist measure as a new bill (HR 3529) on Dec. 19 and passed it by a vote of 224-193 the next day. Only nine Democrats crossed party lines to support the bill. (*House vote 509, p. H-174*)

The stated purpose of the vote was to offer a bipartisan alternative that could pass both the House and Senate. But the move was mostly theater designed to bring pressure on Daschle to allow a floor vote on the measure and then blame him for its demise.

"A bad deal is worse than no deal at all," Daschle said. Democrats blocked GOP efforts to bring up the bill by unanimous consent, and Republicans refused to allow Democrats to salvage parts of it they supported, such as extension of unemployment benefits or expiring tax provisions. "The stimulus is dormant," Daschle said Dec. 20. "Our hope is that it can be revived early next year." ◆

Ban on Internet Tax Extended

The high-tech industry won a difficult victory Nov. 15 when the Senate cleared a bill to reinstate a moratorium on Internet-only taxes through Nov. 1, 2003. The legislation, which the House had passed Oct. 16, revived a moratorium that expired Oct. 21 when senators bogged down over the separate question of whether state sales taxes should apply to electronic commerce. President Bush signed the bill (HR 1552 — PL 107-75) on Nov. 28.

The Senate vote was welcome relief to the battered technology industry, which argued that failure to extend the moratorium would lead to new taxes that could crush the Internet economy during an economic slowdown. "The American economy and the high-tech industry benefit from the Senate's extension of the Internet tax ban," said Bill Archey, president and chief executive officer of the American Electronics Association, a large high-tech trade group.

The Bush administration had endorsed a simple extension of the moratorium, saying it would allow time to study the effects of e-commerce on local sales tax collections and ensure that the growth of the Internet would continue.

However, some lawmakers said the decision to put off the sales tax issue would leave states in need of more federal aid to fund police, fire departments and other essential services. "It will be hard to say no to states when they come here and ask for money when we take away a revenue source," said Sen. George V. Voinovich, R-Ohio.

Sens. Michael B. Enzi, R-Wyo., and Byron L. Dorgan, D-N.D., offered a compromise to extend the ban on Internet taxes until Dec. 31, 2005, while allowing states to develop a uniform sales tax system for Internet transactions. If at least 20 states adopted the uniform system, the bill would have allowed them to begin collecting taxes on all e-commerce. But supporters of a straight moratorium prevailed.

Background

The Internet tax question was one of the most lobbied technology issues before Congress. It pitted the high-tech sector against the nation's approximately 7,500 state and local governments. States and localities, led by groups such as the National Governors' Association (NGA), said the growth of e-commerce was siphoning customers from brick-and-mortar businesses and eroding tax revenues. Retailers and commercial real-estate interests aligned themselves with state and local governments, saying the Internet should not continue to operate as a tax-free zone.

But collecting taxes on sales conducted over the Internet was difficult. Transactions could occur across several states, with a purchaser in one state linking to a computer in a second location that linked to a retailer in a third state. In a

BoxScore

Bill:
HR 1552 — PL 107-75
Legislative Action:
House passed HR 1552 (H Rept 107-240) by voice vote Oct. 16.
Senate cleared HR 1552 by voice vote Nov. 15.
President signed Nov. 28.

1992 case, *Quill Corp. v. North Dakota*, the Supreme Court ruled that states could not force vendors to collect sales taxes unless the purchaser lived in a state where the company had a physical presence, such as a retail store.

Nineteen states had passed laws based on a model from the NGA to create a simplified system for collecting taxes from "remote sellers" located in any of the member states. The governors wanted congressional endorsement for such a compact, while the high-tech industry argued that extra charges could crush the Internet economy during an economic recession.

Unable to find a solution acceptable to both the states and the industry, Congress put the sales tax issue aside in 1998 and passed a three-year moratorium (PL 105-277) that applied to all new taxes specifically imposed on Internet access and commerce. *(1998 Almanac, p. 21-19)*

Legislative Action

House Action

The House Judiciary Committee's Commercial Law Subcommittee approved a five-year extension of the moratorium by voice vote Aug. 2. The bill, backed by House GOP leaders and the high-tech industry, would have permanently banned taxes on Internet access charges and closed a loophole in existing law that allowed 11 states to continue charging fees that were enacted before 1998.

The full Judiciary Committee approved the bill (H Rept 107-240) by voice vote in a contentious markup Oct. 10, but only after reducing the extension to two years, dropping the permanent ban on Internet access taxes and allowing the 11 states to continue charging their fees for the time being. The changes were made in an amendment by Spencer Bachus, R-Ala., which was adopted, 19-15.

Another amendment by Bachus, stating that Congress should approve a sales tax compact once 25 states had agreed to join, was ruled out of order.

The House passed the bill Oct. 16 by voice vote under suspension of the rules, an expedited procedure that requires a two-thirds majority and bars amendments.

Senate Action

The Senate cleared the bill by voice vote Nov. 15, nearly four weeks after the moratorium had been allowed to expire. Senators had been unable to break an impasse over the state sales tax issue.

Many lawmakers sympathetic to the high-tech sector, including John McCain, R-Ariz., and Ron Wyden, D-Ore., favored a simple moratorium extension, though they were

divided on how long it should last. But Dorgan said he would not agree to extend the moratorium for more than nine months unless the tax collection issue was addressed. "They will need unanimous consent to extend the moratorium, and I would not agree to a five-year or even a two-year extension because we need to force the issue of solving the other problems," Dorgan said Oct. 9.

Once the moratorium expired Oct. 21, state and local governments were technically free to start levying charges on Internet access and other online services, though none did. "I don't think Western civilization is going to end . . . but there's certainly a chance for economic mischief at a time when the economy is fragile," Wyden said.

Several local government organizations that had opposed the two-year extension publicly changed their stance and endorsed it. Joined by several telecommunications and marketing groups, the U.S. Conference of Mayors, National Confer-ence of State Legislatures, National Association of Counties and National League of Cities wrote Senate Majority Leader Tom Daschle, D-S.D., and Minority Leader Trent Lott, R-Miss., saying a simple two-year extension of the moratorium would allow for more negotiation on sales taxes.

During the floor debate Nov. 15, Enzi tried to strengthen the states' hands by offering his amendment to encourage the formation of a compact if 20 states agreed. The proposal was tabled (killed), 57-43. (*Senate vote 341, p. S-70*)

Opponents argued that the amendment was so loosely worded that it could lead to taxes being levied every time a person accessed content on the Internet. They also questioned whether endorsing the compact essentially would allow 20 like-minded states to reverse any Supreme Court decision. "I can see this concept of 20 states getting together and ganging up on the rest used fairly regularly, if it's used here," said Judd Gregg, R-N.H. ◆

Chapter 19

TRADE

Fresh Push for Fast Track

President Bush entered office with a global trade agenda that included a hemispherewide free-trade zone and a new round of world trade talks. The first stop, however, was Capitol Hill. Bush hoped to win renewed fast-track authority from Congress, which would allow him to negotiate trade deals with a guarantee of swift legislative action and no amendments. Fast track had expired in 1994, and Congress had rejected President Bill Clinton's requests for an extension.

With the fresh determination of a new president, Bush renamed his top legislative priority "trade promotion authority," lobbied for the loyalty of his party in a time of war against terrorism, and eked out a one-vote victory for the bill (HR 3005) on the House floor Dec. 6. The Senate Finance Committee approved the measure shortly afterward, but Majority Leader Tom Daschle, D-S.D., put off floor action until 2002.

Fast-track authority had been granted to presidents beginning with Gerald Ford. Clinton and Bush both argued that its demise had slowed U.S. progress in global trade talks and undermined the nation's credibility abroad.

Democrats posed the main obstacles to renewing fast track, fearing that free-trade agreements with less-developed countries could weaken labor standards and environmental protection in the United States. They were joined by a small but significant group of Republicans, primarily from industrial districts.

House GOP leaders began their fast-track campaign for the year in June, introducing a five-year extension. House Speaker J. Dennis Hastert, R-Ill., in an effort to firm up support, repeatedly scheduled floor action, only to reverse himself when it became clear the measure would not pass. After Sept. 11, the White House renewed its push, portraying free trade as a critical part of the war on terrorism, though the approach angered Democrats who saw it as an attempt to gain partisan advantage at a time when both parties were stressing national unity. The administration's target of enacting a bill before the World Trade Organization talks in Doha, Qatar, in November came and went.

By early December, both sides were ready for a showdown. House Ways and Means Committee Chairman Bill Thomas, R-Calif., had marked up a fast-track bill (HR 3005) on Oct. 9 with the help of a handful of pro-trade Democrats. The bill included some labor and environmental protection as negotiating goals in trade agreements, as many Democrats had sought.

But it did not include what for most Democrats was essential: a requirement that trade deals eligible for fast track include sanctions or other mechanisms to enforce labor and environmental provisions.

BoxScore

Bill:
HR 3005
Legislative Action:
House passed HR 3005 (H Rept 107-249, Part 1), 215-214, on Dec. 6.
Senate Finance Committee approved HR 3005, amended (S Rept 107-139), 18-3, on Dec. 12.

In the week leading up to the House vote, GOP leaders focused their lobbying on wavering Republicans rather than trying to attract more Democrats. The strategy succeeded — barely — handing Bush a significant victory by the narrowest of margins.

In the Senate, Finance Committee Chairman Max Baucus, D-Mont., and ranking Republican Charles E. Grassley of Iowa marked up a version similar to the House-passed bill, blocking all amendments. That set the stage for floor action, though it left Democrats largely dissatisfied.

Highlights

The following are highlights of the House-passed bill:

● **Consultation.** The president would be required to notify and consult with Congress 90 calendar days before initiating bilateral or multilateral trade negotiations. The U.S. trade representative would have to consult with relevant congressional committees, a newly created congressional oversight group and the Agriculture committees before initialing a trade agreement. If the administration failed to consult with Congress, both chambers could pass a resolution of disapproval that would make the bill implementing the agreement ineligible for fast-track consideration.

The president would have to notify Congress 90 days before signing a trade agreement; 60 days after signing it, he would have to submit a list of expected changes in U.S. law.

● **Congressional oversight.** The new congressional oversight group would be composed of the chairmen and ranking members of the Ways and Means and Finance committees, plus three additional members of those committees and the chairmen and ranking members of committees with jurisdiction over laws affected by the specific trade agreement. Members of the group would be accredited as official advisers to U.S. negotiators conducting trade talks.

● **Legislative procedures.** Once legislation to implement a trade agreement was submitted, Congress would have 90 legislative days to act: 45 days for House committee consideration, 15 days for the House to vote, 15 days for Senate committee consideration and 15 days for the Senate to vote. No amendments would be allowed, and a single, up-or-down floor vote would be required in each chamber.

● **Negotiating objectives.** The "principal trade negotiating objectives" for agreements subject to fast-track approval would include assurances that signatory countries would effectively enforce their labor and environmental laws. Overall negotiating objectives included reciprocal market access, reducing or eliminating trade barriers, ensuring that trade and environment are mutually supportive, and promoting respect for worker rights and the rights of children consistent with International Labor Organization (ILO) core labor standards.

Background

As in previous years, the debate over fast track pitted mostly Republican free-traders, who wanted a bill focused on trade issues, against a mostly Democratic group seeking to ensure that trade agreements included enforceable labor and environmental standards. Some members from both parties also were concerned about diminishing congressional oversight through fast track.

Fast track was created under the 1974 Trade Act (PL 93-618), which provided expedited procedures for congressional approval of non-tariff trade agreements. The president had to give 90 days' notice before entering into a trade pact and had to consult with appropriate congressional committees. Congress had 90 days to vote up or down on implementing the legislation. (*1974 Almanac, p. 553*)

A 1979 law (PL 96-39) implementing the Tokyo Round of multilateral trade negotiations extended fast-track procedures until Jan. 3, 1988. Fast track was reauthorized again under the 1988 omnibus trade bill (PL 100-418) through May 31, 1991, with a possible two-year extension, barring disapproval by either chamber. The extension was contingent on the president submitting progress reports to Congress on the negotiations. (*1988 Almanac, p. 209; 1979 Almanac, p. 293*)

In 1991, Congress defeated an attempt to disapprove the two-year extension. The White House lobbied heavily for the extension to enable President George Bush to continue talks on the General Agreement on Tariffs and Trade (GATT) and begin talks on a U.S.-Mexico free-trade pact, which ultimately led to the North American Free Trade Agreement (NAFTA). (*1991 Almanac, p. 118*)

In 1993, with Clinton in the White House, Congress extended fast-track authority through April 15, 1994 (PL 103-49), for the sole purpose of completing the GATT agreement. Clinton wanted the bill enacted before he attended a summit of industrial nations in Tokyo in July. The focus on GATT allowed him to avoid a fight with Congress over broader fast-track authority. (*1993 Almanac, p. 182*)

Clinton tried but failed to get a long-term extension as part of the 1994 legislation (PL 103-465) implementing the GATT agreement. Republicans objected to Clinton's attempt to include labor and environmental requirements for trade talks. The following year, the House Ways and Means Committee approved a reauthorization good through Dec. 31, 1999, with a possible two-year extension. Clinton wanted the renewal to facilitate talks with Chile, but objected to provisions that would have barred trade negotiations from dealing with labor and environmental issues. (*1995 Almanac, p. 2-94; 1994 Almanac, p. 123*)

In 1997, the Senate easily passed a bill acceptable to Clinton, but the House version was shelved after Clinton was unable to rally support from Democrats, who were under strong pressure from organized labor to defeat the measure. In 1998, the House defeated an attempt by Clinton to renew fast-track procedures. Opponents had turned the debate into a referendum on NAFTA, dooming the bill. The Senate Finance Committee approved a trade bill that included renewal of fast-track authority, but the full Senate never considered it. (*1998 Almanac, p. 23-3; 1997 Almanac, p. 2-85*)

Bush Takes Up the Campaign

The start of the Bush administration brought a renewed push for fast track. Though Congress had little appetite for another debate, Robert B. Zoellick, the president's pick for U.S. trade representative, proposed an aggressive timetable. "In the absence of this authority, other countries have been moving forward with trade agreements while America has stalled," Zoellick told the Senate Finance Committee during his confirmation hearing Jan. 30. "We cannot afford to stand still — or be mired in partisan division — while other nations seize the mantle of leadership of trade from the United States."

Zoellick's agenda included negotiations on a Free Trade Area of the Americas, as well as bilateral talks on trade expansion deals with Chile and Singapore and the formidable task of launching a new multilateral round of WTO negotiations.

Underlying the debate were questions about the effects of trade on U.S. industries and products, and a sense that the United States had been getting shortchanged globally for its willingness to open markets. Republicans and Democrats alike voiced concerns about industries ranging from agriculture to steel, and called on Zoellick to put the United States on an equal footing with other nations in future negotiations.

Baucus warned Zoellick that fast track would not pass without addressing these "legitimate" concerns. "This is not a political issue. This is a substantive issue of importance to many members of Congress, including me," said Baucus, who was then the committee's ranking member, before the Democrats' takeover of the Senate in June.

In the Senate, a group of Republicans led by Pat Roberts of Kansas had introduced a bill (S 599) to permanently revive fast-track authority. Phil Gramm, R-Texas, introduced a similar measure (S 136) to extend the authority through 2004. Neither bill mentioned labor or environmental standards. Though Grassley agreed with their approach, he acknowledged after a bipartisan session with Bush on April 2 that the Democrats' demands would have to be addressed. "I'm one of those that would really not want to deal with labor and environment," he said, but "the practical aspects are, we won't have a bill if we don't deal with it."

Seeking to gain the support of pro-trade "New Democrats," the administration on May 10 released a set of "principles" that included several proposals for protecting children, labor rights and the environment in the context of trade negotiations — including strengthening the ILO so that its core labor standards were enforceable and using multilateral bank financing as an incentive for countries to abide by those norms. On the environment, the administration stressed enhancing countries' ability to preserve their environment, rather than punishing them for failing to do so.

The main difference with the New Democrats concerned the use of economic sanctions to punish violations of labor and environmental standards in trade deals. The Democratic group said sanctions had to be an option; the president's principles did not mention them.

Legislative Action

The jockeying to put together a House bill got under way in earnest June 13, when Thomas and Ways and Means Trade Subcommittee Chairman Philip M. Crane, R-Ill., unveiled a straight renewal of fast track (HR 2149) for agree-

ments reached before June 2007 involving trade in goods, services, agriculture, electronic commerce, intellectual property and investments. Republicans acknowledged that the bill — conspicuously lacking any mention of labor or environmental conditions — was intended primarily to gauge how many votes they would have to get outside their own party, and how much compromise would be necessary.

On July 26, the House Ways and Means Committee approved a bill to implement the U.S.-Jordan trade agreement (HR 2603), a step Republicans hoped would win over some wavering Democrats. Negotiated in 2000 under Clinton, the Jordan pact was the first U.S. bilateral trade agreement to include enforceable requirements on labor and environment in its text, rather than in side agreements. Sander M. Levin of Michigan, the ranking Democrat on the Ways and Means Trade Subcommittee, had suggested that Congress endorse the agreement as a "building block" in creating a consensus on trade authority. (*U.S.-Jordan pact, p. 19-6*)

To keep Republicans in the fold, however, Thomas acted only after receiving assurances from U.S. and Jordanian trade negotiators that neither country intended to use sanctions to punish the other for labor or environmental infractions — a move that made many Democrats uneasy.

The House passed the Jordan bill July 31, but GOP leaders still lacked the votes to pass the fast-track bill, and floor action was postponed until after the August recess. (The Jordan bill was subsequently enacted on Sept. 28.)

The Sept. 11 terrorist attacks added new impetus to the administration's push for trade authority. In back-to-back speeches the week of Sept. 24, Zoellick portrayed liberalized trade as a patriotic imperative, suggesting later that the opposition was coming from "protectionists," or members who were "held back for other rather narrow interests, reasons, some of them related to the understandable politics of where they get their money."

The statements left Charles B. Rangel of New York, the ranking Democrat on the Ways and Means Committee, fuming. He demanded a "public apology" and jettisoned Republican plans for a markup of the fast-track bill the week of Oct. 1. "There's no question that Zoellick crossed the line," said Robert T. Matsui, D-Calif., a leading pro-trader on the Ways and Means Committee. "I was very disappointed."

House Committee Action

After a few days' delay to calm the situation, the House Ways and Means Committee took up a revised version of Thomas' bill Oct. 9, approving the measure (HR 3005 — H Rept 107-249, Part 1), 26-13, nearly along party lines.

Thomas had introduced the bill Oct. 3, together with three centrist Democrats who helped draft it — Cal Dooley of California, William J. Jefferson of Louisiana and John Tanner of Tennessee. Thomas confirmed that his focus was to secure a GOP base of support while attracting just enough Democrats to form a House majority. "Bipartisan is, you reach out to those people who are reachable," he said.

In a major departure from the bill Thomas introduced in June, the new bill stated that a "principal negotiating objective" for trade talks would be getting assurances that participating countries would effectively enforce their existing labor and environmental laws. The bill was silent on enforcement mechanisms, but stated that labor and environmental

provisions would be subject to the same "demonstrably effective" trade remedies used to enforce other parts of a trade pact. The details would be left to the negotiators.

Thomas' bill also sought to involve Congress more closely in trade negotiations, establishing a bipartisan oversight panel for each trade negotiation and requiring the president to consult with the group before, during and after the trade talks. If the president failed to involve Congress, lawmakers could disqualify the trade agreement from fast-track consideration by winning adoption of a disapproval resolution in both the House and Senate.

The committee rejected a Democratic substitute, written by Levin and Rangel, 12-26. Their alternative proposed different negotiating objectives depending on whether an agreement involved two countries, a geographical region, or a group of nations in the multilateral WTO. To receive fast-track consideration, regional and bilateral agreements would have to bind the participants to enforce domestic labor laws that conformed to core standards set by the ILO: the right to associate and bargain collectively and bans on discrimination and child and slave labor. The agreement also would have to ensure that the participating countries could enforce their environmental laws and uphold environmental agreements without violating trade rules.

The committee rejected, by voice vote, an amendment by Lloyd Doggett, D-Texas, and Jim McDermott, D-Wash., to create a procedural point of order — potentially blocking congressional approval — against any trade agreement with investment rules that did not protect U.S. laws, regulations and treaties from challenge by foreign corporations claiming unfair trade.

House Floor Action

On Dec. 6, after months of wrangling, the House passed the fast-track bill by a razor-thin vote of 215-214. The balloting ran neck and neck and was held open while last-minute deals were struck with Republicans from the textile South. It was the fourth time since July that the Speaker had scheduled a vote on the bill. (*House vote 481, p. H-164*)

The Democratic alternative by Levin and Rangel was rejected on a 162-267 procedural vote. (*House vote 480, p. H-164*)

The bill drew 194 Republicans, about 30 more than usual, largely because GOP leaders promised to take care of key interests, such as agriculture, textiles and steel, in future trade pacts. The leadership also argued that a defeat would undermine the president during a time of war. Republicans Jim DeMint of South Carolina and Robin Hayes of North Carolina changed their positions and supported the bill after party leaders pledged to try to change the sub-Saharan African and Caribbean Basin trade preference law (PL 106-200) enacted in 2000 to help protect textile dyeing and finishing industries in their districts. The promise also extended to the Andean nations trade bill (HR 3009), which had passed the House but was pending in the Senate.

The ranks of Democratic supporters, meanwhile, dwindled to 21 — about half the number that supported the failed 1997 effort to extend fast track under Clinton. Many members of the pro-trade New Democrat Coalition said the bill was out of date, focusing on manufacturing and agriculture rather than on issues such as antitrust and intellectual

property. They also were concerned that U.S. laws on the environment, antitrust, and food safety were becoming vulnerable to challenge as "non-tariff barriers to trade," raising the possibility that they could be nullified by trade pacts.

Other Democrats said they could not support the bill without first passing an economic stimulus measure (HR 3090) that GOP leaders were promising would include help for workers laid off after Sept. 11. Nor were Democrats satisfied with a separate bill (HR 3008), passed 420-3, earlier in the day to expand Trade Adjustment Assistance designed to retrain and relocate workers displaced by trade actions. (*House vote 477, p. H-164*)

Senate Committee Action

After waiting for the House vote, the Finance Committee met Dec. 12 to approve its version of the bill (HR 3005 — S Rept 107-139). The 18-3 vote belied the undercurrent of dissatisfaction with the bill and with the manner in which it was handled.

Baucus and Grassley — by then, chairman and ranking member of the committee, respectively — presented a bill based on the House measure, with minor changes to make it more palatable to Democrats in the areas of labor, congressional review and dumping. They made it clear they would reject all amendments, putting off for the floor contentious issues such as Democrats' demands for much tougher labor and dumping provisions.

The initial markup was cut short by Robert C. Byrd, D-W.Va., who invoked a procedural rule cutting off committee discussion two hours after the Senate had convened. Byrd said he took the action because he had been denied a

chance to go before the committee and argue against the bill, which he said would undermine Congress' constitutional authority on trade pacts.

The hasty markup generated so much Democratic dissent that Baucus quickly scheduled a second session. Among the most frustrated was John Kerry, D-Mass., who had come with amendments to tighten labor and environmental provisions, as well as on aid to displaced workers.

The following three amendments were considered when the committee met again Dec. 18; all were rejected by voice vote:

• A proposal by Kerry to change a NAFTA provision that allowed foreign companies to file lawsuits against U.S. states and cities if their laws or ordinances were thought to impede trade. Kerry wanted to deny foreign investors greater protection than was available to U.S. investors.

• An amendment by Kent Conrad, D-N.D., to give the Finance and Ways and Means committees 10 days to review pending trade agreements before the U.S. trade representative could sign them.

• A second Conrad amendment to allow corrections to be made to a trade agreement when mistakes were discovered, even if Congress had already approved it.

Daschle already had announced he would not bring the bill to the Senate floor until 2002, but even ardent fast-track opponents conceded Bush would ultimately win. "It's passed. It passed the House; it's going to pass the Senate," said John D. Rockefeller IV, D-W.Va., who was angry over the administration's lack of action against countries that dumped low-priced steel on the U.S. market. "All we have now is to fight on the edges," he said. ◆

U.S.-Jordan Trade Bill Clears

With the Bush administration portraying trade as a key component in building a coalition against terrorism, Congress on Sept. 24 cleared a long-delayed bill implementing the 2000 U.S.-Jordan trade pact (HR 2603 — PL 107-43). The pact was the first U.S. bilateral trade agreement to include labor and environmental requirements.

House Republicans and Senate Democrats guided the legislation, which authorized the necessary changes in U.S. tariff laws, through the House Ways and Means and Senate Finance committees July 26. GOP reluctance to endorse the pact because of the environmental and labor provisions was mostly alleviated by an exchange of letters on July 23 between U.S. Trade Representative Robert B. Zoellick and his Jordanian counterpart, Ambassador Marwan Muasher, in which both sides pledged to avoid the use of sanctions in enforcing provisions. Though they were wary of the letters, Democrats praised the pact as setting a precedent.

BoxScore

Bill:
HR 2603 — PL 107-43

Legislative Action:

House passed HR 2603 (H Rept 107-176, Part 1) by voice vote July 31.

Senate cleared HR 2603 by voice vote Sept. 24.

President signed Sept. 28.

The House passed the bill easily July 31, but Sen. Phil Gramm, R-Texas, vowed to block it unless the labor and environmental provisions were dropped altogether. Gramm finally withdrew his objections after Sept. 11, but the hopes of free-trade advocates that the bill would smooth the way for enactment of a broader measure guaranteeing expedited treatment for trade agreements did not materialize. (*Trade, p. 19-3*)

Highlights

The bill changed U.S. laws to conform to the trade agreement, which contained the following elements:

• **Tariffs.** The United States and Jordan agreed to eliminate tariffs on virtually all trade between the two countries over 10 years.

• **Labor standards.** Both countries agreed to abide by core labor standards and pledged not to lower those standards to enhance trade.

• **Environmental protection.** The two countries agreed to eliminate tariffs on environmental goods and to avoid lowering environmental laws to promote trade.

• **Services.** Jordan agreed to give U.S. companies access to the services sector. Jordanian service companies already had full access to the U.S. market.

Background

The U.S.-Jordan Free Trade Agreement was negotiated by the Clinton administration and signed Oct. 24, 2000. Although trade with Jordan was relatively minimal, totalling just $386 million in 2000, Democrats saw the pact as a major breakthrough: It was the first time bilateral commitments on workplace and environmental rules were included in the text of a U.S. bilateral trade agreement, making them enforceable by sanctions. Most Republicans opposed the provisions, arguing that trade pacts were not appropriate vehicles for addressing social policy issues.

Reluctant to set such a precedent, the Bush administration refrained from submitting the pact to the 107th Congress for months. It did so only after the exchange of letters in which the two countries stated that, given "the wide range of our bilateral ties and the spirit of collaboration that characterizes our relations," they would seek to resolve any differences about the agreement through means "that will help to secure compliance without recourse to traditional sanctions."

House GOP leaders hoped the bill would serve as a confidence-building measure to spur negotiations with centrist Democrats on Bush's top trade goal, renewal of fast-track negotiating authority. Fast track, which the new administration had renamed "trade promotion authority," guaranteed that Congress would accept or reject trade agreements but would not try to alter them. Democrats wanted to require the inclusion of sanctions to enforce workplace and environmental commitments under such pacts; Republicans were equally determined that such issues not be subject to sanctions. House Ways and Means Committee Chairman Bill Thomas, R-Calif., hoped the example of the Jordan pact would reassure both sides.

After the Sept. 11 attacks, administration officials pressed for quick enactment of the bill, arguing that trade was a key element in the campaign to build a global coalition against terrorism, and stressing the importance of Jordan's King Abdullah as a Muslim ally in the effort.

Legislative Action

House Committee Action

Following the exchange of letters, Thomas introduced the bill on July 24 and won voice vote approval in the committee two days later (HR 2603 — H Rept 107-176, Part 1).

Thomas called the letters "a prerequisite for moving the legislation," and added that it should serve as a "flashlight in the darkness" as lawmakers searched for common ground on trade promotion authority. But many Democrats disagreed. Sander M. Levin of Michigan, the ranking Democrat on the Ways and Means Trade Subcommittee and the leading voice

in his party on trade, called the letters "unfortunate, unwise and unnecessary."

"You really made unnecessary the whole idea of fast track," Democrat Jim McDermott of Washington said during the markup. McDermott said that rather than giving Congress a way to help shape trade agreements, as Democrats said any fast-track grant should, the letters showed that the Bush administration's philosophy was, "If we don't like something, we'll just take it out."

House Floor Action

The House passed the bill by voice vote July 31 under suspension of the rules, a procedure allowing no amendments.

Senate Committee Action

The Senate Finance Committee approved a companion bill (S 643 — S Rept 107-59) by voice vote July 26. It was the second try. Chairman Max Baucus, D-Mont., had called a markup on July 17, hoping for quick action on the bill, but dissatisfied Republicans refused to stay long enough to give him a quorum. Gramm and other Republicans who adamantly opposed the use of sanctions for violations of labor or environmental commitments took scant comfort from the non-binding letters exchanged between Zoellick and Muasher. Calling the letters "comical and insulting," Gramm said the Jordan agreement's provisions could threaten U.S. sovereignty and tie Congress' and the president's hands by allowing other countries to penalize the United States for its workplace or environmental laws. He promised to hold up the bill until the provisions were dropped altogether.

Republicans also were annoyed at Baucus for supporting the revival of fast-track authority in principle but declining to set a timetable for moving such a bill. Baucus was able to persuade Frank H. Murkowski, R-Alaska, to withdraw an amendment that would have attached trade negotiating authority provisions to the Jordan bill.

For the rest of the week, Baucus was unable to obtain the unanimous consent required for the committee to meet informally to cast such a vote.

Senate Floor Action

After Sept. 11, the administration treated trade — especially with Middle East allies — as a key part of the anti-terrorism agenda. At the urging of Zoellick and national security adviser Condoleezza Rice, Gramm cautiously dropped his objections, and the Senate passed the House U.S.-Jordan trade bill (HR 2603) by voice vote Sept. 24, clearing the measure for Bush's signature.

"I am doing this today because we have a crisis in the world," Gramm said. "We need to reaffirm our relationship with Jordan, a critical country in a very important part of the world, when we are at this very moment beginning to look toward a war with terrorism." But he and other Republicans insisted the measure would not set a precedent for future negotiations or for a fast-track bill.

Democrats disagreed. "I hope that by including labor and environmental provisions in the Jordan agreement, we will set a precedent for future trade agreements," Baucus said. ◆

No Deal on High-Tech Exports

A long-standing conflict over which agencies should control exports of "dual-use" technologies stymied efforts to rewrite the nation's export control laws in the first session. Dual-use items are those with both civilian and military applications. The latest standoff pitted a Senate more sympathetic to high-tech exporters against a House that was split between lawmakers who focused on commerce and those whose top priority was national security.

The Senate passed a bill (S 149) on Sept. 6 that aimed to relax existing restrictions and put the Commerce Department in charge of export controls. The House International Relations Committee approved a measure (HR 2581) Aug. 1 that sought to tighten export restrictions and give more control to the State and Defense departments. Before that bill could come to the floor, however, it faced scrutiny from at least four other panels: Agriculture, Armed Services, Energy and Commerce, and Select Intelligence.

Both bills included tougher penalties for willful violations of export curbs. In return, both would remove existing restrictions on items that could be readily obtained abroad or were being mass-marketed domestically. And both would allow the president to override those exceptions for national security or foreign policy reasons.

The Export Administration Act (PL 96-72) had expired in 1994. Export controls had been kept in place since then by short-term extensions and executive order. The export control law allowed the executive branch to block the export of high-tech equipment, such as supercomputers, high-accuracy machine tools and semiconductor manufacturing equipment, that could be used to construct advanced weapons or weapons of mass destruction. Technology industry lobbyists said the export control system was out of date and harmful to U.S. businesses, often blocking the export of devices readily available on world markets.

With no consensus in sight on how to rewrite the law, the House passed two temporary extensions, neither of which was taken up by the Senate.

Background

Despite revolutionary advancements in technology, the law regulating exports of dual-use technology had not been rewritten in 22 years. Congress had tried off and on for seven years to update the Cold War-era law but was unable to reconcile the demands of the high-tech industry — which wanted looser restrictions, especially on technologies that were available to mass-market consumers — and defense hawks — who feared that looser restrictions would allow U.S. technologies to reach hostile nations such as Iran, Iraq and Libya.

After the last authorization lapsed in 1994, President

BoxScore

Bills:
S 149, HR 2581
Legislative Action:
House International Relations Committee approved HR 2581 (H Rept 107-297, Part 1), 26-7, on Aug. 1.
Senate passed S 149 (S Rept 107-10), 85-14, on Sept. 6.

Bill Clinton regulated exports of dual-use technology through executive orders and waivers. Interest in reauthorizing the act was revived after allegations in 1998 that China had improved its long-range missiles with technology gleaned from launching U.S. commercial satellites. But several Senate committee chairmen blocked the legislation on both national security and jurisdictional grounds. (*1999 Almanac, p. 23-9*)

Instead, a stopgap reauthorization (PL 106-508) was enacted in 2000, but it was due to expire in August and did not include the tougher penalties for export violations that sponsors said were needed. (*2000 Almanac, p. 20-27*)

Supporters of a long-term fix for the system argued that the extensions provided by executive order did not carry as much authority as the original Export Administration Act. For example, the International Emergency Economic Powers Act (PL 95-223), which provided the authority Clinton used as the basis for his orders, had lower penalties for civil and criminal violations than did the Export Administration Act. (*1977 Almanac, p. 412*)

A bipartisan group of Senate Banking panel members reintroduced the more expansive bill in January, hopeful that President Bush would help advance their cause. During his campaign, Bush endorsed the idea of a new export control system with tighter controls for "truly sensitive" technologies and lower barriers for those that were widely available.

Legislative Action

Senate Committee Action

The Senate Banking Committee approved a bill (S 149 — S Rept 107-10) on March 22 to reauthorize the export control law for at least three years. The legislation, approved 19-1, proposed an entirely new set of export controls, eliminating restrictions on the export of technologies that were mass-marketed or otherwise widely available, while significantly increasing penalties for those who knowingly violated the remaining controls. "We have to build a higher fence around a smaller number of things," said Chairman Phil Gramm, R-Texas. He described the measure as finding an appropriate balance between protecting national security and enabling the nation's technology companies to be robust international competitors.

Top administration officials had met with Banking Committee members in the preceding months to suggest changes in the legislation, including giving the president the ability to bar exports of specific technologies when he decided their shipment abroad would pose a national security risk.

"The biggest change we made was putting in a provision that the president has the final say-so on everything," said Michael B. Enzi, R-Wyo., the bill's chief Senate proponent. "We thought if we had that, along with an endorsement from the administration, it would solve all the problems."

The administration did its part March 21, when national security adviser Condoleezza Rice sent Gramm a letter declaring: "With these changes, [the bill] represents a positive step towards the reform of the U.S. export control system supported by the president." Supporters hoped White House support would give the legislation new life.

The committee gave voice vote approval to an amendment by Robert F. Bennett, R-Utah, to repeal a requirement in the fiscal 1998 defense authorization law (PL 105-85) to use a measurement of "millions of theoretical operations per second" (MTOPS) in determining where computers could be exported. Bennett noted that the Defense Department, General Accounting Office and Defense Science Board had concluded that the MTOPS system was obsolete and no longer valid as a means of measuring a computer's power.

A separate amendment approved by voice vote would terminate the law in September 2004 if the administration had not reported to Congress by then on the statute's effectiveness.

Senate Floor Action

The Senate passed the bill, 85-14, on Sept. 6. (*Senate vote 275, p. S-57*)

Attempts to bring the measure up earlier in the year had been blocked by Richard C. Shelby, R-Ala., chairman of the Intelligence Committee. Shelby, along with the chairmen of the Armed Services, Foreign Relations and Commerce and Governmental Affairs committees, said the bill would compromise U.S. defense interests for commercial goals.

But after concluding that passage by a large majority was inevitable — the bill had the enthusiastic backing of both party leaderships, as well as the Bush administration — a handful of defense hawks cut several deals on language they said would better protect national security. They then allowed the bill to come to a vote, although the changes they secured were insufficient to win their support.

"It is a more dangerous world out there than ever before, and we've got to be more careful than ever that we don't export dangerous items to dangerous people," said Republican Fred Thompson of Tennessee. "The interest of national security dwarfs — dwarfs — the interests of trade and commerce."

A Sept. 4 test vote signaled that senators had little appetite for such an approach, however. By 74-19, the Senate tabled (killed) a Thompson amendment to lengthen the timetable for agencies to review applications for export licenses. (*Senate vote 274, p. S-57*)

With the bill headed for passage, Thompson and fellow opponents quickly negotiated whatever changes they could. After hours of meetings with the bill's sponsors, they won voice-vote adoption of two amendments. One, by Thompson, narrowed the range of products that would be decontrolled because of their availability abroad. The amendment changed the bill's definition of foreign availability so that only technologies of "comparable quality" to those produced in the United States would trigger the removal of export restrictions.

The other, by Jon Kyl, R-Ariz., would give Commerce authority to cut off exports of sensitive technologies to countries that refused to supply information verifying the uses of the items once they had been shipped.

Sponsors and critics agreed to write joint letters to the president on two issues they could not resolve. They agreed to ask the administration to review its policies on "deemed exports" — sensitive information passed to foreign nationals — and develop new regulations to deal with them. They also agreed to request that national security agencies have a greater role in the process of classifying high-tech products.

Opponents also wanted the bill to create a commission to study the national security implications of U.S. high-tech export policy. The proposal died in a dispute over who should appoint the members and what their specific mandate should be.

House Committee Action

The House International Relations Committee approved a multi-year extension (HR 2581 — H Rept 107-297, Part 1), by a vote of 26-7, on Aug. 1.

But the panel's debate made clear that the standoff between those primarily interested in furthering commerce and those whose top priority was national security had not abated in the seven years since the most recent long-term version of the law (PL 96-72) expired. The committee adopted 25 amendments to tighten the regulation of dual-use exports and to bolster the Defense and State departments' roles in decisions about which technologies could be exported, and to what countries.

"Part of our job is not only to ensure that commerce flows merrily along, but that we take care to provide for the common defense," said Chairman Henry J. Hyde, R-Ill., who joined with ranking Democrat Tom Lantos of California to push many of the amendments.

Robert Menendez, D-N.J., described the altered House bill as "so overwhelmingly weighted in a defense-oriented proposition that it strangulates the commercial enterprises." Rather than wage an uphill fight to try to minimize the changes, however, he said he decided to allow the bill to emerge from the committee "as bad as possible."

The panel accepted only one amendment to relax export controls. Adopted by voice vote, it would shift control over satellite exports from State back to Commerce. Control was handed to State in 1999, after Congress concluded that launches of U.S.-made satellites from China had given Beijing access to sensitive technologies. Sponsor Howard L. Berman, D-Calif., attributed a 30 percent drop in the U.S. share of the communications satellite market in the past year to State's decisions.

"If we destroy the commercial satellite industry in this country, we will not be able to build military satellites," said Dana Rohrabacher, R-Calif., who was otherwise an advocate of the tighter national security controls.

Other amendments included proposals by:

• Hyde, adopted 29-5, to ease the test the president had to apply before overriding a decision by Commerce and preventing an export.

• Lantos, adopted 25-8, to bar export of torture devices or untested pharmaceutical products for the purpose of human experimentation abroad.

• Hyde, adopted 30-7, to restrict exports of items that the State, Defense and Commerce departments agreed could contribute to the proliferation of weapons of mass destruction or undermine the regional stability of the United States or a U.S. ally.

Short-Term Extension

To buy time for the broader bill, the House passed a three-month extension (HR 2602), good through Nov. 20, by voice vote July 30. But Enzi objected to clearing the stopgap bill, saying it would be better to let the statute lapse while Congress debated a long-term rewrite. Majority Leader Tom Daschle, D-S.D., agreed.

On Aug. 17, Bush used his powers under the International Emergency Economic Powers Act to signed a new executive order regulating high-tech exports.

With four additional committees still to act on the multiyear House bill (HR 2581), the House on Nov. 27 passed by voice vote a fresh short-term measure (HR 3189) to extend the Export Administration Act through April 20, 2002. Sponsors said they wanted to prevent the export of technology, such as supercomputers, high-accuracy machine tools and semiconductor manufacturing equipment, that could be used to make advanced weapons.

Supporters argued that the Sept. 11 terrorist attacks made it more urgent to extend the law, but Enzi again insisted he would rather see the law lapse than support another short-term extension. ◆

China Keeps Normal Trade Status

The House decisively rejected an attempt in July to suspend normal trade relations with China for a year. Congress had agreed in 2000 to grant China permanent status as a normal U.S. trading partner once it had joined the World Trade Organization (WTO). China had not yet been admitted to the WTO, however, and that put the issue back on the congressional agenda.

Because of the delay in the WTO's action, President Bush granted yet another one-year waiver of a 1974 law restricting normal trade relations with certain communist countries. The waiver — and with it, normal trade status — had been granted to Beijing each year since 1980.

Bush's action triggered what had become an annual debate in Congress on China's economic, military, labor and human rights policies. The immediate focus was a resolution to disapprove of the presidential waiver. Although Congress was never expected to agree to the resolution, the debate allowed lawmakers to address several contentious issues on the House floor. Topping the list was the collision of a Navy surveillance plane and a Chinese military jet over the South China Sea on April 1, and the subsequent 10-day detention of 24 U.S. crew members. The incarceration of several Chinese-born U.S. scholars, continued human rights abuses and concern regarding Chinese treatment of Taiwan also provoked controversy.

Background

Chinese goods had entered the United States under reduced tariff rates since 1980, after President Jimmy Carter re-established trade ties with Beijing. Under the Jackson-Vanik amendment to the 1974 Trade Act (PL 93-618), the president had to renew the low rates annually. However, the WTO, established in 1995, required member nations to grant one another's products "permanent normal trade relations status," unless they were willing to forgo the benefits of

BoxScore

Bill:

H J Res 50

Legislative Action:

House rejected H J Res 50, 169-259, on July 19.

more open trade with a particular country. In November 1999, U.S. Trade Representative Charlene Barshefsky and Chinese Premier Zhu Rongji reached an agreement to drastically cut tariffs, quotas and other trade barriers on U.S. exports to China. In return, the United States agreed to support China's entry into the WTO.

To fulfill that agreement, President Bill Clinton sought legislation from Congress that would remove China permanently from the list of communist countries subject to Jackson-Vanik. With strong support from business leaders — particularly those in the high-tech and agriculture sectors — a skeptical House and a generally gridlocked Senate cleared a bill in 2000 (PL 106-286) that permanently applied the same low tariff rates to Chinese imports as those already applied to goods from all but a handful of countries. The new trade status was to take effect once China joined the WTO. (*2000 Almanac, p. 20-3*)

The need for one more annual waiver — due to the delay in China's WTO entry — seemed like a formality as the 107th Congress began. But the surveillance plane incident brought a wave of anger in Congress. Vote counters in both parties said the House might vote to disapprove of the waiver, though the Senate seemed likely to stand pat. By midsummer, tensions over the incident had waned noticeably, and the resolution instead became the vehicle for a lively debate over China's human rights record and foreign policy.

Meanwhile, Chinese and WTO negotiators managed to resolve differences — particularly over the degree to which China was allowed to subsidize its agricultural sector — and China was admitted into the WTO on Nov. 11.

Legislative Action

The House rejected the resolution of disapproval (H J Res 50) by a vote of 169-259 on July 19. The Ways and

Means Committee had reported the resolution unfavorably on July 12. *(House vote 255, p. H-90)*

Although GOP leaders signaled that they were using the vote to gauge support for other elements of Bush's trade agenda, primarily his bid to regain fast-track negotiating authority, most members viewed it more as a referendum on China in particular than on globalization in general.

"This is a very free vote for members now," said Robert T. Matsui of California, who led the effort to win the votes of fellow Democrats for the permanent trade relationship with China in 2000. "I think all the other trade bills are separate."

Opponents such as Bill Pascrell Jr., D-N.J., condemned China's human rights record. Pascrell urged his colleagues to "take a small step, a temporary step and revoke" Beijing's trade status.

But free-trade advocates argued that advances by U.S. trade negotiators to pave the way for China to join the WTO rendered pointless the need to suspend the relationship for a few weeks. "Passage of this would be not only ironical, but possibly counterproductive," Sander M. Levin, D-Mich., said. "We need to continue the path that we have set: one of active engagement, but also of vigorous alertness and pressure."

Still, some said they were inspired by the stopgap nature of the decision to use their vote to signal distaste for China's record of religious and political repression, the recent detention of Chinese scholars with U.S. ties on espionage charges and Beijing's behavior over the surveillance plane incident in April. "I recognize that this is largely a symbolic action,"

said Benjamin L. Cardin, D-Md., who had voted for the law to create permanent normal trade relations, previously known as most favored nation (MFN) status. But "standing on its own, using human rights as a test . . . China is not entitled to have MFN status," Cardin added.

In addition to Cardin, 20 other members who had voted for permanent normal trade in 2000 voted for the resolution. However, 39 lawmakers who opposed the permanent grant in 2000 swung the other way and voted to support the one-year extension. Bob Clement, D-Tenn., had argued that a permanent trade relationship would deprive the United States of a key means of leverage over China. This time, he argued that "a policy of principled, purposeful engagement with China remains the best way to advance U.S. interests."

Staunch critics of China used the same arguments they had made for years against engaging the communist nation. Dana Rohrabacher, R-Calif., who sponsored the resolution of disapproval, said lawmakers should support it "to protect our country's national security, as well as to call attention to the gross violations that now are taking place on the mainland of China."

Majority Whip Tom DeLay, R-Texas, did not vote on the trade resolution, but he gave the House an additional chance to register dismay with China. On July 18, the day before the vote, he won adoption, 424-6, of an amendment to the State Department appropriations bill (HR 2500) to prevent funds from being spent to compensate China for costs associated with its detention of the U.S. crew of the surveillance plane. *(House vote 241, p. H-86)* ◆

Vietnam Trade Agreement Clears

Congress readily cleared legislation allowing the president to extend normal trade relations to Vietnam on an annual basis, thus implementing a U.S.-Vietnam bilateral trade agreement reached in 2000. Vietnam's National Assembly ratified the agreement Nov. 28, 2001.

The legislation effectively approved a trade agreement brokered by the Clinton administration in July 2000. Such approval was required under the Jackson-Vanik amendment to the 1974 Trade Act (PL 93-618) before the president could extend normal trade status to certain communist countries, including Vietnam. President Bush signed the measure (H J Res 51 — PL 107-52) on Oct. 16.

Although trade with Vietnam was minimal, the measure's easy enactment symbolized a new level of cordiality between the two former enemies. Since 1998, Vietnam had received narrower, annual waivers effectively allowing federal aid to flow to U.S. companies doing business there. A joint resolution that would have overturned the latest such waiver (H J Res 55) was rejected by the House on June 26.

Shortly before passing the normal trade relations measure

BoxScore

Bill:
H J Res 51 — PL 107-52
Legislative Action:
House passed H J Res 51
(H Rept 107-198) by voice
vote Sept. 6.
Senate cleared H J Res 51,
88-12, on Oct. 3.
President signed Oct. 16.

Sept. 6, the House expressed its concern over Vietnam's human rights record by making non-humanitarian aid conditional on substantial improvements. The Senate did not act on that measure.

Background

The United States imposed a trade embargo on Vietnam during the Vietnam War, and most tariffs remained prohibitively high for a quarter century. But since the early 1990s, the United States had taken a number of steps to improve relations with Vietnam.

Citing the progress made in accounting for prisoners of war and servicemen missing in action, President Bill Clinton lifted the trade embargo in 1994. A liaison office was opened later that year, and in 1995 diplomatic relations were re-established.

Normalizing U.S. trade with Vietnam was viewed as an important step in bringing that country fully into the world community. In July 2000, Clinton concluded an agreement with Vietnam to allow goods from that country to receive the same favorable tariff treatment as those from all but five

countries: Afghanistan, Cuba, North Korea, Laos and Yugoslavia. In return, Vietnam pledged to take a number of steps to open its markets for U.S. goods. The agreement did not cover textiles and apparel. Bush submitted the agreement to Congress for approval on June 8.

Under the 1974 Jackson-Vanik amendment, the president could waive provisions barring favorable tariff treatment for goods from a communist country; the waiver was only good for one year, and Congress had 60 days to block it using expedited rules. To qualify for such a waiver, a country had to have a trade agreement with the United States. (*1974 Almanac, p. 553*)

The U.S.-Vietnam bilateral trade agreement signed in 2000 was a three-year pact, with automatic extensions after that unless either party renounced the agreement. Each extension required presidential determination that Vietnam was satisfactorily providing reciprocal trade treatment to U.S. exports. Vietnam agreed to take five major steps regarding U.S. goods, services and investment: lower its own tariffs, eliminate non-tariff barriers, protect U.S. intellectual property rights, open its markets to U.S. service and investment companies and make its labor force available to U.S. manufacturing ventures.

Trade with Vietnam was not especially valuable in economic terms. In 2000, U.S. imports from Vietnam totaled $822 million and U.S. exports totaled $368 million — combined, just one-twentieth of 1 percent of all trade by the United States.

Legislative Action

House Action

The House Ways and Means Committee approved a one-year grant of nondiscriminatory trade treatment to products from Vietnam (H J Res 51 — H Rept 107-198) by voice vote July 26.

The full House passed the measure by voice vote Sept. 6. Immediately beforehand, members voted 410-1 to pass a bill (HR 2833) that would prohibit non-humanitarian aid to Vietnam unless the president certified to Congress that Hanoi had made substantial progress on human rights. (*House vote 335, p. H-114*)

While some members, such as Jennifer Dunn, R-Wash., said it was time to stop thinking about Vietnam as a war, others — like Michael R. McNulty, D-N.Y., whose brother was killed in Vietnam — argued that the country had not done an adequate job of accounting for missing U.S. personnel.

In separate action, the House on July 26 rejected a measure (H J Res 55) that would have voided an executive order by Bush allowing U.S. companies doing business in Vietnam to qualify for federal aid, including import and export financing. Until normal trade ties were extended, such an order was the principal way for the president to promote trade with Vietnam. The joint resolution was defeated, 91-324. (*House vote 275, p. H-98*)

Senate Action

The Senate Finance Committee approved its version of the legislation allowing non-discriminatory tariffs on Vietnamese goods (S J Res 16 — S Rept 107-49) by voice vote July 17. The measure was shepherded through by two prominent Vietnam War veterans — Democrat John Kerry of Massachusetts and Republican John McCain of Arizona — who argued that the legislation would encourage one of the last remaining communist nations to move toward a market-based system.

The Senate took up the House-passed measure Oct. 3 and cleared it, 88-12. Debate was minimal, and those voting against the proposal generally fell into two camps: those who argued that Vietnam's human rights record did not yet merit the reward of normal U.S. trade relations, and those who wanted to use their vote to signal displeasure with the federal regulation of fish imported from Vietnam. (*Senate vote 291, p. S-61*)

Senators from the Mississippi Delta lambasted a decision by the Food and Drug Administration to allow basa fish from the Mekong Delta to be labeled catfish, a move that helped create a surge in low-priced imports of that species at the expense of domestic catfish farmers. ◆

Chapter 20

TRANSPORTATION

Airlines Get $15 Billion in Aid

Within two weeks of the Sept. 11 terrorist attacks, Congress cleared and the president signed a $15 billion package to help stabilize the nation's airline industry. The bill provided $5 billion in cash and up to $10 billion in loan guarantees. President Bush signed it into law (HR 2926 — PL 107-42) on Sept. 22.

The measure limited the liability of the two airlines whose planes were used in the attacks and created a new system in the Justice Department through which victims of the crashes and their families could receive compensation. The funding was classified as mandatory spending, essentially an entitlement. The bill did not include $3 billion requested by the administration for airline and airport security improvements, but it stated Congress' commitment to act quickly on the issue and affirmed Bush's announced decision to use $3 billion of the $40 billion in emergency appropriations enacted Sept. 18 for airport security (PL 107-38).

Republicans stymied efforts by Democrats and organized labor to include help for as many as 100,000 airline employees who faced layoffs in the aftermath of the attacks. House Speaker J. Dennis Hastert, R-Ill., and Minority Leader Richard A. Gephardt, D-Mo., said legislation to address labor issues would be on the floor the week of Sept. 24. Though help for displaced workers became part of an economic stimulus bill (HR 3090) passed by the House in October, that measure remained stalled at the end of the year.

BoxScore

Bill:
HR 2926 — PL 107-42
Legislative Action:
House passed HR 2926, 356-54, on Sept. 21.
Senate cleared HR 2926 by voice vote Sept. 21, after passing an identical bill (S 1450), 96-1.
President signed Sept. 22.

Highlights

The main elements of the airline assistance bill were:

● **Cash assistance.** $5 billion in immediate cash assistance — $4.5 billion for passenger airlines and $500 million for cargo carriers — to compensate for losses stemming from the Sept. 11 attacks, including the shutdown of the nation's air system and any incremental losses incurred through the end of the year.

To receive cash aid, airlines had to provide proof of their losses to the Transportation Department and General Accounting Office (GAO). Payments were to be based on the lesser of either actual losses or a pro-rata share based on a carrier's percentage of industrywide mileage multiplied by its seats or cargo tonnage.

● **Loan guarantees.** Up to $10 billion in loan guarantees or other credit assistance to passenger airlines. A four-member Air Transportation Stabilization Board — composed of the secretary of Transportation, Federal Reserve chairman, secretary of the Treasury, and comptroller general of the GAO — was created to review and approve applications. Airlines were eligible only if they agreed to freeze compensation for their top executives for two years.

● **Airline liability.** Limited liability for American Airlines and United Airlines, whose aircraft were hijacked. The airlines were made liable for deaths and property damage on the ground due to the attacks only up to the limits of their insurance. All lawsuits against the two airlines were routed through a single federal court — the U.S. District Court for the Southern District of New York.

● **Victim compensation.** Those injured in the attacks and the families of those killed (including people on the four aircraft and those on the ground) could seek compensation through one of two mechanisms — through lawsuits filed in the federal court or through a new Justice Department compensation program to be administered by a special master appointed by the attorney general. The special master had to determine compensation levels for claimants within 120 days of the time a claim was filed. Claimants did not have to prove negligence of any party. Upon filing a claim, however, individuals waived their right to seek any compensation through lawsuits filed in federal court.

● **Future liability.** The Transportation Department could limit the liability of U.S. airlines in any terrorist attacks within the following six months to $100 million, with the federal government assuming responsibility for the rest.

● **Aircraft insurance.** For the next six months, the Transportation Department could use funds from the federal aviation "war risk" insurance program to reimburse U.S. airlines for higher insurance premiums resulting from the Sept. 11 attacks. Following the attacks, many insurance companies notified airlines of huge premium increases. The war risk insurance program provides federal insurance to commercial aircraft that fly overseas into high-risk areas for foreign policy and national security needs — such as to ferry troops and equipment to war zones — when commercial insurance for such flights is not available on reasonable terms. The program's revolving fund is financed by premiums paid by airlines that receive coverage under the program.

● **Airline taxes.** Interest penalties on airlines for failing to pay certain aviation taxes on time (including employment taxes, and fuel and ticket excise taxes) were waived.

Background

The U.S. airline industry had suffered major financial losses due to the economic slowdown and resulting reductions in business travel even before Sept. 11. The terrorist attacks greatly magnified those losses, threatening the continued stability and viability of the U.S. aviation system — an industry that normally constituted 10 percent of the nation's gross domestic product.

U.S. airlines were expected to lose almost $5 billion through the end of the year as a direct result of the federal government's two-day shutdown of the nation's aviation system and its immediate aftermath. Continuing deep losses were projected after that, as fearful passengers avoided air travel and airlines absorbed the costs of increased security measures. Already, Midway Airlines had gone out of business and most other airlines had slashed their flight schedules. Industry representatives estimated that total layoffs could exceed 100,000 and that several U.S. airlines might end up in bankruptcy unless they received financial aid quickly.

In a Sept. 19 letter to Treasury Secretary Paul H. O'Neill, Morgan Stanley directors Gerry Pasciucco and Nelson Walsh said the attacks had virtually closed U.S. capital markets to airlines. They said funding sources would remain closed unless Congress helped the airlines recover. "Even then, access is likely to be severely limited until the path to a more normalized airline system becomes clearer," they wrote. The airlines initially asked for a $24 billion aid package, then trimmed the amount to $17.5 billion. Negotiators from the House, Senate, White House and Transportation Department whittled that request down to $15 billion.

Legislative Action

The aviation assistance bill bypassed the normal committee process and was brought directly to the House and Senate floors. The House passed the bill, 356-54, on Sept. 21, and the Senate cleared it by voice vote the same day. The Senate had earlier passed an identical measure (S 1450), 96-1. (*House vote 348, p. H-120; Senate vote 284, p. S-60*)

An initial effort to pass an emergency aid bill in the early morning hours of Sept. 15 were blocked by members asking for more time. Others said the measure would set a bad precedent, encouraging other industries affected by the attacks to seek aid.

The package that became law was then negotiated by Roy Blunt of Missouri, the House Republicans' chief deputy whip; Senate Majority Leader Tom Daschle, D-S.D.; Senate Commerce Committee Chairman Ernest F. Hollings, D-S.C.; and Office of Management and Budget Director Mitchell E. Daniels Jr. They hoped to limit the bill to financial aid for the airlines, but faced pressure from Republicans to include liability protection for the carriers — particularly American and United — and from Democrats to protect airline workers.

A deal reached the night of Sept. 20 collapsed the next day after some lawmakers had second thoughts about protecting the airlines from liability. The administration originally proposed giving $5 billion to the airlines but without loan guarantees. Blunt said in a Sept. 21 interview that the administration offered a compromise proposal that included a board to oversee the loan guarantees and ensure that the loans did not go to airlines that were financially insolvent.

Lawmakers were emphatic that the bill not be considered a bailout for an industry that was suffering financially long before the terrorist attacks. "We ought to respond to events from Tuesday [Sept. 11] forward, not the underlying problems that the airline industry may have created for itself prior to that," said Sen. Christopher J. Dodd, D-Conn.

A number of Democrats took to the House floor to complain that the bill omitted aid for laid-off workers. "The airline industry is taking advantage of us. We're chumps," said Corrine Brown of Florida. Blunt and House Transportation Committee Chairman Don Young, R-Alaska, himself a longtime labor supporter, said Congress should first help to stabilize the airline system before addressing labor and other issues. "We have to get this done as soon as possible or we will not have an aviation system," Young said Sept. 19. ◆

Law Federalizes Airport Security

Two months after terrorists hijacked commercial airliners and crashed them into the World Trade Center and the Pentagon, President Bush went to Washington Reagan National Airport to sign sweeping aviation security legislation.

The new law (S 1447 — PL 107-71), signed Nov. 19, turned responsibility for airport security over to the federal government. Within a year, the thousands of low-wage contract workers who screened baggage and passengers in the nation's airports were to be replaced with federal employees, hired, trained and supervised by the Transportation Department. After three years, airports could hire private security firms, but only with the agreement of the Transportation Department and only if the private screeners met the same standards as federal employees. The bill also included a pilot program to try private security at five airports after the one-year phase-in period.

Transportation Secretary Norman Y. Mineta called the bill "a major milestone in the creation of a consistent, high-quality, nationwide aviation security force." The bill's final language was a victory for Ernest F. Hollings, D-S.C., chairman of the Senate Commerce, Science and Transportation Committee, who had long favored federalizing all aviation security.

The measure, written largely in negotiations among lawmakers and with the White House, did not go through committee in either chamber. The Senate acted first, unanimously passing a bill Oct. 11 that called for full federalization of airport security.

House GOP leaders, however, emphatically opposed the Senate approach. Majority Whip Tom DeLay and Majority Leader Dick Armey — both Texas Republicans — argued that federalizing the work force would not make flying safer. They said it would simply increase the rolls of labor unions that supported the Democratic Party, and expand the size and reach of government, which was anathema to conservatives. With a critical boost from Bush, House GOP leaders passed a bill Nov. 1 that gave the president the choice of hiring government employees or private contract workers.

DeLay vowed to block any bill that would make more than 20 percent of screeners federal employees.

But in the post-Sept. 11 atmosphere, the public was less interested in ideological battles than in safety, and polls indicated that a majority wanted airport screeners to be federal workers. John McCain, R-Ariz., a leading sponsor of the Senate bill, criticized House leaders' concern over expanding union rolls. "The policemen and firemen that died at the World Trade Center were union members, and I think a lot of them voted for Republicans," McCain said.

House leaders also were undercut by White House signals that, while Bush preferred their bill, he was eager for any bill and would be willing to sign the Senate measure.

After weeks of debate, the House ultimately backed down on the key issue of federalization, clearing the way for enactment of the bill.

BoxScore

Bill:
S 1447 — PL 107-71
Legislative Action:
Senate passed S 1447, 100-0, on Oct. 11.
House passed HR 3150, 286-139, on Nov. 1; it later passed S 1447 by voice vote after substituting text of HR 3150.
Senate adopted the conference report (H Rept 107-296) by voice vote Nov. 16.
House cleared the bill, 410-9, on Nov. 16.
President signed Nov. 19.

eration should be put under the Transportation or Justice department.

Major airlines, which had resisted federalization in the past, now supported the idea. "We would very much like to see the federalization of the airport screening process," said Michael D. Wascom, a spokesman for the Air Transport Association, which represented the largest carriers. "Frankly, it's time for the federal government to take that responsibility." Wascom said airlines also favored more air marshals. "This situation was of such a colossal nature, it requires a colossal response," he said. Deborah McElroy, president of the Regional Airline Association, also endorsed the concept. "This is clearly a national defense issue," she said.

Democrats and some Republicans agreed, arguing that anything less than federalization would fail to reassure the public about airline safety.

While Bush agreed that the government should take responsibility for aviation security, he did not want the more than 20,000 people who actually checked baggage and passengers to be federal employees protected by civil service rules. The White House argued it would be too difficult to discipline or fire them. For many Republicans, such an expansion of the federal work force also was in direct conflict with their goal of reducing the size of government.

Security companies and the Service Employees International Union, which represented many airport workers, lobbied against federalizing the jobs. The union representing government employees — the American Federation of Government Employees — supported the step.

Until these issues could be resolved, Bush authorized state governors to call up National Guard members and, after they were trained by the Federal Aviation Administration (FAA), station them at airport security points at federal expense. The FAA also took a number of interim steps. Only airports with tough new procedures were allowed to reopen. Vehicles had to be under greater surveillance; larger numbers of police had to be on hand. Curbside and off-site baggage check-ins were halted. Only ticketed passengers could go to gates. All knives, even plastic ones, were banned.

Highlights

The new aviation security law included provisions to:
- **Federal workers.** Federalize all airport baggage and passenger screening within one year of enactment. Airports could choose private screeners after three years.
- **Checked baggage.** Require all checked baggage to be screened within 60 days of enactment, with explosive detection systems for all checked baggage by December 2002.
- **Air marshals.** Require more armed air marshals on flights and strengthened cockpit doors.
- **Pilot program.** After the one-year phase-in period, allow one airport from each of the five federal size categories to apply to have a pilot program with private security.
- **Passenger fee.** Institute a $2.50 passenger fee per leg on commercial flights, capped at $5 per one-way trip, to help pay for new security measures.
- **Authorization.** Authorize $1.5 billion to reimburse airports for the increased costs of security since Sept. 11. It also authorized $500 million for airlines to upgrade cockpit doors; those funds had already been appropriated under the $40 billion emergency supplemental (PL 107-38) enacted Sept. 18.

Background

For years, some lawmakers and law enforcement experts had warned that airport security was inadequate, relying as it did largely on low-paid private contract workers who scanned hundreds of bags and passengers an hour. But the ability of hijackers to board the three jets used in the Sept. 11 attacks on the World Trade Center and the Pentagon, as well as a fourth jet that crashed in Pennsylvania, galvanized public and congressional opinion. The main questions became whether screeners should be federal employees or contract workers under federal supervision, and whether the op-

Prior Legislation

Under prior law, aviation security was a three-level system: The FAA provided threat information, handled security policies and regulations, and evaluated the system's effectiveness. The nation's approximately 450 commercial airports were responsible for their buildings and grounds, including providing local law enforcement and protecting secure areas. The airlines were responsible for securing their aircraft and screening passengers, baggage and freight.

The system was governed by three laws. The first, enacted in 1974 (PL 93-366), required airports to have law enforcement authorities, prohibited weapons and explosives aboard aircraft, and required screening of passengers and

baggage. (*1974 Almanac, p. 275*)

In 1990, a year and a half after Libyan terrorists brought down Pan Am Flight 103 over Lockerbie, Scotland, killing 270, Congress cleared two aviation safety bills. One (PL 101-370) extended a program that allowed the FAA to fine airlines and pilots who violated air safety guidelines. The other (PL 101-604) strengthened federal aviation security measures by creating new safety related positions in the Transportation Department, requiring new personnel standards for airport security employees and accelerating the FAA's security research program. (*1990 Almanac, p. 389*)

Six years later, Congress increased safety funding in the fiscal 1997 transportation appropriations bill (PL 104-205). The bill gave the FAA a $354 million increase for operations to hire 867 additional safety related personnel, but reduced aviation facilities and equipment spending, leaving the overall FAA spending level roughly the same as in fiscal 1996. The increased safety spending followed the fatal crashes of ValuJet Flight 592 in the Florida Everglades and TWA Flight 800 over the Atlantic Ocean off New York. (*1996 Almanac, p. 10-74*)

Legislative Action

Senate Floor Action

The Senate passed its bill (S 1447) by a unanimous vote of 100-0 the evening of Oct. 11, after nearly two weeks of deadlock on the question of airport security workers. (*Senate vote 295, p. S-62*)

Under the bill, personnel who manned checkpoints at the 142 largest of the nation's 420 commercial passenger airports would be federal employees. Smaller airports could use a combination of federal employees and state or local law enforcement officers. "There is no Swiss cheese approach here," rumbled Hollings, the bill's chief sponsor. "Every hole is covered, and we're totally federal, as far as I'm concerned."

As passed, the bill contained provisions to:

• Give the Justice Department full responsibility for airport security, from air traffic operations to baggage screening.

• Make security screeners federal employees within the Justice Department, subject to criminal background checks and a training program. They would not be able to strike.

• Require airliners to be outfitted with cockpit doors that could be opened only by the flight deck crew, and allow trained pilots to carry arms, if they chose to.

• Require federal air marshals on all domestic flights.

• Assess airlines a per passenger fee of $2.50 per flight segment to pay for the new security system.

Democrats tried to expand the bill to include financial help for laid-off aviation workers, but they gave up after failing to end debate on an amendment by Jean Carnahan, D-Mo., and Majority Leader Tom Daschle, D-S.D. The vote was 56-44, short of the 60 votes needed to invoke cloture. The amendment would have provided $1.9 billion to pay for an extra 20 weeks of unemployment benefits and 12 months of health insurance benefits for those laid off in the weeks following the Sept. 11 attacks. The proposal had been modified from a $3.1 billion package (S 1454) introduced following the attacks. (*Senate vote 293, p. S-62*)

"We've got 140,000 workers out there, and we're very concerned about them," Carnahan said Oct. 9. "They need some confidence in their lives right now, and that's the least we can do for them. They were the hardest hit, and the first hit, and I think we need to show our intent to do something by doing this now."

But Republicans objected to adding the labor provisions. "We think it's very important that this be aviation security only," said Kay Bailey Hutchison of Texas.

Democrats' withdrawal of the Carnahan amendment automatically ended consideration of a proposal by Phil Gramm, R-Texas, to allow drilling for oil and gas in Alaska's Arctic National Wildlife Refuge (ANWR). Gramm had offered his amendment in retaliation for the labor proposal.

Democrats also agreed not to pursue an amendment that would have added more than $3 billion to help Amtrak pay for better security, repair tunnels and buy new equipment. Instead, Hollings and Joseph R. Biden Jr., D-Del., introduced a bill (S 1530) to give Amtrak $3.2 billion in emergency spending and extend Amtrak's reauthorization to the end of fiscal 2003. It went no further in the first session.

The Senate bill was modified by more than 20 amendments, all adopted by voice vote. The most significant, by Republicans Conrad Burns of Montana and Mike DeWine of Ohio, put oversight of airport security in the Justice Department, rather than the Transportation Department. Others included proposals to allow, but not require, the FAA to let properly trained flight deck crew members carry firearms for self-defense, require the X-ray screening of all bags, create a deputy secretary for transportation security within the Transportation Department, and require existing airline and airport employees to undergo security checks.

A Senate GOP aide said the White House had offered a compromise that would require no more than 25 percent of the screeners to be federal employees, while giving the Transportation secretary flexibility to increase the number of federal security employees as needed. Senate Republicans countered with a minimum of 60 percent federal employees, and the same flexibility for the Transportation secretary, and the deal collapsed, the aide said.

House Floor Action

With last-minute lobbying from Bush and the strong hand of DeLay, House GOP leaders succeeded Nov. 1 in blocking the Senate bill and instead passing legislation (HR 3150) that would give Bush the option of having private or federal employees at airport checkpoints. The vote was 286-139. (*House vote 425, p. H-144*)

In the key test, the House rejected, 214-218, a Democratic substitute that contained the Senate language federalizing aviation security workers. (*House vote 423, p. H-144*)

As passed, the bill contained provisions to:

• Create a Transportation Security Administration within the Transportation Department with responsibility for security issues.

• "Deputize" security workers as federal agents, but allow the president to decide whether to use federal employees or contract workers. They would be subject to background checks and training, and would be prohibited from striking.

• Direct the newly formed security agency to take steps to secure cockpit doors, and allow trained pilots to carry arms if they chose to.

• Require airlines to collect up to $2.50 per one-way trip from passengers for the increased security.

As late as Oct. 28, White House Chief of Staff Andrew H. Card Jr. said publicly that Bush would probably sign the Senate bill if it were sent to him. "I suspect that he wouldn't want to have to sign it, but he would," Card said. But under pressure from DeLay and other House GOP leaders, Bush pitched in to actively support the leadership bill, telephoning and meeting with undecided members.

The rule for floor debate allowed the leadership to add a manager's amendment that included provisions likely to win votes. One provision, aimed at protecting credit card companies from having to refund ticket costs, required air carriers to honor tickets of airlines that had flights disrupted by the terrorist attacks or that went bankrupt. Another limited liability from the Sept. 11 attacks for Boeing Co.; the Port Authority of New York and New Jersey, which built and operated the World Trade Center; jet engine manufacturers General Electric Co. and Pratt & Whitney, and security companies that staffed the airport checkpoints through which the hijackers boarded.

The House voted, 379-50, to remove one last-minute amendment that would have partially lifted a salary cap on the top executives of airlines applying for federal aid in the wake of the terrorist attacks. (*House vote 420, p. H-144*)

Conference/Final Action

With the holidays approaching and continued public fears over air travel, House and Senate conferees agreed Nov. 15 that, within a year, baggage and passenger screening at all commercial airports would be in the hands of federal workers hired and supervised by the Transportation Department. The Senate adopted the conference report (H Rept 107-296) by voice vote Nov. 16, and the House cleared the bill later the same day, 410-9. (*House vote 448, p. H-154*)

The turning point came with the crash Nov. 12 of an American Airlines flight in Queens, New York. While the crash investigation pointed to an accident, rather than a terrorist attack, it further convinced Senate Minority Leader Trent Lott, R-Miss., who was in New York that day, that prompt action was necessary. "There was a realization that a terrorist action could happen anywhere," a Senate GOP aide recounted later. Others quickly joined the call for action. "We need to act swiftly," Marianne McInerney, executive director of the National Business Travel Association, told the Senate Governmental Affairs Committee. "Passenger traffic is now down 28 percent, and security is still not under control. Imagine what it will be like when most of those passengers return."

By Nov. 14, Lott had presented a proposal to Hollings and DeLay that developed into the centerpiece of the final deal. Lott proposed to place federalized security workers at airports for four years, after which airport authorities could choose to replace them with private screeners. The House countered with a proposal to require federal screeners for two years, and the two sides agreed to split the difference with a one-year transition to a federal work force that would be kept in place for at least two more years.

While the final bill was viewed as a victory for the Senate, House Republicans pointed to the decision to place the new security agency in the Transportation Department, rather than in Justice. They also stressed that airports would be able to opt out of the federalization plan.

Bush, too, expressed satisfaction over the choice of the Transportation Department. In a statement, he said the agreement would give the government "the flexibility to ensure a safe transition to a new aviation security system and will ultimately offer local authorities an option to employ the highest quality work force — public or private."

Under the bill:

● **Passenger and baggage screeners.** Federal screeners were to replace private contractors over a yearlong "transition" period. Three years after enactment, airport authorities could replace federal screeners with private contractors, if the Transportation Department agreed. The private screeners would have to meet the same standards as federal employees.

Airports that received permission three years after enactment to hire local police or private security companies, rather than using federal employees, would receive government grants to pay for it. If they could save money by doing so, while still meeting federal security standards, they could pocket the difference.

● **Pilot program.** In addition to allowing airports to opt out of hiring federal screeners, the bill allowed five — one in each size category based on passenger boardings — to apply to the Transportation Department to use private contract screeners. Supporters said that would enable other airports to determine whether a private or federalized security system was best and could encourage them to go with private forces. Airports that wanted to go with private screeners had to give preference to U.S.-owned companies.

● **Oversight.** The new Transportation Security Administration would focus on all modes of transportation and would be run by an undersecretary of Transportation, who would have "unprecedented" authority to set new rules, said John L. Mica, R-Fla., chairman of the House Transportation Subcommittee on Aviation.

● **Passenger fee.** The added security would be partly paid for by a $2.50 ticket fee for each leg of a flight, with a $5 limit on a one-way trip. Mica said the surcharge would raise approximately $1.6 billion a year for security upgrades, with airlines putting in up to an additional $1 billion annually.

● **Liability limits.** Conferees included the liability limits sought by the House for the Port Authority of New York and New Jersey, and for the Boeing Co. and General Electric Co. But they left out the companies that screened passengers at airports where the hijackers boarded the planes.

Some House Republicans criticized what they saw as their leaders' misguided tactics. "We, as House Republicans, had allowed this to be focused as 'Republicans hate unions and government workers,' and 'Democrats want to make this a law enforcement issue,'" said John Shadegg of Arizona, a conservative and one of nine Republicans to vote against the conference report. "We put it in a partisan or philosophical framework that party precinct workers might understand, but not the average American."

House Republican Conference Chairman J.C. Watts Jr. of Oklahoma agreed the message should have stayed on safety concerns. "Don't let this become big-government-versus-smaller-government issues," he said. "This is not what this is about. This is about safety and security for people that use the airports." ◆

Provisions of the Aviation Security Law

The following are the major provisions of the aviation security law (PL 107-71) signed by President Bush on Nov. 19.

Passenger and Bag Screeners

The new law made the federal government directly responsible for airport passenger and baggage screening, relieving the airlines of this responsibility.

• **Federal work force.** Within one year of enactment, the bill required that all airport screeners be federal employees — with airports subsequently allowed to opt out of the federal screening system and instead use private screeners.

• **Opt-out option.** Once the system was totally federalized, up to five airports would be permitted to resume use of private screeners in a two-year pilot program. At the end of that two-year period, other airports would be permitted to opt out and use non-federal screeners — provided that the Transportation Department found the airport's non-federal screeners provided an equal or higher level of security.

• **Federal supervision.** All screening activities — whether by federal employees, private contractors or state or local law enforcement — had to be supervised directly by uniformed federal officers employed by a new Transportation Security Administration. A federal law enforcement officer had to be stationed at each screening checkpoint.

• **Contractor eligibility.** Eligibility to provide private screeners at U.S. airports was limited to U.S. companies, if they were available. Companies would be barred from contracts if they violated screener hiring, training or background standards, or if repeated security failures occurred.

• **Baggage screening.** Within 60 days of enactment, all checked baggage had to be screened by X-ray equipment or other means. By the end of December 2002, all checked baggage was to be screened using explosive-detection equipment.

Employment, Training and Performance Standards

• **Citizenship requirement.** All screeners — federal or private — had to be U.S. citizens and have a functional ability to speak, read and write English.

• **Employee standards, pay.** Background and criminal history checks were required for all screeners. The law required screeners to adhere to stringent new training and performance standards, and to wear common, federally issued uniforms. Pay levels were to be set by the Transportation Department.

• **Firing.** Federal supervisors could fire individual screeners for poor performance, regardless of whether the screener was a federal employee or a contract worker.

• **No strike provision.** Federal screeners could unionize, but they were barred from striking.

• **Passenger profiling.** The Transportation Department could implement certain additional passenger and baggage screening procedures — including the enhanced use of computer profiling to screen passengers, the use of technologies that could identify persons who might pose a danger to aircraft, and the sharing of information with law enforcement and intelligence agencies to identify those on passenger lists who might be a threat.

• **"Trusted passengers."** The Transportation Department was authorized to establish requirements for airlines to implement a "trusted passenger" screening program for the expedited screening of certain regular passengers.

• **Restricted area access.** The Transportation Department, acting through its new security office, was required to conduct background and criminal history checks on all personnel authorized to enter restricted areas of an airport. All individuals and vehicles seeking access to restricted areas — including those of food-service companies — also had to be screened and inspected. The department was authorized to deploy law enforcement personnel to bolster the security of restricted areas and patrol the perimeters of airports, and to provide assistance to enhance communications among airport security personnel about potential threats.

Aircraft and Crew Security

The bill contained numerous provisions to increase security aboard commercial airlines, including requiring the Transportation Department to expand the federal air marshal program.

• **Air marshals.** Air marshals were required on all "high risk" flights. Airlines were required to provide free seating for federal air marshals, even if that meant bumping another passenger, and they had to provide free seating on a space-available basis for air marshals returning from active duty. The bill did not grant a hiring preference for laid-off airline pilots, although it waived age limitations for laid-off pilots and other airline crew members who applied to become air marshals.

• **Cockpit security.** Cockpit doors had to be fortified and locked during flights, and further restrictions had to be placed on access to an airliner's cockpit during flights.

• **Guns.** Pilots were allowed to have guns in the cockpit under certain circumstances, and law enforcement officers from other agencies could travel with guns to assist air marshals.

• **Crew communications.** The Transportation Department was authorized to develop and implement ways to equip aircraft with switches so that cabin crews could discreetly notify the pilots of hijackings, as well as with cameras or other devices to allow pilots in the cockpit to monitor activities in the aircraft cabin.

• **Transponders.** The department also was authorized to develop a way to prevent radar transponders from being turned off during a hijacking.

• **Cell phones.** Steps were required to ensure that emergency calls could be made by telephones in aircraft as well as in passenger trains.

• **Training.** Flight crews were required to get enhanced training to combat hijackers.

• **Liability exemption.** The bill exempted airline passengers and crews from legal liability for actions they might take in trying to thwart what they "reasonably believed" was a hijacking attempt, and it exempted airline employees from liability for disclosing "suspicious" activities, if done in good faith.

Transportation Security Administration

• **Agency.** The bill established a new Transportation Security Administration within the Transportation Department to be responsible for day-to-day security operations involving all modes of transportation — including civil aviation, rail, highway and water transport. The agency would be headed by an undersecretary of Transportation for security, to be appointed by the president and confirmed by the Senate.

• **Responsibilities.** The new agency was responsible for developing standards for the hiring of passenger and baggage screeners, performing background checks on screeners and persons with access to secure areas of airports, the training and testing of screeners, and directly supervising those screeners. The agency also was given responsibility for administering the federal air marshal program.

• **Oversight board.** The bill established a Transportation Securi-

ty Oversight Board — composed of representatives from the departments of Transportation, Defense, Justice and Treasury, as well as the CIA, the National Security Council and the Office of Homeland Security.

The board was given responsibility for sharing transportation intelligence information, as well as for overseeing the activities of the Transportation Security Administration.

Other Provisions

• **Passenger fees.** Passengers were required to pay a $2.50 per ticket fee each time they boarded an aircraft, with a maximum fee of $5 per one-way trip. The fee was to help pay for the federal government's cost of passenger screening.

• **Airline fees.** The Transportation Department also was authorized to collect funds from airlines, up to the amount each airline paid for security in calendar year 2000.

• **Authorization.** The measure authorized $500 million for airlines to upgrade cockpit doors and make other cockpit security improvements. The funds already had been provided from the $40 billion appropriated by Congress for emergency response (PL 107-38). The bill also authorized $1.5 billion to reimburse airports for the increased costs of security since the Sept. 11 attacks.

• **Airport improvement grants.** All primary airports were allowed to use their fiscal 2002 federal airport improvement grants for certain law enforcement expenses; general aviation airports could use their airport grants for any expense.

• **Legal liability.** The bill broadened the liability limits enacted Sept. 22 as part of the Air Transportation Safety and System Stabilization Act (PL 107-42) to companies that built the airliners involved in the terrorist attacks, as well as to companies that built airliner components, such as engines, the owners and operators of airports involved, state port authorities, and anyone with a property interest in the World Trade Center. Those parties would be liable for the resulting deaths and property damage only up to the limits of their insurance coverage. Claims against the City of New York were limited to its insurance coverage or $350 million, whichever was greater.

• **Flying schools.** The bill required background checks on all persons seeking flying lessons on certain aircraft or who sought training through flight simulators.

• **International flights.** All U.S. and foreign airlines destined for the United States had to electronically submit a detailed crew and passenger manifest to the U.S. Customs Service before landing.

• **Honoring other tickets.** For the following 18 months, airlines were required to make a practicable effort to honor the tickets of other airlines that had filed for bankruptcy. ◆

Appendix A

CONGRESS
AND ITS MEMBERS

Glossary of Congressional Terms

Act — The term for legislation once it has passed both chambers of Congress and has been signed by the president or passed over his veto, thus becoming law. Also used in parliamentary terminology for a bill that has been passed by one house and engrossed. (*Also see engrossed bill.*)

Adjournment sine die — Adjournment without a fixed day for reconvening — literally, "adjournment without a day." Usually used to connote the final adjournment of a session of Congress. A session can continue until noon Jan. 3 of the following year, when, under the 20th Amendment to the Constitution, it automatically terminates. Both chambers must agree to a concurrent resolution for either chamber to adjourn for more than three days.

Adjournment to a day certain — Adjournment under a motion or resolution that fixes the next time of meeting. Under the Constitution, neither chamber can adjourn for more than three days without the concurrence of the other. A session of Congress is not ended by adjournment to a day certain.

Amendment — A proposal by a member of Congress to alter the language, provisions or stipulations in a bill or in another amendment. An amendment usually is printed, debated and voted upon in the same manner as a bill.

Amendment in the nature of a substitute — Usually an amendment that seeks to replace the entire text of a bill by striking out everything after the enacting clause and inserting a new version of the bill. An amendment in the nature of a substitute can also refer to an amendment that replaces a large portion of the text of a bill.

Appeal — A member's challenge of a ruling or decision made by the presiding officer of the chamber. A senator can appeal to members of the Senate to override the decision. If carried by a majority vote, the appeal nullifies the chair's ruling. In the House, the decision of the Speaker traditionally has been final; seldom are there appeals to the members to reverse the Speaker's stand. To appeal a ruling is considered an attack on the Speaker.

Appropriations bill — A bill that gives legal authority to spend or obligate money from the Treasury. The Constitution disallows money to be drawn from the Treasury "but in Consequence of Appropriations made by Law."

By congressional custom, an appropriations bill originates in the House. It is not supposed to be considered by the full House or Senate until a related measure authorizing the funding is enacted. An appropriations bill grants the actual budget authority approved by the authorization bill, though not necessarily the full amount permissible under the authorization.

If the 13 regular appropriations bills are not enacted by the start of the fiscal year, Congress must pass a stopgap spending bill or the departments and agencies covered by the unfinished bills must shut down.

About half of all budget authority, notably that for Social Security and interest on the federal debt, does not require annual appropriations; those programs exist under permanent appropriations. (*Also see authorization bill, budget authority, budget process, supplemental appropriations bill.*)

Authorization bill — Basic, substantive legislation that establishes or continues the legal operation of a federal program or agency either indefinitely or for a specific period of time, or which

sanctions a particular type of obligation or expenditure. Under the rules of both chambers, appropriations for a program or agency may not be considered until the program has been authorized, although this requirement is often waived.

An authorization sets the maximum amount of funds that can be given to a program or agency, although sometimes it merely authorizes "such sums as may be necessary." (*Also see backdoor spending authority.*)

Backdoor spending authority — Budget authority provided in legislation outside the normal appropriations process. The most common forms of backdoor spending are borrowing authority, contract authority, entitlements and loan guarantees that commit the government to payments of principal and interest on loans — such as guaranteed student loans — made by banks or other private lenders. Loan guarantees result in actual outlays only when there is a default by the borrower.

In some cases, such as interest on the public debt, a permanent appropriation is provided that becomes available without further action by Congress.

Bills — Most legislative proposals before Congress are in the form of bills and are designated according to the chamber in which they originate — HR in the House of Representatives or S in the Senate — and by a number assigned in the order in which they are introduced during the two-year period of a congressional term.

"Public bills" deal with general questions and become public laws if they are cleared by Congress and signed by the president. "Private bills" deal with individual matters, such as claims against the government, immigration and naturalization cases or land titles, and become private laws if approved and signed. (*Also see private bills, resolution.*)

Bills introduced — In both the House and Senate, any number of members may join in introducing a single bill or resolution. The first member listed is the sponsor of the bill, and all subsequent members listed are cosponsors.

Many bills are committee bills and are introduced under the name of the chairman of the committee or subcommittee. All appropriations bills fall into this category. A committee frequently holds hearings on a number of related bills and may agree to one of them or to an entirely new bill. (*Also see clean bill.*)

Bills referred — After a bill is introduced, it is referred to the committee or committees that have jurisdiction over the subject with which the bill is concerned. Under the standing rules of the House and Senate, bills are referred by the Speaker in the House and by the presiding officer in the Senate. In practice, the House and Senate parliamentarians act for these officials and refer the vast majority of bills. (*Also see discharge a committee.*)

Borrowing authority — Statutory authority that permits a federal agency to incur obligations and make payments for specified purposes with borrowed money.

Budget — The document sent to Congress by the president early each year estimating government revenue and expenditures for the ensuing fiscal year.

Budget Act — The common name for the Congressional Budget and Impoundment Control Act of 1974, which established the

current budget process and created the Congressional Budget Office. The act also put limits on presidential authority to spend appropriated money. It has undergone several major revisions since 1974. (*Also see budget process, impoundments.*)

Budget authority — Authority for federal agencies to enter into obligations that result in immediate or future outlays. The basic forms of budget authority are appropriations, contract authority and borrowing authority. Budget authority may be classified by (1) the period of availability (one-year, multiple-year or without a time limitation), (2) the timing of congressional action (current or permanent) or (3) the manner of determining the amount available (definite or indefinite). (*Also see appropriations, outlays.*)

Budget process — The annual budget process was created by the Congressional Budget and Impoundment Control Act of 1974, with a timetable that was modified in 1990. Under the law, the president must submit his proposed budget by the first Monday in February. Congress is supposed to complete an annual budget resolution by April 15, setting guidelines for congressional action on spending and tax measures.

Budget rules enacted in the 1990 Budget Enforcement Act and updated in 1993 and 1997 set caps on discretionary spending through fiscal 2002. The caps could be adjusted annually to account for changes in the economy and other limited factors. In addition, pay-as-you-go (PAYGO) rules required that any tax cut, new entitlement program or expansion of existing entitlement benefits that would increase a deficit be offset by an increase in taxes or a cut in entitlement spending.

The rules held Congress harmless for budget-deficit increases that lawmakers did not explicitly cause — for example, increases due to a recession or to an expansion in the number of beneficiaries qualifying for Medicare or food stamps. PAYGO did not apply when there was a budget surplus.

If Congress exceeded the discretionary spending caps in its appropriations bills, the law required an across-the-board cut — known as a sequester — in non-exempt discretionary spending accounts. If Congress violated the PAYGO rules, entitlement programs were subject to a sequester. Supplemental appropriations were subject to similar controls, with the proviso that if both Congress and the president agreed, spending designated as an emergency could exceed the caps.

Budget resolution — A concurrent resolution that is passed by both chambers of Congress but does not require the president's signature. The measure sets a strict ceiling on discretionary budget authority, along with non-binding recommendations about how the spending should be allocated. The budget resolution may also contain "reconciliation instructions" requiring authorizing and tax-writing committees to propose changes in existing law to meet deficit-reduction goals. The Budget Committee in each chamber then bundles those proposals into a reconciliation bill and sends it to the floor. (*Also see reconciliation.*)

By request — A phrase used when a senator or representative introduces a bill at the request of an executive agency or private organization but does not necessarily endorse the legislation.

Calendar — An agenda or list of business awaiting possible action by each chamber. The House uses six legislative calendars. They are the Consent, Corrections, Discharge, House, Private and Union calendars. (*Also see individual listings.*)

In the Senate, all legislative matters reported from committee go on one calendar. They are listed there in the order in which committees report them or the Senate places them on the calendar, but they may be called up out of order by the majority leader, either by obtaining unanimous consent of the Senate or by a motion to call up a bill. The Senate also has one non-legislative calendar, which is used for treaties and nominations. (*Also see executive calendar.*)

Call of the calendar — Senate bills that are not brought up for debate by a motion, unanimous consent or a unanimous consent agreement are brought before the Senate for action when the calendar listing them is "called." Bills must be called in the order listed. Measures considered by this method usually are non-controversial, and debate on the bill and any proposed amendments is limited to five minutes for each senator.

Chamber — The meeting place for the membership of either the House or the Senate; also the membership of the House or Senate meeting as such.

Clean bill — Frequently after a committee has finished a major revision of a bill, one of the committee members, usually the chairman, will assemble the changes and what is left of the original bill into a new measure and introduce it as a "clean bill." The revised measure, which is given a new number, is referred back to the committee, which reports it to the floor for consideration. This often is a timesaver, as committee-recommended changes in a clean bill do not have to be considered and voted on by the chamber. Reporting a clean bill also protects committee amendments that could be subject to points of order concerning germaneness.

Clerk of the House — An officer of the House of Representatives who supervises its records and legislative business. Many former administrative duties were transferred in 1992 to a new position, the director of non-legislative and financial services.

Cloture — The process by which a filibuster can be ended in the Senate other than by unanimous consent. A motion for cloture can apply to any measure before the Senate, including a proposal to change the chamber's rules. A cloture motion requires the signatures of 16 senators to be introduced. To end a filibuster, the cloture motion must obtain the votes of three-fifths of the entire Senate membership (60 if there are no vacancies), except when the filibuster is against a proposal to amend the standing rules of the Senate and a two-thirds vote of senators present and voting is required.

The cloture request is put to a roll call vote one hour after the Senate meets on the second day following introduction of the motion. If approved, cloture limits each senator to one hour of debate. The bill or amendment in question comes to a final vote after 30 hours of consideration, including debate time and the time it takes to conduct roll calls, quorum calls and other procedural motions. (*Also see filibuster.*)

Committee — A division of the House or Senate that prepares legislation for action by the parent chamber or makes investigations as directed by the parent chamber.

There are several types of committees. Most standing committees are divided into subcommittees, which study legislation, hold hearings and report bills, with or without amendments, to the full committee. Only the full committee can report legislation for action by the House or Senate. (*Also see standing, oversight, select and special committees.*)

Committee of the Whole — The working title of what is formally "The Committee of the Whole House [of Representatives] on the State of the Union." The membership is composed of all House members sitting as a committee. Any 100 members who are present on the floor of the chamber to consider legislation com-

prise a quorum of the committee. Any legislation, however, must first have passed through the regular legislative or appropriations committee and have been placed on the calendar.

Technically, the Committee of the Whole considers only bills directly or indirectly appropriating money, authorizing appropriations or involving taxes or charges on the public. Because the Committee of the Whole need number only 100 representatives, a quorum is more readily attained and legislative business is expedited. Before 1971, members' positions were not individually recorded on votes taken in the Committee of the Whole.

When the full House resolves itself into the Committee of the Whole, it replaces the Speaker with a "chairman." A measure is debated and amendments may be proposed, with votes on amendments as needed. *(Also see five-minute rule.)*

When the committee completes its work on the measure, it dissolves itself by "rising." The Speaker returns, and the chairman of the Committee of the Whole reports to the House that the committee's work has been completed. At this time, members may demand a roll call vote on any amendment adopted in the Committee of the Whole. The final vote is on passage of the legislation.

In 1993 and 1994, the four delegates from the territories and the resident commissioner of Puerto Rico were allowed to vote on questions before the Committee of the Whole. If their votes were decisive in the outcome, however, the matter was automatically re-voted, with the delegates and resident commissioner ineligible. They could vote on final passage of bills or on separate votes demanded after the Committee of the Whole rises. This limited voting right was rescinded in 1995.

Committee veto — A requirement added to a few statutes directing that certain policy directives by an executive department or agency be reviewed by certain congressional committees before they are implemented. Under common practice, the government department or agency and the committees involved are expected to reach a consensus before the directives are carried out. *(Also see legislative veto.)*

Concurrent resolution — A concurrent resolution, designated H Con Res or S Con Res, must be adopted by both chambers, but it is not sent to the president for approval and, therefore, does not have the force of law. A concurrent resolution, for example, is used to fix the time for adjournment of a Congress. It is also used to express the sense of Congress on a foreign policy or domestic issue. The annual budget resolution is a concurrent resolution.

Conference — A meeting between representatives of the House and the Senate to reconcile differences between the two chambers on provisions of a bill. Members of the conference committee are appointed by the Speaker and the presiding officer of the Senate.

A majority of the conferees for each chamber must agree on a compromise, reflected in a "conference report" before the final bill can go back to both chambers for approval. When the conference report goes to the floor, it is difficult to amend. If it is not approved by both chambers, the bill may go back to conference under certain situations, or a new conference may be convened. Many rules and informal practices govern the conduct of conference committees.

Bills that are passed by both chambers with only minor differences need not be sent to conference. Either chamber may "concur" with the other's amendments, completing action on the legislation. Sometimes leaders of the committees of jurisdiction work out an informal compromise instead of having a formal conference. *(Also see custody of the papers.)*

Confirmations — *(See nominations.)*

Congressional Record — The daily, printed account of proceedings in both the House and Senate chambers, showing substantially verbatim debate, statements and a record of floor action. Highlights of legislative and committee action are given in a Daily Digest section of the Record, and members are entitled to have their extraneous remarks printed in an appendix known as "Extension of Remarks." Members may edit and revise remarks made on the floor during debate, although the House in 1995 limited members to technical or grammatical changes.

The Congressional Record provides a way to distinguish remarks spoken on the floor of the House and Senate from undelivered speeches. In the Senate, all speeches, articles and other matter that members insert in the Record without actually reading them on the floor are set off by large black dots, or bullets. However, a loophole allows a member to avoid the bulleting if he or she delivers any portion of the speech in person. In the House, undelivered speeches and other material are printed in a distinctive typeface. The record is also available in electronic form. *(Also see Journal.)*

Congressional terms of office — Terms normally begin on Jan. 3 of the year following a general election. Terms are two years for representatives and six years for senators. Representatives elected in special elections are sworn in for the remainder of a term. Under most state laws, a person may be appointed to fill a Senate vacancy and serve until a successor is elected; the successor serves until the end of the term applying to the vacant seat.

Consent Calendar — Members of the House may place on this calendar most bills on the Union or House Calendar that are considered non-controversial. Bills on the Consent Calendar normally are called on the first and third Mondays of each month. On the first occasion that a bill is called in this manner, consideration may be blocked by the objection of any member. The second time, if there are three objections, the bill is stricken from the Consent Calendar. If fewer than three members object, the bill is given immediate consideration.

A member may also postpone action on the bill by asking that the measure be passed over "without prejudice." In that case, no objection is recorded against the bill and its status on the Consent Calendar remains unchanged. A bill stricken from the Consent Calendar remains on the Union or House Calendar. The Consent Calendar has seldom been used in recent years.

Continuing resolution — A joint resolution, cleared by Congress and signed by the president, to provide new budget authority for federal agencies and programs until the regular appropriations bills have been enacted. Also known as "CRs" or continuing appropriation, continuing resolutions are used to keep agencies operating when, as often happens, Congress fails to finish the regular appropriations process by the start of the new fiscal year.

The CR usually specifies a maximum rate at which an agency may incur obligations, based on the rate of the prior year, the president's budget request or an appropriations bill passed by either or both chambers of Congress but not yet enacted.

Contract authority — Budget authority contained in an authorization bill that permits the federal government to enter into contracts or other obligations for future payments from funds not yet appropriated by Congress. The assumption is that funds will be provided in a subsequent appropriations act. *(Also see budget authority.)*

Corrections Calendar, Corrections Day — A House calendar established in 1995 to speed consideration of bills aimed at eliminating burdensome or unnecessary regulations. Bills on the Cor-

rections Calendar can be called up on the second and fourth Tuesday of each month, called Corrections Day. They are subject to one hour of debate without amendment, and require a three-fifths majority for passage. (*Also see calendar.*)

Correcting recorded votes — Rules prohibit members from changing their votes after the result has been announced. Occasionally, however, a member may announce hours, days or months after a vote has been taken that he or she was "incorrectly recorded." In the Senate, a request to change one's vote almost always receives unanimous consent, so long as it does not change the outcome. In the House, members are prohibited from changing votes if they were tallied by the electronic voting system.

Cosponsor — (*See bills introduced.*)

Current services estimates — Estimated budget authority and outlays for federal programs and operations for the forthcoming fiscal year based on continuation of existing levels of service without policy changes but with adjustments for inflation and for demographic changes that affect programs. These estimates, accompanied by the underlying economic and policy assumptions upon which they are based, are transmitted by the president to Congress when the budget is submitted.

Custody of the papers — To reconcile differences between the House and Senate versions of a bill, a conference may be arranged. The chamber with "custody of the papers" — the engrossed bill, engrossed amendments, messages of transmittal — is the only body empowered to request the conference. By custom, the chamber that asks for a conference is the last to act on the conference report.

Custody of the papers sometimes is manipulated to ensure that a particular chamber acts either first or last on the conference report. (*Also see conference.*)

Deferral — Executive branch action to defer, or delay, the spending of appropriated money. The 1974 Congressional Budget and Impoundment Control Act requires a special message from the president to Congress reporting a proposed deferral of spending. Deferrals may not extend beyond the end of the fiscal year in which the message is transmitted. A federal district court in 1986 struck down the president's authority to defer spending for policy reasons; the ruling was upheld by a federal appeals court in 1987. Congress can prohibit proposed deferrals by enacting a law doing so; most often, cancellations of proposed deferrals are included in appropriations bills. (*Also see rescission.*)

Dilatory motion — A motion made for the purpose of killing time and preventing action on a bill or amendment. House rules outlaw dilatory motions, but enforcement is largely within the discretion of the Speaker or chairman of the Committee of the Whole. The Senate does not have a rule barring dilatory motions except under cloture.

Discharge a committee — Occasionally, attempts are made to relieve a committee of jurisdiction over a bill that is before it. This is attempted more often in the House than in the Senate, and the procedure rarely is successful.

In the House, if a committee does not report a bill within 30 days after the measure is referred to it, any member may file a discharge motion. Once offered, the motion is treated as a petition needing the signatures of a majority of members (218 if there are no vacancies). After the required signatures have been obtained, there is a delay of seven days.

Thereafter, on the second and fourth Mondays of each month,

except during the last six days of a session, any member who has signed the petition must be recognized, if he or she so desires, to move that the committee be discharged. Debate on the motion to discharge is limited to 20 minutes. If the motion is carried, consideration of the bill becomes a matter of high privilege.

If a resolution to consider a bill is held up in the Rules Committee for more than seven legislative days, any member may enter a motion to discharge the committee. The motion is handled like any other discharge petition in the House. Occasionally, to expedite non-controversial legislative business, a committee is discharged by unanimous consent of the House, and a petition is not required. In 1993, the signatures on pending discharge petitions — previously kept secret — were made a matter of public record. (*For Senate procedure, see discharge resolution.*)

Discharge Calendar — The House calendar to which motions to discharge committees are referred when they have the required number of signatures (218) and are awaiting floor action. (*Also see calendar.*)

Discharge petition — (*See discharge a committee.*)

Discharge resolution — In the Senate, a special motion that any senator may introduce to relieve a committee from consideration of a bill before it. The resolution can be called up for Senate approval or disapproval in the same manner as any other Senate business. (*For House procedure, see discharge a committee.*)

Discretionary spending caps — (*See budget process.*)

Division of a question for voting — A practice that is more common in the Senate but also used in the House whereby a member may demand a division of an amendment or a motion for purposes of voting. Where an amendment or motion can be divided, the individual parts are voted on separately when a member demands a division. This procedure occurs most often during the consideration of conference reports.

Enacting clause — Key phrase in bills beginning, "Be it enacted by the Senate and House of Representatives . . ." A successful motion to strike it from legislation kills the measure.

Engrossed bill — The final copy of a bill as passed by one chamber, with the text as amended by floor action and certified by the clerk of the House or the secretary of the Senate.

Enrolled bill — The final copy of a bill that has been passed in identical form by both chambers. It is certified by an officer of the chamber of origin (clerk of the House or secretary of the Senate) and then sent on for the signatures of the House Speaker, the Senate president pro tempore and the president of the United States. An enrolled bill is printed on parchment.

Entitlement program — A federal program that guarantees a certain level of benefits to people or other entities who meet requirements set by law. Examples include Social Security and unemployment benefits. Some entitlements have permanent appropriations; others are funded under annual appropriations bills. In either case, it is mandatory for Congress to provide the money.

Executive Calendar — A non-legislative calendar in the Senate that lists presidential documents such as treaties and nominations. (*Also see calendar.*)

Executive document — A document, usually a treaty, sent to the Senate by the president for consideration or approval. Execu-

tive documents are referred to committee in the same manner as other measures. Unlike legislative documents, treaties do not die at the end of a Congress but remain "live" proposals until acted on by the Senate or withdrawn by the president.

Executive session — A meeting of a Senate or House committee (or occasionally of either chamber) that only its members may attend. Witnesses regularly appear at committee meetings in executive session — for example, Defense Department officials during presentations of classified defense information. Other members of Congress may be invited, but the public and news media are not allowed to attend.

Filibuster — A time-delaying tactic associated with the Senate and used by a minority in an effort to prevent a vote on a bill or amendment that probably would pass if voted upon directly. The most common method is to take advantage of the Senate's rules permitting unlimited debate, but other forms of parliamentary maneuvering may be used.

The stricter rules of the House make filibusters more difficult, but delaying tactics are employed occasionally through various procedural devices allowed by House rules. *(Also see cloture.)*

Fiscal year — Financial operations of the government are carried out in a 12-month fiscal year, beginning on Oct. 1 and ending on Sept. 30. The fiscal year carries the date of the calendar year in which it ends. (From fiscal 1844 to fiscal 1976, the fiscal year began July 1 and ended the following June 30.)

Five-minute rule — A debate-limiting rule of the House that is invoked when the House sits as the Committee of the Whole. Under the rule, a member offering an amendment and a member opposing it are each allowed to speak for five minutes. Debate is then closed. In practice, amendments regularly are debated for more than 10 minutes, with members gaining the floor by offering pro forma amendments or obtaining unanimous consent to speak longer than five minutes. *(Also see Committee of the Whole, hour rule, strike out the last word.)*

Floor manager — A member who has the task of steering legislation through floor debate and amendment to a final vote in the House or the Senate. Floor managers usually are chairmen or ranking members of the committee that reported the bill. Managers are responsible for apportioning the debate time granted to supporters of the bill. The ranking minority member of the committee normally apportions time for the minority party's participation in the debate.

Frank — A member's facsimile signature, which is used on envelopes in lieu of stamps for the member's official outgoing mail. The "franking privilege" is the right to send mail postage-free.

Germane — Pertaining to the subject matter of the measure at hand. All House amendments must be germane to the bill being considered. The Senate requires that amendments be germane when they are proposed to general appropriations bills or to bills being considered once cloture has been adopted or, frequently, when the Senate is proceeding under a unanimous consent agreement placing a time limit on consideration of a bill. The 1974 budget act also requires that amendments to concurrent budget resolutions be germane.

In the House, floor debate must be germane, and the first three hours of debate each day in the Senate must be germane to the pending business.

Gramm-Rudman-Hollings Deficit Reduction Act — *(See sequester.)*

Grandfather clause — A provision that exempts people or other entities already engaged in an activity from rules or legislation affecting that activity.

Hearings — Committee sessions for taking testimony from witnesses. At hearings on legislation, witnesses usually include specialists, government officials and spokesmen for individuals or entities affected by the bill or bills under study. Hearings related to special investigations bring forth a variety of witnesses. Committees sometimes use their subpoena power to summon reluctant witnesses. The public and news media may attend open hearings but are barred from closed, or "executive," hearings. The vast majority of hearings are open to the public. *(Also see executive session.)*

Hold-harmless clause — A provision added to legislation to ensure that recipients of federal funds do not receive less in a future year than they did in the current year if a new formula for allocating funds authorized in the legislation would result in a reduction to the recipients. This clause has been used most often to soften the impact of sudden reductions in federal grants.

Hopper — Box on House clerk's desk into which members deposit bills and resolutions to introduce them.

Hour rule — A provision in the rules of the House that permits one hour of debate time for each member on amendments debated in the House of Representatives sitting as the House. Therefore, the House normally amends bills while sitting as the Committee of the Whole, where the five-minute rule on amendments operates.

House as in the Committee of the Whole — A procedure that can be used to expedite consideration of certain measures such as continuing resolutions and, when there is debate, private bills. The procedure can be invoked only with the unanimous consent of the House or a rule from the Rules Committee and has procedural elements of both the House sitting as the House of Representatives, such as the Speaker presiding and the previous question motion being in order, and the House sitting as the Committee of the Whole, with the five-minute rule being in order. *(See Committee of the Whole.)*

House Calendar — A listing for action by the House of public bills that do not directly or indirectly appropriate money or raise revenue. *(Also see calendar.)*

Immunity — The constitutional privilege of members of Congress to make verbal statements on the floor and in committee for which they cannot be sued or arrested for slander or libel. Also, freedom from arrest while traveling to or from sessions of Congress or on official business. Members in this status may only be arrested for treason, felonies or a breach of the peace, as defined by congressional manuals.

Joint committee — A committee composed of a specified number of members of both the House and Senate. A joint committee may be investigative or research-oriented, an example of the latter being the Joint Economic Committee. Others have housekeeping duties; examples include the joint committees on Printing and on the Library of Congress.

Joint resolution — Like a bill, a joint resolution, designated H J Res or S J Res, requires the approval of both chambers and the

signature of the president, and has the force of law if approved. There is no practical difference between a bill and a joint resolution. A joint resolution generally is used to deal with a limited matter such as a single appropriation.

Joint resolutions are also used to propose amendments to the Constitution. In that case they require a two-thirds majority in both chambers. They do not require a presidential signature, but they must be ratified by three-fourths of the states to become a part of the Constitution. (*Also see concurrent resolution, resolution.*)

Journal — The official record of the proceedings of the House and Senate. The Journal records the actions taken in each chamber, but, unlike the Congressional Record, it does not include the substantially verbatim report of speeches, debates, statements and the like.

Law — An act of Congress that has been signed by the president or passed, over his veto, by Congress. Public bills, when signed, become public laws and are cited by the letters PL and a hyphenated number. The number before the hyphen corresponds to the Congress, and the one or more digits after the hyphen refer to the numerical sequence in which the president signed the bills during that Congress. Private bills, when signed, become private laws. (*Also see bills, private bills.*)

Legislative day — The "day" extending from the time either chamber meets after an adjournment until the time it next adjourns. Because the House normally adjourns from day to day, legislative days and calendar days usually coincide. But in the Senate, a legislative day may, and frequently does, extend over several calendar days. (*Also see recess.*)

Line-item veto — Presidential authority to strike individual items from appropriations bills, which presidents since Ulysses S. Grant have sought. Congress gave the president a form of the power in 1996 (PL 104-130), but this "enhanced rescission authority" was struck down by the Supreme Court in 1998 as unconstitutional because it allowed the president to change laws on his own.

Loan guarantees — Loans to third parties for which the federal government guarantees the repayment of principal or interest, in whole or in part, to the lender in the event of default.

Lobby — A group seeking to influence the passage or defeat of legislation. Originally the term referred to people frequenting the lobbies or corridors of legislative chambers to speak to lawmakers.

The definition of a lobby and the activity of lobbying is a matter of differing interpretation. By some definitions, lobbying is limited to direct attempts to influence lawmakers through personal interviews and persuasion. Under other definitions, lobbying includes attempts at indirect, or "grass-roots," influence, such as persuading members of a group to write or visit their district's representative and state's senators or attempting to create a climate of opinion favorable to a desired legislative goal.

The right to attempt to influence legislation is based on the First Amendment to the Constitution, which says Congress shall make no law abridging the right of the people "to petition the government for a redress of grievances."

Majority leader — Floor leader for the majority party in each chamber. In the Senate, in consultation with the minority leader, the majority leader directs the legislative schedule for the chamber. He or she is also his party's spokesperson and chief strategist. In the House, the majority leader is second to the Speaker in the majority party's leadership and serves as the party's legislative strategist. (*Also see Speaker, whip.*)

Manual — The official handbook in each chamber prescribing in detail its organization, procedures and operations.

Marking up a bill — Going through the contents of a piece of legislation in committee or subcommittee to, for example, consider the provisions, act on amendments to provisions and proposed revisions to the language, and insert new sections and phraseology. If the bill is extensively amended, the committee's version may be introduced as a separate (or "clean") bill, with a new number, before being considered by the full House or Senate. (*Also see clean bill.*)

Minority leader — Floor leader for the minority party in each chamber.

Morning hour — The time set aside at the beginning of each legislative day for the consideration of regular, routine business. The "hour" is of indefinite duration in the House, where it is rarely used. In the Senate, it is the first two hours of a session following an adjournment, as distinguished from a recess. The morning hour can be terminated earlier if the morning business has been completed.

Business includes such matters as messages from the president, communications from the heads of departments, messages from the House, the presentation of petitions, reports of standing and select committees and the introduction of bills and resolutions.

During the first hour of the morning hour in the Senate, no motion to proceed to the consideration of any bill on the calendar is in order except by unanimous consent. During the second hour, motions can be made but must be decided without debate. Senate committees may meet while the Senate conducts the morning hour.

Motion — In the House or Senate chamber, a request by a member to institute any one of a wide array of parliamentary actions. He or she "moves" for a certain procedure, such as the consideration of a measure. The precedence of motions, and whether they are debatable, is set forth in the House and Senate manuals.

Nominations — Presidential appointments to office subject to Senate confirmation. Although most nominations win quick Senate approval, some are controversial and become the topic of hearings and debate. Sometimes senators object to appointees for patronage reasons — for example, when a nomination to a local federal job is made without consulting the senators of the state concerned. In some situations a senator may object that the nominee is "personally obnoxious" to him. Usually other senators join in blocking such appointments out of courtesy to their colleagues. (*Also see senatorial courtesy.*)

One-minute speeches — Addresses by House members at the beginning of a legislative day. The speeches may cover any subject but are limited to one minute's duration.

Outlays — Actual spending that flows from the liquidation of budget authority. Outlays associated with appropriations bills and other legislation are estimates of future spending made by the Congressional Budget Office (CBO) and the White House's Office of Management and Budget (OMB). CBO's estimates govern bills for the purpose of congressional floor debate, while OMB's numbers govern when it comes to determining whether legislation exceeds spending caps.

Outlays in a given fiscal year may result from budget authority provided in the current year or in previous years. (*Also see budget authority, budget process.*)

Override a veto — If the president vetoes a bill and sends it

back to Congress with his objections, Congress may try to override his veto and enact the bill into law. Neither chamber is required to attempt to override a veto. The override of a veto requires a recorded vote with a two-thirds majority of those present and voting in each chamber. The question put to each chamber is: "Shall the bill pass, the objections of the president to the contrary notwithstanding?" (*Also see pocket veto, veto.*)

Oversight committee — A congressional committee or designated subcommittee that is charged with general oversight of one or more federal agencies' programs and activities. Usually, the oversight panel for a particular agency is also the authorizing committee for that agency's programs and operations.

Pair — A voluntary, informal arrangement that two lawmakers, usually on opposite sides of an issue, make on recorded votes. In many cases the result is to subtract a vote from each side, with no effect on the outcome.

Pairs are not authorized in the rules of either chamber, are not counted in tabulating the final result and have no official standing. However, members pairing are identified in the Congressional Record, along with their positions on such votes, if known. A member who expects to be absent for a vote can pair with a member who plans to vote, with the latter agreeing to withhold his or her vote.

There are three types of pairs:

(1) A live pair involves a member who is present for a vote and another who is absent. The member in attendance votes and then withdraws the vote, announcing that he or she has a live pair with colleague "X" and stating how the two members would have voted, one in favor, the other opposed. A live pair may affect the outcome of a closely contested vote, since it subtracts one "yea" or one "nay" from the final tally. A live pair may cover one or several specific issues.

(2) A general pair, widely used in the House, does not entail any arrangement between two members and does not affect the vote. Members who expect to be absent notify the clerk that they wish to make a general pair. Each member then is paired with another desiring a pair, and their names are listed in the Congressional Record. The member may or may not be paired with another taking the opposite position, and no indication of how the members would have voted is given.

(3) A specific pair is similar to a general pair, except that the opposing stands of the two members are identified and printed in the Congressional Record.

Pay-as-you go (PAYGO) rules — (*See budget process.*)

Petition — A request or plea sent to one or both chambers from an organization or private citizens' group seeking support for particular legislation or favorable consideration of a matter not yet receiving congressional attention. Petitions are referred to appropriate committees. In the House, a petition signed by a majority of members (218) can discharge a bill from a committee. (*Also see discharge a committee.*)

Pocket veto — The act of the president in withholding his approval of a bill after Congress has adjourned. When Congress is in session, a bill becomes law without the president's signature if he does not act upon it within 10 days, excluding Sundays, from the time he receives it. But if Congress adjourns sine die within that 10-day period, the bill will die even if the president does not formally veto it.

The Supreme Court in 1986 agreed to decide whether the president could pocket veto a bill during recesses and between sessions of the same Congress or only between Congresses. The justices in

1987 declared the case moot, however, because the bill in question was invalid once the case reached the court. (*Also see adjournment sine die, veto.*)

Point of order — An objection raised by a member that the chamber is departing from rules governing its conduct of business. The objector cites the rule violated, with the chair sustaining his or her objection if correctly made. Order is restored by the chair's suspending proceedings of the chamber until it conforms to the prescribed "order of business."

Both chambers have procedures for overcoming a point of order, either by vote or, what is most common in the House, by including language in the rule for floor consideration that waives a point of order against a given bill. (*Also see rules.*)

President of the Senate — Under the Constitution, the vice president of the United States presides over the Senate. In his absence, the president pro tempore, or a senator designated by the president pro tempore, presides over the chamber.

President pro tempore — The chief officer of the Senate in the absence of the vice president — literally, but loosely, the president for a time. The president pro tempore is elected by his fellow senators. Recent practice has been to elect the senator of the majority party with the longest period of continuous service.

Previous question — A motion for the previous question, when carried, has the effect of cutting off all debate, preventing the offering of further amendments and forcing a vote on the pending matter. In the House, a motion for the previous question is not permitted in the Committee of the Whole, unless a rule governing debate provides otherwise. The motion for the previous question is a debate-limiting device and is not in order in the Senate.

Printed amendment — A House rule guarantees five minutes of floor debate in support and five minutes in opposition, and no other debate time, on amendments printed in the Congressional Record at least one day prior to the amendment's consideration in the Committee of the Whole.

In the Senate, while amendments may be submitted for printing, they have no parliamentary standing or status. An amendment submitted for printing in the Senate, however, may be called up by any senator.

Private bill — A bill dealing with individual matters such as claims against the government, immigration or land titles. When a private bill is before the chamber, two members may block its consideration, thereby recommitting the bill to committee. The backers still have recourse, however. The measure can be put into an "omnibus claims bill" — several private bills rolled into one. As with any bill, no part of an omnibus claims bill may be deleted without a vote. When the private bill goes back to the House floor in this form, it can be deleted from the omnibus bill only by majority vote.

Private Calendar — The House calendar for private bills. The Private Calendar must be called on the first Tuesday of each month, and the Speaker may call it on the third Tuesday of each month as well. (*Also see calendar, private bill.*)

Privileged questions — The order in which bills, motions and other legislative measures are considered on the floor of the Senate and House is governed by strict priorities. A motion to table, for instance, is more privileged than a motion to recommit. Thus, if a member moves to recommit a bill to committee for further consideration, another member can supersede the first action by moving

to table it, and a vote will occur on the motion to table (or kill) before the motion to recommit. A motion to adjourn is considered "of the highest privilege" and must be considered before virtually any other motion.

Pro forma amendment — (*See strike out the last word.*)

Public Laws — (*See law.*)

Questions of privilege — These are matters affecting members of Congress individually or collectively. Matters affecting the rights, safety, dignity and integrity of proceedings of the House or Senate as a whole are questions of privilege in both chambers.

Questions involving individual members are called questions of "personal privilege." A member rising to ask a question of personal privilege is given precedence over almost all other proceedings. For instance, if a member feels that he or she has been improperly impugned in comments by another member, he or she can immediately demand to be heard on the floor on a question of personal privilege. An annotation in the House rules points out that the privilege rests primarily on the Constitution, which gives members a conditional immunity from arrest and an unconditional freedom to speak in the House.

In 1993, the House changed its rules to allow the Speaker to delay for two legislative days the floor consideration of a question of the privileges of the House unless it is offered by the majority leader or minority leader.

Quorum — The number of members whose presence is necessary for the transaction of business. In the Senate and House, it is a majority of the membership. In the Committee of the Whole House, a quorum is 100. If a point of order is made that a quorum is not present, the only business that is in order is either a motion to adjourn or a motion to direct the sergeant-at-arms to request the attendance of absentees. In practice, however, both chambers conduct much of their business without a quorum present. (*Also see Committee of the Whole House.*)

Reading of bills — Traditional parliamentary procedure required bills to be read three times before they were passed. This custom is of little modern significance. Normally a bill is considered to have its first reading when it is introduced and printed, by title, in the Congressional Record. In the House, a bill's second reading comes when floor consideration begins. (The actual reading of a bill is most likely to occur at this point, if at all.) The second reading in the Senate is supposed to occur on the legislative day after the measure is introduced, but before it is referred to committee. The third reading (again, usually by title) takes place when floor action has been completed on amendments.

Recess — A recess, as distinguished from adjournment, does not end a legislative day and therefore does not interrupt unfinished business. (The rules in each chamber set forth certain matters to be taken up and disposed of at the beginning of each legislative day.) The House usually adjourns from day to day. The Senate often recesses, thus meeting on the same legislative day for several calendar days or even weeks at a time.

Recognition — The power of recognition of a member is lodged in the Speaker of the House and the presiding officer of the Senate. The presiding officer names the member to speak first when two or more members simultaneously request recognition. The order of recognition is governed by precedents and tradition for many situations. In the Senate, for instance, the majority leader has the right to be recognized first.

Recommit to committee — A motion, made on the floor after a bill has been debated, to return it to the committee that reported it. If approved, recommittal usually is considered a death blow to the bill. In the House, the right to offer a motion to recommit is guaranteed to the minority leader or someone he or she designates.

A motion to recommit may include instructions to the committee to report the bill again with specific amendments or by a certain date. Or the instructions may direct that a particular study be made, with no definite deadline for further action.

If the recommittal motion includes instructions to "report the bill back forthwith" and the motion is adopted, floor action on the bill continues with the changes directed by the instructions automatically incorporated into the bill; the committee does not actually reconsider the legislation.

Reconciliation — The 1974 budget act created a "reconciliation" procedure for bringing existing tax and spending laws into conformity with ceilings set in the congressional budget resolution. Under the procedure, the budget resolution sets specific deficit-reduction targets and instructs tax-writing and authorizing committees to propose changes in existing law to meet those targets. Those recommendations are consolidated without change by the Budget committees into an omnibus reconciliation bill, which then must be considered and approved by both chambers of Congress.

Special rules in the Senate limit debate on a reconciliation bill to 20 hours and bar extraneous or non-germane amendments. (*Also see budget resolution, sequester.*)

Reconsider a vote — Until it is disposed of, a motion to reconsider the vote by which an action was taken has the effect of putting the action in abeyance. In the Senate, the motion can be made only by a member who voted on the prevailing side of the original question or by a member who did not vote at all. In the House, it can be made only by a member on the prevailing side.

A common practice in the Senate after close votes on an issue is a motion to reconsider, followed by a motion to table the motion to reconsider. On this motion to table, senators vote as they voted on the original question, which allows the motion to table to prevail, assuming there are no switches. That closes the matter, and further motions to reconsider are not entertained.

In the House, as a routine precaution, a motion to reconsider usually is made every time a measure is passed. Such a motion almost always is tabled immediately, thus shutting off the possibility of future reconsideration except by unanimous consent.

Motions to reconsider must be entered in the Senate within the next two days the Senate is in session after the original vote has been taken. In the House, they must be entered either on the same day or on the next succeeding day the House is in session. Sometimes on a close vote, a member will switch his or her vote to be eligible to offer a motion to reconsider.

Recorded vote — A vote upon which each member's stand is individually made known. In the Senate, this is accomplished through a roll call of the entire membership, to which each senator on the floor must answer "yea," "nay" or "present." Since January 1973, the House has used an electronic voting system for recorded votes, including yea-and-nay votes formerly taken by roll calls.

When not required by the Constitution, a recorded vote can be obtained on questions in the House on the demand of one-fifth (44 members) of a quorum or one-fourth (25) of a quorum in the Committee of the Whole. Recorded votes are required in the House for appropriations, budget and tax bills. (*Also see yeas and nays.*)

Report — Both a verb and a noun as a congressional term. A

committee that has been examining a bill referred to it by the parent chamber "reports" its findings and recommendations to the chamber when it completes consideration and returns the measure. The process is called "reporting" a bill. In some cases, a bill is reported without a written report.

A "report" is the document setting forth the committee's explanation of its action. Senate and House reports are numbered separately and are designated S Rept or H Rept. When a committee report is not unanimous, the dissenting committee members may file a statement of their views, called minority or dissenting views and referred to as a minority report. Members in disagreement with some provisions of a bill may file additional or supplementary views. Sometimes a bill is reported without a committee recommendation.

Legislative committees occasionally submit adverse reports. However, when a committee is opposed to a bill, it usually fails to report the bill at all. Some laws require that committee reports — favorable or adverse — be made.

Rescission — Cancellation of budget authority that was previously appropriated but has not yet been spent.

Resolution — A "simple" resolution, designated H Res or S Res, deals with matters entirely within the prerogatives of a single chamber. It requires neither passage by the other chamber nor approval by the president, and it does not have the force of law. Most resolutions deal with the rules or procedures of one chamber. They are also used to express the sentiments of a single chamber, such as condolences to the family of a deceased member, or to comment on foreign policy or executive business. A simple resolution is the vehicle for a "rule" from the House Rules Committee. (*Also see concurrent and joint resolutions, rules.*)

Rider — An amendment, usually not germane, that its sponsor hopes to get through more easily by including it in other legislation. A rider becomes law if the bill to which it is attached is enacted. Amendments providing legislative directives in appropriations bills are examples of riders, though technically legislation is banned from appropriations bills.

The House, unlike the Senate, has a strict germaneness rule; thus, riders usually are Senate devices to get legislation enacted quickly or to bypass lengthy House consideration and, possibly, opposition.

Rules — Each chamber has a body of rules and precedents that govern the conduct of business. These rules deal with issues such as duties of officers, the order of business, admission to the floor, parliamentary procedures on handling amendments and voting, and jurisdictions of committees. They are normally changed only at the start of each Congress.

In the House, a rule may also be a resolution reported by the Rules Committee to govern the handling of a particular bill on the floor. The committee may report a rule, also called a special order, in the form of a simple resolution. If the House adopts the resolution, the temporary rule becomes as valid as any standing rule and lapses only after action has been completed on the measure to which it pertains.

The rule sets the time limit on general debate. It may also waive points of order against provisions of the bill in question such as non-germane language or against certain amendments expected on the floor. It may even forbid all amendments or all amendments except those proposed by the legislative committee that handled the bill. In this instance, it is known as a "closed" rule as opposed to an "open" rule, which puts no limitation on floor amendments, thus leaving the bill completely open to alteration by the adoption of germane amendments. (*Also see point of order.*)

Secretary of the Senate — Chief administrative officer of the Senate, responsible for overseeing the duties of Senate employees, educating Senate pages, administering oaths, overseeing the registration of lobbyists and handling other tasks necessary for the continuing operation of the Senate. (*Also see Clerk of the House.*)

Select or special committee — A committee set up for a special purpose and, usually, for a limited time by resolution of either the House or Senate. Most special committees are investigative and lack legislative authority: Legislation is not referred to them, and they cannot report bills to their parent chambers.

Senatorial courtesy — A general practice with no written rule — sometimes referred to as "the courtesy of the Senate" — applied to consideration of executive nominations. Generally, it means that nominations from a state are not to be confirmed unless they have been approved by the senators of the president's party of that state, with other senators following their colleagues' lead in the attitude they take toward consideration of such nominations. (*Also see nominations.*)

Sequester — Automatic, across-the-board spending cuts, generally triggered after the close of a session by a report issued by the Office of Management and Budget. Under the 1985 Gramm-Rudman anti-deficit law, modified in 1987, a year-end sequester was triggered if the deficit exceeded a pre-set maximum. However, the Budget Enforcement Act of 1990, updated in 1993 and 1997, effectively replaced that procedure through fiscal 2002.

Instead, if Congress exceeds an annual cap on discretionary budget authority or outlays, a sequester is triggered for all eligible discretionary spending to make up the difference. If Congress violates pay-as-you-go rules by allowing the net effect of legislated changes in mandatory spending and taxes to increase the deficit, a sequester is triggered for all non-exempt entitlement programs. Similar procedures apply to supplemental appropriations bills. (*Also see budget process.*)

Sine die — (*See adjournment sine die.*)

Speaker — The presiding officer of the House of Representatives, selected by his party caucus and formally elected by the whole House. While both parties nominate candidates, choice by the majority party is tantamount to election. In 1995, House rules were changed to limit the Speaker to four consecutive terms.

Special session — A session of Congress after it has adjourned sine die, completing its regular session. Special sessions are convened by the president.

Spending authority — The 1974 budget act defines spending authority as borrowing authority, contract authority and entitlement authority for which budget authority is not provided in advance by appropriation acts.

Sponsor — (*See bills introduced.*)

Standing committees — Committees that are permanently established by House and Senate rules. The standing committees of the House were reorganized in 1974, with some changes in jurisdictions and titles made when Republicans took control of the House in 1995. The last major realignment of Senate committees was in 1977. The standing committees are legislative committees: Legislation may be referred to them, and they may report bills and resolutions to their parent chambers.

Standing vote — A non-recorded vote used in both the House and Senate. (A standing vote is also called a division vote.) Members in favor of a proposal stand and are counted by the presiding officer. Then members opposed stand and are counted. There is no record of how individual members voted.

Statutes at large — A chronological arrangement of the laws enacted in each session of Congress. Though indexed, the laws are not arranged by subject matter, and there is no indication of how they changed previously enacted laws. (*Also see law, U.S. Code.*)

Strike from the Record — A member of the House who is offended by remarks made on the House floor may move that the offending words be "taken down" for the Speaker's cognizance and then expunged from the debate as published in the Congressional Record.

Strike out the last word — A motion whereby a House member is entitled to speak for five minutes on an amendment then being debated by the chamber. A member gains recognition from the chair by moving to "strike out the last word" of the amendment or section of the bill under consideration. The motion is pro forma, requires no vote and does not change the amendment being debated. (*Also see five-minute rule.*)

Substitute — A motion, amendment or entire bill introduced in place of the pending legislative business. Passage of the substitute kills the original measure by supplanting it. The substitute may also be amended. (*Also see amendment in the nature of a substitute.*)

Supplemental appropriations bill — Legislation appropriating funds after the regular annual appropriations bill for a federal department or agency has been enacted. Supplemental appropriations bills often arrive about halfway through the fiscal year, when needs that Congress and the president did not anticipate (or may not have wanted to fund) become pressing. In recent years, supplementals have been driven by spending to help victims of natural disasters and to carry out peacekeeping commitments.

Suspend the rules — A time-saving procedure for passing bills in the House. The wording of the motion, which may be made by any member recognized by the Speaker, is: "I move to suspend the rules and pass the bill . . ." A favorable vote by two-thirds of those present is required for passage. Debate is limited to 40 minutes, and no amendments from the floor are permitted. If a two-thirds favorable vote is not attained, the bill may be considered later under regular procedures. The suspension procedure is in order every Monday and Tuesday and is intended to be reserved for non-controversial bills.

Table a bill — Motions to table, or to "lay on the table," are used to block or kill amendments or other parliamentary questions. When approved, a tabling motion is considered the final disposition of that issue. One of the most widely used parliamentary procedures, the motion to table is not debatable, and adoption requires a simple majority vote.

In the Senate, however, different language sometimes is used. The motion may be worded to let a bill "lie on the table," perhaps for subsequent "picking up." This motion is more flexible, keeping the bill pending for later action, if desired. Tabling motions on amendments are effective debate-ending devices in the Senate.

Treaties — Executive proposals — in the form of resolutions of ratification — which must be submitted to the Senate for approval by two-thirds of the senators present. Treaties are normally sent to the Foreign Relations Committee for scrutiny before the Senate takes action. Foreign Relations has jurisdiction over all treaties, regardless of the subject matter. Treaties are read three times and debated on the floor in much the same manner as legislative proposals. After approval by the Senate, treaties are formally ratified by the president.

Trust funds — Funds collected and used by the federal government for carrying out specific purposes and programs according to terms of a trust agreement or statute such as the Social Security and unemployment compensation trust funds. Such funds are administered by the government in a fiduciary capacity and are not available for the general purposes of the government.

Unanimous consent — A procedure used to expedite floor action. Proceedings of the House or Senate and action on legislation often take place upon the unanimous consent of the chamber, whether or not a rule of the chamber is being violated. It is frequently used in a routine fashion, such as by a senator requesting the unanimous consent of the Senate to have specified members of his or her staff present on the floor during debate on a specific amendment. A single member's objection blocks a unanimous consent request.

Unanimous consent agreement — A device used in the Senate to expedite legislation. Much of the Senate's legislative business, dealing with both minor and controversial issues, is conducted through unanimous consent or unanimous consent agreements. On major legislation, such agreements usually are printed and transmitted to all senators in advance of floor debate. Once agreed to, they are binding on all members unless the Senate, by unanimous consent, agrees to modify them. An agreement may list the order in which various bills are to be considered; specify the length of time for debate on bills and contested amendments and when they are to be voted upon; and, frequently, require that all amendments introduced be germane to the bill under consideration.

In this regard, unanimous consent agreements are similar to the "rules" issued by the House Rules Committee for bills pending in the House.

Union Calendar — Bills that directly or indirectly appropriate money or raise revenue are placed on this House calendar according to the date they are reported from committee. (*Also see calendar.*)

U.S. Code — A consolidation and codification of the general and permanent laws of the United States arranged by subject under 50 titles, the first six dealing with general or political subjects, and the other 44 alphabetically arranged from agriculture to war. The U.S. Code is updated annually, and a new set of bound volumes is published every six years. (*Also see law, statutes at large.*)

Veto — Disapproval by the president of a bill or joint resolution (other than one proposing an amendment to the Constitution). When Congress is in session, the president must veto a bill within 10 days, excluding Sundays, after he has received it; otherwise, it becomes law without his signature. When the president vetoes a bill, he returns it to the chamber of origin along with a message stating his objections. (*Also see pocket veto, override a veto.*)

Voice vote — In either the House or Senate, members answer "aye" or "no" in chorus, and the presiding officer decides the result. The term is also used loosely to indicate action by unanimous consent or without objection. (*Also see yeas and nays.*)

Whip — In effect, the assistant majority or minority leader, in either the House or Senate. His or her job is to help marshal votes in support of party strategy and legislation.

Without objection — Used in lieu of a vote on non-controversial motions, amendments or bills that may be passed in either chamber if no member voices an objection.

Yeas and nays — The Constitution requires that yea-and-nay votes be taken and recorded when requested by one-fifth of the members present. In the House, the Speaker determines whether one-fifth of the members present requested a vote. In the Senate, practice requires only 11 members. The Constitution requires the yeas and nays on a veto override attempt. (*Also see recorded vote.*)

Yielding — When a member has been recognized to speak, no other member may speak unless he or she obtains permission from the member recognized. This permission is called yielding and usually is requested in the form, "Will the gentleman (or gentlelady) yield to me?" While this activity occasionally is seen in the Senate, the Senate has no rule or practice to parcel out time.

In the House, the floor manager of a bill usually apportions debate time by yielding specific amounts of time to members who have requested it. ◆

Members of the 107th Congress, First Session . . .

(As of Dec. 20, 2001)

Representatives
R 222; D 211; I 2

— A —

Abercrombie, Neil, D-Hawaii (1)
Ackerman, Gary L., D-N.Y. (5)
Aderholt, Robert B., R-Ala. (4)
Akin, Todd, R-Mo. (2)
Allen, Tom, D-Maine (1)
Andrews, Robert E., D-N.J. (1)
Armey, Dick, R-Texas (26)

— B —

Baca, Joe, D-Calif. (42)
Bachus, Spencer, R-Ala. (6)
Baird, Brian, D-Wash. (3)
Baker, Richard H., R-La. (6)
Baldacci, John, D-Maine (2)
Baldwin, Tammy, D-Wis. (2)
Ballenger, Cass, R-N.C. (10)
Barcia, James A., D-Mich. (5)
Barr, Bob, R-Ga. (7)
Barrett, Thomas M., D-Wis. (5)
Bartlett, Roscoe G., R-Md. (6)
Barton, Joe L., R-Texas (6)
Bass, Charles, R-N.H. (2)
Becerra, Xavier, D-Calif. (30)
Bentsen, Ken, D-Texas (25)
Bereuter, Doug, R-Neb. (1)
Berkley, Shelley, D-Nev. (1)
Berman, Howard L., D-Calif. (26)
Berry, Marion, D-Ark. (1)
Biggert, Judy, R-Ill. (13)
Bilirakis, Michael, R-Fla. (9)
Bishop, Sanford D. Jr., D-Ga. (2)
Blagojevich, Rod R., D-Ill. (5)
Blumenauer, Earl, D-Ore. (3)
Blunt, Roy, R-Mo. (7)
Boehlert, Sherwood, R-N.Y. (23)
Boehner, John A., R-Ohio (8)
Bonilla, Henry, R-Texas (23)
Bonior, David E., D-Mich. (10)
Bono, Mary, R-Calif. (44)
Boozman, John, R-Ark. (3)
Borski, Robert A., D-Pa. (3)
Boswell, Leonard L., D-Iowa (3)
Boucher, Rick, D-Va. (9)
Boyd, Allen, D-Fla. (2)
Brady, Kevin, R-Texas (8)
Brady, Robert A., D-Pa. (1)
Brown, Corrine, D-Fla. (3)
Brown, Henry E. Jr., R-S.C. (1)
Brown, Sherrod, D-Ohio (13)
Bryant, Ed, R-Tenn. (7)
Burr, Richard M., R-N.C. (5)
Burton, Dan, R-Ind. (6)
Buyer, Steve, R-Ind. (5)

— C —

Callahan, Sonny, R-Ala. (1)
Calvert, Ken, R-Calif. (43)
Camp, Dave, R-Mich. (4)
Cannon, Christopher B., R-Utah (3)
Cantor, Eric, R-Va. (7)
Capito, Shelley Moore, R-W.Va. (2)
Capps, Lois, D-Calif. (22)
Capuano, Michael E., D-Mass. (8)
Cardin, Benjamin L., D-Md. (3)
Carson, Brad, D-Okla. (2)
Carson, Julia, D-Ind. (10)
Castle, Michael N., R-Del. (AL)
Chabot, Steve, R-Ohio (1)
Chambliss, Saxby, R-Ga. (8)
Clay, William Lacy, D-Mo. (1)
Clayton, Eva, D-N.C. (1)
Clement, Bob, D-Tenn. (5)
Clyburn, James E., D-S.C. (6)
Coble, Howard, R-N.C. (6)
Collins, Mac, R-Ga. (3)
Combest, Larry, R-Texas (19)
Condit, Gary A., D-Calif. (18)
Conyers, John Jr., D-Mich. (14)
Cooksey, John, R-La. (5)
Costello, Jerry F., D-Ill. (12)
Cox, Christopher, R-Calif. (47)

Coyne, William J., D-Pa. (14)
Cramer, Robert E. "Bud," D-Ala. (5)
Crane, Philip M., R-Ill. (8)
Crenshaw, Ander, R-Fla. (4)
Crowley, Joseph, D-N.Y. (7)
Cubin, Barbara, R-Wyo. (AL)
Culberson, John, R-Texas (7)
Cummings, Elijah E., D-Md. (7)
Cunningham, Randy "Duke," R-Calif. (51)

— D —

Davis, Danny K., D-Ill. (7)
Davis, Jim, D-Fla. (11)
Davis, Jo Ann, R-Va. (1)
Davis, Susan A., D-Calif. (49)
Davis, Thomas M. III, R-Va. (11)
Deal, Nathan, R-Ga. (9)
DeFazio, Peter A., D-Ore. (4)
DeGette, Diana, D-Colo. (1)
Delahunt, Bill, D-Mass. (10)
DeLauro, Rosa, D-Conn. (3)
DeLay, Tom, R-Texas (22)
DeMint, Jim, R-S.C. (4)
Deutsch, Peter, D-Fla. (20)
Diaz-Balart, Lincoln, R-Fla. (21)
Dicks, Norm, D-Wash. (6)
Dingell, John D., D-Mich. (16)
Doggett, Lloyd, D-Texas (10)
Dooley, Cal, D-Calif. (20)
Doolittle, John T., R-Calif. (4)
Doyle, Mike, D-Pa. (18)
Dreier, David, R-Calif. (28)
Duncan, John J. "Jimmy" Jr., R-Tenn. (2)
Dunn, Jennifer, R-Wash. (8)

— E —

Edwards, Chet, D-Texas (11)
Ehlers, Vernon J., R-Mich. (3)
Ehrlich, Robert L. Jr., R-Md. (2)
Emerson, Jo Ann, R-Mo. (8)
Engel, Eliot L., D-N.Y. (17)
English, Phil, R-Pa. (21)
Eshoo, Anna G., D-Calif. (14)
Etheridge, Bob, D-N.C. (2)
Evans, Lane, D-Ill. (17)
Everett, Terry, R-Ala. (2)

— F —

Farr, Sam, D-Calif. (17)
Fattah, Chaka, D-Pa. (2)
Ferguson, Mike, R-N.J. (7)
Filner, Bob, D-Calif. (50)
Flake, Jeff, R-Ariz. (1)
Fletcher, Ernie, R-Ky. (6)
Foley, Mark, R-Fla. (16)
Forbes, Randy, R-Va. (4)
Ford, Harold E. Jr., D-Tenn. (9)
Fossella, Vito J., R-N.Y. (13)
Frank, Barney, D-Mass. (4)
Frelinghuysen, Rodney, R-N.J. (11)
Frost, Martin, D-Texas (24)

— G —

Gallegly, Elton, R-Calif. (23)
Ganske, Greg, R-Iowa (4)
Gekas, George W., R-Pa. (17)
Gephardt, Richard A., D-Mo. (3)
Gibbons, Jim, R-Nev. (2)
Gilchrest, Wayne T., R-Md. (1)
Gillmor, Paul E., R-Ohio (5)
Gilman, Benjamin A., R-N.Y. (20)
Gonzalez, Charlie, D-Texas (20)
Goode, Virgil H. Jr., I-Va. (5)
Goodlatte, Robert W., R-Va. (6)
Gordon, Bart, D-Tenn. (6)
Goss, Porter J., R-Fla. (14)
Graham, Lindsey, R-S.C. (3)
Granger, Kay, R-Texas (12)
Graves, Sam, R-Mo. (6)
Green, Gene, D-Texas (29)
Green, Mark, R-Wis. (8)
Greenwood, James C., R-Pa. (8)
Grucci, Felix J. Jr., R-N.Y. (1)
Gutierrez, Luis V., D-Ill. (4)
Gutknecht, Gil, R-Minn. (1)

— H —

Hall, Ralph M., D-Texas (4)
Hall, Tony P., D-Ohio (3)
Hansen, James V., R-Utah (1)
Harman, Jane, D-Calif. (36)
Hart, Melissa A., R-Pa. (4)
Hastert, J. Dennis, R-Ill. (14)
Hastings, Alcee L., D-Fla. (23)
Hastings, Doc, R-Wash. (4)
Hayes, Robin, R-N.C. (8)
Hayworth, J.D., R-Ariz. (6)
Hefley, Joel, R-Colo. (5)
Herger, Wally, R-Calif. (2)
Hill, Baron P., D-Ind. (9)
Hilleary, Van, R-Tenn. (4)
Hilliard, Earl F., D-Ala. (7)
Hinchey, Maurice D., D-N.Y. (26)
Hinojosa, Rubén, D-Texas (15)
Hobson, David L., R-Ohio (7)
Hoeffel, Joseph M., D-Pa. (13)
Hoekstra, Peter, R-Mich. (2)
Holden, Tim, D-Pa. (6)
Holt, Rush D., D-N.J. (12)
Honda, Michael M., D-Calif. (15)
Hooley, Darlene, D-Ore. (5)
Horn, Steve, R-Calif. (38)
Hostettler, John, R-Ind. (8)
Houghton, Amo, R-N.Y. (31)
Hoyer, Steny H., D-Md. (5)
Hulshof, Kenny, R-Mo. (9)
Hunter, Duncan, R-Calif. (52)
Hyde, Henry J., R-Ill. (6)

— I, J —

Inslee, Jay, D-Wash. (1)
Isakson, Johnny, R-Ga. (6)
Israel, Steve, D-N.Y. (2)
Issa, Darrell, R-Calif. (48)
Istook, Ernest, R-Okla. (5)
Jackson, Jesse L. Jr., D-Ill. (2)
Jackson-Lee, Sheila, D-Texas (18)
Jefferson, William J., D-La. (2)
Jenkins, Bill, R-Tenn. (1)
John, Chris, D-La. (7)
Johnson, Eddie Bernice, D-Texas (30)
Johnson, Nancy L., R-Conn. (6)
Johnson, Sam, R-Texas (3)
Johnson, Timothy V., R-Ill. (15)
Jones, Stephanie Tubbs, D-Ohio (11)
Jones, Walter B., R-N.C. (3)

— K —

Kanjorski, Paul E., D-Pa. (11)
Kaptur, Marcy, D-Ohio (9)
Keller, Ric, R-Fla. (8)
Kelly, Sue W., R-N.Y. (19)
Kennedy, Mark, R-Minn. (2)
Kennedy, Patrick J., D-R.I. (1)
Kerns, Brian, R-Ind. (7)
Kildee, Dale E., D-Mich. (9)
Kilpatrick, Carolyn Cheeks, D-Mich. (15)
Kind, Ron, D-Wis. (3)
King, Peter T., R-N.Y. (3)
Kingston, Jack, R-Ga. (1)
Kirk, Mark Steven, R-Ill. (10)
Kleczka, Gerald D., D-Wis. (4)
Knollenberg, Joe, R-Mich. (11)
Kolbe, Jim, R-Ariz. (5)
Kucinich, Dennis J., D-Ohio (10)

— L —

LaFalce, John J., D-N.Y. (29)
LaHood, Ray, R-Ill. (18)
Lampson, Nick, D-Texas (9)
Langevin, Jim, D-R.I. (2)
Lantos, Tom, D-Calif. (12)
Largent, Steve, R-Okla. (1)
Larsen, Rick, D-Wash. (2)
Larson, John B., D-Conn. (1)
Latham, Tom, R-Iowa (5)
LaTourette, Steven C., R-Ohio (19)
Leach, Jim, R-Iowa (1)
Lee, Barbara, D-Calif. (9)
Levin, Sander M., D-Mich. (12)
Lewis, Jerry, R-Calif. (40)
Lewis, John, D-Ga. (5)
Lewis, Ron, R-Ky. (2)

Linder, John, R-Ga. (11)
Lipinski, William O., D-Ill. (3)
LoBiondo, Frank A., R-N.J. (2)
Lofgren, Zoe, D-Calif. (16)
Lowey, Nita M., D-N.Y. (18)
Lucas, Frank D., R-Okla. (6)
Lucas, Ken, D-Ky. (4)
Luther, Bill, D-Minn. (6)
Lynch, Stephen F., D-Mass. (9)

— M —

Maloney, Carolyn B., D-N.Y. (14)
Maloney, Jim, D-Conn. (5)
Manzullo, Donald, R-Ill. (16)
Markey, Edward J., D-Mass. (7)
Mascara, Frank R., D-Pa. (20)
Matheson, Jim, D-Utah (2)
Matsui, Robert T., D-Calif. (5)
McCarthy, Carolyn, D-N.Y. (4)
McCarthy, Karen, D-Mo. (5)
McCollum, Betty, D-Minn. (4)
McCrery, Jim, R-La. (4)
McDermott, Jim, D-Wash. (7)
McGovern, Jim, D-Mass. (3)
McHugh, John M., R-N.Y. (24)
McInnis, Scott, R-Colo. (3)
McIntyre, Mike, D-N.C. (7)
McKeon, Howard P. "Buck," R-Calif. (25)
McKinney, Cynthia A., D-Ga. (4)
McNulty, Michael R., D-N.Y. (21)
Meehan, Martin T., D-Mass. (5)
Meek, Carrie P., D-Fla. (17)
Meeks, Gregory W., D-N.Y. (6)
Menendez, Robert, D-N.J. (13)
Mica, John L., R-Fla. (7)
Millender-McDonald, Juanita, D-Calif. (37)
Miller, Dan, R-Fla. (13)
Miller, Gary G., R-Calif. (41)
Miller, George, D-Calif. (7)
Miller, Jeff, R-Fla. (1)
Mink, Patsy T., D-Hawaii (2)
Mollohan, Alan B., D-W.Va. (1)
Moore, Dennis, D-Kan. (3)
Moran, James P., D-Va. (8)
Moran, Jerry, R-Kan. (1)
Morella, Constance A., R-Md. (8)
Murtha, John P., D-Pa. (12)
Myrick, Sue, R-N.C. (9)

— N —

Nadler, Jerrold, D-N.Y. (8)
Napolitano, Grace F., D-Calif. (34)
Neal, Richard E., D-Mass. (2)
Nethercutt, George, R-Wash. (5)
Ney, Bob, R-Ohio (18)
Northup, Anne M., R-Ky. (3)
Norwood, Charlie, R-Ga. (10)
Nussle, Jim, R-Iowa (2)

— O —

Oberstar, James L., D-Minn. (8)
Obey, David R., D-Wis. (7)
Olver, John W., D-Mass. (1)
Ortiz, Solomon P., D-Texas (27)
Osborne, Tom, R-Neb. (3)
Ose, Doug, R-Calif. (3)
Otter, C. L. "Butch," R-Idaho (1)
Owens, Major R., D-N.Y. (11)
Oxley, Michael G., R-Ohio (4)

— P —

Pallone, Frank Jr., D-N.J. (6)
Pascrell, Bill Jr., D-N.J. (8)
Pastor, Ed, D-Ariz. (2)
Paul, Ron, R-Texas (14)
Payne, Donald M., D-N.J. (10)
Pelosi, Nancy, D-Calif. (8)
Pence, Mike, R-Ind. (2)
Peterson, Collin C., D-Minn. (7)
Peterson, John E., R-Pa. (5)
Petri, Tom, R-Wis. (6)
Phelps, David, D-Ill. (19)
Pickering, Charles W. "Chip" Jr., R-Miss. (3)
Pitts, Joe, R-Pa. (16)
Platts, Todd R., R-Pa. (19)
Pombo, Richard W., R-Calif. (11)
Pomeroy, Earl, D-N.D. (AL)
Portman, Rob, R-Ohio (2)

. . . Governors, Supreme Court, Cabinet-Rank Officers

Price, David E., D-N.C. (4)
Pryce, Deborah, R-Ohio (15)
Putnam, Adam H., R-Fla. (12)

— Q, R —

Quinn, Jack, R-N.Y. (30)
Radanovich, George P., R-Calif. (19)
Rahall, Nick J. II, D-W.Va. (3)
Ramstad, Jim, R-Minn. (3)
Rangel, Charles B., D-N.Y. (15)
Regula, Ralph, R-Ohio (16)
Rehberg, Denny, R-Mont. (AL)
Reyes, Silvestre, D-Texas (16)
Reynolds, Thomas M., R-N.Y. (27)
Riley, Bob, R-Ala. (3)
Rivers, Lynn, D-Mich. (13)
Rodriguez, Ciro D., D-Texas (28)
Roemer, Tim, D-Ind. (3)
Rogers, Harold, R-Ky. (5)
Rogers, Mike, R-Mich. (8)
Rohrabacher, Dana, R-Calif. (45)
Ros-Lehtinen, Ileana, R-Fla. (18)
Ross, Mike, D-Ark. (4)
Rothman, Steven R., D-N.J. (9)
Roukema, Marge, R-N.J. (5)
Roybal-Allard, Lucille, D-Calif. (33)
Royce, Ed, R-Calif. (39)
Rush, Bobby L., D-Ill. (1)
Ryan, Paul D., R-Wis. (1)
Ryun, Jim, R-Kan. (2)

— S —

Sabo, Martin Olav, D-Minn. (5)
Sanchez, Loretta, D-Calif. (46)
Sanders, Bernard, I-Vt. (AL)
Sandlin, Max, D-Texas (1)
Sawyer, Tom, D-Ohio (14)
Saxton, H. James, R-N.J. (3)
Schaffer, Bob, R-Colo. (4)
Schakowsky, Jan, D-Ill. (9)
Schiff, Adam B., D-Calif. (27)
Schrock, Ed, R-Va. (2)
Scott, Robert C., D-Va. (3)
Sensenbrenner, F. James Jr., R-Wis. (9)
Serrano, Jose E., D-N.Y. (16)
Sessions, Pete, R-Texas (5)
Shadegg, John, R-Ariz. (4)
Shaw, E. Clay Jr., R-Fla. (22)
Shays, Christopher, R-Conn. (4)
Sherman, Brad, D-Calif. (24)
Sherwood, Donald L., R-Pa. (10)
Shimkus, John, R-Ill. (20)
Shows, Ronnie, D-Miss. (4)
Shuster, Bill, R-Pa. (9)
Simmons, Rob, R-Conn. (2)
Simpson, Mike, R-Idaho (2)
Skeen, Joe, R-N.M. (2)
Skelton, Ike, D-Mo. (4)
Slaughter, Louise M., D-N.Y. (28)
Smith, Adam, D-Wash. (9)
Smith, Christopher H., R-N.J. (4)
Smith, Lamar, R-Texas (21)
Smith, Nick, R-Mich. (7)
Snyder, Vic, D-Ark. (2)
Solis, Hilda L., D-Calif. (31)
Souder, Mark, R-Ind. (4)
Spratt, John M. Jr., D-S.C. (5)
Stark, Pete, D-Calif. (13)
Stearns, Cliff, R-Fla. (6)
Stenholm, Charles W., D-Texas (17)
Strickland, Ted, D-Ohio (6)
Stump, Bob, R-Ariz. (3)
Stupak, Bart, D-Mich. (1)
Sununu, John E., R-N.H. (1)
Sweeney, John E., R-N.Y. (22)

— T —

Tancredo, Tom, R-Colo. (6)
Tanner, John, D-Tenn. (8)
Tauscher, Ellen O., D-Calif. (10)
Tauzin, Billy, R-La. (3)
Taylor, Charles H., R-N.C. (11)
Taylor, Gene, D-Miss. (5)
Terry, Lee, R-Neb. (2)
Thomas, Bill, R-Calif. (21)
Thompson, Bennie, D-Miss. (2)
Thompson, Mike, D-Calif. (1)
Thornberry, William M. "Mac," R-Texas (13)

Thune, John, R-S.D. (AL)
Thurman, Karen L., D-Fla. (5)
Tiahrt, Todd, R-Kan. (4)
Tiberi, Pat, R-Ohio (12)
Tierney, John F., D-Mass. (6)
Toomey, Patrick J., R-Pa. (15)
Towns, Edolphus, D-N.Y. (10)
Traficant, James A. Jr., D-Ohio (17)
Turner, Jim, D-Texas (2)

— U, V —

Udall, Mark, D-Colo. (2)
Udall, Tom, D-N.M. (3)
Upton, Fred, R-Mich. (6)
Velázquez, Nydia M., D-N.Y. (12)
Visclosky, Peter J., D-Ind. (1)
Vitter, David, R-La. (1)

— W —

Walden, Greg, R-Ore. (2)
Walsh, James T., R-N.Y. (25)
Wamp, Zach, R-Tenn. (3)
Waters, Maxine, D-Calif. (35)
Watkins, Wes, R-Okla. (3)
Watson, Diane, D-Calif. (32)
Watt, Melvin, D-N.C. (12)
Watts, J.C. Jr., R-Okla. (4)
Waxman, Henry A., D-Calif. (29)
Weiner, Anthony, D-N.Y. (9)
Weldon, Curt, R-Pa. (7)
Weldon, Dave, R-Fla. (15)
Weller, Jerry, R-Ill. (11)
Wexler, Robert, D-Fla. (19)
Whitfield, Edward, R-Ky. (1)
Wicker, Roger, R-Miss. (1)
Wilson, Heather A., R-N.M. (1)
Wilson, Joe, R-S.C. (2)
Wolf, Frank R., R-Va. (10)
Woolsey, Lynn, D-Calif. (6)
Wu, David, D-Ore. (1)
Wynn, Albert R., D-Md. (4)

— X, Y, Z —

Young, C.W. Bill, R-Fla. (10)
Young, Don, R-Alaska (AL)

Delegates

Acevedo-Vilá, Aníbal, D-P.R.
Christensen, Donna M.C., D-Virgin Is.
Faleomavaega, Eni F.H., D-Am. Samoa
Norton, Eleanor Holmes, D-D.C.
Underwood, Robert A., D-Guam

Senators
R 49; D 50; I 1

Akaka, Daniel K., D-Hawaii
Allard, Wayne, R-Colo.
Allen, George F., R-Va.
Baucus, Max, D-Mont.
Bayh, Evan, D-Ind.
Bennett, Robert F., R-Utah
Biden, Joseph R. Jr., D-Del.
Bingaman, Jeff, D-N.M.
Bond, Christopher S., R-Mo.
Boxer, Barbara, D-Calif.
Breaux, John B., D-La.
Brownback, Sam, R-Kan.
Bunning, Jim, R-Ky.
Burns, Conrad, R-Mont.
Byrd, Robert C., D-W.Va.
Campbell, Ben Nighthorse, R-Colo.
Cantwell, Maria, D-Wash.
Carnahan, Jean, D-Mo.
Carper, Thomas R., D-Del.
Chafee, Lincoln, R-R.I.
Cleland, Max, D-Ga.
Clinton, Hillary Rodham, D-N.Y.
Cochran, Thad, R-Miss.
Collins, Susan, R-Maine
Conrad, Kent, D-N.D.
Corzine, Jon, D-N.J.
Craig, Larry E., R-Idaho
Crapo, Michael D., R-Idaho
Daschle, Tom, D-S.D.
Dayton, Mark, D-Minn.

DeWine, Mike, R-Ohio
Dodd, Christopher J., D-Conn.
Domenici, Pete V., R-N.M.
Dorgan, Byron L., D-N.D.
Durbin, Richard J., D-Ill.
Edwards, John, D-N.C.
Ensign, John, R-Nev.
Enzi, Michael B., R-Wyo.
Feingold, Russell D., D-Wis.
Feinstein, Dianne, D-Calif.
Fitzgerald, Peter G., R-Ill.
Frist, Bill, R-Tenn.
Graham, Bob, D-Fla.
Gramm, Phil, R-Texas
Grassley, Charles E., R-Iowa
Gregg, Judd, R-N.H.
Hagel, Chuck, R-Neb.
Harkin, Tom, D-Iowa
Hatch, Orrin G., R-Utah
Helms, Jesse, R-N.C.
Hollings, Ernest F., D-S.C.
Hutchinson, Tim, R-Ark.
Hutchison, Kay Bailey, R-Texas
Inhofe, James M., R-Okla.
Inouye, Daniel K., D-Hawaii
Jeffords, James M., I-Vt.
Johnson, Tim, D-S.D.
Kennedy, Edward M., D-Mass.
Kerry, John, D-Mass.
Kohl, Herb, D-Wis.
Kyl, Jon, R-Ariz.
Landrieu, Mary L., D-La.
Leahy, Patrick J., D-Vt.
Levin, Carl, D-Mich.
Lieberman, Joseph I., D-Conn.
Lincoln, Blanche, D-Ark.
Lott, Trent, R-Miss.
Lugar, Richard G., R-Ind.
McCain, John, R-Ariz.
McConnell, Mitch, R-Ky.
Mikulski, Barbara A., D-Md.
Miller, Zell, D-Ga.
Murkowski, Frank H., R-Alaska
Murray, Patty, D-Wash.
Nelson, Ben, D-Neb.
Nelson, Bill, D-Fla.
Nickles, Don, R-Okla.
Reed, Jack, D-R.I.
Reid, Harry, D-Nev.
Roberts, Pat, R-Kan.
Rockefeller, John D. IV, D-W.Va.
Santorum, Rick, R-Pa.
Sarbanes, Paul S., D-Md.
Schumer, Charles E., D-N.Y.
Sessions, Jeff, R-Ala.
Shelby, Richard C., R-Ala.
Smith, Gordon H., R-Ore.
Smith, Robert C., R-N.H.
Snowe, Olympia J., R-Maine
Specter, Arlen, R-Pa.
Stabenow, Debbie, D-Mich.
Stevens, Ted, R-Alaska
Thomas, Craig, R-Wyo.
Thompson, Fred, R-Tenn.
Thurmond, Strom, R-S.C.
Torricelli, Robert G., D-N.J.
Voinovich, George V., R-Ohio
Warner, John W., R-Va.
Wellstone, Paul, D-Minn.
Wyden, Ron, D-Ore.

Governors
R 29; D 19; I 2

Ala. — Donald Siegelman, D
Alaska — Tony Knowles, D
Ariz. — Jane Dee Hull, R
Ark. — Mike Huckabee, R
Calif. — Gray Davis, D
Colo. — Bill Owens, R
Conn. — John G. Rowland, R
Del. — Ruth Ann Minner, D
Fla. — Jeb Bush, R
Ga. — Roy Barnes, D
Hawaii — Benjamin J. Cayetano, D
Idaho — Dirk Kempthorne, R
Ill. — George Ryan, R
Ind. — Frank L. O'Bannon, D
Iowa — Tom Vilsack, D
Kan. — Bill Graves, R

Ky. — Paul E. Patton, D
La. — Mike Foster, R
Maine — Angus King, I
Md. — Parris N. Glendening, D
Mass. — Jane Swift, R
Mich. — John Engler, R
Minn. — Jesse Ventura, I
Miss. — Ronnie Musgrove, D
Mo. — Bob Holden, D
Mont. — Judy Martz, R
Neb. — Mike Johanns, R
Nev. — Kenny Guinn, R
N.H. — Jeanne Shaheen, D
N.J. — Donald T. DiFrancesco, R
N.M. — Gary E. Johnson, R
N.Y. — George E. Pataki, R
N.C. — Michael F. Easley, D
N.D. — John Hoeven, R
Ohio — Bob Taft, R
Okla. — Frank Keating, R
Ore. — John Kitzhaber, D
Pa. — Mark Schweiker, R
R.I. — Lincoln C. Almond, R
S.C. — Jim Hodges, D
S.D. — William J. Janklow, R
Tenn. — Don Sundquist, R
Texas — Rick Perry, R
Utah — Michael O. Leavitt, R
Vt. — Howard Dean, D
Va. — James S. Gilmore III, R
Wash. — Gary Locke, D
W.Va. — Bob Wise, D
Wis. — Scott McCallum, R
Wyo. — Jim Geringer, R

Supreme Court

Rehnquist, William H. — Va., Chief Justice
Breyer, Stephen G. — Mass.
Ginsburg, Ruth Bader — N.Y.
Kennedy, Anthony M. — Calif.
O'Connor, Sandra Day — Ariz.
Scalia, Antonin — Va.
Souter, David H. — N.H.
Stevens, John Paul — Ill.
Thomas, Clarence — Ga.

Cabinet

Abraham, Spencer — Energy
Ashcroft, John — Attorney General
Chao, Elaine L. — Labor
Evans, Donald L. — Commerce
Powell, Colin L. — State
Martinez, Mel — HUD
Mineta, Norman Y. — Transportation
Norton, Gale A. — Interior
O'Neill, Paul H. — Treasury
Paige, Rod — Education
Principi, Anthony J. — Veterans Affairs
Rumsfeld, Donald H. — Defense
Thompson, Tommy G. — HHS
Veneman, Ann M. — Agriculture

Other Executive Branch Officers

Cheney, Dick — Vice President
Card, Andrew H. Jr. — Chief of Staff
Daniels, Mitchell E. Jr. — OMB Director
Lindsey, Lawrence — Chairman, National Economic Council
Negroponte, John D. — U.N. Representative
Rice, Condoleezza — National Security Adviser
Tenet, George J. — Director of Central Intelligence
Whitman, Christine Todd — EPA Administrator
Zoellick, Robert B. — U.S. Trade Representative

Appendix B

VOTE STUDIES

Bush Gets Off to Strong Start

A president who began his term with his very legitimacy questioned ended up winning a higher annual share of congressional victories than any of the previous six presidents.

Of the 120 votes on which George W. Bush staked out a clear position during 2001, he got his way all but 16 times. That 87 percent success rate is the best since 1965, when Lyndon B. Johnson won 93 percent of the votes he asked for.

The presidential support rate does not measure how many of a chief executive's initiatives advance in a single year — let alone become law — or how many lawmakers side with the president. It only assesses how frequently Congress votes the way the president wanted. Congressional Quarterly looks at every vote on the House and Senate floors, determines whether the president had taken a clear position beforehand and notes the outcome. Since 1953, when CQ started tracking the figure, presidential support in Congress ranged from Johnson's high in 1965, when he pushed through much of his Great Society program with the help of the most lopsided majority of fellow Democrats since the New Deal, to the low of 36 percent of another Democrat, Bill Clinton, when he faced off in 1995 against the first Republican Congress in four decades.

Bush's first-year success might appear surprising for someone who lost the popular vote in the presidential election and confronted a Congress so closely divided between the two parties. Yet explanations are not hard to find. As the year began, the political stage was set for Republicans to move on their agenda, starting with the confirmation of the new president's Cabinet. Later, the worst attack ever on American soil drove lawmakers of both parties to stand by the nation's leader. And all year, Bush helped to buoy his success rate with his strategies for handling Capitol Hill.

When Bush was inaugurated, he was blessed with one-party government. For the first time since 1954, the GOP controlled not only the White House but also the House of Representatives and the Senate — albeit only with the assurance of Vice President Dick Cheney's vote to break a 50-50 tie. "They magnified the advantage of a small numerical majority," said Steven Schier, professor of political science at Minnesota's Carleton College. "Republicans were able to dominate the agenda. They had remarkable party unity. . . . In the Senate, they were able to pick off a few Democrats."

After eight years of chafing against a Democratic president, Republicans arrived for the 107th Congress keen to work with the White House to enact a GOP agenda. This pent-up desire was most easily exercised in the House, where Speaker J. Dennis Hastert, R-Ill., grabbed issues at the top of Bush's domestic platform, such as cutting taxes and overhauling federal education programs, and put them on the schedule. Early on, Bush also got his way on social initiatives important to both him and most Republicans, such as elevating the legal standing of a fetus and pre-venting foreign aid from supporting abortion.

At the same time, the Republican leadership kept off the floor many of the Democrats' priorities, such as an increase in the minimum wage, as well as many bills the president opposed, such as the year's initial versions of a patients' bill of rights.

Following the Sept. 11 terrorist attacks, Bush's popularity soared and lawmakers cleaved to the commander-in-chief; few voted against his wishes. After the attacks, he won 11 of the 12 votes in the House and 30 of 31 votes in the Senate on which he made his position clear. In this period, he also was aided by the loyalty of his Republican allies in Congress. In the Senate, 49 Republicans, although in the minority, were able to quash the Democrats' initiatives by denying them the 60 votes required to limit debate, thereby preventing legislation that Bush opposed from getting to a final vote. Democrats, for example, failed four times to bring about an end to debate on their farm bill (S 1731).

Only for a brief period did Bush's success in Congress slip: the nine legislative weeks after James M. Jeffords of Vermont left the GOP and gave control of the Senate to the Democrats until Sept. 11. Of the dozen Senate votes during that period on which Bush took a position — excluding nine votes to confirm presidential nominees — Bush lost five, a 58 percent Senate support score. Those summertime rebuffs were some of the highest-profile setbacks for the president in the year, including passage of a patients' rights bill he had vowed to veto (S 1052) and the rejection of Bush's plan to distribute federal vouchers to subsidize private school tuition.

Interestingly, Bush's support drooped in the GOP House during the summer as well; his view prevailed a comparatively low 72 percent of the time between Memorial Day and the terrorist attacks, when he lost five of 18 votes, including on proposals to allow more oil drilling in the Gulf of Mexico, permit Mexican trucks on American roads and lessen standards for arsenic in drinking water.

Economic vs. Domestic Issues

Support for the president's views varied by issue. He had the most success on economic policy, winning 92 percent of the time he made his views plain on a tax, budget, appropriations or trade question. His support score on purely domestic issues slid to 73 percent; on defense and foreign policy votes, it was 71 percent.

Occasionally, Bush's defeats were evanescent. While in July the House voted, against his wishes, to stop prosecuting Americans who illegally travel to Cuba, for example, the provision was ultimately left out of the fiscal 2002 Treasury-Postal Service appropriations law (PL 107-67). The new president's fate offered a faint echo of his predecessor, Clinton, whose positions often were spurned by the GOP House but prevailed in the final bill.

When Congress voted the way Bush

PRESIDENTIAL SUCCESS ▶ **History**

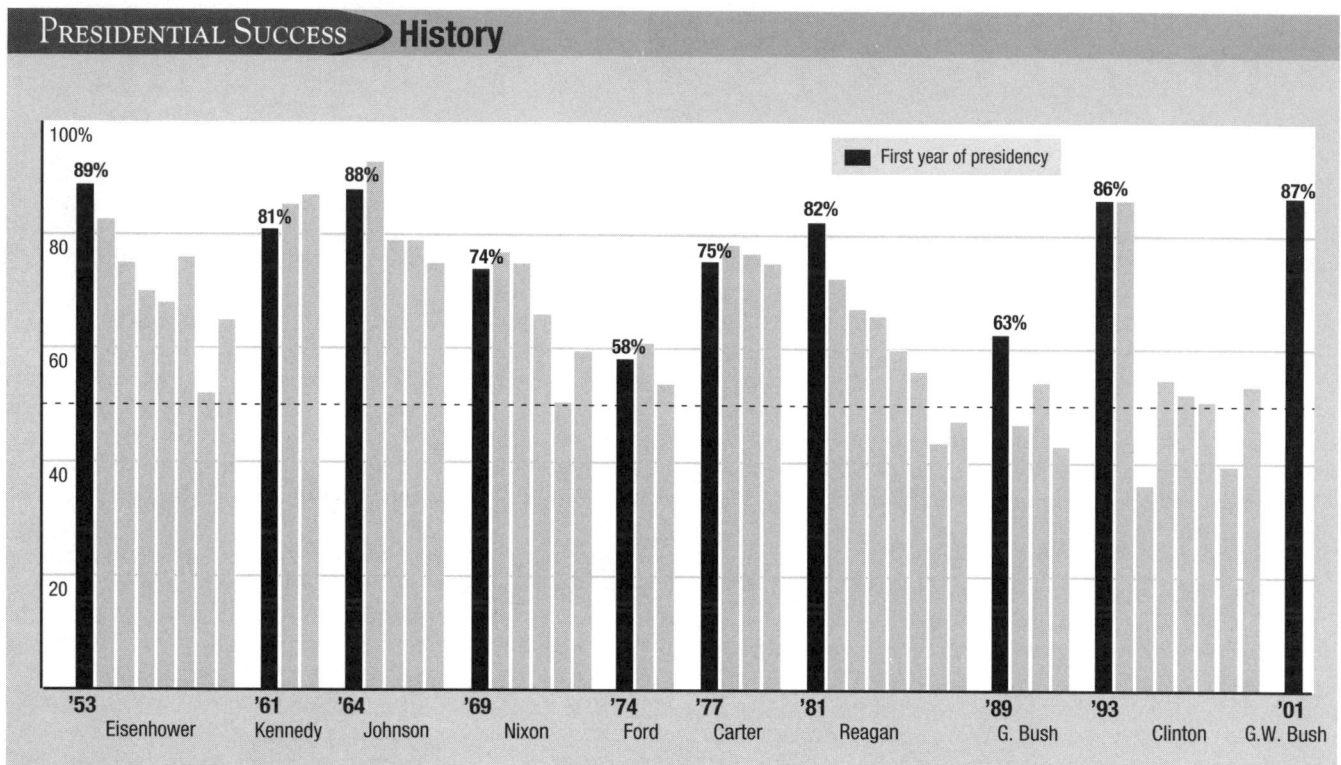

2001 Data	
Senate	68 victories
	9 defeats
House	36 victories
	7 defeats
Total Bush success rate:	87%

For More Information

Top scorers . . . . p. B-5
Lists of votes . . . . pp. B-12, B-13
House members' scores . . . . . p. B-14
Senators' scores . . . . p. B-16

wanted, it generally did so by healthy margins. But some of the year's key votes were decided by razor-thin edges in the president's favor, highlighting how narrowly divided the Congress was and how Bush's future success rates could hinge on the outcome of the next midterm election. In the House, nine Bush victories — on issues including trade expansion, the budget and family planning — would have been defeats had nine or fewer lawmakers switched sides and voted against the president's position. Four Senate victories, three of them on education, would have been lost had three or fewer senators who backed Bush opposed him instead.

The modern-era presidents studied by CQ typically racked up high shares of presidential support in their first years, largely because of the cache of votes the Senate cast at the start of each administration on presidential nominees. Clinton, too, achieved an 86 percent support rate his first year, thanks to Senate confirmations and a Democratic majority Congress in 1993. In 2001, confirmations accounted for 36 percent of all the presidential support votes; Bush won every one. Excluding confirmations, he succeeded 79 percent of the time he made it plain what he wanted.

The Art of Compromise

Beyond party control and wartime patriotism, Bush's score benefitted from his style for dealing with Congress — a blend of compromise, careful selection of battles and tactical shifts.

Reprising a formula he developed with the state Legislature during his six years as governor of Texas, Bush's signature strategy on Capitol Hill was to begin by outlining his desires in broad terms, rather then detailed legislative language. Then, after concluding that he had achieved the best outcome possible given the will of Congress, Bush often chose to declare the final compromise a victory — even when some of the principles he set out were scrapped or some of his desires were ignored.

For example, he embraced a law (PL 107-16) that, although delivering the deepest tax cut in two decades, came up $290 billion short of the mark he initially said was "just right." Congress spurned Bush's campaign call for school vouchers, but when he signed the education overhaul (PL 107-110), he hailed it as "a great symbol of what is possible in Washington when good people come together to do what's right."

That approach was fine with many Democrats. "How much is Bush and how much was Democrat priorities?" asked Jerry Hart, a senior aide in the House minority whip's office. "He talks and espouses the conservative agenda. The reality is much different in the end. Bush is willing to compromise. As long as the formula works for him, we keep walking away with provisions that Democrats want."

Second, Bush selected a rather narrow universe of issues to take a stand on. "The administration chose its agenda carefully and maximized its rate of success," Schier said.

While many disagreements played out behind the scenes, Bush pronounced an unambiguous up-or-down preference in advance of only 43 House roll calls. By contrast, Clinton laid out his position twice as often, an average of 86 House presi-

Leading Scorers: Presidential Support

Support indicates those who in 2001 voted most often for President Bush's position. **Opposition** shows those who voted most often against the president's position. Scores are based on actual votes cast; members are listed alphabetically when their scores are tied. Members who missed half or more of the votes are not listed.

Senate Support

Republicans		Democrats	
Gregg, N.H.	100%	Miller, Ga.	82%
Lugar, Ind.	100	Breaux, La.	77
Murkowski, Alaska	100	Landrieu, La.	74
Bond, Mo.	99	Nelson, Neb.	74
Brownback, Kan.	99	Carper, Del.	72
Enzi, Wyo.	99	Baucus, Mont.	71
Frist, Tenn.	99	Byrd, W.Va.	71
Gramm, Texas	99	Carnahan, Mo.	71
Grassley, Iowa	99	Feinstein, Calif.	71
Kyl, Ariz.	99	Johnson, S.D.	71
Roberts, Kan.	99	Lincoln, Ark.	71
Thompson, Tenn.	99		

Senate Opposition

Republicans		Democrats	
Chafee, R.I.	16%	Wellstone, Minn.	41%
Snowe, Maine	16	Dayton, Minn.	40
Specter, Pa.	13	Clinton, N.Y.	39
Collins, Maine	12	Feingold, Wis.	39
McCain, Ariz.	9	Durbin, Ill.	38
Hutchinson, Ark.	8	Hollings, S.C.	38
Smith, Ore.	7	Leahy, Vt.	38
DeWine, Ohio	5	Corzine, N.J.	37
Inhofe, Okla.	5	Harkin, Iowa	37
Voinovich, Ohio	5	Sarbanes, Md.	37

House Support

Republicans		Democrats	
Baker, La.	100%	Hall, Texas	86%
Callahan, Ala.	100	Lucas, Ky.	81
Dreier, Calif.	100	Traficant, Ohio	81
Miller, Calif.	100	John, La.	69
Armey, Texas	98	Cramer, Ala.	67
Bachus, Ala.	98	Shows, Miss.	64
Boehner, Ohio	98	Lipinski, Ill.	61
Bryant, Tenn.	98	Ortiz, Texas	58
DeLay, Texas	98	Skelton, Mo.	56
Knollenberg, Mich.	98	Gordon, Tenn.	54
Linder, Ga.	98	Dooley, Calif.	53
McCrery, La.	98	Stenholm, Texas	53
McInnis, Colo.	98	Clement, Tenn.	52
McKeon, Calif.	98	McIntyre, N.C.	52
Northup, Ky.	98		
Oxley, Ohio	98		
Schrock, Va.	98		
Skeen, N.M.	98		
Watts, Okla.	98		

House Opposition

Republicans		Democrats	
Paul, Texas	51%	Conyers, Mich.	93%
Morella, Md.	47	Frank, Mass.	91
Leach, Iowa	40	Brown, Ohio	88
Gilman, N.Y.	38	Filner, Calif.	88
Ramstad, Minn.	35	Lee, Calif.	88
Shays, Conn.	35	Olver, Mass.	88
Castle, Del.	33	Payne, N.J.	88
Gilchrest, Md.	33	Rivers, Mich.	88
Johnson, Conn.	30	Waters, Calif.	88
Smith, N.J.	30	Watt, N.C.	88
		Sabo, Minn.	86
		Scott, Va.	86
		Woolsey, Calif.	86

dential support votes a year in his presidency.

Many of the most contentious and pivotal votes occurred when members had no clear presidential position in hand. Of the 23 "key votes" CQ identified for 2001 — because they were on matters of major public controversy, matters of presidential or political power, or of potentially great impact on the nation and the lives of Americans — Bush took a clear-cut position on only 16 of them.

When Bush did take a firm stand, it usually was in favor of what Congress had drafted and was therefore inclined to approve. He called for a "yes" vote on 86 of the year's 120 presidential support votes, or 72 percent.

Bush rarely drew a line in the sand, issuing explicit veto threats only against spending levels he viewed as excessive and four other distinct proposals that Congress considered during the year: to restrict Mexican trucks on U.S. roads, to allow aid to international family planning groups that promote or perform abortions, to expand use of stem cells and to open managed care plans to more lawsuits. He got his way on each and did not veto a bill.

"What he decides are his bottom line things are few. Other stuff, he's not going to lose points off his popularity to get them," concluded George Kundanis, a top aide to House Minority Leader Richard A. Gephardt, D-Mo.

Finally, Bush changed course from week to week, lobbying hard on points, then backing away from them, to nudge legislation along. Like a tacking sailboat, the White House would typically first push to the right for a strongly conservative measure in the House, where GOP numbers and party discipline could help him achieve that. Later he would move back to the center, lobbying for a compromise that often was different from his original desire.

Bush initially opposed the federalization of airport security workers, helping the Republicans win a hard-fought victory in the House. Yet he later embraced the final version of the aviation security package (PL 107-71) even though it included the very federalization he opposed. This granted Bush two victories in the CQ study, albeit for different points of view.

Bush's "House hat is different than his Senate hat. In the House, he pushes the envelope as far as it will go. He takes what he can get from the Senate, and then he pushes for compromise," said Ilona Nickels, a Washington-based scholar at Indiana University's Center on Congress. "This president practices the art of the possible rather than the art of the perfect." ◆

Pattern of Partisanship Persists

The early betting was that moderates would play a key role in the closely divided 107th Congress. The dramatic effect of a single senator's decision in May to switch parties might seem to validate the prediction. Yet when it came to voting on legislation, centrists of both parties had relatively little influence.

Frustrated by partisanship in the Senate, which kept both Democrats and Republicans close to their leadership, and deftly handled by the GOP leadership in the House, moderates seldom had a decisive effect on legislation.

Though briefly emboldened by Vermont Sen. James M. Jeffords' defection from the GOP, moderates found themselves bound tighter to their parties and to President Bush's legislative agenda after the Sept. 11 terrorist attacks.

"It has been quite a year," said Sen. Lincoln Chafee, R-R.I., who was closely watched by his colleagues after Jeffords turned control of the Senate over to Democrats. "This fall, the focus changed dramatically, with the pressures to vote for the president."

Even before Sept. 11, the growing partisanship in the Senate — historically seen as the more deliberative body — had reduced the flexibility of the moderates. Overall, the narrow party divisions in that chamber led to an increase in party-line voting to 55 percent in 2001 from 49 percent the year before. That level remained largely consistent throughout 2001, even after Jeffords' switch.

In the House, by contrast, the percent of party unity votes dropped to 40 percent in 2001, the fourth consecutive year of decline.

Congressional Quarterly's assessment of party unity is based on the percentage of those roll-call votes that pitted a majority of Republicans against a majority of Democrats.

The razor-thin split in the Senate —50-50 under Republicans; 50-49 after the Democrats took over — heightened the pressures to conform to party wishes and often left the centrists with little leverage to sway their colleagues. During negotiations on the ill-fated economic stimulus bill, for example, a bipartisan group of centrists led by Sen. John B. Breaux, D-La., offered their own alternative to the highly partisan bill passed by the House. But talks with Democratic leaders in the Senate stalled, and the bill was left hanging at the end of the session.

Academic observers of Congress attribute the trend in the House to a leadership team that had grown into the job it had had since 1999, and in the Senate to the tactics of Majority Leader Tom Daschle, D-S.D.

"It all goes back to Tom Daschle, who is an extremely ef-fective majority leader in terms of keeping his people together," said Burdett Loomis, a political science professor at the University of Kansas. "Numbers may not quite tell you the whole story, but I think that there's somewhat less confrontation and better management in the House."

There were some intensely partisan battles in both chambers over the economic stimulus package, energy legislation and campaign finance proposals. Indeed, one reason some House Democrats could join their Republican counterparts on certain votes was the knowledge that a Democratic-led Senate would block House-passed legislation.

"The challenges of Senate leadership are so substantially different than the House," said Gary W. Copeland, director of the Carl Albert Center at the University of Oklahoma. A one-vote margin in a chamber that is by nature fractious makes Daschle's job particularly tough, Albert says. "To have some control over his party, that's got to be a success."

A Disciplined House

House GOP moderates credited their leaders, especially Speaker J. Dennis Hastert of Illinois, with maintaining cohesion. Teamwork, along with the period of bipartisan unity immediately after Sept. 11, helped reduce partisan voting.

"Hastert has done an outstanding job of building the team concept," said Sherwood Boehlert, R-N.Y. "There's a greater appreciation that we're all in this together." Boehlert, who had voted against the GOP position more than a third of the time in recent years, broke with his party on just 21 percent of party unity votes in 2001.

Hastert's work, coupled with the effectiveness of Majority Whip Tom DeLay, R-Texas, on a number of high-profile votes, meant House Republicans could practically ensure victory without making concessions to Democrats.

"If there's a big story in the House, it is the ability of [the leadership] to capture the moderates a much higher percentage of the time," Loomis said.

Because GOP leaders generally could count on most, if not all, of their members staying with the party on crucial votes, they did not need to attract large numbers of Democrats to ensure success.

Democrats who voted most frequently with Republicans often were attracted to Bush's conservative agenda. Three members of the "Blue Dog" coalition, a group of mostly Southern, fiscally conservative House Democrats, crossed party lines more than half the time. It was the largest such group in the coalition's brief history. Democrat Ralph M. Hall of Texas voted with Republicans most often, at 75 percent of the time.

But the Blue Dogs were crucial to the outcome on only one party unity vote in 2001. The cohesiveness of the Republican caucus was enough.

That left the moderates with relatively little clout. Chris John, D-La., a Blue Dog co-chairman, for example, expressed disappointment at what he saw as a lack of political sensitivity by the Bush administration when it backed a vote on a second economic stimulus package (HR 3529). Though members of the group did not want to oppose tax cuts, they felt they had to vote against the bill because it would add to the deficit.

"They're going to wound some of their friends on this side by forcing us to vote again on this," John said hours before the Dec. 20 vote.

Ways and Means Committee Chairman Bill Thomas, R-Calif., was roundly criticized by Democrats for excluding all but a few of them in talks on a fast-track trade bill (HR 3005), but the strategy reflected the voting situation in that body. Passage of the fast-track bill, as well as both versions of the economic stimulus package and a critical early vote on the Bush tax cut plan, was achieved in the House without courting Democrats.

Even when they prevailed, moderates could find themselves coming away empty-handed. When House GOP leaders wrote a rule that blocked floor consideration of a bipartisan campaign-finance bill, moderate Republicans joined with Democrats to defeat the rule on a largely party-line vote. The move effectively killed campaign finance legislation for the year. So while the moderates got their vote, the GOP leadership kept a bill they opposed from passing. (Supporters ended the year nearing their goal of 218 signatures on a discharge petition that would force the bill back onto the floor in the second session.)

Conservative Democrats did cause some heartache for their leaders. Georgia Democrat Zell Miller often joined Senate Republicans on crucial votes, providing early Democratic support for Bush's tax cut package.

Bucking the Party

The familiar faces topping the 2001 list of Democrats and Republicans in both chambers most likely to oppose their party on partisan votes remained little changed from previous years. What did change in many cases was the frequency of their opposition.

The quintessential Senate centrist in 2001 was Chafee. On votes that split the parties he voted with each 50 percent of the time. Chafee led the list of Senate Republicans voting against their party, as he did in 2000. But that year, his opposition score was a much higher 63 percent. Chafee said that prior years, when Republicans enjoyed as much as a five-seat majority, provided "a little bit of breathing room" on votes.

The pressure was greatest at the start of 2001, when every Republican vote was critical to maintaining a majority. After Jeffords' switch, Chafee said, GOP leaders still needed his vote, though they used a lighter touch. "It's not as heavy-

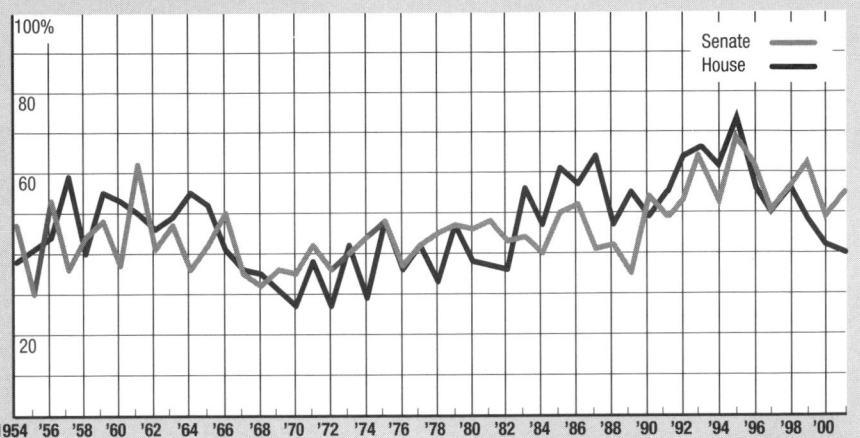

PARTY UNITY ▶ Partisan Voting by Chamber

The percentage of recorded floor votes in each chamber on which a majority of one party voted against a majority of the other party.

Senate
House

1954 '56 '58 '60 '62 '64 '66 '68 '70 '72 '74 '76 '78 '80 '82 '84 '86 '88 '90 '92 '94 '96 '98 '00

handed as in the past because they saw what the results can be," he said.

In the House, 11 Republicans voted against a majority of their colleagues at least 30 percent of the time in 1999. In 2001, just one met that threshold: Constance A. Morella of Maryland, a perennial cross-vote leader. But her opposition score, like Chafee's, dropped — from 50 percent in 2000 to 39 percent in 2001.

She attributes that to a disciplined legislative process that helped avoid fractious floor debates, particularly on appropriations bills. "It has been unusual to have found so many points of agreement," Morella said in a November interview. Specifically, she said some appropriations bills, which often generate intense debate and a multitude of party-line votes, went smoothly.

In 2000, six of the 13 annual spending bills were passed on party unity votes, including the typically contentious Commerce-Justice-State measure. In 2001, none were.

Even before Sept. 11, appropriations bills moved through the House without much rancor, in part because Democratic and Republican appropriators were given a clear budget outline by the Bush administration and congressional leaders. In addition, there was a noticeable lack of legislative riders on spending bills, a troublesome feature of previous years. The fiscal 2002 Commerce-Justice-State bill (PL 107-77) passed the House 408-19 on July 18.

One piece of legislation that drew partisan debate but emerged with a bipartisan vote was the education bill proposed by Bush and signed into law Jan. 8, 2002 (PL 107-110).

2001 Data

	PARTISAN VOTES	TOTAL VOTES	PERCENTAGE
Senate	210	380	55%
House	204	507	40%

For More Information

Top scorers. . . . . p. B-8
Background and data . . . . p. B-17
List of votes . . . . p. B-18
Senators' scores. . . . . p. B-19
House members' scores . . . . . p. B-20

Leading Scorers: Party Unity

Support indicates those who in 2001 voted most consistently with their party's majority against the other party. **Opposition** shows those who voted most often against their party's major- ity. Scores are based on votes cast; members are listed alpha- betically when their scores are tied. Members who missed half or more of the votes are not listed.

Senate Support

Republicans		Democrats	
Allard, Colo.	98%	Dayton, Minn.	99%
Helms, N.C.	98	Reed, R.I.	99
Kyl, Ariz.	98	Sarbanes, Md.	99
Lott, Miss.	98	Wellstone, Minn.	99
McConnell, Ky.	98	Akaka, Hawaii	98
Thurmond, S.C.	98	Boxer, Calif.	98
Bunning, Ky.	97	Cantwell, Wash.	98
Frist, Tenn.	97	Daschle, S.D.	98
Thomas, Wyo.	97	Dodd, Conn.	98
		Inouye, Hawaii	98
		Kerry, Mass.	98
		Leahy, Vt.	98
		Levin, Mich.	98
		Mikulski, Md.	98

Senate Opposition

Republicans		Democrats	
Chafee, R.I.	50%	Miller, Ga.	58%
Specter, Pa.	40	Nelson, Neb.	42
Snowe, Maine	36	Breaux, La.	41
Collins, Maine	33	Baucus, Mont.	33
McCain, Ariz.	33	Cleland, Ga.	22
		Torricelli, N.J.	22

House Support

Republicans		Democrats	
Boehner, Ohio	99%	Coyne, Pa.	99%
Bonilla, Texas	99	Filner, Calif.	99
Callahan, Ala.	99	Schakowsky, Ill.	99
Crane, Ill.	99	Solis, Calif.	99
Knollenberg, Mich.	99	Brown, Ohio	98
Oxley, Ohio	99	Miller, Calif.	98
Smith, Texas	99	Nadler, N.Y.	98
Tauzin, La.	99	Olver, Mass.	98
Thornberry, Texas	99	Woolsey, Calif.	98
Watts, Okla.	99		

House Opposition

Republicans		Democrats	
Morella, Md.	39%	Traficant, Ohio	91%
Leach, Iowa	27	Hall, Texas	75
Shays, Conn.	25	Lucas, Ky.	53
Gilman, N.Y.	24	Cramer, Ala.	50
Johnson, Conn.	24	John, La.	48
Ramstad, Minn.	23	Shows, Miss.	47
Boehlert, N.Y.	21	Stenholm, Texas	47
Castle, Del.	21	Taylor, Miss.	44
Paul, Texas	21	Skelton, Mo.	39
		Lipinski, Ill.	38

But the formula for success in that instance — a White House-backed process that brought together both parties in the beginning and kept them talking — was all but forgotten during much of the remainder of 2001.

With Congress heading into an election year, observers said the prospect of less partisanship in both bodies was slim, despite continuing support for the administration's effort to attack terrorism.

The Senate, in particular, was expected to see divisive debates under Daschle, the highest-ranking Democrat in the nation. Daschle was expected to use his position to help his party prepare for the midterm election, and Republicans to focus on him as a target for attack.

"Democrats undoubtedly see this as a critical opportunity for them and, I would think, try to be pretty aggressive in dividing the two parties," Copeland said. ◆

Voting Rate Edges Higher

Members of the House and Senate increased their overall voting participation record in a session extended to fulfill the legislative duties of a war Congress.

The overall participation rate for both chambers in 2001 was 96.5 percent. That was a slight increase from the 94.4 percent registered in 2000, a busy election year that often drew members away from Washington, and a small jump from the 96 percent scored in 1993, the last year in which Congress worked with a new president.

The increase in voting participation — measured by how often members vote "yea" or "nay" on roll call votes — likely was due in part to members taking advantage of the slower travel pace afforded them in a non-election year. Participation scores tended to dip in election years as members were forced to choose between campaigning and voting. This was evident in the slight decrease in scores during the 2000 election year.

The average score for the two chambers did not rise above 90 percent until 1975, and it has not slipped below 90 percent since 1980. In the past decade, lawmakers have been disciplined about voting, and scores have generally hovered around 95 percent.

In 2001, House members voted 96.2 percent of the time on yea-or-nay votes, slightly above the 94.1 percent scored in 2000. The House took 507 yea-or-nay votes in 2001, significantly fewer than the 600 held in 2000, and adjourned on Dec. 20. The session in 2000 lasted until Dec. 15, although members took a one-week break for the election.

Senators maintained a voting participation record of 98.2 percent in 2001, compared with 96.9 percent in 2000. The Senate took 380 yea-or-nay votes in 2001, a significant increase from the 298 in 2000. The 2001 Senate session lasted until Dec. 20. Like the House, the Senate adjourned on Dec. 15 in 2000.

In 1993, the first year of President Bill Clinton's administration and a new Congress, the Senate took 395 votes and the House took 597 votes. (*1993 Almanac, p. 31-C*)

Senate Outpaces House

The 98.2 percent average voting participation record in the Senate was 2 percent higher than the average House member's score. Senators registered a higher voting participation record only once in the past decade. In 1997, the Senate averaged 98.7 percent on 82 fewer votes. The 2001 participation rate also tied the 98.2 score the Senate achieved in 1996.

The two senators with the lowest scores in 2000 rebounded with dramatic increases in 2001. The unsuccessful presidential campaign of John McCain, R-Ariz., had given him career-low scores of 78 percent in 2000 and 64 percent in 1999. Focusing on the Senate full time, McCain increased his overall participation score to 96 percent in 2001.

The voting participation record of Joseph I. Lieberman of Connecticut, the Democratic vice presidential nominee in 2000, dropped from 99 percent in 1999 to 79 percent the next year. Following the congressional recess in August 2000 — and about the time he hit the campaign trail — Lieberman voted on only four of 67 votes. By contrast, Lieberman missed only six votes in 2001, giving him an overall participation record of 96 percent, higher than the 95 percent average he has maintained since 1995. (*2000 Almanac, p. B-9*)

Age posed no obstacle for the guardians of the Senate in voting participation in 2001. Robert C. Byrd, D-W.Va., who turned 84 in November, and Strom Thurmond, R-S.C., the oldest member of the Senate at age 99, maintained high scores, 100 and 98 percent, respectively. Eighty-year-old Jesse Helms, R-N.C., who suffered health problems, had a voting participation score of 92.

Freshmen Mark

The average freshman participation scores in both the House and Senate exceeded each chamber's overall average. Freshmen members in the House scored 98 percent, while the newest members of the Senate came close to a perfect voting record with a score of 99 percent.

Freshmen members Brian Kerns, R-Ind., Jim Langevin, D-R.I., and Mike Ross, D-Ark., had perfect scores, voting

2001 Data

	RECORDED VOTES	PARTICIPATION RATE
Senate	380	98.2%
House	507	96.2%
Total	887	96.5%

For More Information

House members' scores..... p. B-22
Senators' scores .... p. B-24

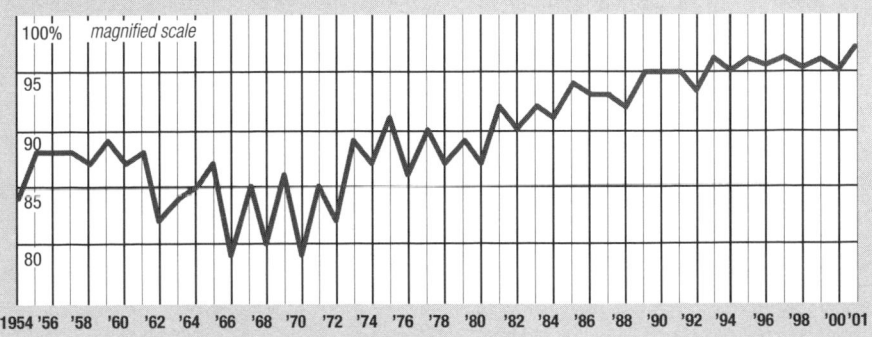

VOTING PARTICIPATION ▶ **History**

How often individual members voted "yea" or "nay" on roll call votes on the floor of the House or Senate.

on all 507 yea-or-nay votes. Two members elected during 2001 also maintained perfect scores, although they were not called on to cast as many votes as some of their veteran colleagues.

Jeff Miller, R-Fla., who replaced retiring member Joe Scarborough, R-Fla., and was sworn in Oct. 23, was eligible for 116 votes. Joe Wilson, R-S.C., who was sworn in Dec. 19 after the death of Floyd D. Spence, R-S.C., was eligible for nine.

Geographic Limits

While 2001 was not an election year, affording more time in Washington and requiring fewer trips home to campaign, geographic distance have accounted for the Alaska delegation's relatively low scores.

Republican Sens. Frank H. Murkowski and Ted Stevens had participation scores of 93 percent and 88 percent, respectively. Republican Rep. Don Young maintained a 79 percent. Each member's score was lower than the number posted in 2000.

Despite having to travel even farther, the participation records of the members from Hawaii, Democratic Sens. Daniel K. Akaka (96) and Daniel K. Inouye (95) and Democratic Reps. Neil Abercrombie (94) and Patsy T. Mink (97) were all more than 90 percent.

Rep. Barbara Cubin, R-Wyo., had a 60 percent voting participation score, due to extended absences throughout the year as she cared for her ailing husband.

A Perfect Mark

Thirteen senators had perfect participation scores. They were Evan Bayh, D-Ind.; Byrd; Lincoln Chafee, R-R.I.; Thad Cochran, R-Miss.; Susan Collins, R-Maine; Mike DeWine, R-Ohio; Russell D. Feingold, D-Wis.; Charles E. Grassley, R-Iowa; Carl Levin, D-Mich.;

Richard G. Lugar, R-Ind.; Jack Reed, D-R.I.; Harry Reid, D-Nev.; and Olympia J. Snowe, R-Maine.

Grassley kept a perfect participation score for the eighth consecutive year. Grassley's streak, the longest active in the Senate, began July 20, 1993, and stood at 3,111 consecutive votes at the end of the session. Grassley trailed former Sen. William Proxmire, D-Wis. (1957-89), who ended his career with a 22-year perfect participation streak.

The only senator to score lower than 90 percent was Stevens with 88. Sen. Pete V. Domenici, R-N.M., had a score of 90.

The number of House members who maintained perfect participation scores more than doubled in 2001, to 14. They were Marion Berry, D-Ark.; Sherwood Boehlert, R-N.Y.; Benjamin L. Cardin, D-Md.; Kerns; Dale E. Kildee, D-Mich.; Langevin; Frank A. LoBiondo, R-N.J.; Jeff Miller; Jerry Moran, R-Kan.; Ross; Paul D. Ryan, R-Wis.; Bud Shuster, R-Pa.; Fred Upton, R-Mich.; and Wilson.

Moran had maintained a 100 percent voting participation score since 1997; Upton had held his perfect score four years in a row.

Shuster's perfect score was based on just seven votes. He retired from the House on Feb. 2 after serving for less than a month of the 2001 session. His successor, his son Bill, had a voting participation score of 97.

Illness took its toll on several members of the House, and it was reflected in their voting scores.

Joe Moakley, D-Mass., who died May 28, three months after announcing he had incurable leukemia, was eligible for 148 votes and had a score of 46 percent. Spence, who died Aug. 16 and was eligible for 329 votes, had a record of 66 percent. Norman Sisisky, D-Va., who died March 29 and was eligible for 69 votes, had a score of 71 percent.

Retiring members of the House had some of the lowest scores in 2001. Asa Hutchinson, R-Ark., who resigned Aug. 6 to head the Drug Enforcement Administration, was eligible for 329 votes and had a record of 82 percent. Scarborough, who resigned Sept. 6 and was eligible for 331 votes, had a score of 84 percent.

The overall voting participation average for retiring House members in 2000 was 90 percent.

Three returning members fell at or below the 80 percent mark: William O. Lipinski, D-Ill. (80 percent); Young (79 percent); and Cubin (60 percent).

Members just below a 90 percent score included Xavier Becerra, D-Calif. (85); Dan Burton, R-Ind. (86); John Conyers Jr., D-Mich. (87); and Pete Stark, D-Calif. (85).

Speaker J. Dennis Hastert, R-Ill., cast 69 votes, a participation score of 14 percent. This score is slightly lower than past years. The Speaker votes only on symbolic issues or issues of critical importance to his party. ◆

CQ Vote Study Guide

Congressional Quarterly has conducted studies analyzing the voting behavior of members of Congress since 1945. This is how the studies are carried out:

● **Selecting votes.** CQ bases its vote studies on all roll call votes on which members were asked to vote "yea" or "nay." In 2001 there were 380 such votes in the Senate and 507 in the House. The study excludes quorum calls (there were five in the House in 2001) because they require only that members vote "present."

The totals do include House votes to approve the Journal (30 in 2001) and Senate votes to instruct the sergeant at arms to request members' presence in the chamber (two in 2001).

The presidential support and party unity studies are based on votes selected from the total according to the criteria described on pages B-11 and B-17.

● **Individual scores.** Members' scores in the accompanying charts are based only on the votes each member actually cast. The same method is used for leading scorers on pages B-5 and B-8.

● **Overall scores.** For consistency with previous years, graphs and breakdowns by chamber, party and region are based on all yea-or-nay votes. In those cases, absences lower scores. *(Methodology, 1987 Almanac, p. 22-C)*

● **Rounding.** Scores are rounded to the nearest percentage point, although rounding is not used to bring any score up to 100 percent.

Presidential Support Background

Congressional Quarterly selects roll call votes for its presidential support study based on statements made by the president or his authorized spokesmen.

Members' **support** shows the percentage of the time members voted *in agreement* with the president on these votes. **Opposition** shows the percentage of the time members voted *against* the president's position.

Presidential **success** is the percentage of the selected votes on which the president prevailed. Absences lower parties' scores. Scores for 2000 are given for comparison.

Presidential Success by Issue

"Economic affairs" includes votes on trade and on omnibus and supplemental spending bills, which may fund both domestic and defense/foreign policy programs. "Average" includes Senate confirmation votes.

	Defense/Foreign Policy		Domestic		Economic Affairs		Average	
	2001	2000	2001	2000	2001	2000	2001	2000
Senate	67%	67%	68%	33%	89%	40%	88%	65%
House	75	40	78	49	94	55	84	49
Average	71	46	73	44	92	52	87	55

Average Presidential Support by Party

	Support						Opposition			
	Republicans		Democrats				Republicans		Democrats	
	2001	2000	2001	2000			2001	2000	2001	2000
Senate	94%	46%	66%	89%		**Senate**	4%	52%	32%	8%
House	86	27	31	73		**House**	12	69	67	23

Average Presidential Support by Region *

	Support									Opposition							
	East		West		South		Midwest			East		West		South		Midwest	
	2001	2000	2001	2000	2001	2000	2001	2000		2001	2000	2001	2000	2001	2000	2001	2000
Republicans									Republicans								
Senate	91%	57%	93%	45%	94%	42%	96%	48%	**Senate**	9%	41%	3%	52%	3%	57%	3%	52%
House	80	37	86	25	88	23	84	28	**House**	18	58	11	70	9	73	14	69
Democrats									Democrats								
Senate	65	89	65	88	69	87	65	90	**Senate**	34	6	32	6	28	12	34	9
House	29	78	29	77	37	67	29	69	**House**	69	18	69	19	60	31	68	25

Presidential Success-Rate History

Average score for both chambers of Congress

Eisenhower		Johnson		Ford				Clinton	
1953	89.0%	1964	88.0%	1974	58.2%	1983	67.1	1993	86.4%
1954	82.8	1965	93.0	1975	61.0	1984	65.8	1994	86.4
1955	75.0	1966	79.0	1976	53.8	1985	59.9	1995	36.2
1956	70.0	1967	79.0			1986	56.1	1996	55.1
1957	68.0	1968	75.0	**Carter**		1987	43.5	1997	53.6
1958	76.0			1977	75.4%	1988	47.4	1998	50.6
1959	52.0	**Nixon**		1978	78.3			1999	37.8
1960	65.0	1969	74.0%	1979	76.8	**Bush**		2000	55.0
		1970	77.0	1980	75.1	1989	62.6%	**Bush**	
Kennedy		1971	75.0			1990	46.8	2001	87.0%
1961	81.0%	1972	66.0	**Reagan**		1991	54.2		
1962	85.4	1973	50.6	1981	82.4%	1992	43.0		
1963	87.1	1974	59.6	1982	72.4				

* **Regions:** Congressional Quarterly defines regions of the United States as follows: **East:** Conn., Del., Maine, Md., Mass., N.H., N.J., N.Y., Pa., R.I., Vt., W.Va. **West:** Alaska, Ariz., Calif., Colo., Hawaii, Idaho, Mont., Nev., N.M., Ore., Utah, Wash., Wyo. **South:** Ala., Ark., Fla., Ga., Ky., La., Miss., N.C., Okla., S.C., Tenn., Texas, Va. **Midwest:** Ill., Ind., Iowa, Kan., Mich., Minn., Mo., Neb., N.D., Ohio, S.D., Wis.

2001 House Presidential Position Votes

The following is a list of 43 House roll-call votes in 2001 on which the president took a clear position. Votes are listed by roll-call number in broad categories and identified by topic.

Domestic Policy

18 Victories

Vote Number	Description
88	Fetal protection
130	Education (testing)
144	Education
145	Education
216	Prescription drugs (imports)
254	Faith-based initiatives
302	Human cloning
304	Human cloning
317	Environment (ANWR)
320	Energy
329	Patients' rights (liability)
332	Patients' rights
386	Crime (anti-terrorism)
398	Crime (anti-terrorism)
423	Aviation security
425	Aviation security
497	Education
501	Crime (anti-terrorism)

5 Defeats

Vote Number	Description
135	Education (vouchers)
181	Energy (Gulf drilling)
217	Prescription drugs (imports)
288	Environment (arsenic)
371	Agriculture (farm bill)

Defense and Foreign Policy

3 Victories

Vote Number	Description
115	Family planning
271	Cuba embargo
342	Defense (use of force)

1 Defeat

Vote Number	Description
270	Cuba travel

Economic Affairs and Trade

15 Victories

Vote Number	Description
45	Taxes (Income tax cuts)
70	Budget
75	Taxes (family benefits)
84	Taxes (estate tax repeal)
104	Budget
118	Taxes (reconciliation)
149	Taxes (reconciliation)
176	Appropriations
255	Trade (China)
256	Appropriations
275	Trade (Vietnam)
341	Appropriations
404	Taxes (stimulus)
481	Trade authority
509	Taxes (stimulus)

1 Defeat

Vote Number	Description
193	Trade (Mexican trucks)

House Success Score

Victories	36
Defeats	7
Total	43
Success rate	83.7%

2001 Senate Presidential Position Votes

The following is a list of 77 Senate roll-call votes in 2001 on which the president took a clear position. Votes are listed by roll-call number in broad categories and identified by topic.

Domestic Policy

15 Victories

Vote Number	Description
87	Environment (brownfields)
103	Education (class size)
108	Education (construction)
174	Education (testing)
176	Education (Title I)
180	Education (comparability)
183	Education (testing)
184	Education (block grants)
192	Education
302	Crime (anti-terrorism)
313	Crime (anti-terrorism)
368	Farm bill (cloture)
371	Education
372	Farm bill (cloture)
377	Farm bill (cloture)

7 Defeats

Vote Number	Description
30	Bankruptcy (table)
43	Campaign finance (table)
179	Education (vouchers)
219	Patients' rights
220	Patients' rights
261	Farm aid (table)
374	Farm bill (table)

Defense and Foreign Policy

2 Victories

Vote Number	Description
281	Defense (use of force)
291	Trade (Vietnam)

1 Defeat

Vote Number	Description
276	International law (table)

Economic Affairs and Trade

8 Victories

Vote Number	Description
98	Budget
165	Taxes (reconciliation)
170	Taxes (reconciliation)
228	Appropriations
280	Appropriations
336	Budget
338	Taxes (stimulus)
357	Appropriations

1 Defeat

Vote Number	Description
69	Taxes

Nominations

43 Victories (0 Defeats)

Vote Number	Description	Vote Number	Description
1	Mitchell E. Daniels Jr.	270	William J. Riley
2	Anthony J. Principi	271	Sarah V. Hart
3	Mel Martinez	272	Robert S. Mueller III
4	Tommy G. Thompson	282	Sharon Prost
5	Norman Y. Mineta	283	Reggie B. Walton
6	Gale A. Norton	285	Kirk Van Tine
7	Christine Todd Whitman	297	Barrington D. Parker Jr.
8	John Ashcroft	298	Michael P. Mills
9	Robert B. Zoellick	307	James H. Payne
13	Joe M. Allbaugh	308	Karen K. Caldwell
14	John M. Duncan	309	Laurie Smith Camp
92	John Robert Bolton	310	Claire V. Eagan
166	Howard H. Baker Jr.	322	Larry R. Hicks
167	Theodore B. Olson	325	M. Christina Armijo
168	Viet D. Dinh	326	Karon O. Bowdre
169	Michael Chertoff	327	Stephen P. Friot
242	John D. Graham	333	Terry L. Wooten
243	Roger W. Ferguson Jr.	335	Edith Brown Clement
244	Roger L. Gregory	353	Harris L. Hartz
245	Sam E. Haddon	361	John D. Bates
246	Richard Cebull	370	Frederick J. Martone
264	Asa Hutchinson		

Senate Success Score

Victories	68
Defeats	9
Total	77
Success rate	88.3%

Key

Presidential Support and Opposition: House

1. Presidential Support Score. Percentage of recorded votes cast in 2001 on which President Bush took a position and on which the member voted "yea" or "nay" in agreement with the president's position. Failure to vote did not lower an individual's score.

2. Presidential Opposition Score. Percentage of recorded votes cast in 2001 on which President Bush took a position and on which the member voted "yea" or "nay" in disagreement with the president's position. Failure to vote did not lower an individual's score.

3. Participation in Presidential Support Votes. Percentage of the 43 recorded House votes on which President Bush took a position and on which a member was present and voted "yea" or "nay."

[1] John Boozman, R-Ark., was sworn in Nov. 29, replacing Asa Hutchinson, R-Ark., who resigned effective Aug. 6. Boozman was eligible for 51 votes in 2001. Hutchinson was eligible for 329; his voting participation score was 82 percent.

[2] Diane Watson, D-Calif., was sworn in June 7, replacing Julian C. Dixon, who died Dec. 8, 2000. Watson was eligible for 356 votes in 2001.

[3] Jeff Miller, R-Fla., was sworn in Oct. 23, replacing Joe Scarborough, R-Fla., who resigned effective Sept. 6. Miller was eligible for 116 votes in 2001. Scarborough was eligible for 331; his voting participation score was 84 percent.

[4] Stephen F. Lynch, D-Mass., was sworn in Oct. 23, replacing Joe Moakley, D-Mass., who died May 28. Lynch was eligible for 116 votes in 2001. Moakley was eligible for 148; his voting participation score was 46 percent.

[5] Bill Shuster, R-Pa., was sworn in May 17, replacing Bud Shuster, R-Pa., who resigned effective Feb. 2. Bill Shuster was eligible for 394 votes in 2001. Bud Shuster was eligible for seven; his voting participation score was 100 percent.

[6] Joe Wilson, R-S.C., was sworn in Dec. 19, replacing Floyd D. Spence, R-S.C., who died Aug. 16. Wilson was eligible for nine votes in 2001. Spence was eligible for 329; his voting participation score was 66 percent.

[7] Randy Forbes, R-Va., was sworn in June 26, replacing Norman Sisisky, D-Va., who died March 29. Forbes was eligible for 322 votes in 2001. Sisisky was eligible for 69; his voting participation score was 71 percent.

	1	2	3
ALABAMA			
1 *Callahan*	100	0	93
2 *Everett*	93	7	98
3 *Riley*	90	10	91
4 *Aderholt*	85	15	95
5 Cramer	67	33	98
6 *Bachus*	97	3	93
7 Hilliard	21	79	100
ALASKA			
AL *Young*	86	14	84
ARIZONA			
1 *Flake*	77	23	100
2 Pastor	21	79	100
3 *Stump*	88	12	98
4 *Shadegg*	84	16	100
5 *Kolbe*	84	16	100
6 *Hayworth*	91	9	100
ARKANSAS			
1 Berry	40	60	100
2 Snyder	33	67	93
3 *Boozman* [1]	100	0	100
4 Ross	37	63	100
CALIFORNIA			
1 Thompson	31	69	98
2 *Herger*	90	10	98
3 *Ose*	81	19	100
4 *Doolittle*	91	9	100
5 Matsui	28	72	100
6 Woolsey	14	86	100
7 Miller	23	77	100
8 Pelosi	28	72	100
9 Lee	12	88	100
10 Tauscher	40	60	100
11 *Pombo*	84	16	100
12 Lantos	26	74	98
13 Stark	19	81	86
14 Eshoo	33	67	100
15 Honda	24	76	98
16 Lofgren	30	70	100
17 Farr	24	76	95
18 Condit	47	53	100
19 *Radanovich*	93	7	100
20 Dooley	53	47	100
21 *Thomas*	90	10	95
22 Capps	36	64	98
23 *Gallegly*	91	9	100
24 Sherman	33	67	100
25 *McKeon*	98	2	98
26 Berman	38	62	98
27 Schiff	40	60	100
28 *Dreier*	100	0	98
29 Waxman	32	68	95
30 Becerra	27	73	93
31 Solis	17	83	98
32 Watson, D. [2]	17	83	100
33 Roybal-Allard	24	76	98
34 Napolitano	24	76	98
35 Waters	12	88	95
36 Harman	40	60	98
37 Millender-McD.	26	74	98
38 *Horn*	74	26	98

	1	2	3
39 *Royce*	84	16	100
40 *Lewis*	97	3	91
41 *Miller*	100	0	100
42 Baca	31	69	98
43 *Calvert*	93	7	98
44 *Bono*	84	16	100
45 *Rohrabacher*	86	14	100
46 Sanchez	24	76	98
47 *Cox*	93	7	93
48 *Issa*	88	12	100
49 Davis	40	60	100
50 Filner	12	88	98
51 *Cunningham*	95	5	100
52 *Hunter*	88	12	98
COLORADO			
1 DeGette	23	77	100
2 Udall	30	70	100
3 *McInnis*	98	2	95
4 *Schaffer*	74	26	100
5 *Hefley*	81	19	98
6 *Tancredo*	77	23	100
CONNECTICUT			
1 Larson	22	78	95
2 *Simmons*	77	23	100
3 DeLauro	26	74	100
4 *Shays*	65	35	100
5 Maloney	42	58	100
6 *Johnson*	70	30	100
DELAWARE			
AL *Castle*	67	33	100
FLORIDA			
1 *Miller* [3]	100	0	100
2 Boyd	44	56	95
3 Brown	24	76	98
4 *Crenshaw*	91	9	100
5 Thurman	26	74	100
6 *Stearns*	83	17	98
7 *Mica*	95	5	100
8 *Keller*	95	5	98
9 *Bilirakis*	86	14	98
10 *Young*	91	9	100
11 Davis	42	58	100
12 *Putnam*	90	10	98
13 *Miller*	87	13	91
14 *Goss*	95	5	100
15 *Weldon*	77	23	100
16 *Foley*	81	19	100
17 Meek	27	73	86
18 *Ros-Lehtinen*	87	13	88
19 Wexler	27	73	93
20 Deutsch	37	63	100
21 *Diaz-Balart*	88	12	100
22 *Shaw*	95	5	100
23 Hastings	18	82	91
GEORGIA			
1 *Kingston*	93	7	100
2 Bishop	50	50	98
3 *Collins*	86	14	98
4 McKinney	15	85	91
5 Lewis	15	85	95
6 *Isakson*	90	10	98
7 *Barr*	91	9	100
8 *Chambliss*	93	7	98
9 *Deal*	93	7	98
10 *Norwood*	88	12	100
11 *Linder*	98	2	93
HAWAII			
1 Abercrombie	35	65	93
2 Mink	21	79	100
IDAHO			
1 *Otter*	81	19	100
2 *Simpson*	88	12	100
ILLINOIS			
1 Rush	26	74	91
2 Jackson	16	84	100
3 Lipinski	61	39	65
4 Gutierrez	28	72	100
5 Blagojevich	37	63	100
6 *Hyde*	88	12	100
7 Davis	17	83	98
8 *Crane*	93	7	98
9 Schakowsky	17	83	98
10 *Kirk*	74	26	100
11 *Weller*	93	7	100
12 Costello	37	63	100
13 *Biggert*	84	16	100

ND Northern Democrats   SD Southern Democrats

Member	1	2	3
14 Hastert	100	0	60
15 Johnson	74	26	100
16 Manzullo	77	23	100
17 Evans	26	74	100
18 LaHood	74	26	100
19 Phelps	49	51	100
20 Shimkus	86	14	100

INDIANA

Member	1	2	3
1 Visclosky	33	67	91
2 Pence	91	9	100
3 Roemer	42	58	100
4 Souder	86	14	100
5 Buyer	93	7	100
6 Burton	87	13	88
7 Kerns	88	12	100
8 Hostettler	85	15	95
9 Hill	34	66	95
10 Carson	26	74	100

IOWA

Member	1	2	3
1 Leach	60	40	98
2 Nussle	88	12	100
3 Boswell	37	63	100
4 Ganske	71	29	98
5 Latham	90	10	98

KANSAS

Member	1	2	3
1 Moran	77	23	100
2 Ryun	91	9	100
3 Moore	40	60	98
4 Tiahrt	88	12	100

KENTUCKY

Member	1	2	3
1 Whitfield	93	7	100
2 Lewis	93	7	100
3 Northup	98	2	100
4 Lucas	81	19	98
5 Rogers	93	7	98
6 Fletcher	93	7	98

LOUISIANA

Member	1	2	3
1 Vitter	93	7	98
2 Jefferson	44	56	100
3 Tauzin	95	5	100
4 McCrery	98	2	95
5 Cooksey	95	5	93
6 Baker	100	0	93
7 John	69	31	98

MAINE

Member	1	2	3
1 Allen	28	72	100
2 Baldacci	26	74	100

MARYLAND

Member	1	2	3
1 Gilchrest	67	33	100
2 Ehrlich	93	7	93
3 Cardin	35	65	100
4 Wynn	31	69	98
5 Hoyer	30	70	100
6 Bartlett	74	26	100
7 Cummings	19	81	100
8 Morella	53	47	100

MASSACHUSETTS

Member	1	2	3
1 Olver	12	88	95
2 Neal	26	74	98
3 McGovern	16	84	100
4 Frank	9	91	100
5 Meehan	29	71	98
6 Tierney	19	81	100
7 Markey	26	74	100
8 Capuano	17	83	95
9 Lynch [4]	37	63	100
10 Delahunt	21	79	98

MICHIGAN

Member	1	2	3
1 Stupak	31	69	98
2 Hoekstra	74	26	100
3 Ehlers	81	19	100
4 Camp	91	9	100
5 Barcia	40	60	98
6 Upton	77	23	100
7 Smith	81	19	100
8 Rogers	88	12	100
9 Kildee	37	63	100
10 Bonior	19	81	98
11 Knollenberg	98	2	95
12 Levin	30	70	100
13 Rivers	12	88	98
14 Conyers	7	93	95
15 Kilpatrick	15	85	91
16 Dingell	29	71	95

MINNESOTA

Member	1	2	3
1 Gutknecht	84	16	100
2 Kennedy	86	14	100
3 Ramstad	65	35	100
4 McCollum	28	72	100
5 Sabo	14	86	100
6 Luther	25	75	93
7 Peterson	42	58	100
8 Oberstar	34	66	95

MISSISSIPPI

Member	1	2	3
1 Wicker	95	5	100
2 Thompson	29	71	98
3 Pickering	84	16	100
4 Shows	64	36	98
5 Taylor	45	55	98

MISSOURI

Member	1	2	3
1 Clay	21	79	98
2 Akin	86	14	100
3 Gephardt	29	71	98
4 Skelton	56	44	95
5 McCarthy	29	71	95
6 Graves	90	10	98
7 Blunt	95	5	95
8 Emerson	83	17	98
9 Hulshof	95	5	98

MONTANA

Member	1	2	3
AL Rehberg	88	12	100

NEBRASKA

Member	1	2	3
1 Bereuter	83	17	98
2 Terry	91	9	100
3 Osborne	88	12	100

NEVADA

Member	1	2	3
1 Berkley	37	63	100
2 Gibbons	93	7	98

NEW HAMPSHIRE

Member	1	2	3
1 Sununu	95	5	98
2 Bass	79	21	100

NEW JERSEY

Member	1	2	3
1 Andrews	35	65	100
2 LoBiondo	79	21	100
3 Saxton	82	18	93
4 Smith	70	30	100
5 Roukema	80	20	95
6 Pallone	28	72	100
7 Ferguson	88	12	100
8 Pascrell	37	63	100
9 Rothman	27	73	95
10 Payne	12	88	100
11 Frelinghuysen	88	12	100
12 Holt	35	65	100
13 Menendez	30	70	100

NEW MEXICO

Member	1	2	3
1 Wilson	88	12	98
2 Skeen	98	2	100
3 Udall	23	77	100

NEW YORK

Member	1	2	3
1 Grucci	93	7	100
2 Israel	48	52	98
3 King	93	7	95
4 McCarthy	44	56	100
5 Ackerman	29	71	95
6 Meeks	20	80	95
7 Crowley	30	70	100
8 Nadler	21	79	100
9 Weiner	26	74	100
10 Towns	34	66	95
11 Owens	17	83	98
12 Velázquez	26	74	100
13 Fossella	93	7	100
14 Maloney	33	67	100
15 Rangel	23	77	100
16 Serrano	29	71	98
17 Engel	35	65	93
18 Lowey	28	72	100
19 Kelly	77	23	100
20 Gilman	62	38	98
21 McNulty	36	64	98
22 Sweeney	83	17	98
23 Boehlert	74	26	100
24 McHugh	88	12	98
25 Walsh	88	12	100
26 Hinchey	21	79	100
27 Reynolds	93	7	100
28 Slaughter	29	71	98
29 LaFalce	40	60	100

Member	1	2	3
30 Quinn	85	15	91
31 Houghton	73	27	86

NORTH CAROLINA

Member	1	2	3
1 Clayton	19	81	98
2 Etheridge	44	56	100
3 Jones	78	22	95
4 Price	35	65	100
5 Burr	93	7	100
6 Coble	86	14	100
7 McIntyre	52	48	98
8 Hayes	91	9	100
9 Myrick	95	5	100
10 Ballenger	93	7	93
11 Taylor	86	14	98
12 Watt	12	88	98

NORTH DAKOTA

Member	1	2	3
AL Pomeroy	35	65	100

OHIO

Member	1	2	3
1 Chabot	81	19	100
2 Portman	93	7	100
3 Hall	40	60	93
4 Oxley	98	2	98
5 Gillmor	90	10	95
6 Strickland	26	74	100
7 Hobson	88	12	100
8 Boehner	98	2	100
9 Kaptur	23	77	91
10 Kucinich	23	77	100
11 Jones	20	80	95
12 Tiberi	95	5	100
13 Brown	12	88	98
14 Sawyer	26	74	100
15 Pryce	86	14	100
16 Regula	88	12	100
17 Traficant	81	19	98
18 Ney	79	21	100
19 LaTourette	86	14	98

OKLAHOMA

Member	1	2	3
1 Largent	88	12	98
2 Carson	51	49	100
3 Watkins	95	5	100
4 Watts	98	2	100
5 Istook	95	5	98
6 Lucas	88	12	100

OREGON

Member	1	2	3
1 Wu	30	70	100
2 Walden	91	9	100
3 Blumenauer	19	81	84
4 DeFazio	19	81	100
5 Hooley	36	64	98

PENNSYLVANIA

Member	1	2	3
1 Brady	33	67	100
2 Fattah	22	78	95
3 Borski	42	58	100
4 Hart	88	12	100
5 Peterson	93	7	100
6 Holden	40	60	100
7 Weldon	80	20	95
8 Greenwood	79	21	100
9 Shuster [5]	89	11	95
10 Sherwood	93	7	100
11 Kanjorski	47	53	100
12 Murtha	47	53	100
13 Hoeffel	36	64	98
14 Coyne	20	80	93
15 Toomey	93	7	100
16 Pitts	91	9	100
17 Gekas	93	7	98
18 Doyle	40	60	100
19 Platts	86	14	98
20 Mascara	47	53	100
21 English	81	19	100

RHODE ISLAND

Member	1	2	3
1 Kennedy	29	71	98
2 Langevin	35	65	100

SOUTH CAROLINA

Member	1	2	3
1 Brown	88	12	100
2 Wilson [6]	100	0	100
3 Graham	84	16	100
4 DeMint	95	5	100
5 Spratt	33	67	98
6 Clyburn	33	67	100

SOUTH DAKOTA

Member	1	2	3
AL Thune	81	19	100

TENNESSEE

Member	1	2	3
1 Jenkins	91	9	100
2 Duncan	76	24	98
3 Wamp	88	12	100
4 Hilleary	86	14	98
5 Clement	52	48	98
6 Gordon	54	46	95
7 Bryant	98	2	100
8 Tanner	48	52	98
9 Ford	38	62	98

TEXAS

Member	1	2	3
1 Sandlin	40	60	100
2 Turner	44	56	100
3 Johnson	91	9	100
4 Hall	86	14	100
5 Sessions	91	9	100
6 Barton	86	14	98
7 Culberson	95	5	100
8 Brady	90	10	98
9 Lampson	34	66	95
10 Doggett	29	71	98
11 Edwards	47	53	100
12 Granger	88	12	100
13 Thornberry	95	5	100
14 Paul	49	51	91
15 Hinojosa	33	67	98
16 Reyes	37	63	100
17 Stenholm	53	47	100
18 Jackson-Lee	16	84	100
19 Combest	88	12	100
20 Gonzalez	32	68	95
21 Smith	95	5	98
22 DeLay	98	2	95
23 Bonilla	95	5	100
24 Frost	36	64	98
25 Bentsen	33	67	98
26 Armey	98	2	100
27 Ortiz	58	42	100
28 Rodriguez	31	69	98
29 Green	33	67	100
30 Johnson	26	74	100

UTAH

Member	1	2	3
1 Hansen	93	7	93
2 Matheson	51	49	100
3 Cannon	95	5	98

VERMONT

Member	1	2	3
AL Sanders	16	84	100

VIRGINIA

Member	1	2	3
1 Davis, Jo Ann	86	14	100
2 Schrock	98	2	100
3 Scott	14	86	100
4 Forbes [7]	93	7	100
5 Goode	79	21	100
6 Goodlatte	91	9	100
7 Cantor	95	5	100
8 Moran	40	60	100
9 Boucher	33	67	100
10 Wolf	86	14	98
11 Davis, T.	88	12	100

WASHINGTON

Member	1	2	3
1 Inslee	33	67	100
2 Larsen	42	58	100
3 Baird	30	70	100
4 Hastings	93	7	100
5 Nethercutt	93	7	100
6 Dicks	36	64	98
7 McDermott	21	79	98
8 Dunn	87	13	93
9 Smith	43	57	98

WEST VIRGINIA

Member	1	2	3
1 Mollohan	45	55	98
2 Capito	79	21	100
3 Rahall	33	67	98

WISCONSIN

Member	1	2	3
1 Ryan	86	14	100
2 Baldwin	22	78	95
3 Kind	28	72	100
4 Kleczka	23	77	100
5 Barrett	23	77	100
6 Petri	83	17	98
7 Obey	29	71	98
8 Green	91	9	100
9 Sensenbrenner	77	23	100

WYOMING

Member	1	2	3
AL Cubin	89	11	65

Southern states - Ala., Ark, Fla., Ga., Ky., La., Miss., N.C., Okla., S.C., Tenn., Texas, Va.

State / Senator	1	2	3
ALABAMA			
Shelby	97	3	100
Sessions	97	3	100
ALASKA			
Stevens	97	3	100
Murkowski	100	0	92
ARIZONA			
McCain	91	9	87
Kyl	99	1	99
ARKANSAS			
Hutchinson	92	8	97
Lincoln	71	29	97
CALIFORNIA			
Feinstein	71	29	100
Boxer	64	36	96
COLORADO			
Campbell	96	4	97
Allard	97	3	100
CONNECTICUT			
Dodd	66	34	99
Lieberman	69	31	100
DELAWARE			
Biden	65	35	97
Carper	72	28	99
FLORIDA			
Graham	67	33	99
Nelson	70	30	99
GEORGIA			
Cleland	70	30	99
Miller	82	18	92
HAWAII			
Inouye	66	34	92
Akaka	70	30	92
IDAHO			
Craig	97	3	97
Crapo	96	4	96
ILLINOIS			
Fitzgerald	96	4	99
Durbin	62	38	99
INDIANA			
Lugar	100	0	100
Bayh	69	31	100
IOWA			
Grassley	99	1	100
Harkin	63	37	99
KANSAS			
Brownback	99	1	95
Roberts	99	1	100
KENTUCKY			
McConnell	97	3	100
Bunning	96	4	99
LOUISIANA			
Breaux	77	23	95
Landrieu	74	26	96
MAINE			
Snowe	84	16	100
Collins	88	12	100
MARYLAND			
Sarbanes	63	37	99
Mikulski	66	34	100
MASSACHUSETTS			
Kennedy	66	34	99
Kerry	65	35	96
MICHIGAN			
Levin	65	35	100
Stabenow	64	36	99
MINNESOTA			
Wellstone	59	41	99
Dayton	60	40	100
MISSISSIPPI			
Cochran	96	4	100
Lott	96	4	96
MISSOURI			
Bond	99	1	96
Carnahan	71	29	97
MONTANA			
Burns	97	3	100
Baucus	71	29	99
NEBRASKA			
Hagel	96	4	97
Nelson	74	26	99
NEVADA			
Reid	65	35	100
Ensign	97	3	97
NEW HAMPSHIRE			
Smith	97	3	100
Gregg	100	0	100
NEW JERSEY			
Torricelli	67	33	94
Corzine	63	37	99
NEW MEXICO			
Domenici	96	4	88
Bingaman	68	32	99
NEW YORK			
Schumer	65	35	100
Clinton	61	39	100
NORTH CAROLINA			
Helms	96	4	88
Edwards	67	33	99
NORTH DAKOTA			
Conrad	66	34	100
Dorgan	68	32	97
OHIO			
DeWine	95	5	100
Voinovich	95	5	96
OKLAHOMA			
Nickles	96	4	100
Inhofe	95	5	95
OREGON			
Wyden	64	36	99
Smith	93	7	99
PENNSYLVANIA			
Specter	87	13	100
Santorum	97	3	99
RHODE ISLAND			
Reed	64	36	100
Chafee	84	16	100
SOUTH CAROLINA			
Thurmond	97	3	99
Hollings	62	38	100
SOUTH DAKOTA			
Daschle	69	31	100
Johnson	71	29	97
TENNESSEE			
Thompson	99	1	99
Frist	99	1	96
TEXAS			
Gramm	99	1	90
Hutchison	96	4	100
UTAH			
Hatch	97	3	95
Bennett	96	4	99
VERMONT			
Leahy	62	38	99
Jeffords[1]	80	20	91
VIRGINIA			
Warner	96	4	100
Allen	97	3	97
WASHINGTON			
Murray	65	35	96
Cantwell	64	36	100
WEST VIRGINIA			
Byrd	71	29	100
Rockefeller	66	34	95
WISCONSIN			
Kohl	69	31	97
Feingold	61	39	100
WYOMING			
Thomas	97	3	95
Enzi	99	1	99

Key

Democrats • **Republicans**
Independents

ND Northern Democrats SD Southern Democrats

Southern states - Ala., Ark., Fla., Ga., Ky., La., Miss., N.C., Okla., S.C., Tenn., Texas, Va.

Presidential Support and Opposition: Senate

1. Presidential Support Score. Percentage of recorded votes cast in 2001 on which President Bush took a position and on which the senator voted "yea" or "nay" in agreement with the president's position. Failure to vote did not lower an individual's score.

2. Presidential Opposition Score. Percentage of recorded votes cast in 2001 on which President Bush took a position and on which the senator voted "yea" or "nay" in disagreement with the president's position. Failure to vote did not lower an individual's score.

3. Participation in Presidential Support Votes. Percentage of the 77 recorded Senate votes on which President Bush took a position and on which the senator was present and voted "yea" or "nay."

[1] James M. Jeffords of Vermont switched party affiliation from Republican to Independent effective June 6, 2001.

Party Unity Background

Roll call votes used for the party unity study are those on which a majority of voting Democrats opposed a majority of voting Republicans.

Support is the percentage of the time that members voted *in agreement* with a majority of their party on these party unity votes.

Opposition is the percentage of the time members voted *against* a majority of their party on party unity votes.

Averages below show the average of members' scores by party, chamber and region.

(Party switchers are accounted for; failure to vote lowers support and opposition scores for chambers and parties.)

Average Party Unity Scores by Chamber

Support	Republicans		Democrats		Opposition	Republicans		Democrats	
	2001	2000	2001	2000		2001	2000	2001	2000
Senate	88%	89%	89%	88%	Senate	10%	9%	10%	10%
House	91	88	83	82	House	6	10	14	13

Average Party Support/Opposition by Region*

Senate	Support	Opposition	House	Support	Opposition
Northern Republicans	86%	12%	Northern Republicans	90%	8%
Southern Republicans	92	7	Southern Republicans	93	4
Northern Democrats	91	8	Northern Democrats	86	11
Southern Democrats	78	21	Southern Democrats	75	22

*Southern Democrats and Republicans are those from Ala., Ark., Fla., Ga., Ky., La., Miss., N.C., Okla., S.C., Tenn., Texas, Va. All others are considered Northern.

2001 Party Victories

The number of times each party won on party unity votes:

	Senate	House	Total
Republicans won	115	177	292
Democrats won	95	27	122

Unanimous Voting by Parties

The number of times each party voted unanimously on party unity votes:

Senate		House		Total	
	2001	2000	2001	2000	2001	2000
Republicans voted unanimously	55	19	66	67	121	86
Democrats voted unanimously	37	52	1	1	38	53

Party Unity Average Scores by Year

Average score by party in both chambers of Congress:

Year	Republicans	Democrats	Year	Republicans	Democrats
1966	67%	61%	1984	72%	74%
1967	71	66	1985	75	79
1968	63	57	1986	71	78
1969	62	62	1987	74	81
1970	59	57	1988	73	79
1971	66	62	1989	73	81
1972	64	57	1990	74	81
1973	68	68	1991	78	81
1974	62	63	1992	79	79
1975	70	69	1993	84	85
1976	66	65	1994	83	83
1977	70	67	1995	91	80
1978	67	64	1996	87	80
1979	72	69	1997	88	82
1980	70	68	1998	86	83
1981	76	69	1999	86	84
1982	71	72	2000	87	83
1983	74	76	2001	90	85

2001 Party Unity Votes

Following are the votes, by roll call number, on which a majority of Democrats voted against a majority of Republicans.

House
(204 of 507 "yea/nay" votes)

2	40	82	106	138	182	228	255	284	309	332	380	442	480
3	41	83	107	141	183	232	260	285	311	345	382	445	481
4	42	84	108	144	184	234	262	286	312	346	383	446	487
22	43	85	115	146	190	235	263	287	314	347	384	447	488
23	44	87	116	148	191	238	264	288	315	351	400	454	506
24	45	88	117	149	193	239	268	289	316	352	401	456	507
25	57	89	118	164	201	240	269	294	317	353	402	457	508
29	65	94	119	169	203	242	270	295	319	354	403	460	509
33	67	95	120	170	205	244	271	296	320	356	404	461	512
34	69	97	125	173	207	247	273	300	325	357	419	462	
35	70	98	130	175	209	250	277	302	326	358	421	463	
36	71	100	132	177	210	251	278	303	328	365	423	464	
37	73	103	135	178	216	252	279	304	329	366	424	476	
38	74	104	136	180	218	253	280	306	330	368	425	478	
39	75	105	137	181	225	254	282	307	331	369	441	479	

Senate
(210 of 380 "yea/nay" votes)

8	34	56	76	103	122	141	157	181	204	229	286	347	377
15	37	57	77	104	123	142	158	184	206	231	293	348	379
16	38	58	78	105	124	143	160	185	207	232	294	354	
17	39	59	79	106	125	144	161	186	210	235	303	355	
18	41	60	81	107	126	145	162	187	211	238	306	357	
19	42	62	82	108	127	146	163	188	212	242	314	358	
20	43	63	83	110	130	147	165	189	214	250	316	362	
21	44	64	84	112	132	148	167	190	215	252	318	363	
22	46	65	86	114	133	149	170	191	216	253	319	365	
23	47	66	92	115	134	150	171	194	217	254	323	366	
24	48	67	93	116	135	151	172	196	218	255	328	367	
25	49	68	94	117	136	152	173	197	219	259	329	368	
27	51	69	96	118	137	153	174	199	220	261	330	372	
28	52	71	98	119	138	154	178	200	221	266	337	374	
30	53	73	99	120	139	155	179	202	222	267	338	375	
32	54	75	100	121	140	156	180	203	227	273	341	376	

Proportion of Partisan Roll Calls

How often a majority of Democrats voted against a majority of Republicans:

Year	House	Senate	Year	House	Senate	Year	House	Senate	Year	House	Senate
1958	40%	4%	1969	31%	36%	1980	38%	46%	1991	55%	49%
1959	55	48	1970	27	35	1981	37	48	1992	64	53
1960	53	37	1971	38	42	1982	36	43	1993	65	67
1961	50	62	1972	27	36	1983	56	44	1994	62	52
1962	46	41	1973	42	40	1984	47	40	1995	73	69
1963	49	47	1974	29	44	1985	61	50	1996	56	62
1964	55	36	1975	48	48	1986	57	52	1997	50	50
1965	52	42	1976	36	37	1987	64	41	1998	56	56
1966	41	50	1977	42	42	1988	47	42	1999	47	63
1967	36	35	1978	33	45	1989	55	35	2000	43	49
1968	35	32	1979	47	47	1990	49	54	2001	40	55

Key

| Democrats • | **Republicans** |
| *Independents* | |

	1	2	3
ALABAMA			
Shelby	88	12	99
Sessions	95	5	96
ALASKA			
Stevens	88	12	82
Murkowski	94	6	91
ARIZONA			
McCain	67	33	99
Kyl	98	2	100
ARKANSAS			
Hutchinson	88	12	100
Lincoln	79	21	99
CALIFORNIA			
Feinstein	85	15	98
Boxer	98	2	97
COLORADO			
Campbell	89	11	99
Allard	98	2	99
CONNECTICUT			
Dodd	98	2	98
Lieberman	93	7	100
DELAWARE			
Biden	94	6	99
Carper	80	20	99
FLORIDA			
Graham	94	6	100
Nelson	92	8	100
GEORGIA			
Cleland	78	22	99
Miller	42	58	96
HAWAII			
Inouye	98	2	95
Akaka	98	2	95
IDAHO			
Craig	96	4	100
Crapo	94	6	97
ILLINOIS			
Fitzgerald	79	21	93
Durbin	95	5	99
INDIANA			
Lugar	92	8	100
Bayh	82	18	100

	1	2	3
IOWA			
Grassley	93	7	100
Harkin	97	3	99
KANSAS			
Brownback	94	6	99
Roberts	95	5	99
KENTUCKY			
McConnell	98	2	100
Bunning	97	3	99
LOUISIANA			
Breaux	59	41	99
Landrieu	81	19	98
MAINE			
Snowe	64	36	100
Collins	67	33	100
MARYLAND			
Sarbanes	99	1	100
Mikulski	98	2	100
MASSACHUSETTS			
Kennedy	97	3	98
Kerry	98	2	98
MICHIGAN			
Levin	98	2	100
Stabenow	96	4	100
MINNESOTA			
Wellstone	99	1	100
Dayton	99	1	99
MISSISSIPPI			
Cochran	84	16	100
Lott	98	2	98
MISSOURI			
Bond	94	6	98
Carnahan	85	15	98
MONTANA			
Burns	96	4	97
Baucus	67	33	99
NEBRASKA			
Hagel	92	8	99
Nelson	58	42	100
NEVADA			
Reid	96	4	100
Ensign	88	12	98

	1	2	3
NEW HAMPSHIRE			
Smith	96	4	99
Gregg	96	4	99
NEW JERSEY			
Torricelli	78	22	100
Corzine	96	4	100
NEW MEXICO			
Domenici	89	11	90
Bingaman	91	9	99
NEW YORK			
Schumer	92	8	99
Clinton	97	3	99
NORTH CAROLINA			
Helms	98	2	94
Edwards	91	9	99
NORTH DAKOTA			
Conrad	90	10	100
Dorgan	91	9	99
OHIO			
DeWine	83	17	100
Voinovich	92	8	99
OKLAHOMA			
Nickles	96	4	99
Inhofe	96	4	97
OREGON			
Wyden	90	10	100
Smith	82	18	99
PENNSYLVANIA			
Specter	60	40	100
Santorum	95	5	98
RHODE ISLAND			
Reed	99	1	100
Chafee	50	50	100
SOUTH CAROLINA			
Thurmond	98	2	99
Hollings	95	5	99
SOUTH DAKOTA			
Daschle	98	2	100
Johnson	87	13	100
TENNESSEE			
Thompson	91	9	100
Frist	97	3	98

	1	2	3
TEXAS			
Gramm	96	4	95
Hutchison	90	10	99
UTAH			
Hatch	95	5	99
Bennett	96	4	99
VERMONT			
Leahy	98	2	99
Jeffords [1]	85	15	98
VIRGINIA			
Warner	85	15	99
Allen	93	7	99
WASHINGTON			
Murray	96	4	99
Cantwell	98	2	99
WEST VIRGINIA			
Byrd	86	14	100
Rockefeller	97	3	99
WISCONSIN			
Kohl	89	11	95
Feingold	89	11	100
WYOMING			
Thomas	97	3	98
Enzi	95	5	98

ND Northern Democrats   SD Southern Democrats

Southern states - Ala., Ark., Fla., Ga., Ky., La., Miss., N.C., Okla., S.C., Tenn., Texas, Va.

Party Unity and Party Opposition: Senate

1. Party Unity. Percentage of recorded party unity votes in 2001 on which a senator voted "yea" or "nay" in agreement with a majority of his or her party. (Party unity roll calls are those on which a majority of voting Democrats opposed a majority of voting Republicans.) Percentages are based on votes cast; thus, failure to vote did not lower a member's score.

2. Party Opposition. Percentage of recorded party unity votes in 2001 on which a senator voted "yea" or "nay" in disagreement with a majority of his or her party. Percentages are based on votes cast; thus, failure to vote did not lower a member's score.

3. Participation in Party Unity Votes. Percentage of the 210 recorded Senate party unity votes in 2001 on which a senator was present and voted "yea" or "nay."

[1] James M. Jeffords of Vermont switched his party affiliation from Republican to Independent effective June 6, 2001. His party unity score is calculated based on votes with Democrats from that date. As a Republican, Jeffords voted with his party on 72 of 118 party unity votes, or 61 percent of the time.

Party Unity and Party Opposition: House

1. Party Unity. Percentage of recorded party unity votes in 2001 on which a member voted "yea" or "nay" in agreement with a majority of his or her party. (Party unity votes are those on which a majority of voting Democrats opposed a majority of voting Republicans.) Percentages are based on votes cast; thus, failure to vote did not lower a member's score.

2. Party Opposition. Percentage of recorded party unity votes in 2001 on which a member voted "yea" or "nay" in disagreement with a majority of his or her party. Percentages are based on votes cast; thus, failure to vote did not lower a member's score.

3. Participation in Party Unity Votes. Percentage of the 204 recorded House party unity votes in 2001 on which a member was present and voted "yea" or "nay."

[1] John Boozman, R-Ark., was sworn in Nov. 29, replacing Asa Hutchinson, R-Ark., who resigned effective Aug. 6. Boozman was eligible for 17 party unity votes in 2001. Hutchinson was eligible for 151 party unity votes; his party unity score was 96 percent.

[2] Diane Watson, D-Calif., was sworn in June 7, replacing Julian C. Dixon, who died Dec. 8, 2000. Watson was eligible for 138 party unity votes in 2001.

[3] Jeff Miller, R-Fla., was sworn in Oct. 23, replacing Joe Scarborough, R-Fla., who resigned effective Sept. 6. Miller was eligible for 35 party unity votes in 2001. Scarborough was eligible for 151 party unity votes; his party unity score was 88 percent.

[4] Stephen F. Lynch, D-Mass., was sworn in Oct. 23, replacing Joe Moakley, D-Mass., who died May 28. Lynch was eligible for 35 party unity votes in 2001. Moakley was eligible for 66 party unity votes; his party unity score was 95 percent.

[5] Bill Shuster, R-Pa., was sworn in May 17, replacing Bud Shuster, R-Pa., who resigned effective Feb. 2. Bill Shuster was eligible for 156 party unity votes in 2001. Bud Shuster was eligible for three party unity votes; his party unity score was 100 percent.

[6] Joe Wilson, R-S.C., was sworn in Dec. 19, replacing Floyd D. Spence, R-S.C., who died Aug. 16. Wilson was eligible for five party unity votes in 2001. Spence was eligible for 151 party unity votes; his party unity score was 97 percent.

[7] Randy Forbes, R-Va., was sworn in June 26, replacing Norman Sisisky, D-Va., who died March 29. Forbes was eligible for 126 party unity votes in 2001. Sisisky was eligible for 26 party unity votes; his party unity score was 71 percent.

Key

Democrats • **Republicans**
Independents

	1	2	3
ALABAMA			
1 Callahan	99	1	91
2 Everett	97	3	95
3 Riley	97	3	91
4 Aderholt	96	4	95
5 Cramer	50	50	94
6 Bachus	96	4	95
7 Hilliard	86	14	99
ALASKA			
AL Young	98	2	85
ARIZONA			
1 Flake	90	10	99
2 Pastor	89	11	100
3 Stump	98	2	97
4 Shadegg	96	4	100
5 Kolbe	91	9	99
6 Hayworth	98	2	100
ARKANSAS			
1 Berry	65	35	100
2 Snyder	75	25	95
3 Boozman [1]	100	0	100
4 Ross	70	30	100
CALIFORNIA			
1 Thompson	88	12	99
2 Herger	97	3	99
3 Ose	90	10	99
4 Doolittle	97	3	99
5 Matsui	92	8	99
6 Woolsey	98	2	100
7 Miller	98	2	98
8 Pelosi	97	3	99
9 Lee	97	3	99
10 Tauscher	84	16	99
11 Pombo	96	4	99
12 Lantos	96	4	98
13 Stark	97	3	84
14 Eshoo	90	10	99
15 Honda	95	5	99
16 Lofgren	87	13	100
17 Farr	96	4	99
18 Condit	75	25	99
19 Radanovich	96	4	97
20 Dooley	67	33	96
21 Thomas	95	5	96
22 Capps	92	8	98
23 Gallegly	96	4	99
24 Sherman	92	8	100
25 McKeon	99	1	99
26 Berman	92	8	96
27 Schiff	83	17	99
28 Dreier	97	3	100
29 Waxman	95	5	97
30 Becerra	97	3	91
31 Solis	99	1	99
32 Watson, D. [2]	95	5	93
33 Roybal-Allard	95	5	97
34 Napolitano	96	4	99
35 Waters	96	4	99
36 Harman	84	16	99
37 Millender-McD.	95	5	97
38 Horn	80	20	99

	1	2	3
39 Royce	93	7	99
40 Lewis	97	3	92
41 Miller	99	1	100
42 Baca	89	11	99
43 Calvert	98	2	98
44 Bono	92	8	99
45 Rohrabacher	93	7	99
46 Sanchez	88	12	99
47 Cox	96	4	92
48 Issa	96	4	96
49 Davis	89	11	99
50 Filner	99	1	99
51 Cunningham	96	4	100
52 Hunter	95	5	96
COLORADO			
1 DeGette	96	4	99
2 Udall	96	4	100
3 McInnis	95	5	92
4 Schaffer	91	9	97
5 Hefley	92	8	95
6 Tancredo	94	6	99
CONNECTICUT			
1 Larson	88	12	99
2 Simmons	83	17	100
3 DeLauro	95	5	99
4 Shays	75	25	99
5 Maloney	79	21	99
6 Johnson	76	24	98
DELAWARE			
AL Castle	79	21	99
FLORIDA			
1 Miller [3]	100	0	100
2 Boyd	70	30	97
3 Brown	92	8	99
4 Crenshaw	97	3	100
5 Thurman	88	12	99
6 Stearns	93	7	99
7 Mica	98	2	99
8 Keller	97	3	96
9 Bilirakis	91	9	99
10 Young	96	4	98
11 Davis	79	21	99
12 Putnam	98	2	95
13 Miller	94	6	93
14 Goss	97	3	100
15 Weldon	95	5	99
16 Foley	89	11	100
17 Meek	89	11	92
18 Ros-Lehtinen	94	6	88
19 Wexler	94	6	91
20 Deutsch	91	9	99
21 Diaz-Balart	94	6	97
22 Shaw	92	8	99
23 Hastings	91	9	92
GEORGIA			
1 Kingston	98	2	98
2 Bishop	71	29	96
3 Collins	98	2	99
4 McKinney	94	6	94
5 Lewis	97	3	96
6 Isakson	97	3	99
7 Barr	96	4	99
8 Chambliss	98	2	97
9 Deal	98	2	98
10 Norwood	96	4	96
11 Linder	99	1	94
HAWAII			
1 Abercrombie	79	21	97
2 Mink	93	7	99
IDAHO			
1 Otter	96	4	100
2 Simpson	98	2	100
ILLINOIS			
1 Rush	91	9	90
2 Jackson	95	5	99
3 Lipinski	62	38	78
4 Gutierrez	95	5	96
5 Blagojevich	90	10	100
6 Hyde	95	5	99
7 Davis	97	3	100
8 Crane	99	1	99
9 Schakowsky	99	1	99
10 Kirk	85	15	99
11 Weller	96	4	99
12 Costello	72	28	99
13 Biggert	90	10	100

ND Northern Democrats SD Southern Democrats

	1	2	3
14 Hastert	100	0	28
15 Johnson	85	15	99
16 Manzullo	94	6	99
17 Evans	93	7	99
18 LaHood	90	10	99
19 Phelps	64	36	99
20 Shimkus	95	5	100

INDIANA

	1	2	3
1 Visclosky	86	14	94
2 Pence	97	3	100
3 Roemer	73	27	99
4 Souder	96	4	99
5 Buyer	97	3	99
6 Burton	97	3	93
7 Kerns	98	2	100
8 Hostettler	94	6	97
9 Hill	72	28	98
10 Carson	95	5	94

IOWA

	1	2	3
1 Leach	73	27	97
2 Nussle	95	5	99
3 Boswell	78	22	99
4 Ganske	84	16	98
5 Latham	97	3	97

KANSAS

	1	2	3
1 Moran	90	10	100
2 Ryun	99	1	100
3 Moore	77	23	99
4 Tiahrt	97	3	99

KENTUCKY

	1	2	3
1 Whitfield	96	4	99
2 Lewis	98	2	99
3 Northup	99	1	99
4 Lucas	47	53	100
5 Rogers	96	4	99
6 Fletcher	97	3	99

LOUISIANA

	1	2	3
1 Vitter	98	2	99
2 Jefferson	87	13	97
3 Tauzin	99	1	99
4 McCrery	98	2	98
5 Cooksey	98	2	95
6 Baker	99	1	95
7 John	52	48	98

MAINE

	1	2	3
1 Allen	96	4	99
2 Baldacci	92	8	100

MARYLAND

	1	2	3
1 Gilchrest	86	14	100
2 Ehrlich	90	10	97
3 Cardin	89	11	100
4 Wynn	88	12	99
5 Hoyer	91	9	98
6 Bartlett	91	9	99
7 Cummings	95	5	98
8 Morella	61	39	98

MASSACHUSETTS

	1	2	3
1 Olver	98	2	99
2 Neal	92	8	97
3 McGovern	97	3	99
4 Frank	97	3	99
5 Meehan	97	3	95
6 Tierney	98	2	99
7 Markey	96	4	99
8 Capuano	96	4	99
9 Lynch[4]	97	3	100
10 Delahunt	94	6	93

MICHIGAN

	1	2	3
1 Stupak	81	19	92
2 Hoekstra	91	9	100
3 Ehlers	88	12	100
4 Camp	96	4	99
5 Barcia	71	29	99
6 Upton	88	12	100
7 Smith	93	7	98
8 Rogers	95	5	100
9 Kildee	88	12	100
10 Bonior	93	7	98
11 Knollenberg	99	1	98
12 Levin	93	7	100
13 Rivers	92	8	97
14 Conyers	96	4	92
15 Kilpatrick	93	7	97
16 Dingell	88	12	95

MINNESOTA

	1	2	3
1 Gutknecht	94	6	99
2 Kennedy	93	7	100
3 Ramstad	77	23	100
4 McCollum	96	4	100
5 Sabo	91	9	99
6 Luther	94	6	97
7 Peterson	63	37	96
8 Oberstar	87	13	99

MISSISSIPPI

	1	2	3
1 Wicker	99	1	99
2 Thompson	87	13	98
3 Pickering	95	5	99
4 Shows	53	47	93
5 Taylor	56	44	99

MISSOURI

	1	2	3
1 Clay	95	5	97
2 Akin	97	3	100
3 Gephardt	94	6	96
4 Skelton	61	39	94
5 McCarthy	92	8	99
6 Graves	96	4	100
7 Blunt	98	2	97
8 Emerson	90	10	98
9 Hulshof	94	6	99

MONTANA

	1	2	3
AL Rehberg	96	4	99

NEBRASKA

	1	2	3
1 Bereuter	90	10	98
2 Terry	95	5	100
3 Osborne	94	6	100

NEVADA

	1	2	3
1 Berkley	88	12	99
2 Gibbons	97	3	98

NEW HAMPSHIRE

	1	2	3
1 Sununu	93	7	98
2 Bass	85	15	99

NEW JERSEY

	1	2	3
1 Andrews	88	12	99
2 LoBiondo	82	18	100
3 Saxton	88	12	99
4 Smith	84	16	99
5 Roukema	83	17	94
6 Pallone	93	7	100
7 Ferguson	87	13	99
8 Pascrell	87	13	99
9 Rothman	91	9	90
10 Payne	98	2	97
11 Frelinghuysen	89	11	99
12 Holt	92	8	100
13 Menendez	89	11	99

NEW MEXICO

	1	2	3
1 Wilson	94	6	99
2 Skeen	98	2	99
3 Udall	96	4	99

NEW YORK

	1	2	3
1 Grucci	91	9	99
2 Israel	82	18	97
3 King	92	8	99
4 McCarthy	83	17	99
5 Ackerman	94	6	89
6 Meeks	94	6	92
7 Crowley	89	11	99
8 Nadler	98	2	98
9 Weiner	95	5	100
10 Towns	91	9	91
11 Owens	98	2	95
12 Velázquez	96	4	96
13 Fossella	92	8	97
14 Maloney	90	10	100
15 Rangel	91	9	97
16 Serrano	92	8	92
17 Engel	94	6	93
18 Lowey	96	4	99
19 Kelly	80	20	100
20 Gilman	76	24	98
21 McNulty	87	13	99
22 Sweeney	92	8	99
23 Boehlert	79	21	100
24 McHugh	89	11	96
25 Walsh	92	8	98
26 Hinchey	96	4	99
27 Reynolds	94	6	99
28 Slaughter	96	4	97
29 LaFalce	90	10	100

	1	2	3
30 Quinn	87	13	90
31 Houghton	84	16	87

NORTH CAROLINA

	1	2	3
1 Clayton	95	5	98
2 Etheridge	83	17	99
3 Jones	88	12	98
4 Price	88	12	100
5 Burr	95	5	99
6 Coble	95	5	100
7 McIntyre	70	30	99
8 Hayes	98	2	100
9 Myrick	96	4	97
10 Ballenger	97	3	97
11 Taylor	97	3	97
12 Watt	96	4	98

NORTH DAKOTA

	1	2	3
AL Pomeroy	78	22	99

OHIO

	1	2	3
1 Chabot	94	6	100
2 Portman	98	2	99
3 Hall	73	27	90
4 Oxley	99	1	96
5 Gillmor	95	5	97
6 Strickland	89	11	99
7 Hobson	95	5	99
8 Boehner	99	1	97
9 Kaptur	89	11	92
10 Kucinich	89	11	100
11 Jones	97	3	96
12 Tiberi	97	3	100
13 Brown	98	2	100
14 Sawyer	96	4	100
15 Pryce	93	7	99
16 Regula	95	5	100
17 Traficant	9	91	99
18 Ney	91	9	99
19 LaTourette	88	12	98

OKLAHOMA

	1	2	3
1 Largent	95	5	93
2 Carson	68	32	99
3 Watkins	98	2	99
4 Watts	99	1	98
5 Istook	95	5	96
6 Lucas	98	2	99

OREGON

	1	2	3
1 Wu	81	19	99
2 Walden	97	3	100
3 Blumenauer	89	11	92
4 DeFazio	96	4	95
5 Hooley	89	11	99

PENNSYLVANIA

	1	2	3
1 Brady	92	8	98
2 Fattah	95	5	97
3 Borski	86	14	99
4 Hart	93	7	99
5 Peterson	96	4	96
6 Holden	71	29	98
7 Weldon	88	12	94
8 Greenwood	86	14	98
9 Shuster[5]	95	5	96
10 Sherwood	94	6	99
11 Kanjorski	75	25	100
12 Murtha	66	34	97
13 Hoeffel	91	9	99
14 Coyne	99	1	96
15 Toomey	93	7	99
16 Pitts	96	4	99
17 Gekas	96	4	99
18 Doyle	78	22	100
19 Platts	91	9	95
20 Mascara	75	25	100
21 English	89	11	99

RHODE ISLAND

	1	2	3
1 Kennedy	93	7	97
2 Langevin	90	10	100

SOUTH CAROLINA

	1	2	3
1 Brown	97	3	99
2 Wilson[6]	100	0	100
3 Graham	93	7	99
4 DeMint	98	2	100
5 Spratt	82	18	99
6 Clyburn	84	16	99

SOUTH DAKOTA

	1	2	3
AL Thune	92	8	99

TENNESSEE

	1	2	3
1 Jenkins	96	4	100
2 Duncan	91	9	100
3 Wamp	95	5	100
4 Hilleary	95	5	99
5 Clement	73	27	95
6 Gordon	66	34	96
7 Bryant	98	2	100
8 Tanner	64	36	99
9 Ford	83	17	95

TEXAS

	1	2	3
1 Sandlin	79	21	99
2 Turner	69	31	100
3 Johnson, Sam	97	3	99
4 Hall	25	75	100
5 Sessions	99	1	99
6 Barton	98	2	92
7 Culberson	99	1	99
8 Brady	98	2	99
9 Lampson	83	17	96
10 Doggett	92	8	99
11 Edwards	72	28	99
12 Granger	97	3	99
13 Thornberry	99	1	100
14 Paul	79	21	95
15 Hinojosa	85	15	96
16 Reyes	81	19	96
17 Stenholm	53	47	100
18 Jackson-Lee	93	7	99
19 Combest	98	2	99
20 Gonzalez	86	14	95
21 Smith	99	1	94
22 DeLay	99	1	99
23 Bonilla	99	1	100
24 Frost	83	17	94
25 Bentsen	75	25	98
26 Armey	98	2	98
27 Ortiz	66	34	99
28 Rodriguez	88	12	99
29 Green	80	20	99
30 Johnson	88	12	97

UTAH

	1	2	3
1 Hansen	98	2	95
2 Matheson	67	33	100
3 Cannon	99	1	98

VERMONT

	1	2	3
AL Sanders	97	3	99

VIRGINIA

	1	2	3
1 Davis, Jo Ann	92	8	99
2 Schrock	99	1	99
3 Scott	94	6	100
4 Forbes[7]	97	3	99
5 Goode	92	8	99
6 Goodlatte	97	3	100
7 Cantor	98	2	99
8 Moran	79	21	98
9 Boucher	82	18	97
10 Wolf	95	5	98
11 Davis, T.	90	10	98

WASHINGTON

	1	2	3
1 Inslee	91	9	98
2 Larsen	80	20	100
3 Baird	87	13	98
4 Hastings	98	2	98
5 Nethercutt	98	2	98
6 Dicks	82	18	98
7 McDermott	94	6	95
8 Dunn	95	5	94
9 Smith	80	20	98

WEST VIRGINIA

	1	2	3
1 Mollohan	65	35	97
2 Capito	89	11	100
3 Rahall	77	23	98

WISCONSIN

	1	2	3
1 Ryan	92	8	100
2 Baldwin	97	3	96
3 Kind	87	13	100
4 Kleczka	91	9	99
5 Barrett	94	6	100
6 Petri	90	10	99
7 Obey	94	6	99
8 Green	94	6	100
9 Sensenbrenner	91	9	98

WYOMING

	1	2	3
AL Cubin	98	2	64

Southern states - Ala., Ark., Fla., Ga., Ky., La., Miss., N.C., Okla., S.C., Tenn., Texas, Va.

Voting Participation: House

1. Voting Participation. Percentage of 507 recorded votes in 2001 on which a representative voted "yea" or "nay."

2. Voting Participation (without Journal votes). Percentage of 477 recorded votes in 2001 on which a member voted "yea" or "nay." In this version of the study, 30 votes on approval of the House Journal were excluded.

Absences because of illness. *Congressional Quarterly no longer designates members who missed votes because of illness. In the past, notations to that effect were based on official statements published in the Congressional Record, but these were found to be inconsistently used.*

Rounding. *Scores are rounded to the nearest percentage, except that no scores are rounded up to 100 percent. Members with a 100 percent score participated in all recorded votes for which they were eligible.*

[1] *John Boozman, R-Ark., was sworn in Nov. 29, replacing Asa Hutchinson, R-Ark., who resigned effective Aug. 6. Boozman was eligible for 51 votes in 2001. Hutchinson was eligible for 329; his voting participation score was 82 percent.*

[2] *Diane Watson, D-Calif., was sworn in June 7, replacing Julian C. Dixon, who died Dec. 8, 2000. Watson was eligible for 356 votes in 2001.*

[3] *Jeff Miller, R-Fla., was sworn in Oct. 23, replacing Joe Scarborough, R-Fla., who resigned effective Sept. 6. Miller was eligible for 116 votes in 2001. Scarborough was eligible for 331; his voting participation score was 84 percent.*

[4] *Stephen F. Lynch, D-Mass., was sworn in Oct. 23, replacing Joe Moakley, D-Mass., who died May 28. Lynch was eligible for 116 votes in 2001. Moakley was eligible for 148; his voting participation score was 46 percent.*

[5] *Bill Shuster, R-Pa., was sworn in May 17, replacing Bud Shuster, R-Pa., who resigned effective Feb. 2. Bill Shuster was eligible for 394 votes in 2001. Bud Shuster was eligible for seven; his voting participation score was 100 percent.*

[6] *Joe Wilson, R-S.C., was sworn in Dec. 19, replacing Floyd D. Spence, R-S.C., who died Aug. 16. Wilson was eligible for nine votes in 2001. Spence was eligible for 329; his voting participation score was 66 percent.*

[7] *Randy Forbes, R-Va., was sworn in June 26, replacing Norman Sisisky, D-Va., who died March 29. Forbes was eligible for 322 votes in 2001. Sisisky was eligible for 69; his voting participation score was 71 percent.*

Key

Democrats • **Republicans**
Independents

	1	2
ALABAMA		
1 *Callahan*	92	92
2 *Everett*	95	95
3 *Riley*	88	87
4 *Aderholt*	97	97
5 Cramer	95	95
6 *Bachus*	95	96
7 Hilliard	99	99
ALASKA		
AL *Young*	79	81
ARIZONA		
1 *Flake*	98	99
2 Pastor	99	99
3 *Stump*	98	98
4 *Shadegg*	99	99
5 *Kolbe*	99	99
6 *Hayworth*	99	99
ARKANSAS		
1 Berry	100	100
2 Snyder	95	95
3 *Boozman* [1]	98	98
4 Ross	100	100
CALIFORNIA		
1 Thompson	99	99
2 *Herger*	97	98
3 *Ose*	99	99
4 *Doolittle*	97	97
5 Matsui	98	98
6 Woolsey	97	97
7 Miller	95	96
8 Pelosi	96	96
9 Lee	98	98
10 Tauscher	99	99
11 *Pombo*	98	98
12 Lantos	95	96
13 Stark	85	85
14 Eshoo	99	99
15 Honda	99	99
16 Lofgren	97	97
17 Farr	99	99
18 Condit	99	99
19 *Radanovich*	93	94
20 Dooley	93	93
21 *Thomas*	96	96
22 Capps	98	97
23 *Gallegly*	97	97
24 Sherman	98	98
25 *McKeon*	99	99
26 Berman	92	92
27 Schiff	99	99
28 *Dreier*	99	99
29 Waxman	94	94
30 Becerra	85	85
31 Solis	97	97
32 Watson, D. [2]	95	96
33 Roybal-Allard	97	97
34 Napolitano	98	99
35 Waters	93	93
36 Harman	97	98
37 Millender-McD.	94	94
38 *Horn*	98	98

	1	2
39 *Royce*	97	97
40 *Lewis*	91	92
41 *Miller*	97	97
42 Baca	98	98
43 *Calvert*	97	97
44 *Bono*	97	97
45 *Rohrabacher*	99	99
46 Sanchez	94	94
47 *Cox*	90	90
48 *Issa*	97	96
49 Davis	99	99
50 Filner	97	97
51 *Cunningham*	98	99
52 *Hunter*	93	94
COLORADO		
1 DeGette	95	95
2 Udall	98	98
3 *McInnis*	93	93
4 *Schaffer*	94	95
5 *Hefley*	96	96
6 *Tancredo*	94	99
CONNECTICUT		
1 Larson	97	97
2 *Simmons*	99	99
3 DeLauro	99	99
4 *Shays*	98	98
5 Maloney	96	97
6 *Johnson*	96	97
DELAWARE		
AL *Castle*	99	99
FLORIDA		
1 *Miller* [3]	100	100
2 Boyd	98	98
3 Brown	93	93
4 *Crenshaw*	99	99
5 Thurman	99	99
6 *Stearns*	97	97
7 *Mica*	98	98
8 *Keller*	95	95
9 *Bilirakis*	98	98
10 *Young*	96	97
11 Davis	99	99
12 *Putnam*	94	94
13 *Miller*	92	91
14 *Goss*	98	99
15 *Weldon*	99	99
16 *Foley*	98	98
17 Meek	88	88
18 *Ros-Lehtinen*	91	90
19 Wexler	89	90
20 Deutsch	99	99
21 *Diaz-Balart*	96	96
22 *Shaw*	97	97
23 Hastings	92	91
GEORGIA		
1 *Kingston*	94	94
2 Bishop	95	95
3 *Collins*	98	98
4 McKinney	92	93
5 Lewis	95	95
6 *Isakson*	99	99
7 *Barr*	95	95
8 *Chambliss*	97	97
9 *Deal*	96	96
10 *Norwood*	96	97
11 *Linder*	95	95
HAWAII		
1 Abercrombie	94	95
2 Mink	97	97
IDAHO		
1 *Otter*	99	99
2 *Simpson*	99	99
ILLINOIS		
1 Rush	89	89
2 Jackson	99	99
3 Lipinski	80	80
4 Gutierrez	94	94
5 Blagojevich	98	98
6 *Hyde*	98	98
7 Davis	97	97
8 *Crane*	97	98
9 Schakowsky	97	97
10 *Kirk*	98	99
11 *Weller*	98	99
12 Costello	99	99
13 *Biggert*	99	99

ND Northern Democrats   SD Southern Democrats

		1	2
14	*Hastert*	14	14
15	*Johnson*	99	99
16	*Manzullo*	98	98
17	Evans	98	98
18	*LaHood*	98	98
19	Phelps	99	99
20	*Shimkus*	99	99
INDIANA			
1	Visclosky	95	95
2	*Pence*	99	99
3	Roemer	99	99
4	*Souder*	95	95
5	*Buyer*	94	94
6	*Burton*	86	86
7	*Kerns*	100	100
8	*Hostettler*	93	93
9	Hill	97	97
10	Carson	92	92
IOWA			
1	Leach	95	96
2	*Nussle*	98	98
3	Boswell	99	99
4	Ganske	94	95
5	*Latham*	96	96
KANSAS			
1	*Moran*	100	100
2	*Ryun*	99	99
3	Moore	99	99
4	*Tiahrt*	98	98
KENTUCKY			
1	*Whitfield*	98	99
2	*Lewis*	99	99
3	*Northup*	99	99
4	Lucas	99	99
5	*Rogers*	97	97
6	*Fletcher*	98	98
LOUISIANA			
1	*Vitter*	96	96
2	Jefferson	93	94
3	*Tauzin*	98	98
4	*McCrery*	96	97
5	*Cooksey*	93	93
6	*Baker*	95	95
7	John	97	97
MAINE			
1	Allen	97	97
2	Baldacci	99	99
MARYLAND			
1	*Gilchrest*	99	99
2	*Ehrlich*	94	94
3	Cardin	100	100
4	Wynn	98	97
5	Hoyer	98	98
6	*Bartlett*	99	99
7	Cummings	96	97
8	*Morella*	97	97
MASSACHUSETTS			
1	Olver	98	98
2	Neal	95	95
3	McGovern	98	98
4	Frank	97	97
5	Meehan	94	94
6	Tierney	98	99
7	Markey	98	98
8	Capuano	96	96
9	Lynch [4]	98	100
10	Delahunt	92	92
MICHIGAN			
1	Stupak	94	95
2	*Hoekstra*	98	98
3	*Ehlers*	99	99
4	*Camp*	99	99
5	Barcia	98	98
6	*Upton*	100	100
7	*Smith*	97	97
8	*Rogers*	99	99
9	Kildee	100	100
10	Bonior	95	96
11	*Knollenberg*	98	98
12	Levin	99	99
13	Rivers	97	97
14	Conyers	87	87
15	Kilpatrick	91	92
16	Dingell	94	94

		1	2
MINNESOTA			
1	*Gutknecht*	99	99
2	*Kennedy*	99	99
3	*Ramstad*	99	99
4	McCollum	98	99
5	Sabo	97	98
6	Luther	94	94
7	Peterson	95	95
8	Oberstar	99	99
MISSISSIPPI			
1	*Wicker*	98	99
2	Thompson	96	96
3	*Pickering*	98	99
4	Shows	95	95
5	Taylor	99	99
MISSOURI			
1	Clay	96	97
2	*Akin*	99	99
3	Gephardt	91	92
4	Skelton	97	97
5	McCarthy	98	98
6	*Graves*	99	99
7	*Blunt*	95	95
8	*Emerson*	97	97
9	*Hulshof*	96	96
MONTANA			
AL	*Rehberg*	99	99
NEBRASKA			
1	*Bereuter*	98	98
2	*Terry*	98	98
3	*Osborne*	99	99
NEVADA			
1	Berkley	98	98
2	*Gibbons*	96	96
NEW HAMPSHIRE			
1	*Sununu*	98	98
2	*Bass*	99	99
NEW JERSEY			
1	Andrews	98	98
2	*LoBiondo*	100	100
3	*Saxton*	97	97
4	*Smith*	99	99
5	*Roukema*	91	91
6	Pallone	99	99
7	*Ferguson*	95	96
8	Pascrell	98	97
9	Rothman	90	90
10	Payne	94	95
11	*Frelinghuysen*	99	99
12	Holt	99	99
13	Menendez	97	97
NEW MEXICO			
1	*Wilson*	98	98
2	*Skeen*	99	99
3	Udall	99	99
NEW YORK			
1	*Grucci*	98	98
2	Israel	98	98
3	*King*	99	99
4	McCarthy	99	99
5	Ackerman	87	87
6	Meeks	90	90
7	Crowley	98	98
8	Nadler	95	96
9	Weiner	97	97
10	Towns	90	90
11	Owens	92	92
12	Velázquez	95	95
13	*Fossella*	92	92
14	Maloney	97	97
15	Rangel	95	96
16	Serrano	93	93
17	Engel	90	91
18	Lowey	97	97
19	*Kelly*	98	99
20	Gilman	98	99
21	McNulty	98	98
22	*Sweeney*	93	93
23	*Boehlert*	100	100
24	*McHugh*	95	95
25	Walsh	97	97
26	Hinchey	97	97
27	*Reynolds*	98	99
28	Slaughter	95	96
29	LaFalce	99	99

		1	2
30	*Quinn*	90	90
31	*Houghton*	89	88
NORTH CAROLINA			
1	Clayton	98	98
2	Etheridge	99	99
3	*Jones*	96	97
4	Price	98	99
5	*Burr*	98	99
6	*Coble*	99	99
7	McIntyre	98	98
8	*Hayes*	99	99
9	*Myrick*	97	97
10	*Ballenger*	96	96
11	*Taylor*	91	91
12	Watt	98	97
NORTH DAKOTA			
AL	Pomeroy	97	97
OHIO			
1	*Chabot*	99	99
2	*Portman*	97	97
3	Hall	90	91
4	*Oxley*	95	96
5	*Gillmor*	95	95
6	Strickland	98	98
7	*Hobson*	99	99
8	*Boehner*	95	96
9	Kaptur	92	92
10	Kucinich	98	98
11	Jones	89	89
12	*Tiberi*	98	98
13	Brown	99	99
14	Sawyer	99	99
15	*Pryce*	97	98
16	*Regula*	99	99
17	Traficant	98	98
18	*Ney*	96	96
19	*LaTourette*	93	93
OKLAHOMA			
1	*Largent*	92	92
2	Carson	98	99
3	*Watkins*	98	98
4	*Watts*	96	96
5	*Istook*	93	93
6	*Lucas*	98	98
OREGON			
1	Wu	99	99
2	*Walden*	99	99
3	Blumenauer	94	94
4	DeFazio	92	92
5	Hooley	99	99
PENNSYLVANIA			
1	Brady	96	96
2	Fattah	93	94
3	Borski	98	98
4	*Hart*	98	98
5	*Peterson*	97	96
6	Holden	98	98
7	*Weldon*	92	92
8	*Greenwood*	96	96
9	*Shuster* [5]	97	98
10	*Sherwood*	98	98
11	Kanjorski	99	99
12	Murtha	94	95
13	Hoeffel	98	98
14	Coyne	95	96
15	*Toomey*	96	96
16	*Pitts*	99	99
17	*Gekas*	99	99
18	Doyle	99	99
19	*Platts*	94	95
20	Mascara	99	99
21	*English*	98	99
RHODE ISLAND			
1	Kennedy	97	97
2	Langevin	100	100
SOUTH CAROLINA			
1	*Brown*	99	99
2	*Wilson* [6]	100	100
3	*Graham*	99	99
4	*DeMint*	99	99
5	Spratt	99	99
6	Clyburn	99	99
SOUTH DAKOTA			
AL	*Thune*	99	99

		1	2
TENNESSEE			
1	*Jenkins*	99	99
2	*Duncan*	99	99
3	*Wamp*	98	97
4	*Hilleary*	96	96
5	Clement	94	95
6	Gordon	92	93
7	*Bryant*	99	99
8	Tanner	98	99
9	Ford	95	95
TEXAS			
1	Sandlin	99	99
2	Turner	99	99
3	*Johnson, Sam*	96	97
4	Hall	99	99
5	*Sessions*	96	96
6	Barton	92	92
7	*Culberson*	97	98
8	*Brady*	97	97
9	Lampson	97	97
10	Doggett	99	99
11	Edwards	98	99
12	*Granger*	95	96
13	*Thornberry*	99	99
14	*Paul*	94	94
15	Hinojosa	95	96
16	Reyes	92	92
17	Stenholm	99	99
18	Jackson-Lee	96	96
19	*Combest*	99	99
20	Gonzalez	95	95
21	*Smith*	95	95
22	*DeLay*	95	96
23	*Bonilla*	99	99
24	Frost	96	96
25	Bentsen	98	98
26	*Armey*	98	99
27	Ortiz	97	97
28	Rodriguez	99	99
29	Green	99	99
30	Johnson	93	93
UTAH			
1	*Hansen*	94	94
2	Matheson	99	99
3	*Cannon*	93	93
VERMONT			
AL	*Sanders*	95	96
VIRGINIA			
1	*Davis, Jo Ann*	99	99
2	*Schrock*	99	99
3	Scott	98	98
4	*Forbes* [7]	99	99
5	*Goode*	98	98
6	*Goodlatte*	99	99
7	*Cantor*	98	99
8	Moran	97	97
9	Boucher	94	95
10	*Wolf*	98	98
11	*Davis, T.*	97	97
WASHINGTON			
1	Inslee	98	98
2	Larsen	99	99
3	Baird	98	98
4	*Hastings*	96	96
5	*Nethercutt*	98	98
6	Dicks	98	98
7	McDermott	97	97
8	*Dunn*	94	94
9	Smith	97	97
WEST VIRGINIA			
1	Mollohan	93	93
2	*Capito*	99	99
3	Rahall	97	97
WISCONSIN			
1	*Ryan*	100	100
2	Baldwin	97	97
3	Kind	99	99
4	Kleczka	98	98
5	Barrett	99	99
6	Petri	99	99
7	Obey	96	97
8	*Green*	99	99
9	Sensenbrenner	99	99
WYOMING			
AL	*Cubin*	60	61

Southern states - Ala., Ark., Fla., Ga., Ky., La., Miss., N.C., Okla., S.C., Tenn., Texas, Va.

Key

Democrats • **Republicans**
Independents

ALABAMA	1	2
Shelby	99	99
Sessions	96	97
ALASKA		
Stevens	88	88
Murkowski	93	93
ARIZONA		
McCain	96	96
Kyl	99	99
ARKANSAS		
Hutchinson	99	99
Lincoln	99	99
CALIFORNIA		
Feinstein	98	98
Boxer	97	97
COLORADO		
Campbell	99	99
Allard	99	99
CONNECTICUT		
Dodd	97	98
Lieberman	98	98
DELAWARE		
Biden	98	98
Carper	99	99
FLORIDA		
Graham	99	99
Nelson	99	99
GEORGIA		
Cleland	99	99
Miller	95	95
HAWAII		
Inouye	95	95
Akaka	96	96
IDAHO		
Craig	99	99
Crapo	97	97
ILLINOIS		
Fitzgerald	94	94
Durbin	99	99
INDIANA		
Lugar	100	100
Bayh	100	100

IOWA	1	2
Grassley	100	100
Harkin	99	99
KANSAS		
Brownback	98	98
Roberts	98	99
KENTUCKY		
McConnell	99	99
Bunning	98	98
LOUISIANA		
Breaux	98	98
Landrieu	98	98
MAINE		
Snowe	100	100
Collins	100	100
MARYLAND		
Sarbanes	99	99
Mikulski	99	99
MASSACHUSETTS		
Kennedy	97	97
Kerry	98	98
MICHIGAN		
Levin	100	100
Stabenow	99	99
MINNESOTA		
Wellstone	99	99
Dayton	99	99
MISSISSIPPI		
Cochran	100	100
Lott	98	98
MISSOURI		
Bond	97	97
Carnahan	98	98
MONTANA		
Burns	97	97
Baucus	99	99
NEBRASKA		
Hagel	98	98
Nelson	99	99
NEVADA		
Reid	100	100
Ensign	97	97

NEW HAMPSHIRE	1	2
Smith	98	98
Gregg	98	98
NEW JERSEY		
Torricelli	96	96
Corzine	99	99
NEW MEXICO		
Domenici	91	90
Bingaman	99	99
NEW YORK		
Schumer	99	99
Clinton	99	99
NORTH CAROLINA		
Helms	92	92
Edwards	99	99
NORTH DAKOTA		
Conrad	99	99
Dorgan	99	99
OHIO		
DeWine	100	100
Voinovich	97	97
OKLAHOMA		
Nickles	99	99
Inhofe	96	96
OREGON		
Wyden	99	99
Smith	98	98
PENNSYLVANIA		
Specter	99	99
Santorum	98	98
RHODE ISLAND		
Reed	100	100
Chafee	100	100
SOUTH CAROLINA		
Thurmond	98	98
Hollings	99	99
SOUTH DAKOTA		
Daschle	99	99
Johnson	99	99
TENNESSEE		
Thompson	99	99
Frist	97	97

TEXAS	1	2
Gramm	96	96
Hutchison	98	98
UTAH		
Hatch	98	98
Bennett	99	99
VERMONT		
Leahy	98	98
Jeffords[1]	95	95
VIRGINIA		
Warner	99	99
Allen	99	99
WASHINGTON		
Murray	98	98
Cantwell	99	99
WEST VIRGINIA		
Byrd	100	100
Rockefeller	99	99
WISCONSIN		
Kohl	96	96
Feingold	100	100
WYOMING		
Thomas	96	96
Enzi	98	98

ND Northern Democrats SD Southern Democrats

Southern states - Ala., Ark., Fla., Ga., Ky., La., Miss., N.C., Okla., S.C., Tenn., Texas, Va.

Voting Participation: Senate

1. Voting Participation. Percentage of 380 recorded votes in 2001 on which a senator voted "yea" or "nay."

2. Voting Participation (without motions to instruct). Percentage of 378 recorded votes in 2001 on which a senator voted "yea" or "nay." In this version of the study, two votes to instruct the sergeant at arms to request the attendance of absent senators were excluded.

Absences because of illness. Congressional Quarterly no longer designates members who missed votes because of illness. In the past, notations to that effect were based on official statements published in the Congressional Record, but these were found to be inconsistently used.

Rounding. Scores are rounded to the nearest percentage, except that no scores are rounded up to 100 percent. Senators with a 100 percent score participated in all recorded votes for which they were eligible.

[1] James M. Jeffords of Vermont switched party affiliation from Republican to Independent effective June 6, 2001.

Appendix C

KEY VOTES

A Year of Grudging Compromise

When Congress is this narrowly divided, there are two basic strategies for getting things done: Resist negotiating too much and hold your own party together, then hope you can pick up enough members from the other party to win; or compromise enough to have solid support from the middle of both parties and risk hating the final product.

In the first session of the 107th Congress, congressional leaders from both parties showed a strong preference for the first option — with decidedly mixed results.

The strategy helped Republicans get a $1.35 trillion tax cut through Congress, and it helped Democrats temporarily upend Republican dominance of the agenda by pushing overhauls of managed care and campaign finance laws through the Senate.

But the charge-ahead approach has risks, and it can fail easily. Democrats could not attract any Republicans to their version of an economic stimulus bill or a "homeland security" package in the Senate, and Republicans could not even hold enough of their own side together to move their preferred campaign finance bill through the House.

The key votes for 2001, as selected by the editors of Congressional Quarterly, illustrate that gamble. Republican and Democratic leaders mostly tried to move their agendas with a bare minimum of bipartisan support, and sometimes suffered the consequences.

Still, it was a gamble neither side could resist.

The House GOP leadership did it regularly, and the Senate Democratic leadership, having secured its first Senate majority in more than six years in June, used the strategy in an effort to put its own stamp on the congressional agenda.

Political scientists say constant showdowns may be inevitable in a Senate with a one-seat margin of control and a House with a four-seat majority. After the near tie in the 2000 elections, leaders of both parties said the results represented a mandate for cooperation. In reality, however, the effect was just the opposite. With control of the House and Senate within reach for either side in 2002, the parties have spent most of their energy trying to satisfy their political bases.

"We're getting a permanent, very competitive kind of national politics," said Merle Black, a professor of political science at Emory University.

There were two exceptions to the pattern. After Sept. 11, lawmakers briefly moved beyond bare-minimum alliances and passed an urgent series of bills that were designed to attract both sides and were intended to deal with the consequences of war. As a group of votes on such matters as the

How CQ Picks Key Votes

Since 1945, Congressional Quarterly has selected a series of key votes on major issues of the year.

An issue is judged to be a key vote by the extent to which it represents:
- a matter of major controversy
- a matter of presidential or political power
- a matter of potentially great impact on the nation and lives of Americans.

For each group of related votes on an issue, one key vote is usually chosen — one that, in the opinion of CQ editors, was most important in determining the outcome.

use of military force and the extent of aid to a reeling airline industry, these bills offered a glimpse of uncommon unity bred of a national crisis.

The other exception was the education overhaul bill (HR 1). From the beginning, President Bush insisted that the bill be written to win strong support from both parties. And he signaled that he would accept almost any compromise necessary to accomplish that, short of abandoning his centerpiece proposal: annual testing in reading and math in third through eighth grades to measure students' progress and hold schools "accountable" if they fell short.

The result was that nearly everything about the bill was a compromise, and even the most critical moment in the life of the bill proved anticlimactic. Republicans and Democrats negotiated most of the provisions early on so they built — and held — an unassailable coalition of bipartisan support.

But the matter of testing remained a point of controversy for die-hards on the left and the right, and it was not until two House members made a concerted effort to strip testing from the bill that supporters realized the strength of their position.

The surprisingly wide margin with which bill supporters defeated an amendment to remove the testing requirement showed lawmakers that the bill's passage was inevitable, and it provided an example of how much safer the path could be when bipartisanship is an early goal.

Hits and Misses

It was not always necessary, however, to assemble such a broad coalition to pass major legislation.

Republicans proved it was possible to hold the line and draw just enough converts from the other side to win when they passed the deepest tax cut in 20 years (PL 107-16).

In the Senate, 12 centrist Democrats — notably Max Baucus of Montana, the top Democrat on the Finance Committee — sided with Republicans on the critical vote. In the House, 28 Democrats voted for the bill, but only 10 sided with Republicans on the most crucial House vote: passage of legislation (HR 3) that reduced personal income tax rates by $958 billion through fiscal 2011, three-fifths of Bush's goal.

But the tax cut showed that the strategy could cut both ways.

Democrats forced Bush to scale back his original plan for $1.62 trillion in tax cuts over 10 years when the Senate approved an amendment to the fiscal 2002 budget resolution (H Con Res 83) that reduced the plan by $448 billion.

Democrats muscled the amendment through the Senate

by winning over three Republicans, including James M. Jeffords of Vermont who later left the Republican Party for the same reasons he supported the Democratic amendment. The Republicans, he said, refused to increase education spending and to guarantee as much special-education funding as he wanted.

House Republicans, meanwhile, routinely passed legislation by cutting just enough deals to keep their own troops happy and win over a few from the Democratic side of the aisle.

That strategy worked in blocking a Clinton administration rule governing workplace ergonomics. It also allowed House Republicans to approve fast-track trade negotiating authority (HR 3005), winning 21 Democratic votes, barely enough to compensate for the loss of 23 Republicans. And it allowed Republicans to squeeze through their version of an economic stimulus package (HR 3090).

Both parties employed the strategy to pass competing versions of the patients' bill of rights (HR 2563, S 1052), seemingly guaranteeing more deadlock on an issue that had been stalemated for years.

Senate Democrats won the support of nine Republicans for their version, which had the benefit of a prominent Republican cosponsor, John McCain of Arizona. House Republicans responded by ramming through a bill Bush brokered with Charlie Norwood, R-Ga., who had played a leading role in every attempt to pass the legislation.

It was another McCain alliance with Democrats that pushed campaign finance legislation (S 27) through the Senate in April, over the opposition of Republican leaders who had the majority at the time.

Both parties found, however, that their ability to form such alliances would only carry them so far. When it was time for the House to take up the campaign finance legislation (HR 2356), Republican leaders, who had found a few Democratic allies for their alternative (HR 2360), could not even hold their own ranks at a critical moment.

The rule to set the terms for floor consideration was shot down, with the help of 19 Republicans and one Independent, and House Speaker J. Dennis Hastert, R-Ill., said he had no plans to bring it back up.

Senate Democrats, meanwhile, found no Republican allies for their economic stimulus plan or the homeland security package championed by Senate Appropriations Committee Chairman Robert C. Byrd, D-W.Va.

Even when the bare-majority approach did work, it could be short-lived.

When the Senate unanimously passed an aviation security bill (S 1447) that would have put federal workers in charge of screening passengers and baggage, House Majority Whip Tom DeLay, R-Texas, and Majority Leader Dick Armey, R-Texas, persuaded the House to reject it Nov. 1 in favor of a version (HR 3150) that would have let the president decide whether to use federal employees or contract workers.

Their fight lost steam two days later, however, when a passenger got through a privately run security checkpoint at Chicago's O'Hare International Airport with seven knives, a stun gun and a can labeled "pepper spray."

The final version of the legislation (PL 107-71) required that airport baggage and passenger screening be federalized within a year.

8 Ashcroft Nomination

Within hours of his nomination, Attorney General John Ashcroft emerged as the most controversial pick for President Bush's Cabinet. Opponents and supporters waged a vigorous and sometimes nasty debate for a month over whether Ashcroft was too deeply ideological to be the nation's top law enforcement official, leading to the closest vote of any successful Cabinet nomination in decades.

Liberal interest groups, including People for the American Way and the Leadership Conference on Civil Rights, mobilized against him, hoping to re-create their 1987 defeat of the Supreme Court nomination of Robert Bork. Conservative groups, such as the American Conservative Union, joined forces to defend Ashcroft and others.

The divisiveness of the debate provided an early challenge to the Bush administration's pledge to "change the tone in Washington," but the implications of the vote went beyond political symbolism. Bush was seeking to assert his authority after winning a controversial election, and Democrats were eager to demonstrate their own power to shape the national agenda as 50-50 partners in the Senate.

Ashcroft had served one term as a senator from Missouri and was defeated for re-election in 2000. During his time in the Senate, Ashcroft established himself as a strong voice for the conservative movement, introducing legislation to ban most abortions and voting against gun control, for example. He briefly toyed with running for president.

Opponents also tried to make much of a 1998 interview Ashcroft granted to Southern Partisan, published by the League of the South, a group that supported Southern independence and that some accused of promoting racist views. A quote from the article made it appear Ashcroft endorsed the group's agenda; Ashcroft said he had no knowledge of the League's activities.

Ashcroft's opponents also questioned his opposition to President Bill Clinton's judicial nominations, focusing in particular on his efforts as a senator in 1999 to block the nomination of Ronnie L. White, a Missouri Supreme Court Justice whom Clinton had chosen for a federal judgeship. White had written dissents in several capital cases, which Ashcroft said made him unfit to be a federal judge because he "voted to give clearly guilty murders new trials." White's supporters argued that Ashcroft only opposed White leading up to his close re-election bid, when the death penalty and prosecuting murderers could be a useful political tool.

During two days of grilling by his former colleagues on the Senate Judiciary Committee, Ashcroft was repeatedly questioned about whether he could set aside his personal views, on abortion for example, and enforce laws such as one protecting abortion providers from violent protesters. "I think it's fair to say that I know the difference between an enactment role and an enforcement role," he said.

Despite such assurances, Democrats on the committee were not convinced. "It's very hard to change your stripes or change your spots," said Dianne Feinstein, D-Calif.

But Republicans held their 50 members and picked up a few Democrats. Russell D. Feingold, D-Wis., was the only Democrat to vote for Ashcroft's nomination during committee consideration. He said he wanted to give Ashcroft the benefit of the doubt on questions of his character and the intentions behind his actions as a senator.

Finally, on Feb. 1, the Senate confirmed Ashcroft as Attorney General by a vote of 58-42: R 50-0; D 8-42 (ND 6-35, SD 2-7). Eight Democrats joined unanimous Republicans in voting for him. But Democrats had made an important point about their ability to hang together against enormous political pressure to let the president choose his Cabinet. By keeping the nomination from getting 60 votes — a threshold majority that Senate procedures require to end debate on contentious legislation and force a vote — Democrats proved they would be a force in future debates, including the shaping of the Bush tax plan in the spring. (*Senate vote 8, p. C-18*)

15 Ergonomics Rules

Republicans had long opposed the idea of workplace rules on ergonomics, and when the Clinton administration published one in the fall of 2000, the business community set a top priority of getting rid of it. But it was only through a stealth campaign in the first months of the Bush administration and the use of a little-noticed 1996 congressional review law that GOP leaders were able to overturn the regulation before Democrats had time to marshal a defense.

The ergonomics regulation had taken effect Jan. 16, and enforcement would have begun Oct. 14. It required employers to educate their workers about ways to prevent injuries from repetitive motion such as typing, sorting or lifting heavy loads. If a worker reported an injury, the rule required employers to reconfigure their workplaces in order to prevent a recurrence. Workers who reported injuries lasting seven days or longer would have been able to receive compensation of up to 90 percent of their salary for as long as 90 days if they were unable to work.

Organized labor had sought such rules for more than a decade, but business groups said the Clinton regulation would cost U.S. companies more than $100 billion a year. In the fall of 2000, Republicans tried to include language in the fiscal 2001 Labor-HHS-Education spending bill (PL 106-554) barring the Occupational Safety and Health Administration (OSHA) from finalizing the ergonomics policy. But the Democratic White House outmatched Republicans by allowing OSHA to publish the final rule while the labor spending bill was still mired in negotiations.

The behind-the-scenes campaign to defeat the rule in Jan-uary and February of 2001 was orchestrated by Don Nickles, R-Okla., who was the assistant majority leader of the Senate at the time, in concert with a coalition of business groups.

Nickles' weapon was a 1996 law, the Congressional Review Act, which he had written with Harry Reid, D-Nev., and tucked into a broader regulatory overhaul measure that was enacted as part of a bill raising the debt limit (PL 104-121).

The law allowed Congress to overturn a major regulation within a certain time limit if both houses passed a joint resolution of disapproval by a simple majority vote. The law limited debate and amendments, and further prohibited the administration from writing a new rule in "substantially the same form" as one that Congress rejected.

Nickles and the business groups concentrated on winning over centrist Democrats, such as John B. Breaux of Louisiana, with a pitch that the ergonomics rule would be onerous for business, particularly for small business. Eventually, six Democrats crossed over, five of them from the South, enabling Republicans to pass a resolution of disapproval (S J Res 6 — PL 107-5), 56-44: R 50-0; D 6-44 (ND 1-40; SD 5-4). (*Senate vote 15, p. C-18*)

The House sealed the fate of the ergonomics rule by passing the resolution the following day. Democrats were thunderstruck. "I'm still trying to figure out what the hell happened," said one Democratic aide after the Senate vote.

64 Campaign Finance

The Senate embarked March 19 on the first wide-open debate of campaign finance laws in almost a decade. That it happened at all was a testament to the determination and political skills of John McCain, R-Ariz., and Russell D. Feingold, D-Wis., who had long labored to bring their campaign finance bill (S 27) to a vote.

The arrival of a Senate debate on campaign finance ended years of stall tactics by opponents of the legislation, who had succeeded in keeping the matter off the floor through a mix of filibusters and threats. The House had twice passed a bill similar to the one McCain and Feingold proposed, so it was widely believed Senate passage would ensure that campaign finance laws would be rewritten for the first time in nearly 30 years.

As floor debate began, the question was whether McCain and Feingold could hold together the fragile bipartisan coalition that had allowed them to force the extraordinary two-week debate in the first place. The Senate's Republican leadership had long opposed the legislation, as had powerful outside interests on the left and the right.

But as the battle neared, the Democrats, who had always been the chief proponents of a McCain-Feingold bill, suddenly got nervous. In particular, Democrats were preparing to bolt and bring down the bill over amendments related to the issue of "hard money," the contributions to individual political candidates. The primary goal of the McCain-Feingold legislation was to ban the large and unregulated "soft money" contributions to political parties that the two sponsors viewed as corrupting the political system. But to get support for closing off that pipeline of cash, McCain and Feingold knew they would have to address demands from some in Congress to raise the limits on hard money. The

limits on direct-to-candidate contributions had stood at $1,000 per candidate per election since 1974, and Republicans, who had long raised more hard money than Democrats, demanded it be raised.

Democrats balked. The Democratic Party had come to rely on soft money to make up for the GOP's hard-money advantage, and Democrats were increasingly worried that banning it would put them at a financial disadvantage. Raising the limits on hard money at the same time, in their view, would make matters even worse.

"Raising hard money [limits] will split our caucus big time," said Tom Daschle, D-S.D., who was then minority leader. "It's so anti-reform, and secondly, it so greatly advantages Republicans."

Daschle reluctantly voted for a compromise, hammered out by Fred Thompson, R-Tenn., and Dianne Feinstein, D-Calif., to double the limit on contributions to candidates to $2,000 per election and raise the limit on contributions to national parties to $25,000 per year. But 16 members of his caucus said no, and some continued to complain about the deal.

Republicans accused Democrats of hypocrisy, of looking for an excuse to vote against a soft-money ban now that it seemed likely to become law. "It sounds like people who are looking for the exit sign in the tall grass," Thompson said.

That accusation stung, and it ultimately helped save the bill. Even with elements of their base opposed to the bill and their own careers perhaps at stake, Democrats found they had painted themselves into a corner. Saying no to McCain-Feingold was no longer an option. "We've taken so strong a position as a party in favor of this bill and against soft money that we've got to stay the course," said Joseph I. Lieberman, D-Conn.

On April 2, the Senate passed the bill, believing at the time that the House already had the votes to endorse the Senate action. Only three Democrats voted no, but 12 Republicans crossed over to support the legislation. The vote was 59-41: R 12-38; D 47-3 (ND 40-1, SD 7-2). McCain and Feingold had won the first round. (*Senate vote 64, p. C-18*)

69 Budget Resolution

That the House would pass President Bush's $1.6 trillion 10-year tax cut was never in serious doubt, but the Senate's 50-50 split put the bill's fate in that chamber in the hands of a few moderates of both parties who preferred a smaller figure. The fiscal 2002 congressional budget resolution (H Con Res 83), which set the parameters for the size of the tax cut and provided filibuster protection in the Senate for the subsequent tax cut legislation, became a key battleground.

The tax cut was Bush's campaign centerpiece and the first crucial test of his Capitol Hill clout following a bitterly contested electoral victory. His hopes for securing all of the tax cut he sought were dashed when a handful of Republicans defected on an amendment to the budget resolution offered by Tom Harkin, D-Iowa, to reduce the tax cut by $448 billion — with the amount to be divided evenly between education funding and additional reduction of the national debt. The budget that ultimately emerged from the Senate called for a tax cut of $1.27 tril-

lion. The Senate adopted Harkin's amendment April 4 on a key vote of 53-47: R 4-46; D 49-1 (ND 41-0, SD 8-1). (*Senate vote 69, p. C-18*)

Senate Budget Committee Chairman Pete V. Domenici, R-N.M., had been unable to move a budget resolution through a panel divided 11-11, forcing the GOP to use special budget rules allowing the measure to go directly before the Senate after April 1. In the weeks leading to the floor debate, Bush tried to pressure Senate Democrats by appearing in campaign-style rallies for the tax cut in states such as Louisiana, Georgia, South Dakota and Montana. Those states, all easily carried by Bush, were represented respectively by Democrats Mary L. Landrieu, Max Cleland, Tim Johnson and Max Baucus — all of whom faced re-election in 2002.

The drama continued through the start of the Senate debate, during which there was more action behind the scenes than on the floor. Vice President Dick Cheney, White House budget director Mitchell E. Daniels Jr. and other White House officials descended on the Capitol to hunt for Democratic defections and to press Republican moderates to commit to Bush's plan.

John B. Breaux, D-La., who had been the subject of intense personal lobbying by Bush, took the lead among Senate moderates in trying to limit the size of Bush's tax cut. While floor debate continued, he held a news conference to unveil his own $1.25 trillion tax cut proposal as a starting point for negotiation. Breaux promised that at least one Republican would join him at the press event. He knew Lincoln Chafee, R-R.I., was on board, but because Georgia Democrat Zell Miller had pledged his support for Bush's plan, Breaux needed one more Republican to turn the tide.

In the moments leading up to the news conference, moderate Republican James M. Jeffords of Vermont had been in another room of the Capitol, in the end stages of several days of talks with Senate GOP leaders and White House negotiators. Jeffords was pressing for a deal to increase special education funding, a pet cause of his, but his fellow Republicans declined to meet his demands.

Jeffords' dramatic arrival at Breaux's side after the conference was under way signaled the demise of Bush's hopes for getting all of his tax cut into the budget resolution. (A few weeks later, Jeffords would leave the GOP, handing control of the Senate to the Democrats.)

Breaux's amendment was never put to a vote. Instead, senators left the conference to vote on the Harkin amendment, which was adopted with the help of Republicans Chafee, Jeffords and Arlen Specter of Pennsylvania. When it was clear the amendment would be adopted, then-Majority Leader Trent Lott, R-Miss., switched from a "no" to a "yes" for a procedural reason: It allowed him to move to reconsider the vote later in the debate if he could find enough people to switch. But that never happened.

With the size of the tax cut reduced, moderate Democrats joined the bandwagon in droves and the budget resolution passed, 65-35.

In the wake of the Senate's action, news media accounts tended to portray it as a loss for Bush and an episode mishandled by White House strategists. In the end, the conference report on the budget called for a $1.35 trillion tax cut — more than three-quarters of what initially came before the Senate.

165 Tax Cuts

Nowhere did the vagaries of the 50-50 Senate, which lasted from January through May, create more of a high-stakes balancing act than in the writing of the 2001 tax cut law.

With the economy already showing signs of weakness as the year began, a broad majority existed in Congress for devoting some of the surplus to a potentially stimulative tax cut. But there the agreement ended — not only between the two parties but also, especially in the Senate, within the Republican as well as Democratic caucuses. The multifaceted dynamic guaranteed that a bipartisan compromise, written to appeal to moderate senators in each party, was the only way to assure that President Bush would win the broad tax cut that was the top priority for his first year in office.

The first threshold question — how deep to cut — was settled in the fiscal 2002 budget resolution. Effectively written by the centrists, it set a limit of $1.35 trillion through fiscal 2011 by saying anything above that would have to muster the support of 60 senators, a political impossibility at the time.

At that point, Republican leaders considered advancing a bill designed to reflect Bush's wishes as closely as possible given the budget restraint, in the hope it could be pushed to passage with almost exclusively GOP votes. At the same time, Democratic leaders considered mounting a campaign to stop the drive for tax legislation outright, principally by refusing to cooperate with the GOP. Instead, a package designed to win over moderates in both parties was cobbled together by the leaders of the Finance Committee, Charles E. Grassley, R-Iowa, and Max Baucus, D-Mont. While following the outline of Bush's plan, it was modified to stay within the confines of the budget. (The rate cuts, for example, were not as deep as the president wanted.) Room was made for additional provisions designed to appeal to the more liberal Republicans, such as allowing poorer parents to claim part of the child tax credit, and more conservative Democrats, primarily an expansion of tax breaks for education.

The key moment came May 23, when the Senate passed the bill, 62-38: R 50-0; D 12-38 (ND 7-34, SD 5-4). *(Senate vote 165, p. C-18)*

The vote showed that Grassley and Baucus had found the formula for a tax package that could claim to have "broad bipartisan support." Not only did their trade-offs succeed in sustaining the support of all Republicans, it also reflected the year's apogee of prominence for the centrist Democrats, a dozen of whom (24 percent of all Democratic senators) voted for the legislation.

The tally also signaled that the deepest tax cut in a generation would happen, and that Bush would score his first big legislative triumph, sooner than almost anyone had predicted. Only 24 days elapsed between when the ceiling for the tax cut was set and when the Senate cleared the legislation (PL 107-16) — blindingly fast for such wide-ranging, expensive and politically precarious legislation.

The same dozen Democrats who voted for the original bill voted for the final version as well, a reflection of how closely the latter resembled the former. To make sure of that, two of the four lawmakers who cut the deal with the White House were Baucus and John B. Breaux of Louisiana, a leader of centrist Senate Democrats. Baucus and five other Democrats who backed the bill were up for re-election in 2002, and all of

them expected competitive races. Only two Democrats seen as vulnerable in 2002, Iowa's Tom Harkin and Minnesota's Paul Wellstone, voted "no" May 23.

Two Republicans who embraced the initial bill spurned the final deal, however: John McCain of Arizona, who opposed deep tax cuts when he ran against Bush for the party's 2000 presidential nomination, and fiscal moderate Lincoln Chafee of Rhode Island. But another pivotal moderate, James M. Jeffords of Vermont, supported the package — his vote for initial Senate passage coming before he announced he was abandoning the GOP to become an Independent, thereby giving Senate control to the Democrats.

As a result, the climactic vote for the tax cut also stands as a high-water mark for the short-lived period — the first since 1954 — of unilateral Republican control of the legislative and executive branches.

220 Patients' Rights

Immediately after becoming Senate majority leader in June, Tom Daschle, D-S.D., said a patients' bill of rights, left on the back burner by Republicans during the first part of the year, would be the first major piece of legislation he would bring to the floor. So on June 19, Democrats began debate on a broad managed-care overhaul bill (S 1052) drafted by Edward M. Kennedy, D-Mass., John McCain, R-Ariz., and John Edwards, D-N.C. To ensure a vote on final passage, Daschle threatened to keep the Senate in session through the July 4 recess, if necessary, to finish.

The Kennedy-McCain-Edwards measure was designed with all the provisions that patients' rights advocates had been pushing for years, including requirements that plans cover visits to specialists and emergency rooms, as well as a stipulation that insurers be prohibited from imposing restrictions on what doctors could tell their patients about treatment options.

The biggest controversy, as always, was over liability. The bill propsed, for the first time, to allow patients to sue their health plans in federal court for damages if harmed or injured by a health plan's coverage decision.

The bill would cap civil damages at $5 million in federal court, but economic and non-economic damages would be unlimited.

The debate, and resulting vote, put Republicans in a tough position. Polls had shown that a managed-care overhaul was popular with voters, but businesses and the insurance industry lobbied heavily against it. A Republican version encompassing broad "principles" laid out by the Bush administration clearly did not have the votes to pass.

But Democrats also faced a complex strategic calculation in bringing the bill to a vote. They knew Bush would oppose their version, and, indeed, the White House issued a veto threat during the first week of debate. That meant a choice for Daschle and his party. They had to decide whether to call Bush's bluff and pass a bill anyway, or try to work it out in advance in order to ensure his signature. They chose the former course, partly because they figured that the bill they passed would be their opening bid in a conference to reconcile it with whatever was produced by the GOP-controlled House.

During the two weeks of Senate debate, Republicans proposed amendment after amendment designed to change the bill's liability provisions. Most of them failed. However, GOP moderates were successful in attaching amendments designed to make the bill more acceptable to business, especially large employers.

One such amendment, sponsored by Olympia J. Snowe, R-Maine, would allow employers who appointed a "designated decision maker" for medical decisions to be shielded from lawsuits. Big business groups and their Republican allies had seized on the issue, painting the bill as one that would make large employers — not just less-popular insurance companies — vulnerable to higher costs. As Minority Whip Don Nickles, R-Okla., said: "Employers beware. There's language in this bill that will bankrupt you."

The Snowe amendment gave some cover to Republicans who were concerned about the bill's potential effect on employers. Along with three Republicans, Democrat Ernest F. Hollings of South Carolina opposed her amendment.

But on final passage Daschle — in his first big test as majority leader — held his caucus together, with no Democrats opposing the bill. It passed June 29 by a vote of 59-36: R 9-35; D 50-0 (ND 41-0, SD 9-0); I 0-1. (*Senate vote 220, p. C-19*)

In addition to McCain, eight Republicans voted for the final product, including three who were up for re-election in 2002: Susan Collins of Maine, Gordon H. Smith of Oregon and John W. Warner of Virginia. Republican-turned-Independent James M. Jeffords of Vermont — the senator whose famous party switch enabled Democrats to bring the measure to the floor in the first place — was not among the supporters.

273 Farm Bill

As its opening foray into rewriting what both parties viewed as a badly flawed farm law, the Senate engaged in a surprisingly partisan fight over how much short-term relief to provide producers — transforming the debate into one that was at least as much about fiscal discipline as about agriculture policy.

Farm bill differences are usually regional in nature, but an uncertain surplus picture, combined with the political pressure of drafting a new law heading into an election year, led Republican and Democratic leaders to stake out different positions on the question of how much to boost direct government payments to farmers beyond the subsidies they were already due.

Democrats, newly in control of the Senate, wanted to spend $7.4 billion, painting themselves as the better advocates for the nation's farmers. Republicans, backed by a veto threat from President Bush, cloaked themselves in the mantle of fiscal restraint as they fought successfully to keep the bill within the confines of the fiscal 2002 budget resolution (H Con Res 83), which set aside $5.5 billion for the supplemental farm package.

The turning point came as Congress was pressing to clear a path to its monthlong August recess. Agriculture Committee Chairman Tom Harkin, D-Iowa, called up his $7.4 billion version of the bill and — when it became clear Republican leaders were intent on stopping the additional

$1.9 billion in funding — moved to invoke cloture, thereby curtailing the debate and limiting amendments.

Harkin needed 60 votes to get his way, but he came up 11 short on the key vote Aug. 3. Only two Republicans took his side in favor of the more generous package, and they were offset by two Democrats who voted with the GOP. The tally was 49-48: R 2-46; D 46-2 (ND 37-2, SD 9-0); I 1-0. (*Senate vote 273, p. C-19*)

By showing that the Democrats could not muster the three-fifths majority needed to get their way, the vote signaled that Republicans, although in the minority, had sufficient muscle to help Bush hold the line on spending.

In the end, however, the outcome was dictated by bureaucratic deadline as much as political will. Under the budget resolution, the Department of Agriculture had only until Sept. 30 to provide whatever extra aid Congress authorized during fiscal 2001, and newly authorized government checks can take weeks to process and deliver. As a result, many believed that the opportunity to provide supplemental assistance would be lost if Congress did not act before its August break.

Harkin and Majority Leader Tom Daschle, D-S.D., initially saw the time constraint as leverage that would help persuade Bush and Republicans to drop their resistance to the more generous package.

Republicans saw the same deadline as a way to compel the Democrats to drop a proposal that — in the face of a veto threat and clear opposition from the House, which had given voice vote approval to the less costly plan — could not quickly become law.

Once it became evident to Democrats that their pressure tactics were not working, they suggested they might wait and continue their fight in September. But hours after their bid to limit debate failed, they gave up and allowed the Senate to clear the House-passed measure (HR 2213) by voice vote.

Still, the midyear farm aid law (PL 107-25) marked the fourth time in as many years that Congress had stepped in to provide direct payments to farmers — a total of $31.5 billion since 1997 — on top of federal support they received under the 1996 farm law (PL 104-127), which had been geared toward weaning farmers from federal subsidies and providing them instead with fixed payments to help them adjust to a more free-market-oriented system.

281 Use of Force Resolution

Unified in its anger over the Sept. 11 terrorist attacks at the World Trade Center and Pentagon, the Senate acted swiftly in unanimously approving a resolution (S J Res 23) giving President Bush the power to pursue and punish the perpetrators.

The resolution authorized the president to "use all necessary and appropriate force against those nations, organizations or persons he determined planned, authorized, committed or aided" the attacks or against the nations that harbored the terrorists. The Senate adopted the resolution by a vote of 98-0: R 47-0; D 50-0 (ND 41-0, SD 9-0); I 1-0. (*Senate vote 281, p. C-19*)

Congress gave Bush free rein to pursue his subsequent military campaign against alleged mastermind Osama bin

Laden and his al Qaeda terrorist network, as well as the Taliban regime in Afghanistan that sheltered the group. But the resolution blurred the lines separating the president's and Congress' respective constitutional roles in initiating military hostilities.

Lawmakers also put off a debate over whether Bush's plan to conduct a global war against terrorism extended to countries beyond Afghanistan, particularly Iraq.

Conservatives, such as Republican Policy Committee Chairman Larry E. Craig of Idaho, argued for passing a declaration of war or a broad resolution to give Bush unfettered power to prosecute terrorism around the world.

"I'm not for putting a lot of strings on it," said Republican Jon Kyl of Arizona, a member of the Senate Intelligence Committee. "Are we going to be able to give the president enough flexibility to act if we put a lot of restrictions in legislation?"

That view was shared by the White House, which initially proposed that it also be granted "all necessary and appropriate force" to "deter and pre-empt any future acts of terrorism or aggression against the United States."

But many lawmakers, especially Democrats, believed that would go too far and would infringe on congressional authority. They feared that an open-ended commitment would come back to haunt them, much as an earlier generation came to lament its support for the 1964 Gulf of Tonkin resolution (PL 88-408).

That resolution was cited by the Johnson and Nixon administrations as congressional authorization for waging the Vietnam War.

Senate Foreign Relations Committee Chairman Joseph R. Biden Jr., D-Del., said lawmakers had struck an appropriate balance between the two branches of government while ensuring congressional prerogative.

"We gave the president all the authority he needed without giving up our constitutional right to decide whether force should be used," Biden said.

286 Base Closings

The Senate approved President Bush's proposal to close surplus military bases after repeatedly rejecting requests by President Bill Clinton for nearly identical legislation. But in a bid to ease House concerns, the Senate delayed the start of the process until 2005.

Lawmakers repeatedly had fought efforts to shutter bases, fearing that installations economically important to their states might be targeted. But in September, 14 senators made an about-face on the issue, supporting Bush where they had opposed Clinton either for political reasons or in the belief that their bases would be on the hit list.

Clinton and Bush made the same argument for closing more bases: The Pentagon was wasting billions of dollars trying to maintain unnecessary facilities. But a new argument was offered during debate on the fiscal 2002 defense authorization bill (S 1438). Base-closing proponents said the savings were even more important as the military waged war against terrorism and faced new duties in homeland defense after the Sept. 11 terrorist attacks.

Base-closing opponents, led by Jim Bunning, R-Ky., challenged the Pentagon's statement that previous clos-

ings had yielded significant savings. They said another round would be ill-timed amid a recession and as the services were deciding what deployments might be needed to fight terrorism.

The key vote occurred on an amendment by Bunning to delete the base-closing provision from the defense bill. It was tabled (killed) by a vote of 53-47: R 21-28; D 31-19 (ND 25-16; SD 6-3); I 1-0. (*Senate vote 286, p. C-19*)

Although Democrats provided the majority of the support for an initiative by a Republican president, the difference between this vote and the Senate's 63-35 rejection of a similar proposal in June 2000 was the number of members — eight Republicans and six Democrats — who switched from opposition to support.

John W. Warner of Virginia, ranking Republican on the Senate Armed Services Committee, had voted against Clinton's plans although he acknowledged that additional bases needed to be closed. He argued that Clinton had politicized the process in 1995 by ordering the Air Force to have private contractors take over aircraft overhaul depots in vote-rich California and Texas, even though the base-closing commission had recommended they be shut down.

Other lawmakers switched because bases that once looked vulnerable now appeared safe. Majority Leader Tom Daschle, whose state of South Dakota was home to Ellsworth Air Force Base, voted against closure in 2000 amid talk that Ellsworth might be a target. But the base's future seemed more certain when the Air Force announced in June that it was one of two at which B-1 bomber operations would be consolidated. This time, Daschle voted for base closings.

313 Anti-Terrorism

In the Senate, all the real debate on the anti-terrorism package proposed by Attorney General John Ashcroft took place behind closed doors. Some members privately expressed concern about the breadth of the bill, but the power of a popular president and public fears of more terrorist attacks helped push it to passage with very few changes and only one senator voting no.

The debate over the Bush administration's tactics in the home-front war on terrorism would continue on Capitol Hill, but the lopsided vote in the Senate sent an important signal early on that Congress would give wide latitude to the White House in dealing with the crisis.

On Sept. 19, Ashcroft asked Congress to give him broader powers to investigate acts of terrorism and other crimes. He argued that limitations in existing law tied his hands and made it far too difficult to track the culprits of the Sept. 11 attack and their associates. He wanted to update the laws to make it easier to track Internet communications, get nationwide search warrants for terrorism investigations, authorize more secret searches of a suspect's residence, and indefinitely detain aliens he believed were national security risks. He also wanted investigators to be able to give information to intelligence agents and receive information in turn.

Almost as soon as the request arrived on Capitol Hill, senators began closed-door discussions on the provisions.

The talks, led by Judiciary Committee Chairman Patrick J. Leahy, D-Vt., and the panel's ranking Republican, Orrin G. Hatch of Utah, included administration representatives nearly from the start.

That was in contrast to the House, where Judiciary Committee Chairman F. James Sensenbrenner Jr., R-Wis., negotiated largely among committee members to come up with a bill. Although the House Judiciary Committee produced a bipartisan bill, it was never brought to the floor. Members instead voted on a bill much closer to the measure finally agreed upon by the Senate negotiators.

After weeks of negotiations, and several breakdowns, Leahy and others announced Oct. 4 that they had reached a deal. The agreement gave the administration most of what it sought, although senators did delete a provision that would have allowed U.S. government officials to use the results of unconstitutional wiretaps by foreign governments.

The bill incorporating the deal (S 1510) was introduced by Majority Leader Tom Daschle, D-S.D., on Oct. 4. It skipped committee and went straight to the floor, where it passed 96-1 on Oct. 11 with less than three hours of actual debate. Daschle told his colleagues to vote against amendments offered by Russell D. Feingold, D-Wis., not because he opposed the substance of the amendments but in order to preserve the carefully negotiated compromise with the administration. Feingold was the only dissenting vote.

After the House passed its version Oct. 12, members spent about a week working out a compromise. The final bill (HR 3162) included much of the Senate bill but also contained a key House-passed end to the authorization for many of the most contentious parts of the bill after four years.

The Senate took up the final bill Oct. 25, the day after the House passed it. The Senate cleared the bill for the president 98-1: R 49-0; D 48-1 (ND 40-1, SD 8-0); I 1-0. The president signed it the next day. Feingold again was the only no vote; Mary L. Landrieu, D-La., did not vote. (*Senate vote 313, p. C-19*)

33 Ergonomics Rules

House Republican leaders were eager to follow their Senate counterparts in overturning a controversial Clinton administration regulation on workplace ergonomics. After weeks of careful groundwork, Republicans had sprung their trap in the Senate on March 6 before Democrats could respond with a procedural defense. They had an easier time in the House the next day, where the GOP controlled the rules more tightly.

The debate over ergonomics and repetitive motion injuries in factories and offices had been going on for more than a decade. Democrats, with their staunch support of organized labor, generally favored new rules; Republicans generally opposed the idea, since it could cost business dearly.

The Clinton administration published a final ergonomics rule in the fall of 2000, pre-empting a Republican effort to block the rule in the fiscal 2001 Labor-HHS-Education spending bill (PL 106-554).

House Republicans were eager to push through a repeal as one of the first acts of the session.

The ergonomics regulation had taken effect Jan. 16 and enforcement would have begun Oct. 14. It required employers to educate workers about ways to prevent injuries from repetitive motion such as typing, sorting or lifting heavy loads. It required employers to make changes in their workplaces if a worker reported a repetitive motion injury. Business groups, which said the requirement would have cost U.S. companies more than $100 billion a year, made it a top goal to overturn the rule before it took effect.

Working behind the scenes, House Republicans and business groups persuaded some centrist Democrats to support overturning the regulation using a little-noticed 1996 law, the Congressional Review Act, which was enacted as part of a debt-limit extension (PL 104-121).

When the House took up the bill March 7, 16 Democrats, 14 of them from the South, supported overturning the ergonomics regulation, more than offsetting the 13 Republicans, many of them from the Northeast and upper Midwest, who sided with labor and voted to keep the regulation. The vote was 223-206: R 206-13; D 16-192 (ND 2-152; SD 14-40); I 1-1. (*House vote 33, p. C-20*)

Some centrist Democrats justified their votes in 2001 against the Clinton-era regulation by saying they would push for legislation that would require the Labor Department to issue narrower ergonomics policies. However, those bills (S 598, HR 598) did not move through either chamber.

Democrats were particularly frustrated that Republicans used the Congressional Review Act because it also banned the administration from writing another regulation that had "substantially the same form."

Later in the year, Labor Secretary Elaine L. Chao held hearings on the ergonomics issue, but the agency did not issue a new round of worker safety regulations that employers would have to implement.

45 Tax Cuts

With Republicans simultaneously controlling the Capitol and the White House for the first time in five decades, and with evidence of an economic downturn already apparent, a tax cut in 2001 seemed to be a certainty as the year began. Its potential scope and speed remained largely unknown, however, until the narrow but united majority of Republicans won a vote that displayed the House's ability to deliver to President Bush the type of tax cut that was the centerpiece of his campaign.

The Constitution stipulates that revenue bills must originate in the House, so it always was certain the debate on the Bush tax plan would start in the more receptive of the two

congressional chambers. It was left to House GOP leaders — and in particular Bill Thomas, R-Calif., the new chairman of the Ways and Means Committee — to decide how best to leverage a bipartisan willingness to cut taxes. As the year began, Democratic leaders had lined up behind a $900 million plan — signaling they were willing to go more than halfway toward Bush's $1.6 trillion-over-10-years package.

But rather than easing into the tax cut issue with negotiations on a broad package or an easy vote on a minimally controversial tax cut — or simply waiting until the administration had settled its macro disputes over fiscal policy — the GOP took a decidedly different tack: It arranged to make the year's most politically difficult vote on taxes the first vote on taxes. By vaulting past the most difficult hurdle first, party leaders theorized, they would help build a sense of inevitability for the deepest tax cut in a generation.

The day after the president sent his first budget outline to Congress, and without any consultation with Democrats, the House GOP started moving its version of Bush's most contentious and costly tax proposal: the first across-the-board reduction of personal income tax rates in 15 years, with the sharpest reduction for those with the highest incomes. The Republican legislation (HR 3) would have reduced revenues by $958 billion through fiscal 2011, three-fifths the total of Bush's entire proposal.

The bill presented the House not only with its first vote on the new president's platform, but also with a vote on the central element of his economic program. The vote March 8 to pass the measure was 230-198: R 219-0; D 10-197 (ND 3-150; SD 7-47); I 1-1. (*House vote 45, p. C-20*)

The vote sent a host of signals not only about the fate of the Bush tax package, but also about the nature of partisanship in the House and the continued differences between the House and Senate.

House GOP leaders learned that their caucus was united behind the Bush tax cut. They learned that, even with the narrowest majority since the 83rd Congress, they could push through one of the most contentious bills of the year without even pretending to collaborate across the aisle — and that more than a handful of Democrats would vote with them anyway. (Most of the 10 who did so had just been re-elected in politically competitive districts; the House votes on other central elements of the Bush plan — tax relief for parents and ending the estate tax — drew many more Democratic votes; 28 Democrats eventually voted for the reconciliation package that became law in June.)

The rate cut vote also showed House GOP leaders that their main argument, that quick action was needed to deliver a boost to a sagging economy, could triumph over the two most politically potent counterarguments. Liberals maintained that the Bush tax cut, especially the personal income rate cut, was inappropriately tilted to the rich. Most of the party's conservatives argued that it was wrong to cut taxes before setting an overall budget framework that could balance the demands on what was, at the time, a robust federal surplus.

Business lobbyists and others hoping to include their special interests in the tax bill also took a lesson from the vote: Their priorities would have to wait because the House GOP was only interested in writing its own version of the president's program.

Finally, the clarity of the vote allowed House leaders early in the year to pass off to the Senate the job of balancing all the debate's competing pressures. The Senate's 50-50 split at the time, combined with rules that essentially require any proposal of controversy to win 60 supporters, always meant it would be the true proving ground for the tax cut fight.

130 Education

President Bush's education overhaul plan turned almost entirely on an idea that had enemies in both parties: annual testing in reading and math for children in grades 3 through 8. So when Reps. Peter Hoekstra, R-Mich., and Barney Frank, D-Mass., teamed up in May to try to delete that element from the House education overhaul bill (HR 1), the White House knew it had a fight on its hands.

There would have been little point to the overhaul bill without the annual testing. The idea was to hold states, school districts and schools accountable for how much students learn, with rewards for the best schools and penalties for the worst. To do that, there had to be a yardstick for measuring students' progress. Annual tests were the best available yardstick, supporters of the Bush plan said, and they were essential to allow the bill's multilayered "accountability" system to work.

It quickly became clear, however, that the annual testing offered something for everyone to hate. Conservatives thought it was a backdoor way to establish the national test they all feared, just four years after they defeated President Bill Clinton's plans for voluntary national tests in reading and math. Liberals argued that children were being forced to take too many tests already, and warned that standardized tests were unfair to poor and minority students.

It was a powerful undercurrent of opposition, and even though the education bill had been approved by the House Education and the Workforce Committee by a strong bipartisan vote of 41-7, the nervousness about testing was seen as a bomb that could explode at any time. When Hoekstra and Frank announced they would offer an amendment on the House floor to remove the testing requirement, administration officials feared the bomb was about to go off.

The alliance of Hoekstra, a conservative, and Frank, a liberal, captured the wide spectrum of opposition to the annual tests. Both argued that the tests would impose an unfair mandate on the states and that they would represent a heavy-handed federal role in education, which traditionally was a state and local responsibility.

All along, the Bush administration and the House bill's main authors — Education and the Workforce Chairman John A. Boehner, R-Ohio, and top Democrat George Miller of California — had to negotiate with Republicans and Democrats to keep them from offering divisive amendments that could destroy the bill's fragile bipartisan support. They swung into action to make sure Hoekstra and Frank did not attract enough support to cut out the bill's centerpiece.

White House Chief of Staff Andrew H. Card Jr. and presidential adviser Karl Rove discouraged conservatives from voting for the amendment. Boehner and Miller spoke passionately on behalf of the testing provision. The Busi-

ness Roundtable sent out an e-mail alert asking its members to urge lawmakers to oppose the amendment, warning that it would "take the teeth out of the bill."

Ultimately, the vote was not as close as the bill's supporters had feared. The Hoekstra-Frank amendment was rejected May 22 by a vote of 173-255: R 52-166; D 119-89 (ND 91-63; SD 28-26); I 2-0. However, the amendment did draw the support of 119 Democrats, including some of the most powerful ones in the House: Minority Leader Richard A. Gephardt of Missouri, Minority Whip David E. Bonior of Michigan and David R. Obey of Wisconsin, the ranking member of the Appropriations Committee. (*House vote 130, p. C-20*)

Still, the fact that the testing survived the onslaught of so many opponents was a defining moment for the education bill. At that moment, it became clear that nothing could stand in the bill's way — because even the most unpopular provision was not fatal.

228 Campaign Finance

Plenty of members, Republicans and Democrats alike, had qualms about the campaign finance legislation that reached the House floor July 12. But when the bill (HR 2356) came crashing down, tangled in a dispute over the rule for debate, each side blamed the other for the failure.

There was room for both parties to portray events in the light that best suited them. In the end, there were no votes for or against the bill in the House, nothing to put members clearly on record. The vote on the rule was very much open to interpretation.

In the weeks leading up to the debate, the sponsors of the campaign finance bill, Democrat Martin T. Meehan of Massachusetts and Republican Christopher Shays of Connecticut, had worked to fine-tune their bill so that it closely matched the Senate-passed version (S 27) sponsored by John McCain, R-Ariz., and Russell D. Feingold, D-Wis. The goal was to avoid a conference committee, where supporters of the bill feared hostile Republican leaders would have another chance to kill it.

But from the start, a critical Senate compromise dogged Democrats in the House. In exchange for banning "soft money," the unregulated contributions to political parties, McCain and Feingold had agreed to raise the limits on "hard money," or direct-to-candidate contributions. Democrats already were having second thoughts about banning soft money as the 2002 midterm elections approached. Raising the limits on hard money, where the GOP has long had the edge, gave them one more reason to say no to the bill.

The fractures were most visible in the 36-member Congressional Black Caucus, whose members said soft money was crucial to get-out-the-vote and voter registration efforts in minority communities.

Republican leaders, who opposed Shays-Meehan, unveiled a rival bill aimed at those fears, driving another wedge into the Democratic caucus. The bill (HR 2360) would have capped, rather than banned, soft money.

Meanwhile, House Minority Leader Richard A. Gephardt, D-Mo., who had taken flak for not fighting visibly enough for Shays-Meehan, lobbied his caucus to stay

behind the bill. He was still working to secure votes when the dispute over the rule for debate came to a head July 12.

Shays and Meehan had asked the House Rules Committee to bundle 14 last-minute changes to their bill — aimed mostly at bringing it in line with the Senate version — into a single "manager's amendment." The Rules Committee refused and said each of the changes would be voted on separately on the floor.

Shays, Meehan and their supporters angrily accused the Republican leadership of trying to bring down the bill with a complicated, obstacle-strewn rule. Republicans countered that Democrats were looking for a face-saving way to scuttle the bill because they did not have the votes to pass it.

Speaker J. Dennis Hastert, R-Ill., offered to compromise on the rule, but he withdrew after conservatives in his caucus demanded that the original rule go forward. In the end, the rule for debating campaign finance legislation in the House was rejected 203-228: R 201-19; D 1-208 (ND 1-154; SD 0-54); I 1-1. It was the first time Hastert lost a vote on a rule, which is typically seen as a matter of party loyalty from which members have little room to deviate. (*House vote 228, p. C-20*)

With the defeat of the rule, campaign finance dropped from the House agenda; Hastert promptly said he had no intention of giving the debate another chance. Shays-Meehan supporters quickly began collecting signatures on a "discharge petition" to force the bill back to the floor under rules more to their liking, and by Sept. 11, they were just nine names short of the 218 they needed. Then the terrorist attacks put it all on hold. The petition was good for the duration of the 107th Congress, so Shays and Meehan had time for another push in 2002, but that would be an election year, which could further complicate their efforts.

288 Arsenic Standards

Early in the spring when President Bush was coming under fire from environmental lobbyists for his industry-favoring policies, there was one decision that became a rallying cry — EPA Administrator Christine Todd Whitman's announcement that stricter standards for arsenic in drinking water would be delayed.

Arsenic occurred naturally in the soil and water, but it also was released by some industrial processes. Studies had linked long-term exposure to arsenic in drinking water to cancer of the bladder, lungs, skin, kidney, liver and prostate. Polls showed that most people roundly supported a Clinton administration regulation that would have lowered the allowable standard from 50 parts per billion — the level that had been permitted for decades — to 10 parts per billion. The lower standard had been recommended by the European Union and the World Health Organization.

The dangers of arsenic were not a new topic for Congress. Five years earlier, lawmakers had directed the administration to study the health risks associated with arsenic as part of its safe drinking water amendments (PL 104-182).

Mining and chemical companies opposed the more stringent Clinton regulations. They had argued that science did not support such a tough policy. The regulation also was opposed by officials from many of the 3,000 towns that would have to update their water systems.

When Whitman insisted that the regulation be put on hold, she said the EPA should take the time to make sure the policy, which was not slated to take effect until 2006, was founded in science, though she herself supported the more stringent standard.

Environmentalists pounced on her announcement as a sign that the White House was abandoning the policy and, as many lobbyists put it, trying to allow more cancer-causing chemicals in the public's water.

The Bush administration had delayed or reversed several orders and regulations that Clinton had issued in the waning days of his term, but none of Bush's decisions resonated like arsenic. Amid a flood of news stories and polls, it was clear that the new administration had miscalculated. Congress was not long in making the point that Bush had gone too far.

On July 27, House Democrats succeeded in attaching an amendment to the fiscal 2002 VA-HUD appropriations bill (HR 2620) to prohibit the EPA from weakening the Clinton standards for arsenic in drinking water.

The amendment, offered by Minority Whip David E. Bonior, D-Mich., was adopted 218-189, with 19 Republicans crossing party lines to support the provision: R 19-182; D 198-6 (ND 151-2; SD 47-4); I 1-1. (*House vote 288, p. C-20*)

The administration did not admit defeat, but it retreated in the following months. At the EPA's request, the National Academy of Sciences studied the issue and its report, completed in September, found that arsenic in drinking water was more harmful to humans than previous studies had indicated. The report suggested that the government consider arsenic limits even more restrictive than those proposed by Clinton.

Following this report, Whitman announced on Oct. 31 that the EPA would, after all, adopt the Clinton standard.

Although the dispute had become moot, the final VA-HUD bill (PL 107-73) included the House language, which banned the EPA from spending federal funds to weaken the Clinton standards.

302 Human Cloning

The House drew a new line on how far it was willing to go in restricting biomedical research July 31, passing a comprehensive ban on cloning human embryos either for reproductive purposes or to develop medical treatments.

The 265-162 vote for the ban (HR 2505), sponsored by Dave Weldon, R-Fla., reflected the growing discomfort many lawmakers felt with the prospect of scientists creating human embryos so their cells could be harvested for medical purposes.

But the precise extent of the discomfort was evident just before the vote on the Weldon measure, when the House in a key vote rejected a substitute amendment by James C. Greenwood, R-Pa., that would have outlawed cloning for the purpose of starting a pregnancy but allowed it to create tissue for medical research. The amendment was defeated, 178-249: R 25-194; D 153-53 (ND 118-35; SD 35-18); I 0-2. (*House vote 302, p. C-20*)

The cloning votes were intertwined with the separate but related issue of whether the government should fund stem cell research.

Researchers in 1998 had announced the ability to isolate primitive human stem cells from days-old embryos. The so-called master cells were capable of evolving into bone, muscle and virtually every kind of human tissue, giving researchers hope they might be able to develop healthy replacement cells to cure such afflictions as juvenile diabetes, spinal cord injuries and Parkinson's disease.

However, the field was controversial because extracting stem cells involved destroying embryos — an act that anti-abortion forces equated with taking a life. Stem cells currently were extracted from leftover embryos developed through in vitro fertilization. Research opponents maintained that human embryos soon could be cloned solely for the purpose of supplying stem cells, pointing to plans by the Worcester, Mass., biotechnology company Advanced Cell Technologies to conduct such "therapeutic cloning."

The Greenwood substitute served as a referendum on that procedure. Supporters suggested that the extraction of stem cells offered a high-resolution view of early human development that might force Congress to change its position on when life begins. During an often emotional four hours of debate, some noted that the act of making cells divide in a petri dish alone would not ensure that they developed into an embryo unless they were implanted in a womb. They urged members not to impose what they considered onerous new regulations, such as the Weldon ban, on a still-developing field.

The substitute lost by an unexpectedly large margin thanks to intense lobbying by anti-abortion groups, which dubbed the Greenwood provision a "clone to kill" bill. Some skeptics also questioned how one could practically enforce the Greenwood provision and ensure that an embryo created for research purposes was not later implanted in a surrogate mother without violating doctor-patient confidentiality agreements.

The cloning debate did not break precisely along the lines of past abortion votes. Fifty-three Democrats joined with 194 Republicans and two Independents to reject the Greenwood measure. Some lawmakers on both sides of the debate expressed discomfort afterward at having to assimilate complicated technical information and parse the differences between what the Weldon and Greenwood measures would do. Greenwood and biotechnology industry officials suggested the outcome ironically would give lawmakers more leeway to support embryonic stem cell research, allowing conservatives to support the medical promise of using stem cells from leftover embryos in fertility clinics and still appear to be taking a firm line against human cloning.

The separate congressional debate over funding stem cell research was settled in August, when President Bush endorsed limited federal funding for the work.

317 Drilling in ANWR

The issue of whether to open the coast of Alaska's Arctic National Wildlife Refuge (ANWR) to oil and natural gas exploration had divided lawmakers and pitted environmentalists against oil companies and Alaska officials for more than 40 years. Despite the West Coast's electricity crunch earlier in 2001, environmentalists were confident they had the upper hand, pointing to polls showing that a majority of

Americans opposed drilling in the distant refuge because of the potential ecological harm.

However, the House defeat of a proposal to ban drilling showed how the combined lobbying of the White House, House Republican leaders, energy industries and labor unions could outmaneuver and overwhelm environmental groups.

Environmentalists described the coastal plain as an important birthing place for caribou, a feeding ground for snow geese and a den site for polar bears. They also noted it would take as long as 10 years to begin piping oil from the refuge, and that even then, it would be of little help to California and other states that got less than 1 percent of their power from oil-fired plants.

However, Bush decided earlier in his administration to publicly talk up the benefits of ANWR as a way to help wean the United States from its dependence on foreign oil. He appointed Vice President Dick Cheney to head an energy task force that recommended in May that a portion of the refuge be opened for exploration.

The House Resources Committee subsequently included the ANWR language in a bill that was combined with three other measures to form an omnibus energy package (HR 4) developed in response to the Cheney task force's report. Environmentalists and their allies in Congress promised to remove the language on ANWR, arguing that opening the refuge would permanently alter it no matter how carefully the work was done.

But proponents of drilling framed the debate in economic rather than environmental terms. The International Brotherhood of Teamsters ran a series of radio advertisements claiming that opening the refuge would create as many as 750,000 jobs.

Environmentalists disputed the figures, but the idea of stimulating employment through increased domestic energy production as unemployment began creeping higher for the first time in years resonated with some undecided lawmakers. "I was moved by the prospects . . . for some jobs," said Jack Quinn, R-N.Y., a moderate with close ties to organized labor.

To win over other lawmakers concerned about the possible environmental damage, House Republican leaders encouraged them to support two amendments that critics said were intended to provide political cover. One would split future oil and gas royalties evenly between the state of Alaska and the federal government, instead of giving Alaska 90 percent.

The other would limit the ground that could be covered by oil production facilities in the refuge to 2,000 acres. Both amendments were adopted.

However, the decisive amendment by Edward J. Markey, D-Mass., to remove the ANWR language from the bill was rejected, 206-223: R 34-186; D 171-36 (ND 141-13; SD 30-23); I 1-1. (*House vote 317, p. C-20*)

After the vote, opponents of drilling were consoled by its dim prospects in the Senate, where Democrats held the majority and put off energy legislation for the year. But ANWR supporters in the House lamented that their intensive lobbying did not register. "It was a tough coalition to beat," Markey said after the vote, "the oil and gas industry, the building trades, the president of the United States and millions of dollars of lobbying."

329 Patients' Rights

One of the most intriguing parts of the managed-care story in 2001 was how the bill came to the House floor in the first place. After the Senate passed its bill in June, House leaders promised to bring patients' rights legislation to a vote before the August recess.

Beyond that, they were stuck. The White House, House Speaker J. Dennis Hastert, R-Ill., and other GOP leaders liked a bill (HR 2315) produced by Ernie Fletcher, R-Ky. But it did not have enough support for House passage.

The more popular measure was one (HR 2563) sponsored by Republicans Charlie Norwood of Georgia and Greg Ganske of Iowa and Democrat John D. Dingell of Michigan. It would expand Americans' ability to sue health plans in federal courts and allow plaintiffs to collect civil damages of up to $5 million and unlimited economic and non-economic damages. Patients also could sue insurers in state courts, with damage caps set by individual states. For years, federal employee benefits law had limited such suits to federal courts, and damages were limited to the cost of denied care.

House leaders were never happy that Norwood, a dentist, and Ganske, a surgeon, were in the other camp, but they had come to accept it as a fact of managed-care politics.

On Aug. 1, Norwood appeared in the White House briefing room with the president and announced a "compromise." Dingell and Ganske were furious. House leaders were jubilant: The measure produced by Norwood and the president was one they could support.

The key provision concerned liability. The deal would allow suits in state courts over medical decisions and cap liability at $1.5 million for non-economic damages and $1.5 million for punitive damages, which would be allowed only if a plan had ignored the decision of an independent review panel.

Hastert quickly brought the Ganske-Dingell bill to the floor the next day with the intention of having the Norwood-Bush deal offered as an amendment. But the House burst into a fiercely partisan and sometimes personal debate, with Ganske accusing Norwood of "free-lancing" and Norwood defending himself by saying his deal with Bush was the only way to get a managed-care bill enacted.

When the Norwood amendment itself came up, the tension was palpable. Said Ganske: "This is the nitty-gritty of the debate. We have sort of been fooling around until we get to the Norwood amendment."

Both sides worked furiously to win votes. The White House and insurance companies lobbied for adoption of the amendment; the American Medical Association and some state officials, who feared the Norwood-Bush deal would pre-empt state laws, worked against it.

Dingell, Ganske and their supporters argued that the Norwood-Bush deal was more beneficial to insurance companies than to consumers.

The Norwood-Bush deal was criticized by all sides — conservatives, moderates and Democrats. Many who voted for it said they did so just to get a bill to conference. Ultimately, the amendment was successful because it did one thing no patients' rights legislation had done: It gave much-needed cover to Republicans who wanted to vote for a patients' rights bill while also supporting their president.

The amendment was adopted Aug. 2, 218-213: R 214-6; D

3-206 (ND 2-153; SD 1-53); I 1-1. (*House vote 329, p. C-22*)

Three GOP members who had cosponsored the original Norwood-Dingell-Ganske bill followed Norwood: Bob Barr of Georgia, Benjamin A. Gilman of New York and Steve Horn of California.

The bill, as amended, passed the House, 226-203, shortly after.

For his part, Norwood insisted the deal he cut with Bush was not the final word, and suggested changes could be made in conference. "I know this isn't the final bill, and so do you," he told his colleagues. "I know there are words that need to be changed."

342 Defense

Intent on pursuing Osama bin Laden and rooting out terrorism after the Sept. 11 attacks, the House overwhelmingly approved a resolution (H J Res 64) giving President Bush the authority to punish those behind the assaults — with one lone voice of dissent.

The vote, which reflected the strong bipartisan anger stemming from the attacks, was 420-1: R 214-0; D 204-1 (ND 150-1; SD 54-0); I 2-0. (*House vote 342, p. C-22*)

Following the vote, the House passed an identical Senate resolution (S J Res 23) by voice vote, clearing it for the president.

The resolution authorized the president to "use all necessary and appropriate force against those nations, organizations or persons he determined planned, authorized, committed or aided" the attacks or the nations that harbored them.

In clearing the measure, Congress gave Bush the power to launch the subsequent military campaign against the Taliban regime in Afghanistan, suspected of protecting bin Laden and the al Qaeda terrorist network. Left unclear were answers to the longtime questions about the constitutional roles of the president and Congress in initiating military operations.

Rep. Barbara Lee, D-Calif., voted against the resolution after attending a prayer service at the Washington National Cathedral. Lee cited the words of the Rev. Nathan D. Baxter, an Episcopal priest and the Cathedral dean, who counseled, "Let us also pray for divine wisdom as our leaders consider the necessary actions for national security, that despite our grief we may not become the evil we deplore."

Said Lee, whose district included Berkeley, with its longstanding anti-war perspective: "Somebody has to say this in the U.S. Congress. And if we all vote in one way, no one does that."

Lawmakers put off debate over whether Bush's global war against terrorism extended beyond Afghanistan to countries such as Iraq.

Conservatives, such as Bob Barr, R-Ga., had argued for passing a declaration of war or a broad resolution to give the president unlimited power to prosecute terrorism around the world. That view was shared by the White House, which initially proposed that it also be granted "all necessary and appropriate force" to "deter and pre-empt any future acts of terrorism or aggression against the United States."

But many lawmakers, particularly Democrats, believed that went too far. They feared that an open-ended commitment would come back to haunt them, much as an earlier generation came to regret its support for the 1964 Gulf of Tonkin resolution (PL 88-408). That resolution was cited by the Johnson and Nixon administrations as congressional authorization for waging the Vietnam War.

"We need to tread very cautiously," said Alcee L. Hastings, D-Fla. "We shouldn't cave in and say 'fire at will.' "

366 Farm Bill

The debate over how to rebuild the federal safety net under the farm economy while it was in the middle of a devastating downturn led to one of the clearer choices in the House this year between taking an "old" or a "new" approach.

Farm-state lawmakers and commodity groups sought to enhance the array of subsidies available to those who grew grains and oilseeds. But urban and suburban members, who typically stayed in the background during farm bill debates, joined with conservation and sportsmen's groups to mount a serious challenge to that system by proposing conservation programs from which all farmers could benefit.

The debate occurred on a farm bill (HR 2646) being written to update the 1996 farm law (PL 104-127), enacted during the heyday of the congressional "Republican revolution." The aim then was to wean farmers from the federal subsidies that were among the longest lasting legacies of the New Deal, but that goal went largely unmet as falling crop prices worldwide compelled Congress to provide supplementary aid almost every year since.

Republican House Agriculture Committee Chairman Larry Combest and ranking Democrat Charles W. Stenholm, both Texans, proposed abandoning the 1996 law and providing an additional $73.5 billion over the next 10 years for farm programs, three-fifths of it to subsidize farmers of the nation's major export commodities: corn, wheat, soybeans, other grains and oilseeds, rice and cotton. The benefits of doing so would be concentrated mostly on the large, profitable farms of the Great Plains, Upper Midwest and deep South.

The alternative was to expand the reach, rather than the generosity, of federal farm aid by increasing the spending on conservation programs — such as those that paid farmers to idle environmentally sensitive land and to protect wildlife and wetlands — which were not confined to any particular region or type of farm.

This drew the support of environmentalists, anti-sprawl groups and sportsmen's organizations. Wisconsin Democrat Ron Kind, a member of the Agriculture panel, teamed up with two leading environmentalists among House Republicans, Sherwood Boehlert of New York and Wayne T. Gilchrest of Maryland, as well as Michigan Democrat John D. Dingell, arguably the most powerful advocate of gun owners' rights in the House, to propose taking $19 billion of the subsidy payments in the Combest-Stenholm bill and spending it instead on conservation.

As the vote approached, the White House signaled sympathy with the environmentalist approach, releasing a report that emphasized the importance of conservation programs and issuing a harsh critique of the commodity-centric Agri-

culture Committee measure. With the new approach gaining momentum, Combest threatened to scuttle the entire bill if the Kind-Boehlert-Dingell amendment was adopted.

Although their plan drew bipartisan support — one-quarter of the Republicans voted for it, as did seven out of 10 Democrats — it was narrowly rejected the night of Oct. 4. The key vote was 200-226: R 54-161; D 145-64 (ND 132-23; SD 13-41); I 1-1. (*House vote 366, p. C-22*)

With the alternative swept aside, the House voted overwhelmingly the next day to pass the more traditional, subsidy-focused farm bill. But the closeness of the vote helped shape the Senate debate later in the year, and seemed destined to influence the outcome when a compromise was written in 2002.

Even in failure, the amendment's proponents "changed American farm politics forever," said Mike Casey of the Environmental Working Group, which lobbied hard for the plan. "They basically said suburban America and Northeast coastal areas have a stake in what farm policy looks like, and never again are farm-state legislators going to be able to say, 'We are the committee; we know what we're doing; shut up and sit down.'"

398 Anti-Terrorism

Overwhelming votes of support in the House for anti-terrorism legislation in October belied the measure's troubled path. A group of Democrats and Republicans voiced misgivings that the legislation sought by the Bush administration sacrificed civil liberties for greater police powers, and the group even drew up a bipartisan alternative, though it went nowhere.

In the end, the vast majority of House members supported the drive to give the Bush administration greater powers to track, investigate and prosecute those accused of terrorism and other crimes.

Attorney General John Ashcroft first went to Congress just eight days after the Sept. 11 attacks with a request for a package of broad new authorities that would allow his investigators to track communications over the Internet, secretly search a suspect's home and obtain a nationwide warrant for searches in terrorism investigations.

Liberal groups immediately denounced the move as a power grab, noting that much of the enhanced authority had been requested by previous administrations — and rejected by Congress — well before the terrorist attacks. Some conservatives also said they were worried the administration was reaching too far. Ashcroft and others defended the request, saying the new dangers that terrorism posed required new tools for law enforcement.

House Judiciary Committee Chairman F. James Sensenbrenner Jr., R-Wis., staked his committee's claim on the Ashcroft proposal, arguing that it should proceed through the regular legislative process. He won approval from the GOP House leadership to take the bill through committee, so long as it moved quickly to the floor.

Sensenbrenner began negotiations with his committee's ranking Democrat, John Conyers Jr. of Michigan, and others. They came up with a compromise bill that dropped some of the most controversial proposals in the administration's package, such as provisions to broaden the circum-

stances under which secret searches of suspects' property and the indefinite detention of aliens would be allowed. The Judiciary Committee then met and approved the bill (HR 2975) unanimously, a rare occurrence for the normally fractious committee.

In the meantime, top members of the Senate Judiciary Committee were negotiating their own version of the bill, this time with Justice Department and White House participation. These negotiations produced a bill much more to the administration's liking, a bill the Senate passed after little real debate.

As the House prepared to debate the Judiciary Committee's version, the White House began to pressure the GOP leadership and Sensenbrenner to bring to the floor a package closer to Ashcroft's proposal. In the wake of the strong Senate vote, House leaders complied, scuttling the committee provisions in favor of language closer to the Senate bill.

They did retain one key provision from the committee to end the authority for certain sections of the bill. The "sunset" was set at five years. After the rule to bring the substitute bill to the floor was narrowly adopted, 214-208, the House passed the revised bill (HR 2975), 337-79.

At that point, it was clear the administration would get what it wanted. On Oct. 24, after negotiations with the Senate, the House brought a final version of the bill (HR 3162) to the floor. It gave the administration broader authority to do secret searches, for example, but it retained the House-passed sunsets, shortened to four years. The House passed it 357-66: R 211-3; D 145-62 (ND 103-50; SD 42-12); I 1-1. (*House vote 398, p. C-22*)

The Senate cleared it the next day. President Bush signed the bill into law (PL 107-56) on Oct. 26.

423 Aviation Security

After the Sept. 11 terrorist attacks, it seemed only a matter of time before Congress would remove the low-paid private security personnel who screened passengers and baggage at the nation's airports and put federal workers in charge — something airlines had resisted for decades, citing higher costs.

While many members of Congress were ready to let the federal government assume the responsibility and cost in the wake of the attacks, a group of House conservatives stood in the way, led by Texas Republicans Dick Armey, the majority leader, and Tom DeLay, the majority whip. Creating as many as 28,000 new federal jobs would not guarantee better security, they argued, but it would increase the size of the federal government and the membership of federal employee unions largely loyal to Democrats.

The debate tied up House action on a broad aviation security package for more than six weeks as Armey and DeLay refused to budge. A bill (HR 3150) eventually drafted by the Transportation and Infrastructure Committee would have given the president the option of having private or government screeners.

When the Senate passed an aviation security bill of its own (S 1447) on Oct. 11 to make all screeners federal employees, it appeared the House Republican effort was doomed. The Senate bill passed 100-0, showing the broad support for federalization. President Bush, though he said he preferred having a choice on airport security, indicated

he would sign the Senate bill if the House passed it.

Facing a big loss, and amid intensive lobbying for federalization by airline pilots and organized labor, Armey and DeLay persuaded the White House to support their effort. Bush, along with Transportation Secretary Norman Y. Mineta and Rep. John L. Mica, R-Fla., chairman of the House Transportation Subcommittee on Aviation, lobbied intensively. They targeted members who had not announced their support for the Republican bill, including conservative Southern "Blue Dog" Democrats and undecided New Yorkers who wanted additional help for New York City.

DeLay and Armey persuaded the Rules Committee to design a floor procedure that allowed a vote on the Senate bill first, which Democrats wanted. But it also allowed the Republicans to offer a manager's amendment that they could alter at the last minute to include whatever deals they reached with wavering members for their support. When the amendment finally was offered, it included liability limits for several organizations affected by the attacks, including Boeing Co., the Port Authority of New York and New Jersey, which built and operated the World Trade Center, and jet engine manufacturers General Electric Co. and Pratt & Whitney. It included security waivers for passengers carrying musical instruments and even a provision that would have required airlines to carry live animals, such as baby chicks, in their freight.

In the end, the strategy worked. The House voted on Nov. 1 to reject the Senate bill, 214-218: R 8-211; D 205-6 (ND 154-3; SD 51-3); I 1-1. *(House vote 423, p. C-22)*

Three of the six dissenting Democrats — Luis V. Gutierrez and Rod R. Blagojevich of Illinois and Solomon P. Ortiz of Texas — represented districts with large immigrant populations. They said they voted against the Senate bill because of a requirement that screeners be U.S. citizens for five years.

The vote showed the tactical skill of DeLay and Armey and their ability to persuade the administration to back their play. But Bush's support was as short-lived as the House victory. In conference with the Senate, Republicans agreed to make all airport screeners federal employees, and Bush signed the bill Nov. 19, three days after Congress cleared it.

481 Fast-Track Trade Authority

Securing fast-track trade negotiating authority from Congress was one of President Bush's top priorities, but convincing lawmakers to go along was expected to be a challenge. The decades-old authority, which had been granted to presidents beginning with Gerald Ford but was abruptly withheld from President Bill Clinton in 1994, allowed the executive branch to negotiate trade agreements and then bring them to Congress for an up-or-down vote without amendments and under mandatory deadlines.

Opposition to the legislation (HR 3005), which the Bush White House renamed trade promotion authority, cut across regional lines. Democrats had become the main obstacle to its passage. They feared that free-trade agreements with less-developed countries could weaken labor standards and envi-

ronmental protection in the United States and its trading partners. Democrats were joined in this view by a small but significant group of Republicans who primarily represent industrial districts.

Republican leaders in the House began their fast-track campaign for the year in June. In an effort to firm up votes, Speaker J. Dennis Hastert, R-Ill., called for a vote before the August recess, but when it became clear the measure would not pass, the vote was canceled. In late September, the issue returned as the White House portrayed free trade as an important part of the war on terrorism, but that backfired as a public relations gambit and Democrats easily blocked a fast-track markup. In November, GOP leaders tentatively scheduled another floor vote, but again put it off.

In early December, both sides dug in for a showdown. House Ways and Means Committee Chairman Bill Thomas, R-Calif., had marked up a fast-track bill Oct. 9 with the help of three pro-trade Democrats — Cal Dooley of California, William J. Jefferson of Louisiana and John Tanner of Tennessee. That was enough for Thomas to call it a bipartisan measure. Also, it included some labor and environmental protection as negotiating goals in trade agreements, a provision that many Democrats sought.

But most pro-trade Democrats, who were members of the New Democratic Coalition, still did not like the bill because they said it was out of date. They said it was too focused on manufacturing and agriculture trade when other issues, such as antitrust and intellectual property, had become just as important.

In the week leading up to the House vote, GOP leaders decided to focus their lobbying on wavering Republicans rather than trying to attract more Democrats, which had been a failed strategy of the past. The shift proved to be pivotal.

The lobbying was intense. Select Republicans were invited to travel with Bush on Air Force One and were promised projects and provisions in the trade bill and other measures. Republican Reps. Jim DeMint of South Carolina and Robin Hayes of North Carolina changed their positions and supported the bill after party leaders pledged to try changing the sub-Saharan African and Caribbean Basin trade preference law (PL 106-200) enacted in 2001, to help protect textile dyeing and finishing industries in their districts. The promise also extended to the Andean nations trade bill (HR 3009), which had been passed by the House but was pending in the Senate.

As tough as the lobbying got, the debate kept pace. On the floor Dec. 6, Republican leaders infuriated Democrats by saying that rejecting fast-track would undermine Bush's standing in the global community in the midst of a war. Some Democrats, including pro-traders from high-technology districts suffering from increased unemployment, said they could not support the bill without an economic stimulus measure (HR 3090) to help workers laid off after Sept. 11, a measure that had stalled.

The vote ran neck and neck and was held open while final deals were struck with Republicans from the textile South. The moment the yeas edged past the nays, the vote was closed and victory was declared, 215-214: R 194-23; D 21-189 (ND 7-150; SD 14-39); I 0-2. *(House vote 481, p. C-22)* ◆

ALABAMA	8	15	64	69	165
Shelby	Y	Y	N	N	Y
Sessions	Y	Y	N	N	Y
ALASKA					
Stevens	Y	Y	Y	N	Y
Murkowski	Y	Y	N	N	Y
ARIZONA					
McCain	Y	Y	Y	N	Y
Kyl	Y	Y	N	N	Y
ARKANSAS					
Hutchinson	Y	Y	N	N	Y
Lincoln	N	Y	Y	Y	Y
CALIFORNIA					
Feinstein	N	N	Y	Y	Y
Boxer	N	N	Y	Y	N
COLORADO					
Campbell	Y	Y	N	N	Y
Allard	Y	Y	N	N	Y
CONNECTICUT					
Dodd	Y	N	Y	Y	N
Lieberman	N	N	Y	Y	N
DELAWARE					
Carper	N	N	Y	Y	N
Biden	N	N	Y	Y	N
FLORIDA					
Graham	N	N	Y	Y	N
Nelson	N	N	Y	Y	N
GEORGIA					
Miller	Y	Y	Y	N	Y
Cleland	N	N	Y	Y	Y
HAWAII					
Inouye	N	N	Y	Y	N
Akaka	N	N	Y	Y	N
IDAHO					
Craig	Y	Y	N	N	Y
Crapo	Y	Y	N	N	Y
ILLINOIS					
Durbin	N	N	Y	Y	N
Fitzgerald	Y	Y	Y	N	Y
INDIANA					
Lugar	Y	Y	Y	N	Y
Bayh	N	N	Y	Y	N

IOWA	8	15	64	69	165
Grassley	Y	Y	N	N	Y
Harkin	N	N	Y	Y	N
KANSAS					
Brownback	Y	Y	N	N	Y
Roberts	Y	Y	N	N	Y
KENTUCKY					
McConnell	Y	Y	N	N	Y
Bunning	Y	Y	N	N	Y
LOUISIANA					
Breaux	Y	Y	N	Y	Y
Landrieu	N	Y	Y	Y	Y
MAINE					
Snowe	Y	Y	Y	N	Y
Collins	Y	Y	Y	N	Y
MARYLAND					
Sarbanes	N	N	Y	Y	N
Mikulski	N	N	Y	Y	N
MASSACHUSETTS					
Kennedy	N	N	Y	Y	N
Kerry	N	N	Y	Y	N
MICHIGAN					
Levin	N	N	Y	Y	N
Stabenow	N	N	Y	Y	N
MINNESOTA					
Wellstone	N	N	Y	Y	N
Dayton	N	N	Y	Y	N
MISSISSIPPI					
Cochran	Y	Y	Y	N	Y
Lott	Y	Y	N	Y	Y
MISSOURI					
Bond	Y	Y	N	N	Y
Carnahan	N	N	Y	Y	N
MONTANA					
Baucus	N	Y	Y	Y	Y
Burns	Y	Y	N	N	Y
NEBRASKA					
Nelson	Y	N	N	Y	Y
Hagel	Y	Y	N	N	Y
NEVADA					
Reid	N	N	Y	Y	N
Ensign	Y	Y	N	N	Y

NEW HAMPSHIRE	8	15	64	69	165
Smith	Y	Y	N	N	Y
Gregg	Y	Y	N	N	Y
NEW JERSEY					
Corzine	N	N	Y	Y	N
Torricelli	N	N	Y	Y	Y
NEW MEXICO					
Domenici	Y	Y	Y	N	Y
Bingaman	N	N	Y	Y	N
NEW YORK					
Clinton	N	N	Y	Y	N
Schumer	N	N	Y	Y	N
NORTH CAROLINA					
Helms	Y	Y	N	N	Y
Edwards	N	N	Y	Y	N
NORTH DAKOTA					
Conrad	Y	N	Y	Y	N
Dorgan	Y	N	Y	Y	N
OHIO					
DeWine	Y	Y	N	N	Y
Voinovich	Y	Y	N	N	Y
OKLAHOMA					
Nickles	Y	Y	N	N	Y
Inhofe	Y	Y	N	N	Y
OREGON					
Wyden	N	N	Y	Y	N
Smith	Y	Y	N	N	Y
PENNSYLVANIA					
Specter	Y	Y	Y	N	Y
Santorum	Y	Y	N	N	Y
RHODE ISLAND					
Reed	N	N	Y	Y	N
Chafee	Y	Y	Y	Y	Y
SOUTH CAROLINA					
Thurmond	Y	Y	N	N	Y
Hollings	N	Y	N	Y	N
SOUTH DAKOTA					
Daschle	N	N	Y	Y	N
Johnson	N	N	Y	Y	Y
TENNESSEE					
Thompson	Y	Y	Y	N	Y
Frist	Y	Y	N	N	Y

Key

Y	Voted for (yea).
#	Paired for.
+	Announced for.
N	Voted against (nay).
X	Paired against.
–	Announced against.
P	Voted "present."
C	Voted "present" to avoid possible conflict of interest.
?	Did not vote or otherwise make a position known.

Democrats **Republicans**
Independents

TEXAS	8	15	64	69	165
Gramm	Y	Y	N	N	Y
Hutchison	Y	Y	N	N	Y
UTAH					
Hatch	Y	Y	N	N	Y
Bennett	Y	Y	N	N	Y
VERMONT					
Leahy	N	N	Y	Y	N
Jeffords [1]	Y	Y	Y	Y	Y
VIRGINIA					
Warner	Y	Y	N	N	Y
Allen	Y	Y	N	N	Y
WASHINGTON					
Cantwell	N	N	Y	Y	N
Murray	N	N	Y	Y	N
WEST VIRGINIA					
Byrd	Y	N	Y	Y	N
Rockefeller	N	N	Y	Y	N
WISCONSIN					
Kohl	N	N	Y	Y	N
Feingold	Y	N	Y	Y	N
WYOMING					
Thomas	Y	Y	N	N	Y
Enzi	Y	Y	N	N	Y

ND Northern Democrats   SD Southern Democrats

Southern states - Ala., Ark., Fla., Ga., Ky., La., Miss., N.C., Okla., S.C., Tenn., Texas, Va.

Following are Senate votes from 2001 selected by Congressional Quarterly as key votes.

8. Ashcroft Nomination/Confirmation. Confirmation of President Bush's nomination of John Ashcroft of Missouri to be attorney general. Confirmed 58-42: R 50-0; D 8-42 (ND 6-35, SD 2-7). A "yea" was a vote in support of the president's position. Feb. 1, 2001.

15. S J Res 6. Ergonomics Rule Disapproval/Passage. Passage of the joint resolution that would provide for congressional disapproval of the ergonomics rule submitted by the Labor Department during the Clinton administration, stating the rule would have no force or effect. Passed 56-44: R 50-0; D 6-44 (ND 1-40, SD 5-4). March 6, 2001.

64. S 27. Campaign Finance Overhaul/Passage. Passage of the bill that would ban "soft-money" donations to political parties, prohibit corporate and union general treasury funds from being spent on issue ads, and require disclosure of individuals who pay for issue ads that run within 60 days of a general election or 30 days of a primary. It also would prevent certain issue ads from targeting specific candidates within the 60-day and 30-day periods. The bill, as amended, would increase the individual contribution limit per candidate to $2,000 per election, the individual limit to national parties to $25,000 per year and the individual aggregate limit to $37,500 per year. Passed 59-41: R 12-38; D 47-3 (ND 40-1, SD 7-2). April 2, 2001.

69. H Con Res 83. Fiscal 2002 Budget Resolution/Education Spending. Harkin, D-Iowa, amendment to the Domenici, R-N.M., substitute amendment. The Harkin amendment would reduce the size of the tax cut by $448 billion and would increase education spending by $224 billion over 10 years. It also would provide for an increase of approximately $224 billion for debt reduction over 10 years. Adopted 53-47: R 4-46; D 49-1 (ND 41-0, SD 8-1). A "nay" was a vote in support of the president's position. April 4, 2001.

165. HR 1836. Tax Cut Reconciliation/Passage. Passage of the bill that would reduce income tax rates and make other tax cuts totaling $1.35 trillion over 11 years. The bill would reduce rates in the top four income tax brackets, retain the 15 percent bracket and create a new 10 percent bracket. It would set the standard deduction for married couples and the income eligible for the 15 percent rate bracket at double that of singles beginning in 2005; gradually repeal the estate tax; double the $500 per child tax credit by 2011; and make the research and development credit permanent. Annual limits on contributions to Individual Retirement Accounts would increase to $5,000 by 2011. Passed 62-38: R 50-0; D 12-38 (ND 7-34, SD 5-4). A "yea" was a vote in support of the president's position. May 23, 2001.

[1] Sen. James M. Jeffords of Vermont left the Republican Party to become an Independent, effective at the close of business June 5. The first vote for which he was eligible as an Independent was Vote 171.

	220	273	281	286	313
ALABAMA					
Shelby	N	N	Y	Y	Y
Sessions	N	N	Y	N	Y
ALASKA					
Stevens	N	N	Y	Y	Y
Murkowski	?	?	Y	Y	Y
ARIZONA					
McCain	Y	N	N	Y	N
Kyl	N	N	Y	N	Y
ARKANSAS					
Hutchinson	N	Y	Y	N	Y
Lincoln	N	Y	Y	Y	Y
CALIFORNIA					
Feinstein	Y	Y	Y	Y	Y
Boxer	Y	Y	Y	Y	Y
COLORADO					
Campbell	N	N	Y	N	Y
Allard	N	N	N	N	Y
CONNECTICUT					
Dodd	Y	Y	Y	Y	Y
Lieberman	Y	Y	Y	Y	Y
DELAWARE					
Carper	Y	Y	Y	Y	Y
Biden	Y	Y	Y	Y	Y
FLORIDA					
Graham	Y	Y	Y	Y	Y
Nelson	Y	Y	Y	Y	Y
GEORGIA					
Miller	Y	Y	Y	Y	Y
Cleland	Y	Y	Y	Y	Y
HAWAII					
Inouye	Y	Y	Y	Y	Y
Akaka	?	?	?	?	?
IDAHO					
Craig	N	N	Y	N	Y
Crapo	N	N	Y	N	Y
ILLINOIS					
Durbin	Y	Y	Y	Y	Y
Fitzgerald	N	N	N	Y	Y
INDIANA					
Lugar	Y	N	Y	N	Y
Bayh	Y	Y	Y	N	Y
IOWA					
Grassley	N	N	Y	N	Y
Harkin	Y	Y	Y	Y	Y
KANSAS					
Brownback	N	N	Y	N	Y
Roberts	N	N	Y	?	Y
KENTUCKY					
McConnell	N	N	Y	N	Y
Bunning	N	N	Y	Y	Y
LOUISIANA					
Breaux	Y	Y	Y	Y	Y
Landrieu	Y	Y	Y	Y	Y
MAINE					
Snowe	Y	Y	Y	N	Y
Collins	Y	Y	Y	N	Y
MARYLAND					
Sarbanes	Y	Y	Y	Y	Y
Mikulski	Y	Y	Y	Y	Y
MASSACHUSETTS					
Kennedy	Y	Y	Y	Y	Y
Kerry	Y	Y	Y	Y	Y
MICHIGAN					
Levin	Y	Y	Y	Y	Y
Stabenow	Y	Y	Y	Y	Y
MINNESOTA					
Wellstone	Y	Y	Y	Y	Y
Dayton	Y	Y	Y	N	Y
MISSISSIPPI					
Cochran	N	N	Y	N	Y
Lott	N	N	Y	N	Y
MISSOURI					
Bond	N	N	Y	N	?
Carnahan	Y	Y	Y	Y	Y
MONTANA					
Baucus	Y	Y	Y	Y	Y
Burns	N	N	Y	N	Y
NEBRASKA					
Nelson	Y	Y	Y	Y	Y
Hagel	Y	N	Y	Y	Y
NEVADA					
Reid	Y	Y	Y	Y	Y
Ensign	N	N	?	?	?
NEW HAMPSHIRE					
Smith	Y	N	N	N	Y
Gregg	Y	N	Y	N	Y
NEW JERSEY					
Corzine	Y	Y	Y	Y	Y
Torricelli	Y	Y	Y	Y	Y
NEW MEXICO					
Domenici	N	N	Y	N	Y
Bingaman	Y	Y	Y	Y	Y
NEW YORK					
Clinton	Y	Y	Y	N	Y
Schumer	Y	Y	Y	N	Y
NORTH CAROLINA					
Helms	–	?	?	?	?
Edwards	N	Y	Y	Y	Y
NORTH DAKOTA					
Conrad	Y	Y	Y	Y	Y
Dorgan	Y	Y	Y	Y	Y
OHIO					
DeWine	N	N	Y	N	Y
Voinovich	Y	N	N	N	Y
OKLAHOMA					
Nickles	N	N	N	N	Y
Inhofe	N	N	Y	N	Y
OREGON					
Wyden	Y	Y	Y	Y	Y
Smith	Y	N	Y	N	Y
PENNSYLVANIA					
Specter	Y	Y	Y	N	Y
Santorum	N	N	Y	N	Y
RHODE ISLAND					
Reed	Y	Y	Y	Y	Y
Chafee	Y	Y	Y	Y	Y
SOUTH CAROLINA					
Thurmond	N	N	Y	N	Y
Hollings	Y	Y	Y	N	Y
SOUTH DAKOTA					
Daschle	Y	N	Y	Y	Y
Johnson	Y	Y	Y	Y	Y
TENNESSEE					
Thompson	N	N	Y	N	Y
Frist	N	N	Y	N	Y
TEXAS					
Gramm	N	N	Y	Y	N
Hutchison	N	N	Y	N	Y
UTAH					
Hatch	N	N	Y	N	Y
Bennett	N	N	Y	Y	Y
VERMONT					
Leahy	Y	Y	Y	Y	Y
Jeffords	Y	Y	Y	Y	Y
VIRGINIA					
Warner	N	N	Y	N	Y
Allen	N	N	Y	N	Y
WASHINGTON					
Cantwell	Y	Y	Y	Y	Y
Murray	Y	Y	Y	Y	Y
WEST VIRGINIA					
Byrd	Y	Y	Y	Y	Y
Rockefeller	Y	Y	Y	Y	Y
WISCONSIN					
Kohl	Y	Y	Y	Y	Y
Feingold	Y	N	Y	N	Y
WYOMING					
Thomas	N	N	Y	N	Y
Enzi	N	N	Y	N	Y

Key

Y Voted for (yea).
Paired for.
+ Announced for.
N Voted against (nay).
X Paired against.
– Announced against.
P Voted "present."
C Voted "present" to avoid possible conflict of interest.
? Did not vote or otherwise make a position known.

• Democrats **Republicans**
Independents

ND Northern Democrats   SD Southern Democrats

Southern states - Ala., Ark., Fla., Ga., Ky., La., Miss., N.C., Okla., S.C., Tenn., Texas, Va.

220. S 1052. Patients' Rights/Passage. Passage of the bill that would provide federal protections, such as access to specialty and emergency room care, and allow patients to appeal a health plan organization's decision on coverage and treatment. It also would allow patients to sue health insurers in state courts over quality-of-care claims and at the federal level over administrative or non-medical coverage disputes. Federal-level economic and non-economic damages would not be capped, and punitive damages would be capped at $5 million. State damages would be determined by state law. The bill, as amended, would exempt from federal lawsuits all employers and plan sponsors with self-insured and self-administered health plans, including multi-employer "Taft-Hartley" plans, who act as their own designated decision makers. It also would require the administrative appeals process to be exhausted for patients before a lawsuit is filed in connection with a denial of claim for benefits. Passed 59-36: R 9-35; D 50-0 (ND 41-0, SD 9-0); I 0-1. A "nay" was a vote in support of the president's position. June 29, 2001.

273. S 1246. Fiscal 2001 Supplemental Agriculture Assistance/ Cloture. Motion to invoke cloture (thus limiting debate) on the bill that would authorize $7.4 billion in additional economic assistance to farmers in fiscal 2001. Motion rejected 49-48: R 2-46; D 46-2 (ND 37-2, SD 9-0); I 1-0. Three-fifths of the total Senate (60) is required to invoke cloture. Aug. 3, 2001.

281. S J Res 23. Use of Force Authorization/Passage. Passage of the joint resolution that would authorize the president to use all necessary and appropriate force against the nations, organizations or people he determines planned, authorized, committed or aided the terrorist attacks that occurred Sept. 11, 2001, or that harbored such organizations or people, to prevent future acts of terrorism against the United States. Passed 98-0: R 47-0; D 50-0 (ND 41-0, SD 9-0); I 1-0. A "yea" was a vote in support of the president's position. Sept. 14, 2001.

286. S 1438. Fiscal 2002 Defense Authorization/Base Closures. Warner, R-Va., motion to table (kill) the Bunning, R-Ky., amendment that would strike the provision in the bill which authorizes an additional round of base realignment and closures in 2003. Motion agreed to 53-47: R 21-28; D 31-19 (ND 25-16, SD 6-3); I 1-0. Sept. 25, 2001.

313. HR 3162. Anti-Terrorism Authority/Passage. Passage of the bill that would expand law enforcement's power to investigate suspected terrorists. The bill would allow disclosure of wiretap information among certain government officials, authorize limited disclosure of secret grand jury information to certain government officials, and allow the detention of foreigners suspected of having ties to terrorism. It also would make it easier for law enforcement to track voice and Internet communications using surveillance techniques and would strengthen laws to combat money laundering. Most of the bill's intelligence-gathering provisions would sunset after four years. Passed (thus cleared for the president) 98-1: R 49-0; D 48-1 (ND 40-1, SD 8-0); I 1-0. A "yea" was a vote in support of the president's position. Oct. 25, 2001.

Following are House votes from 2001 selected by Congressional Quarterly as key votes.

33. S J Res 6. Ergonomics Rule Disapproval/Passage. Passage of the joint resolution that would provide for congressional disapproval of the ergonomics rule submitted by the Labor Department during the Clinton administration, stating the rule would have no force or effect. Passed 223-206: R 206-13; D 16-192 (ND 2-152, SD 14-40); I 1-1. March 7, 2001.

45. HR 3. Income Tax Reduction/Passage. Passage of the bill that would lower federal income taxes by restructuring the five existing tax brackets into four — 10 percent, 15 percent, 25 percent and 33 percent. Passed 230-198: R 219-0; D 10-197 (ND 3-150, SD 7-47); I 1-1. A "yea" was a vote in support of the president's position. March 8, 2001.

130. HR 1. ESEA Reauthorization/Testing Requirement. Hoekstra, R-Mich., amendment that would strike provisions mandating state reading and math tests for students in grades 3 through 8. The amendment would retain current law requiring states to test students in all subjects in which the states have developed standards. Rejected 173-255: R 52-166; D 119-89 (ND 91-63, SD 28-26); I 2-0. A "nay" was a vote in support of the president's position. May 22, 2001.

228. HR 2356. Campaign Finance Overhaul/Rule. Adoption of the rule (H Res 188) to provide for House floor consideration of the bill that would ban "soft-money" donations to national political parties but allow up to $10,000 in soft-money donations to state and local parties for voter registration and get-out-the-vote activity. The bill would prevent issue ads from targeting specific candidates within 60 days of a general election or 30 days of a primary. The bill also would maintain the current individual contribution limit of $1,000 per election for House candidates but raise it to $2,000 for Senate candidates. Both limits would be indexed for inflation. Rejected 203-228: R 201-19; D 1-208 (ND 1-154, SD 0-54); I 1-1. July 12, 2001.

288. HR 2620. Fiscal 2002 VA-HUD Appropriations/Arsenic Standards. Bonior, D-Mich., amendment that would ban use of funds in the bill to delay national drinking water regulations for arsenic or to further a rule to raise arsenic levels under those regulations. Adopted 218-189: R 19-182; D 198-6 (ND 151-2, SD 47-4); I 1-1. A "nay" was a vote in support of the president's position. July 27, 2001.

302. HR 2505. Human Cloning Ban/Substitute. Greenwood, R-Pa., substitute amendment that would ban human cloning to begin a pregnancy but allow the cloning of embryos for medical research as long as a researcher registers with the Department of Health and Human Services. The bill would make it illegal to receive or transport the products of cloning if they would be used to begin a pregnancy. The ban on reproductive cloning would expire in 10 years. Rejected 178-249: R 25-194; D 153-53 (ND 118-35, SD 35-18); I 0-2. A "nay" was a vote in support of the president's position. July 31, 2001.

317. HR 4. Energy Plan/ANWR Drilling Ban. Markey, D-Mass., amendment that would maintain the current prohibition on oil drilling in the Arctic National Wildlife Refuge by striking language opening the reserve up to development. Rejected 206-223: R 34-186; D 171-36 (ND 141-13, SD 30-23); I 1-1. A "nay" was a vote in support of the president's position. Aug. 1, 2001.

[1] *Rep. Diane Watson, D-Calif. was sworn in June 7. The first vote for which she was eligible was Vote 155.*

[2] *The Speaker votes only at his discretion, usually to break a tie or to emphasize the importance of a matter.*

[3] *Rep. Joe Moakley, D-Mass., died May 28. The last vote for which he was eligible was Vote 149.*

[4] *Rep. Bill Shuster, R-Pa., was sworn in May 17. The first vote for which he was eligible was Vote 123. He replaced Rep. Bud Shuster, R, who resigned Feb. 3. The last vote for which Bud Shuster was eligible was Vote 8.*

[5] *Rep. Randy Forbes, R-Va., was sworn in June 26. The first vote for which he was eligible was Vote 190. He replaced Rep. Norman Sisisky, D, who died March 29. The last vote for which Sisisky was eligible was Vote 70.*

Key

Y	Voted for (yea).
#	Paired for.
+	Announced for.
N	Voted against (nay).
X	Paired against.
−	Announced against.
P	Voted "present."
C	Voted "present" to avoid possible conflict of interest.
?	Did not vote or otherwise make a position known.

Democrats **Republicans**
Independents

	33	45	130	228	288	302	317
ALABAMA							
1 *Callahan*	Y	Y	N	Y	?	N	N
2 *Everett*	Y	Y	N	Y	N	N	N
3 *Riley*	Y	Y	Y	Y	N	N	N
4 *Aderholt*	Y	Y	N	Y	N	N	N
5 Cramer	Y	Y	N	N	Y	N	N
6 *Bachus*	Y	Y	N	Y	N	N	N
7 Hilliard	N	N	Y	N	Y	Y	N
ALASKA							
AL *Young*	Y	Y	N	Y	?	N	N
ARIZONA							
1 *Flake*	Y	Y	Y	Y	N	N	N
2 Pastor	N	N	Y	N	Y	Y	Y
3 *Stump*	Y	Y	N	Y	N	N	N
4 *Shadegg*	Y	Y	Y	Y	N	N	N
5 *Kolbe*	Y	Y	N	Y	N	Y	N
6 *Hayworth*	Y	Y	N	Y	N	N	N
ARKANSAS							
1 Berry	N	N	Y	N	Y	N	N
2 Snyder	N	N	N	N	Y	Y	Y
3 *Hutchinson*	Y	Y	N	Y	N	−	?
4 Ross	N	N	Y	N	Y	Y	N
CALIFORNIA							
1 Thompson	N	N	Y	N	Y	Y	Y
2 *Herger*	Y	Y	N	Y	N	N	N
3 *Ose*	Y	Y	N	Y	N	Y	N
4 *Doolittle*	Y	Y	Y	Y	N	N	N
5 Matsui	N	N	Y	N	Y	Y	Y
6 Woolsey	N	N	Y	N	Y	Y	Y
7 Miller, George	N	N	N	N	Y	Y	Y
8 Pelosi	N	N	N	N	Y	Y	Y
9 Lee	N	N	Y	N	Y	Y	Y
10 Tauscher	N	N	N	N	Y	Y	Y
11 *Pombo*	Y	Y	Y	Y	N	N	N
12 Lantos	N	N	N	N	Y	Y	Y
13 Stark	N	N	N	Y	?	?	?
14 Eshoo	N	N	N	N	Y	Y	Y
15 Honda	N	N	N	N	Y	Y	Y
16 Lofgren	N	N	N	N	Y	Y	Y
17 Farr	N	N	Y	N	Y	Y	Y
18 Condit	N	Y	N	N	Y	N	Y
19 *Radanovich*	Y	Y	N	Y	N	N	N
20 Dooley	Y	N	N	N	N	Y	N
21 *Thomas*	Y	Y	N	−	Y	N	N
22 Capps	N	N	N	N	Y	Y	Y
23 *Gallegly*	Y	Y	N	Y	N	N	N
24 Sherman	N	N	N	N	Y	Y	Y
25 *McKeon*	Y	Y	N	Y	N	N	N
26 Berman	N	N	N	N	Y	Y	Y
27 Schiff	N	N	N	N	Y	Y	Y
28 *Dreier*	Y	Y	N	Y	N	N	N
29 Waxman	N	N	Y	N	Y	Y	Y
30 Becerra	−	N	Y	N	Y	Y	Y
31 Solis	N	N	Y	N	Y	Y	Y
32 Watson [1]				N	Y	Y	Y
33 Roybal-Allard	N	N	Y	N	Y	Y	Y
34 Napolitano	N	N	Y	N	Y	Y	Y
35 Waters	N	N	Y	N	Y	Y	Y
36 Harman	N	N	N	N	Y	Y	Y
37 Millender-McD.	N	N	N	N	Y	Y	Y
38 *Horn*	N	Y	N	Y	N	Y	Y

	33	45	130	228	288	302	317
39 *Royce*	Y	Y	N	Y	N	N	N
40 *Lewis*	Y	Y	N	+	N	N	N
41 *Miller, Gary*	Y	Y	N	Y	N	N	N
42 Baca	N	N	Y	N	Y	Y	Y
43 *Calvert*	Y	Y	N	Y	N	N	N
44 *Bono*	Y	Y	N	Y	N	N	N
45 *Rohrabacher*	Y	Y	N	Y	N	N	N
46 Sanchez	N	N	Y	N	Y	N	N
47 *Cox*	Y	Y	N	Y	N	N	N
48 *Issa*	Y	Y	N	Y	N	N	N
49 Davis	N	N	N	N	Y	Y	Y
50 Filner	N	N	Y	N	Y	Y	Y
51 *Cunningham*	Y	Y	N	Y	N	N	N
52 *Hunter*	Y	Y	N	Y	N	N	N
COLORADO							
1 DeGette	N	N	N	N	Y	Y	Y
2 Udall	N	N	N	N	Y	Y	Y
3 *McInnis*	Y	Y	N	Y	?	N	N
4 *Schaffer*	Y	Y	Y	Y	N	N	N
5 *Hefley*	Y	Y	Y	Y	N	N	N
6 *Tancredo*	Y	Y	Y	Y	N	N	N
CONNECTICUT							
1 Larson	N	N	Y	N	Y	Y	Y
2 *Simmons*	Y	Y	N	Y	N	Y	Y
3 DeLauro	N	N	Y	N	Y	Y	Y
4 *Shays*	Y	Y	N	N	Y	Y	Y
5 Maloney	N	N	N	N	Y	Y	Y
6 *Johnson*	Y	Y	N	N	Y	Y	Y
DELAWARE							
AL *Castle*	Y	Y	N	Y	N	Y	Y
FLORIDA							
1 *Scarborough*	Y	Y	Y	N	N	N	N
2 Boyd	Y	N	Y	N	Y	Y	N
3 Brown	N	N	Y	N	Y	Y	Y
4 *Crenshaw*	Y	Y	N	N	N	N	N
5 Thurman	N	N	N	N	Y	Y	Y
6 *Stearns*	Y	Y	Y	N	N	N	N
7 *Mica*	Y	Y	Y	Y	N	N	N
8 *Keller*	Y	Y	N	Y	?	N	N
9 *Bilirakis*	Y	Y	N	Y	N	N	N
10 *Young*	Y	Y	N	Y	N	N	N
11 Davis	N	N	Y	N	Y	Y	Y
12 *Putnam*	Y	Y	N	Y	N	N	N
13 *Miller, D.*	Y	Y	N	Y	?	N	N
14 *Goss*	Y	Y	N	Y	N	N	N
15 *Weldon*	Y	Y	Y	Y	N	N	N
16 *Foley*	Y	Y	N	Y	N	Y	Y
17 Meek	N	N	N	N	Y	Y	Y
18 *Ros-Lehtinen*	Y	Y	N	Y	?	N	N
19 Wexler	N	N	N	N	Y	Y	Y
20 Deutsch	N	N	N	N	Y	Y	Y
21 *Diaz-Balart*	Y	Y	N	Y	N	N	N
22 *Shaw*	Y	Y	N	Y	N	N	N
23 Hastings	N	N	N	N	Y	?	Y
GEORGIA							
1 *Kingston*	Y	Y	N	Y	N	N	N
2 Bishop	N	Y	N	N	N	N	N
3 *Collins*	Y	Y	N	Y	?	N	N
4 McKinney	N	N	Y	N	Y	Y	Y
5 Lewis	N	N	Y	N	Y	Y	Y
6 *Isakson*	Y	Y	N	Y	N	N	N
7 *Barr*	Y	Y	N	Y	N	N	N
8 *Chambliss*	Y	Y	N	Y	N	N	N
9 *Deal*	Y	Y	N	Y	N	N	N
10 *Norwood*	Y	Y	N	Y	N	N	N
11 *Linder*	Y	Y	N	Y	?	N	N
HAWAII							
1 Abercrombie	N	N	+	N	Y	N	Y
2 Mink	N	N	Y	N	Y	N	Y
IDAHO							
1 *Otter*	Y	Y	N	Y	N	N	N
2 *Simpson*	Y	Y	N	Y	N	N	N
ILLINOIS							
1 Rush	N	N	N	N	Y	Y	Y
2 Jackson	N	N	N	Y	Y	Y	Y
3 Lipinski	N	N	N	N	?	?	?
4 Gutierrez	N	N	N	N	Y	Y	Y
5 Blagojevich	N	N	Y	N	Y	Y	Y
6 *Hyde*	Y	Y	Y	Y	N	N	N
7 Davis	N	N	N	N	Y	Y	Y
8 *Crane*	Y	Y	N	Y	N	N	N
9 Schakowsky	N	N	Y	N	Y	Y	Y
10 *Kirk*	Y	Y	N	Y	N	Y	Y
11 *Weller*	Y	Y	N	Y	N	N	N
12 Costello	N	N	Y	N	Y	N	Y
13 *Biggert*	Y	Y	N	Y	N	Y	Y

ND Northern Democrats   SD Southern Democrats

	33	45	130	228	288	302	317
14 *Hastert* [2]	Y	Y	N	Y			N
15 *Johnson*	Y	Y	N	Y	N	N	Y
16 *Manzullo*	Y	Y	Y	Y	N	N	N
17 Evans	N	N	Y	N	Y	Y	Y
18 *LaHood*	Y	Y	N	Y	N	N	Y
19 Phelps	N	N	Y	N	Y	N	N
20 *Shimkus*	Y	Y	N	Y	N	N	N
INDIANA							
1 Visclosky	N	N	N	N	Y	Y	Y
2 *Pence*	Y	Y	Y	Y	N	N	N
3 Roemer	N	N	N	N	Y	N	Y
4 *Souder*	Y	Y	Y	N	N	N	N
5 *Buyer*	Y	Y	N	Y	N	N	N
6 *Burton*	Y	Y	N	Y	N	N	N
7 *Kerns*	Y	Y	Y	Y	N	N	N
8 *Hostettler*	Y	Y	Y	Y	N	N	N
9 Hill	N	N	Y	N	Y	N	Y
10 Carson	N	N	N	N	Y	Y	Y
IOWA							
1 *Leach*	Y	Y	N	N	Y	Y	Y
2 *Nussle*	Y	Y	N	Y	N	N	N
3 Boswell	N	N	Y	N	Y	Y	Y
4 *Ganske*	Y	Y	Y	N	Y	N	N
5 *Latham*	Y	Y	N	Y	N	N	N
KANSAS							
1 *Moran*	Y	Y	Y	Y	N	N	N
2 *Ryun*	Y	Y	Y	Y	N	N	N
3 Moore	N	N	N	–	Y	Y	Y
4 *Tiahrt*	Y	Y	N	Y	N	N	N
KENTUCKY							
1 *Whitfield*	Y	Y	N	Y	N	N	N
2 *Lewis*	Y	Y	N	Y	N	N	N
3 *Northup*	Y	Y	N	Y	N	N	N
4 Lucas	N	Y	N	N	N	N	N
5 *Rogers*	Y	Y	–	Y	N	N	N
6 *Fletcher*	Y	Y	N	Y	N	N	N
LOUISIANA							
1 *Vitter*	Y	Y	Y	Y	N	N	N
2 Jefferson	N	N	Y	N	Y	N	N
3 *Tauzin*	Y	Y	N	Y	N	N	N
4 *McCrery*	Y	Y	N	Y	?	N	N
5 *Cooksey*	Y	Y	N	Y	N	N	N
6 *Baker*	Y	Y	N	Y	N	N	N
7 John	Y	N	N	N	Y	N	N
MAINE							
1 Allen	N	N	N	N	Y	Y	Y
2 Baldacci	N	N	N	N	Y	Y	Y
MARYLAND							
1 *Gilchrest*	Y	Y	Y	Y	N	Y	Y
2 *Ehrlich*	Y	Y	N	Y	N	N	N
3 Cardin	N	N	N	N	Y	Y	Y
4 Wynn	N	N	N	N	Y	Y	Y
5 Hoyer	N	N	N	N	Y	Y	Y
6 *Bartlett*	Y	Y	Y	Y	N	N	Y
7 Cummings	N	N	Y	N	Y	Y	Y
8 *Morella*	Y	Y	N	N	Y	Y	Y
MASSACHUSETTS							
1 Olver	N	N	Y	N	Y	Y	Y
2 Neal	N	N	Y	N	Y	Y	Y
3 McGovern	N	N	Y	N	Y	Y	Y
4 Frank	N	N	Y	N	Y	Y	Y
5 Meehan	N	N	N	N	Y	Y	Y
6 Tierney	N	N	Y	N	Y	Y	Y
7 Markey	N	N	Y	N	Y	Y	Y
8 Capuano	N	N	Y	N	Y	Y	Y
9 Moakley [3]	N	N	?				
10 Delahunt	N	N	Y	N	Y	N	Y
MICHIGAN							
1 Stupak	?	?	Y	N	Y	N	Y
2 *Hoekstra*	Y	Y	Y	Y	N	N	N
3 *Ehlers*	Y	Y	N	Y	N	N	Y
4 *Camp*	Y	Y	N	Y	N	N	N
5 Barcia	N	N	Y	N	Y	N	Y
6 *Upton*	Y	Y	N	N	N	N	N
7 *Smith*	Y	Y	Y	Y	N	N	N
8 *Rogers*	Y	Y	N	Y	N	N	N
9 Kildee	N	N	N	N	Y	N	Y
10 Bonior	N	N	Y	N	Y	N	Y
11 *Knollenberg*	Y	Y	N	Y	N	N	N
12 Levin	N	N	N	N	Y	Y	Y
13 Rivers	N	N	Y	N	Y	Y	Y
14 Conyers	N	N	Y	N	Y	Y	Y
15 Kilpatrick	N	N	Y	N	Y	Y	Y
16 Dingell	N	N	N	N	Y	Y	Y
MINNESOTA							
1 *Gutknecht*	Y	Y	Y	Y	N	N	N
2 *Kennedy*	Y	Y	Y	Y	N	N	Y
3 *Ramstad*	Y	Y	Y	Y	Y	Y	Y
4 McCollum	N	N	Y	N	Y	Y	Y
5 Sabo	N	N	Y	N	Y	Y	Y
6 Luther	N	N	Y	N	Y	Y	Y
7 Peterson	N	Y	Y	N	Y	N	N
8 Oberstar	N	N	Y	N	Y	N	N
MISSISSIPPI							
1 *Wicker*	Y	Y	N	Y	N	N	N
2 Thompson	N	N	Y	N	Y	Y	N
3 *Pickering*	Y	Y	Y	Y	N	N	N
4 Shows	+	+	N	N	N	N	N
5 Taylor	Y	N	N	N	Y	N	N
MISSOURI							
1 Clay	N	N	Y	N	Y	Y	Y
2 *Akin*	Y	Y	Y	Y	N	N	N
3 Gephardt	N	N	Y	N	Y	Y	Y
4 Skelton	Y	?	N	N	Y	N	N
5 McCarthy	N	N	Y	N	Y	Y	Y
6 *Graves*	Y	Y	N	Y	N	N	N
7 *Blunt*	Y	Y	N	Y	N	N	N
8 *Emerson*	Y	Y	N	Y	N	N	N
9 *Hulshof*	Y	Y	N	Y	N	N	N
MONTANA							
AL *Rehberg*	Y	Y	N	Y	N	N	N
NEBRASKA							
1 *Bereuter*	Y	Y	Y	Y	N	N	N
2 *Terry*	Y	Y	Y	Y	N	N	N
3 *Osborne*	Y	Y	N	Y	N	N	N
NEVADA							
1 Berkley	N	N	Y	N	Y	Y	Y
2 *Gibbons*	Y	Y	N	Y	N	N	N
NEW HAMPSHIRE							
1 *Sununu*	Y	Y	N	Y	?	N	N
2 *Bass*	Y	Y	N	N	N	Y	Y
NEW JERSEY							
1 Andrews	N	N	N	N	Y	Y	Y
2 *LoBiondo*	N	Y	N	N	Y	N	Y
3 *Saxton*	N	Y	N	Y	Y	N	Y
4 *Smith*	N	Y	N	Y	Y	N	Y
5 *Roukema*	Y	Y	N	N	N	N	Y
6 Pallone	N	N	Y	N	Y	Y	Y
7 *Ferguson*	N	Y	N	Y	Y	N	Y
8 Pascrell	N	N	Y	N	Y	N	Y
9 Rothman	N	N	Y	N	Y	Y	Y
10 Payne	N	N	Y	N	Y	Y	Y
11 *Frelinghuysen*	Y	Y	N	Y	Y	N	Y
12 Holt	N	N	N	N	Y	Y	Y
13 Menendez	N	N	Y	N	Y	Y	Y
NEW MEXICO							
1 *Wilson*	Y	Y	N	Y	N	Y	N
2 *Skeen*	Y	Y	N	Y	N	N	N
3 Udall	N	N	N	N	Y	Y	Y
NEW YORK							
1 *Grucci*	N	Y	N	Y	N	N	N
2 Israel	N	N	N	N	Y	Y	Y
3 *King*	N	Y	N	Y	N	N	N
4 McCarthy	N	N	N	N	Y	N	Y
5 Ackerman	N	?	Y	N	Y	Y	Y
6 Meeks	N	N	Y	N	Y	Y	Y
7 Crowley	N	N	N	N	Y	Y	Y
8 Nadler	N	N	N	N	Y	Y	Y
9 Weiner	N	N	Y	N	Y	Y	Y
10 Towns	N	N	Y	N	Y	Y	N
11 Owens	N	N	Y	N	Y	Y	Y
12 Velázquez	N	N	Y	N	Y	Y	Y
13 *Fossella*	Y	Y	N	Y	N	N	N
14 Maloney	N	N	N	N	Y	Y	Y
15 Rangel	N	N	Y	N	Y	Y	Y
16 Serrano	N	N	N	N	Y	Y	Y
17 Engel	N	N	N	N	Y	Y	Y
18 Lowey	N	N	Y	N	Y	Y	Y
19 *Kelly*	Y	Y	N	Y	Y	Y	Y
20 *Gilman*	N	Y	Y	Y	Y	Y	Y
21 McNulty	N	N	N	N	Y	N	Y
22 *Sweeney*	Y	Y	N	Y	N	N	Y
23 *Boehlert*	N	Y	N	N	N	Y	Y
24 *McHugh*	N	Y	N	Y	N	N	N
25 *Walsh*	Y	Y	N	Y	N	N	Y
26 Hinchey	N	N	N	N	Y	Y	Y
27 *Reynolds*	Y	Y	N	Y	N	N	N
28 Slaughter	N	N	N	N	+	Y	Y
29 LaFalce	N	N	Y	N	Y	N	Y
30 *Quinn*	N	Y	N	Y	?	N	N
31 *Houghton*	Y	Y	N	N	N	Y	Y
NORTH CAROLINA							
1 Clayton	N	N	Y	N	Y	Y	Y
2 Etheridge	N	N	N	N	Y	Y	Y
3 *Jones*	Y	Y	Y	Y	N	N	N
4 Price	N	N	N	N	Y	Y	Y
5 *Burr*	Y	Y	N	Y	N	N	N
6 *Coble*	Y	Y	Y	Y	N	N	N
7 McIntyre	Y	Y	N	N	Y	N	Y
8 *Hayes*	Y	Y	N	Y	N	N	N
9 *Myrick*	Y	Y	Y	Y	N	N	N
10 *Ballenger*	Y	+	N	Y	N	N	N
11 *Taylor*	Y	Y	N	Y	?	N	N
12 Watt	N	N	Y	N	?	Y	Y
NORTH DAKOTA							
AL Pomeroy	N	N	N	N	Y	N	Y
OHIO							
1 *Chabot*	Y	Y	Y	Y	N	N	N
2 *Portman*	Y	Y	N	Y	N	N	N
3 Hall	N	N	N	N	Y	N	Y
4 *Oxley*	+	Y	N	Y	N	N	N
5 *Gillmor*	Y	Y	N	Y	N	N	N
6 Strickland	N	N	Y	N	Y	Y	Y
7 *Hobson*	Y	Y	N	Y	N	N	N
8 *Boehner*	Y	Y	N	Y	N	N	N
9 Kaptur	N	N	Y	N	Y	N	Y
10 Kucinich	N	N	N	N	Y	N	Y
11 Jones	N	N	Y	N	Y	+	Y
12 *Tiberi*	Y	Y	N	Y	N	N	N
13 Brown	N	N	Y	N	Y	Y	Y
14 Sawyer	N	N	Y	N	Y	Y	Y
15 *Pryce*	Y	Y	N	Y	N	Y	N
16 *Regula*	Y	Y	N	Y	N	N	N
17 Traficant	N	Y	N	Y	N	N	N
18 *Ney*	Y	Y	Y	Y	N	N	N
19 *LaTourette*	Y	Y	N	Y	N	N	N
OKLAHOMA							
1 *Largent*	Y	Y	N	Y	?	N	N
2 Carson	Y	N	N	N	Y	N	N
3 *Watkins*	Y	Y	N	Y	N	N	N
4 *Watts*	Y	Y	N	Y	N	N	N
5 *Istook*	Y	Y	Y	Y	N	N	N
6 *Lucas*	Y	Y	Y	Y	N	N	N
OREGON							
1 Wu	N	N	Y	N	Y	N	Y
2 *Walden*	Y	Y	N	Y	N	N	N
3 Blumenauer	N	N	Y	N	+	Y	Y
4 DeFazio	N	N	Y	N	Y	N	Y
5 Hooley	N	N	N	N	Y	Y	Y
PENNSYLVANIA							
1 Brady	N	N	Y	N	Y	Y	N
2 Fattah	N	N	Y	N	Y	Y	Y
3 Borski	N	N	Y	N	Y	N	Y
4 *Hart*	Y	Y	N	Y	Y	N	N
5 *Peterson*	Y	Y	N	Y	N	N	N
6 Holden	N	N	Y	N	Y	N	Y
7 *Weldon*	N	Y	N	Y	N	N	N
8 *Greenwood*	Y	Y	N	Y	N	Y	Y
9 *Shuster, Bill* [4]			N	Y	N	N	N
10 *Sherwood*	Y	Y	N	Y	N	N	N
11 Kanjorski	N	N	N	N	Y	N	N
12 Murtha	N	N	Y	N	Y	N	N
13 Hoeffel	N	N	N	N	Y	Y	Y
14 Coyne	N	N	Y	N	Y	Y	Y
15 *Toomey*	Y	Y	Y	Y	N	N	N
16 *Pitts*	Y	Y	Y	Y	N	N	N
17 *Gekas*	Y	Y	N	Y	N	N	N
18 Doyle	N	N	Y	N	Y	N	Y
19 *Platts*	Y	Y	N	Y	N	N	N
20 Mascara	N	N	N	N	Y	N	N
21 *English*	Y	Y	N	Y	Y	N	N
RHODE ISLAND							
1 Kennedy	N	N	N	N	Y	Y	Y
2 Langevin	N	N	Y	N	Y	N	Y
SOUTH CAROLINA							
1 *Brown*	Y	Y	N	Y	N	N	N
2 *Spence*	Y	Y	N	Y	?	?	?
3 *Graham*	Y	Y	Y	N	N	N	N
4 *DeMint*	Y	Y	N	Y	N	N	N
5 Spratt	Y	N	N	N	Y	Y	+
6 Clyburn	Y	N	Y	N	Y	Y	N
SOUTH DAKOTA							
AL *Thune*	Y	Y	N	Y	N	N	N
TENNESSEE							
1 *Jenkins*	Y	Y	N	Y	N	N	N
2 *Duncan*	Y	Y	Y	Y	N	N	N
3 *Wamp*	Y	Y	N	N	N	N	N
4 *Hilleary*	Y	Y	N	Y	N	N	N
5 Clement	Y	Y	N	N	Y	N	Y
6 Gordon	N	Y	N	N	Y	N	Y
7 *Bryant*	Y	Y	N	Y	N	N	N
8 Tanner	Y	N	N	N	Y	N	N
9 Ford	N	N	N	N	Y	Y	Y
TEXAS							
1 Sandlin	N	N	N	N	Y	Y	N
2 Turner	Y	N	N	N	Y	N	N
3 *Johnson, Sam*	Y	Y	Y	Y	N	N	N
4 Hall	Y	Y	N	N	N	N	N
5 *Sessions*	Y	Y	N	Y	N	N	N
6 *Barton*	Y	Y	Y	Y	N	N	N
7 *Culberson*	Y	Y	N	Y	N	N	N
8 *Brady*	Y	Y	N	Y	N	N	N
9 Lampson	N	N	N	N	Y	Y	Y
10 Doggett	N	N	N	N	Y	Y	Y
11 Edwards	N	N	N	N	Y	N	N
12 *Granger*	Y	Y	N	Y	N	Y	N
13 *Thornberry*	Y	Y	N	Y	N	N	N
14 *Paul*	Y	Y	Y	?	N	N	N
15 Hinojosa	N	N	Y	N	?	Y	Y
16 Reyes	N	N	Y	N	Y	Y	N
17 Stenholm	Y	N	N	N	N	N	N
18 Jackson-Lee	N	N	Y	N	Y	Y	Y
19 *Combest*	Y	Y	N	Y	N	N	N
20 Gonzalez	N	N	Y	N	Y	Y	Y
21 *Smith*	Y	Y	N	Y	?	N	N
22 *DeLay*	Y	Y	N	Y	N	N	N
23 *Bonilla*	Y	Y	N	Y	N	N	N
24 Frost	N	N	Y	N	?	Y	Y
25 Bentsen	N	N	N	N	Y	Y	Y
26 *Armey*	Y	Y	N	Y	N	N	N
27 Ortiz	N	N	Y	N	Y	N	N
28 Rodriguez	N	N	Y	N	Y	Y	Y
29 Green	N	N	Y	N	Y	Y	N
30 Johnson, E.B.	N	N	Y	N	Y	Y	Y
UTAH							
1 *Hansen*	Y	Y	?	Y	?	N	N
2 Matheson	N	N	N	N	Y	N	Y
3 *Cannon*	Y	Y	N	Y	N	N	N
VERMONT							
AL Sanders	N	N	Y	N	Y	N	Y
VIRGINIA							
1 *Davis, Jo Ann*	Y	Y	Y	Y	N	N	N
2 *Schrock*	Y	Y	N	Y	N	N	N
3 Scott	N	N	Y	N	Y	Y	Y
4 Sisisky [5]	Y	N					
4 *Forbes* [5]				Y	N	N	N
5 *Goode*	Y	Y	Y	Y	N	N	N
6 *Goodlatte*	Y	Y	N	Y	N	N	N
7 *Cantor*	Y	Y	Y	Y	N	N	N
8 Moran	N	N	N	N	Y	Y	Y
9 Boucher	N	N	Y	N	Y	Y	Y
10 *Wolf*	Y	Y	N	N	?	N	N
11 *Davis, T.*	Y	Y	N	Y	N	N	Y
WASHINGTON							
1 Inslee	N	N	N	N	Y	Y	Y
2 Larsen	N	N	N	N	Y	Y	Y
3 Baird	N	N	N	N	Y	Y	Y
4 *Hastings*	Y	Y	N	Y	N	N	N
5 *Nethercutt*	Y	Y	N	Y	N	N	N
6 Dicks	N	N	N	N	Y	Y	Y
7 McDermott	N	N	N	N	Y	Y	Y
8 *Dunn*	Y	Y	N	Y	–	N	Y
9 Smith	N	N	N	N	Y	Y	Y
WEST VIRGINIA							
1 Mollohan	N	N	Y	N	Y	N	N
2 *Capito*	Y	Y	N	Y	N	N	N
3 Rahall	N	N	N	N	Y	N	Y
WISCONSIN							
1 *Ryan*	Y	Y	Y	Y	N	N	N
2 Baldwin	N	N	Y	N	Y	Y	Y
3 Kind	N	N	N	N	Y	Y	Y
4 Kleczka	N	N	Y	N	Y	Y	Y
5 Barrett	N	N	Y	N	Y	Y	Y
6 *Petri*	N	Y	N	N	N	N	Y
7 Obey	N	N	Y	N	Y	Y	Y
8 *Green*	Y	Y	N	Y	N	N	N
9 *Sensenbrenner*	Y	Y	Y	Y	N	N	Y
WYOMING							
AL *Cubin*	Y	Y	?	Y	?	N	N

Southern states - Ala., Ark., Fla., Ga., Ky., La., Miss., N.C., Okla., S.C., Tenn., Texas, Va.

329. HR 2563. Patients' Rights/HMO Liability. Norwood, R-Ga., amendment that would limit liability and damage awards when a patient is harmed by denial of health care. It would allow a patient to sue a health maintenance organization in state court but federal, not state, law would govern. An employer could remove cases to federal court. It would limit non-economic damages to $1.5 million. Punitive damages would be limited to the same amount and only allowed when a decision-maker fails to abide by a grant of benefits by an independent medical reviewer. A patient could seek court reviews when an independent reviewer finds against him, but the patient would be required to produce clear and convincing evidence to overturn the decision. Adopted 218-213: R 214-6; D 3-206 (ND 2-153, SD 1-53); I 1-1. A "yea" was a vote in support of the president's position. Aug. 2, 2001.

342. H J Res 64. Use of Force Authorization/Passage. Passage of the joint resolution that would authorize the president to use all necessary and appropriate force against the nations, organizations or people he determines planned, authorized, committed or aided the terrorist attacks that occurred Sept. 11, 2001, or that harbored such organizations or people, to prevent future acts of terrorism against the United States. Passed 420-1: R 214-0; D 204-1 (ND 150-1, SD 54-0); I 2-0. (Under a unanimous consent agreement, the House subsequently passed an identical Senate resolution (S J Res 23), clearing the measure for the president.) A "yea" was a vote in support of the president's position. Sept. 14, 2001.

366. HR 2646. Farm Bill/Conservation. Boehlert, R-N.Y., amendment that would shift $1.9 billion from the bill's fixed and countercyclical payments to farm and undeveloped land conservation programs, including the Farm and Ranchland Protection Program and the Wildlife Habitat Incentives Program. The measure also would increase the amount of land that could be included in various preservation programs. Rejected 200-226: R 54-161; D 145-64 (ND 132-23, SD 13-41); I 1-1. Oct. 4, 2001.

398. HR 3162. Anti-Terrorism Authority/Passage. Sensenbrenner, R-Wis., motion to suspend the rules and pass the bill that would expand law enforcement's power to investigate suspected terrorists. The bill would allow disclosure of wiretap information among certain government officials, authorize limited disclosure of secret grand jury information to certain government officials, and authorize the detention of foreigners with suspected ties to terrorism. It also would make it easier for law enforcement to track voice and Internet communications using surveillance techniques and would strengthen laws to combat money laundering. Most of the bill's intelligence-gathering provisions would sunset after four years. Motion agreed to 357-66: R 211-3; D 145-62 (ND 103-50, SD 42-12); I 1-1. A two-thirds majority of those present and voting (282 in this case) is required for passage under suspension of the rules. A "yea" was a vote in support of the president's position. Oct. 24, 2001.

423. HR 3150. Aviation Security/Democratic Substitute. Oberstar, D-Minn., amendment that would federalize passenger and baggage screeners at the country's 140 largest airports and give the Justice Department responsibility for airport and airline security. It would contain additional security provisions similar to those in the underlying bill but would not broaden liability caps. Rejected 214-218: R 8-211; D 205-6 (ND 154-3, SD 51-3); I 1-1. A "nay" was a vote in support of the president's position. Nov. 1, 2001.

481. HR 3005. Trade Promotion Authority/Passage. Passage of the bill to allow expedited negotiation and implementation of trade agreements between the executive branch and foreign countries. The bill would include provisions requiring increased consultations with Congress on any proposed changes of tariffs for imports of sensitive agriculture products and on trade disparities for textile products. Passed 215-214: R 194-23; D 21-189 (ND 7-150, SD 14-39); I 0-2. A "yea" was a vote in support of the president's position. Dec. 6, 2001.

[1] *Rep. John Boozman, R-Ark., was sworn in Nov. 29. The first vote for which he was eligible was Vote 460. He replaced Rep. Asa Hutchinson, R, who resigned Aug. 6. The last vote for which Hutchinson was eligible was Vote 332.*

[2] *Rep. Jeff Miller, R-Fla., was sworn in Oct. 23. The first vote for which he was eligible was Vote 396. He replaced Rep. Joe Scarborough, R, who resigned Sept. 6. The last vote for which Scarborough was eligible was Vote 334.*

[3] *The Speaker votes only at his discretion, usually to break a tie or to emphasize the importance of a matter.*

[4] *Rep. Stephen F. Lynch, D-Mass. was sworn in Oct. 23. The first vote for which he was eligible was Vote 396.*

[5] *Rep. Floyd D. Spence, R-S.C., died Aug. 16. The last vote for which he was eligible was Vote 332.*

Key

Y	Voted for (yea).
#	Paired for.
+	Announced for.
N	Voted against (nay).
X	Paired against.
–	Announced against.
P	Voted "present."
C	Voted "present" to avoid possible conflict of interest.
?	Did not vote or otherwise make a position known.

Democrats   *Republicans*

Independents

	329	342	366	398	423	481
ALABAMA						
1 *Callahan*	Y	Y	N	Y	N	Y
2 *Everett*	Y	Y	N	Y	N	Y
3 *Riley*	Y	Y	N	Y	N	Y
4 *Aderholt*	Y	Y	N	Y	N	N
5 Cramer	N	Y	N	N	N	N
6 *Bachus*	Y	Y	N	Y	N	Y
7 Hilliard	N	Y	N	N	Y	N
ALASKA						
AL *Young*	Y	Y	N	?	N	?
ARIZONA						
1 *Flake*	Y	Y	N	Y	N	Y
2 Pastor	N	Y	N	Y	N	N
3 *Stump*	Y	Y	N	Y	N	Y
4 *Shadegg*	Y	Y	N	Y	N	Y
5 *Kolbe*	Y	Y	Y	Y	N	Y
6 *Hayworth*	Y	Y	N	Y	N	Y
ARKANSAS						
1 Berry	N	Y	N	Y	Y	N
2 Snyder	N	Y	N	Y	Y	Y
3 *Hutchinson* [1]	Y					
4 *Boozman* [1]						Y
4 Ross	N	Y	N	Y	Y	N
CALIFORNIA						
1 Thompson	N	Y	Y	Y	Y	N
2 *Herger*	Y	Y	N	Y	N	Y
3 *Ose*	Y	Y	N	Y	N	Y
4 *Doolittle*	Y	Y	N	Y	N	Y
5 Matsui	N	Y	Y	Y	Y	N
6 Woolsey	N	Y	Y	N	Y	N
7 Miller, George	N	Y	Y	N	Y	N
8 Pelosi	N	Y	Y	Y	Y	N
9 Lee	N	N	Y	N	Y	N
10 Tauscher	N	Y	Y	Y	Y	Y
11 *Pombo*	Y	Y	N	Y	N	Y
12 Lantos	N	Y	Y	Y	Y	N
13 Stark	N	Y	Y	N	Y	N
14 Eshoo	N	Y	Y	Y	Y	N
15 Honda	N	Y	Y	N	Y	N
16 Lofgren	N	Y	Y	Y	Y	N
17 Farr	N	?	Y	N	Y	N
18 Condit	N	Y	N	Y	N	N
19 *Radanovich*	Y	Y	N	Y	N	Y
20 Dooley	N	Y	N	Y	N	Y
21 *Thomas*	Y	Y	N	Y	N	Y
22 Capps	N	Y	Y	Y	Y	N
23 *Gallegly*	Y	Y	N	Y	N	Y
24 Sherman	N	Y	Y	Y	Y	N
25 *McKeon*	Y	Y	N	Y	N	Y
26 Berman	N	Y	Y	Y	Y	N
27 Schiff	N	Y	Y	Y	Y	N
28 *Dreier*	Y	Y	N	Y	N	Y
29 Waxman	N	Y	Y	Y	Y	N
30 Becerra	N	Y	Y	Y	Y	N
31 Solis	N	Y	Y	Y	Y	N
32 Watson	N	Y	Y	N	Y	N
33 Royal-Allard	N	Y	Y	Y	Y	N
34 Napolitano	N	Y	Y	Y	Y	N
35 Waters	N	Y	Y	N	Y	N
36 Harman	N	Y	Y	Y	Y	Y
37 Millender-McD.	N	Y	Y	Y	Y	N
38 *Horn*	Y	Y	N	Y	N	Y

	329	342	366	398	423	481
39 *Royce*	Y	Y	N	Y	N	Y
40 *Lewis*	Y	Y	N	Y	N	Y
41 *Miller, Gary*	Y	Y	N	Y	N	Y
42 Baca	N	Y	N	Y	N	Y
43 *Calvert*	Y	Y	N	Y	N	Y
44 *Bono*	Y	Y	N	Y	N	Y
45 *Rohrabacher*	Y	Y	Y	Y	N	Y
46 Sanchez	N	?	Y	N	Y	N
47 *Cox*	Y	Y	N	Y	N	Y
48 *Issa*	Y	Y	N	Y	N	Y
49 Davis	N	Y	Y	Y	Y	Y
50 Filner	N	Y	Y	N	Y	N
51 *Cunningham*	Y	Y	N	Y	N	Y
52 *Hunter*	Y	Y	N	Y	N	Y
COLORADO						
1 DeGette	N	Y	Y	N	Y	N
2 Udall	N	Y	Y	N	Y	N
3 *McInnis*	Y	Y	N	Y	N	Y
4 *Schaffer*	Y	Y	N	Y	N	Y
5 *Hefley*	Y	Y	N	Y	N	Y
6 *Tancredo*	Y	Y	N	Y	N	Y
CONNECTICUT						
1 Larson	N	Y	Y	Y	Y	N
2 *Simmons*	Y	Y	Y	Y	N	N
3 DeLauro	N	Y	Y	Y	Y	N
4 *Shays*	Y	Y	Y	Y	N	Y
5 Maloney	N	Y	Y	Y	Y	N
6 *Johnson*	Y	Y	Y	Y	N	Y
DELAWARE						
AL *Castle*	Y	Y	Y	Y	N	Y
FLORIDA						
1 *Scarborough* [2]	Y					
1 *Miller, J.* [2]				Y	N	Y
2 Boyd	N	Y	N	Y	Y	Y
3 Brown	N	Y	Y	Y	Y	N
4 *Crenshaw*	Y	Y	N	Y	N	Y
5 Thurman	N	Y	N	Y	Y	N
6 *Stearns*	Y	Y	N	Y	N	Y
7 *Mica*	Y	Y	N	Y	N	Y
8 *Keller*	Y	Y	N	Y	N	Y
9 *Bilirakis*	Y	Y	?	Y	N	Y
10 *Young*	Y	Y	N	Y	N	Y
11 Davis	N	Y	Y	Y	Y	Y
12 *Putnam*	Y	Y	N	Y	N	Y
13 *Miller, D.*	Y	Y	Y	Y	N	Y
14 *Goss*	Y	Y	N	Y	N	Y
15 *Weldon*	Y	Y	N	Y	N	Y
16 *Foley*	Y	Y	N	Y	N	N
17 Meek	N	Y	N	N	Y	?
18 *Ros-Lehtinen*	Y	Y	N	Y	N	Y
19 Wexler	N	Y	Y	Y	Y	N
20 Deutsch	N	Y	Y	Y	Y	N
21 *Diaz-Balart*	Y	Y	N	Y	N	Y
22 *Shaw*	Y	Y	N	Y	N	Y
23 Hastings	N	Y	N	N	Y	N
GEORGIA						
1 *Kingston*	Y	Y	N	Y	N	Y
2 Bishop	N	Y	N	Y	Y	N
3 *Collins*	Y	Y	?	Y	N	Y
4 McKinney	N	Y	N	N	Y	N
5 Lewis	N	Y	Y	N	Y	N
6 *Isakson*	Y	Y	N	Y	N	Y
7 *Barr*	Y	Y	N	Y	N	Y
8 *Chambliss*	Y	Y	N	Y	N	Y
9 *Deal*	Y	Y	N	Y	N	Y
10 *Norwood*	Y	Y	N	Y	N	Y
11 *Linder*	Y	Y	N	Y	N	Y
HAWAII						
1 Abercrombie	N	Y	Y	?	Y	N
2 Mink	N	Y	N	N	Y	N
IDAHO						
1 *Otter*	Y	Y	N	N	N	Y
2 *Simpson*	Y	Y	N	Y	N	Y
ILLINOIS						
1 Rush	N	Y	N	N	Y	N
2 Jackson	N	Y	Y	N	Y	N
3 Lipinski	?	?	N	Y	Y	N
4 Gutierrez	N	Y	Y	N	Y	N
5 Blagojevich	N	Y	N	N	Y	N
6 *Hyde*	Y	Y	N	Y	N	Y
7 Davis	N	Y	Y	N	Y	N
8 *Crane*	Y	Y	N	Y	N	Y
9 Schakowsky	N	Y	Y	N	Y	N
10 *Kirk*	Y	Y	Y	Y	N	Y
11 *Weller*	Y	Y	N	Y	N	Y
12 Costello	N	Y	N	Y	N	Y

ND Northern Democrats   SD Southern Democrats

	329	342	366	398	423	481
13 *Biggert*	Y	Y	Y	Y	N	Y
14 *Hastert*[3]	Y	Y	N		N	Y
15 *Johnson*	N	Y	N	Y	N	Y
16 *Manzullo*	Y	Y	N	Y	N	Y
17 Evans	N	Y	N	Y	Y	N
18 *LaHood*	Y	Y	N	Y	N	Y
19 Phelps	N	Y	N	Y	Y	N
20 *Shimkus*	Y	Y	N	Y	N	Y
INDIANA						
1 Visclosky	N	Y	?	N	Y	N
2 *Pence*	Y	Y	N	Y	N	Y
3 Roemer	N	Y	Y	Y	Y	N
4 *Souder*	Y	Y	N	Y	N	Y
5 *Buyer*	Y	Y	N	Y	N	Y
6 *Burton*	Y	Y	–	?	N	Y
7 *Kerns*	Y	Y	N	Y	N	Y
8 *Hostettler*	Y	Y	N	Y	N	?
9 Hill	N	Y	N	?	Y	Y
10 Carson	N	Y	Y	Y	Y	N
IOWA						
1 *Leach*	N	Y	N	Y	Y	Y
2 *Nussle*	Y	Y	N	Y	N	Y
3 Boswell	N	Y	N	Y	Y	N
4 *Ganske*	N	Y	N	Y	Y	Y
5 *Latham*	Y	Y	N	Y	N	Y
KANSAS						
1 *Moran*	Y	Y	N	Y	N	Y
2 *Ryun*	Y	Y	N	Y	N	Y
3 Moore	N	Y	N	Y	Y	Y
4 *Tiahrt*	Y	Y	N	Y	N	Y
KENTUCKY						
1 *Whitfield*	Y	Y	N	Y	N	Y
2 *Lewis*	Y	Y	N	Y	N	Y
3 *Northup*	Y	Y	N	Y	N	Y
4 Lucas	Y	Y	N	Y	Y	Y
5 *Rogers*	Y	Y	N	Y	N	N
6 *Fletcher*	Y	Y	N	Y	N	Y
LOUISIANA						
1 *Vitter*	Y	Y	N	Y	N	Y
2 Jefferson	N	Y	Y	Y	Y	Y
3 *Tauzin*	Y	Y	N	Y	N	Y
4 *McCrery*	Y	Y	N	Y	N	Y
5 *Cooksey*	Y	Y	N	Y	N	Y
6 *Baker*	Y	Y	N	Y	N	Y
7 John	N	Y	N	Y	Y	Y
MAINE						
1 Allen	N	Y	Y	Y	Y	N
2 Baldacci	N	Y	Y	Y	Y	N
MARYLAND						
1 *Gilchrest*	Y	Y	Y	Y	N	Y
2 *Ehrlich*	Y	Y	Y	Y	N	Y
3 Cardin	N	Y	Y	Y	Y	N
4 Wynn	N	Y	Y	Y	Y	N
5 Hoyer	N	Y	Y	Y	Y	N
6 *Bartlett*	Y	Y	N	Y	N	N
7 Cummings	N	Y	Y	N	Y	N
8 *Morella*	N	Y	Y	Y	Y	Y
MASSACHUSETTS						
1 Olver	N	Y	Y	N	Y	N
2 Neal	N	Y	Y	Y	Y	N
3 McGovern	N	Y	Y	N	Y	N
4 Frank	N	Y	Y	N	Y	N
5 Meehan	N	Y	Y	Y	Y	N
6 Tierney	N	Y	Y	N	Y	N
7 Markey	N	Y	Y	Y	Y	N
8 Capuano	N	Y	Y	N	Y	N
9 Lynch[4]				Y	Y	N
10 Delahunt	N	Y	Y	Y	Y	N
MICHIGAN						
1 Stupak	N	Y	Y	Y	Y	N
2 *Hoekstra*	Y	Y	Y	Y	N	N
3 *Ehlers*	Y	Y	Y	Y	N	Y
4 *Camp*	Y	Y	N	Y	N	Y
5 Barcia	N	Y	N	Y	Y	N
6 *Upton*	Y	Y	Y	Y	N	Y
7 *Smith*	Y	Y	N	Y	N	Y
8 *Rogers*	Y	Y	N	Y	N	Y
9 Kildee	N	Y	Y	Y	Y	N
10 Bonior	N	Y	Y	N	Y	N
11 *Knollenberg*	Y	Y	N	Y	N	Y
12 Levin	N	Y	N	Y	Y	N
13 Rivers	N	Y	Y	N	Y	N
14 Conyers	N	?	Y	N	Y	N
15 Kilpatrick	N	?	Y	?	Y	N
16 Dingell	N	Y	Y	N	Y	N

	329	342	366	398	423	481
MINNESOTA						
1 *Gutknecht*	Y	Y	N	Y	N	Y
2 *Kennedy*	Y	Y	N	Y	N	Y
3 *Ramstad*	Y	Y	Y	Y	Y	Y
4 McCollum	N	Y	Y	Y	Y	N
5 Sabo	N	Y	N	N	Y	N
6 Luther	N	Y	Y	Y	Y	N
7 Peterson	Y	Y	N	N	Y	N
8 Oberstar	N	Y	Y	N	Y	N
MISSISSIPPI						
1 *Wicker*	Y	Y	N	Y	N	Y
2 Thompson	N	Y	N	N	Y	N
3 *Pickering*	Y	Y	N	Y	N	Y
4 Shows	N	Y	N	Y	Y	N
5 Taylor	N	Y	N	Y	Y	N
MISSOURI						
1 Clay	N	Y	Y	?	Y	N
2 *Akin*	Y	Y	N	Y	N	Y
3 Gephardt	N	Y	Y	Y	Y	N
4 Skelton	N	Y	N	Y	Y	Y
5 McCarthy	N	Y	Y	Y	Y	N
6 *Graves*	Y	Y	N	Y	N	Y
7 *Blunt*	Y	Y	N	Y	N	Y
8 *Emerson*	Y	Y	N	Y	Y	Y
9 *Hulshof*	Y	Y	N	Y	N	Y
MONTANA						
AL *Rehberg*	Y	Y	N	Y	N	Y
NEBRASKA						
1 *Bereuter*	Y	Y	N	Y	N	Y
2 *Terry*	Y	Y	N	Y	N	Y
3 *Osborne*	Y	Y	N	Y	N	Y
NEVADA						
1 Berkley	N	Y	N	Y	Y	N
2 *Gibbons*	Y	Y	?	Y	N	Y
NEW HAMPSHIRE						
1 *Sununu*	Y	Y	Y	Y	N	Y
2 *Bass*	Y	Y	Y	Y	N	Y
NEW JERSEY						
1 Andrews	N	Y	Y	Y	Y	N
2 *LoBiondo*	Y	Y	Y	Y	N	N
3 *Saxton*	Y	?	Y	Y	N	Y
4 *Smith*	N	Y	Y	Y	Y	N
5 *Roukema*	N	Y	Y	Y	Y	?
6 Pallone	N	Y	Y	Y	Y	N
7 *Ferguson*	Y	Y	Y	Y	N	Y
8 Pascrell	N	Y	Y	Y	Y	N
9 Rothman	N	Y	Y	Y	Y	N
10 Payne	N	Y	Y	N	Y	N
11 *Frelinghuysen*	Y	Y	Y	Y	N	Y
12 Holt	N	Y	Y	Y	Y	N
13 Menendez	N	Y	Y	Y	Y	N
NEW MEXICO						
1 *Wilson*	Y	?	N	Y	N	Y
2 *Skeen*	Y	Y	N	Y	N	Y
3 Udall	N	Y	Y	N	Y	N
NEW YORK						
1 *Grucci*	Y	Y	Y	Y	N	Y
2 Israel	N	Y	Y	Y	Y	N
3 *King*	Y	?	Y	Y	N	Y
4 McCarthy	N	Y	Y	Y	Y	N
5 Ackerman	N	Y	Y	Y	Y	N
6 Meeks	N	Y	Y	Y	Y	N
7 Crowley	N	Y	Y	Y	Y	N
8 Nadler	N	Y	Y	N	Y	N
9 Weiner	N	Y	Y	Y	Y	N
10 Towns	N	Y	Y	Y	Y	N
11 Owens	N	Y	Y	N	Y	N
12 Velázquez	N	Y	Y	N	Y	N
13 *Fossella*	Y	Y	Y	Y	N	Y
14 Maloney	N	Y	Y	Y	Y	N
15 Rangel	N	Y	Y	Y	Y	N
16 Serrano	N	Y	Y	N	Y	N
17 Engel	N	Y	Y	Y	Y	N
18 Lowey	N	Y	Y	Y	Y	N
19 *Kelly*	Y	Y	Y	Y	N	Y
20 *Gilman*	Y	Y	Y	Y	N	N
21 McNulty	N	Y	Y	Y	Y	N
22 *Sweeney*	Y	Y	Y	Y	N	Y
23 *Boehlert*	Y	Y	Y	Y	N	Y
24 *McHugh*	Y	Y	Y	Y	N	N
25 *Walsh*	Y	Y	Y	Y	N	N
26 Hinchey	N	Y	Y	Y	Y	N
27 *Reynolds*	Y	Y	Y	Y	N	Y
28 Slaughter	N	Y	Y	Y	Y	N
29 LaFalce	N	Y	Y	Y	Y	N

	329	342	366	398	423	481
30 *Quinn*	Y	Y	Y	Y	N	?
31 *Houghton*	Y	Y	?	Y	N	Y
NORTH CAROLINA						
1 Clayton	N	Y	N	N	Y	N
2 Etheridge	N	Y	N	Y	Y	Y
3 *Jones*	Y	Y	N	Y	N	N
4 Price	N	Y	Y	Y	Y	N
5 *Burr*	Y	Y	N	Y	N	Y
6 *Coble*	Y	Y	N	Y	N	N
7 McIntyre	N	Y	N	Y	Y	N
8 *Hayes*	Y	Y	N	Y	N	Y
9 *Myrick*	Y	Y	N	Y	N	Y
10 *Ballenger*	Y	?	N	Y	N	Y
11 *Taylor*	Y	Y	N	Y	N	N
12 Watt	N	Y	N	N	Y	N
NORTH DAKOTA						
AL Pomeroy	N	Y	N	Y	Y	N
OHIO						
1 *Chabot*	Y	Y	N	Y	N	Y
2 *Portman*	Y	Y	N	Y	N	Y
3 Hall	N	Y	N	Y	Y	N
4 *Oxley*	Y	Y	N	Y	N	Y
5 *Gillmor*	Y	Y	N	Y	N	Y
6 Strickland	N	Y	Y	Y	Y	N
7 *Hobson*	Y	Y	N	Y	N	Y
8 *Boehner*	Y	Y	N	Y	N	Y
9 Kaptur	N	Y	Y	Y	Y	N
10 Kucinich	N	Y	Y	N	Y	N
11 Jones	N	Y	Y	N	Y	N
12 *Tiberi*	Y	Y	N	Y	N	Y
13 Brown	N	Y	Y	N	Y	N
14 Sawyer	N	Y	Y	Y	Y	N
15 *Pryce*	Y	Y	Y	Y	N	Y
16 *Regula*	Y	Y	N	Y	N	N
17 Traficant	Y	Y	N	Y	N	N
18 *Ney*	Y	Y	Y	N	N	Y
19 *LaTourette*	Y	Y	Y	Y	N	N
OKLAHOMA						
1 *Largent*	Y	Y	N	Y	N	Y
2 Carson	N	Y	N	Y	Y	Y
3 *Watkins*	Y	Y	N	Y	N	Y
4 *Watts*	Y	Y	N	Y	N	Y
5 *Istook*	Y	Y	N	Y	N	Y
6 *Lucas*	Y	Y	N	Y	N	Y
OREGON						
1 Wu	N	Y	Y	N	Y	N
2 *Walden*	Y	Y	N	Y	N	Y
3 Blumenauer	N	Y	Y	N	Y	N
4 DeFazio	N	Y	Y	N	Y	N
5 Hooley	N	Y	Y	Y	Y	N
PENNSYLVANIA						
1 Brady	N	Y	Y	Y	Y	N
2 Fattah	N	Y	Y	Y	Y	N
3 Borski	N	Y	Y	Y	Y	N
4 *Hart*	Y	Y	Y	Y	N	Y
5 *Peterson*	Y	Y	N	Y	N	Y
6 Holden	N	Y	Y	Y	Y	N
7 *Weldon*	Y	Y	Y	Y	N	N
8 *Greenwood*	Y	Y	Y	Y	N	Y
9 *Shuster, Bill*	Y	Y	Y	Y	N	Y
10 *Sherwood*	Y	Y	Y	Y	N	Y
11 Kanjorski	N	Y	Y	Y	Y	N
12 Murtha	N	Y	Y	Y	Y	N
13 Hoeffel	N	Y	Y	Y	Y	N
14 Coyne	N	Y	Y	N	Y	N
15 *Toomey*	Y	Y	Y	Y	N	Y
16 *Pitts*	Y	Y	N	Y	N	Y
17 *Gekas*	Y	Y	N	Y	N	Y
18 Doyle	N	Y	Y	Y	Y	N
19 *Platts*	Y	Y	N	Y	N	Y
20 Mascara	N	Y	Y	Y	Y	N
21 *English*	Y	Y	N	Y	N	Y
RHODE ISLAND						
1 Kennedy	N	Y	Y	Y	Y	N
2 Langevin	N	Y	Y	Y	Y	N
SOUTH CAROLINA						
1 *Brown*	Y	Y	N	Y	N	Y
2 *Spence*[5]	?					
3 *Graham*	Y	Y	N	Y	N	N
4 *DeMint*	Y	Y	N	Y	N	Y
5 Spratt	N	Y	N	Y	Y	N
6 Clyburn	N	Y	N	Y	Y	N
SOUTH DAKOTA						
AL *Thune*	Y	Y	N	Y	N	Y

	329	342	366	398	423	481
TENNESSEE						
1 *Jenkins*	Y	Y	N	Y	N	Y
2 *Duncan*	Y	Y	N	Y	N	N
3 *Wamp*	Y	Y	N	Y	N	Y
4 *Hilleary*	Y	Y	N	Y	N	Y
5 Clement	N	Y	N	Y	Y	N
6 Gordon	N	Y	N	Y	Y	N
7 *Bryant*	Y	Y	N	Y	N	Y
8 Tanner	N	Y	N	Y	Y	Y
9 Ford	N	Y	N	Y	Y	N
TEXAS						
1 Sandlin	N	Y	N	Y	Y	N
2 Turner	N	Y	N	Y	Y	N
3 *Johnson, Sam*	Y	Y	N	Y	N	Y
4 Hall	N	Y	N	Y	N	Y
5 *Sessions*	Y	Y	N	Y	N	Y
6 *Barton*	Y	Y	N	Y	N	Y
7 *Culberson*	Y	Y	N	Y	N	Y
8 *Brady*	Y	Y	N	Y	N	Y
9 Lampson	N	Y	N	Y	Y	N
10 Doggett	N	Y	Y	Y	Y	N
11 Edwards	N	Y	N	Y	Y	N
12 *Granger*	Y	Y	N	Y	N	Y
13 *Thornberry*	Y	Y	N	Y	N	Y
14 *Paul*	?	Y	N	N	N	N
15 Hinojosa	N	Y	N	Y	Y	Y
16 Reyes	N	Y	N	Y	Y	N
17 Stenholm	N	Y	N	Y	Y	Y
18 Jackson-Lee	N	Y	Y	N	Y	N
19 *Combest*	Y	Y	N	Y	N	Y
20 Gonzalez	N	Y	N	Y	Y	N
21 *Smith*	Y	Y	N	Y	N	Y
22 *DeLay*	Y	Y	N	Y	N	Y
23 *Bonilla*	Y	Y	N	Y	N	Y
24 Frost	N	Y	N	Y	Y	N
25 Bentsen	N	Y	N	Y	Y	Y
26 *Armey*	Y	Y	N	Y	N	Y
27 Ortiz	N	Y	N	Y	N	Y
28 Rodriguez	N	Y	N	Y	Y	N
29 Green	N	Y	Y	Y	Y	N
30 Johnson, E.B.	N	Y	Y	N	Y	N
UTAH						
1 *Hansen*	Y	Y	N	+	N	Y
2 Matheson	N	Y	N	Y	Y	Y
3 *Cannon*	Y	Y	N	Y	N	Y
VERMONT						
AL *Sanders*	N	Y	Y	N	Y	N
VIRGINIA						
1 *Davis, Jo Ann*	Y	Y	N	Y	N	Y
2 *Schrock*	Y	Y	N	Y	N	Y
3 Scott	N	Y	N	N	Y	N
4 *Forbes*	Y	Y	N	Y	N	Y
5 *Goode*	Y	Y	N	Y	N	N
6 *Goodlatte*	Y	Y	N	Y	N	Y
7 *Cantor*	Y	Y	N	Y	N	Y
8 Moran	N	Y	Y	Y	Y	Y
9 Boucher	N	Y	Y	N	Y	N
10 *Wolf*	Y	Y	Y	Y	Y	Y
11 *Davis, T.*	Y	Y	Y	Y	N	Y
WASHINGTON						
1 Inslee	N	Y	Y	Y	Y	N
2 Larsen	N	Y	Y	Y	Y	N
3 Baird	N	Y	Y	Y	Y	N
4 *Hastings*	Y	Y	N	Y	N	Y
5 *Nethercutt*	Y	Y	N	Y	N	Y
6 Dicks	N	Y	Y	Y	Y	N
7 McDermott	N	Y	Y	N	Y	N
8 *Dunn*	Y	Y	N	Y	–	Y
9 Smith	N	Y	Y	Y	Y	N
WEST VIRGINIA						
1 Mollohan	N	Y	Y	N	Y	N
2 *Capito*	Y	Y	Y	Y	N	N
3 Rahall	N	Y	Y	N	Y	N
WISCONSIN						
1 *Ryan*	Y	Y	Y	Y	N	Y
2 Baldwin	N	Y	Y	N	Y	N
3 Kind	N	Y	Y	Y	Y	N
4 Kleczka	N	Y	Y	Y	Y	N
5 Barrett	N	Y	Y	N	Y	N
6 *Petri*	Y	+	Y	Y	N	Y
7 Obey	N	Y	Y	Y	Y	N
8 *Green*	Y	Y	Y	Y	N	Y
9 *Sensenbrenner*	Y	Y	Y	Y	N	Y
WYOMING						
AL *Cubin*	Y	Y	N	?	N	Y

Southern states - Ala., Ark., Fla., Ga., Ky., La., Miss., N.C., Okla., S.C., Tenn., Texas, Va.

Appendix D

TEXTS

As Senate Convenes, Daschle and Lott Express Hope a Consensus Can Be Found

Following are the remarks of Vice President Al Gore and Sens. Tom Daschle, D-S.D., and Trent Lott, R-Miss., as the Senate convened Jan. 3 for the 107th Congress. Transcript from the Congressional Record.

GORE: The majority leader, Sen. Daschle, is recognized.

(APPLAUSE)

DASCHLE: Mr. President, on behalf of the entire Senate, but especially this senator, let me welcome you back to the Senate.

This is a historic day. Never before in the history of our nation have we had a 50-50 Senate. I welcome and congratulate all 11 of our newly elected senators and the family members and friends who are here to share this important day with them.

Years after he left the White House, Harry Truman wrote that the decade he spent in this Senate were the happiest years of his life. As our new colleagues begin their Senate careers, we hope that they, too, are beginning what will be the happiest years of their lives.

Several of our departing colleagues are also here with us today. To them we say, thank you. Thank you for sharing with us and with our nation some of the best years of your lives. Thank you for the contributions you have made to our nation during your years of public life. And thank you for the important contributions you will continue to make in the coming years. It has been a pleasure and an honor to work with each of you.

The writer Thomas Wolfe said that America is a place where miracles not only happen, they happen all the time. Today we experience one of those miracles: the peaceful transition of power from one Congress to the other. Some people say that it will take another miracle for this Congress and administration to find a way to work together.

As we begin this historic Congress,

let us resolve that we will work in good faith, with each other, to do the people's business. That is our pledge from this side of the aisle, and we know that our colleagues on the other side of the aisle feel as we do.

Finally, on a personal note, it is a high honor to have the privilege of officially opening this Senate. When I first ran for Democratic leader six years ago, I thought that if I won, I would be majority leader.

I must confess that in six years as minority leader, I had a moment or two when I wondered if that day would ever arrive. But I assure you I intend to savor every one of the next 17 days.

(LAUGHTER)

I know we are all looking forward to a bipartisan and a productive 107th Congress that will serve our country well. It is an honor to be a part of this Congress and to be able to work once again with my friend and my colleague, Sen. Lott.

And I would now ask unanimous consent that the Republican leader be permitted to speak.

GORE: Without objection, it is so ordered. The minority leader, Sen. Lott, is recognized.

(APPLAUSE)

LOTT: Thank you, Mr. President.

I appreciate the courtesy of the distinguished majority leader for this opportunity to speak.

I want to extend also the appreciation of the Senate and a grateful nation to the presiding officer, the vice president of the United States, for the service that he has given to our country.

(APPLAUSE)

GORE: Thank you, thank you.

The chair will remind the Senate that boisterous demonstrations are against the rules.

(LAUGHTER)

LOTT: It is obvious, Mr. President, that you still maintain your sense of humor.

I want to thank you for your leadership and also for the example that you have set through a very difficult time. You took the appropriate step, and now we're prepared to move into a transition and to a new administration.

Here in the Senate also, we are having a historic experience. I would like to welcome all of the new senators that are joining us here today. I congratulate them. I look forward to working with the new senators on both sides of the aisle.

As Sen. Daschle said, I also extend, again, our appreciation to the senators that may be in the chamber that are retiring or leaving the Senate, who have served, most of them, for at least six years and some for much longer than that. They have done a lot to make this country a better place to live.

I also extend our appreciation to the extended family of the Senate, our staff members new and old, and to the families that are here in the gallery today.

I realize we should not be referring to those in the gallery, but there are a lot of people that have made an awful lot of contributions and sacrifices to make this day possible for us in the chamber. So we have a lot of people we need to thank, and also to realize that we are in a position where we can make this an even better country.

To the new members, I urge them to take a look around and think about the challenges and the opportunities they will have here. It is a unique institution, created by the founders of this Republic. Quite often, we are frustrated with the rules — frustrated even today, that we're going through this unique situation — but they had a lot of foresight.

They created this unique Senate that makes sure that we take the time to think through an issue and to have full debate.

And while sometimes we believe, on one side or the other, that we did not have an ample opportunity for debate, I am sure we are going to work together to find a way to give everybody that opportunity over the next six years.

For those of us that have been here a few years, we also face new challenges here. We have one today. I must say that it is the first time I have ever been referred to as the minority leader. And while it beats certain alternatives, I like the other title better.

But we're showing here today — and I hope we will show during the next 17 days, and more importantly, during the months beyond that — that we will always find a way to work together.

It is quite often not easy to find consensus, as is forced upon us quite often in the Senate, but we must strive for it.

Quite often, Sen. Daschle and I do our very best to find a logical solution to a problem, and we have 98 other senators that may not agree with us, but we will continue to work together to make this great Republic — the best and the most outstanding the minds of men have ever created — work as it should.

I look around the chamber, on both sides of the aisle, and I see men and women with the potential to raise this country up to an even higher level, to our highest and our best.

I will work, as the leader of my party, and in 17 days the majority leader of the Senate, to find a way to make that possible.

One bit of information from a housekeeping standpoint: We will have some housekeeping resolutions here in a moment that we will do. One of them is to begin the introduction of bills on Jan. 22. Senators should be prepared to have amendments or bills ready.

Sen. Daschle and I have already talked about the fact that we will do the usual five alternating from one side to the other. We will do that for the first 20 bills. There will be a lot of other announcements that Sen. Daschle and I will make.

So thank you for this opportunity. I thank you on my side of the aisle for this leadership role. Together we will go forward.

I yield the floor, Mr. President. ◆

Clinton Bids Farewell, Looks Ahead At His Future and That of the Nation

Following is President Bill Clinton's Jan. 18 address to the nation. Transcript provided by eMediaMillWorks Inc.

My fellow citizens: Tonight is my last opportunity to speak to you from the Oval Office as your president. I am profoundly grateful to you for twice giving me the honor to serve, to work for you and with you to prepare our nation for the 21st century. And I'm grateful to Vice President Gore, to my Cabinet secretaries and to all those who have served with me for the last eight years.

This has been a time of dramatic transformation, and you have risen to every new challenge. You have made our social fabric stronger, our families healthier and safer, our people more prosperous. You, the American people, have made our passage into the global information age an era of great American renewal.

In all the work I have done as president, every decision I have made, every executive action I have taken, every bill I have proposed and signed, I've tried to give all Americans the tools and conditions to build the future of our dreams, in a good society, with a strong economy, a cleaner environment and a freer, safer, more prosperous world. I have steered my course by our enduring values: opportunity for all; responsibility from all; a community of all Americans. I have sought to give America a new kind of government: smaller, more modern, more effective, full of ideas and policies appropriate to this new time, always putting people first, always focusing on the future.

Working together, America has done well. Our economy is breaking records, with more than 22 million new jobs, the lowest unemployment in 30 years, the highest home ownership ever, the longest expansion in history.

Our families and communities are stronger. Thirty-five million Americans have used the family leave law. Eight million have moved off welfare. Crime is at a 25-year low. Over 10 million Americans receive more college aid, and more people than ever are going to college. Our schools are better — higher standards, greater accountability and larger investments have brought higher test scores and higher graduation rates.

More than 3 million children have health insurance now, and more than 7 million Americans have been lifted out of poverty. Incomes are rising across the board. Our air and water are cleaner. Our food and drinking water are safer. And more of our precious land has been preserved, in the continental United States, than at any time in 100 years. America has been a force for peace and prosperity in every corner of the globe.

I'm very grateful to be able to turn over the reins of leadership to a new president with America in such a strong position to meet the challenges of the future.

Tonight, I want to leave you with three thoughts about our future. First, America must maintain our record of fiscal responsibility. Through our last four budgets, we've turned record deficits to record surpluses, and we've been able to pay down $600 billion of our national debt, on track to be debt-free by the end of the decade for the first time since 1835.

Staying on that course will bring lower interest rates, greater prosperity and the opportunity to meet our big challenges. If we choose wisely, we can pay down the debt, deal with the retirement of the baby boomers, invest more in our future and provide tax relief.

Second, because the world is more connected every day in every way, America's security and prosperity require us to continue to lead in the world. At this remarkable moment in history, more people live in freedom that ever before. Our alliances are stronger than ever. People all around the world look to America to be a force for peace and prosperity, freedom and security. The global economy is giving more of our own people, and billions around the world, the chance to work and live and raise their families with dignity.

But the forces of integration that have created these good opportunities also make us more subject to global forces of destruction, to terrorism, organized crime and narcotrafficking, the spread of deadly weapons and disease, the degradation of the global environment. The expansion of trade hasn't fully closed the gap between those of us who live on the cutting edge of the global economy and the billions around the world who live on the knife's edge of survival.

This global gap requires more than compassion. It requires action. Global poverty is a powder keg that could be ignited by our indifference.

In his first inaugural address, Thomas Jefferson warned of entangling alliances. But in our times, America cannot and must not disentangle itself from the world. If we want the world to embody our shared values, then we must assume a shared responsibility.

If the wars of the 20th century, especially the recent ones in Kosovo and Bosnia, have taught us anything, it is that we achieve our aims by defending our values and leading the forces of freedom and peace. We must embrace boldly and resolutely that duty to lead, to stand with our allies in word and deed, and to put a human face on the global economy so that expanded trade benefits all people in all nations, lifting lives and hopes all across the world.

Third, we must remember that America cannot lead in the world unless here at home we weave the threads of our coat of many colors into the fabric of one America. As we become ever more diverse, we must work harder to unite around our common values and our common humanity.

We must work harder to overcome our differences. In our hearts and in our laws, we must treat all our people with fairness and dignity, regardless of their race, religion, gender or sexual orientation and regardless of when

they arrived in our country, always moving toward the more perfect union of our founders' dreams.

Hillary, Chelsea and I join all Americans in wishing our very best to the next president, George W. Bush, to his family and his administration in meeting these challenges and in leading freedom's march in this new century.

As for me, I'll leave the presidency more idealistic, more full of hope than the day I arrived and more confident than ever that America's best days lie ahead. My days in this office are nearly through, but my days of service, I hope, are not. In the years ahead, I will never hold a position higher or a covenant more sacred than that of president of the United States. But there is no title I will wear more proudly than that of citizen.

Thank you. God bless you, and God bless America. ◆

Bush Pledges to Seek Unity; Appeals for Compassion, Renewed Sense of Civic Duty

The following is the Jan. 20 inaugural address of George W. Bush, the 43rd president. Transcript provided by the White House.

Chief Justice [William H.] Rehnquist, President [Jimmy] Carter, President [George] Bush, President [Bill] Clinton, distinguished guests and my fellow citizens: The peaceful transfer of authority is rare in history, yet common in our country. With a simple oath, we affirm old traditions and make new beginnings.

As I begin, I thank President Clinton for his service to our nation. And I thank Vice President [Al] Gore for a contest conducted with spirit and ended with grace.

I am honored and humbled to stand here, where so many of America's leaders have come before me, and so many will follow.

We have a place, all of us, in a long story — a story we continue, but whose end we will not see. It is the story of a new world that became a friend and liberator of the old; a story of a slave-holding society that became a servant of freedom; the story of a power that went into the world to protect but not possess, to defend but not to conquer.

It is the American story — a story of flawed and fallible people, united across the generations by grand and enduring ideals.

The grandest of these ideals is an unfolding American promise that everyone belongs, that everyone deserves a chance, that no insignificant person was ever born.

Americans are called to enact this promise in our lives and in our laws. And though our nation has sometimes halted, and sometimes delayed, we must follow no other course.

Through much of the last century, America's faith in freedom and democracy was a rock in a raging sea. Now it is a seed upon the wind, taking root in many nations.

Our democratic faith is more than the creed of our country, it is the inborn hope of our humanity, an ideal we carry but do not own, a trust we bear and pass along. And even after nearly 225 years, we have a long way yet to travel.

While many of our citizens prosper, others doubt the promise, even the justice, of our own country. The ambitions of some Americans are limited by failing schools and hidden prejudice and the circumstances of their birth. And sometimes our differences run so deep, it seems we share a continent, but not a country.

We do not accept this, and we will not allow it. Our unity, our union, is the serious work of leaders and citizens in every generation. And this is my solemn pledge: I will work to build a single nation of justice and opportunity.

I know this is in our reach because we are guided by a power larger than ourselves who creates us equal in His image. And we are confident in principles that unite and lead us onward.

America has never been united by blood or birth or soil. We are bound by ideals that move us beyond our backgrounds, lift us above our interests and teach us what it means to be citizens. Every child must be taught these principles. Every citizen must uphold them. And every immigrant, by embracing these ideals, makes our country more, not less, American.

Today, we affirm a new commitment to live out our nation's promise through civility, courage, compassion and character.

America, at its best, matches a commitment to principle with a concern for civility. A civil society demands from each of us good will and respect, fair dealing and forgiveness.

Some seem to believe that our politics can afford to be petty because, in a time of peace, the stakes of our debates appear small.

But the stakes for America are never small. If our country does not lead the cause of freedom, it will not be led. If we do not turn the hearts of children toward knowledge and character, we will lose their gifts and undermine their idealism. If we permit our economy to drift and decline, the vulnerable will suffer most.

We must live up to the calling we share. Civility is not a tactic or a sentiment. It is the determined choice of trust over cynicism, of community over chaos. And this commitment, if we keep it, is a way to shared accomplishment.

America, at its best, is also courageous.

Our national courage has been clear in times of depression and war, when defending common dangers defined our common good. Now we must choose if the example of our fathers and mothers will inspire us or condemn us. We must show courage in a time of blessing by confronting problems instead of passing them on to future generations.

Together, we will reclaim America's schools, before ignorance and apathy claim more young lives.

We will reform Social Security and Medicare, sparing our children from struggles we have the power to prevent. And we will reduce taxes, to recover the momentum of our economy and reward the effort and enterprise of working Americans.

We will build our defenses beyond challenge, lest weakness invite challenge.

We will confront weapons of mass destruction, so that a new century is spared new horrors.

The enemies of liberty and our country should make no mistake: America remains engaged in the world by history and by choice, shaping a balance of power that favors freedom. We will defend our allies and our interests. We will show purpose without arrogance. We will meet aggression and bad faith with resolve and strength.

And to all nations, we will speak for the values that gave our nation birth.

America, at its best, is compassionate. In the quiet of American conscience, we know that deep, persistent poverty is unworthy of our nation's promise.

And whatever our views of its cause, we can agree that children at risk are not at fault. Abandonment and abuse are not acts of God, they are failures of love.

And the proliferation of prisons, however necessary, is no substitute for hope and order in our souls.

Where there is suffering, there is duty. Americans in need are not strangers, they are citizens; not problems, but priorities. And all of us are diminished when any are hopeless.

Government has great responsibilities for public safety and public health, for civil rights and common schools. Yet compassion is the work of a nation, not just a government.

And some needs and hurts are so deep they will only respond to a mentor's touch or a pastor's prayer. Church and charity, synagogue and mosque lend our communities their humanity, and they will have an honored place in our plans and in our laws.

Many in our country do not know the pain of poverty, but we can listen to those who do.

And I can pledge our nation to a goal: When we see that wounded traveler on the road to Jericho, we will not pass to the other side.

America, at its best, is a place where personal responsibility is valued and expected.

Encouraging responsibility is not a search for scapegoats, it is a call to conscience. And though it requires sacrifice, it brings a deeper fulfillment. We find the fullness of life not only in options, but in commitments. And we find that children and community are the commitments that set us free.

Our public interest depends on private character, on civic duty and family bonds and basic fairness, on uncounted, unhonored acts of decency which give direction to our freedom.

Sometimes in life we are called to do great things. But as a saint of our times has said, every day we are called to do small things with great love. The most important tasks of a democracy are done by everyone.

I will live and lead by these principles: to advance my convictions with civility; to pursue the public interest with courage; to speak for greater justice and compassion; to call for responsibility and try to live it as well.

In all these ways, I will bring the values of our history to the care of our times.

What you do is as important as anything government does. I ask you to seek a common good beyond your comfort; to defend needed reforms against easy attacks; to serve your nation, beginning with your neighbor. I ask you to be citizens: citizens, not spectators; citizens, not subjects; responsible citizens, building communities of service and a nation of character.

Americans are generous and strong and decent, not because we believe in ourselves, but because we hold beliefs beyond ourselves. When this spirit of citizenship is missing, no government program can replace it. When this spirit is present, no wrong can stand against it.

After the Declaration of Independence was signed, Virginia statesman John Page wrote to Thomas Jefferson: "We know the race is not to the swift nor the battle to the strong. Do you not think an angel rides in the whirlwind and directs this storm?"

Much time has passed since Jefferson arrived for his inauguration. The years and changes accumulate. But the themes of this day he would know: our nation's grand story of courage and its simple dream of dignity.

We are not this story's author, who fills time and eternity with his purpose. Yet his purpose is achieved in our duty, and our duty is fulfilled in service to one another.

Never tiring, never yielding, never finishing, we renew that purpose today, to make our country more just and generous, to affirm the dignity of our lives and every life.

This work continues. This story goes on. And an angel still rides in the whirlwind and directs this storm.

God bless you all, and God bless America. ◆

Lott Says Education Bill Comes First and Foremost With Bush; New Tax Code Next in Priority

Following are excerpts from a Jan. 24 speech by Senate Majority Leader Trent Lott, R-Miss., to the U.S. Chamber of Commerce. Transcript by eMediaMill-Works, Inc.

Let me talk about the agenda, talk about the things that we know the president's going to bring to this Congress and that we're going to deal with. . . .

You know for sure that education is right out the gate, number one. It's S 1 in the Senate, it's the first thing the president has sent up to us in a package, and we're going to work very hard to follow his blueprint and fundamentally change education in America. I'm the son of a schoolteacher, a lady that taught for 19 years. I went to public schools all my life from the 1st grade all the way through law school, and so did my wife, and so did my children. So I practice what I preach, unlike some people in this city.

But I also know that in certain ways we've lost ground in education. In some respects, education is doing a fantastic job. In others, it's not doing what it should. It's unequal. We have lost ground in fundamentals like reading, science and math. We have got to start thinking outside the box.

Some people say, if we just have more teachers and we just have nicer buildings, everything will be fine. No. No, it is about learning. It's not just about teaching. It's about what happens to the child. How can we make sure that our children are going to be able to read, and that they do it in a safe, drug-free school; that there is an opportunity for teachers that need help with more training can get that training? Quite often, you know, it's not the teacher's fault that he or she has not had an opportunity to get the training they need to be able to make use of computers. . . .

This is not going to be a deal. The way it usually works in Washington,

you just throw more money at the problem and say: "Good luck. By the way, here are all these strings. You must do it this way." No. We're going to have confidence in parents, teachers, administrators at the local level. There will be more money. It'll be targeted in certain areas like reading. But for the most part, more flexibility and accountability. . . .

And if you have any doubt that President Bush is committed to this, you should hear him speak. He speaks with knowledge, compassion and determination. We're going to make a difference in education in America, and that will be good for business. . . .

Cutting Taxes

Tax policy, surely this is going to be probably the second thing to, you know, actually come to the Congress with a proposal. And it will be about trying to make the tax code fairer by eliminating the marriage penalty tax and other things we've talked about, phasing out and hopefully eliminating the death tax.

But here is the area where you've got to be helpful. And I do think the across-the-board rate cuts will have the greatest impact on economic growth. But those of you that are in the business of creating jobs and dealing with the tax code and dealing with what you need for growth and jobs creation, again, you need to be involved in helping support the right kind of tax cut, not one that just addresses this little problem, that little problem, but how is it going to affect the overall economy? . . .

The president absolutely is committed to doing what's necessary for Medicare reform. We are going to have to have a prescription drug plan in America. I still have fundamental problems with — and I think he does — just saying to everybody, "We're going to subsidize your prescription drug needs." Why? A lot of people don't

need that subsidy.

He would like for us even to move quickly to address the needs of our elderly seniors by allowing the states the ability to design some programs to address this area. . . . We've got some great people already thinking about it. It's nice to have a doctor, Bill Frist [R-Tenn.], that will be working in that area. . . . We are going to have to deal with the Patients' Bill of Rights issue. But again, I think what we need there is a process to get a result and not just get a lawsuit. And we are going to have to deal with the scope and how we put it into place. . . .

Social Security, clearly he's going to make some recommendations on that. I still think it makes good sense to maybe have a blue-ribbon commission to take a look at that over a short period of time, include people like [former Sens.] Pat Moynihan [D-N.Y.] and Bill Roth [R-Del.] and the current members, Chuck Grassley [R-Iowa] and Max Baucus [D-Mont.], and maybe, you know, [former Sens.] Bob Kerrey [D-Neb.] and Bob Dole [R-Kan.]. I think they could come back with some pretty good ideas pretty quickly. And make it a base closure-type process: Here's the proposal, the president has to send it to us up or down, and we have to vote on it up or down.

But in the case of Social Security, with just three or four changes, we could protect that program for 90 years. We know what it is. We know how it can be done — I mean, just having an accurate CPI [consumer price index]. I thought we got very close to doing that two or three years ago. . . .

And then one thing I think we'll do pretty quickly is take a good, hard look at the Pentagon. We have lost ground in readiness. We are not meeting our needs for modernization. Morale is not what it should be, although it's better today than it was two weeks ago.

But I think Secretary of Defense

[Donald H.] Rumsfeld and President Bush are not just going to go in there and say, "Oh, geez, let's put billions of dollars in all these programs." I think they're going to take a good, serious, comprehensive look at where we are and where we want to be, in two years and in 20 years, and then they're going to come back and start seeing how we get there.

I had an opportunity to talk to the president last night in depth about a number of these issues, and I said, "You know, I think this idea of, you know, taking a good, long look at the Pentagon and making some changes and maybe changing the decisions on some of the programs, even if they might affect some that I feel very strongly about, is the right way to go."

I believe that two years from now, the men and women in our military will feel confident that we know about them; we care about them; they're going to have decent pay; they're going to have decent retirement; they're going to have decent health benefits; but most importantly, they're going to have what they need to do the job then and in the future. That is big, that's important, and I know President Bush is committed to that.

Now, one thing that may actually move faster in the legislative process, that's not in that agenda that he always enunciates, but one that clearly he understands, and has risen to the surface, is the need for national energy policy. Do we need it? Are some people getting the message that we're going to have to do a better job about exploration and making use of oil and gas and clean coal technology, maybe gold, too, I guess, and incentives for using other resources, conservation? But a national policy, we haven't had it.

I'm going to say it — I guess you're not supposed to say that here, but the extremists in this area have shut us down in many ways. And for us to be dependent on foreign oil, OPEC oil, Iraqi oil, without a policy of how we're going to deal with the short-term problem in California that could soon affect us all, but more importantly where are we going to be 10 years from now, that's unacceptable.

And when I look at the flow chart for the legislative schedule this year, we could have a national energy policy bill ready to go next week. You think Frank Murkowski [R-Alaska] hasn't got one in his coat pocket? He's walking around with it right now. Well, it would have to be massaged a little bit to address current problems. Will it be changed as we go along? Sure. But I think that when we start really looking at the calendar for the year, and when we can do things and when will they be ready, it takes a little time in the case of education. I hope clearly that bill is ready to go by the first of March. But they'll need to have some hearings, they'll have to have a markup.

But if we find a window in there of a week or so, the national energy policy could be a bill that we would move quicker than we would have expected, because of the change in the circumstances, and because some of these other bills may take a little longer. So there, again, that affects you as individuals, as ratepayers, as business and corporate leaders. Your companies are paying the bill. And if you don't have the power — I mean if the lights go out in Silicon Valley, there's a problem. . . .

Aviation and Railroads

Transportation. I feel very strongly about that. We've done some good work, you know. We've had the Tea 21 and the Air 21, and we've got to make sure that that money that we got going with Air 21 for aviation is used, used responsibly, as soon as possible; that we get good people to join — Norm Mineta in Transportation, at FAA — and that we really go forward with making sure that our transportation system in America, across the board and in aviation, that we have the facilities that are needed and that it is safe. And I think that that will receive a high priority.

But you can go down the list. Clearly, we will still — we've got to do the Amtrak bill because we promised we would do that. And I personally am for national rail passenger systems.

There are some in Congress that say, "It won't work. It will never work. It'll cost too much money. Let's kill it now." I don't think that's the way to go. And I want us to have a transportation system that includes our roads and air and rail and ports and harbors, all of it. And that's a part of America being able to be competitive in the future.

And also, I hope we can come up with a national rail passenger system that is clean, fast, efficient, doesn't waste money, that's responsible in how they operate their company, and that the people would use it. Now, if we can't do it, if they waste money on some of the ridiculous requirements of the past, or if the people in America don't ride them, then, you know, we won't have a national rail passenger system. But I think it's worth the effort.

And there'll be other areas we'll work on, from housing to other health care issues. And I'm sure there are many other bills that we didn't finish last year, or maybe you're thinking about for this year, that we will take up as we go along. . . .

But the main point I want to make today is, I feel renewed and invigorated. The Senate is going to be closely divided, as you well know. The Senate is always a difficult place to manage and to move forward. It's very easy in the Senate to delay a bill, kill a bill. If you're working from a negative standpoint, you can do a lot of mischief.

But I tried my very best this year to set the right tone and set up the right atmosphere in the Senate. We could be haggling right now over Rule 25 or Rule 22 or Rule 14 or reconciliation rules, but I didn't think that was the wise thing for the Senate, for this new president or for the American people.

And in ways that maybe are not obvious, it has affected the tone. It has affected some things that I've done, have been done or things that have not been done. Sometime in the Senate, if you just withhold from a shrill reaction or from an objection, that is a major accomplishment. That's one of the reasons I've worried about the nominations. And I continue to talk to Sen. [Tom] Daschle [D-S.D.] and to Sen. [Patrick J.] Leahy [D-Vt.] within the hour, saying, "Be careful. We've got, you know, this bipartisan tone that we've set, let's don't let this die aborning." You know, to ask legitimate questions, to have full debate, that's fine. Words are words, and we have to all spread them on the record. But actions and votes matter. . . .

And I'm optimistic. I'm excited that we're going to be able to get a lot of that done. Now, look, you know me, I've been here 28 years. I was the whip in the House. I used to be not just a spear catcher, I threw a few.

I know about partisanship, and I'm not dreaming. I'm not in the bliss basement. . . . Look, are we going to have some good fights? Healthy debates? Sure. Now, will I feel that the Democrats have, you know, broken faith with us here or there or the other? Perhaps. But, you know, different times require different approaches and different actions.

I am convinced you have to be a realist, but I'm also convinced that if you have a vision for your country, if you have a president that can rise above it and set a different tone and keep pushing ahead, and will stand and fight when he needs to, you can transform this place. We have seen it happen before. I'm excited that it could happen again, and it could be this year.

Thank you very much. ◆

Bush's First Press Conference Focuses on Foreign Policy, Budget and Clinton Pardons

Following are excerpts of President Bush's news conference Feb. 22, his first since taking office. Transcript provided by the White House.

BUSH: Good afternoon. It's been about a month now since I've taken office, and I thought it appropriate to come by and have a press conference. Before I do so, though, I'd like to make a few comments.

One of my missions has been to change the tone here in the nation's capital to encourage civil discourse. I think we're making pretty good progress. I want to thank the Democrats and the Republicans who have been coming up to the White House to hear me make my case. I appreciate their responsiveness. I just hope they vote for my agenda that I'll be submitting next week in a budget address to the Congress.

I have a reasonable and balanced budget. It meets growing needs with a responsible rate of increase in spending. It funds priorities. And my administration has no higher priority than education.

Yesterday I announced that the Department of Education will receive the largest percentage increase of any department in the federal government, a little more than an 11 percent increase. But with new money will come high expectations. We must insist on results and support programs that work. It is in the best interests of American children that we reform our public schools by having strong accountability at its core.

Our budget will honor commitments of America's senior citizens. Social Security and Medicare funds will be protected for Social Security and Medicare. We're now spending $216 billion on Medicare. Under my budget, Medicare spending will increase by more than $21 billion in 2002. My budget also locks away $2.6 trillion of the $5.6 trillion surplus for Social Se-

curity over the next 10 years.

Our budget is fiscally responsible. If enacted, it will reduce debt by an unprecedented amount over the next four years. Altogether, about 60 percent of the projected federal surplus will be used to fund priorities and to reduce debt.

After we've funded our priorities, after we pay down an unprecedented amount of debt, we'll still have money left over, which leaves us with two options — first is to spend it on bigger government, or to return it to the taxpayers who earned it. I believe it should be returned to the taxpayers. It's the people's money, and the government ought to be passing it back after it's met priorities.

It is also necessary because these are uncertain times — increasing layoffs, growing consumer debt, lower consumer confidence — and lower taxes will help our economy. This will be a responsible and fair budget that reflects the nation's priorities. I invite the American people to listen to what I have to say to the Congress.

I will be glad to answer any questions you have. . . .

Q: Do you believe that pardons were for sale in the Clinton White House? And what specifically do you think should be done to look into, to investigate the circumstances of the president's brother-in-law accepting money to lobby him on pardons?

BUSH: As far as this White House is concerned, it's time to go forward. I have too much to do to get a budget passed, to get reforms passed for education, to get a tax cut passed, to strengthen the military, than to be worrying about decisions that my predecessor made.

I understand there's going to be some people on Capitol Hill that are going to be asking questions. That's their right to do so. But I can assure you our White House is moving forward. And to the extent the Justice

Department looks into this matter, it will be done in a non-political way. During John Ashcroft's confirmation process, I said that the Justice Department will conduct its business in a non-political way, and we will do so. . . .

Q: Mr. President, do you think that U.S.-Russian relations have been damaged by the new spy case? And secondly, are the Russians showing any flexibility on a missile defense system?

BUSH: I intend to deal with Mr. Putin [the Russian president] in a very straightforward way, to be up front with him on all matters. I am, of course, disturbed about the espionage — the alleged espionage that took place. I'm mindful that there are people who don't particularly care what America stands for, and people who are interested in our secrets.

Secondly, I was pleased to see comments from Russian leadership that talked about missile defense. It is a — their words indicate that they recognize that there are new threats in the post-Cold War era; threats that require theater-based anti-ballistic missile systems. I felt those words were encouraging.

When I meet with Mr. Putin I'm going to talk to him about exactly what he meant by those words. We have no meeting set up yet, I might add. But I took that to be encouraging, Steve. It reminded me of what happened after I met with Mr. Ivanov [the Russian foreign minister]. Shortly thereafter, Mr. Putin also talked about theater-based systems and the ability to intercept missiles on launch. And to me, it's indicative of his recognition of the realities of the true threats in the post-Cold War era — threats from an accidental launch, or threats as a result of a leader in what they call a rogue nation, trying to hold ourselves or our allies or Russia, for that matter, hostage. So I was pleased with what I saw.

Q: Sir, the secretary of State is departing for the Middle East tomorrow.

One of the things that he will be discussing with Middle East leaders is the possibility of modifying sanctions on Iraq, and I'm wondering what message he will take from this administration to leaders in the Middle East in the area of sanctions that matter, sanctions that are effective on the regime, but do not carry with them the same level of criticism that current sanctions have had in that they affect the Iraqi civilian population more than they do the regime, sir.

BUSH: We're reviewing all policy in all regions of the world, and one of the areas we've been spending a lot of time on is the Persian Gulf and the Middle East. The secretary of State is going to go listen to our allies as to how best to effect a policy, the primary goal of which will be to say to [Iraqi President] Saddam Hussein, we won't tolerate you developing weapons of mass destruction and we expect you to leave your neighbors alone.

I have said that the sanction regime is like Swiss cheese. That meant that they weren't very effective. And we're going to review current sanction policy, and review options as to how to make the sanctions work.

But the primary goal is to make it clear to Saddam that we expect him to be a peaceful neighbor in the region and we expect him not to develop weapons of mass destruction. And if we find him doing so, there will be a consequence. We took action last week, and it may be on your mind as to that decision I made. The mission was twofold — one was to send him a clear message that this administration will remain engaged in that part of the world. I think we accomplished that mission. We got his attention.

And secondly, the mission was to degrade his capacity to harm our pilots who might be flying in the no-fly zone. And we accomplished that mission, as well. . . .

Q: Mr. President, if I can go back to the controversy surrounding former President Clinton and Sen. Hillary Rodham Clinton [D-N.Y.] — are you at all concerned that these controversies are serving as a distraction for your administration's agenda? . . .

Bush: As I've said earlier, I've got a lot of work to do, and I think I've got the Congress' attention. I certainly hope so.

There has been a lot of discussion about tax relief, and I'm pleased with the progress being made on that important subject. There's a lot of hot debate that have already taken place, and we've just begun to make the case. I'm beginning to travel around the country to important states — all the states are important, of course, but some states may be more important than others right now in trying to convince some lawmakers to hear the message of the people.

This is an issue that affects everybody who pays taxes. Congress is listening to the debate. They're participating in the debate. There's a lot of discussion about education reform on the Hill, and I'm confident that the focus will be the right focus. And my speech Tuesday night I hope will help keep the focus on the agenda. . . .

Q: You said that your $1.6 trillion tax cut is reasonable and responsible within the outlines of the budget you're going to present. If, when that gets to Congress, things start getting layered on to it, like corporate tax cuts, capital gains, would you still support it? And if it reached your desk at a higher level, would you sign it?

BUSH: I'm going to resist the Christmas tree effect of tax policy. I don't want people putting ornaments on my plan. I have made it clear to the business interests that the best tax policy is one that reduces the taxes on the people, and I hope they listen to me and I hope they help me get the tax plan through that I have proposed.

And the reason I feel so strongly about that is, one, a marginal cut will help the economy. Secondly, I am deeply concerned about high energy prices and their effect on the working people in the country.

I am concerned about consumer debt. I know there's a lot of talk in Washington about paying down the national debt, and that's fine and good, and our budget will do so. But I am very concerned about the fact that a lot of consumers in our country have got high consumer debt. And I believe we need to share some of their money with them so they can help manage their own personal finances. And I will resist the temptation by folks to pile on their pet projects on to our tax cut.

Q: But if they do pile on?

BUSH: Well, first of all, I'm not willing to admit defeat right here before I've begun to fight. . . . I think I've got a pretty good case, and I think that many of the business interests will hear that case. . . .

Q: Mr. President, to follow up on your answer on the tax question, perhaps looking at it the other way, some people are saying that perhaps it's too large a tax cut.

BUSH: Some are saying it's too small, some are saying it's too large, and I'm saying it's just right.

Q: You were not willing to be flexible in terms of people who want to increase the size. Are you willing to be flexible with people who want to lower the size of your tax cut?

BUSH: I think it's just right. We've thought long and hard about the right number. This is a well-planned-out tax relief package that addresses the concerns of working Americans. . . . There is a choice we have to make: Once we meet priorities, do we increase the size of the government, or do we increase the amount of money in the pockets of the people who are working for a living? It is the right size, and it is the right time for tax relief in the country.

Q: Mr. President, you've talked a lot about areas of the budget that are going to increase — education; today you talked about Medicare; you've talked before a little bit about defense. You haven't talked much about the areas where, to come in with a budget that's going to be responsible, you'll have to do some cuts. . . .

BUSH: Let me remind you, and the people who are listening, that accounting in Washington is a little different than the way . . . the average person accounts. This is a town where if you don't increase the budget by an expected number, it's considered a cut.

We're going to slow the rate of growth of the budget down. It should come to no surprise to anybody that my budget is going to say loud and clear that the rate of growth of the budget, for example, from last year, was excessive. . . . I will be glad to explain some of the slowdowns and some of the increases and perhaps a decrease or two after we put the budget out. ◆

Bush Says Budget Would Pay Down Debt While Aiding Schools, Retirees, Military

Following is a transcript of President Bush's address to a joint session of Congress on Feb. 27. Transcript provided by eMediaMillWorks Inc.

Thank you very much. Thank you very much. Thank you.

Mr. Speaker, Mr. Vice President, members of Congress, it's a great privilege to be here to outline a new budget and a new approach for governing our great country.

I thank you for your invitation to speak here tonight. I know Congress had to formally invite me, and it could have been a close vote.

So, Mr. Vice President, I appreciate you being here to break the tie.

I want to thank so many of you who have accepted my invitation to come to the White House to discuss important issues. We're off to a good start.

I will continue to meet with you and ask for your input. You have been kind and candid, and I thank you for making a new president feel welcome.

The last time I visited the Capitol, I came to take an oath. On the steps of this building, I pledged to honor our Constitution and laws. And I asked you to join me in setting a tone of civility and respect in Washington.

I hope America is noticing the difference, because we are making progress. Together we are changing the tone in the nation's capital. And this spirit of respect and cooperation is vital, because, in the end, we will be judged not only by what we say or how we say it, we will be judged by what we are able to accomplish.

America today is a nation with great challenges, but greater resources. An artist using statistics as a brush could paint two very different pictures of our country. One would have warning signs: increasing layoffs, rising energy prices, too many failing schools, persistent poverty, the stubborn vestiges of racism.

Another picture would be full of blessings: a balanced budget, big surpluses, a military that is second to none, a country at peace with its neighbors, technology that is revolutionizing the world, and our greatest strength: concerned citizens who care for our country and care for each other.

Neither picture is complete in and of itself. And tonight I challenge and invite Congress to work with me to use the resources of one picture to repaint the other, to direct the advantages of our time to solve the problems of our people.

Some of these resources will come from government — some, but not all. Year after year in Washington, budget debates seem to come down to an old, tired argument: on one side, those who want more government, regardless of the cost; on the other, those who want less government, regardless of the need.

We should leave those arguments to the last century and chart a different course.

Government has a role and an important role. Yet too much government crowds out initiative and hard work, private charity and the private economy. Our new governing vision says government should be active, but limited; engaged, but not overbearing.

And my budget is based on that philosophy. It is reasonable, and it is responsible. It meets our obligations, and funds our growing needs.

We increase spending next year for Social Security and Medicare and other entitlement programs by $81 billion. We have increased spending for discretionary programs by a very responsible 4 percent above the rate of inflation. My plan pays down an unprecedented amount of our national debt. And then when money is still left over, my plan returns it to the people who earned it in the first place.

A budget's impact is counted in dollars but measured in lives. Excellent schools, quality health care, a secure retirement, a cleaner environment, a stronger defense — these are all important needs, and we fund them.

The highest percentage increase in our budget should go to our children's education. Education is my top priority, and by supporting this budget, you will make it yours as well.

Reading is the foundation of all learning, so during the next five years, we triple spending, adding $5 billion to help every child in America learn to read. Values are important, so we've tripled funding for character education to teach our children not only reading and writing, but right from wrong.

We've increased funding to train and recruit teachers, because we know a good education starts with a good teacher. And I have a wonderful partner in this effort.

I like teachers so much I married one. Laura has begun a new effort to recruit Americans to the profession that will shape our future: teaching. She will travel across America to promote sound teaching practices and early reading skills in our schools and in programs such as Head Start.

When it comes to our schools, dollars alone do not always make the difference. Funding is important and so is reform, so we must tie funding to higher standards and accountability, for results.

I believe in local control of schools. We should not and we will not run public schools from Washington, D.C.

Yet when the federal government spends tax dollars, we must insist on results. Children should be tested on basic reading and math skills every year between grades three and eight. Measuring is the only way to know whether all our children are learning. And I want to know, because I refuse to leave any child behind in America.

Critics of testing contend it distracts from learning. They talk about "teaching to the test." But let's put that logic to the test. If you test a child on basic math and reading skills, and you are "teaching to the test," you are teaching math and reading. And that's the whole idea.

As standards rise, local schools will need more flexibility to meet them. So we must streamline the dozens of fed-

eral education programs into five and let states spend money in those categories as they see fit.

Schools will be given a reasonable chance to improve and the support to do so. Yet if they don't, if they continue to fail, we must give parents and students different options: a better public school, a private school, tutoring or a charter school.

In the end, every child in a bad situation must be given a better choice, because when it comes to our children, failure is simply not an option.

Another priority in my budget is to keep the vital promises of Medicare and Social Security, and together we will do so. To meet the health care needs of all America's seniors, we double the Medicare budget over the next 10 years.

My budget dedicates $238 billion to Medicare next year alone, enough to fund all current programs and to begin a new prescription drug benefit for low-income seniors. No senior in America should have to choose between buying food and buying prescriptions.

To make sure the retirement savings of America's seniors are not diverted to any other program, my budget protects all $2.6 trillion of the Social Security surplus for Social Security and for Social Security alone.

My budget puts a priority on access to health care without telling Americans what doctor they have to see or what coverage they must choose.

Many working Americans do not have health care coverage, so we will help them buy their own insurance with refundable tax credits.

And to provide quality care in low-income neighborhoods, over the next five years we will double the number of people served at community health care centers.

And we will address the concerns of those who have health coverage yet worry their insurance company doesn't care and will not pay.

Together, this Congress and this president will find common ground to make sure doctors make medical decisions and patients get the health care they deserve with a patients' bill of rights.

When it comes to their health, people want to get the medical care they need, not be forced to go to court because they didn't get it. We will ensure access to the courts for those with legitimate claims. But first, let's put in place a strong, independent review so we promote quality health care, not frivolous lawsuits.

My budget also increases funding for medical research, which gives hope to many who struggle with serious disease. Our prayers tonight are with one of your own who is engaged in his own fight against cancer, a fine representative and a good man, Congressman Joe Moakley. God bless you, Joe.

And I can think of no more appropriate tribute to Joe than to have the Congress finish the job of doubling the budget for the National Institutes of Health.

My New Freedom Initiative for Americans with disabilities funds new technologies, expands opportunities to work and makes our society more welcoming. For the more than 50 million Americans with disabilities, we must continue to break down barriers to equality.

The budget I propose to you also supports the people who keep our country strong and free, the men and women who serve in the United States military.

I am requesting $5.7 billion in increased military pay and benefits and health care and housing. Our men and women in uniform give America their best, and we owe them our support.

America's veterans honored their commitment to our country through their military service. I will honor our commitment to them with a billion dollar increase to ensure better access to quality care and faster decisions on benefit claims.

My budget will improve our environment by accelerating the cleanup of toxic brownfields. And I propose we make a major investment in conservation by fully funding the Land and Water Conservation Fund.

Our national parks have a special place in our country's life. Our parks are places of great natural beauty and history. As good stewards, we must leave them better than we found them, so I propose providing $4.9 billion over five years for the upkeep of these national treasures.

And my budget adopts a hopeful new approach to help the poor and the disadvantaged. We must encourage and support the work of charities and faith-based and community groups that offer help and love one person at a time.

These groups are working in every neighborhood in America to fight homelessness and addiction and domestic violence, to provide a hot meal or a mentor or a safe haven for our children. Government should welcome these groups to apply for funds, not discriminate against them.

Government cannot be replaced by charities or volunteers. Government should not fund religious activities.

But our nation should support the good works of these good people who are helping their neighbors in need. So I propose allowing all taxpayers, whether they itemize or not, to deduct their charitable contributions. Estimates show this could encourage as much as $14 billion a year in new charitable giving, money that will save and change lives.

Our budget provides more than $700 million over the next 10 years for a Federal Compassion Capital Fund with a focused and noble mission: to provide a mentor to the more than 1 million children with a parent in prison and to support other local efforts to fight illiteracy, teen pregnancy, drug addiction and other difficult problems.

With us tonight is the mayor of Philadelphia. Please help me welcome Mayor John Street. Mayor Street has encouraged faith-based and community organizations to make a significant difference in Philadelphia. He's invited me to his city this summer to see compassion in action.

I'm personally aware of just how effective the mayor is. Mayor Street's a Democrat. Let the record show, I lost his city, big time.

But some things are bigger than politics, so I look forward to coming to your city to see your faith-based programs in action.

As government promotes compassion, it also must promote justice. Too many of our citizens have cause to doubt our nation's justice when the law points a finger of suspicion at groups instead of individuals. All our citizens are created equal and must be

treated equally.

Earlier today, I asked John Ashcroft, the attorney general, to develop specific recommendations to end racial profiling. It's wrong, and we will end it in America.

In so doing, we will not hinder the work of our nation's brave police officers. They protect us every day, often at great risk. But by stopping the abuses of a few, we will add to the public confidence our police officers earn and deserve.

My budget has funded a responsible increase in our ongoing operations. It has funded our nation's important priorities. It has protected Social Security and Medicare. And our surpluses are big enough that there is still money left over.

Many of you have talked about the need to pay down our national debt. I listened, and I agree.

We owe it to our children and grandchildren to act now, and I hope you will join me to pay down $2 trillion in debt during the next 10 years. At the end of those 10 years, we will have paid down all the debt that is available to retire.

That is more debt repaid more quickly than has ever been repaid by any nation at any time in history.

We should also prepare for the unexpected, for the uncertainties of the future. We should approach our nation's budget as any prudent family would, with a contingency fund for emergencies or additional spending needs.

For example, after a strategic review, we may need to increase defense spending, we may need to increase spending for our farmers or additional money to reform Medicare. And so my budget sets aside almost a trillion dollars over 10 years for additional needs. That is one trillion additional reasons you can feel comfortable supporting this budget.

We have increased our budget at a responsible 4 percent. We have funded our priorities. We paid down all the available debt. We have prepared for contingencies. And we still have money left over.

Yogi Berra once said, "When you come to a fork in the road, take it." Now we come to a fork in the road. We have two choices. Even though we have already met our needs, we could spend the money on more and bigger government. That's the road our nation has traveled in recent years.

Last year, government spending shot up 8 percent. That's far more than our economy grew, far more than personal income grew and far more than the rate of inflation. If you continue on that road, you will spend the surplus and have to dip into Social Security to pay other bills. Unrestrained government spending is a dangerous road to deficits, so we must take a different path.

The other choice is to let the American people spend their own money to meet their own needs.

I hope you'll join me in standing firmly on the side of the people. You see, the growing surplus exists because taxes are too high, and government is charging more than it needs. The people of America have been overcharged, and, on their behalf, I'm here asking for a refund.

Some say my tax plan is too big. Others say it's too small. I respectfully disagree. This plan is just right.

I didn't throw darts at a board to come up with a number for tax relief. I didn't take a poll or develop an arbitrary formula that might sound good. I looked at problems in the tax code and calculated the cost to fix them.

A tax rate of 15 percent is too high for those who earned low wages, so we must lower the rate to 10 percent. No one should pay more than a third of the money they earn in federal income taxes, so we lowered the top rate to 33 percent.

This reform will be welcome relief for America's small businesses, which often pay taxes at the highest rate. And help for small business means jobs for Americans.

We simplified the tax code by reducing the number of tax rates from the current five rates to four lower ones: 10 percent, 15, 25 and 33 percent. In my plan, no one is targeted in or targeted out. Everyone who pays income taxes will get relief.

Our government should not tax and thereby discourage marriage, so we reduced the marriage penalty.

I want to help families rear and support their children, so we doubled the child credit to $1,000 per child.

It's not fair to tax the same earnings twice, once when you earn them and again when you die, so we must repeal the death tax.

These changes add up to significant help. A typical family with two children will save $1,600 a year on their federal income taxes.

Now, $1,600 may not sound like a lot to some, but it means a lot to many families: $1,600 buys gas for two cars for an entire year. It pays tuition for a year at a community college. It pays the average family grocery bill for three months. That's real money.

With us tonight, representing many American families, are Steven and Josefina Ramos. They are from Pennsylvania, but they could be from any one of your districts. Steven is a network administrator for a school district. Josefina is a Spanish teacher at a charter school. And they have a 2-year-old daughter.

Steven and Josefina tell me they pay almost $8,000 a year in federal income taxes. My plan will save them more than $2,000.

Let me tell you what Steven says: "$2,000 a year means a lot to my family. If we had this money, it would help us reach our goal of paying off our personal debt in two years' time." After that, Steven and Josefina want to start saving for Lianna's college education.

My attitude is, government should never stand in the way of families achieving their dreams.

And as we debate this issue, always remember: The surplus is not the government's money; the surplus is the people's money.

For lower-income families, my tax plan restores basic fairness. Right now, complicated tax rules punish hard work. A waitress supporting two children on $25,000 a year can lose nearly half of every additional dollar she earns above the $25,000. Her overtime, her hardest hours, are taxed at nearly 50 percent. This sends a terrible message: You will never get ahead.

But America's message must be different. We must honor hard work, never punish it.

With tax relief, overtime will no longer be overtax time for the waitress.

People with the smallest incomes will get the highest percentage of reductions, and millions of additional

American families will be removed from the income tax rolls entirely.

Tax relief is right, and tax relief is urgent. The long economic expansion that began almost 10 years ago is faltering. Lower interest rates will eventually help, but we cannot assume they will do the job all by themselves.

Forty years ago, and then 20 years ago, two presidents, one Democrat, one Republican, John F. Kennedy and Ronald Reagan, advocated tax cuts to, in President Kennedy's words, "get this country moving again."

They knew then what we must do now: To create economic growth and opportunity, we must put money back into the hands of the people who buy goods and create jobs.

We must act quickly. The chairman of the Federal Reserve has testified before Congress that tax cuts often come too late to stimulate economic recovery. So I want to work with you to give our economy an important jump start by making tax relief retroactive.

We must act now because it is the right thing to do. We must also act now because we have other things to do. We must show courage to confront and resolve tough challenges: to restructure our nation's defenses, to meet our growing need for energy, and to reform Medicare and Social Security.

America has a window of opportunity to extend and secure our present peace by promoting a distinctly American internationalism. We will work with our allies and friends to be a force for good and a champion of freedom. We will work for free markets, free trade and freedom from oppression. Nations making progress toward freedom will find America is their friend.

We will promote our values. We'll promote the peace. And we need a strong military to keep the peace.

But our military was shaped to confront the challenges of the past, so I have asked the secretary of defense to review America's armed forces and prepare to transform them to meet emerging threats.

My budget makes a down payment on the research and development that will be required. Yet, in our broader transformation effort, we must put strategy first, then spending. Our defense vision will drive our defense budget, not the other way around.

Our nation also needs a clear strategy to confront the threats of the 21st century, threats that are more widespread and less certain. They range from terrorists who threaten with bombs to tyrants and rogue nations intent on developing weapons of mass destruction.

To protect our own people, our allies and friends, we must develop and we must deploy effective missile defenses. And as we transform our military, we can discard Cold War relics and reduce our own nuclear forces to reflect today's needs. A strong America is the world's best hope for peace and freedom.

Yet the cause of freedom rests on more than our ability to defend ourselves and our allies. Freedom is exported every day as we ship goods and products that improve the lives of millions of people. Free trade brings greater political and personal freedom.

Each of the previous five presidents has had the ability to negotiate far-reaching trade agreements. Tonight, I ask you to give me the strong hand of presidential trade promotion authority and to do so quickly.

As we meet tonight, many citizens are struggling with the high cost of energy. We have a serious energy problem that demands a national energy policy.

The West is confronting a major energy shortage that has resulted in high prices and uncertainty. I have asked federal agencies to work with California officials to help speed construction of new energy sources. And I have directed Vice President [Dick] Cheney, Commerce Secretary [Don] Evans, Energy Secretary [Spencer] Abraham and other senior members of my administration to develop a national energy policy.

Our energy demand outstrips our supply. We can produce more energy at home while protecting our environment, and we must. We can produce more electricity to meet demand, and we must. We can promote alternative energy sources and conservation, and we must. America must become more energy independent, and we will.

Perhaps the biggest test of our foresight and courage will be reforming Medicare and Social Security.

Medicare's finances are strained and its coverage is outdated. Ninety-nine percent of employer-provided health plans offer some form of prescription drug coverage. Medicare does not.

The framework for reform has been developed by Sens. [Bill] Frist [R-Tenn.] and [John B.] Breaux [D-La.] and Congressman [Bill] Thomas [R-Calif.], and now is the time to act.

Medicare must be modernized, and we must make sure that every senior on Medicare can choose a health care plan that offers prescription drugs.

Seven years from now, the Baby Boom generation will begin to claim Social Security benefits. Everyone in this chamber knows that Social Security is not prepared to fully fund their retirement, and we only have a couple of years to get prepared.

Without reform, this country will one day awaken to a stark choice: either a drastic rise in payroll taxes, or a radical cut in retirement benefits. There's a better way.

This spring I will form a presidential commission to reform Social Security. The commission will make its recommendations by next fall. Reform should be based on these principles: It must preserve the benefits of all current retirees and those nearing retirement. It must return Social Security to sound financial footing. And it must offer personal savings accounts to younger workers who want them.

Social Security now offers workers a return of less than 2 percent on the money they pay into the system. To save the system, we must increase that by allowing younger workers to make safe, sound investments that yield a higher rate of return.

Ownership, access to wealth, and independence should not be the privilege of a few. They are the hope of every American, and we must make them the foundation of Social Security.

By confronting the tough challenge of reform, by being responsible with our budget, we can earn the trust of the American people. And we can add to that trust by enacting fair and balanced election and campaign reforms.

The agenda I have set before you tonight is worthy of a great nation. America is a nation at peace, but not a nation at rest. Much has been given to us and much is expected.

Let us agree to bridge old divides.

But let us also agree that our good will must be dedicated to great goals. Bipartisanship is more than minding our manners, it is doing our duty.

No one can speak in this Capitol and not be awed by its history. At so many turning points, debates in these chambers have reflected the collected or divided conscience of our country. And when we walk through Statuary Hall and see those men and women of marble, we are reminded of their courage and achievement.

Yet America's purpose is never found only in statues or history. America's purpose always stands before us.

Our generation must show courage in a time of blessing as our nation has always shown in times of crisis. And our courage, issue by issue, can gather to greatness and serve our country. This is the privilege and responsibility we share. And if we work together, we can prove that public service is noble.

We all came here for a reason. We all have things we want to accomplish and promises to keep. *Juntos podemos*, together we can.

We can make Americans proud of their government. Together, we can share in the credit of making our country more prosperous and generous and just, and earn from our conscience and from our fellow citizens, the highest possible praise, "Well done, good and faithful servants."

Thank you all. Good night, and God bless. ◆

Democratic Rebuttal to Bush's Speech Emphasizes Social Security, Medicare

Following is a transcript of the Democratic response to President Bush's address Feb. 27 to a joint session of Congress. The speakers are House Minority Leader Richard A. Gephardt, D-Mo., and Senate Minority Leader Tom Daschle, D-S.D. Transcript provided by eMediaMillWorks Inc.

GEPHARDT: Good evening. I'm Dick Gephardt from Missouri, Democratic leader in the House of Representatives.

DASCHLE: And I'm Tom Daschle of South Dakota, the Democratic leader in the Senate.

Tonight, our nation's Capitol was filled with hope as our new president spoke to Congress for the first time about his priorities for America. Now we'd like to take a few minutes to speak to the American people, to those we are fortunate to represent in South Dakota and Missouri and across America, the hard-working Americans who deserve a booming and vibrant economy, the seniors who seek security in retirement after a lifetime of hard work.

We want to speak to the teachers and students who are striving to master the ideas of a new century in crowded classrooms built in the last century, and to all Americans who want to know that in the halls of our government, their voices are heard and their priorities matter.

We believe, as they do, that America's prosperity must work for all Americans. When President Bush proposes ideas that bring us closer to that goal, like his literacy initiative or increases in military pay, we will work with him, and work hard, to turn those ideas into laws. When he makes proposals with which we disagree, we'll work with him to find common ground.

But when he insists on proposals that threaten the prosperity of all Americans or that harm Social Security or Medicare, we will fight, and fight hard, to put the interests of working families first.

Tonight we begin a debate that will profoundly affect the strength of America's working families for years, perhaps generations, to come. The prosperity that you have built these last eight years has given us all a chance to live better lives at every age. But this opportunity will be squandered if we repeat the mistakes of a generation ago.

In 1981, Dick and I sat in the House chamber when another new president talked to the American people about stimulating our economy. The words spoken that evening were strikingly similar to the message we heard tonight. We were promised that if we gave huge tax cuts to the wealthiest Americans, the benefits would trickle down, deficits would disappear and the economy would flourish.

Congress supported that experiment. It was a huge mistake. As President Bush's own Treasury secretary, Paul O'Neill, said recently, it put America "in a ditch that was horrendous."

Deficits skyrocketed. The national debt quadrupled. High interest rates choked American industries. Unemployment soared. Working families struggled to meet their mortgages, to pay for health care and save for college.

It took us 18 years, four acts of Congress, and a lot of hard work by the American people to get out of that ditch. But working together, we turned record deficits into record surpluses. Freed from the dead weight of deficits, you did what Americans do best. You worked hard; you created the longest economic expansion in history.

And now America has a choice. What shall we do with the blessings of our new prosperity? Our first priority must be to continue paying down the trillions of dollars in federal debt Washington ran up in the 1980s. We can't just pass this debt onto our children, not when we have the ability to pay it off.

By paying down the debt, we'll also keep interest rates low, which will mean real savings for every American family. We agree with the president.

We want a significant tax cut this year.

But we want a different kind — a tax cut that is part of a responsible budget, that lets us pay off the debt and invest in America's future, one that is fair to all Americans. President Bush's plan doesn't do those things.

Think about your own family budget. Imagine you hadn't saved for your retirement, when you owed money on your credit cards and you couldn't afford health insurance, then you're told you might get some extra money sometime down the road. What would you do?

Under the president's approach, you would spend the money immediately — money that you might never see — without taking care of your debts, your medical bills or your retirement. You wouldn't do that, and neither should we. But that's exactly what the president proposed tonight.

Let's take a closer look: First, the president's tax plan is far more expensive than the $1.6 trillion he claimed.

When you add the interest on the debt and all the other hidden costs, the true cost of the president's tax cut is well over $2 trillion. It will consume nearly all of the available surplus, at the expense of prescription drug coverage, education, defense and other critical priorities.

Even worse, instead of strengthening Social Security and Medicare, the president's plan actually takes money from both programs, and that is irresponsible, and it's wrong.

Worse still, the president's plan depends far too heavily on a 10-year budget estimate, which is no more reliable than a 10-year weather forecast. And there's no room for error.

Nobody's crystal ball is that good. Just ask Texas. Two years ago, using rosy forecasts, then-Gov. Bush signed a budget that cut taxes by $1.8 billion. But his budget projections were wrong. And today, Texas faces a serious budget shortfall.

If his budget predictions now are as faulty as they were then, his tax cut would bring huge deficits, increase the

national debt and put our economy back in the ditch.

Finally, the president's plan is deeply unfair to middle-income Americans. The wealthiest 1 percent, people who make an average of over $900,000 a year, get 43 percent of the president's tax cut. The president also wants to eliminate the estate tax for the wealthiest of the wealthy.

Democrats want to make it easier for you to pass on your family farm and small business to the next generation, and our estate tax plan does that.

But the president's proposal provides so much to America's wealthiest families that they themselves are calling it a mistake. Bill Gates Sr., Warren Buffett, members of the Rockefeller family have said that it gives so much to so few that it will actually force tax increases or cuts in Social Security and Medicare and other essential programs. They're right, and the president's estate tax cut is only part of the reason.

Let us be clear: All Americans deserve a tax cut. But surely, the wealthiest among us should not get it at the expense of working families. There's a better way.

GEPHARDT: Thank you, Tom.

Democrats have a better plan, a balanced plan that treats the national budget the way you treat your household budget.

Our plan provides $900 billion in tax cuts for all Americans. Our plan protects every dollar of the Social Security and Medicare trust funds. It strengthens Medicare and adds an affordable prescription drug benefit so seniors don't have to choose between food and medicine. It strengthens Social Security rather than subjecting it to a volatile stock market, so that it will be there, not only for the baby boomers, but for their children and their grandchildren.

Our plan enables us to keep paying down the national debt, the debt we ran up in the '80s, so we can keep interest rates low and keep our economy growing. And it invests in the future of our country, by making sure every child can get an excellent education at a first-rate public school.

The president touched on many of these goals tonight, but we can't accomplish any of them if we spend the entire surplus on the president's tax cut. If what the president said tonight sounded too good to be true, it probably is.

Education is one of our highest priorities, and we believe that strengthening public schools is one of our greatest challenges. The president has made education an important part of his agenda, and, in this, he has our support.

We have differences with his plan. Like most Americans, we don't support spending public money for private school vouchers, and we will never support a reduction in the federal commitment to underserved children and communities.

We'll work with the president to increase literacy, demand accountability and improve every public school. But with tax cuts consuming almost all of the projected surplus, he cannot possibly keep his commitment to leave no child behind.

Millions of seniors depend on Social Security and Medicare, and we have a responsibility to preserve and protect them. We made promises. We need to keep them.

The president said he's dedicated to preserving Social Security and Medicare. We take him at his word. But the president's plan threatens these critical programs.

His plan fails to set aside the resources Social Security and Medicare will need in the future and uses them instead to pay for his tax cut.

All seniors need prescription drug coverage. Democrats believe we should use part of the surplus to provide a reliable, affordable Medicare prescription drug benefit for all seniors. The president has a different approach. His plan excludes millions of middle-income seniors who don't have prescription coverage and need it.

We want to work with the president to solve the prescription drug problem the right way. But we can't add a Medicare prescription drug benefit, we can't improve public schools, we can't address any of our highest priorities if the president does not scale back the excesses of his tax plan.

President Bush's numbers just don't add up. Ours do. His plan leaves no money for anything except tax cuts. Ours does. Our plan is better. It invests in the greatest needs and highest priorities of our country.

The conversation we begin tonight is more than a struggle over this year's budget; it's really about our future. It's about the most important decisions this generation of Americans will make for a very long time to come.

Our country is strong. But we can make it stronger by fighting for stronger families with a higher minimum wage, a patients' bill of rights, safer schools, safer streets and a cleaner environment; by fighting for a stronger economy with a budget that extends the greatest economic expansion in American history; by fighting for a stronger democracy with real campaign finance reform and a renewed commitment to fair and modern elections.

The challenge of writing a budget that is fair and responsible is considerable, but we face other challenges just as great.

All across America, too many people have lost faith in the fundamental principle of democracy, the principle of one person, one vote. We must act to restore their confidence. We should not leave this session of Congress without reforming our election process. Our democracy depends on it.

In addition, too many in Washington and too many Americans have lost faith in the possibility of principled compromise. With Congress so closely divided, some would say that finding common ground is simply impossible. We refuse to believe that. We are determined to steer our country on a more productive course.

We recognize that the president campaigned on an agenda. So did we.

Where our agendas coincide, let's make quick progress for the people. Where our agendas differ, we ask the president to demonstrate his leadership by reaching out for the benefit of all Americans. If he extends his hand, we will grasp it. Tonight, we extend ours.

The things that are most meaningful in our lives often require real effort to meet others halfway: business partnerships, friendships, marriages. It's the same with our democracy. We can do what the people sent us here to do if the president is willing to join us in the middle.

We believe that making America better is the greatest work of all. It is to that task that we pledge ourselves tonight. ◆

Jeffords Says 'Substantive Reservations' About President's Agenda Prompted His Split With GOP

Following is a transcript of Sen. James M. Jeffords' May 24 announcement in Burlington, Vt., that he is leaving the Republican Party to become an independent. Transcript provided by eMediaMillWorks Inc.

JEFFORDS: Good morning, everyone.

Anyone that knows me knows I love Vermont. Vermont has always been known for its independence and social conscience. It was the first state to outlaw slavery in its constitution. It proudly elected Matthew Lyon to Congress, notwithstanding his flouting of the Sedition Act.

It sacrificed a higher share of its sons in the Civil War than perhaps any other state in the Union. And I recall Vermont Sen. Ralph Flanders' dramatic statement 50 years ago, helping to bring the close on the McCarthy hearings — a sorry chapter in our history.

Today's chapter is of much smaller consequence. But I think it appropriate that I share my thoughts with my fellow Vermonters.

For the past several weeks, I have been struggling with a very difficult decision. It's difficult on a personal level, but even more difficult because of the larger impact in the Senate and also the nation. I have been talking with my family and a few close advisers about whether or not I should remain a Republican.

I do not approach this question lightly. I have spent a lifetime in the Republican Party and served 12 years in what I believe is the longest continuously held Republican seat in history. I ran for re-election as a Republican just this past fall, and had no thoughts whatsoever, then, about changing parties.

The party I grew up in was the party of George Aiken, Ernest Gibson, Ralph Flanders, Winston Prouty and Bob Stafford. These names may not mean much today outside Vermont, but each served Vermont as a Republican senator in the 20th century.

I became a Republican, not because I was born into the party, but because of the kind of fundamental principles that these and many Republicans stood for: moderation, tolerance, fiscal responsibility. Their party — our party — was the party of Lincoln.

To be sure, we had our differences in the Vermont Republican Party, but even our more conservative leaders were in many ways progressive.

Our former governor, Dean Davis, championed Act 250, which preserved our environmental heritage.

And Vermont's Calvin Coolidge, our nation's 30th president, could point with pride to his state's willingness to sacrifice in the service of others. Aiken and Gibson and Flanders and Prouty and Bob Stafford were all Republicans, but they were Vermonters first. They spoke their minds, often to the dismay of their party leaders, and did their best to guide the party in the direction of those fundamental principles they believed in.

For 26 years in Washington, first in the House of Representatives and now in the Senate, I have tried to do the same, but I can no longer do so as a Republican. Increasingly, I find myself in disagreement with my party.

I understand that many people are more conservative than I am, and they form the Republican Party. Given the changing nature of the national party, it has become a struggle for our leaders to deal with me and for me to deal with them. Indeed, the party's electoral success has underscored the dilemma that I face within the party.

In the past, without the presidency, the various wings of the Republican Party in Congress have had some freedom to argue and influence and ultimately to shape the party's agenda. The election of President Bush changed that dramatically.

We don't live in a parliamentary system, but it is only natural to expect that people like myself, who have been honored with positions of leadership, will largely support the president's agenda.

And yet, more and more, I find I cannot. Those who don't know me may have thought I took pleasure in resisting the president's budget or that I enjoyed the limelight. Nothing could be further from the truth. I had serious substantive reservations about that budget, as you all know, and the decisions it set in place for the future.

Looking ahead, I can see more and more instances where I'll disagree with the president on very fundamental issues — the issues of choice, the direction of the judiciary, tax and spending decisions, missile defense, energy and the environment, and a host of other issues, large and small.

The largest for me is education. I come from the state of Justin Smith Morrill, a U.S. senator from Vermont who gave America its land grant college system. His Republican Party stood for opportunity for all, for opening the doors of public school education to every American child.

Now, for some, success seems to be measured by the number of students moved out of the public schools.

In order to best represent my state of Vermont, my own conscience and principles I have stood for my whole life, I will leave the Republican Party and become an Independent.

(Applause.)

Control of the Senate will be changed by my decision.

AUDIENCE: Thank you, Jeff. Thank you, Jeff. Thank you, Jeff.

JEFFORDS: I'm sorry for that interruption, but I understand it.

I will make this change and will caucus with the Democrats for organizational purposes once the conference report on the tax bill is sent to the

president. I gave my word to the president that I would not intercept or try to intervene in the signing of that bill.

My colleagues, many of them my friends for years, may find it difficult in their hearts to befriend me any longer. Many of my supporters will be disappointed, and some of my staffers will see their lives upended. I regret this very much.

Having made my decision, the weight that has been lifted from my shoulders now hangs heavy on my heart, but I was not elected to this office to be something that I am not. This comes as no surprise to Vermonters, because independence is the Vermont way.

My friends back home have supported and encouraged my independence. I appreciate the support they have shown when they have agreed with me, and their patience when they have not. I will ask their support and patience again, which I understand will be very difficult for a number of my close friends.

I have informed President Bush, Vice President [Dick] Cheney and Sen. [Trent] Lott [R-Miss.] of my decision.

They are good people with whom I disagree. They have been fair and decent to me, and I have informed Sen. [Tom] Daschle [D-S.D.] also of my decision. Three of these four men disagree with my decision, but I hope each understood my reasons. And it's quite entirely possible that the fourth one, with my independence, may have second thoughts down the road. But anyway, that's the way it is.

I have changed my party label, but I have not changed my beliefs. Indeed, my decision is about affirming the principles that have shaped my career. I hope that the people of Vermont will understand it. I hope in time that my colleagues will as well. I am confident that it is the right decision.

Yes?

Q: Sen. Jeffords, what do you say to those people who, only six months ago, voted for you as a Republican?

JEFFORDS: Right. I understand, and I'm sorry that I had no expectation of it.

Q: (Off mike) . . . you were his campaign chairman, obviously?

JEFFORDS: I was not the campaign chairman, but that's a small point. I believed at the time and had hoped at the time that those of us that are the moderates of the party, not just myself — and I speak, I'm sure, for many moderates in the party who had high hopes when the president spoke of education and when he gave his dedication to education — that we would be able to follow him, and I praise the president for his education package.

And that's the problem that I have with it. Because there are terrible problems out there that will have to be solved, and that is why in the budget process, I stood up and said, no, we can't give all this money back. We have too many high priorities — education, number one.

We have got to provide the resources for the president's plan. If the resources are not there, it's going to be misery in the school systems. And I told this to the president personally. So it's no secret that I have these feelings.

But I could not, after that, see the direction of the budgetary process — and you know I stood up against that, and we succeeded in getting some $300 billion extra to spend. But it's not being directed under the budget process to education.

Q: Do you feel the president has not lived up to his campaign promises?

JEFFORDS: Well, I don't know — I don't ever remember specifically a promise to fund. He gave us a promise to get us new direction in education. But new direction without funding is really no useful direction at all.

Q: Senator, much has been made of the way the Bush White House and the Republican leadership in Congress have treated you. Has their treatment — personal treatment of you had anything to do with your decision?

JEFFORDS: Oh, nothing whatsoever. It gets laughable at times, and you get upset with it — like Vermont, the national school teacher, those kind of things. But that had nothing to do with it. Nothing at all.

Q: When did you make your decision?

JEFFORDS: I'm sorry?

Q: When did you make your decision?

JEFFORDS: I made my decision yesterday on the way down, really. And I'll tell you why — "Why did you wait that long?" I promised my moderates. I met with the moderates yesterday, and it was the most emotional time that I have ever had in my life, with my closest friends urging me not to do what I was going to do because it affected their lives very substantially.

I know, for instance, the chairman of the Finance Committee has dreamed all his life of being chairman. He's chairman a couple of weeks, and now he will be no longer the chairman.

All the way down the line, I could see the anguish and the disappointment as I talked. So I told them I would not make my final decision until I had time on the way to Vermont to decide, and I did leave it open. But I could not justify not going forward.

STAFF: Last question.

Q: Senator, last week, the chairman of the Vermont Republican Party said he'd be terribly surprised if the idea of leaving the party had even crossed your mind. What have you done today to Republican leaders . . . ?

JEFFORDS: I've communicated with them, either I or my staff have. I've had conversations with them on the phone to make sure they understood what I was doing and why I was doing it.

STAFF: Thank you very much. Thank you very much. ◆

Daschle, Lott Express Optimism, Vow to Keep 'Working Together' As They Trade Leadership Posts

Following is a transcript of the remarks that Sens. Tom Daschle, D-S.D., and Trent Lott, R-Miss., made on the floor June 6 as they reversed roles — Daschle became majority leader, and Lott became minority leader. Transcript provided by eMediaMillWorks Inc.

DASCHLE: I want to thank the distinguished senator from South Carolina, [Republican] Strom Thurmond, for his service to our country and to this body as president pro tempore.

And I want to offer my hearty congratulations to Sen. Robert C. Byrd [D-W.Va.] in returning to this high position [as president pro tem] this morning.

Between the two men, the Senate enjoys 90 years of public service. The wisdom that they have given us is beyond measure.

I want to thank my partner and my counterpart, Sen. [Trent] Lott. This is the second time this year Sen. Lott and I have switched roles. To us, this is just another in a series of challenges he and I have faced already this year and yet another example of our ability to face these challenges together.

Every time we've been presented with these challenges, we've come through with our working relationship and our friendship not only intact but, in my view, strengthened. It is my hope and my expectation that we will continue to be able to work in this manner.

Finally, there is another person who deserves special recognition, and that is Sen. [James M.] Jeffords [I-Vt.]. Last week, I was deeply touched by Sen. Jeffords' courageous decision, his eloquent words. The senator from Vermont has always commanded bipartisan respect because of the work that he does. Regardless of where he sits in this chamber, that is work which will continue, and America will be better for it.

This indeed is a humbling moment for me. I'm honored to serve as majority leader, but I also recognize that the majority is slim. This is still one of the most closely divided Senates in all of history, and we have just witnessed something that has never before happened in all of Senate history, the change of power during a session of Congress.

At a time when Americans are evenly divided about their choice of leaders, they are united in their demand for action. Polarized positions are an indulgence, an indulgence that the Senate cannot afford and our nation will not tolerate.

Republicans and Democrats come to this floor with different philosophies, different agendas. We believe in the power of ideas together, Republicans and Democrats. We believe in fashioning those ideas into sound public policy, Republicans and Democrats.

The debate on that policy is what I like to call the noise of democracy. Sometimes it's not a very stereophonic sound, sometimes there is too much sound from the right or from the left, but it is a sound that in my view is a beautiful noise, especially in comparison to the noise of violence we see in so many streets and in so many places all over the world today.

In this divided government, in spite of the passion with which we hold these ideas, in spite of the fervor with which we come to the floor to represent them, we are required to find common ground and seek meaningful bipartisanship.

As I've said before, real bipartisanship is not a mathematical formula; it is a spirit. It is not simply finding a way to 50 plus one. It is a way of working together that tolerates debate. It means seeking principled compromise and respecting the right of each senator to speak his or her mind and to vote his or her conscience.

I believe that in this Senate, at this time, on this historic occasion, each of us has something to prove. We need to prove to the American people that we can overcome the lines that all too often divide us. We need to prove that we can do the work the American people have sent us to do.

I came to the Congress 22 years ago. I had the good fortune of having many mentors, some who I remember so vividly because they continue to guide me today.

Those who are my friends know that one in particular continues to guide me in ways that I articulate on so many occasions. His name was Claude Pepper, a congressman from Florida, once a senator in this body. He told me once on a cold December afternoon that as fervent and as passionate a Democrat as he was, that it wasn't really whether you were a "D" or an "R" that mattered, it's whether you were a "C" or "D." It's whether you were constructive or destructive in the political and legislative process.

I hope I can prove to my colleagues on this side of the aisle that I can be a constructive leader. I hope that we all recognize the difference between constructive and destructive politics and legislative work. I hope in living up to the expectations of the American people and people like Claude Pepper that we can be constructive Republicans and constructive Democrats in dealing with a bipartisan solution to the agenda that we know must be addressed in this body beginning today.

I thank my colleagues for their trust. I thank my colleagues for their friendship. I'm prepared to go to work. I yield the floor.

LOTT: Mr. President, let me first join Sen. Daschle in expressing my personal appreciation and great admiration for Sen. Thurmond, for the job he has done for so many years for the people of South Carolina and, yes, the people of America.

Today, he is in his beloved South Carolina with the president of the

United States. Actually, I believe they're in Bedford, Va., for the dedication of a memorial for those who lost their lives in Normandy.

As our colleagues know, Sen. Thurmond landed at Normandy and served so honorably there, and the energy and strength that he exhibited there continues to this very day in the Senate. He is a legend in his own time, and we all admire and appreciate him so much.

Also, I want to congratulate Sen. Byrd for assuming this position of president pro tem of the Senate. He certainly is going to need no briefing on the rules. He is the paragon of the rules in the Senate. He is the guardian of the rules; he certainly knows them. He will administer them fairly, and he will preside in the chair in a way that we all will appreciate and will admire.

So to you, Sen. Byrd, Mr. President, thank you for what you have done and for what I know you will do as the president pro tempore of the Senate.

I also want to thank our staff members. There are so many people I'd like to recognize that have served the Senate during the period of time that I have been majority leader. The officers, those that are here day in and day out into the night, do such a great job for the Senate, for the senators and for our country, and to all of you, I express my appreciation.

I particularly want to express appreciation to our staff assistants; Elizabeth Letchworth, who has been secretary of the majority, now secretary of the minority; and to Marty Paone, who has served as secretary of the minority and will be secretary of the majority. They have the answers that we need in the Senate. We can always rely on them as to what the schedule may be, based on what the leaders have told them and when the votes will occur, and they do so much to make our life and our job easier here.

But primarily I want to extend my congratulations also to my partner and my friend, Tom Daschle, as majority leader. I also extend to him my hand of continued friendship and commitment to work with him for the interest of the American people. I know he will do an excellent job. I think he has set a very positive tone in his opening remarks, and I told him so when I congratulated him as we shook hands.

We have worked together in the past, over the past five years, when I've been the majority leader, through some good times and some tremendous legislative achievements and through some tough times. And sometimes we have been criticized for that, but most of the time I think people understood that we maintain a working relationship, and we did the best we could, as we saw on our jobs and what we thought was right for the Senate and right for the American people.

The good times, we will remember and try to repeat. The bad times have already been forgotten. But there have been clear examples of where we have worked together in a bipartisan way, for the interest of the American people, and it covers the gamut. It has been on financial issues, on transportation and on trade. At times, sometimes, when we had opposition in our own parties — but we came together because we thought a result was very important.

I know that Sen. Daschle will find sometimes that the weight of this job will be as heavy as the weight of Atlas when he carried the Earth on his shoulders. And I hope that, on occasion, I can help make that weight a little lighter.

Of course, at one point, Atlas tricked Hercules and dumped that burden off on Hercules. But later on, another trick was employed, and Atlas wound up with this weight back on him, as he was fated to do. Now what is the moral of that story?

(LAUGHTER)

The moral is this job will be tough. We're all going to try to make it bearable and easier for you. And of course, I'm hoping someday the weight will come back where it was fated to be.

(LAUGHTER)

I'm proud of things we have accomplished in the Senate over the past five years. I recall almost exactly five years ago when I became majority leader for a variety of reasons. We were tangled up and couldn't decide how to move things like insurance portability, minimum wage, chemical weapons treaty. And I felt like the first thing I had to try to do was to get things sort of stood up and moving again. And I had to make some tough decisions, again, which weren't always popular on this side, but which were always tolerated and, in many cases, encouraged by my colleagues on the Republican side of the House.

In fact, we got those things done. People said, 'Well, you'll never get this untangled.' Well, in that year, 1995, we actually did pass the insurance portability. We did pass safe drinking water legislation.

We did pass a minimum wage increase with some small business tax relief included. We completed our appropriations bills. And we had a very good year, and I think — I know — that Sen. Daschle and I felt good about it. I think most American people did.

I do think we have made a difference in the country over the past six years since we have been in the majority. And I acknowledge that a good portion of that time, obviously, we had a Democrat in the White House, but we have gone from having deficits every year and growing debts to now having the challenge of, how do you deal with balanced budgets and surpluses?

It's so different. In fact, sometimes I think it's more difficult when you've got what appears to be a surplus, and everybody's saying, "Use it here, there or somewhere else." At least when you were having deficits you could say, "Well, we just don't have enough for all those things."

But we have gone to balanced budgets. We have stopped the raid on Social Security. We have moved people from welfare to the dignity and independence of work. We have lower taxes on families and job creations. We have started to restore America's military strength. And we returned education dollars to parents and teachers and communities. We passed the soldier's bill of rights, the juvenile justice reform. We're working on education reform.

And there's a long list, which I will ask, Mr. President, unanimous consent that I include in the record of important bills that we have passed over the past five years.

BYRD: Without objection, it is so ordered.

LOTT: But now we have a challenge before us that is different for me and will be different for Sen. Daschle: Can we come together? Can we find a way to work with this president, President Bush, and find common ground, even on the bill that's pending before us now, education?

We all say we want education reform. And we want a responsible increase in the spending that will go for education. The American people say they want it — the people in every state, the president and so do we. And yet, we haven't gotten it done yet. Can we come together on education? I think we can. It's going to take work. It's going to take some sacrifice.

Sen. [Edward M.] Kennedy [D-Mass.] is going to continue to push it aggressively. And he's probably going to have to cast some votes he doesn't particularly like, and so am I, and so will Sen. [Judd] Gregg [R-N.H.].

But can we do no less? Can we afford not to finally make progress on education reform and take some steps for the federal government to be helpful in improving education in America? I believe we can do it. It may take a little more time. But that will be our first test. And I pledge to work with the managers and with Sen. Daschle to make that happen.

We have a lot of other important issues that we're going to have to deal with this year. Sen. Daschle noted yesterday we have 13 appropriations bills and a supplemental appropriations bill to do to keep the government operating. We have 59 days, estimated, I guess, to get it done.

It's going to take a pretty good lift. I hope we don't have 100 amendments on every appropriations bill like we did last year, and I hope we can find a way to show fiscal restraint and get these bills done.

Obviously, there's going to be health-related issues. How do we deal with patients' bill of rights? How can we deal with this important question of prescription drugs to make sure that the elderly poor get the help they need? Can we come together on Medicare reform? Can we take the lead from [Democrat Daniel Patrick] Moynihan, former senator from New York, on Social Security?

Will we be able to really address energy needs in this country? Will we be taking partisan positions and trying to assess blame? Will we be trying to find how little can we do, or can we come together and have a real national energy policy that will hopefully help this year but, more importantly, will make sure we don't have this problem in five years or 10 years? And defense continues to be something we're going to have to focus on.

So we have a full agenda. I don't think a lot will change. Sen. Daschle will get recognized. He'll be the majority leader, and I'll be the minority leader, the Republican leader. He'll call up the bills, and we will take advantage of our rights in the minority to offer amendments — as certainly the other side has — and sometimes, we'll offer substitutes. But we commit and pledge our best efforts to finding a way to make it work and to pass important legislation to address these issues that are needed by the American people.

It's not about personalities. I still believe that government is about ideas and about issues, so it's not really that important what role we serve in. What is important is what do we do for the people that we serve? What legacy will we leave for the next generation?

I believe we can get it done. We've got a lot of work to do. Let's get started — and I, again, pledge to you my support and cooperation, Sen. Daschle. ◆

Joint Resolutions Authorize Military Retaliation, Condemn Terrorist Attacks

Following is the joint resolution (S J Res 23) passed by the Senate and cleared by the House on Sept. 14, in response to the tragedy of Sept. 11:

To authorize the use of United States Armed Forces against those responsible for the recent attacks launched against the United States.

Whereas, on September 11, 2001, acts of despicable violence were committed against the United States and its citizens; and

Whereas, such acts render it both necessary and appropriate that the United States exercise its rights to self-defense and to protect United States citizens both at home and abroad; and

Whereas, in light of the threat to the national security and foreign policy of the United States posed by these grave acts of violence; and

Whereas, such acts continue to pose an unusual and extraordinary threat to the national security and foreign policy of the United States,

Whereas the President has authority under the Constitution to take action to deter and prevent acts of international terrorism against the United States.

Resolved by the Senate and the House of Representatives of the United States of America in Congress assembled,

SECTION 1. SHORT TITLE

This joint resolution may be cited as the "Authorization for Use of Military Force."

SECTION 2. AUTHORIZATION FOR USE OF UNITED STATES ARMED FORCES

(a) That the President is authorized to use all necessary and appropriate force against those nations, organizations, or persons he determines planned, authorized, committed, or aided the terrorist attacks that occurred on September 11, 2001, or harbored such organizations or persons, in order to prevent any future acts of international terrorism against the United States by such nations, organizations or persons.

(b) War Powers Resolution Requirements

(1) Specific Statutory Authorization — Consistent with section 8(a)(1) of the War Powers Resolution, the Congress declares that this section is intended to constitute specific statutory authorization within the meaning of section 5(b) of the War Powers Resolution.

(2) Applicability of Other Requirements — Nothing in this resolution supersedes any requirement of the War Powers Resolution.

Following is the joint resolution (H J Res 61, S J Res 22) passed by both chambers Sept. 12:

Expressing the sense of the Senate and House of Representatives regarding the terrorist attacks launched against the United States on September 11, 2001.

Whereas on September 11, 2001, terrorists hijacked and destroyed four civilian aircraft, crashing two of them into the towers of the World Trade Center in New York City, and a third into the Pentagon outside Washington, D.C.;

Whereas thousands of innocent Americans were killed and injured as a result of these attacks, including the passengers and crew of the four aircraft, workers in the World Trade Center and in the Pentagon, rescue workers, and bystanders;

Whereas these attacks destroyed both towers of the World Trade Center, as well as adjacent buildings, and seriously damaged the Pentagon; and

Whereas these attacks were by far the deadliest terrorist attacks ever launched against the United States, and, by targeting symbols of American strength and success, clearly were intended to intimidate our nation and weaken its resolve: Now, therefore, be it resolved by the Senate and House of Representatives of the United States of America in Congress assembled, that Congress:

(1) condemns in the strongest possible terms the terrorists who planned and carried out the September 11, 2001, attacks against the United States, as well as their sponsors;

(2) extends its deepest condolences to the victims of these heinous and cowardly attacks, as well as to their families, friends, and loved ones;

(3) is certain that the people of the United States will stand united as our Nation begins the process of recovering and rebuilding in the aftermath of these tragic acts;

(4) commends the heroic actions of the rescue workers, volunteers, and state and local officials who responded to these tragic events with courage, determination, and skill;

(5) declares that these premeditated attacks struck not only at the people of America, but also at the symbols and structures of our economic and military strength, and that the United States is entitled to respond under international law;

(6) thanks those foreign leaders and individuals who have expressed solidarity with the United States in the aftermath of the attacks, and asks them to continue to stand with the United States in the war against international terrorism;

(7) commits to support increased resources in the war to eradicate terrorism;

(8) supports the determination of the President, in close consultation with Congress, to bring to justice and punish the perpetrators of these attacks as well as their sponsors; and

(9) declares that September 12, 2001, shall be a National Day of Unity and Mourning, and that when Congress adjourns today, it stands adjourned out of respect to the victims of the terrorist attacks. ◆

Bush Calls Upon Americans To Unite in 'Monumental Struggle Of Good vs. Evil' After Terrorist Attacks

Following are President Bush's remarks in Sarasota, Fla., on Sept. 11. Transcript provided by Federal Document Clearing House:

Ladies and gentlemen, this is a difficult moment for America. I, unfortunately, will be going back to Washington after my remarks. Secretary Rod Paige and the lieutenant governor will take the podium and discuss education.

I do want to thank the folks here at the Booker Elementary School for their hospitality.

Today we've had a national tragedy. Two airplanes have crashed into the World Trade Center in an apparent terrorist attack on our country. I have spoken to the vice president, to the governor of New York, to the director of the FBI, and I've ordered that the full resources of the federal government go to help the victims and their families, and to conduct a full-scale investigation to hunt down and to find those folks who committed this act.

Terrorism against our nation will not stand.

And now if you join me in a moment of silence.

May God bless the victims, their families and America. Thank you very much.

Following are President Bush's remarks upon arriving at Barksdale Air Force Base in Louisiana on Sept. 11. Transcript provided by Federal Document Clearing House:

Freedom itself was attacked this morning by a faceless coward. And freedom will be defended.

I want to reassure the American people that the full resources of the federal government are working to assist local authorities to save lives and to help the victims of these attacks.

Make no mistake: The United States will hunt down and punish those responsible for these cowardly acts.

I've been in regular contact with the vice president, the secretary of Defense, the national security team and my Cabinet. We have taken all appropriate security precautions to protect the American people. Our military at home and around the world is on high alert status, and we have taken the necessary security precautions to continue the functions of your government.

We have been in touch with the leaders of Congress and with world leaders to assure them that we will do whatever is necessary to protect America and Americans.

I ask the American people to join me in saying a thanks for all the folks who have been fighting hard to rescue our fellow citizens and to join me in saying a prayer for the victims and their families.

The resolve of our great nation is being tested. But make no mistake, we will show the world that we will pass this test.

God bless.

Following is President Bush's address to the nation from the White House on Sept. 11. Transcript provided by Federal Document Clearing House:

Good evening.

Today, our fellow citizens, our way of life, our very freedom came under attack in a series of deliberate and deadly terrorist acts. The victims were in airplanes or in their offices: secretaries, businessmen and women, military and federal workers, moms and dads, friends and neighbors.

Thousands of lives were suddenly ended by evil, despicable acts of terror. The pictures of airplanes flying into buildings, fires burning, huge structures collapsing have filled us with disbelief, terrible sadness and a quiet, unyielding anger.

These acts of mass murder were intended to frighten our nation into chaos and retreat. But they have failed. Our country is strong. A great people has been moved to defend a great nation.

Terrorist attacks can shake the foundations of our biggest buildings, but they cannot touch the foundation of America. These acts shatter steel, but they cannot dent the steel of American resolve.

America was targeted for attack because we're the brightest beacon for freedom and opportunity in the world. And no one will keep that light from shining.

Today, our nation saw evil, the very worst of human nature, and we responded with the best of America, with the daring of our rescue workers, with the caring for strangers and neighbors who came to give blood and help in any way they could.

Immediately following the first attack, I implemented our government's emergency response plans. Our military is powerful, and it's prepared.

Our emergency teams are working in New York City and Washington, D.C., to help with local rescue efforts. Our first priority is to get help to those who have been injured and to take every precaution to protect our citizens at home and around the world from further attacks.

The functions of our government continue without interruption. Federal agencies in Washington which had to be evacuated today are reopening for essential personnel tonight and will be open for business tomorrow.

Our financial institutions remain strong, and the American economy will be open for business as well.

The search is under way for those who are behind these evil acts. I've directed the full resources for our intelligence and law enforcement communi-

ties to find those responsible and bring them to justice. We will make no distinction between the terrorists who committed these acts and those who harbor them.

I appreciate so very much the members of Congress who have joined me in strongly condemning these attacks. And on behalf of the American people, I thank the many world leaders who have called to offer their condolences and assistance.

America and our friends and allies join with all those who want peace and security in the world and we stand together to win the war against terrorism.

Tonight I ask for your prayers for all those who grieve, for the children whose worlds have been shattered, for all whose sense of safety and security has been threatened. And I pray they will be comforted by a power greater than any of us spoken through the ages in Psalm 23: "Even though I walk through the valley of the shadow of death, I fear no evil for you are with me."

This is a day when all Americans from every walk of life unite in our resolve for justice and peace. America has stood down enemies before, and we will do so this time.

None of us will ever forget this day, yet we go forward to defend freedom and all that is good and just in our world.

Thank you. Good night and God bless America.

Following are remarks by President Bush after a meeting with his national security team Sept. 12. Transcript provided by Federal Document Clearing House:

I just completed a meeting with our national security team, and we've received the latest intelligence updates.

The deliberate and deadly attacks which were carried out yesterday against our country were more than acts of terror. They were acts of war. This will require our country to unite in steadfast determination and resolve. Freedom and democracy are under attack.

The American people need to know we're facing a different enemy than we have ever faced. This enemy hides in shadows and has no regard for human life. This is an enemy who preys on in-

nocent and unsuspecting people, then runs for cover, but it won't be able to run for cover forever. This is an enemy that tries to hide, but it won't be able to hide forever. This is an enemy that thinks its harbors are safe, but they won't be safe forever. This enemy attacked not just our people but all freedom-loving people everywhere in the world.

The United States of America will use all our resources to conquer this enemy. We will rally the world. We will be patient. We'll be focused, and we will be steadfast in our determination. This battle will take time and resolve, but make no mistake about it, we will win.

The federal government and all our agencies are conducting business, but it is not business as usual. We are operating on heightened security alert. America is going forward, and as we do so, we must remain keenly aware of the threats to our country.

Those in authority should take appropriate precautions to protect our citizens. But we will not allow this enemy to win the war by changing our way of life or restricting our freedoms.

This morning, I am sending to Congress a request for emergency funding authority so that we are prepared to spend whatever it takes to rescue victims, to help the citizens of New York City and Washington, D.C., respond to this tragedy, and to protect our national security.

I want to thank the members of Congress for their unity and support. America is united. The freedom-loving nations of the world stand by our side. This will be a monumental struggle of good versus evil, but good will prevail.

Thank you very much.

Following are President Bush's remarks while inspecting the damage at the Pentagon Sept. 12. Transcript provided by the White House:

I am so grateful to the people who are working here.

We're here to say thanks to not only the workers on this site, but the workers who are doing the same work in New York City. I want to say thanks to the folks who have given blood to the Red Cross. I want to say thanks for the hun-

dreds of thousands of Americans who pray for the victims and their families.

[Defense] Secretary [Donald] Rumsfeld told me, when I talked to him, that he felt the blast shake the Pentagon — even though he was on the other side of the building, the building rocked. And now I know why.

Coming here makes me sad, on the one hand; it also makes me angry. Our country will, however, not be cowed by terrorists, by people who don't share the same values we share, by people who are willing to destroy people's lives because we embrace freedom. The nation mourns, but our government will go on, the country will function. We are on high alert for possible activity.

But coming here confirms what the Secretary and I both know: that this is a great nation. People here working hard prove it, people out here working their hearts out to answer families' questions, to remove the rubble and debris from this office. I want to thank everybody not only on this site, but all across America, for responding so generously, so kindly, in their prayers, in their contributions of love and their willingness to help in any way they can.

Following are excerpts from President Bush's exchange with reporters Sept. 13, following his telephone conversation Sept. 13 with New York City Mayor Rudolph Giuliani and New York Gov. George Pataki. Transcript provided by the White House:

I've been on the phone this morning . . . with leaders from around the world who express their solidarity with this nation's intention to rout out and to whip terrorism.

They understand, fully understand that an act of war was declared on the United States of America. . . . Many of the leaders understand it could have easily have happened to them.

Secondly, they understand that, unlike previous war, this enemy likes to hide. They heard my call loud and clear, to those who feel like they can provide safe harbor for the terrorists, that we will hold them responsible, as well. And they join me in understanding not only the concept of the enemy, but that the enemy is a different type of enemy.

They join me also in solidarity about holding those who fund them, who harbor them, who encourage them, responsible for their activities.

I'm pleased with the outpouring of support. [Chinese President] Jiang Zemin, [Russian President] Vladimir Putin; had a great visit this morning with His Royal Highness, Prince Abdullah of Saudi Arabia. . . . And there is universal support for the American people, sadness in their voice; but understanding that we have just seen the first war of the 21st Century. And there is universal approval of the statements I have made, and I am confident there will be universal approval of the actions this government takes.

Q: Mr. President, if this is a different kind of war it might require, perhaps, a different kind of coalition. Many people believe that for a real war on terrorism to work you'll need cooperation from governments that haven't necessarily done so in the past — specifically Pakistan and Afghanistan. Have you made any progress on that front, and do you have a message for those —

BUSH: I would refer you to the statements that the Pakistani leader gave about his . . . willingness to work with the United States. And I appreciate that statement, and now we'll just find out what that means, won't we? . . .

Q: Mr. President, how confident are you that [Saudi extremist] Osama bin Laden is behind these attacks? Do you know what his whereabouts are? And, secondly, what kind of support are you looking for from Congress, in terms of your willingness to act?

BUSH: We are — we will not discuss intelligence matters, how we gather intelligence and what we know — about anybody. When our government acts, you'll be informed.

We had a great meeting yesterday here in the Cabinet Room with leadership of the House and the Senate. I was touched by their response, their encouragement and their willingness to work together. . . .

Secondly, progress is being made on a supplemental [spending bill]. I thought that was very swift action and I'm most appreciative, again, of Sen. [Tom] Daschle and Rep. [Richard A.] Gephardt, as well as my Republican colleagues, for really showing solidarity again and uniting the nation. . . .

You know, through the tears of sadness I see an opportunity. Make no mistake about it, this nation is sad. But we're also tough and resolute. And now is an opportunity to do generations a favor, by coming together and whipping terrorism; hunting it down, finding it and holding them accountable. The nation must understand, this is now the focus of my administration. . . .

Following are remarks by President Bush at the Washington Cathedral on Sept. 14:

We are here in the middle hour of our grief. So many have suffered so great a loss, and today we express our nation's sorrow. We come before God to pray for the missing and the dead, and for those who love them.

On Tuesday, our country was attacked with deliberate and massive cruelty. We have seen the images of fire and ashes, and bent steel.

Now come the names, the list of casualties we are only beginning to read. They are the names of men and women who began their day at a desk or in an airport, busy with life. They are the names of people who faced death, and in their last moments called home to say: Be brave, and I love you.

They are the names of passengers who defied their murderers, and prevented the murder of others on the ground. They are the names of men and women who wore the uniform of the United States, and died at their posts.

They are the names of rescuers, the ones whom death found running up the stairs and into the fires to help others. We will read all these names. We will linger over them, and learn their stories, and many Americans will weep.

To the children and parents and spouses and families and friends of the lost, we offer the deepest sympathy of the nation. And I assure you, you are not alone.

Just three days removed from these events, Americans do not yet have the distance of history. But our responsibility to history is already clear: to answer these attacks and rid the world of evil.

War has been waged against us by stealth and deceit and murder. This nation is peaceful, but fierce when stirred to anger. This conflict was begun on the timing and terms of others. It will end in a way, and at an hour, of our choosing.

Our purpose as a nation is firm. Yet our wounds as a people are recent and unhealed, and lead us to pray. In many of our prayers this week, there is a searching, and an honesty. At St. Patrick's Cathedral in New York on Tuesday, a woman said, "I prayed to God to give us a sign that He is still here." Others have prayed for the same, searching hospital to hospital, carrying pictures of those still missing.

God's signs are not always the ones we look for. We learn in tragedy that his purposes are not always our own. Yet the prayers of private suffering, whether in our homes or in this great cathedral, are known and heard, and understood.

There are prayers that help us last through the day, or endure the night. There are prayers of friends and strangers that give us strength for the journey. And there are prayers that yield our will to a will greater than our own.

This world He created is of moral design. Grief and tragedy and hatred are only for a time. Goodness, remembrance and love have no end.

And the Lord of life holds all who die, and all who mourn.

It is said that adversity introduces us to ourselves. This is true of a nation as well. In this trial, we have been reminded, and the world has seen, that our fellow Americans are generous and kind, resourceful and brave. We see our national character in rescuers working past exhaustion; in long lines of blood donors; in thousands of citizens who have asked to work and serve in any way possible.

And we have seen our national character in eloquent acts of sacrifice. Inside the World Trade Center, one man who could have saved himself stayed until the end at the side of his quadriplegic friend. A beloved priest died giving the last rites to a firefighter. Two office workers, finding a disabled stranger, carried her down 68 floors to safety. A group of men drove through the night from Dallas to Washington to bring skin grafts for burn victims.

In these acts, and in many others, Americans showed a deep commitment to one another, and an abiding love for our country. Today, we feel what Franklin Roosevelt called the warm courage of national unity. This is a unity of every faith, and every background.

It has joined together political parties in both houses of Congress. It is evident in services of prayer and candlelight vigils, and American flags, which are displayed in pride and wave in defiance.

Our unity is a kinship of grief, and a steadfast resolve to prevail against our enemies. And this unity against terror is now extending across the world.

America is a nation full of good fortune, with so much to be grateful for. But we are not spared from suffering. In every generation, the world has produced enemies of human freedom. They have attacked America, because we are freedom's home and defender. And the commitment of our fathers is now the calling of our time.

On this national day of prayer and remembrance, we ask almighty God to watch over our nation, and grant us patience and resolve in all that is to come. We pray that He will comfort and console those who now walk in sorrow. We thank Him for each life we now must mourn, and the promise of a life to come.

As we have been assured, neither death nor life, nor angels nor principalities nor powers, nor things present nor things to come, nor height nor depth, can separate us from God's love. May He bless the souls of the departed. May He comfort our own. And may He always guide our country.

God bless America. ◆

Bush Issues Ultimatum to Taliban, Calls Upon Nation and World To Unite and Destroy Terrorism

Following is President Bush's speech Sept. 20 to a joint session of Congress and to the American people. Transcript provided by the White House:

Mr. Speaker, Mr. President Pro Tempore, members of Congress, and fellow Americans:

In the normal course of events, Presidents come to this chamber to report on the state of the Union. Tonight, no such report is needed. It has already been delivered by the American people.

We have seen it in the courage of passengers, who rushed terrorists to save others on the ground — passengers like an exceptional man named Todd Beamer. And would you please help me to welcome his wife, Lisa Beamer, here tonight.

We have seen the state of our Union in the endurance of rescuers, working past exhaustion. We have seen the unfurling of flags, the lighting of candles, the giving of blood, the saying of prayers — in English, Hebrew, and Arabic.

We have seen the decency of a loving and giving people who have made the grief of strangers their own.

My fellow citizens, for the last nine days, the entire world has seen for itself the state of our Union — and it is strong.

Tonight we are a country awakened to danger and called to defend freedom. Our grief has turned to anger, and anger to resolution. Whether we bring our enemies to justice, or bring justice to our enemies, justice will be done.

I thank the Congress for its leadership at such an important time. All of America was touched on the evening of the tragedy to see Republicans and Democrats joined together on the steps of this Capitol, singing "God Bless America." And you did more than sing; you acted, by delivering $40 billion to rebuild our communities and meet the needs of our military.

Speaker [J. Dennis] Hastert [R-Ill.], Minority Leader [Richard A.] Gephardt [D-Mo.], Majority Leader [Tom] Daschle [D-S.D.] and Senator [Trent] Lott [R-Miss.], I thank you for your friendship, for your leadership and for your service to our country. And on behalf of the American people, I thank the world for its outpouring of support. America will never forget the sounds of our National Anthem playing at Buckingham Palace, on the streets of Paris, and at Berlin's Brandenburg Gate.

We will not forget South Korean children gathering to pray outside our embassy in Seoul, or the prayers of sympathy offered at a mosque in Cairo. We will not forget moments of silence and days of mourning in Australia and Africa and Latin America.

Nor will we forget the citizens of 80 other nations who died with our own: dozens of Pakistanis; more than 130 Israelis; more than 250 citizens of India; men and women from El Salvador, Iran, Mexico and Japan; and hundreds of British citizens. America has no truer friend than Great Britain.

Once again, we are joined together in a great cause — so honored the British prime minister has crossed an ocean to show his unity of purpose with America. Thank you for coming, friend.

On Sept. 11, enemies of freedom committed an act of war against our country. Americans have known wars — but for the past 136 years, they have been wars on foreign soil, except for one Sunday in 1941. Americans have known the casualties of war — but not at the center of a great city on a peaceful morning. Americans have known surprise attacks — but never before on thousands of civilians. All of this was brought upon us in a single day — and night fell on a different world, a world where freedom itself is under attack.

Americans have many questions tonight. Americans are asking: Who attacked our country? The evidence we have gathered all points to a collection of loosely affiliated terrorist organizations known as al Qaeda. They are the same murderers indicted for bombing American embassies in Tanzania and Kenya, and responsible for bombing the USS *Cole*.

Al Qaeda is to terror what the Mafia is to crime. But its goal is not making money; its goal is remaking the world — and imposing its radical beliefs on people everywhere.

The terrorists practice a fringe form of Islamic extremism that has been rejected by Muslim scholars and the vast majority of Muslim clerics — a fringe movement that perverts the peaceful teachings of Islam. The terrorists' directive commands them to kill Christians and Jews, to kill all Americans, and make no distinction among military and civilians, including women and children.

This group and its leader — a person named Osama bin Laden — are linked to many other organizations in different countries, including the Egyptian Islamic Jihad and the Islamic Movement of Uzbekistan. There are thousands of these terrorists in more than 60 countries. They are recruited from their own nations and neighborhoods and brought to camps in places like Afghanistan, where they are trained in the tactics of terror. They are sent back to their homes or sent to hide in countries around the world to plot evil and destruction.

The leadership of al Qaeda has great influence in Afghanistan and supports the Taliban regime in controlling most of that country. In Afghanistan, we see al Qaeda's vision for the world. Afghanistan's people have been brutalized — many are starving and many have fled. Women are not allowed to attend school. You can be jailed for owning a television. Religion can be practiced only as their

leaders dictate. A man can be jailed in Afghanistan if his beard is not long enough.

The United States respects the people of Afghanistan — after all, we are currently its largest source of humanitarian aid — but we condemn the Taliban regime. It is not only repressing its own people, it is threatening people everywhere by sponsoring and sheltering and supplying terrorists. By aiding and abetting murder, the Taliban regime is committing murder.

And tonight, the United States of America makes the following demands on the Taliban: Deliver to United States authorities all the leaders of al Qaeda who hide in your land. Release all foreign nationals, including American citizens, you have unjustly imprisoned. Protect foreign journalists, diplomats and aid workers in your country. Close immediately and permanently every terrorist training camp in Afghanistan, and hand over every terrorist, and every person in their support structure, to appropriate authorities. Give the United States full access to terrorist training camps, so we can make sure they are no longer operating.

These demands are not open to negotiation or discussion. The Taliban must act, and act immediately. They will hand over the terrorists, or they will share in their fate. I also want to speak tonight directly to Muslims throughout the world. We respect your faith. It's practiced freely by many millions of Americans, and by millions more in countries that America counts as friends. Its teachings are good and peaceful, and those who commit evil in the name of Allah blaspheme the name of Allah. The terrorists are traitors to their own faith, trying, in effect, to hijack Islam itself. The enemy of America is not our many Muslim friends; it is not our many Arab friends. Our enemy is a radical network of terrorists and every government that supports them.

Our war on terror begins with al Qaeda, but it does not end there. It will not end until every terrorist group of global reach has been found, stopped and defeated.

Americans are asking, why do they hate us? They hate what we see right here in this chamber — a democratically elected government. Their leaders are self-appointed. They hate our freedoms — our freedom of religion, our freedom of speech, our freedom to vote and assemble and disagree with each other. They want to overthrow existing governments in many Muslim countries, such as Egypt, Saudi Arabia and Jordan. They want to drive Israel out of the Middle East. They want to drive Christians and Jews out of vast regions of Asia and Africa.

These terrorists kill not merely to end lives, but to disrupt and end a way of life. With every atrocity, they hope that America grows fearful, retreating from the world and forsaking our friends. They stand against us, because we stand in their way.

We are not deceived by their pretenses to piety. We have seen their kind before. They are the heirs of all the murderous ideologies of the 20th century. By sacrificing human life to serve their radical visions — by abandoning every value except the will to power — they follow in the path of fascism, and Nazism, and totalitarianism. And they will follow that path all the way, to where it ends: in history's unmarked grave of discarded lies.

A Lengthy Campaign

Americans are asking: How will we fight and win this war? We will direct every resource at our command — every means of diplomacy, every tool of intelligence, every instrument of law enforcement, every financial influence and every necessary weapon of war — to the disruption and to the defeat of the global terror network.

This war will not be like the war against Iraq a decade ago, with a decisive liberation of territory and a swift conclusion. It will not look like the air war above Kosovo two years ago, where no ground troops were used and not a single American was lost in combat.

Our response involves far more than instant retaliation and isolated strikes. Americans should not expect one battle, but a lengthy campaign, unlike any other we have ever seen. It may include dramatic strikes, visible on TV, and covert operations, secret even in success. We will starve terrorists of funding, turn them one against another, drive them from place to place, until there is no refuge or no rest. And we will pursue nations that provide aid or safe haven to terrorism. Every nation, in every region, now has a decision to make. Either you are with us, or you are with the terrorists. From this day forward, any nation that continues to harbor or support terrorism will be regarded by the United States as a hostile regime.

Our nation has been put on notice: We are not immune from attack. We will take defensive measures against terrorism to protect Americans. Today, dozens of federal departments and agencies, as well as state and local governments, have responsibilities affecting homeland security. These efforts must be coordinated at the highest level. So tonight I announce the creation of a Cabinet-level position reporting directly to me — the Office of Homeland Security.

And tonight I also announce a distinguished American to lead this effort, to strengthen American security: a military veteran, an effective governor, a true patriot, a trusted friend — Pennsylvania's Tom Ridge. He will lead, oversee and coordinate a comprehensive national strategy to safeguard our country against terrorism and respond to any attacks that may come.

These measures are essential. But the only way to defeat terrorism as a threat to our way of life is to stop it, eliminate it, and destroy it where it grows.

Many will be involved in this effort, from FBI agents to intelligence operatives to the reservists we have called to active duty. All deserve our thanks, and all have our prayers. And tonight, a few miles from the damaged Pentagon, I have a message for our military: Be ready. I've called the Armed Forces to alert, and there is a reason. The hour is coming when America will act, and you will make us proud.

This is not, however, just America's fight. And what is at stake is not just America's freedom. This is the world's fight. This is civilization's fight. This is the fight of all who believe in progress and pluralism, tolerance and freedom.

We ask every nation to join us. We will ask, and we will need, the help of police forces, intelligence services and banking systems around the world. The United States is grateful that many nations and many international organiza-

tions have already responded — with sympathy and with support. Nations from Latin America, to Asia, to Africa, to Europe, to the Islamic world. Perhaps the NATO Charter reflects best the attitude of the world: An attack on one is an attack on all. The civilized world is rallying to America's side. They understand that if this terror goes unpunished, their own cities, their own citizens may be next.

Terror, unanswered, can not only bring down buildings, it can threaten the stability of legitimate governments. And you know what — we're not going to allow it.

Americans are asking: What is expected of us? I ask you to live your lives, and hug your children. I know many citizens have fears tonight, and I ask you to be calm and resolute, even in the face of a continuing threat. I ask you to uphold the values of America, and remember why so many have come here. We are in a fight for our principles, and our first responsibility is to live by them. No one should be singled out for unfair treatment or unkind words because of their ethnic background or religious faith.

I ask you to continue to support the victims of this tragedy with your contributions. Those who want to give can go to a central source of information, libertyunites.org, to find the names of groups providing direct help in New York, Pennsylvania, and Virginia.

The thousands of FBI agents who are now at work in this investigation may need your cooperation, and I ask you to give it.

I ask for your patience, with the delays and inconveniences that may accompany tighter security; and for your patience in what will be a long struggle.

I ask your continued participation and confidence in the American economy. Terrorists attacked a symbol of American prosperity. They did not touch its source. America is successful because of the hard work, and creativity, and enterprise of our people. These were the true strengths of our economy before Sept. 11th, and they are our strengths today.

And finally, please continue praying for the victims of terror and their families, for those in uniform and for our great country. Prayer has comforted us in sorrow, and will help strengthen us for the journey ahead.

Tonight I thank my fellow Americans for what you have already done and for what you will do. And ladies and gentlemen of the Congress, I thank you, their representatives, for what you have already done and for what we will do together.

Tonight, we face new and sudden national challenges. We will come together to improve air safety, to dramatically expand the number of air marshals on domestic flights, and take new measures to prevent hijacking. We will come together to promote stability and keep our airlines flying, with direct assistance during this emergency.

We will come together to give law enforcement the additional tools it needs to track down terror here at home. We will come together to strengthen our intelligence capabilities to know the plans of terrorists before they act, and find them before they strike. We will come together to take active steps that strengthen America's economy, and put our people back to work.

Tonight we welcome two leaders who embody the extraordinary spirit of all New Yorkers: Governor George Pataki and Mayor Rudolph Giuliani. As a symbol of America's resolve, my administration will work with Congress, and these two leaders, to show the world that we will rebuild New York City.

After all that has just passed — all the lives taken and all the possibilities and hopes that died with them — it is natural to wonder if America's future is one of fear. Some speak of an age of terror. I know there are struggles ahead, and dangers to face. But this country will define our times, not be defined by them. As long as the United States of America is determined and strong, this will not be an age of terror; this will be an age of liberty, here and across the world.

Great harm has been done to us. We have suffered great loss. And in our grief and anger we have found our mission and our moment. Freedom and fear are at war. The advance of human freedom — the great achievement of our time and the great hope of every time — now depends on us. Our nation — this generation — will lift a dark threat of violence from our people and our future. We will rally the world to this cause by our efforts, by our courage.

We will not tire, we will not falter and we will not fail. It is my hope that in the months and years ahead, life will return almost to normal. We'll go back to our lives and routines, and that is good. Even grief recedes with time and grace. But our resolve must not pass. Each of us will remember what happened that day, and to whom it happened. We'll remember the moment the news came — where we were and what we were doing. Some will remember an image of a fire, or a story of rescue. Some will carry memories of a face and a voice gone forever.

And I will carry this: It is the police shield of a man named George Howard, who died at the World Trade Center trying to save others. It was given to me by his mom, Arlene, as a proud memorial to her son. This is my reminder of lives that ended, and a task that does not end.

I will not forget this wound to our country or those who inflicted it. I will not yield; I will not rest; I will not relent in waging this struggle for freedom and security for the American people.

The course of this conflict is not known, yet its outcome is certain. Freedom and fear, justice and cruelty, have always been at war, and we know that God is not neutral between them.

Fellow citizens, we'll meet violence with patient justice — assured of the rightness of our cause, and confident of the victories to come. In all that lies before us, may God grant us wisdom, and may He watch over the United States of America. Thank you. ◆

Bush Announces Military Action Against Terrorist Infrastructure in Afghanistan

Following is President Bush's statement Oct. 7 announcing the beginning of attacks in Afghanistan. Text provided by the White House.

Good afternoon. On my orders, the United States military has begun strikes against al Qaeda terrorist training camps and military installations of the Taliban regime in Afghanistan. These carefully targeted actions are designed to disrupt the use of Afghanistan as a terrorist base of operations, and to attack the military capability of the Taliban regime.

We are joined in this operation by our staunch friend, Great Britain. Other close friends, including Canada, Australia, Germany and France, have pledged forces as the operation unfolds. More than 40 countries in the Middle East, Africa, Europe and across Asia have granted air transit or landing rights. Many more have shared intelligence. We are supported by the collective will of the world.

More than two weeks ago, I gave Taliban leaders a series of clear and specific demands: Close terrorist training camps; hand over leaders of the al Qaeda network; and return all foreign nationals, including American citizens, unjustly detained in your country. None of these demands were met. And now the Taliban will pay a price. By destroying camps and disrupting communications, we will make it more difficult for the terror network to train new recruits and coordinate their evil plans.

Initially, the terrorists may burrow deeper into caves and other entrenched hiding places. Our military action is also designed to clear the way for sustained, comprehensive and relentless operations to drive them out and bring them to justice.

At the same time, the oppressed people of Afghanistan will know the generosity of America and our allies. As we strike military targets, we'll also drop food, medicine and supplies to the starving and suffering men and women and children of Afghanistan.

The United States of America is a friend to the Afghan people, and we are the friends of almost a billion worldwide who practice the Islamic faith. The United States of America is an enemy of those who aid terrorists and of the barbaric criminals who profane a great religion by committing murder in its name.

This military action is a part of our campaign against terrorism, another front in a war that has already been joined through diplomacy, intelligence, the freezing of financial assets and the arrests of known terrorists by law enforcement agents in 38 countries. Given the nature and reach of our enemies, we will win this conflict by the patient accumulation of successes, by meeting a series of challenges with determination and will and purpose.

Today we focus on Afghanistan, but the battle is broader. Every nation has a choice to make. In this conflict, there is no neutral ground. If any government sponsors the outlaws and killers of innocents, they have become outlaws and murderers, themselves. And they will take that lonely path at their own peril.

I'm speaking to you today from the Treaty Room of the White House, a place where American presidents have worked for peace. We're a peaceful nation. Yet, as we have learned, so suddenly and so tragically, there can be no peace in a world of sudden terror. In the face of today's new threat, the only way to pursue peace is to pursue those who threaten it.

We did not ask for this mission, but we will fulfill it. The name of today's military operation is Enduring Freedom. We defend not only our precious freedoms, but also the freedom of people everywhere to live and raise their children free from fear.

I know many Americans feel fear today. And our government is taking strong precautions. All law enforcement and intelligence agencies are working aggressively around America, around the world and around the clock. At my request, many governors have activated the National Guard to strengthen airport security. We have called up Reserves to reinforce our military capability and strengthen the protection of our homeland.

In the months ahead, our patience will be one of our strengths — patience with the long waits that will result from tighter security; patience and understanding that it will take time to achieve our goals; patience in all the sacrifices that may come.

Today, those sacrifices are being made by members of our Armed Forces who now defend us so far from home, and by their proud and worried families. A commander in chief sends America's sons and daughters into a battle in a foreign land only after the greatest care and a lot of prayer. We ask a lot of those who wear our uniform. We ask them to leave their loved ones, to travel great distances, to risk injury, even to be prepared to make the ultimate sacrifice of their lives. They are dedicated, they are honorable; they represent the best of our country. And we are grateful.

To all the men and women in our military — every sailor, every soldier, every airman, every Coast Guardsman, every Marine — I say this: Your mission is defined; your objectives are clear; your goal is just. You have my full confidence, and you will have every tool you need to carry out your duty.

I recently received a touching letter that says a lot about the state of America in these difficult times — a letter from a fourth-grade girl, with a father in the military: "As much as I don't want my Dad to fight," she wrote, "I'm willing to give him to you."

This is a precious gift, the greatest she could give. This young girl knows what America is all about. Since Sept. 11, an entire generation of young Americans has gained new understanding of the value of freedom, and its cost in duty and in sacrifice. The battle is now joined on many fronts. We will not waver; we will not tire; we will not falter; and we will not fail. Peace and freedom will prevail.

Thank you. May God continue to bless America. ◆

Appendix E

PUBLIC LAWS

Public Laws — 106th Congress

Public laws 106-171 through 106-563, enacted in the second session of the 106th Congress, were published in the previous edition of the CQ Almanac. (2000 Almanac, p. E-3)

PL 106-564 (HR 3756) Establish a standard time zone for Guam and the Commonwealth of the Northern Mariana Islands. Introduced by UNDERWOOD, D-Guam, on Feb. 29, 2000. House passed, under suspension of the rules, Oct. 10. Senate passed Dec. 15. President signed Dec. 23, 2000.

PL 106-565 (HR 4907) Establish the Jamestown 400th Commemoration Commission. Introduced by BATE-MAN, R-Va., on July 20, 2000. House passed, under suspension of the rules Oct. 30. Senate passed Dec. 15. President signed Dec. 23, 2000.

PL 106-566 (S 1694) Direct the secretary of the Interior to conduct a study on the reclamation and reuse of water and wastewater in Hawaii. Introduced by AKAKA, D-Hawaii, on Oct. 6, 1999. Senate Energy and Natural Resources reported, amended, March 9, 2000 (S Rept 106-234). Senate passed, amended, April 13. House Resources reported, with amendment, Sept. 18 (H Rept 106-857). House passed, with amendments, under suspension of rules, Oct. 24. Senate agreed to House amendments Dec. 7. President signed Dec. 23, 2000.

PL 106-567 (HR 5630) Authorize appropriations for fiscal 2001 for intelligence and intelligence-related activities, the Community Management Account and the Central Intelligence Agency Retirement and Disability System. Introduced by GOSS, R-Fla., on Nov. 13, 2000. House Select Intelligence discharged. House passed Nov. 13. Senate passed, with amendments, Dec. 6. House agreed to Senate amendments Dec. 11. President signed Dec. 27, 2000.

PL 106-568 (HR 5528) Authorize the construction of a Wakpa Sica Reconciliation Place in Fort Pierre, S.D. Introduced by THUNE, R-S.D., on Oct. 24, 2000. House passed, amended, under suspension of the rules, Oct. 26. Senate passed Dec. 11. President signed Dec. 27, 2000.

PL 106-569 (HR 5640) Expand home ownership in the United States. Introduced by LEACH, R-Iowa, on Dec. 5, 2000. House passed, under suspension of the rules, Dec. 5. Senate passed Dec. 7. President signed Dec. 27, 2000.

PL 106-570 (S 2943) Authorize additional assistance for international malaria control. Introduced by HELMS, R-N.C., on July 27, 2000. Senate Foreign Relations reported July 27 (no written report). Senate passed Oct. 19. House passed, amended, under suspension of the rules, Oct. 27. Senate agreed to House amendments, with amendment, Dec. 14. House agreed to Senate amendment Dec. 15. President signed Dec. 27, 2000.

PL 106-571 (HR 207) Amend Title 5, U.S. Code, to provide that physicians' comparability allowances be treated as part of basic pay for retirement purposes. Introduced by MORELLA, R-Md., on Jan. 6, 1999. House passed, amended, under suspension of the rules, Oct. 31, 2000. Senate passed Dec. 15. President signed Dec. 28, 2000.

PL 106-572 (HR 2816) Establish a grant program to assist state and local law enforcement in deterring, investigating and prosecuting computer crimes. Introduced by SALMON, R-Ariz., on Sept. 8, 1999. House Judiciary discharged. House passed, amended, Dec. 15, 2000. Senate passed Dec. 15. President signed Dec. 28, 2000.

PL 106-573 (HR 3594) Repeal revisions to the tax code related to the installment method of accounting. Introduced by HERGER, R-Calif., on Feb. 8, 2000. House passed, under suspension of the rules, Dec. 15. Senate passed Dec. 15. President signed Dec. 28, 2000.

PL 106-574 (HR 4020) Authorize an expansion of the boundaries of Sequoia National Park to include Dillonwood Giant Sequoia Grove. Introduced by RADANOVICH, R-Calif., on March 16, 2000. House passed, amended, under suspension of the rules, Oct. 31. Senate passed, with amendment, Dec. 15. House agreed to Senate amendment Dec. 15. President signed Dec. 28, 2000.

PL 106-575 (HR 4656) Authorize the Forest Service to convey certain lands in the Lake Tahoe Basin to the Washoe County School District for use as an elementary school site. Introduced by GIBBONS, R-Nev., on June 14, 2000. House Resources reported Sept. 22 (H Rept 106-885). House failed to pass, under suspension of the rules, Oct. 12. House passed Oct. 24. Senate passed Dec. 15. President signed Dec. 28, 2000.

PL 106-576 (S 1761) Direct the secretary of the Interior, through the Bureau of Reclamation, to conserve and enhance the water supplies of the Lower Rio Grande Valley. Introduced by HUTCHISON, R-Texas, on Oct. 21, 1999. Senate Energy and Natural Resources discharged. Senate passed, amended, Oct. 27, 2000. House passed, with amendment, under sus-

pension of the rules, Dec. 4. Senate agreed to House amendment Dec. 15. President signed Dec. 28, 2000.

PL 106-577 (S 2749) Establish the California Trail Interpretive Center in Elko, Nev., to facilitate the interpretation of the development and use of trails in the settling of the western portion of the United States. Introduced by REID, D-Nev., on June 19, 2000. Senate Energy and Natural Resources reported Sept. 29 (S Rept 106-441). Senate passed Oct. 5. House passed, with amendment, under suspension of the rules, Oct. 24. Senate agreed to House amendment Dec. 15. President signed Dec. 28, 2000.

PL 106-578 (S 2924) Strengthen the enforcement of federal statutes relating to false identification. Introduced by COLLINS, R-Maine, on July 26, 2000. Senate Judiciary reported, amended, Sept. 28 (no written report). Senate passed, amended, Oct. 31. House Ju-

diciary discharged. House passed, with amendment, Dec. 15. Senate agreed to House amendment Dec. 15. President signed Dec. 28, 2000.

PL 106-579 (S 3181) Establish the White House Commission on the National Moment of Remembrance. Introduced by HAGEL, R-Neb., on Oct. 10, 2000. Senate Judiciary discharged. Senate passed Oct. 27. House passed Dec. 15. President signed Dec. 28, 2000.

PL 106-580 (HR 1795) Amend the Public Health Service Act to establish the National Institute of Biomedical Imaging and Engineering. Introduced by BURR, R-N.C., on May 13, 1999. House Commerce reported, amended, Sept. 26, 2000 (H Rept 106-889). House passed, amended, under suspension of the rules, Sept. 27. Senate passed Dec. 15. President signed Dec. 29, 2000. ◆

Public Laws — 107th Congress

PL 107-1 (H J Res 7) Recognize the 90th birthday of Ronald Reagan. Introduced by COX, R-Calif., on Jan. 31, 2001. House passed, under suspension of the rules, Feb. 6. Senate passed Feb. 6. President signed Feb. 15, 2001.

PL 107-2 (HR 559) Designate the U.S. courthouse located at 1 Courthouse Way in Boston, Mass., as the "John Joseph Moakley United States Courthouse." Introduced by McGOVERN, D-Mass., on Feb. 13, 2001. House passed Feb. 14. Senate passed Feb. 15. President signed March 13, 2001.

PL 107-3 (S 279) Affect the representation of the Senate majority and minority membership of the Joint Economic Committee. Introduced by LOTT, R-Miss., on Feb. 7, 2001. Senate passed Feb. 7. House passed Feb. 14. President signed, March 13, 2001.

PL 107-4 (H J Res 19) Provide for the appointment of Walter E. Massey as a citizen regent of the Board of Regents of the Smithsonian Institution. Introduced by JOHNSON, R-Texas, on Feb. 13, 2001. House Administration discharged. House passed Feb. 28. Senate passed March 1. President signed March 16, 2001.

PL 107-5 (S J Res 6) Provide for congressional disapproval of the rule submitted by the Department of Labor under Chapter 8, Title 5, U.S. Code, relating to ergonomics. Introduced by NICKLES, R-Okla., on March 1, 2001. Senate Health, Education, Labor and Pensions discharged March 5. Senate passed March 6. House passed March 7. President signed March 20, 2001.

PL 107-6 (HR 132) Designate the facility of the U.S. Postal Service at 620 Jacaranda St., Lanai City, Hawaii, as the "Goro Hokama Post Office Building." Introduced by MINK, D-Hawaii, on Jan. 3, 2001. House passed, under suspension of the rules, Feb. 7. Senate passed March 21, 2001. President signed April 12, 2001.

PL 107-7 (HR 395) Designate the facility of the U.S. Postal Service located at 2305 Minton Road in West Melbourne, Florida, as the "Ronald W. Reagan Post Office of West Melbourne, Florida." Introduced by WELDON, R-Fla., on Feb. 6, 2001. House passed, under suspension of the rules, Feb. 6. Senate passed March 21. President signed April 12, 2001.

PL 107-8 (HR 256) Extend for 11 additional months the period for which Chapter 12, Title 11 of the U.S. Code is re-enacted. Introduced by SMITH, R-Mich., on Jan. 30, 2001. House Judiciary reported Feb. 26 (H Rept 107-2). House passed, under suspension of the rules, Feb. 28. Senate passed April 26. President signed May 11, 2001.

PL 107-9 (S 700) Establish a federal interagency task force for the purpose of coordinating actions to prevent the outbreak of bovine spongiform encephalopathy (commonly known as "mad cow disease") and foot-and-mouth disease in the United States. Introduced by CAMPBELL, R-Colo., on April 4, 2001. Senate passed, amended, April 5. House passed May 9. President signed May 24, 2001.

PL 107-10 (HR 428) Authorize the secretary of State to endorse and obtain observer status for Taiwan at the annual summit of the World Health Organization. Introduced by BROWN, D-Ohio, on Feb. 6, 2001. House passed, amended, under suspension of the rules, April 24. Senate Foreign Relations discharged. Senate passed, with amendment, May 9. House agreed to Senate amendment, under suspension of the rules, May 15. President signed May 28, 2001.

PL 107-11 (HR 1696) Expedite the construction of the World War II memorial in the District of Columbia. Introduced by STUMP, R-Ariz., on May 3, 2001. House passed, under suspension of the rules, May 15. Senate Energy and Natural Resources discharged. Senate passed, with amendment, May 21. House agreed to Senate amendment, under suspension of the rules, May 22. President signed May 28, 2001.

PL 107-12 (HR 802) Authorize the Public Safety Officer Medal of Valor. Introduced by SMITH, R-Texas, on Feb. 28, 2001. House Judiciary reported March 12 (H Rept 107-15). House passed, under suspension of the rules, March 22. Senate Judiciary reported May 10 (no written report). Senate passed May 14. President signed May 30, 2001.

PL 107-13 (HR 581) Authorize the secretaries of Agriculture and the Interior to use funds appropriated for wildland fire management in the Department of the Interior and Related Agencies Fiscal 2001 Appropriations Act, to reimburse the U.S. Fish and Wildlife Service and the National Marine Fisheries Service to facilitate the interagency cooperation required under the Endangered Species Act of 1973 in connection with wildland fire management. Introduced by HEFLEY, R-Colo., on Feb. 13, 2001. House Resources reported April 3 (H Rept 107-35). House passed, amended, May 9. Senate Environment and Public Works reported May 23 (no written report.) Senate passed May 24. President signed June 3, 2001.

PL 107-14 (HR 801) Amend Title 38, U.S. Code, to expand eligibility for CHAMPVA, and to provide for family coverage and retroactive expansion of the in-

crease in maximum benefits under Servicemembers' Group Life Insurance. Introduced by SMITH, R-N.J., on Feb. 28, 2001. House Veterans' Affairs reported, amended, March 26 (H Rept 107-27). House passed, amended, under suspension of the rules, March 27. Senate Veterans' Affairs discharged. Senate passed, with amendments, May 24. House agreed to Senate amendments May 24. President signed June 5, 2001.

PL 107-15 (HR 1727) Amend the Taxpayer Relief Act of 1997 to provide for consistent treatment of survivor benefits for public safety officers killed in the line of duty. Introduced by RAMSTAD, R-Minn., on May 3, 2001. House Ways and Means reported, amended, May 15 (H Rept 107-65). House passed, amended, May 15. Senate passed May 22. President signed June 5, 2001.

PL 107-16 (HR 1836) Provide for reconciliation pursuant to Section 104 of the concurrent resolution on the budget for fiscal 2002. Introduced by THOMAS, R-Calif., on May 15, 2001. House Rules reported May 15 (H Rept 107-68). House passed May 16. Senate passed, with amendment, May 23. Conference report filed in the House on May 26 (H Rept 107-84). House agreed to conference report May 26. Senate agreed to conference report May 26. President signed June 7, 2001.

PL 107-17 (HR 1914) Extend for four additional months the period for which Chapter 12, Title 11 of the U.S. Code is re-enacted. Introduced by SMITH, R-Mich., on May 17, 2001. House passed, under suspension of the rules, June 6. Senate passed June 8. President signed June 26, 2001.

PL 107-18 (S 1029) Clarify the authority of the Department of Housing and Urban Development with respect to the use of fees during fiscal 2001 for the manufactured housing program. Introduced by SARBANES, D-Md., on June 13, 2001. Senate passed June 13. House passed, under suspension of the rules, June 20. President signed July 5, 2001.

PL 107-19 (S 657) Authorize funding for the National 4-H Program Centennial Initiative. Introduced by LUGAR, R-Ind., on March, 29, 2001. Senate Agriculture, Nutrition and Forestry discharged. Senate passed, amended, June 19. House passed, under suspension of the rules, June 25. President signed July 10, 2001.

PL 107-20 (HR 2216) Make supplemental appropriations for the fiscal year ending Sept. 30, 2001. Introduced by YOUNG, R-Fla., on June 19, 2001. House Appropriations reported June 19 (H Rept 107-102). House passed, amended, June 20. Senate passed, with amendment, July 10. Conference report filed in the House on July 19 (H Rept 107-148). House agreed to conference report July 20. Senate agreed to conference report July 20. President signed July 24, 2001.

PL 107-21 (S 360) Honor Paul D. Coverdell. Introduced by LOTT, R-Miss., on Feb. 15, 2001. Senate passed Feb. 15. House passed, under suspension of the rules, July 17. President signed July 26, 2001.

PL 107-22 (S 1190) Amend the Internal Revenue Code of 1986 to rename the education individual retirement accounts as the "Coverdell Education Savings Account." Introduced by LOTT, R-Miss., on July 18, 2001. Senate passed July 18. House Ways and Means discharged. House passed July 23. President signed July 26, 2001.

PL 107-23 (S 468) Designate the federal building at 6230 Van Nuys Blvd.,Van Nuys, Calif., as the "James C. Corman Federal Building." Introduced by FEINSTEIN, D-Calif., on March 6, 2001. Senate Environment and Public Works reported May 23 (no written report). Senate passed May 24. House passed, under suspension of the rules, July 23. President signed Aug. 3, 2001.

PL 107-24 (HR 1954) Extend the authorities of the Iran and Libya Sanctions Act of 1996 until Aug. 5, 2006. Introduced by GILMAN, R-N.Y., on May 23, 2001. House International Relations reported, amended, June 22 (H Rept 107-107, Part 1). House Ways and Means reported, amended, July 16 (H Rept 107-107, Part 2). House Financial Services and House Government Reform discharged. House passed, amended, under suspension of the rules, July 26. Senate passed July 27. President signed Aug. 3, 2001.

PL 107-25 (HR 2213) Respond to the continuing economic crisis adversely affecting U.S. agricultural producers. Introduced by COMBEST, R-Texas, on June 19, 2001. House Agriculture reported, amended, June 26 (H Rept 107-111). House passed, amended, under suspension of the rules, June 26. Senate Agriculture, Nutrition, and Forestry discharged. Senate passed Aug. 3. President signed Aug. 13, 2001.

PL 107-26 (HR 2131) Reauthorize the Tropical Forest Conservation Act of 1998 through fiscal 2004. Introduced by PORTMAN, R-Ohio, on June 12, 2001. House International Relations reported, amended, June 28 (H Rept 107-119). House passed, amended, under suspension of the rules, July 10. Senate Foreign Relations discharged. Senate passed July 23. President signed Aug. 17, 2001.

PL 107-27 (HR 93) Amend Title 5, U.S. Code, to provide that the mandatory separation age for federal firefighters be made the same as the age that applies with respect to federal law enforcement officers. Introduced by GALLEGLY, R-Calif., on Jan. 3, 2001. House passed, amended, under suspension of the rules, Jan. 30. Senate Governmental Affairs reported Aug. 2 (no written report). Senate passed Aug. 3. President signed Aug. 20, 2001.

PL 107-28 (HR 271) Direct the secretary of the Interior to convey a former Bureau of Land Management administrative site to the city of Carson City, Nev., for use as a senior center. Introduced by GIBBONS, R-Nev., on Jan. 30, 2001. House Resources reported July 10 (H Rept 107-122). House passed, under suspension of the rules, July 23. Senate passed Aug. 3. President signed Aug. 20, 2001.

PL 107-29 (HR 364) Designate the facility of the U.S. Postal Service located at 5927 S.W. 70th St. in Miami, Fla., as the "Marjory Williams Scrivens Post Office." Introduced by MEEKS, D-Fla., on Jan. 31, 2001. House passed, under suspension of the rules, March 14. Senate Governmental Affairs reported Aug. 2 (no written report). Senate passed Aug. 3. President signed Aug. 20, 2001.

PL 107-30 (HR 427) Provide further protections for the watershed of the Little Sandy River as part of the Bull Run Watershed Management Unit, Ore. Introduced by BLUMENAUER, D-Ore., on Feb. 6, 2001. House Resources reported July 23 (H Rept 107-151, Part 1). House Agriculture discharged. House passed, under suspension of the rules, July 23. Senate passed Aug. 3. President signed Aug. 20, 2001.

PL 107-31 (HR 558) Designate the federal building and U.S. courthouse located at 504 W. Hamilton St. in Allentown, Pa., as the "Edward N. Cahn Federal Building and U.S. Courthouse." Introduced by TOOMEY, R-Pa., on Feb. 12, 2001. House passed, under suspension of the rules, Feb. 28. Senate Environment and Public Works discharged. Senate passed Aug. 3. President signed Aug. 20, 2001.

PL 107-32 (HR 821) Designate the facility of the U.S. Postal Service located at 1030 S. Church St., Asheboro, N.C., as the "W. Joe Trogdon Post Office Building." Introduced by COBLE, R-N.C., on March 1, 2001. House passed, under suspension of the rules, March 14. Senate Governmental Affairs reported Aug. 2 (no written report). Senate passed Aug. 3. President signed Aug. 20, 2001.

PL 107-33 (HR 988) Designate the U.S. courthouse located at 40 Centre St., New York, N.Y., as the "Thurgood Marshall U.S. Courthouse." Introduced by ENGEL, D-N.Y., on March 13, 2001. House Transportation and Infrastructure reported July 26 (H Rept 107-166). House passed Aug. 2. Senate passed Aug. 3. President signed Aug. 20, 2001.

PL 107-34 (HR 1183) Designate the facility of the U.S. Postal Service located at 113 S. Main St., Sylvania, Ga., as the "G. Elliot Hagan Post Office Building." Introduced by KINGSTON, R-Ga., on March 22, 2001. House passed, under suspension of the rules, June 5. Senate Governmental Affairs reported Aug. 2 (no written report). Senate passed Aug. 3. President signed Aug. 20, 2001.

PL 107-35 (HR 1753) Designate the facility of the U.S. Postal Service located at 419 Rutherford Ave., N.E., Roanoke, Va., as the "M. Caldwell Butler Post Office Building." Introduced by GOODLATTE, R-Va., on May 8, 2001. House passed, under suspension of the rules, June 20. Senate Governmental Affairs reported Aug. 2 (no written report). Senate passed Aug. 3. President signed Aug. 20, 2001.

PL 107-36 (HR 2043) Designate the facility of the U.S. Postal Service located at 2719 South Webster St., Kokomo, Ind., as the "Elwood Haynes 'Bud' Hillis Post Office Building." Introduced by BUYER, R-Ind., on May 26, 2001. House passed, under suspension of the rules, June 5. Senate Governmental Affairs reported Aug. 2 (no written report). Senate passed Aug. 3. President signed Aug. 20, 2001.

PL 107-37 (HR 2882) Provide for the expedited payments of certain benefits for a public safety officer who was killed or suffered a catastrophic injury as a direct and proximate result of a personal injury sustained in the line of duty in connection with the terrorist attacks of Sept. 11, 2001. Introduced by NADLER, D-N.Y., on Sept. 13. House Judiciary discharged. House passed Sept. 13. Senate passed Sept. 13. President signed Sept. 18, 2001.

PL 107-38 (HR 2888) Make emergency supplemental appropriations for fiscal 2001 for additional disaster assistance, for anti-terrorism initiatives, and for assistance in the recovery from the tragedy that occurred Sept. 11, 2001. Introduced by YOUNG, R-Fla., on Sept. 14, 2001. House passed Sept. 14. Senate passed Sept. 14. President signed Sept. 18, 2001.

PL 107-39 (S J Res 22) Express the sense of the Senate and House of Representatives regarding the terrorist attacks launched against the United States on Sept. 11, 2001. Introduced by DASCHLE, D-S.D., on Sept. 12, 2001. Senate passed Sept. 12. House passed Sept. 13. President signed Sept. 18, 2001.

PL 107-40 (S J Res 23) Authorize the use of United States armed forces against those responsible for the recent attacks launched against the United States. Introduced by DASCHLE, D-S.D., on Sept. 14, 2001. Senate passed Sept. 14. House passed Sept. 14. President signed Sept. 18, 2001.

PL 107-41 (HR 2133) Establish a commission for the purpose of encouraging and providing for the commemoration of the 50th anniversary of the Supreme Court decision in Brown v. Board of Education. Introduced by RYUN, R-Kan., on June 12, 2001. House passed, amended, under suspension of the rules, June 27. Senate Judiciary reported, with amendments (no written report) Aug. 2. Senate passed, with amendments, Aug. 3. House agreed to Senate amendments, under suspension of the rules, Sept. 10. President signed Sept. 18, 2001.

PL 107-42 (HR 2926) Preserve the continued viability of the United States air transportation system. Introduced by YOUNG, R-Alaska, on Sept. 21, 2001. Senate passed Sept. 21. House passed Sept. 21. President signed Sept. 22, 2001.

PL 107-43 (HR 2603) Implement the agreement establishing a United States-Jordan free trade area. Introduced by THOMAS, R-Calif., on July 24, 2001. House Ways and Means reported, amended July 31 (H Rept 107-176, Part 1). House Judiciary discharged. House passed, amended, under suspension of the rules, July 31. Senate Finance discharged. Senate passed Sept. 24. President signed Sept. 28, 2001.

PL 107-44 (H J Res 65) Make continuing appropriations for fiscal 2002. Introduced by YOUNG, R-Fla., on Sept. 24, 2001. House passed Sept. 24. Senate passed Sept. 25. President signed Sept. 28, 2001.

PL 107-45 (S 1424) Amend the Immigration and Nationality Act to provide permanent authority for the admission of "S" visa non-immigrants. Introduced by KENNEDY, D-Mass., on Sept. 13, 2001. Senate passed Sept. 13. House passed Sept. 15. President signed Oct. 1, 2001.

PL 107-46 (S 248) Amend the Admiral James W. Nance and Meg Donovan Foreign Relations Authorization Act, Fiscal Years 2000 and 2001, to adjust a condition on the payment of arrearages to the United Nations that sets the maximum share of any United Nations peacekeeping operation's budget that may be assessed of any country. Introduced by HELMS, R-N.C., on Feb. 6, 2001. Senate Foreign Relations reported Feb. 7 (no written report). Senate passed Feb. 7. House passed, under suspension of the rules, Sept. 24. President signed Oct. 5, 2001.

PL 107-47 (HR 2510) Extend the expiration date of the Defense Production Act of 1950. Introduced by KING, R-N.Y., on July 17, 2001. House Financial Services reported July 30 (H Rept 107-173). House passed, under suspension of the rules, Sept. 5. Senate Banking, Housing, and Urban Affairs discharged. Senate passed, with amendment, Sept. 21. House agreed to Senate amendment, with amendments, Sept. 25. Senate agreed to House amendments Sept. 26. President signed Oct. 5, 2001.

PL 107-48 (H J Res 68) Make further continuing appropriations for fiscal 2002. Introduced by YOUNG, R-Fla., on Oct. 11, 2001. House Appropriations discharged. House passed Oct. 11. Senate passed Oct. 12. President signed Oct. 12, 2001.

PL 107-49 (HR 1583) Designate the federal building and United States courthouse located at 121 West Spring St., New Albany, Ind., as the "Lee H. Hamilton Federal Building and United States Courthouse." Introduced by HILL, D-Ind., on April 25, 2001. House

passed, under suspension of the rules, Sept. 24. Senate passed Sept. 25. President signed Oct. 15, 2001.

PL 107-50 (HR 1860) Reauthorize the Small Business Technology Transfer Program. Introduced by EHLERS, R-Mich., on May 16, 2001. House Small Business reported, amended, on Sept. 21 (H Rept 107-213, Part 1). House Science discharged. House passed, under suspension of the rules, Sept. 24. Senate passed Sept. 26. President signed Oct. 15, 2001.

PL 107-51 (H J Res 42) Memorialize fallen firefighters by lowering the American flag to half-staff in honor of the National Fallen Firefighters Memorial Service in Emittsburg, Md. Introduced by CASTLE, R-Del., on March 29, 2001. House passed, amended, under suspension of the rules, Oct. 2. Senate passed Oct. 4. President signed Oct. 16, 2001.

PL 107-52 (H J Res 51) Approve the extension of nondiscriminatory treatment with respect to the products of the Socialist Republic of Vietnam. Introduced by ARMEY, R-Texas, on June 12, 2001. House Ways and Means reported Sept. 5 (H Rept 107-198). House passed Sept. 6. Senate passed Oct. 3. President signed Oct. 16, 2001.

PL 107-53 (H J Res 69) Make further continuing appropriations for fiscal 2002. Introduced by YOUNG, R-Fla., on Oct. 17, 2001. House Appropriations discharged. House passed Oct. 17. Senate passed Oct. 17. President signed Oct. 22, 2001.

PL 107-54 (S J Res 19) Provide for the reappointment of Anne d'Harnoncourt as a citizen regent of the Board of Regents of the Smithsonian Institution. Introduced by COCHRAN, R-Miss., on July 12, 2001. Senate Rules and Administration reported Aug. 2 (no written report). Senate passed Sept. 13. House passed, under suspension of the rules, Oct. 9. President signed Oct. 24, 2001.

PL 107-55 (S J Res 20) Provide for the appointment of Roger W. Sant as a citizen regent of the Board of Regents of the Smithsonian Institution. Introduced by COCHRAN, R-Miss., on July 12, 2001. Senate Rules and Administration reported Aug. 2 (no written report). Senate passed Sept. 13. House passed, under suspension of the rules, Oct. 9. President signed Oct. 24, 2001.

PL 107-56 (HR 3162) Deter and punish terrorist acts in the United States and around the world and enhance law enforcement investigatory tools. Introduced by SENSENBRENNER, R-Wis., on Oct. 23, 2001. House passed, under suspension of the rules, Oct. 24. Senate passed Oct. 25. President signed Oct. 26, 2001.

PL 107-57 (S 1465) Authorize the president to exercise waivers of foreign assistance restrictions with respect to Pakistan through Sept. 30, 2003. Introduced by

BROWNBACK, R-Kan., on Sept. 25, 2001. Senate Foreign Relations reported, amended, Oct. 4 (no written report). Senate passed, amended, Oct. 4. House passed, under suspension of the rules, Oct. 16. President signed Oct. 27, 2001.

PL 107-58 (H J Res 70) Make further continuing appropriations for fiscal 2002. Introduced by YOUNG, R-Fla., on Oct. 24, 2001. House passed Oct. 25. Senate passed Oct. 25. President signed Oct. 31, 2001.

PL 107-59 (HR 146) Authorize the secretary of the Interior to study the suitability and feasibility of designating the Great Falls Historic District in Paterson, N.J., as a unit of the National Park System. Introduced by PASCRELL, D-N.J., on Jan. 3, 2001. House Resources reported April 24 (H Rept 107-47). House passed May 9. Senate Energy and Natural Resources reported Oct. 1 (S Rept 107-74). Senate passed Oct. 17. President signed Nov. 5, 2001.

PL 107-60 (HR 1000) Adjust the boundary of the William Howard Taft National Historic Site in Ohio and authorize an exchange of land in connection with the site. Introduced by PORTMAN, R-Ohio, on March 13, 2001. House Resources reported, amended, June 6 (H Rept 107-88). House passed, under suspension of the rules, June 6. Senate Energy and Natural Resources reported Oct. 1 (S Rept 107-76). Senate passed Oct. 17. President signed Nov. 5, 2001.

PL 107-61 (HR 1161) Authorize the American Friends of the Czech Republic to establish a memorial to honor Tomas G. Masaryk in the District of Columbia. Introduced by GILMAN, R-N.Y., on March 22, 2001. House Resources reported, amended, Sept. 28 (H Rept 107-221). House passed, under suspension of the rules, Oct. 2. Senate passed Oct. 17. President signed Nov. 5, 2001.

PL 107-62 (HR 1668) Authorize the Adams Memorial Foundation to establish a commemorative work on federal land in the District of Columbia and its environs to honor former President John Adams and his family. Introduced by ROEMER, D-Ind., on May 1, 2001. House passed, amended, under suspension of the rules, June 25. Senate Energy and Natural Resources reported Oct. 1 (S Rept 107-77). Senate passed Oct.17. President signed Nov. 5, 2001.

PL 107-63 (HR 2217) Make appropriations for the Department of the Interior and related agencies for the fiscal year ending Sept. 30, 2002. Introduced by SKEEN, R-N.M., on June 19, 2001. House Appropriations reported June 19 (H Rept 107-103). House passed, with amendments, June 21. Senate Appropriations reported, with amendments, June 29 (S Rept 107-36). Senate passed, with amendments, July 12. Conference report filed in the House, on Oct. 11 (H Rept 107-234). House agreed to conference re-

port Oct. 17. Senate agreed to conference report Oct. 17. President signed Nov. 5, 2001.

PL 107-64 (HR 2904) Make appropriations for military construction, family housing and base realignment and closure for the Department of Defense for the fiscal year ending Sept. 30, 2002. Introduced by HOBSON, R-Ohio, on Sept. 20, 2001. House Appropriations reported Sept. 20 (H Rept 107-207). House passed Sept. 21. Senate Appropriations discharged. Senate passed, amended, Sept. 26. Conference report filed in the House on Oct. 16 (H Rept 107-246). House agreed to conference report Oct. 17. Senate agreed to conference report Oct. 18. President signed Nov. 5, 2001.

PL 107-65 (HR 182) Amend the Wild and Scenic Rivers Act to designate a segment of the Eight Mile River in Connecticut for study for potential addition to the National Wild and Scenic Rivers System. Introduced by SIMMONS, R-Conn., Jan. 3, 2001. House Resources reported, amended, April 3 (H Rept 107-36). House passed, amended, under suspension of the rules, May 1. Senate Energy and Natural Resources reported Oct. 1 (S Rept 107-75). Senate passed Oct. 17. President signed Nov. 6, 2001.

PL 107-66 (HR 2311) Make appropriations for energy and water development for the fiscal year ending Sept. 30, 2002. Introduced by CALLAHAN, R-Ala., on June 26, 2001. House Appropriations reported June 26, (H Rept 107-112). House passed, amended, June 28. Senate Appropriations Committee discharged. Senate passed, with amendments, July 19. Conference report filed in the House on Oct. 30 (H Rept 107-258). House agreed to conference report Nov. 1. Senate agreed to conference report Nov. 1. President signed Nov. 12, 2001.

PL 107-67 (HR 2590) Make appropriations for the Treasury Department, the U.S. Postal Service, the Executive Office of the President, and certain Independent Agencies, for the fiscal year ending Sept. 30, 2002. Introduced by ISTOOK, R-Okla., on July 23, 2001. House Appropriations reported July 23 (H Rept 107-152). House passed, with amendments, July 25. Senate Appropriations discharged. Senate passed, amended, Sept. 19. Conference report filed in the House on Oct. 26 (H Rept 107-253). House agreed to conference report Oct. 31. Senate agreed to conference report Nov. 1. President signed Nov. 12, 2001.

PL 107-68 (HR 2647) Make appropriations for the legislative branch for the fiscal year ending Sept. 30, 2002. Introduced by TAYLOR, R-N.C., on July 26, 2001. House Appropriations reported July 26 (H Rept 107-169). House passed, with amendments, July 31. Senate passed, with amendments, July 31. Conference report filed in the House on Oct. 30 (H Rept 107-259). House agreed to conference report Nov. 1. Senate agreed to conference report Nov. 1. President signed Nov. 12, 2001.

PL 107-69 (HR 2925) Amend the Reclamation Recreation Management Act of 1992 to provide for the security of dams, facilities and resources under the jurisdiction of the Bureau of Reclamation. Introduced by CALVERT, R-Calif., on Sept. 21, 2001. House Resources reported, amended, Oct. 3 (no written report). House passed, amended, under suspension of the rules, Oct. 23. Senate passed Oct. 30. President signed Nov. 12, 2001.

PL 107-70 (H J Res 74) Make further continuing appropriations for fiscal 2002. Introduced by YOUNG, R-Fla., on Nov. 15, 2001. House Appropriations discharged. House passed Nov. 15. Senate passed Nov. 15. President signed Nov. 17, 2001.

PL 107-71 (S 1447) Improve aviation security. Introduced by HOLLINGS, D-S.C., on Sept. 21, 2001. Senate passed, amended, Oct. 11. House passed, amended, Nov. 6. Conference report filed in the House on Nov. 16 (H Rept 107-296). Senate agreed to conference report Nov. 16. House agreed to conference report Nov. 16. President signed Nov. 19, 2001.

PL 107-72 (HR 768) Amend the Improving America's Schools Act of 1994 to extend the favorable treatment of need-based education aid under the antitrust laws. Introduced by SMITH, R-Texas, on Feb. 28, 2001. House Judiciary reported April 3 (H Rept 107-32). House passed, under suspension of the rules, April 3. Senate Health, Education, Labor, and Pensions discharged. Senate Judiciary discharged. Senate passed, amended, Oct. 3. House agreed to Senate amendments, under suspension of the rules, Nov. 6. President signed Nov. 20, 2001.

PL 107-73 (HR 2620) Make appropriations for the departments of Veterans Affairs and Housing and Urban Development, and for independent agencies, boards, commissions, corporations and offices for the fiscal year ending Sept. 30, 2002. Introduced by WALSH, R-N.Y., on July 25, 2001. House Appropriations reported July 25 (H Rept 107-159). House passed, amended, July 31. Senate passed, with amendment, Aug. 2. Conference report filed in the House on Nov. 6 (H Rept 107-272). House agreed to conference report Nov. 8. Senate agreed to conference report Nov. 8. President signed Nov. 26, 2001.

PL 107-74 (HR 1042) Prevent the elimination of certain reports. Introduced by GRUCCI, R-N.Y., on March 15, 2001. House passed, amended, under suspension of the rules, March 21. Senate Governmental Affairs reported Oct. 31 (S Rept 107-90). Senate passed Nov. 15. President signed Nov. 28, 2001.

PL 107-75 (HR 1552) Extend the moratorium enacted by the Internet Tax Freedom Act through Nov. 1, 2003. Introduced by COX, R-Calif., on April 24, 2001. House Judiciary reported, amended, Oct. 16 (H Rept 107-240). House passed, amended, under sus-

pension of the rules, Oct. 16. Senate passed Nov. 15. President signed Nov. 28, 2001.

PL 107-76 (HR 2330) Make appropriations for agriculture, rural development, Food and Drug Administration, and related agencies' programs for the fiscal year ending Sept. 30, 2002. Introduced by BONILLA, R-Texas, on June 27, 2001. House Appropriations reported June 27 (H Rept 107-116). House passed, amended, July 11. Senate Appropriations discharged. Senate passed, with amendment, Oct. 25. Conference report filed in the House on Nov. 9 (H Rept 107-275). House agreed to conference report Nov. 13. Senate agreed to conference report Nov. 15. President signed Nov. 28, 2001.

PL 107-77 (HR 2500) Make appropriations for the departments of Commerce, Justice, State, and the Judiciary, and related agencies for the fiscal year ending Sept. 30, 2002. Introduced by WOLF, R-Va., on July 13, 2001. House Appropriations reported July 13 (H Rept 107-139). House passed, amended, July 18. Senate passed, with amendments, Sept. 13. Senate amended its amendment Sept. 21. Conference report filed in the House on Nov. 9 (H Rept 107-278). House agreed to conference report Nov. 14. Senate agreed to conference report Nov. 15. President signed Nov. 28, 2001.

PL 107-78 (HR 2924) Provide authority to the Federal Power Marketing Administrations to reduce vandalism and destruction of property. Introduced by CALVERT, R-Calif., on Sept. 21, 2001. House Resources reported Oct. 3 (no written report). House passed, amended, under suspension of the rules, Oct. 23. Senate passed Nov. 15. President signed Nov. 28, 2001.

PL 107-79 (H J Res 76) Make further continuing appropriations for fiscal 2002. Introduced by YOUNG, R-Fla., on Dec. 5, 2001. House Appropriations discharged. House passed Dec. 5. Senate passed Dec. 5. President signed Dec. 7, 2001.

PL 107-80 (S 1459) Designate the federal building and U.S. courthouse located at 550 West Fort St., Boise, Idaho, as the "James A. McClure Federal Building and U.S. Courthouse." Introduced by CRAPO, R-Idaho, on Sept. 25, 2001. Senate Environment and Public Works reported Nov. 8 (no written report). Senate passed Nov. 15. House passed, under suspension of the rules, Nov. 27. President signed Dec. 12, 2001.

PL 107-81 (S 1573) Authorize provision of education and health assistance to the women and children of Afghanistan. Introduced by HUTCHISON, R-Texas, on Oct. 25, 2001. Senate passed, amended, Nov. 15. House passed, under suspension of the rules, Nov. 27. President signed Dec. 12, 2001.

PL 107-82 (HR 2291) Extend the authorization of the Drug-Free Communities Support Program for an addi-

tional five years and authorize a National Community Antidrug Coalition Institute. Introduced by PORTMAN, R-Ohio, on June 21, 2001. House Government Reform reported July 30 (H Rept 107-175, Part 1). House Energy and Commerce discharged. House passed under suspension of the rules, Sept. 5. Senate passed Nov. 29. President signed Dec. 14, 2001.

PL 107-83 (H J Res 78) Make further continuing appropriations for fiscal 2002. Introduced by YOUNG, R-Fla., on Dec. 12, 2001. House Appropriations discharged. House passed Dec. 13. Senate passed Dec. 14. President signed Dec. 15, 2001.

PL 107-84 (HR 717) Amend the Public Health Service Act to provide for research and services with respect to Duchenne muscular dystrophy. Introduced by WICKER, R-Miss., on Feb. 14, 2001. House Energy and Commerce reported, amended, Sept. 5 (H Rept 107-195). House passed, under suspension of the rules, Sept. 24. Senate Health, Education, Labor, and Pensions reported, amended, Oct. 30 (no written report). Senate passed, Nov. 15. House agreed to Senate amendment Nov. 29. President signed Dec. 18, 2001.

PL 107-85 (HR 1766) Designate the facility of the U.S. Postal Service at 4270 John Marr Drive, Annandale, Va., as the "Stan Parris Post Office Building." Introduced by WOLF, R-Va., on May 8, 2001. House passed, under suspension of the rules, Sept. 10. Senate Governmental Affairs reported Nov. 16 (no written report). Senate passed Nov. 30. President signed Dec. 18, 2001.

PL 107-86 (HR 2261) Designate the facility of the U.S. Postal Service at 2853 Candler Road, Decatur, Ga., as the "Earl T. Shinhoster Post Office." Introduced by McKINNEY, D-Ga., on June 20, 2001. House passed, under suspension of the rules, Oct. 16. Senate Governmental Affairs reported Nov. 16 (no written report). Senate passed Nov. 30. President signed Dec. 18, 2001.

PL 107-87 (HR 2299) Make appropriations for the Department of Transportation and related agencies for the fiscal year ending Sept. 30, 2002. Introduced by ROGERS, R-Ky., on June 22, 2001. House Appropriations reported June 22 (H Rept 107-108). House passed, amended, June 26. Senate Appropriations discharged. Senate passed, with amendment, Aug. 1. Conference report filed in the House on Nov. 30 (H Rept 107-308). House agreed to conference report Nov. 30. Senate agreed to conference report Dec. 4. President signed Dec. 18, 2001.

PL 107-88 (HR 2454) Designate the facility of the U.S. Postal Service at 5472 Crenshaw Blvd. in Los Angeles as the "Congressman Julian C. Dixon Post Office Building." Introduced by WATSON, D-Calif., on July 10, 2001. House passed, amended, under suspension of the rules, Oct. 16. Senate Governmental Af-

fairs reported Nov. 16 (no written report). Senate passed Nov. 30. President signed Dec. 18, 2001.

PL 107-89 (H J Res 71) Amend Title 36, U.S. Code, to designate Sept. 11 as Patriot Day. Introduced by FOSSELLA, R-N.Y., on Oct. 25, 2001. House passed Oct. 25. Senate Judiciary discharged. Senate passed Nov. 30. President signed Dec. 18, 2001.

PL 107-90 (HR 10) Provide for pension reform. Introduced by PORTMAN, R-Ohio, on March 14, 2001. House Ways and Means reported, amended, May 1 (H Rept 107-51, Part 1). House Education and the Workforce reported, amended, May 1 (H Rept 107-51, Part 2). House passed, amended, May 2. Senate passed, with amendments, Dec. 5. House agreed to Senate amendments, under suspension of the rules, Dec. 11. President signed Dec. 21, 2001.

PL 107-91 (HR 1230) Provide for the establishment of the Detroit River International Wildlife Refuge in Michigan. Introduced by DINGELL, D-Mich., on March 27, 2001. House Resources reported, amended, Nov. 5 (H Rept 107-270). House passed, under suspensions of the rules, Nov. 27. Senate Environment and Public Works discharged. Senate passed Dec. 8. President signed Dec. 21, 2001.

PL 107-92 (HR 1761) Designate the facility of the U.S. Postal Service at 8588 Richmond Highway, Alexandria, Va., as the "Herb Harris Post Office Building." Introduced by MORAN, D-Va., on May 8, 2001. House passed, amended, under suspension of the rules, Sept. 10. Senate Governmental Affairs discharged. Senate passed Dec. 6. President signed Dec. 21, 2001.

PL 107-93 (HR 2061) Amend the charter of Southeastern University of the District of Columbia. Introduced by NORTON, D-D.C., on June 5, 2001. House passed, under suspension of the rules, Sept. 20. Senate Governmental Affairs reported Nov. 29 (S Rept 107-102). Senate passed Dec. 6. President signed Dec. 21, 2001.

PL 107-94 (HR 2540) Amend Title 38, U.S. Code, to provide a cost of living adjustment in the rates of disability compensation for veterans with service-related disabilities and in the rates of dependency and indemnity compensation for survivors of such veterans. Introduced by SMITH, R-N.J., on July 18, 2001. House Veterans' Affairs reported, amended, July 24 (H Rept 107-156). House passed, amended, under suspension of the rules, July 31. Senate Veterans' Affairs discharged. Senate passed, with amendments, Nov. 15. House agreed to Senate amendments Dec. 11. President signed Dec. 21, 2001.

PL 107-95 (HR 2716) Amend Title 38, U.S. Code, to revise, improve and consolidate provisions of law providing benefits and services for homeless veterans.

Introduced by SMITH, R-N.J., on Aug. 2, 2001. House Veterans' Affairs reported, amended, Oct. 16 (H Rept 107-241, Part 1). House Financial Services discharged. House passed, amended, under suspension of the rules, Oct. 16. Senate passed, with amendment, Dec. 6, 2001. House agreed to Senate amendment Dec. 11. President signed Dec. 21, 2001.

PL 107-96 (HR 2944) Make appropriations for the government of the District of Columbia and other activities chargeable in whole or in part against the revenues of the District for the fiscal year ending Sept. 30, 2002. Introduced by KNOLLENBERG, R-Mich., on Sept. 24, 2001. House Appropriations reported Sept. 24 (H Rept 107-216). House passed, amended, Sept. 25. Senate Appropriations discharged. Senate passed, with amendment, Nov. 7. Conference report filed in the House on Dec. 5 (H Rept 107-321). House agreed to conference report Dec. 6. Senate agreed to conference report Dec. 7. President signed Dec. 21, 2001.

PL 107-97 (H J Res 79) Make further continuing appropriations for fiscal 2002. Introduced by YOUNG, R-Fla., on Dec. 19, 2001. House passed Dec. 20. Senate passed Dec. 20. President signed Dec. 21, 2001.

PL 107-98 (H J Res 80) Appoint the day for convening the second session of the 107th Congress. Introduced by ARMEY, R-Texas, on Dec. 20, 2001. House passed Dec. 20. Senate passed Dec. 20. President signed Dec. 21, 2001.

PL 107-99 (S 494) Provide for a transition to democracy and promote economic recovery in Zimbabwe. Introduced by FRIST, R-Tenn., on March 8, 2001. Senate Foreign Relations reported, amended, July 16 (no written report). Senate passed, amended, Aug. 1. House International Relations reported, with amendment, Dec. 4 (H Rept 107-312, Part 1). House Financial Services discharged. House passed, with amendment, under suspension of the rules, Dec. 4. Senate agreed to House amendment Dec. 11. President signed Dec. 21, 2001.

PL 107-100 (S 1196) Amend the Small Business Investment Act of 1958. Introduced by BOND, R-Mo., on July 18, 2001. Senate Small Business reported Aug. 28 (S Rept 107-55). Senate passed, amended, Nov. 15. House passed, with amendment, Nov. 16. Senate agreed to House amendment with amendment Dec. 8. House agreed to Senate amendment, Dec. 11. President signed Dec. 21, 2001.

PL 107-101 (S J Res 26) Provide for the appointment of Patricia Q. Stonesifer as a citizen regent of the Board of Regents of the Smithsonian Institution. Introduced by COCHRAN, R-Miss., on Oct. 17, 2001. Senate Rules and Administration discharge. Senate passed Nov. 29. House passed, under suspension of the rules, Dec. 11. President signed Dec. 21, 2001.

PL 107-102 (HR 483) Modify the use of the trust land and resources of the Confederated Tribes of the Warm Springs Reservation of Oregon. Introduced by WALDEN, R-Ore., on Feb. 6, 2001. House Resources reported, amended, Oct. 30 (H Rept 107-257). House passed, amended, under suspension of the rules, Oct. 30. Senate Indian Affairs discharged. Senate passed Dec. 13. President signed Dec. 27, 2001.

PL 107-103 (HR 1291) Amend Title 38, U.S. Code, to increase the amount of education benefits for veterans under the Montgomery GI Bill. Introduced by SMITH, R-N.J., on March 29, 2001. House passed, under suspension of the rules, June 19. Senate Veterans' Affairs discharged. Senate passed, with amendments, Dec. 8. House agreed to Senate amendments with an amendment, Dec. 11. Senate agreed to House amendment Dec. 13. President signed Dec. 27, 2001.

PL 107-104 (HR 2559) Amend Chapter 90 of Title 5, U.S. Code, relating to federal long-term care insurance. Introduced by SCARBOROUGH, R-Fla., on July 18, 2001. House Judiciary reported Oct. 11 (H Rept 107-235, Part 1). House passed, under suspension of the rules, Oct. 30. Senate Governmental Affairs reported Nov. 27 (S Rept 107-128). Senate passed Dec. 17. President signed Dec. 27, 2001.

PL 107-105 (HR 3323) Ensure that covered entities comply with standards for electronic health care transactions and code sets adopted under Part C of Title XI of the Social Security Act. Introduced by HOBSON, R-Ohio, Nov. 16, 2001. House passed, amended, under suspension of the rules, Dec. 4. Senate passed Dec. 12. President signed Dec. 27, 2001.

PL 107-106 (HR 3442) Establish the National Museum of African American History and Culture Plan for Action Presidential Commission to develop a plan of action for establishing and maintaining the National Museum of African American History and Culture in Washington, D.C. Introduced by LEWIS, D-Ga., on Dec. 11, 2001. House passed, under suspension of the rules, Dec. 11. Senate passed Dec. 17. President signed Dec. 28, 2001.

PL 107-107 (S 1438) Authorize appropriations for fiscal 2002 for military activities of the Department of Defense, military constructions, and defense activities of the Department of Energy, and prescribe personnel strengths for the armed forces. Introduced by LEVIN, D-Mich., on Sept. 19, 2001. Senate passed, amended, Oct. 2. House passed, with an amendment, Oct. 17. Conference report filed in the House on Dec. 12 (H Rept 107-333). House agreed to conference report Dec. 13. Senate agreed to conference report Dec. 13. President signed Dec. 28, 2001.

PL 107-108 (HR 2883) Authorize appropriations for fiscal 2002 for intelligence and intelligence-related activities of the U.S. government, the Community Management Account, and the Central Intelligence Agency Retire-

ment and Disability System. Introduced by GOSS, R-Fla., on Sept. 13, 2001. House Intelligence reported, amended, Sept. 26 (H Rept 107-219). House passed, amended, Oct. 5. Senate passed, with an amendment, Nov. 8. Conference report filed in the House on Dec. 6 (H Rept 107-328). House agreed to conference report Dec. 12. Senate agreed to conference report Dec. 13. President signed Dec. 28, 2001.

PL 107-109 (S 1789) Amend the Federal Food, Drug and Cosmetic Act to improve the safety and efficacy of pharmaceuticals for children. Introduced by DODD, D-Conn., on Dec. 8, 2001. Senate passed Dec. 12. House passed, under suspension of the rules, Dec. 18. President signed Jan. 4, 2002.

PL 107-110 (HR 1) Amend the Elementary and Secondary Education Act of 1965 (ESEA) to revise, reauthorize and consolidate various programs, and authorize appropriations for ESEA programs through fiscal 2007. Introduced by BOEHNER, R-Ohio, on March 22, 2001. House Education and the Workforce reported, amended, May 14 (H Rept 107-63, Part I). House Judiciary discharged May 15. House passed, amended, May 23. Senate passed, with amendments, June 14. Conference report filed in the House on Dec. 13 (H Rept 107-334). House agreed to conference report Dec. 13. Senate agreed to conference report Dec. 18. President signed Jan. 8, 2002.

PL 107-111 (HR 643) Reauthorize the African Elephant Conservation Act of 1997. Introduced by GILCHREST, R-Md., on Feb. 14, 2001. House Resources reported, amended, June 12 (H Rept 107-93). House passed, under suspension of the rules, June 12. Senate Environment and Public Works reported Nov. 30 (S Rept 107-104). Senate passed Dec. 18. President signed Jan. 8, 2002.

PL 107-112 (HR 645) Reauthorize the Rhinoceros and Tiger Conservation Act of 1994. Introduced by GILCHREST, R-Md., on Feb. 14, 2001. House Resources reported, amended, June 25 (H Rept 107-109). House passed, under suspension of the rules, June 25. Senate Environment and Public Works reported Nov. 30 (S Rept 107-105). Senate passed Dec. 18. President signed Jan. 8, 2002.

PL 107-113 (HR 2199) Amend the National Capital Revitalization and Self-Government Improvement Act of 1997 to permit any federal law enforcement agency to enter into a cooperative agreement with the Metropolitan Police Department of the District of Columbia to assist the department in carrying out crime prevention and law enforcement activities in the District if deemed appropriate by the chief of the department and the U.S. Attorney for the District of Columbia. Introduced by NORTON, D-D.C., on June 14, 2001. House Government Reform reported July 25 (no written report). House passed, under suspension of the rules, Sept. 25. Senate Governmental Affairs reported Nov. 29 (S Rept 107-103). Senate passed, with an amendment, Dec. 11. House agreed to Senate amendment, under suspension of the rules, Dec. 19. President signed Jan. 8, 2002.

PL 107-114 (HR 2657) Amend Title 11, District of Columbia Code, to redesignate the Family Division of the Superior Court of the District of Columbia as the Family Court of the Superior Court, to recruit and retain trained and experienced judges to serve in the family court, and to promote consistency and efficiency in the assignment of judges to the family court and in the actions and proceedings of the court. Introduced by DeLAY, R-Texas, on July 26, 2001. House passed, under suspension of the rules, Sept. 20. Senate Governmental Affairs reported, amended, Dec. 5 (S Rept 107-108). Senate passed, with an amendment, Dec. 14. House agreed to Senate amendment, under suspension of the rules, Dec. 19. President signed Jan. 8, 2002.

PL 107-115 (HR 2506) Make appropriations for foreign operations, export financing, and related programs for the fiscal year ending Sept. 30, 2002. Introduced by KOLBE, R-Ariz., on July 17, 2001. House Appropriations reported July 17 (H Rept 107-142). House passed, amended, July 24. Senate Appropriations reported, with amendment, Sept. 4 (S Rept 107-58). Senate passed, with amendments, Oct. 24. Conference report filed in the House on Dec. 19 (H Rept 107-345). House agreed to conference report Dec. 19. Senate agreed to conference report Dec. 20. President signed Jan. 10, 2002.

PL 107-116 (HR 3061) Make appropriations for the Departments of Labor, Health and Human Services, and Education, and related agencies for the fiscal year ending Sept. 30, 2002. Introduced by REGULA, R-Ohio, on Oct. 9, 2001. House Appropriations reported Oct. 9 (H Rept 107-229). House passed, amended, Oct. 11. Senate passed, with amendment, Nov. 6. Conference report filed in the House on Dec. 19 (H Rept 107-342). House agreed to conference report Dec. 19. Senate agreed to conference report Dec. 20. President signed Jan. 10, 2002.

PL 107-117 (HR 3338) Make appropriations for the Department of Defense for the fiscal year ending Sept. 30, 2002. Introduced by LEWIS, R-Calif., on Nov. 19, 2001. House Appropriations reported Nov. 19 (H Rept 107-298). House passed, amended, Nov. 28. Senate Appropriations reported, with amendment, Dec. 5 (S Rept 107-109). Senate passed, with amendment, Dec. 7. Conference report filed in the House Dec. 19 (H Rept 107-350). House agreed to conference report Dec. 20. Senate agreed to conference report Dec. 20. President signed Jan. 10, 2002.

PL 107-118 (HR 2869) Provide certain relief for small businesses from liability under the Comprehension Environmental Response, Compensation, and Liability Act of 1980, and amend the act to promote the cleanup and reuse of brownfields, provide financial assistance for brownfields revitalization, and enhance state response programs. Introduced by GILLMOR, R-Ohio, on Sept. 10, 2001. House passed, amended, under suspension of the rules, Dec. 20. Senate passed Dec. 20. President signed Jan. 11, 2002.

PL 107-119 (S 1202) Amend the Ethics in Government Act of 1978 to extend the authorization of appropriations for the Office of Government Ethics through fiscal 2006. Introduced by LIEBERMAN, D-Conn., on July 19, 2001. Senate Governmental Affairs reported Oct. 30 (S Rept 107-88). Senate passed Nov. 15. House passed, under suspension of the rules, Dec. 20. President signed Jan. 15, 2002.

PL 107-120 (S 1714) Provide for the installation of a plaque to honor Dr. James Harvey Early in the Williamsburg, Ky., Post Office Building. Introduced by McCONNELL, R-Ky., on Nov. 15, 2001. Senate Governmental Affairs discharged Dec. 6. Senate passed Dec. 6. House passed, under suspension of the rules, Dec. 20. President signed Jan. 15, 2002.

PL 107-121 (S 1741) Amend Title XIX of the Social Security Act to clarify that Indian women with breast or cervical cancer who are eligible for health services provided under a medical care program of the Indian Health Service or of a tribal organization are included in the optional Medicaid eligibility category of breast or cervical cancer patients added by the Breast and Cervical Prevention and Treatment Act of 2000. Introduced by BINGAMAN, D-N.M., on Nov. 28, 2001. Senate passed Nov. 28. House passed, under suspension of the rules, Dec. 20. President signed Jan. 15, 2002.

PL 107-122 (S 1793) Provide the secretary of Education with specific waiver authority to respond to conditions in the national emergency declared by the president on Sept. 14, 2001. Introduced by COLLINS, R-Maine, on Dec. 10, 2001. Senate Health, Education, Labor and Pensions reported Dec. 12 (no written report). Senate passed Dec. 14. House passed, under suspension of the rules, Dec. 20. President signed Jan. 15, 2002.

PL 107-123 (HR 1088) Amend the Securities Exchange Act of 1934 to reduce fees collected by the Securities and Exchange Commission. Introduced by FOSSELLA, R-N.Y., on March 19, 2001. House Financial Services reported, amended, May 1 (H Rept 107-52, Part 1). House Government Reform discharged May 25. House passed June 14. Senate passed Dec. 20. President signed Jan. 16, 2002.

PL 107-124 (HR 2277) Provide for work authorization for nonimmigrant spouses of treaty traders and treaty investors. Introduced by GEKAS, R-Pa., on June 21, 2001. House Judiciary reported Aug. 2 (H Rept 107-187). House passed, under suspension of the rules, Sept. 5. Senate Judiciary reported Dec. 13 (no written report). Senate passed Dec. 20. President signed Jan. 16, 2002.

PL 107-125 (HR 2278) Provide for work authorization for nonimmigrant spouses of intracompany transferees, and reduce the period of time during which certain intracompany transferees have to be continuously employed before applying for admission to the United States. Introduced by GEKAS, R-Pa., on June 21, 2001. House Judiciary reported Aug. 2 (H Rept 107-188). House

passed, under suspension of the rules, Sept. 5. Senate Judiciary reported Dec. 13 (no written report). Senate passed Dec. 20. President signed Jan. 16, 2002.

PL 107-126 (HR 2336) Make permanent the authority to redact financial disclosure statements of judicial employees and judicial officers. Introduced by COBLE, R-N.C., on June 27, 2001. House Judiciary reported Oct. 12 (H Rept 107-239). House passed, under suspension of the rules, Oct. 16. Senate Governmental Affairs reported Dec. 7 (S Rept 107-111). Senate passed, with amendments, Dec. 11. House agreed to Senate amendments, under suspension of the rules, Dec. 20. President signed Jan. 16, 2002.

PL 107-127 (HR 2751) Authorize the president to award a gold medal on behalf of the Congress to Gen. Henry H. Shelton and provide for the production of bronze duplicates of such medal for sale to the public. Introduced by ETHERIDGE, D-N.C., on Aug. 2, 2001. House passed, amended, under suspension of the rules, Dec. 19. Senate passed Dec. 20. President signed Jan. 16, 2002.

PL 107-128 (HR 3030) Extend the "Basic Pilot" employment verification system. Introduced by LATHAM, R-Iowa, on Oct. 4, 2001. House Judiciary reported, amended, Nov. 30 (H Rept 107-310, Part 1). House Education and the Workforce discharged Nov. 30. House passed, under suspension of the rules, Dec. 11. Senate passed Dec. 20. President signed Jan. 16, 2002.

PL 107-129 (HR 3248) Designate the facility of the U.S. Postal Service located at 65 North Main St., Cranbury, N.J., as the "Todd Beamer Post Office Building." Introduced by HOLT, D-N.J., on Nov. 7, 2001. House passed, under suspension of the rules, Dec. 5. Senate Governmental Affairs discharged Dec. 20. Senate passed Dec. 20. President signed Jan. 16, 2002.

PL 107-130 (HR 3334) Designate the Richard J. Guadagno Headquarters and Visitors Center at Humboldt Bay National Wildlife Refuge, Calif. Introduced by THOMPSON, D-Calif., on Nov. 16, 2001. House Resources reported Dec. 5 (H Rept 107-319). House passed, under suspension of the rules, Dec. 18. Senate passed Dec. 20. President signed Jan. 16, 2002.

PL 107-131 (HR 3346) Amend the Internal Revenue Code of 1986 to simplify reporting requirements relating to higher education tuition and related expenses. Introduced by MANZULLO, R-Ill., on Nov. 27, 2001. House passed, under suspension of the rules, Dec. 4. Senate passed Dec. 20. President signed Jan. 16, 2002.

PL 107-132 (HR 3348) Designate the National Foreign Affairs Training Center as the George P. Shultz National Foreign Affairs Training Center. Introduced by HYDE, R-Ill., on Nov. 27, 2001. House passed, under suspension of the rules, Dec. 5. Senate Foreign Relations discharged Dec. 20. Senate passed Dec. 20. President signed Jan. 16, 2002.

PL 107-133 (HR 2873) Extend and amend the Promoting

Safe and Stable Families program under Title IV-B, Subpart 2 of the Social Security Act, and provide new authority to support programs for mentoring children of incarcerated parents; amend the Foster Care Independent Living program under Title IV-E of the act to provide for education and training vouchers for youths aging out of foster care. Introduced by HERGER, R-Calif., on Sept. 10, 2001. House Ways and Means reported, amended Nov. 13 (H Rept 107-281). House passed, under suspension of the rules, Nov. 13. Senate passed Dec. 13. President signed Jan. 17, 2002.

PL 107-134 (HR 2884) Amend the Internal Revenue Code of 1986 to provide tax relief for victims of the Sept. 11 terrorist attacks. Introduced by THOMAS, R-Calif., on Sept. 13, 2001. House Ways and Means discharged Sept. 13. House passed, Sept. 13. Senate Finance discharged Nov. 16. Senate passed, with amendments, Nov. 16. House agreed to Senate amendments with amendment Dec. 13. Senate agreed to House amendment with amendment Dec. 20. House agreed to Senate amendment Dec. 20. President signed, Jan. 23, 2002.

PL 107-135 (HR 3447) Amend Title 38, U.S. Code, to enhance the authority of the secretary of Veterans Affairs (VA) to recruit and retain qualified nurses for the Veterans Health Administration, provide an additional basis for establishing the inability of veterans to defray expenses of necessary medical care, and enhance certain VA health care programs. Introduced by SMITH, R-N.J., on Dec. 11, 2001. House passed, under suspension of the rules, Dec. 11. Senate passed Dec. 20. President signed Jan. 23, 2002.

PL 107-136 (HR 3392) Name the national cemetery in Saratoga, N.Y., the Gerald B. H. Solomon Saratoga National Cemetery. Introduced by HASTERT, R-Ill., on Dec. 4, 2001. House passed, under suspension of the rules, Dec. 4. Senate Veterans' Affairs discharged Dec. 20. Senate passed Dec. 20. President signed Jan. 24, 2002. ◆

Appendix H

HOUSE ROLL CALL VOTES

House Roll Call Votes By Bill Number

House Bills

H Con Res 14, H-6
H Con Res 15, H-6
H Con Res 27, H-12
H Con Res 31, H-16
H Con Res 39, H-12
H Con Res 41, H-24
H Con Res 43, H-24
H Con Res 47, H-16
H Con Res 56, H-50
H Con Res 66, H-32
H Con Res 83, H-28, H-30, H-36, H-40, H-42
H Con Res 91, H-38
H Con Res 95, H-38
H Con Res 100, H-58
H Con Res 102, H-162
H Con Res 145, H-62
H Con Res 154, H-64
H Con Res 161, H-70
H Con Res 163, H-64
H Con Res 168, H-78
H Con Res 170, H-78
H Con Res 174, H-78
H Con Res 190, H-102
H Con Res 211, H-150
H Con Res 217, H-132
H Con Res 228, H-152
H Con Res 232, H-162
H Con Res 233, H-140
H Con Res 239, H-152
H Con Res 242, H-160
H Con Res 243, H-140
H Con Res 244, H-128
H Con Res 248, H-132
H Con Res 257, H-150
H Con Res 262, H-148
H Con Res 280, H-162
H Con Res 281, H-166
H Con Res 282, H-168

H J Res 7, H-8
H J Res 36, H-84
H J Res 41, H-36
H J Res 42, H-124
H J Res 50, H-90
H J Res 55, H-98
H J Res 61, H-116
H J Res 64, H-118
H J Res 65, H-120
H J Res 70, H-138
H J Res 71, H-138
H J Res 75, H-174

H Res 5, H-4
H Res 28, H-8
H Res 34, H-10
H Res 54, H-14
H Res 56, H-32
H Res 67, H-24
H Res 84, H-28
H Res 91, H-32

H Res 97, H-60
H Res 99, H-70
H Res 116, H-44
H Res 124, H-64
H Res 160, H-70
H Res 166, H-70
H Res 172, H-72
H Res 191, H-102
H Res 195, H-84
H Res 212, H-102
H Res 233, H-114
H Res 250, H-128
H Res 298, H-162
H Res 305, H-162
H Res 314, H-170

HR 1, H-48, H-50, H-52, H-54, H-86, H-170
HR 2, H-10
HR 3, H-18, H-20
HR 4, H-106, H-108, H-110
HR 6, H-30
HR 7, H-90
HR 8, H-32, H-34
HR 10, H-38, H-166
HR 93, H-6
HR 132, H-8
HR 169, H-124
HR 223, H-22
HR 247, H-26
HR 256, H-12
HR 327, H-22
HR 333, H-14
HR 428, H-36, H-44
HR 503, H-36
HR 524, H-10
HR 554, H-10
HR 558, H-12
HR 586, H-44
HR 621, H-12
HR 622, H-48
HR 624, H-16
HR 642, H-34
HR 700, H-60
HR 717, H-120
HR 724, H-16
HR 725, H-22
HR 727, H-16
HR 768, H-32, H-146
HR 801, H-28
HR 802, H-26
HR 811, H-28
HR 834, H-22
HR 852, H-146
HR 861, H-22
HR 1022, H-168
HR 1042, H-24
HR 1088, H-62
HR 1098, H-24
HR 1099, H-26
HR 1140, H-106
HR 1157, H-60
HR 1209, H-58

HR 1259, H-156
HR 1291, H-64
HR 1408, H-146
HR 1447, H-146
HR 1646, H-42, H-46, H-48
HR 1696, H-44
HR 1699, H-58
HR 1727, H-44
HR 1761, H-116
HR 1766, H-116
HR 1831, H-52
HR 1836, H-46, H-54, H-56
HR 1885, H-50
HR 1892, H-92
HR 1914, H-58
HR 1954, H-98
HR 1992, H-128
HR 2043, H-58
HR 2052, H-60
HR 2133, H-72
HR 2137, H-92
HR 2199, H-172
HR 2216, H-64, H-66, H-82, H-92
HR 2217, H-66, H-68, H-134
HR 2272, H-134
HR 2291, H-114
HR 2299, H-70, H-72, H-160
HR 2311, H-72, H-74, H-76, H-142
HR 2330, H-76, H-78, H-80, H-150
HR 2356, H-82
HR 2382, H-166
HR 2500, H-84, H-86, H-88, H-150
HR 2505, H-104, H-106
HR 2506, H-92, H-94, H-172
HR 2540, H-104
HR 2541, H-150
HR 2559, H-140
HR 2563, H-110, H-112
HR 2586, H-122
HR 2590, H-94, H-96, H-98, H-140
HR 2620, H-98, H-100, H-102, H-104, H-148
HR 2646, H-124, H-126
HR 2647, H-104, H-142
HR 2657, H-118, H-172
HR 2669, H-152
HR 2722, H-156
HR 2833, H-114
HR 2882, H-116
HR 2884, H-116
HR 2887, H-152
HR 2888, H-118
HR 2904, H-120, H-124, H-134
HR 2910, H-140
HR 2924, H-136
HR 2926, H-120
HR 2944, H-120, H-122, H-164
HR 2975, H-132
HR 2998, H-146
HR 3004, H-134
HR 3005, H-164
HR 3008, H-164
HR 3054, H-172

HR 3061, H-130, H-148, H-172
HR 3086, H-136
HR 3090, H-136, H-138
HR 3129, H-164
HR 3150, H-142, H-144
HR 3160, H-136
HR 3162, H-136
HR 3167, H-148
HR 3209, H-168
HR 3210, H-158
HR 3275, H-172
HR 3295, H-166, H-168
HR 3323, H-160
HR 3338, H-156, H-158, H-170, H-174
HR 3348, H-160
HR 3379, H-172
HR 3391, H-160
HR 3448, H-168
HR 3529, H-174
HR 3009, H-154

Senate Bills

S 360, H-84
S 468, H-92
S 494, H-160
S 1438, H-134, H-170
S 1447, H-154
S 1762, H-174

S Con Res 44, H-156
S Con Res 77, H-156

S J Res 6, H-16, H-18

Key

Y	Voted for (yea).
#	Paired for.
+	Announced for.
N	Voted against (nay).
X	Paired against.
−	Announced against.
P	Voted "present."
C	Voted "present" to avoid possible conflict of interest.
?	Did not vote or otherwise make a position known.

•
Democrats   **Republicans**
Independents

1. Quorum Call.* 429 responded. Jan. 3, 2001.

2. Election of the Speaker. Nomination of J. Dennis Hastert, R-Ill., and Richard A. Gephardt, D-Mo., for Speaker of the House of Representatives for the 107th Congress. Hastert elected 222-207: R 220-0; D 1-206 (ND 1-151, SD 0-55); I 1-1. A "Y" on the chart represents a vote for Hastert; an "N" represents a vote for Gephardt, except for Gene Taylor, D-Miss., who voted for John P. Murtha, D-Pa. A majority of the votes cast for a person by name (215 in this case) is needed for election. All members-elect are eligible to vote on the election of the Speaker. Jan. 3, 2001.

3. H Res 5. Rules of the House/Motion to Commit. Moakley, D-Mass., motion to commit the resolution to set the rules for the 107th Congress to a select committee consisting of the majority and minority leaders. Motion rejected 199-213: R 0-210; D 198-2 (ND 145-1, SD 53-1); I 1-1. Jan. 3, 2001.

4. H Res 5. Rules of the House/Adoption. Adoption of the resolution that would set the rules for the 107th Congress. The rules would create a Financial Services Committee to replace the existing Banking Committee and prohibit the inclusion of arguments in motions to instruct conferees and motions to recommit a conference report. Adopted 215-206: R 213-0; D 1-205 (ND 1-150, SD 0-55); I 1-1. Jan. 3, 2001.

* CQ does not include quorum calls in its vote charts.

[1] Was not sworn in yet, and thus was not eligible to vote.

		2	3	4
ALABAMA				
1	*Callahan*	Y	N	Y
2	*Everett*	Y	N	Y
3	*Riley*	Y	?	?
4	*Aderholt*	Y	N	Y
5	Cramer	N	Y	N
6	*Bachus*	Y	N	Y
7	Hilliard	N	Y	N
ALASKA				
AL	*Young*	Y	N	Y
ARIZONA				
1	*Flake*	Y	N	Y
2	Pastor	N	Y	N
3	*Stump*	Y	N	Y
4	*Shadegg*	Y	N	Y
5	*Kolbe*	Y	N	Y
6	*Hayworth*	Y	N	Y
ARKANSAS				
1	Berry	N	Y	N
2	Snyder	N	N	N
3	*Hutchinson*	Y	N	Y
4	Ross	N	Y	N
CALIFORNIA				
1	Thompson	N	Y	N
2	*Herger*	Y	N	Y
3	*Ose*	Y	N	Y
4	*Doolittle*	Y	N	Y
5	Matsui	N	Y	N
6	Woolsey	N	Y	N
7	Miller, George	N	Y	N
8	Pelosi	N	Y	N
9	Lee	N	Y	N
10	Tauscher	N	Y	N
11	*Pombo*	Y	N	Y
12	Lantos	N	Y	N
13	Stark [1]	?	?	?
14	Eshoo	N	Y	N
15	Honda	N	Y	N
16	Lofgren	N	Y	N
17	Farr	N	Y	N
18	Condit	N	Y	N
19	*Radanovich*	Y	N	Y
20	Dooley	N	Y	N
21	*Thomas*	Y	?	?
22	Capps	N	Y	N
23	*Gallegly*	Y	N	Y
24	Sherman	N	Y	N
25	*McKeon*	Y	N	Y
26	Berman	N	Y	N
27	Schiff	N	Y	N
28	*Dreier*	Y	N	Y
29	Waxman	N	Y	N
30	Becerra	N	Y	N
31	Solis	N	Y	N
32	Vacant			
33	Roybal-Allard	N	Y	N
34	Napolitano	N	Y	N
35	Waters	N	Y	N
36	Harman	N	Y	N
37	Millender-McD.	N	Y	N
38	*Horn*	Y	N	Y

		2	3	4
39	*Royce*	Y	N	Y
40	*Lewis*	Y	N	Y
41	*Miller, Gary*	Y	N	Y
42	Baca	N	Y	N
43	*Calvert*	Y	N	Y
44	*Bono*	Y	N	Y
45	*Rohrabacher*	Y	N	Y
46	Sanchez	N	Y	N
47	*Cox*	Y	N	Y
48	*Issa*	Y	N	Y
49	Davis	N	Y	N
50	Filner	N	Y	N
51	*Cunningham*	Y	N	Y
52	*Hunter*	Y	?	Y
COLORADO				
1	DeGette	N	Y	N
2	Udall	N	Y	N
3	*McInnis*	Y	N	Y
4	*Schaffer*	Y	N	Y
5	*Hefley*	Y	?	?
6	*Tancredo*	Y	N	Y
CONNECTICUT				
1	Larson	N	Y	N
2	*Simmons*	Y	N	Y
3	DeLauro	N	Y	N
4	*Shays*	Y	N	Y
5	Maloney	N	Y	N
6	*Johnson*	Y	N	Y
DELAWARE				
AL	*Castle*	Y	N	Y
FLORIDA				
1	*Scarborough*	Y	N	Y
2	Boyd	N	Y	N
3	Brown	N	?	N
4	*Crenshaw*	Y	N	Y
5	Thurman	N	Y	N
6	*Stearns*	Y	N	Y
7	*Mica*	Y	N	Y
8	*Keller*	Y	?	?
9	*Bilirakis*	Y	N	Y
10	*Young*	Y	N	Y
11	Davis	N	Y	N
12	*Putnam*	Y	N	Y
13	*Miller*	Y	N	Y
14	*Goss*	Y	N	Y
15	*Weldon*	Y	N	Y
16	*Foley*	Y	N	Y
17	Meek	N	Y	N
18	*Ros-Lehtinen*	Y	N	Y
19	Wexler	N	Y	N
20	Deutsch	N	Y	N
21	*Diaz-Balart*	Y	N	Y
22	*Shaw*	Y	N	Y
23	Hastings	N	Y	N
GEORGIA				
1	*Kingston*	Y	N	Y
2	Bishop	N	Y	N
3	*Collins*	Y	N	Y
4	McKinney	N	Y	N
5	Lewis	N	Y	N
6	*Isakson*	Y	N	Y
7	*Barr*	Y	?	Y
8	*Chambliss*	Y	N	Y
9	*Deal*	Y	N	Y
10	*Norwood*	Y	N	Y
11	*Linder*	Y	N	Y
HAWAII				
1	Abercrombie	N	Y	N
2	Mink	N	Y	N
IDAHO				
1	*Otter*	Y	N	Y
2	*Simpson*	Y	N	Y
ILLINOIS				
1	Rush	N	?	N
2	Jackson	N	Y	N
3	Lipinski [1]	?	?	?
4	Gutierrez [1]	?	?	?
5	Blagojevich	N	Y	N
6	*Hyde*	Y	N	Y
7	Davis	N	Y	N
8	*Crane*	Y	N	Y
9	Schakowsky	N	Y	N
10	*Kirk*	Y	?	Y
11	*Weller*	Y	N	Y
12	Costello	N	Y	N
13	*Biggert*	Y	N	Y

ND Northern Democrats   SD Southern Democrats

	2	3	4
14 *Hastert*	P		
15 *Johnson*	Y	N	?
16 *Manzullo*	Y	N	Y
17 Evans	N	Y	N
18 *LaHood*	Y	N	Y
19 Phelps	N	Y	N
20 *Shimkus*	Y	N	Y

INDIANA

	2	3	4
1 Visclosky	N	Y	N
2 *Pence*	Y	N	Y
3 Roemer	N	Y	N
4 *Souder*	Y	N	Y
5 *Buyer*	Y	N	Y
6 *Burton*	Y	N	Y
7 *Kerns*	Y	N	Y
8 *Hostettler*	Y	N	Y
9 Hill	N	Y	N
10 Carson	N	?	?

IOWA

	2	3	4
1 *Leach*	Y	N	Y
2 *Nussle*	Y	N	Y
3 Boswell	N	Y	N
4 *Ganske*	Y	N	Y
5 *Latham*	Y	N	Y

KANSAS

	2	3	4
1 *Moran*	Y	N	Y
2 *Ryun*	Y	N	Y
3 Moore	N	Y	N
4 *Tiahrt*	Y	N	Y

KENTUCKY

	2	3	4
1 *Whitfield*	Y	N	Y
2 *Lewis*	Y	N	Y
3 *Northup*	Y	N	Y
4 Lucas	N	Y	N
5 *Rogers*	Y	N	Y
6 *Fletcher*	Y	N	Y

LOUISIANA

	2	3	4
1 *Vitter*	Y	N	Y
2 Jefferson	N	Y	N
3 *Tauzin*	Y	N	Y
4 *McCrery*	Y	N	Y
5 *Cooksey*	Y	N	Y
6 *Baker*	Y	N	Y
7 John	N	Y	N

MAINE

	2	3	4
1 Allen	N	Y	N
2 Baldacci	N	Y	N

MARYLAND

	2	3	4
1 *Gilchrest*	Y	N	Y
2 *Ehrlich*	Y	N	Y
3 Cardin	N	Y	N
4 Wynn	N	Y	N
5 Hoyer	N	Y	N
6 *Bartlett*	Y	N	Y
7 Cummings	N	?	N
8 *Morella*	Y	N	Y

MASSACHUSETTS

	2	3	4
1 Olver	N	Y	N
2 Neal	N	Y	N
3 McGovern	N	Y	N
4 Frank	N	Y	N
5 Meehan	N	Y	N
6 Tierney	N	Y	N
7 Markey	N	Y	N
8 Capuano	N	Y	N
9 Moakley	N	Y	N
10 Delahunt	N	Y	N

MICHIGAN

	2	3	4
1 Stupak	N	Y	N
2 *Hoekstra*	Y	N	Y
3 *Ehlers*	Y	N	Y
4 *Camp*	Y	N	Y
5 Barcia	N	Y	N
6 *Upton*	Y	N	Y
7 *Smith*	Y	N	Y
8 *Rogers*	Y	N	Y
9 Kildee	N	Y	N
10 Bonior	N	Y	N
11 *Knollenberg*	Y	N	Y
12 Levin	N	Y	N
13 Rivers	N	Y	N
14 Conyers	N	?	N
15 Kilpatrick	N	Y	N
16 Dingell	N	Y	N

MINNESOTA

	2	3	4
1 *Gutknecht*	Y	N	Y
2 *Kennedy*	Y	N	Y
3 *Ramstad*	Y	N	Y
4 McCollum	N	Y	N
5 Sabo	N	Y	N
6 Luther	N	Y	N
7 Peterson	N	Y	N
8 Oberstar	N	Y	N

MISSISSIPPI

	2	3	4
1 *Wicker*	Y	N	Y
2 Thompson	N	Y	N
3 *Pickering*	Y	N	Y
4 Shows	N	Y	N
5 Taylor	N	Y	N

MISSOURI

	2	3	4
1 Clay	N	Y	N
2 *Akin*	Y	N	Y
3 Gephardt	P	Y	N
4 Skelton	N	Y	N
5 McCarthy	N	Y	N
6 *Graves*	Y	N	Y
7 *Blunt*	Y	N	Y
8 *Emerson*	Y	N	Y
9 *Hulshof*	Y	N	Y

MONTANA

	2	3	4
AL *Rehberg*	Y	N	Y

NEBRASKA

	2	3	4
1 *Bereuter*	Y	N	Y
2 *Terry*	Y	N	Y
3 *Osborne*	Y	N	Y

NEVADA

	2	3	4
1 Berkley	N	Y	N
2 *Gibbons*	Y	N	Y

NEW HAMPSHIRE

	2	3	4
1 *Sununu*	Y	N	Y
2 *Bass*	Y	N	Y

NEW JERSEY

	2	3	4
1 Andrews	N	Y	N
2 *LoBiondo*	Y	N	Y
3 *Saxton*	Y	N	Y
4 *Smith*	Y	N	Y
5 *Roukema*	Y	N	Y
6 Pallone	N	Y	N
7 *Ferguson*	Y	N	?
8 Pascrell	N	Y	N
9 Rothman	N	Y	N
10 Payne	N	Y	N
11 *Frelinghuysen*	Y	N	Y
12 Holt	N	Y	N
13 Menendez	N	Y	N

NEW MEXICO

	2	3	4
1 *Wilson*	Y	?	Y
2 *Skeen*	Y	N	Y
3 Udall	N	Y	N

NEW YORK

	2	3	4
1 *Grucci*	Y	N	Y
2 Israel	N	Y	N
3 *King*	Y	N	Y
4 McCarthy	N	Y	N
5 Ackerman	N	Y	N
6 Meeks	N	Y	N
7 Crowley	N	Y	N
8 Nadler	N	Y	N
9 Weiner	N	Y	N
10 Towns	N	Y	N
11 Owens	N	Y	N
12 Velázquez	N	Y	N
13 *Fossella*	Y	N	Y
14 Maloney	N	Y	N
15 Rangel	N	Y	N
16 Serrano	N	Y	N
17 Engel	N	Y	N
18 Lowey	N	Y	N
19 *Kelly*	Y	N	Y
20 *Gilman*	Y	N	Y
21 McNulty	N	Y	N
22 *Sweeney*	Y	N	Y
23 *Boehlert*	Y	N	Y
24 *McHugh*	Y	N	Y
25 *Walsh*	Y	N	Y
26 Hinchey	N	Y	N
27 *Reynolds*	Y	N	Y
28 Slaughter	N	Y	N
29 LaFalce	N	Y	N

	2	3	4
30 Quinn	Y	N	Y
31 Houghton	Y	N	Y

NORTH CAROLINA

	2	3	4
1 Clayton	N	Y	N
2 Etheridge	N	Y	N
3 *Jones*	Y	N	Y
4 Price	N	Y	N
5 *Burr*	Y	N	Y
6 *Coble*	Y	N	Y
7 McIntyre	N	Y	N
8 *Hayes*	Y	N	Y
9 *Myrick*	Y	N	Y
10 *Ballenger*	Y	N	Y
11 *Taylor*	Y	N	Y
12 Watt	N	Y	N

NORTH DAKOTA

	2	3	4
AL Pomeroy	N	Y	N

OHIO

	2	3	4
1 *Chabot*	Y	N	Y
2 *Portman*	Y	N	Y
3 Hall	N	Y	N
4 *Oxley*	Y	N	Y
5 *Gillmor*	Y	N	Y
6 Strickland	N	?	N
7 *Hobson*	Y	N	Y
8 *Boehner*	Y	N	Y
9 Kaptur	N	Y	N
10 Kucinich	N	Y	N
11 Jones	N	Y	N
12 *Tiberi*	Y	N	Y
13 Brown	N	Y	N
14 Sawyer	N	Y	N
15 *Pryce*	Y	N	Y
16 *Regula*	Y	N	Y
17 Traficant	Y	N	Y
18 *Ney*	Y	N	Y
19 *LaTourette*	Y	N	Y

OKLAHOMA

	2	3	4
1 *Largent*	Y	N	Y
2 Carson	N	Y	N
3 *Watkins*	Y	N	Y
4 *Watts*	Y	?	?
5 *Istook*	Y	N	Y
6 *Lucas*	Y	N	Y

OREGON

	2	3	4
1 Wu	N	Y	N
2 *Walden*	Y	N	Y
3 Blumenauer	N	Y	N
4 DeFazio	N	Y	N
5 Hooley	N	Y	N

PENNSYLVANIA

	2	3	4
1 Brady	N	Y	N
2 Fattah	N	Y	N
3 Borski	N	Y	N
4 *Hart*	Y	N	Y
5 *Peterson*	Y	N	Y
6 Holden	N	Y	N
7 *Weldon*	Y	N	Y
8 *Greenwood*	Y	N	Y
9 *Shuster*	Y	N	Y
10 *Sherwood*	Y	N	Y
11 Kanjorski	N	Y	N
12 Murtha	N	?	?
13 Hoeffel	N	Y	N
14 Coyne	N	?	N
15 *Toomey*	Y	N	Y
16 *Pitts*	Y	N	Y
17 *Gekas*	Y	N	Y
18 Doyle	N	Y	N
19 *Platts*	Y	N	Y
20 Mascara	N	Y	N
21 *English*	Y	N	Y

RHODE ISLAND

	2	3	4
1 Kennedy	N	Y	N
2 Langevin	N	Y	N

SOUTH CAROLINA

	2	3	4
1 *Brown*	Y	N	Y
2 *Spence*	Y	N	Y
3 *Graham*	Y	N	Y
4 *DeMint*	Y	N	Y
5 Spratt	N	Y	N
6 Clyburn	N	Y	N

SOUTH DAKOTA

	2	3	4
AL *Thune*	Y	N	Y

TENNESSEE

	2	3	4
1 *Jenkins*	Y	N	Y
2 *Duncan*	Y	N	Y
3 *Wamp*	Y	N	Y
4 *Hilleary*	Y	N	Y
5 Clement	N	Y	N
6 Gordon	N	Y	N
7 *Bryant*	Y	N	Y
8 Tanner	N	Y	N
9 Ford	N	Y	N

TEXAS

	2	3	4
1 Sandlin	N	Y	N
2 Turner	N	Y	N
3 *Johnson, Sam*	Y	N	Y
4 Hall	N	Y	N
5 *Sessions*	Y	N	Y
6 *Barton*	Y	N	Y
7 *Culberson*	Y	?	Y
8 *Brady*	Y	N	Y
9 Lampson	N	Y	N
10 Doggett	N	Y	N
11 Edwards	N	Y	N
12 *Granger*	Y	N	Y
13 *Thornberry*	Y	N	Y
14 Paul	N	Y	N
15 Hinojosa	N	Y	N
16 Reyes	N	Y	N
17 Stenholm	N	Y	N
18 Jackson-Lee	N	Y	N
19 *Combest*	Y	N	Y
20 Gonzalez	N	Y	N
21 *Smith*	Y	N	Y
22 *DeLay*	Y	N	Y
23 *Bonilla*	Y	N	Y
24 Frost	N	Y	N
25 Bentsen	N	Y	N
26 *Armey*	Y	N	Y
27 Ortiz	N	Y	N
28 Rodriguez	N	Y	N
29 Green	N	Y	N
30 Johnson, E.B.	N	Y	N

UTAH

	2	3	4
1 *Hansen*	Y	N	Y
2 Matheson	N	Y	N
3 *Cannon*	Y	N	Y

VERMONT

	2	3	4
AL *Sanders*	N	Y	N

VIRGINIA

	2	3	4
1 *Davis, Jo Ann*	Y	N	Y
2 *Schrock*	Y	N	Y
3 Scott	N	Y	N
4 Sisisky	N	Y	N
5 *Goode*	Y	N	Y
6 *Goodlatte*	Y	N	Y
7 *Cantor*	Y	N	Y
8 Moran	N	Y	N
9 Boucher	N	Y	N
10 *Wolf*	Y	N	Y
11 *Davis, T.*	Y	N	Y

WASHINGTON

	2	3	4
1 Inslee	N	Y	N
2 Larsen	N	Y	N
3 Baird	N	Y	N
4 *Hastings*	Y	N	Y
5 *Nethercutt*	Y	N	Y
6 Dicks	N	Y	N
7 McDermott	N	Y	N
8 *Dunn*	Y	N	Y
9 Smith	N	Y	N

WEST VIRGINIA

	2	3	4
1 Mollohan	N	Y	N
2 *Capito*	Y	N	Y
3 Rahall	N	Y	N

WISCONSIN

	2	3	4
1 *Ryan*	Y	N	Y
2 Baldwin	N	Y	N
3 Kind	N	Y	N
4 Kleczka	N	Y	N
5 Barrett	N	Y	N
6 *Petri*	Y	N	Y
7 Obey	N	Y	N
8 *Green*	Y	N	Y
9 *Sensenbrenner*	Y	N	Y

WYOMING

	2	3	4
AL *Cubin*	Y	N	Y

Southern states - Ala., Ark., Fla., Ga., Ky., La., Miss., N.C., Okla., S.C., Tenn., Texas, Va.

Key

Y	Voted for (yea).
#	Paired for.
+	Announced for.
N	Voted against (nay).
X	Paired against.
−	Announced against.
P	Voted "present."
C	Voted "present" to avoid possible conflict of interest.
?	Did not vote or otherwise make a position known.

Democrats **Republicans**
Independents

5. HR 93. Firefighters Retirement/Passage. LaTourette, R-Ohio, motion to suspend the rules and pass the bill that would increase the mandatory retirement age for federal firefighters from 55 to 57, bringing it in line with the retirement age for federal law enforcement officers. Motion agreed to 401-0: R 205-0; D 194-0 (ND 143-0, SD 51-0); I 2-0. A two-thirds majority of those present and voting (268 in this case) is required for passage under suspension of the rules. Jan. 30, 2001.

6. H Con Res 14. Holocaust Remembrance/Adoption. Ney, R-Ohio, motion to suspend the rules and adopt the resolution permitting the use of the rotunda of the U.S. Capitol for a ceremony as part of the commemoration of the days of remembrance of victims of the Holocaust. Motion agreed to 407-0: R 209-0; D 196-0 (ND 145-0, SD 51-0); I 2-0. A two-thirds majority of those present and voting (272 in this case) is required for adoption under suspension of the rules. Jan. 31, 2001.

7. H Con Res 15. Indian Earthquake/Adoption. Hyde, R-Ill., motion to suspend the rules and adopt the resolution expressing sympathy for the victims of the earthquake that struck India on Jan. 26, 2001, and support for ongoing aid efforts. Motion agreed to 406-1: R 208-1; D 196-0 (ND 147-0, SD 49-0); I 2-0. A two-thirds majority of those present and voting (272 in this case) is required for adoption under suspension of the rules. Jan. 31, 2001.

8. Procedural Motion/Journal. Approval of the Journal of the House for Tuesday, Jan. 30, 2001. Approved 382-19: R 200-4; D 181-15 (ND 132-13, SD 49-2); I 1-0. Jan. 31, 2001.

	5	6	7	8
ALABAMA				
1 *Callahan*	?	?	?	?
2 *Everett*	+	+	+	+
3 *Riley*	Y	Y	Y	Y
4 *Aderholt*	Y	Y	Y	Y
5 Cramer	Y	Y	Y	Y
6 *Bachus*	?	?	?	?
7 Hilliard	Y	Y	Y	Y
ALASKA				
AL *Young*	?	Y	Y	Y
ARIZONA				
1 *Flake*	Y	Y	Y	Y
2 Pastor	Y	Y	Y	Y
3 *Stump*	Y	Y	Y	Y
4 *Shadegg*	Y	Y	Y	Y
5 *Kolbe*	Y	Y	Y	Y
6 *Hayworth*	Y	Y	Y	Y
ARKANSAS				
1 Berry	Y	Y	Y	Y
2 Snyder	Y	Y	Y	Y
3 *Hutchinson*	Y	Y	Y	Y
4 Ross	Y	Y	Y	Y
CALIFORNIA				
1 Thompson	Y	Y	Y	N
2 *Herger*	Y	Y	Y	Y
3 *Ose*	Y	Y	Y	Y
4 *Doolittle*	Y	Y	Y	Y
5 Matsui	Y	Y	Y	Y
6 Woolsey	Y	Y	Y	Y
7 Miller, George	Y	Y	Y	Y
8 Pelosi	Y	Y	Y	?
9 Lee	Y	Y	Y	Y
10 Tauscher	Y	Y	Y	Y
11 *Pombo*	Y	Y	Y	Y
12 Lantos	?	?	?	?
13 Stark	?	Y	Y	N
14 Eshoo	Y	Y	Y	Y
15 Honda	Y	Y	Y	Y
16 Lofgren	Y	Y	Y	Y
17 Farr	Y	Y	Y	Y
18 Condit	Y	Y	Y	Y
19 *Radanovich*	Y	Y	Y	Y
20 Dooley	Y	Y	Y	Y
21 *Thomas*	?	Y	Y	Y
22 Capps	Y	Y	Y	Y
23 *Gallegly*	Y	Y	Y	Y
24 Sherman	Y	Y	Y	Y
25 *McKeon*	Y	Y	Y	Y
26 Berman	Y	?	?	?
27 Schiff	Y	Y	Y	Y
28 *Dreier*	Y	Y	Y	Y
29 Waxman	Y	Y	Y	Y
30 Becerra	?	?	?	?
31 Solis	Y	Y	Y	Y
33 Roybal-Allard	Y	Y	Y	Y
34 Napolitano	Y	Y	Y	Y
35 Waters	Y	Y	Y	N
36 Harman	Y	Y	Y	Y
37 Millender-McD.	Y	Y	Y	Y
38 *Horn*	Y	Y	Y	Y
39 *Royce*	Y	Y	Y	Y

	5	6	7	8
40 *Lewis*	Y	Y	Y	Y
41 *Miller, Gary*	Y	?	?	?
42 Baca	Y	Y	Y	Y
43 *Calvert*	Y	Y	Y	Y
44 *Bono*	?	?	?	?
45 *Rohrabacher*	Y	Y	Y	Y
46 Sanchez	+	Y	Y	Y
47 *Cox*	Y	?	Y	Y
48 *Issa*	Y	Y	Y	Y
49 Davis	Y	Y	Y	Y
50 Filner	Y	Y	Y	N
51 *Cunningham*	Y	Y	Y	Y
52 *Hunter*	Y	Y	Y	Y
COLORADO				
1 DeGette	?	Y	Y	Y
2 Udall	Y	Y	Y	Y
3 *McInnis*	Y	Y	Y	Y
4 *Schaffer*	Y	Y	Y	N
5 *Hefley*	Y	Y	Y	Y
6 *Tancredo*	Y	Y	Y	Y
CONNECTICUT				
1 Larson	Y	Y	Y	Y
2 *Simmons*	Y	Y	Y	Y
3 DeLauro	Y	Y	Y	Y
4 *Shays*	Y	Y	Y	Y
5 Maloney	Y	Y	Y	Y
6 *Johnson*	Y	Y	Y	Y
DELAWARE				
AL *Castle*	Y	Y	Y	Y
FLORIDA				
1 *Scarborough*	Y	Y	Y	Y
2 Boyd	Y	Y	Y	Y
3 Brown	Y	Y	Y	Y
4 *Crenshaw*	Y	Y	Y	Y
5 Thurman	Y	Y	?	Y
6 *Stearns*	Y	Y	Y	Y
7 *Mica*	Y	Y	Y	Y
8 *Keller*	Y	Y	Y	Y
9 *Bilirakis*	Y	Y	Y	Y
10 *Young*	Y	Y	Y	Y
11 Davis	Y	Y	Y	Y
12 *Putnam*	Y	Y	Y	Y
13 *Miller*	Y	Y	Y	Y
14 *Goss*	Y	Y	Y	Y
15 *Weldon*	Y	Y	Y	Y
16 *Foley*	Y	Y	Y	Y
17 Meek	?	Y	?	Y
18 *Ros-Lehtinen*	?	?	?	?
19 Wexler	?	?	?	?
20 Deutsch	Y	Y	Y	Y
21 *Diaz-Balart*	Y	Y	Y	Y
22 *Shaw*	Y	Y	Y	Y
23 Hastings	Y	Y	Y	Y
GEORGIA				
1 *Kingston*	Y	Y	Y	Y
2 Bishop	Y	Y	Y	Y
3 *Collins*	Y	Y	Y	Y
4 McKinney	Y	Y	Y	Y
5 Lewis	Y	?	?	?
6 *Isakson*	Y	Y	Y	Y
7 *Barr*	Y	Y	Y	Y
8 *Chambliss*	Y	Y	Y	Y
9 *Deal*	Y	Y	Y	Y
10 *Norwood*	Y	Y	Y	Y
11 *Linder*	Y	Y	Y	Y
HAWAII				
1 Abercrombie	Y	+	+	+
2 Mink	Y	Y	Y	Y
IDAHO				
1 *Otter*	Y	Y	Y	Y
2 *Simpson*	Y	Y	Y	Y
ILLINOIS				
1 Rush	?	?	?	?
2 Jackson	Y	Y	Y	Y
3 Lipinski	?	Y	Y	Y
4 Gutierrez	?	Y	Y	N
5 Blagojevich	Y	Y	Y	Y
6 *Hyde*	Y	Y	Y	Y
7 Davis	Y	Y	Y	Y
8 *Crane*	Y	Y	Y	N
9 Schakowsky	Y	Y	Y	Y
10 *Kirk*	Y	Y	Y	?
11 *Weller*	Y	Y	Y	N
12 Costello	Y	Y	Y	N
13 *Biggert*	Y	Y	Y	Y

ND Northern Democrats   SD Southern Democrats

	5	6	7	8
14 *Hastert*				
15 *Johnson*	Y	Y	Y	Y
16 *Manzullo*	Y	Y	Y	Y
17 Evans	Y	Y	Y	Y
18 *LaHood*	Y	Y	Y	Y
19 Phelps	Y	Y	Y	Y
20 *Shimkus*	Y	Y	Y	Y

INDIANA

	5	6	7	8
1 Visclosky	Y	Y	Y	Y
2 *Pence*	Y	Y	Y	Y
3 Roemer	Y	Y	Y	Y
4 *Souder*	Y	Y	Y	Y
5 *Buyer*	Y	Y	Y	?
6 *Burton*	Y	Y	Y	Y
7 *Kerns*	Y	Y	Y	Y
8 *Hostettler*	Y	Y	Y	Y
9 Hill	Y	Y	Y	Y
10 Carson	?	?	?	?

IOWA

	5	6	7	8
1 *Leach*	?	?	?	?
2 *Nussle*	Y	Y	Y	Y
3 Boswell	Y	Y	Y	Y
4 *Ganske*	Y	?	?	?
5 *Latham*	Y	Y	Y	Y

KANSAS

	5	6	7	8
1 *Moran*	Y	Y	Y	Y
2 *Ryun*	Y	Y	Y	Y
3 Moore	Y	Y	Y	N
4 *Tiahrt*	Y	Y	Y	Y

KENTUCKY

	5	6	7	8
1 *Whitfield*	Y	Y	Y	Y
2 *Lewis*	Y	Y	Y	Y
3 *Northup*	Y	Y	Y	Y
4 Lucas	Y	Y	Y	Y
5 *Rogers*	Y	Y	Y	Y
6 *Fletcher*	Y	Y	Y	Y

LOUISIANA

	5	6	7	8
1 *Vitter*	?	?	?	?
2 Jefferson	Y	Y	Y	Y
3 *Tauzin*	Y	Y	Y	Y
4 *McCrery*	Y	Y	Y	Y
5 *Cooksey*	Y	Y	Y	Y
6 *Baker*	Y	Y	Y	Y
7 John	Y	Y	Y	Y

MAINE

	5	6	7	8
1 Allen	Y	Y	Y	Y
2 Baldacci	Y	Y	Y	Y

MARYLAND

	5	6	7	8
1 *Gilchrest*	Y	Y	Y	Y
2 *Ehrlich*	Y	Y	Y	Y
3 Cardin	Y	Y	Y	Y
4 Wynn	Y	Y	Y	Y
5 Hoyer	Y	Y	Y	Y
6 *Bartlett*	Y	Y	?	Y
7 Cummings	Y	Y	Y	Y
8 *Morella*	Y	Y	Y	Y

MASSACHUSETTS

	5	6	7	8
1 Olver	Y	Y	Y	Y
2 Neal	?	Y	Y	Y
3 McGovern	Y	Y	Y	Y
4 Frank	Y	Y	Y	Y
5 Meehan	Y	Y	Y	Y
6 Tierney	Y	Y	Y	Y
7 Markey	Y	Y	Y	Y
8 Capuano	Y	Y	Y	?
9 Moakley	?	Y	Y	Y
10 Delahunt	Y	Y	Y	Y

MICHIGAN

	5	6	7	8
1 Stupak	Y	Y	Y	N
2 *Hoekstra*	Y	Y	Y	Y
3 *Ehlers*	Y	Y	Y	Y
4 *Camp*	Y	Y	Y	Y
5 Barcia	Y	Y	Y	Y
6 *Upton*	Y	Y	Y	Y
7 *Smith*	Y	Y	Y	Y
8 *Rogers*	Y	Y	Y	Y
9 Kildee	Y	Y	Y	Y
10 Bonior	Y	Y	Y	Y
11 *Knollenberg*	Y	Y	Y	Y
12 Levin	Y	Y	Y	Y
13 Rivers	Y	Y	Y	Y
14 Conyers	Y	Y	Y	Y
15 Kilpatrick	Y	Y	Y	Y
16 Dingell	Y	Y	Y	Y

MINNESOTA

	5	6	7	8
1 *Gutknecht*	Y	Y	Y	Y
2 *Kennedy*	Y	Y	Y	Y
3 *Ramstad*	Y	Y	Y	N
4 McCollum	Y	Y	Y	Y
5 Sabo	Y	Y	Y	N
6 Luther	Y	Y	Y	Y
7 Peterson	Y	Y	Y	Y
8 Oberstar	Y	Y	Y	N

MISSISSIPPI

	5	6	7	8
1 *Wicker*	Y	Y	Y	Y
2 Thompson	Y	Y	Y	N
3 *Pickering*	Y	Y	Y	Y
4 Shows	Y	Y	Y	Y
5 Taylor	Y	Y	Y	N

MISSOURI

	5	6	7	8
1 Clay	Y	Y	Y	Y
2 *Akin*	Y	Y	Y	Y
3 Gephardt	Y	?	?	?
4 Skelton	Y	Y	Y	Y
5 McCarthy	Y	Y	Y	Y
6 *Graves*	Y	Y	Y	Y
7 *Blunt*	Y	Y	Y	Y
8 *Emerson*	Y	Y	Y	Y
9 *Hulshof*	Y	Y	Y	Y

MONTANA

	5	6	7	8
AL *Rehberg*	Y	Y	Y	Y

NEBRASKA

	5	6	7	8
1 *Bereuter*	Y	Y	Y	Y
2 *Terry*	Y	Y	Y	Y
3 *Osborne*	Y	Y	Y	Y

NEVADA

	5	6	7	8
1 Berkley	Y	Y	Y	Y
2 *Gibbons*	Y	Y	Y	Y

NEW HAMPSHIRE

	5	6	7	8
1 *Sununu*	Y	Y	Y	Y
2 *Bass*	+	Y	Y	Y

NEW JERSEY

	5	6	7	8
1 Andrews	Y	Y	Y	Y
2 *LoBiondo*	Y	Y	Y	Y
3 *Saxton*	Y	Y	Y	?
4 *Smith*	Y	Y	Y	Y
5 *Roukema*	Y	Y	Y	Y
6 Pallone	Y	Y	Y	Y
7 *Ferguson*	Y	Y	Y	Y
8 Pascrell	Y	Y	Y	Y
9 Rothman	Y	Y	Y	Y
10 Payne	Y	Y	Y	Y
11 *Frelinghuysen*	Y	Y	Y	Y
12 Holt	Y	Y	Y	Y
13 Menendez	Y	Y	Y	Y

NEW MEXICO

	5	6	7	8
1 *Wilson*	Y	Y	Y	Y
2 *Skeen*	Y	Y	Y	Y
3 Udall	Y	Y	Y	Y

NEW YORK

	5	6	7	8
1 *Grucci*	Y	Y	Y	Y
2 Israel	Y	Y	Y	Y
3 *King*	Y	Y	Y	Y
4 McCarthy	Y	Y	Y	Y
5 Ackerman	Y	Y	Y	Y
6 Meeks	Y	Y	Y	Y
7 Crowley	Y	Y	Y	Y
8 Nadler	Y	Y	Y	Y
9 Weiner	Y	Y	Y	Y
10 Towns	Y	Y	Y	Y
11 Owens	Y	Y	Y	Y
12 Velázquez	Y	Y	Y	Y
13 *Fossella*	?	Y	Y	Y
14 Maloney	Y	Y	Y	Y
15 Rangel	Y	Y	Y	Y
16 Serrano	Y	Y	Y	Y
17 Engel	Y	Y	Y	Y
18 Lowey	Y	Y	Y	Y
19 *Kelly*	Y	Y	Y	Y
20 *Gilman*	Y	Y	Y	Y
21 McNulty	Y	Y	Y	Y
22 *Sweeney*	Y	Y	Y	Y
23 *Boehlert*	Y	Y	Y	Y
24 *McHugh*	Y	Y	Y	Y
25 *Walsh*	Y	Y	Y	Y
26 Hinchey	Y	Y	Y	Y
27 *Reynolds*	Y	Y	Y	Y
28 Slaughter	Y	Y	Y	Y
29 LaFalce	Y	Y	Y	Y
30 Quinn	Y	Y	Y	Y
31 Houghton	?	Y	Y	Y

NORTH CAROLINA

	5	6	7	8
1 Clayton	Y	Y	Y	Y
2 Etheridge	Y	Y	Y	Y
3 *Jones*	Y	Y	Y	?
4 Price	Y	Y	Y	Y
5 *Burr*	Y	Y	Y	Y
6 *Coble*	Y	Y	Y	Y
7 McIntyre	Y	Y	Y	Y
8 *Hayes*	Y	Y	Y	Y
9 *Myrick*	Y	Y	Y	Y
10 *Ballenger*	?	Y	Y	Y
11 *Taylor*	Y	Y	Y	Y
12 Watt	Y	Y	Y	Y

NORTH DAKOTA

	5	6	7	8
AL Pomeroy	Y	Y	Y	Y

OHIO

	5	6	7	8
1 *Chabot*	Y	Y	Y	Y
2 *Portman*	Y	Y	Y	Y
3 Hall	Y	Y	Y	Y
4 *Oxley*	?	?	?	?
5 *Gillmor*	Y	Y	Y	Y
6 Strickland	Y	?	Y	Y
7 *Hobson*	?	Y	Y	Y
8 *Boehner*	Y	Y	Y	?
9 Kaptur	Y	Y	Y	Y
10 Kucinich	Y	Y	Y	N
11 Jones	Y	Y	Y	Y
12 *Tiberi*	Y	Y	Y	Y
13 Brown	Y	Y	Y	Y
14 Sawyer	Y	Y	Y	Y
15 *Pryce*	Y	Y	Y	Y
16 *Regula*	Y	Y	Y	Y
17 Traficant	Y	Y	Y	Y
18 *Ney*	Y	Y	Y	Y
19 *LaTourette*	Y	Y	Y	Y

OKLAHOMA

	5	6	7	8
1 *Largent*	Y	Y	Y	Y
2 Carson	Y	Y	Y	Y
3 *Watkins*	Y	Y	Y	Y
4 *Watts*	Y	Y	Y	Y
5 *Istook*	Y	Y	Y	Y
6 *Lucas*	Y	Y	Y	Y

OREGON

	5	6	7	8
1 Wu	Y	Y	Y	Y
2 *Walden*	Y	Y	Y	Y
3 Blumenauer	Y	Y	Y	Y
4 DeFazio	?	?	?	?
5 Hooley	Y	Y	Y	Y

PENNSYLVANIA

	5	6	7	8
1 Brady	Y	Y	Y	Y
2 Fattah	Y	Y	Y	Y
3 Borski	Y	Y	Y	Y
4 *Hart*	Y	Y	Y	Y
5 *Peterson*	Y	Y	Y	Y
6 Holden	Y	Y	Y	Y
7 *Weldon*	Y	Y	Y	Y
8 *Greenwood*	Y	Y	Y	Y
9 *Shuster*	Y	Y	Y	Y
10 *Sherwood*	Y	Y	Y	Y
11 Kanjorski	Y	Y	Y	Y
12 Murtha	Y	Y	Y	Y
13 Hoeffel	Y	Y	Y	Y
14 Coyne	Y	Y	Y	Y
15 *Toomey*	Y	Y	Y	Y
16 *Pitts*	Y	?	Y	Y
17 *Gekas*	Y	Y	Y	Y
18 Doyle	Y	Y	Y	Y
19 *Platts*	Y	Y	Y	Y
20 Mascara	Y	Y	Y	Y
21 *English*	Y	Y	Y	Y

RHODE ISLAND

	5	6	7	8
1 Kennedy	Y	?	Y	Y
2 Langevin	Y	Y	Y	Y

SOUTH CAROLINA

	5	6	7	8
1 *Brown*	Y	Y	Y	Y
2 *Spence*	Y	Y	Y	Y
3 *Graham*	Y	Y	Y	Y
4 *DeMint*	Y	Y	Y	Y
5 Spratt	Y	Y	Y	Y
6 Clyburn	Y	Y	Y	Y

SOUTH DAKOTA

	5	6	7	8
AL *Thune*	Y	Y	Y	Y

TENNESSEE

	5	6	7	8
1 *Jenkins*	Y	Y	Y	Y
2 *Duncan*	Y	Y	Y	Y
3 *Wamp*	Y	Y	Y	Y
4 *Hilleary*	Y	Y	?	?
5 Clement	Y	Y	Y	Y
6 Gordon	Y	Y	Y	Y
7 *Bryant*	Y	Y	Y	Y
8 Tanner	Y	Y	Y	Y
9 Ford	Y	Y	Y	Y

TEXAS

	5	6	7	8
1 Sandlin	Y	Y	Y	Y
2 Turner	Y	Y	Y	Y
3 *Johnson, Sam*	Y	Y	Y	Y
4 Hall	Y	Y	Y	Y
5 *Sessions*	Y	Y	Y	Y
6 *Barton*	Y	Y	Y	Y
7 *Culberson*	Y	Y	Y	Y
8 *Brady*	Y	Y	Y	Y
9 Lampson	Y	Y	Y	Y
10 Doggett	Y	Y	Y	Y
11 Edwards	Y	Y	Y	Y
12 *Granger*	Y	Y	Y	Y
13 *Thornberry*	Y	Y	Y	Y
14 *Paul*	Y	Y	N	Y
15 Hinojosa	?	?	?	?
16 Reyes	Y	Y	Y	Y
17 Stenholm	Y	Y	Y	Y
18 Jackson-Lee	Y	Y	Y	Y
19 *Combest*	Y	Y	Y	Y
20 Gonzalez	Y	Y	Y	Y
21 *Smith*	Y	Y	Y	Y
22 *DeLay*	Y	Y	Y	?
23 *Bonilla*	Y	Y	Y	Y
24 Frost	Y	Y	Y	Y
25 Bentsen	Y	Y	Y	Y
26 *Armey*	Y	Y	Y	Y
27 Ortiz	?	?	?	?
28 Rodriguez	Y	Y	Y	Y
29 Green	Y	Y	Y	Y
30 Johnson, E.B.	Y	Y	Y	Y

UTAH

	5	6	7	8
1 *Hansen*	Y	Y	Y	Y
2 Matheson	Y	Y	Y	Y
3 *Cannon*	?	Y	Y	Y

VERMONT

	5	6	7	8
AL *Sanders*	Y	Y	Y	?

VIRGINIA

	5	6	7	8
1 *Davis, Jo Ann*	Y	Y	Y	Y
2 *Schrock*	Y	Y	Y	Y
3 Scott	Y	Y	Y	Y
4 Sisisky	Y	Y	Y	Y
5 *Goode*	Y	Y	Y	Y
6 *Goodlatte*	Y	Y	Y	Y
7 *Cantor*	Y	Y	Y	Y
8 Moran	Y	Y	Y	?
9 Boucher	Y	Y	Y	Y
10 *Wolf*	Y	Y	Y	Y
11 *Davis, T.*	Y	Y	Y	Y

WASHINGTON

	5	6	7	8
1 Inslee	Y	Y	Y	Y
2 Larsen	Y	Y	Y	Y
3 Baird	Y	Y	Y	N
4 *Hastings*	Y	Y	Y	Y
5 *Nethercutt*	Y	Y	Y	Y
6 Dicks	Y	Y	Y	Y
7 McDermott	Y	Y	Y	N
8 *Dunn*	Y	Y	Y	Y
9 Smith	Y	Y	Y	Y

WEST VIRGINIA

	5	6	7	8
1 Mollohan	?	?	?	?
2 *Capito*	Y	Y	Y	Y
3 Rahall	Y	Y	Y	Y

WISCONSIN

	5	6	7	8
1 *Ryan*	Y	Y	Y	Y
2 Baldwin	Y	Y	Y	Y
3 Kind	Y	Y	Y	Y
4 Kleczka	Y	Y	Y	Y
5 Barrett	Y	Y	Y	Y
6 *Petri*	Y	Y	Y	Y
7 Obey	Y	Y	Y	Y
8 *Green*	Y	Y	Y	Y
9 *Sensenbrenner*	Y	Y	Y	Y

WYOMING

	5	6	7	8
AL *Cubin*	Y	Y	Y	Y

Southern states - Ala., Ark., Fla., Ga., Ky., La., Miss., N.C., Okla., S.C., Tenn., Texas, Va.

Key

Y	Voted for (yea).
#	Paired for.
+	Announced for.
N	Voted against (nay).
X	Paired against.
–	Announced against.
P	Voted "present."
C	Voted "present" to avoid possible conflict of interest.
?	Did not vote or otherwise make a position known.

Democrats **Republicans**
Independents

9. H J Res 7. Reagan's 90th Birthday/Passage. Platts, R-Pa., motion to suspend the rules and pass the resolution that extends best wishes and birthday greetings of the Congress to former President Ronald Reagan on his 90th birthday. Motion agreed to 410-0: R 209-0; D 199-0 (ND 146-0, SD 53-0); I 2-0. A two-thirds majority of those present and voting (274 in this case) is required for passage under suspension of the rules. Feb. 6, 2001.

10. H Res 28. Catholic Schools/Adoption. Tiberi, R-Ohio, motion to suspend the rules and adopt the resolution expressing House support for the goals of Catholic Schools Week and congratulating Catholic schools, students, parents and teachers for their contributions to education. Motion agreed to 412-0: R 206-0; D 204-0 (ND 150-0, SD 54-0); I 2-0. A two-thirds majority of those present and voting (275 in this case) is required for adoption under suspension of the rules. Feb. 6, 2001.

11. HR 132. Goro Hokama Post Office/Passage. Miller, R-Fla., motion to suspend the rules and pass the bill that would name a post office in Lanai City, Hawaii, the "Goro Hokama Post Office Building." Motion agreed to 413-0: R 207-0; D 204-0 (ND 151-0, SD 53-0); I 2-0. A two-thirds majority of those present and voting (276 in this case) is required for passage under suspension of the rules. Feb. 7, 2001.

	9	10	11
ALABAMA			
1 *Callahan*	Y	Y	Y
2 *Everett*	Y	Y	Y
3 *Riley*	Y	Y	Y
4 *Aderholt*	Y	Y	Y
5 Cramer	Y	Y	Y
6 *Bachus*	Y	Y	Y
7 Hilliard	Y	Y	Y
ALASKA			
AL *Young*	Y	Y	?
ARIZONA			
1 *Flake*	Y	Y	Y
2 Pastor	Y	Y	Y
3 *Stump*	Y	Y	Y
4 *Shadegg*	Y	Y	Y
5 *Kolbe*	Y	Y	Y
6 *Hayworth*	Y	Y	Y
ARKANSAS			
1 Berry	Y	Y	Y
2 Snyder	Y	Y	Y
3 *Hutchinson*	Y	Y	Y
4 Ross	Y	Y	Y
CALIFORNIA			
1 Thompson	Y	Y	Y
2 *Herger*	Y	Y	Y
3 *Ose*	Y	Y	Y
4 *Doolittle*	Y	Y	?
5 Matsui	Y	Y	Y
6 Woolsey	P	Y	Y
7 Miller, George	Y	Y	Y
8 Pelosi	Y	Y	Y
9 Lee	P	Y	Y
10 Tauscher	Y	Y	Y
11 *Pombo*	Y	Y	Y
12 Lantos	Y	Y	Y
13 Stark	P	Y	Y
14 Eshoo	Y	Y	Y
15 Honda	Y	Y	Y
16 Lofgren	Y	Y	Y
17 Farr	Y	Y	Y
18 Condit	Y	Y	Y
19 *Radanovich*	Y	Y	Y
20 Dooley	Y	Y	Y
21 *Thomas*	Y	Y	Y
22 Capps	Y	Y	Y
23 *Gallegly*	Y	Y	Y
24 Sherman	Y	Y	Y
25 *McKeon*	Y	Y	Y
26 Berman	Y	Y	Y
27 Schiff	Y	Y	Y
28 *Dreier*	Y	Y	Y
29 Waxman	Y	Y	Y
30 Becerra	?	?	?
31 Solis	Y	Y	Y
32 Vacant			
33 Roybal-Allard	Y	Y	Y
34 Napolitano	Y	Y	Y
35 Waters	P	Y	Y
36 Harman	Y	Y	Y
37 Millender-McD.	Y	Y	Y
38 *Horn*	Y	Y	Y

	9	10	11
39 *Royce*	Y	Y	Y
40 *Lewis*	Y	Y	Y
41 *Miller, Gary*	Y	Y	Y
42 Baca	Y	Y	Y
43 *Calvert*	Y	?	?
44 *Bono*	?	?	?
45 *Rohrabacher*	Y	Y	Y
46 Sanchez	P	Y	Y
47 *Cox*	Y	Y	Y
48 *Issa*	Y	Y	Y
49 Davis	Y	Y	Y
50 Filner	Y	Y	Y
51 *Cunningham*	Y	Y	Y
52 *Hunter*	Y	Y	Y
COLORADO			
1 DeGette	Y	Y	Y
2 Udall	Y	Y	Y
3 *McInnis*	?	?	Y
4 *Schaffer*	Y	Y	Y
5 *Hefley*	?	?	Y
6 *Tancredo*	Y	Y	Y
CONNECTICUT			
1 Larson	Y	Y	Y
2 *Simmons*	Y	Y	Y
3 DeLauro	Y	Y	Y
4 *Shays*	Y	Y	Y
5 Maloney	Y	Y	Y
6 *Johnson*	Y	Y	Y
DELAWARE			
AL *Castle*	Y	Y	Y
FLORIDA			
1 *Scarborough*	Y	Y	Y
2 Boyd	Y	Y	Y
3 Brown	?	?	Y
4 *Crenshaw*	Y	Y	Y
5 Thurman	Y	Y	Y
6 *Stearns*	Y	Y	Y
7 *Mica*	Y	Y	Y
8 *Keller*	Y	Y	Y
9 *Bilirakis*	Y	Y	Y
10 *Young*	Y	Y	Y
11 Davis	Y	Y	Y
12 *Putnam*	Y	Y	Y
13 *Miller*	Y	Y	Y
14 *Goss*	Y	Y	Y
15 *Weldon*	Y	?	Y
16 *Foley*	Y	Y	Y
17 Meek	Y	Y	Y
18 *Ros-Lehtinen*	Y	Y	Y
19 Wexler	Y	Y	Y
20 Deutsch	Y	Y	Y
21 *Diaz-Balart*	Y	Y	Y
22 *Shaw*	Y	Y	Y
23 Hastings	Y	Y	Y
GEORGIA			
1 *Kingston*	Y	Y	Y
2 Bishop	Y	Y	Y
3 *Collins*	Y	Y	Y
4 McKinney	Y	Y	Y
5 Lewis	Y	Y	Y
6 *Isakson*	Y	Y	Y
7 *Barr*	Y	Y	Y
8 *Chambliss*	Y	Y	Y
9 *Deal*	Y	Y	Y
10 *Norwood*	Y	Y	Y
11 *Linder*	Y	Y	Y
HAWAII			
1 Abercrombie	Y	Y	Y
2 Mink	Y	Y	Y
IDAHO			
1 *Otter*	Y	Y	Y
2 *Simpson*	Y	Y	Y
ILLINOIS			
1 Rush	Y	Y	Y
2 Jackson	Y	Y	Y
3 Lipinski	Y	Y	Y
4 Gutierrez	Y	Y	Y
5 Blagojevich	Y	Y	Y
6 *Hyde*	Y	Y	Y
7 Davis	Y	Y	Y
8 *Crane*	Y	Y	Y
9 Schakowsky	Y	Y	Y
10 *Kirk*	Y	Y	Y
11 *Weller*	Y	Y	Y
12 Costello	Y	Y	Y
13 *Biggert*	Y	Y	Y

ND Northern Democrats   SD Southern Democrats

The vote columns are headed **9**, **10**, **11**.

#	Name	9	10	11
14	Hastert	Y		
15	Johnson	Y	Y	Y
16	Manzullo	Y	Y	Y
17	Evans	Y	Y	?
18	LaHood	Y	Y	Y
19	Phelps	Y	Y	Y
20	Shimkus	Y	Y	Y

INDIANA

#	Name	9	10	11
1	Visclosky	Y	Y	Y
2	Pence	Y	Y	Y
3	Roemer	Y	Y	Y
4	Souder	Y	Y	Y
5	Buyer	?	?	?
6	Burton	Y	Y	Y
7	Kerns	Y	Y	Y
8	Hostettler	Y	Y	Y
9	Hill	Y	Y	Y
10	Carson	Y	Y	Y

IOWA

#	Name	9	10	11
1	Leach	Y	Y	Y
2	Nussle	Y	Y	Y
3	Boswell	Y	Y	Y
4	Ganske	Y	Y	Y
5	Latham	Y	Y	Y

KANSAS

#	Name	9	10	11
1	Moran	Y	Y	Y
2	Ryun	Y	Y	Y
3	Moore	Y	Y	Y
4	Tiahrt	Y	Y	Y

KENTUCKY

#	Name	9	10	11
1	Whitfield	Y	Y	Y
2	Lewis	Y	Y	Y
3	Northup	Y	Y	Y
4	Lucas	Y	Y	Y
5	Rogers	?	?	?
6	Fletcher	Y	Y	Y

LOUISIANA

#	Name	9	10	11
1	Vitter	Y	Y	Y
2	Jefferson	Y	Y	Y
3	Tauzin	Y	Y	Y
4	McCrery	Y	Y	Y
5	Cooksey	Y	?	Y
6	Baker	Y	Y	Y
7	John	Y	Y	Y

MAINE

#	Name	9	10	11
1	Allen	Y	Y	Y
2	Baldacci	Y	Y	Y

MARYLAND

#	Name	9	10	11
1	Gilchrest	Y	Y	Y
2	Ehrlich	Y	Y	Y
3	Cardin	Y	Y	Y
4	Wynn	Y	Y	Y
5	Hoyer	Y	Y	Y
6	Bartlett	Y	Y	Y
7	Cummings	Y	Y	Y
8	Morella	Y	Y	?

MASSACHUSETTS

#	Name	9	10	11
1	Olver	Y	Y	Y
2	Neal	Y	Y	Y
3	McGovern	Y	Y	Y
4	Frank	Y	Y	Y
5	Meehan	Y	Y	?
6	Tierney	Y	Y	Y
7	Markey	Y	Y	Y
8	Capuano	Y	Y	Y
9	Moakley	?	?	?
10	Delahunt	Y	Y	Y

MICHIGAN

#	Name	9	10	11
1	Stupak	Y	Y	Y
2	Hoekstra	Y	Y	Y
3	Ehlers	Y	Y	Y
4	Camp	Y	Y	Y
5	Barcia	Y	Y	Y
6	Upton	Y	Y	Y
7	Smith	Y	Y	Y
8	Rogers	Y	Y	Y
9	Kildee	Y	Y	Y
10	Bonior	Y	Y	Y
11	Knollenberg	Y	Y	Y
12	Levin	Y	Y	Y
13	Rivers	Y	Y	Y
14	Conyers	?	?	?
15	Kilpatrick	Y	Y	Y
16	Dingell	Y	Y	Y

MINNESOTA

#	Name	9	10	11
1	Gutknecht	Y	Y	Y
2	Kennedy	Y	Y	Y
3	Ramstad	Y	Y	Y
4	McCollum	Y	Y	Y
5	Sabo	Y	Y	Y
6	Luther	Y	Y	Y
7	Peterson	Y	Y	Y
8	Oberstar	Y	Y	Y

MISSISSIPPI

#	Name	9	10	11
1	Wicker	Y	Y	Y
2	Thompson	Y	Y	Y
3	Pickering	Y	Y	Y
4	Shows	Y	Y	Y
5	Taylor	Y	Y	Y

MISSOURI

#	Name	9	10	11
1	Clay	Y	Y	Y
2	Akin	Y	Y	Y
3	Gephardt	Y	Y	Y
4	Skelton	Y	Y	Y
5	McCarthy	Y	Y	Y
6	Graves	+	Y	Y
7	Blunt	Y	Y	Y
8	Emerson	Y	Y	Y
9	Hulshof	Y	Y	Y

MONTANA

#	Name	9	10	11
AL	Rehberg	Y	Y	Y

NEBRASKA

#	Name	9	10	11
1	Bereuter	Y	Y	Y
2	Terry	Y	Y	Y
3	Osborne	+	Y	Y

NEVADA

#	Name	9	10	11
1	Berkley	Y	Y	Y
2	Gibbons	Y	Y	Y

NEW HAMPSHIRE

#	Name	9	10	11
1	Sununu	Y	Y	Y
2	Bass	Y	Y	Y

NEW JERSEY

#	Name	9	10	11
1	Andrews	Y	Y	Y
2	LoBiondo	Y	Y	Y
3	Saxton	Y	Y	Y
4	Smith	Y	Y	Y
5	Roukema	Y	Y	Y
6	Pallone	Y	Y	Y
7	Ferguson	Y	Y	Y
8	Pascrell	Y	Y	Y
9	Rothman	Y	?	Y
10	Payne	Y	Y	Y
11	Frelinghuysen	Y	Y	Y
12	Holt	Y	Y	Y
13	Menendez	Y	Y	Y

NEW MEXICO

#	Name	9	10	11
1	Wilson	Y	Y	Y
2	Skeen	Y	Y	Y
3	Udall	Y	Y	Y

NEW YORK

#	Name	9	10	11
1	Grucci	+	+	+
2	Israel	Y	Y	Y
3	King	Y	Y	Y
4	McCarthy	Y	Y	Y
5	Ackerman	Y	Y	Y
6	Meeks	Y	Y	Y
7	Crowley	Y	Y	Y
8	Nadler	Y	Y	Y
9	Weiner	Y	Y	Y
10	Towns	Y	Y	Y
11	Owens	Y	Y	Y
12	Velázquez	Y	Y	Y
13	Fossella	Y	Y	Y
14	Maloney	?	?	Y
15	Rangel	Y	Y	Y
16	Serrano	Y	Y	Y
17	Engel	Y	Y	Y
18	Lowey	Y	Y	Y
19	Kelly	Y	Y	Y
20	Gilman	Y	Y	Y
21	McNulty	Y	Y	Y
22	Sweeney	Y	Y	Y
23	Boehlert	Y	Y	Y
24	McHugh	Y	Y	Y
25	Walsh	Y	Y	Y
26	Hinchey	Y	Y	Y
27	Reynolds	Y	Y	Y
28	Slaughter	Y	Y	Y
29	LaFalce	Y	Y	Y
30	Quinn	?	?	Y
31	Houghton	?	Y	Y

NORTH CAROLINA

#	Name	9	10	11
1	Clayton	Y	Y	Y
2	Etheridge	Y	Y	Y
3	Jones	Y	Y	Y
4	Price	Y	Y	Y
5	Burr	Y	Y	Y
6	Coble	Y	Y	Y
7	McIntyre	Y	Y	Y
8	Hayes	Y	Y	Y
9	Myrick	Y	Y	Y
10	Ballenger	Y	Y	Y
11	Taylor	Y	Y	Y
12	Watt	Y	Y	Y

NORTH DAKOTA

#	Name	9	10	11
AL	Pomeroy	Y	Y	Y

OHIO

#	Name	9	10	11
1	Chabot	Y	Y	Y
2	Portman	Y	Y	Y
3	Hall	Y	Y	Y
4	Oxley	Y	Y	Y
5	Gillmor	Y	Y	Y
6	Strickland	Y	Y	Y
7	Hobson	Y	Y	Y
8	Boehner	Y	Y	Y
9	Kaptur	Y	Y	Y
10	Kucinich	Y	Y	Y
11	Jones	Y	Y	Y
12	Tiberi	Y	Y	Y
13	Brown	Y	Y	Y
14	Sawyer	Y	Y	Y
15	Pryce	Y	Y	Y
16	Regula	Y	?	Y
17	Traficant	Y	Y	Y
18	Ney	Y	Y	Y
19	LaTourette	Y	Y	Y

OKLAHOMA

#	Name	9	10	11
1	Largent	Y	Y	Y
2	Carson	Y	Y	Y
3	Watkins	Y	Y	Y
4	Watts	Y	Y	Y
5	Istook	Y	Y	?
6	Lucas	Y	Y	Y

OREGON

#	Name	9	10	11
1	Wu	Y	Y	Y
2	Walden	Y	Y	Y
3	Blumenauer	Y	Y	Y
4	DeFazio	P	Y	Y
5	Hooley	Y	Y	Y

PENNSYLVANIA

#	Name	9	10	11
1	Brady	Y	Y	Y
2	Fattah	Y	?	Y
3	Borski	Y	Y	Y
4	Hart	Y	Y	Y
5	Peterson	Y	Y	Y
6	Holden	Y	Y	Y
7	Weldon	Y	Y	Y
8	Greenwood	?	?	?
9	Vacant			
10	Sherwood	Y	Y	Y
11	Kanjorski	Y	Y	Y
12	Murtha	Y	Y	Y
13	Hoeffel	Y	Y	Y
14	Coyne	Y	Y	Y
15	Toomey	Y	Y	Y
16	Pitts	Y	Y	Y
17	Gekas	Y	Y	Y
18	Doyle	Y	Y	Y
19	Platts	Y	Y	Y
20	Mascara	Y	Y	Y
21	English	Y	Y	Y

RHODE ISLAND

#	Name	9	10	11
1	Kennedy	Y	Y	Y
2	Langevin	Y	Y	Y

SOUTH CAROLINA

#	Name	9	10	11
1	Brown	Y	Y	Y
2	Spence	Y	Y	Y
3	Graham	Y	Y	Y
4	DeMint	Y	Y	Y
5	Spratt	Y	Y	Y
6	Clyburn	Y	Y	Y

SOUTH DAKOTA

#	Name	9	10	11
AL	Thune	Y	Y	Y

TENNESSEE

#	Name	9	10	11
1	Jenkins	Y	Y	Y
2	Duncan	Y	Y	Y
3	Wamp	Y	Y	Y
4	Hilleary	Y	Y	Y
5	Clement	Y	Y	?
6	Gordon	Y	Y	Y
7	Bryant	Y	Y	Y
8	Tanner	Y	Y	Y
9	Ford	Y	Y	Y

TEXAS

#	Name	9	10	11
1	Sandlin	Y	Y	Y
2	Turner	Y	Y	Y
3	Johnson, Sam	Y	Y	Y
4	Hall	Y	Y	Y
5	Sessions	Y	Y	Y
6	Barton	Y	Y	Y
7	Culberson	Y	Y	Y
8	Brady	Y	Y	Y
9	Lampson	Y	Y	Y
10	Doggett	Y	Y	Y
11	Edwards	Y	Y	Y
12	Granger	Y	Y	Y
13	Thornberry	Y	Y	Y
14	Paul	Y	P	Y
15	Hinojosa	Y	Y	Y
16	Reyes	Y	Y	Y
17	Stenholm	Y	Y	Y
18	Jackson-Lee	Y	Y	Y
19	Combest	Y	Y	Y
20	Gonzalez	Y	Y	Y
21	Smith	Y	Y	Y
22	DeLay	Y	Y	Y
23	Bonilla	Y	Y	Y
24	Frost	Y	Y	Y
25	Bentsen	Y	Y	Y
26	Armey	Y	Y	Y
27	Ortiz	Y	Y	Y
28	Rodriguez	Y	Y	?
29	Green	Y	Y	Y
30	Johnson, E.B.	P	Y	Y

UTAH

#	Name	9	10	11
1	Hansen	Y	Y	Y
2	Matheson	Y	Y	Y
3	Cannon	?	?	?

VERMONT

#	Name	9	10	11
AL	Sanders	Y	Y	Y

VIRGINIA

#	Name	9	10	11
1	Davis, Jo Ann	Y	Y	Y
2	Schrock	Y	Y	Y
3	Scott	Y	Y	Y
4	Sisisky	Y	Y	Y
5	Goode	Y	Y	Y
6	Goodlatte	Y	Y	Y
7	Cantor	Y	Y	Y
8	Moran	Y	Y	Y
9	Boucher	Y	Y	Y
10	Wolf	Y	Y	Y
11	Davis, T.	Y	Y	Y

WASHINGTON

#	Name	9	10	11
1	Inslee	Y	Y	Y
2	Larsen	Y	Y	Y
3	Baird	Y	Y	?
4	Hastings	Y	Y	Y
5	Nethercutt	Y	Y	Y
6	Dicks	Y	Y	Y
7	McDermott	Y	Y	Y
8	Dunn	Y	Y	Y
9	Smith	Y	Y	Y

WEST VIRGINIA

#	Name	9	10	11
1	Mollohan	Y	Y	Y
2	Capito	Y	Y	+
3	Rahall	Y	Y	Y

WISCONSIN

#	Name	9	10	11
1	Ryan	Y	Y	Y
2	Baldwin	Y	Y	Y
3	Kind	Y	Y	Y
4	Kleczka	Y	Y	Y
5	Barrett	Y	Y	Y
6	Petri	Y	Y	Y
7	Obey	Y	Y	Y
8	Green	Y	Y	Y
9	Sensenbrenner	Y	Y	Y

WYOMING

#	Name	9	10	11
AL	Cubin	Y	Y	Y

Southern states - Ala., Ark., Fla., Ga., Ky., La., Miss., N.C., Okla., S.C., Tenn., Texas, Va.

12. H Res 34. Sharon Congratulations/Adoption. Hyde, R-Ill., motion to suspend the rules and adopt the resolution that congratulates Ariel Sharon on his election as prime minister of Israel and urges Palestinian Authority President Yasser Arafat to use his influence and resources to see that violence in the Middle East is brought to an end. Motion agreed to 410-1: R 210-1; D 198-0 (ND 147-0, SD 51-0); I 2-0. A two-thirds majority of those present and voting (274 in this case) is required for adoption under suspension of the rules. Feb. 13, 2001.

13. HR 2. Social Security 'Lockbox'/Passage. Sessions, R-Texas, motion to suspend the rules and pass the bill that would ensure that the surpluses in the Social Security and Medicare hospital insurance trust funds are used to pay down the public debt, pending enactment of legislation to overhaul those programs. The requirement would be enforced through points of order. Motion agreed to 407-2: R 211-0; D 194-2 (ND 144-2, SD 50-0); I 2-0. A two-thirds majority of those present and voting (273 in this case) is required for passage under suspension of the rules. Feb. 13, 2001.

14. HR 524. E-Commerce/Passage. Boehlert, R-Ohio, motion to suspend the rules and pass the bill that would authorize the National Institute of Standards and Technology to help small- and medium-sized manufacturers use electronic commerce. Motion agreed to 409-6: R 200-6; D 207-0 (ND 153-0, SD 54-0); I 2-0. A two-thirds majority of those present and voting (277 in this case) is required for passage under suspension of the rules. Feb. 14, 2001.

15. HR 554. Railroad Accident Assistance/Passage. Passage of the bill that would require the National Transportation Safety Board (NTSB) to establish a program to help the families of railroad accident victims. The bill would prohibit lawyers or their agents from making unsolicited contacts with families or injured passengers for 45 days after an accident. Passed 404-4: R 200-4; D 202-0 (ND 150-0, SD 52-0); I 2-0. Feb. 14, 2001.

Key

Y	Voted for (yea).
#	Paired for.
+	Announced for.
N	Voted against (nay).
X	Paired against.
–	Announced against.
P	Voted "present."
C	Voted "present" to avoid possible conflict of interest.
?	Did not vote or otherwise make a position known.

Democrats **Republicans**
Independents

	12	13	14	15
ALABAMA				
1 *Callahan*	Y	Y	Y	Y
2 *Everett*	Y	Y	Y	Y
3 *Riley*	Y	Y	Y	Y
4 *Aderholt*	Y	Y	Y	Y
5 Cramer	Y	Y	Y	Y
6 *Bachus*	Y	Y	Y	Y
7 Hilliard	Y	Y	Y	Y
ALASKA				
AL *Young*	?	?	?	?
ARIZONA				
1 *Flake*	Y	Y	N	N
2 Pastor	Y	Y	Y	Y
3 *Stump*	Y	Y	Y	Y
4 *Shadegg*	Y	Y	Y	Y
5 *Kolbe*	Y	Y	Y	Y
6 *Hayworth*	Y	Y	Y	Y
ARKANSAS				
1 Berry	Y	Y	Y	Y
2 Snyder	Y	P	Y	Y
3 *Hutchinson*	Y	Y	Y	Y
4 Ross	Y	Y	Y	Y
CALIFORNIA				
1 Thompson	Y	Y	Y	Y
2 *Herger*	Y	Y	Y	Y
3 *Ose*	Y	Y	Y	Y
4 *Doolittle*	?	?	Y	Y
5 Matsui	Y	Y	Y	Y
6 Woolsey	Y	Y	Y	Y
7 Miller, George	?	?	Y	Y
8 Pelosi	Y	Y	Y	Y
9 Lee	Y	Y	Y	Y
10 Tauscher	Y	Y	Y	Y
11 *Pombo*	Y	Y	Y	Y
12 Lantos	Y	Y	Y	Y
13 Stark	Y	Y	Y	Y
14 Eshoo	Y	Y	Y	Y
15 Honda	Y	Y	Y	Y
16 Lofgren	Y	Y	Y	Y
17 Farr	Y	Y	Y	Y
18 Condit	Y	Y	Y	Y
19 *Radanovich*	Y	Y	Y	Y
20 Dooley	Y	Y	Y	Y
21 *Thomas*	Y	Y	Y	Y
22 Capps	+	Y	Y	Y
23 *Gallegly*	Y	Y	Y	Y
24 Sherman	Y	Y	Y	Y
25 *McKeon*	Y	Y	Y	Y
26 Berman	Y	Y	Y	Y
27 Schiff	Y	Y	Y	Y
28 *Dreier*	Y	Y	Y	Y
29 Waxman	Y	Y	Y	Y
30 Becerra	+	+	Y	Y
31 Solis	Y	Y	Y	Y
32 Vacant				
33 Roybal-Allard	Y	Y	Y	Y
34 Napolitano	Y	Y	Y	Y
35 Waters	Y	Y	Y	Y
36 Harman	Y	Y	Y	Y
37 Millender-McD.	Y	Y	Y	Y
38 *Horn*	Y	Y	Y	Y

	12	13	14	15
39 *Royce*	Y	Y	Y	?
40 *Lewis*	Y	Y	?	?
41 *Miller, Gary*	Y	Y	Y	Y
42 Baca	Y	Y	Y	Y
43 *Calvert*	Y	Y	Y	Y
44 *Bono*	?	?	?	?
45 *Rohrabacher*	?	Y	Y	Y
46 Sanchez	Y	Y	Y	Y
47 *Cox*	Y	Y	Y	Y
48 *Issa*	Y	Y	Y	Y
49 Davis	Y	Y	Y	Y
50 Filner	Y	N	Y	Y
51 *Cunningham*	Y	Y	Y	Y
52 *Hunter*	Y	Y	Y	Y
COLORADO				
1 DeGette	Y	Y	Y	Y
2 Udall	Y	Y	Y	Y
3 *McInnis*	Y	Y	Y	Y
4 *Schaffer*	Y	Y	N	N
5 *Hefley*	Y	Y	Y	Y
6 *Tancredo*	Y	Y	N	N
CONNECTICUT				
1 Larson	Y	Y	Y	Y
2 *Simmons*	Y	Y	Y	Y
3 DeLauro	Y	Y	Y	Y
4 *Shays*	Y	Y	Y	Y
5 Maloney	Y	Y	Y	Y
6 *Johnson*	Y	Y	Y	Y
DELAWARE				
AL *Castle*	Y	Y	Y	Y
FLORIDA				
1 *Scarborough*	Y	Y	Y	Y
2 Boyd	Y	Y	Y	Y
3 Brown	?	?	Y	Y
4 *Crenshaw*	Y	Y	Y	Y
5 Thurman	Y	Y	Y	Y
6 *Stearns*	Y	Y	Y	Y
7 *Mica*	Y	Y	Y	Y
8 *Keller*	Y	Y	Y	Y
9 *Bilirakis*	Y	Y	Y	Y
10 *Young*	Y	Y	Y	Y
11 Davis	Y	Y	Y	Y
12 *Putnam*	Y	Y	+	Y
13 *Miller*	Y	Y	Y	Y
14 *Goss*	Y	Y	Y	Y
15 *Weldon*	Y	Y	Y	Y
16 *Foley*	Y	Y	Y	?
17 Meek	Y	Y	Y	?
18 *Ros-Lehtinen*	Y	Y	Y	Y
19 Wexler	Y	Y	Y	Y
20 Deutsch	Y	Y	Y	Y
21 *Diaz-Balart*	Y	Y	Y	Y
22 *Shaw*	Y	Y	Y	Y
23 Hastings	Y	Y	Y	Y
GEORGIA				
1 *Kingston*	Y	Y	Y	Y
2 Bishop	Y	Y	Y	Y
3 *Collins*	Y	Y	N	Y
4 McKinney	?	?	Y	Y
5 Lewis	Y	Y	Y	Y
6 *Isakson*	Y	Y	Y	Y
7 *Barr*	Y	Y	Y	Y
8 *Chambliss*	Y	Y	Y	Y
9 *Deal*	Y	Y	Y	Y
10 *Norwood*	Y	Y	Y	Y
11 *Linder*	Y	Y	Y	Y
HAWAII				
1 Abercrombie	Y	Y	Y	Y
2 Mink	Y	P	Y	Y
IDAHO				
1 *Otter*	Y	Y	Y	Y
2 *Simpson*	Y	Y	Y	Y
ILLINOIS				
1 Rush	Y	Y	Y	Y
2 Jackson	Y	Y	Y	Y
3 Lipinski	Y	Y	Y	Y
4 Gutierrez	Y	Y	Y	?
5 Blagojevich	Y	Y	Y	Y
6 *Hyde*	Y	Y	Y	Y
7 Davis	Y	Y	Y	Y
8 *Crane*	Y	Y	Y	Y
9 Schakowsky	Y	Y	Y	Y
10 *Kirk*	Y	Y	Y	Y
11 *Weller*	Y	Y	Y	Y
12 Costello	Y	Y	Y	Y
13 *Biggert*	Y	Y	Y	Y

ND Northern Democrats   SD Southern Democrats

Member	12	13	14	15
14 Hastert				
15 Johnson	Y	Y	Y	Y
16 Manzullo	Y	Y	Y	Y
17 Evans	Y	Y	Y	Y
18 LaHood	Y	Y	Y	Y
19 Phelps	Y	Y	Y	Y
20 Shimkus	?	?	Y	Y
INDIANA				
1 Visclosky	Y	Y	Y	Y
2 Pence	Y	Y	Y	Y
3 Roemer	Y	Y	Y	Y
4 Souder	+	+	Y	Y
5 Buyer	Y	Y	Y	Y
6 Burton	+	+	+	+
7 Kerns	Y	Y	Y	Y
8 Hostettler	Y	Y	N	Y
9 Hill	Y	Y	Y	Y
10 Carson	Y	Y	Y	Y
IOWA				
1 Leach	Y	Y	Y	Y
2 Nussle	Y	Y	Y	Y
3 Boswell	Y	Y	Y	Y
4 Ganske	Y	Y	Y	Y
5 Latham	Y	Y	Y	Y
KANSAS				
1 Moran	Y	Y	Y	Y
2 Ryun	Y	Y	Y	Y
3 Moore	Y	Y	Y	Y
4 Tiahrt	Y	Y	Y	Y
KENTUCKY				
1 Whitfield	Y	Y	Y	Y
2 Lewis	Y	Y	Y	Y
3 Northup	Y	Y	Y	Y
4 Lucas	Y	Y	Y	Y
5 Rogers	Y	Y	Y	Y
6 Fletcher	Y	Y	Y	Y
LOUISIANA				
1 Vitter	Y	Y	Y	Y
2 Jefferson	Y	Y	Y	Y
3 Tauzin	Y	Y	Y	Y
4 McCrery	Y	Y	Y	Y
5 Cooksey	?	?	?	?
6 Baker	Y	Y	Y	Y
7 John	Y	Y	Y	Y
MAINE				
1 Allen	Y	Y	Y	Y
2 Baldacci	Y	Y	Y	Y
MARYLAND				
1 Gilchrest	Y	Y	Y	?
2 Ehrlich	Y	Y	Y	Y
3 Cardin	Y	Y	Y	Y
4 Wynn	Y	Y	Y	Y
5 Hoyer	Y	Y	Y	Y
6 Bartlett	Y	Y	Y	Y
7 Cummings	Y	Y	Y	Y
8 Morella	Y	Y	Y	Y
MASSACHUSETTS				
1 Olver	Y	Y	Y	Y
2 Neal	Y	Y	Y	Y
3 McGovern	Y	Y	Y	Y
4 Frank	Y	Y	Y	Y
5 Meehan	Y	Y	Y	Y
6 Tierney	Y	Y	Y	Y
7 Markey	Y	Y	Y	Y
8 Capuano	Y	Y	Y	Y
9 Moakley	Y	Y	Y	Y
10 Delahunt	Y	Y	Y	Y
MICHIGAN				
1 Stupak	Y	Y	Y	Y
2 Hoekstra	Y	Y	Y	Y
3 Ehlers	Y	Y	Y	Y
4 Camp	Y	Y	Y	Y
5 Barcia	Y	Y	Y	Y
6 Upton	Y	Y	Y	Y
7 Smith	Y	?	Y	Y
8 Rogers	Y	Y	Y	Y
9 Kildee	Y	Y	Y	Y
10 Bonior	?	?	Y	Y
11 Knollenberg	Y	Y	Y	Y
12 Levin	Y	Y	Y	Y
13 Rivers	Y	Y	Y	Y
14 Conyers	Y	Y	Y	Y
15 Kilpatrick	Y	Y	Y	Y
16 Dingell	Y	Y	Y	Y
MINNESOTA				
1 Gutknecht	Y	Y	Y	Y
2 Kennedy	Y	Y	Y	Y
3 Ramstad	Y	Y	Y	Y
4 McCollum	Y	Y	Y	Y
5 Sabo	Y	P	Y	Y
6 Luther	Y	Y	Y	Y
7 Peterson	Y	Y	Y	Y
8 Oberstar	Y	Y	Y	Y
MISSISSIPPI				
1 Wicker	Y	Y	Y	Y
2 Thompson	Y	Y	Y	Y
3 Pickering	Y	Y	Y	Y
4 Shows	Y	Y	Y	Y
5 Taylor	Y	Y	Y	Y
MISSOURI				
1 Clay	Y	Y	Y	Y
2 Akin	Y	Y	Y	Y
3 Gephardt	?	?	Y	Y
4 Skelton	Y	Y	Y	Y
5 McCarthy	Y	Y	Y	Y
6 Graves	Y	Y	Y	Y
7 Blunt	Y	Y	Y	Y
8 Emerson	Y	Y	Y	Y
9 Hulshof	Y	Y	Y	Y
MONTANA				
AL Rehberg	Y	Y	Y	Y
NEBRASKA				
1 Bereuter	Y	Y	Y	Y
2 Terry	Y	Y	Y	Y
3 Osborne	Y	Y	Y	Y
NEVADA				
1 Berkley	Y	Y	Y	Y
2 Gibbons	Y	Y	Y	Y
NEW HAMPSHIRE				
1 Sununu	Y	Y	Y	Y
2 Bass	Y	Y	Y	Y
NEW JERSEY				
1 Andrews	Y	Y	Y	Y
2 LoBiondo	Y	Y	Y	Y
3 Saxton	Y	Y	Y	Y
4 Smith	Y	Y	Y	Y
5 Roukema	Y	Y	Y	Y
6 Pallone	Y	Y	Y	Y
7 Ferguson	Y	Y	Y	Y
8 Pascrell	Y	Y	Y	Y
9 Rothman	Y	Y	Y	Y
10 Payne	Y	?	Y	Y
11 Frelinghuysen	Y	Y	Y	Y
12 Holt	Y	Y	Y	Y
13 Menendez	Y	Y	Y	Y
NEW MEXICO				
1 Wilson	Y	Y	Y	Y
2 Skeen	Y	Y	Y	Y
3 Udall	Y	Y	Y	Y
NEW YORK				
1 Grucci	Y	Y	Y	Y
2 Israel	Y	Y	Y	Y
3 King	Y	Y	Y	Y
4 McCarthy	Y	Y	Y	Y
5 Ackerman	?	?	?	?
6 Meeks	Y	Y	Y	Y
7 Crowley	Y	Y	Y	Y
8 Nadler	Y	N	Y	Y
9 Weiner	Y	Y	Y	Y
10 Towns	Y	Y	?	?
11 Owens	Y	Y	Y	Y
12 Velázquez	Y	Y	Y	Y
13 Fossella	Y	Y	Y	?
14 Maloney	Y	Y	Y	Y
15 Rangel	Y	Y	Y	Y
16 Serrano	Y	Y	Y	Y
17 Engel	Y	Y	Y	Y
18 Lowey	?	?	Y	Y
19 Kelly	Y	Y	Y	Y
20 Gilman	Y	Y	Y	Y
21 McNulty	Y	Y	Y	Y
22 Sweeney	Y	Y	Y	Y
23 Boehlert	Y	Y	Y	Y
24 McHugh	Y	Y	Y	Y
25 Walsh	Y	Y	Y	Y
26 Hinchey	Y	P	Y	Y
27 Reynolds	Y	Y	Y	Y
28 Slaughter	Y	Y	Y	?
29 LaFalce	Y	Y	Y	Y
30 Quinn	Y	Y	Y	Y
31 Houghton	Y	Y	Y	Y
NORTH CAROLINA				
1 Clayton	Y	Y	Y	Y
2 Etheridge	Y	Y	Y	Y
3 Jones	Y	Y	Y	Y
4 Price	Y	Y	Y	Y
5 Burr	Y	Y	Y	Y
6 Coble	Y	Y	Y	Y
7 McIntyre	Y	Y	Y	Y
8 Hayes	Y	Y	Y	Y
9 Myrick	Y	Y	Y	Y
10 Ballenger	Y	Y	Y	Y
11 Taylor	Y	Y	Y	Y
12 Watt	Y	Y	Y	Y
NORTH DAKOTA				
AL Pomeroy	Y	Y	Y	Y
OHIO				
1 Chabot	Y	Y	Y	Y
2 Portman	Y	Y	Y	Y
3 Hall	Y	Y	Y	Y
4 Oxley	Y	Y	Y	Y
5 Gillmor	Y	Y	Y	Y
6 Strickland	Y	Y	Y	Y
7 Hobson	Y	Y	Y	Y
8 Boehner	Y	Y	Y	Y
9 Kaptur	Y	Y	Y	Y
10 Kucinich	Y	Y	Y	Y
11 Jones	Y	Y	Y	Y
12 Tiberi	Y	Y	Y	Y
13 Brown	Y	Y	Y	Y
14 Sawyer	Y	Y	Y	?
15 Pryce	Y	Y	Y	Y
16 Regula	Y	Y	Y	Y
17 Traficant	Y	Y	Y	Y
18 Ney	Y	Y	Y	Y
19 LaTourette	Y	Y	Y	Y
OKLAHOMA				
1 Largent	Y	Y	Y	Y
2 Carson	Y	Y	Y	Y
3 Watkins	Y	Y	?	?
4 Watts	Y	Y	Y	Y
5 Istook	Y	Y	?	?
6 Lucas	Y	Y	Y	Y
OREGON				
1 Wu	Y	Y	Y	Y
2 Walden	Y	Y	Y	Y
3 Blumenauer	Y	Y	Y	Y
4 DeFazio	Y	Y	Y	Y
5 Hooley	Y	Y	Y	Y
PENNSYLVANIA				
1 Brady	Y	Y	Y	Y
2 Fattah	?	Y	Y	Y
3 Borski	Y	Y	Y	Y
4 Hart	Y	Y	Y	Y
5 Peterson	Y	Y	Y	Y
6 Holden	Y	Y	Y	Y
7 Weldon	Y	Y	Y	Y
8 Greenwood	Y	Y	Y	Y
9 Vacant				
10 Sherwood	Y	Y	Y	Y
11 Kanjorski	Y	Y	Y	Y
12 Murtha	Y	Y	Y	Y
13 Hoeffel	Y	Y	Y	Y
14 Coyne	Y	Y	Y	Y
15 Toomey	Y	Y	Y	Y
16 Pitts	Y	Y	Y	Y
17 Gekas	Y	Y	Y	Y
18 Doyle	Y	Y	Y	Y
19 Platts	Y	Y	Y	Y
20 Mascara	Y	Y	Y	Y
21 English	Y	Y	Y	Y
RHODE ISLAND				
1 Kennedy	Y	Y	Y	Y
2 Langevin	Y	Y	Y	Y
SOUTH CAROLINA				
1 Brown	Y	Y	Y	Y
2 Spence	Y	Y	Y	Y
3 Graham	Y	Y	Y	Y
4 DeMint	Y	Y	Y	Y
5 Spratt	Y	Y	Y	Y
6 Clyburn	Y	Y	Y	?
SOUTH DAKOTA				
AL Thune	Y	Y	Y	Y
TENNESSEE				
1 Jenkins	Y	Y	Y	Y
2 Duncan	Y	Y	Y	Y
3 Wamp	Y	Y	Y	Y
4 Hilleary	Y	Y	Y	Y
5 Clement	Y	Y	Y	Y
6 Gordon	?	?	Y	Y
7 Bryant	Y	Y	Y	Y
8 Tanner	Y	Y	Y	Y
9 Ford	Y	Y	Y	Y
TEXAS				
1 Sandlin	Y	Y	Y	Y
2 Turner	Y	Y	Y	Y
3 Johnson, Sam	Y	Y	Y	Y
4 Hall	Y	Y	Y	Y
5 Sessions	Y	Y	Y	Y
6 Barton	Y	Y	Y	Y
7 Culberson	Y	Y	Y	Y
8 Brady	Y	Y	Y	Y
9 Lampson	Y	Y	Y	Y
10 Doggett	Y	Y	Y	Y
11 Edwards	Y	Y	Y	Y
12 Granger	Y	Y	Y	Y
13 Thornberry	Y	Y	?	?
14 Paul	N	Y	N	N
15 Hinojosa	Y	Y	Y	Y
16 Reyes	Y	Y	Y	Y
17 Stenholm	Y	Y	Y	Y
18 Jackson-Lee	Y	Y	Y	Y
19 Combest	Y	Y	Y	Y
20 Gonzalez	Y	Y	Y	Y
21 Smith	Y	Y	Y	Y
22 DeLay	Y	Y	Y	Y
23 Bonilla	Y	Y	?	Y
24 Frost	Y	Y	Y	Y
25 Bentsen	Y	Y	Y	Y
26 Armey	Y	Y	Y	Y
27 Ortiz	?	?	?	+
28 Rodriguez	Y	Y	Y	Y
29 Green	Y	Y	Y	Y
30 Johnson, E.B.	Y	Y	Y	Y
UTAH				
1 Hansen	Y	Y	Y	Y
2 Matheson	Y	Y	Y	Y
3 Cannon	Y	Y	Y	Y
VERMONT				
AL Sanders	Y	Y	Y	Y
VIRGINIA				
1 Davis, Jo Ann	Y	Y	Y	Y
2 Schrock	Y	Y	Y	Y
3 Scott	Y	Y	Y	Y
4 Sisisky	Y	Y	Y	Y
5 Goode	Y	Y	Y	Y
6 Goodlatte	Y	Y	Y	Y
7 Cantor	Y	Y	Y	Y
8 Moran	Y	Y	Y	Y
9 Boucher	Y	Y	Y	Y
10 Wolf	Y	Y	Y	Y
11 Davis, T.	Y	Y	?	?
WASHINGTON				
1 Inslee	Y	Y	Y	Y
2 Larsen	Y	Y	Y	Y
3 Baird	Y	Y	Y	Y
4 Hastings	Y	Y	Y	Y
5 Nethercutt	Y	Y	Y	Y
6 Dicks	Y	Y	Y	Y
7 McDermott	Y	Y	Y	Y
8 Dunn	Y	Y	Y	Y
9 Smith	Y	Y	Y	Y
WEST VIRGINIA				
1 Mollohan	Y	Y	?	?
2 Capito	Y	Y	?	?
3 Rahall	P	Y	Y	Y
WISCONSIN				
1 Ryan	Y	Y	Y	Y
2 Baldwin	Y	Y	Y	Y
3 Kind	Y	Y	Y	Y
4 Kleczka	Y	Y	Y	Y
5 Barrett	Y	Y	Y	Y
6 Petri	Y	Y	Y	Y
7 Obey	Y	Y	Y	Y
8 Green	Y	Y	Y	Y
9 Sensenbrenner	Y	Y	Y	Y
WYOMING				
AL Cubin	Y	Y	?	?

Southern states - Ala., Ark., Fla., Ga., Ky., La., Miss., N.C., Okla., S.C., Tenn., Texas, Va.

Key

Y	Voted for (yea).
#	Paired for.
+	Announced for.
N	Voted against (nay).
X	Paired against.
–	Announced against.
P	Voted "present."
C	Voted "present" to avoid possible conflict of interest.
?	Did not vote or otherwise make a position known.

Democrats   **Republicans**
Independents

---

16. H Con Res 39. Iraqi Missile Victims' Tribute/Adoption. Weldon, R-Pa., motion to suspend the rules and adopt the resolution honoring 28 U.S. soldiers killed in a 1991 Iraqi missile attack and resolving to support theater missile defense programs. A two-thirds majority of those present and voting (264 in this case) is required for adoption under suspension of the rules. Motion agreed to 395-0: R 198-0; D 196-0 (ND 143-0, SD 53-0); I 1-0. Feb. 27, 2001.

17. HR 256. Farmer Bankruptcy Extension/Passage. Sensenbrenner, R-Wis., motion to suspend the rules and pass the bill that would extend Chapter 12 federal bankruptcy protection for farmers retroactive to July 1, 2000, and through June 1, 2001. A two-thirds majority of those present and voting (274 in this case) is required for passage under suspension of the rules. Motion agreed to 408-2: R 205-2; D 201-0 (ND 148-0, SD 53-0); I 2-0. Feb. 28, 2001.

18. HR 558. Edward N. Cahn Courthouse/Passage. LaTourette, R-Ohio, motion to suspend the rules and pass the bill that would designate a U.S. courthouse in Allentown, Pa., as the "Edward N. Cahn Federal Building and U.S. Courthouse." A two-thirds majority of those present and voting (275 in this case) is required for passage under suspension of the rules. Motion agreed to 412-0: R 209-0; D 201-0 (ND 148-0, SD 53-0); I 2-0. Feb. 28, 2001.

19. HR 621. James C. Corman Federal Building/Passage. LaTourette, R-Ohio, motion to suspend the rules and pass the bill that would designate a federal building in Van Nuys, Calif., as the "James C. Corman Federal Building." A two-thirds majority of those present and voting (276 in this case) is required for passage under suspension of the rules. Motion agreed to 413-0: R 210-0; D 201-0 (ND 148-0, SD 53-0); I 2-0. Feb. 28 2001.

20. H Con Res 27. National Institute of Standards and Technology Tribute/Adoption. Morella, R-Md., motion to suspend the rules and adopt the resolution that would honor the National Institute of Standards and Technology for 100 years of service. A two-thirds majority of those present and voting (276 in this case) is required for adoption under suspension of the rules. Motion agreed to 413-1: R 209-1; D 202-0 (ND 149-0, SD 53-0); I 2-0. Feb. 28, 2001.

	16	17	18	19	20
ALABAMA					
1 *Callahan*	Y	Y	Y	Y	Y
2 *Everett*	Y	Y	Y	Y	Y
3 *Riley*	+	Y	Y	Y	Y
4 *Aderholt*	Y	Y	Y	Y	Y
5 Cramer	?	?	?	?	?
6 *Bachus*	Y	Y	Y	Y	Y
7 Hilliard	Y	Y	Y	Y	
ALASKA					
AL *Young*	Y	Y	Y	Y	Y
ARIZONA					
1 *Flake*	Y	Y	Y	Y	Y
2 Pastor	Y	Y	Y	Y	Y
3 *Stump*	Y	Y	Y	Y	Y
4 *Shadegg*	Y	Y	Y	Y	Y
5 *Kolbe*	Y	Y	Y	Y	Y
6 *Hayworth*	?	Y	Y	Y	Y
ARKANSAS					
1 Berry	Y	Y	Y	Y	Y
2 Snyder	Y	?	?	?	?
3 *Hutchinson*	Y	Y	Y	Y	Y
4 Ross	Y	Y	Y	Y	Y
CALIFORNIA					
1 Thompson	Y	Y	Y	Y	Y
2 *Herger*	Y	Y	Y	Y	Y
3 *Ose*	Y	Y	Y	Y	Y
4 *Doolittle*	Y	?	Y	Y	Y
5 Matsui	Y	Y	Y	Y	Y
6 Woolsey	Y	Y	Y	Y	Y
7 Miller, George	P	Y	Y	Y	Y
8 Pelosi	Y	Y	Y	Y	Y
9 Lee	P	Y	Y	Y	Y
10 Tauscher	Y	Y	Y	Y	Y
11 *Pombo*	Y	Y	Y	Y	Y
12 Lantos	?	Y	Y	Y	Y
13 Stark	Y	Y	Y	Y	Y
14 Eshoo	Y	Y	Y	Y	Y
15 Honda	Y	Y	Y	Y	Y
16 Lofgren	Y	Y	Y	Y	Y
17 Farr	Y	Y	Y	Y	Y
18 Condit	Y	Y	Y	Y	Y
19 *Radanovich*	Y	Y	Y	Y	Y
20 Dooley	Y	Y	Y	Y	Y
21 *Thomas*	+	Y	Y	Y	Y
22 Capps	Y	Y	Y	Y	Y
23 *Gallegly*	Y	Y	Y	Y	Y
24 Sherman	Y	Y	Y	Y	Y
25 *McKeon*	?	Y	Y	Y	Y
26 Berman	Y	Y	Y	Y	Y
27 Schiff	Y	Y	Y	Y	Y
28 *Dreier*	Y	Y	Y	Y	Y
29 Waxman	Y	Y	Y	Y	Y
30 Becerra	+	+	+	+	+
31 Solis	Y	Y	Y	Y	Y
32 Vacant					
33 Roybal-Allard	Y	Y	Y	Y	Y
34 Napolitano	Y	Y	Y	Y	Y
35 Waters	Y	Y	Y	Y	Y
36 Harman	Y	Y	Y	Y	Y
37 Millender-McD.	Y	Y	Y	Y	Y
38 *Horn*	Y	Y	Y	Y	Y

	16	17	18	19	20
39 *Royce*	Y	Y	Y	Y	Y
40 *Lewis*	Y	Y	Y	Y	Y
41 *Miller, Gary*	Y	Y	Y	Y	Y
42 Baca	Y	Y	Y	Y	Y
43 *Calvert*	Y	Y	Y	Y	Y
44 *Bono*	Y	Y	Y	Y	Y
45 *Rohrabacher*	?	N	Y	Y	Y
46 Sanchez	+	Y	Y	Y	Y
47 *Cox*	Y	Y	Y	Y	Y
48 *Issa*	?	Y	Y	Y	Y
49 Davis	Y	Y	Y	Y	Y
50 Filner	Y	Y	Y	Y	Y
51 *Cunningham*	Y	Y	Y	Y	Y
52 *Hunter*	?	Y	Y	Y	Y
COLORADO					
1 DeGette	Y	Y	Y	Y	Y
2 Udall	Y	Y	Y	?	Y
3 *McInnis*	Y	Y	Y	Y	Y
4 *Schaffer*	Y	Y	Y	Y	Y
5 *Hefley*	Y	Y	Y	Y	Y
6 *Tancredo*	+	Y	Y	Y	Y
CONNECTICUT					
1 Larson	Y	Y	Y	Y	Y
2 *Simmons*	Y	Y	Y	Y	Y
3 DeLauro	?	Y	Y	Y	Y
4 *Shays*	Y	Y	Y	Y	Y
5 Maloney	Y	Y	Y	Y	Y
6 *Johnson*	Y	Y	Y	Y	Y
DELAWARE					
AL *Castle*	Y	Y	Y	Y	Y
FLORIDA					
1 *Scarborough*	Y	Y	Y	Y	Y
2 Boyd	Y	Y	Y	Y	Y
3 Brown	Y	Y	Y	Y	Y
4 *Crenshaw*	Y	Y	Y	Y	Y
5 Thurman	Y	Y	Y	Y	Y
6 *Stearns*	Y	Y	Y	Y	Y
7 *Mica*	Y	Y	Y	Y	Y
8 *Keller*	Y	Y	Y	Y	Y
9 *Bilirakis*	Y	Y	Y	Y	Y
10 *Young*	Y	Y	Y	Y	Y
11 Davis	Y	Y	Y	Y	Y
12 *Putnam*	+	Y	Y	Y	Y
13 *Miller*	Y	Y	Y	Y	Y
14 *Goss*	Y	Y	Y	Y	Y
15 *Weldon*	Y	Y	Y	Y	Y
16 *Foley*	Y	Y	Y	Y	Y
17 Meek	Y	Y	Y	Y	Y
18 *Ros-Lehtinen*	?	?	?	?	?
19 Wexler	Y	Y	Y	Y	Y
20 Deutsch	Y	Y	Y	Y	Y
21 *Diaz-Balart*	Y	Y	Y	Y	Y
22 *Shaw*	Y	Y	Y	Y	Y
23 Hastings	Y	Y	Y	Y	Y
GEORGIA					
1 *Kingston*	Y	Y	Y	Y	Y
2 Bishop	Y	Y	Y	Y	Y
3 *Collins*	Y	Y	Y	Y	Y
4 McKinney	Y	Y	Y	Y	Y
5 Lewis	Y	Y	Y	Y	Y
6 *Isakson*	Y	Y	Y	Y	Y
7 *Barr*	Y	Y	Y	Y	Y
8 *Chambliss*	Y	Y	Y	Y	Y
9 *Deal*	Y	Y	Y	Y	Y
10 *Norwood*	Y	Y	Y	Y	Y
11 *Linder*	Y	Y	Y	Y	Y
HAWAII					
1 Abercrombie	Y	Y	Y	Y	Y
2 Mink	Y	Y	Y	Y	Y
IDAHO					
1 *Otter*	Y	+	Y	Y	Y
2 *Simpson*	?	Y	Y	Y	Y
ILLINOIS					
1 Rush	Y	Y	Y	Y	Y
2 Jackson	Y	Y	Y	Y	Y
3 Lipinski	Y	Y	Y	Y	Y
4 Gutierrez	Y	Y	Y	Y	Y
5 Blagojevich	Y	Y	Y	Y	Y
6 *Hyde*	Y	Y	Y	Y	Y
7 Davis	Y	Y	Y	Y	Y
8 *Crane*	Y	Y	Y	Y	Y
9 Schakowsky	Y	Y	Y	Y	Y
10 *Kirk*	Y	Y	Y	Y	Y
11 *Weller*	Y	Y	Y	Y	Y
12 Costello	Y	Y	Y	Y	Y
13 *Biggert*	Y	Y	Y	Y	Y

ND Northern Democrats   SD Southern Democrats

	16	17	18	19	20
14 Hastert					
15 Johnson	Y	Y	Y	Y	Y
16 Manzullo	Y	Y	Y	Y	Y
17 Evans	Y	Y	Y	Y	Y
18 LaHood	Y	Y	Y	Y	Y
19 Phelps	Y	Y	Y	Y	Y
20 Shimkus	Y	Y	Y	Y	Y
INDIANA					
1 Visclosky	Y	Y	Y	Y	Y
2 Pence	Y	Y	Y	Y	Y
3 Roemer	Y	Y	Y	Y	Y
4 Souder	Y	Y	Y	Y	Y
5 Buyer	?	Y	Y	Y	Y
6 Burton	Y	Y	Y	Y	Y
7 Kerns	Y	Y	Y	Y	Y
8 Hostettler	Y	Y	Y	Y	Y
9 Hill	Y	Y	Y	Y	Y
10 Carson	Y	Y	Y	Y	Y
IOWA					
1 Leach	Y	?	?	?	?
2 Nussle	Y	Y	Y	Y	Y
3 Boswell	Y	Y	Y	Y	Y
4 Ganske	Y	?	?	?	?
5 Latham	Y	?	?	?	?
KANSAS					
1 Moran	Y	Y	Y	Y	Y
2 Ryun	Y	Y	Y	Y	Y
3 Moore	Y	+	+	Y	Y
4 Tiahrt	Y	Y	Y	Y	Y
KENTUCKY					
1 Whitfield	Y	Y	Y	Y	Y
2 Lewis	Y	Y	Y	Y	Y
3 Northup	Y	Y	Y	Y	Y
4 Lucas	Y	Y	Y	Y	Y
5 Rogers	Y	Y	Y	Y	Y
6 Fletcher	Y	Y	Y	Y	Y
LOUISIANA					
1 Vitter	?	Y	Y	Y	Y
2 Jefferson	Y	Y	Y	Y	Y
3 Tauzin	Y	Y	Y	Y	Y
4 McCrery	Y	Y	Y	Y	Y
5 Cooksey	Y	Y	Y	Y	Y
6 Baker	Y	Y	Y	Y	Y
7 John	Y	Y	Y	Y	Y
MAINE					
1 Allen	Y	Y	Y	Y	Y
2 Baldacci	Y	Y	Y	Y	Y
MARYLAND					
1 Gilchrest	Y	Y	Y	Y	Y
2 Ehrlich	Y	Y	Y	Y	Y
3 Cardin	Y	Y	Y	Y	Y
4 Wynn	Y	?	?	?	?
5 Hoyer	Y	Y	Y	Y	Y
6 Bartlett	Y	Y	Y	Y	Y
7 Cummings	Y	Y	Y	Y	Y
8 Morella	Y	Y	Y	Y	Y
MASSACHUSETTS					
1 Olver	Y	Y	Y	Y	Y
2 Neal	Y	Y	Y	Y	Y
3 McGovern	Y	Y	Y	Y	Y
4 Frank	Y	Y	Y	Y	Y
5 Meehan	Y	Y	Y	Y	Y
6 Tierney	Y	Y	Y	Y	Y
7 Markey	Y	Y	Y	?	Y
8 Capuano	Y	Y	Y	Y	Y
9 Moakley	Y	Y	Y	Y	Y
10 Delahunt	Y	Y	Y	Y	Y
MICHIGAN					
1 Stupak	Y	Y	Y	Y	Y
2 Hoekstra	Y	Y	Y	Y	Y
3 Ehlers	Y	Y	Y	Y	Y
4 Camp	Y	Y	Y	Y	Y
5 Barcia	Y	Y	Y	Y	Y
6 Upton	Y	Y	Y	Y	Y
7 Smith	Y	Y	Y	Y	Y
8 Rogers	Y	Y	Y	Y	Y
9 Kildee	Y	Y	Y	Y	Y
10 Bonior	Y	Y	Y	Y	Y
11 Knollenberg	Y	Y	Y	Y	Y
12 Levin	Y	Y	Y	Y	Y
13 Rivers	Y	?	?	?	?
14 Conyers	Y	?	?	?	?
15 Kilpatrick	Y	Y	Y	Y	Y
16 Dingell	?	Y	Y	Y	?

	16	17	18	19	20
MINNESOTA					
1 Gutknecht	Y	Y	?	Y	Y
2 Kennedy	Y	Y	Y	Y	Y
3 Ramstad	Y	Y	Y	Y	Y
4 McCollum	Y	Y	Y	Y	Y
5 Sabo	Y	Y	Y	Y	Y
6 Luther	Y	Y	Y	Y	Y
7 Peterson	Y	Y	Y	Y	Y
8 Oberstar	Y	Y	Y	Y	Y
MISSISSIPPI					
1 Wicker	+	Y	Y	Y	Y
2 Thompson	Y	Y	Y	Y	Y
3 Pickering	Y	Y	Y	Y	Y
4 Shows	Y	Y	Y	Y	Y
5 Taylor	Y	Y	Y	Y	Y
MISSOURI					
1 Clay	Y	Y	Y	Y	Y
2 Akin	Y	Y	Y	Y	Y
3 Gephardt	Y	Y	Y	Y	Y
4 Skelton	Y	Y	Y	Y	Y
5 McCarthy	Y	Y	Y	Y	Y
6 Graves	Y	Y	Y	Y	Y
7 Blunt	Y	Y	Y	Y	Y
8 Emerson	Y	Y	Y	Y	Y
9 Hulshof	Y	Y	Y	Y	Y
MONTANA					
AL Rehberg	+	Y	Y	Y	Y
NEBRASKA					
1 Bereuter	Y	Y	Y	Y	Y
2 Terry	Y	?	?	?	?
3 Osborne	Y	Y	Y	Y	Y
NEVADA					
1 Berkley	Y	Y	Y	Y	Y
2 Gibbons	Y	?	?	?	?
NEW HAMPSHIRE					
1 Sununu	Y	Y	Y	Y	Y
2 Bass	Y	Y	Y	Y	Y
NEW JERSEY					
1 Andrews	Y	Y	Y	Y	Y
2 LoBiondo	Y	Y	Y	Y	Y
3 Saxton	Y	Y	Y	Y	Y
4 Smith	Y	Y	Y	Y	Y
5 Roukema	Y	Y	Y	Y	Y
6 Pallone	+	Y	Y	Y	Y
7 Ferguson	Y	Y	Y	Y	Y
8 Pascrell	Y	Y	Y	Y	Y
9 Rothman	?	?	?	?	?
10 Payne	Y	Y	Y	Y	Y
11 Frelinghuysen	Y	Y	Y	Y	Y
12 Holt	Y	Y	Y	Y	Y
13 Menendez	Y	Y	Y	Y	Y
NEW MEXICO					
1 Wilson	?	Y	Y	Y	Y
2 Skeen	Y	Y	Y	Y	Y
3 Udall	Y	Y	Y	Y	Y
NEW YORK					
1 Grucci	Y	Y	Y	Y	Y
2 Israel	Y	Y	Y	Y	Y
3 King	Y	Y	Y	Y	Y
4 McCarthy	Y	Y	Y	Y	Y
5 Ackerman	?	?	?	?	?
6 Meeks	Y	Y	Y	Y	Y
7 Crowley	Y	Y	Y	Y	Y
8 Nadler	Y	Y	Y	Y	Y
9 Weiner	Y	Y	Y	Y	Y
10 Towns	Y	Y	Y	Y	Y
11 Owens	Y	Y	Y	Y	Y
12 Velázquez	Y	Y	Y	Y	Y
13 Fossella	?	?	Y	Y	Y
14 Maloney	Y	Y	Y	Y	Y
15 Rangel	Y	Y	Y	Y	Y
16 Serrano	Y	Y	Y	Y	Y
17 Engel	Y	Y	Y	Y	Y
18 Lowey	Y	Y	Y	Y	Y
19 Kelly	Y	Y	Y	Y	Y
20 Gilman	Y	Y	Y	Y	Y
21 McNulty	Y	Y	Y	Y	Y
22 Sweeney	Y	Y	Y	Y	Y
23 Boehlert	Y	Y	Y	Y	Y
24 McHugh	Y	Y	Y	Y	Y
25 Walsh	Y	Y	Y	Y	Y
26 Hinchey	Y	Y	Y	Y	Y
27 Reynolds	Y	Y	Y	Y	Y
28 Slaughter	Y	Y	Y	Y	Y
29 LaFalce	Y	Y	Y	Y	Y

	16	17	18	19	20
30 Quinn	Y	Y	Y	Y	Y
31 Houghton	Y	Y	Y	Y	Y
NORTH CAROLINA					
1 Clayton	Y	Y	Y	Y	Y
2 Etheridge	Y	Y	Y	Y	Y
3 Jones	Y	Y	Y	Y	Y
4 Price	Y	Y	Y	Y	Y
5 Burr	Y	Y	Y	Y	Y
6 Coble	Y	Y	Y	Y	Y
7 McIntyre	Y	Y	Y	Y	Y
8 Hayes	Y	Y	Y	Y	Y
9 Myrick	?	Y	Y	Y	Y
10 Ballenger	Y	Y	Y	Y	Y
11 Taylor	Y	Y	Y	Y	Y
12 Watt	Y	Y	Y	Y	Y
NORTH DAKOTA					
AL Pomeroy	Y	Y	Y	Y	Y
OHIO					
1 Chabot	Y	Y	Y	Y	Y
2 Portman	Y	Y	Y	Y	Y
3 Hall	Y	Y	Y	Y	Y
4 Oxley	Y	Y	Y	Y	Y
5 Gillmor	Y	Y	Y	Y	Y
6 Strickland	?	Y	Y	Y	Y
7 Hobson	Y	Y	Y	Y	Y
8 Boehner	Y	Y	Y	Y	Y
9 Kaptur	Y	Y	Y	Y	Y
10 Kucinich	Y	Y	Y	Y	Y
11 Jones	Y	Y	Y	Y	Y
12 Tiberi	Y	Y	Y	Y	Y
13 Brown	Y	Y	Y	Y	Y
14 Sawyer	Y	Y	Y	Y	Y
15 Pryce	Y	Y	Y	Y	Y
16 Regula	Y	Y	Y	Y	Y
17 Traficant	Y	Y	Y	Y	Y
18 Ney	Y	+	+	+	+
19 LaTourette	Y	Y	Y	?	?
OKLAHOMA					
1 Largent	Y	Y	Y	Y	Y
2 Carson	Y	Y	Y	Y	Y
3 Watkins	Y	Y	Y	Y	Y
4 Watts	Y	Y	Y	Y	Y
5 Istook	Y	Y	Y	Y	Y
6 Lucas	Y	Y	Y	Y	Y
OREGON					
1 Wu	Y	Y	Y	Y	Y
2 Walden	Y	Y	Y	Y	Y
3 Blumenauer	Y	Y	Y	Y	Y
4 DeFazio	Y	Y	Y	Y	Y
5 Hooley	Y	Y	Y	Y	Y
PENNSYLVANIA					
1 Brady	Y	Y	Y	Y	Y
2 Fattah	Y	Y	Y	Y	Y
3 Borski	Y	Y	Y	Y	Y
4 Hart	Y	?	?	?	?
5 Peterson	Y	Y	Y	Y	Y
6 Holden	Y	Y	Y	Y	Y
7 Weldon	Y	Y	Y	Y	Y
8 Greenwood	Y	Y	Y	Y	Y
9 Vacant					
10 Sherwood	Y	Y	Y	Y	Y
11 Kanjorski	Y	Y	Y	Y	Y
12 Murtha	Y	Y	Y	Y	Y
13 Hoeffel	Y	Y	Y	Y	Y
14 Coyne	?	Y	Y	Y	Y
15 Toomey	Y	Y	Y	Y	Y
16 Pitts	Y	Y	Y	Y	Y
17 Gekas	?	Y	Y	Y	Y
18 Doyle	Y	Y	Y	Y	Y
19 Platts	Y	Y	Y	Y	Y
20 Mascara	Y	Y	Y	Y	Y
21 English	Y	Y	Y	Y	Y
RHODE ISLAND					
1 Kennedy	Y	Y	Y	Y	Y
2 Langevin	Y	Y	Y	Y	Y
SOUTH CAROLINA					
1 Brown	Y	Y	Y	Y	Y
2 Spence	Y	Y	Y	Y	Y
3 Graham	?	Y	Y	Y	Y
4 DeMint	Y	Y	Y	Y	Y
5 Spratt	Y	Y	Y	Y	Y
6 Clyburn	Y	Y	Y	Y	Y
SOUTH DAKOTA					
AL Thune	Y	Y	Y	Y	Y

	16	17	18	19	20
TENNESSEE					
1 Jenkins	Y	Y	Y	Y	Y
2 Duncan	Y	Y	Y	Y	Y
3 Wamp	Y	Y	Y	Y	Y
4 Hilleary	Y	Y	Y	Y	Y
5 Clement	Y	Y	Y	Y	Y
6 Gordon	Y	Y	Y	Y	Y
7 Bryant	Y	Y	Y	Y	Y
8 Tanner	Y	Y	Y	Y	Y
9 Ford	Y	Y	Y	Y	Y
TEXAS					
1 Sandlin	Y	Y	Y	Y	Y
2 Turner	Y	Y	Y	Y	Y
3 Johnson, Sam	Y	Y	Y	Y	Y
4 Hall	Y	Y	Y	Y	Y
5 Sessions	Y	Y	Y	Y	Y
6 Barton	Y	Y	Y	Y	Y
7 Culberson	Y	Y	Y	Y	Y
8 Brady	Y	Y	Y	Y	Y
9 Lampson	Y	Y	Y	Y	Y
10 Doggett	Y	Y	Y	Y	Y
11 Edwards	Y	Y	Y	Y	Y
12 Granger	Y	Y	Y	Y	Y
13 Thornberry	Y	Y	Y	Y	Y
14 Paul	Y	N	Y	Y	N
15 Hinojosa	Y	Y	Y	Y	Y
16 Reyes	Y	Y	Y	Y	Y
17 Stenholm	Y	Y	Y	Y	Y
18 Jackson-Lee	Y	Y	Y	Y	Y
19 Combest	Y	Y	Y	Y	Y
20 Gonzalez	Y	Y	Y	Y	Y
21 Smith	Y	Y	Y	Y	Y
22 DeLay	Y	Y	Y	Y	Y
23 Bonilla	?	Y	Y	Y	Y
24 Frost	Y	Y	Y	Y	Y
25 Bentsen	Y	Y	Y	Y	Y
26 Armey	Y	Y	Y	Y	Y
27 Ortiz	Y	Y	Y	Y	Y
28 Rodriguez	Y	Y	Y	Y	Y
29 Green	Y	Y	Y	Y	Y
30 Johnson, E.B.	Y	Y	Y	Y	Y
UTAH					
1 Hansen	Y	?	?	Y	Y
2 Matheson	Y	Y	Y	Y	Y
3 Cannon	Y	Y	Y	Y	Y
VERMONT					
AL Sanders	?	Y	Y	Y	Y
VIRGINIA					
1 Davis, Jo Ann	Y	Y	Y	Y	Y
2 Schrock	Y	Y	Y	Y	Y
3 Scott	Y	Y	Y	Y	Y
4 Sisisky	Y	Y	Y	Y	Y
5 Goode	Y	Y	Y	Y	Y
6 Goodlatte	Y	Y	Y	Y	Y
7 Cantor	Y	Y	Y	Y	Y
8 Moran	?	Y	Y	Y	Y
9 Boucher	Y	Y	Y	Y	Y
10 Wolf	Y	Y	Y	Y	Y
11 Davis, T.	Y	Y	Y	Y	Y
WASHINGTON					
1 Inslee	?	Y	Y	Y	Y
2 Larsen	Y	Y	Y	Y	Y
3 Baird	Y	Y	Y	Y	Y
4 Hastings	Y	Y	Y	Y	Y
5 Nethercutt	Y	Y	Y	Y	Y
6 Dicks	Y	Y	Y	Y	Y
7 McDermott	Y	Y	Y	Y	Y
8 Dunn	Y	Y	Y	Y	Y
9 Smith	Y	?	?	Y	Y
WEST VIRGINIA					
1 Mollohan	Y	Y	Y	Y	Y
2 Capito	Y	Y	Y	Y	Y
3 Rahall	Y	?	?	?	?
WISCONSIN					
1 Ryan	Y	Y	Y	Y	Y
2 Baldwin	Y	Y	Y	Y	Y
3 Kind	Y	Y	Y	Y	Y
4 Kleczka	Y	Y	Y	Y	Y
5 Barrett	Y	Y	Y	Y	Y
6 Petri	Y	Y	Y	Y	Y
7 Obey	Y	Y	Y	Y	Y
8 Green	Y	Y	Y	Y	Y
9 Sensenbrenner	Y	Y	Y	Y	Y
WYOMING					
AL Cubin	Y	Y	Y	Y	Y

Southern states - Ala., Ark., Fla., Ga., Ky., La., Miss., N.C., Okla., S.C., Tenn., Texas, Va.

Key

Y	Voted for (yea).
#	Paired for.
+	Announced for.
N	Voted against (nay).
X	Paired against.
−	Announced against.
P	Voted "present."
C	Voted "present" to avoid possible conflict of interest.
?	Did not vote or otherwise make a position known.

Democrats • ***Republicans***
Independents

21. H Res 54. African-American Pioneer Tribute/Adoption. Schaffer, R-Colo., motion to suspend the rules and adopt the resolution that would honor African-American pioneers including those in Dearfield, Colo. A two-thirds majority of those present and voting (274 in this case) is required for adoption under suspension of the rules. Motion agreed to 411-0: R 207-0; D 202-0 (ND 150-0, SD 52-0); I 2-0. Feb. 28, 2001.

22. HR 333. Bankruptcy Overhaul/Rule. Adoption of the rule (H Res 71) to provide for House floor consideration of the bill that would require debtors able to repay $10,000 or 25 percent of their debts over five years to file under Chapter 13, which requires a reorganization of debts under a repayment plan, instead of seeking to discharge their debts under Chapter 7. Adopted 281-132: R 212-1; D 68-130 (ND 39-108, SD 29-22); I 1-1. March 1, 2001.

23. HR 333. Bankruptcy Overhaul/Democratic Substitute. Jackson-Lee, D-Texas, substitute amendment that would allow debtors to deduct additional medical and child-care expenses before determining their eligibility for Chapter 7; expand the definition of family farmer; change the standards for calculating median income; and include debtor privacy provisions. Rejected 160-258: R 1-211; D 158-46 (ND 128-23, SD 30-23); I 1-1. March 1, 2001.

24. HR 333. Bankruptcy Overhaul/Recommit. Conyers, D-Mich., motion to recommit the bill to the House Judiciary Committee with instructions to add language prohibiting the issuance of credit cards to individuals under age 21 unless a child has independent means or a parent co-signs. Motion rejected 165-253: R 4-209; D 160-43 (ND 129-21, SD 31-22); I 1-1. March 1, 2001.

25. HR 333. Bankruptcy Overhaul/Passage. Passage of the bill that would require debtors able to repay $10,000 or 25 percent of their debts over five years to file under Chapter 13, which requires a reorganization of debts under a repayment plan, instead of seeking to discharge their debts under Chapter 7. The bill would also make permanent Chapter 12 bankruptcy relief for farmers. Passed 306-108: R 212-0; D 93-107 (ND 52-95, SD 41-12); I 1-1. March 1, 2001.

	21	22	23	24	25
ALABAMA					
1 *Callahan*	Y	Y	N	N	Y
2 *Everett*	Y	Y	N	N	Y
3 *Riley*	Y	Y	N	N	Y
4 *Aderholt*	Y	Y	N	N	Y
5 Cramer	?	?	?	?	?
6 *Bachus*	Y	Y	N	N	Y
7 Hilliard	Y	N	Y	N	N
ALASKA					
AL *Young*	Y	Y	N	N	Y
ARIZONA					
1 *Flake*	Y	Y	N	N	Y
2 Pastor	Y	Y	Y	Y	Y
3 *Stump*	Y	Y	N	N	Y
4 *Shadegg*	Y	Y	N	N	Y
5 *Kolbe*	Y	Y	N	N	Y
6 *Hayworth*	Y	Y	N	N	Y
ARKANSAS					
1 Berry	Y	Y	N	N	Y
2 Snyder	?	?	?	?	?
3 *Hutchinson*	Y	Y	N	N	Y
4 Ross	Y	Y	N	N	Y
CALIFORNIA					
1 Thompson	Y	N	Y	Y	Y
2 *Herger*	Y	Y	N	N	Y
3 *Ose*	Y	Y	N	N	Y
4 *Doolittle*	Y	Y	N	N	Y
5 Matsui	Y	N	Y	Y	N
6 Woolsey	Y	N	Y	Y	N
7 Miller, George	Y	N	Y	Y	N
8 Pelosi	Y	N	Y	Y	N
9 Lee	Y	N	Y	Y	N
10 Tauscher	Y	Y	N	N	Y
11 *Pombo*	Y	Y	N	N	Y
12 Lantos	Y	N	Y	Y	N
13 Stark	Y	N	Y	Y	N
14 Eshoo	Y	N	Y	Y	N
15 Honda	Y	N	Y	Y	N
16 Lofgren	Y	N	N	N	N
17 Farr	Y	N	Y	Y	N
18 Condit	Y	N	N	N	Y
19 *Radanovich*	Y	Y	N	N	Y
20 Dooley	Y	Y	N	N	Y
21 *Thomas*	Y	Y	N	N	Y
22 Capps	Y	N	Y	Y	Y
23 *Gallegly*	Y	Y	N	N	Y
24 Sherman	Y	N	Y	Y	Y
25 *McKeon*	Y	Y	N	N	Y
26 Berman	Y	N	Y	Y	N
27 Schiff	Y	N	Y	Y	N
28 *Dreier*	Y	Y	N	N	Y
29 Waxman	Y	N	Y	Y	N
30 Becerra	+	N	Y	Y	N
31 Solis	Y	N	Y	Y	Y
32 Vacant					
33 Roybal-Allard	Y	N	Y	Y	N
34 Napolitano	Y	N	Y	Y	N
35 Waters	Y	N	Y	Y	N
36 Harman	Y	Y	N	N	Y
37 Millender-McD.	Y	N	Y	Y	N
38 *Horn*	Y	Y	N	N	Y
39 *Royce*	Y	Y	N	N	Y
40 *Lewis*	Y	Y	N	N	Y
41 *Miller, Gary*	Y	Y	N	N	Y
42 Baca	Y	N	Y	Y	Y
43 *Calvert*	Y	Y	N	N	Y
44 *Bono*	Y	Y	N	N	Y
45 *Rohrabacher*	Y	Y	N	N	Y
46 Sanchez	Y	N	N	N	N
47 *Cox*	Y	Y	N	N	Y
48 *Issa*	Y	Y	N	N	Y
49 Davis	Y	N	Y	Y	N
50 Filner	Y	N	Y	Y	N
51 *Cunningham*	Y	Y	N	N	Y
52 *Hunter*	Y	Y	N	N	Y
COLORADO					
1 DeGette	Y	N	Y	Y	N
2 Udall	Y	N	Y	Y	N
3 *McInnis*	Y	Y	N	N	Y
4 *Schaffer*	Y	Y	N	N	Y
5 *Hefley*	Y	Y	N	N	Y
6 *Tancredo*	Y	Y	N	N	Y
CONNECTICUT					
1 Larson	Y	Y	Y	Y	Y
2 *Simmons*	Y	Y	N	N	Y
3 DeLauro	Y	N	Y	Y	N
4 *Shays*	Y	Y	N	N	Y
5 Maloney	Y	N	Y	N	Y
6 *Johnson*	Y	N	N	N	Y
DELAWARE					
AL *Castle*	Y	Y	N	N	Y
FLORIDA					
1 *Scarborough*	Y	Y	N	N	Y
2 Boyd	Y	Y	N	N	Y
3 Brown	Y	N	Y	Y	N
4 *Crenshaw*	Y	Y	N	N	Y
5 Thurman	Y	N	Y	Y	N
6 *Stearns*	?	Y	N	N	Y
7 *Mica*	Y	Y	N	N	Y
8 *Keller*	Y	Y	N	N	Y
9 *Bilirakis*	Y	Y	N	N	Y
10 *Young*	Y	Y	N	N	Y
11 Davis	Y	Y	Y	Y	Y
12 *Putnam*	Y	Y	N	N	Y
13 *Miller*	Y	Y	N	N	Y
14 *Goss*	Y	Y	N	N	Y
15 *Weldon*	Y	Y	N	N	Y
16 *Foley*	Y	Y	N	N	Y
17 Meek	Y	N	Y	Y	Y
18 *Ros-Lehtinen*	?	?	?	?	?
19 Wexler	Y	N	Y	Y	N
20 Deutsch	Y	N	Y	Y	N
21 *Diaz-Balart*	Y	Y	N	N	Y
22 *Shaw*	Y	Y	N	N	Y
23 Hastings	Y	N	Y	Y	Y
GEORGIA					
1 *Kingston*	Y	?	?	?	+
2 Bishop	Y	Y	Y	N	Y
3 *Collins*	Y	Y	N	N	Y
4 McKinney	Y	?	Y	Y	N
5 Lewis	Y	N	Y	Y	N
6 *Isakson*	Y	Y	N	N	Y
7 *Barr*	Y	Y	N	N	Y
8 *Chambliss*	Y	Y	N	N	Y
9 *Deal*	Y	?	?	?	?
10 *Norwood*	Y	?	?	?	?
11 *Linder*	Y	Y	N	N	Y
HAWAII					
1 Abercrombie	Y	N	Y	Y	N
2 Mink	Y	N	Y	Y	N
IDAHO					
1 *Otter*	Y	Y	N	N	Y
2 *Simpson*	Y	Y	N	N	Y
ILLINOIS					
1 Rush	Y	Y	Y	Y	N
2 Jackson	Y	N	Y	Y	?
3 Lipinski	Y	N	N	Y	Y
4 Gutierrez	Y	N	Y	N	N
5 Blagojevich	Y	N	Y	Y	N
6 *Hyde*	Y	Y	N	N	Y
7 Davis	Y	N	Y	Y	N
8 *Crane*	Y	Y	N	N	Y
9 Schakowsky	Y	N	Y	Y	N
10 *Kirk*	Y	N	Y	N	Y
11 *Weller*	Y	Y	N	N	Y
12 Costello	Y	N	Y	Y	Y
13 *Biggert*	Y	Y	N	N	Y

ND Northern Democrats   SD Southern Democrats

	21	22	23	24	25
14 ***Hastert***					
15 ***Johnson***	Y	Y	N	N	Y
16 ***Manzullo***	Y	Y	N	N	Y
17 Evans	Y	N	Y	Y	N
18 ***LaHood***	Y	Y	N	N	Y
19 Phelps	Y	N	N	Y	Y
20 ***Shimkus***	Y	Y	N	N	Y
INDIANA					
1 Visclosky	Y	N	Y	Y	N
2 ***Pence***	Y	Y	N	N	Y
3 Roemer	Y	Y	N	Y	Y
4 ***Souder***	Y	Y	N	N	Y
5 ***Buyer***	Y	Y	N	N	Y
6 ***Burton***	Y	Y	N	N	Y
7 ***Kerns***	Y	Y	N	N	Y
8 ***Hostettler***	Y	Y	N	N	Y
9 Hill	Y	Y	N	Y	Y
10 Carson	Y	N	Y	Y	N
IOWA					
1 ***Leach***	?	Y	N	N	Y
2 ***Nussle***	Y	Y	N	N	Y
3 Boswell	Y	Y	N	N	Y
4 ***Ganske***	?	Y	N	N	Y
5 ***Latham***	?	Y	N	N	Y
KANSAS					
1 ***Moran***	Y	Y	N	N	Y
2 ***Ryun***	?	Y	N	N	Y
3 Moore	Y	Y	Y	Y	Y
4 ***Tiahrt***	Y	Y	N	N	Y
KENTUCKY					
1 ***Whitfield***	Y	Y	N	N	Y
2 ***Lewis***	Y	Y	N	N	Y
3 ***Northup***	Y	Y	N	N	Y
4 Lucas	Y	Y	N	N	Y
5 ***Rogers***	Y	Y	N	N	Y
6 ***Fletcher***	Y	Y	N	N	Y
LOUISIANA					
1 ***Vitter***	Y	Y	N	N	Y
2 Jefferson	Y	N	Y	Y	Y
3 ***Tauzin***	Y	Y	N	N	Y
4 ***McCrery***	Y	Y	N	N	Y
5 ***Cooksey***	Y	Y	N	N	Y
6 ***Baker***	Y	Y	N	N	Y
7 John	Y	Y	N	N	Y
MAINE					
1 Allen	Y	N	Y	Y	N
2 Baldacci	Y	N	Y	Y	N
MARYLAND					
1 ***Gilchrest***	Y	Y	N	N	Y
2 ***Ehrlich***	Y	Y	N	N	Y
3 Cardin	Y	Y	Y	Y	N
4 Wynn	?	Y	Y	Y	Y
5 Hoyer	Y	?	N	Y	Y
6 ***Bartlett***	Y	Y	N	N	Y
7 Cummings	Y	?	Y	Y	N
8 ***Morella***	Y	Y	N	N	Y
MASSACHUSETTS					
1 Olver	Y	N	Y	Y	N
2 Neal	Y	N	Y	Y	N
3 McGovern	Y	N	Y	Y	N
4 Frank	Y	N	Y	Y	N
5 Meehan	Y	N	Y	Y	N
6 Tierney	Y	N	Y	Y	N
7 Markey	Y	N	Y	Y	N
8 Capuano	Y	N	Y	Y	N
9 Moakley	Y	Y	Y	Y	N
10 Delahunt	Y	N	Y	Y	N
MICHIGAN					
1 Stupak	Y	N	Y	Y	N
2 ***Hoekstra***	Y	Y	N	N	Y
3 ***Ehlers***	Y	Y	N	N	Y
4 ***Camp***	Y	Y	N	N	Y
5 Barcia	Y	Y	Y	Y	Y
6 ***Upton***	Y	Y	N	N	Y
7 ***Smith***	Y	Y	N	N	Y
8 ***Rogers***	Y	Y	N	N	Y
9 Kildee	Y	N	Y	Y	N
10 Bonior	Y	?	Y	Y	N
11 ***Knollenberg***	Y	Y	N	N	Y
12 Levin	Y	N	Y	Y	N
13 Rivers	Y	Y	Y	N	Y
14 Conyers	Y	N	Y	Y	N
15 Kilpatrick	Y	N	Y	Y	N
16 Dingell	?	N	Y	Y	N

	21	22	23	24	25
MINNESOTA					
1 ***Gutknecht***	Y	Y	N	N	Y
2 ***Kennedy***	Y	Y	N	N	Y
3 ***Ramstad***	Y	Y	Y	N	Y
4 McCollum	Y	N	Y	Y	N
5 Sabo	Y	N	Y	Y	N
6 Luther	Y	N	Y	Y	N
7 Peterson	Y	Y	N	Y	?
8 Oberstar	Y	N	Y	Y	N
MISSISSIPPI					
1 ***Wicker***	Y	Y	N	N	Y
2 Thompson	Y	N	Y	Y	N
3 ***Pickering***	Y	Y	N	N	Y
4 Shows	Y	Y	N	N	Y
5 Taylor	Y	Y	N	N	Y
MISSOURI					
1 Clay	Y	N	Y	Y	N
2 ***Akin***	Y	Y	N	N	Y
3 Gephardt	Y	N	Y	?	?
4 Skelton	Y	Y	N	N	Y
5 McCarthy	Y	N	Y	Y	Y
6 ***Graves***	Y	Y	N	N	Y
7 ***Blunt***	Y	Y	N	N	Y
8 ***Emerson***	Y	Y	N	Y	Y
9 ***Hulshof***	Y	Y	N	N	Y
MONTANA					
AL ***Rehberg***	Y	Y	N	N	Y
NEBRASKA					
1 ***Bereuter***	Y	Y	N	N	Y
2 ***Terry***	?	Y	N	N	Y
3 ***Osborne***	Y	Y	N	N	Y
NEVADA					
1 Berkley	Y	Y	Y	Y	Y
2 ***Gibbons***	?	Y	N	N	Y
NEW HAMPSHIRE					
1 ***Sununu***	Y	Y	N	N	Y
2 ***Bass***	Y	Y	N	N	Y
NEW JERSEY					
1 Andrews	Y	N	Y	Y	Y
2 ***LoBiondo***	Y	Y	N	N	Y
3 ***Saxton***	Y	Y	N	N	Y
4 ***Smith***	Y	Y	N	N	Y
5 ***Roukema***	Y	Y	N	N	Y
6 Pallone	Y	Y	Y	Y	Y
7 ***Ferguson***	Y	Y	N	N	Y
8 Pascrell	Y	N	Y	Y	Y
9 Rothman	?	?	?	?	?
10 Payne	Y	N	Y	Y	N
11 ***Frelinghuysen***	Y	Y	N	N	Y
12 Holt	Y	Y	N	Y	Y
13 Menendez	Y	Y	Y	N	Y
NEW MEXICO					
1 ***Wilson***	Y	Y	N	N	Y
2 ***Skeen***	Y	Y	N	N	Y
3 Udall	Y	N	Y	Y	N
NEW YORK					
1 ***Grucci***	Y	Y	N	N	Y
2 Israel	Y	N	Y	Y	Y
3 ***King***	Y	Y	N	N	Y
4 McCarthy	Y	Y	Y	Y	Y
5 Ackerman	?	?	?	?	?
6 Meeks	Y	N	Y	Y	Y
7 Crowley	Y	Y	N	N	Y
8 Nadler	Y	N	Y	Y	N
9 Weiner	Y	N	Y	Y	N
10 Towns	Y	?	Y	Y	?
11 Owens	Y	N	Y	Y	N
12 Velázquez	Y	Y	Y	Y	Y
13 ***Fossella***	Y	Y	N	N	Y
14 Maloney	Y	Y	Y	Y	N
15 Rangel	Y	N	Y	Y	N
16 Serrano	Y	N	Y	Y	N
17 Engel	Y	N	Y	Y	N
18 Lowey	Y	N	Y	Y	N
19 ***Kelly***	Y	Y	N	N	Y
20 ***Gilman***	Y	Y	N	N	+
21 McNulty	Y	N	Y	Y	N
22 ***Sweeney***	Y	Y	N	N	Y
23 ***Boehlert***	Y	Y	N	N	Y
24 ***McHugh***	Y	Y	N	N	Y
25 ***Walsh***	Y	Y	N	N	Y
26 Hinchey	Y	N	Y	Y	N
27 ***Reynolds***	Y	Y	N	N	Y
28 Slaughter	Y	N	Y	Y	N
29 LaFalce	Y	N	Y	Y	N

	21	22	23	24	25
30 ***Quinn***	Y	Y	N	N	Y
31 ***Houghton***	Y	Y	N	N	Y
NORTH CAROLINA					
1 Clayton	Y	N	Y	Y	N
2 Etheridge	Y	Y	Y	Y	Y
3 ***Jones***	Y	Y	N	N	Y
4 Price	Y	Y	Y	Y	Y
5 ***Burr***	Y	Y	N	N	Y
6 ***Coble***	Y	Y	N	N	Y
7 McIntyre	?	Y	Y	Y	Y
8 ***Hayes***	Y	Y	N	N	Y
9 ***Myrick***	Y	Y	N	N	Y
10 ***Ballenger***	Y	Y	N	N	Y
11 ***Taylor***	?	Y	N	N	Y
12 Watt	Y	N	Y	Y	N
NORTH DAKOTA					
AL Pomeroy	Y	N	Y	Y	Y
OHIO					
1 ***Chabot***	Y	Y	N	N	Y
2 ***Portman***	Y	Y	N	N	Y
3 Hall	Y	Y	Y	Y	N
4 ***Oxley***	Y	Y	N	N	Y
5 ***Gillmor***	Y	Y	N	N	Y
6 Strickland	Y	Y	N	Y	Y
7 ***Hobson***	Y	Y	N	N	Y
8 ***Boehner***	Y	Y	N	N	Y
9 Kaptur	Y	N	Y	Y	N
10 Kucinich	Y	N	Y	Y	N
11 Jones	Y	N	Y	Y	N
12 ***Tiberi***	Y	Y	N	N	Y
13 Brown	Y	N	Y	Y	N
14 Sawyer	Y	N	Y	Y	N
15 ***Pryce***	Y	Y	N	N	Y
16 ***Regula***	Y	Y	N	N	Y
17 Traficant	Y	Y	N	N	Y
18 ***Ney***	+	Y	N	N	Y
19 ***LaTourette***	?	Y	N	Y	Y
OKLAHOMA					
1 ***Largent***	Y	Y	N	N	Y
2 Carson	Y	N	N	N	Y
3 ***Watkins***	Y	Y	N	N	Y
4 ***Watts***	Y	Y	N	N	Y
5 ***Istook***	Y	Y	N	N	Y
6 ***Lucas***	Y	Y	N	N	Y
OREGON					
1 Wu	Y	Y	Y	Y	Y
2 ***Walden***	Y	Y	N	N	Y
3 Blumenauer	Y	N	Y	Y	Y
4 DeFazio	Y	N	Y	Y	N
5 Hooley	Y	N	Y	Y	Y
PENNSYLVANIA					
1 Brady	Y	N	Y	Y	N
2 Fattah	Y	N	Y	Y	N
3 Borski	Y	N	Y	Y	N
4 ***Hart***	?	Y	N	N	Y
5 ***Peterson***	Y	Y	N	N	Y
6 Holden	Y	N	Y	Y	Y
7 ***Weldon***	Y	Y	N	Y	Y
8 ***Greenwood***	Y	Y	N	N	Y
9 Vacant					
10 ***Sherwood***	Y	Y	N	N	Y
11 Kanjorski	Y	N	Y	Y	N
12 Murtha	Y	N	Y	Y	N
13 Hoeffel	Y	N	Y	Y	N
14 Coyne	Y	N	Y	Y	N
15 ***Toomey***	Y	?	?	?	?
16 ***Pitts***	Y	Y	N	N	Y
17 ***Gekas***	Y	Y	N	N	Y
18 Doyle	Y	N	Y	Y	N
19 ***Platts***	Y	Y	N	N	Y
20 Mascara	Y	N	Y	Y	N
21 ***English***	Y	Y	N	N	Y
RHODE ISLAND					
1 Kennedy	Y	Y	N	N	Y
2 Langevin	Y	Y	Y	Y	Y
SOUTH CAROLINA					
1 ***Brown***	Y	Y	N	N	Y
2 ***Spence***	Y	Y	N	N	Y
3 ***Graham***	Y	Y	N	N	Y
4 ***DeMint***	Y	Y	N	N	Y
5 Spratt	Y	Y	Y	N	Y
6 Clyburn	Y	N	Y	Y	Y
SOUTH DAKOTA					
AL ***Thune***	Y	Y	N	N	Y

	21	22	23	24	25
TENNESSEE					
1 ***Jenkins***	Y	Y	N	N	Y
2 ***Duncan***	Y	Y	N	Y	Y
3 ***Wamp***	Y	Y	N	N	Y
4 ***Hilleary***	Y	Y	N	N	Y
5 Clement	Y	Y	N	N	Y
6 Gordon	Y	Y	N	N	Y
7 ***Bryant***	Y	Y	N	N	Y
8 Tanner	Y	Y	N	N	Y
9 Ford	Y	Y	N	N	Y
TEXAS					
1 Sandlin	Y	Y	N	N	Y
2 Turner	Y	Y	N	N	Y
3 ***Johnson, Sam***	Y	Y	N	N	Y
4 Hall	Y	Y	N	N	Y
5 ***Sessions***	Y	Y	N	N	Y
6 ***Barton***	Y	Y	N	N	Y
7 ***Culberson***	Y	Y	N	N	Y
8 ***Brady***	Y	Y	N	N	Y
9 Lampson	Y	N	Y	Y	Y
10 Doggett	Y	N	Y	Y	N
11 Edwards	Y	?	N	Y	Y
12 ***Granger***	Y	Y	N	N	Y
13 ***Thornberry***	Y	Y	N	N	Y
14 ***Paul***	Y	Y	N	N	Y
15 Hinojosa	Y	N	Y	N	Y
16 Reyes	Y	Y	Y	Y	Y
17 Stenholm	Y	Y	N	N	Y
18 Jackson-Lee	Y	N	Y	Y	N
19 ***Combest***	Y	Y	N	N	Y
20 Gonzalez	Y	Y	Y	Y	Y
21 ***Smith***	Y	Y	N	N	Y
22 ***DeLay***	Y	Y	N	N	Y
23 ***Bonilla***	Y	Y	N	N	Y
24 Frost	Y	Y	N	Y	Y
25 Bentsen	Y	Y	N	N	Y
26 ***Armey***	Y	Y	N	N	Y
27 Ortiz	Y	Y	Y	Y	Y
28 Rodriguez	Y	N	Y	Y	N
29 Green	Y	N	Y	Y	Y
30 Johnson, E.B.	Y	N	Y	Y	Y
UTAH					
1 ***Hansen***	Y	Y	N	N	Y
2 Matheson	Y	Y	N	N	Y
3 ***Cannon***	Y	Y	?	N	Y
VERMONT					
AL *Sanders*	Y	N	Y	Y	N
VIRGINIA					
1 ***Davis, Jo Ann***	Y	Y	N	N	Y
2 ***Schrock***	Y	Y	N	N	Y
3 Scott	Y	N	Y	Y	N
4 Sisisky	Y	Y	N	N	Y
5 *Goode*	Y	Y	N	N	Y
6 ***Goodlatte***	Y	Y	N	N	Y
7 ***Cantor***	Y	Y	N	N	Y
8 Moran	Y	Y	N	Y	Y
9 Boucher	Y	Y	N	N	Y
10 ***Wolf***	Y	Y	N	N	Y
11 ***Davis, T.***	Y	Y	N	N	Y
WASHINGTON					
1 Inslee	Y	?	?	?	?
2 Larsen	Y	Y	N	N	Y
3 Baird	Y	?	?	?	?
4 ***Hastings***	Y	Y	N	N	Y
5 ***Nethercutt***	Y	Y	N	N	Y
6 Dicks	Y	Y	Y	Y	Y
7 McDermott	Y	−	+	+	−
8 ***Dunn***	Y	+	−	−	+
9 Smith	Y	Y	N	N	Y
WEST VIRGINIA					
1 Mollohan	Y	N	N	N	Y
2 ***Capito***	Y	Y	N	N	Y
3 Rahall	?	Y	Y	Y	N
WISCONSIN					
1 ***Ryan***	Y	Y	N	N	Y
2 Baldwin	Y	N	Y	N	N
3 Kind	Y	Y	Y	N	Y
4 Kleczka	Y	Y	Y	Y	Y
5 Barrett	Y	N	Y	N	N
6 ***Petri***	Y	Y	N	N	Y
7 Obey	Y	N	Y	Y	N
8 ***Green***	Y	Y	N	N	Y
9 ***Sensenbrenner***	Y	Y	N	N	Y
WYOMING					
AL ***Cubin***	Y	Y	N	N	Y

Southern states - Ala., Ark., Fla., Ga., Ky., La., Miss., N.C., Okla., S.C., Tenn., Texas, Va.

26. HR 724. Strategic Petroleum Reserve Correction/Passage. Bass, R-N.H., motion to suspend the rules and pass the bill that would correct an error in legislation signed into law last year re-authorizing the president's authority to operate the Strategic Petroleum Reserve through Sept. 30, 2003. Motion agreed to 400-2: R 200-2; D 199-0 (ND 146-0, SD 53-0); I 1-0. A two-thirds majority of those present and voting (268 in this case) is required for adoption under suspension of the rules. March 6, 2001.

27. HR 727. Electric Bike Reclassification/Passage. Stearns, R-Fla., motion to suspend the rules and pass the bill that would treat low-speed electric bikes as consumer products, the same as pedaled bicycles. Motion agreed to 401-1: R 203-1; D 197-0 (ND 144-0, SD 53-0); I 1-0. A two-thirds majority of those present and voting (268 in this case) is required for passage under suspension of the rules. March 6, 2001.

28. Procedural Motion/Journal. Approval of House Journal of Tuesday, March 6, 2001. Approved 337-72: R 199-11; D 137-61 (ND 99-47, SD 38-14); I 1-0. March 7, 2001.

29. S J Res 6. Ergonomics Rule Disapproval/Rule. Adoption of the rule (H Res 79) to provide for House floor consideration of the joint resolution that would provide for congressional disapproval of the ergonomics rule submitted by the Labor Department during the Clinton administration, stating the rule would have no force or effect. Adopted 222-198: R 216-0; D 5-198 (ND 1-150, SD 4-48); I 1-0. March 7, 2001.

30. H Con Res 31. Donor Awareness/Adoption. Bilirakis, R-Fla., motion to suspend the rules and adopt the resolution that would support National Donor Day and raise awareness of organ and other donor programs. Motion agreed to 418-0: R 210-0; D 206-0 (ND 153-0, SD 53-0); I 2-0. A two-thirds majority of those present and voting (279 in this case) is required for adoption under suspension of the rules. March 7, 2001.

31. HR 624. Organ Donor Funding and Promotion/Passage. Bilirakis, R-Fla., motion to suspend the rules and pass the bill that would authorize $5 million annually over the next five years to help defray travel costs of organ donors if the recipient earns less than $35,000 per year. It also would authorize $15 million in fiscal 2002 for state donor promotion and awareness initiatives. Motion agreed to 404-0: R 197-0; D 205-0 (ND 152-0, SD 53-0); I 2-0. A two-thirds majority of those present and voting (270 in this case) is required for passage under suspension of the rules. March 7, 2001.

32. H Con Res 47. National Guard Tribute/Adoption. Schrock, R-Va., motion to suspend the rules and adopt the resolution that would pay tribute to 21 National Guard members killed in a Georgia airplane crash. Motion agreed to 413-0: R 207-0; D 204-0 (ND 151-0, SD 53-0); I 2-0. A two-thirds majority of those present and voting (276 in this case) is required for adoption under suspension of the rules. March 7, 2001.

Key

Y	Voted for (yea).
#	Paired for.
+	Announced for.
N	Voted against (nay).
X	Paired against.
−	Announced against.
P	Voted "present."
C	Voted "present" to avoid possible conflict of interest.
?	Did not vote or otherwise make a position known.

Democrats **Republicans** *Independents*

	26	27	28	29	30	31	32
ALABAMA							
1 *Callahan*	Y	Y	Y	Y	Y	Y	?
2 *Everett*	Y	Y	Y	Y	Y	Y	Y
3 *Riley*	Y	Y	N	Y	Y	+	Y
4 *Aderholt*	Y	Y	N	Y	Y	Y	Y
5 Cramer	Y	Y	Y	N	Y	Y	Y
6 *Bachus*	Y	Y	Y	Y	Y	Y	Y
7 Hilliard	Y	Y	N	N	Y	Y	Y
ALASKA							
AL *Young*	Y	Y	Y	Y	Y	?	Y
ARIZONA							
1 *Flake*	Y	Y	Y	Y	Y	?	Y
2 Pastor	Y	Y	N	N	Y	Y	Y
3 *Stump*	Y	Y	Y	Y	Y	Y	Y
4 *Shadegg*	Y	Y	Y	Y	Y	?	?
5 *Kolbe*	Y	Y	Y	Y	Y	Y	Y
6 *Hayworth*	Y	Y	Y	Y	Y	Y	Y
ARKANSAS							
1 Berry	Y	Y	N	N	Y	Y	Y
2 Snyder	Y	Y	Y	N	Y	Y	Y
3 *Hutchinson*	Y	Y	Y	Y	Y	Y	Y
4 Ross	Y	Y	N	N	Y	Y	Y
CALIFORNIA							
1 Thompson	Y	Y	N	N	Y	Y	Y
2 *Herger*	Y	Y	Y	Y	Y	?	?
3 *Ose*	Y	Y	Y	Y	Y	Y	Y
4 *Doolittle*	Y	Y	Y	Y	?	?	?
5 Matsui	Y	Y	N	N	Y	Y	Y
6 Woolsey	Y	Y	N	N	Y	Y	Y
7 Miller, George	Y	Y	N	N	Y	Y	Y
8 Pelosi	Y	Y	N	N	Y	Y	Y
9 Lee	Y	Y	N	N	Y	Y	Y
10 Tauscher	Y	Y	N	N	Y	Y	Y
11 *Pombo*	Y	Y	Y	Y	Y	Y	Y
12 Lantos	Y	Y	N	N	Y	Y	Y
13 Stark	Y	N	N	N	Y	Y	Y
14 Eshoo	Y	Y	N	N	Y	Y	Y
15 Honda	Y	Y	N	Y	?	Y	Y
16 Lofgren	Y	Y	N	N	Y	Y	Y
17 Farr	Y	Y	N	N	Y	Y	Y
18 Condit	Y	Y	N	N	Y	Y	Y
19 *Radanovich*	?	Y	Y	Y	Y	Y	Y
20 Dooley	Y	Y	N	N	Y	Y	Y
21 *Thomas*	Y	Y	Y	Y	Y	Y	Y
22 Capps	Y	Y	N	N	Y	Y	Y
23 *Gallegly*	Y	Y	Y	Y	Y	Y	Y
24 Sherman	Y	Y	N	N	Y	Y	Y
25 *McKeon*	Y	Y	Y	Y	Y	Y	Y
26 Berman	Y	Y	N	N	Y	Y	Y
27 Schiff	Y	Y	N	N	Y	Y	Y
28 *Dreier*	Y	Y	Y	Y	Y	Y	Y
29 Waxman	Y	Y	?	N	Y	Y	Y
30 Becerra	+	+	+	−	+	+	+
31 Solis	Y	Y	N	N	Y	Y	Y
32 Vacant							
33 Roybal-Allard	Y	Y	Y	N	Y	Y	Y
34 Napolitano	Y	Y	N	N	Y	Y	Y
35 Waters	Y	Y	N	N	Y	Y	Y
36 Harman	Y	Y	N	N	Y	Y	Y
37 Millender-McD.	Y	Y	N	N	Y	Y	Y
38 *Horn*	Y	Y	Y	Y	Y	Y	Y

	26	27	28	29	30	31	32
39 *Royce*	N	Y	Y	Y	Y	Y	Y
40 *Lewis*	?	?	?	?	?	?	?
41 *Miller, Gary*	Y	Y	Y	Y	Y	Y	Y
42 Baca	Y	N	N	N	Y	Y	Y
43 *Calvert*	Y	Y	Y	Y	Y	Y	Y
44 *Bono*	Y	Y	Y	Y	Y	Y	Y
45 *Rohrabacher*	Y	Y	Y	Y	Y	Y	Y
46 Sanchez	Y	Y	N	Y	Y	Y	?
47 *Cox*	Y	Y	Y	Y	Y	Y	Y
48 *Issa*	Y	Y	Y	Y	Y	Y	Y
49 Davis	Y	Y	N	Y	Y	Y	Y
50 Filner	Y	Y	N	N	Y	Y	Y
51 *Cunningham*	Y	Y	Y	Y	Y	Y	Y
52 *Hunter*	Y	Y	?	Y	Y	Y	Y
COLORADO							
1 DeGette	Y	Y	N	N	Y	Y	Y
2 Udall	Y	Y	N	N	Y	Y	Y
3 *McInnis*	Y	Y	Y	Y	Y	Y	Y
4 *Schaffer*	Y	Y	N	Y	Y	?	Y
5 *Hefley*	Y	Y	Y	Y	Y	Y	Y
6 *Tancredo*	Y	Y	P	Y	Y	Y	Y
CONNECTICUT							
1 Larson	Y	Y	N	N	Y	Y	Y
2 *Simmons*	Y	Y	Y	Y	Y	Y	Y
3 DeLauro	Y	Y	N	N	Y	Y	Y
4 *Shays*	?	?	Y	Y	Y	Y	Y
5 Maloney	+	+	+	N	Y	Y	Y
6 *Johnson*	Y	Y	Y	Y	Y	Y	Y
DELAWARE							
AL *Castle*	Y	Y	Y	Y	Y	Y	Y
FLORIDA							
1 *Scarborough*	Y	Y	Y	Y	Y	Y	Y
2 Boyd	Y	Y	N	Y	Y	Y	Y
3 Brown	Y	Y	N	N	Y	Y	Y
4 *Crenshaw*	Y	Y	N	Y	Y	Y	Y
5 Thurman	Y	Y	N	N	Y	Y	Y
6 *Stearns*	Y	Y	Y	Y	Y	Y	Y
7 *Mica*	Y	Y	Y	Y	Y	Y	Y
8 *Keller*	Y	Y	Y	Y	Y	Y	Y
9 *Bilirakis*	Y	Y	+	Y	Y	Y	Y
10 *Young*	Y	Y	Y	Y	Y	Y	Y
11 Davis	Y	Y	N	N	Y	Y	Y
12 *Putnam*	Y	Y	Y	Y	Y	Y	Y
13 *Miller*	Y	Y	Y	Y	Y	Y	Y
14 *Goss*	Y	Y	Y	Y	Y	Y	Y
15 *Weldon*	Y	Y	Y	Y	Y	Y	Y
16 *Foley*	Y	Y	Y	Y	Y	Y	Y
17 Meek	Y	Y	N	N	Y	Y	Y
18 *Ros-Lehtinen*	Y	Y	Y	Y	Y	Y	Y
19 Wexler	Y	Y	N	N	Y	Y	Y
20 Deutsch	Y	Y	N	N	Y	Y	Y
21 *Diaz-Balart*	?	?	?	Y	Y	Y	Y
22 *Shaw*	Y	Y	Y	Y	Y	Y	Y
23 Hastings	Y	Y	N	N	Y	Y	Y
GEORGIA							
1 *Kingston*	?	?	Y	Y	Y	Y	Y
2 Bishop	Y	Y	?	?	?	?	?
3 *Collins*	Y	Y	Y	Y	Y	Y	Y
4 McKinney	Y	Y	N	N	Y	Y	Y
5 Lewis	Y	Y	N	N	Y	Y	Y
6 *Isakson*	Y	Y	Y	Y	Y	Y	Y
7 *Barr*	Y	Y	Y	Y	Y	?	Y
8 *Chambliss*	Y	Y	Y	Y	Y	Y	Y
9 *Deal*	Y	Y	Y	Y	Y	Y	Y
10 *Norwood*	Y	Y	Y	Y	Y	Y	Y
11 *Linder*	Y	Y	Y	Y	Y	Y	Y
HAWAII							
1 Abercrombie	Y	Y	N	Y	Y	Y	Y
2 Mink	Y	Y	N	Y	Y	Y	Y
IDAHO							
1 *Otter*	Y	Y	Y	Y	Y	Y	Y
2 *Simpson*	Y	Y	Y	Y	Y	Y	Y
ILLINOIS							
1 Rush	Y	Y	N	Y	Y	Y	?
2 Jackson	Y	Y	N	Y	Y	Y	Y
3 Lipinski	?	?	N	Y	Y	Y	Y
4 Gutierrez	Y	N	N	N	Y	Y	Y
5 Blagojevich	Y	Y	N	Y	Y	Y	Y
6 *Hyde*	?	?	Y	Y	Y	Y	Y
7 Davis	Y	Y	N	Y	Y	Y	Y
8 *Crane*	Y	Y	N	Y	Y	Y	Y
9 Schakowsky	Y	Y	N	N	Y	Y	Y
10 *Kirk*	Y	Y	Y	Y	Y	Y	Y
11 *Weller*	Y	Y	N	Y	Y	Y	Y
12 Costello	Y	Y	N	N	Y	Y	Y
13 *Biggert*	Y	Y	Y	Y	Y	Y	Y

ND Northern Democrats   SD Southern Democrats

	26	27	28	29	30	31	32
14 ***Hastert***							
15 ***Johnson***	Y	Y	Y	Y	Y	Y	Y
16 ***Manzullo***	Y	Y	Y	Y	Y	Y	Y
17 Evans	Y	Y	Y	N	Y	Y	Y
18 ***LaHood***	Y	Y	Y	Y	Y	Y	Y
19 Phelps	Y	Y	Y	N	Y	Y	Y
20 ***Shimkus***	Y	Y	Y	Y	Y	Y	Y
INDIANA							
1 Visclosky	Y	Y	N	N	Y	Y	Y
2 ***Pence***	Y	Y	Y	Y	Y	Y	Y
3 Roemer	Y	Y	Y	N	Y	Y	Y
4 ***Souder***	Y	Y	Y	Y	Y	Y	Y
5 ***Buyer***	Y	Y	Y	Y	Y	Y	Y
6 ***Burton***	Y	Y	Y	Y	Y	Y	Y
7 ***Kerns***	Y	Y	Y	Y	Y	Y	Y
8 ***Hostettler***	Y	Y	Y	Y	Y	Y	Y
9 Hill	Y	Y	N	N	Y	Y	Y
10 Carson	Y	Y	Y	N	Y	Y	Y
IOWA							
1 ***Leach***	Y	Y	Y	Y	Y	Y	Y
2 ***Nussle***	Y	Y	Y	Y	Y	Y	Y
3 Boswell	Y	Y	Y	N	Y	Y	Y
4 ***Ganske***	Y	Y	Y	Y	Y	Y	Y
5 ***Latham***	Y	Y	Y	Y	Y	Y	Y
KANSAS							
1 ***Moran***	Y	Y	Y	Y	Y	Y	Y
2 ***Ryun***	Y	Y	Y	Y	Y	Y	Y
3 Moore	Y	+	N	N	Y	Y	Y
4 ***Tiahrt***	Y	Y	Y	Y	Y	Y	Y
KENTUCKY							
1 ***Whitfield***	Y	Y	Y	Y	Y	Y	Y
2 ***Lewis***	Y	Y	Y	Y	Y	Y	Y
3 ***Northup***	Y	Y	Y	Y	Y	Y	Y
4 Lucas	Y	Y	Y	N	Y	Y	Y
5 ***Rogers***	Y	Y	Y	Y	Y	Y	Y
6 ***Fletcher***	Y	Y	Y	Y	Y	Y	Y
LOUISIANA							
1 ***Vitter***	Y	Y	Y	Y	Y	Y	Y
2 Jefferson	Y	Y	Y	N	Y	Y	Y
3 ***Tauzin***	Y	Y	Y	Y	Y	?	Y
4 ***McCrery***	Y	Y	?	Y	Y	Y	Y
5 ***Cooksey***	Y	Y	Y	Y	Y	Y	?
6 ***Baker***	Y	Y	Y	Y	Y	Y	Y
7 John	Y	Y	Y	N	Y	Y	Y
MAINE							
1 Allen	Y	Y	N	N	Y	Y	Y
2 Baldacci	+	+	Y	N	Y	Y	Y
MARYLAND							
1 ***Gilchrest***	Y	Y	Y	Y	Y	?	Y
2 ***Ehrlich***	Y	Y	Y	Y	Y	Y	Y
3 Cardin	Y	Y	Y	N	Y	Y	Y
4 Wynn	Y	Y	Y	N	Y	Y	Y
5 Hoyer	Y	Y	Y	N	Y	Y	Y
6 ***Bartlett***	Y	Y	Y	Y	Y	Y	Y
7 Cummings	Y	Y	Y	N	Y	Y	Y
8 ***Morella***	Y	Y	Y	Y	Y	Y	Y
MASSACHUSETTS							
1 Olver	Y	Y	N	N	Y	Y	Y
2 Neal	Y	Y	Y	N	Y	Y	Y
3 McGovern	Y	Y	N	N	Y	Y	Y
4 Frank	Y	Y	Y	N	Y	Y	Y
5 Meehan	Y	Y	N	N	Y	Y	Y
6 Tierney	Y	Y	Y	N	Y	Y	Y
7 Markey	Y	Y	Y	N	Y	Y	Y
8 Capuano	Y	Y	–	N	Y	Y	Y
9 Moakley	?	?	?	N	Y	Y	Y
10 Delahunt	Y	Y	Y	N	Y	Y	Y
MICHIGAN							
1 Stupak	?	?	?	?	?	?	?
2 ***Hoekstra***	Y	Y	Y	Y	Y	Y	Y
3 ***Ehlers***	Y	Y	Y	Y	Y	Y	Y
4 ***Camp***	Y	Y	Y	Y	Y	Y	Y
5 Barcia	Y	Y	Y	N	Y	Y	Y
6 ***Upton***	Y	Y	Y	Y	Y	Y	Y
7 ***Smith***	Y	Y	Y	Y	Y	+	Y
8 ***Rogers***	Y	Y	Y	Y	Y	Y	Y
9 Kildee	Y	Y	Y	N	Y	Y	Y
10 Bonior	Y	?	N	N	Y	Y	Y
11 ***Knollenberg***	Y	Y	Y	Y	Y	Y	Y
12 Levin	Y	Y	Y	N	Y	Y	Y
13 Rivers	Y	Y	Y	N	Y	Y	Y
14 Conyers	Y	Y	Y	N	Y	Y	Y
15 Kilpatrick	Y	Y	Y	N	Y	Y	Y
16 Dingell	Y	Y	Y	?	Y	Y	Y

	26	27	28	29	30	31	32
MINNESOTA							
1 ***Gutknecht***	Y	Y	N	Y	Y	Y	Y
2 ***Kennedy***	Y	Y	Y	Y	Y	Y	Y
3 ***Ramstad***	Y	Y	N	Y	Y	Y	Y
4 McCollum	Y	Y	Y	N	Y	Y	Y
5 Sabo	Y	Y	N	N	Y	Y	Y
6 Luther	Y	Y	Y	N	Y	Y	Y
7 Peterson	Y	Y	N	N	Y	Y	Y
8 Oberstar	Y	Y	N	N	Y	Y	Y
MISSISSIPPI							
1 ***Wicker***	Y	Y	Y	Y	Y	Y	Y
2 Thompson	Y	Y	N	N	Y	Y	Y
3 ***Pickering***	Y	Y	Y	Y	Y	Y	Y
4 Shows	?	?	?	?	?	?	?
5 Taylor	Y	Y	N	Y	Y	Y	Y
MISSOURI							
1 Clay	Y	Y	N	N	Y	Y	Y
2 ***Akin***	Y	Y	Y	Y	Y	Y	Y
3 Gephardt	Y	Y	N	N	Y	Y	Y
4 Skelton	Y	Y	Y	N	Y	Y	Y
5 McCarthy	Y	Y	Y	N	Y	Y	Y
6 ***Graves***	Y	Y	Y	Y	Y	Y	Y
7 ***Blunt***	Y	Y	Y	Y	Y	Y	Y
8 ***Emerson***	Y	Y	Y	Y	Y	Y	Y
9 ***Hulshof***	Y	Y	N	Y	Y	Y	Y
MONTANA							
AL ***Rehberg***	Y	Y	Y	Y	Y	Y	Y
NEBRASKA							
1 ***Bereuter***	Y	Y	Y	Y	Y	Y	Y
2 ***Terry***	Y	Y	Y	Y	Y	Y	Y
3 ***Osborne***	Y	Y	Y	Y	Y	Y	Y
NEVADA							
1 Berkley	Y	Y	Y	N	Y	Y	Y
2 ***Gibbons***	Y	Y	Y	Y	Y	Y	Y
NEW HAMPSHIRE							
1 ***Sununu***	?	?	Y	Y	Y	Y	Y
2 ***Bass***	Y	Y	Y	Y	Y	Y	Y
NEW JERSEY							
1 Andrews	Y	Y	Y	N	Y	Y	Y
2 ***LoBiondo***	Y	Y	N	Y	Y	Y	Y
3 ***Saxton***	Y	Y	Y	Y	Y	Y	Y
4 ***Smith***	Y	Y	Y	Y	Y	Y	Y
5 ***Roukema***	?	?	?	?	?	?	Y
6 Pallone	Y	Y	N	N	Y	Y	Y
7 ***Ferguson***	Y	Y	Y	Y	Y	Y	Y
8 Pascrell	Y	Y	Y	N	Y	Y	Y
9 Rothman	Y	Y	Y	N	Y	Y	Y
10 Payne	Y	Y	Y	N	Y	Y	Y
11 ***Frelinghuysen***	Y	Y	Y	Y	Y	Y	Y
12 Holt	Y	Y	N	N	Y	Y	Y
13 Menendez	Y	Y	N	N	Y	Y	Y
NEW MEXICO							
1 ***Wilson***	Y	Y	Y	Y	Y	Y	Y
2 ***Skeen***	Y	Y	Y	Y	Y	Y	Y
3 Udall	Y	Y	N	N	Y	Y	Y
NEW YORK							
1 ***Grucci***	Y	Y	Y	Y	Y	Y	Y
2 Israel	Y	Y	Y	N	Y	Y	Y
3 ***King***	Y	Y	Y	Y	Y	Y	Y
4 McCarthy	Y	Y	Y	N	Y	Y	Y
5 Ackerman	?	?	?	?	?	?	?
6 Meeks	Y	Y	Y	N	Y	Y	Y
7 Crowley	Y	Y	Y	N	Y	Y	Y
8 Nadler	Y	Y	Y	N	Y	Y	Y
9 Weiner	Y	Y	N	N	Y	Y	Y
10 Towns	Y	Y	Y	N	Y	Y	Y
11 Owens	Y	Y	Y	N	Y	Y	Y
12 Velázquez	Y	Y	N	N	Y	Y	Y
13 ***Fossella***	Y	Y	Y	Y	Y	Y	Y
14 Maloney	Y	Y	Y	N	Y	Y	Y
15 Rangel	Y	Y	?	N	Y	Y	Y
16 Serrano	Y	Y	Y	N	Y	Y	Y
17 Engel	Y	Y	Y	N	Y	Y	Y
18 Lowey	Y	Y	Y	N	Y	Y	Y
19 ***Kelly***	Y	Y	Y	Y	Y	Y	Y
20 ***Gilman***	Y	Y	Y	Y	Y	Y	Y
21 McNulty	Y	Y	N	N	Y	Y	Y
22 ***Sweeney***	?	?	N	Y	Y	Y	Y
23 ***Boehlert***	Y	Y	Y	Y	Y	Y	Y
24 ***McHugh***	Y	Y	Y	Y	Y	Y	Y
25 ***Walsh***	?	?	?	?	Y	Y	Y
26 Hinchey	Y	Y	?	N	Y	Y	Y
27 ***Reynolds***	Y	Y	Y	Y	Y	Y	Y
28 Slaughter	+	+	?	N	Y	Y	Y
29 LaFalce	Y	Y	N	N	Y	Y	Y

	26	27	28	29	30	31	32
30 ***Quinn***	Y	Y	Y	Y	Y	Y	Y
31 ***Houghton***	?	?	Y	Y	Y	Y	Y
NORTH CAROLINA							
1 Clayton	Y	Y	Y	N	Y	Y	Y
2 Etheridge	Y	Y	Y	N	Y	Y	Y
3 ***Jones***	+	+	Y	Y	Y	Y	Y
4 Price	Y	Y	Y	N	Y	Y	Y
5 ***Burr***	Y	Y	?	Y	Y	Y	Y
6 ***Coble***	Y	Y	Y	Y	Y	Y	Y
7 McIntyre	Y	Y	Y	N	Y	Y	Y
8 ***Hayes***	Y	Y	Y	Y	Y	Y	Y
9 ***Myrick***	Y	Y	Y	Y	Y	Y	Y
10 ***Ballenger***	Y	Y	Y	Y	Y	Y	Y
11 ***Taylor***	?	?	Y	Y	Y	Y	Y
12 Watt	Y	Y	N	N	Y	Y	Y
NORTH DAKOTA							
AL Pomeroy	Y	Y	Y	N	Y	Y	Y
OHIO							
1 ***Chabot***	Y	Y	Y	Y	Y	Y	Y
2 ***Portman***	Y	Y	Y	Y	Y	Y	Y
3 Hall	Y	Y	Y	N	Y	Y	Y
4 ***Oxley***	Y	Y	Y	Y	+	+	+
5 ***Gillmor***	Y	Y	Y	Y	Y	Y	Y
6 Strickland	Y	Y	N	N	Y	Y	Y
7 ***Hobson***	Y	Y	Y	Y	Y	Y	Y
8 ***Boehner***	Y	Y	Y	Y	Y	Y	Y
9 Kaptur	Y	Y	Y	N	Y	Y	Y
10 Kucinich	Y	Y	N	N	Y	Y	Y
11 Jones	Y	Y	N	N	Y	Y	Y
12 ***Tiberi***	Y	Y	Y	Y	?	?	?
13 Brown	Y	Y	N	N	Y	Y	Y
14 Sawyer	Y	Y	Y	N	Y	Y	Y
15 ***Pryce***	Y	Y	Y	Y	?	?	?
16 ***Regula***	Y	Y	Y	Y	Y	Y	Y
17 Traficant	Y	Y	Y	Y	Y	Y	Y
18 ***Ney***	Y	Y	Y	Y	Y	Y	Y
19 ***LaTourette***	Y	Y	Y	Y	?	?	?
OKLAHOMA							
1 ***Largent***	Y	Y	Y	Y	Y	?	Y
2 Carson	Y	Y	Y	Y	Y	Y	Y
3 ***Watkins***	Y	Y	Y	Y	Y	Y	Y
4 ***Watts***	Y	Y	Y	Y	Y	Y	Y
5 ***Istook***	Y	Y	Y	Y	Y	?	Y
6 ***Lucas***	Y	Y	Y	Y	Y	Y	Y
OREGON							
1 Wu	Y	Y	Y	N	Y	Y	Y
2 ***Walden***	Y	Y	Y	Y	Y	Y	Y
3 Blumenauer	Y	Y	Y	N	Y	Y	Y
4 DeFazio	Y	Y	N	N	Y	Y	Y
5 Hooley	Y	Y	Y	N	Y	Y	Y
PENNSYLVANIA							
1 Brady	Y	Y	N	N	Y	Y	Y
2 Fattah	Y	Y	Y	N	Y	Y	Y
3 Borski	Y	Y	N	N	Y	Y	Y
4 ***Hart***	Y	Y	Y	Y	Y	Y	Y
5 ***Peterson***	Y	Y	Y	Y	Y	Y	Y
6 Holden	Y	Y	Y	N	Y	Y	Y
7 ***Weldon***	Y	Y	Y	Y	Y	Y	Y
8 ***Greenwood***	Y	Y	Y	Y	Y	Y	Y
9 Vacant							
10 ***Sherwood***	Y	Y	Y	Y	Y	Y	Y
11 Kanjorski	Y	Y	Y	N	Y	Y	Y
12 Murtha	Y	Y	Y	N	Y	Y	Y
13 Hoeffel	+	+	Y	N	Y	Y	Y
14 Coyne	Y	Y	Y	N	Y	Y	Y
15 ***Toomey***	Y	Y	Y	Y	Y	Y	Y
16 ***Pitts***	Y	Y	Y	Y	Y	Y	Y
17 ***Gekas***	Y	Y	Y	Y	Y	Y	Y
18 Doyle	Y	Y	Y	N	Y	Y	Y
19 ***Platts***	Y	Y	Y	Y	Y	Y	Y
20 Mascara	Y	Y	Y	N	Y	Y	Y
21 ***English***	Y	?	N	Y	Y	Y	Y
RHODE ISLAND							
1 Kennedy	?	?	Y	N	Y	Y	Y
2 Langevin	Y	Y	N	N	Y	Y	Y
SOUTH CAROLINA							
1 ***Brown***	Y	Y	Y	Y	Y	Y	Y
2 ***Spence***	Y	Y	Y	Y	Y	Y	Y
3 ***Graham***	Y	Y	Y	Y	Y	Y	Y
4 ***DeMint***	Y	Y	Y	Y	Y	Y	Y
5 Spratt	Y	Y	Y	N	Y	Y	Y
6 Clyburn	Y	Y	Y	N	Y	Y	Y
SOUTH DAKOTA							
AL ***Thune***	Y	Y	Y	Y	Y	Y	Y

	26	27	28	29	30	31	32
TENNESSEE							
1 ***Jenkins***	Y	Y	Y	Y	Y	Y	Y
2 ***Duncan***	Y	Y	Y	Y	Y	Y	Y
3 ***Wamp***	?	?	Y	Y	Y	Y	Y
4 ***Hilleary***	?	?	Y	Y	Y	Y	Y
5 Clement	Y	Y	Y	N	Y	Y	Y
6 Gordon	Y	Y	Y	N	Y	Y	Y
7 ***Bryant***	Y	Y	Y	Y	Y	Y	Y
8 Tanner	Y	Y	Y	N	Y	Y	Y
9 Ford	Y	Y	N	N	Y	Y	Y
TEXAS							
1 Sandlin	Y	Y	N	N	Y	Y	Y
2 Turner	Y	Y	Y	Y	Y	Y	Y
3 ***Johnson, Sam***	Y	Y	Y	Y	?	?	?
4 Hall	Y	Y	Y	Y	Y	Y	Y
5 ***Sessions***	Y	Y	Y	Y	Y	Y	Y
6 ***Barton***	Y	Y	Y	Y	Y	Y	Y
7 ***Culberson***	Y	Y	Y	Y	Y	Y	Y
8 ***Brady***	?	Y	Y	Y	Y	Y	Y
9 Lampson	Y	Y	Y	N	Y	Y	Y
10 Doggett	Y	Y	Y	N	Y	Y	Y
11 Edwards	Y	Y	Y	?	Y	Y	Y
12 ***Granger***	Y	Y	Y	Y	Y	Y	Y
13 ***Thornberry***	Y	Y	Y	Y	Y	Y	Y
14 ***Paul***	N	N	Y	Y	Y	?	Y
15 Hinojosa	Y	Y	Y	N	Y	Y	Y
16 Reyes	Y	Y	Y	N	Y	Y	Y
17 Stenholm	Y	Y	N	N	Y	Y	Y
18 Jackson-Lee	Y	Y	Y	N	Y	Y	Y
19 ***Combest***	Y	Y	Y	Y	Y	Y	Y
20 Gonzalez	Y	Y	N	N	Y	Y	Y
21 ***Smith***	Y	Y	Y	Y	Y	Y	Y
22 ***DeLay***	Y	Y	Y	Y	Y	Y	Y
23 ***Bonilla***	Y	Y	Y	Y	Y	Y	Y
24 Frost	Y	Y	N	N	Y	Y	Y
25 Bentsen	Y	Y	Y	N	Y	Y	Y
26 ***Armey***	Y	Y	Y	Y	Y	Y	Y
27 Ortiz	Y	Y	Y	N	Y	Y	Y
28 Rodriguez	Y	Y	Y	N	Y	Y	Y
29 Green	Y	Y	N	N	Y	Y	Y
30 Johnson, E.B.	Y	Y	Y	N	Y	Y	Y
UTAH							
1 ***Hansen***	Y	Y	Y	Y	Y	Y	Y
2 Matheson	Y	Y	Y	N	Y	Y	Y
3 ***Cannon***	Y	Y	Y	Y	?	Y	Y
VERMONT							
AL *Sanders*	?	?	?	?	Y	Y	Y
VIRGINIA							
1 ***Davis, Jo Ann***	Y	Y	Y	Y	Y	Y	Y
2 ***Schrock***	Y	Y	Y	Y	Y	Y	Y
3 Scott	?	?	N	N	Y	Y	Y
4 Sisisky	Y	Y	Y	N	Y	Y	Y
5 *Goode*	Y	Y	Y	Y	Y	Y	Y
6 ***Goodlatte***	Y	Y	Y	Y	Y	Y	Y
7 ***Cantor***	Y	Y	Y	Y	Y	Y	Y
8 Moran	Y	Y	Y	N	Y	Y	Y
9 Boucher	Y	Y	?	N	Y	Y	Y
10 ***Wolf***	Y	Y	Y	Y	Y	Y	Y
11 ***Davis, T.***	Y	Y	Y	Y	Y	Y	Y
WASHINGTON							
1 Inslee	Y	Y	Y	N	Y	Y	Y
2 Larsen	Y	Y	N	N	Y	Y	Y
3 Baird	Y	Y	N	N	Y	Y	Y
4 ***Hastings***	Y	Y	Y	Y	Y	Y	Y
5 ***Nethercutt***	Y	Y	Y	Y	Y	Y	Y
6 Dicks	Y	Y	N	?	Y	Y	Y
7 McDermott	Y	Y	N	N	Y	Y	Y
8 ***Dunn***	Y	Y	Y	Y	Y	Y	Y
9 Smith	Y	Y	Y	N	Y	Y	Y
WEST VIRGINIA							
1 Mollohan	Y	Y	Y	N	Y	Y	Y
2 ***Capito***	Y	Y	Y	Y	Y	Y	Y
3 Rahall	Y	Y	Y	N	Y	Y	Y
WISCONSIN							
1 ***Ryan***	Y	Y	Y	Y	Y	Y	Y
2 Baldwin	Y	Y	Y	N	Y	Y	Y
3 Kind	Y	Y	Y	N	Y	Y	Y
4 Kleczka	Y	Y	Y	N	Y	Y	Y
5 Barrett	Y	Y	Y	N	Y	Y	Y
6 ***Petri***	Y	Y	Y	Y	Y	Y	Y
7 Obey	Y	Y	Y	N	Y	Y	Y
8 ***Green***	+	Y	Y	Y	Y	Y	Y
9 ***Sensenbrenner***	Y	Y	Y	Y	Y	Y	Y
WYOMING							
AL ***Cubin***	Y	Y	Y	Y	Y	?	?

Southern states - Ala., Ark., Fla., Ga., Ky., La., Miss., N.C., Okla., S.C., Tenn., Texas, Va.

Key

Y	Voted for (yea).
#	Paired for.
+	Announced for.
N	Voted against (nay).
X	Paired against.
–	Announced against.
P	Voted "present."
C	Voted "present" to avoid possible conflict of interest.
?	Did not vote or otherwise make a position known.

Democrats   ***Republicans***
Independents

33. S J Res 6. Ergonomics Rule Disapproval/Passage. Passage of the joint resolution that would provide for congressional disapproval of the ergonomics rule submitted by the Labor Department during the Clinton administration, stating the rule would have no force or effect. Passed 223-206: R 206-13; D 16-192 (ND 2-152, SD 14-40); I 1-1. March 7, 2001.

34. Procedural Motion/Journal. Approval of the House Journal of Wednesday, March 7, 2001. Approved 230-180: R 206-4; D 23-175 (ND 16-129, SD 7-46); I 1-1. March 8, 2001.

35. Procedural Motion/Adjourn. Hill, D-Ind., motion to adjourn. Motion rejected 174-241: R 1-210; D 172-30 (ND 129-21, SD 43-9); I 1-1. March 8, 2001.

36. Procedural Motion/Adjourn. Sandlin, D-Texas, motion to adjourn. Motion rejected 171-251: R 0-213; D 170-37 (ND 127-26, SD 43-11); I 1-1. March 8, 2001.

37. HR 3. Income Tax Reduction/Previous Question. Reynolds, R-N.Y., motion to order the previous question (thus ending debate and possibility of amendment) on adoption of the rule (H Res 83) to provide for House floor consideration of the measure that would lower federal income taxes by restructuring the five existing tax brackets into four — 10, 15, 25 and 33 percent. Motion agreed to 220-204: R 215-0; D 4-203 (ND 2-151, SD 2-52); I 1-1. March 8, 2001.

38. HR 3. Income Tax Reduction/Previous Question Reconsideration. Reynolds, R-N.Y., motion to table (kill) the John, D-La., motion to reconsider the vote on the motion to order the previous question (thus ending debate and possibility of amendment) on adoption of the rule (H Res 83) to provide for House floor consideration of the bill that would lower federal income taxes by restructuring the five existing tax brackets into four — 10, 15, 25 and 33 percent. Motion agreed to 217-205: R 214-0; D 2-204 (ND 2-150, SD 0-54); I 1-1. March 8, 2001.

39. HR 3. Income Tax Reduction/Rule. Adoption of the rule (H Res 83) to provide for House floor consideration of the bill that would lower federal income taxes by restructuring the five existing tax brackets into four — 10, 15, 25 and 33 percent. Adopted 220-204: R 216-0; D 3-203 (ND 2-150, SD 1-53); I 1-1. March 8, 2001.

	33	34	35	36	37	38	39
ALABAMA							
1 *Callahan*	Y	Y	N	N	Y	Y	?
2 *Everett*	Y	Y	N	N	Y	Y	Y
3 *Riley*	Y	Y	N	N	Y	Y	Y
4 *Aderholt*	Y	N	N	N	Y	Y	Y
5 Cramer	Y	N	Y	N	N	N	N
6 *Bachus*	Y	Y	N	N	Y	Y	Y
7 Hilliard	N	N	Y	N	N	N	N
ALASKA							
AL *Young*	Y	?	?	N	Y	Y	Y
ARIZONA							
1 *Flake*	Y	Y	N	N	Y	Y	Y
2 Pastor	N	N	N	N	N	N	N
3 *Stump*	Y	Y	N	N	Y	Y	Y
4 *Shadegg*	Y	Y	N	N	Y	Y	Y
5 *Kolbe*	Y	Y	N	N	Y	Y	Y
6 *Hayworth*	Y	Y	N	N	Y	Y	Y
ARKANSAS							
1 Berry	N	N	Y	Y	N	N	N
2 Snyder	N	N	Y	Y	N	N	N
3 *Hutchinson*	Y	Y	N	?	Y	Y	Y
4 Ross	N	N	Y	Y	N	N	N
CALIFORNIA							
1 Thompson	N	N	Y	Y	N	N	N
2 *Herger*	Y	Y	N	N	Y	Y	Y
3 *Ose*	Y	Y	N	N	Y	Y	Y
4 *Doolittle*	Y	Y	N	N	Y	Y	Y
5 Matsui	N	N	Y	N	N	N	N
6 Woolsey	N	N	Y	N	N	N	N
7 Miller, George	N	N	Y	N	N	N	N
8 Pelosi	N	N	Y	N	N	N	N
9 Lee	N	N	Y	N	N	N	N
10 Tauscher	N	N	Y	N	N	N	N
11 *Pombo*	Y	Y	N	N	Y	Y	Y
12 Lantos	N	N	Y	N	N	N	N
13 Stark	N	N	Y	N	N	N	N
14 Eshoo	N	N	Y	N	N	N	N
15 Honda	N	N	Y	N	N	N	N
16 Lofgren	N	N	N	N	N	N	N
17 Farr	N	N	Y	N	N	N	N
18 Condit	N	N	Y	N	N	N	N
19 *Radanovich*	Y	Y	Y	N	Y	Y	Y
20 Dooley	Y	N	N	N	N	N	N
21 *Thomas*	Y	Y	N	N	Y	Y	Y
22 Capps	N	N	Y	N	N	N	N
23 *Gallegly*	Y	Y	N	N	Y	Y	Y
24 Sherman	N	N	Y	N	N	N	N
25 *McKeon*	Y	Y	N	N	Y	Y	Y
26 Berman	N	N	Y	N	N	N	N
27 Schiff	N	N	Y	N	N	N	N
28 *Dreier*	Y	Y	N	N	Y	Y	Y
29 Waxman	N	Y	?	N	N	N	N
30 Becerra	–	N	Y	N	N	N	N
31 Solis	N	N	Y	N	N	N	N
32 Vacant							
33 Roybal-Allard	N	N	Y	N	N	N	N
34 Napolitano	N	N	Y	N	N	N	N
35 Waters	N	N	Y	N	N	N	N
36 Harman	N	N	Y	N	N	N	N
37 Millender-McD.	N	N	Y	N	N	N	N
38 *Horn*	N	Y	N	N	Y	Y	Y

	33	34	35	36	37	38	39
39 *Royce*	Y	Y	N	N	Y	Y	Y
40 *Lewis*	Y	?	?	?	?	?	?
41 *Miller, Gary*	Y	Y	N	N	Y	Y	Y
42 Baca	N	N	Y	N	N	N	N
43 *Calvert*	Y	Y	N	N	Y	Y	Y
44 *Bono*	Y	Y	N	N	Y	Y	Y
45 *Rohrabacher*	Y	Y	N	N	Y	Y	Y
46 Sanchez	N	N	Y	N	N	N	N
47 *Cox*	Y	Y	N	N	Y	Y	Y
48 *Issa*	Y	Y	N	N	+	+	Y
49 Davis	N	N	Y	N	N	N	N
50 Filner	N	N	Y	N	N	N	N
51 *Cunningham*	Y	Y	N	N	Y	Y	Y
52 *Hunter*	Y	Y	N	N	Y	Y	Y
COLORADO							
1 DeGette	N	N	Y	N	N	N	N
2 Udall	N	N	Y	N	N	N	N
3 *McInnis*	Y	Y	N	N	Y	Y	Y
4 *Schaffer*	Y	N	N	N	Y	Y	Y
5 *Hefley*	Y	Y	N	N	Y	Y	Y
6 *Tancredo*	Y	P	N	N	Y	Y	Y
CONNECTICUT							
1 Larson	N	N	Y	N	N	N	–
2 *Simmons*	Y	Y	N	N	Y	Y	Y
3 DeLauro	N	?	Y	N	N	N	N
4 *Shays*	Y	?	N	N	Y	Y	Y
5 Maloney	N	Y	Y	N	N	N	N
6 *Johnson*	Y	Y	N	N	Y	Y	Y
DELAWARE							
AL *Castle*	Y	Y	N	N	Y	Y	Y
FLORIDA							
1 *Scarborough*	Y	Y	N	N	Y	Y	Y
2 Boyd	Y	Y	Y	Y	N	N	N
3 Brown	N	N	Y	N	N	N	N
4 *Crenshaw*	Y	Y	N	N	Y	Y	Y
5 Thurman	N	N	Y	N	N	N	N
6 *Stearns*	Y	Y	N	N	Y	Y	Y
7 *Mica*	Y	Y	N	N	Y	Y	Y
8 *Keller*	Y	Y	N	N	Y	Y	Y
9 *Bilirakis*	Y	Y	N	N	Y	Y	Y
10 *Young*	Y	Y	N	N	Y	Y	Y
11 Davis	N	?	?	N	N	N	N
12 *Putnam*	Y	Y	N	N	Y	Y	Y
13 *Miller*	Y	Y	N	N	Y	Y	Y
14 *Goss*	Y	Y	N	N	Y	Y	Y
15 *Weldon*	Y	Y	N	N	Y	Y	Y
16 *Foley*	Y	Y	N	N	Y	Y	Y
17 Meek	N	N	Y	N	N	N	N
18 *Ros-Lehtinen*	Y	Y	N	N	Y	Y	Y
19 Wexler	N	N	Y	N	N	N	N
20 Deutsch	N	N	Y	N	N	N	N
21 *Diaz-Balart*	Y	Y	N	N	Y	Y	Y
22 *Shaw*	Y	Y	N	N	Y	Y	Y
23 Hastings	N	Y	Y	N	N	N	N
GEORGIA							
1 *Kingston*	Y	Y	N	N	Y	Y	Y
2 Bishop	N	N	Y	N	N	N	N
3 *Collins*	Y	Y	N	N	Y	Y	Y
4 McKinney	N	N	Y	N	N	N	N
5 Lewis	N	N	Y	N	N	N	N
6 *Isakson*	Y	Y	N	N	Y	Y	Y
7 *Barr*	Y	Y	N	N	Y	Y	Y
8 *Chambliss*	Y	Y	N	N	Y	Y	Y
9 *Deal*	Y	Y	N	N	Y	Y	Y
10 *Norwood*	Y	Y	N	N	Y	Y	Y
11 *Linder*	Y	Y	N	N	Y	Y	Y
HAWAII							
1 Abercrombie	N	Y	N	N	N	N	N
2 Mink	N	N	Y	N	N	N	N
IDAHO							
1 *Otter*	Y	Y	N	N	Y	Y	Y
2 *Simpson*	Y	Y	N	N	Y	Y	Y
ILLINOIS							
1 Rush	N	N	Y	N	N	N	N
2 Jackson	N	N	Y	N	N	N	N
3 Lipinski	N	N	N	N	Y	N	N
4 Gutierrez	N	?	Y	N	N	N	N
5 Blagojevich	N	N	Y	N	N	N	N
6 *Hyde*	Y	Y	N	N	Y	Y	Y
7 Davis	N	N	Y	N	N	N	N
8 *Crane*	Y	Y	N	N	Y	Y	Y
9 Schakowsky	N	N	Y	N	N	N	N
10 *Kirk*	Y	Y	N	N	Y	Y	Y
11 *Weller*	Y	Y	N	N	Y	Y	Y
12 Costello	N	N	N	N	N	N	N
13 *Biggert*	Y	Y	N	N	Y	Y	Y

ND Northern Democrats   SD Southern Democrats

	33	34	35	36	37	38	39
14 ***Hastert***	Y						
15 ***Johnson***	Y	Y	N	N	Y	Y	Y
16 ***Manzullo***	Y	Y	N	N	Y	Y	Y
17 Evans	N	N	Y	Y	N	N	N
18 ***LaHood***	Y	Y	N	N	Y	Y	Y
19 Phelps	N	N	Y	Y	N	N	N
20 ***Shimkus***	Y	Y	N	N	Y	Y	Y
INDIANA							
1 Visclosky	N	N	Y	Y	N	N	N
2 ***Pence***	Y	Y	N	N	Y	Y	Y
3 Roemer	N	N	N	N	N	N	N
4 ***Souder***	Y	Y	N	N	Y	Y	Y
5 ***Buyer***	Y	Y	N	N	Y	Y	Y
6 ***Burton***	Y	Y	N	N	Y	Y	Y
7 ***Kerns***	Y	Y	N	N	Y	Y	Y
8 ***Hostettler***	Y	Y	N	N	Y	Y	Y
9 Hill	N	N	Y	Y	N	N	N
10 Carson	N	N	Y	Y	N	N	N
IOWA							
1 ***Leach***	Y	Y	N	N	Y	Y	Y
2 ***Nussle***	Y	Y	N	N	Y	?	Y
3 Boswell	N	N	Y	Y	N	N	N
4 ***Ganske***	Y	Y	N	N	Y	Y	Y
5 ***Latham***	Y	Y	N	N	Y	Y	Y
KANSAS							
1 ***Moran***	Y	Y	N	N	Y	Y	Y
2 ***Ryun***	Y	Y	N	N	Y	Y	Y
3 Moore	N	N	Y	N	N	N	N
4 ***Tiahrt***	Y	Y	N	–	Y	Y	Y
KENTUCKY							
1 ***Whitfield***	Y	Y	N	N	Y	Y	Y
2 ***Lewis***	Y	Y	N	N	Y	Y	Y
3 ***Northup***	Y	Y	–	N	Y	Y	Y
4 Lucas	N	N	Y	Y	N	N	N
5 ***Rogers***	Y	Y	N	N	Y	Y	Y
6 ***Fletcher***	Y	Y	N	N	Y	Y	Y
LOUISIANA							
1 ***Vitter***	Y	Y	N	?	Y	Y	Y
2 Jefferson	N	N	Y	Y	N	N	N
3 ***Tauzin***	Y	Y	?	N	Y	Y	Y
4 ***McCrery***	Y	Y	N	?	Y	Y	Y
5 ***Cooksey***	Y	Y	N	N	Y	Y	Y
6 ***Baker***	Y	Y	N	N	Y	Y	Y
7 John	Y	N	Y	Y	Y	N	N
MAINE							
1 Allen	N	N	Y	Y	N	N	N
2 Baldacci	N	N	N	N	N	N	N
MARYLAND							
1 ***Gilchrest***	Y	Y	N	N	Y	Y	Y
2 ***Ehrlich***	Y	Y	N	N	Y	Y	Y
3 Cardin	N	N	Y	Y	N	N	N
4 Wynn	N	N	Y	Y	N	N	N
5 Hoyer	N	N	Y	Y	N	N	N
6 ***Bartlett***	Y	Y	N	N	Y	Y	Y
7 Cummings	N	?	Y	Y	N	N	N
8 ***Morella***	Y	Y	N	N	Y	?	Y
MASSACHUSETTS							
1 Olver	N	N	Y	Y	N	N	N
2 Neal	N	N	Y	Y	N	N	N
3 McGovern	N	N	Y	Y	N	N	N
4 Frank	N	N	Y	Y	N	N	N
5 Meehan	N	N	Y	Y	N	N	N
6 Tierney	N	?	Y	Y	N	N	N
7 Markey	N	N	Y	Y	N	N	N
8 Capuano	N	N	Y	Y	N	N	N
9 Moakley	N	Y	Y	Y	N	N	N
10 Delahunt	N	N	?	Y	N	N	N
MICHIGAN							
1 Stupak	?	?	?	?	?	?	?
2 ***Hoekstra***	Y	Y	N	N	Y	Y	Y
3 ***Ehlers***	Y	Y	N	N	Y	Y	Y
4 ***Camp***	Y	Y	N	N	Y	Y	Y
5 Barcia	N	N	N	N	N	N	N
6 ***Upton***	Y	Y	N	N	Y	Y	Y
7 ***Smith***	Y	Y	N	N	Y	Y	Y
8 ***Rogers***	Y	Y	N	N	Y	Y	Y
9 Kildee	N	Y	Y	Y	N	N	N
10 Bonior	N	?	Y	Y	N	N	N
11 ***Knollenberg***	Y	Y	N	N	Y	Y	Y
12 Levin	N	N	Y	Y	N	N	N
13 Rivers	N	N	Y	Y	N	N	N
14 Conyers	N	Y	Y	Y	N	N	N
15 Kilpatrick	N	N	Y	Y	Y	N	N
16 Dingell	N	Y	Y	Y	N	N	N

	33	34	35	36	37	38	39
MINNESOTA							
1 ***Gutknecht***	Y	Y	N	N	Y	Y	Y
2 ***Kennedy***	Y	Y	N	N	Y	Y	Y
3 ***Ramstad***	Y	N	N	N	Y	Y	Y
4 McCollum	N	N	Y	Y	N	N	N
5 Sabo	N	N	Y	Y	N	N	N
6 Luther	N	N	Y	Y	N	N	N
7 Peterson	N	N	Y	Y	N	N	N
8 Oberstar	N	N	Y	Y	N	N	N
MISSISSIPPI							
1 ***Wicker***	Y	Y	N	N	Y	Y	Y
2 Thompson	N	N	Y	Y	N	N	N
3 ***Pickering***	Y	Y	N	N	?	Y	Y
4 Shows	?	?	?	?	?	?	?
5 Taylor	Y	N	Y	Y	N	N	N
MISSOURI							
1 Clay	N	N	Y	Y	N	N	N
2 ***Akin***	Y	Y	N	N	Y	Y	Y
3 Gephardt	N	N	Y	Y	N	N	N
4 Skelton	Y	?	?	?	?	?	?
5 McCarthy	N	N	Y	Y	N	N	N
6 ***Graves***	Y	Y	N	N	Y	Y	Y
7 ***Blunt***	Y	Y	N	N	Y	Y	Y
8 ***Emerson***	Y	Y	N	N	Y	Y	Y
9 ***Hulshof***	Y	N	N	N	Y	Y	Y
MONTANA							
AL ***Rehberg***	Y	Y	N	N	Y	Y	Y
NEBRASKA							
1 ***Bereuter***	Y	Y	N	N	Y	Y	Y
2 ***Terry***	Y	Y	N	N	Y	Y	Y
3 ***Osborne***	Y	Y	N	N	Y	Y	Y
NEVADA							
1 Berkley	N	N	Y	Y	N	N	N
2 ***Gibbons***	Y	Y	N	N	Y	Y	Y
NEW HAMPSHIRE							
1 ***Sununu***	Y	Y	N	N	Y	Y	Y
2 ***Bass***	Y	Y	N	N	Y	Y	Y
NEW JERSEY							
1 Andrews	N	N	Y	Y	N	N	N
2 ***LoBiondo***	N	Y	N	N	Y	Y	Y
3 ***Saxton***	N	Y	?	N	Y	Y	Y
4 ***Smith***	N	Y	?	N	Y	Y	Y
5 ***Roukema***	Y	Y	N	N	Y	Y	Y
6 Pallone	N	N	Y	Y	N	N	N
7 ***Ferguson***	N	Y	N	N	Y	Y	Y
8 Pascrell	N	N	Y	Y	N	N	N
9 Rothman	N	N	Y	Y	N	N	N
10 Payne	N	Y	Y	Y	N	N	N
11 ***Frelinghuysen***	Y	Y	N	N	Y	Y	Y
12 Holt	N	N	Y	Y	N	N	N
13 Menendez	N	N	Y	Y	N	N	N
NEW MEXICO							
1 ***Wilson***	Y	Y	N	N	Y	Y	Y
2 ***Skeen***	Y	Y	N	N	Y	Y	Y
3 Udall	N	N	Y	Y	N	N	N
NEW YORK							
1 ***Grucci***	N	Y	N	N	Y	Y	Y
2 Israel	N	N	Y	Y	N	N	N
3 ***King***	N	Y	N	N	Y	Y	Y
4 McCarthy	N	N	Y	Y	N	N	N
5 Ackerman	N	?	?	?	?	?	?
6 Meeks	N	N	Y	Y	N	N	N
7 Crowley	N	N	Y	Y	N	N	N
8 Nadler	N	N	Y	Y	N	N	N
9 Weiner	N	N	Y	Y	N	N	N
10 Towns	N	N	Y	Y	N	N	N
11 Owens	N	?	Y	Y	N	N	N
12 Velázquez	N	N	Y	Y	N	N	N
13 ***Fossella***	Y	Y	N	N	Y	Y	Y
14 Maloney	N	Y	Y	Y	N	N	N
15 Rangel	N	N	Y	Y	N	N	N
16 Serrano	N	N	Y	Y	N	N	N
17 Engel	N	N	Y	Y	N	N	N
18 Lowey	N	N	Y	Y	N	N	N
19 ***Kelly***	Y	Y	N	N	Y	Y	Y
20 ***Gilman***	N	Y	N	N	Y	Y	Y
21 McNulty	N	N	Y	Y	N	N	N
22 ***Sweeney***	Y	Y	N	N	Y	Y	Y
23 ***Boehlert***	N	Y	N	N	Y	Y	Y
24 ***McHugh***	N	Y	N	N	Y	Y	Y
25 ***Walsh***	Y	Y	N	N	Y	Y	Y
26 Hinchey	N	N	Y	Y	N	N	N
27 ***Reynolds***	Y	Y	N	N	Y	Y	Y
28 Slaughter	N	N	Y	Y	N	N	N
29 LaFalce	N	N	Y	Y	N	N	N

	33	34	35	36	37	38	39
30 ***Quinn***	N	Y	N	N	Y	Y	Y
31 ***Houghton***	Y	Y	N	N	Y	Y	Y
NORTH CAROLINA							
1 Clayton	N	N	N	Y	N	N	N
2 Etheridge	N	N	N	N	N	N	N
3 ***Jones***	Y	?	N	N	Y	Y	Y
4 Price	N	N	Y	Y	N	N	N
5 ***Burr***	Y	?	N	N	Y	Y	Y
6 ***Coble***	Y	Y	N	N	Y	Y	Y
7 McIntyre	Y	N	Y	Y	N	N	N
8 ***Hayes***	Y	Y	N	N	Y	Y	Y
9 ***Myrick***	Y	Y	N	N	Y	Y	Y
10 ***Ballenger***	Y	Y	N	N	Y	Y	Y
11 ***Taylor***	Y	Y	N	N	Y	Y	Y
12 Watt	N	N	Y	Y	N	N	N
NORTH DAKOTA							
AL Pomeroy	N	N	Y	Y	N	N	N
OHIO							
1 ***Chabot***	Y	Y	N	N	Y	Y	Y
2 ***Portman***	Y	Y	N	N	Y	Y	Y
3 Hall	N	N	Y	Y	N	N	N
4 ***Oxley***	+	Y	N	N	Y	Y	Y
5 ***Gillmor***	Y	Y	N	N	Y	Y	Y
6 Strickland	N	N	Y	Y	N	N	N
7 ***Hobson***	Y	Y	N	N	Y	Y	Y
8 ***Boehner***	Y	Y	N	N	Y	Y	Y
9 Kaptur	N	N	Y	Y	N	N	N
10 Kucinich	N	N	N	N	N	N	N
11 Jones	N	N	Y	Y	N	N	N
12 ***Tiberi***	Y	Y	N	N	Y	Y	Y
13 Brown	N	N	Y	Y	N	N	N
14 Sawyer	N	N	Y	Y	N	N	N
15 ***Pryce***	Y	Y	N	N	Y	Y	Y
16 ***Regula***	Y	Y	N	N	Y	Y	Y
17 Traficant	N	Y	N	N	Y	Y	Y
18 ***Ney***	Y	Y	N	N	Y	Y	Y
19 ***LaTourette***	Y	?	?	N	Y	Y	Y
OKLAHOMA							
1 ***Largent***	Y	Y	N	N	Y	Y	Y
2 Carson	Y	N	Y	Y	N	N	N
3 ***Watkins***	Y	Y	N	N	Y	Y	Y
4 ***Watts***	Y	Y	N	N	Y	Y	Y
5 ***Istook***	Y	Y	N	N	Y	Y	Y
6 ***Lucas***	Y	Y	N	N	Y	Y	Y
OREGON							
1 Wu	N	Y	N	N	N	N	N
2 ***Walden***	Y	Y	N	N	Y	Y	Y
3 Blumenauer	N	N	N	N	N	N	N
4 DeFazio	N	N	Y	Y	N	N	N
5 Hooley	N	N	N	N	N	N	N
PENNSYLVANIA							
1 Brady	N	N	Y	Y	N	N	N
2 Fattah	N	?	?	Y	N	N	N
3 Borski	N	N	Y	Y	N	N	N
4 ***Hart***	Y	Y	N	N	Y	Y	Y
5 ***Peterson***	Y	Y	N	?	?	Y	Y
6 Holden	N	N	Y	Y	N	N	N
7 ***Weldon***	N	Y	N	N	Y	Y	Y
8 ***Greenwood***	Y	Y	N	N	Y	Y	Y
9 Vacant							
10 ***Sherwood***	Y	Y	N	N	Y	Y	Y
11 Kanjorski	N	N	Y	Y	N	N	N
12 Murtha	N	N	N	N	N	N	N
13 Hoeffel	N	N	Y	Y	N	N	N
14 Coyne	N	?	Y	Y	N	N	N
15 ***Toomey***	Y	Y	N	N	Y	Y	Y
16 ***Pitts***	Y	Y	N	N	Y	Y	Y
17 ***Gekas***	Y	Y	N	N	Y	Y	Y
18 Doyle	N	N	Y	Y	N	N	N
19 ***Platts***	Y	?	N	N	Y	Y	Y
20 Mascara	N	N	Y	Y	N	N	N
21 ***English***	Y	Y	N	N	Y	Y	Y
RHODE ISLAND							
1 Kennedy	N	N	Y	Y	N	N	N
2 Langevin	N	N	Y	Y	N	N	N
SOUTH CAROLINA							
1 ***Brown***	Y	Y	N	N	Y	Y	Y
2 ***Spence***	Y	Y	N	N	Y	Y	Y
3 ***Graham***	Y	Y	N	N	Y	Y	Y
4 ***DeMint***	Y	Y	N	N	Y	Y	Y
5 Spratt	Y	N	Y	Y	N	N	N
6 Clyburn	Y	Y	Y	Y	N	N	N
SOUTH DAKOTA							
AL ***Thune***	Y	Y	N	N	Y	Y	Y

	33	34	35	36	37	38	39
TENNESSEE							
1 ***Jenkins***	Y	Y	N	N	Y	Y	Y
2 ***Duncan***	Y	Y	N	N	Y	Y	Y
3 ***Wamp***	Y	Y	N	N	Y	Y	Y
4 ***Hilleary***	Y	Y	N	N	Y	Y	Y
5 Clement	Y	N	Y	Y	N	N	N
6 Gordon	N	Y	N	N	N	N	N
7 ***Bryant***	Y	Y	N	N	Y	Y	Y
8 Tanner	Y	N	Y	Y	N	N	N
9 Ford	N	N	Y	Y	N	N	N
TEXAS							
1 Sandlin	N	N	Y	Y	N	N	N
2 Turner	Y	N	Y	Y	N	N	N
3 ***Johnson, Sam***	Y	Y	N	N	Y	Y	Y
4 Hall	Y	Y	N	N	Y	N	Y
5 ***Sessions***	Y	Y	N	N	Y	Y	Y
6 ***Barton***	Y	?	N	N	Y	Y	Y
7 ***Culberson***	Y	Y	N	N	Y	Y	Y
8 ***Brady***	Y	Y	N	N	Y	Y	Y
9 Lampson	N	N	Y	Y	N	N	N
10 Doggett	N	N	Y	Y	N	N	N
11 Edwards	N	Y	N	N	N	N	N
12 ***Granger***	Y	Y	N	N	Y	Y	Y
13 ***Thornberry***	Y	Y	N	N	Y	Y	Y
14 ***Paul***	Y	Y	N	N	Y	Y	Y
15 Hinojosa	N	N	Y	Y	N	N	N
16 Reyes	N	N	N	Y	N	N	N
17 Stenholm	Y	N	Y	Y	N	N	N
18 Jackson-Lee	N	N	Y	Y	N	N	N
19 ***Combest***	Y	Y	N	N	Y	Y	Y
20 Gonzalez	N	N	Y	Y	N	N	N
21 ***Smith***	Y	Y	N	N	Y	Y	Y
22 ***DeLay***	Y	Y	N	N	Y	Y	Y
23 ***Bonilla***	Y	Y	N	N	Y	Y	Y
24 Frost	N	N	Y	Y	N	N	N
25 Bentsen	N	N	Y	N	N	N	N
26 ***Armey***	Y	Y	N	N	Y	Y	Y
27 Ortiz	N	Y	Y	Y	N	N	N
28 Rodriguez	N	N	Y	Y	N	N	N
29 Green	N	N	N	N	N	N	N
30 Johnson, E.B.	N	N	Y	Y	N	N	N
UTAH							
1 ***Hansen***	Y	Y	N	N	Y	Y	Y
2 Matheson	N	N	N	N	N	N	N
3 ***Cannon***	Y	Y	N	N	Y	Y	Y
VERMONT							
AL *Sanders*	N	N	Y	Y	N	N	N
VIRGINIA							
1 ***Davis, Jo Ann***	Y	Y	N	N	Y	Y	Y
2 ***Schrock***	Y	Y	N	N	Y	Y	Y
3 Scott	N	N	N	N	N	N	N
4 Sisisky	Y	N	Y	Y	N	N	N
5 *Goode*	Y	Y	N	N	Y	Y	Y
6 ***Goodlatte***	Y	Y	N	N	Y	Y	Y
7 ***Cantor***	Y	Y	N	N	Y	Y	Y
8 Moran	N	N	?	Y	N	N	N
9 Boucher	N	N	Y	Y	N	N	N
10 ***Wolf***	Y	Y	N	N	Y	Y	Y
11 ***Davis, T.***	Y	Y	N	N	Y	Y	Y
WASHINGTON							
1 Inslee	N	N	Y	Y	N	N	N
2 Larsen	N	N	Y	Y	N	N	N
3 Baird	N	N	Y	Y	N	N	N
4 ***Hastings***	Y	Y	?	N	Y	Y	Y
5 ***Nethercutt***	Y	Y	N	N	Y	Y	Y
6 Dicks	N	N	Y	N	N	N	N
7 McDermott	N	N	Y	Y	N	?	N
8 ***Dunn***	Y	Y	N	N	Y	Y	Y
9 Smith	N	N	Y	Y	N	N	N
WEST VIRGINIA							
1 Mollohan	N	Y	N	N	N	N	N
2 ***Capito***	Y	Y	N	N	Y	Y	Y
3 Rahall	N	N	N	N	N	N	N
WISCONSIN							
1 ***Ryan***	Y	Y	N	N	Y	Y	Y
2 Baldwin	N	N	Y	Y	N	N	N
3 Kind	N	N	N	Y	N	N	N
4 Kleczka	N	Y	N	N	N	N	N
5 Barrett	N	N	N	N	N	N	N
6 ***Petri***	N	Y	N	N	Y	Y	Y
7 Obey	N	N	Y	N	N	N	N
8 ***Green***	Y	Y	N	N	Y	Y	Y
9 ***Sensenbrenner***	Y	Y	N	N	Y	Y	Y
WYOMING							
AL ***Cubin***	Y	Y	N	N	Y	?	?

Southern states - Ala., Ark., Fla., Ga., Ky., La., Miss., N.C., Okla., S.C., Tenn., Texas, Va.

Key

40. HR 3. Income Tax Reduction/Rule Reconsideration. Reynolds, R-N.Y., motion to table (kill) the Pryce, R-Ohio, motion to reconsider the vote on adoption of the rule (H Res 83) to provide for House floor consideration of the bill that would lower federal income taxes by restructuring five tax brackets into four — 10 percent, 15 percent, 25 percent and 33 percent. Motion agreed to 221-197: R 215-0; D 5-196 (ND 4-146, SD 1-50); I 1-1. March 8, 2001.

41. Procedural Motion/Adjourn. Hill, D-Ind., motion to adjourn. Motion rejected 160-253: R 0-209; D 159-43 (ND 117-34, SD 42-9); I 1-1. March 8, 2001.

42. HR 3. Income Tax Reduction/Democratic Substitute. Rangel, D-N.Y., substitute amendment that would create a new 12 percent tax rate to be phased in over three years; expand the earned income tax credit; double the married couple deduction; and adjust the alternative minimum tax so that filers would receive the rate reduction benefits. Rejected 155-273: R 0-219; D 154-53 (ND 117-36, SD 37-17); I 1-1. March 8, 2001.

43. HR 3. Income Tax Reduction/Substitute Amendment Reconsideration. Thomas, R-Calif., motion to table (kill) the Berry, D-Ark., motion to reconsider the vote on the Rangel, D-N.Y., substitute amendment that would create a new 12 percent tax rate to be phased in over three years; expand the earned income tax credit; double the married couple deduction; and adjust the alternative minimum tax so that filers would receive the rate reduction benefits. Motion agreed to 228-197: R 216-0; D 11-196 (ND 6-147, SD 5-49); I 1-1. March 8, 2001.

44. HR 3. Income Tax Reduction/Recommit. Stenholm, D-Texas, motion to recommit the bill to the House Ways and Means Committee with instructions not to report the bill back until April 15, 2001, unless Congress has completed action on the concurrent budget resolution for fiscal 2002. Motion rejected 204-221: R 0-218; D 203-2 (ND 151-1, SD 52-1); I 1-1. March 8, 2001.

45. HR 3. Income Tax Reduction/Passage. Passage of the bill that would lower federal income taxes by restructuring the five existing tax brackets into four — 10 percent, 15 percent, 25 percent and 33 percent. Passed 230-198: R 219-0; D 10-197 (ND 3-150, SD 7-47); I 1-1. A "yea" was a vote in support of the president's position. March 8, 2001.

	40	41	42	43	44	45
ALABAMA						
1 *Callahan*	Y	N	N	Y	N	Y
2 *Everett*	Y	N	N	Y	N	Y
3 *Riley*	Y	N	N	Y	N	Y
4 *Aderholt*	Y	N	N	Y	Y	Y
5 Cramer	N	Y	Y	Y	Y	Y
6 *Bachus*	Y	?	N	Y	N	Y
7 Hilliard	N	Y	Y	N	Y	N
ALASKA						
AL *Young*	Y	N	N	Y	N	Y
ARIZONA						
1 *Flake*	Y	N	N	Y	N	Y
2 Pastor	N	N	N	N	Y	N
3 *Stump*	Y	N	N	Y	N	Y
4 *Shadegg*	Y	N	N	Y	N	Y
5 *Kolbe*	Y	N	N	Y	N	Y
6 *Hayworth*	Y	N	N	Y	N	Y
ARKANSAS						
1 Berry	N	Y	N	N	Y	N
2 Snyder	N	Y	N	Y	Y	N
3 *Hutchinson*	Y	N	N	Y	N	Y
4 Ross	N	Y	N	N	Y	N
CALIFORNIA						
1 Thompson	N	Y	N	N	Y	N
2 *Herger*	Y	N	N	Y	N	Y
3 *Ose*	Y	N	N	Y	N	Y
4 *Doolittle*	Y	N	N	Y	N	Y
5 Matsui	N	Y	Y	N	Y	N
6 Woolsey	N	Y	N	N	Y	N
7 Miller, George	N	Y	Y	N	Y	N
8 Pelosi	N	Y	Y	N	Y	N
9 Lee	N	Y	N	N	Y	N
10 Tauscher	N	Y	N	N	Y	N
11 *Pombo*	Y	N	N	Y	N	Y
12 Lantos	N	Y	Y	N	Y	N
13 Stark	N	Y	Y	N	Y	N
14 Eshoo	N	Y	N	N	Y	N
15 Honda	N	N	Y	N	Y	N
16 Lofgren	N	N	Y	N	Y	N
17 Farr	N	Y	Y	N	Y	N
18 Condit	N	Y	Y	Y	Y	Y
19 *Radanovich*	Y	N	N	Y	N	Y
20 Dooley	N	N	N	Y	N	N
21 *Thomas*	Y	N	N	Y	N	Y
22 Capps	N	Y	Y	N	Y	N
23 *Gallegly*	Y	N	N	Y	N	Y
24 Sherman	N	N	N	N	Y	N
25 *McKeon*	Y	N	N	Y	N	Y
26 Berman	N	Y	Y	N	Y	N
27 Schiff	N	Y	N	N	Y	N
28 *Dreier*	Y	N	N	Y	N	Y
29 Waxman	N	Y	Y	N	Y	N
30 Becerra	N	Y	Y	N	Y	N
31 Solis	N	Y	Y	N	Y	N
32 Vacant						
33 Roybal-Allard	N	Y	Y	N	Y	N
34 Napolitano	N	Y	Y	N	Y	N
35 Waters	N	Y	Y	N	Y	N
36 Harman	N	Y	N	N	Y	N
37 Millender-McD.	N	Y	Y	N	Y	N
38 *Horn*	Y	N	N	Y	N	Y

	40	41	42	43	44	45
39 *Royce*	Y	N	N	Y	N	Y
40 *Lewis*	?	?	?	?	?	Y
41 *Miller, Gary*	Y	N	N	Y	N	Y
42 Baca	N	Y	N	Y	N	N
43 *Calvert*	Y	N	N	Y	N	Y
44 *Bono*	Y	N	N	Y	N	Y
45 *Rohrabacher*	Y	N	N	Y	N	Y
46 Sanchez	N	Y	N	N	Y	N
47 *Cox*	Y	N	N	Y	N	Y
48 *Issa*	Y	N	N	Y	N	Y
49 Davis	N	Y	Y	N	Y	N
50 Filner	N	Y	N	N	Y	N
51 *Cunningham*	Y	N	N	Y	N	Y
52 *Hunter*	Y	N	N	Y	N	Y
COLORADO						
1 DeGette	N	Y	Y	N	Y	N
2 Udall	N	Y	Y	N	Y	N
3 *McInnis*	Y	N	N	Y	N	Y
4 *Schaffer*	Y	N	N	Y	N	Y
5 *Hefley*	Y	N	N	Y	N	Y
6 *Tancredo*	Y	N	N	Y	N	Y
CONNECTICUT						
1 Larson	N	Y	Y	N	Y	N
2 *Simmons*	Y	N	N	Y	N	Y
3 DeLauro	N	Y	Y	N	Y	N
4 *Shays*	Y	N	N	Y	N	Y
5 Maloney	N	?	Y	N	Y	N
6 *Johnson*	Y	N	N	Y	N	Y
DELAWARE						
AL *Castle*	Y	N	N	Y	N	Y
FLORIDA						
1 *Scarborough*	Y	N	N	Y	N	Y
2 Boyd	N	Y	Y	Y	N	Y
3 Brown	N	Y	N	N	Y	N
4 *Crenshaw*	Y	N	N	Y	N	Y
5 Thurman	N	N	N	N	Y	N
6 *Stearns*	Y	N	N	Y	N	Y
7 *Mica*	Y	N	N	Y	N	Y
8 *Keller*	Y	N	N	Y	N	Y
9 *Bilirakis*	Y	N	N	Y	N	Y
10 *Young*	Y	N	N	Y	N	Y
11 Davis	N	N	N	Y	Y	N
12 *Putnam*	Y	N	N	Y	N	Y
13 *Miller*	Y	N	N	Y	N	Y
14 *Goss*	Y	N	N	Y	N	Y
15 *Weldon*	Y	N	N	Y	N	Y
16 *Foley*	Y	N	N	Y	N	Y
17 Meek	N	Y	Y	N	Y	N
18 *Ros-Lehtinen*	Y	N	N	Y	N	Y
19 Wexler	N	Y	Y	N	Y	N
20 Deutsch	N	Y	Y	N	Y	N
21 *Diaz-Balart*	Y	N	N	Y	N	Y
22 *Shaw*	Y	N	N	Y	N	Y
23 Hastings	N	Y	Y	N	Y	N
GEORGIA						
1 *Kingston*	Y	N	N	Y	N	Y
2 Bishop	N	Y	Y	N	?	Y
3 *Collins*	Y	N	N	Y	N	Y
4 McKinney	N	Y	Y	N	Y	N
5 Lewis	N	Y	Y	N	Y	N
6 *Isakson*	Y	N	N	Y	N	Y
7 *Barr*	Y	N	N	Y	N	Y
8 *Chambliss*	Y	N	N	Y	N	Y
9 *Deal*	Y	N	N	Y	N	Y
10 *Norwood*	Y	N	N	Y	N	Y
11 *Linder*	Y	N	N	Y	N	Y
HAWAII						
1 Abercrombie	N	N	Y	N	Y	N
2 Mink	N	Y	Y	N	Y	N
IDAHO						
1 *Otter*	Y	N	N	Y	N	Y
2 *Simpson*	Y	N	N	Y	N	Y
ILLINOIS						
1 Rush	N	Y	N	N	Y	N
2 Jackson	N	Y	N	N	Y	N
3 Lipinski	N	Y	Y	N	Y	N
4 Gutierrez	N	Y	N	N	Y	N
5 Blagojevich	N	Y	Y	N	Y	N
6 *Hyde*	Y	N	N	Y	N	Y
7 Davis	N	Y	Y	N	Y	N
8 *Crane*	Y	N	N	Y	N	Y
9 Schakowsky	N	Y	Y	N	Y	N
10 *Kirk*	Y	N	N	Y	N	Y
11 *Weller*	Y	N	N	Y	N	Y
12 Costello	N	N	N	N	Y	N
13 *Biggert*	Y	N	N	Y	N	Y

ND Northern Democrats   SD Southern Democrats

	40	41	42	43	44	45
14 ***Hastert***			N	Y	N	Y
15 ***Johnson***	Y	N	N	Y	N	Y
16 ***Manzullo***	Y	N	N	Y	N	Y
17 Evans	N	N	Y	N	Y	N
18 ***LaHood***	Y	N	N	Y	N	Y
19 Phelps	N	Y	N	N	Y	N
20 ***Shimkus***	Y	N	N	Y	N	Y

INDIANA	40	41	42	43	44	45
1 Visclosky	N	Y	N	N	Y	N
2 ***Pence***	Y	N	N	Y	N	Y
3 Roemer	N	N	Y	N	Y	N
4 ***Souder***	Y	N	N	Y	N	Y
5 ***Buyer***	Y	N	N	Y	N	Y
6 ***Burton***	Y	N	N	Y	N	Y
7 ***Kerns***	Y	N	N	Y	N	Y
8 ***Hostettler***	Y	N	N	Y	N	Y
9 Hill	N	Y	N	Y	Y	N
10 Carson	N	Y	Y	N	Y	N

IOWA	40	41	42	43	44	45
1 ***Leach***	Y	N	N	Y	N	Y
2 ***Nussle***	Y	N	N	Y	N	Y
3 Boswell	N	Y	Y	N	Y	N
4 ***Ganske***	Y	N	N	Y	N	Y
5 ***Latham***	Y	N	N	Y	N	Y

KANSAS	40	41	42	43	44	45
1 ***Moran***	Y	N	N	Y	N	Y
2 ***Ryun***	Y	N	N	Y	N	Y
3 Moore	N	N	N	Y	Y	N
4 ***Tiahrt***	Y	N	N	Y	N	Y

KENTUCKY	40	41	42	43	44	45
1 ***Whitfield***	Y	N	N	Y	N	Y
2 ***Lewis***	Y	N	N	Y	N	Y
3 ***Northup***	Y	N	N	Y	N	Y
4 Lucas	N	Y	N	Y	Y	Y
5 ***Rogers***	Y	N	N	Y	N	Y
6 ***Fletcher***	Y	N	N	Y	N	Y

LOUISIANA	40	41	42	43	44	45
1 ***Vitter***	Y	N	N	Y	N	Y
2 Jefferson	N	Y	Y	N	Y	N
3 ***Tauzin***	Y	N	N	Y	N	Y
4 ***McCrery***	Y	N	N	Y	N	Y
5 ***Cooksey***	Y	N	N	Y	N	Y
6 ***Baker***	Y	N	N	Y	N	Y
7 John	N	Y	Y	N	Y	N

MAINE	40	41	42	43	44	45
1 Allen	N	Y	Y	N	Y	N
2 Baldacci	N	Y	Y	N	Y	N

MARYLAND	40	41	42	43	44	45
1 ***Gilchrest***	Y	N	N	Y	N	Y
2 ***Ehrlich***	Y	N	N	Y	N	Y
3 Cardin	N	Y	Y	N	Y	N
4 Wynn	N	Y	Y	N	Y	N
5 Hoyer	N	Y	Y	N	Y	N
6 ***Bartlett***	Y	N	N	Y	N	Y
7 Cummings	N	Y	Y	N	Y	N
8 ***Morella***	Y	?	N	Y	N	Y

MASSACHUSETTS	40	41	42	43	44	45
1 Olver	N	Y	Y	N	Y	N
2 Neal	N	N	Y	N	Y	N
3 McGovern	N	Y	Y	N	Y	N
4 Frank	N	Y	Y	N	Y	N
5 Meehan	N	Y	Y	N	Y	N
6 Tierney	N	Y	Y	N	Y	N
7 Markey	N	Y	Y	N	Y	N
8 Capuano	N	Y	Y	N	Y	N
9 Moakley	?	?	Y	N	Y	N
10 Delahunt	N	Y	Y	N	Y	N

MICHIGAN	40	41	42	43	44	45
1 Stupak	?	?	?	?	?	?
2 ***Hoekstra***	Y	N	N	Y	N	Y
3 ***Ehlers***	Y	N	N	Y	N	Y
4 ***Camp***	Y	N	N	Y	N	Y
5 Barcia	N	N	Y	N	Y	N
6 ***Upton***	Y	N	N	Y	N	Y
7 ***Smith***	Y	N	N	Y	N	Y
8 ***Rogers***	Y	N	N	Y	N	Y
9 Kildee	N	Y	Y	N	Y	N
10 Bonior	N	Y	Y	N	Y	N
11 ***Knollenberg***	Y	?	N	Y	N	Y
12 Levin	N	Y	Y	N	Y	N
13 Rivers	N	N	Y	N	Y	N
14 Conyers	N	Y	N	N	Y	N
15 Kilpatrick	N	Y	Y	N	Y	N
16 Dingell	N	Y	Y	N	Y	N

MINNESOTA	40	41	42	43	44	45
1 ***Gutknecht***	Y	?	N	Y	N	Y
2 ***Kennedy***	Y	N	N	Y	N	Y
3 ***Ramstad***	Y	N	N	Y	N	Y
4 McCollum	N	Y	Y	N	Y	N
5 Sabo	N	Y	Y	N	Y	N
6 Luther	N	Y	Y	N	Y	N
7 Peterson	Y	Y	N	Y	Y	Y
8 Oberstar	N	N	Y	N	Y	N

MISSISSIPPI	40	41	42	43	44	45
1 ***Wicker***	Y	N	N	Y	N	Y
2 Thompson	N	Y	N	N	Y	N
3 ***Pickering***	Y	N	N	Y	N	Y
4 Shows	?	?	?	?	?	?
5 Taylor	N	Y	N	N	Y	N

MISSOURI	40	41	42	43	44	45
1 Clay	N	Y	Y	N	Y	N
2 ***Akin***	Y	N	N	Y	N	Y
3 Gephardt	N	Y	Y	N	Y	N
4 Skelton	?	?	?	?	?	?
5 McCarthy	N	Y	Y	N	Y	N
6 ***Graves***	Y	N	N	Y	N	Y
7 ***Blunt***	Y	N	N	Y	N	Y
8 ***Emerson***	Y	N	N	Y	N	Y
9 ***Hulshof***	Y	N	N	Y	N	Y

MONTANA	40	41	42	43	44	45
AL ***Rehberg***	Y	N	N	Y	N	Y

NEBRASKA	40	41	42	43	44	45
1 ***Bereuter***	Y	?	N	Y	N	Y
2 ***Terry***	Y	N	N	Y	N	Y
3 ***Osborne***	Y	N	N	Y	N	Y

NEVADA	40	41	42	43	44	45
1 Berkley	N	Y	Y	N	Y	N
2 ***Gibbons***	Y	N	N	Y	N	Y

NEW HAMPSHIRE	40	41	42	43	44	45
1 ***Sununu***	Y	N	N	Y	N	Y
2 ***Bass***	Y	N	N	Y	N	Y

NEW JERSEY	40	41	42	43	44	45
1 Andrews	N	Y	N	N	Y	N
2 ***LoBiondo***	Y	N	N	Y	N	Y
3 ***Saxton***	Y	N	N	Y	N	Y
4 ***Smith***	Y	N	N	Y	N	Y
5 ***Roukema***	Y	N	N	Y	N	Y
6 Pallone	N	Y	Y	N	Y	N
7 ***Ferguson***	Y	N	N	Y	N	Y
8 Pascrell	N	Y	Y	N	Y	N
9 Rothman	N	Y	Y	N	Y	N
10 Payne	N	Y	Y	N	Y	N
11 ***Frelinghuysen***	Y	N	N	Y	N	Y
12 Holt	N	Y	Y	N	Y	N
13 Menendez	N	Y	Y	N	Y	N

NEW MEXICO	40	41	42	43	44	45
1 ***Wilson***	Y	N	N	Y	N	Y
2 ***Skeen***	Y	N	N	Y	N	Y
3 Udall	N	N	Y	N	Y	N

NEW YORK	40	41	42	43	44	45
1 ***Grucci***	Y	N	N	Y	N	Y
2 Israel	N	Y	Y	N	Y	N
3 ***King***	Y	N	N	Y	N	Y
4 McCarthy	N	Y	Y	N	Y	N
5 Ackerman	?	?	?	?	?	?
6 Meeks	N	Y	N	N	Y	N
7 Crowley	N	Y	Y	N	Y	N
8 Nadler	N	Y	Y	N	Y	N
9 Weiner	N	Y	Y	N	Y	N
10 Towns	N	Y	N	N	Y	N
11 Owens	N	Y	Y	N	Y	N
12 Velázquez	N	Y	Y	N	Y	N
13 ***Fossella***	Y	N	N	Y	N	Y
14 Maloney	N	Y	Y	N	Y	N
15 Rangel	N	Y	Y	N	Y	N
16 Serrano	N	Y	N	N	Y	N
17 Engel	N	N	Y	N	Y	N
18 Lowey	N	Y	Y	N	Y	N
19 ***Kelly***	Y	N	N	Y	N	Y
20 ***Gilman***	Y	N	N	Y	N	Y
21 McNulty	N	Y	Y	N	Y	N
22 ***Sweeney***	Y	N	N	Y	N	Y
23 ***Boehlert***	Y	N	N	Y	N	Y
24 ***McHugh***	Y	N	N	Y	N	Y
25 ***Walsh***	Y	N	N	Y	N	Y
26 Hinchey	N	Y	Y	N	Y	N
27 ***Reynolds***	Y	N	N	Y	N	Y
28 Slaughter	N	Y	Y	N	Y	N
29 LaFalce	N	Y	Y	N	Y	N
30 ***Quinn***	Y	N	N	Y	N	Y
31 ***Houghton***	Y	N	N	Y	N	Y

NORTH CAROLINA	40	41	42	43	44	45
1 Clayton	N	Y	Y	N	Y	N
2 Etheridge	N	N	Y	N	Y	N
3 ***Jones***	Y	N	N	Y	N	Y
4 Price	N	N	Y	N	Y	N
5 ***Burr***	Y	N	N	Y	N	Y
6 ***Coble***	Y	N	N	Y	N	Y
7 McIntyre	N	Y	Y	N	Y	Y
8 ***Hayes***	Y	N	N	Y	N	Y
9 ***Myrick***	Y	N	N	Y	N	Y
10 ***Ballenger***	Y	N	N	?	?	?
11 ***Taylor***	Y	N	N	Y	N	Y
12 Watt	N	Y	Y	N	Y	N

NORTH DAKOTA	40	41	42	43	44	45
AL Pomeroy	N	Y	Y	N	Y	N

OHIO	40	41	42	43	44	45
1 ***Chabot***	Y	N	N	Y	N	Y
2 ***Portman***	Y	N	N	Y	N	Y
3 Hall	N	Y	Y	N	Y	N
4 ***Oxley***	Y	N	N	Y	N	Y
5 ***Gillmor***	Y	N	N	Y	N	Y
6 Strickland	?	Y	Y	N	Y	N
7 ***Hobson***	Y	N	N	Y	N	Y
8 ***Boehner***	Y	N	N	Y	N	Y
9 Kaptur	N	Y	N	N	?	N
10 Kucinich	N	N	Y	N	Y	N
11 Jones	N	Y	N	N	Y	N
12 ***Tiberi***	Y	N	N	Y	N	Y
13 Brown	N	Y	Y	N	Y	N
14 Sawyer	N	N	Y	N	Y	N
15 ***Pryce***	Y	N	N	Y	N	Y
16 ***Regula***	Y	N	N	Y	N	Y
17 Traficant	Y	N	N	Y	N	Y
18 ***Ney***	Y	N	N	Y	N	Y
19 ***LaTourette***	Y	N	N	Y	N	Y

OKLAHOMA	40	41	42	43	44	45
1 ***Largent***	?	N	N	Y	N	Y
2 Carson	N	Y	Y	N	Y	N
3 ***Watkins***	Y	N	N	Y	N	Y
4 ***Watts***	Y	N	N	Y	N	Y
5 ***Istook***	Y	N	N	Y	N	Y
6 ***Lucas***	Y	N	N	Y	N	Y

OREGON	40	41	42	43	44	45
1 Wu	N	N	Y	N	Y	N
2 ***Walden***	Y	N	N	Y	N	Y
3 Blumenauer	N	N	Y	N	Y	N
4 DeFazio	N	Y	Y	N	Y	N
5 Hooley	N	N	Y	N	Y	N

PENNSYLVANIA	40	41	42	43	44	45
1 Brady	N	Y	N	N	Y	N
2 Fattah	N	Y	N	N	Y	N
3 Borski	N	Y	N	N	Y	N
4 ***Hart***	Y	N	N	Y	N	Y
5 ***Peterson***	Y	N	N	Y	N	Y
6 Holden	N	Y	N	N	Y	N
7 ***Weldon***	Y	N	N	Y	N	Y
8 ***Greenwood***	?	?	N	Y	N	Y
9 Vacant						
10 ***Sherwood***	Y	N	N	Y	N	Y
11 Kanjorski	N	Y	N	N	Y	N
12 Murtha	N	N	N	N	Y	N
13 Hoeffel	N	N	N	N	Y	N
14 Coyne	?	Y	Y	N	Y	N
15 ***Toomey***	Y	N	N	Y	N	Y
16 ***Pitts***	Y	?	N	Y	N	Y
17 ***Gekas***	Y	N	N	Y	N	Y
18 Doyle	N	Y	Y	N	Y	N
19 ***Platts***	Y	N	N	Y	N	Y
20 Mascara	N	Y	Y	N	Y	N
21 ***English***	Y	N	N	Y	N	Y

RHODE ISLAND	40	41	42	43	44	45
1 Kennedy	N	Y	Y	N	Y	N
2 Langevin	N	Y	Y	N	Y	N

SOUTH CAROLINA	40	41	42	43	44	45
1 ***Brown***	Y	N	N	Y	N	Y
2 ***Spence***	Y	N	N	Y	N	Y
3 ***Graham***	Y	N	N	Y	N	Y
4 ***DeMint***	Y	N	N	Y	N	Y
5 Spratt	N	?	Y	N	Y	N
6 Clyburn	N	Y	N	N	Y	N

SOUTH DAKOTA	40	41	42	43	44	45
AL ***Thune***	Y	N	N	Y	N	Y

TENNESSEE	40	41	42	43	44	45
1 ***Jenkins***	Y	N	N	Y	N	Y
2 ***Duncan***	Y	N	N	Y	N	Y
3 ***Wamp***	Y	N	N	Y	N	Y
4 ***Hilleary***	Y	N	N	Y	N	Y
5 Clement	N	Y	Y	N	Y	Y
6 Gordon	N	N	Y	N	Y	Y
7 ***Bryant***	Y	N	N	Y	N	Y
8 Tanner	N	Y	N	N	Y	N
9 Ford	N	Y	N	N	Y	N

TEXAS	40	41	42	43	44	45
1 Sandlin	N	Y	N	N	Y	N
2 Turner	N	Y	Y	N	Y	N
3 ***Johnson, Sam***	Y	N	N	Y	N	Y
4 Hall	Y	N	N	Y	N	Y
5 ***Sessions***	Y	N	N	?	N	Y
6 ***Barton***	Y	N	N	Y	N	Y
7 ***Culberson***	Y	N	N	Y	N	Y
8 ***Brady***	Y	N	N	Y	N	Y
9 Lampson	N	Y	Y	N	Y	N
10 Doggett	N	Y	N	N	Y	N
11 Edwards	N	N	Y	N	Y	N
12 ***Granger***	Y	N	N	Y	N	Y
13 ***Thornberry***	Y	N	N	Y	N	Y
14 ***Paul***	Y	N	N	Y	N	Y
15 Hinojosa	?	Y	Y	N	Y	N
16 Reyes	N	Y	Y	N	Y	N
17 Stenholm	N	Y	N	N	Y	N
18 Jackson-Lee	N	Y	Y	N	Y	N
19 ***Combest***	Y	N	N	Y	N	Y
20 Gonzalez	N	Y	Y	N	Y	N
21 ***Smith***	Y	N	N	Y	N	Y
22 ***DeLay***	Y	N	N	Y	N	Y
23 ***Bonilla***	Y	N	N	Y	N	Y
24 Frost	?	?	Y	N	Y	N
25 Bentsen	?	?	N	N	Y	N
26 ***Armey***	Y	N	N	?	N	Y
27 Ortiz	N	Y	Y	N	Y	N
28 Rodriguez	N	Y	Y	N	Y	N
29 Green	N	N	Y	N	Y	N
30 Johnson, E.B.	N	Y	Y	N	Y	N

UTAH	40	41	42	43	44	45
1 ***Hansen***	Y	N	N	Y	N	Y
2 Matheson	N	N	N	N	Y	N
3 ***Cannon***	Y	N	N	Y	N	Y

VERMONT	40	41	42	43	44	45
AL *Sanders*	N	Y	Y	N	Y	N

VIRGINIA	40	41	42	43	44	45
1 ***Davis, Jo Ann***	Y	N	N	Y	N	Y
2 ***Schrock***	Y	N	N	Y	N	Y
3 Scott	N	N	Y	N	Y	N
4 Sisisky	N	Y	N	N	Y	N
5 *Goode*	Y	N	N	Y	N	Y
6 ***Goodlatte***	Y	N	N	Y	N	Y
7 ***Cantor***	Y	N	N	Y	N	Y
8 Moran	N	Y	Y	N	Y	N
9 Boucher	N	Y	Y	N	Y	N
10 ***Wolf***	Y	N	N	Y	N	Y
11 ***Davis, T.***	Y	?	N	Y	N	Y

WASHINGTON	40	41	42	43	44	45
1 Inslee	N	N	Y	N	Y	N
2 Larsen	N	Y	Y	N	Y	N
3 Baird	N	Y	Y	N	Y	N
4 ***Hastings***	Y	N	N	Y	N	Y
5 ***Nethercutt***	Y	N	N	Y	N	Y
6 Dicks	Y	N	Y	N	Y	N
7 McDermott	N	Y	N	N	Y	N
8 ***Dunn***	Y	N	N	Y	N	Y
9 Smith	N	Y	Y	N	Y	N

WEST VIRGINIA	40	41	42	43	44	45
1 Mollohan	N	N	N	N	Y	N
2 ***Capito***	Y	N	N	Y	N	Y
3 Rahall	N	N	N	N	Y	N

WISCONSIN	40	41	42	43	44	45
1 ***Ryan***	Y	N	N	Y	N	Y
2 Baldwin	N	Y	Y	N	Y	N
3 Kind	N	N	Y	N	Y	N
4 Kleczka	N	N	Y	N	Y	N
5 Barrett	N	N	Y	N	Y	N
6 ***Petri***	Y	N	N	Y	N	Y
7 Obey	N	N	Y	N	Y	N
8 ***Green***	Y	N	N	Y	N	Y
9 ***Sensenbrenner***	Y	N	N	Y	N	Y

WYOMING	40	41	42	43	44	45
AL ***Cubin***	?	?	N	Y	N	Y

Southern states - Ala., Ark., Fla., Ga., Ky., La., Miss., N.C., Okla., S.C., Tenn., Texas, Va.

Key

Y	Voted for (yea).
#	Paired for.
+	Announced for.
N	Voted against (nay).
X	Paired against.
–	Announced against.
P	Voted "present."
C	Voted "present" to avoid possible conflict of interest.
?	Did not vote or otherwise make a position known.

Democrats **Republicans**
Independents

46. HR 834. National Trails Purchasing Power/Passage. Hansen, R-Utah, motion to suspend the rules and pass the bill that would authorize federal agencies to purchase private property along nine national trail routes from owners willing to sell. Motion agreed to 409-3: R 209-3; D 198-0 (ND 144-0, SD 54-0); I 2-0. A two-thirds majority of those present and voting (275 in this case) is required for passage under suspension of the rules. March 13, 2001.

47. HR 223. Clear Creek Land Sale/Passage. Hansen, R-Utah, motion to suspend the rules and pass the bill that would extend until May 19, 2015, the time Clear Creek County, Colo., officials have to finish selling 7,300 acres of former Bureau of Land Management property. Motion agreed to 413-0: R 212-0; D 199-0 (ND 145-0, SD 54-0); I 2-0. A two-thirds majority of those present and voting (276 in this case) is required for passage under suspension of the rules. March 13, 2001.

48. HR 725. "Made in America" Products/Passage. Stearns, R-Fla., motion to suspend the rules and pass the bill that would direct the Commerce Department to establish a toll-free phone number to confirm that a product is "Made in America." Motion agreed to 407-3: R 207-3; D 198-0 (ND 148-0, SD 50-0); I 2-0. A two-thirds majority of those present and voting (274 in this case) is required for passage under suspension of the rules. March 14, 2001.

49. HR 861. Arbitration Language Correction/Passage. Sensenbrenner, R-Wis., motion to suspend the rules and pass the bill that would correct minor grammatical errors in Title 9, Section 10 of the U.S. Code, related to federal court arbitration proceedings. A two-thirds majority of those present and voting (276 in this case) is required for passage under suspension of the rules. Motion agreed to 413-0: R 211-0; D 200-0 (ND 149-0, SD 51-0); I 2-0. March 14, 2001.

50. HR 327. Small Business Paperwork Reduction/Passage. Passage of the bill that would reduce small business paperwork by requiring federal agencies to increase efforts in this area, ordering the Office of Management and Budget to publish regulations in the Federal Register and on its Web site, appointing liaisons within agencies, and establishing an inter-agency task force. Passed 418-0: R 210-0; D 206-0 (ND 152-0, SD 54-0); I 2-0. March 15, 2001.

	46	47	48	49	50
ALABAMA					
1 *Callahan*	Y	Y	Y	Y	Y
2 *Everett*	Y	Y	Y	Y	Y
3 *Riley*	Y	Y	Y	Y	Y
4 *Aderholt*	Y	Y	Y	Y	Y
5 Cramer	Y	Y	Y	Y	Y
6 *Bachus*	Y	Y	Y	Y	Y
7 Hilliard	Y	Y	Y	Y	Y
ALASKA					
AL *Young*	Y	Y	Y	Y	Y
ARIZONA					
1 *Flake*	N	Y	N	Y	Y
2 Pastor	Y	Y	Y	Y	Y
3 *Stump*	Y	Y	Y	Y	Y
4 *Shadegg*	Y	Y	Y	Y	Y
5 *Kolbe*	Y	Y	Y	Y	Y
6 *Hayworth*	Y	Y	Y	Y	Y
ARKANSAS					
1 Berry	Y	Y	Y	Y	Y
2 Snyder	Y	Y	Y	Y	Y
3 *Hutchinson*	Y	Y	Y	Y	Y
4 Ross	Y	Y	Y	Y	Y
CALIFORNIA					
1 Thompson	Y	Y	Y	Y	Y
2 *Herger*	Y	Y	Y	Y	Y
3 *Ose*	Y	Y	Y	Y	Y
4 *Doolittle*	Y	Y	Y	Y	Y
5 Matsui	Y	Y	Y	Y	Y
6 Woolsey	Y	Y	Y	Y	Y
7 Miller, George	Y	Y	?	?	Y
8 Pelosi	?	Y	Y	Y	Y
9 Lee	Y	Y	?	Y	Y
10 Tauscher	Y	Y	Y	Y	Y
11 *Pombo*	Y	Y	Y	Y	Y
12 Lantos	Y	Y	Y	Y	Y
13 Stark	Y	Y	Y	Y	Y
14 Eshoo	Y	Y	Y	Y	Y
15 Honda	Y	Y	Y	Y	Y
16 Lofgren	?	?	Y	Y	Y
17 Farr	Y	Y	Y	Y	Y
18 Condit	Y	Y	Y	Y	Y
19 *Radanovich*	Y	Y	Y	Y	Y
20 Dooley	Y	Y	Y	Y	Y
21 *Thomas*	Y	Y	Y	Y	Y
22 Capps	Y	Y	Y	Y	Y
23 *Gallegly*	Y	Y	Y	Y	Y
24 Sherman	Y	Y	Y	Y	Y
25 *McKeon*	Y	Y	Y	Y	Y
26 Berman	Y	Y	Y	Y	Y
27 Schiff	Y	Y	Y	Y	Y
28 *Dreier*	Y	Y	Y	Y	Y
29 Waxman	Y	Y	Y	Y	Y
30 Becerra	+	+	+	+	Y
31 Solis	Y	Y	Y	Y	Y
32 Vacant					
33 Roybal-Allard	Y	Y	Y	Y	Y
34 Napolitano	Y	Y	Y	Y	Y
35 Waters	Y	Y	Y	Y	Y
36 Harman	Y	Y	Y	Y	Y
37 Millender-McD.	Y	Y	Y	Y	Y
38 Horn	Y	Y	Y	Y	Y

	46	47	48	49	50
39 *Royce*	Y	Y	Y	Y	Y
40 *Lewis*	Y	?	Y	Y	Y
41 *Miller, Gary*	Y	Y	Y	Y	Y
42 Baca	Y	Y	Y	Y	Y
43 *Calvert*	Y	Y	Y	Y	Y
44 *Bono*	Y	Y	Y	Y	Y
45 *Rohrabacher*	Y	Y	Y	Y	Y
46 Sanchez	Y	Y	Y	Y	Y
47 *Cox*	?	?	Y	Y	Y
48 *Issa*	Y	Y	Y	Y	Y
49 Davis	Y	Y	Y	Y	Y
50 Filner	Y	Y	Y	Y	Y
51 *Cunningham*	Y	Y	Y	Y	Y
52 *Hunter*	Y	Y	?	Y	Y
COLORADO					
1 DeGette	Y	Y	Y	Y	Y
2 Udall	Y	Y	Y	Y	Y
3 *McInnis*	Y	Y	Y	Y	Y
4 *Schaffer*	Y	Y	N	Y	?
5 *Hefley*	Y	Y	Y	Y	Y
6 *Tancredo*	Y	Y	Y	Y	Y
CONNECTICUT					
1 Larson	Y	Y	Y	Y	Y
2 *Simmons*	Y	Y	Y	Y	Y
3 DeLauro	Y	Y	Y	Y	Y
4 *Shays*	Y	Y	Y	Y	Y
5 Maloney	Y	Y	Y	Y	Y
6 *Johnson*	Y	Y	Y	Y	Y
DELAWARE					
AL *Castle*	Y	Y	Y	Y	Y
FLORIDA					
1 *Scarborough*	Y	Y	Y	Y	?
2 Boyd	Y	Y	Y	Y	?
3 Brown	Y	Y	?	?	Y
4 *Crenshaw*	Y	Y	Y	Y	Y
5 Thurman	Y	Y	Y	Y	Y
6 *Stearns*	Y	Y	Y	Y	Y
7 *Mica*	Y	Y	Y	Y	Y
8 *Keller*	?	?	?	?	?
9 *Bilirakis*	Y	+	Y	Y	Y
10 *Young*	Y	Y	Y	Y	Y
11 Davis	Y	Y	Y	Y	Y
12 *Putnam*	Y	Y	Y	Y	Y
13 *Miller*	Y	Y	Y	Y	Y
14 *Goss*	Y	Y	Y	Y	Y
15 *Weldon*	Y	Y	Y	Y	Y
16 *Foley*	Y	Y	Y	Y	Y
17 Meek	Y	Y	?	?	Y
18 *Ros-Lehtinen*	?	?	?	Y	Y
19 Wexler	Y	Y	Y	Y	Y
20 Deutsch	Y	Y	Y	Y	Y
21 *Diaz-Balart*	Y	Y	Y	Y	Y
22 *Shaw*	Y	Y	Y	Y	Y
23 Hastings	?	?	Y	Y	Y
GEORGIA					
1 *Kingston*	Y	Y	Y	Y	Y
2 Bishop	Y	Y	Y	Y	Y
3 *Collins*	Y	Y	Y	Y	Y
4 McKinney	Y	Y	Y	Y	Y
5 Lewis	Y	Y	Y	Y	Y
6 *Isakson*	Y	Y	Y	Y	Y
7 *Barr*	?	Y	Y	Y	Y
8 *Chambliss*	Y	Y	Y	Y	Y
9 *Deal*	Y	Y	Y	Y	Y
10 *Norwood*	Y	Y	Y	Y	Y
11 *Linder*	Y	Y	Y	Y	Y
HAWAII					
1 Abercrombie	Y	Y	Y	Y	Y
2 Mink	Y	Y	Y	Y	Y
IDAHO					
1 *Otter*	Y	Y	Y	Y	Y
2 *Simpson*	Y	Y	Y	Y	Y
ILLINOIS					
1 Rush	Y	Y	Y	Y	Y
2 Jackson	Y	Y	Y	Y	Y
3 Lipinski	Y	Y	Y	Y	Y
4 Gutierrez	Y	Y	Y	Y	Y
5 Blagojevich	Y	Y	Y	Y	Y
6 *Hyde*	Y	Y	Y	Y	Y
7 Davis	Y	Y	?	Y	Y
8 *Crane*	Y	Y	Y	Y	Y
9 Schakowsky	Y	Y	Y	Y	Y
10 *Kirk*	+	Y	Y	Y	Y
11 *Weller*	Y	Y	Y	Y	Y
12 Costello	Y	Y	Y	Y	Y
13 *Biggert*	Y	Y	Y	Y	Y

ND Northern Democrats   SD Southern Democrats

Vote columns: **46 47 48 49 50**

	46	47	48	49	50
14 *Hastert*					
15 *Johnson*	Y	Y	Y	Y	Y
16 *Manzullo*	Y	Y	Y	Y	Y
17 Evans	Y	Y	Y	Y	?
18 *LaHood*	Y	Y	Y	Y	Y
19 Phelps	Y	Y	Y	Y	Y
20 *Shimkus*	Y	Y	Y	Y	Y

INDIANA

	46	47	48	49	50
1 Visclosky	Y	Y	Y	Y	Y
2 *Pence*	Y	Y	Y	Y	Y
3 Roemer	Y	Y	Y	Y	Y
4 *Souder*	Y	Y	Y	Y	Y
5 *Buyer*	Y	Y	Y	Y	Y
6 *Burton*	Y	Y	Y	Y	Y
7 *Kerns*	Y	Y	Y	Y	Y
8 *Hostettler*	Y	Y	Y	Y	Y
9 Hill	Y	Y	Y	Y	Y
10 Carson	Y	Y	Y	Y	Y

IOWA

	46	47	48	49	50
1 Leach	Y	Y	Y	Y	Y
2 *Nussle*	Y	Y	Y	Y	Y
3 Boswell	Y	Y	Y	Y	Y
4 *Ganske*	Y	Y	Y	Y	?
5 *Latham*	Y	Y	Y	Y	Y

KANSAS

	46	47	48	49	50
1 *Moran*	Y	Y	Y	Y	Y
2 *Ryun*	Y	Y	Y	Y	Y
3 Moore	Y	Y	Y	Y	Y
4 *Tiahrt*	Y	Y	Y	Y	Y

KENTUCKY

	46	47	48	49	50
1 *Whitfield*	Y	Y	Y	Y	Y
2 *Lewis*	Y	Y	Y	Y	Y
3 *Northup*	Y	Y	Y	Y	Y
4 Lucas	Y	Y	Y	Y	Y
5 *Rogers*	Y	Y	Y	Y	Y
6 *Fletcher*	Y	Y	Y	Y	Y

LOUISIANA

	46	47	48	49	50
1 *Vitter*	Y	Y	Y	Y	Y
2 Jefferson	Y	Y	?	Y	Y
3 *Tauzin*	Y	Y	Y	Y	Y
4 *McCrery*	Y	Y	Y	Y	Y
5 *Cooksey*	Y	Y	Y	Y	Y
6 *Baker*	Y	Y	Y	Y	Y
7 John	Y	Y	Y	Y	Y

MAINE

	46	47	48	49	50
1 Allen	Y	Y	Y	Y	Y
2 Baldacci	Y	Y	Y	Y	Y

MARYLAND

	46	47	48	49	50
1 *Gilchrest*	Y	Y	Y	Y	Y
2 *Ehrlich*	Y	Y	Y	Y	Y
3 Cardin	Y	Y	Y	Y	Y
4 Wynn	Y	Y	Y	Y	Y
5 Hoyer	Y	Y	Y	Y	Y
6 *Bartlett*	Y	Y	Y	Y	Y
7 Cummings	Y	Y	Y	Y	Y
8 *Morella*	Y	Y	Y	Y	Y

MASSACHUSETTS

	46	47	48	49	50
1 Olver	Y	Y	Y	Y	Y
2 Neal	?	?	Y	Y	Y
3 McGovern	Y	Y	Y	Y	Y
4 Frank	Y	Y	Y	Y	Y
5 Meehan	Y	Y	Y	Y	Y
6 Tierney	Y	Y	Y	Y	Y
7 Markey	Y	Y	Y	Y	Y
8 Capuano	Y	Y	Y	Y	Y
9 Moakley	?	?	?	?	?
10 Delahunt	Y	Y	Y	Y	Y

MICHIGAN

	46	47	48	49	50
1 Stupak	Y	Y	Y	Y	Y
2 *Hoekstra*	Y	Y	Y	Y	?
3 *Ehlers*	Y	Y	Y	Y	Y
4 *Camp*	Y	Y	Y	Y	Y
5 Barcia	Y	Y	Y	Y	Y
6 *Upton*	Y	Y	Y	Y	Y
7 *Smith*	Y	Y	Y	Y	Y
8 *Rogers*	Y	Y	Y	Y	Y
9 Kildee	Y	Y	Y	Y	Y
10 Bonior	Y	Y	Y	Y	Y
11 *Knollenberg*	Y	Y	Y	Y	Y
12 Levin	Y	Y	Y	Y	Y
13 Rivers	Y	Y	Y	Y	Y
14 Conyers	Y	Y	Y	Y	Y
15 Kilpatrick	Y	Y	Y	Y	Y
16 Dingell	Y	Y	Y	Y	Y

MINNESOTA

	46	47	48	49	50
1 *Gutknecht*	Y	Y	Y	Y	Y
2 *Kennedy*	Y	Y	Y	Y	Y
3 *Ramstad*	Y	Y	Y	Y	Y
4 McCollum	Y	Y	Y	Y	Y
5 Sabo	Y	Y	Y	Y	Y
6 Luther	Y	Y	Y	Y	Y
7 Peterson	Y	Y	Y	Y	Y
8 Oberstar	Y	Y	Y	Y	Y

MISSISSIPPI

	46	47	48	49	50
1 *Wicker*	Y	Y	Y	Y	Y
2 Thompson	Y	Y	Y	Y	Y
3 *Pickering*	Y	Y	Y	Y	Y
4 Shows	Y	Y	Y	Y	Y
5 Taylor	Y	Y	Y	Y	Y

MISSOURI

	46	47	48	49	50
1 Clay	Y	Y	Y	Y	Y
2 *Akin*	Y	Y	Y	Y	Y
3 Gephardt	?	?	Y	Y	?
4 Skelton	Y	Y	Y	Y	Y
5 McCarthy	Y	Y	Y	Y	Y
6 *Graves*	?	?	Y	Y	Y
7 *Blunt*	Y	Y	Y	Y	Y
8 *Emerson*	Y	Y	Y	Y	Y
9 *Hulshof*	Y	Y	Y	Y	Y

MONTANA

	46	47	48	49	50
AL *Rehberg*	Y	Y	Y	Y	Y

NEBRASKA

	46	47	48	49	50
1 *Bereuter*	Y	Y	Y	Y	Y
2 *Terry*	Y	Y	Y	Y	Y
3 *Osborne*	Y	Y	Y	Y	Y

NEVADA

	46	47	48	49	50
1 Berkley	Y	Y	Y	Y	Y
2 *Gibbons*	Y	Y	Y	Y	Y

NEW HAMPSHIRE

	46	47	48	49	50
1 *Sununu*	Y	Y	Y	Y	Y
2 *Bass*	Y	Y	Y	Y	Y

NEW JERSEY

	46	47	48	49	50
1 Andrews	Y	Y	Y	Y	Y
2 *LoBiondo*	Y	Y	Y	Y	Y
3 *Saxton*	Y	Y	?	?	Y
4 *Smith*	Y	Y	?	?	Y
5 *Roukema*	Y	Y	?	?	Y
6 Pallone	Y	Y	Y	Y	Y
7 *Ferguson*	Y	Y	?	?	Y
8 Pascrell	Y	Y	Y	Y	Y
9 Rothman	Y	Y	Y	Y	Y
10 Payne	Y	Y	Y	Y	Y
11 *Frelinghuysen*	Y	Y	?	?	Y
12 Holt	Y	Y	?	?	Y
13 Menendez	Y	Y	Y	Y	Y

NEW MEXICO

	46	47	48	49	50
1 *Wilson*	Y	Y	Y	Y	Y
2 *Skeen*	Y	Y	Y	Y	Y
3 Udall	Y	Y	Y	Y	Y

NEW YORK

	46	47	48	49	50
1 *Grucci*	Y	Y	Y	Y	Y
2 Israel	Y	Y	Y	Y	Y
3 *King*	Y	Y	Y	Y	Y
4 McCarthy	Y	Y	Y	Y	Y
5 Ackerman	?	?	?	?	?
6 Meeks	?	?	Y	Y	Y
7 Crowley	Y	Y	Y	Y	Y
8 Nadler	Y	Y	Y	Y	Y
9 Weiner	Y	Y	Y	Y	Y
10 Towns	?	?	?	?	Y
11 Owens	Y	Y	Y	Y	Y
12 Velázquez	Y	Y	Y	Y	Y
13 *Fossella*	Y	Y	Y	Y	Y
14 Maloney	Y	Y	Y	Y	Y
15 Rangel	Y	Y	Y	Y	Y
16 Serrano	Y	Y	Y	Y	Y
17 Engel	Y	Y	Y	Y	Y
18 Lowey	?	?	Y	Y	Y
19 *Kelly*	Y	Y	Y	Y	Y
20 *Gilman*	Y	Y	Y	Y	Y
21 McNulty	Y	Y	Y	Y	Y
22 *Sweeney*	Y	Y	Y	Y	Y
23 *Boehlert*	Y	Y	Y	Y	Y
24 *McHugh*	Y	Y	Y	Y	Y
25 *Walsh*	Y	Y	Y	Y	Y
26 Hinchey	Y	Y	Y	Y	Y
27 *Reynolds*	Y	Y	Y	Y	Y
28 Slaughter	Y	Y	Y	Y	Y
29 LaFalce	Y	Y	Y	Y	Y

	46	47	48	49	50
30 *Quinn*	Y	Y	Y	Y	Y
31 *Houghton*	Y	Y	Y	Y	Y

NORTH CAROLINA

	46	47	48	49	50
1 Clayton	Y	Y	Y	Y	Y
2 Etheridge	Y	Y	Y	Y	Y
3 *Jones*	Y	Y	Y	Y	?
4 Price	Y	Y	Y	Y	Y
5 *Burr*	Y	Y	Y	Y	Y
6 *Coble*	Y	Y	Y	Y	Y
7 McIntyre	Y	Y	Y	Y	Y
8 *Hayes*	Y	Y	Y	Y	Y
9 *Myrick*	Y	Y	Y	Y	Y
10 *Ballenger*	Y	Y	Y	Y	Y
11 *Taylor*	Y	Y	Y	Y	Y
12 Watt	Y	Y	Y	Y	Y

NORTH DAKOTA

	46	47	48	49	50
AL Pomeroy	?	?	Y	Y	Y

OHIO

	46	47	48	49	50
1 *Chabot*	Y	Y	Y	Y	Y
2 *Portman*	Y	Y	Y	Y	Y
3 Hall	Y	Y	Y	Y	Y
4 *Oxley*	Y	Y	Y	Y	Y
5 *Gillmor*	Y	Y	Y	Y	Y
6 Strickland	Y	Y	Y	Y	Y
7 *Hobson*	Y	Y	Y	Y	Y
8 *Boehner*	Y	Y	Y	Y	Y
9 Kaptur	Y	Y	Y	Y	Y
10 Kucinich	Y	Y	Y	Y	Y
11 Jones	Y	Y	Y	Y	Y
12 *Tiberi*	Y	Y	Y	Y	Y
13 Brown	Y	Y	Y	Y	Y
14 Sawyer	Y	Y	Y	Y	Y
15 *Pryce*	Y	Y	Y	Y	Y
16 *Regula*	Y	Y	Y	Y	Y
17 Traficant	Y	Y	Y	Y	Y
18 *Ney*	Y	Y	Y	Y	Y
19 *LaTourette*	Y	Y	Y	Y	Y

OKLAHOMA

	46	47	48	49	50
1 *Largent*	Y	Y	Y	Y	?
2 Carson	Y	Y	Y	Y	Y
3 *Watkins*	Y	Y	Y	Y	Y
4 *Watts*	Y	Y	Y	Y	Y
5 *Istook*	Y	Y	Y	Y	Y
6 *Lucas*	Y	Y	Y	Y	Y

OREGON

	46	47	48	49	50
1 Wu	Y	Y	Y	Y	Y
2 *Walden*	Y	Y	Y	Y	Y
3 Blumenauer	Y	Y	Y	Y	Y
4 DeFazio	Y	Y	Y	Y	Y
5 Hooley	Y	Y	Y	Y	Y

PENNSYLVANIA

	46	47	48	49	50
1 Brady	Y	Y	Y	Y	Y
2 Fattah	Y	Y	Y	Y	Y
3 Borski	Y	Y	Y	Y	Y
4 Hart	Y	Y	Y	Y	Y
5 *Peterson*	Y	Y	Y	Y	Y
6 Holden	Y	Y	Y	Y	Y
7 *Weldon*	Y	Y	Y	Y	Y
8 *Greenwood*	Y	Y	Y	Y	Y
9 Vacant					
10 *Sherwood*	Y	Y	Y	Y	Y
11 Kanjorski	Y	Y	Y	Y	Y
12 Murtha	Y	Y	Y	Y	Y
13 Hoeffel	Y	Y	Y	Y	Y
14 Coyne	Y	Y	Y	Y	Y
15 *Toomey*	Y	Y	Y	Y	Y
16 *Pitts*	Y	Y	Y	Y	Y
17 *Gekas*	Y	Y	Y	Y	Y
18 Doyle	Y	Y	Y	Y	Y
19 *Platts*	Y	Y	Y	Y	Y
20 Mascara	Y	Y	Y	Y	Y
21 *English*	Y	Y	Y	Y	Y

RHODE ISLAND

	46	47	48	49	50
1 Kennedy	Y	Y	Y	Y	Y
2 Langevin	Y	Y	Y	Y	Y

SOUTH CAROLINA

	46	47	48	49	50
1 *Brown*	Y	Y	Y	Y	Y
2 *Spence*	Y	Y	Y	Y	Y
3 *Graham*	Y	Y	Y	Y	Y
4 *DeMint*	Y	Y	Y	Y	Y
5 Spratt	Y	Y	Y	Y	Y
6 Clyburn	Y	Y	Y	Y	Y

SOUTH DAKOTA

	46	47	48	49	50
AL *Thune*	Y	Y	Y	Y	Y

TENNESSEE

	46	47	48	49	50
1 *Jenkins*	Y	Y	Y	Y	Y
2 *Duncan*	Y	Y	Y	Y	Y
3 *Wamp*	Y	Y	Y	Y	Y
4 *Hilleary*	Y	Y	Y	Y	?
5 Clement	Y	Y	Y	Y	Y
6 Gordon	Y	Y	Y	Y	Y
7 *Bryant*	Y	Y	Y	Y	Y
8 Tanner	Y	Y	Y	Y	Y
9 Ford	Y	Y	Y	Y	Y

TEXAS

	46	47	48	49	50
1 Sandlin	Y	Y	Y	Y	Y
2 Turner	Y	Y	Y	Y	Y
3 *Johnson, Sam*	Y	Y	Y	Y	Y
4 Hall	Y	Y	Y	Y	Y
5 *Sessions*	Y	Y	Y	Y	Y
6 *Barton*	Y	Y	?	?	Y
7 *Culberson*	Y	Y	Y	Y	Y
8 *Brady*	Y	Y	Y	Y	Y
9 Lampson	Y	Y	Y	Y	Y
10 Doggett	Y	Y	Y	Y	Y
11 Edwards	Y	Y	?	?	Y
12 *Granger*	Y	Y	Y	Y	Y
13 *Thornberry*	Y	Y	Y	Y	Y
14 *Paul*	N	Y	N	Y	Y
15 Hinojosa	Y	Y	Y	Y	Y
16 Reyes	Y	Y	Y	Y	Y
17 Stenholm	Y	Y	Y	Y	Y
18 Jackson-Lee	Y	Y	Y	Y	Y
19 *Combest*	Y	Y	Y	Y	Y
20 Gonzalez	Y	Y	Y	Y	Y
21 *Smith*	Y	Y	Y	Y	Y
22 *DeLay*	Y	Y	Y	Y	Y
23 *Bonilla*	Y	Y	Y	Y	Y
24 Frost	Y	Y	Y	Y	Y
25 Bentsen	Y	Y	Y	Y	Y
26 *Armey*	Y	Y	Y	Y	Y
27 Ortiz	Y	Y	Y	Y	Y
28 Rodriguez	Y	Y	Y	Y	Y
29 Green	Y	Y	Y	Y	Y
30 Johnson, E.B.	Y	Y	?	?	Y

UTAH

	46	47	48	49	50
1 *Hansen*	Y	Y	Y	Y	Y
2 Matheson	+	+	Y	Y	Y
3 *Cannon*	?	?	?	?	?

VERMONT

	46	47	48	49	50
AL *Sanders*	Y	Y	Y	Y	Y

VIRGINIA

	46	47	48	49	50
1 *Davis, Jo Ann*	N	Y	Y	Y	Y
2 *Schrock*	Y	Y	Y	Y	Y
3 Scott	Y	Y	Y	Y	Y
4 Sisisky	Y	Y	Y	Y	Y
5 *Goode*	Y	Y	Y	Y	Y
6 *Goodlatte*	Y	Y	Y	Y	Y
7 *Cantor*	Y	Y	Y	Y	Y
8 Moran	Y	Y	Y	Y	Y
9 Boucher	Y	Y	Y	Y	Y
10 *Wolf*	Y	Y	Y	Y	Y
11 *Davis, T.*	Y	Y	Y	Y	?

WASHINGTON

	46	47	48	49	50
1 Inslee	Y	Y	Y	Y	Y
2 Larsen	Y	Y	Y	Y	Y
3 Baird	Y	Y	Y	Y	Y
4 *Hastings*	Y	Y	Y	Y	Y
5 *Nethercutt*	Y	Y	Y	Y	Y
6 Dicks	Y	Y	Y	Y	Y
7 McDermott	Y	Y	Y	Y	Y
8 *Dunn*	Y	Y	Y	Y	Y
9 Smith	Y	Y	Y	Y	Y

WEST VIRGINIA

	46	47	48	49	50
1 Mollohan	Y	Y	Y	Y	Y
2 *Capito*	Y	Y	Y	Y	Y
3 Rahall	Y	Y	Y	Y	Y

WISCONSIN

	46	47	48	49	50
1 *Ryan*	Y	Y	Y	Y	Y
2 Baldwin	Y	Y	Y	Y	Y
3 Kind	Y	Y	Y	Y	Y
4 Kleczka	Y	Y	Y	Y	Y
5 Barrett	Y	Y	Y	Y	Y
6 *Petri*	Y	Y	Y	Y	Y
/ Obey	Y	Y	Y	Y	Y
8 *Green*	Y	Y	Y	Y	Y
9 *Sensenbrenner*	Y	Y	Y	Y	Y

WYOMING

	46	47	48	49	50
AL *Cubin*	Y	Y	Y	Y	Y

Southern states - Ala., Ark., Fla., Ga., Ky., La., Miss., N.C., Okla., S.C., Tenn., Texas, Va.

Key

Y	Voted for (yea).
#	Paired for.
+	Announced for.
N	Voted against (nay).
X	Paired against.
−	Announced against.
P	Voted "present."
C	Voted "present" to avoid possible conflict of interest.
?	Did not vote or otherwise make a position known.

Democrats   *Republicans*
Independents

51. H Res 67. Tuberculosis Awareness/Adoption. Ballenger, R-N.C., motion to suspend the rules and adopt the resolution that would support more funds in the fiscal 2002 foreign aid budget to prevent the spread of tuberculosis. Motion agreed to 405-2: R 209-1; D 195-0 (ND 143-0, SD 52-0); I 1-1. A two-thirds majority of those present and voting (272 in this case) is required for adoption under suspension of the rules. March 20, 2001.

52. H Con Res 41. El Salvador Earthquake Assistance/Adoption. Ballenger, R-N.C., motion to suspend the rules and adopt the resolution that would offer sympathy and support, including encouraging additional international aid, to El Salvador earthquake victims. Motion agreed to 405-1: R 209-1; D 194-0 (ND 143-0, SD 51-0); I 2-0. A two-thirds majority of those present and voting (271 in this case) is required for adoption under suspension of the rules. March 20, 2001.

53. H Con Res 43. Black Americans in Congress/Adoption. Ney, R-Ohio, motion to suspend the rules and adopt the resolution that would authorize a revised edition of the House-printed biographical and historical report "Black Americans in Congress, 1870-1989." Motion agreed to 414-1: R 208-1; D 204-0 (ND 152-0, SD 52-0); I 2-0. A two-thirds majority of those present and voting (277 in this case) is required for adoption under suspension of the rules. March 21, 2001.

54. HR 1042. Science Reports Preservation/Passage. Grucci, R-N.Y., motion to suspend the rules and pass the bill that would exempt 29 reports required to be submitted to the House Science Committee from elimination by the Federal Reports Elimination and Sunset Act of 1995. Motion agreed to 414-2: R 208-1; D 204-1 (ND 153-0, SD 51-1); I 2-0. A two-thirds majority of those present and voting (278 in this case) is required for passage under suspension of the rules. March 21, 2001.

55. HR 1098. Maritime Changes/Passage. LoBiondo, R-N.J., motion to suspend the rules and pass the bill that would authorize certain maritime changes, such as allowing $500,000 for an addition to the American Merchant Marine Memorial Wall of Honor in San Pedro, Calif., ensuring the recording of maritime liens on all U.S. flag vessels, and providing special treatment for certain named vessels, including exempting some from U.S. maritime regulations. Motion agreed to 415-3: R 209-2; D 204-1 (ND 153-0, SD 51-1); I 2-0. A two-thirds majority of those present and voting (279 in this case) is required for passage under suspension of the rules. March 21, 2001.

56. Procedural Motion/Adjourn. LaFalce, D-N.Y., motion to adjourn. Motion rejected 71-336: R 0-210; D 71-125 (ND 56-92, SD 15-33); I 0-1. March 22, 2001.

	51	52	53	54	55	56
ALABAMA						
1 *Callahan*	Y	Y	Y	Y	Y	N
2 *Everett*	Y	Y	Y	Y	Y	N
3 *Riley*	Y	Y	Y	Y	Y	N
4 *Aderholt*	Y	Y	Y	Y	Y	N
5 Cramer	?	?	Y	Y	Y	N
6 *Bachus*	Y	Y	Y	Y	Y	N
7 Hilliard	Y	Y	Y	Y	Y	Y
ALASKA						
AL *Young*	Y	Y	Y	Y	Y	N
ARIZONA						
1 *Flake*	Y	Y	Y	Y	N	N
2 Pastor	Y	Y	Y	Y	Y	N
3 *Stump*	Y	Y	Y	Y	Y	N
4 *Shadegg*	Y	Y	Y	Y	Y	N
5 *Kolbe*	Y	Y	Y	Y	Y	N
6 *Hayworth*	Y	Y	Y	Y	Y	N
ARKANSAS						
1 Berry	Y	Y	Y	Y	Y	Y
2 Snyder	Y	Y	Y	Y	Y	N
3 *Hutchinson*	Y	Y	Y	Y	Y	N
4 Ross	Y	Y	Y	Y	Y	N
CALIFORNIA						
1 Thompson	Y	Y	Y	Y	Y	N
2 *Herger*	Y	Y	Y	Y	Y	N
3 Ose	Y	Y	Y	Y	Y	N
4 *Doolittle*	Y	Y	Y	Y	Y	N
5 Matsui	?	?	Y	Y	Y	Y
6 Woolsey	Y	Y	+	Y	Y	Y
7 Miller, George	Y	Y	Y	Y	Y	Y
8 Pelosi	Y	Y	Y	Y	Y	Y
9 Lee	Y	Y	Y	Y	Y	Y
10 Tauscher	Y	Y	Y	Y	Y	Y
11 *Pombo*	Y	Y	Y	Y	Y	N
12 Lantos	Y	Y	Y	Y	Y	Y
13 Stark	Y	Y	Y	Y	Y	Y
14 Eshoo	Y	Y	Y	Y	Y	N
15 Honda	Y	Y	Y	Y	Y	N
16 Lofgren	Y	Y	Y	Y	Y	N
17 Farr	Y	Y	Y	Y	Y	N
18 Condit	Y	Y	Y	Y	Y	Y
19 *Radanovich*	Y	Y	Y	Y	Y	N
20 Dooley	Y	Y	Y	Y	Y	?
21 *Thomas*	?	Y	Y	Y	Y	Y
22 Capps	Y	Y	Y	Y	Y	Y
23 *Gallegly*	Y	Y	Y	Y	Y	N
24 Sherman	Y	Y	Y	Y	Y	N
25 *McKeon*	Y	Y	Y	Y	Y	N
26 Berman	Y	Y	Y	Y	Y	N
27 Schiff	Y	Y	Y	Y	Y	N
28 *Dreier*	Y	Y	Y	Y	Y	N
29 Waxman	Y	Y	Y	Y	Y	N
30 Becerra	?	?	?	?	?	?
31 Solis	Y	Y	Y	Y	Y	N
32 Vacant						
33 Roybal-Allard	Y	Y	Y	Y	Y	Y
34 Napolitano	Y	Y	Y	Y	Y	N
35 Waters	Y	Y	Y	Y	Y	N
36 Harman	Y	Y	Y	Y	Y	N
37 Millender-McD.	?	?	Y	Y	Y	N
38 *Horn*	Y	Y	Y	Y	Y	N

	51	52	53	54	55	56
39 *Royce*	Y	Y	Y	Y	Y	N
40 *Lewis*	Y	Y	Y	Y	Y	N
41 *Miller, Gary*	Y	Y	Y	Y	Y	N
42 Baca	Y	Y	Y	Y	Y	N
43 *Calvert*	Y	Y	Y	Y	Y	N
44 *Bono*	Y	Y	Y	Y	Y	N
45 *Rohrabacher*	Y	Y	Y	Y	Y	N
46 Sanchez	Y	Y	Y	Y	Y	N
47 *Cox*	Y	Y	Y	Y	Y	N
48 *Issa*	Y	Y	Y	Y	Y	N
49 Davis	Y	Y	Y	Y	Y	N
50 Filner	+	+	Y	Y	Y	Y
51 *Cunningham*	Y	Y	Y	Y	Y	N
52 *Hunter*	Y	Y	Y	Y	Y	N
COLORADO						
1 DeGette	Y	Y	Y	Y	Y	N
2 Udall	Y	Y	Y	Y	Y	Y
3 *McInnis*	Y	Y	Y	Y	Y	N
4 *Schaffer*	Y	Y	Y	Y	Y	N
5 *Hefley*	Y	Y	N	N	Y	N
6 *Tancredo*	Y	Y	Y	Y	Y	N
CONNECTICUT						
1 Larson	Y	Y	Y	Y	Y	N
2 *Simmons*	Y	Y	?	Y	Y	N
3 DeLauro	Y	Y	Y	Y	Y	N
4 *Shays*	Y	Y	Y	Y	Y	?
5 Maloney	Y	Y	Y	Y	Y	N
6 *Johnson*	Y	Y	Y	Y	Y	N
DELAWARE						
AL *Castle*	Y	Y	Y	Y	Y	N
FLORIDA						
1 *Scarborough*	?	?	?	?	?	?
2 Boyd	Y	Y	Y	Y	Y	N
3 Brown	?	?	?	?	?	?
4 *Crenshaw*	Y	Y	Y	Y	Y	N
5 Thurman	Y	Y	Y	Y	Y	N
6 *Stearns*	Y	Y	Y	Y	Y	N
7 *Mica*	Y	Y	?	?	?	N
8 *Keller*	?	?	+	+	+	N
9 *Bilirakis*	Y	Y	Y	Y	Y	N
10 *Young*	Y	Y	Y	Y	Y	N
11 Davis	Y	Y	Y	Y	Y	N
12 *Putnam*	Y	Y	Y	Y	Y	?
13 *Miller*	Y	Y	Y	Y	Y	N
14 Goss	Y	Y	Y	Y	Y	N
15 *Weldon*	Y	Y	?	?	?	N
16 *Foley*	Y	Y	Y	Y	Y	N
17 Meek	Y	Y	Y	Y	Y	Y
18 *Ros-Lehtinen*	Y	Y	Y	Y	Y	N
19 Wexler	Y	Y	Y	Y	Y	?
20 Deutsch	Y	Y	Y	Y	Y	N
21 *Diaz-Balart*	Y	Y	Y	Y	Y	N
22 *Shaw*	Y	Y	Y	Y	Y	N
23 Hastings	Y	Y	Y	Y	Y	Y
GEORGIA						
1 *Kingston*	Y	Y	Y	Y	Y	N
2 Bishop	Y	Y	Y	Y	Y	N
3 *Collins*	Y	Y	?	Y	Y	N
4 McKinney	Y	Y	Y	Y	Y	N
5 Lewis	Y	Y	Y	Y	Y	Y
6 *Isakson*	Y	Y	Y	Y	Y	N
7 *Barr*	Y	Y	Y	Y	Y	N
8 *Chambliss*	Y	Y	Y	Y	Y	N
9 *Deal*	Y	Y	Y	Y	Y	N
10 *Norwood*	Y	Y	Y	Y	Y	N
11 *Linder*	Y	Y	Y	Y	Y	N
HAWAII						
1 Abercrombie	Y	Y	Y	Y	Y	N
2 Mink	Y	Y	Y	Y	Y	Y
IDAHO						
1 *Otter*	Y	Y	Y	Y	Y	N
2 *Simpson*	Y	Y	Y	Y	Y	N
ILLINOIS						
1 Rush	?	?	Y	Y	Y	N
2 Jackson	Y	Y	Y	Y	Y	N
3 Lipinski	Y	Y	Y	Y	Y	N
4 Gutierrez	Y	Y	Y	Y	Y	N
5 Blagojevich	Y	Y	Y	Y	Y	N
6 *Hyde*	Y	Y	Y	Y	Y	N
7 Davis	Y	Y	Y	Y	Y	N
8 *Crane*	Y	Y	Y	Y	Y	N
9 Schakowsky	Y	Y	Y	Y	Y	N
10 *Kirk*	Y	Y	Y	Y	Y	N
11 *Weller*	Y	Y	Y	Y	Y	N
12 Costello	Y	Y	Y	Y	Y	N
13 *Biggert*	Y	Y	Y	Y	Y	N

ND Northern Democrats   SD Southern Democrats

	51	52	53	54	55	56
14 ***Hastert***						
15 ***Johnson***	Y	Y	Y	Y	Y	N
16 ***Manzullo***	?	?	Y	Y	Y	N
17 Evans	Y	Y	Y	Y	Y	N
18 ***LaHood***	Y	Y	Y	Y	Y	N
19 Phelps	Y	Y	Y	Y	Y	N
20 ***Shimkus***	Y	Y	Y	Y	Y	N
INDIANA						
1 Visclosky	Y	Y	Y	Y	Y	N
2 ***Pence***	Y	Y	Y	Y	Y	N
3 Roemer	Y	Y	Y	Y	Y	N
4 ***Souder***	Y	Y	Y	Y	Y	N
5 ***Buyer***	Y	Y	Y	Y	Y	N
6 ***Burton***	Y	Y	Y	Y	Y	N
7 ***Kerns***	Y	Y	Y	Y	Y	N
8 ***Hostettler***	Y	Y	Y	Y	Y	N
9 Hill	Y	Y	Y	Y	Y	Y
10 Carson	Y	Y	Y	Y	Y	Y
IOWA						
1 ***Leach***	Y	Y	Y	Y	Y	N
2 ***Nussle***	Y	Y	Y	Y	Y	N
3 Boswell	Y	Y	Y	Y	Y	N
4 ***Ganske***	Y	Y	Y	Y	Y	N
5 ***Latham***	Y	Y	Y	Y	Y	N
KANSAS						
1 ***Moran***	Y	Y	Y	Y	Y	N
2 ***Ryun***	Y	Y	Y	Y	Y	N
3 Moore	Y	Y	Y	Y	Y	N
4 ***Tiahrt***	+	+	Y	Y	Y	N
KENTUCKY						
1 ***Whitfield***	Y	Y	Y	Y	Y	N
2 ***Lewis***	Y	Y	Y	Y	Y	N
3 ***Northup***	Y	Y	Y	Y	Y	N
4 Lucas	Y	Y	Y	Y	Y	N
5 ***Rogers***	Y	Y	Y	Y	Y	N
6 ***Fletcher***	Y	Y	Y	Y	Y	N
LOUISIANA						
1 ***Vitter***	?	?	Y	Y	Y	N
2 Jefferson	Y	Y	Y	Y	Y	Y
3 ***Tauzin***	Y	Y	Y	Y	Y	N
4 ***McCrery***	Y	Y	Y	Y	Y	N
5 ***Cooksey***	Y	Y	Y	Y	Y	N
6 ***Baker***	Y	Y	Y	Y	Y	N
7 John	Y	Y	Y	Y	Y	N
MAINE						
1 Allen	Y	Y	Y	Y	Y	Y
2 Baldacci	Y	Y	Y	Y	Y	Y
MARYLAND						
1 ***Gilchrest***	Y	Y	Y	Y	Y	N
2 ***Ehrlich***	Y	Y	Y	Y	Y	N
3 Cardin	Y	Y	Y	Y	Y	N
4 Wynn	Y	Y	Y	Y	Y	N
5 Hoyer	Y	Y	Y	Y	Y	N
6 ***Bartlett***	Y	Y	Y	Y	Y	N
7 Cummings	Y	Y	Y	Y	Y	N
8 ***Morella***	Y	Y	Y	?	Y	?
MASSACHUSETTS						
1 Olver	Y	Y	Y	Y	Y	Y
2 Neal	Y	Y	Y	Y	Y	Y
3 McGovern	Y	Y	Y	Y	Y	Y
4 Frank	Y	Y	Y	Y	Y	Y
5 Meehan	Y	Y	Y	Y	Y	N
6 Tierney	Y	Y	Y	Y	Y	N
7 Markey	Y	Y	Y	Y	Y	N
8 Capuano	Y	Y	Y	Y	Y	Y
9 Moakley	?	?	?	?	?	?
10 Delahunt	Y	Y	Y	Y	Y	Y
MICHIGAN						
1 Stupak	?	?	Y	Y	Y	Y
2 ***Hoekstra***	Y	Y	Y	Y	Y	N
3 ***Ehlers***	Y	Y	Y	Y	Y	N
4 ***Camp***	Y	Y	Y	Y	Y	N
5 Barcia	Y	Y	Y	Y	Y	N
6 ***Upton***	Y	Y	Y	Y	Y	N
7 ***Smith***	Y	Y	Y	Y	Y	N
8 ***Rogers***	Y	Y	Y	Y	Y	N
9 Kildee	Y	Y	Y	Y	Y	N
10 Bonior	Y	Y	Y	Y	Y	Y
11 ***Knollenberg***	Y	Y	Y	Y	Y	N
12 Levin	Y	Y	Y	Y	Y	N
13 Rivers	Y	Y	Y	Y	Y	N
14 Conyers	Y	Y	Y	Y	Y	Y
15 Kilpatrick	Y	Y	Y	Y	Y	Y
16 Dingell	Y	Y	Y	Y	Y	N

	51	52	53	54	55	56
MINNESOTA						
1 ***Gutknecht***	Y	Y	Y	Y	Y	N
2 ***Kennedy***	Y	Y	Y	+	Y	N
3 ***Ramstad***	Y	Y	Y	Y	Y	N
4 McCollum	Y	Y	Y	Y	Y	N
5 Sabo	Y	Y	Y	Y	Y	N
6 Luther	Y	Y	Y	Y	Y	N
7 Peterson	Y	Y	Y	Y	Y	Y
8 Oberstar	Y	Y	Y	Y	Y	Y
MISSISSIPPI						
1 ***Wicker***	Y	Y	Y	Y	Y	N
2 Thompson	Y	Y	Y	Y	Y	N
3 ***Pickering***	Y	Y	Y	Y	Y	?
4 Shows	Y	Y	Y	Y	Y	N
5 Taylor	Y	Y	Y	N	N	N
MISSOURI						
1 Clay	Y	Y	Y	Y	Y	Y
2 ***Akin***	Y	Y	Y	Y	Y	N
3 Gephardt	Y	Y	Y	Y	Y	Y
4 Skelton	Y	Y	Y	Y	Y	N
5 McCarthy	Y	Y	Y	Y	Y	N
6 ***Graves***	Y	Y	Y	Y	Y	N
7 ***Blunt***	Y	Y	Y	Y	Y	N
8 ***Emerson***	Y	Y	Y	Y	Y	N
9 ***Hulshof***	Y	Y	Y	Y	Y	N
MONTANA						
AL ***Rehberg***	Y	Y	Y	Y	Y	N
NEBRASKA						
1 ***Bereuter***	Y	Y	Y	Y	Y	N
2 ***Terry***	Y	Y	Y	Y	Y	N
3 ***Osborne***	Y	Y	Y	Y	Y	N
NEVADA						
1 Berkley	Y	Y	Y	Y	Y	Y
2 ***Gibbons***	Y	Y	Y	Y	Y	N
NEW HAMPSHIRE						
1 ***Sununu***	Y	Y	Y	Y	Y	N
2 ***Bass***	Y	Y	Y	Y	Y	N
NEW JERSEY						
1 Andrews	Y	Y	Y	Y	Y	Y
2 ***LoBiondo***	Y	Y	Y	Y	Y	N
3 ***Saxton***	Y	Y	Y	Y	Y	N
4 ***Smith***	Y	Y	Y	Y	Y	N
5 ***Roukema***	Y	Y	Y	Y	Y	N
6 Pallone	Y	Y	Y	Y	Y	N
7 ***Ferguson***	Y	Y	Y	Y	Y	N
8 Pascrell	Y	Y	Y	Y	Y	N
9 Rothman	?	?	?	?	?	?
10 Payne	Y	Y	Y	Y	Y	Y
11 ***Frelinghuysen***	Y	Y	Y	Y	Y	N
12 Holt	Y	Y	Y	Y	Y	N
13 Menendez	Y	Y	Y	Y	Y	N
NEW MEXICO						
1 ***Wilson***	Y	Y	Y	Y	Y	N
2 ***Skeen***	Y	Y	Y	Y	Y	N
3 Udall	Y	Y	Y	Y	Y	N
NEW YORK						
1 ***Grucci***	Y	Y	Y	Y	Y	N
2 Israel	Y	Y	Y	Y	Y	Y
3 ***King***	Y	Y	Y	Y	Y	N
4 McCarthy	Y	Y	Y	Y	Y	N
5 Ackerman	Y	?	?	Y	Y	?
6 Meeks	Y	Y	Y	Y	Y	N
7 Crowley	Y	Y	Y	Y	Y	Y
8 Nadler	Y	Y	Y	Y	Y	Y
9 Weiner	Y	Y	Y	Y	Y	Y
10 Towns	Y	Y	Y	Y	Y	Y
11 Owens	?	?	Y	Y	Y	?
12 Velázquez	Y	Y	Y	Y	Y	N
13 ***Fossella***	Y	Y	Y	Y	Y	N
14 Maloney	Y	Y	Y	Y	Y	N
15 Rangel	Y	Y	Y	Y	Y	N
16 Serrano	?	Y	Y	Y	Y	N
17 Engel	Y	Y	Y	Y	Y	N
18 Lowey	Y	Y	Y	Y	Y	Y
19 ***Kelly***	Y	Y	Y	Y	Y	N
20 ***Gilman***	Y	Y	Y	Y	Y	N
21 McNulty	Y	Y	Y	Y	Y	Y
22 ***Sweeney***	Y	Y	Y	Y	Y	N
23 ***Boehlert***	Y	Y	Y	Y	Y	N
24 ***McHugh***	Y	Y	?	?	?	N
25 ***Walsh***	Y	Y	Y	Y	Y	N
26 Hinchey	Y	Y	Y	Y	Y	N
27 ***Reynolds***	Y	Y	Y	Y	Y	N
28 Slaughter	Y	Y	Y	Y	Y	Y
29 LaFalce	Y	Y	Y	Y	Y	Y

	51	52	53	54	55	56
30 ***Quinn***	Y	Y	Y	Y	Y	N
31 ***Houghton***	Y	Y	Y	Y	Y	N
NORTH CAROLINA						
1 Clayton	Y	Y	Y	Y	Y	Y
2 Etheridge	Y	Y	Y	Y	Y	N
3 ***Jones***	Y	Y	Y	Y	Y	N
4 Price	Y	Y	Y	Y	Y	Y
5 ***Burr***	Y	Y	Y	Y	Y	N
6 ***Coble***	Y	Y	Y	Y	Y	N
7 McIntyre	Y	Y	Y	Y	Y	Y
8 ***Hayes***	Y	Y	Y	Y	Y	N
9 ***Myrick***	Y	Y	Y	Y	Y	N
10 ***Ballenger***	Y	Y	Y	Y	Y	N
11 ***Taylor***	?	?	?	?	?	N
12 Watt	Y	Y	Y	Y	Y	N
NORTH DAKOTA						
AL Pomeroy	Y	Y	Y	Y	Y	N
OHIO						
1 ***Chabot***	Y	Y	Y	Y	Y	N
2 ***Portman***	Y	Y	Y	Y	Y	?
3 Hall	Y	Y	Y	Y	Y	Y
4 ***Oxley***	Y	Y	Y	Y	Y	N
5 ***Gillmor***	Y	Y	Y	Y	Y	N
6 Strickland	Y	Y	Y	Y	Y	N
7 ***Hobson***	Y	Y	Y	Y	Y	N
8 ***Boehner***	Y	Y	Y	Y	Y	N
9 Kaptur	Y	Y	Y	Y	Y	N
10 Kucinich	Y	Y	Y	Y	Y	N
11 Jones	Y	Y	Y	Y	Y	?
12 ***Tiberi***	Y	Y	Y	Y	Y	N
13 Brown	Y	Y	Y	Y	Y	N
14 Sawyer	Y	Y	Y	Y	Y	N
15 ***Pryce***	Y	Y	Y	Y	Y	N
16 ***Regula***	Y	Y	Y	Y	Y	N
17 Traficant	Y	Y	Y	Y	Y	N
18 ***Ney***	Y	Y	Y	Y	Y	N
19 ***LaTourette***	Y	Y	Y	Y	Y	N
OKLAHOMA						
1 ***Largent***	Y	Y	Y	Y	Y	N
2 Carson	Y	Y	Y	Y	Y	Y
3 ***Watkins***	Y	Y	Y	Y	Y	N
4 ***Watts***	Y	Y	Y	Y	Y	N
5 ***Istook***	Y	Y	Y	Y	Y	N
6 ***Lucas***	Y	Y	Y	Y	Y	N
OREGON						
1 Wu	Y	Y	Y	Y	Y	N
2 ***Walden***	Y	Y	Y	Y	Y	N
3 Blumenauer	Y	Y	Y	Y	Y	N
4 DeFazio	Y	Y	Y	Y	Y	Y
5 Hooley	Y	Y	Y	Y	Y	N
PENNSYLVANIA						
1 Brady	?	?	Y	Y	Y	N
2 Fattah	?	?	Y	Y	Y	N
3 Borski	Y	Y	Y	Y	Y	N
4 ***Hart***	Y	Y	Y	Y	Y	N
5 ***Peterson***	Y	Y	Y	Y	Y	N
6 Holden	Y	Y	Y	Y	Y	N
7 ***Weldon***	Y	Y	Y	Y	Y	N
8 ***Greenwood***	Y	Y	Y	Y	Y	N
9 Vacant						
10 ***Sherwood***	Y	Y	Y	Y	Y	N
11 Kanjorski	Y	Y	Y	Y	Y	Y
12 Murtha	?	?	Y	Y	Y	N
13 Hoeffel	Y	Y	Y	Y	Y	N
14 Coyne	Y	Y	Y	Y	Y	Y
15 ***Toomey***	Y	Y	Y	Y	Y	?
16 ***Pitts***	Y	Y	Y	Y	Y	N
17 ***Gekas***	Y	Y	Y	Y	Y	?
18 Doyle	Y	Y	Y	Y	Y	?
19 ***Platts***	Y	Y	Y	Y	Y	N
20 Mascara	Y	Y	Y	Y	Y	N
21 ***English***	Y	Y	Y	Y	Y	N
RHODE ISLAND						
1 Kennedy	Y	Y	Y	Y	Y	Y
2 Langevin	Y	Y	Y	Y	Y	Y
SOUTH CAROLINA						
1 ***Brown***	Y	Y	Y	Y	Y	N
2 ***Spence***	Y	Y	Y	Y	Y	N
3 ***Graham***	Y	Y	Y	Y	Y	N
4 ***DeMint***	Y	Y	Y	Y	Y	N
5 Spratt	Y	Y	Y	Y	Y	N
6 Clyburn	Y	Y	Y	Y	Y	Y
SOUTH DAKOTA						
AL ***Thune***	Y	Y	Y	Y	Y	N

	51	52	53	54	55	56
TENNESSEE						
1 ***Jenkins***	Y	Y	Y	Y	Y	N
2 ***Duncan***	Y	Y	Y	Y	Y	N
3 ***Wamp***	Y	Y	Y	Y	Y	N
4 ***Hilleary***	?	?	Y	Y	Y	N
5 Clement	Y	Y	Y	Y	Y	N
6 Gordon	Y	?	?	?	?	?
7 ***Bryant***	Y	Y	Y	Y	Y	N
8 Tanner	Y	Y	Y	Y	Y	N
9 Ford	Y	Y	Y	Y	Y	N
TEXAS						
1 Sandlin	Y	Y	Y	Y	Y	Y
2 Turner	Y	Y	Y	Y	Y	N
3 ***Johnson, Sam***	Y	Y	Y	Y	Y	N
4 Hall	Y	Y	Y	Y	Y	N
5 ***Sessions***	Y	Y	?	?	?	N
6 ***Barton***	Y	Y	Y	Y	Y	N
7 ***Culberson***	Y	Y	Y	Y	Y	N
8 ***Brady***	Y	Y	Y	Y	Y	N
9 Lampson	Y	Y	Y	Y	Y	Y
10 Doggett	Y	Y	Y	Y	Y	N
11 Edwards	Y	Y	Y	Y	Y	?
12 ***Granger***	Y	Y	Y	Y	Y	N
13 ***Thornberry***	Y	Y	Y	Y	Y	N
14 ***Paul***	N	N	N	Y	N	N
15 Hinojosa	Y	Y	Y	Y	Y	N
16 Reyes	Y	Y	Y	Y	Y	N
17 Stenholm	Y	Y	Y	Y	Y	N
18 Jackson-Lee	Y	Y	Y	Y	Y	Y
19 ***Combest***	Y	Y	Y	Y	Y	N
20 Gonzalez	Y	Y	Y	Y	Y	Y
21 ***Smith***	Y	Y	Y	Y	Y	N
22 ***DeLay***	Y	Y	Y	Y	Y	N
23 ***Bonilla***	Y	Y	Y	Y	Y	N
24 Frost	Y	Y	Y	Y	Y	N
25 Bentsen	Y	Y	Y	Y	Y	N
26 ***Armey***	Y	Y	Y	Y	Y	N
27 Ortiz	Y	Y	Y	Y	Y	N
28 Rodriguez	Y	Y	Y	Y	Y	N
29 Green	Y	Y	Y	Y	Y	N
30 Johnson, E.B.	Y	Y	Y	Y	Y	?
UTAH						
1 ***Hansen***	Y	Y	Y	Y	Y	N
2 Matheson	Y	Y	Y	Y	Y	N
3 ***Cannon***	?	?	?	?	?	?
VERMONT						
AL *Sanders*	Y	Y	Y	Y	Y	?
VIRGINIA						
1 ***Davis, Jo Ann***	Y	Y	Y	Y	Y	N
2 ***Schrock***	Y	Y	Y	Y	Y	N
3 Scott	Y	Y	Y	Y	Y	?
4 Sisisky	?	?	?	?	?	?
5 *Goode*	N	Y	Y	Y	Y	N
6 ***Goodlatte***	Y	Y	Y	Y	Y	N
7 ***Cantor***	Y	Y	Y	Y	Y	N
8 Moran	Y	Y	Y	Y	Y	N
9 Boucher	Y	Y	Y	Y	Y	N
10 ***Wolf***	Y	Y	Y	Y	Y	N
11 ***Davis, T.***	Y	Y	Y	Y	Y	N
WASHINGTON						
1 Inslee	Y	Y	Y	Y	Y	Y
2 Larsen	Y	Y	Y	Y	Y	N
3 Baird	Y	Y	Y	Y	Y	Y
4 ***Hastings***	Y	Y	Y	Y	Y	N
5 ***Nethercutt***	Y	Y	Y	Y	Y	N
6 Dicks	Y	Y	Y	Y	Y	N
7 McDermott	Y	Y	Y	Y	Y	Y
8 ***Dunn***	Y	?	Y	Y	Y	N
9 Smith	Y	Y	Y	Y	Y	N
WEST VIRGINIA						
1 Mollohan	Y	Y	Y	Y	Y	N
2 ***Capito***	Y	Y	Y	Y	Y	N
3 Rahall	Y	Y	Y	Y	Y	N
WISCONSIN						
1 ***Ryan***	Y	Y	Y	Y	Y	N
2 Baldwin	Y	Y	Y	Y	Y	N
3 Kind	Y	Y	Y	Y	Y	N
4 Kleczka	Y	Y	Y	Y	Y	N
5 Barrett	Y	Y	Y	Y	Y	N
6 ***Petri***	Y	Y	Y	Y	Y	N
7 Obey	Y	Y	Y	Y	Y	Y
8 ***Green***	Y	Y	Y	Y	Y	N
9 ***Sensenbrenner***	Y	Y	Y	Y	Y	N
WYOMING						
AL ***Cubin***	Y	Y	Y	Y	Y	N

Southern states - Ala., Ark., Fla., Ga., Ky., La., Miss., N.C., Okla., S.C., Tenn., Texas, Va.

57. HR 247. Mobile Home Shelters/Rule. Adoption of the rule (H Res 93) to provide for House floor consideration of the bill that would allow community block grants to be used for the construction of tornado and storm shelters in manufactured housing communities. Adopted 246-169: R 212-0; D 33-168 (ND 21-130, SD 12-38); I 1-1. March 22, 2001.

58. HR 1099. Miscellaneous Coast Guard Changes/Passage. LoBiondo, R-N.J., motion to suspend the rules and pass the bill that would authorize safety, personnel, and other changes in the U.S. Coast Guard. The measure would increase civil penalties against negligent vessel operators and authorize more vessels for immigration patrols. A two-thirds majority of those present and voting (277 in this case) is required for passage under suspension of the rules. Motion agreed to 415-0: R 212-0; D 201-0 (ND 151-0, SD 50-0); I 2-0. March 22, 2001.

59. HR 802. Law Enforcement Medals/Passage. Sensenbrenner, R-Wis., motion to suspend the rules and pass the bill that would authorize the president to award a Medal of Valor annually to up to five public safety officers who perform acts above and beyond the call of duty. Motion agreed to 414-0: R 211-0; D 201-0 (ND 150-0, SD 51-0); I 2-0. A two-thirds majority of those present and voting (276 in this case) is required for passage under suspension of the rules. March 22, 2001.

60. HR 247. Mobile Home Shelters/Buy American. Traficant, D-Ohio, amendment that would express the sense of the Congress that federally funded materials purchased for the construction of tornado and storm shelters should be American-made. Adopted 396-0: R 201-0; D 193-0 (ND 145-0, SD 48-0); I 2-0. March 22, 2001.

61. HR 247. Mobile Home Shelters/Passage. Passage of the bill that would allow community block grants to be used for the construction of tornado and storm shelters in manufactured housing communities. Passed 401-6: R 200-6; D 199-0 (ND 149-0, SD 50-0); I 2-0. March 22, 2001.

	57	58	59	60	61
ALABAMA					
1 *Callahan*	Y	Y	Y	Y	Y
2 *Everett*	Y	Y	Y	Y	Y
3 *Riley*	Y	Y	Y	Y	Y
4 *Aderholt*	Y	Y	Y	Y	Y
5 Cramer	Y	Y	Y	Y	Y
6 *Bachus*	Y	Y	Y	Y	Y
7 Hilliard	N	Y	Y	Y	Y
ALASKA					
AL *Young*	Y	Y	Y	Y	Y
ARIZONA					
1 *Flake*	Y	Y	Y	Y	N
2 Pastor	N	Y	Y	Y	Y
3 *Stump*	Y	Y	Y	Y	N
4 *Shadegg*	Y	Y	Y	Y	N
5 *Kolbe*	Y	Y	Y	Y	Y
6 *Hayworth*	Y	Y	Y	Y	Y
ARKANSAS					
1 Berry	Y	Y	Y	Y	Y
2 Snyder	Y	Y	Y	Y	Y
3 *Hutchinson*	Y	Y	Y	Y	Y
4 Ross	Y	Y	Y	Y	Y
CALIFORNIA					
1 Thompson	N	Y	Y	Y	Y
2 *Herger*	Y	Y	Y	Y	Y
3 *Ose*	Y	Y	Y	Y	Y
4 *Doolittle*	Y	Y	Y	Y	Y
5 Matsui	N	Y	Y	Y	Y
6 Woolsey	N	Y	Y	Y	Y
7 Miller, George	N	Y	Y	Y	Y
8 Pelosi	N	Y	Y	Y	Y
9 Lee	N	Y	Y	Y	Y
10 Tauscher	N	Y	Y	Y	Y
11 *Pombo*	Y	Y	Y	Y	Y
12 Lantos	N	Y	Y	Y	?
13 Stark	N	Y	Y	Y	Y
14 Eshoo	Y	Y	Y	Y	Y
15 Honda	N	Y	Y	Y	Y
16 Lofgren	N	Y	Y	Y	Y
17 Farr	N	Y	Y	Y	Y
18 Condit	N	Y	Y	Y	Y
19 *Radanovich*	Y	Y	Y	Y	Y
20 Dooley	N	Y	Y	Y	Y
21 *Thomas*	Y	Y	Y	Y	Y
22 Capps	N	Y	Y	Y	Y
23 *Gallegly*	Y	Y	Y	Y	Y
24 Sherman	N	Y	Y	Y	Y
25 *McKeon*	Y	Y	Y	Y	Y
26 Berman	N	Y	Y	?	Y
27 Schiff	Y	Y	Y	Y	Y
28 *Dreier*	Y	Y	Y	Y	Y
29 Waxman	N	Y	Y	Y	Y
30 Becerra	?	?	?	?	?
31 Solis	N	Y	Y	Y	Y
32 Vacant					
33 Roybal-Allard	N	Y	Y	Y	Y
34 Napolitano	N	Y	Y	Y	Y
35 Waters	N	Y	Y	Y	Y
36 Harman	N	Y	Y	Y	Y
37 Millender-McD.	N	Y	Y	Y	Y
38 *Horn*	Y	?	Y	Y	Y

	57	58	59	60	61
39 *Royce*	Y	Y	Y	Y	Y
40 *Lewis*	Y	Y	Y	Y	Y
41 *Miller, Gary*	Y	Y	Y	Y	Y
42 Baca	N	Y	Y	Y	Y
43 *Calvert*	Y	Y	Y	?	?
44 *Bono*	Y	Y	Y	Y	Y
45 *Rohrabacher*	Y	Y	Y	Y	Y
46 Sanchez	N	Y	Y	Y	Y
47 *Cox*	Y	Y	Y	?	?
48 *Issa*	Y	Y	Y	Y	Y
49 Davis	N	Y	Y	Y	Y
50 Filner	N	Y	Y	Y	Y
51 *Cunningham*	Y	Y	Y	?	?
52 *Hunter*	Y	Y	Y	Y	Y
COLORADO					
1 DeGette	N	Y	Y	Y	Y
2 Udall	N	Y	Y	Y	Y
3 *McInnis*	Y	Y	Y	Y	Y
4 *Schaffer*	Y	Y	Y	Y	Y
5 *Hefley*	Y	Y	Y	Y	Y
6 *Tancredo*	Y	Y	Y	?	Y
CONNECTICUT					
1 Larson	N	Y	Y	Y	Y
2 *Simmons*	Y	Y	Y	Y	Y
3 DeLauro	N	Y	Y	Y	Y
4 *Shays*	Y	Y	Y	Y	Y
5 Maloney	Y	Y	Y	Y	Y
6 *Johnson*	Y	Y	Y	?	Y
DELAWARE					
AL *Castle*	Y	Y	Y	Y	Y
FLORIDA					
1 *Scarborough*	?	?	?	?	?
2 Boyd	N	Y	Y	Y	Y
3 Brown	?	?	?	?	?
4 *Crenshaw*	Y	Y	Y	Y	Y
5 Thurman	N	Y	Y	Y	Y
6 *Stearns*	Y	Y	Y	Y	Y
7 *Mica*	Y	Y	Y	Y	Y
8 *Keller*	Y	Y	Y	Y	Y
9 *Bilirakis*	Y	Y	Y	Y	Y
10 *Young*	Y	Y	Y	Y	Y
11 Davis	N	Y	Y	?	Y
12 *Putnam*	Y	Y	Y	Y	Y
13 *Miller*	Y	Y	Y	Y	Y
14 *Goss*	Y	Y	Y	Y	?
15 *Weldon*	Y	Y	Y	Y	Y
16 *Foley*	Y	Y	Y	Y	Y
17 Meek	N	Y	Y	Y	Y
18 *Ros-Lehtinen*	Y	Y	Y	Y	Y
19 Wexler	N	Y	Y	Y	Y
20 Deutsch	N	Y	Y	Y	Y
21 *Diaz-Balart*	Y	Y	Y	?	+
22 *Shaw*	Y	Y	Y	Y	Y
23 Hastings	N	Y	Y	Y	Y
GEORGIA					
1 *Kingston*	Y	Y	Y	Y	Y
2 Bishop	N	Y	Y	Y	Y
3 *Collins*	Y	Y	Y	Y	N
4 McKinney	N	Y	Y	Y	Y
5 Lewis	N	Y	Y	Y	Y
6 *Isakson*	Y	Y	Y	Y	Y
7 *Barr*	Y	Y	Y	Y	Y
8 *Chambliss*	Y	Y	Y	Y	Y
9 *Deal*	Y	Y	Y	Y	Y
10 *Norwood*	Y	Y	Y	Y	Y
11 *Linder*	Y	Y	Y	Y	Y
HAWAII					
1 Abercrombie	N	Y	Y	Y	Y
2 Mink	N	Y	Y	Y	Y
IDAHO					
1 *Otter*	Y	Y	Y	Y	Y
2 *Simpson*	Y	Y	Y	+	+
ILLINOIS					
1 Rush	N	Y	Y	Y	Y
2 Jackson	N	Y	Y	Y	Y
3 Lipinski	N	Y	Y	Y	Y
4 Gutierrez	N	Y	Y	Y	Y
5 Blagojevich	N	Y	Y	Y	Y
6 *Hyde*	Y	Y	Y	Y	Y
7 Davis	N	Y	Y	Y	Y
8 *Crane*	Y	Y	Y	Y	Y
9 Schakowsky	N	Y	Y	Y	Y
10 *Kirk*	Y	Y	Y	Y	Y
11 *Weller*	Y	Y	Y	Y	Y
12 Costello	N	Y	Y	Y	Y
13 *Biggert*	Y	Y	Y	Y	Y

ND Northern Democrats   SD Southern Democrats

	57	58	59	60	61
14 ***Hastert***					
15 ***Johnson***	Y	Y	Y	Y	Y
16 ***Manzullo***	Y	Y	Y	Y	Y
17 Evans	N	Y	Y	Y	Y
18 ***LaHood***	Y	Y	Y	Y	Y
19 Phelps	N	Y	Y	Y	Y
20 ***Shimkus***	Y	Y	Y	Y	Y
INDIANA					
1 Visclosky	N	Y	Y	Y	Y
2 ***Pence***	Y	Y	Y	Y	Y
3 Roemer	N	Y	Y	Y	Y
4 ***Souder***	Y	Y	Y	Y	Y
5 ***Buyer***	Y	Y	Y	Y	Y
6 ***Burton***	Y	Y	Y	Y	Y
7 ***Kerns***	Y	Y	Y	Y	Y
8 ***Hostettler***	Y	Y	Y	Y	Y
9 Hill	N	Y	Y	Y	Y
10 Carson	N	Y	Y	Y	Y
IOWA					
1 ***Leach***	Y	Y	Y	Y	Y
2 ***Nussle***	Y	Y	Y	Y	Y
3 Boswell	Y	Y	Y	Y	Y
4 ***Ganske***	Y	Y	Y	Y	Y
5 ***Latham***	Y	Y	Y	Y	Y
KANSAS					
1 ***Moran***	Y	Y	Y	Y	Y
2 ***Ryun***	Y	Y	Y	Y	Y
3 Moore	Y	Y	Y	Y	Y
4 ***Tiahrt***	Y	Y	Y	Y	Y
KENTUCKY					
1 ***Whitfield***	Y	Y	Y	Y	Y
2 ***Lewis***	Y	Y	Y	Y	Y
3 ***Northup***	Y	Y	Y	Y	Y
4 Lucas	Y	Y	Y	Y	Y
5 ***Rogers***	Y	Y	Y	Y	Y
6 ***Fletcher***	Y	Y	Y	?	?
LOUISIANA					
1 ***Vitter***	Y	Y	Y	Y	Y
2 Jefferson	N	Y	Y	Y	Y
3 ***Tauzin***	Y	Y	Y	Y	Y
4 ***McCrery***	Y	Y	Y	Y	Y
5 ***Cooksey***	Y	Y	Y	Y	Y
6 ***Baker***	Y	Y	Y	Y	Y
7 John	N	Y	Y	Y	Y
MAINE					
1 Allen	N	Y	Y	Y	Y
2 Baldacci	N	Y	Y	Y	Y
MARYLAND					
1 ***Gilchrest***	Y	Y	Y	Y	Y
2 ***Ehrlich***	Y	Y	Y	Y	Y
3 Cardin	Y	Y	Y	Y	Y
4 Wynn	N	Y	Y	Y	Y
5 Hoyer	N	Y	Y	Y	Y
6 ***Bartlett***	Y	Y	Y	Y	Y
7 Cummings	N	Y	Y	Y	Y
8 ***Morella***	?	?	?	?	Y
MASSACHUSETTS					
1 Olver	N	Y	Y	Y	Y
2 Neal	N	Y	Y	Y	Y
3 McGovern	N	Y	Y	Y	Y
4 Frank	N	Y	Y	Y	Y
5 Meehan	N	Y	Y	Y	Y
6 Tierney	N	Y	Y	Y	Y
7 Markey	N	Y	Y	Y	Y
8 Capuano	N	Y	Y	Y	Y
9 Moakley	?	?	?	?	?
10 Delahunt	N	Y	Y	Y	Y
MICHIGAN					
1 Stupak	N	Y	Y	Y	Y
2 ***Hoekstra***	Y	Y	Y	Y	Y
3 ***Ehlers***	Y	Y	?	Y	Y
4 ***Camp***	Y	Y	Y	Y	Y
5 Barcia	Y	Y	Y	Y	Y
6 ***Upton***	Y	Y	Y	Y	Y
7 ***Smith***	Y	Y	Y	?	?
8 ***Rogers***	Y	Y	Y	Y	Y
9 Kildee	N	Y	Y	Y	Y
10 Bonior	N	Y	Y	Y	Y
11 ***Knollenberg***	Y	Y	Y	Y	Y
12 Levin	N	Y	Y	Y	Y
13 Rivers	N	Y	Y	Y	Y
14 Conyers	N	Y	Y	Y	Y
15 Kilpatrick	N	Y	Y	Y	Y
16 Dingell	N	Y	Y	Y	Y

	57	58	59	60	61
MINNESOTA					
1 ***Gutknecht***	Y	Y	Y	Y	Y
2 ***Kennedy***	Y	Y	Y	Y	Y
3 ***Ramstad***	Y	Y	Y	Y	Y
4 McCollum	Y	Y	Y	?	Y
5 Sabo	N	Y	Y	Y	Y
6 Luther	Y	Y	Y	Y	Y
7 Peterson	Y	Y	Y	Y	Y
8 Oberstar	N	Y	Y	Y	Y
MISSISSIPPI					
1 ***Wicker***	Y	Y	Y	Y	Y
2 Thompson	N	Y	Y	Y	Y
3 ***Pickering***	Y	Y	Y	Y	Y
4 Shows	N	Y	Y	Y	Y
5 Taylor	N	Y	Y	Y	Y
MISSOURI					
1 Clay	N	Y	Y	Y	Y
2 ***Akin***	Y	Y	Y	Y	Y
3 Gephardt	N	Y	Y	Y	Y
4 Skelton	Y	Y	Y	Y	Y
5 McCarthy	N	Y	Y	Y	Y
6 ***Graves***	Y	Y	Y	Y	Y
7 ***Blunt***	?	Y	Y	Y	Y
8 ***Emerson***	Y	Y	Y	Y	Y
9 ***Hulshof***	Y	Y	Y	Y	Y
MONTANA					
AL ***Rehberg***	Y	Y	Y	Y	Y
NEBRASKA					
1 ***Bereuter***	Y	Y	Y	Y	Y
2 ***Terry***	Y	Y	Y	Y	Y
3 ***Osborne***	Y	Y	Y	Y	Y
NEVADA					
1 Berkley	N	Y	Y	Y	Y
2 ***Gibbons***	Y	Y	Y	Y	Y
NEW HAMPSHIRE					
1 ***Sununu***	Y	Y	Y	Y	Y
2 ***Bass***	Y	Y	Y	Y	Y
NEW JERSEY					
1 Andrews	N	Y	Y	Y	Y
2 ***LoBiondo***	Y	Y	Y	Y	Y
3 ***Saxton***	Y	Y	Y	Y	Y
4 ***Smith***	Y	Y	Y	Y	Y
5 ***Roukema***	Y	Y	Y	Y	Y
6 Pallone	N	Y	Y	Y	Y
7 ***Ferguson***	Y	Y	Y	Y	Y
8 Pascrell	N	Y	Y	Y	Y
9 Rothman	?	?	?	?	?
10 Payne	N	Y	Y	?	Y
11 ***Frelinghuysen***	Y	Y	Y	Y	Y
12 Holt	N	Y	Y	Y	Y
13 Menendez	N	Y	Y	Y	Y
NEW MEXICO					
1 ***Wilson***	Y	Y	Y	Y	Y
2 ***Skeen***	Y	Y	Y	Y	Y
3 Udall	N	Y	Y	Y	Y
NEW YORK					
1 ***Grucci***	Y	Y	Y	Y	Y
2 Israel	N	Y	Y	Y	Y
3 ***King***	Y	Y	Y	Y	Y
4 McCarthy	Y	Y	Y	Y	Y
5 Ackerman	?	?	?	?	?
6 Meeks	N	Y	Y	Y	Y
7 Crowley	N	Y	Y	Y	Y
8 Nadler	N	Y	Y	Y	Y
9 Weiner	N	Y	Y	Y	Y
10 Towns	N	Y	Y	Y	Y
11 Owens	N	Y	Y	Y	Y
12 Velázquez	N	Y	Y	Y	Y
13 ***Fossella***	Y	Y	Y	Y	Y
14 Maloney	N	Y	Y	Y	Y
15 Rangel	N	Y	Y	?	Y
16 Serrano	N	Y	Y	Y	Y
17 Engel	N	Y	Y	Y	Y
18 Lowey	N	Y	Y	Y	Y
19 ***Kelly***	Y	Y	Y	Y	Y
20 ***Gilman***	Y	Y	Y	Y	Y
21 McNulty	N	Y	Y	Y	Y
22 ***Sweeney***	Y	Y	Y	Y	Y
23 ***Boehlert***	Y	Y	Y	Y	Y
24 ***McHugh***	Y	Y	Y	Y	Y
25 ***Walsh***	Y	Y	Y	Y	Y
26 Hinchey	N	Y	Y	Y	Y
27 ***Reynolds***	Y	Y	Y	Y	Y
28 Slaughter	N	Y	Y	Y	Y
29 LaFalce	N	Y	Y	Y	Y

	57	58	59	60	61
30 ***Quinn***	Y	Y	Y	Y	Y
31 ***Houghton***	Y	Y	Y	Y	Y
NORTH CAROLINA					
1 Clayton	N	Y	Y	Y	Y
2 Etheridge	N	?	Y	Y	Y
3 ***Jones***	Y	Y	Y	Y	Y
4 Price	N	Y	Y	Y	Y
5 ***Burr***	Y	Y	Y	Y	Y
6 ***Coble***	Y	Y	Y	Y	Y
7 McIntyre	N	Y	Y	Y	Y
8 ***Hayes***	Y	Y	Y	Y	Y
9 ***Myrick***	?	Y	Y	Y	Y
10 ***Ballenger***	Y	Y	Y	Y	Y
11 ***Taylor***	Y	Y	Y	Y	Y
12 Watt	N	Y	Y	Y	Y
NORTH DAKOTA					
AL Pomeroy	Y	Y	Y	Y	Y
OHIO					
1 ***Chabot***	Y	Y	Y	Y	Y
2 ***Portman***	?	?	?	?	?
3 Hall	Y	Y	Y	?	Y
4 ***Oxley***	Y	Y	Y	Y	Y
5 ***Gillmor***	Y	Y	Y	Y	Y
6 Strickland	Y	Y	Y	Y	Y
7 ***Hobson***	Y	Y	Y	Y	Y
8 ***Boehner***	Y	Y	Y	Y	Y
9 Kaptur	Y	Y	Y	Y	Y
10 Kucinich	N	Y	Y	Y	Y
11 Jones	?	?	?	?	?
12 ***Tiberi***	Y	Y	Y	Y	Y
13 Brown	N	Y	Y	Y	Y
14 Sawyer	N	Y	Y	Y	Y
15 ***Pryce***	Y	Y	Y	Y	Y
16 ***Regula***	Y	Y	Y	Y	Y
17 Traficant	Y	Y	Y	Y	Y
18 ***Ney***	Y	Y	?	Y	Y
19 ***LaTourette***	Y	Y	Y	Y	Y
OKLAHOMA					
1 ***Largent***	Y	Y	Y	Y	Y
2 Carson	N	Y	Y	Y	Y
3 ***Watkins***	Y	Y	Y	Y	Y
4 ***Watts***	Y	Y	Y	?	?
5 ***Istook***	Y	?	Y	Y	Y
6 ***Lucas***	Y	Y	Y	Y	Y
OREGON					
1 Wu	Y	Y	Y	Y	Y
2 ***Walden***	Y	Y	Y	Y	Y
3 Blumenauer	N	Y	Y	Y	Y
4 DeFazio	N	Y	Y	Y	Y
5 Hooley	N	Y	Y	Y	Y
PENNSYLVANIA					
1 Brady	N	Y	Y	Y	Y
2 Fattah	N	Y	Y	Y	Y
3 Borski	N	Y	Y	Y	Y
4 ***Hart***	Y	Y	Y	Y	Y
5 ***Peterson***	Y	Y	Y	Y	Y
6 Holden	N	Y	Y	Y	Y
7 ***Weldon***	Y	Y	Y	Y	Y
8 ***Greenwood***	Y	Y	Y	Y	Y
9 Vacant					
10 ***Sherwood***	Y	Y	Y	Y	Y
11 Kanjorski	N	Y	Y	Y	Y
12 Murtha	N	Y	Y	Y	Y
13 Hoeffel	Y	Y	Y	Y	?
14 Coyne	N	Y	Y	Y	Y
15 ***Toomey***	?	?	?	?	?
16 ***Pitts***	Y	Y	Y	Y	Y
17 ***Gekas***	Y	Y	Y	Y	Y
18 Doyle	N	Y	Y	Y	Y
19 ***Platts***	Y	Y	Y	Y	Y
20 Mascara	N	Y	Y	Y	Y
21 ***English***	Y	Y	Y	Y	Y
RHODE ISLAND					
1 Kennedy	N	Y	Y	Y	Y
2 Langevin	N	Y	Y	Y	Y
SOUTH CAROLINA					
1 ***Brown***	Y	Y	?	Y	Y
2 ***Spence***	Y	Y	Y	Y	Y
3 ***Graham***	Y	Y	Y	Y	Y
4 ***DeMint***	Y	Y	Y	Y	Y
5 Spratt	N	Y	Y	Y	Y
6 Clyburn	N	Y	Y	Y	Y
SOUTH DAKOTA					
AL ***Thune***	Y	Y	Y	Y	Y

	57	58	59	60	61
TENNESSEE					
1 ***Jenkins***	Y	Y	Y	Y	Y
2 ***Duncan***	Y	Y	Y	Y	N
3 ***Wamp***	Y	Y	Y	Y	Y
4 ***Hilleary***	Y	Y	Y	Y	Y
5 Clement	?	Y	Y	Y	Y
6 Gordon	?	?	?	?	?
7 ***Bryant***	Y	Y	Y	Y	Y
8 Tanner	N	Y	Y	Y	Y
9 Ford	N	Y	Y	Y	Y
TEXAS					
1 Sandlin	Y	Y	Y	Y	Y
2 Turner	Y	Y	Y	Y	Y
3 ***Johnson, Sam***	Y	Y	Y	Y	Y
4 Hall	N	Y	Y	Y	Y
5 ***Sessions***	Y	Y	Y	Y	Y
6 ***Barton***	Y	Y	Y	Y	Y
7 ***Culberson***	Y	Y	Y	Y	Y
8 ***Brady***	Y	Y	Y	Y	Y
9 Lampson	Y	Y	Y	Y	Y
10 Doggett	N	Y	Y	Y	Y
11 Edwards	N	Y	Y	Y	Y
12 ***Granger***	Y	Y	Y	Y	Y
13 ***Thornberry***	Y	Y	Y	Y	Y
14 ***Paul***	Y	Y	Y	Y	N
15 Hinojosa	N	Y	Y	Y	Y
16 Reyes	N	Y	Y	?	Y
17 Stenholm	N	Y	Y	Y	Y
18 Jackson-Lee	N	Y	Y	Y	Y
19 ***Combest***	Y	Y	Y	Y	Y
20 Gonzalez	N	Y	Y	Y	Y
21 ***Smith***	Y	Y	Y	Y	Y
22 ***DeLay***	Y	Y	Y	Y	Y
23 ***Bonilla***	Y	Y	Y	Y	Y
24 Frost	N	Y	Y	Y	Y
25 Bentsen	N	Y	Y	?	?
26 ***Armey***	Y	Y	Y	?	Y
27 Ortiz	Y	Y	Y	Y	Y
28 Rodriguez	Y	Y	Y	Y	Y
29 Green	Y	Y	Y	Y	Y
30 Johnson, E.B.	?	?	?	?	?
UTAH					
1 ***Hansen***	Y	Y	Y	Y	Y
2 Matheson	Y	Y	Y	Y	Y
3 ***Cannon***	?	?	?	?	?
VERMONT					
AL *Sanders*	N	Y	Y	Y	Y
VIRGINIA					
1 ***Davis, Jo Ann***	Y	Y	Y	Y	Y
2 ***Schrock***	Y	Y	Y	Y	Y
3 Scott	N	Y	Y	Y	Y
4 Sisisky	?	?	?	?	?
5 *Goode*	Y	Y	Y	Y	Y
6 ***Goodlatte***	Y	Y	Y	Y	Y
7 ***Cantor***	Y	Y	Y	Y	Y
8 Moran	N	Y	Y	Y	Y
9 Boucher	N	Y	Y	Y	Y
10 ***Wolf***	Y	Y	Y	?	Y
11 ***Davis, T.***	Y	Y	Y	Y	Y
WASHINGTON					
1 Inslee	N	Y	Y	Y	Y
2 Larsen	N	Y	Y	Y	Y
3 Baird	N	Y	Y	Y	Y
4 ***Hastings***	Y	Y	Y	?	?
5 ***Nethercutt***	Y	Y	Y	Y	Y
6 Dicks	Y	Y	Y	Y	Y
7 McDermott	N	Y	?	?	Y
8 ***Dunn***	Y	Y	Y	Y	Y
9 Smith	N	Y	Y	Y	Y
WEST VIRGINIA					
1 Mollohan	N	Y	Y	Y	Y
2 ***Capito***	Y	Y	Y	Y	Y
3 Rahall	N	Y	Y	Y	Y
WISCONSIN					
1 ***Ryan***	Y	Y	Y	Y	Y
2 Baldwin	N	Y	Y	Y	Y
3 Kind	N	Y	Y	Y	Y
4 Kleczka	N	Y	Y	Y	Y
5 Barrett	N	Y	Y	Y	Y
6 ***Petri***	Y	Y	Y	Y	Y
7 Obey	N	Y	Y	Y	Y
8 ***Green***	Y	Y	Y	Y	Y
9 ***Sensenbrenner***	Y	Y	Y	Y	Y
WYOMING					
AL ***Cubin***	Y	Y	Y	Y	Y

Southern states - Ala., Ark., Fla., Ga., Ky., La., Miss., N.C., Okla., S.C., Tenn., Texas, Va.

WWW.CQ.COM

2001 CQ ALMANAC — H-27

Key

Y	Voted for (yea).
#	Paired for.
+	Announced for.
N	Voted against (nay).
X	Paired against.
–	Announced against.
P	Voted "present."
C	Voted "present" to avoid possible conflict of interest.
?	Did not vote or otherwise make a position known.

Democrats   **Republicans**
Independents

62. H Res 84. House Committee Funding/Adoption. Adoption of the resolution that would provide $203.5 million in the 107th Congress for 18 House standing committees and the Permanent Select Committee on Intelligence — $20 million (11 percent) more than they received in the 106th. Total funding includes nearly $99.7 million for these 19 committees in 2001 and $103.8 million in 2002. (The Appropriations Committee is not covered by this resolution because it is funded through the legislative branch appropriations bill.) Adopted 357-61: R 201-14; D 154-47 (ND 110-38, SD 44-9); I 2-0. March 27, 2001.

63. HR 801. Veterans' Benefits/Passage. Smith, R-N.J., motion to suspend the rules and pass the bill that would expand and increase funds for several Veterans Affairs Department programs, including those related to veterans' educational, retirement, life insurance and death benefits. Motion agreed to 417-0: R 214-0; D 201-0 (ND 149-0, SD 52-0); I 2-0. A two-thirds majority of those present and voting (278 in this case) is required for passage under suspension of the rules. March 27, 2001.

64. HR 811. Veterans' Health Care Facilities/Passage. Smith, R-N.J., motion to suspend the rules and pass the bill that would authorize $550 million in construction funding in fiscal 2002-03 to improve veterans' health care facilities. Motion agreed to 417-0: R 214-0; D 201-0 (ND 148-0, SD 53-0); I 2-0. A two-thirds majority of those present and voting (278 in this case) is required for passage under suspension of the rules. March 27, 2001.

65. H Con Res 83. Fiscal 2002 Budget Resolution/Rule. Adoption of the rule (H Res 100) to provide for House floor consideration of the concurrent resolution that would set broad spending and revenue targets. Adopted 282-130: R 211-1; D 70-128 (ND 51-98, SD 19-30); I 1-1. March 28, 2001.

66. H Con Res 83. Fiscal 2002 Budget Resolution/Kucinich Substitute. Kucinich, D-Ohio, substitute amendment on behalf of the Congressional Progressive Caucus that calls for using one-third of the available on-budget surplus over 10 years for reducing the public debt, one-third for cutting taxes, and one-third for increasing non-defense discretionary spending, especially in the areas of education and health care. The amendment would cut proposed fiscal 2002 defense spending by $66 billion. Rejected 79-343: R 0-217; D 78-125 (ND 67-85, SD 11-40); I 1-1. March 28, 2001.

67. H Con Res 83. Fiscal 2002 Budget Resolution/Stenholm Substitute. Stenholm, D-Texas, substitute amendment on behalf of the Blue Dog Coalition that would cover five years, not 10 years as in the underlying resolution. The substitute calls for using half the projected on-budget surplus over five years for reducing the public debt, one-quarter for increasing priority discretionary spending projects, and one-quarter for tax cuts. Rejected 204-221: R 12-206; D 191-14 (ND 138-14, SD 53-0); I 1-1. March 28, 2001.

68. H Con Res 83. Fiscal 2002 Budget Resolution/Flake Substitute. Flake, R-Ariz., substitute amendment on behalf of the Republican Study Committee that would provide $6.7 billion less in fiscal 2002 discretionary spending than the underlying resolution, and would cut taxes by $2.2 trillion over 10 years. The amendment would increase fiscal 2002 defense spending by $25 billion, compared to the underlying resolution. Rejected 81-341: R 79-139; D 1-201 (ND 0-152, SD 1-49); I 1-1. March 28, 2001.

	62	63	64	65	66	67	68
ALABAMA							
1 Callahan	Y	Y	Y	?	N	N	N
2 Everett	Y	Y	Y	Y	N	N	Y
3 Riley	Y	Y	Y	Y	N	N	Y
4 Aderholt	Y	Y	Y	Y	N	N	Y
5 Cramer	Y	Y	Y	Y	N	Y	N
6 Bachus	Y	Y	Y	Y	N	N	Y
7 Hilliard	Y	Y	Y	N	Y	Y	N
ALASKA							
AL Young	Y	Y	Y	?	N	N	N
ARIZONA							
1 Flake	Y	Y	Y	Y	N	N	Y
2 Pastor	Y	Y	Y	Y	N	Y	N
3 Stump	Y	Y	Y	Y	N	N	N
4 Shadegg	Y	Y	Y	Y	N	N	Y
5 Kolbe	Y	Y	Y	Y	N	N	N
6 Hayworth	Y	Y	Y	Y	N	N	Y
ARKANSAS							
1 Berry	Y	Y	Y	N	N	Y	N
2 Snyder	Y	Y	Y	Y	N	Y	N
3 Hutchinson	Y	Y	Y	Y	N	N	N
4 Ross	Y	Y	Y	N	N	Y	N
CALIFORNIA							
1 Thompson	N	Y	Y	Y	N	Y	N
2 Herger	Y	Y	Y	Y	N	N	Y
3 Ose	Y	Y	Y	Y	N	N	N
4 Doolittle	Y	Y	Y	Y	N	N	Y
5 Matsui	Y	Y	Y	Y	N	Y	N
6 Woolsey	Y	Y	Y	N	Y	Y	N
7 Miller, George	Y	Y	Y	N	Y	Y	N
8 Pelosi	Y	Y	Y	N	Y	Y	N
9 Lee	Y	Y	Y	N	Y	Y	N
10 Tauscher	N	Y	Y	N	N	Y	N
11 Pombo	Y	Y	Y	Y	N	N	Y
12 Lantos	Y	Y	Y	Y	N	Y	N
13 Stark	Y	Y	Y	N	Y	Y	N
14 Eshoo	Y	Y	Y	Y	N	Y	N
15 Honda	N	Y	Y	N	Y	Y	N
16 Lofgren	Y	Y	Y	N	Y	Y	N
17 Farr	Y	Y	Y	N	Y	Y	N
18 Condit	N	Y	Y	N	N	Y	N
19 Radanovich	Y	Y	Y	?	N	N	N
20 Dooley	N	Y	Y	N	N	Y	N
21 Thomas	Y	Y	Y	Y	N	N	N
22 Capps	Y	Y	Y	N	N	Y	N
23 Gallegly	Y	Y	Y	Y	N	N	N
24 Sherman	Y	Y	Y	N	N	Y	N
25 McKeon	Y	Y	Y	Y	N	N	N
26 Berman	Y	Y	Y	N	N	Y	N
27 Schiff	N	Y	Y	N	N	Y	N
28 Dreier	Y	Y	Y	Y	N	N	Y
29 Waxman	Y	Y	Y	N	Y	Y	N
30 Becerra	+	+	+	–	+	+	–
31 Solis	Y	Y	Y	N	Y	Y	N
32 Vacant							
33 Roybal-Allard	Y	Y	Y	N	Y	Y	N
34 Napolitano	Y	Y	Y	N	Y	Y	N
35 Waters	N	Y	Y	N	Y	Y	N
36 Harman	N	Y	Y	N	N	Y	N
37 Millender-McD.	Y	Y	Y	N	Y	Y	N
38 Horn	Y	Y	Y	N	N	N	N

	62	63	64	65	66	67	68
39 Royce	N	Y	Y	Y	N	N	Y
40 Lewis	Y	Y	Y	Y	N	N	N
41 Miller, Gary	Y	Y	Y	Y	N	N	Y
42 Baca	Y	Y	Y	N	N	Y	N
43 Calvert	Y	Y	Y	Y	N	N	N
44 Bono	Y	Y	Y	Y	N	N	N
45 Rohrabacher	Y	Y	Y	Y	N	N	Y
46 Sanchez	N	Y	N	N	N	Y	N
47 Cox	Y	Y	Y	?	N	N	N
48 Issa	Y	Y	Y	Y	N	N	Y
49 Davis	N	Y	Y	N	N	Y	N
50 Filner	N	Y	Y	N	Y	Y	N
51 Cunningham	Y	Y	Y	Y	N	N	N
52 Hunter	Y	Y	Y	Y	N	N	Y
COLORADO							
1 DeGette	Y	Y	Y	N	Y	N	N
2 Udall	?	Y	Y	N	Y	Y	N
3 McInnis	Y	Y	Y	Y	N	N	N
4 Schaffer	N	Y	Y	Y	N	N	Y
5 Hefley	N	Y	Y	Y	N	N	Y
6 Tancredo	N	Y	Y	Y	N	N	Y
CONNECTICUT							
1 Larson	Y	Y	Y	Y	N	N	N
2 Simmons	Y	Y	Y	Y	N	N	N
3 DeLauro	Y	Y	Y	Y	N	N	N
4 Shays	Y	Y	Y	Y	N	N	N
5 Maloney	Y	Y	Y	N	N	Y	N
6 Johnson	Y	Y	Y	Y	N	N	N
DELAWARE							
AL Castle	Y	Y	Y	N	N	N	N
FLORIDA							
1 Scarborough	N	Y	Y	Y	N	Y	Y
2 Boyd	N	Y	Y	?	N	Y	N
3 Brown	Y	Y	Y	N	Y	Y	N
4 Crenshaw	Y	Y	Y	Y	N	N	N
5 Thurman	N	Y	Y	N	N	Y	N
6 Stearns	+	+	+	Y	N	Y	Y
7 Mica	Y	Y	Y	Y	N	N	N
8 Keller	Y	Y	Y	Y	N	N	N
9 Bilirakis	Y	Y	Y	Y	N	N	N
10 Young	Y	Y	Y	Y	N	N	N
11 Davis	Y	Y	Y	N	N	Y	N
12 Putnam	Y	Y	Y	Y	N	N	N
13 Miller	Y	Y	Y	Y	N	N	N
14 Goss	Y	Y	Y	Y	N	N	N
15 Weldon	Y	Y	Y	Y	N	N	N
16 Foley	Y	Y	Y	N	N	N	N
17 Meek	Y	Y	Y	N	?	Y	N
18 Ros-Lehtinen	Y	Y	Y	Y	N	N	N
19 Wexler	Y	Y	Y	N	N	Y	N
20 Deutsch	N	Y	Y	N	N	Y	N
21 Diaz-Balart	Y	Y	Y	Y	N	N	N
22 Shaw	?	?	?	+	–	–	Y
23 Hastings	Y	Y	Y	N	Y	Y	N
GEORGIA							
1 Kingston	N	Y	Y	Y	N	N	N
2 Bishop	Y	Y	Y	N	N	Y	N
3 Collins	Y	Y	?	Y	N	N	N
4 McKinney	Y	Y	Y	?	Y	Y	?
5 Lewis	Y	Y	Y	N	Y	Y	N
6 Isakson	Y	Y	Y	Y	N	N	N
7 Barr	Y	Y	Y	Y	N	N	Y
8 Chambliss	Y	Y	Y	Y	N	N	N
9 Deal	?	?	?	Y	N	N	Y
10 Norwood	Y	Y	Y	Y	N	N	Y
11 Linder	Y	Y	Y	Y	N	N	N
HAWAII							
1 Abercrombie	Y	Y	Y	Y	N	Y	N
2 Mink	Y	Y	Y	?	?	?	?
IDAHO							
1 Otter	Y	Y	Y	Y	N	N	Y
2 Simpson	Y	Y	Y	Y	N	N	N
ILLINOIS							
1 Rush	Y	Y	Y	N	Y	Y	N
2 Jackson	Y	Y	Y	N	Y	Y	N
3 Lipinski	Y	Y	Y	N	N	Y	N
4 Gutierrez	Y	Y	Y	N	Y	Y	N
5 Blagojevich	Y	Y	Y	N	N	Y	N
6 Hyde	Y	Y	Y	Y	N	N	N
7 Davis	Y	Y	Y	N	Y	Y	N
8 Crane	Y	Y	Y	Y	N	N	Y
9 Schakowsky	Y	Y	Y	N	Y	Y	N
10 Kirk	Y	Y	Y	Y	N	N	N
11 Weller	Y	Y	Y	Y	N	N	N
12 Costello	Y	Y	Y	N	N	Y	N
13 Biggert	Y	Y	Y	Y	N	N	N

ND Northern Democrats   SD Southern Democrats

	62	63	64	65	66	67	68
14 ***Hastert***	Y	Y	Y	Y	N	N	N
15 ***Johnson***	Y	Y	Y	Y	N	N	N
16 ***Manzullo***	Y	Y	Y	Y	N	N	Y
17 Evans	Y	Y	Y	N	N	N	N
18 ***LaHood***	Y	Y	Y	Y	N	N	N
19 Phelps	N	Y	Y	Y	N	Y	N
20 ***Shimkus***	Y	Y	Y	Y	N	Y	Y
INDIANA							
1 Visclosky	Y	Y	Y	N	N	Y	N
2 ***Pence***	Y	Y	Y	Y	N	N	Y
3 Roemer	N	Y	Y	Y	N	Y	N
4 ***Souder***	Y	Y	Y	Y	N	N	?
5 ***Buyer***	Y	Y	Y	Y	N	N	N
6 ***Burton***	Y	Y	Y	?	N	N	Y
7 ***Kerns***	Y	Y	Y	Y	N	N	N
8 ***Hostettler***	Y	Y	Y	Y	N	N	Y
9 Hill	N	Y	Y	Y	N	Y	N
10 Carson	Y	Y	Y	N	Y	Y	N
IOWA							
1 ***Leach***	Y	Y	Y	Y	N	N	N
2 ***Nussle***	Y	?	Y	Y	N	N	N
3 Boswell	Y	Y	Y	Y	N	Y	N
4 ***Ganske***	Y	Y	Y	Y	N	N	N
5 ***Latham***	Y	Y	Y	Y	N	N	N
KANSAS							
1 ***Moran***	Y	Y	Y	Y	N	N	N
2 ***Ryun***	Y	Y	Y	Y	N	N	Y
3 Moore	N	Y	Y	Y	N	Y	N
4 ***Tiahrt***	Y	Y	Y	Y	N	N	Y
KENTUCKY							
1 ***Whitfield***	Y	Y	Y	Y	N	N	N
2 ***Lewis***	Y	Y	Y	Y	N	N	Y
3 ***Northup***	Y	Y	Y	Y	N	N	N
4 Lucas	N	Y	Y	Y	N	Y	N
5 ***Rogers***	Y	Y	Y	Y	N	N	N
6 ***Fletcher***	Y	Y	Y	Y	N	N	N
LOUISIANA							
1 ***Vitter***	Y	Y	Y	Y	N	N	Y
2 Jefferson	Y	Y	Y	N	Y	Y	N
3 ***Tauzin***	Y	Y	Y	Y	N	N	N
4 ***McCrery***	Y	Y	Y	Y	N	N	N
5 ***Cooksey***	Y	Y	Y	Y	N	N	N
6 ***Baker***	Y	Y	Y	Y	N	N	N
7 John	Y	+	Y	N	N	Y	N
MAINE							
1 Allen	Y	Y	Y	N	N	Y	N
2 Baldacci	Y	Y	Y	N	N	Y	N
MARYLAND							
1 ***Gilchrest***	Y	Y	Y	Y	N	N	N
2 ***Ehrlich***	Y	Y	Y	Y	N	N	N
3 Cardin	Y	Y	Y	Y	N	Y	N
4 Wynn	Y	Y	Y	Y	Y	Y	N
5 Hoyer	Y	Y	Y	N	N	Y	N
6 ***Bartlett***	Y	Y	Y	Y	N	N	Y
7 Cummings	Y	Y	Y	Y	Y	Y	N
8 ***Morella***	Y	Y	Y	Y	N	Y	N
MASSACHUSETTS							
1 Olver	Y	Y	Y	N	Y	Y	N
2 Neal	Y	Y	Y	N	N	Y	N
3 McGovern	Y	Y	Y	N	Y	Y	N
4 Frank	Y	Y	Y	N	Y	Y	N
5 Meehan	Y	Y	Y	N	N	Y	N
6 Tierney	Y	Y	Y	N	Y	Y	N
7 Markey	Y	Y	Y	N	Y	Y	N
8 Capuano	Y	Y	Y	N	Y	Y	N
9 Moakley	?	?	?	N	Y	Y	N
10 Delahunt	Y	Y	Y	N	Y	Y	N
MICHIGAN							
1 Stupak	Y	Y	Y	N	N	Y	N
2 ***Hoekstra***	Y	Y	Y	Y	N	N	Y
3 ***Ehlers***	Y	Y	Y	Y	N	N	N
4 ***Camp***	Y	Y	Y	Y	N	N	Y
5 Barcia	Y	Y	Y	Y	N	Y	N
6 ***Upton***	Y	Y	Y	Y	N	Y	N
7 ***Smith***	Y	Y	Y	Y	N	Y	N
8 ***Rogers***	Y	Y	Y	Y	N	N	N
9 Kildee	Y	Y	Y	N	N	Y	N
10 Bonior	?	?	?	Y	Y	Y	N
11 ***Knollenberg***	Y	Y	Y	Y	N	N	N
12 Levin	Y	Y	Y	N	N	Y	N
13 Rivers	Y	Y	?	Y	N	Y	N
14 Conyers	Y	Y	Y	N	Y	Y	N
15 Kilpatrick	Y	Y	Y	N	Y	Y	N
16 Dingell	Y	Y	Y	Y	N	Y	N
MINNESOTA							
1 ***Gutknecht***	Y	Y	Y	Y	N	N	N
2 ***Kennedy***	Y	Y	Y	Y	N	N	N
3 ***Ramstad***	Y	Y	Y	Y	N	N	N
4 McCollum	Y	Y	Y	N	Y	Y	N
5 Sabo	Y	Y	Y	N	N	Y	N
6 Luther	N	Y	Y	N	N	Y	N
7 Peterson	N	Y	Y	N	Y	Y	N
8 Oberstar	Y	Y	Y	N	Y	Y	N
MISSISSIPPI							
1 ***Wicker***	Y	Y	Y	Y	N	N	N
2 Thompson	Y	Y	Y	N	N	Y	N
3 ***Pickering***	Y	Y	Y	Y	N	N	N
4 Shows	Y	Y	Y	Y	N	Y	N
5 Taylor	N	Y	Y	Y	N	Y	N
MISSOURI							
1 Clay	Y	Y	Y	N	Y	Y	N
2 ***Akin***	Y	Y	Y	Y	N	N	Y
3 Gephardt	Y	Y	Y	N	Y	Y	N
4 Skelton	Y	Y	Y	Y	N	Y	N
5 McCarthy	Y	Y	Y	Y	N	Y	N
6 ***Graves***	Y	Y	Y	Y	N	N	N
7 ***Blunt***	Y	Y	Y	Y	N	N	Y
8 ***Emerson***	Y	Y	Y	Y	N	Y	N
9 ***Hulshof***	N	Y	Y	Y	N	N	N
MONTANA							
AL ***Rehberg***	Y	Y	Y	Y	N	N	N
NEBRASKA							
1 ***Bereuter***	Y	Y	Y	Y	N	N	N
2 ***Terry***	Y	Y	Y	Y	N	N	Y
3 ***Osborne***	Y	Y	Y	Y	N	N	N
NEVADA							
1 Berkley	N	Y	Y	Y	N	Y	N
2 ***Gibbons***	Y	Y	Y	Y	N	N	Y
NEW HAMPSHIRE							
1 ***Sununu***	Y	Y	Y	Y	N	N	Y
2 ***Bass***	Y	Y	Y	Y	N	N	N
NEW JERSEY							
1 Andrews	N	Y	Y	N	N	Y	N
2 ***LoBiondo***	Y	Y	Y	Y	N	N	N
3 ***Saxton***	Y	Y	Y	Y	N	N	N
4 ***Smith***	Y	Y	Y	Y	N	N	N
5 ***Roukema***	Y	Y	Y	Y	N	N	N
6 Pallone	Y	Y	Y	N	Y	Y	N
7 ***Ferguson***	Y	Y	Y	Y	N	N	N
8 Pascrell	Y	Y	Y	Y	N	Y	N
9 Rothman	?	?	?	?	?	?	?
10 Payne	Y	Y	Y	N	Y	Y	N
11 ***Frelinghuysen***	Y	Y	Y	Y	N	N	N
12 Holt	N	Y	Y	N	N	Y	N
13 Menendez	Y	Y	Y	Y	N	Y	N
NEW MEXICO							
1 ***Wilson***	Y	Y	Y	Y	N	N	N
2 ***Skeen***	Y	Y	Y	Y	N	N	N
3 Udall	N	Y	Y	N	N	N	N
NEW YORK							
1 ***Grucci***	Y	Y	Y	Y	N	N	N
2 Israel	N	Y	Y	Y	N	Y	N
3 ***King***	Y	Y	Y	Y	N	N	N
4 McCarthy	N	Y	Y	Y	N	Y	N
5 Ackerman	?	?	?	N	Y	Y	N
6 Meeks	Y	Y	Y	N	Y	Y	N
7 Crowley	Y	Y	Y	Y	N	Y	N
8 Nadler	Y	Y	Y	N	Y	Y	N
9 Weiner	Y	Y	Y	N	Y	N	N
10 Towns	Y	Y	Y	N	N	N	N
11 Owens	?	?	?	N	Y	Y	N
12 Velázquez	Y	Y	Y	N	Y	Y	N
13 ***Fossella***	Y	Y	Y	Y	N	N	N
14 Maloney	Y	Y	Y	Y	Y	Y	N
15 Rangel	Y	Y	Y	?	Y	Y	N
16 Serrano	Y	Y	Y	N	Y	Y	N
17 Engel	Y	Y	Y	Y	Y	Y	N
18 Lowey	Y	Y	Y	N	Y	Y	N
19 ***Kelly***	Y	Y	Y	Y	N	Y	N
20 ***Gilman***	Y	Y	Y	Y	N	N	N
21 McNulty	Y	Y	Y	N	Y	Y	N
22 ***Sweeney***	Y	Y	Y	Y	N	N	N
23 ***Boehlert***	Y	Y	Y	Y	N	N	N
24 ***McHugh***	Y	Y	Y	Y	N	N	N
25 ***Walsh***	Y	Y	Y	Y	N	N	N
26 Hinchey	Y	Y	Y	N	Y	Y	N
27 ***Reynolds***	Y	Y	Y	?	N	N	Y
28 Slaughter	N	Y	Y	N	Y	Y	N
29 LaFalce	Y	Y	Y	N	N	Y	N
30 ***Quinn***	Y	Y	Y	Y	N	N	N
31 ***Houghton***	Y	Y	Y	Y	N	N	N
NORTH CAROLINA							
1 Clayton	Y	Y	Y	N	Y	Y	N
2 Etheridge	Y	Y	Y	Y	N	Y	N
3 ***Jones***	N	Y	Y	Y	N	N	Y
4 Price	Y	Y	Y	N	N	Y	N
5 ***Burr***	Y	Y	Y	Y	N	N	N
6 ***Coble***	Y	Y	Y	Y	N	N	N
7 McIntyre	Y	Y	Y	N	N	Y	N
8 ***Hayes***	Y	Y	Y	Y	N	N	N
9 ***Myrick***	Y	Y	Y	Y	N	N	Y
10 ***Ballenger***	Y	Y	Y	Y	N	N	N
11 ***Taylor***	Y	Y	Y	Y	N	N	N
12 Watt	Y	Y	Y	N	Y	Y	N
NORTH DAKOTA							
AL Pomeroy	Y	Y	Y	Y	N	Y	N
OHIO							
1 ***Chabot***	?	?	?	Y	N	N	Y
2 ***Portman***	Y	Y	Y	Y	N	N	Y
3 Hall	Y	Y	Y	Y	N	N	N
4 ***Oxley***	Y	Y	Y	Y	N	N	N
5 ***Gillmor***	Y	Y	Y	Y	N	N	N
6 Strickland	N	Y	Y	Y	N	N	N
7 ***Hobson***	Y	Y	Y	Y	N	N	N
8 ***Boehner***	Y	Y	Y	Y	N	N	Y
9 Kaptur	Y	Y	Y	?	N	N	N
10 Kucinich	N	Y	Y	Y	Y	N	N
11 Jones	Y	Y	Y	N	Y	Y	N
12 ***Tiberi***	Y	Y	Y	Y	N	N	Y
13 Brown	N	Y	Y	N	Y	Y	N
14 Sawyer	Y	Y	Y	N	N	Y	N
15 ***Pryce***	Y	Y	Y	Y	N	N	N
16 ***Regula***	Y	Y	Y	Y	N	N	N
17 Traficant	Y	Y	Y	Y	N	N	N
18 ***Ney***	Y	Y	Y	Y	N	N	N
19 ***LaTourette***	Y	Y	Y	Y	N	N	N
OKLAHOMA							
1 ***Largent***	N	Y	Y	Y	N	N	Y
2 Carson	N	Y	Y	N	N	Y	N
3 ***Watkins***	Y	Y	Y	Y	N	N	N
4 ***Watts***	Y	Y	Y	Y	N	N	N
5 ***Istook***	Y	Y	Y	Y	N	N	Y
6 ***Lucas***	Y	Y	Y	Y	N	N	Y
OREGON							
1 Wu	N	Y	Y	N	Y	Y	N
2 ***Walden***	Y	Y	Y	Y	N	N	N
3 Blumenauer	Y	Y	Y	N	Y	Y	N
4 DeFazio	N	Y	Y	N	Y	Y	N
5 Hooley	N	Y	Y	N	N	Y	N
PENNSYLVANIA							
1 Brady	Y	Y	Y	Y	Y	Y	N
2 Fattah	Y	Y	Y	N	Y	Y	N
3 Borski	Y	Y	Y	Y	N	Y	N
4 ***Hart***	Y	Y	Y	Y	N	N	N
5 ***Peterson***	Y	Y	Y	Y	N	N	N
6 Holden	Y	Y	Y	Y	N	Y	N
7 ***Weldon***	Y	Y	Y	Y	N	N	N
8 ***Greenwood***	Y	Y	Y	Y	N	N	N
9 Vacant							
10 ***Sherwood***	Y	Y	Y	Y	N	N	N
11 Kanjorski	Y	Y	Y	N	N	Y	N
12 Murtha	Y	Y	Y	Y	N	Y	N
13 Hoeffel	Y	Y	Y	N	N	Y	N
14 Coyne	Y	Y	Y	N	Y	Y	N
15 ***Toomey***	N	Y	Y	Y	N	N	Y
16 ***Pitts***	Y	Y	Y	Y	N	N	Y
17 ***Gekas***	Y	Y	Y	Y	N	N	N
18 Doyle	Y	Y	Y	Y	N	Y	N
19 ***Platts***	Y	Y	Y	Y	N	N	N
20 Mascara	Y	Y	Y	Y	N	Y	N
21 ***English***	Y	Y	Y	Y	N	N	N
RHODE ISLAND							
1 Kennedy	Y	Y	Y	N	N	Y	N
2 Langevin	N	Y	Y	N	N	Y	N
SOUTH CAROLINA							
1 ***Brown***	Y	Y	Y	Y	N	N	N
2 ***Spence***	Y	Y	Y	Y	N	N	Y
3 ***Graham***	Y	Y	Y	Y	N	N	Y
4 ***DeMint***	N	Y	Y	Y	N	N	Y
5 Spratt	Y	Y	Y	N	N	Y	N
6 Clyburn	Y	Y	Y	N	N	Y	N
SOUTH DAKOTA							
AL ***Thune***	Y	Y	Y	Y	N	N	N
TENNESSEE							
1 ***Jenkins***	Y	Y	Y	Y	N	N	N
2 ***Duncan***	N	Y	Y	Y	N	Y	N
3 ***Wamp***	Y	Y	Y	Y	N	N	Y
4 ***Hilleary***	N	Y	Y	Y	N	N	N
5 Clement	Y	Y	Y	Y	N	Y	N
6 Gordon	Y	Y	Y	?	N	Y	?
7 ***Bryant***	Y	Y	Y	Y	N	N	Y
8 Tanner	N	Y	Y	N	N	Y	N
9 Ford	Y	Y	Y	Y	N	Y	N
TEXAS							
1 Sandlin	Y	Y	Y	N	N	Y	N
2 Turner	Y	Y	Y	Y	N	Y	N
3 ***Johnson, Sam***	Y	Y	Y	Y	N	N	Y
4 Hall	Y	Y	Y	Y	N	Y	Y
5 ***Sessions***	Y	Y	Y	Y	N	N	Y
6 ***Barton***	Y	Y	Y	Y	N	N	Y
7 ***Culberson***	Y	Y	Y	Y	N	N	Y
8 ***Brady***	Y	Y	Y	Y	N	N	Y
9 Lampson	?	?	?	?	?	?	?
10 Doggett	N	Y	Y	Y	N	Y	N
11 Edwards	Y	Y	Y	N	N	Y	N
12 ***Granger***	Y	Y	Y	Y	N	N	N
13 ***Thornberry***	Y	Y	Y	Y	N	N	N
14 ***Paul***	N	Y	Y	Y	N	N	N
15 Hinojosa	Y	Y	Y	Y	N	Y	N
16 Reyes	Y	Y	Y	?	N	Y	N
17 Stenholm	Y	Y	Y	Y	N	Y	N
18 Jackson-Lee	Y	Y	Y	N	Y	Y	N
19 ***Combest***	Y	Y	Y	Y	N	N	N
20 Gonzalez	Y	Y	Y	Y	N	Y	N
21 ***Smith***	Y	Y	Y	Y	N	N	N
22 ***DeLay***	Y	Y	Y	Y	–	N	Y
23 ***Bonilla***	Y	Y	Y	Y	N	N	N
24 Frost	Y	Y	Y	Y	N	Y	N
25 Bentsen	Y	Y	Y	N	N	Y	N
26 ***Armey***	Y	Y	Y	Y	N	N	N
27 Ortiz	Y	Y	Y	Y	N	Y	N
28 Rodriguez	Y	Y	Y	Y	N	Y	N
29 Green	N	Y	Y	N	N	Y	N
30 Johnson, E.B.	Y	Y	Y	N	Y	Y	N
UTAH							
1 ***Hansen***	Y	Y	Y	Y	N	N	Y
2 Matheson	N	Y	Y	Y	N	Y	N
3 ***Cannon***	Y	Y	Y	Y	N	N	Y
VERMONT							
AL *Sanders*	Y	Y	Y	N	Y	Y	N
VIRGINIA							
1 ***Davis, Jo Ann***	Y	Y	Y	Y	N	Y	Y
2 ***Schrock***	Y	Y	Y	Y	N	N	Y
3 Scott	Y	Y	Y	N	N	Y	N
4 Sisisky	?	?	?	?	?	?	?
5 *Goode*	Y	Y	Y	Y	N	N	Y
6 ***Goodlatte***	Y	Y	Y	Y	N	N	Y
7 ***Cantor***	Y	Y	Y	Y	N	N	Y
8 Moran	Y	Y	Y	N	N	Y	N
9 Boucher	Y	Y	Y	Y	?	Y	N
10 ***Wolf***	Y	Y	Y	Y	N	N	N
11 ***Davis, T.***	Y	Y	Y	Y	N	N	N
WASHINGTON							
1 Inslee	N	Y	Y	Y	N	Y	N
2 Larsen	N	Y	Y	Y	N	Y	N
3 Baird	N	Y	Y	Y	N	Y	N
4 ***Hastings***	Y	Y	Y	Y	N	N	N
5 ***Nethercutt***	Y	Y	Y	Y	N	N	Y
6 Dicks	Y	Y	Y	N	N	Y	N
7 McDermott	Y	Y	Y	N	Y	Y	N
8 ***Dunn***	Y	Y	Y	Y	N	N	Y
9 Smith	N	Y	Y	Y	N	Y	N
WEST VIRGINIA							
1 Mollohan	Y	Y	Y	N	N	Y	N
2 ***Capito***	Y	Y	Y	Y	N	N	N
3 Rahall	Y	Y	Y	Y	N	N	N
WISCONSIN							
1 ***Ryan***	Y	Y	Y	Y	N	N	Y
2 Baldwin	?	?	?	?	?	?	?
3 Kind	N	Y	Y	N	N	Y	N
4 Kleczka	Y	Y	Y	?	N	Y	N
5 Barrett	N	Y	Y	Y	N	Y	N
6 ***Petri***	Y	Y	Y	Y	N	N	Y
7 Obey	Y	Y	Y	N	N	Y	N
8 ***Green***	Y	Y	Y	Y	N	N	N
9 ***Sensenbrenner***	Y	Y	Y	Y	N	N	Y
WYOMING							
AL ***Cubin***	Y	Y	Y	Y	N	N	Y

Southern states - Ala., Ark., Fla., Ga., Ky., La., Miss., N.C., Okla., S.C., Tenn., Texas, Va.

69. H Con Res 83. Fiscal 2002 Budget Resolution/Democratic Substitute. Spratt, D-S.C., substitute amendment that calls for dividing the non-Social Security, non-Medicare, 10-year surplus into approximately one-third for spending, one-third for cutting taxes, and one-third for reducing the debt and providing additional Medicare and Social Security resources. The plan calls for $270.6 billion more in non-defense discretionary spending than the budget resolution over 10 years. In 2002, it calls for $18.6 billion more in non-defense discretionary spending than the resolution, and $2.7 billion more in defense discretionary spending. Rejected 183-243: R 0-219; D 182-23 (ND 138-15,SD 44-8); I 1-1. March 28, 2001.

70. H Con Res 83. Fiscal 2002 Budget Resolution/Adoption. Adoption of the concurrent resolution that would set broad spending and revenue targets. The resolution calls for cutting taxes by $1.6 trillion over 10 years and reducing the publicly held debt over the same period by $2.3 trillion. The resolution calls for $660.6 billion in discretionary spending for fiscal 2002. It calls for a $13.8 billion increase in defense spending over fiscal 2001, $11.3 billion more in non-defense spending. The resolution would permit additional tax cuts if the Congressional Budget Office increases its projected on-budget surplus estimates. Adopted 222-205: R 218-2; D 3-202 (ND 2-151, SD 1-51); I 1-1. A "yea" was a vote in support of the president's position. March 28, 2001.

71. HR 6. Marriage Tax Reduction/Rule. Adoption of the rule (H Res 104) to provide for House floor consideration of the bill that would reduce taxes by $399.2 billion through 2011. Adopted 249-171: R 213-0; D 35-170 (ND 18-135, SD 17-35); I 1-1. March 29, 2001.

72. Procedural Motion/Journal. Approval of the House Journal of Wednesday, March 28, 2001. Approved 354-62: R 199-10; D 153-52 (ND 116-38, SD 37-14); I 2-0. March 29, 2001.

73. HR 6. Marriage Tax Reduction/Democratic Substitute. Rangel, D-N.Y., substitute amendment, that would reduce taxes by $585.5 billion through 2011. The plan would create a new 12 percent bracket for the the first $20,000 of a couple's taxable income and $10,000 for single taxpayers. It would increase the standard deduction for married couples filing jointly to twice that of individuals filing singly. The amendment also would simplify and expand the earned-income tax credit for low-income earners. Rejected 196-231: R 0-218; D 195-12 (ND 146-8, SD 49-4); I 1-1. March 29, 2001.

74. HR 6. Marriage Tax Reduction/Recommit. Rangel, D-N.Y., motion to recommit the bill to the House Ways and Means Committee with instructions to report the measure back to the House with an amendment providing a tax rebate for those with tax liability and those eligible for the earned-income tax credit in 2000 of $300 for singles and $600 for married couples. Motion rejected 184-240: R 0-216; D 183-23 (ND 140-13, SD 43-10); I 1-1. March 29, 2001.

75. HR 6. Marriage Tax Reduction/Passage. Passage of the bill that would reduce taxes by $399.2 billion through 2011 by allowing married couples filing jointly to claim a standard deduction twice that for a single filer, increase the amount of a married couple's income subject to the lowest tax bracket to twice that of a single filer, and allow low-income filers to make more money and still qualify for the earned-income tax credit. It also would gradually double the child tax credit to $1,000. Passed 282-144: R 217-0; D 64-143 (ND 40-114, SD 24-29); I 1-1. A "yea" was a vote in support of the president's position. March 29, 2001.

¹ Rep. Norman Sisisky, D-Va., died March 29. The last vote for which he was eligible was Vote 70.

Key

Y	Voted for (yea).
#	Paired for.
+	Announced for.
N	Voted against (nay).
X	Paired against.
−	Announced against.
P	Voted "present."
C	Voted "present" to avoid possible conflict of interest.
?	Did not vote or otherwise make a position known.

Democrats • **Republicans**
Independents

	69	70	71	72	73	74	75
ALABAMA							
1 *Callahan*	N	Y	Y	Y	N	N	Y
2 *Everett*	N	Y	?	Y	N	N	Y
3 *Riley*	N	Y	Y	Y	N	N	Y
4 *Aderholt*	N	Y	Y	Y	N	N	Y
5 Cramer	Y	N	Y	Y	Y	Y	Y
6 *Bachus*	N	Y	Y	Y	N	N	Y
7 Hilliard	Y	N	N	N	Y	Y	N
ALASKA							
AL *Young*	N	Y	?	?	N	N	Y
ARIZONA							
1 *Flake*	N	Y	Y	Y	N	N	Y
2 Pastor	Y	N	N	Y	Y	Y	N
3 *Stump*	N	Y	Y	Y	N	N	Y
4 *Shadegg*	N	Y	Y	Y	N	N	Y
5 *Kolbe*	N	Y	Y	Y	N	N	Y
6 *Hayworth*	N	Y	Y	Y	N	N	Y
ARKANSAS							
1 Berry	N	N	Y	Y	N	Y	Y
2 Snyder	Y	N	Y	Y	Y	N	N
3 *Hutchinson*	N	Y	Y	Y	N	?	?
4 Ross	N	N	Y	Y	Y	Y	Y
CALIFORNIA							
1 Thompson	Y	N	N	N	Y	Y	N
2 *Herger*	N	Y	Y	Y	N	N	Y
3 *Ose*	N	Y	Y	Y	N	N	Y
4 *Doolittle*	N	Y	Y	Y	N	N	Y
5 Matsui	Y	N	N	Y	Y	Y	N
6 Woolsey	Y	N	N	Y	Y	Y	N
7 Miller, George	Y	N	N	N	Y	Y	N
8 Pelosi	Y	N	?	Y	Y	Y	N
9 Lee	Y	N	N	N	Y	Y	N
10 Tauscher	Y	N	N	Y	Y	Y	N
11 *Pombo*	N	Y	Y	Y	N	N	Y
12 Lantos	Y	N	N	Y	Y	Y	N
13 Stark	Y	N	N	N	Y	Y	N
14 Eshoo	Y	N	Y	Y	Y	Y	N
15 Honda	Y	N	N	Y	Y	Y	N
16 Lofgren	Y	N	N	Y	Y	Y	N
17 Farr	Y	N	N	Y	Y	Y	N
18 Condit	Y	Y	N	Y	Y	N	Y
19 *Radanovich*	N	Y	Y	?	N	N	Y
20 Dooley	Y	Y	Y	Y	Y	Y	N
21 *Thomas*	N	Y	Y	Y	N	N	Y
22 Capps	Y	N	N	Y	Y	Y	N
23 *Gallegly*	N	Y	Y	Y	N	N	Y
24 Sherman	Y	N	N	Y	Y	Y	N
25 *McKeon*	N	Y	Y	Y	N	N	Y
26 Berman	Y	N	N	Y	Y	Y	N
27 Schiff	N	N	Y	Y	Y	Y	Y
28 *Dreier*	N	Y	Y	Y	N	N	Y
29 Waxman	Y	N	N	Y	Y	Y	N
30 Becerra	+	−	N	Y	Y	Y	N
31 Solis	Y	N	N	Y	Y	Y	N
32 Vacant							
33 Roybal-Allard	Y	N	N	Y	Y	Y	N
34 Napolitano	Y	N	N	Y	Y	Y	N
35 Waters	Y	N	N	Y	Y	Y	N
36 Harman	N	N	N	Y	Y	Y	Y
37 Millender-McD.	Y	N	N	Y	Y	Y	N
38 *Horn*	N	Y	Y	Y	N	N	Y

	69	70	71	72	73	74	75
39 *Royce*	N	Y	Y	?	N	N	Y
40 *Lewis*	N	Y	Y	Y	N	N	Y
41 *Miller, Gary*	N	Y	Y	Y	N	N	Y
42 Baca	Y	N	N	Y	Y	Y	N
43 *Calvert*	N	Y	Y	Y	N	N	Y
44 *Bono*	N	Y	Y	Y	N	N	Y
45 *Rohrabacher*	N	Y	Y	Y	N	N	Y
46 Sanchez	Y	N	N	Y	Y	Y	N
47 *Cox*	N	Y	Y	Y	N	N	Y
48 *Issa*	N	Y	Y	Y	N	N	Y
49 Davis	Y	N	Y	Y	Y	Y	Y
50 Filner	Y	N	N	N	Y	Y	N
51 *Cunningham*	N	Y	Y	Y	N	N	Y
52 *Hunter*	N	Y	Y	Y	N	N	Y
COLORADO							
1 DeGette	Y	N	N	Y	Y	Y	N
2 Udall	Y	N	N	N	Y	Y	Y
3 *McInnis*	N	Y	Y	Y	N	N	Y
4 *Schaffer*	N	Y	Y	Y	N	N	Y
5 *Hefley*	N	N	N	N	N	N	Y
6 *Tancredo*	N	Y	Y	Y	N	N	Y
CONNECTICUT							
1 Larson	Y	N	N	Y	Y	Y	N
2 *Simmons*	N	Y	Y	Y	N	N	Y
3 DeLauro	Y	N	N	Y	Y	Y	N
4 *Shays*	N	Y	Y	Y	N	N	Y
5 Maloney	Y	N	N	Y	Y	Y	Y
6 *Johnson*	N	Y	?	?	N	N	Y
DELAWARE							
AL *Castle*	N	Y	Y	Y	N	N	Y
FLORIDA							
1 *Scarborough*	N	Y	Y	Y	N	N	Y
2 Boyd	Y	N	N	Y	Y	Y	Y
3 Brown	Y	N	N	N	Y	Y	N
4 *Crenshaw*	N	Y	Y	Y	N	N	Y
5 Thurman	Y	N	N	Y	Y	Y	N
6 *Stearns*	N	Y	Y	Y	N	N	Y
7 *Mica*	N	Y	Y	Y	N	N	Y
8 *Keller*	N	Y	Y	Y	N	N	Y
9 *Bilirakis*	N	Y	Y	Y	N	N	Y
10 *Young*	N	Y	Y	Y	N	N	Y
11 Davis	Y	N	N	Y	Y	Y	Y
12 *Putnam*	N	Y	Y	Y	N	N	Y
13 *Miller*	N	Y	Y	Y	N	N	Y
14 *Goss*	N	Y	Y	Y	N	N	Y
15 *Weldon*	N	Y	Y	Y	N	N	Y
16 *Foley*	N	Y	Y	Y	N	N	Y
17 Meek	Y	N	N	?	Y	Y	N
18 *Ros-Lehtinen*	N	Y	?	?	?	?	?
19 Wexler	Y	N	N	Y	Y	Y	N
20 Deutsch	Y	N	N	Y	Y	Y	N
21 *Diaz-Balart*	N	Y	Y	Y	N	N	Y
22 *Shaw*	N	Y	Y	Y	N	N	Y
23 Hastings	Y	N	N	N	Y	Y	N
GEORGIA							
1 *Kingston*	N	Y	Y	Y	N	N	Y
2 Bishop	Y	N	Y	Y	N	Y	Y
3 *Collins*	N	Y	Y	Y	N	N	Y
4 McKinney	Y	N	N	Y	Y	Y	N
5 Lewis	Y	N	N	N	Y	Y	N
6 *Isakson*	N	Y	Y	Y	N	N	Y
7 *Barr*	N	Y	Y	N	N	N	Y
8 *Chambliss*	N	Y	Y	Y	N	N	Y
9 *Deal*	N	Y	Y	Y	N	N	Y
10 *Norwood*	N	Y	Y	N	N	N	Y
11 *Linder*	N	Y	Y	Y	N	N	Y
HAWAII							
1 Abercrombie	Y	N	N	Y	Y	Y	N
2 Mink	Y	N	N	Y	Y	Y	N
IDAHO							
1 *Otter*	N	Y	Y	Y	N	N	Y
2 *Simpson*	N	Y	Y	Y	N	N	Y
ILLINOIS							
1 Rush	Y	N	N	Y	Y	Y	N
2 Jackson	Y	N	N	Y	Y	Y	N
3 Lipinski	N	N	N	Y	N	N	Y
4 Gutierrez	Y	N	N	Y	Y	Y	N
5 Blagojevich	Y	N	Y	Y	Y	Y	Y
6 *Hyde*	N	Y	Y	Y	N	N	Y
7 Davis	Y	N	N	Y	Y	Y	N
8 *Crane*	N	Y	N	N	N	N	Y
9 Schakowsky	Y	N	N	Y	Y	Y	N
10 *Kirk*	N	Y	Y	Y	N	N	Y
11 *Weller*	N	Y	Y	?	N	N	Y
12 Costello	N	N	N	N	N	Y	Y
13 *Biggert*	N	Y	Y	Y	N	N	Y

ND Northern Democrats   SD Southern Democrats

	69	70	71	72	73	74	75
14 ***Hastert***		Y					Y
15 ***Johnson***	N	Y	Y	Y	N	N	Y
16 ***Manzullo***	N	Y	Y	Y	N	N	Y
17 Evans	Y	N	N	Y	Y	Y	N
18 ***LaHood***	N	Y	Y	Y	N	N	Y
19 Phelps	N	N	N	Y	Y	Y	Y
20 ***Shimkus***	N	Y	Y	Y	N	N	Y
INDIANA							
1 Visclosky	N	N	N	N	N	Y	N
2 ***Pence***	N	Y	Y	Y	N	N	Y
3 Roemer	N	N	Y	Y	Y	N	Y
4 ***Souder***	N	Y	Y	Y	N	N	Y
5 ***Buyer***	N	Y	Y	Y	N	N	Y
6 ***Burton***	N	Y	Y	Y	N	N	Y
7 ***Kerns***	N	Y	Y	Y	N	N	Y
8 ***Hostettler***	N	Y	Y	Y	N	N	Y
9 Hill	N	N	N	Y	Y	Y	Y
10 Carson	Y	N	N	Y	Y	Y	Y
IOWA							
1 ***Leach***	N	Y	?	?	N	N	Y
2 ***Nussle***	N	Y	Y	?	N	N	Y
3 Boswell	Y	N	Y	Y	Y	N	Y
4 ***Ganske***	N	Y	Y	Y	N	N	Y
5 ***Latham***	N	Y	Y	Y	N	N	Y
KANSAS							
1 ***Moran***	N	Y	Y	Y	N	N	Y
2 ***Ryun***	N	Y	Y	Y	N	N	Y
3 Moore	N	N	N	Y	Y	Y	Y
4 ***Tiahrt***	N	Y	Y	Y	N	N	Y
KENTUCKY							
1 ***Whitfield***	N	Y	Y	Y	N	N	Y
2 ***Lewis***	N	Y	Y	Y	N	N	Y
3 ***Northup***	N	Y	Y	Y	N	N	Y
4 Lucas	N	N	Y	Y	N	N	Y
5 ***Rogers***	N	Y	Y	Y	N	N	Y
6 ***Fletcher***	N	Y	Y	Y	N	N	Y
LOUISIANA							
1 ***Vitter***	N	Y	Y	Y	N	N	Y
2 Jefferson	Y	N	N	N	Y	Y	N
3 ***Tauzin***	N	Y	Y	Y	N	N	Y
4 ***McCrery***	N	Y	Y	Y	N	N	Y
5 ***Cooksey***	N	Y	Y	Y	N	N	Y
6 ***Baker***	N	Y	Y	Y	N	N	Y
7 John	N	N	N	N	Y	Y	Y
MAINE							
1 Allen	Y	N	N	Y	Y	Y	N
2 Baldacci	Y	N	N	N	Y	Y	N
MARYLAND							
1 ***Gilchrest***	N	Y	Y	Y	N	N	Y
2 ***Ehrlich***	N	Y	Y	Y	N	N	Y
3 Cardin	Y	N	N	Y	Y	N	N
4 Wynn	Y	N	N	Y	Y	Y	Y
5 Hoyer	Y	N	N	Y	Y	Y	N
6 ***Bartlett***	N	Y	Y	Y	N	N	Y
7 Cummings	Y	N	N	Y	Y	Y	N
8 ***Morella***	N	Y	Y	Y	N	N	Y
MASSACHUSETTS							
1 Olver	Y	N	N	Y	Y	Y	N
2 Neal	Y	N	N	Y	Y	Y	N
3 McGovern	Y	N	N	N	Y	Y	N
4 Frank	Y	N	N	Y	Y	Y	N
5 Meehan	Y	N	N	Y	Y	Y	N
6 Tierney	Y	N	N	Y	Y	Y	N
7 Markey	Y	N	N	Y	Y	Y	N
8 Capuano	Y	N	N	N	N	Y	N
9 Moakley	Y	N	N	Y	Y	Y	N
10 Delahunt	Y	N	N	Y	Y	Y	N
MICHIGAN							
1 Stupak	Y	N	N	N	Y	?	N
2 ***Hoekstra***	N	Y	Y	Y	N	N	Y
3 ***Ehlers***	N	Y	Y	Y	N	N	Y
4 ***Camp***	N	Y	Y	Y	N	N	Y
5 Barcia	Y	N	Y	Y	N	N	Y
6 ***Upton***	N	Y	Y	Y	N	N	Y
7 ***Smith***	N	Y	Y	Y	N	N	Y
8 ***Rogers***	N	Y	Y	Y	N	N	Y
9 Kildee	Y	N	N	Y	Y	Y	N
10 Bonior	Y	N	N	N	Y	Y	N
11 ***Knollenberg***	N	Y	Y	Y	N	N	Y
12 Levin	Y	N	N	Y	Y	Y	N
13 Rivers	N	N	N	Y	Y	N	N
14 Conyers	Y	N	N	Y	Y	Y	N
15 Kilpatrick	Y	N	N	Y	Y	Y	N
16 Dingell	Y	N	N	Y	Y	Y	N
MINNESOTA							
1 ***Gutknecht***	N	Y	Y	N	N	N	Y
2 ***Kennedy***	N	Y	Y	N	N	N	Y
3 ***Ramstad***	N	Y	Y	N	N	N	Y
4 McCollum	Y	N	N	Y	Y	Y	N
5 Sabo	Y	N	N	N	Y	Y	N
6 Luther	Y	N	N	Y	Y	Y	Y
7 Peterson	Y	N	N	Y	Y	N	N
8 Oberstar	Y	N	N	N	Y	Y	N
MISSISSIPPI							
1 ***Wicker***	N	Y	Y	Y	N	N	Y
2 Thompson	Y	N	N	N	Y	Y	N
3 ***Pickering***	N	Y	Y	Y	N	N	Y
4 Shows	N	N	Y	Y	Y	N	Y
5 Taylor	N	N	N	N	N	N	Y
MISSOURI							
1 Clay	Y	N	N	Y	Y	Y	Y
2 ***Akin***	N	Y	Y	Y	N	N	Y
3 Gephardt	Y	N	N	Y	Y	Y	N
4 Skelton	Y	N	N	Y	Y	Y	Y
5 McCarthy	Y	N	N	Y	Y	Y	N
6 ***Graves***	N	Y	Y	Y	N	N	Y
7 ***Blunt***	N	Y	Y	?	N	N	Y
8 ***Emerson***	N	Y	Y	Y	N	N	Y
9 ***Hulshof***	N	Y	Y	Y	N	N	Y
MONTANA							
AL ***Rehberg***	N	Y	Y	Y	N	N	Y
NEBRASKA							
1 ***Bereuter***	N	Y	Y	Y	N	N	Y
2 ***Terry***	N	Y	Y	Y	N	N	Y
3 ***Osborne***	N	Y	Y	Y	N	N	Y
NEVADA							
1 Berkley	Y	N	Y	Y	Y	Y	Y
2 ***Gibbons***	N	Y	Y	N	N	N	Y
NEW HAMPSHIRE							
1 ***Sununu***	N	Y	Y	Y	N	N	Y
2 ***Bass***	N	Y	Y	Y	N	N	Y
NEW JERSEY							
1 Andrews	Y	N	N	Y	Y	Y	N
2 ***LoBiondo***	N	Y	Y	N	N	N	Y
3 ***Saxton***	N	Y	Y	Y	N	N	Y
4 ***Smith***	N	Y	Y	Y	N	N	Y
5 ***Roukema***	N	Y	Y	Y	N	N	Y
6 Pallone	Y	N	N	N	Y	Y	N
7 ***Ferguson***	N	Y	Y	Y	N	N	Y
8 Pascrell	Y	N	Y	Y	Y	Y	N
9 Rothman	?	?	?	?	?	?	?
10 Payne	Y	N	N	Y	Y	Y	N
11 ***Frelinghuysen***	N	Y	Y	Y	N	N	Y
12 Holt	Y	N	Y	N	Y	Y	Y
13 Menendez	Y	N	N	N	Y	Y	N
NEW MEXICO							
1 ***Wilson***	N	Y	Y	Y	N	N	Y
2 ***Skeen***	N	Y	Y	Y	N	N	Y
3 Udall	Y	N	N	N	Y	Y	N
NEW YORK							
1 ***Grucci***	N	Y	Y	Y	N	N	Y
2 Israel	Y	N	N	Y	Y	N	Y
3 ***King***	N	Y	Y	Y	N	N	Y
4 McCarthy	Y	N	Y	Y	Y	N	Y
5 Ackerman	Y	N	N	Y	Y	Y	N
6 Meeks	Y	N	N	Y	Y	Y	N
7 Crowley	Y	N	N	Y	Y	Y	N
8 Nadler	Y	N	N	Y	Y	Y	N
9 Weiner	Y	N	N	Y	Y	Y	N
10 Towns	N	N	N	Y	Y	Y	Y
11 Owens	Y	N	N	Y	Y	Y	N
12 Velázquez	Y	N	N	Y	Y	Y	N
13 ***Fossella***	N	Y	Y	Y	N	N	Y
14 Maloney	Y	N	N	Y	Y	Y	N
15 Rangel	Y	N	Y	Y	Y	Y	N
16 Serrano	Y	N	N	Y	Y	Y	N
17 Engel	Y	N	N	Y	Y	Y	Y
18 Lowey	Y	N	N	Y	Y	Y	N
19 ***Kelly***	N	Y	Y	Y	N	N	Y
20 ***Gilman***	N	Y	Y	Y	N	N	+
21 McNulty	Y	N	N	N	Y	Y	N
22 ***Sweeney***	N	Y	Y	Y	N	N	Y
23 ***Boehlert***	N	Y	Y	Y	N	N	Y
24 ***McHugh***	N	Y	Y	Y	N	N	Y
25 ***Walsh***	N	Y	Y	Y	N	N	Y
26 Hinchey	Y	N	N	N	Y	Y	N
27 ***Reynolds***	N	Y	?	?	N	N	Y
28 Slaughter	Y	N	N	N	Y	Y	N
29 LaFalce	Y	N	N	N	Y	Y	N
30 ***Quinn***	N	Y	Y	Y	N	N	Y
31 ***Houghton***	N	Y	Y	Y	N	N	Y
NORTH CAROLINA							
1 Clayton	Y	N	N	Y	Y	Y	N
2 Etheridge	Y	N	N	Y	Y	Y	Y
3 ***Jones***	N	Y	Y	Y	N	N	Y
4 Price	Y	N	N	Y	Y	Y	N
5 ***Burr***	N	Y	Y	Y	N	N	Y
6 ***Coble***	N	Y	Y	Y	N	N	Y
7 McIntyre	Y	N	N	Y	Y	Y	Y
8 ***Hayes***	N	Y	Y	Y	N	N	Y
9 ***Myrick***	N	Y	Y	Y	N	N	Y
10 ***Ballenger***	N	Y	Y	Y	N	N	Y
11 ***Taylor***	N	Y	Y	Y	N	N	Y
12 Watt	Y	N	N	N	Y	Y	N
NORTH DAKOTA							
AL Pomeroy	Y	N	N	N	Y	Y	N
OHIO							
1 ***Chabot***	N	Y	Y	Y	N	N	Y
2 ***Portman***	N	Y	Y	Y	N	N	Y
3 Hall	Y	N	Y	Y	Y	Y	N
4 ***Oxley***	N	Y	Y	Y	N	N	Y
5 ***Gillmor***	N	Y	Y	Y	N	N	Y
6 Strickland	Y	N	N	Y	Y	Y	N
7 ***Hobson***	N	Y	Y	Y	N	N	Y
8 ***Boehner***	N	Y	Y	Y	N	N	Y
9 Kaptur	N	N	N	Y	Y	Y	N
10 Kucinich	Y	N	N	N	Y	Y	N
11 Jones	Y	N	N	N	Y	Y	N
12 ***Tiberi***	N	Y	Y	Y	N	N	Y
13 Brown	Y	N	N	Y	Y	Y	N
14 Sawyer	Y	N	N	Y	Y	Y	N
15 ***Pryce***	N	Y	Y	Y	N	N	Y
16 ***Regula***	N	Y	Y	Y	N	N	Y
17 Traficant	N	Y	Y	Y	N	N	Y
18 ***Ney***	N	Y	Y	Y	N	–	Y
19 ***LaTourette***	N	Y	Y	Y	N	N	Y
OKLAHOMA							
1 ***Largent***	N	Y	Y	Y	N	N	Y
2 Carson	Y	N	N	Y	Y	Y	Y
3 ***Watkins***	N	Y	Y	Y	N	N	Y
4 ***Watts***	N	Y	Y	Y	N	N	Y
5 ***Istook***	N	Y	Y	Y	N	N	Y
6 ***Lucas***	N	Y	Y	Y	N	N	Y
OREGON							
1 Wu	Y	N	N	N	Y	Y	Y
2 ***Walden***	N	Y	Y	Y	N	N	Y
3 Blumenauer	Y	N	N	Y	Y	Y	N
4 DeFazio	Y	N	N	N	Y	Y	N
5 Hooley	Y	N	N	N	Y	Y	Y
PENNSYLVANIA							
1 Brady	Y	N	N	N	Y	Y	N
2 Fattah	Y	N	N	Y	Y	Y	N
3 Borski	Y	N	N	N	Y	Y	N
4 ***Hart***	N	Y	Y	Y	N	N	Y
5 ***Peterson***	N	Y	Y	Y	N	N	Y
6 Holden	Y	N	N	Y	Y	Y	Y
7 ***Weldon***	N	Y	Y	Y	N	N	Y
8 ***Greenwood***	N	Y	Y	Y	N	N	Y
9 Vacant							
10 ***Sherwood***	N	Y	Y	Y	N	N	Y
11 Kanjorski	Y	N	N	N	N	Y	N
12 Murtha	Y	N	N	Y	N	Y	N
13 Hoeffel	Y	N	N	Y	Y	Y	N
14 Coyne	Y	N	N	Y	Y	Y	N
15 ***Toomey***	N	Y	Y	Y	N	N	Y
16 ***Pitts***	N	Y	Y	Y	N	N	Y
17 ***Gekas***	N	Y	Y	Y	N	N	Y
18 Doyle	Y	N	N	Y	Y	Y	Y
19 ***Platts***	N	Y	Y	Y	N	N	Y
20 Mascara	Y	N	N	Y	Y	Y	Y
21 ***English***	N	Y	Y	N	N	N	Y
RHODE ISLAND							
1 Kennedy	Y	N	N	Y	Y	Y	N
2 Langevin	Y	N	N	Y	Y	Y	Y
SOUTH CAROLINA							
1 ***Brown***	N	Y	Y	Y	N	N	Y
2 ***Spence***	N	Y	Y	Y	N	N	Y
3 ***Graham***	N	Y	Y	Y	N	N	Y
4 ***DeMint***	N	Y	Y	Y	N	N	Y
5 Spratt	Y	N	N	Y	Y	Y	N
6 Clyburn	Y	N	N	N	Y	Y	N
SOUTH DAKOTA							
AL ***Thune***	N	Y	Y	Y	N	N	Y
TENNESSEE							
1 ***Jenkins***	N	Y	Y	Y	N	N	Y
2 ***Duncan***	N	Y	Y	Y	N	N	Y
3 ***Wamp***	N	Y	Y	Y	N	N	Y
4 ***Hilleary***	N	Y	Y	N	N	N	Y
5 Clement	Y	N	N	Y	Y	Y	Y
6 Gordon	?	?	?	?	Y	Y	Y
7 ***Bryant***	N	Y	Y	Y	N	N	Y
8 Tanner	N	N	N	N	Y	N	N
9 Ford	Y	N	Y	Y	Y	Y	Y
TEXAS							
1 Sandlin	Y	N	Y	Y	Y	Y	Y
2 Turner	Y	N	Y	N	Y	Y	Y
3 ***Johnson, Sam***	N	Y	Y	Y	N	N	Y
4 Hall	N	Y	N	Y	Y	N	Y
5 ***Sessions***	N	Y	Y	Y	N	N	Y
6 ***Barton***	N	Y	Y	Y	N	N	Y
7 ***Culberson***	N	Y	Y	Y	N	N	Y
8 ***Brady***	N	Y	Y	Y	N	N	Y
9 Lampson	?	?	?	?	?	?	?
10 Doggett	Y	N	N	Y	N	Y	N
11 Edwards	Y	N	N	Y	Y	Y	Y
12 ***Granger***	N	Y	Y	Y	N	N	Y
13 ***Thornberry***	N	Y	Y	Y	N	N	Y
14 ***Paul***	N	N	Y	Y	N	N	Y
15 Hinojosa	Y	N	Y	Y	Y	Y	N
16 Reyes	Y	N	Y	Y	Y	Y	N
17 Stenholm	Y	N	N	N	Y	N	N
18 Jackson-Lee	Y	N	N	N	Y	Y	N
19 ***Combest***	N	Y	Y	Y	N	N	Y
20 Gonzalez	Y	N	Y	Y	Y	Y	N
21 ***Smith***	N	Y	Y	Y	N	N	Y
22 ***DeLay***	N	Y	Y	Y	N	N	Y
23 ***Bonilla***	N	Y	Y	Y	N	N	Y
24 Frost	Y	N	Y	Y	Y	Y	N
25 Bentsen	Y	N	N	Y	Y	Y	N
26 ***Armey***	N	Y	Y	Y	N	N	Y
27 Ortiz	Y	N	Y	Y	Y	Y	N
28 Rodriguez	Y	N	Y	Y	Y	Y	Y
29 Green	Y	N	N	Y	Y	Y	N
30 Johnson, E.B.	Y	N	N	N	Y	Y	N
UTAH							
1 ***Hansen***	N	Y	Y	Y	N	N	Y
2 Matheson	N	N	N	Y	N	N	Y
3 ***Cannon***	N	Y	Y	Y	N	N	Y
VERMONT							
AL *Sanders*	Y	N	N	Y	Y	Y	N
VIRGINIA							
1 ***Davis, Jo Ann***	N	Y	Y	Y	N	N	Y
2 ***Schrock***	N	Y	Y	Y	N	N	Y
3 Scott	Y	N	N	Y	Y	Y	N
4 Sisisky [1]	?	?					
5 *Goode*	N	Y	Y	Y	N	N	Y
6 ***Goodlatte***	N	Y	Y	Y	N	N	Y
7 ***Cantor***	N	Y	Y	Y	N	N	Y
8 Moran	Y	N	N	Y	Y	Y	N
9 Boucher	Y	N	N	Y	Y	N	Y
10 ***Wolf***	N	Y	Y	Y	N	N	Y
11 ***Davis, T.***	N	Y	Y	Y	N	N	Y
WASHINGTON							
1 Inslee	Y	N	N	Y	Y	Y	N
2 Larsen	Y	N	N	Y	Y	Y	Y
3 Baird	Y	N	N	N	Y	Y	Y
4 ***Hastings***	N	Y	Y	Y	N	N	Y
5 ***Nethercutt***	N	Y	Y	Y	N	N	Y
6 Dicks	Y	N	N	Y	Y	Y	N
7 McDermott	Y	N	N	N	Y	Y	N
8 ***Dunn***	N	Y	Y	Y	N	N	Y
9 Smith	Y	N	Y	Y	Y	Y	Y
WEST VIRGINIA							
1 Mollohan	Y	N	N	Y	Y	Y	N
2 ***Capito***	N	Y	Y	Y	N	N	Y
3 Rahall	N	N	N	Y	Y	Y	N
WISCONSIN							
1 ***Ryan***	N	Y	Y	Y	N	N	Y
2 Baldwin	?	?	?	?	?	?	?
3 Kind	Y	N	N	Y	Y	Y	N
4 Kleczka	Y	N	N	Y	Y	Y	N
5 Barrett	Y	N	N	Y	Y	Y	Y
6 ***Petri***	N	Y	Y	Y	N	N	Y
7 Obey	Y	N	N	N	Y	Y	N
8 ***Green***	N	Y	Y	Y	N	N	Y
9 ***Sensenbrenner***	N	Y	Y	Y	N	N	Y
WYOMING							
AL ***Cubin***	N	Y	Y	Y	N	N	Y

Southern states - Ala., Ark., Fla., Ga., Ky., La., Miss., N.C., Okla., S.C., Tenn., Texas, Va.

Key

76. HR 768. Student Financial Aid/Passage. Sensenbrenner, R-Wis., motion to suspend the rules and pass the bill that would make permanent an antitrust exemption that allows universities to agree on common standards of need when awarding financial aid to students. Motion agreed to 414-0: R 209-0; D 203-0 (ND 150-0, SD 53-0); I 2-0. A two-thirds majority of those present and voting (276 in this case) is required for passage under suspension of the rules. April 3, 2001.

77. H Res 91. Cuba Human Rights/Adoption. Ros-Lehtinen, R-Fla., motion to suspend the rules and adopt the resolution that would express the sense of the House condemning Cuba for human rights violations and urge the president to seek a similar resolution at a U.N. Human Rights Commission meeting in Geneva. Motion agreed to 347-44: R 209-1; D 137-42 (ND 98-35, SD 39-7); I 1-1. A two-thirds majority of those present and voting (261 in this case) is required for adoption under suspension of the rules. April 3, 2001.

78. H Res 56. China Human Rights/Adoption. Ros-Lehtinen, R-Fla., motion to suspend the rules and adopt the resolution that would urge U.S. representatives at a U.N. Human Rights Commission meeting to seek a resolution calling for the end of human rights violations in China and Tibet. Motion agreed to 406-6: R 209-2; D 195-4 (ND 147-1, SD 48-3); I 2-0. A two-thirds majority of those present and voting (275 in this case) is required for adoption under suspension of the rules. April 3, 2001.

79. H Con Res 66. Women in Congress Report/Adoption. Ney, R-Ohio, motion to suspend the rules and adopt the concurrent resolution that would authorize an updated version of the House report titled "Women in Congress, 1917-1990." Motion agreed to 414-1: R 212-1; D 200-0 (ND 149-0, SD 51-0); I 2-0. A two-thirds majority of those present and voting (277 in this case) is required for adoption under suspension of the rules. April 4, 2001.

80. HR 8. Estate Tax Relief/Rule. Adoption of the rule (H Res 111) to provide for House floor consideration of the bill that would lower revenue by $185.6 billion over 10 years by reducing the estate, gift and generation-skipping taxes annually, cutting the top rate from 55 percent to 39 percent, with a complete repeal by 2011. Adopted 413-12: R 217-0; D 194-12 (ND 143-9, SD 51-3); I 2-0. April 4, 2001.

	76	77	78	79	80
ALABAMA					
1 *Callahan*	Y	Y	Y	Y	Y
2 *Everett*	Y	Y	Y	Y	Y
3 *Riley*	Y	Y	?	Y	Y
4 *Aderholt*	Y	Y	Y	Y	Y
5 Cramer	Y	Y	Y	Y	Y
6 *Bachus*	Y	Y	Y	Y	Y
7 Hilliard	Y	N	N	Y	N
ALASKA					
AL *Young*	Y	Y	Y	?	Y
ARIZONA					
1 *Flake*	Y	Y	Y	Y	Y
2 Pastor	Y	Y	Y	Y	Y
3 *Stump*	Y	Y	Y	Y	Y
4 *Shadegg*	Y	Y	Y	Y	Y
5 *Kolbe*	Y	Y	Y	Y	Y
6 *Hayworth*	Y	Y	Y	Y	Y
ARKANSAS					
1 Berry	Y	Y	Y	Y	Y
2 Snyder	Y	Y	Y	Y	Y
3 *Hutchinson*	Y	Y	Y	Y	Y
4 Ross	Y	Y	Y	Y	Y
CALIFORNIA					
1 Thompson	Y	Y	Y	Y	Y
2 *Herger*	Y	Y	Y	Y	Y
3 *Ose*	Y	Y	Y	Y	Y
4 *Doolittle*	Y	Y	Y	Y	Y
5 Matsui	Y	Y	Y	?	Y
6 Woolsey	?	?	?	?	?
7 Miller, George	Y	N	Y	Y	Y
8 Pelosi	Y	P	Y	Y	Y
9 Lee	Y	N	Y	Y	N
10 Tauscher	Y	Y	Y	Y	Y
11 *Pombo*	Y	Y	Y	Y	Y
12 Lantos	Y	Y	Y	Y	Y
13 Stark	Y	N	Y	Y	Y
14 Eshoo	Y	Y	Y	Y	Y
15 Honda	Y	Y	Y	Y	Y
16 Lofgren	Y	Y	Y	Y	Y
17 Farr	Y	P	Y	Y	Y
18 Condit	Y	Y	Y	Y	Y
19 *Radanovich*	Y	Y	Y	Y	Y
20 Dooley	Y	N	Y	Y	Y
21 *Thomas*	Y	Y	Y	Y	Y
22 Capps	Y	Y	Y	Y	Y
23 *Gallegly*	Y	Y	Y	Y	Y
24 Sherman	Y	Y	Y	Y	Y
25 *McKeon*	Y	Y	Y	Y	Y
26 Berman	Y	Y	Y	Y	Y
27 Schiff	Y	Y	Y	Y	Y
28 *Dreier*	Y	Y	Y	Y	Y
29 Waxman	Y	Y	Y	Y	Y
30 Becerra	?	?	?	?	?
31 Solis	Y	Y	Y	Y	Y
32 Vacant					
33 Roybal-Allard	Y	Y	Y	Y	Y
34 Napolitano	Y	P	Y	Y	Y
35 Waters	Y	N	N	Y	Y
36 Harman	Y	Y	Y	Y	Y
37 Millender-McD.	Y	Y	Y	Y	Y
38 *Horn*	Y	Y	Y	Y	Y

	76	77	78	79	80
39 *Royce*	Y	Y	Y	Y	Y
40 *Lewis*	Y	Y	Y	Y	Y
41 *Miller, Gary*	Y	Y	Y	Y	Y
42 Baca	Y	Y	Y	Y	Y
43 *Calvert*	Y	Y	Y	Y	Y
44 *Bono*	Y	Y	Y	Y	Y
45 *Rohrabacher*	Y	Y	Y	Y	Y
46 Sanchez	Y	Y	Y	Y	Y
47 *Cox*	Y	Y	Y	Y	Y
48 *Issa*	Y	Y	Y	Y	Y
49 Davis	Y	Y	Y	Y	Y
50 Filner	Y	N	Y	N	
51 *Cunningham*	?	?	Y	Y	Y
52 *Hunter*	Y	Y	Y	Y	Y
COLORADO					
1 DeGette	Y	Y	Y	Y	Y
2 Udall	Y	Y	Y	N	
3 *McInnis*	Y	Y	Y	Y	Y
4 *Schaffer*	Y	Y	Y	Y	Y
5 *Hefley*	Y	Y	Y	Y	Y
6 *Tancredo*	Y	Y	Y	Y	Y
CONNECTICUT					
1 Larson	Y	P	Y	Y	Y
2 *Simmons*	Y	Y	Y	Y	Y
3 DeLauro	Y	Y	Y	Y	Y
4 *Shays*	Y	Y	Y	Y	Y
5 Maloney	Y	Y	Y	Y	Y
6 *Johnson*	Y	Y	Y	Y	Y
DELAWARE					
AL *Castle*	Y	?	Y	Y	Y
FLORIDA					
1 *Scarborough*	+	+	Y	Y	
2 Boyd	Y	Y	Y	Y	Y
3 Brown	Y	P	Y	Y	Y
4 *Crenshaw*	Y	Y	Y	Y	Y
5 Thurman	Y	Y	P	Y	Y
6 *Stearns*	Y	Y	Y	Y	Y
7 *Mica*	Y	Y	Y	Y	Y
8 *Keller*	Y	Y	Y	Y	Y
9 *Bilirakis*	Y	Y	Y	Y	Y
10 *Young*	Y	Y	Y	Y	Y
11 Davis	Y	Y	Y	Y	Y
12 *Putnam*	Y	Y	Y	Y	Y
13 *Miller*	Y	Y	Y	Y	Y
14 *Goss*	Y	Y	Y	Y	Y
15 *Weldon*	Y	Y	Y	Y	Y
16 *Foley*	Y	Y	Y	Y	Y
17 Meek	Y	Y	Y	?	Y
18 *Ros-Lehtinen*	Y	Y	Y	Y	Y
19 Wexler	Y	Y	Y	Y	Y
20 Deutsch	Y	Y	Y	Y	Y
21 *Diaz-Balart*	Y	Y	Y	Y	Y
22 *Shaw*	Y	Y	Y	Y	Y
23 Hastings	Y	Y	N	Y	Y
GEORGIA					
1 *Kingston*	?	?	?	Y	Y
2 Bishop	Y	P	Y	Y	Y
3 *Collins*	?	Y	Y	Y	Y
4 McKinney	?	?	Y	?	N
5 Lewis	Y	N	Y	Y	Y
6 *Isakson*	Y	Y	Y	Y	Y
7 *Barr*	Y	Y	Y	Y	Y
8 *Chambliss*	Y	Y	Y	Y	Y
9 *Deal*	Y	Y	Y	Y	Y
10 *Norwood*	Y	Y	Y	Y	Y
11 *Linder*	Y	Y	Y	Y	Y
HAWAII					
1 Abercrombie	Y	Y	Y	Y	Y
2 Mink	Y	Y	Y	Y	Y
IDAHO					
1 *Otter*	Y	Y	Y	Y	Y
2 *Simpson*	Y	Y	Y	Y	Y
ILLINOIS					
1 Rush	?	?	?	?	?
2 Jackson	Y	N	Y	Y	Y
3 Lipinski	Y	Y	Y	Y	Y
4 Gutierrez	Y	Y	Y	Y	Y
5 Blagojevich	Y	Y	Y	Y	Y
6 *Hyde*	Y	Y	Y	Y	Y
7 Davis	Y	P	Y	Y	Y
8 *Crane*	Y	Y	P	Y	Y
9 Schakowsky	Y	N	?	Y	Y
10 *Kirk*	Y	Y	Y	Y	?
11 *Weller*	Y	Y	Y	Y	Y
12 Costello	Y	Y	Y	Y	Y
13 *Biggert*	Y	Y	Y	Y	Y

ND Northern Democrats   SD Southern Democrats

Member	76	77	78	79	80
14 Hastert					
15 *Johnson*	Y	Y	Y	Y	Y
16 *Manzullo*	Y	Y	Y	Y	Y
17 Evans	Y	Y	Y	Y	Y
18 *LaHood*	Y	Y	Y	Y	Y
19 Phelps	Y	Y	Y	Y	Y
20 *Shimkus*	Y	Y	Y	Y	Y
INDIANA					
1 Visclosky	Y	Y	Y	Y	Y
2 *Pence*	Y	Y	Y	Y	Y
3 Roemer	Y	Y	Y	Y	Y
4 *Souder*	Y	Y	Y	Y	Y
5 *Buyer*	Y	Y	Y	Y	Y
6 *Burton*	Y	Y	Y	Y	Y
7 *Kerns*	Y	Y	Y	Y	Y
8 *Hostettler*	Y	Y	Y	Y	Y
9 Hill	Y	Y	Y	Y	Y
10 Carson	Y	Y	Y	Y	Y
IOWA					
1 *Leach*	Y	Y	Y	Y	Y
2 *Nussle*	Y	Y	Y	Y	Y
3 Boswell	Y	Y	Y	Y	Y
4 *Ganske*	Y	Y	Y	Y	Y
5 *Latham*	?	?	?	?	?
KANSAS					
1 *Moran*	Y	Y	Y	Y	Y
2 *Ryun*	Y	Y	Y	Y	Y
3 Moore	Y	Y	Y	Y	Y
4 *Tiahrt*	Y	Y	Y	Y	Y
KENTUCKY					
1 *Whitfield*	Y	Y	Y	?	Y
2 *Lewis*	Y	Y	Y	Y	Y
3 *Northup*	Y	Y	Y	Y	Y
4 Lucas	Y	Y	Y	Y	Y
5 *Rogers*	Y	Y	Y	Y	Y
6 *Fletcher*	Y	Y	Y	Y	Y
LOUISIANA					
1 *Vitter*	Y	Y	Y	Y	Y
2 Jefferson	Y	N	Y	Y	Y
3 *Tauzin*	Y	Y	Y	Y	Y
4 *McCrery*	Y	Y	Y	Y	Y
5 *Cooksey*	Y	Y	Y	Y	Y
6 *Baker*	Y	Y	Y	Y	Y
7 John	Y	Y	Y	Y	Y
MAINE					
1 Allen	Y	Y	Y	Y	Y
2 Baldacci	Y	Y	Y	Y	Y
MARYLAND					
1 *Gilchrest*	Y	Y	Y	Y	Y
2 *Ehrlich*	Y	Y	Y	Y	Y
3 Cardin	Y	Y	Y	Y	Y
4 Wynn	Y	N	Y	Y	Y
5 Hoyer	Y	Y	Y	Y	Y
6 *Bartlett*	Y	Y	Y	Y	Y
7 Cummings	Y	N	Y	Y	Y
8 *Morella*	Y	Y	Y	Y	Y
MASSACHUSETTS					
1 Olver	Y	N	Y	Y	Y
2 Neal	Y	Y	Y	Y	Y
3 McGovern	Y	N	Y	Y	Y
4 Frank	Y	Y	Y	Y	Y
5 Meehan	Y	Y	Y	Y	Y
6 Tierney	Y	P	Y	?	Y
7 Markey	Y	Y	Y	Y	Y
8 Capuano	Y	P	Y	Y	Y
9 Moakley	?	?	?	Y	Y
10 Delahunt	Y	P	Y	Y	Y
MICHIGAN					
1 Stupak	Y	Y	Y	Y	Y
2 *Hoekstra*	Y	Y	Y	Y	Y
3 *Ehlers*	Y	Y	Y	Y	Y
4 *Camp*	Y	Y	Y	Y	Y
5 Barcia	Y	P	Y	Y	Y
6 *Upton*	Y	Y	Y	Y	Y
7 *Smith*	Y	Y	N	Y	Y
8 *Rogers*	Y	Y	Y	Y	Y
9 Kildee	Y	Y	Y	Y	Y
10 Bonior	Y	Y	Y	Y	Y
11 *Knollenberg*	Y	Y	Y	Y	Y
12 Levin	Y	Y	Y	Y	Y
13 Rivers	Y	Y	Y	Y	Y
14 Conyers	Y	N	Y	Y	Y
15 Kilpatrick	Y	N	Y	Y	Y
16 Dingell	Y	Y	Y	Y	Y

Member	76	77	78	79	80
MINNESOTA					
1 *Gutknecht*	Y	Y	Y	Y	Y
2 *Kennedy*	Y	Y	Y	Y	Y
3 *Ramstad*	Y	Y	Y	Y	Y
4 McCollum	Y	P	Y	Y	Y
5 Sabo	Y	N	Y	Y	Y
6 Luther	Y	Y	Y	Y	Y
7 Peterson	Y	P	Y	Y	Y
8 Oberstar	Y	N	Y	Y	Y
MISSISSIPPI					
1 *Wicker*	Y	Y	Y	Y	Y
2 Thompson	Y	N	Y	Y	N
3 *Pickering*	Y	Y	Y	Y	Y
4 Shows	Y	Y	Y	Y	Y
5 Taylor	Y	Y	Y	Y	Y
MISSOURI					
1 Clay	Y	N	Y	Y	Y
2 *Akin*	Y	Y	Y	Y	Y
3 Gephardt	Y	Y	Y	Y	Y
4 Skelton	Y	Y	Y	Y	Y
5 McCarthy	Y	Y	Y	Y	Y
6 *Graves*	Y	Y	Y	Y	Y
7 *Blunt*	Y	Y	Y	Y	Y
8 *Emerson*	Y	Y	Y	Y	Y
9 *Hulshof*	?	?	?	Y	Y
MONTANA					
AL *Rehberg*	Y	Y	Y	Y	Y
NEBRASKA					
1 *Bereuter*	Y	Y	Y	+	Y
2 *Terry*	Y	Y	Y	Y	Y
3 *Osborne*	Y	Y	Y	Y	Y
NEVADA					
1 Berkley	Y	Y	Y	Y	Y
2 *Gibbons*	Y	Y	Y	Y	Y
NEW HAMPSHIRE					
1 *Sununu*	Y	Y	Y	Y	Y
2 *Bass*	Y	Y	Y	Y	Y
NEW JERSEY					
1 Andrews	Y	Y	Y	Y	Y
2 *LoBiondo*	Y	Y	Y	Y	Y
3 *Saxton*	Y	Y	Y	Y	Y
4 *Smith*	Y	Y	Y	Y	Y
5 *Roukema*	Y	Y	Y	Y	Y
6 Pallone	Y	Y	Y	Y	Y
7 *Ferguson*	Y	Y	Y	Y	Y
8 Pascrell	Y	Y	Y	Y	Y
9 Rothman	Y	Y	Y	Y	Y
10 Payne	Y	N	Y	Y	Y
11 *Frelinghuysen*	Y	Y	Y	Y	Y
12 Holt	Y	Y	Y	Y	Y
13 Menendez	Y	Y	Y	Y	Y
NEW MEXICO					
1 *Wilson*	Y	Y	Y	Y	Y
2 *Skeen*	Y	Y	Y	Y	Y
3 Udall	Y	Y	Y	Y	Y
NEW YORK					
1 *Grucci*	Y	Y	Y	Y	Y
2 Israel	Y	Y	Y	Y	Y
3 *King*	Y	Y	Y	Y	Y
4 McCarthy	Y	Y	Y	Y	Y
5 Ackerman	Y	Y	Y	Y	Y
6 Meeks	Y	N	Y	Y	Y
7 Crowley	Y	Y	Y	Y	Y
8 Nadler	Y	N	Y	Y	N
9 Weiner	Y	Y	Y	Y	Y
10 Towns	Y	N	Y	Y	Y
11 Owens	Y	P	Y	Y	N
12 Velázquez	Y	N	Y	Y	Y
13 *Fossella*	Y	Y	Y	?	Y
14 Maloney	+	+	Y	Y	Y
15 Rangel	Y	N	Y	Y	Y
16 Serrano	Y	N	Y	Y	Y
17 Engel	Y	Y	Y	Y	Y
18 Lowey	Y	P	Y	Y	Y
19 *Kelly*	Y	Y	Y	Y	Y
20 *Gilman*	Y	Y	Y	Y	Y
21 McNulty	Y	Y	Y	Y	Y
22 *Sweeney*	Y	Y	Y	Y	Y
23 *Boehlert*	Y	Y	Y	Y	Y
24 *McHugh*	Y	Y	Y	Y	Y
25 *Walsh*	Y	Y	Y	Y	Y
26 Hinchey	Y	N	P	Y	Y
27 *Reynolds*	Y	Y	Y	Y	Y
28 Slaughter	Y	P	Y	Y	Y
29 LaFalce	Y	Y	Y	Y	Y

Member	76	77	78	79	80
30 *Quinn*	Y	Y	Y	Y	Y
31 *Houghton*	Y	Y	Y	Y	Y
NORTH CAROLINA					
1 Clayton	Y	P	Y	Y	Y
2 Etheridge	Y	Y	Y	Y	Y
3 *Jones*	Y	Y	Y	Y	Y
4 Price	Y	Y	Y	Y	Y
5 *Burr*	Y	Y	Y	Y	Y
6 *Coble*	Y	Y	Y	Y	Y
7 McIntyre	Y	Y	Y	Y	Y
8 *Hayes*	Y	Y	Y	Y	Y
9 *Myrick*	Y	Y	Y	Y	Y
10 *Ballenger*	Y	Y	Y	Y	Y
11 *Taylor*	Y	Y	Y	Y	Y
12 Watt	Y	P	P	Y	Y
NORTH DAKOTA					
AL Pomeroy	Y	Y	Y	Y	Y
OHIO					
1 *Chabot*	Y	Y	Y	Y	Y
2 *Portman*	Y	Y	Y	Y	Y
3 Hall	Y	Y	Y	Y	Y
4 *Oxley*	Y	Y	Y	Y	Y
5 *Gillmor*	Y	Y	Y	Y	Y
6 Strickland	Y	Y	Y	Y	Y
7 *Hobson*	Y	Y	Y	Y	Y
8 *Boehner*	Y	Y	Y	Y	Y
9 Kaptur	Y	Y	Y	Y	Y
10 Kucinich	Y	N	P	Y	Y
11 Jones	Y	N	Y	Y	Y
12 *Tiberi*	Y	Y	Y	Y	Y
13 Brown	Y	Y	Y	Y	Y
14 Sawyer	Y	Y	Y	Y	Y
15 *Pryce*	Y	Y	Y	Y	Y
16 *Regula*	Y	Y	Y	Y	Y
17 Traficant	Y	Y	Y	Y	Y
18 *Ney*	Y	Y	Y	Y	Y
19 *LaTourette*	Y	Y	Y	Y	Y
OKLAHOMA					
1 *Largent*	Y	Y	Y	Y	Y
2 Carson	Y	Y	Y	Y	Y
3 *Watkins*	Y	Y	Y	Y	Y
4 *Watts*	Y	Y	Y	Y	Y
5 *Istook*	?	?	Y	Y	Y
6 *Lucas*	Y	Y	Y	Y	Y
OREGON					
1 Wu	Y	Y	Y	Y	N
2 *Walden*	+	+	+	Y	Y
3 Blumenauer	Y	P	Y	Y	Y
4 DeFazio	Y	P	Y	Y	N
5 Hooley	Y	Y	Y	Y	Y
PENNSYLVANIA					
1 Brady	Y	Y	Y	Y	Y
2 Fattah	Y	N	Y	?	Y
3 Borski	Y	Y	Y	Y	Y
4 *Hart*	Y	Y	Y	Y	Y
5 *Peterson*	Y	Y	Y	Y	Y
6 Holden	Y	Y	Y	Y	Y
7 *Weldon*	Y	Y	Y	Y	Y
8 *Greenwood*	Y	Y	Y	Y	Y
9 Vacant					
10 *Sherwood*	Y	Y	Y	Y	Y
11 Kanjorski	Y	Y	Y	Y	Y
12 Murtha	Y	Y	Y	Y	Y
13 Hoeffel	Y	N	Y	Y	Y
14 Coyne	Y	N	Y	Y	Y
15 *Toomey*	Y	Y	Y	Y	Y
16 *Pitts*	Y	Y	Y	Y	Y
17 *Gekas*	Y	Y	Y	Y	Y
18 Doyle	Y	Y	Y	Y	Y
19 *Platts*	Y	Y	Y	Y	Y
20 Mascara	Y	Y	Y	Y	Y
21 *English*	Y	Y	Y	Y	Y
RHODE ISLAND					
1 Kennedy	Y	Y	Y	?	?
2 Langevin	Y	Y	Y	Y	Y
SOUTH CAROLINA					
1 *Brown*	Y	Y	Y	Y	Y
2 *Spence*	Y	Y	Y	Y	Y
3 *Graham*	Y	Y	Y	Y	Y
4 *DeMint*	Y	Y	Y	Y	Y
5 Spratt	Y	Y	Y	Y	Y
6 Clyburn	Y	N	N	Y	Y
SOUTH DAKOTA					
AL *Thune*	Y	Y	Y	Y	Y

Member	76	77	78	79	80
TENNESSEE					
1 *Jenkins*	Y	Y	Y	Y	Y
2 *Duncan*	Y	Y	Y	Y	Y
3 *Wamp*	Y	Y	Y	Y	Y
4 *Hilleary*	Y	Y	Y	Y	Y
5 Clement	Y	Y	Y	Y	Y
6 Gordon	Y	Y	Y	?	Y
7 *Bryant*	Y	Y	Y	Y	Y
8 Tanner	Y	Y	Y	Y	Y
9 Ford	Y	Y	Y	Y	Y
TEXAS					
1 Sandlin	Y	Y	Y	Y	Y
2 Turner	Y	Y	Y	Y	Y
3 *Johnson, Sam*	Y	Y	Y	?	Y
4 Hall	Y	Y	Y	Y	Y
5 *Sessions*	Y	Y	Y	Y	Y
6 *Barton*	Y	Y	Y	Y	Y
7 *Culberson*	+	Y	Y	Y	Y
8 *Brady*	Y	Y	Y	Y	Y
9 Lampson	Y	N	Y	Y	Y
10 Doggett	Y	Y	Y	Y	Y
11 Edwards	Y	Y	Y	Y	Y
12 *Granger*	Y	Y	Y	Y	Y
13 *Thornberry*	Y	Y	Y	Y	Y
14 *Paul*	Y	N	N	N	Y
15 Hinojosa	Y	Y	Y	Y	Y
16 Reyes	Y	Y	Y	Y	Y
17 Stenholm	Y	Y	Y	Y	Y
18 Jackson-Lee	Y	?	Y	Y	Y
19 *Combest*	Y	Y	Y	Y	Y
20 Gonzalez	Y	N	Y	Y	Y
21 *Smith*	Y	Y	Y	Y	Y
22 *DeLay*	Y	Y	Y	Y	Y
23 *Bonilla*	Y	Y	Y	Y	Y
24 Frost	Y	Y	Y	Y	Y
25 Bentsen	Y	Y	Y	Y	Y
26 *Armey*	Y	Y	Y	Y	Y
27 Ortiz	Y	P	Y	Y	Y
28 Rodriguez	Y	P	Y	Y	Y
29 Green	Y	Y	Y	Y	Y
30 Johnson, E.B.	Y	Y	Y	Y	Y
UTAH					
1 *Hansen*	Y	Y	Y	Y	Y
2 Matheson	Y	Y	Y	Y	Y
3 *Cannon*	Y	Y	Y	Y	Y
VERMONT					
AL *Sanders*	Y	N	Y	Y	Y
VIRGINIA					
1 *Davis, Jo Ann*	Y	Y	Y	Y	Y
2 *Schrock*	Y	Y	Y	Y	Y
3 Scott	Y	Y	Y	Y	Y
4 Vacant					
5 Goode	Y	Y	Y	Y	Y
6 *Goodlatte*	Y	Y	Y	Y	Y
7 *Cantor*	Y	Y	Y	Y	Y
8 Moran	Y	P	Y	Y	Y
9 Boucher	Y	Y	Y	Y	Y
10 *Wolf*	?	?	?	Y	Y
11 *Davis, T.*	Y	Y	Y	Y	Y
WASHINGTON					
1 Inslee	Y	N	Y	Y	Y
2 Larsen	Y	Y	Y	Y	Y
3 Baird	Y	N	Y	Y	N
4 *Hastings*	Y	Y	Y	Y	Y
5 *Nethercutt*	Y	Y	Y	Y	Y
6 Dicks	Y	Y	Y	Y	Y
7 McDermott	Y	N	Y	Y	Y
8 *Dunn*	Y	Y	Y	Y	Y
9 Smith	Y	Y	Y	Y	Y
WEST VIRGINIA					
1 Mollohan	?	?	?	Y	Y
2 *Capito*	Y	Y	Y	Y	Y
3 Rahall	Y	Y	Y	Y	Y
WISCONSIN					
1 *Ryan*	Y	Y	Y	Y	Y
2 Baldwin	Y	N	Y	Y	Y
3 Kind	Y	Y	Y	Y	Y
4 Kleczka	Y	N	Y	Y	N
5 Barrett	Y	N	Y	Y	Y
6 *Petri*	Y	Y	Y	Y	Y
7 Obey	Y	?	Y	Y	Y
8 *Green*	Y	Y	Y	Y	Y
9 *Sensenbrenner*	Y	Y	Y	Y	Y
WYOMING					
AL *Cubin*	Y	Y	Y	Y	Y

Southern states - Ala., Ark., Fla., Ga., Ky., La., Miss., N.C., Okla., S.C., Tenn., Texas, Va.

Key

Y	Voted for (yea).
#	Paired for.
+	Announced for.
N	Voted against (nay).
X	Paired against.
−	Announced against.
P	Voted "present."
C	Voted "present" to avoid possible conflict of interest.
?	Did not vote or otherwise make a position known.

Democrats   **Republicans**
Independents

81. HR 642. Chesapeake Bay Office Reauthorization/Passage. Gilchrest, R-Md., motion to suspend the rules and pass the bill that would reauthorize the Chesapeake Bay office of the National Oceanic and Atmospheric Administration; authorize $6 million for its operation annually through fiscal 2006; establish a small-grants, restoration program; and call for a five-year study of the bay's ecosystem. Motion agreed to 406-13: R 200-13; D 204-0 (ND 150-0, SD 54-0); I 2-0. A two-thirds majority of those present and voting (280 in this case) is required for passage under suspension of the rules. April 4, 2001.

82. HR 8. Estate Tax Relief/Democratic Substitute. Rangel, D-N.Y., substitute amendment that would lower revenue by $39.2 billion over 10 years. The estate tax exemption would be increased from $675,000 to $2 million ($4 million for married couples) in 2002, rising to $2.5 million by 2010. The amendment would retain current-law "step-up basis" provisions, and replace the credit for estate taxes paid to a state with a deduction. Rejected 201-227: R 3-215; D 197-11 (ND 147-7, SD 50-4); I 1-1. April 4, 2001.

83. HR 8. Estate Tax Relief/Recommit. Pomeroy, D-N.D., motion to recommit the bill to the House Ways and Means Committee with instructions to report the measure back with a substitute amendment that would include increasing the estate and gift tax exemption with the goal of exempting 99 percent of all farms and two-thirds of all others currently subject to the tax. Motion rejected 192-235: R 0-218; D 191-16 (ND 144-10, SD 47-6); I 1-1. April 4, 2001.

84. HR 8. Estate Tax Relief/Passage. Passage of the bill that would lower revenue by $185.6 billion over 10 years by reducing the estate, gift and generation-skipping taxes annually, cutting the top rate from 55 percent to 39 percent, with a complete repeal by 2011. Beginning in 2002, the unified gift and estate credit would be replaced with an exemption allowing estates to be taxed at the lowest rate (18 percent, instead of 37 percent). Beginning in 2011, individuals inheriting more than $1.3 million ($3 million for spouses), would be required to pay capital gains taxes on any increase in value from the time the asset was acquired by the deceased until it was sold by the heir. Passed 274-154: R 215-3; D 58-150 (ND 35-119, SD 23-31); I 1-1. A "yea" was a vote in support of the president's position. April 4, 2001.

	81	82	83	84
ALABAMA				
1 *Callahan*	Y	N	N	Y
2 *Everett*	Y	N	N	Y
3 *Riley*	Y	N	N	Y
4 *Aderholt*	Y	N	N	Y
5 Cramer	Y	Y	N	Y
6 *Bachus*	Y	N	N	Y
7 Hilliard	Y	N	N	N
ALASKA				
AL *Young*	Y	N	N	Y
ARIZONA				
1 *Flake*	N	N	N	Y
2 Pastor	Y	Y	Y	N
3 *Stump*	Y	N	N	Y
4 *Shadegg*	Y	N	N	Y
5 *Kolbe*	Y	N	N	Y
6 *Hayworth*	Y	N	N	Y
ARKANSAS				
1 Berry	Y	Y	Y	Y
2 Snyder	Y	Y	Y	N
3 *Hutchinson*	Y	N	N	Y
4 Ross	Y	Y	Y	Y
CALIFORNIA				
1 Thompson	Y	Y	Y	Y
2 *Herger*	Y	N	N	Y
3 *Ose*	Y	N	N	Y
4 *Doolittle*	Y	N	N	Y
5 Matsui	Y	Y	Y	N
6 Woolsey	?	Y	Y	N
7 Miller, George	Y	Y	Y	N
8 Pelosi	Y	Y	Y	N
9 Lee	Y	N	Y	N
10 Tauscher	Y	Y	Y	Y
11 *Pombo*	Y	N	N	Y
12 Lantos	Y	Y	Y	N
13 Stark	Y	Y	Y	N
14 Eshoo	Y	Y	Y	N
15 Honda	Y	Y	Y	Y
16 Lofgren	Y	Y	Y	N
17 Farr	Y	Y	Y	N
18 Condit	Y	Y	N	Y
19 *Radanovich*	Y	N	N	Y
20 Dooley	Y	Y	Y	Y
21 *Thomas*	Y	N	N	Y
22 Capps	Y	Y	Y	Y
23 *Gallegly*	Y	N	N	Y
24 Sherman	Y	Y	Y	N
25 *McKeon*	Y	N	N	Y
26 Berman	Y	Y	Y	N
27 Schiff	Y	Y	Y	N
28 *Dreier*	Y	N	N	Y
29 Waxman	Y	Y	Y	N
30 Becerra	?	?	?	?
31 Solis	Y	Y	Y	N
32 Vacant				
33 Roybal-Allard	Y	Y	Y	N
34 Napolitano	Y	Y	Y	N
35 Waters	Y	Y	Y	N
36 Harman	Y	Y	Y	Y
37 Millender-McD.	Y	Y	Y	N
38 *Horn*	Y	N	N	Y

	81	82	83	84
39 *Royce*	N	N	N	Y
40 *Lewis*	Y	N	N	Y
41 *Miller, Gary*	Y	N	N	Y
42 *Baca*	Y	Y	Y	Y
43 *Calvert*	Y	N	N	Y
44 *Bono*	Y	N	N	Y
45 *Rohrabacher*	Y	N	N	Y
46 Sanchez	Y	Y	Y	Y
47 *Cox*	Y	N	N	Y
48 *Issa*	Y	N	N	Y
49 Davis	?	Y	Y	Y
50 Filner	Y	Y	Y	N
51 *Cunningham*	Y	Y	Y	N
52 *Hunter*	Y	N	N	Y
COLORADO				
1 DeGette	Y	Y	Y	N
2 Udall	Y	Y	Y	N
3 *McInnis*	Y	N	N	Y
4 *Schaffer*	N	N	N	Y
5 *Hefley*	Y	N	N	Y
6 *Tancredo*	N	N	N	Y
CONNECTICUT				
1 Larson	Y	Y	Y	N
2 *Simmons*	Y	N	N	Y
3 DeLauro	Y	Y	Y	N
4 *Shays*	Y	N	N	Y
5 Maloney	Y	Y	Y	Y
6 *Johnson*	Y	N	N	Y
DELAWARE				
AL *Castle*	Y	Y	N	N
FLORIDA				
1 *Scarborough*	N	N	N	Y
2 Boyd	Y	Y	Y	Y
3 Brown	Y	Y	Y	N
4 *Crenshaw*	Y	N	N	Y
5 Thurman	Y	Y	Y	N
6 *Stearns*	N	N	N	Y
7 *Mica*	Y	N	N	Y
8 *Keller*	Y	N	N	Y
9 *Bilirakis*	Y	N	N	Y
10 *Young*	Y	N	N	Y
11 Davis	Y	Y	Y	N
12 *Putnam*	Y	N	N	Y
13 *Miller*	Y	N	N	Y
14 *Goss*	Y	N	N	Y
15 *Weldon*	Y	N	N	Y
16 *Foley*	Y	N	N	Y
17 Meek	Y	Y	Y	N
18 *Ros-Lehtinen*	Y	N	N	Y
19 Wexler	Y	Y	Y	N
20 Deutsch	Y	Y	Y	N
21 *Diaz-Balart*	Y	N	N	Y
22 *Shaw*	Y	N	N	Y
23 Hastings	Y	Y	Y	N
GEORGIA				
1 *Kingston*	Y	N	N	Y
2 Bishop	Y	Y	Y	Y
3 *Collins*	Y	N	N	Y
4 McKinney	Y	Y	Y	N
5 Lewis	Y	Y	Y	N
6 *Isakson*	Y	N	N	Y
7 *Barr*	Y	N	N	Y
8 *Chambliss*	Y	N	N	Y
9 *Deal*	Y	N	N	Y
10 *Norwood*	Y	N	N	Y
11 *Linder*	Y	N	N	Y
HAWAII				
1 Abercrombie	Y	N	N	Y
2 Mink	Y	Y	Y	N
IDAHO				
1 *Otter*	Y	N	N	Y
2 *Simpson*	Y	N	N	Y
ILLINOIS				
1 Rush	?	Y	Y	N
2 Jackson	Y	N	Y	N
3 Lipinski	Y	Y	N	Y
4 Gutierrez	Y	Y	Y	N
5 Blagojevich	Y	Y	Y	N
6 *Hyde*	Y	N	N	Y
7 Davis	Y	Y	Y	N
8 *Crane*	Y	N	N	Y
9 Schakowsky	Y	Y	Y	N
10 *Kirk*	Y	N	N	Y
11 *Weller*	Y	N	N	Y
12 Costello	Y	Y	N	Y
13 *Biggert*	Y	N	N	Y

ND Northern Democrats   SD Southern Democrats

	81	82	83	84
14 *Hastert*				
15 *Johnson*	Y	N	N	Y
16 *Manzullo*	Y	N	N	Y
17 *Evans*	Y	Y	N	N
18 *LaHood*	Y	N	N	Y
19 Phelps	Y	Y	Y	Y
20 *Shimkus*	Y	N	N	Y

INDIANA

	81	82	83	84
1 Visclosky	Y	Y	Y	N
2 *Pence*	Y	N	N	Y
3 Roemer	Y	Y	Y	N
4 *Souder*	Y	N	N	Y
5 *Buyer*	Y	N	N	Y
6 *Burton*	Y	N	N	Y
7 *Kerns*	Y	N	N	Y
8 *Hostettler*	Y	N	N	Y
9 Hill	Y	Y	Y	N
10 Carson	Y	Y	Y	N

IOWA

	81	82	83	84
1 *Leach*	?	N	N	Y
2 *Nussle*	Y	N	N	Y
3 Boswell	Y	Y	Y	Y
4 *Ganske*	Y	N	N	Y
5 *Latham*	?	?	?	?

KANSAS

	81	82	83	84
1 *Moran*	Y	N	N	Y
2 *Ryun*	Y	N	N	Y
3 Moore	Y	Y	Y	Y
4 *Tiahrt*	Y	N	N	Y

KENTUCKY

	81	82	83	84
1 *Whitfield*	Y	N	N	Y
2 *Lewis*	Y	N	N	Y
3 *Northup*	Y	N	N	Y
4 Lucas	Y	Y	Y	Y
5 *Rogers*	Y	N	N	Y
6 *Fletcher*	Y	N	N	Y

LOUISIANA

	81	82	83	84
1 *Vitter*	Y	N	N	Y
2 Jefferson	Y	Y	Y	Y
3 *Tauzin*	Y	N	N	Y
4 *McCrery*	Y	N	N	Y
5 *Cooksey*	Y	N	N	Y
6 *Baker*	Y	N	N	Y
7 John	Y	Y	Y	Y

MAINE

	81	82	83	84
1 Allen	Y	Y	Y	N
2 Baldacci	Y	Y	Y	N

MARYLAND

	81	82	83	84
1 *Gilchrest*	Y	N	N	Y
2 *Ehrlich*	Y	N	N	Y
3 Cardin	Y	Y	Y	N
4 Wynn	Y	Y	Y	N
5 Hoyer	Y	Y	Y	N
6 *Bartlett*	Y	N	N	Y
7 Cummings	Y	Y	Y	N
8 *Morella*	Y	Y	Y	N

MASSACHUSETTS

	81	82	83	84
1 Olver	Y	Y	Y	N
2 Neal	Y	Y	Y	N
3 McGovern	Y	Y	Y	N
4 Frank	Y	Y	Y	N
5 Meehan	Y	Y	Y	N
6 Tierney	Y	Y	Y	N
7 Markey	Y	Y	Y	N
8 Capuano	Y	Y	Y	N
9 Moakley	Y	Y	Y	N
10 Delahunt	Y	Y	Y	N

MICHIGAN

	81	82	83	84
1 Stupak	Y	Y	Y	N
2 *Hoekstra*	Y	N	N	Y
3 *Ehlers*	Y	N	N	Y
4 *Camp*	Y	N	N	Y
5 Barcia	Y	Y	N	Y
6 *Upton*	Y	N	N	Y
7 *Smith*	Y	N	N	Y
8 *Rogers*	Y	N	N	Y
9 Kildee	Y	Y	Y	N
10 Bonior	Y	Y	Y	N
11 *Knollenberg*	Y	N	N	Y
12 Levin	Y	Y	Y	N
13 Rivers	Y	Y	Y	N
14 Conyers	Y	Y	Y	N
15 Kilpatrick	Y	Y	Y	N
16 Dingell	Y	Y	Y	N

MINNESOTA

	81	82	83	84
1 *Gutknecht*	Y	N	N	Y
2 *Kennedy*	Y	N	N	Y
3 *Ramstad*	Y	N	N	Y
4 McCollum	Y	Y	Y	N
5 Sabo	Y	Y	Y	N
6 Luther	Y	Y	Y	N
7 Peterson	Y	Y	Y	N
8 Oberstar	Y	Y	Y	N

MISSISSIPPI

	81	82	83	84
1 *Wicker*	Y	N	N	Y
2 Thompson	Y	N	N	Y
3 *Pickering*	Y	N	N	Y
4 Shows	Y	Y	N	Y
5 Taylor	Y	Y	Y	N

MISSOURI

	81	82	83	84
1 Clay	Y	Y	Y	N
2 *Akin*	N	N	N	Y
3 Gephardt	Y	Y	Y	N
4 Skelton	Y	Y	Y	N
5 McCarthy	Y	Y	Y	N
6 *Graves*	Y	N	N	Y
7 *Blunt*	Y	N	N	Y
8 *Emerson*	Y	N	N	Y
9 *Hulshof*	Y	N	N	Y

MONTANA

	81	82	83	84
AL *Rehberg*	Y	N	N	Y

NEBRASKA

	81	82	83	84
1 *Bereuter*	Y	Y	N	Y
2 *Terry*	Y	N	N	Y
3 *Osborne*	Y	N	N	Y

NEVADA

	81	82	83	84
1 Berkley	Y	Y	Y	Y
2 *Gibbons*	Y	N	N	Y

NEW HAMPSHIRE

	81	82	83	84
1 *Sununu*	Y	N	N	Y
2 *Bass*	Y	N	N	Y

NEW JERSEY

	81	82	83	84
1 Andrews	Y	Y	N	Y
2 *LoBiondo*	Y	N	N	Y
3 *Saxton*	Y	N	N	Y
4 *Smith*	Y	N	N	Y
5 *Roukema*	Y	N	N	Y
6 Pallone	Y	Y	Y	N
7 *Ferguson*	Y	N	N	Y
8 Pascrell	Y	Y	Y	N
9 Rothman	Y	Y	Y	N
10 Payne	Y	Y	Y	N
11 *Frelinghuysen*	Y	N	N	Y
12 Holt	Y	Y	Y	N
13 Menendez	Y	Y	Y	N

NEW MEXICO

	81	82	83	84
1 *Wilson*	Y	N	N	Y
2 *Skeen*	Y	N	N	Y
3 Udall	Y	Y	Y	N

NEW YORK

	81	82	83	84
1 *Grucci*	Y	N	N	Y
2 Israel	Y	Y	Y	Y
3 *King*	Y	N	N	Y
4 McCarthy	Y	Y	Y	N
5 Ackerman	Y	Y	Y	N
6 Meeks	Y	Y	Y	N
7 Crowley	Y	Y	Y	N
8 Nadler	Y	Y	Y	N
9 Weiner	Y	Y	Y	N
10 Towns	Y	N	N	Y
11 Owens	Y	Y	Y	N
12 Velázquez	Y	Y	Y	N
13 *Fossella*	Y	N	N	Y
14 Maloney	Y	Y	Y	N
15 Rangel	Y	Y	Y	N
16 Serrano	Y	Y	Y	N
17 Engel	Y	Y	Y	N
18 Lowey	Y	Y	Y	N
19 *Kelly*	Y	N	N	Y
20 *Gilman*	Y	N	N	Y
21 McNulty	Y	Y	Y	N
22 *Sweeney*	?	N	N	Y
23 *Boehlert*	Y	N	N	Y
24 *McHugh*	Y	N	N	Y
25 *Walsh*	Y	N	N	Y
26 Hinchey	Y	Y	Y	N
27 *Reynolds*	Y	N	N	Y
28 Slaughter	Y	Y	Y	N
29 LaFalce	Y	Y	Y	N

	81	82	83	84
30 *Quinn*	Y	N	N	Y
31 *Houghton*	Y	N	N	N

NORTH CAROLINA

	81	82	83	84
1 Clayton	Y	Y	Y	N
2 Etheridge	Y	Y	Y	Y
3 *Jones*	N	N	N	Y
4 Price	Y	Y	Y	N
5 *Burr*	Y	N	N	Y
6 *Coble*	N	N	N	Y
7 McIntyre	Y	Y	Y	Y
8 *Hayes*	Y	N	N	Y
9 *Myrick*	Y	N	N	Y
10 *Ballenger*	Y	N	N	Y
11 *Taylor*	Y	N	N	Y
12 Watt	Y	Y	Y	N

NORTH DAKOTA

	81	82	83	84
AL Pomeroy	Y	Y	Y	N

OHIO

	81	82	83	84
1 *Chabot*	Y	N	N	Y
2 *Portman*	Y	N	N	Y
3 Hall	Y	Y	Y	N
4 *Oxley*	Y	N	N	Y
5 *Gillmor*	Y	N	N	Y
6 Strickland	Y	Y	Y	N
7 *Hobson*	Y	N	N	Y
8 *Boehner*	?	N	N	Y
9 Kaptur	Y	Y	Y	N
10 Kucinich	Y	Y	Y	N
11 Jones	Y	Y	Y	N
12 *Tiberi*	Y	N	N	Y
13 Brown	Y	Y	Y	N
14 Sawyer	Y	Y	Y	N
15 *Pryce*	Y	N	N	Y
16 *Regula*	Y	N	N	Y
17 Traficant	Y	N	N	Y
18 *Ney*	Y	N	N	Y
19 *LaTourette*	Y	N	N	Y

OKLAHOMA

	81	82	83	84
1 *Largent*	Y	N	N	Y
2 Carson	Y	Y	Y	Y
3 *Watkins*	Y	N	N	Y
4 *Watts*	Y	N	N	Y
5 *Istook*	Y	N	N	Y
6 *Lucas*	Y	N	N	Y

OREGON

	81	82	83	84
1 Wu	Y	Y	Y	N
2 *Walden*	Y	N	N	Y
3 Blumenauer	Y	Y	Y	N
4 DeFazio	Y	Y	Y	N
5 Hooley	Y	Y	Y	Y

PENNSYLVANIA

	81	82	83	84
1 Brady	Y	Y	Y	N
2 Fattah	Y	Y	Y	N
3 Borski	?	Y	Y	N
4 *Hart*	Y	N	N	Y
5 *Peterson*	Y	N	N	Y
6 Holden	Y	Y	Y	N
7 *Weldon*	Y	N	N	Y
8 *Greenwood*	Y	N	N	Y
9 Vacant				
10 *Sherwood*	Y	N	N	Y
11 Kanjorski	Y	N	N	Y
12 Murtha	Y	N	N	Y
13 Hoeffel	Y	Y	Y	N
14 Coyne	Y	Y	Y	N
15 *Toomey*	N	N	N	Y
16 *Pitts*	Y	N	N	Y
17 *Gekas*	Y	N	N	Y
18 Doyle	Y	Y	Y	N
19 *Platts*	Y	N	N	Y
20 Mascara	Y	Y	Y	Y
21 *English*	N	N	N	Y

RHODE ISLAND

	81	82	83	84
1 Kennedy	?	?	?	?
2 Langevin	Y	Y	Y	N

SOUTH CAROLINA

	81	82	83	84
1 *Brown*	Y	N	N	Y
2 *Spence*	Y	N	N	Y
3 *Graham*	Y	N	N	Y
4 *DeMint*	Y	N	N	Y
5 Spratt	Y	Y	Y	N
6 Clyburn	Y	N	N	Y

SOUTH DAKOTA

	81	82	83	84
AL *Thune*	Y	N	N	Y

TENNESSEE

	81	82	83	84
1 *Jenkins*	Y	N	N	Y
2 *Duncan*	Y	N	N	Y
3 *Wamp*	Y	N	N	Y
4 *Hilleary*	Y	N	N	Y
5 Clement	Y	Y	Y	Y
6 Gordon	Y	N	N	Y
7 *Bryant*	Y	N	N	Y
8 Tanner	Y	Y	Y	Y
9 Ford	Y	Y	Y	Y

TEXAS

	81	82	83	84
1 Sandlin	Y	Y	Y	Y
2 Turner	Y	Y	Y	N
3 *Johnson, Sam*	Y	N	N	Y
4 Hall	Y	N	N	Y
5 *Sessions*	Y	N	N	Y
6 *Barton*	Y	N	N	Y
7 *Culberson*	Y	N	N	Y
8 *Brady*	Y	N	N	Y
9 Lampson	Y	Y	Y	Y
10 Doggett	Y	Y	Y	N
11 Edwards	Y	Y	Y	N
12 *Granger*	Y	N	N	Y
13 *Thornberry*	Y	N	N	Y
14 *Paul*	N	N	N	Y
15 Hinojosa	Y	Y	Y	Y
16 Reyes	Y	Y	Y	Y
17 Stenholm	Y	Y	Y	Y
18 Jackson-Lee	Y	Y	Y	N
19 *Combest*	Y	N	N	Y
20 Gonzalez	Y	Y	Y	N
21 *Smith*	Y	N	N	Y
22 *DeLay*	Y	N	N	Y
23 *Bonilla*	Y	N	N	Y
24 Frost	Y	Y	Y	N
25 Bentsen	Y	Y	Y	N
26 *Armey*	?	N	N	Y
27 Ortiz	Y	Y	Y	Y
28 Rodriguez	Y	Y	Y	N
29 Green	Y	Y	+	N
30 Johnson, E.B.	Y	Y	Y	N

UTAH

	81	82	83	84
1 *Hansen*	Y	N	N	Y
2 Matheson	Y	Y	N	Y
3 *Cannon*	?	N	N	Y

VERMONT

	81	82	83	84
AL *Sanders*	Y	Y	Y	N

VIRGINIA

	81	82	83	84
1 *Davis, Jo Ann*	Y	N	N	Y
2 *Schrock*	Y	N	N	Y
3 Scott	Y	Y	Y	N
4 Vacant				
5 Goode	Y	N	N	Y
6 *Goodlatte*	Y	N	N	Y
7 *Cantor*	Y	N	N	Y
8 Moran	Y	Y	Y	N
9 Boucher	Y	Y	Y	Y
10 *Wolf*	Y	N	N	Y
11 *Davis, T.*	Y	N	N	Y

WASHINGTON

	81	82	83	84
1 Inslee	Y	Y	Y	N
2 Larsen	Y	Y	Y	Y
3 Baird	Y	Y	Y	Y
4 *Hastings*	Y	N	N	Y
5 *Nethercutt*	Y	N	N	Y
6 Dicks	Y	Y	Y	N
7 McDermott	Y	Y	Y	N
8 *Dunn*	Y	N	N	Y
9 Smith	Y	Y	Y	Y

WEST VIRGINIA

	81	82	83	84
1 Mollohan	Y	Y	Y	N
2 *Capito*	Y	N	N	Y
3 Rahall	Y	Y	Y	Y

WISCONSIN

	81	82	83	84
1 *Ryan*	Y	N	N	Y
2 Baldwin	Y	Y	Y	N
3 Kind	Y	Y	Y	N
4 Kleczka	Y	Y	Y	N
5 Barrett	Y	Y	Y	N
6 *Petri*	Y	N	N	Y
7 Obey	Y	Y	Y	N
8 *Green*	Y	N	N	Y
9 *Sensenbrenner*	N	N	N	Y

WYOMING

	81	82	83	84
AL *Cubin*	Y	N	N	Y

Southern states - Ala., Ark., Fla., Ga., Ky., La., Miss., N.C., Okla., S.C., Tenn., Texas, Va.

85. H Con Res 83. Fiscal 2002 Budget Resolution/Motion to Instruct.
Spratt, D-S.C., motion to instruct conferees to insist that the conference report include language that would increase education funding to the maximum feasible; provide that Medicare prescription drug coverage costs not be taken from the Federal Hospital Insurance Trust Fund surplus; increase Medicare prescription drug coverage funding to the level set by the Senate amendment; and insist that the on-budget surplus for any fiscal year not be less than that year's Federal Hospital Insurance Trust Fund surplus. Motion rejected 200-207: R 3-204; D 196-2 (ND 145-1, SD 51-1); I 1-1. April 24. 2001.

86. HR 428. Taiwan Participation/Passage.
Leach, R-Iowa, motion to suspend the rules and pass the bill that would encourage Taiwan's participation in the World Health Organization and would direct the secretary of State to initiate a U.S. plan to obtain observer status for Taiwan at the annual summit of the WHO. Motion agreed to 407-0: R 208-0; D 197-0 (ND 145-0, SD 52-0); I 2-0. A two-thirds majority of those present and voting (272 in this case) is required for passage under suspension of the rules. April 24, 2001.

87. H J Res 41. Tax Limitation Constitutional Amendment/Passage.
Passage of the joint resolution to propose a constitutional amendment to require a two-thirds majority vote of the entire House and Senate to pass any legislation that increases federal revenues by more than a "de minimis" amount, except in times of war or military conflict threatening national security. Rejected 232-189: R 204-11; D 27-177 (ND 14-137, SD 13-40); I 1-1. A two-thirds majority vote of those present and voting (281 in this case) is required to pass a joint resolution proposing an amendment to the Constitution. April 25, 2001.

88. HR 503. Fetal Protection/Democratic Substitute.
Lofgren, D-Calif., substitute amendment that would make assault on a pregnant woman a federal crime. Under the substitute, a perpetrator could be subject to up to 20 years' imprisonment for an assault causing prenatal injury and up to life imprisonment for an assault causing termination of the pregnancy. Rejected 196-229: R 27-191; D 168-37 (ND 126-26, SD 42-11); I 1-1. A "nay" was a vote in support of the president's position. April 26, 2001.

89. HR 503. Fetal Protection/Passage.
Passage of the bill that would make it a criminal offense to injure or kill a fetus during the commission of a violent federal crime. The measure would establish criminal penalties, equal to those that would apply if the injury or death occurred to the pregnant woman, for those who harm a fetus, regardless of the perpetrator's knowledge of the pregnancy or intent to harm the fetus. The bill states that its provisions should not be interpreted to apply to consensual abortion or to a woman's actions with respect to her pregnancy. The death penalty could not be imposed under this bill. Passed 252-172: R 198-21; D 53-150 (ND 35-115, SD 18-35); I 1-1. April 26, 2001.

Key

Y	Voted for (yea).
#	Paired for.
+	Announced for.
N	Voted against (nay).
X	Paired against.
−	Announced against.
P	Voted "present."
C	Voted "present" to avoid possible conflict of interest.
?	Did not vote or otherwise make a position known.

Democrats   **Republicans**
Independents

	85	86	87	88	89
ALABAMA					
1 *Callahan*	N	Y	Y	N	Y
2 *Everett*	N	Y	Y	N	Y
3 *Riley*	N	Y	Y	N	Y
4 *Aderholt*	N	Y	Y	N	Y
5 Cramer	Y	Y	N	N	Y
6 *Bachus*	N	Y	Y	N	Y
7 Hilliard	Y	Y	N	Y	N
ALASKA					
AL *Young*	N	Y	Y	N	Y
ARIZONA					
1 *Flake*	N	Y	Y	N	Y
2 Pastor	Y	Y	N	Y	N
3 *Stump*	N	Y	Y	N	Y
4 *Shadegg*	N	Y	Y	N	Y
5 *Kolbe*	N	Y	Y	Y	N
6 *Hayworth*	N	Y	Y	N	Y
ARKANSAS					
1 Berry	Y	Y	Y	N	Y
2 Snyder	Y	Y	N	Y	N
3 *Hutchinson*	N	Y	Y	N	Y
4 Ross	Y	Y	N	Y	Y
CALIFORNIA					
1 Thompson	Y	Y	N	Y	N
2 *Herger*	N	Y	Y	N	Y
3 *Ose*	N	Y	Y	Y	N
4 *Doolittle*	N	Y	Y	N	Y
5 Matsui	Y	Y	N	Y	N
6 Woolsey	Y	Y	N	Y	N
7 Miller, George	Y	Y	N	Y	N
8 Pelosi	Y	Y	N	Y	N
9 Lee	Y	Y	N	Y	N
10 Tauscher	Y	Y	N	Y	N
11 *Pombo*	N	Y	Y	N	Y
12 Lantos	Y	Y	N	?	−
13 Stark	?	?	N	Y	N
14 Eshoo	Y	Y	N	Y	N
15 Honda	Y	Y	N	Y	N
16 Lofgren	Y	Y	N	Y	N
17 Farr	Y	Y	N	Y	N
18 Condit	N	Y	Y	N	Y
19 *Radanovich*	N	Y	Y	N	Y
20 Dooley	Y	Y	N	Y	N
21 *Thomas*	N	Y	N	N	Y
22 Capps	+	+	−	+	−
23 *Gallegly*	N	Y	Y	N	Y
24 Sherman	Y	Y	Y	Y	N
25 *McKeon*	N	Y	Y	N	Y
26 Berman	Y	?	N	Y	N
27 Schiff	+	+	N	Y	N
28 *Dreier*	N	Y	N	N	Y
29 Waxman	Y	Y	N	Y	N
30 Becerra	Y	Y	N	Y	N
31 Solis	Y	Y	N	Y	N
32 Vacant					
33 Roybal-Allard	?	?	?	?	?
34 Napolitano	Y	Y	N	Y	N
35 Waters	Y	Y	N	Y	N
36 Harman	Y	Y	Y	Y	N
37 Millender-McD.	Y	Y	N	Y	N
38 *Horn*	N	Y	Y	N	Y

	85	86	87	88	89
39 *Royce*	N	Y	Y	N	Y
40 *Lewis*	N	Y	Y	N	Y
41 *Miller, Gary*	N	Y	Y	N	Y
42 Baca	Y	Y	N	Y	N
43 *Calvert*	N	Y	Y	N	Y
44 *Bono*	N	Y	Y	Y	N
45 *Rohrabacher*	N	Y	Y	N	Y
46 Sanchez	N	Y	Y	N	Y
47 *Cox*	N	Y	Y	N	Y
48 *Issa*	N	Y	Y	N	Y
49 Davis	+	+	N	Y	N
50 Filner	+	+	N	Y	N
51 *Cunningham*	N	Y	Y	N	Y
52 *Hunter*	?	?	Y	N	Y
COLORADO					
1 DeGette	Y	Y	N	Y	N
2 Udall	Y	Y	N	Y	N
3 *McInnis*	N	Y	Y	N	Y
4 *Schaffer*	N	Y	Y	N	Y
5 *Hefley*	N	Y	Y	N	Y
6 *Tancredo*	N	Y	Y	N	Y
CONNECTICUT					
1 Larson	Y	Y	N	Y	N
2 *Simmons*	N	Y	Y	Y	N
3 DeLauro	Y	Y	N	Y	N
4 *Shays*	N	Y	Y	Y	N
5 Maloney	Y	Y	Y	Y	N
6 *Johnson*	N	Y	N	Y	N
DELAWARE					
AL *Castle*	N	Y	Y	Y	Y
FLORIDA					
1 *Scarborough*	N	Y	Y	N	Y
2 Boyd	Y	Y	N	Y	N
3 Brown	?	?	N	Y	N
4 *Crenshaw*	N	Y	Y	N	Y
5 Thurman	Y	Y	N	Y	N
6 *Stearns*	N	Y	Y	N	Y
7 *Mica*	−	+	Y	N	Y
8 *Keller*	N	Y	Y	N	Y
9 *Bilirakis*	N	Y	Y	N	Y
10 *Young*	N	Y	Y	N	Y
11 Davis	Y	Y	N	Y	N
12 *Putnam*	N	Y	Y	N	Y
13 *Miller*	N	Y	Y	N	Y
14 *Goss*	N	Y	Y	N	Y
15 *Weldon*	N	Y	Y	N	Y
16 *Foley*	N	Y	Y	Y	N
17 Meek	Y	Y	N	?	?
18 *Ros-Lehtinen*	N	Y	Y	N	Y
19 Wexler	Y	Y	N	Y	N
20 Deutsch	Y	Y	N	Y	N
21 *Diaz-Balart*	N	Y	Y	N	Y
22 *Shaw*	N	Y	Y	N	Y
23 Hastings	Y	Y	N	Y	N
GEORGIA					
1 *Kingston*	N	Y	Y	N	Y
2 Bishop	Y	Y	Y	Y	Y
3 *Collins*	N	Y	Y	N	Y
4 McKinney	?	?	N	Y	N
5 Lewis	Y	Y	N	Y	N
6 *Isakson*	N	Y	Y	N	Y
7 *Barr*	N	Y	Y	N	Y
8 *Chambliss*	N	Y	Y	N	Y
9 *Deal*	N	Y	Y	N	Y
10 *Norwood*	N	Y	Y	N	Y
11 *Linder*	?	?	Y	N	Y
HAWAII					
1 Abercrombie	+	+	N	Y	N
2 Mink	Y	Y	N	Y	N
IDAHO					
1 *Otter*	N	Y	Y	N	Y
2 *Simpson*	N	Y	Y	N	Y
ILLINOIS					
1 Rush	Y	Y	N	Y	P
2 Jackson	Y	Y	N	Y	N
3 Lipinski	Y	Y	N	N	Y
4 Gutierrez	Y	Y	?	Y	N
5 Blagojevich	Y	Y	N	Y	N
6 *Hyde*	N	Y	N	N	Y
7 Davis	Y	Y	N	Y	N
8 *Crane*	N	Y	Y	N	Y
9 Schakowsky	Y	Y	N	Y	N
10 *Kirk*	N	Y	Y	Y	N
11 *Weller*	−	+	Y	N	Y
12 Costello	Y	Y	N	N	Y
13 *Biggert*	N	Y	Y	N	Y

ND Northern Democrats   SD Southern Democrats

	85	86	87	88	89
14 ***Hastert***			Y		Y
15 ***Johnson***	N	Y	Y	N	Y
16 ***Manzullo***	N	Y	Y	N	Y
17 Evans	Y	Y	N	Y	N
18 ***LaHood***	N	Y	Y	N	Y
19 Phelps	Y	Y	N	N	Y
20 ***Shimkus***	N	Y	Y	N	Y
INDIANA					
1 Visclosky	Y	Y	N	N	N
2 ***Pence***	N	Y	Y	N	Y
3 Roemer	Y	Y	Y	N	Y
4 ***Souder***	N	Y	Y	N	Y
5 ***Buyer***	N	Y	Y	N	Y
6 ***Burton***	N	Y	Y	N	Y
7 ***Kerns***	N	Y	Y	N	Y
8 ***Hostettler***	N	Y	N	N	Y
9 Hill	Y	Y	N	Y	Y
10 Carson	Y	Y	N	Y	N
IOWA					
1 ***Leach***	N	Y	Y	?	?
2 ***Nussle***	N	Y	Y	N	Y
3 Boswell	Y	Y	Y	Y	N
4 ***Ganske***	Y	Y	Y	N	Y
5 ***Latham***	N	Y	Y	N	Y
KANSAS					
1 ***Moran***	N	Y	Y	N	Y
2 ***Ryun***	N	Y	Y	N	Y
3 Moore	Y	Y	N	Y	N
4 ***Tiahrt***	N	Y	Y	N	Y
KENTUCKY					
1 ***Whitfield***	?	?	Y	N	Y
2 ***Lewis***	N	Y	Y	N	Y
3 ***Northup***	N	Y	Y	N	Y
4 Lucas	Y	Y	Y	N	Y
5 ***Rogers***	N	Y	Y	N	Y
6 ***Fletcher***	N	Y	Y	N	Y
LOUISIANA					
1 ***Vitter***	?	?	?	N	Y
2 Jefferson	Y	Y	N	Y	N
3 ***Tauzin***	N	Y	Y	N	Y
4 ***McCrery***	N	Y	Y	N	Y
5 ***Cooksey***	N	Y	?	N	Y
6 ***Baker***	N	Y	Y	N	Y
7 John	Y	Y	Y	N	Y
MAINE					
1 Allen	Y	Y	N	Y	N
2 Baldacci	Y	Y	N	Y	N
MARYLAND					
1 ***Gilchrest***	N	Y	Y	N	Y
2 ***Ehrlich***	N	Y	Y	N	Y
3 Cardin	Y	Y	N	Y	N
4 Wynn	Y	Y	N	Y	N
5 Hoyer	Y	Y	N	Y	N
6 ***Bartlett***	N	Y	Y	N	Y
7 Cummings	Y	Y	N	Y	N
8 ***Morella***	Y	Y	N	Y	N
MASSACHUSETTS					
1 Olver	Y	Y	N	Y	N
2 Neal	Y	Y	N	Y	Y
3 McGovern	Y	Y	N	Y	N
4 Frank	Y	Y	N	Y	N
5 Meehan	Y	Y	N	Y	N
6 Tierney	Y	Y	N	Y	N
7 Markey	Y	Y	N	Y	N
8 Capuano	Y	Y	N	Y	N
9 Moakley	?	?	?	?	?
10 Delahunt	Y	Y	N	Y	N
MICHIGAN					
1 Stupak	Y	Y	N	N	Y
2 ***Hoekstra***	N	Y	Y	N	Y
3 ***Ehlers***	N	Y	Y	N	Y
4 ***Camp***	N	Y	Y	N	Y
5 Barcia	Y	Y	Y	N	Y
6 ***Upton***	Y	Y	Y	Y	Y
7 ***Smith***	N	Y	Y	N	Y
8 ***Rogers***	N	Y	Y	N	Y
9 Kildee	Y	Y	N	N	Y
10 Bonior	Y	Y	N	Y	Y
11 ***Knollenberg***	N	Y	Y	N	Y
12 Levin	Y	Y	N	Y	N
13 Rivers	Y	Y	N	Y	N
14 Conyers	Y	Y	N	Y	N
15 Kilpatrick	Y	Y	N	Y	N
16 Dingell	Y	Y	N	Y	Y
MINNESOTA					
1 ***Gutknecht***	N	Y	Y	N	Y
2 ***Kennedy***	N	Y	Y	N	Y
3 ***Ramstad***	N	Y	Y	N	Y
4 McCollum	Y	Y	N	Y	N
5 Sabo	Y	Y	N	Y	N
6 Luther	Y	Y	N	Y	N
7 Peterson	Y	Y	N	N	Y
8 Oberstar	Y	Y	N	N	Y
MISSISSIPPI					
1 ***Wicker***	N	Y	Y	N	Y
2 Thompson	Y	Y	N	Y	N
3 ***Pickering***	N	Y	Y	N	Y
4 Shows	Y	Y	Y	N	Y
5 Taylor	Y	Y	Y	N	Y
MISSOURI					
1 Clay	Y	Y	N	Y	N
2 ***Akin***	N	Y	Y	N	Y
3 Gephardt	Y	Y	N	Y	N
4 Skelton	Y	Y	Y	N	Y
5 McCarthy	Y	Y	N	Y	N
6 ***Graves***	N	Y	Y	N	Y
7 ***Blunt***	N	Y	Y	N	Y
8 ***Emerson***	N	Y	Y	N	Y
9 ***Hulshof***	N	Y	Y	N	Y
MONTANA					
AL ***Rehberg***	N	Y	Y	N	Y
NEBRASKA					
1 ***Bereuter***	N	Y	N	N	Y
2 ***Terry***	N	Y	Y	N	Y
3 ***Osborne***	N	Y	Y	N	Y
NEVADA					
1 Berkley	Y	Y	Y	Y	N
2 ***Gibbons***	N	Y	Y	N	Y
NEW HAMPSHIRE					
1 ***Sununu***	N	Y	Y	N	Y
2 ***Bass***	N	Y	Y	Y	N
NEW JERSEY					
1 Andrews	Y	Y	Y	Y	N
2 ***LoBiondo***	N	Y	Y	N	Y
3 ***Saxton***	N	Y	Y	N	Y
4 ***Smith***	N	Y	Y	N	Y
5 ***Roukema***	N	Y	Y	Y	N
6 Pallone	Y	Y	Y	Y	N
7 ***Ferguson***	N	Y	Y	N	Y
8 Pascrell	Y	Y	N	Y	N
9 Rothman	Y	Y	N	Y	N
10 Payne	?	?	N	Y	N
11 ***Frelinghuysen***	N	Y	Y	Y	N
12 Holt	Y	Y	N	Y	N
13 Menendez	Y	Y	N	Y	N
NEW MEXICO					
1 ***Wilson***	N	Y	Y	N	Y
2 ***Skeen***	N	Y	Y	N	Y
3 Udall	Y	Y	N	Y	N
NEW YORK					
1 ***Grucci***	N	Y	Y	N	Y
2 Israel	Y	Y	N	Y	N
3 ***King***	N	Y	Y	N	Y
4 McCarthy	Y	Y	Y	Y	N
5 Ackerman	Y	Y	N	Y	N
6 Meeks	Y	Y	N	Y	N
7 Crowley	Y	Y	N	Y	Y
8 Nadler	Y	Y	N	Y	N
9 Weiner	Y	Y	N	Y	N
10 Towns	Y	Y	N	Y	N
11 Owens	Y	Y	N	Y	N
12 Velázquez	Y	Y	N	Y	N
13 ***Fossella***	N	Y	Y	N	Y
14 Maloney	Y	Y	N	Y	N
15 Rangel	Y	Y	N	Y	Y
16 Serrano	Y	Y	N	Y	N
17 Engel	Y	Y	N	Y	N
18 Lowey	Y	Y	N	Y	N
19 ***Kelly***	N	Y	Y	Y	N
20 ***Gilman***	N	Y	Y	Y	N
21 McNulty	Y	Y	N	N	Y
22 ***Sweeney***	N	Y	Y	Y	Y
23 ***Boehlert***	N	Y	N	Y	N
24 ***McHugh***	?	?	?	N	Y
25 ***Walsh***	N	Y	Y	Y	N
26 Hinchey	Y	Y	N	Y	N
27 ***Reynolds***	N	Y	Y	N	Y
28 Slaughter	Y	Y	N	Y	N
29 LaFalce	Y	Y	N	N	Y
30 ***Quinn***	N	Y	Y	N	Y
31 ***Houghton***	N	Y	N	Y	N
NORTH CAROLINA					
1 Clayton	Y	Y	N	Y	N
2 Etheridge	Y	Y	Y	Y	N
3 ***Jones***	N	Y	Y	N	Y
4 Price	Y	Y	N	Y	N
5 ***Burr***	N	Y	Y	N	Y
6 ***Coble***	N	Y	Y	N	Y
7 McIntyre	Y	Y	Y	N	Y
8 ***Hayes***	N	Y	Y	N	Y
9 ***Myrick***	?	?	Y	N	Y
10 ***Ballenger***	N	Y	Y	N	Y
11 ***Taylor***	?	?	Y	N	Y
12 Watt	Y	Y	N	Y	N
NORTH DAKOTA					
AL Pomeroy	Y	Y	N	Y	Y
OHIO					
1 ***Chabot***	N	Y	Y	N	Y
2 ***Portman***	N	Y	Y	N	Y
3 Hall	Y	Y	?	N	Y
4 ***Oxley***	N	Y	Y	N	Y
5 ***Gillmor***	N	Y	N	N	Y
6 Strickland	Y	Y	N	Y	N
7 ***Hobson***	N	Y	Y	Y	Y
8 ***Boehner***	N	Y	Y	N	Y
9 Kaptur	Y	Y	N	Y	Y
10 Kucinich	Y	Y	N	N	Y
11 Jones	Y	Y	N	N	–
12 ***Tiberi***	N	Y	Y	N	Y
13 Brown	Y	Y	N	Y	N
14 Sawyer	Y	Y	N	Y	N
15 ***Pryce***	N	Y	Y	Y	Y
16 ***Regula***	N	Y	Y	N	Y
17 Traficant	Y	Y	Y	N	Y
18 ***Ney***	N	Y	Y	N	Y
19 ***LaTourette***	N	Y	Y	N	Y
OKLAHOMA					
1 ***Largent***	N	Y	Y	N	Y
2 Carson	Y	Y	N	Y	N
3 ***Watkins***	N	Y	Y	N	Y
4 ***Watts***	N	Y	+	N	Y
5 ***Istook***	?	Y	Y	N	Y
6 ***Lucas***	N	Y	Y	N	Y
OREGON					
1 Wu	Y	Y	N	Y	N
2 ***Walden***	N	Y	Y	N	Y
3 Blumenauer	Y	Y	N	Y	N
4 DeFazio	Y	Y	N	Y	N
5 Hooley	Y	Y	N	Y	N
PENNSYLVANIA					
1 Brady	Y	Y	N	Y	N
2 Fattah	Y	Y	N	Y	N
3 Borski	Y	Y	N	N	Y
4 ***Hart***	N	Y	Y	N	Y
5 ***Peterson***	N	Y	Y	N	Y
6 Holden	?	?	N	N	Y
7 ***Weldon***	N	Y	Y	N	Y
8 ***Greenwood***	N	Y	Y	Y	N
9 Vacant					
10 ***Sherwood***	N	Y	Y	N	Y
11 Kanjorski	Y	Y	N	N	Y
12 Murtha	Y	Y	N	N	Y
13 Hoeffel	Y	Y	N	Y	N
14 Coyne	Y	Y	N	Y	N
15 ***Toomey***	N	Y	Y	N	Y
16 ***Pitts***	N	Y	Y	N	Y
17 ***Gekas***	N	Y	Y	N	Y
18 Doyle	Y	Y	N	N	Y
19 ***Platts***	N	Y	Y	N	Y
20 Mascara	Y	Y	N	N	Y
21 ***English***	N	Y	Y	N	Y
RHODE ISLAND					
1 Kennedy	Y	Y	N	Y	N
2 Langevin	Y	Y	N	N	Y
SOUTH CAROLINA					
1 ***Brown***	N	Y	Y	N	Y
2 ***Spence***	N	Y	Y	N	Y
3 ***Graham***	N	Y	Y	N	Y
4 ***DeMint***	N	Y	Y	N	Y
5 Spratt	Y	Y	N	Y	Y
6 Clyburn	Y	Y	N	Y	Y
SOUTH DAKOTA					
AL ***Thune***	N	Y	Y	N	Y
TENNESSEE					
1 ***Jenkins***	N	Y	Y	N	Y
2 ***Duncan***	N	Y	Y	N	Y
3 ***Wamp***	N	Y	Y	N	Y
4 ***Hilleary***	N	Y	Y	N	Y
5 Clement	Y	Y	N	N	Y
6 Gordon	Y	Y	Y	Y	Y
7 ***Bryant***	N	Y	Y	N	Y
8 Tanner	Y	Y	N	Y	Y
9 Ford	Y	Y	N	Y	N
TEXAS					
1 Sandlin	Y	Y	Y	Y	N
2 Turner	Y	Y	N	Y	Y
3 ***Johnson, Sam***	N	Y	Y	N	Y
4 Hall	N	Y	Y	N	Y
5 ***Sessions***	N	Y	Y	N	Y
6 ***Barton***	N	Y	Y	N	Y
7 ***Culberson***	N	Y	Y	N	Y
8 ***Brady***	N	Y	Y	N	Y
9 Lampson	Y	Y	N	Y	N
10 Doggett	Y	Y	N	Y	N
11 Edwards	Y	Y	N	Y	N
12 ***Granger***	N	Y	Y	Y	Y
13 ***Thornberry***	N	Y	Y	N	Y
14 ***Paul***	N	Y	Y	N	N
15 Hinojosa	Y	Y	N	Y	N
16 Reyes	Y	Y	N	Y	N
17 Stenholm	Y	Y	N	N	Y
18 Jackson-Lee	Y	Y	N	Y	N
19 ***Combest***	N	Y	Y	N	Y
20 Gonzalez	Y	Y	N	Y	N
21 ***Smith***	?	?	?	N	Y
22 ***DeLay***	N	Y	Y	N	Y
23 ***Bonilla***	N	Y	Y	N	Y
24 Frost	Y	Y	N	Y	N
25 Bentsen	Y	Y	N	Y	N
26 ***Armey***	N	Y	Y	N	Y
27 Ortiz	Y	Y	N	N	Y
28 Rodriguez	Y	Y	N	Y	N
29 Green	Y	Y	Y	Y	N
30 Johnson, E.B.	Y	Y	N	Y	N
UTAH					
1 ***Hansen***	N	Y	Y	N	Y
2 Matheson	Y	Y	N	Y	Y
3 ***Cannon***	N	Y	Y	N	Y
VERMONT					
AL *Sanders*	Y	Y	N	Y	N
VIRGINIA					
1 ***Davis, Jo Ann***	N	Y	Y	N	Y
2 ***Schrock***	N	Y	Y	N	Y
3 Scott	Y	Y	N	Y	N
4 Vacant					
5 *Goode*	N	Y	Y	N	Y
6 ***Goodlatte***	N	Y	Y	N	Y
7 ***Cantor***	–	+	Y	N	Y
8 Moran	Y	Y	?	Y	N
9 Boucher	Y	Y	N	Y	N
10 ***Wolf***	N	Y	Y	N	Y
11 ***Davis, T.***	N	Y	Y	N	Y
WASHINGTON					
1 Inslee	Y	Y	N	Y	N
2 Larsen	Y	Y	N	Y	N
3 Baird	Y	Y	N	Y	N
4 ***Hastings***	N	Y	Y	N	Y
5 ***Nethercutt***	N	Y	Y	N	Y
6 Dicks	Y	Y	N	Y	N
7 McDermott	Y	Y	N	Y	N
8 ***Dunn***	N	Y	Y	Y	Y
9 Smith	Y	Y	N	Y	N
WEST VIRGINIA					
1 Mollohan	Y	Y	N	N	Y
2 ***Capito***	N	Y	Y	N	Y
3 Rahall	Y	Y	N	N	Y
WISCONSIN					
1 ***Ryan***	N	Y	Y	N	Y
2 Baldwin	Y	Y	N	Y	N
3 Kind	Y	Y	N	Y	Y
4 Kleczka	Y	Y	N	Y	N
5 Barrett	Y	Y	N	Y	N
6 ***Petri***	N	Y	Y	N	Y
7 Obey	Y	Y	N	Y	Y
8 ***Green***	N	Y	Y	N	Y
9 ***Sensenbrenner***	N	Y	Y	N	Y
WYOMING					
AL ***Cubin***	N	Y	Y	N	Y

Southern states - Ala., Ark., Fla., Ga., Ky., La., Miss., N.C., Okla., S.C., Tenn., Texas, Va.

Key

Y	Voted for (yea).
#	Paired for.
+	Announced for.
N	Voted against (nay).
X	Paired against.
−	Announced against.
P	Voted "present."
C	Voted "present" to avoid possible conflict of interest.
?	Did not vote or otherwise make a position known.

● Democrats   **Republicans**   Independents

---

90. H Con Res 91. Autism Awareness/Adoption. Greenwood, R-Pa., motion to suspend the rules and adopt the concurrent resolution that would recognize the importance of raising awareness of autism and express support for additional federal funding to support research on the disorder. Motion agreed to 418-1: R 214-1; D 202-0 (ND 149-0, SD 53-0); I 2-0. A two-thirds majority of those present and voting (280 in this case) is required for adoption under suspension of the rules. May 1, 2001.

91. H Con Res 95. Charter School Awareness/Adoption. Keller, R-Fla., motion to suspend the rules and adopt the concurrent resolution that would express the sense of Congress in support of establishing a National Charter Schools Week. Motion agreed to 404-6: R 215-0; D 187-6 (ND 136-5, SD 51-1); I 2-0. A two-thirds majority of those present and voting (274 in this case) is required for adoption under suspension of the rules. May 1, 2001.

92. HR 10. Pension and Retirement Incentives/Rule. Adoption of the rule (H Res 127) to provide for House floor consideration of the bill that would increase the amount individuals may contribute to traditional and Roth Individual Retirement Accounts (IRAs) and to 401(k) and similar plans and ease the ability of employees to take pension plans with them when they change jobs. Adopted 404-24: R 217-0; D 186-23 (ND 136-19, SD 50-4); I 1-1. May 2, 2001.

93. Procedural Motion/Journal. Approval of the House Journal of Tuesday, May 1, 2001. Approved 377-47: R 204-11; D 171-36 (ND 124-30, SD 47-6); I 2-0. May 2, 2001.

94. HR 10. Pension and Retirement Incentives/Democratic Substitute. Neal, D-Mass., substitute amendment that would add provisions to the bill giving a refundable tax credit of up to $1,000 to low- and middle-income employees who contribute to IRAs and employer-sponsored retirement pension plans including 401(k) and similar plans. The amendment also would allow a three-year tax credit for small employers of 50 percent of the costs incurred in establishing such pension plans and would offer them a 50 percent credit for certain employer contributions to retirement plans on behalf of non-highly paid workers. Rejected 207-223: R 0-219; D 207-2 (ND 153-2, SD 54-0); I 0-2. May 2, 2001.

95. HR 10. Pension and Retirement Incentives/Recommit. Sanders, I-Vt., motion to recommit the bill to the House Education and the Workforce and Ways and Means committees with instructions to add an amendment that would require companies that convert to a cash balance pension system to allow employees the choice to remain in their old pension plans. Motion rejected 153-276: R 1-217; D 151-58 (ND 123-32, SD 28-26); I 1-1. May 2, 2001.

96. HR 10. Pension and Retirement Incentives/Passage. Passage of the bill that would increase the amount individuals may contribute to traditional and Roth IRAs and to 401(k) and similar plans and ease the ability of employees to take pension plans with them when they change jobs. The bill would increase from $2,000 to $5,000 the limit on annual IRA contributions by 2004. Those age 50 and older could contribute up to $5,000 annually to the accounts beginning in 2002. Beginning in 2005, contribution limits would be indexed for inflation. Passed 407-24: R 219-1; D 187-22 (ND 133-22, SD 54-0); I 1-1. May 2, 2001.

97. Procedural Motion/Adjourn. Bonior, D-Mich., motion to adjourn. Motion rejected 157-250: R 0-204; D 156-45 (ND 117-32, SD 39-13); I 1-1. May 3, 2001.

	90	91	92	93	94	95	96	97
ALABAMA								
1 *Callahan*	Y	Y	Y	Y	N	N	Y	N
2 *Everett*	Y	Y	Y	N	N	N	Y	N
3 *Riley*	Y	Y	Y	N	N	N	Y	N
4 *Aderholt*	Y	Y	Y	N	N	N	Y	N
5 Cramer	Y	Y	Y	Y	N	Y	N	Y
6 *Bachus*	Y	Y	Y	Y	N	N	Y	N
7 Hilliard	Y	N	N	N	Y	Y	Y	Y
ALASKA								
AL *Young*	Y	Y	Y	Y	N	N	Y	?
ARIZONA								
1 *Flake*	Y	Y	Y	N	N	N	Y	N
2 Pastor	Y	Y	Y	N	Y	Y	Y	Y
3 *Stump*	Y	Y	Y	Y	N	N	Y	N
4 *Shadegg*	Y	Y	Y	N	N	N	Y	N
5 *Kolbe*	Y	Y	Y	N	N	N	Y	N
6 *Hayworth*	Y	Y	Y	N	N	N	Y	N
ARKANSAS								
1 Berry	Y	Y	Y	Y	Y	N	Y	Y
2 Snyder	Y	Y	Y	Y	Y	N	Y	Y
3 *Hutchinson*	Y	Y	Y	?	N	N	Y	?
4 Ross	Y	Y	Y	Y	Y	N	Y	Y
CALIFORNIA								
1 Thompson	Y	Y	Y	N	Y	Y	Y	Y
2 *Herger*	Y	Y	Y	Y	N	N	Y	N
3 *Ose*	Y	Y	Y	Y	N	N	Y	N
4 *Doolittle*	Y	Y	Y	N	N	N	Y	N
5 Matsui	Y	Y	N	Y	Y	Y	N	Y
6 Woolsey	Y	Y	Y	Y	Y	Y	N	Y
7 Miller, George	Y	Y	Y	N	Y	Y	N	Y
8 Pelosi	Y	Y	Y	Y	Y	Y	N	Y
9 Lee	Y	P	N	Y	Y	Y	N	Y
10 Tauscher	Y	Y	Y	Y	Y	Y	N	Y
11 *Pombo*	Y	Y	Y	Y	N	N	Y	N
12 Lantos	Y	Y	Y	Y	Y	Y	Y	Y
13 Stark	Y	N	N	N	Y	Y	N	Y
14 Eshoo	Y	Y	Y	Y	Y	Y	N	Y
15 Honda	Y	Y	Y	Y	Y	Y	N	Y
16 Lofgren	Y	Y	Y	Y	Y	Y	Y	N
17 Farr	Y	Y	Y	Y	Y	Y	N	Y
18 Condit	Y	Y	Y	N	Y	N	Y	Y
19 *Radanovich*	Y	Y	Y	Y	N	N	Y	N
20 Dooley	Y	Y	Y	Y	Y	N	Y	Y
21 *Thomas*	Y	Y	Y	Y	N	N	Y	N
22 Capps	Y	Y	Y	Y	Y	Y	N	Y
23 *Gallegly*	Y	Y	Y	Y	N	N	Y	N
24 Sherman	Y	Y	Y	Y	Y	N	Y	Y
25 *McKeon*	Y	Y	Y	Y	N	N	Y	N
26 Berman	Y	Y	Y	Y	Y	Y	N	Y
27 Schiff	Y	Y	Y	Y	Y	Y	N	Y
28 *Dreier*	Y	Y	Y	Y	N	N	Y	N
29 Waxman	Y	Y	Y	Y	Y	Y	N	Y
30 Becerra	Y	Y	Y	Y	Y	Y	Y	Y
31 Solis	Y	Y	Y	Y	Y	Y	Y	Y
32 Vacant								
33 Roybal-Allard	Y	Y	Y	Y	Y	Y	Y	N
34 Napolitano	Y	Y	Y	Y	Y	Y	Y	N
35 Waters	Y	N	N	N	Y	Y	N	Y
36 Harman	Y	Y	Y	Y	Y	N	Y	N
37 Millender-McD.	+	+	Y	Y	Y	Y	Y	Y
38 *Horn*	Y	Y	Y	Y	N	Y	N	N
39 *Royce*	Y	Y	Y	Y	N	?	Y	N
40 *Lewis*	Y	Y	Y	Y	N	N	Y	N
41 *Miller, Gary*	Y	Y	Y	Y	N	N	Y	N
42 Baca	Y	Y	Y	Y	Y	Y	Y	Y
43 *Calvert*	Y	Y	Y	Y	N	N	Y	N
44 *Bono*	Y	Y	Y	Y	N	N	Y	N
45 *Rohrabacher*	Y	Y	Y	N	N	N	Y	N
46 Sanchez	Y	Y	Y	Y	N	Y	N	Y
47 *Cox*	Y	Y	Y	Y	N	N	Y	N
48 *Issa*	Y	Y	Y	Y	N	N	Y	N
49 Davis	Y	Y	Y	Y	N	Y	Y	Y
50 Filner	Y	Y	N	Y	N	Y	N	Y
51 *Cunningham*	Y	Y	Y	Y	N	N	Y	N
52 *Hunter*	Y	Y	Y	Y	N	N	Y	N
COLORADO								
1 DeGette	Y	Y	Y	Y	Y	Y	Y	Y
2 Udall	Y	Y	Y	N	Y	Y	Y	Y
3 *McInnis*	Y	Y	Y	Y	N	N	Y	N
4 *Schaffer*	Y	Y	Y	N	N	N	Y	N
5 *Hefley*	Y	Y	Y	N	N	N	Y	N
6 *Tancredo*	Y	Y	Y	P	N	N	Y	N
CONNECTICUT								
1 Larson	Y	Y	Y	Y	Y	Y	Y	Y
2 *Simmons*	Y	Y	Y	Y	N	N	Y	N
3 DeLauro	Y	Y	Y	Y	Y	Y	Y	Y
4 *Shays*	Y	Y	Y	N	N	N	Y	N
5 *Maloney*	Y	Y	Y	Y	Y	Y	Y	Y
6 *Johnson*	Y	Y	?	?	N	N	Y	N
DELAWARE								
AL *Castle*	Y	Y	Y	Y	N	N	Y	N
FLORIDA								
1 *Scarborough*	Y	Y	Y	Y	N	N	Y	N
2 Boyd	Y	Y	Y	Y	Y	N	Y	Y
3 Brown	Y	Y	Y	Y	Y	Y	Y	Y
4 *Crenshaw*	Y	Y	Y	Y	N	N	Y	N
5 Thurman	Y	Y	Y	Y	Y	Y	Y	Y
6 *Stearns*	Y	Y	Y	N	N	N	Y	N
7 *Mica*	Y	Y	Y	Y	N	N	Y	N
8 *Keller*	Y	Y	Y	Y	N	N	Y	N
9 *Bilirakis*	Y	Y	Y	Y	N	N	Y	N
10 *Young*	?	?	Y	Y	N	N	Y	?
11 Davis	Y	Y	Y	Y	Y	N	Y	?
12 *Putnam*	Y	Y	Y	Y	N	N	Y	N
13 *Miller*	Y	Y	Y	Y	N	N	Y	N
14 *Goss*	Y	Y	Y	Y	N	N	Y	N
15 *Weldon*	Y	Y	Y	Y	N	N	Y	N
16 *Foley*	Y	Y	Y	Y	N	N	Y	N
17 Meek	Y	Y	Y	Y	Y	N	Y	N
18 *Ros-Lehtinen*	Y	Y	Y	Y	N	N	Y	N
19 Wexler	Y	Y	Y	Y	Y	Y	Y	Y
20 Deutsch	Y	Y	N	Y	Y	Y	Y	Y
21 *Diaz-Balart*	Y	Y	Y	Y	N	N	Y	N
22 *Shaw*	Y	Y	Y	Y	N	N	Y	N
23 Hastings	Y	Y	N	N	Y	Y	Y	Y
GEORGIA								
1 *Kingston*	Y	Y	Y	Y	N	N	Y	N
2 Bishop	Y	Y	Y	Y	Y	N	Y	Y
3 *Collins*	Y	Y	Y	Y	N	N	Y	N
4 McKinney	Y	Y	Y	Y	Y	Y	Y	N
5 Lewis	Y	Y	Y	Y	Y	Y	Y	Y
6 *Isakson*	Y	Y	Y	Y	N	N	Y	N
7 *Barr*	Y	Y	Y	Y	N	N	Y	N
8 *Chambliss*	Y	Y	Y	Y	N	N	Y	N
9 *Deal*	Y	Y	Y	Y	N	N	Y	N
10 *Norwood*	Y	Y	Y	Y	N	N	Y	N
11 *Linder*	Y	Y	Y	Y	N	N	Y	N
HAWAII								
1 Abercrombie	Y	Y	Y	Y	Y	Y	Y	N
2 Mink	Y	Y	Y	Y	Y	Y	Y	Y
IDAHO								
1 *Otter*	Y	Y	Y	Y	N	N	Y	N
2 *Simpson*	Y	Y	Y	Y	N	N	Y	N
ILLINOIS								
1 Rush	Y	Y	Y	Y	Y	Y	N	Y
2 Jackson	Y	Y	Y	Y	Y	Y	N	N
3 Lipinski	Y	Y	Y	Y	Y	N	Y	N
4 Gutierrez	?	?	Y	Y	Y	Y	Y	Y
5 Blagojevich	Y	Y	Y	Y	Y	Y	Y	N
6 *Hyde*	Y	Y	Y	Y	N	N	Y	?
7 Davis	Y	Y	Y	Y	Y	Y	Y	N
8 *Crane*	Y	Y	Y	N	N	N	Y	N
9 Schakowsky	Y	Y	Y	Y	Y	Y	Y	N
10 *Kirk*	Y	Y	Y	Y	N	N	Y	N
11 *Weller*	Y	Y	Y	Y	N	N	Y	N
12 Costello	Y	Y	Y	N	Y	N	Y	N
13 *Biggert*	Y	Y	Y	Y	N	N	Y	N

ND Northern Democrats   SD Southern Democrats

	90	91	92	93	94	95	96	97
14 ***Hastert***							Y	
15 ***Johnson***	Y	Y	Y	Y	N	N	Y	N
16 ***Manzullo***	Y	Y	Y	Y	N	N	Y	N
17 Evans	Y	Y	Y	Y	Y	Y	Y	Y
18 ***LaHood***	Y	Y	Y	Y	N	N	Y	N
19 Phelps	Y	Y	Y	Y	Y	Y	Y	Y
20 ***Shimkus***	Y	Y	Y	Y	N	N	Y	N
INDIANA								
1 Visclosky	Y	Y	N	N	Y	Y	Y	N
2 ***Pence***	Y	Y	Y	Y	N	N	Y	N
3 Roemer	Y	Y	Y	Y	Y	N	Y	N
4 ***Souder***	Y	Y	Y	Y	N	N	Y	N
5 ***Buyer***	?	?	Y	Y	N	N	Y	N
6 ***Burton***	Y	Y	Y	Y	N	N	Y	N
7 ***Kerns***	Y	Y	Y	Y	N	N	Y	N
8 ***Hostettler***	Y	Y	Y	Y	N	N	Y	N
9 Hill	Y	Y	Y	Y	Y	N	Y	Y
10 Carson	Y	Y	Y	Y	Y	Y	Y	N
IOWA								
1 ***Leach***	Y	Y	Y	Y	N	N	Y	N
2 ***Nussle***	Y	Y	Y	Y	N	N	Y	?
3 Boswell	Y	Y	Y	Y	Y	N	Y	Y
4 ***Ganske***	?	?	Y	Y	N	N	Y	N
5 ***Latham***	Y	Y	Y	Y	N	N	Y	N
KANSAS								
1 ***Moran***	Y	Y	Y	Y	N	N	Y	N
2 ***Ryun***	Y	Y	Y	Y	N	N	Y	N
3 Moore	Y	Y	Y	N	Y	N	Y	Y
4 ***Tiahrt***	Y	Y	+	+	N	N	Y	N
KENTUCKY								
1 ***Whitfield***	Y	Y	Y	Y	N	N	Y	N
2 ***Lewis***	Y	Y	Y	Y	N	N	Y	N
3 ***Northup***	Y	Y	Y	Y	N	N	Y	N
4 Lucas	Y	Y	Y	Y	Y	N	Y	Y
5 ***Rogers***	Y	Y	Y	Y	N	N	Y	N
6 ***Fletcher***	Y	Y	Y	Y	N	N	Y	N
LOUISIANA								
1 ***Vitter***	Y	Y	Y	Y	N	N	Y	N
2 Jefferson	Y	Y	Y	?	Y	Y	Y	Y
3 ***Tauzin***	Y	Y	Y	Y	N	N	Y	?
4 ***McCrery***	Y	Y	Y	Y	N	N	Y	N
5 ***Cooksey***	Y	Y	Y	Y	N	N	Y	N
6 ***Baker***	Y	Y	Y	Y	N	N	Y	N
7 John	?	?	Y	Y	Y	N	Y	Y
MAINE								
1 Allen	Y	?	Y	Y	Y	Y	Y	Y
2 Baldacci	Y	Y	Y	Y	Y	Y	Y	Y
MARYLAND								
1 ***Gilchrest***	Y	Y	Y	Y	N	N	Y	N
2 ***Ehrlich***	Y	Y	Y	Y	N	N	Y	N
3 Cardin	Y	Y	Y	Y	Y	N	Y	Y
4 Wynn	Y	Y	Y	Y	Y	N	Y	Y
5 Hoyer	Y	Y	Y	Y	Y	N	Y	Y
6 ***Bartlett***	Y	Y	Y	Y	N	N	Y	N
7 Cummings	Y	Y	Y	Y	Y	Y	Y	Y
8 ***Morella***	Y	Y	Y	Y	N	N	Y	N
MASSACHUSETTS								
1 Olver	Y	Y	N	Y	Y	Y	N	Y
2 Neal	Y	Y	N	N	Y	N	N	Y
3 McGovern	Y	Y	N	Y	Y	Y	Y	?
4 Frank	Y	Y	N	Y	Y	Y	N	Y
5 Meehan	Y	Y	Y	Y	Y	Y	Y	Y
6 Tierney	Y	N	N	Y	Y	Y	Y	Y
7 Markey	Y	Y	Y	N	Y	Y	Y	Y
8 Capuano	Y	N	Y	N	Y	Y	Y	N
9 Moakley	?	?	?	?	?	?	?	?
10 Delahunt	Y	Y	Y	Y	Y	Y	Y	?
MICHIGAN								
1 Stupak	Y	Y	Y	N	Y	Y	Y	Y
2 ***Hoekstra***	Y	Y	Y	Y	N	N	Y	N
3 ***Ehlers***	Y	Y	Y	Y	N	N	Y	N
4 ***Camp***	Y	Y	Y	Y	N	N	Y	N
5 Barcia	Y	Y	Y	Y	Y	Y	Y	N
6 ***Upton***	Y	Y	Y	Y	N	N	Y	N
7 ***Smith***	Y	Y	Y	Y	N	N	Y	N
8 ***Rogers***	Y	Y	Y	Y	N	N	Y	N
9 Kildee	Y	Y	Y	Y	Y	Y	Y	N
10 Bonior	Y	P	Y	Y	Y	Y	Y	Y
11 ***Knollenberg***	Y	Y	Y	Y	N	N	Y	N
12 Levin	Y	Y	Y	Y	Y	Y	Y	Y
13 Rivers	Y	P	Y	Y	Y	Y	Y	N
14 Conyers	Y	Y	N	Y	Y	Y	N	Y
15 Kilpatrick	Y	Y	Y	Y	Y	Y	Y	?
16 Dingell	Y	Y	Y	Y	Y	Y	Y	Y

	90	91	92	93	94	95	96	97
MINNESOTA								
1 ***Gutknecht***	Y	Y	Y	Y	N	Y	N	N
2 ***Kennedy***	Y	Y	Y	N	N	N	Y	N
3 ***Ramstad***	Y	Y	Y	N	N	N	Y	N
4 McCollum	Y	Y	Y	Y	Y	Y	Y	Y
5 Sabo	Y	Y	N	N	Y	Y	N	Y
6 Luther	Y	Y	Y	Y	Y	Y	Y	Y
7 Peterson	Y	Y	Y	N	N	Y	Y	Y
8 Oberstar	Y	Y	N	N	Y	Y	N	Y
MISSISSIPPI								
1 ***Wicker***	Y	Y	Y	Y	N	N	Y	?
2 Thompson	Y	Y	Y	N	Y	Y	Y	Y
3 ***Pickering***	Y	Y	Y	Y	N	N	Y	N
4 Shows	Y	Y	Y	Y	Y	N	Y	Y
5 Taylor	Y	Y	Y	N	Y	N	Y	Y
MISSOURI								
1 Clay	Y	Y	Y	Y	Y	Y	Y	+
2 ***Akin***	Y	Y	Y	Y	N	N	Y	N
3 Gephardt	Y	Y	Y	Y	Y	Y	Y	Y
4 Skelton	Y	Y	Y	Y	Y	Y	Y	Y
5 McCarthy	Y	Y	Y	Y	Y	N	Y	Y
6 ***Graves***	Y	Y	Y	Y	N	N	Y	N
7 ***Blunt***	Y	Y	Y	Y	N	N	Y	N
8 ***Emerson***	Y	Y	Y	Y	N	N	Y	?
9 ***Hulshof***	Y	Y	Y	N	N	N	Y	?
MONTANA								
AL ***Rehberg***	Y	Y	Y	Y	N	N	Y	N
NEBRASKA								
1 ***Bereuter***	Y	Y	Y	Y	N	N	Y	N
2 ***Terry***	Y	Y	Y	Y	N	N	Y	N
3 ***Osborne***	Y	Y	Y	Y	N	N	Y	N
NEVADA								
1 Berkley	Y	?	Y	Y	Y	Y	Y	Y
2 ***Gibbons***	Y	Y	Y	Y	N	N	Y	N
NEW HAMPSHIRE								
1 ***Sununu***	Y	Y	Y	Y	N	N	Y	N
2 ***Bass***	Y	Y	Y	Y	N	N	Y	N
NEW JERSEY								
1 Andrews	Y	Y	Y	Y	Y	N	Y	Y
2 ***LoBiondo***	Y	Y	Y	N	N	N	Y	N
3 ***Saxton***	Y	Y	Y	Y	N	N	Y	N
4 ***Smith***	Y	Y	Y	Y	N	N	Y	N
5 ***Roukema***	Y	Y	Y	Y	N	N	Y	N
6 Pallone	Y	Y	Y	N	Y	Y	Y	Y
7 ***Ferguson***	Y	Y	Y	Y	N	N	Y	N
8 Pascrell	Y	Y	Y	Y	Y	Y	Y	Y
9 Rothman	?	?	Y	N	Y	Y	Y	N
10 Payne	Y	Y	Y	Y	Y	Y	N	Y
11 ***Frelinghuysen***	Y	Y	Y	Y	N	N	Y	N
12 Holt	Y	Y	Y	Y	Y	Y	Y	Y
13 Menendez	Y	Y	Y	Y	Y	Y	Y	Y
NEW MEXICO								
1 ***Wilson***	Y	Y	Y	Y	N	N	Y	N
2 ***Skeen***	Y	Y	Y	Y	N	N	Y	N
3 Udall	Y	Y	Y	N	Y	Y	Y	Y
NEW YORK								
1 ***Grucci***	Y	Y	Y	Y	N	N	Y	N
2 Israel	Y	Y	Y	Y	Y	N	Y	Y
3 ***King***	Y	Y	Y	Y	N	N	Y	N
4 McCarthy	Y	Y	Y	Y	Y	N	Y	N
5 Ackerman	Y	N	Y	Y	Y	Y	Y	Y
6 Meeks	Y	Y	Y	?	Y	Y	Y	Y
7 Crowley	Y	N	Y	Y	Y	N	Y	Y
8 Nadler	Y	Y	Y	Y	Y	Y	Y	Y
9 Weiner	+	+	Y	Y	Y	Y	Y	Y
10 Towns	Y	Y	Y	Y	Y	Y	Y	Y
11 Owens	Y	P	N	Y	Y	Y	N	Y
12 Velázquez	Y	Y	Y	Y	Y	Y	Y	Y
13 ***Fossella***	Y	Y	Y	Y	N	N	Y	N
14 Maloney	Y	Y	Y	Y	Y	Y	Y	Y
15 Rangel	Y	Y	Y	Y	Y	Y	N	N
16 Serrano	?	?	Y	Y	Y	Y	Y	Y
17 Engel	Y	Y	Y	Y	Y	Y	Y	Y
18 Lowey	Y	Y	Y	Y	Y	Y	Y	Y
19 ***Kelly***	Y	Y	Y	Y	N	N	Y	N
20 ***Gilman***	Y	Y	Y	Y	N	N	Y	N
21 McNulty	Y	Y	Y	N	Y	Y	Y	Y
22 ***Sweeney***	Y	Y	Y	N	N	N	Y	N
23 ***Boehlert***	Y	Y	Y	Y	N	N	Y	N
24 ***McHugh***	Y	Y	Y	Y	N	N	Y	N
25 ***Walsh***	Y	Y	Y	Y	N	N	Y	N
26 Hinchey	Y	Y	N	N	Y	Y	N	Y
27 ***Reynolds***	Y	Y	Y	Y	N	N	Y	N
28 Slaughter	Y	Y	Y	N	Y	Y	Y	Y
29 LaFalce	Y	Y	Y	Y	Y	Y	N	Y

	90	91	92	93	94	95	96	97
30 ***Quinn***	Y	Y	Y	Y	N	N	Y	N
31 ***Houghton***	Y	Y	Y	Y	N	N	Y	?
NORTH CAROLINA								
1 Clayton	Y	Y	Y	Y	Y	Y	Y	Y
2 Etheridge	Y	Y	Y	N	Y	N	Y	Y
3 ***Jones***	Y	Y	Y	Y	N	N	Y	N
4 Price	Y	Y	Y	Y	Y	N	Y	N
5 ***Burr***	Y	Y	Y	Y	N	N	Y	N
6 ***Coble***	Y	Y	Y	Y	N	N	Y	N
7 McIntyre	Y	Y	Y	Y	Y	N	Y	Y
8 ***Hayes***	Y	Y	Y	Y	N	N	Y	N
9 ***Myrick***	Y	Y	Y	Y	N	N	Y	N
10 ***Ballenger***	Y	Y	Y	Y	N	N	Y	N
11 ***Taylor***	Y	Y	Y	Y	N	N	Y	N
12 Watt	Y	Y	N	Y	Y	Y	Y	N
NORTH DAKOTA								
AL Pomeroy	Y	Y	Y	Y	Y	N	Y	Y
OHIO								
1 ***Chabot***	Y	Y	Y	Y	N	N	Y	N
2 ***Portman***	Y	Y	Y	Y	N	N	Y	N
3 Hall	Y	Y	Y	Y	Y	Y	Y	Y
4 ***Oxley***	Y	Y	Y	Y	N	N	Y	N
5 ***Gillmor***	Y	Y	Y	Y	N	N	Y	N
6 Strickland	Y	Y	Y	N	Y	Y	Y	Y
7 ***Hobson***	?	+	Y	Y	N	N	Y	N
8 ***Boehner***	Y	Y	Y	Y	N	N	Y	N
9 Kaptur	Y	Y	Y	Y	Y	Y	Y	Y
10 Kucinich	Y	P	Y	Y	Y	Y	N	Y
11 Jones	Y	P	Y	Y	Y	Y	Y	Y
12 ***Tiberi***	Y	Y	Y	Y	N	N	Y	N
13 Brown	Y	Y	Y	Y	Y	Y	Y	Y
14 Sawyer	Y	Y	Y	Y	Y	Y	Y	Y
15 ***Pryce***	Y	Y	Y	Y	N	N	Y	N
16 ***Regula***	Y	Y	Y	Y	N	N	Y	N
17 Traficant	Y	Y	Y	Y	N	N	Y	N
18 ***Ney***	Y	Y	Y	Y	N	N	Y	N
19 ***LaTourette***	Y	Y	Y	Y	N	N	Y	N
OKLAHOMA								
1 ***Largent***	Y	Y	Y	Y	N	N	Y	?
2 Carson	Y	Y	Y	Y	Y	Y	Y	Y
3 ***Watkins***	Y	Y	Y	Y	N	N	Y	N
4 ***Watts***	Y	Y	Y	Y	N	N	Y	N
5 ***Istook***	Y	Y	Y	Y	N	N	Y	N
6 ***Lucas***	Y	Y	Y	Y	N	N	Y	N
OREGON								
1 Wu	Y	Y	Y	N	Y	N	Y	N
2 ***Walden***	Y	Y	Y	Y	N	N	Y	N
3 Blumenauer	Y	Y	Y	Y	Y	Y	Y	Y
4 DeFazio	Y	Y	N	Y	Y	Y	Y	Y
5 Hooley	Y	Y	Y	N	Y	Y	Y	Y
PENNSYLVANIA								
1 Brady	Y	Y	Y	N	Y	N	Y	Y
2 Fattah	Y	Y	Y	Y	Y	Y	Y	Y
3 Borski	Y	Y	Y	N	Y	N	Y	N
4 ***Hart***	Y	Y	Y	Y	N	N	Y	N
5 ***Peterson***	Y	Y	Y	Y	N	N	Y	N
6 Holden	Y	Y	Y	Y	Y	Y	Y	N
7 ***Weldon***	Y	Y	Y	Y	N	N	Y	N
8 ***Greenwood***	Y	Y	Y	Y	N	N	Y	N
9 Vacant								
10 ***Sherwood***	Y	Y	Y	Y	N	N	Y	N
11 Kanjorski	Y	Y	Y	Y	Y	Y	Y	Y
12 Murtha	Y	Y	Y	Y	Y	Y	Y	?
13 Hoeffel	Y	Y	Y	Y	Y	N	Y	Y
14 Coyne	Y	Y	Y	Y	Y	Y	Y	?
15 ***Toomey***	Y	Y	Y	Y	N	N	Y	N
16 ***Pitts***	Y	Y	Y	Y	N	N	Y	N
17 ***Gekas***	Y	Y	Y	Y	N	N	Y	N
18 Doyle	Y	Y	Y	Y	Y	Y	Y	Y
19 ***Platts***	Y	Y	Y	Y	N	N	Y	N
20 Mascara	Y	Y	Y	Y	Y	Y	Y	N
21 ***English***	Y	Y	Y	N	N	N	Y	N
RHODE ISLAND								
1 Kennedy	Y	Y	Y	Y	Y	Y	Y	Y
2 Langevin	Y	Y	Y	Y	Y	Y	Y	Y
SOUTH CAROLINA								
1 ***Brown***	Y	Y	Y	Y	N	N	Y	N
2 ***Spence***	Y	Y	Y	Y	N	N	Y	N
3 ***Graham***	Y	Y	Y	Y	N	N	Y	N
4 ***DeMint***	Y	Y	Y	Y	N	N	Y	N
5 Spratt	Y	Y	Y	Y	Y	Y	Y	Y
6 Clyburn	Y	Y	Y	Y	Y	Y	Y	Y
SOUTH DAKOTA								
AL ***Thune***	Y	Y	Y	Y	N	N	Y	N

	90	91	92	93	94	95	96	97
TENNESSEE								
1 ***Jenkins***	Y	Y	Y	Y	N	N	Y	N
2 ***Duncan***	Y	Y	Y	Y	N	N	Y	N
3 ***Wamp***	Y	Y	Y	Y	N	N	Y	N
4 ***Hilleary***	Y	Y	Y	Y	N	N	Y	N
5 Clement	Y	Y	Y	Y	Y	N	Y	N
6 Gordon	Y	Y	Y	Y	Y	N	Y	N
7 ***Bryant***	Y	Y	Y	Y	N	N	Y	N
8 Tanner	Y	Y	Y	Y	Y	N	Y	Y
9 Ford	Y	Y	Y	Y	Y	N	Y	Y
TEXAS								
1 Sandlin	Y	Y	Y	Y	Y	N	Y	Y
2 Turner	Y	Y	Y	Y	Y	N	Y	N
3 ***Johnson, Sam***	Y	Y	Y	Y	N	N	Y	N
4 Hall	Y	Y	Y	Y	Y	N	Y	Y
5 ***Sessions***	Y	Y	Y	Y	N	N	Y	?
6 ***Barton***	Y	Y	Y	Y	N	N	Y	N
7 ***Culberson***	Y	Y	Y	Y	N	N	Y	N
8 ***Brady***	Y	Y	Y	Y	N	N	Y	N
9 Lampson	Y	Y	Y	Y	Y	N	Y	Y
10 Doggett	Y	Y	Y	Y	Y	Y	Y	Y
11 Edwards	Y	Y	Y	Y	Y	Y	Y	N
12 ***Granger***	Y	Y	Y	Y	N	N	Y	N
13 ***Thornberry***	Y	Y	Y	Y	N	N	Y	N
14 ***Paul***	N	Y	Y	Y	N	N	Y	N
15 Hinojosa	Y	Y	Y	Y	Y	N	Y	Y
16 Reyes	Y	Y	Y	Y	Y	Y	Y	Y
17 Stenholm	Y	Y	Y	N	Y	N	Y	Y
18 Jackson-Lee	Y	Y	Y	Y	Y	Y	Y	Y
19 ***Combest***	Y	Y	Y	Y	N	N	Y	N
20 Gonzalez	Y	Y	Y	Y	Y	N	Y	Y
21 ***Smith***	Y	Y	Y	Y	N	N	Y	N
22 ***DeLay***	Y	Y	Y	Y	N	N	Y	?
23 ***Bonilla***	Y	Y	Y	Y	N	N	Y	N
24 Frost	Y	Y	Y	Y	Y	Y	Y	Y
25 Bentsen	Y	Y	Y	Y	Y	Y	Y	Y
26 ***Armey***	Y	Y	Y	Y	N	N	Y	?
27 Ortiz	Y	Y	Y	Y	Y	Y	Y	?
28 Rodriguez	Y	Y	Y	Y	Y	Y	Y	N
29 Green	Y	Y	Y	Y	Y	Y	Y	N
30 Johnson, E.B.	Y	P	Y	Y	Y	Y	Y	Y
UTAH								
1 ***Hansen***	Y	Y	Y	Y	N	N	Y	N
2 Matheson	Y	Y	Y	Y	Y	N	Y	Y
3 ***Cannon***	Y	Y	Y	Y	N	N	Y	N
VERMONT								
AL *Sanders*	Y	Y	N	Y	N	Y	N	Y
VIRGINIA								
1 ***Davis, Jo Ann***	Y	Y	Y	Y	N	N	Y	N
2 ***Schrock***	Y	Y	Y	Y	N	N	Y	N
3 Scott	Y	Y	Y	Y	Y	Y	Y	Y
4 Vacant								
5 *Goode*	Y	Y	Y	Y	N	N	Y	N
6 ***Goodlatte***	Y	Y	Y	Y	N	N	Y	N
7 ***Cantor***	Y	Y	Y	Y	N	N	Y	N
8 Moran	Y	Y	Y	Y	Y	N	Y	N
9 Boucher	Y	Y	Y	Y	Y	Y	Y	Y
10 ***Wolf***	Y	Y	Y	Y	N	N	Y	N
11 ***Davis, T.***	Y	Y	Y	Y	N	N	Y	?
WASHINGTON								
1 Inslee	Y	Y	Y	Y	Y	Y	Y	Y
2 Larsen	Y	Y	Y	Y	Y	Y	Y	Y
3 Baird	Y	Y	Y	Y	Y	N	Y	Y
4 ***Hastings***	Y	Y	Y	Y	N	N	Y	N
5 ***Nethercutt***	Y	Y	Y	Y	N	N	Y	N
6 Dicks	Y	Y	Y	Y	Y	Y	Y	Y
7 McDermott	Y	Y	N	N	Y	Y	N	N
8 ***Dunn***	Y	Y	Y	Y	N	N	Y	N
9 Smith	?	?	Y	Y	Y	N	Y	Y
WEST VIRGINIA								
1 Mollohan	Y	Y	Y	Y	Y	Y	Y	N
2 ***Capito***	Y	Y	Y	Y	N	N	Y	N
3 Rahall	Y	Y	Y	Y	Y	Y	Y	N
WISCONSIN								
1 ***Ryan***	Y	Y	Y	Y	N	N	Y	N
2 Baldwin	Y	Y	Y	Y	Y	Y	Y	Y
3 Kind	Y	Y	Y	Y	Y	Y	Y	N
4 Kleczka	Y	Y	Y	Y	Y	Y	Y	N
5 Barrett	Y	Y	Y	Y	Y	Y	Y	Y
6 ***Petri***	Y	Y	Y	Y	N	N	Y	N
7 Obey	Y	Y	N	Y	Y	Y	N	Y
8 ***Green***	Y	Y	Y	Y	N	N	Y	N
9 ***Sensenbrenner***	Y	Y	Y	Y	N	N	Y	N
WYOMING								
AL ***Cubin***	Y	Y	Y	Y	N	N	Y	N

Southern states - Ala., Ark., Fla., Ga., Ky., La., Miss., N.C., Okla., S.C., Tenn., Texas, Va.

Key

Y	Voted for (yea).
#	Paired for.
+	Announced for.
N	Voted against (nay).
X	Paired against.
–	Announced against.
P	Voted "present."
C	Voted "present" to avoid possible conflict of interest.
?	Did not vote or otherwise make a position known.

Democrats **Republicans**
Independents

98. Procedural Motion/Adjourn. Capuano, D-Mass., motion to adjourn. Rejected 171-239: R 1-207; D 169-31 (ND 127-23, SD 42-8); I 1-1. May 3, 2001.

99. Procedural Motion/Journal. Approval of the House Journal of Wednesday, May 2, 2001. Approved 299-107: R 191-15; D 106-92 (ND 73-76, SD 33-16); I 2-0. May 4, 2001 (in the Congressional Record dated May 3).

100. H Con Res 83. Fiscal 2002 Budget Resolution/Waiver. Adoption of the rule (H Res 131) that would waive the two-thirds majority vote requirement for same-day consideration of a rule reported by the House Rules Committee on May 8, 2001, on the conference report to the concurrent budget resolution. Adopted 214-200: R 212-0; D 1-199 (ND 1-146, SD 0-53); I 1-1. May 8, 2001.

101. H Con Res 83. Fiscal 2002 Budget Resolution/Rule to Recommit. Adoption of the rule (H Res 134) that would recommit to the conference committee the concurrent budget resolution. Adopted 409-1: R 212-0; D 195-1 (ND 143-1, SD 52-0); I 2-0. May 8, 2001.

102. Procedural Motion/Journal. Approval of the House Journal of Tuesday, May 8, 2001. Approved 335-70: R 196-14; D 137-56 (ND 94-47, SD 43-9); I 2-0. May 9, 2001.

103. H Con Res 83. Fiscal 2002 Budget Resolution/Rule. Adoption of the rule (H Res 136) to waive points of order and to provide for House floor consideration of the conference report to the concurrent resolution on the budget. Adopted 218-208: R 216-0; D 1-207 (ND 1-153, SD 0-54); I 1-1. May 9, 2001.

	98	99	100	101	102	103
ALABAMA						
1 *Callahan*	?	?	Y	Y	Y	Y
2 *Everett*	N	Y	Y	Y	Y	Y
3 *Riley*	N	Y	Y	Y	N	Y
4 *Aderholt*	N	N	Y	Y	N	Y
5 Cramer	N	Y	N	Y	Y	N
6 *Bachus*	N	N	Y	Y	Y	Y
7 Hilliard	Y	N	N	Y	N	N
ALASKA						
AL *Young*	N	Y	Y	Y	?	Y
ARIZONA						
1 *Flake*	N	Y	Y	Y	Y	Y
2 Pastor	Y	N	N	Y	Y	N
3 *Stump*	N	Y	?	?	?	+
4 *Shadegg*	N	Y	Y	Y	Y	Y
5 *Kolbe*	N	Y	Y	Y	Y	Y
6 *Hayworth*	N	Y	Y	Y	Y	Y
ARKANSAS						
1 Berry	Y	Y	N	Y	Y	N
2 Snyder	Y	Y	N	Y	Y	N
3 *Hutchinson*	N	Y	Y	Y	Y	Y
4 Ross	Y	Y	N	Y	Y	N
CALIFORNIA						
1 Thompson	Y	N	N	Y	N	N
2 *Herger*	N	Y	Y	Y	Y	Y
3 *Ose*	N	Y	Y	Y	Y	Y
4 *Doolittle*	N	Y	Y	Y	Y	Y
5 Matsui	Y	Y	N	Y	Y	N
6 Woolsey	Y	Y	N	Y	Y	N
7 Miller, George	Y	N	?	Y	N	N
8 Pelosi	Y	Y	N	Y	Y	N
9 Lee	Y	N	N	Y	N	N
10 Tauscher	Y	N	N	Y	Y	N
11 *Pombo*	N	Y	Y	Y	Y	Y
12 Lantos	Y	N	N	Y	N	N
13 Stark	?	?	N	Y	N	N
14 Eshoo	Y	Y	N	Y	Y	N
15 Honda	Y	Y	N	Y	Y	N
16 Lofgren	Y	Y	N	Y	N	N
17 Farr	Y	N	N	Y	N	N
18 Condit	N	N	N	Y	Y	N
19 *Radanovich*	N	Y	Y	Y	Y	Y
20 Dooley	N	Y	N	?	Y	N
21 *Thomas*	N	Y	Y	Y	Y	Y
22 Capps	Y	N	N	Y	Y	N
23 *Gallegly*	N	Y	Y	Y	Y	Y
24 Sherman	Y	Y	N	Y	Y	N
25 *McKeon*	N	Y	Y	Y	Y	Y
26 Berman	Y	Y	N	Y	Y	N
27 Schiff	Y	Y	N	Y	Y	N
28 *Dreier*	N	Y	Y	Y	Y	Y
29 Waxman	Y	Y	N	Y	Y	N
30 Becerra	?	?	N	Y	Y	N
31 Solis	Y	Y	N	Y	Y	N
32 Vacant						
33 Roybal-Allard	Y	Y	N	Y	Y	N
34 Napolitano	Y	Y	N	Y	?	N
35 Waters	Y	N	N	Y	N	N
36 Harman	Y	Y	N	Y	N	N
37 Millender-McD.	Y	Y	N	Y	Y	N
38 *Horn*	N	Y	Y	Y	Y	Y

	98	99	100	101	102	103
39 *Royce*	N	Y	Y	Y	Y	Y
40 *Lewis*	N	Y	Y	Y	Y	Y
41 *Miller, Gary*	N	Y	Y	Y	Y	Y
42 Baca	Y	Y	N	Y	N	N
43 *Calvert*	N	Y	Y	Y	Y	Y
44 *Bono*	N	Y	Y	Y	Y	Y
45 *Rohrabacher*	N	Y	Y	Y	Y	Y
46 Sanchez	N	N	N	Y	N	N
47 *Cox*	N	Y	Y	Y	Y	Y
48 *Issa*	N	Y	Y	+	Y	Y
49 Davis	Y	Y	N	Y	N	N
50 Filner	+	–	N	Y	N	N
51 *Cunningham*	N	Y	Y	Y	Y	Y
52 *Hunter*	N	Y	Y	Y	Y	Y
COLORADO						
1 DeGette	Y	Y	N	?	Y	N
2 Udall	Y	N	N	Y	N	N
3 *McInnis*	N	Y	Y	Y	Y	Y
4 *Schaffer*	N	N	Y	Y	Y	Y
5 *Hefley*	?	?	Y	Y	N	Y
6 *Tancredo*	N	N	Y	Y	P	Y
CONNECTICUT						
1 Larson	Y	Y	N	Y	Y	N
2 *Simmons*	N	Y	Y	Y	Y	Y
3 DeLauro	Y	Y	N	Y	Y	N
4 *Shays*	N	Y	Y	Y	Y	Y
5 Maloney	N	N	Y	N	?	N
6 *Johnson*	N	Y	Y	Y	Y	Y
DELAWARE						
AL *Castle*	Y	Y	Y	Y	Y	Y
FLORIDA						
1 *Scarborough*	N	Y	Y	Y	Y	Y
2 Boyd	Y	Y	N	Y	Y	N
3 Brown	Y	N	N	Y	N	N
4 *Crenshaw*	N	Y	Y	Y	Y	Y
5 Thurman	Y	N	N	Y	N	N
6 *Stearns*	N	Y	Y	Y	Y	Y
7 *Mica*	N	Y	Y	Y	Y	Y
8 *Keller*	N	Y	Y	Y	Y	Y
9 *Bilirakis*	N	Y	Y	Y	Y	Y
10 *Young*	N	Y	Y	Y	Y	Y
11 Davis	Y	Y	N	Y	N	N
12 *Putnam*	N	Y	Y	Y	Y	Y
13 *Miller*	N	Y	Y	Y	Y	Y
14 *Goss*	N	Y	Y	Y	Y	Y
15 *Weldon*	N	Y	Y	Y	Y	Y
16 *Foley*	N	Y	Y	Y	Y	Y
17 Meek	Y	Y	N	Y	Y	N
18 *Ros-Lehtinen*	N	Y	Y	Y	Y	Y
19 Wexler	Y	Y	N	Y	N	N
20 Deutsch	Y	Y	N	Y	N	N
21 *Diaz-Balart*	N	Y	Y	Y	Y	Y
22 *Shaw*	N	Y	Y	Y	Y	Y
23 Hastings	Y	N	N	Y	N	N
GEORGIA						
1 *Kingston*	N	Y	Y	Y	Y	Y
2 Bishop	Y	Y	N	Y	Y	N
3 *Collins*	N	Y	Y	Y	Y	Y
4 McKinney	N	N	Y	Y	Y	N
5 Lewis	Y	N	N	Y	Y	N
6 *Isakson*	N	Y	Y	Y	Y	Y
7 *Barr*	N	Y	Y	Y	Y	Y
8 *Chambliss*	N	Y	Y	Y	Y	Y
9 *Deal*	N	Y	Y	Y	N	Y
10 *Norwood*	N	Y	Y	Y	Y	Y
11 *Linder*	N	Y	Y	Y	Y	Y
HAWAII						
1 Abercrombie	Y	N	N	Y	?	N
2 Mink	Y	Y	N	Y	Y	N
IDAHO						
1 *Otter*	N	Y	Y	Y	Y	Y
2 *Simpson*	N	Y	Y	Y	Y	Y
ILLINOIS						
1 Rush	Y	Y	N	Y	Y	N
2 Jackson	N	N	N	Y	Y	N
3 Lipinski	N	Y	N	Y	Y	N
4 Gutierrez	Y	N	–	+	Y	N
5 Blagojevich	N	Y	N	Y	Y	N
6 *Hyde*	N	Y	Y	Y	Y	Y
7 Davis	Y	N	N	Y	Y	N
8 *Crane*	N	N	Y	Y	?	Y
9 Schakowsky	Y	N	N	Y	?	N
10 *Kirk*	N	Y	Y	Y	Y	Y
11 *Weller*	N	Y	Y	Y	N	Y
12 Costello	N	N	?	?	N	N
13 *Biggert*	N	Y	Y	Y	Y	Y

ND Northern Democrats SD Southern Democrats

	98	99	100	101	102	103
14 ***Hastert***	N					
15 ***Johnson***	N	Y	Y	Y	Y	Y
16 ***Manzullo***	N	Y	Y	Y	Y	Y
17 Evans	Y	Y	N	Y	Y	N
18 ***LaHood***	N	Y	?	?	Y	Y
19 Phelps	Y	N	N	Y	N	N
20 ***Shimkus***	N	Y	Y	Y	Y	Y
INDIANA						
1 Visclosky	Y	N	N	Y	N	N
2 ***Pence***	N	Y	Y	Y	Y	Y
3 Roemer	Y	Y	N	Y	Y	N
4 ***Souder***	N	Y	Y	Y	Y	Y
5 ***Buyer***	N	Y	Y	Y	Y	Y
6 ***Burton***	N	Y	Y	Y	Y	Y
7 ***Kerns***	N	Y	Y	Y	Y	Y
8 ***Hostettler***	N	Y	Y	Y	Y	Y
9 Hill	Y	N	N	Y	Y	N
10 Carson	Y	N	N	Y	Y	N
IOWA						
1 ***Leach***	N	Y	Y	Y	Y	Y
2 ***Nussle***	N	Y	Y	Y	Y	Y
3 Boswell	Y	Y	N	Y	Y	N
4 ***Ganske***	N	Y	Y	Y	Y	Y
5 ***Latham***	N	N	Y	Y	Y	Y
KANSAS						
1 ***Moran***	N	Y	Y	Y	Y	Y
2 ***Ryun***	N	Y	Y	Y	Y	Y
3 Moore	Y	N	N	Y	N	N
4 ***Tiahrt***	N	Y	Y	Y	Y	Y
KENTUCKY						
1 ***Whitfield***	N	Y	Y	Y	?	Y
2 ***Lewis***	N	Y	Y	Y	Y	Y
3 ***Northup***	N	Y	Y	Y	Y	Y
4 Lucas	Y	Y	N	Y	Y	N
5 ***Rogers***	N	Y	Y	Y	Y	Y
6 ***Fletcher***	N	Y	Y	Y	Y	Y
LOUISIANA						
1 ***Vitter***	N	Y	Y	Y	Y	Y
2 Jefferson	Y	N	N	Y	Y	N
3 ***Tauzin***	N	Y	Y	Y	Y	Y
4 ***McCrery***	?	?	Y	Y	Y	Y
5 ***Cooksey***	N	Y	Y	Y	Y	Y
6 ***Baker***	N	Y	Y	Y	Y	Y
7 John	Y	Y	N	Y	Y	N
MAINE						
1 Allen	Y	N	?	?	?	N
2 Baldacci	Y	N	N	Y	Y	N
MARYLAND						
1 ***Gilchrest***	N	Y	Y	Y	Y	Y
2 ***Ehrlich***	N	Y	Y	Y	Y	Y
3 Cardin	Y	Y	N	Y	Y	N
4 Wynn	Y	Y	N	Y	Y	N
5 Hoyer	Y	Y	N	Y	Y	N
6 ***Bartlett***	N	Y	Y	Y	Y	Y
7 Cummings	Y	Y	N	Y	Y	N
8 ***Morella***	N	Y	Y	Y	Y	Y
MASSACHUSETTS						
1 Olver	Y	N	N	Y	N	N
2 Neal	Y	N	N	Y	Y	N
3 McGovern	Y	N	N	Y	N	N
4 Frank	Y	Y	N	Y	Y	N
5 Meehan	Y	N	N	Y	Y	N
6 Tierney	Y	Y	N	Y	Y	N
7 Markey	Y	Y	N	Y	Y	N
8 Capuano	Y	N	N	N	N	N
9 Moakley	?	?	N	Y	?	N
10 Delahunt	Y	N	N	Y	?	N
MICHIGAN						
1 Stupak	Y	N	N	Y	N	N
2 ***Hoekstra***	N	Y	Y	Y	Y	Y
3 ***Ehlers***	N	Y	Y	Y	Y	Y
4 ***Camp***	N	Y	Y	Y	Y	Y
5 Barcia	N	Y	N	Y	Y	N
6 ***Upton***	N	Y	Y	Y	Y	Y
7 ***Smith***	N	Y	Y	Y	Y	Y
8 ***Rogers***	N	Y	Y	Y	Y	Y
9 Kildee	Y	Y	N	Y	Y	N
10 Bonior	Y	N	N	Y	N	N
11 ***Knollenberg***	N	Y	Y	Y	Y	Y
12 Levin	Y	N	N	Y	Y	N
13 Rivers	Y	Y	?	?	?	?
14 Conyers	Y	N	N	Y	?	N
15 Kilpatrick	Y	N	N	Y	N	N
16 Dingell	Y	N	N	Y	N	N

	98	99	100	101	102	103
MINNESOTA						
1 ***Gutknecht***	N	N	Y	Y	N	Y
2 ***Kennedy***	N	N	Y	Y	N	Y
3 ***Ramstad***	N	N	Y	Y	N	Y
4 McCollum	Y	Y	N	Y	?	N
5 Sabo	Y	N	N	Y	N	N
6 Luther	Y	Y	N	Y	Y	N
7 Peterson	Y	N	N	Y	?	N
8 Oberstar	Y	N	N	Y	N	N
MISSISSIPPI						
1 ***Wicker***	N	N	Y	Y	Y	Y
2 Thompson	Y	N	N	Y	N	N
3 ***Pickering***	N	Y	Y	Y	Y	Y
4 Shows	N	Y	N	Y	Y	N
5 Taylor	Y	N	N	Y	N	N
MISSOURI						
1 Clay	Y	N	N	Y	N	N
2 ***Akin***	N	Y	Y	Y	Y	Y
3 Gephardt	Y	N	N	Y	?	N
4 Skelton	Y	Y	N	Y	Y	N
5 McCarthy	+	+	N	Y	Y	N
6 ***Graves***	N	Y	Y	Y	Y	Y
7 ***Blunt***	N	Y	Y	Y	Y	Y
8 ***Emerson***	N	Y	Y	Y	Y	Y
9 ***Hulshof***	?	?	Y	Y	N	Y
MONTANA						
AL ***Rehberg***	N	Y	Y	Y	Y	Y
NEBRASKA						
1 ***Bereuter***	N	Y	Y	Y	Y	Y
2 ***Terry***	N	Y	Y	Y	Y	Y
3 ***Osborne***	N	Y	Y	Y	Y	Y
NEVADA						
1 Berkley	Y	Y	N	Y	Y	N
2 ***Gibbons***	N	Y	Y	Y	Y	Y
NEW HAMPSHIRE						
1 ***Sununu***	N	Y	Y	Y	Y	Y
2 ***Bass***	N	Y	Y	Y	Y	Y
NEW JERSEY						
1 Andrews	Y	Y	N	Y	Y	N
2 ***LoBiondo***	N	N	Y	Y	N	Y
3 ***Saxton***	N	Y	Y	Y	Y	Y
4 ***Smith***	N	Y	Y	Y	Y	Y
5 ***Roukema***	N	Y	Y	Y	Y	Y
6 Pallone	Y	N	N	Y	N	N
7 ***Ferguson***	N	Y	Y	Y	Y	Y
8 Pascrell	Y	Y	N	Y	Y	N
9 Rothman	Y	Y	N	Y	Y	N
10 Payne	Y	Y	N	Y	Y	N
11 ***Frelinghuysen***	N	Y	Y	Y	Y	Y
12 Holt	Y	Y	N	Y	Y	N
13 Menendez	Y	N	N	Y	N	N
NEW MEXICO						
1 ***Wilson***	N	Y	Y	Y	Y	Y
2 ***Skeen***	N	Y	Y	Y	Y	Y
3 Udall	Y	N	N	Y	N	N
NEW YORK						
1 ***Grucci***	?	?	Y	Y	Y	Y
2 Israel	Y	Y	N	Y	Y	N
3 ***King***	N	Y	Y	Y	Y	Y
4 McCarthy	N	Y	N	Y	Y	N
5 Ackerman	?	?	?	?	N	N
6 Meeks	Y	N	N	Y	Y	N
7 Crowley	Y	N	N	Y	N	N
8 Nadler	Y	Y	N	Y	Y	N
9 Weiner	Y	N	N	Y	Y	N
10 Towns	Y	N	N	Y	N	N
11 Owens	Y	Y	N	Y	Y	N
12 Velázquez	Y	N	N	Y	N	N
13 ***Fossella***	N	Y	Y	Y	Y	Y
14 Maloney	Y	Y	N	Y	Y	N
15 Rangel	N	Y	N	Y	Y	N
16 Serrano	Y	Y	N	Y	Y	N
17 Engel	Y	N	N	Y	Y	N
18 Lowey	Y	Y	N	Y	Y	N
19 ***Kelly***	N	Y	Y	Y	Y	Y
20 ***Gilman***	N	Y	Y	Y	Y	Y
21 McNulty	Y	N	N	Y	N	N
22 ***Sweeney***	N	N	?	?	N	Y
23 ***Boehlert***	N	Y	Y	Y	Y	Y
24 ***McHugh***	N	Y	Y	Y	Y	Y
25 ***Walsh***	N	Y	Y	Y	Y	Y
26 Hinchey	Y	N	N	Y	N	N
27 ***Reynolds***	N	Y	Y	Y	Y	Y
28 Slaughter	Y	?	N	Y	Y	N
29 LaFalce	Y	N	N	Y	N	N

	98	99	100	101	102	103
30 ***Quinn***	N	Y	Y	Y	Y	Y
31 ***Houghton***	N	Y	Y	Y	Y	Y
NORTH CAROLINA						
1 Clayton	Y	Y	N	Y	Y	N
2 Etheridge	Y	Y	N	Y	Y	N
3 ***Jones***	?	?	Y	Y	Y	Y
4 Price	Y	Y	N	Y	Y	N
5 ***Burr***	N	Y	Y	Y	Y	Y
6 ***Coble***	N	Y	Y	Y	Y	Y
7 McIntyre	Y	Y	N	Y	Y	N
8 ***Hayes***	N	Y	Y	Y	Y	Y
9 ***Myrick***	N	Y	Y	Y	Y	Y
10 ***Ballenger***	N	Y	Y	Y	Y	Y
11 ***Taylor***	?	?	?	?	Y	Y
12 Watt	Y	Y	N	Y	Y	N
NORTH DAKOTA						
AL Pomeroy	Y	N	N	Y	N	?
OHIO						
1 ***Chabot***	N	Y	Y	Y	Y	Y
2 ***Portman***	N	Y	Y	Y	Y	Y
3 Hall	Y	Y	N	?	?	N
4 ***Oxley***	N	Y	Y	Y	Y	Y
5 ***Gillmor***	N	Y	Y	Y	Y	Y
6 Strickland	Y	N	N	Y	N	N
7 ***Hobson***	N	Y	Y	Y	Y	Y
8 ***Boehner***	N	Y	Y	Y	Y	Y
9 Kaptur	Y	N	N	Y	Y	N
10 Kucinich	N	N	N	Y	N	N
11 Jones	Y	N	?	?	N	N
12 ***Tiberi***	N	Y	Y	Y	Y	Y
13 Brown	Y	N	N	Y	N	N
14 Sawyer	Y	Y	N	Y	Y	N
15 ***Pryce***	N	Y	Y	Y	Y	Y
16 ***Regula***	N	Y	Y	Y	Y	Y
17 Traficant	N	Y	Y	Y	Y	Y
18 ***Ney***	N	Y	Y	Y	Y	Y
19 ***LaTourette***	N	Y	Y	Y	Y	Y
OKLAHOMA						
1 ***Largent***	?	?	Y	Y	Y	Y
2 Carson	Y	Y	N	Y	Y	N
3 ***Watkins***	N	Y	Y	Y	Y	Y
4 ***Watts***	N	Y	Y	Y	Y	Y
5 ***Istook***	N	Y	Y	Y	Y	Y
6 ***Lucas***	N	Y	Y	Y	Y	Y
OREGON						
1 Wu	N	N	N	Y	Y	N
2 ***Walden***	N	Y	Y	Y	Y	Y
3 Blumenauer	N	Y	N	Y	Y	N
4 DeFazio	Y	N	N	Y	N	N
5 Hooley	Y	N	N	Y	N	N
PENNSYLVANIA						
1 Brady	Y	N	N	Y	N	N
2 Fattah	N	Y	N	?	Y	N
3 Borski	Y	N	N	Y	N	N
4 ***Hart***	N	Y	Y	Y	Y	Y
5 ***Peterson***	N	Y	+	Y	Y	Y
6 Holden	N	Y	N	Y	Y	N
7 ***Weldon***	?	?	Y	?	Y	?
8 ***Greenwood***	N	Y	Y	Y	Y	Y
9 Vacant						
10 ***Sherwood***	N	Y	Y	Y	Y	Y
11 Kanjorski	N	N	N	Y	Y	N
12 Murtha	N	Y	N	Y	Y	N
13 Hoeffel	Y	Y	N	Y	Y	N
14 Coyne	Y	Y	N	Y	Y	N
15 ***Toomey***	N	Y	Y	Y	Y	Y
16 ***Pitts***	N	Y	Y	Y	Y	Y
17 ***Gekas***	N	Y	Y	Y	Y	Y
18 Doyle	Y	Y	N	Y	Y	N
19 ***Platts***	N	Y	Y	Y	Y	Y
20 Mascara	N	Y	N	Y	Y	N
21 ***English***	N	N	Y	Y	N	Y
RHODE ISLAND						
1 Kennedy	Y	N	N	Y	N	N
2 Langevin	Y	N	N	Y	N	N
SOUTH CAROLINA						
1 ***Brown***	N	Y	Y	Y	Y	Y
2 ***Spence***	N	Y	Y	Y	Y	Y
3 ***Graham***	N	Y	Y	Y	Y	Y
4 ***DeMint***	N	Y	Y	Y	Y	Y
5 Spratt	Y	Y	N	Y	?	N
6 Clyburn	Y	Y	N	Y	Y	N
SOUTH DAKOTA						
AL ***Thune***	N	Y	Y	Y	Y	Y

	98	99	100	101	102	103
TENNESSEE						
1 ***Jenkins***	N	Y	Y	Y	Y	Y
2 ***Duncan***	N	Y	Y	Y	Y	Y
3 ***Wamp***	N	Y	Y	Y	Y	Y
4 ***Hilleary***	N	N	Y	Y	N	Y
5 Clement	Y	N	N	?	Y	N
6 Gordon	?	?	N	Y	Y	N
7 ***Bryant***	N	Y	Y	Y	Y	Y
8 Tanner	Y	N	N	Y	Y	N
9 Ford	Y	Y	N	Y	Y	N
TEXAS						
1 Sandlin	Y	Y	N	Y	Y	N
2 Turner	Y	?	N	Y	Y	N
3 ***Johnson, Sam***	?	?	Y	Y	Y	Y
4 Hall	N	Y	N	Y	Y	N
5 ***Sessions***	N	Y	Y	Y	Y	Y
6 ***Barton***	N	Y	Y	Y	?	Y
7 ***Culberson***	N	Y	Y	Y	?	Y
8 ***Brady***	N	Y	Y	Y	Y	Y
9 Lampson	Y	Y	?	Y	Y	N
10 Doggett	Y	N	N	Y	Y	N
11 Edwards	?	?	N	Y	Y	N
12 ***Granger***	N	Y	Y	Y	Y	Y
13 ***Thornberry***	N	Y	Y	Y	Y	Y
14 ***Paul***	N	Y	?	Y	Y	Y
15 Hinojosa	?	?	N	Y	Y	N
16 Reyes	N	Y	N	Y	Y	N
17 Stenholm	Y	N	N	Y	N	N
18 Jackson-Lee	N	Y	N	Y	N	N
19 ***Combest***	N	Y	Y	Y	Y	Y
20 Gonzalez	Y	N	N	Y	Y	N
21 ***Smith***	N	Y	Y	Y	Y	Y
22 ***DeLay***	N	?	Y	Y	?	Y
23 ***Bonilla***	N	Y	Y	Y	Y	Y
24 Frost	Y	N	N	?	Y	N
25 Bentsen	Y	Y	N	Y	Y	N
26 ***Armey***	?	?	Y	Y	Y	Y
27 Ortiz	N	Y	N	Y	Y	N
28 Rodriguez	Y	Y	N	Y	Y	N
29 Green	N	Y	N	Y	Y	N
30 Johnson, E.B.	Y	N	N	Y	N	N
UTAH						
1 ***Hansen***	N	Y	Y	Y	Y	Y
2 Matheson	Y	N	N	Y	Y	N
3 ***Cannon***	N	Y	Y	Y	Y	Y
VERMONT						
AL *Sanders*	Y	Y	N	Y	Y	N
VIRGINIA						
1 ***Davis, Jo Ann***	N	Y	Y	Y	Y	Y
2 ***Schrock***	N	Y	Y	Y	Y	Y
3 Scott	Y	N	N	Y	Y	N
4 Vacant						
5 *Goode*	N	Y	Y	Y	Y	Y
6 ***Goodlatte***	N	Y	Y	Y	Y	Y
7 ***Cantor***	N	Y	Y	Y	Y	Y
8 Moran	Y	Y	N	Y	?	N
9 Boucher	?	?	N	Y	Y	N
10 ***Wolf***	N	Y	Y	Y	Y	Y
11 ***Davis, T.***	N	Y	Y	Y	Y	Y
WASHINGTON						
1 Inslee	Y	Y	?	?	Y	N
2 Larsen	Y	N	N	Y	N	N
3 Baird	Y	N	N	Y	?	N
4 ***Hastings***	N	Y	Y	Y	Y	Y
5 ***Nethercutt***	N	Y	Y	Y	Y	Y
6 Dicks	Y	N	N	Y	N	N
7 McDermott	Y	N	–	+	N	N
8 ***Dunn***	N	Y	Y	Y	Y	Y
9 Smith	Y	Y	N	Y	Y	N
WEST VIRGINIA						
1 Mollohan	N	Y	N	Y	Y	N
2 ***Capito***	N	Y	Y	Y	Y	Y
3 Rahall	N	Y	N	Y	Y	N
WISCONSIN						
1 ***Ryan***	N	Y	Y	Y	Y	Y
2 Baldwin	Y	Y	N	Y	Y	N
3 Kind	Y	Y	N	Y	Y	N
4 Kleczka	N	Y	N	Y	Y	N
5 Barrett	Y	N	N	Y	Y	N
6 ***Petri***	N	Y	Y	Y	Y	Y
7 Obey	Y	N	N	Y	?	N
8 ***Green***	N	Y	Y	Y	Y	Y
9 ***Sensenbrenner***	?	?	Y	Y	Y	Y
WYOMING						
AL ***Cubin***	N	Y	?	?	?	?

Southern states - Ala., Ark., Fla., Ga., Ky., La., Miss., N.C., Okla., S.C., Tenn., Texas, Va.

Key

Y	Voted for (yea).
#	Paired for.
+	Announced for.
N	Voted against (nay).
X	Paired against.
–	Announced against.
P	Voted "present."
C	Voted "present" to avoid possible conflict of interest.
?	Did not vote or otherwise make a position known.

•

Democrats   **Republicans**
Independents

104. H Con Res 83. Fiscal 2002 Budget Resolution/Conference Report. Adoption of the conference report on the concurrent budget resolution that calls for approximately $1.35 trillion in tax cuts through fiscal 2011; in the Senate, $100 billion of that would only be available in fiscal 2001 through 2002. The resolution would limit discretionary spending to $661.3 billion, with a target of $325.1 billion for defense and $336.2 billion for non-defense programs. Adopted (thus sent to the Senate) 221-207: R 214-3; D 6-203 (ND 2-153, SD 4-50); I 1-1. A "yea" was a vote in support of the president's position. May 9, 2001.

105. HR 1646. State Department Authorization/Rule. Adoption of the rule (H Res 138) to provide for House floor consideration of the bill that would authorize $8.2 billion in appropriations for fiscal 2002 and "such funds as may be necessary" for fiscal 2003 for the Department of State and for foreign broadcasting operations. Adopted 226-192: R 212-1; D 13-190 (ND 8-142, SD 5-48); I 1-1. May 10, 2001.

106. HR 1646. State Department Authorization/International Prosecution Protection. DeLay, R-Texas, amendment that would protect U.S. citizens acting on behalf of the government from prosecution by the International Criminal Court until the Senate ratifies the treaty establishing the court. Adopted 282-137: R 205-4; D 76-132 (ND 48-106, SD 28-26); I 1-1. May 10, 2001.

107. HR 1646. State Department Authorization/U.N. Back Payments. Hyde, R-Ill., amendment that would require that the United States be restored to its seat on the U.N. Human Rights Commission before the release of a final payment of $244 million in U.N. back dues. Adopted 252-165: R 189-21; D 62-143 (ND 38-113, SD 24-30); I 1-1. May 10, 2001.

108. HR 1646. State Department Authorization/UNESCO Participation. Tancredo, R-Colo., amendment that would strike language authorizing a $67 million payment required for the United States to rejoin the U.N. Educational Scientific and Cultural Organization and language urging the president to renew U.S. participation in the organization. Rejected 193-225: R 183-27; D 9-197 (ND 4-148, SD 5-49); I 1-1. May 10, 2001.

	104	105	106	107	108
ALABAMA					
1 *Callahan*	Y	Y	Y	Y	Y
2 *Everett*	Y	Y	Y	Y	Y
3 *Riley*	Y	Y	Y	Y	Y
4 *Aderholt*	Y	Y	Y	Y	Y
5 Cramer	Y	N	Y	N	N
6 *Bachus*	Y	Y	Y	N	Y
7 Hilliard	N	N	N	N	N
ALASKA					
AL *Young*	Y	?	Y	Y	Y
ARIZONA					
1 *Flake*	Y	Y	Y	Y	Y
2 Pastor	N	N	N	N	N
3 *Stump*	+	?	?	?	?
4 *Shadegg*	Y	Y	Y	Y	Y
5 *Kolbe*	Y	Y	Y	N	N
6 *Hayworth*	Y	Y	Y	Y	Y
ARKANSAS					
1 Berry	N	N	Y	Y	N
2 Snyder	N	N	N	N	N
3 *Hutchinson*	Y	Y	Y	N	Y
4 Ross	N	N	Y	Y	N
CALIFORNIA					
1 Thompson	N	N	N	N	N
2 *Herger*	Y	Y	Y	Y	Y
3 *Ose*	Y	N	Y	Y	Y
4 *Doolittle*	Y	Y	Y	Y	Y
5 Matsui	N	N	N	N	N
6 Woolsey	N	N	N	N	N
7 Miller, George	N	N	N	N	N
8 Pelosi	N	N	N	N	N
9 Lee	N	Y	N	N	N
10 Tauscher	N	Y	N	N	N
11 *Pombo*	Y	Y	Y	Y	Y
12 Lantos	N	Y	N	Y	N
13 Stark	N	N	N	N	N
14 Eshoo	N	N	N	N	?
15 Honda	N	N	N	N	N
16 Lofgren	N	N	N	N	N
17 Farr	N	N	N	N	N
18 Condit	Y	N	Y	Y	N
19 *Radanovich*	Y	Y	Y	Y	Y
20 Dooley	N	N	Y	Y	N
21 *Thomas*	Y	Y	Y	Y	Y
22 Capps	N	N	N	N	N
23 *Gallegly*	Y	Y	Y	Y	Y
24 Sherman	N	N	Y	Y	N
25 *McKeon*	Y	Y	Y	Y	Y
26 Berman	N	N	N	N	N
27 Schiff	N	Y	Y	N	N
28 *Dreier*	Y	Y	Y	Y	Y
29 Waxman	N	N	N	N	N
30 Becerra	N	N	N	N	N
31 Solis	N	N	N	N	N
32 Vacant					
33 Roybal-Allard	N	N	N	?	N
34 Napolitano	N	N	N	N	N
35 Waters	N	N	N	N	N
36 Harman	N	N	Y	Y	N
37 Millender-McD.	N	N	N	N	N
38 *Horn*	Y	Y	Y	Y	N

	104	105	106	107	108
39 *Royce*	Y	Y	Y	Y	Y
40 *Lewis*	Y	Y	Y	Y	Y
41 *Miller, Gary*	Y	Y	Y	Y	Y
42 Baca	N	N	Y	Y	N
43 *Calvert*	Y	Y	Y	Y	Y
44 *Bono*	Y	Y	Y	Y	Y
45 *Rohrabacher*	Y	Y	Y	Y	Y
46 Sanchez	N	N	Y	N	N
47 *Cox*	Y	Y	Y	Y	Y
48 *Issa*	Y	Y	Y	Y	Y
49 Davis	N	N	Y	N	N
50 Filner	N	N	N	N	N
51 *Cunningham*	Y	Y	Y	Y	Y
52 *Hunter*	Y	?	?	?	?
COLORADO					
1 DeGette	N	N	N	N	N
2 Udall	N	N	N	N	N
3 *McInnis*	Y	Y	Y	Y	Y
4 *Schaffer*	Y	Y	Y	Y	Y
5 *Hefley*	N	Y	Y	Y	Y
6 *Tancredo*	Y	Y	Y	Y	Y
CONNECTICUT					
1 Larson	N	N	N	N	N
2 *Simmons*	Y	Y	Y	Y	Y
3 DeLauro	N	N	N	N	N
4 *Shays*	Y	Y	Y	N	N
5 Maloney	N	N	Y	Y	N
6 *Johnson*	Y	Y	N	N	Y
DELAWARE					
AL *Castle*	Y	Y	Y	N	N
FLORIDA					
1 *Scarborough*	Y	Y	Y	Y	Y
2 Boyd	N	Y	N	Y	N
3 Brown	N	N	N	N	N
4 *Crenshaw*	Y	Y	Y	Y	Y
5 Thurman	N	N	Y	N	N
6 *Stearns*	Y	Y	Y	Y	Y
7 *Mica*	Y	Y	Y	Y	Y
8 *Keller*	Y	Y	Y	Y	Y
9 *Bilirakis*	Y	Y	Y	Y	Y
10 *Young*	Y	Y	Y	Y	Y
11 Davis	N	N	N	N	N
12 *Putnam*	Y	Y	Y	Y	Y
13 *Miller*	?	Y	Y	Y	Y
14 *Goss*	Y	Y	Y	N	Y
15 *Weldon*	Y	Y	Y	Y	Y
16 *Foley*	Y	Y	Y	Y	Y
17 Meek	N	N	N	N	N
18 *Ros-Lehtinen*	Y	?	?	?	?
19 Wexler	N	N	N	N	N
20 Deutsch	N	N	N	N	N
21 *Diaz-Balart*	Y	Y	+	+	+
22 *Shaw*	Y	Y	Y	Y	N
23 Hastings	N	N	N	N	N
GEORGIA					
1 *Kingston*	Y	Y	Y	Y	Y
2 Bishop	N	N	Y	Y	N
3 *Collins*	Y	Y	Y	Y	Y
4 McKinney	N	N	N	N	N
5 Lewis	N	N	N	N	N
6 *Isakson*	Y	Y	Y	Y	Y
7 *Barr*	Y	Y	Y	Y	Y
8 *Chambliss*	Y	Y	Y	Y	Y
9 *Deal*	Y	Y	Y	Y	Y
10 *Norwood*	Y	Y	Y	Y	Y
11 *Linder*	Y	Y	Y	Y	Y
HAWAII					
1 Abercrombie	N	–	N	Y	N
2 Mink	N	N	N	N	N
IDAHO					
1 *Otter*	Y	Y	Y	Y	Y
2 *Simpson*	Y	Y	Y	Y	Y
ILLINOIS					
1 Rush	N	N	N	N	N
2 Jackson	N	N	N	N	N
3 Lipinski	N	Y	Y	Y	N
4 Gutierrez	N	N	N	N	N
5 Blagojevich	N	N	N	N	N
6 *Hyde*	Y	Y	Y	Y	Y
7 Davis	N	N	N	N	N
8 *Crane*	Y	Y	Y	Y	Y
9 Schakowsky	N	N	N	N	N
10 *Kirk*	Y	Y	Y	Y	N
11 *Weller*	Y	Y	Y	Y	Y
12 Costello	N	N	Y	Y	N
13 *Biggert*	Y	Y	Y	N	Y

ND Northern Democrats   SD Southern Democrats

	104	105	106	107	108
14 ***Hastert***	Y				
15 ***Johnson***	Y	Y	Y	Y	Y
16 ***Manzullo***	Y	Y	Y	Y	Y
17 Evans	N	N	N	N	N
18 ***LaHood***	Y	Y	Y	Y	Y
19 Phelps	N	N	Y	Y	N
20 ***Shimkus***	Y	Y	Y	Y	Y
INDIANA					
1 Visclosky	N	N	Y	Y	N
2 ***Pence***	Y	Y	Y	Y	Y
3 Roemer	N	N	Y	Y	N
4 ***Souder***	Y	Y	Y	Y	Y
5 ***Buyer***	Y	Y	Y	Y	Y
6 ***Burton***	Y	Y	Y	Y	Y
7 ***Kerns***	Y	Y	Y	Y	Y
8 ***Hostettler***	Y	Y	Y	Y	Y
9 Hill	N	N	Y	Y	N
10 Carson	N	N	N	N	N
IOWA					
1 ***Leach***	Y	Y	N	N	N
2 ***Nussle***	Y	Y	Y	Y	Y
3 Boswell	N	N	Y	N	N
4 ***Ganske***	Y	Y	Y	Y	N
5 ***Latham***	Y	Y	?	?	?
KANSAS					
1 ***Moran***	Y	Y	Y	Y	Y
2 ***Ryun***	Y	Y	Y	Y	Y
3 Moore	N	N	Y	Y	N
4 ***Tiahrt***	Y	Y	Y	Y	Y
KENTUCKY					
1 ***Whitfield***	Y	Y	Y	Y	N
2 ***Lewis***	Y	Y	Y	Y	Y
3 ***Northup***	Y	Y	Y	Y	Y
4 Lucas	Y	N	Y	Y	N
5 ***Rogers***	Y	Y	Y	Y	Y
6 ***Fletcher***	Y	Y	Y	Y	Y
LOUISIANA					
1 ***Vitter***	Y	Y	Y	Y	Y
2 Jefferson	N	N	N	N	N
3 ***Tauzin***	Y	Y	Y	Y	Y
4 ***McCrery***	Y	Y	Y	Y	Y
5 ***Cooksey***	Y	Y	Y	Y	Y
6 ***Baker***	Y	Y	Y	Y	Y
7 John	Y	N	Y	N	N
MAINE					
1 Allen	N	N	N	?	?
2 Baldacci	N	N	N	N	N
MARYLAND					
1 ***Gilchrest***	Y	Y	Y	Y	N
2 ***Ehrlich***	Y	Y	Y	Y	N
3 Cardin	N	N	N	N	N
4 Wynn	N	N	N	N	N
5 Hoyer	N	N	N	P	N
6 ***Bartlett***	Y	Y	Y	Y	Y
7 Cummings	N	N	N	N	N
8 ***Morella***	Y	Y	N	N	N
MASSACHUSETTS					
1 Olver	N	N	N	N	N
2 Neal	N	N	N	N	N
3 McGovern	N	N	N	N	N
4 Frank	N	N	N	N	N
5 Meehan	N	N	N	N	N
6 Tierney	N	N	N	N	N
7 Markey	N	N	N	N	N
8 Capuano	N	N	N	Y	N
9 Moakley	N	?	?	?	?
10 Delahunt	N	?	N	N	N
MICHIGAN					
1 Stupak	N	N	Y	Y	N
2 ***Hoekstra***	Y	Y	Y	Y	Y
3 ***Ehlers***	Y	Y	Y	N	N
4 ***Camp***	Y	Y	Y	Y	Y
5 Barcia	N	Y	Y	Y	N
6 ***Upton***	Y	Y	Y	Y	Y
7 ***Smith***	Y	Y	Y	N	N
8 ***Rogers***	Y	Y	Y	Y	Y
9 Kildee	N	N	Y	Y	N
10 Bonior	N	N	N	N	N
11 ***Knollenberg***	Y	Y	Y	Y	Y
12 Levin	N	N	N	N	N
13 Rivers	?	?	?	?	?
14 Conyers	N	N	N	N	N
15 Kilpatrick	N	N	N	N	N
16 Dingell	N	N	Y	Y	N

	104	105	106	107	108
MINNESOTA					
1 ***Gutknecht***	Y	Y	Y	Y	Y
2 ***Kennedy***	Y	Y	Y	Y	Y
3 ***Ramstad***	Y	Y	Y	Y	Y
4 McCollum	N	N	N	N	N
5 Sabo	N	N	N	N	N
6 Luther	N	N	N	N	N
7 Peterson	N	Y	Y	Y	Y
8 Oberstar	N	N	N	N	N
MISSISSIPPI					
1 ***Wicker***	Y	Y	Y	Y	Y
2 Thompson	N	N	N	N	N
3 ***Pickering***	Y	Y	Y	Y	Y
4 Shows	N	Y	Y	Y	Y
5 Taylor	N	Y	Y	Y	Y
MISSOURI					
1 Clay	N	N	Y	N	N
2 ***Akin***	Y	Y	Y	Y	Y
3 Gephardt	N	N	N	Y	N
4 Skelton	N	N	Y	Y	Y
5 McCarthy	N	N	N	N	N
6 ***Graves***	Y	Y	Y	Y	Y
7 ***Blunt***	Y	Y	Y	Y	Y
8 ***Emerson***	Y	Y	?	?	?
9 ***Hulshof***	Y	Y	Y	Y	Y
MONTANA					
AL ***Rehberg***	Y	Y	Y	Y	Y
NEBRASKA					
1 ***Bereuter***	Y	Y	Y	N	Y
2 ***Terry***	Y	Y	Y	Y	Y
3 ***Osborne***	Y	Y	Y	Y	Y
NEVADA					
1 Berkley	N	N	N	N	N
2 ***Gibbons***	Y	Y	Y	Y	Y
NEW HAMPSHIRE					
1 ***Sununu***	Y	Y	Y	Y	Y
2 ***Bass***	N	Y	Y	Y	Y
NEW JERSEY					
1 Andrews	N	N	Y	Y	N
2 ***LoBiondo***	Y	Y	Y	Y	Y
3 ***Saxton***	Y	Y	Y	Y	Y
4 ***Smith***	Y	Y	Y	Y	Y
5 ***Roukema***	Y	Y	Y	Y	N
6 Pallone	N	N	Y	N	N
7 ***Ferguson***	Y	Y	Y	Y	Y
8 Pascrell	N	N	Y	N	N
9 Rothman	N	N	Y	N	N
10 Payne	N	N	N	N	N
11 ***Frelinghuysen***	Y	Y	Y	Y	Y
12 Holt	N	N	N	N	N
13 Menendez	N	?	Y	Y	N
NEW MEXICO					
1 ***Wilson***	Y	Y	Y	Y	Y
2 ***Skeen***	Y	Y	Y	Y	Y
3 Udall	N	N	N	N	N
NEW YORK					
1 ***Grucci***	Y	Y	Y	Y	Y
2 Israel	N	N	N	Y	N
3 ***King***	Y	Y	Y	Y	Y
4 McCarthy	N	N	N	Y	N
5 Ackerman	N	N	N	N	N
6 Meeks	N	N	N	N	N
7 Crowley	N	N	N	N	N
8 Nadler	N	N	N	N	N
9 Weiner	N	Y	N	N	N
10 Towns	N	N	N	N	N
11 Owens	N	N	N	N	N
12 Velázquez	N	N	N	N	N
13 ***Fossella***	Y	Y	Y	Y	Y
14 Maloney	N	N	N	N	N
15 Rangel	N	N	N	N	N
16 Serrano	N	N	N	N	N
17 Engel	N	?	N	N	N
18 Lowey	N	N	N	N	N
19 ***Kelly***	Y	Y	Y	N	N
20 ***Gilman***	Y	Y	Y	Y	Y
21 McNulty	N	N	Y	N	N
22 ***Sweeney***	Y	Y	Y	Y	N
23 ***Boehlert***	Y	Y	Y	N	Y
24 ***McHugh***	Y	Y	Y	N	Y
25 ***Walsh***	Y	Y	Y	N	N
26 Hinchey	N	N	N	N	N
27 ***Reynolds***	Y	Y	Y	Y	Y
28 Slaughter	N	N	N	N	N
29 LaFalce	N	N	N	N	N

	104	105	106	107	108
30 ***Quinn***	Y	Y	Y	Y	N
31 ***Houghton***	Y	Y	N	N	N
NORTH CAROLINA					
1 Clayton	N	N	N	N	N
2 Etheridge	N	N	Y	Y	N
3 ***Jones***	Y	Y	Y	Y	Y
4 Price	N	N	Y	N	N
5 ***Burr***	Y	Y	Y	Y	Y
6 ***Coble***	Y	Y	Y	Y	Y
7 McIntyre	N	N	Y	Y	Y
8 ***Hayes***	Y	Y	Y	Y	Y
9 ***Myrick***	Y	Y	Y	Y	Y
10 ***Ballenger***	Y	Y	Y	Y	Y
11 ***Taylor***	Y	Y	Y	Y	Y
12 Watt	N	N	N	N	N
NORTH DAKOTA					
AL Pomeroy	N	N	N	N	N
OHIO					
1 ***Chabot***	Y	Y	Y	Y	Y
2 ***Portman***	Y	Y	Y	Y	+
3 Hall	N	N	N	N	N
4 ***Oxley***	Y	Y	Y	Y	Y
5 ***Gillmor***	Y	Y	Y	Y	Y
6 Strickland	N	N	Y	N	N
7 ***Hobson***	Y	Y	Y	Y	Y
8 ***Boehner***	Y	Y	Y	Y	Y
9 Kaptur	N	N	Y	Y	N
10 Kucinich	N	N	N	N	N
11 Jones	N	N	N	N	N
12 ***Tiberi***	Y	Y	Y	Y	Y
13 Brown	N	N	N	N	N
14 Sawyer	N	N	N	N	N
15 ***Pryce***	Y	Y	Y	Y	N
16 ***Regula***	Y	Y	Y	Y	Y
17 Traficant	Y	Y	Y	Y	Y
18 ***Ney***	Y	Y	Y	Y	N
19 ***LaTourette***	Y	Y	Y	Y	Y
OKLAHOMA					
1 ***Largent***	Y	Y	Y	Y	Y
2 Carson	N	N	Y	Y	N
3 ***Watkins***	Y	Y	Y	Y	Y
4 ***Watts***	Y	Y	Y	Y	Y
5 ***Istook***	Y	Y	Y	Y	Y
6 ***Lucas***	Y	Y	Y	Y	Y
OREGON					
1 Wu	N	N	N	N	N
2 ***Walden***	Y	Y	Y	Y	Y
3 Blumenauer	N	N	N	N	N
4 DeFazio	N	N	Y	Y	N
5 Hooley	N	N	N	Y	N
PENNSYLVANIA					
1 Brady	N	N	Y	N	N
2 Fattah	N	N	N	N	N
3 Borski	N	N	N	N	N
4 ***Hart***	Y	Y	Y	Y	Y
5 ***Peterson***	Y	Y	Y	Y	Y
6 Holden	N	N	Y	Y	N
7 ***Weldon***	Y	Y	?	Y	Y
8 ***Greenwood***	Y	Y	Y	Y	N
9 Vacant					
10 ***Sherwood***	Y	Y	Y	Y	Y
11 Kanjorski	N	N	Y	Y	N
12 Murtha	N	N	Y	N	N
13 Hoeffel	N	N	N	N	N
14 Coyne	N	N	N	N	N
15 ***Toomey***	Y	Y	Y	Y	Y
16 ***Pitts***	Y	Y	Y	Y	Y
17 ***Gekas***	Y	Y	Y	Y	Y
18 Doyle	N	N	Y	Y	N
19 ***Platts***	Y	Y	Y	Y	Y
20 Mascara	N	N	Y	Y	N
21 ***English***	Y	Y	Y	Y	N
RHODE ISLAND					
1 Kennedy	N	N	N	N	N
2 Langevin	N	N	Y	Y	N
SOUTH CAROLINA					
1 ***Brown***	Y	Y	Y	Y	Y
2 ***Spence***	Y	Y	Y	Y	Y
3 ***Graham***	Y	Y	Y	Y	N
4 ***DeMint***	Y	Y	Y	Y	Y
5 Spratt	N	N	Y	Y	N
6 Clyburn	N	N	N	N	N
SOUTH DAKOTA					
AL ***Thune***	Y	Y	Y	+	Y

	104	105	106	107	108
TENNESSEE					
1 ***Jenkins***	Y	Y	Y	Y	Y
2 ***Duncan***	Y	Y	Y	Y	Y
3 ***Wamp***	Y	Y	Y	Y	Y
4 ***Hilleary***	Y	Y	Y	Y	Y
5 Clement	N	–	N	N	N
6 Gordon	N	Y	Y	Y	N
7 ***Bryant***	Y	Y	Y	Y	Y
8 Tanner	N	N	Y	Y	N
9 Ford	N	N	N	N	N
TEXAS					
1 Sandlin	N	N	Y	N	N
2 Turner	N	N	Y	Y	N
3 ***Johnson, Sam***	Y	Y	Y	Y	Y
4 Hall	Y	Y	Y	Y	Y
5 ***Sessions***	Y	Y	Y	Y	Y
6 ***Barton***	Y	Y	Y	Y	Y
7 ***Culberson***	Y	Y	Y	Y	Y
8 ***Brady***	Y	Y	Y	Y	Y
9 Lampson	N	N	N	Y	N
10 Doggett	N	N	N	N	N
11 Edwards	N	N	Y	Y	N
12 ***Granger***	Y	Y	Y	Y	Y
13 ***Thornberry***	Y	Y	Y	Y	Y
14 ***Paul***	N	Y	P	Y	Y
15 Hinojosa	N	N	N	N	N
16 Reyes	N	N	Y	Y	N
17 Stenholm	N	N	Y	Y	Y
18 Jackson-Lee	N	N	Y	N	N
19 ***Combest***	Y	Y	Y	Y	Y
20 Gonzalez	N	N	N	N	N
21 ***Smith***	Y	Y	Y	Y	Y
22 ***DeLay***	Y	Y	Y	Y	Y
23 ***Bonilla***	Y	Y	Y	Y	Y
24 Frost	N	N	Y	Y	N
25 Bentsen	N	N	Y	Y	N
26 ***Armey***	Y	Y	Y	Y	Y
27 Ortiz	N	N	Y	Y	N
28 Rodriguez	N	N	N	N	N
29 Green	N	N	Y	Y	N
30 Johnson, E.B.	N	N	N	N	N
UTAH					
1 ***Hansen***	Y	Y	Y	Y	Y
2 Matheson	N	N	Y	Y	N
3 ***Cannon***	Y	Y	Y	Y	Y
VERMONT					
AL *Sanders*	N	N	N	N	N
VIRGINIA					
1 ***Davis, Jo Ann***	Y	Y	Y	Y	Y
2 ***Schrock***	Y	Y	Y	Y	Y
3 Scott	N	N	N	N	N
4 Vacant					
5 *Goode*	Y	Y	Y	Y	Y
6 ***Goodlatte***	Y	Y	Y	N	Y
7 ***Cantor***	Y	Y	Y	Y	Y
8 Moran	N	N	N	N	N
9 Boucher	N	N	Y	N	N
10 ***Wolf***	Y	Y	Y	Y	Y
11 ***Davis, T.***	Y	Y	Y	N	N
WASHINGTON					
1 Inslee	N	N	Y	N	N
2 Larsen	N	N	Y	N	N
3 Baird	N	N	N	N	N
4 ***Hastings***	Y	Y	Y	Y	Y
5 ***Nethercutt***	Y	Y	Y	Y	Y
6 Dicks	N	N	Y	N	N
7 McDermott	N	N	N	N	N
8 ***Dunn***	Y	Y	Y	Y	Y
9 Smith	N	N	Y	N	N
WEST VIRGINIA					
1 Mollohan	N	N	Y	N	N
2 ***Capito***	Y	Y	Y	Y	Y
3 Rahall	N	N	Y	N	N
WISCONSIN					
1 ***Ryan***	Y	Y	Y	Y	Y
2 Baldwin	N	N	N	N	N
3 Kind	N	N	N	Y	N
4 Kleczka	N	N	N	N	N
5 Barrett	N	N	N	N	N
6 ***Petri***	Y	Y	Y	N	Y
7 Obey	N	N	N	N	N
8 ***Green***	Y	Y	Y	Y	Y
9 ***Sensenbrenner***	Y	?	?	?	?
WYOMING					
AL ***Cubin***	?	?	?	?	?

Southern states - Ala., Ark., Fla., Ga., Ky., La., Miss., N.C., Okla., S.C., Tenn., Texas, Va.

Key

Y	Voted for (yea).
#	Paired for.
+	Announced for.
N	Voted against (nay).
X	Paired against.
–	Announced against.
P	Voted "present."
C	Voted "present" to avoid possible conflict of interest.
?	Did not vote or otherwise make a position known.

•

Democrats   **Republicans**
Independents

109. HR 1696. World World II Memorial/Passage. Stump, R-Ariz., motion to suspend the rules and pass the bill that would direct the American Battle Monuments Commission to expeditiously begin construction of the World War II Memorial at the Rainbow Pool on the National Mall. The bill states that the monument's previously approved design and siting are final, meet all applicable laws, and are not subject to administrative or judicial review. Motion agreed to 400-15: R 209-3; D 189-12 (ND 137-11, SD 52-1); I 2-0. A two-thirds majority of those present and voting (277 in this case) is required for passage under suspension of the rules. May 15, 2001.

110. H Res 116. Law Officer Tribute/Adoption. Otter, R-Idaho, motion to suspend the rules and adopt the resolution that would honor law enforcement officers killed or disabled in the line of duty. Motion agreed to 416-0: R 213-0; D 201-0 (ND 149-0, SD 52-0); I 2-0. A two-thirds majority of those present and voting (278 in this case) is required for adoption under suspension of the rules. May 15, 2001.

111. HR 1727. Police Survivor Benefits/Passage. Ramstad, R-Minn., motion to suspend the rules and pass the bill that would extend tax-exempt status to annuities paid to survivors of public safety officers killed in the line of duty before Dec. 31, 1996, the same benefit given to survivors of officers killed after that date. Motion agreed to 419-0: R 214-0; D 203-0 (ND 150-0, SD 53-0); I 2-0. A two-thirds majority of those present and voting (280 in this case) is required for passage under suspension of the rules. May 15, 2001.

112. HR 586. Foster Care Benefits/Passage. Lewis, R-Ky., motion to suspend the rules and pass the bill that would extend tax-exempt status to foster care payments made by any placement agency licensed, certified or designated by a state. The bill also would eliminate the requirement that the exemption apply only to payments made for the care of individuals younger than age 19. Motion agreed to 420-0: R 215-0; D 203-0 (ND 150-0, SD 53-0); I 2-0. A two-thirds majority of those present and voting (280 in this case) is required for passage under suspension of the rules. May 15, 2001.

113. HR 428. Taiwan Participation/Concur with Senate Amendment. Leach, R-Iowa, motion to suspend the rules and concur with a Senate amendment to the bill that would direct the secretary of State to work on a plan to help Taiwan win observer status at the World Health Organization. Motion agreed to 415-0: R 213-0; D 200-0 (ND 148-0, SD 52-0); I 2-0. A two-thirds majority of those present and voting (277 in this case) is required for passage under suspension of the rules. May 15, 2001.

114. Procedural Motion/Journal. Approval of the House Journal of Tuesday, May 15, 2001. Approved 348-53: R 188-12; D 159-41 (ND 114-36, SD 45-5); I 1-0. May 16, 2001.

	109	110	111	112	113	114
ALABAMA						
1 *Callahan*	Y	Y	Y	Y	Y	Y
2 *Everett*	Y	Y	Y	Y	Y	Y
3 *Riley*	Y	Y	Y	Y	Y	Y
4 *Aderholt*	Y	Y	Y	Y	Y	N
5 Cramer	Y	Y	Y	Y	Y	Y
6 *Bachus*	Y	Y	Y	Y	Y	Y
7 Hilliard	Y	Y	Y	Y	Y	N
ALASKA						
AL *Young*	Y	Y	Y	Y	Y	?
ARIZONA						
1 *Flake*	Y	Y	Y	Y	Y	Y
2 Pastor	Y	Y	Y	Y	Y	Y
3 *Stump*	Y	Y	Y	Y	Y	Y
4 *Shadegg*	Y	Y	Y	Y	Y	Y
5 *Kolbe*	Y	Y	Y	Y	Y	Y
6 *Hayworth*	Y	Y	Y	Y	Y	Y
ARKANSAS						
1 Berry	Y	Y	Y	Y	Y	Y
2 Snyder	N	Y	Y	Y	Y	Y
3 *Hutchinson*	Y	Y	Y	Y	Y	?
4 Ross	Y	Y	Y	Y	Y	Y
CALIFORNIA						
1 Thompson	Y	Y	Y	Y	Y	N
2 *Herger*	Y	Y	Y	Y	Y	Y
3 *Ose*	Y	Y	Y	Y	Y	Y
4 *Doolittle*	Y	Y	Y	Y	Y	Y
5 Matsui	Y	Y	Y	Y	Y	Y
6 Woolsey	Y	Y	Y	Y	Y	Y
7 Miller, George	N	Y	Y	Y	Y	N
8 Pelosi	Y	Y	Y	Y	Y	Y
9 Lee	N	Y	Y	Y	Y	Y
10 Tauscher	Y	Y	Y	Y	Y	Y
11 *Pombo*	Y	Y	Y	Y	Y	Y
12 Lantos	Y	Y	Y	Y	Y	Y
13 Stark	N	Y	Y	Y	Y	N
14 Eshoo	Y	Y	Y	Y	Y	Y
15 Honda	Y	Y	Y	Y	Y	Y
16 Lofgren	Y	Y	Y	Y	Y	Y
17 Farr	Y	Y	Y	Y	Y	Y
18 Condit	Y	Y	Y	Y	Y	Y
19 *Radanovich*	Y	Y	Y	Y	Y	Y
20 Dooley	Y	Y	Y	Y	Y	Y
21 *Thomas*	Y	Y	Y	Y	Y	?
22 Capps	Y	Y	Y	Y	Y	Y
23 *Gallegly*	Y	Y	Y	Y	Y	Y
24 Sherman	Y	Y	Y	Y	Y	Y
25 *McKeon*	Y	Y	Y	Y	Y	Y
26 Berman	N	Y	Y	Y	Y	Y
27 Schiff	Y	Y	Y	Y	Y	Y
28 *Dreier*	Y	Y	Y	Y	Y	Y
29 Waxman	N	Y	Y	Y	Y	Y
30 Becerra	Y	Y	Y	Y	Y	Y
31 Solis	Y	Y	Y	Y	Y	Y
32 Vacant						
33 Roybal-Allard	Y	Y	Y	Y	Y	Y
34 Napolitano	Y	Y	Y	Y	Y	Y
35 Waters	Y	Y	Y	Y	Y	N
36 Harman	Y	Y	Y	Y	Y	Y
37 Millender-McD.	Y	Y	Y	Y	Y	Y
38 *Horn*	Y	?	Y	Y	Y	Y

	109	110	111	112	113	114
39 *Royce*	Y	Y	Y	Y	Y	Y
40 *Lewis*	Y	Y	Y	Y	Y	Y
41 *Miller, Gary*	Y	Y	Y	Y	Y	Y
42 Baca	Y	Y	Y	Y	Y	Y
43 *Calvert*	Y	Y	Y	Y	Y	Y
44 *Bono*	Y	Y	Y	Y	Y	Y
45 *Rohrabacher*	Y	Y	Y	Y	Y	Y
46 Sanchez	+	+	+	+	+	Y
47 *Cox*	Y	Y	Y	Y	Y	Y
48 *Issa*	Y	Y	Y	Y	Y	Y
49 Davis	Y	Y	Y	Y	Y	Y
50 Filner	Y	Y	Y	Y	Y	N
51 *Cunningham*	Y	Y	Y	Y	Y	Y
52 *Hunter*	Y	Y	Y	Y	Y	?
COLORADO						
1 DeGette	Y	Y	Y	Y	Y	Y
2 Udall	Y	Y	Y	Y	Y	N
3 *McInnis*	?	?	?	Y	Y	Y
4 *Schaffer*	Y	Y	Y	Y	Y	Y
5 *Hefley*	Y	Y	Y	Y	Y	N
6 *Tancredo*	Y	Y	Y	Y	Y	P
CONNECTICUT						
1 Larson	Y	Y	Y	Y	Y	Y
2 *Simmons*	Y	Y	Y	Y	Y	Y
3 DeLauro	Y	Y	Y	Y	Y	Y
4 *Shays*	Y	Y	Y	Y	Y	Y
5 Maloney	Y	Y	Y	Y	Y	Y
6 *Johnson*	Y	Y	Y	Y	?	Y
DELAWARE						
AL *Castle*	Y	Y	Y	Y	Y	Y
FLORIDA						
1 *Scarborough*	Y	Y	Y	Y	Y	?
2 Boyd	Y	Y	Y	Y	Y	+
3 Brown	Y	Y	Y	Y	Y	Y
4 *Crenshaw*	Y	Y	Y	Y	Y	Y
5 Thurman	Y	Y	Y	Y	Y	Y
6 *Stearns*	Y	Y	Y	Y	Y	Y
7 *Mica*	Y	Y	Y	Y	Y	Y
8 *Keller*	Y	Y	Y	Y	Y	Y
9 *Bilirakis*	Y	Y	Y	Y	Y	Y
10 *Young*	?	?	?	?	?	Y
11 Davis	Y	Y	Y	Y	Y	Y
12 *Putnam*	Y	Y	Y	Y	Y	Y
13 *Miller*	Y	Y	Y	Y	Y	Y
14 *Goss*	Y	Y	Y	Y	Y	Y
15 *Weldon*	Y	Y	Y	Y	Y	Y
16 *Foley*	Y	Y	Y	Y	Y	Y
17 Meek	Y	Y	Y	Y	Y	Y
18 *Ros-Lehtinen*	?	?	?	?	?	?
19 Wexler	Y	Y	Y	Y	Y	Y
20 Deutsch	Y	Y	Y	Y	Y	Y
21 *Diaz-Balart*	Y	Y	Y	Y	Y	Y
22 *Shaw*	Y	Y	Y	Y	Y	Y
23 Hastings	Y	Y	Y	Y	Y	N
GEORGIA						
1 *Kingston*	Y	Y	Y	Y	Y	Y
2 Bishop	Y	Y	Y	Y	?	Y
3 *Collins*	Y	Y	Y	Y	Y	?
4 McKinney	Y	Y	Y	Y	Y	Y
5 Lewis	Y	Y	Y	Y	Y	N
6 *Isakson*	Y	Y	Y	Y	Y	Y
7 *Barr*	Y	Y	Y	Y	Y	Y
8 *Chambliss*	Y	Y	Y	Y	Y	Y
9 *Deal*	Y	Y	Y	Y	Y	Y
10 *Norwood*	Y	Y	Y	Y	Y	Y
11 *Linder*	Y	Y	Y	Y	Y	?
HAWAII						
1 Abercrombie	Y	Y	Y	Y	Y	Y
2 Mink	Y	Y	Y	Y	Y	Y
IDAHO						
1 *Otter*	Y	Y	Y	Y	Y	Y
2 *Simpson*	Y	Y	Y	Y	Y	Y
ILLINOIS						
1 Rush	Y	Y	Y	Y	Y	Y
2 Jackson	Y	Y	Y	Y	Y	Y
3 Lipinski	Y	Y	Y	Y	Y	Y
4 Gutierrez	Y	Y	Y	Y	Y	N
5 Blagojevich	Y	Y	Y	Y	Y	Y
6 *Hyde*	Y	Y	Y	Y	Y	Y
7 Davis	Y	Y	Y	Y	Y	Y
8 *Crane*	Y	Y	Y	Y	Y	N
9 Schakowsky	Y	Y	Y	Y	Y	Y
10 *Kirk*	Y	Y	Y	Y	Y	Y
11 *Weller*	Y	Y	Y	Y	?	N
12 Costello	Y	Y	Y	Y	Y	N
13 *Biggert*	Y	Y	?	Y	Y	Y

ND Northern Democrats   SD Southern Democrats

	109	110	111	112	113	114
14 ***Hastert***						
15 ***Johnson***	Y	Y	Y	Y	Y	Y
16 ***Manzullo***	Y	Y	Y	Y	Y	Y
17 Evans	Y	Y	Y	Y	Y	Y
18 ***LaHood***	Y	Y	Y	Y	Y	Y
19 Phelps	Y	Y	Y	Y	Y	Y
20 ***Shimkus***	Y	Y	Y	Y	Y	Y
INDIANA						
1 Visclosky	Y	Y	Y	Y	Y	N
2 ***Pence***	Y	Y	Y	Y	Y	Y
3 Roemer	Y	Y	Y	Y	Y	N
4 ***Souder***	?	?	?	?	?	Y
5 ***Buyer***	Y	Y	Y	Y	Y	Y
6 ***Burton***	Y	Y	Y	Y	Y	Y
7 ***Kerns***	Y	Y	Y	Y	Y	Y
8 ***Hostettler***	Y	Y	Y	Y	Y	Y
9 Hill	Y	Y	Y	Y	Y	Y
10 Carson	Y	Y	Y	Y	Y	Y
IOWA						
1 ***Leach***	Y	Y	Y	Y	Y	Y
2 ***Nussle***	Y	Y	Y	Y	Y	Y
3 Boswell	Y	Y	Y	Y	Y	Y
4 ***Ganske***	Y	Y	Y	Y	Y	Y
5 ***Latham***	Y	Y	Y	Y	Y	Y
KANSAS						
1 ***Moran***	Y	Y	Y	Y	Y	Y
2 ***Ryun***	Y	Y	Y	Y	Y	Y
3 Moore	Y	Y	Y	Y	Y	N
4 ***Tiahrt***	Y	Y	Y	Y	Y	Y
KENTUCKY						
1 ***Whitfield***	?	Y	Y	Y	Y	Y
2 ***Lewis***	Y	Y	Y	Y	Y	Y
3 ***Northup***	Y	Y	Y	Y	Y	Y
4 Lucas	Y	Y	Y	Y	Y	Y
5 ***Rogers***	Y	Y	Y	Y	Y	Y
6 ***Fletcher***	Y	Y	Y	Y	Y	Y
LOUISIANA						
1 ***Vitter***	Y	Y	Y	Y	Y	Y
2 Jefferson	Y	Y	Y	Y	Y	?
3 ***Tauzin***	Y	Y	Y	Y	Y	Y
4 ***McCrery***	Y	Y	Y	Y	Y	Y
5 ***Cooksey***	Y	Y	Y	Y	Y	Y
6 ***Baker***	Y	Y	Y	Y	Y	Y
7 John	Y	Y	Y	Y	Y	Y
MAINE						
1 Allen	?	?	?	?	?	Y
2 Baldacci	Y	Y	Y	Y	Y	Y
MARYLAND						
1 ***Gilchrest***	N	Y	Y	Y	Y	Y
2 ***Ehrlich***	Y	Y	Y	Y	Y	Y
3 Cardin	Y	Y	Y	Y	Y	Y
4 Wynn	Y	Y	Y	Y	Y	Y
5 Hoyer	Y	Y	Y	Y	Y	Y
6 ***Bartlett***	Y	Y	Y	Y	Y	Y
7 Cummings	Y	Y	Y	Y	Y	Y
8 ***Morella***	Y	Y	Y	Y	Y	Y
MASSACHUSETTS						
1 Olver	Y	Y	Y	Y	Y	Y
2 Neal	Y	Y	Y	Y	Y	Y
3 McGovern	Y	Y	Y	Y	Y	Y
4 Frank	Y	Y	Y	Y	?	Y
5 Meehan	Y	Y	Y	Y	Y	Y
6 Tierney	Y	Y	Y	Y	Y	Y
7 Markey	Y	Y	Y	Y	Y	Y
8 Capuano	Y	Y	Y	Y	?	N
9 Moakley	Y	Y	Y	Y	Y	?
10 Delahunt	Y	Y	Y	Y	Y	Y
MICHIGAN						
1 Stupak	N	Y	Y	Y	Y	N
2 ***Hoekstra***	Y	Y	Y	Y	Y	Y
3 ***Ehlers***	Y	Y	Y	Y	Y	Y
4 ***Camp***	Y	Y	Y	Y	Y	Y
5 Barcia	Y	Y	Y	Y	Y	Y
6 ***Upton***	Y	Y	Y	Y	Y	Y
7 ***Smith***	Y	Y	Y	Y	Y	Y
8 ***Rogers***	Y	Y	Y	Y	Y	Y
9 Kildee	Y	Y	Y	Y	Y	Y
10 Bonior	Y	Y	Y	Y	Y	N
11 ***Knollenberg***	Y	Y	Y	Y	Y	Y
12 Levin	Y	Y	Y	Y	Y	Y
13 Rivers	Y	Y	Y	Y	Y	Y
14 Conyers	Y	Y	Y	Y	Y	Y
15 Kilpatrick	Y	Y	Y	Y	Y	Y
16 Dingell	Y	Y	Y	Y	Y	Y

	109	110	111	112	113	114
MINNESOTA						
1 ***Gutknecht***	Y	Y	Y	Y	Y	N
2 ***Kennedy***	Y	Y	Y	Y	Y	N
3 ***Ramstad***	Y	Y	Y	Y	Y	N
4 McCollum	Y	Y	Y	Y	Y	Y
5 Sabo	Y	Y	Y	Y	Y	N
6 Luther	Y	Y	Y	Y	Y	Y
7 Peterson	Y	Y	Y	Y	Y	N
8 Oberstar	N	Y	Y	Y	Y	N
MISSISSIPPI						
1 ***Wicker***	Y	Y	Y	Y	Y	?
2 Thompson	Y	Y	Y	Y	Y	N
3 ***Pickering***	Y	Y	Y	Y	Y	Y
4 Shows	Y	Y	Y	Y	Y	Y
5 Taylor	Y	Y	Y	Y	Y	N
MISSOURI						
1 Clay	N	Y	Y	Y	Y	Y
2 ***Akin***	Y	Y	Y	Y	Y	Y
3 Gephardt	Y	Y	Y	Y	Y	N
4 Skelton	Y	Y	Y	Y	Y	Y
5 McCarthy	Y	Y	Y	Y	Y	Y
6 ***Graves***	Y	Y	Y	Y	Y	Y
7 ***Blunt***	Y	Y	Y	Y	Y	?
8 ***Emerson***	Y	Y	Y	Y	Y	Y
9 ***Hulshof***	Y	Y	Y	Y	Y	Y
MONTANA						
AL ***Rehberg***	Y	Y	Y	Y	Y	Y
NEBRASKA						
1 ***Bereuter***	N	Y	Y	Y	Y	?
2 ***Terry***	Y	Y	Y	Y	Y	Y
3 ***Osborne***	Y	Y	Y	Y	Y	Y
NEVADA						
1 Berkley	Y	Y	Y	Y	Y	Y
2 ***Gibbons***	Y	Y	Y	Y	Y	Y
NEW HAMPSHIRE						
1 ***Sununu***	Y	Y	Y	Y	Y	Y
2 ***Bass***	Y	Y	Y	Y	Y	Y
NEW JERSEY						
1 Andrews	Y	Y	Y	Y	Y	Y
2 ***LoBiondo***	Y	Y	Y	Y	Y	N
3 ***Saxton***	Y	Y	Y	Y	Y	Y
4 ***Smith***	Y	Y	Y	Y	Y	Y
5 ***Roukema***	Y	Y	Y	Y	Y	?
6 Pallone	Y	Y	Y	Y	Y	N
7 ***Ferguson***	Y	Y	Y	Y	Y	Y
8 Pascrell	Y	Y	Y	Y	Y	Y
9 Rothman	Y	Y	Y	Y	Y	Y
10 Payne	Y	Y	Y	Y	Y	Y
11 ***Frelinghuysen***	Y	Y	Y	Y	Y	Y
12 Holt	Y	Y	Y	Y	Y	Y
13 Menendez	Y	Y	Y	Y	Y	N
NEW MEXICO						
1 ***Wilson***	Y	Y	Y	Y	Y	Y
2 ***Skeen***	Y	Y	Y	Y	Y	Y
3 Udall	Y	Y	Y	Y	Y	N
NEW YORK						
1 ***Grucci***	Y	Y	Y	Y	Y	Y
2 Israel	Y	Y	Y	Y	Y	Y
3 ***King***	Y	Y	Y	Y	Y	Y
4 McCarthy	Y	Y	Y	Y	Y	Y
5 Ackerman	Y	Y	Y	Y	Y	Y
6 Meeks	Y	Y	Y	Y	Y	Y
7 Crowley	Y	Y	Y	Y	Y	N
8 Nadler	Y	Y	Y	Y	Y	?
9 Weiner	Y	Y	Y	Y	Y	N
10 Towns	Y	Y	Y	Y	Y	Y
11 Owens	Y	Y	Y	Y	Y	Y
12 Velázquez	Y	Y	Y	Y	Y	Y
13 ***Fossella***	Y	Y	Y	Y	Y	?
14 Maloney	Y	Y	Y	Y	Y	Y
15 Rangel	Y	Y	Y	Y	Y	?
16 Serrano	Y	Y	Y	Y	Y	Y
17 Engel	Y	Y	Y	Y	Y	Y
18 Lowey	Y	Y	Y	Y	Y	N
19 ***Kelly***	Y	Y	Y	Y	Y	Y
20 ***Gilman***	Y	Y	Y	Y	Y	Y
21 McNulty	Y	Y	Y	Y	Y	Y
22 ***Sweeney***	Y	Y	Y	Y	Y	?
23 ***Boehlert***	Y	Y	Y	Y	Y	Y
24 ***McHugh***	Y	Y	Y	Y	Y	Y
25 ***Walsh***	Y	Y	Y	Y	Y	Y
26 Hinchey	N	Y	Y	Y	Y	?
27 ***Reynolds***	Y	Y	Y	Y	Y	Y
28 Slaughter	?	?	?	?	?	N
29 LaFalce	N	Y	Y	Y	Y	N

	109	110	111	112	113	114
30 ***Quinn***	Y	Y	Y	Y	?	Y
31 ***Houghton***	Y	Y	Y	Y	Y	Y
NORTH CAROLINA						
1 Clayton	Y	Y	Y	Y	Y	Y
2 Etheridge	Y	Y	Y	Y	Y	Y
3 ***Jones***	Y	Y	Y	Y	Y	Y
4 Price	Y	Y	Y	Y	Y	Y
5 ***Burr***	Y	Y	Y	Y	Y	?
6 ***Coble***	Y	Y	Y	Y	Y	Y
7 McIntyre	+	+	+	+	+	Y
8 ***Hayes***	Y	Y	Y	Y	Y	Y
9 ***Myrick***	Y	Y	Y	Y	Y	Y
10 ***Ballenger***	Y	Y	Y	Y	Y	Y
11 ***Taylor***	N	Y	Y	Y	Y	Y
12 Watt	Y	Y	Y	Y	Y	Y
NORTH DAKOTA						
AL Pomeroy	Y	Y	Y	Y	Y	Y
OHIO						
1 ***Chabot***	Y	Y	Y	Y	Y	Y
2 ***Portman***	?	Y	Y	Y	Y	Y
3 Hall	?	?	?	?	?	?
4 ***Oxley***	Y	Y	Y	Y	Y	Y
5 ***Gillmor***	Y	Y	Y	Y	Y	N
6 Strickland	Y	Y	Y	Y	Y	N
7 ***Hobson***	Y	Y	Y	Y	Y	Y
8 ***Boehner***	Y	Y	Y	?	Y	Y
9 Kaptur	Y	Y	Y	Y	Y	Y
10 Kucinich	Y	Y	Y	Y	Y	N
11 Jones	Y	Y	Y	Y	Y	N
12 ***Tiberi***	Y	Y	Y	Y	Y	Y
13 Brown	Y	Y	Y	Y	Y	Y
14 Sawyer	Y	Y	Y	Y	Y	Y
15 ***Pryce***	Y	Y	Y	Y	Y	Y
16 ***Regula***	Y	Y	Y	Y	Y	Y
17 Traficant	Y	Y	Y	Y	Y	Y
18 ***Ney***	Y	Y	Y	Y	Y	Y
19 ***LaTourette***	Y	Y	Y	Y	Y	Y
OKLAHOMA						
1 ***Largent***	Y	Y	Y	Y	Y	Y
2 Carson	Y	Y	Y	Y	Y	Y
3 ***Watkins***	Y	Y	Y	Y	Y	Y
4 ***Watts***	Y	Y	Y	Y	Y	?
5 ***Istook***	Y	?	Y	Y	Y	Y
6 ***Lucas***	Y	Y	Y	Y	Y	Y
OREGON						
1 Wu	Y	Y	Y	Y	Y	Y
2 ***Walden***	Y	Y	Y	Y	Y	Y
3 Blumenauer	Y	Y	Y	Y	Y	Y
4 DeFazio	Y	Y	Y	Y	Y	N
5 Hooley	Y	Y	Y	Y	Y	Y
PENNSYLVANIA						
1 Brady	?	?	?	?	?	N
2 Fattah	?	?	?	?	?	Y
3 Borski	Y	Y	Y	Y	Y	N
4 ***Hart***	Y	Y	Y	Y	Y	Y
5 ***Peterson***	Y	Y	Y	Y	Y	Y
6 Holden	Y	Y	Y	Y	Y	Y
7 ***Weldon***	Y	Y	Y	Y	Y	Y
8 ***Greenwood***	Y	Y	Y	Y	Y	Y
9 Vacant						
10 ***Sherwood***	Y	Y	Y	Y	Y	Y
11 Kanjorski	Y	Y	Y	Y	Y	Y
12 Murtha	Y	Y	Y	Y	Y	Y
13 Hoeffel	Y	Y	Y	Y	Y	Y
14 Coyne	Y	Y	Y	Y	Y	?
15 ***Toomey***	Y	Y	Y	Y	Y	Y
16 ***Pitts***	Y	Y	Y	Y	Y	Y
17 ***Gekas***	Y	Y	Y	Y	Y	Y
18 Doyle	Y	Y	Y	Y	Y	Y
19 ***Platts***	+	Y	Y	Y	Y	Y
20 Mascara	Y	Y	Y	Y	Y	Y
21 ***English***	Y	Y	Y	Y	Y	N
RHODE ISLAND						
1 Kennedy	Y	Y	Y	Y	Y	N
2 Langevin	Y	Y	Y	Y	Y	Y
SOUTH CAROLINA						
1 ***Brown***	Y	Y	Y	Y	Y	Y
2 ***Spence***	Y	Y	Y	Y	Y	Y
3 ***Graham***	Y	Y	Y	Y	Y	Y
4 ***DeMint***	Y	Y	Y	Y	Y	Y
5 Spratt	Y	Y	Y	Y	Y	Y
6 Clyburn	Y	Y	Y	Y	Y	Y
SOUTH DAKOTA						
AL ***Thune***	Y	Y	Y	Y	Y	Y

	109	110	111	112	113	114
TENNESSEE						
1 ***Jenkins***	Y	Y	Y	Y	Y	Y
2 ***Duncan***	Y	Y	Y	Y	Y	Y
3 ***Wamp***	Y	Y	Y	Y	Y	Y
4 ***Hilleary***	Y	Y	Y	Y	Y	N
5 Clement	Y	Y	Y	Y	Y	?
6 Gordon	Y	?	Y	Y	Y	Y
7 ***Bryant***	Y	Y	Y	Y	Y	Y
8 Tanner	Y	Y	Y	Y	Y	Y
9 Ford	Y	Y	Y	Y	Y	Y
TEXAS						
1 Sandlin	Y	Y	Y	Y	Y	Y
2 Turner	Y	Y	Y	Y	Y	Y
3 ***Johnson, Sam***	Y	Y	Y	Y	Y	?
4 Hall	Y	Y	Y	Y	Y	Y
5 ***Sessions***	Y	Y	Y	Y	Y	Y
6 ***Barton***	Y	Y	Y	Y	Y	Y
7 ***Culberson***	Y	Y	Y	Y	Y	Y
8 ***Brady***	Y	Y	Y	Y	Y	Y
9 Lampson	Y	Y	Y	Y	Y	Y
10 Doggett	Y	Y	Y	Y	Y	Y
11 Edwards	Y	Y	Y	Y	Y	Y
12 ***Granger***	Y	Y	Y	Y	Y	Y
13 ***Thornberry***	Y	Y	Y	Y	Y	Y
14 ***Paul***	Y	Y	Y	Y	Y	Y
15 Hinojosa	Y	Y	Y	Y	Y	Y
16 Reyes	Y	Y	Y	Y	Y	Y
17 Stenholm	Y	Y	Y	Y	Y	Y
18 Jackson-Lee	Y	Y	Y	Y	Y	Y
19 ***Combest***	Y	Y	Y	Y	Y	Y
20 Gonzalez	Y	Y	Y	Y	Y	Y
21 ***Smith***	Y	Y	Y	Y	Y	Y
22 ***DeLay***	Y	Y	Y	Y	Y	Y
23 ***Bonilla***	Y	Y	Y	Y	Y	Y
24 Frost	Y	Y	Y	Y	Y	Y
25 Bentsen	Y	Y	Y	Y	Y	Y
26 ***Armey***	Y	Y	Y	Y	Y	Y
27 Ortiz	Y	Y	Y	Y	Y	Y
28 Rodriguez	Y	Y	Y	Y	Y	Y
29 Green	Y	Y	Y	Y	Y	Y
30 Johnson, E.B.	Y	Y	Y	Y	Y	+
UTAH						
1 ***Hansen***	Y	Y	Y	Y	Y	Y
2 Matheson	Y	Y	Y	Y	Y	Y
3 ***Cannon***	Y	Y	Y	Y	Y	Y
VERMONT						
AL *Sanders*	Y	Y	Y	Y	Y	?
VIRGINIA						
1 ***Davis, Jo Ann***	Y	Y	Y	Y	Y	Y
2 ***Schrock***	Y	Y	Y	Y	Y	Y
3 Scott	Y	Y	Y	Y	Y	Y
4 Vacant						
5 *Goode*	Y	Y	Y	Y	Y	Y
6 ***Goodlatte***	Y	Y	Y	Y	Y	Y
7 ***Cantor***	Y	Y	Y	Y	Y	Y
8 Moran	Y	Y	Y	Y	Y	Y
9 Boucher	Y	Y	Y	Y	Y	Y
10 ***Wolf***	Y	Y	Y	Y	Y	Y
11 ***Davis, T.***	Y	Y	Y	Y	Y	Y
WASHINGTON						
1 Inslee	Y	Y	Y	Y	Y	Y
2 Larsen	Y	Y	Y	Y	Y	N
3 Baird	Y	Y	Y	Y	Y	N
4 ***Hastings***	Y	Y	Y	Y	Y	Y
5 ***Nethercutt***	Y	Y	Y	Y	Y	Y
6 Dicks	Y	Y	Y	Y	Y	Y
7 McDermott	Y	Y	Y	Y	Y	N
8 ***Dunn***	Y	Y	Y	Y	Y	?
9 Smith	Y	Y	Y	Y	Y	Y
WEST VIRGINIA						
1 Mollohan	?	?	Y	Y	Y	Y
2 ***Capito***	Y	Y	Y	Y	Y	Y
3 Rahall	Y	Y	Y	Y	Y	Y
WISCONSIN						
1 ***Ryan***	Y	Y	Y	Y	Y	Y
2 Baldwin	Y	Y	Y	Y	Y	Y
3 Kind	Y	Y	Y	Y	Y	Y
4 Kleczka	Y	Y	Y	Y	Y	Y
5 Barrett	Y	Y	Y	Y	Y	Y
6 ***Petri***	Y	Y	Y	Y	Y	Y
7 Obey	?	Y	Y	Y	Y	Y
8 ***Green***	Y	Y	Y	Y	Y	Y
9 ***Sensenbrenner***	Y	Y	Y	Y	Y	Y
WYOMING						
AL ***Cubin***	Y	Y	Y	Y	Y	Y

Southern states - Ala., Ark., Fla., Ga., Ky., La., Miss., N.C., Okla., S.C., Tenn., Texas, Va.

Key

Y	Voted for (yea).
#	Paired for.
+	Announced for.
N	Voted against (nay).
X	Paired against.
–	Announced against.
P	Voted "present."
C	Voted "present" to avoid possible conflict of interest.
?	Did not vote or otherwise make a position known.

Democrats **Republicans**
Independents

---

115. HR 1646. State Department Authorization/Family Planning Funding. Hyde, R- Ill., amendment that would remove language reversing President Bush's restrictions on funding to foreign family planning groups that provide abortion services, counseling or advocacy. Adopted 218-210: R 185-33; D 32-176 (ND 23-131, SD 9-45); I 1-1. A "yea" was a vote in support of the president's position. May 16, 2001.

116. HR 1836. Tax-Cut Reconciliation Bill/Rule. Adoption of the rule (H Res 142) to provide for House floor consideration of a tax-cut reconciliation bill. Adopted 220-207: R 217-0; D 2-206 (ND 1-154, SD 1-52); I 1-1. May 16, 2001.

117. HR 1836. Tax-Cut Reconciliation Bill/Democratic Substitute. Rangel, D-N.Y., substitute amendment that would provide a one-time, retroactive rebate and reduce the smallest income tax bracket to 12 percent. The amendment would increase the amount of income that one can earn and still qualify for the earned-income tax credit, and increase the standard deduction for married couples. Rejected 188-239: R 0-218; D 187-20 (ND 144-10, SD 43-10); I 1-1. May 16, 2001.

118. HR 1836. Tax-Cut Reconciliation Bill/Passage. Passage of the bill that would cut all income tax rates for a total of $958.3 billion in cuts over 11 years. The bill would convert the five existing tax rate brackets, which range from 15 percent to 39.6 percent, to a system of four brackets with rates of 10 percent, 15 percent, 25 percent and 33 percent. Passed 230-197: R 216-0; D 13-196 (ND 4-151, SD 9-45); I 1-1. A "yea" was a vote in support of the president's position. May 16, 2001.

119. HR 1646. State Department Authorization/Lebanon Assistance. Lantos, D-Calif., amendment that would bar U.S. military training or economic assistance to Lebanon unless that country militarily occupies and secures its border with Israel. Adopted 216-210: R 94-123; D 121-86 (ND 84-69, SD 37-17); I 1-1. May 16, 2001.

120. HR 1646. State Department Authorization/Recommit. Hastings, D-Fla., motion to recommit the bill to the House International Relations Committee with instructions to add an amendment that would require the creation of a special envoy for Korea within the State Department. Motion rejected 189-239: R 0-218; D 188-20 (ND 142-12, SD 46-8); I 1-1. May 16, 2001.

	115	116	117	118	119	120
ALABAMA						
1 *Callahan*	Y	Y	N	Y	N	N
2 *Everett*	Y	Y	N	Y	N	N
3 *Riley*	Y	Y	N	Y	Y	N
4 *Aderholt*	Y	Y	N	Y	N	N
5 Cramer	N	N	?	Y	Y	Y
6 *Bachus*	Y	Y	N	Y	N	N
7 Hilliard	N	N	Y	N	Y	Y
ALASKA						
AL *Young*	Y	Y	N	Y	N	N
ARIZONA						
1 *Flake*	Y	Y	N	Y	Y	N
2 Pastor	N	N	Y	N	Y	Y
3 *Stump*	Y	Y	N	Y	N	N
4 *Shadegg*	Y	Y	N	Y	Y	N
5 *Kolbe*	N	Y	N	Y	N	N
6 *Hayworth*	Y	Y	N	Y	Y	N
ARKANSAS						
1 Berry	Y	N	N	N	N	Y
2 Snyder	N	N	Y	N	N	N
3 *Hutchinson*	Y	Y	N	Y	N	N
4 Ross	N	N	N	N	Y	Y
CALIFORNIA						
1 Thompson	N	N	N	N	Y	Y
2 *Herger*	Y	Y	N	Y	N	N
3 *Ose*	N	Y	N	Y	N	N
4 *Doolittle*	Y	Y	N	Y	N	N
5 Matsui	N	N	N	N	Y	N
6 Woolsey	N	N	Y	N	N	Y
7 Miller, George	N	N	Y	N	N	Y
8 Pelosi	N	N	Y	N	N	Y
9 Lee	N	N	Y	N	N	Y
10 Tauscher	N	N	Y	N	Y	N
11 *Pombo*	Y	Y	N	Y	Y	N
12 Lantos	N	N	Y	N	N	Y
13 Stark	N	N	Y	N	N	Y
14 Eshoo	N	N	Y	N	N	Y
15 Honda	N	N	Y	N	Y	Y
16 Lofgren	N	N	Y	N	N	Y
17 Farr	N	N	Y	N	N	Y
18 Condit	N	N	N	Y	Y	Y
19 *Radanovich*	Y	Y	N	Y	N	N
20 Dooley	N	N	Y	N	Y	Y
21 *Thomas*	N	Y	N	Y	N	N
22 Capps	N	N	N	N	N	Y
23 *Gallegly*	Y	Y	N	Y	Y	N
24 Sherman	N	N	N	N	Y	Y
25 *McKeon*	Y	Y	N	Y	N	N
26 Berman	N	N	Y	N	Y	Y
27 Schiff	N	N	N	N	Y	Y
28 *Dreier*	Y	Y	N	Y	N	N
29 Waxman	N	N	Y	N	Y	Y
30 Becerra	N	N	Y	N	N	Y
31 Solis	N	N	Y	N	Y	Y
32 Vacant						
33 Roybal-Allard	N	N	Y	N	N	Y
34 Napolitano	N	N	+	N	N	Y
35 Waters	N	N	Y	N	N	Y
36 Harman	N	N	N	N	Y	Y
37 Millender-McD.	N	N	Y	N	Y	Y
38 *Horn*	N	Y	N	+	N	N

	115	116	117	118	119	120
39 *Royce*	Y	Y	N	Y	N	N
40 *Lewis*	Y	Y	N	Y	N	N
41 *Miller, Gary*	Y	Y	N	Y	N	N
42 Baca	N	N	N	N	Y	N
43 *Calvert*	Y	Y	N	Y	N	N
44 *Bono*	Y	Y	N	Y	N	N
45 *Rohrabacher*	Y	Y	N	Y	N	N
46 Sanchez	N	N	Y	N	N	Y
47 *Cox*	Y	Y	N	Y	N	N
48 *Issa*	Y	Y	N	Y	N	N
49 Davis	N	N	Y	N	Y	Y
50 Filner	N	N	Y	N	Y	Y
51 *Cunningham*	Y	Y	N	Y	N	N
52 *Hunter*	Y	Y	N	Y	Y	N
COLORADO						
1 DeGette	N	N	Y	N	Y	Y
2 Udall	N	N	Y	N	Y	Y
3 *McInnis*	Y	Y	N	Y	N	N
4 *Schaffer*	Y	Y	N	Y	N	N
5 *Hefley*	Y	Y	N	Y	Y	N
6 *Tancredo*	Y	Y	N	Y	Y	N
CONNECTICUT						
1 Larson	N	N	Y	N	Y	Y
2 *Simmons*	N	Y	N	Y	N	N
3 DeLauro	N	N	Y	N	Y	Y
4 *Shays*	N	Y	N	Y	Y	N
5 Maloney	N	N	Y	N	Y	Y
6 *Johnson*	N	Y	N	Y	N	N
DELAWARE						
AL *Castle*	N	Y	N	Y	N	N
FLORIDA						
1 *Scarborough*	Y	Y	N	Y	Y	N
2 Boyd	N	N	N	N	Y	Y
3 Brown	N	N	Y	N	Y	Y
4 *Crenshaw*	Y	Y	N	Y	N	N
5 Thurman	N	N	N	N	Y	Y
6 *Stearns*	Y	Y	N	Y	N	N
7 *Mica*	Y	Y	N	Y	N	N
8 *Keller*	Y	Y	N	Y	N	N
9 *Bilirakis*	Y	Y	N	Y	N	N
10 *Young*	Y	Y	N	Y	N	N
11 Davis	N	N	Y	N	Y	N
12 *Putnam*	Y	Y	N	Y	N	N
13 *Miller*	N	Y	N	Y	N	N
14 *Goss*	Y	Y	N	Y	N	N
15 *Weldon*	Y	Y	N	Y	N	N
16 *Foley*	N	Y	N	Y	Y	N
17 Meek	N	N	Y	N	Y	Y
18 *Ros-Lehtinen*	?	Y	N	Y	Y	N
19 Wexler	N	?	Y	N	Y	Y
20 Deutsch	N	N	Y	N	Y	Y
21 *Diaz-Balart*	Y	Y	N	Y	Y	N
22 *Shaw*	Y	Y	N	Y	Y	N
23 Hastings	N	N	Y	N	Y	Y
GEORGIA						
1 *Kingston*	Y	Y	N	Y	Y	N
2 Bishop	N	N	Y	Y	Y	Y
3 *Collins*	Y	Y	N	Y	N	N
4 McKinney	N	N	N	N	N	Y
5 Lewis	N	N	Y	N	Y	Y
6 *Isakson*	N	Y	N	Y	N	N
7 *Barr*	Y	Y	N	Y	N	N
8 *Chambliss*	Y	Y	N	Y	N	N
9 *Deal*	Y	Y	N	Y	N	N
10 *Norwood*	Y	Y	N	Y	N	N
11 *Linder*	Y	Y	N	Y	N	N
HAWAII						
1 Abercrombie	N	N	Y	Y	N	Y
2 Mink	N	N	Y	N	N	Y
IDAHO						
1 *Otter*	Y	Y	N	Y	Y	N
2 *Simpson*	Y	Y	N	Y	N	N
ILLINOIS						
1 Rush	N	N	Y	N	N	Y
2 Jackson	N	N	N	N	N	N
3 Lipinski	Y	N	N	N	N	N
4 Gutierrez	N	N	Y	N	Y	Y
5 Blagojevich	N	N	Y	Y	Y	Y
6 *Hyde*	Y	Y	N	Y	N	N
7 Davis	N	N	Y	N	Y	Y
8 *Crane*	Y	Y	N	Y	N	N
9 Schakowsky	N	N	Y	–	Y	Y
10 *Kirk*	N	Y	N	Y	Y	N
11 *Weller*	Y	Y	N	Y	Y	N
12 Costello	Y	N	N	N	Y	Y
13 *Biggert*	N	Y	N	Y	N	N

ND Northern Democrats   SD Southern Democrats

	115	116	117	118	119	120
14 ***Hastert***	Y	Y		Y		
15 ***Johnson***	Y	Y	N	Y	Y	N
16 ***Manzullo***	Y	Y	N	Y	Y	N
17 Evans	N	N	Y	N	Y	Y
18 ***LaHood***	Y	Y	N	Y	N	N
19 Phelps	Y	N	?	N	Y	N
20 ***Shimkus***	Y	Y	N	Y	N	N
INDIANA						
1 Visclosky	N	N	Y	N	Y	Y
2 ***Pence***	Y	Y	N	Y	Y	N
3 Roemer	Y	N	Y	N	N	Y
4 ***Souder***	Y	Y	N	Y	Y	N
5 ***Buyer***	Y	Y	N	Y	N	N
6 ***Burton***	Y	Y	N	Y	N	N
7 ***Kerns***	Y	Y	N	Y	N	N
8 ***Hostettler***	Y	Y	N	Y	N	N
9 Hill	N	N	N	N	Y	Y
10 Carson	N	N	Y	N	N	Y
IOWA						
1 ***Leach***	N	Y	N	Y	N	N
2 ***Nussle***	Y	Y	N	Y	Y	N
3 Boswell	N	N	Y	N	Y	Y
4 ***Ganske***	Y	Y	N	Y	N	N
5 ***Latham***	Y	Y	N	Y	N	N
KANSAS						
1 ***Moran***	Y	Y	N	Y	Y	N
2 ***Ryun***	Y	Y	N	Y	Y	N
3 Moore	N	N	Y	N	Y	Y
4 ***Tiahrt***	Y	Y	N	Y	Y	N
KENTUCKY						
1 ***Whitfield***	Y	Y	N	Y	N	N
2 ***Lewis***	Y	?	N	Y	N	N
3 ***Northup***	Y	Y	N	Y	N	N
4 Lucas	Y	N	N	Y	Y	N
5 ***Rogers***	Y	Y	N	Y	N	N
6 ***Fletcher***	Y	Y	N	Y	Y	N
LOUISIANA						
1 ***Vitter***	Y	Y	N	Y	Y	N
2 Jefferson	N	N	Y	N	Y	Y
3 ***Tauzin***	Y	Y	N	Y	N	N
4 ***McCrery***	Y	Y	N	Y	N	N
5 ***Cooksey***	Y	Y	N	+	N	N
6 ***Baker***	Y	Y	N	Y	N	N
7 John	Y	N	Y	Y	N	N
MAINE						
1 Allen	N	N	Y	N	N	Y
2 Baldacci	N	N	Y	N	N	Y
MARYLAND						
1 ***Gilchrest***	N	Y	N	Y	N	N
2 ***Ehrlich***	–	Y	N	Y	Y	N
3 Cardin	N	N	Y	N	Y	Y
4 Wynn	N	N	Y	N	Y	Y
5 Hoyer	N	N	Y	N	Y	Y
6 ***Bartlett***	Y	Y	N	Y	Y	N
7 Cummings	N	N	Y	N	N	Y
8 ***Morella***	N	Y	N	Y	Y	N
MASSACHUSETTS						
1 Olver	N	N	Y	N	N	Y
2 Neal	N	N	Y	N	Y	Y
3 McGovern	N	N	Y	N	N	Y
4 Frank	N	N	Y	N	N	Y
5 Meehan	N	N	Y	N	Y	Y
6 Tierney	N	N	Y	N	N	Y
7 Markey	N	N	Y	N	Y	Y
8 Capuano	N	N	Y	N	N	Y
9 Moakley	?	?	Y	N	?	Y
10 Delahunt	N	N	Y	N	Y	Y
MICHIGAN						
1 Stupak	Y	N	Y	N	Y	Y
2 ***Hoekstra***	Y	Y	N	Y	N	N
3 ***Ehlers***	Y	Y	N	Y	N	N
4 ***Camp***	Y	Y	N	Y	Y	N
5 Barcia	Y	N	Y	N	N	Y
6 ***Upton***	N	Y	N	Y	N	N
7 ***Smith***	Y	Y	N	Y	N	N
8 ***Rogers***	Y	Y	N	Y	N	N
9 Kildee	Y	N	Y	N	N	Y
10 Bonior	N	N	Y	N	N	Y
11 ***Knollenberg***	Y	Y	N	Y	N	N
12 Levin	N	N	Y	N	N	Y
13 Rivers	N	N	Y	N	N	N
14 Conyers	N	N	Y	N	N	Y
15 Kilpatrick	N	N	Y	N	N	Y
16 Dingell	N	N	Y	N	N	Y

	115	116	117	118	119	120
MINNESOTA						
1 ***Gutknecht***	Y	Y	N	Y	N	N
2 ***Kennedy***	Y	Y	N	Y	N	N
3 ***Ramstad***	N	Y	N	Y	Y	N
4 McCollum	N	N	Y	N	Y	Y
5 Sabo	N	N	Y	N	N	Y
6 Luther	N	N	Y	N	N	Y
7 Peterson	Y	N	N	N	Y	N
8 Oberstar	Y	N	Y	N	N	Y
MISSISSIPPI						
1 ***Wicker***	Y	Y	N	Y	N	N
2 Thompson	N	N	Y	N	N	Y
3 ***Pickering***	Y	Y	N	Y	Y	N
4 Shows	Y	N	N	Y	Y	N
5 Taylor	Y	N	N	N	Y	N
MISSOURI						
1 Clay	N	N	Y	N	N	Y
2 ***Akin***	Y	Y	N	Y	N	N
3 Gephardt	N	N	Y	N	N	Y
4 Skelton	Y	N	Y	N	Y	Y
5 McCarthy	N	N	Y	N	N	Y
6 ***Graves***	Y	Y	N	Y	Y	N
7 ***Blunt***	Y	Y	N	Y	Y	N
8 ***Emerson***	Y	Y	N	Y	Y	N
9 ***Hulshof***	Y	Y	N	Y	N	N
MONTANA						
AL ***Rehberg***	Y	Y	N	Y	N	N
NEBRASKA						
1 ***Bereuter***	Y	Y	N	Y	N	N
2 ***Terry***	Y	Y	N	Y	Y	N
3 ***Osborne***	Y	Y	N	Y	N	N
NEVADA						
1 Berkley	N	N	Y	N	Y	Y
2 ***Gibbons***	Y	Y	N	Y	N	N
NEW HAMPSHIRE						
1 ***Sununu***	Y	Y	N	Y	N	N
2 ***Bass***	N	Y	N	Y	N	N
NEW JERSEY						
1 Andrews	N	N	Y	N	Y	Y
2 ***LoBiondo***	Y	Y	N	Y	Y	N
3 ***Saxton***	Y	Y	N	Y	Y	N
4 ***Smith***	Y	Y	N	Y	Y	N
5 ***Roukema***	N	Y	N	Y	Y	N
6 Pallone	N	N	Y	N	Y	Y
7 ***Ferguson***	Y	Y	N	Y	Y	N
8 Pascrell	N	N	Y	N	N	Y
9 Rothman	N	N	Y	N	Y	Y
10 Payne	N	N	Y	N	N	Y
11 ***Frelinghuysen***	N	Y	N	Y	Y	N
12 Holt	N	N	Y	N	Y	Y
13 Menendez	N	N	Y	N	Y	Y
NEW MEXICO						
1 ***Wilson***	Y	Y	N	Y	N	N
2 ***Skeen***	Y	Y	N	Y	?	N
3 Udall	N	N	Y	N	Y	Y
NEW YORK						
1 ***Grucci***	Y	Y	N	Y	Y	N
2 Israel	N	N	Y	N	Y	Y
3 ***King***	Y	Y	N	Y	Y	N
4 McCarthy	N	N	Y	N	Y	Y
5 Ackerman	N	N	Y	N	Y	Y
6 Meeks	N	N	Y	N	Y	Y
7 Crowley	N	N	Y	N	Y	Y
8 Nadler	N	N	Y	N	Y	Y
9 Weiner	N	N	Y	N	Y	Y
10 Towns	N	N	Y	N	Y	Y
11 Owens	N	N	Y	N	Y	Y
12 Velázquez	N	N	Y	N	Y	Y
13 ***Fossella***	Y	Y	N	Y	Y	N
14 Maloney	N	N	Y	N	Y	Y
15 Rangel	N	Y	Y	N	Y	Y
16 Serrano	N	N	Y	N	N	Y
17 Engel	N	N	Y	N	Y	Y
18 Lowey	N	N	Y	N	Y	Y
19 ***Kelly***	N	Y	N	Y	Y	N
20 ***Gilman***	N	Y	N	Y	Y	N
21 McNulty	N	N	Y	N	Y	N
22 ***Sweeney***	N	Y	N	Y	Y	N
23 ***Boehlert***	N	Y	N	Y	N	N
24 ***McHugh***	Y	Y	N	Y	N	N
25 ***Walsh***	Y	Y	N	Y	N	N
26 Hinchey	N	N	Y	N	N	Y
27 ***Reynolds***	Y	Y	N	Y	Y	N
28 Slaughter	N	N	Y	N	Y	Y
29 LaFalce	Y	N	Y	N	Y	Y

	115	116	117	118	119	120
30 ***Quinn***	Y	Y	N	Y	N	N
31 ***Houghton***	N	Y	N	Y	N	N
NORTH CAROLINA						
1 Clayton	N	N	Y	N	N	Y
2 Etheridge	N	N	Y	N	Y	Y
3 ***Jones***	Y	Y	N	Y	N	N
4 Price	N	N	Y	N	N	Y
5 ***Burr***	Y	Y	N	Y	Y	N
6 ***Coble***	Y	Y	N	Y	Y	N
7 McIntyre	Y	N	Y	Y	Y	Y
8 ***Hayes***	Y	Y	N	Y	N	N
9 ***Myrick***	Y	Y	N	Y	N	N
10 ***Ballenger***	Y	Y	N	Y	Y	N
11 ***Taylor***	Y	Y	N	Y	N	N
12 Watt	N	N	Y	N	N	Y
NORTH DAKOTA						
AL Pomeroy	N	N	Y	N	N	Y
OHIO						
1 ***Chabot***	Y	Y	N	Y	Y	N
2 ***Portman***	Y	Y	N	Y	Y	N
3 Hall	Y	N	Y	N	N	Y
4 ***Oxley***	Y	Y	N	Y	N	N
5 ***Gillmor***	Y	Y	N	Y	N	N
6 Strickland	N	N	Y	N	Y	Y
7 ***Hobson***	Y	Y	N	Y	Y	N
8 ***Boehner***	Y	Y	N	Y	N	N
9 Kaptur	N	N	Y	N	N	Y
10 Kucinich	Y	N	Y	N	N	Y
11 Jones	N	N	Y	N	Y	Y
12 ***Tiberi***	Y	Y	N	Y	Y	N
13 Brown	N	N	Y	N	Y	Y
14 Sawyer	N	N	Y	N	N	Y
15 ***Pryce***	N	Y	N	Y	N	N
16 ***Regula***	Y	Y	N	Y	N	N
17 Traficant	Y	N	N	Y	N	N
18 ***Ney***	Y	Y	N	Y	N	N
19 ***LaTourette***	Y	Y	N	Y	N	N
OKLAHOMA						
1 ***Largent***	Y	Y	N	Y	N	N
2 Carson	N	N	Y	N	Y	Y
3 ***Watkins***	Y	Y	N	Y	N	N
4 ***Watts***	Y	Y	N	Y	N	N
5 ***Istook***	Y	Y	N	Y	Y	N
6 ***Lucas***	Y	Y	N	Y	N	N
OREGON						
1 Wu	N	N	Y	N	Y	Y
2 ***Walden***	N	Y	N	Y	Y	N
3 Blumenauer	N	N	Y	N	N	N
4 DeFazio	N	N	Y	N	N	Y
5 Hooley	–	N	Y	N	Y	Y
PENNSYLVANIA						
1 Brady	N	N	Y	N	?	?
2 Fattah	N	N	Y	N	Y	Y
3 Borski	Y	N	Y	N	?	?
4 ***Hart***	Y	Y	N	Y	Y	N
5 ***Peterson***	Y	Y	N	Y	N	N
6 Holden	Y	N	N	N	Y	Y
7 ***Weldon***	Y	Y	N	Y	N	N
8 ***Greenwood***	N	Y	N	Y	N	N
9 Vacant						
10 ***Sherwood***	Y	Y	N	Y	Y	N
11 Kanjorski	Y	N	N	N	N	Y
12 Murtha	Y	N	N	N	N	N
13 Hoeffel	N	N	Y	N	Y	Y
14 Coyne	N	N	Y	N	Y	Y
15 ***Toomey***	Y	Y	N	Y	N	N
16 ***Pitts***	Y	Y	N	Y	Y	N
17 ***Gekas***	Y	Y	N	Y	N	N
18 Doyle	Y	N	Y	N	Y	Y
19 ***Platts***	Y	Y	N	Y	Y	N
20 Mascara	Y	N	Y	N	Y	Y
21 ***English***	Y	Y	N	Y	Y	N
RHODE ISLAND						
1 Kennedy	N	N	Y	N	Y	Y
2 Langevin	Y	N	Y	N	Y	Y
SOUTH CAROLINA						
1 ***Brown***	Y	Y	N	Y	Y	N
2 ***Spence***	Y	Y	N	Y	Y	N
3 ***Graham***	Y	Y	N	Y	Y	N
4 ***DeMint***	Y	Y	N	Y	N	N
5 Spratt	N	N	Y	N	Y	Y
6 Clyburn	N	N	Y	N	Y	Y
SOUTH DAKOTA						
AL ***Thune***	Y	Y	N	Y	Y	N

	115	116	117	118	119	120
TENNESSEE						
1 ***Jenkins***	Y	Y	N	Y	N	N
2 ***Duncan***	Y	Y	N	Y	Y	N
3 ***Wamp***	Y	Y	N	Y	Y	N
4 ***Hilleary***	Y	Y	N	Y	Y	N
5 Clement	N	N	Y	Y	N	Y
6 Gordon	N	N	N	Y	Y	Y
7 ***Bryant***	Y	Y	N	Y	Y	N
8 Tanner	N	N	Y	N	N	Y
9 Ford	N	N	Y	N	N	Y
TEXAS						
1 Sandlin	N	N	Y	N	Y	Y
2 Turner	N	N	Y	N	Y	N
3 ***Johnson, Sam***	Y	Y	N	Y	Y	N
4 Hall	Y	Y	N	Y	Y	N
5 ***Sessions***	Y	Y	N	Y	N	N
6 ***Barton***	Y	Y	N	Y	N	N
7 ***Culberson***	Y	Y	N	Y	N	N
8 ***Brady***	Y	Y	N	Y	N	N
9 Lampson	N	N	Y	N	Y	Y
10 Doggett	N	N	N	N	N	Y
11 Edwards	N	N	Y	N	Y	Y
12 ***Granger***	N	Y	N	Y	N	N
13 ***Thornberry***	Y	Y	N	Y	N	N
14 ***Paul***	Y	Y	N	Y	Y	N
15 Hinojosa	N	N	Y	N	N	Y
16 Reyes	N	N	Y	N	Y	Y
17 Stenholm	Y	N	N	N	Y	N
18 Jackson-Lee	N	N	Y	N	Y	Y
19 ***Combest***	Y	Y	N	Y	N	N
20 Gonzalez	N	N	Y	N	Y	Y
21 ***Smith***	Y	Y	N	Y	N	N
22 ***DeLay***	Y	Y	N	Y	Y	N
23 ***Bonilla***	Y	Y	N	Y	Y	N
24 Frost	N	N	Y	N	Y	Y
25 Bentsen	N	N	Y	N	Y	Y
26 ***Armey***	Y	Y	N	Y	Y	N
27 Ortiz	Y	N	Y	N	N	Y
28 Rodriguez	N	N	Y	N	Y	Y
29 Green	N	N	Y	N	Y	Y
30 Johnson, E.B.	N	N	Y	N	N	Y
UTAH						
1 ***Hansen***	Y	?	N	Y	N	N
2 Matheson	N	N	Y	N	Y	Y
3 ***Cannon***	Y	Y	N	?	N	N
VERMONT						
AL *Sanders*	N	N	Y	N	N	Y
VIRGINIA						
1 ***Davis, Jo Ann***	Y	Y	N	Y	Y	N
2 ***Schrock***	Y	Y	N	Y	Y	N
3 Scott	N	N	Y	N	Y	Y
4 Vacant						
5 *Goode*	Y	Y	N	Y	Y	N
6 ***Goodlatte***	Y	Y	N	Y	N	N
7 ***Cantor***	Y	Y	N	Y	Y	N
8 Moran	N	N	Y	N	N	Y
9 Boucher	N	N	Y	N	N	Y
10 ***Wolf***	Y	Y	N	Y	N	N
11 ***Davis, T.***	N	Y	N	Y	Y	N
WASHINGTON						
1 Inslee	N	N	Y	N	Y	Y
2 Larsen	N	N	Y	N	Y	Y
3 Baird	N	N	Y	N	N	N
4 ***Hastings***	Y	Y	N	Y	N	N
5 ***Nethercutt***	Y	Y	N	Y	N	N
6 Dicks	N	N	Y	N	N	Y
7 McDermott	N	N	Y	N	N	Y
8 ***Dunn***	N	Y	N	Y	N	N
9 Smith	N	N	Y	N	N	Y
WEST VIRGINIA						
1 Mollohan	Y	N	Y	N	N	N
2 ***Capito***	N	Y	N	Y	N	N
3 Rahall	Y	N	N	N	N	Y
WISCONSIN						
1 ***Ryan***	Y	Y	N	Y	Y	N
2 Baldwin	N	N	Y	N	N	Y
3 Kind	N	N	Y	N	N	Y
4 Kleczka	N	N	Y	N	N	Y
5 Barrett	N	N	Y	N	N	Y
6 ***Petri***	Y	Y	N	Y	N	N
7 Obey	N	N	Y	N	N	Y
8 ***Green***	Y	Y	N	Y	N	N
9 ***Sensenbrenner***	Y	Y	N	Y	Y	N
WYOMING						
AL ***Cubin***	Y	?	?	?	?	?

Southern states - Ala., Ark., Fla., Ga., Ky., La., Miss., N.C., Okla., S.C., Tenn., Texas, Va.

Key

Y	Voted for (yea).
#	Paired for.
+	Announced for.
N	Voted against (nay).
X	Paired against.
–	Announced against.
P	Voted "present."
C	Voted "present" to avoid possible conflict of interest.
?	Did not vote or otherwise make a position known.

Democrats **Republicans**
Independents

121. HR 1646. State Department Authorization/Passage. Passage of the bill that would authorize $8.2 billion in appropriations for fiscal 2002 and unspecified funds for fiscal 2003 for the Department of State and for foreign broadcasting operations. Passed 352-73: R 180-36; D 172-35 (ND 124-29, SD 48-6); I 0-2. May 16, 2001.

122. Procedural Motion/Journal. Approval of the House Journal of Wednesday, May 16, 2001. Approved 336-68: R 194-11; D 141-57 (ND 102-46, SD 39-11); I 1-0. May 17, 2001.

123. HR 622. Adoption Tax Credits/Rule. Adoption of the rule (H Res 141) to waive points of order and to provide for House floor consideration of a bill that would increase tax credits provided to families that adopt children. Adopted 415-1: R 210-0; D 203-1 (ND 150-1, SD 53-0); I 2-0. May 17, 2001.

124. HR 622. Adoption Tax Credits/Passage. Passage of a bill that would increase the tax credit for those who adopt children and make the credit permanent. Passed 420-0: R 213-0; D 205-0 (ND 151-0, SD 54-0); I 2-0. May 17, 2001.

125. HR 1. ESEA Reauthorization/Rule. Adoption of the rule (H Res 143) to provide for House floor consideration of the bill that would reauthorize the Elementary and Secondary Education Act for five years and consolidate or eliminate 34 programs. Adopted 219-201: R 217-0; D 1-200 (ND 1-149, SD 0-51); I 1-1. May 17, 2001.

[1] *Rep. Bill Shuster, R-Pa., was sworn in May 17, 2001. The first vote for which he was eligible was vote 123.*

	121	122	123	124	125
ALABAMA					
1 *Callahan*	Y	Y	Y	Y	Y
2 *Everett*	N	Y	Y	Y	Y
3 *Riley*	Y	Y	Y	Y	Y
4 *Aderholt*	Y	N	Y	Y	Y
5 Cramer	Y	Y	Y	Y	N
6 *Bachus*	Y	Y	Y	Y	Y
7 Hilliard	Y	N	Y	Y	N
ALASKA					
AL *Young*	Y	?	Y	Y	Y
ARIZONA					
1 *Flake*	N	Y	Y	Y	Y
2 Pastor	Y	N	Y	Y	N
3 *Stump*	Y	Y	Y	Y	Y
4 *Shadegg*	Y	Y	Y	Y	Y
5 *Kolbe*	Y	Y	Y	Y	Y
6 *Hayworth*	Y	?	Y	Y	Y
ARKANSAS					
1 Berry	N	Y	Y	Y	N
2 Snyder	Y	Y	Y	Y	N
3 *Hutchinson*	Y	N	Y	Y	Y
4 Ross	Y	Y	Y	Y	N
CALIFORNIA					
1 Thompson	Y	N	Y	Y	N
2 *Herger*	Y	?	Y	Y	Y
3 *Ose*	Y	Y	Y	Y	Y
4 *Doolittle*	N	Y	Y	Y	Y
5 Matsui	Y	Y	Y	Y	N
6 Woolsey	Y	Y	Y	Y	N
7 Miller, George	N	Y	Y	Y	N
8 Pelosi	Y	Y	Y	Y	N
9 Lee	N	N	Y	Y	N
10 Tauscher	N	Y	Y	Y	N
11 *Pombo*	N	Y	Y	Y	Y
12 Lantos	Y	Y	Y	Y	N
13 Stark	N	N	N	Y	N
14 Eshoo	Y	Y	Y	Y	N
15 Honda	Y	Y	Y	Y	N
16 Lofgren	Y	Y	Y	Y	N
17 Farr	Y	Y	Y	Y	N
18 Condit	Y	N	?	?	?
19 *Radanovich*	Y	Y	?	Y	Y
20 Dooley	Y	Y	Y	Y	N
21 *Thomas*	Y	Y	Y	Y	N
22 Capps	Y	Y	Y	Y	N
23 *Gallegly*	Y	Y	Y	Y	Y
24 Sherman	Y	Y	Y	Y	N
25 *McKeon*	Y	Y	Y	Y	Y
26 Berman	Y	Y	Y	Y	N
27 Schiff	Y	Y	Y	Y	N
28 *Dreier*	Y	Y	Y	Y	Y
29 Waxman	Y	Y	Y	Y	N
30 Becerra	Y	Y	Y	Y	N
31 Solis	N	Y	Y	Y	N
32 Vacant					
33 Roybal-Allard	Y	?	Y	Y	N
34 Napolitano	Y	Y	Y	Y	N
35 Waters	Y	N	Y	Y	?
36 Harman	Y	Y	Y	Y	N
37 Millender-McD.	Y	Y	Y	Y	N
38 *Horn*	Y	Y	Y	Y	Y

	121	122	123	124	125
39 *Royce*	N	Y	Y	Y	Y
40 *Lewis*	Y	Y	Y	Y	Y
41 *Miller, Gary*	Y	Y	Y	Y	Y
42 Baca	Y	Y	Y	Y	N
43 *Calvert*	Y	Y	Y	Y	Y
44 *Bono*	Y	Y	Y	Y	Y
45 *Rohrabacher*	N	Y	Y	Y	Y
46 Sanchez	Y	N	Y	Y	N
47 *Cox*	Y	Y	Y	?	Y
48 *Issa*	N	Y	Y	Y	Y
49 Davis	Y	Y	Y	Y	N
50 Filner	N	N	Y	Y	N
51 *Cunningham*	Y	Y	Y	Y	Y
52 *Hunter*	Y	?	?	?	?
COLORADO					
1 DeGette	N	Y	Y	Y	N
2 Udall	N	Y	Y	Y	N
3 *McInnis*	N	Y	Y	Y	N
4 *Schaffer*	N	N	Y	Y	Y
5 *Hefley*	N	N	Y	Y	Y
6 *Tancredo*	N	P	Y	Y	Y
CONNECTICUT					
1 Larson	Y	Y	Y	Y	Y
2 *Simmons*	Y	Y	Y	Y	Y
3 DeLauro	Y	N	Y	Y	N
4 *Shays*	Y	Y	Y	Y	Y
5 Maloney	Y	Y	Y	Y	N
6 *Johnson*	Y	?	Y	Y	Y
DELAWARE					
AL *Castle*	N	Y	Y	Y	Y
FLORIDA					
1 *Scarborough*	Y	Y	Y	Y	Y
2 Boyd	Y	Y	Y	Y	N
3 Brown	Y	N	Y	Y	N
4 *Crenshaw*	Y	Y	Y	Y	Y
5 Thurman	Y	N	Y	Y	N
6 *Stearns*	N	Y	Y	Y	Y
7 *Mica*	Y	Y	Y	Y	Y
8 *Keller*	Y	Y	Y	Y	Y
9 *Bilirakis*	Y	Y	?	Y	Y
10 *Young*	Y	Y	Y	Y	Y
11 Davis	Y	Y	Y	Y	N
12 *Putnam*	N	Y	Y	Y	Y
13 *Miller*	Y	Y	Y	Y	Y
14 *Goss*	Y	Y	Y	Y	Y
15 *Weldon*	N	Y	Y	Y	Y
16 *Foley*	Y	Y	Y	Y	Y
17 Meek	Y	Y	Y	Y	N
18 *Ros-Lehtinen*	Y	Y	Y	Y	Y
19 Wexler	Y	Y	Y	Y	N
20 Deutsch	Y	Y	Y	Y	N
21 *Diaz-Balart*	Y	Y	Y	Y	Y
22 *Shaw*	+	Y	Y	Y	Y
23 Hastings	N	Y	N	Y	N
GEORGIA					
1 *Kingston*	Y	Y	Y	Y	Y
2 Bishop	Y	Y	Y	Y	?
3 *Collins*	Y	Y	Y	Y	Y
4 McKinney	N	?	Y	Y	N
5 Lewis	Y	Y	?	Y	N
6 *Isakson*	Y	Y	Y	Y	Y
7 *Barr*	N	Y	Y	Y	Y
8 *Chambliss*	Y	Y	Y	Y	Y
9 *Deal*	Y	Y	Y	Y	Y
10 *Norwood*	Y	Y	Y	Y	Y
11 *Linder*	Y	Y	Y	Y	Y
HAWAII					
1 Abercrombie	Y	Y	Y	Y	N
2 Mink	Y	Y	Y	Y	N
IDAHO					
1 *Otter*	N	Y	Y	Y	Y
2 *Simpson*	Y	Y	Y	Y	Y
ILLINOIS					
1 Rush	Y	Y	Y	Y	N
2 Jackson	N	Y	Y	Y	N
3 Lipinski	Y	Y	Y	Y	N
4 Gutierrez	Y	N	Y	Y	N
5 Blagojevich	Y	Y	Y	Y	N
6 *Hyde*	Y	Y	Y	Y	Y
7 Davis	N	Y	Y	Y	N
8 *Crane*	Y	N	Y	Y	Y
9 Schakowsky	Y	Y	Y	Y	N
10 *Kirk*	Y	Y	Y	Y	Y
11 *Weller*	Y	?	Y	Y	Y
12 Costello	Y	N	Y	Y	N
13 *Biggert*	Y	Y	Y	Y	Y

ND Northern Democrats   SD Southern Democrats

	121	122	123	124	125
14 ***Hastert***					Y
15 ***Johnson***	Y	Y	Y	Y	Y
16 ***Manzullo***	Y	Y	Y	Y	Y
17 Evans	Y	N	Y	Y	N
18 ***LaHood***	N	N	Y	Y	Y
19 Phelps	Y	Y	Y	Y	N
20 ***Shimkus***	Y	Y	Y	Y	Y
INDIANA					
1 Visclosky	Y	N	Y	Y	N
2 ***Pence***	N	Y	+	Y	Y
3 Roemer	N	Y	Y	Y	N
4 ***Souder***	Y	Y	Y	Y	Y
5 ***Buyer***	Y	Y	Y	Y	Y
6 ***Burton***	Y	Y	Y	Y	Y
7 ***Kerns***	N	Y	Y	Y	Y
8 ***Hostettler***	N	Y	Y	Y	Y
9 Hill	Y	Y	Y	Y	N
10 Carson	N	Y	Y	Y	N
IOWA					
1 ***Leach***	Y	?	Y	Y	Y
2 ***Nussle***	Y	Y	Y	Y	Y
3 Boswell	Y	Y	Y	Y	N
4 ***Ganske***	Y	?	?	?	?
5 ***Latham***	Y	Y	Y	Y	Y
KANSAS					
1 ***Moran***	N	Y	Y	Y	Y
2 ***Ryun***	Y	Y	Y	Y	Y
3 Moore	Y	N	Y	Y	N
4 ***Tiahrt***	Y	Y	Y	Y	Y
KENTUCKY					
1 ***Whitfield***	Y	Y	Y	Y	Y
2 ***Lewis***	Y	Y	Y	Y	Y
3 ***Northup***	Y	Y	Y	Y	Y
4 Lucas	Y	Y	Y	Y	N
5 ***Rogers***	Y	Y	Y	Y	Y
6 ***Fletcher***	Y	Y	Y	Y	Y
LOUISIANA					
1 ***Vitter***	Y	Y	Y	Y	Y
2 Jefferson	Y	?	Y	Y	N
3 ***Tauzin***	Y	Y	Y	Y	Y
4 ***McCrery***	Y	Y	Y	Y	Y
5 ***Cooksey***	Y	Y	?	Y	Y
6 ***Baker***	Y	Y	Y	Y	Y
7 John	Y	Y	Y	Y	N
MAINE					
1 Allen	Y	Y	Y	Y	N
2 Baldacci	Y	Y	Y	Y	N
MARYLAND					
1 ***Gilchrest***	Y	Y	Y	Y	Y
2 ***Ehrlich***	Y	Y	Y	Y	Y
3 Cardin	Y	Y	Y	Y	N
4 Wynn	Y	Y	Y	Y	N
5 Hoyer	Y	Y	Y	Y	N
6 ***Bartlett***	Y	Y	Y	Y	Y
7 Cummings	N	N	Y	Y	N
8 ***Morella***	Y	Y	Y	Y	Y
MASSACHUSETTS					
1 Olver	Y	N	Y	Y	N
2 Neal	Y	Y	Y	Y	N
3 McGovern	Y	N	Y	Y	N
4 Frank	Y	Y	Y	Y	N
5 Meehan	Y	Y	Y	Y	N
6 Tierney	Y	Y	?	Y	N
7 Markey	Y	Y	Y	Y	N
8 Capuano	Y	N	Y	Y	N
9 Moakley	Y	?	Y	Y	N
10 Delahunt	Y	Y	Y	Y	N
MICHIGAN					
1 Stupak	Y	N	Y	Y	N
2 ***Hoekstra***	Y	Y	Y	Y	Y
3 ***Ehlers***	Y	Y	Y	Y	Y
4 ***Camp***	Y	Y	Y	Y	Y
5 Barcia	Y	Y	Y	Y	N
6 ***Upton***	N	Y	Y	Y	Y
7 ***Smith***	Y	Y	Y	Y	Y
8 ***Rogers***	Y	Y	Y	Y	Y
9 Kildee	Y	Y	Y	Y	N
10 Bonior	N	N	Y	Y	N
11 ***Knollenberg***	N	Y	Y	Y	Y
12 Levin	Y	Y	Y	Y	N
13 Rivers	Y	Y	Y	Y	N
14 Conyers	N	Y	Y	Y	N
15 Kilpatrick	N	?	?	?	?
16 Dingell	Y	Y	Y	Y	N
MINNESOTA					
1 ***Gutknecht***	Y	N	Y	Y	Y
2 ***Kennedy***	Y	N	Y	Y	Y
3 ***Ramstad***	Y	N	Y	Y	Y
4 McCollum	Y	Y	Y	Y	N
5 Sabo	?	N	Y	Y	N
6 Luther	Y	Y	Y	Y	N
7 Peterson	Y	N	Y	Y	N
8 Oberstar	Y	N	Y	Y	N
MISSISSIPPI					
1 ***Wicker***	Y	?	Y	Y	Y
2 Thompson	N	N	Y	Y	?
3 ***Pickering***	Y	Y	Y	Y	Y
4 Shows	Y	Y	Y	Y	N
5 Taylor	N	N	Y	Y	N
MISSOURI					
1 Clay	N	Y	Y	Y	N
2 ***Akin***	N	Y	Y	Y	Y
3 Gephardt	Y	Y	Y	Y	N
4 Skelton	Y	Y	Y	Y	N
5 McCarthy	Y	Y	Y	Y	N
6 ***Graves***	Y	Y	Y	Y	Y
7 ***Blunt***	N	Y	Y	Y	Y
8 ***Emerson***	N	Y	Y	Y	Y
9 ***Hulshof***	Y	Y	Y	Y	Y
MONTANA					
AL ***Rehberg***	Y	Y	Y	Y	Y
NEBRASKA					
1 ***Bereuter***	Y	Y	Y	Y	Y
2 ***Terry***	Y	Y	Y	Y	Y
3 ***Osborne***	Y	Y	Y	Y	Y
NEVADA					
1 Berkley	Y	Y	Y	Y	N
2 ***Gibbons***	Y	Y	Y	Y	Y
NEW HAMPSHIRE					
1 ***Sununu***	N	Y	Y	Y	Y
2 ***Bass***	Y	Y	Y	Y	Y
NEW JERSEY					
1 Andrews	Y	Y	Y	Y	N
2 ***LoBiondo***	Y	N	Y	Y	Y
3 ***Saxton***	Y	Y	Y	Y	Y
4 ***Smith***	Y	Y	Y	Y	Y
5 ***Roukema***	Y	Y	Y	Y	Y
6 Pallone	Y	N	Y	Y	N
7 ***Ferguson***	Y	Y	Y	Y	Y
8 Pascrell	Y	Y	Y	Y	N
9 Rothman	Y	N	Y	Y	N
10 Payne	N	Y	Y	Y	N
11 ***Frelinghuysen***	Y	Y	Y	Y	Y
12 Holt	Y	N	Y	Y	N
13 Menendez	Y	N	Y	Y	N
NEW MEXICO					
1 ***Wilson***	Y	Y	Y	Y	Y
2 ***Skeen***	Y	Y	Y	Y	Y
3 Udall	Y	N	Y	Y	N
NEW YORK					
1 ***Grucci***	Y	Y	Y	Y	Y
2 Israel	Y	Y	Y	Y	N
3 ***King***	Y	Y	Y	Y	Y
4 McCarthy	Y	Y	Y	Y	N
5 Ackerman	Y	Y	Y	Y	N
6 Meeks	N	Y	Y	Y	?
7 Crowley	Y	N	Y	Y	N
8 Nadler	Y	N	Y	Y	N
9 Weiner	Y	Y	Y	Y	N
10 Towns	Y	Y	Y	Y	N
11 Owens	Y	Y	Y	Y	N
12 Velázquez	Y	Y	Y	Y	N
13 ***Fossella***	Y	Y	Y	Y	Y
14 Maloney	Y	Y	Y	Y	N
15 Rangel	Y	?	Y	Y	N
16 Serrano	Y	Y	Y	Y	N
17 Engel	Y	Y	Y	Y	N
18 Lowey	Y	Y	Y	Y	N
19 ***Kelly***	Y	Y	Y	Y	Y
20 ***Gilman***	Y	+	+	+	Y
21 McNulty	Y	N	Y	Y	N
22 ***Sweeney***	Y	N	Y	Y	Y
23 ***Boehlert***	Y	Y	Y	Y	Y
24 ***McHugh***	Y	Y	Y	Y	Y
25 ***Walsh***	Y	Y	Y	Y	Y
26 Hinchey	Y	N	Y	Y	N
27 ***Reynolds***	Y	Y	Y	Y	Y
28 Slaughter	N	N	Y	Y	N
29 LaFalce	Y	N	Y	Y	N
30 ***Quinn***	Y	Y	Y	Y	Y
31 ***Houghton***	Y	Y	Y	Y	Y
NORTH CAROLINA					
1 Clayton	Y	Y	Y	Y	N
2 Etheridge	Y	Y	Y	Y	N
3 ***Jones***	N	Y	Y	Y	Y
4 Price	Y	Y	Y	Y	N
5 ***Burr***	Y	Y	Y	Y	Y
6 ***Coble***	Y	Y	Y	Y	Y
7 McIntyre	Y	Y	Y	Y	N
8 ***Hayes***	Y	Y	Y	Y	Y
9 ***Myrick***	Y	Y	Y	Y	Y
10 ***Ballenger***	Y	Y	Y	Y	Y
11 ***Taylor***	Y	Y	Y	Y	Y
12 Watt	Y	Y	Y	Y	N
NORTH DAKOTA					
AL Pomeroy	Y	N	Y	Y	N
OHIO					
1 ***Chabot***	Y	Y	Y	Y	Y
2 ***Portman***	Y	Y	Y	Y	Y
3 Hall	Y	N	Y	Y	N
4 ***Oxley***	Y	Y	Y	Y	Y
5 ***Gillmor***	Y	Y	Y	Y	Y
6 Strickland	Y	N	Y	Y	N
7 ***Hobson***	Y	Y	Y	Y	Y
8 ***Boehner***	Y	Y	Y	Y	Y
9 Kaptur	Y	N	Y	Y	N
10 Kucinich	N	N	Y	Y	N
11 Jones	N	N	Y	Y	N
12 ***Tiberi***	Y	Y	Y	Y	Y
13 Brown	Y	Y	Y	Y	N
14 Sawyer	Y	Y	Y	Y	N
15 ***Pryce***	Y	Y	Y	Y	Y
16 ***Regula***	Y	Y	Y	Y	Y
17 Traficant	Y	Y	Y	Y	Y
18 ***Ney***	Y	Y	Y	Y	Y
19 ***LaTourette***	Y	Y	Y	Y	Y
OKLAHOMA					
1 ***Largent***	Y	Y	?	?	Y
2 Carson	Y	Y	Y	Y	N
3 ***Watkins***	N	Y	Y	Y	Y
4 ***Watts***	Y	Y	Y	Y	Y
5 ***Istook***	Y	Y	Y	Y	Y
6 ***Lucas***	N	?	?	?	?
OREGON					
1 Wu	Y	N	Y	Y	N
2 ***Walden***	Y	Y	Y	Y	Y
3 Blumenauer	Y	Y	Y	Y	N
4 DeFazio	N	N	Y	Y	N
5 Hooley	Y	Y	Y	Y	N
PENNSYLVANIA					
1 Brady	?	?	?	?	?
2 Fattah	Y	Y	Y	Y	N
3 Borski	?	?	?	?	?
4 ***Hart***	Y	Y	Y	Y	Y
5 ***Peterson***	Y	Y	Y	Y	Y
6 Holden	Y	Y	Y	Y	N
7 ***Weldon***	Y	Y	Y	Y	Y
8 ***Greenwood***	Y	Y	Y	Y	Y
9 ***Shuster, Bill***[1]			Y	Y	Y
10 ***Sherwood***	Y	Y	Y	Y	Y
11 Kanjorski	Y	Y	Y	Y	N
12 Murtha	Y	Y	Y	Y	N
13 Hoeffel	Y	Y	Y	Y	N
14 Coyne	Y	Y	Y	Y	N
15 ***Toomey***	Y	Y	Y	Y	Y
16 ***Pitts***	Y	Y	Y	Y	Y
17 ***Gekas***	Y	Y	Y	Y	Y
18 Doyle	Y	?	Y	Y	N
19 ***Platts***	Y	Y	Y	Y	Y
20 Mascara	Y	Y	Y	Y	N
21 ***English***	Y	?	Y	Y	Y
RHODE ISLAND					
1 Kennedy	Y	Y	Y	+	N
2 Langevin	Y	Y	Y	Y	N
SOUTH CAROLINA					
1 ***Brown***	Y	Y	Y	Y	Y
2 ***Spence***	Y	Y	Y	Y	Y
3 ***Graham***	Y	Y	Y	Y	Y
4 ***DeMint***	Y	Y	Y	Y	Y
5 Spratt	Y	Y	Y	Y	N
6 Clyburn	Y	Y	Y	Y	N
SOUTH DAKOTA					
AL ***Thune***	Y	Y	Y	Y	Y
TENNESSEE					
1 ***Jenkins***	Y	Y	Y	Y	Y
2 ***Duncan***	N	Y	Y	Y	Y
3 ***Wamp***	Y	Y	Y	Y	Y
4 ***Hilleary***	Y	Y	Y	Y	Y
5 Clement	Y	Y	Y	Y	N
6 Gordon	Y	?	Y	Y	N
7 ***Bryant***	Y	Y	Y	Y	Y
8 Tanner	N	N	Y	Y	N
9 Ford	Y	Y	Y	Y	N
TEXAS					
1 Sandlin	Y	Y	Y	Y	N
2 Turner	Y	Y	Y	Y	N
3 ***Johnson, Sam***	Y	Y	Y	Y	Y
4 Hall	Y	Y	Y	Y	N
5 ***Sessions***	Y	Y	Y	Y	Y
6 ***Barton***	Y	Y	Y	Y	Y
7 ***Culberson***	Y	Y	Y	Y	Y
8 ***Brady***	Y	Y	Y	Y	Y
9 Lampson	Y	Y	Y	Y	N
10 Doggett	Y	Y	Y	Y	N
11 Edwards	Y	Y	Y	Y	N
12 ***Granger***	Y	Y	Y	Y	Y
13 ***Thornberry***	Y	Y	Y	Y	Y
14 ***Paul***	N	Y	Y	Y	Y
15 Hinojosa	Y	Y	Y	Y	N
16 Reyes	Y	Y	Y	Y	N
17 Stenholm	Y	N	Y	Y	N
18 Jackson-Lee	Y	N	Y	Y	N
19 ***Combest***	N	Y	Y	Y	Y
20 Gonzalez	Y	Y	Y	Y	N
21 ***Smith***	?	Y	Y	Y	Y
22 ***DeLay***	Y	Y	Y	Y	Y
23 ***Bonilla***	Y	Y	Y	Y	Y
24 Frost	Y	N	Y	Y	N
25 Bentsen	Y	Y	Y	Y	N
26 ***Armey***	Y	Y	Y	Y	Y
27 Ortiz	Y	Y	Y	Y	N
28 Rodriguez	Y	Y	Y	Y	N
29 Green	Y	Y	Y	Y	N
30 Johnson, E.B.	Y	N	Y	Y	N
UTAH					
1 ***Hansen***	Y	Y	Y	Y	Y
2 Matheson	Y	Y	Y	Y	N
3 ***Cannon***	Y	Y	Y	Y	Y
VERMONT					
AL *Sanders*	N	?	Y	Y	N
VIRGINIA					
1 ***Davis, Jo Ann***	Y	Y	Y	Y	Y
2 ***Schrock***	Y	Y	Y	Y	Y
3 Scott	Y	Y	Y	Y	N
5 *Goode*	N	Y	Y	Y	Y
4 Vacant					
6 ***Goodlatte***	Y	Y	Y	Y	Y
7 ***Cantor***	Y	Y	Y	Y	Y
8 Moran	N	Y	Y	Y	–
9 Boucher	Y	?	Y	Y	N
10 ***Wolf***	Y	Y	Y	Y	Y
11 ***Davis, T.***	Y	Y	Y	Y	Y
WASHINGTON					
1 Inslee	N	Y	Y	Y	N
2 Larsen	Y	N	Y	Y	N
3 Baird	N	N	Y	Y	N
4 ***Hastings***	Y	Y	Y	Y	Y
5 ***Nethercutt***	Y	Y	Y	Y	Y
6 Dicks	N	Y	Y	Y	N
7 McDermott	N	N	Y	Y	N
8 ***Dunn***	Y	Y	Y	Y	Y
9 Smith	Y	Y	Y	Y	N
WEST VIRGINIA					
1 Mollohan	N	Y	Y	Y	N
2 ***Capito***	Y	Y	Y	Y	Y
3 Rahall	N	Y	Y	Y	N
WISCONSIN					
1 ***Ryan***	Y	Y	Y	Y	Y
2 Baldwin	Y	Y	Y	Y	N
3 Kind	Y	Y	Y	Y	N
4 Kleczka	N	?	Y	Y	N
5 Barrett	Y	Y	Y	Y	N
6 ***Petri***	N	Y	Y	Y	Y
7 Obey	Y	N	Y	Y	N
8 ***Green***	Y	Y	Y	Y	Y
9 ***Sensenbrenner***	N	Y	Y	Y	Y
WYOMING					
AL ***Cubin***	?	?	?	?	?

Southern states - Ala., Ark., Fla., Ga., Ky., La., Miss., N.C., Okla., S.C., Tenn., Texas, Va.

Key

Y	Voted for (yea).
#	Paired for.
+	Announced for.
N	Voted against (nay).
X	Paired against.
−	Announced against.
P	Voted "present."
C	Voted "present" to avoid possible conflict of interest.
?	Did not vote or otherwise make a position known.

Democrats   **Republicans**
Independents

126. H Con Res 56. Pearl Harbor Remembrance Day/Adoption. La-Tourette, R-Ohio, motion to suspend the rules and adopt the concurrent resolution expressing the sense of Congress regarding National Pearl Harbor Remembrance Day on the 60th anniversary of the Dec. 7, 1941, attack. Motion agreed to 368-0: R 184-0; D 183-0 (ND 131-0, SD 52-0); I 1-0. A two-thirds majority of those present and voting (246 in this case) is required for adoption under suspension of the rules. May 21, 2001.

127. HR 1885. Immigrant Residency Extension/Passage. Sensenbrenner, R-Wis., motion to suspend the rules and pass the bill that would extend for four months a law allowing some immigrants to remain in the country while pursuing legal residency. Motion agreed to 336-43: R 152-40; D 184-2 (ND 133-1, SD 51-1); I 0-1. A two-thirds majority of those present and voting (253 in this case) is required for passage under suspension of the rules. May 21, 2001.

128. HR 1. ESEA Reauthorization/Student CPR Training. Capps, D-Calif., amendment that would allow schools to use Title IV funding to provide CPR training to students. Adopted 421-2: R 213-2; D 206-0 (ND 153-0, SD 53-0); I 2-0. May 22, 2001.

129. HR 1. ESEA Reauthorization/Education Spending. Graves, R-Mo., amendment that would express the sense of Congress that 95 percent of all federal education funds should be spent by school districts directly on improving the educational performance of students. Adopted 422-0: R 214-0; D 206-0 (ND 152-0, SD 54-0); I 2-0. May 22, 2001.

130. HR 1. ESEA Reauthorization/Testing Requirement. Hoekstra, R-Mich., amendment that would strike provisions mandating state reading and math tests for students in grades 3 through 8. The amendment would retain current law that requires states to test student in all subjects in which the states have developed standards. Rejected 173-255: R 52-166; D 119-89 (ND 91-63, SD 28-26); I 2-0. A "nay" was a vote in support of the president's position. May 22, 2001.

131. HR 1. ESEA Reauthorization/Resource Officer Funding. Dunn, R-Wash., amendment that would lift a limit in the bill on funds that local education agencies could spend on law enforcement and security activities, including the hiring and training of school resource officers. Adopted 420-3: R 213-3; D 205-0 (ND 153-0, SD 52-0); I 2-0. May 22, 2001.

132. HR 1. ESEA Reauthorization/100 School Districts. Tiberi, R-Ohio, amendment that would allow up to 100 school districts to apply for education block grants in exchange for improving students' academic performance. No more than two districts from each state could apply for the grants. Adopted 217-209: R 213-4; D 3-204 (ND 1-152, SD 2-52); I 1-1. May 22, 2001.

133. HR 1. ESEA Reauthorization/Military Recruitment Visits. Vitter, R-La., amendment that would require secondary schools receiving federal funding to allow military recruiting visits on school grounds. Adopted 366-57: R 215-2; D 150-54 (ND 101-50, SD 49-4); I 1-1. May 22, 2001.

	126	127	128	129	130	131	132	133
ALABAMA								
1 *Callahan*	Y	Y	Y	Y	N	Y	Y	Y
2 *Everett*	Y	N	Y	Y	N	Y	Y	Y
3 *Riley*	+	−	Y	Y	Y	Y	Y	Y
4 *Aderholt*	Y	N	Y	Y	N	Y	Y	Y
5 Cramer	Y	Y	Y	Y	N	Y	N	Y
6 *Bachus*	Y	N	Y	Y	N	Y	Y	Y
7 Hilliard	Y	Y	Y	Y	Y	Y	N	Y
ALASKA								
AL *Young*	Y	Y	Y	Y	N	Y	Y	Y
ARIZONA								
1 *Flake*	Y	Y	Y	Y	Y	Y	Y	Y
2 Pastor	?	Y	Y	Y	Y	Y	N	N
3 *Stump*	Y	N	Y	Y	N	Y	Y	Y
4 *Shadegg*	Y	Y	Y	Y	Y	Y	Y	Y
5 *Kolbe*	Y	Y	Y	Y	Y	Y	Y	Y
6 *Hayworth*	?	Y	Y	Y	N	Y	Y	Y
ARKANSAS								
1 Berry	Y	Y	Y	Y	Y	Y	N	Y
2 Snyder	Y	Y	Y	Y	N	Y	N	Y
3 *Hutchinson*	?	Y	Y	Y	N	Y	Y	Y
4 Ross	Y	Y	Y	Y	Y	Y	N	Y
CALIFORNIA								
1 Thompson	Y	Y	Y	Y	Y	Y	N	N
2 *Herger*	Y	N	Y	Y	N	Y	Y	Y
3 *Ose*	Y	Y	Y	Y	N	Y	Y	Y
4 *Doolittle*	Y	Y	Y	Y	N	Y	Y	Y
5 Matsui	Y	Y	Y	Y	Y	Y	N	Y
6 Woolsey	Y	Y	Y	Y	Y	Y	N	N
7 Miller, George	Y	Y	Y	Y	Y	Y	N	N
8 Pelosi	Y	Y	Y	Y	Y	Y	N	N
9 Lee	Y	Y	Y	Y	Y	Y	N	N
10 Tauscher	Y	Y	Y	Y	N	Y	N	Y
11 *Pombo*	Y	Y	Y	Y	N	Y	Y	Y
12 Lantos	?	?	Y	Y	N	Y	N	Y
13 Stark	Y	Y	Y	Y	N	Y	N	N
14 Eshoo	Y	Y	Y	Y	N	Y	N	N
15 Honda	Y	Y	Y	Y	N	Y	N	N
16 Lofgren	Y	Y	Y	Y	N	Y	N	N
17 Farr	Y	Y	Y	Y	N	Y	N	N
18 Condit	Y	Y	Y	Y	N	Y	N	Y
19 *Radanovich*	Y	Y	Y	Y	N	Y	Y	Y
20 Dooley	Y	Y	Y	Y	N	Y	N	Y
21 *Thomas*	Y	Y	Y	Y	N	Y	Y	Y
22 Capps	Y	Y	Y	Y	N	Y	N	Y
23 *Gallegly*	Y	Y	Y	Y	N	Y	Y	Y
24 Sherman	Y	Y	Y	Y	Y	Y	N	Y
25 *McKeon*	Y	Y	Y	Y	N	Y	N	Y
26 Berman	Y	Y	Y	Y	N	Y	N	Y
27 Schiff	Y	Y	Y	Y	N	Y	N	Y
28 *Dreier*	Y	Y	Y	Y	N	Y	Y	Y
29 Waxman	?	?	Y	Y	N	Y	N	Y
30 Becerra	Y	Y	Y	Y	N	Y	N	Y
31 Solis	Y	Y	Y	Y	N	Y	N	N
32 Vacant								
33 Roybal-Allard	Y	Y	Y	Y	Y	Y	N	N
34 Napolitano	Y	Y	Y	Y	N	Y	N	Y
35 Waters	?	?	Y	Y	Y	Y	N	N
36 Harman	Y	Y	Y	Y	N	Y	N	Y
37 Millender-McD.	Y	Y	Y	Y	N	Y	N	Y
38 *Horn*	Y	Y	Y	Y	N	Y	Y	Y

	126	127	128	129	130	131	132	133
39 *Royce*	Y	N	Y	Y	N	Y	Y	Y
40 *Lewis*	Y	Y	Y	Y	N	Y	Y	Y
41 *Miller, Gary*	Y	Y	Y	Y	N	Y	Y	Y
42 Baca	Y	Y	Y	Y	N	Y	N	Y
43 *Calvert*	Y	Y	Y	Y	N	Y	Y	Y
44 *Bono*	Y	Y	Y	Y	N	Y	Y	Y
45 *Rohrabacher*	Y	N	Y	Y	N	Y	Y	Y
46 Sanchez	?	?	Y	Y	Y	N	Y	Y
47 *Cox*	?	?	Y	Y	N	Y	Y	Y
48 *Issa*	Y	Y	Y	Y	N	Y	Y	Y
49 Davis	Y	Y	Y	Y	N	Y	N	Y
50 *Filner*	Y	Y	Y	Y	Y	N	Y	N
51 *Cunningham*	Y	Y	Y	Y	Y	Y	Y	Y
52 *Hunter*	Y	N	Y	Y	N	Y	Y	Y
COLORADO								
1 DeGette	Y	Y	Y	Y	N	Y	N	N
2 Udall	Y	Y	Y	Y	N	Y	N	Y
3 *McInnis*	Y	Y	Y	Y	N	Y	Y	Y
4 *Schaffer*	Y	N	Y	Y	N	Y	Y	Y
5 *Hefley*	Y	N	Y	Y	Y	Y	Y	Y
6 *Tancredo*	Y	N	Y	Y	N	Y	Y	Y
CONNECTICUT								
1 Larson	Y	Y	Y	Y	N	Y	N	Y
2 *Simmons*	Y	Y	Y	Y	N	Y	Y	Y
3 DeLauro	Y	Y	Y	Y	Y	Y	N	Y
4 *Shays*	Y	Y	Y	Y	N	Y	Y	Y
5 Maloney	Y	Y	Y	Y	N	Y	N	Y
6 *Johnson*	Y	Y	Y	Y	N	Y	N	Y
DELAWARE								
AL *Castle*	Y	Y	Y	Y	N	Y	Y	Y
FLORIDA								
1 *Scarborough*	?	?	Y	?	Y	Y	Y	Y
2 Boyd	Y	Y	Y	Y	N	Y	N	Y
3 Brown	Y	Y	Y	Y	Y	Y	N	Y
4 *Crenshaw*	Y	Y	Y	Y	N	Y	Y	Y
5 Thurman	Y	Y	Y	Y	Y	Y	N	Y
6 *Stearns*	Y	N	Y	Y	N	Y	Y	Y
7 *Mica*	Y	N	Y	Y	N	Y	Y	Y
8 *Keller*	Y	Y	Y	Y	N	Y	Y	Y
9 *Bilirakis*	Y	Y	Y	Y	N	Y	Y	Y
10 *Young*	Y	Y	Y	Y	N	Y	Y	Y
11 Davis	Y	Y	Y	Y	N	Y	N	Y
12 *Putnam*	Y	N	Y	Y	N	Y	Y	Y
13 *Miller*	Y	Y	Y	Y	N	Y	Y	Y
14 *Goss*	Y	Y	Y	Y	N	Y	Y	Y
15 *Weldon*	Y	N	Y	Y	N	Y	Y	Y
16 *Foley*	Y	Y	Y	Y	N	Y	Y	Y
17 Meek	Y	Y	Y	Y	Y	Y	N	?
18 *Ros-Lehtinen*	Y	Y	Y	Y	N	Y	Y	Y
19 Wexler	Y	Y	Y	Y	N	Y	N	Y
20 Deutsch	Y	Y	Y	Y	N	Y	N	Y
21 *Diaz-Balart*	Y	Y	Y	Y	N	Y	Y	Y
22 *Shaw*	Y	Y	Y	Y	N	Y	Y	Y
23 Hastings	Y	Y	Y	Y	Y	Y	N	Y
GEORGIA								
1 *Kingston*	?	?	Y	Y	N	Y	Y	Y
2 Bishop	Y	Y	Y	Y	N	Y	N	Y
3 *Collins*	Y	Y	Y	Y	N	Y	Y	Y
4 McKinney	Y	Y	?	Y	Y	Y	N	N
5 Lewis	?	?	Y	Y	Y	Y	N	N
6 *Isakson*	Y	Y	Y	Y	N	Y	Y	Y
7 *Barr*	?	?	Y	Y	N	Y	Y	Y
8 *Chambliss*	Y	N	Y	Y	N	Y	Y	Y
9 *Deal*	Y	N	Y	Y	N	Y	Y	Y
10 *Norwood*	Y	N	Y	Y	N	Y	Y	Y
11 *Linder*	Y	Y	Y	Y	N	Y	Y	Y
HAWAII								
1 Abercrombie	?	?	?	?	?	?	?	?
2 Mink	Y	Y	Y	Y	Y	Y	N	Y
IDAHO								
1 *Otter*	?	?	Y	Y	N	Y	Y	Y
2 *Simpson*	?	?	Y	Y	N	Y	Y	Y
ILLINOIS								
1 Rush	Y	Y	Y	Y	N	Y	N	N
2 Jackson	Y	Y	Y	Y	N	Y	N	N
3 Lipinski	Y	Y	Y	Y	N	Y	N	Y
4 Gutierrez	Y	Y	Y	Y	N	Y	N	Y
5 Blagojevich	Y	Y	Y	Y	N	Y	N	Y
6 *Hyde*	Y	Y	Y	Y	N	Y	Y	Y
7 Davis	Y	Y	Y	Y	N	Y	N	N
8 *Crane*	Y	Y	Y	Y	N	Y	Y	Y
9 Schakowsky	?	Y	Y	Y	Y	N	N	N
10 *Kirk*	Y	Y	Y	Y	N	Y	Y	Y
11 *Weller*	Y	Y	Y	Y	N	Y	Y	Y
12 Costello	Y	Y	Y	Y	N	Y	N	Y
13 *Biggert*	Y	Y	Y	Y	N	Y	Y	Y

ND Northern Democrats   SD Southern Democrats

	126	127	128	129	130	131	132	133
14 ***Hastert***					N			
15 ***Johnson***	?	Y	Y	Y	N	Y	Y	Y
16 ***Manzullo***	Y	Y	Y	Y	Y	Y	Y	Y
17 Evans	Y	Y	Y	Y	Y	Y	N	Y
18 ***LaHood***	Y	Y	Y	Y	N	Y	Y	Y
19 Phelps	?	?	Y	Y	Y	Y	N	Y
20 ***Shimkus***	Y	Y	Y	Y	N	Y	Y	Y
INDIANA								
1 Visclosky	Y	N	Y	Y	N	Y	N	Y
2 ***Pence***	Y	Y	Y	Y	Y	Y	Y	Y
3 Roemer	Y	Y	Y	Y	N	Y	N	Y
4 ***Souder***	Y	Y	N	Y	Y	N	Y	Y
5 ***Buyer***	Y	Y	Y	Y	N	Y	Y	Y
6 ***Burton***	Y	N	Y	Y	N	Y	Y	Y
7 ***Kerns***	Y	N	Y	Y	Y	Y	Y	Y
8 ***Hostettler***	?	?	Y	Y	Y	Y	Y	Y
9 Hill	?	?	Y	Y	Y	Y	N	Y
10 Carson	Y	Y	Y	Y	N	Y	N	Y
IOWA								
1 ***Leach***	Y	Y	Y	Y	N	Y	Y	Y
2 ***Nussle***	Y	Y	Y	Y	N	Y	Y	Y
3 Boswell	Y	Y	Y	Y	Y	Y	N	Y
4 ***Ganske***	Y	?	Y	Y	Y	Y	Y	Y
5 ***Latham***	Y	Y	Y	Y	N	Y	Y	Y
KANSAS								
1 ***Moran***	Y	Y	Y	Y	Y	Y	Y	Y
2 ***Ryun***	Y	Y	Y	Y	Y	Y	Y	Y
3 Moore	Y	Y	Y	Y	N	Y	N	Y
4 ***Tiahrt***	Y	Y	Y	Y	N	Y	Y	Y
KENTUCKY								
1 ***Whitfield***	Y	Y	Y	Y	N	Y	Y	Y
2 ***Lewis***	?	Y	Y	Y	N	Y	Y	Y
3 ***Northup***	Y	Y	Y	Y	N	Y	Y	Y
4 Lucas	Y	Y	Y	Y	N	Y	N	Y
5 ***Rogers***	?	?	+	+	–	+	Y	Y
6 ***Fletcher***	Y	Y	Y	Y	N	Y	Y	Y
LOUISIANA								
1 ***Vitter***	?	Y	Y	Y	Y	Y	Y	Y
2 Jefferson	Y	Y	Y	Y	Y	Y	N	Y
3 ***Tauzin***	Y	Y	Y	Y	N	Y	Y	Y
4 ***McCrery***	Y	Y	Y	Y	N	Y	Y	Y
5 ***Cooksey***	Y	Y	Y	Y	N	Y	Y	Y
6 ***Baker***	Y	N	Y	Y	N	Y	Y	Y
7 John	Y	Y	Y	Y	N	Y	N	Y
MAINE								
1 Allen	Y	Y	Y	Y	N	Y	N	Y
2 Baldacci	Y	Y	Y	Y	N	Y	N	Y
MARYLAND								
1 ***Gilchrest***	Y	Y	Y	Y	Y	Y	Y	N
2 ***Ehrlich***	Y	Y	Y	Y	N	Y	Y	Y
3 Cardin	Y	Y	Y	Y	N	Y	N	Y
4 Wynn	Y	Y	Y	Y	N	Y	N	Y
5 Hoyer	Y	Y	Y	Y	N	Y	N	Y
6 ***Bartlett***	Y	N	Y	Y	Y	Y	Y	Y
7 Cummings	Y	Y	Y	Y	Y	Y	N	Y
8 ***Morella***	Y	Y	Y	Y	N	Y	N	Y
MASSACHUSETTS								
1 Olver	Y	Y	Y	Y	Y	Y	N	?
2 Neal	?	?	Y	Y	Y	Y	N	N
3 McGovern	Y	Y	Y	Y	Y	Y	N	N
4 Frank	Y	Y	Y	Y	Y	Y	?	?
5 Meehan	Y	Y	Y	Y	N	Y	N	N
6 Tierney	Y	Y	Y	Y	Y	Y	N	N
7 Markey	Y	Y	Y	Y	Y	Y	N	N
8 Capuano	Y	Y	Y	Y	Y	Y	N	Y
9 Moakley	?	?	?	?	?	?	?	?
10 Delahunt	Y	Y	Y	Y	Y	Y	N	N
MICHIGAN								
1 Stupak	Y	Y	Y	Y	Y	Y	N	Y
2 ***Hoekstra***	Y	Y	Y	Y	Y	Y	Y	Y
3 ***Ehlers***	Y	Y	Y	Y	N	Y	Y	Y
4 ***Camp***	Y	Y	Y	Y	N	Y	Y	Y
5 Barcia	Y	Y	Y	Y	Y	Y	N	Y
6 ***Upton***	Y	Y	Y	Y	N	Y	Y	Y
7 ***Smith***	Y	Y	Y	Y	Y	Y	Y	Y
8 ***Rogers***	Y	Y	Y	Y	N	Y	Y	Y
9 Kildee	Y	Y	Y	Y	N	Y	N	Y
10 Bonior	Y	Y	Y	Y	Y	Y	N	Y
11 ***Knollenberg***	Y	Y	Y	Y	N	Y	Y	Y
12 Levin	?	?	Y	Y	N	Y	N	Y
13 Rivers	Y	Y	Y	Y	Y	Y	N	N
14 Conyers	Y	Y	Y	Y	Y	Y	N	?
15 Kilpatrick	Y	Y	Y	Y	Y	Y	N	N
16 Dingell	Y	Y	Y	Y	N	Y	N	Y

	126	127	128	129	130	131	132	133
MINNESOTA								
1 ***Gutknecht***	?	N	Y	Y	Y	Y	Y	Y
2 ***Kennedy***	Y	Y	Y	Y	Y	Y	Y	Y
3 ***Ramstad***	Y	Y	Y	Y	Y	Y	Y	Y
4 McCollum	Y	Y	Y	Y	Y	Y	N	Y
5 Sabo	Y	Y	Y	Y	Y	Y	N	N
6 Luther	Y	Y	Y	Y	Y	Y	N	Y
7 Peterson	Y	Y	Y	Y	Y	?	N	Y
8 Oberstar	Y	Y	Y	Y	Y	Y	N	N
MISSISSIPPI								
1 ***Wicker***	Y	Y	Y	Y	N	Y	Y	Y
2 Thompson	Y	Y	Y	Y	Y	Y	N	Y
3 ***Pickering***	Y	Y	Y	+	Y	Y	Y	Y
4 Shows	Y	Y	Y	Y	N	Y	N	Y
5 Taylor	Y	N	Y	Y	N	Y	Y	Y
MISSOURI								
1 Clay	?	?	Y	Y	Y	Y	N	Y
2 ***Akin***	Y	Y	Y	Y	Y	Y	Y	Y
3 Gephardt	Y	Y	Y	Y	Y	Y	N	Y
4 Skelton	Y	Y	Y	Y	N	Y	N	Y
5 McCarthy	Y	Y	Y	Y	Y	Y	N	Y
6 ***Graves***	?	N	Y	Y	N	Y	Y	Y
7 ***Blunt***	Y	Y	Y	Y	N	Y	Y	Y
8 ***Emerson***	?	?	Y	Y	N	Y	Y	Y
9 ***Hulshof***	?	?	Y	Y	N	Y	Y	Y
MONTANA								
AL ***Rehberg***	Y	Y	Y	Y	N	Y	Y	Y
NEBRASKA								
1 ***Bereuter***	Y	N	Y	Y	Y	Y	Y	Y
2 ***Terry***	Y	Y	Y	Y	Y	Y	Y	Y
3 ***Osborne***	Y	Y	Y	Y	N	Y	Y	Y
NEVADA								
1 Berkley	?	?	Y	Y	Y	Y	N	N
2 ***Gibbons***	Y	Y	Y	Y	N	Y	Y	Y
NEW HAMPSHIRE								
1 ***Sununu***	Y	Y	Y	Y	N	Y	Y	Y
2 ***Bass***	Y	Y	Y	Y	N	Y	Y	Y
NEW JERSEY								
1 Andrews	Y	Y	Y	Y	N	Y	N	Y
2 ***LoBiondo***	Y	N	Y	Y	N	Y	Y	Y
3 ***Saxton***	Y	N	Y	Y	N	Y	Y	Y
4 ***Smith***	Y	Y	Y	Y	N	Y	Y	Y
5 ***Roukema***	Y	N	Y	Y	N	Y	Y	Y
6 Pallone	Y	Y	Y	Y	Y	Y	N	Y
7 ***Ferguson***	Y	Y	Y	Y	N	Y	Y	Y
8 Pascrell	+	+	Y	Y	Y	Y	N	Y
9 Rothman	Y	Y	Y	Y	Y	Y	N	Y
10 Payne	Y	Y	Y	Y	Y	Y	N	N
11 ***Frelinghuysen***	Y	Y	Y	Y	N	Y	Y	Y
12 Holt	Y	Y	Y	Y	N	Y	N	N
13 Menendez	Y	Y	Y	Y	Y	Y	N	Y
NEW MEXICO								
1 ***Wilson***	Y	Y	Y	Y	N	Y	Y	Y
2 ***Skeen***	Y	Y	Y	Y	N	Y	Y	Y
3 Udall	Y	Y	Y	Y	N	Y	N	Y
NEW YORK								
1 ***Grucci***	Y	Y	Y	Y	N	Y	Y	Y
2 Israel	Y	Y	Y	Y	N	Y	N	Y
3 ***King***	Y	Y	Y	Y	N	Y	Y	Y
4 McCarthy	Y	Y	Y	?	N	Y	N	Y
5 Ackerman	Y	Y	Y	Y	Y	Y	N	Y
6 Meeks	Y	Y	Y	Y	Y	Y	N	N
7 Crowley	Y	Y	Y	Y	N	Y	N	Y
8 Nadler	Y	Y	Y	Y	N	Y	N	N
9 Weiner	?	?	Y	Y	Y	Y	N	N
10 Towns	?	?	Y	Y	Y	Y	N	Y
11 Owens	?	?	?	?	Y	Y	N	Y
12 Velázquez	Y	Y	Y	Y	Y	Y	N	N
13 ***Fossella***	?	?	Y	Y	N	Y	Y	Y
14 Maloney	Y	Y	Y	Y	N	Y	N	Y
15 Rangel	Y	Y	Y	Y	Y	Y	N	Y
16 Serrano	Y	Y	Y	Y	N	Y	N	Y
17 Engel	Y	Y	Y	Y	N	Y	N	Y
18 Lowey	Y	Y	Y	Y	Y	Y	N	N
19 ***Kelly***	?	?	Y	Y	N	Y	Y	Y
20 ***Gilman***	Y	Y	Y	Y	Y	Y	N	Y
21 McNulty	Y	Y	Y	Y	N	Y	N	Y
22 ***Sweeney***	?	?	Y	Y	N	Y	Y	Y
23 ***Boehlert***	Y	Y	Y	Y	N	Y	N	Y
24 ***McHugh***	Y	Y	Y	Y	N	Y	Y	Y
25 ***Walsh***	Y	Y	?	Y	N	Y	Y	Y
26 Hinchey	?	?	Y	Y	N	Y	N	N
27 ***Reynolds***	Y	Y	Y	Y	N	Y	Y	Y
28 Slaughter	Y	Y	Y	Y	N	Y	N	N
29 LaFalce	Y	Y	Y	Y	Y	Y	N	Y

	126	127	128	129	130	131	132	133
30 ***Quinn***	Y	Y	Y	Y	N	Y	Y	Y
31 ***Houghton***	Y	Y	Y	Y	N	Y	Y	Y
NORTH CAROLINA								
1 Clayton	Y	Y	Y	Y	Y	Y	N	Y
2 Etheridge	Y	Y	Y	Y	N	Y	N	Y
3 ***Jones***	Y	N	Y	Y	Y	Y	Y	Y
4 Price	Y	Y	Y	Y	N	Y	N	Y
5 ***Burr***	Y	Y	Y	Y	N	Y	Y	Y
6 ***Coble***	Y	N	Y	Y	Y	Y	Y	Y
7 McIntyre	Y	Y	Y	Y	N	Y	N	Y
8 ***Hayes***	Y	N	Y	Y	N	Y	Y	Y
9 ***Myrick***	Y	Y	Y	Y	Y	Y	Y	Y
10 ***Ballenger***	Y	N	Y	Y	N	Y	Y	Y
11 ***Taylor***	?	?	Y	Y	N	Y	Y	Y
12 Watt	Y	Y	Y	Y	Y	Y	N	N
NORTH DAKOTA								
AL Pomeroy	Y	Y	Y	Y	N	Y	N	Y
OHIO								
1 ***Chabot***	Y	Y	Y	Y	Y	Y	Y	Y
2 ***Portman***	Y	Y	Y	Y	N	Y	Y	Y
3 Hall	Y	Y	Y	Y	N	Y	N	Y
4 ***Oxley***	Y	Y	Y	Y	N	Y	Y	Y
5 ***Gillmor***	Y	Y	Y	Y	N	Y	Y	Y
6 Strickland	?	?	Y	Y	Y	Y	N	Y
7 ***Hobson***	?	?	Y	Y	N	Y	Y	Y
8 ***Boehner***	Y	Y	Y	Y	N	Y	Y	Y
9 Kaptur	Y	Y	Y	Y	Y	Y	N	Y
10 Kucinich	Y	Y	Y	Y	N	Y	N	N
11 Jones	Y	Y	Y	Y	Y	Y	N	N
12 ***Tiberi***	?	?	Y	Y	N	Y	Y	Y
13 Brown	Y	Y	Y	Y	Y	Y	N	Y
14 Sawyer	Y	Y	Y	Y	Y	Y	N	Y
15 ***Pryce***	Y	Y	Y	Y	N	Y	Y	Y
16 ***Regula***	Y	Y	Y	Y	N	Y	Y	Y
17 Traficant	Y	Y	Y	Y	N	Y	Y	Y
18 ***Ney***	+	+	Y	Y	Y	Y	Y	Y
19 ***LaTourette***	Y	Y	Y	Y	N	Y	Y	Y
OKLAHOMA								
1 ***Largent***	?	?	Y	Y	N	Y	Y	Y
2 Carson	?	Y	Y	Y	N	Y	N	Y
3 ***Watkins***	Y	Y	Y	Y	N	Y	Y	Y
4 ***Watts***	+	+	Y	Y	N	Y	Y	Y
5 ***Istook***	Y	Y	Y	Y	Y	Y	Y	Y
6 ***Lucas***	Y	Y	Y	Y	Y	Y	Y	Y
OREGON								
1 Wu	Y	Y	Y	Y	Y	Y	N	N
2 ***Walden***	Y	Y	Y	Y	N	Y	Y	Y
3 Blumenauer	?	?	Y	Y	Y	Y	N	N
4 DeFazio	Y	Y	Y	Y	Y	Y	N	N
5 Hooley	Y	Y	Y	Y	N	Y	N	N
PENNSYLVANIA								
1 Brady	Y	Y	Y	Y	Y	Y	N	N
2 Fattah	Y	Y	Y	Y	Y	Y	N	N
3 Borski	Y	Y	Y	Y	Y	Y	N	Y
4 ***Hart***	?	?	Y	Y	N	Y	Y	Y
5 ***Peterson***	?	?	Y	Y	N	Y	Y	Y
6 Holden	Y	Y	Y	Y	Y	Y	N	Y
7 ***Weldon***	Y	Y	Y	Y	N	Y	Y	Y
8 ***Greenwood***	Y	Y	?	?	N	Y	Y	Y
9 ***Shuster, Bill***	Y	Y	Y	Y	N	Y	Y	Y
10 ***Sherwood***	Y	Y	Y	Y	N	Y	Y	Y
11 Kanjorski	Y	Y	Y	Y	N	Y	N	Y
12 Murtha	Y	Y	Y	Y	Y	Y	N	Y
13 Hoeffel	Y	Y	Y	Y	N	Y	N	Y
14 Coyne	?	?	Y	Y	Y	Y	N	N
15 ***Toomey***	?	?	Y	Y	Y	Y	Y	Y
16 ***Pitts***	Y	Y	Y	Y	Y	Y	Y	Y
17 ***Gekas***	Y	Y	Y	Y	N	Y	Y	Y
18 Doyle	Y	Y	Y	Y	Y	Y	N	Y
19 ***Platts***	Y	Y	Y	Y	N	Y	Y	Y
20 Mascara	Y	Y	Y	Y	N	Y	N	Y
21 ***English***	Y	Y	Y	Y	N	Y	Y	Y
RHODE ISLAND								
1 Kennedy	Y	Y	Y	Y	N	Y	N	Y
2 Langevin	Y	Y	Y	Y	Y	Y	N	Y
SOUTH CAROLINA								
1 ***Brown***	Y	Y	Y	Y	N	Y	Y	Y
2 ***Spence***	Y	N	Y	Y	N	Y	Y	Y
3 ***Graham***	Y	Y	Y	Y	Y	Y	Y	Y
4 ***DeMint***	Y	Y	Y	Y	N	Y	Y	?
5 Spratt	Y	Y	Y	Y	N	Y	N	Y
6 Clyburn	Y	Y	Y	Y	Y	Y	N	Y
SOUTH DAKOTA								
AL ***Thune***	?	?	Y	Y	N	Y	Y	Y

	126	127	128	129	130	131	132	133
TENNESSEE								
1 ***Jenkins***	Y	Y	Y	Y	N	Y	Y	Y
2 ***Duncan***	Y	N	Y	Y	Y	Y	Y	Y
3 ***Wamp***	?	?	Y	Y	N	Y	Y	Y
4 ***Hilleary***	?	?	Y	Y	N	Y	Y	Y
5 Clement	Y	Y	Y	Y	N	Y	N	Y
6 Gordon	Y	?	Y	Y	N	Y	N	Y
7 ***Bryant***	Y	Y	Y	Y	N	Y	Y	Y
8 Tanner	Y	Y	Y	Y	N	Y	N	Y
9 Ford	Y	Y	Y	Y	N	?	N	Y
TEXAS								
1 Sandlin	Y	Y	Y	Y	N	Y	N	Y
2 Turner	Y	Y	Y	Y	N	Y	N	Y
3 ***Johnson, Sam***	Y	N	N	Y	Y	N	Y	Y
4 Hall	Y	Y	Y	Y	N	Y	Y	Y
5 ***Sessions***	Y	N	Y	Y	N	Y	Y	Y
6 ***Barton***	Y	Y	Y	Y	Y	Y	Y	Y
7 ***Culberson***	Y	N	Y	Y	N	Y	Y	Y
8 ***Brady***	Y	Y	Y	Y	N	Y	Y	Y
9 Lampson	Y	Y	Y	Y	N	Y	N	Y
10 Doggett	Y	Y	Y	Y	N	Y	N	Y
11 Edwards	Y	Y	Y	Y	N	Y	N	Y
12 ***Granger***	Y	Y	Y	Y	N	+	+	Y
13 ***Thornberry***	Y	Y	Y	Y	N	Y	Y	Y
14 ***Paul***	Y	Y	Y	Y	Y	Y	Y	N
15 Hinojosa	Y	Y	Y	Y	Y	Y	N	Y
16 Reyes	Y	Y	Y	Y	Y	Y	N	Y
17 Stenholm	Y	Y	Y	Y	N	Y	N	Y
18 Jackson-Lee	Y	Y	Y	Y	Y	Y	N	Y
19 ***Combest***	Y	N	Y	Y	N	Y	Y	Y
20 Gonzalez	Y	Y	Y	Y	Y	Y	N	Y
21 ***Smith***	Y	Y	Y	Y	N	Y	Y	Y
22 ***DeLay***	Y	Y	Y	Y	N	Y	Y	Y
23 ***Bonilla***	Y	Y	Y	Y	N	Y	Y	Y
24 Frost	Y	Y	Y	Y	Y	Y	N	Y
25 Bentsen	Y	Y	Y	Y	N	Y	N	Y
26 ***Armey***	Y	Y	Y	Y	N	Y	Y	Y
27 Ortiz	Y	Y	Y	Y	Y	Y	N	Y
28 Rodriguez	Y	Y	Y	Y	Y	?	N	Y
29 Green	Y	Y	Y	Y	Y	Y	N	Y
30 Johnson, E.B.	Y	Y	Y	Y	Y	Y	N	Y
UTAH								
1 ***Hansen***	?	?	?	?	?	?	?	?
2 Matheson	Y	Y	Y	Y	N	Y	N	Y
3 ***Cannon***	Y	Y	Y	Y	N	Y	Y	Y
VERMONT								
AL *Sanders*	?	?	Y	Y	Y	Y	N	N
VIRGINIA								
1 ***Davis, Jo Ann***	Y	Y	Y	Y	Y	Y	Y	Y
2 ***Schrock***	Y	Y	Y	Y	N	Y	Y	Y
3 Scott	Y	Y	Y	Y	Y	Y	N	N
4 Vacant								
5 *Goode*	Y	N	Y	Y	Y	Y	Y	Y
6 ***Goodlatte***	Y	N	Y	Y	N	Y	Y	Y
7 ***Cantor***	Y	Y	Y	Y	Y	Y	Y	Y
8 Moran	Y	Y	Y	Y	N	Y	N	Y
9 Boucher	Y	Y	Y	Y	Y	Y	N	Y
10 ***Wolf***	Y	Y	Y	Y	N	Y	Y	Y
11 ***Davis, T.***	Y	Y	Y	Y	N	Y	Y	Y
WASHINGTON								
1 Inslee	Y	Y	Y	Y	N	Y	N	Y
2 Larsen	Y	Y	Y	Y	N	Y	N	Y
3 Baird	Y	Y	Y	Y	Y	Y	N	Y
4 ***Hastings***	Y	Y	Y	Y	N	Y	Y	Y
5 ***Nethercutt***	Y	N	Y	Y	N	Y	Y	Y
6 Dicks	Y	Y	Y	Y	N	Y	N	Y
7 McDermott	Y	Y	Y	Y	Y	Y	N	N
8 ***Dunn***	Y	Y	Y	Y	N	Y	Y	Y
9 Smith	Y	Y	Y	Y	N	Y	N	Y
WEST VIRGINIA								
1 Mollohan	?	?	Y	Y	Y	Y	N	Y
2 ***Capito***	Y	Y	Y	Y	N	Y	Y	Y
3 Rahall	?	?	Y	Y	N	Y	N	Y
WISCONSIN								
1 ***Ryan***	Y	Y	Y	Y	Y	Y	Y	Y
2 Baldwin	Y	Y	Y	Y	Y	Y	N	N
3 Kind	Y	Y	Y	Y	N	Y	N	Y
4 Kleczka	Y	Y	Y	Y	Y	Y	N	Y
5 Barrett	+	Y	Y	Y	Y	Y	N	Y
6 ***Petri***	Y	Y	Y	Y	N	Y	Y	Y
7 Obey	Y	Y	Y	Y	Y	Y	N	Y
8 ***Green***	Y	Y	Y	Y	N	Y	Y	Y
9 ***Sensenbrenner***	Y	Y	Y	Y	Y	Y	Y	Y
WYOMING								
AL ***Cubin***	?	?	?	?	?	?	?	?

Southern states - Ala., Ark., Fla., Ga., Ky., La., Miss., N.C., Okla., S.C., Tenn., Texas, Va.

Key

134. HR 1831. Small Polluter Protection/Passage. Gillmor, R-Ohio, motion to suspend the rules and pass the bill that would protect businesses that contributed small amounts of mildly hazardous waste or ordinary garbage to a superfund site from EPA action and from lawsuits filed by third parties. Passed 419-0: R 215-0; D 202-0 (ND 149-0, SD 53-0); I 2-0. A two-thirds majority of those present and voting (280 in this case) is required for passage under suspension of the rules. May 22, 2001.

135. HR 1. ESEA Reauthorization/School Vouchers. Armey, R-Texas, amendment that would provide federal funding for students who attend schools that are dangerous or have been low-performing for three years to attend private schools, including religious schools. Crime victims also would be provided funding for alternative schools. Rejected 155-273: R 152-68; D 2-204 (ND 1-153, SD 1-51); I 1-1. A "yea" was a vote in support of the president's position. May 23, 2001.

136. HR 1. ESEA Reauthorization/Pilot School Choice Program. Armey, R-Texas, amendment would authorize $50 million for five school choice demonstration projects to fund low-income students' attendance at private or public schools. Rejected 186-241: R 182-37; D 3-203 (ND 2-151, SD 1-52); I 1-1. May 23, 2001.

137. HR 1. ESEA Reauthorization/75 Percent Funding Shift. Hoekstra, R-Mich., amendment that would increase the amount of federal funding school districts would be allowed to transfer between programs from 50 percent to 75 percent. The states would have to approve the transfers. Rejected 191-236: R 189-29; D 1-206 (ND 1-152, SD 0-54); I 1-1. May 23, 2001.

138. HR 1. ESEA Reauthorization/Disabled Student Discipline. Norwood, R-Ga., amendment that would require states to require school district policies allowing school personnel to discipline disabled students who carry weapons in school, possess, use or sell illegal drugs, or assault other students in the same way they discipline non-disabled students. Disabled students could avoid sanctions if they demonstrated the offense occurred out of innocence or ignorance. Continuing education services would no longer be required for sanctioned students, though the district could opt to provide services. Adopted 246-181: R 201-16; D 44-164 (ND 22-132, SD 22-32); I 1-1. May 23, 2001.

139. HR 1. ESEA Reauthorization/School Improvement Reports. Stearns, R-Fla., amendment that would require state education departments to submit annual reports identifying schools that are not making adequate improvement. Adopted 361-67: R 156-62; D 204-4 (ND 150-4, SD 54-0); I 1-1. May 23, 2001.

140. HR 1. ESEA Reauthorization/Use American Steel. Traficant, D-Ohio, amendment that would express the sense of Congress that all construction resulting from the bill must use American-made steel and comply with the Buy American Act. Adopted 415-9: R 208-8; D 205-1 (ND 152-1, SD 53-0); I 2-0. May 23, 2001.

141. HR 1. ESEA Reauthorization/Immunity for Discipline. Brady, R-Texas, amendment that would provide more extensive immunity from lawsuits for school officials that engage in reasonable actions to maintain order. Adopted 239-189: R 208-11; D 30-177 (ND 19-134, SD 11-43); I 1-1. May 23, 2001.

	134	135	136	137	138	139	140	141
ALABAMA								
1 *Callahan*	Y	Y	Y	Y	Y	Y	Y	Y
2 *Everett*	Y	Y	Y	Y	Y	N	Y	Y
3 *Riley*	Y	Y	Y	Y	Y	Y	Y	Y
4 *Aderholt*	Y	Y	Y	Y	Y	Y	Y	Y
5 Cramer	Y	N	N	N	Y	Y	N	Y
6 *Bachus*	Y	Y	Y	Y	Y	N	Y	Y
7 Hilliard	Y	N	N	N	N	Y	Y	N
ALASKA								
AL *Young*	Y	Y	Y	Y	Y	Y	Y	Y
ARIZONA								
1 *Flake*	Y	Y	N	Y	Y	N	N	Y
2 Pastor	Y	N	N	N	N	Y	Y	N
3 *Stump*	Y	Y	Y	Y	Y	N	Y	Y
4 *Shadegg*	Y	Y	Y	Y	Y	N	N	Y
5 *Kolbe*	Y	Y	Y	Y	Y	N	N	Y
6 *Hayworth*	Y	Y	Y	Y	Y	N	Y	Y
ARKANSAS								
1 Berry	Y	N	N	N	Y	Y	Y	N
2 Snyder	Y	N	N	N	Y	Y	Y	N
3 *Hutchinson*	Y	N	?	?	?	?	?	Y
4 Ross	Y	N	N	N	N	Y	Y	N
CALIFORNIA								
1 Thompson	Y	N	N	N	Y	Y	Y	Y
2 *Herger*	Y	Y	Y	Y	Y	Y	Y	Y
3 *Ose*	Y	N	Y	N	Y	Y	Y	Y
4 *Doolittle*	Y	Y	Y	Y	Y	Y	Y	Y
5 Matsui	Y	N	N	N	N	Y	Y	N
6 Woolsey	Y	N	N	N	N	Y	Y	N
7 Miller, George	Y	N	N	N	N	Y	Y	N
8 Pelosi	Y	N	N	N	N	Y	Y	N
9 Lee	Y	N	N	N	N	Y	Y	N
10 Tauscher	Y	N	N	N	N	Y	Y	N
11 *Pombo*	Y	N	Y	Y	Y	Y	Y	Y
12 Lantos	Y	N	N	N	N	Y	Y	N
13 Stark	Y	N	N	N	N	Y	N	N
14 Eshoo	Y	N	N	N	N	Y	Y	N
15 Honda	Y	N	N	N	N	Y	Y	N
16 Lofgren	Y	N	N	N	N	Y	Y	N
17 Farr	Y	N	N	N	N	Y	Y	N
18 Condit	Y	N	N	N	Y	Y	Y	Y
19 *Radanovich*	Y	Y	Y	Y	Y	Y	Y	Y
20 Dooley	Y	N	N	N	Y	Y	Y	?
21 *Thomas*	Y	Y	Y	Y	Y	Y	Y	Y
22 Capps	Y	N	N	N	N	Y	Y	N
23 *Gallegly*	Y	Y	Y	Y	Y	Y	Y	Y
24 Sherman	Y	N	N	N	N	Y	Y	N
25 *McKeon*	Y	Y	Y	Y	Y	Y	Y	Y
26 Berman	Y	N	N	N	N	Y	Y	N
27 Schiff	Y	N	N	N	N	Y	Y	Y
28 *Dreier*	Y	Y	Y	Y	Y	Y	N	Y
29 Waxman	Y	N	N	N	N	Y	Y	N
30 Becerra	Y	N	N	N	N	Y	Y	N
31 Solis	?	N	N	N	N	Y	Y	N
32 Vacant								
33 Roybal-Allard	Y	N	N	N	N	Y	Y	N
34 Napolitano	Y	N	N	N	N	Y	Y	N
35 Waters	Y	N	N	N	N	N	Y	N
36 Harman	Y	N	N	N	Y	Y	Y	Y
37 Millender-McD.	Y	N	N	N	N	Y	Y	N
38 *Horn*	Y	N	N	N	Y	Y	Y	Y

	134	135	136	137	138	139	140	141
39 *Royce*	Y	Y	Y	Y	Y	Y	Y	Y
40 *Lewis*	Y	Y	Y	N	Y	Y	Y	Y
41 *Miller, Gary*	Y	Y	Y	Y	Y	Y	Y	Y
42 Baca	Y	N	N	N	Y	Y	Y	N
43 *Calvert*	Y	Y	Y	Y	Y	Y	Y	Y
44 *Bono*	Y	Y	Y	Y	Y	Y	Y	Y
45 *Rohrabacher*	Y	Y	Y	Y	Y	Y	Y	Y
46 Sanchez	Y	N	N	N	N	Y	Y	N
47 *Cox*	Y	Y	Y	Y	Y	N	Y	Y
48 *Issa*	Y	N	Y	Y	Y	Y	Y	Y
49 Davis	Y	N	N	N	N	Y	Y	N
50 Filner	Y	N	N	N	N	Y	N	N
51 *Cunningham*	Y	Y	Y	Y	Y	Y	Y	Y
52 *Hunter*	Y	Y	Y	Y	Y	Y	Y	Y
COLORADO								
1 DeGette	Y	N	N	N	N	Y	Y	N
2 Udall	Y	N	N	N	N	Y	Y	N
3 *McInnis*	Y	Y	Y	Y	Y	Y	Y	Y
4 *Schaffer*	Y	Y	Y	Y	Y	N	Y	Y
5 *Hefley*	Y	Y	Y	Y	Y	N	Y	Y
6 *Tancredo*	Y	Y	Y	Y	Y	N	Y	Y
CONNECTICUT								
1 Larson	Y	N	N	N	N	Y	Y	N
2 *Simmons*	Y	N	Y	N	Y	Y	Y	Y
3 DeLauro	Y	N	N	N	N	Y	Y	N
4 *Shays*	Y	Y	Y	Y	Y	Y	Y	Y
5 Maloney	Y	N	N	N	N	Y	Y	N
6 *Johnson*	Y	N	N	N	N	Y	Y	Y
DELAWARE								
AL *Castle*	Y	N	N	N	N	Y	Y	Y
FLORIDA								
1 *Scarborough*	Y	Y	Y	Y	Y	N	Y	Y
2 Boyd	Y	N	N	N	Y	Y	Y	Y
3 Brown	Y	N	N	N	N	Y	Y	N
4 *Crenshaw*	Y	Y	Y	Y	Y	Y	Y	Y
5 Thurman	Y	N	N	N	N	Y	Y	N
6 *Stearns*	Y	Y	Y	Y	Y	Y	Y	Y
7 *Mica*	Y	Y	Y	Y	Y	N	Y	Y
8 *Keller*	Y	Y	Y	Y	Y	Y	Y	Y
9 *Bilirakis*	Y	N	Y	Y	Y	N	Y	Y
10 *Young*	Y	N	Y	Y	Y	N	Y	Y
11 Davis	Y	N	N	N	N	Y	Y	N
12 *Putnam*	Y	Y	Y	Y	Y	N	Y	Y
13 *Miller*	Y	Y	Y	Y	Y	Y	Y	Y
14 *Goss*	Y	Y	Y	Y	Y	Y	Y	Y
15 *Weldon*	Y	Y	Y	Y	Y	Y	Y	Y
16 *Foley*	Y	Y	Y	Y	Y	Y	Y	Y
17 Meek	Y	N	N	N	N	Y	Y	N
18 *Ros-Lehtinen*	Y	Y	Y	Y	Y	Y	Y	Y
19 Wexler	Y	N	N	N	N	Y	Y	N
20 Deutsch	Y	N	N	N	N	Y	Y	N
21 *Diaz-Balart*	Y	Y	Y	Y	Y	Y	Y	Y
22 *Shaw*	Y	Y	Y	Y	Y	Y	Y	Y
23 Hastings	Y	N	N	N	N	Y	Y	N
GEORGIA								
1 *Kingston*	Y	Y	Y	Y	Y	Y	Y	Y
2 Bishop	Y	N	N	N	Y	Y	Y	Y
3 *Collins*	?	Y	Y	Y	Y	N	Y	Y
4 McKinney	Y	N	N	N	N	Y	Y	N
5 Lewis	Y	N	N	N	N	Y	Y	N
6 *Isakson*	Y	Y	Y	Y	Y	Y	Y	Y
7 *Barr*	Y	Y	Y	Y	Y	Y	Y	Y
8 *Chambliss*	Y	Y	Y	Y	Y	Y	Y	Y
9 *Deal*	Y	Y	Y	Y	Y	Y	Y	Y
10 *Norwood*	Y	Y	Y	Y	Y	Y	Y	Y
11 *Linder*	Y	Y	Y	Y	Y	Y	Y	Y
HAWAII								
1 Abercrombie	?	N	N	N	N	Y	Y	N
2 Mink	Y	N	N	N	N	Y	Y	N
IDAHO								
1 *Otter*	Y	Y	Y	Y	Y	Y	Y	Y
2 *Simpson*	Y	N	Y	Y	Y	Y	Y	Y
ILLINOIS								
1 Rush	?	N	N	N	N	Y	Y	N
2 Jackson	Y	N	N	N	N	Y	Y	N
3 Lipinski	Y	Y	Y	N	Y	Y	Y	Y
4 Gutierrez	Y	N	N	N	N	Y	Y	N
5 Blagojevich	Y	N	N	N	N	Y	Y	N
6 *Hyde*	Y	Y	Y	Y	Y	Y	Y	Y
7 Davis	Y	N	N	N	N	Y	Y	N
8 *Crane*	Y	Y	Y	Y	Y	Y	N	Y
9 Schakowsky	Y	N	N	N	N	Y	Y	N
10 *Kirk*	Y	N	N	N	N	Y	Y	Y
11 *Weller*	Y	Y	Y	Y	Y	Y	Y	Y
12 Costello	Y	N	N	N	N	Y	Y	N
13 *Biggert*	Y	N	N	Y	Y	Y	Y	Y

ND Northern Democrats   SD Southern Democrats

	134	135	136	137	138	139	140	141
14 ***Hastert***		Y	Y					
15 ***Johnson***	Y	N	N	N	Y	Y	Y	N
16 ***Manzullo***	Y	Y	Y	Y	Y	N	Y	N
17 Evans	Y	N	N	N	N	Y	Y	N
18 ***LaHood***	Y	N	Y	Y	N	Y	Y	Y
19 Phelps	Y	N	N	N	Y	Y	Y	Y
20 ***Shimkus***	Y	N	Y	Y	Y	Y	Y	Y
INDIANA								
1 Visclosky	Y	?	?	?	?	?	?	?
2 ***Pence***	Y	Y	Y	Y	Y	N	Y	Y
3 Roemer	Y	N	N	N	N	Y	Y	Y
4 ***Souder***	Y	Y	Y	Y	N	Y	Y	Y
5 ***Buyer***	Y	Y	Y	Y	Y	Y	Y	Y
6 ***Burton***	Y	Y	Y	Y	Y	Y	Y	Y
7 ***Kerns***	Y	Y	Y	Y	Y	N	Y	Y
8 ***Hostettler***	Y	N	N	Y	Y	N	Y	Y
9 Hill	Y	N	N	N	Y	Y	Y	N
10 Carson	Y	N	N	N	N	Y	Y	N
IOWA								
1 ***Leach***	Y	N	N	N	N	Y	Y	Y
2 ***Nussle***	Y	Y	Y	Y	Y	Y	Y	Y
3 Boswell	Y	N	N	N	Y	Y	Y	N
4 ***Ganske***	Y	N	Y	Y	Y	Y	Y	Y
5 ***Latham***	Y	Y	Y	Y	Y	Y	Y	Y
KANSAS								
1 ***Moran***	Y	N	N	Y	Y	N	Y	Y
2 ***Ryun***	Y	Y	Y	Y	Y	Y	Y	Y
3 Moore	Y	N	N	N	N	Y	Y	N
4 ***Tiahrt***	Y	Y	Y	Y	Y	N	Y	Y
KENTUCKY								
1 ***Whitfield***	Y	Y	Y	Y	Y	N	Y	Y
2 ***Lewis***	Y	Y	Y	Y	Y	Y	Y	Y
3 ***Northup***	Y	Y	Y	Y	Y	Y	Y	Y
4 Lucas	Y	N	N	N	Y	Y	Y	Y
5 ***Rogers***	Y	Y	Y	Y	Y	Y	Y	Y
6 ***Fletcher***	Y	Y	Y	Y	Y	Y	Y	Y
LOUISIANA								
1 ***Vitter***	Y	Y	Y	Y	Y	Y	Y	Y
2 Jefferson	Y	N	N	N	N	Y	Y	N
3 ***Tauzin***	Y	Y	Y	Y	Y	Y	Y	Y
4 ***McCrery***	Y	Y	Y	Y	Y	Y	Y	Y
5 ***Cooksey***	Y	Y	Y	Y	Y	N	Y	Y
6 ***Baker***	Y	Y	Y	Y	Y	Y	?	Y
7 John	Y	?	N	N	Y	Y	?	Y
MAINE								
1 Allen	Y	N	N	N	N	Y	Y	N
2 Baldacci	Y	N	N	N	N	Y	Y	N
MARYLAND								
1 ***Gilchrest***	Y	N	Y	Y	Y	N	Y	Y
2 ***Ehrlich***	Y	Y	Y	Y	Y	Y	Y	N
3 Cardin	Y	N	N	N	N	Y	Y	N
4 Wynn	Y	N	N	N	N	Y	Y	Y
5 Hoyer	?	N	N	N	N	Y	Y	N
6 ***Bartlett***	Y	Y	Y	Y	Y	Y	Y	Y
7 Cummings	Y	N	N	N	N	Y	Y	N
8 ***Morella***	Y	N	N	N	N	Y	Y	N
MASSACHUSETTS								
1 Olver	Y	N	N	N	N	Y	Y	N
2 Neal	Y	N	N	N	N	Y	Y	N
3 McGovern	Y	N	N	N	N	Y	Y	N
4 Frank	?	N	N	N	N	N	Y	N
5 Meehan	Y	N	N	N	N	Y	Y	N
6 Tierney	Y	N	N	N	N	Y	Y	N
7 Markey	Y	N	N	N	N	Y	Y	N
8 Capuano	Y	N	N	N	Y	Y	Y	N
9 Moakley	?	?	?	?	?	?	?	?
10 Delahunt	Y	N	N	N	N	Y	Y	N
MICHIGAN								
1 Stupak	Y	N	N	N	N	Y	Y	N
2 ***Hoekstra***	Y	Y	N	Y	Y	Y	Y	Y
3 ***Ehlers***	Y	Y	Y	Y	Y	Y	Y	Y
4 ***Camp***	Y	Y	Y	Y	Y	Y	Y	Y
5 Barcia	Y	N	N	N	N	Y	Y	N
6 ***Upton***	Y	N	Y	Y	Y	Y	Y	Y
7 ***Smith***	Y	Y	Y	Y	Y	Y	Y	Y
8 ***Rogers***	Y	N	N	Y	Y	N	Y	Y
9 Kildee	Y	N	N	N	N	Y	Y	N
10 Bonior	Y	N	N	N	N	Y	Y	N
11 ***Knollenberg***	Y	Y	Y	Y	Y	Y	Y	Y
12 Levin	Y	N	N	N	N	Y	Y	N
13 Rivers	Y	N	N	N	N	Y	Y	N
14 Conyers	Y	N	N	N	N	N	Y	N
15 Kilpatrick	Y	N	N	N	N	Y	Y	N
16 Dingell	Y	N	N	N	N	Y	Y	N

	134	135	136	137	138	139	140	141
MINNESOTA								
1 ***Gutknecht***	Y	Y	Y	Y	Y	Y	Y	Y
2 ***Kennedy***	Y	N	Y	Y	Y	Y	Y	Y
3 ***Ramstad***	Y	N	N	Y	Y	N	Y	Y
4 McCollum	Y	N	N	N	N	Y	Y	N
5 Sabo	Y	N	N	N	N	Y	Y	N
6 Luther	Y	N	N	N	N	Y	Y	N
7 Peterson	Y	N	N	N	N	Y	Y	Y
8 Oberstar	Y	N	N	N	N	Y	Y	N
MISSISSIPPI								
1 ***Wicker***	Y	Y	Y	Y	Y	Y	Y	Y
2 Thompson	Y	N	N	N	N	Y	Y	N
3 ***Pickering***	Y	Y	Y	Y	Y	N	Y	Y
4 Shows	Y	N	N	N	Y	Y	Y	Y
5 Taylor	Y	N	N	N	Y	Y	Y	Y
MISSOURI								
1 Clay	Y	N	N	N	N	Y	Y	N
2 ***Akin***	Y	Y	Y	Y	Y	Y	Y	Y
3 Gephardt	Y	N	N	N	N	Y	Y	N
4 Skelton	Y	N	N	N	Y	Y	Y	Y
5 McCarthy	Y	N	N	N	N	Y	Y	N
6 ***Graves***	Y	N	N	Y	Y	Y	Y	Y
7 ***Blunt***	Y	N	N	Y	Y	N	Y	Y
8 ***Emerson***	Y	N	N	Y	Y	Y	Y	Y
9 ***Hulshof***	Y	N	N	Y	Y	Y	Y	Y
MONTANA								
AL ***Rehberg***	Y	N	N	Y	Y	Y	Y	Y
NEBRASKA								
1 ***Bereuter***	Y	N	N	Y	Y	N	Y	Y
2 ***Terry***	Y	Y	Y	Y	Y	Y	Y	N
3 ***Osborne***	Y	N	N	N	Y	Y	Y	Y
NEVADA								
1 Berkley	Y	N	N	N	N	Y	Y	N
2 ***Gibbons***	Y	N	Y	Y	Y	Y	Y	Y
NEW HAMPSHIRE								
1 ***Sununu***	Y	Y	Y	Y	Y	Y	Y	Y
2 ***Bass***	Y	Y	Y	Y	Y	Y	Y	Y
NEW JERSEY								
1 Andrews	Y	N	N	N	N	Y	Y	N
2 ***LoBiondo***	Y	N	N	N	Y	Y	Y	Y
3 ***Saxton***	Y	N	Y	N	Y	Y	Y	Y
4 ***Smith***	Y	N	Y	N	Y	Y	Y	Y
5 ***Roukema***	Y	N	N	N	Y	Y	Y	Y
6 Pallone	Y	N	N	N	N	Y	Y	N
7 ***Ferguson***	Y	N	Y	Y	N	Y	Y	Y
8 Pascrell	Y	N	N	N	N	Y	Y	N
9 Rothman	Y	N	N	N	N	Y	Y	N
10 Payne	Y	N	N	N	N	Y	Y	N
11 ***Frelinghuysen***	Y	Y	Y	N	N	Y	Y	Y
12 Holt	Y	N	N	N	Y	Y	Y	N
13 Menendez	Y	N	N	N	Y	Y	Y	N
NEW MEXICO								
1 ***Wilson***	Y	N	Y	N	Y	Y	Y	Y
2 ***Skeen***	Y	Y	N	N	Y	Y	Y	Y
3 Udall	Y	N	N	N	N	Y	Y	N
NEW YORK								
1 ***Grucci***	Y	N	Y	Y	Y	Y	Y	Y
2 Israel	Y	N	N	N	N	Y	Y	N
3 ***King***	Y	Y	Y	Y	Y	N	Y	Y
4 McCarthy	Y	N	N	N	N	Y	Y	N
5 Ackerman	Y	N	N	N	N	Y	Y	N
6 Meeks	Y	N	N	N	N	Y	Y	N
7 Crowley	Y	N	N	N	N	Y	Y	N
8 Nadler	Y	N	N	N	N	Y	Y	N
9 Weiner	Y	N	N	N	N	Y	Y	N
10 Towns	Y	N	N	N	N	Y	Y	N
11 Owens	Y	N	N	N	N	Y	Y	N
12 Velázquez	Y	N	N	N	N	Y	Y	N
13 ***Fossella***	Y	Y	Y	Y	Y	N	Y	Y
14 Maloney	Y	N	N	N	N	Y	Y	N
15 Rangel	?	N	N	N	N	Y	Y	N
16 Serrano	Y	N	N	N	N	Y	Y	N
17 Engel	Y	N	N	N	N	Y	Y	N
18 Lowey	Y	N	N	N	N	Y	Y	N
19 ***Kelly***	Y	N	Y	N	Y	Y	Y	Y
20 ***Gilman***	Y	N	N	N	N	Y	?	N
21 McNulty	Y	N	N	N	N	Y	Y	N
22 ***Sweeney***	Y	N	Y	Y	Y	Y	Y	Y
23 ***Boehlert***	Y	N	N	N	N	N	Y	Y
24 ***McHugh***	Y	N	N	N	N	Y	Y	Y
25 ***Walsh***	Y	Y	Y	N	N	N	Y	Y
26 Hinchey	Y	N	N	N	N	Y	Y	N
27 ***Reynolds***	Y	N	Y	Y	Y	Y	Y	Y
28 Slaughter	Y	N	N	N	N	Y	Y	N
29 LaFalce	Y	N	N	N	Y	Y	Y	N

	134	135	136	137	138	139	140	141
30 ***Quinn***	Y	N	N	N	N	Y	Y	Y
31 ***Houghton***	Y	N	N	N	N	Y	Y	Y
NORTH CAROLINA								
1 Clayton	Y	N	N	N	N	Y	Y	N
2 Etheridge	Y	N	N	N	N	Y	Y	N
3 ***Jones***	Y	Y	Y	Y	Y	N	Y	Y
4 Price	Y	N	N	N	N	Y	Y	N
5 ***Burr***	Y	N	N	Y	Y	Y	Y	Y
6 ***Coble***	Y	Y	Y	Y	Y	N	Y	Y
7 McIntyre	Y	N	N	N	N	Y	Y	N
8 ***Hayes***	Y	Y	Y	Y	Y	N	Y	Y
9 ***Myrick***	Y	Y	Y	Y	Y	N	Y	Y
10 ***Ballenger***	Y	Y	Y	Y	Y	Y	Y	Y
11 ***Taylor***	Y	Y	Y	Y	Y	Y	Y	Y
12 Watt	Y	N	N	N	N	Y	Y	N
NORTH DAKOTA								
AL Pomeroy	Y	N	N	N	N	Y	Y	N
OHIO								
1 ***Chabot***	Y	Y	Y	Y	Y	Y	Y	Y
2 ***Portman***	Y	Y	Y	Y	Y	Y	Y	Y
3 Hall	Y	N	N	N	Y	Y	Y	Y
4 ***Oxley***	Y	Y	Y	Y	Y	Y	Y	Y
5 ***Gillmor***	Y	N	Y	N	Y	N	Y	Y
6 Strickland	Y	N	N	N	N	Y	Y	N
7 ***Hobson***	Y	N	Y	Y	Y	Y	Y	Y
8 ***Boehner***	Y	Y	Y	Y	Y	Y	Y	Y
9 Kaptur	Y	N	N	N	N	Y	Y	N
10 Kucinich	Y	N	N	N	N	Y	Y	N
11 Jones	Y	N	N	N	N	Y	Y	N
12 ***Tiberi***	Y	Y	Y	Y	Y	Y	Y	Y
13 Brown	Y	N	N	N	N	Y	Y	N
14 Sawyer	Y	N	N	N	N	Y	Y	N
15 ***Pryce***	Y	N	Y	Y	N	Y	Y	Y
16 ***Regula***	Y	N	Y	N	Y	Y	Y	Y
17 Traficant	Y	N	Y	Y	Y	Y	Y	Y
18 ***Ney***	Y	N	N	N	Y	Y	Y	Y
19 ***LaTourette***	Y	N	Y	N	Y	Y	Y	Y
OKLAHOMA								
1 ***Largent***	Y	Y	Y	Y	Y	N	Y	Y
2 Carson	Y	N	N	N	Y	Y	Y	N
3 ***Watkins***	Y	Y	Y	Y	Y	Y	Y	Y
4 ***Watts***	Y	Y	Y	Y	Y	N	Y	Y
5 ***Istook***	Y	Y	Y	Y	Y	Y	Y	Y
6 ***Lucas***	Y	N	Y	Y	Y	Y	Y	Y
OREGON								
1 Wu	Y	N	N	N	Y	Y	Y	Y
2 ***Walden***	Y	N	Y	Y	Y	N	Y	Y
3 Blumenauer	Y	N	N	N	N	N	Y	N
4 DeFazio	Y	N	N	N	N	Y	Y	N
5 Hooley	Y	N	N	N	N	Y	Y	N
PENNSYLVANIA								
1 Brady	Y	N	N	N	N	Y	Y	N
2 Fattah	Y	N	N	N	N	Y	Y	N
3 Borski	Y	N	N	N	N	Y	Y	Y
4 ***Hart***	Y	Y	Y	Y	Y	Y	Y	Y
5 ***Peterson***	Y	Y	Y	Y	Y	Y	Y	Y
6 Holden	Y	N	N	N	Y	Y	Y	Y
7 ***Weldon***	Y	N	Y	Y	Y	Y	Y	Y
8 ***Greenwood***	Y	Y	Y	Y	Y	Y	Y	Y
9 ***Shuster, Bill***	Y	N	N	Y	Y	N	Y	Y
10 ***Sherwood***	Y	Y	Y	Y	?	Y	Y	Y
11 Kanjorski	Y	N	N	N	N	Y	Y	Y
12 Murtha	Y	N	N	N	N	Y	Y	N
13 Hoeffel	Y	N	N	N	N	Y	Y	N
14 Coyne	Y	N	N	N	N	Y	Y	N
15 ***Toomey***	Y	Y	Y	Y	Y	N	Y	Y
16 ***Pitts***	Y	Y	Y	Y	Y	Y	Y	Y
17 ***Gekas***	Y	N	N	Y	Y	Y	Y	Y
18 Doyle	Y	N	N	N	N	Y	Y	N
19 ***Platts***	Y	N	N	Y	Y	Y	Y	Y
20 Mascara	Y	N	N	N	N	Y	Y	N
21 ***English***	Y	N	Y	Y	Y	Y	Y	N
RHODE ISLAND								
1 Kennedy	Y	N	?	?	N	Y	?	N
2 Langevin	Y	N	N	N	N	Y	Y	N
SOUTH CAROLINA								
1 ***Brown***	Y	Y	Y	Y	Y	Y	Y	Y
2 ***Spence***	Y	Y	Y	Y	Y	Y	Y	Y
3 ***Graham***	?	Y	Y	Y	Y	N	Y	Y
4 ***DeMint***	?	Y	Y	Y	Y	Y	Y	Y
5 Spratt	Y	N	N	N	Y	Y	Y	Y
6 Clyburn	?	N	N	N	N	Y	Y	N
SOUTH DAKOTA								
AL ***Thune***	Y	N	N	Y	Y	Y	Y	Y

	134	135	136	137	138	139	140	141
TENNESSEE								
1 ***Jenkins***	Y	Y	Y	Y	Y	N	Y	Y
2 ***Duncan***	Y	Y	Y	Y	Y	N	Y	Y
3 ***Wamp***	Y	N	Y	Y	Y	N	Y	Y
4 ***Hilleary***	Y	Y	Y	Y	Y	Y	Y	Y
5 Clement	Y	N	N	N	Y	Y	Y	Y
6 Gordon	Y	N	N	N	Y	Y	Y	N
7 ***Bryant***	Y	Y	Y	Y	Y	N	Y	Y
8 Tanner	Y	?	?	N	Y	Y	Y	N
9 Ford	Y	N	N	N	N	Y	Y	N
TEXAS								
1 Sandlin	Y	N	N	N	N	Y	Y	N
2 Turner	Y	N	N	N	Y	Y	Y	N
3 ***Johnson, Sam***	Y	Y	Y	Y	Y	N	Y	Y
4 Hall	Y	Y	Y	N	Y	Y	Y	Y
5 ***Sessions***	Y	Y	Y	Y	N	Y	Y	Y
6 ***Barton***	Y	Y	Y	Y	Y	Y	N	Y
7 ***Culberson***	Y	Y	Y	Y	Y	N	Y	Y
8 ***Brady***	Y	Y	Y	Y	Y	Y	Y	Y
9 Lampson	Y	N	N	N	Y	Y	Y	N
10 Doggett	Y	N	N	N	N	Y	Y	N
11 Edwards	Y	N	N	N	Y	Y	Y	N
12 ***Granger***	Y	Y	Y	Y	Y	Y	Y	Y
13 ***Thornberry***	Y	Y	Y	Y	Y	N	Y	Y
14 ***Paul***	Y	N	N	Y	Y	N	N	N
15 Hinojosa	Y	N	N	N	N	Y	Y	N
16 Reyes	Y	N	N	N	N	Y	Y	N
17 Stenholm	Y	N	N	N	Y	Y	Y	Y
18 Jackson-Lee	Y	N	N	N	N	Y	Y	N
19 ***Combest***	Y	Y	Y	Y	Y	Y	Y	Y
20 Gonzalez	Y	N	N	N	N	Y	Y	N
21 ***Smith***	Y	Y	Y	Y	Y	Y	Y	Y
22 ***DeLay***	Y	Y	Y	Y	Y	Y	Y	Y
23 ***Bonilla***	Y	Y	Y	Y	Y	N	Y	Y
24 Frost	Y	N	N	N	N	Y	Y	N
25 Bentsen	Y	N	N	N	N	Y	Y	N
26 ***Armey***	Y	Y	Y	Y	Y	Y	N	Y
27 Ortiz	Y	N	N	N	N	Y	Y	N
28 Rodriguez	Y	N	N	N	N	Y	Y	N
29 Green	Y	N	N	N	Y	Y	Y	N
30 Johnson, E.B.	Y	N	N	N	N	Y	Y	N
UTAH								
1 ***Hansen***	?	Y	Y	Y	Y	N	Y	Y
2 Matheson	Y	N	N	N	Y	Y	Y	Y
3 ***Cannon***	Y	Y	Y	Y	Y	N	Y	Y
VERMONT								
AL *Sanders*	Y	N	N	N	N	Y	Y	N
VIRGINIA								
1 ***Davis, Jo Ann***	Y	Y	Y	Y	Y	N	Y	Y
2 ***Schrock***	Y	Y	Y	Y	Y	Y	Y	Y
3 Scott	Y	N	N	N	N	Y	Y	N
4 Vacant								
5 *Goode*	Y	Y	Y	Y	Y	N	Y	Y
6 ***Goodlatte***	Y	Y	Y	Y	Y	Y	Y	Y
7 ***Cantor***	Y	Y	Y	Y	Y	Y	Y	Y
8 Moran	Y	N	N	N	Y	Y	Y	N
9 Boucher	Y	N	N	N	N	Y	Y	N
10 ***Wolf***	Y	Y	Y	Y	Y	Y	Y	Y
11 ***Davis, T.***	Y	N	N	Y	Y	N	Y	Y
WASHINGTON								
1 Inslee	Y	N	N	N	N	Y	Y	N
2 Larsen	Y	N	N	N	N	Y	Y	N
3 Baird	Y	N	N	N	Y	Y	Y	Y
4 ***Hastings***	Y	Y	Y	Y	Y	N	Y	Y
5 ***Nethercutt***	Y	Y	Y	Y	Y	N	Y	Y
6 Dicks	Y	N	N	N	Y	Y	Y	Y
7 McDermott	Y	N	N	N	N	Y	Y	N
8 ***Dunn***	Y	Y	Y	Y	Y	Y	Y	Y
9 Smith	Y	N	N	N	Y	Y	Y	Y
WEST VIRGINIA								
1 Mollohan	Y	N	N	N	Y	Y	Y	Y
2 ***Capito***	Y	N	Y	Y	Y	Y	Y	Y
3 Rahall	Y	N	N	N	Y	Y	Y	N
WISCONSIN								
1 ***Ryan***	Y	Y	Y	Y	Y	Y	Y	Y
2 Baldwin	Y	N	N	N	N	Y	Y	N
3 Kind	Y	N	N	N	N	Y	Y	N
4 Kleczka	Y	N	N	N	N	Y	Y	N
5 Barrett	Y	N	N	N	N	Y	Y	N
6 ***Petri***	Y	Y	Y	Y	Y	N	Y	Y
7 Obey	Y	N	N	N	N	Y	Y	N
8 ***Green***	Y	Y	Y	Y	Y	Y	Y	Y
9 ***Sensenbrenner***	Y	Y	Y	Y	Y	N	Y	Y
WYOMING								
AL ***Cubin***	?	?	?	?	?	?	?	?

Southern states - Ala., Ark., Fla., Ga., Ky., La., Miss., N.C., Okla., S.C., Tenn., Texas, Va.

Key

Y	Voted for (yea).
#	Paired for.
+	Announced for.
N	Voted against (nay).
X	Paired against.
−	Announced against.
P	Voted "present."
C	Voted "present" to avoid possible conflict of interest.
?	Did not vote or otherwise make a position known.

Democrats   **Republicans**   *Independents*

---

142. HR 1. ESEA Reauthorization/Impact Aid. Kirk, R-Ill., amendment that would express the sense of Congress that the Senate, House and Bush administration should work together to provide more assistance to school districts with a small tax base because of a large federal presence. Adopted 425-3: R 216-2; D 207-1 (ND 153-1, SD 54-0); I 2-0. May 23, 2001.

143. HR 1. ESEA Reauthorization/Reduced Funding. Cox, R-Calif., amendment that would reduce the overall funding level in the bill by 11.5 percent to $20.5 billion for fiscal 2002. Maximum funding levels in each subsequent year could not exceed a 3.5 percent increase over the previous year's funding. Rejected 101-326: R 98-120; D 2-205 (ND 2-151, SD 0-54); I 1-1. May 23, 2001.

144. HR 1. ESEA Reauthorization/Motion to Recommit. Owens, D-N.Y., motion to recommit the bill to the House Education and the Workforce Committee with instructions to add language authorizing $2 billion for school construction. Motion rejected 207-223: R 2-218; D 204-4 (ND 152-2, SD 52-2); I 1-1. A "nay" was a vote in support of the president's position. May 23, 2001.

145. HR 1. ESEA Reauthorization/Passage. Passage of the bill that would authorize $22.8 billion in education funding. The centerpiece of the bill would require states to test students in math and reading annually in grades 3 through 8. The bill also would authorize funding for disadvantaged students to meet higher standards, professional development for teachers, funding to states for innovative strategies, safe and drug-free schools programs and education technology programs. Passed 384-45: R 186-34; D 197-10 (ND 146-7, SD 51-3); I 1-1. A "yea" was a vote in support of the president's position. May 23, 2001.

146. HR 1836. Tax-Cut Reconciliation Bill/Motion to Instruct. Stark, D-Calif., motion to instruct conferees to insist that the conference report not include phase-ins longer than five years, delayed effective dates, or sunsets. The conference report should include "marriage penalty" relief, estate-tax relief, increasing the per-child tax credit, pension reform and permanent extension of the research tax credit. Motion rejected 198-210: R 1-205; D 196-4 (ND 145-3, SD 51-1); I 1-1. May 23, 2001.

147. Procedural Motion/Journal. Approval of the House Journal of Wednesday, May 23, 2001. Approved 336-71: R 193-15; D 141-56 (ND 103-44, SD 38-12); I 2-0. May 24, 2001.

	142	143	144	145	146	147
ALABAMA						
1 *Callahan*	Y	N	N	Y	N	Y
2 *Everett*	Y	N	N	Y	N	Y
3 *Riley*	Y	N	N	Y	N	N
4 *Aderholt*	Y	N	N	Y	N	N
5 Cramer	Y	N	Y	Y	Y	Y
6 *Bachus*	Y	N	N	Y	N	Y
7 Hilliard	Y	N	Y	N	Y	N
ALASKA						
AL *Young*	Y	Y	N	Y	?	?
ARIZONA						
1 *Flake*	Y	Y	N	N	N	Y
2 Pastor	Y	N	Y	Y	Y	Y
3 *Stump*	Y	Y	N	Y	N	Y
4 *Shadegg*	Y	Y	N	N	N	Y
5 *Kolbe*	Y	N	N	Y	N	Y
6 *Hayworth*	Y	Y	N	Y	N	Y
ARKANSAS						
1 Berry	Y	N	Y	Y	Y	Y
2 Snyder	Y	N	Y	Y	Y	Y
3 *Hutchinson*	?	?	N	Y	N	Y
4 Ross	Y	N	Y	Y	Y	Y
CALIFORNIA						
1 Thompson	Y	N	Y	Y	Y	N
2 *Herger*	Y	Y	N	N	N	Y
3 *Ose*	Y	N	N	Y	N	Y
4 *Doolittle*	Y	Y	N	N	N	Y
5 Matsui	Y	N	Y	Y	Y	Y
6 Woolsey	Y	N	Y	Y	Y	Y
7 Miller, George	Y	N	Y	Y	Y	N
8 Pelosi	Y	N	Y	Y	Y	Y
9 Lee	Y	N	Y	Y	Y	N
10 Tauscher	Y	N	Y	Y	Y	Y
11 *Pombo*	Y	Y	N	N	N	Y
12 Lantos	Y	N	Y	Y	Y	Y
13 Stark	Y	N	Y	Y	Y	N
14 Eshoo	Y	N	Y	Y	Y	Y
15 Honda	Y	N	Y	Y	Y	Y
16 Lofgren	Y	N	Y	Y	Y	Y
17 Farr	Y	N	Y	Y	Y	Y
18 Condit	Y	N	Y	Y	N	N
19 *Radanovich*	Y	Y	N	Y	Y	Y
20 Dooley	Y	N	Y	Y	?	Y
21 *Thomas*	Y	N	N	Y	N	Y
22 Capps	Y	N	Y	Y	Y	Y
23 *Gallegly*	Y	N	N	Y	N	Y
24 Sherman	Y	N	Y	Y	Y	Y
25 *McKeon*	Y	N	N	Y	N	Y
26 Berman	Y	N	Y	Y	Y	Y
27 Schiff	Y	N	Y	Y	Y	Y
28 *Dreier*	Y	N	N	Y	N	Y
29 Waxman	Y	N	Y	Y	Y	Y
30 Becerra	Y	N	Y	Y	?	?
31 Solis	Y	N	Y	Y	Y	Y
32 Vacant						
33 Roybal-Allard	Y	N	Y	Y	Y	Y
34 Napolitano	Y	N	Y	Y	Y	Y
35 Waters	Y	N	Y	N	Y	N
36 Harman	Y	N	Y	Y	Y	Y
37 Millender-McD.	Y	N	Y	Y	Y	Y
38 *Horn*	Y	N	N	Y	N	Y

	142	143	144	145	146	147
39 *Royce*	Y	Y	N	Y	N	Y
40 *Lewis*	Y	Y	N	Y	N	Y
41 *Miller, Gary*	Y	Y	N	Y	N	Y
42 Baca	Y	N	Y	Y	N	Y
43 *Calvert*	Y	N	N	Y	N	Y
44 *Bono*	Y	N	N	Y	N	Y
45 *Rohrabacher*	Y	Y	N	N	N	Y
46 Sanchez	Y	N	Y	Y	N	Y
47 *Cox*	Y	Y	N	Y	N	Y
48 *Issa*	Y	Y	N	Y	N	Y
49 Davis	Y	N	Y	Y	Y	Y
50 Filner	Y	N	Y	N	Y	N
51 *Cunningham*	Y	N	N	Y	N	Y
52 *Hunter*	Y	Y	N	Y	N	Y
COLORADO						
1 DeGette	Y	N	Y	Y	Y	Y
2 Udall	Y	N	Y	Y	Y	Y
3 *McInnis*	Y	Y	N	Y	N	Y
4 *Schaffer*	Y	Y	N	N	N	N
5 *Hefley*	Y	Y	N	N	N	N
6 *Tancredo*	Y	Y	N	N	N	P
CONNECTICUT						
1 Larson	Y	Y	Y	?	Y	?
2 *Simmons*	Y	N	N	Y	N	Y
3 DeLauro	Y	N	Y	Y	Y	Y
4 *Shays*	Y	N	N	Y	N	Y
5 Maloney	Y	N	Y	Y	Y	Y
6 *Johnson*	Y	N	Y	Y	N	Y
DELAWARE						
AL *Castle*	Y	N	N	Y	N	Y
FLORIDA						
1 *Scarborough*	Y	Y	N	N	?	Y
2 Boyd	Y	N	Y	Y	Y	Y
3 Brown	Y	N	Y	Y	Y	Y
4 *Crenshaw*	Y	N	N	Y	N	Y
5 Thurman	Y	N	Y	Y	Y	Y
6 *Stearns*	Y	Y	N	N	N	Y
7 *Mica*	Y	Y	N	Y	N	Y
8 *Keller*	Y	N	N	Y	N	Y
9 *Bilirakis*	Y	N	N	Y	N	Y
10 *Young*	Y	N	N	Y	N	?
11 Davis	Y	N	Y	Y	Y	Y
12 *Putnam*	Y	N	N	Y	N	Y
13 *Miller*	Y	Y	N	Y	N	Y
14 *Goss*	Y	N	N	Y	N	Y
15 *Weldon*	Y	Y	N	N	N	Y
16 *Foley*	Y	Y	N	Y	N	Y
17 Meek	Y	N	Y	Y	Y	?
18 *Ros-Lehtinen*	Y	N	N	Y	N	Y
19 Wexler	Y	N	Y	Y	Y	?
20 Deutsch	Y	N	Y	Y	Y	Y
21 *Diaz-Balart*	Y	N	N	Y	N	?
22 *Shaw*	Y	N	N	Y	?	Y
23 Hastings	Y	N	Y	Y	N	N
GEORGIA						
1 *Kingston*	Y	Y	N	Y	N	Y
2 Bishop	Y	N	Y	Y	Y	Y
3 *Collins*	Y	N	Y	N	Y	Y
4 McKinney	Y	N	Y	Y	Y	Y
5 Lewis	Y	N	Y	Y	Y	Y
6 *Isakson*	Y	N	N	Y	N	Y
7 *Barr*	Y	N	N	Y	N	Y
8 *Chambliss*	Y	N	N	Y	?	Y
9 *Deal*	Y	N	N	Y	N	Y
10 *Norwood*	Y	Y	N	Y	N	Y
11 *Linder*	Y	Y	N	Y	N	Y
HAWAII						
1 Abercrombie	Y	N	Y	Y	Y	Y
2 Mink	Y	N	Y	Y	Y	N
IDAHO						
1 *Otter*	Y	Y	N	Y	N	Y
2 *Simpson*	Y	N	N	Y	N	Y
ILLINOIS						
1 Rush	Y	?	Y	Y	Y	Y
2 Jackson	Y	N	Y	Y	Y	Y
3 Lipinski	Y	N	Y	Y	Y	Y
4 Gutierrez	Y	N	Y	Y	Y	Y
5 Blagojevich	Y	N	Y	Y	Y	Y
6 *Hyde*	Y	N	N	Y	N	Y
7 Davis	Y	N	Y	Y	Y	Y
8 *Crane*	Y	Y	N	N	N	N
9 Schakowsky	Y	N	Y	Y	Y	Y
10 *Kirk*	Y	N	N	Y	N	Y
11 *Weller*	Y	N	N	Y	N	N
12 Costello	Y	N	Y	Y	N	Y
13 *Biggert*	Y	N	N	Y	N	Y

ND Northern Democrats   SD Southern Democrats

	142	143	144	145	146	147
14 *Hastert*			N	Y		
15 *Johnson*	Y	N	N	Y	N	Y
16 *Manzullo*	Y	Y	N	Y	N	?
17 Evans	Y	N	Y	Y	Y	Y
18 *LaHood*	Y	N	N	N	?	Y
19 Phelps	Y	N	Y	Y	Y	N
20 *Shimkus*	Y	Y	N	Y	N	Y
INDIANA						
1 Visclosky	?	?	?	?	?	N
2 *Pence*	Y	Y	N	N	N	Y
3 Roemer	Y	N	Y	Y	Y	Y
4 *Souder*	Y	Y	N	N	N	?
5 *Buyer*	Y	N	N	Y	N	Y
6 *Burton*	Y	Y	N	Y	N	?
7 *Kerns*	Y	Y	N	N	N	Y
8 *Hostettler*	Y	Y	N	N	N	Y
9 Hill	Y	N	Y	Y	Y	Y
10 Carson	Y	N	Y	Y	Y	Y
IOWA						
1 *Leach*	Y	N	N	Y	N	Y
2 *Nussle*	Y	Y	N	Y	N	Y
3 Boswell	Y	N	Y	Y	Y	Y
4 *Ganske*	Y	N	N	Y	N	Y
5 *Latham*	Y	N	N	Y	N	Y
KANSAS						
1 *Moran*	Y	N	N	N	N	Y
2 *Ryun*	Y	Y	N	N	N	Y
3 Moore	Y	N	Y	Y	Y	N
4 *Tiahrt*	Y	Y	N	Y	N	Y
KENTUCKY						
1 *Whitfield*	Y	N	N	Y	?	Y
2 *Lewis*	Y	Y	N	N	N	Y
3 *Northup*	Y	N	N	Y	N	Y
4 Lucas	Y	N	Y	Y	Y	Y
5 *Rogers*	Y	N	N	Y	N	Y
6 *Fletcher*	Y	N	N	Y	N	Y
LOUISIANA						
1 *Vitter*	Y	Y	N	Y	N	Y
2 Jefferson	Y	N	Y	Y	Y	N
3 *Tauzin*	Y	N	N	Y	N	Y
4 *McCrery*	Y	Y	N	Y	N	?
5 *Cooksey*	Y	N	N	Y	N	Y
6 *Baker*	Y	Y	N	Y	N	Y
7 John	Y	N	Y	Y	Y	Y
MAINE						
1 Allen	Y	N	Y	Y	Y	Y
2 Baldacci	Y	N	Y	Y	Y	N
MARYLAND						
1 *Gilchrest*	Y	N	N	N	N	Y
2 *Ehrlich*	Y	Y	N	Y	N	Y
3 Cardin	Y	N	Y	Y	Y	Y
4 Wynn	Y	N	Y	Y	Y	Y
5 Hoyer	Y	N	Y	Y	Y	Y
6 *Bartlett*	Y	Y	N	N	N	Y
7 Cummings	Y	N	Y	Y	Y	Y
8 *Morella*	Y	N	Y	Y	N	Y
MASSACHUSETTS						
1 Olver	Y	N	Y	Y	Y	N
2 Neal	Y	N	Y	Y	Y	N
3 McGovern	Y	N	Y	Y	Y	N
4 Frank	Y	N	Y	N	Y	Y
5 Meehan	Y	N	Y	Y	Y	Y
6 Tierney	Y	N	Y	Y	Y	Y
7 Markey	Y	N	Y	Y	Y	Y
8 Capuano	Y	N	Y	Y	Y	N
9 Moakley	?	?	?	?	?	?
10 Delahunt	Y	N	Y	Y	Y	Y
MICHIGAN						
1 Stupak	Y	N	Y	Y	Y	N
2 *Hoekstra*	Y	Y	N	N	N	N
3 *Ehlers*	Y	N	N	Y	N	Y
4 *Camp*	Y	Y	N	Y	N	Y
5 Barcia	Y	N	Y	Y	Y	Y
6 *Upton*	N	N	N	Y	N	Y
7 *Smith*	Y	Y	N	Y	N	Y
8 *Rogers*	Y	Y	N	Y	N	Y
9 Kildee	Y	N	Y	Y	Y	Y
10 Bonior	Y	N	Y	Y	Y	N
11 *Knollenberg*	Y	Y	N	Y	N	Y
12 Levin	Y	N	Y	Y	Y	N
13 Rivers	Y	N	Y	N	Y	Y
14 Conyers	Y	N	Y	N	Y	Y
15 Kilpatrick	Y	N	Y	Y	Y	Y
16 Dingell	Y	N	Y	Y	Y	Y

	142	143	144	145	146	147
MINNESOTA						
1 *Gutknecht*	Y	Y	N	Y	N	N
2 *Kennedy*	Y	Y	N	Y	N	N
3 *Ramstad*	Y	Y	N	Y	N	N
4 McCollum	Y	N	Y	Y	Y	Y
5 Sabo	Y	N	N	N	Y	N
6 Luther	Y	N	Y	Y	Y	Y
7 Peterson	Y	N	N	Y	N	N
8 Oberstar	Y	N	Y	Y	Y	N
MISSISSIPPI						
1 *Wicker*	Y	N	N	Y	N	Y
2 Thompson	Y	N	Y	Y	Y	N
3 *Pickering*	Y	N	N	Y	N	Y
4 Shows	Y	N	Y	Y	Y	Y
5 Taylor	Y	N	N	Y	Y	N
MISSOURI						
1 Clay	Y	N	Y	Y	Y	Y
2 *Akin*	Y	Y	N	N	N	Y
3 Gephardt	Y	N	Y	Y	Y	N
4 Skelton	Y	N	Y	Y	Y	Y
5 McCarthy	Y	N	Y	Y	Y	Y
6 *Graves*	Y	N	N	Y	N	Y
7 *Blunt*	Y	Y	N	Y	N	Y
8 *Emerson*	Y	N	N	Y	N	Y
9 *Hulshof*	Y	Y	N	Y	N	N
MONTANA						
AL *Rehberg*	Y	N	N	Y	N	Y
NEBRASKA						
1 *Bereuter*	Y	N	N	Y	?	Y
2 *Terry*	Y	N	N	Y	N	Y
3 *Osborne*	Y	N	N	Y	N	Y
NEVADA						
1 Berkley	Y	N	Y	Y	Y	Y
2 *Gibbons*	Y	N	N	Y	N	Y
NEW HAMPSHIRE						
1 *Sununu*	Y	N	N	Y	N	Y
2 *Bass*	Y	N	N	Y	N	Y
NEW JERSEY						
1 Andrews	Y	N	Y	Y	Y	Y
2 *LoBiondo*	Y	N	N	Y	N	N
3 *Saxton*	Y	N	N	Y	N	Y
4 *Smith*	Y	N	N	Y	N	Y
5 *Roukema*	Y	N	N	Y	N	Y
6 Pallone	Y	N	Y	Y	Y	N
7 *Ferguson*	Y	N	N	Y	N	Y
8 Pascrell	Y	Y	Y	Y	Y	Y
9 Rothman	Y	N	Y	Y	Y	Y
10 Payne	Y	N	Y	N	Y	Y
11 *Frelinghuysen*	Y	N	N	Y	N	Y
12 Holt	Y	N	Y	Y	Y	Y
13 Menendez	Y	N	Y	Y	Y	?
NEW MEXICO						
1 *Wilson*	Y	N	N	Y	?	Y
2 *Skeen*	Y	N	N	Y	N	Y
3 Udall	Y	N	Y	Y	Y	N
NEW YORK						
1 *Grucci*	Y	N	N	Y	N	Y
2 Israel	Y	N	Y	Y	Y	Y
3 *King*	Y	N	N	Y	N	Y
4 McCarthy	Y	N	Y	Y	Y	Y
5 Ackerman	Y	N	Y	Y	Y	Y
6 Meeks	Y	N	Y	Y	Y	N
7 Crowley	Y	N	Y	Y	Y	N
8 Nadler	Y	N	Y	Y	Y	?
9 Weiner	Y	N	Y	Y	Y	Y
10 Towns	Y	N	Y	Y	Y	Y
11 Owens	Y	N	Y	Y	Y	Y
12 Velázquez	Y	N	Y	Y	Y	?
13 *Fossella*	Y	N	N	Y	N	Y
14 Maloney	Y	N	Y	Y	Y	Y
15 Rangel	Y	N	Y	Y	Y	N
16 Serrano	Y	N	Y	Y	Y	Y
17 Engel	Y	N	Y	Y	Y	Y
18 Lowey	Y	N	Y	Y	Y	Y
19 *Kelly*	Y	N	N	Y	N	Y
20 *Gilman*	Y	N	N	Y	N	Y
21 McNulty	Y	N	Y	Y	Y	N
22 *Sweeney*	Y	N	N	Y	N	N
23 *Boehlert*	Y	N	N	Y	N	Y
24 *McHugh*	Y	N	N	Y	N	Y
25 *Walsh*	Y	N	N	Y	N	Y
26 Hinchey	Y	N	Y	Y	Y	N
27 *Reynolds*	Y	N	N	Y	N	Y
28 Slaughter	Y	N	Y	Y	Y	N
29 LaFalce	Y	N	Y	Y	Y	Y

	142	143	144	145	146	147
30 *Quinn*	Y	N	N	Y	N	Y
31 *Houghton*	Y	N	N	Y	N	Y
NORTH CAROLINA						
1 Clayton	Y	N	Y	Y	Y	Y
2 Etheridge	Y	N	Y	Y	Y	Y
3 *Jones*	Y	Y	N	N	N	Y
4 Price	Y	N	Y	Y	Y	Y
5 *Burr*	Y	N	N	Y	N	Y
6 *Coble*	Y	Y	N	Y	N	Y
7 McIntyre	Y	N	Y	Y	Y	Y
8 *Hayes*	Y	N	N	Y	N	Y
9 *Myrick*	Y	Y	N	Y	N	Y
10 *Ballenger*	Y	N	N	Y	N	Y
11 *Taylor*	Y	Y	N	Y	N	Y
12 Watt	Y	N	Y	N	Y	Y
NORTH DAKOTA						
AL Pomeroy	Y	N	Y	Y	Y	N
OHIO						
1 *Chabot*	Y	Y	N	Y	N	Y
2 *Portman*	Y	Y	N	Y	N	Y
3 Hall	Y	N	Y	Y	Y	?
4 *Oxley*	Y	N	N	Y	?	Y
5 *Gillmor*	Y	N	N	Y	N	?
6 Strickland	Y	N	Y	Y	Y	N
7 *Hobson*	Y	N	N	Y	N	Y
8 *Boehner*	Y	N	N	Y	N	Y
9 Kaptur	Y	N	Y	Y	Y	Y
10 Kucinich	Y	N	Y	Y	Y	N
11 Jones	Y	N	Y	Y	Y	N
12 *Tiberi*	Y	Y	N	Y	N	Y
13 Brown	Y	N	Y	Y	Y	N
14 Sawyer	Y	N	Y	Y	Y	Y
15 *Pryce*	Y	N	N	Y	N	Y
16 *Regula*	Y	N	N	Y	N	Y
17 Traficant	Y	N	Y	Y	N	Y
18 *Ney*	Y	N	N	Y	N	Y
19 *LaTourette*	Y	N	N	Y	N	?
OKLAHOMA						
1 *Largent*	Y	Y	N	Y	?	Y
2 Carson	Y	N	Y	Y	Y	Y
3 *Watkins*	Y	N	N	Y	N	Y
4 *Watts*	Y	N	N	Y	N	Y
5 *Istook*	Y	Y	N	Y	N	Y
6 *Lucas*	Y	N	N	Y	N	Y
OREGON						
1 Wu	Y	N	Y	Y	Y	Y
2 *Walden*	Y	N	N	Y	N	Y
3 Blumenauer	Y	N	Y	Y	Y	Y
4 DeFazio	Y	N	Y	Y	Y	N
5 Hooley	Y	N	Y	Y	Y	Y
PENNSYLVANIA						
1 Brady	Y	N	Y	Y	Y	N
2 Fattah	Y	N	Y	Y	Y	Y
3 Borski	Y	N	Y	Y	Y	N
4 *Hart*	Y	N	N	Y	N	Y
5 *Peterson*	Y	N	N	Y	N	Y
6 Holden	Y	N	Y	Y	Y	Y
7 *Weldon*	Y	N	N	Y	N	Y
8 *Greenwood*	Y	N	N	Y	N	Y
9 *Shuster, Bill*	Y	N	N	Y	N	Y
10 *Sherwood*	Y	N	N	Y	N	Y
11 Kanjorski	Y	N	Y	Y	Y	Y
12 Murtha	Y	N	Y	Y	?	?
13 Hoeffel	Y	N	Y	Y	Y	Y
14 Coyne	Y	N	Y	Y	Y	Y
15 *Toomey*	Y	Y	N	Y	N	Y
16 *Pitts*	Y	Y	N	N	N	Y
17 *Gekas*	Y	N	N	Y	N	Y
18 Doyle	Y	N	Y	Y	Y	Y
19 *Platts*	Y	N	N	Y	N	Y
20 Mascara	Y	N	Y	Y	Y	Y
21 *English*	Y	N	N	Y	N	N
RHODE ISLAND						
1 Kennedy	Y	N	Y	Y	Y	Y
2 Langevin	Y	N	Y	Y	Y	Y
SOUTH CAROLINA						
1 *Brown*	Y	N	N	Y	N	Y
2 *Spence*	Y	Y	N	Y	N	Y
3 *Graham*	Y	Y	N	Y	?	Y
4 *DeMint*	Y	Y	N	N	N	Y
5 Spratt	Y	N	Y	Y	Y	Y
6 Clyburn	Y	N	Y	Y	Y	Y
SOUTH DAKOTA						
AL *Thune*	Y	N	N	Y	N	Y

	142	143	144	145	146	147
TENNESSEE						
1 *Jenkins*	Y	N	N	Y	N	Y
2 *Duncan*	Y	Y	N	N	N	Y
3 *Wamp*	Y	N	N	Y	N	Y
4 *Hilleary*	Y	N	N	Y	N	N
5 Clement	Y	N	Y	Y	?	Y
6 Gordon	Y	N	Y	Y	Y	Y
7 *Bryant*	Y	Y	N	Y	N	Y
8 Tanner	Y	N	Y	Y	Y	N
9 Ford	Y	N	Y	Y	Y	Y
TEXAS						
1 Sandlin	Y	N	Y	Y	Y	Y
2 Turner	Y	N	Y	Y	Y	N
3 *Johnson, Sam*	Y	Y	N	N	N	Y
4 Hall	Y	N	N	Y	N	Y
5 *Sessions*	Y	Y	N	N	N	Y
6 *Barton*	Y	Y	N	Y	N	Y
7 *Culberson*	Y	Y	N	Y	?	Y
8 *Brady*	Y	Y	N	Y	N	Y
9 Lampson	Y	N	Y	Y	Y	Y
10 Doggett	Y	N	Y	Y	Y	N
11 Edwards	Y	N	Y	Y	Y	Y
12 *Granger*	Y	Y	N	Y	N	Y
13 *Thornberry*	Y	Y	N	Y	N	Y
14 *Paul*	Y	Y	N	N	N	Y
15 Hinojosa	Y	N	Y	Y	Y	?
16 Reyes	Y	N	Y	Y	Y	Y
17 Stenholm	Y	N	Y	Y	Y	N
18 Jackson-Lee	Y	N	Y	Y	Y	?
19 *Combest*	Y	Y	N	Y	N	Y
20 Gonzalez	Y	N	Y	Y	Y	Y
21 *Smith*	Y	Y	N	Y	N	Y
22 *DeLay*	Y	Y	N	Y	N	Y
23 *Bonilla*	Y	N	N	Y	N	Y
24 Frost	Y	N	Y	Y	?	Y
25 Bentsen	Y	N	Y	Y	Y	Y
26 *Armey*	Y	Y	N	Y	N	Y
27 Ortiz	Y	N	Y	Y	Y	Y
28 Rodriguez	Y	N	Y	Y	Y	Y
29 Green	Y	N	Y	Y	Y	N
30 Johnson, E.B.	Y	N	Y	Y	Y	N
UTAH						
1 *Hansen*	Y	Y	N	Y	N	Y
2 Matheson	Y	N	Y	Y	Y	Y
3 *Cannon*	Y	Y	N	Y	?	Y
VERMONT						
AL *Sanders*	Y	N	Y	Y	Y	Y
VIRGINIA						
1 *Davis, Jo Ann*	Y	Y	N	Y	N	Y
2 *Schrock*	Y	N	N	Y	N	Y
3 Scott	Y	N	Y	N	Y	N
4 Vacant						
5 *Goode*	Y	Y	N	N	N	Y
6 *Goodlatte*	Y	Y	N	Y	N	Y
7 *Cantor*	Y	Y	N	Y	N	Y
8 Moran	Y	N	Y	Y	Y	Y
9 Boucher	Y	N	Y	Y	Y	Y
10 *Wolf*	Y	N	N	Y	N	Y
11 *Davis, T.*	Y	N	N	Y	N	Y
WASHINGTON						
1 Inslee	Y	N	Y	Y	Y	Y
2 Larsen	Y	N	Y	Y	Y	N
3 Baird	Y	N	Y	Y	Y	N
4 *Hastings*	Y	Y	N	Y	N	Y
5 *Nethercutt*	Y	N	N	Y	N	?
6 Dicks	Y	N	Y	Y	?	Y
7 McDermott	Y	N	Y	Y	Y	N
8 *Dunn*	Y	N	N	Y	N	Y
9 Smith	Y	N	Y	Y	?	Y
WEST VIRGINIA						
1 Mollohan	Y	N	Y	Y	Y	Y
2 *Capito*	Y	N	N	Y	N	Y
3 Rahall	Y	N	Y	Y	?	?
WISCONSIN						
1 *Ryan*	Y	Y	N	Y	N	Y
2 Baldwin	Y	N	Y	Y	Y	Y
3 Kind	Y	N	Y	Y	Y	Y
4 Kleczka	Y	N	Y	Y	Y	Y
5 Barrett	Y	N	Y	Y	Y	Y
6 *Petri*	Y	N	N	Y	N	Y
7 Obey	N	N	Y	Y	Y	Y
8 *Green*	Y	N	N	Y	N	Y
9 *Sensenbrenner*	N	Y	N	N	N	Y
WYOMING						
AL *Cubin*	?	?	?	?	?	?

Southern states - Ala., Ark., Fla., Ga., Ky., La., Miss., N.C., Okla., S.C., Tenn., Texas, Va.

Key

Y	Voted for (yea).
#	Paired for.
+	Announced for.
N	Voted against (nay).
X	Paired against.
−	Announced against.
P	Voted "present."
C	Voted "present" to avoid possible conflict of interest.
?	Did not vote or otherwise make a position known.

Democrats **Republicans**
Independents

148. HR 1836. Tax Cut Reconciliation/Rule. Adoption of the rule (H Res 153) to provide for House floor consideration of the conference report on the tax reconciliation bill. Adopted 213-177: R 209-0; D 3-176 (ND 2-132, SD 1-44); I 1-1. May 26, 2001.

149. HR 1836. Tax Cut Reconciliation Bill/Conference Report. Adoption of the conference report on the bill that would reduce taxes by $1.35 trillion through fiscal 2011 through income tax rate cuts, relief of the "marriage penalty," a phaseout of the federal estate tax, doubling the child tax credit, and providing incentives for retirement savings. A new 10 percent tax rate would be created retroactive to Jan. 1. The bill would double the $500-per-child tax credit by 2010 and make it refundable; raise the estate tax exemption to $1 million in 2002 and repeal the tax in 2010; increase the standard deduction for married couples to double that of singles over five years, beginning in 2005; and increase annual contributions limits for Individual Retirement Accounts. The bill's provisions would expire Dec. 31, 2010. Adopted (thus sent to the Senate) 240-154: R 211-0; D 28-153 (ND 17-118, SD 11-35); I 1-1. A "yea" was a vote in support of the president's position. May 26, 2001.

		148	149
ALABAMA			
1	*Callahan*	Y	Y
2	*Everett*	Y	Y
3	*Riley*	Y	Y
4	*Aderholt*	Y	Y
5	Cramer	N	Y
6	*Bachus*	Y	Y
7	Hilliard	N	N
ALASKA			
AL	*Young*	Y	Y
ARIZONA			
1	*Flake*	Y	Y
2	Pastor	N	N
3	*Stump*	Y	Y
4	*Shadegg*	Y	Y
5	*Kolbe*	Y	Y
6	*Hayworth*	Y	Y
ARKANSAS			
1	Berry	N	N
2	Snyder	N	N
3	*Hutchinson*	Y	Y
4	Ross	N	Y
CALIFORNIA			
1	Thompson	N	N
2	*Herger*	Y	Y
3	Ose	+	Y
4	*Doolittle*	Y	Y
5	Matsui	N	N
6	Woolsey	N	N
7	Miller, George	N	N
8	Pelosi	N	N
9	Lee	N	N
10	Tauscher	N	Y
11	*Pombo*	Y	Y
12	Lantos	N	N
13	Stark	N	N
14	Eshoo	N	N
15	Honda	?	?
16	Lofgren	N	N
17	Farr	N	N
18	Condit	Y	Y
19	*Radanovich*	Y	Y
20	Dooley	N	Y
21	*Thomas*	Y	Y
22	Capps	N	Y
23	*Gallegly*	Y	Y
24	Sherman	N	N
25	*McKeon*	Y	Y
26	Berman	N	N
27	Schiff	N	Y
28	*Dreier*	Y	Y
29	Waxman	?	?
30	Becerra	?	?
31	Solis	N	N
32	Vacant		
33	Roybal-Allard	N	N
34	Napolitano	N	N
35	Waters	?	?
36	Harman	N	N
37	Millender-McD.	?	?
38	*Horn*	Y	Y

		148	149
39	*Royce*	Y	Y
40	*Lewis*	Y	Y
41	*Miller, Gary*	Y	Y
42	Baca	?	?
43	*Calvert*	Y	Y
44	*Bono*	Y	Y
45	*Rohrabacher*	Y	Y
46	Sanchez	N	N
47	*Cox*	Y	Y
48	*Issa*	Y	Y
49	Davis	N	N
50	Filner	N	N
51	*Cunningham*	Y	Y
52	*Hunter*	Y	Y
COLORADO			
1	DeGette	N	N
2	Udall	N	N
3	*McInnis*	Y	Y
4	*Schaffer*	Y	Y
5	*Hefley*	?	Y
6	*Tancredo*	Y	Y
CONNECTICUT			
1	Larson	N	N
2	*Simmons*	Y	Y
3	DeLauro	N	N
4	*Shays*	Y	Y
5	Maloney	N	N
6	*Johnson*	Y	Y
DELAWARE			
AL	*Castle*	Y	Y
FLORIDA			
1	*Scarborough*	?	?
2	Boyd	?	?
3	Brown	N	N
4	*Crenshaw*	Y	Y
5	Thurman	N	N
6	*Stearns*	Y	Y
7	*Mica*	Y	Y
8	*Keller*	Y	Y
9	*Bilirakis*	Y	Y
10	*Young*	Y	Y
11	Davis	N	N
12	*Putnam*	Y	Y
13	*Miller*	Y	Y
14	*Goss*	Y	Y
15	*Weldon*	Y	Y
16	*Foley*	Y	Y
17	Meek	?	?
18	*Ros-Lehtinen*	Y	Y
19	Wexler	N	N
20	Deutsch	N	N
21	*Diaz-Balart*	Y	Y
22	*Shaw*	Y	Y
23	Hastings	?	N
GEORGIA			
1	*Kingston*	Y	Y
2	Bishop	?	?
3	*Collins*	Y	Y
4	McKinney	N	N
5	Lewis	N	N
6	*Isakson*	?	?
7	*Barr*	Y	Y
8	*Chambliss*	Y	Y
9	*Deal*	Y	Y
10	*Norwood*	Y	Y
11	*Linder*	Y	Y
HAWAII			
1	Abercrombie	N	Y
2	Mink	N	N
IDAHO			
1	*Otter*	Y	Y
2	*Simpson*	Y	Y
ILLINOIS			
1	Rush	?	?
2	Jackson	N	N
3	Lipinski	?	?
4	Gutierrez	N	N
5	Blagojevich	N	N
6	*Hyde*	Y	Y
7	Davis	N	N
8	*Crane*	Y	Y
9	Schakowsky	N	N
10	*Kirk*	Y	Y
11	*Weller*	Y	Y
12	Costello	N	N
13	*Biggert*	Y	Y

ND Northern Democrats   SD Southern Democrats

	148	149
14 Hastert	Y	Y
15 Johnson	Y	Y
16 Manzullo	Y	Y
17 Evans	N	N
18 LaHood	Y	Y
19 Phelps	N	N
20 Shimkus	Y	Y
INDIANA		
1 Visclosky	N	N
2 Pence	Y	Y
3 Roemer	N	Y
4 Souder	Y	Y
5 Buyer	Y	Y
6 Burton	Y	Y
7 Kerns	Y	Y
8 Hostettler	Y	Y
9 Hill	N	N
10 Carson	N	N
IOWA		
1 Leach	Y	Y
2 Nussle	Y	Y
3 Boswell	N	N
4 Ganske	Y	Y
5 Latham	Y	Y
KANSAS		
1 Moran	Y	Y
2 Ryun	Y	Y
3 Moore	N	N
4 Tiahrt	Y	Y
KENTUCKY		
1 Whitfield	Y	Y
2 Lewis	Y	Y
3 Northup	Y	Y
4 Lucas	N	N
5 Rogers	Y	Y
6 Fletcher	Y	Y
LOUISIANA		
1 Vitter	Y	Y
2 Jefferson	N	N
3 Tauzin	Y	Y
4 McCrery	Y	Y
5 Cooksey	Y	Y
6 Baker	Y	Y
7 John	N	Y
MAINE		
1 Allen	N	N
2 Baldacci	N	N
MARYLAND		
1 Gilchrest	Y	Y
2 Ehrlich	Y	Y
3 Cardin	N	N
4 Wynn	?	?
5 Hoyer	N	N
6 Bartlett	Y	Y
7 Cummings	N	N
8 Morella	Y	Y
MASSACHUSETTS		
1 Olver	N	N
2 Neal	N	N
3 McGovern	N	N
4 Frank	N	N
5 Meehan	N	N
6 Tierney	N	N
7 Markey	N	N
8 Capuano	N	N
9 Moakley	?	?
10 Delahunt	N	N
MICHIGAN		
1 Stupak	N	N
2 Hoekstra	Y	Y
3 Ehlers	Y	Y
4 Camp	Y	Y
5 Barcia	N	Y
6 Upton	Y	Y
7 Smith	Y	Y
8 Rogers	Y	Y
9 Kildee	N	N
10 Bonlor	N	N
11 Knollenberg	Y	Y
12 Levin	N	N
13 Rivers	N	N
14 Conyers	N	N
15 Kilpatrick	N	N
16 Dingell	N	N
MINNESOTA		
1 Gutknecht	Y	Y
2 Kennedy	Y	Y
3 Ramstad	Y	Y
4 McCollum	N	N
5 Sabo	N	N
6 Luther	N	N
7 Peterson	N	Y
8 Oberstar	?	?
MISSISSIPPI		
1 Wicker	Y	Y
2 Thompson	N	N
3 Pickering	Y	Y
4 Shows	N	Y
5 Taylor	N	N
MISSOURI		
1 Clay	N	N
2 Akin	Y	Y
3 Gephardt	N	N
4 Skelton	?	N
5 McCarthy	—	—
6 Graves	Y	Y
7 Blunt	Y	Y
8 Emerson	Y	Y
9 Hulshof	Y	Y
MONTANA		
AL Rehberg	Y	Y
NEBRASKA		
1 Bereuter	Y	Y
2 Terry	Y	Y
3 Osborne	Y	Y
NEVADA		
1 Berkley	N	Y
2 Gibbons	Y	Y
NEW HAMPSHIRE		
1 Sununu	Y	Y
2 Bass	Y	Y
NEW JERSEY		
1 Andrews	N	N
2 LoBiondo	Y	Y
3 Saxton	Y	Y
4 Smith	Y	Y
5 Roukema	Y	Y
6 Pallone	N	N
7 Ferguson	Y	Y
8 Pascrell	N	N
9 Rothman	N	N
10 Payne	N	N
11 Frelinghuysen	Y	Y
12 Holt	N	N
13 Menendez	N	N
NEW MEXICO		
1 Wilson	Y	Y
2 Skeen	Y	Y
3 Udall	N	N
NEW YORK		
1 Grucci	Y	Y
2 Israel	N	Y
3 King	?	?
4 McCarthy	N	Y
5 Ackerman	?	?
6 Meeks	N	N
7 Crowley	N	N
8 Nadler	N	N
9 Weiner	N	N
10 Towns	?	?
11 Owens	N	N
12 Velázquez	N	N
13 Fossella	Y	Y
14 Maloney	N	N
15 Rangel	N	N
16 Serrano	N	N
17 Engel	N	N
18 Lowey	N	N
19 Kelly	Y	Y
20 Gilman	Y	Y
21 McNulty	N	N
22 Sweeney	Y	Y
23 Boehlert	Y	Y
24 McHugh	Y	Y
25 Walsh	?	?
26 Hinchey	N	N
27 Reynolds	Y	Y
28 Slaughter	N	N
29 LaFalce	N	N
30 Quinn	?	?
31 Houghton	Y	?
NORTH CAROLINA		
1 Clayton	?	?
2 Etheridge	N	N
3 Jones	?	?
4 Price	N	N
5 Burr	Y	Y
6 Coble	Y	Y
7 McIntyre	?	?
8 Hayes	Y	Y
9 Myrick	Y	Y
10 Ballenger	Y	Y
11 Taylor	Y	Y
12 Watt	N	N
NORTH DAKOTA		
AL Pomeroy	N	N
OHIO		
1 Chabot	Y	Y
2 Portman	Y	Y
3 Hall	?	?
4 Oxley	Y	Y
5 Gillmor	?	?
6 Strickland	N	N
7 Hobson	Y	Y
8 Boehner	Y	Y
9 Kaptur	?	?
10 Kucinich	N	N
11 Jones	N	N
12 Tiberi	Y	Y
13 Brown	N	N
14 Sawyer	N	N
15 Pryce	Y	Y
16 Regula	Y	Y
17 Traficant	Y	Y
18 Ney	Y	Y
19 LaTourette	Y	Y
OKLAHOMA		
1 Largent	Y	Y
2 Carson	N	Y
3 Watkins	Y	Y
4 Watts	Y	Y
5 Istook	Y	Y
6 Lucas	Y	Y
OREGON		
1 Wu	N	N
2 Walden	Y	Y
3 Blumenauer	?	?
4 DeFazio	N	N
5 Hooley	N	Y
PENNSYLVANIA		
1 Brady	N	N
2 Fattah	N	N
3 Borski	N	N
4 Hart	Y	Y
5 Peterson	Y	Y
6 Holden	N	N
7 Weldon	Y	Y
8 Greenwood	Y	Y
9 Shuster, Bill	Y	Y
10 Sherwood	Y	Y
11 Kanjorski	N	N
12 Murtha	N	N
13 Hoeffel	?	?
14 Coyne	?	?
15 Toomey	Y	Y
16 Pitts	Y	Y
17 Gekas	Y	Y
18 Doyle	N	N
19 Platts	Y	Y
20 Mascara	N	N
21 English	Y	Y
RHODE ISLAND		
1 Kennedy	N	N
2 Langevin	N	N
SOUTH CAROLINA		
1 Brown	Y	Y
2 Spence	Y	?
3 Graham	Y	Y
4 DeMint	Y	Y
5 Spratt	N	N
6 Clyburn	N	N
SOUTH DAKOTA		
AL Thune	Y	Y
TENNESSEE		
1 Jenkins	Y	Y
2 Duncan	Y	Y
3 Wamp	Y	Y
4 Hilleary	Y	Y
5 Clement	N	Y
6 Gordon	N	Y
7 Bryant	Y	Y
8 Tanner	N	N
9 Ford	N	N
TEXAS		
1 Sandlin	N	Y
2 Turner	N	Y
3 Johnson, Sam	Y	Y
4 Hall	Y	Y
5 Sessions	Y	Y
6 Barton	?	Y
7 Culberson	Y	Y
8 Brady	?	Y
9 Lampson	N	N
10 Doggett	?	?
11 Edwards	N	N
12 Granger	Y	Y
13 Thornberry	Y	Y
14 Paul	Y	Y
15 Hinojosa	N	N
16 Reyes	N	N
17 Stenholm	N	N
18 Jackson-Lee	N	N
19 Combest	Y	Y
20 Gonzalez	N	N
21 Smith	Y	Y
22 DeLay	Y	Y
23 Bonilla	Y	Y
24 Frost	N	N
25 Bentsen	?	?
26 Armey	Y	Y
27 Ortiz	N	N
28 Rodriguez	?	?
29 Green	N	N
30 Johnson, E.B.	N	N
UTAH		
1 Hansen	Y	Y
2 Matheson	N	Y
3 Cannon	Y	Y
VERMONT		
AL Sanders	N	N
VIRGINIA		
1 Davis, Jo Ann	Y	Y
2 Schrock	Y	Y
3 Scott	N	N
4 Vacant		
5 Goode	Y	Y
6 Goodlatte	Y	Y
7 Cantor	Y	Y
8 Moran	N	N
9 Boucher	N	N
10 Wolf	Y	Y
11 Davis, T.	Y	Y
WASHINGTON		
1 Inslee	N	N
2 Larsen	N	Y
3 Baird	N	N
4 Hastings	Y	Y
5 Nethercutt	Y	Y
6 Dicks	N	N
7 McDermott	?	—
8 Dunn	Y	Y
9 Smith	N	N
WEST VIRGINIA		
1 Mollohan	N	N
2 Capito	Y	Y
3 Rahall	?	?
WISCONSIN		
1 Ryan	Y	Y
2 Baldwin	N	N
3 Kind	N	N
4 Kleczka	N	N
5 Barrett	N	N
6 Petri	Y	Y
7 Obey	N	N
8 Green	Y	Y
9 Sensenbrenner	Y	Y
WYOMING		
AL Cubin	?	?

Southern states - Ala., Ark., Fla., Ga., Ky., La., Miss., N.C., Okla., S.C., Tenn., Texas, Va.

Key

150. H Con Res 100. Child Identification/Adoption. Osborne, R-Neb., motion to suspend the rules and adopt the resolution that would commend the American Football Coaches Association and Clear Channel Communications for supplying parents with child identification kits to gather data that can help in locating missing, kidnapped and runaway children. Motion agreed to 405-0: R 208-0; D 196-0 (ND 144-0, SD 52-0); I 1-0. A two-thirds majority of those present and voting (270 in this case) is required for adoption under suspension of the rules. June 5, 2001.

151. HR 2043. Elwood Hillis Post Office/Passage. Otter, R-Idaho, motion to suspend the rules and pass the bill that would designate a post office in Kokomo, Ind., as the "Elwood Haynes 'Bud' Hillis Post Office Building." Motion agreed to 407-0: R 210-0; D 196-0 (ND 144-0, SD 52-0); I 1-0. A two-thirds majority of those present and voting (272 in this case) is required for passage under suspension of the rules. June 5, 2001.

152. HR 1209. Children's Visa Expansion/Passage. Sensenbrenner, R-Wis., motion to suspend the rules and pass the bill that would amend the Immigration and Nationality Act so that the age of an alien applying for permanent residency status would be based on the application's filing date rather than its processing date. Motion agreed to 416-0: R 213-0; D 202-0 (ND 148-0, SD 54-0); I 1-0. A two-thirds majority of those present and voting (278 in this case) is required for passage under suspension of the rules. June 6, 2001.

153. HR 1914. Farmer Bankruptcy Extension/Passage. Sensenbrenner, R-Wis., motion to suspend the rules and pass the bill that would extend Chapter 12 federal bankruptcy protection for farmers retroactive to June 1, 2001, and through Oct. 1, 2001. Motion agreed to 411-1: R 210-1; D 200-0 (ND 147-0, SD 53-0); I 1-0. A two-thirds majority of those present and voting (275 in this case) is required for passage under suspension of the rules. June 6, 2001.

154. Procedural Motion/Journal. Approval of the House Journal of Wednesday, June 6, 2001. Approved 362-36: R 199-10; D 161-26 (ND 117-23, SD 44-3); I 2-0. June 7, 2001.

155. HR 1699. Coast Guard Authorization/Passage. Passage of the bill to authorize $5.3 billion in fiscal 2002 for Coast Guard programs and activities, including $3.7 billion for operation and maintenance and $659 million for facilities, vessels and other equipment. Passed 411-3: R 210-3; D 199-0 (ND 148-0, SD 51-0); I 2-0. June 7, 2001.

[1] *Rep. Diane Watson, D-Calif., was sworn in June 7. The first vote for which she was eligible was Vote 155.*

[2] *Rep. Joe Moakley, D-Mass., died May 28. The last vote for which he was eligible was Vote 149.*

	150	151	152	153	154	155
ALABAMA						
1 Callahan	Y	Y	Y	Y	Y	Y
2 Everett	Y	Y	Y	Y	Y	Y
3 Riley	Y	Y	Y	Y	Y	Y
4 Aderholt	Y	Y	Y	Y	N	Y
5 Cramer	Y	Y	Y	Y	Y	Y
6 Bachus	Y	Y	Y	Y	Y	Y
7 Hilliard	Y	Y	Y	Y	Y	Y
ALASKA						
AL Young	Y	Y	Y	Y	Y	Y
ARIZONA						
1 Flake	Y	Y	Y	Y	Y	Y
2 Pastor	Y	Y	Y	Y	N	Y
3 Stump	Y	Y	Y	Y	Y	Y
4 Shadegg	Y	Y	Y	Y	Y	Y
5 Kolbe	Y	Y	Y	Y	Y	Y
6 Hayworth	Y	Y	Y	Y	Y	Y
ARKANSAS						
1 Berry	Y	Y	Y	Y	Y	Y
2 Snyder	Y	Y	Y	Y	Y	Y
3 Hutchinson	Y	Y	Y	Y	Y	?
4 Ross	Y	Y	Y	Y	Y	Y
CALIFORNIA						
1 Thompson	Y	Y	Y	Y	N	Y
2 Herger	Y	Y	Y	Y	Y	Y
3 Ose	Y	Y	Y	Y	Y	Y
4 Doolittle	?	?	Y	Y	Y	Y
5 Matsui	?	?	Y	Y	Y	Y
6 Woolsey	Y	Y	Y	?	Y	Y
7 Miller, George	Y	Y	Y	Y	?	?
8 Pelosi	Y	Y	Y	Y	Y	Y
9 Lee	Y	Y	Y	Y	Y	Y
10 Tauscher	Y	Y	Y	Y	Y	Y
11 Pombo	?	?	Y	Y	N	Y
12 Lantos	Y	Y	Y	Y	Y	Y
13 Stark	Y	Y	Y	Y	Y	Y
14 Eshoo	Y	Y	+	+	Y	Y
15 Honda	Y	Y	Y	Y	Y	Y
16 Lofgren	Y	Y	Y	Y	Y	?
17 Farr	Y	Y	Y	Y	Y	Y
18 Condit	Y	Y	Y	Y	Y	Y
19 Radanovich	Y	Y	Y	Y	Y	Y
20 Dooley	Y	Y	Y	Y	?	Y
21 Thomas	Y	Y	Y	Y	Y	Y
22 Capps	Y	Y	Y	Y	Y	Y
23 Gallegly	Y	Y	Y	Y	Y	Y
24 Sherman	?	?	Y	Y	Y	Y
25 McKeon	Y	Y	Y	Y	Y	Y
26 Berman	Y	Y	Y	Y	Y	Y
27 Schiff	Y	Y	Y	Y	Y	Y
28 Dreier	Y	Y	Y	Y	Y	Y
29 Waxman	Y	Y	?	?	Y	Y
30 Becerra	Y	Y	Y	Y	Y	Y
31 Solis	+	+	+	+	+	+
32 Watson[1]						Y
33 Roybal-Allard	Y	Y	Y	Y	Y	Y
34 Napolitano	Y	Y	Y	Y	Y	Y
35 Waters	?	?	?	?	Y	Y
36 Harman	Y	Y	?	?	Y	Y
37 Millender-McD.	?	?	?	?	Y	Y
38 Horn	Y	Y	Y	Y	Y	Y

	150	151	152	153	154	155
39 Royce	Y	Y	Y	Y	Y	Y
40 Lewis	Y	Y	Y	Y	Y	Y
41 Miller, Gary	Y	Y	Y	Y	Y	Y
42 Baca	Y	Y	Y	Y	Y	Y
43 Calvert	Y	Y	Y	Y	Y	Y
44 Bono	Y	Y	Y	Y	Y	Y
45 Rohrabacher	Y	Y	Y	Y	Y	Y
46 Sanchez	Y	Y	Y	Y	Y	Y
47 Cox	Y	Y	?	?	?	Y
48 Issa	Y	Y	Y	Y	Y	Y
49 Davis	Y	Y	Y	Y	Y	Y
50 Filner	Y	Y	Y	Y	Y	Y
51 Cunningham	Y	Y	Y	Y	N	Y
52 Hunter	Y	Y	Y	Y	Y	Y
COLORADO						
1 DeGette	Y	Y	Y	Y	Y	Y
2 Udall	Y	Y	Y	Y	?	?
3 McInnis	Y	Y	Y	Y	Y	Y
4 Schaffer	Y	Y	Y	Y	N	N
5 Hefley	Y	Y	Y	Y	N	Y
6 Tancredo	Y	Y	Y	Y	?	N
CONNECTICUT						
1 Larson	Y	Y	Y	Y	Y	Y
2 Simmons	Y	Y	Y	Y	Y	+
3 DeLauro	Y	Y	Y	Y	Y	Y
4 Shays	Y	Y	Y	Y	Y	Y
5 Maloney	Y	Y	Y	Y	Y	Y
6 Johnson	Y	Y	Y	Y	?	Y
DELAWARE						
AL Castle	Y	Y	Y	Y	Y	Y
FLORIDA						
1 Scarborough	?	?	Y	Y	Y	Y
2 Boyd	Y	Y	Y	Y	Y	Y
3 Brown	?	?	Y	Y	Y	Y
4 Crenshaw	Y	Y	Y	Y	Y	Y
5 Thurman	Y	Y	Y	Y	Y	Y
6 Stearns	Y	Y	Y	Y	Y	Y
7 Mica	Y	Y	Y	Y	Y	Y
8 Keller	Y	Y	Y	Y	Y	Y
9 Bilirakis	Y	Y	Y	Y	Y	Y
10 Young	Y	Y	Y	Y	Y	Y
11 Davis	Y	Y	Y	Y	?	Y
12 Putnam	Y	Y	Y	Y	Y	?
13 Miller	Y	Y	Y	Y	Y	Y
14 Goss	Y	Y	Y	Y	Y	Y
15 Weldon	Y	Y	Y	Y	Y	Y
16 Foley	Y	Y	Y	Y	Y	Y
17 Meek	Y	Y	Y	Y	Y	Y
18 Ros-Lehtinen	Y	Y	Y	Y	Y	Y
19 Wexler	?	?	Y	Y	?	?
20 Deutsch	Y	Y	Y	Y	Y	Y
21 Diaz-Balart	Y	Y	Y	Y	Y	Y
22 Shaw	Y	Y	Y	Y	Y	Y
23 Hastings	Y	Y	Y	Y	Y	Y
GEORGIA						
1 Kingston	?	?	Y	Y	Y	Y
2 Bishop	Y	Y	Y	Y	Y	Y
3 Collins	Y	Y	Y	Y	Y	Y
4 McKinney	Y	Y	Y	Y	Y	Y
5 Lewis	Y	Y	Y	Y	Y	Y
6 Isakson	Y	Y	Y	Y	Y	Y
7 Barr	Y	Y	Y	Y	Y	Y
8 Chambliss	Y	Y	Y	Y	Y	Y
9 Deal	Y	Y	Y	Y	Y	Y
10 Norwood	Y	Y	Y	Y	Y	Y
11 Linder	Y	Y	Y	Y	?	Y
HAWAII						
1 Abercrombie	Y	Y	Y	Y	Y	Y
2 Mink	?	?	Y	Y	Y	Y
IDAHO						
1 Otter	Y	Y	Y	Y	Y	Y
2 Simpson	Y	Y	Y	Y	Y	Y
ILLINOIS						
1 Rush	Y	Y	Y	Y	Y	Y
2 Jackson	Y	Y	Y	Y	Y	Y
3 Lipinski	Y	Y	Y	Y	Y	Y
4 Gutierrez	Y	Y	Y	Y	Y	Y
5 Blagojevich	Y	Y	Y	Y	Y	Y
6 Hyde	Y	Y	Y	Y	Y	Y
7 Davis	Y	Y	Y	Y	Y	Y
8 Crane	Y	Y	Y	Y	N	Y
9 Schakowsky	Y	Y	Y	Y	Y	Y
10 Kirk	Y	Y	Y	Y	Y	Y
11 Weller	Y	Y	Y	Y	N	Y
12 Costello	Y	Y	Y	Y	N	Y
13 Biggert	Y	Y	Y	Y	Y	Y

ND Northern Democrats   SD Southern Democrats

Voting record (roll-call votes 150–155)

ILLINOIS (continued)

District / Member	150	151	152	153	154	155
14 *Hastert*						
15 *Johnson*	Y	+	Y	Y	Y	Y
16 *Manzullo*	Y	Y	Y	Y	Y	Y
17 Evans	Y	Y	Y	Y	Y	Y
18 *LaHood*	Y	Y	Y	Y	Y	Y
19 Phelps	Y	Y	Y	Y	Y	Y
20 *Shimkus*	Y	Y	Y	Y	Y	Y

INDIANA

District / Member	150	151	152	153	154	155
1 Visclosky	Y	Y	Y	Y	N	Y
2 *Pence*	Y	Y	Y	Y	Y	Y
3 Roemer	Y	Y	Y	Y	Y	Y
4 *Souder*	Y	Y	Y	Y	Y	Y
5 *Buyer*	Y	Y	?	?	Y	Y
6 *Burton*	?	?	?	?	?	?
7 *Kerns*	Y	Y	Y	Y	Y	Y
8 *Hostettler*	Y	Y	Y	Y	Y	Y
9 Hill	Y	Y	Y	Y	Y	Y
10 Carson	Y	Y	Y	Y	Y	Y

IOWA

District / Member	150	151	152	153	154	155
1 *Leach*	Y	Y	Y	Y	Y	Y
2 *Nussle*	Y	Y	Y	Y	Y	Y
3 Boswell	Y	Y	Y	Y	Y	Y
4 Ganske	Y	Y	Y	Y	Y	Y
5 Latham	Y	Y	Y	Y	Y	Y

KANSAS

District / Member	150	151	152	153	154	155
1 *Moran*	Y	Y	Y	Y	Y	Y
2 *Ryun*	Y	Y	Y	Y	Y	Y
3 Moore	Y	Y	Y	Y	N	Y
4 Tiahrt	Y	Y	Y	Y	Y	Y

KENTUCKY

District / Member	150	151	152	153	154	155
1 *Whitfield*	Y	Y	Y	Y	Y	Y
2 Lewis	Y	Y	Y	Y	+	+
3 *Northup*	Y	Y	Y	Y	Y	Y
4 Lucas	Y	Y	Y	Y	Y	Y
5 *Rogers*	Y	Y	Y	Y	Y	Y
6 *Fletcher*	Y	Y	Y	Y	Y	Y

LOUISIANA

District / Member	150	151	152	153	154	155
1 *Vitter*	Y	Y	Y	Y	Y	Y
2 Jefferson	Y	Y	Y	?	?	?
3 *Tauzin*	Y	Y	Y	Y	Y	?
4 *McCrery*	Y	Y	Y	Y	Y	Y
5 *Cooksey*	Y	Y	Y	Y	Y	Y
6 *Baker*	Y	Y	Y	Y	Y	Y
7 John	Y	Y	Y	Y	Y	Y

MAINE

District / Member	150	151	152	153	154	155
1 Allen	Y	Y	Y	Y	Y	Y
2 Baldacci	Y	Y	Y	Y	Y	Y

MARYLAND

District / Member	150	151	152	153	154	155
1 *Gilchrest*	Y	Y	Y	Y	Y	Y
2 *Ehrlich*	?	?	Y	Y	Y	Y
3 Cardin	Y	Y	Y	Y	Y	Y
4 Wynn	Y	Y	Y	Y	Y	Y
5 Hoyer	Y	Y	Y	Y	?	Y
6 *Bartlett*	Y	Y	Y	Y	Y	Y
7 Cummings	Y	Y	Y	Y	Y	Y
8 *Morella*	Y	Y	Y	Y	Y	Y

MASSACHUSETTS

District / Member	150	151	152	153	154	155
1 Olver	Y	Y	Y	Y	?	Y
2 Neal	Y	Y	Y	Y	Y	Y
3 McGovern	Y	Y	Y	Y	Y	Y
4 Frank	Y	Y	Y	Y	Y	Y
5 Meehan	Y	Y	Y	Y	Y	Y
6 Tierney	Y	Y	Y	Y	Y	Y
7 Markey	Y	Y	Y	Y	Y	Y
8 Capuano	Y	Y	Y	Y	N	Y
9 Vacant [2]						
10 Delahunt	Y	Y	Y	Y	Y	Y

MICHIGAN

District / Member	150	151	152	153	154	155
1 Stupak	Y	Y	Y	Y	N	Y
2 *Hoekstra*	Y	Y	Y	Y	Y	Y
3 *Ehlers*	Y	Y	Y	Y	Y	Y
4 *Camp*	Y	Y	Y	Y	Y	Y
5 Barcia	Y	Y	Y	Y	Y	Y
6 *Upton*	Y	Y	Y	Y	Y	Y
7 *Smith*	Y	Y	Y	Y	Y	Y
8 *Rogers*	Y	Y	Y	Y	Y	Y
9 Kildee	Y	Y	Y	Y	Y	Y
10 Bonlor	Y	Y	Y	Y	Y	Y
11 *Knollenberg*	Y	Y	Y	Y	Y	Y
12 Levin	Y	Y	Y	Y	Y	Y
13 Rivers	Y	Y	Y	Y	Y	Y
14 Conyers	Y	Y	Y	Y	Y	Y
15 Kilpatrick	Y	Y	Y	Y	Y	Y
16 Dingell	Y	Y	?	?	Y	?

MINNESOTA

District / Member	150	151	152	153	154	155
1 *Gutknecht*	Y	Y	Y	Y	Y	Y
2 *Kennedy*	Y	Y	Y	Y	Y	Y
3 *Ramstad*	Y	Y	Y	Y	N	Y
4 McCollum	Y	Y	Y	Y	Y	Y
5 Sabo	Y	Y	Y	Y	?	Y
6 Luther	Y	Y	Y	Y	Y	Y
7 Peterson	Y	Y	Y	Y	N	Y
8 Oberstar	Y	Y	Y	Y	N	Y

MISSISSIPPI

District / Member	150	151	152	153	154	155
1 *Wicker*	Y	Y	Y	Y	Y	Y
2 Thompson	Y	Y	Y	Y	N	Y
3 *Pickering*	Y	Y	Y	Y	Y	Y
4 Shows	Y	Y	Y	Y	Y	Y
5 Taylor	Y	Y	Y	Y	N	Y

MISSOURI

District / Member	150	151	152	153	154	155
1 Clay	Y	Y	Y	Y	Y	Y
2 *Akin*	Y	Y	Y	Y	Y	Y
3 Gephardt	Y	Y	Y	Y	Y	Y
4 Skelton	Y	Y	Y	Y	Y	Y
5 McCarthy	Y	Y	Y	Y	Y	Y
6 *Graves*	Y	Y	Y	Y	Y	Y
7 *Blunt*	Y	Y	Y	Y	Y	Y
8 *Emerson*	Y	Y	Y	Y	Y	Y
9 *Hulshof*	Y	Y	Y	Y	N	Y

MONTANA

District / Member	150	151	152	153	154	155
AL *Rehberg*	Y	Y	Y	Y	Y	Y

NEBRASKA

District / Member	150	151	152	153	154	155
1 *Bereuter*	Y	Y	Y	Y	Y	Y
2 *Terry*	Y	Y	Y	Y	Y	Y
3 *Osborne*	Y	Y	Y	Y	Y	Y

NEVADA

District / Member	150	151	152	153	154	155
1 Berkley	Y	Y	Y	Y	Y	Y
2 *Gibbons*	Y	Y	Y	Y	Y	Y

NEW HAMPSHIRE

District / Member	150	151	152	153	154	155
1 *Sununu*	Y	Y	Y	Y	Y	Y
2 *Bass*	Y	Y	Y	Y	Y	Y

NEW JERSEY

District / Member	150	151	152	153	154	155
1 Andrews	Y	Y	Y	Y	Y	Y
2 *LoBiondo*	Y	Y	Y	Y	N	Y
3 *Saxton*	Y	Y	Y	Y	Y	Y
4 *Smith*	Y	Y	Y	Y	Y	Y
5 *Roukema*	Y	Y	Y	Y	Y	Y
6 Pallone	Y	Y	Y	Y	N	Y
7 *Ferguson*	Y	Y	?	?	?	?
8 Pascrell	Y	Y	Y	Y	Y	Y
9 Rothman	Y	Y	Y	Y	Y	Y
10 Payne	?	?	Y	Y	Y	Y
11 *Frelinghuysen*	Y	Y	Y	Y	Y	Y
12 Holt	Y	Y	Y	Y	?	Y
13 Menendez	Y	Y	Y	Y	N	Y

NEW MEXICO

District / Member	150	151	152	153	154	155
1 *Wilson*	Y	Y	Y	Y	Y	Y
2 *Skeen*	Y	Y	Y	Y	Y	Y
3 Udall	Y	Y	Y	Y	N	Y

NEW YORK

District / Member	150	151	152	153	154	155
1 *Grucci*	Y	Y	Y	Y	Y	Y
2 Israel	Y	Y	Y	Y	Y	Y
3 *King*	Y	Y	Y	Y	Y	Y
4 McCarthy	Y	Y	Y	Y	Y	Y
5 Ackerman	?	?	Y	Y	Y	Y
6 Meeks	Y	Y	Y	Y	Y	Y
7 Crowley	Y	Y	Y	Y	N	Y
8 Nadler	Y	Y	Y	Y	Y	Y
9 Weiner	Y	Y	Y	Y	Y	Y
10 Towns	Y	Y	Y	Y	?	?
11 Owens	Y	Y	Y	Y	Y	Y
12 Velázquez	Y	Y	Y	Y	Y	Y
13 *Fossella*	Y	Y	Y	Y	Y	Y
14 Maloney	Y	Y	Y	Y	Y	Y
15 Rangel	Y	Y	Y	Y	?	Y
16 Serrano	Y	Y	Y	Y	Y	Y
17 Engel	?	?	Y	Y	?	Y
18 Lowey	Y	Y	Y	Y	Y	Y
19 *Kelly*	Y	Y	Y	Y	Y	Y
20 Gilman	Y	Y	Y	Y	Y	Y
21 McNulty	Y	Y	Y	Y	Y	Y
22 *Sweeney*	Y	Y	Y	Y	N	Y
23 *Boehlert*	Y	Y	Y	Y	Y	Y
24 *McHugh*	Y	Y	Y	Y	Y	Y
25 *Walsh*	Y	Y	Y	?	Y	Y
26 Hinchey	Y	Y	Y	Y	Y	Y
27 *Reynolds*	Y	Y	Y	Y	Y	Y
28 Slaughter	Y	Y	Y	Y	Y	Y
29 LaFalce	Y	Y	Y	Y	Y	Y
30 Quinn	Y	Y	Y	Y	Y	Y
31 Houghton	Y	Y	?	?	Y	Y

NORTH CAROLINA

District / Member	150	151	152	153	154	155
1 Clayton	Y	Y	Y	Y	Y	Y
2 Etheridge	Y	Y	Y	Y	Y	Y
3 *Jones*	Y	Y	Y	Y	Y	Y
4 Price	Y	Y	Y	Y	Y	Y
5 *Burr*	Y	Y	Y	Y	Y	Y
6 *Coble*	Y	Y	Y	Y	Y	Y
7 McIntyre	Y	Y	Y	Y	Y	Y
8 *Hayes*	Y	Y	Y	Y	Y	Y
9 *Myrick*	Y	Y	Y	Y	Y	Y
10 *Ballenger*	Y	Y	Y	Y	Y	Y
11 *Taylor*	?	?	Y	Y	?	Y
12 Watt	Y	Y	Y	Y	Y	Y

NORTH DAKOTA

District / Member	150	151	152	153	154	155
AL Pomeroy	Y	Y	Y	Y	Y	Y

OHIO

District / Member	150	151	152	153	154	155
1 *Chabot*	Y	Y	Y	Y	Y	Y
2 *Portman*	Y	Y	Y	Y	Y	Y
3 Hall	Y	Y	Y	Y	Y	Y
4 *Oxley*	Y	Y	Y	Y	Y	Y
5 *Gillmor*	?	?	Y	Y	Y	Y
6 Strickland	Y	Y	Y	Y	Y	Y
7 *Hobson*	Y	Y	Y	Y	Y	Y
8 *Boehner*	Y	Y	Y	Y	Y	Y
9 Kaptur	Y	Y	Y	Y	Y	Y
10 Kucinich	Y	Y	Y	Y	N	Y
11 Jones	Y	Y	Y	?	?	
12 *Tiberi*	Y	Y	Y	Y	Y	Y
13 Brown	Y	Y	Y	Y	Y	Y
14 Sawyer	?	?	Y	Y	Y	Y
15 *Pryce*	Y	Y	Y	Y	Y	Y
16 *Regula*	Y	Y	Y	Y	Y	Y
17 Traficant	Y	Y	Y	Y	Y	Y
18 *Ney*	Y	Y	Y	Y	Y	Y
19 *LaTourette*	Y	Y	Y	Y	Y	Y

OKLAHOMA

District / Member	150	151	152	153	154	155
1 *Largent*	Y	Y	Y	Y	Y	Y
2 Carson	Y	Y	Y	?	Y	Y
3 *Watkins*	Y	Y	Y	?	Y	Y
4 *Watts*	Y	Y	Y	Y	Y	Y
5 *Istook*	Y	Y	Y	Y	Y	Y
6 *Lucas*	Y	Y	Y	Y	Y	Y

OREGON

District / Member	150	151	152	153	154	155
1 Wu	Y	Y	Y	Y	N	Y
2 *Walden*	Y	Y	Y	Y	Y	Y
3 Blumenauer	Y	Y	Y	Y	Y	Y
4 DeFazio	Y	Y	Y	Y	N	Y
5 Hooley	Y	Y	Y	Y	Y	Y

PENNSYLVANIA

District / Member	150	151	152	153	154	155
1 Brady	Y	Y	Y	Y	N	Y
2 Fattah	Y	Y	Y	Y	Y	Y
3 Borski	Y	Y	Y	Y	N	Y
4 *Hart*	?	?	Y	Y	Y	Y
5 *Peterson*	?	?	Y	Y	Y	Y
6 Holden	Y	Y	Y	Y	Y	Y
7 *Weldon*	?	?	Y	Y	Y	Y
8 *Greenwood*	Y	Y	Y	Y	?	Y
9 *Shuster, Bill*	Y	Y	Y	Y	Y	Y
10 *Sherwood*	Y	Y	Y	Y	Y	Y
11 Kanjorski	Y	Y	Y	Y	Y	Y
12 Murtha	Y	Y	Y	Y	Y	Y
13 Hoeffel	Y	Y	Y	Y	Y	Y
14 Coyne	Y	Y	Y	Y	?	Y
15 *Toomey*	Y	Y	Y	Y	Y	Y
16 *Pitts*	Y	Y	Y	Y	Y	Y
17 *Gekas*	Y	Y	Y	Y	Y	Y
18 Doyle	Y	Y	Y	Y	Y	Y
19 *Platts*	Y	Y	Y	Y	Y	Y
20 Mascara	Y	Y	Y	Y	Y	Y
21 *English*	Y	Y	Y	?	Y	Y

RHODE ISLAND

District / Member	150	151	152	153	154	155
1 Kennedy	Y	Y	Y	Y	Y	Y
2 Langevin	Y	Y	Y	Y	Y	Y

SOUTH CAROLINA

District / Member	150	151	152	153	154	155
1 *Brown*	Y	Y	Y	Y	Y	Y
2 *Spence*	?	Y	Y	Y	Y	Y
3 *Graham*	Y	Y	Y	Y	Y	Y
4 *DeMint*	Y	Y	Y	Y	Y	Y
5 Spratt	Y	Y	Y	Y	Y	Y
6 Clyburn	Y	Y	Y	Y	Y	Y

SOUTH DAKOTA

District / Member	150	151	152	153	154	155
AL *Thune*	Y	Y	Y	Y	Y	Y

TENNESSEE

District / Member	150	151	152	153	154	155
1 *Jenkins*	Y	Y	Y	Y	Y	Y
2 *Duncan*	Y	Y	Y	Y	Y	Y
3 *Wamp*	Y	Y	Y	Y	Y	Y
4 *Hilleary*	Y	Y	Y	Y	Y	Y
5 Clement	Y	Y	Y	Y	Y	Y
6 Gordon	Y	Y	Y	Y	Y	Y
7 *Bryant*	Y	Y	Y	Y	Y	Y
8 Tanner	Y	Y	Y	Y	Y	Y
9 Ford	Y	Y	Y	Y	N	Y

TEXAS

District / Member	150	151	152	153	154	155
1 Sandlin	Y	Y	Y	Y	Y	Y
2 Turner	Y	Y	Y	Y	?	?
3 *Johnson, Sam*	Y	Y	Y	Y	Y	Y
4 Hall	Y	Y	Y	Y	Y	Y
5 *Sessions*	Y	Y	Y	Y	Y	Y
6 *Barton*	Y	Y	Y	Y	Y	Y
7 *Culberson*	Y	Y	Y	Y	Y	Y
8 *Brady*	Y	Y	Y	Y	Y	Y
9 Lampson	Y	Y	Y	Y	Y	Y
10 Doggett	Y	Y	Y	Y	Y	Y
11 Edwards	Y	Y	Y	Y	?	Y
12 *Granger*	Y	Y	Y	Y	Y	Y
13 *Thornberry*	Y	Y	Y	Y	Y	Y
14 *Paul*	Y	Y	Y	N	Y	N
15 Hinojosa	Y	Y	Y	Y	Y	Y
16 Reyes	Y	Y	Y	Y	Y	Y
17 Stenholm	Y	Y	Y	Y	?	Y
18 Jackson-Lee	Y	Y	Y	Y	Y	Y
19 *Combest*	Y	Y	Y	Y	Y	Y
20 Gonzalez	Y	Y	Y	Y	Y	Y
21 *Smith*	Y	Y	Y	Y	Y	Y
22 *DeLay*	Y	Y	Y	Y	Y	Y
23 *Bonilla*	Y	Y	Y	Y	Y	Y
24 Frost	Y	Y	Y	Y	Y	Y
25 Bentsen	Y	Y	Y	Y	Y	Y
26 *Armey*	Y	Y	Y	Y	Y	Y
27 Ortiz	Y	Y	Y	Y	Y	Y
28 Rodriguez	Y	Y	Y	Y	Y	Y
29 Green	Y	Y	Y	Y	Y	Y
30 Johnson, E.B.	Y	Y	Y	Y	Y	Y

UTAH

District / Member	150	151	152	153	154	155
1 *Hansen*	Y	Y	Y	Y	Y	Y
2 Matheson	Y	Y	Y	Y	Y	Y
3 *Cannon*	Y	Y	Y	Y	Y	Y

VERMONT

District / Member	150	151	152	153	154	155
AL *Sanders*	Y	Y	Y	Y	Y	Y

VIRGINIA

District / Member	150	151	152	153	154	155
1 *Davis, Jo Ann*	Y	Y	Y	Y	Y	Y
2 *Schrock*	Y	Y	Y	Y	Y	Y
3 Scott	Y	Y	Y	Y	Y	Y
4 Vacant						
5 *Goode*	?	?	?	?	Y	Y
6 *Goodlatte*	Y	Y	?	?	Y	Y
7 *Cantor*	Y	Y	Y	?	Y	Y
8 Moran	Y	Y	Y	Y	Y	Y
9 Boucher	Y	Y	Y	Y	Y	Y
10 *Wolf*	Y	Y	Y	Y	Y	Y
11 *Davis, T.*	Y	Y	Y	Y	Y	Y

WASHINGTON

District / Member	150	151	152	153	154	155
1 Inslee	Y	Y	Y	Y	Y	Y
2 Larsen	Y	Y	Y	Y	N	Y
3 Baird	?	?	Y	Y	Y	Y
4 *Hastings*	Y	Y	Y	Y	Y	Y
5 *Nethercutt*	Y	Y	?	?	Y	Y
6 Dicks	Y	Y	Y	Y	Y	Y
7 McDermott	Y	Y	Y	Y	N	Y
8 *Dunn*	Y	Y	Y	Y	Y	Y
9 Smith	Y	Y	Y	Y	Y	Y

WEST VIRGINIA

District / Member	150	151	152	153	154	155
1 Mollohan	Y	Y	Y	Y	Y	Y
2 *Capito*	Y	Y	Y	Y	Y	Y
3 Rahall	Y	Y	Y	Y	Y	Y

WISCONSIN

District / Member	150	151	152	153	154	155
1 *Ryan*	Y	Y	Y	Y	Y	Y
2 Baldwin	Y	Y	Y	Y	Y	Y
3 Kind	Y	Y	Y	Y	Y	Y
4 Kleczka	Y	Y	Y	Y	Y	Y
5 Barrett	Y	Y	Y	Y	Y	Y
6 *Petri*	Y	Y	Y	Y	Y	Y
7 Obey	Y	Y	Y	Y	?	Y
8 *Green*	Y	Y	Y	Y	Y	Y
9 *Sensenbrenner*	Y	Y	Y	Y	Y	Y

WYOMING

District / Member	150	151	152	153	154	155
AL *Cubin*	Y	Y	Y	Y	Y	Y

Southern states - Ala., Ark., Fla., Ga., Ky., La., Miss., N.C., Okla., S.C., Tenn., Texas, Va.

Key

Y Voted for (yea).
Paired for.
+ Announced for.
N Voted against (nay).
X Paired against.
− Announced against.
P Voted "present."
C Voted "present" to avoid possible conflict of interest.
? Did not vote or otherwise make a position known.

Democrats   ***Republicans***
Independents

156. HR 700. Asian Elephants/Passage. Gilchrest, R-Md., motion to suspend the rules and pass the bill that would reauthorize through fiscal 2007 the Asian Elephant Conservation Act, which calls for up to $5 million annually in appropriations to the Interior Department's Multi-National Species Conservation Fund to conserve Asian elephants. Motion agreed to 401-15: R 197-14; D 202-1 (ND 152-0, SD 50-1); I 2-0. A two-thirds majority of those present and voting (278 in this case) is required for passage under suspension of the rules. June 12, 2001.

157. H Res 97. Shirley Chisholm Tribute/Adoption. Morella, R-Md., motion to suspend the rules and adopt the resolution that would honor the work and achievements of former Rep. Shirley Anita Chisholm, the first African-American woman to serve in Congress. Motion agreed to 415-0: R 210-0; D 203-0 (ND 152-0, SD 51-0); I 2-0. A two-thirds majority of those present and voting (277 in this case) is required for adoption under suspension of the rules. June 12, 2001.

158. Procedural Motion/Journal. Approval of the House Journal of Tuesday, June 12, 2001. Approved 374-42: R 201-13; D 171-29 (ND 125-24, SD 46-5); I 2-0. June 13, 2001.

159. HR 1157. Salmon Restocking/Passage. Passage of the bill that would authorize $200 million annually through fiscal 2004 to the states and Indian tribes of Alaska, California, Idaho, Oregon and Washington for salmon conservation and restoration projects. It would require states and localities to offer matching funds to receive federal assistance. Passed 418-6: R 211-6; D 205-0 (ND 154-0, SD 51-0); I 2-0. June 13, 2001.

160. HR 2052. Sudan Relief/Passage. Passage of the bill that would support relief programs and condemn human rights abuses in Sudan. Companies trading securities in the United States would have to disclose their Sudan operations in filings with the Securities and Exchange Commission. It also calls for the Bush administration to facilitate the peace process, support additional forms of direct relief, and spend $10 million from the fiscal 2001 foreign operations appropriations law (PL 106-429) for humanitarian assistance in Sudan. Passed 422-2: R 215-2; D 205-0 (ND 152-0, SD 53-0); I 2-0. June 13, 2001.

	156	157	158	159	160
ALABAMA					
1 *Callahan*	Y	Y	Y	Y	Y
2 *Everett*	Y	Y	Y	Y	Y
3 *Riley*	Y	Y	Y	Y	Y
4 *Aderholt*	Y	Y	N	Y	Y
5 Cramer	Y	Y	Y	Y	Y
6 *Bachus*	Y	Y	Y	Y	Y
7 Hilliard	Y	Y	N	Y	Y
ALASKA					
AL *Young*	Y	Y	?	Y	Y
ARIZONA					
1 *Flake*	N	Y	Y	N	N
2 Pastor	Y	Y	Y	Y	Y
3 *Stump*	N	Y	Y	Y	Y
4 *Shadegg*	N	Y	Y	Y	Y
5 *Kolbe*	Y	Y	Y	Y	Y
6 *Hayworth*	Y	Y	Y	Y	Y
ARKANSAS					
1 Berry	Y	Y	Y	Y	Y
2 Snyder	Y	Y	Y	Y	Y
3 *Hutchinson*	Y	Y	?	Y	Y
4 Ross	Y	Y	Y	Y	Y
CALIFORNIA					
1 Thompson	Y	Y	N	Y	Y
2 *Herger*	N	Y	Y	Y	Y
3 *Ose*	Y	Y	Y	Y	Y
4 *Doolittle*	Y	Y	Y	Y	Y
5 Matsui	Y	Y	Y	Y	Y
6 Woolsey	Y	Y	Y	Y	Y
7 Miller, George	Y	Y	?	Y	Y
8 Pelosi	Y	Y	Y	Y	Y
9 Lee	Y	Y	Y	Y	Y
10 Tauscher	Y	Y	Y	Y	Y
11 *Pombo*	Y	Y	Y	Y	Y
12 Lantos	Y	Y	Y	Y	Y
13 Stark	Y	Y	N	Y	Y
14 Eshoo	Y	Y	Y	Y	Y
15 Honda	Y	Y	Y	Y	Y
16 Lofgren	Y	Y	Y	Y	Y
17 Farr	Y	Y	Y	Y	Y
18 Condit	Y	Y	Y	Y	Y
19 *Radanovich*	Y	Y	Y	Y	Y
20 Dooley	Y	Y	Y	Y	Y
21 *Thomas*	Y	Y	Y	Y	Y
22 Capps	Y	Y	Y	Y	Y
23 *Gallegly*	Y	Y	Y	Y	Y
24 Sherman	Y	Y	Y	Y	Y
25 *McKeon*	Y	Y	Y	Y	Y
26 Berman	Y	Y	Y	Y	Y
27 Schiff	Y	Y	Y	Y	Y
28 *Dreier*	Y	Y	Y	Y	Y
29 Waxman	Y	Y	Y	Y	Y
30 Becerra	Y	Y	Y	?	Y
31 Solis	Y	Y	Y	Y	Y
32 Watson	Y	Y	?	Y	Y
33 Roybal-Allard	Y	Y	Y	Y	Y
34 Napolitano	Y	Y	Y	Y	Y
35 Waters	Y	Y	N	Y	Y
36 Harman	Y	Y	Y	Y	Y
37 Millender-McD.	Y	Y	Y	Y	Y
38 *Horn*	Y	Y	Y	Y	Y

	156	157	158	159	160
39 *Royce*	?	?	Y	N	Y
40 *Lewis*	Y	Y	Y	Y	Y
41 *Miller, Gary*	Y	Y	Y	Y	Y
42 Baca	Y	Y	Y	Y	Y
43 *Calvert*	Y	Y	Y	Y	Y
44 *Bono*	Y	Y	Y	Y	Y
45 *Rohrabacher*	Y	Y	Y	Y	Y
46 Sanchez	Y	Y	Y	Y	Y
47 *Cox*	Y	Y	Y	Y	Y
48 *Issa*	Y	Y	Y	Y	Y
49 Davis	Y	Y	Y	Y	Y
50 Filner	Y	Y	N	Y	+
51 *Cunningham*	?	?	Y	Y	Y
52 *Hunter*	Y	Y	Y	Y	Y
COLORADO					
1 DeGette	Y	Y	?	Y	Y
2 Udall	?	?	N	Y	Y
3 *McInnis*	Y	Y	Y	Y	Y
4 *Schaffer*	N	Y	N	N	Y
5 *Hefley*	Y	Y	N	Y	Y
6 *Tancredo*	Y	Y	P	Y	Y
CONNECTICUT					
1 Larson	Y	Y	Y	Y	Y
2 *Simmons*	Y	Y	Y	Y	Y
3 DeLauro	Y	Y	Y	Y	Y
4 *Shays*	Y	Y	Y	Y	Y
5 Maloney	Y	Y	Y	Y	Y
6 *Johnson*	Y	Y	Y	Y	Y
DELAWARE					
AL *Castle*	Y	Y	Y	Y	Y
FLORIDA					
1 *Scarborough*	Y	Y	Y	Y	Y
2 Boyd	Y	Y	Y	Y	Y
3 Brown	Y	Y	Y	Y	Y
4 *Crenshaw*	Y	Y	Y	Y	Y
5 Thurman	Y	Y	Y	Y	Y
6 *Stearns*	Y	Y	Y	Y	Y
7 *Mica*	Y	Y	Y	Y	Y
8 *Keller*	Y	Y	Y	Y	Y
9 *Bilirakis*	Y	Y	Y	Y	Y
10 *Young*	Y	?	Y	Y	Y
11 Davis	Y	Y	Y	Y	Y
12 *Putnam*	Y	Y	Y	Y	Y
13 *Miller*	Y	Y	Y	Y	Y
14 *Goss*	Y	Y	Y	Y	Y
15 *Weldon*	Y	Y	Y	Y	Y
16 *Foley*	Y	Y	Y	Y	Y
17 Meek	Y	Y	Y	Y	Y
18 *Ros-Lehtinen*	Y	Y	Y	Y	Y
19 Wexler	Y	Y	Y	Y	Y
20 Deutsch	Y	Y	Y	Y	Y
21 *Diaz-Balart*	?	?	Y	Y	Y
22 *Shaw*	Y	Y	Y	Y	Y
23 Hastings	Y	Y	N	Y	Y
GEORGIA					
1 *Kingston*	?	?	Y	Y	Y
2 Bishop	Y	Y	Y	Y	Y
3 *Collins*	N	Y	Y	Y	Y
4 McKinney	Y	Y	Y	Y	Y
5 Lewis	Y	Y	N	Y	Y
6 *Isakson*	Y	Y	Y	Y	Y
7 *Barr*	Y	Y	Y	Y	Y
8 *Chambliss*	Y	Y	Y	Y	Y
9 *Deal*	Y	Y	Y	Y	Y
10 *Norwood*	Y	Y	Y	Y	Y
11 *Linder*	Y	?	Y	Y	Y
HAWAII					
1 Abercrombie	Y	Y	+	+	Y
2 Mink	Y	Y	Y	Y	Y
IDAHO					
1 *Otter*	Y	Y	Y	Y	Y
2 *Simpson*	Y	Y	Y	Y	Y
ILLINOIS					
1 Rush	?	?	?	Y	?
2 Jackson	Y	Y	Y	Y	Y
3 Lipinski	Y	Y	Y	Y	Y
4 Gutierrez	Y	Y	N	Y	Y
5 Blagojevich	Y	Y	Y	Y	Y
6 *Hyde*	Y	Y	Y	Y	Y
7 Davis	Y	Y	Y	Y	Y
8 *Crane*	Y	Y	N	Y	Y
9 Schakowsky	Y	Y	Y	Y	Y
10 *Kirk*	Y	Y	Y	Y	Y
11 *Weller*	Y	Y	N	Y	Y
12 Costello	Y	Y	N	Y	Y
13 *Biggert*	Y	Y	Y	Y	Y

ND Northern Democrats   SD Southern Democrats

	156	157	158	159	160
14 ***Hastert***					
15 ***Johnson***	Y	Y	Y	Y	Y
16 ***Manzullo***	Y	Y	Y	Y	Y
17 Evans	Y	Y	Y	Y	Y
18 ***LaHood***	Y	Y	Y	Y	Y
19 Phelps	Y	Y	Y	Y	Y
20 ***Shimkus***	Y	Y	Y	Y	Y
INDIANA					
1 Visclosky	Y	Y	N	Y	Y
2 ***Pence***	?	+	Y	Y	Y
3 Roemer	Y	Y	Y	Y	Y
4 ***Souder***	Y	Y	Y	Y	Y
5 ***Buyer***	Y	Y	Y	Y	Y
6 ***Burton***	+	?	Y	Y	Y
7 ***Kerns***	N	Y	Y	Y	Y
8 ***Hostettler***	N	Y	Y	N	Y
9 Hill	Y	Y	Y	Y	Y
10 Carson	Y	Y	Y	Y	Y
IOWA					
1 ***Leach***	Y	Y	Y	Y	Y
2 ***Nussle***	Y	Y	Y	Y	Y
3 Boswell	Y	Y	Y	Y	Y
4 ***Ganske***	Y	Y	Y	Y	Y
5 ***Latham***	Y	Y	Y	Y	Y
KANSAS					
1 ***Moran***	Y	Y	Y	Y	Y
2 ***Ryun***	Y	Y	Y	Y	Y
3 Moore	Y	Y	N	Y	Y
4 ***Tiahrt***	N	Y	Y	Y	Y
KENTUCKY					
1 ***Whitfield***	Y	Y	Y	Y	Y
2 ***Lewis***	Y	Y	Y	Y	Y
3 ***Northup***	Y	Y	Y	Y	Y
4 Lucas	Y	Y	Y	Y	Y
5 ***Rogers***	Y	Y	Y	Y	Y
6 ***Fletcher***	Y	Y	Y	Y	Y
LOUISIANA					
1 ***Vitter***	Y	Y	Y	Y	Y
2 Jefferson	Y	Y	?	Y	Y
3 ***Tauzin***	Y	Y	Y	Y	Y
4 ***McCrery***	Y	Y	Y	Y	Y
5 ***Cooksey***	Y	Y	Y	Y	Y
6 ***Baker***	Y	Y	Y	Y	Y
7 John	Y	Y	Y	?	Y
MAINE					
1 Allen	Y	Y	Y	Y	+
2 Baldacci	Y	Y	Y	Y	Y
MARYLAND					
1 ***Gilchrest***	Y	Y	Y	Y	Y
2 ***Ehrlich***	Y	Y	Y	Y	Y
3 Cardin	Y	Y	Y	Y	Y
4 Wynn	Y	Y	Y	Y	Y
5 Hoyer	Y	Y	Y	Y	Y
6 ***Bartlett***	Y	Y	Y	Y	Y
7 Cummings	Y	Y	Y	Y	Y
8 ***Morella***	Y	Y	Y	Y	?
MASSACHUSETTS					
1 Olver	Y	Y	Y	Y	Y
2 Neal	Y	Y	Y	Y	Y
3 McGovern	Y	Y	Y	Y	Y
4 Frank	Y	Y	Y	Y	Y
5 Meehan	Y	Y	Y	Y	Y
6 Tierney	Y	Y	Y	Y	Y
7 Markey	Y	Y	Y	Y	Y
8 Capuano	Y	Y	N	Y	Y
9 Vacant					
10 Delahunt	Y	Y	Y	Y	Y
MICHIGAN					
1 Stupak	Y	Y	N	Y	Y
2 ***Hoekstra***	Y	Y	Y	Y	Y
3 ***Ehlers***	Y	Y	Y	Y	Y
4 ***Camp***	Y	Y	Y	Y	Y
5 Barcia	Y	Y	Y	Y	Y
6 ***Upton***	Y	Y	Y	Y	Y
7 ***Smith***	Y	Y	Y	Y	Y
8 ***Rogers***	Y	Y	Y	Y	Y
9 Kildee	Y	Y	Y	Y	Y
10 Bonior	Y	Y	Y	Y	Y
11 ***Knollenberg***	Y	Y	Y	Y	Y
12 Levin	Y	Y	Y	Y	Y
13 Rivers	Y	Y	Y	Y	Y
14 Conyers	Y	Y	Y	Y	Y
15 Kilpatrick	Y	Y	Y	Y	Y
16 Dingell	Y	Y	?	Y	?

	156	157	158	159	160
MINNESOTA					
1 ***Gutknecht***	Y	Y	N	Y	Y
2 ***Kennedy***	Y	Y	N	Y	Y
3 ***Ramstad***	Y	Y	N	Y	Y
4 McCollum	Y	Y	Y	Y	Y
5 Sabo	Y	Y	N	Y	Y
6 Luther	Y	Y	Y	Y	Y
7 Peterson	Y	Y	Y	Y	Y
8 Oberstar	Y	Y	N	Y	Y
MISSISSIPPI					
1 ***Wicker***	Y	Y	Y	Y	Y
2 Thompson	Y	Y	N	Y	Y
3 ***Pickering***	Y	Y	Y	Y	Y
4 Shows	Y	Y	Y	Y	Y
5 Taylor	Y	Y	N	Y	Y
MISSOURI					
1 Clay	Y	Y	Y	Y	Y
2 ***Akin***	N	Y	Y	Y	Y
3 Gephardt	Y	Y	Y	Y	Y
4 Skelton	Y	Y	?	Y	Y
5 McCarthy	Y	Y	Y	Y	Y
6 ***Graves***	Y	Y	Y	Y	Y
7 ***Blunt***	Y	Y	Y	Y	Y
8 ***Emerson***	Y	Y	Y	Y	Y
9 ***Hulshof***	Y	Y	N	Y	Y
MONTANA					
AL ***Rehberg***	Y	Y	Y	Y	Y
NEBRASKA					
1 ***Bereuter***	Y	Y	Y	Y	Y
2 ***Terry***	Y	Y	Y	Y	Y
3 ***Osborne***	Y	Y	N	Y	Y
NEVADA					
1 Berkley	Y	Y	Y	Y	Y
2 ***Gibbons***	Y	Y	Y	Y	Y
NEW HAMPSHIRE					
1 ***Sununu***	Y	Y	Y	Y	Y
2 ***Bass***	Y	Y	Y	Y	Y
NEW JERSEY					
1 Andrews	Y	Y	Y	Y	Y
2 ***LoBiondo***	Y	Y	N	Y	Y
3 ***Saxton***	Y	Y	Y	Y	Y
4 ***Smith***	Y	Y	Y	Y	Y
5 ***Roukema***	Y	Y	Y	Y	Y
6 Pallone	Y	Y	N	Y	Y
7 ***Ferguson***	?	?	?	?	?
8 Pascrell	Y	Y	Y	Y	Y
9 Rothman	Y	Y	Y	Y	Y
10 Payne	Y	Y	Y	Y	Y
11 ***Frelinghuysen***	Y	Y	Y	Y	Y
12 Holt	Y	Y	Y	Y	Y
13 Menendez	Y	Y	N	Y	Y
NEW MEXICO					
1 ***Wilson***	Y	Y	Y	Y	Y
2 ***Skeen***	Y	Y	Y	Y	Y
3 Udall	Y	Y	N	Y	Y
NEW YORK					
1 ***Grucci***	Y	Y	Y	Y	Y
2 Israel	Y	Y	Y	Y	Y
3 ***King***	Y	Y	Y	Y	Y
4 McCarthy	Y	Y	Y	Y	Y
5 Ackerman	Y	Y	Y	Y	Y
6 Meeks	Y	Y	Y	Y	Y
7 Crowley	Y	Y	N	Y	Y
8 Nadler	Y	Y	Y	Y	Y
9 Weiner	Y	Y	Y	Y	Y
10 Towns	Y	Y	Y	Y	Y
11 Owens	Y	Y	Y	Y	Y
12 Velázquez	?	?	Y	Y	Y
13 ***Fossella***	Y	Y	?	?	?
14 Maloney	Y	Y	Y	Y	Y
15 Rangel	Y	Y	Y	Y	Y
16 Serrano	Y	Y	Y	Y	Y
17 Engel	Y	Y	Y	Y	Y
18 Lowey	Y	Y	Y	Y	Y
19 ***Kelly***	Y	Y	Y	Y	Y
20 ***Gilman***	Y	Y	Y	Y	Y
21 McNulty	Y	Y	N	Y	Y
22 ***Sweeney***	Y	Y	N	Y	Y
23 ***Boehlert***	Y	Y	Y	Y	Y
24 ***McHugh***	Y	Y	Y	Y	Y
25 ***Walsh***	?	Y	Y	Y	Y
26 Hinchey	Y	Y	Y	Y	Y
27 ***Reynolds***	Y	Y	Y	Y	Y
28 Slaughter	Y	Y	Y	Y	Y
29 LaFalce	Y	Y	Y	Y	Y

	156	157	158	159	160
30 ***Quinn***	Y	Y	Y	Y	Y
31 ***Houghton***	Y	Y	Y	Y	Y
NORTH CAROLINA					
1 Clayton	Y	Y	Y	Y	Y
2 Etheridge	Y	Y	Y	Y	Y
3 ***Jones***	Y	Y	Y	Y	Y
4 Price	Y	Y	Y	Y	Y
5 ***Burr***	Y	Y	Y	Y	Y
6 ***Coble***	N	Y	Y	Y	Y
7 McIntyre	Y	Y	Y	Y	Y
8 ***Hayes***	Y	Y	Y	Y	Y
9 ***Myrick***	Y	Y	Y	Y	Y
10 ***Ballenger***	Y	Y	Y	Y	Y
11 ***Taylor***	Y	Y	Y	Y	Y
12 Watt	Y	Y	Y	Y	Y
NORTH DAKOTA					
AL Pomeroy	Y	Y	Y	Y	Y
OHIO					
1 ***Chabot***	Y	Y	Y	Y	Y
2 ***Portman***	Y	Y	Y	Y	Y
3 Hall	Y	Y	Y	Y	Y
4 ***Oxley***	Y	Y	Y	Y	Y
5 ***Gillmor***	Y	Y	Y	Y	Y
6 Strickland	Y	Y	Y	Y	Y
7 ***Hobson***	Y	Y	Y	Y	Y
8 ***Boehner***	Y	Y	Y	Y	Y
9 Kaptur	Y	Y	Y	Y	Y
10 Kucinich	Y	Y	N	Y	Y
11 Jones	Y	Y	Y	Y	Y
12 ***Tiberi***	Y	Y	Y	Y	Y
13 Brown	Y	Y	Y	Y	Y
14 Sawyer	Y	Y	Y	Y	Y
15 ***Pryce***	Y	Y	Y	Y	Y
16 ***Regula***	Y	Y	Y	Y	Y
17 Traficant	Y	Y	Y	Y	Y
18 ***Ney***	Y	Y	Y	Y	Y
19 ***LaTourette***	Y	Y	Y	Y	Y
OKLAHOMA					
1 ***Largent***	?	?	?	Y	Y
2 Carson	Y	Y	Y	Y	Y
3 ***Watkins***	Y	Y	Y	Y	Y
4 ***Watts***	Y	Y	Y	Y	Y
5 ***Istook***	Y	Y	Y	Y	Y
6 ***Lucas***	Y	Y	Y	Y	Y
OREGON					
1 Wu	Y	Y	Y	Y	Y
2 ***Walden***	Y	Y	Y	Y	Y
3 Blumenauer	Y	Y	Y	Y	Y
4 DeFazio	Y	Y	N	Y	Y
5 Hooley	Y	Y	Y	Y	Y
PENNSYLVANIA					
1 Brady	Y	Y	N	Y	Y
2 Fattah	Y	Y	Y	Y	Y
3 Borski	Y	Y	N	Y	Y
4 ***Hart***	Y	Y	Y	Y	Y
5 ***Peterson***	Y	Y	Y	Y	Y
6 Holden	Y	Y	Y	Y	Y
7 ***Weldon***	Y	Y	Y	?	Y
8 ***Greenwood***	Y	Y	Y	Y	Y
9 ***Shuster, Bill***	Y	Y	Y	Y	Y
10 ***Sherwood***	Y	Y	Y	Y	Y
11 Kanjorski	Y	Y	Y	Y	Y
12 Murtha	Y	Y	Y	Y	Y
13 Hoeffel	Y	Y	Y	Y	Y
14 Coyne	Y	Y	Y	Y	Y
15 ***Toomey***	N	Y	Y	Y	Y
16 ***Pitts***	Y	Y	Y	Y	Y
17 ***Gekas***	Y	Y	Y	Y	Y
18 Doyle	Y	Y	Y	Y	Y
19 ***Platts***	Y	Y	Y	Y	Y
20 Mascara	Y	Y	Y	Y	Y
21 ***English***	Y	Y	N	Y	Y
RHODE ISLAND					
1 Kennedy	Y	Y	Y	Y	Y
2 Langevin	Y	Y	Y	Y	Y
SOUTH CAROLINA					
1 ***Brown***	Y	Y	Y	Y	Y
2 ***Spence***	Y	Y	Y	Y	Y
3 ***Graham***	Y	Y	Y	Y	Y
4 ***DeMint***	Y	Y	Y	Y	Y
5 Spratt	Y	Y	Y	Y	Y
6 Clyburn	Y	Y	Y	Y	Y
SOUTH DAKOTA					
AL ***Thune***	Y	Y	Y	Y	Y

	156	157	158	159	160
TENNESSEE					
1 ***Jenkins***	Y	Y	Y	Y	Y
2 ***Duncan***	Y	Y	Y	Y	Y
3 ***Wamp***	Y	Y	Y	Y	Y
4 ***Hilleary***	Y	Y	Y	Y	Y
5 Clement	Y	Y	Y	Y	Y
6 Gordon	Y	Y	Y	Y	Y
7 ***Bryant***	Y	Y	Y	Y	Y
8 Tanner	?	?	?	?	Y
9 Ford	Y	Y	Y	Y	Y
TEXAS					
1 Sandlin	Y	Y	Y	Y	Y
2 Turner	Y	Y	Y	Y	Y
3 ***Johnson, Sam***	Y	Y	Y	Y	Y
4 Hall	N	Y	Y	Y	Y
5 ***Sessions***	Y	Y	Y	Y	Y
6 ***Barton***	Y	Y	Y	Y	Y
7 ***Culberson***	N	Y	Y	Y	Y
8 ***Brady***	Y	Y	Y	N	Y
9 Lampson	Y	Y	Y	Y	Y
10 Doggett	Y	Y	Y	Y	Y
11 Edwards	Y	Y	Y	Y	Y
12 ***Granger***	Y	Y	Y	Y	Y
13 ***Thornberry***	Y	Y	Y	Y	Y
14 ***Paul***	N	Y	Y	N	N
15 Hinojosa	Y	Y	Y	Y	Y
16 Reyes	Y	Y	Y	Y	Y
17 Stenholm	Y	Y	Y	Y	Y
18 Jackson-Lee	?	?	Y	Y	Y
19 ***Combest***	Y	Y	Y	Y	Y
20 Gonzalez	Y	Y	Y	Y	Y
21 ***Smith***	Y	Y	Y	Y	Y
22 ***DeLay***	Y	Y	Y	Y	Y
23 ***Bonilla***	Y	Y	Y	Y	Y
24 Frost	Y	Y	Y	Y	Y
25 Bentsen	Y	Y	Y	Y	Y
26 ***Armey***	Y	Y	Y	Y	Y
27 Ortiz	Y	Y	Y	Y	Y
28 Rodriguez	Y	Y	Y	Y	Y
29 Green	Y	Y	Y	Y	Y
30 Johnson, E.B.	?	?	?	?	?
UTAH					
1 ***Hansen***	Y	Y	Y	Y	Y
2 Matheson	Y	Y	Y	Y	Y
3 ***Cannon***	Y	Y	Y	Y	Y
VERMONT					
AL *Sanders*	Y	Y	Y	Y	Y
VIRGINIA					
1 ***Davis, Jo Ann***	Y	Y	Y	Y	Y
2 ***Schrock***	Y	Y	Y	Y	Y
3 Scott	Y	Y	Y	Y	Y
4 Vacant					
5 *Goode*	Y	Y	Y	Y	Y
6 ***Goodlatte***	Y	Y	Y	Y	Y
7 ***Cantor***	Y	Y	Y	Y	Y
8 Moran	Y	Y	Y	Y	Y
9 Boucher	Y	Y	Y	Y	Y
10 ***Wolf***	Y	Y	Y	Y	Y
11 ***Davis, T.***	Y	Y	Y	Y	Y
WASHINGTON					
1 Inslee	Y	Y	Y	Y	Y
2 Larsen	Y	Y	N	Y	Y
3 Baird	Y	Y	Y	Y	Y
4 ***Hastings***	Y	Y	Y	Y	Y
5 ***Nethercutt***	Y	Y	Y	Y	Y
6 Dicks	Y	Y	Y	Y	Y
7 McDermott	Y	Y	N	Y	Y
8 ***Dunn***	Y	Y	Y	Y	Y
9 Smith	Y	Y	Y	Y	Y
WEST VIRGINIA					
1 Mollohan	?	?	Y	Y	Y
2 ***Capito***	Y	Y	Y	Y	Y
3 Rahall	Y	Y	Y	Y	Y
WISCONSIN					
1 ***Ryan***	Y	Y	Y	Y	Y
2 Baldwin	Y	Y	Y	Y	Y
3 Kind	Y	Y	Y	Y	Y
4 Kleczka	Y	Y	Y	Y	Y
5 Barrett	Y	Y	Y	Y	Y
6 ***Petri***	Y	Y	Y	Y	Y
7 Obey	Y	Y	Y	Y	Y
8 ***Green***	Y	Y	Y	Y	Y
9 ***Sensenbrenner***	Y	Y	Y	Y	Y
WYOMING					
AL ***Cubin***	Y	Y	Y	Y	Y

Southern states - Ala., Ark., Fla., Ga., Ky., La., Miss., N.C., Okla., S.C., Tenn., Texas, Va.

Y   Voted for (yea).
\#   Paired for.
\+   Announced for.
N   Voted against (nay).
X   Paired against.
−   Announced against.
P   Voted "present."
C   Voted "present" to avoid possible conflict of interest.
?   Did not vote or otherwise make a position known.

Democrats   **Republicans**
Independents

161. H Con Res 145. Afghan Human Rights/Adoption. Adoption of the concurrent resolution that would condemn the Taliban regime's forcing of Hindus in Afghanistan to wear symbols identifying them as Hindu and would call for the policy's revocation. It also urges Pakistan to push the Taliban to revoke the policy and supports humanitarian assistance for the Afghan people. Adopted 420-0: R 215-0; D 203-0 (ND 152-0, SD 51-0); I 2-0. June 13, 2001.

162. HR 1088. SEC Fees and Salaries/Previous Question. Linder, R-Ga., motion to order the previous question (thus ending debate and possibility of amendment) on adoption of the rule (H Res 161) to provide for House floor consideration of the bill that would reduce Securities and Exchange Commission fees by $14 billion over 10 years and allow for an increase in SEC employee compensation. Motion agreed to 418-1: R 215-0; D 201-1 (ND 150-1, SD 51-0); I 2-0. June 14, 2001.

163. HR 1088. SEC Fees and Salaries/Rule. Adoption of the rule (H Res 161) to provide for House floor consideration of the bill that would reduce Securities and Exchange Commission fees by $14 billion over 10 years and allow for an increase in SEC employee compensation. Adopted 408-12: R 214-1; D 192-11 (ND 144-9, SD 48-2); I 2-0. June 14, 2001.

164. HR 1088. SEC Fees and Salaries/Democratic Substitute. LaFalce, D-N.Y., substitute amendment that would reduce SEC securities transaction fees (Section 31 fees) at a cost of $4.8 billion over 10 years. It also would provide for SEC employee compensation parity with other federal banking regulators. Rejected 126-299: R 0-215; D 125-83 (ND 101-54, SD 24-29); I 1-1. June 14, 2001.

165. HR 1088. SEC Fees and Salaries/Passage. Passage of the bill that would reduce Securities and Exchange Commission fees by $14 billion over 10 years and allow for an increase in SEC employee compensation. The measure would lower SEC fees for securities registrations and transactions, merger and tender offers, and single stock future assessments. It also would eliminate the Trust Indenture Act filing fee. The measure would require the agency to adjust registration and transaction fees annually after fiscal 2002 for changing market conditions. It also would change fees' budgetary treatment to record them as "offsetting collections." A new demonstration project would allow the commission to raise employee pay and benefits to levels comparable with other federal bank regulatory agencies. Passed 404-22: R 214-2; D 188-20 (ND 139-17, SD 49-3); I 2-0. June 14, 2001.

	161	162	163	164	165
ALABAMA					
1 *Callahan*	Y	Y	Y	N	Y
2 *Everett*	Y	Y	Y	N	Y
3 *Riley*	Y	Y	Y	N	Y
4 *Aderholt*	Y	Y	Y	N	Y
5 Cramer	Y	Y	Y	N	Y
6 *Bachus*	Y	Y	Y	N	Y
7 Hilliard	Y	Y	N	Y	Y
ALASKA					
AL *Young*	Y	?	?	N	Y
ARIZONA					
1 *Flake*	Y	Y	Y	N	Y
2 Pastor	Y	Y	Y	Y	Y
3 *Stump*	Y	Y	Y	N	Y
4 *Shadegg*	Y	Y	Y	N	Y
5 *Kolbe*	Y	Y	Y	N	Y
6 *Hayworth*	Y	Y	Y	N	Y
ARKANSAS					
1 Berry	Y	Y	Y	N	Y
2 Snyder	Y	Y	Y	N	Y
3 *Hutchinson*	Y	Y	Y	N	Y
4 Ross	Y	Y	Y	N	Y
CALIFORNIA					
1 Thompson	Y	Y	Y	Y	Y
2 *Herger*	Y	Y	Y	N	Y
3 *Ose*	Y	Y	Y	N	Y
4 *Doolittle*	Y	Y	Y	N	Y
5 Matsui	Y	Y	Y	Y	Y
6 Woolsey	Y	Y	Y	Y	Y
7 Miller, George	Y	Y	Y	Y	Y
8 Pelosi	Y	Y	Y	Y	Y
9 Lee	Y	Y	Y	Y	N
10 Tauscher	Y	Y	Y	N	Y
11 *Pombo*	Y	Y	Y	N	Y
12 Lantos	Y	Y	Y	Y	Y
13 Stark	Y	Y	Y	Y	N
14 Eshoo	Y	Y	Y	Y	Y
15 Honda	Y	Y	Y	Y	Y
16 Lofgren	Y	Y	Y	N	Y
17 Farr	Y	Y	Y	Y	Y
18 Condit	Y	Y	Y	N	Y
19 *Radanovich*	Y	Y	Y	N	Y
20 Dooley	Y	Y	Y	N	Y
21 *Thomas*	Y	Y	Y	N	Y
22 Capps	Y	Y	Y	N	Y
23 *Gallegly*	Y	Y	Y	N	Y
24 Sherman	Y	Y	Y	N	Y
25 *McKeon*	Y	Y	Y	N	Y
26 Berman	Y	Y	Y	Y	Y
27 Schiff	Y	Y	Y	Y	Y
28 *Dreier*	Y	Y	Y	N	Y
29 Waxman	Y	Y	Y	Y	Y
30 Becerra	Y	Y	Y	Y	Y
31 Solis	Y	Y	Y	Y	Y
32 Watson	Y	Y	Y	Y	Y
33 Roybal-Allard	Y	Y	Y	Y	Y
34 Napolitano	Y	Y	Y	Y	Y
35 Waters	Y	Y	N	Y	N
36 Harman	Y	Y	Y	Y	Y
37 Millender-McD.	Y	Y	Y	Y	Y
38 *Horn*	Y	Y	Y	N	Y

	161	162	163	164	165
39 *Royce*	Y	Y	Y	N	Y
40 *Lewis*	Y	Y	Y	N	Y
41 *Miller, Gary*	Y	Y	Y	N	Y
42 Baca	Y	Y	Y	Y	Y
43 *Calvert*	Y	Y	Y	N	Y
44 *Bono*	Y	Y	Y	N	Y
45 *Rohrabacher*	Y	Y	Y	N	Y
46 Sanchez	Y	Y	Y	N	Y
47 *Cox*	Y	Y	Y	N	Y
48 *Issa*	Y	Y	Y	N	Y
49 Davis	Y	Y	Y	N	Y
50 Filner	Y	Y	Y	Y	N
51 *Cunningham*	Y	Y	Y	N	Y
52 *Hunter*	Y	Y	Y	N	Y
COLORADO					
1 DeGette	Y	?	?	Y	Y
2 Udall	Y	Y	Y	Y	Y
3 *McInnis*	Y	Y	Y	N	Y
4 *Schaffer*	Y	Y	Y	N	Y
5 *Hefley*	Y	Y	Y	N	Y
6 *Tancredo*	Y	Y	Y	N	Y
CONNECTICUT					
1 Larson	+	Y	Y	Y	Y
2 *Simmons*	Y	Y	Y	N	Y
3 DeLauro	Y	Y	Y	Y	Y
4 *Shays*	Y	Y	Y	N	Y
5 Maloney	Y	Y	Y	N	Y
6 *Johnson*	Y	Y	Y	N	Y
DELAWARE					
AL *Castle*	Y	Y	Y	N	Y
FLORIDA					
1 *Scarborough*	Y	Y	Y	N	Y
2 Boyd	Y	Y	Y	Y	Y
3 Brown	Y	?	?	Y	Y
4 *Crenshaw*	Y	Y	Y	N	Y
5 Thurman	Y	Y	Y	Y	N
6 *Stearns*	Y	Y	Y	N	Y
7 *Mica*	Y	Y	Y	N	Y
8 *Keller*	Y	Y	Y	N	Y
9 *Bilirakis*	Y	Y	Y	N	Y
10 *Young*	Y	Y	Y	N	Y
11 Davis	Y	Y	Y	N	Y
12 *Putnam*	Y	Y	Y	N	Y
13 *Miller*	Y	Y	Y	N	Y
14 *Goss*	Y	Y	Y	N	Y
15 *Weldon*	Y	Y	Y	N	Y
16 *Foley*	Y	Y	Y	N	Y
17 Meek	?	Y	Y	Y	Y
18 *Ros-Lehtinen*	Y	Y	Y	N	Y
19 Wexler	Y	Y	Y	N	Y
20 Deutsch	Y	Y	Y	N	Y
21 *Diaz-Balart*	Y	Y	Y	N	Y
22 *Shaw*	Y	Y	Y	N	Y
23 Hastings	Y	Y	Y	Y	Y
GEORGIA					
1 *Kingston*	Y	Y	Y	N	Y
2 Bishop	Y	Y	Y	N	Y
3 *Collins*	Y	Y	Y	N	Y
4 McKinney	Y	Y	Y	Y	Y
5 Lewis	Y	Y	Y	Y	Y
6 *Isakson*	Y	Y	Y	N	Y
7 *Barr*	Y	Y	Y	N	Y
8 *Chambliss*	Y	Y	Y	N	Y
9 *Deal*	Y	Y	Y	N	Y
10 *Norwood*	Y	Y	Y	N	Y
11 *Linder*	Y	Y	Y	N	Y
HAWAII					
1 Abercrombie	Y	Y	Y	Y	Y
2 Mink	Y	Y	Y	Y	Y
IDAHO					
1 *Otter*	Y	Y	Y	N	Y
2 *Simpson*	Y	Y	Y	N	Y
ILLINOIS					
1 Rush	Y	Y	Y	N	Y
2 Jackson	Y	Y	Y	Y	Y
3 Lipinski	Y	Y	Y	N	Y
4 Gutierrez	Y	Y	Y	N	Y
5 Blagojevich	Y	Y	Y	N	Y
6 *Hyde*	Y	Y	Y	N	Y
7 Davis	Y	Y	Y	N	Y
8 *Crane*	Y	Y	Y	N	Y
9 Schakowsky	Y	Y	Y	Y	Y
10 *Kirk*	Y	Y	Y	N	Y
11 *Weller*	Y	Y	Y	N	Y
12 Costello	Y	Y	N	N	Y
13 *Biggert*	Y	Y	Y	N	Y

ND Northern Democrats   SD Southern Democrats

	161	162	163	164	165
14 ***Hastert***					
15 ***Johnson***	Y	Y	Y	N	Y
16 ***Manzullo***	Y	Y	Y	N	Y
17 Evans	Y	Y	Y	Y	Y
18 ***LaHood***	Y	Y	Y	N	Y
19 Phelps	Y	Y	Y	N	Y
20 ***Shimkus***	Y	Y	Y	N	Y
INDIANA					
1 Visclosky	Y	Y	N	Y	N
2 ***Pence***	Y	Y	Y	N	Y
3 Roemer	Y	Y	Y	N	Y
4 ***Souder***	Y	Y	Y	N	Y
5 ***Buyer***	Y	Y	Y	N	Y
6 ***Burton***	Y	Y	N	N	N
7 ***Kerns***	Y	Y	Y	N	Y
8 ***Hostettler***	?	Y	Y	N	Y
9 Hill	?	Y	Y	N	Y
10 Carson	Y	+	Y	Y	Y
IOWA					
1 ***Leach***	Y	Y	Y	N	Y
2 ***Nussle***	Y	Y	Y	N	Y
3 Boswell	Y	Y	Y	Y	Y
4 ***Ganske***	Y	Y	Y	N	Y
5 ***Latham***	Y	Y	Y	N	Y
KANSAS					
1 ***Moran***	Y	Y	Y	N	Y
2 ***Ryun***	Y	Y	Y	N	Y
3 Moore	Y	Y	Y	N	Y
4 ***Tiahrt***	Y	Y	Y	N	Y
KENTUCKY					
1 ***Whitfield***	Y	?	?	N	Y
2 ***Lewis***	Y	Y	Y	N	Y
3 ***Northup***	Y	Y	Y	N	Y
4 Lucas	Y	Y	Y	N	Y
5 ***Rogers***	Y	Y	Y	N	Y
6 ***Fletcher***	Y	Y	Y	N	Y
LOUISIANA					
1 ***Vitter***	Y	Y	Y	N	Y
2 Jefferson	Y	Y	Y	N	?
3 ***Tauzin***	Y	Y	Y	N	Y
4 ***McCrery***	Y	Y	Y	N	Y
5 ***Cooksey***	Y	Y	Y	N	Y
6 ***Baker***	Y	Y	Y	N	Y
7 John	Y	Y	?	N	Y
MAINE					
1 Allen	+	Y	Y	Y	Y
2 Baldacci	Y	Y	Y	Y	Y
MARYLAND					
1 ***Gilchrest***	Y	Y	Y	N	Y
2 ***Ehrlich***	Y	Y	Y	N	Y
3 Cardin	Y	Y	Y	Y	Y
4 Wynn	Y	Y	Y	Y	Y
5 Hoyer	Y	Y	Y	Y	Y
6 ***Bartlett***	Y	Y	Y	N	Y
7 Cummings	Y	?	Y	Y	Y
8 ***Morella***	Y	Y	Y	N	Y
MASSACHUSETTS					
1 Olver	Y	Y	Y	Y	N
2 Neal	Y	Y	Y	Y	Y
3 McGovern	Y	Y	Y	Y	Y
4 Frank	Y	Y	N	Y	Y
5 Meehan	Y	Y	Y	Y	Y
6 Tierney	Y	Y	Y	Y	N
7 Markey	Y	Y	Y	Y	N
8 Capuano	Y	Y	Y	Y	Y
9 Vacant					
10 Delahunt	Y	Y	Y	Y	N
MICHIGAN					
1 Stupak	Y	Y	Y	Y	Y
2 ***Hoekstra***	?	Y	Y	N	Y
3 ***Ehlers***	Y	Y	Y	N	Y
4 ***Camp***	Y	Y	Y	N	Y
5 Barcia	Y	Y	Y	N	Y
6 ***Upton***	Y	Y	Y	N	Y
7 ***Smith***	Y	Y	Y	N	Y
8 ***Rogers***	Y	Y	Y	N	Y
9 Kildee	Y	Y	Y	Y	Y
10 Bonior	Y	Y	Y	Y	Y
11 ***Knollenberg***	Y	Y	Y	N	Y
12 Levin	Y	Y	Y	Y	Y
13 Rivers	Y	Y	Y	Y	Y
14 Conyers	Y	Y	Y	Y	Y
15 Kilpatrick	Y	Y	Y	Y	Y
16 Dingell	Y	Y	Y	Y	N

	161	162	163	164	165
MINNESOTA					
1 ***Gutknecht***	Y	Y	Y	N	Y
2 ***Kennedy***	Y	Y	Y	N	Y
3 ***Ramstad***	Y	Y	Y	N	Y
4 McCollum	Y	Y	Y	Y	Y
5 Sabo	Y	Y	Y	Y	Y
6 Luther	Y	Y	Y	Y	Y
7 Peterson	Y	Y	Y	N	Y
8 Oberstar	Y	Y	Y	Y	Y
MISSISSIPPI					
1 ***Wicker***	Y	Y	Y	N	Y
2 Thompson	Y	Y	Y	Y	Y
3 ***Pickering***	Y	Y	Y	N	Y
4 Shows	Y	Y	Y	N	Y
5 Taylor	Y	Y	N	Y	N
MISSOURI					
1 Clay	Y	Y	Y	Y	Y
2 ***Akin***	Y	Y	Y	N	Y
3 Gephardt	Y	Y	Y	Y	Y
4 Skelton	Y	Y	Y	Y	Y
5 McCarthy	Y	Y	Y	Y	Y
6 ***Graves***	Y	Y	Y	N	Y
7 ***Blunt***	Y	Y	Y	N	Y
8 ***Emerson***	Y	Y	Y	N	Y
9 ***Hulshof***	Y	Y	Y	N	Y
MONTANA					
AL ***Rehberg***	Y	Y	Y	N	Y
NEBRASKA					
1 ***Bereuter***	Y	Y	Y	N	Y
2 ***Terry***	Y	Y	Y	N	Y
3 ***Osborne***	Y	Y	Y	N	Y
NEVADA					
1 Berkley	Y	Y	Y	N	Y
2 ***Gibbons***	Y	Y	Y	N	Y
NEW HAMPSHIRE					
1 ***Sununu***	Y	Y	Y	N	Y
2 ***Bass***	Y	Y	Y	N	Y
NEW JERSEY					
1 Andrews	Y	Y	Y	N	Y
2 ***LoBiondo***	Y	Y	Y	N	Y
3 ***Saxton***	Y	Y	Y	N	Y
4 ***Smith***	Y	Y	Y	N	Y
5 ***Roukema***	Y	Y	Y	N	Y
6 Pallone	Y	Y	Y	N	Y
7 ***Ferguson***	?	?	?	?	?
8 Pascrell	Y	Y	Y	N	Y
9 Rothman	Y	Y	Y	N	Y
10 Payne	Y	Y	Y	Y	Y
11 ***Frelinghuysen***	Y	Y	Y	N	Y
12 Holt	Y	Y	Y	N	Y
13 Menendez	Y	Y	Y	N	Y
NEW MEXICO					
1 ***Wilson***	Y	Y	Y	N	Y
2 ***Skeen***	Y	Y	Y	N	Y
3 Udall	Y	Y	Y	Y	Y
NEW YORK					
1 ***Grucci***	Y	Y	Y	N	Y
2 Israel	Y	Y	Y	N	Y
3 ***King***	Y	Y	Y	N	Y
4 McCarthy	Y	Y	Y	N	Y
5 Ackerman	Y	Y	Y	N	Y
6 Meeks	Y	Y	Y	N	Y
7 Crowley	Y	Y	Y	N	Y
8 Nadler	Y	Y	Y	N	Y
9 Weiner	Y	Y	Y	N	Y
10 Towns	Y	Y	Y	N	Y
11 Owens	Y	Y	Y	Y	Y
12 Velázquez	Y	Y	?	N	Y
13 ***Fossella***	?	Y	Y	N	Y
14 Maloney	Y	Y	Y	N	Y
15 Rangel	Y	Y	Y	N	Y
16 Serrano	Y	Y	Y	Y	Y
17 Engel	Y	?	Y	N	Y
18 Lowey	?	Y	Y	N	Y
19 ***Kelly***	Y	Y	Y	N	Y
20 ***Gilman***	Y	Y	Y	N	Y
21 McNulty	Y	Y	Y	N	Y
22 ***Sweeney***	Y	Y	Y	N	Y
23 ***Boehlert***	Y	Y	Y	N	Y
24 ***McHugh***	Y	Y	Y	N	Y
25 ***Walsh***	Y	Y	Y	N	Y
26 Hinchey	Y	Y	Y	Y	Y
27 ***Reynolds***	Y	Y	Y	N	Y
28 Slaughter	Y	Y	Y	Y	Y
29 LaFalce	Y	Y	N	Y	N

	161	162	163	164	165
30 ***Quinn***	Y	Y	Y	N	Y
31 ***Houghton***	Y	?	?	?	?
NORTH CAROLINA					
1 Clayton	Y	Y	Y	Y	N
2 Etheridge	Y	Y	Y	Y	Y
3 ***Jones***	Y	Y	Y	N	Y
4 Price	Y	Y	Y	Y	Y
5 ***Burr***	?	Y	Y	N	Y
6 ***Coble***	Y	Y	Y	N	Y
7 McIntyre	Y	Y	Y	N	Y
8 ***Hayes***	Y	Y	Y	N	Y
9 ***Myrick***	Y	Y	Y	N	Y
10 ***Ballenger***	Y	Y	Y	N	Y
11 ***Taylor***	Y	Y	Y	N	Y
12 Watt	Y	Y	Y	Y	Y
NORTH DAKOTA					
AL Pomeroy	Y	Y	Y	Y	Y
OHIO					
1 ***Chabot***	Y	Y	Y	N	Y
2 ***Portman***	Y	Y	Y	N	Y
3 Hall	Y	Y	Y	N	Y
4 ***Oxley***	Y	Y	Y	N	Y
5 ***Gillmor***	Y	Y	Y	N	Y
6 Strickland	Y	Y	Y	N	Y
7 ***Hobson***	Y	Y	Y	N	Y
8 ***Boehner***	Y	Y	Y	N	Y
9 Kaptur	Y	Y	Y	Y	N
10 Kucinich	Y	Y	Y	N	N
11 Jones	Y	?	?	?	N
12 ***Tiberi***	Y	Y	Y	N	Y
13 Brown	Y	Y	Y	Y	Y
14 Sawyer	Y	Y	Y	Y	Y
15 ***Pryce***	Y	Y	Y	N	Y
16 ***Regula***	Y	Y	Y	N	Y
17 Traficant	Y	Y	Y	N	Y
18 ***Ney***	Y	Y	Y	N	Y
19 ***LaTourette***	Y	Y	Y	N	Y
OKLAHOMA					
1 ***Largent***	Y	Y	Y	N	Y
2 Carson	Y	Y	Y	N	Y
3 ***Watkins***	Y	Y	Y	N	Y
4 ***Watts***	Y	Y	Y	–	Y
5 ***Istook***	Y	Y	Y	N	Y
6 ***Lucas***	Y	Y	Y	?	Y
OREGON					
1 Wu	Y	Y	N	N	Y
2 ***Walden***	Y	Y	Y	N	Y
3 Blumenauer	Y	Y	Y	N	Y
4 DeFazio	Y	Y	N	Y	N
5 Hooley	Y	Y	Y	Y	Y
PENNSYLVANIA					
1 Brady	Y	Y	Y	Y	Y
2 Fattah	Y	Y	Y	Y	Y
3 Borski	Y	Y	Y	Y	Y
4 ***Hart***	Y	Y	Y	N	Y
5 ***Peterson***	Y	Y	Y	N	Y
6 Holden	Y	Y	Y	Y	Y
7 ***Weldon***	Y	Y	Y	N	Y
8 ***Greenwood***	Y	Y	Y	N	?
9 ***Shuster, Bill***	Y	Y	Y	N	Y
10 ***Sherwood***	Y	Y	Y	N	Y
11 Kanjorski	Y	N	N	Y	N
12 Murtha	Y	Y	Y	Y	Y
13 Hoeffel	Y	Y	Y	Y	Y
14 Coyne	Y	Y	Y	Y	Y
15 ***Toomey***	Y	Y	Y	N	Y
16 ***Pitts***	Y	Y	Y	N	Y
17 ***Gekas***	Y	Y	Y	N	Y
18 Doyle	Y	Y	Y	Y	Y
19 ***Platts***	Y	Y	Y	N	Y
20 Mascara	Y	Y	Y	Y	Y
21 ***English***	Y	Y	Y	N	Y
RHODE ISLAND					
1 Kennedy	Y	Y	Y	Y	Y
2 Langevin	Y	Y	Y	Y	Y
SOUTH CAROLINA					
1 ***Brown***	Y	Y	Y	N	Y
2 ***Spence***	Y	Y	Y	N	Y
3 ***Graham***	Y	Y	Y	N	Y
4 ***DeMint***	Y	Y	Y	N	Y
5 Spratt	Y	Y	Y	Y	Y
6 Clyburn	Y	Y	Y	Y	Y
SOUTH DAKOTA					
AL ***Thune***	Y	Y	Y	N	Y

	161	162	163	164	165
TENNESSEE					
1 ***Jenkins***	Y	Y	Y	N	Y
2 ***Duncan***	Y	Y	Y	N	N
3 ***Wamp***	Y	Y	Y	N	Y
4 ***Hilleary***	Y	Y	Y	N	Y
5 Clement	Y	Y	Y	N	Y
6 Gordon	Y	Y	Y	N	Y
7 ***Bryant***	Y	Y	Y	N	Y
8 Tanner	Y	Y	Y	N	Y
9 Ford	?	Y	Y	N	Y
TEXAS					
1 Sandlin	Y	Y	Y	N	Y
2 Turner	Y	Y	Y	Y	Y
3 ***Johnson, Sam***	Y	Y	Y	N	Y
4 Hall	Y	Y	Y	N	Y
5 ***Sessions***	Y	Y	Y	N	Y
6 ***Barton***	Y	Y	Y	N	Y
7 ***Culberson***	Y	Y	Y	N	Y
8 ***Brady***	Y	Y	Y	N	Y
9 Lampson	Y	Y	Y	Y	Y
10 Doggett	Y	Y	Y	Y	Y
11 Edwards	Y	Y	Y	Y	Y
12 ***Granger***	Y	Y	Y	N	Y
13 ***Thornberry***	Y	Y	Y	N	Y
14 ***Paul***	Y	Y	Y	N	Y
15 Hinojosa	Y	Y	Y	N	Y
16 Reyes	Y	Y	Y	N	Y
17 Stenholm	Y	Y	Y	N	Y
18 Jackson-Lee	Y	Y	Y	Y	Y
19 ***Combest***	Y	Y	Y	N	Y
20 Gonzalez	Y	Y	Y	N	Y
21 ***Smith***	Y	Y	Y	N	Y
22 ***DeLay***	Y	Y	Y	N	Y
23 ***Bonilla***	Y	Y	Y	N	Y
24 Frost	Y	?	?	N	Y
25 Bentsen	Y	Y	Y	N	Y
26 ***Armey***	Y	Y	Y	N	Y
27 Ortiz	Y	Y	Y	N	Y
28 Rodriguez	Y	Y	Y	Y	Y
29 Green	Y	Y	Y	Y	Y
30 Johnson, E.B.	?	?	?	?	?
UTAH					
1 ***Hansen***	Y	Y	Y	N	Y
2 Matheson	Y	Y	Y	Y	Y
3 ***Cannon***	Y	Y	Y	N	Y
VERMONT					
AL *Sanders*	Y	Y	Y	Y	Y
VIRGINIA					
1 ***Davis, Jo Ann***	Y	Y	Y	N	Y
2 ***Schrock***	Y	Y	Y	N	Y
3 Scott	Y	Y	Y	Y	Y
4 Vacant					
5 *Goode*	Y	Y	Y	N	Y
6 ***Goodlatte***	Y	Y	Y	N	Y
7 ***Cantor***	Y	Y	Y	N	Y
8 Moran	Y	Y	Y	N	Y
9 Boucher	Y	Y	Y	N	Y
10 ***Wolf***	Y	Y	Y	N	Y
11 ***Davis, T.***	Y	Y	Y	N	Y
WASHINGTON					
1 Inslee	Y	Y	Y	Y	Y
2 Larsen	Y	Y	Y	N	Y
3 Baird	Y	Y	Y	N	Y
4 ***Hastings***	Y	Y	Y	N	Y
5 ***Nethercutt***	Y	Y	Y	N	Y
6 Dicks	Y	Y	Y	Y	Y
7 McDermott	Y	Y	Y	Y	Y
8 ***Dunn***	Y	Y	Y	N	Y
9 Smith	Y	Y	Y	N	Y
WEST VIRGINIA					
1 Mollohan	Y	Y	Y	Y	Y
2 ***Capito***	Y	Y	Y	N	Y
3 Rahall	Y	Y	N	N	Y
WISCONSIN					
1 ***Ryan***	Y	Y	Y	N	Y
2 Baldwin	Y	Y	Y	Y	Y
3 Kind	Y	Y	Y	Y	Y
4 Kleczka	Y	Y	Y	N	Y
5 Barrett	Y	Y	Y	Y	Y
6 ***Petri***	Y	Y	Y	N	Y
7 Obey	Y	Y	Y	Y	N
8 ***Green***	Y	Y	Y	N	Y
9 ***Sensenbrenner***	Y	Y	Y	N	Y
WYOMING					
AL ***Cubin***	Y	?	?	?	?

Southern states - Ala., Ark., Fla., Ga., Ky., La., Miss., N.C., Okla., S.C., Tenn., Texas, Va.

166. HR 1291. Military Education Benefits/Passage. Smith, R-N.J., motion to suspend the rules and pass the bill that would increase education benefits under the Montgomery GI Bill for military veterans pursuing full-time study through fiscal 2004. Assistance for veterans with three years or more of service would increase from $650 per month to $1,100 over three years. Benefits for those with two years of service and four years of reserve duty would increase from $528 per month to $894. Motion agreed to 416-0: R 212-0; D 203-0 (ND 150-0, SD 53-0); I 1-0. A two-thirds majority of those present and voting (278 in this case) is required for passage under suspension of the rules. June 19, 2001.

167. H Con Res 154. National Guard Tribute/Adoption. Thornberry, R-Texas, motion to suspend the rules and adopt the concurrent resolution that would pay tribute to Army National Guard combat units deployed in support of Army operations in Bosnia and recognize the importance of all National Guard and Reserve units to U.S. security. Motion agreed to 417-0: R 212-0; D 203-0 (ND 150-0, SD 53-0); I 2-0. A two-thirds majority of those present and voting (278 in this case) is required for adoption under suspension of the rules. June 19, 2001.

168. H Con Res 163. Juneteenth Tribute/Adoption. Shays, R-Conn., motion to suspend the rules and adopt the concurrent resolution that would recognize the significance of Juneteenth, the annual celebration marking June 19, 1865, the day slaves in Galveston, Texas, heard of their emancipation. Motion agreed to 415-0: R 210-0; D 203-0 (ND 150-0, SD 53-0); I 2-0. A two-thirds majority of those present and voting (277 in this case) is required for adoption under suspension of the rules. June 19, 2001.

169. HR 2216. Fiscal 2001 Supplemental Appropriations/Previous Question. Myrick, R-N.C., motion to order the previous question (thus ending debate and possibility of amendment) on adoption of the rule (H Res 171) to provide for House floor consideration of the bill that would appropriate a net $6.5 billion in supplemental, discretionary funds, including $5.5 billion for national defense and $473 million in emergency spending. Motion agreed to 222-205: R 218-0; D 3-204 (ND 2-152, SD 1-52); I 1-1. June 20, 2001.

170. HR 2216. Fiscal 2001 Supplemental Appropriations/Rule. Adoption of the rule (H Res 171) to provide for House floor consideration of the bill that would appropriate a net $6.5 billion in supplemental, discretionary funds, including $5.5 billion for national defense and $473 million in emergency spending. Adopted 223-205: R 218-1; D 4-203 (ND 2-151, SD 2-52); I 1-1. June 20, 2001.

171. H Res 124. Youth Tribute/Adoption. Castle, R-Del., motion to suspend the rules and adopt the resolution that would recognize the importance of America's youth, support American Youth Day, and encourage participation in activities furthering the five promises of America's Promise-The Alliance for Youth. Motion agreed to 424-0: R 215-0; D 207-0 (ND 153-0, SD 54-0); I 2-0. A two-thirds majority of those present and voting (283 in this case) is required for adoption under suspension of the rules. June 20, 2001.

172. HR 2216. Fiscal 2001 Supplemental Appropriations/Air Force Operations. DeFazio, D-Ore., amendment that would cut by $24.5 million the Air Force operation and maintenance account. Rejected 50-376: R 4-213; D 45-162 (ND 42-112, SD 3-50); I 1-1. June 20, 2001.

Key

Y	Voted for (yea).
#	Paired for.
+	Announced for.
N	Voted against (nay).
X	Paired against.
–	Announced against.
P	Voted "present."
C	Voted "present" to avoid possible conflict of interest.
?	Did not vote or otherwise make a position known.

Democrats • *Republicans*
Independents

	166	167	168	169	170	171	172
ALABAMA							
1 *Callahan*	Y	Y	Y	Y	Y	Y	N
2 *Everett*	Y	Y	Y	Y	Y	Y	N
3 *Riley*	Y	Y	Y	Y	Y	Y	N
4 *Aderholt*	Y	Y	Y	Y	Y	Y	N
5 Cramer	Y	Y	N	N	N	Y	N
6 *Bachus*	Y	Y	Y	Y	Y	Y	N
7 Hilliard	Y	Y	N	N	N	Y	N
ALASKA							
AL *Young*	Y	Y	Y	Y	Y	Y	N
ARIZONA							
1 *Flake*	Y	Y	Y	Y	Y	Y	?
2 Pastor	Y	Y	N	N	N	Y	N
3 *Stump*	Y	Y	Y	Y	Y	Y	N
4 *Shadegg*	Y	Y	Y	Y	Y	Y	N
5 *Kolbe*	Y	Y	Y	Y	Y	Y	N
6 *Hayworth*	Y	Y	Y	Y	Y	Y	N
ARKANSAS							
1 Berry	Y	Y	N	N	N	Y	N
2 Snyder	Y	Y	N	N	N	Y	N
3 *Hutchinson*	Y	Y	?	Y	Y	Y	N
4 Ross	Y	Y	N	N	N	Y	N
CALIFORNIA							
1 Thompson	Y	Y	N	N	N	Y	N
2 *Herger*	Y	Y	Y	Y	Y	Y	N
3 *Ose*	Y	Y	Y	Y	Y	Y	N
4 *Doolittle*	Y	Y	Y	Y	Y	Y	N
5 Matsui	Y	Y	N	N	N	Y	N
6 Woolsey	Y	Y	N	N	Y	Y	Y
7 Miller, George	Y	Y	N	N	Y	Y	Y
8 Pelosi	Y	Y	N	N	N	Y	N
9 Lee	Y	Y	N	N	Y	Y	Y
10 Tauscher	Y	Y	N	N	N	Y	N
11 *Pombo*	Y	Y	Y	Y	Y	Y	N
12 Lantos	Y	Y	N	N	N	Y	N
13 Stark	Y	Y	N	N	N	Y	Y
14 Eshoo	Y	Y	–	–	Y	Y	N
15 Honda	Y	Y	N	N	N	Y	N
16 Lofgren	Y	Y	N	N	N	Y	N
17 Farr	Y	Y	N	N	N	Y	N
18 Condit	Y	Y	N	N	N	Y	N
19 *Radanovich*	Y	Y	?	Y	Y	Y	N
20 Dooley	Y	Y	N	?	N	Y	N
21 *Thomas*	Y	Y	Y	Y	Y	Y	N
22 Capps	Y	Y	N	N	N	Y	N
23 *Gallegly*	Y	Y	Y	Y	Y	Y	N
24 Sherman	Y	Y	N	N	N	Y	N
25 *McKeon*	Y	Y	Y	Y	Y	Y	N
26 Berman	Y	Y	N	N	N	Y	N
27 Schiff	Y	Y	N	N	?	Y	N
28 *Dreier*	Y	Y	Y	Y	Y	Y	N
29 Waxman	Y	Y	N	N	N	Y	N
30 Becerra	Y	Y	N	N	N	Y	N
31 Solis	Y	Y	N	N	Y	Y	Y
32 Watson	Y	Y	N	N	N	Y	N
33 Roybal-Allard	Y	Y	N	N	N	Y	N
34 Napolitano	Y	Y	N	N	N	Y	N
35 Waters	Y	Y	N	N	N	Y	N
36 Harman	Y	Y	N	N	N	Y	N
37 Millender-McD.	Y	Y	N	N	N	Y	N
38 *Horn*	Y	Y	Y	Y	Y	Y	N

	166	167	168	169	170	171	172
39 *Royce*	Y	Y	Y	Y	Y	Y	N
40 *Lewis*	Y	Y	Y	Y	Y	Y	N
41 *Miller, Gary*	Y	Y	Y	Y	Y	Y	N
42 Baca	Y	Y	Y	N	N	Y	N
43 *Calvert*	Y	Y	Y	Y	Y	Y	N
44 *Bono*	Y	Y	Y	Y	Y	Y	N
45 *Rohrabacher*	Y	Y	Y	Y	Y	Y	Y
46 Sanchez	Y	Y	N	N	N	Y	N
47 *Cox*	?	?	?	?	?	?	?
48 *Issa*	Y	Y	Y	Y	Y	Y	N
49 Davis	Y	Y	N	N	N	Y	N
50 Filner	P	Y	Y	N	N	Y	Y
51 *Cunningham*	Y	Y	Y	Y	Y	Y	N
52 *Hunter*	Y	Y	Y	Y	Y	Y	N
COLORADO							
1 DeGette	Y	Y	N	N	N	Y	Y
2 Udall	Y	Y	N	N	N	Y	Y
3 *McInnis*	Y	Y	Y	Y	Y	Y	N
4 *Schaffer*	Y	Y	Y	Y	Y	Y	N
5 *Hefley*	Y	Y	Y	Y	Y	Y	N
6 *Tancredo*	Y	Y	Y	Y	Y	Y	N
CONNECTICUT							
1 Larson	Y	Y	N	N	Y	Y	N
2 *Simmons*	Y	Y	Y	Y	Y	Y	N
3 DeLauro	Y	Y	N	N	Y	Y	N
4 *Shays*	Y	Y	Y	Y	Y	Y	Y
5 Maloney	Y	Y	N	N	N	Y	N
6 *Johnson*	Y	Y	Y	Y	Y	Y	N
DELAWARE							
AL *Castle*	Y	Y	Y	Y	Y	Y	N
FLORIDA							
1 *Scarborough*	Y	Y	Y	Y	Y	Y	N
2 Boyd	Y	Y	N	N	N	Y	N
3 Brown	Y	Y	N	N	N	Y	N
4 *Crenshaw*	Y	Y	Y	Y	Y	Y	N
5 Thurman	Y	Y	N	N	N	Y	N
6 *Stearns*	Y	Y	Y	Y	Y	Y	N
7 *Mica*	Y	Y	Y	Y	Y	Y	N
8 *Keller*	Y	Y	Y	Y	Y	Y	N
9 *Bilirakis*	Y	Y	Y	Y	Y	Y	N
10 *Young*	Y	Y	Y	Y	Y	Y	N
11 Davis	Y	Y	N	N	N	Y	N
12 *Putnam*	Y	Y	Y	Y	Y	Y	N
13 *Miller*	Y	Y	Y	Y	Y	Y	N
14 *Goss*	Y	Y	Y	Y	Y	Y	N
15 *Weldon*	Y	Y	Y	Y	Y	Y	N
16 *Foley*	Y	Y	Y	Y	Y	Y	N
17 Meek	Y	Y	N	N	N	Y	N
18 *Ros-Lehtinen*	Y	Y	Y	Y	Y	Y	N
19 Wexler	Y	Y	N	N	N	Y	N
20 Deutsch	Y	Y	N	N	N	Y	N
21 *Diaz-Balart*	Y	Y	Y	Y	Y	Y	N
22 *Shaw*	Y	Y	Y	Y	Y	Y	N
23 Hastings	Y	Y	N	N	N	Y	N
GEORGIA							
1 *Kingston*	Y	Y	Y	Y	Y	Y	N
2 Bishop	Y	Y	N	N	N	Y	N
3 *Collins*	Y	Y	Y	Y	Y	Y	N
4 McKinney	Y	Y	N	N	N	Y	Y
5 Lewis	Y	Y	N	N	N	Y	N
6 *Isakson*	Y	Y	Y	Y	Y	Y	N
7 *Barr*	Y	Y	Y	Y	Y	Y	N
8 *Chambliss*	Y	Y	Y	Y	Y	Y	N
9 *Deal*	Y	Y	Y	Y	Y	Y	N
10 *Norwood*	Y	Y	Y	Y	Y	Y	N
11 *Linder*	Y	Y	Y	Y	Y	Y	N
HAWAII							
1 Abercrombie	Y	Y	Y	Y	Y	Y	N
2 Mink	Y	Y	N	N	N	Y	N
IDAHO							
1 *Otter*	Y	Y	Y	Y	Y	Y	N
2 *Simpson*	Y	Y	Y	Y	Y	Y	N
ILLINOIS							
1 Rush	Y	Y	N	N	N	Y	?
2 Jackson	Y	Y	N	N	N	Y	N
3 Lipinski	Y	Y	N	N	N	Y	N
4 Gutierrez	Y	Y	N	N	N	Y	N
5 Blagojevich	Y	Y	N	N	N	Y	N
6 *Hyde*	Y	Y	Y	Y	Y	Y	N
7 Davis	Y	Y	N	N	N	Y	N
8 *Crane*	Y	Y	Y	Y	Y	Y	N
9 Schakowsky	Y	Y	N	N	N	Y	N
10 *Kirk*	Y	Y	Y	Y	Y	Y	N
11 *Weller*	Y	Y	Y	Y	Y	Y	N
12 Costello	Y	Y	N	N	N	Y	N
13 *Biggert*	Y	Y	Y	Y	Y	Y	N

ND Northern Democrats   SD Southern Democrats

	166	167	168	169	170	171	172
14 ***Hastert***					Y		
15 ***Johnson***	Y	Y	Y	Y	Y	Y	N
16 ***Manzullo***	Y	?	Y	Y	Y	Y	N
17 Evans	Y	Y	Y	N	N	Y	N
18 ***LaHood***	Y	Y	Y	Y	Y	Y	N
19 Phelps	Y	Y	Y	N	N	Y	N
20 ***Shimkus***	Y	Y	Y	Y	Y	Y	N
INDIANA							
1 Visclosky	Y	Y	Y	N	N	Y	N
2 ***Pence***	Y	Y	Y	Y	Y	Y	N
3 Roemer	Y	Y	Y	N	N	Y	N
4 ***Souder***	Y	Y	Y	Y	Y	Y	N
5 ***Buyer***	Y	Y	Y	Y	Y	Y	N
6 ***Burton***	Y	Y	Y	Y	Y	Y	N
7 ***Kerns***	Y	Y	Y	Y	Y	Y	N
8 ***Hostettler***	Y	Y	Y	Y	Y	Y	N
9 Hill	Y	Y	Y	N	N	Y	N
10 Carson	Y	Y	Y	N	N	Y	N
IOWA							
1 ***Leach***	Y	Y	Y	Y	Y	Y	N
2 ***Nussle***	Y	Y	Y	Y	Y	Y	N
3 Boswell	Y	Y	Y	N	N	Y	N
4 ***Ganske***	Y	Y	Y	Y	Y	Y	N
5 ***Latham***	Y	Y	Y	Y	Y	Y	N
KANSAS							
1 ***Moran***	Y	Y	Y	Y	Y	Y	N
2 ***Ryun***	Y	Y	Y	Y	Y	Y	N
3 Moore	Y	Y	Y	N	N	Y	N
4 ***Tiahrt***	Y	Y	Y	Y	Y	Y	N
KENTUCKY							
1 ***Whitfield***	Y	Y	Y	Y	Y	Y	N
2 ***Lewis***	Y	Y	Y	Y	Y	Y	N
3 ***Northup***	Y	Y	Y	Y	Y	Y	N
4 Lucas	Y	Y	Y	N	N	Y	N
5 ***Rogers***	Y	Y	Y	Y	Y	Y	N
6 ***Fletcher***	Y	Y	Y	Y	Y	?	N
LOUISIANA							
1 ***Vitter***	Y	Y	Y	Y	Y	Y	N
2 Jefferson	Y	Y	Y	N	N	Y	?
3 ***Tauzin***	Y	Y	Y	Y	Y	Y	N
4 ***McCrery***	Y	Y	Y	Y	Y	Y	N
5 ***Cooksey***	Y	Y	Y	Y	Y	Y	N
6 ***Baker***	Y	Y	Y	Y	Y	Y	N
7 John	Y	Y	Y	N	N	Y	N
MAINE							
1 Allen	Y	Y	Y	N	N	Y	N
2 Baldacci	Y	Y	Y	N	N	Y	N
MARYLAND							
1 ***Gilchrest***	Y	Y	Y	Y	Y	Y	N
2 ***Ehrlich***	Y	Y	Y	Y	Y	Y	N
3 Cardin	Y	Y	Y	N	N	Y	N
4 Wynn	Y	Y	Y	N	N	Y	N
5 Hoyer	Y	Y	Y	N	N	Y	N
6 ***Bartlett***	Y	Y	Y	Y	Y	Y	N
7 Cummings	Y	Y	Y	N	N	Y	N
8 ***Morella***	Y	Y	Y	Y	Y	Y	N
MASSACHUSETTS							
1 Olver	Y	Y	Y	N	N	Y	N
2 Neal	Y	Y	Y	N	N	Y	N
3 McGovern	Y	Y	Y	N	N	Y	Y
4 Frank	Y	Y	Y	N	N	Y	Y
5 Meehan	Y	Y	Y	N	N	Y	N
6 Tierney	Y	Y	Y	N	N	Y	Y
7 Markey	Y	Y	Y	N	N	Y	Y
8 Capuano	Y	Y	Y	N	N	Y	N
9 Vacant							
10 Delahunt	Y	Y	Y	N	N	Y	N
MICHIGAN							
1 Stupak	Y	Y	Y	N	N	Y	N
2 ***Hoekstra***	Y	Y	Y	Y	Y	Y	N
3 ***Ehlers***	Y	Y	Y	Y	Y	Y	N
4 ***Camp***	Y	Y	Y	Y	Y	Y	N
5 Barcia	Y	Y	Y	N	N	Y	N
6 ***Upton***	Y	Y	Y	Y	Y	Y	N
7 ***Smith***	Y	Y	Y	Y	Y	Y	N
8 ***Rogers***	Y	Y	Y	Y	Y	Y	N
9 Kildee	Y	Y	Y	N	N	Y	N
10 Bonior	Y	Y	Y	N	N	Y	Y
11 ***Knollenberg***	Y	Y	Y	Y	Y	Y	N
12 Levin	Y	Y	Y	N	N	Y	N
13 Rivers	Y	Y	Y	N	N	Y	Y
14 Conyers	Y	Y	Y	N	?	Y	Y
15 Kilpatrick	Y	Y	Y	N	N	Y	N
16 Dingell	Y	Y	Y	N	N	Y	N

	166	167	168	169	170	171	172
MINNESOTA							
1 ***Gutknecht***	Y	Y	Y	Y	Y	Y	N
2 ***Kennedy***	Y	Y	Y	Y	Y	Y	N
3 ***Ramstad***	Y	Y	Y	Y	Y	Y	N
4 McCollum	Y	Y	Y	N	N	Y	N
5 Sabo	Y	Y	Y	N	N	Y	N
6 Luther	Y	Y	Y	N	N	Y	Y
7 Peterson	Y	Y	Y	N	N	Y	N
8 Oberstar	Y	Y	Y	N	N	Y	Y
MISSISSIPPI							
1 ***Wicker***	Y	Y	Y	Y	Y	Y	N
2 Thompson	Y	Y	Y	N	N	Y	N
3 ***Pickering***	Y	Y	Y	Y	Y	Y	N
4 Shows	Y	Y	Y	N	N	Y	N
5 Taylor	Y	Y	Y	N	N	Y	N
MISSOURI							
1 Clay	Y	Y	Y	N	N	Y	N
2 ***Akin***	Y	Y	Y	Y	Y	Y	N
3 Gephardt	?	?	?	N	N	Y	N
4 Skelton	Y	Y	Y	N	N	Y	N
5 McCarthy	+	+	+	N	N	Y	N
6 ***Graves***	Y	Y	Y	Y	Y	Y	N
7 ***Blunt***	Y	Y	Y	Y	Y	Y	N
8 ***Emerson***	Y	Y	Y	Y	Y	Y	N
9 ***Hulshof***	Y	Y	Y	Y	Y	Y	N
MONTANA							
AL ***Rehberg***	Y	Y	Y	Y	Y	Y	N
NEBRASKA							
1 ***Bereuter***	Y	Y	Y	Y	Y	Y	N
2 ***Terry***	Y	Y	Y	Y	Y	Y	N
3 ***Osborne***	Y	Y	Y	Y	Y	Y	N
NEVADA							
1 Berkley	Y	Y	Y	N	N	?	N
2 ***Gibbons***	+	+	+	Y	Y	Y	N
NEW HAMPSHIRE							
1 ***Sununu***	Y	Y	Y	Y	Y	Y	N
2 ***Bass***	Y	Y	Y	Y	Y	Y	N
NEW JERSEY							
1 Andrews	Y	Y	Y	N	N	Y	N
2 ***LoBiondo***	Y	Y	Y	Y	Y	Y	N
3 ***Saxton***	Y	Y	Y	Y	Y	Y	N
4 ***Smith***	Y	Y	Y	Y	Y	Y	N
5 ***Roukema***	Y	Y	Y	Y	Y	Y	N
6 Pallone	Y	Y	Y	N	N	Y	N
7 ***Ferguson***	Y	Y	Y	Y	Y	Y	N
8 Pascrell	Y	Y	Y	N	N	Y	N
9 Rothman	Y	Y	Y	N	N	Y	N
10 Payne	Y	Y	Y	N	N	Y	Y
11 ***Frelinghuysen***	Y	Y	Y	Y	Y	Y	N
12 Holt	Y	Y	Y	N	N	Y	Y
13 Menendez	Y	Y	Y	N	N	Y	N
NEW MEXICO							
1 ***Wilson***	Y	Y	Y	Y	Y	Y	N
2 ***Skeen***	Y	Y	Y	Y	Y	Y	N
3 Udall	Y	Y	Y	N	N	Y	N
NEW YORK							
1 ***Grucci***	Y	Y	Y	Y	Y	Y	N
2 Israel	Y	Y	Y	N	N	Y	N
3 ***King***	Y	Y	Y	Y	Y	Y	N
4 McCarthy	Y	Y	Y	N	N	Y	N
5 Ackerman	Y	Y	Y	N	N	Y	N
6 Meeks	Y	Y	Y	N	N	Y	N
7 Crowley	Y	Y	Y	N	N	Y	N
8 Nadler	Y	Y	Y	N	N	Y	Y
9 Weiner	Y	Y	Y	N	N	Y	N
10 Towns	Y	Y	Y	N	N	Y	Y
11 Owens	Y	Y	Y	N	N	Y	N
12 Velázquez	Y	Y	Y	N	N	Y	Y
13 ***Fossella***	Y	Y	Y	Y	Y	Y	N
14 Maloney	Y	Y	Y	N	N	Y	Y
15 Rangel	Y	Y	Y	N	N	Y	N
16 Serrano	Y	Y	Y	N	N	Y	N
17 Engel	Y	Y	Y	N	N	Y	N
18 Lowey	Y	Y	Y	N	N	Y	N
19 ***Kelly***	Y	Y	Y	Y	Y	?	N
20 ***Gilman***	Y	Y	Y	Y	Y	Y	N
21 McNulty	Y	Y	Y	N	N	Y	N
22 ***Sweeney***	?	?	?	Y	Y	Y	N
23 ***Boehlert***	Y	Y	Y	Y	Y	Y	N
24 ***McHugh***	Y	Y	Y	Y	Y	Y	N
25 ***Walsh***	Y	Y	Y	Y	Y	Y	N
26 Hinchey	?	?	?	N	N	Y	Y
27 ***Reynolds***	Y	Y	Y	Y	Y	Y	N
28 Slaughter	Y	Y	Y	N	N	Y	Y
29 LaFalce	Y	Y	Y	N	N	Y	N

	166	167	168	169	170	171	172
30 ***Quinn***	Y	Y	Y	Y	Y	Y	N
31 ***Houghton***	Y	Y	Y	?	?	?	?
NORTH CAROLINA							
1 Clayton	Y	Y	Y	N	N	Y	N
2 Etheridge	Y	Y	Y	?	N	Y	N
3 ***Jones***	Y	Y	Y	Y	N	Y	N
4 Price	Y	Y	Y	N	N	Y	N
5 ***Burr***	Y	Y	Y	Y	Y	Y	N
6 ***Coble***	Y	Y	Y	Y	Y	Y	N
7 McIntyre	Y	Y	Y	N	N	Y	N
8 ***Hayes***	Y	Y	Y	Y	Y	Y	N
9 ***Myrick***	Y	Y	?	Y	Y	Y	N
10 ***Ballenger***	Y	Y	Y	Y	Y	Y	N
11 ***Taylor***	Y	Y	Y	Y	Y	Y	N
12 Watt	Y	Y	Y	N	N	Y	Y
NORTH DAKOTA							
AL Pomeroy	Y	Y	Y	N	N	Y	N
OHIO							
1 ***Chabot***	Y	Y	Y	Y	Y	Y	N
2 ***Portman***	Y	Y	Y	Y	Y	Y	N
3 Hall	Y	Y	Y	N	N	Y	N
4 ***Oxley***	Y	Y	Y	Y	Y	Y	N
5 ***Gillmor***	Y	Y	Y	Y	Y	Y	N
6 Strickland	Y	Y	Y	N	N	Y	N
7 ***Hobson***	Y	Y	Y	Y	Y	Y	N
8 ***Boehner***	Y	Y	Y	Y	Y	Y	N
9 Kaptur	Y	Y	Y	N	N	Y	?
10 Kucinich	Y	Y	Y	N	N	Y	Y
11 Jones	?	?	?	N	N	Y	N
12 ***Tiberi***	Y	Y	Y	Y	Y	Y	N
13 Brown	Y	Y	Y	N	N	Y	Y
14 Sawyer	Y	Y	Y	N	N	Y	N
15 ***Pryce***	Y	Y	Y	Y	Y	Y	N
16 ***Regula***	Y	Y	Y	Y	Y	Y	N
17 Traficant	Y	Y	Y	Y	Y	Y	N
18 ***Ney***	Y	Y	Y	Y	Y	Y	N
19 ***LaTourette***	Y	Y	Y	Y	Y	Y	N
OKLAHOMA							
1 ***Largent***	Y	Y	Y	Y	Y	Y	N
2 Carson	Y	Y	Y	N	Y	Y	N
3 ***Watkins***	Y	Y	Y	Y	Y	Y	N
4 ***Watts***	Y	Y	Y	Y	Y	Y	N
5 ***Istook***	Y	Y	Y	Y	Y	Y	N
6 ***Lucas***	Y	Y	Y	Y	Y	Y	N
OREGON							
1 Wu	Y	Y	Y	N	N	Y	Y
2 ***Walden***	Y	Y	Y	Y	Y	Y	N
3 Blumenauer	Y	Y	Y	N	N	Y	Y
4 DeFazio	Y	Y	Y	N	N	Y	Y
5 Hooley	Y	Y	Y	N	N	Y	Y
PENNSYLVANIA							
1 Brady	Y	Y	Y	N	N	Y	N
2 Fattah	Y	Y	Y	N	N	Y	N
3 Borski	Y	Y	Y	N	N	Y	N
4 ***Hart***	Y	Y	Y	Y	Y	Y	N
5 ***Peterson***	?	?	?	Y	Y	Y	N
6 Holden	Y	Y	Y	N	N	Y	N
7 ***Weldon***	Y	Y	Y	Y	Y	Y	N
8 ***Greenwood***	Y	Y	Y	Y	Y	Y	N
9 ***Shuster, Bill***	Y	Y	Y	Y	Y	Y	N
10 ***Sherwood***	Y	Y	Y	Y	Y	Y	N
11 Kanjorski	Y	Y	Y	N	N	Y	N
12 Murtha	Y	Y	?	N	N	Y	N
13 Hoeffel	Y	Y	Y	N	N	Y	N
14 Coyne	Y	Y	Y	N	N	Y	N
15 ***Toomey***	Y	Y	Y	Y	Y	Y	N
16 ***Pitts***	Y	Y	Y	Y	Y	Y	N
17 ***Gekas***	Y	Y	Y	Y	Y	Y	N
18 Doyle	Y	Y	Y	N	N	Y	N
19 ***Platts***	Y	Y	Y	Y	Y	Y	N
20 Mascara	Y	Y	Y	N	N	Y	N
21 ***English***	?	Y	Y	Y	Y	Y	N
RHODE ISLAND							
1 Kennedy	Y	Y	Y	N	N	Y	N
2 Langevin	Y	Y	Y	N	N	Y	N
SOUTH CAROLINA							
1 ***Brown***	Y	Y	Y	Y	Y	Y	N
2 ***Spence***	Y	Y	Y	Y	Y	Y	N
3 ***Graham***	Y	Y	Y	Y	Y	Y	N
4 ***DeMint***	Y	Y	Y	Y	Y	Y	N
5 Spratt	Y	Y	Y	N	N	Y	N
6 Clyburn	Y	Y	Y	N	N	Y	N
SOUTH DAKOTA							
AL ***Thune***	Y	Y	Y	Y	Y	Y	N

	166	167	168	169	170	171	172
TENNESSEE							
1 ***Jenkins***	Y	Y	Y	Y	Y	Y	N
2 ***Duncan***	Y	Y	Y	Y	Y	Y	Y
3 ***Wamp***	Y	Y	Y	Y	Y	Y	N
4 ***Hilleary***	Y	Y	Y	Y	Y	Y	N
5 Clement	Y	Y	Y	N	N	Y	N
6 Gordon	Y	Y	Y	Y	N	Y	N
7 ***Bryant***	Y	Y	Y	Y	Y	Y	N
8 Tanner	Y	Y	Y	N	N	Y	N
9 Ford	Y	Y	Y	N	N	Y	N
TEXAS							
1 Sandlin	Y	Y	Y	N	N	Y	N
2 Turner	Y	Y	Y	N	N	Y	N
3 ***Johnson, Sam***	Y	Y	Y	Y	Y	Y	N
4 Hall	Y	Y	Y	N	N	Y	N
5 ***Sessions***	Y	Y	Y	Y	Y	Y	N
6 ***Barton***	Y	Y	Y	Y	Y	Y	N
7 ***Culberson***	Y	Y	Y	Y	Y	Y	N
8 ***Brady***	Y	Y	Y	Y	Y	Y	N
9 Lampson	Y	Y	Y	N	N	Y	N
10 Doggett	Y	Y	Y	N	N	Y	Y
11 Edwards	Y	Y	Y	N	N	Y	N
12 ***Granger***	Y	Y	Y	Y	Y	Y	N
13 ***Thornberry***	Y	Y	Y	Y	Y	Y	N
14 ***Paul***	Y	Y	Y	Y	Y	Y	Y
15 Hinojosa	Y	Y	Y	N	N	Y	N
16 Reyes	Y	Y	Y	N	N	Y	N
17 Stenholm	Y	Y	Y	N	Y	Y	N
18 Jackson-Lee	Y	Y	Y	N	N	Y	N
19 ***Combest***	Y	Y	Y	Y	Y	Y	N
20 Gonzalez	Y	Y	Y	N	N	Y	N
21 ***Smith***	Y	Y	Y	Y	Y	Y	N
22 ***DeLay***	Y	Y	Y	Y	Y	?	N
23 ***Bonilla***	Y	Y	Y	Y	Y	Y	N
24 Frost	Y	Y	Y	N	N	Y	N
25 Bentsen	Y	Y	Y	N	N	Y	N
26 ***Armey***	Y	Y	Y	Y	Y	Y	N
27 Ortiz	Y	Y	Y	N	N	Y	N
28 Rodriguez	Y	Y	Y	N	N	Y	N
29 Green	Y	Y	Y	N	N	Y	N
30 Johnson, E.B.	Y	Y	Y	N	N	Y	N
UTAH							
1 ***Hansen***	Y	Y	Y	Y	Y	Y	N
2 Matheson	Y	Y	Y	N	N	Y	N
3 ***Cannon***	?	?	?	Y	Y	Y	N
VERMONT							
AL *Sanders*	?	Y	Y	N	N	Y	Y
VIRGINIA							
1 ***Davis, Jo Ann***	Y	Y	Y	Y	Y	Y	N
2 ***Schrock***	Y	Y	Y	Y	Y	Y	N
3 Scott	?	?	?	N	N	Y	N
4 Vacant							
5 *Goode*	Y	Y	Y	Y	Y	Y	N
6 ***Goodlatte***	Y	Y	Y	Y	Y	Y	N
7 ***Cantor***	Y	Y	Y	Y	Y	Y	N
8 Moran	Y	Y	Y	N	N	Y	N
9 Boucher	Y	Y	Y	N	N	Y	N
10 ***Wolf***	Y	Y	Y	Y	Y	Y	N
11 ***Davis, T.***	?	?	?	Y	Y	Y	N
WASHINGTON							
1 Inslee	Y	Y	Y	N	N	Y	N
2 Larsen	Y	Y	Y	N	N	Y	N
3 Baird	Y	Y	Y	N	N	Y	Y
4 ***Hastings***	Y	Y	Y	Y	Y	Y	N
5 ***Nethercutt***	Y	Y	Y	Y	Y	Y	N
6 Dicks	Y	Y	Y	N	N	Y	N
7 McDermott	Y	Y	Y	N	N	Y	Y
8 ***Dunn***	Y	Y	Y	Y	Y	Y	N
9 Smith	Y	?	Y	N	?	?	N
WEST VIRGINIA							
1 Mollohan	Y	Y	Y	N	N	Y	N
2 ***Capito***	Y	Y	Y	Y	Y	Y	N
3 Rahall	Y	Y	Y	N	N	Y	N
WISCONSIN							
1 ***Ryan***	Y	Y	Y	Y	Y	Y	N
2 Baldwin	Y	Y	Y	N	N	Y	Y
3 Kind	Y	Y	Y	N	N	Y	Y
4 Kleczka	Y	Y	Y	N	N	Y	N
5 Barrett	Y	Y	Y	N	N	Y	Y
6 ***Petri***	Y	Y	Y	Y	Y	Y	N
7 Obey	?	?	?	N	N	Y	N
8 ***Green***	Y	Y	Y	Y	Y	Y	N
9 ***Sensenbrenner***	Y	Y	Y	Y	Y	Y	N
WYOMING							
AL ***Cubin***	?	?	?	Y	Y	Y	N

Southern states - Ala., Ark., Fla., Ga., Ky., La., Miss., N.C., Okla., S.C., Tenn., Texas, Va.

173. HR 2216. Fiscal 2001 Supplemental Appropriations/Anti-Drug Efforts. Obey, D-Wis., amendment that would increase by $30.5 million the High Intensity Drug Trafficking Areas program. Rejected 212-216: R 5-213; D 206-2 (ND 153-1, SD 53-1); I 1-1. June 20, 2001.

174. HR 2216. Fiscal 2001 Supplemental Appropriations/Disaster Relief. Toomey, R-Pa., amendment that would strike the bill's $389 million rescission in Federal Emergency Management Agency (FEMA) disaster relief funds and enact a 0.33 percent across-the-board reduction in fiscal 2001 non-defense discretionary spending. The reduction would save about $1 billion, enough to offset non-defense, non-Veterans portions of the bill not currently offset and to replace the lost FEMA rescission savings. Rejected 65-362: R 61-156; D 3-205 (ND 1-153, SD 2-52); I 1-1. June 20, 2001.

175. HR 2216. Fiscal 2001 Supplemental Appropriations/Recommit. Obey, D-Wis., motion to recommit the bill to the House Appropriations Committee with instructions to report it back with amendments to strike the $389 million rescission from the FEMA disaster relief fund while complying with all applicable budget constraints. Motion rejected 209-218: R 1-216; D 207-1 (ND 153-1, SD 54-0); I 1-1. June 20, 2001.

176. HR 2216. Fiscal 2001 Supplemental Appropriations/Passage. Passage of the bill that would appropriate a net $6.5 billion in supplemental, discretionary funds including $5.5 billion for national defense and $473 million in emergency spending. The bill actually calls for about $8 billion in total additional funds but provides for $1.5 billion in offsets and rescissions from prior appropriations. It includes $389 million in emergency natural-disaster aid, $300 million for low-income energy assistance, $161 million for the Title I Education for the Disadvantaged program, $116 million for the Treasury Department to issue tax rebate checks, and $62 million for House members' representational allowances. Passed 341-87: R 199-19; D 141-67 (ND 96-58, SD 45-9); I 1-1. A "yea" was a vote in support of the president's position. June 20, 2001.

177. HR 2217. Fiscal 2002 Interior Appropriations/Arts and Humanities. Slaughter, D-N.Y., amendment that would provide increases of $10 million for the National Endowment for the Arts, $3 million for the National Endowment for the Humanities, and $2 million for the Institute of Museums and Library Services and offset the costs by a reduction of less than 0.3 percent in Department of the Interior and U.S. Forest Service administrative costs. Adopted 221-193: R 33-178; D 187-14 (ND 143-5, SD 44-9); I 1-1. June 21, 2001.

178. HR 2217. Fiscal 2002 Interior Appropriations/Energy Efficiency. Sanders, I-Vt., amendment that would provide increases of $24 million for weatherization assistance, $12 million for payments in lieu of taxes, and $12 million for other energy efficiency programs, and offset the costs by a $52 million cut in fossil fuel energy research and development. Rejected 153-262: R 44-166; D 108-95 (ND 95-56, SD 13-39); I 1-1 June 21, 2001.

179. HR 2217. Fiscal 2002 Interior Appropriations/Recreational Fees. DeFazio, D-Ore., amendment that would eliminate the Recreational Fee Demonstration Program. Rejected 129-287: R 32-179; D 96-107 (ND 82-69, SD 14-38); I 1-1 June 21, 2001.

Key

Y	Voted for (yea).
#	Paired for.
+	Announced for.
N	Voted against (nay).
X	Paired against.
–	Announced against.
P	Voted "present."
C	Voted "present" to avoid possible conflict of interest.
?	Did not vote or otherwise make a position known.

Democrats • ***Republicans***
Independents

	173	174	175	176	177	178	179
ALABAMA							
1 *Callahan*	N	N	N	Y	?	?	?
2 *Everett*	N	N	N	Y	?	?	?
3 *Riley*	N	N	N	Y	?	?	?
4 *Aderholt*	N	N	N	Y	?	?	?
5 Cramer	Y	N	Y	Y	?	?	?
6 *Bachus*	N	N	N	Y	?	?	?
7 Hilliard	Y	N	Y	Y	Y	N	N
ALASKA							
AL *Young*	N	N	N	Y	N	N	N
ARIZONA							
1 *Flake*	N	Y	N	N	N	N	Y
2 Pastor	Y	N	Y	Y	Y	Y	N
3 *Stump*	N	N	N	Y	N	N	Y
4 *Shadegg*	N	Y	N	N	N	N	Y
5 *Kolbe*	N	N	N	Y	Y	N	N
6 *Hayworth*	N	Y	N	Y	N	N	Y
ARKANSAS							
1 Berry	Y	N	Y	Y	Y	Y	N
2 Snyder	Y	N	Y	Y	Y	Y	N
3 *Hutchinson*	N	N	N	Y	N	N	N
4 Ross	Y	N	Y	Y	Y	N	N
CALIFORNIA							
1 Thompson	Y	N	Y	Y	Y	Y	Y
2 *Herger*	N	Y	N	Y	N	?	Y
3 *Ose*	Y	N	N	Y	N	N	N
4 *Doolittle*	N	Y	N	N	N	N	Y
5 Matsui	Y	N	Y	Y	Y	Y	N
6 Woolsey	Y	N	Y	N	Y	Y	Y
7 Miller, George	Y	N	Y	N	Y	Y	Y
8 Pelosi	Y	N	Y	Y	Y	N	N
9 Lee	Y	N	Y	N	Y	Y	Y
10 Tauscher	Y	N	Y	Y	Y	N	N
11 *Pombo*	N	Y	N	N	N	N	N
12 Lantos	Y	N	Y	Y	Y	Y	N
13 Stark	Y	N	Y	N	Y	Y	Y
14 Eshoo	Y	N	Y	Y	Y	Y	N
15 Honda	Y	N	Y	N	Y	Y	Y
16 Lofgren	Y	N	Y	N	Y	N	N
17 Farr	Y	N	Y	Y	Y	Y	Y
18 Condit	Y	N	Y	Y	Y	N	N
19 *Radanovich*	N	N	N	Y	N	N	N
20 Dooley	Y	N	Y	Y	N	N	N
21 *Thomas*	N	N	N	Y	N	N	N
22 Capps	Y	N	Y	Y	Y	N	Y
23 *Gallegly*	N	N	N	Y	N	N	Y
24 Sherman	Y	N	Y	Y	Y	Y	N
25 *McKeon*	N	N	N	Y	N	Y	N
26 Berman	Y	N	Y	Y	Y	Y	N
27 Schiff	Y	N	Y	Y	Y	N	Y
28 *Dreier*	N	N	N	Y	N	N	Y
29 Waxman	Y	N	Y	Y	Y	Y	N
30 Becerra	Y	N	Y	Y	Y	Y	Y
31 Solis	Y	N	Y	N	Y	Y	Y
32 Watson	Y	N	Y	N	Y	Y	N
33 Roybal-Allard	Y	N	Y	Y	?	N	Y
34 Napolitano	Y	N	Y	Y	Y	Y	Y
35 Waters	Y	N	Y	N	Y	Y	Y
36 Harman	Y	N	Y	Y	Y	N	N
37 Millender-McD.	Y	N	Y	Y	Y	Y	N
38 *Horn*	N	Y	N	Y	Y	N	N

	173	174	175	176	177	178	179
39 *Royce*	N	Y	?	N	N	N	N
40 *Lewis*	N	N	N	Y	N	N	Y
41 *Miller, Gary*	N	N	N	Y	N	N	N
42 Baca	Y	N	Y	Y	+	N	N
43 *Calvert*	N	N	N	Y	N	N	N
44 *Bono*	N	N	N	Y	N	N	Y
45 *Rohrabacher*	N	N	N	Y	?	N	N
46 Sanchez	Y	N	Y	Y	Y	N	N
47 *Cox*	?	?	?	?	?	?	?
48 *Issa*	N	N	N	N	N	N	N
49 Davis	Y	N	Y	Y	Y	Y	Y
50 Filner	Y	N	N	Y	Y	Y	Y
51 *Cunningham*	N	N	N	Y	N	N	N
52 *Hunter*	N	N	N	Y	N	N	Y
COLORADO							
1 DeGette	Y	N	Y	N	Y	Y	Y
2 Udall	Y	N	Y	N	Y	Y	Y
3 *McInnis*	N	N	N	Y	?	?	?
4 *Schaffer*	N	Y	N	N	N	N	Y
5 *Hefley*	N	N	N	N	N	N	N
6 *Tancredo*	N	Y	N	N	N	N	Y
CONNECTICUT							
1 Larson	Y	N	Y	Y	Y	Y	N
2 *Simmons*	N	N	N	Y	Y	Y	N
3 DeLauro	Y	N	Y	Y	Y	Y	N
4 *Shays*	N	Y	N	N	Y	Y	N
5 Maloney	Y	N	Y	Y	Y	N	N
6 *Johnson*	N	N	N	Y	Y	Y	N
DELAWARE							
AL *Castle*	N	Y	N	Y	Y	Y	N
FLORIDA							
1 *Scarborough*	N	Y	N	Y	N	Y	N
2 Boyd	Y	N	Y	Y	Y	N	N
3 Brown	Y	N	Y	Y	Y	N	N
4 *Crenshaw*	N	N	N	Y	N	N	N
5 Thurman	Y	N	Y	Y	Y	N	N
6 *Stearns*	N	Y	N	Y	N	N	N
7 *Mica*	N	N	N	Y	N	N	N
8 *Keller*	N	Y	N	Y	N	N	N
9 *Bilirakis*	N	N	N	Y	?	N	N
10 *Young*	N	N	N	Y	N	N	N
11 Davis	Y	N	Y	Y	Y	N	N
12 *Putnam*	N	N	N	Y	N	N	N
13 *Miller*	N	Y	N	N	N	N	N
14 *Goss*	N	N	N	Y	N	N	N
15 *Weldon*	N	N	N	Y	N	N	N
16 *Foley*	N	N	N	Y	Y	N	N
17 Meek	Y	N	Y	Y	Y	Y	N
18 *Ros-Lehtinen*	N	N	N	Y	N	N	N
19 Wexler	Y	N	Y	Y	Y	Y	Y
20 Deutsch	Y	N	Y	N	Y	Y	Y
21 *Diaz-Balart*	N	N	N	Y	N	N	N
22 *Shaw*	N	N	N	Y	N	N	N
23 Hastings	Y	N	Y	N	Y	N	N
GEORGIA							
1 *Kingston*	N	Y	N	N	N	N	N
2 Bishop	Y	N	Y	Y	Y	N	N
3 *Collins*	N	N	N	Y	N	N	Y
4 McKinney	Y	N	Y	N	Y	Y	Y
5 Lewis	Y	N	Y	Y	Y	?	?
6 *Isakson*	N	N	N	Y	N	N	N
7 *Barr*	N	N	N	N	N	N	N
8 *Chambliss*	N	N	N	Y	N	N	N
9 *Deal*	N	N	N	Y	N	N	N
10 *Norwood*	N	N	N	Y	N	N	N
11 *Linder*	N	N	N	Y	N	N	N
HAWAII							
1 Abercrombie	Y	N	Y	Y	Y	Y	N
2 Mink	Y	N	Y	N	Y	Y	Y
IDAHO							
1 *Otter*	N	Y	N	Y	N	N	N
2 *Simpson*	N	N	N	Y	N	N	N
ILLINOIS							
1 Rush	?	?	?	?	?	?	?
2 Jackson	Y	N	Y	N	Y	Y	Y
3 Lipinski	Y	N	Y	Y	Y	Y	Y
4 Gutierrez	Y	N	Y	Y	Y	Y	Y
5 Blagojevich	Y	N	Y	Y	Y	Y	Y
6 *Hyde*	N	N	N	Y	N	N	N
7 Davis	Y	N	Y	Y	Y	Y	Y
8 *Crane*	N	Y	N	N	N	N	N
9 Schakowsky	Y	N	Y	N	Y	Y	Y
10 *Kirk*	N	N	N	Y	Y	Y	N
11 *Weller*	N	N	N	Y	N	N	N
12 Costello	Y	N	Y	N	Y	N	N
13 *Biggert*	N	N	N	Y	N	N	N

ND Northern Democrats   SD Southern Democrats

	173	174	175	176	177	178	179
14 ***Hastert***					N		
15 ***Johnson***	N	N	N	Y	Y	Y	Y
16 ***Manzullo***	N	N	N	N	N	N	Y
17 Evans	Y	N	Y	Y	Y	N	Y
18 ***LaHood***	N	N	N	Y	Y	Y	N
19 Phelps	Y	N	Y	Y	N	N	N
20 ***Shimkus***	N	N	N	Y	N	N	N
INDIANA							
1 Visclosky	Y	N	Y	Y	Y	N	N
2 ***Pence***	N	Y	N	Y	N	N	N
3 Roemer	Y	N	Y	Y	Y	Y	N
4 ***Souder***	N	?	N	Y	N	N	N
5 ***Buyer***	N	N	N	Y	N	N	N
6 ***Burton***	N	N	N	Y	N	N	N
7 ***Kerns***	N	N	N	Y	N	N	N
8 ***Hostettler***	N	Y	N	Y	N	N	N
9 Hill	Y	N	Y	Y	Y	N	Y
10 Carson	Y	N	Y	N	Y	Y	Y
IOWA							
1 ***Leach***	N	N	N	Y	Y	Y	N
2 ***Nussle***	N	Y	N	Y	N	Y	N
3 Boswell	Y	N	Y	Y	Y	Y	Y
4 ***Ganske***	N	N	N	Y	N	Y	N
5 ***Latham***	N	N	N	Y	N	N	N
KANSAS							
1 ***Moran***	Y	N	N	Y	N	N	Y
2 ***Ryun***	N	Y	N	Y	N	N	N
3 Moore	Y	N	Y	Y	Y	Y	N
4 ***Tiahrt***	N	Y	N	Y	N	N	N
KENTUCKY							
1 ***Whitfield***	N	N	N	Y	N	N	N
2 ***Lewis***	N	N	N	Y	N	N	N
3 ***Northup***	N	N	N	Y	N	N	N
4 Lucas	Y	N	Y	Y	N	N	N
5 ***Rogers***	N	N	N	Y	N	N	N
6 ***Fletcher***	N	N	N	Y	N	N	N
LOUISIANA							
1 ***Vitter***	N	Y	N	Y	N	N	N
2 Jefferson	Y	N	Y	Y	Y	Y	Y
3 ***Tauzin***	N	Y	N	Y	N	N	N
4 ***McCrery***	N	N	N	Y	N	N	N
5 ***Cooksey***	N	N	N	Y	N	N	N
6 ***Baker***	N	Y	N	Y	N	N	N
7 John	Y	Y	Y	Y	N	N	N
MAINE							
1 Allen	Y	N	Y	Y	Y	N	Y
2 Baldacci	Y	N	Y	Y	Y	N	Y
MARYLAND							
1 ***Gilchrest***	N	N	N	Y	N	N	N
2 ***Ehrlich***	N	N	N	Y	N	N	N
3 Cardin	Y	N	Y	Y	Y	N	N
4 Wynn	Y	N	Y	Y	Y	N	Y
5 Hoyer	Y	N	Y	Y	Y	N	N
6 ***Bartlett***	N	Y	N	Y	N	N	N
7 Cummings	Y	N	Y	Y	Y	Y	Y
8 ***Morella***	N	N	N	Y	Y	Y	N
MASSACHUSETTS							
1 Olver	Y	N	Y	N	Y	N	N
2 Neal	Y	N	Y	N	Y	?	?
3 McGovern	Y	N	Y	N	Y	Y	Y
4 Frank	Y	N	Y	N	Y	Y	N
5 Meehan	Y	N	Y	N	Y	Y	N
6 Tierney	Y	N	Y	Y	Y	Y	N
7 Markey	Y	N	Y	N	Y	Y	Y
8 Capuano	Y	N	Y	N	Y	Y	Y
9 Vacant							
10 Delahunt	Y	N	Y	N	Y	Y	N
MICHIGAN							
1 Stupak	Y	N	Y	N	Y	N	N
2 ***Hoekstra***	Y	Y	N	N	N	N	N
3 ***Ehlers***	N	N	N	N	Y	N	N
4 ***Camp***	N	N	N	Y	N	N	N
5 Barcia	Y	N	Y	Y	Y	N	Y
6 ***Upton***	Y	N	N	N	N	N	N
7 ***Smith***	N	Y	N	N	N	N	N
8 ***Rogers***	N	N	N	Y	Y	N	N
9 Kildee	Y	N	Y	Y	Y	Y	Y
10 Bonior	Y	N	Y	N	Y	N	N
11 ***Knollenberg***	N	N	N	Y	N	N	N
12 Levin	Y	N	Y	Y	Y	Y	N
13 Rivers	Y	N	Y	N	Y	Y	N
14 Conyers	Y	N	Y	N	Y	Y	Y
15 Kilpatrick	Y	N	Y	Y	+	N	N
16 Dingell	Y	N	Y	N	?	Y	N

	173	174	175	176	177	178	179
MINNESOTA							
1 ***Gutknecht***	N	N	N	Y	N	N	N
2 ***Kennedy***	N	Y	N	Y	N	Y	N
3 ***Ramstad***	N	Y	N	N	Y	Y	Y
4 McCollum	Y	N	Y	Y	Y	Y	Y
5 Sabo	Y	N	Y	Y	Y	N	N
6 Luther	Y	N	Y	N	Y	Y	Y
7 Peterson	Y	N	Y	Y	Y	Y	Y
8 Oberstar	Y	N	Y	Y	Y	N	N
MISSISSIPPI							
1 ***Wicker***	N	N	N	Y	N	N	N
2 Thompson	Y	N	Y	Y	Y	N	N
3 ***Pickering***	N	N	N	Y	N	N	N
4 Shows	Y	N	Y	Y	N	N	Y
5 Taylor	Y	N	Y	Y	N	N	Y
MISSOURI							
1 Clay	Y	N	Y	Y	Y	N	Y
2 ***Akin***	N	Y	N	Y	N	N	N
3 Gephardt	Y	N	Y	Y	Y	Y	Y
4 Skelton	Y	N	Y	Y	N	N	N
5 McCarthy	Y	N	Y	Y	Y	Y	N
6 ***Graves***	N	N	N	Y	N	N	Y
7 ***Blunt***	N	Y	N	Y	N	N	N
8 ***Emerson***	N	N	N	Y	N	Y	Y
9 ***Hulshof***	N	Y	N	Y	N	Y	Y
MONTANA							
AL ***Rehberg***	N	N	N	Y	N	N	N
NEBRASKA							
1 ***Bereuter***	N	N	N	Y	Y	Y	N
2 ***Terry***	N	N	N	N	N	N	Y
3 ***Osborne***	N	N	N	Y	N	N	N
NEVADA							
1 Berkley	Y	N	Y	Y	Y	N	Y
2 ***Gibbons***	N	N	N	Y	N	N	N
NEW HAMPSHIRE							
1 ***Sununu***	N	N	N	Y	N	Y	Y
2 ***Bass***	N	N	N	Y	Y	Y	Y
NEW JERSEY							
1 Andrews	Y	N	Y	Y	Y	Y	N
2 ***LoBiondo***	N	N	N	Y	Y	Y	Y
3 ***Saxton***	N	N	N	Y	N	Y	Y
4 ***Smith***	N	N	N	Y	N	Y	Y
5 ***Roukema***	N	N	N	Y	Y	Y	N
6 Pallone	Y	N	Y	Y	Y	Y	Y
7 ***Ferguson***	N	N	N	Y	N	Y	Y
8 Pascrell	Y	N	Y	Y	Y	Y	Y
9 Rothman	Y	N	Y	N	Y	Y	Y
10 Payne	Y	N	Y	N	Y	Y	Y
11 ***Frelinghuysen***	N	N	N	Y	N	N	N
12 Holt	Y	N	Y	Y	Y	Y	Y
13 Menendez	Y	N	Y	Y	Y	Y	Y
NEW MEXICO							
1 ***Wilson***	N	N	N	Y	N	N	N
2 ***Skeen***	N	N	N	Y	N	N	N
3 Udall	Y	N	Y	Y	Y	Y	Y
NEW YORK							
1 ***Grucci***	N	N	N	Y	Y	Y	N
2 Israel	Y	N	Y	Y	Y	?	?
3 ***King***	N	N	N	Y	N	Y	N
4 McCarthy	Y	N	Y	Y	Y	Y	N
5 Ackerman	Y	N	Y	Y	Y	Y	Y
6 Meeks	Y	N	Y	N	Y	Y	Y
7 Crowley	Y	N	Y	N	Y	Y	N
8 Nadler	Y	N	Y	N	Y	Y	Y
9 Weiner	Y	N	Y	N	Y	Y	N
10 Towns	Y	N	Y	Y	Y	Y	Y
11 Owens	Y	N	Y	N	Y	Y	Y
12 Velázquez	Y	N	Y	Y	Y	Y	Y
13 ***Fossella***	N	N	N	Y	Y	N	N
14 Maloney	Y	N	Y	Y	Y	N	Y
15 Rangel	Y	N	Y	Y	Y	Y	Y
16 Serrano	Y	N	Y	Y	Y	?	?
17 Engel	Y	N	Y	Y	Y	Y	Y
18 Lowey	Y	N	Y	Y	Y	Y	N
19 ***Kelly***	N	N	N	Y	Y	Y	N
20 ***Gilman***	N	N	N	Y	Y	Y	N
21 McNulty	Y	N	Y	Y	Y	Y	Y
22 ***Sweeney***	N	N	N	Y	N	Y	N
23 ***Boehlert***	N	N	N	Y	Y	Y	N
24 ***McHugh***	N	N	N	Y	Y	Y	N
25 ***Walsh***	N	N	N	Y	N	Y	N
26 Hinchey	Y	N	Y	N	Y	N	Y
27 ***Reynolds***	N	N	N	Y	N	N	N
28 Slaughter	Y	N	Y	N	Y	Y	Y
29 LaFalce	Y	N	Y	N	Y	Y	Y

	173	174	175	176	177	178	179
30 ***Quinn***	N	N	N	Y	Y	Y	N
31 ***Houghton***	?	?	?	?	?	?	?
NORTH CAROLINA							
1 Clayton	Y	N	Y	Y	Y	N	Y
2 Etheridge	Y	N	Y	Y	Y	Y	Y
3 ***Jones***	Y	Y	Y	Y	N	N	Y
4 Price	Y	N	Y	Y	Y	N	N
5 ***Burr***	N	Y	N	Y	N	N	N
6 ***Coble***	N	N	N	Y	N	N	N
7 McIntyre	Y	N	Y	Y	N	Y	N
8 ***Hayes***	N	N	N	Y	N	N	N
9 ***Myrick***	N	Y	N	Y	N	N	N
10 ***Ballenger***	N	N	N	Y	Y	N	N
11 ***Taylor***	N	N	N	Y	N	N	N
12 Watt	Y	N	Y	N	Y	Y	Y
NORTH DAKOTA							
AL Pomeroy	Y	N	Y	Y	Y	N	N
OHIO							
1 ***Chabot***	N	Y	N	N	N	N	Y
2 ***Portman***	N	Y	N	Y	N	N	N
3 Hall	Y	N	Y	N	Y	Y	Y
4 ***Oxley***	N	N	N	Y	N	N	N
5 ***Gillmor***	N	N	N	Y	N	N	N
6 Strickland	Y	N	Y	Y	Y	N	Y
7 ***Hobson***	N	N	N	Y	N	N	N
8 ***Boehner***	N	N	N	Y	N	N	N
9 Kaptur	?	?	?	?	?	?	?
10 Kucinich	Y	N	Y	N	Y	Y	Y
11 Jones	Y	N	Y	N	Y	Y	Y
12 ***Tiberi***	N	N	N	Y	N	N	N
13 Brown	Y	N	Y	N	Y	Y	N
14 Sawyer	Y	N	Y	Y	Y	Y	N
15 ***Pryce***	N	N	N	Y	Y	N	N
16 ***Regula***	N	N	N	Y	N	N	N
17 Traficant	N	N	N	Y	N	N	N
18 ***Ney***	N	N	N	Y	N	N	Y
19 ***LaTourette***	N	N	N	Y	N	N	N
OKLAHOMA							
1 ***Largent***	N	Y	N	Y	N	N	N
2 Carson	Y	N	Y	Y	Y	N	Y
3 ***Watkins***	N	N	N	Y	N	N	N
4 ***Watts***	N	Y	N	Y	N	N	N
5 ***Istook***	N	Y	N	Y	N	N	N
6 ***Lucas***	N	N	N	Y	N	N	N
OREGON							
1 Wu	Y	Y	Y	N	Y	Y	Y
2 ***Walden***	N	N	N	Y	N	N	Y
3 Blumenauer	Y	N	Y	N	Y	Y	Y
4 DeFazio	Y	N	Y	N	P	Y	Y
5 Hooley	Y	N	Y	N	Y	Y	Y
PENNSYLVANIA							
1 Brady	Y	N	Y	Y	Y	N	Y
2 Fattah	Y	N	Y	Y	?	N	Y
3 Borski	Y	N	Y	Y	Y	N	N
4 ***Hart***	N	N	N	Y	N	N	N
5 ***Peterson***	N	N	N	Y	N	N	N
6 Holden	Y	N	Y	Y	Y	N	N
7 ***Weldon***	N	N	N	Y	Y	Y	N
8 ***Greenwood***	N	N	N	Y	Y	N	N
9 ***Shuster, Bill***	N	N	N	Y	N	N	N
10 ***Sherwood***	N	N	N	Y	N	Y	N
11 Kanjorski	Y	N	Y	Y	Y	N	N
12 Murtha	Y	N	Y	Y	Y	N	N
13 Hoeffel	Y	N	Y	Y	Y	N	N
14 Coyne	Y	N	Y	N	Y	N	Y
15 ***Toomey***	N	Y	N	Y	N	N	N
16 ***Pitts***	N	Y	N	Y	N	N	N
17 ***Gekas***	N	N	N	Y	N	N	N
18 Doyle	Y	N	Y	Y	Y	N	N
19 ***Platts***	N	N	N	Y	N	Y	N
20 Mascara	Y	N	Y	Y	Y	N	N
21 ***English***	N	N	N	Y	N	N	N
RHODE ISLAND							
1 Kennedy	Y	N	Y	N	Y	N	N
2 Langevin	Y	N	Y	Y	Y	Y	Y
SOUTH CAROLINA							
1 ***Brown***	N	N	N	Y	N	N	N
2 ***Spence***	N	N	N	Y	N	N	N
3 ***Graham***	N	N	N	Y	N	N	N
4 ***DeMint***	N	Y	N	Y	N	N	N
5 Spratt	Y	N	Y	Y	Y	N	N
6 Clyburn	Y	N	Y	Y	Y	N	N
SOUTH DAKOTA							
AL ***Thune***	N	N	N	Y	N	N	N

	173	174	175	176	177	178	179
TENNESSEE							
1 ***Jenkins***	N	N	N	Y	N	N	N
2 ***Duncan***	N	Y	N	N	N	N	N
3 ***Wamp***	N	N	N	Y	N	N	N
4 ***Hilleary***	N	N	N	Y	N	N	N
5 Clement	Y	N	Y	Y	Y	N	N
6 Gordon	Y	N	Y	Y	Y	N	N
7 ***Bryant***	N	N	N	Y	N	N	N
8 Tanner	Y	N	Y	Y	N	Y	N
9 Ford	Y	N	Y	Y	Y	Y	N
TEXAS							
1 Sandlin	Y	N	Y	Y	Y	N	N
2 Turner	Y	N	Y	Y	N	N	N
3 ***Johnson, Sam***	N	Y	N	Y	N	N	N
4 Hall	N	Y	Y	Y	N	N	Y
5 ***Sessions***	N	Y	N	Y	N	N	Y
6 ***Barton***	N	Y	N	Y	N	N	N
7 ***Culberson***	N	Y	N	Y	N	N	N
8 ***Brady***	N	N	N	Y	N	N	N
9 Lampson	Y	N	Y	N	Y	N	N
10 Doggett	Y	N	Y	N	Y	Y	Y
11 Edwards	Y	N	Y	Y	Y	N	N
12 ***Granger***	N	N	N	Y	N	N	N
13 ***Thornberry***	N	Y	N	Y	N	N	N
14 ***Paul***	N	Y	N	N	N	Y	Y
15 Hinojosa	Y	N	Y	Y	Y	Y	N
16 Reyes	Y	N	Y	Y	Y	N	N
17 Stenholm	Y	N	Y	Y	N	N	N
18 Jackson-Lee	Y	N	Y	N	Y	N	Y
19 ***Combest***	N	N	N	Y	N	N	N
20 Gonzalez	Y	N	Y	Y	Y	N	N
21 ***Smith***	N	N	N	Y	N	N	N
22 ***DeLay***	N	Y	N	Y	N	N	N
23 ***Bonilla***	N	N	N	Y	N	N	N
24 Frost	Y	N	Y	Y	Y	N	N
25 Bentsen	Y	N	Y	N	Y	N	N
26 ***Armey***	N	N	N	Y	N	N	N
27 Ortiz	Y	N	Y	Y	Y	N	N
28 Rodriguez	Y	N	Y	Y	Y	Y	N
29 Green	Y	N	Y	N	Y	N	N
30 Johnson, E.B.	Y	N	Y	Y	Y	N	N
UTAH							
1 ***Hansen***	N	N	N	Y	N	Y	N
2 Matheson	Y	N	Y	Y	N	N	N
3 ***Cannon***	N	Y	N	Y	N	Y	N
VERMONT							
AL *Sanders*	Y	N	Y	N	Y	Y	Y
VIRGINIA							
1 ***Davis, Jo Ann***	N	Y	N	Y	N	N	N
2 ***Schrock***	N	N	N	Y	N	N	N
3 Scott	Y	N	Y	Y	Y	N	N
4 Vacant							
5 *Goode*	N	Y	N	Y	N	N	N
6 ***Goodlatte***	N	Y	N	Y	N	N	N
7 ***Cantor***	N	Y	N	Y	N	N	N
8 Moran	Y	N	Y	Y	Y	N	N
9 Boucher	Y	N	Y	Y	Y	N	Y
10 ***Wolf***	N	N	N	Y	N	N	N
11 ***Davis, T.***	N	N	N	Y	Y	Y	N
WASHINGTON							
1 Inslee	Y	N	Y	Y	Y	Y	Y
2 Larsen	Y	N	Y	Y	Y	N	Y
3 Baird	Y	N	Y	Y	Y	Y	N
4 ***Hastings***	N	N	N	Y	N	N	N
5 ***Nethercutt***	N	N	N	Y	N	N	N
6 Dicks	Y	N	Y	Y	Y	N	N
7 McDermott	Y	N	Y	N	Y	Y	Y
8 ***Dunn***	N	Y	N	Y	N	N	N
9 Smith	Y	N	Y	Y	Y	N	N
WEST VIRGINIA							
1 Mollohan	Y	N	Y	Y	Y	N	N
2 ***Capito***	N	N	N	Y	N	N	N
3 Rahall	Y	N	Y	Y	Y	N	Y
WISCONSIN							
1 ***Ryan***	N	N	N	Y	N	Y	N
2 Baldwin	Y	N	Y	N	Y	Y	N
3 Kind	Y	N	Y	N	Y	Y	N
4 Kleczka	Y	N	Y	N	Y	Y	N
5 Barrett	Y	N	Y	N	Y	Y	N
6 ***Petri***	N	N	N	N	N	Y	N
7 Obey	Y	N	Y	N	Y	N	N
8 ***Green***	N	Y	N	Y	N	Y	N
9 ***Sensenbrenner***	N	N	N	N	N	Y	N
WYOMING							
AL ***Cubin***	N	Y	N	Y	?	?	?

Southern states - Ala., Ark., Fla., Ga., Ky., La., Miss., N.C., Okla., S.C., Tenn., Texas, Va.

Key

Y	Voted for (yea).
#	Paired for.
+	Announced for.
N	Voted against (nay).
X	Paired against.
–	Announced against.
P	Voted "present."
C	Voted "present" to avoid possible conflict of interest.
?	Did not vote or otherwise make a position known.

Democrats **Republicans** *Independents*

180. HR 2217. Fiscal 2002 Interior Appropriations/Monument Protection. Rahall, D-W.Va., amendment that would prohibit spending funds for oil and gas leasing and development within national monument boundaries except for monuments already authorizing such activity. Adopted 242-173: R 47-164; D 194-8 (ND 149-1, SD 45-7); I 1-1. June 21, 2001.

181. HR 2217. Fiscal 2002 Interior Appropriations/Gulf Energy. Davis, D-Fla., amendment that would prohibit spending funds for oil and gas development before April 1, 2002, in an area of the Gulf of Mexico known as Lease Sale 181. Adopted 247-164: R 70-139; D 176-24 (ND 142-6, SD 34-18); I 1-1. A "nay" was a vote in support of the president's position.. June 21, 2001.

182. HR 2217. Fiscal 2002 Interior Appropriations/Mining Regulations. Inslee, D-Wash., amendment that would prohibit spending funds to suspend or revise final regulations amending environmental mining rules and published in the Nov. 21, 2000, Federal Register. Adopted 216-194: R 28-179; D 187-14 (ND 143-6, SD 44-8); I 1-1. June 21, 2001.

183. HR 2217. Fiscal 2002 Interior Appropriations/Biscayne Lease. Deutsch, D-Fla., amendment that would prohibit spending funds to compensate Interior Department staff to extend leases, standstill agreements, or a March 30, 2001, settlement agreement, related to seven campsite leases in Biscayne National Park, Florida. Rejected 187-222: R 3-203; D 183-18 (ND 143-6, SD 40-12); I 1-1. June 21, 2001.

184. HR 2217. Fiscal 2002 Interior Appropriations/NEA Funding. Stearns, R-Fla, amendment that would reduce funding for the National Endowment for the Arts by $10 million and increase energy conservation programs by $10 million. Rejected 145-264: R 137-70; D 7-193 (ND 1-147, SD 6-46); I 1-1. June 21, 2001.

185. HR 2217. Fiscal 2002 Interior Appropriations/Passage. Passage of the bill that would appropriate $18.9 billion for the Interior Department, related agencies and cultural programs in fiscal 2002. Passed 376-32: R 177-30; D 198-1 (ND 148-0, SD 50-1); I 1-1. June 21, 2001.

Member	180	181	182	183	184	185
ALABAMA						
1 *Callahan*	?	?	?	?	?	?
2 *Everett*	?	?	?	?	?	?
3 *Riley*	?	?	?	?	?	?
4 *Aderholt*	?	?	?	?	?	?
5 *Cramer*	?	?	?	?	?	?
6 *Bachus*	?	?	?	?	?	?
7 Hilliard	Y	Y	Y	N	N	Y
ALASKA						
AL *Young*	N	N	N	N	Y	Y
ARIZONA						
1 *Flake*	N	N	N	N	Y	N
2 Pastor	Y	Y	Y	Y	N	Y
3 *Stump*	N	N	N	N	Y	Y
4 *Shadegg*	N	N	N	N	Y	N
5 *Kolbe*	N	N	N	N	N	Y
6 *Hayworth*	N	N	N	N	Y	Y
ARKANSAS						
1 Berry	N	Y	N	N	N	N
2 Snyder	Y	Y	Y	Y	N	Y
3 *Hutchinson*	N	Y	N	N	N	Y
4 Ross	Y	Y	N	N	N	Y
CALIFORNIA						
1 Thompson	Y	Y	Y	Y	N	Y
2 *Herger*	N	N	N	Y	N	Y
3 *Ose*	N	Y	N	N	N	Y
4 *Doolittle*	N	N	N	N	Y	Y
5 Matsui	Y	Y	Y	Y	N	Y
6 Woolsey	Y	Y	Y	Y	N	Y
7 Miller, George	Y	Y	Y	Y	N	Y
8 Pelosi	Y	Y	Y	Y	N	Y
9 Lee	Y	Y	Y	Y	N	Y
10 Tauscher	Y	Y	Y	Y	N	Y
11 *Pombo*	N	N	N	N	Y	Y
12 Lantos	Y	Y	Y	Y	N	Y
13 Stark	Y	Y	Y	Y	N	Y
14 Eshoo	Y	Y	Y	Y	N	Y
15 Honda	Y	Y	Y	Y	N	Y
16 Lofgren	Y	Y	Y	Y	N	Y
17 Farr	Y	Y	Y	Y	N	Y
18 Condit	Y	Y	Y	N	N	Y
19 *Radanovich*	N	N	N	N	Y	Y
20 Dooley	Y	N	Y	Y	N	Y
21 *Thomas*	N	N	N	N	Y	Y
22 Capps	Y	Y	Y	Y	N	Y
23 *Gallegly*	N	Y	N	N	N	Y
24 Sherman	Y	Y	Y	Y	N	Y
25 *McKeon*	N	N	N	N	N	Y
26 Berman	Y	?	?	?	?	?
27 Schiff	Y	Y	Y	Y	N	Y
28 *Dreier*	N	N	N	N	N	Y
29 Waxman	Y	Y	Y	Y	N	Y
30 Becerra	?	Y	Y	Y	N	Y
31 Solis	Y	Y	Y	Y	N	Y
32 Watson	Y	Y	Y	Y	N	?
33 Roybal-Allard	Y	Y	Y	Y	N	Y
34 Napolitano	Y	Y	Y	Y	N	Y
35 Waters	Y	Y	Y	Y	N	Y
36 Harman	Y	Y	Y	Y	N	Y
37 Millender-McD.	Y	Y	Y	Y	N	Y
38 Horn	Y	Y	Y	Y	N	Y
39 *Royce*	N	N	N	N	N	Y
40 *Lewis*	N	N	N	N	N	Y
41 *Miller, Gary*	N	N	N	N	N	Y
42 Baca	Y	Y	Y	Y	N	Y
43 *Calvert*	N	?	?	?	?	?
44 *Bono*	N	N	N	N	N	Y
45 *Rohrabacher*	N	N	N	N	N	Y
46 Sanchez	Y	Y	Y	Y	N	Y
47 *Cox*	?	?	?	?	?	?
48 *Issa*	N	N	N	N	N	Y
49 Davis	Y	Y	Y	Y	N	Y
50 Filner	Y	Y	Y	Y	N	Y
51 *Cunningham*	N	N	N	N	N	Y
52 *Hunter*	N	N	N	N	Y	Y
COLORADO						
1 DeGette	Y	Y	Y	Y	N	Y
2 Udall	Y	Y	Y	Y	N	Y
3 *McInnis*	?	?	?	?	?	Y
4 *Schaffer*	N	N	N	N	Y	Y
5 *Hefley*	N	N	N	N	Y	N
6 *Tancredo*	N	N	N	N	Y	Y
CONNECTICUT						
1 Larson	Y	Y	Y	Y	N	Y
2 *Simmons*	Y	N	Y	N	N	Y
3 DeLauro	Y	Y	Y	Y	N	Y
4 *Shays*	Y	Y	Y	Y	N	Y
5 Maloney	Y	Y	Y	Y	N	Y
6 *Johnson*	Y	Y	N	Y	N	Y
DELAWARE						
AL *Castle*	Y	Y	Y	N	N	Y
FLORIDA						
1 *Scarborough*	Y	Y	Y	N	Y	?
2 Boyd	Y	Y	Y	N	N	Y
3 Brown	Y	Y	Y	N	N	Y
4 *Crenshaw*	N	Y	N	N	N	Y
5 Thurman	Y	Y	Y	N	N	Y
6 *Stearns*	N	Y	N	N	Y	N
7 *Mica*	N	N	N	N	N	Y
8 *Keller*	N	Y	N	N	Y	Y
9 *Bilirakis*	Y	Y	N	N	N	Y
10 *Young*	N	Y	N	Y	N	Y
11 Davis	Y	Y	Y	Y	N	Y
12 *Putnam*	N	Y	N	N	Y	Y
13 *Miller*	N	Y	N	Y	N	Y
14 *Goss*	N	Y	N	Y	N	Y
15 *Weldon*	N	Y	N	N	N	Y
16 *Foley*	Y	Y	N	Y	N	Y
17 Meek	Y	Y	Y	N	N	Y
18 *Ros-Lehtinen*	N	Y	N	N	N	Y
19 Wexler	Y	Y	Y	Y	N	Y
20 Deutsch	Y	Y	Y	Y	N	Y
21 *Diaz-Balart*	N	Y	N	N	N	Y
22 *Shaw*	N	Y	N	N	N	Y
23 Hastings	Y	Y	Y	N	N	Y
GEORGIA						
1 *Kingston*	N	N	N	N	Y	Y
2 Bishop	Y	Y	Y	N	N	Y
3 *Collins*	N	N	N	N	Y	Y
4 McKinney	Y	Y	Y	Y	N	Y
5 Lewis	?	?	?	?	?	?
6 *Isakson*	N	N	N	N	N	Y
7 *Barr*	N	N	N	N	Y	Y
8 *Chambliss*	N	N	N	N	Y	Y
9 *Deal*	N	N	N	N	Y	Y
10 *Norwood*	N	N	N	N	Y	Y
11 *Linder*	N	?	N	N	Y	Y
HAWAII						
1 Abercrombie	Y	Y	Y	N	N	Y
2 Mink	Y	Y	Y	Y	N	Y
IDAHO						
1 *Otter*	N	N	N	N	Y	N
2 *Simpson*	N	N	N	N	Y	N
ILLINOIS						
1 Rush	?	?	?	?	?	?
2 Jackson	Y	Y	Y	Y	N	Y
3 Lipinski	Y	N	Y	N	N	Y
4 Gutierrez	Y	Y	Y	Y	N	Y
5 Blagojevich	Y	Y	Y	Y	N	Y
6 *Hyde*	Y	N	N	N	Y	Y
7 Davis	Y	Y	Y	Y	N	Y
8 *Crane*	N	N	N	N	Y	N
9 Schakowsky	Y	Y	Y	Y	N	Y
10 *Kirk*	Y	N	N	N	N	Y
11 *Weller*	N	Y	N	N	Y	Y
12 Costello	Y	Y	Y	Y	N	Y
13 *Biggert*	N	N	N	N	Y	Y

ND Northern Democrats   SD Southern Democrats

	180	181	182	183	184	185
14 ***Hastert***						
15 ***Johnson***	Y	Y	Y	N	N	Y
16 ***Manzullo***	N	Y	N	N	Y	Y
17 Evans	Y	Y	Y	Y	N	Y
18 ***LaHood***	Y	Y	N	N	N	Y
19 Phelps	Y	Y	N	Y	N	Y
20 ***Shimkus***	N	N	N	N	Y	Y
INDIANA						
1 Visclosky	Y	Y	Y	Y	N	Y
2 ***Pence***	N	N	N	N	Y	Y
3 Roemer	Y	Y	Y	Y	N	Y
4 ***Souder***	N	N	N	N	Y	Y
5 ***Buyer***	N	N	N	N	Y	Y
6 ***Burton***	N	N	N	N	Y	Y
7 ***Kerns***	N	Y	N	N	Y	Y
8 ***Hostettler***	N	N	N	N	Y	N
9 Hill	Y	Y	Y	Y	N	Y
10 Carson	Y	Y	Y	Y	N	Y
IOWA						
1 ***Leach***	Y	Y	Y	N	N	Y
2 ***Nussle***	Y	N	N	N	Y	Y
3 Boswell	Y	N	Y	N	N	Y
4 ***Ganske***	Y	Y	Y	N	Y	Y
5 ***Latham***	Y	N	N	N	Y	Y
KANSAS						
1 ***Moran***	N	N	N	N	Y	N
2 ***Ryun***	N	N	N	N	Y	N
3 Moore	Y	Y	Y	Y	N	Y
4 ***Tiahrt***	N	N	N	N	Y	Y
KENTUCKY						
1 ***Whitfield***	N	N	N	N	Y	N
2 ***Lewis***	N	N	N	N	Y	Y
3 ***Northup***	Y	N	N	N	Y	Y
4 Lucas	Y	Y	N	Y	Y	Y
5 ***Rogers***	N	N	N	N	Y	Y
6 ***Fletcher***	N	N	N	N	Y	Y
LOUISIANA						
1 ***Vitter***	N	N	N	N	Y	Y
2 Jefferson	Y	N	Y	Y	N	Y
3 ***Tauzin***	N	N	N	N	Y	Y
4 ***McCrery***	N	N	N	N	Y	Y
5 ***Cooksey***	N	N	N	N	Y	Y
6 ***Baker***	N	N	?	?	?	?
7 John	N	N	N	N	N	Y
MAINE						
1 Allen	Y	Y	Y	Y	N	Y
2 Baldacci	Y	Y	Y	Y	N	Y
MARYLAND						
1 ***Gilchrest***	N	Y	N	N	N	Y
2 ***Ehrlich***	N	Y	N	N	N	Y
3 Cardin	Y	Y	Y	Y	N	Y
4 Wynn	Y	Y	Y	Y	N	Y
5 Hoyer	Y	Y	Y	Y	N	Y
6 ***Bartlett***	Y	Y	N	N	Y	Y
7 Cummings	Y	Y	Y	Y	N	Y
8 ***Morella***	Y	Y	Y	N	N	Y
MASSACHUSETTS						
1 Olver	Y	Y	Y	Y	N	Y
2 Neal	?	?	?	?	?	?
3 McGovern	Y	Y	Y	Y	N	Y
4 Frank	Y	Y	Y	Y	N	Y
5 Meehan	Y	?	?	?	?	?
6 Tierney	Y	Y	Y	Y	N	Y
7 Markey	Y	Y	Y	Y	N	Y
8 Capuano	Y	Y	Y	Y	N	Y
9 Vacant						
10 Delahunt	Y	Y	Y	Y	N	Y
MICHIGAN						
1 Stupak	Y	Y	Y	Y	N	Y
2 ***Hoekstra***	N	Y	N	N	Y	Y
3 ***Ehlers***	Y	Y	Y	N	N	Y
4 ***Camp***	N	Y	N	N	Y	Y
5 Barcia	Y	Y	Y	Y	N	Y
6 ***Upton***	Y	Y	Y	N	Y	Y
7 ***Smith***	N	N	N	N	Y	N
8 ***Rogers***	N	Y	N	N	N	Y
9 Kildee	Y	Y	Y	Y	N	Y
10 Bonior	Y	Y	Y	Y	N	Y
11 ***Knollenberg***	N	N	N	N	Y	Y
12 Levin	Y	Y	Y	Y	N	Y
13 Rivers	Y	Y	Y	Y	N	Y
14 Conyers	Y	Y	Y	Y	N	Y
15 Kilpatrick	Y	Y	Y	Y	N	Y
16 Dingell	Y	N	Y	Y	N	Y
MINNESOTA						
1 ***Gutknecht***	N	N	N	N	Y	Y
2 ***Kennedy***	Y	N	N	N	Y	Y
3 ***Ramstad***	Y	Y	Y	N	N	Y
4 McCollum	Y	Y	Y	Y	N	Y
5 Sabo	Y	Y	Y	Y	N	Y
6 Luther	Y	Y	Y	Y	N	Y
7 Peterson	Y	Y	Y	Y	N	Y
8 Oberstar	Y	Y	Y	Y	N	Y
MISSISSIPPI						
1 ***Wicker***	N	N	N	N	Y	Y
2 Thompson	Y	Y	Y	N	N	Y
3 ***Pickering***	N	N	N	N	Y	Y
4 Shows	N	N	Y	Y	Y	Y
5 Taylor	N	N	Y	Y	Y	Y
MISSOURI						
1 Clay	Y	Y	Y	Y	N	Y
2 ***Akin***	N	N	N	N	Y	Y
3 Gephardt	Y	Y	Y	Y	N	Y
4 Skelton	Y	Y	Y	Y	Y	Y
5 McCarthy	Y	Y	Y	Y	N	Y
6 ***Graves***	N	N	N	N	Y	Y
7 ***Blunt***	N	N	N	N	Y	Y
8 ***Emerson***	N	N	N	N	Y	N
9 ***Hulshof***	N	N	N	N	Y	Y
MONTANA						
AL ***Rehberg***	N	N	N	N	N	Y
NEBRASKA						
1 ***Bereuter***	N	N	N	N	N	Y
2 ***Terry***	N	N	N	N	N	Y
3 ***Osborne***	N	N	N	N	N	Y
NEVADA						
1 Berkley	Y	Y	N	Y	N	Y
2 ***Gibbons***	N	N	N	N	Y	N
NEW HAMPSHIRE						
1 ***Sununu***	Y	Y	Y	N	N	Y
2 ***Bass***	Y	N	Y	N	N	Y
NEW JERSEY						
1 Andrews	Y	Y	Y	Y	N	Y
2 ***LoBiondo***	Y	Y	Y	N	N	Y
3 ***Saxton***	Y	Y	Y	N	N	Y
4 ***Smith***	Y	Y	Y	N	Y	Y
5 ***Roukema***	Y	Y	?	?	?	?
6 Pallone	Y	Y	Y	Y	N	Y
7 ***Ferguson***	Y	Y	Y	N	N	Y
8 Pascrell	Y	Y	Y	Y	N	Y
9 Rothman	Y	Y	Y	Y	N	Y
10 Payne	Y	Y	Y	Y	N	Y
11 ***Frelinghuysen***	Y	Y	Y	N	N	Y
12 Holt	Y	Y	Y	Y	N	Y
13 Menendez	Y	Y	Y	Y	N	Y
NEW MEXICO						
1 ***Wilson***	N	N	N	N	Y	Y
2 ***Skeen***	N	N	N	N	Y	Y
3 Udall	Y	Y	Y	Y	N	Y
NEW YORK						
1 ***Grucci***	Y	N	N	N	N	Y
2 Israel	?	?	?	?	?	?
3 ***King***	Y	N	N	N	Y	Y
4 McCarthy	Y	Y	Y	Y	?	Y
5 Ackerman	Y	Y	Y	Y	N	Y
6 Meeks	Y	?	Y	Y	N	Y
7 Crowley	Y	Y	Y	Y	N	Y
8 Nadler	Y	Y	Y	Y	N	Y
9 Weiner	Y	Y	Y	Y	N	Y
10 Towns	Y	Y	Y	Y	N	Y
11 Owens	Y	Y	Y	Y	N	Y
12 Velázquez	Y	Y	Y	Y	N	Y
13 ***Fossella***	Y	Y	N	N	N	Y
14 Maloney	Y	Y	Y	Y	N	Y
15 Rangel	Y	Y	Y	Y	N	Y
16 Serrano	?	?	?	?	?	?
17 Engel	Y	Y	Y	Y	N	Y
18 Lowey	Y	Y	Y	Y	N	Y
19 ***Kelly***	Y	Y	Y	N	N	Y
20 ***Gilman***	Y	Y	Y	N	N	Y
21 McNulty	Y	Y	Y	Y	N	Y
22 ***Sweeney***	N	Y	N	N	N	Y
23 ***Boehlert***	Y	Y	Y	N	N	Y
24 ***McHugh***	Y	Y	N	N	N	Y
25 ***Walsh***	Y	Y	N	N	Y	Y
26 Hinchey	Y	Y	Y	Y	N	Y
27 ***Reynolds***	N	N	N	N	N	Y
28 Slaughter	Y	Y	Y	Y	N	Y
29 LaFalce	Y	Y	Y	Y	N	Y
30 ***Quinn***	Y	Y	Y	N	N	Y
31 ***Houghton***	?	?	?	?	?	?
NORTH CAROLINA						
1 Clayton	Y	Y	Y	Y	N	Y
2 Etheridge	Y	Y	Y	Y	N	Y
3 ***Jones***	N	Y	N	N	Y	N
4 Price	Y	Y	Y	Y	N	Y
5 ***Burr***	N	N	N	N	N	Y
6 ***Coble***	N	N	N	N	Y	Y
7 McIntyre	Y	Y	Y	Y	Y	Y
8 ***Hayes***	N	N	N	N	Y	Y
9 ***Myrick***	N	Y	N	N	Y	Y
10 ***Ballenger***	N	N	N	N	N	Y
11 ***Taylor***	N	N	N	N	Y	Y
12 Watt	Y	Y	Y	Y	N	Y
NORTH DAKOTA						
AL Pomeroy	Y	Y	Y	Y	N	Y
OHIO						
1 ***Chabot***	N	Y	N	N	Y	Y
2 ***Portman***	N	Y	N	N	N	Y
3 Hall	Y	Y	Y	Y	N	Y
4 ***Oxley***	N	N	N	N	Y	Y
5 ***Gillmor***	Y	N	N	N	N	Y
6 Strickland	Y	Y	Y	Y	N	Y
7 ***Hobson***	N	N	N	N	N	Y
8 ***Boehner***	N	N	?	N	Y	Y
9 Kaptur	?	?	?	?	?	?
10 Kucinich	Y	Y	Y	Y	N	Y
11 Jones	Y	Y	Y	Y	N	Y
12 ***Tiberi***	N	N	N	N	N	Y
13 Brown	Y	Y	Y	Y	N	Y
14 Sawyer	Y	Y	Y	Y	N	Y
15 ***Pryce***	Y	N	N	N	N	Y
16 ***Regula***	N	N	N	N	N	Y
17 Traficant	N	N	N	N	N	Y
18 ***Ney***	Y	N	N	N	Y	Y
19 ***LaTourette***	N	N	N	N	N	Y
OKLAHOMA						
1 ***Largent***	N	N	N	N	Y	Y
2 Carson	Y	N	Y	Y	N	Y
3 ***Watkins***	N	N	N	N	Y	Y
4 ***Watts***	N	N	N	N	Y	Y
5 ***Istook***	N	N	N	N	Y	Y
6 ***Lucas***	N	N	N	N	Y	Y
OREGON						
1 Wu	Y	Y	Y	Y	N	Y
2 ***Walden***	N	N	N	N	N	Y
3 Blumenauer	Y	Y	Y	Y	N	Y
4 DeFazio	Y	Y	Y	Y	N	Y
5 Hooley	Y	Y	Y	Y	N	Y
PENNSYLVANIA						
1 Brady	Y	Y	Y	Y	N	Y
2 Fattah	Y	Y	Y	Y	N	Y
3 Borski	Y	Y	Y	Y	N	Y
4 ***Hart***	N	N	N	N	N	Y
5 ***Peterson***	N	N	N	N	?	Y
6 Holden	Y	Y	N	Y	N	Y
7 ***Weldon***	Y	Y	Y	N	N	Y
8 ***Greenwood***	Y	Y	Y	N	N	Y
9 ***Shuster, Bill***	N	N	N	N	Y	Y
10 ***Sherwood***	N	N	N	N	N	Y
11 Kanjorski	Y	Y	Y	Y	N	Y
12 Murtha	Y	Y	N	N	N	Y
13 Hoeffel	Y	Y	Y	Y	N	Y
14 Coyne	Y	Y	Y	Y	N	Y
15 ***Toomey***	N	N	N	N	Y	N
16 ***Pitts***	N	N	N	?	Y	Y
17 ***Gekas***	N	N	N	N	N	Y
18 Doyle	Y	Y	Y	Y	N	Y
19 ***Platts***	N	Y	N	N	N	Y
20 Mascara	Y	Y	Y	Y	N	Y
21 ***English***	N	Y	Y	N	N	Y
RHODE ISLAND						
1 Kennedy	Y	Y	Y	Y	N	Y
2 Langevin	Y	Y	Y	Y	N	Y
SOUTH CAROLINA						
1 ***Brown***	N	N	N	N	Y	Y
2 ***Spence***	N	N	N	N	Y	Y
3 ***Graham***	N	Y	N	?	Y	Y
4 ***DeMint***	N	N	N	N	Y	Y
5 Spratt	Y	Y	Y	Y	N	Y
6 Clyburn	Y	Y	Y	N	N	Y
SOUTH DAKOTA						
AL ***Thune***	N	N	N	N	N	Y
TENNESSEE						
1 ***Jenkins***	N	N	N	N	Y	Y
2 ***Duncan***	N	N	N	N	Y	Y
3 ***Wamp***	N	N	N	N	Y	Y
4 ***Hilleary***	N	N	N	N	Y	Y
5 Clement	Y	Y	Y	Y	N	Y
6 Gordon	Y	Y	Y	Y	N	Y
7 ***Bryant***	N	N	N	N	Y	Y
8 Tanner	N	Y	N	Y	Y	Y
9 Ford	Y	Y	Y	Y	N	?
TEXAS						
1 Sandlin	Y	N	N	N	N	Y
2 Turner	Y	N	Y	Y	N	Y
3 ***Johnson, Sam***	N	N	N	N	Y	N
4 Hall	N	N	N	Y	Y	Y
5 ***Sessions***	N	N	N	N	Y	N
6 ***Barton***	N	N	N	N	Y	Y
7 ***Culberson***	N	N	N	N	Y	N
8 ***Brady***	N	N	N	N	Y	Y
9 Lampson	Y	N	Y	Y	N	Y
10 Doggett	Y	N	Y	Y	N	Y
11 Edwards	Y	N	Y	Y	N	Y
12 ***Granger***	N	N	N	N	N	Y
13 ***Thornberry***	N	N	N	N	Y	N
14 ***Paul***	N	Y	N	N	Y	N
15 Hinojosa	Y	Y	Y	Y	N	Y
16 Reyes	Y	N	Y	Y	N	Y
17 Stenholm	N	N	N	Y	N	Y
18 Jackson-Lee	Y	Y	Y	Y	N	Y
19 ***Combest***	N	N	N	N	Y	Y
20 Gonzalez	Y	N	Y	Y	N	Y
21 ***Smith***	N	N	N	N	Y	Y
22 ***DeLay***	N	N	N	N	Y	Y
23 ***Bonilla***	N	N	N	N	Y	Y
24 Frost	Y	Y	Y	Y	N	Y
25 Bentsen	Y	N	Y	Y	N	Y
26 ***Armey***	N	N	N	N	Y	Y
27 Ortiz	Y	N	Y	Y	N	Y
28 Rodriguez	Y	N	Y	Y	N	Y
29 Green	Y	N	Y	Y	N	Y
30 Johnson, E.B.	Y	Y	Y	Y	N	Y
UTAH						
1 ***Hansen***	N	N	N	N	Y	Y
2 Matheson	Y	Y	Y	Y	N	Y
3 ***Cannon***	N	N	N	N	Y	N
VERMONT						
AL *Sanders*	Y	Y	Y	Y	N	Y
VIRGINIA						
1 ***Davis, Jo Ann***	Y	N	N	N	Y	Y
2 ***Schrock***	N	N	N	N	Y	Y
3 Scott	Y	Y	Y	Y	N	Y
4 Vacant						
5 *Goode*	N	N	N	N	Y	N
6 ***Goodlatte***	N	N	N	N	Y	N
7 ***Cantor***	N	N	N	N	Y	Y
8 Moran	Y	Y	Y	Y	N	Y
9 Boucher	Y	Y	Y	Y	N	Y
10 ***Wolf***	N	N	N	N	N	Y
11 ***Davis, T.***	N	Y	N	N	N	Y
WASHINGTON						
1 Inslee	Y	Y	Y	Y	N	Y
2 Larsen	Y	Y	Y	Y	N	Y
3 Baird	Y	Y	Y	Y	N	Y
4 ***Hastings***	N	N	N	N	Y	Y
5 ***Nethercutt***	N	N	N	N	Y	Y
6 Dicks	Y	Y	Y	Y	N	Y
7 McDermott	Y	Y	Y	Y	N	Y
8 ***Dunn***	N	Y	N	N	Y	Y
9 Smith	Y	Y	Y	Y	N	Y
WEST VIRGINIA						
1 Mollohan	Y	N	N	Y	N	Y
2 ***Capito***	Y	Y	N	N	N	Y
3 Rahall	Y	Y	Y	Y	N	Y
WISCONSIN						
1 ***Ryan***	N	Y	N	N	Y	Y
2 Baldwin	Y	Y	Y	Y	N	Y
3 Kind	Y	Y	Y	Y	N	Y
4 Kleczka	Y	Y	Y	Y	N	Y
5 Barrett	Y	Y	Y	Y	N	Y
6 ***Petri***	Y	Y	N	N	Y	N
7 Obey	Y	Y	Y	Y	N	Y
8 ***Green***	N	Y	N	N	Y	N
9 ***Sensenbrenner***	N	N	N	N	Y	N
WYOMING						
AL ***Cubin***	?	?	?	?	?	?

Southern states - Ala., Ark., Fla., Ga., Ky., La., Miss., N.C., Okla., S.C., Tenn., Texas, Va.

186. H Res 160. China Detention/Adoption. Smith, R-N.J., motion to suspend the rules and adopt the resolution that would condemn the Chinese government's detention and treatment of five U.S.-based scholars, urge President Bush to push for their release and urge China to release a U.S.-based businessman on medical parole. Motion agreed to 379-0: R 193-0; D 184-0 (ND 136-0, SD 48-0); I 2-0. A two-thirds majority of those present and voting (253 in this case) is required for adoption under suspension of the rules. June 25, 2001.

187. H Res 99. Hezbollah Abduction/Adoption. Smith, R-N.J., motion to suspend the rules and adopt the resolution that would urge Lebanon, Syria and Iran to push Hezbollah to allow Red Cross staff to visit four Israelis abducted by the group in Lebanon last fall. Motion agreed to 379-0: R 193-0; D 184-0 (ND 136-0, SD 48-0); I 2-0. A two-thirds majority of those present and voting (253 in this case) is required for adoption under suspension of the rules. June 25, 2001.

188. H Con Res 161. Khobar Towers Bombing/Adoption. McHugh, R-N.Y., motion to suspend the rules and adopt the concurrent resolution that would honor 19 U.S. servicemen killed in a terrorist bombing of Khobar Towers in Saudi Arabia on June 25, 1996. Motion agreed to 379-0: R 193-0; D 184-0 (ND 136-0, SD 48-0); I 2-0. A two-thirds majority of those present and voting (253 in this case) is required for adoption under suspension of the rules. June 25, 2001.

189. Procedural Motion/Journal. Approval of the House journal of Monday, June 25, 2001. Approved 346-45: R 190-13; D 155-32 (ND 112-26, SD 43-6); I 1-0. June 26, 2001.

190. HR 2299. Fiscal 2002 Transportation Appropriations/Question of Consideration. Question of whether the House should consider the rule (H Res 178) to provide for House floor consideration of the bill that would appropriate $59.1 billion for transportation programs for fiscal 2002. Agreed to consider 219-202: R 214-2; D 4-199 (ND 3-147, SD 1-52); I 1-1. June 26, 2001.

191. HR 2299. Fiscal 2002 Transportation Appropriations/Rule. Adoption of the rule (H Res 178) to provide for House floor consideration of the bill that would appropriate $59.1 billion for transportation programs for fiscal 2002. Adopted 219-205: R 217-0; D 1-204 (ND 1-153, SD 0-51); I 1-1. June 26, 2001.

192. H Res 166. Houston Relief/Adoption. Cooksey, R-La., motion to suspend the rules and adopt the resolution that would recognize those who provided relief and service to the people of Houston and surrounding areas in the wake of Tropical Storm Allison. Motion agreed to 411-0: R 207-0; D 202-0 (ND 152-0, SD 50-0); I 2-0. June 26, 2001. A two-thirds majority of those present and voting (274 in this case) is required for adoption under suspension of the rules. June 26, 2001.

¹ Rep. Randy Forbes, R-Va., was sworn in June 26, 2001. The first vote for which he was eligible was Vote 190.

Key

Y	Voted for (yea).
#	Paired for.
+	Announced for.
N	Voted against (nay).
X	Paired against.
−	Announced against.
P	Voted "present."
C	Voted "present" to avoid possible conflict of interest.
?	Did not vote or otherwise make a position known.

Democrats   **Republicans**   *Independents*

ALABAMA
	186	187	188	189	190	191	192
1 Callahan	Y	Y	Y	Y	Y	Y	Y
2 Everett	Y	Y	Y	Y	Y	Y	Y
3 Riley	Y	Y	Y	Y	Y	Y	Y
4 Aderholt	Y	Y	Y	N	Y	Y	Y
5 Cramer	Y	Y	Y	N	N	Y	Y
6 Bachus	Y	Y	Y	Y	Y	Y	Y
7 Hilliard	Y	Y	Y	N	N	?	?

ALASKA
	186	187	188	189	190	191	192
AL Young	Y	Y	Y	?	Y	Y	Y

ARIZONA
	186	187	188	189	190	191	192
1 Flake	Y	Y	Y	Y	Y	Y	Y
2 Pastor	Y	Y	Y	N	N	N	Y
3 Stump	Y	Y	Y	Y	Y	Y	Y
4 Shadegg	?	?	?	Y	Y	Y	Y
5 Kolbe	Y	Y	Y	Y	Y	Y	Y
6 Hayworth	Y	Y	Y	Y	Y	Y	Y

ARKANSAS
	186	187	188	189	190	191	192
1 Berry	Y	Y	Y	N	N	N	Y
2 Snyder	Y	Y	Y	N	N	N	Y
3 Hutchinson	?	?	?	Y	Y	Y	Y
4 Ross	Y	Y	Y	N	N	N	Y

CALIFORNIA
	186	187	188	189	190	191	192
1 Thompson	Y	Y	Y	N	N	N	Y
2 Herger	Y	Y	Y	?	Y	Y	Y
3 Ose	Y	Y	Y	Y	Y	Y	Y
4 Doolittle	Y	Y	Y	?	?	Y	Y
5 Matsui	Y	Y	Y	N	N	N	Y
6 Woolsey	Y	Y	Y	N	N	N	Y
7 Miller, George	Y	Y	Y	N	N	N	Y
8 Pelosi	?	?	?	?	N	N	Y
9 Lee	Y	Y	Y	N	N	N	Y
10 Tauscher	Y	Y	Y	Y	?	N	Y
11 Pombo	Y	Y	Y	Y	Y	Y	Y
12 Lantos	?	Y	Y	N	N	N	Y
13 Stark	Y	Y	Y	N	N	N	Y
14 Eshoo	Y	Y	Y	N	N	N	Y
15 Honda	Y	Y	Y	N	N	N	Y
16 Lofgren	Y	Y	Y	N	N	N	Y
17 Farr	Y	Y	Y	N	N	N	Y
18 Condit	Y	Y	Y	N	N	N	Y
19 Radanovich	Y	Y	Y	Y	Y	Y	Y
20 Dooley	Y	Y	Y	Y	N	N	?
21 Thomas	Y	Y	Y	N	N	N	Y
22 Capps	Y	Y	Y	N	N	N	Y
23 Gallegly	Y	Y	Y	Y	Y	Y	Y
24 Sherman	Y	Y	Y	N	N	N	Y
25 McKeon	Y	Y	Y	Y	Y	Y	?
26 Berman	Y	Y	Y	N	N	N	Y
27 Schiff	Y	Y	Y	N	N	N	Y
28 Dreier	Y	Y	Y	Y	Y	Y	Y
29 Waxman	?	?	?	?	N	N	Y
30 Becerra	Y	Y	Y	N	N	N	Y
31 Solis	Y	Y	Y	N	N	N	Y
32 Watson	Y	Y	Y	−	N	N	Y
33 Roybal-Allard	Y	Y	Y	N	N	N	Y
34 Napolitano	Y	Y	Y	N	N	N	Y
35 Waters	Y	Y	Y	N	N	N	Y
36 Harman	Y	Y	Y	N	N	N	Y
37 Millender-McD.	?	?	?	N	N	N	Y
38 Horn	Y	Y	Y	Y	Y	Y	Y
39 Royce	Y	Y	Y	Y	Y	Y	Y
40 Lewis	Y	Y	Y	Y	Y	Y	Y
41 Miller, Gary	Y	Y	Y	Y	Y	Y	?
42 Baca	Y	Y	Y	Y	N	N	Y
43 Calvert	Y	Y	Y	Y	Y	Y	?
44 Bono	Y	Y	Y	Y	Y	Y	Y
45 Rohrabacher	Y	Y	Y	Y	Y	Y	Y
46 Sanchez	+	+	+	N	N	N	Y
47 Cox	Y	Y	Y	?	Y	Y	Y
48 Issa	Y	Y	Y	Y	Y	Y	Y
49 Davis	Y	Y	Y	Y	N	N	Y
50 Filner	Y	Y	Y	N	N	N	Y
51 Cunningham	Y	Y	Y	Y	Y	Y	?
52 Hunter	Y	Y	Y	Y	Y	Y	Y

COLORADO
	186	187	188	189	190	191	192
1 DeGette	Y	Y	Y	N	Y	N	Y
2 Udall	Y	Y	Y	N	N	N	Y
3 McInnis	Y	Y	Y	Y	Y	Y	Y
4 Schaffer	Y	Y	Y	N	Y	Y	Y
5 Hefley	Y	Y	Y	N	Y	Y	Y
6 Tancredo	Y	Y	Y	P	Y	Y	Y

CONNECTICUT
	186	187	188	189	190	191	192
1 Larson	Y	Y	Y	N	N	N	Y
2 Simmons	?	?	?	Y	Y	Y	Y
3 DeLauro	Y	Y	Y	N	N	N	Y
4 Shays	Y	Y	Y	Y	Y	Y	Y
5 Maloney	+	+	+	+	?	N	Y
6 Johnson	Y	Y	Y	Y	Y	Y	Y

DELAWARE
	186	187	188	189	190	191	192
AL Castle	Y	Y	Y	Y	Y	Y	Y

FLORIDA
	186	187	188	189	190	191	192
1 Scarborough	Y	Y	Y	Y	Y	Y	Y
2 Boyd	Y	Y	Y	N	N	N	Y
3 Brown	Y	Y	Y	N	N	N	Y
4 Crenshaw	Y	Y	Y	Y	Y	Y	Y
5 Thurman	Y	Y	Y	N	N	N	Y
6 Stearns	Y	Y	Y	Y	Y	Y	Y
7 Mica	Y	Y	Y	Y	Y	Y	Y
8 Keller	Y	Y	Y	Y	Y	Y	Y
9 Bilirakis	Y	Y	Y	Y	Y	Y	Y
10 Young	Y	Y	Y	Y	Y	Y	Y
11 Davis	Y	Y	Y	Y	N	N	Y
12 Putnam	?	?	?	?	?	?	?
13 Miller	Y	Y	Y	Y	Y	Y	Y
14 Goss	Y	Y	Y	Y	Y	Y	Y
15 Weldon	Y	Y	Y	Y	Y	Y	Y
16 Foley	?	?	?	Y	Y	Y	Y
17 Meek	Y	Y	Y	N	N	N	Y
18 Ros-Lehtinen	Y	Y	Y	Y	Y	Y	Y
19 Wexler	Y	Y	Y	N	N	N	Y
20 Deutsch	Y	Y	Y	N	N	N	Y
21 Diaz-Balart	?	?	?	Y	Y	Y	Y
22 Shaw	Y	Y	Y	Y	Y	Y	Y
23 Hastings	Y	Y	Y	N	N	N	Y

GEORGIA
	186	187	188	189	190	191	192
1 Kingston	Y	Y	Y	N	Y	Y	Y
2 Bishop	Y	Y	Y	N	N	N	Y
3 Collins	Y	Y	Y	Y	Y	Y	Y
4 McKinney	Y	Y	Y	N	N	N	Y
5 Lewis	Y	Y	Y	N	N	N	Y
6 Isakson	Y	Y	Y	Y	Y	Y	Y
7 Barr	Y	Y	Y	Y	Y	Y	Y
8 Chambliss	Y	Y	Y	Y	Y	Y	Y
9 Deal	Y	Y	Y	Y	Y	Y	Y
10 Norwood	Y	Y	Y	Y	Y	Y	Y
11 Linder	Y	Y	Y	Y	Y	Y	Y

HAWAII
	186	187	188	189	190	191	192
1 Abercrombie	Y	Y	Y	N	Y	N	Y
2 Mink	Y	Y	Y	N	N	N	Y

IDAHO
	186	187	188	189	190	191	192
1 Otter	Y	Y	Y	Y	Y	Y	Y
2 Simpson	Y	Y	Y	Y	Y	Y	Y

ILLINOIS
	186	187	188	189	190	191	192
1 Rush	Y	Y	Y	N	N	N	Y
2 Jackson	Y	Y	Y	N	N	N	Y
3 Lipinski	?	?	?	N	N	N	Y
4 Gutierrez	Y	Y	Y	N	N	N	Y
5 Blagojevich	Y	Y	Y	N	N	N	Y
6 Hyde	Y	Y	Y	Y	Y	Y	Y
7 Davis	Y	Y	Y	N	N	N	Y
8 Crane	Y	Y	Y	?	Y	Y	Y
9 Schakowsky	Y	Y	Y	?	N	N	Y
10 Kirk	Y	Y	Y	Y	Y	Y	Y
11 Weller	Y	Y	Y	N	Y	Y	Y
12 Costello	Y	Y	Y	N	N	N	Y
13 Biggert	Y	Y	Y	Y	Y	Y	Y

ND Northern Democrats   SD Southern Democrats

	186	187	188	189	190	191	192
14 ***Hastert***							
15 ***Johnson***	Y	Y	Y	Y	Y	Y	Y
16 ***Manzullo***	Y	Y	Y	Y	Y	Y	Y
17 Evans	Y	Y	Y	Y	N	N	Y
18 ***LaHood***	Y	Y	Y	Y	Y	Y	Y
19 Phelps	Y	Y	Y	Y	N	N	Y
20 ***Shimkus***	?	?	?	Y	Y	Y	Y
INDIANA							
1 Visclosky	Y	Y	Y	N	N	N	Y
2 ***Pence***	Y	Y	Y	Y	Y	Y	Y
3 Roemer	Y	Y	Y	Y	N	N	Y
4 ***Souder***	Y	Y	Y	Y	Y	Y	Y
5 ***Buyer***	Y	Y	Y	Y	Y	Y	Y
6 ***Burton***	?	?	?	?	?	?	?
7 ***Kerns***	Y	Y	Y	Y	Y	Y	Y
8 ***Hostettler***	Y	Y	Y	Y	Y	Y	Y
9 Hill	Y	Y	Y	Y	N	N	Y
10 Carson	+	+	+	Y	N	N	Y
IOWA							
1 ***Leach***	Y	Y	Y	Y	Y	Y	Y
2 ***Nussle***	Y	Y	Y	Y	Y	Y	Y
3 Boswell	Y	Y	Y	Y	N	N	Y
4 ***Ganske***	Y	Y	Y	Y	Y	Y	Y
5 ***Latham***	Y	Y	Y	N	Y	Y	Y
KANSAS							
1 ***Moran***	Y	Y	Y	Y	Y	Y	Y
2 ***Ryun***	Y	Y	Y	?	Y	Y	Y
3 Moore	Y	?	Y	N	N	N	Y
4 ***Tiahrt***	Y	Y	Y	Y	Y	Y	Y
KENTUCKY							
1 ***Whitfield***	Y	Y	Y	Y	Y	Y	Y
2 ***Lewis***	Y	Y	Y	Y	Y	Y	Y
3 ***Northup***	Y	Y	Y	Y	Y	Y	Y
4 Lucas	Y	Y	Y	Y	N	N	Y
5 ***Rogers***	Y	Y	Y	Y	Y	Y	Y
6 ***Fletcher***	Y	Y	Y	Y	Y	Y	Y
LOUISIANA							
1 ***Vitter***	Y	Y	Y	Y	Y	Y	Y
2 Jefferson	Y	Y	Y	Y	N	N	Y
3 ***Tauzin***	Y	Y	Y	Y	Y	Y	Y
4 ***McCrery***	Y	Y	Y	Y	Y	Y	Y
5 ***Cooksey***	Y	Y	Y	Y	Y	Y	Y
6 ***Baker***	Y	Y	Y	Y	Y	Y	Y
7 John	?	?	?	?	N	N	Y
MAINE							
1 Allen	Y	Y	Y	Y	N	N	Y
2 Baldacci	Y	Y	Y	Y	N	N	Y
MARYLAND							
1 ***Gilchrest***	Y	Y	Y	Y	Y	Y	Y
2 ***Ehrlich***	?	?	?	?	Y	Y	Y
3 Cardin	Y	Y	Y	Y	N	N	Y
4 Wynn	Y	Y	Y	Y	N	N	Y
5 Hoyer	Y	Y	Y	Y	N	N	Y
6 ***Bartlett***	Y	Y	Y	Y	Y	Y	Y
7 Cummings	Y	Y	Y	?	N	N	Y
8 ***Morella***	Y	Y	Y	Y	N	Y	Y
MASSACHUSETTS							
1 Olver	Y	Y	Y	Y	N	N	Y
2 Neal	?	?	?	Y	N	N	Y
3 McGovern	?	?	?	Y	N	N	Y
4 Frank	Y	Y	Y	Y	N	N	Y
5 Meehan	Y	Y	Y	Y	N	N	Y
6 Tierney	Y	Y	Y	Y	N	N	Y
7 Markey	Y	Y	Y	Y	N	N	Y
8 Capuano	Y	Y	Y	N	N	N	Y
9 Vacant							
10 Delahunt	Y	Y	Y	Y	N	N	Y
MICHIGAN							
1 Stupak	Y	Y	?	N	N	N	Y
2 ***Hoekstra***	?	?	?	Y	Y	Y	Y
3 ***Ehlers***	Y	Y	Y	Y	Y	Y	Y
4 ***Camp***	Y	Y	Y	Y	Y	Y	Y
5 Barcia	Y	Y	Y	Y	N	N	Y
6 ***Upton***	Y	Y	Y	Y	Y	Y	Y
7 ***Smith***	?	?	?	?	Y	Y	Y
8 ***Rogers***	Y	Y	Y	Y	Y	Y	Y
9 Kildee	Y	Y	Y	Y	N	N	Y
10 Bonior	Y	Y	Y	N	N	N	Y
11 ***Knollenberg***	Y	Y	Y	Y	Y	Y	Y
12 Levin	Y	Y	Y	Y	N	N	Y
13 Rivers	Y	Y	Y	Y	N	N	Y
14 Conyers	Y	Y	Y	Y	N	N	Y
15 Kilpatrick	Y	Y	Y	Y	N	N	Y
16 Dingell	Y	Y	Y	Y	N	N	Y

	186	187	188	189	190	191	192
MINNESOTA							
1 ***Gutknecht***	Y	Y	Y	N	Y	Y	Y
2 ***Kennedy***	Y	Y	Y	N	Y	Y	Y
3 ***Ramstad***	Y	Y	Y	N	Y	Y	?
4 McCollum	Y	Y	Y	Y	N	N	Y
5 Sabo	Y	Y	Y	N	N	N	Y
6 Luther	Y	Y	Y	Y	N	N	Y
7 Peterson	?	?	?	N	N	N	Y
8 Oberstar	Y	Y	Y	N	N	N	Y
MISSISSIPPI							
1 ***Wicker***	Y	Y	Y	N	Y	Y	Y
2 Thompson	Y	Y	Y	N	N	N	Y
3 ***Pickering***	Y	Y	Y	Y	Y	Y	Y
4 Shows	Y	Y	Y	Y	N	N	Y
5 Taylor	Y	Y	Y	N	N	N	Y
MISSOURI							
1 Clay	Y	Y	Y	?	N	N	Y
2 ***Akin***	+	+	+	Y	Y	Y	Y
3 Gephardt	?	?	?	Y	N	N	Y
4 Skelton	Y	Y	Y	Y	N	N	Y
5 McCarthy	Y	Y	Y	Y	N	N	Y
6 ***Graves***	Y	Y	Y	Y	Y	Y	Y
7 ***Blunt***	?	?	?	Y	Y	Y	Y
8 ***Emerson***	Y	Y	Y	Y	Y	Y	Y
9 ***Hulshof***	?	?	?	Y	Y	Y	Y
MONTANA							
AL ***Rehberg***	Y	Y	Y	Y	Y	Y	Y
NEBRASKA							
1 ***Bereuter***	Y	Y	Y	Y	Y	Y	Y
2 ***Terry***	Y	Y	Y	Y	Y	Y	Y
3 ***Osborne***	Y	Y	?	Y	Y	Y	Y
NEVADA							
1 Berkley	?	?	?	Y	N	N	Y
2 ***Gibbons***	Y	Y	Y	Y	Y	Y	Y
NEW HAMPSHIRE							
1 ***Sununu***	?	?	?	Y	Y	Y	Y
2 ***Bass***	Y	Y	Y	Y	Y	Y	Y
NEW JERSEY							
1 Andrews	Y	Y	Y	Y	N	N	Y
2 ***LoBiondo***	Y	Y	Y	N	Y	Y	Y
3 ***Saxton***	Y	Y	Y	Y	Y	Y	Y
4 ***Smith***	Y	Y	Y	Y	Y	Y	Y
5 ***Roukema***	Y	Y	Y	Y	Y	Y	Y
6 Pallone	Y	Y	Y	N	N	N	Y
7 ***Ferguson***	Y	Y	Y	Y	Y	Y	Y
8 Pascrell	Y	Y	Y	Y	N	N	Y
9 Rothman	Y	Y	Y	Y	Y	N	?
10 Payne	Y	Y	Y	?	?	?	?
11 ***Frelinghuysen***	Y	Y	Y	Y	Y	Y	Y
12 Holt	Y	Y	Y	N	N	N	Y
13 Menendez	Y	Y	Y	N	N	N	Y
NEW MEXICO							
1 ***Wilson***	Y	Y	Y	Y	Y	Y	Y
2 ***Skeen***	Y	Y	Y	Y	Y	Y	Y
3 Udall	Y	Y	Y	N	N	N	Y
NEW YORK							
1 ***Grucci***	Y	Y	Y	Y	Y	Y	Y
2 Israel	Y	Y	Y	Y	N	N	Y
3 ***King***	Y	Y	Y	Y	Y	Y	Y
4 McCarthy	Y	Y	Y	Y	N	N	Y
5 Ackerman	Y	Y	Y	Y	N	N	Y
6 Meeks	Y	Y	Y	Y	N	N	Y
7 Crowley	Y	Y	Y	Y	N	N	Y
8 Nadler	?	?	?	Y	N	N	Y
9 Weiner	+	+	+	+	N	N	Y
10 Towns	Y	Y	Y	?	N	N	Y
11 Owens	?	?	?	?	N	N	Y
12 Velázquez	Y	Y	Y	N	N	N	Y
13 ***Fossella***	?	?	?	?	Y	Y	Y
14 Maloney	Y	Y	Y	Y	N	N	Y
15 Rangel	?	?	?	Y	N	N	Y
16 Serrano	Y	Y	Y	Y	N	N	Y
17 Engel	Y	Y	Y	Y	N	N	Y
18 Lowey	Y	Y	Y	Y	N	N	Y
19 ***Kelly***	Y	Y	Y	N	Y	Y	Y
20 ***Gilman***	Y	Y	Y	Y	Y	Y	Y
21 McNulty	Y	Y	Y	Y	N	N	Y
22 ***Sweeney***	Y	Y	Y	N	Y	Y	Y
23 ***Boehlert***	Y	Y	Y	Y	Y	Y	Y
24 ***McHugh***	Y	Y	Y	Y	Y	Y	Y
25 ***Walsh***	Y	Y	Y	Y	Y	Y	Y
26 Hinchey	Y	Y	Y	?	N	N	Y
27 ***Reynolds***	Y	Y	Y	Y	Y	Y	Y
28 Slaughter	Y	Y	Y	?	N	N	Y
29 LaFalce	Y	Y	Y	Y	N	N	Y

	186	187	188	189	190	191	192
30 ***Quinn***	Y	Y	Y	Y	Y	Y	Y
31 ***Houghton***	Y	Y	Y	Y	Y	Y	Y
NORTH CAROLINA							
1 Clayton	Y	Y	Y	Y	N	N	Y
2 Etheridge	Y	Y	Y	Y	N	N	Y
3 ***Jones***	Y	Y	Y	Y	Y	Y	Y
4 Price	Y	Y	Y	?	N	N	Y
5 ***Burr***	Y	Y	Y	Y	Y	Y	Y
6 ***Coble***	+	+	+	Y	Y	Y	Y
7 McIntyre	Y	Y	Y	Y	N	N	Y
8 ***Hayes***	Y	Y	Y	Y	Y	Y	Y
9 ***Myrick***	Y	Y	Y	Y	Y	Y	Y
10 ***Ballenger***	Y	Y	Y	Y	Y	Y	Y
11 ***Taylor***	?	?	?	Y	Y	Y	Y
12 Watt	Y	Y	Y	Y	N	N	?
NORTH DAKOTA							
AL Pomeroy	?	?	?	Y	N	N	Y
OHIO							
1 ***Chabot***	Y	Y	Y	Y	Y	Y	Y
2 ***Portman***	Y	Y	Y	Y	Y	Y	Y
3 Hall	Y	Y	Y	Y	N	N	Y
4 ***Oxley***	Y	Y	Y	Y	Y	Y	Y
5 ***Gillmor***	Y	Y	Y	Y	Y	Y	Y
6 Strickland	Y	Y	Y	Y	N	N	Y
7 ***Hobson***	Y	Y	Y	Y	Y	Y	Y
8 ***Boehner***	Y	Y	Y	Y	Y	Y	Y
9 Kaptur	?	?	?	?	?	?	?
10 Kucinich	Y	Y	Y	N	N	N	Y
11 Jones	Y	Y	Y	Y	N	N	Y
12 ***Tiberi***	Y	Y	Y	Y	Y	Y	Y
13 Brown	Y	Y	Y	Y	N	N	Y
14 Sawyer	Y	Y	Y	Y	N	N	Y
15 ***Pryce***	?	?	?	?	Y	Y	Y
16 ***Regula***	Y	Y	Y	Y	Y	Y	Y
17 Traficant	Y	Y	Y	Y	Y	Y	Y
18 ***Ney***	Y	Y	Y	Y	Y	Y	Y
19 ***LaTourette***	?	?	?	?	?	?	?
OKLAHOMA							
1 ***Largent***	Y	Y	Y	?	Y	Y	Y
2 Carson	Y	Y	Y	Y	N	N	Y
3 ***Watkins***	Y	Y	Y	Y	Y	Y	Y
4 ***Watts***	Y	Y	Y	Y	Y	Y	Y
5 ***Istook***	?	?	?	?	Y	Y	Y
6 ***Lucas***	Y	Y	Y	Y	Y	Y	Y
OREGON							
1 Wu	Y	Y	Y	N	N	N	Y
2 ***Walden***	Y	Y	Y	Y	Y	Y	Y
3 Blumenauer	Y	Y	Y	Y	N	N	Y
4 DeFazio	Y	Y	Y	N	N	N	Y
5 Hooley	?	?	?	Y	Y	N	Y
PENNSYLVANIA							
1 Brady	Y	Y	Y	N	N	N	Y
2 Fattah	Y	Y	Y	?	N	N	Y
3 Borski	Y	Y	Y	N	N	N	Y
4 ***Hart***	Y	Y	Y	Y	Y	Y	Y
5 ***Peterson***	Y	Y	Y	Y	Y	Y	Y
6 Holden	Y	Y	Y	Y	N	N	Y
7 ***Weldon***	Y	Y	Y	Y	Y	Y	Y
8 ***Greenwood***	Y	Y	Y	Y	Y	Y	Y
9 ***Shuster, Bill***	Y	Y	Y	Y	Y	Y	Y
10 ***Sherwood***	Y	Y	Y	Y	Y	Y	Y
11 Kanjorski	Y	Y	Y	Y	N	N	Y
12 Murtha	Y	Y	Y	Y	N	N	Y
13 Hoeffel	Y	Y	Y	Y	N	N	Y
14 Coyne	Y	Y	Y	Y	N	N	Y
15 ***Toomey***	?	?	?	?	Y	Y	Y
16 ***Pitts***	Y	Y	Y	Y	Y	Y	Y
17 ***Gekas***	Y	Y	Y	Y	Y	Y	Y
18 Doyle	Y	Y	Y	?	N	N	Y
19 ***Platts***	?	?	?	?	?	?	?
20 Mascara	Y	Y	Y	Y	N	N	Y
21 ***English***	Y	Y	Y	Y	Y	Y	Y
RHODE ISLAND							
1 Kennedy	Y	Y	Y	Y	N	N	Y
2 Langevin	Y	Y	Y	Y	N	N	Y
SOUTH CAROLINA							
1 ***Brown***	Y	Y	Y	Y	Y	Y	Y
2 ***Spence***	?	?	?	Y	Y	Y	Y
3 ***Graham***	Y	Y	Y	Y	Y	Y	Y
4 ***DeMint***	Y	Y	Y	Y	Y	Y	Y
5 Spratt	Y	Y	Y	Y	N	N	Y
6 Clyburn	Y	Y	Y	Y	N	N	Y
SOUTH DAKOTA							
AL ***Thune***	Y	Y	Y	Y	Y	Y	Y

	186	187	188	189	190	191	192
TENNESSEE							
1 ***Jenkins***	Y	Y	Y	Y	Y	Y	?
2 ***Duncan***	Y	Y	Y	Y	Y	Y	?
3 ***Wamp***	Y	Y	Y	Y	Y	Y	?
4 ***Hilleary***	Y	Y	Y	Y	Y	Y	?
5 Clement	?	?	?	?	?	?	?
6 Gordon	?	?	?	Y	N	N	Y
7 ***Bryant***	Y	Y	Y	Y	Y	Y	?
8 Tanner	Y	Y	Y	Y	N	N	Y
9 Ford	+	+	+	Y	N	N	Y
TEXAS							
1 Sandlin	Y	Y	Y	Y	N	N	Y
2 Turner	Y	Y	Y	Y	N	N	?
3 ***Johnson, Sam***	Y	Y	Y	Y	Y	Y	Y
4 Hall	Y	Y	Y	Y	Y	N	Y
5 ***Sessions***	?	?	?	Y	Y	Y	Y
6 ***Barton***	Y	Y	Y	Y	Y	Y	Y
7 ***Culberson***	Y	Y	Y	Y	Y	Y	Y
8 ***Brady***	?	?	Y	Y	Y	Y	Y
9 Lampson	Y	Y	Y	Y	N	N	Y
10 Doggett	Y	Y	Y	Y	N	N	Y
11 Edwards	Y	Y	Y	Y	N	N	Y
12 ***Granger***	Y	Y	Y	Y	Y	Y	Y
13 ***Thornberry***	Y	Y	Y	Y	Y	Y	Y
14 ***Paul***	?	?	?	Y	Y	Y	Y
15 Hinojosa	?	?	?	?	N	?	Y
16 Reyes	Y	Y	Y	Y	N	N	Y
17 Stenholm	Y	Y	Y	Y	N	N	Y
18 Jackson-Lee	Y	Y	Y	Y	N	N	Y
19 ***Combest***	Y	Y	Y	Y	Y	Y	Y
20 Gonzalez	Y	Y	Y	Y	N	N	Y
21 ***Smith***	Y	Y	Y	Y	Y	Y	Y
22 ***DeLay***	Y	Y	Y	Y	Y	Y	Y
23 ***Bonilla***	Y	Y	Y	Y	Y	Y	Y
24 Frost	Y	Y	Y	Y	N	N	Y
25 Bentsen	Y	Y	Y	Y	N	N	Y
26 ***Armey***	Y	Y	Y	Y	Y	Y	Y
27 Ortiz	Y	Y	Y	Y	N	N	Y
28 Rodriguez	Y	Y	Y	Y	N	N	Y
29 Green	Y	Y	Y	Y	N	N	Y
30 Johnson, E.B.	Y	Y	Y	Y	N	N	Y
UTAH							
1 ***Hansen***	Y	Y	Y	Y	Y	Y	Y
2 Matheson	Y	Y	Y	Y	N	N	Y
3 ***Cannon***	Y	Y	Y	Y	Y	Y	Y
VERMONT							
AL *Sanders*	Y	Y	Y	?	N	N	Y
VIRGINIA							
1 ***Davis, Jo Ann***	Y	Y	Y	Y	Y	Y	Y
2 ***Schrock***	Y	Y	Y	Y	Y	Y	Y
3 Scott	Y	Y	Y	Y	N	N	Y
4 ***Forbes*** [1]						Y	Y
5 *Goode*	Y	Y	Y	Y	Y	Y	Y
6 ***Goodlatte***	Y	Y	Y	Y	Y	Y	Y
7 ***Cantor***	Y	Y	Y	Y	Y	Y	Y
8 Moran	Y	Y	Y	Y	N	N	Y
9 Boucher	?	?	?	?	N	N	Y
10 ***Wolf***	Y	Y	Y	Y	Y	Y	Y
11 ***Davis, T.***	Y	Y	Y	Y	N	Y	Y
WASHINGTON							
1 Inslee	Y	Y	Y	Y	N	N	Y
2 Larsen	Y	Y	Y	?	N	N	Y
3 Baird	Y	Y	Y	N	N	N	Y
4 ***Hastings***	Y	Y	Y	Y	Y	Y	Y
5 ***Nethercutt***	Y	Y	Y	Y	Y	Y	Y
6 Dicks	Y	Y	Y	Y	N	N	Y
7 McDermott	Y	Y	Y	N	N	N	Y
8 ***Dunn***	Y	Y	Y	Y	Y	Y	Y
9 Smith	Y	Y	Y	Y	?	N	Y
WEST VIRGINIA							
1 Mollohan	Y	Y	Y	Y	N	N	Y
2 ***Capito***	Y	Y	Y	Y	Y	Y	Y
3 Rahall	Y	Y	Y	Y	N	N	Y
WISCONSIN							
1 ***Ryan***	Y	Y	Y	Y	Y	Y	Y
2 Baldwin	Y	Y	Y	Y	N	N	Y
3 Kind	Y	Y	Y	Y	N	N	Y
4 Kleczka	Y	Y	Y	Y	N	N	Y
5 Barrett	Y	Y	Y	Y	N	N	Y
6 ***Petri***	Y	Y	Y	Y	Y	Y	Y
7 Obey	Y	Y	Y	Y	N	N	Y
8 ***Green***	Y	Y	Y	Y	Y	Y	Y
9 ***Sensenbrenner***	Y	Y	Y	Y	Y	Y	Y
WYOMING							
AL ***Cubin***	Y	Y	Y	Y	Y	Y	Y

Southern states - Ala., Ark., Fla., Ga., Ky., La., Miss., N.C., Okla., S.C., Tenn., Texas, Va.

Key

Y	Voted for (yea).
#	Paired for.
+	Announced for.
N	Voted against (nay).
X	Paired against.
–	Announced against.
P	Voted "present."
C	Voted "present" to avoid possible conflict of interest.
?	Did not vote or otherwise make a position known.

Democrats   **Republicans**
Independents

---

193. HR 2299. Fiscal 2002 Transportation Appropriations/Motor Carriers. Sabo, D-Minn., amendment that would bar funds to process applications from Mexican motor carriers for authority to operate beyond current U.S. commercial zones near the U.S.-Mexico border. Adopted 285-143: R 82-134; D 201-9 (ND 152-4, SD 49-5); I 2-0. A "nay" was a vote in support of the president's position. June 26, 2001.

194. HR 2299. Fiscal 2002 Transportation Appropriations/Passage. Passage of the bill that would appropriate $59.1 billion for transportation programs for fiscal 2002, including: $32.7 billion for federal highway programs; $13.3 billion for the Federal Aviation Administration; $6.7 billion for mass transit; $5.0 billion for the U.S. Coast Guard; and $684 million for railroads. Passed 426-1: R 215-1; D 209-0 (ND 155-0, SD 54-0); I 2-0. June 26, 2001.

195. Procedural Motion/Journal. Approval of the House Journal of Tuesday, June 26, 2001. Approved 368-49: R 197-14; D 169-35 (ND 124-27, SD 45-8); I 2-0. June 27, 2001.

196. HR 2311. Fiscal 2002 Energy and Water Appropriations/Rule. Adoption of the rule (H Res 180) to provide for House floor consideration of the bill that would appropriate $23.7 billion for the Energy Department, the Army Corps of Engineers, water projects and other independent agencies in fiscal 2002. Adopted 425-1: R 216-1; D 207-0 (ND 154-0, SD 53-0); I 2-0. June 27, 2001.

197. H Res 172. Firefighter Tribute/Adoption. J. Davis, R-Va., motion to suspend the rules and adopt the resolution that would pay tribute to John J. Downing, Brian Fahey and Harry Ford, firefighters killed in the line of duty June 17, 2001. Motion agreed to 424-0: R 217-0; D 205-0 (ND 152-0, SD 53-0); I 2-0. A two-thirds majority of those present and voting (283 in this case) is required for adoption under suspension of the rules. June 27, 2001.

198. HR 2133. Brown Decision/Passage. Morella, R-Md., motion to suspend the rules and pass the bill that would authorize a total of $250,000 in funding for fiscal years 2003 and 2004 to establish a commission to help commemorate the 50th anniversary of the Supreme Court's decision in *Brown v. Board of Education*. Motion agreed to 414-2: R 211-2; D 201-0 (ND 149-0, SD 52-0); I 2-0. A two-thirds majority of those present and voting (278 in this case) is required for passage under suspension of the rules. June 27, 2001.

		193	194	195	196	197	198
ALABAMA							
1	*Callahan*	N	Y	Y	Y	Y	?
2	*Everett*	N	Y	Y	Y	Y	Y
3	*Riley*	N	Y	Y	Y	Y	Y
4	*Aderholt*	N	Y	N	Y	Y	Y
5	Cramer	Y	Y	Y	Y	Y	Y
6	*Bachus*	N	Y	Y	Y	Y	Y
7	Hilliard	Y	Y	N	Y	Y	Y
ALASKA							
AL	*Young*	Y	Y	?	Y	Y	Y
ARIZONA							
1	*Flake*	N	Y	Y	Y	Y	N
2	Pastor	N	Y	Y	Y	Y	Y
3	*Stump*	N	Y	Y	Y	Y	Y
4	*Shadegg*	N	Y	Y	Y	Y	Y
5	*Kolbe*	N	Y	Y	Y	Y	Y
6	*Hayworth*	N	Y	Y	Y	Y	Y
ARKANSAS							
1	Berry	Y	Y	Y	Y	Y	Y
2	Snyder	Y	Y	Y	Y	Y	Y
3	*Hutchinson*	N	Y	?	Y	Y	Y
4	Ross	Y	Y	Y	Y	Y	Y
CALIFORNIA							
1	Thompson	Y	Y	N	Y	Y	Y
2	*Herger*	N	Y	Y	Y	Y	Y
3	*Ose*	N	Y	Y	Y	Y	Y
4	*Doolittle*	Y	Y	Y	Y	Y	?
5	Matsui	Y	Y	Y	Y	Y	?
6	Woolsey	Y	?	Y	Y	Y	Y
7	Miller, George	Y	Y	N	Y	Y	Y
8	Pelosi	Y	Y	Y	Y	Y	Y
9	Lee	Y	Y	Y	Y	Y	Y
10	Tauscher	Y	Y	Y	Y	Y	Y
11	*Pombo*	Y	Y	Y	?	?	?
12	Lantos	Y	Y	Y	Y	Y	Y
13	Stark	Y	Y	Y	Y	Y	Y
14	Eshoo	Y	Y	Y	Y	Y	Y
15	Honda	Y	Y	Y	Y	Y	Y
16	Lofgren	Y	Y	Y	Y	Y	Y
17	Farr	Y	Y	Y	Y	Y	Y
18	Condit	Y	Y	Y	Y	Y	Y
19	*Radanovich*	N	Y	Y	Y	Y	Y
20	Dooley	N	Y	Y	Y	Y	Y
21	*Thomas*	N	Y	Y	Y	Y	Y
22	Capps	Y	Y	Y	Y	Y	Y
23	*Gallegly*	Y	Y	Y	Y	Y	Y
24	Sherman	Y	Y	Y	Y	Y	Y
25	*McKeon*	N	Y	Y	Y	Y	Y
26	Berman	Y	Y	Y	Y	Y	Y
27	Schiff	Y	Y	Y	Y	Y	Y
28	*Dreier*	N	Y	Y	Y	Y	Y
29	Waxman	Y	Y	Y	Y	Y	Y
30	Becerra	Y	Y	Y	Y	Y	Y
31	Solis	Y	Y	Y	Y	Y	Y
32	Watson	Y	Y	Y	Y	Y	Y
33	Roybal-Allard	Y	Y	Y	Y	Y	Y
34	Napolitano	Y	Y	Y	Y	Y	Y
35	Waters	Y	Y	Y	N	Y	Y
36	Harman	Y	Y	Y	Y	Y	Y
37	Millender-McD.	Y	Y	?	Y	Y	Y
38	*Horn*	Y	Y	Y	Y	Y	Y

		193	194	195	196	197	198
39	*Royce*	Y	Y	Y	Y	Y	Y
40	*Lewis*	N	Y	Y	Y	Y	Y
41	*Miller, Gary*	N	Y	Y	Y	Y	Y
42	Baca	Y	Y	Y	Y	Y	Y
43	*Calvert*	Y	Y	Y	Y	Y	Y
44	*Bono*	Y	Y	Y	Y	Y	Y
45	*Rohrabacher*	Y	Y	Y	Y	Y	Y
46	Sanchez	Y	Y	Y	Y	Y	Y
47	*Cox*	N	Y	Y	Y	Y	Y
48	*Issa*	N	Y	Y	Y	Y	Y
49	Davis	Y	Y	Y	Y	Y	Y
50	Filner	Y	Y	N	Y	Y	Y
51	*Cunningham*	Y	Y	Y	Y	Y	Y
52	*Hunter*	Y	Y	Y	Y	Y	Y
COLORADO							
1	DeGette	Y	Y	Y	Y	Y	Y
2	Udall	Y	Y	N	Y	Y	Y
3	*McInnis*	N	Y	Y	Y	Y	Y
4	*Schaffer*	Y	Y	N	Y	Y	Y
5	*Hefley*	Y	Y	N	Y	Y	Y
6	*Tancredo*	Y	Y	P	Y	Y	Y
CONNECTICUT							
1	Larson	Y	Y	Y	Y	Y	Y
2	*Simmons*	N	Y	Y	Y	Y	Y
3	DeLauro	Y	Y	Y	Y	Y	Y
4	*Shays*	Y	Y	Y	Y	Y	Y
5	Maloney	Y	Y	Y	Y	Y	Y
6	*Johnson*	N	Y	Y	Y	Y	Y
DELAWARE							
AL	*Castle*	Y	Y	Y	Y	Y	Y
FLORIDA							
1	*Scarborough*	Y	Y	?	Y	Y	Y
2	Boyd	Y	Y	Y	Y	Y	Y
3	Brown	Y	Y	Y	Y	Y	Y
4	*Crenshaw*	Y	Y	Y	Y	Y	Y
5	Thurman	Y	Y	Y	Y	Y	Y
6	*Stearns*	Y	Y	Y	Y	Y	Y
7	*Mica*	Y	Y	Y	Y	Y	Y
8	*Keller*	N	Y	Y	Y	Y	Y
9	*Bilirakis*	Y	Y	Y	Y	Y	Y
10	*Young*	N	Y	Y	Y	Y	Y
11	Davis	Y	Y	Y	Y	Y	Y
12	*Putnam*	?	?	?	?	?	?
13	*Miller*	N	Y	Y	Y	Y	Y
14	*Goss*	N	Y	Y	Y	Y	Y
15	*Weldon*	Y	Y	Y	Y	Y	Y
16	*Foley*	Y	Y	Y	Y	Y	Y
17	Meek	Y	Y	Y	?	?	?
18	*Ros-Lehtinen*	Y	Y	Y	Y	Y	Y
19	Wexler	Y	Y	Y	Y	Y	Y
20	Deutsch	Y	Y	Y	Y	Y	Y
21	*Diaz-Balart*	N	Y	Y	Y	Y	Y
22	*Shaw*	N	Y	Y	Y	Y	Y
23	Hastings	Y	Y	N	Y	Y	Y
GEORGIA							
1	*Kingston*	N	Y	Y	Y	Y	Y
2	Bishop	Y	Y	Y	Y	Y	Y
3	*Collins*	Y	Y	Y	Y	Y	Y
4	McKinney	Y	Y	Y	Y	Y	Y
5	Lewis	Y	Y	N	Y	Y	Y
6	*Isakson*	N	Y	Y	Y	Y	Y
7	*Barr*	Y	Y	Y	Y	Y	Y
8	*Chambliss*	Y	Y	Y	Y	Y	Y
9	*Deal*	Y	Y	Y	Y	Y	Y
10	*Norwood*	Y	Y	Y	Y	Y	Y
11	*Linder*	N	Y	Y	Y	Y	Y
HAWAII							
1	Abercrombie	Y	Y	Y	Y	Y	Y
2	Mink	Y	Y	Y	Y	Y	Y
IDAHO							
1	*Otter*	N	Y	Y	Y	Y	Y
2	*Simpson*	N	Y	Y	Y	Y	Y
ILLINOIS							
1	Rush	Y	Y	Y	Y	Y	Y
2	Jackson	Y	Y	Y	Y	Y	Y
3	Lipinski	Y	Y	Y	Y	Y	Y
4	Gutierrez	Y	Y	Y	Y	Y	Y
5	Blagojevich	Y	Y	Y	Y	Y	Y
6	*Hyde*	Y	Y	Y	Y	Y	Y
7	Davis	Y	Y	Y	Y	Y	Y
8	*Crane*	N	Y	N	Y	Y	Y
9	Schakowsky	Y	Y	Y	Y	Y	Y
10	*Kirk*	Y	Y	Y	Y	Y	Y
11	*Weller*	Y	Y	N	Y	Y	Y
12	Costello	Y	Y	N	Y	Y	Y
13	*Biggert*	N	Y	Y	Y	Y	Y

ND Northern Democrats   SD Southern Democrats

	193	194	195	196	197	198
14 ***Hastert***						
15 ***Johnson***	Y	Y	Y	Y	Y	Y
16 ***Manzullo***	Y	Y	Y	Y	Y	Y
17 Evans	Y	Y	Y	Y	Y	Y
18 ***LaHood***	Y	Y	Y	Y	Y	Y
19 Phelps	Y	Y	Y	Y	Y	Y
20 ***Shimkus***	Y	Y	Y	Y	Y	Y
INDIANA						
1 Visclosky	Y	Y	N	Y	Y	Y
2 ***Pence***	N	Y	Y	Y	Y	Y
3 Roemer	Y	Y	Y	Y	Y	Y
4 ***Souder***	Y	Y	Y	Y	Y	Y
5 ***Buyer***	Y	Y	Y	Y	Y	Y
6 ***Burton***	?	?	?	?	?	?
7 ***Kerns***	N	Y	Y	Y	Y	Y
8 ***Hostettler***	N	Y	Y	Y	Y	Y
9 Hill	Y	Y	Y	Y	Y	Y
10 Carson	Y	Y	Y	Y	Y	Y
IOWA						
1 ***Leach***	Y	Y	Y	Y	Y	Y
2 ***Nussle***	Y	Y	Y	Y	Y	Y
3 Boswell	Y	Y	Y	Y	Y	?
4 ***Ganske***	Y	Y	Y	Y	Y	Y
5 ***Latham***	N	Y	N	Y	Y	Y
KANSAS						
1 ***Moran***	Y	Y	Y	Y	Y	Y
2 ***Ryun***	N	Y	Y	Y	Y	Y
3 Moore	Y	Y	N	Y	Y	Y
4 ***Tiahrt***	N	Y	Y	Y	Y	Y
KENTUCKY						
1 ***Whitfield***	N	Y	?	Y	Y	Y
2 ***Lewis***	N	Y	Y	Y	Y	Y
3 ***Northup***	N	Y	Y	Y	Y	Y
4 Lucas	Y	Y	Y	Y	Y	Y
5 ***Rogers***	N	Y	Y	Y	Y	Y
6 ***Fletcher***	N	Y	Y	Y	Y	Y
LOUISIANA						
1 ***Vitter***	N	Y	Y	Y	Y	Y
2 Jefferson	Y	Y	Y	Y	Y	Y
3 ***Tauzin***	Y	Y	Y	Y	Y	Y
4 ***McCrery***	N	Y	Y	Y	Y	Y
5 ***Cooksey***	N	Y	Y	Y	Y	Y
6 ***Baker***	N	Y	Y	Y	Y	Y
7 John	Y	Y	Y	Y	Y	Y
MAINE						
1 Allen	Y	Y	Y	Y	Y	?
2 Baldacci	Y	Y	Y	Y	Y	Y
MARYLAND						
1 ***Gilchrest***	N	Y	Y	Y	Y	Y
2 ***Ehrlich***	N	Y	Y	Y	Y	Y
3 Cardin	Y	Y	Y	Y	Y	Y
4 Wynn	Y	Y	Y	Y	Y	Y
5 Hoyer	Y	Y	Y	Y	Y	Y
6 ***Bartlett***	N	Y	Y	Y	Y	Y
7 Cummings	Y	Y	Y	Y	Y	Y
8 ***Morella***	Y	Y	Y	Y	Y	Y
MASSACHUSETTS						
1 Olver	Y	Y	Y	Y	Y	Y
2 Neal	Y	Y	Y	Y	Y	Y
3 McGovern	Y	Y	Y	Y	Y	Y
4 Frank	Y	Y	Y	Y	Y	?
5 Meehan	Y	Y	Y	Y	Y	Y
6 Tierney	Y	Y	Y	Y	Y	Y
7 Markey	Y	Y	Y	Y	Y	Y
8 Capuano	Y	Y	N	Y	Y	Y
9 Vacant						
10 Delahunt	Y	Y	Y	Y	Y	Y
MICHIGAN						
1 Stupak	Y	Y	N	Y	Y	Y
2 ***Hoekstra***	Y	Y	Y	Y	Y	Y
3 ***Ehlers***	N	Y	Y	Y	Y	Y
4 ***Camp***	Y	Y	Y	Y	Y	Y
5 Barcia	Y	Y	Y	Y	Y	Y
6 ***Upton***	Y	Y	Y	Y	Y	Y
7 ***Smith***	N	Y	Y	Y	Y	Y
8 ***Rogers***	N	Y	Y	Y	Y	Y
9 Kildee	Y	Y	Y	Y	Y	Y
10 Bonior	Y	Y	N	Y	Y	Y
11 ***Knollenberg***	N	Y	Y	Y	Y	Y
12 Levin	Y	Y	Y	Y	Y	Y
13 Rivers	Y	Y	Y	Y	Y	Y
14 Conyers	Y	Y	Y	Y	Y	Y
15 Kilpatrick	Y	Y	Y	Y	Y	Y
16 Dingell	Y	Y	Y	Y	Y	Y

	193	194	195	196	197	198
MINNESOTA						
1 ***Gutknecht***	Y	Y	N	Y	Y	Y
2 ***Kennedy***	N	Y	N	Y	Y	Y
3 ***Ramstad***	N	Y	N	Y	Y	Y
4 McCollum	Y	Y	Y	Y	Y	Y
5 Sabo	Y	Y	N	Y	Y	Y
6 Luther	Y	Y	Y	Y	Y	Y
7 Peterson	Y	Y	N	Y	Y	Y
8 Oberstar	Y	Y	N	Y	Y	Y
MISSISSIPPI						
1 ***Wicker***	N	Y	Y	Y	Y	Y
2 Thompson	Y	Y	N	Y	Y	Y
3 ***Pickering***	Y	Y	Y	Y	Y	Y
4 Shows	Y	Y	Y	Y	Y	Y
5 Taylor	Y	Y	N	Y	Y	Y
MISSOURI						
1 Clay	Y	Y	Y	Y	Y	Y
2 ***Akin***	N	Y	Y	Y	Y	Y
3 Gephardt	Y	Y	N	Y	Y	Y
4 Skelton	Y	Y	Y	Y	Y	Y
5 McCarthy	Y	Y	Y	Y	Y	Y
6 ***Graves***	N	Y	Y	Y	Y	Y
7 ***Blunt***	N	Y	Y	Y	Y	Y
8 ***Emerson***	N	Y	?	Y	Y	Y
9 ***Hulshof***	N	Y	N	Y	Y	Y
MONTANA						
AL ***Rehberg***	N	Y	Y	Y	Y	Y
NEBRASKA						
1 ***Bereuter***	N	Y	Y	Y	Y	Y
2 ***Terry***	N	Y	Y	Y	Y	Y
3 ***Osborne***	N	Y	Y	Y	Y	Y
NEVADA						
1 Berkley	Y	Y	Y	Y	Y	Y
2 ***Gibbons***	N	Y	Y	Y	Y	Y
NEW HAMPSHIRE						
1 ***Sununu***	N	Y	Y	Y	Y	Y
2 ***Bass***	N	Y	Y	Y	Y	Y
NEW JERSEY						
1 Andrews	Y	Y	Y	Y	?	?
2 ***LoBiondo***	Y	Y	N	Y	Y	Y
3 ***Saxton***	Y	Y	Y	Y	Y	Y
4 ***Smith***	Y	Y	Y	Y	Y	Y
5 ***Roukema***	Y	Y	Y	Y	Y	Y
6 Pallone	Y	Y	N	Y	Y	Y
7 ***Ferguson***	Y	Y	Y	Y	Y	Y
8 Pascrell	Y	Y	Y	Y	Y	Y
9 Rothman	Y	Y	Y	Y	Y	Y
10 Payne	Y	Y	Y	Y	Y	Y
11 ***Frelinghuysen***	N	Y	Y	Y	Y	Y
12 Holt	Y	Y	Y	Y	Y	Y
13 Menendez	Y	Y	N	Y	Y	Y
NEW MEXICO						
1 ***Wilson***	N	Y	Y	Y	Y	Y
2 ***Skeen***	N	Y	Y	Y	Y	Y
3 Udall	Y	Y	N	Y	Y	Y
NEW YORK						
1 ***Grucci***	Y	Y	Y	Y	Y	Y
2 Israel	Y	Y	Y	Y	Y	Y
3 ***King***	Y	Y	Y	Y	Y	Y
4 McCarthy	Y	Y	Y	Y	Y	Y
5 Ackerman	Y	Y	Y	Y	Y	Y
6 Meeks	Y	Y	Y	Y	Y	Y
7 Crowley	Y	Y	Y	Y	Y	Y
8 Nadler	Y	Y	Y	Y	Y	Y
9 Weiner	Y	Y	Y	Y	Y	Y
10 Towns	Y	Y	Y	Y	Y	Y
11 Owens	Y	Y	Y	Y	Y	?
12 Velázquez	N	Y	Y	Y	Y	Y
13 ***Fossella***	Y	Y	Y	Y	Y	Y
14 Maloney	Y	Y	Y	Y	Y	Y
15 Rangel	Y	Y	?	Y	Y	Y
16 Serrano	N	Y	Y	Y	Y	Y
17 Engel	Y	Y	Y	Y	Y	Y
18 Lowey	Y	Y	Y	Y	Y	Y
19 ***Kelly***	Y	Y	Y	Y	Y	Y
20 ***Gilman***	Y	Y	Y	Y	Y	Y
21 McNulty	Y	Y	N	Y	Y	Y
22 ***Sweeney***	?	?	N	Y	Y	Y
23 ***Boehlert***	Y	Y	Y	Y	Y	Y
24 ***McHugh***	Y	Y	Y	Y	Y	Y
25 ***Walsh***	N	Y	Y	Y	Y	Y
26 Hinchey	Y	Y	Y	?	Y	Y
27 ***Reynolds***	N	Y	Y	Y	Y	Y
28 Slaughter	Y	Y	?	Y	Y	Y
29 LaFalce	Y	Y	Y	Y	Y	Y

	193	194	195	196	197	198
30 ***Quinn***	Y	Y	?	Y	Y	Y
31 ***Houghton***	N	Y	Y	Y	Y	Y
NORTH CAROLINA						
1 Clayton	Y	Y	?	Y	Y	Y
2 Etheridge	Y	Y	Y	Y	Y	Y
3 ***Jones***	Y	Y	Y	Y	Y	Y
4 Price	Y	Y	Y	Y	Y	Y
5 ***Burr***	N	Y	Y	Y	Y	Y
6 ***Coble***	N	Y	Y	Y	Y	Y
7 McIntyre	Y	Y	Y	Y	Y	Y
8 ***Hayes***	N	Y	Y	Y	Y	Y
9 ***Myrick***	N	Y	Y	Y	Y	Y
10 ***Ballenger***	N	Y	Y	Y	Y	Y
11 ***Taylor***	N	Y	Y	Y	Y	Y
12 Watt	Y	Y	Y	Y	Y	Y
NORTH DAKOTA						
AL Pomeroy	Y	Y	Y	Y	Y	Y
OHIO						
1 ***Chabot***	Y	Y	Y	Y	Y	Y
2 ***Portman***	N	Y	Y	Y	Y	Y
3 Hall	Y	Y	Y	Y	Y	Y
4 ***Oxley***	N	Y	Y	Y	Y	Y
5 ***Gillmor***	N	Y	Y	Y	Y	Y
6 Strickland	Y	Y	Y	Y	Y	Y
7 ***Hobson***	N	Y	Y	Y	Y	Y
8 ***Boehner***	N	Y	Y	Y	Y	Y
9 Kaptur	Y	Y	Y	Y	?	Y
10 Kucinich	Y	Y	N	Y	Y	Y
11 Jones	Y	Y	Y	Y	Y	Y
12 ***Tiberi***	N	Y	Y	Y	Y	Y
13 Brown	Y	Y	Y	Y	Y	Y
14 Sawyer	Y	Y	Y	Y	Y	Y
15 ***Pryce***	N	Y	Y	Y	Y	Y
16 ***Regula***	N	Y	Y	Y	Y	Y
17 Traficant	Y	Y	Y	Y	Y	Y
18 ***Ney***	Y	Y	Y	Y	Y	Y
19 ***LaTourette***	?	?	Y	Y	Y	Y
OKLAHOMA						
1 ***Largent***	N	Y	Y	Y	Y	Y
2 Carson	Y	Y	N	Y	Y	Y
3 ***Watkins***	N	Y	Y	Y	Y	Y
4 ***Watts***	N	Y	Y	Y	Y	Y
5 ***Istook***	N	Y	Y	Y	Y	Y
6 ***Lucas***	Y	Y	Y	Y	Y	Y
OREGON						
1 Wu	Y	Y	N	?	?	?
2 ***Walden***	N	Y	Y	Y	Y	Y
3 Blumenauer	Y	Y	Y	Y	Y	Y
4 DeFazio	Y	Y	N	Y	Y	Y
5 Hooley	Y	Y	N	Y	Y	Y
PENNSYLVANIA						
1 Brady	Y	Y	N	Y	Y	Y
2 Fattah	Y	Y	?	Y	Y	Y
3 Borski	Y	Y	N	Y	Y	Y
4 ***Hart***	Y	Y	Y	Y	Y	Y
5 ***Peterson***	N	Y	Y	Y	Y	Y
6 Holden	Y	Y	Y	Y	Y	Y
7 ***Weldon***	Y	Y	Y	Y	Y	Y
8 ***Greenwood***	N	Y	Y	Y	Y	Y
9 ***Shuster, Bill***	Y	Y	Y	Y	Y	Y
10 ***Sherwood***	Y	Y	Y	Y	Y	?
11 Kanjorski	Y	Y	Y	Y	Y	Y
12 Murtha	Y	Y	Y	Y	Y	Y
13 Hoeffel	Y	Y	Y	Y	Y	Y
14 Coyne	Y	Y	Y	Y	Y	Y
15 ***Toomey***	N	Y	Y	Y	Y	Y
16 ***Pitts***	N	Y	Y	Y	Y	Y
17 ***Gekas***	N	Y	Y	Y	Y	Y
18 Doyle	Y	Y	Y	Y	Y	Y
19 ***Platts***	?	?	?	?	?	?
20 Mascara	Y	Y	Y	Y	Y	Y
21 ***English***	Y	Y	N	Y	Y	Y
RHODE ISLAND						
1 Kennedy	Y	Y	Y	Y	Y	Y
2 Langevin	Y	Y	Y	Y	Y	Y
SOUTH CAROLINA						
1 ***Brown***	N	Y	Y	Y	Y	Y
2 ***Spence***	N	Y	Y	Y	Y	Y
3 ***Graham***	N	Y	Y	Y	Y	Y
4 ***DeMint***	N	Y	Y	Y	Y	Y
5 Spratt	Y	Y	Y	Y	Y	Y
6 Clyburn	Y	Y	N	Y	Y	Y
SOUTH DAKOTA						
AL ***Thune***	Y	Y	Y	N	Y	Y

	193	194	195	196	197	198
TENNESSEE						
1 ***Jenkins***	N	Y	Y	Y	Y	Y
2 ***Duncan***	Y	Y	Y	Y	Y	Y
3 ***Wamp***	N	Y	Y	Y	Y	Y
4 ***Hilleary***	Y	Y	N	Y	Y	Y
5 Clement	Y	Y	Y	Y	Y	Y
6 Gordon	Y	Y	Y	Y	Y	Y
7 ***Bryant***	N	Y	Y	Y	Y	Y
8 Tanner	Y	Y	Y	Y	Y	Y
9 Ford	Y	Y	N	Y	Y	Y
TEXAS						
1 Sandlin	Y	Y	Y	Y	Y	Y
2 Turner	Y	Y	Y	Y	Y	?
3 ***Johnson, Sam***	N	Y	Y	Y	Y	?
4 Hall	Y	Y	Y	Y	Y	Y
5 ***Sessions***	Y	Y	Y	Y	Y	Y
6 ***Barton***	N	Y	Y	Y	Y	Y
7 ***Culberson***	N	Y	Y	Y	Y	Y
8 ***Brady***	N	Y	Y	Y	Y	Y
9 Lampson	Y	Y	Y	Y	Y	Y
10 Doggett	Y	Y	Y	Y	Y	Y
11 Edwards	Y	Y	Y	Y	Y	Y
12 ***Granger***	N	Y	Y	Y	Y	Y
13 ***Thornberry***	N	Y	Y	Y	Y	Y
14 ***Paul***	N	N	Y	Y	Y	N
15 Hinojosa	N	Y	Y	Y	Y	Y
16 Reyes	N	Y	Y	Y	Y	Y
17 Stenholm	N	Y	Y	Y	Y	Y
18 Jackson-Lee	Y	Y	Y	Y	Y	Y
19 ***Combest***	Y	Y	Y	Y	Y	Y
20 Gonzalez	N	Y	Y	Y	Y	Y
21 ***Smith***	N	Y	Y	Y	Y	Y
22 ***DeLay***	N	Y	Y	Y	Y	Y
23 ***Bonilla***	N	Y	Y	Y	Y	Y
24 Frost	Y	Y	Y	Y	Y	Y
25 Bentsen	Y	Y	Y	Y	Y	Y
26 ***Armey***	N	Y	Y	Y	Y	Y
27 Ortiz	N	Y	Y	Y	Y	Y
28 Rodriguez	Y	Y	Y	Y	Y	Y
29 Green	Y	Y	Y	Y	Y	Y
30 Johnson, E.B.	Y	Y	Y	Y	Y	Y
UTAH						
1 ***Hansen***	N	Y	Y	Y	Y	Y
2 Matheson	Y	Y	Y	Y	Y	Y
3 ***Cannon***	N	Y	Y	Y	Y	Y
VERMONT						
AL *Sanders*	Y	Y	Y	Y	Y	Y
VIRGINIA						
1 ***Davis, Jo Ann***	Y	Y	Y	Y	Y	Y
2 ***Schrock***	N	Y	Y	Y	Y	Y
3 Scott	Y	Y	Y	Y	Y	Y
4 ***Forbes***	N	Y	Y	Y	Y	Y
5 *Goode*	Y	Y	Y	Y	Y	Y
6 ***Goodlatte***	Y	Y	Y	Y	Y	Y
7 ***Cantor***	N	Y	Y	Y	Y	Y
8 Moran	Y	Y	Y	Y	Y	Y
9 Boucher	Y	Y	Y	Y	Y	Y
10 ***Wolf***	Y	Y	Y	Y	Y	Y
11 ***Davis, T.***	N	Y	Y	Y	Y	Y
WASHINGTON						
1 Inslee	Y	Y	Y	Y	Y	Y
2 Larsen	Y	Y	N	Y	Y	Y
3 Baird	Y	Y	N	Y	Y	Y
4 ***Hastings***	N	Y	Y	Y	Y	Y
5 ***Nethercutt***	N	Y	Y	Y	Y	Y
6 Dicks	Y	Y	Y	Y	Y	Y
7 McDermott	Y	Y	Y	Y	Y	Y
8 ***Dunn***	N	Y	Y	Y	Y	Y
9 Smith	Y	Y	Y	Y	Y	Y
WEST VIRGINIA						
1 Mollohan	Y	Y	Y	Y	Y	Y
2 ***Capito***	Y	Y	Y	Y	Y	Y
3 Rahall	Y	Y	?	Y	Y	Y
WISCONSIN						
1 ***Ryan***	Y	Y	Y	Y	Y	Y
2 Baldwin	Y	Y	Y	Y	Y	Y
3 Kind	Y	Y	Y	Y	Y	Y
4 Kleczka	Y	Y	Y	Y	Y	Y
5 Barrett	Y	Y	Y	Y	Y	Y
6 ***Petri***	N	Y	Y	Y	Y	Y
7 Obey	Y	Y	Y	Y	?	Y
8 ***Green***	Y	Y	Y	Y	Y	Y
9 ***Sensenbrenner***	Y	Y	Y	Y	Y	Y
WYOMING						
AL ***Cubin***	N	Y	Y	Y	Y	Y

Southern states - Ala., Ark., Fla., Ga., Ky., La., Miss., N.C., Okla., S.C., Tenn., Texas, Va.

Key

Y	Voted for (yea).
#	Paired for.
+	Announced for.
N	Voted against (nay).
X	Paired against.
−	Announced against.
P	Voted "present."
C	Voted "present" to avoid possible conflict of interest.
?	Did not vote or otherwise make a position known.

Democrats **Republicans** *Independents*

199. HR 2311. Fiscal 2002 Energy and Water Appropriations/Renewable Programs. Tancredo, R-Colo., amendment that would increase by $8.9 million renewable energy programs at the Energy Department and offset the cost with a decrease of $9.9 million from general investigation funds of the Army Corps of Engineers. Rejected 39-372: R 27-179; D 11-192 (ND 9-142, SD 2-50); I 1-1. June 28, 2001.

200. HR 2311. Fiscal 2002 Energy and Water Appropriations/Beach Protection. Tancredo, R-Colo., amendment that would strike language in the bill that would provide for beach replenishment and coastal protection projects to be paid for with 65 percent federal and 35 percent local funds. Rejected 84-333: R 44-164; D 39-168 (ND 36-118, SD 3-50); I 1-1. June 28, 2001.

201. HR 2311. Fiscal 2002 Energy and Water Appropriations/Energy Supply. Hinchey, D-N.Y., amendment that would increase by $50 million renewable alternative energy programs at the Energy Department and offset the cost with a decrease by $60 million for weapons activities from the National Nuclear Security Administration Stockpile Stewardship program. Rejected 163-258: R 18-192; D 144-65 (ND 124-31, SD 20-34); I 1-1. June 28, 2001.

202. HR 2311. Fiscal 2002 Energy and Water Appropriations/Non-Proliferation. Kucinich, D-Ohio, amendment that would increase by $66 million nuclear non-proliferation activities and decrease by $122.5 million funding for the National Ignition Facility. Rejected 91-331: R 8-202; D 82-128 (ND 77-79, SD 5-49); I 1-1. June 28, 2001.

203. HR 2311. Fiscal 2002 Energy and Water Appropriations/Lake Drilling. Bonior, D-Mich., amendment that would ban oil and gas drilling in the Great Lakes, Lake Saint Clair, and the Saint Mary's, Saint Clair, Detroit, Niagara and Saint Lawrence Rivers. Adopted 265-157: R 70-140; D 194-16 (ND 153-3, SD 41-13); I 1-1. June 28, 2001.

204. HR 2311. Fiscal 2002 Energy and Water Appropriations/Yucca Study. Berkley, D-Nev., amendment that would transfer $500,000 from nuclear waste disposal funds to the Nuclear Waste Technical Review Board to study the Energy Department's activities relating to the transportation of radioactive waste and spent nuclear fuel to Yucca Mountain. It also would authorize conducting hearings, obtaining testimony, and gathering other evidence from the department. Rejected 102-321: R 9-203; D 92-117 (ND 83-73, SD 9-44); I 1-1. June 28, 2001.

	199	200	201	202	203	204
ALABAMA						
1 *Callahan*	N	N	N	N	N	N
2 *Everett*	N	N	N	N	N	N
3 *Riley*	N	N	N	N	N	N
4 *Aderholt*	N	N	N	N	N	N
5 Cramer	N	N	N	N	Y	N
6 *Bachus*	N	N	N	N	Y	N
7 Hilliard	N	N	Y	Y	Y	N
ALASKA						
AL *Young*	?	?	?	?	?	N
ARIZONA						
1 *Flake*	Y	Y	N	N	N	N
2 Pastor	N	N	Y	N	Y	N
3 *Stump*	N	N	N	N	N	N
4 *Shadegg*	Y	Y	N	N	N	N
5 *Kolbe*	N	Y	N	N	N	N
6 *Hayworth*	N	Y	N	N	N	N
ARKANSAS						
1 Berry	N	N	N	N	Y	N
2 Snyder	N	Y	N	N	Y	N
3 *Hutchinson*	N	N	N	N	N	N
4 Ross	N	N	N	N	N	N
CALIFORNIA						
1 Thompson	N	N	Y	N	Y	Y
2 *Herger*	N	N	N	N	N	N
3 *Ose*	N	N	N	N	N	N
4 *Doolittle*	N	N	N	N	N	N
5 Matsui	N	N	N	Y	Y	Y
6 Woolsey	N	N	Y	Y	Y	Y
7 Miller, George	N	Y	Y	Y	Y	N
8 Pelosi	N	N	Y	Y	Y	Y
9 Lee	Y	Y	Y	Y	Y	Y
10 Tauscher	N	N	N	N	Y	Y
11 *Pombo*	N	N	N	N	N	N
12 Lantos	N	N	Y	Y	Y	Y
13 Stark	N	Y	Y	Y	Y	Y
14 Eshoo	N	Y	Y	Y	Y	Y
15 Honda	N	N	Y	Y	Y	Y
16 Lofgren	N	Y	Y	N	Y	N
17 Farr	N	Y	Y	Y	Y	N
18 Condit	N	N	N	N	Y	N
19 *Radanovich*	Y	?	?	?	?	N
20 Dooley	?	?	N	Y	N	N
21 *Thomas*	?	?	?	?	?	?
22 Capps	N	N	Y	N	Y	Y
23 *Gallegly*	N	N	N	N	N	N
24 Sherman	N	Y	Y	N	Y	Y
25 *McKeon*	N	N	N	N	N	N
26 Berman	N	N	Y	N	Y	Y
27 Schiff	N	N	N	N	N	Y
28 *Dreier*	N	N	N	N	N	N
29 Waxman	?	N	Y	N	Y	Y
30 Becerra	N	N	Y	N	Y	Y
31 Solis	N	Y	Y	N	Y	Y
32 Watson	N	N	Y	N	Y	Y
33 Roybal-Allard	N	N	Y	N	Y	Y
34 Napolitano	N	N	Y	N	Y	Y
35 Waters	Y	Y	Y	Y	Y	Y
36 Harman	?	N	N	N	Y	N
37 Millender-McD.	N	N	Y	N	Y	Y
38 *Horn*	N	N	N	N	N	N

	199	200	201	202	203	204
39 *Royce*	N	N	N	N	N	N
40 *Lewis*	N	N	N	N	N	N
41 *Miller, Gary*	N	Y	N	N	N	N
42 Baca	N	N	Y	N	Y	Y
43 *Calvert*	N	N	N	N	N	N
44 *Bono*	N	N	N	N	N	N
45 *Rohrabacher*	N	N	N	N	N	N
46 Sanchez	N	N	N	N	N	N
47 *Cox*	N	N	N	N	N	N
48 *Issa*	N	N	N	N	N	N
49 Davis	N	N	Y	N	Y	Y
50 Filner	N	N	Y	Y	Y	Y
51 *Cunningham*	N	N	N	N	N	N
52 *Hunter*	N	N	N	N	N	N
COLORADO						
1 DeGette	Y	Y	Y	Y	Y	N
2 Udall	Y	Y	Y	Y	Y	Y
3 *McInnis*	N	N	N	N	Y	N
4 *Schaffer*	Y	Y	Y	N	N	N
5 *Hefley*	Y	Y	N	N	N	N
6 *Tancredo*	Y	Y	N	N	N	N
CONNECTICUT						
1 Larson	N	N	Y	N	Y	N
2 *Simmons*	N	N	Y	N	Y	N
3 DeLauro	N	N	N	N	Y	N
4 *Shays*	Y	Y	Y	N	Y	Y
5 Maloney	N	N	N	N	Y	N
6 *Johnson*	N	Y	Y	N	Y	N
DELAWARE						
AL *Castle*	N	N	N	N	Y	N
FLORIDA						
1 *Scarborough*	N	N	N	N	N	N
2 Boyd	N	N	N	N	Y	N
3 Brown	N	N	Y	N	Y	N
4 *Crenshaw*	N	N	N	N	N	N
5 Thurman	N	N	N	N	Y	N
6 *Stearns*	N	N	N	N	Y	N
7 *Mica*	−	N	N	N	N	N
8 *Keller*	N	N	N	N	N	N
9 *Bilirakis*	N	N	N	N	N	N
10 *Young*	N	N	N	N	Y	N
11 Davis	N	N	Y	N	Y	N
12 *Putnam*	?	?	?	?	?	?
13 *Miller*	N	N	N	N	N	N
14 *Goss*	N	N	N	N	Y	N
15 *Weldon*	N	N	N	N	Y	N
16 *Foley*	N	Y	N	N	Y	N
17 Meek	N	N	Y	N	Y	Y
18 *Ros-Lehtinen*	N	N	N	?	?	?
19 Wexler	N	N	N	Y	Y	Y
20 Deutsch	N	N	Y	Y	Y	N
21 *Diaz-Balart*	N	N	N	N	Y	N
22 *Shaw*	N	N	N	N	Y	N
23 Hastings	N	N	Y	N	Y	Y
GEORGIA						
1 *Kingston*	N	N	N	N	N	N
2 Bishop	N	N	N	N	N	N
3 *Collins*	N	N	N	N	N	N
4 McKinney	Y	Y	Y	Y	Y	Y
5 Lewis	N	N	N	N	Y	N
6 *Isakson*	N	N	N	N	N	N
7 *Barr*	N	Y	N	N	N	N
8 *Chambliss*	N	N	N	N	N	N
9 *Deal*	N	N	N	N	N	N
10 *Norwood*	N	N	N	N	N	N
11 *Linder*	N	N	N	N	N	N
HAWAII						
1 Abercrombie	N	N	N	N	Y	Y
2 Mink	N	N	Y	Y	Y	Y
IDAHO						
1 *Otter*	N	Y	N	N	N	N
2 *Simpson*	N	N	N	N	N	N
ILLINOIS						
1 Rush	N	N	Y	Y	Y	Y
2 Jackson	N	N	Y	Y	Y	Y
3 Lipinski	N	N	N	N	Y	N
4 Gutierrez	N	N	Y	N	Y	Y
5 Blagojevich	N	N	N	N	Y	Y
6 *Hyde*	?	N	N	N	Y	N
7 Davis	N	N	Y	Y	Y	Y
8 *Crane*	N	N	N	N	N	N
9 Schakowsky	N	N	Y	Y	Y	Y
10 *Kirk*	N	N	N	N	Y	N
11 *Weller*	N	N	N	N	N	N
12 Costello	N	N	N	N	Y	N
13 *Biggert*	Y	N	N	N	Y	N

ND Northern Democrats   SD Southern Democrats

	199	200	201	202	203	204
14 ***Hastert***						
15 ***Johnson***	N	Y	Y	N	Y	N
16 ***Manzullo***	N	N	N	N	N	N
17 Evans	N	N	Y	Y	Y	Y
18 ***LaHood***	N	N	N	N	Y	N
19 Phelps	N	N	N	N	Y	N
20 ***Shimkus***	N	N	N	N	N	N
INDIANA						
1 Visclosky	N	N	Y	N	Y	N
2 ***Pence***	Y	Y	N	N	N	N
3 Roemer	N	N	Y	N	Y	N
4 ***Souder***	N	N	N	N	N	Y
5 ***Buyer***	?	?	?	N	N	N
6 ***Burton***	?	?	?	?	?	?
7 ***Kerns***	N	Y	N	N	N	N
8 ***Hostettler***	N	Y	N	N	N	N
9 Hill	N	Y	N	N	Y	Y
10 Carson	N	N	Y	Y	Y	N
IOWA						
1 ***Leach***	?	?	?	?	?	Y
2 ***Nussle***	N	N	N	N	Y	N
3 Boswell	Y	N	Y	N	Y	Y
4 ***Ganske***	N	N	N	N	Y	N
5 ***Latham***	N	N	N	N	N	N
KANSAS						
1 ***Moran***	Y	Y	N	N	N	N
2 ***Ryun***	N	?	N	N	N	N
3 Moore	N	Y	Y	Y	Y	Y
4 ***Tiahrt***	N	Y	N	N	N	N
KENTUCKY						
1 ***Whitfield***	N	N	N	N	N	N
2 ***Lewis***	N	N	N	N	N	N
3 ***Northup***	N	N	N	N	N	N
4 Lucas	N	N	N	N	Y	N
5 ***Rogers***	N	N	N	N	N	N
6 ***Fletcher***	N	N	N	N	?	N
LOUISIANA						
1 ***Vitter***	N	N	N	N	N	N
2 Jefferson	N	N	Y	N	N	N
3 ***Tauzin***	N	N	N	N	N	N
4 ***McCrery***	N	N	N	N	N	N
5 ***Cooksey***	N	N	N	N	N	N
6 ***Baker***	N	N	N	N	N	N
7 John	N	N	N	N	N	N
MAINE						
1 Allen	N	N	Y	Y	Y	N
2 Baldacci	N	N	Y	Y	Y	N
MARYLAND						
1 ***Gilchrest***	Y	Y	N	N	Y	N
2 ***Ehrlich***	–	–	–	–	Y	N
3 Cardin	N	N	Y	N	Y	N
4 Wynn	N	N	Y	N	Y	N
5 Hoyer	N	N	Y	N	Y	N
6 ***Bartlett***	Y	Y	N	N	Y	N
7 Cummings	N	N	Y	Y	Y	N
8 ***Morella***	N	N	Y	N	Y	N
MASSACHUSETTS						
1 Olver	N	N	Y	Y	Y	Y
2 Neal	N	Y	Y	Y	Y	Y
3 McGovern	N	Y	Y	Y	Y	Y
4 Frank	N	Y	Y	Y	Y	Y
5 Meehan	N	Y	Y	Y	Y	N
6 Tierney	N	N	Y	Y	Y	N
7 Markey	N	N	Y	Y	Y	Y
8 Capuano	N	N	Y	N	Y	Y
9 Vacant						
10 Delahunt	N	N	Y	N	Y	N
MICHIGAN						
1 Stupak	N	N	Y	N	Y	Y
2 ***Hoekstra***	N	N	N	N	Y	N
3 ***Ehlers***	Y	N	Y	N	Y	N
4 ***Camp***	N	N	N	N	Y	N
5 Barcia	N	N	Y	N	Y	N
6 ***Upton***	N	Y	N	N	Y	N
7 ***Smith***	Y	Y	Y	N	N	N
8 ***Rogers***	N	N	N	N	N	N
9 Kildee	N	Y	Y	Y	Y	N
10 Bonior	N	N	Y	Y	Y	N
11 ***Knollenberg***	N	N	N	N	N	N
12 Levin	N	N	Y	Y	Y	N
13 Rivers	Y	Y	Y	Y	Y	Y
14 Conyers	N	N	Y	Y	Y	Y
15 Kilpatrick	N	N	Y	N	Y	N
16 Dingell	N	N	N	N	Y	Y
MINNESOTA						
1 ***Gutknecht***	Y	N	N	N	Y	N
2 ***Kennedy***	N	N	N	N	Y	N
3 ***Ramstad***	Y	Y	Y	N	Y	N
4 McCollum	Y	Y	Y	Y	Y	Y
5 Sabo	N	Y	Y	Y	Y	N
6 Luther	Y	Y	Y	Y	Y	Y
7 Peterson	N	Y	N	N	Y	N
8 Oberstar	N	N	Y	Y	Y	Y
MISSISSIPPI						
1 ***Wicker***	N	N	N	N	N	N
2 Thompson	N	N	N	N	Y	N
3 ***Pickering***	Y	N	N	N	N	N
4 Shows	N	N	N	N	N	N
5 Taylor	N	N	N	N	N	N
MISSOURI						
1 Clay	N	Y	Y	Y	Y	N
2 ***Akin***	N	N	N	N	N	N
3 Gephardt	N	N	Y	N	Y	Y
4 Skelton	N	N	N	N	Y	N
5 McCarthy	N	N	Y	Y	Y	Y
6 ***Graves***	N	Y	N	N	N	N
7 ***Blunt***	N	N	N	N	N	N
8 ***Emerson***	N	N	N	N	N	N
9 ***Hulshof***	N	N	N	N	N	Y
MONTANA						
AL ***Rehberg***	N	N	N	N	N	N
NEBRASKA						
1 ***Bereuter***	N	Y	N	N	N	N
2 ***Terry***	Y	Y	N	N	N	N
3 ***Osborne***	Y	N	N	N	N	N
NEVADA						
1 Berkley	N	N	Y	N	Y	Y
2 ***Gibbons***	N	Y	N	N	N	Y
NEW HAMPSHIRE						
1 ***Sununu***	Y	Y	N	N	N	N
2 ***Bass***	N	Y	Y	N	N	N
NEW JERSEY						
1 Andrews	N	N	Y	Y	Y	N
2 ***LoBiondo***	N	N	Y	Y	Y	N
3 ***Saxton***	N	N	N	N	N	N
4 ***Smith***	N	N	N	Y	Y	Y
5 ***Roukema***	N	N	Y	N	Y	N
6 Pallone	N	N	Y	Y	Y	N
7 ***Ferguson***	N	N	Y	Y	Y	Y
8 Pascrell	N	N	Y	N	Y	Y
9 Rothman	N	N	Y	Y	Y	N
10 Payne	N	N	Y	Y	Y	N
11 ***Frelinghuysen***	N	N	N	N	N	N
12 Holt	Y	N	Y	N	Y	Y
13 Menendez	N	N	Y	N	Y	Y
NEW MEXICO						
1 ***Wilson***	N	N	N	N	Y	N
2 ***Skeen***	N	N	N	N	N	N
3 Udall	Y	Y	Y	N	Y	Y
NEW YORK						
1 ***Grucci***	–	N	N	N	N	N
2 Israel	N	N	N	N	Y	Y
3 ***King***	N	N	N	N	N	N
4 McCarthy	N	N	Y	N	Y	Y
5 Ackerman	N	N	Y	N	Y	Y
6 Meeks	N	N	Y	N	Y	N
7 Crowley	N	N	Y	N	Y	Y
8 Nadler	N	N	Y	Y	Y	Y
9 Weiner	N	N	Y	Y	Y	Y
10 Towns	N	N	Y	N	Y	Y
11 Owens	?	?	Y	Y	Y	Y
12 Velázquez	N	N	Y	Y	Y	Y
13 ***Fossella***	N	N	N	N	Y	N
14 Maloney	N	N	Y	Y	Y	Y
15 Rangel	N	N	Y	Y	Y	Y
16 Serrano	?	N	Y	Y	Y	N
17 Engel	N	N	Y	N	Y	Y
18 Lowey	N	N	Y	N	Y	Y
19 ***Kelly***	N	Y	Y	N	Y	N
20 ***Gilman***	N	N	N	N	Y	N
21 McNulty	N	N	Y	Y	Y	N
22 ***Sweeney***	N	N	N	N	Y	N
23 ***Boehlert***	N	N	Y	N	Y	N
24 ***McHugh***	N	N	N	N	Y	N
25 ***Walsh***	N	N	N	N	Y	N
26 Hinchey	Y	N	Y	Y	Y	Y
27 ***Reynolds***	N	N	N	N	Y	N
28 Slaughter	N	N	Y	N	Y	Y
29 LaFalce	N	N	Y	Y	Y	N
30 ***Quinn***	N	N	N	N	Y	N
31 ***Houghton***	N	N	N	N	N	?
NORTH CAROLINA						
1 Clayton	?	N	Y	N	Y	N
2 Etheridge	N	N	N	N	Y	N
3 ***Jones***	N	N	N	N	Y	N
4 Price	N	N	Y	N	Y	N
5 ***Burr***	N	N	N	N	N	N
6 ***Coble***	N	N	N	N	N	N
7 McIntyre	N	N	N	N	Y	N
8 ***Hayes***	N	N	N	N	N	N
9 ***Myrick***	N	N	N	N	N	N
10 ***Ballenger***	N	N	N	N	N	N
11 ***Taylor***	N	N	N	N	N	N
12 Watt	N	N	Y	N	Y	N
NORTH DAKOTA						
AL Pomeroy	N	N	N	N	Y	N
OHIO						
1 ***Chabot***	N	Y	N	N	Y	N
2 ***Portman***	N	N	N	N	Y	N
3 Hall	N	N	Y	N	Y	Y
4 ***Oxley***	N	N	N	N	N	N
5 ***Gillmor***	N	N	N	N	Y	N
6 Strickland	N	N	Y	Y	Y	N
7 ***Hobson***	N	N	N	N	N	N
8 ***Boehner***	N	N	N	N	N	N
9 Kaptur	N	N	Y	Y	Y	N
10 Kucinich	N	N	Y	Y	Y	Y
11 Jones	N	N	Y	Y	Y	Y
12 ***Tiberi***	N	Y	N	Y	N	N
13 Brown	N	N	Y	Y	Y	N
14 Sawyer	N	N	Y	Y	Y	Y
15 ***Pryce***	N	N	N	N	N	N
16 ***Regula***	N	N	N	N	Y	N
17 Traficant	N	N	N	N	Y	N
18 ***Ney***	N	N	N	Y	Y	N
19 ***LaTourette***	N	N	N	N	Y	N
OKLAHOMA						
1 ***Largent***	N	Y	N	N	N	N
2 Carson	N	N	N	N	N	N
3 ***Watkins***	N	N	N	N	N	N
4 ***Watts***	N	N	N	N	N	N
5 ***Istook***	N	N	N	N	N	N
6 ***Lucas***	N	N	N	N	N	N
OREGON						
1 Wu	N	N	Y	Y	Y	Y
2 ***Walden***	N	N	N	N	N	N
3 Blumenauer	N	Y	Y	Y	Y	Y
4 DeFazio	N	Y	Y	Y	Y	Y
5 Hooley	N	Y	Y	Y	Y	Y
PENNSYLVANIA						
1 Brady	N	N	N	N	Y	N
2 Fattah	N	N	Y	Y	Y	N
3 Borski	N	N	N	N	Y	N
4 ***Hart***	N	N	N	N	N	N
5 ***Peterson***	N	N	N	N	N	N
6 Holden	N	N	N	N	Y	N
7 ***Weldon***	N	N	N	N	N	?
8 ***Greenwood***	?	?	N	N	Y	N
9 ***Shuster, Bill***	N	N	N	N	N	N
10 ***Sherwood***	N	N	N	N	N	N
11 Kanjorski	N	N	N	N	Y	N
12 Murtha	N	N	N	N	N	N
13 Hoeffel	N	N	Y	N	Y	N
14 Coyne	N	N	Y	N	Y	N
15 ***Toomey***	Y	Y	N	Y	N	N
16 ***Pitts***	Y	Y	N	N	N	N
17 ***Gekas***	N	N	N	N	N	N
18 Doyle	N	N	N	N	Y	N
19 ***Platts***	?	?	?	?	?	?
20 Mascara	N	N	N	N	Y	N
21 ***English***	N	N	N	N	Y	N
RHODE ISLAND						
1 Kennedy	N	N	Y	Y	Y	Y
2 Langevin	N	N	N	N	Y	N
SOUTH CAROLINA						
1 ***Brown***	N	N	N	N	Y	N
2 ***Spence***	N	N	N	N	N	N
3 ***Graham***	N	N	N	N	N	N
4 ***DeMint***	N	N	N	N	N	N
5 Spratt	N	N	N	N	Y	?
6 Clyburn	N	N	N	N	Y	N
SOUTH DAKOTA						
AL ***Thune***	N	N	N	N	N	N
TENNESSEE						
1 ***Jenkins***	N	N	N	N	N	N
2 ***Duncan***	N	N	N	N	N	N
3 ***Wamp***	N	N	N	N	Y	N
4 ***Hilleary***	N	N	N	N	Y	N
5 Clement	N	N	N	N	Y	N
6 Gordon	N	N	N	N	Y	N
7 ***Bryant***	N	Y	N	N	N	Y
8 Tanner	N	N	N	N	Y	N
9 Ford	N	N	N	N	Y	N
TEXAS						
1 Sandlin	N	N	N	N	N	N
2 Turner	N	N	N	N	N	N
3 ***Johnson, Sam***	N	N	N	N	N	N
4 Hall	N	N	N	N	N	N
5 ***Sessions***	N	N	N	N	N	N
6 ***Barton***	?	?	?	?	?	?
7 ***Culberson***	N	N	N	N	N	N
8 ***Brady***	N	N	N	N	N	N
9 Lampson	N	N	N	N	N	N
10 Doggett	Y	Y	Y	Y	Y	Y
11 Edwards	N	N	N	N	N	N
12 ***Granger***	N	N	N	N	N	N
13 ***Thornberry***	N	N	N	N	N	N
14 ***Paul***	Y	Y	Y	Y	N	N
15 Hinojosa	N	N	Y	N	Y	N
16 Reyes	N	N	N	N	Y	Y
17 Stenholm	N	N	N	N	N	N
18 Jackson-Lee	N	N	Y	N	Y	N
19 ***Combest***	N	N	N	N	N	N
20 Gonzalez	N	N	Y	N	Y	N
21 ***Smith***	?	?	?	?	?	?
22 ***DeLay***	N	Y	N	N	N	N
23 ***Bonilla***	?	N	N	N	N	N
24 Frost	N	N	Y	N	Y	Y
25 Bentsen	N	N	N	N	N	N
26 ***Armey***	N	N	N	N	N	N
27 Ortiz	N	N	N	N	Y	N
28 Rodriguez	N	N	Y	N	Y	N
29 Green	N	N	N	N	N	N
30 Johnson, E.B.	N	N	Y	N	Y	Y
UTAH						
1 ***Hansen***	N	N	N	N	N	N
2 Matheson	N	Y	N	N	Y	N
3 ***Cannon***	Y	Y	N	N	N	N
VERMONT						
AL *Sanders*	N	N	Y	Y	Y	Y
VIRGINIA						
1 ***Davis, Jo Ann***	Y	N	N	N	Y	N
2 ***Schrock***	N	N	N	N	N	N
3 Scott	N	N	Y	N	Y	N
4 ***Forbes***	N	N	N	N	N	N
5 *Goode*	Y	Y	N	N	N	N
6 ***Goodlatte***	N	Y	N	N	N	N
7 ***Cantor***	N	N	N	N	N	N
8 Moran	?	?	Y	Y	Y	N
9 Boucher	N	N	N	N	Y	N
10 ***Wolf***	N	N	N	N	N	N
11 ***Davis, T.***	N	N	N	N	Y	N
WASHINGTON						
1 Inslee	N	Y	Y	N	Y	Y
2 Larsen	N	Y	Y	N	Y	N
3 Baird	N	N	Y	Y	Y	N
4 ***Hastings***	N	N	N	N	N	N
5 ***Nethercutt***	N	N	N	N	N	N
6 Dicks	N	N	N	N	Y	N
7 McDermott	N	N	Y	Y	Y	N
8 ***Dunn***	N	N	N	N	N	N
9 Smith	N	Y	Y	Y	N	N
WEST VIRGINIA						
1 Mollohan	N	N	N	N	N	N
2 ***Capito***	N	N	N	N	Y	N
3 Rahall	N	N	Y	Y	Y	Y
WISCONSIN						
1 ***Ryan***	N	N	N	Y	Y	N
2 Baldwin	N	Y	Y	Y	Y	Y
3 Kind	N	Y	Y	Y	Y	N
4 Kleczka	N	N	Y	Y	Y	N
5 Barrett	N	N	Y	Y	Y	N
6 ***Petri***	N	Y	Y	N	Y	N
7 Obey	N	N	Y	Y	Y	Y
8 ***Green***	N	N	N	N	Y	N
9 ***Sensenbrenner***	Y	Y	Y	N	Y	N
WYOMING						
AL ***Cubin***	N	Y	N	N	N	N

Southern states - Ala., Ark., Fla., Ga., Ky., La., Miss., N.C., Okla., S.C., Tenn., Texas, Va.

Key

Y	Voted for (yea).
#	Paired for.
+	Announced for.
N	Voted against (nay).
X	Paired against.
–	Announced against.
P	Voted "present."
C	Voted "present" to avoid possible conflict of interest.
?	Did not vote or otherwise make a position known.

Democrats **Republicans**
Independents

---

205. HR 2311. Fiscal 2002 Energy and Water Appropriations/Gulfstream Gas. Davis, D-Fla., amendment that would strike language in the bill that would prohibit the Federal Energy Regulatory Commission from using funds to finance the Gulfstream Natural Gas Project, a natural gas pipeline from Alabama to Florida. Rejected 210-213: R 39-172; D 170-40 (ND 131-25, SD 39-15); I 1-1. June 28, 2001.

206. HR 2311. Fiscal 2002 Energy and Water Appropriations/Passage. Passage of the bill that would appropriate $23.7 billion for the Energy Department, the Army Corps of Engineers, water projects and other independent agencies in fiscal 2002, $148 million more than fiscal 2001. Of this total, $18.7 billion is provided to the Energy Department and $4.5 billion to the Corps of Engineers. Passed 405-15: R 199-13; D 204-2 (ND 152-2, SD 52-0); I 2-0. June 28, 2001.

207. HR 2330. Fiscal 2002 Agriculture Appropriations/Rule. Adoption of the rule (H Res 183) to provide for House floor consideration of the bill that would appropriate $74.4 billion in fiscal 2002 for agriculture programs, including $15.7 billion for discretionary spending. Adopted 222-194: R 211-1; D 10-192 (ND 8-142, SD 2-50); I 1-1. June 28, 2001.

208. HR 2330. Fiscal 2002 Agriculture Appropriations/Drug Applications. Brown, D-Ohio, amendment that would provide $2.5 million for carrying out FDA duties regarding abbreviated applications for approving new drugs and $250,000 for public education programs about such approvals. Adopted 324-89: R 117-88; D 205-1 (ND 153-0, SD 52-1); I 2-0. June 28, 2001.

209. HR 2330. Fiscal 2002 Agriculture Appropriations/Antibiotics. Brown, D-Ohio, amendment that would provide $5 million for carrying out FDA duties regarding antibiotic drugs. Adopted 271-140: R 64-139; D 206-0 (ND 152-0, SD 54-0); I 1-1. June 28, 2001.

210. HR 2330. Fiscal 2002 Agriculture Appropriations/Food Labeling. Engel, D-N.Y., amendment that would provide $250,000 for carrying out FDA duties regarding food labeling. Adopted 291-115: R 90-112; D 200-2 (ND 149-1, SD 51-1); I 1-1. June 28, 2001.

	205	206	207	208	209	210
ALABAMA						
1 *Callahan*	N	Y	Y	?	?	?
2 *Everett*	N	Y	Y	?	?	?
3 *Riley*	N	Y	Y	N	N	Y
4 *Aderholt*	N	Y	Y	Y	N	Y
5 Cramer	N	Y	N	Y	Y	Y
6 *Bachus*	N	Y	Y	N	Y	Y
7 Hilliard	N	Y	N	Y	Y	Y
ALASKA						
AL *Young*	N	Y	Y	Y	N	N
ARIZONA						
1 *Flake*	N	N	Y	N	N	N
2 Pastor	N	Y	N	Y	Y	Y
3 *Stump*	N	Y	Y	N	N	N
4 *Shadegg*	N	Y	Y	N	N	N
5 *Kolbe*	N	Y	Y	N	N	N
6 *Hayworth*	N	Y	Y	N	N	N
ARKANSAS						
1 Berry	N	Y	N	Y	Y	Y
2 Snyder	Y	Y	N	Y	Y	Y
3 *Hutchinson*	N	Y	Y	N	N	N
4 Ross	Y	Y	N	Y	Y	Y
CALIFORNIA						
1 Thompson	Y	Y	N	Y	Y	Y
2 *Herger*	N	Y	Y	N	N	N
3 *Ose*	N	Y	Y	N	N	Y
4 *Doolittle*	N	Y	Y	N	N	N
5 Matsui	Y	Y	N	Y	Y	Y
6 Woolsey	Y	Y	N	Y	Y	Y
7 Miller, George	N	Y	N	Y	Y	Y
8 Pelosi	Y	Y	N	Y	Y	Y
9 Lee	Y	Y	N	Y	Y	Y
10 Tauscher	Y	Y	N	Y	Y	Y
11 *Pombo*	N	Y	N	N	N	N
12 Lantos	Y	Y	N	Y	Y	Y
13 Stark	N	Y	N	Y	Y	Y
14 Eshoo	Y	Y	N	Y	Y	Y
15 Honda	Y	Y	N	Y	Y	Y
16 Lofgren	Y	Y	N	Y	Y	Y
17 Farr	N	Y	N	Y	Y	?
18 Condit	N	Y	N	Y	Y	Y
19 *Radanovich*	N	Y	Y	N	N	N
20 Dooley	Y	Y	N	Y	Y	Y
21 *Thomas*	?	?	?	?	?	?
22 Capps	Y	Y	N	Y	Y	Y
23 *Gallegly*	N	Y	Y	N	N	N
24 Sherman	Y	Y	N	Y	Y	Y
25 *McKeon*	N	Y	Y	N	N	N
26 Berman	N	Y	N	Y	Y	Y
27 Schiff	Y	Y	N	Y	Y	Y
28 *Dreier*	N	Y	Y	N	N	N
29 Waxman	Y	Y	N	Y	Y	Y
30 Becerra	Y	Y	N	Y	Y	Y
31 Solis	Y	Y	N	Y	Y	Y
32 Watson	Y	Y	N	Y	Y	Y
33 Roybal-Allard	N	Y	N	Y	Y	Y
34 Napolitano	Y	Y	N	Y	Y	Y
35 Waters	Y	Y	N	Y	Y	Y
36 Harman	Y	Y	N	Y	Y	Y
37 Millender-McD.	Y	Y	N	Y	Y	Y
38 *Horn*	N	Y	Y	Y	Y	Y

	205	206	207	208	209	210
39 *Royce*	N	Y	Y	Y	Y	Y
40 *Lewis*	N	Y	Y	N	N	Y
41 *Miller, Gary*	N	Y	Y	N	N	N
42 Baca	Y	Y	N	Y	Y	Y
43 *Calvert*	N	Y	Y	N	Y	Y
44 *Bono*	N	Y	Y	Y	Y	?
45 *Rohrabacher*	N	Y	Y	N	N	Y
46 Sanchez	Y	Y	N	Y	Y	Y
47 *Cox*	Y	Y	Y	Y	Y	Y
48 *Issa*	N	Y	Y	N	N	N
49 Davis	Y	Y	N	Y	Y	Y
50 Filner	Y	Y	N	Y	Y	Y
51 *Cunningham*	N	Y	Y	Y	Y	Y
52 *Hunter*	N	Y	Y	N	N	N
COLORADO						
1 DeGette	Y	Y	N	Y	Y	Y
2 Udall	Y	Y	N	Y	Y	Y
3 *McInnis*	N	Y	N	?	?	?
4 *Schaffer*	N	N	Y	?	?	?
5 *Hefley*	N	Y	Y	Y	Y	Y
6 *Tancredo*	N	N	Y	Y	N	N
CONNECTICUT						
1 Larson	Y	Y	N	Y	Y	Y
2 *Simmons*	N	Y	Y	Y	Y	Y
3 DeLauro	Y	Y	N	Y	Y	Y
4 *Shays*	Y	N	Y	Y	Y	Y
5 Maloney	Y	Y	N	Y	Y	Y
6 *Johnson*	Y	Y	Y	Y	Y	Y
DELAWARE						
AL *Castle*	Y	Y	Y	Y	Y	N
FLORIDA						
1 *Scarborough*	Y	N	Y	N	N	Y
2 Boyd	Y	Y	Y	Y	Y	N
3 Brown	Y	Y	N	Y	Y	Y
4 *Crenshaw*	Y	Y	Y	N	N	N
5 Thurman	Y	Y	N	Y	Y	Y
6 *Stearns*	Y	N	Y	Y	Y	Y
7 *Mica*	N	Y	Y	N	N	N
8 *Keller*	Y	Y	Y	N	N	N
9 *Bilirakis*	Y	Y	Y	Y	N	N
10 *Young*	Y	Y	N	N	N	N
11 Davis	Y	?	N	Y	Y	Y
12 *Putnam*	?	?	?	?	?	?
13 *Miller*	Y	Y	Y	N	N	N
14 *Goss*	Y	Y	Y	N	N	N
15 *Weldon*	Y	Y	Y	Y	Y	Y
16 *Foley*	Y	Y	Y	Y	Y	Y
17 Meek	Y	Y	?	Y	Y	Y
18 *Ros-Lehtinen*	+	?	?	?	?	?
19 Wexler	Y	Y	N	Y	Y	Y
20 Deutsch	Y	Y	N	Y	Y	Y
21 *Diaz-Balart*	Y	Y	Y	?	?	?
22 *Shaw*	Y	Y	Y	Y	Y	Y
23 Hastings	Y	Y	N	Y	Y	Y
GEORGIA						
1 *Kingston*	N	Y	Y	N	N	N
2 Bishop	N	Y	N	Y	Y	Y
3 *Collins*	N	Y	Y	N	N	N
4 McKinney	Y	Y	N	Y	Y	Y
5 Lewis	Y	Y	N	Y	Y	Y
6 *Isakson*	N	Y	Y	N	N	N
7 *Barr*	N	Y	N	N	N	N
8 *Chambliss*	N	Y	Y	N	N	N
9 *Deal*	N	Y	Y	N	N	N
10 *Norwood*	N	Y	N	N	N	N
11 *Linder*	N	Y	Y	N	N	N
HAWAII						
1 Abercrombie	N	Y	N	Y	Y	Y
2 Mink	N	Y	N	Y	Y	Y
IDAHO						
1 *Otter*	N	Y	Y	N	N	N
2 *Simpson*	N	Y	Y	N	N	N
ILLINOIS						
1 Rush	Y	Y	N	Y	Y	Y
2 Jackson	Y	Y	N	Y	Y	Y
3 Lipinski	Y	Y	N	Y	Y	Y
4 Gutierrez	Y	?	N	Y	Y	Y
5 Blagojevich	Y	Y	N	Y	Y	Y
6 *Hyde*	N	Y	Y	Y	Y	Y
7 Davis	Y	Y	N	Y	Y	Y
8 *Crane*	N	Y	Y	N	N	N
9 Schakowsky	Y	Y	N	Y	Y	Y
10 *Kirk*	N	Y	Y	Y	Y	Y
11 *Weller*	N	Y	Y	Y	Y	Y
12 Costello	Y	Y	N	Y	Y	Y
13 *Biggert*	N	Y	Y	N	N	N

ND Northern Democrats   SD Southern Democrats

	205	206	207	208	209	210
14 ***Hastert***			Y			
15 ***Johnson***	N	Y	Y	Y	Y	Y
16 ***Manzullo***	N	Y	Y	Y	Y	Y
17 Evans	Y	Y	N	Y	Y	Y
18 ***LaHood***	Y	Y	Y	Y	Y	Y
19 Phelps	Y	Y	N	Y	Y	Y
20 ***Shimkus***	N	Y	Y	Y	Y	Y
INDIANA						
1 Visclosky	N	Y	N	Y	Y	Y
2 ***Pence***	N	Y	Y	N	N	Y
3 Roemer	Y	Y	N	Y	Y	Y
4 ***Souder***	N	Y	Y	N	N	Y
5 ***Buyer***	Y	Y	Y	N	N	N
6 ***Burton***	?	?	?	?	?	?
7 ***Kerns***	N	Y	Y	N	N	N
8 ***Hostettler***	N	N	Y	N	N	Y
9 Hill	Y	Y	N	Y	Y	Y
10 Carson	Y	Y	N	Y	Y	Y
IOWA						
1 ***Leach***	Y	Y	Y	Y	Y	Y
2 ***Nussle***	N	Y	Y	Y	Y	Y
3 Boswell	Y	Y	N	Y	Y	Y
4 ***Ganske***	Y	Y	Y	Y	Y	Y
5 ***Latham***	N	Y	Y	N	N	N
KANSAS						
1 ***Moran***	N	N	Y	Y	N	Y
2 ***Ryun***	N	Y	Y	N	N	N
3 Moore	Y	Y	N	Y	Y	Y
4 ***Tiahrt***	N	Y	Y	Y	N	Y
KENTUCKY						
1 ***Whitfield***	N	Y	Y	Y	N	Y
2 ***Lewis***	N	Y	Y	Y	N	Y
3 ***Northup***	N	Y	Y	Y	N	N
4 Lucas	Y	Y	N	Y	Y	Y
5 ***Rogers***	N	Y	Y	Y	N	Y
6 ***Fletcher***	N	Y	Y	Y	Y	Y
LOUISIANA						
1 ***Vitter***	N	Y	Y	N	N	N
2 Jefferson	Y	Y	N	Y	Y	?
3 ***Tauzin***	N	Y	Y	Y	N	N
4 ***McCrery***	N	Y	Y	Y	N	N
5 ***Cooksey***	N	Y	Y	Y	Y	N
6 ***Baker***	N	Y	Y	Y	?	?
7 John	N	Y	N	Y	Y	?
MAINE						
1 Allen	Y	Y	N	Y	Y	Y
2 Baldacci	Y	Y	Y	Y	Y	Y
MARYLAND						
1 ***Gilchrest***	Y	Y	Y	Y	Y	Y
2 ***Ehrlich***	Y	Y	Y	Y	Y	Y
3 Cardin	Y	Y	N	Y	Y	Y
4 Wynn	Y	Y	N	Y	Y	Y
5 Hoyer	Y	Y	N	Y	Y	Y
6 ***Bartlett***	Y	Y	Y	Y	Y	Y
7 Cummings	Y	Y	N	Y	Y	Y
8 ***Morella***	Y	Y	Y	Y	Y	Y
MASSACHUSETTS						
1 Olver	Y	Y	N	Y	Y	Y
2 Neal	N	Y	N	Y	Y	Y
3 McGovern	Y	Y	N	Y	Y	Y
4 Frank	N	Y	N	Y	Y	Y
5 Meehan	Y	Y	N	?	?	?
6 Tierney	Y	Y	N	Y	Y	Y
7 Markey	N	Y	N	Y	Y	Y
8 Capuano	Y	Y	N	Y	Y	Y
9 Vacant						
10 Delahunt	N	Y	N	Y	Y	Y
MICHIGAN						
1 Stupak	Y	Y	N	Y	Y	Y
2 ***Hoekstra***	N	Y	Y	Y	N	Y
3 ***Ehlers***	Y	Y	Y	N	N	N
4 ***Camp***	Y	Y	Y	Y	N	N
5 Barcia	Y	Y	N	Y	Y	Y
6 ***Upton***	Y	Y	Y	Y	N	N
7 ***Smith***	N	Y	Y	Y	N	N
8 ***Rogers***	N	Y	Y	Y	Y	Y
9 Kildee	Y	Y	N	Y	Y	Y
10 Bonior	Y	Y	?	?	?	?
11 ***Knollenberg***	N	Y	Y	N	N	N
12 Levin	Y	Y	N	Y	Y	Y
13 Rivers	Y	Y	N	Y	Y	Y
14 Conyers	Y	Y	?	Y	Y	?
15 Kilpatrick	Y	Y	N	Y	Y	Y
16 Dingell	Y	Y	?	Y	Y	Y
MINNESOTA						
1 ***Gutknecht***	N	Y	Y	Y	Y	Y
2 ***Kennedy***	N	Y	Y	Y	Y	Y
3 ***Ramstad***	Y	Y	Y	Y	Y	Y
4 McCollum	Y	?	N	Y	Y	Y
5 Sabo	N	Y	N	Y	Y	Y
6 Luther	Y	Y	N	Y	Y	Y
7 Peterson	N	Y	N	Y	Y	N
8 Oberstar	Y	Y	N	Y	Y	Y
MISSISSIPPI						
1 ***Wicker***	N	Y	Y	Y	N	N
2 Thompson	N	Y	N	Y	Y	Y
3 ***Pickering***	N	Y	Y	Y	N	Y
4 Shows	Y	Y	N	Y	Y	Y
5 Taylor	Y	Y	N	Y	Y	Y
MISSOURI						
1 Clay	Y	Y	N	Y	Y	Y
2 ***Akin***	N	Y	Y	N	N	Y
3 Gephardt	Y	Y	N	Y	Y	Y
4 Skelton	Y	Y	Y	Y	Y	Y
5 McCarthy	Y	Y	N	Y	Y	Y
6 ***Graves***	N	Y	Y	N	N	N
7 ***Blunt***	N	Y	Y	N	N	N
8 ***Emerson***	N	Y	Y	Y	N	N
9 ***Hulshof***	N	Y	Y	Y	N	Y
MONTANA						
AL ***Rehberg***	N	Y	Y	Y	N	N
NEBRASKA						
1 ***Bereuter***	N	Y	Y	Y	N	N
2 ***Terry***	N	Y	Y	Y	Y	Y
3 ***Osborne***	N	Y	Y	N	N	N
NEVADA						
1 Berkley	Y	N	N	Y	Y	Y
2 ***Gibbons***	N	N	Y	N	N	N
NEW HAMPSHIRE						
1 ***Sununu***	Y	Y	Y	Y	N	Y
2 ***Bass***	N	Y	Y	Y	Y	Y
NEW JERSEY						
1 Andrews	Y	N	N	Y	Y	Y
2 ***LoBiondo***	N	Y	Y	Y	Y	Y
3 ***Saxton***	N	Y	Y	Y	Y	Y
4 ***Smith***	N	Y	Y	Y	Y	Y
5 ***Roukema***	N	Y	Y	?	?	?
6 Pallone	Y	Y	N	Y	Y	Y
7 ***Ferguson***	N	Y	Y	N	N	Y
8 Pascrell	Y	Y	N	Y	Y	Y
9 Rothman	Y	Y	N	Y	Y	Y
10 Payne	Y	Y	N	Y	Y	Y
11 ***Frelinghuysen***	N	Y	Y	N	N	N
12 Holt	Y	Y	N	Y	Y	Y
13 Menendez	Y	Y	N	Y	Y	Y
NEW MEXICO						
1 ***Wilson***	N	Y	Y	Y	Y	N
2 ***Skeen***	N	Y	Y	N	N	N
3 Udall	Y	Y	N	Y	Y	Y
NEW YORK						
1 ***Grucci***	N	Y	Y	N	N	Y
2 Israel	Y	Y	N	Y	Y	Y
3 ***King***	N	Y	Y	Y	Y	Y
4 McCarthy	Y	Y	N	Y	Y	Y
5 Ackerman	Y	Y	N	Y	Y	Y
6 Meeks	Y	Y	N	Y	Y	Y
7 Crowley	Y	Y	N	Y	Y	Y
8 Nadler	Y	Y	N	Y	Y	Y
9 Weiner	Y	Y	N	Y	Y	Y
10 Towns	Y	Y	N	Y	Y	Y
11 Owens	Y	Y	?	Y	Y	Y
12 Velázquez	Y	Y	N	Y	Y	Y
13 ***Fossella***	N	Y	Y	?	?	?
14 Maloney	Y	Y	Y	Y	Y	Y
15 Rangel	Y	Y	N	Y	Y	Y
16 Serrano	Y	Y	N	Y	Y	Y
17 Engel	Y	Y	N	Y	?	Y
18 Lowey	Y	Y	N	Y	Y	Y
19 ***Kelly***	N	Y	Y	Y	N	Y
20 ***Gilman***	+	Y	Y	Y	Y	Y
21 McNulty	Y	Y	N	Y	Y	Y
22 ***Sweeney***	N	Y	Y	N	N	N
23 ***Boehlert***	N	Y	Y	Y	Y	N
24 ***McHugh***	N	Y	Y	Y	Y	Y
25 ***Walsh***	N	Y	Y	N	N	N
26 Hinchey	N	Y	Y	Y	Y	Y
27 ***Reynolds***	N	Y	Y	Y	Y	Y
28 Slaughter	Y	Y	?	Y	Y	Y
29 LaFalce	Y	Y	N	Y	Y	Y
30 ***Quinn***	N	Y	Y	Y	Y	Y
31 ***Houghton***	?	?	?	?	?	?
NORTH CAROLINA						
1 Clayton	Y	Y	N	Y	Y	Y
2 Etheridge	Y	Y	N	Y	Y	Y
3 ***Jones***	Y	Y	Y	Y	N	Y
4 Price	Y	Y	N	Y	Y	Y
5 ***Burr***	Y	Y	Y	N	N	N
6 ***Coble***	N	Y	Y	N	N	N
7 McIntyre	N	Y	N	Y	Y	Y
8 ***Hayes***	N	Y	Y	N	N	N
9 ***Myrick***	Y	Y	Y	N	N	Y
10 ***Ballenger***	N	Y	Y	N	N	N
11 ***Taylor***	N	Y	Y	Y	N	N
12 Watt	Y	Y	N	Y	Y	Y
NORTH DAKOTA						
AL Pomeroy	Y	Y	N	Y	Y	Y
OHIO						
1 ***Chabot***	N	Y	Y	N	N	N
2 ***Portman***	N	Y	Y	N	N	N
3 Hall	Y	Y	N	?	?	?
4 ***Oxley***	N	Y	Y	N	N	N
5 ***Gillmor***	N	Y	Y	Y	N	N
6 Strickland	Y	Y	N	Y	Y	Y
7 ***Hobson***	N	Y	Y	Y	N	Y
8 ***Boehner***	N	Y	Y	N	N	N
9 Kaptur	Y	Y	N	Y	Y	Y
10 Kucinich	Y	Y	N	Y	Y	Y
11 Jones	Y	Y	N	Y	Y	Y
12 ***Tiberi***	N	Y	Y	Y	N	Y
13 Brown	Y	Y	N	Y	Y	Y
14 Sawyer	Y	Y	N	Y	Y	Y
15 ***Pryce***	N	Y	Y	Y	N	N
16 ***Regula***	N	Y	Y	Y	Y	N
17 Traficant	N	Y	Y	Y	Y	Y
18 ***Ney***	N	Y	Y	Y	Y	Y
19 ***LaTourette***	N	Y	Y	Y	Y	Y
OKLAHOMA						
1 ***Largent***	Y	Y	?	?	?	?
2 Carson	Y	Y	N	Y	Y	Y
3 ***Watkins***	Y	Y	Y	N	N	N
4 ***Watts***	Y	Y	Y	N	N	N
5 ***Istook***	Y	Y	Y	N	N	N
6 ***Lucas***	Y	Y	Y	N	N	N
OREGON						
1 Wu	N	Y	Y	Y	Y	Y
2 ***Walden***	N	Y	Y	Y	N	N
3 Blumenauer	Y	Y	N	Y	Y	Y
4 DeFazio	Y	Y	N	Y	Y	Y
5 Hooley	Y	Y	N	Y	Y	Y
PENNSYLVANIA						
1 Brady	Y	Y	N	Y	Y	Y
2 Fattah	Y	Y	N	Y	Y	?
3 Borski	Y	Y	N	Y	Y	Y
4 ***Hart***	N	Y	Y	Y	N	Y
5 ***Peterson***	N	Y	Y	Y	N	N
6 Holden	N	Y	Y	Y	Y	Y
7 ***Weldon***	?	?	?	?	?	?
8 ***Greenwood***	Y	Y	Y	N	N	N
9 ***Shuster, Bill***	N	Y	Y	N	N	N
10 ***Sherwood***	N	Y	Y	Y	N	Y
11 Kanjorski	N	Y	N	Y	Y	Y
12 Murtha	N	Y	N	Y	Y	Y
13 Hoeffel	Y	Y	N	Y	Y	Y
14 Coyne	Y	Y	N	Y	Y	Y
15 ***Toomey***	N	Y	Y	Y	N	Y
16 ***Pitts***	N	Y	Y	N	N	Y
17 ***Gekas***	N	Y	Y	N	N	Y
18 Doyle	Y	Y	N	Y	Y	Y
19 ***Platts***	?	?	?	?	?	?
20 Mascara	Y	Y	N	Y	Y	Y
21 ***English***	N	Y	Y	Y	Y	Y
RHODE ISLAND						
1 Kennedy	Y	Y	N	Y	Y	Y
2 Langevin	Y	Y	N	Y	Y	Y
SOUTH CAROLINA						
1 ***Brown***	N	Y	Y	N	N	N
2 ***Spence***	N	Y	Y	N	Y	Y
3 ***Graham***	N	Y	Y	Y	Y	Y
4 ***DeMint***	N	Y	Y	N	N	N
5 Spratt	Y	Y	N	Y	Y	Y
6 Clyburn	N	Y	N	Y	Y	Y
SOUTH DAKOTA						
AL ***Thune***	N	N	Y	Y	N	Y
TENNESSEE						
1 ***Jenkins***	N	Y	Y	Y	N	N
2 ***Duncan***	N	Y	Y	Y	N	Y
3 ***Wamp***	N	Y	Y	Y	N	N
4 ***Hilleary***	N	Y	Y	Y	N	Y
5 Clement	Y	Y	N	Y	Y	Y
6 Gordon	N	Y	N	?	Y	Y
7 ***Bryant***	N	Y	Y	N	N	N
8 Tanner	N	Y	N	Y	Y	Y
9 Ford	Y	Y	N	Y	Y	Y
TEXAS						
1 Sandlin	Y	Y	N	Y	Y	Y
2 Turner	Y	Y	N	Y	Y	Y
3 ***Johnson, Sam***	N	Y	Y	N	N	N
4 Hall	Y	Y	Y	N	Y	Y
5 ***Sessions***	N	Y	Y	N	N	N
6 ***Barton***	?	?	?	?	?	?
7 ***Culberson***	N	Y	Y	N	N	Y
8 ***Brady***	N	Y	Y	Y	N	Y
9 Lampson	Y	Y	N	Y	Y	Y
10 Doggett	Y	?	N	Y	Y	Y
11 Edwards	N	Y	N	Y	Y	Y
12 ***Granger***	N	Y	Y	N	N	N
13 ***Thornberry***	N	Y	Y	N	N	N
14 ***Paul***	N	N	Y	Y	Y	N
15 Hinojosa	Y	Y	N	Y	Y	Y
16 Reyes	Y	Y	N	Y	Y	Y
17 Stenholm	Y	Y	N	Y	Y	Y
18 Jackson-Lee	Y	Y	N	Y	Y	Y
19 ***Combest***	N	Y	N	N	N	N
20 Gonzalez	Y	Y	N	Y	Y	Y
21 ***Smith***	?	?	?	?	?	?
22 ***DeLay***	N	Y	Y	N	N	N
23 ***Bonilla***	N	Y	Y	N	N	N
24 Frost	Y	Y	N	Y	Y	Y
25 Bentsen	N	Y	N	Y	Y	Y
26 ***Armey***	N	Y	Y	N	N	N
27 Ortiz	N	Y	N	Y	Y	Y
28 Rodriguez	Y	Y	N	Y	Y	Y
29 Green	N	Y	N	Y	Y	Y
30 Johnson, E.B.	N	Y	N	Y	Y	Y
UTAH						
1 ***Hansen***	N	Y	Y	Y	Y	N
2 Matheson	Y	Y	N	Y	Y	Y
3 ***Cannon***	N	Y	Y	Y	N	N
VERMONT						
AL *Sanders*	Y	Y	N	Y	Y	Y
VIRGINIA						
1 ***Davis, Jo Ann***	N	Y	Y	Y	Y	Y
2 ***Schrock***	N	Y	Y	N	N	N
3 Scott	Y	Y	N	Y	Y	Y
4 ***Forbes***	N	Y	Y	Y	Y	Y
5 *Goode*	N	Y	Y	Y	N	N
6 ***Goodlatte***	N	Y	Y	Y	Y	N
7 ***Cantor***	N	Y	Y	N	N	N
8 Moran	Y	Y	N	Y	Y	Y
9 Boucher	Y	Y	?	Y	Y	Y
10 ***Wolf***	N	Y	Y	Y	N	Y
11 ***Davis, T.***	N	Y	Y	Y	Y	Y
WASHINGTON						
1 Inslee	Y	Y	N	Y	Y	Y
2 Larsen	Y	Y	Y	Y	Y	Y
3 Baird	Y	Y	N	Y	Y	Y
4 ***Hastings***	N	Y	Y	N	N	N
5 ***Nethercutt***	N	Y	Y	N	N	N
6 Dicks	N	Y	N	Y	Y	Y
7 McDermott	Y	Y	N	Y	Y	Y
8 ***Dunn***	N	Y	Y	N	N	N
9 Smith	Y	Y	N	Y	Y	Y
WEST VIRGINIA						
1 Mollohan	N	Y	N	Y	Y	Y
2 ***Capito***	N	Y	Y	Y	Y	Y
3 Rahall	N	Y	?	Y	Y	Y
WISCONSIN						
1 ***Ryan***	N	Y	Y	Y	Y	Y
2 Baldwin	Y	Y	N	Y	Y	Y
3 Kind	Y	Y	N	Y	Y	Y
4 Kleczka	Y	Y	N	Y	Y	Y
5 Barrett	Y	Y	N	Y	Y	Y
6 ***Petri***	N	Y	Y	Y	Y	Y
7 Obey	Y	Y	N	Y	Y	Y
8 ***Green***	N	Y	Y	Y	Y	Y
9 ***Sensenbrenner***	N	N	Y	Y	Y	Y
WYOMING						
AL ***Cubin***	N	Y	Y	N	N	N

Southern states - Ala., Ark., Fla., Ga., Ky., La., Miss., N.C., Okla., S.C., Tenn., Texas, Va.

Key

Y	Voted for (yea).
#	Paired for.
+	Announced for.
N	Voted against (nay).
X	Paired against.
−	Announced against.
P	Voted "present."
C	Voted "present" to avoid possible conflict of interest.
?	Did not vote or otherwise make a position known.

•

Democrats   **Republicans**
Independents

---

211. H Con Res 170. Faith-Based Support/Adoption. Whitfield, R-Ky., motion to suspend the rules and adopt the concurrent resolution that would express the sense of Congress that corporations should increase their support of faith-based organizations and should not adopt policies barring the company from giving to such organizations merely because they are faith-based. Motion agreed to 391-17: R 210-0; D 179-17 (ND 129-16, SD 50-1); I 2-0. A two-thirds majority of those present and voting (272 in this case) is required for adoption under suspension of the rules. July 10, 2001.

212. H Con Res 168. Torture Victims' Support/Adoption. Ros-Lehtinen, R-Fla., motion to suspend the rules and adopt the concurrent resolution that would honor torture victims in the United States and abroad annually on the occasion of the U.N. International Day in Support of Victims of Torture. Motion agreed to 409-0: R 207-0; D 200-0 (ND 148-0, SD 52-0); I 2-0. A two-thirds majority of those present and voting (273 in this case) is required for adoption under suspension of the rules. July 10, 2001.

213. H Con Res 174. Navajo Tribute/Adoption. Ney, R-Ohio, motion to suspend the rules and adopt the concurrent resolution that would allow use of the Capitol Rotunda on July 26, 2001, to present congressional gold medals to the original 29 Navajo Code Talkers. Motion agreed to 409-0: R 208-0; D 199-0 (ND 147-0, SD 52-0); I 2-0. A two-thirds majority of those present and voting (273 in this case) is required for adoption under suspension of the rules. July 10, 2001.

214. Procedural Motion/Journal. Approval of the House Journal of Tuesday, July 10, 2001. Approved 366-42: R 194-12; D 170-30 (ND 123-25, SD 47-5); I 2-0. July 11, 2001.

215. Procedural Motion/Adjourn. McNulty, D-N.Y., motion to adjourn. Motion rejected 11-405: R 3-211; D 8-192 (ND 8-138, SD 0-54); I 0-2. July 11, 2001.

216. HR 2330. Fiscal 2002 Agriculture Appropriations/Drug Re-Imports. Sanders, I-Vt., amendment that would bar using funds in the bill to enforce a provision in the Food, Drug and Cosmetic Act that forbids the re-importation of drugs originally manufactured in the United States by anyone but the manufacturer. Rejected 159-267: R 35-182; D 123-84 (ND 95-58, SD 28-26); I 1-1. A "nay" was a vote in support of the president's position. July 11, 2001.

	211	212	213	214	215	216
ALABAMA						
1 *Callahan*	Y	Y	Y	Y	N	N
2 *Everett*	Y	Y	Y	Y	N	N
3 *Riley*	+	+	+	?	?	−
4 *Aderholt*	Y	Y	Y	N	N	N
5 Cramer	Y	Y	Y	Y	N	Y
6 *Bachus*	Y	Y	Y	Y	N	N
7 Hilliard	Y	Y	Y	N	N	N
ALASKA						
AL *Young*	?	?	?	Y	N	N
ARIZONA						
1 *Flake*	Y	Y	Y	Y	N	Y
2 Pastor	Y	Y	Y	Y	N	Y
3 *Stump*	Y	Y	Y	Y	N	N
4 *Shadegg*	Y	Y	Y	Y	N	Y
5 *Kolbe*	Y	Y	Y	Y	N	Y
6 *Hayworth*	Y	Y	Y	Y	N	N
ARKANSAS						
1 Berry	Y	Y	Y	Y	N	Y
2 Snyder	P	Y	Y	Y	N	Y
3 *Hutchinson*	Y	Y	Y	?	?	N
4 Ross	Y	Y	Y	Y	N	Y
CALIFORNIA						
1 Thompson	Y	Y	Y	N	N	N
2 *Herger*	Y	Y	Y	Y	N	N
3 *Ose*	Y	Y	Y	Y	N	N
4 *Doolittle*	Y	Y	Y	Y	N	N
5 Matsui	Y	Y	Y	Y	N	N
6 Woolsey	Y	Y	Y	Y	N	Y
7 Miller, George	?	?	?	Y	N	Y
8 Pelosi	Y	Y	Y	Y	N	Y
9 Lee	Y	Y	Y	Y	N	Y
10 Tauscher	Y	Y	Y	Y	N	N
11 *Pombo*	Y	Y	Y	Y	N	N
12 Lantos	Y	Y	?	Y	N	Y
13 Stark	N	Y	Y	N	N	Y
14 Eshoo	Y	Y	Y	Y	N	N
15 Honda	N	Y	Y	Y	N	N
16 Lofgren	Y	Y	Y	Y	N	N
17 Farr	Y	Y	Y	N	N	N
18 Condit	Y	Y	Y	Y	N	Y
19 *Radanovich*	Y	Y	Y	Y	N	N
20 Dooley	Y	Y	Y	Y	N	?
21 *Thomas*	Y	Y	Y	Y	N	N
22 Capps	Y	Y	Y	Y	N	Y
23 *Gallegly*	Y	Y	Y	Y	N	N
24 Sherman	Y	Y	Y	Y	N	N
25 *McKeon*	Y	Y	Y	Y	N	N
26 Berman	Y	Y	Y	Y	N	N
27 Schiff	Y	Y	Y	Y	N	Y
28 *Dreier*	Y	Y	Y	Y	N	N
29 Waxman	Y	Y	Y	Y	N	N
30 Becerra	Y	Y	Y	Y	N	N
31 Solis	Y	Y	Y	Y	N	N
32 Watson	Y	Y	Y	Y	N	Y
33 Roybal-Allard	Y	Y	Y	Y	N	N
34 Napolitano	Y	Y	Y	Y	N	N
35 Waters	?	?	?	N	N	N
36 Harman	Y	Y	Y	Y	N	N
37 Millender-McD.	?	?	?	Y	N	N
38 *Horn*	Y	Y	Y	Y	N	N

	211	212	213	214	215	216
39 *Royce*	Y	Y	Y	Y	N	Y
40 *Lewis*	?	?	?	?	?	−
41 *Miller, Gary*	Y	Y	Y	Y	N	N
42 Baca	Y	Y	Y	Y	N	N
43 *Calvert*	Y	Y	Y	Y	N	N
44 *Bono*	Y	Y	Y	Y	N	N
45 *Rohrabacher*	Y	Y	Y	Y	N	N
46 Sanchez	Y	Y	Y	Y	N	N
47 *Cox*	Y	?	Y	Y	N	N
48 *Issa*	Y	Y	Y	Y	N	N
49 Davis	Y	Y	Y	Y	N	N
50 Filner	Y	Y	Y	−	+	Y
51 *Cunningham*	Y	Y	Y	Y	N	N
52 *Hunter*	Y	Y	Y	?	N	Y
COLORADO						
1 DeGette	N	Y	Y	Y	N	N
2 Udall	Y	Y	Y	N	N	N
3 *McInnis*	Y	Y	Y	Y	N	N
4 *Schaffer*	Y	Y	Y	N	N	Y
5 *Hefley*	Y	Y	Y	N	N	N
6 *Tancredo*	Y	Y	Y	P	N	Y
CONNECTICUT						
1 Larson	?	Y	Y	Y	N	N
2 *Simmons*	Y	Y	Y	Y	N	N
3 DeLauro	Y	Y	Y	Y	N	Y
4 *Shays*	Y	Y	Y	Y	N	Y
5 Maloney	Y	Y	Y	Y	N	N
6 *Johnson*	Y	Y	Y	Y	N	N
DELAWARE						
AL *Castle*	Y	Y	Y	Y	N	Y
FLORIDA						
1 *Scarborough*	?	?	?	?	N	Y
2 Boyd	Y	Y	Y	Y	N	N
3 Brown	Y	Y	Y	N	N	N
4 *Crenshaw*	Y	Y	Y	Y	N	N
5 Thurman	Y	Y	Y	Y	N	Y
6 *Stearns*	Y	Y	Y	N	N	N
7 *Mica*	Y	Y	Y	Y	N	N
8 *Keller*	Y	+	Y	Y	N	N
9 *Bilirakis*	Y	Y	Y	N	N	N
10 *Young*	Y	Y	Y	Y	N	N
11 Davis	Y	Y	Y	Y	N	N
12 *Putnam*	Y	Y	Y	Y	N	N
13 *Miller*	Y	Y	Y	Y	N	N
14 *Goss*	Y	Y	Y	Y	N	N
15 *Weldon*	Y	Y	Y	N	N	N
16 *Foley*	Y	Y	Y	Y	N	N
17 Meek	Y	Y	Y	Y	N	N
18 *Ros-Lehtinen*	Y	Y	Y	Y	N	N
19 Wexler	Y	Y	Y	Y	N	Y
20 Deutsch	Y	Y	Y	Y	N	N
21 *Diaz-Balart*	Y	Y	Y	Y	N	N
22 *Shaw*	Y	Y	Y	N	N	N
23 Hastings	Y	Y	Y	N	N	Y
GEORGIA						
1 *Kingston*	Y	Y	Y	Y	N	N
2 Bishop	Y	Y	Y	Y	N	N
3 *Collins*	Y	Y	Y	Y	N	N
4 McKinney	N	Y	Y	Y	N	Y
5 Lewis	Y	Y	Y	Y	N	Y
6 *Isakson*	Y	Y	Y	Y	N	N
7 *Barr*	Y	Y	Y	Y	N	N
8 *Chambliss*	Y	Y	Y	Y	N	N
9 *Deal*	Y	Y	Y	Y	N	N
10 *Norwood*	Y	Y	Y	?	N	N
11 *Linder*	Y	Y	Y	Y	N	N
HAWAII						
1 Abercrombie	Y	Y	Y	Y	N	Y
2 Mink	Y	Y	Y	Y	N	Y
IDAHO						
1 *Otter*	Y	Y	Y	Y	N	Y
2 *Simpson*	Y	Y	Y	Y	N	N
ILLINOIS						
1 Rush	Y	Y	Y	Y	N	N
2 Jackson	N	Y	Y	Y	N	Y
3 Lipinski	Y	Y	Y	Y	N	N
4 Gutierrez	Y	Y	?	?	N	Y
5 Blagojevich	Y	Y	Y	Y	N	Y
6 *Hyde*	Y	Y	Y	Y	N	N
7 Davis	Y	Y	Y	Y	N	Y
8 *Crane*	Y	Y	Y	N	N	N
9 Schakowsky	N	Y	Y	Y	N	Y
10 *Kirk*	Y	Y	Y	Y	N	N
11 *Weller*	Y	Y	Y	N	N	N
12 Costello	Y	Y	Y	N	N	Y
13 *Biggert*	Y	Y	Y	Y	N	N

ND Northern Democrats   SD Southern Democrats

	211	212	213	214	215	216
14 ***Hastert***						
15 ***Johnson***	Y	Y	Y	Y	N	Y
16 ***Manzullo***	Y	Y	Y	Y	N	N
17 Evans	?	Y	Y	Y	?	Y
18 ***LaHood***	Y	Y	Y	Y	N	N
19 Phelps	Y	Y	Y	Y	N	N
20 ***Shimkus***	Y	Y	?	Y	N	N
INDIANA						
1 Visclosky	Y	Y	Y	N	N	N
2 ***Pence***	Y	Y	Y	Y	N	N
3 Roemer	Y	Y	Y	Y	?	Y
4 ***Souder***	Y	Y	Y	Y	N	N
5 ***Buyer***	Y	Y	Y	Y	N	N
6 ***Burton***	Y	Y	Y	Y	N	Y
7 ***Kerns***	Y	Y	Y	Y	N	N
8 ***Hostettler***	Y	Y	Y	Y	N	N
9 Hill	Y	Y	Y	Y	N	Y
10 Carson	+	+	+	P	N	Y
IOWA						
1 ***Leach***	Y	Y	Y	Y	N	Y
2 ***Nussle***	Y	Y	Y	Y	N	N
3 Boswell	Y	Y	Y	Y	N	Y
4 ***Ganske***	Y	Y	Y	Y	N	N
5 ***Latham***	Y	Y	Y	N	N	N
KANSAS						
1 ***Moran***	Y	Y	Y	N	N	Y
2 ***Ryun***	Y	Y	Y	Y	N	N
3 Moore	Y	Y	Y	Y	N	N
4 ***Tiahrt***	Y	Y	Y	Y	N	Y
KENTUCKY						
1 ***Whitfield***	Y	Y	Y	Y	N	N
2 ***Lewis***	Y	Y	Y	Y	N	N
3 ***Northup***	Y	Y	Y	Y	N	N
4 Lucas	Y	Y	Y	Y	N	N
5 ***Rogers***	Y	Y	Y	Y	N	N
6 ***Fletcher***	Y	Y	Y	Y	N	N
LOUISIANA						
1 ***Vitter***	Y	Y	Y	Y	N	N
2 Jefferson	Y	Y	Y	Y	N	N
3 ***Tauzin***	Y	Y	Y	Y	N	N
4 ***McCrery***	Y	Y	Y	Y	N	N
5 ***Cooksey***	Y	Y	Y	Y	N	N
6 ***Baker***	Y	Y	Y	Y	N	N
7 John	Y	Y	Y	Y	N	N
MAINE						
1 Allen	P	Y	Y	Y	N	Y
2 Baldacci	Y	Y	Y	Y	N	Y
MARYLAND						
1 ***Gilchrest***	Y	Y	Y	Y	N	Y
2 ***Ehrlich***	Y	Y	Y	Y	N	N
3 Cardin	Y	Y	Y	Y	N	N
4 Wynn	Y	Y	Y	Y	N	Y
5 Hoyer	Y	Y	Y	?	N	N
6 ***Bartlett***	Y	Y	Y	Y	N	N
7 Cummings	Y	Y	Y	Y	N	Y
8 ***Morella***	Y	Y	Y	Y	N	N
MASSACHUSETTS						
1 Olver	N	Y	Y	Y	N	Y
2 Neal	Y	Y	Y	Y	N	Y
3 McGovern	Y	Y	Y	Y	N	Y
4 Frank	N	Y	Y	Y	Y	Y
5 Meehan	Y	Y	Y	Y	N	Y
6 Tierney	P	Y	Y	Y	N	Y
7 Markey	Y	Y	Y	Y	N	Y
8 Capuano	?	?	?	?	?	?
9 Vacant						
10 Delahunt	Y	Y	Y	Y	N	Y
MICHIGAN						
1 Stupak	Y	Y	Y	N	N	N
2 ***Hoekstra***	Y	Y	Y	Y	N	N
3 ***Ehlers***	Y	Y	Y	Y	N	N
4 ***Camp***	Y	Y	Y	Y	N	N
5 Barcia	Y	Y	Y	Y	N	N
6 ***Upton***	Y	Y	Y	Y	N	N
7 ***Smith***	Y	Y	Y	Y	N	Y
8 ***Rogers***	Y	Y	Y	?	N	N
9 Kildee	Y	Y	Y	Y	N	Y
10 Bonior	Y	Y	Y	Y	N	Y
11 ***Knollenberg***	Y	Y	Y	?	?	?
12 Levin	Y	Y	Y	Y	N	N
13 Rivers	N	Y	Y	Y	N	Y
14 Conyers	N	Y	Y	Y	Y	Y
15 Kilpatrick	Y	Y	Y	Y	N	N
16 Dingell	N	Y	Y	?	?	?

	211	212	213	214	215	216
MINNESOTA						
1 ***Gutknecht***	Y	Y	Y	N	N	Y
2 ***Kennedy***	+	+	+	N	N	N
3 ***Ramstad***	Y	Y	Y	N	N	Y
4 McCollum	Y	Y	Y	Y	N	N
5 Sabo	Y	Y	Y	N	N	Y
6 Luther	Y	Y	Y	Y	N	Y
7 Peterson	Y	Y	Y	N	N	Y
8 Oberstar	Y	Y	Y	N	N	Y
MISSISSIPPI						
1 ***Wicker***	?	?	?	Y	N	N
2 Thompson	Y	Y	Y	N	N	N
3 ***Pickering***	Y	Y	Y	Y	N	N
4 Shows	Y	Y	Y	Y	N	Y
5 Taylor	?	?	?	N	N	Y
MISSOURI						
1 Clay	Y	Y	Y	Y	Y	Y
2 ***Akin***	Y	Y	Y	Y	N	N
3 Gephardt	Y	Y	Y	Y	N	Y
4 Skelton	Y	Y	Y	Y	N	Y
5 McCarthy	Y	Y	Y	Y	N	N
6 ***Graves***	Y	Y	Y	Y	N	N
7 ***Blunt***	Y	Y	Y	Y	N	N
8 ***Emerson***	Y	Y	Y	Y	N	Y
9 ***Hulshof***	?	?	?	Y	N	N
MONTANA						
AL ***Rehberg***	Y	Y	Y	Y	N	N
NEBRASKA						
1 ***Bereuter***	Y	Y	Y	Y	N	Y
2 ***Terry***	Y	Y	Y	Y	N	N
3 ***Osborne***	Y	Y	Y	Y	N	N
NEVADA						
1 Berkley	Y	Y	Y	Y	N	N
2 ***Gibbons***	Y	Y	Y	Y	N	Y
NEW HAMPSHIRE						
1 ***Sununu***	Y	Y	Y	Y	N	N
2 ***Bass***	Y	Y	Y	Y	N	N
NEW JERSEY						
1 Andrews	Y	Y	Y	Y	N	Y
2 ***LoBiondo***	Y	Y	Y	N	N	N
3 ***Saxton***	Y	Y	Y	Y	N	N
4 ***Smith***	Y	Y	Y	Y	N	N
5 ***Roukema***	Y	Y	Y	Y	N	N
6 Pallone	Y	Y	Y	N	N	Y
7 ***Ferguson***	Y	Y	Y	Y	N	N
8 Pascrell	Y	Y	Y	Y	N	N
9 Rothman	Y	Y	Y	Y	N	Y
10 Payne	Y	Y	Y	Y	N	Y
11 ***Frelinghuysen***	Y	Y	Y	Y	N	N
12 Holt	Y	Y	Y	Y	Y	N
13 Menendez	Y	Y	Y	N	N	N
NEW MEXICO						
1 ***Wilson***	Y	Y	Y	Y	N	Y
2 ***Skeen***	Y	Y	Y	Y	N	N
3 Udall	Y	Y	Y	N	N	Y
NEW YORK						
1 ***Grucci***	Y	Y	Y	Y	N	N
2 Israel	Y	Y	Y	Y	N	Y
3 ***King***	Y	Y	Y	Y	N	N
4 McCarthy	Y	Y	Y	Y	N	N
5 Ackerman	Y	Y	Y	Y	N	Y
6 Meeks	Y	Y	Y	Y	N	Y
7 Crowley	Y	Y	Y	N	N	Y
8 Nadler	Y	Y	Y	Y	?	Y
9 Weiner	Y	Y	Y	Y	N	Y
10 Towns	Y	Y	Y	Y	N	N
11 Owens	Y	Y	Y	Y	N	Y
12 Velázquez	Y	Y	Y	Y	N	N
13 ***Fossella***	Y	Y	Y	Y	N	N
14 Maloney	Y	Y	Y	Y	?	Y
15 Rangel	Y	Y	Y	Y	N	Y
16 Serrano	Y	Y	Y	Y	N	Y
17 Engel	?	?	?	?	?	Y
18 Lowey	Y	Y	Y	Y	N	N
19 ***Kelly***	Y	Y	Y	Y	N	N
20 ***Gilman***	Y	Y	Y	Y	N	N
21 McNulty	Y	Y	Y	N	Y	Y
22 ***Sweeney***	Y	Y	Y	Y	N	N
23 ***Boehlert***	Y	Y	Y	Y	N	N
24 ***McHugh***	Y	Y	Y	Y	N	N
25 ***Walsh***	Y	Y	Y	Y	N	N
26 Hinchey	N	Y	Y	Y	N	Y
27 ***Reynolds***	Y	Y	Y	?	N	N
28 Slaughter	Y	Y	Y	Y	N	Y
29 LaFalce	Y	Y	Y	Y	N	Y

	211	212	213	214	215	216
30 ***Quinn***	Y	Y	Y	Y	N	N
31 ***Houghton***	Y	Y	Y	Y	N	N
NORTH CAROLINA						
1 Clayton	Y	Y	Y	?	N	N
2 Etheridge	Y	Y	Y	Y	N	N
3 ***Jones***	Y	Y	Y	?	N	N
4 Price	Y	Y	Y	Y	N	N
5 ***Burr***	Y	Y	Y	Y	N	N
6 ***Coble***	Y	Y	Y	Y	N	N
7 McIntyre	Y	Y	Y	Y	N	N
8 ***Hayes***	Y	Y	Y	Y	N	N
9 ***Myrick***	Y	Y	Y	Y	?	N
10 ***Ballenger***	Y	Y	Y	?	N	N
11 ***Taylor***	Y	Y	Y	Y	N	N
12 Watt	Y	Y	Y	Y	N	Y
NORTH DAKOTA						
AL Pomeroy	Y	Y	Y	Y	N	Y
OHIO						
1 ***Chabot***	Y	Y	Y	Y	N	Y
2 ***Portman***	Y	Y	Y	Y	N	N
3 Hall	Y	Y	Y	Y	N	Y
4 ***Oxley***	Y	Y	Y	Y	N	N
5 ***Gillmor***	Y	Y	Y	Y	N	N
6 Strickland	Y	Y	Y	N	N	Y
7 ***Hobson***	Y	Y	Y	Y	N	N
8 ***Boehner***	Y	Y	Y	Y	N	N
9 Kaptur	Y	Y	Y	Y	N	Y
10 Kucinich	Y	Y	Y	N	N	Y
11 Jones	Y	Y	Y	N	N	Y
12 ***Tiberi***	Y	Y	Y	Y	Y	N
13 Brown	Y	Y	Y	Y	N	Y
14 Sawyer	Y	Y	Y	Y	N	Y
15 ***Pryce***	Y	Y	Y	Y	N	N
16 ***Regula***	Y	Y	Y	Y	N	N
17 Traficant	Y	Y	Y	Y	N	N
18 ***Ney***	Y	Y	Y	Y	N	N
19 ***LaTourette***	Y	Y	Y	Y	N	N
OKLAHOMA						
1 ***Largent***	Y	Y	Y	Y	N	Y
2 Carson	Y	Y	Y	Y	N	Y
3 ***Watkins***	Y	Y	Y	Y	N	N
4 ***Watts***	+	+	+	Y	N	N
5 ***Istook***	Y	Y	Y	Y	N	N
6 ***Lucas***	Y	Y	?	Y	N	N
OREGON						
1 Wu	Y	Y	Y	N	N	Y
2 ***Walden***	Y	Y	Y	Y	N	N
3 Blumenauer	Y	Y	Y	Y	N	N
4 DeFazio	Y	Y	Y	N	Y	Y
5 Hooley	Y	Y	Y	Y	N	Y
PENNSYLVANIA						
1 Brady	Y	Y	Y	N	N	Y
2 Fattah	Y	Y	Y	Y	N	Y
3 Borski	Y	Y	Y	N	N	N
4 ***Hart***	Y	Y	Y	Y	N	N
5 ***Peterson***	Y	Y	Y	Y	N	N
6 Holden	Y	Y	Y	Y	N	N
7 ***Weldon***	Y	Y	Y	?	?	N
8 ***Greenwood***	Y	Y	Y	Y	N	N
9 ***Shuster, Bill***	Y	Y	Y	Y	N	N
10 ***Sherwood***	Y	Y	Y	Y	N	N
11 Kanjorski	Y	Y	Y	Y	N	N
12 Murtha	Y	Y	Y	Y	N	N
13 Hoeffel	Y	Y	Y	Y	N	N
14 Coyne	?	?	?	?	?	?
15 ***Toomey***	?	?	?	Y	N	N
16 ***Pitts***	Y	Y	Y	Y	N	N
17 ***Gekas***	Y	?	Y	Y	Y	N
18 Doyle	Y	Y	Y	Y	N	N
19 ***Platts***	Y	Y	Y	Y	N	Y
20 Mascara	Y	Y	Y	Y	N	Y
21 ***English***	Y	Y	Y	N	N	N
RHODE ISLAND						
1 Kennedy	Y	+	Y	Y	N	Y
2 Langevin	Y	Y	Y	Y	N	Y
SOUTH CAROLINA						
1 ***Brown***	Y	Y	Y	Y	N	N
2 ***Spence***	Y	Y	Y	Y	N	N
3 ***Graham***	Y	Y	Y	Y	N	N
4 ***DeMint***	Y	Y	Y	Y	N	N
5 Spratt	Y	Y	Y	Y	N	Y
6 Clyburn	Y	Y	Y	Y	N	N
SOUTH DAKOTA						
AL ***Thune***	Y	Y	Y	Y	N	Y

	211	212	213	214	215	216
TENNESSEE						
1 ***Jenkins***	Y	Y	Y	Y	N	N
2 ***Duncan***	Y	Y	Y	Y	N	N
3 ***Wamp***	Y	Y	Y	Y	N	N
4 ***Hilleary***	Y	Y	Y	Y	N	N
5 Clement	Y	Y	Y	Y	N	Y
6 Gordon	Y	Y	Y	Y	N	N
7 ***Bryant***	Y	Y	Y	Y	N	N
8 Tanner	Y	Y	Y	Y	N	N
9 Ford	Y	Y	Y	Y	N	N
TEXAS						
1 Sandlin	Y	Y	Y	Y	N	Y
2 Turner	Y	Y	Y	Y	N	Y
3 ***Johnson, Sam***	Y	Y	Y	Y	N	N
4 Hall	Y	Y	Y	Y	N	N
5 ***Sessions***	Y	Y	Y	Y	N	N
6 ***Barton***	Y	Y	Y	Y	N	N
7 ***Culberson***	Y	Y	Y	Y	N	N
8 ***Brady***	Y	Y	Y	Y	N	N
9 Lampson	Y	Y	Y	Y	N	Y
10 Doggett	Y	Y	Y	Y	N	Y
11 Edwards	Y	Y	Y	Y	N	N
12 ***Granger***	Y	Y	Y	Y	N	N
13 ***Thornberry***	Y	Y	Y	Y	N	N
14 ***Paul***	?	?	?	?	?	?
15 Hinojosa	Y	Y	Y	Y	N	Y
16 Reyes	Y	Y	Y	Y	N	Y
17 Stenholm	Y	Y	Y	Y	N	Y
18 Jackson-Lee	?	?	?	Y	N	Y
19 ***Combest***	Y	Y	Y	Y	N	N
20 Gonzalez	Y	Y	Y	Y	N	N
21 ***Smith***	Y	Y	Y	Y	N	N
22 ***DeLay***	Y	Y	Y	Y	N	N
23 ***Bonilla***	Y	Y	Y	Y	N	N
24 Frost	Y	Y	Y	Y	N	N
25 Bentsen	Y	Y	Y	Y	N	N
26 ***Armey***	Y	Y	Y	Y	N	N
27 Ortiz	Y	Y	Y	Y	N	Y
28 Rodriguez	Y	Y	Y	Y	N	Y
29 Green	Y	Y	Y	N	N	Y
30 Johnson, E.B.	Y	Y	Y	Y	N	N
UTAH						
1 ***Hansen***	Y	Y	Y	Y	N	N
2 Matheson	Y	Y	Y	Y	N	N
3 ***Cannon***	?	?	?	Y	N	N
VERMONT						
AL *Sanders*	Y	Y	Y	Y	N	Y
VIRGINIA						
1 ***Davis, Jo Ann***	Y	Y	Y	Y	N	N
2 ***Schrock***	Y	Y	Y	Y	N	N
3 Scott	Y	Y	Y	Y	N	Y
4 ***Forbes***	Y	Y	Y	Y	N	N
5 *Goode*	Y	Y	Y	Y	N	N
6 ***Goodlatte***	Y	Y	Y	Y	N	Y
7 ***Cantor***	Y	Y	Y	?	N	N
8 Moran	Y	Y	Y	Y	N	N
9 Boucher	Y	Y	Y	?	N	N
10 ***Wolf***	Y	Y	Y	Y	N	N
11 ***Davis, T.***	Y	Y	Y	Y	N	N
WASHINGTON						
1 Inslee	N	Y	Y	Y	N	N
2 Larsen	Y	Y	Y	N	N	N
3 Baird	N	Y	Y	N	N	Y
4 ***Hastings***	Y	Y	Y	Y	N	Y
5 ***Nethercutt***	Y	Y	Y	Y	N	N
6 Dicks	Y	Y	Y	Y	N	N
7 McDermott	N	Y	Y	N	Y	Y
8 ***Dunn***	Y	Y	Y	Y	N	N
9 Smith	Y	Y	Y	Y	N	N
WEST VIRGINIA						
1 Mollohan	Y	Y	Y	Y	N	Y
2 ***Capito***	Y	Y	Y	Y	N	Y
3 Rahall	Y	Y	Y	Y	N	Y
WISCONSIN						
1 ***Ryan***	Y	Y	Y	Y	N	N
2 Baldwin	Y	Y	Y	Y	N	Y
3 Kind	Y	Y	Y	Y	N	Y
4 Kleczka	Y	Y	Y	Y	N	Y
5 Barrett	Y	Y	Y	Y	N	Y
6 ***Petri***	Y	Y	Y	Y	N	Y
7 Obey	N	Y	Y	Y	N	N
8 ***Green***	Y	Y	Y	Y	N	N
9 ***Sensenbrenner***	Y	Y	Y	Y	N	Y
WYOMING						
AL ***Cubin***	Y	Y	Y	Y	N	N

Southern states - Ala., Ark., Fla., Ga., Ky., La., Miss., N.C., Okla., S.C., Tenn., Texas, Va.

Key

Y	Voted for (yea).
#	Paired for.
+	Announced for.
N	Voted against (nay).
X	Paired against.
–	Announced against.
P	Voted "present."
C	Voted "present" to avoid possible conflict of interest.
?	Did not vote or otherwise make a position known.

Democrats   ***Republicans***
Independents

217. HR 2330. Fiscal 2002 Agriculture Appropriations/Drug Imports. Gutknecht, R-Minn., amendment that would bar using funds in the bill to prevent individuals not in the prescription drug importation business from importing drugs that appear to be approved by the Food and Drug Administration and do not appear to be narcotics. Adopted 324-101: R 149-68; D 173-33 (ND 127-26, SD 46-7); I 2-0. A "nay" was a vote in support of the president's position. July 11, 2001.

218. HR 2330. Fiscal 2002 Agriculture Appropriations/Engineered Fish. Kucinich, D-Ohio, amendment that would bar using funds in the bill to approve an application for an animal drug to create genetically engineered fish. Rejected 145-279: R 13-203; D 130-76 (ND 108-44, SD 22-32); I 2-0. July 11, 2001.

219. HR 2330. Fiscal 2002 Agriculture Appropriations/Wool and Mohair. Weiner, D-N.Y., amendment that would bar using funds in the bill to pay salaries of personnel to make payments to wool or mohair producers for the 2000 or 2001 marketing years. Rejected 155-272: R 79-139; D 76-131 (ND 69-84, SD 7-47); I 0-2. July 11, 2001.

220. HR 2330. Fiscal 2002 Agriculture Appropriations/Market Access Program. Royce, R-Calif., amendment that would bar the use of federal funds in the bill to pay for any new allocations under the market access program or to pay for any staff salaries to award such allocations. Rejected 85-341: R 61-157; D 24-182 (ND 22-132, SD 2-50); I 0-2. July 11, 2001.

221. HR 2330. Fiscal 2002 Agriculture Appropriations/Passage. Passage of the bill that would appropriate $74.4 billion in fiscal 2002 for agriculture programs. It includes $22 billion for the food stamp program, $10.1 billion for child nutrition programs, $4.6 billion for Rural Electric and Telecommunications Loans, $4.5 billion for Rural Housing Loans, and $4.1 billion for Women, Infants and Children. It also includes $3 billion for the Federal Crop Insurance Corporation, $1.2 billion for the Food and Drug Administration, $1.1 billion for the Agricultural Research Service and $720 million for the Food Safety and Inspection Service. Passed 414-16: R 205-14; D 207-2 (ND 154-1, SD 53-1); I 2-0. July 11, 2001.

222. Procedural Motion/Journal. Approval of the House Journal of Wednesday, July 11, 2001. Approved 362-50: R 194-13; D 166-37 (ND 119-32, SD 47-5); I 2-0. July 12, 2001.

Member	217	218	219	220	221	222
ALABAMA						
1 *Callahan*	N	N	N	N	Y	Y
2 *Everett*	N	N	N	N	Y	Y
3 *Riley*	–	–	N	N	Y	Y
4 *Aderholt*	Y	N	N	N	Y	N
5 Cramer	Y	N	N	Y	Y	Y
6 *Bachus*	Y	N	N	Y	Y	Y
7 Hilliard	Y	N	N	N	Y	N
ALASKA						
AL *Young*	Y	Y	N	N	Y	?
ARIZONA						
1 *Flake*	Y	N	Y	Y	N	Y
2 Pastor	Y	Y	N	N	Y	Y
3 *Stump*	Y	N	Y	N	Y	Y
4 *Shadegg*	Y	N	Y	Y	Y	Y
5 *Kolbe*	Y	N	Y	N	Y	Y
6 *Hayworth*	Y	N	Y	Y	Y	Y
ARKANSAS						
1 Berry	Y	N	N	N	Y	Y
2 Snyder	Y	Y	N	N	Y	Y
3 *Hutchinson*	N	N	Y	N	Y	?
4 Ross	Y	N	N	N	Y	Y
CALIFORNIA						
1 Thompson	Y	Y	N	N	Y	N
2 *Herger*	N	N	?	N	Y	Y
3 *Ose*	Y	N	N	N	Y	Y
4 *Doolittle*	N	N	N	N	Y	Y
5 Matsui	Y	Y	N	N	Y	Y
6 Woolsey	Y	Y	N	N	Y	Y
7 Miller, George	N	Y	N	N	Y	Y
8 Pelosi	N	Y	N	N	Y	Y
9 Lee	Y	Y	N	N	Y	Y
10 Tauscher	Y	Y	N	N	Y	Y
11 *Pombo*	N	N	N	N	Y	Y
12 Lantos	Y	N	Y	N	Y	?
13 Stark	Y	Y	Y	N	N	N
14	N	Y	N	N	Y	Y
15 Honda	N	Y	N	N	Y	Y
16 Lofgren	N	N	Y	N	Y	Y
17 Farr	N	Y	N	N	Y	Y
18 Condit	Y	N	N	N	Y	Y
19 *Radanovich*	N	N	N	N	Y	Y
20 Dooley	N	N	N	N	Y	Y
21 *Thomas*	N	N	N	N	Y	?
22 Capps	Y	Y	N	N	Y	Y
23 *Gallegly*	N	N	N	N	Y	Y
24 Sherman	N	Y	N	N	Y	Y
25 *McKeon*	N	N	N	N	Y	Y
26 Berman	N	N	Y	N	Y	Y
27 Schiff	Y	Y	N	N	Y	Y
28 *Dreier*	N	N	N	N	Y	Y
29 Waxman	N	N	Y	N	Y	Y
30 Becerra	Y	N	N	N	Y	N
31 Solis	Y	Y	N	N	Y	Y
32 Watson	Y	?	N	N	Y	Y
33 Roybal-Allard	Y	N	N	N	Y	Y
34 Napolitano	Y	Y	N	N	Y	Y
35 Waters	Y	Y	N	Y	Y	Y
36 Harman	Y	Y	N	N	Y	Y
37 Millender-McD.	Y	N	Y	N	Y	Y
38 Horn	Y	N	N	Y	Y	Y
39 *Royce*	Y	N	Y	Y	N	Y
40 *Lewis*	–	–	–	–	+	?
41 *Miller, Gary*	N	N	Y	N	Y	Y
42 Baca	Y	Y	N	N	Y	Y
43 *Calvert*	Y	N	N	N	Y	Y
44 *Bono*	Y	N	N	N	Y	Y
45 *Rohrabacher*	Y	N	Y	Y	N	Y
46 Sanchez	Y	N	Y	N	Y	Y
47 *Cox*	Y	N	Y	N	Y	?
48 *Issa*	Y	N	N	N	Y	Y
49 Davis	Y	Y	N	N	Y	Y
50 Filner	Y	Y	Y	Y	Y	N
51 *Cunningham*	N	N	Y	N	Y	Y
52 *Hunter*	N	N	N	N	Y	Y
COLORADO						
1 DeGette	N	Y	N	Y	Y	Y
2 Udall	N	Y	N	Y	Y	Y
3 *McInnis*	Y	N	N	Y	Y	Y
4 *Schaffer*	Y	N	N	Y	N	Y
5 *Hefley*	Y	N	N	N	N	N
6 *Tancredo*	Y	N	Y	N	Y	P
CONNECTICUT						
1 Larson	Y	N	N	N	Y	Y
2 *Simmons*	Y	N	N	Y	Y	Y
3 DeLauro	Y	N	N	N	Y	Y
4 *Shays*	Y	N	Y	N	Y	Y
5 Maloney	Y	Y	Y	N	Y	Y
6 *Johnson*	Y	Y	Y	N	Y	Y
DELAWARE						
AL *Castle*	Y	N	Y	Y	Y	Y
FLORIDA						
1 *Scarborough*	Y	N	Y	Y	N	Y
2 Boyd	Y	N	N	N	Y	Y
3 Brown	Y	Y	N	N	Y	Y
4 *Crenshaw*	Y	N	N	N	Y	Y
5 Thurman	Y	Y	N	N	Y	Y
6 *Stearns*	Y	N	Y	Y	Y	Y
7 *Mica*	Y	N	N	N	Y	Y
8 *Keller*	N	N	Y	Y	Y	Y
9 *Bilirakis*	N	N	N	N	Y	Y
10 *Young*	Y	N	N	N	Y	Y
11 Davis	Y	N	N	N	Y	Y
12 *Putnam*	Y	N	N	N	Y	Y
13 *Miller*	Y	N	Y	Y	Y	Y
14 *Goss*	Y	N	N	N	Y	Y
15 *Weldon*	Y	N	N	N	Y	Y
16 *Foley*	Y	N	N	N	Y	Y
17 Meek	Y	Y	N	N	Y	Y
18 *Ros-Lehtinen*	Y	N	N	N	Y	Y
19 Wexler	Y	Y	N	N	Y	Y
20 Deutsch	Y	N	Y	N	Y	Y
21 *Diaz-Balart*	Y	N	N	N	Y	Y
22 *Shaw*	Y	N	Y	Y	Y	?
23 Hastings	Y	Y	N	Y	Y	N
GEORGIA						
1 *Kingston*	Y	N	N	N	Y	Y
2 Bishop	Y	N	N	N	Y	Y
3 *Collins*	N	N	N	N	Y	Y
4 McKinney	?	Y	Y	N	Y	Y
5 Lewis	Y	N	Y	?	Y	N
6 *Isakson*	Y	N	N	N	Y	Y
7 *Barr*	Y	N	Y	Y	Y	Y
8 *Chambliss*	Y	N	N	N	Y	Y
9 *Deal*	N	N	N	N	Y	Y
10 *Norwood*	N	N	N	N	Y	Y
11 *Linder*	Y	N	Y	Y	Y	Y
HAWAII						
1 Abercrombie	Y	N	N	N	Y	?
2 Mink	Y	Y	N	N	Y	Y
IDAHO						
1 *Otter*	Y	N	N	N	Y	Y
2 *Simpson*	Y	N	N	N	Y	Y
ILLINOIS						
1 Rush	N	N	N	N	Y	Y
2 Jackson	Y	Y	N	N	Y	Y
3 Lipinski	Y	Y	Y	N	Y	Y
4 Gutierrez	Y	Y	N	N	Y	Y
5 Blagojevich	Y	Y	N	N	Y	Y
6 *Hyde*	Y	N	N	N	Y	Y
7 Davis	Y	Y	N	N	Y	Y
8 *Crane*	N	N	Y	N	N	N
9 Schakowsky	Y	Y	Y	N	Y	Y
10 *Kirk*	Y	N	Y	N	Y	Y
11 *Weller*	N	N	N	N	Y	N
12 Costello	Y	N	Y	N	Y	Y
13 *Biggert*	N	N	Y	N	Y	Y

ND Northern Democrats   SD Southern Democrats

	217	218	219	220	221	222
14 ***Hastert***						
15 ***Johnson***	Y	N	N	N	Y	Y
16 ***Manzullo***	Y	N	Y	?	Y	Y
17 Evans	Y	Y	Y	N	Y	Y
18 ***LaHood***	Y	N	N	N	Y	Y
19 Phelps	Y	N	N	N	Y	Y
20 ***Shimkus***	Y	N	Y	N	Y	Y
INDIANA						
1 Visclosky	N	N	N	N	Y	N
2 ***Pence***	N	N	N	N	Y	Y
3 Roemer	Y	Y	Y	N	Y	Y
4 ***Souder***	N	N	Y	N	Y	Y
5 ***Buyer***	N	N	N	N	Y	Y
6 ***Burton***	Y	Y	Y	N	Y	Y
7 ***Kerns***	N	N	Y	N	Y	Y
8 ***Hostettler***	N	N	Y	Y	N	Y
9 Hill	Y	N	N	N	Y	Y
10 Carson	Y	Y	N	N	Y	Y
IOWA						
1 ***Leach***	Y	N	N	N	Y	?
2 ***Nussle***	Y	N	N	N	Y	Y
3 Boswell	Y	N	N	N	Y	Y
4 ***Ganske***	Y	N	N	N	Y	Y
5 ***Latham***	Y	N	N	N	Y	Y
KANSAS						
1 ***Moran***	Y	N	N	N	Y	N
2 ***Ryun***	N	N	N	N	Y	Y
3 Moore	Y	N	Y	N	Y	Y
4 ***Tiahrt***	Y	N	N	N	Y	Y
KENTUCKY						
1 ***Whitfield***	Y	N	N	N	Y	Y
2 ***Lewis***	N	N	N	N	Y	Y
3 ***Northup***	Y	N	N	N	Y	Y
4 Lucas	Y	N	N	N	Y	Y
5 ***Rogers***	N	N	N	N	Y	Y
6 ***Fletcher***	Y	N	N	N	Y	Y
LOUISIANA						
1 ***Vitter***	Y	N	N	N	Y	Y
2 Jefferson	N	Y	N	N	Y	Y
3 ***Tauzin***	N	N	N	N	Y	Y
4 ***McCrery***	N	N	N	N	Y	Y
5 ***Cooksey***	Y	N	N	N	Y	Y
6 ***Baker***	N	N	N	N	Y	Y
7 John	N	N	N	N	Y	Y
MAINE						
1 Allen	Y	Y	N	N	Y	Y
2 Baldacci	Y	Y	Y	N	Y	Y
MARYLAND						
1 ***Gilchrest***	Y	Y	N	N	Y	Y
2 ***Ehrlich***	N	N	Y	Y	Y	Y
3 Cardin	Y	Y	Y	Y	Y	Y
4 Wynn	Y	Y	N	N	Y	Y
5 Hoyer	Y	Y	N	N	Y	Y
6 ***Bartlett***	Y	N	N	Y	Y	Y
7 Cummings	Y	Y	Y	N	Y	Y
8 ***Morella***	Y	Y	Y	Y	Y	Y
MASSACHUSETTS						
1 Olver	Y	Y	N	N	Y	Y
2 Neal	Y	N	Y	N	Y	Y
3 McGovern	Y	Y	N	N	Y	N
4 Frank	Y	Y	Y	N	Y	Y
5 Meehan	Y	Y	Y	Y	Y	Y
6 Tierney	Y	Y	Y	Y	Y	Y
7 Markey	N	N	Y	N	Y	Y
8 Capuano	?	?	?	?	?	N
9 Vacant						
10 Delahunt	Y	N	N	N	Y	Y
MICHIGAN						
1 Stupak	N	N	Y	N	Y	N
2 ***Hoekstra***	Y	N	Y	Y	Y	Y
3 ***Ehlers***	Y	Y	Y	Y	Y	Y
4 ***Camp***	N	N	Y	N	Y	Y
5 Barcia	Y	Y	Y	N	Y	Y
6 ***Upton***	N	N	Y	N	Y	Y
7 ***Smith***	Y	N	N	N	Y	Y
8 ***Rogers***	Y	N	Y	N	Y	Y
9 Kildee	Y	Y	N	N	Y	Y
10 Bonior	Y	Y	N	N	Y	N
11 ***Knollenberg***	?	?	N	N	Y	Y
12 Levin	Y	N	N	N	Y	Y
13 Rivers	Y	Y	Y	Y	Y	Y
14 Conyers	Y	N	?	N	Y	Y
15 Kilpatrick	Y	N	N	N	Y	Y
16 Dingell	?	?	N	N	Y	Y
MINNESOTA						
1 ***Gutknecht***	Y	Y	N	N	Y	N
2 ***Kennedy***	Y	N	N	N	Y	N
3 ***Ramstad***	Y	Y	Y	Y	Y	N
4 McCollum	N	Y	N	N	Y	Y
5 Sabo	Y	Y	N	N	Y	N
6 Luther	Y	Y	Y	Y	Y	Y
7 Peterson	Y	Y	N	N	Y	N
8 Oberstar	Y	Y	N	N	Y	N
MISSISSIPPI						
1 ***Wicker***	Y	N	N	N	Y	Y
2 Thompson	Y	N	N	N	Y	N
3 ***Pickering***	Y	N	N	N	Y	Y
4 Shows	Y	N	N	N	Y	Y
5 Taylor	Y	N	Y	Y	Y	N
MISSOURI						
1 Clay	Y	Y	Y	N	Y	Y
2 ***Akin***	Y	N	Y	Y	Y	Y
3 Gephardt	Y	N	N	N	Y	N
4 Skelton	Y	N	N	N	Y	Y
5 McCarthy	N	N	N	N	Y	Y
6 ***Graves***	N	N	N	N	Y	Y
7 ***Blunt***	N	N	N	N	Y	Y
8 ***Emerson***	Y	N	N	N	Y	Y
9 ***Hulshof***	N	N	N	N	Y	Y
MONTANA						
AL ***Rehberg***	Y	N	N	N	Y	Y
NEBRASKA						
1 ***Bereuter***	Y	N	Y	N	Y	Y
2 ***Terry***	Y	N	Y	N	Y	Y
3 ***Osborne***	Y	N	N	N	Y	Y
NEVADA						
1 Berkley	Y	Y	Y	Y	Y	Y
2 ***Gibbons***	Y	N	N	N	Y	Y
NEW HAMPSHIRE						
1 ***Sununu***	N	N	Y	Y	Y	Y
2 ***Bass***	Y	N	Y	Y	N	Y
NEW JERSEY						
1 Andrews	Y	Y	Y	Y	Y	Y
2 ***LoBiondo***	N	Y	Y	Y	Y	N
3 ***Saxton***	N	N	Y	N	Y	Y
4 ***Smith***	Y	Y	Y	Y	Y	?
5 ***Roukema***	N	Y	Y	Y	Y	Y
6 Pallone	Y	Y	Y	Y	Y	Y
7 ***Ferguson***	N	N	Y	Y	Y	Y
8 Pascrell	N	Y	Y	N	Y	Y
9 Rothman	Y	Y	Y	Y	Y	Y
10 Payne	Y	Y	Y	Y	Y	Y
11 ***Frelinghuysen***	N	N	Y	Y	Y	Y
12 Holt	N	N	Y	Y	Y	Y
13 Menendez	Y	Y	Y	N	Y	N
NEW MEXICO						
1 ***Wilson***	Y	N	N	N	Y	Y
2 ***Skeen***	N	N	N	N	Y	Y
3 Udall	Y	Y	N	N	Y	N
NEW YORK						
1 ***Grucci***	N	N	N	Y	Y	Y
2 Israel	Y	Y	Y	N	Y	Y
3 ***King***	Y	N	N	N	Y	Y
4 McCarthy	Y	Y	Y	N	Y	Y
5 Ackerman	Y	Y	Y	N	Y	Y
6 Meeks	Y	Y	N	N	Y	Y
7 Crowley	Y	N	Y	N	Y	N
8 Nadler	Y	Y	Y	N	Y	Y
9 Weiner	Y	N	Y	Y	Y	Y
10 Towns	N	N	Y	N	Y	Y
11 Owens	Y	Y	Y	N	Y	Y
12 Velázquez	Y	Y	Y	N	Y	N
13 ***Fossella***	Y	N	Y	Y	Y	Y
14 Maloney	Y	Y	Y	N	Y	Y
15 Rangel	Y	Y	Y	N	Y	?
16 Serrano	Y	Y	N	N	Y	Y
17 Engel	Y	Y	Y	N	Y	Y
18 Lowey	Y	Y	Y	N	Y	Y
19 ***Kelly***	Y	N	Y	Y	Y	Y
20 ***Gilman***	Y	N	N	N	Y	Y
21 McNulty	Y	Y	Y	N	Y	N
22 ***Sweeney***	Y	N	N	N	Y	N
23 ***Boehlert***	Y	N	N	N	Y	Y
24 ***McHugh***	Y	N	N	N	Y	Y
25 ***Walsh***	Y	N	N	N	Y	Y
26 Hinchey	Y	Y	N	N	Y	N
27 ***Reynolds***	Y	N	N	N	Y	Y
28 Slaughter	Y	Y	Y	N	Y	Y
29 LaFalce	Y	N	Y	N	Y	Y
30 ***Quinn***	Y	N	N	N	Y	Y
31 ***Houghton***	N	N	N	N	Y	Y
NORTH CAROLINA						
1 Clayton	Y	N	N	N	Y	+
2 Etheridge	N	N	N	N	Y	Y
3 ***Jones***	Y	N	N	N	Y	Y
4 Price	N	N	N	N	Y	Y
5 ***Burr***	N	N	N	N	Y	Y
6 ***Coble***	Y	N	N	Y	Y	Y
7 McIntyre	Y	N	N	N	Y	Y
8 ***Hayes***	Y	N	N	N	Y	Y
9 ***Myrick***	N	N	N	N	Y	Y
10 ***Ballenger***	Y	N	N	N	Y	Y
11 ***Taylor***	Y	N	N	Y	Y	Y
12 Watt	Y	N	N	N	Y	Y
NORTH DAKOTA						
AL Pomeroy	Y	N	N	N	Y	Y
OHIO						
1 ***Chabot***	Y	N	Y	Y	Y	Y
2 ***Portman***	Y	N	Y	Y	Y	Y
3 Hall	Y	N	N	Y	Y	Y
4 ***Oxley***	N	?	N	N	Y	Y
5 ***Gillmor***	Y	N	N	N	Y	Y
6 Strickland	Y	Y	N	N	Y	Y
7 ***Hobson***	Y	N	N	N	Y	Y
8 ***Boehner***	N	N	N	N	Y	Y
9 Kaptur	Y	Y	N	N	Y	Y
10 Kucinich	Y	Y	N	Y	Y	N
11 Jones	Y	Y	?	?	Y	Y
12 ***Tiberi***	N	N	Y	Y	Y	Y
13 Brown	Y	Y	N	Y	Y	N
14 Sawyer	Y	Y	N	N	Y	Y
15 ***Pryce***	N	N	Y	N	Y	Y
16 ***Regula***	Y	N	N	N	Y	Y
17 Traficant	Y	N	N	N	Y	Y
18 ***Ney***	Y	N	N	N	Y	Y
19 ***LaTourette***	Y	N	N	N	Y	Y
OKLAHOMA						
1 ***Largent***	Y	N	N	N	Y	Y
2 Carson	Y	N	N	N	Y	Y
3 ***Watkins***	Y	N	N	N	Y	?
4 ***Watts***	N	N	N	N	Y	Y
5 ***Istook***	Y	N	Y	Y	Y	Y
6 ***Lucas***	Y	N	N	N	Y	Y
OREGON						
1 Wu	Y	Y	Y	N	Y	N
2 ***Walden***	Y	N	N	N	Y	Y
3 Blumenauer	Y	Y	Y	N	Y	Y
4 DeFazio	Y	Y	N	N	Y	N
5 Hooley	Y	Y	N	N	Y	Y
PENNSYLVANIA						
1 Brady	Y	Y	N	N	Y	N
2 Fattah	Y	Y	Y	N	Y	?
3 Borski	N	Y	Y	N	Y	N
4 ***Hart***	Y	N	N	N	Y	Y
5 ***Peterson***	N	N	N	N	Y	Y
6 Holden	Y	N	N	N	Y	Y
7 ***Weldon***	Y	Y	N	N	Y	Y
8 ***Greenwood***	N	N	Y	N	Y	Y
9 ***Shuster, Bill***	Y	N	Y	N	Y	Y
10 ***Sherwood***	Y	N	N	N	Y	Y
11 Kanjorski	Y	Y	N	N	Y	Y
12 Murtha	Y	N	N	N	Y	?
13 Hoeffel	N	Y	Y	N	Y	Y
14 Coyne	?	?	Y	N	Y	Y
15 ***Toomey***	Y	N	Y	Y	N	Y
16 ***Pitts***	N	N	N	N	Y	Y
17 ***Gekas***	Y	N	N	N	Y	Y
18 Doyle	Y	N	N	Y	Y	Y
19 ***Platts***	Y	N	N	N	Y	?
20 Mascara	Y	N	N	N	Y	Y
21 ***English***	Y	N	Y	Y	Y	N
RHODE ISLAND						
1 Kennedy	Y	Y	N	N	Y	Y
2 Langevin	Y	Y	Y	N	Y	Y
SOUTH CAROLINA						
1 ***Brown***	Y	N	Y	Y	Y	Y
2 ***Spence***	N	N	N	N	Y	?
3 ***Graham***	Y	N	Y	Y	Y	Y
4 ***DeMint***	Y	N	Y	Y	Y	Y
5 Spratt	Y	N	N	N	Y	Y
6 Clyburn	Y	N	N	N	Y	Y
SOUTH DAKOTA						
AL ***Thune***	Y	N	N	N	Y	Y
TENNESSEE						
1 ***Jenkins***	Y	N	N	N	Y	Y
2 ***Duncan***	Y	N	Y	Y	Y	Y
3 ***Wamp***	Y	N	Y	Y	Y	N
4 ***Hilleary***	Y	N	N	N	Y	Y
5 Clement	Y	Y	N	N	Y	Y
6 Gordon	Y	N	N	N	Y	Y
7 ***Bryant***	N	N	N	N	Y	Y
8 Tanner	N	N	N	N	Y	Y
9 Ford	Y	N	N	N	Y	Y
TEXAS						
1 Sandlin	Y	Y	N	N	Y	Y
2 Turner	Y	N	N	?	Y	Y
3 ***Johnson, Sam***	N	N	N	N	Y	Y
4 Hall	Y	N	N	N	Y	Y
5 ***Sessions***	N	N	N	N	Y	Y
6 ***Barton***	Y	N	N	N	Y	Y
7 ***Culberson***	N	N	Y	Y	Y	?
8 ***Brady***	Y	N	N	N	Y	Y
9 Lampson	Y	Y	N	N	Y	Y
10 Doggett	Y	Y	Y	Y	N	Y
11 Edwards	Y	Y	N	N	Y	Y
12 ***Granger***	Y	N	N	N	Y	Y
13 ***Thornberry***	Y	N	N	N	Y	Y
14 ***Paul***	?	?	?	?	?	?
15 Hinojosa	Y	Y	N	N	Y	Y
16 Reyes	Y	Y	N	N	Y	Y
17 Stenholm	Y	N	N	N	Y	Y
18 Jackson-Lee	Y	Y	N	N	Y	Y
19 ***Combest***	Y	N	N	N	Y	Y
20 Gonzalez	Y	Y	N	N	Y	Y
21 ***Smith***	Y	N	N	N	Y	Y
22 ***DeLay***	N	N	N	Y	Y	Y
23 ***Bonilla***	N	N	N	N	Y	Y
24 Frost	Y	N	N	N	Y	Y
25 Bentsen	Y	Y	N	N	Y	Y
26 ***Armey***	N	N	Y	Y	Y	Y
27 Ortiz	Y	Y	N	N	Y	Y
28 Rodriguez	Y	Y	N	N	Y	Y
29 Green	Y	Y	N	N	Y	Y
30 Johnson, E.B.	N	N	N	N	Y	Y
UTAH						
1 ***Hansen***	Y	N	N	N	Y	Y
2 Matheson	N	N	N	N	Y	Y
3 ***Cannon***	Y	N	N	N	Y	Y
VERMONT						
AL *Sanders*	Y	Y	N	N	Y	Y
VIRGINIA						
1 ***Davis, Jo Ann***	Y	N	Y	Y	Y	Y
2 ***Schrock***	Y	N	Y	N	Y	Y
3 Scott	Y	Y	N	N	Y	Y
4 ***Forbes***	Y	N	Y	N	Y	Y
5 *Goode*	Y	Y	N	N	Y	Y
6 ***Goodlatte***	Y	N	N	N	Y	Y
7 ***Cantor***	N	N	Y	Y	Y	Y
8 Moran	N	N	Y	N	Y	Y
9 Boucher	Y	N	N	N	Y	Y
10 ***Wolf***	Y	N	N	N	Y	Y
11 ***Davis, T.***	N	N	Y	N	Y	Y
WASHINGTON						
1 Inslee	Y	Y	Y	N	Y	Y
2 Larsen	Y	Y	N	N	Y	N
3 Baird	Y	Y	Y	N	Y	N
4 ***Hastings***	Y	N	N	N	Y	Y
5 ***Nethercutt***	N	N	N	N	Y	Y
6 Dicks	Y	Y	N	N	Y	Y
7 McDermott	Y	Y	N	N	Y	N
8 ***Dunn***	Y	N	N	N	Y	Y
9 Smith	N	Y	Y	N	Y	Y
WEST VIRGINIA						
1 Mollohan	Y	N	N	N	Y	Y
2 ***Capito***	Y	N	N	N	Y	Y
3 Rahall	Y	N	N	N	Y	Y
WISCONSIN						
1 ***Ryan***	Y	N	Y	N	Y	Y
2 Baldwin	Y	Y	Y	N	Y	N
3 Kind	Y	Y	Y	Y	Y	Y
4 Kleczka	Y	Y	N	Y	Y	Y
5 Barrett	Y	Y	Y	Y	Y	Y
6 ***Petri***	Y	N	Y	Y	Y	Y
7 Obey	N	Y	N	N	Y	Y
8 ***Green***	Y	Y	Y	N	N	Y
9 ***Sensenbrenner***	Y	N	Y	Y	N	Y
WYOMING						
AL ***Cubin***	Y	N	N	Y	Y	Y

Southern states - Ala., Ark., Fla., Ga., Ky., La., Miss., N.C., Okla., S.C., Tenn., Texas, Va.

Key

Y	Voted for (yea).
#	Paired for.
+	Announced for.
N	Voted against (nay).
X	Paired against.
–	Announced against.
P	Voted "present."
C	Voted "present" to avoid possible conflict of interest.
?	Did not vote or otherwise make a position known.

Democrats · **Republicans**
Independents

223. Procedural Motion/Adjourn. McNulty, D-N.Y., motion to adjourn. Motion rejected 7-412: R 1-211; D 6-199 (ND 4-148, SD 2-51); I 0-2. July 12, 2001.

224. HR 2216. Fiscal 2001 Supplemental Appropriations/Agree to Conference. Young, R-Fla., motion that the House disagree to the Senate amendment and agree to a conference on the bill that would appropriate $6.5 billion in supplemental discretionary funds, including $5.5 billion for national defense and $473 million in emergency spending. Motion agreed to 423-3: R 215-0; D 206-3 (ND 153-3, SD 53-0); I 2-0. July 12, 2001.

225. HR 2216. Fiscal 2001 Supplemental Appropriations/Motion to Instruct. Obey, D-Wis., motion to instruct House conferees to insist that the conference report does not include any provision rescinding Federal Emergency Management Agency (FEMA) disaster relief funds. It also would insist that conferees agree to Senate provisions appropriating another $35 million to the Animal and Plant Health Inspection Service for programs related to mad-cow disease and hoof-and-mouth disease and another $84 million for claims under the Radiation Exposure Compensation Act. Motion rejected 205-219: R 2-215; D 202-3 (ND 148-3, SD 54-0); I 1-1. July 12, 2001.

226. Procedural Motion/Adjourn. McNulty, D-N.Y., motion to adjourn. Motion rejected 6-418: R 0-217; D 6-199 (ND 6-145, SD 0-54); I 0-2. July 12, 2001.

227. Quorum Call.* 422 members responded (11 members did not respond). July 12, 2001.

228. HR 2356. Campaign Finance Overhaul/Rule. Adoption of the rule (H Res 188) to provide for House floor consideration of the bill that would ban "soft money" donations to national political parties but allow up to $10,000 in soft-money donations to state and local parties for voter registration and get-out-the vote activity. The bill would prevent issue ads from targeting specific candidates within 60 days of a general election or 30 days of a primary. The bill also would maintain the current individual contribution limit of $1,000 per election for House candidates but raise it to $2,000 for Senate candidates, both of which would be indexed for inflation. Rejected 203-228: R 201-19; D 1-208 (ND 1-154, SD 0-54); I 1-1. July 12, 2001.

* CQ does not include quorum calls in its vote charts.

		223	224	225	226	228
ALABAMA						
1	*Callahan*	N	Y	N	N	Y
2	*Everett*	N	Y	N	N	Y
3	*Riley*	N	Y	N	N	Y
4	*Aderholt*	N	Y	N	N	Y
5	Cramer	N	Y	Y	N	N
6	*Bachus*	N	Y	N	N	Y
7	Hilliard	?	Y	Y	N	N
ALASKA						
AL	*Young*	?	Y	N	N	Y
ARIZONA						
1	*Flake*	N	Y	N	N	Y
2	Pastor	N	Y	Y	N	N
3	*Stump*	N	Y	N	N	Y
4	*Shadegg*	N	Y	N	N	Y
5	*Kolbe*	N	Y	N	N	Y
6	*Hayworth*	N	Y	N	N	Y
ARKANSAS						
1	Berry	N	Y	Y	N	N
2	Snyder	N	Y	Y	N	N
3	*Hutchinson*	?	Y	N	N	Y
4	Ross	N	Y	Y	N	N
CALIFORNIA						
1	Thompson	N	Y	Y	N	N
2	*Herger*	N	Y	N	N	Y
3	*Ose*	N	Y	N	N	Y
4	*Doolittle*	N	Y	N	N	Y
5	Matsui	N	Y	Y	N	N
6	Woolsey	N	Y	Y	N	N
7	Miller, George	N	Y	?	N	N
8	Pelosi	N	Y	Y	N	N
9	Lee	N	Y	Y	N	N
10	Tauscher	N	Y	Y	N	N
11	*Pombo*	N	Y	N	N	Y
12	Lantos	N	Y	Y	N	N
13	Stark	N	Y	Y	N	N
14	Eshoo	N	Y	Y	N	N
15	Honda	N	Y	Y	N	N
16	Lofgren	N	Y	Y	N	N
17	Farr	N	Y	Y	N	N
18	Condit	N	Y	Y	N	N
19	*Radanovich*	N	Y	N	N	Y
20	Dooley	N	Y	Y	?	N
21	*Thomas*	N	Y	N	N	Y
22	Capps	N	Y	Y	N	N
23	*Gallegly*	N	Y	N	N	Y
24	Sherman	N	Y	Y	N	N
25	*McKeon*	N	Y	N	N	Y
26	Berman	N	Y	?	?	N
27	Schiff	N	Y	Y	N	N
28	*Dreier*	N	Y	N	N	Y
29	Waxman	N	Y	Y	N	N
30	Becerra	N	Y	Y	N	N
31	Solis	N	Y	Y	N	N
32	Watson	N	Y	Y	?	N
33	Roybal-Allard	N	Y	Y	N	N
34	Napolitano	N	Y	Y	N	N
35	Waters	N	Y	Y	N	N
36	Harman	N	Y	Y	N	N
37	Millender-McD.	N	Y	Y	N	N
38	*Horn*	?	Y	N	N	Y
39	*Royce*	N	Y	N	N	Y
40	*Lewis*	?	+	–	?	+
41	*Miller, Gary*	N	Y	N	N	Y
42	Baca	N	Y	Y	N	N
43	*Calvert*	N	Y	N	N	Y
44	*Bono*	N	Y	N	N	Y
45	*Rohrabacher*	N	Y	N	N	Y
46	Sanchez	N	Y	+	N	N
47	*Cox*	?	Y	N	N	Y
48	*Issa*	N	Y	N	N	Y
49	Davis	N	Y	Y	N	N
50	Filner	Y	N	Y	N	N
51	*Cunningham*	N	Y	N	N	Y
52	*Hunter*	N	Y	N	N	Y
COLORADO						
1	DeGette	N	Y	Y	N	N
2	Udall	N	Y	Y	N	N
3	*McInnis*	N	Y	N	N	Y
4	*Schaffer*	N	Y	N	N	Y
5	*Hefley*	N	Y	N	N	Y
6	*Tancredo*	N	Y	N	N	Y
CONNECTICUT						
1	Larson	N	Y	Y	N	N
2	*Simmons*	N	Y	N	N	N
3	DeLauro	N	Y	Y	N	N
4	*Shays*	N	Y	N	N	N
5	Maloney	N	Y	Y	N	N
6	*Johnson*	N	Y	N	N	N
DELAWARE						
AL	*Castle*	N	Y	N	N	N
FLORIDA						
1	*Scarborough*	N	?	N	N	N
2	Boyd	N	Y	Y	N	N
3	Brown	N	Y	N	N	N
4	*Crenshaw*	N	Y	N	N	Y
5	Thurman	N	Y	Y	N	N
6	*Stearns*	N	Y	N	N	Y
7	*Mica*	N	Y	N	N	Y
8	*Keller*	N	Y	N	N	Y
9	*Bilirakis*	N	Y	N	N	Y
10	*Young*	N	Y	N	N	Y
11	Davis	N	Y	Y	N	N
12	*Putnam*	N	Y	–	N	Y
13	*Miller*	N	Y	N	N	Y
14	*Goss*	N	Y	N	N	Y
15	*Weldon*	N	Y	N	N	Y
16	Foley	N	+	N	N	Y
17	Meek	N	Y	Y	N	N
18	*Ros-Lehtinen*	N	Y	N	N	Y
19	Wexler	N	Y	Y	N	N
20	Deutsch	N	Y	Y	N	N
21	*Diaz-Balart*	N	Y	N	N	Y
22	*Shaw*	?	Y	N	N	Y
23	Hastings	Y	Y	Y	N	N
GEORGIA						
1	*Kingston*	N	Y	N	N	Y
2	Bishop	N	Y	Y	N	N
3	*Collins*	N	Y	N	N	Y
4	McKinney	N	Y	Y	N	N
5	Lewis	N	Y	Y	N	N
6	*Isakson*	N	Y	N	N	Y
7	*Barr*	N	Y	N	N	Y
8	*Chambliss*	N	Y	N	N	Y
9	*Deal*	N	Y	N	N	Y
10	*Norwood*	N	Y	N	N	Y
11	*Linder*	N	Y	N	N	Y
HAWAII						
1	Abercrombie	N	Y	N	N	N
2	Mink	N	Y	Y	N	N
IDAHO						
1	*Otter*	N	Y	N	N	Y
2	*Simpson*	N	Y	N	N	Y
ILLINOIS						
1	Rush	N	Y	Y	N	N
2	Jackson	N	Y	Y	N	N
3	Lipinski	N	Y	Y	N	N
4	Gutierrez	N	Y	Y	N	N
5	Blagojevich	N	Y	Y	N	N
6	*Hyde*	N	Y	N	N	Y
7	Davis	N	Y	Y	N	N
8	*Crane*	N	Y	N	N	Y
9	Schakowsky	N	Y	Y	N	N
10	*Kirk*	N	Y	?	N	Y
11	*Weller*	N	Y	N	N	Y
12	Costello	N	Y	Y	N	N
13	*Biggert*	N	Y	N	N	Y

ND Northern Democrats   SD Southern Democrats

	223	224	225	226	228
14 ***Hastert***					Y
15 ***Johnson***	N	Y	N	N	Y
16 ***Manzullo***	N	Y	N	N	Y
17 Evans	N	Y	Y	N	N
18 ***LaHood***	N	Y	N	N	Y
19 Phelps	N	Y	Y	N	N
20 ***Shimkus***	N	Y	N	N	Y
INDIANA					
1 Visclosky	N	Y	Y	N	N
2 ***Pence***	N	Y	N	N	Y
3 Roemer	N	Y	Y	N	N
4 ***Souder***	N	Y	N	N	N
5 ***Buyer***	N	Y	N	N	Y
6 ***Burton***	N	Y	N	N	Y
7 ***Kerns***	N	Y	N	N	Y
8 ***Hostettler***	N	Y	N	N	Y
9 Hill	N	Y	Y	N	N
10 Carson	Y	Y	Y	N	N
IOWA					
1 ***Leach***	N	Y	N	N	N
2 ***Nussle***	N	Y	N	N	Y
3 Boswell	N	Y	Y	N	N
4 ***Ganske***	N	Y	N	N	N
5 ***Latham***	N	Y	N	N	Y
KANSAS					
1 ***Moran***	N	Y	N	N	Y
2 ***Ryun***	N	Y	N	N	Y
3 Moore	N	Y	Y	N	?
4 ***Tiahrt***	N	Y	N	N	Y
KENTUCKY					
1 ***Whitfield***	N	Y	N	N	Y
2 ***Lewis***	N	Y	N	N	Y
3 ***Northup***	N	Y	N	N	Y
4 Lucas	N	Y	Y	N	N
5 ***Rogers***	N	Y	N	N	Y
6 ***Fletcher***	N	Y	N	N	Y
LOUISIANA					
1 ***Vitter***	N	Y	N	N	Y
2 Jefferson	N	?	Y	N	N
3 ***Tauzin***	N	Y	N	N	Y
4 ***McCrery***	N	Y	N	N	Y
5 ***Cooksey***	N	Y	N	N	Y
6 ***Baker***	N	Y	N	N	Y
7 John	N	Y	Y	N	N
MAINE					
1 Allen	N	Y	Y	N	N
2 Baldacci	N	Y	Y	N	N
MARYLAND					
1 ***Gilchrest***	N	Y	N	N	Y
2 ***Ehrlich***	N	Y	N	N	Y
3 Cardin	N	Y	Y	N	N
4 Wynn	?	Y	Y	N	N
5 Hoyer	N	Y	Y	N	N
6 ***Bartlett***	N	Y	N	N	Y
7 Cummings	N	Y	Y	N	N
8 ***Morella***	N	?	N	N	N
MASSACHUSETTS					
1 Olver	N	Y	Y	N	N
2 Neal	N	Y	Y	N	N
3 McGovern	N	Y	Y	N	N
4 Frank	N	Y	Y	N	N
5 Meehan	N	Y	Y	N	N
6 Tierney	N	Y	Y	N	N
7 Markey	N	Y	Y	N	N
8 Capuano	N	Y	Y	N	N
9 Vacant					
10 Delahunt	N	Y	Y	N	N
MICHIGAN					
1 Stupak	N	Y	Y	N	N
2 ***Hoekstra***	N	Y	N	N	Y
3 ***Ehlers***	N	Y	N	N	Y
4 ***Camp***	N	Y	N	N	Y
5 Barcia	N	Y	Y	N	N
6 ***Upton***	N	Y	N	N	N
7 ***Smith***	N	Y	N	N	Y
8 ***Rogers***	N	Y	N	N	Y
9 Kildee	N	Y	Y	N	N
10 Bonior	N	Y	Y	N	N
11 ***Knollenberg***	N	Y	N	N	Y
12 Levin	N	Y	Y	N	N
13 Rivers	N	Y	Y	N	N
14 Conyers	N	Y	Y	Y	N
15 Kilpatrick	N	Y	Y	?	N
16 Dingell	N	Y	Y	N	N

	223	224	225	226	228
MINNESOTA					
1 ***Gutknecht***	N	Y	N	N	Y
2 ***Kennedy***	N	Y	N	N	Y
3 ***Ramstad***	N	Y	N	N	Y
4 McCollum	N	Y	Y	N	N
5 Sabo	N	Y	Y	N	N
6 Luther	N	Y	Y	N	N
7 Peterson	N	Y	Y	N	N
8 Oberstar	N	Y	Y	N	N
MISSISSIPPI					
1 ***Wicker***	N	Y	N	N	Y
2 Thompson	N	Y	Y	N	N
3 ***Pickering***	N	Y	N	N	Y
4 Shows	N	Y	Y	N	N
5 Taylor	N	Y	Y	N	N
MISSOURI					
1 Clay	N	Y	Y	N	N
2 ***Akin***	N	Y	N	N	Y
3 Gephardt	?	Y	Y	N	N
4 Skelton	N	Y	Y	N	N
5 McCarthy	N	Y	Y	N	N
6 ***Graves***	N	Y	N	N	Y
7 ***Blunt***	N	Y	N	N	Y
8 ***Emerson***	N	Y	N	N	Y
9 ***Hulshof***	N	Y	N	N	Y
MONTANA					
AL ***Rehberg***	N	Y	N	N	Y
NEBRASKA					
1 ***Bereuter***	N	Y	N	N	Y
2 ***Terry***	N	Y	N	N	Y
3 ***Osborne***	N	Y	N	N	Y
NEVADA					
1 Berkley	N	Y	Y	N	N
2 ***Gibbons***	N	Y	N	N	Y
NEW HAMPSHIRE					
1 ***Sununu***	N	Y	N	N	Y
2 ***Bass***	?	Y	N	N	N
NEW JERSEY					
1 Andrews	N	Y	Y	N	N
2 ***LoBiondo***	N	Y	N	N	N
3 ***Saxton***	N	Y	N	N	Y
4 ***Smith***	Y	Y	N	N	Y
5 ***Roukema***	N	Y	N	N	N
6 Pallone	N	Y	Y	N	N
7 ***Ferguson***	N	Y	N	N	Y
8 Pascrell	N	Y	Y	N	N
9 Rothman	N	Y	Y	N	N
10 Payne	N	Y	Y	N	N
11 ***Frelinghuysen***	N	Y	N	N	Y
12 Holt	N	Y	Y	N	N
13 Menendez	N	Y	Y	N	N
NEW MEXICO					
1 ***Wilson***	N	Y	N	N	Y
2 ***Skeen***	N	Y	N	N	Y
3 Udall	N	Y	Y	N	N
NEW YORK					
1 ***Grucci***	N	Y	N	N	Y
2 Israel	N	Y	Y	Y	N
3 ***King***	N	Y	N	N	Y
4 McCarthy	N	Y	Y	N	N
5 Ackerman	N	Y	Y	N	N
6 Meeks	N	Y	Y	N	N
7 Crowley	N	Y	Y	N	N
8 Nadler	N	Y	Y	N	N
9 Weiner	N	Y	Y	N	N
10 Towns	Y	Y	Y	N	N
11 Owens	N	Y	Y	N	N
12 Velázquez	N	Y	Y	N	N
13 ***Fossella***	N	Y	N	N	Y
14 Maloney	N	Y	Y	N	N
15 Rangel	N	Y	Y	N	N
16 Serrano	N	Y	Y	Y	N
17 Engel	N	Y	Y	N	N
18 Lowey	N	Y	Y	N	N
19 ***Kelly***	N	Y	N	N	Y
20 ***Gilman***	N	Y	N	N	Y
21 McNulty	Y	Y	Y	Y	N
22 ***Sweeney***	N	Y	N	N	Y
23 ***Boehlert***	N	Y	N	N	N
24 ***McHugh***	N	Y	N	?	Y
25 ***Walsh***	N	Y	N	N	Y
26 Hinchey	N	Y	Y	N	N
27 ***Reynolds***	N	Y	N	N	Y
28 Slaughter	N	Y	Y	N	N
29 LaFalce	N	Y	Y	N	N

	223	224	225	226	228
30 ***Quinn***	N	Y	N	N	Y
31 ***Houghton***	N	Y	N	N	N
NORTH CAROLINA					
1 Clayton	N	Y	Y	N	N
2 Etheridge	N	Y	Y	N	N
3 ***Jones***	N	Y	N	N	Y
4 Price	N	Y	Y	N	N
5 ***Burr***	N	Y	N	N	Y
6 ***Coble***	N	Y	N	N	Y
7 McIntyre	N	Y	Y	N	N
8 ***Hayes***	N	Y	N	N	Y
9 ***Myrick***	N	Y	N	N	Y
10 ***Ballenger***	N	Y	N	N	Y
11 ***Taylor***	N	Y	N	N	Y
12 Watt	N	Y	Y	N	N
NORTH DAKOTA					
AL Pomeroy	N	Y	?	?	N
OHIO					
1 ***Chabot***	N	Y	N	N	Y
2 ***Portman***	N	Y	N	N	Y
3 Hall	?	Y	Y	Y	N
4 ***Oxley***	N	Y	N	N	Y
5 ***Gillmor***	N	Y	N	N	Y
6 Strickland	N	Y	Y	N	N
7 ***Hobson***	N	Y	N	N	Y
8 ***Boehner***	N	Y	N	N	Y
9 Kaptur	N	Y	Y	N	N
10 Kucinich	N	Y	Y	N	N
11 Jones	N	Y	Y	N	N
12 ***Tiberi***	N	Y	N	N	Y
13 Brown	N	Y	Y	N	N
14 Sawyer	N	Y	Y	N	N
15 ***Pryce***	N	Y	N	N	Y
16 ***Regula***	N	Y	N	N	Y
17 Traficant	N	Y	N	N	Y
18 ***Ney***	N	Y	N	N	Y
19 ***LaTourette***	N	Y	N	N	Y
OKLAHOMA					
1 ***Largent***	N	Y	N	N	Y
2 Carson	N	Y	Y	N	N
3 ***Watkins***	N	Y	N	N	Y
4 ***Watts***	N	Y	N	N	Y
5 ***Istook***	N	Y	N	N	Y
6 ***Lucas***	N	Y	N	N	Y
OREGON					
1 Wu	N	N	Y	N	N
2 ***Walden***	N	Y	N	N	Y
3 Blumenauer	N	Y	Y	N	N
4 DeFazio	N	N	Y	N	N
5 Hooley	N	Y	Y	N	N
PENNSYLVANIA					
1 Brady	N	Y	Y	N	N
2 Fattah	?	Y	Y	N	N
3 Borski	N	Y	Y	N	N
4 ***Hart***	N	Y	N	N	Y
5 ***Peterson***	N	Y	N	N	Y
6 Holden	N	Y	Y	N	N
7 ***Weldon***	N	Y	N	N	Y
8 ***Greenwood***	N	Y	N	N	Y
9 ***Shuster, Bill***	N	Y	N	N	Y
10 ***Sherwood***	N	Y	N	N	Y
11 Kanjorski	N	Y	Y	N	N
12 Murtha	N	Y	N	N	N
13 Hoeffel	N	Y	Y	N	N
14 Coyne	N	Y	Y	N	N
15 ***Toomey***	N	Y	N	N	Y
16 ***Pitts***	N	Y	N	N	Y
17 ***Gekas***	N	Y	N	N	Y
18 Doyle	N	Y	Y	N	N
19 ***Platts***	N	Y	N	N	Y
20 Mascara	N	Y	Y	N	N
21 ***English***	N	Y	N	N	Y
RHODE ISLAND					
1 Kennedy	N	Y	Y	N	N
2 Langevin	N	Y	Y	N	N
SOUTH CAROLINA					
1 ***Brown***	N	Y	N	N	Y
2 ***Spence***	?	?	N	N	Y
3 ***Graham***	N	Y	N	N	N
4 ***DeMint***	N	Y	N	N	Y
5 Spratt	N	Y	Y	N	N
6 Clyburn	N	Y	Y	N	N
SOUTH DAKOTA					
AL ***Thune***	N	Y	N	N	Y

	223	224	225	226	228
TENNESSEE					
1 ***Jenkins***	N	Y	Y	N	Y
2 ***Duncan***	N	Y	N	N	Y
3 ***Wamp***	N	Y	N	N	N
4 ***Hilleary***	N	Y	N	N	Y
5 Clement	N	Y	Y	N	N
6 Gordon	N	Y	Y	N	N
7 ***Bryant***	N	Y	N	N	Y
8 Tanner	N	Y	Y	N	N
9 Ford	N	Y	Y	N	N
TEXAS					
1 Sandlin	N	Y	Y	N	N
2 Turner	N	Y	Y	N	N
3 ***Johnson, Sam***	N	Y	N	N	Y
4 Hall	N	Y	Y	N	N
5 ***Sessions***	N	Y	N	N	Y
6 ***Barton***	N	Y	N	N	Y
7 ***Culberson***	N	Y	N	N	Y
8 ***Brady***	N	Y	N	N	Y
9 Lampson	N	Y	Y	N	N
10 Doggett	N	Y	Y	N	N
11 Edwards	N	Y	Y	N	N
12 ***Granger***	N	Y	N	N	Y
13 ***Thornberry***	N	Y	N	N	Y
14 ***Paul***	?	?	?	?	?
15 Hinojosa	N	Y	Y	N	N
16 Reyes	N	Y	Y	N	N
17 Stenholm	N	Y	Y	N	N
18 Jackson-Lee	N	Y	Y	N	N
19 ***Combest***	N	Y	N	N	Y
20 Gonzalez	N	Y	Y	N	N
21 ***Smith***	N	Y	N	N	Y
22 ***DeLay***	N	Y	N	N	Y
23 ***Bonilla***	N	Y	N	N	Y
24 Frost	N	Y	Y	N	N
25 Bentsen	Y	Y	Y	N	N
26 ***Armey***	N	Y	N	N	Y
27 Ortiz	N	Y	Y	N	N
28 Rodriguez	N	Y	Y	N	N
29 Green	N	Y	Y	N	N
30 Johnson, E.B.	N	Y	Y	N	N
UTAH					
1 ***Hansen***	N	Y	N	N	Y
2 Matheson	N	Y	Y	N	N
3 ***Cannon***	N	Y	N	N	Y
VERMONT					
AL *Sanders*	N	Y	Y	N	N
VIRGINIA					
1 ***Davis, Jo Ann***	N	Y	N	N	Y
2 ***Schrock***	N	Y	N	N	Y
3 Scott	N	Y	Y	N	N
4 ***Forbes***	N	Y	N	N	Y
5 *Goode*	N	Y	N	N	Y
6 ***Goodlatte***	N	Y	N	N	Y
7 ***Cantor***	N	Y	N	N	Y
8 Moran	N	Y	Y	N	N
9 Boucher	N	Y	Y	N	N
10 ***Wolf***	N	Y	N	N	N
11 ***Davis, T.***	N	Y	N	N	Y
WASHINGTON					
1 Inslee	N	Y	Y	N	N
2 Larsen	N	Y	Y	N	N
3 Baird	N	Y	Y	N	N
4 ***Hastings***	N	Y	N	N	Y
5 ***Nethercutt***	N	Y	N	N	Y
6 Dicks	N	Y	Y	N	N
7 McDermott	N	Y	?	N	N
8 ***Dunn***	N	Y	N	N	Y
9 Smith	N	Y	Y	N	N
WEST VIRGINIA					
1 Mollohan	N	Y	Y	N	N
2 ***Capito***	N	Y	N	N	Y
3 Rahall	N	Y	Y	N	N
WISCONSIN					
1 ***Ryan***	N	Y	N	N	Y
2 Baldwin	N	Y	Y	N	N
3 Kind	N	Y	Y	N	N
4 Kleczka	N	Y	Y	N	N
5 Barrett	N	Y	Y	N	N
6 ***Petri***	N	Y	N	N	Y
7 Obey	N	Y	Y	N	N
8 ***Green***	N	Y	N	N	Y
9 ***Sensenbrenner***	N	Y	N	?	Y
WYOMING					
AL ***Cubin***	N	Y	N	N	Y

Southern states - Ala., Ark., Fla., Ga., Ky., La., Miss., N.C., Okla., S.C., Tenn., Texas, Va.

Key

Y   Voted for (yea).
Paired for.
+   Announced for.
N   Voted against (nay).
X   Paired against.
−   Announced against.
P   Voted "present."
C   Voted "present" to avoid possible conflict of interest.
?   Did not vote or otherwise make a position known.

•

Democrats   **Republicans**
Independents

229. S 360. Paul Coverdell Tribute/Passage. Hyde, R-Ill., motion to suspend the rules and pass the bill that would name the U.S. Peace Corps headquarters and World Wise Schools Program after the late Sen. Paul Coverdell, R-Ga. (1993-2000), and authorize $10 million for the University of Georgia to construct a facility named the "Paul D. Coverdell Building." Motion agreed to 330-61: R 197-8; D 132-53 (ND 89-48, SD 43-5); I 1-0. A two-thirds majority of those present and voting (261 in this case) is required for passage under suspension of the rules. July 17, 2001.

230. H Res 195. Missile Test/Adoption. Hunter, R-Calif., motion to suspend the rules and adopt the resolution that would honor the U.S. military and defense contractors for the successful July 14, 2001, missile defense interceptor test. Motion agreed to 321-77: R 207-2; D 113-75 (ND 73-65, SD 40-10); I 1-0. A two-thirds majority of those present and voting (266 in this case) is required for adoption under suspension of the rules. July 17, 2001.

231. H J Res 36. Flag Desecration/Watt Substitute. Watt, D-N.C., substitute amendment to declare that Congress shall have the power to prohibit the physical desecration of the U.S. flag, but only in a manner consistent with the First Amendment of the Constitution. Rejected 100-324: R 5-214; D 94-109 (ND 73-79, SD 21-30); I 1-1. July 17, 2001.

232. H J Res 36. Flag Desecration/Passage. Passage of the joint resolution to propose a Constitutional amendment stating that Congress shall have the power to prohibit physical desecration of the U.S. flag. Passed 298-125: R 207-11; D 90-113 (ND 56-96, SD 34-17); I 1-1. A two-thirds majority vote of those present and voting (282 in this case) is required to pass a joint resolution proposing an amendment to the Constitution. July 17, 2001.

233. HR 2500. Fiscal 2002 Commerce-Justice-State Appropriations/ Lab Seizures. Lucas, R-Okla., amendment that would increase by $11.7 million the Community Oriented Policing Services' methamphetamine lab seizures program, offset by a cut in funding for international broadcasting operations. Rejected 187-227: R 84-123; D 102-103 (ND 73-80, SD 29-23); I 1-1. July 17, 2001.

234. HR 2500. Fiscal 2002 Commerce-Justice-State Appropriations/ Economic Development. Hinchey, D-N.Y., amendment that would increase funds for the Economic Development Administration by $73 million and reduce prison construction funding by the same amount. Rejected 172-244: R 22-190; D 148-54 (ND 121-31, SD 27-23); I 2-0. July 17, 2001.

235. HR 2500. Fiscal 2002 Commerce-Justice-State Appropriations/ Abortion Ban. DeGette, D-Colo., amendment that would strike language prohibiting the use of funds for abortion services in federal prisons. Rejected 169-253: R 17-198; D 151-54 (ND 118-35, SD 33-19); I 1-1. July 17, 2001.

	229	230	231	232	233	234	235
ALABAMA							
1 *Callahan*	Y	Y	N	Y	?	N	N
2 *Everett*	Y	Y	N	Y	N	N	N
3 *Riley*	+	+	N	+	+	−	−
4 *Aderholt*	Y	Y	N	Y	Y	N	N
5 Cramer	Y	Y	N	N	N	N	N
6 *Bachus*	Y	Y	N	Y	N	N	N
7 Hilliard	Y	N	Y	Y	Y	Y	Y
ALASKA							
AL *Young*	Y	Y	N	Y	N	N	N
ARIZONA							
1 *Flake*	N	Y	N	N	N	N	N
2 Pastor	Y	N	Y	N	N	Y	Y
3 *Stump*	Y	Y	N	N	N	N	N
4 *Shadegg*	Y	Y	Y	N	N	N	N
5 *Kolbe*	Y	Y	Y	−	N	N	N
6 *Hayworth*	Y	N	Y	Y	Y	N	N
ARKANSAS							
1 Berry	Y	Y	N	Y	N	N	N
2 Snyder	Y	Y	N	N	N	N	N
3 *Hutchinson*	?	Y	N	Y	N	N	N
4 Ross	Y	Y	N	Y	Y	N	N
CALIFORNIA							
1 Thompson	N	N	N	N	Y	N	Y
2 *Herger*	?	?	N	Y	N	N	N
3 *Ose*	Y	Y	N	Y	N	N	N
4 *Doolittle*	Y	Y	N	Y	N	N	N
5 Matsui	Y	Y	Y	N	Y	Y	Y
6 Woolsey	Y	N	N	N	Y	Y	Y
7 Miller, George	N	N	N	N	Y	Y	Y
8 Pelosi	Y	P	Y	N	N	Y	Y
9 Lee	N	N	N	N	Y	Y	Y
10 Tauscher	Y	Y	Y	N	Y	N	Y
11 *Pombo*	Y	Y	Y	Y	N	N	N
12 Lantos	Y	Y	Y	Y	N	Y	N
13 Stark	N	N	N	N	Y	Y	Y
14 Eshoo	N	N	N	N	Y	Y	Y
15 Honda	N	N	N	N	N	Y	Y
16 Lofgren	N	Y	N	N	Y	Y	Y
17 Farr	N	N	N	N	Y	Y	Y
18 Condit	Y	Y	N	Y	Y	N	Y
19 *Radanovich*	Y	Y	N	Y	Y	N	N
20 Dooley	N	Y	N	Y	Y	N	Y
21 *Thomas*	Y	Y	N	Y	N	N	Y
22 Capps	Y	Y	N	N	Y	N	Y
23 *Gallegly*	Y	Y	Y	N	Y	N	N
24 Sherman	N	Y	N	N	Y	N	Y
25 *McKeon*	Y	Y	N	Y	N	N	N
26 Berman	?	?	Y	N	Y	N	Y
27 Schiff	?	?	?	?	N	N	Y
28 *Dreier*	Y	Y	N	N	N	N	N
29 Waxman	N	Y	Y	N	Y	Y	Y
30 Becerra	P	Y	Y	N	Y	Y	Y
31 Solis	Y	N	N	Y	N	Y	Y
32 Watson	N	Y	N	N	Y	Y	Y
33 Roybal-Allard	Y	Y	Y	N	N	N	Y
34 Napolitano	N	Y	N	N	Y	N	Y
35 Waters	?	?	Y	N	Y	Y	Y
36 Harman	Y	?	N	Y	N	N	Y
37 Millender-McD.	Y	Y	Y	Y	N	Y	Y
38 Horn	Y	Y	N	Y	N	N	Y

	229	230	231	232	233	234	235
39 *Royce*	N	Y	N	Y	N	N	N
40 *Lewis*	Y	Y	N	Y	N	N	N
41 *Miller, Gary*	Y	Y	N	Y	Y	N	N
42 Baca	Y	Y	N	Y	N	Y	Y
43 *Calvert*	Y	Y	N	Y	N	N	N
44 *Bono*	Y	Y	N	Y	N	N	N
45 *Rohrabacher*	Y	Y	N	Y	N	N	N
46 Sanchez	Y	Y	N	Y	N	N	N
47 *Cox*	Y	Y	N	Y	N	N	N
48 *Issa*	Y	Y	N	Y	N	N	N
49 Davis	Y	Y	N	N	Y	Y	Y
50 Filner	Y	N	N	N	Y	Y	Y
51 *Cunningham*	Y	Y	N	Y	N	N	N
52 *Hunter*	Y	Y	N	Y	N	N	N
COLORADO							
1 DeGette	?	?	N	N	Y	Y	Y
2 Udall	?	?	Y	N	N	Y	Y
3 *McInnis*	?	?	N	Y	N	N	N
4 *Schaffer*	N	Y	N	Y	N	N	N
5 *Hefley*	Y	Y	N	Y	N	Y	N
6 *Tancredo*	N	Y	N	Y	N	N	N
CONNECTICUT							
1 Larson	Y	Y	Y	Y	N	Y	Y
2 *Simmons*	Y	Y	N	Y	N	N	Y
3 DeLauro	N	Y	N	N	N	Y	Y
4 *Shays*	P	Y	N	N	N	Y	Y
5 Maloney	Y	Y	N	Y	Y	Y	Y
6 *Johnson*	Y	Y	N	Y	N	Y	Y
DELAWARE							
AL *Castle*	Y	Y	N	Y	N	N	N
FLORIDA							
1 *Scarborough*	?	?	N	N	Y	N	N
2 Boyd	Y	Y	N	Y	N	N	N
3 Brown	Y	N	N	N	Y	N	Y
4 *Crenshaw*	Y	Y	N	Y	N	N	N
5 Thurman	Y	Y	N	Y	N	Y	N
6 *Stearns*	Y	Y	N	Y	N	Y	N
7 *Mica*	Y	Y	N	Y	N	N	N
8 *Keller*	Y	Y	N	Y	N	N	N
9 *Bilirakis*	Y	Y	N	Y	N	N	N
10 *Young*	Y	Y	N	Y	N	N	N
11 Davis	Y	Y	N	Y	N	Y	N
12 *Putnam*	?	?	N	Y	N	N	N
13 *Miller*	Y	Y	N	Y	N	N	N
14 *Goss*	Y	Y	N	Y	N	N	N
15 *Weldon*	Y	Y	N	Y	N	N	N
16 *Foley*	Y	Y	N	Y	N	N	N
17 Meek	Y	N	Y	N	N	Y	Y
18 *Ros-Lehtinen*	Y	Y	N	Y	N	N	N
19 Wexler	Y	Y	N	N	N	Y	Y
20 Deutsch	Y	Y	N	Y	N	Y	Y
21 *Diaz-Balart*	Y	Y	N	Y	N	N	N
22 *Shaw*	Y	Y	N	Y	?	Y	N
23 Hastings	N	N	Y	N	N	Y	Y
GEORGIA							
1 *Kingston*	Y	Y	N	Y	N	N	N
2 Bishop	?	?	?	?	?	?	?
3 *Collins*	Y	Y	N	N	N	N	N
4 McKinney	Y	N	Y	N	Y	Y	Y
5 Lewis	Y	N	Y	N	Y	Y	Y
6 *Isakson*	Y	Y	N	N	N	N	N
7 *Barr*	Y	Y	N	Y	N	N	N
8 *Chambliss*	Y	Y	N	Y	?	?	N
9 *Deal*	Y	Y	N	Y	N	N	N
10 *Norwood*	Y	Y	N	Y	N	N	N
11 *Linder*	Y	Y	N	Y	N	N	N
HAWAII							
1 Abercrombie	N	Y	Y	N	N	Y	Y
2 Mink	N	Y	N	N	Y	Y	Y
IDAHO							
1 *Otter*	Y	Y	N	Y	N	N	N
2 *Simpson*	Y	Y	N	Y	N	N	N
ILLINOIS							
1 Rush	Y	N	Y	Y	Y	Y	Y
2 Jackson	N	N	Y	N	N	Y	Y
3 Lipinski	Y	Y	N	Y	N	Y	N
4 Gutierrez	N	N	Y	N	Y	Y	Y
5 Blagojevich	Y	Y	Y	Y	Y	Y	Y
6 *Hyde*	Y	Y	N	Y	N	N	N
7 Davis	Y	N	Y	N	Y	Y	Y
8 *Crane*	Y	Y	N	Y	N	N	N
9 Schakowsky	N	N	N	N	Y	Y	Y
10 *Kirk*	Y	Y	N	Y	N	N	N
11 *Weller*	Y	Y	N	Y	N	N	N
12 Costello	Y	Y	N	Y	N	Y	N
13 *Biggert*	Y	Y	N	Y	N	Y	N

ND Northern Democrats   SD Southern Democrats

	229	230	231	232	233	234	235
14 ***Hastert***							
15 Johnson	Y	Y	N	Y	Y	N	N
16 Manzullo	Y	Y	N	Y	Y	N	N
17 Evans	Y	Y	Y	N	Y	Y	Y
18 ***LaHood***	Y	Y	N	Y	N	N	N
19 Phelps	Y	Y	N	Y	N	N	N
20 ***Shimkus***	Y	Y	N	Y	N	N	N
INDIANA							
1 Visclosky	N	N	Y	N	N	N	Y
2 ***Pence***	Y	Y	N	Y	N	N	N
3 Roemer	Y	Y	N	Y	Y	N	N
4 ***Souder***	Y	Y	N	Y	Y	N	N
5 ***Buyer***	Y	Y	N	Y	N	N	N
6 ***Burton***	Y	Y	N	Y	N	N	N
7 ***Kerns***	N	Y	N	Y	Y	N	N
8 ***Hostettler***	?	?	N	Y	Y	N	N
9 Hill	Y	Y	N	N	Y	Y	N
10 Carson	Y	Y	N	N	N	Y	Y
IOWA							
1 ***Leach***	Y	Y	Y	N	N	N	N
2 ***Nussle***	Y	Y	N	Y	N	N	N
3 Boswell	Y	Y	N	Y	Y	N	Y
4 ***Ganske***	Y	Y	N	Y	N	N	N
5 ***Latham***	Y	Y	N	Y	N	N	N
KANSAS							
1 ***Moran***	Y	Y	N	Y	Y	Y	N
2 ***Ryun***	Y	Y	N	Y	Y	N	N
3 Moore	Y	Y	N	N	Y	Y	N
4 ***Tiahrt***	Y	Y	N	Y	N	N	N
KENTUCKY							
1 ***Whitfield***	Y	Y	N	Y	N	Y	N
2 ***Lewis***	Y	Y	N	Y	Y	N	N
3 ***Northup***	Y	Y	N	Y	Y	N	N
4 Lucas	Y	Y	N	Y	N	N	N
5 ***Rogers***	Y	Y	N	Y	?	N	N
6 ***Fletcher***	Y	Y	N	Y	N	N	N
LOUISIANA							
1 ***Vitter***	+	+	N	Y	N	N	N
2 Jefferson	?	?	?	?	Y	Y	Y
3 ***Tauzin***	Y	Y	N	Y	N	N	N
4 ***McCrery***	Y	Y	N	Y	N	N	N
5 ***Cooksey***	Y	Y	N	Y	N	N	N
6 ***Baker***	Y	Y	N	Y	N	N	N
7 John	Y	Y	N	Y	Y	N	N
MAINE							
1 Allen	Y	N	Y	N	N	Y	Y
2 Baldacci	Y	N	N	Y	Y	Y	Y
MARYLAND							
1 ***Gilchrest***	Y	Y	N	N	N	N	Y
2 ***Ehrlich***	Y	Y	N	Y	?	?	N
3 Cardin	Y	N	Y	N	N	N	Y
4 Wynn	Y	N	N	Y	N	Y	Y
5 Hoyer	Y	Y	Y	N	N	Y	?
6 ***Bartlett***	Y	Y	N	Y	N	N	N
7 Cummings	Y	Y	Y	Y	Y	Y	Y
8 ***Morella***	Y	Y	N	Y	N	N	Y
MASSACHUSETTS							
1 Olver	N	N	Y	N	N	Y	Y
2 Neal	?	N	Y	Y	?	Y	N
3 McGovern	N	N	Y	Y	N	Y	Y
4 Frank	N	N	Y	N	N	Y	Y
5 Meehan	N	N	Y	N	N	Y	Y
6 Tierney	N	N	Y	N	N	Y	Y
7 Markey	N	N	Y	N	N	Y	Y
8 Capuano	N	N	Y	N	N	Y	Y
9 Vacant							
10 Delahunt	?	?	?	?	?	?	?
MICHIGAN							
1 Stupak	Y	N	N	Y	Y	Y	N
2 ***Hoekstra***	P	N	N	N	N	N	N
3 ***Ehlers***	Y	Y	N	N	N	N	N
4 ***Camp***	Y	Y	N	Y	Y	N	N
5 Barcia	Y	Y	N	Y	Y	N	N
6 ***Upton***	Y	Y	N	Y	Y	N	N
7 ***Smith***	Y	Y	N	Y	N	N	N
8 ***Rogers***	Y	Y	N	Y	Y	N	N
9 Kildee	Y	Y	N	Y	N	Y	N
10 Bonior	P	N	Y	N	Y	Y	N
11 ***Knollenberg***	Y	Y	N	Y	N	N	N
12 Levin	N	N	N	N	N	N	Y
13 Rivers	N	N	N	N	Y	Y	Y
14 Conyers	N	N	N	N	N	Y	Y
15 Kilpatrick	Y	N	Y	N	N	Y	Y
16 Dingell	Y	P	N	N	N	Y	Y

	229	230	231	232	233	234	235
MINNESOTA							
1 ***Gutknecht***	Y	Y	N	Y	Y	N	N
2 ***Kennedy***	N	Y	N	Y	Y	N	N
3 ***Ramstad***	N	Y	N	Y	Y	N	N
4 McCollum	N	N	Y	N	N	Y	Y
5 Sabo	N	N	Y	N	Y	Y	Y
6 Luther	N	N	N	Y	Y	Y	Y
7 Peterson	Y	Y	N	N	N	Y	N
8 Oberstar	N	N	N	N	N	Y	N
MISSISSIPPI							
1 ***Wicker***	Y	Y	N	Y	Y	N	N
2 Thompson	Y	Y	Y	Y	Y	Y	Y
3 ***Pickering***	Y	Y	N	Y	Y	N	N
4 Shows	Y	Y	N	Y	Y	N	N
5 Taylor	Y	Y	N	Y	Y	N	N
MISSOURI							
1 Clay	Y	N	Y	N	Y	Y	Y
2 ***Akin***	Y	Y	N	Y	N	N	N
3 Gephardt	?	?	?	?	?	?	?
4 Skelton	Y	Y	N	Y	N	N	N
5 McCarthy	N	N	Y	N	Y	Y	Y
6 ***Graves***	Y	Y	N	Y	Y	Y	N
7 ***Blunt***	Y	Y	N	Y	?	?	?
8 ***Emerson***	Y	Y	N	Y	Y	Y	N
9 ***Hulshof***	Y	Y	N	Y	Y	Y	N
MONTANA							
AL ***Rehberg***	Y	Y	N	Y	Y	N	N
NEBRASKA							
1 ***Bereuter***	Y	Y	N	Y	N	N	N
2 ***Terry***	Y	Y	N	Y	Y	N	N
3 ***Osborne***	Y	Y	N	Y	Y	N	N
NEVADA							
1 Berkley	N	Y	N	Y	Y	Y	Y
2 ***Gibbons***	Y	Y	N	Y	N	N	N
NEW HAMPSHIRE							
1 ***Sununu***	Y	Y	N	Y	Y	N	N
2 ***Bass***	Y	Y	N	Y	N	N	Y
NEW JERSEY							
1 Andrews	Y	Y	N	Y	Y	Y	Y
2 ***LoBiondo***	Y	Y	N	Y	Y	N	N
3 ***Saxton***	Y	Y	N	Y	Y	N	N
4 ***Smith***	Y	Y	N	Y	N	Y	N
5 ***Roukema***	Y	Y	N	Y	N	N	Y
6 Pallone	Y	Y	N	Y	N	Y	Y
7 ***Ferguson***	Y	Y	N	Y	N	Y	N
8 Pascrell	Y	Y	N	Y	Y	Y	N
9 Rothman	Y	Y	N	Y	N	Y	Y
10 Payne	N	N	Y	N	N	Y	Y
11 ***Frelinghuysen***	Y	Y	N	Y	N	N	Y
12 Holt	Y	N	N	N	N	Y	Y
13 Menendez	P	Y	N	Y	N	Y	Y
NEW MEXICO							
1 ***Wilson***	Y	Y	N	Y	Y	Y	N
2 ***Skeen***	Y	Y	N	Y	N	N	N
3 Udall	Y	N	Y	N	Y	Y	N
NEW YORK							
1 ***Grucci***	Y	Y	N	Y	N	Y	N
2 Israel	Y	?	Y	N	Y	N	Y
3 ***King***	Y	Y	N	Y	N	N	N
4 McCarthy	Y	Y	N	Y	Y	Y	Y
5 Ackerman	Y	N	N	N	N	Y	Y
6 Meeks	Y	N	Y	N	Y	?	Y
7 Crowley	Y	P	N	Y	N	Y	N
8 Nadler	N	N	Y	N	N	Y	Y
9 Weiner	Y	N	Y	N	N	Y	Y
10 Towns	?	?	Y	Y	N	Y	Y
11 Owens	+	−	+	−	N	Y	Y
12 Velázquez	Y	N	N	N	Y	Y	Y
13 ***Fossella***	Y	Y	N	Y	N	N	N
14 Maloney	Y	Y	Y	N	Y	Y	Y
15 Rangel	Y	N	Y	N	N	Y	Y
16 Serrano	Y	Y	N	N	N	N	Y
17 Engel	Y	Y	Y	N	N	Y	Y
18 Lowey	Y	Y	Y	N	N	Y	Y
19 ***Kelly***	Y	Y	N	Y	N	Y	Y
20 ***Gilman***	Y	Y	N	Y	N	Y	Y
21 McNulty	Y	Y	N	Y	Y	Y	N
22 ***Sweeney***	Y	Y	N	Y	N	N	N
23 ***Boehlert***	Y	Y	N	Y	N	Y	Y
24 ***McHugh***	Y	Y	N	Y	?	?	?
25 ***Walsh***	Y	Y	N	Y	N	N	N
26 Hinchey	N	N	Y	N	Y	Y	Y
27 ***Reynolds***	Y	Y	N	Y	Y	N	N
28 Slaughter	N	N	Y	N	Y	Y	Y
29 LaFalce	N	N	Y	N	Y	Y	N

	229	230	231	232	233	234	235
30 ***Quinn***	Y	Y	N	Y	Y	N	N
31 ***Houghton***	Y	Y	N	Y	N	N	Y
NORTH CAROLINA							
1 Clayton	P	N	Y	N	Y	Y	Y
2 Etheridge	Y	Y	Y	Y	Y	N	N
3 ***Jones***	Y	Y	N	Y	N	N	N
4 Price	N	Y	Y	N	Y	N	Y
5 ***Burr***	Y	?	N	Y	Y	N	N
6 ***Coble***	Y	Y	N	Y	Y	N	N
7 McIntyre	Y	Y	N	Y	Y	Y	N
8 ***Hayes***	Y	Y	N	Y	N	N	N
9 ***Myrick***	Y	Y	N	Y	?	?	?
10 ***Ballenger***	Y	Y	N	Y	+	−	−
11 ***Taylor***	Y	Y	N	Y	N	N	N
12 Watt	P	N	Y	N	N	Y	Y
NORTH DAKOTA							
AL Pomeroy	Y	Y	N	Y	Y	Y	N
OHIO							
1 ***Chabot***	Y	Y	N	Y	Y	N	N
2 ***Portman***	Y	Y	N	Y	N	N	N
3 Hall	Y	Y	N	N	N	N	N
4 ***Oxley***	Y	Y	N	Y	N	N	N
5 ***Gillmor***	Y	Y	N	Y	N	N	N
6 Strickland	Y	Y	N	Y	Y	Y	Y
7 ***Hobson***	Y	Y	N	Y	N	N	N
8 ***Boehner***	Y	Y	N	Y	?	?	N
9 Kaptur	Y	N	N	Y	N	Y	N
10 Kucinich	Y	N	N	Y	N	Y	N
11 Jones	P	N	Y	N	N	Y	Y
12 ***Tiberi***	Y	Y	N	Y	N	N	N
13 Brown	N	N	N	Y	N	Y	Y
14 Sawyer	?	N	Y	N	Y	Y	Y
15 ***Pryce***	Y	Y	N	Y	N	N	N
16 ***Regula***	Y	Y	N	Y	N	N	N
17 Traficant	Y	Y	N	Y	Y	N	N
18 ***Ney***	Y	Y	N	Y	Y	Y	N
19 ***LaTourette***	?	?	N	Y	N	Y	N
OKLAHOMA							
1 ***Largent***	Y	Y	N	Y	Y	N	N
2 Carson	Y	Y	N	Y	Y	Y	N
3 ***Watkins***	?	?	N	Y	Y	N	N
4 ***Watts***	Y	Y	N	Y	Y	N	N
5 ***Istook***	Y	Y	N	Y	Y	N	N
6 ***Lucas***	Y	Y	N	Y	Y	N	N
OREGON							
1 Wu	N	Y	N	N	N	N	Y
2 ***Walden***	Y	Y	N	Y	Y	N	N
3 Blumenauer	Y	N	Y	N	Y	Y	Y
4 DeFazio	N	P	Y	N	Y	Y	Y
5 Hooley	Y	Y	Y	N	Y	N	Y
PENNSYLVANIA							
1 Brady	Y	Y	Y	N	Y	Y	Y
2 Fattah	N	Y	N	Y	Y	Y	Y
3 Borski	Y	Y	Y	N	N	N	N
4 ***Hart***	Y	Y	N	Y	Y	Y	N
5 ***Peterson***	Y	Y	N	Y	Y	Y	N
6 Holden	Y	Y	N	Y	Y	Y	N
7 ***Weldon***	Y	Y	N	Y	N	Y	N
8 ***Greenwood***	Y	Y	Y	N	N	N	Y
9 ***Shuster, Bill***	Y	Y	N	Y	N	N	N
10 ***Sherwood***	Y	Y	N	Y	?	N	N
11 Kanjorski	Y	Y	N	Y	N	Y	Y
12 Murtha	Y	Y	N	Y	N	Y	N
13 Hoeffel	Y	Y	Y	N	N	Y	Y
14 Coyne	?	?	Y	N	N	Y	Y
15 ***Toomey***	Y	Y	N	Y	Y	N	N
16 ***Pitts***	Y	Y	N	Y	N	N	N
17 ***Gekas***	Y	Y	N	Y	N	N	N
18 Doyle	Y	Y	N	Y	N	Y	N
19 ***Platts***	?	Y	N	Y	Y	N	N
20 Mascara	Y	Y	N	Y	N	Y	N
21 ***English***	Y	Y	N	Y	N	Y	N
RHODE ISLAND							
1 Kennedy	N	Y	Y	N	N	N	Y
2 Langevin	Y	Y	N	Y	Y	Y	N
SOUTH CAROLINA							
1 ***Brown***	Y	Y	N	Y	Y	N	N
2 ***Spence***	?	?	?	?	?	?	?
3 ***Graham***	Y	Y	N	Y	N	N	N
4 ***DeMint***	Y	Y	N	Y	N	N	N
5 Spratt	Y	Y	N	Y	N	N	Y
6 Clyburn	Y	N	Y	N	N	Y	Y
SOUTH DAKOTA							
AL ***Thune***	Y	Y	N	Y	Y	Y	N

	229	230	231	232	233	234	235
TENNESSEE							
1 ***Jenkins***	Y	Y	N	Y	N	N	N
2 ***Duncan***	Y	Y	N	Y	Y	N	N
3 ***Wamp***	Y	Y	N	Y	Y	N	N
4 ***Hilleary***	Y	Y	N	Y	Y	N	N
5 Clement	Y	Y	N	Y	Y	N	N
6 Gordon	Y	Y	N	Y	Y	Y	Y
7 ***Bryant***	?	?	N	Y	Y	N	N
8 Tanner	Y	Y	Y	N	Y	Y	Y
9 Ford	Y	Y	N	Y	Y	Y	Y
TEXAS							
1 Sandlin	Y	Y	Y	Y	Y	?	Y
2 Turner	Y	Y	N	Y	Y	N	N
3 ***Johnson, Sam***	Y	Y	N	Y	N	N	N
4 Hall	Y	Y	N	Y	N	N	N
5 ***Sessions***	Y	Y	N	Y	Y	N	N
6 ***Barton***	Y	Y	N	Y	Y	N	N
7 ***Culberson***	Y	Y	N	Y	N	N	N
8 ***Brady***	Y	Y	N	Y	N	N	N
9 Lampson	Y	Y	Y	Y	Y	Y	N
10 Doggett	N	N	N	N	Y	N	Y
11 Edwards	Y	Y	N	Y	Y	N	N
12 ***Granger***	Y	Y	N	Y	N	N	N
13 ***Thornberry***	Y	Y	N	Y	Y	N	N
14 ***Paul***	N	N	Y	N	N	Y	N
15 Hinojosa	P	Y	N	Y	N	Y	Y
16 Reyes	?	?	?	?	?	?	?
17 Stenholm	Y	Y	N	Y	N	N	N
18 Jackson-Lee	Y	P	Y	N	N	Y	Y
19 ***Combest***	Y	Y	N	Y	N	N	N
20 Gonzalez	Y	Y	Y	N	N	Y	Y
21 ***Smith***	Y	Y	N	Y	N	N	N
22 ***DeLay***	Y	Y	N	Y	N	N	N
23 ***Bonilla***	Y	Y	N	Y	N	N	N
24 Frost	N	Y	N	Y	N	Y	Y
25 Bentsen	Y	Y	N	Y	Y	Y	Y
26 ***Armey***	Y	Y	N	Y	N	N	N
27 Ortiz	Y	Y	N	Y	N	Y	N
28 Rodriguez	Y	Y	N	Y	Y	Y	Y
29 Green	Y	Y	N	Y	N	N	Y
30 Johnson, E.B.	Y	Y	Y	N	N	Y	Y
UTAH							
1 ***Hansen***	Y	Y	N	Y	Y	N	N
2 Matheson	Y	Y	Y	N	Y	N	Y
3 ***Cannon***	Y	Y	N	Y	?	N	N
VERMONT							
AL *Sanders*	?	?	Y	N	Y	Y	Y
VIRGINIA							
1 ***Davis, Jo Ann***	Y	Y	N	Y	Y	N	N
2 ***Schrock***	Y	Y	N	Y	N	N	N
3 Scott	Y	Y	Y	N	N	Y	Y
4 ***Forbes***	Y	Y	N	Y	N	N	N
5 *Goode*	Y	Y	N	Y	N	Y	N
6 ***Goodlatte***	Y	Y	N	Y	Y	N	N
7 ***Cantor***	Y	Y	N	Y	N	N	N
8 Moran	N	Y	Y	N	N	N	Y
9 Boucher	Y	Y	Y	N	N	?	Y
10 ***Wolf***	Y	Y	N	Y	N	N	N
11 ***Davis, T.***	Y	Y	N	Y	N	N	N
WASHINGTON							
1 Inslee	Y	Y	Y	N	Y	N	Y
2 Larsen	Y	N	Y	N	Y	N	Y
3 Baird	Y	N	N	Y	N	Y	Y
4 ***Hastings***	Y	Y	N	Y	Y	N	N
5 ***Nethercutt***	Y	Y	N	Y	Y	N	N
6 Dicks	Y	Y	Y	N	Y	N	Y
7 McDermott	N	N	N	N	Y	?	Y
8 ***Dunn***	Y	Y	N	Y	Y	N	N
9 Smith	Y	Y	N	Y	Y	N	Y
WEST VIRGINIA							
1 Mollohan	Y	Y	N	Y	N	N	N
2 ***Capito***	Y	Y	N	Y	Y	Y	N
3 Rahall	N	Y	N	Y	Y	Y	N
WISCONSIN							
1 ***Ryan***	Y	Y	N	Y	N	N	N
2 Baldwin	N	N	Y	N	N	Y	Y
3 Kind	?	Y	Y	N	Y	Y	Y
4 Kleczka	?	?	Y	N	N	Y	N
5 Barrett	P	N	Y	N	Y	Y	Y
6 ***Petri***	P	Y	N	N	N	N	N
7 Obey	N	P	Y	N	N	Y	N
8 ***Green***	Y	Y	N	Y	Y	N	N
9 ***Sensenbrenner***	Y	Y	N	Y	Y	N	N
WYOMING							
AL ***Cubin***	Y	Y	N	Y	N	N	N

Southern states - Ala., Ark., Fla., Ga., Ky., La., Miss., N.C., Okla., S.C., Tenn., Texas, Va.

Key

Y Voted for (yea).
\# Paired for.
+ Announced for.
N Voted against (nay).
X Paired against.
– Announced against.
P Voted "present."
C Voted "present" to avoid possible conflict of interest.
? Did not vote or otherwise make a position known.

•

Democrats   **Republicans**
Independents

236. Procedural Motion/Journal. Approval of the House Journal of Tuesday, July 17, 2001. Approved 372-47: R 193-16; D 177-31 (ND 128-26, SD 49-5); I 2-0. July 18, 2001.

237. HR 1. ESEA Reauthorization/Agree to Conference. Boehner, R-Ohio, motion that the House disagree to the Senate amendment and agree to a conference on the bill that would authorize $22.8 billion in education funding. Motion agreed to 424-5: R 214-3; D 209-1 (ND 155-1, SD 54-0); I 1-1. July 18, 2001.

238. HR 1. ESEA Reauthorization/Motion to Instruct. Boehner, R-Ohio, motion to table (kill) the Baldacci, D-Maine, motion to instruct House conferees to agree to provide full funding for part B of the Individuals with Disabilities Education Act (PL 94-142) to provide a free, appropriate public education for children with disabilities. The instructions also would call for ensuring that the on-budget surplus is not less than the Federal Hospital Insurance Trust Fund surplus. Motion agreed to 296-126: R 197-16; D 99-109 (ND 67-87, SD 32-22); I 0-1. July 18, 2001.

239. HR 2500. Fiscal 2002 Commerce-Justice-State Appropriations/Census Data Content. Maloney, D-N.Y., amendment that would increase by $500,000 the Census Bureau's data content and products account and reduce by the same amount funding to pay for collecting and publishing statistics for other periodic censuses. Rejected 209-217: R 2-213; D 206-3 (ND 155-1, SD 51-2); I 1-1. July 18, 2001.

240. HR 2500. Fiscal 2002 Commerce-Justice-State Appropriations/Census Data Processing. Maloney, D-N.Y., amendment that would increase by $2 million the Census Bureau's automated data processing and telecommunications support account and reduce by the same amount funding to pay for collecting and publishing statistics for other periodic censuses. Rejected 215-215: R 5-213; D 209-1 (ND 155-1, SD 54-0); I 1-1. July 18, 2001.

241. HR 2500. Fiscal 2002 Commerce-Justice-State Appropriations/China Payment. DeLay, R-Texas, amendment that would prohibit use of funds in the bill to negotiate or pay any request or claim by China for reimbursement of costs associated with the detention of the crew of the U.S. Navy EP-3 airplane or with the return of the aircraft to the United States. Adopted 424-6: R 219-0; D 203-6 (ND 151-5, SD 52-1); I 2-0. July 18, 2001.

242. HR 2500. Fiscal 2002 Commerce-Justice-State Appropriations/Deportation of Aliens. Jackson-Lee, D-Texas, amendment that would prohibit use of funds in the bill to deport aliens for conviction of a crime if they entered into a plea agreement before April 1997 or if they requested discretionary relief after June 25, 2001. Rejected 189-242: R 6-213; D 182-28 (ND 145-11, SD 37-17); I 1-1. July 18, 2001.

	236	237	238	239	240	241	242
ALABAMA							
1 *Callahan*	Y	Y	Y	N	N	Y	N
2 *Everett*	Y	Y	Y	N	N	Y	N
3 *Riley*	?	?	?	?	?	?	?
4 *Aderholt*	N	Y	Y	N	N	Y	N
5 Cramer	Y	Y	Y	Y	Y	Y	N
6 *Bachus*	Y	Y	Y	N	N	Y	N
7 Hilliard	N	Y	N	Y	Y	Y	Y
ALASKA							
AL *Young*	?	Y	Y	N	N	Y	N
ARIZONA							
1 *Flake*	Y	Y	Y	N	N	Y	N
2 Pastor	Y	Y	Y	Y	Y	Y	Y
3 *Stump*	Y	Y	Y	N	N	Y	N
4 *Shadegg*	Y	Y	Y	N	N	Y	N
5 *Kolbe*	Y	Y	Y	N	N	Y	N
6 *Hayworth*	Y	Y	Y	N	N	Y	N
ARKANSAS							
1 Berry	Y	Y	Y	Y	Y	Y	N
2 Snyder	Y	Y	N	Y	Y	Y	N
3 *Hutchinson*	?	Y	Y	?	?	Y	N
4 Ross	Y	Y	Y	Y	Y	Y	N
CALIFORNIA							
1 Thompson	N	Y	N	Y	Y	Y	Y
2 *Herger*	Y	Y	Y	N	N	Y	N
3 *Ose*	Y	Y	Y	N	N	Y	N
4 *Doolittle*	Y	Y	Y	N	N	Y	N
5 Matsui	Y	Y	Y	Y	Y	Y	Y
6 Woolsey	Y	Y	N	Y	Y	Y	Y
7 Miller, George	Y	Y	N	Y	Y	Y	Y
8 Pelosi	Y	Y	Y	Y	Y	Y	Y
9 Lee	Y	Y	N	Y	Y	Y	Y
10 Tauscher	Y	Y	N	Y	Y	Y	N
11 *Pombo*	N	Y	N	N	N	Y	N
12 Lantos	Y	Y	N	Y	Y	Y	Y
13 Stark	Y	Y	N	Y	Y	Y	N
14 Eshoo	Y	Y	N	Y	Y	Y	Y
15 Honda	Y	Y	N	Y	Y	Y	Y
16 Lofgren	Y	Y	N	Y	Y	Y	Y
17 Farr	Y	Y	Y	Y	Y	Y	Y
18 Condit	Y	Y	Y	Y	Y	Y	Y
19 *Radanovich*	Y	Y	N	N	N	Y	N
20 Dooley	Y	Y	Y	Y	Y	Y	Y
21 *Thomas*	Y	Y	Y	N	N	Y	N
22 Capps	Y	Y	N	Y	Y	Y	Y
23 *Gallegly*	Y	Y	Y	N	N	Y	N
24 Sherman	Y	Y	Y	Y	Y	Y	Y
25 *McKeon*	Y	Y	Y	N	N	Y	N
26 Berman	Y	Y	N	Y	Y	Y	Y
27 Schiff	Y	Y	N	Y	Y	Y	Y
28 *Dreier*	Y	Y	Y	N	N	Y	N
29 Waxman	Y	Y	N	Y	Y	Y	Y
30 Becerra	Y	Y	N	Y	Y	Y	Y
31 Solis	Y	Y	N	Y	Y	Y	Y
32 Watson	Y	Y	N	Y	Y	Y	Y
33 Roybal-Allard	Y	Y	N	Y	Y	Y	Y
34 Napolitano	Y	Y	Y	Y	Y	Y	Y
35 Waters	N	Y	Y	Y	Y	Y	Y
36 Harman	Y	Y	N	Y	Y	Y	Y
37 Millender-McD.	Y	Y	N	Y	Y	Y	Y
38 *Horn*	Y	Y	Y	N	N	Y	N

	236	237	238	239	240	241	242
39 *Royce*	Y	Y	Y	N	N	Y	N
40 *Lewis*	Y	Y	Y	N	N	Y	N
41 *Miller, Gary*	Y	Y	Y	N	N	Y	N
42 Baca	Y	Y	N	Y	Y	Y	Y
43 *Calvert*	Y	Y	Y	N	N	Y	N
44 *Bono*	Y	Y	Y	N	N	Y	N
45 *Rohrabacher*	Y	Y	Y	N	N	Y	N
46 Sanchez	Y	Y	N	Y	Y	Y	Y
47 *Cox*	Y	Y	Y	N	N	Y	N
48 *Issa*	Y	Y	Y	N	N	Y	N
49 Davis	Y	Y	N	Y	Y	Y	Y
50 Filner	N	Y	N	Y	Y	Y	Y
51 *Cunningham*	Y	Y	Y	N	N	Y	N
52 *Hunter*	Y	Y	Y	N	N	Y	N
COLORADO							
1 DeGette	Y	Y	N	Y	Y	Y	Y
2 Udall	N	Y	Y	Y	Y	Y	Y
3 *McInnis*	Y	Y	Y	N	N	Y	N
4 *Schaffer*	N	Y	N	N	N	Y	N
5 *Hefley*	N	Y	N	Y	N	Y	N
6 *Tancredo*	P	Y	Y	N	N	Y	N
CONNECTICUT							
1 Larson	Y	Y	Y	Y	Y	Y	Y
2 *Simmons*	Y	Y	Y	N	N	Y	Y
3 DeLauro	Y	Y	Y	Y	Y	Y	Y
4 *Shays*	Y	Y	N	N	N	Y	N
5 Maloney	?	Y	N	Y	Y	Y	Y
6 *Johnson*	Y	Y	Y	N	N	Y	N
DELAWARE							
AL *Castle*	Y	Y	Y	N	N	Y	N
FLORIDA							
1 *Scarborough*	Y	N	Y	N	N	Y	Y
2 Boyd	Y	Y	Y	Y	Y	Y	N
3 Brown	Y	Y	Y	Y	Y	Y	Y
4 *Crenshaw*	Y	Y	Y	N	N	Y	N
5 Thurman	Y	Y	N	Y	N	Y	N
6 *Stearns*	Y	Y	N	N	N	Y	N
7 *Mica*	Y	Y	Y	N	N	Y	N
8 *Keller*	Y	Y	Y	N	N	Y	N
9 *Bilirakis*	Y	Y	N	N	N	Y	N
10 *Young*	Y	Y	Y	N	N	Y	N
11 Davis	Y	Y	N	Y	N	Y	N
12 *Putnam*	Y	Y	N	N	N	Y	N
13 *Miller*	Y	Y	Y	N	N	Y	N
14 *Goss*	?	Y	N	N	N	Y	N
15 *Weldon*	Y	Y	Y	?	N	Y	N
16 *Foley*	Y	Y	Y	N	N	Y	N
17 Meek	Y	Y	Y	Y	Y	Y	Y
18 *Ros-Lehtinen*	Y	Y	N	N	N	Y	Y
19 Wexler	Y	Y	N	Y	Y	Y	Y
20 Deutsch	Y	Y	N	Y	Y	Y	Y
21 *Diaz-Balart*	Y	Y	N	N	N	Y	Y
22 *Shaw*	Y	Y	Y	N	N	Y	N
23 Hastings	Y	Y	Y	Y	N	Y	Y
GEORGIA							
1 *Kingston*	Y	Y	Y	N	N	Y	N
2 Bishop	Y	Y	Y	Y	Y	Y	Y
3 *Collins*	Y	Y	Y	N	N	Y	N
4 McKinney	Y	Y	N	Y	Y	Y	Y
5 Lewis	Y	Y	N	Y	Y	Y	Y
6 *Isakson*	Y	Y	N	N	N	Y	N
7 *Barr*	Y	Y	Y	N	N	Y	N
8 *Chambliss*	Y	Y	Y	N	N	Y	N
9 *Deal*	Y	Y	Y	N	N	Y	N
10 *Norwood*	Y	Y	Y	N	N	Y	N
11 *Linder*	Y	Y	Y	N	N	Y	N
HAWAII							
1 Abercrombie	Y	Y	Y	Y	Y	Y	Y
2 Mink	Y	Y	N	Y	N	Y	N
IDAHO							
1 *Otter*	Y	Y	Y	N	N	Y	N
2 *Simpson*	Y	Y	Y	N	N	Y	N
ILLINOIS							
1 Rush	Y	Y	Y	Y	Y	Y	Y
2 Jackson	Y	Y	Y	Y	Y	Y	Y
3 Lipinski	Y	Y	Y	Y	Y	Y	Y
4 Gutierrez	N	Y	N	Y	Y	Y	Y
5 Blagojevich	Y	Y	Y	Y	Y	Y	Y
6 *Hyde*	Y	Y	Y	N	N	Y	N
7 Davis	Y	Y	Y	Y	Y	Y	Y
8 *Crane*	?	Y	N	N	N	Y	N
9 Schakowsky	Y	Y	N	Y	Y	Y	Y
10 *Kirk*	Y	Y	N	N	N	Y	N
11 *Weller*	N	Y	Y	N	N	Y	N
12 Costello	N	Y	Y	Y	Y	Y	Y
13 *Biggert*	Y	Y	Y	N	N	Y	N

ND Northern Democrats   SD Southern Democrats

	236	237	238	239	240	241	242
14 ***Hastert***							
15 ***Johnson***	Y	Y	Y	N	N	Y	N
16 ***Manzullo***	Y	Y	Y	N	N	Y	N
17 Evans	Y	Y	N	Y	Y	Y	Y
18 ***LaHood***	Y	Y	Y	N	N	Y	N
19 Phelps	Y	Y	Y	Y	Y	Y	N
20 ***Shimkus***	Y	Y	Y	N	N	Y	N
INDIANA							
1 Visclosky	N	Y	Y	Y	Y	Y	N
2 ***Pence***	Y	Y	Y	N	N	Y	N
3 Roemer	Y	Y	N	Y	Y	Y	N
4 ***Souder***	Y	Y	Y	N	N	Y	N
5 ***Buyer***	Y	Y	Y	N	N	Y	N
6 ***Burton***	Y	Y	Y	N	N	Y	N
7 ***Kerns***	Y	Y	Y	N	N	Y	N
8 ***Hostettler***	Y	N	Y	N	N	Y	N
9 Hill	Y	Y	N	Y	Y	Y	N
10 Carson	Y	Y	Y	Y	Y	Y	Y
IOWA							
1 ***Leach***	Y	Y	Y	N	N	Y	N
2 ***Nussle***	Y	Y	Y	N	N	Y	N
3 Boswell	Y	Y	Y	Y	Y	Y	Y
4 ***Ganske***	Y	Y	Y	N	N	Y	N
5 ***Latham***	Y	Y	Y	N	N	Y	N
KANSAS							
1 ***Moran***	N	Y	N	N	N	Y	N
2 ***Ryun***	Y	Y	Y	N	N	Y	N
3 Moore	Y	Y	N	Y	Y	Y	Y
4 ***Tiahrt***	N	N	Y	N	N	Y	N
KENTUCKY							
1 ***Whitfield***	Y	Y	Y	N	N	Y	N
2 ***Lewis***	Y	Y	Y	N	N	Y	N
3 ***Northup***	Y	Y	Y	N	N	Y	N
4 Lucas	Y	Y	Y	Y	Y	Y	N
5 ***Rogers***	Y	Y	Y	N	N	Y	N
6 ***Fletcher***	Y	Y	Y	Y	N	Y	N
LOUISIANA							
1 ***Vitter***	Y	Y	Y	N	N	Y	N
2 Jefferson	Y	Y	Y	?	Y	Y	Y
3 ***Tauzin***	Y	Y	Y	N	N	Y	N
4 ***McCrery***	Y	Y	Y	N	N	Y	N
5 ***Cooksey***	Y	Y	Y	N	N	Y	N
6 ***Baker***	Y	Y	Y	N	N	Y	N
7 John	Y	Y	Y	Y	Y	Y	N
MAINE							
1 Allen	Y	Y	N	Y	Y	Y	Y
2 Baldacci	Y	Y	N	Y	Y	Y	Y
MARYLAND							
1 ***Gilchrest***	Y	Y	Y	N	N	Y	N
2 ***Ehrlich***	Y	Y	Y	N	N	Y	N
3 Cardin	Y	Y	N	Y	Y	Y	Y
4 Wynn	Y	Y	N	Y	Y	Y	Y
5 Hoyer	Y	Y	Y	Y	Y	Y	Y
6 ***Bartlett***	Y	Y	Y	N	N	Y	N
7 Cummings	Y	Y	Y	Y	Y	Y	Y
8 ***Morella***	Y	Y	Y	Y	Y	Y	Y
MASSACHUSETTS							
1 Olver	Y	Y	Y	Y	Y	Y	Y
2 Neal	Y	Y	Y	Y	Y	Y	Y
3 McGovern	N	Y	N	Y	Y	Y	Y
4 Frank	Y	Y	N	Y	Y	Y	Y
5 Meehan	Y	Y	Y	Y	Y	Y	Y
6 Tierney	Y	Y	N	Y	Y	Y	Y
7 Markey	Y	Y	N	Y	Y	Y	N
8 Capuano	N	Y	N	Y	Y	Y	Y
9 Vacant							
10 Delahunt	Y	Y	N	Y	Y	Y	Y
MICHIGAN							
1 Stupak	N	Y	Y	Y	Y	Y	N
2 ***Hoekstra***	Y	Y	N	N	N	Y	N
3 ***Ehlers***	Y	Y	Y	N	N	Y	N
4 ***Camp***	Y	Y	Y	N	N	Y	N
5 Barcia	Y	Y	N	Y	Y	Y	Y
6 ***Upton***	Y	Y	Y	N	N	Y	N
7 ***Smith***	Y	Y	Y	N	N	Y	N
8 ***Rogers***	Y	Y	Y	N	N	Y	N
9 Kildee	Y	Y	N	Y	Y	Y	Y
10 Bonior	Y	Y	N	Y	Y	Y	Y
11 ***Knollenberg***	Y	Y	Y	N	N	Y	N
12 Levin	Y	Y	N	Y	Y	Y	Y
13 Rivers	Y	Y	N	Y	Y	Y	Y
14 Conyers	Y	Y	N	Y	Y	Y	Y
15 Kilpatrick	Y	Y	Y	Y	Y	Y	Y
16 Dingell	Y	Y	N	Y	Y	Y	Y

	236	237	238	239	240	241	242
MINNESOTA							
1 ***Gutknecht***	N	Y	Y	N	N	Y	N
2 ***Kennedy***	N	Y	N	N	N	Y	N
3 ***Ramstad***	N	Y	N	N	N	Y	N
4 McCollum	Y	Y	N	Y	Y	Y	Y
5 Sabo	N	N	Y	Y	Y	Y	Y
6 Luther	Y	Y	N	Y	Y	Y	Y
7 Peterson	N	Y	Y	Y	Y	Y	Y
8 Oberstar	N	Y	Y	Y	Y	Y	Y
MISSISSIPPI							
1 ***Wicker***	N	Y	Y	N	N	Y	N
2 Thompson	N	Y	Y	Y	Y	Y	Y
3 ***Pickering***	Y	Y	Y	N	N	Y	N
4 Shows	Y	Y	N	Y	Y	?	N
5 Taylor	N	Y	N	Y	Y	Y	N
MISSOURI							
1 Clay	Y	Y	Y	Y	Y	N	Y
2 ***Akin***	Y	Y	Y	N	N	Y	N
3 Gephardt	Y	Y	N	Y	Y	Y	Y
4 Skelton	Y	Y	N	Y	Y	Y	N
5 McCarthy	Y	Y	N	Y	Y	Y	Y
6 ***Graves***	Y	Y	Y	N	N	Y	N
7 ***Blunt***	Y	Y	Y	N	N	Y	N
8 ***Emerson***	Y	Y	Y	N	N	Y	N
9 ***Hulshof***	Y	Y	Y	N	N	Y	N
MONTANA							
AL ***Rehberg***	Y	Y	N	N	N	Y	N
NEBRASKA							
1 ***Bereuter***	Y	Y	N	N	N	Y	N
2 ***Terry***	Y	Y	Y	N	N	Y	N
3 ***Osborne***	Y	Y	Y	N	N	Y	N
NEVADA							
1 Berkley	Y	Y	Y	Y	Y	Y	Y
2 ***Gibbons***	?	?	?	N	N	Y	N
NEW HAMPSHIRE							
1 ***Sununu***	Y	Y	N	N	N	Y	N
2 ***Bass***	Y	Y	N	N	N	Y	N
NEW JERSEY							
1 Andrews	Y	Y	Y	Y	Y	Y	Y
2 ***LoBiondo***	N	Y	Y	N	N	Y	N
3 ***Saxton***	Y	Y	Y	N	N	Y	N
4 ***Smith***	Y	Y	Y	N	N	Y	N
5 ***Roukema***	Y	Y	Y	N	N	Y	N
6 Pallone	N	Y	Y	Y	Y	Y	Y
7 ***Ferguson***	Y	Y	N	N	N	Y	N
8 Pascrell	Y	Y	Y	Y	Y	Y	Y
9 Rothman	Y	Y	Y	Y	Y	Y	Y
10 Payne	Y	Y	N	Y	Y	Y	Y
11 ***Frelinghuysen***	Y	Y	Y	N	N	Y	N
12 Holt	Y	Y	N	Y	Y	Y	Y
13 Menendez	N	Y	Y	Y	Y	Y	Y
NEW MEXICO							
1 ***Wilson***	Y	Y	Y	N	Y	Y	N
2 ***Skeen***	Y	Y	Y	N	N	Y	N
3 Udall	N	Y	N	Y	Y	Y	Y
NEW YORK							
1 ***Grucci***	Y	Y	Y	N	N	Y	Y
2 Israel	Y	Y	N	Y	Y	Y	Y
3 ***King***	Y	Y	Y	N	N	Y	Y
4 McCarthy	Y	Y	N	Y	Y	Y	Y
5 Ackerman	Y	Y	Y	Y	Y	N	Y
6 Meeks	Y	Y	Y	Y	Y	Y	Y
7 Crowley	Y	Y	N	Y	Y	Y	Y
8 Nadler	Y	Y	N	Y	Y	Y	Y
9 Weiner	Y	Y	N	Y	Y	Y	Y
10 Towns	Y	Y	Y	Y	Y	Y	Y
11 Owens	Y	Y	N	Y	Y	Y	Y
12 Velázquez	Y	Y	Y	Y	Y	Y	Y
13 ***Fossella***	N	Y	Y	N	N	Y	N
14 Maloney	Y	Y	N	Y	Y	Y	Y
15 Rangel	Y	Y	Y	Y	Y	Y	Y
16 Serrano	Y	Y	Y	Y	Y	Y	Y
17 Engel	Y	Y	N	Y	Y	Y	Y
18 Lowey	Y	Y	Y	Y	Y	Y	Y
19 ***Kelly***	Y	Y	N	N	N	Y	N
20 ***Gilman***	Y	Y	Y	–	N	Y	N
21 McNulty	N	Y	N	Y	Y	Y	Y
22 ***Sweeney***	Y	Y	Y	N	N	Y	N
23 ***Boehlert***	Y	Y	Y	N	N	Y	N
24 ***McHugh***	Y	Y	Y	N	N	Y	N
25 ***Walsh***	Y	Y	?	N	N	Y	N
26 Hinchey	Y	Y	?	Y	Y	Y	Y
27 ***Reynolds***	Y	Y	Y	N	N	Y	N
28 Slaughter	Y	Y	N	Y	Y	Y	Y
29 LaFalce	Y	Y	N	Y	Y	Y	Y

	236	237	238	239	240	241	242
30 ***Quinn***	Y	Y	Y	N	N	Y	N
31 ***Houghton***	Y	Y	Y	N	N	Y	N
NORTH CAROLINA							
1 Clayton	Y	Y	N	Y	Y	Y	Y
2 Etheridge	Y	Y	N	Y	Y	Y	Y
3 ***Jones***	Y	Y	Y	N	N	Y	N
4 Price	Y	Y	Y	Y	Y	Y	Y
5 ***Burr***	Y	Y	Y	N	N	Y	N
6 ***Coble***	Y	Y	Y	N	N	Y	N
7 McIntyre	Y	Y	Y	Y	Y	Y	N
8 ***Hayes***	Y	Y	Y	N	N	Y	N
9 ***Myrick***	?	?	?	N	N	Y	N
10 ***Ballenger***	Y	Y	Y	N	N	Y	N
11 ***Taylor***	Y	Y	Y	N	N	Y	N
12 Watt	Y	Y	N	Y	Y	Y	Y
NORTH DAKOTA							
AL Pomeroy	Y	Y	Y	Y	Y	Y	Y
OHIO							
1 ***Chabot***	Y	Y	Y	N	N	Y	N
2 ***Portman***	Y	Y	Y	N	N	Y	N
3 Hall	Y	Y	N	Y	Y	Y	N
4 ***Oxley***	+	Y	+	N	N	Y	N
5 ***Gillmor***	Y	Y	Y	N	N	Y	N
6 Strickland	N	Y	Y	Y	Y	Y	Y
7 ***Hobson***	Y	Y	Y	N	N	Y	N
8 ***Boehner***	Y	Y	Y	N	N	Y	N
9 Kaptur	Y	Y	Y	Y	Y	Y	Y
10 Kucinich	N	Y	N	Y	Y	Y	Y
11 Jones	N	Y	N	Y	Y	Y	Y
12 ***Tiberi***	Y	Y	Y	N	N	Y	N
13 Brown	Y	Y	N	Y	Y	Y	Y
14 Sawyer	Y	Y	N	Y	Y	Y	Y
15 ***Pryce***	Y	Y	Y	N	N	Y	N
16 ***Regula***	Y	Y	Y	N	N	Y	N
17 Traficant	Y	Y	Y	N	N	Y	N
18 ***Ney***	Y	Y	Y	N	N	Y	N
19 ***LaTourette***	Y	Y	Y	N	N	Y	N
OKLAHOMA							
1 ***Largent***	Y	Y	Y	N	N	Y	N
2 Carson	Y	Y	N	Y	Y	Y	N
3 ***Watkins***	Y	Y	Y	N	N	Y	N
4 ***Watts***	Y	Y	Y	N	N	Y	N
5 ***Istook***	?	Y	Y	N	N	Y	N
6 ***Lucas***	Y	Y	Y	N	N	Y	N
OREGON							
1 Wu	N	Y	N	Y	Y	Y	Y
2 ***Walden***	Y	Y	Y	N	N	Y	N
3 Blumenauer	Y	Y	N	Y	Y	Y	Y
4 DeFazio	N	Y	N	Y	Y	Y	Y
5 Hooley	Y	Y	N	Y	Y	Y	Y
PENNSYLVANIA							
1 Brady	N	Y	?	Y	Y	Y	Y
2 Fattah	Y	Y	Y	Y	Y	Y	Y
3 Borski	N	Y	N	Y	Y	Y	Y
4 ***Hart***	Y	Y	Y	N	N	Y	N
5 ***Peterson***	Y	Y	Y	N	N	Y	N
6 Holden	Y	Y	Y	Y	Y	Y	N
7 ***Weldon***	Y	Y	Y	N	N	Y	N
8 ***Greenwood***	Y	Y	N	N	N	Y	N
9 ***Shuster, Bill***	Y	Y	Y	N	N	Y	N
10 ***Sherwood***	Y	Y	Y	N	N	Y	N
11 Kanjorski	Y	Y	Y	Y	Y	Y	Y
12 Murtha	?	Y	Y	Y	Y	Y	Y
13 Hoeffel	Y	Y	N	Y	Y	Y	Y
14 Coyne	Y	Y	N	Y	Y	Y	Y
15 ***Toomey***	Y	Y	Y	N	N	Y	N
16 ***Pitts***	Y	Y	?	N	N	Y	N
17 ***Gekas***	Y	Y	Y	N	N	Y	N
18 Doyle	Y	Y	N	Y	Y	Y	Y
19 ***Platts***	Y	Y	N	N	N	Y	N
20 Mascara	Y	Y	Y	Y	Y	Y	Y
21 ***English***	N	Y	Y	N	N	Y	N
RHODE ISLAND							
1 Kennedy	Y	Y	Y	Y	Y	Y	Y
2 Langevin	Y	Y	N	Y	Y	Y	Y
SOUTH CAROLINA							
1 ***Brown***	Y	Y	Y	N	N	Y	N
2 ***Spence***	?	?	?	?	?	?	?
3 ***Graham***	Y	Y	Y	N	N	Y	N
4 ***DeMint***	Y	Y	Y	N	N	Y	N
5 Spratt	Y	Y	Y	Y	Y	Y	N
6 Clyburn	Y	Y	Y	Y	Y	Y	Y
SOUTH DAKOTA							
AL ***Thune***	Y	Y	N	N	N	Y	N

	236	237	238	239	240	241	242
TENNESSEE							
1 ***Jenkins***	Y	Y	Y	N	N	Y	N
2 ***Duncan***	Y	Y	Y	N	N	Y	N
3 ***Wamp***	N	Y	Y	N	N	Y	N
4 ***Hilleary***	N	Y	Y	N	N	Y	N
5 Clement	Y	Y	Y	Y	Y	Y	Y
6 Gordon	Y	Y	Y	Y	Y	Y	N
7 ***Bryant***	Y	Y	Y	N	N	Y	N
8 Tanner	Y	Y	Y	Y	Y	Y	N
9 Ford	Y	Y	N	Y	Y	Y	Y
TEXAS							
1 Sandlin	Y	Y	N	Y	Y	Y	Y
2 Turner	Y	Y	Y	Y	Y	Y	N
3 ***Johnson, Sam***	Y	Y	Y	N	N	Y	N
4 Hall	Y	Y	Y	N	Y	Y	Y
5 ***Sessions***	Y	Y	Y	N	N	Y	N
6 ***Barton***	Y	Y	Y	N	N	Y	N
7 ***Culberson***	?	Y	Y	N	N	Y	N
8 ***Brady***	Y	Y	Y	N	N	Y	N
9 Lampson	Y	Y	Y	Y	Y	Y	Y
10 Doggett	Y	Y	N	Y	Y	Y	Y
11 Edwards	Y	Y	Y	Y	Y	Y	Y
12 ***Granger***	Y	Y	Y	N	N	Y	N
13 ***Thornberry***	Y	Y	Y	N	N	Y	N
14 ***Paul***	Y	Y	Y	?	N	Y	N
15 Hinojosa	Y	Y	N	Y	Y	Y	N
16 Reyes	Y	Y	Y	Y	Y	Y	Y
17 Stenholm	Y	Y	Y	N	Y	Y	Y
18 Jackson-Lee	Y	Y	N	Y	Y	Y	Y
19 ***Combest***	Y	Y	Y	N	N	Y	N
20 Gonzalez	Y	Y	N	Y	Y	Y	Y
21 ***Smith***	Y	Y	Y	N	N	Y	N
22 ***DeLay***	Y	Y	Y	N	N	Y	N
23 ***Bonilla***	Y	Y	Y	N	N	Y	N
24 Frost	Y	Y	Y	Y	Y	Y	Y
25 Bentsen	Y	Y	N	Y	Y	Y	Y
26 ***Armey***	Y	Y	Y	N	N	Y	N
27 Ortiz	Y	Y	Y	Y	Y	Y	Y
28 Rodriguez	Y	Y	Y	Y	Y	Y	Y
29 Green	Y	Y	N	Y	Y	Y	Y
30 Johnson, E.B.	N	Y	Y	Y	Y	Y	Y
UTAH							
1 ***Hansen***	Y	Y	Y	N	N	Y	N
2 Matheson	Y	Y	Y	Y	Y	Y	Y
3 ***Cannon***	Y	Y	Y	N	N	Y	N
VERMONT							
AL *Sanders*	Y	Y	N	Y	Y	Y	Y
VIRGINIA							
1 ***Davis, Jo Ann***	Y	Y	?	N	N	Y	N
2 ***Schrock***	Y	Y	Y	N	N	Y	N
3 Scott	N	Y	Y	Y	Y	Y	Y
4 ***Forbes***	Y	Y	Y	N	N	Y	N
5 *Goode*	Y	N	?	N	N	Y	N
6 ***Goodlatte***	Y	Y	Y	N	N	Y	N
7 ***Cantor***	Y	Y	Y	N	N	Y	N
8 Moran	Y	Y	Y	Y	Y	Y	Y
9 Boucher	Y	Y	Y	Y	Y	Y	Y
10 ***Wolf***	Y	Y	Y	N	N	Y	N
11 ***Davis, T.***	Y	Y	Y	N	N	Y	N
WASHINGTON							
1 Inslee	Y	Y	N	Y	Y	Y	Y
2 Larsen	N	Y	Y	Y	Y	Y	Y
3 Baird	Y	Y	N	Y	Y	Y	Y
4 ***Hastings***	Y	Y	Y	N	N	Y	N
5 ***Nethercutt***	Y	Y	Y	N	N	Y	N
6 Dicks	Y	Y	Y	Y	Y	Y	Y
7 McDermott	N	Y	N	Y	Y	N	Y
8 ***Dunn***	Y	Y	Y	N	N	Y	N
9 Smith	Y	Y	Y	Y	Y	Y	Y
WEST VIRGINIA							
1 Mollohan	Y	Y	Y	Y	Y	Y	Y
2 ***Capito***	Y	Y	Y	N	N	Y	N
3 Rahall	Y	Y	N	Y	Y	Y	Y
WISCONSIN							
1 ***Ryan***	Y	Y	Y	N	N	Y	N
2 Baldwin	Y	Y	N	Y	Y	Y	Y
3 Kind	Y	Y	N	Y	Y	Y	Y
4 Kleczka	Y	Y	N	Y	Y	Y	Y
5 Barrett	Y	Y	N	Y	Y	Y	Y
6 ***Petri***	Y	Y	Y	N	N	Y	N
7 Obey	Y	Y	Y	Y	Y	Y	Y
8 ***Green***	Y	Y	Y	N	N	Y	N
9 ***Sensenbrenner***	Y	Y	Y	N	N	Y	N
WYOMING							
AL ***Cubin***	Y	Y	Y	N	N	Y	N

Southern states - Ala., Ark., Fla., Ga., Ky., La., Miss., N.C., Okla., S.C., Tenn., Texas, Va.

Key

Y	Voted for (yea).
#	Paired for.
+	Announced for.
N	Voted against (nay).
X	Paired against.
−	Announced against.
P	Voted "present."
C	Voted "present" to avoid possible conflict of interest.
?	Did not vote or otherwise make a position known.

Democrats ***Republicans***
Independents

243. HR 2500. Fiscal 2002 Commerce-Justice-State Appropriations/ War Prisoners. Rohrabacher, R-Calif., amendment that would prohibit the use of funds in the bill for filing a court motion opposing a civil action against a Japanese individual or company for compensation where the plaintiff alleges slavery or forced labor while an American prisoner of war during World War II. Adopted 395-33: R 192-26; D 201-7 (ND 150-5, SD 51-2); I 2-0. July 18, 2001.

244. HR 2500. Fiscal 2002 Commerce-Justice-State Appropriations/ Background Checks. Moran, D-Va., amendment that would prohibit the use of funds in the bill to destroy national instant criminal background check system records within 90 days of their creation. Rejected 161-268: R 14-205; D 147-61 (ND 125-30, SD 22-31); I 0-2. July 18, 2001.

245. HR 2500. Fiscal 2002 Commerce-Justice-State Appropriations/ U.N. Contributions. Paul, R-Texas, amendment that would prohibit the use of funds in the bill for U.S. contributions to the United Nations or any of its affiliates. Rejected 62-364: R 56-164; D 5-199 (ND 3-148, SD 2-51); I 1-1. July 18, 2001.

246. HR 2500. Fiscal 2002 Commerce-Justice-State Appropriations/ U.N. Peacekeepers. Paul, R-Texas, amendment that would prohibit the use of funds in the bill for U.S. contributions to U.N. peacekeeping efforts. Rejected 71-359: R 67-153; D 3-205 (ND 2-153, SD 1-52); I 1-1. July 18, 2001.

247. HR 2500. Fiscal 2002 Commerce-Justice-State Appropriations/ WTO Proceedings. Waters, D-Calif., amendment that would prohibit the use of funds in the bill to start a World Trade Organization action challenging a law of a country not belonging to the Organization for Economic Cooperation and Development. Rejected 123-306: R 2-218; D 120-87 (ND 92-63, SD 28-24); I 1-1. July 18, 2001.

248. HR 2500. Fiscal 2002 Commerce-Justice-State Appropriations/ Passage. Passage of the bill that would appropriate $41.5 billion for the departments of Commerce, Justice and State and the federal judiciary and related agencies in fiscal 2002. Passed 408-19: R 203-16; D 203-3 (ND 150-3, SD 53-0); I 2-0. July 18, 2001.

249. Procedural Motion/Journal. Approval of the House journal of Wednesday, July 18, 2001. Approved 368-52: R 196-19; D 170-33 (ND 122-30, SD 48-3); I 2-0. July 19, 2001.

	243	244	245	246	247	248	249
ALABAMA							
1 *Callahan*	N	N	N	Y	N	Y	Y
2 *Everett*	Y	N	Y	N	Y	N	Y
3 *Riley*	Y	N	Y	Y	N	Y	N
4 *Aderholt*	Y	N	Y	N	Y	N	Y
5 Cramer	Y	N	N	N	Y	Y	Y
6 *Bachus*	Y	N	N	N	N	Y	Y
7 Hilliard	N	N	N	N	Y	Y	N
ALASKA							
AL *Young*	Y	N	Y	Y	N	Y	?
ARIZONA							
1 *Flake*	N	N	N	N	N	N	Y
2 Pastor	Y	Y	N	N	Y	Y	Y
3 *Stump*	N	N	Y	Y	N	Y	Y
4 *Shadegg*	Y	N	Y	N	Y	Y	Y
5 *Kolbe*	N	N	N	N	N	Y	Y
6 *Hayworth*	Y	N	N	Y	N	Y	Y
ARKANSAS							
1 Berry	Y	N	N	N	Y	Y	Y
2 Snyder	Y	N	N	N	N	Y	Y
3 *Hutchinson*	Y	N	N	N	N	Y	Y
4 Ross	Y	N	N	N	Y	Y	Y
CALIFORNIA							
1 Thompson	Y	N	N	N	N	Y	N
2 *Herger*	Y	N	N	N	N	Y	Y
3 *Ose*	Y	N	N	N	N	Y	Y
4 *Doolittle*	Y	N	Y	N	Y	N	Y
5 Matsui	Y	Y	N	N	N	Y	Y
6 Woolsey	Y	Y	N	Y	Y	Y	Y
7 Miller, George	Y	Y	N	N	Y	Y	N
8 Pelosi	Y	Y	N	N	Y	Y	Y
9 Lee	Y	Y	N	N	Y	Y	N
10 Tauscher	Y	Y	N	N	N	Y	Y
11 *Pombo*	Y	N	Y	N	Y	N	Y
12 Lantos	Y	Y	N	N	Y	Y	Y
13 Stark	Y	Y	N	N	Y	N	Y
14 Eshoo	Y	Y	N	N	N	Y	Y
15 Honda	Y	Y	N	N	N	Y	Y
16 Lofgren	Y	Y	N	N	N	Y	Y
17 Farr	Y	Y	N	N	Y	Y	Y
18 Condit	Y	N	N	N	N	Y	Y
19 *Radanovich*	Y	N	Y	N	Y	N	Y
20 Dooley	Y	Y	N	N	N	Y	Y
21 *Thomas*	Y	N	N	N	N	Y	Y
22 Capps	Y	Y	N	N	N	Y	Y
23 *Gallegly*	Y	N	N	N	N	Y	Y
24 Sherman	Y	Y	N	N	N	Y	Y
25 *McKeon*	Y	N	N	N	N	Y	Y
26 Berman	Y	Y	N	N	N	Y	Y
27 Schiff	Y	Y	N	N	N	Y	Y
28 *Dreier*	N	N	N	N	N	Y	Y
29 Waxman	Y	Y	N	N	Y	Y	Y
30 Becerra	Y	Y	N	N	Y	Y	Y
31 Solis	Y	Y	?	N	Y	Y	Y
32 Watson	Y	Y	N	N	Y	Y	Y
33 Roybal-Allard	Y	Y	N	N	Y	Y	Y
34 Napolitano	Y	Y	N	N	Y	Y	Y
35 Waters	Y	Y	N	N	Y	N	N
36 Harman	Y	Y	N	N	N	Y	?
37 Millender-McD.	+	+	−	−	+	Y	Y
38 *Horn*	Y	Y	N	N	N	Y	Y

	243	244	245	246	247	248	249
39 *Royce*	Y	N	Y	Y	N	N	Y
40 *Lewis*	Y	N	N	N	N	Y	Y
41 *Miller, Gary*	Y	N	N	N	N	Y	Y
42 Baca	Y	N	N	N	N	Y	Y
43 *Calvert*	Y	N	N	N	N	Y	Y
44 *Bono*	Y	N	N	N	N	Y	Y
45 *Rohrabacher*	Y	N	N	N	N	Y	Y
46 Sanchez	Y	Y	N	N	Y	Y	Y
47 *Cox*	N	N	N	N	N	N	Y
48 *Issa*	Y	N	N	N	N	Y	Y
49 Davis	Y	Y	N	N	N	Y	Y
50 Filner	Y	Y	N	Y	Y	Y	N
51 *Cunningham*	Y	N	N	N	N	Y	Y
52 *Hunter*	Y	N	N	Y	N	Y	Y
COLORADO							
1 DeGette	Y	Y	N	N	Y	?	Y
2 Udall	Y	Y	N	N	Y	Y	Y
3 *McInnis*	Y	N	N	N	Y	Y	Y
4 *Schaffer*	N	N	Y	N	N	N	N
5 *Hefley*	Y	N	Y	N	N	N	N
6 *Tancredo*	Y	N	Y	N	N	N	P
CONNECTICUT							
1 Larson	Y	Y	N	N	N	?	Y
2 *Simmons*	Y	N	N	N	N	Y	Y
3 DeLauro	Y	Y	N	N	N	Y	Y
4 *Shays*	Y	Y	N	N	N	?	Y
5 Maloney	Y	Y	N	N	N	Y	Y
6 *Johnson*	Y	N	N	N	N	Y	Y
DELAWARE							
AL *Castle*	N	Y	N	N	N	Y	Y
FLORIDA							
1 *Scarborough*	Y	?	Y	Y	N	N	Y
2 Boyd	Y	N	N	N	N	Y	Y
3 Brown	Y	Y	N	N	Y	Y	Y
4 *Crenshaw*	Y	N	N	N	N	Y	Y
5 Thurman	Y	N	N	N	N	Y	Y
6 *Stearns*	Y	N	N	N	Y	N	Y
7 *Mica*	Y	N	N	N	N	Y	Y
8 *Keller*	Y	N	Y	N	Y	Y	Y
9 *Bilirakis*	Y	N	Y	Y	N	Y	Y
10 *Young*	N	N	N	N	N	N	Y
11 Davis	Y	N	N	N	N	Y	Y
12 *Putnam*	Y	N	N	N	N	Y	Y
13 *Miller*	Y	N	N	N	N	Y	Y
14 *Goss*	Y	N	N	N	N	Y	Y
15 *Weldon*	Y	N	Y	N	N	N	Y
16 *Foley*	Y	N	Y	Y	N	Y	Y
17 Meek	Y	Y	N	N	Y	Y	?
18 *Ros-Lehtinen*	Y	N	N	N	N	Y	Y
19 Wexler	Y	Y	N	N	Y	Y	Y
20 Deutsch	Y	N	N	N	N	Y	Y
21 *Diaz-Balart*	Y	N	N	N	N	Y	Y
22 *Shaw*	Y	N	N	N	N	Y	Y
23 Hastings	N	Y	N	N	Y	Y	Y
GEORGIA							
1 *Kingston*	Y	N	Y	Y	N	Y	Y
2 Bishop	Y	N	N	N	N	Y	Y
3 *Collins*	Y	N	Y	N	Y	N	Y
4 McKinney	Y	N	N	N	Y	Y	?
5 Lewis	Y	Y	N	N	Y	Y	Y
6 *Isakson*	Y	N	N	N	N	Y	Y
7 *Barr*	Y	N	Y	N	Y	N	Y
8 *Chambliss*	Y	N	N	N	N	Y	Y
9 *Deal*	N	N	N	N	N	Y	Y
10 *Norwood*	Y	N	Y	N	Y	N	Y
11 *Linder*	Y	N	N	N	N	Y	Y
HAWAII							
1 Abercrombie	Y	Y	N	N	Y	Y	Y
2 Mink	Y	Y	N	N	Y	Y	Y
IDAHO							
1 *Otter*	Y	N	Y	Y	N	Y	Y
2 *Simpson*	Y	N	N	N	N	Y	Y
ILLINOIS							
1 Rush	Y	Y	N	N	Y	Y	Y
2 Jackson	Y	Y	N	N	Y	Y	Y
3 Lipinski	Y	N	N	Y	N	Y	Y
4 Gutierrez	Y	Y	N	N	Y	Y	Y
5 Blagojevich	Y	Y	N	N	Y	Y	Y
6 *Hyde*	N	N	N	N	N	Y	Y
7 Davis	Y	Y	N	N	Y	Y	Y
8 *Crane*	Y	N	Y	N	Y	N	Y
9 Schakowsky	Y	Y	N	N	Y	Y	Y
10 *Kirk*	N	N	N	N	N	Y	Y
11 *Weller*	Y	N	N	N	N	Y	Y
12 Costello	Y	N	N	N	N	Y	N
13 *Biggert*	Y	N	N	N	N	Y	Y

ND Northern Democrats   SD Southern Democrats

	243	244	245	246	247	248	249
14 ***Hastert***							
15 ***Johnson***	Y	N	N	N	N	Y	Y
16 ***Manzullo***	Y	N	Y	Y	N	Y	Y
17 Evans	Y	Y	N	N	Y	Y	Y
18 ***LaHood***	Y	N	N	N	N	Y	Y
19 Phelps	Y	N	N	N	N	Y	Y
20 ***Shimkus***	Y	N	N	N	N	Y	Y
INDIANA							
1 Visclosky	Y	Y	N	N	Y	Y	N
2 ***Pence***	Y	N	Y	Y	N	Y	Y
3 Roemer	Y	Y	N	N	N	Y	Y
4 ***Souder***	N	N	N	N	N	Y	Y
5 ***Buyer***	Y	N	N	N	N	Y	Y
6 ***Burton***	Y	N	Y	Y	N	Y	Y
7 ***Kerns***	Y	N	Y	Y	N	Y	Y
8 ***Hostettler***	Y	N	Y	Y	N	N	Y
9 Hill	Y	N	N	N	N	Y	Y
10 Carson	Y	Y	N	N	Y	Y	Y
IOWA							
1 ***Leach***	Y	Y	N	N	N	Y	?
2 ***Nussle***	Y	N	N	N	N	Y	Y
3 Boswell	Y	N	N	N	N	Y	Y
4 ***Ganske***	Y	N	N	N	N	Y	Y
5 ***Latham***	Y	N	N	N	N	Y	Y
KANSAS							
1 ***Moran***	Y	N	Y	Y	N	N	N
2 ***Ryun***	Y	N	Y	Y	N	Y	Y
3 Moore	Y	Y	N	N	N	Y	Y
4 ***Tiahrt***	Y	N	N	Y	N	Y	Y
KENTUCKY							
1 ***Whitfield***	Y	N	N	N	N	Y	N
2 ***Lewis***	Y	N	Y	N	N	Y	Y
3 ***Northup***	Y	N	N	N	N	Y	Y
4 Lucas	Y	N	N	N	N	Y	Y
5 ***Rogers***	Y	N	N	N	N	Y	Y
6 ***Fletcher***	Y	N	N	N	N	Y	Y
LOUISIANA							
1 ***Vitter***	Y	N	N	N	N	Y	Y
2 Jefferson	Y	Y	N	N	?	Y	Y
3 ***Tauzin***	Y	N	N	N	N	Y	Y
4 ***McCrery***	Y	N	N	N	N	Y	Y
5 ***Cooksey***	Y	N	N	N	N	Y	Y
6 ***Baker***	Y	N	N	N	N	Y	Y
7 John	Y	N	N	N	N	Y	Y
MAINE							
1 Allen	Y	Y	N	N	Y	Y	Y
2 Baldacci	Y	Y	N	N	Y	Y	Y
MARYLAND							
1 ***Gilchrest***	N	N	N	N	N	Y	Y
2 ***Ehrlich***	Y	N	N	N	N	Y	Y
3 Cardin	Y	Y	N	N	Y	Y	Y
4 Wynn	Y	Y	N	N	Y	Y	Y
5 Hoyer	Y	Y	N	N	Y	Y	Y
6 ***Bartlett***	Y	N	Y	Y	N	Y	Y
7 Cummings	Y	Y	N	N	Y	Y	Y
8 ***Morella***	Y	Y	N	N	Y	Y	Y
MASSACHUSETTS							
1 Olver	Y	Y	N	N	Y	Y	Y
2 Neal	Y	Y	N	N	N	Y	Y
3 McGovern	Y	Y	N	N	Y	Y	Y
4 Frank	Y	Y	N	N	N	Y	Y
5 Meehan	Y	Y	N	N	Y	Y	Y
6 Tierney	Y	Y	N	N	Y	?	Y
7 Markey	Y	Y	N	N	N	Y	Y
8 Capuano	Y	Y	N	N	Y	Y	N
9 Vacant							
10 Delahunt	Y	Y	N	N	N	Y	N
MICHIGAN							
1 Stupak	Y	N	N	N	Y	Y	N
2 ***Hoekstra***	Y	N	N	N	N	Y	Y
3 ***Ehlers***	Y	N	N	N	N	Y	Y
4 ***Camp***	Y	N	N	N	N	Y	Y
5 Barcia	Y	N	Y	N	Y	Y	Y
6 ***Upton***	Y	N	N	N	N	Y	Y
7 ***Smith***	N	N	N	Y	N	N	Y
8 ***Rogers***	Y	N	N	N	N	Y	Y
9 Kildee	Y	Y	N	N	Y	Y	Y
10 Bonior	Y	N	N	N	Y	Y	Y
11 ***Knollenberg***	Y	N	N	N	N	Y	Y
12 Levin	Y	Y	N	N	N	Y	Y
13 Rivers	Y	Y	N	N	Y	Y	Y
14 Conyers	Y	Y	N	N	Y	N	Y
15 Kilpatrick	Y	Y	N	N	Y	Y	Y
16 Dingell	Y	N	N	N	N	Y	Y
MINNESOTA							
1 ***Gutknecht***	Y	N	N	Y	N	Y	N
2 ***Kennedy***	Y	N	N	N	N	Y	N
3 ***Ramstad***	Y	Y	N	N	N	Y	N
4 McCollum	Y	Y	N	N	Y	Y	Y
5 Sabo	Y	Y	N	N	Y	Y	N
6 Luther	Y	Y	N	N	Y	Y	Y
7 Peterson	Y	N	Y	Y	N	Y	N
8 Oberstar	Y	N	N	N	Y	Y	N
MISSISSIPPI							
1 ***Wicker***	Y	N	N	N	N	Y	N
2 Thompson	Y	Y	N	N	Y	Y	N
3 ***Pickering***	Y	N	N	N	N	Y	Y
4 Shows	Y	N	N	N	N	Y	N
5 Taylor	Y	N	Y	Y	N	Y	N
MISSOURI							
1 Clay	Y	Y	N	N	Y	Y	Y
2 ***Akin***	Y	N	Y	Y	N	Y	Y
3 Gephardt	Y	Y	N	N	Y	Y	N
4 Skelton	Y	N	N	N	N	Y	Y
5 McCarthy	Y	Y	N	N	Y	Y	Y
6 ***Graves***	Y	N	N	N	N	Y	Y
7 ***Blunt***	N	N	N	N	N	Y	Y
8 ***Emerson***	Y	N	N	N	N	Y	Y
9 ***Hulshof***	Y	N	N	Y	N	Y	N
MONTANA							
AL ***Rehberg***	Y	N	N	N	N	Y	Y
NEBRASKA							
1 ***Bereuter***	Y	N	N	N	N	Y	Y
2 ***Terry***	Y	N	N	N	N	Y	Y
3 ***Osborne***	Y	N	N	N	N	Y	Y
NEVADA							
1 Berkley	Y	Y	N	N	Y	Y	?
2 ***Gibbons***	Y	N	Y	N	N	Y	Y
NEW HAMPSHIRE							
1 ***Sununu***	Y	N	N	N	N	Y	Y
2 ***Bass***	Y	N	N	N	N	Y	Y
NEW JERSEY							
1 Andrews	Y	Y	N	N	Y	Y	Y
2 ***LoBiondo***	Y	N	N	N	N	Y	N
3 ***Saxton***	Y	N	N	N	N	Y	Y
4 ***Smith***	Y	Y	N	N	N	Y	Y
5 ***Roukema***	Y	Y	N	N	N	Y	Y
6 Pallone	Y	Y	N	N	Y	Y	N
7 ***Ferguson***	Y	Y	N	N	N	Y	Y
8 Pascrell	Y	Y	N	N	N	Y	Y
9 Rothman	Y	Y	N	N	N	Y	Y
10 Payne	N	Y	N	N	Y	Y	Y
11 ***Frelinghuysen***	Y	N	N	N	N	Y	Y
12 Holt	Y	Y	N	N	N	Y	N
13 Menendez	Y	Y	N	N	N	Y	N
NEW MEXICO							
1 ***Wilson***	Y	N	N	N	N	Y	Y
2 ***Skeen***	Y	N	N	N	N	Y	Y
3 Udall	Y	Y	N	N	Y	Y	N
NEW YORK							
1 ***Grucci***	Y	Y	N	N	N	Y	Y
2 Israel	Y	Y	N	N	N	Y	Y
3 ***King***	Y	Y	N	N	N	Y	Y
4 McCarthy	Y	Y	N	N	Y	Y	Y
5 Ackerman	Y	Y	N	N	N	Y	Y
6 Meeks	N	Y	N	N	Y	Y	?
7 Crowley	Y	Y	N	N	Y	Y	N
8 Nadler	Y	Y	?	N	Y	Y	Y
9 Weiner	Y	Y	N	N	Y	Y	Y
10 Towns	Y	Y	N	N	Y	Y	Y
11 Owens	Y	Y	?	N	Y	Y	Y
12 Velázquez	Y	Y	N	N	Y	Y	Y
13 ***Fossella***	Y	N	N	N	N	Y	N
14 Maloney	Y	Y	N	N	Y	Y	Y
15 Rangel	Y	Y	N	N	Y	Y	Y
16 Serrano	Y	Y	N	N	Y	Y	Y
17 Engel	Y	Y	N	N	Y	Y	?
18 Lowey	Y	Y	N	N	Y	Y	Y
19 ***Kelly***	Y	N	N	N	N	Y	Y
20 ***Gilman***	Y	N	N	N	N	Y	Y
21 McNulty	Y	N	N	N	Y	Y	N
22 ***Sweeney***	Y	N	N	N	N	Y	Y
23 ***Boehlert***	Y	N	N	N	N	Y	Y
24 ***McHugh***	Y	N	N	N	N	Y	Y
25 ***Walsh***	Y	N	N	N	N	Y	Y
26 Hinchey	Y	Y	?	N	Y	Y	N
27 ***Reynolds***	Y	N	N	N	N	Y	Y
28 Slaughter	Y	Y	N	N	N	Y	N
29 LaFalce	Y	Y	N	N	Y	Y	Y
30 ***Quinn***	Y	Y	N	N	N	Y	Y
31 ***Houghton***	N	N	N	N	N	Y	Y
NORTH CAROLINA							
1 Clayton	Y	Y	N	N	Y	Y	Y
2 Etheridge	Y	N	N	N	N	Y	Y
3 ***Jones***	Y	N	Y	Y	N	Y	Y
4 Price	Y	Y	N	N	N	Y	Y
5 ***Burr***	Y	N	N	N	N	Y	Y
6 ***Coble***	Y	N	Y	Y	N	Y	Y
7 McIntyre	Y	N	N	N	N	Y	Y
8 ***Hayes***	Y	N	N	N	N	Y	Y
9 ***Myrick***	Y	N	N	Y	N	Y	Y
10 ***Ballenger***	Y	N	N	N	N	Y	Y
11 ***Taylor***	Y	N	Y	Y	N	Y	Y
12 Watt	Y	Y	N	N	Y	Y	Y
NORTH DAKOTA							
AL Pomeroy	Y	N	N	N	N	Y	Y
OHIO							
1 ***Chabot***	Y	N	N	N	N	Y	Y
2 ***Portman***	Y	N	N	N	N	Y	Y
3 Hall	Y	Y	N	N	N	Y	Y
4 ***Oxley***	Y	N	N	N	N	Y	Y
5 ***Gillmor***	Y	N	N	N	N	Y	N
6 Strickland	Y	N	N	N	Y	Y	Y
7 ***Hobson***	Y	N	N	N	N	Y	Y
8 ***Boehner***	Y	N	N	N	N	Y	Y
9 Kaptur	Y	Y	N	N	Y	Y	Y
10 Kucinich	Y	Y	N	N	Y	Y	N
11 Jones	Y	Y	N	N	Y	Y	Y
12 ***Tiberi***	Y	N	Y	Y	N	Y	Y
13 Brown	Y	Y	N	N	Y	Y	Y
14 Sawyer	Y	Y	N	N	Y	Y	Y
15 ***Pryce***	Y	N	N	N	N	Y	Y
16 ***Regula***	Y	N	N	N	N	Y	Y
17 Traficant	Y	N	Y	Y	N	Y	Y
18 ***Ney***	Y	N	Y	Y	N	Y	Y
19 ***LaTourette***	Y	N	N	Y	N	Y	Y
OKLAHOMA							
1 ***Largent***	N	N	N	N	N	Y	Y
2 Carson	Y	N	N	N	N	Y	Y
3 ***Watkins***	?	N	N	N	N	Y	Y
4 ***Watts***	N	N	N	N	N	Y	Y
5 ***Istook***	Y	N	Y	N	N	Y	?
6 ***Lucas***	Y	N	Y	Y	N	Y	Y
OREGON							
1 Wu	Y	Y	N	N	N	Y	Y
2 ***Walden***	Y	N	N	N	N	Y	Y
3 Blumenauer	N	Y	N	N	N	Y	Y
4 DeFazio	Y	N	N	N	Y	Y	N
5 Hooley	Y	Y	N	N	N	Y	Y
PENNSYLVANIA							
1 Brady	Y	Y	N	N	Y	Y	N
2 Fattah	Y	Y	N	N	Y	Y	Y
3 Borski	Y	Y	N	N	N	Y	N
4 ***Hart***	Y	N	N	N	N	Y	Y
5 ***Peterson***	Y	N	N	N	N	Y	Y
6 Holden	Y	N	N	N	N	Y	Y
7 ***Weldon***	Y	N	N	N	N	Y	Y
8 ***Greenwood***	Y	N	N	N	N	Y	Y
9 ***Shuster, Bill***	Y	N	Y	Y	N	Y	Y
10 ***Sherwood***	Y	N	N	N	N	Y	Y
11 Kanjorski	Y	N	N	N	N	Y	Y
12 Murtha	Y	N	N	N	N	Y	Y
13 Hoeffel	Y	Y	N	N	N	Y	Y
14 Coyne	Y	Y	N	N	Y	Y	Y
15 ***Toomey***	Y	N	N	N	N	Y	Y
16 ***Pitts***	Y	N	N	N	N	Y	Y
17 ***Gekas***	Y	N	N	N	N	Y	Y
18 Doyle	Y	Y	N	N	Y	Y	Y
19 ***Platts***	Y	N	N	N	N	Y	?
20 Mascara	Y	N	N	N	N	Y	Y
21 ***English***	?	N	N	N	N	Y	N
RHODE ISLAND							
1 Kennedy	Y	Y	N	N	Y	Y	Y
2 Langevin	Y	Y	N	N	Y	Y	Y
SOUTH CAROLINA							
1 ***Brown***	Y	N	N	N	N	Y	Y
2 ***Spence***	?	?	?	?	?	?	?
3 ***Graham***	Y	N	N	N	N	Y	Y
4 ***DeMint***	Y	N	Y	Y	N	Y	Y
5 Spratt	Y	N	N	N	N	Y	Y
6 Clyburn	Y	Y	N	N	Y	Y	Y
SOUTH DAKOTA							
AL ***Thune***	Y	N	N	N	N	Y	Y
TENNESSEE							
1 ***Jenkins***	Y	N	N	Y	N	Y	Y
2 ***Duncan***	Y	N	Y	Y	N	N	Y
3 ***Wamp***	Y	N	N	Y	N	Y	N
4 ***Hilleary***	Y	N	N	Y	N	Y	N
5 Clement	Y	N	N	N	Y	Y	Y
6 Gordon	Y	N	N	N	N	Y	Y
7 ***Bryant***	Y	N	N	Y	N	Y	Y
8 Tanner	Y	N	N	N	N	Y	Y
9 Ford	Y	Y	N	N	Y	Y	Y
TEXAS							
1 Sandlin	Y	N	N	N	Y	Y	Y
2 Turner	Y	N	N	N	Y	Y	Y
3 ***Johnson, Sam***	Y	N	N	Y	N	Y	Y
4 Hall	Y	N	Y	N	N	Y	Y
5 ***Sessions***	Y	N	Y	Y	N	Y	Y
6 ***Barton***	Y	N	Y	Y	N	Y	Y
7 ***Culberson***	Y	N	Y	N	N	Y	Y
8 ***Brady***	Y	N	N	N	N	Y	Y
9 Lampson	Y	N	N	N	Y	Y	Y
10 Doggett	Y	Y	N	N	N	Y	Y
11 Edwards	Y	N	N	N	N	Y	Y
12 ***Granger***	N	N	N	N	N	Y	Y
13 ***Thornberry***	Y	N	N	N	N	Y	Y
14 ***Paul***	Y	N	Y	Y	Y	N	Y
15 Hinojosa	?	?	?	?	?	?	?
16 Reyes	Y	N	N	N	Y	Y	Y
17 Stenholm	Y	N	N	N	N	Y	Y
18 Jackson-Lee	Y	Y	N	N	Y	Y	Y
19 ***Combest***	N	N	Y	Y	N	Y	Y
20 Gonzalez	Y	Y	N	N	Y	Y	Y
21 ***Smith***	Y	N	N	N	N	Y	Y
22 ***DeLay***	Y	N	Y	Y	N	Y	Y
23 ***Bonilla***	Y	N	N	Y	N	Y	Y
24 Frost	Y	N	N	N	N	Y	Y
25 Bentsen	Y	Y	N	N	N	Y	Y
26 ***Armey***	Y	N	Y	N	N	Y	Y
27 Ortiz	Y	N	N	N	Y	Y	Y
28 Rodriguez	Y	Y	N	N	Y	Y	Y
29 Green	Y	N	N	N	Y	Y	Y
30 Johnson, E.B.	Y	Y	N	N	Y	Y	Y
UTAH							
1 ***Hansen***	N	N	N	N	N	Y	Y
2 Matheson	Y	N	N	N	N	Y	Y
3 ***Cannon***	N	N	Y	Y	N	Y	Y
VERMONT							
AL *Sanders*	Y	N	N	N	Y	Y	Y
VIRGINIA							
1 ***Davis, Jo Ann***	Y	N	N	Y	N	Y	Y
2 ***Schrock***	Y	N	N	N	N	Y	Y
3 Scott	Y	Y	N	N	Y	Y	Y
4 ***Forbes***	Y	N	N	N	N	Y	Y
5 *Goode*	Y	N	Y	Y	N	Y	Y
6 ***Goodlatte***	Y	N	N	N	N	Y	Y
7 ***Cantor***	Y	N	N	N	N	Y	Y
8 Moran	Y	Y	N	N	N	Y	Y
9 Boucher	Y	N	N	N	N	Y	Y
10 ***Wolf***	Y	N	N	N	N	Y	Y
11 ***Davis, T.***	N	Y	N	N	N	Y	Y
WASHINGTON							
1 Inslee	Y	Y	N	N	N	Y	Y
2 Larsen	Y	N	N	N	N	Y	N
3 Baird	Y	N	N	N	N	Y	N
4 ***Hastings***	Y	N	N	Y	N	Y	Y
5 ***Nethercutt***	N	N	N	Y	N	Y	Y
6 Dicks	N	Y	N	N	N	Y	Y
7 McDermott	Y	Y	N	N	N	Y	N
8 ***Dunn***	Y	N	N	N	N	Y	Y
9 Smith	N	N	N	N	N	Y	Y
WEST VIRGINIA							
1 Mollohan	Y	N	N	N	N	Y	Y
2 ***Capito***	Y	N	N	N	N	Y	Y
3 Rahall	Y	N	N	N	Y	Y	Y
WISCONSIN							
1 ***Ryan***	Y	N	N	N	N	Y	Y
2 Baldwin	Y	Y	N	N	Y	Y	Y
3 Kind	Y	N	N	N	N	Y	Y
4 Kleczka	Y	Y	N	N	N	Y	Y
5 Barrett	Y	Y	N	N	Y	Y	Y
6 ***Petri***	N	N	N	N	N	N	Y
7 Obey	Y	N	N	N	Y	Y	Y
8 ***Green***	Y	N	N	N	N	Y	Y
9 ***Sensenbrenner***	N	N	Y	Y	N	N	Y
WYOMING							
AL ***Cubin***	N	N	Y	Y	N	Y	Y

Southern states - Ala., Ark., Fla., Ga., Ky., La., Miss., N.C., Okla., S.C., Tenn., Texas, Va.

250. HR 7. Faith-Based Initiatives/Previous Question. Pryce, R-Ohio, motion to order the previous question (thus ending debate and possibility of amendment) on adoption of the rule (H Res 196) on the bill that would allow religious organizations to compete with other non-governmental groups for federal funds to provide an expanded list of social services without abandoning their religious character; the bill also would provide $13.3 billion in tax breaks for charitable giving over 10 years. Motion agreed to 228-199: R 217-1; D 10-197 (ND 5-150, SD 5-47); I 1-1. July 19, 2001.

251. HR 7. Faith-Based Initiatives/Rule. Adoption of the rule (H Res 196) to provide for House floor consideration of the faith-based initiatives bill. Adopted 233-194: R 218-0; D 14-193 (ND 5-150, SD 9-43); I 1-1. July 19, 2001.

252. HR 7. Faith-Based Initiatives/Democratic Substitute. Rangel, D-N.Y., substitute amendment that would forbid federally funded religious social service providers from employment discrimination based on religion. It would disallow the pre-emption of any state or local civil rights law by any bill provision. It also would prohibit religious groups from conducting sectarian activities at the same time and place that they carry out federally funded social programs and would strike a bill provision allowing indirect aid to be used for religious purposes. It would offset the bill's tax break by reducing by 0.2 percent the rate reduction given to individuals in the top bracket in the recently enacted tax package. Rejected 168-261: R 0-220; D 167-40 (ND 131-23, SD 36-17); I 1-1. July 19, 2001.

253. HR 7. Faith-Based Initiatives/Recommit. Conyers, D-Mich., motion to recommit the bill to the Judiciary Committee with instructions to add language stating that federally funded religious service providers cannot discriminate based on religion and that no provisions supercede state or local civil rights laws. Motion rejected 195-234: R 4-216; D 190-17 (ND 147-7, SD 43-10); I 1-1. July 19, 2001.

254. HR 7. Faith-Based Initiatives/Passage. Passage of the bill that would allow religious organizations to compete with other non-governmental groups for federal funds to provide an expanded list of social services without abandoning their religious character; the bill also would provide $13.3 billion in tax breaks for charitable giving over 10 years. Passed 233-198: R 217-4; D 15-193 (ND 8-147, SD 7-46); I 1-1. A "yea" was a vote in support of the president's position. July 19, 2001.

255. H J Res 50. China NTR Disapproval/Passage. Passage of the joint resolution to deny the president's request to provide normal trade relations (formerly known as most-favored-nation trade status) for items produced in China for the period July 2001 through July 2002. Rejected 169-259: R 62-157; D 105-102 (ND 89-65, SD 16-37); I 2-0. A "nay" was a vote in support of the president's position. July 19, 2001.

Key

Y	Voted for (yea).
#	Paired for.
+	Announced for.
N	Voted against (nay).
X	Paired against.
−	Announced against.
P	Voted "present."
C	Voted "present" to avoid possible conflict of interest.
?	Did not vote or otherwise make a position known.

Democrats   **Republicans**
Independents

	250	251	252	253	254	255
ALABAMA						
1 *Callahan*	Y	Y	N	N	Y	N
2 *Everett*	Y	Y	N	N	Y	Y
3 *Riley*	Y	Y	N	N	Y	Y
4 *Aderholt*	Y	Y	N	N	Y	Y
5 Cramer	N	N	N	N	Y	N
6 *Bachus*	Y	Y	N	N	Y	N
7 Hilliard	N	N	Y	Y	N	Y
ALASKA						
AL *Young*	Y	Y	N	N	Y	Y
ARIZONA						
1 *Flake*	Y	Y	N	N	Y	N
2 Pastor	N	N	Y	Y	N	Y
3 *Stump*	Y	Y	N	N	N	N
4 *Shadegg*	Y	Y	N	N	Y	N
5 *Kolbe*	Y	Y	N	N	Y	N
6 *Hayworth*	Y	Y	N	N	Y	Y
ARKANSAS						
1 Berry	N	N	N	Y	N	N
2 Snyder	N	N	N	Y	N	N
3 *Hutchinson*	Y	Y	N	N	Y	N
4 Ross	N	N	N	N	N	Y
CALIFORNIA						
1 Thompson	N	N	N	Y	N	N
2 *Herger*	Y	Y	N	N	Y	N
3 *Ose*	Y	Y	N	N	Y	N
4 *Doolittle*	Y	Y	N	N	Y	N
5 Matsui	N	N	?	Y	N	N
6 Woolsey	N	N	Y	Y	N	Y
7 Miller, George	N	N	Y	Y	N	Y
8 Pelosi	N	N	Y	Y	N	Y
9 Lee	N	N	Y	Y	N	Y
10 Tauscher	N	N	N	Y	N	N
11 *Pombo*	Y	Y	N	N	Y	Y
12 Lantos	N	N	Y	Y	N	Y
13 Stark	N	N	Y	Y	N	Y
14 Eshoo	N	N	Y	Y	N	N
15 Honda	N	N	Y	Y	N	N
16 Lofgren	N	N	N	Y	N	N
17 Farr	N	N	Y	Y	N	N
18 Condit	N	N	Y	Y	Y	Y
19 *Radanovich*	Y	Y	N	N	Y	Y
20 Dooley	N	N	Y	Y	N	N
21 *Thomas*	Y	Y	N	N	Y	N
22 Capps	N	N	Y	Y	N	N
23 *Gallegly*	Y	Y	N	N	Y	N
24 Sherman	N	N	N	Y	N	Y
25 *McKeon*	Y	Y	N	N	Y	N
26 Berman	N	N	Y	Y	N	N
27 Schiff	N	N	N	Y	N	N
28 *Dreier*	Y	Y	N	N	Y	N
29 Waxman	N	N	Y	Y	N	N
30 Becerra	N	N	Y	Y	N	N
31 Solis	N	N	Y	Y	N	Y
32 Watson	N	N	Y	Y	N	N
33 Roybal-Allard	N	N	Y	Y	N	Y
34 Napolitano	N	N	Y	Y	N	N
35 Waters	N	N	Y	Y	N	Y
36 Harman	N	N	Y	Y	N	N
37 Millender-McD.	N	N	Y	Y	N	Y
38 *Horn*	Y	Y	N	N	Y	N
39 *Royce*	Y	Y	N	N	Y	Y
40 *Lewis*	Y	Y	N	N	Y	Y
41 *Miller, Gary*	Y	Y	N	N	Y	N
42 Baca	N	N	Y	Y	N	Y
43 *Calvert*	Y	Y	N	N	Y	N
44 *Bono*	Y	Y	N	N	Y	N
45 *Rohrabacher*	Y	Y	N	N	Y	N
46 Sanchez	N	N	N	Y	N	Y
47 *Cox*	Y	Y	N	N	Y	N
48 *Issa*	Y	Y	N	N	Y	N
49 Davis	N	N	N	Y	N	N
50 Filner	N	N	Y	Y	N	N
51 *Cunningham*	N	Y	N	Y	Y	N
52 *Hunter*	Y	Y	N	N	Y	Y
COLORADO						
1 DeGette	N	N	Y	Y	N	N
2 Udall	N	N	Y	Y	N	Y
3 *McInnis*	Y	Y	N	N	Y	N
4 *Schaffer*	Y	Y	N	N	Y	Y
5 *Hefley*	Y	Y	N	N	Y	Y
6 *Tancredo*	Y	Y	N	N	Y	Y
CONNECTICUT						
1 Larson	N	N	Y	Y	N	N
2 *Simmons*	Y	Y	N	N	Y	N
3 DeLauro	N	N	Y	Y	N	N
4 *Shays*	Y	Y	N	Y	Y	N
5 Maloney	N	N	Y	Y	N	N
6 *Johnson*	Y	?	N	N	Y	N
DELAWARE						
AL *Castle*	Y	Y	N	N	Y	N
FLORIDA						
1 *Scarborough*	Y	Y	N	N	Y	Y
2 Boyd	N	N	Y	Y	N	N
3 Brown	N	N	Y	Y	N	Y
4 *Crenshaw*	Y	Y	N	N	Y	N
5 Thurman	N	N	Y	Y	N	N
6 *Stearns*	Y	Y	N	N	Y	Y
7 *Mica*	Y	Y	N	N	Y	N
8 *Keller*	Y	Y	N	N	Y	N
9 *Bilirakis*	Y	Y	N	N	Y	Y
10 *Young*	Y	Y	N	N	Y	N
11 Davis	N	N	Y	Y	N	N
12 *Putnam*	Y	Y	N	N	Y	N
13 *Miller*	Y	Y	N	N	Y	N
14 *Goss*	Y	Y	N	N	Y	N
15 *Weldon*	Y	Y	N	N	Y	Y
16 *Foley*	Y	Y	N	N	Y	N
17 Meek	N	N	Y	Y	N	N
18 *Ros-Lehtinen*	Y	Y	N	N	Y	Y
19 Wexler	N	N	Y	Y	N	Y
20 Deutsch	N	N	Y	Y	N	N
21 *Diaz-Balart*	Y	Y	N	N	Y	Y
22 *Shaw*	Y	Y	N	N	Y	N
23 Hastings	N	N	Y	Y	N	Y
GEORGIA						
1 *Kingston*	Y	Y	N	N	Y	Y
2 Bishop	N	Y	Y	Y	N	N
3 *Collins*	Y	Y	N	N	Y	Y
4 McKinney	?	?	?	?	?	?
5 Lewis	N	N	Y	Y	N	N
6 *Isakson*	Y	Y	N	N	Y	N
7 *Barr*	Y	Y	N	N	Y	Y
8 *Chambliss*	Y	Y	N	N	Y	Y
9 *Deal*	Y	Y	N	N	Y	Y
10 *Norwood*	?	?	N	N	Y	Y
11 *Linder*	Y	Y	N	N	Y	N
HAWAII						
1 Abercrombie	N	N	Y	Y	N	Y
2 Mink	N	N	Y	Y	N	Y
IDAHO						
1 *Otter*	Y	Y	N	N	Y	N
2 *Simpson*	Y	Y	N	N	Y	N
ILLINOIS						
1 Rush	N	N	Y	Y	N	Y
2 Jackson	N	N	Y	Y	N	Y
3 Lipinski	Y	Y	N	N	Y	Y
4 Gutierrez	N	N	Y	Y	N	Y
5 Blagojevich	N	N	Y	Y	N	N
6 *Hyde*	Y	Y	N	N	Y	Y
7 Davis	N	N	Y	Y	N	Y
8 *Crane*	Y	Y	N	N	Y	N
9 Schakowsky	N	N	Y	Y	N	Y
10 *Kirk*	Y	Y	N	N	Y	N
11 *Weller*	Y	Y	N	N	Y	N
12 Costello	N	N	N	Y	N	Y
13 *Biggert*	Y	Y	N	N	Y	N

ND Northern Democrats   SD Southern Democrats

	250	251	252	253	254	255
14 *Hastert*					Y	N
15 *Johnson*	Y	Y	N	N	Y	N
16 *Manzullo*	Y	Y	N	N	N	N
17 Evans	N	N	Y	Y	N	Y
18 *LaHood*	Y	Y	N	N	Y	N
19 Phelps	N	N	N	N	Y	Y
20 *Shimkus*	Y	Y	N	N	Y	N
INDIANA						
1 Visclosky	N	N	Y	Y	N	Y
2 *Pence*	Y	Y	N	N	Y	N
3 Roemer	N	N	Y	Y	N	N
4 *Souder*	Y	Y	N	N	Y	Y
5 *Buyer*	Y	Y	N	N	Y	N
6 *Burton*	Y	Y	N	N	Y	Y
7 *Kerns*	Y	Y	N	N	Y	N
8 *Hostettler*	Y	Y	N	N	Y	Y
9 Hill	N	N	Y	Y	N	N
10 Carson	N	N	Y	Y	N	Y
IOWA						
1 *Leach*	Y	Y	N	Y	Y	N
2 *Nussle*	Y	Y	N	N	Y	N
3 Boswell	N	N	Y	Y	N	N
4 *Ganske*	Y	Y	N	N	Y	N
5 *Latham*	Y	Y	N	N	Y	N
KANSAS						
1 *Moran*	Y	Y	N	N	Y	N
2 *Ryun*	Y	Y	N	N	Y	N
3 Moore	N	N	N	Y	N	N
4 *Tiahrt*	Y	Y	N	N	Y	N
KENTUCKY						
1 *Whitfield*	Y	Y	N	N	Y	N
2 *Lewis*	Y	Y	N	N	Y	N
3 *Northup*	Y	Y	N	N	Y	N
4 Lucas	N	Y	N	N	Y	N
5 *Rogers*	Y	Y	N	N	Y	Y
6 *Fletcher*	Y	Y	N	N	Y	N
LOUISIANA						
1 *Vitter*	Y	Y	N	N	Y	N
2 Jefferson	N	N	Y	Y	N	N
3 *Tauzin*	Y	Y	N	N	Y	N
4 *McCrery*	Y	Y	N	N	Y	N
5 *Cooksey*	Y	Y	N	N	Y	N
6 *Baker*	Y	Y	N	N	Y	N
7 John	Y	N	N	N	N	N
MAINE						
1 Allen	N	N	Y	Y	N	N
2 Baldacci	N	N	Y	Y	N	Y
MARYLAND						
1 *Gilchrest*	Y	Y	N	N	Y	N
2 *Ehrlich*	Y	Y	N	N	Y	Y
3 Cardin	N	N	Y	Y	N	Y
4 Wynn	N	N	Y	Y	N	Y
5 Hoyer	N	N	Y	Y	N	Y
6 *Bartlett*	?	Y	N	N	Y	Y
7 Cummings	N	N	Y	Y	N	Y
8 *Morella*	Y	Y	N	Y	N	N
MASSACHUSETTS						
1 Olver	N	N	Y	Y	N	Y
2 Neal	N	N	Y	Y	N	N
3 McGovern	N	N	Y	Y	N	N
4 Frank	N	N	Y	Y	N	Y
5 Meehan	N	N	Y	?	N	N
6 Tierney	N	N	Y	Y	N	Y
7 Markey	N	N	Y	Y	N	Y
8 Capuano	N	N	Y	Y	N	Y
9 Vacant						
10 Delahunt	N	N	Y	Y	N	Y
MICHIGAN						
1 Stupak	N	N	Y	Y	N	Y
2 *Hoekstra*	Y	Y	N	N	Y	N
3 *Ehlers*	Y	Y	N	N	Y	N
4 *Camp*	Y	Y	N	N	Y	N
5 Barcia	N	N	Y	Y	N	Y
6 *Upton*	Y	Y	N	N	Y	N
7 *Smith*	Y	Y	N	N	Y	N
8 *Rogers*	Y	Y	N	N	Y	N
9 Kildee	N	N	Y	Y	N	Y
10 Bonior	N	N	Y	Y	N	Y
11 *Knollenberg*	Y	Y	N	N	Y	N
12 Levin	N	N	Y	Y	N	N
13 Rivers	N	N	Y	Y	N	Y
14 Conyers	N	N	Y	Y	N	N
15 Kilpatrick	N	N	Y	Y	N	Y
16 Dingell	N	N	Y	Y	N	Y

	250	251	252	253	254	255
MINNESOTA						
1 *Gutknecht*	Y	Y	N	N	Y	N
2 *Kennedy*	Y	Y	N	N	Y	N
3 *Ramstad*	Y	Y	N	N	Y	N
4 McCollum	N	N	Y	Y	N	Y
5 Sabo	N	N	Y	Y	N	Y
6 Luther	N	N	Y	Y	N	N
7 Peterson	N	N	N	N	N	Y
8 Oberstar	N	N	N	Y	N	N
MISSISSIPPI						
1 *Wicker*	Y	Y	N	N	Y	N
2 Thompson	N	N	Y	Y	N	Y
3 *Pickering*	Y	Y	N	N	Y	Y
4 Shows	Y	Y	N	N	Y	N
5 Taylor	Y	N	N	N	N	Y
MISSOURI						
1 Clay	N	N	Y	Y	N	Y
2 *Akin*	Y	Y	N	N	Y	Y
3 Gephardt	N	N	Y	Y	N	Y
4 Skelton	N	Y	N	N	Y	N
5 McCarthy	N	N	Y	Y	N	N
6 *Graves*	Y	Y	N	N	Y	N
7 *Blunt*	Y	Y	N	N	Y	N
8 *Emerson*	Y	Y	N	N	Y	N
9 *Hulshof*	Y	Y	N	N	Y	N
MONTANA						
AL *Rehberg*	Y	Y	N	N	Y	N
NEBRASKA						
1 *Bereuter*	Y	Y	N	N	Y	N
2 *Terry*	Y	Y	N	N	Y	N
3 *Osborne*	Y	Y	N	N	Y	N
NEVADA						
1 Berkley	N	N	Y	Y	N	Y
2 *Gibbons*	Y	Y	N	N	Y	N
NEW HAMPSHIRE						
1 *Sununu*	Y	Y	N	N	Y	N
2 *Bass*	Y	Y	N	N	Y	N
NEW JERSEY						
1 Andrews	N	N	Y	Y	N	N
2 *LoBiondo*	Y	Y	N	N	Y	Y
3 *Saxton*	Y	Y	N	N	Y	?
4 *Smith*	Y	Y	N	N	Y	Y
5 *Roukema*	Y	Y	N	N	Y	N
6 Pallone	N	N	Y	Y	N	Y
7 *Ferguson*	Y	Y	N	N	Y	N
8 Pascrell	N	N	Y	Y	N	Y
9 Rothman	N	N	Y	Y	N	Y
10 Payne	N	N	Y	Y	N	Y
11 *Frelinghuysen*	Y	Y	N	N	Y	N
12 Holt	N	N	Y	Y	N	N
13 Menendez	N	N	Y	Y	N	Y
NEW MEXICO						
1 *Wilson*	Y	Y	N	N	Y	N
2 *Skeen*	Y	Y	N	N	Y	N
3 Udall	N	N	Y	Y	N	Y
NEW YORK						
1 *Grucci*	Y	Y	N	N	Y	N
2 Israel	N	N	N	Y	N	N
3 *King*	Y	Y	N	N	Y	Y
4 McCarthy	N	N	Y	Y	N	N
5 Ackerman	N	N	Y	Y	N	N
6 Meeks	N	N	Y	Y	N	N
7 Crowley	N	N	Y	Y	N	N
8 Nadler	N	N	Y	Y	N	Y
9 Weiner	N	N	Y	Y	N	N
10 Towns	N	N	Y	Y	N	Y
11 Owens	N	N	Y	Y	N	Y
12 Velázquez	N	N	Y	Y	N	Y
13 *Fossella*	Y	Y	N	N	Y	N
14 Maloney	N	N	Y	Y	N	N
15 Rangel	N	N	Y	Y	N	Y
16 Serrano	N	N	Y	Y	N	N
17 Engel	?	?	?	?	?	?
18 Lowey	N	N	Y	Y	N	N
19 *Kelly*	Y	Y	N	N	Y	N
20 *Gilman*	Y	Y	N	N	Y	Y
21 McNulty	N	N	Y	Y	N	N
22 *Sweeney*	Y	Y	N	N	Y	N
23 *Boehlert*	Y	Y	N	N	Y	N
24 *McHugh*	Y	Y	N	N	Y	N
25 *Walsh*	Y	Y	N	N	Y	N
26 Hinchey	N	N	Y	Y	N	Y
27 *Reynolds*	Y	Y	N	N	Y	N
28 Slaughter	N	N	Y	Y	N	N
29 LaFalce	N	N	Y	Y	Y	N

	250	251	252	253	254	255
30 *Quinn*	Y	Y	N	N	Y	Y
31 *Houghton*	Y	Y	N	N	Y	N
NORTH CAROLINA						
1 Clayton	N	N	Y	Y	N	Y
2 Etheridge	N	N	Y	Y	N	N
3 *Jones*	Y	Y	N	N	Y	Y
4 Price	N	N	Y	Y	N	N
5 *Burr*	Y	Y	N	N	Y	Y
6 *Coble*	Y	Y	N	N	Y	Y
7 McIntyre	Y	Y	N	N	Y	Y
8 *Hayes*	Y	Y	N	N	Y	Y
9 *Myrick*	Y	Y	N	N	Y	N
10 *Ballenger*	Y	Y	N	N	Y	N
11 *Taylor*	Y	Y	N	N	Y	Y
12 Watt	N	N	Y	Y	N	N
NORTH DAKOTA						
AL Pomeroy	N	N	Y	Y	N	N
OHIO						
1 *Chabot*	Y	Y	N	N	Y	N
2 *Portman*	Y	Y	N	N	Y	N
3 Hall	Y	Y	N	N	Y	Y
4 *Oxley*	Y	Y	N	N	Y	N
5 *Gillmor*	Y	Y	N	N	Y	Y
6 Strickland	N	N	N	N	Y	Y
7 *Hobson*	Y	Y	N	N	Y	Y
8 *Boehner*	Y	Y	N	N	Y	N
9 Kaptur	N	N	Y	Y	N	Y
10 Kucinich	N	N	Y	Y	N	Y
11 Jones	N	N	Y	Y	N	Y
12 *Tiberi*	Y	Y	N	N	Y	N
13 Brown	N	N	Y	Y	N	Y
14 Sawyer	N	N	Y	Y	N	Y
15 *Pryce*	Y	Y	N	N	Y	N
16 *Regula*	Y	Y	N	N	Y	Y
17 Traficant	Y	Y	N	N	Y	Y
18 *Ney*	Y	Y	N	N	Y	Y
19 *LaTourette*	Y	Y	N	N	Y	Y
OKLAHOMA						
1 *Largent*	Y	Y	N	N	Y	N
2 Carson	N	N	Y	Y	N	N
3 *Watkins*	Y	Y	N	N	Y	N
4 *Watts*	Y	Y	N	N	Y	N
5 *Istook*	Y	Y	N	N	Y	N
6 *Lucas*	Y	Y	N	N	Y	N
OREGON						
1 Wu	Y	N	Y	Y	N	Y
2 *Walden*	Y	Y	N	N	Y	N
3 Blumenauer	N	N	Y	Y	N	?
4 DeFazio	N	N	Y	Y	N	Y
5 Hooley	N	N	Y	Y	N	N
PENNSYLVANIA						
1 Brady	N	N	Y	Y	N	Y
2 Fattah	N	N	Y	Y	N	Y
3 Borski	N	N	Y	Y	N	Y
4 *Hart*	Y	Y	N	N	Y	Y
5 *Peterson*	Y	Y	N	N	Y	N
6 Holden	N	N	Y	Y	N	Y
7 *Weldon*	Y	Y	N	N	Y	N
8 *Greenwood*	Y	Y	N	N	Y	N
9 *Shuster, Bill*	Y	Y	N	N	Y	N
10 *Sherwood*	Y	Y	N	N	Y	N
11 Kanjorski	N	N	Y	Y	N	Y
12 Murtha	N	N	N	Y	N	N
13 Hoeffel	N	N	N	Y	N	Y
14 Coyne	N	N	Y	Y	N	Y
15 *Toomey*	Y	Y	N	N	Y	N
16 *Pitts*	Y	Y	N	N	Y	N
17 *Gekas*	Y	Y	N	N	Y	N
18 Doyle	N	N	Y	Y	N	Y
19 *Platts*	Y	Y	N	N	Y	N
20 Mascara	N	N	Y	Y	N	Y
21 *English*	Y	Y	N	N	Y	N
RHODE ISLAND						
1 Kennedy	N	N	Y	Y	N	Y
2 Langevin	N	N	Y	Y	N	Y
SOUTH CAROLINA						
1 *Brown*	Y	Y	N	N	Y	N
2 *Spence*	?	?	?	?	?	?
3 *Graham*	Y	Y	N	N	Y	Y
4 *DeMint*	Y	Y	N	N	Y	N
5 Spratt	N	N	Y	Y	N	Y
6 Clyburn	N	N	Y	Y	N	N
SOUTH DAKOTA						
AL *Thune*	Y	Y	N	N	Y	N

	250	251	252	253	254	255
TENNESSEE						
1 *Jenkins*	Y	Y	N	N	Y	Y
2 *Duncan*	Y	Y	N	N	Y	Y
3 *Wamp*	Y	Y	N	N	Y	Y
4 *Hilleary*	Y	Y	N	N	Y	Y
5 Clement	N	Y	N	Y	Y	N
6 Gordon	N	Y	Y	Y	Y	N
7 *Bryant*	Y	Y	N	N	Y	N
8 Tanner	N	N	Y	Y	N	N
9 Ford	N	Y	Y	Y	N	N
TEXAS						
1 Sandlin	N	N	N	Y	N	Y
2 Turner	N	N	N	N	N	N
3 *Johnson, Sam*	Y	Y	N	N	Y	N
4 Hall	Y	Y	N	N	Y	N
5 *Sessions*	Y	Y	N	N	Y	N
6 *Barton*	Y	Y	N	N	Y	Y
7 *Culberson*	Y	Y	N	N	Y	N
8 *Brady*	Y	Y	N	N	Y	N
9 Lampson	N	N	Y	Y	N	N
10 Doggett	N	N	N	Y	N	N
11 Edwards	N	N	Y	Y	N	N
12 *Granger*	Y	Y	N	N	Y	N
13 *Thornberry*	Y	Y	N	N	Y	N
14 *Paul*	Y	Y	N	N	N	N
15 Hinojosa	?	?	N	Y	N	N
16 Reyes	N	N	Y	Y	N	Y
17 Stenholm	N	N	N	N	N	N
18 Jackson-Lee	N	Y	Y	Y	N	Y
19 *Combest*	Y	Y	N	N	Y	N
20 Gonzalez	N	N	Y	Y	N	N
21 *Smith*	Y	Y	N	N	Y	N
22 *DeLay*	Y	Y	N	N	Y	?
23 *Bonilla*	Y	Y	N	N	Y	N
24 Frost	N	N	Y	Y	N	N
25 Bentsen	N	N	N	Y	N	N
26 *Armey*	Y	Y	N	N	Y	N
27 Ortiz	N	N	Y	Y	N	N
28 Rodriguez	N	N	Y	Y	N	N
29 Green	N	N	Y	Y	N	Y
30 Johnson, E.B.	N	N	Y	Y	N	N
UTAH						
1 *Hansen*	Y	Y	N	N	Y	Y
2 Matheson	Y	Y	Y	Y	N	N
3 *Cannon*	Y	Y	N	N	Y	N
VERMONT						
AL *Sanders*	N	N	Y	Y	N	Y
VIRGINIA						
1 *Davis, Jo Ann*	Y	Y	N	N	Y	Y
2 *Schrock*	Y	Y	N	N	Y	N
3 Scott	N	N	Y	Y	N	Y
4 *Forbes*	Y	Y	N	N	Y	N
5 *Goode*	Y	Y	N	N	Y	Y
6 *Goodlatte*	Y	Y	N	N	Y	N
7 *Cantor*	Y	Y	N	N	Y	N
8 Moran	N	N	Y	Y	N	N
9 Boucher	N	N	Y	Y	N	N
10 *Wolf*	Y	Y	N	N	Y	Y
11 *Davis, T.*	Y	Y	N	N	Y	N
WASHINGTON						
1 Inslee	N	N	Y	Y	N	N
2 Larsen	N	N	Y	Y	N	N
3 Baird	N	N	Y	Y	N	N
4 *Hastings*	Y	Y	N	N	Y	N
5 *Nethercutt*	Y	Y	N	N	Y	N
6 Dicks	N	N	Y	Y	N	N
7 McDermott	N	N	N	Y	N	N
8 *Dunn*	Y	Y	N	N	Y	N
9 Smith	N	N	Y	Y	N	N
WEST VIRGINIA						
1 Mollohan	N	N	N	N	Y	Y
2 *Capito*	Y	Y	N	N	Y	Y
3 Rahall	N	N	Y	Y	N	Y
WISCONSIN						
1 *Ryan*	Y	Y	N	N	Y	N
2 Baldwin	N	N	Y	Y	N	Y
3 Kind	N	N	Y	Y	N	N
4 Kleczka	N	N	Y	Y	N	N
5 Barrett	N	N	Y	Y	N	N
6 *Petri*	Y	Y	N	N	Y	N
7 Obey	N	N	Y	Y	N	Y
8 *Green*	Y	Y	N	N	Y	N
9 *Sensenbrenner*	Y	Y	N	N	Y	Y
WYOMING						
AL *Cubin*	Y	Y	N	N	Y	Y

Southern states - Ala., Ark., Fla., Ga., Ky., La., Miss., N.C., Okla., S.C., Tenn., Texas, Va.

Key

256. HR 2216. Fiscal 2001 Supplemental Appropriations/Conference Report. Adoption of the conference report on the $6.5 billion bill, which would provide $5.8 billion for the military, primarily for readiness, training and operations. The agreement includes $389 million for disaster aid, $300 million for low-income energy assistance, $161 million for the Title I, Education for the Disadvantaged program, and $116 million for mailing tax rebate checks. Adopted (thus sent to the Senate) 375-30: R 190-18; D 184-11 (ND 135-11, SD 49-0); I 1-1. A "yea" was a vote in support of the president's position. July 20, 2001.

257. HR 2137. Criminal Law Technical Corrections/Passage. Sensenbrenner, R-Wis., motion to suspend the rules and pass the bill that would make over 60 technical changes to various criminal statutes. Motion agreed to 374-0: R 195-0; D 177-0 (ND 125-0, SD 52-0); I 2-0. A two-thirds majority of those present and voting (250 in this case) is required for passage under suspension of the rules. July 23, 2001.

258. HR 1892. Immigrant Affidavit/Passage. Sensenbrenner, R-Wis., motion to suspend the rules and pass the bill that would authorize close family members of a sponsor of a permanent residency application to sign an affidavit of financial support if the sponsor dies and if the attorney general decides the application should not be revoked. Motion agreed to 379-0: R 199-0; D 178-0 (ND 126-0, SD 52-0); I 2-0. A two-thirds majority of those present and voting (253 in this case) is required for passage under suspension of the rules. July 23, 2001.

259. S 468. James Corman Building/Passage. Cooksey, R-La., motion to suspend the rules and pass the bill that would name a federal building in Van Nuys, Calif., the "James C. Corman Federal Building." Motion agreed to 381-0: R 200-0; D 179-0 (ND 127-0, SD 52-0); I 2-0. A two-thirds majority of those present and voting (254 in this case) is required for passage under suspension of the rules. July 23, 2001.

260. HR 2506. Fiscal 2002 Foreign Operations Appropriations/Ex-Im Bank. Visclosky, D-Ind., amendment that would reduce funding for the Export-Import Bank's subsidy account by $15 million and its administrative expenses by $3 million. It would increase by $18 million the Child Survival and Health Programs Fund, with $13 million going toward HIV/AIDS funding and $5 million toward Vulnerable Children programs. Adopted 258-162: R 87-128; D 169-34 (ND 124-26, SD 45-8); I 2-0. July 24, 2001.

261. HR 2506. Fiscal 2002 Foreign Operations Appropriations/Ex-Im Bank. Paul, R-Texas, amendment that would eliminate the subsidy appropriation account for the Export-Import Bank. Rejected 47-375: R 40-177; D 6-197 (ND 2-149, SD 4-48); I 1-1. July 24, 2001.

	256	257	258	259	260	261
ALABAMA						
1 *Callahan*	Y	?	?	?	N	N
2 *Everett*	Y	Y	Y	Y	N	N
3 *Riley*	Y	+	+	+	Y	N
4 *Aderholt*	Y	Y	Y	Y	Y	N
5 Cramer	Y	Y	Y	Y	N	N
6 *Bachus*	Y	Y	Y	Y	Y	N
7 Hilliard	Y	Y	Y	Y	Y	Y
ALASKA						
AL *Young*	?	Y	Y	Y	Y	N
ARIZONA						
1 *Flake*	N	Y	Y	Y	Y	Y
2 Pastor	Y	Y	Y	Y	N	N
3 *Stump*	Y	Y	Y	Y	N	N
4 *Shadegg*	N	Y	Y	Y	N	Y
5 *Kolbe*	Y	Y	Y	Y	N	N
6 *Hayworth*	Y	Y	Y	Y	Y	Y
ARKANSAS						
1 Berry	Y	Y	Y	Y	Y	N
2 Snyder	Y	Y	Y	Y	N	N
3 *Hutchinson*	Y	Y	Y	Y	?	N
4 Ross	Y	Y	Y	Y	Y	N
CALIFORNIA						
1 Thompson	Y	Y	Y	Y	Y	N
2 *Herger*	Y	?	Y	Y	N	Y
3 *Ose*	Y	Y	Y	Y	N	N
4 *Doolittle*	Y	Y	Y	Y	Y	Y
5 Matsui	Y	Y	Y	Y	Y	N
6 Woolsey	Y	Y	Y	Y	Y	N
7 Miller, George	Y	Y	Y	Y	N	N
8 Pelosi	Y	?	?	?	Y	N
9 Lee	N	Y	Y	Y	Y	N
10 Tauscher	Y	Y	Y	Y	N	N
11 *Pombo*	Y	Y	Y	Y	Y	Y
12 Lantos	Y	Y	Y	Y	Y	N
13 Stark	N	?	?	?	Y	N
14 Eshoo	Y	Y	Y	Y	N	N
15 Honda	Y	Y	Y	Y	N	N
16 Lofgren	Y	Y	Y	Y	N	N
17 Farr	Y	Y	Y	Y	N	N
18 Condit	Y	Y	Y	Y	N	N
19 *Radanovich*	Y	Y	Y	Y	N	N
20 Dooley	Y	Y	Y	Y	N	N
21 *Thomas*	?	Y	Y	Y	N	N
22 Capps	Y	+	+	+	Y	N
23 *Gallegly*	Y	?	?	?	?	?
24 Sherman	Y	?	?	?	Y	N
25 *McKeon*	Y	Y	Y	Y	N	N
26 Berman	Y	?	?	?	Y	N
27 Schiff	Y	Y	Y	Y	Y	N
28 *Dreier*	?	Y	Y	Y	N	N
29 Waxman	Y	?	?	?	Y	N
30 Becerra	Y	Y	Y	Y	Y	N
31 Solis	Y	+	+	+	Y	N
32 Watson	Y	Y	Y	Y	Y	N
33 Roybal-Allard	Y	+	+	+	Y	N
34 Napolitano	Y	Y	Y	Y	Y	N
35 Waters	Y	?	?	?	Y	N
36 Harman	Y	Y	Y	Y	N	N
37 Millender-McD.	Y	Y	Y	Y	N	N
38 *Horn*	Y	Y	Y	Y	+	N

	256	257	258	259	260	261
39 *Royce*	N	Y	Y	Y	Y	Y
40 *Lewis*	Y	Y	Y	Y	N	N
41 *Miller, Gary*	Y	?	?	?	N	N
42 Baca	Y	?	?	?	Y	N
43 *Calvert*	Y	Y	Y	Y	N	N
44 *Bono*	Y	Y	Y	Y	N	N
45 *Rohrabacher*	Y	Y	Y	Y	Y	N
46 Sanchez	Y	Y	Y	Y	N	N
47 *Cox*	Y	Y	Y	Y	N	Y
48 *Issa*	Y	Y	Y	Y	N	N
49 Davis	Y	Y	Y	Y	N	N
50 Filner	–	Y	Y	Y	Y	N
51 *Cunningham*	Y	Y	Y	Y	N	N
52 *Hunter*	Y	?	?	Y	Y	Y
COLORADO						
1 DeGette	Y	?	?	?	?	?
2 Udall	Y	Y	Y	Y	Y	N
3 *McInnis*	Y	Y	Y	Y	Y	N
4 *Schaffer*	N	Y	Y	Y	Y	Y
5 *Hefley*	Y	Y	Y	Y	N	N
6 *Tancredo*	N	Y	Y	Y	Y	Y
CONNECTICUT						
1 Larson	Y	Y	Y	Y	N	N
2 *Simmons*	Y	Y	Y	Y	N	N
3 DeLauro	Y	Y	Y	Y	N	N
4 *Shays*	N	Y	Y	Y	N	N
5 Maloney	Y	Y	Y	Y	N	N
6 *Johnson*	Y	Y	Y	Y	N	N
DELAWARE						
AL *Castle*	Y	Y	Y	Y	N	N
FLORIDA						
1 *Scarborough*	Y	?	?	?	?	?
2 Boyd	Y	Y	Y	Y	Y	N
3 Brown	?	Y	Y	Y	N	N
4 *Crenshaw*	Y	Y	Y	Y	N	N
5 Thurman	Y	Y	Y	Y	N	N
6 *Stearns*	Y	Y	Y	Y	N	N
7 *Mica*	Y	Y	Y	Y	N	N
8 *Keller*	Y	Y	Y	Y	N	N
9 *Bilirakis*	Y	Y	Y	Y	Y	N
10 *Young*	Y	Y	Y	Y	N	N
11 Davis	Y	Y	Y	Y	N	N
12 *Putnam*	Y	Y	Y	Y	N	N
13 *Miller*	?	Y	Y	Y	N	N
14 *Goss*	Y	Y	Y	Y	N	N
15 *Weldon*	N	Y	Y	Y	N	N
16 *Foley*	Y	Y	Y	Y	N	N
17 Meek	Y	Y	Y	Y	N	N
18 *Ros-Lehtinen*	Y	Y	Y	Y	N	N
19 Wexler	Y	Y	Y	Y	N	N
20 Deutsch	Y	Y	Y	Y	N	N
21 *Diaz-Balart*	Y	Y	Y	Y	N	N
22 *Shaw*	Y	Y	Y	Y	N	N
23 Hastings	Y	Y	Y	Y	Y	N
GEORGIA						
1 *Kingston*	Y	Y	Y	Y	N	N
2 Bishop	Y	Y	Y	Y	N	N
3 *Collins*	Y	Y	Y	Y	N	N
4 McKinney	?	Y	Y	Y	Y	Y
5 Lewis	?	Y	Y	Y	N	N
6 *Isakson*	Y	Y	Y	Y	N	N
7 *Barr*	Y	?	?	?	Y	Y
8 *Chambliss*	Y	?	?	?	N	N
9 *Deal*	Y	?	?	?	N	N
10 *Norwood*	Y	Y	Y	Y	N	N
11 *Linder*	Y	Y	Y	Y	N	N
HAWAII						
1 Abercrombie	Y	+	+	+	Y	N
2 Mink	Y	Y	Y	Y	Y	N
IDAHO						
1 *Otter*	Y	Y	Y	Y	N	Y
2 *Simpson*	Y	Y	Y	Y	N	N
ILLINOIS						
1 Rush	Y	?	?	?	Y	N
2 Jackson	Y	Y	Y	Y	Y	N
3 Lipinski	?	?	?	?	?	?
4 Gutierrez	Y	?	?	?	Y	N
5 Blagojevich	Y	Y	Y	Y	Y	N
6 *Hyde*	Y	Y	Y	Y	N	N
7 Davis	Y	Y	Y	Y	Y	N
8 *Crane*	?	?	?	?	N	Y
9 Schakowsky	Y	+	+	?	Y	N
10 *Kirk*	Y	Y	Y	Y	N	N
11 *Weller*	Y	Y	Y	Y	N	N
12 Costello	Y	Y	Y	Y	Y	N
13 *Biggert*	Y	Y	Y	Y	N	N

ND Northern Democrats   SD Southern Democrats

	256	257	258	259	260	261
14 ***Hastert***						
15 ***Johnson***	Y	Y	Y	Y	N	N
16 ***Manzullo***	Y	+	+	+	N	N
17 Evans	Y	Y	Y	Y	Y	N
18 ***LaHood***	Y	Y	Y	Y	Y	N
19 Phelps	Y	Y	Y	Y	Y	N
20 ***Shimkus***	Y	Y	Y	Y	Y	N
INDIANA						
1 Visclosky	Y	Y	Y	Y	Y	N
2 ***Pence***	Y	Y	Y	Y	Y	Y
3 Roemer	N	+	+	+	Y	N
4 ***Souder***	Y	Y	Y	Y	N	N
5 ***Buyer***	Y	Y	Y	Y	Y	N
6 ***Burton***	+	Y	Y	Y	N	Y
7 ***Kerns***	Y	Y	Y	Y	N	N
8 ***Hostettler***	Y	Y	Y	Y	Y	Y
9 Hill	Y	Y	Y	Y	Y	N
10 Carson	Y	?	?	?	Y	N
IOWA						
1 ***Leach***	Y	Y	Y	Y	N	N
2 ***Nussle***	Y	+	+	+	N	N
3 Boswell	Y	Y	Y	Y	N	N
4 ***Ganske***	Y	Y	Y	Y	N	N
5 ***Latham***	Y	Y	Y	Y	N	N
KANSAS						
1 ***Moran***	Y	Y	Y	Y	Y	N
2 ***Ryun***	Y	+	+	+	N	N
3 Moore	+	Y	Y	Y	N	N
4 ***Tiahrt***	Y	Y	Y	Y	N	N
KENTUCKY						
1 ***Whitfield***	Y	Y	Y	Y	Y	N
2 ***Lewis***	Y	Y	Y	Y	N	N
3 ***Northup***	Y	Y	Y	Y	N	N
4 Lucas	?	Y	Y	Y	Y	N
5 ***Rogers***	Y	Y	Y	Y	Y	N
6 ***Fletcher***	Y	Y	Y	Y	N	N
LOUISIANA						
1 ***Vitter***	Y	Y	Y	Y	N	N
2 Jefferson	Y	?	?	?	Y	N
3 ***Tauzin***	Y	?	?	?	N	N
4 ***McCrery***	?	Y	Y	Y	N	N
5 ***Cooksey***	Y	Y	Y	Y	N	N
6 ***Baker***	Y	Y	Y	Y	N	N
7 John	Y	Y	Y	Y	Y	N
MAINE						
1 Allen	Y	Y	Y	Y	Y	N
2 Baldacci	Y	Y	Y	Y	Y	N
MARYLAND						
1 ***Gilchrest***	Y	Y	Y	Y	N	N
2 ***Ehrlich***	?	Y	Y	Y	N	N
3 Cardin	Y	Y	Y	Y	Y	N
4 Wynn	Y	Y	?	?	Y	N
5 Hoyer	Y	Y	Y	Y	Y	N
6 ***Bartlett***	Y	Y	Y	Y	N	Y
7 Cummings	Y	Y	Y	Y	Y	N
8 ***Morella***	Y	Y	Y	Y	N	N
MASSACHUSETTS						
1 Olver	Y	Y	Y	Y	Y	N
2 Neal	Y	Y	Y	Y	Y	N
3 McGovern	Y	Y	Y	Y	Y	N
4 Frank	N	Y	Y	Y	Y	N
5 Meehan	Y	Y	Y	Y	?	?
6 Tierney	Y	Y	Y	Y	Y	N
7 Markey	Y	Y	Y	Y	Y	N
8 Capuano	Y	Y	Y	Y	Y	N
9 Vacant						
10 Delahunt	Y	?	?	?	?	?
MICHIGAN						
1 Stupak	N	Y	Y	Y	Y	N
2 ***Hoekstra***	N	?	Y	Y	Y	Y
3 ***Ehlers***	N	?	Y	Y	N	N
4 ***Camp***	Y	Y	Y	Y	N	N
5 Barcia	?	Y	Y	Y	Y	N
6 ***Upton***	N	Y	Y	Y	Y	N
7 ***Smith***	N	Y	Y	Y	Y	Y
8 ***Rogers***	Y	Y	Y	Y	Y	N
9 Kildee	Y	Y	Y	Y	Y	N
10 Bonior	Y	Y	Y	Y	Y	N
11 ***Knollenberg***	Y	Y	Y	Y	N	N
12 Levin	Y	Y	Y	Y	Y	N
13 Rivers	Y	Y	Y	Y	Y	N
14 Conyers	N	Y	Y	Y	Y	Y
15 Kilpatrick	Y	+	+	+	+	–
16 Dingell	Y	Y	Y	Y	Y	N

	256	257	258	259	260	261
MINNESOTA						
1 ***Gutknecht***	Y	Y	Y	Y	Y	N
2 ***Kennedy***	Y	Y	Y	Y	Y	N
3 ***Ramstad***	Y	Y	Y	Y	N	N
4 McCollum	Y	Y	Y	Y	Y	N
5 Sabo	Y	?	?	Y	?	N
6 Luther	Y	Y	Y	Y	Y	N
7 Peterson	Y	Y	Y	Y	Y	N
8 Oberstar	?	Y	Y	Y	Y	N
MISSISSIPPI						
1 ***Wicker***	Y	Y	Y	Y	N	N
2 Thompson	Y	Y	Y	Y	Y	N
3 ***Pickering***	Y	Y	Y	Y	Y	N
4 Shows	Y	Y	Y	Y	Y	N
5 Taylor	Y	Y	Y	Y	Y	Y
MISSOURI						
1 Clay	Y	Y	Y	Y	Y	N
2 ***Akin***	Y	Y	Y	Y	Y	Y
3 Gephardt	Y	Y	Y	Y	Y	N
4 Skelton	?	Y	Y	Y	Y	N
5 McCarthy	Y	Y	Y	Y	Y	N
6 ***Graves***	?	Y	Y	Y	N	N
7 ***Blunt***	Y	Y	Y	Y	N	N
8 ***Emerson***	Y	Y	Y	Y	Y	N
9 ***Hulshof***	?	Y	Y	Y	Y	N
MONTANA						
AL ***Rehberg***	Y	Y	Y	Y	Y	N
NEBRASKA						
1 ***Bereuter***	Y	Y	Y	Y	N	N
2 ***Terry***	Y	Y	Y	Y	N	N
3 ***Osborne***	Y	Y	Y	Y	N	N
NEVADA						
1 Berkley	Y	Y	Y	Y	Y	N
2 ***Gibbons***	Y	Y	Y	Y	Y	Y
NEW HAMPSHIRE						
1 ***Sununu***	Y	Y	Y	Y	N	N
2 ***Bass***	Y	Y	Y	Y	Y	Y
NEW JERSEY						
1 Andrews	Y	Y	Y	Y	Y	N
2 ***LoBiondo***	Y	Y	Y	Y	N	N
3 ***Saxton***	Y	Y	Y	Y	N	N
4 ***Smith***	Y	Y	Y	Y	Y	N
5 ***Roukema***	Y	Y	Y	Y	N	N
6 Pallone	Y	Y	Y	Y	Y	N
7 ***Ferguson***	Y	Y	Y	Y	N	N
8 Pascrell	Y	+	+	+	Y	N
9 Rothman	Y	Y	Y	Y	Y	N
10 Payne	Y	Y	Y	Y	Y	N
11 ***Frelinghuysen***	Y	Y	Y	Y	N	N
12 Holt	Y	Y	Y	Y	Y	N
13 Menendez	Y	+	+	+	N	N
NEW MEXICO						
1 ***Wilson***	Y	Y	Y	Y	N	N
2 ***Skeen***	Y	Y	Y	Y	N	N
3 Udall	Y	Y	Y	Y	Y	N
NEW YORK						
1 ***Grucci***	Y	Y	Y	Y	Y	N
2 Israel	Y	Y	Y	Y	N	N
3 ***King***	Y	Y	Y	Y	Y	N
4 McCarthy	Y	Y	Y	Y	Y	N
5 Ackerman	Y	Y	Y	Y	Y	N
6 Meeks	Y	?	Y	Y	Y	N
7 Crowley	Y	Y	Y	Y	Y	N
8 Nadler	Y	Y	Y	Y	Y	N
9 Weiner	Y	Y	Y	Y	Y	N
10 Towns	Y	Y	Y	Y	Y	N
11 Owens	Y	Y	Y	Y	Y	N
12 Velázquez	Y	Y	Y	Y	Y	N
13 ***Fossella***	Y	?	?	?	Y	N
14 Maloney	Y	Y	Y	Y	Y	N
15 Rangel	Y	Y	Y	Y	Y	N
16 Serrano	Y	Y	Y	Y	Y	N
17 Engel	?	?	?	?	Y	N
18 Lowey	Y	Y	Y	Y	Y	N
19 ***Kelly***	Y	Y	Y	Y	Y	N
20 ***Gilman***	Y	Y	Y	Y	N	N
21 McNulty	Y	Y	Y	Y	Y	N
22 ***Sweeney***	Y	Y	Y	Y	Y	N
23 ***Boehlert***	Y	Y	Y	Y	Y	N
24 ***McHugh***	Y	Y	Y	Y	Y	N
25 ***Walsh***	Y	Y	Y	Y	N	N
26 Hinchey	Y	Y	Y	Y	Y	N
27 ***Reynolds***	Y	?	?	?	Y	N
28 Slaughter	Y	Y	Y	Y	Y	N
29 LaFalce	Y	Y	Y	Y	N	N

	256	257	258	259	260	261
30 ***Quinn***	Y	Y	Y	Y	Y	N
31 ***Houghton***	Y	Y	Y	Y	N	N
NORTH CAROLINA						
1 Clayton	Y	Y	Y	Y	Y	N
2 Etheridge	Y	Y	Y	Y	Y	N
3 ***Jones***	Y	Y	Y	Y	Y	Y
4 Price	Y	Y	Y	Y	Y	N
5 ***Burr***	Y	?	Y	Y	N	N
6 ***Coble***	Y	Y	Y	Y	Y	Y
7 McIntyre	Y	Y	Y	Y	Y	N
8 ***Hayes***	Y	Y	Y	Y	N	N
9 ***Myrick***	Y	Y	Y	Y	N	N
10 ***Ballenger***	Y	Y	Y	Y	N	N
11 ***Taylor***	Y	?	?	?	N	Y
12 Watt	Y	Y	Y	Y	Y	N
NORTH DAKOTA						
AL Pomeroy	Y	Y	Y	Y	N	N
OHIO						
1 ***Chabot***	N	Y	Y	Y	Y	Y
2 ***Portman***	Y	Y	Y	Y	N	N
3 Hall	Y	Y	Y	Y	Y	N
4 ***Oxley***	Y	Y	Y	Y	N	N
5 ***Gillmor***	Y	?	Y	Y	N	N
6 Strickland	Y	Y	Y	Y	Y	N
7 ***Hobson***	Y	Y	Y	Y	N	N
8 ***Boehner***	Y	Y	Y	Y	N	N
9 Kaptur	Y	Y	Y	Y	Y	N
10 Kucinich	N	Y	Y	Y	Y	N
11 Jones	Y	+	+	+	Y	N
12 ***Tiberi***	Y	Y	Y	Y	N	N
13 Brown	Y	Y	Y	Y	Y	N
14 Sawyer	Y	Y	Y	Y	Y	N
15 ***Pryce***	Y	Y	Y	Y	N	N
16 ***Regula***	Y	Y	Y	Y	Y	N
17 Traficant	?	Y	Y	Y	Y	Y
18 ***Ney***	Y	Y	Y	?	Y	Y
19 ***LaTourette***	Y	Y	Y	Y	Y	N
OKLAHOMA						
1 ***Largent***	Y	Y	Y	Y	Y	N
2 Carson	Y	Y	Y	Y	N	N
3 ***Watkins***	Y	Y	Y	Y	Y	N
4 ***Watts***	Y	Y	Y	Y	N	N
5 ***Istook***	?	?	?	?	N	N
6 ***Lucas***	Y	Y	Y	Y	N	N
OREGON						
1 Wu	Y	Y	Y	Y	Y	N
2 ***Walden***	Y	Y	Y	Y	N	N
3 Blumenauer	?	Y	Y	Y	N	N
4 DeFazio	N	Y	Y	Y	Y	N
5 Hooley	Y	Y	Y	Y	N	N
PENNSYLVANIA						
1 Brady	Y	Y	Y	Y	Y	N
2 Fattah	?	?	?	?	Y	N
3 Borski	Y	Y	Y	Y	Y	N
4 ***Hart***	Y	Y	Y	Y	Y	N
5 ***Peterson***	Y	Y	Y	Y	Y	N
6 Holden	Y	Y	Y	Y	Y	N
7 ***Weldon***	Y	Y	Y	Y	Y	N
8 ***Greenwood***	Y	Y	Y	Y	N	N
9 ***Shuster, Bill***	Y	Y	Y	Y	Y	N
10 ***Sherwood***	Y	Y	Y	Y	Y	N
11 Kanjorski	Y	Y	Y	Y	Y	N
12 Murtha	Y	Y	Y	Y	Y	N
13 Hoeffel	Y	Y	Y	Y	Y	N
14 Coyne	Y	Y	Y	Y	Y	N
15 ***Toomey***	Y	Y	Y	Y	N	N
16 ***Pitts***	Y	Y	Y	Y	N	N
17 ***Gekas***	Y	Y	Y	Y	Y	N
18 Doyle	Y	?	?	?	Y	N
19 ***Platts***	Y	Y	Y	Y	Y	Y
20 Mascara	Y	Y	Y	Y	Y	N
21 ***English***	Y	Y	Y	Y	Y	N
RHODE ISLAND						
1 Kennedy	Y	Y	Y	Y	Y	N
2 Langevin	Y	Y	Y	Y	Y	N
SOUTH CAROLINA						
1 ***Brown***	Y	Y	Y	Y	Y	N
2 ***Spence***	?	?	?	?	?	?
3 ***Graham***	Y	Y	Y	Y	Y	N
4 ***DeMint***	Y	Y	Y	Y	Y	N
5 Spratt	Y	Y	Y	Y	Y	N
6 Clyburn	Y	Y	Y	Y	Y	N
SOUTH DAKOTA						
AL ***Thune***	Y	Y	Y	Y	Y	N

	256	257	258	259	260	261
TENNESSEE						
1 ***Jenkins***	Y	Y	Y	Y	Y	N
2 ***Duncan***	N	Y	Y	Y	Y	Y
3 ***Wamp***	Y	Y	Y	Y	Y	Y
4 ***Hilleary***	Y	Y	Y	Y	Y	Y
5 Clement	Y	Y	Y	Y	Y	N
6 Gordon	?	Y	Y	Y	Y	N
7 ***Bryant***	Y	Y	Y	Y	N	N
8 Tanner	Y	Y	Y	Y	Y	N
9 Ford	Y	Y	Y	Y	Y	N
TEXAS						
1 Sandlin	Y	Y	Y	Y	Y	N
2 Turner	Y	Y	Y	Y	Y	N
3 ***Johnson, Sam***	Y	Y	Y	Y	N	N
4 Hall	Y	Y	Y	Y	N	N
5 ***Sessions***	Y	Y	Y	Y	N	N
6 ***Barton***	N	Y	Y	Y	Y	N
7 ***Culberson***	Y	Y	Y	Y	Y	Y
8 ***Brady***	Y	Y	Y	Y	N	N
9 Lampson	Y	Y	Y	Y	Y	N
10 Doggett	Y	Y	Y	Y	Y	N
11 Edwards	Y	Y	Y	Y	Y	Y
12 ***Granger***	Y	Y	Y	Y	N	N
13 ***Thornberry***	Y	Y	Y	Y	N	N
14 ***Paul***	N	Y	Y	Y	Y	Y
15 Hinojosa	Y	Y	Y	Y	Y	N
16 Reyes	Y	Y	Y	Y	?	?
17 Stenholm	Y	Y	Y	Y	N	?
18 Jackson-Lee	Y	Y	Y	Y	Y	N
19 ***Combest***	Y	Y	Y	Y	N	N
20 Gonzalez	Y	Y	Y	Y	N	N
21 ***Smith***	Y	Y	Y	Y	N	N
22 ***DeLay***	?	Y	Y	Y	N	Y
23 ***Bonilla***	Y	Y	Y	Y	N	N
24 Frost	Y	Y	Y	Y	Y	N
25 Bentsen	Y	Y	Y	Y	N	N
26 ***Armey***	N	Y	Y	Y	Y	Y
27 Ortiz	Y	Y	Y	Y	Y	N
28 Rodriguez	Y	Y	Y	Y	Y	N
29 Green	Y	Y	Y	Y	Y	N
30 Johnson, E.B.	Y	Y	Y	Y	Y	N
UTAH						
1 ***Hansen***	Y	?	?	?	N	N
2 Matheson	Y	?	Y	Y	Y	N
3 ***Cannon***	Y	Y	Y	Y	Y	N
VERMONT						
AL *Sanders*	N	Y	Y	Y	Y	N
VIRGINIA						
1 ***Davis, Jo Ann***	Y	Y	Y	Y	Y	N
2 ***Schrock***	Y	Y	Y	Y	N	N
3 Scott	Y	Y	Y	Y	Y	N
4 ***Forbes***	Y	Y	Y	Y	N	N
5 *Goode*	Y	Y	Y	Y	Y	Y
6 ***Goodlatte***	Y	Y	Y	Y	N	N
7 ***Cantor***	Y	Y	Y	Y	Y	N
8 Moran	Y	Y	Y	Y	N	N
9 Boucher	Y	?	?	?	Y	N
10 ***Wolf***	Y	Y	Y	Y	Y	N
11 ***Davis, T.***	Y	Y	Y	Y	N	N
WASHINGTON						
1 Inslee	Y	Y	Y	Y	N	N
2 Larsen	Y	Y	Y	Y	N	N
3 Baird	Y	Y	Y	Y	N	N
4 ***Hastings***	Y	?	?	?	?	?
5 ***Nethercutt***	Y	Y	Y	Y	N	N
6 Dicks	Y	Y	Y	Y	N	N
7 McDermott	Y	Y	Y	Y	N	N
8 ***Dunn***	Y	Y	Y	Y	N	N
9 Smith	Y	Y	Y	Y	N	N
WEST VIRGINIA						
1 Mollohan	Y	?	?	?	Y	N
2 ***Capito***	Y	Y	Y	Y	Y	N
3 Rahall	Y	Y	Y	Y	Y	N
WISCONSIN						
1 ***Ryan***	Y	Y	Y	Y	Y	N
2 Baldwin	Y	Y	Y	Y	Y	N
3 Kind	N	Y	Y	Y	N	N
4 Kleczka	N	?	?	?	Y	N
5 Barrett	N	Y	Y	Y	Y	N
6 ***Petri***	N	Y	Y	Y	Y	Y
7 Obey	Y	Y	Y	Y	Y	N
8 ***Green***	Y	+	+	+	Y	N
9 ***Sensenbrenner***	N	Y	Y	Y	Y	Y
WYOMING						
AL ***Cubin***	Y	Y	Y	Y	N	N

Southern states - Ala., Ark., Fla., Ga., Ky., La., Miss., N.C., Okla., S.C., Tenn., Texas, Va.

Key

Y	Voted for (yea).
#	Paired for.
+	Announced for.
N	Voted against (nay).
X	Paired against.
−	Announced against.
P	Voted "present."
C	Voted "present" to avoid possible conflict of interest.
?	Did not vote or otherwise make a position known.

Democrats **Republicans** *Independents*

262. HR 2506. Fiscal 2002 Foreign Operations Appropriations/ Global Health. Lee, D-Calif., amendment that would increase the U.S. contribution to the Child Survival and Health Programs Fund by $60 million to fight HIV/AIDS, malaria and tuberculosis, and reduce the Andean Counterdrug Initiative by $38 million and foreign military financing by $22 million. Rejected 188-240: R 15-204; D 172-35 (ND 141-12, SD 31-23); I 1-1. July 24, 2001.

263. HR 2506. Fiscal 2002 Foreign Operations Appropriations/ Global Health. McGovern, D-Mass., amendment that would increase the Infectious Diseases account by $50 million and the Child Survival and Maternal Health account by $50 million and reduce funding for the Andean Counterdrug Initiative by $100 million. Rejected 179-249: R 22-197; D 156-51 (ND 131-22, SD 25-29); I 1-1. July 24, 2001.

264. HR 2506. Fiscal 2002 Foreign Operations Appropriations/ Tuberculosis. Brown, D-Ohio, amendment that would increase the Child Survival and Health Programs account by $20 million to fight tuberculosis and decrease funding for the Multilateral Investment Guarantee Agency by $10 million and the Asian Development Fund by $10 million. Adopted 268-159: R 64-153; D 203-5 (ND 152-3, SD 51-2); I 1-1. July 24, 2001.

265. HR 2506. Fiscal 2002 Foreign Operations Appropriations/Human Trafficking. Smith, R-N.J., amendment that would earmark $10 million for human trafficking prevention programs, $10 million to help trafficking victims, and $10 million for other countries' anti-trafficking efforts. Adopted 427-0: R 216-0; D 209-0 (ND 155-0, SD 54-0); I 2-0. July 24, 2001.

266. HR 2506. Fiscal 2002 Foreign Operations Appropriations/Passage. Passage of the bill that would appropriate $15.2 billion in fiscal 2002 for foreign operations, $304 million more than fiscal 2001, including $676 million for the Andean Counterdrug Initiative and $474 million for international HIV/AIDS programs. Passed 381-46: R 181-35; D 199-10 (ND 149-6, SD 50-4); I 1-1. July 24, 2001.

267. HR 2590. Fiscal 2002 Treasury Appropriations/Previous Question. Linder, R-Ga., motion to order the previous question (thus ending debate and the possibility of amendment) on adoption of the rule (H Res 206) to provide for House floor consideration of the bill that would appropriate $32.7 billion in fiscal 2002 for the Treasury Department, U.S. Postal Service, various offices of the Executive Office of the President and certain independent agencies. Motion agreed to 293-129: R 152-63; D 141-64 (ND 101-51, SD 40-13); I 0-2. (Subsequently, the rule was adopted by voice vote.) July 25, 2001.

	262	263	264	265	266	267
ALABAMA						
1 *Callahan*	N	N	N	Y	Y	Y
2 *Everett*	N	N	N	Y	N	N
3 *Riley*	N	N	N	Y	Y	N
4 *Aderholt*	N	N	N	Y	Y	N
5 Cramer	N	N	Y	Y	Y	Y
6 *Bachus*	N	N	Y	Y	Y	Y
7 Hilliard	Y	N	Y	Y	Y	Y
ALASKA						
AL *Young*	N	N	?	?	?	Y
ARIZONA						
1 *Flake*	Y	Y	Y	Y	N	Y
2 Pastor	Y	Y	Y	Y	Y	Y
3 *Stump*	N	N	N	Y	Y	N
4 *Shadegg*	N	N	N	Y	Y	Y
5 *Kolbe*	N	N	N	Y	Y	Y
6 *Hayworth*	N	N	N	Y	Y	N
ARKANSAS						
1 Berry	N	N	Y	Y	N	N
2 Snyder	N	N	Y	Y	Y	?
3 *Hutchinson*	N	N	N	Y	Y	?
4 Ross	N	N	Y	Y	Y	N
CALIFORNIA						
1 Thompson	Y	Y	Y	Y	Y	Y
2 *Herger*	N	N	N	Y	N	Y
3 *Ose*	N	N	N	Y	Y	N
4 *Doolittle*	N	N	Y	Y	Y	Y
5 Matsui	Y	Y	Y	Y	Y	Y
6 Woolsey	Y	Y	Y	Y	Y	Y
7 Miller, George	Y	Y	Y	Y	Y	Y
8 Pelosi	Y	Y	Y	Y	Y	Y
9 Lee	Y	Y	Y	Y	Y	Y
10 Tauscher	N	N	Y	Y	Y	Y
11 *Pombo*	N	N	N	Y	N	Y
12 Lantos	Y	Y	Y	Y	Y	?
13 Stark	Y	Y	Y	Y	N	Y
14 Eshoo	Y	Y	Y	Y	Y	Y
15 Honda	Y	Y	Y	Y	Y	N
16 Lofgren	Y	Y	Y	Y	Y	Y
17 Farr	Y	Y	Y	Y	Y	Y
18 Condit	Y	Y	Y	Y	N	Y
19 *Radanovich*	N	N	N	?	Y	Y
20 Dooley	Y	N	Y	Y	Y	Y
21 *Thomas*	N	N	N	Y	Y	Y
22 Capps	Y	Y	Y	Y	Y	N
23 *Gallegly*	N	N	Y	Y	Y	Y
24 Sherman	Y	Y	Y	Y	Y	Y
25 *McKeon*	N	N	N	Y	Y	Y
26 Berman	Y	Y	Y	Y	Y	Y
27 Schiff	Y	Y	Y	Y	Y	N
28 *Dreier*	N	N	N	Y	Y	Y
29 Waxman	Y	Y	Y	Y	Y	Y
30 Becerra	Y	Y	Y	Y	Y	N
31 Solis	Y	Y	Y	Y	Y	N
32 Watson	Y	Y	Y	Y	Y	Y
33 Roybal-Allard	Y	Y	Y	Y	Y	Y
34 Napolitano	Y	Y	Y	Y	Y	N
35 Waters	Y	Y	Y	Y	Y	Y
36 Harman	Y	Y	Y	Y	Y	Y
37 Millender-McD.	Y	Y	Y	Y	Y	Y
38 *Horn*	Y	N	Y	Y	Y	Y

	262	263	264	265	266	267
39 *Royce*	Y	N	Y	Y	N	N
40 *Lewis*	N	N	N	Y	Y	?
41 *Miller, Gary*	N	N	N	Y	Y	Y
42 Baca	Y	Y	Y	Y	Y	Y
43 *Calvert*	N	N	N	Y	Y	Y
44 *Bono*	N	N	Y	Y	Y	Y
45 *Rohrabacher*	Y	Y	Y	Y	N	Y
46 Sanchez	N	Y	Y	Y	Y	Y
47 *Cox*	N	N	N	Y	Y	Y
48 *Issa*	N	N	Y	Y	Y	Y
49 Davis	Y	N	Y	Y	Y	N
50 Filner	Y	Y	Y	Y	Y	Y
51 *Cunningham*	N	N	N	Y	N	Y
52 *Hunter*	N	N	Y	Y	Y	Y
COLORADO						
1 DeGette	Y	Y	Y	Y	Y	Y
2 Udall	Y	Y	Y	Y	Y	N
3 *McInnis*	N	N	N	Y	Y	Y
4 *Schaffer*	N	N	Y	Y	N	N
5 *Hefley*	N	N	N	Y	N	Y
6 *Tancredo*	N	Y	N	Y	N	N
CONNECTICUT						
1 Larson	Y	Y	Y	Y	Y	Y
2 *Simmons*	N	N	N	Y	Y	Y
3 DeLauro	Y	Y	Y	Y	Y	Y
4 *Shays*	Y	Y	N	Y	Y	Y
5 Maloney	N	N	Y	Y	Y	N
6 *Johnson*	N	N	N	Y	Y	Y
DELAWARE						
AL *Castle*	N	N	N	Y	Y	Y
FLORIDA						
1 *Scarborough*	?	?	?	?	?	?
2 Boyd	N	N	Y	Y	Y	Y
3 Brown	Y	Y	Y	Y	Y	Y
4 *Crenshaw*	N	N	N	Y	Y	Y
5 Thurman	N	N	Y	Y	Y	Y
6 *Stearns*	N	N	Y	Y	N	N
7 *Mica*	N	N	N	Y	Y	N
8 *Keller*	N	N	N	Y	Y	N
9 *Bilirakis*	N	N	N	Y	Y	N
10 *Young*	N	N	N	Y	Y	?
11 Davis	N	N	N	Y	Y	Y
12 *Putnam*	N	N	N	Y	Y	Y
13 *Miller*	N	N	N	Y	Y	Y
14 *Goss*	N	N	N	Y	Y	Y
15 *Weldon*	N	N	N	Y	N	Y
16 *Foley*	N	N	Y	Y	Y	Y
17 Meek	Y	Y	Y	Y	Y	Y
18 *Ros-Lehtinen*	N	N	N	Y	Y	Y
19 Wexler	Y	Y	Y	Y	Y	Y
20 Deutsch	Y	Y	Y	Y	Y	Y
21 *Diaz-Balart*	N	N	N	Y	Y	Y
22 *Shaw*	N	N	N	Y	Y	Y
23 Hastings	Y	Y	Y	Y	Y	Y
GEORGIA						
1 *Kingston*	N	N	N	Y	Y	Y
2 Bishop	Y	N	Y	Y	Y	Y
3 *Collins*	N	N	N	Y	N	Y
4 McKinney	Y	Y	Y	Y	Y	N
5 Lewis	Y	Y	Y	Y	Y	Y
6 *Isakson*	N	N	N	Y	Y	Y
7 *Barr*	N	N	N	Y	N	Y
8 *Chambliss*	N	N	N	Y	Y	N
9 *Deal*	N	N	Y	Y	Y	Y
10 *Norwood*	N	Y	N	Y	Y	Y
11 *Linder*	N	N	N	Y	Y	Y
HAWAII						
1 Abercrombie	Y	Y	Y	Y	Y	Y
2 Mink	Y	Y	Y	Y	Y	Y
IDAHO						
1 *Otter*	N	N	N	Y	N	Y
2 *Simpson*	N	N	N	Y	Y	Y
ILLINOIS						
1 Rush	Y	Y	Y	Y	Y	Y
2 Jackson	Y	Y	Y	Y	Y	Y
3 Lipinski	?	?	?	?	?	?
4 Gutierrez	Y	Y	Y	Y	Y	Y
5 Blagojevich	Y	Y	Y	Y	Y	N
6 *Hyde*	N	N	N	Y	Y	?
7 Davis	Y	Y	Y	Y	Y	Y
8 *Crane*	N	N	N	Y	Y	Y
9 Schakowsky	Y	Y	Y	Y	Y	Y
10 *Kirk*	N	N	N	Y	Y	Y
11 *Weller*	N	N	N	Y	Y	Y
12 Costello	N	N	Y	Y	Y	N
13 *Biggert*	N	N	N	Y	Y	Y

ND Northern Democrats   SD Southern Democrats

	262	263	264	265	266	267
14 ***Hastert***	N	N				
15 ***Johnson***	N	N	N	Y	Y	N
16 ***Manzullo***	N	Y	N	Y	Y	Y
17 Evans	Y	Y	Y	Y	Y	N
18 ***LaHood***	N	N	N	Y	Y	N
19 Phelps	N	N	Y	Y	N	N
20 ***Shimkus***	N	N	Y	Y	Y	N
INDIANA						
1 Visclosky	Y	Y	Y	Y	Y	Y
2 ***Pence***	N	N	N	Y	Y	Y
3 Roemer	Y	Y	Y	Y	N	Y
4 ***Souder***	N	N	N	Y	Y	Y
5 ***Buyer***	N	N	Y	Y	Y	Y
6 ***Burton***	N	N	Y	Y	Y	Y
7 ***Kerns***	N	N	Y	Y	N	N
8 ***Hostettler***	N	N	Y	Y	N	N
9 Hill	Y	Y	Y	Y	Y	N
10 Carson	Y	Y	Y	Y	Y	Y
IOWA						
1 ***Leach***	Y	Y	Y	Y	Y	N
2 ***Nussle***	Y	N	N	Y	Y	Y
3 Boswell	N	N	Y	Y	Y	N
4 ***Ganske***	Y	Y	Y	Y	Y	Y
5 ***Latham***	N	N	N	Y	Y	N
KANSAS						
1 ***Moran***	N	N	Y	Y	Y	Y
2 ***Ryun***	N	N	N	Y	N	Y
3 Moore	Y	Y	Y	Y	Y	N
4 ***Tiahrt***	N	N	Y	Y	Y	Y
KENTUCKY						
1 ***Whitfield***	N	N	N	Y	Y	Y
2 ***Lewis***	N	N	N	Y	Y	N
3 ***Northup***	N	N	N	Y	Y	N
4 Lucas	Y	Y	Y	Y	Y	N
5 ***Rogers***	N	N	N	Y	Y	Y
6 ***Fletcher***	N	N	N	Y	Y	Y
LOUISIANA						
1 ***Vitter***	N	N	N	Y	Y	N
2 Jefferson	Y	Y	Y	Y	Y	Y
3 ***Tauzin***	N	N	N	Y	Y	Y
4 ***McCrery***	N	N	N	Y	Y	Y
5 ***Cooksey***	N	N	N	Y	Y	Y
6 ***Baker***	N	N	N	Y	Y	Y
7 John	N	N	N	Y	Y	Y
MAINE						
1 Allen	Y	Y	Y	Y	Y	Y
2 Baldacci	Y	Y	Y	Y	Y	Y
MARYLAND						
1 ***Gilchrest***	N	N	Y	Y	Y	Y
2 ***Ehrlich***	N	N	N	Y	Y	Y
3 Cardin	N	N	Y	Y	Y	Y
4 Wynn	Y	Y	Y	Y	Y	Y
5 Hoyer	Y	N	Y	Y	Y	Y
6 ***Bartlett***	N	N	Y	Y	Y	N
7 Cummings	Y	Y	Y	Y	Y	Y
8 ***Morella***	Y	Y	Y	Y	Y	Y
MASSACHUSETTS						
1 Olver	Y	Y	Y	Y	Y	Y
2 Neal	Y	Y	Y	Y	Y	Y
3 McGovern	Y	Y	Y	Y	Y	?
4 Frank	Y	Y	Y	Y	Y	Y
5 Meehan	Y	Y	Y	Y	Y	N
6 Tierney	Y	Y	Y	Y	Y	N
7 Markey	Y	Y	Y	Y	Y	Y
8 Capuano	Y	Y	Y	Y	Y	Y
9 Vacant						
10 Delahunt	?	?	Y	Y	Y	Y
MICHIGAN						
1 Stupak	Y	Y	Y	Y	Y	N
2 ***Hoekstra***	N	Y	Y	Y	Y	Y
3 ***Ehlers***	Y	N	Y	Y	Y	Y
4 ***Camp***	N	N	N	Y	Y	Y
5 Barcia	Y	Y	Y	Y	Y	N
6 ***Upton***	N	Y	Y	Y	Y	Y
7 ***Smith***	N	N	N	Y	Y	Y
8 ***Rogers***	N	N	N	Y	Y	N
9 Kildee	Y	Y	Y	Y	Y	N
10 Bonior	Y	Y	Y	Y	Y	Y
11 ***Knollenberg***	N	N	N	Y	Y	Y
12 Levin	Y	N	Y	Y	Y	Y
13 Rivers	Y	Y	Y	Y	Y	N
14 Conyers	Y	Y	Y	Y	Y	Y
15 Kilpatrick	+	+	Y	Y	Y	Y
16 Dingell	N	N	Y	Y	Y	N
MINNESOTA						
1 ***Gutknecht***	N	Y	N	Y	Y	Y
2 ***Kennedy***	N	Y	N	Y	Y	N
3 ***Ramstad***	Y	Y	N	Y	Y	Y
4 McCollum	Y	Y	Y	Y	Y	Y
5 Sabo	Y	Y	Y	Y	Y	Y
6 Luther	Y	Y	Y	Y	Y	N
7 Peterson	N	N	Y	Y	Y	N
8 Oberstar	Y	Y	Y	Y	Y	Y
MISSISSIPPI						
1 ***Wicker***	N	N	N	Y	Y	Y
2 Thompson	Y	Y	Y	Y	Y	Y
3 ***Pickering***	N	N	N	Y	Y	Y
4 Shows	N	N	Y	Y	Y	N
5 Taylor	N	N	Y	Y	N	Y
MISSOURI						
1 Clay	Y	Y	Y	Y	Y	Y
2 ***Akin***	N	N	N	Y	Y	Y
3 Gephardt	Y	Y	Y	Y	Y	Y
4 Skelton	Y	N	Y	Y	Y	?
5 McCarthy	Y	Y	Y	Y	Y	Y
6 ***Graves***	N	N	N	Y	Y	N
7 ***Blunt***	N	N	N	Y	Y	Y
8 ***Emerson***	N	Y	N	Y	Y	N
9 ***Hulshof***	Y	Y	Y	Y	Y	N
MONTANA						
AL ***Rehberg***	N	N	N	Y	Y	N
NEBRASKA						
1 ***Bereuter***	N	N	N	Y	Y	Y
2 ***Terry***	N	N	N	Y	Y	N
3 ***Osborne***	N	N	Y	Y	Y	Y
NEVADA						
1 Berkley	Y	Y	Y	Y	Y	N
2 ***Gibbons***	N	N	N	Y	Y	N
NEW HAMPSHIRE						
1 ***Sununu***	N	N	N	Y	Y	Y
2 ***Bass***	N	N	N	Y	Y	Y
NEW JERSEY						
1 Andrews	Y	Y	Y	Y	Y	Y
2 ***LoBiondo***	N	N	Y	Y	Y	N
3 ***Saxton***	N	N	Y	Y	Y	Y
4 ***Smith***	N	N	Y	Y	Y	Y
5 ***Roukema***	N	N	N	Y	Y	Y
6 Pallone	Y	Y	Y	Y	Y	Y
7 ***Ferguson***	N	N	N	Y	Y	N
8 Pascrell	Y	Y	Y	Y	Y	Y
9 Rothman	Y	N	Y	Y	Y	Y
10 Payne	Y	Y	Y	Y	Y	Y
11 ***Frelinghuysen***	N	N	N	Y	Y	Y
12 Holt	Y	Y	Y	Y	Y	N
13 Menendez	Y	N	Y	Y	Y	Y
NEW MEXICO						
1 ***Wilson***	N	N	Y	Y	Y	Y
2 ***Skeen***	N	N	N	Y	Y	Y
3 Udall	Y	Y	Y	Y	Y	N
NEW YORK						
1 ***Grucci***	N	N	N	Y	Y	Y
2 Israel	Y	Y	Y	Y	Y	N
3 ***King***	N	N	N	Y	Y	Y
4 McCarthy	Y	Y	Y	Y	Y	Y
5 Ackerman	Y	Y	Y	Y	Y	Y
6 Meeks	Y	Y	Y	Y	Y	Y
7 Crowley	Y	Y	Y	Y	Y	Y
8 Nadler	Y	Y	Y	Y	Y	Y
9 Weiner	Y	Y	Y	Y	Y	Y
10 Towns	Y	Y	Y	Y	Y	Y
11 Owens	Y	Y	Y	Y	Y	Y
12 Velázquez	Y	Y	Y	Y	Y	N
13 ***Fossella***	N	N	Y	Y	Y	N
14 Maloney	Y	Y	Y	Y	Y	N
15 Rangel	Y	Y	Y	Y	Y	Y
16 Serrano	Y	Y	Y	Y	Y	Y
17 Engel	Y	Y	Y	Y	Y	Y
18 Lowey	Y	Y	Y	Y	Y	Y
19 ***Kelly***	N	Y	Y	Y	Y	N
20 ***Gilman***	N	N	N	Y	Y	Y
21 McNulty	Y	Y	Y	Y	Y	Y
22 ***Sweeney***	N	N	N	Y	Y	Y
23 ***Boehlert***	N	Y	N	Y	Y	Y
24 ***McHugh***	N	N	N	Y	Y	Y
25 ***Walsh***	N	N	N	Y	Y	Y
26 Hinchey	Y	Y	Y	Y	Y	Y
27 ***Reynolds***	N	N	N	Y	Y	Y
28 Slaughter	Y	Y	Y	Y	Y	Y
29 LaFalce	Y	Y	N	Y	Y	Y
30 ***Quinn***	N	N	N	Y	Y	Y
31 ***Houghton***	N	N	N	Y	Y	Y
NORTH CAROLINA						
1 Clayton	Y	Y	Y	Y	Y	Y
2 Etheridge	Y	Y	Y	Y	Y	N
3 ***Jones***	N	N	Y	Y	N	Y
4 Price	Y	Y	Y	Y	Y	N
5 ***Burr***	N	N	N	Y	Y	N
6 ***Coble***	N	N	N	Y	Y	N
7 McIntyre	N	N	Y	Y	Y	N
8 ***Hayes***	N	N	N	Y	N	N
9 ***Myrick***	N	N	N	Y	Y	Y
10 ***Ballenger***	N	N	N	Y	Y	Y
11 ***Taylor***	N	N	N	Y	N	Y
12 Watt	Y	Y	Y	Y	Y	Y
NORTH DAKOTA						
AL Pomeroy	N	Y	N	Y	Y	N
OHIO						
1 ***Chabot***	N	N	Y	Y	Y	N
2 ***Portman***	N	N	N	Y	Y	Y
3 Hall	Y	Y	Y	Y	Y	Y
4 ***Oxley***	N	N	N	Y	Y	Y
5 ***Gillmor***	N	N	Y	Y	Y	Y
6 Strickland	Y	Y	Y	Y	Y	N
7 ***Hobson***	N	N	N	Y	Y	Y
8 ***Boehner***	N	N	N	Y	Y	Y
9 Kaptur	Y	Y	Y	Y	N	N
10 Kucinich	Y	Y	Y	Y	Y	N
11 Jones	Y	Y	Y	Y	Y	Y
12 ***Tiberi***	N	N	Y	Y	Y	Y
13 Brown	Y	Y	Y	Y	Y	N
14 Sawyer	Y	Y	Y	Y	Y	Y
15 ***Pryce***	N	N	N	Y	Y	Y
16 ***Regula***	N	N	N	Y	Y	Y
17 Traficant	N	N	N	Y	Y	Y
18 ***Ney***	N	N	N	Y	Y	Y
19 ***LaTourette***	N	N	N	Y	Y	Y
OKLAHOMA						
1 ***Largent***	N	Y	Y	Y	Y	Y
2 Carson	N	N	Y	Y	Y	N
3 ***Watkins***	N	N	Y	Y	N	Y
4 ***Watts***	N	N	N	Y	Y	Y
5 ***Istook***	N	N	N	Y	Y	Y
6 ***Lucas***	N	N	N	Y	N	Y
OREGON						
1 Wu	Y	Y	Y	Y	Y	N
2 ***Walden***	N	N	N	Y	Y	Y
3 Blumenauer	Y	Y	Y	Y	Y	Y
4 DeFazio	Y	Y	Y	Y	Y	Y
5 Hooley	Y	Y	Y	Y	Y	N
PENNSYLVANIA						
1 Brady	Y	Y	Y	Y	Y	Y
2 Fattah	Y	Y	Y	Y	Y	Y
3 Borski	Y	Y	Y	Y	Y	Y
4 ***Hart***	N	N	N	Y	Y	N
5 ***Peterson***	N	N	N	Y	Y	Y
6 Holden	N	N	Y	Y	Y	Y
7 ***Weldon***	N	N	Y	Y	Y	Y
8 ***Greenwood***	N	N	N	Y	Y	Y
9 ***Shuster, Bill***	N	N	N	Y	Y	N
10 ***Sherwood***	N	N	N	Y	Y	N
11 Kanjorski	Y	N	Y	Y	Y	Y
12 Murtha	Y	N	Y	Y	Y	Y
13 Hoeffel	Y	Y	Y	Y	Y	Y
14 Coyne	Y	Y	Y	Y	Y	Y
15 ***Toomey***	N	Y	Y	Y	N	N
16 ***Pitts***	N	N	Y	Y	Y	N
17 ***Gekas***	N	N	N	Y	Y	N
18 Doyle	Y	Y	Y	Y	Y	Y
19 ***Platts***	N	N	Y	Y	Y	N
20 Mascara	N	N	Y	Y	Y	N
21 ***English***	N	N	Y	Y	Y	N
RHODE ISLAND						
1 Kennedy	Y	Y	Y	Y	Y	Y
2 Langevin	Y	Y	Y	Y	Y	N
SOUTH CAROLINA						
1 ***Brown***	N	N	N	Y	Y	Y
2 ***Spence***	?	?	?	?	?	?
3 ***Graham***	N	N	N	Y	Y	Y
4 ***DeMint***	N	N	N	Y	Y	N
5 Spratt	Y	N	Y	Y	Y	Y
6 Clyburn	Y	Y	Y	Y	Y	Y
SOUTH DAKOTA						
AL ***Thune***	N	N	Y	Y	Y	N
TENNESSEE						
1 ***Jenkins***	N	N	N	Y	N	N
2 ***Duncan***	N	Y	Y	Y	N	Y
3 ***Wamp***	N	N	Y	Y	Y	Y
4 ***Hilleary***	N	N	Y	Y	N	N
5 Clement	Y	N	Y	Y	Y	Y
6 Gordon	Y	Y	Y	Y	Y	Y
7 ***Bryant***	N	N	N	Y	Y	N
8 Tanner	N	N	Y	Y	N	Y
9 Ford	Y	Y	Y	Y	Y	Y
TEXAS						
1 Sandlin	Y	Y	Y	Y	Y	N
2 Turner	N	N	Y	Y	Y	N
3 ***Johnson, Sam***	N	N	N	Y	?	Y
4 Hall	N	N	Y	Y	N	Y
5 ***Sessions***	N	N	N	Y	Y	Y
6 ***Barton***	N	N	N	Y	Y	Y
7 ***Culberson***	N	N	N	Y	Y	Y
8 ***Brady***	N	N	N	Y	Y	N
9 Lampson	Y	Y	Y	Y	Y	Y
10 Doggett	Y	Y	Y	Y	Y	Y
11 Edwards	N	N	Y	Y	Y	N
12 ***Granger***	N	N	N	Y	Y	Y
13 ***Thornberry***	N	N	N	Y	Y	Y
14 ***Paul***	Y	Y	Y	Y	N	N
15 Hinojosa	N	N	Y	Y	Y	Y
16 Reyes	N	N	?	Y	Y	Y
17 Stenholm	N	N	N	Y	Y	Y
18 Jackson-Lee	Y	Y	Y	Y	Y	Y
19 ***Combest***	N	N	N	Y	N	Y
20 Gonzalez	N	N	Y	Y	Y	Y
21 ***Smith***	N	N	N	Y	Y	Y
22 ***DeLay***	N	N	N	Y	Y	Y
23 ***Bonilla***	N	N	N	Y	Y	Y
24 Frost	N	N	Y	Y	Y	Y
25 Bentsen	Y	N	Y	Y	Y	Y
26 ***Armey***	N	N	N	Y	Y	Y
27 Ortiz	N	N	Y	Y	Y	Y
28 Rodriguez	Y	Y	Y	Y	Y	Y
29 Green	Y	N	Y	Y	Y	Y
30 Johnson, E.B.	Y	Y	Y	Y	Y	Y
UTAH						
1 ***Hansen***	N	N	N	Y	N	Y
2 Matheson	Y	Y	Y	Y	Y	N
3 ***Cannon***	N	N	N	Y	Y	Y
VERMONT						
AL *Sanders*	Y	Y	Y	Y	Y	N
VIRGINIA						
1 ***Davis, Jo Ann***	N	N	Y	Y	Y	N
2 ***Schrock***	N	N	N	Y	Y	Y
3 Scott	Y	Y	Y	Y	Y	Y
4 ***Forbes***	N	N	N	Y	Y	N
5 *Goode*	N	N	N	Y	N	N
6 ***Goodlatte***	N	N	N	Y	N	Y
7 ***Cantor***	N	N	N	Y	Y	Y
8 Moran	N	N	Y	Y	Y	Y
9 Boucher	Y	Y	Y	Y	Y	Y
10 ***Wolf***	N	N	N	Y	Y	Y
11 ***Davis, T.***	N	N	N	Y	Y	Y
WASHINGTON						
1 Inslee	Y	Y	Y	Y	Y	N
2 Larsen	Y	Y	Y	Y	Y	N
3 Baird	Y	Y	Y	Y	Y	N
4 ***Hastings***	?	?	?	?	?	Y
5 ***Nethercutt***	N	N	N	Y	Y	Y
6 Dicks	Y	Y	Y	Y	Y	Y
7 McDermott	Y	Y	Y	Y	Y	Y
8 ***Dunn***	N	N	N	Y	Y	Y
9 Smith	Y	Y	Y	Y	Y	N
WEST VIRGINIA						
1 Mollohan	Y	N	Y	Y	Y	Y
2 ***Capito***	N	N	N	Y	Y	N
3 Rahall	Y	Y	Y	Y	N	Y
WISCONSIN						
1 ***Ryan***	N	N	Y	Y	Y	N
2 Baldwin	Y	Y	Y	Y	Y	N
3 Kind	Y	Y	Y	Y	Y	N
4 Kleczka	Y	Y	Y	Y	Y	N
5 Barrett	Y	Y	Y	Y	Y	N
6 ***Petri***	N	N	N	Y	N	N
7 Obey	Y	Y	Y	Y	Y	Y
8 ***Green***	Y	Y	N	Y	Y	N
9 ***Sensenbrenner***	N	N	Y	Y	N	Y
WYOMING						
AL ***Cubin***	N	N	N	Y	N	Y

Southern states - Ala., Ark., Fla., Ga., Ky., La., Miss., N.C., Okla., S.C., Tenn., Texas, Va.

Key

268. HR 2590. Fiscal 2002 Treasury Appropriations/Vice President's Utilities. Inslee, D-Wash., amendment that would strike a provision that allows the U.S. Navy to pay electric and other utility bills for the vice president's residence. Rejected 141-285: R 0-219; D 140-65 (ND 109-45, SD 31-20); I 1-1. July 25, 2001.

269. HR 2590. Fiscal 2002 Treasury Appropriations/Vice President's Events. Hinchey, D-N.Y., amendment that would strike a provision that allows the U.S. Navy to accept donated goods, including food and beverages, for use at official events at the vice president's residence. Rejected 151-274: R 0-219; D 150-54 (ND 117-36, SD 33-18); I 1-1. July 25, 2001.

270. HR 2590. Fiscal 2002 Treasury Appropriations/Cuba Travel. Flake, R-Ariz., substitute amendment to the Smith, R-N.J., amendment. The Flake amendment would prohibit the use of funds in the bill to enforce travel restrictions on U.S. citizens to Cuba. The Smith amendment would make the same prohibition but would go into effect only after the president has certified to Congress that Cuba has released all political prisoners and has returned to the U.S. government all individuals sought by it on charges of air piracy, drug trafficking and murder. Adopted 240-186: R 67-151; D 172-34 (ND 131-22, SD 41-12); I 1-1. A "nay" was a vote in support of the president's position. (Subsequently, the Smith amendment, as amended, was adopted by voice vote.) July 25, 2001.

271. HR 2590. Fiscal 2002 Treasury Appropriations/Cuba Embargo. Rangel, D-N.Y., amendment that would prohibit the use of funds in the bill to carry out the U.S. economic embargo of Cuba. Rejected 201-227: R 40-179; D 160-47 (ND 124-30, SD 36-17); I 1-1. A "nay" was a vote in support of the president's position. July 25, 2001.

272. HR 2590. Fiscal 2002 Treasury Appropriations/IRS Bonuses. Traficant, D-Ohio, amendment that would prohibit the use of funds in the bill for bonuses and incentive payments to senior management at the Internal Revenue Service. Rejected 24-401: R 20-197; D 4-202 (ND 3-150, SD 1-52); I 0-2. July 25, 2001.

273. HR 2590. Fiscal 2002 Treasury Appropriations/Social Security Report. Filner, D-Calif., amendment that would prohibit the use of funds in the bill for carrying out the final report of President Bush's Commission to Strengthen Social Security. Rejected 188-238: R 0-217; D 187-20 (ND 143-11, SD 44-9); I 1-1. July 25, 2001.

	268	269	270	271	272	273
ALABAMA						
1 *Callahan*	N	N	N	N	N	N
2 *Everett*	N	N	N	N	N	N
3 *Riley*	N	N	N	N	N	N
4 *Aderholt*	N	N	Y	N	N	N
5 Cramer	N	N	Y	N	N	N
6 *Bachus*	N	N	N	N	?	?
7 Hilliard	N	N	Y	Y	N	Y
ALASKA						
AL *Young*	N	N	N	N	Y	N
ARIZONA						
1 *Flake*	N	N	Y	Y	N	N
2 Pastor	Y	N	Y	Y	N	Y
3 *Stump*	N	N	N	N	N	N
4 *Shadegg*	N	N	N	N	N	N
5 *Kolbe*	N	N	Y	N	N	N
6 *Hayworth*	N	N	N	N	N	N
ARKANSAS						
1 Berry	Y	N	Y	Y	N	N
2 Snyder	?	?	?	?	?	?
3 *Hutchinson*	N	N	N	N	N	N
4 Ross	N	N	Y	Y	N	Y
CALIFORNIA						
1 Thompson	N	N	Y	Y	N	Y
2 *Herger*	N	N	Y	N	N	N
3 *Ose*	N	N	N	N	N	N
4 *Doolittle*	N	N	N	N	N	N
5 Matsui	N	N	N	N	N	Y
6 Woolsey	Y	Y	Y	Y	N	Y
7 Miller, George	Y	Y	Y	Y	N	Y
8 Pelosi	Y	Y	Y	Y	N	Y
9 Lee	Y	Y	Y	Y	N	Y
10 Tauscher	Y	Y	Y	Y	N	Y
11 *Pombo*	N	N	N	N	N	N
12 Lantos	Y	Y	Y	Y	N	Y
13 Stark	Y	Y	Y	Y	N	Y
14 Eshoo	Y	Y	Y	Y	N	Y
15 Honda	Y	Y	Y	Y	N	Y
16 Lofgren	Y	Y	Y	Y	N	Y
17 Farr	Y	Y	Y	Y	N	Y
18 Condit	N	N	Y	Y	N	Y
19 *Radanovich*	N	N	N	Y	N	N
20 Dooley	N	N	Y	Y	N	N
21 *Thomas*	N	N	N	N	N	N
22 Capps	Y	Y	Y	Y	N	Y
23 *Gallegly*	N	N	N	N	N	N
24 Sherman	Y	Y	N	N	N	Y
25 *McKeon*	N	N	N	N	N	N
26 Berman	N	N	Y	N	N	Y
27 Schiff	Y	Y	Y	N	N	N
28 *Dreier*	N	N	N	N	N	N
29 Waxman	Y	Y	Y	Y	N	Y
30 Becerra	Y	Y	Y	Y	N	Y
31 Solis	Y	Y	Y	Y	N	Y
32 Watson	Y	Y	Y	Y	Y	Y
33 Roybal-Allard	Y	Y	Y	Y	N	Y
34 Napolitano	Y	Y	Y	Y	N	Y
35 Waters	Y	?	Y	Y	N	Y
36 Harman	Y	Y	Y	Y	N	Y
37 Millender-McD.	Y	Y	Y	Y	N	Y
38 Horn	N	N	Y	N	N	N

	268	269	270	271	272	273
39 *Royce*	N	N	N	N	N	N
40 *Lewis*	N	N	N	N	N	N
41 *Miller, Gary*	N	N	N	N	N	N
42 Baca	Y	N	N	Y	N	Y
43 *Calvert*	N	N	N	N	N	N
44 *Bono*	N	N	Y	N	Y	N
45 *Rohrabacher*	N	N	Y	N	Y	N
46 Sanchez	Y	N	Y	N	N	N
47 *Cox*	N	N	N	N	N	N
48 *Issa*	N	N	Y	N	N	N
49 Davis	Y	Y	Y	Y	N	Y
50 Filner	Y	Y	Y	Y	N	Y
51 *Cunningham*	N	N	N	N	N	N
52 *Hunter*	N	N	N	N	N	N
COLORADO						
1 DeGette	Y	Y	Y	Y	N	Y
2 Udall	Y	Y	Y	Y	N	Y
3 *McInnis*	N	N	N	N	N	N
4 *Schaffer*	N	N	N	N	N	N
5 *Hefley*	N	N	N	N	N	N
6 *Tancredo*	N	N	N	Y	N	N
CONNECTICUT						
1 Larson	Y	N	Y	Y	N	Y
2 *Simmons*	N	N	Y	N	N	N
3 DeLauro	Y	Y	Y	Y	N	Y
4 *Shays*	N	N	Y	N	Y	N
5 Maloney	Y	Y	Y	N	N	N
6 *Johnson*	N	N	Y	N	N	N
DELAWARE						
AL *Castle*	N	N	Y	N	N	N
FLORIDA						
1 *Scarborough*	?	?	?	?	?	?
2 Boyd	Y	Y	N	N	N	N
3 Brown	Y	Y	Y	Y	N	N
4 *Crenshaw*	N	N	N	N	N	N
5 Thurman	Y	Y	Y	Y	N	Y
6 *Stearns*	N	N	N	N	N	N
7 *Mica*	N	N	N	N	N	N
8 *Keller*	N	N	N	N	N	N
9 *Bilirakis*	N	N	N	Y	N	N
10 *Young*	N	N	N	N	N	N
11 Davis	N	Y	N	N	N	Y
12 *Putnam*	N	N	N	N	N	N
13 *Miller*	N	N	N	N	N	N
14 *Goss*	N	N	N	N	N	N
15 *Weldon*	N	N	N	N	N	N
16 *Foley*	N	N	N	N	N	N
17 Meek	Y	Y	N	N	N	Y
18 *Ros-Lehtinen*	N	N	N	N	N	N
19 Wexler	N	Y	N	N	N	N
20 Deutsch	Y	Y	N	N	N	Y
21 *Diaz-Balart*	N	N	N	N	N	N
22 *Shaw*	N	N	N	N	N	N
23 Hastings	N	Y	N	N	N	Y
GEORGIA						
1 *Kingston*	N	N	N	N	N	N
2 Bishop	Y	N	Y	Y	N	Y
3 *Collins*	N	N	N	N	N	N
4 McKinney	Y	Y	Y	Y	N	Y
5 Lewis	Y	Y	Y	Y	N	Y
6 *Isakson*	N	N	Y	N	N	N
7 *Barr*	N	N	N	N	N	N
8 *Chambliss*	N	N	N	N	N	N
9 *Deal*	N	N	N	N	N	N
10 *Norwood*	N	N	N	N	N	N
11 *Linder*	N	N	N	N	N	N
HAWAII						
1 Abercrombie	N	N	Y	N	Y	N
2 Mink	N	N	Y	Y	N	Y
IDAHO						
1 *Otter*	N	N	Y	N	Y	N
2 *Simpson*	N	N	Y	N	N	N
ILLINOIS						
1 Rush	Y	Y	Y	Y	N	Y
2 Jackson	Y	Y	Y	Y	N	Y
3 Lipinski	?	?	?	?	?	?
4 Gutierrez	Y	Y	Y	Y	N	Y
5 Blagojevich	N	N	N	N	N	Y
6 *Hyde*	N	N	N	N	N	N
7 Davis	Y	Y	Y	Y	N	Y
8 *Crane*	N	N	N	N	N	N
9 Schakowsky	Y	Y	Y	Y	N	Y
10 *Kirk*	N	N	N	N	N	N
11 *Weller*	N	N	N	N	N	N
12 Costello	N	N	Y	Y	N	Y
13 *Biggert*	N	Y	Y	N	Y	N

	268	269	270	271	272	273
14 ***Hastert***						
15 ***Johnson***	N	N	Y	Y	N	N
16 ***Manzullo***	N	N	Y	Y	N	N
17 Evans	N	N	Y	Y	N	Y
18 ***LaHood***	N	N	Y	Y	N	N
19 Phelps	N	N	Y	Y	N	Y
20 ***Shimkus***	N	N	Y	Y	N	N
INDIANA						
1 Visclosky	Y	Y	N	N	N	Y
2 ***Pence***	N	N	N	N	N	N
3 Roemer	Y	Y	Y	Y	N	N
4 ***Souder***	N	N	N	N	N	N
5 ***Buyer***	N	N	N	N	N	N
6 ***Burton***	N	N	N	N	N	N
7 ***Kerns***	N	N	N	N	N	N
8 ***Hostettler***	N	N	Y	N	N	N
9 Hill	N	Y	Y	Y	N	N
10 Carson	N	N	Y	Y	N	Y
IOWA						
1 ***Leach***	N	N	Y	Y	N	N
2 ***Nussle***	N	N	Y	Y	N	N
3 Boswell	Y	Y	Y	Y	N	Y
4 ***Ganske***	N	N	Y	Y	N	N
5 ***Latham***	N	N	Y	Y	N	N
KANSAS						
1 ***Moran***	N	N	Y	Y	N	N
2 ***Ryun***	N	N	N	N	N	N
3 Moore	N	Y	Y	Y	N	N
4 ***Tiahrt***	N	N	Y	N	N	N
KENTUCKY						
1 ***Whitfield***	N	N	Y	N	N	N
2 ***Lewis***	N	N	N	N	N	N
3 ***Northup***	N	N	N	N	N	N
4 Lucas	N	Y	N	N	N	Y
5 ***Rogers***	N	N	N	N	N	N
6 ***Fletcher***	N	N	Y	N	N	N
LOUISIANA						
1 ***Vitter***	N	N	N	N	N	N
2 Jefferson	Y	N	Y	Y	N	Y
3 ***Tauzin***	N	N	N	N	N	N
4 ***McCrery***	N	N	N	N	N	N
5 ***Cooksey***	N	N	?	N	N	N
6 ***Baker***	N	N	N	N	Y	N
7 John	Y	Y	Y	Y	N	N
MAINE						
1 Allen	Y	Y	Y	Y	N	N
2 Baldacci	Y	Y	Y	Y	N	Y
MARYLAND						
1 ***Gilchrest***	N	N	Y	Y	N	N
2 ***Ehrlich***	N	N	N	N	N	N
3 Cardin	N	N	Y	N	N	Y
4 Wynn	N	N	Y	Y	N	Y
5 Hoyer	Y	Y	Y	N	N	Y
6 ***Bartlett***	N	N	N	N	N	N
7 Cummings	N	Y	Y	Y	N	Y
8 ***Morella***	N	N	Y	Y	N	N
MASSACHUSETTS						
1 Olver	Y	Y	Y	Y	N	Y
2 Neal	Y	Y	Y	Y	N	Y
3 McGovern	Y	Y	Y	Y	?	Y
4 Frank	Y	Y	Y	Y	N	Y
5 Meehan	Y	Y	Y	Y	N	Y
6 Tierney	N	Y	Y	Y	N	Y
7 Markey	Y	Y	Y	Y	N	Y
8 Capuano	Y	Y	Y	Y	N	Y
9 Vacant						
10 Delahunt	N	N	Y	Y	N	Y
MICHIGAN						
1 Stupak	N	N	Y	Y	N	Y
2 ***Hoekstra***	N	N	Y	N	N	N
3 ***Ehlers***	N	N	Y	N	N	N
4 ***Camp***	N	N	Y	N	N	N
5 Barcia	Y	N	Y	Y	N	Y
6 ***Upton***	N	N	Y	Y	N	N
7 ***Smith***	N	N	Y	N	N	N
8 ***Rogers***	N	N	N	N	N	N
9 Kildee	Y	Y	Y	Y	N	Y
10 Bonior	Y	Y	Y	Y	N	Y
11 ***Knollenberg***	N	N	N	N	N	?
12 Levin	Y	Y	Y	Y	N	Y
13 Rivers	Y	Y	Y	Y	N	Y
14 Conyers	?	?	Y	Y	N	Y
15 Kilpatrick	N	Y	Y	Y	N	Y
16 Dingell	Y	Y	Y	Y	N	Y

	268	269	270	271	272	273
MINNESOTA						
1 ***Gutknecht***	N	N	N	N	N	N
2 ***Kennedy***	N	N	N	N	N	N
3 ***Ramstad***	N	N	Y	Y	N	N
4 McCollum	Y	Y	Y	Y	N	Y
5 Sabo	N	Y	Y	Y	N	Y
6 Luther	Y	Y	Y	Y	N	Y
7 Peterson	N	N	Y	Y	N	N
8 Oberstar	N	Y	Y	Y	N	Y
MISSISSIPPI						
1 ***Wicker***	N	N	N	N	N	N
2 Thompson	Y	N	Y	Y	N	Y
3 ***Pickering***	N	N	Y	N	N	N
4 Shows	Y	N	Y	N	N	Y
5 Taylor	Y	N	Y	Y	N	N
MISSOURI						
1 Clay	Y	Y	Y	Y	N	Y
2 ***Akin***	N	N	N	N	N	N
3 Gephardt	Y	Y	N	N	N	Y
4 Skelton	N	N	N	N	N	N
5 McCarthy	Y	Y	Y	Y	N	Y
6 ***Graves***	N	N	Y	Y	N	N
7 ***Blunt***	N	N	N	N	N	N
8 ***Emerson***	N	N	Y	Y	N	N
9 ***Hulshof***	N	N	N	N	N	N
MONTANA						
AL ***Rehberg***	N	N	Y	Y	N	N
NEBRASKA						
1 ***Bereuter***	N	N	Y	Y	N	N
2 ***Terry***	N	N	N	N	N	N
3 ***Osborne***	N	N	Y	Y	N	N
NEVADA						
1 Berkley	Y	Y	N	N	N	Y
2 ***Gibbons***	N	N	N	N	Y	N
NEW HAMPSHIRE						
1 ***Sununu***	N	N	Y	N	N	N
2 ***Bass***	N	N	Y	N	N	N
NEW JERSEY						
1 Andrews	Y	Y	N	N	N	Y
2 ***LoBiondo***	N	N	N	N	N	N
3 ***Saxton***	N	N	N	N	N	N
4 ***Smith***	N	N	N	N	N	N
5 ***Roukema***	N	N	N	N	N	N
6 Pallone	Y	Y	N	N	N	Y
7 ***Ferguson***	N	N	N	N	N	N
8 Pascrell	Y	Y	N	N	N	Y
9 Rothman	Y	Y	N	N	N	Y
10 Payne	Y	Y	Y	Y	N	Y
11 ***Frelinghuysen***	N	N	N	N	N	N
12 Holt	Y	Y	Y	Y	N	Y
13 Menendez	Y	Y	N	N	N	Y
NEW MEXICO						
1 ***Wilson***	N	N	N	N	N	N
2 ***Skeen***	N	N	N	N	N	N
3 Udall	Y	Y	Y	Y	N	Y
NEW YORK						
1 ***Grucci***	N	N	N	N	N	N
2 Israel	N	N	N	N	N	Y
3 ***King***	N	N	N	N	N	N
4 McCarthy	N	Y	N	Y	N	Y
5 Ackerman	Y	Y	N	N	N	Y
6 Meeks	Y	Y	?	Y	N	Y
7 Crowley	Y	Y	N	N	N	Y
8 Nadler	N	Y	Y	Y	N	Y
9 Weiner	Y	Y	Y	Y	N	Y
10 Towns	Y	Y	Y	Y	N	Y
11 Owens	Y	Y	Y	Y	N	Y
12 Velázquez	Y	Y	Y	Y	N	Y
13 ***Fossella***	N	N	N	N	N	N
14 Maloney	Y	Y	Y	Y	N	Y
15 Rangel	Y	Y	Y	Y	N	Y
16 Serrano	N	Y	Y	Y	N	Y
17 Engel	N	N	N	N	N	Y
18 Lowey	Y	Y	Y	Y	N	Y
19 ***Kelly***	N	N	N	N	N	N
20 ***Gilman***	N	N	N	N	N	N
21 McNulty	N	N	Y	Y	N	Y
22 ***Sweeney***	N	N	N	N	N	N
23 ***Boehlert***	N	N	Y	N	N	N
24 ***McHugh***	N	N	N	N	N	N
25 ***Walsh***	N	N	N	N	N	N
26 Hinchey	Y	Y	Y	Y	Y	Y
27 ***Reynolds***	N	N	N	N	N	N
28 Slaughter	Y	Y	Y	Y	N	Y
29 LaFalce	Y	Y	Y	Y	N	Y

	268	269	270	271	272	273
30 ***Quinn***	N	N	N	N	N	N
31 ***Houghton***	N	N	Y	Y	N	N
NORTH CAROLINA						
1 Clayton	N	Y	Y	Y	N	Y
2 Etheridge	Y	Y	Y	N	N	Y
3 ***Jones***	N	N	N	N	Y	N
4 Price	Y	Y	Y	Y	N	Y
5 ***Burr***	N	N	N	N	N	N
6 ***Coble***	N	N	N	N	Y	N
7 McIntyre	N	Y	Y	N	N	Y
8 ***Hayes***	N	N	N	N	N	N
9 ***Myrick***	N	N	N	N	N	N
10 ***Ballenger***	N	N	N	N	N	N
11 ***Taylor***	N	N	N	N	N	N
12 Watt	Y	N	Y	Y	N	Y
NORTH DAKOTA						
AL Pomeroy	Y	Y	Y	Y	N	Y
OHIO						
1 ***Chabot***	N	N	N	N	N	N
2 ***Portman***	N	N	N	N	N	N
3 Hall	N	N	N	Y	N	Y
4 ***Oxley***	N	N	N	N	N	N
5 ***Gillmor***	N	N	N	N	N	N
6 Strickland	Y	Y	Y	Y	N	Y
7 ***Hobson***	N	N	N	N	N	N
8 ***Boehner***	N	N	N	N	N	N
9 Kaptur	Y	Y	Y	Y	N	Y
10 Kucinich	N	Y	Y	Y	N	Y
11 Jones	Y	Y	Y	Y	N	Y
12 ***Tiberi***	N	N	Y	N	N	N
13 Brown	Y	Y	Y	Y	N	Y
14 Sawyer	Y	Y	Y	Y	N	Y
15 ***Pryce***	N	N	N	N	N	N
16 ***Regula***	N	N	N	N	N	N
17 Traficant	N	N	N	N	Y	N
18 ***Ney***	N	N	Y	N	Y	N
19 ***LaTourette***	N	N	N	N	Y	N
OKLAHOMA						
1 ***Largent***	N	N	Y	Y	N	N
2 Carson	Y	Y	Y	Y	N	Y
3 ***Watkins***	N	N	N	N	?	N
4 ***Watts***	N	N	N	N	N	N
5 ***Istook***	N	N	N	N	N	N
6 ***Lucas***	N	N	N	N	N	N
OREGON						
1 Wu	Y	Y	N	N	N	Y
2 ***Walden***	N	N	N	N	N	N
3 Blumenauer	N	N	?	?	?	?
4 DeFazio	Y	Y	Y	Y	N	Y
5 Hooley	Y	N	Y	Y	N	Y
PENNSYLVANIA						
1 Brady	Y	Y	Y	N	N	Y
2 Fattah	Y	Y	Y	Y	N	Y
3 Borski	N	Y	Y	N	N	Y
4 ***Hart***	N	N	N	N	N	N
5 ***Peterson***	N	N	Y	Y	N	N
6 Holden	N	N	Y	N	N	Y
7 ***Weldon***	N	N	Y	N	N	N
8 ***Greenwood***	N	N	Y	Y	N	N
9 ***Shuster, Bill***	N	N	N	N	N	N
10 ***Sherwood***	N	N	Y	N	N	N
11 Kanjorski	N	N	Y	Y	N	Y
12 Murtha	N	N	Y	N	N	Y
13 Hoeffel	N	Y	Y	Y	N	Y
14 Coyne	Y	Y	Y	Y	N	Y
15 ***Toomey***	N	N	Y	N	N	N
16 ***Pitts***	N	N	N	N	N	N
17 ***Gekas***	N	N	N	N	N	N
18 Doyle	N	N	Y	Y	N	Y
19 ***Platts***	N	N	Y	N	N	N
20 Mascara	N	Y	Y	N	N	Y
21 ***English***	N	N	Y	Y	N	N
RHODE ISLAND						
1 Kennedy	Y	Y	N	N	N	Y
2 Langevin	Y	Y	Y	Y	N	Y
SOUTH CAROLINA						
1 ***Brown***	N	N	Y	Y	N	N
2 ***Spence***	?	?	?	?	?	?
3 ***Graham***	N	N	N	N	N	N
4 ***DeMint***	N	N	N	N	N	N
5 Spratt	Y	Y	Y	N	N	Y
6 Clyburn	N	N	Y	Y	N	Y
SOUTH DAKOTA						
AL ***Thune***	N	N	Y	Y	N	N

	268	269	270	271	272	273
TENNESSEE						
1 ***Jenkins***	N	N	N	N	N	N
2 ***Duncan***	N	N	N	N	Y	N
3 ***Wamp***	N	N	Y	N	N	N
4 ***Hilleary***	N	N	Y	N	Y	N
5 Clement	Y	Y	Y	Y	N	Y
6 Gordon	N	Y	Y	N	N	Y
7 ***Bryant***	N	N	N	N	N	N
8 Tanner	Y	N	Y	Y	N	N
9 Ford	Y	Y	Y	Y	N	Y
TEXAS						
1 Sandlin	Y	Y	Y	Y	N	Y
2 Turner	Y	Y	Y	Y	N	Y
3 ***Johnson, Sam***	N	N	N	N	N	N
4 Hall	N	N	N	N	Y	N
5 ***Sessions***	N	N	N	N	Y	N
6 ***Barton***	N	N	N	N	N	N
7 ***Culberson***	N	N	N	N	N	N
8 ***Brady***	N	N	Y	Y	N	N
9 Lampson	N	Y	Y	Y	N	Y
10 Doggett	Y	Y	Y	Y	N	Y
11 Edwards	Y	Y	Y	Y	N	Y
12 ***Granger***	N	N	N	N	N	N
13 ***Thornberry***	N	N	N	N	N	N
14 ***Paul***	N	N	Y	Y	Y	N
15 Hinojosa	Y	Y	Y	Y	N	Y
16 Reyes	N	N	N	N	N	Y
17 Stenholm	N	N	Y	Y	N	N
18 Jackson-Lee	Y	N	Y	Y	N	Y
19 ***Combest***	N	N	Y	Y	N	N
20 Gonzalez	?	?	Y	Y	N	Y
21 ***Smith***	N	N	N	N	N	N
22 ***DeLay***	N	N	N	N	N	N
23 ***Bonilla***	N	N	N	N	N	N
24 Frost	Y	Y	N	N	N	Y
25 Bentsen	N	Y	Y	Y	N	Y
26 ***Armey***	N	N	N	N	N	N
27 Ortiz	N	N	N	N	N	Y
28 Rodriguez	N	Y	Y	Y	N	Y
29 Green	Y	Y	N	N	N	Y
30 Johnson, E.B.	+	+	Y	Y	N	Y
UTAH						
1 ***Hansen***	N	N	N	N	Y	N
2 Matheson	Y	Y	Y	Y	N	Y
3 ***Cannon***	N	N	N	N	N	N
VERMONT						
AL *Sanders*	Y	Y	Y	Y	N	Y
VIRGINIA						
1 ***Davis, Jo Ann***	N	N	N	N	N	N
2 ***Schrock***	N	N	N	N	N	N
3 Scott	N	Y	Y	Y	N	Y
4 ***Forbes***	N	N	N	N	N	N
5 *Goode*	N	N	N	N	N	N
6 ***Goodlatte***	N	N	N	N	N	N
7 ***Cantor***	N	N	N	N	N	N
8 Moran	Y	Y	Y	Y	N	N
9 Boucher	N	N	Y	Y	N	Y
10 ***Wolf***	N	N	N	N	N	N
11 ***Davis, T.***	N	N	N	N	N	N
WASHINGTON						
1 Inslee	Y	Y	Y	Y	N	Y
2 Larsen	Y	Y	Y	Y	N	Y
3 Baird	Y	Y	Y	Y	N	Y
4 ***Hastings***	N	N	N	N	N	N
5 ***Nethercutt***	N	N	Y	Y	N	N
6 Dicks	N	Y	Y	Y	N	Y
7 McDermott	Y	N	Y	Y	N	Y
8 ***Dunn***	N	N	N	N	N	N
9 Smith	Y	Y	Y	Y	N	N
WEST VIRGINIA						
1 Mollohan	N	N	N	N	N	Y
2 ***Capito***	N	N	N	N	N	N
3 Rahall	N	Y	Y	Y	N	Y
WISCONSIN						
1 ***Ryan***	N	N	Y	Y	N	N
2 Baldwin	Y	Y	Y	Y	N	Y
3 Kind	Y	Y	Y	Y	N	N
4 Kleczka	Y	Y	Y	Y	N	Y
5 Barrett	Y	Y	Y	Y	N	Y
6 ***Petri***	N	N	N	N	N	N
7 Obey	Y	Y	Y	Y	N	Y
8 ***Green***	N	N	N	N	N	N
9 ***Sensenbrenner***	N	N	N	N	N	N
WYOMING						
AL ***Cubin***	N	N	N	N	N	N

Southern states - Ala., Ark., Fla., Ga., Ky., La., Miss., N.C., Okla., S.C., Tenn., Texas, Va.

274. HR 2590. Fiscal 2002 Treasury Appropriations/Passage. Passage of the bill that would appropriate $32.7 billion in fiscal 2002 for the Treasury Department, U.S. Postal Service, various offices of the Executive Office of the President and certain independent agencies, a $1.1 billion increase over fiscal 2001 spending. The total includes $9.5 billion for the Internal Revenue Service and $2.7 billion for the Customs Service. The measure provides that all federal employees would receive a 4.6 percent pay raise. It also would prohibit payments under federal employee health plans for abortions except in the case of rape, incest or when the woman's life is endangered. Passed 334-94: R 172-47; D 161-46 (ND 121-33, SD 40-13); I 1-1. July 25, 2001.

275. H J Res 55. Vietnam Trade/Passage. Passage of the joint resolution to disapprove the presidential waiver that allows U.S. trade credits and guarantees for companies that do business with Vietnam through July 2, 2002. Rejected 91-324: R 56-152; D 33-172 (ND 23-129, SD 10-43); I 2-0. A "nay" was a vote in support of the president's position. July 26, 2001.

276. HR 1954. Iran and Libya Sanctions/Passage. Gilman, R-N.Y., motion to suspend the rules and pass the bill that would revise and extend for five years the Iran-Libya Sanctions Act (PL 104-172), thereby allowing the president to impose sanctions on domestic and foreign individuals and companies that invest more than $20 million annually in Iranian and Libyan oil and gas industries. Motion agreed to 409-6: R 207-1; D 200-5 (ND 149-3, SD 51-2); I 2-0. A two-thirds majority of those present and voting (277 in this case) is required for passage under suspension of the rules. July 26, 2001.

277. HR 2620. Fiscal 2002 VA-HUD Appropriations/Consideration of Rule. Adoption of the resolution (H Res 209) that would waive the two-thirds vote requirement for same day consideration of the rule (H Res 210) to provide for House floor consideration of the bill that would appropriate $112.7 billion in fiscal 2002 for the departments of Veterans Affairs and Housing and Urban Development and other independent agencies. Adopted 216-200: R 211-0; D 4-199 (ND 2-149, SD 2-50); I 1-1. July 26, 2001.

278. HR 2620. Fiscal 2002 VA-HUD Appropriations/Previous Question. Pryce, R-Ohio, motion to order the previous question (thus ending debate and possibility of amendment) on adoption of the rule (H Res 210) to provide for House floor consideration of the bill that would appropriate $112.7 billion in fiscal year 2002 for the departments of Veterans Affairs and Housing and Urban Development and other independent agencies. Motion agreed to 220-204: R 217-0; D 2-203 (ND 1-152, SD 1-51); I 1-1. July 26, 2001.

279. HR 2620. Fiscal 2002 VA-HUD Appropriations/Rule. Adoption of the rule (H Res 210) to provide for House floor consideration of the bill that would appropriate $112.7 billion in fiscal 2002 for the departments of Veterans Affairs and Housing and Urban Development and other independent agencies. Adopted 228-195: R 189-26; D 38-168 (ND 27-127, SD 11-41); I 1-1. July 26, 2001.

	274	275	276	277	278	279
ALABAMA						
1 *Callahan*	Y	N	Y	Y	Y	Y
2 *Everett*	Y	Y	Y	Y	Y	Y
3 *Riley*	Y	Y	Y	Y	Y	Y
4 *Aderholt*	Y	Y	Y	Y	Y	Y
5 Cramer	Y	N	Y	N	N	Y
6 *Bachus*	Y	?	Y	Y	?	Y
7 Hilliard	Y	N	N	N	N	N
ALASKA						
AL *Young*	Y	Y	Y	Y	Y	Y
ARIZONA						
1 *Flake*	Y	Y	Y	Y	Y	N
2 Pastor	Y	N	Y	N	N	N
3 *Stump*	Y	Y	Y	Y	Y	Y
4 *Shadegg*	N	N	Y	Y	Y	N
5 *Kolbe*	Y	N	Y	Y	Y	Y
6 *Hayworth*	N	Y	Y	Y	Y	Y
ARKANSAS						
1 Berry	N	Y	Y	N	N	N
2 Snyder	?	?	?	?	N	N
3 *Hutchinson*	Y	N	Y	Y	Y	Y
4 Ross	N	Y	Y	N	N	N
CALIFORNIA						
1 Thompson	Y	N	Y	N	N	N
2 *Herger*	N	N	Y	Y	Y	N
3 *Ose*	Y	N	Y	Y	Y	Y
4 *Doolittle*	Y	Y	Y	Y	Y	Y
5 Matsui	Y	N	Y	N	N	N
6 Woolsey	Y	N	Y	N	N	N
7 Miller, George	Y	N	Y	N	N	N
8 Pelosi	Y	N	Y	N	N	N
9 Lee	Y	N	Y	N	N	N
10 Tauscher	Y	N	Y	N	N	N
11 *Pombo*	Y	Y	Y	Y	Y	Y
12 Lantos	Y	N	Y	N	N	N
13 Stark	Y	N	Y	N	N	N
14 Eshoo	Y	N	Y	N	N	N
15 Honda	Y	Y	Y	N	N	N
16 Lofgren	Y	N	Y	N	N	N
17 Farr	Y	N	Y	N	N	N
18 Condit	Y	N	Y	N	N	N
19 *Radanovich*	Y	N	?	Y	Y	Y
20 Dooley	Y	N	N	N	N	N
21 *Thomas*	Y	N	Y	Y	Y	Y
22 Capps	Y	N	Y	N	N	N
23 *Gallegly*	Y	N	Y	Y	Y	Y
24 Sherman	Y	N	Y	N	N	N
25 *McKeon*	Y	N	Y	Y	Y	Y
26 Berman	Y	N	Y	N	N	N
27 Schiff	N	N	Y	N	N	N
28 *Dreier*	Y	N	Y	Y	Y	Y
29 Waxman	Y	N	Y	N	N	N
30 Becerra	Y	N	Y	N	N	N
31 Solis	Y	Y	Y	N	N	N
32 Watson	Y	Y	Y	N	N	N
33 Roybal-Allard	Y	N	Y	N	N	N
34 Napolitano	Y	N	Y	N	N	N
35 Waters	Y	N	Y	?	N	N
36 Harman	Y	N	Y	N	N	N
37 Millender-McD.	Y	N	Y	N	N	N
38 *Horn*	Y	N	Y	Y	Y	N

	274	275	276	277	278	279
39 *Royce*	N	Y	Y	Y	Y	Y
40 *Lewis*	Y	N	Y	Y	Y	Y
41 *Miller, Gary*	Y	N	Y	Y	Y	Y
42 Baca	Y	Y	Y	N	N	N
43 *Calvert*	Y	N	Y	Y	Y	Y
44 *Bono*	Y	N	Y	Y	Y	Y
45 *Rohrabacher*	N	Y	Y	Y	Y	Y
46 Sanchez	Y	Y	Y	N	N	N
47 *Cox*	N	Y	Y	Y	Y	Y
48 *Issa*	Y	N	Y	Y	Y	Y
49 Davis	N	N	N	N	N	N
50 Filner	Y	N	N	N	N	N
51 *Cunningham*	Y	N	Y	Y	Y	Y
52 *Hunter*	Y	?	?	Y	Y	Y
COLORADO						
1 DeGette	Y	N	Y	N	N	N
2 Udall	N	N	Y	N	N	N
3 *McInnis*	N	N	Y	Y	Y	Y
4 *Schaffer*	N	Y	Y	?	Y	N
5 *Hefley*	N	N	Y	Y	Y	Y
6 *Tancredo*	N	Y	Y	?	Y	N
CONNECTICUT						
1 Larson	Y	N	Y	N	N	Y
2 *Simmons*	Y	N	Y	Y	Y	Y
3 DeLauro	Y	N	Y	N	N	N
4 *Shays*	N	N	Y	N	N	N
5 Maloney	Y	N	N	N	N	N
6 *Johnson*	Y	N	Y	Y	Y	Y
DELAWARE						
AL *Castle*	Y	N	Y	Y	Y	N
FLORIDA						
1 *Scarborough*	?	Y	Y	Y	Y	Y
2 Boyd	Y	N	Y	N	N	N
3 Brown	Y	N	Y	N	N	Y
4 *Crenshaw*	N	N	Y	Y	Y	Y
5 Thurman	N	N	Y	N	N	N
6 *Stearns*	N	N	Y	Y	N	N
7 *Mica*	Y	N	Y	Y	Y	Y
8 *Keller*	Y	N	Y	Y	Y	Y
9 *Bilirakis*	Y	N	Y	Y	Y	Y
10 *Young*	Y	Y	Y	Y	Y	Y
11 Davis	Y	N	Y	N	N	N
12 *Putnam*	N	N	Y	Y	Y	Y
13 *Miller*	Y	N	Y	Y	Y	Y
14 *Goss*	Y	N	Y	Y	Y	Y
15 *Weldon*	N	N	Y	Y	Y	Y
16 *Foley*	Y	N	Y	Y	Y	Y
17 Meek	Y	N	Y	N	N	Y
18 *Ros-Lehtinen*	Y	N	Y	Y	Y	Y
19 Wexler	N	N	N	N	N	N
20 Deutsch	N	N	N	N	N	N
21 *Diaz-Balart*	N	Y	Y	Y	Y	Y
22 *Shaw*	Y	N	Y	Y	Y	Y
23 Hastings	Y	Y	Y	N	N	N
GEORGIA						
1 *Kingston*	Y	N	Y	Y	Y	Y
2 Bishop	Y	N	Y	N	N	N
3 *Collins*	Y	Y	Y	Y	Y	Y
4 McKinney	Y	N	N	N	?	N
5 Lewis	Y	N	Y	N	N	N
6 *Isakson*	Y	N	Y	Y	Y	Y
7 *Barr*	N	Y	Y	Y	Y	Y
8 *Chambliss*	Y	?	Y	Y	Y	Y
9 *Deal*	Y	?	?	Y	Y	Y
10 *Norwood*	Y	Y	Y	Y	Y	Y
11 *Linder*	Y	N	Y	Y	Y	Y
HAWAII						
1 Abercrombie	Y	N	Y	N	Y	N
2 Mink	Y	Y	Y	N	N	N
IDAHO						
1 *Otter*	Y	Y	Y	Y	Y	N
2 *Simpson*	Y	N	Y	Y	Y	Y
ILLINOIS						
1 Rush	Y	N	N	N	N	N
2 Jackson	Y	N	Y	N	N	N
3 Lipinski	?	?	?	?	?	?
4 Gutierrez	Y	N	N	N	N	N
5 Blagojevich	Y	N	Y	N	N	N
6 *Hyde*	Y	N	Y	Y	Y	Y
7 Davis	Y	N	N	N	N	N
8 *Crane*	N	N	Y	Y	Y	Y
9 Schakowsky	Y	N	Y	N	N	N
10 *Kirk*	Y	N	Y	Y	Y	Y
11 *Weller*	Y	N	Y	Y	Y	Y
12 Costello	N	N	Y	N	N	N
13 *Biggert*	Y	N	Y	Y	Y	Y

ND Northern Democrats   SD Southern Democrats

	274	275	276	277	278	279
14 ***Hastert***					Y	Y
15 ***Johnson***	N	N	Y	Y	Y	N
16 ***Manzullo***	Y	N	Y	Y	Y	Y
17 Evans	N	N	Y	N	N	N
18 ***LaHood***	Y	N	Y	Y	Y	Y
19 Phelps	N	N	Y	N	N	N
20 ***Shimkus***	N	N	Y	Y	Y	Y
INDIANA						
1 Visclosky	Y	Y	Y	N	N	Y
2 ***Pence***	Y	N	Y	Y	Y	N
3 Roemer	Y	N	Y	N	N	N
4 ***Souder***	Y	Y	Y	Y	Y	?
5 ***Buyer***	Y	Y	Y	Y	Y	Y
6 ***Burton***	Y	Y	Y	Y	Y	Y
7 ***Kerns***	N	N	Y	Y	Y	N
8 ***Hostettler***	N	N	Y	Y	Y	N
9 Hill	N	N	Y	N	N	N
10 Carson	Y	N	Y	N	N	N
IOWA						
1 ***Leach***	Y	N	Y	Y	Y	Y
2 ***Nussle***	Y	N	Y	Y	Y	Y
3 Boswell	N	N	Y	N	N	N
4 ***Ganske***	Y	N	Y	Y	Y	Y
5 ***Latham***	Y	N	Y	Y	Y	Y
KANSAS						
1 ***Moran***	N	N	Y	Y	Y	Y
2 ***Ryun***	N	N	Y	Y	Y	Y
3 Moore	Y	N	Y	N	N	N
4 ***Tiahrt***	Y	N	Y	Y	Y	Y
KENTUCKY						
1 ***Whitfield***	Y	N	Y	Y	Y	Y
2 ***Lewis***	Y	N	Y	Y	Y	Y
3 ***Northup***	Y	N	Y	?	Y	Y
4 Lucas	N	N	Y	N	N	N
5 ***Rogers***	Y	N	Y	Y	Y	Y
6 ***Fletcher***	Y	?	?	Y	Y	Y
LOUISIANA						
1 ***Vitter***	Y	N	Y	Y	Y	Y
2 Jefferson	Y	N	Y	N	N	N
3 ***Tauzin***	Y	N	Y	Y	Y	Y
4 ***McCrery***	Y	N	Y	Y	Y	Y
5 ***Cooksey***	Y	N	Y	Y	Y	?
6 ***Baker***	N	N	Y	Y	Y	Y
7 John	Y	N	Y	N	N	N
MAINE						
1 Allen	Y	N	Y	N	N	N
2 Baldacci	Y	N	Y	N	N	Y
MARYLAND						
1 ***Gilchrest***	Y	N	Y	Y	Y	Y
2 ***Ehrlich***	Y	?	?	?	Y	Y
3 Cardin	Y	N	Y	N	N	N
4 Wynn	Y	Y	Y	N	N	N
5 Hoyer	Y	N	Y	N	N	N
6 ***Bartlett***	N	Y	Y	Y	Y	N
7 Cummings	Y	N	Y	N	N	N
8 ***Morella***	Y	N	Y	Y	Y	Y
MASSACHUSETTS						
1 Olver	Y	N	Y	N	N	N
2 Neal	Y	N	Y	N	N	Y
3 McGovern	Y	N	Y	N	N	N
4 Frank	Y	N	Y	N	N	N
5 Meehan	Y	N	Y	N	N	N
6 Tierney	Y	N	Y	N	N	N
7 Markey	Y	N	Y	N	N	N
8 Capuano	Y	N	Y	N	N	N
9 Vacant						
10 Delahunt	Y	N	Y	N	N	N
MICHIGAN						
1 Stupak	Y	Y	Y	N	N	Y
2 ***Hoekstra***	N	Y	Y	Y	Y	N
3 ***Ehlers***	Y	N	Y	Y	Y	Y
4 ***Camp***	Y	N	Y	Y	Y	Y
5 Barcia	N	Y	Y	N	N	Y
6 ***Upton***	N	N	Y	Y	Y	Y
7 ***Smith***	N	N	Y	Y	Y	N
8 ***Rogers***	Y	Y	Y	Y	Y	Y
9 Kildee	N	N	Y	N	N	N
10 Bonior	Y	Y	P	N	N	N
11 ***Knollenberg***	Y	N	Y	Y	Y	Y
12 Levin	Y	N	Y	N	N	N
13 Rivers	Y	Y	Y	N	N	N
14 Conyers	N	Y	N	N	N	N
15 Kilpatrick	Y	N	Y	N	N	N
16 Dingell	Y	N	Y	N	N	N
MINNESOTA						
1 ***Gutknecht***	Y	Y	Y	Y	Y	Y
2 ***Kennedy***	Y	N	Y	Y	Y	Y
3 ***Ramstad***	N	N	Y	Y	Y	N
4 McCollum	Y	N	Y	N	N	N
5 Sabo	Y	N	Y	N	N	Y
6 Luther	N	N	Y	N	N	N
7 Peterson	N	N	Y	N	N	N
8 Oberstar	Y	N	Y	N	N	N
MISSISSIPPI						
1 ***Wicker***	Y	N	Y	Y	Y	Y
2 Thompson	Y	N	Y	N	N	N
3 ***Pickering***	N	Y	Y	Y	Y	Y
4 Shows	N	Y	Y	N	N	N
5 Taylor	N	Y	Y	N	N	Y
MISSOURI						
1 Clay	Y	N	Y	N	N	N
2 ***Akin***	Y	N	Y	Y	Y	N
3 Gephardt	Y	N	Y	N	N	N
4 Skelton	Y	N	Y	N	N	N
5 McCarthy	Y	N	Y	N	N	N
6 ***Graves***	Y	N	Y	Y	Y	Y
7 ***Blunt***	Y	?	?	Y	Y	Y
8 ***Emerson***	Y	?	?	Y	Y	Y
9 ***Hulshof***	Y	N	Y	Y	Y	Y
MONTANA						
AL ***Rehberg***	Y	N	Y	Y	Y	Y
NEBRASKA						
1 ***Bereuter***	Y	N	Y	Y	Y	Y
2 ***Terry***	Y	N	Y	Y	Y	Y
3 ***Osborne***	Y	N	Y	Y	Y	Y
NEVADA						
1 Berkley	N	N	Y	N	N	N
2 ***Gibbons***	Y	N	Y	Y	Y	Y
NEW HAMPSHIRE						
1 ***Sununu***	Y	N	Y	Y	Y	Y
2 ***Bass***	Y	N	Y	Y	Y	Y
NEW JERSEY						
1 Andrews	N	Y	Y	N	N	N
2 ***LoBiondo***	Y	Y	Y	Y	Y	Y
3 ***Saxton***	Y	N	Y	Y	Y	Y
4 ***Smith***	N	Y	Y	Y	Y	Y
5 ***Roukema***	Y	N	Y	Y	Y	Y
6 Pallone	Y	N	Y	N	N	N
7 ***Ferguson***	Y	N	Y	Y	Y	Y
8 Pascrell	Y	N	Y	N	N	Y
9 Rothman	Y	Y	Y	N	N	N
10 Payne	Y	N	Y	N	N	N
11 ***Frelinghuysen***	Y	N	Y	Y	Y	Y
12 Holt	Y	N	Y	N	N	N
13 Menendez	N	Y	Y	N	N	N
NEW MEXICO						
1 ***Wilson***	Y	N	Y	Y	Y	Y
2 ***Skeen***	Y	N	Y	Y	Y	Y
3 Udall	N	N	Y	?	N	N
NEW YORK						
1 ***Grucci***	Y	N	Y	Y	Y	Y
2 Israel	N	N	Y	N	N	N
3 ***King***	Y	N	?	Y	Y	Y
4 McCarthy	Y	N	Y	N	N	Y
5 Ackerman	Y	N	Y	N	N	N
6 Meeks	Y	N	Y	N	N	N
7 Crowley	Y	N	Y	N	N	N
8 Nadler	Y	N	Y	N	N	N
9 Weiner	Y	N	Y	N	N	N
10 Towns	Y	N	Y	N	N	N
11 Owens	Y	N	Y	N	N	N
12 Velázquez	Y	N	Y	N	N	N
13 ***Fossella***	Y	N	Y	Y	Y	Y
14 Maloney	N	N	Y	N	N	N
15 Rangel	Y	N	Y	N	N	N
16 Serrano	Y	N	Y	N	N	N
17 Engel	Y	N	Y	N	N	N
18 Lowey	Y	N	Y	N	N	N
19 ***Kelly***	Y	N	Y	Y	Y	Y
20 ***Gilman***	Y	Y	Y	Y	Y	Y
21 McNulty	Y	+	+	−	N	Y
22 ***Sweeney***	Y	N	Y	Y	Y	Y
23 ***Boehlert***	Y	N	Y	Y	Y	Y
24 ***McHugh***	Y	N	Y	Y	Y	Y
25 ***Walsh***	Y	N	Y	Y	Y	Y
26 Hinchey	Y	N	Y	N	N	N
27 ***Reynolds***	Y	N	Y	Y	Y	Y
28 Slaughter	Y	N	Y	N	N	Y
29 LaFalce	Y	N	N	N	N	N
30 ***Quinn***	Y	N	Y	Y	Y	Y
31 ***Houghton***	Y	?	?	?	?	?
NORTH CAROLINA						
1 Clayton	Y	N	Y	N	N	?
2 Etheridge	N	N	Y	N	N	N
3 ***Jones***	N	?	?	Y	Y	N
4 Price	Y	N	Y	N	N	Y
5 ***Burr***	Y	N	Y	Y	Y	Y
6 ***Coble***	N	Y	Y	Y	Y	Y
7 McIntyre	Y	Y	Y	N	N	N
8 ***Hayes***	Y	Y	Y	Y	Y	Y
9 ***Myrick***	Y	N	Y	?	Y	Y
10 ***Ballenger***	Y	Y	Y	Y	Y	Y
11 ***Taylor***	Y	Y	Y	Y	Y	Y
12 Watt	Y	Y	Y	N	N	N
NORTH DAKOTA						
AL Pomeroy	N	N	Y	N	N	N
OHIO						
1 ***Chabot***	N	Y	Y	Y	Y	N
2 ***Portman***	Y	N	Y	Y	Y	Y
3 Hall	Y	N	Y	N	N	N
4 ***Oxley***	Y	N	Y	Y	Y	Y
5 ***Gillmor***	Y	N	Y	Y	Y	Y
6 Strickland	N	Y	Y	N	N	N
7 ***Hobson***	Y	N	Y	Y	Y	Y
8 ***Boehner***	Y	N	Y	Y	Y	?
9 Kaptur	Y	P	Y	N	N	Y
10 Kucinich	N	Y	Y	N	N	N
11 Jones	Y	N	Y	N	?	N
12 ***Tiberi***	Y	N	Y	Y	Y	Y
13 Brown	N	Y	Y	N	N	N
14 Sawyer	Y	N	Y	N	N	N
15 ***Pryce***	Y	N	Y	Y	Y	Y
16 ***Regula***	Y	N	Y	Y	Y	Y
17 Traficant	Y	Y	Y	Y	Y	Y
18 ***Ney***	Y	N	Y	Y	Y	Y
19 ***LaTourette***	Y	N	Y	Y	Y	Y
OKLAHOMA						
1 ***Largent***	Y	N	Y	Y	Y	N
2 Carson	N	N	Y	?	N	N
3 ***Watkins***	Y	N	Y	Y	Y	Y
4 ***Watts***	Y	N	Y	Y	Y	Y
5 ***Istook***	Y	N	Y	?	Y	Y
6 ***Lucas***	Y	N	Y	Y	Y	Y
OREGON						
1 Wu	N	N	Y	N	N	Y
2 ***Walden***	N	N	Y	Y	Y	Y
3 Blumenauer	?	?	?	?	?	?
4 DeFazio	N	N	Y	N	N	N
5 Hooley	Y	N	Y	N	N	N
PENNSYLVANIA						
1 Brady	Y	N	Y	N	N	Y
2 Fattah	Y	N	Y	N	N	Y
3 Borski	Y	N	Y	N	N	Y
4 ***Hart***	Y	N	Y	Y	Y	Y
5 ***Peterson***	Y	N	Y	Y	Y	Y
6 Holden	Y	Y	Y	N	N	Y
7 ***Weldon***	Y	Y	Y	Y	Y	Y
8 ***Greenwood***	Y	N	Y	Y	Y	Y
9 ***Shuster, Bill***	Y	N	Y	Y	Y	Y
10 ***Sherwood***	Y	N	Y	Y	Y	Y
11 Kanjorski	Y	N	Y	N	N	Y
12 Murtha	Y	N	Y	N	N	Y
13 Hoeffel	Y	N	Y	N	N	Y
14 Coyne	Y	N	Y	N	N	N
15 ***Toomey***	N	N	Y	Y	Y	N
16 ***Pitts***	N	Y	Y	Y	Y	N
17 ***Gekas***	Y	−	+	Y	Y	Y
18 Doyle	Y	N	Y	N	N	Y
19 ***Platts***	Y	N	Y	Y	Y	Y
20 Mascara	Y	N	Y	N	N	Y
21 ***English***	Y	N	Y	Y	Y	Y
RHODE ISLAND						
1 Kennedy	Y	Y	Y	N	N	N
2 Langevin	N	N	Y	N	N	N
SOUTH CAROLINA						
1 ***Brown***	Y	Y	Y	Y	Y	Y
2 ***Spence***	?	?	?	?	?	?
3 ***Graham***	Y	Y	Y	Y	Y	Y
4 ***DeMint***	Y	N	Y	Y	Y	Y
5 Spratt	Y	N	Y	N	N	N
6 Clyburn	Y	N	Y	N	N	N
SOUTH DAKOTA						
AL ***Thune***	N	N	Y	Y	Y	Y
TENNESSEE						
1 ***Jenkins***	Y	Y	Y	Y	Y	Y
2 ***Duncan***	N	Y	Y	Y	Y	Y
3 ***Wamp***	Y	Y	Y	Y	Y	Y
4 ***Hilleary***	N	Y	Y	Y	Y	Y
5 Clement	Y	N	Y	N	N	N
6 Gordon	Y	N	Y	N	N	N
7 ***Bryant***	Y	N	Y	Y	Y	Y
8 Tanner	Y	N	Y	N	N	N
9 Ford	Y	N	Y	N	N	N
TEXAS						
1 Sandlin	N	N	Y	N	N	N
2 Turner	N	N	Y	N	N	N
3 ***Johnson, Sam***	Y	Y	Y	Y	Y	N
4 Hall	N	Y	Y	Y	Y	Y
5 ***Sessions***	N	N	Y	Y	Y	Y
6 ***Barton***	Y	Y	Y	Y	?	?
7 ***Culberson***	Y	Y	Y	Y	Y	Y
8 ***Brady***	Y	N	Y	Y	Y	Y
9 Lampson	Y	N	Y	N	N	Y
10 Doggett	Y	N	Y	N	N	N
11 Edwards	Y	N	Y	N	N	N
12 ***Granger***	Y	N	Y	Y	Y	Y
13 ***Thornberry***	Y	N	Y	Y	Y	Y
14 ***Paul***	N	Y	N	Y	Y	Y
15 Hinojosa	Y	N	Y	N	N	Y
16 Reyes	Y	N	Y	N	N	N
17 Stenholm	Y	N	Y	N	N	N
18 Jackson-Lee	Y	Y	Y	N	?	?
19 ***Combest***	Y	N	Y	Y	Y	Y
20 Gonzalez	Y	N	Y	N	N	N
21 ***Smith***	Y	N	Y	Y	Y	Y
22 ***DeLay***	Y	N	Y	Y	Y	Y
23 ***Bonilla***	Y	Y	Y	Y	Y	Y
24 Frost	Y	N	Y	N	N	N
25 Bentsen	Y	N	Y	N	N	Y
26 ***Armey***	Y	N	Y	?	Y	Y
27 Ortiz	Y	N	Y	N	N	Y
28 Rodriguez	Y	N	Y	N	N	N
29 Green	Y	Y	Y	N	N	N
30 Johnson, E.B.	Y	N	Y	N	N	N
UTAH						
1 ***Hansen***	Y	N	Y	Y	Y	Y
2 Matheson	N	N	Y	N	N	N
3 ***Cannon***	Y	N	Y	Y	Y	Y
VERMONT						
AL *Sanders*	Y	Y	Y	N	N	N
VIRGINIA						
1 ***Davis, Jo Ann***	Y	Y	Y	Y	Y	Y
2 ***Schrock***	Y	N	Y	Y	Y	Y
3 Scott	Y	N	Y	N	N	N
4 ***Forbes***	Y	N	Y	Y	Y	Y
5 *Goode*	N	Y	Y	Y	Y	Y
6 ***Goodlatte***	N	N	Y	Y	Y	Y
7 ***Cantor***	Y	N	Y	Y	Y	Y
8 Moran	Y	N	Y	N	N	Y
9 Boucher	Y	N	Y	N	N	N
10 ***Wolf***	Y	Y	Y	Y	Y	Y
11 ***Davis, T.***	Y	Y	Y	Y	Y	Y
WASHINGTON						
1 Inslee	N	N	Y	N	N	N
2 Larsen	N	N	Y	N	N	N
3 Baird	Y	N	Y	N	N	N
4 ***Hastings***	Y	N	Y	Y	Y	Y
5 ***Nethercutt***	Y	N	Y	Y	Y	Y
6 Dicks	Y	N	Y	N	N	Y
7 McDermott	Y	N	Y	N	N	N
8 ***Dunn***	Y	N	Y	Y	Y	Y
9 Smith	N	N	Y	N	N	N
WEST VIRGINIA						
1 Mollohan	Y	N	Y	N	N	Y
2 ***Capito***	Y	N	Y	Y	Y	Y
3 Rahall	Y	N	N	N	N	Y
WISCONSIN						
1 ***Ryan***	Y	N	Y	Y	Y	N
2 Baldwin	N	N	Y	N	N	N
3 Kind	N	N	Y	N	N	N
4 Kleczka	Y	N	Y	N	N	N
5 Barrett	N	N	Y	N	N	N
6 ***Petri***	N	N	Y	Y	Y	Y
7 Obey	Y	N	Y	N	N	N
8 ***Green***	N	Y	Y	Y	Y	Y
9 ***Sensenbrenner***	N	N	Y	Y	Y	Y
WYOMING						
AL ***Cubin***	Y	?	?	?	?	?

Southern states - Ala., Ark., Fla., Ga., Ky., La., Miss., N.C., Okla., S.C., Tenn., Texas, Va.

Key

Y	Voted for (yea).
#	Paired for.
+	Announced for.
N	Voted against (nay).
X	Paired against.
−	Announced against.
P	Voted "present."
C	Voted "present" to avoid possible conflict of interest.
?	Did not vote or otherwise make a position known.

Democrats **Republicans**
Independents

280. HR 2620. Fiscal 2002 VA-HUD Appropriations/Motion to Rise. Frank, D-Mass., motion to rise from the Committee of the Whole. Motion rejected 189-230: R 1-212; D 187-17 (ND 138-13, SD 49-4); I 1-1. July 26, 2001.

281. HR 2620. Fiscal 2002 VA-HUD Appropriations/Veterans Benefits. Foley, R-Fla., amendment that would increase by $25 million VA funding to help that department reduce its backlog of pending benefits claims and reduce by $92 million National Science Foundation funding for polar and Antarctic research. Rejected 107-311: R 75-136; D 32-173 (ND 24-128, SD 8-45); I 0-2. July 26, 2001.

282. HR 2620. Fiscal 2002 VA-HUD Appropriations/Section 8 Vouchers. Nadler, D-N.Y., amendment that would increase by $195 million section 8 assistance to fund 34,000 more incremental vouchers and increase by $4.8 million VA state grants for additional extended-care facilities construction. It would reduce by $200 million the HUD Downpayment Assistance Initiative. Rejected 139-284: R 2-213; D 136-70 (ND 104-48, SD 32-22); I 1-1. July 26, 2001.

283. HR 2620. Fiscal 2002 VA-HUD Appropriations/Distressed Housing. Davis, D-Ill., amendment that would increase by $100 million funding for HUD's Revitalization of Severely Distressed Public Housing account and reduce by the same amount its Public Housing Capital Fund account. Rejected 60-360: R 3-211; D 57-147 (ND 44-106, SD 13-41); I 0-2. July 26, 2001.

284. HR 2620. Fiscal 2002 VA-HUD Appropriations/Youthbuild. Velázquez, D-N.Y., amendment that would increase by $10 million HUD funding for the Youthbuild program and reduce by $10 million funding for HUD salaries and expenses. Adopted 216-209: R 17-200; D 198-8 (ND 147-5, SD 51-3); I 1-1. July 26, 2001.

285. HR 2620. Fiscal 2002 VA-HUD Appropriations/Homelessness Aid. LaFalce, D-N.Y., amendment that would increase by $122.6 million homeless assistance grants and reduce by $100 million the HUD Downpayment Assistance Initiative and by $22.6 million HUD salaries and expenses. Rejected 124-300: R 1-215; D 122-84 (ND 101-51, SD 21-33); I 1-1. July 26, 2001.

	280	281	282	283	284	285
ALABAMA						
1 *Callahan*	N	N	N	N	N	N
2 *Everett*	N	N	N	N	N	N
3 *Riley*	N	N	N	N	N	N
4 *Aderholt*	N	N	N	N	N	N
5 *Cramer*	N	N	N	N	Y	N
6 *Bachus*	N	N	N	N	N	N
7 Hilliard	Y	N	N	Y	N	N
ALASKA						
AL *Young*	N	N	N	N	N	N
ARIZONA						
1 *Flake*	N	Y	N	N	N	N
2 Pastor	Y	N	Y	N	Y	Y
3 *Stump*	N	N	N	N	N	N
4 *Shadegg*	N	Y	N	N	N	N
5 *Kolbe*	N	N	N	N	N	N
6 *Hayworth*	N	Y	N	N	N	N
ARKANSAS						
1 Berry	Y	N	Y	N	Y	N
2 Snyder	Y	N	Y	N	Y	N
3 *Hutchinson*	?	Y	N	N	N	N
4 Ross	Y	N	Y	Y	Y	Y
CALIFORNIA						
1 Thompson	N	N	Y	N	Y	Y
2 *Herger*	N	Y	N	N	N	N
3 *Ose*	N	N	N	N	N	N
4 *Doolittle*	N	N	N	N	N	N
5 Matsui	Y	N	N	N	Y	Y
6 Woolsey	Y	N	Y	N	Y	N
7 Miller, George	Y	N	Y	N	Y	Y
8 Pelosi	Y	N	Y	Y	Y	Y
9 Lee	Y	N	Y	Y	Y	Y
10 Tauscher	Y	Y	Y	Y	Y	N
11 *Pombo*	N	N	N	N	N	N
12 Lantos	Y	N	Y	N	Y	Y
13 Stark	?	?	?	?	?	?
14 Eshoo	Y	N	N	N	Y	N
15 Honda	Y	N	Y	Y	Y	Y
16 Lofgren	Y	N	N	N	Y	Y
17 Farr	Y	N	Y	N	Y	Y
18 Condit	Y	Y	N	Y	N	N
19 *Radanovich*	?	N	N	N	N	N
20 Dooley	Y	N	N	N	N	N
21 *Thomas*	N	N	N	N	N	N
22 Capps	Y	N	Y	N	Y	Y
23 *Gallegly*	N	Y	N	N	N	N
24 Sherman	Y	N	Y	N	Y	Y
25 *McKeon*	N	?	N	N	N	N
26 Berman	Y	N	Y	?	Y	Y
27 Schiff	Y	N	Y	N	Y	N
28 *Dreier*	N	N	N	N	N	N
29 Waxman	Y	N	Y	N	Y	Y
30 Becerra	Y	N	Y	N	Y	Y
31 Solis	Y	N	Y	Y	Y	Y
32 Watson	Y	N	Y	Y	Y	Y
33 Roybal-Allard	Y	N	Y	N	Y	Y
34 Napolitano	Y	N	N	N	Y	N
35 Waters	Y	N	Y	Y	Y	Y
36 Harman	Y	N	Y	N	Y	N
37 Millender-McD.	Y	N	Y	N	Y	N
38 *Horn*	N	N	N	N	Y	N

	280	281	282	283	284	285
39 *Royce*	N	N	N	N	N	N
40 *Lewis*	N	N	N	N	N	N
41 *Miller, Gary*	N	N	N	N	N	N
42 Baca	Y	N	N	Y	N	N
43 *Calvert*	N	N	N	N	N	N
44 *Bono*	N	N	N	N	N	N
45 *Rohrabacher*	N	N	N	N	N	N
46 Sanchez	Y	N	Y	N	N	N
47 *Cox*	N	N	N	N	N	N
48 *Issa*	N	N	N	N	N	N
49 Davis	Y	N	N	N	Y	Y
50 Filner	Y	N	Y	Y	Y	Y
51 *Cunningham*	N	N	N	N	N	N
52 *Hunter*	N	?	N	N	N	N
COLORADO						
1 DeGette	Y	N	N	Y	Y	N
2 Udall	Y	N	Y	Y	Y	Y
3 *McInnis*	N	N	N	N	N	N
4 *Schaffer*	N	Y	N	N	Y	Y
5 *Hefley*	Y	N	N	N	N	N
6 *Tancredo*	N	Y	Y	N	N	N
CONNECTICUT						
1 Larson	Y	N	N	N	Y	N
2 *Simmons*	N	Y	N	N	N	N
3 DeLauro	Y	N	Y	N	Y	Y
4 *Shays*	N	N	N	Y	N	N
5 Maloney	N	Y	N	N	Y	N
6 *Johnson*	N	Y	N	N	N	N
DELAWARE						
AL *Castle*	N	N	N	N	N	N
FLORIDA						
1 *Scarborough*	N	Y	N	N	N	N
2 Boyd	Y	Y	Y	N	Y	Y
3 Brown	Y	N	Y	N	Y	N
4 *Crenshaw*	N	N	N	N	N	N
5 Thurman	Y	Y	Y	N	Y	N
6 *Stearns*	N	Y	N	N	N	N
7 *Mica*	N	Y	N	N	N	N
8 *Keller*	N	Y	N	N	N	N
9 *Bilirakis*	N	Y	N	N	N	N
10 *Young*	N	N	N	N	N	N
11 Davis	Y	Y	Y	N	Y	N
12 *Putnam*	N	Y	N	N	N	N
13 *Miller*	?	?	?	?	?	?
14 *Goss*	N	N	N	N	N	N
15 *Weldon*	N	N	N	N	N	N
16 *Foley*	N	Y	N	N	N	N
17 Meek	Y	N	N	N	Y	N
18 *Ros-Lehtinen*	N	Y	N	N	N	N
19 Wexler	Y	N	Y	Y	Y	Y
20 Deutsch	Y	Y	N	N	Y	Y
21 *Diaz-Balart*	N	Y	N	N	N	N
22 *Shaw*	N	N	N	N	N	N
23 Hastings	Y	N	N	N	Y	N
GEORGIA						
1 *Kingston*	N	Y	N	N	N	N
2 Bishop	Y	N	N	Y	Y	Y
3 *Collins*	N	N	N	Y	Y	Y
4 McKinney	?	N	Y	Y	Y	Y
5 Lewis	Y	N	Y	Y	Y	Y
6 *Isakson*	N	N	N	N	N	N
7 *Barr*	N	Y	N	N	N	N
8 *Chambliss*	N	N	N	N	N	N
9 *Deal*	N	N	N	N	N	N
10 *Norwood*	N	N	N	N	N	N
11 *Linder*	?	?	?	?	?	?
HAWAII						
1 Abercrombie	N	N	Y	N	Y	Y
2 Mink	Y	N	Y	Y	Y	N
IDAHO						
1 *Otter*	N	Y	N	?	N	N
2 *Simpson*	N	Y	N	N	N	N
ILLINOIS						
1 Rush	Y	N	Y	Y	Y	N
2 Jackson	Y	N	Y	Y	Y	Y
3 Lipinski	?	?	?	?	?	?
4 Gutierrez	Y	Y	Y	Y	Y	Y
5 Blagojevich	Y	N	Y	Y	Y	Y
6 *Hyde*	N	N	N	N	N	N
7 Davis	N	N	Y	Y	Y	Y
8 *Crane*	N	Y	N	N	N	N
9 Schakowsky	Y	N	Y	Y	Y	Y
10 *Kirk*	N	N	N	N	N	N
11 *Weller*	N	N	N	N	N	N
12 Costello	N	Y	N	Y	Y	N
13 *Biggert*	N	N	N	N	N	N

ND Northern Democrats   SD Southern Democrats

	280	281	282	283	284	285
14 **Hastert**					N	
15 **Johnson**	N	Y	N	N	Y	N
16 **Manzullo**	N	Y	N	N	Y	N
17 Evans	N	Y	Y	Y	Y	Y
18 **LaHood**	N	N	N	N	N	N
19 Phelps	N	N	N	N	Y	N
20 **Shimkus**	N	N	N	N	N	N
INDIANA						
1 Visclosky	Y	Y	Y	N	Y	Y
2 **Pence**	N	Y	N	N	N	N
3 Roemer	N	N	Y	N	Y	N
4 **Souder**	N	N	N	N	N	N
5 **Buyer**	N	N	N	N	N	N
6 **Burton**	N	N	N	N	N	N
7 **Kerns**	N	Y	N	N	N	N
8 **Hostettler**	N	Y	N	N	N	N
9 Hill	Y	N	N	N	Y	N
10 Carson	Y	N	Y	Y	Y	Y
IOWA						
1 **Leach**	N	N	N	N	Y	N
2 **Nussle**	N	N	N	N	N	N
3 Boswell	N	Y	Y	N	Y	Y
4 **Ganske**	N	N	N	N	N	N
5 **Latham**	N	N	N	N	N	N
KANSAS						
1 **Moran**	N	Y	N	N	Y	N
2 **Ryun**	N	N	N	N	N	N
3 Moore	Y	N	N	N	Y	N
4 **Tiahrt**	N	N	N	N	N	N
KENTUCKY						
1 **Whitfield**	N	N	N	N	N	N
2 **Lewis**	N	Y	N	N	N	N
3 **Northup**	N	–	N	N	N	N
4 Lucas	Y	N	Y	Y	Y	Y
5 **Rogers**	N	N	N	N	N	N
6 **Fletcher**	N	Y	N	N	N	N
LOUISIANA						
1 **Vitter**	N	N	N	N	N	N
2 Jefferson	Y	N	Y	N	Y	N
3 **Tauzin**	N	N	N	N	N	N
4 **McCrery**	N	N	N	N	N	N
5 **Cooksey**	N	N	N	N	N	N
6 **Baker**	N	N	N	N	N	N
7 John	Y	N	N	N	Y	N
MAINE						
1 Allen	Y	N	Y	N	Y	Y
2 Baldacci	Y	N	Y	N	Y	Y
MARYLAND						
1 **Gilchrest**	N	N	N	N	N	N
2 **Ehrlich**	N	N	N	N	N	N
3 Cardin	Y	N	N	N	Y	N
4 Wynn	Y	N	N	Y	N	N
5 Hoyer	Y	N	N	N	N	N
6 **Bartlett**	N	N	N	N	N	N
7 Cummings	Y	N	N	Y	Y	Y
8 **Morella**	N	N	N	N	N	N
MASSACHUSETTS						
1 Olver	Y	N	Y	N	Y	Y
2 Neal	Y	N	N	N	Y	Y
3 McGovern	Y	N	N	N	Y	Y
4 Frank	Y	N	N	N	Y	Y
5 Meehan	Y	N	Y	?	Y	Y
6 Tierney	Y	N	N	N	Y	Y
7 Markey	Y	N	N	N	Y	Y
8 Capuano	Y	N	N	N	Y	Y
9 Vacant						
10 Delahunt	Y	N	N	N	Y	Y
MICHIGAN						
1 Stupak	Y	N	N	N	Y	N
2 **Hoekstra**	N	N	N	N	N	N
3 **Ehlers**	N	N	N	N	N	N
4 **Camp**	N	N	N	N	N	N
5 Barcia	Y	N	N	N	Y	N
6 **Upton**	N	N	N	N	N	N
7 **Smith**	N	N	N	N	N	N
8 **Rogers**	N	N	N	N	N	N
9 Kildee	Y	Y	N	Y	Y	N
10 Bonior	Y	N	Y	Y	Y	Y
11 **Knollenberg**	N	N	N	N	N	N
12 Levin	Y	N	Y	N	Y	Y
13 Rivers	Y	N	Y	N	Y	N
14 Conyers	Y	N	N	Y	Y	Y
15 Kilpatrick	Y	N	Y	Y	Y	Y
16 Dingell	Y	Y	N	N	Y	N
MINNESOTA						
1 **Gutknecht**	N	N	N	N	N	N
2 **Kennedy**	N	N	N	N	N	N
3 **Ramstad**	N	Y	N	N	Y	N
4 McCollum	Y	N	Y	N	Y	Y
5 Sabo	Y	N	N	N	Y	Y
6 Luther	Y	N	Y	N	Y	Y
7 Peterson	Y	N	Y	N	Y	N
8 Oberstar	Y	N	Y	N	Y	Y
MISSISSIPPI						
1 **Wicker**	N	N	N	N	N	N
2 Thompson	Y	N	N	Y	Y	N
3 **Pickering**	N	N	N	N	N	N
4 Shows	N	N	Y	N	Y	N
5 Taylor	Y	N	N	N	Y	N
MISSOURI						
1 Clay	Y	N	Y	Y	Y	Y
2 **Akin**	N	Y	N	N	N	N
3 Gephardt	Y	Y	N	Y	Y	Y
4 Skelton	Y	N	Y	N	Y	N
5 McCarthy	Y	N	N	N	Y	N
6 **Graves**	N	N	N	N	N	N
7 **Blunt**	N	N	N	N	N	N
8 **Emerson**	N	N	N	N	Y	N
9 **Hulshof**	N	N	N	N	N	N
MONTANA						
AL **Rehberg**	N	N	N	N	N	N
NEBRASKA						
1 **Bereuter**	N	N	N	N	Y	N
2 **Terry**	N	N	N	N	N	N
3 **Osborne**	N	N	N	N	Y	N
NEVADA						
1 Berkley	Y	N	Y	N	Y	Y
2 **Gibbons**	N	N	N	N	N	N
NEW HAMPSHIRE						
1 **Sununu**	N	N	N	N	N	N
2 **Bass**	N	–	N	N	N	N
NEW JERSEY						
1 Andrews	Y	N	N	Y	Y	N
2 **LoBiondo**	N	Y	N	N	N	N
3 **Saxton**	N	Y	N	N	N	N
4 **Smith**	N	N	N	N	N	N
5 **Roukema**	N	N	N	N	N	N
6 Pallone	Y	N	Y	N	Y	N
7 **Ferguson**	N	Y	N	N	N	N
8 Pascrell	Y	Y	Y	N	Y	Y
9 Rothman	Y	N	Y	N	Y	N
10 Payne	Y	N	Y	Y	Y	Y
11 **Frelinghuysen**	N	N	N	N	N	N
12 Holt	Y	N	Y	Y	N	Y
13 Menendez	N	N	Y	N	Y	N
NEW MEXICO						
1 **Wilson**	N	N	N	N	Y	N
2 **Skeen**	N	Y	N	N	N	N
3 Udall	Y	Y	Y	Y	Y	Y
NEW YORK						
1 **Grucci**	N	N	N	N	N	N
2 Israel	Y	Y	N	N	Y	Y
3 **King**	N	Y	N	N	N	N
4 McCarthy	Y	Y	Y	Y	Y	Y
5 Ackerman	Y	Y	Y	N	Y	Y
6 Meeks	?	N	Y	N	Y	N
7 Crowley	Y	Y	Y	N	Y	Y
8 Nadler	Y	N	Y	N	Y	Y
9 Weiner	Y	Y	Y	N	Y	Y
10 Towns	Y	N	Y	Y	Y	N
11 Owens	Y	N	Y	Y	Y	Y
12 Velázquez	Y	N	Y	Y	Y	Y
13 **Fossella**	N	Y	N	N	Y	N
14 Maloney	Y	N	Y	N	Y	Y
15 Rangel	Y	Y	Y	N	Y	Y
16 Serrano	Y	N	Y	N	Y	Y
17 Engel	Y	Y	Y	N	Y	Y
18 Lowey	Y	N	Y	N	Y	Y
19 **Kelly**	N	Y	N	N	N	N
20 **Gilman**	N	Y	N	N	N	N
21 McNulty	Y	N	Y	N	Y	Y
22 **Sweeney**	N	N	N	N	N	N
23 **Boehlert**	N	N	N	N	N	N
24 **McHugh**	N	N	N	N	N	N
25 **Walsh**	N	N	N	N	N	N
26 Hinchey	Y	N	Y	N	Y	N
27 **Reynolds**	N	N	N	N	N	N
28 Slaughter	Y	N	Y	N	Y	N
29 LaFalce	Y	N	Y	N	Y	Y
30 **Quinn**	N	N	N	N	N	N
31 **Houghton**	N	N	N	N	N	N
NORTH CAROLINA						
1 Clayton	Y	N	N	N	Y	Y
2 Etheridge	Y	N	Y	N	Y	Y
3 **Jones**	N	Y	N	N	Y	N
4 Price	Y	N	Y	N	Y	Y
5 **Burr**	N	N	N	N	Y	N
6 **Coble**	N	Y	N	N	N	N
7 McIntyre	Y	N	Y	N	Y	Y
8 **Hayes**	N	Y	N	N	N	N
9 **Myrick**	N	Y	N	Y	N	N
10 **Ballenger**	N	N	N	N	N	N
11 **Taylor**	N	N	N	N	N	N
12 Watt	Y	N	Y	N	Y	Y
NORTH DAKOTA						
AL Pomeroy	Y	N	N	N	Y	N
OHIO						
1 **Chabot**	N	Y	N	N	Y	N
2 **Portman**	N	N	N	N	N	N
3 Hall	?	?	?	?	?	?
4 **Oxley**	N	N	N	N	N	N
5 **Gillmor**	N	N	N	N	N	N
6 Strickland	Y	Y	Y	N	Y	Y
7 **Hobson**	N	N	N	N	N	N
8 **Boehner**	N	N	N	N	N	N
9 Kaptur	Y	N	Y	Y	Y	Y
10 Kucinich	Y	N	Y	Y	Y	Y
11 Jones	Y	N	Y	N	Y	Y
12 **Tiberi**	N	Y	Y	N	N	N
13 Brown	Y	N	Y	N	Y	Y
14 Sawyer	Y	N	Y	N	Y	Y
15 **Pryce**	N	N	N	N	N	N
16 **Regula**	N	N	N	N	N	N
17 Traficant	N	Y	N	N	N	N
18 **Ney**	N	Y	N	N	N	N
19 **LaTourette**	N	N	N	N	N	N
OKLAHOMA						
1 **Largent**	N	N	N	N	N	N
2 Carson	Y	N	N	Y	Y	N
3 **Watkins**	N	N	N	N	N	N
4 **Watts**	N	N	N	N	N	N
5 **Istook**	?	?	N	N	N	N
6 **Lucas**	N	N	N	N	N	N
OREGON						
1 Wu	Y	N	Y	N	Y	Y
2 **Walden**	N	N	N	N	N	N
3 Blumenauer	?	?	?	?	?	?
4 DeFazio	Y	N	Y	N	Y	Y
5 Hooley	Y	N	Y	N	Y	Y
PENNSYLVANIA						
1 Brady	Y	N	Y	Y	Y	Y
2 Fattah	Y	N	Y	Y	Y	Y
3 Borski	Y	N	N	N	Y	Y
4 **Hart**	N	Y	N	N	N	N
5 **Peterson**	N	N	N	N	N	N
6 Holden	Y	N	N	N	Y	N
7 **Weldon**	N	N	N	N	N	N
8 **Greenwood**	N	Y	N	N	N	N
9 **Shuster, Bill**	N	N	N	N	N	N
10 **Sherwood**	N	N	N	N	N	N
11 Kanjorski	Y	N	N	N	Y	Y
12 Murtha	Y	N	N	N	Y	N
13 Hoeffel	Y	N	N	Y	Y	N
14 Coyne	Y	N	Y	N	Y	Y
15 **Toomey**	N	Y	N	N	N	N
16 **Pitts**	N	Y	N	N	N	N
17 **Gekas**	N	Y	N	N	N	N
18 Doyle	Y	N	N	Y	N	N
19 **Platts**	N	N	N	N	N	N
20 Mascara	Y	N	N	N	Y	N
21 **English**	N	N	N	N	N	N
RHODE ISLAND						
1 Kennedy	Y	N	Y	N	Y	Y
2 Langevin	Y	N	Y	N	Y	Y
SOUTH CAROLINA						
1 **Brown**	N	N	N	N	N	N
2 **Spence**	?	?	?	?	?	?
3 **Graham**	N	N	N	N	N	N
4 **DeMint**	N	Y	N	N	N	N
5 Spratt	Y	N	Y	N	Y	N
6 Clyburn	Y	N	N	Y	N	N
SOUTH DAKOTA						
AL **Thune**	N	N	N	N	N	N
TENNESSEE						
1 **Jenkins**	N	Y	N	N	N	N
2 **Duncan**	N	Y	N	N	N	N
3 **Wamp**	N	N	N	N	N	N
4 **Hilleary**	N	Y	N	?	N	N
5 Clement	Y	N	N	N	Y	N
6 Gordon	N	N	N	N	Y	Y
7 **Bryant**	N	Y	N	N	N	N
8 Tanner	Y	N	Y	N	Y	N
9 Ford	Y	N	Y	N	Y	N
TEXAS						
1 Sandlin	Y	Y	Y	Y	Y	Y
2 Turner	Y	Y	N	N	Y	N
3 **Johnson, Sam**	N	N	N	N	N	N
4 Hall	N	?	N	N	Y	N
5 **Sessions**	N	Y	N	N	N	N
6 **Barton**	N	N	N	N	N	N
7 **Culberson**	N	N	N	N	N	N
8 **Brady**	N	N	N	N	N	N
9 Lampson	Y	N	N	Y	Y	Y
10 Doggett	Y	N	Y	N	Y	N
11 Edwards	Y	Y	N	N	Y	N
12 **Granger**	N	N	N	N	N	N
13 **Thornberry**	N	N	N	N	N	N
14 **Paul**	N	Y	N	N	N	N
15 Hinojosa	Y	N	Y	N	Y	N
16 Reyes	Y	N	Y	N	Y	N
17 Stenholm	Y	N	Y	N	Y	N
18 Jackson-Lee	Y	N	Y	N	Y	Y
19 **Combest**	N	N	?	N	N	N
20 Gonzalez	Y	N	Y	N	Y	N
21 **Smith**	N	N	N	N	N	N
22 **DeLay**	N	N	N	N	N	N
23 **Bonilla**	N	Y	N	N	N	N
24 Frost	Y	N	Y	N	Y	Y
25 Bentsen	Y	N	N	N	Y	Y
26 **Armey**	N	N	N	N	N	N
27 Ortiz	Y	N	Y	N	Y	N
28 Rodriguez	Y	N	N	N	Y	N
29 Green	Y	N	N	N	Y	Y
30 Johnson, E.B.	Y	N	N	Y	Y	N
UTAH						
1 **Hansen**	N	Y	N	N	N	N
2 Matheson	Y	N	N	N	Y	Y
3 **Cannon**	N	Y	N	N	N	N
VERMONT						
AL Sanders	Y	N	Y	N	Y	Y
VIRGINIA						
1 **Davis, Jo Ann**	N	Y	N	Y	N	N
2 **Schrock**	N	Y	N	N	N	N
3 Scott	Y	N	Y	Y	Y	Y
4 **Forbes**	N	Y	N	N	N	N
5 Goode	N	N	N	N	N	N
6 **Goodlatte**	N	Y	N	N	N	N
7 **Cantor**	N	Y	N	N	N	N
8 Moran	Y	N	Y	N	N	N
9 Boucher	Y	N	Y	N	Y	N
10 **Wolf**	N	N	N	N	N	N
11 **Davis, T.**	N	N	N	N	N	N
WASHINGTON						
1 Inslee	Y	N	N	N	Y	N
2 Larsen	Y	Y	Y	N	Y	N
3 Baird	Y	Y	N	N	Y	N
4 **Hastings**	N	Y	N	N	N	N
5 **Nethercutt**	?	?	?	?	?	?
6 Dicks	Y	N	Y	N	Y	N
7 McDermott	Y	N	Y	N	Y	Y
8 **Dunn**	N	Y	N	N	Y	N
9 Smith	Y	N	Y	N	Y	Y
WEST VIRGINIA						
1 Mollohan	N	N	Y	N	Y	Y
2 **Capito**	N	Y	N	N	Y	N
3 Rahall	Y	N	Y	Y	Y	Y
WISCONSIN						
1 **Ryan**	N	N	N	N	N	N
2 Baldwin	Y	N	Y	N	Y	Y
3 Kind	Y	N	Y	N	Y	N
4 Kleczka	N	N	Y	N	Y	Y
5 Barrett	Y	N	Y	N	Y	Y
6 **Petri**	N	N	N	N	N	N
7 Obey	Y	N	Y	N	Y	Y
8 **Green**	N	N	N	N	N	N
9 **Sensenbrenner**	N	N	N	N	N	N
WYOMING						
AL **Cubin**	?	?	?	?	?	?

Southern states - Ala., Ark., Fla., Ga., Ky., La., Miss., N.C., Okla., S.C., Tenn., Texas, Va.

286. HR 2620. Fiscal 2002 VA-HUD Appropriations/Downpayment Assistance. Frank, D-Mass., amendment that would strike a $200 million earmark in the HOME program for the Downpayment Assistance Initiative but keep the funding in the program. Rejected 163-247: R 0-203; D 162-43 (ND 133-20, SD 29-23); I 1-1. July 27, 2001.

287. HR 2620. Fiscal 2002 VA-HUD Appropriations/Anti-Drug Program. Kaptur, D-Ohio, amendment that would provide $175 million for HUD's public housing drug elimination program and reduce by the same amount the Downpayment Assistance Initiative. Rejected 197-213: R 17-187; D 179-25 (ND 139-13, SD 40-12); I 1-1. July 27, 2001.

288. HR 2620. Fiscal 2002 VA-HUD Appropriations/Arsenic Standards. Bonior, D-Mich., amendment that would ban use of funds in the bill to delay national drinking water regulations for arsenic or to further a rule to raise arsenic levels under those regulations. Adopted 218-189: R 19-182; D 198-6 (ND 151-2, SD 47-4); I 1-1. A "nay" was a vote in support of the president's position. July 27, 2001.

289. HR 2620. Fiscal 2002 VA-HUD Appropriations/EPA Enforcement. Menendez, D-N.J., amendment that would restore $25 million for EPA enforcement that would be cut under the bill, and reduce administrative expenses for agencies other than the EPA and the Department of Veterans Affairs (VA) by $25 million. Rejected 182-214: R 5-191; D 176-22 (ND 137-10, SD 39-12); I 1-1. July 27, 2001.

290. H Res 212. Racism Conference/Adoption. Ballenger, R-N.C., motion to suspend the rules and adopt the resolution that would encourage participants at the U.N. World Conference Against Racism, Racial Discrimination, Xenophobia, and Related Intolerance to tackle those and similar discrimination issues. It also would recognize the need for a global framework to address such issues and praise South Africa for hosting the conference. Motion agreed to 408-3: R 213-1; D 194-2 (ND 145-1, SD 49-1); I 1-0. A two-thirds majority of those present and voting (274 in this case) is required for adoption under suspension of the rules. July 30, 2001.

291. H Res 191. Israeli Abduction/Adoption. Ballenger, R-N.C., motion to suspend the rules and adopt the resolution that would call for the United Nations to transfer to Israel all material evidence in the investigation into the Oct. 7, 2000, abduction of three Israeli soldiers by Hezbollah forces, including an unedited videotape. Motion agreed to 411-4: R 212-1; D 198-3 (ND 147-3, SD 51-0); I 1-0. A two-thirds majority of those present and voting (277 in this case) is required for adoption under suspension of the rules. July 30, 2001.

292. H Con Res 190. Substance Addiction/Adoption. Morella, R-Md., motion to suspend the rules and adopt the concurrent resolution that would support National Alcohol and Drug Addiction Recovery Month, recognized in September each year. Motion agreed to 418-0: R 216-0; D 201-0 (ND 149-0, SD 52-0); I 1-0. A two-thirds majority of those present and voting (279 in this case) is required for adoption under suspension of the rules. July 30, 2001.

293. HR 2620. Fiscal 2002 VA-HUD Appropriations/Sewer Improvements. Barcia, D-Mich., amendment that would increase by $140 million EPA water improvement grants to improve municipal combined and sanitary sewer systems and reduce sewage overflow during heavy rains, and reduce the superfund program by the same amount. Rejected 99-325: R 30-187; D 69-136 (ND 58-94, SD 11-42); I 0-2. July 30, 2001.

Key

Y	Voted for (yea).
#	Paired for.
+	Announced for.
N	Voted against (nay).
X	Paired against.
–	Announced against.
P	Voted "present."
C	Voted "present" to avoid possible conflict of interest.
?	Did not vote or otherwise make a position known.

Democrats **Republicans**
Independents

		286	287	288	289	290	291	292	293
ALABAMA									
1	*Callahan*	?	?	?	?	Y	Y	Y	N
2	*Everett*	N	N	N	N	Y	Y	Y	N
3	*Riley*	N	N	N	N	Y	Y	Y	N
4	*Aderholt*	N	N	N	N	Y	Y	Y	N
5	Cramer	N	Y	N	N	Y	Y	Y	N
6	*Bachus*	N	N	N	N	Y	Y	Y	N
7	Hilliard	N	N	Y	Y	Y	Y	Y	N
ALASKA									
AL	*Young*	?	?	?	?	Y	Y	Y	N
ARIZONA									
1	*Flake*	N	N	N	N	Y	Y	Y	N
2	Pastor	Y	Y	Y	Y	Y	Y	Y	N
3	*Stump*	N	N	N	N	Y	Y	Y	N
4	*Shadegg*	N	N	N	N	Y	Y	Y	N
5	*Kolbe*	N	N	N	N	Y	Y	Y	N
6	*Hayworth*	N	N	N	N	Y	Y	Y	Y
ARKANSAS									
1	Berry	N	N	Y	Y	Y	Y	Y	Y
2	Snyder	N	N	Y	Y	?	?	N	Y
3	*Hutchinson*	N	Y	N	N	Y	Y	Y	N
4	Ross	Y	N	Y	N	Y	Y	Y	N
CALIFORNIA									
1	Thompson	Y	Y	Y	Y	Y	Y	Y	Y
2	*Herger*	N	N	N	N	Y	Y	Y	N
3	*Ose*	N	N	N	N	Y	Y	Y	N
4	*Doolittle*	N	N	N	N	Y	Y	Y	N
5	Matsui	Y	Y	Y	Y	Y	Y	Y	N
6	Woolsey	Y	Y	Y	Y	Y	Y	Y	Y
7	Miller, George	Y	Y	Y	Y	Y	Y	Y	Y
8	Pelosi	Y	Y	Y	Y	Y	Y	Y	N
9	Lee	Y	Y	Y	Y	Y	Y	Y	Y
10	Tauscher	Y	Y	Y	Y	Y	Y	Y	Y
11	*Pombo*	N	N	N	N	Y	Y	Y	N
12	Lantos	Y	Y	Y	Y	Y	Y	Y	N
13	Stark	Y	Y	Y	Y	?	?	?	?
14	Eshoo	Y	Y	Y	Y	Y	Y	Y	N
15	Honda	Y	Y	Y	Y	Y	Y	Y	Y
16	Lofgren	Y	N	Y	Y	Y	Y	Y	N
17	Farr	Y	Y	Y	Y	Y	Y	Y	Y
18	Condit	Y	Y	Y	Y	Y	Y	Y	N
19	*Radanovich*	N	N	N	N	Y	Y	Y	?
20	Dooley	N	Y	N	Y	Y	Y	Y	N
21	*Thomas*	N	N	–	N	Y	Y	Y	N
22	Capps	Y	Y	Y	Y	Y	Y	Y	N
23	*Gallegly*	N	N	N	N	Y	Y	Y	N
24	Sherman	Y	N	Y	Y	Y	Y	Y	Y
25	*McKeon*	N	N	N	N	Y	Y	Y	N
26	Berman	Y	Y	Y	?	Y	Y	Y	N
27	Schiff	Y	Y	Y	Y	Y	Y	Y	N
28	*Dreier*	N	N	N	N	Y	Y	Y	N
29	Waxman	Y	Y	Y	Y	Y	Y	Y	Y
30	Becerra	Y	Y	Y	Y	Y	Y	Y	N
31	Solis	Y	Y	Y	Y	Y	Y	Y	N
32	Watson	Y	Y	Y	Y	Y	Y	Y	N
33	Roybal-Allard	Y	Y	Y	Y	Y	Y	Y	N
34	Napolitano	Y	Y	Y	Y	Y	Y	Y	N
35	Waters	Y	Y	Y	Y	?	?	Y	N
36	Harman	N	Y	Y	Y	Y	Y	Y	N
37	Millender-McD.	Y	Y	Y	Y	Y	Y	Y	N
38	Horn	N	N	N	N	Y	Y	Y	N

		286	287	288	289	290	291	292	293
39	*Royce*	N	N	N	N	Y	Y	Y	N
40	*Lewis*	N	N	N	N	Y	Y	Y	N
41	*Miller, Gary*	N	N	N	N	Y	Y	Y	N
42	Baca	Y	Y	Y	+	+	+	+	N
43	*Calvert*	N	N	N	N	Y	Y	Y	N
44	*Bono*	N	N	N	N	Y	Y	Y	N
45	*Rohrabacher*	N	N	N	Y	?	Y	Y	Y
46	Sanchez	N	N	N	Y	Y	Y	Y	N
47	*Cox*	N	N	N	Y	Y	?	Y	N
48	Issa	N	N	N	N	Y	Y	Y	N
49	Davis	Y	Y	Y	Y	Y	Y	Y	N
50	Filner	Y	Y	Y	Y	Y	Y	Y	N
51	*Cunningham*	N	N	N	N	Y	Y	Y	N
52	*Hunter*	N	N	N	N	Y	Y	Y	N
COLORADO									
1	DeGette	N	Y	Y	Y	?	?	?	N
2	Udall	Y	Y	Y	Y	?	?	?	Y
3	*McInnis*	?	?	?	?	Y	Y	Y	N
4	*Schaffer*	N	N	N	N	?	?	?	N
5	*Hefley*	N	N	N	N	?	?	?	N
6	*Tancredo*	N	N	N	N	Y	Y	Y	N
CONNECTICUT									
1	Larson	Y	Y	Y	?	Y	Y	Y	Y
2	*Simmons*	N	N	Y	N	Y	Y	Y	N
3	DeLauro	Y	Y	Y	Y	Y	Y	Y	N
4	*Shays*	N	N	N	Y	Y	Y	Y	N
5	Maloney	Y	Y	Y	Y	Y	Y	Y	N
6	*Johnson*	N	Y	N	Y	Y	Y	Y	N
DELAWARE									
AL	*Castle*	N	N	Y	N	Y	Y	Y	Y
FLORIDA									
1	*Scarborough*	?	N	Y	N	Y	Y	Y	N
2	Boyd	Y	Y	Y	Y	Y	Y	Y	N
3	Brown	Y	Y	Y	Y	Y	Y	Y	N
4	*Crenshaw*	N	N	N	N	Y	Y	Y	N
5	Thurman	Y	Y	Y	Y	Y	Y	Y	N
6	*Stearns*	N	N	N	N	Y	Y	Y	N
7	*Mica*	N	N	N	N	Y	Y	Y	N
8	*Keller*	?	?	?	?	Y	Y	Y	N
9	*Bilirakis*	N	N	N	N	Y	Y	Y	N
10	*Young*	N	N	N	N	Y	Y	Y	N
11	Davis	Y	Y	Y	Y	Y	Y	Y	N
12	*Putnam*	N	N	N	N	Y	Y	Y	N
13	*Miller*	?	?	?	?	Y	Y	Y	N
14	*Goss*	N	N	N	N	Y	Y	Y	N
15	*Weldon*	N	N	N	N	Y	Y	Y	N
16	*Foley*	N	N	N	N	Y	Y	Y	N
17	Meek	Y	Y	Y	Y	Y	Y	Y	N
18	*Ros-Lehtinen*	?	?	?	?	Y	Y	Y	N
19	Wexler	Y	Y	Y	Y	Y	Y	Y	N
20	Deutsch	Y	Y	Y	Y	Y	Y	Y	N
21	*Diaz-Balart*	N	N	N	?	Y	Y	Y	N
22	*Shaw*	N	N	N	N	Y	Y	Y	N
23	Hastings	Y	Y	Y	Y	Y	Y	Y	N
GEORGIA									
1	*Kingston*	N	Y	N	N	Y	Y	Y	N
2	Bishop	N	N	Y	Y	Y	Y	Y	N
3	*Collins*	N	N	?	?	Y	Y	Y	N
4	McKinney	Y	Y	Y	Y	N	Y	Y	Y
5	Lewis	Y	Y	Y	Y	Y	Y	Y	Y
6	*Isakson*	N	N	N	N	Y	Y	Y	N
7	*Barr*	N	Y	N	N	P	P	Y	N
8	*Chambliss*	N	N	N	N	Y	Y	Y	N
9	*Deal*	N	N	N	N	Y	Y	Y	N
10	*Norwood*	N	N	N	N	Y	Y	Y	N
11	*Linder*	?	?	?	?	Y	Y	Y	N
HAWAII									
1	Abercrombie	Y	Y	Y	Y	Y	Y	Y	N
2	Mink	Y	Y	Y	Y	Y	Y	Y	N
IDAHO									
1	*Otter*	N	N	N	N	Y	Y	Y	Y
2	*Simpson*	N	N	N	N	Y	Y	Y	N
ILLINOIS									
1	Rush	Y	Y	Y	Y	Y	Y	Y	Y
2	Jackson	Y	Y	Y	Y	Y	Y	Y	Y
3	Lipinski	?	?	?	?	?	?	?	?
4	Gutierrez	Y	Y	Y	Y	Y	Y	Y	N
5	Blagojevich	Y	Y	Y	Y	Y	Y	Y	Y
6	*Hyde*	N	N	N	N	Y	Y	Y	N
7	Davis	Y	Y	Y	Y	Y	Y	Y	Y
8	*Crane*	N	N	N	N	Y	Y	Y	N
9	Schakowsky	Y	Y	Y	Y	Y	Y	Y	N
10	*Kirk*	N	N	N	N	Y	Y	Y	N
11	*Weller*	N	N	N	N	Y	Y	Y	N
12	Costello	Y	Y	N	Y	Y	Y	Y	N
13	*Biggert*	N	N	N	N	Y	Y	Y	N

ND Northern Democrats   SD Southern Democrats

	286	287	288	289	290	291	292	293
14 ***Hastert***								
15 ***Johnson***	N	Y	N	N	Y	Y	Y	N
16 ***Manzullo***	N	N	N	N	Y	Y	Y	N
17 Evans	Y	Y	Y	Y	Y	Y	Y	N
18 ***LaHood***	N	N	N	N	Y	Y	Y	N
19 Phelps	N	N	Y	N	Y	Y	Y	N
20 ***Shimkus***	N	N	N	N	Y	Y	Y	N
INDIANA								
1 Visclosky	Y	Y	Y	Y	Y	Y	Y	N
2 ***Pence***	N	N	N	N	Y	Y	Y	N
3 Roemer	Y	Y	Y	Y	Y	Y	Y	N
4 ***Souder***	N	Y	N	N	Y	Y	Y	Y
5 ***Buyer***	N	N	N	N	Y	Y	Y	N
6 ***Burton***	N	N	N	N	Y	Y	Y	N
7 ***Kerns***	N	N	N	N	Y	Y	Y	Y
8 ***Hostettler***	N	N	N	N	Y	Y	Y	N
9 Hill	N	N	Y	Y	Y	Y	Y	N
10 Carson	Y	Y	Y	Y	P	Y	Y	Y
IOWA								
1 ***Leach***	N	Y	Y	N	Y	Y	Y	N
2 ***Nussle***	N	N	N	N	Y	Y	Y	N
3 Boswell	N	Y	Y	?	Y	Y	Y	Y
4 ***Ganske***	N	N	Y	N	Y	Y	Y	N
5 ***Latham***	N	N	N	N	Y	Y	Y	N
KANSAS								
1 ***Moran***	N	N	N	N	Y	Y	Y	Y
2 ***Ryun***	N	N	N	N	Y	Y	Y	N
3 Moore	Y	Y	Y	Y	Y	Y	Y	Y
4 ***Tiahrt***	N	N	N	N	Y	Y	Y	N
KENTUCKY								
1 ***Whitfield***	N	Y	N	N	Y	Y	Y	N
2 ***Lewis***	N	N	N	N	Y	Y	Y	N
3 ***Northup***	N	N	N	N	Y	Y	Y	N
4 Lucas	N	Y	N	N	Y	Y	Y	N
5 ***Rogers***	N	N	N	N	Y	Y	Y	N
6 ***Fletcher***	N	N	N	N	Y	Y	Y	N
LOUISIANA								
1 ***Vitter***	N	N	N	N	Y	Y	Y	N
2 Jefferson	Y	Y	Y	Y	?	?	?	?
3 ***Tauzin***	N	N	N	N	Y	Y	Y	N
4 ***McCrery***	N	N	?	?	Y	Y	Y	N
5 ***Cooksey***	N	N	N	N	Y	Y	Y	N
6 ***Baker***	N	N	N	N	?	Y	Y	N
7 John	N	Y	Y	N	Y	Y	Y	N
MAINE								
1 Allen	Y	Y	Y	Y	Y	Y	Y	Y
2 Baldacci	Y	Y	Y	Y	Y	Y	Y	N
MARYLAND								
1 ***Gilchrest***	N	N	N	N	Y	Y	Y	N
2 ***Ehrlich***	N	N	N	N	Y	Y	Y	N
3 Cardin	Y	Y	Y	Y	Y	Y	Y	Y
4 Wynn	N	N	Y	Y	Y	Y	Y	N
5 Hoyer	Y	Y	Y	Y	Y	Y	Y	Y
6 ***Bartlett***	N	N	N	N	Y	Y	Y	Y
7 Cummings	Y	Y	Y	Y	Y	Y	Y	N
8 ***Morella***	N	Y	Y	Y	Y	Y	Y	Y
MASSACHUSETTS								
1 Olver	Y	Y	Y	Y	Y	Y	Y	Y
2 Neal	Y	Y	Y	Y	Y	Y	Y	Y
3 McGovern	Y	Y	Y	Y	Y	Y	Y	Y
4 Frank	Y	Y	Y	Y	Y	Y	Y	Y
5 Meehan	Y	Y	Y	Y	Y	Y	Y	Y
6 Tierney	Y	?	Y	Y	Y	Y	Y	Y
7 Markey	Y	Y	Y	Y	Y	Y	Y	Y
8 Capuano	Y	Y	Y	N	Y	Y	Y	Y
9 Vacant								
10 Delahunt	Y	Y	Y	Y	Y	Y	Y	Y
MICHIGAN								
1 Stupak	N	Y	Y	Y	Y	Y	Y	Y
2 ***Hoekstra***	N	N	N	N	Y	Y	Y	N
3 ***Ehlers***	N	N	N	N	Y	Y	Y	N
4 ***Camp***	N	N	N	?	Y	Y	Y	Y
5 Barcia	Y	Y	Y	Y	Y	Y	Y	Y
6 ***Upton***	N	N	N	N	Y	Y	Y	Y
7 ***Smith***	N	N	N	?	Y	Y	Y	Y
8 ***Rogers***	N	N	N	N	Y	Y	Y	Y
9 Kildee	Y	Y	Y	Y	Y	Y	Y	Y
10 Bonior	Y	Y	Y	Y	Y	Y	Y	Y
11 ***Knollenberg***	N	N	N	N	Y	Y	Y	N
12 Levin	Y	Y	Y	Y	Y	Y	Y	Y
13 Rivers	Y	Y	Y	Y	?	Y	Y	Y
14 Conyers	Y	Y	Y	Y	N	N	Y	?
15 Kilpatrick	Y	Y	Y	+	Y	Y	Y	N
16 Dingell	Y	Y	Y	Y	Y	N	Y	Y

	286	287	288	289	290	291	292	293
MINNESOTA								
1 ***Gutknecht***	N	N	N	N	Y	Y	Y	N
2 ***Kennedy***	N	N	N	N	Y	Y	Y	N
3 ***Ramstad***	N	Y	Y	Y	Y	Y	Y	N
4 McCollum	Y	Y	Y	Y	Y	Y	Y	N
5 Sabo	Y	Y	Y	Y	Y	Y	Y	N
6 Luther	Y	Y	Y	Y	Y	Y	Y	N
7 Peterson	N	N	Y	N	Y	Y	Y	N
8 Oberstar	Y	Y	Y	Y	Y	Y	Y	N
MISSISSIPPI								
1 ***Wicker***	N	N	N	N	Y	Y	Y	N
2 Thompson	N	N	Y	Y	Y	Y	Y	N
3 ***Pickering***	N	N	N	N	Y	Y	Y	Y
4 Shows	N	Y	N	Y	Y	Y	Y	Y
5 Taylor	N	N	Y	Y	Y	Y	Y	Y
MISSOURI								
1 Clay	Y	Y	Y	Y	Y	Y	Y	N
2 ***Akin***	N	N	N	N	Y	Y	Y	N
3 Gephardt	Y	Y	Y	Y	Y	Y	Y	Y
4 Skelton	Y	N	Y	N	Y	Y	Y	N
5 McCarthy	Y	Y	Y	Y	Y	Y	Y	Y
6 ***Graves***	N	N	N	N	Y	Y	Y	N
7 ***Blunt***	N	N	N	N	Y	Y	Y	N
8 ***Emerson***	N	N	N	N	Y	Y	Y	N
9 ***Hulshof***	N	N	N	N	Y	Y	Y	N
MONTANA								
AL ***Rehberg***	N	N	N	N	Y	Y	Y	N
NEBRASKA								
1 ***Bereuter***	N	N	N	N	Y	Y	Y	N
2 ***Terry***	N	N	N	N	Y	Y	Y	Y
3 ***Osborne***	N	N	N	N	Y	Y	Y	N
NEVADA								
1 Berkley	Y	Y	Y	Y	Y	Y	?	N
2 ***Gibbons***	N	N	N	N	Y	Y	Y	N
NEW HAMPSHIRE								
1 ***Sununu***	?	?	?	?	Y	Y	Y	N
2 ***Bass***	N	N	N	N	Y	Y	Y	N
NEW JERSEY								
1 Andrews	N	Y	Y	Y	Y	Y	Y	N
2 ***LoBiondo***	N	Y	Y	N	Y	Y	Y	N
3 ***Saxton***	N	N	Y	N	Y	Y	Y	N
4 ***Smith***	N	Y	Y	N	Y	Y	Y	N
5 ***Roukema***	N	N	N	?	Y	Y	Y	N
6 Pallone	Y	Y	Y	Y	Y	Y	Y	N
7 ***Ferguson***	N	N	Y	N	Y	Y	Y	N
8 Pascrell	Y	Y	Y	Y	Y	Y	Y	Y
9 Rothman	Y	Y	Y	Y	Y	Y	Y	Y
10 Payne	Y	Y	Y	Y	Y	Y	Y	?
11 ***Frelinghuysen***	N	N	Y	N	Y	Y	Y	N
12 Holt	Y	Y	Y	Y	Y	Y	Y	N
13 Menendez	Y	Y	Y	Y	Y	Y	Y	N
NEW MEXICO								
1 ***Wilson***	N	N	N	N	Y	Y	Y	N
2 ***Skeen***	N	N	N	N	Y	Y	Y	N
3 Udall	Y	Y	Y	Y	Y	Y	Y	N
NEW YORK								
1 ***Grucci***	N	N	N	N	Y	Y	Y	N
2 Israel	Y	Y	Y	Y	Y	Y	Y	N
3 ***King***	N	N	N	N	Y	Y	Y	N
4 McCarthy	Y	Y	Y	Y	Y	Y	Y	Y
5 Ackerman	Y	Y	Y	Y	Y	Y	Y	N
6 Meeks	Y	Y	Y	Y	Y	Y	Y	N
7 Crowley	Y	Y	Y	Y	Y	Y	Y	N
8 Nadler	Y	Y	Y	Y	Y	Y	Y	N
9 Weiner	Y	Y	Y	Y	Y	Y	Y	N
10 Towns	Y	Y	Y	Y	Y	Y	Y	N
11 Owens	Y	Y	Y	Y	Y	Y	Y	N
12 Velázquez	Y	Y	Y	Y	Y	Y	Y	N
13 ***Fossella***	N	Y	N	N	Y	Y	Y	Y
14 Maloney	Y	Y	Y	Y	Y	Y	Y	Y
15 Rangel	Y	Y	Y	Y	Y	Y	Y	N
16 Serrano	Y	Y	Y	Y	Y	Y	Y	N
17 Engel	N	Y	Y	Y	Y	Y	Y	N
18 Lowey	Y	Y	Y	Y	Y	Y	Y	N
19 ***Kelly***	N	N	Y	Y	Y	Y	Y	Y
20 ***Gilman***	N	Y	Y	N	Y	Y	Y	N
21 McNulty	Y	Y	Y	Y	Y	Y	Y	N
22 ***Sweeney***	N	N	N	N	Y	Y	Y	N
23 ***Boehlert***	N	N	N	Y	Y	Y	Y	N
24 ***McHugh***	N	N	N	N	Y	Y	Y	N
25 ***Walsh***	N	N	N	N	Y	Y	Y	N
26 Hinchey	Y	Y	Y	Y	Y	Y	Y	N
27 ***Reynolds***	N	N	N	N	Y	Y	Y	N
28 Slaughter	+	+	+	+	Y	Y	Y	N
29 LaFalce	Y	Y	Y	Y	Y	Y	Y	N

	286	287	288	289	290	291	292	293
30 ***Quinn***	?	?	?	?	Y	Y	Y	N
31 ***Houghton***	N	N	N	N	Y	Y	Y	N
NORTH CAROLINA								
1 Clayton	N	Y	Y	Y	Y	Y	Y	N
2 Etheridge	Y	Y	Y	Y	Y	Y	Y	Y
3 ***Jones***	N	N	N	N	Y	Y	Y	N
4 Price	Y	Y	Y	Y	Y	Y	Y	N
5 ***Burr***	N	N	N	N	Y	Y	Y	N
6 ***Coble***	N	N	N	N	Y	Y	Y	N
7 McIntyre	Y	Y	Y	Y	Y	Y	Y	N
8 ***Hayes***	N	N	N	N	Y	Y	Y	N
9 ***Myrick***	N	N	N	N	Y	Y	Y	N
10 ***Ballenger***	N	N	N	N	Y	Y	Y	Y
11 ***Taylor***	?	?	?	?	Y	Y	Y	N
12 Watt	?	?	?	?	Y	Y	Y	N
NORTH DAKOTA								
AL Pomeroy	Y	N	Y	?	Y	Y	Y	Y
OHIO								
1 ***Chabot***	N	N	N	N	Y	Y	Y	Y
2 ***Portman***	N	N	N	N	Y	Y	Y	N
3 Hall	Y	Y	Y	Y	Y	Y	Y	N
4 ***Oxley***	N	N	N	N	Y	Y	Y	N
5 ***Gillmor***	N	N	N	N	Y	Y	Y	N
6 Strickland	Y	Y	Y	Y	Y	Y	Y	Y
7 ***Hobson***	N	N	N	N	Y	Y	Y	N
8 ***Boehner***	N	N	N	?	Y	Y	Y	N
9 Kaptur	Y	Y	Y	Y	Y	Y	Y	N
10 Kucinich	Y	Y	Y	Y	Y	Y	Y	N
11 Jones	Y	Y	Y	Y	Y	Y	Y	N
12 ***Tiberi***	N	N	N	N	Y	Y	Y	N
13 Brown	Y	Y	Y	Y	Y	Y	Y	N
14 Sawyer	Y	Y	Y	Y	Y	Y	Y	Y
15 ***Pryce***	N	N	N	N	Y	Y	Y	N
16 ***Regula***	N	N	N	N	Y	Y	Y	N
17 Traficant	N	N	N	N	Y	Y	Y	N
18 ***Ney***	N	N	N	N	Y	Y	Y	N
19 ***LaTourette***	N	N	N	N	Y	Y	Y	Y
OKLAHOMA								
1 ***Largent***	?	?	?	?	Y	Y	Y	N
2 Carson	N	Y	Y	N	Y	Y	Y	N
3 ***Watkins***	N	N	N	N	Y	Y	Y	N
4 ***Watts***	N	N	N	N	Y	Y	Y	N
5 ***Istook***	N	N	N	N	Y	Y	Y	?
6 ***Lucas***	N	N	N	N	Y	Y	Y	N
OREGON								
1 Wu	Y	Y	Y	Y	Y	Y	Y	N
2 ***Walden***	N	N	N	N	Y	Y	Y	N
3 Blumenauer	+	+	+	+	Y	Y	Y	N
4 DeFazio	Y	Y	Y	?	Y	Y	Y	N
5 Hooley	Y	Y	Y	Y	Y	Y	Y	N
PENNSYLVANIA								
1 Brady	Y	Y	Y	Y	Y	Y	Y	Y
2 Fattah	Y	Y	Y	Y	Y	Y	?	N
3 Borski	Y	Y	Y	Y	Y	Y	Y	N
4 ***Hart***	N	N	Y	N	Y	Y	Y	Y
5 ***Peterson***	N	N	N	N	Y	Y	Y	N
6 Holden	N	Y	Y	Y	Y	Y	Y	N
7 ***Weldon***	N	N	N	N	Y	Y	Y	N
8 ***Greenwood***	N	N	N	N	Y	?	Y	N
9 ***Shuster, Bill***	N	N	N	N	Y	Y	Y	N
10 ***Sherwood***	N	N	N	N	Y	Y	Y	N
11 Kanjorski	N	N	Y	Y	Y	Y	Y	Y
12 Murtha	N	N	Y	N	Y	Y	Y	N
13 Hoeffel	Y	Y	Y	Y	Y	Y	Y	N
14 Coyne	Y	Y	Y	Y	Y	Y	Y	Y
15 ***Toomey***	N	N	N	N	Y	Y	Y	N
16 ***Pitts***	N	N	N	N	Y	Y	Y	N
17 ***Gekas***	N	N	N	N	Y	Y	Y	N
18 Doyle	N	N	Y	N	Y	Y	Y	Y
19 ***Platts***	N	N	N	N	Y	Y	Y	N
20 Mascara	N	Y	Y	Y	Y	Y	Y	Y
21 ***English***	N	N	Y	N	Y	Y	Y	Y
RHODE ISLAND								
1 Kennedy	Y	Y	Y	Y	Y	Y	Y	Y
2 Langevin	Y	N	Y	Y	Y	Y	Y	Y
SOUTH CAROLINA								
1 ***Brown***	N	N	N	N	Y	Y	Y	N
2 ***Spence***	?	?	?	?	?	?	?	?
3 ***Graham***	N	N	N	N	Y	Y	Y	N
4 ***DeMint***	N	N	N	N	Y	Y	Y	N
5 Spratt	N	N	Y	Y	Y	Y	Y	N
6 Clyburn	N	N	Y	Y	Y	Y	Y	N
SOUTH DAKOTA								
AL ***Thune***	N	N	N	N	Y	Y	Y	Y

	286	287	288	289	290	291	292	293
TENNESSEE								
1 ***Jenkins***	N	N	N	N	Y	Y	Y	N
2 ***Duncan***	N	N	N	N	Y	Y	Y	Y
3 ***Wamp***	N	N	N	N	Y	Y	Y	N
4 ***Hilleary***	N	N	N	?	Y	Y	Y	N
5 Clement	N	Y	Y	Y	Y	Y	Y	N
6 Gordon	Y	Y	Y	Y	Y	Y	Y	N
7 ***Bryant***	N	N	N	N	Y	Y	Y	N
8 Tanner	Y	Y	Y	N	Y	Y	Y	N
9 Ford	Y	Y	Y	Y	Y	Y	Y	N
TEXAS								
1 Sandlin	Y	Y	Y	N	Y	Y	Y	Y
2 Turner	N	Y	Y	N	Y	Y	Y	N
3 ***Johnson, Sam***	N	N	N	N	Y	Y	Y	N
4 Hall	N	N	N	N	Y	Y	Y	Y
5 ***Sessions***	N	N	N	N	Y	Y	Y	N
6 ***Barton***	N	N	N	Y	Y	Y	Y	N
7 ***Culberson***	N	N	N	N	Y	Y	Y	N
8 ***Brady***	N	N	N	N	Y	Y	Y	N
9 Lampson	Y	Y	Y	N	Y	Y	Y	N
10 Doggett	Y	Y	Y	Y	Y	Y	Y	N
11 Edwards	N	N	Y	Y	Y	Y	Y	Y
12 ***Granger***	N	Y	N	N	Y	Y	Y	N
13 ***Thornberry***	N	N	N	N	Y	Y	Y	N
14 ***Paul***	N	N	N	N	N	N	Y	N
15 Hinojosa	Y	Y	?	?	Y	Y	Y	N
16 Reyes	Y	Y	Y	Y	Y	Y	Y	N
17 Stenholm	N	N	N	N	?	?	Y	N
18 Jackson-Lee	Y	Y	Y	Y	Y	Y	Y	N
19 ***Combest***	N	N	N	N	Y	Y	Y	N
20 Gonzalez	Y	Y	Y	Y	Y	Y	Y	N
21 ***Smith***	?	?	?	?	Y	Y	Y	N
22 ***DeLay***	N	N	N	N	Y	Y	Y	N
23 ***Bonilla***	N	N	N	N	Y	Y	Y	N
24 Frost	?	?	?	?	Y	Y	Y	N
25 Bentsen	Y	Y	Y	N	Y	Y	Y	N
26 ***Armey***	N	N	N	N	Y	Y	Y	N
27 Ortiz	N	Y	Y	Y	Y	Y	Y	N
28 Rodriguez	N	Y	Y	Y	Y	Y	Y	N
29 Green	Y	Y	Y	Y	Y	Y	Y	N
30 Johnson, E.B.	N	Y	Y	Y	P	Y	Y	N
UTAH								
1 ***Hansen***	?	?	?	?	?	?	?	?
2 Matheson	Y	Y	Y	N	Y	Y	Y	N
3 ***Cannon***	N	N	N	N	Y	Y	Y	N
VERMONT								
AL *Sanders*	Y	Y	Y	Y	Y	Y	Y	N
VIRGINIA								
1 ***Davis, Jo Ann***	N	N	N	N	Y	Y	Y	N
2 ***Schrock***	N	N	N	N	Y	Y	Y	N
3 Scott	Y	Y	Y	Y	Y	Y	Y	Y
4 ***Forbes***	N	N	N	N	Y	Y	Y	N
5 *Goode*	N	N	N	N	?	?	?	N
6 ***Goodlatte***	N	N	N	N	Y	Y	Y	Y
7 ***Cantor***	N	N	N	N	Y	Y	Y	Y
8 Moran	Y	Y	Y	Y	Y	Y	Y	Y
9 Boucher	N	Y	Y	Y	Y	Y	Y	N
10 ***Wolf***	?	?	?	?	Y	Y	Y	N
11 ***Davis, T.***	N	N	N	N	Y	Y	Y	N
WASHINGTON								
1 Inslee	Y	Y	Y	Y	Y	Y	Y	Y
2 Larsen	N	Y	Y	Y	Y	Y	Y	Y
3 Baird	Y	Y	Y	Y	Y	Y	Y	Y
4 ***Hastings***	N	N	N	N	Y	Y	Y	N
5 ***Nethercutt***	N	N	N	N	Y	Y	Y	N
6 Dicks	Y	Y	Y	Y	Y	Y	Y	Y
7 McDermott	Y	Y	Y	Y	Y	Y	Y	N
8 ***Dunn***	–	–	–	–	Y	Y	Y	N
9 Smith	Y	Y	Y	Y	Y	Y	Y	Y
WEST VIRGINIA								
1 Mollohan	N	Y	Y	N	?	Y	Y	N
2 ***Capito***	N	N	N	N	Y	Y	Y	N
3 Rahall	Y	Y	Y	Y	Y	N	Y	N
WISCONSIN								
1 ***Ryan***	N	N	N	N	Y	Y	Y	N
2 Baldwin	Y	Y	Y	Y	Y	Y	Y	N
3 Kind	Y	Y	Y	Y	Y	Y	Y	N
4 Kleczka	N	Y	Y	Y	?	Y	Y	N
5 Barrett	Y	Y	Y	Y	Y	Y	Y	N
6 ***Petri***	N	N	N	N	Y	Y	Y	Y
7 Obey	Y	Y	Y	Y	Y	Y	Y	N
8 ***Green***	N	N	N	N	Y	Y	Y	N
9 ***Sensenbrenner***	N	N	N	N	Y	Y	Y	Y
WYOMING								
AL ***Cubin***	?	?	?	?	?	?	Y	N

Southern states - Ala., Ark., Fla., Ga., Ky., La., Miss., N.C., Okla., S.C., Tenn., Texas, Va.

294. HR 2620. Fiscal 2002 VA-HUD Appropriations/Project Impact. Capps, D-Calif., amendment that would designate $25 million of FEMA emergency planning and assistance funding for Project Impact, which funds pre-disaster hazard mitigation efforts. Rejected 190-231: R 29-184; D 160-46 (ND 128-25, SD 32-21); I 1-1. July 30, 2001.

295. HR 2620. Fiscal 2002 VA-HUD Appropriations/Insurance Premiums. Frank, D-Mass., amendment that would prohibit the use of funds to establish, charge or collect mortgage insurance premiums for the FHA multi-family program in an amount more than the cost of the insurance and would reduce by $5 million funding for Operation Safe Home. Rejected 212-212: R 6-211; D 204-1 (ND 152-1, SD 52-0); I 2-0. July 30, 2001.

296. HR 2620. Fiscal 2002 VA-HUD Appropriations/Recommit. Boyd, D-Fla., motion to recommit the bill to the House Appropriations Committee with instructions to add language increasing funding for VA medical care programs by an amount adequate to fully fund the cost of all currently authorized services including those under the Veterans Millennium Health Care Act (PL 106-117). Motion rejected 196-230: R 0-218; D 195-11 (ND 146-7, SD 49-4); I 1-1. July 30, 2001.

297. HR 2620. Fiscal 2002 VA-HUD Appropriations/Passage. Passage of the bill that would appropriate $112.7 billion in fiscal 2002 for the departments of Veterans Affairs (VA) and Housing and Urban Development (HUD) and other independent agencies. The bill would appropriate $51.3 billion for VA programs and benefits, $30 billion for HUD, $7.5 billion for the EPA, $15 billion for the National Aeronautics and Space Administration, and $3.6 billion for the Federal Emergency Management Agency programs, including $1.3 billion in "emergency" disaster relief. Passed 336-89: R 203-15; D 132-73 (ND 94-59, SD 38-14); I 1-1. July 31, 2001 (in the session that began and the Congressional Record dated July 30, 2001).

298. HR 2647. Fiscal 2002 Legislative Branch Appropriations/Passage. Passage of the bill that would appropriate $2.2 billion in fiscal 2002 for legislative branch operations, including $124 million for the Capitol Police and $882 million for the House of Representatives. Passed 380-38: R 195-21; D 184-16 (ND 142-9, SD 42-7); I 1-1. July 31, 2001.

299. Procedural Motion/Journal. Approval of the House Journal of Monday, July 30, 2001. Approved 359-44: R 190-17; D 167-27 (ND 122-25, SD 45-2); I 2-0. July 31, 2001.

300. HR 2505. Human Cloning Ban/Rule. Adoption of the rule (H Res 214) to provide for House floor consideration of the bill that would prohibit human cloning for any purpose. Adopted 239-188: R 204-15; D 34-172 (ND 23-130, SD 11-42); I 1-1. July 31, 2001.

301. HR 2540. Veterans Programs/Passage. Smith, R-N.J., motion to suspend the rules and pass the bill that would authorize a cost of living raise for various veterans' benefits, expand disability compensation for Persian Gulf War veterans with undiagnosed illnesses, and make other changes to Veteran Affairs programs. Additional illnesses for which Gulf veterans could receive benefits include chronic fatigue syndrome, fibromyalgia, and chronic multi-symptom illness. Motion agreed to 422-0: R 218-0; D 202-0 (ND 151-0, SD 51-0); I 2-0. A two-thirds majority of those present and voting (282 in this case) is required for passage under suspension of the rules. July 31, 2001.

Key

Y	Voted for (yea).
#	Paired for.
+	Announced for.
N	Voted against (nay).
X	Paired against.
−	Announced against.
P	Voted "present."
C	Voted "present" to avoid possible conflict of interest.
?	Did not vote or otherwise make a position known.

Democrats **Republicans** *Independents*

	294	295	296	297	298	299	300	301
ALABAMA								
1 *Callahan*	N	N	N	Y	Y	Y	Y	Y
2 *Everett*	N	N	N	Y	Y	Y	Y	Y
3 *Riley*	N	N	N	Y	Y	Y	Y	+
4 *Aderholt*	N	N	N	Y	Y	Y	Y	Y
5 Cramer	N	Y	Y	Y	Y	Y	N	Y
6 *Bachus*	N	Y	N	Y	Y	Y	Y	Y
7 Hilliard	N	Y	Y	N	Y	N	N	Y
ALASKA								
AL *Young*	N	N	N	Y	Y	Y	Y	Y
ARIZONA								
1 *Flake*	N	N	N	N	?	?	Y	Y
2 Pastor	N	Y	Y	Y	Y	Y	N	Y
3 *Stump*	N	N	N	Y	Y	Y	Y	Y
4 *Shadegg*	N	N	N	N	Y	Y	Y	Y
5 *Kolbe*	N	N	N	Y	Y	Y	N	Y
6 *Hayworth*	N	N	N	Y	Y	Y	Y	Y
ARKANSAS								
1 Berry	Y	Y	Y	Y	Y	Y	Y	Y
2 Snyder	Y	Y	Y	Y	Y	Y	N	Y
3 *Hutchinson*	N	N	N	Y	?	?	?	?
4 Ross	N	Y	Y	Y	Y	Y	N	Y
CALIFORNIA								
1 Thompson	Y	Y	Y	Y	Y	N	N	Y
2 *Herger*	N	N	N	Y	+	Y	Y	Y
3 *Ose*	Y	N	N	Y	Y	Y	Y	Y
4 *Doolittle*	N	N	N	Y	Y	Y	Y	Y
5 Matsui	Y	Y	Y	Y	Y	Y	N	Y
6 Woolsey	Y	Y	Y	Y	Y	Y	N	Y
7 Miller, George	Y	Y	Y	N	Y	N	Y	Y
8 Pelosi	Y	Y	Y	N	Y	Y	N	Y
9 Lee	Y	Y	Y	N	Y	N	N	Y
10 Tauscher	Y	Y	Y	Y	Y	Y	N	Y
11 *Pombo*	N	N	N	Y	Y	Y	Y	Y
12 Lantos	Y	Y	Y	Y	Y	Y	N	Y
13 Stark	?	?	?	?	?	?	?	?
14 Eshoo	Y	Y	Y	N	Y	Y	N	Y
15 Honda	Y	Y	Y	N	Y	Y	N	Y
16 Lofgren	Y	Y	Y	Y	Y	Y	N	Y
17 Farr	Y	Y	Y	Y	Y	Y	N	Y
18 Condit	Y	Y	Y	Y	Y	Y	N	Y
19 *Radanovich*	?	N	N	Y	Y	Y	Y	Y
20 Dooley	Y	Y	Y	Y	Y	Y	N	Y
21 *Thomas*	N	N	N	Y	Y	Y	Y	Y
22 Capps	Y	Y	Y	Y	Y	N	N	Y
23 *Gallegly*	?	N	N	Y	Y	Y	Y	Y
24 Sherman	Y	Y	Y	Y	Y	Y	N	Y
25 *McKeon*	N	N	N	Y	Y	Y	N	Y
26 Berman	Y	Y	Y	Y	Y	Y	N	Y
27 Schiff	Y	Y	Y	Y	Y	N	Y	Y
28 *Dreier*	N	N	N	Y	Y	Y	Y	Y
29 Waxman	Y	Y	Y	Y	Y	Y	N	Y
30 Becerra	Y	Y	Y	N	Y	Y	N	Y
31 Solis	Y	Y	Y	Y	Y	Y	N	Y
32 Watson	Y	Y	Y	Y	Y	Y	N	Y
33 Roybal-Allard	Y	Y	Y	Y	Y	Y	N	Y
34 Napolitano	Y	Y	Y	Y	Y	Y	N	Y
35 Waters	Y	Y	Y	N	Y	N	N	Y
36 Harman	Y	Y	Y	Y	Y	Y	N	Y
37 Millender-McD.	Y	Y	Y	Y	+	+	N	Y
38 *Horn*	N	N	Y	Y	Y	Y	N	Y

	294	295	296	297	298	299	300	301
39 *Royce*	N	N	N	Y	N	N	Y	Y
40 *Lewis*	N	N	N	Y	Y	?	Y	Y
41 *Miller, Gary*	N	N	N	Y	Y	?	Y	Y
42 Baca	Y	Y	Y	Y	Y	Y	N	Y
43 *Calvert*	N	N	N	Y	Y	?	Y	Y
44 *Bono*	Y	N	N	Y	Y	Y	N	Y
45 *Rohrabacher*	N	N	N	Y	Y	Y	Y	Y
46 Sanchez	Y	Y	Y	Y	Y	Y	N	Y
47 *Cox*	N	N	N	Y	Y	Y	Y	Y
48 *Issa*	N	N	N	Y	Y	Y	Y	Y
49 Davis	Y	Y	Y	N	Y	N	N	Y
50 Filner	Y	Y	Y	N	Y	N	N	Y
51 *Cunningham*	N	N	N	Y	Y	Y	Y	Y
52 *Hunter*	N	N	N	Y	?	?	Y	Y
COLORADO								
1 DeGette	Y	Y	Y	N	Y	N	N	Y
2 Udall	Y	Y	Y	N	Y	N	N	Y
3 *McInnis*	N	N	N	Y	Y	Y	Y	Y
4 *Schaffer*	N	N	N	N	N	N	Y	Y
5 *Hefley*	N	N	N	N	N	N	Y	Y
6 *Tancredo*	N	N	N	N	N	P	Y	Y
CONNECTICUT								
1 Larson	Y	Y	Y	Y	Y	Y	N	Y
2 *Simmons*	N	N	N	Y	Y	Y	Y	Y
3 DeLauro	Y	Y	Y	N	Y	N	N	Y
4 *Shays*	N	N	N	Y	Y	Y	N	Y
5 Maloney	Y	Y	Y	Y	Y	Y	N	Y
6 *Johnson*	N	N	N	Y	Y	Y	N	Y
DELAWARE								
AL *Castle*	Y	N	N	N	Y	Y	N	Y
FLORIDA								
1 *Scarborough*	N	N	N	Y	Y	Y	Y	Y
2 Boyd	Y	Y	Y	N	Y	Y	N	Y
3 Brown	N	Y	Y	Y	Y	Y	N	Y
4 *Crenshaw*	N	N	N	Y	Y	Y	Y	Y
5 Thurman	Y	Y	Y	N	Y	N	N	Y
6 *Stearns*	N	N	N	Y	Y	Y	Y	Y
7 *Mica*	N	N	N	Y	Y	Y	Y	Y
8 *Keller*	N	N	N	Y	Y	?	Y	Y
9 *Bilirakis*	N	Y	N	Y	Y	Y	Y	Y
10 *Young*	N	N	N	Y	Y	Y	Y	Y
11 Davis	N	Y	Y	Y	Y	Y	N	Y
12 *Putnam*	N	N	N	Y	Y	Y	Y	Y
13 *Miller*	N	N	N	Y	Y	Y	Y	Y
14 *Goss*	N	N	N	Y	Y	?	Y	Y
15 *Weldon*	Y	N	N	Y	Y	Y	Y	Y
16 *Foley*	N	N	N	Y	Y	Y	Y	Y
17 Meek	Y	Y	N	Y	Y	Y	N	Y
18 *Ros-Lehtinen*	N	N	N	Y	Y	Y	Y	Y
19 Wexler	Y	Y	Y	N	Y	Y	N	Y
20 Deutsch	Y	Y	Y	N	Y	N	N	Y
21 *Diaz-Balart*	N	N	N	Y	Y	Y	Y	Y
22 *Shaw*	N	N	N	Y	Y	Y	Y	Y
23 Hastings	N	Y	?	?	?	?	?	?
GEORGIA								
1 *Kingston*	N	N	N	Y	Y	Y	Y	Y
2 Bishop	N	Y	Y	Y	Y	Y	N	Y
3 *Collins*	N	N	N	Y	Y	Y	Y	Y
4 McKinney	Y	Y	Y	?	?	N	N	Y
5 Lewis	N	Y	Y	N	Y	N	N	Y
6 *Isakson*	N	N	N	Y	Y	Y	Y	Y
7 *Barr*	Y	N	N	Y	N	Y	Y	Y
8 *Chambliss*	N	N	N	Y	Y	Y	Y	Y
9 *Deal*	N	N	N	Y	Y	Y	Y	Y
10 *Norwood*	N	N	N	Y	?	?	Y	Y
11 *Linder*	N	N	N	Y	Y	Y	Y	Y
HAWAII								
1 Abercrombie	Y	Y	N	Y	Y	Y	N	Y
2 Mink	N	Y	Y	Y	Y	Y	N	Y
IDAHO								
1 *Otter*	N	N	N	Y	Y	Y	Y	Y
2 *Simpson*	Y	N	N	Y	Y	Y	Y	Y
ILLINOIS								
1 Rush	Y	Y	Y	N	Y	?	N	Y
2 Jackson	Y	Y	Y	N	Y	N	N	Y
3 Lipinski	?	?	?	?	?	?	?	?
4 Gutierrez	Y	Y	Y	N	Y	N	N	Y
5 Blagojevich	Y	Y	Y	N	Y	N	N	Y
6 *Hyde*	N	N	N	Y	Y	Y	Y	Y
7 Davis	Y	Y	Y	N	Y	N	N	Y
8 *Crane*	N	N	N	Y	N	Y	Y	Y
9 Schakowsky	Y	Y	Y	N	Y	N	N	Y
10 *Kirk*	N	N	N	Y	Y	Y	N	Y
11 *Weller*	N	N	N	Y	Y	Y	Y	Y
12 Costello	Y	Y	Y	N	N	N	Y	Y
13 *Biggert*	N	N	N	Y	Y	Y	Y	Y

ND Northern Democrats   SD Southern Democrats

	294	295	296	297	298	299	300	301
14 ***Hastert***							Y	
15 ***Johnson***	N	N	N	Y	N	Y	Y	Y
16 ***Manzullo***	N	N	N	Y	Y	Y	Y	Y
17 Evans	N	Y	Y	Y	Y	Y	N	Y
18 ***LaHood***	N	N	N	Y	Y	Y	?	Y
19 Phelps	N	Y	Y	Y	N	Y	Y	Y
20 ***Shimkus***	N	N	N	Y	N	Y	Y	Y
INDIANA								
1 Visclosky	N	Y	Y	Y	Y	N	N	Y
2 ***Pence***	N	N	N	Y	Y	Y	Y	Y
3 Roemer	Y	Y	Y	N	Y	N	Y	Y
4 ***Souder***	N	N	N	Y	Y	Y	Y	Y
5 ***Buyer***	N	N	N	Y	Y	Y	Y	Y
6 ***Burton***	N	N	N	Y	Y	Y	Y	Y
7 ***Kerns***	N	N	N	Y	Y	Y	Y	Y
8 ***Hostettler***	N	N	N	N	Y	Y	Y	Y
9 Hill	N	Y	Y	Y	Y	Y	N	Y
10 Carson	Y	Y	Y	N	Y	Y	N	Y
IOWA								
1 ***Leach***	N	N	N	Y	Y	Y	Y	Y
2 ***Nussle***	N	N	N	Y	Y	Y	Y	Y
3 Boswell	Y	Y	Y	Y	Y	Y	N	Y
4 ***Ganske***	Y	N	N	Y	Y	Y	Y	Y
5 ***Latham***	Y	N	N	Y	Y	N	Y	Y
KANSAS								
1 ***Moran***	Y	N	N	Y	N	N	Y	Y
2 ***Ryun***	N	N	N	Y	N	Y	Y	Y
3 Moore	Y	Y	Y	N	N	N	N	Y
4 ***Tiahrt***	N	N	N	Y	Y	Y	Y	Y
KENTUCKY								
1 ***Whitfield***	N	N	N	Y	Y	Y	Y	Y
2 ***Lewis***	N	N	N	Y	Y	Y	Y	Y
3 ***Northup***	N	N	N	Y	Y	Y	Y	Y
4 Lucas	Y	Y	Y	Y	N	Y	Y	Y
5 ***Rogers***	N	N	N	Y	Y	Y	Y	Y
6 ***Fletcher***	N	N	N	Y	Y	Y	Y	Y
LOUISIANA								
1 ***Vitter***	N	N	N	Y	Y	Y	Y	Y
2 Jefferson	?	?	?	?	Y	?	N	Y
3 ***Tauzin***	N	N	N	Y	Y	Y	Y	Y
4 ***McCrery***	N	N	N	Y	Y	Y	Y	Y
5 ***Cooksey***	N	N	N	Y	Y	Y	Y	Y
6 ***Baker***	N	N	N	Y	Y	Y	Y	Y
7 John	Y	?	Y	N	Y	Y	Y	Y
MAINE								
1 Allen	Y	Y	Y	N	Y	Y	N	Y
2 Baldacci	N	Y	Y	Y	Y	Y	N	Y
MARYLAND								
1 ***Gilchrest***	N	N	N	Y	Y	Y	Y	Y
2 ***Ehrlich***	N	N	N	Y	Y	Y	Y	Y
3 Cardin	Y	Y	Y	N	Y	Y	N	Y
4 Wynn	N	Y	Y	Y	Y	Y	N	Y
5 Hoyer	Y	Y	Y	Y	Y	Y	N	Y
6 ***Bartlett***	Y	N	N	Y	Y	Y	Y	Y
7 Cummings	Y	Y	Y	Y	Y	Y	N	Y
8 ***Morella***	N	Y	N	Y	Y	Y	Y	Y
MASSACHUSETTS								
1 Olver	Y	Y	Y	N	Y	Y	N	Y
2 Neal	Y	Y	Y	Y	?	?	N	Y
3 McGovern	Y	Y	Y	N	Y	Y	N	Y
4 Frank	Y	Y	Y	N	Y	Y	N	Y
5 Meehan	Y	Y	Y	Y	Y	Y	N	Y
6 Tierney	Y	Y	Y	N	Y	Y	N	Y
7 Markey	Y	Y	Y	N	Y	Y	N	Y
8 Capuano	Y	Y	Y	N	Y	N	N	Y
9 Vacant								
10 Delahunt	Y	Y	Y	N	Y	Y	N	Y
MICHIGAN								
1 Stupak	N	Y	Y	N	Y	N	Y	Y
2 ***Hoekstra***	N	N	N	N	N	N	Y	Y
3 ***Ehlers***	Y	N	N	Y	Y	Y	Y	Y
4 ***Camp***	Y	N	N	Y	Y	Y	Y	Y
5 Barcia	N	Y	Y	Y	N	Y	Y	Y
6 ***Upton***	Y	N	N	Y	Y	Y	N	Y
7 ***Smith***	?	N	N	Y	Y	Y	Y	Y
8 ***Rogers***	N	N	N	Y	Y	Y	Y	Y
9 Kildee	Y	Y	Y	Y	Y	Y	Y	Y
10 Bonior	Y	Y	Y	Y	Y	Y	N	Y
11 ***Knollenberg***	N	N	N	Y	Y	Y	Y	Y
12 Levin	Y	Y	Y	Y	Y	Y	N	Y
13 Rivers	Y	Y	Y	Y	Y	Y	N	Y
14 Conyers	Y	Y	Y	N	Y	Y	N	Y
15 Kilpatrick	N	Y	Y	Y	Y	Y	N	Y
16 Dingell	Y	Y	Y	Y	Y	Y	N	Y

	294	295	296	297	298	299	300	301
MINNESOTA								
1 ***Gutknecht***	N	N	N	Y	Y	N	Y	Y
2 ***Kennedy***	N	N	N	Y	Y	N	Y	Y
3 ***Ramstad***	N	Y	N	Y	Y	N	N	Y
4 McCollum	Y	Y	Y	Y	Y	Y	N	Y
5 Sabo	Y	Y	N	N	Y	N	N	Y
6 Luther	Y	Y	Y	Y	N	Y	N	Y
7 Peterson	Y	Y	Y	Y	Y	N	Y	Y
8 Oberstar	Y	Y	Y	N	Y	N	Y	Y
MISSISSIPPI								
1 ***Wicker***	N	N	N	Y	Y	Y	Y	Y
2 Thompson	N	Y	Y	N	Y	N	N	?
3 ***Pickering***	N	N	N	Y	Y	Y	Y	Y
4 Shows	Y	Y	Y	Y	N	Y	Y	Y
5 Taylor	Y	Y	Y	Y	N	?	Y	Y
MISSOURI								
1 Clay	Y	Y	Y	Y	Y	Y	N	Y
2 ***Akin***	N	N	N	Y	Y	Y	Y	Y
3 Gephardt	Y	Y	Y	N	Y	?	N	Y
4 Skelton	Y	Y	Y	Y	Y	Y	Y	Y
5 McCarthy	Y	Y	Y	N	Y	Y	N	Y
6 ***Graves***	N	N	N	Y	Y	Y	Y	Y
7 ***Blunt***	N	N	N	Y	Y	Y	Y	Y
8 ***Emerson***	Y	N	N	Y	Y	Y	Y	Y
9 ***Hulshof***	N	N	N	Y	N	N	Y	Y
MONTANA								
AL ***Rehberg***	N	N	N	Y	Y	Y	Y	Y
NEBRASKA								
1 ***Bereuter***	Y	N	N	Y	Y	Y	Y	Y
2 ***Terry***	N	N	N	Y	Y	Y	Y	Y
3 ***Osborne***	Y	N	N	N	Y	Y	Y	Y
NEVADA								
1 Berkley	Y	Y	Y	Y	Y	Y	N	Y
2 ***Gibbons***	Y	N	N	Y	Y	Y	Y	Y
NEW HAMPSHIRE								
1 ***Sununu***	N	N	N	Y	Y	Y	Y	Y
2 ***Bass***	Y	N	N	Y	Y	Y	N	Y
NEW JERSEY								
1 Andrews	N	Y	Y	Y	Y	Y	N	Y
2 ***LoBiondo***	N	N	N	Y	Y	N	Y	Y
3 ***Saxton***	?	?	N	Y	Y	Y	Y	Y
4 ***Smith***	N	N	N	Y	Y	Y	Y	Y
5 ***Roukema***	N	N	N	Y	Y	Y	N	Y
6 Pallone	Y	Y	Y	Y	Y	Y	N	Y
7 ***Ferguson***	N	N	N	Y	Y	Y	Y	Y
8 Pascrell	Y	Y	Y	Y	Y	Y	N	Y
9 Rothman	Y	Y	Y	N	Y	Y	N	Y
10 Payne	?	?	?	?	Y	Y	N	?
11 ***Frelinghuysen***	N	N	N	Y	Y	Y	Y	Y
12 Holt	N	Y	Y	Y	Y	Y	N	Y
13 Menendez	Y	Y	Y	N	Y	N	N	Y
NEW MEXICO								
1 ***Wilson***	N	N	N	Y	Y	Y	Y	Y
2 ***Skeen***	N	N	N	Y	Y	Y	Y	Y
3 Udall	Y	Y	Y	Y	Y	N	N	Y
NEW YORK								
1 ***Grucci***	N	N	N	Y	Y	Y	Y	Y
2 Israel	Y	Y	Y	Y	N	Y	N	Y
3 ***King***	N	N	N	Y	Y	Y	Y	Y
4 McCarthy	Y	Y	Y	Y	Y	N	Y	Y
5 Ackerman	Y	Y	Y	N	Y	Y	N	Y
6 Meeks	Y	Y	Y	Y	Y	Y	N	Y
7 Crowley	Y	Y	Y	Y	Y	N	N	Y
8 Nadler	Y	Y	Y	N	Y	Y	N	Y
9 Weiner	Y	Y	Y	Y	Y	Y	N	Y
10 Towns	Y	Y	Y	N	Y	?	N	Y
11 Owens	Y	Y	Y	N	Y	Y	N	Y
12 Velázquez	Y	Y	Y	N	Y	N	N	Y
13 ***Fossella***	N	N	N	Y	Y	N	Y	Y
14 Maloney	Y	Y	Y	N	Y	Y	N	Y
15 Rangel	Y	Y	N	Y	Y	Y	N	Y
16 Serrano	N	Y	Y	Y	Y	Y	N	Y
17 Engel	Y	Y	Y	Y	Y	Y	N	Y
18 Lowey	Y	Y	Y	Y	Y	Y	N	Y
19 ***Kelly***	Y	N	N	Y	Y	?	Y	Y
20 ***Gilman***	N	N	N	Y	Y	Y	N	Y
21 McNulty	N	Y	Y	N	Y	N	Y	Y
22 ***Sweeney***	N	N	N	Y	Y	N	Y	Y
23 ***Boehlert***	Y	N	N	Y	Y	Y	Y	Y
24 ***McHugh***	N	N	N	Y	Y	Y	Y	Y
25 ***Walsh***	N	N	N	Y	Y	Y	Y	Y
26 Hinchey	Y	Y	Y	N	Y	Y	N	Y
27 ***Reynolds***	N	N	N	Y	Y	?	Y	Y
28 Slaughter	Y	Y	Y	Y	Y	?	N	Y
29 LaFalce	N	Y	Y	Y	Y	Y	N	Y

	294	295	296	297	298	299	300	301
30 ***Quinn***	N	N	N	Y	Y	Y	Y	Y
31 ***Houghton***	Y	N	N	Y	Y	Y	Y	Y
NORTH CAROLINA								
1 Clayton	Y	Y	Y	Y	Y	Y	N	Y
2 Etheridge	Y	Y	Y	Y	Y	Y	N	Y
3 ***Jones***	N	Y	N	Y	N	Y	Y	Y
4 Price	Y	Y	Y	Y	Y	Y	N	Y
5 ***Burr***	N	N	N	Y	Y	Y	Y	Y
6 ***Coble***	N	N	N	Y	Y	Y	Y	Y
7 McIntyre	Y	Y	Y	Y	Y	Y	Y	Y
8 ***Hayes***	N	N	N	Y	Y	Y	Y	Y
9 ***Myrick***	Y	N	N	Y	Y	Y	Y	Y
10 ***Ballenger***	N	N	N	Y	Y	Y	Y	Y
11 ***Taylor***	N	N	N	Y	Y	Y	Y	Y
12 Watt	Y	Y	Y	Y	Y	Y	N	Y
NORTH DAKOTA								
AL Pomeroy	Y	Y	Y	N	Y	Y	Y	Y
OHIO								
1 ***Chabot***	N	N	N	Y	Y	Y	Y	Y
2 ***Portman***	N	N	N	Y	Y	Y	Y	Y
3 Hall	Y	Y	Y	N	Y	Y	Y	Y
4 ***Oxley***	N	N	N	Y	Y	Y	Y	Y
5 ***Gillmor***	N	N	N	Y	Y	Y	Y	Y
6 Strickland	Y	Y	Y	Y	Y	Y	N	Y
7 ***Hobson***	N	N	N	Y	Y	Y	Y	Y
8 ***Boehner***	N	N	N	Y	Y	Y	Y	Y
9 Kaptur	Y	Y	Y	Y	Y	Y	N	Y
10 Kucinich	Y	Y	Y	Y	Y	N	Y	Y
11 Jones	N	Y	Y	Y	+	+	–	+
12 ***Tiberi***	N	N	N	Y	Y	Y	Y	Y
13 Brown	Y	Y	Y	N	Y	Y	N	Y
14 Sawyer	Y	Y	Y	Y	Y	Y	N	Y
15 ***Pryce***	N	N	N	Y	Y	Y	Y	Y
16 ***Regula***	N	N	N	Y	Y	Y	Y	Y
17 Traficant	N	N	N	Y	Y	Y	Y	Y
18 ***Ney***	N	N	N	Y	Y	Y	Y	Y
19 ***LaTourette***	N	N	N	Y	Y	Y	Y	Y
OKLAHOMA								
1 ***Largent***	N	N	N	Y	Y	Y	Y	Y
2 Carson	N	Y	Y	Y	Y	Y	Y	Y
3 ***Watkins***	N	N	N	Y	Y	Y	Y	Y
4 ***Watts***	N	N	N	Y	Y	Y	Y	Y
5 ***Istook***	?	?	?	?	Y	Y	Y	Y
6 ***Lucas***	N	N	N	Y	Y	Y	Y	Y
OREGON								
1 Wu	Y	Y	Y	Y	Y	N	Y	?
2 ***Walden***	N	N	N	Y	Y	Y	Y	Y
3 Blumenauer	Y	Y	Y	N	Y	Y	N	Y
4 DeFazio	Y	Y	Y	Y	Y	N	N	Y
5 Hooley	Y	Y	Y	Y	Y	Y	N	Y
PENNSYLVANIA								
1 Brady	Y	Y	Y	Y	Y	Y	N	Y
2 Fattah	Y	Y	Y	Y	Y	Y	N	Y
3 Borski	Y	Y	Y	Y	Y	Y	N	Y
4 ***Hart***	N	N	N	Y	Y	Y	Y	Y
5 ***Peterson***	N	N	N	Y	Y	Y	Y	Y
6 Holden	N	Y	Y	Y	Y	Y	Y	Y
7 ***Weldon***	N	N	N	Y	Y	Y	Y	Y
8 ***Greenwood***	N	N	N	Y	Y	Y	Y	Y
9 ***Shuster, Bill***	N	N	N	Y	Y	Y	Y	Y
10 ***Sherwood***	?	N	N	Y	Y	Y	Y	Y
11 Kanjorski	N	Y	Y	Y	Y	Y	N	Y
12 Murtha	N	Y	N	Y	Y	Y	N	Y
13 Hoeffel	Y	Y	Y	Y	Y	Y	N	Y
14 Coyne	Y	Y	Y	Y	Y	Y	N	Y
15 ***Toomey***	N	N	N	N	N	Y	Y	Y
16 ***Pitts***	N	N	N	Y	N	Y	Y	Y
17 ***Gekas***	N	N	N	Y	Y	Y	Y	Y
18 Doyle	N	Y	Y	Y	Y	Y	Y	Y
19 ***Platts***	N	N	N	Y	Y	N	Y	Y
20 Mascara	N	Y	Y	Y	Y	Y	Y	Y
21 ***English***	N	N	N	Y	Y	N	Y	Y
RHODE ISLAND								
1 Kennedy	N	Y	Y	Y	Y	Y	N	Y
2 Langevin	Y	Y	Y	Y	Y	Y	Y	Y
SOUTH CAROLINA								
1 ***Brown***	N	N	N	Y	Y	Y	Y	Y
2 ***Spence***	?	?	?	?	?	?	?	?
3 ***Graham***	N	N	N	Y	Y	Y	Y	Y
4 ***DeMint***	N	N	N	Y	Y	Y	Y	Y
5 Spratt	Y	Y	Y	Y	Y	Y	N	Y
6 Clyburn	N	Y	Y	Y	Y	Y	N	Y
SOUTH DAKOTA								
AL ***Thune***	Y	N	N	Y	Y	Y	Y	Y

	294	295	296	297	298	299	300	301
TENNESSEE								
1 ***Jenkins***	N	N	N	Y	Y	Y	Y	Y
2 ***Duncan***	N	N	N	Y	Y	Y	Y	Y
3 ***Wamp***	N	N	N	Y	Y	N	Y	Y
4 ***Hilleary***	N	N	N	Y	Y	Y	Y	Y
5 Clement	Y	Y	Y	Y	Y	Y	N	Y
6 Gordon	Y	Y	N	Y	?	?	N	?
7 ***Bryant***	Y	N	N	Y	Y	Y	Y	Y
8 Tanner	N	Y	Y	N	Y	Y	N	Y
9 Ford	N	Y	Y	N	Y	Y	N	Y
TEXAS								
1 Sandlin	N	Y	Y	Y	Y	Y	N	Y
2 Turner	Y	Y	Y	Y	Y	Y	Y	Y
3 ***Johnson, Sam***	N	N	N	Y	Y	Y	Y	Y
4 Hall	N	Y	Y	Y	Y	Y	Y	Y
5 ***Sessions***	N	N	N	Y	Y	Y	Y	Y
6 ***Barton***	N	N	N	Y	Y	Y	Y	Y
7 ***Culberson***	N	N	N	Y	Y	Y	Y	Y
8 ***Brady***	N	N	N	Y	Y	Y	Y	Y
9 Lampson	Y	Y	Y	Y	Y	Y	N	Y
10 Doggett	Y	Y	Y	N	N	Y	N	Y
11 Edwards	Y	Y	Y	Y	Y	Y	N	Y
12 ***Granger***	N	N	N	Y	Y	Y	N	Y
13 ***Thornberry***	N	N	N	Y	Y	Y	Y	Y
14 ***Paul***	N	N	N	N	N	Y	Y	Y
15 Hinojosa	Y	Y	Y	N	Y	Y	N	Y
16 Reyes	Y	Y	Y	N	Y	Y	N	Y
17 Stenholm	N	Y	Y	N	Y	Y	Y	Y
18 Jackson-Lee	Y	Y	Y	Y	Y	Y	N	Y
19 ***Combest***	N	N	N	Y	Y	Y	Y	Y
20 Gonzalez	Y	Y	Y	Y	Y	Y	N	Y
21 ***Smith***	N	N	N	Y	Y	Y	Y	Y
22 ***DeLay***	N	N	N	Y	Y	Y	Y	Y
23 ***Bonilla***	N	N	N	Y	Y	Y	Y	Y
24 Frost	N	Y	Y	Y	Y	Y	N	Y
25 Bentsen	Y	Y	N	Y	Y	Y	N	Y
26 ***Armey***	N	N	N	Y	Y	Y	Y	Y
27 Ortiz	Y	Y	Y	Y	Y	Y	Y	Y
28 Rodriguez	N	Y	Y	Y	Y	Y	N	Y
29 Green	N	Y	Y	Y	N	Y	N	Y
30 Johnson, E.B.	N	Y	Y	Y	+	+	N	Y
UTAH								
1 ***Hansen***	?	?	?	?	Y	Y	Y	Y
2 Matheson	Y	Y	Y	Y	Y	Y	Y	Y
3 ***Cannon***	N	N	N	Y	Y	Y	Y	Y
VERMONT								
AL *Sanders*	Y	Y	Y	N	Y	Y	N	Y
VIRGINIA								
1 ***Davis, Jo Ann***	Y	Y	N	Y	Y	Y	Y	Y
2 ***Schrock***	N	N	N	Y	Y	Y	Y	Y
3 Scott	Y	Y	Y	Y	?	?	N	Y
4 ***Forbes***	N	N	N	Y	Y	Y	Y	Y
5 *Goode*	N	Y	N	Y	N	Y	Y	Y
6 ***Goodlatte***	Y	N	N	Y	N	Y	Y	Y
7 ***Cantor***	N	N	N	Y	Y	Y	Y	Y
8 Moran	Y	Y	N	Y	Y	Y	N	Y
9 Boucher	N	Y	Y	Y	Y	Y	N	Y
10 ***Wolf***	N	N	N	Y	Y	Y	Y	Y
11 ***Davis, T.***	N	N	N	Y	Y	Y	Y	Y
WASHINGTON								
1 Inslee	Y	Y	Y	Y	Y	Y	N	Y
2 Larsen	Y	Y	Y	Y	Y	N	N	Y
3 Baird	Y	Y	Y	Y	Y	Y	N	Y
4 ***Hastings***	N	N	N	Y	Y	Y	Y	Y
5 ***Nethercutt***	N	N	N	Y	Y	Y	Y	Y
6 Dicks	Y	Y	Y	Y	Y	Y	N	Y
7 McDermott	Y	Y	Y	N	Y	N	N	Y
8 ***Dunn***	Y	N	N	Y	Y	Y	Y	Y
9 Smith	Y	Y	Y	N	Y	Y	N	Y
WEST VIRGINIA								
1 Mollohan	N	Y	N	Y	Y	Y	Y	Y
2 ***Capito***	Y	N	N	Y	Y	Y	Y	Y
3 Rahall	Y	Y	N	Y	Y	Y	Y	Y
WISCONSIN								
1 ***Ryan***	N	N	N	N	N	Y	Y	Y
2 Baldwin	Y	Y	Y	N	Y	Y	N	Y
3 Kind	Y	Y	Y	N	N	N	N	Y
4 Kleczka	Y	Y	Y	N	Y	Y	N	Y
5 Barrett	Y	Y	Y	N	N	Y	N	Y
6 ***Petri***	N	N	N	N	N	Y	Y	Y
7 Obey	Y	Y	Y	N	Y	Y	N	Y
8 ***Green***	N	N	N	Y	N	Y	Y	Y
9 ***Sensenbrenner***	N	N	N	N	N	N	Y	Y
WYOMING								
AL ***Cubin***	N	N	N	Y	Y	?	Y	Y

Southern states - Ala., Ark., Fla., Ga., Ky., La., Miss., N.C., Okla., S.C., Tenn., Texas, Va.

Key

Y	Voted for (yea).
#	Paired for.
+	Announced for.
N	Voted against (nay).
X	Paired against.
–	Announced against.
P	Voted "present."
C	Voted "present" to avoid possible conflict of interest.
?	Did not vote or otherwise make a position known.

Democrats **Republicans**
Independents

---

302. HR 2505. Human Cloning Ban/Substitute. Greenwood, R-Pa., substitute amendment that would ban human cloning to begin a pregnancy but allow the cloning of embryos for medical research as long as a researcher registers with the Department of Health and Human Services. The bill would make it illegal to receive or transport the products of cloning if they would be used to begin a pregnancy. The ban on reproductive cloning would expire in 10 years. Rejected 178-249: R 25-194; D 153-53 (ND 118-35, SD 35-18); I 0-2. A "nay" was a vote in support of the president's position. July 31, 2001.

303. HR 2505. Human Cloning Ban/Recommit. Lofgren, D-Calif., motion to recommit the bill to the House Judiciary Committee with instructions to add an amendment providing that the bill shall not prohibit human cloning related to the development of treatments for various diseases, including Parkinson's, cancer, and heart disease. The instructions specify that the product of the cloning process could not used to begin a pregnancy. Motion rejected 175-251: R 19-200; D 156-49 (ND 120-33, SD 36-16); I 0-2. July 31, 2001.

304. HR 2505. Human Cloning Ban/Passage. Passage of the bill that would prohibit human cloning for any purpose. The bill would make it illegal for any person or organization to perform, attempt or participate in human cloning; it would ban receiving, shipping or importing cloned embryos or products made from them. The bill includes civil and criminal penalties including up to 10 years imprisonment and fines of more than $1 million. Passed 265-162: R 200-19; D 63-143 (ND 36-117, SD 27-26); I 2-0. A "yea" was a vote in support of the president's position. July 31, 2001.

305. HR 1140. Railroad Retirement/Passage. Young, R-Alaska, motion to suspend the rules and pass the bill that would allow railroad retirement assets to be invested in private securities. It also would reduce the payroll tax on railroads and makes other changes in the railroad retirement system. Motion agreed to 384-33: R 184-31; D 198-2 (ND 149-0, SD 49-2); I 2-0. A two-thirds majority of those present and voting (278 in this case) is required for passage under suspension of the rules. July 31, 2001.

306. HR 4. Energy Plan/Previous Question. Hastings, R-Wash., motion to order the previous question (thus ending debate and possibility of amendment) on adoption of the rule (H Res 216) to provide for House floor consideration of the bill that would make numerous changes to the nation's energy policies. Motion agreed to 221-208: R 219-0; D 1-207 (ND 1-154, SD 0-53); I 1-1. Aug. 1, 2001.

307. HR 4. Energy Plan/Rule. Adoption of the rule (H Res 216) to provide for House floor consideration of the bill that would make numerous changes to the nation's energy policies, including those in the areas of production, conservation, taxes and research. Adopted 220-206: R 218-0; D 1-205 (ND 1-153, SD 0-52); I 1-1. Aug. 1, 2001.

308. Procedural Motion/Journal. Approval of the House Journal of Tuesday, July 31, 2001. Approved 343-65: R 194-18; D 148-47 (ND 108-38, SD 40-9); I 1-0. Aug. 1, 2001.

309. HR 4. Energy Plan/Additional Studies. Tauzin, R-La., amendment that would make various changes to the bill, including the authorization of numerous studies and analyses on turning municipal waste into fuel; developing nuclear reactors at existing Energy Department sites; linking education to energy conservation; and increasing the market share for renewable fuels. Adopted 281-148: R 218-1; D 62-146 (ND 27-127, SD 35-19); I 1-1. Aug. 1, 2001.

	302	303	304	305	306	307	308	309
ALABAMA								
1 *Callahan*	N	N	Y	Y	Y	Y	Y	Y
2 *Everett*	N	N	Y	Y	Y	Y	Y	Y
3 *Riley*	N	N	Y	Y	Y	Y	Y	Y
4 *Aderholt*	N	N	Y	Y	Y	Y	N	Y
5 Cramer	N	N	Y	?	N	N	N	Y
6 *Bachus*	N	N	Y	Y	Y	Y	N	Y
7 Hilliard	Y	Y	N	Y	N	N	N	Y
ALASKA								
AL *Young*	N	N	Y	Y	Y	Y	Y	Y
ARIZONA								
1 *Flake*	N	N	Y	N	Y	Y	Y	Y
2 Pastor	Y	Y	N	Y	N	N	Y	N
3 *Stump*	N	N	Y	N	Y	Y	Y	Y
4 *Shadegg*	N	N	Y	N	Y	Y	Y	Y
5 *Kolbe*	Y	Y	Y	N	Y	Y	Y	Y
6 *Hayworth*	N	N	Y	Y	Y	Y	Y	Y
ARKANSAS								
1 Berry	N	N	Y	N	N	N	Y	Y
2 Snyder	Y	Y	N	Y	N	N	Y	Y
3 *Hutchinson*	?	?	?	?	?	?	?	?
4 Ross	Y	Y	Y	Y	N	N	Y	Y
CALIFORNIA								
1 Thompson	Y	Y	N	Y	N	N	N	N
2 *Herger*	N	N	Y	N	Y	Y	Y	Y
3 *Ose*	Y	Y	N	Y	Y	Y	Y	Y
4 *Doolittle*	N	N	Y	Y	Y	Y	Y	Y
5 Matsui	Y	Y	N	Y	N	N	N	N
6 Woolsey	Y	Y	N	Y	N	N	N	N
7 Miller, George	Y	Y	N	Y	N	N	N	N
8 Pelosi	Y	Y	N	Y	N	N	N	N
9 Lee	Y	Y	N	Y	N	N	N	N
10 Tauscher	Y	Y	N	Y	N	N	N	N
11 *Pombo*	N	N	Y	Y	Y	Y	Y	Y
12 Lantos	Y	Y	N	Y	N	N	Y	N
13 Stark	?	?	?	?	?	?	?	?
14 Eshoo	Y	Y	N	Y	N	N	N	N
15 Honda	Y	Y	N	Y	N	N	?	N
16 Lofgren	Y	Y	N	Y	N	N	Y	N
17 Farr	Y	Y	N	Y	N	N	N	Y
18 Condit	Y	Y	N	Y	N	N	Y	Y
19 *Radanovich*	N	N	Y	Y	Y	Y	Y	Y
20 Dooley	Y	Y	N	Y	N	N	Y	N
21 *Thomas*	Y	N	Y	N	Y	N	Y	N
22 Capps	Y	Y	N	Y	N	N	N	N
23 *Gallegly*	N	N	Y	Y	Y	Y	Y	Y
24 Sherman	Y	Y	N	Y	N	N	N	N
25 *McKeon*	N	N	Y	Y	Y	Y	Y	Y
26 Berman	Y	Y	N	Y	N	N	N	N
27 Schiff	Y	Y	N	Y	N	N	N	N
28 *Dreier*	N	N	Y	Y	Y	Y	Y	Y
29 Waxman	Y	Y	N	Y	N	N	N	N
30 Becerra	Y	Y	N	Y	N	N	Y	N
31 Solis	Y	Y	N	Y	N	N	N	N
32 Watson	Y	Y	N	+	N	N	N	N
33 Roybal-Allard	Y	Y	N	Y	N	N	N	N
34 Napolitano	Y	Y	N	Y	N	N	N	N
35 Waters	Y	Y	N	Y	N	N	N	N
36 Harman	Y	Y	N	Y	N	N	N	N
37 Millender-McD.	Y	Y	N	Y	N	N	N	N
38 *Horn*	Y	Y	N	Y	Y	Y	Y	Y

	302	303	304	305	306	307	308	309
39 *Royce*	N	N	Y	Y	Y	Y	Y	Y
40 *Lewis*	N	N	Y	Y	Y	Y	Y	Y
41 *Miller, Gary*	N	N	Y	N	Y	Y	Y	Y
42 Baca	Y	Y	N	Y	N	N	Y	Y
43 *Calvert*	N	N	Y	Y	Y	Y	Y	Y
44 *Bono*	Y	Y	Y	Y	Y	Y	Y	Y
45 *Rohrabacher*	Y	Y	Y	Y	Y	Y	Y	Y
46 Sanchez	Y	Y	N	Y	N	N	N	N
47 *Cox*	N	N	Y	N	Y	Y	Y	Y
48 *Issa*	N	N	Y	Y	Y	Y	Y	Y
49 Davis	Y	Y	N	Y	N	N	N	N
50 Filner	Y	Y	N	Y	N	N	N	N
51 *Cunningham*	N	N	Y	Y	Y	Y	Y	Y
52 *Hunter*	N	N	Y	Y	Y	Y	Y	Y
COLORADO								
1 DeGette	Y	Y	N	Y	N	N	N	N
2 Udall	Y	Y	N	Y	N	N	N	N
3 *McInnis*	N	N	Y	Y	Y	Y	Y	Y
4 *Schaffer*	N	N	Y	N	Y	Y	N	Y
5 *Hefley*	N	N	Y	N	Y	Y	N	Y
6 *Tancredo*	N	N	Y	N	Y	Y	P	Y
CONNECTICUT								
1 Larson	Y	Y	N	Y	N	N	Y	N
2 *Simmons*	Y	Y	N	Y	Y	Y	Y	Y
3 DeLauro	Y	Y	N	Y	N	N	N	N
4 *Shays*	Y	Y	N	Y	Y	N	N	Y
5 Maloney	Y	Y	N	Y	N	N	N	N
6 *Johnson*	Y	Y	N	Y	Y	Y	Y	Y
DELAWARE								
AL *Castle*	Y	Y	N	Y	Y	Y	Y	Y
FLORIDA								
1 *Scarborough*	N	N	Y	Y	Y	Y	Y	Y
2 Boyd	Y	Y	Y	Y	N	N	Y	Y
3 Brown	Y	Y	N	Y	N	N	?	N
4 *Crenshaw*	N	N	Y	Y	Y	Y	Y	Y
5 Thurman	Y	Y	N	Y	N	N	N	N
6 *Stearns*	N	N	Y	Y	Y	Y	+	Y
7 *Mica*	N	N	Y	Y	Y	Y	Y	Y
8 *Keller*	N	N	Y	Y	Y	Y	Y	Y
9 *Bilirakis*	N	N	Y	Y	Y	Y	Y	Y
10 *Young*	N	N	Y	Y	Y	Y	Y	Y
11 Davis	Y	Y	N	Y	N	N	Y	Y
12 *Putnam*	N	N	Y	Y	Y	Y	Y	Y
13 *Miller*	Y	Y	N	Y	Y	N	N	Y
14 *Goss*	N	N	Y	Y	Y	Y	Y	Y
15 *Weldon*	N	N	Y	Y	Y	Y	Y	Y
16 *Foley*	N	N	Y	Y	Y	Y	Y	Y
17 Meek	Y	Y	N	Y	N	N	N	N
18 *Ros-Lehtinen*	N	N	Y	Y	Y	Y	Y	Y
19 Wexler	Y	Y	N	N	N	N	N	N
20 Deutsch	Y	Y	N	Y	N	N	N	N
21 *Diaz-Balart*	N	N	Y	Y	Y	Y	Y	Y
22 *Shaw*	N	N	Y	Y	Y	Y	Y	Y
23 Hastings	?	?	?	?	?	?	?	N
GEORGIA								
1 *Kingston*	N	N	Y	Y	Y	Y	Y	Y
2 Bishop	N	N	Y	Y	N	N	Y	Y
3 *Collins*	N	N	Y	Y	Y	Y	Y	Y
4 McKinney	N	?	Y	N	N	N	N	Y
5 Lewis	Y	Y	N	Y	N	N	Y	Y
6 *Isakson*	N	N	Y	Y	Y	Y	Y	Y
7 *Barr*	N	N	Y	Y	Y	Y	Y	Y
8 *Chambliss*	N	N	Y	Y	Y	Y	Y	Y
9 *Deal*	N	N	Y	Y	Y	Y	Y	Y
10 *Norwood*	N	N	Y	Y	Y	Y	Y	Y
11 *Linder*	N	N	Y	Y	Y	Y	Y	Y
HAWAII								
1 Abercrombie	N	Y	N	Y	Y	N	N	Y
2 Mink	N	N	Y	Y	N	N	Y	Y
IDAHO								
1 *Otter*	N	N	Y	Y	Y	Y	Y	Y
2 *Simpson*	N	N	Y	Y	Y	Y	Y	Y
ILLINOIS								
1 Rush	Y	Y	N	Y	N	N	Y	N
2 Jackson	Y	Y	N	Y	N	N	Y	N
3 Lipinski	?	?	?	?	N	N	?	Y
4 Gutierrez	Y	Y	N	N	N	N	N	N
5 Blagojevich	Y	Y	N	Y	N	N	Y	N
6 *Hyde*	N	N	Y	?	Y	Y	Y	Y
7 Davis	Y	Y	N	Y	N	N	Y	N
8 *Crane*	N	N	Y	Y	Y	Y	N	Y
9 Schakowsky	Y	Y	N	Y	N	N	N	N
10 *Kirk*	Y	Y	N	Y	Y	Y	Y	Y
11 *Weller*	N	N	Y	Y	Y	Y	Y	Y
12 Costello	N	N	Y	Y	N	N	N	Y
13 *Biggert*	Y	N	Y	N	Y	Y	Y	Y

ND Northern Democrats   SD Southern Democrats

	302	303	204	305	306	307	308	309
14 ***Hastert***								
15 ***Johnson***	N	N	Y	Y	Y	Y	Y	Y
16 ***Manzullo***	N	N	Y	Y	Y	Y	?	Y
17 Evans	Y	Y	N	Y	N	N	Y	N
18 ***LaHood***	N	N	Y	Y	Y	Y	Y	Y
19 Phelps	N	N	Y	Y	N	N	?	Y
20 ***Shimkus***	N	N	Y	Y	Y	Y	Y	Y
INDIANA								
1 Visclosky	Y	Y	N	Y	N	N	N	N
2 ***Pence***	N	N	Y	N	Y	Y	Y	Y
3 Roemer	N	N	Y	Y	N	N	Y	N
4 ***Souder***	N	N	Y	Y	Y	Y	Y	Y
5 ***Buyer***	N	N	Y	Y	Y	Y	Y	Y
6 ***Burton***	N	N	Y	Y	Y	Y	Y	Y
7 ***Kerns***	N	N	Y	Y	Y	Y	Y	Y
8 ***Hostettler***	N	N	Y	Y	Y	Y	Y	Y
9 Hill	N	N	Y	Y	N	N	Y	Y
10 Carson	Y	Y	N	Y	N	N	N	N
IOWA								
1 ***Leach***	Y	Y	N	?	Y	Y	Y	Y
2 ***Nussle***	N	N	Y	Y	Y	Y	Y	Y
3 Boswell	Y	Y	N	Y	N	N	Y	N
4 ***Ganske***	N	N	Y	Y	Y	Y	Y	Y
5 ***Latham***	N	N	Y	Y	Y	Y	Y	Y
KANSAS								
1 ***Moran***	N	N	Y	Y	Y	Y	N	Y
2 ***Ryun***	N	N	Y	Y	Y	Y	Y	Y
3 Moore	Y	Y	N	Y	N	N	N	Y
4 ***Tiahrt***	N	N	Y	Y	Y	Y	Y	Y
KENTUCKY								
1 ***Whitfield***	N	N	Y	Y	Y	Y	P	Y
2 ***Lewis***	N	N	Y	Y	Y	Y	Y	Y
3 ***Northup***	N	N	Y	Y	Y	Y	Y	Y
4 Lucas	N	N	Y	Y	N	N	Y	Y
5 ***Rogers***	N	N	Y	Y	Y	Y	Y	Y
6 ***Fletcher***	N	N	Y	Y	Y	Y	Y	Y
LOUISIANA								
1 ***Vitter***	N	N	Y	Y	Y	Y	?	Y
2 Jefferson	N	Y	Y	Y	N	N	Y	Y
3 ***Tauzin***	N	N	Y	Y	Y	Y	Y	Y
4 ***McCrery***	N	N	Y	Y	Y	Y	Y	Y
5 ***Cooksey***	N	N	Y	Y	Y	Y	Y	Y
6 ***Baker***	N	N	Y	Y	Y	Y	Y	Y
7 John	N	N	Y	Y	N	N	Y	Y
MAINE								
1 Allen	Y	Y	N	Y	N	N	Y	Y
2 Baldacci	Y	Y	N	Y	N	N	?	Y
MARYLAND								
1 ***Gilchrest***	Y	N	N	Y	Y	Y	Y	Y
2 ***Ehrlich***	N	N	Y	Y	Y	Y	Y	Y
3 Cardin	Y	Y	N	Y	N	N	Y	N
4 Wynn	Y	Y	Y	Y	N	N	Y	Y
5 Hoyer	Y	Y	N	Y	N	N	Y	N
6 ***Bartlett***	N	N	Y	Y	Y	Y	Y	Y
7 Cummings	Y	Y	N	Y	N	N	Y	Y
8 ***Morella***	Y	Y	N	Y	Y	Y	Y	Y
MASSACHUSETTS								
1 Olver	Y	Y	N	Y	N	N	Y	N
2 Neal	Y	Y	N	Y	N	N	Y	N
3 McGovern	Y	Y	N	Y	N	N	N	N
4 Frank	Y	Y	N	Y	N	N	Y	N
5 Meehan	Y	Y	N	Y	N	N	Y	N
6 Tierney	Y	Y	N	Y	N	N	Y	N
7 Markey	Y	Y	N	?	N	N	N	N
8 Capuano	Y	Y	N	Y	N	N	N	N
9 Vacant								
10 Delahunt	N	N	N	Y	N	N	Y	N
MICHIGAN								
1 Stupak	N	N	Y	Y	N	N	N	Y
2 ***Hoekstra***	N	N	Y	N	Y	Y	Y	Y
3 ***Ehlers***	N	N	Y	Y	Y	Y	Y	Y
4 ***Camp***	N	N	Y	Y	Y	Y	Y	Y
5 Barcia	N	N	Y	Y	N	N	Y	Y
6 ***Upton***	N	N	Y	Y	Y	Y	Y	Y
7 ***Smith***	N	N	Y	N	Y	?	Y	Y
8 ***Rogers***	N	N	Y	Y	Y	Y	Y	Y
9 Kildee	N	N	Y	Y	N	N	Y	N
10 Bonior	N	N	Y	Y	N	N	Y	N
11 ***Knollenberg***	N	N	Y	Y	Y	Y	Y	Y
12 Levin	Y	Y	N	Y	N	N	Y	N
13 Rivers	Y	Y	N	Y	N	N	Y	N
14 Conyers	Y	Y	N	Y	N	N	N	N
15 Kilpatrick	Y	Y	N	Y	N	N	?	N
16 Dingell	Y	Y	N	Y	N	?	?	N

	302	303	204	305	306	307	308	309
MINNESOTA								
1 ***Gutknecht***	N	N	Y	Y	Y	Y	N	Y
2 ***Kennedy***	N	N	Y	Y	Y	Y	N	Y
3 ***Ramstad***	Y	Y	N	Y	Y	Y	N	Y
4 McCollum	Y	Y	N	Y	N	N	Y	N
5 Sabo	Y	Y	N	Y	N	N	N	N
6 Luther	Y	Y	N	Y	N	N	Y	N
7 Peterson	N	N	Y	?	N	N	N	Y
8 Oberstar	N	N	Y	Y	N	N	N	N
MISSISSIPPI								
1 ***Wicker***	N	N	Y	Y	Y	Y	N	Y
2 Thompson	Y	Y	Y	Y	N	N	N	Y
3 ***Pickering***	N	N	Y	Y	Y	Y	Y	Y
4 Shows	N	N	Y	Y	N	N	Y	Y
5 Taylor	N	N	Y	N	N	N	N	Y
MISSOURI								
1 Clay	Y	Y	N	Y	N	N	Y	N
2 ***Akin***	N	N	Y	Y	Y	Y	Y	Y
3 Gephardt	Y	Y	N	Y	N	N	N	N
4 Skelton	N	N	Y	Y	N	N	Y	N
5 McCarthy	Y	Y	N	Y	N	N	Y	N
6 ***Graves***	N	N	Y	Y	Y	Y	Y	Y
7 ***Blunt***	N	N	Y	Y	Y	Y	Y	Y
8 ***Emerson***	N	N	Y	Y	Y	Y	Y	Y
9 ***Hulshof***	N	N	Y	Y	Y	Y	N	Y
MONTANA								
AL ***Rehberg***	N	N	Y	Y	Y	Y	Y	Y
NEBRASKA								
1 ***Bereuter***	N	N	Y	Y	Y	Y	Y	Y
2 ***Terry***	N	N	Y	Y	Y	Y	Y	Y
3 ***Osborne***	N	N	Y	Y	Y	Y	Y	Y
NEVADA								
1 Berkley	Y	Y	N	Y	N	N	Y	N
2 ***Gibbons***	N	N	Y	Y	Y	Y	Y	Y
NEW HAMPSHIRE								
1 ***Sununu***	N	N	Y	N	Y	Y	Y	Y
2 ***Bass***	Y	Y	N	Y	Y	Y	Y	Y
NEW JERSEY								
1 Andrews	Y	Y	N	Y	N	N	?	N
2 ***LoBiondo***	N	N	Y	Y	Y	Y	N	Y
3 ***Saxton***	N	N	Y	Y	Y	Y	Y	Y
4 ***Smith***	N	N	Y	Y	Y	Y	Y	Y
5 ***Roukema***	N	N	Y	Y	Y	Y	Y	Y
6 Pallone	Y	Y	N	Y	N	N	N	N
7 ***Ferguson***	N	N	Y	Y	Y	Y	Y	Y
8 Pascrell	N	N	Y	Y	N	N	Y	Y
9 Rothman	Y	Y	N	Y	N	N	Y	N
10 Payne	Y	Y	N	Y	N	N	Y	N
11 ***Frelinghuysen***	N	N	Y	N	Y	Y	Y	Y
12 Holt	Y	Y	N	Y	N	N	Y	N
13 Menendez	Y	Y	N	Y	N	N	N	N
NEW MEXICO								
1 ***Wilson***	Y	N	Y	Y	Y	Y	Y	Y
2 ***Skeen***	N	N	Y	Y	Y	Y	Y	Y
3 Udall	Y	Y	N	Y	N	N	N	N
NEW YORK								
1 ***Grucci***	N	N	Y	Y	Y	Y	Y	Y
2 Israel	Y	Y	Y	Y	N	N	Y	N
3 ***King***	N	N	Y	Y	Y	Y	Y	Y
4 McCarthy	N	Y	Y	Y	N	N	Y	Y
5 Ackerman	Y	Y	N	Y	N	N	Y	N
6 Meeks	Y	Y	N	Y	N	N	Y	N
7 Crowley	Y	Y	N	Y	N	N	N	N
8 Nadler	Y	Y	N	?	N	N	Y	N
9 Weiner	Y	Y	N	Y	N	N	Y	N
10 Towns	Y	Y	N	Y	N	N	N	N
11 Owens	Y	Y	N	Y	N	N	Y	N
12 Velázquez	Y	Y	N	Y	N	N	N	N
13 ***Fossella***	N	N	Y	Y	Y	Y	N	Y
14 Maloney	Y	Y	N	Y	N	N	Y	N
15 Rangel	Y	Y	N	Y	N	N	Y	N
16 Serrano	Y	Y	N	Y	N	N	Y	N
17 Engel	Y	Y	N	Y	N	N	Y	N
18 Lowey	Y	Y	N	Y	N	N	Y	N
19 ***Kelly***	Y	Y	Y	Y	Y	Y	Y	Y
20 ***Gilman***	Y	Y	N	Y	Y	Y	?	Y
21 McNulty	N	N	Y	Y	N	N	N	N
22 ***Sweeney***	N	N	Y	Y	Y	Y	N	Y
23 ***Boehlert***	Y	Y	N	Y	Y	Y	Y	Y
24 ***McHugh***	N	N	Y	Y	Y	Y	Y	Y
25 ***Walsh***	N	N	Y	Y	Y	Y	Y	Y
26 Hinchey	Y	Y	N	Y	N	N	N	N
27 ***Reynolds***	N	N	Y	Y	Y	Y	Y	Y
28 Slaughter	Y	Y	N	Y	N	N	N	N
29 LaFalce	N	N	Y	Y	N	N	?	N

	302	303	204	305	306	307	308	309
30 ***Quinn***	N	N	Y	Y	Y	Y	Y	Y
31 ***Houghton***	Y	Y	N	Y	Y	Y	Y	Y
NORTH CAROLINA								
1 Clayton	Y	Y	N	Y	N	N	?	N
2 Etheridge	Y	Y	N	Y	N	N	Y	N
3 ***Jones***	N	N	Y	N	Y	Y	Y	Y
4 Price	Y	Y	N	Y	N	N	Y	N
5 ***Burr***	N	N	Y	Y	Y	Y	Y	Y
6 ***Coble***	N	N	Y	Y	Y	Y	Y	Y
7 McIntyre	N	N	Y	Y	N	N	Y	N
8 ***Hayes***	N	N	Y	Y	Y	Y	Y	Y
9 ***Myrick***	N	N	Y	N	Y	Y	Y	Y
10 ***Ballenger***	N	N	Y	N	Y	Y	Y	Y
11 ***Taylor***	N	N	Y	Y	Y	Y	Y	Y
12 Watt	Y	Y	N	Y	N	N	Y	N
NORTH DAKOTA								
AL Pomeroy	N	N	Y	Y	N	N	Y	Y
OHIO								
1 ***Chabot***	N	N	Y	N	Y	Y	Y	Y
2 ***Portman***	N	N	Y	Y	Y	Y	Y	Y
3 Hall	N	N	Y	Y	N	N	Y	?
4 ***Oxley***	N	N	Y	+	Y	Y	Y	Y
5 ***Gillmor***	N	N	Y	Y	Y	Y	N	Y
6 Strickland	Y	Y	Y	Y	N	N	N	N
7 ***Hobson***	N	N	Y	Y	Y	Y	Y	Y
8 ***Boehner***	N	N	Y	Y	Y	Y	Y	Y
9 Kaptur	N	N	N	Y	N	N	Y	N
10 Kucinich	N	N	Y	Y	N	N	Y	N
11 Jones	+	+	−	+	N	N	N	N
12 ***Tiberi***	N	N	Y	Y	Y	Y	Y	Y
13 Brown	Y	Y	N	Y	N	N	Y	N
14 Sawyer	Y	Y	N	Y	N	N	Y	N
15 ***Pryce***	Y	N	N	Y	Y	Y	Y	Y
16 ***Regula***	N	N	Y	Y	Y	Y	?	Y
17 Traficant	N	N	Y	Y	Y	Y	Y	Y
18 ***Ney***	N	N	Y	Y	Y	Y	Y	Y
19 ***LaTourette***	N	N	Y	Y	Y	Y	Y	Y
OKLAHOMA								
1 ***Largent***	N	N	Y	N	Y	Y	Y	Y
2 Carson	N	N	Y	Y	N	N	Y	Y
3 ***Watkins***	N	N	Y	Y	Y	Y	Y	Y
4 ***Watts***	N	N	Y	Y	Y	Y	Y	Y
5 ***Istook***	N	N	Y	Y	Y	Y	Y	Y
6 ***Lucas***	N	N	Y	Y	Y	Y	Y	Y
OREGON								
1 Wu	N	N	Y	Y	N	N	Y	N
2 ***Walden***	N	N	Y	Y	Y	Y	Y	Y
3 Blumenauer	Y	Y	N	Y	N	N	Y	N
4 DeFazio	N	Y	N	Y	N	N	N	N
5 Hooley	Y	Y	N	Y	N	N	N	N
PENNSYLVANIA								
1 Brady	Y	Y	N	Y	N	N	N	N
2 Fattah	Y	Y	N	Y	N	N	Y	N
3 Borski	N	N	Y	Y	N	N	N	N
4 ***Hart***	N	N	Y	Y	Y	Y	Y	Y
5 ***Peterson***	N	N	Y	Y	Y	Y	Y	Y
6 Holden	N	N	Y	Y	N	N	N	Y
7 ***Weldon***	N	N	Y	Y	Y	Y	Y	Y
8 ***Greenwood***	Y	Y	N	Y	Y	Y	Y	Y
9 ***Shuster, Bill***	N	N	Y	Y	Y	Y	Y	Y
10 ***Sherwood***	N	N	Y	Y	Y	Y	Y	Y
11 Kanjorski	N	N	Y	Y	N	N	Y	N
12 Murtha	N	N	Y	Y	N	N	Y	N
13 Hoeffel	Y	Y	N	Y	N	N	Y	N
14 Coyne	Y	Y	N	Y	N	N	Y	N
15 ***Toomey***	N	N	Y	?	Y	Y	Y	Y
16 ***Pitts***	N	N	Y	N	Y	Y	Y	Y
17 ***Gekas***	N	N	Y	Y	Y	Y	Y	Y
18 Doyle	N	N	Y	Y	N	N	Y	Y
19 ***Platts***	N	N	Y	Y	Y	Y	N	Y
20 Mascara	N	N	Y	Y	N	N	Y	Y
21 ***English***	N	N	Y	Y	Y	Y	N	Y
RHODE ISLAND								
1 Kennedy	Y	Y	N	Y	N	N	Y	N
2 Langevin	N	N	Y	Y	N	N	Y	N
SOUTH CAROLINA								
1 ***Brown***	N	N	Y	Y	Y	Y	Y	Y
2 ***Spence***	?	?	?	?	?	?	?	?
3 ***Graham***	N	N	Y	Y	Y	Y	Y	Y
4 ***DeMint***	N	N	Y	N	Y	Y	Y	Y
5 Spratt	Y	Y	Y	Y	N	N	Y	N
6 Clyburn	Y	Y	Y	Y	N	N	Y	Y
SOUTH DAKOTA								
AL ***Thune***	N	N	Y	Y	Y	Y	Y	Y

	302	303	204	305	306	307	308	309
TENNESSEE								
1 ***Jenkins***	N	N	Y	Y	Y	Y	Y	Y
2 ***Duncan***	N	N	Y	Y	Y	Y	Y	Y
3 ***Wamp***	N	N	Y	Y	Y	Y	N	Y
4 ***Hilleary***	N	N	Y	Y	Y	Y	Y	Y
5 Clement	N	N	Y	Y	N	N	Y	Y
6 Gordon	N	N	Y	Y	N	N	Y	Y
7 ***Bryant***	N	N	Y	Y	Y	Y	Y	Y
8 Tanner	N	Y	Y	Y	N	N	N	N
9 Ford	Y	Y	Y	Y	N	−	Y	N
TEXAS								
1 Sandlin	Y	Y	N	Y	N	N	Y	Y
2 Turner	N	N	Y	Y	N	N	Y	Y
3 ***Johnson, Sam***	N	N	Y	N	Y	Y	Y	Y
4 Hall	N	N	Y	Y	N	N	Y	Y
5 ***Sessions***	N	N	Y	Y	Y	Y	Y	Y
6 ***Barton***	N	N	Y	Y	Y	Y	Y	Y
7 ***Culberson***	N	N	Y	Y	Y	Y	Y	Y
8 ***Brady***	N	N	Y	Y	Y	Y	Y	Y
9 Lampson	Y	Y	N	Y	N	N	Y	Y
10 Doggett	Y	Y	N	Y	N	N	Y	N
11 Edwards	N	N	Y	Y	N	N	Y	Y
12 ***Granger***	Y	N	Y	Y	Y	Y	Y	Y
13 ***Thornberry***	N	N	Y	Y	Y	Y	Y	Y
14 ***Paul***	N	N	N	N	Y	Y	Y	N
15 Hinojosa	Y	Y	N	Y	N	N	Y	Y
16 Reyes	Y	Y	Y	Y	N	N	Y	Y
17 Stenholm	N	N	Y	N	N	N	N	Y
18 Jackson-Lee	Y	Y	N	Y	N	N	?	Y
19 ***Combest***	N	N	Y	Y	Y	Y	Y	Y
20 Gonzalez	Y	Y	N	Y	N	N	Y	Y
21 ***Smith***	N	N	Y	Y	Y	Y	Y	Y
22 ***DeLay***	N	N	Y	N	Y	Y	Y	Y
23 ***Bonilla***	N	N	Y	Y	Y	Y	Y	Y
24 Frost	Y	Y	N	Y	N	N	?	N
25 Bentsen	Y	Y	N	Y	N	N	Y	Y
26 ***Armey***	N	N	Y	Y	Y	Y	Y	Y
27 Ortiz	N	N	Y	Y	N	N	Y	Y
28 Rodriguez	Y	Y	N	Y	N	N	N	Y
29 Green	Y	Y	Y	Y	N	N	Y	Y
30 Johnson, E.B.	Y	Y	N	Y	N	N	Y	Y
UTAH								
1 ***Hansen***	N	N	Y	Y	Y	Y	Y	Y
2 Matheson	N	N	Y	Y	N	N	Y	N
3 ***Cannon***	N	N	Y	Y	Y	Y	Y	Y
VERMONT								
AL *Sanders*	N	N	Y	Y	N	N	?	N
VIRGINIA								
1 ***Davis, Jo Ann***	N	N	Y	Y	Y	Y	Y	Y
2 ***Schrock***	N	N	Y	Y	Y	Y	Y	Y
3 Scott	Y	Y	N	Y	N	N	Y	Y
4 ***Forbes***	N	N	Y	Y	Y	Y	Y	Y
5 *Goode*	N	N	Y	Y	Y	Y	Y	Y
6 ***Goodlatte***	N	N	Y	Y	Y	Y	Y	Y
7 ***Cantor***	N	N	Y	Y	Y	Y	Y	Y
8 Moran	Y	Y	N	?	N	N	Y	N
9 Boucher	Y	Y	N	Y	N	N	Y	Y
10 ***Wolf***	N	N	Y	Y	Y	Y	Y	Y
11 ***Davis, T.***	N	N	Y	Y	Y	Y	Y	Y
WASHINGTON								
1 Inslee	Y	Y	N	Y	N	N	Y	N
2 Larsen	Y	N	Y	Y	N	N	N	Y
3 Baird	Y	Y	N	Y	N	N	N	N
4 ***Hastings***	N	N	Y	Y	Y	Y	Y	Y
5 ***Nethercutt***	N	N	Y	Y	Y	Y	Y	Y
6 Dicks	Y	Y	N	Y	N	N	?	N
7 McDermott	Y	Y	N	Y	N	N	N	N
8 ***Dunn***	N	N	Y	Y	Y	Y	Y	Y
9 Smith	Y	Y	N	Y	N	N	Y	Y
WEST VIRGINIA								
1 Mollohan	N	N	Y	Y	N	N	Y	N
2 ***Capito***	N	N	Y	Y	Y	Y	Y	Y
3 Rahall	N	N	Y	Y	N	N	Y	N
WISCONSIN								
1 ***Ryan***	N	N	Y	Y	Y	Y	Y	Y
2 Baldwin	Y	Y	N	Y	N	N	Y	N
3 Kind	Y	Y	N	Y	N	N	Y	N
4 Kleczka	Y	Y	N	Y	N	N	Y	N
5 Barrett	Y	Y	N	Y	N	N	Y	N
6 ***Petri***	N	N	Y	Y	Y	Y	Y	Y
7 Obey	Y	Y	N	Y	N	N	Y	N
8 ***Green***	N	N	Y	Y	Y	Y	Y	Y
9 ***Sensenbrenner***	N	N	Y	N	Y	Y	Y	Y
WYOMING								
AL ***Cubin***	N	N	Y	Y	Y	Y	Y	Y

Southern states - Ala., Ark., Fla., Ga., Ky., La., Miss., N.C., Okla., S.C., Tenn., Texas, Va.

310. HR 4. Energy Plan/Renewable Programs. Bono, R-Calif., amendment that would authorize $10 million annually through fiscal 2006 for a partnership program involving the EPA, the Energy Department and private industry to promote and conduct public outreach on renewable and alternative energy. Adopted 411-15: R 204-12; D 205-3 (ND 151-3, SD 54-0); I 2-0. Aug. 1, 2001.

311. HR 4. Energy Plan/CAFE Standards. Boehlert, R-N.Y., amendment that would require a combined corporate average fuel efficiency (CAFE) standard for passenger automobiles and light trucks, including sport-utility vehicles, of 26 miles per gallon in 2005 and 2006 and 27.5 miles per gallon in 2007 and beyond. It also would offer incentives for alternative fuel vehicles and require the secretary of Transportation to use his authority to ensure automobile and truck safety. Rejected 160-269: R 36-182; D 123-86 (ND 107-48, SD 16-38); I 1-1. Aug. 1, 2001.

312. HR 4. Energy Plan/California Gas. Green, D-Texas, amendment that would block the state of California from preventing the Federal Energy Regulatory Commission from ensuring low-cost natural gas transmission inside the state. Rejected 154-275: R 123-95; D 31-178 (ND 10-145, SD 21-33); I 0-2. Aug. 1, 2001.

313. HR 4. Energy Plan/Oxygen Limits. Cox, R-Calif., amendment that would give California a waiver from a federal law requiring that reformulated gasoline contain at least 2 percent oxygen, provided the state achieves equivalent or greater emissions reductions. Rejected 125-300: R 44-173; D 80-126 (ND 73-79, SD 7-47); I 1-1. Aug. 1, 2001.

314. HR 4. Energy Plan/Electricity Rates. Waxman, D-Calif., amendment that would require the Federal Energy Regulatory Commission to impose cost-of-service rates on electricity generators selling power in Western states for 18 months. Power plants coming online after Jan. 1, 2001, would be exempted. Rejected 154-274: R 3-216; D 150-57 (ND 128-25, SD 22-32); I 1-1. Aug. 1, 2001.

315. HR 4. Energy Plan/ANWR Drilling Receipts. Sununu, R-N.H., amendment that would require that receipts from new oil and gas drilling in the Arctic National Wildlife Refuge be split, with 50 percent going to Alaska and the rest evenly divided between a new federal fund for renewable energy research and development and one for the elimination of the maintenance and improvement backlog on federal lands. Adopted 241-186: R 200-18; D 40-167 (ND 17-136, SD 23-31); I 1-1. Aug. 1, 2001.

316. HR 4. Energy Plan/ANWR Size Limit. Sununu, R-N.H., amendment that would limit oil and gas drilling operations in the Arctic National Wildlife Refuge to 2,000 acres of total surface area. Adopted 228-201: R 186-34; D 41-166 (ND 17-136, SD 24-30); I 1-1. Aug. 1, 2001.

317. HR 4. Energy Plan/ANWR Drilling Ban. Markey, D-Mass., amendment that would maintain the current prohibition on oil drilling in the Arctic National Wildlife Refuge by striking language opening the reserve up to development. Rejected 206-223: R 34-186; D 171-36 (ND 141-13, SD 30-23); I 1-1. A "nay" was a vote in support of the president's position. Aug. 1, 2001.

Key

Y	Voted for (yea).
#	Paired for.
+	Announced for.
N	Voted against (nay).
X	Paired against.
–	Announced against.
P	Voted "present."
C	Voted "present" to avoid possible conflict of interest.
?	Did not vote or otherwise make a position known.

● Democrats **Republicans**
Independents

	310	311	312	313	314	315	316	317
ALABAMA								
1 *Callahan*	Y	N	N	N	Y	Y	N	
2 *Everett*	Y	N	Y	N	N	Y	Y	N
3 *Riley*	Y	N	N	N	Y	Y	N	
4 *Aderholt*	Y	N	N	N	Y	Y	N	
5 Cramer	Y	N	Y	N	N	Y	Y	N
6 *Bachus*	Y	N	Y	N	N	Y	Y	N
7 Hilliard	Y	N	N	N	N	N	N	
ALASKA								
AL *Young*	Y	N	Y	N	N	Y	Y	N
ARIZONA								
1 *Flake*	N	N	N	Y	N	Y	N	N
2 Pastor	Y	N	N	N	N	N	N	Y
3 *Stump*	Y	N	N	N	Y	N	Y	N
4 *Shadegg*	Y	N	N	Y	N	Y	Y	N
5 *Kolbe*	Y	N	Y	Y	N	Y	Y	N
6 *Hayworth*	Y	N	Y	N	N	Y	Y	N
ARKANSAS								
1 Berry	Y	N	N	N	N	Y	Y	N
2 Snyder	Y	Y	N	N	N	N	N	Y
3 *Hutchinson*	?	?	?	?	?	?	?	?
4 Ross	Y	N	N	N	N	Y	Y	N
CALIFORNIA								
1 Thompson	Y	Y	N	Y	Y	N	N	Y
2 *Herger*	Y	N	N	Y	N	Y	Y	N
3 *Ose*	Y	N	N	Y	N	Y	Y	N
4 *Doolittle*	Y	N	N	N	Y	N	N	
5 Matsui	Y	N	N	Y	Y	N	N	Y
6 Woolsey	Y	Y	Y	Y	Y	N	N	Y
7 Miller, George	Y	Y	N	Y	Y	N	N	Y
8 Pelosi	Y	Y	N	Y	Y	N	N	Y
9 Lee	Y	Y	N	Y	Y	N	N	Y
10 Tauscher	Y	Y	N	Y	Y	N	N	Y
11 *Pombo*	Y	N	N	N	Y	N	Y	N
12 Lantos	Y	Y	N	Y	Y	N	N	Y
13 Stark	?	?	?	?	?	?	?	?
14 Eshoo	Y	Y	N	Y	Y	N	N	Y
15 Honda	Y	Y	N	Y	Y	N	N	Y
16 Lofgren	Y	Y	N	Y	Y	N	N	Y
17 Farr	Y	Y	N	Y	Y	N	N	Y
18 Condit	Y	N	Y	N	Y	N	N	Y
19 *Radanovich*	Y	N	N	Y	N	Y	Y	N
20 Dooley	Y	Y	N	Y	N	Y	N	Y
21 *Thomas*	Y	N	N	N	Y	N	Y	N
22 Capps	Y	Y	N	Y	Y	N	N	Y
23 *Gallegly*	Y	N	Y	Y	Y	Y	Y	N
24 Sherman	Y	Y	N	Y	Y	N	N	Y
25 *McKeon*	Y	N	Y	N	N	Y	Y	N
26 Berman	Y	Y	N	Y	Y	N	N	Y
27 Schiff	Y	Y	N	Y	Y	N	N	Y
28 *Dreier*	Y	N	Y	N	N	Y	Y	N
29 Waxman	Y	Y	N	Y	Y	N	N	Y
30 Becerra	Y	Y	N	Y	Y	N	N	Y
31 Solis	Y	Y	N	?	Y	N	N	Y
32 Watson	Y	Y	N	Y	Y	N	N	Y
33 Roybal-Allard	Y	Y	N	Y	Y	N	N	Y
34 Napolitano	Y	Y	N	Y	Y	N	N	Y
35 Waters	Y	Y	N	Y	Y	N	N	Y
36 Harman	Y	Y	N	Y	Y	N	N	Y
37 Millender-McD.	Y	Y	N	Y	Y	N	N	Y
38 *Horn*	Y	Y	N	N	Y	N	N	Y

	310	311	312	313	314	315	316	317
39 *Royce*	Y	N	N	Y	N	Y	Y	N
40 *Lewis*	Y	N	N	Y	N	Y	Y	N
41 *Miller, Gary*	Y	N	N	Y	Y	Y	N	
42 Baca	Y	N	Y	Y	Y	N	N	
43 *Calvert*	Y	N	N	N	Y	Y	N	
44 *Bono*	Y	N	N	Y	N	Y	Y	N
45 *Rohrabacher*	Y	N	N	Y	N	Y	Y	N
46 Sanchez	Y	Y	N	Y	Y	N	N	Y
47 *Cox*	Y	N	N	Y	N	Y	Y	N
48 *Issa*	Y	N	Y	Y	N	Y	Y	N
49 Davis	Y	Y	N	Y	Y	Y	N	Y
50 Filner	N	Y	N	Y	N	N	N	
51 *Cunningham*	Y	N	N	Y	N	Y	Y	N
52 *Hunter*	Y	N	N	Y	Y	Y	Y	N
COLORADO								
1 DeGette	Y	Y	N	Y	Y	N	N	Y
2 Udall	Y	Y	N	Y	N	N	N	Y
3 *McInnis*	Y	N	N	N	N	Y	N	
4 *Schaffer*	N	N	N	N	Y	N	Y	N
5 *Hefley*	Y	Y	Y	N	N	Y	Y	N
6 *Tancredo*	Y	N	Y	N	N	Y	Y	N
CONNECTICUT								
1 Larson	Y	Y	N	Y	Y	N	N	Y
2 *Simmons*	Y	N	N	Y	N	N	N	Y
3 DeLauro	Y	Y	N	Y	Y	N	N	Y
4 *Shays*	Y	Y	N	Y	N	N	N	Y
5 Maloney	Y	Y	N	N	N	N	N	Y
6 *Johnson*	Y	Y	N	Y	N	N	N	Y
DELAWARE								
AL *Castle*	Y	N	Y	N	N	Y	N	Y
FLORIDA								
1 *Scarborough*	Y	Y	N	Y	Y	Y	Y	N
2 Boyd	Y	Y	N	N	Y	Y	Y	N
3 Brown	Y	N	N	N	N	N	Y	Y
4 *Crenshaw*	Y	N	N	N	N	Y	Y	N
5 Thurman	Y	Y	N	Y	Y	N	N	Y
6 *Stearns*	Y	N	N	N	Y	Y	N	
7 *Mica*	Y	N	N	N	N	Y	Y	N
8 *Keller*	Y	N	N	N	N	Y	Y	N
9 *Bilirakis*	Y	Y	N	N	Y	Y	Y	N
10 *Young*	Y	Y	N	N	N	Y	Y	N
11 Davis	Y	N	Y	Y	N	Y	N	Y
12 *Putnam*	Y	N	N	N	Y	Y	N	
13 *Miller*	Y	N	Y	N	N	Y	Y	N
14 Goss	Y	N	N	N	Y	Y	N	
15 *Weldon*	Y	N	N	N	N	Y	Y	N
16 *Foley*	Y	N	N	N	Y	Y	N	
17 Meek	Y	N	N	Y	Y	N	N	
18 *Ros-Lehtinen*	Y	Y	N	Y	N	Y	N	
19 Wexler	Y	Y	N	N	Y	N	N	Y
20 Deutsch	Y	Y	N	Y	N	Y	N	Y
21 *Diaz-Balart*	Y	N	Y	?	N	Y	Y	N
22 *Shaw*	Y	N	Y	N	N	Y	Y	N
23 Hastings	Y	N	N	N	N	N	N	Y
GEORGIA								
1 *Kingston*	Y	N	N	Y	N	Y	Y	N
2 Bishop	Y	N	N	N	N	Y	Y	N
3 *Collins*	N	N	Y	N	Y	N	Y	N
4 McKinney	Y	Y	N	Y	N	N	N	
5 Lewis	Y	Y	N	Y	N	N	N	
6 *Isakson*	Y	N	N	N	Y	Y	N	
7 *Barr*	N	N	N	N	N	Y	Y	N
8 *Chambliss*	Y	N	N	N	N	Y	Y	N
9 *Deal*	Y	N	N	Y	N	Y	Y	N
10 *Norwood*	Y	?	?	N	N	Y	Y	N
11 *Linder*	Y	N	N	Y	N	Y	Y	N
HAWAII								
1 Abercrombie	Y	Y	N	N	Y	N	N	Y
2 Mink	Y	Y	N	Y	N	N	N	Y
IDAHO								
1 *Otter*	N	N	Y	N	N	Y	N	N
2 *Simpson*	Y	N	N	N	N	Y	N	N
ILLINOIS								
1 Rush	Y	N	Y	N	Y	N	N	
2 Jackson	Y	Y	N	Y	N	N	N	
3 Lipinski	Y	N	N	?	?	?	?	?
4 Gutierrez	Y	N	N	N	N	N	N	
5 Blagojevich	Y	N	Y	N	N	Y	N	
6 *Hyde*	Y	N	N	N	N	Y	Y	N
7 Davis	Y	N	N	N	N	Y	N	
8 *Crane*	Y	N	N	N	Y	N	Y	N
9 Schakowsky	Y	Y	N	Y	N	N	N	
10 *Kirk*	Y	Y	N	Y	N	Y	N	
11 *Weller*	Y	N	Y	N	N	Y	N	
12 Costello	N	N	N	N	N	Y	N	
13 *Biggert*	Y	N	Y	N	Y	Y	N	

ND Northern Democrats   SD Southern Democrats

	310	311	312	313	314	315	316	317
14 ***Hastert***							Y	N
15 ***Johnson***	Y	Y	Y	N	N	N	N	Y
16 ***Manzullo***	Y	N	Y	N	N	Y	Y	N
17 Evans	Y	Y	Y	N	Y	N	N	Y
18 ***LaHood***	Y	Y	Y	N	N	Y	N	Y
19 Phelps	Y	N	N	N	N	N	N	N
20 ***Shimkus***	Y	N	Y	N	N	Y	Y	N
INDIANA								
1 Visclosky	Y	N	N	N	Y	N	Y	Y
2 ***Pence***	N	N	Y	N	N	Y	Y	N
3 Roemer	Y	N	N	N	N	N	N	Y
4 ***Souder***	Y	N	Y	N	N	?	Y	N
5 ***Buyer***	Y	N	Y	N	N	Y	Y	N
6 ***Burton***	Y	N	N	N	N	Y	Y	N
7 ***Kerns***	N	N	Y	N	N	Y	Y	N
8 ***Hostettler***	N	N	Y	Y	N	Y	Y	N
9 Hill	Y	N	N	N	N	N	Y	Y
10 Carson	Y	N	N	N	Y	N	N	Y
IOWA								
1 ***Leach***	Y	Y	N	N	N	N	N	Y
2 ***Nussle***	Y	N	Y	N	N	Y	Y	N
3 Boswell	Y	N	Y	N	N	N	N	Y
4 ***Ganske***	Y	Y	N	N	N	Y	Y	N
5 ***Latham***	Y	N	N	N	N	Y	Y	N
KANSAS								
1 ***Moran***	Y	N	N	N	N	Y	Y	N
2 ***Ryun***	Y	N	Y	N	N	Y	Y	N
3 Moore	Y	N	N	N	N	N	N	Y
4 ***Tiahrt***	Y	N	Y	N	N	Y	Y	N
KENTUCKY								
1 ***Whitfield***	Y	N	Y	N	N	Y	Y	N
2 ***Lewis***	Y	N	Y	N	N	Y	Y	N
3 ***Northup***	Y	N	Y	N	N	Y	Y	N
4 Lucas	Y	N	Y	N	N	Y	Y	N
5 ***Rogers***	Y	N	N	N	N	Y	Y	N
6 ***Fletcher***	Y	N	N	N	N	Y	Y	N
LOUISIANA								
1 ***Vitter***	Y	N	Y	N	N	Y	Y	N
2 Jefferson	Y	N	N	N	N	N	N	N
3 ***Tauzin***	Y	N	Y	N	N	Y	Y	N
4 ***McCrery***	Y	N	Y	?	N	Y	Y	N
5 ***Cooksey***	Y	N	N	N	N	Y	Y	N
6 ***Baker***	Y	N	Y	N	N	Y	Y	N
7 John	Y	N	Y	N	N	Y	Y	N
MAINE								
1 Allen	Y	Y	N	Y	Y	N	N	Y
2 Baldacci	Y	Y	N	Y	Y	N	N	Y
MARYLAND								
1 ***Gilchrest***	Y	Y	Y	N	N	Y	N	Y
2 ***Ehrlich***	Y	N	Y	N	N	Y	Y	N
3 Cardin	Y	Y	N	N	Y	N	N	Y
4 Wynn	Y	Y	N	N	Y	N	N	Y
5 Hoyer	?	N	N	N	Y	N	N	Y
6 ***Bartlett***	Y	N	Y	N	N	Y	Y	Y
7 Cummings	Y	Y	N	N	Y	N	N	Y
8 ***Morella***	Y	Y	N	N	N	N	N	Y
MASSACHUSETTS								
1 Olver	Y	Y	N	Y	Y	N	N	Y
2 Neal	Y	Y	N	Y	Y	N	N	Y
3 McGovern	Y	Y	N	Y	Y	N	N	Y
4 Frank	Y	Y	N	Y	Y	N	N	Y
5 Meehan	Y	Y	N	Y	Y	N	N	Y
6 Tierney	Y	Y	N	Y	Y	N	N	Y
7 Markey	Y	Y	N	Y	Y	N	N	Y
8 Capuano	Y	Y	N	Y	Y	N	N	Y
9 Vacant								
10 Delahunt	Y	Y	N	N	Y	N	N	Y
MICHIGAN								
1 Stupak	Y	N	N	Y	Y	Y	Y	Y
2 ***Hoekstra***	Y	N	Y	N	N	Y	Y	N
3 ***Ehlers***	Y	Y	N	N	N	Y	N	Y
4 ***Camp***	Y	N	Y	N	N	Y	Y	N
5 Barcia	Y	N	N	N	Y	N	N	Y
6 ***Upton***	Y	N	Y	N	N	Y	Y	N
7 ***Smith***	Y	N	N	N	N	Y	Y	N
8 ***Rogers***	Y	N	N	N	N	Y	Y	N
9 Kildee	Y	N	N	N	N	N	N	Y
10 Bonior	Y	N	N	N	Y	N	N	Y
11 ***Knollenberg***	Y	N	N	N	N	Y	Y	N
12 Levin	Y	N	N	N	Y	N	N	Y
13 Rivers	Y	N	N	N	Y	N	N	Y
14 Conyers	Y	N	N	?	?	?	N	Y
15 Kilpatrick	Y	N	N	N	Y	N	N	Y
16 Dingell	Y	N	Y	N	Y	N	N	Y

	310	311	312	313	314	315	316	317
MINNESOTA								
1 ***Gutknecht***	Y	N	Y	N	N	Y	Y	N
2 ***Kennedy***	Y	N	N	N	N	Y	Y	Y
3 ***Ramstad***	Y	Y	N	N	N	N	N	Y
4 McCollum	Y	N	Y	N	Y	N	N	Y
5 Sabo	Y	Y	N	N	Y	N	N	Y
6 Luther	Y	Y	N	N	Y	N	N	Y
7 Peterson	Y	N	Y	N	N	Y	Y	N
8 Oberstar	N	Y	N	N	Y	Y	N	N
MISSISSIPPI								
1 ***Wicker***	Y	N	N	N	N	Y	Y	N
2 Thompson	Y	N	N	N	Y	N	N	N
3 ***Pickering***	Y	N	Y	N	N	Y	Y	N
4 Shows	Y	N	Y	N	N	Y	Y	N
5 Taylor	Y	Y	Y	N	N	Y	Y	N
MISSOURI								
1 Clay	Y	N	Y	N	Y	N	N	Y
2 ***Akin***	Y	N	N	Y	N	Y	Y	N
3 Gephardt	Y	N	N	N	Y	N	N	Y
4 Skelton	Y	N	N	N	N	Y	Y	N
5 McCarthy	Y	N	N	N	Y	N	N	Y
6 ***Graves***	Y	N	N	N	N	N	Y	N
7 ***Blunt***	Y	N	N	N	N	Y	Y	N
8 ***Emerson***	Y	N	N	N	N	Y	Y	N
9 ***Hulshof***	Y	N	N	N	N	Y	Y	N
MONTANA								
AL ***Rehberg***	Y	N	N	N	N	Y	Y	N
NEBRASKA								
1 ***Bereuter***	Y	Y	Y	N	N	Y	Y	N
2 ***Terry***	Y	N	Y	N	N	Y	Y	N
3 ***Osborne***	Y	N	N	N	N	Y	Y	N
NEVADA								
1 Berkley	Y	Y	N	N	N	N	N	Y
2 ***Gibbons***	Y	N	N	Y	N	Y	Y	N
NEW HAMPSHIRE								
1 ***Sununu***	Y	N	Y	Y	N	Y	Y	N
2 ***Bass***	Y	N	Y	N	N	Y	N	Y
NEW JERSEY								
1 Andrews	Y	Y	N	N	Y	N	N	Y
2 ***LoBiondo***	Y	Y	N	N	N	N	N	Y
3 ***Saxton***	Y	Y	N	N	N	N	N	Y
4 ***Smith***	Y	Y	N	Y	N	N	N	Y
5 ***Roukema***	Y	Y	N	N	N	Y	N	Y
6 Pallone	Y	Y	N	Y	Y	N	N	Y
7 ***Ferguson***	Y	Y	N	N	N	N	N	Y
8 Pascrell	Y	Y	N	Y	Y	Y	Y	Y
9 Rothman	Y	Y	N	Y	Y	N	N	Y
10 Payne	Y	Y	N	Y	Y	N	N	Y
11 ***Frelinghuysen***	Y	Y	N	N	N	Y	N	Y
12 Holt	Y	Y	N	Y	Y	N	N	Y
13 Menendez	Y	Y	N	N	N	N	N	Y
NEW MEXICO								
1 ***Wilson***	Y	N	Y	N	N	Y	Y	N
2 ***Skeen***	Y	N	Y	N	N	Y	Y	N
3 Udall	Y	Y	N	N	N	N	N	Y
NEW YORK								
1 ***Grucci***	?	N	N	Y	N	Y	Y	N
2 Israel	Y	Y	N	Y	Y	N	N	Y
3 ***King***	Y	Y	Y	Y	N	Y	Y	N
4 McCarthy	Y	Y	N	Y	Y	N	Y	Y
5 Ackerman	Y	Y	N	Y	Y	N	N	Y
6 Meeks	Y	N	N	Y	Y	N	N	Y
7 Crowley	Y	N	N	Y	Y	N	?	Y
8 Nadler	Y	Y	N	Y	Y	N	N	Y
9 Weiner	Y	Y	N	Y	Y	N	N	Y
10 Towns	Y	N	N	Y	Y	N	N	N
11 Owens	Y	N	N	N	Y	N	N	Y
12 Velázquez	Y	Y	N	N	Y	N	N	Y
13 ***Fossella***	Y	N	Y	Y	N	Y	Y	N
14 Maloney	Y	Y	N	N	Y	N	N	Y
15 Rangel	Y	Y	N	Y	Y	N	N	Y
16 Serrano	Y	Y	N	Y	Y	N	N	Y
17 Engel	Y	Y	N	N	Y	N	N	Y
18 Lowey	Y	Y	N	Y	Y	N	N	Y
19 ***Kelly***	Y	Y	N	Y	N	Y	N	Y
20 ***Gilman***	Y	Y	Y	Y	N	N	N	Y
21 McNulty	Y	Y	N	Y	Y	N	N	Y
22 ***Sweeney***	Y	N	Y	N	N	Y	Y	Y
23 ***Boehlert***	Y	Y	N	N	N	Y	N	Y
24 ***McHugh***	Y	N	Y	N	N	Y	Y	N
25 ***Walsh***	Y	N	N	N	N	Y	N	Y
26 Hinchey	Y	Y	N	Y	Y	N	N	Y
27 ***Reynolds***	Y	Y	N	N	N	Y	Y	N
28 Slaughter	Y	Y	N	Y	Y	N	N	Y
29 LaFalce	Y	Y	N	Y	Y	N	N	Y

	310	311	312	313	314	315	316	317
30 ***Quinn***	Y	N	N	Y	N	Y	Y	N
31 ***Houghton***	Y	Y	Y	Y	N	N	N	Y
NORTH CAROLINA								
1 Clayton	Y	Y	N	N	Y	N	N	Y
2 Etheridge	Y	N	N	N	Y	N	N	Y
3 ***Jones***	N	N	N	N	N	Y	Y	N
4 Price	Y	Y	N	N	N	N	N	Y
5 ***Burr***	Y	N	Y	N	N	Y	Y	N
6 ***Coble***	N	N	Y	N	N	Y	Y	N
7 McIntyre	Y	N	N	N	N	N	N	Y
8 ***Hayes***	Y	N	Y	N	N	Y	Y	N
9 ***Myrick***	Y	N	Y	N	N	Y	Y	N
10 ***Ballenger***	Y	N	N	N	N	Y	Y	N
11 ***Taylor***	Y	N	Y	N	N	Y	Y	N
12 Watt	Y	Y	N	N	N	N	N	Y
NORTH DAKOTA								
AL Pomeroy	Y	N	N	N	Y	N	N	Y
OHIO								
1 ***Chabot***	Y	N	Y	N	N	Y	Y	N
2 ***Portman***	Y	N	N	N	N	Y	Y	N
3 Hall	Y	N	N	N	N	Y	N	Y
4 ***Oxley***	?	N	Y	N	N	Y	Y	N
5 ***Gillmor***	Y	N	Y	N	N	Y	Y	N
6 Strickland	Y	N	N	N	Y	N	N	Y
7 ***Hobson***	Y	N	N	N	N	Y	Y	N
8 ***Boehner***	Y	N	Y	N	N	Y	Y	N
9 Kaptur	Y	N	N	N	Y	Y	N	Y
10 Kucinich	Y	Y	N	Y	Y	N	N	Y
11 Jones	Y	N	N	N	Y	N	N	Y
12 ***Tiberi***	Y	N	Y	N	N	Y	Y	N
13 Brown	Y	Y	Y	N	Y	N	N	Y
14 Sawyer	Y	Y	Y	Y	Y	N	N	Y
15 ***Pryce***	Y	N	Y	N	N	Y	Y	N
16 ***Regula***	Y	N	Y	N	N	Y	Y	N
17 Traficant	Y	N	N	N	N	Y	Y	N
18 ***Ney***	Y	N	Y	N	N	Y	Y	N
19 ***LaTourette***	Y	Y	N	N	N	Y	Y	N
OKLAHOMA								
1 ***Largent***	?	N	Y	Y	N	Y	Y	N
2 Carson	Y	N	N	N	N	Y	Y	N
3 ***Watkins***	Y	N	Y	N	N	Y	Y	N
4 ***Watts***	Y	N	Y	N	N	Y	Y	N
5 ***Istook***	Y	N	Y	N	N	Y	Y	N
6 ***Lucas***	Y	N	Y	N	N	Y	Y	N
OREGON								
1 Wu	Y	Y	N	N	Y	N	N	Y
2 ***Walden***	Y	N	Y	N	N	Y	Y	N
3 Blumenauer	Y	Y	N	Y	Y	N	N	Y
4 DeFazio	Y	Y	N	Y	Y	N	N	Y
5 Hooley	Y	Y	N	N	Y	N	N	Y
PENNSYLVANIA								
1 Brady	Y	N	N	N	Y	N	Y	N
2 Fattah	Y	Y	N	Y	Y	N	N	Y
3 Borski	Y	Y	N	N	N	N	N	Y
4 ***Hart***	Y	N	Y	N	N	Y	Y	N
5 ***Peterson***	Y	N	Y	Y	N	Y	Y	N
6 Holden	Y	N	N	N	N	Y	Y	Y
7 ***Weldon***	Y	Y	Y	N	N	Y	Y	N
8 ***Greenwood***	Y	Y	N	N	N	Y	N	Y
9 ***Shuster, Bill***	Y	N	Y	N	N	Y	Y	N
10 ***Sherwood***	Y	N	N	N	N	Y	Y	N
11 Kanjorski	Y	Y	N	N	N	Y	Y	N
12 Murtha	Y	N	N	N	N	Y	Y	N
13 Hoeffel	Y	Y	N	N	Y	N	N	Y
14 Coyne	Y	Y	N	N	Y	N	N	Y
15 ***Toomey***	Y	N	Y	N	N	Y	Y	N
16 ***Pitts***	Y	N	Y	N	N	Y	Y	N
17 ***Gekas***	Y	N	Y	N	N	Y	Y	N
18 Doyle	Y	N	N	N	N	Y	Y	Y
19 ***Platts***	Y	Y	N	N	N	Y	Y	N
20 Mascara	Y	N	N	N	N	Y	Y	N
21 ***English***	Y	Y	N	N	N	Y	Y	N
RHODE ISLAND								
1 Kennedy	Y	Y	N	N	Y	N	N	Y
2 Langevin	Y	Y	N	N	Y	N	N	Y
SOUTH CAROLINA								
1 ***Brown***	Y	N	Y	N	N	Y	Y	N
2 ***Spence***	?	?	?	?	?	?	?	?
3 ***Graham***	Y	N	Y	N	N	Y	Y	N
4 ***DeMint***	Y	N	Y	N	N	Y	Y	N
5 Spratt	Y	N	N	N	N	N	N	+
6 Clyburn	Y	N	N	N	Y	N	N	N
SOUTH DAKOTA								
AL ***Thune***	Y	N	N	N	N	Y	Y	N

	310	311	312	313	314	315	316	317
TENNESSEE								
1 ***Jenkins***	Y	N	Y	N	N	Y	Y	N
2 ***Duncan***	Y	N	Y	N	N	Y	N	N
3 ***Wamp***	Y	N	Y	N	N	Y	Y	N
4 ***Hilleary***	Y	N	N	N	N	Y	Y	N
5 Clement	Y	N	N	N	Y	N	N	Y
6 Gordon	Y	N	N	N	Y	N	Y	Y
7 ***Bryant***	Y	N	N	N	N	Y	Y	N
8 Tanner	Y	N	Y	N	N	Y	Y	N
9 Ford	Y	N	N	N	Y	N	N	Y
TEXAS								
1 Sandlin	Y	N	Y	N	N	Y	Y	N
2 Turner	Y	N	Y	N	N	N	Y	N
3 ***Johnson, Sam***	N	N	Y	N	N	N	N	N
4 Hall	Y	N	Y	N	N	Y	N	N
5 ***Sessions***	Y	N	Y	N	N	Y	Y	N
6 ***Barton***	Y	N	Y	N	N	Y	Y	N
7 ***Culberson***	Y	N	Y	N	N	Y	Y	N
8 ***Brady***	Y	N	Y	N	N	Y	Y	N
9 Lampson	Y	Y	Y	N	N	N	N	Y
10 Doggett	Y	Y	N	Y	Y	N	N	Y
11 Edwards	Y	N	Y	N	N	Y	Y	N
12 ***Granger***	Y	N	Y	N	N	Y	Y	N
13 ***Thornberry***	Y	N	Y	N	N	Y	Y	N
14 ***Paul***	N	N	N	Y	N	N	N	N
15 Hinojosa	Y	N	N	N	Y	N	N	Y
16 Reyes	Y	N	Y	N	N	Y	Y	N
17 Stenholm	Y	N	Y	N	N	Y	N	N
18 Jackson-Lee	Y	N	Y	N	N	Y	Y	Y
19 ***Combest***	Y	N	Y	N	N	Y	Y	N
20 Gonzalez	Y	Y	Y	N	N	Y	Y	Y
21 ***Smith***	Y	N	Y	N	N	Y	Y	N
22 ***DeLay***	Y	N	Y	N	N	Y	Y	N
23 ***Bonilla***	Y	N	Y	N	N	Y	Y	N
24 Frost	Y	N	N	N	Y	N	N	Y
25 Bentsen	Y	N	Y	N	N	N	N	Y
26 ***Armey***	Y	N	Y	N	N	Y	Y	N
27 Ortiz	Y	N	Y	N	N	Y	Y	N
28 Rodriguez	Y	N	N	N	Y	Y	Y	Y
29 Green	Y	N	Y	N	N	Y	Y	N
30 Johnson, E.B.	Y	N	Y	N	N	Y	Y	Y
UTAH								
1 ***Hansen***	Y	N	Y	N	N	Y	Y	N
2 Matheson	Y	N	N	Y	N	N	N	Y
3 ***Cannon***	Y	N	Y	N	N	Y	Y	N
VERMONT								
AL *Sanders*	Y	Y	N	Y	Y	N	N	Y
VIRGINIA								
1 ***Davis, Jo Ann***	Y	N	Y	N	N	Y	Y	N
2 ***Schrock***	Y	N	N	N	N	Y	Y	N
3 Scott	Y	N	N	N	Y	Y	Y	Y
4 ***Forbes***	Y	N	N	N	N	Y	Y	N
5 *Goode*	Y	N	N	N	N	Y	Y	N
6 ***Goodlatte***	Y	N	N	N	N	Y	Y	N
7 ***Cantor***	Y	N	N	N	N	Y	Y	N
8 Moran	Y	Y	N	Y	Y	N	N	Y
9 Boucher	Y	N	N	Y	Y	N	N	Y
10 ***Wolf***	Y	N	Y	N	N	Y	Y	N
11 ***Davis, T.***	Y	N	N	N	N	Y	Y	Y
WASHINGTON								
1 Inslee	Y	Y	N	N	Y	N	N	Y
2 Larsen	Y	Y	N	N	Y	N	N	Y
3 Baird	Y	Y	N	Y	Y	N	N	Y
4 ***Hastings***	Y	N	N	N	N	Y	Y	N
5 ***Nethercutt***	Y	N	Y	N	N	Y	Y	N
6 Dicks	Y	Y	N	N	Y	N	N	Y
7 McDermott	Y	Y	N	Y	Y	N	N	Y
8 ***Dunn***	Y	N	N	N	N	Y	Y	Y
9 Smith	Y	Y	N	N	Y	N	N	Y
WEST VIRGINIA								
1 Mollohan	Y	N	N	N	N	Y	Y	N
2 ***Capito***	Y	N	N	N	N	Y	Y	N
3 Rahall	Y	N	N	N	Y	N	N	Y
WISCONSIN								
1 ***Ryan***	Y	N	N	N	N	Y	Y	N
2 Baldwin	Y	Y	N	N	Y	N	N	Y
3 Kind	Y	Y	N	N	N	N	N	Y
4 Kleczka	Y	Y	N	N	Y	N	N	Y
5 Barrett	Y	Y	N	N	Y	N	N	Y
6 ***Petri***	Y	N	Y	N	N	Y	Y	Y
7 Obey	Y	Y	N	N	Y	N	N	Y
8 ***Green***	Y	N	N	N	N	Y	Y	N
9 ***Sensenbrenner***	Y	N	Y	Y	N	N	Y	Y
WYOMING								
AL ***Cubin***	Y	N	Y	Y	N	Y	Y	N

Southern states - Ala., Ark., Fla., Ga., Ky., La., Miss., N.C., Okla., S.C., Tenn., Texas, Va.

318. HR 4. Energy Plan/Great Lakes Drilling. Rogers, R-Mich., amendment that would express the sense of Congress that states along the Great Lakes should enact prohibitions against offshore oil and gas drilling or maintain existing ones. Adopted 345-85: R 149-71; D 194-14 (ND 152-2, SD 42-12); I 2-0. Aug. 1, 2001.

319. HR 4. Energy Plan/Recommit. Thurman, D-Fla., motion to recommit the bill to the House Ways and Means Committee with instructions to add language providing that tax reductions should be contingent on sufficient non-Social Security, non-Medicare surpluses. Motion rejected 206-223: R 1-218; D 204-4 (ND 153-1, SD 51-3); I 1-1. Aug. 2, 2001 (in the session that began and the Congressional Record dated Aug. 1, 2001).

320. HR 4. Energy Plan/Passage. Passage of the bill that would make numerous changes to the nation's energy policies including those in the areas of production, conservation, taxes and research. The bill includes allowing oil and gas drilling in the Arctic National Wildlife Refuge; offering incentives for offshore drilling; funding nuclear energy, clean coal, and oil and gas research; extending tax credits for energy-efficiency and coal technology; and raising fuel efficiency standards for sport-utility vehicles and light trucks. It would provide $33.5 billion in tax credits and deductions over 10 years to encourage energy production and conservation. Passed 240-189: R 203-16; D 36-172 (ND 16-138, SD 20-34); I 1-1. A "yea" was a vote in support of the president's position. Aug. 2, 2001 (in the session that began and the Congressional Record dated Aug. 1, 2001).

321. Procedural Motion/Journal. Approval of the House Journal of Wednesday, Aug. 1, 2001. Approved 331-76: R 191-17; D 138-59 (ND 98-45, SD 40-14); I 2-0. Aug. 2, 2001.

322. Procedural Motion/Adjourn. McNulty, D-N.Y., motion to adjourn. Motion rejected 55-363: R 0-212; D 55-149 (ND 44-108, SD 11-41); I 0-2. Aug. 2, 2001.

323. Procedural Motion/Adjourn. McNulty, D-N.Y., motion to adjourn. Motion rejected 56-355: R 0-208; D 56-146 (ND 41-107, SD 15-39); I 0-1. Aug. 2, 2001.

324. Quorum Call. * 418 members responded. Aug. 2, 2001.

325. HR 2563. Patients' Rights/Previous Question. Goss, R-Fla., motion to order the previous question (thus ending debate and possibility of amendment) on adoption of the rule (H Res 219) to provide for House floor consideration of the bill that would provide federal health care protections, such as access to specialty and emergency room care, and require that health maintenance organizations have an appeals process for patients who are denied care. Motion agreed to 222-205: R 219-0; D 2-204 (ND 2-151, SD 0-53); I 1-1. Aug. 2, 2001.

CQ does not include quorum calls in its vote charts.

Key

Y	Voted for (yea).
#	Paired for.
+	Announced for.
N	Voted against (nay).
X	Paired against.
–	Announced against.
P	Voted "present."
C	Voted "present" to avoid possible conflict of interest.
?	Did not vote or otherwise make a position known.

Democrats • *Republicans*
Independents

	318	319	320	321	322	323	325
ALABAMA							
1 *Callahan*	N	N	Y	Y	N	N	Y
2 *Everett*	Y	N	Y	Y	N	N	Y
3 *Riley*	N	N	Y	Y	N	N	Y
4 *Aderholt*	N	N	Y	N	N	N	Y
5 Cramer	Y	N	Y	N	N	N	N
6 *Bachus*	Y	N	Y	Y	N	N	Y
7 Hilliard	N	Y	Y	N	N	Y	N
ALASKA							
AL *Young*	Y	N	Y	?	?	?	Y
ARIZONA							
1 *Flake*	N	N	Y	Y	N	N	Y
2 Pastor	Y	Y	N	Y	N	N	N
3 *Stump*	N	N	Y	Y	N	N	Y
4 *Shadegg*	N	N	Y	Y	N	N	Y
5 *Kolbe*	N	N	Y	Y	N	N	Y
6 *Hayworth*	Y	N	Y	Y	N	N	Y
ARKANSAS							
1 Berry	Y	Y	N	Y	Y	Y	N
2 Snyder	Y	Y	N	Y	N	N	N
3 *Hutchinson*	?	?	?	?	?	?	Y
4 Ross	Y	Y	Y	Y	N	Y	N
CALIFORNIA							
1 Thompson	Y	Y	N	N	N	N	N
2 *Herger*	N	N	Y	Y	N	N	Y
3 *Ose*	Y	N	Y	Y	N	N	Y
4 *Doolittle*	N	N	Y	Y	N	N	Y
5 Matsui	Y	Y	N	Y	N	N	N
6 Woolsey	Y	Y	N	Y	N	?	N
7 Miller, George	Y	N	Y	?	Y	Y	N
8 Pelosi	Y	Y	N	Y	N	N	N
9 Lee	Y	Y	N	N	N	Y	N
10 Tauscher	Y	Y	N	Y	Y	Y	N
11 *Pombo*	N	N	Y	Y	N	N	Y
12 Lantos	Y	Y	N	Y	N	Y	N
13 Stark	?	?	?	?	?	?	N
14 Eshoo	Y	Y	N	?	Y	N	N
15 Honda	Y	Y	N	Y	N	N	N
16 Lofgren	Y	Y	N	Y	N	N	N
17 Farr	Y	Y	N	Y	Y	Y	N
18 Condit	Y	Y	N	N	N	N	N
19 *Radanovich*	N	N	Y	Y	?	N	Y
20 Dooley	N	Y	Y	N	N	N	N
21 *Thomas*	Y	N	Y	N	N	N	N
22 Capps	Y	Y	N	Y	N	N	N
23 *Gallegly*	Y	N	Y	Y	N	N	Y
24 Sherman	Y	Y	N	Y	N	N	N
25 *McKeon*	Y	N	Y	Y	N	N	Y
26 Berman	Y	Y	N	Y	N	?	N
27 Schiff	Y	Y	N	Y	N	N	N
28 *Dreier*	Y	N	Y	Y	N	N	Y
29 Waxman	Y	Y	N	Y	Y	Y	N
30 Becerra	Y	Y	N	Y	N	N	N
31 Solis	Y	Y	N	Y	Y	N	N
32 Watson	Y	Y	N	Y	Y	Y	N
33 Roybal-Allard	Y	Y	N	Y	N	N	N
34 Napolitano	Y	Y	N	Y	N	N	N
35 Waters	Y	Y	N	Y	Y	N	N
36 Harman	Y	Y	N	Y	N	N	N
37 Millender-McD.	Y	Y	N	Y	N	N	?
38 *Horn*	Y	N	Y	Y	N	N	Y

	318	319	320	321	322	323	325
39 *Royce*	Y	N	Y	Y	N	N	?
40 *Lewis*	N	N	?	Y	N	N	Y
41 *Miller, Gary*	N	N	Y	Y	N	N	Y
42 Baca	Y	Y	Y	Y	N	N	N
43 *Calvert*	N	N	Y	Y	N	N	Y
44 *Bono*	Y	N	Y	Y	N	N	Y
45 *Rohrabacher*	N	N	Y	Y	N	N	Y
46 Sanchez	Y	Y	N	Y	N	N	N
47 *Cox*	Y	N	Y	Y	N	?	Y
48 *Issa*	Y	N	Y	Y	N	N	Y
49 Davis	Y	Y	Y	Y	N	N	N
50 Filner	Y	Y	N	Y	Y	Y	N
51 *Cunningham*	Y	N	Y	Y	N	N	Y
52 *Hunter*	Y	N	Y	Y	N	?	Y
COLORADO							
1 DeGette	Y	Y	N	Y	N	Y	N
2 Udall	Y	Y	N	N	N	N	N
3 *McInnis*	N	N	Y	Y	N	N	Y
4 *Schaffer*	N	N	Y	Y	N	N	Y
5 *Hefley*	N	N	Y	N	N	N	Y
6 *Tancredo*	N	N	Y	P	N	N	Y
CONNECTICUT							
1 Larson	Y	Y	N	Y	N	N	N
2 *Simmons*	Y	N	Y	Y	N	N	Y
3 DeLauro	Y	Y	N	Y	Y	Y	N
4 *Shays*	Y	N	N	Y	N	N	Y
5 Maloney	Y	Y	N	Y	N	?	N
6 *Johnson*	Y	N	N	?	?	N	Y
DELAWARE							
AL *Castle*	Y	N	N	Y	N	N	Y
FLORIDA							
1 *Scarborough*	Y	N	Y	Y	N	N	Y
2 Boyd	Y	Y	N	Y	N	Y	N
3 Brown	Y	Y	N	Y	N	N	N
4 *Crenshaw*	Y	N	Y	Y	N	N	Y
5 Thurman	Y	Y	N	Y	N	N	N
6 *Stearns*	Y	N	Y	N	N	N	Y
7 *Mica*	N	N	Y	Y	N	N	Y
8 *Keller*	Y	N	Y	Y	N	N	Y
9 *Bilirakis*	Y	N	Y	N	N	N	Y
10 *Young*	Y	N	Y	?	N	N	Y
11 Davis	Y	Y	N	Y	N	N	N
12 *Putnam*	Y	N	Y	Y	N	N	Y
13 *Miller*	N	N	Y	N	N	N	Y
14 *Goss*	Y	N	Y	N	N	N	Y
15 *Weldon*	Y	N	Y	N	N	N	Y
16 *Foley*	Y	N	Y	N	N	N	Y
17 Meek	Y	Y	N	Y	N	N	N
18 *Ros-Lehtinen*	Y	N	Y	Y	N	N	Y
19 Wexler	Y	N	N	N	N	N	N
20 Deutsch	Y	Y	N	N	N	N	N
21 *Diaz-Balart*	Y	N	Y	Y	N	N	Y
22 *Shaw*	Y	N	Y	N	N	Y	N
23 Hastings	Y	Y	N	N	N	Y	N
GEORGIA							
1 *Kingston*	N	N	Y	Y	N	N	N
2 Bishop	Y	Y	Y	Y	N	N	N
3 *Collins*	N	N	Y	N	N	N	Y
4 McKinney	Y	Y	N	Y	N	N	?
5 Lewis	Y	Y	N	Y	N	N	N
6 *Isakson*	Y	N	Y	Y	N	N	Y
7 *Barr*	N	N	Y	N	N	N	Y
8 *Chambliss*	Y	N	Y	Y	N	N	Y
9 *Deal*	N	N	Y	N	N	N	Y
10 *Norwood*	Y	N	Y	?	?	?	Y
11 *Linder*	Y	N	Y	?	?	?	Y
HAWAII							
1 Abercrombie	Y	Y	N	Y	N	N	N
2 Mink	Y	Y	N	Y	Y	Y	N
IDAHO							
1 *Otter*	N	N	Y	Y	N	N	Y
2 *Simpson*	N	N	Y	Y	N	N	Y
ILLINOIS							
1 Rush	Y	Y	N	Y	N	N	N
2 Jackson	Y	Y	N	Y	Y	N	N
3 Lipinski	?	?	?	?	?	?	?
4 Gutierrez	Y	Y	N	Y	N	N	N
5 Blagojevich	Y	Y	N	Y	N	N	N
6 *Hyde*	Y	N	Y	Y	N	N	Y
7 Davis	Y	Y	N	Y	N	N	N
8 *Crane*	N	N	Y	?	N	N	Y
9 Schakowsky	Y	Y	N	N	N	Y	N
10 *Kirk*	Y	N	N	Y	N	N	Y
11 *Weller*	Y	N	Y	Y	N	N	Y
12 Costello	Y	Y	N	N	N	N	N
13 *Biggert*	Y	N	Y	Y	N	N	Y

ND Northern Democrats   SD Southern Democrats

	318	319	320	321	322	323	325
14 ***Hastert***	Y	N	Y				
15 ***Johnson***	Y	N	N	Y	N	N	Y
16 ***Manzullo***	N	N	Y	Y	N	N	Y
17 Evans	Y	Y	N	Y	N	Y	N
18 ***LaHood***	Y	N	Y	Y	N	N	Y
19 Phelps	Y	Y	Y	N	N	N	N
20 ***Shimkus***	N	N	Y	Y	N	N	Y
INDIANA							
1 Visclosky	Y	Y	Y	N	N	N	N
2 ***Pence***	Y	N	Y	Y	N	N	Y
3 Roemer	Y	Y	N	Y	N	N	N
4 ***Souder***	Y	N	Y	Y	N	N	Y
5 ***Buyer***	Y	N	Y	Y	N	N	Y
6 ***Burton***	Y	N	Y	Y	N	N	Y
7 ***Kerns***	Y	N	Y	Y	N	N	Y
8 ***Hostettler***	N	N	Y	Y	N	N	Y
9 Hill	Y	Y	N	Y	N	?	N
10 Carson	Y	Y	N	Y	N	N	N
IOWA							
1 ***Leach***	Y	Y	N	?	N	N	Y
2 ***Nussle***	Y	N	Y	Y	?	N	Y
3 Boswell	Y	Y	N	Y	N	N	N
4 ***Ganske***	Y	N	Y	Y	N	N	Y
5 ***Latham***	Y	N	Y	Y	N	N	Y
KANSAS							
1 ***Moran***	Y	N	Y	N	N	N	Y
2 ***Ryun***	N	N	Y	?	N	N	Y
3 Moore	Y	Y	N	N	N	N	N
4 ***Tiahrt***	Y	N	Y	Y	N	N	Y
KENTUCKY							
1 ***Whitfield***	Y	N	Y	Y	N	N	Y
2 ***Lewis***	N	N	Y	Y	N	N	Y
3 ***Northup***	Y	N	Y	Y	N	N	Y
4 Lucas	Y	Y	Y	Y	N	N	N
5 ***Rogers***	N	N	Y	Y	N	N	Y
6 ***Fletcher***	Y	N	Y	Y	N	N	Y
LOUISIANA							
1 ***Vitter***	N	N	Y	Y	N	N	Y
2 Jefferson	Y	Y	Y	Y	Y	Y	N
3 ***Tauzin***	Y	N	Y	Y	N	N	Y
4 ***McCrery***	N	N	Y	Y	N	N	Y
5 ***Cooksey***	N	N	Y	?	N	N	Y
6 ***Baker***	N	N	Y	Y	N	N	Y
7 John	N	Y	Y	Y	N	N	N
MAINE							
1 Allen	Y	Y	N	N	N	N	N
2 Baldacci	Y	Y	N	N	N	N	N
MARYLAND							
1 ***Gilchrest***	Y	N	Y	?	?	?	Y
2 ***Ehrlich***	Y	N	Y	Y	N	N	Y
3 Cardin	Y	Y	N	Y	N	N	N
4 Wynn	Y	Y	N	Y	N	N	N
5 Hoyer	Y	Y	N	Y	N	N	N
6 ***Bartlett***	Y	N	Y	Y	N	N	Y
7 Cummings	Y	Y	N	?	?	N	N
8 ***Morella***	Y	N	N	Y	N	N	Y
MASSACHUSETTS							
1 Olver	Y	Y	N	?	Y	Y	N
2 Neal	Y	Y	N	Y	N	N	N
3 McGovern	Y	Y	N	N	Y	Y	N
4 Frank	Y	Y	N	Y	Y	Y	N
5 Meehan	Y	Y	N	Y	N	N	N
6 Tierney	Y	Y	N	Y	Y	Y	N
7 Markey	Y	Y	N	?	Y	N	N
8 Capuano	Y	Y	N	N	Y	Y	N
9 Vacant							
10 Delahunt	Y	Y	N	Y	N	N	N
MICHIGAN							
1 Stupak	Y	Y	N	N	N	Y	N
2 ***Hoekstra***	Y	N	Y	Y	N	N	Y
3 ***Ehlers***	Y	N	Y	Y	N	N	Y
4 ***Camp***	Y	N	Y	Y	N	N	Y
5 Barcia	Y	Y	Y	Y	N	N	N
6 ***Upton***	Y	N	Y	Y	N	N	Y
7 ***Smith***	Y	N	Y	Y	N	N	Y
8 ***Rogers***	Y	N	Y	N	N	N	Y
9 Kildee	Y	Y	N	Y	N	N	N
10 Bonior	Y	Y	N	N	Y	Y	N
11 ***Knollenberg***	Y	N	Y	Y	N	N	Y
12 Levin	Y	Y	N	Y	N	N	N
13 Rivers	Y	Y	N	Y	N	N	N
14 Conyers	Y	Y	N	Y	Y	Y	N
15 Kilpatrick	Y	Y	N	Y	N	N	N
16 Dingell	Y	Y	Y	?	Y	Y	N
MINNESOTA							
1 ***Gutknecht***	Y	N	Y	N	N	N	Y
2 ***Kennedy***	Y	N	Y	N	N	N	Y
3 ***Ramstad***	Y	N	Y	N	N	N	Y
4 McCollum	Y	Y	N	Y	N	Y	N
5 Sabo	Y	Y	N	N	Y	N	N
6 Luther	Y	Y	N	Y	N	N	N
7 Peterson	Y	Y	N	N	N	?	Y
8 Oberstar	Y	Y	N	N	Y	Y	N
MISSISSIPPI							
1 ***Wicker***	N	N	Y	Y	N	N	Y
2 Thompson	Y	Y	Y	N	N	N	N
3 ***Pickering***	N	N	Y	Y	N	N	Y
4 Shows	N	N	Y	Y	N	Y	N
5 Taylor	N	Y	N	N	N	N	N
MISSOURI							
1 Clay	Y	Y	N	?	Y	Y	?
2 ***Akin***	N	N	Y	Y	N	N	Y
3 Gephardt	Y	Y	N	N	Y	Y	N
4 Skelton	Y	Y	N	Y	N	N	N
5 McCarthy	Y	Y	N	Y	N	N	N
6 ***Graves***	N	N	Y	Y	N	N	Y
7 ***Blunt***	Y	N	Y	Y	N	N	Y
8 ***Emerson***	N	N	Y	Y	N	?	Y
9 ***Hulshof***	N	N	Y	N	N	N	Y
MONTANA							
AL ***Rehberg***	Y	N	Y	Y	N	N	Y
NEBRASKA							
1 ***Bereuter***	N	N	Y	Y	N	N	Y
2 ***Terry***	N	N	Y	Y	N	N	Y
3 ***Osborne***	Y	N	Y	Y	N	N	Y
NEVADA							
1 Berkley	Y	Y	N	Y	N	N	N
2 ***Gibbons***	N	N	Y	Y	N	N	Y
NEW HAMPSHIRE							
1 ***Sununu***	Y	N	Y	Y	N	N	Y
2 ***Bass***	Y	N	N	Y	N	N	Y
NEW JERSEY							
1 Andrews	Y	Y	N	?	Y	N	N
2 ***LoBiondo***	Y	N	N	N	N	N	Y
3 ***Saxton***	Y	N	N	Y	N	N	Y
4 ***Smith***	Y	N	N	Y	N	N	Y
5 ***Roukema***	Y	N	Y	Y	N	N	Y
6 Pallone	Y	Y	N	N	N	N	N
7 ***Ferguson***	Y	N	Y	Y	N	N	Y
8 Pascrell	Y	Y	N	Y	N	N	N
9 Rothman	Y	Y	N	N	N	N	N
10 Payne	Y	Y	N	Y	N	N	N
11 ***Frelinghuysen***	Y	N	Y	Y	N	N	Y
12 Holt	Y	Y	N	Y	N	N	N
13 Menendez	Y	Y	N	N	Y	N	N
NEW MEXICO							
1 ***Wilson***	Y	N	Y	Y	N	N	Y
2 ***Skeen***	Y	N	Y	Y	N	N	Y
3 Udall	Y	Y	N	N	N	N	N
NEW YORK							
1 ***Grucci***	Y	N	Y	Y	N	N	Y
2 Israel	Y	Y	N	Y	N	N	N
3 ***King***	N	N	Y	Y	N	N	Y
4 McCarthy	Y	Y	N	Y	N	N	N
5 Ackerman	Y	Y	N	Y	N	N	N
6 Meeks	Y	Y	N	Y	N	N	N
7 Crowley	Y	Y	N	N	N	N	N
8 Nadler	Y	Y	N	Y	N	Y	N
9 Weiner	Y	Y	N	N	Y	N	N
10 Towns	Y	Y	Y	Y	Y	N	N
11 Owens	Y	Y	N	Y	Y	N	N
12 Velázquez	Y	Y	N	N	Y	Y	N
13 ***Fossella***	Y	N	Y	N	N	N	Y
14 Maloney	Y	Y	N	Y	N	N	N
15 Rangel	Y	Y	N	Y	N	N	N
16 Serrano	Y	Y	N	Y	N	N	N
17 Engel	Y	Y	N	Y	N	N	N
18 Lowey	Y	Y	N	Y	N	N	N
19 ***Kelly***	Y	N	Y	Y	N	N	Y
20 ***Gilman***	Y	N	N	Y	N	N	Y
21 McNulty	Y	Y	N	N	Y	Y	N
22 ***Sweeney***	Y	N	Y	N	N	N	Y
23 ***Boehlert***	Y	N	N	Y	N	N	Y
24 ***McHugh***	Y	N	Y	Y	N	N	Y
25 ***Walsh***	Y	N	Y	Y	N	N	Y
26 Hinchey	Y	Y	N	Y	Y	Y	N
27 ***Reynolds***	Y	N	Y	Y	N	N	Y
28 Slaughter	Y	Y	N	N	N	Y	N
29 LaFalce	Y	Y	N	Y	Y	Y	N
30 ***Quinn***	Y	N	Y	Y	N	N	Y
31 ***Houghton***	N	N	N	Y	N	N	Y
NORTH CAROLINA							
1 Clayton	Y	Y	N	Y	N	N	N
2 Etheridge	Y	Y	N	Y	N	Y	N
3 ***Jones***	N	N	Y	Y	N	N	Y
4 Price	Y	Y	N	Y	N	Y	N
5 ***Burr***	Y	N	Y	Y	N	N	Y
6 ***Coble***	N	N	Y	Y	N	N	Y
7 McIntyre	Y	Y	N	Y	N	N	N
8 ***Hayes***	Y	N	Y	Y	N	N	Y
9 ***Myrick***	Y	N	Y	Y	N	N	Y
10 ***Ballenger***	Y	N	Y	Y	N	N	Y
11 ***Taylor***	N	N	Y	Y	N	N	Y
12 Watt	Y	Y	N	Y	N	N	N
NORTH DAKOTA							
AL Pomeroy	Y	Y	N	Y	N	N	N
OHIO							
1 ***Chabot***	Y	N	Y	Y	N	N	Y
2 ***Portman***	Y	N	Y	Y	N	N	Y
3 Hall	Y	Y	N	Y	N	N	N
4 ***Oxley***	Y	N	Y	Y	N	N	Y
5 ***Gillmor***	Y	N	Y	N	N	N	Y
6 Strickland	Y	Y	N	N	N	N	N
7 ***Hobson***	N	N	Y	Y	N	N	Y
8 ***Boehner***	N	N	Y	Y	N	?	Y
9 Kaptur	Y	Y	N	N	Y	Y	N
10 Kucinich	Y	Y	N	N	N	N	N
11 Jones	Y	Y	N	N	Y	N	N
12 ***Tiberi***	Y	N	Y	Y	N	N	Y
13 Brown	Y	Y	N	N	N	N	N
14 Sawyer	Y	Y	N	Y	N	N	N
15 ***Pryce***	Y	N	Y	Y	N	N	Y
16 ***Regula***	Y	N	Y	Y	N	N	Y
17 Traficant	Y	N	Y	Y	N	N	Y
18 ***Ney***	Y	–	Y	Y	N	N	Y
19 ***LaTourette***	Y	N	Y	Y	N	N	Y
OKLAHOMA							
1 ***Largent***	N	N	Y	Y	N	N	Y
2 Carson	N	Y	Y	Y	Y	N	N
3 ***Watkins***	N	N	Y	Y	N	N	Y
4 ***Watts***	N	N	Y	Y	N	N	Y
5 ***Istook***	Y	N	Y	Y	N	?	Y
6 ***Lucas***	N	N	Y	Y	N	N	Y
OREGON							
1 Wu	Y	Y	N	N	N	N	N
2 ***Walden***	Y	N	Y	Y	N	N	Y
3 Blumenauer	Y	Y	N	Y	N	N	N
4 DeFazio	Y	Y	N	N	Y	Y	N
5 Hooley	Y	Y	N	Y	N	N	N
PENNSYLVANIA							
1 Brady	Y	Y	Y	N	N	N	N
2 Fattah	Y	Y	N	?	Y	N	N
3 Borski	Y	Y	N	N	Y	Y	N
4 ***Hart***	Y	N	Y	Y	N	N	Y
5 ***Peterson***	Y	N	Y	Y	N	N	Y
6 Holden	Y	Y	Y	?	N	N	N
7 ***Weldon***	Y	N	Y	Y	N	N	Y
8 ***Greenwood***	Y	N	Y	Y	N	N	Y
9 ***Shuster, Bill***	Y	N	Y	Y	N	N	Y
10 ***Sherwood***	Y	N	Y	Y	N	N	Y
11 Kanjorski	Y	Y	Y	Y	N	N	N
12 Murtha	Y	Y	Y	Y	N	N	N
13 Hoeffel	Y	Y	N	Y	N	N	N
14 Coyne	Y	Y	N	Y	Y	N	N
15 ***Toomey***	N	N	Y	Y	N	N	Y
16 ***Pitts***	Y	N	Y	Y	N	N	Y
17 ***Gekas***	Y	N	Y	Y	N	N	Y
18 Doyle	Y	Y	Y	Y	N	N	N
19 ***Platts***	Y	N	Y	N	N	N	Y
20 Mascara	Y	Y	Y	Y	N	N	N
21 ***English***	Y	N	Y	N	N	N	Y
RHODE ISLAND							
1 Kennedy	Y	Y	N	Y	N	N	N
2 Langevin	Y	Y	N	Y	Y	Y	N
SOUTH CAROLINA							
1 ***Brown***	Y	N	Y	Y	N	N	Y
2 ***Spence***	?	?	?	?	?	?	?
3 ***Graham***	Y	N	Y	Y	N	N	Y
4 ***DeMint***	N	N	Y	Y	N	N	Y
5 Spratt	Y	Y	N	Y	?	Y	N
6 Clyburn	Y	Y	Y	Y	N	N	N
SOUTH DAKOTA							
AL ***Thune***	Y	N	Y	Y	N	N	Y
TENNESSEE							
1 ***Jenkins***	Y	N	Y	Y	N	N	Y
2 ***Duncan***	N	N	Y	Y	N	N	Y
3 ***Wamp***	Y	N	Y	N	N	N	Y
4 ***Hilleary***	Y	N	Y	Y	N	N	Y
5 Clement	Y	Y	N	Y	Y	N	N
6 Gordon	Y	Y	N	Y	?	N	N
7 ***Bryant***	Y	N	Y	Y	N	N	Y
8 Tanner	Y	Y	N	N	N	N	N
9 Ford	Y	Y	N	Y	N	N	N
TEXAS							
1 Sandlin	N	Y	Y	Y	Y	Y	N
2 Turner	N	Y	Y	N	N	N	N
3 ***Johnson, Sam***	N	N	Y	Y	N	N	Y
4 Hall	Y	N	Y	Y	N	N	N
5 ***Sessions***	N	N	Y	Y	N	N	Y
6 ***Barton***	N	N	Y	Y	N	N	Y
7 ***Culberson***	Y	N	Y	Y	N	N	Y
8 ***Brady***	N	N	Y	Y	N	N	Y
9 Lampson	N	Y	Y	Y	N	N	N
10 Doggett	Y	Y	N	N	Y	Y	N
11 Edwards	Y	Y	Y	Y	N	N	N
12 ***Granger***	Y	N	Y	Y	N	N	Y
13 ***Thornberry***	N	N	Y	Y	N	N	Y
14 ***Paul***	N	N	N	Y	N	N	Y
15 Hinojosa	Y	Y	N	Y	N	N	N
16 Reyes	Y	Y	N	Y	N	N	N
17 Stenholm	N	Y	N	N	N	N	N
18 Jackson-Lee	N	Y	Y	N	N	N	N
19 ***Combest***	N	N	Y	Y	N	N	Y
20 Gonzalez	Y	Y	N	Y	Y	N	N
21 ***Smith***	Y	N	Y	Y	N	N	Y
22 ***DeLay***	Y	N	Y	Y	N	?	Y
23 ***Bonilla***	Y	N	Y	Y	N	N	Y
24 Frost	Y	Y	N	Y	Y	Y	N
25 Bentsen	N	Y	N	Y	N	N	N
26 ***Armey***	Y	N	Y	Y	N	N	Y
27 Ortiz	Y	Y	Y	Y	N	N	N
28 Rodriguez	Y	Y	N	Y	N	Y	N
29 Green	N	Y	Y	Y	N	N	N
30 Johnson, E.B.	Y	Y	N	N	N	Y	N
UTAH							
1 ***Hansen***	N	N	Y	Y	N	N	Y
2 Matheson	Y	Y	Y	N	N	N	N
3 ***Cannon***	Y	N	Y	Y	N	N	Y
VERMONT							
AL *Sanders*	Y	Y	N	Y	N	?	N
VIRGINIA							
1 ***Davis, Jo Ann***	Y	N	Y	Y	N	N	Y
2 ***Schrock***	Y	N	Y	Y	N	N	Y
3 Scott	Y	Y	N	N	N	N	N
4 ***Forbes***	Y	N	Y	Y	N	N	Y
5 *Goode*	Y	N	Y	Y	N	N	Y
6 ***Goodlatte***	Y	N	Y	Y	N	N	Y
7 ***Cantor***	Y	N	Y	Y	N	N	Y
8 Moran	Y	Y	N	Y	N	N	N
9 Boucher	Y	Y	Y	Y	N	N	N
10 ***Wolf***	Y	N	Y	Y	N	N	Y
11 ***Davis, T.***	Y	N	Y	Y	N	N	Y
WASHINGTON							
1 Inslee	Y	Y	N	Y	N	N	N
2 Larsen	Y	Y	N	N	?	N	N
3 Baird	Y	Y	N	N	Y	Y	N
4 ***Hastings***	N	N	Y	Y	N	N	Y
5 ***Nethercutt***	Y	N	Y	Y	N	N	Y
6 Dicks	Y	Y	N	Y	Y	Y	N
7 McDermott	Y	Y	N	N	N	N	N
8 ***Dunn***	Y	N	Y	Y	N	?	Y
9 Smith	N	Y	N	Y	N	N	N
WEST VIRGINIA							
1 Mollohan	Y	Y	Y	?	N	N	N
2 ***Capito***	Y	N	Y	Y	N	N	Y
3 Rahall	Y	Y	N	Y	N	N	N
WISCONSIN							
1 ***Ryan***	Y	N	Y	Y	N	N	Y
2 Baldwin	Y	Y	N	Y	N	N	N
3 Kind	Y	Y	N	Y	N	N	N
4 Kleczka	Y	Y	N	Y	N	?	N
5 Barrett	Y	Y	N	N	N	N	N
6 ***Petri***	Y	N	N	Y	N	N	Y
7 Obey	Y	Y	N	N	Y	Y	N
8 ***Green***	Y	N	Y	Y	N	N	Y
9 ***Sensenbrenner***	Y	N	Y	Y	N	N	Y
WYOMING							
AL ***Cubin***	N	N	Y	Y	N	N	Y

Southern states - Ala., Ark., Fla., Ga., Ky., La., Miss., N.C., Okla., S.C., Tenn., Texas, Va.

326. HR 2563. Patients' Rights/Rule. Adoption of the rule (H Res 219) to provide for House floor consideration of the bill that would provide federal health care protections, such as access to specialty and emergency room care, and require that health maintenance organizations have an appeals process for patients who are denied care. Adopted 222-205: R 220-0; D 1-204 (ND 1-151, SD 0-53); I 1-1. Aug. 2, 2001.

327. Procedural Motion/Adjourn. McNulty, D-N.Y., motion to adjourn. Motion rejected 55-356: R 0-211; D 55-143 (ND 45-100, SD 10-43); I 0-2. Aug. 2, 2001.

328. HR 2563. Patients' Rights/Medical Savings Accounts. Thomas, R-Calif., amendment that would cut section 511, which details caps limiting the number of medical savings accounts, and replace it with language lifting current restrictions on such accounts. It also would allow the setting up of association health plans, through which businesses could combine their resources to negotiate lower cost insurance plans, which would be regulated by federal law. Adopted 236-194: R 217-2; D 18-191 (ND 14-141, SD 4-50); I 1-1. Aug. 2, 2001.

329. HR 2563. Patients' Rights/HMO Liability. Norwood, R-Ga., amendment that would limit liability and damage awards when a patient is harmed by denial of health care. It would allow a patient to sue a health maintenance organization in state court but federal, not state, law would govern. An employer could remove cases to federal court. It would limit non-economic damages to $1.5 million. Punitive damages would be limited to the same amount and only allowed when a decision-maker fails to abide by a grant of benefits by an independent medical reviewer. A patient could seek court reviews when an independent reviewer finds against him, but the patient would be required to produce clear and convincing evidence to overturn the decision. Adopted 218-213: R 214-6; D 3-206 (ND 2-153, SD 1-53); I 1-1. A "yea" was a vote in support of the president's position. Aug. 2, 2001.

330. HR 2563. Patients' Rights/Medical Malpractice. Thomas, R-Calif., amendment that would require a plaintiff to begin a lawsuit within two years of discovering an injury and mandate that all health care actions be filed within five years of the injury. These requirements would pre-empt other tort law. It would limit non-economic damage awards to $250,000, divide damages with multiple defendants based on responsibility, and allow evidence of collateral source benefits. It also would restrict punitive damages including a limit on recovery to the greater of twice the amount of economic damages or $250,000. Rejected 207-221: R 201-18; D 5-202 (ND 2-151, SD 3-51); I 1-1. Aug. 2, 2001.

331. HR 2563. Patients' Rights/Recommit. Berry, D-Ark., motion to recommit the bill to the House Ways and Means, Energy and Commerce, and Education and the Workforce committees with instructions to revert to the bill's text prior to amendment. Motion rejected 208-220: R 3-216; D 204-3 (ND 151-2, SD 53-1); I 1-1. Aug. 2, 2001.

332. HR 2563. Patients' Rights/Passage. Passage of the bill that would provide federal health care protections, such as access to specialty and emergency room care, and require that health maintenance organizations (HMOs) have an appeals process for patients who are denied care. A patient denied care could sue an HMO in state and federal court but first must exhaust internal and external appeals processes. Federal law would govern a state court suit and an employer could remove certain cases to federal court. Economic damages would not be limited but non-economic and punitive damages would both be capped at $1.5 million. An employer could select a "designated decision maker" to assume liability. The bill would reauthorize and lift current law restrictions on medical savings accounts and allow association health plans. Passed 226-203: R 220-0; D 5-202 (ND 3-150, SD 2-52); I 1-1. A "yea" was a vote in support of the president's position. Aug. 2, 2001.

Key

Y	Voted for (yea).
#	Paired for.
+	Announced for.
N	Voted against (nay).
X	Paired against.
−	Announced against.
P	Voted "present."
C	Voted "present" to avoid possible conflict of interest.
?	Did not vote or otherwise make a position known.

Democrats ***Republicans***
Independents

	326	327	328	329	330	331	332
ALABAMA							
1 *Callahan*	Y	N	Y	Y	Y	N	Y
2 *Everett*	Y	N	Y	Y	Y	N	Y
3 *Riley*	Y	N	Y	Y	Y	N	Y
4 *Aderholt*	Y	N	Y	Y	Y	N	Y
5 Cramer	N	N	N	Y	N	Y	Y
6 *Bachus*	Y	N	Y	Y	Y	N	Y
7 Hilliard	N	Y	N	N	N	Y	N
ALASKA							
AL *Young*	Y	N	Y	Y	Y	N	Y
ARIZONA							
1 *Flake*	Y	N	Y	Y	Y	N	Y
2 Pastor	N	N	N	N	N	Y	N
3 *Stump*	Y	?	Y	Y	Y	N	Y
4 *Shadegg*	Y	N	Y	Y	Y	N	Y
5 *Kolbe*	Y	N	Y	Y	Y	N	Y
6 *Hayworth*	Y	N	Y	Y	Y	N	Y
ARKANSAS							
1 Berry	N	Y	N	N	N	Y	N
2 Snyder	N	N	N	N	N	Y	N
3 *Hutchinson*	Y	?	Y	Y	Y	N	Y
4 Ross	N	Y	N	N	N	Y	N
CALIFORNIA							
1 Thompson	N	N	Y	N	?	?	?
2 *Herger*	Y	N	Y	Y	Y	N	Y
3 *Ose*	Y	N	Y	Y	Y	N	Y
4 *Doolittle*	Y	N	Y	Y	Y	N	Y
5 Matsui	N	N	N	N	N	Y	N
6 Woolsey	N	N	N	N	N	Y	N
7 Miller, George	N	Y	N	N	N	Y	N
8 Pelosi	N	N	N	N	N	Y	N
9 Lee	N	Y	N	N	N	Y	N
10 Tauscher	N	N	N	N	N	Y	N
11 *Pombo*	Y	N	Y	Y	Y	N	Y
12 Lantos	N	Y	N	N	N	Y	N
13 Stark	N	N	N	N	N	Y	N
14 Eshoo	N	N	N	N	N	Y	N
15 Honda	N	N	N	N	N	Y	N
16 Lofgren	N	Y	N	N	N	Y	N
17 Farr	N	Y	N	N	N	Y	N
18 Condit	N	N	Y	N	N	Y	N
19 *Radanovich*	Y	N	Y	Y	Y	N	Y
20 Dooley	N	?	Y	N	N	Y	N
21 *Thomas*	Y	N	Y	Y	Y	N	Y
22 Capps	N	Y	N	N	N	Y	N
23 *Gallegly*	Y	N	Y	Y	Y	N	Y
24 Sherman	N	N	N	N	N	Y	N
25 *McKeon*	Y	N	Y	Y	Y	N	Y
26 Berman	N	N	N	N	N	Y	N
27 Schiff	N	N	N	N	N	Y	N
28 *Dreier*	Y	N	Y	Y	Y	N	Y
29 Waxman	N	Y	N	N	N	Y	N
30 Becerra	N	N	N	N	N	Y	N
31 Solis	N	Y	N	N	N	Y	?
32 Watson	N	Y	N	N	N	Y	N
33 Royal-Allard	N	N	N	N	N	Y	N
34 Napolitano	N	N	N	N	N	Y	N
35 Waters	N	N	N	N	N	Y	N
36 Harman	N	?	Y	N	N	Y	N
37 Millender-McD.	N	N	N	N	N	Y	N
38 *Horn*	Y	?	Y	Y	Y	N	Y

	326	327	328	329	330	331	332
39 *Royce*	Y	N	Y	Y	Y	N	Y
40 *Lewis*	Y	N	Y	Y	Y	N	Y
41 *Miller, Gary*	Y	N	Y	Y	Y	N	Y
42 Baca	N	N	N	N	N	Y	N
43 *Calvert*	Y	N	Y	Y	Y	N	Y
44 *Bono*	Y	N	Y	Y	Y	N	Y
45 *Rohrabacher*	Y	N	Y	Y	Y	N	Y
46 Sanchez	N	N	N	N	N	Y	N
47 *Cox*	Y	?	Y	Y	Y	N	Y
48 *Issa*	Y	N	?	Y	Y	N	Y
49 Davis	N	N	N	N	N	Y	N
50 Filner	N	Y	N	N	N	Y	N
51 *Cunningham*	Y	N	Y	Y	Y	N	Y
52 *Hunter*	Y	?	Y	Y	Y	N	Y
COLORADO							
1 DeGette	N	Y	N	N	N	Y	N
2 Udall	N	Y	N	N	N	Y	N
3 *McInnis*	Y	N	Y	Y	Y	N	Y
4 *Schaffer*	Y	N	Y	Y	Y	N	Y
5 *Hefley*	Y	N	Y	Y	Y	N	Y
6 *Tancredo*	Y	N	Y	Y	Y	N	Y
CONNECTICUT							
1 Larson	N	N	N	N	N	Y	N
2 *Simmons*	Y	N	Y	Y	Y	N	Y
3 DeLauro	N	Y	N	N	N	Y	N
4 *Shays*	Y	N	Y	Y	Y	N	Y
5 Maloney	N	Y	N	N	N	Y	N
6 *Johnson*	Y	N	Y	Y	Y	N	Y
DELAWARE							
AL *Castle*	Y	N	Y	Y	Y	N	Y
FLORIDA							
1 *Scarborough*	Y	?	Y	Y	Y	N	Y
2 Boyd	−	N	N	N	N	Y	N
3 Brown	N	N	N	N	N	Y	N
4 *Crenshaw*	Y	N	Y	Y	Y	N	Y
5 Thurman	N	N	N	N	N	Y	N
6 *Stearns*	Y	N	Y	Y	Y	N	Y
7 *Mica*	Y	N	Y	Y	Y	N	Y
8 *Keller*	Y	N	Y	Y	Y	N	Y
9 *Bilirakis*	Y	N	Y	Y	Y	N	Y
10 *Young*	Y	N	Y	Y	Y	N	Y
11 Davis	N	N	N	N	N	Y	N
12 *Putnam*	Y	N	Y	Y	Y	N	Y
13 *Miller*	Y	N	Y	Y	Y	N	Y
14 *Goss*	Y	N	Y	Y	Y	N	Y
15 *Weldon*	Y	N	Y	Y	Y	N	Y
16 *Foley*	Y	N	Y	Y	Y	N	Y
17 Meek	N	N	N	N	N	Y	N
18 *Ros-Lehtinen*	Y	N	Y	Y	Y	N	Y
19 Wexler	N	N	N	N	N	Y	N
20 Deutsch	N	N	N	N	N	Y	N
21 *Diaz-Balart*	Y	N	Y	Y	Y	N	Y
22 *Shaw*	Y	N	Y	Y	Y	N	Y
23 Hastings	N	Y	N	N	N	Y	N
GEORGIA							
1 *Kingston*	Y	N	Y	Y	Y	N	Y
2 Bishop	N	N	N	N	N	Y	N
3 *Collins*	Y	?	Y	Y	Y	N	Y
4 McKinney	N	N	N	N	N	Y	N
5 Lewis	N	N	N	N	N	Y	N
6 *Isakson*	Y	N	Y	Y	Y	N	Y
7 *Barr*	Y	N	Y	Y	Y	N	Y
8 *Chambliss*	Y	N	Y	Y	Y	N	Y
9 *Deal*	Y	N	Y	Y	Y	N	Y
10 *Norwood*	Y	N	Y	Y	Y	N	Y
11 *Linder*	Y	N	Y	Y	Y	N	Y
HAWAII							
1 Abercrombie	N	N	N	N	N	Y	N
2 Mink	N	Y	N	N	N	Y	N
IDAHO							
1 *Otter*	Y	N	Y	Y	Y	N	Y
2 *Simpson*	Y	N	Y	Y	Y	N	Y
ILLINOIS							
1 Rush	N	N	N	N	N	Y	N
2 Jackson	N	N	N	N	N	Y	N
3 Lipinski	?	?	?	?	?	?	?
4 Gutierrez	N	?	N	N	N	Y	N
5 Blagojevich	N	N	N	N	N	Y	N
6 *Hyde*	Y	N	Y	Y	Y	N	Y
7 Davis	N	N	N	N	N	Y	N
8 *Crane*	Y	N	Y	Y	Y	N	Y
9 Schakowsky	N	Y	N	N	N	Y	N
10 *Kirk*	Y	N	Y	Y	Y	N	Y
11 *Weller*	Y	N	Y	Y	Y	N	Y
12 Costello	N	N	N	N	N	Y	N
13 *Biggert*	Y	N	Y	Y	Y	N	Y

ND Northern Democrats   SD Southern Democrats

	326	327	328	329	330	331	332
14 ***Hastert***			Y	Y		N	Y
15 ***Johnson***	Y	N	Y	N	N	N	Y
16 ***Manzullo***	Y	N	Y	Y	Y	N	Y
17 Evans	N	N	N	N	N	Y	N
18 ***LaHood***	Y	N	Y	Y	Y	N	Y
19 Phelps	N	N	Y	N	N	Y	N
20 ***Shimkus***	Y	N	Y	Y	Y	N	Y
INDIANA							
1 Visclosky	N	N	N	N	N	Y	N
2 ***Pence***	Y	N	Y	Y	Y	N	Y
3 Roemer	N	N	N	N	N	Y	N
4 ***Souder***	Y	N	Y	Y	Y	N	Y
5 ***Buyer***	Y	N	Y	Y	Y	N	Y
6 ***Burton***	Y	N	Y	Y	Y	N	Y
7 ***Kerns***	Y	N	Y	Y	Y	N	Y
8 ***Hostettler***	Y	N	Y	Y	Y	N	Y
9 Hill	N	N	N	N	N	Y	N
10 Carson	N	N	N	N	N	Y	N
IOWA							
1 ***Leach***	Y	N	Y	N	Y	Y	Y
2 ***Nussle***	Y	N	Y	Y	Y	N	Y
3 Boswell	N	N	N	N	N	Y	N
4 ***Ganske***	Y	N	?	N	N	Y	Y
5 ***Latham***	Y	N	Y	Y	Y	N	Y
KANSAS							
1 ***Moran***	Y	N	Y	Y	Y	N	Y
2 ***Ryun***	Y	N	Y	Y	Y	N	Y
3 Moore	N	N	N	N	N	Y	N
4 ***Tiahrt***	Y	N	Y	Y	Y	N	Y
KENTUCKY							
1 ***Whitfield***	Y	N	Y	Y	Y	N	Y
2 ***Lewis***	Y	N	Y	Y	Y	N	Y
3 ***Northup***	Y	N	Y	Y	Y	N	Y
4 Lucas	N	N	Y	Y	Y	N	Y
5 ***Rogers***	Y	N	Y	Y	Y	N	Y
6 ***Fletcher***	Y	N	Y	Y	Y	N	Y
LOUISIANA							
1 ***Vitter***	Y	N	Y	Y	Y	N	Y
2 Jefferson	N	Y	N	N	N	Y	N
3 ***Tauzin***	Y	N	Y	Y	Y	N	Y
4 ***McCrery***	Y	N	Y	Y	Y	N	Y
5 ***Cooksey***	Y	N	Y	Y	Y	N	Y
6 ***Baker***	Y	N	Y	Y	Y	N	Y
7 John	N	N	N	N	N	Y	N
MAINE							
1 Allen	N	Y	N	N	N	Y	N
2 Baldacci	N	N	N	N	N	Y	N
MARYLAND							
1 ***Gilchrest***	Y	N	Y	Y	Y	N	Y
2 ***Ehrlich***	Y	N	N	Y	N	N	Y
3 Cardin	N	N	N	N	N	Y	N
4 Wynn	N	N	N	N	N	Y	N
5 Hoyer	N	N	N	N	N	Y	N
6 ***Bartlett***	Y	N	Y	Y	Y	N	Y
7 Cummings	N	N	N	N	N	Y	N
8 ***Morella***	Y	N	N	N	N	Y	Y
MASSACHUSETTS							
1 Olver	N	Y	N	N	N	Y	N
2 Neal	N	N	N	N	N	Y	N
3 McGovern	N	Y	N	N	N	Y	N
4 Frank	N	Y	N	N	N	Y	N
5 Meehan	N	N	N	N	N	Y	N
6 Tierney	N	Y	N	N	N	Y	N
7 Markey	N	N	N	N	?	Y	N
8 Capuano	N	Y	N	N	N	Y	N
9 Vacant							
10 Delahunt	N	Y	N	N	N	Y	N
MICHIGAN							
1 Stupak	N	Y	N	N	N	?	N
2 ***Hoekstra***	Y	N	Y	Y	Y	N	Y
3 ***Ehlers***	Y	N	Y	Y	Y	N	Y
4 ***Camp***	Y	N	Y	Y	Y	N	Y
5 Barcia	N	N	Y	N	N	Y	N
6 ***Upton***	Y	N	Y	Y	Y	N	Y
7 ***Smith***	Y	N	Y	Y	Y	N	Y
8 ***Rogers***	Y	N	Y	Y	Y	N	Y
9 Kildee	N	N	N	N	N	Y	N
10 Bonior	N	Y	N	N	N	Y	N
11 ***Knollenberg***	Y	N	Y	Y	Y	N	Y
12 Levin	N	N	N	N	N	Y	N
13 Rivers	N	N	N	N	N	Y	N
14 Conyers	N	Y	N	N	N	Y	N
15 Kilpatrick	N	N	N	N	N	Y	N
16 Dingell	N	Y	N	N	N	Y	N
MINNESOTA							
1 ***Gutknecht***	Y	N	Y	Y	Y	N	Y
2 ***Kennedy***	Y	N	Y	Y	Y	N	Y
3 ***Ramstad***	Y	N	Y	Y	Y	N	Y
4 McCollum	N	N	N	N	N	Y	N
5 Sabo	N	N	N	N	N	Y	N
6 Luther	N	N	N	N	N	Y	N
7 Peterson	?	?	Y	Y	Y	N	Y
8 Oberstar	N	Y	N	N	N	Y	N
MISSISSIPPI							
1 ***Wicker***	Y	N	Y	Y	N	N	Y
2 Thompson	N	N	N	N	N	Y	N
3 ***Pickering***	Y	N	Y	Y	Y	N	Y
4 Shows	N	N	N	N	N	Y	N
5 Taylor	N	Y	N	N	N	Y	N
MISSOURI							
1 Clay	?	Y	N	N	N	Y	N
2 ***Akin***	Y	N	Y	Y	Y	N	Y
3 Gephardt	N	?	N	N	N	Y	N
4 Skelton	N	N	N	N	N	Y	N
5 McCarthy	N	N	N	N	N	Y	N
6 ***Graves***	Y	N	Y	Y	Y	N	Y
7 ***Blunt***	Y	N	Y	Y	Y	N	Y
8 ***Emerson***	Y	N	Y	Y	N	N	Y
9 ***Hulshof***	Y	N	Y	Y	Y	N	Y
MONTANA							
AL ***Rehberg***	Y	N	Y	Y	Y	N	Y
NEBRASKA							
1 ***Bereuter***	Y	N	Y	Y	Y	N	Y
2 ***Terry***	Y	N	Y	Y	N	N	Y
3 ***Osborne***	Y	N	Y	Y	Y	N	Y
NEVADA							
1 Berkley	N	N	N	N	N	Y	N
2 ***Gibbons***	Y	N	Y	Y	Y	N	Y
NEW HAMPSHIRE							
1 ***Sununu***	Y	N	Y	Y	Y	N	Y
2 ***Bass***	Y	N	Y	Y	Y	N	Y
NEW JERSEY							
1 Andrews	N	N	N	N	N	Y	N
2 ***LoBiondo***	Y	N	Y	Y	Y	N	Y
3 ***Saxton***	Y	N	Y	Y	Y	N	Y
4 ***Smith***	Y	N	Y	N	Y	N	Y
5 ***Roukema***	Y	N	Y	N	Y	N	Y
6 Pallone	N	N	N	N	N	Y	N
7 ***Ferguson***	Y	N	Y	Y	Y	N	Y
8 Pascrell	?	N	N	N	N	Y	N
9 Rothman	N	N	N	N	N	Y	N
10 Payne	N	N	N	N	N	Y	N
11 ***Frelinghuysen***	Y	N	Y	Y	Y	N	Y
12 Holt	N	N	N	N	N	Y	N
13 Menendez	N	?	N	N	N	Y	N
NEW MEXICO							
1 ***Wilson***	Y	N	Y	Y	Y	N	Y
2 ***Skeen***	Y	N	Y	Y	Y	N	Y
3 Udall	N	N	N	N	N	Y	N
NEW YORK							
1 ***Grucci***	Y	N	Y	Y	N	N	Y
2 Israel	N	N	N	N	N	Y	N
3 ***King***	Y	N	Y	Y	N	N	Y
4 McCarthy	N	N	N	N	N	Y	N
5 Ackerman	N	N	N	N	N	Y	N
6 Meeks	N	N	N	N	N	Y	N
7 Crowley	N	N	N	N	N	Y	N
8 Nadler	N	Y	N	N	N	Y	N
9 Weiner	N	N	N	N	N	Y	N
10 Towns	N	Y	N	N	N	Y	N
11 Owens	N	Y	N	N	N	Y	N
12 Velázquez	N	Y	N	N	N	Y	N
13 ***Fossella***	Y	N	Y	Y	Y	N	Y
14 Maloney	N	N	N	N	N	Y	N
15 Rangel	N	N	N	N	N	Y	N
16 Serrano	N	N	N	N	N	Y	N
17 Engel	N	N	N	N	N	Y	N
18 Lowey	N	N	N	N	N	Y	N
19 ***Kelly***	Y	N	Y	Y	Y	N	Y
20 ***Gilman***	Y	N	Y	Y	N	N	Y
21 McNulty	N	Y	N	N	N	Y	N
22 ***Sweeney***	Y	N	Y	Y	Y	N	Y
23 ***Boehlert***	Y	N	Y	Y	Y	N	Y
24 ***McHugh***	Y	N	Y	Y	Y	N	Y
25 ***Walsh***	Y	N	Y	Y	Y	N	Y
26 Hinchey	N	Y	N	N	N	Y	N
27 ***Reynolds***	Y	N	Y	Y	Y	N	Y
28 Slaughter	N	Y	N	N	N	Y	N
29 LaFalce	N	Y	N	N	N	Y	N
30 ***Quinn***	Y	N	Y	Y	Y	N	Y
31 ***Houghton***	Y	N	Y	Y	Y	N	Y
NORTH CAROLINA							
1 Clayton	N	N	N	N	N	Y	N
2 Etheridge	N	N	N	N	N	Y	N
3 ***Jones***	Y	N	Y	Y	Y	N	Y
4 Price	N	N	N	N	N	Y	N
5 ***Burr***	Y	N	Y	Y	Y	N	Y
6 ***Coble***	Y	N	Y	Y	Y	N	Y
7 McIntyre	N	N	N	N	N	Y	N
8 ***Hayes***	Y	N	Y	Y	Y	N	Y
9 ***Myrick***	Y	N	Y	Y	Y	N	Y
10 ***Ballenger***	Y	N	Y	Y	Y	N	Y
11 ***Taylor***	Y	N	Y	Y	Y	N	Y
12 Watt	N	N	N	N	N	Y	N
NORTH DAKOTA							
AL Pomeroy	N	N	N	N	N	Y	N
OHIO							
1 ***Chabot***	Y	N	Y	Y	Y	N	Y
2 ***Portman***	Y	N	Y	Y	Y	N	Y
3 Hall	N	N	N	N	N	Y	N
4 ***Oxley***	Y	N	Y	Y	Y	N	Y
5 ***Gillmor***	Y	N	Y	Y	Y	N	Y
6 Strickland	N	Y	N	N	N	Y	N
7 ***Hobson***	Y	N	Y	Y	Y	N	Y
8 ***Boehner***	Y	?	Y	Y	Y	N	Y
9 Kaptur	N	Y	N	N	N	Y	N
10 Kucinich	N	N	N	N	N	Y	N
11 Jones	N	N	N	N	N	Y	N
12 ***Tiberi***	Y	N	Y	Y	Y	N	Y
13 Brown	N	Y	N	N	N	Y	N
14 Sawyer	N	N	N	N	N	Y	N
15 ***Pryce***	Y	N	Y	Y	Y	N	Y
16 ***Regula***	Y	N	Y	Y	Y	N	Y
17 Traficant	Y	N	Y	Y	Y	N	Y
18 ***Ney***	Y	N	Y	Y	Y	N	Y
19 ***LaTourette***	Y	N	Y	Y	N	N	Y
OKLAHOMA							
1 ***Largent***	Y	N	Y	Y	Y	N	Y
2 Carson	N	N	N	N	N	Y	N
3 ***Watkins***	Y	N	Y	Y	Y	N	Y
4 ***Watts***	Y	N	Y	Y	Y	N	Y
5 ***Istook***	Y	N	Y	Y	N	N	Y
6 ***Lucas***	Y	N	Y	Y	Y	N	Y
OREGON							
1 Wu	N	N	N	N	N	Y	N
2 ***Walden***	Y	N	Y	Y	Y	N	Y
3 Blumenauer	N	N	N	N	N	Y	N
4 DeFazio	N	Y	N	N	N	Y	N
5 Hooley	N	N	N	N	N	Y	N
PENNSYLVANIA							
1 Brady	N	N	N	N	N	Y	N
2 Fattah	N	N	N	N	N	Y	N
3 Borski	N	Y	N	N	N	Y	N
4 ***Hart***	Y	N	Y	Y	Y	N	Y
5 ***Peterson***	Y	N	Y	Y	Y	N	Y
6 Holden	N	N	N	N	N	Y	N
7 ***Weldon***	Y	N	Y	Y	Y	?	Y
8 ***Greenwood***	Y	N	Y	Y	Y	N	Y
9 ***Shuster, Bill***	Y	N	Y	Y	Y	N	Y
10 ***Sherwood***	Y	N	Y	Y	Y	N	Y
11 Kanjorski	N	N	N	N	N	Y	N
12 Murtha	N	N	Y	N	N	Y	N
13 Hoeffel	N	N	N	N	N	Y	N
14 Coyne	N	N	N	N	N	Y	N
15 ***Toomey***	Y	N	Y	Y	Y	N	Y
16 ***Pitts***	Y	N	Y	Y	Y	N	Y
17 ***Gekas***	Y	N	Y	Y	Y	N	Y
18 Doyle	N	N	N	N	N	Y	N
19 ***Platts***	Y	N	Y	Y	Y	N	Y
20 Mascara	N	N	Y	N	N	Y	N
21 ***English***	Y	N	Y	Y	Y	N	Y
RHODE ISLAND							
1 Kennedy	N	N	N	N	N	Y	N
2 Langevin	N	Y	N	N	N	Y	N
SOUTH CAROLINA							
1 ***Brown***	Y	N	Y	Y	Y	N	Y
2 ***Spence***	?	?	?	?	?	?	?
3 ***Graham***	Y	N	Y	Y	N	N	Y
4 ***DeMint***	Y	N	Y	Y	Y	N	Y
5 Spratt	N	Y	N	N	N	Y	N
6 Clyburn	N	N	N	N	N	Y	N
SOUTH DAKOTA							
AL ***Thune***	Y	N	Y	Y	Y	N	Y
TENNESSEE							
1 ***Jenkins***	Y	N	Y	Y	N	N	Y
2 ***Duncan***	Y	N	Y	Y	N	N	Y
3 ***Wamp***	Y	N	Y	Y	Y	N	Y
4 ***Hilleary***	Y	N	Y	Y	Y	N	Y
5 Clement	N	N	N	N	N	Y	N
6 Gordon	N	N	N	N	N	Y	N
7 ***Bryant***	Y	N	Y	Y	Y	N	Y
8 Tanner	N	N	N	N	N	Y	N
9 Ford	N	N	N	N	N	Y	N
TEXAS							
1 Sandlin	N	Y	N	N	N	Y	N
2 Turner	N	N	N	N	N	Y	N
3 ***Johnson, Sam***	Y	N	Y	Y	Y	N	Y
4 Hall	N	N	Y	N	N	Y	N
5 ***Sessions***	Y	N	Y	Y	Y	N	Y
6 ***Barton***	Y	N	Y	Y	Y	N	Y
7 ***Culberson***	Y	N	Y	Y	Y	N	Y
8 ***Brady***	Y	N	Y	Y	Y	N	Y
9 Lampson	N	N	N	N	N	Y	N
10 Doggett	N	Y	N	N	N	Y	N
11 Edwards	N	N	N	N	N	Y	N
12 ***Granger***	Y	N	Y	Y	Y	N	Y
13 ***Thornberry***	Y	N	Y	Y	Y	N	Y
14 ***Paul***	Y	N	Y	?	?	?	?
15 Hinojosa	N	N	N	N	N	Y	N
16 Reyes	N	Y	N	N	N	Y	N
17 Stenholm	N	N	N	N	Y	Y	N
18 Jackson-Lee	N	N	N	N	N	Y	N
19 ***Combest***	Y	N	Y	Y	Y	N	Y
20 Gonzalez	N	N	N	N	N	Y	N
21 ***Smith***	Y	N	Y	Y	Y	N	Y
22 ***DeLay***	Y	N	Y	Y	Y	N	Y
23 ***Bonilla***	Y	N	Y	Y	Y	N	Y
24 Frost	N	N	N	N	N	Y	N
25 Bentsen	N	N	N	N	N	Y	N
26 ***Armey***	Y	N	Y	Y	Y	N	Y
27 Ortiz	N	N	N	N	N	Y	N
28 Rodriguez	N	N	N	N	N	Y	N
29 Green	N	N	N	N	N	Y	N
30 Johnson, E.B.	N	N	N	N	N	Y	N
UTAH							
1 ***Hansen***	Y	N	Y	Y	Y	N	Y
2 Matheson	N	?	N	N	N	Y	N
3 ***Cannon***	Y	?	Y	Y	Y	N	Y
VERMONT							
AL *Sanders*	N	N	N	N	N	Y	N
VIRGINIA							
1 ***Davis, Jo Ann***	Y	N	Y	Y	Y	N	Y
2 ***Schrock***	Y	N	Y	Y	Y	N	Y
3 Scott	N	N	N	N	N	Y	N
4 ***Forbes***	Y	N	Y	Y	Y	N	Y
5 *Goode*	Y	N	Y	Y	Y	N	Y
6 ***Goodlatte***	Y	N	Y	Y	Y	N	Y
7 ***Cantor***	Y	N	Y	Y	Y	N	Y
8 Moran	N	N	Y	N	N	Y	N
9 Boucher	N	?	N	N	N	Y	N
10 ***Wolf***	Y	N	Y	Y	Y	N	Y
11 ***Davis, T.***	Y	N	Y	Y	Y	N	Y
WASHINGTON							
1 Inslee	N	N	N	N	N	Y	N
2 Larsen	N	N	Y	N	N	Y	N
3 Baird	N	Y	N	N	N	Y	N
4 ***Hastings***	Y	N	Y	Y	Y	N	Y
5 ***Nethercutt***	Y	N	Y	Y	N	N	Y
6 Dicks	N	N	N	N	N	Y	N
7 McDermott	N	?	N	N	N	Y	N
8 ***Dunn***	Y	N	Y	Y	Y	N	Y
9 Smith	N	?	Y	N	N	Y	Y
WEST VIRGINIA							
1 Mollohan	N	N	N	N	N	Y	N
2 ***Capito***	Y	N	Y	Y	Y	N	Y
3 Rahall	N	N	N	N	N	Y	N
WISCONSIN							
1 ***Ryan***	Y	N	Y	Y	Y	N	Y
2 Baldwin	N	N	N	N	N	Y	N
3 Kind	N	N	N	N	N	Y	N
4 Kleczka	N	N	N	N	N	Y	N
5 Barrett	N	N	N	N	N	Y	N
6 ***Petri***	Y	N	Y	Y	Y	N	Y
7 Obey	N	Y	N	N	N	Y	N
8 ***Green***	Y	N	Y	Y	Y	N	Y
9 ***Sensenbrenner***	Y	N	Y	Y	Y	N	Y
WYOMING							
AL ***Cubin***	Y	N	Y	Y	Y	N	Y

Southern states - Ala., Ark., Fla., Ga., Ky., La., Miss., N.C., Okla., S.C., Tenn., Texas, Va.

Key

Y	Voted for (yea).
#	Paired for.
+	Announced for.
N	Voted against (nay).
X	Paired against.
−	Announced against.
P	Voted "present."
C	Voted "present" to avoid possible conflict of interest.
?	Did not vote or otherwise make a position known.

•

Democrats   ***Republicans***
Independents

333. HR 2291. Anti-Drug Efforts/Passage. Souder, R-Ind., motion to suspend the rules and pass the bill that would authorize $414 million in grant funding to extend through fiscal 2007 the Drug-Free Communities Support Program. It would allow local anti-drug coalitions to receive funding beyond their original five-year grants, fund mentoring efforts, authorize the establishment of an institute to train and assess coalitions, and cap the program's administrative costs at 6 percent of its annual funding. Motion agreed to 402-1: R 209-1; D 191-0 (ND 143-0, SD 48-0); I 2-0. A two-thirds majority of those present and voting (269 in this case) is required for passage under suspension of the rules. Sept. 5, 2001.

334. H Res 233. U.S.-Mexico Relations/Adoption. Hyde, R-Ill., motion to suspend the rules and adopt the resolution that would acknowledge the important partnership between the United States and Mexico and support Mexican President Vicente Fox. Motion agreed to 407-0: R 211-0; D 194-0 (ND 144-0, SD 50-0); I 2-0. A two-thirds majority of those present and voting (272 in this case) is required for adoption under suspension of the rules. Sept. 5, 2001.

335. HR 2833. Vietnam Rights/Passage. Passage of the bill that would set up a commission to monitor human rights in Vietnam and condition that country's future non-humanitarian aid on achieving "substantial progress" toward specified human rights goals including the release of political and religious prisoners and an end to government involvement in human trafficking. The secretary of the Treasury would be required to consider human rights violations when deciding whether to support or oppose multilateral aid to Vietnam by international financial institutions. The bill would authorize $2 million per year in fiscal 2002 and 2003 to support human rights and democracy in Vietnam. Passed 410-1: R 208-1; D 200-0 (ND 148-0, SD 52-0); I 2-0. Sept. 6, 2001.

[1] *Rep. Asa Hutchinson, R-Ark., resigned Aug. 6, 2001, to become administrator of the Drug Enforcement Agency. The last vote for which he was eligible was vote 332.*

[2] *Rep. Joe Scarborough, R-Fla., resigned effective Sept. 6, 2001. The last vote for which he was eligible was vote 334.*

[3] *Rep. Floyd D. Spence, R-S.C., died Aug. 16, 2001. The last vote for which he was eligible was vote 332.*

		333	334	335
ALABAMA				
1	*Callahan*	Y	Y	Y
2	*Everett*	Y	Y	Y
3	*Riley*	Y	?	Y
4	*Aderholt*	Y	Y	Y
5	Cramer	Y	Y	Y
6	*Bachus*	Y	Y	Y
7	Hilliard	Y	Y	Y
ALASKA				
AL	*Young*	?	?	?
ARIZONA				
1	*Flake*	N	Y	Y
2	Pastor	Y	Y	Y
3	*Stump*	Y	Y	Y
4	*Shadegg*	Y	Y	Y
5	*Kolbe*	Y	Y	Y
6	*Hayworth*	Y	Y	Y
ARKANSAS				
1	Berry	Y	Y	Y
2	Snyder	Y	Y	Y
3	Vacant[1]			
4	Ross	Y	Y	Y
CALIFORNIA				
1	Thompson	Y	Y	Y
2	*Herger*	Y	Y	Y
3	*Ose*	Y	Y	Y
4	*Doolittle*	Y	Y	Y
5	Matsui	Y	Y	Y
6	Woolsey	Y	Y	Y
7	Miller, George	Y	Y	Y
8	Pelosi	Y	Y	Y
9	Lee	Y	Y	Y
10	Tauscher	Y	Y	Y
11	*Pombo*	Y	Y	Y
12	Lantos	Y	Y	Y
13	Stark	Y	Y	Y
14	Eshoo	Y	Y	Y
15	Honda	Y	Y	Y
16	Lofgren	Y	Y	Y
17	Farr	Y	Y	Y
18	Condit	Y	Y	Y
19	*Radanovich*	Y	Y	Y
20	Dooley	Y	Y	Y
21	*Thomas*	Y	Y	Y
22	Capps	Y	Y	Y
23	*Gallegly*	Y	Y	Y
24	Sherman	?	?	?
25	*McKeon*	Y	Y	Y
26	Berman	Y	Y	Y
27	Schiff	Y	Y	Y
28	*Dreier*	Y	Y	Y
29	Waxman	Y	Y	Y
30	Becerra	Y	Y	Y
31	Solis	Y	Y	Y
32	Watson	Y	Y	Y
33	Roybal-Allard	Y	Y	Y
34	Napolitano	Y	Y	Y
35	Waters	Y	Y	Y
36	Harman	Y	Y	Y
37	Millender-McD.	Y	Y	Y
38	*Horn*	?	?	?

		333	334	335
39	*Royce*	Y	Y	Y
40	*Lewis*	Y	Y	Y
41	*Miller, Gary*	Y	Y	Y
42	Baca	Y	Y	Y
43	*Calvert*	Y	Y	Y
44	*Bono*	Y	Y	Y
45	*Rohrabacher*	Y	Y	Y
46	Sanchez	Y	Y	Y
47	*Cox*	Y	Y	Y
48	*Issa*	Y	Y	Y
49	Davis	Y	Y	Y
50	Filner	Y	Y	Y
51	*Cunningham*	Y	Y	Y
52	*Hunter*	Y	Y	Y
COLORADO				
1	DeGette	?	Y	Y
2	Udall	Y	Y	Y
3	*McInnis*	Y	Y	Y
4	*Schaffer*	Y	Y	Y
5	*Hefley*	Y	Y	Y
6	*Tancredo*	Y	Y	Y
CONNECTICUT				
1	Larson	Y	Y	Y
2	*Simmons*	Y	Y	Y
3	DeLauro	Y	Y	Y
4	*Shays*	Y	Y	Y
5	Maloney	Y	Y	Y
6	*Johnson*	Y	Y	Y
DELAWARE				
AL	*Castle*	Y	Y	Y
FLORIDA				
1	*Scarborough*[2]	Y	Y	
2	Boyd	Y	Y	Y
3	Brown	Y	Y	Y
4	*Crenshaw*	Y	Y	Y
5	Thurman	Y	Y	Y
6	*Stearns*	Y	Y	Y
7	*Mica*	+	Y	Y
8	*Keller*	Y	Y	Y
9	*Bilirakis*	Y	Y	Y
10	*Young*	Y	Y	Y
11	Davis	Y	Y	Y
12	*Putnam*	Y	Y	Y
13	*Miller*	Y	Y	Y
14	*Goss*	Y	Y	Y
15	*Weldon*	Y	Y	Y
16	*Foley*	+	+	Y
17	Meek	Y	Y	?
18	*Ros-Lehtinen*	Y	Y	Y
19	Wexler	Y	Y	Y
20	Deutsch	Y	Y	Y
21	*Diaz-Balart*	Y	Y	Y
22	*Shaw*	Y	Y	Y
23	Hastings	?	?	?
GEORGIA				
1	*Kingston*	Y	Y	Y
2	Bishop	Y	Y	Y
3	*Collins*	Y	Y	Y
4	McKinney	Y	Y	Y
5	Lewis	Y	Y	Y
6	*Isakson*	Y	Y	Y
7	*Barr*	Y	Y	Y
8	*Chambliss*	Y	Y	Y
9	*Deal*	Y	Y	Y
10	*Norwood*	Y	Y	Y
11	*Linder*	Y	Y	Y
HAWAII				
1	Abercrombie	Y	Y	Y
2	Mink	Y	Y	Y
IDAHO				
1	*Otter*	Y	Y	Y
2	*Simpson*	Y	Y	Y
ILLINOIS				
1	Rush	Y	Y	Y
2	Jackson	Y	Y	Y
3	Lipinski	?	?	?
4	Gutierrez	Y	Y	Y
5	Blagojevich	Y	Y	Y
6	*Hyde*	Y	Y	Y
7	Davis	Y	Y	?
8	*Crane*	?	?	?
9	Schakowsky	Y	Y	Y
10	*Kirk*	Y	Y	Y
11	*Weller*	Y	Y	Y
12	Costello	Y	Y	Y
13	*Biggert*	Y	Y	Y

ND Northern Democrats   SD Southern Democrats

	333	334	335
14 Hastert			
15 *Johnson*	Y	Y	Y
16 *Manzullo*	Y	Y	Y
17 Evans	Y	Y	Y
18 *LaHood*	Y	Y	Y
19 Phelps	Y	Y	Y
20 *Shimkus*	Y	Y	Y

INDIANA

	333	334	335
1 Visclosky	Y	Y	Y
2 *Pence*	Y	Y	Y
3 Roemer	Y	Y	Y
4 *Souder*	Y	Y	Y
5 *Buyer*	Y	Y	Y
6 *Burton*	Y	Y	Y
7 *Kerns*	Y	Y	Y
8 *Hostettler*	Y	Y	Y
9 Hill	Y	Y	Y
10 Carson	?	?	Y

IOWA

	333	334	335
1 Leach	Y	Y	Y
2 *Nussle*	Y	Y	Y
3 Boswell	Y	Y	Y
4 *Ganske*	Y	Y	Y
5 *Latham*	Y	Y	Y

KANSAS

	333	334	335
1 *Moran*	Y	Y	Y
2 *Ryun*	Y	Y	Y
3 Moore	Y	Y	Y
4 *Tiahrt*	Y	Y	Y

KENTUCKY

	333	334	335
1 *Whitfield*	Y	Y	Y
2 *Lewis*	Y	Y	Y
3 *Northup*	Y	Y	Y
4 Lucas	Y	Y	Y
5 *Rogers*	Y	Y	Y
6 *Fletcher*	Y	Y	Y

LOUISIANA

	333	334	335
1 *Vitter*	Y	Y	Y
2 Jefferson	Y	Y	Y
3 *Tauzin*	Y	Y	Y
4 *McCrery*	Y	Y	Y
5 *Cooksey*	Y	Y	Y
6 *Baker*	Y	Y	Y
7 John	Y	Y	Y

MAINE

	333	334	335
1 Allen	Y	Y	Y
2 Baldacci	Y	Y	Y

MARYLAND

	333	334	335
1 *Gilchrest*	Y	Y	Y
2 *Ehrlich*	Y	Y	Y
3 Cardin	Y	Y	Y
4 Wynn	Y	Y	Y
5 Hoyer	Y	Y	Y
6 *Bartlett*	Y	Y	Y
7 Cummings	Y	Y	Y
8 *Morella*	Y	Y	Y

MASSACHUSETTS

	333	334	335
1 Olver	Y	Y	Y
2 Neal	Y	Y	Y
3 McGovern	Y	Y	Y
4 Frank	?	?	?
5 Meehan	Y	Y	Y
6 Tierney	Y	Y	Y
7 Markey	Y	Y	Y
8 Capuano	Y	Y	Y
9 Vacant			
10 Delahunt	Y	Y	Y

MICHIGAN

	333	334	335
1 Stupak	Y	Y	Y
2 *Hoekstra*	Y	Y	Y
3 *Ehlers*	Y	Y	Y
4 *Camp*	Y	Y	Y
5 Barcia	Y	Y	Y
6 *Upton*	Y	Y	Y
7 *Smith*	Y	Y	Y
8 *Rogers*	Y	Y	Y
9 Kildee	Y	Y	Y
10 Bonior	Y	Y	Y
11 *Knollenberg*	Y	Y	Y
12 Levin	Y	Y	Y
13 Rivers	Y	Y	Y
14 Conyers	Y	Y	?
15 Kilpatrick	Y	Y	Y
16 Dingell	Y	Y	Y

MINNESOTA

	333	334	335
1 *Gutknecht*	Y	Y	Y
2 *Kennedy*	Y	Y	Y
3 *Ramstad*	Y	Y	Y
4 McCollum	Y	Y	Y
5 Sabo	Y	Y	Y
6 Luther	Y	Y	Y
7 Peterson	Y	Y	Y
8 Oberstar	Y	Y	Y

MISSISSIPPI

	333	334	335
1 *Wicker*	Y	Y	Y
2 Thompson	Y	Y	Y
3 *Pickering*	Y	Y	Y
4 Shows	Y	Y	Y
5 Taylor	Y	Y	Y

MISSOURI

	333	334	335
1 Clay	Y	Y	Y
2 *Akin*	Y	Y	Y
3 Gephardt	Y	Y	Y
4 Skelton	Y	Y	Y
5 McCarthy	Y	Y	Y
6 *Graves*	Y	Y	Y
7 *Blunt*	Y	Y	Y
8 *Emerson*	Y	Y	Y
9 *Hulshof*	Y	Y	Y

MONTANA

	333	334	335
AL *Rehberg*	Y	Y	Y

NEBRASKA

	333	334	335
1 *Bereuter*	Y	Y	Y
2 *Terry*	Y	Y	Y
3 *Osborne*	Y	Y	Y

NEVADA

	333	334	335
1 Berkley	Y	Y	Y
2 *Gibbons*	Y	Y	Y

NEW HAMPSHIRE

	333	334	335
1 *Sununu*	Y	Y	Y
2 *Bass*	Y	Y	Y

NEW JERSEY

	333	334	335
1 Andrews	Y	Y	Y
2 *LoBiondo*	Y	Y	Y
3 *Saxton*	Y	Y	Y
4 *Smith*	Y	Y	Y
5 *Roukema*	Y	Y	Y
6 Pallone	Y	Y	Y
7 *Ferguson*	Y	Y	Y
8 Pascrell	+	+	Y
9 Rothman	Y	Y	Y
10 Payne	Y	Y	Y
11 *Frelinghuysen*	Y	Y	Y
12 Holt	Y	Y	Y
13 Menendez	Y	Y	Y

NEW MEXICO

	333	334	335
1 *Wilson*	Y	Y	Y
2 *Skeen*	Y	Y	Y
3 Udall	Y	Y	Y

NEW YORK

	333	334	335
1 *Grucci*	Y	Y	Y
2 Israel	Y	Y	Y
3 *King*	Y	Y	Y
4 McCarthy	Y	Y	Y
5 Ackerman	Y	Y	Y
6 Meeks	Y	Y	Y
7 Crowley	Y	Y	Y
8 Nadler	?	?	Y
9 Weiner	Y	Y	Y
10 Towns	Y	Y	Y
11 Owens	Y	Y	Y
12 Velázquez	Y	Y	Y
13 *Fossella*	Y	Y	Y
14 Maloney	Y	Y	Y
15 Rangel	?	?	Y
16 Serrano	Y	Y	Y
17 Engel	Y	Y	Y
18 Lowey	Y	Y	Y
19 *Kelly*	Y	Y	Y
20 *Gilman*	Y	Y	Y
21 McNulty	?	?	Y
22 *Sweeney*	Y	Y	Y
23 *Boehlert*	Y	Y	Y
24 *McHugh*	Y	Y	Y
25 *Walsh*	Y	Y	Y
26 Hinchey	?	?	Y
27 *Reynolds*	Y	Y	Y
28 Slaughter	Y	Y	Y
29 LaFalce	Y	Y	Y
30 *Quinn*	Y	Y	Y
31 Houghton	Y	Y	Y

NORTH CAROLINA

	333	334	335
1 Clayton	Y	Y	Y
2 Etheridge	+	+	Y
3 *Jones*	Y	Y	?
4 Price	Y	Y	Y
5 *Burr*	Y	Y	Y
6 *Coble*	Y	Y	Y
7 McIntyre	Y	Y	Y
8 *Hayes*	?	?	+
9 *Myrick*	Y	Y	Y
10 *Ballenger*	Y	Y	Y
11 *Taylor*	Y	Y	Y
12 Watt	Y	Y	Y

NORTH DAKOTA

	333	334	335
AL Pomeroy	Y	Y	Y

OHIO

	333	334	335
1 *Chabot*	Y	Y	Y
2 *Portman*	Y	Y	?
3 Hall	Y	Y	Y
4 *Oxley*	Y	Y	?
5 *Gillmor*	Y	Y	?
6 Strickland	Y	Y	Y
7 *Hobson*	Y	Y	Y
8 *Boehner*	Y	Y	Y
9 Kaptur	Y	Y	?
10 Kucinich	Y	Y	Y
11 Jones	Y	Y	Y
12 *Tiberi*	Y	Y	Y
13 Brown	Y	Y	Y
14 Sawyer	Y	Y	Y
15 *Pryce*	Y	Y	Y
16 *Regula*	Y	Y	Y
17 Traficant	?	?	?
18 *Ney*	Y	Y	Y
19 *LaTourette*	Y	Y	Y

OKLAHOMA

	333	334	335
1 *Largent*	Y	Y	Y
2 Carson	Y	Y	Y
3 *Watkins*	Y	Y	Y
4 *Watts*	Y	Y	+
5 *Istook*	Y	Y	Y
6 *Lucas*	Y	Y	Y

OREGON

	333	334	335
1 *Wu*	Y	Y	Y
2 *Walden*	Y	Y	Y
3 Blumenauer	Y	Y	Y
4 DeFazio	?	?	Y
5 Hooley	Y	Y	Y

PENNSYLVANIA

	333	334	335
1 Brady	Y	Y	Y
2 Fattah	Y	Y	Y
3 Borski	Y	Y	Y
4 *Hart*	Y	Y	Y
5 *Peterson*	Y	Y	Y
6 Holden	Y	Y	Y
7 *Weldon*	Y	Y	Y
8 *Greenwood*	Y	Y	Y
9 *Shuster, Bill*	Y	Y	Y
10 *Sherwood*	Y	Y	Y
11 Kanjorski	Y	Y	Y
12 Murtha	Y	?	Y
13 Hoeffel	Y	Y	Y
14 Coyne	Y	Y	Y
15 *Toomey*	Y	Y	Y
16 *Pitts*	Y	Y	Y
17 *Gekas*	Y	Y	Y
18 Doyle	Y	Y	Y
19 *Platts*	Y	Y	Y
20 Mascara	Y	Y	Y
21 *English*	Y	Y	Y

RHODE ISLAND

	333	334	335
1 Kennedy	Y	Y	Y
2 Langevin	Y	Y	Y

SOUTH CAROLINA

	333	334	335
1 *Brown*	Y	Y	Y
2 Vacant[3]			
3 *Graham*	Y	Y	Y
4 *DeMint*	Y	Y	Y
5 Spratt	Y	Y	Y
6 Clyburn	Y	Y	Y

SOUTH DAKOTA

	333	334	335
AL *Thune*	Y	Y	Y

TENNESSEE

	333	334	335
1 *Jenkins*	Y	Y	Y
2 *Duncan*	Y	Y	Y
3 *Wamp*	Y	Y	Y
4 *Hilleary*	Y	Y	Y
5 Clement	Y	Y	Y
6 Gordon	Y	Y	Y
7 *Bryant*	Y	Y	Y
8 Tanner	Y	Y	Y
9 Ford	Y	Y	Y

TEXAS

	333	334	335
1 Sandlin	Y	Y	Y
2 Turner	Y	Y	Y
3 *Johnson, Sam*	Y	Y	Y
4 Hall	Y	Y	Y
5 *Sessions*	Y	Y	Y
6 *Barton*	?	?	Y
7 *Culberson*	Y	Y	Y
8 *Brady*	Y	Y	Y
9 Lampson	?	?	Y
10 Doggett	Y	Y	Y
11 Edwards	Y	Y	Y
12 *Granger*	Y	Y	Y
13 *Thornberry*	Y	Y	Y
14 *Paul*	?	Y	N
15 Hinojosa	Y	Y	Y
16 Reyes	?	?	Y
17 Stenholm	Y	Y	Y
18 Jackson-Lee	+	Y	Y
19 *Combest*	Y	Y	Y
20 Gonzalez	Y	Y	Y
21 *Smith*	Y	Y	Y
22 *DeLay*	?	?	Y
23 *Bonilla*	Y	Y	Y
24 Frost	Y	Y	Y
25 Bentsen	Y	Y	Y
26 *Armey*	Y	Y	Y
27 Ortiz	Y	Y	Y
28 Rodriguez	Y	Y	Y
29 Green	+	Y	Y
30 Johnson, E.B.	Y	Y	Y

UTAH

	333	334	335
1 *Hansen*	Y	Y	Y
2 Matheson	Y	Y	Y
3 *Cannon*	Y	Y	Y

VERMONT

	333	334	335
AL *Sanders*	Y	Y	Y

VIRGINIA

	333	334	335
1 *Davis, Jo Ann*	Y	Y	Y
2 *Schrock*	Y	Y	Y
3 Scott	Y	Y	Y
4 *Forbes*	Y	Y	Y
5 *Goode*	Y	Y	Y
6 *Goodlatte*	Y	Y	Y
7 *Cantor*	Y	Y	Y
8 Moran	Y	Y	Y
9 Boucher	Y	Y	Y
10 *Wolf*	Y	Y	Y
11 *Davis, T.*	Y	Y	Y

WASHINGTON

	333	334	335
1 Inslee	Y	Y	Y
2 Larsen	Y	Y	Y
3 Baird	Y	Y	Y
4 *Hastings*	Y	Y	Y
5 *Nethercutt*	Y	Y	Y
6 Dicks	Y	Y	Y
7 McDermott	Y	Y	Y
8 *Dunn*	Y	Y	Y
9 Smith	Y	Y	Y

WEST VIRGINIA

	333	334	335
1 Mollohan	?	?	?
2 *Capito*	Y	Y	Y
3 Rahall	Y	Y	Y

WISCONSIN

	333	334	335
1 *Ryan*	Y	Y	Y
2 Baldwin	Y	Y	Y
3 Kind	Y	Y	Y
4 Kleczka	Y	Y	Y
5 Barrett	Y	Y	Y
6 *Petri*	Y	Y	Y
7 Obey	Y	Y	Y
8 *Green*	Y	Y	Y
9 *Sensenbrenner*	Y	Y	Y

WYOMING

	333	334	335
AL *Cubin*	Y	Y	Y

Southern states - Ala., Ark., Fla., Ga., Ky., La., Miss., N.C., Okla., S.C., Tenn., Texas, Va.

Key

Y	Voted for (yea).
#	Paired for.
+	Announced for.
N	Voted against (nay).
X	Paired against.
–	Announced against.
P	Voted "present."
C	Voted "present" to avoid possible conflict of interest.
?	Did not vote or otherwise make a position known.

•

Democrats   **Republicans**
Independents

336. HR 1766. Stan Parris Building/Passage. T. Davis, R-Va., motion to suspend the rules and pass the bill that would name a U.S. Postal Service building in Annandale, Va., the "Stan Parris Post Office Building." Motion agreed to 362-0: R 185-0; D 176-0 (ND 125-0, SD 51-0); I 1-0. A two-thirds majority of those present and voting (242 in this case) is required for passage under suspension of the rules. Sept. 10, 2001.

337. HR 1761. Herb Harris Building/Passage. T. Davis, R-Va., motion to suspend the rules and pass the bill that would name a U.S. Postal Service building in Alexandria, Va., the "Herb E. Harris Post Office Building." Motion agreed to 365-0: R 185-0; D 179-0 (ND 127-0, SD 52-0); I 1-0. A two-thirds majority of those present and voting (244 in this case) is required for passage under suspension of the rules. Sept. 10, 2001.

338. H J Res 61. Terrorist Attacks/Passage. Passage of the joint resolution that would express the sense of Congress that the Senate and the House condemn the terrorists who planned and carried out the Sept. 11, 2001, attacks against the United States, as well as their sponsors; extend deepest condolences to the victims and their families; commend the actions of rescue workers, volunteers and officials responding to the scene; commit support of increased resources to eradicate terrorism; and declare Sept. 12, 2001, as a national day of unity and mourning. Passed 408-0: R 211-0; D 195-0 (ND 142-0, SD 53-0); I 2-0. (Under a unanimous consent agreement, following Senate passage of an identical resolution (S J Res 22), the House was considered to have passed the Senate resolution.) Sept. 13, 2001 (in the session that began and the Congressional Record dated Sept. 11).

339. HR 2882. Officer Payments/Passage. Passage of the bill that would require Public Safety Officer Benefit payments to be made to beneficiaries of officers killed or suffering a catastrophic injury within 30 days that a public agency certifies such injuries occurred in the line of duty while responding to the Sept. 11, 2001, attacks. Passed 413-0: R 210-0; D 201-0 (ND 149-0, SD 52-0); I 2-0. Sept. 13, 2001.

340. HR 2884. Attack Victims' Taxes/Passage. Passage of the bill that would lower estate and income tax liability for individuals killed during the Sept. 11, 2001, terrorist attacks against the United States. It would reduce by more than half their estate tax liability. It also would exempt them from paying income taxes in the year they died and exempt assistance money from the Federal Emergency Management Agency. Commercial airline payments of $25,000 to passengers killed also would be exempt from income. Passed 418-0: R 214-0; D 202-0 (ND 148-0, SD 54-0); I 2-0. Sept. 13, 2001.

	336	337	338	339	340
ALABAMA					
1 *Callahan*	Y	Y	Y	Y	Y
2 *Everett*	Y	Y	Y	Y	Y
3 *Riley*	Y	Y	Y	Y	Y
4 *Aderholt*	Y	Y	Y	Y	Y
5 Cramer	Y	Y	Y	Y	Y
6 *Bachus*	Y	Y	Y	Y	Y
7 Hilliard	Y	Y	Y	Y	Y
ALASKA					
AL *Young*	Y	Y	Y	?	Y
ARIZONA					
1 *Flake*	Y	Y	Y	Y	Y
2 Pastor	Y	Y	Y	Y	Y
3 *Stump*	Y	Y	Y	Y	Y
4 *Shadegg*	Y	Y	Y	Y	Y
5 *Kolbe*	Y	Y	Y	Y	Y
6 *Hayworth*	Y	Y	Y	Y	Y
ARKANSAS					
1 Berry	Y	Y	Y	Y	Y
2 Snyder	Y	Y	Y	Y	Y
3 Vacant					
4 Ross	Y	Y	Y	Y	Y
CALIFORNIA					
1 Thompson	Y	Y	Y	Y	Y
2 *Herger*	Y	Y	Y	Y	Y
3 *Ose*	Y	Y	Y	Y	Y
4 *Doolittle*	?	?	Y	Y	Y
5 Matsui	Y	Y	Y	Y	Y
6 Woolsey	Y	Y	Y	Y	Y
7 Miller, George	Y	Y	Y	Y	Y
8 Pelosi	Y	Y	Y	Y	?
9 Lee	Y	Y	Y	Y	Y
10 Tauscher	Y	Y	Y	Y	Y
11 *Pombo*	Y	Y	Y	Y	Y
12 Lantos	?	?	Y	Y	Y
13 Stark	?	?	Y	Y	Y
14 Eshoo	Y	Y	Y	Y	Y
15 Honda	Y	Y	Y	Y	Y
16 Lofgren	Y	Y	Y	Y	Y
17 Farr	Y	Y	Y	Y	Y
18 Condit	Y	Y	Y	Y	Y
19 *Radanovich*	?	?	Y	Y	Y
20 Dooley	Y	Y	Y	Y	Y
21 *Thomas*	Y	Y	Y	Y	Y
22 Capps	Y	Y	Y	Y	Y
23 *Gallegly*	Y	Y	Y	Y	Y
24 Sherman	Y	Y	Y	Y	Y
25 *McKeon*	Y	Y	Y	Y	?
26 Berman	?	?	Y	Y	Y
27 Schiff	Y	Y	Y	Y	Y
28 *Dreier*	Y	Y	Y	Y	Y
29 Waxman	?	?	Y	Y	Y
30 Becerra	Y	Y	Y	Y	Y
31 Solis	Y	Y	Y	Y	Y
32 Watson	Y	Y	Y	Y	Y
33 Roybal-Allard	Y	Y	Y	Y	Y
34 Napolitano	Y	Y	Y	Y	Y
35 Waters	Y	Y	Y	Y	Y
36 Harman	Y	Y	Y	Y	Y
37 Millender-McD.	Y	Y	Y	Y	Y
38 *Horn*	Y	Y	Y	Y	Y

	336	337	338	339	340
39 *Royce*	?	?	?	?	?
40 *Lewis*	Y	Y	Y	Y	Y
41 *Miller, Gary*	Y	?	Y	Y	Y
42 Baca	Y	Y	Y	Y	Y
43 *Calvert*	Y	Y	Y	Y	Y
44 *Bono*	Y	Y	Y	Y	Y
45 *Rohrabacher*	Y	Y	Y	Y	Y
46 Sanchez	Y	Y	Y	Y	Y
47 *Cox*	Y	Y	Y	Y	Y
48 *Issa*	Y	Y	Y	Y	Y
49 Davis	Y	Y	Y	Y	Y
50 Filner	Y	Y	Y	Y	Y
51 *Cunningham*	Y	Y	Y	Y	Y
52 *Hunter*	Y	Y	Y	Y	Y
COLORADO					
1 DeGette	?	Y	Y	Y	Y
2 Udall	Y	Y	Y	Y	Y
3 *McInnis*	Y	Y	Y	Y	Y
4 *Schaffer*	?	?	Y	Y	Y
5 *Hefley*	Y	Y	Y	Y	Y
6 *Tancredo*	Y	Y	Y	Y	Y
CONNECTICUT					
1 Larson	Y	Y	Y	Y	Y
2 *Simmons*	Y	Y	Y	Y	Y
3 DeLauro	Y	Y	Y	Y	Y
4 *Shays*	Y	Y	Y	Y	Y
5 Maloney	Y	Y	Y	Y	Y
6 *Johnson*	Y	Y	Y	Y	Y
DELAWARE					
AL *Castle*	Y	Y	Y	Y	Y
FLORIDA					
1 Vacant					
2 Boyd	Y	Y	Y	Y	Y
3 Brown	Y	Y	Y	Y	Y
4 *Crenshaw*	?	?	Y	Y	Y
5 Thurman	Y	Y	Y	Y	Y
6 *Stearns*	?	?	Y	Y	Y
7 *Mica*	?	?	Y	Y	Y
8 *Keller*	Y	Y	Y	Y	Y
9 *Bilirakis*	Y	Y	Y	Y	Y
10 *Young*	Y	Y	Y	Y	Y
11 Davis	Y	Y	Y	Y	Y
12 *Putnam*	Y	Y	Y	Y	Y
13 *Miller*	?	?	Y	Y	Y
14 *Goss*	Y	Y	Y	Y	Y
15 *Weldon*	Y	Y	Y	Y	Y
16 *Foley*	?	?	Y	Y	Y
17 Meek	Y	Y	Y	Y	Y
18 *Ros-Lehtinen*	Y	Y	Y	Y	Y
19 Wexler	Y	Y	Y	Y	Y
20 Deutsch	?	?	Y	Y	Y
21 *Diaz-Balart*	Y	Y	Y	Y	Y
22 *Shaw*	Y	Y	Y	Y	Y
23 Hastings	Y	Y	Y	Y	Y
GEORGIA					
1 *Kingston*	Y	Y	Y	Y	Y
2 Bishop	Y	Y	Y	Y	Y
3 *Collins*	Y	Y	?	Y	Y
4 McKinney	Y	Y	Y	Y	Y
5 Lewis	Y	Y	Y	Y	Y
6 *Isakson*	Y	Y	Y	Y	Y
7 *Barr*	?	?	Y	Y	Y
8 *Chambliss*	?	?	Y	Y	Y
9 *Deal*	?	?	Y	Y	Y
10 *Norwood*	Y	Y	Y	Y	Y
11 *Linder*	Y	Y	Y	Y	Y
HAWAII					
1 Abercrombie	Y	Y	Y	Y	Y
2 Mink	Y	Y	Y	Y	Y
IDAHO					
1 *Otter*	Y	Y	Y	Y	Y
2 *Simpson*	Y	Y	Y	Y	Y
ILLINOIS					
1 Rush	Y	Y	Y	Y	Y
2 Jackson	Y	Y	Y	Y	Y
3 Lipinski	?	?	?	?	?
4 Gutierrez	?	?	Y	Y	Y
5 Blagojevich	?	?	Y	Y	Y
6 *Hyde*	Y	Y	Y	Y	Y
7 Davis	?	?	?	?	?
8 *Crane*	Y	Y	Y	Y	Y
9 Schakowsky	Y	Y	Y	Y	Y
10 *Kirk*	Y	Y	Y	Y	Y
11 *Weller*	Y	Y	Y	Y	Y
12 Costello	Y	Y	Y	Y	Y
13 *Biggert*	Y	Y	Y	Y	Y

ND Northern Democrats   SD Southern Democrats

	336	337	338	339	340
14 Hastert					
15 Johnson	Y	Y	Y	Y	Y
16 Manzullo	Y	Y	Y	Y	Y
17 Evans	?	Y	Y	Y	Y
18 LaHood	Y	Y	Y	Y	Y
19 Phelps	Y	Y	Y	Y	Y
20 Shimkus	Y	Y	Y	Y	Y
INDIANA					
1 Visclosky	Y	Y	Y	Y	Y
2 Pence	Y	Y	Y	Y	Y
3 Roemer	Y	Y	Y	Y	Y
4 Souder	?	?	?	Y	Y
5 Buyer	Y	Y	Y	Y	Y
6 Burton	Y	Y	Y	Y	Y
7 Kerns	Y	Y	Y	Y	Y
8 Hostettler	Y	Y	Y	Y	Y
9 Hill	Y	Y	Y	Y	Y
10 Carson	?	?	Y	Y	Y
IOWA					
1 Leach	Y	Y	Y	Y	Y
2 Nussle	Y	Y	Y	Y	Y
3 Boswell	Y	Y	Y	Y	Y
4 Ganske	?	?	Y	Y	Y
5 Latham	Y	Y	Y	Y	Y
KANSAS					
1 Moran	Y	Y	Y	Y	Y
2 Ryun	Y	Y	Y	Y	Y
3 Moore	Y	Y	Y	Y	Y
4 Tiahrt	Y	Y	Y	Y	Y
KENTUCKY					
1 Whitfield	Y	Y	Y	Y	Y
2 Lewis	Y	Y	Y	Y	Y
3 Northup	Y	Y	Y	Y	Y
4 Lucas	Y	Y	Y	Y	Y
5 Rogers	Y	Y	Y	Y	Y
6 Fletcher	Y	Y	Y	Y	Y
LOUISIANA					
1 Vitter	Y	Y	Y	Y	Y
2 Jefferson	Y	Y	Y	Y	Y
3 Tauzin	?	?	Y	Y	Y
4 McCrery	Y	Y	Y	Y	Y
5 Cooksey	?	?	Y	Y	Y
6 Baker	Y	Y	Y	Y	Y
7 John	Y	Y	Y	Y	Y
MAINE					
1 Allen	Y	Y	Y	Y	Y
2 Baldacci	Y	Y	Y	Y	Y
MARYLAND					
1 Gilchrest	Y	Y	Y	Y	Y
2 Ehrlich	Y	Y	Y	Y	Y
3 Cardin	Y	Y	Y	Y	Y
4 Wynn	Y	Y	Y	Y	Y
5 Hoyer	Y	Y	Y	Y	Y
6 Bartlett	Y	Y	Y	Y	Y
7 Cummings	Y	Y	Y	Y	Y
8 Morella	Y	Y	Y	Y	Y
MASSACHUSETTS					
1 Olver	Y	Y	Y	Y	Y
2 Neal	?	?	Y	Y	Y
3 McGovern	Y	Y	Y	Y	Y
4 Frank	Y	Y	Y	Y	Y
5 Meehan	Y	Y	Y	Y	Y
6 Tierney	Y	Y	Y	Y	Y
7 Markey	Y	Y	Y	Y	Y
8 Capuano	Y	Y	Y	Y	Y
9 Vacant					
10 Delahunt	Y	Y	Y	Y	Y
MICHIGAN					
1 Stupak	?	?	Y	Y	Y
2 Hoekstra	Y	Y	Y	Y	Y
3 Ehlers	Y	Y	Y	Y	Y
4 Camp	?	?	Y	Y	Y
5 Barcia	?	?	Y	Y	Y
6 Upton	Y	Y	Y	Y	Y
7 Smith	Y	Y	Y	Y	Y
8 Rogers	Y	Y	Y	Y	Y
9 Kildee	Y	Y	Y	Y	Y
10 Bonior	Y	Y	Y	Y	Y
11 Knollenberg	?	?	Y	Y	Y
12 Levin	Y	Y	Y	Y	Y
13 Rivers	Y	Y	Y	Y	Y
14 Conyers	?	?	?	?	?
15 Kilpatrick	?	?	?	?	?
16 Dingell	Y	Y	Y	Y	Y

	336	337	338	339	340
MINNESOTA					
1 Gutknecht	Y	Y	Y	Y	Y
2 Kennedy	Y	Y	Y	Y	Y
3 Ramstad	Y	Y	Y	Y	Y
4 McCollum	Y	Y	Y	Y	Y
5 Sabo	Y	Y	Y	Y	Y
6 Luther	Y	Y	Y	Y	Y
7 Peterson	Y	Y	Y	Y	Y
8 Oberstar	Y	Y	Y	Y	Y
MISSISSIPPI					
1 Wicker	Y	Y	Y	Y	Y
2 Thompson	Y	Y	Y	Y	Y
3 Pickering	Y	Y	Y	Y	Y
4 Shows	Y	Y	Y	Y	Y
5 Taylor	Y	Y	Y	Y	Y
MISSOURI					
1 Clay	Y	Y	Y	Y	Y
2 Akin	Y	Y	Y	Y	Y
3 Gephardt	Y	Y	Y	Y	Y
4 Skelton	Y	Y	Y	Y	Y
5 McCarthy	Y	Y	?	Y	Y
6 Graves	Y	Y	Y	Y	Y
7 Blunt	Y	Y	Y	Y	Y
8 Emerson	?	?	Y	Y	Y
9 Hulshof	Y	Y	Y	Y	Y
MONTANA					
AL Rehberg	Y	Y	Y	Y	Y
NEBRASKA					
1 Bereuter	Y	Y	Y	Y	Y
2 Terry	?	?	Y	Y	Y
3 Osborne	Y	Y	Y	Y	Y
NEVADA					
1 Berkley	Y	Y	Y	Y	Y
2 Gibbons	Y	Y	Y	Y	Y
NEW HAMPSHIRE					
1 Sununu	Y	Y	Y	Y	Y
2 Bass	Y	Y	Y	Y	Y
NEW JERSEY					
1 Andrews	Y	Y	Y	Y	Y
2 LoBiondo	Y	Y	Y	Y	Y
3 Saxton	Y	Y	?	?	?
4 Smith	Y	Y	Y	Y	Y
5 Roukema	?	?	Y	Y	Y
6 Pallone	Y	Y	Y	Y	Y
7 Ferguson	?	?	Y	Y	Y
8 Pascrell	Y	Y	Y	Y	Y
9 Rothman	Y	Y	Y	Y	Y
10 Payne	?	?	?	Y	Y
11 Frelinghuysen	Y	Y	Y	Y	Y
12 Holt	Y	Y	Y	Y	Y
13 Menendez	Y	Y	Y	Y	Y
NEW MEXICO					
1 Wilson	Y	Y	Y	Y	Y
2 Skeen	Y	Y	Y	Y	Y
3 Udall	Y	Y	Y	Y	Y
NEW YORK					
1 Grucci	?	?	Y	Y	Y
2 Israel	Y	Y	Y	Y	Y
3 King	Y	Y	Y	Y	Y
4 McCarthy	Y	Y	Y	Y	Y
5 Ackerman	?	?	Y	Y	Y
6 Meeks	?	?	?	?	?
7 Crowley	?	?	?	Y	Y
8 Nadler	Y	Y	?	Y	Y
9 Weiner	?	?	?	Y	Y
10 Towns	?	?	Y	Y	Y
11 Owens	?	?	Y	Y	Y
12 Velázquez	?	?	Y	Y	Y
13 Fossella	?	?	?	Y	Y
14 Maloney	Y	Y	?	?	?
15 Rangel	?	?	?	?	?
16 Serrano	?	?	?	Y	Y
17 Engel	?	?	Y	Y	Y
18 Lowey	?	?	Y	Y	Y
19 Kelly	Y	Y	?	?	?
20 Gilman	Y	Y	Y	Y	Y
21 McNulty	Y	Y	Y	Y	Y
22 Sweeney	?	?	Y	Y	Y
23 Boehlert	Y	Y	Y	Y	Y
24 McHugh	Y	Y	Y	Y	Y
25 Walsh	Y	Y	Y	Y	Y
26 Hinchey	Y	Y	Y	Y	Y
27 Reynolds	Y	Y	Y	Y	Y
28 Slaughter	Y	Y	Y	Y	Y
29 LaFalce	Y	Y	Y	Y	Y

	336	337	338	339	340
30 Quinn	Y	Y	Y	Y	Y
31 Houghton	Y	Y	Y	Y	Y
NORTH CAROLINA					
1 Clayton	Y	Y	Y	Y	Y
2 Etheridge	Y	Y	Y	Y	Y
3 Jones	Y	Y	Y	Y	Y
4 Price	?	?	Y	Y	Y
5 Burr	Y	Y	Y	Y	Y
6 Coble	Y	Y	Y	Y	Y
7 McIntyre	Y	Y	Y	Y	Y
8 Hayes	Y	Y	Y	Y	Y
9 Myrick	Y	Y	Y	Y	Y
10 Ballenger	Y	Y	Y	Y	Y
11 Taylor	?	?	Y	?	Y
12 Watt	Y	Y	Y	?	Y
NORTH DAKOTA					
AL Pomeroy	Y	Y	Y	Y	Y
OHIO					
1 Chabot	Y	Y	Y	Y	Y
2 Portman	Y	Y	Y	Y	Y
3 Hall	Y	Y	Y	Y	Y
4 Oxley	Y	Y	Y	Y	Y
5 Gillmor	Y	Y	Y	Y	Y
6 Strickland	Y	Y	Y	Y	Y
7 Hobson	Y	Y	Y	Y	Y
8 Boehner	?	?	Y	Y	Y
9 Kaptur	Y	Y	Y	Y	Y
10 Kucinich	Y	Y	Y	Y	Y
11 Jones	Y	Y	Y	Y	Y
12 Tiberi	Y	Y	Y	Y	Y
13 Brown	Y	Y	Y	Y	Y
14 Sawyer	Y	Y	Y	Y	Y
15 Pryce	Y	Y	Y	Y	Y
16 Regula	Y	Y	Y	Y	Y
17 Traficant	Y	Y	Y	Y	Y
18 Ney	Y	Y	Y	Y	Y
19 LaTourette	?	?	Y	Y	Y
OKLAHOMA					
1 Largent	?	?	?	?	?
2 Carson	Y	Y	Y	Y	Y
3 Watkins	Y	Y	Y	Y	Y
4 Watts	Y	Y	Y	Y	Y
5 Istook	?	?	Y	Y	Y
6 Lucas	Y	Y	Y	Y	Y
OREGON					
1 Wu	Y	Y	Y	Y	Y
2 Walden	Y	Y	Y	Y	Y
3 Blumenauer	Y	Y	Y	Y	Y
4 DeFazio	?	?	Y	Y	Y
5 Hooley	Y	Y	Y	Y	Y
PENNSYLVANIA					
1 Brady	?	?	Y	Y	Y
2 Fattah	Y	Y	Y	Y	Y
3 Borski	Y	Y	Y	Y	Y
4 Hart	Y	Y	Y	Y	Y
5 Peterson	Y	Y	Y	Y	Y
6 Holden	Y	Y	Y	Y	Y
7 Weldon	?	?	?	Y	Y
8 Greenwood	Y	Y	Y	Y	Y
9 Shuster, Bill	Y	Y	Y	Y	Y
10 Sherwood	Y	Y	Y	Y	Y
11 Kanjorski	Y	Y	Y	Y	Y
12 Murtha	Y	Y	?	Y	Y
13 Hoeffel	Y	Y	Y	Y	Y
14 Coyne	Y	Y	Y	Y	Y
15 Toomey	Y	Y	Y	Y	Y
16 Pitts	Y	Y	Y	Y	Y
17 Gekas	Y	Y	Y	Y	Y
18 Doyle	Y	Y	Y	Y	Y
19 Platts	Y	Y	Y	Y	Y
20 Mascara	Y	Y	Y	Y	Y
21 English	Y	Y	Y	Y	Y
RHODE ISLAND					
1 Kennedy	Y	Y	Y	Y	Y
2 Langevin	Y	Y	Y	Y	Y
SOUTH CAROLINA					
1 Brown	Y	Y	Y	Y	Y
2 Vacant					
3 Graham	Y	Y	Y	Y	Y
4 DeMint	Y	Y	Y	Y	Y
5 Spratt	Y	Y	Y	Y	Y
6 Clyburn	Y	Y	Y	Y	Y
SOUTH DAKOTA					
AL Thune	Y	Y	Y	Y	Y

	336	337	338	339	340
TENNESSEE					
1 Jenkins	Y	Y	Y	Y	Y
2 Duncan	Y	Y	Y	Y	Y
3 Wamp	Y	Y	Y	Y	Y
4 Hilleary	Y	Y	Y	Y	Y
6 Clement	Y	Y	?	Y	Y
7 Bryant	Y	Y	Y	Y	Y
8 Tanner	Y	Y	Y	Y	Y
9 Ford	Y	Y	Y	Y	Y
TEXAS					
1 Sandlin	Y	Y	Y	Y	Y
2 Turner	Y	Y	Y	Y	Y
3 Johnson, Sam	Y	Y	Y	Y	Y
4 Hall	Y	Y	Y	Y	Y
5 Sessions	Y	Y	Y	Y	Y
6 Barton	?	?	Y	Y	Y
7 Culberson	Y	Y	Y	Y	Y
8 Brady	Y	Y	Y	Y	Y
9 Lampson	Y	Y	Y	Y	Y
10 Doggett	Y	Y	Y	Y	Y
11 Edwards	Y	Y	Y	Y	Y
12 Granger	Y	Y	Y	Y	Y
13 Thornberry	Y	Y	Y	Y	Y
14 Paul	Y	Y	Y	Y	Y
15 Hinojosa	Y	Y	Y	Y	Y
16 Reyes	Y	Y	Y	Y	Y
17 Stenholm	Y	Y	Y	Y	Y
18 Jackson-Lee	Y	Y	Y	Y	Y
19 Combest	Y	Y	Y	Y	Y
20 Gonzalez	Y	Y	Y	Y	Y
21 Smith	?	?	Y	Y	Y
22 DeLay	Y	Y	Y	Y	Y
23 Bonilla	Y	Y	Y	Y	Y
24 Frost	Y	Y	Y	Y	Y
25 Bentsen	?	?	Y	Y	Y
26 Armey	Y	Y	Y	Y	Y
27 Ortiz	Y	Y	Y	?	Y
28 Rodriguez	Y	Y	Y	Y	Y
29 Green	Y	Y	Y	Y	Y
30 Johnson, E.B.	Y	Y	Y	Y	Y
UTAH					
1 Hansen	Y	Y	Y	Y	Y
2 Matheson	Y	Y	Y	Y	Y
3 Cannon	Y	Y	Y	Y	Y
VERMONT					
AL Sanders	?	?	Y	Y	Y
VIRGINIA					
1 Davis, Jo Ann	Y	Y	Y	Y	Y
2 Schrock	Y	Y	Y	Y	Y
3 Scott	Y	Y	Y	Y	Y
4 Forbes	Y	Y	Y	Y	Y
5 Goode	Y	Y	Y	Y	Y
6 Goodlatte	Y	Y	Y	Y	Y
7 Cantor	Y	Y	Y	Y	Y
8 Moran	Y	Y	Y	Y	Y
9 Boucher	Y	Y	Y	Y	Y
10 Wolf	Y	Y	Y	Y	Y
11 Davis, T.	Y	Y	Y	Y	Y
WASHINGTON					
1 Inslee	Y	Y	Y	Y	Y
2 Larsen	Y	Y	Y	Y	Y
3 Baird	Y	Y	Y	Y	Y
4 Hastings	Y	Y	Y	Y	Y
5 Nethercutt	Y	Y	Y	Y	Y
6 Dicks	Y	Y	?	Y	Y
7 McDermott	Y	Y	Y	Y	Y
8 Dunn	Y	Y	Y	Y	Y
9 Smith	Y	Y	Y	Y	Y
WEST VIRGINIA					
1 Mollohan	?	?	Y	Y	Y
2 Capito	Y	Y	Y	Y	Y
3 Rahall	?	?	Y	Y	Y
WISCONSIN					
1 Ryan	Y	Y	Y	Y	Y
2 Baldwin	Y	Y	Y	Y	Y
3 Kind	Y	Y	Y	Y	Y
4 Kleczka	Y	Y	Y	Y	Y
5 Barrett	Y	Y	Y	Y	Y
6 Petri	Y	Y	Y	Y	Y
7 Obey	Y	Y	Y	Y	Y
8 Green	Y	Y	Y	Y	Y
9 Sensenbrenner	Y	Y	Y	Y	Y
WYOMING					
AL Cubin	Y	Y	Y	Y	Y

Southern states - Ala., Ark., Fla., Ga., Ky., La., Miss., N.C., Okla., S.C., Tenn., Texas, Va.

Key

Y	Voted for (yea).
#	Paired for.
+	Announced for.
N	Voted against (nay).
X	Paired against.
−	Announced against.
P	Voted "present."
C	Voted "present" to avoid possible conflict of interest.
?	Did not vote or otherwise make a position known.

Democrats   **Republicans**
Independents

341. HR 2888. Emergency Supplemental Appropriations/ Passage. Passage of the bill that would provide $40 billion in emergency supplemental appropriations available for disaster assistance, anti-terrorism initiatives and recovery assistance from the terrorist attacks on the United States that occurred Sept. 11, 2001. Passed 422-0: R 215-0; D 205-0 (ND 151-0, SD 54-0); I 2-0. A "yea" was a vote in support of the president's position. Sept. 14, 2001.

342. H J Res 64. Use of Force Authorization/Passage. Passage of the joint resolution that would authorize the president to use all necessary and appropriate force against the nations, organizations or people that he determines planned, authorized, committed or aided the terrorist attacks that occurred on Sept. 11, 2001, or that harbored such organizations or people, to prevent future acts of terrorism against the United States. Passed 420-1: R 214-0; D 204-1 (ND 150-1, SD 54-0); I 2-0. A "yea" was a vote in support of the president's position. (Under a unanimous consent agreement, the House subsequently passed an identical Senate-passed resolution (S J Res 23), clearing the measure for the president.) Sept. 14, 2001.

343. HR 2657. D.C. Family Court/Passage. Morella, R-Md., motion to suspend the rules and pass the bill that would re-designate the D.C. Superior Court's Family Division as the Family Court and promote recruitment and retention of experienced judges. The bill would extend the terms of new judges from one year to five, require ongoing training, establish a "one family, one judge" rule and expedite existing case backlogs. A two-thirds majority of those present and voting (272 in this case) is required for passage under suspension of the rules. Motion agreed to 408-0: R 208-0; D 198-0 (ND 145-0, SD 53-0); I 2-0. Sept. 20, 2001.

	341	342	343
ALABAMA			
1 *Callahan*	Y	Y	Y
2 *Everett*	Y	Y	Y
3 *Riley*	Y	Y	Y
4 *Aderholt*	Y	Y	Y
5 Cramer	Y	Y	Y
6 *Bachus*	Y	Y	Y
7 Hilliard	Y	Y	Y
ALASKA			
AL *Young*	Y	Y	Y
ARIZONA			
1 *Flake*	Y	Y	Y
2 Pastor	Y	Y	Y
3 *Stump*	Y	Y	Y
4 *Shadegg*	Y	Y	Y
5 *Kolbe*	Y	Y	Y
6 *Hayworth*	Y	Y	Y
ARKANSAS			
1 Berry	Y	Y	Y
2 Snyder	Y	Y	Y
3 Vacant			
4 Ross	Y	Y	Y
CALIFORNIA			
1 Thompson	Y	Y	Y
2 *Herger*	Y	Y	Y
3 *Ose*	Y	Y	Y
4 *Doolittle*	Y	Y	Y
5 Matsui	Y	Y	Y
6 Woolsey	Y	Y	Y
7 Miller, George	Y	Y	Y
8 Pelosi	Y	Y	Y
9 Lee	Y	N	Y
10 Tauscher	Y	Y	Y
11 *Pombo*	Y	Y	Y
12 Lantos	Y	Y	Y
13 Stark	Y	Y	Y
14 Eshoo	Y	Y	Y
15 Honda	Y	Y	Y
16 Lofgren	Y	Y	Y
17 Farr	?	?	Y
18 Condit	Y	Y	Y
19 *Radanovich*	Y	Y	Y
20 Dooley	Y	Y	Y
21 *Thomas*	Y	Y	Y
22 Capps	Y	Y	Y
23 *Gallegly*	Y	Y	Y
24 Sherman	Y	Y	Y
25 *McKeon*	Y	Y	Y
26 Berman	Y	Y	?
27 Schiff	Y	Y	Y
28 *Dreier*	Y	Y	Y
29 Waxman	Y	Y	Y
30 Becerra	Y	Y	Y
31 Solis	Y	Y	Y
32 Watson	Y	Y	Y
33 Roybal-Allard	Y	Y	Y
34 Napolitano	Y	Y	Y
35 Waters	Y	Y	Y
36 Harman	Y	Y	Y
37 Millender-McD.	Y	Y	Y
38 Horn	Y	Y	Y

	341	342	343
39 *Royce*	Y	Y	Y
40 *Lewis*	Y	Y	Y
41 *Miller, Gary*	Y	Y	Y
42 Baca	Y	Y	Y
43 *Calvert*	Y	Y	Y
44 *Bono*	Y	Y	Y
45 *Rohrabacher*	Y	Y	Y
46 Sanchez	Y	?	Y
47 *Cox*	Y	Y	Y
48 *Issa*	Y	Y	Y
49 Davis	Y	Y	Y
50 Filner	Y	Y	Y
51 *Cunningham*	Y	Y	Y
52 *Hunter*	Y	Y	Y
COLORADO			
1 DeGette	Y	Y	?
2 Udall	Y	Y	Y
3 *McInnis*	Y	Y	?
4 *Schaffer*	Y	Y	?
5 *Hefley*	Y	Y	Y
6 *Tancredo*	Y	Y	Y
CONNECTICUT			
1 Larson	Y	Y	Y
2 *Simmons*	Y	Y	Y
3 DeLauro	Y	Y	Y
4 *Shays*	Y	Y	Y
5 Maloney	Y	Y	Y
6 *Johnson*	Y	Y	Y
DELAWARE			
AL *Castle*	Y	Y	Y
FLORIDA			
1 Vacant			
2 Boyd	Y	Y	Y
3 Brown	Y	Y	Y
4 *Crenshaw*	Y	Y	Y
5 Thurman	Y	Y	Y
6 *Stearns*	Y	Y	Y
7 *Mica*	Y	Y	Y
8 *Keller*	Y	Y	Y
9 *Bilirakis*	Y	Y	Y
10 *Young*	Y	Y	Y
11 Davis	Y	Y	Y
12 *Putnam*	Y	Y	Y
13 *Miller*	Y	Y	Y
14 *Goss*	Y	Y	Y
15 *Weldon*	Y	Y	Y
16 *Foley*	Y	Y	Y
17 Meek	Y	Y	Y
18 *Ros-Lehtinen*	Y	Y	Y
19 Wexler	Y	Y	Y
20 Deutsch	Y	Y	Y
21 *Diaz-Balart*	Y	Y	Y
22 *Shaw*	Y	Y	Y
23 Hastings	Y	Y	Y
GEORGIA			
1 *Kingston*	Y	Y	Y
2 Bishop	Y	Y	Y
3 *Collins*	Y	Y	Y
4 McKinney	Y	Y	Y
5 Lewis	Y	Y	Y
6 *Isakson*	Y	Y	Y
7 *Barr*	Y	Y	Y
8 *Chambliss*	Y	Y	Y
9 *Deal*	Y	Y	?
10 *Norwood*	Y	Y	Y
11 *Linder*	?	Y	Y
HAWAII			
1 Abercrombie	Y	Y	Y
2 Mink	Y	Y	Y
IDAHO			
1 *Otter*	Y	Y	Y
2 *Simpson*	Y	Y	Y
ILLINOIS			
1 Rush	Y	Y	?
2 Jackson	Y	Y	Y
3 Lipinski	?	?	Y
4 Gutierrez	Y	Y	Y
5 Blagojevich	Y	Y	Y
6 *Hyde*	Y	Y	Y
7 Davis	+	Y	Y
8 *Crane*	Y	Y	Y
9 Schakowsky	Y	Y	Y
10 *Kirk*	Y	Y	Y
11 *Weller*	Y	Y	Y
12 Costello	Y	Y	Y
13 *Biggert*	Y	Y	Y

ND Northern Democrats   SD Southern Democrats

WWW.CQ.COM

	341	342	343
14 Hastert	Y	Y	
15 Johnson	Y	Y	Y
16 Manzullo	Y	Y	Y
17 Evans	Y	Y	Y
18 LaHood	Y	Y	Y
19 Phelps	Y	Y	Y
20 Shimkus	Y	Y	Y

INDIANA

	341	342	343
1 Visclosky	Y	Y	Y
2 Pence	Y	Y	Y
3 Roemer	Y	Y	Y
4 Souder	Y	Y	Y
5 Buyer	Y	Y	Y
6 Burton	Y	Y	?
7 Kerns	Y	Y	Y
8 Hostettler	Y	Y	?
9 Hill	Y	Y	Y
10 Carson	Y	Y	Y

IOWA

	341	342	343
1 Leach	Y	Y	Y
2 Nussle	Y	Y	Y
3 Boswell	Y	Y	Y
4 Ganske	Y	Y	Y
5 Latham	Y	Y	Y

KANSAS

	341	342	343
1 Moran	Y	Y	Y
2 Ryun	Y	Y	Y
3 Moore	Y	Y	Y
4 Tiahrt	Y	Y	Y

KENTUCKY

	341	342	343
1 Whitfield	Y	Y	Y
2 Lewis	Y	Y	Y
3 Northup	Y	Y	Y
4 Lucas	Y	Y	Y
5 Rogers	Y	Y	Y
6 Fletcher	Y	Y	Y

LOUISIANA

	341	342	343
1 Vitter	Y	Y	Y
2 Jefferson	Y	Y	Y
3 Tauzin	Y	Y	Y
4 McCrery	Y	Y	Y
5 Cooksey	Y	Y	Y
6 Baker	Y	Y	?
7 John	Y	Y	Y

MAINE

	341	342	343
1 Allen	Y	Y	Y
2 Baldacci	Y	Y	Y

MARYLAND

	341	342	343
1 Gilchrest	Y	Y	Y
2 Ehrlich	Y	Y	Y
3 Cardin	Y	Y	Y
4 Wynn	Y	Y	Y
5 Hoyer	Y	Y	Y
6 Bartlett	Y	Y	Y
7 Cummings	Y	Y	Y
8 Morella	Y	Y	Y

MASSACHUSETTS

	341	342	343
1 Olver	Y	Y	Y
2 Neal	Y	Y	Y
3 McGovern	Y	Y	Y
4 Frank	Y	Y	Y
5 Meehan	Y	Y	Y
6 Tierney	Y	Y	Y
7 Markey	Y	Y	Y
8 Capuano	Y	Y	Y
9 Vacant			
10 Delahunt	Y	Y	Y

MICHIGAN

	341	342	343
1 Stupak	Y	Y	?
2 Hoekstra	Y	Y	Y
3 Ehlers	Y	Y	Y
4 Camp	Y	Y	Y
5 Barcia	Y	Y	Y
6 Upton	Y	Y	Y
7 Smith	Y	Y	Y
8 Rogers	Y	Y	Y
9 Kildee	Y	Y	Y
10 Bonlor	Y	Y	Y
11 Knollenberg	Y	Y	Y
12 Levin	Y	Y	Y
13 Rivers	Y	Y	Y
14 Conyers	?	?	Y
15 Kilpatrick	+	?	Y
16 Dingell	Y	Y	?

MINNESOTA

	341	342	343
1 Gutknecht	Y	Y	Y
2 Kennedy	Y	Y	Y
3 Ramstad	Y	Y	Y
4 McCollum	Y	Y	Y
5 Sabo	Y	Y	Y
6 Luther	Y	Y	Y
7 Peterson	Y	Y	Y
8 Oberstar	Y	Y	Y

MISSISSIPPI

	341	342	343
1 Wicker	Y	Y	Y
2 Thompson	Y	Y	Y
3 Pickering	Y	Y	Y
4 Shows	Y	Y	Y
5 Taylor	Y	Y	Y

MISSOURI

	341	342	343
1 Clay	Y	Y	?
2 Akin	Y	Y	Y
3 Gephardt	Y	Y	Y
4 Skelton	Y	Y	Y
5 McCarthy	Y	Y	Y
6 Graves	Y	Y	Y
7 Blunt	Y	Y	Y
8 Emerson	Y	Y	Y
9 Hulshof	Y	Y	Y

MONTANA

	341	342	343
AL Rehberg	Y	Y	Y

NEBRASKA

	341	342	343
1 Bereuter	Y	Y	Y
2 Terry	Y	Y	Y
3 Osborne	Y	Y	Y

NEVADA

	341	342	343
1 Berkley	Y	Y	Y
2 Gibbons	Y	Y	Y

NEW HAMPSHIRE

	341	342	343
1 Sununu	Y	Y	Y
2 Bass	Y	Y	Y

NEW JERSEY

	341	342	343
1 Andrews	Y	Y	Y
2 LoBiondo	Y	Y	Y
3 Saxton	?	?	Y
4 Smith	Y	Y	Y
5 Roukema	Y	Y	Y
6 Pallone	Y	Y	Y
7 Ferguson	Y	Y	Y
8 Pascrell	Y	Y	Y
9 Rothman	Y	Y	Y
10 Payne	Y	Y	Y
11 Frelinghuysen	Y	Y	Y
12 Holt	Y	Y	Y
13 Menendez	Y	Y	Y

NEW MEXICO

	341	342	343
1 Wilson	Y	?	Y
2 Skeen	Y	Y	Y
3 Udall	Y	Y	Y

NEW YORK

	341	342	343
1 Grucci	Y	Y	Y
2 Israel	Y	Y	Y
3 King	Y	?	?
4 McCarthy	Y	Y	Y
5 Ackerman	Y	Y	Y
6 Meeks	Y	Y	Y
7 Crowley	Y	Y	Y
8 Nadler	Y	Y	Y
9 Weiner	Y	Y	Y
10 Towns	Y	Y	?
11 Owens	Y	Y	Y
12 Velázquez	Y	Y	Y
13 Fossella	Y	Y	Y
14 Maloney	Y	Y	Y
15 Rangel	Y	Y	Y
16 Serrano	Y	Y	Y
17 Engel	Y	Y	Y
18 Lowey	Y	Y	Y
19 Kelly	Y	Y	Y
20 Gilman	Y	Y	Y
21 McNulty	Y	Y	Y
22 Sweeney	Y	Y	Y
23 Doehlert	Y	Y	Y
24 McHugh	Y	Y	Y
25 Walsh	Y	Y	Y
26 Hinchey	Y	Y	Y
27 Reynolds	Y	Y	Y
28 Slaughter	Y	Y	Y
29 LaFalce	Y	Y	Y

	341	342	343
30 Quinn	Y	Y	Y
31 Houghton	Y	Y	Y

NORTH CAROLINA

	341	342	343
1 Clayton	Y	Y	Y
2 Etheridge	Y	Y	Y
3 Jones	Y	Y	Y
4 Price	Y	Y	Y
5 Burr	Y	Y	Y
6 Coble	Y	Y	Y
7 McIntyre	Y	Y	Y
8 Hayes	Y	Y	Y
9 Myrick	Y	Y	Y
10 Ballenger	?	?	Y
11 Taylor	Y	Y	Y
12 Watt	Y	Y	Y

NORTH DAKOTA

	341	342	343
AL Pomeroy	Y	Y	Y

OHIO

	341	342	343
1 Chabot	Y	Y	Y
2 Portman	Y	Y	Y
3 Hall	Y	Y	Y
4 Oxley	Y	Y	Y
5 Gillmor	Y	Y	?
6 Strickland	Y	Y	Y
7 Hobson	Y	Y	Y
8 Boehner	Y	Y	Y
9 Kaptur	Y	Y	Y
10 Kucinich	Y	Y	Y
11 Jones	Y	Y	Y
12 Tiberi	Y	Y	Y
13 Brown	Y	Y	Y
14 Sawyer	Y	Y	?
15 Pryce	Y	Y	Y
16 Regula	Y	Y	Y
17 Traficant	Y	Y	Y
18 Ney	Y	Y	Y
19 LaTourette	Y	Y	Y

OKLAHOMA

	341	342	343
1 Largent	Y	Y	Y
2 Carson	Y	Y	Y
3 Watkins	Y	Y	?
4 Watts	Y	Y	Y
5 Istook	Y	Y	Y
6 Lucas	Y	Y	?

OREGON

	341	342	343
1 Wu	Y	Y	Y
2 Walden	Y	Y	Y
3 Blumenauer	Y	Y	Y
4 DeFazio	Y	Y	Y
5 Hooley	Y	Y	Y

PENNSYLVANIA

	341	342	343
1 Brady	Y	Y	Y
2 Fattah	Y	Y	Y
3 Borski	Y	Y	Y
4 Hart	Y	Y	Y
5 Peterson	Y	Y	Y
6 Holden	Y	Y	?
7 Weldon	?	Y	Y
8 Greenwood	Y	Y	Y
9 Shuster, Bill	Y	Y	Y
10 Sherwood	Y	Y	Y
11 Kanjorski	Y	Y	Y
12 Murtha	Y	Y	?
13 Hoeffel	Y	Y	Y
14 Coyne	Y	Y	Y
15 Toomey	Y	Y	Y
16 Pitts	Y	Y	Y
17 Gekas	Y	Y	Y
18 Doyle	Y	Y	Y
19 Platts	Y	Y	Y
20 Mascara	Y	Y	Y
21 English	Y	Y	Y

RHODE ISLAND

	341	342	343
1 Kennedy	Y	Y	Y
2 Langevin	Y	Y	Y

SOUTH CAROLINA

	341	342	343
1 Brown	Y	Y	Y
2 Vacant			
3 Graham	Y	Y	Y
4 DeMint	Y	Y	Y
5 Spratt	Y	Y	Y
6 Clyburn	Y	Y	Y

SOUTH DAKOTA

	341	342	343
AL Thune	Y	Y	Y

TENNESSEE

	341	342	343
1 Jenkins	Y	Y	Y
2 Duncan	Y	Y	Y
3 Wamp	Y	Y	Y
4 Hilleary	Y	Y	Y
5 Clement	Y	Y	Y
6 Gordon	Y	Y	Y
7 Bryant	Y	Y	Y
8 Tanner	Y	Y	Y
9 Ford	Y	Y	Y

TEXAS

	341	342	343
1 Sandlin	Y	Y	Y
2 Turner	Y	Y	Y
3 Johnson, Sam	Y	Y	Y
4 Hall	Y	Y	Y
5 Sessions	Y	Y	Y
6 Barton	Y	Y	Y
7 Culberson	Y	Y	Y
8 Brady	Y	Y	Y
9 Lampson	Y	Y	Y
10 Doggett	Y	Y	Y
11 Edwards	Y	Y	Y
12 Granger	Y	Y	Y
13 Thornberry	Y	Y	Y
14 Paul	Y	Y	Y
15 Hinojosa	Y	Y	Y
16 Reyes	Y	Y	Y
17 Stenholm	Y	Y	Y
18 Jackson-Lee	Y	Y	Y
19 Combest	Y	Y	Y
20 Gonzalez	Y	Y	Y
21 Smith	Y	Y	Y
22 DeLay	Y	Y	Y
23 Bonilla	Y	Y	Y
24 Frost	Y	Y	Y
25 Bentsen	Y	Y	Y
26 Armey	Y	Y	Y
27 Ortiz	Y	Y	+
28 Rodriguez	Y	Y	Y
29 Green	Y	Y	Y
30 Johnson, E.B.	Y	Y	Y

UTAH

	341	342	343
1 Hansen	Y	Y	Y
2 Matheson	Y	Y	Y
3 Cannon	Y	Y	Y

VERMONT

	341	342	343
AL Sanders	Y	Y	Y

VIRGINIA

	341	342	343
1 Davis, Jo Ann	Y	Y	Y
2 Schrock	Y	Y	Y
3 Scott	Y	Y	Y
4 Forbes	Y	Y	Y
5 Goode	Y	Y	Y
6 Goodlatte	Y	Y	Y
7 Cantor	Y	Y	Y
8 Moran	Y	Y	Y
9 Boucher	Y	Y	Y
10 Wolf	Y	Y	Y
11 Davis, T.	Y	Y	Y

WASHINGTON

	341	342	343
1 Inslee	Y	Y	Y
2 Larsen	Y	Y	Y
3 Baird	Y	Y	Y
4 Hastings	Y	Y	Y
5 Nethercutt	Y	Y	Y
6 Dicks	Y	Y	Y
7 McDermott	Y	Y	Y
8 Dunn	Y	Y	Y
9 Smith	Y	Y	Y

WEST VIRGINIA

	341	342	343
1 Mollohan	Y	Y	Y
2 Capito	Y	Y	Y
3 Rahall	Y	Y	Y

WISCONSIN

	341	342	343
1 Ryan	Y	Y	Y
2 Baldwin	Y	Y	Y
3 Kind	Y	Y	+
4 Kleczka	Y	Y	Y
5 Barrett	Y	Y	Y
6 Petri	Y	+	Y
7 Obey	Y	Y	Y
8 Green	Y	Y	Y
9 Sensenbrenner	Y	Y	Y

WYOMING

	341	342	343
AL Cubin	Y	Y	Y

Southern states - Ala., Ark., Fla., Ga., Ky., La., Miss., N.C., Okla., S.C., Tenn., Texas, Va.

344. HR 2904. Fiscal 2002 Military Construction Appropriations/ Passage. Passage of the bill that would provide $10.5 billion for military construction projects including the building of barracks, family housing and medical facilities for fiscal 2002. Passed 401-0: R 207-0; D 192-0 (ND 141-0, SD 51-0); I 2-0. Sept. 21, 2001.

345. HR 2926. Airline Relief/Consideration of the Rule. Adoption of the resolution (H Res 242) that would waive the two-thirds vote requirement for same day consideration of the rule (H Res 244) to provide for House floor consideration of the bill that would provide $5 billion in grants and up to $10 billion in loan guarantees to airline companies to compensate for losses incurred as a result of the Sept. 11, 2001, terrorist attacks. Adopted 303-107: R 209-0; D 93-106 (ND 63-84, SD 30-22); I 1-1. Sept. 21, 2001.

346. HR 2926. Airline Relief/Rule. Adoption of the rule (H Res 244) to provide for House floor consideration of the bill that would provide $5 billion in grants and up to $10 billion in loan guarantees to airline companies to compensate for losses incurred as a result of the Sept. 11, 2001, terrorist attacks. Adopted 285-130: R 210-1; D 74-128 (ND 47-102, SD 27-26); I 1-1. Sept. 21, 2001.

347. HR 2926. Airline Relief/Recommit. DeFazio, D-Ore., motion to recommit the bill to the House Transportation and Infrastructure Committee with instructions to add new sections requiring airlines to cover all health insurance costs for employees for 18 months after separation and ordering that airline passengers be screened by Federal Aviation Administration employees. Motion rejected 174-239: R 0-208; D 173-30 (ND 136-14, SD 37-16); I 1-1. Sept. 21, 2001.

348. HR 2926. Airline Relief/Passage. Passage of the bill that would provide $5 billion in grants and up to $10 billion in loan guarantees to airline companies to compensate for losses incurred as a result of the Sept. 11, 2001, terrorist attacks. The bill would create a federal board to review how the loan guarantees are handled, and establish a fund to compensate victims killed or injured in the attacks, or their survivors. Airlines' liability for damages related to the Sept. 11 attacks would be limited to the amount of insurance coverage they had for such incidents. Passed 356-54: R 201-6; D 155-46 (ND 110-38, SD 45-8); I 0-2. Sept. 21, 2001.

349. HR 717. Muscular Dystrophy Research/Passage. Bilirakis, R-Fla., motion to suspend the rules and pass the bill that would support additional federal research, coordination, information and education on Duchenne and other forms of muscular dystrophy. Motion agreed to 383-0: R 194-0; D 188-0 (ND 136-0, SD 52-0); I 1-0. A two-thirds majority of those present and voting (256 in this case) is required for passage under suspension of the rules. Sept. 24, 2001.

350. H J Res 65. Fiscal 2002 Continuing Appropriations/Passage. Passage of the joint resolution to provide continuing appropriations at current levels through Oct. 16 for all federal departments and programs covered by the fiscal 2002 spending bills not yet enacted. Passed 392-0: R 201-0; D 190-0 (ND 138-0, SD 52-0); I 1-0. Sept. 24, 2001.

351. HR 2944. Fiscal 2002 District of Columbia Appropriations/Rule. Adoption of the rule (H Res 245) to provide for House floor consideration of the bill that would appropriate $398.1 million to the District of Columbia and approve the District's $7.2 billion budget. Adopted 236-183: R 214-3; D 21-179 (ND 7-139, SD 14-40); I 1-1. Sept. 25, 2001.

Key

Y	Voted for (yea).
#	Paired for.
+	Announced for.
N	Voted against (nay).
X	Paired against.
–	Announced against.
P	Voted "present."
C	Voted "present" to avoid possible conflict of interest.
?	Did not vote or otherwise make a position known.

Democrats **Republicans**
Independents

		344	345	346	347	348	349	350	351
ALABAMA									
1	*Callahan*	Y	Y	Y	N	Y	Y	Y	Y
2	*Everett*	Y	Y	Y	N	Y	Y	Y	Y
3	*Riley*	Y	Y	Y	N	Y	Y	Y	Y
4	*Aderholt*	Y	Y	Y	N	Y	Y	Y	Y
5	Cramer	Y	Y	Y	N	Y	Y	Y	Y
6	*Bachus*	Y	Y	Y	N	Y	Y	Y	Y
7	Hilliard	Y	N	N	Y	N	Y	Y	N
ALASKA									
AL	*Young*	Y	Y	Y	N	Y	Y	Y	?
ARIZONA									
1	*Flake*	Y	Y	Y	N	N	Y	Y	Y
2	Pastor	Y	Y	Y	Y	Y	Y	Y	N
3	*Stump*	Y	Y	Y	N	Y	Y	Y	Y
4	*Shadegg*	Y	Y	Y	N	Y	Y	Y	Y
5	*Kolbe*	Y	Y	Y	N	Y	Y	N	Y
6	*Hayworth*	Y	Y	Y	N	Y	?	?	Y
ARKANSAS									
1	Berry	Y	Y	Y	N	Y	Y	Y	Y
2	Snyder	Y	Y	Y	Y	Y	Y	Y	N
3	Vacant								
4	Ross	Y	Y	Y	N	Y	Y	Y	Y
CALIFORNIA									
1	Thompson	Y	Y	N	Y	Y	Y	Y	N
2	*Herger*	Y	Y	Y	N	Y	Y	Y	Y
3	*Ose*	Y	Y	Y	N	Y	Y	Y	Y
4	*Doolittle*	Y	Y	Y	N	Y	?	Y	Y
5	Matsui	Y	Y	Y	Y	Y	Y	Y	N
6	Woolsey	N	N	N	Y	N	Y	Y	N
7	Miller, George	N	N	N	Y	N	Y	Y	N
8	Pelosi	N	N	N	Y	N	Y	Y	N
9	Lee	N	N	N	Y	N	Y	Y	N
10	Tauscher	Y	Y	Y	N	Y	Y	Y	N
11	*Pombo*	Y	Y	Y	N	Y	?	Y	Y
12	Lantos	Y	N	N	Y	N	Y	Y	N
13	Stark	Y	N	N	Y	N	?	?	N
14	Eshoo	Y	N	N	Y	Y	Y	Y	N
15	Honda	Y	Y	Y	Y	Y	Y	Y	N
16	Lofgren	Y	Y	Y	Y	Y	Y	Y	N
17	Farr	N	N	N	Y	Y	Y	Y	?
18	Condit	Y	N	N	Y	N	Y	Y	N
19	*Radanovich*	Y	Y	Y	N	Y	Y	Y	Y
20	Dooley	Y	?	Y	N	Y	Y	Y	Y
21	*Thomas*	Y	Y	Y	N	Y	Y	Y	Y
22	Capps	Y	Y	Y	Y	Y	Y	Y	N
23	*Gallegly*	Y	Y	Y	N	Y	Y	Y	Y
24	Sherman	Y	N	N	Y	Y	Y	Y	N
25	*McKeon*	Y	?	Y	Y	Y	Y	Y	Y
26	Berman	?	?	?	?	?	Y	Y	N
27	Schiff	Y	Y	Y	N	Y	Y	Y	N
28	*Dreier*	Y	Y	Y	N	Y	?	Y	Y
29	Waxman	Y	N	N	Y	N	Y	Y	N
30	Becerra	Y	N	Y	N	N	Y	Y	N
31	Solis	Y	N	N	Y	N	Y	Y	N
32	Watson	Y	Y	Y	Y	Y	Y	Y	?
33	Roybal-Allard	Y	N	N	Y	N	Y	Y	N
34	Napolitano	Y	N	N	Y	Y	Y	Y	N
35	Waters	?	?	N	Y	Y	Y	Y	N
36	Harman	Y	?	N	Y	Y	Y	Y	N
37	Millender-McD.	?	N	N	Y	Y	+	Y	Y
38	*Horn*	Y	Y	Y	N	Y	Y	Y	Y

		344	345	346	347	348	349	350	351
39	*Royce*	Y	Y	Y	N	Y	Y	Y	Y
40	*Lewis*	Y	Y	Y	N	Y	Y	Y	Y
41	*Miller, Gary*	Y	Y	Y	N	Y	?	Y	Y
42	Baca	Y	N	N	Y	Y	Y	Y	N
43	*Calvert*	Y	Y	Y	N	Y	Y	Y	Y
44	*Bono*	Y	Y	Y	N	Y	Y	Y	Y
45	*Rohrabacher*	Y	Y	Y	N	Y	Y	Y	Y
46	Sanchez	Y	Y	Y	?	Y	Y	Y	N
47	*Cox*	Y	?	?	?	?	Y	Y	Y
48	*Issa*	Y	?	?	?	?	Y	Y	Y
49	Davis	Y	N	N	Y	Y	?	?	N
50	Filner	Y	N	N	Y	N	Y	Y	N
51	*Cunningham*	Y	Y	Y	N	Y	Y	Y	Y
52	*Hunter*	Y	Y	Y	N	Y	Y	Y	Y
COLORADO									
1	DeGette	Y	N	N	Y	P	Y	Y	N
2	Udall	Y	N	N	Y	Y	Y	Y	N
3	*McInnis*	Y	Y	Y	N	Y	?	?	Y
4	*Schaffer*	?	?	?	?	?	?	?	Y
5	*Hefley*	Y	?	?	?	?	Y	Y	Y
6	*Tancredo*	Y	Y	Y	N	N	Y	Y	Y
CONNECTICUT									
1	Larson	Y	Y	Y	Y	Y	Y	Y	N
2	*Simmons*	Y	Y	Y	N	Y	Y	Y	Y
3	DeLauro	Y	N	N	Y	Y	Y	Y	N
4	*Shays*	Y	Y	Y	N	Y	Y	Y	Y
5	Maloney	Y	Y	Y	N	Y	Y	Y	Y
6	*Johnson*	Y	Y	Y	N	Y	Y	Y	N
DELAWARE									
AL	*Castle*	Y	?	Y	N	Y	Y	Y	Y
FLORIDA									
1	Vacant								
2	Boyd	Y	N	N	Y	N	Y	Y	N
3	Brown	Y	N	N	Y	N	Y	Y	N
4	*Crenshaw*	Y	Y	Y	N	Y	Y	Y	Y
5	Thurman	Y	N	N	Y	Y	Y	Y	N
6	*Stearns*	Y	Y	Y	N	Y	Y	Y	Y
7	*Mica*	Y	Y	Y	N	Y	Y	Y	Y
8	*Keller*	Y	Y	Y	N	Y	Y	Y	Y
9	*Bilirakis*	Y	Y	Y	N	Y	Y	Y	Y
10	*Young*	Y	Y	Y	N	Y	Y	N	Y
11	Davis	Y	N	N	Y	Y	Y	Y	N
12	*Putnam*	Y	Y	Y	N	Y	Y	Y	Y
13	*Miller*	?	?	?	N	Y	Y	Y	Y
14	Goss	Y	Y	Y	N	Y	Y	Y	Y
15	*Weldon*	+	Y	Y	N	Y	Y	Y	Y
16	*Foley*	Y	Y	Y	N	Y	Y	Y	Y
17	Meek	Y	N	N	Y	Y	Y	Y	N
18	*Ros-Lehtinen*	Y	Y	Y	N	Y	Y	Y	Y
19	Wexler	Y	Y	Y	N	Y	Y	Y	N
20	Deutsch	Y	?	?	?	?	Y	Y	N
21	*Diaz-Balart*	Y	Y	Y	N	Y	Y	Y	Y
22	*Shaw*	Y	Y	Y	N	Y	Y	Y	Y
23	Hastings	Y	N	N	Y	N	Y	Y	N
GEORGIA									
1	*Kingston*	Y	Y	Y	N	Y	Y	Y	Y
2	Bishop	Y	Y	N	Y	Y	Y	Y	Y
3	*Collins*	Y	Y	Y	N	Y	Y	Y	Y
4	McKinney	+	N	N	Y	N	Y	Y	N
5	Lewis	Y	N	N	Y	N	Y	Y	N
6	*Isakson*	Y	Y	Y	N	Y	Y	Y	Y
7	*Barr*	Y	Y	Y	N	Y	Y	Y	Y
8	*Chambliss*	Y	Y	Y	N	Y	Y	Y	Y
9	*Deal*	Y	Y	Y	N	Y	Y	Y	Y
10	*Norwood*	Y	Y	Y	N	Y	Y	Y	Y
11	*Linder*	Y	?	?	?	?	Y	Y	Y
HAWAII									
1	Abercrombie	Y	Y	N	Y	Y	Y	Y	N
2	Mink	Y	N	N	Y	Y	Y	Y	N
IDAHO									
1	*Otter*	Y	Y	Y	N	N	Y	Y	Y
2	*Simpson*	Y	Y	Y	N	Y	Y	Y	Y
ILLINOIS									
1	Rush	Y	N	N	Y	N	Y	?	?
2	Jackson	Y	N	N	Y	N	Y	Y	N
3	Lipinski	Y	N	N	Y	N	Y	Y	N
4	Gutierrez	Y	N	N	Y	N	?	?	N
5	Blagojevich	Y	N	N	Y	N	Y	Y	N
6	*Hyde*	Y	Y	Y	N	Y	Y	Y	Y
7	Davis	Y	N	N	Y	N	Y	Y	N
8	*Crane*	Y	Y	Y	N	Y	Y	Y	Y
9	Schakowsky	Y	N	N	Y	N	Y	Y	N
10	*Kirk*	Y	Y	Y	N	Y	Y	Y	Y
11	*Weller*	Y	Y	Y	N	Y	Y	Y	Y
12	Costello	Y	Y	Y	Y	Y	Y	Y	Y
13	*Biggert*	Y	Y	Y	N	Y	Y	Y	Y

ND Northern Democrats   SD Southern Democrats

	344	345	346	347	348	349	350	351
14 ***Hastert***			Y					
15 ***Johnson***	Y	Y	Y	N	Y	Y	Y	Y
16 ***Manzullo***	Y	Y	Y	N	Y	Y	Y	Y
17 Evans	Y	N	N	Y	Y	Y	Y	N
18 ***LaHood***	Y	Y	Y	N	Y	Y	Y	Y
19 Phelps	Y	Y	Y	N	Y	Y	Y	Y
20 ***Shimkus***	Y	Y	Y	N	Y	Y	Y	Y
INDIANA								
1 Visclosky	Y	N	N	Y	N	?	?	N
2 ***Pence***	Y	Y	Y	N	Y	Y	Y	Y
3 Roemer	Y	Y	Y	Y	Y	Y	Y	N
4 ***Souder***	Y	Y	Y	N	Y	Y	Y	Y
5 ***Buyer***	Y	Y	Y	N	+	?	?	Y
6 ***Burton***	Y	Y	Y	N	Y	Y	Y	Y
7 ***Kerns***	Y	Y	Y	N	Y	Y	Y	Y
8 ***Hostettler***	Y	Y	Y	N	Y	Y	Y	Y
9 Hill	Y	Y	Y	N	Y	Y	Y	N
10 Carson	?	?	?	?	?	Y	Y	N
IOWA								
1 ***Leach***	Y	Y	Y	N	Y	Y	Y	Y
2 ***Nussle***	Y	Y	Y	N	Y	Y	Y	Y
3 Boswell	Y	Y	Y	N	Y	Y	Y	N
4 ***Ganske***	Y	Y	Y	N	Y	Y	Y	Y
5 ***Latham***	Y	Y	Y	N	Y	Y	Y	Y
KANSAS								
1 ***Moran***	Y	Y	Y	N	Y	Y	Y	Y
2 ***Ryun***	Y	Y	Y	N	Y	Y	Y	Y
3 Moore	Y	Y	Y	N	Y	Y	Y	N
4 ***Tiahrt***	Y	Y	Y	N	Y	Y	Y	Y
KENTUCKY								
1 ***Whitfield***	Y	Y	Y	N	Y	Y	Y	Y
2 ***Lewis***	Y	Y	Y	N	Y	Y	Y	Y
3 ***Northup***	Y	Y	Y	N	Y	Y	Y	Y
4 Lucas	Y	Y	Y	N	Y	?	?	Y
5 ***Rogers***	Y	Y	Y	N	Y	Y	Y	Y
6 ***Fletcher***	Y	Y	Y	N	Y	Y	Y	Y
LOUISIANA								
1 ***Vitter***	Y	Y	Y	N	Y	Y	Y	Y
2 Jefferson	Y	N	N	Y	Y	Y	Y	N
3 ***Tauzin***	Y	Y	Y	N	Y	Y	Y	Y
4 ***McCrery***	?	Y	Y	N	Y	Y	Y	Y
5 ***Cooksey***	Y	Y	Y	N	Y	?	?	Y
6 ***Baker***	Y	Y	Y	N	Y	Y	Y	Y
7 John	Y	Y	Y	N	Y	Y	Y	Y
MAINE								
1 Allen	Y	N	N	Y	Y	Y	Y	N
2 Baldacci	Y	Y	Y	Y	Y	Y	Y	N
MARYLAND								
1 ***Gilchrest***	Y	Y	Y	N	Y	Y	Y	Y
2 ***Ehrlich***	?	Y	Y	N	Y	Y	Y	Y
3 Cardin	Y	Y	N	Y	Y	Y	Y	N
4 Wynn	Y	Y	Y	Y	Y	Y	Y	N
5 Hoyer	Y	Y	N	Y	Y	Y	Y	-
6 ***Bartlett***	Y	Y	Y	N	Y	Y	Y	Y
7 Cummings	?	Y	N	Y	Y	Y	Y	N
8 ***Morella***	Y	Y	Y	N	Y	Y	Y	Y
MASSACHUSETTS								
1 Olver	Y	N	N	Y	Y	Y	Y	N
2 Neal	Y	N	N	Y	Y	?	?	N
3 McGovern	Y	Y	Y	Y	Y	Y	Y	N
4 Frank	Y	N	?	Y	N	Y	Y	N
5 Meehan	Y	Y	Y	Y	Y	Y	Y	N
6 Tierney	Y	N	N	Y	N	Y	Y	N
7 Markey	?	N	N	Y	N	Y	Y	N
8 Capuano	Y	N	N	Y	Y	Y	Y	N
9 Vacant								
10 Delahunt	Y	N	N	Y	Y	Y	Y	N
MICHIGAN								
1 Stupak	Y	N	N	Y	N	Y	Y	N
2 ***Hoekstra***	Y	Y	Y	N	Y	Y	Y	Y
3 ***Ehlers***	Y	Y	Y	N	Y	Y	Y	Y
4 ***Camp***	Y	Y	Y	N	Y	Y	Y	Y
5 Barcia	Y	N	N	Y	Y	Y	Y	N
6 ***Upton***	Y	Y	Y	N	Y	Y	Y	Y
7 ***Smith***	Y	Y	Y	N	Y	?	Y	Y
8 ***Rogers***	Y	Y	Y	N	Y	Y	Y	Y
9 Kildee	Y	N	N	Y	Y	Y	Y	N
10 Bonior	Y	N	N	Y	N	Y	Y	N
11 ***Knollenberg***	Y	Y	Y	N	Y	Y	Y	Y
12 Levin	Y	Y	Y	Y	Y	Y	Y	N
13 Rivers	Y	N	N	Y	Y	Y	Y	N
14 Conyers	?	?	?	?	?	Y	Y	?
15 Kilpatrick	Y	N	N	Y	N	Y	Y	N
16 Dingell	?	?	?	?	?	Y	Y	N
MINNESOTA								
1 ***Gutknecht***	Y	Y	Y	N	Y	Y	Y	Y
2 ***Kennedy***	Y	Y	Y	N	Y	Y	Y	Y
3 ***Ramstad***	Y	Y	Y	N	Y	Y	Y	Y
4 McCollum	Y	N	N	Y	Y	Y	Y	N
5 Sabo	Y	Y	Y	N	Y	?	?	N
6 Luther	Y	N	N	Y	Y	Y	Y	N
7 Peterson	Y	N	N	Y	N	?	?	?
8 Oberstar	Y	Y	Y	N	Y	Y	Y	N
MISSISSIPPI								
1 ***Wicker***	Y	Y	Y	N	Y	Y	Y	Y
2 Thompson	Y	N	N	Y	N	Y	Y	N
3 ***Pickering***	Y	Y	Y	N	Y	Y	Y	Y
4 Shows	Y	Y	Y	N	Y	Y	Y	Y
5 Taylor	Y	Y	Y	N	Y	Y	Y	Y
MISSOURI								
1 Clay	Y	N	N	Y	Y	Y	Y	N
2 ***Akin***	Y	Y	Y	N	Y	Y	Y	Y
3 Gephardt	Y	Y	Y	Y	Y	Y	Y	N
4 Skelton	Y	Y	Y	N	Y	Y	Y	N
5 McCarthy	Y	N	N	Y	Y	Y	Y	N
6 ***Graves***	Y	Y	Y	N	Y	Y	Y	Y
7 ***Blunt***	Y	Y	Y	N	Y	?	?	Y
8 ***Emerson***	Y	Y	Y	N	Y	Y	Y	Y
9 ***Hulshof***	Y	Y	Y	N	Y	?	?	Y
MONTANA								
AL ***Rehberg***	Y	Y	Y	N	Y	Y	Y	Y
NEBRASKA								
1 ***Bereuter***	Y	+	+	–	+	Y	Y	Y
2 ***Terry***	Y	Y	Y	N	Y	Y	Y	Y
3 ***Osborne***	Y	Y	Y	N	Y	Y	Y	Y
NEVADA								
1 Berkley	Y	Y	Y	N	Y	Y	Y	N
2 ***Gibbons***	Y	Y	Y	N	Y	Y	Y	Y
NEW HAMPSHIRE								
1 ***Sununu***	Y	Y	Y	N	Y	Y	Y	Y
2 ***Bass***	Y	Y	Y	N	Y	Y	Y	Y
NEW JERSEY								
1 Andrews	Y	Y	Y	Y	Y	Y	Y	N
2 ***LoBiondo***	Y	Y	Y	N	Y	Y	Y	Y
3 ***Saxton***	Y	Y	Y	N	Y	Y	Y	Y
4 ***Smith***	Y	Y	Y	N	Y	Y	Y	Y
5 ***Roukema***	Y	Y	Y	N	Y	Y	Y	Y
6 Pallone	Y	Y	Y	Y	Y	Y	Y	N
7 ***Ferguson***	Y	Y	Y	N	Y	Y	Y	Y
8 Pascrell	Y	Y	Y	Y	Y	Y	Y	N
9 Rothman	Y	Y	N	Y	Y	Y	Y	N
10 Payne	Y	N	N	Y	Y	?	?	N
11 ***Frelinghuysen***	Y	Y	Y	N	Y	Y	Y	Y
12 Holt	Y	N	N	Y	N	Y	Y	N
13 Menendez	Y	Y	Y	Y	Y	Y	Y	N
NEW MEXICO								
1 ***Wilson***	Y	Y	Y	N	Y	Y	Y	Y
2 ***Skeen***	Y	Y	Y	N	Y	Y	Y	Y
3 Udall	+	N	N	Y	Y	Y	Y	N
NEW YORK								
1 ***Grucci***	Y	Y	Y	N	Y	Y	Y	Y
2 Israel	Y	Y	Y	Y	Y	Y	Y	N
3 ***King***	Y	Y	Y	N	Y	Y	Y	Y
4 McCarthy	Y	Y	N	Y	Y	Y	Y	N
5 Ackerman	Y	Y	N	Y	Y	Y	Y	N
6 Meeks	?	Y	Y	Y	Y	Y	Y	N
7 Crowley	Y	Y	Y	Y	Y	?	?	N
8 Nadler	Y	N	N	Y	Y	Y	Y	N
9 Weiner	Y	Y	Y	Y	Y	?	?	N
10 Towns	?	?	?	?	?	?	?	?
11 Owens	Y	N	N	Y	Y	+	+	?
12 Velázquez	Y	N	N	Y	Y	?	?	?
13 ***Fossella***	Y	?	?	?	+	Y	Y	Y
14 Maloney	Y	Y	Y	Y	Y	+	+	N
15 Rangel	Y	Y	N	Y	Y	Y	Y	N
16 Serrano	Y	Y	Y	Y	Y	?	?	?
17 Engel	?	N	N	Y	Y	Y	Y	N
18 Lowey	?	Y	N	Y	Y	Y	Y	N
19 ***Kelly***	Y	Y	Y	N	Y	Y	Y	Y
20 ***Gilman***	Y	Y	Y	N	Y	Y	Y	Y
21 McNulty	Y	Y	N	Y	Y	Y	Y	N
22 ***Sweeney***	Y	Y	Y	N	Y	Y	Y	Y
23 ***Boehlert***	Y	Y	Y	N	Y	Y	Y	Y
24 ***McHugh***	Y	Y	Y	N	Y	Y	Y	Y
25 ***Walsh***	Y	Y	N	N	Y	Y	Y	Y
26 Hinchey	?	N	N	Y	N	Y	Y	N
27 ***Reynolds***	Y	Y	Y	N	Y	Y	Y	Y
28 Slaughter	Y	N	N	Y	Y	Y	Y	N
29 LaFalce	Y	N	N	Y	N	Y	Y	N
30 ***Quinn***	Y	Y	Y	N	Y	Y	Y	Y
31 ***Houghton***	Y	Y	Y	N	Y	Y	Y	Y
NORTH CAROLINA								
1 Clayton	Y	N	N	Y	N	Y	Y	N
2 Etheridge	Y	Y	Y	Y	Y	Y	Y	N
3 ***Jones***	Y	Y	Y	N	Y	Y	Y	Y
4 Price	?	Y	N	Y	Y	Y	Y	N
5 ***Burr***	Y	Y	Y	N	Y	Y	Y	Y
6 ***Coble***	Y	Y	Y	N	Y	Y	Y	Y
7 McIntyre	Y	Y	Y	Y	Y	Y	Y	Y
8 ***Hayes***	Y	Y	Y	N	Y	Y	Y	Y
9 ***Myrick***	Y	Y	Y	N	Y	Y	Y	Y
10 ***Ballenger***	Y	Y	Y	N	Y	Y	Y	Y
11 ***Taylor***	Y	Y	Y	N	Y	Y	Y	Y
12 Watt	Y	N	N	Y	Y	Y	Y	N
NORTH DAKOTA								
AL Pomeroy	Y	Y	Y	Y	Y	?	?	N
OHIO								
1 ***Chabot***	Y	Y	Y	N	Y	Y	Y	Y
2 ***Portman***	Y	Y	Y	N	Y	+	+	Y
3 Hall	Y	Y	Y	Y	Y	Y	Y	Y
4 ***Oxley***	Y	Y	Y	N	Y	+	+	Y
5 ***Gillmor***	Y	Y	Y	?	?	?	?	Y
6 Strickland	Y	N	N	Y	N	Y	Y	N
7 ***Hobson***	Y	Y	Y	?	?	Y	Y	Y
8 ***Boehner***	Y	Y	Y	N	Y	?	?	Y
9 Kaptur	Y	N	N	Y	P	Y	Y	N
10 Kucinich	Y	N	N	Y	N	Y	Y	N
11 Jones	Y	N	N	Y	N	Y	Y	N
12 ***Tiberi***	Y	Y	Y	N	Y	?	?	Y
13 Brown	Y	N	N	Y	N	Y	Y	N
14 Sawyer	Y	Y	N	Y	Y	Y	Y	N
15 ***Pryce***	Y	Y	Y	?	?	Y	Y	Y
16 ***Regula***	Y	Y	Y	N	Y	Y	Y	Y
17 Traficant	Y	Y	Y	N	Y	Y	Y	Y
18 ***Ney***	Y	Y	Y	N	Y	Y	Y	Y
19 ***LaTourette***	Y	Y	Y	N	Y	Y	Y	Y
OKLAHOMA								
1 ***Largent***	Y	Y	Y	N	Y	Y	Y	Y
2 Carson	Y	Y	Y	N	Y	Y	Y	N
3 ***Watkins***	Y	Y	Y	N	Y	Y	Y	Y
4 ***Watts***	+	Y	Y	N	Y	+	+	Y
5 ***Istook***	Y	Y	Y	N	Y	Y	Y	Y
6 ***Lucas***	Y	Y	Y	N	Y	Y	Y	Y
OREGON								
1 Wu	Y	N	N	Y	Y	Y	Y	N
2 ***Walden***	Y	Y	Y	N	Y	+	Y	Y
3 Blumenauer	Y	N	N	Y	N	?	Y	N
4 DeFazio	Y	N	N	Y	N	Y	Y	N
5 Hooley	Y	N	N	Y	Y	Y	Y	N
PENNSYLVANIA								
1 Brady	Y	Y	N	Y	Y	Y	Y	N
2 Fattah	Y	Y	N	Y	Y	Y	Y	N
3 Borski	Y	Y	Y	Y	Y	Y	Y	N
4 ***Hart***	Y	Y	Y	N	Y	Y	Y	Y
5 ***Peterson***	Y	Y	Y	N	Y	Y	Y	Y
6 Holden	?	?	?	?	?	Y	Y	Y
7 ***Weldon***	Y	Y	Y	N	Y	Y	Y	Y
8 ***Greenwood***	?	Y	Y	N	Y	Y	Y	Y
9 ***Shuster, Bill***	Y	Y	Y	N	Y	Y	Y	Y
10 ***Sherwood***	Y	Y	Y	N	Y	Y	Y	Y
11 Kanjorski	Y	Y	Y	N	Y	Y	Y	N
12 Murtha	Y	Y	Y	N	Y	Y	Y	N
13 Hoeffel	Y	Y	N	Y	Y	Y	Y	N
14 Coyne	Y	N	N	Y	N	Y	Y	N
15 ***Toomey***	Y	Y	Y	N	Y	Y	Y	Y
16 ***Pitts***	Y	Y	Y	N	Y	Y	Y	Y
17 ***Gekas***	Y	Y	Y	N	Y	Y	Y	Y
18 Doyle	Y	Y	Y	Y	Y	Y	Y	N
19 ***Platts***	Y	Y	Y	N	Y	Y	Y	Y
20 Mascara	Y	Y	Y	Y	Y	Y	Y	N
21 ***English***	Y	Y	Y	N	Y	Y	Y	Y
RHODE ISLAND								
1 Kennedy	Y	N	N	Y	Y	Y	Y	N
2 Langevin	Y	N	N	Y	Y	Y	Y	N
SOUTH CAROLINA								
1 ***Brown***	Y	Y	Y	N	Y	Y	Y	Y
2 Vacant								
3 ***Graham***	Y	Y	Y	N	Y	Y	Y	Y
4 ***DeMint***	Y	Y	Y	N	Y	+	+	Y
5 Spratt	Y	N	N	Y	Y	Y	Y	N
6 Clyburn	Y	N	N	Y	N	Y	Y	N
SOUTH DAKOTA								
AL ***Thune***	Y	Y	Y	N	Y	Y	Y	Y
TENNESSEE								
1 ***Jenkins***	Y	Y	Y	N	Y	Y	Y	Y
2 ***Duncan***	Y	Y	Y	N	Y	Y	Y	Y
3 ***Wamp***	Y	Y	Y	N	Y	Y	Y	Y
4 ***Hilleary***	Y	Y	Y	N	Y	Y	Y	Y
5 Clement	Y	N	N	Y	Y	Y	Y	N
6 Gordon	Y	Y	N	Y	Y	Y	Y	N
7 ***Bryant***	Y	Y	Y	N	Y	+	+	Y
8 Tanner	Y	Y	Y	N	Y	+	+	Y
9 Ford	Y	Y	Y	Y	Y	Y	Y	N
TEXAS								
1 Sandlin	Y	N	N	Y	Y	Y	Y	N
2 Turner	+	Y	Y	N	Y	Y	Y	N
3 ***Johnson, Sam***	Y	Y	Y	N	Y	Y	Y	Y
4 Hall	Y	Y	N	N	Y	Y	Y	Y
5 ***Sessions***	Y	Y	Y	N	Y	Y	Y	Y
6 ***Barton***	Y	Y	Y	N	Y	Y	Y	Y
7 ***Culberson***	?	Y	Y	N	Y	Y	Y	Y
8 ***Brady***	Y	Y	Y	N	Y	?	?	Y
9 Lampson	Y	Y	Y	Y	Y	Y	Y	N
10 Doggett	Y	N	N	Y	N	Y	Y	N
11 Edwards	Y	Y	Y	Y	Y	Y	Y	N
12 ***Granger***	Y	Y	Y	N	Y	?	?	Y
13 ***Thornberry***	Y	Y	Y	N	Y	Y	Y	Y
14 ***Paul***	?	Y	Y	N	N	?	Y	Y
15 Hinojosa	Y	N	N	Y	Y	Y	Y	N
16 Reyes	Y	Y	Y	Y	Y	Y	Y	N
17 Stenholm	Y	Y	Y	N	Y	Y	Y	Y
18 Jackson-Lee	Y	N	Y	Y	Y	Y	Y	N
19 ***Combest***	Y	Y	Y	N	Y	Y	Y	Y
20 Gonzalez	Y	N	N	Y	Y	Y	Y	N
21 ***Smith***	Y	Y	Y	N	Y	Y	Y	Y
22 ***DeLay***	Y	Y	Y	N	Y	Y	Y	Y
23 ***Bonilla***	Y	Y	Y	N	Y	Y	Y	Y
24 Frost	Y	Y	Y	N	Y	Y	Y	N
25 Bentsen	Y	Y	Y	N	Y	Y	Y	N
26 ***Armey***	Y	Y	Y	N	Y	Y	Y	Y
27 Ortiz	Y	Y	Y	Y	Y	Y	Y	Y
28 Rodriguez	Y	N	N	Y	Y	Y	Y	N
29 Green	Y	Y	Y	Y	Y	Y	Y	N
30 Johnson, E.B.	Y	Y	Y	N	Y	Y	Y	N
UTAH								
1 ***Hansen***	?	Y	Y	N	Y	Y	Y	Y
2 Matheson	Y	Y	Y	N	Y	Y	Y	N
3 ***Cannon***	Y	Y	Y	N	Y	Y	Y	Y
VERMONT								
AL *Sanders*	Y	N	N	Y	N	?	?	N
VIRGINIA								
1 ***Davis, Jo Ann***	Y	Y	Y	N	Y	Y	Y	Y
2 ***Schrock***	Y	Y	Y	N	Y	Y	Y	Y
3 Scott	Y	N	N	Y	N	Y	Y	N
4 ***Forbes***	Y	Y	Y	N	Y	Y	Y	Y
5 *Goode*	Y	Y	Y	N	N	Y	Y	Y
6 ***Goodlatte***	Y	Y	Y	N	Y	Y	Y	Y
7 ***Cantor***	Y	Y	Y	N	Y	Y	Y	Y
8 Moran	Y	?	Y	Y	Y	Y	Y	N
9 Boucher	Y	Y	Y	Y	Y	Y	Y	N
10 ***Wolf***	Y	Y	Y	N	Y	Y	Y	Y
11 ***Davis, T.***	Y	Y	Y	N	Y	Y	Y	Y
WASHINGTON								
1 Inslee	Y	N	N	Y	N	?	?	N
2 Larsen	Y	N	N	Y	Y	Y	Y	N
3 Baird	Y	N	Y	Y	Y	Y	Y	N
4 ***Hastings***	Y	Y	Y	N	Y	Y	Y	Y
5 ***Nethercutt***	Y	Y	Y	N	Y	Y	Y	Y
6 Dicks	Y	Y	Y	Y	Y	Y	Y	N
7 McDermott	Y	N	N	Y	N	Y	Y	N
8 ***Dunn***	Y	Y	Y	N	Y	Y	Y	Y
9 Smith	Y	Y	N	Y	N	Y	Y	N
WEST VIRGINIA								
1 Mollohan	Y	N	N	Y	Y	Y	Y	N
2 ***Capito***	Y	Y	Y	N	Y	Y	Y	Y
3 Rahall	Y	N	N	Y	Y	Y	Y	N
WISCONSIN								
1 ***Ryan***	Y	Y	Y	N	Y	Y	Y	Y
2 Baldwin	Y	N	N	Y	N	Y	Y	N
3 Kind	Y	Y	N	Y	Y	Y	Y	N
4 Kleczka	Y	N	N	Y	Y	Y	Y	Y
5 Barrett	Y	Y	N	Y	Y	Y	Y	N
6 ***Petri***	Y	Y	Y	N	Y	Y	Y	Y
7 Obey	Y	N	N	Y	N	Y	Y	N
8 ***Green***	Y	Y	Y	N	Y	Y	Y	Y
9 ***Sensenbrenner***	Y	Y	Y	N	N	Y	Y	Y
WYOMING								
AL ***Cubin***	?	Y	Y	N	Y	Y	Y	Y

Southern states - Ala., Ark., Fla., Ga., Ky., La., Miss., N.C., Okla., S.C., Tenn., Texas, Va.

352. HR 2944. Fiscal 2002 District of Columbia Appropriations/ Domestic Partner Benefits. Weldon, R-Fla., amendment that would prohibit the use of local as well as federal funds under the bill to extend city employees' health benefits to unmarried domestic partners. Rejected 194-226: R 175-41; D 18-184 (ND 7-141, SD 11-43); I 1-1. Sept. 25, 2001.

353. HR 2944. Fiscal 2002 District of Columbia Appropriations/ Freedom of Association. Norton, D-D.C., amendment to the Hostettler, R-Ind., amendment. The Norton amendment would allow the use of local funds to carry out a D.C. Commission on Human Rights order that the Boy Scouts reinstate two homosexual leaders and compensate them $50,000 each. The Hostettler amendment would ban the use of local or federal funds to carry out the order. Rejected 173-243: R 13-202; D 159-40 (ND 128-18, SD 31-22); I 1-1. Sept. 25, 2001.

354. HR 2944. Fiscal 2002 District of Columbia Appropriations/ Boy Scouts. Hostettler, R-Ind., amendment that would ban the use of local or federal funds under the bill to carry out a D.C. Commission on Human Rights order that the Boy Scouts reinstate two homosexual leaders and compensate them $50,000 each. Adopted 262-152: R 207-8; D 54-143 (ND 27-118, SD 27-25); I 1-1. Sept. 25, 2001.

355. HR 2944. Fiscal 2002 District of Columbia Appropriations/ Passage. Passage of the bill to appropriate $398.1 million to the District of Columbia and approve the District's $7.2 billion budget. Passed 327-88: R 138-76; D 188-11 (ND 143-3, SD 45-8); I 1-1. Sept. 25, 2001.

356. HR 2586. Fiscal 2002 Defense Authorization/Anti-Terrorism and Drug Task Force. Traficant, D-Ohio, amendment that would set up a task force on counterterrorism and drug interdiction by either the Treasury or Justice departments and would allow military personnel to help patrol U.S. borders. Adopted 242-173: R 191-25; D 50-147 (ND 32-112, SD 18-35); I 1-1. Sept. 25, 2001.

357. HR 2586. Fiscal 2002 Defense Authorization/Abortions Overseas. Sanchez, D-Calif., amendment that would allow female military personnel stationed at U.S. bases overseas to undergo an abortion at medical facilities there provided they pay for it themselves and a doctor consents to perform the operation. Rejected 199-217: R 32-184; D 166-32 (ND 122-22, SD 44-10); I 1-1. Sept. 25, 2001.

358. HR 2586. Fiscal 2002 Defense Authorization/Recommit. Bonior, D-Mich., motion to recommit the bill to the House Armed Services Committee with instructions to strike section 331 and restore committee language requiring that the Defense Department allow federal employees to compete with private companies for contracts. Motion rejected 197-221: R 4-212; D 192-8 (ND 140-6, SD 52-2); I 1-1. Sept. 25, 2001.

359. HR 2586. Fiscal 2002 Defense Authorization/Passage. Passage of the bill that would authorize $343 billion for defense programs, including about $125 billion for operations and maintenance, $82 billion for military personnel, $62 billion for weapons procurement, $48 billion for research and development, $13 billion for the Energy Department, and $10 billion for military construction and family housing. The bill also would authorize $7.9 billion for national missile defense programs. Passed 398-17: R 213-1; D 183-16 (ND 130-15, SD 53-1); I 2-0. Sept. 25, 2001.

Key

Y	Voted for (yea).
#	Paired for.
+	Announced for.
N	Voted against (nay).
X	Paired against.
–	Announced against.
P	Voted "present."
C	Voted "present" to avoid possible conflict of interest.
?	Did not vote or otherwise make a position known.

Democrats **Republicans**
Independents

		352	353	354	355	356	357	358	359
ALABAMA									
1	*Callahan*	Y	N	Y	Y	Y	N	N	Y
2	*Everett*	Y	N	Y	N	Y	N	N	Y
3	*Riley*	Y	N	Y	N	Y	N	N	Y
4	*Aderholt*	Y	N	Y	Y	Y	N	N	Y
5	Cramer	Y	N	Y	Y	Y	Y	N	Y
6	*Bachus*	Y	N	Y	Y	Y	N	N	Y
7	Hilliard	N	Y	N	Y	N	Y	Y	Y
ALASKA									
AL	*Young*	Y	N	Y	N	Y	N	N	Y
ARIZONA									
1	*Flake*	Y	N	N	N	N	N	N	Y
2	Pastor	N	N	N	Y	N	Y	Y	Y
3	*Stump*	Y	N	Y	N	Y	N	N	Y
4	*Shadegg*	Y	N	N	N	N	N	N	Y
5	*Kolbe*	N	Y	N	Y	N	Y	N	Y
6	*Hayworth*	Y	N	Y	N	Y	N	N	Y
ARKANSAS									
1	Berry	Y	N	Y	N	N	N	Y	Y
2	Snyder	N	Y	Y	Y	N	Y	Y	Y
3	Vacant								
4	Ross	N	N	Y	Y	N	N	Y	Y
CALIFORNIA									
1	Thompson	N	Y	N	Y	N	Y	Y	Y
2	*Herger*	Y	N	Y	N	Y	N	N	Y
3	*Ose*	N	N	Y	N	Y	N	N	Y
4	*Doolittle*	Y	?	Y	Y	Y	N	N	Y
5	Matsui	N	Y	N	Y	N	Y	Y	Y
6	Woolsey	N	Y	N	Y	N	Y	Y	N
7	Miller, George	N	Y	N	Y	N	Y	Y	N
8	Pelosi	N	Y	N	Y	N	Y	Y	Y
9	Lee	N	Y	?	Y	N	Y	Y	N
10	Tauscher	N	Y	Y	Y	N	Y	Y	Y
11	*Pombo*	Y	N	Y	Y	Y	N	N	Y
12	Lantos	N	Y	N	Y	Y	Y	Y	Y
13	Stark	N	Y	N	Y	N	Y	Y	N
14	Eshoo	N	Y	N	Y	N	Y	Y	Y
15	Honda	N	Y	N	Y	N	Y	Y	Y
16	Lofgren	N	Y	N	Y	N	Y	Y	Y
17	Farr	N	Y	N	Y	N	Y	Y	Y
18	Condit	N	Y	N	Y	N	Y	Y	Y
19	*Radanovich*	Y	N	Y	N	N	N	N	Y
20	Dooley	N	Y	N	Y	N	Y	Y	Y
21	*Thomas*	N	N	Y	N	Y	Y	N	Y
22	Capps	N	Y	N	Y	N	Y	Y	Y
23	*Gallegly*	Y	N	Y	N	Y	N	N	?
24	Sherman	N	Y	N	Y	N	Y	Y	Y
25	*McKeon*	Y	N	Y	Y	Y	N	N	Y
26	Berman	N	Y	N	Y	N	Y	Y	Y
27	Schiff	N	Y	N	Y	N	Y	Y	Y
28	*Dreier*	N	N	Y	N	N	N	N	Y
29	Waxman	N	Y	N	Y	N	Y	Y	Y
30	Becerra	N	Y	N	Y	N	Y	Y	Y
31	Solis	N	Y	N	Y	N	Y	Y	Y
32	Watson	?	?	?	?	?	?	?	?
33	Roybal-Allard	N	Y	N	Y	N	Y	Y	Y
34	Napolitano	N	Y	N	Y	N	Y	Y	Y
35	Waters	N	Y	N	Y	N	Y	N	Y
36	Harman	N	Y	N	Y	N	Y	N	Y
37	Millender-McD.	N	Y	N	Y	N	Y	Y	Y
38	*Horn*	N	N	N	Y	Y	Y	N	Y

		352	353	354	355	356	357	358	359
39	*Royce*	Y	N	Y	N	Y	N	N	Y
40	*Lewis*	N	Y	Y	Y	Y	N	N	Y
41	*Miller, Gary*	Y	N	Y	Y	N	N	N	Y
42	Baca	N	Y	N	Y	N	Y	Y	Y
43	*Calvert*	Y	N	Y	N	Y	N	N	Y
44	*Bono*	N	Y	Y	Y	N	N	N	Y
45	*Rohrabacher*	N	N	Y	Y	N	N	N	Y
46	Sanchez	N	Y	N	Y	N	Y	N	Y
47	*Cox*	Y	N	Y	N	Y	N	N	Y
48	*Issa*	N	N	Y	N	Y	N	N	Y
49	Davis	N	Y	N	Y	N	Y	Y	Y
50	Filner	N	Y	N	Y	N	Y	Y	N
51	*Cunningham*	Y	N	Y	N	Y	N	N	Y
52	*Hunter*	Y	?	?	N	Y	N	N	Y
COLORADO									
1	DeGette	N	Y	N	Y	N	Y	Y	Y
2	Udall	N	Y	N	Y	Y	Y	Y	Y
3	*McInnis*	Y	N	Y	N	?	?	?	?
4	*Schaffer*	Y	N	Y	N	Y	N	N	Y
5	*Hefley*	Y	N	Y	N	Y	N	N	Y
6	*Tancredo*	Y	N	Y	N	Y	N	N	Y
CONNECTICUT									
1	Larson	N	Y	N	Y	N	Y	Y	Y
2	*Simmons*	N	Y	N	Y	Y	Y	N	Y
3	DeLauro	N	Y	N	Y	N	Y	Y	Y
4	*Shays*	N	Y	N	Y	Y	Y	Y	Y
5	Maloney	N	Y	Y	Y	Y	Y	Y	Y
6	*Johnson*	N	N	Y	Y	Y	Y	N	Y
DELAWARE									
AL	*Castle*	N	N	Y	Y	Y	Y	N	Y
FLORIDA									
1	Vacant								
2	Boyd	N	N	Y	Y	N	Y	Y	Y
3	Brown	N	Y	N	Y	N	Y	Y	Y
4	*Crenshaw*	Y	N	Y	Y	Y	N	N	Y
5	Thurman	N	Y	Y	Y	Y	Y	Y	Y
6	*Stearns*	Y	N	N	N	Y	N	N	Y
7	*Mica*	Y	N	Y	Y	N	N	N	Y
8	*Keller*	Y	N	Y	Y	N	N	N	Y
9	*Bilirakis*	Y	N	Y	Y	N	N	N	Y
10	*Young*	Y	N	Y	Y	Y	N	N	Y
11	Davis	N	Y	Y	Y	Y	Y	Y	Y
12	*Putnam*	Y	N	Y	N	N	N	N	Y
13	*Miller*	N	N	Y	Y	N	N	N	Y
14	*Goss*	Y	N	Y	N	Y	N	N	Y
15	*Weldon*	Y	N	Y	N	Y	N	N	Y
16	*Foley*	N	Y	Y	Y	Y	N	N	Y
17	Meek	N	Y	N	Y	N	Y	Y	Y
18	*Ros-Lehtinen*	N	N	Y	Y	N	N	N	Y
19	Wexler	N	Y	N	Y	N	Y	Y	Y
20	Deutsch	N	Y	N	Y	N	Y	Y	Y
21	*Diaz-Balart*	Y	N	Y	Y	N	N	N	Y
22	*Shaw*	N	Y	Y	Y	N	N	N	Y
23	Hastings	N	Y	N	Y	N	Y	Y	Y
GEORGIA									
1	*Kingston*	Y	N	Y	N	Y	N	N	Y
2	Bishop	N	N	Y	Y	Y	Y	Y	Y
3	*Collins*	Y	N	Y	N	Y	N	N	Y
4	McKinney	N	Y	N	Y	N	Y	Y	N
5	Lewis	N	?	?	?	N	Y	Y	Y
6	*Isakson*	Y	N	Y	Y	Y	N	N	Y
7	*Barr*	Y	N	Y	N	Y	N	N	Y
8	*Chambliss*	Y	N	?	Y	N	N	N	Y
9	*Deal*	Y	N	Y	N	Y	N	N	Y
10	*Norwood*	Y	N	Y	N	Y	N	N	Y
11	*Linder*	Y	N	Y	N	Y	N	N	Y
HAWAII									
1	Abercrombie	N	?	?	Y	N	Y	N	Y
2	Mink	N	Y	N	Y	N	Y	Y	Y
IDAHO									
1	*Otter*	Y	N	Y	N	Y	N	N	Y
2	*Simpson*	Y	N	Y	Y	Y	N	N	Y
ILLINOIS									
1	Rush	?	?	?	?	?	?	?	?
2	Jackson	N	Y	N	Y	N	Y	N	Y
3	Lipinski	Y	N	Y	Y	Y	N	Y	Y
4	Gutierrez	N	Y	N	Y	N	Y	Y	Y
5	Blagojevich	N	Y	N	Y	N	Y	Y	Y
6	*Hyde*	Y	N	Y	Y	N	N	N	Y
7	Davis	N	Y	N	Y	N	Y	Y	Y
8	*Crane*	Y	N	Y	N	Y	N	N	Y
9	Schakowsky	N	Y	N	Y	N	Y	Y	N
10	*Kirk*	N	N	Y	Y	Y	Y	N	Y
11	*Weller*	Y	N	Y	Y	Y	N	N	Y
12	Costello	Y	N	Y	Y	Y	N	Y	Y
13	*Biggert*	N	Y	Y	Y	Y	N	N	Y

ND Northern Democrats   SD Southern Democrats

	352	353	354	355	356	357	358	359
14 ***Hastert***								
15 ***Johnson***	Y	N	Y	N	Y	N	N	Y
16 ***Manzullo***	Y	N	Y	N	Y	N	N	Y
17 Evans	N	Y	N	Y	N	Y	Y	Y
18 ***LaHood***	Y	N	Y	Y	Y	N	N	Y
19 Phelps	Y	N	Y	Y	Y	N	Y	Y
20 ***Shimkus***	Y	N	Y	N	Y	N	N	Y
INDIANA								
1 Visclosky	N	Y	N	Y	?	?	?	?
2 ***Pence***	Y	N	Y	N	Y	N	N	Y
3 Roemer	N	N	Y	N	Y	N	Y	Y
4 ***Souder***	Y	N	Y	Y	Y	N	N	Y
5 ***Buyer***	Y	N	Y	Y	N	N	N	Y
6 ***Burton***	Y	N	Y	N	Y	N	N	Y
7 ***Kerns***	Y	N	Y	N	Y	N	N	Y
8 ***Hostettler***	Y	N	Y	Y	Y	N	N	Y
9 Hill	N	Y	N	Y	N	Y	Y	Y
10 Carson	N	Y	N	Y	N	Y	Y	Y
IOWA								
1 ***Leach***	N	Y	N	Y	N	Y	N	Y
2 ***Nussle***	Y	N	Y	Y	Y	N	N	Y
3 Boswell	N	Y	N	Y	Y	Y	Y	Y
4 ***Ganske***	N	N	Y	Y	N	N	N	Y
5 ***Latham***	Y	N	Y	Y	Y	N	N	Y
KANSAS								
1 ***Moran***	Y	N	Y	N	Y	N	N	Y
2 ***Ryun***	Y	N	Y	N	Y	N	N	Y
3 Moore	N	Y	N	Y	N	Y	Y	Y
4 ***Tiahrt***	Y	N	Y	N	Y	N	N	Y
KENTUCKY								
1 ***Whitfield***	Y	N	Y	Y	N	N	N	Y
2 ***Lewis***	Y	N	Y	N	Y	N	Y	Y
3 ***Northup***	Y	N	Y	Y	Y	N	N	Y
4 Lucas	Y	N	Y	N	Y	N	Y	Y
5 ***Rogers***	Y	N	Y	Y	Y	N	N	Y
6 ***Fletcher***	Y	N	Y	Y	Y	N	N	Y
LOUISIANA								
1 ***Vitter***	Y	N	Y	Y	Y	N	N	Y
2 Jefferson	N	Y	N	Y	N	Y	Y	Y
3 ***Tauzin***	Y	N	Y	Y	Y	N	N	Y
4 ***McCrery***	N	N	Y	Y	Y	N	N	Y
5 ***Cooksey***	?	N	Y	Y	Y	N	N	Y
6 ***Baker***	Y	N	Y	Y	Y	N	N	Y
7 John	Y	N	Y	Y	Y	N	Y	Y
MAINE								
1 Allen	N	Y	N	Y	N	Y	Y	Y
2 Baldacci	N	Y	N	Y	N	Y	Y	Y
MARYLAND								
1 ***Gilchrest***	N	N	Y	Y	Y	Y	N	Y
2 ***Ehrlich***	N	N	Y	Y	N	Y	N	Y
3 Cardin	N	Y	N	Y	N	Y	Y	Y
4 Wynn	N	Y	N	Y	N	Y	Y	Y
5 Hoyer	N	Y	N	Y	N	Y	Y	Y
6 ***Bartlett***	Y	N	Y	N	Y	N	N	Y
7 Cummings	N	Y	N	Y	N	Y	Y	Y
8 ***Morella***	N	Y	N	Y	Y	Y	N	Y
MASSACHUSETTS								
1 Olver	N	Y	N	Y	N	Y	Y	N
2 Neal	N	Y	N	Y	N	Y	Y	Y
3 McGovern	N	Y	N	Y	N	Y	Y	Y
4 Frank	N	Y	N	Y	N	Y	Y	N
5 Meehan	N	Y	N	Y	N	Y	Y	Y
6 Tierney	N	Y	N	Y	N	Y	Y	N
7 Markey	N	Y	N	Y	N	Y	Y	Y
8 Capuano	N	Y	N	Y	N	Y	Y	Y
9 Vacant								
10 Delahunt	N	Y	N	Y	N	Y	Y	Y
MICHIGAN								
1 Stupak	N	Y	Y	Y	N	N	Y	Y
2 ***Hoekstra***	Y	N	Y	Y	Y	N	N	Y
3 ***Ehlers***	Y	N	Y	Y	N	N	N	Y
4 ***Camp***	Y	N	Y	Y	Y	N	N	Y
5 Barcia	N	N	Y	Y	Y	N	Y	Y
6 ***Upton***	Y	N	Y	Y	Y	N	N	Y
7 ***Smith***	Y	N	Y	?	N	N	N	Y
8 ***Rogers***	Y	N	Y	Y	Y	N	N	Y
9 Kildee	N	Y	N	Y	Y	N	Y	Y
10 Bonior	N	Y	N	Y	N	Y	Y	Y
11 ***Knollenberg***	Y	N	Y	Y	Y	N	N	Y
12 Levin	N	Y	N	Y	N	Y	Y	Y
13 Rivers	N	Y	N	Y	Y	Y	Y	Y
14 Conyers	N	Y	N	Y	?	?	Y	N
15 Kilpatrick	N	Y	N	Y	N	Y	Y	Y
16 Dingell	N	Y	N	Y	N	Y	Y	Y

	352	353	354	355	356	357	358	359
MINNESOTA								
1 ***Gutknecht***	Y	N	Y	Y	Y	N	N	Y
2 ***Kennedy***	Y	N	Y	N	Y	N	N	Y
3 ***Ramstad***	Y	N	Y	Y	Y	Y	N	Y
4 McCollum	N	Y	N	Y	N	Y	Y	Y
5 Sabo	N	Y	N	Y	N	Y	Y	Y
6 Luther	N	Y	N	Y	Y	Y	Y	Y
7 Peterson	?	?	?	?	?	?	?	?
8 Oberstar	N	Y	Y	Y	N	N	Y	Y
MISSISSIPPI								
1 ***Wicker***	Y	N	Y	N	Y	N	N	Y
2 Thompson	N	Y	N	Y	N	Y	Y	Y
3 ***Pickering***	Y	N	Y	N	Y	N	N	Y
4 Shows	Y	N	Y	N	Y	N	N	Y
5 Taylor	Y	N	Y	N	Y	N	Y	Y
MISSOURI								
1 Clay	N	Y	N	Y	N	Y	Y	Y
2 ***Akin***	Y	N	Y	N	Y	N	N	Y
3 Gephardt	N	Y	N	Y	Y	Y	Y	Y
4 Skelton	N	N	Y	N	N	N	Y	Y
5 McCarthy	N	Y	N	Y	Y	Y	Y	Y
6 ***Graves***	Y	N	Y	N	Y	N	N	Y
7 ***Blunt***	Y	N	Y	N	Y	N	N	Y
8 ***Emerson***	Y	N	Y	Y	Y	N	N	Y
9 ***Hulshof***	Y	N	Y	Y	Y	N	N	Y
MONTANA								
AL ***Rehberg***	+	N	Y	Y	Y	N	N	Y
NEBRASKA								
1 ***Bereuter***	Y	N	Y	Y	N	N	N	Y
2 ***Terry***	Y	N	Y	Y	N	N	N	Y
3 ***Osborne***	Y	N	Y	Y	N	N	N	Y
NEVADA								
1 Berkley	N	Y	N	Y	N	Y	Y	Y
2 ***Gibbons***	Y	N	Y	Y	Y	N	N	Y
NEW HAMPSHIRE								
1 ***Sununu***	Y	N	Y	Y	Y	N	N	Y
2 ***Bass***	N	N	Y	Y	Y	Y	N	Y
NEW JERSEY								
1 Andrews	N	Y	N	Y	N	Y	Y	Y
2 ***LoBiondo***	Y	N	Y	Y	Y	N	N	Y
3 ***Saxton***	Y	N	Y	Y	Y	N	N	Y
4 ***Smith***	Y	N	Y	N	Y	N	N	Y
5 ***Roukema***	Y	N	Y	Y	Y	Y	N	Y
6 Pallone	N	Y	N	Y	Y	Y	Y	Y
7 ***Ferguson***	N	N	Y	Y	Y	N	N	Y
8 Pascrell	N	Y	Y	Y	Y	Y	Y	Y
9 Rothman	N	Y	N	Y	Y	Y	Y	Y
10 Payne	N	Y	N	Y	N	Y	Y	Y
11 ***Frelinghuysen***	N	N	Y	Y	Y	Y	N	Y
12 Holt	N	Y	N	Y	N	Y	Y	Y
13 Menendez	N	Y	Y	Y	N	Y	Y	Y
NEW MEXICO								
1 ***Wilson***	Y	N	Y	Y	N	N	N	Y
2 ***Skeen***	Y	N	Y	Y	N	N	N	Y
3 Udall	N	Y	N	Y	Y	Y	Y	Y
NEW YORK								
1 ***Grucci***	Y	N	Y	Y	Y	N	N	Y
2 Israel	N	Y	N	Y	Y	Y	Y	Y
3 ***King***	Y	N	Y	Y	Y	N	N	Y
4 McCarthy	N	Y	N	Y	Y	Y	Y	Y
5 Ackerman	N	Y	N	Y	N	Y	Y	Y
6 Meeks	?	?	?	?	?	?	?	?
7 Crowley	N	Y	N	Y	N	Y	Y	Y
8 Nadler	N	Y	N	Y	?	?	?	?
9 Weiner	N	Y	N	Y	N	Y	Y	Y
10 Towns	?	?	?	?	?	?	?	?
11 Owens	?	?	?	?	?	N	Y	N
12 Velázquez	?	?	?	?	?	?	?	?
13 ***Fossella***	Y	N	Y	N	Y	N	N	Y
14 Maloney	N	Y	N	Y	N	Y	Y	Y
15 Rangel	N	Y	N	?	N	Y	Y	Y
16 Serrano	?	?	?	?	?	?	?	?
17 Engel	N	Y	N	Y	?	?	?	?
18 Lowey	N	Y	N	Y	Y	Y	Y	Y
19 ***Kelly***	N	Y	N	Y	Y	Y	N	Y
20 ***Gilman***	N	Y	N	Y	Y	Y	Y	Y
21 McNulty	N	N	Y	Y	Y	N	Y	Y
22 ***Sweeney***	N	N	Y	Y	Y	N	N	Y
23 ***Boehlert***	N	Y	Y	Y	Y	Y	N	Y
24 ***McHugh***	Y	N	Y	Y	Y	N	N	Y
25 ***Walsh***	Y	N	Y	Y	Y	N	N	Y
26 Hinchey	N	Y	N	Y	N	Y	Y	Y
27 ***Reynolds***	Y	N	Y	Y	Y	N	N	Y
28 Slaughter	N	Y	N	Y	N	Y	Y	Y
29 LaFalce	N	Y	N	Y	N	N	Y	Y

	352	353	354	355	356	357	358	359
30 ***Quinn***	Y	N	Y	Y	Y	N	N	Y
31 ***Houghton***	N	Y	N	Y	Y	Y	N	Y
NORTH CAROLINA								
1 Clayton	N	Y	N	Y	N	Y	Y	Y
2 Etheridge	N	Y	N	Y	Y	Y	Y	Y
3 ***Jones***	Y	N	Y	N	Y	N	Y	Y
4 Price	N	Y	N	Y	Y	Y	Y	Y
5 ***Burr***	Y	N	Y	Y	Y	N	N	Y
6 ***Coble***	Y	N	Y	N	Y	N	N	Y
7 McIntyre	Y	N	Y	Y	Y	N	Y	Y
8 ***Hayes***	Y	N	Y	N	Y	N	N	Y
9 ***Myrick***	Y	N	Y	Y	Y	N	N	Y
10 ***Ballenger***	Y	N	Y	Y	Y	N	N	Y
11 ***Taylor***	Y	N	Y	Y	Y	N	N	Y
12 Watt	N	Y	N	Y	N	Y	Y	Y
NORTH DAKOTA								
AL Pomeroy	N	N	Y	Y	Y	Y	Y	Y
OHIO								
1 ***Chabot***	Y	N	Y	N	Y	N	N	Y
2 ***Portman***	Y	N	Y	Y	Y	N	N	Y
3 Hall	Y	N	Y	Y	Y	N	Y	Y
4 ***Oxley***	Y	N	Y	Y	N	N	N	Y
5 ***Gillmor***	N	N	Y	Y	Y	N	N	Y
6 Strickland	N	Y	Y	N	Y	Y	Y	Y
7 ***Hobson***	N	N	Y	Y	Y	N	N	Y
8 ***Boehner***	Y	N	Y	Y	N	N	N	Y
9 Kaptur	N	Y	N	Y	Y	Y	Y	Y
10 Kucinich	N	Y	N	Y	N	N	Y	Y
11 Jones	N	Y	N	Y	N	Y	Y	Y
12 ***Tiberi***	Y	N	Y	N	Y	N	N	Y
13 Brown	N	Y	N	Y	N	Y	Y	Y
14 Sawyer	N	Y	N	Y	N	Y	Y	Y
15 ***Pryce***	N	Y	Y	Y	Y	Y	N	Y
16 ***Regula***	N	N	Y	Y	Y	N	N	Y
17 Traficant	Y	N	Y	Y	Y	N	N	Y
18 ***Ney***	Y	N	Y	N	Y	N	N	Y
19 ***LaTourette***	N	N	Y	Y	Y	N	Y	Y
OKLAHOMA								
1 ***Largent***	Y	N	Y	Y	Y	N	N	Y
2 Carson	N	N	Y	Y	Y	Y	Y	Y
3 ***Watkins***	Y	N	Y	N	Y	N	N	Y
4 ***Watts***	Y	N	Y	Y	Y	N	N	Y
5 ***Istook***	Y	N	Y	Y	Y	N	N	Y
6 ***Lucas***	Y	N	Y	Y	Y	N	N	Y
OREGON								
1 Wu	N	Y	N	Y	N	Y	Y	Y
2 ***Walden***	Y	N	Y	Y	Y	Y	N	Y
3 Blumenauer	N	Y	N	Y	N	Y	Y	N
4 DeFazio	N	Y	N	Y	N	Y	Y	Y
5 Hooley	N	Y	N	Y	N	Y	Y	Y
PENNSYLVANIA								
1 Brady	N	Y	N	Y	N	Y	Y	Y
2 Fattah	N	Y	N	Y	N	Y	Y	Y
3 Borski	N	Y	N	Y	N	N	Y	Y
4 ***Hart***	Y	N	Y	N	Y	N	N	Y
5 ***Peterson***	Y	N	Y	Y	?	?	?	?
6 Holden	Y	N	Y	Y	N	N	Y	Y
7 ***Weldon***	Y	?	?	?	Y	N	N	Y
8 ***Greenwood***	N	N	Y	Y	Y	Y	N	Y
9 ***Shuster, Bill***	Y	N	Y	–	Y	N	N	Y
10 ***Sherwood***	Y	N	Y	Y	Y	N	N	Y
11 Kanjorski	N	Y	Y	Y	Y	N	Y	Y
12 Murtha	N	N	Y	Y	N	N	N	Y
13 Hoeffel	N	Y	N	Y	N	Y	Y	Y
14 Coyne	N	Y	N	Y	N	Y	Y	Y
15 ***Toomey***	Y	N	Y	Y	Y	N	N	Y
16 ***Pitts***	Y	N	Y	N	Y	N	N	Y
17 ***Gekas***	Y	N	Y	Y	Y	N	N	Y
18 Doyle	N	Y	Y	Y	N	N	Y	Y
19 ***Platts***	Y	N	Y	N	Y	N	N	Y
20 Mascara	Y	N	Y	Y	N	N	Y	Y
21 ***English***	N	N	Y	Y	Y	N	N	Y
RHODE ISLAND								
1 Kennedy	N	Y	N	Y	N	Y	Y	Y
2 Langevin	N	Y	N	Y	Y	N	Y	Y
SOUTH CAROLINA								
1 ***Brown***	Y	N	Y	Y	Y	N	N	Y
2 Vacant								
3 ***Graham***	Y	N	Y	N	Y	N	N	Y
4 ***DeMint***	Y	N	Y	N	Y	N	N	Y
5 Spratt	N	N	Y	Y	Y	Y	Y	Y
6 Clyburn	N	Y	N	Y	N	Y	Y	Y
SOUTH DAKOTA								
AL ***Thune***	Y	N	Y	Y	Y	N	N	Y

	352	353	354	355	356	357	358	359
TENNESSEE								
1 ***Jenkins***	Y	N	Y	N	N	N	N	Y
2 ***Duncan***	Y	N	Y	N	Y	N	N	Y
3 ***Wamp***	Y	N	Y	Y	Y	N	N	Y
4 ***Hilleary***	Y	N	Y	N	Y	N	N	Y
5 Clement	Y	N	?	Y	N	Y	Y	Y
6 Gordon	N	N	Y	N	Y	Y	Y	Y
7 ***Bryant***	Y	N	Y	N	Y	N	N	Y
8 Tanner	Y	N	Y	Y	N	Y	Y	Y
9 Ford	N	Y	N	Y	N	Y	Y	Y
TEXAS								
1 Sandlin	N	N	Y	Y	N	Y	Y	Y
2 Turner	N	N	Y	Y	N	Y	Y	Y
3 ***Johnson, Sam***	Y	N	Y	N	Y	N	N	Y
4 Hall	Y	N	Y	N	Y	N	Y	Y
5 ***Sessions***	Y	N	Y	N	Y	N	N	Y
6 ***Barton***	Y	N	Y	Y	Y	N	N	Y
7 ***Culberson***	Y	N	Y	N	Y	N	N	Y
8 ***Brady***	Y	N	Y	N	Y	N	N	Y
9 Lampson	N	Y	Y	Y	N	Y	Y	Y
10 Doggett	N	Y	N	Y	N	Y	Y	Y
11 Edwards	N	N	Y	Y	N	Y	Y	Y
12 ***Granger***	Y	N	Y	Y	Y	N	N	Y
13 ***Thornberry***	Y	N	Y	N	N	N	N	Y
14 ***Paul***	Y	N	Y	N	N	N	N	N
15 Hinojosa	N	Y	N	Y	N	Y	Y	Y
16 Reyes	N	Y	N	Y	N	Y	Y	Y
17 Stenholm	Y	N	Y	N	Y	N	Y	Y
18 Jackson-Lee	N	Y	N	Y	N	Y	Y	Y
19 ***Combest***	Y	N	Y	N	Y	N	N	Y
20 Gonzalez	N	Y	N	Y	N	Y	Y	Y
21 ***Smith***	Y	N	Y	Y	Y	N	N	Y
22 ***DeLay***	Y	N	Y	Y	Y	N	N	Y
23 ***Bonilla***	Y	N	Y	Y	Y	N	N	Y
24 Frost	N	Y	N	Y	N	Y	Y	Y
25 Bentsen	N	Y	Y	N	Y	Y	Y	Y
26 ***Armey***	Y	N	Y	N	Y	N	N	Y
27 Ortiz	N	N	Y	Y	N	N	Y	Y
28 Rodriguez	N	Y	N	Y	N	Y	Y	Y
29 Green	N	Y	Y	N	N	Y	Y	Y
30 Johnson, E.B.	N	Y	N	Y	N	Y	Y	Y
UTAH								
1 ***Hansen***	Y	N	Y	N	Y	N	N	Y
2 Matheson	N	N	Y	Y	Y	Y	Y	Y
3 ***Cannon***	Y	N	Y	Y	Y	N	N	Y
VERMONT								
AL *Sanders*	N	Y	N	Y	N	Y	Y	Y
VIRGINIA								
1 ***Davis, Jo Ann***	Y	N	Y	N	Y	N	N	Y
2 ***Schrock***	Y	N	Y	N	Y	N	N	Y
3 Scott	N	Y	N	Y	N	Y	Y	Y
4 ***Forbes***	Y	N	Y	N	Y	N	N	Y
5 *Goode*	Y	N	Y	N	Y	N	N	Y
6 ***Goodlatte***	Y	N	Y	N	Y	N	N	Y
7 ***Cantor***	Y	N	Y	N	Y	N	N	Y
8 Moran	N	Y	N	Y	?	Y	N	Y
9 Boucher	N	N	Y	Y	N	Y	Y	Y
10 ***Wolf***	Y	N	Y	Y	Y	N	N	Y
11 ***Davis, T.***	N	N	Y	Y	Y	N	N	Y
WASHINGTON								
1 Inslee	N	Y	N	Y	N	Y	Y	Y
2 Larsen	N	Y	N	Y	N	Y	Y	Y
3 Baird	N	N	Y	Y	N	Y	Y	Y
4 ***Hastings***	Y	N	Y	Y	Y	N	N	Y
5 ***Nethercutt***	Y	N	Y	Y	Y	N	N	Y
6 Dicks	N	Y	N	Y	N	Y	Y	Y
7 McDermott	N	Y	N	Y	N	Y	Y	N
8 ***Dunn***	Y	N	Y	?	Y	Y	N	Y
9 Smith	N	Y	N	Y	N	Y	Y	Y
WEST VIRGINIA								
1 Mollohan	N	N	Y	Y	?	?	N	Y
2 ***Capito***	Y	N	Y	Y	Y	Y	N	Y
3 Rahall	N	N	Y	Y	N	N	Y	Y
WISCONSIN								
1 ***Ryan***	Y	N	Y	N	N	N	N	Y
2 Baldwin	N	Y	N	Y	N	Y	Y	Y
3 Kind	N	Y	Y	Y	Y	Y	Y	Y
4 Kleczka	N	Y	N	Y	N	Y	Y	Y
5 Barrett	N	Y	N	Y	N	Y	Y	Y
6 ***Petri***	Y	N	Y	N	N	N	N	Y
7 Obey	N	?	?	P	N	Y	Y	Y
8 ***Green***	Y	N	Y	N	Y	N	N	Y
9 ***Sensenbrenner***	Y	N	Y	N	Y	N	N	Y
WYOMING								
AL ***Cubin***	Y	N	Y	Y	Y	N	N	?

Southern states - Ala., Ark., Fla., Ga., Ky., La., Miss., N.C., Okla., S.C., Tenn., Texas, Va.

Key

Y	Voted for (yea).
#	Paired for.
+	Announced for.
N	Voted against (nay).
X	Paired against.
−	Announced against.
P	Voted "present."
C	Voted "present" to avoid possible conflict of interest.
?	Did not vote or otherwise make a position known.

Democrats **Republicans** *Independents*

---

360. HR 169. Federal Employees' Protection/Passage. Sensenbrenner, R-Wis., motion to suspend the rules and pass the bill that aims to strengthen federal agencies' compliance with anti-discrimination and whistleblower protection laws by requiring them to pay for employee claims resulting in judgements against them out of their own budgets, better notify employees about relevant laws, and mandate detailed, annual reports to Congress on actions filed against them. Motion agreed to 420-0: R 213-0; D 205-0 (ND 151-0, SD 54-0); I 2-0. A two-thirds majority of those present and voting (280 in this case) is required for passage under suspension of the rules. Oct. 2, 2001.

361. H J Res 42. Firefighter Tribute/Passage. Sensenbrenner, R-Wis., motion to suspend the rules and pass the joint resolution that would require that American flags on all federal office buildings be flown at half-mast one day each year in honor of the National Fallen Firefighters Memorial Service in Emittsburg, Md. Motion agreed to 420-0: R 213-0; D 205-0 (ND 151-0, SD 54-0); I 2-0. A two-thirds majority of those present and voting (280 in this case) is required for passage under suspension of the rules. Oct. 2, 2001.

362. HR 2904. Fiscal 2002 Military Construction/Motion to Instruct. Olver, D-Mass., motion to instruct House conferees to insist on the House position on all items included in the House-passed bill for overseas military construction. The bill would provide $10.5 billion for military construction projects, including the building of barracks, family housing, and medical facilities for fiscal 2002. Motion agreed to 417-1: R 211-1; D 204-0 (ND 151-0, SD 53-0); I 2-0. Oct. 2, 2001.

363. HR 2646. Farm Bill/Renewable Fuels. Boswell, D-Iowa, amendment that would establish a 10-year renewable energy reserve program to purchase and store agricultural products needed to produce bio-energy and renewable fuels. Rejected 100-323: R 8-207; D 91-115 (ND 80-73, SD 11-42); I 1-1. Oct. 3, 2001.

364. HR 2646. Farm Bill/Buy American. Traficant, D-Ohio, amendment that would limit the bill's funding to those persons and entities abiding by the Buy America Act. Adopted 418-5: R 212-3; D 204-2 (ND 151-2, SD 53-0); I 2-0. Oct. 3, 2001.

365. HR 2646. Farm Bill/Loan Gains. Smith, R-Mich., amendment that would require the secretary of Agriculture to consider marketing loan gains, loan deficiency payments, and gains from certificates or crop forfeiture when determining whether the limit on the total amount of payments or gains any person can receive for a single commodity in a crop year has been reached. Rejected 187-238: R 65-151; D 120-87 (ND 113-41, SD 7-46); I 2-0. Oct. 3, 2001.

	360	361	362	363	364	365
ALABAMA						
1 *Callahan*	Y	Y	Y	N	Y	N
2 *Everett*	Y	Y	Y	N	Y	N
3 *Riley*	Y	Y	Y	N	Y	N
4 *Aderholt*	Y	Y	Y	N	Y	N
5 Cramer	Y	Y	Y	N	Y	N
6 *Bachus*	Y	Y	Y	N	Y	N
7 Hilliard	Y	Y	Y	N	Y	N
ALASKA						
AL *Young*	Y	Y	Y	N	Y	N
ARIZONA						
1 *Flake*	Y	Y	Y	N	Y	Y
2 Pastor	Y	Y	Y	N	Y	N
3 *Stump*	Y	Y	Y	N	Y	N
4 *Shadegg*	Y	Y	Y	N	Y	Y
5 *Kolbe*	Y	Y	Y	N	N	N
6 *Hayworth*	Y	Y	Y	N	Y	N
ARKANSAS						
1 Berry	Y	Y	Y	N	Y	N
2 Snyder	Y	Y	Y	N	Y	N
3 Vacant						
4 Ross	Y	Y	Y	N	Y	N
CALIFORNIA						
1 Thompson	Y	Y	Y	Y	Y	N
2 *Herger*	Y	Y	Y	N	Y	N
3 *Ose*	Y	Y	Y	N	Y	N
4 *Doolittle*	Y	Y	Y	N	Y	N
5 Matsui	Y	Y	Y	N	Y	N
6 Woolsey	Y	Y	Y	Y	Y	Y
7 Miller, George	Y	Y	Y	Y	Y	Y
8 Pelosi	Y	Y	Y	Y	Y	Y
9 Lee	Y	Y	Y	Y	Y	Y
10 Tauscher	Y	Y	Y	Y	Y	N
11 *Pombo*	Y	Y	Y	N	Y	N
12 Lantos	Y	Y	Y	N	Y	Y
13 Stark	Y	Y	N	N	Y	Y
14 Eshoo	Y	Y	Y	N	Y	Y
15 Honda	Y	Y	Y	Y	Y	Y
16 Lofgren	Y	Y	Y	Y	Y	Y
17 Farr	Y	Y	Y	Y	Y	Y
18 Condit	Y	Y	Y	N	Y	N
19 *Radanovich*	Y	Y	Y	N	Y	N
20 Dooley	Y	Y	Y	N	Y	N
21 *Thomas*	Y	Y	Y	N	Y	N
22 Capps	Y	Y	Y	N	Y	Y
23 *Gallegly*	Y	Y	Y	N	Y	N
24 Sherman	Y	Y	Y	N	Y	N
25 *McKeon*	Y	Y	Y	N	Y	N
26 Berman	Y	Y	Y	N	Y	N
27 Schiff	Y	Y	Y	Y	Y	N
28 *Dreier*	Y	Y	Y	N	N	Y
29 Waxman	Y	Y	Y	N	Y	Y
30 Becerra	Y	Y	Y	N	Y	Y
31 Solis	Y	Y	Y	Y	Y	Y
32 Watson	Y	Y	Y	Y	Y	Y
33 Roybal-Allard	Y	Y	Y	Y	Y	Y
34 Napolitano	Y	Y	Y	N	Y	Y
35 Waters	Y	Y	Y	Y	Y	Y
36 Harman	Y	Y	Y	N	Y	N
37 Millender-McD.	Y	Y	Y	+	+	N
38 *Horn*	Y	Y	Y	N	Y	N
39 *Royce*	Y	Y	Y	N	Y	Y
40 *Lewis*	Y	Y	Y	N	Y	N
41 *Miller, Gary*	Y	Y	Y	N	Y	Y
42 Baca	Y	Y	Y	N	Y	N
43 *Calvert*	Y	Y	Y	N	Y	N
44 *Bono*	Y	Y	Y	N	Y	N
45 *Rohrabacher*	Y	Y	Y	N	Y	N
46 Sanchez	Y	Y	Y	Y	Y	Y
47 *Cox*	Y	Y	Y	N	Y	N
48 *Issa*	Y	Y	Y	N	Y	N
49 Davis	Y	Y	Y	Y	Y	Y
50 Filner	Y	Y	Y	Y	Y	Y
51 *Cunningham*	Y	Y	Y	N	Y	N
52 *Hunter*	?	Y	Y	N	Y	N
COLORADO						
1 DeGette	Y	Y	Y	Y	Y	Y
2 Udall	Y	Y	Y	Y	Y	Y
3 *McInnis*	Y	Y	Y	N	Y	Y
4 *Schaffer*	?	?	?	N	Y	N
5 *Hefley*	Y	Y	Y	N	Y	Y
6 *Tancredo*	Y	Y	Y	N	Y	Y
CONNECTICUT						
1 Larson	Y	Y	Y	N	Y	Y
2 *Simmons*	Y	Y	Y	N	Y	Y
3 DeLauro	Y	Y	Y	N	Y	Y
4 *Shays*	Y	Y	Y	N	Y	Y
5 Maloney	Y	Y	Y	N	Y	Y
6 *Johnson*	Y	Y	Y	N	Y	Y
DELAWARE						
AL *Castle*	Y	Y	Y	N	Y	N
FLORIDA						
1 Vacant						
2 Boyd	Y	Y	Y	N	Y	N
3 Brown	Y	Y	Y	N	Y	N
4 *Crenshaw*	Y	Y	Y	N	Y	N
5 Thurman	Y	Y	Y	Y	Y	N
6 *Stearns*	Y	Y	Y	N	Y	Y
7 *Mica*	Y	Y	Y	N	Y	Y
8 *Keller*	Y	Y	Y	N	Y	Y
9 *Bilirakis*	Y	Y	Y	N	Y	Y
10 *Young*	Y	Y	Y	N	Y	N
11 Davis	Y	Y	Y	N	Y	N
12 *Putnam*	Y	Y	Y	N	Y	N
13 *Miller*	Y	Y	Y	N	Y	N
14 *Goss*	Y	Y	Y	N	Y	Y
15 *Weldon*	Y	Y	Y	N	Y	N
16 *Foley*	Y	Y	Y	N	Y	N
17 Meek	Y	Y	Y	N	Y	N
18 *Ros-Lehtinen*	Y	Y	Y	N	Y	N
19 Wexler	Y	Y	Y	N	Y	N
20 Deutsch	Y	Y	Y	N	Y	N
21 *Diaz-Balart*	Y	Y	Y	N	Y	N
22 *Shaw*	Y	Y	Y	N	Y	N
23 Hastings	Y	Y	Y	N	Y	N
GEORGIA						
1 *Kingston*	Y	Y	Y	N	Y	N
2 Bishop	Y	Y	Y	N	Y	N
3 *Collins*	Y	Y	Y	N	Y	N
4 McKinney	Y	Y	Y	Y	Y	Y
5 Lewis	Y	Y	Y	Y	Y	Y
6 *Isakson*	Y	Y	Y	N	Y	N
7 *Barr*	Y	Y	Y	N	Y	N
8 *Chambliss*	Y	Y	Y	N	Y	N
9 *Deal*	Y	Y	Y	N	Y	N
10 *Norwood*	Y	Y	Y	N	Y	N
11 *Linder*	Y	Y	Y	N	Y	Y
HAWAII						
1 Abercrombie	Y	Y	Y	N	Y	Y
2 Mink	Y	Y	Y	N	Y	N
IDAHO						
1 *Otter*	Y	Y	Y	P	Y	N
2 *Simpson*	Y	?	Y	N	Y	N
ILLINOIS						
1 Rush	Y	Y	Y	Y	Y	Y
2 Jackson	Y	Y	Y	Y	Y	Y
3 Lipinski	?	?	?	N	Y	Y
4 Gutierrez	Y	Y	Y	N	Y	Y
5 Blagojevich	Y	Y	Y	Y	Y	N
6 *Hyde*	Y	Y	Y	N	Y	N
7 Davis	Y	Y	Y	Y	Y	Y
8 *Crane*	Y	Y	Y	N	Y	Y
9 Schakowsky	Y	Y	Y	Y	Y	Y
10 *Kirk*	Y	Y	Y	N	Y	N
11 *Weller*	Y	Y	Y	N	Y	N
12 Costello	Y	Y	Y	N	Y	N
13 *Biggert*	Y	Y	Y	N	Y	Y

ND Northern Democrats   SD Southern Democrats

	360	361	362	363	364	365
14 ***Hastert***						
15 ***Johnson***	Y	Y	Y	N	Y	N
16 ***Manzullo***	Y	Y	Y	N	Y	N
17 Evans	Y	Y	Y	Y	Y	N
18 ***LaHood***	Y	Y	Y	N	Y	N
19 Phelps	Y	Y	Y	N	Y	N
20 ***Shimkus***	Y	Y	Y	N	Y	N
INDIANA						
1 Visclosky	Y	Y	Y	N	Y	N
2 ***Pence***	Y	Y	Y	N	Y	N
3 Roemer	Y	Y	Y	N	Y	N
4 ***Souder***	Y	Y	Y	N	Y	N
5 ***Buyer***	Y	Y	Y	N	Y	N
6 ***Burton***	Y	Y	Y	N	Y	N
7 ***Kerns***	Y	Y	Y	N	Y	N
8 ***Hostettler***	Y	Y	Y	N	Y	Y
9 Hill	Y	Y	Y	N	Y	N
10 Carson	Y	Y	Y	N	Y	N
IOWA						
1 ***Leach***	Y	Y	Y	Y	Y	Y
2 ***Nussle***	Y	Y	Y	N	Y	N
3 Boswell	Y	Y	Y	Y	Y	Y
4 ***Ganske***	Y	Y	Y	N	Y	N
5 ***Latham***	Y	Y	Y	N	Y	N
KANSAS						
1 ***Moran***	Y	Y	Y	N	Y	Y
2 ***Ryun***	Y	Y	Y	N	Y	N
3 Moore	Y	Y	Y	Y	Y	Y
4 ***Tiahrt***	Y	Y	Y	N	Y	Y
KENTUCKY						
1 ***Whitfield***	Y	Y	Y	N	Y	N
2 ***Lewis***	Y	Y	Y	N	Y	N
3 ***Northup***	Y	Y	Y	N	Y	N
4 Lucas	Y	Y	Y	N	Y	N
5 ***Rogers***	Y	Y	Y	N	Y	N
6 ***Fletcher***	Y	Y	Y	N	Y	N
LOUISIANA						
1 ***Vitter***	Y	Y	Y	N	Y	N
2 Jefferson	Y	Y	Y	N	Y	N
3 ***Tauzin***	Y	Y	Y	N	Y	N
4 ***McCrery***	Y	Y	Y	N	Y	N
5 ***Cooksey***	Y	Y	Y	N	Y	N
6 ***Baker***	Y	Y	Y	N	Y	N
7 John	Y	Y	Y	N	Y	N
MAINE						
1 Allen	Y	Y	Y	N	Y	Y
2 Baldacci	Y	Y	Y	N	Y	Y
MARYLAND						
1 ***Gilchrest***	Y	Y	Y	N	Y	Y
2 ***Ehrlich***	Y	Y	Y	N	Y	Y
3 Cardin	Y	Y	Y	Y	Y	Y
4 Wynn	Y	Y	Y	Y	Y	N
5 Hoyer	Y	Y	Y	N	Y	N
6 ***Bartlett***	Y	Y	Y	Y	Y	Y
7 Cummings	Y	Y	Y	Y	Y	N
8 ***Morella***	Y	Y	Y	Y	Y	Y
MASSACHUSETTS						
1 Olver	Y	Y	Y	Y	Y	Y
2 Neal	Y	Y	Y	Y	Y	Y
3 McGovern	Y	Y	Y	Y	Y	Y
4 Frank	Y	Y	Y	Y	Y	Y
5 Meehan	Y	Y	Y	Y	Y	Y
6 Tierney	Y	Y	Y	N	Y	Y
7 Markey	Y	Y	Y	Y	Y	Y
8 Capuano	Y	Y	Y	Y	Y	Y
9 Vacant						
10 Delahunt	Y	Y	Y	Y	Y	Y
MICHIGAN						
1 Stupak	Y	Y	Y	Y	Y	Y
2 ***Hoekstra***	Y	Y	Y	N	Y	N
3 ***Ehlers***	Y	Y	Y	Y	Y	Y
4 ***Camp***	Y	Y	Y	N	Y	N
5 Barcia	Y	Y	Y	N	Y	Y
6 ***Upton***	Y	Y	Y	N	Y	N
7 ***Smith***	Y	Y	Y	N	Y	Y
8 ***Rogers***	Y	Y	Y	N	Y	N
9 Kildee	Y	Y	Y	N	Y	Y
10 Bonior	Y	Y	Y	N	Y	Y
11 ***Knollenberg***	Y	Y	Y	N	Y	N
12 Levin	Y	Y	Y	N	Y	N
13 Rivers	Y	Y	Y	Y	Y	Y
14 Conyers	Y	Y	Y	Y	Y	Y
15 Kilpatrick	Y	Y	Y	N	Y	N
16 Dingell	Y	Y	Y	Y	Y	N

	360	361	362	363	364	365
MINNESOTA						
1 ***Gutknecht***	Y	Y	Y	N	Y	N
2 ***Kennedy***	Y	Y	Y	N	Y	N
3 ***Ramstad***	Y	Y	Y	Y	Y	Y
4 McCollum	Y	Y	Y	Y	Y	N
5 Sabo	Y	Y	Y	Y	Y	N
6 Luther	Y	Y	Y	Y	Y	Y
7 Peterson	Y	Y	Y	Y	Y	N
8 Oberstar	Y	Y	Y	Y	Y	N
MISSISSIPPI						
1 ***Wicker***	Y	Y	Y	N	Y	N
2 Thompson	Y	Y	Y	N	Y	N
3 ***Pickering***	?	?	?	N	Y	N
4 Shows	Y	Y	Y	N	Y	N
5 Taylor	Y	Y	Y	N	Y	N
MISSOURI						
1 Clay	Y	Y	Y	N	Y	Y
2 ***Akin***	Y	Y	Y	N	Y	N
3 Gephardt	Y	Y	Y	Y	Y	Y
4 Skelton	Y	Y	Y	N	Y	N
5 McCarthy	Y	Y	Y	Y	Y	Y
6 ***Graves***	Y	Y	Y	N	Y	N
7 ***Blunt***	Y	Y	Y	N	Y	N
8 ***Emerson***	Y	Y	Y	N	Y	N
9 ***Hulshof***	Y	Y	Y	N	Y	N
MONTANA						
AL ***Rehberg***	Y	Y	Y	N	Y	N
NEBRASKA						
1 ***Bereuter***	Y	Y	Y	Y	Y	N
2 ***Terry***	Y	Y	Y	N	Y	N
3 ***Osborne***	Y	Y	Y	N	Y	N
NEVADA						
1 Berkley	Y	Y	Y	N	Y	N
2 ***Gibbons***	Y	Y	Y	N	Y	N
NEW HAMPSHIRE						
1 ***Sununu***	Y	Y	Y	N	Y	Y
2 ***Bass***	Y	Y	Y	N	Y	Y
NEW JERSEY						
1 Andrews	Y	Y	Y	N	Y	Y
2 ***LoBiondo***	Y	Y	Y	N	Y	Y
3 ***Saxton***	Y	Y	Y	N	?	N
4 ***Smith***	Y	Y	Y	N	Y	Y
5 ***Roukema***	Y	Y	Y	N	Y	Y
6 Pallone	Y	Y	Y	Y	Y	N
7 ***Ferguson***	Y	Y	Y	N	Y	Y
8 Pascrell	Y	Y	Y	Y	Y	Y
9 Rothman	Y	Y	Y	Y	Y	N
10 Payne	Y	Y	Y	Y	Y	Y
11 ***Frelinghuysen***	Y	Y	Y	N	Y	Y
12 Holt	Y	Y	Y	Y	Y	Y
13 Menendez	Y	Y	Y	N	Y	Y
NEW MEXICO						
1 ***Wilson***	Y	Y	Y	N	Y	N
2 ***Skeen***	Y	Y	Y	N	Y	N
3 Udall	Y	Y	Y	Y	Y	Y
NEW YORK						
1 ***Grucci***	Y	Y	Y	Y	Y	N
2 Israel	Y	Y	Y	Y	Y	Y
3 ***King***	Y	Y	Y	N	Y	N
4 McCarthy	Y	Y	Y	N	Y	Y
5 Ackerman	Y	Y	Y	N	Y	Y
6 Meeks	Y	Y	Y	N	Y	Y
7 Crowley	Y	Y	Y	Y	Y	Y
8 Nadler	Y	Y	Y	Y	Y	Y
9 Weiner	Y	Y	Y	Y	Y	Y
10 Towns	?	?	?	N	Y	Y
11 Owens	Y	Y	Y	N	Y	Y
12 Velázquez	Y	Y	Y	N	Y	Y
13 ***Fossella***	Y	Y	Y	N	Y	Y
14 Maloney	Y	Y	Y	Y	Y	Y
15 Rangel	Y	Y	Y	N	Y	N
16 Serrano	Y	Y	Y	Y	Y	N
17 Engel	?	?	?	?	?	?
18 Lowey	Y	Y	Y	Y	Y	Y
19 ***Kelly***	Y	Y	Y	N	Y	Y
20 ***Gilman***	Y	Y	Y	N	Y	Y
21 McNulty	Y	Y	Y	Y	Y	Y
22 ***Sweeney***	Y	Y	Y	N	Y	N
23 ***Boehlert***	Y	Y	Y	N	Y	N
24 ***McHugh***	Y	Y	Y	N	Y	N
25 ***Walsh***	Y	Y	Y	N	Y	N
26 Hinchey	Y	Y	Y	N	Y	Y
27 ***Reynolds***	Y	Y	Y	N	Y	N
28 Slaughter	Y	Y	Y	Y	Y	Y
29 LaFalce	Y	Y	Y	Y	Y	Y

	360	361	362	363	364	365
30 ***Quinn***	Y	Y	Y	N	Y	N
31 ***Houghton***	?	?	?	?	?	?
NORTH CAROLINA						
1 Clayton	Y	Y	Y	Y	Y	Y
2 Etheridge	Y	Y	Y	N	Y	N
3 ***Jones***	Y	Y	+	N	Y	N
4 Price	Y	Y	Y	N	Y	N
5 ***Burr***	Y	Y	Y	N	Y	N
6 ***Coble***	Y	Y	Y	N	Y	N
7 McIntyre	Y	Y	Y	N	Y	N
8 ***Hayes***	Y	Y	Y	N	Y	N
9 ***Myrick***	Y	Y	Y	N	Y	N
10 ***Ballenger***	Y	Y	Y	N	Y	N
11 ***Taylor***	?	?	?	N	Y	N
12 Watt	Y	Y	Y	Y	Y	Y
NORTH DAKOTA						
AL Pomeroy	Y	Y	Y	Y	Y	Y
OHIO						
1 ***Chabot***	Y	Y	Y	N	Y	Y
2 ***Portman***	Y	Y	Y	N	Y	N
3 Hall	Y	Y	Y	N	Y	N
4 ***Oxley***	Y	Y	Y	N	Y	N
5 ***Gillmor***	Y	Y	Y	N	Y	N
6 Strickland	Y	Y	Y	Y	Y	Y
7 ***Hobson***	Y	Y	Y	N	Y	N
8 ***Boehner***	Y	Y	Y	N	Y	N
9 Kaptur	?	?	?	?	Y	Y
10 Kucinich	Y	Y	Y	Y	Y	Y
11 Jones	+	+	+	Y	Y	Y
12 ***Tiberi***	Y	Y	Y	N	Y	N
13 Brown	Y	Y	Y	Y	Y	Y
14 Sawyer	Y	Y	Y	N	Y	Y
15 ***Pryce***	Y	Y	Y	N	Y	N
16 ***Regula***	Y	Y	Y	N	Y	N
17 Traficant	Y	Y	Y	N	Y	N
18 ***Ney***	Y	Y	Y	N	Y	Y
19 ***LaTourette***	Y	Y	Y	N	Y	Y
OKLAHOMA						
1 ***Largent***	Y	Y	Y	N	Y	N
2 Carson	Y	Y	Y	Y	Y	N
3 ***Watkins***	Y	Y	Y	N	Y	N
4 ***Watts***	Y	Y	Y	N	Y	N
5 ***Istook***	Y	Y	Y	N	Y	Y
6 ***Lucas***	Y	Y	Y	N	Y	N
OREGON						
1 Wu	Y	Y	Y	N	Y	N
2 ***Walden***	Y	Y	Y	N	Y	N
3 Blumenauer	Y	Y	Y	N	Y	Y
4 DeFazio	Y	Y	Y	Y	Y	Y
5 Hooley	Y	Y	Y	N	Y	Y
PENNSYLVANIA						
1 Brady	Y	Y	Y	Y	Y	Y
2 Fattah	Y	Y	Y	N	Y	Y
3 Borski	Y	Y	Y	N	Y	Y
4 ***Hart***	Y	Y	Y	N	Y	Y
5 ***Peterson***	Y	Y	Y	N	Y	Y
6 Holden	Y	Y	Y	N	Y	Y
7 ***Weldon***	Y	Y	Y	?	?	?
8 ***Greenwood***	Y	Y	Y	N	Y	N
9 ***Shuster, Bill***	Y	Y	Y	N	Y	N
10 ***Sherwood***	Y	Y	Y	N	Y	Y
11 Kanjorski	Y	Y	Y	N	Y	Y
12 Murtha	Y	Y	Y	N	Y	Y
13 Hoeffel	Y	Y	Y	Y	Y	Y
14 Coyne	Y	Y	Y	N	Y	Y
15 ***Toomey***	Y	Y	Y	N	Y	Y
16 ***Pitts***	Y	Y	Y	N	Y	Y
17 ***Gekas***	Y	Y	Y	N	Y	Y
18 Doyle	Y	Y	Y	N	Y	Y
19 ***Platts***	Y	Y	Y	N	Y	Y
20 Mascara	Y	Y	Y	N	Y	Y
21 ***English***	Y	Y	Y	N	Y	N
RHODE ISLAND						
1 Kennedy	Y	Y	Y	Y	Y	Y
2 Langevin	Y	Y	Y	Y	Y	Y
SOUTH CAROLINA						
1 ***Brown***	Y	Y	Y	N	Y	N
2 Vacant						
3 ***Graham***	Y	Y	Y	N	Y	N
4 ***DeMint***	Y	Y	Y	N	Y	Y
5 Spratt	Y	Y	Y	N	Y	N
6 Clyburn	Y	Y	Y	N	Y	N
SOUTH DAKOTA						
AL ***Thune***	Y	Y	Y	N	Y	Y

	360	361	362	363	364	365
TENNESSEE						
1 ***Jenkins***	Y	Y	Y	N	Y	N
2 ***Duncan***	Y	Y	Y	N	Y	Y
3 ***Wamp***	Y	Y	Y	N	Y	Y
4 ***Hilleary***	Y	Y	Y	N	Y	N
5 Clement	Y	Y	Y	N	Y	N
6 Gordon	Y	Y	Y	N	Y	N
7 ***Bryant***	Y	Y	Y	N	Y	N
8 Tanner	Y	Y	Y	N	Y	N
9 Ford	Y	Y	Y	N	Y	N
TEXAS						
1 Sandlin	Y	Y	Y	Y	Y	N
2 Turner	Y	Y	Y	N	Y	N
3 ***Johnson, Sam***	Y	Y	Y	N	Y	N
4 Hall	Y	Y	Y	Y	Y	N
5 ***Sessions***	Y	Y	Y	N	Y	N
6 ***Barton***	Y	Y	Y	N	Y	N
7 ***Culberson***	Y	Y	Y	N	Y	N
8 ***Brady***	Y	Y	Y	N	Y	N
9 Lampson	Y	Y	Y	N	Y	N
10 Doggett	Y	Y	?	N	Y	Y
11 Edwards	Y	Y	Y	N	Y	N
12 ***Granger***	Y	Y	?	N	Y	N
13 ***Thornberry***	Y	Y	Y	N	Y	N
14 ***Paul***	Y	Y	N	N	Y	Y
15 Hinojosa	Y	Y	Y	N	Y	N
16 Reyes	Y	Y	Y	?	?	?
17 Stenholm	Y	Y	Y	N	Y	N
18 Jackson-Lee	Y	Y	Y	Y	Y	N
19 ***Combest***	Y	Y	Y	N	Y	N
20 Gonzalez	Y	Y	Y	N	Y	N
21 ***Smith***	Y	Y	Y	N	Y	N
22 ***DeLay***	Y	Y	Y	N	Y	Y
23 ***Bonilla***	Y	Y	Y	N	Y	N
24 Frost	Y	Y	Y	N	Y	N
25 Bentsen	Y	Y	Y	N	Y	N
26 ***Armey***	Y	Y	Y	N	N	Y
27 Ortiz	Y	Y	Y	N	Y	N
28 Rodriguez	Y	Y	Y	N	Y	N
29 Green	Y	Y	Y	N	Y	Y
30 Johnson, E.B.	Y	Y	Y	Y	Y	N
UTAH						
1 ***Hansen***	Y	Y	Y	N	Y	N
2 Matheson	Y	Y	Y	N	Y	N
3 ***Cannon***	Y	Y	Y	N	Y	N
VERMONT						
AL *Sanders*	Y	Y	Y	Y	Y	Y
VIRGINIA						
1 ***Davis, Jo Ann***	Y	Y	Y	N	Y	N
2 ***Schrock***	Y	Y	Y	N	Y	N
3 Scott	Y	Y	Y	N	Y	N
4 ***Forbes***	Y	Y	Y	N	Y	N
5 *Goode*	Y	Y	Y	N	Y	Y
6 ***Goodlatte***	Y	Y	Y	N	Y	N
7 ***Cantor***	Y	Y	Y	N	Y	N
8 Moran	Y	Y	Y	Y	Y	Y
9 Boucher	Y	Y	Y	N	Y	N
10 ***Wolf***	Y	Y	Y	N	Y	N
11 ***Davis, T.***	Y	Y	Y	N	Y	Y
WASHINGTON						
1 Inslee	Y	Y	Y	Y	Y	Y
2 Larsen	Y	Y	Y	N	Y	N
3 Baird	Y	Y	Y	N	Y	Y
4 ***Hastings***	Y	Y	Y	N	Y	N
5 ***Nethercutt***	Y	Y	Y	N	Y	N
6 Dicks	Y	Y	Y	Y	Y	Y
7 McDermott	Y	Y	Y	Y	N	Y
8 ***Dunn***	Y	Y	Y	N	Y	N
9 Smith	Y	Y	Y	Y	Y	Y
WEST VIRGINIA						
1 Mollohan	Y	Y	Y	?	?	?
2 ***Capito***	Y	Y	Y	N	Y	N
3 Rahall	Y	Y	Y	Y	Y	Y
WISCONSIN						
1 ***Ryan***	Y	Y	Y	N	Y	N
2 Baldwin	Y	Y	Y	N	Y	Y
3 Kind	Y	Y	Y	N	Y	Y
4 Kleczka	Y	Y	Y	N	Y	Y
5 Barrett	Y	Y	Y	N	Y	Y
6 ***Petri***	Y	Y	Y	N	Y	Y
7 Obey	Y	Y	Y	Y	Y	Y
8 ***Green***	Y	Y	Y	N	Y	N
9 ***Sensenbrenner***	Y	Y	Y	N	Y	Y
WYOMING						
AL ***Cubin***	Y	Y	Y	N	Y	N

Southern states - Ala., Ark., Fla., Ga., Ky., La., Miss., N.C., Okla., S.C., Tenn., Texas, Va.

Key

Y   Voted for (yea).
\#   Paired for.
\+   Announced for.
N   Voted against (nay).
X   Paired against.
−   Announced against.
P   Voted "present."
C   Voted "present" to avoid possible conflict of interest.
?   Did not vote or otherwise make a position known.

•

Democrats   **Republicans**
Independents

366. HR 2646. Farm Bill/Farm Conservation. Boehlert, R-N.Y., amendment that would shift $1.9 billion from the bill's fixed and countercyclical payments to farm and undeveloped land conservation programs, including the Farmland and Ranchland Protection Program and the Wildlife Habitat Incentives Program. The measure also would increase the amount of land that could be included in various preservation programs. Rejected 200-226: R 54-161; D 145-64 (ND 132-23, SD 13-41); I 1-1. Oct. 4, 2001.

367. HR 2646. Farm Bill/Sugar Subsidy. Miller, R-Fla., amendment that would reduce the loan rates for raw cane sugar by 1 cent, increase the forfeiture penalty by 1 cent per pound and authorize up to $300 million in resulting savings for conservation and environmental stewardship programs, with a priority for Everglades restoration. Rejected 177-239: R 105-107; D 72-130 (ND 62-87, SD 10-43); I 0-2. Oct. 4, 2001.

368. HR 2646. Farm Bill/National Dairy Compact. Sanders, I-Vt., amendment that would create a framework allowing for a nationwide dairy compact in which all states that have already voted to join a dairy compact would be members. Any other state could opt to join. Rejected 194-224: R 60-152, D 132-72 (ND 107-44; SD 25-28); I 2-0. Oct. 4, 2001.

369. HR 2646. Farm Bill/Rural Improvement Grants. Clayton, D-N.C., amendment that would shift $100 million in fixed payments for agricultural producers to several rural grants, including $45 million annually for rural strategic planning initiatives; $45 million annually for community water assistance grants; and $10 million annually for the value-added grants program. Adopted 235-183: R 59-153; D 174-30 (ND 143-8, SD 31-22); I 2-0. Oct. 4, 2001.

370. HR 2646. Farm Bill/Fruit Labels. Bono, R-Calif., amendment that would require retailers of fresh fruits, vegetables or any other perishable agricultural commodity to label fresh produce with its country of origin. Adopted 296-121: R 119-92; D 175-29 (ND 138-13, SD 37-16); I 2-0. Oct. 4, 2001.

	366	367	368	369	370
ALABAMA					
1 *Callahan*	N	?	?	?	?
2 *Everett*	N	N	N	N	Y
3 *Riley*	N	N	N	N	Y
4 *Aderholt*	N	N	N	N	Y
5 *Cramer*	N	N	N	N	N
6 *Bachus*	N	N	N	N	Y
7 Hilliard	N	N	N	N	Y
ALASKA					
AL *Young*	N	N	?	?	?
ARIZONA					
1 *Flake*	N	Y	N	N	N
2 Pastor	Y	N	Y	Y	N
3 *Stump*	N	N	N	N	N
4 *Shadegg*	N	Y	N	N	N
5 *Kolbe*	Y	Y	N	N	N
6 *Hayworth*	N	Y	N	Y	Y
ARKANSAS					
1 Berry	N	N	N	N	Y
2 Snyder	N	Y	Y	Y	Y
3 Vacant					
4 Ross	N	N	N	N	Y
CALIFORNIA					
1 Thompson	Y	N	N	Y	Y
2 *Herger*	N	N	N	Y	Y
3 *Ose*	N	N	N	N	N
4 *Doolittle*	N	N	N	N	N
5 Matsui	Y	N	Y	Y	Y
6 Woolsey	Y	N	Y	Y	Y
7 Miller, George	Y	Y	Y	Y	Y
8 Pelosi	Y	N	Y	Y	Y
9 Lee	Y	N	Y	Y	Y
10 Tauscher	Y	Y	Y	Y	Y
11 *Pombo*	N	N	N	N	N
12 Lantos	Y	Y	Y	Y	N
13 Stark	Y	N	Y	Y	Y
14 Eshoo	Y	Y	Y	Y	Y
15 Honda	Y	N	Y	Y	Y
16 Lofgren	Y	N	Y	Y	Y
17 Farr	Y	N	Y	Y	Y
18 Condit	N	N	Y	Y	Y
19 *Radanovich*	N	N	N	N	Y
20 Dooley	N	Y	N	Y	N
21 *Thomas*	N	Y	N	N	Y
22 Capps	Y	Y	Y	Y	Y
23 *Gallegly*	N	Y	N	N	Y
24 Sherman	Y	Y	Y	Y	Y
25 *McKeon*	N	N	N	N	N
26 Berman	Y	Y	Y	Y	Y
27 Schiff	Y	Y	N	Y	Y
28 *Dreier*	N	Y	N	N	N
29 Waxman	Y	Y	Y	Y	Y
30 Becerra	Y	N	Y	Y	Y
31 Solis	Y	N	N	Y	Y
32 Watson	Y	N	Y	Y	Y
33 Roybal-Allard	Y	N	Y	Y	Y
34 Napolitano	Y	N	Y	Y	Y
35 Waters	Y	N	Y	Y	Y
36 Harman	Y	N	Y	Y	Y
37 Millender-McD.	Y	−	Y	Y	Y
38 *Horn*	N	Y	Y	Y	Y

	366	367	368	369	370
39 *Royce*	N	Y	N	Y	Y
40 *Lewis*	N	N	N	N	Y
41 *Miller, Gary*	N	N	N	N	Y
42 Baca	N	N	N	Y	Y
43 *Calvert*	N	N	N	N	Y
44 *Bono*	N	Y	N	N	Y
45 *Rohrabacher*	Y	Y	N	Y	Y
46 Sanchez	N	Y	Y	Y	Y
47 *Cox*	N	Y	N	N	Y
48 *Issa*	N	Y	?	?	?
49 Davis	Y	Y	Y	Y	Y
50 Filner	Y	N	Y	Y	Y
51 *Cunningham*	N	N	N	N	Y
52 *Hunter*	N	N	N	N	Y
COLORADO					
1 DeGette	Y	Y	Y	Y	Y
2 Udall	Y	N	N	Y	Y
3 *McInnis*	N	Y	N	N	Y
4 *Schaffer*	N	N	N	N	N
5 *Hefley*	N	Y	N	N	Y
6 *Tancredo*	N	Y	N	N	N
CONNECTICUT					
1 Larson	Y	Y	Y	Y	Y
2 *Simmons*	Y	Y	Y	Y	Y
3 DeLauro	Y	Y	Y	Y	Y
4 *Shays*	Y	Y	N	Y	Y
5 Maloney	Y	Y	Y	Y	Y
6 *Johnson*	Y	Y	Y	Y	Y
DELAWARE					
AL *Castle*	Y	Y	Y	Y	N
FLORIDA					
1 Vacant					
2 Boyd	N	N	Y	N	Y
3 Brown	Y	N	Y	Y	Y
4 *Crenshaw*	N	N	N	N	Y
5 Thurman	N	N	Y	Y	Y
6 *Stearns*	N	N	N	N	Y
7 *Mica*	N	N	N	N	Y
8 *Keller*	N	Y	N	N	N
9 *Bilirakis*	Y	Y	N	Y	Y
10 *Young*	N	Y	N	N	Y
11 Davis	Y	N	Y	Y	Y
12 *Putnam*	N	N	N	N	Y
13 *Miller*	Y	Y	N	N	Y
14 *Goss*	Y	Y	N	N	Y
15 *Weldon*	N	N	N	N	Y
16 *Foley*	N	N	Y	Y	Y
17 Meek	N	N	Y	Y	Y
18 *Ros-Lehtinen*	N	N	N	N	Y
19 Wexler	Y	?	?	?	?
20 Deutsch	Y	Y	Y	Y	Y
21 *Diaz-Balart*	N	N	N	N	Y
22 *Shaw*	Y	N	N	N	Y
23 Hastings	N	N	Y	Y	Y
GEORGIA					
1 *Kingston*	N	Y	N	N	N
2 Bishop	N	N	N	N	Y
3 *Collins*	?	N	Y	N	Y
4 McKinney	N	Y	Y	Y	Y
5 Lewis	Y	N	Y	Y	Y
6 *Isakson*	N	Y	N	N	Y
7 *Barr*	N	Y	N	N	Y
8 *Chambliss*	N	N	N	N	Y
9 *Deal*	N	N	N	N	Y
10 *Norwood*	N	N	Y	N	Y
11 *Linder*	N	Y	N	N	Y
HAWAII					
1 Abercrombie	Y	N	Y	Y	Y
2 Mink	N	N	Y	Y	Y
IDAHO					
1 *Otter*	N	N	N	N	N
2 *Simpson*	N	N	N	N	N
ILLINOIS					
1 Rush	N	Y	Y	Y	Y
2 Jackson	Y	Y	Y	Y	Y
3 Lipinski	N	Y	N	Y	Y
4 Gutierrez	Y	Y	Y	Y	Y
5 Blagojevich	N	Y	Y	Y	Y
6 *Hyde*	N	Y	N	N	Y
7 Davis	Y	Y	Y	Y	Y
8 *Crane*	N	Y	N	N	N
9 Schakowsky	Y	Y	Y	Y	Y
10 *Kirk*	Y	Y	N	Y	Y
11 *Weller*	N	N	N	N	N
12 Costello	N	N	N	N	Y
13 *Biggert*	Y	Y	N	N	Y

ND Northern Democrats   SD Southern Democrats

	366	367	368	369	370
14 ***Hastert***	N				
15 ***Johnson***	N	N	N	N	N
16 ***Manzullo***	N	Y	N	N	N
17 Evans	N	N	N	N	Y
18 ***LaHood***	N	N	N	N	Y
19 Phelps	N	N	N	N	Y
20 ***Shimkus***	N	N	N	N	Y
INDIANA					
1 Visclosky	?	?	?	?	?
2 ***Pence***	N	Y	N	N	N
3 Roemer	Y	N	Y	Y	Y
4 ***Souder***	N	Y	N	N	N
5 ***Buyer***	N	N	N	N	Y
6 ***Burton***	?	?	?	?	?
7 ***Kerns***	N	Y	N	N	N
8 ***Hostettler***	N	Y	N	N	N
9 Hill	N	N	N	N	Y
10 Carson	Y	N	Y	Y	Y
IOWA					
1 ***Leach***	N	N	N	N	N
2 ***Nussle***	N	N	N	N	N
3 Boswell	N	N	N	Y	N
4 ***Ganske***	N	N	N	N	N
5 ***Latham***	N	N	N	N	N
KANSAS					
1 ***Moran***	N	N	N	N	N
2 ***Ryun***	N	N	N	N	N
3 Moore	N	Y	N	Y	Y
4 ***Tiahrt***	N	N	N	N	N
KENTUCKY					
1 ***Whitfield***	N	N	Y	N	Y
2 ***Lewis***	N	N	Y	N	N
3 ***Northup***	N	Y	N	Y	N
4 Lucas	N	N	N	N	N
5 ***Rogers***	N	N	Y	Y	Y
6 ***Fletcher***	N	N	N	N	N
LOUISIANA					
1 ***Vitter***	N	N	Y	N	N
2 Jefferson	Y	N	N	Y	Y
3 ***Tauzin***	N	N	N	N	Y
4 ***McCrery***	N	Y	N	N	N
5 ***Cooksey***	N	N	Y	N	Y
6 ***Baker***	N	N	Y	N	N
7 John	N	N	N	N	Y
MAINE					
1 Allen	Y	Y	Y	Y	Y
2 Baldacci	Y	N	Y	Y	Y
MARYLAND					
1 ***Gilchrest***	Y	N	Y	Y	N
2 ***Ehrlich***	Y	Y	N	Y	N
3 Cardin	Y	N	Y	Y	Y
4 Wynn	Y	N	Y	Y	Y
5 Hoyer	Y	N	Y	Y	Y
6 ***Bartlett***	N	Y	Y	Y	Y
7 Cummings	Y	N	Y	Y	Y
8 ***Morella***	Y	Y	Y	Y	Y
MASSACHUSETTS					
1 Olver	Y	N	?	?	?
2 Neal	Y	N	Y	Y	Y
3 McGovern	Y	N	Y	Y	N
4 Frank	Y	Y	N	Y	N
5 Meehan	Y	Y	Y	Y	Y
6 Tierney	Y	Y	N	Y	Y
7 Markey	Y	Y	N	Y	Y
8 Capuano	Y	N	Y	Y	Y
9 Vacant					
10 Delahunt	Y	N	N	Y	Y
MICHIGAN					
1 Stupak	Y	N	Y	Y	Y
2 ***Hoekstra***	Y	Y	N	N	Y
3 ***Ehlers***	Y	Y	Y	Y	Y
4 ***Camp***	N	N	N	N	Y
5 Barcia	N	N	N	Y	Y
6 ***Upton***	Y	Y	Y	Y	Y
7 ***Smith***	N	N	N	N	N
8 ***Rogers***	N	N	N	N	Y
9 Kildee	Y	N	Y	Y	Y
10 Bonior	Y	N	Y	Y	Y
11 ***Knollenberg***	N	N	N	N	N
12 Levin	N	N	Y	Y	Y
13 Rivers	Y	N	Y	Y	Y
14 Conyers	Y	Y	Y	Y	Y
15 Kilpatrick	Y	N	Y	Y	Y
16 Dingell	Y	N	N	Y	Y

	366	367	368	369	370
MINNESOTA					
1 ***Gutknecht***	N	N	N	N	N
2 ***Kennedy***	N	N	N	N	N
3 ***Ramstad***	Y	Y	N	N	N
4 McCollum	Y	N	N	Y	Y
5 Sabo	N	N	N	Y	N
6 Luther	Y	N	Y	Y	Y
7 Peterson	N	N	N	N	N
8 Oberstar	Y	N	Y	Y	Y
MISSISSIPPI					
1 ***Wicker***	N	N	N	N	Y
2 Thompson	N	N	N	Y	Y
3 ***Pickering***	N	N	Y	N	Y
4 Shows	N	N	Y	N	Y
5 Taylor	N	N	Y	N	Y
MISSOURI					
1 Clay	Y	Y	N	Y	Y
2 ***Akin***	N	N	N	N	N
3 Gephardt	Y	N	Y	Y	Y
4 Skelton	N	N	N	N	Y
5 McCarthy	Y	Y	N	N	N
6 ***Graves***	N	N	N	N	N
7 ***Blunt***	N	N	N	N	N
8 ***Emerson***	N	N	Y	N	Y
9 ***Hulshof***	N	N	N	N	N
MONTANA					
AL ***Rehberg***	N	N	N	N	Y
NEBRASKA					
1 ***Bereuter***	N	N	Y	N	N
2 ***Terry***	N	N	N	N	N
3 ***Osborne***	N	N	N	N	N
NEVADA					
1 Berkley	N	Y	N	Y	Y
2 ***Gibbons***	?	?	?	?	?
NEW HAMPSHIRE					
1 ***Sununu***	Y	Y	N	Y	N
2 ***Bass***	Y	Y	Y	Y	N
NEW JERSEY					
1 Andrews	Y	Y	Y	Y	Y
2 ***LoBiondo***	Y	Y	Y	Y	Y
3 ***Saxton***	Y	Y	Y	Y	Y
4 ***Smith***	Y	Y	N	Y	Y
5 ***Roukema***	Y	Y	Y	Y	?
6 Pallone	Y	Y	Y	Y	Y
7 ***Ferguson***	Y	Y	Y	Y	Y
8 Pascrell	Y	Y	Y	Y	Y
9 Rothman	Y	N	Y	Y	Y
10 Payne	Y	N	Y	Y	Y
11 ***Frelinghuysen***	Y	Y	Y	Y	Y
12 Holt	Y	Y	Y	Y	Y
13 Menendez	Y	N	Y	Y	Y
NEW MEXICO					
1 ***Wilson***	N	N	N	Y	N
2 ***Skeen***	N	N	N	N	Y
3 Udall	Y	N	N	Y	Y
NEW YORK					
1 ***Grucci***	Y	N	Y	Y	Y
2 Israel	Y	N	Y	Y	Y
3 ***King***	Y	Y	Y	Y	Y
4 McCarthy	Y	Y	Y	Y	Y
5 Ackerman	Y	N	Y	Y	Y
6 Meeks	Y	Y	Y	Y	Y
7 Crowley	Y	N	Y	Y	Y
8 Nadler	Y	Y	Y	Y	Y
9 Weiner	Y	Y	Y	Y	Y
10 Towns	Y	N	Y	Y	Y
11 Owens	Y	Y	Y	Y	Y
12 Velázquez	Y	Y	Y	Y	Y
13 ***Fossella***	Y	Y	Y	Y	Y
14 Maloney	Y	Y	Y	Y	Y
15 Rangel	Y	N	Y	Y	Y
16 Serrano	Y	?	?	?	?
17 Engel	Y	N	Y	Y	Y
18 Lowey	Y	Y	Y	Y	Y
19 ***Kelly***	Y	Y	Y	Y	Y
20 ***Gilman***	Y	N	Y	Y	Y
21 McNulty	Y	Y	Y	Y	Y
22 ***Sweeney***	Y	N	Y	Y	Y
23 ***Boehlert***	Y	Y	Y	Y	Y
24 ***McHugh***	Y	Y	Y	Y	Y
25 ***Walsh***	Y	N	N	Y	N
26 Hinchey	Y	Y	Y	Y	Y
27 ***Reynolds***	Y	Y	Y	Y	N
28 Slaughter	Y	Y	Y	Y	Y
29 LaFalce	Y	?	Y	Y	Y

	366	367	368	369	370
30 ***Quinn***	Y	Y	Y	Y	Y
31 ***Houghton***	?	?	?	?	?
NORTH CAROLINA					
1 Clayton	N	N	Y	Y	Y
2 Etheridge	N	N	Y	Y	N
3 ***Jones***	N	N	Y	N	Y
4 Price	Y	N	Y	Y	N
5 ***Burr***	N	N	N	N	N
6 ***Coble***	N	N	Y	Y	Y
7 McIntyre	N	N	N	Y	N
8 ***Hayes***	N	N	N	N	N
9 ***Myrick***	N	Y	N	N	N
10 ***Ballenger***	N	N	N	N	N
11 ***Taylor***	N	N	Y	N	Y
12 Watt	N	N	Y	Y	Y
NORTH DAKOTA					
AL Pomeroy	N	N	N	Y	Y
OHIO					
1 ***Chabot***	N	Y	N	N	Y
2 ***Portman***	N	Y	N	N	Y
3 Hall	N	Y	N	Y	Y
4 ***Oxley***	N	N	N	N	N
5 ***Gillmor***	N	N	N	N	N
6 Strickland	Y	N	Y	Y	Y
7 ***Hobson***	N	Y	Y	Y	Y
8 ***Boehner***	N	N	N	N	N
9 Kaptur	Y	N	Y	Y	Y
10 Kucinich	Y	N	Y	Y	Y
11 Jones	Y	Y	Y	Y	Y
12 ***Tiberi***	N	Y	N	N	Y
13 Brown	Y	Y	Y	Y	Y
14 Sawyer	Y	Y	Y	Y	Y
15 ***Pryce***	Y	Y	Y	N	Y
16 ***Regula***	N	Y	Y	Y	Y
17 Traficant	N	N	N	Y	Y
18 ***Ney***	Y	Y	Y	N	N
19 ***LaTourette***	Y	Y	Y	Y	N
OKLAHOMA					
1 ***Largent***	N	Y	N	N	N
2 Carson	N	N	Y	N	Y
3 ***Watkins***	N	N	N	N	Y
4 ***Watts***	N	N	N	N	Y
5 ***Istook***	N	?	N	Y	Y
6 ***Lucas***	N	N	N	N	N
OREGON					
1 Wu	Y	N	N	Y	Y
2 ***Walden***	N	N	N	N	Y
3 Blumenauer	Y	Y	N	Y	Y
4 DeFazio	Y	N	N	Y	Y
5 Hooley	Y	N	Y	Y	Y
PENNSYLVANIA					
1 Brady	Y	N	Y	Y	Y
2 Fattah	Y	N	Y	Y	Y
3 Borski	Y	Y	Y	Y	Y
4 ***Hart***	Y	Y	Y	Y	Y
5 ***Peterson***	N	Y	Y	Y	N
6 Holden	Y	N	Y	Y	Y
7 ***Weldon***	Y	Y	Y	Y	Y
8 ***Greenwood***	Y	Y	Y	Y	N
9 ***Shuster, Bill***	Y	Y	Y	Y	N
10 ***Sherwood***	Y	Y	Y	Y	N
11 Kanjorski	Y	Y	Y	Y	Y
12 Murtha	Y	?	?	?	?
13 Hoeffel	Y	Y	Y	Y	Y
14 Coyne	Y	Y	Y	Y	N
15 ***Toomey***	Y	Y	N	Y	Y
16 ***Pitts***	N	Y	Y	Y	Y
17 ***Gekas***	N	Y	Y	Y	Y
18 Doyle	Y	Y	Y	Y	Y
19 ***Platts***	N	Y	Y	Y	Y
20 Mascara	Y	N	Y	Y	Y
21 ***English***	N	Y	Y	N	Y
RHODE ISLAND					
1 Kennedy	Y	N	Y	Y	Y
2 Langevin	Y	Y	Y	Y	Y
SOUTH CAROLINA					
1 ***Brown***	N	Y	N	Y	Y
2 Vacant					
3 ***Graham***	N	N	N	N	Y
4 ***DeMint***	N	Y	N	N	N
5 Spratt	N	N	Y	Y	Y
6 Clyburn	N	N	Y	Y	Y
SOUTH DAKOTA					
AL ***Thune***	N	N	N	N	Y

	366	367	368	369	370
TENNESSEE					
1 ***Jenkins***	N	N	Y	Y	Y
2 ***Duncan***	N	Y	Y	Y	Y
3 ***Wamp***	N	Y	N	N	Y
4 ***Hilleary***	N	Y	N	N	Y
5 Clement	N	Y	Y	N	N
6 Gordon	N	Y	N	Y	Y
7 ***Bryant***	N	N	Y	N	Y
8 Tanner	N	N	N	N	N
9 Ford	N	N	N	Y	Y
TEXAS					
1 Sandlin	N	N	Y	Y	Y
2 Turner	N	N	N	Y	Y
3 ***Johnson, Sam***	N	N	N	N	N
4 Hall	N	N	N	N	N
5 ***Sessions***	N	N	N	N	N
6 ***Barton***	N	N	N	N	Y
7 ***Culberson***	N	Y	N	N	N
8 ***Brady***	N	N	N	N	N
9 Lampson	N	N	N	N	N
10 Doggett	Y	Y	N	Y	Y
11 Edwards	N	Y	N	N	N
12 ***Granger***	N	N	N	N	N
13 ***Thornberry***	N	N	N	N	N
14 ***Paul***	N	Y	N	Y	N
15 Hinojosa	N	N	N	N	N
16 Reyes	N	N	N	Y	N
17 Stenholm	N	N	N	N	N
18 Jackson-Lee	Y	N	Y	Y	Y
19 ***Combest***	N	N	N	N	N
20 Gonzalez	N	N	N	N	N
21 ***Smith***	N	N	N	N	Y
22 ***DeLay***	N	Y	N	N	Y
23 ***Bonilla***	N	N	N	N	N
24 Frost	N	N	N	Y	Y
25 Bentsen	N	N	N	N	N
26 ***Armey***	N	Y	N	N	N
27 Ortiz	N	N	N	Y	N
28 Rodriguez	N	N	N	N	Y
29 Green	Y	N	Y	N	Y
30 Johnson, E.B.	Y	N	N	Y	Y
UTAH					
1 ***Hansen***	N	–	N	N	Y
2 Matheson	N	Y	N	Y	Y
3 ***Cannon***	N	N	N	N	N
VERMONT					
AL *Sanders*	Y	N	Y	Y	Y
VIRGINIA					
1 ***Davis, Jo Ann***	N	Y	Y	N	Y
2 ***Schrock***	N	Y	N	N	N
3 Scott	N	Y	Y	Y	Y
4 ***Forbes***	N	N	N	N	Y
5 *Goode*	N	N	Y	Y	Y
6 ***Goodlatte***	N	Y	N	N	N
7 ***Cantor***	N	Y	N	N	N
8 Moran	Y	Y	N	Y	Y
9 Boucher	Y	Y	Y	Y	Y
10 ***Wolf***	Y	Y	Y	N	Y
11 ***Davis, T.***	Y	Y	N	N	N
WASHINGTON					
1 Inslee	Y	N	Y	Y	N
2 Larsen	Y	N	N	N	Y
3 Baird	Y	N	N	Y	Y
4 ***Hastings***	N	N	N	N	Y
5 ***Nethercutt***	N	N	N	N	N
6 Dicks	Y	?	N	Y	Y
7 McDermott	N	Y	Y	Y	Y
8 ***Dunn***	N	Y	N	N	N
9 Smith	Y	N	N	Y	N
WEST VIRGINIA					
1 Mollohan	Y	?	?	?	?
2 ***Capito***	Y	Y	Y	Y	Y
3 Rahall	Y	N	Y	Y	Y
WISCONSIN					
1 ***Ryan***	Y	Y	N	N	N
2 Baldwin	Y	Y	Y	Y	Y
3 Kind	Y	Y	Y	Y	N
4 Kleczka	Y	N	Y	Y	Y
5 Barrett	Y	Y	Y	Y	Y
6 ***Petri***	Y	Y	N	N	N
7 Obey	Y	N	Y	Y	Y
8 ***Green***	Y	Y	N	N	N
9 ***Sensenbrenner***	Y	Y	N	N	Y
WYOMING					
AL ***Cubin***	N	N	N	N	Y

Southern states - Ala., Ark., Fla., Ga., Ky., La., Miss., N.C., Okla., S.C., Tenn., Texas, Va.

Key

Y   Voted for (yea).
\#   Paired for.
\+   Announced for.
N   Voted against (nay).
X   Paired against.
–   Announced against.
P   Voted "present."
C   Voted "present" to avoid possible conflict of interest.
?   Did not vote or otherwise make a position known.

Democrats   **Republicans**
Independents

371. HR 2646. Farm Bill/Passage. Passage of the bill that would authorize $167 billion over 10 years for mandatory, direct spending for farm price support and conservation programs, including a new countercyclical program to help farmers when prices drop below a target level. The bill also would provide $242.9 billion for the food stamp program. Passed 291-120: R 151-58; D 139-61 (ND 90-58, SD 49-3); I 1-1. A "nay" was a vote in support of the president's position. Oct. 5, 2001.

372. H Con Res 244. Flag Pamphlet/Adoption. Ney, R-Ohio, motion to suspend the rules and adopt the concurrent resolution that would authorize the printing of a revised edition of the publication entitled "Our Flag." Motion agreed to 412-0: R 209-0; D 201-0 (ND 149-0, SD 52-0); I 2-0. A two-thirds majority of those present and voting (275 in this case) is required for adoption under suspension of the rules. Oct. 9, 2001.

373. H Res 250. Oil Reserves/Adoption. Barton, R-Texas, motion to suspend the rules and adopt the resolution that would urge the Energy secretary to increase the capacity of the Strategic Petroleum Reserve to 1 billion barrels, fill it to capacity and consider buying from marginal wells. Motion agreed to 409-3: R 207-2; D 200-1 (ND 147-1, SD 53-0); I 2-0. A two-thirds majority of those present and voting (275 in this case) is required for adoption under suspension of the rules. Oct. 9, 2001.

374. HR 1992. Internet Education/Democratic Substitute. Mink, D-Hawaii, substitute amendment that would eliminate the bill's provisions changing a 12-hour requirement of regular instruction or examination for every week of participation in a non-traditional program and easing current prohibitions on incentive payments to individuals recruiting students. Rejected 99-327: R 1-213; D 97-113 (ND 79-77, SD 18-36); I 1-1. Oct. 10, 2001.

375. HR 1992. Internet Education/Passage. Passage of the bill that would allow eligible higher education institutions that offer more than half their courses through telecommunications or permit more than half their students to take correspondence courses, to receive federal financial aid. Passed 354-70: R 211-1; D 141-69 (ND 100-56, SD 41-13); I 2-0. Oct. 10, 2001.

	371	372	373	374	375
ALABAMA					
1 *Callahan*	?	Y	Y	N	Y
2 *Everett*	Y	Y	Y	N	Y
3 *Riley*	Y	Y	Y	N	Y
4 *Aderholt*	Y	Y	Y	N	Y
5 Cramer	Y	Y	Y	N	Y
6 *Bachus*	?	Y	Y	N	Y
7 Hilliard	Y	Y	Y	N	Y
ALASKA					
AL *Young*	Y	Y	Y	N	Y
ARIZONA					
1 *Flake*	N	Y	Y	N	Y
2 Pastor	Y	Y	Y	N	Y
3 *Stump*	Y	Y	Y	N	Y
4 *Shadegg*	N	Y	Y	N	Y
5 *Kolbe*	Y	Y	Y	N	Y
6 *Hayworth*	Y	Y	Y	N	Y
ARKANSAS					
1 Berry	Y	Y	Y	N	Y
2 Snyder	Y	Y	Y	N	Y
3 Vacant					
4 Ross	Y	Y	Y	Y	N
CALIFORNIA					
1 Thompson	Y	Y	Y	N	Y
2 *Herger*	Y	Y	Y	N	Y
3 *Ose*	Y	Y	Y	N	Y
4 *Doolittle*	N	Y	Y	N	Y
5 Matsui	Y	Y	Y	N	Y
6 Woolsey	Y	Y	Y	Y	N
7 Miller, George	N	Y	Y	N	Y
8 Pelosi	Y	Y	Y	N	Y
9 Lee	N	+	+	N	N
10 Tauscher	N	Y	Y	N	Y
11 *Pombo*	Y	Y	Y	N	Y
12 Lantos	Y	Y	Y	N	Y
13 Stark	N	Y	Y	Y	N
14 Eshoo	N	Y	Y	N	Y
15 Honda	N	Y	Y	Y	Y
16 Lofgren	N	Y	Y	N	Y
17 Farr	Y	Y	Y	Y	Y
18 Condit	Y	Y	Y	Y	Y
19 *Radanovich*	Y	?	?	N	Y
20 Dooley	Y	Y	Y	N	Y
21 *Thomas*	Y	Y	Y	Y	Y
22 Capps	Y	Y	Y	Y	Y
23 *Gallegly*	Y	Y	Y	Y	Y
24 Sherman	Y	Y	Y	N	Y
25 *McKeon*	Y	Y	Y	N	Y
26 Berman	N	Y	Y	N	Y
27 Schiff	Y	Y	Y	N	Y
28 *Dreier*	N	Y	Y	N	Y
29 Waxman	?	Y	Y	N	Y
30 Becerra	Y	Y	Y	N	Y
31 Solis	Y	Y	Y	N	Y
32 Watson	Y	Y	Y	Y	Y
33 Roybal-Allard	Y	Y	Y	Y	N
34 Napolitano	Y	Y	Y	N	Y
35 Waters	N	Y	Y	Y	Y
36 Harman	N	Y	Y	N	Y
37 Millender-McD.	Y	Y	Y	N	N
38 *Horn*	Y	Y	Y	N	Y
	371	372	373	374	375
39 *Royce*	N	Y	N	N	Y
40 *Lewis*	Y	Y	Y	N	Y
41 *Miller, Gary*	N	Y	Y	N	Y
42 Baca	Y	Y	Y	Y	N
43 *Calvert*	Y	Y	Y	N	Y
44 *Bono*	Y	?	?	N	Y
45 *Rohrabacher*	N	Y	Y	N	Y
46 Sanchez	N	+	+	N	Y
47 *Cox*	?	Y	Y	N	Y
48 *Issa*	Y	?	?	?	?
49 Davis	N	Y	Y	N	Y
50 Filner	Y	Y	Y	Y	N
51 *Cunningham*	Y	Y	Y	N	Y
52 *Hunter*	Y	Y	Y	N	Y
COLORADO					
1 DeGette	Y	Y	Y	Y	Y
2 Udall	N	Y	Y	Y	Y
3 *McInnis*	N	Y	Y	N	Y
4 *Schaffer*	Y	Y	Y	N	Y
5 *Hefley*	N	Y	N	N	Y
6 *Tancredo*	N	Y	Y	N	Y
CONNECTICUT					
1 Larson	Y	Y	Y	N	Y
2 *Simmons*	N	Y	Y	N	Y
3 DeLauro	Y	Y	Y	Y	Y
4 *Shays*	N	Y	Y	N	Y
5 Maloney	N	Y	Y	Y	Y
6 *Johnson*	N	Y	Y	N	Y
DELAWARE					
AL *Castle*	N	Y	Y	N	Y
FLORIDA					
1 Vacant					
2 Boyd	Y	Y	Y	N	Y
3 Brown	Y	Y	Y	N	N
4 *Crenshaw*	Y	Y	Y	N	Y
5 Thurman	Y	Y	Y	Y	Y
6 *Stearns*	N	Y	Y	N	Y
7 *Mica*	N	Y	Y	N	Y
8 *Keller*	Y	Y	Y	N	Y
9 *Bilirakis*	Y	Y	Y	N	Y
10 *Young*	N	Y	Y	N	Y
11 Davis	Y	Y	Y	N	Y
12 *Putnam*	Y	Y	Y	N	Y
13 *Miller*	N	?	?	?	?
14 *Goss*	N	Y	Y	N	Y
15 *Weldon*	Y	Y	Y	N	Y
16 *Foley*	Y	Y	Y	N	Y
17 Meek	Y	Y	Y	N	N
18 *Ros-Lehtinen*	?	Y	Y	N	Y
19 Wexler	?	Y	Y	Y	Y
20 Deutsch	N	Y	Y	N	Y
21 *Diaz-Balart*	Y	Y	Y	N	Y
22 *Shaw*	N	Y	N	N	Y
23 Hastings	Y	Y	Y	Y	N
GEORGIA					
1 *Kingston*	Y	Y	Y	N	Y
2 Bishop	Y	?	?	N	N
3 *Collins*	Y	Y	Y	N	Y
4 McKinney	Y	?	Y	N	N
5 Lewis	Y	Y	Y	N	Y
6 *Isakson*	Y	Y	Y	N	Y
7 *Barr*	N	Y	Y	N	Y
8 *Chambliss*	Y	Y	Y	N	Y
9 *Deal*	Y	Y	Y	N	Y
10 *Norwood*	Y	?	?	N	Y
11 *Linder*	N	Y	Y	N	Y
HAWAII					
1 Abercrombie	Y	Y	Y	Y	Y
2 Mink	Y	Y	Y	Y	N
IDAHO					
1 *Otter*	Y	Y	Y	N	Y
2 *Simpson*	Y	Y	Y	N	Y
ILLINOIS					
1 Rush	Y	Y	Y	Y	Y
2 Jackson	Y	Y	Y	N	N
3 Lipinski	?	Y	Y	N	Y
4 Gutierrez	Y	Y	Y	N	Y
5 Blagojevich	Y	Y	Y	Y	N
6 *Hyde*	Y	Y	Y	N	Y
7 Davis	Y	Y	Y	N	Y
8 *Crane*	N	Y	Y	N	Y
9 Schakowsky	Y	Y	Y	Y	Y
10 *Kirk*	Y	Y	Y	N	Y
11 *Weller*	Y	Y	Y	N	Y
12 Costello	Y	Y	Y	Y	Y
13 *Biggert*	N	Y	Y	N	Y

ND Northern Democrats   SD Southern Democrats

	371	372	373	374	375
14 ***Hastert***					
15 ***Johnson***	Y	Y	Y	N	Y
16 ***Manzullo***	Y	Y	Y	N	?
17 Evans	Y	Y	Y	Y	N
18 ***LaHood***	Y	?	?	N	Y
19 Phelps	Y	Y	Y	Y	N
20 ***Shimkus***	Y	Y	Y	N	Y
INDIANA					
1 Visclosky	?	Y	Y	Y	N
2 ***Pence***	Y	Y	Y	N	Y
3 Roemer	Y	Y	Y	Y	N
4 ***Souder***	Y	Y	Y	N	Y
5 ***Buyer***	Y	Y	Y	N	Y
6 ***Burton***	+	Y	Y	N	Y
7 ***Kerns***	Y	Y	Y	N	Y
8 ***Hostettler***	Y	Y	Y	N	Y
9 Hill	Y	Y	Y	Y	N
10 Carson	Y	Y	Y	Y	Y
IOWA					
1 ***Leach***	Y	Y	Y	N	Y
2 ***Nussle***	Y	Y	Y	N	Y
3 Boswell	N	Y	Y	N	Y
4 ***Ganske***	Y	Y	Y	N	Y
5 ***Latham***	Y	Y	Y	N	Y
KANSAS					
1 ***Moran***	Y	Y	Y	N	Y
2 ***Ryun***	Y	Y	Y	N	Y
3 Moore	Y	Y	Y	Y	N
4 ***Tiahrt***	Y	Y	Y	N	Y
KENTUCKY					
1 ***Whitfield***	Y	Y	Y	N	Y
2 ***Lewis***	Y	Y	Y	N	Y
3 ***Northup***	N	Y	Y	N	Y
4 Lucas	Y	Y	Y	N	Y
5 ***Rogers***	Y	Y	Y	N	Y
6 ***Fletcher***	Y	Y	Y	N	Y
LOUISIANA					
1 ***Vitter***	Y	Y	Y	N	Y
2 Jefferson	Y	Y	Y	Y	Y
3 ***Tauzin***	Y	Y	Y	N	Y
4 ***McCrery***	Y	Y	Y	N	Y
5 ***Cooksey***	Y	Y	Y	N	Y
6 ***Baker***	?	Y	Y	N	Y
7 John	Y	Y	Y	N	Y
MAINE					
1 Allen	Y	Y	?	N	Y
2 Baldacci	Y	Y	Y	N	Y
MARYLAND					
1 ***Gilchrest***	Y	Y	Y	N	Y
2 ***Ehrlich***	Y	Y	Y	N	Y
3 Cardin	N	Y	Y	Y	Y
4 Wynn	Y	Y	Y	N	Y
5 Hoyer	Y	Y	Y	Y	Y
6 ***Bartlett***	Y	Y	Y	N	Y
7 Cummings	Y	Y	Y	Y	Y
8 ***Morella***	N	Y	Y	Y	N
MASSACHUSETTS					
1 Olver	?	Y	Y	Y	N
2 Neal	N	Y	Y	Y	N
3 McGovern	Y	Y	Y	Y	Y
4 Frank	N	Y	Y	N	N
5 Meehan	N	Y	Y	Y	N
6 Tierney	N	Y	Y	Y	N
7 Markey	N	Y	Y	Y	N
8 Capuano	N	Y	Y	Y	N
9 Vacant					
10 Delahunt	N	Y	?	Y	Y
MICHIGAN					
1 Stupak	Y	Y	Y	N	Y
2 ***Hoekstra***	N	Y	Y	N	Y
3 ***Ehlers***	Y	Y	Y	N	Y
4 ***Camp***	Y	Y	Y	N	Y
5 Barcia	Y	Y	Y	N	Y
6 ***Upton***	Y	Y	Y	N	Y
7 ***Smith***	Y	Y	Y	N	Y
8 ***Rogers***	Y	Y	Y	N	Y
9 Kildee	Y	Y	Y	N	Y
10 Bonior	Y	Y	Y	N	Y
11 ***Knollenberg***	Y	Y	Y	N	Y
12 Levin	Y	Y	Y	Y	Y
13 Rivers	N	Y	Y	Y	N
14 Conyers	N	?	Y	Y	N
15 Kilpatrick	+	Y	Y	N	Y
16 Dingell	Y	Y	Y	Y	Y

	371	372	373	374	375
MINNESOTA					
1 ***Gutknecht***	Y	Y	Y	N	Y
2 ***Kennedy***	Y	Y	Y	N	Y
3 ***Ramstad***	N	Y	Y	N	Y
4 McCollum	Y	Y	Y	Y	Y
5 Sabo	Y	Y	Y	Y	N
6 Luther	Y	Y	Y	Y	Y
7 Peterson	Y	Y	Y	N	Y
8 Oberstar	N	Y	Y	Y	N
MISSISSIPPI					
1 ***Wicker***	Y	Y	Y	N	Y
2 Thompson	?	Y	Y	N	Y
3 ***Pickering***	Y	Y	Y	N	Y
4 Shows	Y	Y	Y	N	Y
5 Taylor	Y	Y	Y	N	Y
MISSOURI					
1 Clay	Y	Y	Y	N	Y
2 ***Akin***	Y	Y	Y	N	Y
3 Gephardt	N	Y	Y	N	Y
4 Skelton	Y	Y	Y	N	N
5 McCarthy	+	Y	Y	Y	Y
6 ***Graves***	Y	Y	Y	N	Y
7 ***Blunt***	Y	Y	Y	N	Y
8 ***Emerson***	Y	Y	Y	N	Y
9 ***Hulshof***	Y	Y	Y	N	Y
MONTANA					
AL ***Rehberg***	Y	Y	Y	N	Y
NEBRASKA					
1 ***Bereuter***	Y	+	+	N	Y
2 ***Terry***	Y	Y	Y	N	Y
3 ***Osborne***	Y	Y	Y	N	Y
NEVADA					
1 Berkley	Y	Y	Y	Y	Y
2 ***Gibbons***	?	Y	Y	N	Y
NEW HAMPSHIRE					
1 ***Sununu***	N	Y	Y	N	Y
2 ***Bass***	N	Y	Y	N	Y
NEW JERSEY					
1 Andrews	Y	Y	Y	N	Y
2 ***LoBiondo***	N	Y	Y	N	Y
3 ***Saxton***	Y	Y	Y	N	Y
4 ***Smith***	Y	Y	Y	N	Y
5 ***Roukema***	N	Y	Y	N	Y
6 Pallone	Y	Y	Y	Y	N
7 ***Ferguson***	N	Y	Y	N	Y
8 Pascrell	Y	Y	Y	N	Y
9 Rothman	N	Y	Y	Y	N
10 Payne	Y	Y	Y	Y	N
11 ***Frelinghuysen***	N	Y	Y	N	Y
12 Holt	Y	Y	Y	Y	N
13 Menendez	N	?	?	N	Y
NEW MEXICO					
1 ***Wilson***	Y	?	?	N	Y
2 ***Skeen***	Y	Y	Y	N	Y
3 Udall	N	Y	Y	Y	N
NEW YORK					
1 ***Grucci***	Y	Y	Y	N	Y
2 Israel	Y	Y	Y	N	Y
3 ***King***	N	Y	Y	N	Y
4 McCarthy	Y	Y	Y	N	Y
5 Ackerman	Y	Y	Y	Y	Y
6 Meeks	Y	Y	Y	N	Y
7 Crowley	Y	Y	Y	N	Y
8 Nadler	N	Y	Y	N	N
9 Weiner	N	Y	Y	Y	Y
10 Towns	Y	Y	Y	N	N
11 Owens	N	Y	Y	N	Y
12 Velázquez	N	?	?	Y	N
13 ***Fossella***	N	Y	Y	N	Y
14 Maloney	N	Y	Y	Y	N
15 Rangel	Y	Y	Y	N	Y
16 Serrano	Y	Y	Y	Y	Y
17 Engel	Y	Y	Y	Y	N
18 Lowey	Y	Y	Y	Y	Y
19 ***Kelly***	Y	Y	Y	N	Y
20 ***Gilman***	Y	Y	Y	N	Y
21 McNulty	N	Y	Y	Y	N
22 ***Sweeney***	Y	Y	Y	N	Y
23 ***Boehlert***	N	Y	Y	N	Y
24 ***McHugh***	N	Y	Y	N	Y
25 ***Walsh***	Y	?	?	N	Y
26 Hinchey	N	Y	Y	Y	N
27 ***Reynolds***	Y	Y	Y	N	Y
28 Slaughter	N	Y	Y	Y	N
29 LaFalce	N	Y	Y	Y	Y

	371	372	373	374	375
30 ***Quinn***	N	Y	Y	N	Y
31 ***Houghton***	?	Y	Y	N	Y
NORTH CAROLINA					
1 Clayton	Y	Y	Y	N	Y
2 Etheridge	Y	Y	Y	Y	Y
3 ***Jones***	Y	Y	Y	N	Y
4 Price	Y	Y	Y	Y	Y
5 ***Burr***	Y	Y	Y	N	Y
6 ***Coble***	Y	Y	Y	N	Y
7 McIntyre	Y	Y	Y	Y	Y
8 ***Hayes***	Y	Y	Y	N	Y
9 ***Myrick***	N	Y	Y	N	Y
10 ***Ballenger***	Y	Y	Y	N	Y
11 ***Taylor***	Y	Y	Y	N	Y
12 Watt	Y	Y	Y	N	Y
NORTH DAKOTA					
AL Pomeroy	Y	Y	Y	N	Y
OHIO					
1 ***Chabot***	N	Y	Y	N	Y
2 ***Portman***	Y	Y	Y	N	Y
3 Hall	Y	Y	Y	N	Y
4 ***Oxley***	Y	Y	Y	N	Y
5 ***Gillmor***	Y	Y	Y	N	Y
6 Strickland	Y	Y	Y	N	Y
7 ***Hobson***	Y	Y	Y	N	Y
8 ***Boehner***	Y	Y	Y	N	Y
9 Kaptur	N	Y	N	N	Y
10 Kucinich	N	Y	Y	N	Y
11 Jones	N	?	?	N	Y
12 ***Tiberi***	Y	Y	Y	N	Y
13 Brown	N	Y	Y	N	Y
14 Sawyer	Y	Y	Y	N	Y
15 ***Pryce***	Y	Y	Y	N	Y
16 ***Regula***	Y	Y	Y	N	Y
17 Traficant	Y	Y	Y	N	Y
18 ***Ney***	Y	Y	Y	N	Y
19 ***LaTourette***	Y	Y	Y	N	Y
OKLAHOMA					
1 ***Largent***	Y	Y	Y	N	Y
2 Carson	Y	Y	Y	Y	Y
3 ***Watkins***	Y	Y	Y	N	Y
4 ***Watts***	Y	Y	Y	N	Y
5 ***Istook***	N	Y	Y	N	Y
6 ***Lucas***	Y	Y	Y	N	Y
OREGON					
1 Wu	Y	Y	Y	N	Y
2 ***Walden***	Y	Y	Y	N	Y
3 Blumenauer	N	Y	Y	N	Y
4 DeFazio	N	Y	Y	Y	N
5 Hooley	Y	Y	Y	N	Y
PENNSYLVANIA					
1 Brady	N	Y	Y	N	N
2 Fattah	N	Y	Y	N	Y
3 Borski	N	Y	Y	Y	N
4 ***Hart***	Y	Y	Y	N	Y
5 ***Peterson***	Y	Y	Y	N	Y
6 Holden	Y	Y	Y	N	Y
7 ***Weldon***	Y	Y	Y	N	Y
8 ***Greenwood***	Y	Y	Y	N	Y
9 ***Shuster, Bill***	Y	Y	Y	N	Y
10 ***Sherwood***	N	Y	Y	N	Y
11 Kanjorski	N	Y	Y	N	Y
12 Murtha	N	Y	Y	N	Y
13 Hoeffel	N	Y	Y	N	Y
14 Coyne	N	Y	Y	Y	N
15 ***Toomey***	N	Y	Y	N	Y
16 ***Pitts***	N	Y	Y	N	Y
17 ***Gekas***	Y	Y	Y	N	Y
18 Doyle	Y	Y	Y	N	Y
19 ***Platts***	Y	Y	Y	N	Y
20 Mascara	Y	Y	Y	N	Y
21 ***English***	Y	Y	Y	N	Y
RHODE ISLAND					
1 Kennedy	Y	Y	Y	N	Y
2 Langevin	Y	Y	Y	N	Y
SOUTH CAROLINA					
1 ***Brown***	Y	Y	Y	N	Y
2 Vacant					
3 ***Graham***	Y	Y	Y	N	Y
4 ***DeMint***	N	Y	Y	N	Y
5 Spratt	Y	Y	Y	N	N
6 Clyburn	Y	Y	Y	N	Y
SOUTH DAKOTA					
AL ***Thune***	Y	Y	Y	N	Y

	371	372	373	374	375
TENNESSEE					
1 ***Jenkins***	Y	Y	Y	N	Y
2 ***Duncan***	?	Y	Y	N	Y
3 ***Wamp***	N	Y	Y	N	Y
4 ***Hilleary***	Y	Y	Y	N	Y
5 Clement	Y	Y	Y	Y	Y
6 Gordon	Y	Y	Y	N	Y
7 ***Bryant***	Y	Y	Y	N	Y
8 Tanner	Y	Y	Y	N	Y
9 Ford	Y	Y	Y	N	Y
TEXAS					
1 Sandlin	Y	Y	Y	Y	N
2 Turner	Y	Y	Y	N	Y
3 ***Johnson, Sam***	Y	Y	Y	N	Y
4 Hall	Y	Y	Y	N	Y
5 ***Sessions***	Y	Y	Y	N	Y
6 ***Barton***	Y	Y	Y	N	Y
7 ***Culberson***	N	Y	Y	N	Y
8 ***Brady***	Y	Y	Y	N	Y
9 Lampson	Y	Y	Y	N	Y
10 Doggett	N	Y	Y	N	Y
11 Edwards	Y	Y	Y	Y	N
12 ***Granger***	Y	Y	Y	N	Y
13 ***Thornberry***	Y	Y	Y	N	Y
14 ***Paul***	N	Y	N	N	Y
15 Hinojosa	Y	Y	Y	N	Y
16 Reyes	Y	Y	Y	N	Y
17 Stenholm	Y	Y	Y	N	Y
18 Jackson-Lee	Y	Y	Y	N	N
19 ***Combest***	Y	Y	Y	N	Y
20 Gonzalez	Y	Y	Y	Y	Y
21 ***Smith***	Y	Y	Y	N	Y
22 ***DeLay***	N	Y	Y	N	Y
23 ***Bonilla***	Y	Y	Y	N	Y
24 Frost	Y	Y	Y	N	Y
25 Bentsen	Y	Y	Y	N	Y
26 ***Armey***	N	Y	Y	N	Y
27 Ortiz	Y	Y	Y	N	Y
28 Rodriguez	Y	Y	Y	Y	N
29 Green	Y	Y	Y	Y	Y
30 Johnson, E.B.	Y	Y	Y	N	N
UTAH					
1 ***Hansen***	Y	Y	Y	N	Y
2 Matheson	Y	Y	Y	N	Y
3 ***Cannon***	Y	Y	Y	N	Y
VERMONT					
AL *Sanders*	N	Y	Y	Y	Y
VIRGINIA					
1 ***Davis, Jo Ann***	Y	Y	Y	N	Y
2 ***Schrock***	N	Y	Y	N	Y
3 Scott	Y	Y	Y	Y	N
4 ***Forbes***	Y	Y	Y	N	Y
5 *Goode*	Y	Y	Y	N	Y
6 ***Goodlatte***	Y	Y	Y	N	Y
7 ***Cantor***	Y	Y	Y	N	Y
8 Moran	N	Y	Y	Y	Y
9 Boucher	Y	Y	Y	N	Y
10 ***Wolf***	Y	Y	Y	N	Y
11 ***Davis, T.***	N	Y	Y	N	?
WASHINGTON					
1 Inslee	Y	Y	Y	N	Y
2 Larsen	Y	Y	Y	N	Y
3 Baird	Y	Y	Y	N	Y
4 ***Hastings***	Y	Y	Y	?	?
5 ***Nethercutt***	Y	Y	Y	N	Y
6 Dicks	Y	Y	Y	N	Y
7 McDermott	N	Y	Y	N	N
8 ***Dunn***	N	Y	Y	N	Y
9 Smith	?	?	?	N	Y
WEST VIRGINIA					
1 Mollohan	?	Y	Y	N	Y
2 ***Capito***	Y	Y	Y	N	Y
3 Rahall	Y	Y	Y	Y	Y
WISCONSIN					
1 ***Ryan***	N	Y	Y	N	Y
2 Baldwin	N	Y	Y	Y	N
3 Kind	N	Y	Y	Y	Y
4 Kleczka	N	Y	Y	Y	N
5 Barrett	N	Y	Y	Y	N
6 ***Petri***	N	Y	Y	N	Y
7 Obey	N	Y	Y	Y	N
8 ***Green***	N	Y	Y	N	Y
9 ***Sensenbrenner***	N	Y	Y	N	Y
WYOMING					
AL ***Cubin***	Y	Y	Y	?	?

Southern states - Ala., Ark., Fla., Ga., Ky., La., Miss., N.C., Okla., S.C., Tenn., Texas, Va.

Key

Y	Voted for (yea).
#	Paired for.
+	Announced for.
N	Voted against (nay).
X	Paired against.
−	Announced against.
P	Voted "present."
C	Voted "present" to avoid possible conflict of interest.
?	Did not vote or otherwise make a position known.

● Democrats   **Republicans**
Independents

376. Quorum Call. * 412 members responded. Oct. 11, 2001.

377. HR 3061. Fiscal 2002 Labor-HHS-Education Appropriations/IDEA. Schaffer, R-Colo., amendment that would add $1.1 billion for programs under the Individuals with Disabilities Education Act (IDEA), offset with reductions from other education programs. Rejected 76-349: R 73-142; D 2-206 (ND 1-153, SD 1-53); I 1-1. Oct. 11, 2001.

378. HR 3061. Fiscal 2002 Labor-HHS-Education Appropriations/Centers for Disease Control. Stearns, R-Fla., amendment that would add $12 million for the Centers for Disease Control and Prevention, offset with a reduction from the Corporation for Public Broadcasting. Rejected 107-312: R 104-108; D 2-203 (ND 0-151, SD 2-52); I 1-1. Oct. 11, 2001.

379. HR 3061. Fiscal 2002 Labor-HHS-Education Appropriations/Abstinence Programs. Istook, R-Okla., amendment that would add $33 million to community-based abstinence education programs. Rejected 106-311: R 97-114; D 8-196 (ND 3-147, SD 5-49); I 1-1. Oct. 11, 2001.

380. HR 3061. Fiscal 2002 Labor-HHS-Education Appropriations/Translators. Istook, R-Okla., amendment that would restrict spending to carry out an executive order that requires federal contractors and other recipients of federal assistance to provide translations of documents for people with limited English language skills. Rejected 156-262: R 148-63; D 7-198 (ND 2-149, SD 5-49); I 1-1. Oct. 11, 2001.

381. HR 3061. Fiscal 2002 Labor-HHS-Education Appropriations/Passage. Passage of the bill that would appropriate $123.1 billion in discretionary spending for the Labor, Health and Human Services and Education departments and related agencies, $11.2 billion more than the fiscal 2001 level. The bill includes $49.3 billion in discretionary funding for education programs. Passed 373-43: R 170-41; D 201-2 (ND 149-0, SD 52-2); I 2-0. Oct. 11, 2001.

* CQ does not include quorum calls in its vote charts.

	377	378	379	380	381
ALABAMA					
1 *Callahan*	N	N	N	N	Y
2 *Everett*	N	N	Y	Y	Y
3 *Riley*	N	Y	Y	Y	Y
4 *Aderholt*	N	Y	Y	Y	Y
5 Cramer	N	N	N	N	Y
6 *Bachus*	N	Y	N	Y	Y
7 Hilliard	N	N	N	N	Y
ALASKA					
AL *Young*	N	N	N	N	Y
ARIZONA					
1 *Flake*	Y	Y	Y	Y	N
2 Pastor	N	N	N	N	Y
3 *Stump*	Y	Y	Y	Y	N
4 *Shadegg*	Y	Y	Y	Y	N
5 *Kolbe*	N	N	N	N	Y
6 *Hayworth*	Y	Y	Y	Y	N
ARKANSAS					
1 Berry	N	N	N	N	Y
2 Snyder	N	N	N	N	Y
3 Vacant					
4 Ross	N	N	N	N	Y
CALIFORNIA					
1 Thompson	N	N	N	N	Y
2 *Herger*	Y	Y	N	Y	N
3 *Ose*	N	N	N	N	Y
4 *Doolittle*	Y	Y	Y	Y	N
5 Matsui	N	N	N	N	Y
6 Woolsey	N	N	N	N	Y
7 Miller, George	N	N	N	N	Y
8 Pelosi	N	N	N	N	Y
9 Lee	N	N	N	N	Y
10 Tauscher	N	N	N	N	Y
11 *Pombo*	Y	Y	Y	Y	N
12 Lantos	N	N	N	N	Y
13 Stark	N	N	N	N	Y
14 Eshoo	N	N	N	N	Y
15 Honda	N	N	N	N	Y
16 Lofgren	N	N	N	N	Y
17 Farr	N	N	N	N	Y
18 Condit	N	N	N	N	Y
19 *Radanovich*	Y	N	Y	Y	Y
20 Dooley	N	N	N	N	Y
21 *Thomas*	N	N	N	N	Y
22 Capps	N	N	N	N	Y
23 *Gallegly*	N	Y	N	Y	Y
24 Sherman	N	N	−	N	Y
25 *McKeon*	N	Y	Y	N	Y
26 Berman	N	N	N	N	Y
27 Schiff	N	N	N	N	Y
28 *Dreier*	N	N	N	N	Y
29 Waxman	N	N	N	N	Y
30 Becerra	N	N	N	N	Y
31 Solis	N	N	N	N	Y
32 Watson	N	N	N	N	Y
33 Royal-Allard	N	N	N	N	Y
34 Napolitano	N	N	N	N	Y
35 Waters	N	N	N	N	?
36 Harman	Y	N	N	Y	Y
37 Millender-McD.	N	N	N	N	Y
38 *Horn*	N	N	N	Y	Y

	377	378	379	380	381
39 *Royce*	Y	Y	Y	Y	N
40 *Lewis*	N	N	N	N	Y
41 *Miller, Gary*	Y	Y	Y	Y	N
42 Baca	N	N	N	N	Y
43 *Calvert*	N	N	N	N	Y
44 *Bono*	N	N	N	N	Y
45 *Rohrabacher*	Y	Y	Y	Y	N
46 Sanchez	N	N	N	N	Y
47 *Cox*	Y	Y	N	N	Y
48 *Issa*	Y	N	Y	Y	Y
49 Davis	N	N	N	N	Y
50 Filner	N	N	N	N	Y
51 *Cunningham*	N	N	N	N	Y
52 *Hunter*	N	Y	Y	Y	N
COLORADO					
1 DeGette	N	N	N	N	Y
2 Udall	N	N	N	N	Y
3 *McInnis*	Y	N	N	N	Y
4 *Schaffer*	Y	Y	Y	Y	N
5 *Hefley*	Y	Y	Y	Y	N
6 *Tancredo*	Y	Y	Y	Y	N
CONNECTICUT					
1 Larson	N	N	N	N	Y
2 *Simmons*	Y	N	N	N	Y
3 DeLauro	N	N	N	N	Y
4 *Shays*	N	N	N	Y	Y
5 Maloney	N	N	N	N	Y
6 *Johnson*	N	N	N	Y	Y
DELAWARE					
AL *Castle*	N	N	N	N	Y
FLORIDA					
1 Vacant					
2 Boyd	N	N	N	N	Y
3 Brown	N	N	N	N	Y
4 *Crenshaw*	N	N	Y	Y	Y
5 Thurman	N	N	N	N	Y
6 *Stearns*	Y	Y	Y	Y	Y
7 *Mica*	N	N	Y	Y	Y
8 *Keller*	N	Y	Y	Y	Y
9 *Bilirakis*	N	N	N	N	Y
10 *Young*	N	N	N	N	Y
11 Davis	N	N	N	N	Y
12 *Putnam*	N	Y	N	Y	Y
13 *Miller*	?	?	?	?	?
14 *Goss*	N	N	N	N	Y
15 *Weldon*	Y	Y	Y	Y	N
16 *Foley*	N	Y	N	N	Y
17 Meek	N	N	N	N	Y
18 *Ros-Lehtinen*	N	N	N	N	Y
19 Wexler	N	N	N	N	Y
20 Deutsch	N	N	N	N	Y
21 *Diaz-Balart*	N	Y	N	N	Y
22 *Shaw*	N	N	N	N	Y
23 Hastings	N	N	N	N	Y
GEORGIA					
1 *Kingston*	?	?	?	?	?
2 Bishop	N	Y	N	Y	Y
3 *Collins*	N	Y	N	Y	Y
4 McKinney	N	N	N	N	Y
5 Lewis	N	N	N	N	Y
6 *Isakson*	N	Y	N	Y	Y
7 *Barr*	N	Y	Y	Y	N
8 *Chambliss*	N	Y	N	Y	Y
9 *Deal*	Y	Y	N	Y	Y
10 *Norwood*	Y	Y	N	Y	Y
11 *Linder*	N	Y	Y	Y	Y
HAWAII					
1 Abercrombie	N	N	N	N	Y
2 Mink	N	N	N	N	Y
IDAHO					
1 *Otter*	N	Y	N	Y	N
2 *Simpson*	N	N	N	N	Y
ILLINOIS					
1 Rush	N	N	N	N	Y
2 Jackson	N	N	N	N	Y
3 Lipinski	N	N	Y	N	Y
4 Gutierrez	N	N	N	N	Y
5 Blagojevich	N	N	N	N	Y
6 *Hyde*	N	N	Y	Y	Y
7 Davis	N	N	N	N	Y
8 *Crane*	N	Y	N	Y	N
9 Schakowsky	N	N	N	N	Y
10 *Kirk*	N	N	N	N	Y
11 *Weller*	N	Y	N	Y	Y
12 Costello	N	N	Y	N	Y
13 *Biggert*	N	N	N	Y	Y

ND Northern Democrats   SD Southern Democrats

District / Member	377	378	379	380	381
14 Hastert					
15 *Johnson*	Y	N	Y	N	Y
16 *Manzullo*	Y	Y	Y	Y	Y
17 Evans	N	N	Y	N	Y
18 *LaHood*	N	N	Y	N	Y
19 Phelps	N	N	Y	N	Y
20 *Shimkus*	N	N	Y	Y	Y
INDIANA					
1 Visclosky	N	N	N	N	Y
2 *Pence*	Y	Y	Y	Y	N
3 Roemer	N	N	N	N	Y
4 *Souder*	Y	N	Y	Y	Y
5 *Buyer*	N	N	Y	N	Y
6 *Burton*	N	Y	Y	Y	Y
7 *Kerns*	Y	Y	Y	Y	Y
8 *Hostettler*	Y	Y	Y	Y	N
9 Hill	N	N	N	N	Y
10 Carson	N	N	N	N	Y
IOWA					
1 *Leach*	N	N	N	Y	Y
2 *Nussle*	N	N	N	N	Y
3 Boswell	N	N	N	N	Y
4 *Ganske*	N	N	Y	Y	Y
5 *Latham*	N	N	N	Y	Y
KANSAS					
1 *Moran*	N	N	Y	Y	N
2 *Ryun*	Y	Y	Y	Y	N
3 Moore	N	N	N	N	Y
4 *Tiahrt*	Y	Y	Y	N	Y
KENTUCKY					
1 *Whitfield*	N	N	Y	Y	Y
2 *Lewis*	N	Y	Y	Y	Y
3 *Northup*	N	N	N	Y	Y
4 Lucas	N	N	Y	Y	Y
5 *Rogers*	N	N	N	N	Y
6 *Fletcher*	N	N	?	Y	Y
LOUISIANA					
1 *Vitter*	Y	Y	Y	Y	N
2 Jefferson	N	N	N	N	Y
3 *Tauzin*	N	Y	Y	Y	Y
4 *McCrery*	N	Y	N	Y	Y
5 *Cooksey*	N	Y	N	Y	Y
6 *Baker*	N	Y	Y	Y	Y
7 John	N	N	N	N	Y
MAINE					
1 Allen	N	N	N	N	Y
2 Baldacci	N	N	N	N	Y
MARYLAND					
1 *Gilchrest*	N	N	N	N	Y
2 *Ehrlich*	N	N	Y	Y	Y
3 Cardin	N	N	N	N	Y
4 Wynn	N	N	N	N	Y
5 Hoyer	N	N	N	N	Y
6 *Bartlett*	Y	Y	Y	Y	N
7 Cummings	N	N	N	N	Y
8 *Morella*	N	N	N	N	Y
MASSACHUSETTS					
1 Olver	N	N	N	N	Y
2 Neal	N	N	N	N	Y
3 McGovern	N	N	N	N	Y
4 Frank	N	N	N	N	?
5 Meehan	N	N	N	N	Y
6 Tierney	N	N	N	N	Y
7 Markey	N	N	N	N	Y
8 Capuano	N	N	N	N	Y
9 Vacant					
10 Delahunt	N	N	N	N	Y
MICHIGAN					
1 Stupak	N	N	N	N	Y
2 *Hoekstra*	Y	Y	N	Y	N
3 *Ehlers*	N	N	N	N	Y
4 *Camp*	N	Y	N	Y	Y
5 Barcia	N	N	N	N	Y
6 *Upton*	N	Y	N	Y	Y
7 *Smith*	N	Y	Y	N	Y
8 *Rogers*	N	N	N	Y	Y
9 Kildee	N	N	N	N	Y
10 Bonlor	N	N	N	N	Y
11 *Knollenberg*	N	N	N	N	Y
12 Levin	N	N	N	N	Y
13 Rivers	N	N	N	N	Y
14 Conyers	N	N	N	N	Y
15 Kilpatrick	N	N	N	N	Y
16 Dingell	N	N	N	N	Y

District / Member	377	378	379	380	381
MINNESOTA					
1 *Gutknecht*	Y	Y	Y	Y	Y
2 *Kennedy*	Y	Y	N	Y	Y
3 *Ramstad*	Y	Y	N	Y	Y
4 McCollum	N	N	N	N	Y
5 Sabo	N	N	N	N	Y
6 Luther	N	N	N	N	Y
7 Peterson	N	N	N	N	Y
8 Oberstar	N	N	N	N	Y
MISSISSIPPI					
1 *Wicker*	N	Y	Y	Y	Y
2 Thompson	N	N	N	N	Y
3 *Pickering*	N	Y	Y	Y	Y
4 Shows	N	Y	Y	Y	Y
5 Taylor	N	N	Y	Y	N
MISSOURI					
1 Clay	N	N	N	N	Y
2 *Akin*	Y	Y	Y	Y	Y
3 Gephardt	N	N	N	N	Y
4 Skelton	N	N	N	N	Y
5 McCarthy	N	N	N	N	Y
6 *Graves*	Y	Y	N	Y	Y
7 *Blunt*	?	?	?	?	?
8 *Emerson*	N	Y	N	Y	Y
9 *Hulshof*	N	Y	N	Y	Y
MONTANA					
AL *Rehberg*	Y	N	N	Y	Y
NEBRASKA					
1 *Bereuter*	N	N	Y	Y	Y
2 *Terry*	N	Y	Y	Y	Y
3 *Osborne*	N	N	N	Y	Y
NEVADA					
1 Berkley	N	N	N	N	Y
2 *Gibbons*	Y	N	N	Y	Y
NEW HAMPSHIRE					
1 *Sununu*	Y	N	N	Y	Y
2 *Bass*	Y	N	N	N	Y
NEW JERSEY					
1 Andrews	N	N	N	N	Y
2 *LoBiondo*	N	Y	N	Y	Y
3 *Saxton*	N	Y	Y	N	Y
4 *Smith*	N	Y	Y	N	N
5 *Roukema*	N	N	N	Y	Y
6 Pallone	N	N	N	N	Y
7 *Ferguson*	N	Y	Y	?	Y
8 Pascrell	N	N	N	N	Y
9 Rothman	N	N	N	N	Y
10 Payne	N	N	N	N	Y
11 *Frelinghuysen*	N	N	N	N	Y
12 Holt	N	N	N	N	Y
13 Menendez	N	N	N	N	Y
NEW MEXICO					
1 *Wilson*	N	N	N	N	Y
2 *Skeen*	N	N	N	Y	Y
3 Udall	N	N	N	N	Y
NEW YORK					
1 *Grucci*	Y	N	Y	Y	Y
2 Israel	N	N	N	N	Y
3 *King*	N	N	N	Y	Y
4 McCarthy	N	N	N	N	Y
5 Ackerman	N	N	N	N	Y
6 Meeks	?	?	?	?	?
7 Crowley	N	N	N	N	Y
8 Nadler	N	?	?	?	?
9 Weiner	N	N	N	N	Y
10 Towns	N	?	?	?	?
11 Owens	N	N	N	N	Y
12 Velázquez	?	?	?	?	?
13 *Fossella*	N	?	?	?	?
14 Maloney	N	N	N	N	Y
15 Rangel	N	N	N	N	Y
16 Serrano	N	N	N	N	Y
17 Engel	N	?	?	?	?
18 Lowey	N	N	N	N	Y
19 *Kelly*	Y	N	N	N	Y
20 *Gilman*	Y	N	N	N	Y
21 McNulty	N	N	N	N	Y
22 *Sweeney*	N	N	N	N	Y
23 *Boehlert*	N	N	N	N	Y
24 *McHugh*	N	?	?	?	?
25 *Walsh*	N	N	N	N	Y
26 Hinchey	N	N	N	N	Y
27 *Reynolds*	N	N	N	N	Y
28 Slaughter	N	N	N	N	Y
29 LaFalce	N	N	N	N	Y

District / Member	377	378	379	380	381
30 *Quinn*	N	N	N	N	Y
31 *Houghton*	N	N	N	N	Y
NORTH CAROLINA					
1 Clayton	N	N	N	N	Y
2 Etheridge	N	N	N	N	Y
3 *Jones*	Y	Y	Y	Y	N
4 Price	N	N	N	N	Y
5 *Burr*	Y	Y	N	Y	Y
6 *Coble*	N	Y	Y	Y	Y
7 McIntyre	N	N	Y	N	Y
8 *Hayes*	N	Y	Y	Y	Y
9 *Myrick*	Y	N	Y	N	Y
10 *Ballenger*	N	N	N	N	Y
11 *Taylor*	Y	Y	Y	Y	Y
12 Watt	N	N	N	N	Y
NORTH DAKOTA					
AL Pomeroy	N	N	N	N	Y
OHIO					
1 *Chabot*	Y	Y	Y	Y	N
2 *Portman*	N	N	N	N	Y
3 Hall	N	N	N	N	Y
4 *Oxley*	N	Y	N	N	Y
5 *Gillmor*	N	?	?	?	?
6 Strickland	N	N	N	N	Y
7 *Hobson*	N	N	N	N	Y
8 *Boehner*	N	N	N	N	Y
9 Kaptur	N	N	N	N	Y
10 Kucinich	N	N	N	N	Y
11 Jones	N	N	N	N	Y
12 *Tiberi*	N	N	Y	N	Y
13 Brown	N	N	N	N	Y
14 Sawyer	N	N	N	N	Y
15 *Pryce*	N	N	N	N	Y
16 *Regula*	N	N	N	N	Y
17 Traficant	N	N	N	N	Y
18 *Ney*	N	N	N	N	Y
19 *LaTourette*	N	N	N	N	Y
OKLAHOMA					
1 *Largent*	Y	Y	Y	Y	Y
2 Carson	N	N	N	N	Y
3 *Watkins*	N	Y	Y	Y	Y
4 *Watts*	N	Y	Y	Y	Y
5 *Istook*	N	N	Y	Y	Y
6 *Lucas*	N	N	N	Y	Y
OREGON					
1 Wu	N	N	N	N	Y
2 *Walden*	N	N	N	Y	Y
3 Blumenauer	N	N	N	N	Y
4 DeFazio	N	N	N	N	Y
5 Hooley	N	N	N	N	Y
PENNSYLVANIA					
1 Brady	N	N	N	N	Y
2 Fattah	N	N	N	N	Y
3 Borski	N	N	N	N	Y
4 *Hart*	N	Y	Y	Y	Y
5 *Peterson*	N	N	Y	N	Y
6 Holden	N	N	N	N	Y
7 *Weldon*	N	N	N	N	Y
8 Greenwood	N	N	N	N	Y
9 *Shuster, Bill*	N	N	N	Y	?
10 *Sherwood*	N	N	Y	N	Y
11 Kanjorski	N	N	N	N	Y
12 Murtha	N	N	N	N	Y
13 Hoeffel	N	N	N	N	Y
14 Coyne	N	N	N	N	Y
15 *Toomey*	Y	Y	N	Y	N
16 *Pitts*	Y	Y	Y	Y	N
17 *Gekas*	N	N	N	N	Y
18 Doyle	N	N	N	N	Y
19 *Platts*	N	N	Y	Y	Y
20 Mascara	N	N	N	N	Y
21 *English*	N	N	N	Y	Y
RHODE ISLAND					
1 Kennedy	N	N	N	N	Y
2 Langevin	N	N	N	N	Y
SOUTH CAROLINA					
1 *Brown*	Y	N	Y	Y	Y
2 Vacant					
3 *Graham*	Y	N	Y	Y	Y
4 *DeMint*	Y	Y	Y	Y	N
5 Spratt	N	N	N	N	Y
6 Clyburn	N	N	N	N	Y
SOUTH DAKOTA					
AL *Thune*	N	N	N	N	Y

District / Member	377	378	379	380	381
TENNESSEE					
1 *Jenkins*	Y	N	Y	Y	Y
2 *Duncan*	N	Y	Y	Y	Y
3 *Wamp*	N	Y	N	Y	Y
4 *Hilleary*	N	Y	Y	Y	Y
5 Clement	N	N	N	N	Y
6 Gordon	N	N	N	N	Y
7 *Bryant*	Y	Y	Y	Y	Y
8 Tanner	N	N	N	N	Y
9 Ford	N	N	N	N	Y
TEXAS					
1 Sandlin	N	N	N	N	Y
2 Turner	N	Y	N	N	Y
3 *Johnson, Sam*	N	Y	Y	Y	N
4 Hall	Y	N	Y	Y	Y
5 *Sessions*	Y	Y	Y	Y	N
6 *Barton*	Y	Y	Y	Y	N
7 *Culberson*	Y	Y	Y	Y	N
8 *Brady*	Y	Y	Y	Y	N
9 Lampson	N	N	N	N	Y
10 Doggett	N	N	N	N	Y
11 Edwards	N	N	N	N	Y
12 *Granger*	N	N	N	N	Y
13 *Thornberry*	Y	Y	N	Y	Y
14 *Paul*	Y	Y	Y	Y	N
15 Hinojosa	N	N	N	N	Y
16 Reyes	N	N	N	N	Y
17 Stenholm	N	N	N	N	N
18 Jackson-Lee	N	N	N	N	N
19 *Combest*	N	Y	Y	Y	N
20 Gonzalez	N	N	N	N	Y
21 *Smith*	N	N	Y	Y	Y
22 *DeLay*	Y	Y	Y	Y	N
23 *Bonilla*	N	N	N	N	Y
24 Frost	N	N	N	N	Y
25 Bentsen	N	N	N	N	Y
26 *Armey*	Y	Y	Y	Y	N
27 Ortiz	N	N	N	N	Y
28 Rodriguez	N	N	N	N	Y
29 Green	N	N	N	N	Y
30 Johnson, E.B.	N	N	N	N	Y
UTAH					
1 *Hansen*	N	N	Y	Y	Y
2 Matheson	N	N	N	N	Y
3 *Cannon*	Y	Y	Y	Y	Y
VERMONT					
AL *Sanders*	N	N	N	N	Y
VIRGINIA					
1 *Davis, Jo Ann*	Y	Y	Y	Y	Y
2 *Schrock*	N	N	Y	Y	Y
3 Scott	N	N	N	N	Y
4 *Forbes*	Y	Y	Y	Y	Y
5 *Goode*	Y	Y	Y	Y	Y
6 *Goodlatte*	N	Y	Y	Y	Y
7 *Cantor*	Y	Y	Y	Y	N
8 Moran	N	N	N	N	Y
9 Boucher	N	N	N	N	Y
10 *Wolf*	N	N	Y	N	Y
11 *Davis, T.*	N	N	N	N	Y
WASHINGTON					
1 Inslee	N	N	N	N	Y
2 Larsen	N	N	N	N	Y
3 Baird	N	N	N	N	Y
4 *Hastings*	N	N	N	N	Y
5 *Nethercutt*	N	N	N	N	Y
6 Dicks	N	N	N	N	Y
7 McDermott	N	N	N	N	Y
8 *Dunn*	N	N	N	N	Y
9 Smith	N	N	N	Y	Y
WEST VIRGINIA					
1 Mollohan	N	N	N	N	Y
2 *Capito*	N	N	N	Y	Y
3 Rahall	N	N	N	N	Y
WISCONSIN					
1 *Ryan*	Y	Y	Y	N	Y
2 Baldwin	N	N	N	N	Y
3 Kind	N	N	N	N	Y
4 Kleczka	N	N	N	N	Y
5 Barrett	N	N	N	N	Y
6 *Petri*	Y	Y	Y	N	Y
7 Obey	N	N	N	N	Y
8 *Green*	Y	Y	Y	N	Y
9 *Sensenbrenner*	Y	Y	Y	Y	N
WYOMING					
AL *Cubin*	N	Y	Y	Y	Y

Southern states - Ala., Ark., Fla., Ga., Ky., La., Miss., N.C., Okla., S.C., Tenn., Texas, Va.

Key

Y	Voted for (yea).
#	Paired for.
+	Announced for.
N	Voted against (nay).
X	Paired against.
–	Announced against.
P	Voted "present."
C	Voted "present" to avoid possible conflict of interest.
?	Did not vote or otherwise make a position known.

Democrats **Republicans**
Independents

382. HR 2975. Anti-Terrorism Authority/Consideration of Rule. Adoption of the resolution (H Res 263) that would waive the two-thirds vote requirement for same day consideration of the rule (H Res 264) to provide for House floor consideration of the bill that would expand law enforcement's power to investigate suspected terrorists. Adopted 216-205: R 209-3; D 6-201 (ND 3-151, SD 3-50); I 1-1. Oct. 12, 2001.

383. HR 2975. Anti-Terrorism Authority/Previous Question. Diaz-Balart, R-Fla., motion to order the previous question (thus ending debate and possibility of amendment) on adoption of the rule (H Res 264) to provide for House floor consideration of the bill that would expand law enforcement's power to investigate suspected terrorists. Motion agreed to 215-207: R 212-0; D 2-206 (ND 1-154, SD 1-52); I 1-1. Oct. 12, 2001.

384. HR 2975. Anti-Terrorism Authority/Rule. Adoption of the rule (H Res 264) that would provide for House floor consideration of the bill that would expand law enforcement's power to investigate suspected terrorists. Adopted 214-208: R 210-3; D 3-204 (ND 1-153, SD 2-51); I 1-1. Oct. 12, 2001.

385. HR 2975. Anti-Terrorism Authority/Recommit. Nadler, D-N.Y., motion to recommit the bill to the House Judiciary Committee with instructions to add language that would restrict the bill's surveillance provisions to terrorism-related investigations. Motion rejected 73-345: R 1-210; D 72-133 (ND 53-99, SD 19-34); I 0-2. Oct. 12, 2001.

386. HR 2975. Anti-Terrorism Authority/Passage. Passage of the bill that would expand law enforcement's power to investigate suspected terrorists. The bill would allow disclosure of wiretap information among certain government officials, authorize limited disclosure of secret grand jury information to certain government officials, and authorize the attorney general to detain foreigners he suspects are tied to terrorism. It also would make it easier for law enforcement to track Internet communications using surveillance techniques. The surveillance provisions would sunset after three years, with a two-year extension if the president finds that the national interest requires it. Most other provisions would expire in 2006. Passed 337-79: R 207-3; D 129-75 (ND 91-60, SD 38-15); I 1-1. A "yea" was a vote in support of the president's position. Oct. 12, 2001.

387. H Con Res 248. God Bless America/Adoption. Castle, R-Del., motion to suspend the rules and adopt the resolution that would express the sense of the Congress that public schools could display "God Bless America" in support of the United States. Adopted 404-0: R 208-0; D 194-0 (ND 143-0, SD 51-0); I 2-0. A two-thirds majority of those present and voting (270 in this case) is required for adoption under suspension of the rules. Oct. 16, 2001.

388. H Con Res 217. U.S.-Australia Relations/Adoption. Hyde, R-Ill., motion to suspend the rules and adopt the resolution that would acknowledge the diplomatic, economic and security importance of the relationship between the United States and Australia, welcome Australian Prime Minister John Howard and honor the 50th anniversary of the two countries' alliance under the ANZUS treaty. Motion agreed to 413-1: R 206-1; D 205-0 (ND 153-0, SD 52-0); I 2-0. A two-thirds majority of those present and voting (276 in this case) is required for adoption under suspension of the rules. Oct. 16, 2001.

	382	383	384	385	386	387	388
ALABAMA							
1 *Callahan*	Y	Y	Y	N	Y	Y	Y
2 *Everett*	Y	Y	Y	N	Y	Y	Y
3 *Riley*	Y	Y	Y	N	Y	Y	Y
4 *Aderholt*	?	?	?	?	?	Y	Y
5 Cramer	N	N	N	N	Y	Y	Y
6 *Bachus*	Y	Y	Y	N	Y	Y	Y
7 Hilliard	N	N	N	Y	N	Y	Y
ALASKA							
AL *Young*	Y	Y	Y	N	Y	Y	Y
ARIZONA							
1 *Flake*	Y	Y	Y	N	Y	Y	Y
2 Pastor	N	N	N	N	N	Y	Y
3 *Stump*	Y	Y	Y	N	Y	Y	Y
4 *Shadegg*	Y	Y	Y	N	Y	Y	Y
5 *Kolbe*	Y	Y	Y	N	Y	Y	Y
6 *Hayworth*	Y	Y	Y	N	Y	Y	Y
ARKANSAS							
1 Berry	N	N	N	N	Y	Y	Y
2 Snyder	N	N	N	Y	Y	Y	Y
3 Vacant							
4 Ross	N	N	N	N	Y	Y	Y
CALIFORNIA							
1 Thompson	N	N	N	N	Y	Y	Y
2 *Herger*	Y	Y	Y	N	Y	Y	Y
3 *Ose*	Y	Y	Y	N	Y	Y	Y
4 *Doolittle*	Y	Y	Y	N	Y	Y	Y
5 Matsui	N	N	N	Y	Y	Y	Y
6 Woolsey	N	N	N	N	N	P	Y
7 Miller, George	N	N	N	N	N	Y	Y
8 Pelosi	N	N	N	N	Y	Y	Y
9 Lee	N	N	N	Y	N	Y	Y
10 Tauscher	N	N	N	Y	Y	Y	Y
11 *Pombo*	Y	Y	Y	N	Y	Y	Y
12 Lantos	N	N	N	N	Y	Y	Y
13 Stark	N	N	N	N	N	Y	Y
14 Eshoo	N	N	N	N	Y	Y	Y
15 Honda	N	N	N	Y	N	P	Y
16 Lofgren	N	N	N	Y	Y	Y	Y
17 Farr	N	N	N	Y	Y	Y	Y
18 Condit	N	N	N	Y	Y	Y	Y
19 *Radanovich*	Y	Y	Y	N	Y	Y	Y
20 Dooley	N	N	N	Y	Y	Y	Y
21 *Thomas*	Y	Y	Y	N	Y	Y	Y
22 Capps	N	N	Y	Y	Y	Y	Y
23 *Gallegly*	Y	Y	Y	N	Y	Y	Y
24 Sherman	N	N	N	Y	Y	Y	Y
25 *McKeon*	Y	Y	Y	N	Y	Y	Y
26 Berman	N	N	N	Y	Y	Y	Y
27 Schiff	N	N	N	N	Y	Y	Y
28 *Dreier*	Y	Y	Y	N	Y	Y	Y
29 Waxman	N	N	N	Y	Y	Y	Y
30 Becerra	N	N	N	N	N	?	?
31 Solis	N	N	N	Y	N	Y	Y
32 Watson	N	N	N	Y	N	Y	Y
33 Roybal-Allard	N	N	N	Y	N	Y	Y
34 Napolitano	N	N	N	?	?	Y	Y
35 Waters	N	N	N	Y	N	Y	Y
36 Harman	N	N	N	?	?	Y	Y
37 Millender-McD.	N	N	N	N	N	Y	Y
38 *Horn*	Y	Y	Y	N	Y	Y	Y

	382	383	384	385	386	387	388
39 *Royce*	Y	Y	Y	N	Y	Y	Y
40 *Lewis*	Y	Y	Y	N	?	Y	Y
41 *Miller, Gary*	Y	Y	Y	N	Y	Y	Y
42 Baca	N	N	N	N	Y	Y	Y
43 *Calvert*	Y	Y	Y	N	Y	Y	Y
44 *Bono*	Y	Y	Y	N	Y	Y	Y
45 *Rohrabacher*	Y	Y	Y	N	Y	Y	Y
46 Sanchez	N	N	N	N	Y	Y	Y
47 *Cox*	Y	Y	Y	N	Y	Y	Y
48 *Issa*	Y	Y	Y	N	Y	Y	Y
49 Davis	N	N	N	N	Y	Y	Y
50 Filner	N	N	N	Y	N	Y	Y
51 *Cunningham*	N	Y	N	N	Y	Y	Y
52 *Hunter*	Y	Y	Y	N	Y	Y	Y
COLORADO							
1 DeGette	N	N	N	Y	N	Y	Y
2 Udall	N	N	N	Y	N	Y	Y
3 *McInnis*	Y	Y	Y	N	Y	Y	Y
4 *Schaffer*	Y	Y	Y	N	Y	Y	Y
5 *Hefley*	Y	Y	Y	N	Y	Y	Y
6 *Tancredo*	Y	Y	Y	N	Y	Y	Y
CONNECTICUT							
1 Larson	N	N	N	N	Y	Y	Y
2 *Simmons*	Y	Y	Y	N	Y	Y	Y
3 DeLauro	N	N	N	N	Y	Y	Y
4 *Shays*	Y	Y	Y	N	Y	Y	Y
5 Maloney	Y	N	N	N	Y	Y	Y
6 *Johnson*	Y	Y	Y	N	Y	Y	Y
DELAWARE							
AL *Castle*	Y	Y	Y	N	Y	Y	Y
FLORIDA							
1 Vacant							
2 Boyd	N	–	–	+	+	Y	Y
3 Brown	N	N	N	N	Y	Y	Y
4 *Crenshaw*	Y	Y	Y	N	Y	Y	Y
5 Thurman	N	N	N	Y	Y	Y	Y
6 *Stearns*	Y	Y	Y	N	Y	Y	Y
7 *Mica*	Y	Y	Y	N	Y	Y	Y
8 *Keller*	Y	Y	Y	N	Y	Y	Y
9 *Bilirakis*	Y	Y	Y	N	Y	Y	Y
10 *Young*	Y	Y	Y	N	Y	Y	Y
11 Davis	N	N	N	N	Y	Y	Y
12 *Putnam*	Y	Y	Y	N	Y	Y	Y
13 *Miller, D.*	?	?	?	?	?	?	?
14 *Goss*	Y	Y	Y	N	Y	Y	Y
15 *Weldon*	Y	Y	Y	N	Y	Y	Y
16 *Foley*	Y	Y	Y	N	Y	Y	Y
17 Meek	N	N	N	N	Y	Y	Y
18 *Ros-Lehtinen*	Y	Y	Y	N	Y	Y	Y
19 Wexler	?	N	N	N	Y	?	?
20 Deutsch	Y	N	N	Y	Y	Y	Y
21 *Diaz-Balart*	Y	Y	Y	N	Y	Y	Y
22 *Shaw*	Y	Y	Y	N	Y	Y	Y
23 Hastings	N	N	N	Y	N	Y	Y
GEORGIA							
1 *Kingston*	Y	Y	Y	N	Y	Y	Y
2 Bishop	N	N	N	N	Y	Y	Y
3 *Collins*	Y	Y	Y	N	Y	Y	Y
4 *McKinney*	N	N	N	Y	N	Y	Y
5 Lewis	N	N	N	Y	N	Y	Y
6 *Isakson*	Y	Y	Y	N	Y	Y	Y
7 *Barr*	Y	Y	Y	N	Y	Y	Y
8 *Chambliss*	Y	Y	Y	N	Y	Y	Y
9 *Deal*	Y	Y	Y	N	Y	Y	Y
10 *Norwood*	Y	Y	Y	N	Y	Y	Y
11 *Linder*	Y	Y	Y	N	Y	Y	Y
HAWAII							
1 Abercrombie	Y	N	N	+	–	Y	Y
2 Mink	N	N	N	Y	N	Y	Y
IDAHO							
1 *Otter*	Y	Y	Y	N	N	Y	Y
2 *Simpson*	Y	Y	Y	N	Y	Y	Y
ILLINOIS							
1 Rush	N	N	N	N	Y	Y	Y
2 Jackson	N	N	N	Y	N	P	Y
3 Lipinski	N	N	N	N	Y	Y	Y
4 Gutierrez	N	N	N	Y	Y	Y	Y
5 Blagojevich	N	N	N	Y	Y	Y	Y
6 *Hyde*	Y	Y	Y	N	Y	Y	Y
7 Davis	N	N	N	Y	Y	Y	Y
8 *Crane*	Y	Y	Y	N	Y	Y	Y
9 Schakowsky	N	N	N	N	P	Y	Y
10 *Kirk*	Y	Y	Y	N	Y	Y	Y
11 *Weller*	Y	Y	Y	N	Y	Y	Y
12 Costello	N	N	N	N	Y	Y	Y
13 *Biggert*	Y	Y	Y	N	Y	Y	Y

ND Northern Democrats SD Southern Democrats

	382	383	384	385	386	387	388
14 ***Hastert***	Y		Y		Y		
15 ***Johnson***	Y	Y	Y	N	Y	Y	Y
16 ***Manzullo***	Y	Y	Y	N	Y	Y	Y
17 Evans	N	N	N	N	Y	Y	Y
18 ***LaHood***	Y	Y	Y	N	N	Y	Y
19 Phelps	N	N	N	N	Y	Y	Y
20 ***Shimkus***	Y	Y	Y	N	Y	Y	Y
INDIANA							
1 Visclosky	N	N	N	Y	N	Y	Y
2 ***Pence***	Y	Y	Y	N	Y	Y	Y
3 Roemer	N	N	N	N	Y	Y	Y
4 ***Souder***	Y	Y	Y	N	Y	Y	Y
5 ***Buyer***	Y	Y	Y	N	Y	Y	Y
6 ***Burton***	Y	Y	Y	N	Y	?	?
7 ***Kerns***	Y	Y	Y	N	Y	Y	Y
8 ***Hostettler***	Y	Y	Y	N	Y	Y	Y
9 Hill	N	N	N	N	Y	Y	Y
10 Carson	N	N	N	N	Y	Y	Y
IOWA							
1 ***Leach***	Y	Y	Y	N	Y	Y	Y
2 ***Nussle***	Y	Y	Y	N	Y	Y	Y
3 Boswell	N	N	N	N	Y	Y	Y
4 ***Ganske***	Y	Y	Y	N	Y	Y	Y
5 ***Latham***	Y	Y	Y	N	Y	Y	Y
KANSAS							
1 ***Moran***	Y	Y	Y	N	Y	Y	Y
2 ***Ryun***	Y	Y	Y	N	Y	Y	Y
3 Moore	N	N	N	N	Y	Y	Y
4 ***Tiahrt***	Y	Y	Y	N	Y	Y	Y
KENTUCKY							
1 ***Whitfield***	Y	Y	Y	N	Y	Y	Y
2 ***Lewis***	Y	Y	Y	N	Y	Y	?
3 ***Northup***	Y	Y	Y	N	Y	Y	Y
4 Lucas	N	N	N	N	Y	Y	Y
5 ***Rogers***	Y	Y	Y	N	Y	Y	Y
6 ***Fletcher***	Y	Y	Y	N	Y	Y	Y
LOUISIANA							
1 ***Vitter***	Y	Y	Y	N	Y	Y	Y
2 Jefferson	N	N	N	Y	N	Y	Y
3 ***Tauzin***	Y	Y	Y	N	Y	Y	Y
4 ***McCrery***	Y	Y	Y	N	Y	Y	Y
5 ***Cooksey***	Y	Y	Y	N	Y	Y	Y
6 ***Baker***	Y	Y	Y	N	Y	Y	Y
7 John	N	N	N	N	Y	Y	Y
MAINE							
1 Allen	N	N	N	N	Y	Y	Y
2 Baldacci	N	N	N	N	Y	Y	Y
MARYLAND							
1 ***Gilchrest***	Y	Y	Y	N	Y	Y	Y
2 ***Ehrlich***	Y	Y	Y	N	Y	?	?
3 Cardin	N	N	N	Y	Y	Y	Y
4 Wynn	N	N	N	Y	Y	Y	Y
5 Hoyer	N	N	N	Y	Y	Y	Y
6 ***Bartlett***	Y	Y	Y	N	Y	Y	Y
7 Cummings	N	N	N	N	N	Y	Y
8 ***Morella***	Y	Y	Y	N	Y	Y	Y
MASSACHUSETTS							
1 Olver	N	N	N	Y	N	Y	Y
2 Neal	N	N	N	N	Y	Y	Y
3 McGovern	N	N	N	N	N	Y	Y
4 Frank	N	N	N	N	N	P	Y
5 Meehan	N	N	N	N	Y	Y	Y
6 Tierney	N	N	N	N	N	?	Y
7 Markey	N	N	N	N	N	Y	Y
8 Capuano	N	N	N	Y	N	P	Y
9 Vacant							
10 Delahunt	N	N	N	Y	N	Y	Y
MICHIGAN							
1 Stupak	N	N	N	N	Y	Y	Y
2 ***Hoekstra***	Y	Y	Y	N	Y	Y	Y
3 ***Ehlers***	Y	Y	Y	N	Y	Y	Y
4 ***Camp***	Y	Y	Y	N	Y	Y	Y
5 Barcia	N	N	N	N	Y	Y	Y
6 ***Upton***	Y	Y	Y	N	Y	Y	Y
7 ***Smith***	Y	Y	Y	N	Y	Y	Y
8 ***Rogers***	Y	Y	Y	N	Y	Y	Y
9 Kildee	N	N	N	N	Y	Y	Y
10 Bonior	N	N	N	Y	N	Y	Y
11 ***Knollenberg***	Y	Y	Y	N	Y	Y	Y
12 Levin	N	N	N	N	Y	Y	Y
13 Rivers	N	N	N	N	N	P	Y
14 Conyers	N	N	N	Y	N	?	?
15 Kilpatrick	N	N	N	Y	N	+	+
16 Dingell	N	N	N	Y	Y	Y	Y

	382	383	384	385	386	387	388
MINNESOTA							
1 ***Gutknecht***	Y	Y	Y	N	Y	Y	Y
2 ***Kennedy***	Y	Y	Y	N	Y	Y	Y
3 ***Ramstad***	Y	Y	Y	N	Y	Y	Y
4 McCollum	N	N	N	Y	Y	Y	Y
5 Sabo	N	N	N	Y	N	Y	Y
6 Luther	N	N	N	N	Y	Y	Y
7 Peterson	N	N	N	N	N	Y	Y
8 Oberstar	N	N	N	Y	N	Y	Y
MISSISSIPPI							
1 ***Wicker***	Y	Y	Y	N	Y	Y	Y
2 Thompson	N	N	N	Y	N	Y	Y
3 ***Pickering***	Y	Y	Y	N	Y	Y	Y
4 Shows	Y	N	Y	N	Y	Y	Y
5 Taylor	N	N	N	N	Y	Y	Y
MISSOURI							
1 Clay	N	N	N	Y	Y	Y	Y
2 ***Akin***	Y	Y	Y	N	Y	Y	Y
3 Gephardt	N	N	N	Y	Y	Y	Y
4 Skelton	N	N	N	N	Y	Y	Y
5 McCarthy	N	N	N	Y	Y	Y	Y
6 ***Graves***	Y	Y	Y	N	Y	Y	Y
7 ***Blunt***	?	?	?	?	?	Y	Y
8 ***Emerson***	Y	Y	Y	N	Y	Y	Y
9 ***Hulshof***	Y	Y	Y	N	Y	Y	Y
MONTANA							
AL ***Rehberg***	Y	Y	Y	N	Y	Y	Y
NEBRASKA							
1 ***Bereuter***	Y	Y	Y	N	Y	Y	Y
2 ***Terry***	Y	Y	Y	N	Y	Y	Y
3 ***Osborne***	Y	Y	Y	N	Y	Y	Y
NEVADA							
1 Berkley	N	N	N	Y	Y	Y	Y
2 ***Gibbons***	Y	Y	Y	N	Y	Y	Y
NEW HAMPSHIRE							
1 ***Sununu***	Y	Y	Y	N	Y	Y	Y
2 ***Bass***	Y	Y	Y	N	Y	Y	Y
NEW JERSEY							
1 Andrews	N	N	N	N	Y	Y	Y
2 ***LoBiondo***	Y	Y	Y	N	Y	Y	Y
3 ***Saxton***	Y	Y	Y	N	Y	Y	Y
4 ***Smith***	Y	Y	Y	N	Y	Y	Y
5 ***Roukema***	Y	Y	Y	N	?	Y	Y
6 Pallone	N	N	N	N	Y	Y	Y
7 ***Ferguson***	Y	Y	Y	N	Y	Y	Y
8 Pascrell	N	N	N	N	Y	Y	Y
9 Rothman	N	N	N	N	Y	Y	Y
10 Payne	N	N	N	N	N	Y	Y
11 ***Frelinghuysen***	Y	Y	Y	N	Y	Y	Y
12 Holt	N	N	N	N	Y	Y	Y
13 Menendez	N	N	N	N	Y	Y	Y
NEW MEXICO							
1 ***Wilson***	Y	Y	Y	N	Y	Y	Y
2 ***Skeen***	Y	Y	Y	N	Y	Y	Y
3 Udall	N	N	N	N	N	Y	Y
NEW YORK							
1 ***Grucci***	Y	Y	Y	N	Y	Y	Y
2 Israel	N	N	N	N	Y	Y	Y
3 ***King***	Y	Y	Y	N	Y	Y	Y
4 McCarthy	N	N	N	N	Y	Y	Y
5 Ackerman	N	N	N	N	N	P	Y
6 Meeks	N	N	N	N	N	Y	Y
7 Crowley	N	N	N	N	Y	Y	Y
8 Nadler	N	N	N	Y	N	P	Y
9 Weiner	N	N	N	N	Y	Y	Y
10 Towns	?	?	?	?	?	Y	Y
11 Owens	N	N	N	Y	N	Y	Y
12 Velázquez	N	N	N	N	N	Y	Y
13 ***Fossella***	Y	Y	Y	N	Y	Y	Y
14 Maloney	N	N	N	N	Y	Y	Y
15 Rangel	N	N	N	N	N	Y	Y
16 Serrano	N	N	N	N	N	Y	Y
17 Engel	N	N	N	Y	Y	Y	Y
18 Lowey	N	N	N	N	Y	Y	Y
19 ***Kelly***	Y	Y	Y	N	Y	Y	Y
20 ***Gilman***	Y	Y	Y	N	Y	Y	Y
21 McNulty	N	N	N	N	Y	Y	Y
22 ***Sweeney***	Y	Y	Y	N	Y	?	?
23 ***Boehlert***	Y	Y	Y	N	Y	Y	Y
24 ***McHugh***	?	?	?	?	+	Y	Y
25 ***Walsh***	Y	Y	Y	N	Y	Y	Y
26 Hinchey	N	N	N	Y	N	Y	Y
27 ***Reynolds***	Y	Y	Y	N	Y	Y	Y
28 Slaughter	N	N	N	Y	Y	Y	Y
29 LaFalce	N	N	N	N	Y	Y	Y

	382	383	384	385	386	387	388
30 ***Quinn***	Y	Y	Y	?	?	Y	Y
31 ***Houghton***	Y	Y	Y	N	Y	Y	Y
NORTH CAROLINA							
1 Clayton	N	N	N	Y	N	Y	Y
2 Etheridge	N	N	N	N	Y	Y	Y
3 ***Jones***	Y	Y	Y	N	Y	Y	Y
4 Price	N	N	N	N	Y	Y	Y
5 ***Burr***	Y	Y	Y	N	Y	Y	Y
6 ***Coble***	Y	Y	Y	N	Y	Y	Y
7 McIntyre	N	N	N	N	Y	Y	Y
8 ***Hayes***	Y	Y	Y	N	Y	Y	Y
9 ***Myrick***	Y	Y	Y	N	Y	Y	Y
10 ***Ballenger***	Y	Y	Y	N	Y	Y	Y
11 ***Taylor***	Y	Y	Y	N	Y	?	?
12 Watt	N	N	N	Y	N	P	Y
NORTH DAKOTA							
AL Pomeroy	N	N	N	N	Y	Y	Y
OHIO							
1 ***Chabot***	Y	Y	N	N	Y	Y	Y
2 ***Portman***	Y	Y	Y	N	Y	Y	Y
3 Hall	N	N	N	N	Y	Y	Y
4 ***Oxley***	Y	Y	Y	N	Y	Y	Y
5 ***Gillmor***	?	?	?	?	?	Y	Y
6 Strickland	N	N	N	N	Y	Y	Y
7 ***Hobson***	Y	Y	Y	N	Y	Y	Y
8 ***Boehner***	Y	Y	Y	N	Y	Y	Y
9 Kaptur	N	N	N	Y	N	Y	Y
10 Kucinich	N	N	N	Y	N	Y	Y
11 Jones	N	N	N	Y	N	Y	Y
12 ***Tiberi***	Y	Y	Y	N	Y	Y	Y
13 Brown	N	N	N	N	N	Y	Y
14 Sawyer	N	N	N	N	Y	Y	Y
15 ***Pryce***	Y	Y	Y	N	Y	?	?
16 ***Regula***	Y	Y	Y	N	Y	Y	Y
17 Traficant	Y	Y	Y	N	Y	Y	Y
18 ***Ney***	Y	Y	Y	N	Y	Y	Y
19 ***LaTourette***	Y	Y	Y	N	Y	?	?
OKLAHOMA							
1 ***Largent***	Y	Y	Y	N	Y	Y	Y
2 Carson	N	N	N	N	Y	Y	Y
3 ***Watkins***	Y	Y	Y	N	Y	Y	Y
4 ***Watts***	Y	Y	Y	N	Y	Y	Y
5 ***Istook***	Y	Y	Y	N	Y	Y	Y
6 ***Lucas***	Y	Y	Y	N	Y	Y	Y
OREGON							
1 Wu	N	N	N	Y	N	Y	Y
2 ***Walden***	Y	Y	Y	N	Y	Y	Y
3 Blumenauer	N	N	N	N	N	Y	Y
4 DeFazio	N	N	N	N	N	Y	Y
5 Hooley	N	N	N	N	Y	Y	Y
PENNSYLVANIA							
1 Brady	N	N	N	Y	Y	Y	Y
2 Fattah	N	N	N	Y	Y	Y	Y
3 Borski	N	N	N	N	Y	Y	Y
4 ***Hart***	Y	Y	Y	N	Y	Y	Y
5 ***Peterson***	Y	Y	Y	N	Y	Y	Y
6 Holden	N	N	N	N	Y	Y	Y
7 ***Weldon***	Y	Y	Y	N	Y	?	?
8 ***Greenwood***	Y	Y	Y	N	Y	Y	Y
9 ***Shuster, Bill***	Y	Y	Y	N	Y	Y	Y
10 ***Sherwood***	Y	Y	Y	N	Y	?	?
11 Kanjorski	N	N	N	N	Y	Y	Y
12 Murtha	N	N	N	N	Y	Y	Y
13 Hoeffel	N	N	N	Y	Y	Y	Y
14 Coyne	N	N	N	Y	N	Y	Y
15 ***Toomey***	Y	Y	Y	N	Y	Y	Y
16 ***Pitts***	Y	Y	Y	N	Y	Y	Y
17 ***Gekas***	Y	Y	Y	N	Y	Y	Y
18 Doyle	N	N	N	N	Y	Y	Y
19 ***Platts***	Y	Y	Y	N	Y	Y	Y
20 Mascara	N	N	N	N	Y	Y	Y
21 ***English***	Y	Y	Y	N	Y	Y	Y
RHODE ISLAND							
1 Kennedy	N	N	N	N	Y	Y	Y
2 Langevin	N	N	N	N	Y	Y	Y
SOUTH CAROLINA							
1 ***Brown***	Y	Y	Y	N	Y	Y	Y
2 Vacant							
3 ***Graham***	Y	Y	Y	N	Y	Y	Y
4 ***DeMint***	Y	Y	Y	N	Y	Y	Y
5 Spratt	N	N	N	N	Y	Y	Y
6 Clyburn	N	N	N	Y	N	Y	Y
SOUTH DAKOTA							
AL ***Thune***	Y	Y	Y	N	Y	Y	Y

	382	383	384	385	386	387	388
TENNESSEE							
1 ***Jenkins***	Y	Y	Y	N	Y	Y	Y
2 ***Duncan***	Y	Y	Y	N	Y	Y	Y
3 ***Wamp***	Y	Y	Y	N	Y	Y	Y
4 ***Hilleary***	Y	Y	Y	N	Y	Y	Y
5 Clement	N	N	N	N	Y	?	?
6 Gordon	N	N	N	N	Y	Y	Y
7 ***Bryant***	Y	Y	Y	N	Y	Y	Y
8 Tanner	N	N	N	N	Y	Y	Y
9 Ford	N	N	N	N	Y	Y	Y
TEXAS							
1 Sandlin	N	N	N	Y	Y	Y	Y
2 Turner	N	N	N	N	Y	Y	Y
3 ***Johnson, Sam***	Y	Y	Y	N	Y	Y	Y
4 Hall	Y	Y	Y	N	Y	Y	Y
5 ***Sessions***	Y	Y	Y	N	Y	Y	Y
6 ***Barton***	?	?	?	?	?	Y	Y
7 ***Culberson***	Y	Y	Y	N	Y	Y	Y
8 ***Brady***	Y	Y	Y	N	Y	Y	Y
9 Lampson	N	N	N	N	Y	Y	Y
10 Doggett	N	N	N	N	N	Y	Y
11 Edwards	N	N	N	N	Y	Y	Y
12 ***Granger***	Y	Y	Y	N	Y	Y	Y
13 ***Thornberry***	Y	Y	Y	N	Y	Y	Y
14 ***Paul***	N	Y	Y	Y	N	Y	N
15 Hinojosa	N	N	N	N	Y	Y	Y
16 Reyes	N	N	N	N	Y	Y	Y
17 Stenholm	N	N	N	N	Y	Y	Y
18 Jackson-Lee	N	N	N	N	N	Y	Y
19 ***Combest***	Y	Y	Y	N	Y	Y	Y
20 Gonzalez	N	N	N	Y	Y	Y	Y
21 ***Smith***	Y	Y	Y	N	Y	Y	Y
22 ***DeLay***	Y	Y	Y	N	Y	Y	Y
23 ***Bonilla***	Y	Y	Y	N	Y	Y	Y
24 Frost	N	N	N	Y	Y	Y	Y
25 Bentsen	N	N	N	N	Y	Y	Y
26 ***Armey***	Y	Y	Y	N	Y	Y	Y
27 Ortiz	N	N	N	N	Y	Y	Y
28 Rodriguez	N	N	N	Y	Y	Y	Y
29 Green	N	N	N	Y	Y	Y	Y
30 Johnson, E.B.	N	N	N	Y	N	Y	Y
UTAH							
1 ***Hansen***	Y	Y	Y	N	Y	Y	Y
2 Matheson	N	N	N	N	Y	Y	Y
3 ***Cannon***	Y	Y	Y	N	Y	Y	Y
VERMONT							
AL *Sanders*	N	N	N	N	N	Y	Y
VIRGINIA							
1 ***Davis, Jo Ann***	Y	Y	Y	N	Y	Y	Y
2 ***Schrock***	+	Y	Y	N	Y	Y	Y
3 Scott	N	N	N	Y	N	Y	Y
4 ***Forbes***	Y	Y	Y	N	Y	Y	Y
5 *Goode*	Y	Y	Y	N	Y	Y	Y
6 ***Goodlatte***	Y	Y	Y	N	Y	Y	Y
7 ***Cantor***	Y	Y	Y	N	Y	Y	Y
8 Moran	N	N	N	N	Y	Y	Y
9 Boucher	N	N	N	Y	N	Y	Y
10 ***Wolf***	Y	Y	Y	N	Y	Y	Y
11 ***Davis, T.***	Y	Y	Y	N	Y	Y	Y
WASHINGTON							
1 Inslee	N	N	N	Y	Y	Y	Y
2 Larsen	N	N	N	N	Y	Y	Y
3 Baird	N	N	N	N	Y	Y	Y
4 ***Hastings***	Y	Y	Y	N	Y	Y	Y
5 ***Nethercutt***	Y	Y	Y	N	Y	Y	Y
6 Dicks	?	N	N	N	Y	Y	Y
7 McDermott	N	N	N	Y	N	Y	Y
8 ***Dunn***	Y	Y	Y	N	Y	Y	Y
9 Smith	N	N	N	N	Y	Y	Y
WEST VIRGINIA							
1 Mollohan	N	N	?	N	Y	Y	Y
2 ***Capito***	Y	Y	Y	N	Y	Y	Y
3 Rahall	N	N	N	Y	N	Y	Y
WISCONSIN							
1 ***Ryan***	Y	Y	Y	N	Y	Y	Y
2 Baldwin	N	N	N	N	N	Y	Y
3 Kind	N	N	N	N	Y	Y	Y
4 Kleczka	N	N	N	N	N	Y	Y
5 Barrett	N	N	N	N	N	Y	Y
6 ***Petri***	N	Y	N	N	Y	Y	Y
7 Obey	N	N	N	N	P	Y	Y
8 ***Green***	Y	Y	Y	N	Y	Y	Y
9 ***Sensenbrenner***	Y	Y	Y	N	Y	Y	Y
WYOMING							
AL ***Cubin***	Y	Y	Y	N	Y	?	?

Southern states - Ala., Ark., Fla., Ga., Ky., La., Miss., N.C., Okla., S.C., Tenn., Texas, Va.

Key

Y Voted for (yea).
\# Paired for.
+ Announced for.
N Voted against (nay).
X Paired against.
− Announced against.
P Voted "present."
C Voted "present" to avoid possible conflict of interest.
? Did not vote or otherwise make a position known.

● Democrats **Republicans** *Independents*

---

389. HR 2272. Reef Preservation/Passage. Hyde, R-Ill., motion to suspend the rules and pass the bill that would allow the president to reduce or restructure the debt of developing countries that agree to spend the resulting savings on coral reef and other coastal marine protection efforts. Motion agreed to 382-32: R 181-27; D 199-5 (ND 151-1, SD 48-4); I 2-0. A two-thirds majority of those present and voting (276 in this case) is required for adoption under suspension of the rules. Oct. 16, 2001.

390. HR 3004. Money Laundering/Passage. Oxley, R-Ohio, motion to suspend the rules and pass the bill that would expand the Treasury Department's ability to fight money laundering. The bill would broaden law enforcement activities in this area, impose additional recordkeeping and other financial safeguards on domestic banks, and place new restrictions or bans on foreign banks that deal with the United States. Motion agreed to 412-1: R 210-1; D 200-0 (ND 149-0, SD 51-0); I 2-0. A two-thirds majority of those present and voting (276 in this case) is required for passage under suspension of the rules. Oct. 17, 2001.

391. S 1438. Fiscal 2002 Defense Authorization/Motion to Close Conference. Stump, R-Ariz., motion to close portions of the conference on the bill that would authorize $343.2 billion for defense programs. Motion agreed to 420-0: R 211-0; D 207-0 (ND 155-0, SD 52-0); I 2-0. Oct. 17, 2001.

392. Procedural Motion/Journal. Approval of the House Journal of Tuesday, Oct. 16, 2001. Approved 365-34: R 191-8; D 172-26 (ND 129-19, SD 43-7); I 2-0. Oct. 17, 2001.

393. HR 2217. Fiscal 2002 Interior Appropriations/Conference Report. Adoption of the conference report on the bill that would appropriate $19.1 billion for the Interior Department, related agencies and cultural programs in fiscal 2002. The bill includes $1.3 billion for conservation efforts, $400 million in emergency funds to fight wildfires, and prohibitions on oil and gas exploration in the Gulf of Mexico and at national monuments. Adopted (thus sent to the Senate) 380-28: R 186-24; D 193-3 (ND 146-1, SD 47-2); I 1-1. Oct. 17, 2001.

394. HR 2904. Fiscal 2002 Military Construction Appropriations/Conference Report. Adoption of the conference report on the bill that would provide $10.5 billion in fiscal 2002 for military construction projects, including the building of barracks, family housing, and medical facilities. Adopted (thus sent to the Senate) 409-1: R 207-1; D 200-0 (ND 149-0, SD 51-0); I 2-0. Oct. 17, 2001.

	389	390	391	392	393	394
ALABAMA						
1 *Callahan*	Y	Y	Y	Y	Y	?
2 *Everett*	Y	Y	Y	Y	Y	?
3 *Riley*	Y	Y	Y	Y	Y	Y
4 *Aderholt*	Y	Y	Y	N	Y	Y
5 Cramer	Y	Y	Y	Y	Y	Y
6 *Bachus*	Y	Y	Y	Y	Y	Y
7 Hilliard	Y	Y	Y	N	Y	Y
ALASKA						
AL *Young*	Y	Y	Y	Y	Y	Y
ARIZONA						
1 *Flake*	N	Y	Y	Y	N	Y
2 Pastor	Y	Y	Y	Y	Y	Y
3 *Stump*	N	Y	Y	Y	Y	Y
4 *Shadegg*	N	Y	Y	Y	Y	Y
5 *Kolbe*	Y	Y	Y	Y	Y	Y
6 *Hayworth*	N	Y	Y	Y	Y	Y
ARKANSAS						
1 Berry	N	Y	Y	Y	N	Y
2 Snyder	Y	Y	Y	Y	Y	Y
3 Vacant						
4 Ross	Y	Y	Y	Y	Y	Y
CALIFORNIA						
1 Thompson	Y	Y	Y	N	Y	Y
2 *Herger*	Y	Y	Y	Y	Y	Y
3 *Ose*	Y	Y	Y	Y	Y	Y
4 *Doolittle*	N	Y	Y	Y	Y	Y
5 Matsui	Y	Y	Y	Y	Y	Y
6 Woolsey	N	Y	Y	Y	Y	Y
7 Miller, George	Y	Y	Y	N	Y	Y
8 Pelosi	Y	Y	Y	?	Y	Y
9 Lee	Y	Y	Y	Y	Y	Y
10 Tauscher	Y	Y	Y	Y	Y	Y
11 *Pombo*	N	Y	Y	Y	Y	Y
12 Lantos	Y	Y	Y	Y	Y	Y
13 Stark	Y	Y	Y	N	Y	Y
14 Eshoo	Y	Y	Y	Y	Y	Y
15 Honda	?	Y	Y	Y	Y	Y
16 Lofgren	Y	Y	Y	Y	Y	Y
17 Farr	Y	Y	Y	Y	Y	Y
18 Condit	Y	Y	Y	Y	Y	Y
19 *Radanovich*	Y	Y	Y	Y	Y	Y
20 Dooley	Y	Y	Y	Y	Y	Y
21 *Thomas*	Y	Y	Y	Y	Y	Y
22 Capps	Y	Y	Y	Y	Y	Y
23 *Gallegly*	Y	Y	Y	Y	Y	Y
24 Sherman	Y	Y	Y	Y	Y	Y
25 *McKeon*	Y	Y	Y	Y	Y	Y
26 Berman	Y	Y	Y	Y	Y	Y
27 Schiff	Y	Y	Y	Y	Y	Y
28 *Dreier*	Y	Y	Y	Y	Y	Y
29 Waxman	Y	Y	Y	Y	Y	Y
30 Becerra	?	Y	Y	Y	Y	Y
31 Solis	Y	Y	Y	Y	Y	Y
32 Watson	Y	Y	Y	Y	Y	Y
33 Roybal-Allard	Y	?	Y	Y	Y	Y
34 Napolitano	Y	Y	Y	Y	Y	Y
35 Waters	Y	Y	Y	N	Y	Y
36 Harman	Y	Y	Y	Y	Y	Y
37 Millender-McD.	Y	Y	Y	Y	Y	Y
38 *Horn*	Y	Y	Y	Y	Y	Y

	389	390	391	392	393	394
39 *Royce*	N	Y	Y	Y	N	Y
40 *Lewis*	Y	Y	Y	Y	Y	Y
41 *Miller, Gary*	N	Y	Y	Y	Y	Y
42 Baca	Y	Y	Y	Y	Y	Y
43 *Calvert*	Y	Y	Y	Y	Y	Y
44 *Bono*	Y	Y	Y	Y	Y	Y
45 *Rohrabacher*	Y	Y	Y	Y	N	Y
46 Sanchez	Y	Y	Y	Y	Y	Y
47 *Cox*	Y	Y	Y	Y	Y	Y
48 *Issa*	Y	+	Y	Y	Y	Y
49 Davis	Y	Y	Y	Y	Y	Y
50 Filner	Y	Y	Y	N	Y	Y
51 *Cunningham*	Y	Y	Y	Y	Y	Y
52 *Hunter*	Y	Y	Y	Y	?	Y
COLORADO						
1 DeGette	Y	Y	Y	Y	Y	Y
2 Udall	Y	Y	Y	Y	Y	Y
3 *McInnis*	Y	Y	Y	Y	Y	Y
4 *Schaffer*	N	Y	Y	N	N	Y
5 *Hefley*	Y	Y	Y	Y	N	Y
6 *Tancredo*	Y	Y	Y	?	N	Y
CONNECTICUT						
1 Larson	Y	Y	Y	Y	Y	Y
2 *Simmons*	Y	Y	Y	Y	Y	Y
3 DeLauro	Y	Y	Y	Y	Y	Y
4 *Shays*	Y	Y	Y	Y	Y	Y
5 Maloney	Y	Y	Y	Y	Y	Y
6 *Johnson*	Y	Y	Y	Y	Y	Y
DELAWARE						
AL *Castle*	Y	Y	Y	Y	Y	Y
FLORIDA						
1 Vacant						
2 Boyd	Y	Y	Y	Y	Y	Y
3 Brown	Y	Y	Y	Y	Y	Y
4 *Crenshaw*	Y	Y	Y	Y	Y	Y
5 Thurman	Y	Y	Y	Y	Y	Y
6 *Stearns*	N	Y	Y	Y	N	Y
7 *Mica*	Y	Y	Y	Y	Y	Y
8 *Keller*	Y	Y	Y	Y	Y	Y
9 *Bilirakis*	Y	Y	Y	Y	Y	?
10 *Young*	Y	Y	Y	Y	Y	Y
11 Davis	Y	Y	Y	Y	Y	Y
12 *Putnam*	Y	Y	Y	Y	Y	Y
13 *Miller, D.*	?	?	?	?	?	?
14 *Goss*	Y	Y	Y	Y	Y	Y
15 *Weldon*	Y	Y	Y	Y	Y	Y
16 *Foley*	Y	Y	Y	?	Y	Y
17 Meek	Y	Y	Y	Y	Y	Y
18 *Ros-Lehtinen*	Y	Y	Y	Y	Y	Y
19 Wexler	?	Y	Y	Y	Y	Y
20 Deutsch	Y	Y	Y	Y	Y	Y
21 *Diaz-Balart*	Y	Y	Y	Y	Y	Y
22 *Shaw*	Y	Y	Y	Y	Y	Y
23 Hastings	Y	Y	Y	N	Y	Y
GEORGIA						
1 *Kingston*	Y	Y	Y	Y	Y	Y
2 Bishop	Y	?	Y	Y	Y	Y
3 *Collins*	N	Y	Y	Y	Y	Y
4 McKinney	Y	Y	Y	Y	Y	Y
5 Lewis	Y	Y	Y	Y	Y	Y
6 *Isakson*	Y	Y	Y	Y	Y	Y
7 *Barr*	N	Y	Y	N	Y	Y
8 *Chambliss*	Y	Y	Y	?	Y	Y
9 *Deal*	Y	Y	Y	Y	Y	Y
10 *Norwood*	N	Y	Y	Y	Y	Y
11 *Linder*	Y	Y	Y	Y	Y	Y
HAWAII						
1 Abercrombie	Y	Y	Y	Y	?	?
2 Mink	Y	Y	Y	Y	Y	Y
IDAHO						
1 *Otter*	Y	Y	Y	Y	Y	Y
2 *Simpson*	Y	Y	Y	Y	Y	Y
ILLINOIS						
1 Rush	Y	Y	Y	Y	Y	Y
2 Jackson	Y	Y	Y	Y	Y	Y
3 Lipinski	Y	Y	Y	Y	Y	Y
4 Gutierrez	Y	Y	Y	Y	Y	Y
5 Blagojevich	Y	Y	Y	Y	+	Y
6 *Hyde*	Y	Y	Y	Y	Y	Y
7 Davis	Y	Y	Y	Y	Y	Y
8 *Crane*	Y	Y	Y	N	N	Y
9 Schakowsky	Y	Y	Y	Y	Y	Y
10 *Kirk*	Y	Y	Y	?	Y	Y
11 *Weller*	Y	Y	Y	N	Y	Y
12 Costello	Y	Y	Y	N	?	Y
13 *Biggert*	Y	Y	Y	Y	Y	Y

ND Northern Democrats   SD Southern Democrats

	389	390	391	392	393	394
14 ***Hastert***						
15 ***Johnson***	Y	Y	Y	Y	Y	Y
16 ***Manzullo***	Y	Y	Y	Y	Y	Y
17 Evans	Y	Y	Y	Y	Y	Y
18 ***LaHood***	Y	Y	Y	Y	Y	Y
19 Phelps	Y	Y	Y	N	?	Y
20 ***Shimkus***	Y	Y	Y	Y	Y	Y
INDIANA						
1 Visclosky	Y	Y	Y	N	Y	Y
2 ***Pence***	Y	Y	Y	Y	Y	Y
3 Roemer	Y	Y	Y	Y	Y	Y
4 ***Souder***	Y	Y	Y	Y	Y	Y
5 ***Buyer***	Y	Y	Y	Y	?	Y
6 ***Burton***	?	+	+	+	+	+
7 ***Kerns***	N	Y	Y	Y	N	Y
8 ***Hostettler***	N	Y	Y	Y	N	Y
9 Hill	Y	Y	Y	Y	?	Y
10 Carson	Y	Y	Y	Y	Y	Y
IOWA						
1 ***Leach***	Y	Y	Y	Y	Y	Y
2 ***Nussle***	Y	Y	Y	Y	Y	Y
3 Boswell	Y	Y	Y	Y	Y	Y
4 ***Ganske***	Y	Y	Y	Y	Y	Y
5 ***Latham***	Y	Y	Y	N	Y	Y
KANSAS						
1 ***Moran***	N	Y	Y	Y	N	Y
2 ***Ryun***	N	Y	Y	Y	N	Y
3 Moore	Y	Y	Y	Y	Y	Y
4 ***Tiahrt***	Y	Y	Y	Y	Y	Y
KENTUCKY						
1 ***Whitfield***	Y	Y	Y	Y	Y	Y
2 ***Lewis***	Y	Y	Y	Y	Y	Y
3 ***Northup***	Y	Y	Y	Y	Y	Y
4 Lucas	Y	Y	Y	?	Y	Y
5 ***Rogers***	Y	Y	Y	Y	Y	?
6 ***Fletcher***	Y	Y	Y	Y	Y	Y
LOUISIANA						
1 ***Vitter***	Y	Y	Y	Y	Y	Y
2 Jefferson	Y	Y	Y	Y	Y	Y
3 ***Tauzin***	Y	Y	Y	Y	Y	Y
4 ***McCrery***	Y	Y	Y	Y	Y	Y
5 ***Cooksey***	Y	Y	Y	Y	Y	Y
6 ***Baker***	Y	Y	Y	Y	Y	Y
7 John	Y	Y	Y	Y	?	Y
MAINE						
1 Allen	Y	Y	Y	Y	?	Y
2 Baldacci	Y	Y	Y	Y	Y	Y
MARYLAND						
1 ***Gilchrest***	Y	Y	Y	Y	Y	Y
2 ***Ehrlich***	?	Y	Y	Y	Y	Y
3 Cardin	Y	Y	Y	Y	Y	Y
4 Wynn	Y	Y	Y	Y	Y	Y
5 Hoyer	Y	Y	Y	Y	Y	Y
6 ***Bartlett***	Y	Y	Y	Y	Y	Y
7 Cummings	Y	Y	Y	Y	Y	Y
8 ***Morella***	Y	Y	Y	Y	Y	Y
MASSACHUSETTS						
1 Olver	Y	Y	Y	N	Y	Y
2 Neal	Y	Y	Y	Y	Y	Y
3 McGovern	Y	Y	Y	Y	Y	Y
4 Frank	Y	Y	Y	Y	Y	Y
5 Meehan	Y	Y	Y	Y	Y	Y
6 Tierney	Y	Y	Y	?	Y	Y
7 Markey	Y	Y	Y	?	Y	Y
8 Capuano	Y	Y	Y	Y	Y	Y
9 Vacant						
10 Delahunt	Y	Y	Y	Y	Y	Y
MICHIGAN						
1 Stupak	Y	Y	Y	Y	Y	Y
2 ***Hoekstra***	Y	Y	Y	?	Y	Y
3 ***Ehlers***	Y	Y	Y	Y	Y	Y
4 ***Camp***	Y	Y	Y	Y	Y	Y
5 Barcia	Y	Y	Y	Y	Y	Y
6 ***Upton***	Y	Y	Y	Y	Y	Y
7 ***Smith***	N	Y	Y	Y	Y	Y
8 ***Rogers***	Y	Y	Y	Y	Y	Y
9 Kildee	Y	Y	Y	Y	Y	Y
10 Bonior	Y	Y	Y	?	Y	Y
11 ***Knollenberg***	Y	Y	Y	Y	Y	Y
12 Levin	Y	Y	Y	Y	Y	Y
13 Rivers	Y	Y	Y	Y	Y	Y
14 Conyers	?	?	?	?	?	?
15 Kilpatrick	?	Y	Y	Y	Y	Y
16 Dingell	Y	Y	Y	Y	Y	Y
MINNESOTA						
1 ***Gutknecht***	Y	Y	Y	Y	Y	Y
2 ***Kennedy***	Y	Y	Y	Y	Y	Y
3 ***Ramstad***	Y	Y	Y	N	Y	Y
4 McCollum	Y	Y	Y	Y	Y	Y
5 Sabo	Y	?	Y	?	Y	Y
6 Luther	Y	Y	Y	Y	Y	Y
7 Peterson	Y	Y	Y	N	?	?
8 Oberstar	Y	Y	Y	N	Y	Y
MISSISSIPPI						
1 ***Wicker***	Y	Y	Y	N	Y	Y
2 Thompson	Y	Y	Y	N	Y	Y
3 ***Pickering***	N	Y	Y	?	Y	Y
4 Shows	N	Y	Y	Y	+	+
5 Taylor	Y	Y	Y	N	Y	Y
MISSOURI						
1 Clay	Y	Y	Y	Y	Y	Y
2 ***Akin***	Y	Y	Y	Y	Y	Y
3 Gephardt	Y	Y	Y	Y	Y	Y
4 Skelton	Y	Y	Y	Y	Y	Y
5 McCarthy	Y	Y	Y	Y	Y	Y
6 ***Graves***	Y	Y	Y	Y	Y	Y
7 ***Blunt***	Y	Y	Y	Y	Y	Y
8 ***Emerson***	Y	Y	Y	Y	N	Y
9 ***Hulshof***	Y	Y	Y	Y	Y	Y
MONTANA						
AL ***Rehberg***	Y	Y	Y	Y	Y	Y
NEBRASKA						
1 ***Bereuter***	Y	Y	Y	Y	Y	Y
2 ***Terry***	Y	Y	Y	Y	Y	Y
3 ***Osborne***	Y	Y	Y	Y	Y	Y
NEVADA						
1 Berkley	Y	Y	Y	Y	Y	Y
2 ***Gibbons***	Y	Y	Y	Y	Y	Y
NEW HAMPSHIRE						
1 ***Sununu***	Y	Y	Y	Y	Y	Y
2 ***Bass***	Y	?	Y	Y	+	Y
NEW JERSEY						
1 Andrews	Y	Y	Y	Y	Y	Y
2 ***LoBiondo***	Y	Y	Y	Y	Y	Y
3 ***Saxton***	Y	Y	Y	Y	Y	Y
4 ***Smith***	Y	Y	Y	Y	Y	Y
5 ***Roukema***	Y	Y	?	?	?	?
6 Pallone	Y	Y	Y	Y	Y	Y
7 ***Ferguson***	Y	Y	Y	Y	Y	Y
8 Pascrell	Y	Y	Y	Y	Y	Y
9 Rothman	Y	Y	Y	Y	Y	Y
10 Payne	Y	Y	Y	Y	Y	Y
11 ***Frelinghuysen***	Y	Y	?	?	Y	Y
12 Holt	Y	Y	Y	Y	Y	Y
13 Menendez	Y	Y	Y	Y	Y	?
NEW MEXICO						
1 ***Wilson***	Y	Y	Y	Y	Y	Y
2 ***Skeen***	Y	Y	Y	Y	Y	Y
3 Udall	Y	Y	Y	Y	Y	Y
NEW YORK						
1 ***Grucci***	Y	Y	Y	Y	Y	Y
2 Israel	Y	Y	Y	Y	Y	Y
3 ***King***	Y	Y	Y	Y	Y	Y
4 McCarthy	Y	Y	Y	Y	+	Y
5 Ackerman	Y	Y	Y	Y	Y	Y
6 Meeks	Y	Y	Y	Y	Y	Y
7 Crowley	Y	Y	Y	Y	Y	Y
8 Nadler	Y	Y	Y	Y	Y	Y
9 Weiner	Y	Y	Y	Y	Y	Y
10 Towns	Y	Y	Y	Y	Y	Y
11 Owens	Y	Y	Y	Y	Y	Y
12 Velázquez	Y	Y	Y	Y	Y	Y
13 ***Fossella***	Y	Y	Y	Y	Y	Y
14 Maloney	Y	Y	Y	Y	Y	Y
15 Rangel	Y	Y	Y	Y	Y	Y
16 Serrano	Y	?	Y	Y	Y	Y
17 Engel	Y	Y	Y	Y	Y	Y
18 Lowey	Y	Y	Y	Y	Y	Y
19 ***Kelly***	Y	Y	Y	?	Y	Y
20 ***Gilman***	Y	Y	Y	Y	Y	Y
21 McNulty	Y	Y	Y	Y	Y	?
22 ***Sweeney***	?	?	?	?	Y	Y
23 ***Boehlert***	Y	Y	Y	Y	Y	Y
24 ***McHugh***	Y	Y	Y	Y	Y	Y
25 ***Walsh***	Y	Y	Y	Y	Y	Y
26 Hinchey	Y	Y	Y	Y	Y	Y
27 ***Reynolds***	Y	Y	Y	?	Y	Y
28 Slaughter	Y	Y	Y	Y	Y	Y
29 LaFalce	Y	Y	Y	Y	Y	?
30 ***Quinn***	Y	Y	Y	Y	Y	Y
31 ***Houghton***	Y	Y	Y	Y	Y	Y
NORTH CAROLINA						
1 Clayton	Y	Y	Y	Y	Y	Y
2 Etheridge	Y	Y	Y	N	Y	Y
3 ***Jones***	Y	Y	Y	?	N	Y
4 Price	Y	?	?	?	?	?
5 ***Burr***	Y	Y	Y	Y	Y	Y
6 ***Coble***	N	Y	Y	Y	Y	Y
7 McIntyre	Y	Y	Y	Y	Y	Y
8 ***Hayes***	Y	Y	Y	Y	Y	Y
9 ***Myrick***	Y	Y	Y	Y	Y	Y
10 ***Ballenger***	Y	Y	Y	Y	Y	Y
11 ***Taylor***	?	Y	Y	Y	Y	Y
12 Watt	Y	Y	Y	Y	Y	Y
NORTH DAKOTA						
AL Pomeroy	Y	Y	Y	Y	Y	Y
OHIO						
1 ***Chabot***	Y	Y	Y	Y	Y	Y
2 ***Portman***	Y	Y	Y	Y	Y	Y
3 Hall	Y	Y	Y	Y	Y	Y
4 ***Oxley***	Y	Y	Y	?	Y	Y
5 ***Gillmor***	Y	Y	Y	Y	Y	Y
6 Strickland	Y	Y	Y	N	Y	Y
7 ***Hobson***	Y	Y	Y	Y	Y	Y
8 ***Boehner***	Y	Y	Y	?	Y	Y
9 Kaptur	Y	?	Y	Y	Y	Y
10 Kucinich	Y	Y	Y	Y	Y	Y
11 Jones	Y	Y	Y	N	Y	Y
12 ***Tiberi***	Y	Y	Y	Y	N	Y
13 Brown	Y	Y	Y	Y	Y	Y
14 Sawyer	Y	Y	Y	Y	Y	Y
15 ***Pryce***	?	Y	Y	Y	Y	Y
16 ***Regula***	Y	Y	Y	Y	Y	?
17 Traficant	Y	Y	Y	Y	Y	Y
18 ***Ney***	Y	Y	Y	Y	Y	Y
19 ***LaTourette***	?	?	?	?	?	?
OKLAHOMA						
1 ***Largent***	Y	Y	Y	Y	Y	Y
2 Carson	Y	Y	Y	Y	?	Y
3 ***Watkins***	Y	Y	Y	Y	Y	Y
4 ***Watts***	Y	Y	Y	Y	Y	Y
5 ***Istook***	Y	Y	Y	Y	Y	Y
6 ***Lucas***	Y	Y	Y	Y	Y	Y
OREGON						
1 Wu	Y	Y	Y	N	N	Y
2 ***Walden***	Y	Y	Y	Y	Y	Y
3 Blumenauer	Y	Y	Y	Y	Y	Y
4 DeFazio	Y	Y	Y	N	Y	Y
5 Hooley	Y	Y	Y	Y	Y	Y
PENNSYLVANIA						
1 Brady	Y	Y	Y	N	Y	Y
2 Fattah	Y	?	Y	N	Y	Y
3 Borski	Y	Y	Y	N	Y	Y
4 ***Hart***	Y	Y	Y	Y	Y	Y
5 ***Peterson***	Y	Y	Y	Y	Y	Y
6 Holden	Y	Y	Y	Y	Y	Y
7 ***Weldon***	?	Y	Y	Y	Y	Y
8 ***Greenwood***	Y	Y	Y	Y	Y	Y
9 ***Shuster, Bill***	Y	Y	Y	Y	Y	Y
10 ***Sherwood***	?	Y	Y	Y	Y	Y
11 Kanjorski	Y	Y	Y	Y	Y	Y
12 Murtha	Y	Y	Y	Y	Y	Y
13 Hoeffel	Y	Y	Y	Y	Y	Y
14 Coyne	Y	Y	Y	Y	Y	Y
15 ***Toomey***	N	Y	Y	Y	N	Y
16 ***Pitts***	Y	Y	Y	Y	Y	Y
17 ***Gekas***	Y	Y	Y	Y	Y	Y
18 Doyle	Y	Y	Y	Y	Y	Y
19 ***Platts***	Y	Y	Y	Y	Y	Y
20 Mascara	Y	Y	Y	Y	Y	Y
21 ***English***	Y	Y	Y	N	Y	Y
RHODE ISLAND						
1 Kennedy	Y	Y	Y	?	Y	Y
2 Langevin	Y	Y	Y	Y	Y	Y
SOUTH CAROLINA						
1 ***Brown***	Y	Y	Y	Y	Y	Y
2 Vacant						
3 ***Graham***	Y	Y	Y	Y	Y	Y
4 ***DeMint***	Y	Y	Y	Y	Y	Y
5 Spratt	Y	Y	Y	Y	Y	Y
6 Clyburn	Y	Y	Y	Y	Y	Y
SOUTH DAKOTA						
AL ***Thune***	Y	Y	Y	Y	Y	Y
TENNESSEE						
1 ***Jenkins***	Y	Y	Y	Y	Y	Y
2 ***Duncan***	N	Y	Y	Y	N	Y
3 ***Wamp***	Y	Y	Y	Y	Y	Y
4 ***Hilleary***	Y	Y	Y	Y	Y	Y
5 Clement	?	Y	Y	Y	Y	Y
6 Gordon	Y	Y	Y	Y	Y	Y
7 ***Bryant***	Y	Y	Y	Y	Y	Y
8 Tanner	Y	Y	Y	Y	Y	Y
9 Ford	Y	Y	Y	N	Y	Y
TEXAS						
1 Sandlin	Y	?	Y	Y	Y	Y
2 Turner	Y	Y	Y	Y	Y	Y
3 ***Johnson, Sam***	N	Y	Y	Y	N	Y
4 Hall	N	Y	Y	Y	N	Y
5 ***Sessions***	Y	Y	Y	Y	Y	Y
6 ***Barton***	N	Y	Y	Y	Y	Y
7 ***Culberson***	N	Y	Y	Y	Y	Y
8 ***Brady***	Y	Y	Y	Y	Y	Y
9 Lampson	Y	Y	Y	Y	Y	Y
10 Doggett	Y	Y	Y	Y	Y	Y
11 Edwards	Y	Y	Y	Y	Y	Y
12 ***Granger***	Y	Y	Y	Y	Y	Y
13 ***Thornberry***	Y	Y	Y	Y	Y	Y
14 ***Paul***	N	N	Y	Y	N	N
15 Hinojosa	Y	Y	Y	Y	Y	Y
16 Reyes	Y	Y	?	?	?	?
17 Stenholm	N	Y	Y	Y	Y	Y
18 Jackson-Lee	Y	Y	Y	Y	Y	Y
19 ***Combest***	Y	Y	Y	?	Y	Y
20 Gonzalez	Y	Y	Y	Y	Y	Y
21 ***Smith***	Y	Y	Y	Y	Y	Y
22 ***DeLay***	Y	Y	Y	Y	Y	Y
23 ***Bonilla***	N	Y	Y	Y	Y	Y
24 Frost	Y	Y	Y	?	Y	Y
25 Bentsen	Y	Y	Y	Y	Y	Y
26 ***Armey***	Y	Y	Y	Y	Y	Y
27 Ortiz	Y	Y	Y	Y	Y	Y
28 Rodriguez	Y	Y	Y	Y	Y	Y
29 Green	Y	Y	Y	Y	Y	Y
30 Johnson, E.B.	Y	Y	Y	Y	Y	Y
UTAH						
1 ***Hansen***	Y	Y	Y	Y	Y	Y
2 Matheson	Y	Y	Y	Y	Y	Y
3 ***Cannon***	Y	Y	Y	Y	Y	Y
VERMONT						
AL *Sanders*	Y	Y	Y	Y	Y	Y
VIRGINIA						
1 ***Davis, Jo Ann***	Y	Y	Y	Y	Y	Y
2 ***Schrock***	Y	Y	Y	Y	Y	Y
3 Scott	Y	Y	Y	N	Y	Y
4 ***Forbes***	Y	Y	Y	Y	Y	Y
5 *Goode*	Y	Y	Y	Y	N	Y
6 ***Goodlatte***	Y	Y	Y	Y	N	Y
7 ***Cantor***	Y	Y	Y	Y	Y	Y
8 Moran	Y	Y	Y	Y	Y	Y
9 Boucher	Y	Y	Y	Y	Y	Y
10 ***Wolf***	Y	Y	Y	Y	Y	Y
11 ***Davis, T.***	Y	Y	Y	Y	Y	Y
WASHINGTON						
1 Inslee	Y	Y	Y	Y	Y	Y
2 Larsen	Y	Y	Y	Y	Y	Y
3 Baird	Y	Y	Y	Y	Y	Y
4 ***Hastings***	Y	Y	Y	Y	Y	Y
5 ***Nethercutt***	Y	Y	Y	Y	Y	Y
6 Dicks	Y	Y	Y	?	Y	Y
7 McDermott	Y	Y	Y	N	Y	Y
8 ***Dunn***	Y	Y	Y	Y	Y	Y
9 Smith	Y	Y	Y	Y	Y	Y
WEST VIRGINIA						
1 Mollohan	Y	Y	Y	Y	Y	Y
2 ***Capito***	Y	Y	Y	Y	Y	Y
3 Rahall	Y	Y	Y	Y	Y	Y
WISCONSIN						
1 ***Ryan***	Y	Y	Y	Y	Y	Y
2 Baldwin	Y	Y	Y	Y	Y	Y
3 Kind	Y	Y	Y	Y	Y	Y
4 Kleczka	Y	?	Y	Y	Y	?
5 Barrett	Y	Y	Y	Y	Y	Y
6 ***Petri***	Y	Y	Y	Y	N	Y
7 Obey	Y	Y	Y	Y	Y	Y
8 ***Green***	Y	Y	Y	Y	N	Y
9 ***Sensenbrenner***	Y	Y	Y	Y	N	Y
WYOMING						
AL ***Cubin***	?	?	?	?	?	?

Southern states - Ala., Ark., Fla., Ga., Ky., La., Miss., N.C., Okla., S.C., Tenn., Texas, Va.

395. HR 3086. Student Loan Aid/Passage. McKeon, R-Calif., motion to suspend the rules and pass the bill that would allow the secretary of Education to waive or change through 2003 the regulatory and administrative requirements of federal student financial aid programs to help students who are on active duty in the armed services or were directly affected by the Sept. 11 terrorist attacks. Motion agreed to 415-0: R 210-0; D 203-0 (ND 150-0, SD 53-0); I 2-0. A two-thirds majority of those present and voting (277 in this case) is required for passage under suspension of the rules. Oct. 23, 2001.

396. HR 3160. Bioterrorism Enforcement/Passage. Tauzin, R-La., motion to suspend the rules and pass the bill that would amend the 1996 Anti-Terrorism and Effective Death Penalty Act to impose new criminal penalties on individuals who unsafely or illegally possess, use or transfer certain controlled biological agents and toxins. It also would require the Department of Health and Human Services to establish new regulations in this area, including additional reporting, registration and handling requirements. Motion agreed to 419-0: R 212-0; D 205-0 (ND 152-0, SD 53-0); I 2-0. A two-thirds majority of those present and voting (280 in this case) is required for passage under suspension of the rules. Oct. 23, 2001.

397. HR 2924. Electricity Protection/Passage. Calvert, R-Calif., motion to suspend the rules and pass the bill that would allow the Western Area and Southeastern and Southwestern power administrations to offer rewards to individuals who provide information or evidence leading to the arrest and prosecution of anyone responsible for causing damage to the nation's electricity plants and transmission lines. Motion agreed to 418-0: R 211-0; D 205-0 (ND 152-0, SD 53-0); I 2-0. A two-thirds majority of those present and voting (279 in this case) is required for passage under suspension of the rules. Oct. 23, 2001.

398. HR 3162. Anti-Terrorism Authority/Passage. Sensenbrenner, R-Wis., motion to suspend the rules and pass the bill that would expand law enforcement's power to investigate suspected terrorists. The bill would allow disclosure of wiretap information among certain government officials, authorize limited disclosure of secret grand jury information, and authorize the detention of foreigners with suspected ties to terrorism. It would make it easier for law enforcement to track voice and Internet communications, and strengthen laws to combat money laundering. Most intelligence-gathering provisions would sunset after four years. Motion agreed to 357-66: R 211-3; D 145-62 (ND 103-50, SD 42-12); I 1-1. A two-thirds majority of those present and voting (282 in this case) is required for passage under suspension of the rules. A "yea" was a vote in support of the president's position. Oct. 24, 2001.

399. Procedural Motion/Journal. Approval of the House Journal of Tuesday, Oct. 23, 2001. Approved 367-48: R 198-12; D 167-36 (ND 121-29, SD 46-7); I 2-0. Oct. 24, 2001.

400. HR 3090. Economic Stimulus/Previous Question. Linder, R-Ga., motion to order the previous question (thus ending debate and possibility of amendment) on adoption of the rule (H Res 270) to provide for House floor consideration of the bill that would grant businesses and individuals $99.5 billion in federal tax cuts in fiscal 2002, and a total $159.4 billion in reductions over 10 years. Motion agreed to 219-207: R 216-0; D 2-206 (ND 1-155, SD 1-51); I 1-1. Oct. 24, 2001.

401. HR 3090. Economic Stimulus/Rule. Adoption of the rule (H Res 270) to provide for House floor consideration of the bill that would grant businesses and individuals $99.5 billion in federal tax cuts in fiscal 2002, and a total $159.4 billion in reductions over 10 years. Adopted 225-199: R 214-0; D 10-198 (ND 9-146, SD 1-52); I 1-1. Oct. 24, 2001.

[1] *Rep. Jeff Miller, R-Fla., was sworn in Oct. 23, 2001. The first vote for which he was eligible was 396.*

[2] *Rep. Stephen F. Lynch, D-Mass., was sworn in Oct. 23, 2001. The first vote for which he was eligible was 396.*

Key

Y	Voted for (yea).
#	Paired for.
+	Announced for.
N	Voted against (nay).
X	Paired against.
−	Announced against.
P	Voted "present."
C	Voted "present" to avoid possible conflict of interest.
?	Did not vote or otherwise make a position known.

•

Democrats **Republicans**
Independents

	395	396	397	398	399	400	401
ALABAMA							
1 *Callahan*	Y	Y	Y	Y	Y	Y	Y
2 *Everett*	Y	Y	Y	Y	Y	Y	Y
3 *Riley*	Y	Y	Y	Y	Y	Y	Y
4 *Aderholt*	Y	Y	Y	Y	Y	Y	Y
5 Cramer	Y	Y	Y	Y	Y	N	N
6 *Bachus*	Y	Y	Y	Y	Y	Y	Y
7 Hilliard	Y	Y	N	N	N	N	N
ALASKA							
AL *Young*	Y	Y	Y	?	Y	Y	Y
ARIZONA							
1 *Flake*	Y	Y	Y	Y	Y	Y	Y
2 Pastor	Y	Y	Y	N	Y	N	N
3 *Stump*	Y	Y	Y	?	Y	Y	Y
4 *Shadegg*	Y	Y	Y	Y	Y	Y	Y
5 *Kolbe*	Y	Y	Y	Y	Y	Y	Y
6 *Hayworth*	Y	Y	Y	Y	Y	Y	Y
ARKANSAS							
1 Berry	Y	Y	Y	Y	Y	N	N
2 Snyder	Y	Y	Y	Y	Y	N	N
3 Vacant							
4 Ross	Y	Y	Y	Y	Y	N	N
CALIFORNIA							
1 Thompson	Y	Y	Y	Y	N	N	N
2 *Herger*	Y	Y	Y	Y	Y	Y	Y
3 *Ose*	Y	Y	Y	Y	Y	Y	Y
4 *Doolittle*	Y	Y	Y	Y	Y	Y	Y
5 Matsui	Y	Y	Y	Y	Y	N	N
6 Woolsey	Y	Y	N	N	N	N	N
7 Miller, George	Y	Y	Y	N	N	N	N
8 Pelosi	Y	Y	Y	N	N	N	N
9 Lee	Y	Y	N	N	N	N	N
10 Tauscher	Y	Y	Y	Y	Y	N	N
11 *Pombo*	Y	Y	Y	Y	Y	Y	Y
12 Lantos	Y	Y	Y	Y	Y	N	N
13 Stark	?	?	?	N	N	N	N
14 Eshoo	Y	Y	Y	Y	Y	N	N
15 Honda	Y	Y	Y	N	N	N	N
16 Lofgren	Y	Y	Y	N	N	N	N
17 Farr	Y	Y	Y	N	N	N	N
18 Condit	Y	Y	Y	Y	N	N	N
19 *Radanovich*	Y	Y	Y	Y	Y	Y	Y
20 Dooley	Y	Y	Y	Y	Y	N	N
21 *Thomas*	Y	Y	Y	Y	Y	N	N
22 Capps	Y	Y	Y	Y	Y	N	N
23 *Gallegly*	Y	Y	Y	Y	Y	Y	Y
24 Sherman	Y	Y	Y	Y	Y	N	N
25 *McKeon*	Y	Y	Y	Y	Y	Y	Y
26 Berman	?	Y	Y	Y	Y	N	N
27 Schiff	Y	Y	Y	Y	Y	N	N
28 *Dreier*	Y	Y	Y	Y	Y	Y	Y
29 Waxman	Y	Y	Y	Y	Y	N	N
30 Becerra	Y	Y	Y	Y	Y	N	N
31 Solis	Y	Y	Y	Y	Y	N	N
32 Watson	Y	Y	Y	N	N	N	N
33 Roybal-Allard	Y	Y	Y	Y	Y	N	N
34 Napolitano	Y	Y	Y	Y	Y	N	N
35 Waters	Y	Y	Y	N	N	N	N
36 Harman	Y	Y	Y	Y	?	N	N
37 Millender-McD.	Y	Y	Y	Y	Y	N	N
38 *Horn*	Y	Y	Y	Y	Y	Y	Y

	395	396	397	398	399	400	401
39 *Royce*	Y	Y	Y	Y	Y	Y	Y
40 *Lewis*	Y	Y	Y	Y	Y	Y	Y
41 *Miller, Gary*	Y	Y	Y	Y	Y	Y	Y
42 Baca	Y	Y	Y	Y	Y	N	N
43 *Calvert*	Y	Y	Y	Y	Y	Y	Y
44 *Bono*	Y	Y	Y	Y	Y	Y	Y
45 *Rohrabacher*	Y	Y	Y	Y	Y	Y	Y
46 Sanchez	?	?	?	Y	Y	N	N
47 *Cox*	Y	Y	Y	Y	Y	Y	Y
48 *Issa*	Y	Y	Y	Y	Y	Y	Y
49 Davis	Y	Y	Y	Y	N	Y	N
50 Filner	Y	Y	N	N	N	N	N
51 *Cunningham*	Y	Y	Y	Y	Y	Y	Y
52 *Hunter*	Y	Y	Y	Y	Y	Y	Y
COLORADO							
1 DeGette	Y	Y	Y	N	Y	N	N
2 Udall	Y	Y	Y	N	?	N	N
3 *McInnis*	?	Y	Y	Y	Y	?	Y
4 *Schaffer*	Y	Y	Y	Y	Y	Y	Y
5 *Hefley*	Y	Y	Y	Y	N	Y	Y
6 *Tancredo*	Y	Y	Y	?	Y	Y	Y
CONNECTICUT							
1 Larson	Y	Y	Y	Y	Y	N	N
2 *Simmons*	Y	Y	Y	Y	Y	Y	Y
3 DeLauro	Y	Y	Y	Y	Y	N	N
4 *Shays*	Y	Y	Y	Y	Y	Y	Y
5 Maloney	Y	Y	Y	Y	Y	N	Y
6 Johnson	Y	Y	Y	Y	Y	Y	Y
DELAWARE							
AL *Castle*	Y	Y	Y	Y	Y	Y	Y
FLORIDA							
1 *Miller, J.* [1]		Y	Y	Y	Y	Y	Y
2 Boyd	Y	Y	Y	Y	Y	N	N
3 Brown	Y	Y	Y	Y	Y	N	N
4 *Crenshaw*	Y	Y	Y	Y	Y	Y	Y
5 Thurman	Y	Y	Y	Y	Y	N	N
6 *Stearns*	+	+	+	Y	Y	Y	Y
7 *Mica*	Y	Y	Y	Y	Y	Y	Y
8 *Keller*	Y	Y	Y	Y	Y	Y	Y
9 *Bilirakis*	?	?	?	?	?	?	?
10 *Young*	Y	Y	Y	Y	Y	?	Y
11 Davis	Y	Y	Y	Y	Y	N	N
12 *Putnam*	Y	Y	Y	Y	Y	Y	Y
13 *Miller, D.*	?	?	?	Y	Y	Y	Y
14 *Goss*	Y	Y	Y	Y	Y	?	Y
15 *Weldon*	Y	Y	Y	Y	Y	Y	Y
16 *Foley*	Y	Y	Y	Y	Y	Y	Y
17 Meek	Y	Y	N	Y	N	N	N
18 *Ros-Lehtinen*	Y	Y	Y	Y	N	N	N
19 Wexler	Y	Y	Y	N	N	N	N
20 Deutsch	Y	Y	Y	Y	Y	N	N
21 *Diaz-Balart*	Y	Y	Y	Y	Y	Y	Y
22 *Shaw*	Y	Y	Y	Y	Y	Y	Y
23 Hastings	Y	Y	N	N	N	N	N
GEORGIA							
1 *Kingston*	Y	Y	Y	Y	Y	Y	Y
2 Bishop	Y	Y	Y	Y	Y	N	N
3 *Collins*	Y	Y	Y	Y	Y	Y	Y
4 McKinney	Y	Y	Y	N	N	N	N
5 Lewis	Y	Y	Y	N	N	N	N
6 *Isakson*	Y	Y	Y	Y	Y	Y	Y
7 *Barr*	Y	Y	Y	Y	Y	Y	Y
8 *Chambliss*	Y	Y	Y	Y	Y	Y	Y
9 *Deal*	Y	Y	Y	Y	Y	Y	Y
10 *Norwood*	Y	Y	Y	Y	Y	Y	Y
11 *Linder*	Y	Y	Y	Y	Y	Y	Y
HAWAII							
1 Abercrombie	Y	Y	Y	?	Y	N	N
2 Mink	Y	Y	Y	N	Y	N	N
IDAHO							
1 *Otter*	Y	Y	Y	N	Y	Y	Y
2 *Simpson*	Y	Y	Y	Y	Y	Y	Y
ILLINOIS							
1 Rush	Y	Y	Y	N	N	N	N
2 Jackson	Y	Y	N	N	N	N	N
3 Lipinski	Y	Y	Y	Y	N	N	N
4 Gutierrez	Y	Y	Y	Y	N	N	N
5 Blagojevich	Y	Y	Y	Y	N	N	N
6 *Hyde*	Y	Y	Y	Y	Y	Y	Y
7 Davis	?	?	?	N	Y	N	N
8 *Crane*	Y	Y	Y	N	Y	Y	Y
9 Schakowsky	Y	Y	N	N	N	N	N
10 *Kirk*	Y	Y	Y	Y	Y	Y	Y
11 *Weller*	Y	Y	Y	Y	N	Y	Y
12 Costello	Y	Y	Y	Y	N	N	N
13 *Biggert*	Y	Y	Y	Y	Y	Y	Y

ND Northern Democrats   SD Southern Democrats

	395	396	397	398	399	400	401
14 ***Hastert***							
15 ***Johnson***	Y	Y	Y	Y	Y	Y	Y
16 ***Manzullo***	Y	Y	Y	Y	Y	Y	Y
17 Evans	Y	Y	Y	Y	Y	N	N
18 ***LaHood***	Y	Y	Y	Y	Y	Y	Y
19 Phelps	Y	Y	Y	Y	Y	N	N
20 ***Shimkus***	Y	Y	Y	Y	Y	Y	Y
INDIANA							
1 Visclosky	Y	Y	Y	N	N	N	N
2 ***Pence***	+	Y	Y	Y	Y	Y	Y
3 Roemer	Y	Y	Y	Y	Y	N	N
4 ***Souder***	Y	Y	Y	Y	Y	Y	Y
5 ***Buyer***	Y	Y	Y	Y	Y	Y	Y
6 ***Burton***	?	?	?	?	?	Y	?
7 ***Kerns***	Y	Y	Y	Y	Y	Y	Y
8 ***Hostettler***	Y	Y	Y	Y	Y	Y	Y
9 Hill	Y	Y	Y	?	?	?	?
10 Carson	Y	Y	Y	Y	Y	N	N
IOWA							
1 ***Leach***	Y	Y	Y	Y	Y	Y	?
2 ***Nussle***	Y	Y	Y	Y	Y	Y	Y
3 Boswell	Y	Y	Y	Y	Y	N	N
4 ***Ganske***	Y	Y	Y	Y	Y	Y	Y
5 ***Latham***	Y	Y	Y	Y	Y	Y	Y
KANSAS							
1 ***Moran***	Y	Y	Y	Y	N	Y	Y
2 ***Ryun***	Y	Y	Y	Y	Y	Y	Y
3 Moore	Y	Y	Y	Y	Y	N	N
4 ***Tiahrt***	Y	Y	Y	Y	Y	Y	Y
KENTUCKY							
1 ***Whitfield***	Y	Y	Y	Y	N	Y	Y
2 ***Lewis***	Y	Y	Y	Y	Y	Y	Y
3 ***Northup***	Y	Y	Y	Y	Y	Y	Y
4 Lucas	Y	Y	Y	Y	Y	N	N
5 ***Rogers***	Y	Y	Y	Y	Y	Y	Y
6 ***Fletcher***	Y	Y	Y	Y	Y	Y	Y
LOUISIANA							
1 ***Vitter***	Y	Y	Y	Y	Y	Y	Y
2 Jefferson	Y	Y	Y	Y	Y	N	N
3 ***Tauzin***	Y	Y	Y	Y	Y	Y	Y
4 ***McCrery***	Y	Y	Y	Y	Y	Y	Y
5 ***Cooksey***	Y	Y	Y	Y	Y	Y	Y
6 ***Baker***	Y	Y	Y	Y	Y	Y	Y
7 John	Y	Y	Y	Y	Y	N	N
MAINE							
1 Allen	Y	Y	Y	Y	Y	N	N
2 Baldacci	Y	Y	Y	Y	Y	N	N
MARYLAND							
1 ***Gilchrest***	Y	Y	Y	Y	Y	Y	Y
2 ***Ehrlich***	Y	Y	Y	Y	Y	Y	Y
3 Cardin	Y	Y	Y	Y	Y	N	N
4 Wynn	Y	Y	Y	Y	Y	N	N
5 Hoyer	Y	Y	Y	Y	Y	N	N
6 ***Bartlett***	Y	Y	Y	Y	Y	Y	Y
7 Cummings	Y	Y	Y	N	Y	N	N
8 ***Morella***	Y	Y	Y	Y	Y	Y	Y
MASSACHUSETTS							
1 Olver	Y	Y	Y	N	N	N	N
2 Neal	Y	Y	Y	Y	Y	N	N
3 McGovern	Y	Y	Y	N	N	N	N
4 Frank	Y	Y	Y	N	Y	N	N
5 Meehan	Y	Y	Y	Y	Y	N	N
6 Tierney	Y	Y	Y	N	Y	N	N
7 Markey	Y	Y	Y	Y	Y	N	N
8 Capuano	Y	Y	Y	N	N	N	N
9 Lynch [2]		Y	Y	Y	Y	N	N
10 Delahunt	Y	Y	Y	Y	Y	N	N
MICHIGAN							
1 Stupak	Y	Y	Y	Y	N	N	N
2 ***Hoekstra***	Y	Y	Y	Y	Y	Y	Y
3 ***Ehlers***	Y	Y	Y	Y	Y	Y	Y
4 ***Camp***	Y	Y	Y	Y	Y	Y	Y
5 Barcia	Y	Y	Y	Y	Y	N	Y
6 ***Upton***	Y	Y	Y	Y	Y	Y	Y
7 ***Smith***	Y	Y	Y	Y	Y	Y	Y
8 ***Rogers***	Y	Y	Y	Y	Y	Y	Y
9 Kildee	Y	Y	Y	Y	Y	N	N
10 Bonior	Y	Y	Y	N	Y	N	N
11 ***Knollenberg***	Y	Y	Y	Y	Y	Y	Y
12 Levin	Y	Y	Y	Y	Y	N	N
13 Rivers	Y	Y	Y	N	Y	N	N
14 Conyers	?	Y	Y	N	Y	N	N
15 Kilpatrick	+	+	+	?	?	N	N
16 Dingell	Y	Y	Y	N	Y	N	N

	395	396	397	398	399	400	401
MINNESOTA							
1 ***Gutknecht***	Y	Y	Y	Y	N	Y	Y
2 ***Kennedy***	Y	Y	Y	Y	Y	Y	Y
3 ***Ramstad***	Y	Y	Y	Y	N	Y	Y
4 McCollum	Y	Y	Y	Y	?	N	N
5 Sabo	Y	Y	Y	N	N	N	N
6 Luther	Y	Y	Y	Y	Y	N	N
7 Peterson	Y	Y	Y	N	N	N	N
8 Oberstar	Y	Y	Y	N	N	N	N
MISSISSIPPI							
1 ***Wicker***	Y	Y	Y	Y	N	Y	Y
2 Thompson	Y	Y	Y	N	N	N	N
3 ***Pickering***	Y	Y	Y	Y	?	Y	Y
4 Shows	Y	Y	Y	Y	Y	N	N
5 Taylor	Y	Y	Y	Y	N	N	N
MISSOURI							
1 Clay	Y	Y	Y	?	?	N	N
2 ***Akin***	Y	Y	Y	Y	Y	Y	Y
3 Gephardt	Y	Y	Y	Y	Y	N	N
4 Skelton	Y	Y	Y	Y	?	N	N
5 McCarthy	Y	Y	Y	Y	Y	N	N
6 ***Graves***	Y	Y	Y	Y	Y	Y	Y
7 ***Blunt***	Y	Y	Y	Y	?	Y	Y
8 ***Emerson***	Y	Y	Y	Y	Y	Y	Y
9 ***Hulshof***	Y	Y	Y	Y	N	Y	Y
MONTANA							
AL ***Rehberg***	Y	Y	Y	Y	Y	Y	Y
NEBRASKA							
1 ***Bereuter***	Y	Y	Y	Y	Y	Y	Y
2 ***Terry***	Y	Y	Y	Y	Y	Y	Y
3 ***Osborne***	Y	Y	Y	Y	Y	Y	Y
NEVADA							
1 Berkley	Y	Y	Y	Y	Y	N	N
2 ***Gibbons***	Y	Y	Y	Y	Y	Y	Y
NEW HAMPSHIRE							
1 ***Sununu***	Y	Y	Y	Y	Y	Y	Y
2 ***Bass***	Y	Y	Y	Y	Y	Y	Y
NEW JERSEY							
1 Andrews	Y	Y	Y	Y	Y	N	N
2 ***LoBiondo***	Y	Y	Y	Y	N	Y	Y
3 ***Saxton***	Y	Y	Y	Y	Y	Y	Y
4 ***Smith***	Y	Y	Y	Y	Y	Y	Y
5 ***Roukema***	Y	Y	Y	Y	Y	Y	Y
6 Pallone	Y	Y	Y	Y	Y	N	N
7 ***Ferguson***	Y	Y	Y	Y	Y	Y	Y
8 Pascrell	Y	Y	Y	Y	Y	N	N
9 Rothman	Y	Y	Y	Y	Y	N	N
10 Payne	Y	Y	Y	N	Y	N	N
11 ***Frelinghuysen***	Y	Y	Y	Y	Y	Y	Y
12 Holt	Y	Y	Y	Y	Y	N	N
13 Menendez	Y	Y	Y	Y	Y	N	N
NEW MEXICO							
1 ***Wilson***	Y	Y	Y	Y	Y	Y	Y
2 ***Skeen***	Y	Y	Y	Y	Y	Y	Y
3 Udall	Y	Y	Y	N	Y	N	N
NEW YORK							
1 ***Grucci***	Y	Y	Y	Y	Y	Y	Y
2 Israel	Y	Y	Y	Y	Y	N	Y
3 ***King***	Y	Y	Y	Y	Y	Y	Y
4 McCarthy	Y	Y	Y	Y	Y	N	N
5 Ackerman	Y	Y	Y	Y	Y	N	N
6 Meeks	Y	Y	Y	Y	Y	N	Y
7 Crowley	Y	Y	Y	Y	Y	N	N
8 Nadler	Y	Y	Y	N	Y	N	N
9 Weiner	Y	Y	Y	Y	Y	N	Y
10 Towns	Y	Y	Y	Y	N	N	N
11 Owens	Y	Y	Y	N	Y	N	N
12 Velázquez	Y	Y	Y	N	Y	N	N
13 ***Fossella***	Y	Y	Y	Y	Y	Y	Y
14 Maloney	Y	Y	Y	Y	Y	N	N
15 Rangel	Y	Y	Y	Y	Y	N	Y
16 Serrano	Y	Y	Y	N	Y	N	N
17 Engel	Y	Y	Y	Y	Y	N	N
18 Lowey	Y	Y	Y	Y	Y	N	N
19 ***Kelly***	Y	Y	Y	Y	Y	Y	Y
20 ***Gilman***	Y	Y	Y	Y	Y	Y	Y
21 McNulty	Y	Y	Y	Y	N	N	N
22 ***Sweeney***	Y	Y	Y	Y	N	Y	Y
23 ***Boehlert***	Y	Y	Y	Y	Y	Y	Y
24 ***McHugh***	Y	Y	Y	Y	Y	Y	Y
25 ***Walsh***	Y	Y	Y	Y	Y	Y	Y
26 Hinchey	Y	Y	Y	Y	N	N	N
27 ***Reynolds***	Y	Y	Y	Y	Y	Y	Y
28 Slaughter	Y	Y	Y	Y	N	N	N
29 LaFalce	Y	Y	Y	Y	N	N	N

	395	396	397	398	399	400	401
30 ***Quinn***	Y	Y	Y	Y	Y	Y	Y
31 ***Houghton***	Y	Y	Y	Y	Y	Y	Y
NORTH CAROLINA							
1 Clayton	Y	Y	Y	N	Y	N	N
2 Etheridge	Y	Y	Y	Y	Y	N	N
3 ***Jones***	Y	Y	Y	Y	Y	Y	Y
4 Price	Y	Y	Y	Y	Y	N	N
5 ***Burr***	Y	Y	Y	Y	Y	Y	Y
6 ***Coble***	Y	Y	Y	Y	Y	Y	Y
7 McIntyre	Y	Y	Y	Y	Y	N	N
8 ***Hayes***	Y	Y	Y	Y	Y	Y	Y
9 ***Myrick***	Y	Y	Y	Y	Y	Y	Y
10 ***Ballenger***	Y	?	?	Y	Y	Y	Y
11 ***Taylor***	?	?	?	Y	Y	Y	Y
12 Watt	Y	Y	Y	N	Y	N	N
NORTH DAKOTA							
AL Pomeroy	Y	+	Y	Y	Y	N	N
OHIO							
1 ***Chabot***	Y	Y	Y	Y	Y	Y	Y
2 ***Portman***	Y	Y	Y	Y	Y	Y	Y
3 Hall	Y	Y	Y	Y	Y	N	N
4 ***Oxley***	Y	Y	Y	Y	Y	Y	Y
5 ***Gillmor***	Y	Y	Y	Y	Y	Y	Y
6 Strickland	Y	Y	Y	Y	N	N	N
7 ***Hobson***	Y	Y	Y	Y	Y	Y	Y
8 ***Boehner***	Y	Y	?	Y	Y	Y	Y
9 Kaptur	Y	Y	Y	Y	Y	N	?
10 Kucinich	Y	Y	Y	N	N	N	N
11 Jones	Y	Y	?	N	Y	N	N
12 ***Tiberi***	Y	Y	Y	Y	Y	Y	Y
13 Brown	Y	Y	Y	N	Y	N	N
14 Sawyer	Y	Y	Y	Y	Y	N	N
15 ***Pryce***	Y	Y	Y	Y	Y	Y	Y
16 ***Regula***	Y	Y	Y	Y	Y	Y	Y
17 Traficant	Y	Y	Y	Y	Y	Y	Y
18 ***Ney***	Y	Y	Y	N	Y	Y	Y
19 ***LaTourette***	Y	Y	Y	Y	Y	Y	Y
OKLAHOMA							
1 ***Largent***	Y	Y	Y	Y	Y	Y	Y
2 Carson	Y	Y	Y	Y	Y	N	N
3 ***Watkins***	Y	Y	Y	Y	Y	Y	Y
4 ***Watts***	Y	Y	Y	Y	Y	Y	Y
5 ***Istook***	Y	Y	Y	Y	Y	Y	Y
6 ***Lucas***	Y	Y	Y	Y	Y	Y	Y
OREGON							
1 Wu	Y	Y	Y	N	N	N	N
2 ***Walden***	Y	Y	Y	Y	Y	Y	Y
3 Blumenauer	Y	Y	Y	N	Y	N	N
4 DeFazio	Y	Y	Y	N	N	N	N
5 Hooley	Y	Y	Y	Y	Y	N	N
PENNSYLVANIA							
1 Brady	Y	Y	Y	Y	N	N	N
2 Fattah	Y	Y	Y	Y	N	N	N
3 Borski	Y	Y	Y	Y	N	N	N
4 ***Hart***	Y	Y	Y	Y	Y	Y	Y
5 ***Peterson***	Y	Y	Y	Y	Y	Y	Y
6 Holden	Y	Y	Y	Y	Y	N	N
7 ***Weldon***	Y	Y	Y	Y	Y	Y	Y
8 ***Greenwood***	Y	Y	Y	Y	Y	Y	Y
9 ***Shuster, Bill***	Y	Y	Y	Y	Y	Y	Y
10 ***Sherwood***	Y	Y	Y	Y	Y	Y	Y
11 Kanjorski	Y	Y	Y	Y	Y	N	N
12 Murtha	Y	Y	Y	Y	Y	N	N
13 Hoeffel	Y	Y	Y	Y	Y	N	N
14 Coyne	Y	Y	Y	N	Y	N	N
15 ***Toomey***	Y	Y	Y	Y	Y	Y	Y
16 ***Pitts***	Y	Y	Y	Y	Y	Y	Y
17 ***Gekas***	Y	Y	Y	Y	Y	Y	?
18 Doyle	Y	Y	Y	Y	Y	N	N
19 ***Platts***	Y	Y	Y	Y	Y	Y	Y
20 Mascara	Y	Y	Y	Y	Y	N	N
21 ***English***	Y	Y	Y	Y	N	Y	Y
RHODE ISLAND							
1 Kennedy	Y	Y	Y	Y	Y	N	N
2 Langevin	Y	Y	Y	Y	Y	N	N
SOUTH CAROLINA							
1 ***Brown***	Y	Y	Y	Y	Y	Y	Y
2 Vacant							
3 ***Graham***	Y	Y	Y	Y	Y	Y	Y
4 ***DeMint***	Y	Y	Y	Y	Y	Y	Y
5 Spratt	Y	Y	Y	Y	Y	N	N
6 Clyburn	Y	Y	Y	Y	Y	N	N
SOUTH DAKOTA							
AL ***Thune***	Y	Y	Y	Y	Y	Y	Y

	395	396	397	398	399	400	401
TENNESSEE							
1 ***Jenkins***	Y	Y	Y	Y	Y	Y	Y
2 ***Duncan***	Y	Y	Y	Y	Y	Y	Y
3 ***Wamp***	Y	Y	Y	Y	Y	Y	Y
4 ***Hilleary***	Y	Y	Y	Y	Y	Y	Y
5 Clement	Y	Y	Y	Y	Y	N	N
6 Gordon	Y	Y	Y	Y	Y	N	N
7 ***Bryant***	Y	Y	Y	Y	Y	Y	Y
8 Tanner	Y	Y	Y	Y	Y	N	N
9 Ford	Y	Y	Y	Y	Y	N	N
TEXAS							
1 Sandlin	Y	Y	Y	Y	Y	N	N
2 Turner	Y	Y	Y	Y	Y	N	N
3 ***Johnson, Sam***	Y	Y	Y	Y	Y	Y	Y
4 Hall	Y	Y	Y	Y	Y	Y	Y
5 ***Sessions***	Y	Y	Y	Y	Y	Y	Y
6 ***Barton***	Y	Y	Y	Y	Y	Y	Y
7 ***Culberson***	Y	Y	Y	Y	Y	Y	Y
8 ***Brady***	Y	Y	Y	Y	Y	Y	Y
9 Lampson	Y	Y	Y	Y	Y	N	N
10 Doggett	Y	Y	Y	Y	Y	N	N
11 Edwards	Y	Y	Y	Y	Y	N	N
12 ***Granger***	Y	Y	Y	Y	Y	Y	Y
13 ***Thornberry***	Y	Y	Y	Y	Y	Y	Y
14 ***Paul***	Y	Y	Y	N	Y	Y	Y
15 Hinojosa	Y	Y	Y	Y	Y	N	N
16 Reyes	?	?	?	Y	Y	?	N
17 Stenholm	Y	Y	Y	Y	Y	N	N
18 Jackson-Lee	Y	Y	Y	N	N	N	N
19 ***Combest***	Y	Y	Y	Y	Y	Y	Y
20 Gonzalez	Y	Y	Y	Y	Y	?	?
21 ***Smith***	Y	Y	Y	Y	Y	Y	Y
22 ***DeLay***	Y	Y	Y	Y	Y	Y	Y
23 ***Bonilla***	Y	Y	Y	Y	Y	Y	Y
24 Frost	Y	Y	Y	Y	Y	N	N
25 Bentsen	Y	Y	Y	Y	Y	N	N
26 ***Armey***	Y	Y	Y	Y	Y	Y	Y
27 Ortiz	Y	Y	Y	Y	Y	N	N
28 Rodriguez	Y	Y	Y	Y	Y	N	N
29 Green	Y	Y	Y	Y	Y	N	N
30 Johnson, E.B.	Y	Y	Y	N	Y	N	N
UTAH							
1 ***Hansen***	Y	Y	Y	+	Y	Y	Y
2 Matheson	Y	Y	Y	Y	Y	N	N
3 ***Cannon***	Y	Y	Y	Y	Y	Y	Y
VERMONT							
AL *Sanders*	Y	Y	Y	N	Y	N	N
VIRGINIA							
1 ***Davis, Jo Ann***	Y	Y	Y	Y	Y	Y	Y
2 ***Schrock***	Y	Y	Y	Y	Y	Y	Y
3 Scott	Y	Y	Y	N	N	N	N
4 ***Forbes***	Y	Y	Y	Y	Y	Y	Y
5 *Goode*	Y	Y	Y	Y	Y	Y	Y
6 ***Goodlatte***	Y	Y	Y	Y	Y	Y	Y
7 ***Cantor***	Y	Y	Y	Y	Y	Y	Y
8 Moran	Y	Y	Y	Y	?	N	N
9 Boucher	Y	Y	Y	N	Y	N	N
10 ***Wolf***	Y	Y	Y	Y	Y	Y	Y
11 ***Davis, T.***	Y	Y	Y	Y	Y	Y	Y
WASHINGTON							
1 Inslee	Y	Y	Y	Y	Y	N	N
2 Larsen	Y	Y	Y	Y	N	N	N
3 Baird	Y	Y	Y	Y	N	N	N
4 ***Hastings***	Y	Y	Y	Y	Y	Y	Y
5 ***Nethercutt***	Y	Y	Y	Y	Y	Y	Y
6 Dicks	Y	Y	Y	Y	Y	N	N
7 McDermott	Y	Y	Y	N	N	N	N
8 ***Dunn***	Y	Y	Y	Y	Y	Y	Y
9 Smith	Y	Y	Y	Y	Y	N	N
WEST VIRGINIA							
1 Mollohan	Y	Y	Y	N	Y	N	Y
2 ***Capito***	Y	Y	Y	Y	Y	Y	Y
3 Rahall	Y	Y	Y	N	N	N	N
WISCONSIN							
1 ***Ryan***	Y	Y	Y	Y	Y	Y	Y
2 Baldwin	Y	Y	Y	N	Y	N	N
3 Kind	Y	Y	Y	Y	Y	N	N
4 Kleczka	Y	Y	Y	Y	Y	N	N
5 Barrett	Y	Y	Y	N	Y	N	N
6 ***Petri***	Y	Y	Y	Y	Y	Y	Y
7 Obey	Y	Y	Y	Y	Y	N	N
8 ***Green***	Y	Y	Y	Y	Y	Y	Y
9 ***Sensenbrenner***	Y	Y	Y	Y	Y	Y	Y
WYOMING							
AL ***Cubin***	?	?	?	?	?	?	?

Southern states - Ala., Ark., Fla., Ga., Ky., La., Miss., N.C., Okla., S.C., Tenn., Texas, Va.

Key

Y	Voted for (yea).
#	Paired for.
+	Announced for.
N	Voted against (nay).
X	Paired against.
–	Announced against.
P	Voted "present."
C	Voted "present" to avoid possible conflict of interest.
?	Did not vote or otherwise make a position known.

Democrats **Republicans**
Independents

402. HR 3090. Economic Stimulus/Democratic Substitute. Rangel, D-N.Y., substitute amendment that would cost $110 billion in fiscal 2002 for individual and business tax reductions, additional unemployment and health insurance benefits, and new spending on school construction, economic development, security enhancements and other domestic programs. It would offset $91 billion of the bill's cost by freezing a reduction in the top individual tax bracket at 38.6 percent. Rejected 166-261: R 0-217; D 165-43 (ND 132-24, SD 33-19); I 1-1. Oct. 24, 2001.

403. HR 3090. Economic Stimulus/Recommit. Turner, D-Texas, motion to recommit the bill to the House Ways and Means Committee with instructions to add language that would lower the bill's tax cuts to the level of funding for anti-terrorism efforts, mandate that provisions are temporary only and are to be offset by other changes in the tax code, and require financial aid to individuals and businesses affected by the Sept. 11 terrorist attacks. Motion rejected 199-230: R 0-218; D 198-11 (ND 147-9, SD 51-2); I 1-1. Oct. 24, 2001.

404. HR 3090. Economic Stimulus/Passage. Passage of the bill that would grant businesses and individuals $99.5 billion in federal tax cuts in fiscal 2002, and a total $159.4 billion in reductions over 10 years. The bill would allow more individuals to receive tax rebates for 2000, accelerate a reduction of the 27 percent tax bracket to 25 percent, lower the capital gains tax rate from 20 percent to 18 percent and eliminate the corporate alternative minimum tax. The bill would provide $3 billion to states for health insurance for the unemployed. Passed 216-214: R 212-7; D 3-206 (ND 1-155, SD 2-51); I 1-1. A "yea" was a vote in support of the president's position. Oct. 24, 2001.

405. H J Res 70. Fiscal 2002 Continuing Appropriations/Passage. Passage of the joint resolution to provide continuing appropriations through Nov. 16 for all federal departments and programs covered by the fiscal 2002 spending bills not yet enacted. Passed 419-0: R 211-0; D 206-0 (ND 154-0, SD 52-0); I 2-0. Oct. 25, 2001.

406. Procedural Motion/Journal. Approval of the House Journal of Wednesday, Oct. 24, 2001. Approved 361-52: R 194-13; D 165-39 (ND 125-27, SD 40-12); I 2-0. Oct. 25, 2001.

407. H J Res 71. Patriot Day/Passage. Passage of the joint resolution that would designate Sept. 11 as "Patriot Day." Passed 407-0: R 202-0; D 203-0 (ND 153-0, SD 50-0); I 2-0. Oct. 25, 2001.

	402	403	404	405	406	407
ALABAMA						
1 *Callahan*	N	N	Y	?	?	?
2 *Everett*	N	N	Y	+	+	+
3 *Riley*	N	N	Y	Y	Y	Y
4 *Aderholt*	N	N	Y	Y	Y	Y
5 Cramer	N	Y	N	Y	Y	Y
6 *Bachus*	N	N	Y	Y	Y	Y
7 Hilliard	Y	Y	N	Y	Y	Y
ALASKA						
AL *Young*	N	N	Y	Y	Y	Y
ARIZONA						
1 *Flake*	N	N	Y	Y	Y	Y
2 Pastor	Y	Y	N	Y	Y	Y
3 *Stump*	N	N	Y	Y	Y	Y
4 *Shadegg*	N	N	Y	Y	Y	Y
5 *Kolbe*	N	N	Y	Y	Y	Y
6 *Hayworth*	N	N	Y	Y	Y	Y
ARKANSAS						
1 Berry	N	Y	N	Y	Y	Y
2 Snyder	N	N	N	Y	Y	Y
3 Vacant						
4 Ross	N	Y	N	Y	Y	Y
CALIFORNIA						
1 Thompson	N	Y	N	Y	N	Y
2 *Herger*	N	N	Y	Y	Y	Y
3 *Ose*	N	N	Y	Y	Y	Y
4 *Doolittle*	N	N	Y	Y	Y	Y
5 Matsui	Y	Y	N	Y	Y	Y
6 Woolsey	Y	Y	N	Y	Y	Y
7 Miller, George	Y	Y	N	Y	N	Y
8 Pelosi	Y	Y	N	Y	Y	Y
9 Lee	Y	N	N	Y	N	Y
10 Tauscher	Y	Y	N	Y	Y	Y
11 *Pombo*	N	N	Y	Y	Y	Y
12 Lantos	Y	Y	N	Y	Y	Y
13 Stark	Y	Y	N	Y	Y	Y
14 Eshoo	Y	Y	N	Y	Y	Y
15 Honda	Y	Y	N	Y	Y	Y
16 Lofgren	Y	Y	N	Y	Y	Y
17 Farr	Y	Y	N	Y	Y	Y
18 Condit	N	N	Y	Y	Y	Y
19 *Radanovich*	N	N	Y	Y	Y	Y
20 Dooley	N	Y	N	Y	Y	Y
21 *Thomas*	N	N	Y	Y	Y	Y
22 Capps	Y	Y	N	Y	Y	Y
23 *Gallegly*	N	N	Y	?	?	?
24 Sherman	Y	Y	N	Y	Y	Y
25 *McKeon*	N	N	Y	Y	Y	Y
26 Berman	Y	Y	N	Y	Y	Y
27 Schiff	N	N	Y	Y	Y	Y
28 *Dreier*	N	N	Y	Y	Y	Y
29 Waxman	Y	Y	N	Y	Y	Y
30 Becerra	Y	Y	N	Y	Y	Y
31 Solis	Y	Y	N	Y	Y	Y
32 Watson	Y	Y	N	Y	Y	Y
33 Roybal-Allard	Y	Y	N	Y	Y	Y
34 Napolitano	Y	Y	N	Y	Y	Y
35 Waters	Y	Y	N	Y	N	?
36 Harman	N	Y	N	Y	Y	Y
37 Millender-McD.	Y	Y	N	Y	Y	Y
38 *Horn*	N	N	Y	Y	Y	Y

	402	403	404	405	406	407
39 *Royce*	N	N	Y	Y	Y	Y
40 *Lewis*	N	N	Y	Y	?	Y
41 *Miller, Gary*	N	N	Y	?	?	?
42 Baca	Y	Y	N	Y	Y	Y
43 *Calvert*	N	N	Y	Y	Y	Y
44 *Bono*	N	N	Y	Y	Y	Y
45 *Rohrabacher*	N	N	Y	Y	Y	Y
46 Sanchez	N	Y	N	Y	Y	Y
47 *Cox*	N	N	Y	Y	Y	Y
48 *Issa*	N	N	Y	Y	Y	Y
49 Davis	Y	Y	N	Y	Y	Y
50 Filner	Y	Y	N	Y	N	Y
51 *Cunningham*	N	N	Y	Y	Y	Y
52 *Hunter*	N	N	Y	Y	Y	Y
COLORADO						
1 DeGette	Y	Y	N	Y	Y	Y
2 Udall	Y	Y	N	Y	Y	Y
3 *McInnis*	N	N	Y	Y	Y	Y
4 *Schaffer*	N	?	Y	Y	N	?
5 *Hefley*	N	N	Y	N	Y	Y
6 *Tancredo*	N	N	Y	Y	Y	Y
CONNECTICUT						
1 Larson	Y	Y	N	Y	Y	Y
2 *Simmons*	N	N	Y	Y	Y	Y
3 DeLauro	Y	Y	N	Y	Y	Y
4 *Shays*	N	N	Y	Y	Y	Y
5 Maloney	Y	Y	N	Y	Y	Y
6 *Johnson*	N	N	Y	Y	Y	Y
DELAWARE						
AL *Castle*	N	N	Y	Y	Y	Y
FLORIDA						
1 *Miller, J.*	N	N	Y	Y	Y	Y
2 Boyd	N	Y	N	Y	Y	Y
3 Brown	Y	Y	N	Y	Y	Y
4 *Crenshaw*	N	N	Y	Y	Y	Y
5 Thurman	Y	Y	N	Y	N	Y
6 *Stearns*	N	N	Y	Y	Y	Y
7 *Mica*	N	N	Y	Y	Y	Y
8 *Keller*	N	N	Y	Y	Y	Y
9 *Bilirakis*	N	N	Y	Y	Y	Y
10 *Young*	N	N	Y	Y	Y	?
11 Davis	Y	Y	N	Y	Y	Y
12 *Putnam*	N	N	Y	Y	Y	Y
13 *Miller, D.*	N	N	Y	Y	Y	Y
14 *Goss*	N	N	Y	Y	Y	Y
15 *Weldon*	N	N	Y	Y	Y	Y
16 *Foley*	N	N	Y	Y	Y	Y
17 Meek	Y	Y	N	Y	Y	Y
18 *Ros-Lehtinen*	N	N	Y	Y	Y	Y
19 Wexler	Y	Y	N	Y	Y	Y
20 Deutsch	Y	Y	N	Y	Y	Y
21 *Diaz-Balart*	N	N	Y	Y	Y	Y
22 *Shaw*	N	N	Y	Y	Y	Y
23 Hastings	Y	Y	N	Y	N	Y
GEORGIA						
1 *Kingston*	N	N	Y	Y	Y	Y
2 Bishop	N	Y	N	Y	Y	Y
3 *Collins*	N	N	Y	Y	Y	Y
4 McKinney	Y	Y	N	Y	Y	Y
5 Lewis	Y	Y	N	Y	N	Y
6 *Isakson*	N	N	Y	Y	Y	Y
7 *Barr*	N	N	Y	?	?	?
8 *Chambliss*	N	N	Y	Y	Y	Y
9 *Deal*	N	N	Y	Y	Y	Y
10 *Norwood*	N	N	Y	Y	Y	Y
11 *Linder*	N	N	Y	?	Y	Y
HAWAII						
1 Abercrombie	N	Y	N	Y	Y	Y
2 Mink	Y	Y	N	Y	Y	Y
IDAHO						
1 *Otter*	N	N	Y	Y	Y	Y
2 *Simpson*	N	N	Y	Y	Y	Y
ILLINOIS						
1 Rush	Y	Y	N	Y	Y	Y
2 Jackson	N	N	N	Y	Y	Y
3 Lipinski	Y	Y	N	Y	N	Y
4 Gutierrez	Y	Y	N	Y	Y	Y
5 Blagojevich	Y	Y	N	Y	Y	Y
6 *Hyde*	N	N	Y	Y	Y	Y
7 Davis	Y	Y	N	Y	Y	Y
8 *Crane*	N	N	Y	N	Y	N
9 Schakowsky	Y	Y	N	Y	Y	Y
10 *Kirk*	N	N	Y	Y	Y	Y
11 *Weller*	N	N	Y	Y	Y	Y
12 Costello	Y	Y	N	Y	N	Y
13 *Biggert*	N	N	Y	Y	Y	Y

ND Northern Democrats   SD Southern Democrats

	402	403	404	405	406	407
14 **Hastert**		N	Y			
15 **Johnson**	N	N	Y	Y	Y	Y
16 **Manzullo**	N	N	Y	Y	Y	Y
17 Evans	Y	Y	N	Y	Y	Y
18 **LaHood**	N	N	N	Y	Y	Y
19 Phelps	N	Y	N	Y	Y	Y
20 **Shimkus**	N	N	Y	Y	Y	Y
INDIANA						
1 Visclosky	Y	Y	N	Y	N	Y
2 **Pence**	N	N	Y	Y	Y	Y
3 Roemer	N	Y	N	Y	Y	Y
4 **Souder**	N	N	Y	Y	Y	?
5 **Buyer**	N	N	Y	Y	Y	Y
6 **Burton**	N	N	Y	Y	Y	Y
7 **Kerns**	N	N	Y	Y	Y	Y
8 **Hostettler**	N	N	Y	Y	Y	Y
9 Hill	?	?	?	Y	Y	Y
10 Carson	Y	Y	N	Y	N	Y
IOWA						
1 **Leach**	N	N	N	Y	Y	Y
2 **Nussle**	N	N	Y	Y	Y	Y
3 Boswell	Y	Y	N	Y	N	Y
4 **Ganske**	N	N	N	Y	Y	Y
5 **Latham**	N	N	Y	Y	Y	Y
KANSAS						
1 **Moran**	N	N	Y	Y	N	Y
2 **Ryun**	N	N	Y	Y	Y	Y
3 Moore	N	Y	N	Y	Y	Y
4 **Tiahrt**	N	N	Y	Y	Y	Y
KENTUCKY						
1 **Whitfield**	N	N	Y	Y	N	Y
2 **Lewis**	N	N	Y	Y	Y	Y
3 **Northup**	N	N	Y	Y	Y	Y
4 Lucas	N	Y	Y	Y	Y	Y
5 **Rogers**	N	N	Y	Y	Y	Y
6 **Fletcher**	N	N	Y	Y	Y	Y
LOUISIANA						
1 **Vitter**	N	N	Y	Y	Y	Y
2 Jefferson	Y	Y	N	Y	Y	Y
3 **Tauzin**	N	N	Y	Y	Y	Y
4 **McCrery**	N	N	Y	Y	Y	Y
5 **Cooksey**	N	N	Y	Y	?	?
6 **Baker**	N	N	Y	Y	Y	Y
7 John	N	Y	N	Y	Y	Y
MAINE						
1 Allen	Y	Y	N	Y	Y	Y
2 Baldacci	Y	Y	N	Y	Y	Y
MARYLAND						
1 **Gilchrest**	N	N	Y	Y	Y	Y
2 **Ehrlich**	N	N	Y	Y	Y	Y
3 Cardin	Y	Y	N	Y	Y	Y
4 Wynn	Y	Y	N	Y	Y	Y
5 Hoyer	Y	Y	N	Y	Y	Y
6 **Bartlett**	N	N	Y	Y	Y	Y
7 Cummings	Y	Y	N	?	?	Y
8 **Morella**	N	N	N	Y	Y	Y
MASSACHUSETTS						
1 Olver	Y	Y	N	Y	N	Y
2 Neal	Y	Y	N	Y	Y	Y
3 McGovern	Y	Y	N	Y	Y	Y
4 Frank	Y	Y	N	Y	Y	Y
5 Meehan	Y	Y	N	Y	Y	Y
6 Tierney	Y	Y	N	Y	Y	Y
7 Markey	Y	Y	N	Y	Y	Y
8 Capuano	Y	Y	N	Y	N	Y
9 Lynch	Y	Y	N	Y	?	Y
10 Delahunt	Y	Y	N	Y	Y	Y
MICHIGAN						
1 Stupak	Y	Y	N	Y	N	Y
2 **Hoekstra**	N	N	Y	Y	Y	?
3 **Ehlers**	N	N	Y	Y	Y	Y
4 **Camp**	N	N	Y	Y	Y	?
5 Barcia	Y	Y	N	Y	Y	Y
6 **Upton**	N	N	Y	Y	Y	Y
7 **Smith**	N	N	N	Y	Y	Y
8 **Rogers**	N	N	Y	Y	Y	Y
9 Kildee	Y	Y	N	Y	Y	Y
10 Bonior	Y	Y	N	Y	Y	Y
11 **Knollenberg**	N	N	Y	Y	Y	Y
12 Levin	Y	Y	N	Y	Y	Y
13 Rivers	Y	Y	N	Y	Y	Y
14 Conyers	Y	Y	N	Y	Y	Y
15 Kilpatrick	Y	Y	N	Y	Y	Y
16 Dingell	Y	Y	N	Y	Y	Y

	402	403	404	405	406	407
MINNESOTA						
1 **Gutknecht**	N	N	Y	Y	N	Y
2 **Kennedy**	N	N	Y	Y	Y	Y
3 **Ramstad**	N	N	Y	Y	N	Y
4 McCollum	Y	Y	N	Y	Y	Y
5 Sabo	Y	Y	N	Y	N	Y
6 Luther	N	Y	N	Y	Y	Y
7 Peterson	N	Y	N	Y	N	Y
8 Oberstar	Y	Y	N	Y	N	Y
MISSISSIPPI						
1 **Wicker**	N	N	Y	Y	N	Y
2 Thompson	Y	Y	N	Y	N	Y
3 **Pickering**	N	N	Y	Y	Y	Y
4 Shows	N	Y	N	Y	Y	Y
5 Taylor	N	Y	N	Y	N	Y
MISSOURI						
1 Clay	Y	Y	N	Y	Y	Y
2 **Akin**	N	N	Y	Y	Y	Y
3 Gephardt	Y	Y	N	Y	Y	Y
4 Skelton	Y	Y	N	Y	Y	Y
5 McCarthy	N	Y	N	Y	Y	Y
6 **Graves**	N	N	Y	Y	Y	Y
7 **Blunt**	N	N	Y	Y	Y	Y
8 **Emerson**	N	N	Y	Y	Y	Y
9 **Hulshof**	N	N	Y	Y	Y	Y
MONTANA						
AL **Rehberg**	N	N	Y	Y	Y	Y
NEBRASKA						
1 **Bereuter**	N	N	Y	Y	Y	Y
2 **Terry**	N	N	Y	Y	Y	Y
3 **Osborne**	N	N	Y	Y	Y	Y
NEVADA						
1 Berkley	Y	Y	N	Y	Y	Y
2 **Gibbons**	N	N	Y	Y	Y	Y
NEW HAMPSHIRE						
1 **Sununu**	N	N	Y	Y	Y	Y
2 **Bass**	N	N	Y	Y	Y	Y
NEW JERSEY						
1 Andrews	Y	Y	N	Y	Y	Y
2 **LoBiondo**	N	N	Y	Y	N	Y
3 **Saxton**	N	N	Y	Y	Y	Y
4 **Smith**	N	N	Y	Y	Y	Y
5 **Roukema**	N	N	Y	Y	Y	?
6 Pallone	Y	Y	N	Y	Y	Y
7 **Ferguson**	N	N	Y	Y	Y	Y
8 Pascrell	Y	Y	N	Y	Y	Y
9 Rothman	Y	Y	N	Y	Y	Y
10 Payne	Y	Y	N	Y	Y	Y
11 **Frelinghuysen**	N	N	Y	Y	Y	Y
12 Holt	Y	Y	N	Y	Y	Y
13 Menendez	Y	Y	N	Y	Y	Y
NEW MEXICO						
1 **Wilson**	N	N	Y	Y	Y	Y
2 **Skeen**	N	N	Y	Y	Y	Y
3 Udall	N	Y	N	Y	Y	Y
NEW YORK						
1 **Grucci**	N	N	Y	Y	Y	Y
2 Israel	Y	Y	N	Y	Y	Y
3 **King**	N	N	Y	Y	Y	Y
4 McCarthy	Y	Y	N	Y	Y	Y
5 Ackerman	Y	Y	N	Y	Y	Y
6 Meeks	Y	Y	N	Y	Y	Y
7 Crowley	Y	Y	N	Y	Y	Y
8 Nadler	Y	Y	N	Y	Y	Y
9 Weiner	Y	Y	N	Y	Y	Y
10 Towns	Y	Y	N	Y	Y	Y
11 Owens	Y	Y	N	Y	Y	Y
12 Velázquez	Y	Y	N	Y	Y	Y
13 **Fossella**	N	N	Y	Y	Y	Y
14 Maloney	Y	Y	N	Y	Y	Y
15 Rangel	Y	Y	N	Y	Y	Y
16 Serrano	Y	Y	N	Y	Y	Y
17 Engel	Y	Y	N	Y	Y	Y
18 Lowey	Y	Y	N	Y	Y	Y
19 **Kelly**	N	N	Y	Y	Y	Y
20 **Gilman**	N	N	Y	Y	Y	Y
21 McNulty	Y	Y	N	Y	N	Y
22 **Sweeney**	N	N	Y	Y	N	Y
23 **Boehlert**	N	N	Y	Y	Y	Y
24 **McHugh**	N	N	Y	Y	Y	Y
25 **Walsh**	N	N	Y	Y	Y	Y
26 Hinchey	Y	Y	N	Y	Y	Y
27 **Reynolds**	N	N	Y	Y	Y	Y
28 Slaughter	Y	Y	N	Y	N	Y
29 LaFalce	Y	Y	N	Y	Y	Y

	402	403	404	405	406	407
30 **Quinn**	N	N	N	Y	Y	Y
31 **Houghton**	N	N	Y	Y	Y	Y
NORTH CAROLINA						
1 Clayton	Y	Y	N	Y	Y	Y
2 Etheridge	Y	Y	N	Y	N	Y
3 **Jones**	N	N	Y	Y	Y	Y
4 Price	Y	Y	N	Y	Y	Y
5 **Burr**	N	N	Y	Y	Y	Y
6 **Coble**	N	N	Y	Y	Y	Y
7 McIntyre	+	Y	N	Y	Y	Y
8 **Hayes**	N	N	Y	Y	Y	Y
9 **Myrick**	N	N	Y	Y	Y	Y
10 **Ballenger**	N	N	Y	?	Y	Y
11 **Taylor**	N	N	Y	Y	Y	?
12 Watt	Y	Y	N	Y	N	Y
NORTH DAKOTA						
AL Pomeroy	Y	Y	N	Y	Y	Y
OHIO						
1 **Chabot**	N	N	Y	Y	Y	Y
2 **Portman**	N	N	Y	Y	Y	Y
3 Hall	N	N	N	Y	Y	Y
4 **Oxley**	N	N	Y	Y	Y	Y
5 **Gillmor**	N	N	Y	Y	N	Y
6 Strickland	Y	Y	N	Y	N	Y
7 **Hobson**	N	N	Y	Y	Y	Y
8 **Boehner**	N	N	Y	Y	Y	Y
9 Kaptur	N	Y	N	Y	Y	Y
10 Kucinich	Y	N	N	Y	N	Y
11 Jones	Y	N	N	Y	?	Y
12 **Tiberi**	N	N	Y	Y	Y	Y
13 Brown	Y	Y	N	Y	Y	Y
14 Sawyer	Y	Y	N	Y	Y	Y
15 **Pryce**	N	N	Y	Y	Y	Y
16 **Regula**	N	N	Y	Y	Y	Y
17 Traficant	N	N	Y	Y	Y	Y
18 **Ney**	N	N	Y	Y	Y	Y
19 **LaTourette**	N	N	Y	Y	Y	Y
OKLAHOMA						
1 **Largent**	N	N	Y	Y	Y	Y
2 Carson	N	Y	N	Y	Y	Y
3 **Watkins**	N	N	Y	Y	Y	Y
4 **Watts**	N	N	Y	Y	Y	Y
5 **Istook**	N	N	Y	?	?	Y
6 **Lucas**	N	N	Y	Y	Y	Y
OREGON						
1 Wu	N	Y	N	Y	N	Y
2 **Walden**	N	N	Y	Y	Y	Y
3 Blumenauer	Y	Y	N	Y	Y	Y
4 DeFazio	Y	Y	N	Y	N	Y
5 Hooley	Y	Y	N	Y	Y	Y
PENNSYLVANIA						
1 Brady	Y	Y	N	Y	N	Y
2 Fattah	Y	Y	N	?	?	?
3 Borski	Y	Y	N	Y	N	Y
4 **Hart**	?	N	Y	Y	Y	Y
5 **Peterson**	N	N	Y	Y	Y	Y
6 Holden	Y	Y	N	Y	Y	Y
7 **Weldon**	N	N	Y	Y	Y	Y
8 **Greenwood**	N	N	Y	Y	Y	Y
9 **Shuster, Bill**	N	N	Y	Y	Y	Y
10 **Sherwood**	N	N	Y	Y	Y	Y
11 Kanjorski	Y	Y	N	Y	Y	Y
12 Murtha	N	N	N	Y	Y	Y
13 Hoeffel	Y	Y	N	?	?	?
14 Coyne	Y	Y	N	Y	Y	Y
15 **Toomey**	N	N	Y	Y	Y	Y
16 **Pitts**	N	N	Y	Y	Y	Y
17 **Gekas**	N	N	Y	Y	Y	Y
18 Doyle	Y	Y	N	Y	Y	Y
19 **Platts**	N	N	Y	Y	Y	Y
20 Mascara	Y	Y	N	Y	Y	Y
21 **English**	N	N	Y	Y	N	Y
RHODE ISLAND						
1 Kennedy	Y	Y	N	Y	Y	Y
2 Langevin	Y	Y	N	Y	Y	Y
SOUTH CAROLINA						
1 **Brown**	N	N	Y	Y	Y	Y
2 Vacant						
3 **Graham**	N	N	Y	Y	Y	Y
4 **DeMint**	N	N	Y	Y	Y	?
5 Spratt	Y	Y	N	Y	Y	Y
6 Clyburn	Y	Y	N	Y	Y	Y
SOUTH DAKOTA						
AL **Thune**	N	N	N	Y	Y	Y

	402	403	404	405	406	407
TENNESSEE						
1 **Jenkins**	N	N	Y	Y	Y	Y
2 **Duncan**	N	N	Y	Y	Y	Y
3 **Wamp**	N	N	Y	Y	Y	Y
4 **Hilleary**	N	N	Y	Y	Y	Y
5 Clement	Y	Y	N	Y	Y	Y
6 Gordon	Y	Y	N	?	?	Y
7 **Bryant**	N	N	Y	Y	Y	Y
8 Tanner	N	Y	N	Y	N	Y
9 Ford	Y	Y	N	Y	N	Y
TEXAS						
1 Sandlin	N	Y	N	Y	Y	Y
2 Turner	N	Y	N	Y	Y	Y
3 **Johnson, Sam**	N	N	Y	Y	?	Y
4 Hall	N	N	Y	Y	Y	Y
5 **Sessions**	N	N	Y	Y	Y	Y
6 **Barton**	N	N	Y	Y	Y	Y
7 **Culberson**	N	N	Y	Y	Y	Y
8 **Brady**	N	N	Y	Y	Y	Y
9 Lampson	Y	Y	N	Y	Y	Y
10 Doggett	N	Y	N	Y	Y	Y
11 Edwards	N	Y	N	Y	Y	Y
12 **Granger**	N	N	Y	Y	Y	Y
13 **Thornberry**	N	N	Y	Y	Y	Y
14 **Paul**	N	N	Y	Y	Y	Y
15 Hinojosa	Y	Y	N	Y	Y	Y
16 Reyes	Y	Y	N	Y	Y	Y
17 Stenholm	N	Y	N	Y	N	Y
18 Jackson-Lee	Y	Y	N	Y	N	?
19 **Combest**	N	N	Y	Y	Y	Y
20 Gonzalez	?	?	?	?	?	?
21 **Smith**	N	N	Y	Y	Y	Y
22 **DeLay**	N	N	Y	Y	Y	?
23 **Bonilla**	N	N	Y	Y	Y	Y
24 Frost	Y	Y	N	Y	Y	Y
25 Bentsen	N	Y	N	Y	Y	Y
26 **Armey**	N	N	Y	Y	Y	Y
27 Ortiz	Y	Y	N	Y	Y	Y
28 Rodriguez	Y	Y	N	Y	Y	Y
29 Green	Y	Y	N	Y	Y	Y
30 Johnson, E.B.	Y	Y	N	Y	Y	?
UTAH						
1 **Hansen**	N	N	Y	Y	Y	Y
2 Matheson	N	Y	N	Y	Y	Y
3 **Cannon**	N	N	Y	Y	Y	Y
VERMONT						
AL *Sanders*	Y	Y	N	Y	Y	Y
VIRGINIA						
1 **Davis, Jo Ann**	N	N	Y	Y	Y	Y
2 **Schrock**	N	N	Y	Y	Y	Y
3 Scott	Y	Y	N	Y	N	Y
4 **Forbes**	N	N	Y	Y	Y	Y
5 *Goode*	N	N	Y	Y	Y	Y
6 **Goodlatte**	N	N	Y	Y	Y	Y
7 **Cantor**	N	N	Y	Y	Y	Y
8 Moran	Y	Y	N	Y	Y	Y
9 Boucher	Y	Y	N	Y	Y	?
10 **Wolf**	N	N	Y	Y	Y	Y
11 **Davis, T.**	N	N	Y	Y	Y	Y
WASHINGTON						
1 Inslee	Y	Y	N	Y	Y	Y
2 Larsen	Y	Y	N	Y	N	Y
3 Baird	Y	Y	N	Y	Y	?
4 **Hastings**	N	N	Y	Y	?	?
5 **Nethercutt**	N	N	Y	Y	Y	Y
6 Dicks	Y	Y	N	Y	Y	Y
7 McDermott	Y	Y	N	Y	N	Y
8 **Dunn**	N	N	Y	Y	Y	Y
9 Smith	Y	Y	N	Y	Y	Y
WEST VIRGINIA						
1 Mollohan	N	N	N	Y	Y	Y
2 **Capito**	N	N	Y	Y	Y	Y
3 Rahall	N	N	N	Y	N	Y
WISCONSIN						
1 **Ryan**	N	N	Y	Y	Y	Y
2 Baldwin	Y	Y	N	Y	Y	Y
3 Kind	N	Y	N	Y	Y	Y
4 Kleczka	Y	Y	N	Y	Y	Y
5 Barrett	Y	Y	N	Y	Y	Y
6 **Petri**	N	N	Y	Y	Y	Y
7 Obey	Y	Y	N	Y	Y	Y
8 **Green**	N	N	Y	Y	Y	Y
9 **Sensenbrenner**	N	N	Y	Y	Y	Y
WYOMING						
AL **Cubin**	?	?	?	?	?	?

Southern states - Ala., Ark., Fla., Ga., Ky., La., Miss., N.C., Okla., S.C., Tenn., Texas, Va.

Key

Y	Voted for (yea).
#	Paired for.
+	Announced for.
N	Voted against (nay).
X	Paired against.
−	Announced against.
P	Voted "present."
C	Voted "present" to avoid possible conflict of interest.
?	Did not vote or otherwise make a position known.

Democrats   **Republicans**
Independents

408. H Con Res 243. Officers' Medal/Adoption. Sensenbrenner, R-Wis., motion to suspend the rules and adopt the resolution that would express the sense of Congress that the medal of valor should be awarded to public safety officers who were killed or demonstrated valor above and beyond the call of duty while responding to the Sept. 11 terrorist attacks. Motion agreed to 409-0: R 206-0; D 201-0 (ND 151-0, SD 50-0); I 2-0. A two-thirds majority of those present and voting (273 in this case) is required for adoption under suspension of the rules. Oct. 30, 2001.

409. HR 2559. Federal Insurance Premiums/Passage. Jo Ann Davis, R-Va., motion to suspend the rules and pass the bill that would exempt from state and local taxation the premiums paid by federal employees for private insurance under the Long-Term Care Security Act. It also would allow those who retire from the federal government but defer their annuities to participate in the insurance program. Motion agreed to 406-1: R 204-1; D 200-0 (ND 151-0, SD 49-0); I 2-0. A two-thirds majority of those present and voting (272 in this case) is required for passage under suspension of the rules. Oct. 30, 2001.

410. HR 2910. Norman Sisisky Building/Passage. Jo Ann Davis, R-Va., motion to suspend the rules and pass the bill that would designate a building in Petersburg, Va., as the "Norman Sisisky Post Office Building." Motion agreed to 405-0: R 203-0; D 200-0 (ND 151-0, SD 49-0); I 2-0. A two-thirds majority of those present and voting (270 in this case) is required for passage under suspension of the rules. Oct. 30, 2001.

411. H Con Res 233. Emergency Personnel Tribute/Adoption. La-Tourette, R-Ohio, motion to suspend the rules and adopt the resolution that would honor the emergency personnel who first responded to the Sept. 11 terrorist attacks, support a presidential proclamation in tribute to them, express regrets to the families of those killed or injured, and support further coordination among federal, state and local governments on emergency preparedness. Motion agreed to 405-0: R 203-0; D 200-0 (ND 150-0, SD 50-0); I 2-0. A two-thirds majority of those present and voting (270 in this case) is required for adoption under suspension of the rules. Oct. 30, 2001.

412. Procedural Motion/Journal. Approval of the House Journal of Tuesday, Oct. 30, 2001. Approved 374-39: R 193-11; D 179-28 (ND 130-24, SD 49-4); I 2-0. Oct. 31, 2001.

413. HR 2590. Fiscal 2002 Treasury-Postal Appropriations/Conference Report. Adoption of the conference report on the bill that would provide $32.8 billion for the Treasury Department, Postal Service, Executive Office of the President and other federal agencies. The bill would increase pay for federal employees by 4.6 percent and maintain current law provisions that ban funding abortions under federal employee health plans but allow funding for contraceptives. Adopted (thus sent to the Senate) 339-85: R 180-35; D 158-49 (ND 118-36, SD 40-13); I 1-1. Oct. 31, 2001.

	408	409	410	411	412	413
ALABAMA						
1 *Callahan*	Y	Y	Y	Y	Y	Y
2 *Everett*	Y	Y	Y	Y	Y	N
3 *Riley*	+	+	+	+	Y	Y
4 *Aderholt*	Y	Y	Y	Y	N	Y
5 Cramer	Y	Y	Y	Y	Y	Y
6 *Bachus*	Y	Y	Y	Y	?	Y
7 Hilliard	Y	Y	Y	Y	N	Y
ALASKA						
AL *Young*	Y	Y	?	Y	Y	Y
ARIZONA						
1 *Flake*	Y	Y	Y	Y	Y	N
2 Pastor	Y	Y	Y	Y	Y	Y
3 *Stump*	Y	Y	Y	Y	Y	N
4 *Shadegg*	Y	Y	Y	Y	Y	Y
5 *Kolbe*	Y	Y	Y	Y	Y	Y
6 *Hayworth*	Y	Y	Y	Y	Y	N
ARKANSAS						
1 Berry	Y	Y	Y	Y	Y	N
2 Snyder	Y	Y	Y	Y	Y	Y
3 Vacant						
4 Ross	Y	Y	Y	Y	Y	N
CALIFORNIA						
1 Thompson	Y	Y	Y	Y	N	Y
2 *Herger*	Y	Y	Y	Y	Y	N
3 *Ose*	Y	Y	Y	Y	Y	Y
4 *Doolittle*	Y	Y	Y	Y	Y	Y
5 Matsui	Y	Y	Y	Y	Y	Y
6 Woolsey	Y	Y	Y	Y	Y	Y
7 Miller, George	Y	Y	Y	Y	Y	Y
8 Pelosi	Y	Y	Y	Y	Y	Y
9 Lee	Y	Y	Y	Y	Y	Y
10 Tauscher	Y	Y	Y	Y	Y	Y
11 *Pombo*	Y	Y	Y	Y	Y	Y
12 Lantos	Y	Y	Y	Y	?	?
13 Stark	Y	Y	Y	Y	Y	Y
14 Eshoo	Y	Y	Y	Y	Y	Y
15 Honda	Y	Y	Y	Y	Y	N
16 Lofgren	Y	Y	Y	Y	Y	Y
17 Farr	Y	Y	Y	Y	Y	Y
18 Condit	Y	Y	Y	Y	Y	Y
19 *Radanovich*	Y	Y	Y	Y	Y	Y
20 Dooley	?	?	?	?	Y	Y
21 *Thomas*	Y	Y	Y	Y	Y	Y
22 Capps	Y	Y	Y	Y	N	Y
23 *Gallegly*	Y	Y	Y	Y	Y	Y
24 Sherman	Y	Y	Y	Y	Y	N
25 *McKeon*	Y	Y	Y	Y	Y	Y
26 Berman	Y	Y	Y	Y	Y	Y
27 Schiff	Y	Y	Y	Y	Y	N
28 *Dreier*	Y	Y	Y	Y	?	Y
29 Waxman	Y	Y	Y	Y	Y	Y
30 Becerra	Y	Y	Y	Y	Y	Y
31 Solis	Y	Y	Y	Y	Y	Y
32 Watson	Y	Y	Y	Y	Y	Y
33 Roybal-Allard	Y	Y	Y	Y	Y	Y
34 Napolitano	Y	Y	Y	Y	Y	N
35 Waters	Y	Y	Y	Y	N	Y
36 Harman	Y	Y	Y	Y	Y	Y
37 Millender-McD.	Y	Y	Y	Y	Y	Y
38 *Horn*	Y	Y	Y	Y	Y	Y

	408	409	410	411	412	413
39 *Royce*	Y	Y	Y	Y	Y	N
40 *Lewis*	Y	Y	Y	Y	Y	Y
41 *Miller, Gary*	Y	Y	Y	Y	Y	Y
42 Baca	Y	Y	Y	Y	Y	Y
43 *Calvert*	Y	Y	Y	Y	Y	Y
44 *Bono*	Y	Y	Y	Y	Y	Y
45 *Rohrabacher*	Y	Y	Y	Y	Y	N
46 Sanchez	Y	Y	Y	Y	N	Y
47 *Cox*	Y	Y	Y	?	?	Y
48 *Issa*	Y	Y	Y	Y	Y	Y
49 Davis	Y	Y	Y	Y	Y	N
50 Filner	Y	Y	Y	N	Y	Y
51 *Cunningham*	Y	Y	Y	Y	Y	Y
52 *Hunter*	Y	Y	?	Y	Y	Y
COLORADO						
1 DeGette	?	?	?	?	?	?
2 Udall	Y	Y	Y	Y	N	Y
3 *McInnis*	Y	Y	Y	Y	Y	Y
4 *Schaffer*	Y	Y	Y	Y	N	N
5 *Hefley*	Y	Y	Y	Y	N	N
6 *Tancredo*	Y	Y	Y	Y	P	N
CONNECTICUT						
1 Larson	Y	Y	Y	Y	Y	Y
2 *Simmons*	Y	Y	Y	Y	Y	Y
3 DeLauro	Y	Y	Y	Y	Y	Y
4 *Shays*	Y	Y	Y	Y	Y	N
5 Maloney	Y	Y	Y	Y	Y	Y
6 *Johnson*	Y	Y	Y	Y	Y	Y
DELAWARE						
AL *Castle*	Y	Y	Y	Y	Y	Y
FLORIDA						
1 *Miller, J.*	Y	Y	Y	Y	Y	Y
2 Boyd	Y	Y	Y	Y	Y	Y
3 Brown	Y	Y	Y	Y	Y	Y
4 *Crenshaw*	Y	Y	Y	Y	Y	Y
5 Thurman	Y	Y	Y	Y	Y	N
6 *Stearns*	Y	Y	Y	Y	Y	N
7 *Mica*	Y	Y	Y	Y	Y	Y
8 *Keller*	?	?	?	?	Y	Y
9 *Bilirakis*	Y	Y	Y	Y	Y	Y
10 *Young*	Y	Y	Y	?	Y	Y
11 Davis	Y	Y	Y	Y	Y	Y
12 *Putnam*	Y	Y	Y	Y	Y	Y
13 *Miller, D.*	Y	Y	Y	Y	Y	Y
14 *Goss*	Y	Y	Y	Y	Y	Y
15 *Weldon*	Y	Y	Y	Y	Y	Y
16 *Foley*	Y	Y	Y	Y	Y	Y
17 Meek	Y	Y	Y	Y	Y	Y
18 *Ros-Lehtinen*	Y	Y	Y	Y	Y	Y
19 Wexler	Y	Y	Y	Y	Y	Y
20 Deutsch	Y	Y	Y	Y	N	Y
21 *Diaz-Balart*	Y	Y	Y	Y	Y	Y
22 *Shaw*	Y	Y	Y	Y	Y	Y
23 Hastings	Y	Y	Y	Y	N	Y
GEORGIA						
1 *Kingston*	Y	Y	Y	Y	Y	Y
2 Bishop	Y	Y	Y	Y	Y	Y
3 *Collins*	Y	Y	Y	Y	Y	Y
4 McKinney	Y	Y	Y	Y	Y	N
5 Lewis	Y	Y	Y	Y	N	Y
6 *Isakson*	Y	Y	Y	Y	Y	Y
7 *Barr*	Y	Y	Y	Y	Y	Y
8 *Chambliss*	Y	Y	Y	Y	Y	Y
9 *Deal*	Y	Y	Y	Y	Y	Y
10 *Norwood*	Y	Y	Y	Y	Y	Y
11 *Linder*	Y	Y	Y	Y	Y	Y
HAWAII						
1 Abercrombie	Y	Y	Y	Y	Y	Y
2 Mink	Y	Y	Y	Y	Y	Y
IDAHO						
1 *Otter*	Y	Y	Y	Y	Y	Y
2 *Simpson*	Y	Y	Y	Y	Y	Y
ILLINOIS						
1 Rush	Y	Y	Y	Y	Y	Y
2 Jackson	Y	Y	Y	Y	Y	Y
3 Lipinski	Y	Y	Y	Y	Y	Y
4 Gutierrez	Y	Y	Y	Y	Y	Y
5 Blagojevich	Y	Y	Y	Y	Y	Y
6 *Hyde*	Y	Y	Y	Y	Y	Y
7 Davis	Y	Y	Y	Y	Y	Y
8 *Crane*	Y	Y	Y	Y	N	N
9 Schakowsky	Y	Y	Y	Y	Y	Y
10 *Kirk*	Y	Y	Y	Y	Y	Y
11 *Weller*	Y	Y	Y	Y	N	Y
12 Costello	Y	Y	Y	Y	N	N
13 *Biggert*	Y	Y	Y	Y	Y	Y

ND Northern Democrats   SD Southern Democrats

	408	409	410	411	412	413
14 ***Hastert***						
15 ***Johnson***	Y	Y	Y	Y	Y	Y
16 ***Manzullo***	Y	Y	Y	Y	Y	Y
17 Evans	Y	Y	?	Y	Y	N
18 ***LaHood***	Y	Y	Y	Y	Y	Y
19 Phelps	Y	Y	Y	Y	Y	N
20 ***Shimkus***	Y	Y	Y	Y	Y	Y
INDIANA						
1 Visclosky	Y	Y	Y	Y	N	Y
2 ***Pence***	Y	Y	Y	Y	Y	Y
3 Roemer	Y	Y	Y	Y	Y	Y
4 ***Souder***	Y	Y	Y	Y	Y	Y
5 ***Buyer***	Y	Y	Y	Y	Y	Y
6 ***Burton***	Y	Y	Y	Y	Y	Y
7 ***Kerns***	Y	Y	Y	Y	Y	N
8 ***Hostettler***	Y	Y	Y	Y	Y	N
9 Hill	Y	Y	Y	Y	Y	N
10 Carson	Y	Y	Y	Y	Y	N
IOWA						
1 ***Leach***	Y	Y	Y	Y	Y	Y
2 ***Nussle***	Y	Y	Y	Y	Y	Y
3 Boswell	Y	Y	Y	Y	Y	N
4 ***Ganske***	Y	Y	Y	?	Y	Y
5 ***Latham***	Y	Y	Y	Y	Y	Y
KANSAS						
1 ***Moran***	Y	Y	Y	Y	N	N
2 ***Ryun***	Y	Y	Y	Y	Y	N
3 Moore	Y	Y	Y	Y	Y	N
4 ***Tiahrt***	Y	Y	Y	Y	Y	Y
KENTUCKY						
1 ***Whitfield***	Y	Y	Y	Y	Y	Y
2 ***Lewis***	Y	Y	Y	Y	Y	Y
3 ***Northup***	+	Y	+	Y	Y	Y
4 Lucas	Y	Y	Y	Y	Y	N
5 ***Rogers***	?	?	?	?	Y	Y
6 ***Fletcher***	Y	Y	Y	Y	Y	Y
LOUISIANA						
1 ***Vitter***	Y	Y	Y	Y	Y	Y
2 Jefferson	Y	Y	Y	Y	Y	Y
3 ***Tauzin***	Y	Y	Y	Y	Y	Y
4 ***McCrery***	?	?	?	?	?	?
5 ***Cooksey***	?	?	?	?	Y	Y
6 ***Baker***	Y	Y	Y	Y	Y	Y
7 John	Y	Y	Y	Y	Y	Y
MAINE						
1 Allen	Y	Y	Y	Y	Y	Y
2 Baldacci	Y	Y	Y	Y	Y	Y
MARYLAND						
1 ***Gilchrest***	Y	Y	Y	Y	Y	Y
2 ***Ehrlich***	Y	Y	Y	Y	Y	Y
3 Cardin	Y	Y	Y	Y	Y	Y
4 Wynn	Y	Y	Y	Y	Y	Y
5 Hoyer	Y	Y	Y	Y	Y	Y
6 ***Bartlett***	Y	Y	Y	Y	Y	Y
7 Cummings	Y	Y	Y	Y	Y	Y
8 ***Morella***	Y	Y	Y	Y	Y	Y
MASSACHUSETTS						
1 Olver	Y	Y	Y	Y	Y	Y
2 Neal	Y	Y	Y	Y	Y	Y
3 McGovern	Y	Y	Y	Y	Y	Y
4 Frank	Y	Y	Y	Y	Y	Y
5 Meehan	Y	Y	Y	Y	Y	Y
6 Tierney	Y	Y	Y	Y	Y	Y
7 Markey	Y	Y	Y	Y	Y	Y
8 Capuano	Y	Y	Y	Y	N	N
9 Lynch	Y	Y	Y	Y	Y	N
10 Delahunt	Y	Y	Y	Y	Y	Y
MICHIGAN						
1 Stupak	Y	Y	Y	Y	N	Y
2 ***Hoekstra***	Y	Y	Y	Y	Y	Y
3 ***Ehlers***	Y	Y	Y	Y	Y	Y
4 ***Camp***	Y	Y	Y	Y	Y	Y
5 Barcia	Y	Y	Y	Y	Y	N
6 ***Upton***	Y	Y	Y	Y	Y	Y
7 ***Smith***	Y	Y	Y	Y	Y	Y
8 ***Rogers***	Y	Y	Y	Y	Y	Y
9 Kildee	Y	Y	Y	Y	Y	N
10 Bonior	Y	Y	Y	Y	Y	Y
11 ***Knollenberg***	Y	Y	Y	Y	Y	Y
12 Levin	Y	Y	Y	Y	Y	Y
13 Rivers	Y	Y	Y	Y	Y	Y
14 Conyers	?	?	?	?	Y	Y
15 Kilpatrick	Y	Y	Y	Y	Y	Y
16 Dingell	Y	Y	Y	Y	Y	Y
MINNESOTA						
1 ***Gutknecht***	Y	Y	Y	Y	N	Y
2 ***Kennedy***	Y	Y	Y	Y	Y	Y
3 ***Ramstad***	Y	Y	Y	Y	N	N
4 McCollum	Y	Y	Y	Y	Y	Y
5 Sabo	Y	Y	Y	Y	N	Y
6 Luther	Y	Y	Y	Y	Y	N
7 Peterson	Y	Y	Y	Y	N	Y
8 Oberstar	Y	Y	Y	Y	N	Y
MISSISSIPPI						
1 ***Wicker***	Y	Y	Y	Y	N	Y
2 Thompson	?	?	?	?	?	?
3 ***Pickering***	Y	Y	Y	Y	Y	N
4 Shows	?	?	?	?	Y	N
5 Taylor	Y	Y	Y	Y	N	N
MISSOURI						
1 Clay	Y	Y	Y	Y	Y	Y
2 ***Akin***	Y	Y	Y	Y	Y	Y
3 Gephardt	Y	Y	Y	Y	Y	Y
4 Skelton	Y	Y	Y	Y	Y	Y
5 McCarthy	Y	Y	Y	Y	Y	Y
6 ***Graves***	Y	Y	Y	Y	Y	N
7 ***Blunt***	Y	Y	Y	Y	?	Y
8 ***Emerson***	Y	Y	Y	Y	Y	Y
9 ***Hulshof***	Y	Y	Y	Y	Y	Y
MONTANA						
AL ***Rehberg***	Y	Y	Y	Y	Y	Y
NEBRASKA						
1 ***Bereuter***	Y	Y	Y	Y	Y	Y
2 ***Terry***	Y	Y	Y	Y	Y	Y
3 ***Osborne***	Y	Y	Y	Y	Y	Y
NEVADA						
1 Berkley	Y	Y	Y	Y	Y	N
2 ***Gibbons***	Y	Y	Y	Y	Y	Y
NEW HAMPSHIRE						
1 ***Sununu***	Y	Y	Y	Y	Y	Y
2 ***Bass***	Y	Y	Y	Y	Y	Y
NEW JERSEY						
1 Andrews	Y	Y	Y	Y	?	?
2 ***LoBiondo***	Y	Y	Y	Y	N	Y
3 ***Saxton***	Y	Y	Y	Y	Y	Y
4 ***Smith***	Y	Y	Y	Y	Y	Y
5 ***Roukema***	Y	Y	Y	Y	Y	Y
6 Pallone	Y	Y	Y	Y	N	Y
7 ***Ferguson***	Y	Y	Y	Y	Y	Y
8 Pascrell	Y	Y	Y	Y	Y	Y
9 Rothman	Y	Y	Y	Y	Y	Y
10 Payne	Y	Y	Y	Y	Y	Y
11 ***Frelinghuysen***	Y	?	Y	Y	Y	Y
12 Holt	Y	Y	Y	Y	N	N
13 Menendez	?	?	?	?	Y	Y
NEW MEXICO						
1 ***Wilson***	Y	Y	Y	Y	Y	Y
2 ***Skeen***	Y	Y	Y	Y	Y	Y
3 Udall	Y	Y	Y	Y	N	N
NEW YORK						
1 ***Grucci***	Y	Y	Y	Y	Y	Y
2 Israel	Y	Y	Y	Y	Y	N
3 ***King***	Y	Y	Y	Y	Y	Y
4 McCarthy	Y	Y	Y	Y	Y	Y
5 Ackerman	Y	Y	Y	Y	Y	Y
6 Meeks	Y	Y	Y	?	Y	Y
7 Crowley	Y	Y	Y	Y	Y	Y
8 Nadler	Y	Y	Y	Y	Y	Y
9 Weiner	Y	Y	Y	Y	Y	Y
10 Towns	Y	Y	Y	Y	Y	Y
11 Owens	Y	Y	Y	Y	Y	Y
12 Velázquez	Y	Y	Y	Y	Y	Y
13 ***Fossella***	Y	Y	Y	Y	Y	Y
14 Maloney	Y	Y	Y	Y	Y	Y
15 Rangel	Y	Y	Y	Y	Y	Y
16 Serrano	Y	Y	Y	Y	Y	Y
17 Engel	Y	Y	Y	Y	Y	Y
18 Lowey	Y	Y	Y	?	Y	Y
19 ***Kelly***	Y	Y	Y	Y	Y	Y
20 ***Gilman***	Y	Y	Y	Y	Y	Y
21 McNulty	Y	Y	Y	Y	Y	Y
22 ***Sweeney***	Y	Y	Y	Y	?	?
23 ***Boehlert***	Y	Y	Y	Y	Y	Y
24 ***McHugh***	?	?	?	?	Y	Y
25 ***Walsh***	Y	Y	Y	Y	Y	Y
26 Hinchey	Y	Y	Y	Y	Y	Y
27 ***Reynolds***	Y	Y	Y	Y	Y	Y
28 Slaughter	Y	Y	Y	Y	Y	Y
29 LaFalce	Y	Y	Y	Y	Y	Y
30 ***Quinn***	Y	Y	?	Y	Y	Y
31 ***Houghton***	Y	Y	Y	Y	Y	Y
NORTH CAROLINA						
1 Clayton	Y	Y	Y	Y	Y	Y
2 Etheridge	Y	Y	Y	Y	Y	N
3 ***Jones***	Y	Y	Y	Y	Y	N
4 Price	Y	Y	Y	Y	Y	Y
5 ***Burr***	Y	Y	Y	Y	Y	Y
6 ***Coble***	Y	Y	Y	Y	Y	N
7 McIntyre	Y	Y	Y	Y	Y	Y
8 ***Hayes***	Y	Y	Y	Y	Y	Y
9 ***Myrick***	Y	Y	Y	Y	Y	Y
10 ***Ballenger***	Y	Y	Y	Y	Y	Y
11 ***Taylor***	Y	Y	Y	Y	Y	Y
12 Watt	Y	Y	Y	Y	Y	Y
NORTH DAKOTA						
AL Pomeroy	Y	Y	Y	Y	Y	Y
OHIO						
1 ***Chabot***	Y	Y	Y	Y	Y	N
2 ***Portman***	Y	Y	Y	Y	?	Y
3 Hall	Y	Y	Y	Y	Y	Y
4 ***Oxley***	Y	Y	Y	Y	Y	Y
5 ***Gillmor***	Y	Y	Y	Y	Y	Y
6 Strickland	Y	Y	Y	Y	N	N
7 ***Hobson***	Y	Y	Y	Y	Y	Y
8 ***Boehner***	Y	Y	Y	Y	Y	Y
9 Kaptur	Y	Y	Y	Y	Y	Y
10 Kucinich	Y	Y	Y	Y	N	N
11 Jones	Y	Y	Y	Y	Y	Y
12 ***Tiberi***	Y	Y	Y	Y	Y	Y
13 Brown	Y	Y	Y	Y	N	N
14 Sawyer	Y	Y	Y	Y	Y	Y
15 ***Pryce***	Y	Y	Y	Y	?	Y
16 ***Regula***	Y	Y	Y	Y	Y	Y
17 Traficant	Y	Y	Y	Y	Y	Y
18 ***Ney***	Y	Y	Y	Y	Y	Y
19 ***LaTourette***	Y	Y	Y	Y	Y	Y
OKLAHOMA						
1 ***Largent***	Y	Y	Y	Y	Y	Y
2 Carson	?	?	?	?	Y	N
3 ***Watkins***	Y	Y	Y	Y	Y	Y
4 ***Watts***	Y	Y	Y	?	?	Y
5 ***Istook***	Y	Y	Y	Y	Y	Y
6 ***Lucas***	Y	Y	Y	Y	Y	Y
OREGON						
1 Wu	Y	Y	Y	Y	Y	N
2 ***Walden***	Y	Y	Y	Y	Y	N
3 Blumenauer	Y	Y	Y	Y	Y	N
4 DeFazio	Y	Y	Y	Y	N	N
5 Hooley	?	?	Y	Y	Y	N
PENNSYLVANIA						
1 Brady	Y	Y	Y	Y	N	Y
2 Fattah	Y	Y	Y	Y	Y	Y
3 Borski	Y	Y	Y	Y	N	Y
4 ***Hart***	Y	Y	Y	Y	Y	Y
5 ***Peterson***	Y	Y	Y	Y	Y	Y
6 Holden	Y	Y	Y	Y	Y	Y
7 ***Weldon***	Y	Y	Y	Y	Y	Y
8 ***Greenwood***	?	?	?	?	Y	Y
9 ***Shuster, Bill***	Y	Y	Y	Y	Y	Y
10 ***Sherwood***	Y	Y	Y	Y	Y	Y
11 Kanjorski	Y	Y	Y	Y	Y	Y
12 Murtha	?	?	?	?	Y	Y
13 Hoeffel	Y	Y	Y	Y	Y	Y
14 Coyne	Y	Y	Y	Y	Y	Y
15 ***Toomey***	Y	Y	Y	Y	Y	N
16 ***Pitts***	Y	Y	Y	Y	Y	N
17 ***Gekas***	Y	Y	Y	Y	Y	Y
18 Doyle	Y	Y	Y	Y	Y	Y
19 ***Platts***	Y	Y	Y	Y	Y	N
20 Mascara	Y	Y	Y	Y	Y	Y
21 ***English***	Y	Y	Y	Y	N	Y
RHODE ISLAND						
1 Kennedy	Y	Y	Y	Y	Y	Y
2 Langevin	Y	Y	Y	Y	Y	N
SOUTH CAROLINA						
1 ***Brown***	Y	Y	Y	Y	Y	Y
2 Vacant						
3 ***Graham***	Y	Y	Y	Y	Y	Y
4 ***DeMint***	Y	Y	Y	Y	Y	Y
5 Spratt	Y	Y	Y	Y	Y	Y
6 Clyburn	Y	Y	Y	Y	Y	Y
SOUTH DAKOTA						
AL ***Thune***	Y	Y	Y	Y	Y	N
TENNESSEE						
1 ***Jenkins***	Y	Y	Y	Y	Y	N
2 ***Duncan***	Y	Y	Y	Y	Y	N
3 ***Wamp***	Y	Y	Y	Y	Y	Y
4 ***Hilleary***	Y	Y	Y	Y	Y	N
5 Clement	Y	Y	Y	Y	Y	Y
6 Gordon	Y	Y	Y	Y	Y	Y
7 ***Bryant***	Y	Y	Y	Y	Y	Y
8 Tanner	Y	Y	Y	Y	Y	Y
9 Ford	Y	Y	Y	Y	Y	Y
TEXAS						
1 Sandlin	Y	?	Y	Y	Y	N
2 Turner	Y	Y	Y	Y	Y	N
3 ***Johnson, Sam***	Y	Y	Y	Y	Y	Y
4 Hall	Y	Y	Y	Y	Y	N
5 ***Sessions***	Y	Y	Y	Y	Y	Y
6 ***Barton***	Y	Y	Y	Y	Y	Y
7 ***Culberson***	Y	Y	Y	Y	Y	Y
8 ***Brady***	?	?	?	?	Y	Y
9 Lampson	Y	Y	Y	Y	Y	Y
10 Doggett	Y	Y	Y	Y	Y	Y
11 Edwards	Y	Y	?	Y	Y	Y
12 ***Granger***	?	?	?	?	?	?
13 ***Thornberry***	Y	Y	Y	Y	Y	Y
14 ***Paul***	Y	N	Y	Y	Y	N
15 Hinojosa	Y	Y	Y	Y	Y	Y
16 Reyes	Y	Y	Y	Y	Y	Y
17 Stenholm	Y	Y	Y	Y	Y	Y
18 Jackson-Lee	Y	Y	Y	Y	Y	Y
19 ***Combest***	Y	Y	Y	Y	Y	Y
20 Gonzalez	Y	Y	Y	Y	Y	Y
21 ***Smith***	Y	Y	Y	Y	Y	Y
22 ***DeLay***	?	?	?	?	?	Y
23 ***Bonilla***	Y	Y	Y	Y	Y	Y
24 Frost	Y	Y	Y	Y	Y	Y
25 Bentsen	Y	Y	Y	Y	Y	Y
26 ***Armey***	Y	Y	Y	Y	?	Y
27 Ortiz	Y	Y	Y	Y	Y	Y
28 Rodriguez	Y	Y	Y	Y	Y	Y
29 Green	Y	Y	Y	Y	Y	Y
30 Johnson, E.B.	Y	Y	Y	Y	Y	Y
UTAH						
1 ***Hansen***	Y	Y	Y	Y	Y	Y
2 Matheson	Y	Y	Y	Y	Y	N
3 ***Cannon***	Y	Y	Y	Y	Y	Y
VERMONT						
AL *Sanders*	Y	Y	Y	Y	Y	Y
VIRGINIA						
1 ***Davis, Jo Ann***	Y	Y	Y	Y	Y	Y
2 ***Schrock***	Y	Y	Y	Y	Y	Y
3 Scott	Y	Y	Y	Y	Y	Y
4 ***Forbes***	Y	Y	Y	Y	Y	Y
5 *Goode*	Y	Y	Y	Y	Y	N
6 ***Goodlatte***	Y	Y	Y	Y	Y	N
7 ***Cantor***	Y	+	Y	Y	Y	Y
8 Moran	Y	Y	Y	Y	Y	Y
9 Boucher	?	?	?	?	Y	Y
10 ***Wolf***	Y	Y	Y	Y	Y	Y
11 ***Davis, T.***	Y	Y	Y	Y	Y	Y
WASHINGTON						
1 Inslee	Y	Y	Y	Y	Y	N
2 Larsen	Y	Y	Y	Y	N	N
3 Baird	Y	Y	Y	Y	N	Y
4 ***Hastings***	Y	Y	Y	Y	Y	Y
5 ***Nethercutt***	Y	Y	Y	Y	Y	Y
6 Dicks	Y	Y	Y	Y	Y	Y
7 McDermott	Y	Y	Y	Y	N	Y
8 ***Dunn***	+	+	+	+	+	+
9 Smith	Y	Y	Y	Y	Y	Y
WEST VIRGINIA						
1 Mollohan	Y	Y	Y	Y	Y	Y
2 ***Capito***	Y	Y	Y	Y	Y	Y
3 Rahall	Y	Y	Y	Y	Y	Y
WISCONSIN						
1 ***Ryan***	Y	Y	Y	Y	Y	Y
2 Baldwin	Y	Y	Y	Y	Y	N
3 Kind	Y	Y	Y	Y	Y	N
4 Kleczka	Y	Y	Y	Y	Y	Y
5 Barrett	Y	Y	Y	Y	Y	N
6 ***Petri***	Y	Y	Y	Y	Y	N
7 Obey	Y	Y	Y	Y	Y	Y
8 ***Green***	Y	Y	Y	Y	Y	N
9 ***Sensenbrenner***	Y	Y	Y	Y	Y	N
WYOMING						
AL ***Cubin***	?	?	?	?	?	Y

Southern states - Ala., Ark., Fla., Ga., Ky., La., Miss., N.C., Okla., S.C., Tenn., Texas, Va.

Key

Y	Voted for (yea).
#	Paired for.
+	Announced for.
N	Voted against (nay).
X	Paired against.
−	Announced against.
P	Voted "present."
C	Voted "present" to avoid possible conflict of interest.
?	Did not vote or otherwise make a position known.

Democrats   **Republicans**
Independents

414. HR 2647. Fiscal 2002 Legislative Branch Appropriations/Rule. Adoption of the rule (H Res 273) to waive points of order and provide for House floor consideration of the conference report on the bill that would appropriate $2.97 billion for legislative branch operations in fiscal 2002. Adopted 423-0: R 215-0; D 206-0 (ND 153-0, SD 53-0); I 2-0. Oct. 31, 2001.

415. HR 2311. Fiscal 2002 Energy-Water Appropriations/Rule. Adoption of the rule (H Res 272) to provide for House floor consideration of the conference report on the bill that would appropriate $24.6 billion in fiscal 2002 for the Energy Department, the Army Corps of Engineers and other agencies, $2.1 billion more than the president's request. Adopted 421-2: R 214-0; D 205-2 (ND 154-2, SD 51-0); I 2-0. Nov. 1, 2001.

416. HR 2311. Fiscal 2002 Energy-Water Appropriations/Conference Report. Adoption of the conference report on the bill that would appropriate $24.6 billion in fiscal 2002 for the Energy Department, the Army Corps of Engineers and other agencies, $2.1 billion more than the president's request. Adopted (thus sent to the Senate) 399-29: R 203-14; D 194-15 (ND 144-13, SD 50-2); I 2-0. Nov. 1, 2001.

417. HR 2647. Fiscal 2002 Legislative Branch Appropriations/Conference Report. Adoption of the conference report on the bill that would appropriate $2.97 billion for legislative branch operations in fiscal 2002. The bill would provide $878 million for House operations and $607 million for the Senate, as well as funding for other congressional agencies including the Capitol Police, the Architect of the Capitol, the Congressional Budget Office and the Library of Congress. It includes a 4.6 percent cost of living increase for congressional staff. Adopted (thus sent to the Senate) 374-52: R 183-33; D 190-18 (ND 144-13, SD 46-5); I 1-1. Nov. 1, 2001.

418. Procedural Motion/Journal. Approval of the House Journal of Wednesday, Oct. 31, 2001. Approved 380-33: R 201-10; D 177-23 (ND 129-21, SD 48-2); I 2-0. Nov. 1, 2001.

419. HR 3150. Aviation Security/Previous Question. Reynolds, R-N.Y., motion to order the previous question (thus ending debate and possibility of amendment) on adoption of the rule (H Res 274) to provide for House floor consideration of the bill that would increase airline and airport security. Motion agreed to 218-207: R 215-1; D 2-205 (ND 1-154, SD 1-51); I 1-1. Nov. 1, 2001.

	414	415	416	417	418	419
ALABAMA						
1 *Callahan*	Y	Y	Y	Y	Y	Y
2 *Everett*	Y	Y	Y	Y	Y	Y
3 *Riley*	Y	Y	Y	Y	Y	Y
4 *Aderholt*	Y	Y	Y	Y	N	Y
5 Cramer	Y	Y	Y	Y	Y	N
6 *Bachus*	Y	Y	Y	Y	Y	Y
7 Hilliard	Y	Y	Y	Y	Y	N
ALASKA						
AL *Young*	Y	?	Y	Y	Y	Y
ARIZONA						
1 *Flake*	Y	Y	N	N	Y	Y
2 Pastor	Y	Y	Y	Y	Y	N
3 *Stump*	Y	Y	Y	Y	Y	Y
4 *Shadegg*	Y	Y	Y	N	Y	Y
5 *Kolbe*	Y	Y	Y	Y	Y	Y
6 *Hayworth*	Y	Y	Y	Y	Y	Y
ARKANSAS						
1 Berry	Y	Y	Y	N	Y	N
2 Snyder	Y	Y	Y	Y	Y	N
3 Vacant						
4 Ross	Y	Y	Y	Y	Y	N
CALIFORNIA						
1 Thompson	Y	Y	Y	Y	N	N
2 *Herger*	Y	?	N	Y	Y	Y
3 *Ose*	Y	Y	Y	Y	Y	Y
4 *Doolittle*	Y	Y	Y	Y	Y	Y
5 Matsui	Y	Y	Y	Y	Y	N
6 Woolsey	?	Y	Y	Y	Y	N
7 Miller, George	Y	Y	Y	Y	Y	N
8 Pelosi	Y	Y	Y	Y	Y	N
9 Lee	Y	Y	Y	Y	Y	N
10 Tauscher	Y	Y	Y	Y	Y	N
11 *Pombo*	Y	Y	Y	Y	Y	Y
12 Lantos	?	Y	Y	Y	Y	N
13 Stark	Y	N	Y	Y	Y	N
14 Eshoo	Y	Y	Y	Y	Y	N
15 Honda	Y	Y	Y	Y	Y	N
16 Lofgren	Y	Y	Y	Y	?	N
17 Farr	Y	Y	Y	Y	Y	N
18 Condit	Y	Y	Y	Y	Y	N
19 *Radanovich*	Y	Y	Y	Y	Y	Y
20 Dooley	Y	Y	Y	Y	Y	N
21 *Thomas*	Y	Y	Y	Y	Y	N
22 Capps	Y	Y	Y	Y	Y	N
23 *Gallegly*	Y	Y	Y	Y	Y	N
24 Sherman	Y	Y	Y	Y	Y	N
25 *McKeon*	Y	Y	Y	Y	Y	Y
26 Berman	Y	Y	Y	Y	Y	N
27 Schiff	Y	Y	Y	Y	Y	N
28 *Dreier*	Y	Y	Y	Y	Y	Y
29 Waxman	Y	Y	Y	Y	Y	N
30 Becerra	Y	Y	Y	Y	Y	N
31 Solis	Y	Y	Y	Y	Y	N
32 Watson	Y	Y	Y	Y	Y	N
33 Roybal-Allard	Y	Y	Y	Y	Y	N
34 Napolitano	Y	Y	Y	Y	Y	Y
35 Waters	Y	Y	Y	Y	N	N
36 Harman	Y	Y	Y	Y	Y	N
37 Millender-McD.	Y	Y	Y	Y	Y	N
38 *Horn*	Y	Y	Y	Y	Y	Y

	414	415	416	417	418	419
39 *Royce*	Y	Y	N	N	Y	Y
40 *Lewis*	Y	Y	Y	Y	Y	Y
41 *Miller, Gary*	Y	Y	Y	Y	Y	Y
42 Baca	Y	Y	Y	Y	Y	N
43 *Calvert*	Y	Y	Y	Y	Y	Y
44 *Bono*	Y	Y	Y	Y	Y	Y
45 *Rohrabacher*	Y	Y	Y	N	Y	Y
46 Sanchez	Y	Y	Y	Y	Y	N
47 *Cox*	Y	Y	Y	Y	Y	Y
48 *Issa*	Y	Y	Y	Y	Y	Y
49 Davis	Y	Y	Y	Y	Y	N
50 Filner	Y	Y	Y	Y	N	N
51 *Cunningham*	Y	Y	Y	Y	Y	Y
52 *Hunter*	Y	Y	Y	Y	Y	Y
COLORADO						
1 DeGette	?	Y	Y	Y	Y	N
2 Udall	Y	Y	Y	N	Y	N
3 *McInnis*	Y	Y	Y	N	Y	Y
4 *Schaffer*	Y	Y	N	N	N	Y
5 *Hefley*	Y	Y	Y	N	N	Y
6 *Tancredo*	Y	Y	N	N	P	Y
CONNECTICUT						
1 Larson	Y	Y	Y	Y	?	N
2 *Simmons*	Y	Y	Y	Y	Y	N
3 DeLauro	Y	Y	Y	Y	Y	N
4 *Shays*	Y	Y	N	N	Y	Y
5 Maloney	Y	Y	Y	Y	Y	N
6 *Johnson*	Y	Y	Y	Y	Y	?
DELAWARE						
AL *Castle*	Y	Y	Y	Y	Y	Y
FLORIDA						
1 *Miller, J.*	Y	Y	Y	Y	Y	Y
2 Boyd	Y	Y	Y	Y	Y	N
3 Brown	Y	?	Y	Y	Y	N
4 *Crenshaw*	Y	Y	Y	Y	Y	Y
5 Thurman	Y	Y	Y	Y	Y	N
6 *Stearns*	Y	N	N	Y	Y	Y
7 *Mica*	Y	Y	Y	Y	Y	Y
8 *Keller*	Y	Y	N	Y	Y	Y
9 *Bilirakis*	Y	Y	Y	Y	Y	Y
10 *Young*	Y	Y	Y	Y	?	Y
11 Davis	Y	Y	Y	Y	Y	Y
12 *Putnam*	Y	Y	Y	Y	Y	Y
13 *Miller, D.*	Y	Y	Y	Y	Y	Y
14 *Goss*	Y	Y	Y	Y	Y	Y
15 *Weldon*	Y	Y	N	N	Y	Y
16 *Foley*	Y	Y	Y	Y	Y	Y
17 Meek	Y	Y	Y	Y	Y	N
18 *Ros-Lehtinen*	Y	Y	Y	Y	Y	Y
19 Wexler	Y	?	Y	Y	Y	N
20 Deutsch	Y	Y	Y	N	Y	N
21 *Diaz-Balart*	Y	Y	Y	Y	Y	Y
22 *Shaw*	Y	Y	Y	Y	Y	Y
23 Hastings	Y	Y	Y	Y	N	N
GEORGIA						
1 *Kingston*	Y	Y	Y	Y	N	N
2 Bishop	Y	Y	Y	Y	Y	N
3 *Collins*	Y	Y	Y	Y	Y	Y
4 McKinney	Y	Y	?	?	?	N
5 Lewis	Y	Y	Y	Y	Y	N
6 *Isakson*	Y	Y	Y	Y	Y	Y
7 *Barr*	Y	Y	Y	N	Y	Y
8 *Chambliss*	Y	Y	Y	Y	Y	Y
9 *Deal*	Y	Y	Y	Y	Y	Y
10 *Norwood*	Y	Y	Y	Y	Y	Y
11 *Linder*	Y	Y	Y	Y	Y	Y
HAWAII						
1 Abercrombie	Y	Y	Y	Y	Y	N
2 Mink	Y	Y	Y	Y	Y	N
IDAHO						
1 *Otter*	Y	Y	Y	Y	Y	Y
2 *Simpson*	Y	Y	Y	Y	Y	Y
ILLINOIS						
1 Rush	Y	Y	Y	Y	Y	N
2 Jackson	Y	Y	Y	Y	Y	N
3 Lipinski	Y	Y	Y	Y	Y	N
4 Gutierrez	Y	Y	Y	Y	Y	N
5 Blagojevich	Y	Y	Y	Y	Y	N
6 *Hyde*	Y	Y	Y	Y	Y	Y
7 Davis	Y	Y	Y	Y	Y	N
8 *Crane*	Y	Y	Y	N	N	Y
9 Schakowsky	Y	Y	Y	Y	Y	N
10 *Kirk*	Y	Y	Y	Y	Y	Y
11 *Weller*	Y	Y	Y	Y	N	Y
12 Costello	Y	Y	Y	N	N	N
13 *Biggert*	Y	Y	Y	Y	Y	Y

ND Northern Democrats   SD Southern Democrats

	414	415	416	417	418	419
14 ***Hastert***						
15 ***Johnson***	Y	Y	Y	Y	Y	Y
16 ***Manzullo***	Y	Y	Y	Y	Y	Y
17 Evans	Y	Y	Y	Y	Y	N
18 ***LaHood***	Y	Y	Y	Y	Y	Y
19 Phelps	Y	Y	Y	Y	Y	N
20 ***Shimkus***	Y	Y	Y	Y	Y	Y
INDIANA						
1 Visclosky	Y	Y	Y	Y	N	N
2 ***Pence***	Y	Y	Y	Y	Y	Y
3 Roemer	Y	Y	Y	Y	Y	N
4 ***Souder***	Y	Y	Y	Y	Y	Y
5 ***Buyer***	Y	Y	Y	Y	Y	Y
6 ***Burton***	Y	Y	Y	Y	Y	Y
7 ***Kerns***	Y	Y	N	N	Y	Y
8 ***Hostettler***	Y	Y	N	Y	Y	Y
9 Hill	Y	Y	Y	Y	N	N
10 Carson	Y	Y	Y	Y	Y	N
IOWA						
1 ***Leach***	Y	Y	Y	Y	Y	Y
2 ***Nussle***	Y	Y	Y	Y	Y	Y
3 Boswell	Y	Y	Y	Y	Y	N
4 ***Ganske***	Y	Y	Y	Y	Y	Y
5 ***Latham***	Y	Y	Y	Y	Y	Y
KANSAS						
1 ***Moran***	Y	Y	Y	N	Y	Y
2 ***Ryun***	Y	Y	Y	N	Y	Y
3 Moore	Y	Y	Y	Y	Y	N
4 ***Tiahrt***	Y	Y	Y	Y	Y	Y
KENTUCKY						
1 ***Whitfield***	Y	Y	Y	Y	N	Y
2 ***Lewis***	Y	Y	Y	Y	Y	Y
3 ***Northup***	Y	Y	Y	Y	Y	Y
4 Lucas	Y	Y	Y	N	Y	N
5 ***Rogers***	Y	Y	Y	Y	Y	Y
6 ***Fletcher***	Y	Y	Y	Y	Y	Y
LOUISIANA						
1 ***Vitter***	Y	Y	Y	Y	Y	Y
2 Jefferson	Y	Y	Y	Y	?	N
3 ***Tauzin***	Y	Y	Y	Y	Y	Y
4 ***McCrery***	?	?	Y	Y	Y	Y
5 ***Cooksey***	Y	Y	Y	Y	Y	Y
6 ***Baker***	Y	Y	Y	Y	Y	Y
7 John	Y	Y	Y	Y	Y	N
MAINE						
1 Allen	Y	Y	Y	Y	Y	N
2 Baldacci	Y	Y	Y	Y	Y	N
MARYLAND						
1 ***Gilchrest***	Y	Y	Y	Y	Y	Y
2 ***Ehrlich***	Y	Y	Y	Y	Y	Y
3 Cardin	Y	Y	Y	Y	Y	N
4 Wynn	Y	Y	Y	Y	Y	N
5 Hoyer	Y	Y	Y	Y	Y	N
6 ***Bartlett***	Y	Y	Y	Y	?	Y
7 Cummings	Y	Y	Y	Y	Y	N
8 ***Morella***	Y	Y	Y	Y	Y	Y
MASSACHUSETTS						
1 Olver	Y	Y	Y	Y	?	N
2 Neal	Y	Y	Y	Y	Y	N
3 McGovern	Y	Y	Y	Y	N	N
4 Frank	Y	Y	Y	Y	Y	N
5 Meehan	Y	Y	Y	Y	Y	N
6 Tierney	Y	Y	Y	Y	Y	N
7 Markey	Y	Y	Y	Y	Y	N
8 Capuano	Y	Y	Y	Y	N	N
9 Lynch	Y	Y	Y	Y	?	N
10 Delahunt	Y	Y	Y	Y	Y	N
MICHIGAN						
1 Stupak	Y	Y	Y	Y	N	N
2 ***Hoekstra***	Y	Y	Y	Y	Y	Y
3 ***Ehlers***	Y	Y	Y	Y	Y	Y
4 ***Camp***	Y	Y	Y	Y	Y	Y
5 Barcia	Y	Y	Y	Y	Y	N
6 ***Upton***	Y	Y	Y	Y	Y	Y
7 ***Smith***	Y	Y	Y	N	Y	Y
8 ***Rogers***	Y	Y	N	Y	Y	Y
9 Kildee	Y	Y	Y	Y	Y	N
10 Bonior	Y	Y	Y	Y	Y	N
11 ***Knollenberg***	Y	Y	Y	Y	Y	Y
12 Levin	Y	Y	Y	Y	Y	N
13 Rivers	Y	Y	Y	Y	Y	N
14 Conyers	Y	Y	N	Y	Y	?
15 Kilpatrick	Y	Y	Y	Y	Y	N
16 Dingell	Y	Y	Y	Y	Y	N

	414	415	416	417	418	419
MINNESOTA						
1 ***Gutknecht***	Y	Y	Y	Y	Y	Y
2 ***Kennedy***	Y	Y	Y	Y	Y	Y
3 ***Ramstad***	Y	Y	Y	Y	N	Y
4 McCollum	Y	Y	Y	Y	Y	N
5 Sabo	Y	Y	Y	Y	N	N
6 Luther	Y	Y	Y	N	Y	N
7 Peterson	Y	Y	Y	Y	N	N
8 Oberstar	Y	Y	Y	Y	N	N
MISSISSIPPI						
1 ***Wicker***	Y	Y	Y	Y	Y	Y
2 Thompson	?	?	?	?	?	?
3 ***Pickering***	Y	Y	Y	Y	Y	Y
4 Shows	Y	Y	Y	Y	Y	N
5 Taylor	Y	Y	Y	–	N	N
MISSOURI						
1 Clay	Y	Y	Y	Y	Y	N
2 ***Akin***	Y	Y	Y	Y	Y	Y
3 Gephardt	Y	Y	Y	Y	Y	N
4 Skelton	Y	Y	Y	Y	Y	N
5 McCarthy	Y	Y	Y	Y	Y	N
6 ***Graves***	Y	Y	Y	N	Y	Y
7 ***Blunt***	Y	Y	Y	Y	Y	Y
8 ***Emerson***	Y	Y	Y	Y	Y	Y
9 ***Hulshof***	Y	Y	Y	N	Y	Y
MONTANA						
AL ***Rehberg***	Y	Y	Y	Y	Y	Y
NEBRASKA						
1 ***Bereuter***	Y	Y	Y	Y	Y	Y
2 ***Terry***	Y	Y	Y	Y	Y	Y
3 ***Osborne***	Y	Y	Y	Y	Y	Y
NEVADA						
1 Berkley	Y	N	N	Y	Y	N
2 ***Gibbons***	Y	Y	N	Y	Y	Y
NEW HAMPSHIRE						
1 ***Sununu***	Y	Y	Y	Y	Y	Y
2 ***Bass***	Y	Y	Y	Y	Y	Y
NEW JERSEY						
1 Andrews	?	Y	N	Y	Y	N
2 ***LoBiondo***	Y	Y	Y	Y	N	Y
3 ***Saxton***	Y	Y	Y	Y	Y	Y
4 ***Smith***	Y	Y	Y	Y	Y	Y
5 ***Roukema***	Y	Y	Y	Y	Y	Y
6 Pallone	Y	Y	Y	Y	Y	N
7 ***Ferguson***	Y	Y	Y	Y	Y	Y
8 Pascrell	Y	Y	Y	Y	Y	N
9 Rothman	Y	Y	Y	Y	Y	N
10 Payne	Y	Y	N	Y	?	N
11 ***Frelinghuysen***	Y	Y	Y	Y	Y	Y
12 Holt	Y	Y	N	N	Y	N
13 Menendez	Y	Y	Y	N	Y	N
NEW MEXICO						
1 ***Wilson***	Y	Y	Y	Y	Y	Y
2 ***Skeen***	Y	Y	Y	Y	Y	Y
3 Udall	Y	Y	Y	N	N	N
NEW YORK						
1 ***Grucci***	Y	Y	Y	Y	Y	Y
2 Israel	Y	Y	Y	N	Y	N
3 ***King***	Y	Y	Y	Y	Y	Y
4 McCarthy	Y	Y	Y	Y	?	N
5 Ackerman	Y	Y	Y	Y	Y	N
6 Meeks	Y	Y	Y	Y	Y	N
7 Crowley	Y	Y	Y	Y	Y	N
8 Nadler	Y	Y	Y	Y	?	N
9 Weiner	Y	Y	Y	Y	Y	N
10 Towns	Y	Y	Y	Y	Y	N
11 Owens	Y	Y	N	Y	Y	N
12 Velázquez	Y	Y	Y	Y	Y	N
13 ***Fossella***	Y	Y	Y	Y	Y	Y
14 Maloney	Y	Y	Y	Y	Y	N
15 Rangel	Y	Y	Y	Y	Y	?
16 Serrano	Y	Y	Y	Y	Y	N
17 Engel	Y	Y	Y	Y	Y	N
18 Lowey	Y	Y	Y	Y	Y	N
19 ***Kelly***	Y	Y	Y	Y	Y	Y
20 ***Gilman***	Y	Y	Y	Y	Y	Y
21 McNulty	Y	Y	Y	Y	Y	N
22 ***Sweeney***	?	Y	Y	Y	Y	Y
23 ***Boehlert***	Y	Y	Y	Y	Y	Y
24 ***McHugh***	Y	Y	Y	Y	Y	Y
25 ***Walsh***	Y	Y	Y	Y	?	Y
26 Hinchey	Y	Y	Y	Y	Y	N
27 ***Reynolds***	Y	Y	Y	Y	Y	Y
28 Slaughter	Y	Y	Y	Y	Y	N
29 LaFalce	Y	Y	Y	Y	Y	N

	414	415	416	417	418	419
30 ***Quinn***	Y	Y	Y	Y	Y	Y
31 ***Houghton***	Y	Y	Y	Y	Y	Y
NORTH CAROLINA						
1 Clayton	Y	Y	Y	Y	Y	N
2 Etheridge	Y	Y	N	Y	Y	N
3 ***Jones***	Y	Y	Y	N	Y	Y
4 Price	Y	Y	Y	Y	Y	N
5 ***Burr***	Y	Y	Y	Y	Y	Y
6 ***Coble***	Y	Y	Y	Y	Y	Y
7 McIntyre	Y	Y	Y	Y	Y	N
8 ***Hayes***	Y	Y	Y	Y	Y	Y
9 ***Myrick***	Y	Y	Y	Y	Y	Y
10 ***Ballenger***	Y	Y	Y	Y	Y	Y
11 ***Taylor***	Y	Y	Y	Y	Y	Y
12 Watt	Y	Y	Y	Y	Y	N
NORTH DAKOTA						
AL Pomeroy	Y	Y	Y	Y	Y	N
OHIO						
1 ***Chabot***	Y	Y	Y	N	Y	Y
2 ***Portman***	Y	Y	Y	Y	Y	Y
3 Hall	Y	?	Y	Y	Y	N
4 ***Oxley***	Y	Y	Y	Y	Y	Y
5 ***Gillmor***	Y	Y	Y	Y	Y	Y
6 Strickland	Y	Y	Y	N	N	N
7 ***Hobson***	Y	Y	Y	Y	Y	Y
8 ***Boehner***	Y	Y	Y	Y	Y	Y
9 Kaptur	Y	Y	Y	Y	Y	N
10 Kucinich	Y	Y	N	N	Y	N
11 Jones	Y	Y	Y	Y	Y	N
12 ***Tiberi***	Y	Y	Y	Y	Y	Y
13 Brown	Y	Y	N	N	N	N
14 Sawyer	Y	Y	Y	Y	Y	N
15 ***Pryce***	Y	Y	Y	Y	?	Y
16 ***Regula***	Y	Y	Y	Y	Y	Y
17 Traficant	Y	Y	Y	Y	Y	Y
18 ***Ney***	Y	Y	Y	Y	Y	Y
19 ***LaTourette***	Y	Y	Y	Y	Y	Y
OKLAHOMA						
1 ***Largent***	Y	Y	Y	Y	Y	Y
2 Carson	Y	Y	Y	Y	Y	N
3 ***Watkins***	Y	Y	Y	Y	Y	Y
4 ***Watts***	Y	Y	Y	Y	Y	Y
5 ***Istook***	Y	Y	Y	Y	Y	Y
6 ***Lucas***	Y	Y	Y	Y	Y	Y
OREGON						
1 Wu	Y	Y	N	Y	Y	N
2 ***Walden***	Y	Y	N	Y	Y	Y
3 Blumenauer	Y	Y	Y	Y	Y	N
4 DeFazio	Y	Y	N	Y	N	N
5 Hooley	Y	Y	Y	Y	Y	N
PENNSYLVANIA						
1 Brady	Y	Y	Y	Y	Y	N
2 Fattah	Y	Y	Y	Y	Y	N
3 Borski	Y	Y	Y	Y	N	N
4 ***Hart***	Y	Y	Y	Y	Y	Y
5 ***Peterson***	Y	Y	Y	Y	Y	Y
6 Holden	Y	Y	Y	Y	Y	N
7 ***Weldon***	Y	Y	Y	Y	Y	Y
8 ***Greenwood***	Y	Y	Y	Y	Y	?
9 ***Shuster, Bill***	Y	Y	Y	Y	Y	Y
10 ***Sherwood***	Y	Y	Y	Y	Y	Y
11 Kanjorski	Y	Y	Y	Y	Y	N
12 Murtha	Y	Y	Y	Y	Y	N
13 Hoeffel	Y	Y	Y	Y	Y	N
14 Coyne	Y	Y	Y	Y	Y	N
15 ***Toomey***	Y	Y	Y	N	Y	Y
16 ***Pitts***	Y	Y	N	N	Y	Y
17 ***Gekas***	Y	Y	Y	?	Y	Y
18 Doyle	Y	Y	Y	Y	Y	N
19 ***Platts***	Y	Y	Y	Y	Y	Y
20 Mascara	Y	Y	Y	Y	Y	N
21 ***English***	Y	Y	Y	Y	N	Y
RHODE ISLAND						
1 Kennedy	Y	Y	Y	Y	Y	N
2 Langevin	Y	Y	Y	Y	Y	N
SOUTH CAROLINA						
1 ***Brown***	Y	Y	Y	Y	Y	Y
2 Vacant						
3 ***Graham***	Y	Y	Y	Y	?	Y
4 ***DeMint***	Y	Y	Y	Y	Y	Y
5 Spratt	Y	Y	Y	Y	Y	N
6 Clyburn	Y	Y	Y	Y	Y	N
SOUTH DAKOTA						
AL ***Thune***	Y	Y	Y	N	Y	Y

	414	415	416	417	418	419
TENNESSEE						
1 ***Jenkins***	Y	Y	Y	Y	Y	Y
2 ***Duncan***	Y	Y	Y	Y	Y	Y
3 ***Wamp***	Y	Y	Y	Y	Y	Y
4 ***Hilleary***	Y	Y	Y	Y	Y	Y
5 Clement	Y	Y	Y	Y	Y	N
6 Gordon	Y	Y	Y	Y	Y	N
7 ***Bryant***	Y	Y	Y	Y	Y	Y
8 Tanner	Y	Y	Y	Y	Y	N
9 Ford	Y	Y	Y	Y	Y	N
TEXAS						
1 Sandlin	Y	Y	Y	Y	Y	N
2 Turner	Y	Y	Y	Y	Y	N
3 ***Johnson, Sam***	Y	Y	Y	Y	Y	Y
4 Hall	Y	Y	Y	Y	Y	Y
5 ***Sessions***	Y	Y	Y	Y	Y	Y
6 ***Barton***	Y	Y	Y	Y	Y	Y
7 ***Culberson***	Y	Y	Y	Y	Y	Y
8 ***Brady***	Y	Y	Y	N	Y	Y
9 Lampson	Y	Y	Y	Y	Y	N
10 Doggett	Y	Y	N	N	Y	N
11 Edwards	Y	Y	Y	Y	?	N
12 ***Granger***	?	Y	Y	Y	Y	Y
13 ***Thornberry***	Y	Y	Y	Y	Y	Y
14 ***Paul***	Y	Y	N	N	Y	Y
15 Hinojosa	Y	Y	Y	Y	Y	N
16 Reyes	Y	Y	Y	Y	Y	N
17 Stenholm	Y	Y	Y	Y	Y	N
18 Jackson-Lee	Y	Y	Y	Y	Y	N
19 ***Combest***	Y	Y	Y	Y	Y	Y
20 Gonzalez	Y	Y	Y	Y	Y	N
21 ***Smith***	Y	Y	Y	Y	Y	Y
22 ***DeLay***	Y	Y	Y	Y	Y	Y
23 ***Bonilla***	Y	Y	Y	Y	Y	Y
24 Frost	Y	Y	Y	Y	Y	N
25 Bentsen	Y	Y	Y	Y	Y	N
26 ***Armey***	Y	Y	Y	Y	Y	Y
27 Ortiz	Y	Y	Y	Y	Y	N
28 Rodriguez	Y	Y	Y	Y	Y	N
29 Green	Y	Y	Y	N	Y	?
30 Johnson, E.B.	Y	Y	Y	Y	Y	N
UTAH						
1 ***Hansen***	Y	Y	Y	Y	Y	Y
2 Matheson	Y	Y	Y	Y	Y	N
3 ***Cannon***	Y	Y	Y	Y	Y	Y
VERMONT						
AL *Sanders*	Y	Y	Y	Y	Y	N
VIRGINIA						
1 ***Davis, Jo Ann***	Y	Y	Y	Y	Y	Y
2 ***Schrock***	Y	Y	Y	Y	Y	Y
3 Scott	Y	Y	Y	Y	Y	N
4 ***Forbes***	Y	Y	Y	Y	Y	Y
5 *Goode*	Y	Y	Y	N	Y	Y
6 ***Goodlatte***	Y	Y	Y	N	Y	Y
7 ***Cantor***	Y	Y	Y	Y	Y	Y
8 Moran	Y	Y	Y	Y	Y	N
9 Boucher	Y	Y	Y	Y	Y	N
10 ***Wolf***	Y	Y	Y	Y	Y	Y
11 ***Davis, T.***	Y	Y	Y	Y	Y	Y
WASHINGTON						
1 Inslee	Y	Y	N	N	Y	N
2 Larsen	Y	Y	Y	Y	N	N
3 Baird	Y	Y	Y	Y	N	N
4 ***Hastings***	Y	Y	Y	Y	Y	Y
5 ***Nethercutt***	Y	Y	Y	Y	Y	Y
6 Dicks	Y	Y	Y	Y	Y	N
7 McDermott	Y	Y	N	Y	N	N
8 ***Dunn***	+	?	?	?	?	?
9 Smith	Y	Y	Y	Y	Y	N
WEST VIRGINIA						
1 Mollohan	Y	Y	Y	Y	Y	N
2 ***Capito***	Y	Y	Y	Y	Y	Y
3 Rahall	Y	Y	Y	Y	Y	N
WISCONSIN						
1 ***Ryan***	Y	Y	Y	N	Y	Y
2 Baldwin	Y	Y	Y	Y	Y	N
3 Kind	Y	Y	Y	N	Y	N
4 Kleczka	Y	Y	Y	Y	Y	N
5 Barrett	Y	Y	Y	N	Y	N
6 ***Petri***	Y	Y	Y	N	Y	Y
7 Obey	Y	Y	N	Y	Y	N
8 ***Green***	Y	Y	Y	N	Y	Y
9 ***Sensenbrenner***	Y	Y	N	N	Y	Y
WYOMING						
AL ***Cubin***	Y	?	?	?	?	Y

Southern states - Ala., Ark., Fla., Ga., Ky., La., Miss., N.C., Okla., S.C., Tenn., Texas, Va.

420. HR 3150. Aviation Security/Amendment to the Rule. Reynolds, R-N.Y., amendment to the Young, R-Alaska, amendment made in order under the rule (H Res 274) to provide for House floor consideration of the bill that would increase airline and airport security. The Reynolds amendment would create a hiring preference for laid-off airline workers as airport screeners, eliminate a provision exempting some compensation from salary and benefits caps in the aviation assistance law enacted in September (PL 107-42), require a preference for U.S.-owned companies in contracts for screening services, and order an itemized list of security expenses by airports seeking reimbursement under the act. Adopted 379-50: R 216-2; D 161-48 (ND 120-36, SD 41-12); I 2-0. (Subsequently, the rule was adopted by voice vote.) Nov. 1, 2001.

421. HR 3150. Aviation Security/Manager's Amendment. Young, R-Alaska, amendment that would add provisions broadening liability caps in the aviation assistance law (PL 107-42) to any party sued as a result of the Sept. 11 terrorist attacks. It also would require that all airport screeners be deputized as federal transportation agents, order the screening of as much baggage as possible for explosives, require additional employee background checks, authorize airports and related service companies to use $1.5 billion for security reimbursement, and order airlines to honor tickets from other carries whose flights were disrupted by terrorism, war or bankruptcy. Adopted 223-202: R 210-6; D 12-195 (ND 6-149, SD 6-46); I 1-1. Nov. 1, 2001.

422. HR 3150. Aviation Security/Motion to Rise. DeFazio, D-Ore., motion to rise from the Committee of the Whole. Motion rejected 11-402: R 0-208; D 11-192 (ND 8-143, SD 3-49); I 0-2. Nov. 1, 2001.

423. HR 3150. Aviation Security/Democratic Substitute. Oberstar, D-Minn., amendment that would federalize passenger and baggage screeners at the country's largest 140 airports and give the Justice Department responsibility for airport and airline security. It includes additional security provisions similar to those in the underlying bill but would not broaden liability caps. Rejected 214-218: R 8-211; D 205-6 (ND 154-3, SD 51-3); I 1-1. A "nay" was a vote in support of the president's position. Nov. 1, 2001.

424. HR 3150. Aviation Security/Recommit. Oberstar, D-Minn., motion to recommit the bill to the House Transportation and Infrastructure Committee with instructions to add language that would create the Transportation Security Administration under the Transportation Department, call for the development of a personnel system to hire and train screeners, and establish rules and standards for screeners to follow. Motion rejected 201-227: R 0-217; D 200-9 (ND 151-4, SD 49-5); I 1-1. Nov. 1, 2001.

425. HR 3150. Aviation Security/Passage. Passage of the bill that would establishes a new security agency within the Transportation Department to assume federal control of U.S. airport security and screening services. Uniformed officers from the agency would directly supervise passenger and baggage screeners, who could be either federal employees or federally trained private contract workers, but who would have to comply with more stringent employment, training and performance standards. Other safeguards would include armed air marshals, anti-hijacking training for flight crews, stronger cockpit doors, law enforcement oversight at screening areas, and background checks for individuals in secure areas. Passengers would pay $2.50 for each segment of a flight to help pay for enhanced security. Passed 286-139: R 211-2; D 74-136 (ND 49-107, SD 25-29); I 1-1. A "yea" was a vote in support of the president's position. Nov. 1, 2001.

Key

Y	Voted for (yea).
#	Paired for.
+	Announced for.
N	Voted against (nay).
X	Paired against.
–	Announced against.
P	Voted "present."
C	Voted "present" to avoid possible conflict of interest.
?	Did not vote or otherwise make a position known.

Democrats **Republicans**
Independents

		420	421	422	423	424	425
ALABAMA							
1	*Callahan*	Y	Y	N	N	N	Y
2	*Everett*	Y	Y	N	N	N	Y
3	*Riley*	Y	Y	N	N	N	?
4	*Aderholt*	Y	Y	N	N	N	Y
5	Cramer	N	Y	N	N	N	Y
6	*Bachus*	Y	Y	N	N	N	Y
7	Hilliard	Y	N	Y	Y	Y	N
ALASKA							
AL	*Young*	Y	Y	N	N	N	Y
ARIZONA							
1	*Flake*	N	N	N	N	N	Y
2	Pastor	N	N	Y	Y	Y	N
3	*Stump*	Y	Y	N	N	N	Y
4	*Shadegg*	Y	Y	N	N	N	Y
5	*Kolbe*	Y	Y	N	N	N	Y
6	*Hayworth*	Y	Y	N	N	N	Y
ARKANSAS							
1	Berry	N	N	N	Y	Y	N
2	Snyder	Y	N	N	Y	Y	Y
3	Vacant						
4	Ross	Y	N	N	Y	Y	Y
CALIFORNIA							
1	Thompson	Y	N	N	Y	Y	N
2	*Herger*	Y	Y	N	N	N	?
3	*Ose*	Y	Y	N	N	N	Y
4	*Doolittle*	Y	Y	N	N	N	Y
5	Matsui	Y	N	N	Y	Y	N
6	Woolsey	N	N	N	Y	Y	N
7	Miller, George	N	N	N	Y	Y	N
8	Pelosi	N	N	N	Y	Y	N
9	Lee	N	N	N	Y	Y	N
10	Tauscher	N	N	N	Y	Y	N
11	*Pombo*	Y	Y	N	N	N	Y
12	Lantos	Y	N	N	Y	Y	N
13	Stark	N	N	N	Y	Y	N
14	Eshoo	Y	N	N	Y	Y	N
15	Honda	Y	N	Y	Y	Y	N
16	Lofgren	Y	N	N	Y	Y	N
17	Farr	Y	N	N	Y	Y	N
18	Condit	Y	N	N	Y	Y	Y
19	*Radanovich*	Y	Y	?	N	N	Y
20	Dooley	Y	N	N	Y	Y	N
21	*Thomas*	Y	Y	N	N	N	Y
22	Capps	Y	N	N	Y	Y	N
23	*Gallegly*	Y	N	N	N	N	Y
24	Sherman	Y	N	N	Y	Y	N
25	*McKeon*	Y	Y	N	N	N	?
26	Berman	Y	N	N	Y	Y	N
27	Schiff	Y	N	N	Y	Y	N
28	*Dreier*	Y	Y	N	N	N	Y
29	Waxman	Y	N	N	Y	Y	N
30	Becerra	Y	N	N	Y	Y	N
31	Solis	Y	N	N	Y	Y	N
32	Watson	Y	N	N	Y	Y	N
33	Roybal-Allard	Y	N	N	Y	Y	N
34	Napolitano	Y	N	N	Y	Y	N
35	Waters	Y	N	N	Y	Y	N
36	Harman	Y	N	N	Y	Y	Y
37	Millender-McD.	Y	N	N	Y	Y	N
38	*Horn*	Y	Y	N	N	N	Y
39	*Royce*	Y	Y	N	N	N	Y
40	*Lewis*	Y	Y	N	N	N	Y
41	*Miller, Gary*	Y	Y	N	N	N	Y
42	Baca	Y	N	N	Y	Y	N
43	*Calvert*	Y	Y	N	N	N	Y
44	*Bono*	Y	Y	N	N	N	Y
45	*Rohrabacher*	Y	Y	N	N	N	Y
46	Sanchez	N	N	N	Y	Y	N
47	*Cox*	Y	Y	N	N	N	Y
48	*Issa*	Y	Y	N	N	N	Y
49	Davis	Y	N	N	Y	Y	N
50	Filner	N	N	N	Y	Y	N
51	*Cunningham*	Y	Y	N	N	N	Y
52	*Hunter*	Y	Y	N	N	N	Y
COLORADO							
1	DeGette	Y	N	N	Y	Y	N
2	Udall	Y	N	N	Y	Y	Y
3	*McInnis*	Y	Y	N	N	N	Y
4	*Schaffer*	Y	Y	N	N	N	Y
5	*Hefley*	Y	Y	N	N	N	Y
6	*Tancredo*	Y	Y	N	N	N	Y
CONNECTICUT							
1	Larson	Y	N	N	Y	Y	N
2	*Simmons*	Y	Y	N	N	N	Y
3	DeLauro	Y	N	N	Y	Y	N
4	*Shays*	Y	Y	N	N	N	Y
5	Maloney	Y	N	?	Y	N	N
6	*Johnson*	Y	Y	N	N	N	Y
DELAWARE							
AL	*Castle*	Y	Y	N	N	N	Y
FLORIDA							
1	*Miller, J.*	Y	Y	N	N	N	Y
2	Boyd	Y	N	N	Y	Y	Y
3	Brown	N	N	Y	Y	Y	N
4	*Crenshaw*	Y	Y	N	N	N	Y
5	Thurman	Y	N	N	Y	Y	N
6	*Stearns*	Y	N	N	N	N	Y
7	*Mica*	Y	Y	N	N	N	Y
8	*Keller*	Y	Y	N	N	N	Y
9	*Bilirakis*	Y	Y	N	N	N	Y
10	*Young*	Y	Y	N	N	N	Y
11	Davis	Y	N	N	Y	Y	Y
12	*Putnam*	Y	Y	N	N	N	Y
13	*Miller, D.*	Y	Y	N	N	N	Y
14	*Goss*	Y	Y	N	N	N	Y
15	*Weldon*	Y	Y	N	N	N	Y
16	*Foley*	Y	Y	?	N	N	Y
17	Meek	Y	N	N	Y	Y	N
18	*Ros-Lehtinen*	Y	Y	N	N	N	Y
19	Wexler	Y	N	N	Y	Y	N
20	Deutsch	N	N	N	Y	Y	N
21	*Diaz-Balart*	Y	Y	N	N	N	Y
22	*Shaw*	Y	Y	?	N	N	Y
23	Hastings	N	N	Y	Y	Y	N
GEORGIA							
1	*Kingston*	Y	Y	N	N	N	Y
2	Bishop	N	N	N	Y	Y	Y
3	*Collins*	Y	Y	N	N	N	Y
4	McKinney	Y	N	N	Y	Y	N
5	Lewis	Y	N	N	Y	Y	N
6	*Isakson*	Y	Y	N	N	N	Y
7	*Barr*	Y	Y	N	N	N	Y
8	*Chambliss*	Y	Y	N	N	N	Y
9	*Deal*	Y	Y	N	N	N	Y
10	*Norwood*	Y	Y	N	N	N	Y
11	*Linder*	Y	Y	N	N	N	Y
HAWAII							
1	Abercrombie	Y	N	N	Y	N	Y
2	Mink	N	N	?	Y	Y	Y
IDAHO							
1	*Otter*	Y	Y	N	N	N	Y
2	*Simpson*	Y	Y	N	N	N	Y
ILLINOIS							
1	Rush	Y	N	N	Y	Y	Y
2	Jackson	N	N	N	Y	Y	N
3	Lipinski	Y	N	N	Y	Y	Y
4	Gutierrez	Y	N	?	N	Y	N
5	Blagojevich	Y	N	N	N	N	Y
6	*Hyde*	Y	Y	N	N	N	Y
7	Davis	Y	N	N	Y	Y	Y
8	*Crane*	Y	Y	N	N	N	Y
9	Schakowsky	Y	N	N	Y	Y	N
10	*Kirk*	Y	Y	N	N	N	Y
11	*Weller*	Y	Y	N	N	N	Y
12	Costello	Y	N	N	Y	Y	N
13	*Biggert*	Y	Y	N	N	N	Y

ND Northern Democrats   SD Southern Democrats

	420	421	422	423	424	425
14 ***Hastert***				N	N	Y
15 ***Johnson***	Y	Y	N	N	N	Y
16 ***Manzullo***	Y	Y	N	N	N	Y
17 Evans	N	N	N	Y	Y	Y
18 ***LaHood***	Y	Y	N	N	N	Y
19 Phelps	Y	N	N	Y	Y	Y
20 ***Shimkus***	Y	Y	N	N	N	Y
INDIANA						
1 Visclosky	N	N	N	Y	Y	N
2 ***Pence***	Y	Y	N	N	N	Y
3 Roemer	Y	N	N	Y	Y	Y
4 ***Souder***	Y	Y	N	N	N	Y
5 ***Buyer***	Y	Y	N	N	N	Y
6 ***Burton***	Y	Y	N	N	N	Y
7 ***Kerns***	Y	Y	N	N	N	Y
8 ***Hostettler***	Y	Y	N	N	N	Y
9 Hill	Y	N	N	Y	Y	N
10 Carson	N	N	N	Y	Y	N
IOWA						
1 ***Leach***	Y	N	N	Y	N	Y
2 ***Nussle***	Y	Y	N	N	N	Y
3 Boswell	Y	N	N	Y	Y	Y
4 ***Ganske***	Y	N	N	Y	?	?
5 ***Latham***	Y	Y	N	N	N	Y
KANSAS						
1 ***Moran***	Y	Y	N	N	N	Y
2 ***Ryun***	Y	Y	N	N	N	Y
3 Moore	Y	N	N	Y	Y	Y
4 ***Tiahrt***	Y	Y	N	N	N	Y
KENTUCKY						
1 ***Whitfield***	Y	Y	N	N	N	Y
2 ***Lewis***	Y	Y	N	N	N	Y
3 ***Northup***	Y	Y	N	N	N	Y
4 Lucas	Y	Y	N	Y	Y	Y
5 ***Rogers***	Y	Y	N	N	N	Y
6 ***Fletcher***	Y	Y	N	N	N	Y
LOUISIANA						
1 ***Vitter***	Y	Y	N	N	N	Y
2 Jefferson	Y	N	N	Y	Y	N
3 ***Tauzin***	Y	Y	N	N	N	Y
4 ***McCrery***	Y	Y	?	N	N	Y
5 ***Cooksey***	Y	Y	N	N	N	Y
6 ***Baker***	Y	Y	N	N	N	Y
7 John	Y	Y	N	Y	Y	Y
MAINE						
1 Allen	Y	N	N	Y	Y	N
2 Baldacci	Y	N	N	Y	Y	N
MARYLAND						
1 ***Gilchrest***	Y	Y	N	N	N	Y
2 ***Ehrlich***	Y	Y	N	N	N	Y
3 Cardin	Y	N	N	Y	Y	Y
4 Wynn	Y	N	N	Y	Y	N
5 Hoyer	Y	N	N	Y	Y	N
6 ***Bartlett***	Y	Y	N	N	N	Y
7 Cummings	N	N	N	Y	Y	N
8 ***Morella***	Y	N	N	Y	N	Y
MASSACHUSETTS						
1 Olver	N	N	N	Y	Y	N
2 Neal	Y	N	N	Y	Y	N
3 McGovern	Y	N	N	Y	Y	N
4 Frank	Y	N	N	Y	Y	N
5 Meehan	Y	N	N	Y	Y	N
6 Tierney	Y	N	N	Y	Y	N
7 Markey	Y	N	N	Y	Y	N
8 Capuano	Y	N	Y	Y	Y	N
9 Lynch	Y	N	N	Y	Y	N
10 Delahunt	Y	N	N	Y	?	?
MICHIGAN						
1 Stupak	N	N	N	Y	Y	N
2 ***Hoekstra***	Y	Y	N	N	N	Y
3 ***Ehlers***	Y	Y	N	N	N	Y
4 ***Camp***	Y	Y	N	N	N	Y
5 Barcia	Y	N	N	Y	Y	N
6 ***Upton***	Y	Y	N	N	N	Y
7 ***Smith***	Y	Y	N	N	N	Y
8 ***Rogers***	Y	Y	N	N	N	Y
9 Kildee	Y	N	N	Y	Y	Y
10 Bonior	Y	N	N	Y	Y	Y
11 ***Knollenberg***	Y	Y	N	N	N	Y
12 Levin	Y	N	N	Y	Y	N
13 Rivers	Y	N	N	Y	Y	N
14 Conyers	N	N	N	Y	Y	N
15 Kilpatrick	N	N	N	Y	Y	N
16 Dingell	N	N	N	Y	Y	Y

	420	421	422	423	424	425
MINNESOTA						
1 ***Gutknecht***	Y	Y	N	N	N	Y
2 ***Kennedy***	Y	Y	N	N	N	Y
3 ***Ramstad***	Y	N	N	Y	N	Y
4 McCollum	N	N	N	Y	Y	Y
5 Sabo	N	N	N	Y	Y	N
6 Luther	Y	N	N	Y	Y	Y
7 Peterson	Y	Y	N	Y	Y	Y
8 Oberstar	N	N	N	Y	Y	N
MISSISSIPPI						
1 ***Wicker***	Y	Y	N	N	N	Y
2 Thompson	?	?	?	Y	Y	N
3 ***Pickering***	Y	Y	N	N	N	Y
4 Shows	Y	N	N	Y	Y	Y
5 Taylor	Y	Y	N	Y	N	Y
MISSOURI						
1 Clay	Y	N	?	Y	Y	N
2 ***Akin***	Y	Y	N	N	N	Y
3 Gephardt	?	N	N	Y	Y	N
4 Skelton	Y	N	N	Y	Y	Y
5 McCarthy	Y	N	N	Y	Y	N
6 ***Graves***	Y	Y	N	N	N	Y
7 ***Blunt***	Y	Y	N	N	N	Y
8 ***Emerson***	Y	Y	N	Y	N	Y
9 ***Hulshof***	Y	Y	N	N	N	Y
MONTANA						
AL ***Rehberg***	Y	Y	N	N	N	Y
NEBRASKA						
1 ***Bereuter***	Y	Y	N	N	N	Y
2 ***Terry***	Y	Y	N	N	N	Y
3 ***Osborne***	Y	Y	N	N	N	Y
NEVADA						
1 Berkley	Y	?	N	Y	Y	N
2 ***Gibbons***	Y	Y	N	N	N	Y
NEW HAMPSHIRE						
1 ***Sununu***	Y	Y	N	N	N	Y
2 ***Bass***	Y	Y	N	N	N	Y
NEW JERSEY						
1 Andrews	N	N	N	Y	Y	Y
2 ***LoBiondo***	Y	Y	N	N	N	Y
3 ***Saxton***	Y	Y	N	N	N	Y
4 ***Smith***	Y	Y	N	Y	N	Y
5 ***Roukema***	Y	Y	N	Y	N	Y
6 Pallone	Y	N	N	Y	Y	N
7 ***Ferguson***	Y	Y	N	N	N	Y
8 Pascrell	Y	N	N	Y	Y	N
9 Rothman	Y	N	N	Y	Y	N
10 Payne	Y	N	N	Y	Y	N
11 ***Frelinghuysen***	Y	Y	N	N	N	Y
12 Holt	Y	N	N	Y	Y	N
13 Menendez	Y	N	N	Y	Y	N
NEW MEXICO						
1 ***Wilson***	Y	Y	N	N	N	Y
2 ***Skeen***	Y	Y	N	N	N	Y
3 Udall	Y	N	N	Y	Y	N
NEW YORK						
1 ***Grucci***	Y	Y	N	N	N	Y
2 Israel	Y	N	N	Y	Y	Y
3 ***King***	Y	Y	N	N	N	Y
4 McCarthy	Y	N	N	Y	Y	N
5 Ackerman	Y	N	N	Y	Y	N
6 Meeks	Y	N	N	Y	Y	N
7 Crowley	Y	N	N	Y	Y	N
8 Nadler	Y	N	N	Y	Y	N
9 Weiner	Y	N	N	Y	Y	N
10 Towns	N	N	N	Y	Y	N
11 Owens	N	N	N	Y	Y	N
12 Velázquez	Y	N	N	Y	Y	N
13 ***Fossella***	Y	Y	N	N	N	Y
14 Maloney	Y	N	Y	Y	Y	Y
15 Rangel	Y	N	Y	Y	Y	N
16 Serrano	Y	N	N	Y	?	Y
17 Engel	Y	N	N	Y	Y	Y
18 Lowey	Y	N	N	Y	Y	N
19 ***Kelly***	Y	Y	N	N	N	Y
20 ***Gilman***	Y	Y	N	N	N	Y
21 McNulty	Y	N	N	Y	Y	N
22 ***Sweeney***	Y	Y	N	N	N	Y
23 ***Boehlert***	Y	Y	N	N	N	Y
24 ***McHugh***	Y	Y	N	N	N	Y
25 ***Walsh***	Y	Y	N	N	N	Y
26 Hinchey	N	N	N	Y	Y	N
27 ***Reynolds***	Y	Y	N	N	N	Y
28 Slaughter	Y	N	N	Y	Y	N
29 LaFalce	Y	N	N	Y	Y	Y

	420	421	422	423	424	425
30 ***Quinn***	Y	Y	N	N	N	Y
31 ***Houghton***	Y	Y	N	N	N	?
NORTH CAROLINA						
1 Clayton	Y	N	N	Y	Y	N
2 Etheridge	Y	N	N	Y	Y	Y
3 ***Jones***	Y	Y	?	N	N	Y
4 Price	Y	N	N	Y	Y	Y
5 ***Burr***	Y	Y	?	N	N	Y
6 ***Coble***	Y	Y	N	N	N	Y
7 McIntyre	N	N	N	Y	Y	Y
8 ***Hayes***	Y	Y	N	N	N	Y
9 ***Myrick***	Y	Y	N	N	N	Y
10 ***Ballenger***	Y	?	N	N	N	Y
11 ***Taylor***	Y	Y	N	N	N	Y
12 Watt	Y	?	N	Y	Y	N
NORTH DAKOTA						
AL Pomeroy	Y	N	N	Y	Y	Y
OHIO						
1 ***Chabot***	Y	Y	N	N	N	Y
2 ***Portman***	Y	Y	N	N	N	Y
3 Hall	Y	N	N	Y	Y	Y
4 ***Oxley***	Y	Y	?	N	N	Y
5 ***Gillmor***	Y	Y	?	N	N	Y
6 Strickland	N	N	N	Y	Y	Y
7 ***Hobson***	Y	Y	N	N	N	Y
8 ***Boehner***	Y	Y	N	N	N	Y
9 Kaptur	Y	N	?	Y	Y	N
10 Kucinich	Y	N	N	Y	Y	N
11 Jones	Y	N	N	Y	Y	N
12 ***Tiberi***	Y	Y	N	N	N	Y
13 Brown	Y	N	N	Y	Y	N
14 Sawyer	Y	N	N	Y	Y	Y
15 ***Pryce***	Y	Y	N	N	N	Y
16 ***Regula***	Y	Y	N	N	N	Y
17 Traficant	Y	Y	N	N	N	Y
18 ***Ney***	Y	Y	N	N	N	Y
19 ***LaTourette***	Y	Y	N	N	N	Y
OKLAHOMA						
1 ***Largent***	Y	Y	N	N	N	Y
2 Carson	Y	N	N	Y	Y	Y
3 ***Watkins***	Y	Y	N	N	N	Y
4 ***Watts***	Y	Y	N	N	N	Y
5 ***Istook***	Y	Y	?	N	?	Y
6 ***Lucas***	Y	Y	N	N	N	Y
OREGON						
1 Wu	Y	N	N	Y	Y	Y
2 ***Walden***	Y	Y	N	N	N	Y
3 Blumenauer	N	N	N	Y	Y	N
4 DeFazio	N	N	Y	Y	Y	N
5 Hooley	Y	N	Y	Y	Y	Y
PENNSYLVANIA						
1 Brady	N	N	N	Y	Y	N
2 Fattah	N	?	N	Y	Y	N
3 Borski	N	N	N	Y	Y	N
4 ***Hart***	Y	Y	N	N	N	Y
5 ***Peterson***	Y	Y	N	N	N	Y
6 Holden	Y	N	N	Y	Y	N
7 ***Weldon***	Y	Y	N	N	N	?
8 ***Greenwood***	Y	Y	N	N	N	Y
9 ***Shuster, Bill***	Y	Y	N	N	N	Y
10 ***Sherwood***	Y	Y	N	N	N	Y
11 Kanjorski	Y	N	N	Y	Y	N
12 Murtha	Y	N	N	Y	Y	N
13 Hoeffel	Y	N	N	Y	Y	Y
14 Coyne	N	N	?	Y	Y	N
15 ***Toomey***	Y	Y	N	N	N	Y
16 ***Pitts***	Y	Y	N	N	N	Y
17 ***Gekas***	Y	Y	N	N	N	Y
18 Doyle	Y	N	N	Y	Y	N
19 ***Platts***	Y	Y	N	N	N	Y
20 Mascara	Y	N	N	Y	Y	N
21 ***English***	Y	Y	N	N	N	Y
RHODE ISLAND						
1 Kennedy	Y	N	N	Y	Y	Y
2 Langevin	Y	N	Y	Y	Y	N
SOUTH CAROLINA						
1 ***Brown***	Y	Y	N	N	N	Y
2 Vacant						
3 ***Graham***	Y	Y	N	N	N	Y
4 ***DeMint***	Y	Y	N	N	N	Y
5 Spratt	Y	N	N	Y	Y	Y
6 Clyburn	Y	N	Y	Y	Y	N
SOUTH DAKOTA						
AL ***Thune***	Y	Y	N	N	N	Y

	420	421	422	423	424	425
TENNESSEE						
1 ***Jenkins***	Y	Y	N	N	N	Y
2 ***Duncan***	Y	Y	N	N	N	Y
3 ***Wamp***	Y	Y	N	N	N	Y
4 ***Hilleary***	Y	Y	N	N	N	Y
5 Clement	Y	N	N	Y	Y	Y
6 Gordon	Y	N	N	Y	Y	Y
7 ***Bryant***	Y	Y	N	N	N	Y
8 Tanner	Y	N	N	Y	Y	Y
9 Ford	Y	N	N	Y	Y	N
TEXAS						
1 Sandlin	Y	N	N	Y	Y	N
2 Turner	Y	N	N	Y	Y	N
3 ***Johnson, Sam***	Y	Y	N	N	N	Y
4 Hall	Y	Y	N	N	N	Y
5 ***Sessions***	Y	Y	N	N	N	Y
6 ***Barton***	Y	Y	N	N	N	Y
7 ***Culberson***	Y	Y	N	N	N	Y
8 ***Brady***	Y	Y	N	N	N	Y
9 Lampson	N	N	N	Y	Y	N
10 Doggett	Y	N	N	Y	Y	N
11 Edwards	N	N	N	Y	Y	Y
12 ***Granger***	Y	Y	N	N	N	Y
13 ***Thornberry***	Y	Y	N	N	N	Y
14 ***Paul***	N	N	N	N	N	N
15 Hinojosa	Y	N	N	Y	Y	N
16 Reyes	Y	N	N	Y	Y	N
17 Stenholm	Y	N	N	Y	N	Y
18 Jackson-Lee	Y	N	N	Y	Y	N
19 ***Combest***	Y	Y	N	N	N	Y
20 Gonzalez	Y	N	N	Y	Y	N
21 ***Smith***	Y	Y	N	N	N	Y
22 ***DeLay***	Y	Y	N	N	N	Y
23 ***Bonilla***	Y	Y	N	N	N	Y
24 Frost	N	N	N	Y	Y	Y
25 Bentsen	Y	N	N	Y	Y	N
26 ***Armey***	Y	Y	N	N	N	Y
27 Ortiz	Y	Y	?	N	N	Y
28 Rodriguez	Y	N	N	Y	Y	N
29 Green	N	N	N	Y	Y	N
30 Johnson, E.B.	Y	N	N	Y	Y	N
UTAH						
1 ***Hansen***	Y	Y	N	N	N	Y
2 Matheson	Y	N	N	Y	Y	Y
3 ***Cannon***	Y	Y	N	N	N	Y
VERMONT						
AL *Sanders*	Y	N	N	Y	Y	N
VIRGINIA						
1 ***Davis, Jo Ann***	Y	Y	N	N	N	Y
2 ***Schrock***	Y	Y	N	N	N	Y
3 Scott	N	N	N	Y	Y	N
4 ***Forbes***	Y	Y	N	N	N	Y
5 *Goode*	Y	Y	N	N	N	Y
6 ***Goodlatte***	Y	Y	N	N	N	Y
7 ***Cantor***	Y	Y	N	N	N	Y
8 Moran	Y	N	N	Y	Y	Y
9 Boucher	N	N	N	Y	Y	Y
10 ***Wolf***	Y	Y	N	Y	N	Y
11 ***Davis, T.***	Y	Y	N	N	N	Y
WASHINGTON						
1 Inslee	Y	Y	N	Y	Y	Y
2 Larsen	Y	Y	N	Y	Y	Y
3 Baird	Y	N	N	Y	Y	N
4 ***Hastings***	Y	Y	N	N	N	Y
5 ***Nethercutt***	Y	Y	N	N	N	Y
6 Dicks	Y	Y	N	Y	Y	Y
7 McDermott	Y	N	N	Y	Y	N
8 ***Dunn***	?	?	?	?	?	?
9 Smith	N	N	N	Y	Y	Y
WEST VIRGINIA						
1 Mollohan	Y	N	N	Y	Y	N
2 ***Capito***	Y	Y	?	N	N	Y
3 Rahall	Y	N	N	Y	Y	N
WISCONSIN						
1 ***Ryan***	Y	Y	N	N	N	Y
2 Baldwin	Y	N	N	Y	Y	Y
3 Kind	Y	N	N	Y	Y	Y
4 Kleczka	Y	N	N	Y	Y	Y
5 Barrett	Y	N	N	Y	Y	Y
6 ***Petri***	Y	Y	N	N	N	Y
7 Obey	Y	N	N	Y	Y	Y
8 ***Green***	Y	Y	N	N	N	Y
9 ***Sensenbrenner***	Y	Y	N	N	N	Y
WYOMING						
AL ***Cubin***	Y	?	N	N	N	Y

Southern states - Ala., Ark., Fla., Ga., Ky., La., Miss., N.C., Okla., S.C., Tenn., Texas, Va.

Key

Y	Voted for (yea).
#	Paired for.
+	Announced for.
N	Voted against (nay).
X	Paired against.
–	Announced against.
P	Voted "present."
C	Voted "present" to avoid possible conflict of interest.
?	Did not vote or otherwise make a position known.

Democrats **Republicans** *Independents*

---

426. HR 768. Student Grant Information/Concur with Senate Amendments. Sensenbrenner, R-Wis., motion to suspend the rules and concur with Senate amendments to the bill that would allow financial aid officers at private universities to collectively discuss need-based grant information, including student award formulas, for seven years without violating anti-trust laws. Motion agreed to 400-0: R 213-0; D 185-0 (ND 134-0, SD 51-0); I 2-0. A two-thirds majority of those present and voting (267 in this case) is required for passage under suspension of the rules. Nov. 6, 2001.

427. HR 1408. Financial Fraud/Passage. Bachus, R-Ala., motion to suspend the rules and pass the bill that would require federal, state and private financial regulators to network their computer databases and share additional information aimed at preventing fraudulent activities. It also would allow the FBI to conduct background checks on individuals seeking insurance and other financial services licenses. Motion agreed to 392-4: R 206-4; D 184-0 (ND 134-0, SD 50-0); I 2-0. A two-thirds majority of those present and voting (264 in this case) is required for passage under suspension of the rules. Nov. 6, 2001.

428. S 1447. Aviation Security/Motion to Instruct. Oberstar, D-Minn., motion to instruct House conferees to resolve as quickly as possible, and not later than Nov. 9, the differences between the House and Senate versions of the bill aimed at increasing airline and airport security. Motion agreed to 397-0: R 210-0; D 185-0 (ND 133-0, SD 52-0); I 2-0. Nov. 6, 2001.

429. HR 2998. Afghan Radio/Passage. Royce, R-Calif., motion to suspend the rules and pass the bill that would authorize $27.5 million through fiscal 2003 to establish and run Radio Free Afghanistan, which would broadcast programming to Afghans in their native languages. Motion agreed to 405-2: R 206-2; D 197-0 (ND 146-0, SD 51-0); I 2-0. A two-thirds majority of those present and voting (272 in this case) is required for passage under suspension of the rules. Nov. 7, 2001.

430. HR 852. Jones-Battisti Building/Passage. Rehberg, R-Mont., motion to suspend the rules and pass the bill that would designate a Youngstown, Ohio, building as the "Nathaniel R. Jones and Frank J. Battisti Federal Building and U.S. Courthouse." Motion agreed to 410-0: R 210-0; D 198-0 (ND 147-0, SD 51-0); I 2-0. A two-thirds majority of those present and voting (274 in this case) is required for passage under suspension of the rules. Nov. 7, 2001.

	426	427	428	429	430
ALABAMA					
1 Callahan	Y	Y	Y	Y	Y
2 Everett	Y	Y	Y	Y	Y
3 Riley	+	+	+	Y	Y
4 Aderholt	Y	Y	Y	Y	Y
5 Cramer	Y	Y	Y	Y	Y
6 Bachus	Y	Y	Y	Y	Y
7 Hilliard	Y	Y	Y	Y	Y
ALASKA					
AL Young	Y	Y	Y	?	?
ARIZONA					
1 Flake	Y	N	Y	Y	Y
2 Pastor	Y	Y	Y	Y	Y
3 Stump	Y	Y	Y	Y	Y
4 Shadegg	Y	Y	Y	Y	Y
5 Kolbe	Y	Y	Y	Y	Y
6 Hayworth	Y	Y	Y	Y	Y
ARKANSAS					
1 Berry	Y	Y	Y	Y	Y
2 Snyder	Y	Y	Y	Y	Y
3 Vacant					
4 Ross	Y	Y	Y	Y	Y
CALIFORNIA					
1 Thompson	Y	Y	Y	Y	Y
2 Herger	Y	Y	Y	Y	Y
3 Ose	Y	Y	Y	Y	Y
4 Doolittle	Y	Y	Y	Y	Y
5 Matsui	Y	Y	Y	Y	Y
6 Woolsey	Y	Y	Y	Y	Y
7 Miller, George	Y	Y	Y	Y	Y
8 Pelosi	Y	Y	Y	Y	Y
9 Lee	Y	Y	Y	Y	Y
10 Tauscher	Y	Y	Y	Y	Y
11 Pombo	Y	Y	Y	Y	Y
12 Lantos	Y	Y	Y	Y	Y
13 Stark	Y	Y	Y	Y	Y
14 Eshoo	Y	Y	Y	Y	Y
15 Honda	Y	Y	Y	Y	Y
16 Lofgren	?	?	?	?	?
17 Farr	Y	Y	Y	Y	Y
18 Condit	Y	Y	Y	Y	Y
19 Radanovich	Y	Y	Y	Y	Y
20 Dooley	Y	Y	Y	Y	Y
21 Thomas	Y	Y	Y	Y	Y
22 Capps	+	+	+	Y	Y
23 Gallegly	Y	Y	Y	Y	Y
24 Sherman	Y	Y	Y	Y	Y
25 McKeon	Y	Y	Y	Y	Y
26 Berman	Y	Y	Y	Y	Y
27 Schiff	Y	Y	Y	Y	Y
28 Dreier	Y	Y	Y	Y	Y
29 Waxman	Y	Y	Y	Y	Y
30 Becerra	Y	Y	Y	Y	Y
31 Solis	Y	Y	Y	Y	Y
32 Watson	Y	Y	Y	Y	Y
33 Roybal-Allard	Y	Y	Y	+	Y
34 Napolitano	?	Y	Y	Y	Y
35 Waters	Y	Y	Y	Y	Y
36 Harman	Y	Y	Y	Y	Y
37 Millender-McD.	Y	Y	Y	Y	Y
38 Horn	Y	Y	Y	Y	Y
39 Royce	Y	Y	Y	Y	Y
40 Lewis	Y	Y	Y	Y	Y
41 Miller, Gary	Y	Y	Y	Y	Y
42 Baca	Y	Y	Y	Y	Y
43 Calvert	Y	Y	Y	Y	Y
44 Bono	Y	Y	Y	Y	Y
45 Rohrabacher	Y	Y	Y	Y	Y
46 Sanchez	Y	Y	Y	Y	Y
47 Cox	Y	Y	Y	Y	Y
48 Issa	Y	Y	Y	Y	Y
49 Davis	Y	Y	Y	Y	Y
50 Filner	Y	Y	Y	Y	Y
51 Cunningham	Y	Y	Y	Y	Y
52 Hunter	Y	Y	Y	Y	Y
COLORADO					
1 DeGette	Y	Y	Y	Y	Y
2 Udall	Y	Y	Y	Y	Y
3 McInnis	Y	Y	Y	Y	Y
4 Schaffer	Y	Y	Y	Y	Y
5 Hefley	Y	Y	Y	Y	Y
6 Tancredo	Y	Y	Y	Y	Y
CONNECTICUT					
1 Larson	Y	Y	Y	Y	Y
2 Simmons	Y	Y	Y	Y	Y
3 DeLauro	Y	Y	Y	Y	Y
4 Shays	+	+	+	Y	Y
5 Maloney	Y	Y	Y	Y	Y
6 Johnson	Y	Y	Y	Y	Y
DELAWARE					
AL Castle	Y	Y	Y	Y	Y
FLORIDA					
1 Miller, J.	Y	Y	Y	Y	Y
2 Boyd	Y	Y	Y	Y	Y
3 Brown	Y	Y	Y	Y	Y
4 Crenshaw	Y	Y	Y	Y	Y
5 Thurman	Y	Y	Y	Y	Y
6 Stearns	Y	Y	Y	Y	Y
7 Mica	Y	Y	Y	Y	Y
8 Keller	Y	Y	Y	Y	Y
9 Bilirakis	Y	Y	Y	Y	Y
10 Young	Y	Y	Y	Y	Y
11 Davis	Y	Y	Y	Y	Y
12 Putnam	Y	Y	Y	Y	Y
13 Miller, D.	Y	Y	Y	Y	Y
14 Goss	Y	Y	Y	Y	Y
15 Weldon	Y	Y	Y	Y	Y
16 Foley	Y	Y	Y	Y	Y
17 Meek	Y	Y	Y	?	?
18 Ros-Lehtinen	Y	Y	Y	Y	Y
19 Wexler	Y	Y	Y	Y	Y
20 Deutsch	Y	Y	Y	Y	Y
21 Diaz-Balart	Y	Y	Y	Y	Y
22 Shaw	Y	Y	Y	Y	Y
23 Hastings	Y	Y	Y	Y	Y
GEORGIA					
1 Kingston	Y	Y	Y	Y	Y
2 Bishop	Y	Y	Y	Y	Y
3 Collins	Y	Y	Y	N	Y
4 McKinney	Y	?	Y	Y	Y
5 Lewis	?	?	?	Y	Y
6 Isakson	Y	Y	Y	Y	Y
7 Barr	Y	Y	Y	Y	Y
8 Chambliss	Y	Y	Y	Y	Y
9 Deal	Y	Y	Y	Y	Y
10 Norwood	Y	Y	Y	Y	Y
11 Linder	Y	?	Y	Y	Y
HAWAII					
1 Abercrombie	Y	Y	Y	Y	Y
2 Mink	Y	Y	Y	Y	Y
IDAHO					
1 Otter	Y	Y	Y	Y	Y
2 Simpson	Y	Y	Y	Y	Y
ILLINOIS					
1 Rush	Y	Y	Y	Y	Y
2 Jackson	Y	Y	Y	Y	Y
3 Lipinski	Y	?	Y	Y	Y
4 Gutierrez	Y	Y	Y	Y	Y
5 Blagojevich	Y	Y	Y	Y	Y
6 Hyde	Y	Y	Y	Y	Y
7 Davis	Y	Y	Y	Y	Y
8 Crane	Y	Y	Y	?	Y
9 Schakowsky	Y	Y	Y	Y	Y
10 Kirk	Y	Y	Y	Y	Y
11 Weller	Y	Y	?	Y	Y
12 Costello	Y	Y	Y	Y	Y
13 Biggert	Y	Y	Y	Y	Y

ND Northern Democrats   SD Southern Democrats

Member	426	427	428	429	430
14 Hastert					
15 Johnson	Y	Y	Y	Y	Y
16 Manzullo	Y	Y	Y	Y	Y
17 Evans	Y	Y	Y	Y	Y
18 LaHood	Y	Y	Y	Y	Y
19 Phelps	Y	Y	Y	Y	Y
20 Shimkus	Y	Y	Y	Y	Y
INDIANA					
1 Visclosky	Y	Y	Y	Y	Y
2 Pence	Y	Y	Y	Y	Y
3 Roemer	Y	Y	Y	Y	Y
4 Souder	Y	Y	Y	Y	Y
5 Buyer	Y	Y	Y	Y	Y
6 Burton	?	?	?	?	?
7 Kerns	Y	Y	Y	Y	Y
8 Hostettler	Y	Y	Y	Y	Y
9 Hill	Y	Y	Y	Y	Y
10 Carson	Y	Y	Y	Y	Y
IOWA					
1 Leach	Y	Y	Y	Y	Y
2 Nussle	Y	Y	Y	Y	Y
3 Boswell	Y	Y	Y	Y	Y
4 Ganske	Y	Y	Y	Y	Y
5 Latham	Y	Y	Y	Y	Y
KANSAS					
1 Moran	Y	Y	Y	Y	Y
2 Ryun	Y	Y	Y	Y	Y
3 Moore	Y	Y	Y	Y	Y
4 Tiahrt	Y	Y	?	Y	Y
KENTUCKY					
1 Whitfield	Y	Y	Y	Y	Y
2 Lewis	Y	Y	Y	Y	Y
3 Northup	Y	Y	Y	Y	Y
4 Lucas	Y	Y	Y	Y	Y
5 Rogers	Y	Y	Y	Y	Y
6 Fletcher	Y	Y	Y	+	+
LOUISIANA					
1 Vitter	Y	Y	Y	Y	Y
2 Jefferson	Y	Y	Y	Y	Y
3 Tauzin	Y	Y	Y	Y	Y
4 McCrery	Y	Y	Y	Y	Y
5 Cooksey	Y	Y	Y	Y	Y
6 Baker	Y	Y	Y	Y	Y
7 John	Y	Y	Y	Y	Y
MAINE					
1 Allen	Y	Y	Y	Y	Y
2 Baldacci	Y	Y	Y	Y	Y
MARYLAND					
1 Gilchrest	Y	Y	Y	Y	Y
2 Ehrlich	Y	Y	Y	?	Y
3 Cardin	Y	Y	Y	Y	Y
4 Wynn	Y	Y	Y	Y	Y
5 Hoyer	Y	Y	Y	Y	Y
6 Bartlett	Y	Y	Y	Y	Y
7 Cummings	Y	Y	Y	Y	Y
8 Morella	Y	Y	Y	Y	Y
MASSACHUSETTS					
1 Olver	Y	Y	Y	Y	Y
2 Neal	Y	Y	Y	Y	Y
3 McGovern	Y	Y	Y	Y	Y
4 Frank	Y	Y	?	Y	Y
5 Meehan	Y	Y	Y	Y	?
6 Tierney	Y	Y	Y	Y	Y
7 Markey	Y	Y	Y	Y	Y
8 Capuano	Y	Y	Y	Y	Y
9 Lynch	Y	Y	Y	Y	Y
10 Delahunt	Y	Y	Y	Y	Y
MICHIGAN					
1 Stupak	Y	Y	Y	Y	Y
2 Hoekstra	Y	Y	Y	Y	Y
3 Ehlers	Y	Y	Y	Y	Y
4 Camp	Y	Y	Y	Y	Y
5 Barcia	Y	Y	Y	Y	Y
6 Upton	Y	Y	Y	Y	Y
7 Smith	Y	Y	Y	Y	Y
8 Rogers	Y	Y	Y	Y	Y
9 Kildee	Y	Y	Y	Y	Y
10 Bonior	?	Y	Y	Y	Y
11 Knollenberg	Y	Y	Y	Y	Y
12 Levin	Y	Y	Y	Y	Y
13 Rivers	Y	Y	Y	Y	Y
14 Conyers	?	?	?	?	?
15 Kilpatrick	+	+	+	+	+
16 Dingell	Y	Y	Y	Y	Y
MINNESOTA					
1 Gutknecht	Y	Y	Y	Y	Y
2 Kennedy	Y	Y	Y	Y	Y
3 Ramstad	Y	Y	Y	Y	Y
4 McCollum	+	+	+	Y	Y
5 Sabo	Y	Y	Y	Y	Y
6 Luther	Y	Y	Y	Y	Y
7 Peterson	Y	Y	Y	Y	Y
8 Oberstar	Y	Y	Y	Y	Y
MISSISSIPPI					
1 Wicker	Y	Y	Y	Y	Y
2 Thompson	Y	Y	Y	Y	Y
3 Pickering	Y	Y	Y	Y	Y
4 Shows	Y	Y	Y	Y	Y
5 Taylor	Y	Y	Y	Y	Y
MISSOURI					
1 Clay	Y	Y	Y	Y	Y
2 Akin	Y	Y	Y	Y	Y
3 Gephardt	Y	Y	Y	Y	Y
4 Skelton	Y	Y	Y	Y	Y
5 McCarthy	Y	Y	Y	Y	Y
6 Graves	Y	Y	Y	Y	Y
7 Blunt	Y	Y	Y	Y	Y
8 Emerson	Y	Y	Y	Y	Y
9 Hulshof	Y	Y	Y	Y	Y
MONTANA					
AL Rehberg	Y	Y	Y	Y	Y
NEBRASKA					
1 Bereuter	Y	Y	Y	Y	Y
2 Terry	Y	Y	Y	Y	Y
3 Osborne	Y	Y	Y	Y	Y
NEVADA					
1 Berkley	Y	Y	Y	Y	Y
2 Gibbons	Y	Y	Y	Y	Y
NEW HAMPSHIRE					
1 Sununu	Y	Y	Y	Y	Y
2 Bass	Y	Y	Y	Y	Y
NEW JERSEY					
1 Andrews	Y	Y	Y	Y	Y
2 LoBiondo	Y	Y	Y	Y	Y
3 Saxton	Y	Y	Y	Y	Y
4 Smith	Y	Y	Y	Y	Y
5 Roukema	Y	Y	Y	Y	Y
6 Pallone	?	?	?	?	?
7 Ferguson	?	?	?	Y	Y
8 Pascrell	?	?	?	Y	Y
9 Rothman	?	?	?	Y	Y
10 Payne	?	?	?	Y	Y
11 Frelinghuysen	Y	Y	Y	Y	Y
12 Holt	Y	Y	Y	Y	Y
13 Menendez	?	?	?	Y	Y
NEW MEXICO					
1 Wilson	Y	Y	Y	Y	Y
2 Skeen	Y	Y	Y	Y	Y
3 Udall	Y	Y	Y	Y	Y
NEW YORK					
1 Grucci	Y	Y	Y	Y	Y
2 Israel	Y	Y	Y	Y	Y
3 King	Y	Y	Y	Y	Y
4 McCarthy	Y	Y	Y	Y	Y
5 Ackerman	?	?	?	Y	Y
6 Meeks	?	?	?	?	?
7 Crowley	?	?	?	Y	Y
8 Nadler	?	?	?	Y	Y
9 Weiner	Y	Y	Y	Y	Y
10 Towns	Y	Y	Y	Y	Y
11 Owens	Y	Y	Y	Y	Y
12 Velázquez	?	?	?	Y	Y
13 Fossella	Y	Y	+	Y	Y
14 Maloney	+	+	+	Y	Y
15 Rangel	Y	Y	Y	Y	Y
16 Serrano	?	?	?	Y	Y
17 Engel	?	?	?	?	?
18 Lowey	?	?	?	Y	Y
19 Kelly	Y	Y	Y	Y	Y
20 Gilman	Y	Y	Y	Y	Y
21 McNulty	?	?	?	Y	Y
22 Sweeney	?	?	?	?	?
23 Boehlert	Y	Y	Y	Y	Y
24 McHugh	Y	Y	Y	Y	Y
25 Walsh	Y	Y	Y	Y	Y
26 Hinchey	Y	Y	Y	Y	Y
27 Reynolds	Y	Y	Y	Y	Y
28 Slaughter	Y	Y	Y	Y	Y
29 LaFalce	Y	Y	Y	Y	Y
30 Quinn	Y	Y	Y	Y	Y
31 Houghton	Y	Y	Y	Y	Y
NORTH CAROLINA					
1 Clayton	Y	Y	Y	Y	Y
2 Etheridge	Y	Y	Y	Y	Y
3 Jones	Y	Y	Y	Y	Y
4 Price	Y	Y	Y	Y	Y
5 Burr	Y	Y	Y	Y	Y
6 Coble	Y	Y	Y	Y	Y
7 McIntyre	Y	Y	Y	Y	Y
8 Hayes	Y	Y	Y	Y	Y
9 Myrick	Y	Y	Y	Y	?
10 Ballenger	Y	Y	Y	?	?
11 Taylor	Y	Y	Y	Y	Y
12 Watt	Y	Y	Y	Y	Y
NORTH DAKOTA					
AL Pomeroy	Y	Y	Y	Y	Y
OHIO					
1 Chabot	Y	Y	Y	Y	Y
2 Portman	Y	Y	Y	Y	Y
3 Hall	Y	Y	Y	Y	Y
4 Oxley	Y	Y	Y	Y	Y
5 Gillmor	Y	Y	Y	Y	Y
6 Strickland	Y	Y	?	?	?
7 Hobson	Y	Y	Y	Y	Y
8 Boehner	Y	Y	Y	Y	Y
9 Kaptur	Y	Y	Y	Y	Y
10 Kucinich	Y	Y	Y	Y	Y
11 Jones	?	?	?	?	?
12 Tiberi	Y	Y	Y	Y	Y
13 Brown	Y	Y	Y	?	?
14 Sawyer	Y	Y	Y	Y	Y
15 Pryce	Y	Y	Y	Y	Y
16 Regula	Y	Y	Y	Y	Y
17 Traficant	Y	Y	Y	Y	Y
18 Ney	Y	Y	Y	Y	Y
19 LaTourette	Y	Y	Y	Y	Y
OKLAHOMA					
1 Largent	Y	?	Y	Y	Y
2 Carson	Y	Y	Y	Y	Y
3 Watkins	Y	?	Y	Y	Y
4 Watts	Y	Y	Y	Y	Y
5 Istook	Y	Y	Y	Y	Y
6 Lucas	Y	Y	Y	Y	Y
OREGON					
1 Wu	Y	Y	Y	Y	Y
2 Walden	Y	Y	Y	Y	Y
3 Blumenauer	Y	Y	Y	Y	Y
4 DeFazio	Y	Y	Y	Y	Y
5 Hooley	Y	Y	Y	Y	Y
PENNSYLVANIA					
1 Brady	?	?	?	Y	Y
2 Fattah	?	?	?	Y	Y
3 Borski	?	?	?	Y	Y
4 Hart	Y	Y	Y	Y	Y
5 Peterson	Y	Y	Y	Y	Y
6 Holden	Y	Y	Y	Y	Y
7 Weldon	Y	Y	Y	Y	Y
8 Greenwood	Y	Y	Y	Y	Y
9 Shuster, Bill	Y	Y	Y	Y	Y
10 Sherwood	Y	Y	Y	Y	Y
11 Kanjorski	Y	Y	Y	?	Y
12 Murtha	Y	Y	Y	Y	Y
13 Hoeffel	Y	Y	Y	Y	Y
14 Coyne	Y	Y	Y	Y	Y
15 Toomey	Y	Y	Y	Y	Y
16 Pitts	Y	Y	Y	Y	Y
17 Gekas	Y	Y	Y	Y	Y
18 Doyle	Y	Y	Y	Y	Y
19 Platts	Y	Y	Y	Y	Y
20 Mascara	Y	Y	Y	Y	Y
21 English	Y	Y	Y	Y	Y
RHODE ISLAND					
1 Kennedy	Y	Y	Y	Y	Y
2 Langevin	Y	Y	Y	Y	Y
SOUTH CAROLINA					
1 Brown	Y	Y	Y	Y	Y
2 Vacant					
3 Graham	Y	Y	Y	Y	Y
4 DeMint	Y	Y	Y	Y	Y
5 Spratt	Y	Y	Y	Y	Y
6 Clyburn	Y	Y	Y	Y	Y
SOUTH DAKOTA					
AL Thune	Y	Y	Y	Y	Y
TENNESSEE					
1 Jenkins	Y	Y	Y	Y	Y
2 Duncan	Y	Y	Y	Y	Y
3 Wamp	Y	Y	Y	Y	Y
4 Hilleary	Y	Y	Y	Y	Y
5 Clement	Y	Y	Y	Y	Y
6 Gordon	Y	Y	Y	Y	Y
7 Bryant	Y	Y	Y	Y	Y
8 Tanner	Y	Y	Y	Y	Y
9 Ford	Y	Y	Y	Y	
TEXAS					
1 Sandlin	Y	Y	Y	Y	Y
2 Turner	Y	Y	Y	Y	Y
3 Johnson, Sam	Y	Y	Y	Y	Y
4 Hall	Y	Y	Y	Y	Y
5 Sessions	?	?	?	?	?
6 Barton	Y	Y	Y	?	Y
7 Culberson	Y	Y	Y	Y	Y
8 Brady	Y	Y	Y	Y	Y
9 Lampson	Y	Y	Y	Y	Y
10 Doggett	Y	Y	Y	Y	Y
11 Edwards	Y	Y	Y	Y	Y
12 Granger	Y	Y	Y	Y	Y
13 Thornberry	Y	Y	Y	Y	Y
14 Paul	Y	N	Y	N	Y
15 Hinojosa	Y	Y	Y	Y	Y
16 Reyes	Y	Y	Y	Y	Y
17 Stenholm	Y	Y	Y	Y	Y
18 Jackson-Lee	+	+	+	+	+
19 Combest	Y	Y	Y	Y	Y
20 Gonzalez	Y	Y	Y	Y	Y
21 Smith	Y	N	Y	Y	Y
22 DeLay	Y	Y	Y	?	?
23 Bonilla	Y	Y	Y	Y	Y
24 Frost	Y	Y	Y	Y	Y
25 Bentsen	Y	Y	Y	Y	Y
26 Armey	Y	Y	Y	Y	Y
27 Ortiz	Y	Y	Y	Y	Y
28 Rodriguez	Y	Y	Y	Y	Y
29 Green	Y	Y	Y	Y	Y
30 Johnson, E.B.	Y	Y	Y	Y	Y
UTAH					
1 Hansen	Y	Y	Y	Y	Y
2 Matheson	Y	Y	Y	Y	Y
3 Cannon	Y	Y	Y	Y	Y
VERMONT					
AL Sanders	Y	Y	Y	Y	Y
VIRGINIA					
1 Davis, Jo Ann	Y	N	Y	Y	Y
2 Schrock	Y	Y	Y	Y	Y
3 Scott	?	?	Y	Y	Y
4 Forbes	Y	Y	Y	Y	Y
5 Goode	Y	Y	Y	Y	Y
6 Goodlatte	Y	Y	Y	Y	Y
7 Cantor	Y	Y	Y	Y	Y
8 Moran	Y	Y	Y	?	?
9 Boucher	Y	Y	Y	Y	Y
10 Wolf	Y	Y	Y	Y	Y
11 Davis, T.	Y	Y	Y	Y	Y
WASHINGTON					
1 Inslee	Y	Y	Y	Y	Y
2 Larsen	Y	Y	Y	Y	Y
3 Baird	Y	Y	Y	Y	Y
4 Hastings	Y	Y	Y	Y	Y
5 Nethercutt	Y	Y	Y	Y	Y
6 Dicks	Y	Y	Y	Y	Y
7 McDermott	Y	Y	Y	Y	Y
8 Dunn	Y	Y	Y	Y	Y
9 Smith	Y	Y	Y	Y	Y
WEST VIRGINIA					
1 Mollohan	Y	Y	Y	Y	Y
2 Capito	Y	Y	Y	Y	Y
3 Rahall	Y	Y	Y	Y	Y
WISCONSIN					
1 Ryan	Y	Y	Y	Y	Y
2 Baldwin	Y	Y	Y	Y	Y
3 Kind	Y	Y	Y	Y	Y
4 Kleczka	Y	Y	Y	Y	Y
5 Barrett	Y	Y	Y	Y	Y
6 Petri	Y	Y	Y	Y	Y
7 Obey	Y	Y	?	Y	Y
8 Green	Y	Y	Y	Y	Y
9 Sensenbrenner	Y	Y	Y	Y	Y
WYOMING					
AL Cubin	?	?	?	?	?

Southern states - Ala., Ark., Fla., Ga., Ky., La., Miss., N.C., Okla., S.C., Tenn., Texas, Va.

Key

Y	Voted for (yea).
#	Paired for.
+	Announced for.
N	Voted against (nay).
X	Paired against.
–	Announced against.
P	Voted "present."
C	Voted "present" to avoid possible conflict of interest.
?	Did not vote or otherwise make a position known.

Democrats **Republicans**
Independents

---

431. HR 3167. NATO Expansion/Passage. Passage of the bill that would support further expansion of the North Atlantic Treaty Organization, authorize military assistance to several eastern European countries and lift assistance restrictions on Slovakia. Passed 372-46: R 190-22; D 182-22 (ND 133-17, SD 49-5); I 0-2. Nov. 7, 2001.

432. H Con Res 262. Trade Protection/Adoption. English, R-Pa., motion to suspend the rules and adopt the concurrent resolution that would express the sense of Congress that President Bush should maintain the U.S. ability to strictly enforce its trade laws at World Trade Organization negotiations including those in Doha, Qatar, and resist agreements that would reduce fair trade regulations. Motion agreed to 410-4: R 206-3; D 202-1 (ND 148-1, SD 54-0); I 2-0. A two-thirds majority of those present and voting (276 in this case) is required for adoption under suspension of the rules. Nov. 7, 2001.

433. Procedural Motion/Journal. Approval of the House Journal of Wednesday, Nov. 7, 2001. Approved 363-47: R 192-16; D 169-31 (ND 124-24, SD 45-7); I 2-0. Nov. 8, 2001.

434. HR 2620. Fiscal 2002 VA-HUD Appropriations/Conference Report. Adoption of the conference report on the bill that would provide $112.7 billion for the departments of Veterans Affairs (VA) and Housing and Urban Development (HUD) and related agencies including the EPA, NASA, and the National Science Foundation. Adopted (thus sent to the Senate) 401-18: R 199-13; D 200-5 (ND 147-4, SD 53-1); I 2-0. Nov. 8, 2001.

435. HR 3061. Fiscal 2002 Labor-HHS-Education Appropriations/Motion to Instruct. Obey, D-Wis., motion to instruct House conferees to insist on the House's position to provide at least $51.7 billion for the Department of Education. Motion agreed to 367-48: R 165-46; D 201-1 (ND 148-0, SD 53-1); I 1-1. Nov. 8, 2001.

	431	432	433	434	435
ALABAMA					
1 *Callahan*	Y	Y	Y	Y	Y
2 *Everett*	N	Y	Y	Y	Y
3 *Riley*	Y	Y	N	Y	Y
4 *Aderholt*	Y	Y	N	Y	Y
5 Cramer	Y	Y	Y	Y	Y
6 *Bachus*	Y	Y	Y	Y	Y
7 Hilliard	Y	Y	N	Y	Y
ALASKA					
AL *Young*	Y	Y	?	Y	Y
ARIZONA					
1 *Flake*	N	N	Y	N	N
2 Pastor	Y	Y	Y	Y	Y
3 *Stump*	N	?	Y	Y	N
4 *Shadegg*	Y	Y	Y	Y	N
5 *Kolbe*	Y	N	Y	Y	Y
6 *Hayworth*	Y	Y	Y	Y	N
ARKANSAS					
1 Berry	Y	Y	Y	N	Y
2 Snyder	N	Y	Y	Y	Y
3 Vacant					
4 Ross	Y	Y	Y	Y	Y
CALIFORNIA					
1 Thompson	Y	Y	N	Y	Y
2 *Herger*	Y	Y	Y	Y	N
3 *Ose*	Y	Y	?	?	?
4 *Doolittle*	Y	Y	Y	Y	N
5 Matsui	Y	Y	Y	Y	Y
6 Woolsey	Y	Y	Y	Y	Y
7 Miller, George	N	Y	N	Y	Y
8 Pelosi	Y	Y	Y	Y	Y
9 Lee	N	Y	Y	Y	Y
10 Tauscher	Y	Y	Y	Y	Y
11 *Pombo*	N	Y	Y	Y	N
12 Lantos	Y	Y	Y	Y	Y
13 Stark	N	Y	Y	Y	Y
14 Eshoo	Y	Y	Y	Y	Y
15 Honda	Y	Y	Y	Y	Y
16 Lofgren	?	?	?	?	?
17 Farr	Y	Y	Y	Y	Y
18 Condit	N	Y	Y	Y	Y
19 *Radanovich*	Y	Y	?	Y	N
20 Dooley	Y	Y	Y	Y	Y
21 *Thomas*	Y	Y	Y	Y	Y
22 Capps	Y	Y	Y	Y	Y
23 *Gallegly*	Y	Y	Y	Y	Y
24 Sherman	N	Y	Y	Y	Y
25 *McKeon*	Y	Y	Y	Y	Y
26 Berman	Y	Y	Y	Y	Y
27 Schiff	Y	Y	Y	Y	Y
28 *Dreier*	Y	N	Y	Y	Y
29 Waxman	N	Y	Y	Y	Y
30 Becerra	Y	Y	Y	Y	Y
31 Solis	Y	Y	Y	Y	Y
32 Watson	Y	Y	Y	Y	Y
33 Roybal-Allard	Y	Y	Y	Y	Y
34 Napolitano	Y	Y	Y	Y	Y
35 Waters	Y	N	N	Y	Y
36 Harman	N	Y	Y	Y	Y
37 Millender-McD.	Y	Y	Y	Y	Y
38 *Horn*	Y	Y	Y	Y	Y

	431	432	433	434	435
39 *Royce*	Y	Y	Y	N	N
40 *Lewis*	Y	Y	Y	Y	Y
41 *Miller, Gary*	Y	Y	Y	Y	Y
42 Baca	Y	Y	Y	Y	Y
43 *Calvert*	Y	Y	Y	Y	Y
44 *Bono*	Y	Y	Y	Y	Y
45 *Rohrabacher*	N	Y	Y	Y	N
46 Sanchez	Y	Y	Y	Y	Y
47 *Cox*	Y	Y	Y	Y	N
48 *Issa*	Y	Y	Y	Y	Y
49 Davis	Y	Y	Y	Y	Y
50 Filner	Y	Y	N	N	Y
51 *Cunningham*	Y	Y	Y	Y	Y
52 *Hunter*	Y	?	Y	Y	N
COLORADO					
1 DeGette	Y	Y	Y	Y	Y
2 Udall	Y	Y	Y	Y	Y
3 *McInnis*	Y	Y	Y	Y	Y
4 *Schaffer*	Y	Y	N	N	N
5 *Hefley*	Y	Y	N	N	N
6 *Tancredo*	N	Y	P	N	N
CONNECTICUT					
1 Larson	+	Y	Y	Y	Y
2 *Simmons*	Y	Y	Y	Y	Y
3 DeLauro	Y	Y	Y	Y	Y
4 *Shays*	Y	Y	N	Y	Y
5 Maloney	Y	Y	?	Y	Y
6 *Johnson*	Y	Y	Y	Y	?
DELAWARE					
AL *Castle*	Y	Y	Y	Y	Y
FLORIDA					
1 *Miller, J.*	Y	Y	Y	Y	Y
2 Boyd	Y	Y	Y	Y	Y
3 Brown	Y	Y	Y	Y	Y
4 *Crenshaw*	Y	Y	Y	Y	Y
5 Thurman	Y	Y	Y	Y	Y
6 *Stearns*	+	Y	Y	Y	N
7 *Mica*	Y	Y	Y	Y	Y
8 *Keller*	Y	Y	Y	Y	Y
9 *Bilirakis*	Y	Y	Y	Y	Y
10 *Young*	Y	Y	Y	Y	Y
11 Davis	Y	Y	Y	Y	Y
12 *Putnam*	Y	Y	Y	Y	N
13 *Miller, D.*	Y	Y	Y	Y	Y
14 *Goss*	Y	Y	Y	Y	Y
15 *Weldon*	Y	Y	N	N	N
16 *Foley*	Y	Y	Y	Y	Y
17 Meek	Y	Y	Y	Y	Y
18 *Ros-Lehtinen*	Y	Y	Y	Y	Y
19 Wexler	Y	Y	Y	Y	Y
20 Deutsch	Y	Y	Y	Y	Y
21 *Diaz-Balart*	Y	Y	Y	Y	Y
22 *Shaw*	Y	Y	Y	Y	Y
23 Hastings	Y	Y	N	Y	Y
GEORGIA					
1 *Kingston*	Y	Y	Y	Y	Y
2 Bishop	Y	Y	Y	Y	Y
3 *Collins*	N	Y	Y	Y	N
4 McKinney	N	Y	Y	Y	Y
5 Lewis	Y	Y	Y	Y	Y
6 *Isakson*	Y	Y	Y	Y	Y
7 *Barr*	N	Y	Y	Y	Y
8 *Chambliss*	Y	Y	Y	Y	Y
9 *Deal*	N	Y	Y	Y	Y
10 *Norwood*	Y	Y	Y	Y	Y
11 *Linder*	Y	Y	Y	Y	Y
HAWAII					
1 Abercrombie	Y	Y	Y	Y	Y
2 Mink	Y	Y	Y	Y	Y
IDAHO					
1 *Otter*	N	Y	Y	?	N
2 *Simpson*	Y	Y	Y	Y	Y
ILLINOIS					
1 Rush	Y	Y	Y	Y	Y
2 Jackson	Y	Y	Y	Y	Y
3 Lipinski	Y	Y	Y	Y	Y
4 Gutierrez	Y	Y	N	Y	Y
5 Blagojevich	Y	Y	Y	Y	Y
6 *Hyde*	Y	Y	Y	Y	Y
7 Davis	Y	Y	Y	Y	Y
8 *Crane*	Y	Y	N	Y	N
9 Schakowsky	?	?	Y	Y	Y
10 *Kirk*	Y	Y	Y	Y	Y
11 *Weller*	Y	Y	N	Y	Y
12 Costello	Y	Y	Y	Y	Y
13 *Biggert*	Y	Y	Y	Y	Y

ND Northern Democrats   SD Southern Democrats

	431	432	433	434	435
14 Hastert					
15 *Johnson*	Y	Y	Y	Y	Y
16 *Manzullo*	Y	Y	Y	Y	Y
17 Evans	Y	Y	Y	Y	?
18 *LaHood*	Y	Y	Y	Y	Y
19 Phelps	Y	Y	Y	Y	Y
20 *Shimkus*	Y	Y	Y	Y	Y
INDIANA					
1 Visclosky	Y	Y	N	Y	Y
2 *Pence*	N	Y	Y	Y	N
3 Roemer	Y	Y	Y	N	Y
4 *Souder*	Y	Y	Y	Y	Y
5 *Buyer*	?	?	Y	Y	Y
6 *Burton*	?	?	?	?	?
7 *Kerns*	N	Y	Y	N	N
8 *Hostettler*	Y	Y	Y	N	N
9 Hill	Y	Y	Y	Y	Y
10 Carson	Y	Y	Y	Y	Y
IOWA					
1 *Leach*	Y	Y	Y	Y	Y
2 *Nussle*	Y	Y	Y	Y	Y
3 Boswell	Y	Y	Y	Y	Y
4 *Ganske*	?	?	?	?	?
5 *Latham*	Y	Y	N	Y	Y
KANSAS					
1 *Moran*	Y	Y	N	Y	Y
2 *Ryun*	Y	Y	Y	Y	N
3 Moore	Y	Y	N	Y	Y
4 *Tiahrt*	Y	Y	Y	Y	N
KENTUCKY					
1 *Whitfield*	Y	Y	N	Y	Y
2 *Lewis*	Y	Y	Y	Y	Y
3 *Northup*	Y	Y	Y	Y	Y
4 Lucas	Y	Y	Y	Y	Y
5 *Rogers*	Y	Y	Y	Y	Y
6 *Fletcher*	Y	Y	Y	Y	Y
LOUISIANA					
1 *Vitter*	Y	Y	Y	Y	Y
2 Jefferson	Y	Y	?	Y	Y
3 *Tauzin*	Y	Y	Y	Y	Y
4 *McCrery*	Y	Y	?	Y	Y
5 *Cooksey*	Y	Y	?	Y	Y
6 *Baker*	Y	Y	Y	Y	Y
7 John	Y	Y	Y	Y	Y
MAINE					
1 Allen	Y	Y	Y	Y	Y
2 Baldacci	Y	Y	Y	Y	?
MARYLAND					
1 *Gilchrest*	Y	?	Y	Y	Y
2 *Ehrlich*	Y	Y	Y	Y	Y
3 Cardin	Y	Y	Y	Y	Y
4 Wynn	Y	Y	Y	Y	Y
5 Hoyer	Y	Y	Y	Y	Y
6 *Bartlett*	N	Y	Y	Y	N
7 Cummings	Y	Y	Y	Y	Y
8 *Morella*	Y	Y	Y	Y	Y
MASSACHUSETTS					
1 Olver	Y	Y	N	Y	Y
2 Neal	Y	Y	Y	Y	Y
3 McGovern	Y	Y	Y	Y	Y
4 Frank	N	Y	Y	Y	Y
5 Meehan	Y	Y	Y	Y	Y
6 Tierney	N	Y	Y	Y	Y
7 Markey	Y	Y	Y	Y	Y
8 Capuano	Y	Y	N	N	Y
9 Lynch	Y	Y	Y	Y	Y
10 Delahunt	Y	Y	?	?	?
MICHIGAN					
1 Stupak	Y	Y	N	Y	Y
2 *Hoekstra*	Y	Y	N	N	Y
3 *Ehlers*	Y	Y	Y	Y	Y
4 *Camp*	Y	Y	Y	Y	Y
5 Barcia	Y	Y	Y	Y	Y
6 *Upton*	Y	Y	Y	Y	Y
7 *Smith*	Y	Y	Y	Y	N
8 *Rogers*	Y	Y	Y	Y	Y
9 Kildee	Y	Y	Y	Y	Y
10 Bonior	Y	Y	?	Y	Y
11 *Knollenberg*	Y	Y	Y	Y	Y
12 Levin	Y	Y	Y	Y	Y
13 Rivers	Y	Y	Y	Y	Y
14 Conyers	?	?	?	?	?
15 Kilpatrick	+	+	+	+	+
16 Dingell	Y	Y	Y	Y	Y
MINNESOTA					
1 *Gutknecht*	Y	Y	Y	Y	Y
2 *Kennedy*	Y	Y	N	Y	Y
3 *Ramstad*	Y	Y	N	Y	Y
4 McCollum	Y	Y	Y	Y	Y
5 Sabo	Y	Y	N	Y	Y
6 Luther	Y	Y	Y	Y	Y
7 Peterson	Y	?	N	Y	Y
8 Oberstar	Y	Y	N	Y	Y
MISSISSIPPI					
1 *Wicker*	Y	Y	Y	Y	?
2 Thompson	Y	Y	N	Y	Y
3 *Pickering*	Y	Y	Y	Y	Y
4 Shows	Y	Y	Y	Y	Y
5 Taylor	Y	Y	N	Y	Y
MISSOURI					
1 Clay	Y	Y	Y	Y	Y
2 *Akin*	N	Y	Y	Y	N
3 Gephardt	Y	Y	?	Y	Y
4 Skelton	Y	Y	Y	Y	Y
5 McCarthy	Y	Y	Y	Y	Y
6 *Graves*	Y	Y	Y	Y	Y
7 *Blunt*	Y	Y	Y	Y	N
8 *Emerson*	Y	Y	Y	Y	Y
9 *Hulshof*	Y	Y	N	Y	Y
MONTANA					
AL *Rehberg*	Y	Y	Y	Y	
NEBRASKA					
1 *Bereuter*	Y	Y	Y	Y	Y
2 *Terry*	Y	Y	Y	Y	Y
3 *Osborne*	Y	Y	Y	Y	Y
NEVADA					
1 Berkley	Y	Y	Y	Y	Y
2 *Gibbons*	Y	Y	Y	Y	Y
NEW HAMPSHIRE					
1 *Sununu*	Y	Y	Y	Y	Y
2 *Bass*	Y	Y	Y	Y	Y
NEW JERSEY					
1 Andrews	Y	Y	Y	Y	Y
2 *LoBiondo*	Y	Y	N	Y	Y
3 *Saxton*	Y	Y	Y	Y	Y
4 *Smith*	Y	Y	Y	Y	Y
5 *Roukema*	Y	Y	Y	Y	Y
6 Pallone	Y	Y	Y	Y	Y
7 *Ferguson*	Y	Y	Y	Y	Y
8 Pascrell	Y	Y	Y	Y	Y
9 Rothman	Y	Y	Y	Y	Y
10 Payne	N	Y	Y	Y	Y
11 *Frelinghuysen*	Y	Y	Y	Y	Y
12 Holt	N	Y	Y	Y	Y
13 Menendez	Y	Y	Y	Y	Y
NEW MEXICO					
1 *Wilson*	Y	Y	Y	Y	Y
2 *Skeen*	Y	Y	Y	Y	Y
3 Udall	Y	Y	N	Y	Y
NEW YORK					
1 *Grucci*	Y	Y	Y	Y	Y
2 Israel	Y	Y	Y	Y	Y
3 *King*	Y	Y	Y	Y	Y
4 McCarthy	Y	Y	Y	Y	Y
5 Ackerman	Y	Y	Y	Y	?
6 Meeks	?	?	Y	Y	Y
7 Crowley	Y	Y	Y	Y	Y
8 Nadler	N	Y	Y	Y	Y
9 Weiner	Y	Y	Y	Y	Y
10 Towns	Y	Y	Y	Y	Y
11 Owens	Y	Y	Y	Y	Y
12 Velázquez	Y	Y	Y	Y	Y
13 *Fossella*	Y	Y	Y	Y	Y
14 Maloney	Y	Y	Y	?	?
15 Rangel	Y	Y	Y	Y	Y
16 Serrano	Y	Y	Y	Y	Y
17 Engel	Y	Y	Y	Y	Y
18 Lowey	Y	Y	?	Y	Y
19 *Kelly*	Y	Y	Y	Y	Y
20 *Gilman*	Y	Y	Y	Y	Y
21 McNulty	Y	Y	N	Y	Y
22 *Sweeney*	?	?	N	Y	Y
23 *Boehlert*	Y	Y	Y	Y	Y
24 *McHugh*	Y	Y	Y	Y	Y
25 *Walsh*	Y	Y	Y	Y	Y
26 Hinchey	N	Y	Y	Y	Y
27 *Reynolds*	Y	Y	Y	Y	Y
28 Slaughter	N	Y	Y	Y	Y
29 LaFalce	Y	?	Y	Y	Y
30 *Quinn*	Y	?	Y	Y	Y
31 *Houghton*	Y	Y	Y	Y	Y
NORTH CAROLINA					
1 Clayton	Y	Y	Y	Y	Y
2 Etheridge	Y	Y	Y	Y	Y
3 *Jones*	N	Y	Y	Y	N
4 Price	Y	Y	Y	Y	Y
5 *Burr*	Y	Y	?	Y	Y
6 *Coble*	N	Y	Y	Y	N
7 McIntyre	Y	Y	Y	Y	Y
8 *Hayes*	Y	Y	Y	Y	Y
9 *Myrick*	Y	Y	Y	Y	N
10 *Ballenger*	Y	Y	Y	Y	Y
11 *Taylor*	Y	Y	Y	Y	Y
12 Watt	N	Y	Y	Y	Y
NORTH DAKOTA					
AL Pomeroy	Y	Y	Y	Y	Y
OHIO					
1 *Chabot*	Y	Y	Y	Y	Y
2 *Portman*	Y	Y	Y	Y	Y
3 Hall	Y	Y	Y	Y	Y
4 *Oxley*	Y	Y	Y	Y	Y
5 *Gillmor*	Y	Y	Y	Y	Y
6 Strickland	Y	Y	N	Y	Y
7 *Hobson*	Y	Y	Y	Y	Y
8 *Boehner*	Y	Y	Y	Y	Y
9 Kaptur	Y	Y	Y	Y	Y
10 Kucinich	Y	Y	N	Y	Y
11 Jones	?	?	Y	Y	Y
12 *Tiberi*	Y	Y	Y	Y	Y
13 Brown	Y	Y	Y	Y	Y
14 Sawyer	Y	Y	Y	Y	Y
15 *Pryce*	Y	Y	Y	Y	Y
16 *Regula*	Y	Y	Y	Y	Y
17 Traficant	Y	Y	?	?	?
18 *Ney*	Y	Y	Y	Y	Y
19 *LaTourette*	Y	Y	Y	Y	Y
OKLAHOMA					
1 *Largent*	Y	Y	Y	?	?
2 Carson	N	Y	Y	Y	Y
3 *Watkins*	Y	Y	Y	Y	Y
4 *Watts*	Y	Y	Y	Y	Y
5 *Istook*	Y	Y	Y	Y	Y
6 *Lucas*	Y	Y	Y	Y	Y
OREGON					
1 Wu	Y	Y	Y	Y	Y
2 *Walden*	Y	Y	Y	Y	Y
3 Blumenauer	N	Y	N	Y	Y
4 DeFazio	N	Y	N	Y	Y
5 Hooley	Y	Y	Y	N	Y
PENNSYLVANIA					
1 Brady	Y	Y	N	Y	Y
2 Fattah	Y	Y	N	Y	Y
3 Borski	Y	Y	N	Y	Y
4 *Hart*	Y	Y	Y	Y	Y
5 *Peterson*	Y	Y	Y	Y	Y
6 Holden	Y	Y	Y	Y	Y
7 *Weldon*	Y	Y	Y	Y	Y
8 *Greenwood*	Y	Y	Y	Y	Y
9 *Shuster, Bill*	Y	Y	Y	Y	Y
10 *Sherwood*	Y	Y	Y	Y	Y
11 Kanjorski	Y	Y	Y	Y	Y
12 Murtha	Y	Y	Y	Y	Y
13 Hoeffel	Y	Y	Y	Y	Y
14 Coyne	Y	Y	Y	Y	Y
15 *Toomey*	Y	Y	Y	N	N
16 *Pitts*	Y	Y	Y	Y	N
17 *Gekas*	Y	Y	Y	Y	Y
18 Doyle	Y	Y	Y	Y	Y
19 *Platts*	Y	Y	Y	Y	Y
20 Mascara	Y	Y	Y	Y	Y
21 *English*	Y	Y	N	Y	Y
RHODE ISLAND					
1 Kennedy	Y	Y	Y	Y	Y
2 Langevin	Y	Y	Y	Y	Y
SOUTH CAROLINA					
1 *Brown*	Y	Y	Y	Y	Y
2 Vacant					
3 *Graham*	Y	Y	Y	Y	Y
4 *DeMint*	Y	Y	Y	Y	N
5 Spratt	Y	Y	Y	Y	Y
6 Clyburn	Y	Y	Y	Y	Y
SOUTH DAKOTA					
AL *Thune*	Y	Y	Y	Y	Y
TENNESSEE					
1 *Jenkins*	Y	Y	Y	Y	Y
2 *Duncan*	N	Y	Y	Y	N
3 *Wamp*	Y	Y	Y	Y	Y
4 *Hilleary*	Y	Y	Y	Y	Y
5 Clement	Y	Y	Y	Y	Y
6 Gordon	Y	Y	Y	Y	Y
7 *Bryant*	Y	Y	Y	Y	Y
8 Tanner	Y	Y	Y	Y	Y
9 Ford	Y	Y	N	Y	Y
TEXAS					
1 Sandlin	Y	Y	Y	Y	Y
2 Turner	Y	Y	Y	Y	Y
3 *Johnson, Sam*	N	Y	Y	Y	N
4 Hall	Y	Y	Y	Y	Y
5 *Sessions*	Y	Y	Y	Y	N
6 *Barton*	Y	Y	Y	Y	N
7 *Culberson*	Y	Y	Y	Y	N
8 *Brady*	Y	Y	Y	Y	N
9 Lampson	Y	Y	Y	Y	Y
10 Doggett	N	Y	Y	Y	Y
11 Edwards	Y	Y	Y	Y	Y
12 *Granger*	Y	Y	Y	Y	Y
13 *Thornberry*	Y	Y	Y	Y	Y
14 *Paul*	N	Y	N	N	N
15 Hinojosa	Y	Y	Y	Y	Y
16 Reyes	Y	Y	Y	Y	Y
17 Stenholm	Y	Y	N	Y	Y
18 Jackson-Lee	Y	Y	Y	Y	Y
19 *Combest*	Y	Y	Y	Y	Y
20 Gonzalez	Y	Y	Y	Y	Y
21 *Smith*	Y	Y	Y	Y	Y
22 *DeLay*	?	?	?	?	?
23 *Bonilla*	Y	Y	Y	Y	Y
24 Frost	Y	Y	?	Y	Y
25 Bentsen	Y	Y	Y	Y	Y
26 *Armey*	Y	Y	Y	Y	Y
27 Ortiz	Y	Y	Y	Y	Y
28 Rodriguez	Y	Y	Y	Y	Y
29 Green	Y	Y	N	Y	Y
30 Johnson, E.B.	Y	Y	Y	Y	Y
UTAH					
1 *Hansen*	Y	Y	Y	Y	Y
2 Matheson	Y	Y	Y	Y	Y
3 *Cannon*	N	Y	Y	Y	Y
VERMONT					
AL *Sanders*	N	Y	Y	Y	Y
VIRGINIA					
1 *Davis, Jo Ann*	N	Y	Y	Y	Y
2 *Schrock*	Y	Y	Y	Y	Y
3 Scott	Y	Y	Y	Y	Y
4 *Forbes*	Y	Y	Y	Y	Y
5 *Goode*	N	Y	Y	Y	N
6 *Goodlatte*	Y	Y	Y	Y	Y
7 *Cantor*	Y	Y	Y	Y	N
8 Moran	Y	Y	Y	Y	Y
9 Boucher	Y	Y	Y	Y	Y
10 *Wolf*	Y	Y	Y	Y	Y
11 *Davis, T.*	Y	Y	?	Y	Y
WASHINGTON					
1 Inslee	Y	Y	Y	Y	Y
2 Larsen	Y	Y	Y	Y	Y
3 Baird	Y	Y	Y	Y	Y
4 *Hastings*	Y	Y	Y	Y	Y
5 *Nethercutt*	Y	Y	Y	Y	Y
6 Dicks	Y	Y	Y	Y	Y
7 McDermott	Y	Y	N	Y	Y
8 *Dunn*	Y	Y	Y	Y	Y
9 Smith	Y	Y	Y	Y	Y
WEST VIRGINIA					
1 Mollohan	Y	Y	Y	Y	Y
2 *Capito*	Y	Y	Y	Y	Y
3 Rahall	Y	Y	Y	Y	Y
WISCONSIN					
1 *Ryan*	Y	Y	Y	Y	Y
2 Baldwin	Y	Y	Y	Y	Y
3 Kind	Y	Y	Y	Y	Y
4 Kleczka	Y	Y	Y	Y	Y
5 Barrett	Y	Y	Y	Y	Y
6 *Petri*	Y	Y	Y	Y	Y
7 Obey	N	Y	Y	Y	Y
8 *Green*	Y	Y	Y	Y	Y
9 *Sensenbrenner*	N	Y	N	N	N
WYOMING					
AL *Cubin*	?	?	?	?	?

Southern states - Ala., Ark., Fla., Ga., Ky., La., Miss., N.C., Okla., S.C., Tenn., Texas, Va.

Key

436. HR 2330. Fiscal 2002 Agriculture Appropriations/Conference Report. Adoption of the conference report on the bill that would provide $75.9 billion, including $16 billion in discretionary funds, in fiscal 2002 for agriculture, rural development and nutrition programs. The agreement includes $23 billion for the food stamp program, $10.1 billion for child nutrition programs and $1 billion for the Agricultural Research Service. Adopted (thus sent to the Senate) 379-33: R 184-26; D 193-7 (ND 145-6, SD 48-1); I 2-0. Nov. 13, 2001.

437. HR 2541. State Department Agents/Passage. Smith, R-N.J., motion to suspend the rules and pass the bill that would increase the law enforcement powers of State Department special agents, including expanding their ability to execute search warrants and subpoenas, make arrests without warrants, and protect all individuals falling under their jurisdiction. Motion agreed to 410-0: R 208-0; D 200-0 (ND 150-0, SD 50-0); I 2-0. A two-thirds majority of those present and voting (274 in this case) is required for passage under suspension of the rules. Nov. 13, 2001.

438. HR 2500. Fiscal 2002 Commerce-Justice-State Appropriations/ Conference Report. Adoption of the conference report on the bill that would provide $41.6 billion in fiscal 2002 for the departments of Commerce, Justice and State, and the federal judiciary and related agencies, $1.9 billion more than fiscal 2001. Adopted (thus sent to the Senate) 411-15: R 201-15; D 208-0 (ND 155-0, SD 53-0); I 2-0. Nov. 14, 2001.

439. H Con Res 211. Burmese Human Rights/Adoption. Smith, R-N.J., motion to suspend the rules and adopt the concurrent resolution that would express the sense of Congress honoring Daw Aung San Suu Kyi on the 10th anniversary of her award of the Nobel Peace Prize and supporting human rights in Burma. Motion agreed to 420-0: R 214-0; D 204-0 (ND 151-0, SD 53-0); I 2-0. A two-thirds majority of those present and voting (280 in this case) is required for adoption under suspension of the rules. Nov. 14, 2001.

440. H Con Res 257. Postal Tribute/Adoption. McHugh, R-N.Y., motion to suspend the rules and adopt the concurrent resolution that would express the sense of Congress commending the work of the U.S. Postal Service and assuring its employees that the government will work to ensure their safety. Motion agreed to 418-0: R 212-0; D 204-0 (ND 151-0, SD 53-0); I 2-0. A two-thirds majority of those present and voting (279 in this case) is required for adoption under suspension of the rules. Nov. 14, 2001.

	436	437	438	439	440
ALABAMA					
1 *Callahan*	Y	Y	Y	Y	Y
2 *Everett*	Y	Y	Y	Y	Y
3 *Riley*	Y	Y	Y	Y	Y
4 *Aderholt*	Y	Y	Y	Y	Y
5 Cramer	Y	Y	Y	Y	Y
6 *Bachus*	Y	Y	Y	Y	Y
7 Hilliard	Y	Y	Y	Y	Y
ALASKA					
AL *Young*	Y	Y	Y	Y	Y
ARIZONA					
1 *Flake*	N	Y	N	Y	Y
2 Pastor	Y	Y	Y	Y	Y
3 *Stump*	Y	Y	Y	Y	Y
4 *Shadegg*	N	Y	Y	Y	Y
5 *Kolbe*	Y	Y	Y	Y	+
6 *Hayworth*	Y	Y	Y	Y	Y
ARKANSAS					
1 Berry	Y	Y	Y	Y	Y
2 Snyder	Y	Y	Y	Y	Y
3 Vacant					
4 Ross	Y	Y	Y	Y	Y
CALIFORNIA					
1 Thompson	Y	Y	Y	Y	Y
2 *Herger*	Y	Y	Y	Y	Y
3 *Ose*	Y	Y	Y	Y	Y
4 *Doolittle*	Y	Y	Y	Y	Y
5 Matsui	Y	Y	Y	Y	Y
6 Woolsey	Y	Y	Y	Y	Y
7 Miller, George	Y	Y	Y	Y	Y
8 Pelosi	Y	Y	Y	?	?
9 Lee	Y	Y	Y	Y	Y
10 Tauscher	Y	Y	Y	Y	Y
11 *Pombo*	Y	Y	Y	Y	Y
12 Lantos	Y	Y	Y	Y	Y
13 Stark	?	?	Y	Y	Y
14 Eshoo	Y	Y	Y	Y	Y
15 Honda	Y	Y	Y	Y	Y
16 Lofgren	Y	Y	Y	Y	Y
17 Farr	Y	Y	Y	Y	Y
18 Condit	Y	Y	Y	Y	Y
19 *Radanovich*	Y	Y	?	?	Y
20 Dooley	Y	Y	Y	Y	Y
21 *Thomas*	Y	Y	Y	Y	Y
22 Capps	Y	Y	Y	Y	Y
23 *Gallegly*	Y	Y	Y	Y	Y
24 Sherman	Y	Y	Y	Y	Y
25 *McKeon*	Y	Y	Y	Y	Y
26 Berman	Y	Y	Y	Y	Y
27 Schiff	Y	Y	Y	Y	Y
28 *Dreier*	Y	Y	Y	Y	Y
29 Waxman	Y	Y	Y	Y	Y
30 Becerra	Y	Y	Y	Y	Y
31 Solis	Y	Y	Y	Y	Y
32 Watson	Y	Y	Y	Y	Y
33 Roybal-Allard	Y	Y	Y	Y	Y
34 Napolitano	?	?	Y	Y	Y
35 Waters	Y	Y	Y	Y	Y
36 Harman	Y	Y	Y	Y	Y
37 Millender-McD.	Y	Y	Y	Y	Y
38 *Horn*	Y	Y	Y	Y	Y

	436	437	438	439	440
39 *Royce*	N	Y	N	Y	Y
40 *Lewis*	Y	Y	Y	Y	Y
41 *Miller, Gary*	N	Y	Y	Y	Y
42 Baca	Y	Y	Y	Y	Y
43 *Calvert*	Y	Y	Y	Y	Y
44 *Bono*	Y	Y	Y	Y	Y
45 *Rohrabacher*	N	Y	N	Y	Y
46 Sanchez	Y	Y	Y	Y	Y
47 *Cox*	?	?	Y	Y	Y
48 *Issa*	Y	Y	Y	Y	Y
49 Davis	Y	Y	Y	Y	Y
50 Filner	+	+	Y	Y	Y
51 *Cunningham*	Y	Y	Y	Y	Y
52 *Hunter*	Y	Y	Y	Y	Y
COLORADO					
1 DeGette	Y	Y	Y	Y	Y
2 Udall	Y	Y	Y	Y	Y
3 *McInnis*	Y	Y	Y	Y	Y
4 *Schaffer*	Y	Y	N	Y	Y
5 *Hefley*	N	Y	N	Y	Y
6 *Tancredo*	N	Y	N	Y	Y
CONNECTICUT					
1 Larson	Y	Y	Y	Y	Y
2 *Simmons*	Y	Y	Y	Y	Y
3 DeLauro	Y	Y	Y	Y	Y
4 *Shays*	N	Y	Y	Y	Y
5 Maloney	Y	Y	Y	Y	Y
6 *Johnson*	Y	Y	Y	Y	Y
DELAWARE					
AL *Castle*	Y	Y	Y	Y	Y
FLORIDA					
1 *Miller, J.*	Y	Y	Y	Y	Y
2 Boyd	Y	Y	Y	Y	Y
3 Brown	Y	Y	Y	Y	Y
4 *Crenshaw*	Y	Y	Y	Y	Y
5 Thurman	Y	Y	Y	Y	Y
6 *Stearns*	Y	Y	Y	Y	Y
7 *Mica*	Y	Y	Y	Y	Y
8 *Keller*	Y	Y	Y	Y	Y
9 *Bilirakis*	Y	Y	Y	Y	Y
10 *Young*	Y	Y	Y	Y	Y
11 Davis	Y	Y	Y	Y	Y
12 *Putnam*	Y	Y	Y	Y	Y
13 *Miller, D.*	Y	Y	Y	Y	Y
14 *Goss*	+	+	Y	+	+
15 *Weldon*	N	Y	Y	Y	Y
16 *Foley*	Y	Y	Y	Y	Y
17 Meek	Y	Y	Y	Y	Y
18 *Ros-Lehtinen*	Y	Y	Y	Y	Y
19 Wexler	?	?	Y	Y	Y
20 Deutsch	Y	Y	Y	Y	Y
21 *Diaz-Balart*	Y	Y	Y	Y	Y
22 *Shaw*	Y	Y	Y	Y	Y
23 Hastings	?	?	?	?	?
GEORGIA					
1 *Kingston*	Y	Y	Y	Y	Y
2 Bishop	Y	Y	Y	Y	Y
3 *Collins*	Y	Y	Y	Y	Y
4 McKinney	Y	Y	Y	Y	Y
5 Lewis	?	?	Y	Y	Y
6 *Isakson*	Y	Y	Y	Y	Y
7 *Barr*	Y	Y	Y	Y	Y
8 *Chambliss*	Y	Y	Y	Y	Y
9 *Deal*	Y	Y	Y	Y	Y
10 *Norwood*	Y	Y	Y	Y	Y
11 *Linder*	Y	Y	Y	Y	Y
HAWAII					
1 Abercrombie	Y	Y	Y	Y	Y
2 Mink	?	?	?	?	?
IDAHO					
1 *Otter*	Y	Y	Y	Y	Y
2 *Simpson*	Y	Y	Y	Y	Y
ILLINOIS					
1 Rush	Y	Y	Y	Y	Y
2 Jackson	Y	Y	Y	Y	Y
3 Lipinski	Y	Y	Y	Y	Y
4 Gutierrez	Y	Y	Y	Y	Y
5 Blagojevich	Y	Y	Y	Y	Y
6 *Hyde*	Y	Y	Y	Y	Y
7 Davis	Y	Y	Y	Y	Y
8 *Crane*	N	Y	Y	Y	Y
9 Schakowsky	Y	Y	Y	Y	Y
10 *Kirk*	Y	Y	Y	Y	Y
11 *Weller*	Y	Y	Y	Y	Y
12 Costello	Y	Y	Y	Y	Y
13 *Biggert*	Y	Y	Y	Y	Y

ND Northern Democrats   SD Southern Democrats

Illinois	436	437	438	439	440
14 Hastert					
15 *Johnson*	Y	Y	Y	Y	Y
16 *Manzullo*	Y	Y	Y	Y	Y
17 Evans	Y	Y	Y	Y	Y
18 *LaHood*	Y	Y	Y	Y	Y
19 Phelps	Y	Y	Y	Y	Y
20 *Shimkus*	Y	Y	Y	Y	Y

INDIANA

	436	437	438	439	440
1 Visclosky	Y	Y	Y	Y	Y
2 *Pence*	Y	Y	Y	Y	Y
3 Roemer	Y	Y	Y	Y	Y
4 *Souder*	Y	Y	Y	Y	Y
5 *Buyer*	Y	Y	Y	Y	Y
6 *Burton*	Y	Y	Y	Y	Y
7 *Kerns*	N	Y	N	Y	Y
8 *Hostettler*	N	Y	N	Y	Y
9 Hill	Y	Y	Y	Y	?
10 Carson	Y	Y	Y	Y	Y

IOWA

	436	437	438	439	440
1 *Leach*	Y	Y	Y	Y	Y
2 *Nussle*	Y	Y	Y	Y	Y
3 Boswell	Y	Y	Y	Y	Y
4 *Ganske*	Y	Y	Y	Y	Y
5 *Latham*	Y	Y	Y	Y	Y

KANSAS

	436	437	438	439	440
1 *Moran*	Y	Y	Y	Y	Y
2 *Ryun*	Y	Y	Y	Y	Y
3 Moore	Y	Y	Y	Y	Y
4 *Tiahrt*	Y	Y	Y	Y	Y

KENTUCKY

	436	437	438	439	440
1 *Whitfield*	Y	Y	Y	Y	Y
2 *Lewis*	Y	Y	Y	Y	Y
3 *Northup*	Y	Y	Y	Y	Y
4 Lucas	Y	Y	Y	Y	Y
5 *Rogers*	Y	Y	Y	Y	Y
6 *Fletcher*	Y	Y	Y	Y	Y

LOUISIANA

	436	437	438	439	440
1 *Vitter*	Y	Y	Y	Y	Y
2 Jefferson	Y	Y	Y	Y	Y
3 *Tauzin*	Y	Y	Y	Y	Y
4 *McCrery*	Y	Y	Y	Y	Y
5 *Cooksey*	Y	Y	Y	Y	Y
6 *Baker*	Y	Y	Y	Y	Y
7 John	Y	Y	Y	Y	Y

MAINE

	436	437	438	439	440
1 Allen	Y	Y	Y	Y	Y
2 Baldacci	Y	Y	Y	Y	Y

MARYLAND

	436	437	438	439	440
1 *Gilchrest*	Y	Y	Y	Y	Y
2 *Ehrlich*	Y	Y	Y	Y	Y
3 Cardin	Y	Y	Y	Y	Y
4 Wynn	Y	Y	Y	Y	Y
5 Hoyer	Y	?	Y	Y	Y
6 *Bartlett*	Y	Y	Y	Y	Y
7 Cummings	Y	Y	Y	Y	Y
8 *Morella*	Y	Y	Y	Y	Y

MASSACHUSETTS

	436	437	438	439	440
1 Olver	Y	Y	Y	Y	Y
2 Neal	Y	Y	Y	Y	Y
3 McGovern	Y	Y	Y	Y	Y
4 Frank	Y	Y	Y	?	?
5 Meehan	Y	Y	Y	Y	Y
6 Tierney	Y	Y	Y	Y	Y
7 Markey	Y	Y	Y	Y	Y
8 Capuano	Y	Y	Y	Y	Y
9 Lynch	Y	Y	Y	Y	Y
10 Delahunt	Y	Y	Y	Y	Y

MICHIGAN

	436	437	438	439	440
1 Stupak	Y	Y	Y	Y	Y
2 *Hoekstra*	Y	Y	Y	Y	Y
3 *Ehlers*	Y	Y	Y	Y	Y
4 *Camp*	Y	Y	Y	Y	Y
5 Barcia	Y	Y	Y	Y	Y
6 *Upton*	Y	Y	Y	Y	Y
7 *Smith*	Y	Y	Y	Y	Y
8 *Rogers*	Y	Y	Y	Y	Y
9 Kildee	Y	Y	Y	Y	Y
10 Bonior	Y	Y	Y	Y	Y
11 *Knollenberg*	Y	Y	Y	Y	?
12 Levin	Y	Y	Y	Y	Y
13 Rivers	Y	Y	Y	Y	Y
14 Conyers	Y	Y	Y	?	Y
15 Kilpatrick	Y	Y	Y	Y	Y
16 Dingell	Y	Y	Y	Y	Y

MINNESOTA

	436	437	438	439	440
1 *Gutknecht*	N	Y	Y	Y	Y
2 *Kennedy*	Y	Y	Y	Y	Y
3 *Ramstad*	Y	Y	Y	Y	Y
4 McCollum	Y	Y	Y	Y	Y
5 Sabo	Y	Y	Y	Y	Y
6 Luther	Y	Y	Y	Y	Y
7 Peterson	Y	Y	Y	Y	Y
8 Oberstar	Y	Y	Y	Y	Y

MISSISSIPPI

	436	437	438	439	440
1 *Wicker*	Y	Y	Y	Y	Y
2 Thompson	Y	Y	Y	Y	Y
3 *Pickering*	Y	Y	Y	Y	Y
4 Shows	Y	Y	Y	Y	Y
5 Taylor	Y	Y	Y	Y	Y

MISSOURI

	436	437	438	439	440
1 Clay	Y	Y	Y	Y	Y
2 *Akin*	N	Y	Y	Y	Y
3 Gephardt	Y	Y	Y	Y	Y
4 Skelton	Y	Y	Y	Y	Y
5 McCarthy	Y	Y	Y	Y	Y
6 *Graves*	Y	Y	Y	Y	Y
7 *Blunt*	Y	Y	Y	Y	Y
8 *Emerson*	Y	Y	Y	Y	Y
9 *Hulshof*	?	?	Y	Y	Y

MONTANA

	436	437	438	439	440
AL *Rehberg*	Y	Y	Y	Y	Y

NEBRASKA

	436	437	438	439	440
1 *Bereuter*	Y	Y	Y	Y	Y
2 *Terry*	Y	Y	Y	Y	Y
3 *Osborne*	Y	Y	Y	Y	Y

NEVADA

	436	437	438	439	440
1 Berkley	Y	Y	Y	Y	Y
2 *Gibbons*	Y	Y	Y	Y	Y

NEW HAMPSHIRE

	436	437	438	439	440
1 *Sununu*	Y	Y	Y	Y	Y
2 *Bass*	N	Y	Y	Y	Y

NEW JERSEY

	436	437	438	439	440
1 Andrews	Y	Y	Y	Y	Y
2 *LoBiondo*	Y	Y	Y	Y	Y
3 *Saxton*	Y	Y	Y	Y	Y
4 *Smith*	Y	Y	Y	Y	Y
5 *Roukema*	Y	Y	Y	Y	Y
6 Pallone	Y	Y	Y	Y	Y
7 *Ferguson*	Y	Y	Y	Y	Y
8 Pascrell	Y	Y	Y	Y	Y
9 Rothman	Y	Y	Y	Y	Y
10 Payne	Y	Y	Y	Y	Y
11 *Frelinghuysen*	Y	Y	Y	Y	Y
12 Holt	Y	Y	Y	Y	Y
13 Menendez	N	Y	Y	Y	Y

NEW MEXICO

	436	437	438	439	440
1 *Wilson*	Y	Y	Y	Y	Y
2 *Skeen*	Y	Y	Y	Y	Y
3 Udall	Y	Y	Y	Y	Y

NEW YORK

	436	437	438	439	440
1 *Grucci*	Y	Y	Y	Y	Y
2 Israel	N	Y	Y	Y	Y
3 *King*	Y	Y	Y	Y	Y
4 McCarthy	Y	Y	Y	Y	Y
5 Ackerman	Y	Y	Y	Y	Y
6 Meeks	Y	Y	?	Y	?
7 Crowley	Y	Y	Y	Y	Y
8 Nadler	Y	Y	Y	Y	Y
9 Weiner	+	+	Y	Y	Y
10 Towns	Y	Y	Y	Y	Y
11 Owens	Y	Y	Y	Y	Y
12 Velázquez	Y	Y	Y	Y	Y
13 *Fossella*	Y	?	Y	Y	Y
14 Maloney	Y	Y	Y	Y	Y
15 Rangel	Y	Y	Y	Y	Y
16 Serrano	Y	Y	Y	Y	Y
17 Engel	Y	Y	Y	Y	Y
18 Lowey	Y	Y	Y	Y	Y
19 *Kelly*	Y	Y	Y	Y	Y
20 *Gilman*	Y	Y	Y	Y	Y
21 McNulty	Y	Y	Y	Y	Y
22 *Sweeney*	Y	Y	Y	Y	Y
23 *Boehlert*	Y	Y	Y	Y	Y
24 *McHugh*	Y	Y	Y	Y	Y
25 *Walsh*	Y	Y	Y	Y	Y
26 Hinchey	Y	Y	Y	Y	Y
27 *Reynolds*	Y	Y	Y	Y	Y
28 Slaughter	Y	Y	Y	Y	Y
29 LaFalce	Y	Y	Y	Y	Y
30 *Quinn*	Y	Y	Y	Y	Y
31 Houghton	Y	Y	Y	Y	Y

NORTH CAROLINA

	436	437	438	439	440
1 Clayton	Y	Y	Y	Y	Y
2 Etheridge	Y	Y	Y	Y	Y
3 *Jones*	Y	Y	N	Y	Y
4 Price	Y	Y	Y	Y	Y
5 *Burr*	Y	Y	Y	Y	Y
6 *Coble*	Y	Y	Y	Y	Y
7 McIntyre	Y	Y	Y	Y	Y
8 *Hayes*	Y	Y	Y	Y	Y
9 *Myrick*	Y	Y	Y	Y	Y
10 *Ballenger*	Y	Y	Y	Y	Y
11 *Taylor*	N	Y	Y	Y	Y
12 Watt	Y	Y	Y	Y	Y

NORTH DAKOTA

	436	437	438	439	440
AL Pomeroy	Y	Y	Y	?	Y

OHIO

	436	437	438	439	440
1 *Chabot*	N	Y	Y	Y	Y
2 *Portman*	Y	Y	Y	Y	Y
3 Hall	Y	Y	Y	Y	Y
4 *Oxley*	Y	Y	Y	Y	Y
5 *Gillmor*	?	?	Y	Y	Y
6 Strickland	Y	Y	Y	Y	Y
7 *Hobson*	Y	Y	Y	Y	Y
8 *Boehner*	Y	Y	Y	Y	Y
9 Kaptur	Y	Y	Y	Y	Y
10 Kucinich	Y	Y	Y	Y	Y
11 Jones	Y	Y	Y	Y	Y
12 *Tiberi*	Y	Y	Y	Y	Y
13 Brown	Y	Y	Y	Y	Y
14 Sawyer	Y	Y	Y	Y	Y
15 *Pryce*	Y	Y	Y	Y	Y
16 *Regula*	Y	Y	Y	Y	Y
17 Traficant	Y	Y	Y	Y	Y
18 *Ney*	Y	Y	Y	Y	Y
19 *LaTourette*	Y	Y	Y	Y	Y

OKLAHOMA

	436	437	438	439	440
1 *Largent*	Y	Y	Y	Y	Y
2 Carson	Y	Y	Y	Y	Y
3 *Watkins*	Y	Y	Y	Y	Y
4 *Watts*	+	+	Y	Y	Y
5 *Istook*	Y	Y	Y	Y	Y
6 *Lucas*	?	?	Y	Y	Y

OREGON

	436	437	438	439	440
1 Wu	Y	Y	Y	Y	?
2 *Walden*	Y	Y	Y	Y	Y
3 Blumenauer	Y	Y	Y	Y	Y
4 DeFazio	Y	Y	Y	Y	Y
5 Hooley	Y	Y	Y	Y	Y

PENNSYLVANIA

	436	437	438	439	440
1 Brady	Y	Y	Y	Y	Y
2 Fattah	Y	Y	Y	Y	Y
3 Borski	Y	Y	Y	Y	Y
4 *Hart*	Y	Y	Y	Y	Y
5 *Peterson*	Y	Y	Y	Y	Y
6 Holden	Y	Y	Y	Y	Y
7 *Weldon*	Y	Y	?	Y	?
8 *Greenwood*	Y	Y	Y	Y	Y
9 *Shuster, Bill*	Y	Y	Y	Y	Y
10 *Sherwood*	?	?	Y	Y	Y
11 Kanjorski	Y	Y	Y	Y	Y
12 Murtha	Y	Y	Y	Y	Y
13 Hoeffel	Y	Y	Y	Y	Y
14 Coyne	Y	Y	Y	Y	Y
15 *Toomey*	N	Y	Y	Y	Y
16 *Pitts*	N	Y	Y	Y	Y
17 *Gekas*	Y	Y	Y	Y	Y
18 Doyle	Y	Y	Y	Y	Y
19 *Platts*	Y	Y	Y	Y	Y
20 Mascara	+	+	Y	Y	Y
21 *English*	Y	Y	Y	Y	Y

RHODE ISLAND

	436	437	438	439	440
1 Kennedy	Y	Y	Y	Y	Y
2 Langevin	Y	Y	Y	Y	Y

SOUTH CAROLINA

	436	437	438	439	440
1 *Brown*	Y	Y	Y	Y	Y
2 Vacant					
3 *Graham*	?	?	Y	Y	Y
4 *DeMint*	Y	Y	Y	Y	Y
5 Spratt	Y	Y	Y	Y	Y
6 Clyburn	Y	Y	Y	Y	Y

SOUTH DAKOTA

	436	437	438	439	440
AL *Thune*	Y	Y	Y	Y	Y

TENNESSEE

	436	437	438	439	440
1 *Jenkins*	Y	Y	Y	Y	Y
2 *Duncan*	Y	Y	N	Y	Y
3 *Wamp*	Y	Y	Y	Y	Y
4 *Hilleary*	Y	Y	Y	Y	Y
5 Clement	Y	Y	Y	Y	Y
6 Gordon	Y	Y	Y	Y	Y
7 *Bryant*	Y	Y	Y	Y	Y
8 Tanner	Y	Y	Y	Y	Y
9 Ford	Y	Y	Y	Y	Y

TEXAS

	436	437	438	439	440
1 Sandlin	Y	Y	Y	Y	Y
2 Turner	Y	Y	Y	Y	Y
3 *Johnson, Sam*	N	Y	Y	Y	Y
4 Hall	Y	Y	Y	Y	Y
5 *Sessions*	Y	Y	N	Y	Y
6 *Barton*	Y	Y	Y	Y	Y
7 *Culberson*	Y	Y	Y	Y	Y
8 *Brady*	Y	Y	Y	Y	Y
9 Lampson	Y	Y	Y	Y	Y
10 Doggett	N	Y	Y	Y	Y
11 Edwards	Y	Y	Y	Y	Y
12 *Granger*	Y	Y	Y	Y	Y
13 *Thornberry*	Y	Y	Y	Y	Y
14 *Paul*	N	Y	N	Y	Y
15 Hinojosa	Y	Y	Y	Y	Y
16 Reyes	?	?	Y	Y	Y
17 Stenholm	Y	Y	Y	Y	Y
18 Jackson-Lee	Y	Y	Y	Y	Y
19 *Combest*	Y	Y	Y	Y	Y
20 Gonzalez	Y	Y	Y	Y	Y
21 *Smith*	Y	Y	Y	Y	Y
22 *DeLay*	Y	Y	Y	Y	Y
23 *Bonilla*	Y	Y	Y	Y	Y
24 Frost	Y	Y	Y	Y	Y
25 Bentsen	Y	Y	Y	Y	Y
26 *Armey*	Y	Y	Y	Y	Y
27 Ortiz	Y	Y	Y	Y	Y
28 Rodriguez	Y	Y	Y	Y	Y
29 Green	Y	Y	Y	Y	Y
30 Johnson, E.B.	?	Y	Y	Y	Y

UTAH

	436	437	438	439	440
1 *Hansen*	Y	Y	Y	Y	Y
2 Matheson	Y	Y	Y	Y	Y
3 *Cannon*	Y	Y	Y	Y	Y

VERMONT

	436	437	438	439	440
AL Sanders	Y	Y	Y	Y	Y

VIRGINIA

	436	437	438	439	440
1 *Davis, Jo Ann*	Y	Y	Y	Y	?
2 *Schrock*	Y	Y	Y	Y	Y
3 Scott	Y	Y	Y	Y	Y
4 *Forbes*	Y	Y	Y	Y	Y
5 *Goode*	Y	Y	Y	Y	Y
6 *Goodlatte*	Y	Y	Y	Y	Y
7 *Cantor*	Y	Y	Y	Y	Y
8 Moran	Y	Y	Y	Y	Y
9 Boucher	Y	Y	Y	Y	Y
10 *Wolf*	Y	Y	Y	Y	Y
11 *Davis, T.*	N	?	Y	?	?

WASHINGTON

	436	437	438	439	440
1 Inslee	Y	Y	Y	Y	Y
2 Larsen	Y	Y	Y	Y	Y
3 Baird	Y	Y	Y	Y	Y
4 *Hastings*	Y	Y	Y	Y	Y
5 *Nethercutt*	Y	Y	Y	Y	Y
6 Dicks	Y	Y	Y	Y	Y
7 McDermott	N	Y	Y	Y	Y
8 *Dunn*	Y	Y	Y	Y	Y
9 Smith	Y	Y	Y	Y	Y

WEST VIRGINIA

	436	437	438	439	440
1 Mollohan	Y	Y	Y	Y	Y
2 *Capito*	Y	Y	Y	Y	Y
3 Rahall	Y	Y	Y	Y	Y

WISCONSIN

	436	437	438	439	440
1 *Ryan*	N	Y	N	Y	Y
2 Baldwin	N	Y	Y	Y	Y
3 Kind	N	Y	Y	Y	Y
4 Kleczka	Y	Y	Y	Y	Y
5 Barrett	N	Y	Y	Y	Y
6 *Petri*	N	N	N	Y	Y
7 Obey	Y	Y	Y	Y	Y
8 *Green*	N	Y	N	Y	Y
9 *Sensenbrenner*	N	N	Y	N	Y

WYOMING

	436	437	438	439	440
AL *Cubin*	?	?	?	?	?

Southern states - Ala., Ark., Fla., Ga., Ky., La., Miss., N.C., Okla., S.C., Tenn., Texas, Va.

Key

Y	Voted for (yea).
#	Paired for.
+	Announced for.
N	Voted against (nay).
X	Paired against.
–	Announced against.
P	Voted "present."
C	Voted "present" to avoid possible conflict of interest.
?	Did not vote or otherwise make a position known.

Democrats **Republicans**
Independents

441. HR 2269. Employee Retirement Advice/Democratic Substitute. Andrews, D-N.J., substitute amendment that would increase requirements for financial advisers, including additional mandatory professional qualifications, full disclosure of conflicts of interest and fees every time they advise employees, and require locating alternative advisers when conflicts of interest exist. It also would increase oversight of the advisers and stiffen penalties for breach of fiduciary duties. Rejected 180-243: R 0-214; D 179-28 (ND 139-15, SD 40-13); I 1-1. Nov. 15, 2001.

442. HR 2269. Employee Retirement Advice/Passage. Passage of the bill that would amend the Employee Retirement Income Security Act (ERISA) and the tax code to allow employers to provide third-party financial advisers to their employees to discuss retirement and pension plans. The bill would require advisers to disclose fees and any potential conflicts of interest to employees and work in their best interest. Passed 280-144: R 215-0; D 64-143 (ND 39-115, SD 25-28); I 1-1. Nov. 15, 2001.

443. H Con Res 228. Children's Aid/Adoption. Herger, R-Calif., motion to suspend the rules and adopt the resolution that would express the sense of Congress that the children who lost a parent or guardian in the Sept. 11 terror attacks should be provided with all necessary assistance and urge agencies to make such assistance a priority. Motion agreed to 418-0: R 210-0; D 206-0 (ND 154-0, SD 52-0); I 2-0. A two-thirds majority of those present and voting (279 in this case) is required for adoption under suspension of the rules. Nov. 15, 2001.

444. HR 2887. Pediatric Drug Tests/Passage. Tauzin, R-La., motion to suspend the rules and pass the bill that would renew through 2007 a statute allowing companies that conduct pediatric testing at the request of the Food and Drug Administration an additional six months of exclusive marketing rights and authorize $200 million in annual awards for universities and others that conduct testing but do not receive such rights. Motion agreed to 338-86: R 212-3; D 125-82 (ND 87-67, SD 38-15); I 1-1. A two-thirds majority of those present and voting (283 in this case) is required for passage under suspension of the rules. Nov. 15, 2001.

445. H Con Res 239. School Prayer/Adoption. Isakson, R-Ga., motion to suspend the rules and adopt the resolution that would express the sense of Congress that schools should allow children time to pray for, or silently reflect upon, the country during the war against terrorism. Motion agreed to 297-125: R 212-3; D 84-121 (ND 45-108, SD 39-13); I 1-1. A two-thirds majority of those present and voting (282 in this case) is required for adoption under suspension of the rules. Nov. 15, 2001.

	441	442	443	444	445
ALABAMA					
1 *Callahan*	N	Y	Y	Y	Y
2 *Everett*	N	Y	Y	Y	Y
3 *Riley*	N	Y	Y	Y	Y
4 *Aderholt*	N	Y	Y	Y	Y
5 Cramer	N	Y	Y	Y	Y
6 *Bachus*	N	Y	Y	Y	Y
7 Hilliard	Y	N	Y	N	Y
ALASKA					
AL *Young*	N	Y	Y	Y	Y
ARIZONA					
1 *Flake*	N	Y	Y	Y	Y
2 Pastor	Y	N	Y	N	N
3 *Stump*	N	Y	Y	Y	Y
4 *Shadegg*	N	Y	Y	Y	Y
5 *Kolbe*	N	Y	Y	Y	Y
6 *Hayworth*	N	Y	Y	Y	Y
ARKANSAS					
1 Berry	Y	Y	Y	N	Y
2 Snyder	N	Y	Y	N	Y
3 Vacant					
4 Ross	Y	N	Y	Y	Y
CALIFORNIA					
1 Thompson	N	Y	Y	Y	N
2 *Herger*	N	Y	Y	Y	Y
3 *Ose*	N	Y	Y	Y	Y
4 *Doolittle*	N	Y	Y	Y	Y
5 Matsui	Y	Y	Y	Y	N
6 Woolsey	Y	N	Y	N	N
7 Miller, George	Y	N	Y	N	N
8 Pelosi	Y	N	Y	Y	N
9 Lee	Y	N	Y	N	N
10 Tauscher	Y	Y	Y	Y	N
11 *Pombo*	N	Y	Y	Y	Y
12 Lantos	Y	N	Y	N	N
13 Stark	Y	N	Y	N	N
14 Eshoo	Y	N	Y	Y	N
15 Honda	Y	N	Y	Y	N
16 Lofgren	Y	N	Y	Y	N
17 Farr	Y	N	Y	N	N
18 Condit	Y	Y	Y	Y	Y
19 *Radanovich*	N	Y	Y	Y	Y
20 Dooley	N	Y	Y	Y	N
21 *Thomas*	N	Y	Y	Y	Y
22 Capps	Y	N	Y	Y	N
23 *Gallegly*	N	Y	Y	Y	Y
24 Sherman	Y	Y	Y	Y	N
25 *McKeon*	N	Y	Y	Y	Y
26 Berman	Y	N	Y	N	N
27 Schiff	Y	Y	Y	Y	N
28 *Dreier*	N	Y	Y	Y	Y
29 Waxman	Y	N	Y	N	N
30 Becerra	?	?	?	?	?
31 Solis	Y	N	Y	N	N
32 Watson	Y	N	Y	N	N
33 Roybal-Allard	Y	N	Y	N	N
34 Napolitano	Y	N	Y	Y	N
35 Waters	Y	N	Y	N	N
36 Harman	Y	Y	Y	Y	N
37 Millender-McD.	Y	N	Y	N	N
38 *Horn*	N	Y	Y	Y	N

	441	442	443	444	445
39 *Royce*	N	Y	?	Y	Y
40 *Lewis*	N	Y	Y	Y	Y
41 *Miller, Gary*	N	Y	Y	Y	Y
42 Baca	Y	N	Y	Y	Y
43 *Calvert*	N	Y	Y	Y	Y
44 *Bono*	N	Y	Y	Y	Y
45 *Rohrabacher*	N	Y	Y	Y	Y
46 Sanchez	Y	Y	Y	N	N
47 *Cox*	N	Y	?	Y	Y
48 *Issa*	N	Y	Y	Y	Y
49 Davis	N	Y	Y	N	N
50 Filner	Y	N	Y	N	N
51 *Cunningham*	N	Y	Y	Y	Y
52 *Hunter*	N	Y	Y	Y	Y
COLORADO					
1 DeGette	Y	N	Y	Y	N
2 Udall	Y	N	Y	N	N
3 *McInnis*	N	Y	Y	Y	Y
4 *Schaffer*	N	Y	Y	Y	Y
5 *Hefley*	N	Y	Y	Y	Y
6 *Tancredo*	N	Y	Y	Y	Y
CONNECTICUT					
1 Larson	N	Y	Y	Y	N
2 *Simmons*	N	Y	?	Y	Y
3 DeLauro	Y	N	Y	N	N
4 *Shays*	N	Y	Y	Y	N
5 Maloney	Y	Y	Y	Y	N
6 *Johnson*	N	Y	Y	Y	N
DELAWARE					
AL *Castle*	N	Y	Y	Y	Y
FLORIDA					
1 *Miller, J.*	N	Y	Y	Y	Y
2 Boyd	N	Y	Y	Y	Y
3 Brown	Y	N	Y	Y	N
4 *Crenshaw*	N	Y	Y	Y	Y
5 Thurman	Y	N	Y	N	P
6 *Stearns*	N	Y	Y	Y	Y
7 *Mica*	N	Y	Y	Y	Y
8 *Keller*	–	+	+	+	+
9 *Bilirakis*	N	Y	Y	Y	Y
10 *Young*	N	Y	Y	Y	Y
11 Davis	N	Y	Y	Y	Y
12 *Putnam*	N	Y	Y	Y	Y
13 *Miller, D.*	N	Y	Y	Y	Y
14 *Goss*	N	Y	Y	Y	Y
15 *Weldon*	N	Y	Y	Y	Y
16 *Foley*	N	Y	Y	Y	Y
17 Meek	Y	N	Y	Y	Y
18 *Ros-Lehtinen*	N	Y	Y	Y	Y
19 Wexler	Y	N	Y	N	N
20 Deutsch	Y	N	Y	N	N
21 *Diaz-Balart*	N	Y	Y	Y	Y
22 *Shaw*	N	Y	Y	Y	Y
23 Hastings	?	?	?	?	?
GEORGIA					
1 *Kingston*	N	Y	Y	Y	Y
2 Bishop	Y	N	Y	Y	Y
3 *Collins*	N	Y	Y	Y	Y
4 McKinney	Y	N	Y	N	Y
5 Lewis	Y	N	Y	N	N
6 *Isakson*	N	Y	Y	Y	Y
7 *Barr*	N	Y	Y	Y	Y
8 *Chambliss*	N	Y	Y	Y	Y
9 *Deal*	N	Y	Y	Y	Y
10 *Norwood*	N	Y	Y	Y	Y
11 *Linder*	N	Y	Y	Y	Y
HAWAII					
1 Abercrombie	Y	N	Y	N	N
2 Mink	Y	N	Y	N	N
IDAHO					
1 *Otter*	N	Y	Y	Y	Y
2 *Simpson*	N	Y	Y	Y	Y
ILLINOIS					
1 Rush	Y	N	Y	Y	Y
2 Jackson	Y	N	Y	N	N
3 Lipinski	Y	N	Y	Y	Y
4 Gutierrez	Y	N	Y	Y	N
5 Blagojevich	Y	N	Y	N	N
6 *Hyde*	N	Y	Y	Y	Y
7 Davis	Y	N	Y	N	N
8 *Crane*	N	Y	Y	Y	Y
9 Schakowsky	Y	N	Y	N	N
10 *Kirk*	N	Y	?	Y	N
11 *Weller*	N	Y	Y	Y	Y
12 Costello	Y	N	Y	Y	Y
13 *Biggert*	N	Y	Y	Y	Y

ND Northern Democrats   SD Southern Democrats

	441	442	443	444	445
14 ***Hastert***					
15 ***Johnson***	N	Y	Y	Y	Y
16 ***Manzullo***	N	Y	Y	Y	Y
17 Evans	Y	N	Y	N	N
18 ***LaHood***	N	Y	Y	Y	Y
19 Phelps	N	N	Y	Y	Y
20 ***Shimkus***	N	Y	Y	Y	Y
INDIANA					
1 Visclosky	Y	N	Y	Y	Y
2 ***Pence***	N	Y	Y	Y	Y
3 Roemer	Y	Y	Y	Y	Y
4 ***Souder***	N	Y	Y	Y	Y
5 ***Buyer***	N	Y	Y	Y	Y
6 ***Burton***	N	Y	Y	Y	Y
7 ***Kerns***	N	Y	Y	Y	Y
8 ***Hostettler***	N	Y	Y	N	N
9 Hill	N	Y	Y	Y	Y
10 Carson	Y	N	Y	Y	N
IOWA					
1 ***Leach***	N	Y	Y	Y	Y
2 ***Nussle***	N	Y	Y	Y	Y
3 Boswell	Y	Y	Y	Y	Y
4 ***Ganske***	?	Y	Y	Y	Y
5 ***Latham***	N	Y	Y	Y	Y
KANSAS					
1 ***Moran***	N	Y	Y	Y	Y
2 ***Ryun***	N	Y	Y	Y	Y
3 Moore	Y	Y	Y	Y	Y
4 ***Tiahrt***	N	Y	Y	Y	Y
KENTUCKY					
1 ***Whitfield***	N	Y	Y	Y	Y
2 ***Lewis***	N	Y	Y	Y	Y
3 ***Northup***	N	Y	Y	Y	Y
4 Lucas	N	Y	Y	Y	Y
5 ***Rogers***	N	Y	Y	Y	Y
6 ***Fletcher***	N	Y	Y	Y	Y
LOUISIANA					
1 ***Vitter***	N	Y	Y	Y	Y
2 Jefferson	Y	N	Y	Y	Y
3 ***Tauzin***	N	Y	Y	Y	Y
4 ***McCrery***	N	Y	?	Y	Y
5 ***Cooksey***	N	Y	Y	Y	Y
6 ***Baker***	N	Y	Y	Y	Y
7 John	N	Y	Y	Y	Y
MAINE					
1 Allen	Y	N	Y	N	N
2 Baldacci	Y	N	Y	N	Y
MARYLAND					
1 ***Gilchrest***	N	Y	Y	Y	Y
2 ***Ehrlich***	N	Y	Y	Y	Y
3 Cardin	N	N	Y	Y	N
4 Wynn	Y	N	Y	Y	N
5 Hoyer	Y	N	Y	Y	N
6 ***Bartlett***	N	Y	Y	Y	Y
7 Cummings	Y	N	Y	N	N
8 ***Morella***	N	Y	Y	Y	Y
MASSACHUSETTS					
1 Olver	Y	N	Y	N	N
2 Neal	Y	Y	Y	Y	N
3 McGovern	Y	N	Y	Y	N
4 Frank	Y	N	Y	N	N
5 Meehan	Y	N	Y	Y	N
6 Tierney	Y	N	Y	N	N
7 Markey	Y	N	Y	N	N
8 Capuano	Y	N	Y	Y	N
9 Lynch	Y	N	Y	Y	N
10 Delahunt	Y	N	Y	Y	N
MICHIGAN					
1 Stupak	Y	N	Y	N	Y
2 ***Hoekstra***	N	Y	Y	Y	Y
3 ***Ehlers***	N	Y	Y	Y	Y
4 ***Camp***	N	Y	Y	Y	Y
5 Barcia	Y	Y	Y	N	Y
6 ***Upton***	N	Y	Y	Y	Y
7 ***Smith***	N	Y	Y	Y	Y
8 ***Rogers***	N	Y	Y	Y	Y
9 Kildee	Y	N	Y	N	Y
10 Bonior	Y	N	Y	N	N
11 ***Knollenberg***	N	Y	Y	Y	Y
12 Levin	Y	N	Y	N	N
13 Rivers	Y	N	Y	Y	N
14 Conyers	Y	N	Y	N	N
15 Kilpatrick	Y	N	Y	N	N
16 Dingell	Y	N	Y	N	N

	441	442	443	444	445
MINNESOTA					
1 ***Gutknecht***	N	Y	Y	N	Y
2 ***Kennedy***	N	Y	Y	Y	Y
3 ***Ramstad***	N	Y	Y	Y	Y
4 McCollum	Y	N	Y	Y	N
5 Sabo	Y	Y	Y	N	N
6 Luther	Y	N	Y	Y	Y
7 Peterson	Y	Y	Y	Y	Y
8 Oberstar	Y	N	Y	N	N
MISSISSIPPI					
1 ***Wicker***	N	Y	Y	Y	Y
2 Thompson	Y	N	Y	N	Y
3 ***Pickering***	N	Y	Y	Y	Y
4 Shows	Y	N	Y	Y	Y
5 Taylor	N	Y	Y	Y	Y
MISSOURI					
1 Clay	Y	N	Y	N	N
2 ***Akin***	N	Y	Y	Y	Y
3 Gephardt	Y	N	Y	Y	Y
4 Skelton	N	Y	Y	Y	Y
5 McCarthy	Y	Y	Y	N	N
6 ***Graves***	N	Y	Y	Y	Y
7 ***Blunt***	N	Y	Y	Y	Y
8 ***Emerson***	N	Y	Y	N	Y
9 ***Hulshof***	N	Y	Y	Y	Y
MONTANA					
AL ***Rehberg***	N	Y	Y	Y	Y
NEBRASKA					
1 ***Bereuter***	N	Y	Y	Y	Y
2 ***Terry***	N	Y	Y	Y	Y
3 ***Osborne***	N	Y	Y	Y	Y
NEVADA					
1 Berkley	Y	N	Y	Y	N
2 ***Gibbons***	N	Y	Y	Y	Y
NEW HAMPSHIRE					
1 ***Sununu***	N	Y	Y	Y	Y
2 ***Bass***	N	Y	Y	Y	Y
NEW JERSEY					
1 Andrews	Y	N	Y	N	N
2 ***LoBiondo***	N	Y	Y	Y	Y
3 ***Saxton***	N	Y	Y	Y	Y
4 ***Smith***	N	Y	Y	Y	Y
5 ***Roukema***	N	Y	Y	Y	Y
6 Pallone	Y	N	Y	N	N
7 ***Ferguson***	N	Y	Y	Y	Y
8 Pascrell	Y	N	Y	Y	N
9 Rothman	Y	N	Y	Y	N
10 Payne	Y	N	Y	N	N
11 ***Frelinghuysen***	N	Y	Y	Y	Y
12 Holt	Y	Y	Y	Y	N
13 Menendez	Y	N	Y	Y	N
NEW MEXICO					
1 ***Wilson***	N	Y	Y	Y	Y
2 ***Skeen***	N	Y	Y	Y	Y
3 Udall	Y	N	Y	Y	N
NEW YORK					
1 ***Grucci***	N	Y	Y	Y	Y
2 Israel	Y	Y	Y	Y	Y
3 ***King***	N	Y	Y	Y	Y
4 McCarthy	Y	Y	Y	Y	Y
5 Ackerman	Y	N	Y	Y	N
6 Meeks	?	?	?	?	?
7 Crowley	Y	Y	Y	N	N
8 Nadler	Y	N	Y	Y	N
9 Weiner	Y	N	Y	Y	N
10 Towns	Y	N	Y	Y	N
11 Owens	Y	N	Y	N	N
12 Velázquez	Y	N	Y	Y	N
13 ***Fossella***	N	Y	Y	Y	Y
14 Maloney	Y	Y	Y	Y	Y
15 Rangel	Y	N	Y	N	N
16 Serrano	Y	N	Y	N	N
17 Engel	Y	N	Y	Y	N
18 Lowey	Y	N	Y	Y	N
19 ***Kelly***	N	Y	Y	Y	Y
20 ***Gilman***	N	Y	Y	Y	Y
21 McNulty	Y	N	Y	Y	Y
22 ***Sweeney***	N	Y	Y	Y	Y
23 ***Boehlert***	N	Y	Y	Y	Y
24 ***McHugh***	N	Y	Y	Y	Y
25 ***Walsh***	N	Y	Y	Y	Y
26 Hinchey	Y	N	Y	Y	N
27 ***Reynolds***	N	Y	Y	Y	Y
28 Slaughter	Y	N	Y	Y	N
29 LaFalce	Y	N	Y	Y	Y

	441	442	443	444	445
30 ***Quinn***	N	Y	Y	Y	Y
31 ***Houghton***	N	Y	Y	Y	Y
NORTH CAROLINA					
1 Clayton	Y	N	Y	Y	N
2 Etheridge	Y	N	Y	Y	Y
3 ***Jones***	N	Y	Y	Y	Y
4 Price	Y	N	Y	Y	Y
5 ***Burr***	N	Y	Y	Y	Y
6 ***Coble***	N	Y	Y	Y	Y
7 McIntyre	Y	Y	Y	Y	Y
8 ***Hayes***	N	Y	Y	Y	Y
9 ***Myrick***	N	Y	Y	Y	Y
10 ***Ballenger***	N	Y	Y	Y	Y
11 ***Taylor***	N	Y	Y	Y	Y
12 Watt	Y	N	Y	Y	N
NORTH DAKOTA					
AL Pomeroy	N	Y	Y	N	Y
OHIO					
1 ***Chabot***	N	Y	Y	Y	Y
2 ***Portman***	N	Y	Y	Y	Y
3 Hall	?	?	?	?	?
4 ***Oxley***	N	Y	Y	Y	Y
5 ***Gillmor***	N	Y	Y	Y	Y
6 Strickland	Y	N	Y	Y	Y
7 ***Hobson***	N	Y	Y	Y	Y
8 ***Boehner***	N	Y	Y	Y	Y
9 Kaptur	Y	N	Y	N	N
10 Kucinich	Y	N	Y	N	N
11 Jones	Y	N	Y	N	N
12 ***Tiberi***	N	Y	Y	Y	Y
13 Brown	Y	N	Y	N	N
14 Sawyer	Y	N	Y	N	N
15 ***Pryce***	N	Y	Y	Y	Y
16 ***Regula***	N	Y	Y	Y	Y
17 Traficant	N	Y	Y	Y	Y
18 ***Ney***	N	Y	Y	Y	Y
19 ***LaTourette***	N	Y	Y	Y	Y
OKLAHOMA					
1 ***Largent***	?	?	?	?	?
2 Carson	Y	Y	Y	Y	Y
3 ***Watkins***	N	Y	Y	Y	Y
4 ***Watts***	N	Y	Y	Y	Y
5 ***Istook***	N	Y	Y	Y	Y
6 ***Lucas***	N	Y	Y	Y	Y
OREGON					
1 Wu	N	Y	Y	N	Y
2 ***Walden***	N	Y	Y	Y	Y
3 Blumenauer	Y	Y	Y	N	N
4 DeFazio	Y	N	Y	N	Y
5 Hooley	Y	Y	Y	Y	Y
PENNSYLVANIA					
1 Brady	Y	N	Y	Y	N
2 Fattah	Y	N	Y	Y	N
3 Borski	Y	N	Y	Y	N
4 ***Hart***	N	Y	Y	Y	Y
5 ***Peterson***	N	Y	Y	Y	Y
6 Holden	Y	N	Y	Y	Y
7 ***Weldon***	N	Y	Y	Y	Y
8 ***Greenwood***	N	Y	Y	Y	Y
9 ***Shuster, Bill***	N	Y	Y	Y	Y
10 ***Sherwood***	N	Y	Y	Y	Y
11 Kanjorski	Y	N	Y	Y	Y
12 Murtha	Y	N	Y	N	Y
13 Hoeffel	Y	N	Y	Y	N
14 Coyne	Y	N	Y	N	N
15 ***Toomey***	N	Y	Y	Y	Y
16 ***Pitts***	N	Y	Y	Y	Y
17 ***Gekas***	N	Y	Y	Y	Y
18 Doyle	Y	N	Y	N	Y
19 ***Platts***	N	Y	Y	Y	Y
20 Mascara	Y	N	Y	Y	Y
21 ***English***	N	Y	Y	Y	Y
RHODE ISLAND					
1 Kennedy	Y	N	Y	N	N
2 Langevin	Y	N	Y	N	Y
SOUTH CAROLINA					
1 ***Brown***	N	Y	Y	Y	Y
2 Vacant					
3 ***Graham***	N	Y	Y	Y	Y
4 ***DeMint***	N	Y	Y	Y	Y
5 Spratt	Y	N	Y	N	Y
6 Clyburn	Y	N	Y	Y	Y
SOUTH DAKOTA					
AL ***Thune***	N	Y	Y	Y	Y

	441	442	443	444	445
TENNESSEE					
1 ***Jenkins***	N	Y	Y	Y	Y
2 ***Duncan***	N	Y	Y	Y	Y
3 ***Wamp***	N	Y	Y	Y	Y
4 ***Hilleary***	N	Y	Y	Y	Y
5 Clement	N	Y	Y	Y	Y
6 Gordon	N	Y	Y	Y	Y
7 ***Bryant***	N	Y	Y	Y	Y
8 Tanner	N	Y	Y	Y	Y
9 Ford	Y	Y	?	Y	Y
TEXAS					
1 Sandlin	Y	Y	Y	N	Y
2 Turner	Y	Y	Y	Y	Y
3 ***Johnson, Sam***	N	Y	Y	Y	Y
4 Hall	N	Y	Y	Y	Y
5 ***Sessions***	N	Y	Y	Y	Y
6 ***Barton***	?	?	?	?	?
7 ***Culberson***	N	Y	Y	Y	Y
8 ***Brady***	N	Y	Y	Y	Y
9 Lampson	Y	N	Y	N	Y
10 Doggett	Y	N	Y	N	N
11 Edwards	Y	N	Y	Y	N
12 ***Granger***	N	Y	Y	Y	Y
13 ***Thornberry***	N	Y	Y	Y	Y
14 ***Paul***	N	Y	Y	N	N
15 Hinojosa	Y	Y	Y	Y	Y
16 Reyes	Y	Y	Y	N	Y
17 Stenholm	N	Y	Y	Y	Y
18 Jackson-Lee	Y	N	Y	Y	N
19 ***Combest***	N	Y	Y	Y	Y
20 Gonzalez	Y	Y	Y	Y	N
21 ***Smith***	N	Y	Y	Y	Y
22 ***DeLay***	N	Y	Y	Y	Y
23 ***Bonilla***	N	Y	Y	Y	Y
24 Frost	Y	Y	Y	Y	Y
25 Bentsen	N	Y	Y	Y	Y
26 ***Armey***	N	Y	Y	Y	Y
27 Ortiz	Y	Y	Y	N	Y
28 Rodriguez	Y	N	Y	Y	N
29 Green	Y	N	Y	N	Y
30 Johnson, E.B.	Y	N	Y	Y	N
UTAH					
1 ***Hansen***	N	Y	Y	Y	Y
2 Matheson	N	Y	Y	Y	Y
3 ***Cannon***	N	Y	Y	Y	Y
VERMONT					
AL *Sanders*	Y	N	Y	N	N
VIRGINIA					
1 ***Davis, Jo Ann***	N	Y	Y	Y	Y
2 ***Schrock***	N	Y	Y	Y	Y
3 Scott	Y	N	Y	Y	N
4 ***Forbes***	N	Y	Y	Y	Y
5 *Goode*	N	Y	Y	Y	Y
6 ***Goodlatte***	N	Y	Y	Y	Y
7 ***Cantor***	N	Y	Y	Y	Y
8 Moran	Y	Y	Y	Y	Y
9 Boucher	Y	N	Y	Y	Y
10 ***Wolf***	N	Y	Y	Y	Y
11 ***Davis, T.***	N	Y	Y	Y	Y
WASHINGTON					
1 Inslee	Y	Y	Y	N	N
2 Larsen	N	Y	Y	Y	Y
3 Baird	N	Y	Y	N	N
4 ***Hastings***	N	Y	Y	Y	Y
5 ***Nethercutt***	N	Y	Y	Y	Y
6 Dicks	Y	Y	Y	Y	N
7 McDermott	Y	N	Y	N	N
8 ***Dunn***	N	Y	Y	Y	Y
9 Smith	N	Y	Y	Y	N
WEST VIRGINIA					
1 Mollohan	Y	N	Y	N	Y
2 ***Capito***	N	Y	Y	Y	Y
3 Rahall	Y	N	Y	Y	Y
WISCONSIN					
1 ***Ryan***	N	Y	Y	Y	Y
2 Baldwin	Y	N	Y	N	N
3 Kind	Y	Y	Y	N	N
4 Kleczka	Y	N	Y	Y	N
5 Barrett	Y	N	Y	N	N
6 ***Petri***	N	Y	Y	Y	Y
7 Obey	Y	N	Y	N	?
8 ***Green***	N	Y	Y	Y	Y
9 ***Sensenbrenner***	N	Y	Y	Y	Y
WYOMING					
AL ***Cubin***	?	?	?	?	?

Southern states - Ala., Ark., Fla., Ga., Ky., La., Miss., N.C., Okla., S.C., Tenn., Texas, Va.

Key

Y	Voted for (yea).
#	Paired for.
+	Announced for.
N	Voted against (nay).
X	Paired against.
–	Announced against.
P	Voted "present."
C	Voted "present" to avoid possible conflict of interest.
?	Did not vote or otherwise make a position known.

Democrats **Republicans** *Independents*

---

446. HR 3009. Andean Trade/Rule. Adoption of the rule (H Res 289) to provide for House floor consideration of the bill that would extend through 2006 the Andean Trade Preference Act, which would grant duty-free status to about 6,000 products from Bolivia, Colombia, Ecuador and Peru, and would eliminate tariffs on some currently exempted goods such as tuna, petroleum products, footwear and sugar. Adopted 225-191: R 198-15; D 27-174 (ND 21-129, SD 6-45); I 0-2. Nov. 16, 2001.

447. HR 3009. Andean Trade/Recommit. Spratt, D-S.C., motion to recommit the bill to the House Ways and Means Committee with instructions to strike all the language after the enacting clause and insert a new section stating that no duty-free status would remain in effect after Dec. 31, 2006. Motion rejected 168-250: R 19-195; D 147-55 (ND 111-40, SD 36-15); I 2-0. (Subsequently, the bill passed by voice vote.) Nov. 16, 2001.

448. S 1447. Aviation Security/Conference Report. Adoption of the conference report on the bill that would establish a new security agency within the Transportation Department to assume federal control of U.S. airport security and screening services. Passenger and baggage screeners would become federal employees within one year of enactment, but the bill sets up a pilot program under which five airports could resume use of private screeners under federal supervision after that time and all airports could switch to private screeners after three years. Passengers would pay a $2.50 boarding charge, with a maximum fee of $5 per trip, to help pay for enhanced security. The bill also would limit legal liability for certain parties sued after the Sept. 11 attacks. Adopted (thus cleared for the president) 410-9: R 208-9; D 200-0 (ND 150-0, SD 50-0); I 2-0. Nov. 16, 2001.

	446	447	448
ALABAMA			
1 *Callahan*	Y	N	Y
2 *Everett*	N	Y	Y
3 *Riley*	Y	N	Y
4 *Aderholt*	Y	N	Y
5 Cramer	N	Y	Y
6 *Bachus*	Y	N	Y
7 Hilliard	N	Y	Y
ALASKA			
AL *Young*	?	N	Y
ARIZONA			
1 *Flake*	+	–	–
2 Pastor	N	Y	Y
3 *Stump*	Y	N	N
4 *Shadegg*	Y	N	N
5 *Kolbe*	Y	N	Y
6 *Hayworth*	Y	N	Y
ARKANSAS			
1 Berry	N	Y	Y
2 Snyder	N	N	Y
3 Vacant			
4 Ross	N	Y	Y
CALIFORNIA			
1 Thompson	N	Y	Y
2 *Herger*	Y	N	Y
3 *Ose*	Y	N	Y
4 *Doolittle*	Y	N	Y
5 Matsui	N	N	Y
6 Woolsey	N	Y	Y
7 Miller, George	N	Y	Y
8 Pelosi	N	Y	Y
9 Lee	N	Y	Y
10 Tauscher	Y	N	Y
11 *Pombo*	Y	N	Y
12 Lantos	?	?	?
13 Stark	N	Y	Y
14 Eshoo	Y	N	Y
15 Honda	N	N	Y
16 Lofgren	Y	N	Y
17 Farr	N	N	Y
18 Condit	N	Y	Y
19 *Radanovich*	Y	N	Y
20 Dooley	Y	N	Y
21 *Thomas*	Y	N	Y
22 Capps	N	Y	Y
23 *Gallegly*	Y	N	Y
24 Sherman	N	Y	Y
25 *McKeon*	Y	N	Y
26 Berman	Y	N	Y
27 Schiff	N	Y	Y
28 *Dreier*	Y	N	Y
29 Waxman	?	?	?
30 Becerra	N	Y	Y
31 Solis	N	Y	Y
32 Watson	N	Y	Y
33 Roybal-Allard	N	Y	Y
34 Napolitano	N	Y	Y
35 Waters	N	Y	Y
36 Harman	N	Y	Y
37 Millender-McD.	–	Y	Y
38 *Horn*	Y	N	Y

	446	447	448
39 *Royce*	Y	N	Y
40 *Lewis*	Y	N	Y
41 *Miller, Gary*	Y	N	Y
42 Baca	N	Y	Y
43 *Calvert*	Y	N	Y
44 *Bono*	?	?	+
45 *Rohrabacher*	Y	Y	Y
46 Sanchez	N	Y	Y
47 *Cox*	Y	N	Y
48 *Issa*	Y	N	Y
49 Davis	N	N	Y
50 Filner	N	Y	Y
51 *Cunningham*	Y	N	Y
52 *Hunter*	Y	Y	Y
COLORADO			
1 DeGette	N	Y	Y
2 Udall	N	Y	Y
3 *McInnis*	Y	N	Y
4 *Schaffer*	Y	N	N
5 *Hefley*	Y	N	Y
6 *Tancredo*	Y	N	Y
CONNECTICUT			
1 Larson	Y	Y	Y
2 *Simmons*	Y	N	Y
3 DeLauro	N	Y	Y
4 *Shays*	Y	N	Y
5 Maloney	N	Y	Y
6 *Johnson*	Y	N	Y
DELAWARE			
AL *Castle*	N	Y	Y
FLORIDA			
1 *Miller, J.*	Y	N	Y
2 Boyd	N	Y	Y
3 Brown	N	Y	Y
4 *Crenshaw*	Y	N	Y
5 Thurman	N	Y	Y
6 *Stearns*	Y	N	Y
7 *Mica*	Y	N	Y
8 *Keller*	Y	N	Y
9 *Bilirakis*	Y	N	Y
10 *Young*	Y	?	Y
11 Davis	N	Y	Y
12 *Putnam*	Y	N	Y
13 *Miller, D.*	Y	N	Y
14 *Goss*	Y	N	Y
15 *Weldon*	Y	N	Y
16 *Foley*	Y	N	Y
17 Meek	?	Y	Y
18 *Ros-Lehtinen*	?	?	?
19 Wexler	N	N	Y
20 Deutsch	N	Y	Y
21 *Diaz-Balart*	Y	N	Y
22 *Shaw*	Y	N	Y
23 Hastings	?	?	?
GEORGIA			
1 *Kingston*	Y	N	Y
2 Bishop	N	Y	Y
3 *Collins*	Y	N	N
4 McKinney	N	Y	Y
5 Lewis	N	Y	Y
6 *Isakson*	Y	N	Y
7 *Barr*	Y	Y	Y
8 *Chambliss*	Y	N	Y
9 *Deal*	Y	N	Y
10 Norwood	N	Y	Y
11 *Linder*	Y	N	Y
HAWAII			
1 Abercrombie	N	Y	Y
2 Mink	N	Y	Y
IDAHO			
1 *Otter*	Y	N	Y
2 *Simpson*	Y	N	Y
ILLINOIS			
1 Rush	N	Y	Y
2 Jackson	N	Y	Y
3 Lipinski	N	Y	Y
4 Gutierrez	N	Y	Y
5 Blagojevich	N	N	Y
6 *Hyde*	Y	N	Y
7 Davis	N	Y	Y
8 *Crane*	Y	N	Y
9 Schakowsky	N	Y	Y
10 *Kirk*	Y	N	Y
11 *Weller*	Y	N	Y
12 Costello	N	Y	Y
13 *Biggert*	Y	N	Y

ND Northern Democrats   SD Southern Democrats

	446	447	448
14 Hastert		N	Y
15 Johnson	Y	N	Y
16 Manzullo	Y	N	Y
17 Evans	N	Y	Y
18 LaHood	Y	N	Y
19 Phelps	N	Y	Y
20 Shimkus	Y	N	Y

INDIANA

	446	447	448
1 Visclosky	N	Y	Y
2 Pence	Y	N	Y
3 Roemer	N	N	Y
4 Souder	Y	N	Y
5 Buyer	Y	N	Y
6 Burton	Y	N	Y
7 Kerns	Y	N	Y
8 Hostettler	Y	N	Y
9 Hill	Y	Y	Y
10 Carson	N	Y	Y

IOWA

	446	447	448
1 Leach	Y	N	Y
2 Nussle	Y	N	Y
3 Boswell	Y	Y	Y
4 Ganske	Y	N	Y
5 Latham	Y	N	Y

KANSAS

	446	447	448
1 Moran	Y	N	Y
2 Ryun	Y	N	Y
3 Moore	N	N	Y
4 Tiahrt	Y	N	Y

KENTUCKY

	446	447	448
1 Whitfield	Y	N	Y
2 Lewis	Y	N	Y
3 Northup	Y	N	Y
4 Lucas	N	N	Y
5 Rogers	N	Y	Y
6 Fletcher	Y	N	Y

LOUISIANA

	446	447	448
1 Vitter	Y	N	Y
2 Jefferson	N	N	Y
3 Tauzin	Y	N	Y
4 McCrery	Y	N	Y
5 Cooksey	Y	N	Y
6 Baker	Y	N	Y
7 John	N	N	Y

MAINE

	446	447	448
1 Allen	N	N	Y
2 Baldacci	N	Y	Y

MARYLAND

	446	447	448
1 Gilchrest	Y	N	Y
2 Ehrlich	Y	N	Y
3 Cardin	N	N	Y
4 Wynn	N	N	Y
5 Hoyer	Y	Y	Y
6 Bartlett	Y	N	Y
7 Cummings	N	N	Y
8 Morella	Y	N	Y

MASSACHUSETTS

	446	447	448
1 Olver	N	Y	Y
2 Neal	N	Y	Y
3 McGovern	N	Y	Y
4 Frank	N	Y	Y
5 Meehan	?	?	?
6 Tierney	N	Y	Y
7 Markey	N	Y	Y
8 Capuano	N	Y	Y
9 Lynch	N	Y	Y
10 Delahunt	N	N	Y

MICHIGAN

	446	447	448
1 Stupak	N	Y	Y
2 Hoekstra	N	Y	Y
3 Ehlers	Y	N	Y
4 Camp	Y	N	Y
5 Barcia	N	?	?
6 Upton	N	N	Y
7 Smith	Y	N	Y
8 Rogers	Y	N	Y
9 Kildee	N	Y	Y
10 Bonior	N	N	Y
11 Knollenberg	Y	N	Y
12 Levin	N	N	Y
13 Rivers	N	Y	Y
14 Conyers	N	Y	Y
15 Kilpatrick	N	Y	Y
16 Dingell	N	Y	Y

MINNESOTA

	446	447	448
1 Gutknecht	Y	N	Y
2 Kennedy	Y	N	Y
3 Ramstad	Y	N	Y
4 McCollum	N	Y	Y
5 Sabo	N	Y	Y
6 Luther	N	Y	Y
7 Peterson	N	Y	Y
8 Oberstar	N	Y	Y

MISSISSIPPI

	446	447	448
1 Wicker	Y	N	Y
2 Thompson	N	?	?
3 Pickering	N	N	Y
4 Shows	N	Y	Y
5 Taylor	N	Y	Y

MISSOURI

	446	447	448
1 Clay	?	N	Y
2 Akin	Y	N	Y
3 Gephardt	N	N	Y
4 Skelton	N	N	Y
5 McCarthy	N	Y	Y
6 Graves	Y	N	Y
7 Blunt	Y	N	Y
8 Emerson	Y	N	Y
9 Hulshof	Y	N	Y

MONTANA

	446	447	448
AL Rehberg	Y	N	Y

NEBRASKA

	446	447	448
1 Bereuter	Y	N	Y
2 Terry	Y	N	Y
3 Osborne	Y	N	Y

NEVADA

	446	447	448
1 Berkley	N	N	Y
2 Gibbons	Y	N	Y

NEW HAMPSHIRE

	446	447	448
1 Sununu	Y	N	Y
2 Bass	Y	N	Y

NEW JERSEY

	446	447	448
1 Andrews	N	Y	Y
2 LoBiondo	Y	N	Y
3 Saxton	Y	N	Y
4 Smith	Y	N	Y
5 Roukema	Y	N	Y
6 Pallone	N	Y	Y
7 Ferguson	Y	N	Y
8 Pascrell	N	Y	Y
9 Rothman	N	Y	Y
10 Payne	N	N	Y
11 Frelinghuysen	Y	N	Y
12 Holt	N	Y	Y
13 Menendez	N	Y	Y

NEW MEXICO

	446	447	448
1 Wilson	Y	N	Y
2 Skeen	Y	N	Y
3 Udall	N	Y	Y

NEW YORK

	446	447	448
1 Grucci	Y	N	Y
2 Israel	N	N	Y
3 King	Y	N	Y
4 McCarthy	N	Y	Y
5 Ackerman	N	N	Y
6 Meeks	?	?	?
7 Crowley	Y	N	Y
8 Nadler	N	Y	Y
9 Weiner	N	Y	Y
10 Towns	N	Y	Y
11 Owens	N	Y	Y
12 Velázquez	N	Y	Y
13 Fossella	Y	N	Y
14 Maloney	N	Y	Y
15 Rangel	Y	N	Y
16 Serrano	N	Y	Y
17 Engel	N	Y	Y
18 Lowey	N	Y	Y
19 Kelly	Y	N	Y
20 Gilman	Y	N	Y
21 McNulty	N	Y	Y
22 Sweeney	Y	N	Y
23 Boehlert	Y	N	Y
24 McHugh	Y	Y	Y
25 Walsh	Y	N	Y
26 Hinchey	N	Y	Y
27 Reynolds	Y	N	Y
28 Slaughter	N	Y	Y
29 LaFalce	N	Y	Y
30 Quinn	Y	?	Y
31 Houghton	Y	N	Y

NORTH CAROLINA

	446	447	448
1 Clayton	N	Y	Y
2 Etheridge	N	Y	Y
3 Jones	N	Y	Y
4 Price	N	Y	Y
5 Burr	N	Y	Y
6 Coble	N	Y	N
7 McIntyre	N	Y	Y
8 Hayes	N	Y	Y
9 Myrick	N	Y	Y
10 Ballenger	Y	Y	Y
11 Taylor	N	Y	N
12 Watt	N	Y	Y

NORTH DAKOTA

	446	447	448
AL Pomeroy	N	N	Y

OHIO

	446	447	448
1 Chabot	Y	N	Y
2 Portman	Y	N	Y
3 Hall	?	?	?
4 Oxley	Y	N	Y
5 Gillmor	Y	N	Y
6 Strickland	N	Y	Y
7 Hobson	Y	N	Y
8 Boehner	Y	N	Y
9 Kaptur	N	Y	Y
10 Kucinich	N	Y	Y
11 Jones	N	Y	Y
12 Tiberi	Y	N	Y
13 Brown	N	Y	Y
14 Sawyer	N	Y	Y
15 Pryce	Y	N	Y
16 Regula	Y	N	Y
17 Traficant	Y	N	Y
18 Ney	Y	N	Y
19 LaTourette	Y	N	Y

OKLAHOMA

	446	447	448
1 Largent	?	N	Y
2 Carson	Y	N	Y
3 Watkins	Y	N	Y
4 Watts	Y	N	Y
5 Istook	Y	N	Y
6 Lucas	Y	N	Y

OREGON

	446	447	448
1 Wu	N	N	Y
2 Walden	Y	N	Y
3 Blumenauer	Y	N	Y
4 DeFazio	N	Y	Y
5 Hooley	Y	Y	Y

PENNSYLVANIA

	446	447	448
1 Brady	N	Y	Y
2 Fattah	N	Y	Y
3 Borski	N	?	?
4 Hart	Y	N	Y
5 Peterson	Y	N	Y
6 Holden	N	Y	Y
7 Weldon	Y	N	Y
8 Greenwood	Y	N	Y
9 Shuster, Bill	Y	N	Y
10 Sherwood	Y	N	Y
11 Kanjorski	N	N	Y
12 Murtha	N	Y	Y
13 Hoeffel	N	N	Y
14 Coyne	N	Y	Y
15 Toomey	Y	N	Y
16 Pitts	Y	N	Y
17 Gekas	Y	N	Y
18 Doyle	N	N	Y
19 Platts	Y	N	Y
20 Mascara	N	Y	Y
21 English	Y	N	Y

RHODE ISLAND

	446	447	448
1 Kennedy	Y	Y	Y
2 Langevin	N	Y	Y

SOUTH CAROLINA

	446	447	448
1 Brown	Y	N	Y
2 Vacant			
3 Graham	N	Y	Y
4 DeMint	N	Y	Y
5 Spratt	N	Y	Y
6 Clyburn	N	Y	Y

SOUTH DAKOTA

	446	447	448
AL Thune	Y	N	Y

TENNESSEE

	446	447	448
1 Jenkins	Y	N	Y
2 Duncan	Y	N	Y
3 Wamp	Y	N	Y
4 Hilleary	Y	N	Y
5 Clement	N	Y	Y
6 Gordon	N	Y	Y
7 Bryant	Y	N	Y
8 Tanner	N	N	Y
9 Ford	N	Y	Y

TEXAS

	446	447	448
1 Sandlin	Y	Y	Y
2 Turner	N	Y	Y
3 Johnson, Sam	Y	N	Y
4 Hall	N	Y	Y
5 Sessions	Y	N	N
6 Barton	Y	N	Y
7 Culberson	Y	N	N
8 Brady	Y	N	N
9 Lampson	N	Y	Y
10 Doggett	N	N	Y
11 Edwards	N	Y	Y
12 Granger	Y	N	Y
13 Thornberry	Y	N	Y
14 Paul	Y	N	N
15 Hinojosa	Y	N	?
16 Reyes	N	Y	Y
17 Stenholm	Y	N	Y
18 Jackson-Lee	N	Y	Y
19 Combest	Y	N	Y
20 Gonzalez	N	Y	Y
21 Smith	Y	N	Y
22 DeLay	Y	N	Y
23 Bonilla	Y	N	Y
24 Frost	N	Y	Y
25 Bentsen	N	N	Y
26 Armey	Y	N	Y
27 Ortiz	N	N	Y
28 Rodriguez	N	N	Y
29 Green	N	Y	Y
30 Johnson, E.B.	?	?	?

UTAH

	446	447	448
1 Hansen	Y	N	Y
2 Matheson	Y	N	Y
3 Cannon	Y	N	Y

VERMONT

	446	447	448
AL Sanders	N	Y	Y

VIRGINIA

	446	447	448
1 Davis, Jo Ann	Y	N	Y
2 Schrock	Y	N	Y
3 Scott	N	Y	Y
4 Forbes	Y	N	Y
5 Goode	N	Y	Y
6 Goodlatte	Y	N	Y
7 Cantor	Y	N	Y
8 Moran	Y	N	Y
9 Boucher	N	Y	Y
10 Wolf	Y	N	Y
11 Davis, T.	Y	N	Y

WASHINGTON

	446	447	448
1 Inslee	Y	N	Y
2 Larsen	Y	N	Y
3 Baird	Y	N	Y
4 Hastings	Y	N	Y
5 Nethercutt	Y	N	Y
6 Dicks	N	N	Y
7 McDermott	N	N	Y
8 Dunn	Y	N	Y
9 Smith	Y	N	Y

WEST VIRGINIA

	446	447	448
1 Mollohan	N	Y	?
2 Capito	Y	N	Y
3 Rahall	N	Y	Y

WISCONSIN

	446	447	448
1 Ryan	Y	N	Y
2 Baldwin	N	Y	Y
3 Kind	Y	N	Y
4 Kleczka	N	Y	Y
5 Barrett	N	Y	Y
6 Petri	Y	N	Y
7 Obey	N	Y	Y
8 Green	Y	N	Y
9 Sensenbrenner	Y	N	Y

WYOMING

	446	447	448
AL Cubin	?	?	Y

Southern states - Ala., Ark., Fla., Ga., Ky., La., Miss., N.C., Okla., S.C., Tenn., Texas, Va.

449. HR 1259. Federal Data Protection/Passage. Morella, R-Md., motion to suspend the rules and pass the bill that would expand the role of the National Institute of Standards and Technology in the protection of sensitive but unclassified information maintained in electronic databases by federal agencies. Motion agreed to 391-4: R 195-4; D 194-0 (ND 147-0, SD 47-0); I 2-0. A two-thirds majority of those present and voting (264 in this case) is required for passage under suspension of the rules. Nov. 27, 2001.

450. S Con Res 44. Pearl Harbor Anniversary/Adoption. Barr, R-Ga., motion to suspend the rules and adopt the concurrent resolution that would mark the 60th anniversary of Japan's bombing of Pearl Harbor, Hawaii, by honoring the U.S. military personnel who were killed and those who survived the Dec. 7, 1941, attack. Motion agreed to 393-0: R 197-0; D 194-0 (ND 147-0, SD 47-0); I 2-0. A two-thirds majority of those present and voting (262 in this case) is required for adoption under suspension of the rules. Nov. 27, 2001.

451. Procedural Motion/Journal. Approval of the House Journal of Tuesday, Nov. 27, 2001. Approved 372-39: R 196-13; D 174-26 (ND 127-22, SD 47-4); I 2-0. Nov. 28, 2001.

452. H Con Res 77. Korean Unity/Adoption. Royce, R-Calif., motion to suspend the rules and adopt the concurrent resolution that would express the sense of Congress to support the timely reunification of families separated 50 years ago because of the division of North Korea and South Korea. Motion agreed to 420-0: R 213-0; D 205-0 (ND 153-0, SD 52-0); I 2-0. A two-thirds majority of those present and voting (280 in this case) is required for adoption under suspension of the rules. Nov. 28, 2001.

453. HR 2722. Conflict Diamonds/Passage. Thomas, R-Calif., motion to suspend the rules and pass the bill that would allow the president to ban imports of rough diamonds if exporting countries fail to take effective measures to halt the conflict diamond trade and to ban imports of polished diamonds and jewelry if he believes they were produced with conflict diamonds. It would allow for penalties for violators, call for reports on the conflict diamond trade and measures taken to stem it, and authorize $5 million in fiscal 2002 and 2003 for assistance to countries implementing new measures under the bill. Motion agreed to 408-6: R 204-6; D 202-0 (ND 151-0, SD 51-0); I 2-0. A two-thirds majority of those present and voting (276 in this case) is required for passage under suspension of the rules. Nov. 28, 2001.

454. HR 3338. Fiscal 2002 Defense Appropriations/Rule. Adoption of the rule (H Res 296) to provide for House floor consideration of the bill that would provide $317.5 billion for the Defense Department for fiscal 2002, about $20 billion more than fiscal 2001. Adopted 216-211: R 214-4; D 1-206 (ND 1-154, SD 0-52); I 1-1. Nov. 28, 2001.

455. Quorum Call.* 409 members responded. Nov. 28, 2001.

456. HR 3338. Fiscal 2002 Defense Appropriations/Ruling of the Chair. Motion to sustain the ruling of the chair that upheld the Lewis, R-Calif., point of order against the Filner, D-Calif., amendment, on the grounds that it would constitute legislation on an appropriations bill. The amendment would order the federal government to pay the difference in salaries for federal employees called to duty in military reserve units and the National Guard since Sept. 11. Motion agreed to 275-141: R 211-0; D 63-140 (ND 44-108, SD 19-32); I 1-1. Nov. 28, 2001.

CQ does not include quorum calls in its vote charts.

Key

Y	Voted for (yea).
#	Paired for.
+	Announced for.
N	Voted against (nay).
X	Paired against.
–	Announced against.
P	Voted "present."
C	Voted "present" to avoid possible conflict of interest.
?	Did not vote or otherwise make a position known.

Democrats **Republicans** *Independents*

Member	449	450	451	452	453	454	456
ALABAMA							
1 *Callahan*	Y	?	Y	Y	Y	Y	Y
2 *Everett*	+	+	+	+	+	Y	Y
3 *Riley*	+	+	Y	Y	Y	Y	Y
4 *Aderholt*	?	?	N	Y	Y	Y	Y
5 Cramer	Y	Y	Y	Y	Y	N	Y
6 *Bachus*	?	?	Y	Y	Y	Y	Y
7 Hilliard	Y	Y	N	Y	Y	N	N
ALASKA							
AL *Young*	Y	Y	Y	Y	Y	Y	Y
ARIZONA							
1 *Flake*	N	Y	Y	Y	N	Y	Y
2 Pastor	Y	Y	Y	Y	Y	N	Y
3 *Stump*	Y	Y	Y	Y	Y	Y	Y
4 *Shadegg*	Y	Y	Y	Y	Y	Y	Y
5 *Kolbe*	Y	Y	Y	Y	Y	Y	Y
6 *Hayworth*	Y	Y	Y	Y	Y	Y	Y
ARKANSAS							
1 Berry	Y	Y	Y	Y	Y	N	N
2 Snyder	Y	Y	Y	Y	N	Y	Y
3 Vacant							
4 Ross	Y	Y	Y	Y	Y	N	N
CALIFORNIA							
1 Thompson	Y	Y	N	Y	Y	N	N
2 *Herger*	Y	Y	Y	Y	Y	Y	Y
3 *Ose*	Y	Y	Y	Y	Y	Y	Y
4 *Doolittle*	Y	Y	Y	Y	Y	Y	Y
5 Matsui	Y	Y	Y	Y	Y	N	N
6 Woolsey	Y	Y	Y	Y	Y	N	N
7 Miller, George	Y	Y	?	Y	Y	N	N
8 Pelosi	Y	Y	?	Y	Y	N	N
9 Lee	Y	Y	Y	Y	Y	N	N
10 Tauscher	Y	Y	Y	Y	Y	N	N
11 *Pombo*	Y	Y	Y	Y	Y	Y	Y
12 Lantos	Y	Y	Y	Y	Y	N	N
13 Stark	Y	Y	Y	Y	Y	N	N
14 Eshoo	Y	Y	Y	Y	Y	N	N
15 Honda	Y	Y	Y	Y	Y	N	N
16 Lofgren	Y	Y	Y	Y	Y	N	N
17 Farr	Y	Y	Y	Y	Y	N	N
18 Condit	Y	Y	Y	Y	Y	N	N
19 *Radanovich*	Y	Y	Y	Y	Y	Y	Y
20 Dooley	Y	Y	Y	Y	Y	N	?
21 *Thomas*	Y	Y	Y	Y	Y	Y	Y
22 Capps	Y	Y	Y	Y	Y	N	N
23 *Gallegly*	Y	Y	Y	Y	Y	Y	Y
24 Sherman	Y	Y	Y	Y	Y	N	N
25 *McKeon*	Y	Y	Y	Y	Y	Y	Y
26 Berman	Y	Y	Y	Y	Y	N	N
27 Schiff	Y	Y	Y	Y	Y	N	N
28 *Dreier*	Y	Y	Y	Y	Y	Y	Y
29 Waxman	Y	Y	Y	Y	Y	N	N
30 Becerra	Y	Y	Y	Y	Y	N	N
31 Solis	Y	Y	Y	Y	Y	N	N
32 Watson	Y	Y	Y	Y	Y	N	N
33 Roybal-Allard	Y	Y	Y	Y	Y	N	N
34 Napolitano	Y	Y	Y	Y	Y	N	N
35 Waters	Y	Y	Y	Y	Y	N	N
36 Harman	Y	Y	Y	Y	Y	N	N
37 Millender-McD.	Y	Y	Y	Y	Y	N	N
38 *Horn*	Y	Y	Y	Y	Y	Y	Y
39 *Royce*	Y	Y	Y	Y	Y	Y	Y
40 *Lewis*	?	?	Y	Y	Y	Y	Y
41 *Miller, Gary*	Y	Y	Y	Y	Y	Y	Y
42 Baca	Y	Y	Y	Y	Y	Y	N
43 *Calvert*	Y	Y	Y	Y	Y	Y	Y
44 *Bono*	Y	Y	Y	Y	Y	Y	Y
45 *Rohrabacher*	Y	Y	Y	Y	Y	Y	Y
46 Sanchez	Y	Y	N	Y	Y	N	N
47 *Cox*	Y	Y	?	Y	Y	Y	Y
48 *Issa*	Y	Y	Y	Y	Y	Y	Y
49 Davis	Y	Y	Y	Y	Y	N	N
50 Filner	Y	Y	N	Y	Y	N	N
51 *Cunningham*	Y	Y	Y	Y	Y	Y	Y
52 *Hunter*	?	?	Y	Y	?	Y	Y
COLORADO							
1 DeGette	Y	Y	Y	Y	Y	N	N
2 Udall	Y	Y	N	Y	Y	N	N
3 *McInnis*	Y	Y	Y	Y	Y	Y	Y
4 *Schaffer*	?	?	N	Y	Y	Y	Y
5 *Hefley*	Y	Y	N	Y	N	Y	Y
6 *Tancredo*	Y	Y	P	Y	Y	Y	Y
CONNECTICUT							
1 Larson	+	+	?	Y	Y	N	Y
2 *Simmons*	Y	Y	Y	Y	Y	Y	Y
3 DeLauro	Y	Y	Y	Y	Y	N	N
4 *Shays*	Y	Y	Y	Y	Y	Y	Y
5 *Maloney*	Y	Y	Y	Y	Y	N	?
6 *Johnson*	?	?	?	?	?	Y	Y
DELAWARE							
AL *Castle*	Y	Y	Y	Y	Y	Y	Y
FLORIDA							
1 *Miller, J.*	Y	Y	Y	Y	Y	Y	Y
2 Boyd	Y	Y	Y	Y	Y	N	Y
3 Brown	?	?	Y	Y	Y	N	Y
4 *Crenshaw*	Y	Y	Y	Y	Y	Y	Y
5 Thurman	Y	Y	Y	Y	Y	N	N
6 *Stearns*	Y	Y	Y	Y	Y	Y	Y
7 *Mica*	Y	Y	Y	Y	Y	Y	Y
8 *Keller*	Y	Y	Y	Y	Y	Y	Y
9 *Bilirakis*	Y	Y	Y	Y	Y	Y	Y
10 *Young*	Y	Y	Y	Y	Y	Y	Y
11 Davis	Y	Y	Y	Y	Y	N	Y
12 *Putnam*	Y	Y	Y	Y	Y	Y	Y
13 *Miller, D.*	Y	Y	Y	Y	Y	Y	Y
14 *Goss*	+	+	Y	Y	Y	Y	Y
15 *Weldon*	Y	Y	Y	Y	Y	Y	Y
16 *Foley*	Y	Y	Y	Y	Y	Y	Y
17 Meek	Y	Y	Y	Y	Y	N	Y
18 *Ros-Lehtinen*	Y	Y	Y	Y	Y	Y	Y
19 Wexler	?	?	?	?	?	?	?
20 Deutsch	Y	Y	Y	Y	Y	N	N
21 *Diaz-Balart*	Y	Y	Y	Y	Y	Y	Y
22 *Shaw*	Y	Y	Y	Y	Y	Y	Y
23 Hastings	Y	Y	N	Y	Y	N	N
GEORGIA							
1 *Kingston*	Y	Y	Y	Y	Y	Y	Y
2 Bishop	Y	Y	Y	Y	Y	N	N
3 *Collins*	Y	Y	Y	Y	Y	N	N
4 McKinney	?	?	Y	Y	Y	N	N
5 Lewis	Y	Y	Y	Y	Y	N	N
6 *Isakson*	Y	Y	Y	Y	Y	Y	Y
7 *Barr*	Y	Y	Y	Y	Y	Y	Y
8 *Chambliss*	?	?	Y	Y	Y	Y	Y
9 *Deal*	Y	Y	Y	Y	Y	Y	Y
10 *Norwood*	?	?	Y	Y	Y	Y	Y
11 *Linder*	Y	Y	Y	Y	Y	Y	Y
HAWAII							
1 Abercrombie	Y	Y	Y	Y	Y	N	Y
2 Mink	Y	Y	Y	Y	Y	N	N
IDAHO							
1 *Otter*	Y	Y	Y	Y	N	Y	Y
2 *Simpson*	Y	Y	Y	Y	Y	Y	Y
ILLINOIS							
1 Rush	Y	Y	Y	Y	Y	N	N
2 Jackson	Y	Y	Y	Y	Y	N	N
3 Lipinski	Y	Y	Y	Y	Y	N	Y
4 Gutierrez	Y	Y	Y	Y	Y	N	N
5 Blagojevich	?	?	Y	Y	Y	N	N
6 *Hyde*	Y	Y	Y	Y	Y	Y	Y
7 Davis	Y	Y	Y	Y	Y	N	N
8 *Crane*	Y	Y	N	Y	Y	N	N
9 Schakowsky	Y	Y	Y	Y	Y	N	N
10 *Kirk*	Y	Y	Y	Y	Y	Y	Y
11 *Weller*	Y	Y	N	Y	Y	N	Y
12 Costello	Y	Y	N	Y	Y	N	Y
13 *Biggert*	Y	Y	Y	Y	Y	Y	Y

ND Northern Democrats   SD Southern Democrats

	449	450	451	452	453	454	456
14 ***Hastert***						Y	Y
15 ***Johnson***	Y	Y	Y	Y	Y	Y	Y
16 ***Manzullo***	Y	Y	Y	Y	Y	Y	Y
17 Evans	Y	Y	Y	Y	Y	N	Y
18 ***LaHood***	?	?	Y	Y	Y	Y	Y
19 Phelps	Y	Y	Y	Y	Y	N	Y
20 ***Shimkus***	Y	Y	Y	Y	Y	Y	Y
INDIANA							
1 Visclosky	Y	Y	N	Y	?	N	Y
2 ***Pence***	Y	Y	Y	Y	Y	Y	Y
3 Roemer	Y	Y	Y	Y	Y	N	Y
4 ***Souder***	Y	Y	Y	Y	Y	Y	Y
5 ***Buyer***	?	?	Y	Y	Y	Y	Y
6 ***Burton***	Y	?	Y	Y	Y	Y	Y
7 ***Kerns***	Y	Y	Y	Y	Y	Y	Y
8 ***Hostettler***	Y	Y	Y	Y	Y	Y	Y
9 Hill	Y	Y	Y	Y	Y	N	Y
10 Carson	?	?	?	?	?	?	?
IOWA							
1 ***Leach***	Y	Y	Y	Y	Y	Y	Y
2 ***Nussle***	Y	Y	Y	Y	Y	Y	Y
3 Boswell	Y	Y	Y	Y	Y	N	Y
4 ***Ganske***	Y	Y	Y	Y	Y	Y	Y
5 ***Latham***	Y	Y	N	Y	Y	Y	Y
KANSAS							
1 ***Moran***	Y	Y	N	Y	Y	Y	Y
2 ***Ryun***	Y	Y	Y	Y	Y	Y	Y
3 Moore	Y	Y	N	Y	Y	N	Y
4 ***Tiahrt***	Y	Y	Y	Y	Y	Y	Y
KENTUCKY							
1 ***Whitfield***	Y	Y	Y	Y	Y	Y	Y
2 ***Lewis***	Y	Y	Y	Y	Y	Y	Y
3 ***Northup***	Y	Y	Y	Y	Y	Y	Y
4 Lucas	Y	Y	Y	Y	Y	N	Y
5 ***Rogers***	Y	Y	Y	Y	Y	Y	Y
6 ***Fletcher***	Y	Y	Y	Y	Y	Y	Y
LOUISIANA							
1 ***Vitter***	Y	Y	Y	Y	Y	Y	Y
2 Jefferson	?	?	Y	Y	Y	N	N
3 ***Tauzin***	Y	Y	Y	Y	Y	Y	Y
4 ***McCrery***	Y	Y	Y	Y	Y	Y	Y
5 ***Cooksey***	Y	Y	Y	Y	Y	Y	Y
6 ***Baker***	Y	Y	Y	Y	Y	Y	Y
7 John	Y	Y	Y	Y	Y	N	Y
MAINE							
1 Allen	Y	Y	Y	Y	Y	N	N
2 Baldacci	Y	Y	Y	Y	Y	N	Y
MARYLAND							
1 ***Gilchrest***	Y	Y	Y	Y	Y	Y	Y
2 ***Ehrlich***	Y	Y	Y	Y	Y	Y	?
3 Cardin	Y	Y	Y	Y	Y	N	Y
4 Wynn	Y	Y	Y	Y	Y	N	N
5 Hoyer	?	?	Y	Y	Y	N	Y
6 ***Bartlett***	Y	Y	Y	Y	Y	Y	Y
7 Cummings	Y	Y	Y	Y	Y	N	N
8 ***Morella***	Y	Y	Y	Y	Y	Y	Y
MASSACHUSETTS							
1 Olver	Y	Y	N	Y	Y	N	N
2 Neal	Y	Y	Y	Y	Y	N	N
3 McGovern	?	?	Y	Y	Y	N	N
4 Frank	Y	Y	Y	Y	Y	N	Y
5 Meehan	Y	Y	Y	Y	Y	N	N
6 Tierney	Y	Y	Y	Y	Y	N	N
7 Markey	Y	Y	Y	Y	Y	N	N
8 Capuano	Y	Y	Y	Y	Y	N	Y
9 Lynch	Y	Y	Y	Y	Y	N	N
10 Delahunt	Y	Y	Y	Y	Y	N	N
MICHIGAN							
1 Stupak	Y	Y	N	Y	Y	N	Y
2 ***Hoekstra***	Y	Y	Y	Y	Y	Y	Y
3 ***Ehlers***	Y	Y	Y	Y	Y	Y	Y
4 ***Camp***	Y	Y	Y	Y	Y	Y	Y
5 Barcia	Y	Y	Y	Y	Y	N	Y
6 ***Upton***	Y	Y	Y	Y	Y	Y	Y
7 ***Smith***	Y	Y	Y	Y	Y	Y	?
8 ***Rogers***	Y	Y	Y	Y	Y	Y	Y
9 Kildee	Y	Y	Y	Y	Y	N	N
10 Bonior	?	?	Y	Y	Y	N	N
11 ***Knollenberg***	?	?	Y	Y	Y	Y	Y
12 Levin	Y	Y	Y	Y	Y	N	N
13 Rivers	Y	Y	Y	Y	Y	N	N
14 Conyers	Y	Y	Y	Y	Y	N	N
15 Kilpatrick	Y	Y	Y	Y	Y	N	Y
16 Dingell	Y	Y	Y	Y	Y	N	N
MINNESOTA							
1 ***Gutknecht***	Y	Y	N	Y	Y	Y	Y
2 ***Kennedy***	Y	Y	N	Y	Y	Y	Y
3 ***Ramstad***	Y	Y	N	Y	Y	Y	Y
4 McCollum	Y	Y	Y	Y	Y	N	N
5 Sabo	Y	Y	N	Y	Y	N	Y
6 Luther	Y	Y	Y	Y	Y	N	N
7 Peterson	Y	Y	N	Y	Y	N	N
8 Oberstar	Y	Y	–	+	+	N	N
MISSISSIPPI							
1 ***Wicker***	Y	Y	N	Y	Y	Y	Y
2 Thompson	Y	Y	N	Y	Y	N	N
3 ***Pickering***	Y	Y	Y	Y	Y	Y	Y
4 Shows	Y	Y	Y	Y	Y	N	N
5 Taylor	Y	Y	N	Y	Y	N	N
MISSOURI							
1 Clay	Y	Y	?	Y	Y	N	N
2 ***Akin***	Y	Y	Y	Y	N	Y	Y
3 Gephardt	?	?	Y	Y	Y	N	N
4 Skelton	Y	Y	Y	Y	Y	N	Y
5 McCarthy	Y	Y	Y	Y	Y	N	N
6 ***Graves***	Y	Y	Y	Y	Y	Y	Y
7 ***Blunt***	Y	Y	Y	Y	Y	Y	Y
8 ***Emerson***	Y	Y	Y	Y	Y	Y	Y
9 ***Hulshof***	Y	Y	Y	Y	Y	Y	Y
MONTANA							
AL ***Rehberg***	Y	Y	Y	Y	Y	Y	Y
NEBRASKA							
1 ***Bereuter***	Y	Y	Y	Y	Y	Y	Y
2 ***Terry***	Y	Y	Y	Y	Y	Y	Y
3 ***Osborne***	Y	Y	Y	Y	Y	Y	Y
NEVADA							
1 Berkley	Y	Y	Y	Y	Y	N	N
2 ***Gibbons***	Y	Y	Y	Y	Y	Y	Y
NEW HAMPSHIRE							
1 ***Sununu***	Y	Y	Y	Y	Y	Y	Y
2 ***Bass***	Y	Y	Y	Y	Y	Y	Y
NEW JERSEY							
1 Andrews	Y	Y	Y	Y	Y	N	Y
2 ***LoBiondo***	Y	Y	N	Y	Y	Y	Y
3 ***Saxton***	Y	Y	Y	Y	Y	Y	Y
4 ***Smith***	Y	Y	Y	Y	Y	Y	Y
5 ***Roukema***	Y	Y	Y	Y	Y	Y	Y
6 Pallone	Y	Y	Y	Y	Y	N	N
7 ***Ferguson***	Y	Y	Y	Y	Y	Y	Y
8 Pascrell	Y	Y	Y	Y	Y	N	Y
9 Rothman	Y	Y	Y	Y	Y	N	Y
10 Payne	Y	Y	Y	Y	Y	N	N
11 ***Frelinghuysen***	Y	Y	Y	Y	Y	Y	?
12 Holt	Y	Y	Y	Y	Y	N	N
13 Menendez	Y	Y	Y	Y	Y	N	N
NEW MEXICO							
1 ***Wilson***	Y	Y	?	Y	Y	Y	Y
2 ***Skeen***	Y	Y	Y	Y	Y	Y	Y
3 Udall	Y	Y	N	Y	Y	N	N
NEW YORK							
1 ***Grucci***	Y	Y	Y	Y	Y	Y	Y
2 Israel	Y	Y	Y	Y	Y	N	N
3 ***King***	Y	Y	Y	Y	Y	Y	Y
4 McCarthy	Y	Y	Y	Y	Y	N	N
5 Ackerman	Y	Y	Y	Y	Y	N	N
6 Meeks	Y	Y	Y	Y	?	N	N
7 Crowley	Y	Y	Y	Y	Y	N	N
8 Nadler	Y	Y	Y	Y	Y	N	N
9 Weiner	Y	Y	Y	Y	Y	N	N
10 Towns	Y	Y	Y	Y	Y	N	N
11 Owens	Y	Y	Y	Y	Y	N	N
12 Velázquez	Y	Y	Y	Y	Y	N	N
13 ***Fossella***	Y	Y	Y	Y	Y	Y	Y
14 Maloney	Y	Y	Y	Y	Y	N	N
15 Rangel	Y	Y	Y	Y	Y	N	Y
16 Serrano	Y	Y	Y	Y	Y	N	N
17 Engel	Y	Y	Y	Y	Y	N	N
18 Lowey	Y	Y	Y	Y	Y	N	N
19 ***Kelly***	Y	Y	N	Y	Y	N	Y
20 ***Gilman***	Y	Y	Y	Y	Y	Y	Y
21 McNulty	Y	Y	Y	Y	Y	N	N
22 ***Sweeney***	?	?	?	?	?	N	Y
23 ***Boehlert***	Y	Y	Y	Y	Y	Y	Y
24 ***McHugh***	Y	Y	Y	Y	Y	Y	Y
25 ***Walsh***	Y	Y	Y	Y	Y	Y	Y
26 Hinchey	Y	Y	N	Y	Y	N	N
27 ***Reynolds***	Y	Y	Y	Y	Y	Y	Y
28 Slaughter	Y	Y	N	Y	Y	N	?
29 LaFalce	Y	Y	Y	Y	Y	N	N
30 ***Quinn***	?	?	?	?	?	?	?
31 ***Houghton***	Y	Y	Y	Y	Y	Y	Y
NORTH CAROLINA							
1 Clayton	Y	Y	Y	Y	Y	N	N
2 Etheridge	Y	Y	Y	Y	Y	N	N
3 ***Jones***	Y	Y	Y	Y	Y	Y	Y
4 Price	Y	Y	Y	Y	Y	N	N
5 ***Burr***	?	?	Y	Y	Y	Y	Y
6 ***Coble***	Y	Y	Y	Y	N	Y	Y
7 McIntyre	Y	Y	Y	Y	Y	N	N
8 ***Hayes***	Y	Y	Y	Y	Y	Y	Y
9 ***Myrick***	Y	Y	Y	Y	Y	Y	Y
10 ***Ballenger***	Y	Y	Y	Y	Y	Y	Y
11 ***Taylor***	Y	Y	Y	Y	N	Y	Y
12 Watt	Y	Y	Y	Y	Y	N	N
NORTH DAKOTA							
AL Pomeroy	Y	Y	Y	Y	Y	N	Y
OHIO							
1 ***Chabot***	Y	Y	Y	Y	Y	Y	Y
2 ***Portman***	Y	Y	Y	Y	Y	Y	Y
3 Hall	Y	Y	Y	Y	Y	N	N
4 ***Oxley***	Y	Y	Y	Y	Y	Y	?
5 ***Gillmor***	Y	Y	Y	Y	Y	Y	Y
6 Strickland	Y	Y	N	Y	Y	N	N
7 ***Hobson***	Y	Y	Y	Y	Y	Y	Y
8 ***Boehner***	Y	Y	Y	Y	Y	Y	Y
9 Kaptur	Y	Y	Y	Y	Y	N	Y
10 Kucinich	Y	Y	N	Y	Y	N	N
11 Jones	?	?	?	?	?	N	N
12 ***Tiberi***	Y	Y	Y	Y	Y	Y	Y
13 Brown	Y	Y	Y	Y	Y	N	N
14 Sawyer	Y	Y	Y	Y	Y	N	Y
15 ***Pryce***	Y	Y	Y	Y	Y	Y	Y
16 ***Regula***	Y	Y	Y	Y	Y	Y	Y
17 Traficant	Y	Y	Y	Y	Y	Y	Y
18 ***Ney***	Y	Y	Y	Y	Y	Y	Y
19 ***LaTourette***	Y	Y	Y	Y	Y	Y	Y
OKLAHOMA							
1 ***Largent***	Y	Y	Y	Y	Y	Y	Y
2 Carson	Y	Y	Y	Y	Y	N	N
3 ***Watkins***	Y	Y	Y	Y	Y	Y	Y
4 ***Watts***	Y	Y	Y	Y	Y	Y	Y
5 ***Istook***	Y	Y	Y	Y	Y	P	Y
6 ***Lucas***	Y	Y	Y	Y	Y	Y	Y
OREGON							
1 Wu	Y	Y	Y	Y	Y	N	Y
2 ***Walden***	Y	Y	Y	Y	Y	Y	Y
3 Blumenauer	Y	Y	Y	Y	Y	N	N
4 DeFazio	?	?	?	?	?	?	?
5 Hooley	Y	Y	Y	Y	Y	N	N
PENNSYLVANIA							
1 Brady	Y	Y	N	Y	Y	N	Y
2 Fattah	Y	Y	Y	Y	Y	N	Y
3 Borski	Y	Y	N	Y	Y	N	Y
4 ***Hart***	Y	Y	Y	Y	Y	Y	Y
5 ***Peterson***	Y	Y	Y	Y	Y	Y	Y
6 Holden	Y	Y	Y	Y	Y	N	Y
7 ***Weldon***	Y	Y	Y	Y	Y	N	Y
8 ***Greenwood***	Y	Y	Y	Y	Y	Y	Y
9 ***Shuster, Bill***	Y	Y	Y	Y	Y	Y	Y
10 ***Sherwood***	Y	Y	Y	Y	Y	Y	Y
11 Kanjorski	Y	Y	Y	Y	Y	N	Y
12 Murtha	?	?	Y	Y	Y	N	Y
13 Hoeffel	Y	Y	Y	Y	Y	N	Y
14 Coyne	Y	Y	Y	Y	Y	N	N
15 ***Toomey***	Y	Y	Y	Y	Y	Y	Y
16 ***Pitts***	Y	Y	Y	Y	Y	Y	Y
17 ***Gekas***	Y	Y	Y	Y	Y	Y	Y
18 Doyle	Y	Y	Y	Y	Y	N	Y
19 ***Platts***	Y	Y	Y	Y	Y	Y	Y
20 Mascara	Y	Y	Y	Y	Y	N	Y
21 ***English***	Y	Y	?	Y	Y	Y	Y
RHODE ISLAND							
1 Kennedy	Y	Y	Y	Y	Y	N	N
2 Langevin	Y	Y	Y	Y	Y	N	N
SOUTH CAROLINA							
1 ***Brown***	Y	Y	Y	Y	Y	Y	Y
2 Vacant							
3 ***Graham***	Y	Y	Y	Y	Y	Y	Y
4 ***DeMint***	Y	Y	Y	Y	Y	Y	Y
5 Spratt	Y	Y	Y	Y	Y	N	N
6 Clyburn	Y	Y	Y	Y	Y	N	N
SOUTH DAKOTA							
AL ***Thune***	Y	Y	Y	Y	Y	Y	Y
TENNESSEE							
1 ***Jenkins***	Y	Y	Y	Y	Y	Y	Y
2 ***Duncan***	Y	Y	Y	Y	Y	Y	Y
3 ***Wamp***	?	?	Y	Y	Y	Y	Y
4 ***Hilleary***	?	?	?	?	?	Y	Y
5 Clement	+	+	Y	Y	Y	N	N
6 Gordon	Y	Y	Y	Y	?	N	N
7 ***Bryant***	Y	Y	Y	Y	Y	Y	Y
8 Tanner	Y	Y	Y	Y	Y	N	Y
9 Ford	?	?	?	?	?	?	?
TEXAS							
1 Sandlin	Y	Y	Y	Y	Y	N	N
2 Turner	Y	Y	Y	Y	Y	N	N
3 ***Johnson, Sam***	Y	Y	Y	Y	Y	Y	Y
4 Hall	Y	Y	Y	Y	Y	N	Y
5 ***Sessions***	Y	Y	Y	Y	Y	Y	Y
6 ***Barton***	Y	Y	Y	Y	Y	Y	Y
7 ***Culberson***	Y	Y	Y	Y	Y	Y	Y
8 ***Brady***	Y	Y	Y	Y	Y	Y	Y
9 Lampson	Y	Y	Y	Y	Y	N	Y
10 Doggett	Y	Y	Y	Y	Y	N	Y
11 Edwards	Y	Y	Y	Y	Y	N	N
12 ***Granger***	Y	Y	Y	Y	Y	Y	Y
13 ***Thornberry***	Y	Y	Y	Y	Y	Y	Y
14 ***Paul***	N	Y	Y	Y	N	Y	Y
15 Hinojosa	Y	Y	+	Y	Y	N	Y
16 Reyes	Y	Y	Y	Y	Y	N	Y
17 Stenholm	Y	Y	Y	Y	Y	N	Y
18 Jackson-Lee	Y	Y	Y	Y	Y	N	N
19 ***Combest***	Y	Y	Y	Y	Y	Y	Y
20 Gonzalez	Y	Y	Y	Y	Y	N	Y
21 ***Smith***	Y	Y	Y	Y	Y	Y	Y
22 ***DeLay***	Y	Y	Y	Y	?	Y	?
23 ***Bonilla***	Y	Y	Y	Y	Y	Y	Y
24 Frost	Y	Y	Y	Y	Y	N	?
25 Bentsen	?	?	Y	Y	Y	N	N
26 ***Armey***	Y	Y	Y	Y	Y	Y	Y
27 Ortiz	Y	Y	Y	Y	Y	N	Y
28 Rodriguez	Y	Y	Y	Y	Y	N	N
29 Green	Y	Y	Y	Y	Y	N	Y
30 Johnson, E.B.	Y	Y	Y	Y	Y	N	N
UTAH							
1 ***Hansen***	N	Y	Y	Y	Y	Y	Y
2 Matheson	Y	Y	Y	Y	Y	N	N
3 ***Cannon***	Y	Y	Y	Y	Y	Y	Y
VERMONT							
AL *Sanders*	Y	Y	Y	Y	Y	N	N
VIRGINIA							
1 ***Davis, Jo Ann***	Y	Y	Y	Y	Y	Y	Y
2 ***Schrock***	Y	Y	Y	Y	Y	Y	Y
3 Scott	Y	Y	Y	Y	Y	N	N
4 ***Forbes***	Y	Y	Y	Y	Y	Y	Y
5 *Goode*	Y	Y	Y	Y	Y	Y	Y
6 ***Goodlatte***	Y	Y	Y	Y	?	Y	Y
7 ***Cantor***	Y	Y	Y	Y	Y	Y	Y
8 Moran	Y	Y	Y	Y	Y	N	N
9 Boucher	Y	Y	Y	Y	Y	N	Y
10 ***Wolf***	Y	Y	Y	Y	Y	Y	Y
11 ***Davis, T.***	Y	Y	Y	Y	Y	Y	?
WASHINGTON							
1 Inslee	Y	Y	Y	Y	Y	N	N
2 Larsen	Y	Y	N	Y	Y	N	N
3 Baird	Y	Y	N	Y	Y	N	N
4 ***Hastings***	Y	Y	Y	Y	Y	Y	Y
5 ***Nethercutt***	Y	Y	Y	Y	Y	Y	Y
6 Dicks	Y	Y	Y	Y	Y	N	Y
7 McDermott	Y	Y	N	Y	Y	N	N
8 ***Dunn***	Y	Y	Y	Y	Y	Y	Y
9 Smith	Y	Y	Y	Y	Y	N	N
WEST VIRGINIA							
1 Mollohan	Y	Y	Y	Y	Y	N	Y
2 ***Capito***	Y	Y	Y	Y	Y	Y	Y
3 Rahall	Y	Y	Y	Y	Y	N	Y
WISCONSIN							
1 ***Ryan***	Y	Y	Y	Y	Y	Y	Y
2 Baldwin	Y	Y	Y	Y	Y	N	N
3 Kind	Y	Y	Y	Y	Y	N	N
4 Kleczka	Y	Y	Y	Y	Y	N	N
5 Barrett	Y	Y	Y	Y	Y	N	N
6 ***Petri***	Y	Y	Y	Y	Y	Y	?
7 Obey	Y	Y	Y	Y	Y	N	Y
8 ***Green***	Y	Y	Y	Y	Y	Y	Y
9 ***Sensenbrenner***	N	Y	Y	Y	Y	Y	Y
WYOMING							
AL ***Cubin***	?	?	?	?	?	Y	?

Southern states - Ala., Ark., Fla., Ga., Ky., La., Miss., N.C., Okla., S.C., Tenn., Texas, Va.

457. HR 3338. Fiscal 2002 Defense Appropriations/Employment Funds. Miller, D-Calif., amendment that would prohibit $1.5 billion in employment funds from being spent on New York City rebuilding efforts. Rejected 201-220: R 14-199; D 186-20 (ND 134-20, SD 52-0); I 1-1. Nov. 28, 2001.

458. HR 3338. Fiscal 2002 Defense Appropriations/Passage. Passage of the bill that would provide $317.5 billion for the Defense Department for fiscal 2002, about $20 billion more than fiscal 2001. The bill would include $7.9 billion for ballistic missile defense, $1.7 billion for a new counterterrorism program, and a 4.6 percent pay increase for military personnel. It also would allocate $20 billion in funding appropriated by the emergency supplemental spending package (PL 107-38) enacted after the Sept. 11 terror attacks, including $7.3 billion for defense. Passed 406-20: R 217-1; D 187-19 (ND 137-17, SD 50-2); I 2-0. Nov. 28, 2001.

459. Procedural Motion/Journal. Approval of the House Journal of Wednesday, Nov. 28, 2001. Approved 349-48: R 192-12; D 156-36 (ND 117-27, SD 39-9); I 1-0. Nov. 29, 2001.

460. HR 3210. Terrorism Insurance/Previous Question. Sessions, R-Texas, motion to order the previous question (thus ending debate and possibility of amendment) on adoption of the rule (H Res 297) to provide for House floor consideration of the bill that would authorize a three-year federal loan program to help the casualty and property insurance industry cover future terrorist-related losses. Motion agreed to 220-204: R 217-0; D 2-203 (ND 1-153, SD 1-50); I 1-1. Nov. 29, 2001.

461. HR 3210. Terrorism Insurance/Rule. Adoption of the rule (H Res 297) to provide for House floor consideration of the bill that would authorize a three-year federal loan program to help the casualty and property insurance industry cover future terrorist-related losses. Adopted 216-202: R 213-1; D 2-200 (ND 1-150, SD 1-50); I 1-1. Nov. 29, 2001.

462. HR 3210. Terrorism Insurance/Democratic Substitute. LaFalce, D-N.Y., substitute amendment that would include provisions similar to the underlying bill regarding loans for the insurance industry in the event of future terrorist-related losses but require the industry to be responsible for a greater portion of initial losses before receiving aid, mandate that providers offer terrorism-related coverage, eliminate restrictions on lawsuits, and allow any provider to receive aid whose losses exceed seven percent of its net premiums. Rejected 197-222: R 7-207; D 189-14 (ND 145-7, SD 44-7); I 1-1. Nov. 29, 2001.

463. HR 3210. Terrorism Insurance/Recommit. LaFalce, D-N.Y., motion to recommit the bill to the House Financial Services Committee with instructions to strike language that restrict lawsuits and liability damages and add language that would ban insurers from passing assessment costs associated with repaying federal loans on to policyholders and require insurers to provide assurances that it will abide by the bill's repayment assessment provisions. Motion rejected 173-243: R 1-212; D 171-30 (ND 136-15, SD 35-15); I 1-1. Nov. 29, 2001.

464. HR 3210. Terrorism Insurance/Passage. Passage of the bill that would authorize a three-year federal loan program to help the casualty and property insurance industry cover future terrorist-related losses. The loans would cover 90 percent of industry-wide losses over $1 billion and would have to be repaid, the initial $20 billion to come from insurance company assessments, the rest up to $100 billion to come from surcharges levied on policyholders. It would restrict terrorist-related lawsuits to federal court, ban punitive damages in such suits and limit non-economic damages and attorney fees. Passed 227-193: R 207-9; D 19-183 (ND 9-143, SD 10-40); I 1-1. Nov. 29, 2001.

[1] *Rep. John Boozman, R-Ark., was sworn in Nov. 29, 2001. The first vote for which he was eligible was 460.*

Key

Y	Voted for (yea).
#	Paired for.
+	Announced for.
N	Voted against (nay).
X	Paired against.
–	Announced against.
P	Voted "present."
C	Voted "present" to avoid possible conflict of interest.
?	Did not vote or otherwise make a position known.

Democrats • **Republicans**
Independents

	457	458	459	460	461	462	463	464
ALABAMA								
1 *Callahan*	N	Y	Y	Y	Y	N	N	Y
2 *Everett*	N	Y	Y	Y	Y	N	N	Y
3 *Riley*	N	Y	Y	Y	Y	N	N	Y
4 *Aderholt*	N	Y	N	Y	Y	N	N	Y
5 Cramer	Y	Y	Y	N	N	N	N	Y
6 *Bachus*	N	Y	Y	Y	Y	N	N	Y
7 Hilliard	Y	Y	N	N	N	Y	Y	N
ALASKA								
AL *Young*	N	Y	?	Y	Y	N	N	Y
ARIZONA								
1 *Flake*	N	Y	Y	Y	Y	N	N	N
2 Pastor	Y	Y	Y	N	N	Y	N	Y
3 *Stump*	N	Y	Y	Y	Y	N	N	Y
4 *Shadegg*	N	Y	Y	Y	Y	N	N	Y
5 *Kolbe*	N	Y	Y	Y	Y	N	N	Y
6 *Hayworth*	N	Y	Y	Y	Y	N	N	Y
ARKANSAS								
1 Berry	Y	Y	Y	N	N	Y	Y	N
2 Snyder	Y	Y	Y	N	N	Y	N	N
3 *Boozman* [1]			Y	Y	N	Y	N	Y
4 Ross	Y	Y	Y	N	N	Y	Y	N
CALIFORNIA								
1 Thompson	Y	Y	N	N	N	Y	N	N
2 *Herger*	N	Y	Y	Y	Y	N	N	Y
3 *Ose*	N	Y	Y	Y	Y	N	N	Y
4 *Doolittle*	N	Y	Y	Y	Y	N	N	Y
5 Matsui	Y	Y	Y	N	N	Y	N	N
6 Woolsey	Y	Y	N	N	N	Y	Y	N
7 Miller, George	Y	N	N	N	N	?	?	N
8 Pelosi	Y	Y	Y	N	N	Y	N	N
9 Lee	Y	N	Y	N	N	Y	Y	N
10 Tauscher	Y	Y	Y	N	N	Y	Y	N
11 *Pombo*	N	Y	Y	Y	Y	N	N	Y
12 Lantos	Y	Y	Y	N	?	Y	Y	N
13 Stark	Y	N	Y	N	N	N	N	N
14 Eshoo	Y	N	Y	N	N	Y	N	N
15 Honda	Y	Y	Y	N	N	Y	Y	N
16 Lofgren	Y	Y	Y	N	N	Y	N	N
17 Farr	Y	Y	Y	N	N	Y	N	N
18 Condit	Y	Y	N	N	Y	Y	N	N
19 *Radanovich*	N	Y	Y	?	N	N	N	Y
20 Dooley	Y	Y	N	N	N	N	Y	N
21 *Thomas*	N	Y	Y	Y	Y	N	N	Y
22 Capps	Y	Y	Y	N	N	Y	N	N
23 *Gallegly*	N	Y	Y	Y	Y	N	N	Y
24 Sherman	Y	Y	Y	N	N	Y	Y	N
25 *McKeon*	N	Y	Y	Y	Y	N	N	Y
26 Berman	Y	Y	Y	N	N	Y	N	N
27 Schiff	Y	Y	Y	N	N	Y	Y	N
28 *Dreier*	N	Y	Y	Y	Y	N	N	Y
29 Waxman	Y	Y	Y	N	N	Y	Y	N
30 Becerra	Y	Y	Y	N	N	Y	N	N
31 Solis	Y	Y	Y	N	N	Y	Y	N
32 Watson	Y	Y	Y	N	N	Y	Y	N
33 Roybal-Allard	Y	Y	Y	N	N	Y	Y	N
34 Napolitano	Y	Y	N	N	N	Y	Y	N
35 Waters	Y	Y	?	N	N	Y	Y	N
36 Harman	Y	Y	Y	N	N	Y	N	N
37 Millender-McD.	Y	Y	N	N	N	Y	Y	N
38 *Horn*	N	Y	Y	?	N	N	N	Y

	457	458	459	460	461	462	463	464
39 *Royce*	N	Y	Y	Y	Y	N	N	Y
40 *Lewis*	N	Y	Y	Y	Y	N	N	Y
41 *Miller, Gary*	N	Y	Y	Y	Y	N	N	Y
42 Baca	Y	Y	Y	N	N	Y	N	Y
43 *Calvert*	N	Y	Y	Y	Y	N	N	Y
44 *Bono*	N	Y	Y	Y	Y	N	N	Y
45 *Rohrabacher*	N	Y	Y	Y	Y	N	N	Y
46 Sanchez	Y	Y	?	N	N	Y	N	N
47 *Cox*	N	Y	Y	Y	Y	N	N	Y
48 *Issa*	N	Y	Y	Y	Y	N	N	Y
49 Davis	Y	Y	Y	N	N	Y	N	N
50 Filner	Y	N	N	N	N	Y	Y	N
51 *Cunningham*	N	Y	?	Y	Y	N	N	Y
52 *Hunter*	N	Y	Y	Y	Y	N	N	Y
COLORADO								
1 DeGette	Y	Y	Y	N	N	Y	Y	N
2 Udall	Y	Y	N	N	N	Y	Y	N
3 *McInnis*	N	Y	Y	Y	Y	N	N	N
4 *Schaffer*	Y	Y	?	Y	Y	N	N	Y
5 *Hefley*	Y	Y	N	Y	Y	N	N	Y
6 *Tancredo*	N	Y	P	Y	Y	N	N	N
CONNECTICUT								
1 Larson	Y	Y	Y	N	N	N	N	Y
2 *Simmons*	N	Y	Y	Y	N	N	Y	Y
3 DeLauro	Y	Y	Y	N	N	Y	N	N
4 *Shays*	N	Y	Y	Y	Y	N	N	Y
5 Maloney	Y	Y	Y	N	N	Y	Y	N
6 *Johnson*	N	Y	?	Y	Y	N	?	Y
DELAWARE								
AL *Castle*	N	Y	Y	Y	Y	N	N	Y
FLORIDA								
1 *Miller, J.*	N	Y	Y	Y	Y	N	N	Y
2 Boyd	Y	Y	Y	N	N	N	Y	N
3 Brown	Y	Y	Y	N	N	N	N	N
4 *Crenshaw*	N	Y	Y	Y	Y	N	N	Y
5 Thurman	Y	Y	N	N	N	N	N	N
6 *Stearns*	N	Y	Y	Y	Y	N	N	Y
7 *Mica*	N	Y	Y	Y	Y	N	N	Y
8 *Keller*	N	Y	Y	Y	Y	N	N	Y
9 *Bilirakis*	Y	Y	Y	Y	Y	N	N	Y
10 *Young*	N	Y	Y	Y	Y	N	N	Y
11 Davis	Y	Y	Y	N	N	Y	N	N
12 *Putnam*	N	Y	Y	Y	Y	N	N	Y
13 *Miller, D.*	N	Y	Y	Y	Y	N	N	Y
14 *Goss*	N	Y	Y	Y	Y	N	N	Y
15 *Weldon*	N	Y	Y	Y	Y	N	N	Y
16 *Foley*	N	Y	Y	Y	Y	N	N	Y
17 Meek	Y	Y	?	N	N	Y	Y	N
18 *Ros-Lehtinen*	N	Y	Y	Y	Y	N	N	Y
19 Wexler	?	?	?	?	?	?	?	?
20 Deutsch	Y	Y	Y	N	N	Y	N	N
21 *Diaz-Balart*	N	Y	Y	Y	Y	N	N	Y
22 *Shaw*	N	Y	Y	Y	Y	N	N	Y
23 Hastings	Y	Y	N	N	N	Y	N	N
GEORGIA								
1 *Kingston*	N	Y	Y	Y	Y	N	N	Y
2 Bishop	Y	Y	Y	N	N	Y	Y	N
3 *Collins*	N	Y	Y	Y	Y	N	N	Y
4 McKinney	Y	N	N	N	N	Y	N	N
5 Lewis	Y	N	N	N	N	Y	N	N
6 *Isakson*	N	Y	Y	Y	Y	N	N	Y
7 *Barr*	N	Y	Y	Y	Y	N	N	Y
8 *Chambliss*	?	Y	Y	Y	Y	?	?	?
9 *Deal*	N	Y	Y	Y	Y	N	N	Y
10 *Norwood*	N	Y	Y	Y	Y	N	N	Y
11 *Linder*	N	Y	Y	Y	Y	N	N	Y
HAWAII								
1 Abercrombie	Y	Y	Y	N	N	Y	Y	N
2 Mink	Y	Y	Y	N	N	Y	Y	N
IDAHO								
1 *Otter*	N	Y	Y	Y	Y	N	N	Y
2 *Simpson*	N	Y	Y	Y	Y	N	N	Y
ILLINOIS								
1 Rush	Y	Y	N	N	Y	N	Y	N
2 Jackson	Y	N	N	N	N	Y	N	N
3 Lipinski	Y	Y	Y	N	N	Y	Y	N
4 Gutierrez	Y	Y	Y	N	N	Y	N	N
5 Blagojevich	Y	Y	N	N	N	Y	Y	N
6 *Hyde*	N	Y	?	Y	Y	N	N	Y
7 Davis	Y	Y	N	N	N	Y	N	N
8 *Crane*	N	Y	N	Y	Y	N	N	Y
9 Schakowsky	Y	Y	Y	N	N	Y	N	N
10 *Kirk*	N	Y	Y	Y	Y	N	N	Y
11 *Weller*	N	Y	N	Y	Y	N	N	Y
12 Costello	Y	Y	N	N	N	N	Y	N
13 *Biggert*	N	Y	Y	Y	Y	N	N	Y

ND Northern Democrats   SD Southern Democrats

	457	458	459	460	461	462	463	464
14 ***Hastert***		Y						
15 ***Johnson***	N	Y	Y	Y	Y	Y	N	Y
16 ***Manzullo***	N	Y	Y	Y	Y	N	N	Y
17 Evans	Y	Y	Y	N	N	Y	Y	N
18 ***LaHood***	N	Y	Y	Y	Y	N	N	Y
19 Phelps	Y	Y	Y	N	N	Y	Y	N
20 ***Shimkus***	N	Y	Y	Y	Y	N	N	Y
INDIANA								
1 Visclosky	Y	Y	N	N	N	Y	Y	N
2 ***Pence***	N	Y	Y	Y	Y	N	N	Y
3 Roemer	Y	Y	Y	N	N	Y	N	N
4 ***Souder***	N	Y	?	Y	Y	N	N	Y
5 ***Buyer***	N	Y	Y	Y	Y	N	N	Y
6 ***Burton***	N	Y	Y	Y	Y	N	N	Y
7 ***Kerns***	N	Y	Y	Y	Y	N	N	Y
8 ***Hostettler***	N	Y	Y	Y	Y	N	N	Y
9 Hill	Y	Y	Y	N	N	Y	N	N
10 Carson	?	?	?	?	?	?	?	?
IOWA								
1 ***Leach***	N	Y	Y	Y	Y	N	N	Y
2 ***Nussle***	N	Y	Y	Y	Y	N	N	Y
3 Boswell	Y	Y	Y	N	N	Y	Y	N
4 ***Ganske***	N	Y	Y	Y	Y	N	N	Y
5 ***Latham***	?	Y	Y	Y	Y	N	N	Y
KANSAS								
1 ***Moran***	N	Y	N	Y	Y	N	N	Y
2 ***Ryun***	N	Y	Y	Y	Y	N	N	Y
3 Moore	Y	Y	N	N	N	Y	N	N
4 ***Tiahrt***	N	Y	Y	Y	Y	N	N	Y
KENTUCKY								
1 ***Whitfield***	N	Y	?	Y	Y	N	N	Y
2 ***Lewis***	N	Y	Y	Y	Y	N	N	Y
3 ***Northup***	N	Y	Y	Y	Y	N	N	Y
4 Lucas	Y	Y	Y	N	Y	N	N	Y
5 ***Rogers***	N	Y	Y	Y	Y	N	N	Y
6 ***Fletcher***	N	Y	Y	Y	Y	N	N	Y
LOUISIANA								
1 ***Vitter***	N	Y	Y	Y	Y	N	N	Y
2 Jefferson	Y	Y	Y	N	N	Y	Y	N
3 ***Tauzin***	N	Y	Y	Y	Y	N	N	Y
4 ***McCrery***	N	Y	Y	Y	Y	N	N	Y
5 ***Cooksey***	N	Y	?	?	?	?	?	?
6 ***Baker***	N	Y	Y	Y	Y	N	N	Y
7 John	Y	Y	Y	N	N	N	N	Y
MAINE								
1 Allen	Y	Y	Y	N	N	Y	Y	N
2 Baldacci	Y	Y	Y	N	N	Y	Y	N
MARYLAND								
1 ***Gilchrest***	N	Y	Y	Y	Y	N	N	Y
2 ***Ehrlich***	N	Y	Y	Y	Y	N	N	Y
3 Cardin	Y	Y	Y	N	N	Y	Y	N
4 Wynn	Y	Y	Y	N	N	Y	Y	N
5 Hoyer	Y	Y	Y	N	N	Y	Y	N
6 ***Bartlett***	N	Y	Y	Y	Y	N	N	Y
7 Cummings	Y	Y	?	N	N	Y	Y	N
8 ***Morella***	N	Y	Y	Y	Y	Y	N	Y
MASSACHUSETTS								
1 Olver	Y	Y	N	N	N	Y	Y	N
2 Neal	Y	Y	Y	N	N	Y	Y	N
3 McGovern	Y	Y	Y	N	N	Y	Y	N
4 Frank	Y	Y	Y	N	N	Y	Y	N
5 Meehan	Y	Y	Y	N	N	Y	Y	N
6 Tierney	Y	Y	Y	N	N	Y	Y	N
7 Markey	Y	Y	Y	N	N	Y	Y	N
8 Capuano	Y	Y	N	N	N	Y	Y	N
9 Lynch	Y	Y	Y	N	N	Y	Y	N
10 Delahunt	Y	N	Y	N	N	Y	Y	N
MICHIGAN								
1 Stupak	Y	Y	N	N	N	Y	Y	N
2 ***Hoekstra***	N	Y	N	Y	Y	N	N	Y
3 ***Ehlers***	N	Y	Y	Y	Y	N	N	Y
4 ***Camp***	N	Y	Y	Y	Y	N	N	Y
5 Barcia	N	Y	Y	N	N	Y	Y	Y
6 ***Upton***	N	Y	Y	Y	Y	N	N	Y
7 ***Smith***	N	Y	Y	Y	Y	N	N	Y
8 ***Rogers***	N	Y	Y	Y	Y	N	N	Y
9 Kildee	Y	Y	Y	N	N	Y	Y	N
10 Bonior	Y	Y	Y	N	N	Y	Y	N
11 ***Knollenberg***	N	Y	Y	Y	Y	N	N	Y
12 Levin	Y	Y	Y	N	N	Y	Y	N
13 Rivers	Y	Y	Y	N	N	Y	Y	N
14 Conyers	Y	N	?	N	N	Y	Y	N
15 Kilpatrick	Y	Y	Y	N	N	Y	N	N
16 Dingell	Y	Y	Y	N	?	Y	Y	N
MINNESOTA								
1 ***Gutknecht***	N	Y	N	Y	Y	N	N	Y
2 ***Kennedy***	Y	Y	N	Y	Y	N	N	Y
3 ***Ramstad***	N	Y	N	Y	Y	N	N	Y
4 McCollum	Y	Y	Y	N	N	Y	Y	N
5 Sabo	Y	Y	N	N	N	Y	Y	N
6 Luther	Y	Y	Y	N	N	Y	Y	N
7 Peterson	Y	Y	N	N	N	N	N	N
8 Oberstar	Y	Y	N	N	N	Y	Y	N
MISSISSIPPI								
1 ***Wicker***	N	Y	N	Y	Y	N	N	Y
2 Thompson	Y	Y	N	N	N	Y	Y	N
3 ***Pickering***	N	Y	Y	Y	Y	N	N	Y
4 Shows	Y	Y	Y	N	N	Y	Y	N
5 Taylor	Y	Y	N	N	N	Y	Y	Y
MISSOURI								
1 Clay	Y	Y	?	N	N	Y	Y	N
2 ***Akin***	N	Y	Y	Y	Y	N	N	Y
3 Gephardt	Y	Y	Y	N	N	Y	Y	N
4 Skelton	Y	Y	Y	N	N	Y	Y	N
5 McCarthy	Y	Y	Y	N	N	Y	Y	N
6 ***Graves***	N	Y	Y	Y	Y	N	N	Y
7 ***Blunt***	N	Y	Y	Y	Y	N	N	Y
8 ***Emerson***	N	Y	Y	Y	Y	N	N	Y
9 ***Hulshof***	N	Y	Y	Y	Y	N	N	Y
MONTANA								
AL ***Rehberg***	N	Y	Y	Y	Y	N	N	Y
NEBRASKA								
1 ***Bereuter***	Y	Y	Y	Y	Y	N	N	Y
2 ***Terry***	N	Y	Y	Y	Y	Y	N	Y
3 ***Osborne***	N	Y	Y	Y	Y	N	N	Y
NEVADA								
1 Berkley	Y	Y	Y	N	N	Y	Y	N
2 ***Gibbons***	N	Y	Y	Y	Y	N	N	Y
NEW HAMPSHIRE								
1 ***Sununu***	N	Y	Y	Y	Y	N	N	Y
2 ***Bass***	N	Y	Y	Y	Y	N	N	Y
NEW JERSEY								
1 Andrews	Y	Y	Y	N	N	Y	Y	N
2 ***LoBiondo***	N	Y	N	Y	Y	N	N	Y
3 ***Saxton***	N	Y	Y	Y	Y	N	N	Y
4 ***Smith***	N	Y	Y	Y	Y	N	N	Y
5 ***Roukema***	N	Y	Y	Y	Y	N	N	Y
6 Pallone	Y	Y	N	N	N	Y	Y	N
7 ***Ferguson***	N	Y	Y	Y	Y	N	N	Y
8 Pascrell	Y	Y	Y	N	N	Y	N	N
9 Rothman	?	?	?	?	?	?	?	?
10 Payne	Y	N	Y	N	N	Y	Y	N
11 ***Frelinghuysen***	N	Y	Y	Y	Y	N	N	Y
12 Holt	Y	Y	Y	N	N	Y	Y	N
13 Menendez	Y	Y	Y	N	N	Y	Y	N
NEW MEXICO								
1 ***Wilson***	Y	Y	Y	Y	Y	N	N	Y
2 ***Skeen***	N	Y	Y	Y	Y	N	N	Y
3 Udall	Y	Y	N	N	N	Y	Y	N
NEW YORK								
1 ***Grucci***	N	Y	Y	Y	Y	N	N	Y
2 Israel	N	Y	Y	N	N	Y	Y	N
3 ***King***	N	Y	Y	Y	Y	N	N	Y
4 McCarthy	N	Y	Y	N	N	Y	Y	N
5 Ackerman	N	Y	Y	N	N	Y	Y	N
6 Meeks	N	Y	Y	N	N	Y	Y	N
7 Crowley	N	Y	Y	N	N	Y	Y	N
8 Nadler	N	N	?	N	N	Y	Y	N
9 Weiner	N	Y	Y	N	N	Y	Y	N
10 Towns	N	Y	N	N	N	Y	Y	Y
11 Owens	N	N	Y	N	N	Y	Y	N
12 Velázquez	N	N	Y	N	N	Y	Y	N
13 ***Fossella***	N	Y	?	Y	Y	N	N	Y
14 Maloney	N	Y	Y	N	N	Y	N	N
15 Rangel	N	Y	Y	N	N	?	?	?
16 Serrano	N	N	Y	N	N	Y	Y	N
17 Engel	N	Y	?	N	N	Y	Y	N
18 Lowey	N	Y	Y	N	N	Y	?	?
19 ***Kelly***	N	Y	Y	Y	Y	N	N	Y
20 ***Gilman***	N	Y	Y	Y	Y	Y	N	Y
21 McNulty	N	Y	N	N	N	Y	Y	N
22 ***Sweeney***	N	Y	Y	Y	Y	N	N	Y
23 ***Boehlert***	N	Y	Y	Y	Y	N	N	Y
24 ***McHugh***	N	Y	Y	Y	Y	N	N	Y
25 ***Walsh***	N	Y	Y	Y	Y	N	N	Y
26 Hinchey	N	N	N	N	N	Y	Y	N
27 ***Reynolds***	N	Y	Y	Y	Y	N	N	Y
28 Slaughter	N	Y	N	N	N	Y	Y	N
29 LaFalce	N	Y	?	N	N	Y	Y	N
30 ***Quinn***	?	?	?	?	?	?	?	?
31 ***Houghton***	N	Y	Y	Y	Y	N	N	Y
NORTH CAROLINA								
1 Clayton	Y	Y	Y	N	N	Y	Y	N
2 Etheridge	Y	Y	N	N	N	Y	N	N
3 ***Jones***	N	Y	Y	Y	Y	N	N	Y
4 Price	Y	Y	Y	N	N	Y	N	N
5 ***Burr***	N	Y	Y	Y	Y	N	N	Y
6 ***Coble***	Y	Y	Y	Y	Y	N	N	Y
7 McIntyre	Y	Y	Y	N	N	Y	Y	N
8 ***Hayes***	N	Y	Y	Y	Y	N	N	Y
9 ***Myrick***	N	Y	?	Y	Y	N	N	Y
10 ***Ballenger***	N	Y	Y	Y	Y	N	N	Y
11 ***Taylor***	N	Y	Y	Y	Y	N	N	Y
12 Watt	Y	Y	Y	N	N	Y	Y	N
NORTH DAKOTA								
AL Pomeroy	Y	Y	Y	N	N	Y	N	N
OHIO								
1 ***Chabot***	N	Y	Y	Y	Y	N	N	Y
2 ***Portman***	N	Y	Y	Y	Y	N	N	Y
3 Hall	Y	Y	?	N	N	Y	Y	Y
4 ***Oxley***	N	Y	Y	Y	Y	N	N	Y
5 ***Gillmor***	N	Y	N	Y	Y	N	N	Y
6 Strickland	Y	Y	Y	N	N	Y	Y	N
7 ***Hobson***	N	Y	Y	Y	Y	N	N	Y
8 ***Boehner***	?	Y	Y	Y	Y	N	?	Y
9 Kaptur	Y	Y	Y	N	N	Y	Y	N
10 Kucinich	Y	Y	N	N	N	Y	Y	N
11 Jones	Y	Y	Y	N	N	Y	Y	N
12 ***Tiberi***	N	Y	Y	Y	Y	N	N	Y
13 Brown	Y	N	Y	N	N	Y	Y	N
14 Sawyer	Y	Y	Y	N	N	Y	Y	N
15 ***Pryce***	N	Y	Y	Y	Y	N	N	Y
16 ***Regula***	N	Y	Y	Y	Y	N	N	Y
17 Traficant	Y	Y	Y	Y	Y	Y	Y	Y
18 ***Ney***	N	Y	Y	Y	Y	N	N	Y
19 ***LaTourette***	Y	Y	Y	Y	Y	Y	Y	Y
OKLAHOMA								
1 ***Largent***	N	Y	Y	Y	Y	N	N	Y
2 Carson	Y	Y	Y	N	N	Y	Y	N
3 ***Watkins***	N	Y	Y	Y	?	N	N	Y
4 ***Watts***	N	Y	Y	Y	Y	N	N	Y
5 ***Istook***	N	Y	Y	Y	N	Y	N	Y
6 ***Lucas***	N	Y	Y	Y	Y	N	N	Y
OREGON								
1 Wu	Y	Y	Y	N	N	Y	N	N
2 ***Walden***	N	Y	Y	Y	Y	N	N	Y
3 Blumenauer	Y	N	Y	N	N	Y	N	N
4 DeFazio	?	?	?	?	?	?	?	?
5 Hooley	Y	Y	Y	N	N	Y	Y	N
PENNSYLVANIA								
1 Brady	Y	Y	N	N	N	Y	Y	N
2 Fattah	Y	Y	Y	N	N	Y	Y	N
3 Borski	Y	Y	N	N	N	Y	Y	N
4 ***Hart***	Y	Y	Y	Y	Y	N	N	Y
5 ***Peterson***	?	Y	Y	Y	Y	N	N	Y
6 Holden	Y	Y	Y	N	N	Y	Y	Y
7 ***Weldon***	N	Y	Y	Y	Y	N	N	Y
8 ***Greenwood***	N	Y	Y	Y	Y	N	?	Y
9 ***Shuster, Bill***	N	Y	Y	Y	Y	N	N	Y
10 ***Sherwood***	N	Y	Y	Y	Y	N	N	Y
11 Kanjorski	Y	Y	Y	N	N	Y	Y	N
12 Murtha	Y	Y	Y	N	N	Y	Y	N
13 Hoeffel	Y	Y	Y	N	N	Y	Y	N
14 Coyne	Y	Y	?	N	N	Y	Y	N
15 ***Toomey***	Y	Y	Y	Y	Y	N	N	Y
16 ***Pitts***	N	Y	Y	Y	Y	N	N	Y
17 ***Gekas***	N	Y	Y	Y	Y	N	N	Y
18 Doyle	Y	Y	Y	N	N	Y	Y	N
19 ***Platts***	N	Y	Y	Y	Y	N	N	N
20 Mascara	Y	Y	Y	N	N	Y	Y	N
21 ***English***	N	Y	Y	Y	Y	N	N	Y
RHODE ISLAND								
1 Kennedy	Y	Y	Y	N	N	Y	Y	N
2 Langevin	Y	Y	Y	N	N	Y	Y	N
SOUTH CAROLINA								
1 ***Brown***	N	Y	Y	Y	Y	N	N	Y
2 Vacant								
3 ***Graham***	N	Y	Y	Y	Y	Y	N	Y
4 ***DeMint***	N	Y	Y	Y	Y	N	N	Y
5 Spratt	Y	Y	Y	N	N	Y	N	N
6 Clyburn	Y	Y	Y	N	N	Y	Y	N
SOUTH DAKOTA								
AL ***Thune***	N	Y	Y	Y	Y	N	N	Y
TENNESSEE								
1 ***Jenkins***	N	Y	Y	Y	Y	N	N	Y
2 ***Duncan***	N	Y	Y	Y	Y	N	N	N
3 ***Wamp***	N	Y	Y	Y	Y	N	N	Y
4 ***Hilleary***	N	Y	Y	Y	Y	N	N	Y
5 Clement	Y	Y	Y	N	N	Y	Y	Y
6 Gordon	Y	Y	Y	N	N	Y	Y	Y
7 ***Bryant***	N	Y	Y	Y	Y	N	N	Y
8 Tanner	Y	Y	Y	N	N	Y	N	Y
9 Ford	?	?	?	?	?	?	?	?
TEXAS								
1 Sandlin	Y	Y	Y	N	N	Y	Y	N
2 Turner	Y	Y	Y	N	N	Y	Y	N
3 ***Johnson, Sam***	N	Y	Y	Y	Y	N	N	Y
4 Hall	Y	Y	Y	Y	N	N	N	Y
5 ***Sessions***	N	Y	Y	Y	Y	N	N	Y
6 ***Barton***	N	Y	Y	Y	Y	N	N	Y
7 ***Culberson***	N	Y	?	Y	Y	N	N	Y
8 ***Brady***	N	Y	Y	Y	Y	N	N	Y
9 Lampson	Y	Y	Y	N	N	Y	Y	N
10 Doggett	Y	Y	Y	N	N	Y	Y	N
11 Edwards	Y	Y	Y	N	N	Y	Y	N
12 ***Granger***	N	Y	Y	Y	Y	N	N	Y
13 ***Thornberry***	N	Y	Y	Y	Y	N	N	Y
14 ***Paul***	Y	N	Y	Y	Y	N	N	N
15 Hinojosa	Y	Y	N	N	N	Y	Y	N
16 Reyes	Y	Y	?	N	N	Y	Y	N
17 Stenholm	Y	Y	Y	N	N	N	N	Y
18 Jackson-Lee	Y	Y	Y	N	N	Y	Y	N
19 ***Combest***	N	Y	Y	Y	Y	N	N	Y
20 Gonzalez	Y	Y	Y	N	N	Y	Y	N
21 ***Smith***	N	Y	Y	Y	Y	N	N	Y
22 ***DeLay***	N	Y	Y	Y	Y	N	N	Y
23 ***Bonilla***	N	Y	Y	Y	Y	N	N	Y
24 Frost	Y	Y	Y	?	?	?	?	?
25 Bentsen	Y	Y	?	N	N	Y	N	N
26 ***Armey***	N	Y	Y	Y	Y	N	N	Y
27 Ortiz	Y	Y	Y	N	N	Y	Y	N
28 Rodriguez	Y	Y	Y	N	N	Y	Y	N
29 Green	Y	Y	Y	N	N	Y	Y	N
30 Johnson, E.B.	Y	Y	N	N	N	Y	Y	N
UTAH								
1 ***Hansen***	N	Y	Y	Y	Y	N	N	Y
2 Matheson	Y	Y	N	N	N	Y	Y	Y
3 ***Cannon***	N	Y	?	Y	Y	N	N	Y
VERMONT								
AL *Sanders*	Y	Y	Y	N	N	Y	Y	N
VIRGINIA								
1 ***Davis, Jo Ann***	Y	Y	Y	Y	Y	N	N	Y
2 ***Schrock***	N	Y	Y	Y	Y	N	N	Y
3 Scott	Y	Y	N	N	N	Y	Y	N
4 ***Forbes***	N	Y	Y	Y	Y	N	N	Y
5 *Goode*	N	Y	?	Y	Y	N	N	Y
6 ***Goodlatte***	N	Y	Y	Y	Y	N	N	Y
7 ***Cantor***	N	Y	Y	Y	Y	N	N	Y
8 Moran	Y	Y	Y	N	N	N	N	Y
9 Boucher	Y	Y	?	N	N	Y	?	?
10 ***Wolf***	N	Y	Y	Y	Y	–	N	Y
11 ***Davis, T.***	N	Y	Y	Y	Y	–	N	Y
WASHINGTON								
1 Inslee	Y	Y	Y	N	N	Y	Y	N
2 Larsen	Y	Y	N	N	N	Y	Y	N
3 Baird	Y	Y	N	N	N	Y	Y	N
4 ***Hastings***	N	Y	Y	Y	Y	N	N	Y
5 ***Nethercutt***	N	Y	Y	Y	Y	N	N	Y
6 Dicks	Y	Y	Y	N	N	Y	Y	N
7 McDermott	Y	N	N	N	N	Y	Y	N
8 ***Dunn***	Y	Y	Y	Y	Y	N	N	Y
9 Smith	Y	Y	Y	N	N	Y	Y	N
WEST VIRGINIA								
1 Mollohan	Y	Y	Y	N	N	Y	Y	N
2 ***Capito***	Y	Y	Y	Y	Y	N	N	Y
3 Rahall	Y	Y	Y	N	N	Y	Y	N
WISCONSIN								
1 ***Ryan***	N	Y	Y	Y	Y	N	N	Y
2 Baldwin	Y	Y	Y	N	N	Y	Y	N
3 Kind	Y	Y	Y	N	N	Y	Y	N
4 Kleczka	Y	Y	Y	N	?	N	Y	N
5 Barrett	Y	Y	Y	N	N	Y	Y	N
6 ***Petri***	N	Y	Y	Y	Y	N	N	N
7 Obey	Y	Y	N	N	N	Y	Y	N
8 ***Green***	N	Y	Y	Y	Y	N	N	Y
9 ***Sensenbrenner***	N	Y	Y	Y	Y	N	N	Y
WYOMING								
AL ***Cubin***	?	?	?	?	?	?	?	?

Southern states - Ala., Ark., Fla., Ga., Ky., La., Miss., N.C., Okla., S.C., Tenn., Texas, Va.

465. HR 2299. Fiscal 2002 Transportation Appropriations/Conference Report. Adoption of the conference report on the bill that would appropriate $59.6 billion for fiscal 2002 transportation programs, $1.5 billion more than fiscal 2001. The total includes $1.25 billion for a security office responsible for passenger and baggage screeners at airports established under the aviation security bill (PL 107-71). It also would allow trucks from Mexico to travel throughout the United States but those trucks would be subject to additional inspection, safety and border controls. Adopted (thus sent to the Senate) 371-11: R 189-9; D 180-2 (ND 130-2, SD 50-0); I 2-0. Nov. 30, 2001.

466. HR 3323. Medicare Electronic Transactions/Passage. Tauzin, R-La., motion to suspend the rules and pass the bill that would require all Medicare providers to meet October 2002 electronic transactions requirements of the Health Insurance Portability and Accountability Act or submit a plan for compliance by 2003 to the Health and Human Services Department. The bill would authorize $44 million to help providers comply with the requirements. Motion agreed to 410-0: R 210-0; D 198-0 (ND 147-0, SD 51-0); I 2-0. A two-thirds majority of those present and voting (274 in this case) is required for passage under suspension of the rules. Dec. 4, 2001.

467. HR 3391. Medicare Regulations/Passage. Johnson, R-Conn., motion to suspend the rules and pass the bill that would streamline Medicare regulations for health care providers, give the Health and Human Service Department additional flexibility and control over private contractors, and mandate additional educational outreach by contractors to providers. Motion agreed to 408-0: R 208-0; D 198-0 (ND 147-0, SD 51-0); I 2-0. A two-thirds majority of those present and voting (272 in this case) is required for passage under suspension of the rules. Dec. 4, 2001.

468. S 494. Zimbabwe Relief/Passage. Royce, R-Calif., motion to suspend the rules and pass the bill that would order the Treasury Department to study ways to relieve Zimbabwe of its U.S. debt, but only after the president certifies that the country has made certain democratic changes. The bill would authorize $26 million to support democratic change in Zimbabwe. Motion agreed to 396-11: R 201-8; D 194-2 (ND 145-0, SD 49-2); I 1-1. A two-thirds majority of those present and voting (272 in this case) is required for passage under suspension of the rules. Dec. 4, 2001.

469. H Con Res 242. International Radio Broadcasts/Adoption. Leach, R-Iowa, motion to suspend the rules and adopt the concurrent resolution that would pay tribute to Radio Free Europe and Radio Liberty for their contributions in promoting democracy in eastern Europe and Russia over the last 50 years. Motion agreed to 404-1: R 204-1; D 198-0 (ND 147-0, SD 51-0); I 2-0. A two-thirds majority of those present and voting (270 in this case) is required for adoption under suspension of the rules. Dec. 5, 2001.

470. HR 3348. George P. Schultz Tribute/Passage. Leach, R-Iowa, motion to suspend the rules and pass the bill that would name Virginia's National Foreign Affairs Training Center after George P. Schultz. Motion agreed to 407-0: R 208-0; D 197-0 (ND 146-0, SD 51-0); I 2-0. A two-thirds majority of those present and voting (272 in this case) is required for passage under suspension of the rules. Dec. 5, 2001.

Key

Y	Voted for (yea).
#	Paired for.
+	Announced for.
N	Voted against (nay).
X	Paired against.
–	Announced against.
P	Voted "present."
C	Voted "present" to avoid possible conflict of interest.
?	Did not vote or otherwise make a position known.

Democrats • **Republicans**
Independents

	465	466	467	468	469	470
ALABAMA						
1 *Callahan*	Y	Y	Y	Y	Y	Y
2 *Everett*	Y	Y	Y	Y	Y	Y
3 *Riley*	Y	+	+	+	Y	Y
4 *Aderholt*	Y	Y	Y	Y	Y	Y
5 Cramer	Y	Y	Y	Y	Y	Y
6 *Bachus*	?	Y	Y	Y	Y	Y
7 Hilliard	Y	Y	Y	Y	Y	Y
ALASKA						
AL *Young*	Y	Y	Y	Y	?	?
ARIZONA						
1 *Flake*	N	Y	Y	Y	Y	Y
2 Pastor	Y	Y	Y	Y	Y	Y
3 *Stump*	Y	Y	Y	Y	Y	Y
4 *Shadegg*	Y	Y	Y	Y	Y	Y
5 *Kolbe*	Y	Y	Y	Y	Y	Y
6 *Hayworth*	Y	Y	Y	Y	Y	Y
ARKANSAS						
1 Berry	Y	Y	Y	N	Y	Y
2 Snyder	Y	Y	Y	Y	Y	Y
3 *Boozman*	Y	Y	Y	?	Y	Y
4 Ross	Y	Y	Y	Y	Y	Y
CALIFORNIA						
1 Thompson	Y	Y	Y	Y	Y	Y
2 *Herger*	Y	Y	Y	Y	Y	Y
3 *Ose*	Y	Y	Y	Y	Y	Y
4 *Doolittle*	Y	Y	Y	Y	Y	Y
5 Matsui	Y	Y	Y	Y	Y	Y
6 Woolsey	Y	Y	Y	Y	Y	Y
7 Miller, George	Y	Y	Y	Y	Y	Y
8 Pelosi	Y	?	?	?	Y	Y
9 Lee	Y	Y	Y	Y	Y	Y
10 Tauscher	Y	Y	Y	Y	Y	Y
11 *Pombo*	Y	Y	Y	Y	Y	Y
12 Lantos	Y	Y	Y	Y	Y	Y
13 Stark	Y	Y	Y	Y	Y	Y
14 Eshoo	Y	Y	Y	Y	Y	Y
15 Honda	Y	Y	Y	Y	Y	Y
16 Lofgren	Y	Y	Y	Y	Y	Y
17 Farr	Y	Y	Y	Y	Y	Y
18 Condit	Y	Y	Y	Y	Y	Y
19 *Radanovich*	Y	?	?	?	Y	Y
20 Dooley	?	Y	Y	Y	Y	Y
21 *Thomas*	Y	Y	Y	Y	?	Y
22 Capps	Y	Y	Y	Y	Y	Y
23 *Gallegly*	?	Y	Y	Y	Y	Y
24 Sherman	Y	Y	Y	Y	Y	Y
25 *McKeon*	Y	Y	Y	Y	Y	Y
26 Berman	?	?	?	?	?	?
27 Schiff	Y	Y	Y	Y	Y	Y
28 *Dreier*	?	Y	Y	Y	Y	Y
29 Waxman	?	?	?	?	?	?
30 Becerra	+	Y	Y	Y	Y	Y
31 Solis	Y	Y	Y	Y	Y	Y
32 Watson	Y	Y	Y	Y	Y	Y
33 Roybal-Allard	Y	Y	Y	Y	Y	Y
34 Napolitano	Y	Y	Y	Y	Y	Y
35 Waters	?	Y	Y	Y	Y	Y
36 Harman	Y	Y	Y	Y	Y	?
37 Millender-McD.	Y	Y	Y	Y	Y	Y
38 *Horn*	Y	Y	Y	Y	Y	Y

	465	466	467	468	469	470
39 *Royce*	N	Y	Y	Y	Y	Y
40 *Lewis*	Y	Y	Y	Y	Y	Y
41 *Miller, Gary*	?	Y	Y	Y	Y	Y
42 Baca	Y	Y	Y	Y	Y	Y
43 *Calvert*	?	Y	Y	Y	Y	Y
44 *Bono*	Y	Y	Y	Y	Y	Y
45 *Rohrabacher*	Y	Y	Y	Y	Y	Y
46 Sanchez	?	Y	Y	Y	?	?
47 *Cox*	Y	Y	Y	Y	Y	Y
48 *Issa*	Y	Y	Y	Y	Y	Y
49 Davis	Y	Y	Y	Y	Y	Y
50 Filner	N	Y	Y	Y	Y	Y
51 *Cunningham*	Y	Y	Y	Y	Y	Y
52 *Hunter*	Y	Y	Y	Y	Y	?
COLORADO						
1 DeGette	Y	Y	Y	Y	Y	Y
2 Udall	Y	Y	Y	Y	Y	Y
3 *McInnis*	N	Y	Y	Y	Y	Y
4 *Schaffer*	N	Y	Y	N	Y	Y
5 *Hefley*	N	Y	Y	Y	?	Y
6 *Tancredo*	N	Y	Y	Y	Y	Y
CONNECTICUT						
1 Larson	Y	Y	Y	Y	Y	Y
2 *Simmons*	Y	Y	Y	Y	Y	Y
3 DeLauro	Y	Y	Y	Y	Y	Y
4 *Shays*	Y	Y	Y	Y	Y	Y
5 Maloney	Y	Y	Y	Y	Y	Y
6 *Johnson*	Y	Y	Y	Y	+	+
DELAWARE						
AL *Castle*	Y	Y	Y	Y	Y	Y
FLORIDA						
1 *Miller, J.*	Y	Y	Y	Y	Y	Y
2 Boyd	?	Y	Y	Y	Y	Y
3 Brown	Y	?	?	?	Y	Y
4 *Crenshaw*	Y	Y	Y	Y	Y	Y
5 Thurman	Y	Y	Y	Y	?	Y
6 *Stearns*	Y	Y	Y	Y	Y	Y
7 *Mica*	Y	Y	Y	Y	Y	Y
8 *Keller*	Y	Y	Y	Y	Y	Y
9 *Bilirakis*	Y	Y	Y	Y	Y	Y
10 *Young*	Y	Y	Y	Y	Y	Y
11 Davis	Y	Y	Y	Y	Y	Y
12 *Putnam*	Y	Y	Y	Y	Y	Y
13 *Miller, D.*	Y	Y	Y	Y	Y	Y
14 *Goss*	Y	Y	Y	Y	Y	Y
15 *Weldon*	Y	Y	Y	Y	Y	Y
16 *Foley*	Y	Y	Y	Y	Y	Y
17 Meek	Y	Y	Y	Y	?	?
18 *Ros-Lehtinen*	?	Y	Y	Y	Y	Y
19 Wexler	Y	Y	Y	Y	Y	Y
20 Deutsch	Y	Y	Y	Y	Y	Y
21 *Diaz-Balart*	?	Y	Y	Y	Y	Y
22 *Shaw*	Y	Y	?	?	Y	Y
23 Hastings	Y	Y	Y	Y	Y	Y
GEORGIA						
1 *Kingston*	Y	Y	Y	Y	?	?
2 Bishop	Y	Y	Y	Y	Y	Y
3 *Collins*	Y	Y	Y	N	Y	Y
4 McKinney	Y	?	?	?	Y	Y
5 Lewis	Y	Y	Y	Y	Y	Y
6 *Isakson*	Y	Y	Y	Y	Y	Y
7 *Barr*	Y	?	?	?	Y	Y
8 *Chambliss*	Y	Y	Y	Y	Y	Y
9 *Deal*	Y	Y	Y	N	Y	Y
10 *Norwood*	Y	Y	Y	Y	Y	Y
11 *Linder*	Y	Y	Y	Y	Y	Y
HAWAII						
1 Abercrombie	Y	Y	Y	Y	Y	Y
2 Mink	Y	Y	Y	Y	Y	Y
IDAHO						
1 *Otter*	Y	Y	Y	Y	Y	Y
2 *Simpson*	Y	Y	Y	Y	Y	Y
ILLINOIS						
1 Rush	Y	?	?	?	Y	Y
2 Jackson	Y	Y	Y	Y	Y	Y
3 Lipinski	?	Y	Y	Y	Y	Y
4 Gutierrez	Y	Y	Y	Y	?	?
5 Blagojevich	Y	?	?	?	Y	Y
6 *Hyde*	Y	Y	Y	Y	Y	Y
7 Davis	Y	Y	Y	Y	Y	Y
8 *Crane*	Y	Y	Y	Y	Y	Y
9 Schakowsky	Y	Y	Y	Y	Y	Y
10 *Kirk*	Y	Y	Y	Y	Y	Y
11 *Weller*	Y	Y	+	Y	Y	Y
12 Costello	Y	Y	Y	Y	Y	Y
13 *Biggert*	Y	Y	Y	Y	Y	Y

ND Northern Democrats   SD Southern Democrats

WWW.CQ.COM

	465	466	467	468	469	470
14 ***Hastert***						
15 ***Johnson***	Y	Y	Y	Y	Y	Y
16 ***Manzullo***	Y	Y	Y	Y	Y	Y
17 Evans	Y	Y	Y	Y	Y	Y
18 ***LaHood***	?	Y	Y	Y	Y	Y
19 Phelps	Y	Y	Y	Y	Y	Y
20 ***Shimkus***	Y	Y	Y	Y	Y	Y
INDIANA						
1 Visclosky	Y	Y	Y	Y	Y	Y
2 ***Pence***	Y	Y	Y	Y	Y	Y
3 Roemer	Y	Y	Y	Y	Y	Y
4 ***Souder***	Y	Y	Y	Y	?	Y
5 ***Buyer***	Y	Y	Y	?	Y	Y
6 ***Burton***	Y	Y	Y	Y	Y	Y
7 ***Kerns***	Y	Y	Y	Y	Y	Y
8 ***Hostettler***	Y	Y	Y	N	?	?
9 Hill	Y	Y	Y	Y	Y	Y
10 Carson	?	Y	Y	Y	Y	Y
IOWA						
1 ***Leach***	Y	Y	Y	Y	Y	Y
2 ***Nussle***	Y	Y	+	Y	Y	Y
3 Boswell	Y	Y	Y	Y	Y	Y
4 ***Ganske***	?	Y	Y	Y	Y	Y
5 ***Latham***	Y	Y	Y	Y	Y	Y
KANSAS						
1 ***Moran***	Y	Y	Y	Y	Y	Y
2 ***Ryun***	Y	Y	Y	Y	Y	Y
3 Moore	Y	Y	Y	Y	Y	Y
4 ***Tiahrt***	Y	Y	Y	Y	Y	Y
KENTUCKY						
1 ***Whitfield***	Y	Y	Y	Y	Y	Y
2 ***Lewis***	Y	Y	Y	Y	Y	Y
3 ***Northup***	Y	Y	Y	Y	Y	Y
4 Lucas	Y	Y	Y	Y	Y	Y
5 ***Rogers***	Y	Y	Y	Y	Y	Y
6 ***Fletcher***	Y	Y	Y	Y	Y	Y
LOUISIANA						
1 ***Vitter***	?	Y	Y	Y	Y	Y
2 Jefferson	Y	Y	Y	Y	Y	Y
3 ***Tauzin***	Y	Y	Y	Y	Y	Y
4 ***McCrery***	Y	Y	Y	Y	Y	Y
5 ***Cooksey***	?	Y	Y	Y	Y	Y
6 ***Baker***	Y	Y	Y	Y	Y	Y
7 John	Y	Y	Y	Y	Y	Y
MAINE						
1 Allen	Y	Y	Y	Y	Y	Y
2 Baldacci	Y	Y	Y	Y	Y	Y
MARYLAND						
1 ***Gilchrest***	Y	Y	Y	Y	Y	Y
2 ***Ehrlich***	Y	Y	Y	Y	Y	Y
3 Cardin	Y	Y	Y	Y	Y	Y
4 Wynn	Y	Y	Y	Y	Y	Y
5 Hoyer	Y	Y	Y	Y	Y	Y
6 ***Bartlett***	Y	Y	Y	Y	Y	Y
7 Cummings	?	Y	Y	Y	?	Y
8 ***Morella***	Y	Y	Y	Y	Y	Y
MASSACHUSETTS						
1 Olver	Y	Y	Y	Y	Y	Y
2 Neal	?	Y	Y	Y	Y	Y
3 McGovern	Y	Y	Y	Y	Y	Y
4 Frank	Y	Y	Y	Y	Y	Y
5 Meehan	?	?	?	?	?	?
6 Tierney	Y	Y	Y	Y	Y	Y
7 Markey	Y	Y	Y	Y	Y	Y
8 Capuano	Y	Y	Y	Y	Y	Y
9 Lynch	Y	Y	Y	Y	Y	Y
10 Delahunt	Y	Y	Y	Y	Y	Y
MICHIGAN						
1 Stupak	Y	Y	Y	Y	Y	Y
2 ***Hoekstra***	Y	Y	Y	Y	Y	Y
3 ***Ehlers***	Y	Y	Y	Y	Y	Y
4 ***Camp***	Y	Y	Y	Y	Y	Y
5 Barcia	N	Y	Y	Y	Y	Y
6 ***Upton***	Y	Y	Y	Y	Y	Y
7 ***Smith***	Y	Y	Y	Y	Y	Y
8 ***Rogers***	Y	Y	Y	Y	Y	Y
9 Kildee	Y	Y	Y	Y	Y	Y
10 Bonior	?	Y	Y	Y	Y	Y
11 ***Knollenberg***	Y	Y	Y	Y	Y	Y
12 Levin	Y	Y	Y	Y	Y	Y
13 Rivers	Y	Y	Y	Y	Y	Y
14 Conyers	?	Y	Y	Y	Y	Y
15 Kilpatrick	Y	Y	Y	?	Y	Y
16 Dingell	Y	Y	Y	Y	Y	Y

	465	466	467	468	469	470
MINNESOTA						
1 ***Gutknecht***	Y	Y	Y	Y	Y	Y
2 ***Kennedy***	Y	Y	Y	Y	Y	Y
3 ***Ramstad***	Y	Y	Y	Y	Y	Y
4 McCollum	Y	Y	Y	Y	Y	Y
5 Sabo	Y	Y	Y	Y	Y	Y
6 Luther	Y	Y	Y	Y	Y	Y
7 Peterson	Y	Y	Y	Y	Y	Y
8 Oberstar	Y	Y	Y	Y	Y	Y
MISSISSIPPI						
1 ***Wicker***	Y	Y	Y	Y	Y	Y
2 Thompson	Y	Y	Y	Y	Y	Y
3 ***Pickering***	Y	Y	Y	Y	Y	Y
4 Shows	Y	Y	Y	Y	Y	Y
5 Taylor	Y	Y	Y	N	Y	Y
MISSOURI						
1 Clay	Y	Y	Y	Y	Y	Y
2 ***Akin***	Y	Y	Y	N	Y	Y
3 Gephardt	?	Y	Y	Y	Y	Y
4 Skelton	Y	Y	Y	Y	Y	Y
5 McCarthy	Y	Y	Y	Y	Y	Y
6 ***Graves***	Y	Y	Y	Y	Y	Y
7 ***Blunt***	Y	Y	Y	Y	Y	Y
8 ***Emerson***	Y	Y	Y	Y	Y	Y
9 ***Hulshof***	Y	Y	Y	Y	Y	Y
MONTANA						
AL ***Rehberg***	Y	Y	Y	Y	Y	Y
NEBRASKA						
1 ***Bereuter***	Y	Y	Y	Y	Y	Y
2 ***Terry***	Y	Y	Y	Y	Y	Y
3 ***Osborne***	Y	Y	Y	Y	Y	Y
NEVADA						
1 Berkley	Y	Y	Y	Y	Y	Y
2 ***Gibbons***	Y	Y	Y	Y	Y	Y
NEW HAMPSHIRE						
1 ***Sununu***	?	Y	Y	Y	Y	Y
2 ***Bass***	Y	Y	Y	Y	Y	Y
NEW JERSEY						
1 Andrews	Y	Y	Y	Y	?	?
2 ***LoBiondo***	Y	Y	Y	Y	Y	Y
3 ***Saxton***	Y	Y	Y	Y	Y	Y
4 ***Smith***	Y	Y	Y	Y	Y	Y
5 ***Roukema***	Y	?	?	?	?	?
6 Pallone	Y	Y	Y	Y	Y	Y
7 ***Ferguson***	Y	Y	Y	Y	Y	Y
8 Pascrell	Y	Y	Y	Y	Y	Y
9 Rothman	?	Y	Y	Y	Y	Y
10 Payne	Y	Y	Y	Y	Y	Y
11 ***Frelinghuysen***	Y	Y	Y	Y	Y	Y
12 Holt	Y	Y	Y	Y	Y	Y
13 Menendez	Y	Y	Y	Y	Y	Y
NEW MEXICO						
1 ***Wilson***	?	Y	Y	Y	Y	Y
2 ***Skeen***	Y	Y	Y	Y	Y	Y
3 Udall	Y	Y	Y	Y	Y	Y
NEW YORK						
1 ***Grucci***	Y	Y	Y	Y	Y	Y
2 Israel	Y	Y	Y	Y	Y	Y
3 ***King***	Y	Y	Y	Y	Y	Y
4 McCarthy	Y	Y	Y	Y	Y	Y
5 Ackerman	Y	Y	Y	Y	Y	Y
6 Meeks	Y	Y	Y	Y	Y	Y
7 Crowley	Y	Y	Y	Y	Y	Y
8 Nadler	Y	Y	Y	Y	Y	Y
9 Weiner	Y	Y	Y	Y	Y	Y
10 Towns	Y	Y	Y	Y	Y	Y
11 Owens	?	Y	Y	Y	Y	Y
12 Velázquez	Y	Y	Y	Y	Y	Y
13 ***Fossella***	Y	Y	Y	Y	Y	Y
14 Maloney	Y	Y	Y	Y	Y	Y
15 Rangel	?	Y	Y	Y	Y	Y
16 Serrano	Y	Y	Y	Y	Y	Y
17 Engel	Y	?	?	?	Y	Y
18 Lowey	?	Y	Y	Y	Y	Y
19 ***Kelly***	Y	Y	Y	Y	Y	Y
20 ***Gilman***	Y	Y	Y	Y	Y	Y
21 McNulty	Y	Y	Y	Y	Y	Y
22 ***Sweeney***	Y	Y	Y	Y	Y	Y
23 ***Boehlert***	Y	Y	Y	Y	Y	Y
24 ***McHugh***	Y	Y	Y	Y	Y	Y
25 ***Walsh***	Y	Y	Y	Y	Y	Y
26 Hinchey	Y	Y	Y	Y	Y	Y
27 ***Reynolds***	Y	Y	Y	Y	Y	Y
28 Slaughter	Y	Y	Y	Y	Y	Y
29 LaFalce	?	Y	Y	Y	Y	Y

	465	466	467	468	469	470
30 ***Quinn***	?	?	?	?	?	?
31 ***Houghton***	Y	?	?	?	Y	Y
NORTH CAROLINA						
1 Clayton	Y	Y	Y	Y	Y	Y
2 Etheridge	Y	Y	Y	Y	Y	Y
3 ***Jones***	?	Y	Y	Y	Y	Y
4 Price	Y	Y	Y	Y	Y	Y
5 ***Burr***	Y	Y	Y	Y	Y	Y
6 ***Coble***	Y	Y	Y	N	Y	Y
7 McIntyre	Y	Y	Y	Y	Y	Y
8 ***Hayes***	Y	Y	Y	Y	Y	Y
9 ***Myrick***	+	Y	Y	Y	Y	Y
10 ***Ballenger***	Y	Y	Y	Y	Y	Y
11 ***Taylor***	?	Y	Y	Y	Y	Y
12 Watt	Y	Y	Y	Y	Y	Y
NORTH DAKOTA						
AL Pomeroy	Y	Y	Y	?	Y	Y
OHIO						
1 ***Chabot***	Y	Y	Y	Y	Y	Y
2 ***Portman***	?	Y	Y	Y	Y	Y
3 Hall	Y	Y	Y	Y	Y	Y
4 ***Oxley***	Y	Y	Y	Y	Y	Y
5 ***Gillmor***	Y	Y	Y	Y	Y	Y
6 Strickland	Y	Y	Y	Y	Y	Y
7 ***Hobson***	Y	Y	Y	Y	Y	Y
8 ***Boehner***	Y	Y	Y	Y	Y	Y
9 Kaptur	Y	Y	Y	Y	Y	Y
10 Kucinich	Y	?	?	?	?	?
11 Jones	Y	+	+	+	Y	Y
12 ***Tiberi***	Y	Y	Y	Y	Y	Y
13 Brown	Y	Y	Y	Y	Y	Y
14 Sawyer	Y	Y	Y	Y	Y	Y
15 ***Pryce***	Y	Y	Y	Y	Y	Y
16 ***Regula***	Y	Y	Y	Y	Y	Y
17 Traficant	Y	Y	Y	Y	Y	Y
18 ***Ney***	Y	Y	Y	Y	?	?
19 ***LaTourette***	?	?	?	?	?	?
OKLAHOMA						
1 ***Largent***	?	Y	Y	Y	Y	Y
2 Carson	Y	Y	Y	Y	Y	Y
3 ***Watkins***	Y	Y	Y	Y	Y	Y
4 ***Watts***	Y	Y	Y	Y	Y	Y
5 ***Istook***	Y	?	?	?	Y	Y
6 ***Lucas***	Y	Y	Y	Y	Y	Y
OREGON						
1 Wu	Y	Y	Y	Y	Y	P
2 ***Walden***	Y	Y	Y	Y	Y	Y
3 Blumenauer	?	Y	Y	Y	Y	Y
4 DeFazio	?	?	?	?	?	?
5 Hooley	Y	Y	Y	Y	Y	Y
PENNSYLVANIA						
1 Brady	Y	Y	Y	Y	Y	Y
2 Fattah	?	Y	Y	Y	Y	Y
3 Borski	Y	Y	Y	Y	Y	Y
4 ***Hart***	Y	Y	Y	Y	Y	Y
5 ***Peterson***	Y	Y	Y	Y	Y	Y
6 Holden	?	Y	Y	Y	Y	Y
7 ***Weldon***	Y	Y	Y	Y	?	?
8 ***Greenwood***	Y	Y	Y	Y	Y	Y
9 ***Shuster, Bill***	Y	Y	Y	Y	Y	Y
10 ***Sherwood***	Y	Y	Y	Y	Y	Y
11 Kanjorski	Y	Y	Y	Y	Y	Y
12 Murtha	Y	Y	Y	Y	Y	Y
13 Hoeffel	Y	Y	Y	Y	Y	Y
14 Coyne	Y	Y	Y	Y	Y	Y
15 ***Toomey***	Y	Y	Y	Y	Y	Y
16 ***Pitts***	Y	Y	Y	Y	Y	Y
17 ***Gekas***	Y	Y	Y	Y	Y	Y
18 Doyle	Y	Y	Y	Y	Y	Y
19 ***Platts***	Y	Y	Y	Y	Y	Y
20 Mascara	Y	Y	Y	Y	Y	Y
21 ***English***	Y	Y	Y	Y	Y	Y
RHODE ISLAND						
1 Kennedy	Y	Y	Y	Y	Y	Y
2 Langevin	Y	Y	Y	Y	Y	Y
SOUTH CAROLINA						
1 ***Brown***	Y	Y	Y	Y	Y	Y
2 Vacant						
3 ***Graham***	Y	Y	Y	Y	Y	Y
4 ***DeMint***	Y	Y	Y	Y	Y	Y
5 Spratt	Y	Y	Y	Y	Y	Y
6 Clyburn	Y	Y	Y	Y	Y	Y
SOUTH DAKOTA						
AL ***Thune***	Y	Y	Y	Y	Y	Y

	465	466	467	468	469	470
TENNESSEE						
1 ***Jenkins***	Y	Y	Y	Y	Y	Y
2 ***Duncan***	Y	Y	Y	Y	Y	Y
3 ***Wamp***	Y	Y	Y	Y	Y	Y
4 ***Hilleary***	Y	Y	Y	Y	Y	Y
5 Clement	Y	Y	Y	Y	Y	Y
6 Gordon	Y	Y	Y	Y	Y	Y
7 ***Bryant***	Y	Y	Y	Y	Y	Y
8 Tanner	Y	Y	Y	Y	Y	Y
9 Ford	?	Y	Y	Y	Y	Y
TEXAS						
1 Sandlin	Y	Y	Y	Y	Y	Y
2 Turner	Y	Y	Y	Y	Y	Y
3 ***Johnson, Sam***	Y	Y	Y	Y	?	?
4 Hall	Y	Y	Y	Y	Y	Y
5 ***Sessions***	Y	Y	Y	Y	Y	Y
6 ***Barton***	Y	Y	Y	Y	Y	Y
7 ***Culberson***	Y	Y	Y	Y	Y	Y
8 ***Brady***	Y	+	Y	Y	Y	Y
9 Lampson	Y	Y	Y	Y	Y	Y
10 Doggett	Y	Y	Y	Y	Y	Y
11 Edwards	Y	Y	Y	Y	Y	Y
12 ***Granger***	Y	Y	Y	Y	Y	Y
13 ***Thornberry***	Y	Y	Y	Y	Y	Y
14 ***Paul***	N	Y	Y	N	N	Y
15 Hinojosa	Y	Y	Y	Y	Y	Y
16 Reyes	Y	?	?	?	?	?
17 Stenholm	Y	Y	Y	Y	Y	Y
18 Jackson-Lee	Y	Y	Y	Y	Y	Y
19 ***Combest***	Y	Y	Y	Y	Y	Y
20 Gonzalez	Y	Y	Y	Y	Y	Y
21 ***Smith***	?	Y	Y	Y	Y	Y
22 ***DeLay***	Y	Y	Y	Y	Y	Y
23 ***Bonilla***	Y	Y	Y	Y	Y	Y
24 Frost	?	Y	Y	Y	Y	Y
25 Bentsen	Y	Y	Y	Y	Y	Y
26 ***Armey***	Y	Y	Y	Y	Y	Y
27 Ortiz	Y	Y	Y	Y	Y	Y
28 Rodriguez	Y	Y	Y	Y	Y	Y
29 Green	Y	Y	Y	Y	Y	Y
30 Johnson, E.B.	Y	Y	Y	Y	Y	Y
UTAH						
1 ***Hansen***	Y	Y	Y	Y	Y	Y
2 Matheson	Y	Y	Y	Y	Y	Y
3 ***Cannon***	Y	Y	Y	Y	Y	Y
VERMONT						
AL *Sanders*	Y	Y	Y	Y	Y	Y
VIRGINIA						
1 ***Davis, Jo Ann***	Y	Y	Y	Y	Y	Y
2 ***Schrock***	Y	Y	Y	Y	Y	Y
3 Scott	Y	Y	Y	Y	Y	Y
4 ***Forbes***	Y	Y	Y	Y	Y	Y
5 *Goode*	Y	Y	Y	N	Y	Y
6 ***Goodlatte***	Y	Y	Y	Y	Y	Y
7 ***Cantor***	Y	Y	Y	Y	Y	Y
8 Moran	Y	Y	Y	Y	Y	Y
9 Boucher	?	Y	Y	Y	Y	Y
10 ***Wolf***	Y	Y	Y	Y	Y	Y
11 ***Davis, T.***	Y	Y	Y	Y	Y	Y
WASHINGTON						
1 Inslee	Y	Y	Y	Y	Y	Y
2 Larsen	Y	Y	Y	Y	Y	Y
3 Baird	Y	Y	Y	Y	Y	Y
4 ***Hastings***	Y	Y	Y	Y	Y	Y
5 ***Nethercutt***	Y	Y	Y	Y	Y	Y
6 Dicks	?	Y	Y	Y	Y	Y
7 McDermott	?	Y	Y	Y	Y	Y
8 ***Dunn***	Y	Y	Y	Y	Y	Y
9 Smith	Y	Y	Y	Y	Y	Y
WEST VIRGINIA						
1 Mollohan	Y	Y	Y	Y	Y	Y
2 ***Capito***	Y	Y	Y	Y	Y	Y
3 Rahall	Y	Y	Y	Y	Y	P
WISCONSIN						
1 ***Ryan***	Y	Y	Y	Y	Y	Y
2 Baldwin	Y	Y	Y	Y	Y	Y
3 Kind	Y	Y	Y	Y	Y	Y
4 Kleczka	Y	Y	Y	Y	Y	Y
5 Barrett	Y	Y	Y	Y	Y	Y
6 ***Petri***	N	Y	Y	Y	Y	Y
7 Obey	Y	Y	Y	Y	Y	Y
8 ***Green***	Y	Y	Y	Y	Y	Y
9 ***Sensenbrenner***	N	Y	Y	N	Y	Y
WYOMING						
AL ***Cubin***	?	?	?	?	?	?

Southern states - Ala., Ark., Fla., Ga., Ky., La., Miss., N.C., Okla., S.C., Tenn., Texas, Va.

Key

Y	Voted for (yea).
#	Paired for.
+	Announced for.
N	Voted against (nay).
X	Paired against.
−	Announced against.
P	Voted "present."
C	Voted "present" to avoid possible conflict of interest.
?	Did not vote or otherwise make a position known.

Democrats   *Republicans*
Independents

471. H Con Res 102. Africa Relief/Adoption. Leach, R-Iowa, motion to suspend the rules and adopt the concurrent resolution that would encourage humanitarian, economic development and other relief assistance in sub-Saharan Africa. Motion agreed to 400-9: R 199-7; D 200-1 (ND 149-0, SD 51-1); I 1-1. A two-thirds majority of those present and voting (273 in this case) is required for adoption under suspension of the rules. Dec. 5, 2001.

472. H Res 298. Veterans Day/Adoption. Morella, R-Md., motion to suspend the rules and adopt the resolution that would express the sense of the House that Nov. 11 should be observed as Veterans Day. Motion agreed to 415-0: R 210-0; D 203-0 (ND 151-0, SD 52-0); I 2-0. A two-thirds majority of those present and voting (277 in this case) is required for adoption under suspension of the rules. Dec. 5, 2001.

473. H Con Res 232. United Airlines Flight 93/Adoption. Mica, R-Fla., motion to suspend the rules and adopt the resolution that would express the sense of Congress to pay tribute to those killed on United Airlines Flight 93, offering condolences to their family and friends, and stating that a memorial plaque in their honor should be placed on the U.S. Capitol grounds. Motion agreed to 415-0: R 211-0; D 202-0 (ND 151-0, SD 51-0); I 2-0. A two-thirds majority of those present and voting (277 in this case) is required for adoption under suspension of the rules. Dec. 5, 2001.

474. H Con Res 280. Israel Terror Attacks/Adoption. Hyde, R-Ill., motion to suspend the rules and adopt the concurrent resolution that would express the sense of Congress condemning recent terrorist attacks in Israel, insisting that the Palestinian Authority act against terrorists groups in its territory and urging President Bush to apply pressure on the Palestinian leadership to ensure that it does. Motion agreed to 384-11: R 206-1; D 177-10 (ND 133-7, SD 44-3); I 1-0. A two-thirds majority of those present and voting (264 in this case) is required for adoption under suspension of the rules. Dec. 5, 2001.

475. Procedural Motion/Hour of Meeting. Armey, R-Texas, motion that when the House adjourns Dec. 5, it reconvene at 9:00 a.m., Dec. 6, 2001. Motion agreed to 322-82: R 203-3; D 117-79 (ND 79-66, SD 38-13); I 2-0. Dec. 5, 2001.

476. H Res 305. Procedural Motion/Suspending the Rules. Adoption of the resolution (H Res 305) to provide for House floor consideration of two bills (HR 3129, HR 3008) under suspension of the rules. Adopted 207-179: R 194-1; D 12-177 (ND 9-134, SD 3-43); I 1-1. Dec. 6, 2001.

	471	472	473	474	475	476
ALABAMA						
1 *Callahan*	Y	Y	Y	Y	Y	Y
2 *Everett*	Y	Y	Y	Y	Y	Y
3 *Riley*	Y	Y	Y	Y	Y	Y
4 *Aderholt*	Y	Y	Y	Y	Y	Y
5 Cramer	Y	Y	Y	Y	Y	?
6 *Bachus*	Y	Y	Y	Y	Y	Y
7 Hilliard	Y	Y	Y	N	N	N
ALASKA						
AL *Young*	?	?	?	?	?	?
ARIZONA						
1 *Flake*	N	Y	Y	Y	Y	Y
2 Pastor	Y	Y	?	Y	Y	N
3 *Stump*	Y	Y	Y	Y	Y	Y
4 *Shadegg*	Y	Y	Y	Y	Y	Y
5 *Kolbe*	Y	Y	Y	Y	Y	Y
6 *Hayworth*	Y	Y	Y	Y	Y	Y
ARKANSAS						
1 Berry	N	Y	Y	Y	N	N
2 Snyder	Y	Y	Y	P	Y	N
3 *Boozman*	Y	Y	Y	Y	Y	Y
4 Ross	Y	Y	Y	Y	Y	N
CALIFORNIA						
1 Thompson	Y	Y	Y	Y	Y	N
2 *Herger*	N	Y	Y	Y	Y	?
3 *Ose*	Y	Y	Y	Y	Y	Y
4 *Doolittle*	Y	Y	Y	Y	Y	?
5 Matsui	Y	Y	Y	Y	Y	N
6 Woolsey	Y	Y	Y	Y	Y	N
7 Miller, George	Y	Y	Y	Y	N	N
8 Pelosi	Y	Y	Y	Y	N	N
9 Lee	Y	Y	Y	P	N	N
10 Tauscher	Y	Y	Y	Y	Y	N
11 *Pombo*	Y	Y	Y	Y	Y	?
12 Lantos	Y	Y	Y	Y	N	N
13 Stark	Y	Y	Y	P	N	N
14 Eshoo	Y	Y	Y	Y	Y	N
15 Honda	Y	Y	Y	Y	N	N
16 Lofgren	Y	Y	Y	Y	Y	N
17 Farr	Y	Y	Y	Y	N	N
18 Condit	Y	Y	Y	Y	N	N
19 *Radanovich*	Y	Y	Y	Y	Y	?
20 Dooley	Y	Y	Y	Y	?	N
21 *Thomas*	Y	Y	Y	Y	Y	Y
22 Capps	Y	Y	Y	Y	N	N
23 *Gallegly*	Y	Y	Y	Y	Y	Y
24 Sherman	Y	Y	Y	Y	N	N
25 *McKeon*	Y	Y	Y	Y	Y	Y
26 Berman	Y	Y	Y	Y	Y	N
27 Schiff	Y	Y	Y	Y	N	N
28 *Dreier*	Y	Y	Y	Y	Y	Y
29 Waxman	?	Y	Y	N	?	?
30 Becerra	Y	Y	Y	N	N	N
31 Solis	Y	Y	Y	Y	N	N
32 Watson	Y	Y	Y	Y	N	N
33 Roybal-Allard	Y	Y	P	N	N	N
34 Napolitano	Y	Y	Y	N	N	N
35 Waters	Y	Y	Y	P	N	N
36 Harman	Y	Y	Y	N	N	N
37 Millender-McD.	Y	Y	Y	N	N	N
38 *Horn*	Y	Y	Y	Y	Y	Y

	471	472	473	474	475	476
39 *Royce*	Y	Y	Y	Y	Y	Y
40 *Lewis*	Y	Y	Y	Y	Y	Y
41 *Miller, Gary*	Y	Y	Y	Y	Y	Y
42 Baca	Y	Y	Y	Y	Y	N
43 *Calvert*	Y	Y	Y	Y	Y	Y
44 *Bono*	Y	Y	Y	Y	Y	Y
45 *Rohrabacher*	N	Y	Y	Y	Y	Y
46 Sanchez	?	?	?	?	?	?
47 *Cox*	Y	Y	Y	Y	Y	Y
48 *Issa*	Y	Y	Y	Y	Y	Y
49 Davis	Y	Y	Y	Y	Y	N
50 Filner	Y	Y	Y	N	N	N
51 *Cunningham*	Y	Y	Y	Y	Y	Y
52 *Hunter*	Y	Y	Y	Y	Y	Y
COLORADO						
1 DeGette	Y	Y	Y	Y	N	N
2 Udall	Y	Y	Y	Y	Y	N
3 *McInnis*	Y	Y	Y	Y	Y	Y
4 *Schaffer*	Y	Y	Y	Y	Y	Y
5 *Hefley*	Y	Y	Y	Y	Y	Y
6 *Tancredo*	Y	Y	Y	Y	Y	Y
CONNECTICUT						
1 Larson	Y	Y	Y	Y	Y	N
2 *Simmons*	Y	Y	Y	Y	Y	Y
3 DeLauro	Y	Y	Y	Y	N	N
4 *Shays*	Y	Y	Y	Y	Y	Y
5 Maloney	Y	Y	Y	Y	?	N
6 *Johnson*	Y	Y	Y	Y	Y	Y
DELAWARE						
AL *Castle*	Y	Y	Y	Y	Y	Y
FLORIDA						
1 *Miller, J.*	Y	Y	Y	Y	Y	Y
2 Boyd	Y	Y	Y	Y	Y	N
3 Brown	Y	Y	Y	Y	Y	N
4 *Crenshaw*	Y	Y	Y	Y	Y	Y
5 Thurman	Y	Y	Y	Y	Y	N
6 *Stearns*	Y	Y	Y	Y	Y	Y
7 *Mica*	Y	Y	Y	Y	Y	Y
8 *Keller*	Y	Y	Y	Y	Y	Y
9 *Bilirakis*	Y	Y	Y	Y	Y	Y
10 *Young*	Y	Y	Y	Y	Y	?
11 Davis	Y	Y	Y	Y	Y	N
12 *Putnam*	Y	Y	Y	Y	Y	Y
13 *Miller, D.*	Y	Y	Y	Y	Y	N
14 *Goss*	Y	Y	Y	Y	Y	Y
15 *Weldon*	Y	Y	Y	Y	Y	Y
16 *Foley*	Y	Y	Y	Y	Y	Y
17 Meek	?	?	?	?	?	?
18 *Ros-Lehtinen*	Y	Y	Y	Y	Y	Y
19 Wexler	Y	Y	Y	Y	Y	?
20 Deutsch	Y	Y	Y	Y	Y	N
21 *Diaz-Balart*	Y	Y	Y	Y	Y	Y
22 *Shaw*	Y	Y	Y	Y	Y	Y
23 Hastings	Y	Y	Y	Y	Y	N
GEORGIA						
1 *Kingston*	?	?	?	?	?	Y
2 Bishop	Y	Y	Y	Y	N	N
3 *Collins*	N	Y	Y	Y	?	Y
4 McKinney	Y	Y	Y	N	N	N
5 Lewis	Y	Y	Y	Y	N	N
6 *Isakson*	Y	Y	Y	Y	Y	Y
7 *Barr*	N	Y	Y	P	Y	Y
8 *Chambliss*	Y	Y	Y	Y	Y	Y
9 *Deal*	Y	Y	Y	P	Y	Y
10 *Norwood*	Y	Y	Y	Y	Y	Y
11 *Linder*	Y	Y	Y	Y	?	Y
HAWAII						
1 Abercrombie	Y	Y	N	N	N	N
2 Mink	Y	Y	N	N	N	N
IDAHO						
1 *Otter*	Y	Y	Y	Y	Y	Y
2 *Simpson*	Y	Y	Y	Y	Y	Y
ILLINOIS						
1 Rush	Y	Y	Y	N	Y	N
2 Jackson	Y	Y	Y	N	Y	N
3 Lipinski	Y	Y	Y	Y	N	N
4 Gutierrez	?	?	?	?	?	?
5 Blagojevich	Y	Y	Y	Y	Y	N
6 *Hyde*	Y	Y	Y	Y	Y	Y
7 Davis	Y	Y	Y	P	Y	N
8 *Crane*	Y	Y	Y	Y	Y	Y
9 Schakowsky	Y	Y	Y	Y	N	N
10 *Kirk*	Y	Y	Y	Y	Y	Y
11 *Weller*	Y	Y	Y	Y	Y	Y
12 Costello	Y	Y	Y	Y	Y	N
13 *Biggert*	Y	Y	Y	Y	Y	Y

ND Northern Democrats   SD Southern Democrats

	471	472	473	474	475	476
14 ***Hastert***						
15 ***Johnson***	Y	Y	Y	Y	Y	Y
16 ***Manzullo***	Y	Y	Y	Y	Y	Y
17 Evans	Y	Y	Y	Y	N	N
18 ***LaHood***	Y	Y	Y	Y	Y	Y
19 Phelps	Y	Y	Y	Y	N	N
20 ***Shimkus***	Y	Y	Y	Y	Y	Y
INDIANA						
1 Visclosky	Y	Y	Y	Y	N	N
2 ***Pence***	Y	Y	Y	Y	Y	Y
3 Roemer	Y	Y	Y	Y	Y	N
4 ***Souder***	Y	Y	Y	Y	Y	?
5 ***Buyer***	Y	Y	Y	Y	Y	Y
6 ***Burton***	Y	Y	Y	Y	Y	Y
7 ***Kerns***	Y	Y	Y	Y	Y	Y
8 ***Hostettler***	?	?	?	?	?	?
9 Hill	Y	Y	Y	Y	N	N
10 Carson	Y	Y	Y	Y	Y	N
IOWA						
1 ***Leach***	Y	Y	Y	Y	Y	Y
2 ***Nussle***	Y	Y	Y	Y	Y	Y
3 Boswell	Y	Y	Y	Y	Y	N
4 ***Ganske***	Y	Y	Y	Y	Y	Y
5 ***Latham***	Y	Y	Y	Y	Y	Y
KANSAS						
1 ***Moran***	Y	Y	Y	Y	N	Y
2 ***Ryun***	Y	Y	Y	Y	Y	Y
3 Moore	Y	Y	Y	Y	N	N
4 ***Tiahrt***	Y	Y	Y	Y	Y	Y
KENTUCKY						
1 ***Whitfield***	Y	Y	Y	Y	Y	Y
2 ***Lewis***	Y	Y	Y	Y	Y	Y
3 ***Northup***	Y	Y	Y	Y	Y	Y
4 Lucas	Y	Y	Y	Y	Y	N
5 ***Rogers***	Y	Y	Y	Y	Y	Y
6 ***Fletcher***	Y	Y	Y	Y	Y	Y
LOUISIANA						
1 ***Vitter***	Y	Y	Y	Y	Y	Y
2 Jefferson	Y	Y	Y	Y	Y	Y
3 ***Tauzin***	Y	Y	Y	Y	Y	Y
4 ***McCrery***	Y	Y	Y	Y	Y	Y
5 ***Cooksey***	Y	Y	Y	Y	Y	Y
6 ***Baker***	Y	Y	Y	Y	Y	Y
7 John	Y	Y	Y	Y	Y	N
MAINE						
1 Allen	Y	Y	Y	Y	Y	N
2 Baldacci	Y	Y	Y	Y	Y	N
MARYLAND						
1 ***Gilchrest***	Y	Y	Y	Y	Y	Y
2 ***Ehrlich***	Y	Y	Y	Y	Y	?
3 Cardin	Y	Y	Y	Y	Y	N
4 Wynn	Y	Y	Y	Y	N	N
5 Hoyer	Y	Y	Y	Y	Y	N
6 ***Bartlett***	Y	Y	Y	P	Y	Y
7 Cummings	Y	Y	Y	Y	Y	?
8 ***Morella***	Y	Y	Y	Y	Y	?
MASSACHUSETTS						
1 Olver	Y	Y	Y	Y	N	N
2 Neal	Y	Y	Y	Y	Y	N
3 McGovern	Y	Y	Y	Y	N	N
4 Frank	Y	Y	Y	Y	Y	N
5 Meehan	?	?	?	?	?	?
6 Tierney	Y	Y	Y	Y	Y	N
7 Markey	Y	?	?	?	?	N
8 Capuano	Y	Y	Y	Y	N	N
9 Lynch	Y	Y	Y	Y	N	N
10 Delahunt	Y	Y	Y	Y	Y	?
MICHIGAN						
1 Stupak	Y	Y	Y	Y	N	N
2 ***Hoekstra***	Y	Y	Y	Y	Y	Y
3 ***Ehlers***	Y	Y	Y	P	Y	Y
4 ***Camp***	?	Y	Y	Y	Y	Y
5 Barcia	Y	Y	Y	Y	Y	N
6 ***Upton***	Y	Y	Y	Y	Y	Y
7 ***Smith***	Y	Y	Y	Y	Y	Y
8 ***Rogers***	Y	Y	Y	Y	Y	Y
9 Kildee	Y	Y	Y	Y	Y	N
10 Bonior	Y	Y	Y	P	N	N
11 ***Knollenberg***	Y	Y	Y	Y	Y	Y
12 Levin	Y	Y	Y	Y	Y	N
13 Rivers	Y	Y	Y	Y	N	N
14 Conyers	Y	Y	Y	P	Y	N
15 Kilpatrick	Y	Y	Y	P	N	N
16 Dingell	Y	Y	Y	N	?	N
MINNESOTA						
1 ***Gutknecht***	Y	Y	Y	Y	Y	Y
2 ***Kennedy***	Y	Y	Y	Y	N	Y
3 ***Ramstad***	Y	Y	Y	Y	Y	Y
4 McCollum	Y	Y	Y	Y	Y	N
5 Sabo	Y	Y	Y	Y	?	?
6 Luther	Y	Y	Y	Y	Y	N
7 Peterson	Y	Y	Y	Y	Y	N
8 Oberstar	Y	Y	Y	Y	N	N
MISSISSIPPI						
1 ***Wicker***	Y	Y	Y	Y	Y	Y
2 Thompson	Y	Y	Y	N	N	N
3 ***Pickering***	Y	Y	Y	Y	Y	?
4 Shows	Y	Y	Y	Y	Y	N
5 Taylor	Y	Y	Y	Y	Y	N
MISSOURI						
1 Clay	Y	Y	Y	P	N	?
2 ***Akin***	Y	Y	Y	Y	Y	Y
3 Gephardt	Y	Y	Y	Y	N	N
4 Skelton	Y	Y	Y	Y	Y	N
5 McCarthy	Y	Y	Y	Y	Y	N
6 ***Graves***	Y	Y	Y	Y	Y	Y
7 ***Blunt***	Y	Y	Y	Y	Y	Y
8 ***Emerson***	Y	Y	Y	Y	Y	Y
9 ***Hulshof***	Y	Y	Y	Y	Y	Y
MONTANA						
AL ***Rehberg***	Y	Y	Y	Y	Y	Y
NEBRASKA						
1 ***Bereuter***	Y	Y	Y	Y	Y	Y
2 ***Terry***	Y	Y	Y	Y	Y	Y
3 ***Osborne***	Y	Y	Y	Y	Y	Y
NEVADA						
1 Berkley	Y	Y	Y	Y	N	N
2 ***Gibbons***	Y	Y	Y	Y	Y	Y
NEW HAMPSHIRE						
1 ***Sununu***	Y	Y	Y	Y	Y	Y
2 ***Bass***	Y	Y	Y	Y	Y	?
NEW JERSEY						
1 Andrews	?	Y	Y	Y	N	N
2 ***LoBiondo***	Y	Y	Y	Y	Y	Y
3 ***Saxton***	?	Y	Y	Y	Y	Y
4 ***Smith***	Y	Y	Y	Y	Y	Y
5 ***Roukema***	?	?	?	?	?	?
6 Pallone	Y	Y	Y	Y	N	N
7 ***Ferguson***	Y	Y	Y	Y	Y	Y
8 Pascrell	Y	Y	Y	Y	?	N
9 Rothman	Y	Y	Y	Y	N	?
10 Payne	Y	Y	Y	P	N	N
11 ***Frelinghuysen***	Y	Y	Y	Y	Y	Y
12 Holt	Y	Y	Y	Y	N	N
13 Menendez	Y	Y	Y	Y	N	N
NEW MEXICO						
1 ***Wilson***	Y	Y	Y	Y	Y	Y
2 ***Skeen***	Y	Y	Y	Y	Y	Y
3 Udall	Y	Y	Y	Y	N	N
NEW YORK						
1 ***Grucci***	Y	Y	Y	Y	Y	Y
2 Israel	Y	Y	Y	Y	N	Y
3 ***King***	Y	Y	Y	Y	Y	Y
4 McCarthy	Y	Y	Y	Y	Y	N
5 Ackerman	Y	Y	Y	Y	N	Y
6 Meeks	Y	Y	Y	Y	N	N
7 Crowley	Y	Y	Y	Y	N	N
8 Nadler	Y	Y	Y	Y	Y	N
9 Weiner	Y	Y	Y	Y	Y	N
10 Towns	Y	Y	Y	Y	Y	N
11 Owens	Y	Y	Y	Y	Y	N
12 Velázquez	Y	Y	Y	Y	N	N
13 ***Fossella***	Y	Y	Y	Y	Y	?
14 Maloney	Y	Y	Y	Y	Y	N
15 Rangel	Y	Y	Y	Y	Y	N
16 Serrano	Y	Y	Y	Y	Y	N
17 Engel	Y	Y	Y	Y	Y	?
18 Lowey	Y	Y	Y	Y	Y	Y
19 ***Kelly***	Y	Y	Y	Y	Y	Y
20 ***Gilman***	Y	Y	Y	Y	N	Y
21 McNulty	Y	Y	Y	Y	Y	N
22 ***Sweeney***	Y	Y	Y	Y	Y	Y
23 ***Boehlert***	Y	Y	Y	Y	Y	Y
24 ***McHugh***	Y	Y	Y	Y	Y	Y
25 ***Walsh***	Y	Y	Y	Y	Y	Y
26 Hinchey	Y	Y	Y	N	N	?
27 ***Reynolds***	Y	Y	Y	Y	Y	Y
28 Slaughter	Y	Y	Y	Y	N	N
29 LaFalce	Y	Y	Y	Y	Y	N
30 ***Quinn***	?	?	?	?	?	?
31 ***Houghton***	Y	Y	Y	Y	Y	Y
NORTH CAROLINA						
1 Clayton	Y	Y	Y	P	N	?
2 Etheridge	Y	Y	Y	Y	Y	N
3 ***Jones***	Y	Y	Y	Y	Y	Y
4 Price	Y	Y	Y	Y	Y	N
5 ***Burr***	Y	Y	Y	Y	Y	Y
6 ***Coble***	Y	Y	Y	Y	Y	Y
7 McIntyre	Y	Y	Y	Y	Y	Y
8 ***Hayes***	Y	?	?	?	?	Y
9 ***Myrick***	Y	Y	Y	Y	Y	Y
10 ***Ballenger***	Y	Y	Y	Y	Y	Y
11 ***Taylor***	Y	Y	Y	Y	Y	Y
12 Watt	Y	Y	Y	P	N	N
NORTH DAKOTA						
AL Pomeroy	Y	Y	Y	Y	Y	N
OHIO						
1 ***Chabot***	Y	Y	Y	Y	Y	Y
2 ***Portman***	Y	Y	Y	Y	Y	Y
3 Hall	Y	Y	Y	Y	Y	?
4 ***Oxley***	Y	Y	Y	Y	Y	Y
5 ***Gillmor***	Y	Y	Y	Y	Y	Y
6 Strickland	Y	Y	Y	Y	N	N
7 ***Hobson***	Y	Y	Y	Y	Y	Y
8 ***Boehner***	Y	Y	Y	Y	Y	?
9 Kaptur	Y	Y	Y	P	N	N
10 Kucinich	?	?	Y	Y	Y	N
11 Jones	Y	Y	Y	Y	N	N
12 ***Tiberi***	Y	Y	Y	Y	Y	Y
13 Brown	Y	Y	Y	Y	N	N
14 Sawyer	Y	Y	Y	Y	N	N
15 ***Pryce***	Y	Y	Y	Y	Y	Y
16 ***Regula***	Y	Y	Y	Y	Y	Y
17 Traficant	Y	Y	Y	Y	Y	Y
18 ***Ney***	?	?	?	?	?	Y
19 ***LaTourette***	?	?	Y	Y	Y	Y
OKLAHOMA						
1 ***Largent***	Y	Y	Y	Y	Y	Y
2 Carson	Y	Y	Y	Y	N	N
3 ***Watkins***	Y	Y	Y	Y	Y	Y
4 ***Watts***	Y	Y	Y	Y	Y	Y
5 ***Istook***	Y	Y	Y	Y	Y	Y
6 ***Lucas***	Y	Y	Y	Y	Y	Y
OREGON						
1 Wu	Y	Y	Y	Y	Y	?
2 ***Walden***	Y	Y	Y	Y	Y	Y
3 Blumenauer	Y	Y	Y	Y	N	Y
4 DeFazio	?	?	?	?	?	N
5 Hooley	Y	Y	Y	Y	Y	N
PENNSYLVANIA						
1 Brady	Y	Y	Y	Y	N	N
2 Fattah	Y	Y	Y	Y	N	N
3 Borski	Y	Y	Y	Y	Y	N
4 ***Hart***	Y	Y	Y	Y	Y	Y
5 ***Peterson***	Y	Y	Y	Y	Y	Y
6 Holden	Y	Y	Y	Y	Y	N
7 ***Weldon***	?	Y	Y	Y	Y	?
8 ***Greenwood***	Y	Y	Y	Y	Y	Y
9 ***Shuster, Bill***	Y	Y	Y	Y	Y	Y
10 ***Sherwood***	Y	Y	Y	Y	Y	Y
11 Kanjorski	Y	Y	Y	Y	Y	N
12 Murtha	Y	Y	Y	Y	?	N
13 Hoeffel	Y	Y	Y	Y	N	N
14 Coyne	Y	Y	Y	Y	Y	N
15 ***Toomey***	Y	Y	Y	Y	Y	Y
16 ***Pitts***	Y	Y	Y	Y	?	Y
17 ***Gekas***	Y	Y	Y	Y	Y	Y
18 Doyle	Y	Y	Y	Y	Y	Y
19 ***Platts***	Y	Y	Y	Y	Y	?
20 Mascara	Y	Y	Y	Y	Y	N
21 ***English***	Y	Y	Y	Y	Y	?
RHODE ISLAND						
1 Kennedy	Y	Y	Y	Y	Y	?
2 Langevin	Y	Y	Y	Y	Y	N
SOUTH CAROLINA						
1 ***Brown***	Y	Y	Y	Y	Y	+
2 Vacant						
3 ***Graham***	Y	Y	Y	Y	Y	Y
4 ***DeMint***	Y	Y	Y	Y	Y	Y
5 Spratt	Y	Y	Y	Y	Y	N
6 Clyburn	Y	Y	Y	Y	N	?
SOUTH DAKOTA						
AL ***Thune***	Y	Y	Y	Y	Y	Y
TENNESSEE						
1 ***Jenkins***	Y	Y	Y	Y	Y	Y
2 ***Duncan***	Y	Y	Y	Y	?	Y
3 ***Wamp***	Y	Y	Y	Y	Y	Y
4 ***Hilleary***	Y	Y	Y	Y	Y	?
5 Clement	Y	Y	Y	Y	N	N
6 Gordon	Y	Y	?	Y	Y	?
7 ***Bryant***	Y	Y	Y	Y	Y	Y
8 Tanner	Y	Y	Y	Y	Y	N
9 Ford	Y	Y	Y	Y	Y	N
TEXAS						
1 Sandlin	Y	Y	Y	Y	N	N
2 Turner	Y	Y	Y	Y	Y	N
3 ***Johnson, Sam***	?	?	?	?	?	?
4 Hall	Y	Y	Y	Y	Y	N
5 ***Sessions***	?	Y	Y	Y	Y	Y
6 ***Barton***	Y	Y	Y	Y	Y	?
7 ***Culberson***	Y	Y	Y	Y	Y	Y
8 ***Brady***	Y	Y	Y	Y	Y	Y
9 Lampson	Y	Y	Y	Y	Y	N
10 Doggett	Y	Y	Y	Y	Y	N
11 Edwards	Y	Y	Y	Y	Y	N
12 ***Granger***	Y	Y	Y	Y	Y	Y
13 ***Thornberry***	Y	Y	Y	Y	Y	Y
14 ***Paul***	N	Y	Y	N	Y	Y
15 Hinojosa	Y	Y	Y	Y	Y	N
16 Reyes	?	?	?	?	?	N
17 Stenholm	Y	Y	Y	Y	Y	N
18 Jackson-Lee	Y	Y	Y	Y	Y	N
19 ***Combest***	Y	Y	Y	Y	Y	Y
20 Gonzalez	Y	Y	Y	Y	Y	–
21 ***Smith***	Y	Y	Y	Y	Y	Y
22 ***DeLay***	Y	Y	Y	Y	Y	Y
23 ***Bonilla***	N	Y	Y	Y	Y	Y
24 Frost	Y	Y	Y	Y	Y	N
25 Bentsen	Y	Y	Y	Y	Y	N
26 ***Armey***	Y	Y	Y	Y	Y	Y
27 Ortiz	Y	Y	Y	Y	Y	N
28 Rodriguez	Y	Y	Y	Y	Y	N
29 Green	Y	Y	Y	Y	Y	N
30 Johnson, E.B.	Y	Y	Y	P	N	N
UTAH						
1 ***Hansen***	Y	Y	Y	Y	Y	Y
2 Matheson	Y	Y	Y	Y	Y	N
3 ***Cannon***	Y	Y	Y	Y	Y	Y
VERMONT						
AL *Sanders*	Y	Y	Y	P	Y	N
VIRGINIA						
1 ***Davis, Jo Ann***	Y	Y	Y	Y	Y	Y
2 ***Schrock***	Y	Y	Y	Y	Y	Y
3 Scott	Y	Y	Y	Y	Y	N
4 ***Forbes***	Y	Y	Y	Y	Y	Y
5 *Goode*	N	Y	Y	Y	Y	Y
6 ***Goodlatte***	Y	Y	Y	Y	Y	Y
7 ***Cantor***	Y	Y	Y	Y	Y	Y
8 Moran	Y	Y	Y	Y	Y	Y
9 Boucher	Y	Y	Y	P	?	?
10 ***Wolf***	Y	Y	Y	Y	Y	Y
11 ***Davis, T.***	Y	Y	Y	Y	?	Y
WASHINGTON						
1 Inslee	Y	Y	Y	Y	Y	N
2 Larsen	Y	Y	Y	Y	N	N
3 Baird	Y	Y	Y	Y	Y	N
4 ***Hastings***	Y	Y	Y	Y	Y	Y
5 ***Nethercutt***	Y	Y	Y	Y	Y	Y
6 Dicks	?	Y	Y	Y	Y	Y
7 McDermott	Y	Y	Y	Y	Y	N
8 ***Dunn***	Y	Y	Y	Y	Y	Y
9 Smith	Y	Y	Y	Y	N	N
WEST VIRGINIA						
1 Mollohan	Y	Y	Y	Y	Y	N
2 ***Capito***	Y	Y	Y	Y	Y	Y
3 Rahall	Y	Y	Y	N	Y	N
WISCONSIN						
1 ***Ryan***	Y	Y	Y	Y	Y	Y
2 Baldwin	Y	Y	Y	Y	Y	N
3 Kind	Y	Y	Y	Y	Y	N
4 Kleczka	Y	Y	Y	Y	Y	N
5 Barrett	Y	Y	Y	Y	Y	N
6 ***Petri***	Y	Y	Y	Y	Y	Y
7 Obey	Y	Y	Y	?	?	N
8 ***Green***	Y	Y	Y	Y	Y	Y
9 ***Sensenbrenner***	Y	Y	Y	Y	Y	Y
WYOMING						
AL ***Cubin***	?	?	?	?	?	?

Southern states - Ala., Ark., Fla., Ga., Ky., La., Miss., N.C., Okla., S.C., Tenn., Texas, Va.

WWW.CQ.COM

2001 CQ ALMANAC — H-163

Key

Y	Voted for (yea).
#	Paired for.
+	Announced for.
N	Voted against (nay).
X	Paired against.
−	Announced against.
P	Voted "present."
C	Voted "present" to avoid possible conflict of interest.
?	Did not vote or otherwise make a position known.

Democrats **Republicans** *Independents*

477. HR 3008. Trade Assistance Expansion/Passage. Thomas, R-Calif., motion to suspend the rules and pass the bill that would reauthorize and extend the Trade Adjustment Assistance program through Sept. 30, 2003. The bill would expand to two years the length of direct benefit payments to workers laid off as a result of trade policies. It also would authorize $2 billion in fiscal 2002 and 2003 to extend unemployment benefits to those laid off as a result of the Sept. 11 attacks. Motion agreed to 420-3: R 211-2; D 207-1 (ND 155-1, SD 52-0); I 2-0. A two-thirds majority of those present and voting (282 in this case) is required for passage under suspension of the rules. Dec. 6, 2001.

478. HR 3129. Customs Service Authorization/Passage. Thomas, R-Calif., motion to suspend the rules and pass the bill that would authorize more than $5 billion through fiscal 2003 for the activities of the U.S. Customs Service, an 18 percent increase over fiscal 2001. Motion rejected 256-168: R 211-2; D 44-165 (ND 19-138, SD 25-27); I 1-1. A two-thirds majority of those present and voting (283 in this case) is required for passage under suspension of the rules. Dec. 6, 2001.

479. HR 3005. Trade Promotion Authority/Rule. Adoption of the rule (H Res 306) to provide for House floor consideration of the bill that would allow expedited negotiation and implementation of trade agreements between the executive branch and foreign countries. Adopted 224-202: R 216-0; D 7-201. (ND 3-152, SD 4-49); I 1-1. Dec. 6, 2001.

480. HR 3005. Trade Promotion Authority/Recommit. Rangel, D-N.Y., motion to recommit the bill to the House Ways and Means Committee with instructions to strike all language after the enacting clause and insert new text that would require the president, when negotiating trade agreements, to insist on binding provisions requiring countries to implement five international labor standards; meet environmental, health and safety provisions; and establish a system of biennial reviews by Congress of trade negotiating authority. Motion rejected 162-267: R 0-217; D 161-49 (ND 122-35, SD 39-14); I 1-1. Dec. 6, 2001.

481. HR 3005. Trade Promotion Authority/Passage. Passage of the bill to allow expedited negotiation and implementation of trade agreements between the executive branch and foreign countries. The bill includes provisions requiring increased consultations with Congress on any proposed changes of tariffs for imports of sensitive agriculture products and on trade disparities for textile products. Passed 215-214: R 194-23; D 21-189 (ND 7-150, SD 14-39); I 0-2. A "yea" was a vote in support of the president's position. Dec. 6, 2001.

482. HR 2944. Fiscal 2002 District of Columbia Appropriations/Conference Report. Adoption of the conference report on the bill that would provide $408 million for the District of Columbia in fiscal 2002, including funds for the city's courts and corrections systems. It also would approve a $7.15 billion budget for the District. Adopted (thus sent to the Senate) 302-84: R 121-67; D 180-16 (ND 137-9, SD 43-7); I 1-1. Dec. 6, 2001.

	477	478	479	480	481	482
ALABAMA						
1 *Callahan*	Y	Y	Y	N	Y	Y
2 *Everett*	Y	Y	Y	N	Y	?
3 *Riley*	Y	Y	Y	N	Y	?
4 *Aderholt*	Y	Y	Y	N	N	Y
5 Cramer	Y	Y	N	Y	N	Y
6 *Bachus*	Y	Y	Y	N	Y	Y
7 Hilliard	Y	N	N	Y	N	Y
ALASKA						
AL *Young*	?	?	?	?	?	?
ARIZONA						
1 *Flake*	N	Y	Y	N	Y	?
2 Pastor	Y	N	N	Y	N	Y
3 *Stump*	Y	Y	Y	N	Y	N
4 *Shadegg*	Y	Y	Y	N	Y	N
5 *Kolbe*	Y	Y	Y	N	Y	Y
6 *Hayworth*	Y	Y	Y	N	Y	N
ARKANSAS						
1 Berry	Y	Y	N	Y	N	N
2 Snyder	Y	Y	N	N	Y	Y
3 *Boozman*	Y	Y	Y	N	Y	N
4 Ross	Y	Y	N	Y	N	Y
CALIFORNIA						
1 Thompson	Y	N	N	Y	N	Y
2 *Herger*	Y	Y	Y	N	Y	N
3 *Ose*	Y	Y	Y	N	Y	Y
4 *Doolittle*	Y	Y	Y	N	Y	Y
5 Matsui	Y	N	N	Y	N	Y
6 Woolsey	Y	N	N	Y	N	Y
7 Miller, George	Y	N	N	Y	N	Y
8 Pelosi	Y	N	N	Y	N	Y
9 Lee	Y	N	N	Y	N	Y
10 Tauscher	Y	N	N	Y	N	Y
11 *Pombo*	Y	Y	Y	N	Y	Y
12 Lantos	Y	N	N	Y	N	Y
13 Stark	Y	N	N	Y	N	Y
14 Eshoo	Y	N	N	Y	N	Y
15 Honda	Y	N	N	Y	N	Y
16 Lofgren	Y	N	N	N	N	?
17 Farr	Y	N	N	Y	N	Y
18 Condit	Y	N	N	Y	N	Y
19 *Radanovich*	Y	Y	Y	N	Y	Y
20 Dooley	Y	N	N	Y	N	Y
21 *Thomas*	Y	Y	Y	N	Y	Y
22 Capps	Y	N	N	Y	N	Y
23 *Gallegly*	Y	Y	Y	N	Y	?
24 Sherman	Y	N	N	Y	N	Y
25 *McKeon*	Y	Y	Y	N	Y	Y
26 Berman	Y	N	N	Y	N	Y
27 Schiff	Y	N	N	Y	N	Y
28 *Dreier*	Y	Y	Y	N	Y	Y
29 Waxman	Y	N	N	Y	N	Y
30 Becerra	Y	N	N	Y	N	Y
31 Solis	Y	N	N	Y	N	Y
32 Watson	Y	N	N	Y	N	Y
33 Roybal-Allard	Y	N	N	Y	N	Y
34 Napolitano	Y	N	N	Y	N	Y
35 Waters	Y	N	N	Y	N	Y
36 Harman	Y	N	N	N	N	Y
37 Millender-McD.	Y	N	N	Y	N	Y
38 *Horn*	Y	Y	Y	N	Y	Y

	477	478	479	480	481	482
39 *Royce*	Y	Y	Y	N	Y	N
40 *Lewis*	Y	Y	Y	N	Y	Y
41 *Miller, Gary*	Y	Y	Y	N	Y	?
42 Baca	Y	N	N	Y	N	Y
43 *Calvert*	Y	Y	Y	N	Y	Y
44 *Bono*	Y	Y	Y	N	Y	Y
45 *Rohrabacher*	Y	Y	Y	N	Y	N
46 Sanchez	Y	N	N	Y	N	Y
47 *Cox*	Y	Y	Y	N	Y	Y
48 *Issa*	Y	Y	Y	N	Y	Y
49 Davis	Y	N	N	Y	Y	Y
50 Filner	P	N	N	Y	N	Y
51 *Cunningham*	Y	Y	Y	N	Y	Y
52 *Hunter*	Y	Y	Y	N	Y	N
COLORADO						
1 DeGette	Y	N	N	Y	N	Y
2 Udall	Y	N	N	Y	N	?
3 *McInnis*	Y	Y	Y	N	Y	?
4 *Schaffer*	Y	Y	Y	N	Y	N
5 *Hefley*	Y	Y	Y	N	Y	N
6 *Tancredo*	Y	Y	Y	N	Y	N
CONNECTICUT						
1 Larson	Y	N	N	Y	N	Y
2 *Simmons*	Y	Y	Y	N	N	Y
3 DeLauro	Y	N	N	N	N	Y
4 *Shays*	Y	Y	Y	N	Y	Y
5 Maloney	Y	Y	N	Y	N	Y
6 *Johnson*	Y	Y	Y	N	Y	Y
DELAWARE						
AL *Castle*	Y	Y	Y	N	Y	Y
FLORIDA						
1 *Miller, J.*	Y	Y	Y	N	Y	N
2 Boyd	Y	Y	N	N	N	Y
3 Brown	Y	N	N	Y	N	Y
4 *Crenshaw*	Y	Y	Y	N	Y	Y
5 Thurman	Y	N	N	N	N	Y
6 *Stearns*	Y	Y	Y	N	Y	N
7 *Mica*	Y	Y	Y	N	Y	Y
8 *Keller*	Y	Y	Y	N	Y	N
9 *Bilirakis*	Y	Y	Y	N	Y	Y
10 *Young*	Y	Y	Y	N	Y	Y
11 Davis	Y	N	N	N	N	Y
12 *Putnam*	Y	Y	Y	N	Y	Y
13 *Miller, D.*	Y	Y	Y	N	Y	Y
14 *Goss*	Y	Y	Y	N	Y	N
15 *Weldon*	Y	Y	Y	N	N	Y
16 *Foley*	Y	Y	Y	N	N	Y
17 Meek	?	?	?	?	?	?
18 *Ros-Lehtinen*	Y	Y	Y	N	Y	Y
19 Wexler	Y	Y	N	Y	N	Y
20 Deutsch	Y	N	N	Y	N	Y
21 *Diaz-Balart*	Y	Y	Y	N	Y	Y
22 *Shaw*	Y	Y	Y	N	Y	Y
23 Hastings	Y	N	N	Y	N	Y
GEORGIA						
1 *Kingston*	Y	Y	Y	N	Y	?
2 Bishop	Y	N	N	Y	N	Y
3 *Collins*	Y	Y	Y	N	Y	Y
4 McKinney	Y	N	N	Y	N	Y
5 Lewis	Y	N	N	Y	N	Y
6 *Isakson*	Y	Y	Y	N	Y	Y
7 *Barr*	Y	Y	Y	N	Y	N
8 *Chambliss*	Y	Y	Y	N	Y	Y
9 *Deal*	Y	Y	Y	N	Y	?
10 *Norwood*	Y	Y	Y	N	N	N
11 *Linder*	Y	Y	Y	N	Y	Y
HAWAII						
1 Abercrombie	N	N	N	Y	N	Y
2 Mink	Y	N	N	Y	N	Y
IDAHO						
1 *Otter*	Y	N	Y	N	Y	N
2 *Simpson*	Y	Y	Y	N	Y	Y
ILLINOIS						
1 Rush	Y	N	N	Y	N	Y
2 Jackson	Y	N	N	Y	N	Y
3 Lipinski	Y	Y	N	Y	N	Y
4 Gutierrez	Y	N	N	Y	N	Y
5 Blagojevich	Y	N	N	Y	N	Y
6 *Hyde*	Y	Y	Y	N	Y	Y
7 Davis	Y	N	N	Y	N	Y
8 *Crane*	Y	Y	Y	N	Y	N
9 Schakowsky	Y	N	N	Y	N	Y
10 *Kirk*	Y	+	Y	N	Y	N
11 *Weller*	Y	Y	Y	N	Y	N
12 Costello	Y	Y	N	Y	N	?
13 *Biggert*	Y	Y	Y	N	Y	Y

ND Northern Democrats   SD Southern Democrats

	477	478	479	480	481	482
14 ***Hastert***				N	Y	
15 ***Johnson***	Y	Y	Y	N	Y	Y
16 ***Manzullo***	Y	Y	Y	N	Y	N
17 Evans	Y	N	N	Y	N	Y
18 ***LaHood***	Y	Y	Y	N	Y	N
19 Phelps	Y	Y	N	Y	N	Y
20 ***Shimkus***	Y	Y	Y	N	Y	N
INDIANA						
1 Visclosky	Y	N	N	N	N	Y
2 ***Pence***	Y	Y	Y	N	Y	?
3 Roemer	Y	N	–	Y	N	N
4 ***Souder***	Y	Y	Y	N	Y	Y
5 ***Buyer***	Y	Y	Y	N	Y	Y
6 ***Burton***	Y	Y	Y	N	Y	Y
7 ***Kerns***	Y	Y	Y	N	Y	N
8 ***Hostettler***	?	?	?	?	?	?
9 Hill	Y	N	N	N	Y	Y
10 Carson	Y	N	N	Y	N	Y
IOWA						
1 ***Leach***	Y	Y	Y	N	Y	Y
2 ***Nussle***	Y	Y	Y	N	Y	Y
3 Boswell	Y	Y	N	Y	N	Y
4 ***Ganske***	Y	Y	Y	N	Y	Y
5 ***Latham***	Y	Y	Y	N	Y	Y
KANSAS						
1 ***Moran***	Y	Y	Y	N	Y	N
2 ***Ryun***	Y	Y	Y	N	Y	N
3 Moore	Y	N	N	Y	Y	N
4 ***Tiahrt***	Y	Y	Y	N	Y	N
KENTUCKY						
1 ***Whitfield***	Y	Y	Y	N	Y	N
2 ***Lewis***	Y	Y	Y	N	Y	Y
3 ***Northup***	Y	Y	Y	N	Y	Y
4 Lucas	Y	Y	N	N	Y	N
5 ***Rogers***	Y	Y	Y	N	N	Y
6 ***Fletcher***	Y	Y	Y	N	Y	Y
LOUISIANA						
1 ***Vitter***	Y	Y	Y	N	Y	Y
2 Jefferson	Y	N	Y	N	Y	Y
3 ***Tauzin***	Y	Y	Y	N	Y	Y
4 ***McCrery***	Y	Y	Y	N	Y	Y
5 ***Cooksey***	Y	Y	Y	N	Y	Y
6 ***Baker***	Y	Y	Y	N	Y	?
7 John	Y	Y	N	N	Y	Y
MAINE						
1 Allen	Y	N	N	Y	N	Y
2 Baldacci	Y	N	N	Y	N	Y
MARYLAND						
1 ***Gilchrest***	Y	Y	Y	N	Y	Y
2 ***Ehrlich***	Y	Y	Y	N	Y	Y
3 Cardin	Y	N	N	Y	N	Y
4 Wynn	Y	N	N	Y	N	Y
5 Hoyer	Y	N	N	Y	N	Y
6 ***Bartlett***	Y	Y	Y	N	N	N
7 Cummings	Y	N	N	Y	N	Y
8 ***Morella***	?	Y	Y	N	Y	Y
MASSACHUSETTS						
1 Olver	Y	N	N	Y	N	N
2 Neal	Y	N	N	Y	N	?
3 McGovern	Y	N	N	Y	N	Y
4 Frank	Y	N	N	Y	N	Y
5 Meehan	Y	N	N	Y	N	Y
6 Tierney	Y	N	N	Y	N	Y
7 Markey	Y	N	N	Y	N	Y
8 Capuano	Y	N	N	Y	N	Y
9 Lynch	Y	N	N	Y	N	Y
10 Delahunt	Y	N	N	Y	N	Y
MICHIGAN						
1 Stupak	Y	N	N	N	N	Y
2 ***Hoekstra***	Y	Y	Y	N	N	N
3 ***Ehlers***	Y	Y	Y	N	Y	Y
4 ***Camp***	Y	Y	Y	N	Y	Y
5 Barcia	Y	N	N	Y	N	Y
6 ***Upton***	Y	Y	Y	N	Y	N
7 ***Smith***	Y	Y	Y	N	Y	?
8 ***Rogers***	Y	Y	Y	N	Y	?
9 Kildee	Y	N	N	Y	N	Y
10 Bonlor	Y	N	N	N	N	?
11 ***Knollenberg***	Y	Y	Y	N	Y	Y
12 Levin	Y	N	N	Y	N	Y
13 Rivers	Y	N	N	N	N	Y
14 Conyers	Y	N	N	Y	N	Y
15 Kilpatrick	Y	N	N	Y	N	N
16 Dingell	Y	N	N	N	N	Y
MINNESOTA						
1 ***Gutknecht***	Y	Y	Y	N	Y	Y
2 ***Kennedy***	Y	Y	Y	N	Y	N
3 ***Ramstad***	Y	Y	Y	N	Y	N
4 McCollum	Y	N	N	Y	N	Y
5 Sabo	Y	N	N	N	N	Y
6 Luther	Y	Y	N	Y	N	Y
7 Peterson	Y	N	N	N	N	N
8 Oberstar	Y	N	N	N	N	Y
MISSISSIPPI						
1 ***Wicker***	Y	Y	Y	N	Y	Y
2 Thompson	Y	N	N	Y	N	Y
3 ***Pickering***	Y	Y	Y	N	Y	N
4 Shows	Y	Y	N	Y	N	N
5 Taylor	Y	Y	N	N	N	N
MISSOURI						
1 Clay	Y	N	N	Y	N	Y
2 ***Akin***	Y	Y	Y	N	Y	N
3 Gephardt	Y	N	N	Y	N	N
4 Skelton	Y	N	N	Y	Y	Y
5 McCarthy	Y	N	N	Y	N	–
6 ***Graves***	Y	Y	Y	N	Y	N
7 ***Blunt***	Y	Y	Y	N	Y	N
8 ***Emerson***	Y	Y	Y	N	Y	?
9 ***Hulshof***	Y	Y	Y	N	Y	Y
MONTANA						
AL ***Rehberg***	Y	Y	Y	N	Y	Y
NEBRASKA						
1 ***Bereuter***	Y	Y	Y	N	Y	?
2 ***Terry***	Y	Y	Y	N	Y	Y
3 ***Osborne***	Y	Y	Y	N	Y	Y
NEVADA						
1 Berkley	Y	N	N	Y	N	Y
2 ***Gibbons***	Y	Y	Y	N	Y	Y
NEW HAMPSHIRE						
1 ***Sununu***	Y	Y	Y	N	Y	Y
2 ***Bass***	Y	Y	Y	N	Y	Y
NEW JERSEY						
1 Andrews	Y	N	?	Y	N	Y
2 ***LoBiondo***	Y	Y	Y	N	N	Y
3 ***Saxton***	Y	Y	Y	N	Y	Y
4 ***Smith***	Y	Y	Y	N	N	N
5 ***Roukema***	?	?	?	?	?	?
6 Pallone	Y	N	N	Y	N	Y
7 ***Ferguson***	Y	Y	Y	N	Y	Y
8 Pascrell	Y	N	N	Y	N	Y
9 Rothman	Y	N	N	Y	N	Y
10 Payne	Y	N	N	Y	N	Y
11 ***Frelinghuysen***	Y	Y	Y	N	Y	Y
12 Holt	Y	N	N	Y	N	Y
13 Menendez	Y	N	N	Y	N	Y
NEW MEXICO						
1 ***Wilson***	Y	Y	Y	N	Y	Y
2 ***Skeen***	Y	Y	Y	N	Y	Y
3 Udall	Y	N	N	Y	N	Y
NEW YORK						
1 ***Grucci***	Y	Y	Y	N	Y	Y
2 Israel	Y	Y	N	Y	N	N
3 ***King***	Y	Y	Y	N	Y	Y
4 McCarthy	Y	N	N	Y	N	+
5 Ackerman	Y	N	N	Y	N	?
6 Meeks	Y	N	N	Y	N	Y
7 Crowley	Y	N	N	Y	N	Y
8 Nadler	Y	N	N	Y	N	Y
9 Weiner	Y	N	N	Y	N	Y
10 Towns	Y	N	N	Y	N	Y
11 Owens	Y	N	N	Y	N	Y
12 Velázquez	Y	N	N	N	N	Y
13 ***Fossella***	Y	Y	Y	N	Y	N
14 Maloney	Y	Y	N	Y	N	Y
15 Rangel	Y	N	N	Y	N	Y
16 Serrano	Y	N	N	Y	N	Y
17 Engel	Y	N	N	Y	N	Y
18 Lowey	Y	N	N	Y	N	Y
19 ***Kelly***	Y	Y	Y	N	Y	?
20 ***Gilman***	Y	Y	Y	N	N	Y
21 McNulty	Y	N	N	Y	N	?
22 ***Sweeney***	Y	Y	Y	N	Y	Y
23 ***Boehlert***	Y	Y	Y	N	Y	Y
24 ***McHugh***	Y	Y	Y	N	N	?
25 ***Walsh***	Y	Y	Y	N	N	Y
26 Hinchey	Y	N	N	Y	N	Y
27 ***Reynolds***	Y	Y	Y	N	Y	Y
28 Slaughter	Y	N	N	Y	N	Y
29 LaFalce	Y	Y	N	Y	N	Y
30 ***Quinn***	?	?	?	?	?	?
31 ***Houghton***	Y	Y	Y	N	Y	Y
NORTH CAROLINA						
1 Clayton	Y	N	N	Y	N	Y
2 Etheridge	Y	Y	N	Y	Y	Y
3 ***Jones***	Y	Y	Y	N	N	N
4 Price	Y	Y	N	Y	N	Y
5 ***Burr***	Y	Y	Y	N	Y	Y
6 ***Coble***	Y	Y	Y	N	N	N
7 McIntyre	Y	Y	N	Y	N	Y
8 ***Hayes***	Y	Y	Y	N	Y	N
9 ***Myrick***	Y	Y	Y	N	Y	Y
10 ***Ballenger***	Y	Y	Y	N	Y	Y
11 ***Taylor***	Y	Y	Y	N	N	?
12 Watt	Y	N	N	Y	N	Y
NORTH DAKOTA						
AL Pomeroy	Y	Y	N	Y	N	Y
OHIO						
1 ***Chabot***	Y	Y	Y	N	Y	N
2 ***Portman***	Y	Y	Y	N	Y	Y
3 Hall	Y	Y	N	Y	N	Y
4 ***Oxley***	Y	Y	Y	N	Y	?
5 ***Gillmor***	Y	Y	Y	N	Y	Y
6 Strickland	Y	N	N	N	N	N
7 ***Hobson***	Y	Y	Y	N	Y	Y
8 ***Boehner***	Y	Y	Y	N	Y	Y
9 Kaptur	Y	Y	N	Y	N	Y
10 Kucinich	Y	N	N	Y	N	Y
11 Jones	Y	N	N	Y	N	Y
12 ***Tiberi***	Y	Y	Y	N	Y	?
13 Brown	Y	N	N	N	N	Y
14 Sawyer	Y	N	N	Y	N	Y
15 ***Pryce***	Y	Y	Y	N	Y	Y
16 ***Regula***	Y	Y	Y	N	N	Y
17 Traficant	Y	Y	Y	N	N	Y
18 ***Ney***	Y	Y	Y	N	Y	Y
19 ***LaTourette***	Y	Y	Y	N	N	Y
OKLAHOMA						
1 ***Largent***	Y	Y	Y	N	Y	?
2 Carson	Y	Y	Y	N	Y	Y
3 ***Watkins***	Y	Y	Y	N	Y	?
4 ***Watts***	Y	Y	Y	N	Y	Y
5 ***Istook***	Y	Y	Y	N	Y	Y
6 ***Lucas***	Y	Y	Y	N	Y	Y
OREGON						
1 Wu	Y	Y	N	N	N	Y
2 ***Walden***	Y	Y	Y	N	Y	Y
3 Blumenauer	Y	N	N	Y	N	Y
4 DeFazio	Y	N	N	Y	N	Y
5 Hooley	Y	N	N	Y	N	Y
PENNSYLVANIA						
1 Brady	Y	N	N	N	N	Y
2 Fattah	Y	N	N	Y	N	Y
3 Borski	Y	N	N	N	N	Y
4 ***Hart***	Y	Y	Y	N	Y	Y
5 ***Peterson***	Y	Y	Y	N	Y	Y
6 Holden	Y	N	N	N	N	Y
7 ***Weldon***	Y	Y	Y	N	N	Y
8 ***Greenwood***	Y	Y	Y	N	Y	Y
9 ***Shuster, Bill***	Y	Y	Y	N	Y	N
10 ***Sherwood***	Y	Y	Y	N	Y	Y
11 Kanjorski	Y	N	N	N	N	Y
12 Murtha	Y	N	N	N	N	?
13 Hoeffel	Y	N	N	Y	N	Y
14 Coyne	Y	N	N	Y	N	?
15 ***Toomey***	Y	Y	Y	N	Y	Y
16 ***Pitts***	Y	Y	Y	N	Y	?
17 ***Gekas***	Y	Y	Y	N	Y	Y
18 Doyle	Y	N	N	N	N	Y
19 ***Platts***	Y	Y	Y	N	Y	N
20 Mascara	Y	N	N	N	N	Y
21 ***English***	Y	Y	Y	N	Y	Y
RHODE ISLAND						
1 Kennedy	Y	N	N	Y	N	Y
2 Langevin	Y	Y	N	Y	N	Y
SOUTH CAROLINA						
1 ***Brown***	+	+	Y	N	Y	Y
2 Vacant						
3 ***Graham***	Y	Y	Y	N	N	Y
4 ***DeMint***	Y	Y	Y	N	Y	N
5 Spratt	Y	Y	N	Y	N	Y
6 Clyburn	?	?	N	Y	N	Y
SOUTH DAKOTA						
AL ***Thune***	Y	Y	Y	N	Y	N
TENNESSEE						
1 ***Jenkins***	Y	Y	Y	N	Y	Y
2 ***Duncan***	Y	Y	Y	N	N	N
3 ***Wamp***	Y	Y	Y	N	Y	N
4 ***Hilleary***	Y	Y	Y	N	Y	N
5 Clement	Y	Y	N	Y	N	Y
6 Gordon	Y	Y	N	Y	N	Y
7 ***Bryant***	Y	Y	Y	N	Y	N
8 Tanner	Y	Y	Y	N	Y	Y
9 Ford	Y	N	N	N	N	Y
TEXAS						
1 Sandlin	Y	N	N	Y	N	Y
2 Turner	Y	N	N	Y	N	N
3 ***Johnson, Sam***	Y	Y	Y	N	Y	N
4 Hall	Y	Y	N	N	Y	?
5 ***Sessions***	Y	Y	Y	N	Y	?
6 ***Barton***	Y	Y	Y	N	Y	?
7 ***Culberson***	Y	Y	Y	N	Y	N
8 ***Brady***	Y	Y	Y	N	Y	N
9 Lampson	Y	N	N	Y	N	Y
10 Doggett	Y	N	N	Y	N	Y
11 Edwards	Y	N	N	Y	N	Y
12 ***Granger***	Y	Y	Y	N	Y	Y
13 ***Thornberry***	Y	Y	Y	N	Y	N
14 ***Paul***	N	N	Y	N	N	N
15 Hinojosa	Y	N	N	Y	Y	Y
16 Reyes	Y	Y	N	Y	N	Y
17 Stenholm	Y	Y	N	N	Y	N
18 Jackson-Lee	Y	N	N	Y	N	Y
19 ***Combest***	Y	Y	Y	N	Y	N
20 Gonzalez	Y	N	N	Y	N	Y
21 ***Smith***	Y	Y	Y	N	Y	Y
22 ***DeLay***	Y	Y	Y	N	Y	Y
23 ***Bonilla***	Y	Y	Y	N	Y	Y
24 Frost	Y	N	N	Y	N	N
25 Bentsen	Y	Y	N	Y	Y	Y
26 ***Armey***	Y	Y	Y	N	Y	?
27 Ortiz	Y	Y	Y	N	Y	Y
28 Rodriguez	Y	N	N	Y	N	?
29 Green	Y	Y	N	Y	N	?
30 Johnson, E.B.	Y	N	N	Y	N	Y
UTAH						
1 ***Hansen***	Y	Y	Y	N	Y	N
2 Matheson	Y	Y	N	N	Y	Y
3 ***Cannon***	Y	Y	Y	N	Y	?
VERMONT						
AL *Sanders*	Y	N	N	Y	N	Y
VIRGINIA						
1 ***Davis, Jo Ann***	Y	Y	Y	N	Y	N
2 ***Schrock***	Y	Y	Y	N	Y	Y
3 Scott	Y	N	N	Y	N	Y
4 ***Forbes***	Y	Y	Y	N	Y	N
5 *Goode*	Y	Y	Y	N	N	N
6 ***Goodlatte***	Y	Y	Y	N	Y	N
7 ***Cantor***	Y	Y	Y	N	Y	Y
8 Moran	Y	Y	N	Y	Y	Y
9 Boucher	Y	N	N	Y	N	Y
10 ***Wolf***	Y	Y	Y	N	Y	Y
11 ***Davis, T.***	Y	Y	Y	N	Y	Y
WASHINGTON						
1 Inslee	Y	N	N	Y	N	Y
2 Larsen	Y	Y	N	N	N	Y
3 Baird	Y	Y	N	Y	N	Y
4 ***Hastings***	Y	Y	Y	N	Y	?
5 ***Nethercutt***	Y	Y	Y	N	Y	Y
6 Dicks	Y	N	Y	N	Y	Y
7 McDermott	Y	N	N	Y	N	Y
8 ***Dunn***	Y	Y	Y	N	Y	Y
9 Smith	Y	Y	N	N	N	?
WEST VIRGINIA						
1 Mollohan	Y	N	N	N	N	Y
2 ***Capito***	Y	Y	Y	N	N	Y
3 Rahall	Y	N	N	N	N	Y
WISCONSIN						
1 ***Ryan***	Y	Y	Y	N	Y	N
2 Baldwin	Y	N	N	N	N	Y
3 Kind	Y	N	N	Y	N	Y
4 Kleczka	Y	N	N	Y	N	Y
5 Barrett	Y	N	N	Y	N	Y
6 ***Petri***	Y	Y	Y	N	Y	N
7 Obey	Y	N	N	Y	N	N
8 ***Green***	Y	Y	Y	N	Y	N
9 ***Sensenbrenner***	Y	Y	Y	N	Y	N
WYOMING						
AL ***Cubin***	?	?	Y	N	Y	?

Southern states - Ala., Ark., Fla., Ga., Ky., La., Miss., N.C., Okla., S.C., Tenn., Texas, Va.

Key

Y	Voted for (yea).
#	Paired for.
+	Announced for.
N	Voted against (nay).
X	Paired against.
−	Announced against.
P	Voted "present."
C	Voted "present" to avoid possible conflict of interest.
?	Did not vote or otherwise make a position known.

Democrats **Republicans** *Independents*

483. H Con Res 281. Johnny Spann Tribute/Adoption. Goss, R-Fla., motion to suspend the rules and adopt the concurrent resolution that would pay tribute to Johnny Micheal Spann, a Central Intelligence Agency officer and the first U.S. citizen killed in combat in Afghanistan. Motion agreed to 401-0: R 202-0; D 197-0 (ND 145-0, SD 52-0); I 2-0. A two-thirds majority of those present and voting (268 in this case) is required for adoption under suspension of the rules. Dec. 11, 2001.

484. HR 3282. Mike Mansfield Building/Passage. LaTourette, R-Ohio, motion to suspend the rules and pass the bill that would name a federal building in Butte, Mont., after the late Sen. Mike Mansfield, D-Mont. Motion agreed to 401-0: R 202-0; D 197-0 (ND 145-0, SD 52-0); I 2-0. A two-thirds majority of those present and voting (268 in this case) is required for adoption under suspension of the rules. Dec. 11, 2001.

485. HR 10. Railroad Retirement/Concur with Senate Amendments. Quinn, R-N.Y., motion to suspend the rules and concur with Senate amendments to the bill that would create a railroad retirement board that would have the authority to invest the pension system's $15.3 billion in Treasury bonds in higher-yielding private equities. The bill also would reduce the payroll tax on railroads and make other changes in the railroad retirement system. Motion agreed to 369-33: R 171-31; D 196-2 (ND 146-0, SD 50-2); I 2-0. A two-thirds majority of those present and voting (268 in this case) is required for passage under suspension of the rules. Dec. 11, 2001.

486. Procedural Motion/Journal. Approval of the House Journal of Tuesday, Dec. 11, 2001. Approved 355-44: R 193-12; D 160-32 (ND 114-26, SD 46-6); I 2-0. Dec. 12, 2001.

487. HR 3295. Election Overhaul/Rule. Adoption of the rule (H Res 311) to provide for House floor consideration of the bill that would overhaul the nation's election procedures, including authorizing $400 million in one-time payments for states and counties to replace or upgrade punch card voting machines. Adopted 223-193: R 206-3; D 16-189 (ND 7-146, SD 9-43); I 1-1. Dec. 12, 2001.

488. HR 3295. Election Overhaul/Recommit. Menendez, D-N.J., motion to recommit the bill to the House Administration Committee with instructions to add language ensuring that Motor Voter Law provisions remain in place, securing provisional voting rights, mandating that within five years voting systems must provide increased opportunities for voters to correct ballot errors, and requiring that election guidelines be developed by the Department of Justice. Motion rejected 197-226: R 1-214; D 195-11 (ND 148-5, SD 47-6); I 1-1. Dec. 12, 2001.

	483	484	485	486	487	488
ALABAMA						
1 *Callahan*	Y	Y	Y	Y	Y	N
2 *Everett*	Y	Y	Y	Y	Y	N
3 *Riley*	+	+	+	Y	Y	N
4 *Aderholt*	Y	Y	Y	Y	Y	N
5 Cramer	Y	Y	Y	Y	N	N
6 *Bachus*	Y	Y	Y	Y	Y	N
7 Hilliard	Y	Y	Y	N	N	Y
ALASKA						
AL *Young*	?	?	?	?	?	?
ARIZONA						
1 *Flake*	Y	Y	N	Y	Y	N
2 Pastor	Y	Y	Y	Y	N	Y
3 *Stump*	Y	Y	Y	Y	Y	N
4 *Shadegg*	Y	Y	N	Y	Y	N
5 *Kolbe*	Y	Y	N	Y	Y	N
6 *Hayworth*	Y	Y	Y	Y	Y	N
ARKANSAS						
1 Berry	Y	Y	Y	Y	Y	Y
2 Snyder	Y	Y	Y	Y	N	Y
3 *Boozman*	Y	Y	Y	Y	Y	N
4 Ross	Y	Y	Y	Y	N	Y
CALIFORNIA						
1 Thompson	Y	Y	Y	N	N	Y
2 *Herger*	Y	Y	N	Y	Y	N
3 *Ose*	Y	Y	Y	Y	Y	N
4 *Doolittle*	Y	Y	Y	Y	Y	N
5 Matsui	?	?	?	Y	N	Y
6 Woolsey	Y	Y	Y	Y	N	Y
7 Miller, George	Y	Y	Y	?	N	Y
8 Pelosi	Y	Y	Y	Y	N	Y
9 Lee	Y	Y	Y	Y	N	Y
10 Tauscher	Y	Y	Y	Y	N	Y
11 *Pombo*	Y	Y	Y	Y	Y	N
12 Lantos	Y	Y	Y	Y	N	Y
13 Stark	Y	Y	Y	?	N	Y
14 Eshoo	Y	Y	Y	Y	N	Y
15 Honda	Y	Y	Y	Y	N	Y
16 Lofgren	Y	Y	Y	Y	N	Y
17 Farr	Y	Y	Y	Y	N	Y
18 Condit	Y	Y	Y	N	N	Y
19 *Radanovich*	?	?	?	Y	Y	N
20 Dooley	?	?	?	?	?	?
21 *Thomas*	Y	Y	Y	Y	Y	N
22 Capps	Y	Y	Y	Y	N	Y
23 *Gallegly*	Y	Y	Y	Y	Y	N
24 Sherman	Y	Y	Y	Y	N	Y
25 *McKeon*	Y	Y	Y	Y	Y	N
26 Berman	?	?	?	Y	N	Y
27 Schiff	Y	Y	Y	Y	N	Y
28 *Dreier*	Y	Y	Y	Y	Y	N
29 Waxman	Y	Y	Y	Y	N	Y
30 Becerra	Y	Y	Y	Y	N	Y
31 Solis	Y	Y	Y	Y	N	Y
32 Watson	Y	Y	Y	Y	N	Y
33 Roybal-Allard	Y	Y	Y	Y	N	Y
34 Napolitano	Y	Y	Y	Y	N	Y
35 Waters	Y	Y	N	N	N	Y
36 Harman	Y	Y	Y	Y	N	Y
37 Millender-McD.	Y	Y	Y	Y	N	Y
38 *Horn*	Y	Y	Y	Y	Y	N

	483	484	485	486	487	488
39 *Royce*	Y	Y	N	Y	Y	N
40 *Lewis*	Y	Y	Y	Y	Y	N
41 *Miller, Gary*	Y	Y	Y	Y	Y	N
42 Baca	Y	Y	Y	Y	N	Y
43 *Calvert*	Y	Y	Y	Y	Y	N
44 *Bono*	Y	Y	Y	Y	Y	N
45 *Rohrabacher*	Y	Y	N	Y	Y	N
46 Sanchez	Y	Y	Y	N	N	Y
47 *Cox*	Y	Y	N	Y	Y	N
48 *Issa*	Y	Y	Y	Y	Y	N
49 Davis	Y	Y	Y	Y	N	Y
50 Filner	Y	Y	Y	N	N	Y
51 *Cunningham*	Y	Y	Y	Y	Y	N
52 *Hunter*	Y	Y	Y	Y	Y	N
COLORADO						
1 DeGette	Y	Y	Y	Y	N	Y
2 Udall	Y	Y	Y	Y	N	Y
3 *McInnis*	Y	Y	Y	Y	Y	N
4 *Schaffer*	Y	Y	N	N	Y	N
5 *Hefley*	Y	Y	N	N	Y	N
6 *Tancredo*	Y	Y	N	P	Y	N
CONNECTICUT						
1 Larson	Y	Y	Y	Y	N	Y
2 *Simmons*	Y	Y	Y	Y	Y	N
3 DeLauro	Y	Y	Y	Y	N	Y
4 *Shays*	Y	Y	N	Y	N	Y
5 Maloney	+	+	+	Y	N	Y
6 *Johnson*	Y	Y	Y	Y	Y	N
DELAWARE						
AL *Castle*	Y	Y	Y	Y	Y	N
FLORIDA						
1 *Miller, J.*	Y	Y	Y	Y	Y	N
2 Boyd	Y	Y	Y	Y	Y	Y
3 Brown	Y	Y	Y	Y	Y	Y
4 *Crenshaw*	Y	Y	Y	Y	Y	N
5 Thurman	Y	Y	Y	Y	N	Y
6 *Stearns*	Y	Y	Y	Y	Y	N
7 *Mica*	Y	Y	Y	Y	Y	N
8 *Keller*	Y	Y	Y	Y	Y	N
9 *Bilirakis*	Y	Y	Y	Y	Y	N
10 *Young*	Y	Y	Y	Y	Y	N
11 Davis	Y	Y	Y	Y	Y	Y
12 *Putnam*	Y	Y	Y	Y	Y	N
13 *Miller, D.*	Y	Y	N	Y	Y	N
14 *Goss*	Y	Y	Y	Y	Y	N
15 *Weldon*	Y	Y	N	?	Y	N
16 *Foley*	Y	Y	Y	Y	Y	N
17 Meek	Y	Y	?	?	Y	Y
18 *Ros-Lehtinen*	Y	Y	Y	Y	Y	N
19 Wexler	Y	Y	Y	Y	N	Y
20 Deutsch	Y	Y	Y	Y	N	Y
21 *Diaz-Balart*	Y	Y	Y	Y	Y	N
22 *Shaw*	Y	Y	Y	Y	Y	N
23 Hastings	Y	Y	N	N	N	Y
GEORGIA						
1 *Kingston*	Y	Y	Y	Y	Y	N
2 Bishop	Y	Y	Y	Y	N	Y
3 *Collins*	Y	Y	Y	Y	Y	N
4 McKinney	Y	Y	Y	Y	N	Y
5 Lewis	Y	Y	Y	Y	N	Y
6 *Isakson*	Y	Y	Y	Y	Y	N
7 *Barr*	?	?	?	Y	Y	N
8 *Chambliss*	Y	Y	Y	Y	Y	N
9 *Deal*	?	?	?	?	Y	N
10 *Norwood*	Y	Y	Y	Y	Y	N
11 *Linder*	Y	Y	Y	Y	Y	N
HAWAII						
1 Abercrombie	Y	Y	Y	Y	N	Y
2 Mink	Y	Y	Y	Y	N	Y
IDAHO						
1 *Otter*	Y	Y	Y	Y	Y	N
2 *Simpson*	Y	Y	Y	Y	Y	N
ILLINOIS						
1 Rush	Y	Y	Y	N	N	Y
2 Jackson	Y	Y	Y	Y	N	Y
3 Lipinski	Y	Y	Y	Y	N	Y
4 Gutierrez	Y	Y	N	N	N	Y
5 Blagojevich	?	?	?	Y	N	Y
6 *Hyde*	Y	Y	Y	Y	Y	N
7 Davis	Y	Y	Y	?	N	Y
8 *Crane*	Y	Y	N	Y	Y	N
9 Schakowsky	Y	Y	Y	Y	N	Y
10 *Kirk*	Y	Y	Y	Y	Y	N
11 *Weller*	Y	Y	Y	Y	Y	N
12 Costello	Y	Y	Y	N	N	Y
13 *Biggert*	Y	Y	Y	Y	Y	N

ND Northern Democrats   SD Southern Democrats

	483	484	485	486	487	488
14 ***Hastert***						
15 ***Johnson***	Y	Y	Y	Y	Y	N
16 ***Manzullo***	Y	Y	Y	Y	Y	N
17 Evans	Y	Y	Y	Y	N	?
18 ***LaHood***	Y	Y	Y	Y	Y	N
19 Phelps	Y	Y	Y	Y	N	Y
20 ***Shimkus***	Y	Y	Y	Y	Y	N
INDIANA						
1 Visclosky	Y	Y	Y	N	N	Y
2 ***Pence***	Y	Y	N	Y	Y	N
3 Roemer	Y	Y	Y	Y	N	Y
4 ***Souder***	?	?	?	Y	Y	N
5 ***Buyer***	Y	Y	Y	?	?	?
6 ***Burton***	Y	Y	Y	Y	Y	N
7 ***Kerns***	Y	Y	Y	Y	Y	N
8 ***Hostettler***	?	?	?	?	?	?
9 Hill	Y	Y	Y	Y	N	Y
10 Carson	Y	Y	Y	Y	N	Y
IOWA						
1 ***Leach***	Y	Y	Y	?	Y	N
2 ***Nussle***	Y	Y	Y	Y	Y	N
3 Boswell	Y	Y	Y	Y	N	Y
4 ***Ganske***	Y	Y	Y	Y	Y	N
5 ***Latham***	Y	Y	Y	Y	Y	N
KANSAS						
1 ***Moran***	Y	Y	Y	N	Y	N
2 ***Ryun***	Y	Y	Y	Y	Y	N
3 Moore	Y	?	Y	N	N	Y
4 ***Tiahrt***	+	+	+	Y	Y	N
KENTUCKY						
1 ***Whitfield***	Y	Y	Y	Y	Y	N
2 ***Lewis***	Y	Y	Y	Y	Y	N
3 ***Northup***	Y	Y	Y	Y	Y	N
4 Lucas	Y	Y	Y	Y	Y	N
5 ***Rogers***	Y	Y	Y	Y	Y	N
6 ***Fletcher***	Y	Y	Y	Y	Y	N
LOUISIANA						
1 ***Vitter***	Y	Y	Y	Y	Y	N
2 Jefferson	?	?	?	Y	N	Y
3 ***Tauzin***	Y	Y	Y	Y	Y	N
4 ***McCrery***	Y	Y	Y	Y	Y	N
5 ***Cooksey***	Y	Y	Y	Y	Y	N
6 ***Baker***	Y	Y	Y	Y	Y	N
7 John	Y	Y	Y	Y	Y	Y
MAINE						
1 Allen	Y	Y	Y	N	N	Y
2 Baldacci	Y	Y	Y	Y	N	Y
MARYLAND						
1 ***Gilchrest***	Y	Y	Y	Y	Y	N
2 ***Ehrlich***	?	?	?	Y	Y	N
3 Cardin	Y	Y	Y	Y	N	Y
4 Wynn	Y	Y	Y	Y	N	Y
5 Hoyer	Y	Y	Y	Y	N	Y
6 ***Bartlett***	Y	Y	Y	Y	Y	N
7 Cummings	Y	Y	Y	Y	N	Y
8 ***Morella***	Y	Y	Y	Y	N	N
MASSACHUSETTS						
1 Olver	Y	Y	Y	Y	N	Y
2 Neal	Y	Y	Y	Y	N	Y
3 McGovern	Y	Y	Y	Y	N	Y
4 Frank	Y	Y	Y	Y	N	Y
5 Meehan	Y	Y	Y	Y	N	Y
6 Tierney	Y	Y	Y	Y	N	Y
7 Markey	Y	Y	Y	Y	N	Y
8 Capuano	+	+	+	N	N	Y
9 Lynch	Y	Y	Y	Y	N	Y
10 Delahunt	?	?	?	?	?	?
MICHIGAN						
1 Stupak	Y	Y	Y	N	N	Y
2 ***Hoekstra***	Y	Y	N	Y	Y	N
3 ***Ehlers***	Y	Y	Y	Y	Y	N
4 ***Camp***	Y	Y	Y	Y	Y	N
5 Barcia	Y	Y	Y	Y	N	Y
6 ***Upton***	Y	Y	Y	Y	Y	N
7 ***Smith***	Y	Y	N	Y	?	N
8 ***Rogers***	Y	Y	Y	Y	Y	N
9 Kildee	Y	Y	Y	Y	N	Y
10 Bonior	Y	Y	Y	N	N	Y
11 ***Knollenberg***	Y	Y	Y	Y	Y	N
12 Levin	Y	Y	Y	Y	N	Y
13 Rivers	Y	Y	Y	Y	N	Y
14 Conyers	Y	Y	Y	?	N	Y
15 Kilpatrick	Y	Y	Y	Y	N	Y
16 Dingell	Y	Y	Y	?	N	Y

	483	484	485	486	487	488
MINNESOTA						
1 ***Gutknecht***	Y	?	Y	N	Y	N
2 ***Kennedy***	Y	Y	Y	N	Y	N
3 ***Ramstad***	Y	Y	Y	N	Y	N
4 McCollum	Y	Y	Y	Y	N	Y
5 Sabo	Y	Y	Y	?	N	Y
6 Luther	?	?	?	?	?	?
7 Peterson	Y	Y	Y	N	N	Y
8 Oberstar	Y	Y	Y	N	N	Y
MISSISSIPPI						
1 ***Wicker***	Y	Y	Y	N	Y	N
2 Thompson	Y	Y	Y	N	N	Y
3 ***Pickering***	Y	Y	Y	Y	Y	N
4 Shows	Y	Y	Y	Y	N	Y
5 Taylor	Y	Y	N	N	N	N
MISSOURI						
1 Clay	Y	Y	Y	?	N	Y
2 ***Akin***	Y	Y	N	Y	Y	N
3 Gephardt	?	?	?	?	?	Y
4 Skelton	Y	Y	Y	Y	N	N
5 McCarthy	Y	Y	Y	Y	N	Y
6 ***Graves***	Y	Y	Y	Y	Y	N
7 ***Blunt***	Y	Y	Y	Y	Y	N
8 ***Emerson***	Y	Y	Y	Y	Y	N
9 ***Hulshof***	Y	Y	Y	Y	Y	N
MONTANA						
AL ***Rehberg***	Y	Y	Y	Y	Y	N
NEBRASKA						
1 ***Bereuter***	Y	Y	Y	Y	Y	N
2 ***Terry***	Y	Y	Y	Y	Y	N
3 ***Osborne***	Y	Y	Y	Y	Y	N
NEVADA						
1 Berkley	Y	Y	Y	Y	N	Y
2 ***Gibbons***	Y	Y	Y	Y	Y	N
NEW HAMPSHIRE						
1 ***Sununu***	Y	Y	N	Y	Y	N
2 ***Bass***	Y	Y	Y	Y	Y	N
NEW JERSEY						
1 Andrews	Y	Y	Y	Y	N	Y
2 ***LoBiondo***	Y	Y	Y	N	Y	N
3 ***Saxton***	Y	Y	Y	Y	Y	N
4 ***Smith***	Y	Y	Y	Y	Y	N
5 ***Roukema***	Y	Y	Y	Y	Y	N
6 Pallone	Y	Y	Y	Y	N	Y
7 ***Ferguson***	Y	Y	Y	Y	Y	N
8 Pascrell	Y	Y	Y	Y	N	Y
9 Rothman	Y	Y	Y	Y	N	Y
10 Payne	Y	Y	Y	Y	N	Y
11 ***Frelinghuysen***	Y	Y	N	Y	Y	N
12 Holt	Y	Y	Y	N	N	Y
13 Menendez	Y	Y	Y	Y	N	Y
NEW MEXICO						
1 ***Wilson***	Y	Y	Y	Y	Y	N
2 ***Skeen***	Y	Y	Y	Y	Y	N
3 Udall	Y	Y	Y	N	N	Y
NEW YORK						
1 ***Grucci***	Y	Y	Y	Y	Y	N
2 Israel	Y	Y	Y	Y	N	Y
3 ***King***	Y	Y	Y	Y	Y	N
4 McCarthy	Y	Y	Y	Y	Y	Y
5 Ackerman	?	?	?	Y	N	Y
6 Meeks	Y	Y	Y	Y	N	Y
7 Crowley	+	+	+	Y	N	Y
8 Nadler	Y	Y	Y	Y	N	Y
9 Weiner	Y	Y	Y	Y	N	Y
10 Towns	Y	Y	Y	Y	N	Y
11 Owens	Y	Y	Y	Y	N	Y
12 Velázquez	Y	Y	Y	Y	N	Y
13 ***Fossella***	+	+	+	?	Y	N
14 Maloney	Y	Y	Y	Y	Y	Y
15 Rangel	Y	Y	Y	Y	N	Y
16 Serrano	Y	Y	Y	Y	N	Y
17 Engel	Y	Y	Y	Y	N	Y
18 Lowey	Y	Y	Y	Y	N	Y
19 ***Kelly***	Y	Y	Y	N	Y	N
20 ***Gilman***	Y	Y	Y	Y	Y	N
21 McNulty	Y	Y	Y	Y	N	Y
22 ***Sweeney***	Y	Y	Y	Y	Y	N
23 ***Boehlert***	Y	Y	Y	Y	Y	N
24 ***McHugh***	Y	Y	Y	Y	Y	N
25 ***Walsh***	Y	Y	?	Y	Y	N
26 Hinchey	Y	Y	Y	?	N	Y
27 ***Reynolds***	Y	Y	Y	Y	Y	N
28 Slaughter	Y	Y	Y	?	N	Y
29 LaFalce	Y	Y	Y	Y	N	Y

	483	484	485	486	487	488
30 ***Quinn***	Y	Y	Y	Y	?	N
31 ***Houghton***	Y	Y	Y	Y	Y	N
NORTH CAROLINA						
1 Clayton	Y	Y	Y	Y	N	Y
2 Etheridge	Y	Y	Y	N	N	Y
3 ***Jones***	Y	Y	N	Y	Y	N
4 Price	Y	Y	Y	Y	N	Y
5 ***Burr***	Y	Y	Y	Y	?	N
6 ***Coble***	Y	Y	Y	Y	Y	N
7 McIntyre	Y	Y	Y	Y	N	Y
8 ***Hayes***	Y	Y	Y	Y	Y	N
9 ***Myrick***	Y	Y	N	Y	Y	N
10 ***Ballenger***	Y	Y	N	?	?	N
11 ***Taylor***	Y	Y	N	Y	Y	N
12 Watt	Y	Y	Y	Y	N	Y
NORTH DAKOTA						
AL Pomeroy	Y	Y	Y	Y	N	Y
OHIO						
1 ***Chabot***	Y	Y	N	Y	Y	N
2 ***Portman***	Y	Y	Y	Y	Y	N
3 Hall	Y	Y	Y	Y	N	Y
4 ***Oxley***	Y	Y	Y	Y	Y	N
5 ***Gillmor***	Y	Y	Y	Y	Y	N
6 Strickland	Y	Y	Y	N	N	Y
7 ***Hobson***	Y	Y	Y	Y	Y	N
8 ***Boehner***	Y	Y	Y	Y	Y	N
9 Kaptur	Y	Y	Y	Y	N	Y
10 Kucinich	Y	Y	Y	N	N	Y
11 Jones	Y	Y	Y	Y	N	Y
12 ***Tiberi***	?	?	?	Y	Y	N
13 Brown	Y	Y	Y	N	N	Y
14 Sawyer	Y	Y	Y	Y	N	Y
15 ***Pryce***	Y	Y	Y	Y	Y	N
16 ***Regula***	Y	Y	Y	Y	Y	N
17 Traficant	Y	Y	Y	Y	Y	N
18 ***Ney***	Y	Y	Y	Y	Y	N
19 ***LaTourette***	Y	Y	Y	Y	Y	N
OKLAHOMA						
1 ***Largent***	Y	Y	N	Y	Y	N
2 Carson	Y	Y	Y	Y	N	Y
3 ***Watkins***	Y	Y	Y	Y	Y	N
4 ***Watts***	Y	Y	Y	Y	Y	N
5 ***Istook***	Y	Y	Y	Y	N	N
6 ***Lucas***	Y	Y	Y	Y	Y	N
OREGON						
1 Wu	Y	Y	Y	Y	N	Y
2 ***Walden***	Y	Y	Y	Y	Y	N
3 Blumenauer	Y	Y	Y	Y	N	Y
4 DeFazio	Y	Y	Y	N	N	Y
5 Hooley	?	Y	Y	N	N	Y
PENNSYLVANIA						
1 Brady	Y	Y	Y	N	N	Y
2 Fattah	Y	Y	Y	Y	N	Y
3 Borski	Y	Y	Y	N	N	Y
4 ***Hart***	Y	Y	Y	Y	Y	N
5 ***Peterson***	Y	Y	Y	Y	Y	N
6 Holden	Y	Y	Y	Y	N	Y
7 ***Weldon***	Y	Y	Y	?	Y	N
8 ***Greenwood***	Y	Y	Y	Y	Y	N
9 ***Shuster, Bill***	Y	Y	Y	Y	Y	N
10 ***Sherwood***	Y	Y	Y	Y	Y	N
11 Kanjorski	Y	Y	Y	Y	N	Y
12 Murtha	Y	Y	Y	Y	Y	Y
13 Hoeffel	Y	Y	Y	Y	N	Y
14 Coyne	Y	Y	Y	?	N	Y
15 ***Toomey***	Y	Y	Y	Y	Y	N
16 ***Pitts***	Y	Y	N	Y	Y	N
17 ***Gekas***	Y	Y	Y	Y	Y	N
18 Doyle	Y	Y	Y	?	N	Y
19 ***Platts***	Y	Y	Y	Y	Y	N
20 Mascara	Y	Y	Y	Y	N	Y
21 ***English***	?	Y	Y	N	Y	N
RHODE ISLAND						
1 Kennedy	Y	Y	Y	Y	N	Y
2 Langevin	Y	Y	Y	Y	N	Y
SOUTH CAROLINA						
1 ***Brown***	Y	Y	Y	Y	Y	N
2 Vacant						
3 ***Graham***	Y	Y	Y	Y	Y	N
4 ***DeMint***	Y	Y	N	Y	Y	N
5 Spratt	Y	Y	Y	Y	N	Y
6 Clyburn	Y	Y	Y	Y	N	Y
SOUTH DAKOTA						
AL ***Thune***	Y	Y	Y	Y	Y	N

	483	484	485	486	487	488
TENNESSEE						
1 ***Jenkins***	Y	Y	Y	Y	Y	N
2 ***Duncan***	Y	Y	Y	Y	Y	N
3 ***Wamp***	?	?	?	Y	Y	N
4 ***Hilleary***	Y	Y	Y	Y	Y	N
5 Clement	Y	Y	Y	Y	N	Y
6 Gordon	Y	Y	Y	Y	N	Y
7 ***Bryant***	Y	Y	Y	Y	Y	N
8 Tanner	Y	Y	Y	Y	N	N
9 Ford	Y	Y	Y	Y	N	Y
TEXAS						
1 Sandlin	Y	Y	Y	Y	N	Y
2 Turner	Y	Y	Y	Y	N	Y
3 ***Johnson, Sam***	Y	Y	N	Y	Y	N
4 Hall	Y	Y	Y	Y	Y	N
5 ***Sessions***	?	?	?	?	Y	N
6 ***Barton***	?	?	?	Y	Y	N
7 ***Culberson***	?	?	?	?	?	N
8 ***Brady***	Y	Y	Y	Y	Y	N
9 Lampson	Y	Y	Y	Y	N	Y
10 Doggett	Y	Y	Y	Y	N	Y
11 Edwards	Y	Y	Y	Y	N	Y
12 ***Granger***	?	?	?	?	?	?
13 ***Thornberry***	Y	Y	Y	Y	Y	N
14 ***Paul***	Y	Y	N	Y	Y	N
15 Hinojosa	Y	Y	Y	Y	N	Y
16 Reyes	Y	Y	Y	Y	N	Y
17 Stenholm	Y	Y	N	N	N	N
18 Jackson-Lee	Y	Y	Y	Y	?	Y
19 ***Combest***	Y	Y	Y	Y	Y	N
20 Gonzalez	?	?	?	?	?	?
21 ***Smith***	Y	Y	Y	Y	?	N
22 ***DeLay***	Y	Y	N	Y	Y	N
23 ***Bonilla***	Y	Y	Y	Y	Y	N
24 Frost	Y	Y	Y	Y	N	Y
25 Bentsen	Y	Y	Y	Y	N	Y
26 ***Armey***	Y	Y	Y	Y	Y	N
27 Ortiz	Y	Y	Y	Y	N	Y
28 Rodriguez	Y	Y	Y	Y	N	Y
29 Green	Y	Y	Y	Y	N	Y
30 Johnson, E.B.	Y	Y	Y	Y	N	Y
UTAH						
1 ***Hansen***	Y	Y	Y	Y	Y	N
2 Matheson	Y	Y	Y	Y	N	Y
3 ***Cannon***	Y	Y	Y	Y	Y	N
VERMONT						
AL *Sanders*	Y	Y	Y	Y	N	Y
VIRGINIA						
1 ***Davis, Jo Ann***	Y	Y	Y	Y	Y	N
2 ***Schrock***	Y	Y	Y	Y	Y	N
3 Scott	Y	Y	Y	Y	N	Y
4 ***Forbes***	Y	Y	Y	Y	Y	N
5 *Goode*	Y	Y	Y	Y	Y	N
6 ***Goodlatte***	Y	Y	Y	Y	Y	N
7 ***Cantor***	Y	Y	Y	?	Y	N
8 Moran	Y	Y	Y	Y	N	Y
9 Boucher	Y	Y	Y	Y	N	Y
10 ***Wolf***	Y	Y	Y	Y	Y	N
11 ***Davis, T.***	Y	Y	Y	Y	Y	N
WASHINGTON						
1 Inslee	Y	Y	Y	Y	N	Y
2 Larsen	Y	Y	Y	N	N	Y
3 Baird	Y	Y	Y	N	N	N
4 ***Hastings***	Y	Y	Y	Y	Y	N
5 ***Nethercutt***	Y	Y	Y	Y	Y	N
6 Dicks	Y	Y	Y	Y	N	Y
7 McDermott	Y	Y	Y	N	N	Y
8 ***Dunn***	Y	Y	Y	Y	Y	N
9 Smith	Y	Y	Y	Y	N	N
WEST VIRGINIA						
1 Mollohan	Y	Y	Y	?	Y	N
2 ***Capito***	Y	Y	Y	Y	Y	N
3 Rahall	Y	Y	Y	Y	N	Y
WISCONSIN						
1 ***Ryan***	Y	Y	Y	Y	Y	N
2 Baldwin	Y	Y	Y	Y	N	Y
3 Kind	Y	Y	Y	Y	N	Y
4 Kleczka	Y	Y	Y	Y	N	Y
5 Barrett	Y	Y	Y	Y	N	Y
6 ***Petri***	Y	Y	Y	Y	Y	N
7 Obey	Y	Y	Y	?	N	Y
8 ***Green***	Y	Y	Y	Y	Y	N
9 ***Sensenbrenner***	Y	Y	N	Y	Y	N
WYOMING						
AL ***Cubin***	?	?	?	?	?	?

Southern states - Ala., Ark., Fla., Ga., Ky., La., Miss., N.C., Okla., S.C., Tenn., Texas, Va.

Key

Y	Voted for (yea).
#	Paired for.
+	Announced for.
N	Voted against (nay).
X	Paired against.
–	Announced against.
P	Voted "present."
C	Voted "present" to avoid possible conflict of interest.
?	Did not vote or otherwise make a position known.

Democrats   **Republicans**   *Independents*

489. HR 3295. Election Overhaul/Passage. Passage of the bill that would overhaul the nation's election procedures, including authorizing $400 million in one-time payments for states and counties to replace or upgrade punch card voting machines. The bill also would authorize $2.25 billion in federal funds to states over three years to improve the administration of elections, mandate minimum federal election standards and establish an Election Assistance Commission to serve as a clearinghouse for information and promulgate additional voluntary standards. Passed 362-63: R 196-20; D 165-42 (ND 122-32, SD 43-10); I 1-1. Dec. 12, 2001.

490. H Con Res 282. Social Security Support/Adoption. Shaw, R-Fla., motion to suspend the rules and adopt the concurrent resolution that would express the sense of Congress in support of the importance of strengthening Social Security and recommending that a presidential panel on the topic find novel ways to protect the program without raising taxes or reducing benefits. Motion agreed to 415-5: R 208-4; D 205-1 (ND 153-0, SD 52-1); I 2-0. A two-thirds majority of those present and voting (280 in this case) is required for adoption under suspension of the rules. Dec. 12, 2001.

491. HR 3209. Terrorist Hoaxes/Passage. Sensenbrenner, R-Wis., motion to suspend the rules and pass the bill that would make hoaxes involving biological agents, chemical weapons and weapons of mass destruction federal crimes if they set off an emergency response by a law enforcement agency. Violators would be subject to criminal and civil penalties, including repayment of response costs. Motion agreed to 423-0: R 214-0; D 207-0 (ND 154-0, SD 53-0); I 2-0. A two-thirds majority of those present and voting (282 in this case) is required for passage under suspension of the rules. Dec. 12, 2001.

492. HR 1022. Half-Staff Flags/Passage. Passage of the bill that would explicitly authorize top local government officials to order the lowering of the U.S. flag to half staff to honor the death of a local public servant or official. Passed 420-0: R 213-0; D 206-0 (ND 153-0, SD 53-0); I 1-0. A three-fifths majority of those present and voting (252 in this case) is required for passage on the corrections calendar. Dec. 12, 2001.

493. HR 3448. Bio-Terrorism Preparedness/Passage. Tauzin, R-La., motion to suspend the rules and pass the bill that would authorize federal, state and local governments to spend up to $2.9 billion in fiscal 2002, and additional amounts in future years, to prepare for and respond to acts of bio-terrorism. The total would include more than $1 billion for the Department of Health and Human Services to increase medicine and vaccine stockpiles, $450 million to expand facilities and labs run by the Centers for Disease Control and Prevention, and funds to safeguard the nation's food and water supplies. Motion agreed to 418-2: R 212-2; D 204-0 (ND 152-0, SD 52-0); I 2-0. A two-thirds majority of those present and voting (280 in this case) is required for passage under suspension of the rules. Dec. 12, 2001.

	489	490	491	492	493
ALABAMA					
1 *Callahan*	Y	Y	Y	Y	Y
2 *Everett*	Y	Y	Y	Y	Y
3 *Riley*	Y	Y	Y	Y	Y
4 *Aderholt*	Y	Y	Y	Y	Y
5 Cramer	Y	Y	Y	Y	Y
6 *Bachus*	Y	Y	Y	Y	Y
7 Hilliard	N	Y	Y	Y	Y
ALASKA					
AL *Young*	?	?	?	?	?
ARIZONA					
1 *Flake*	N	N	Y	Y	Y
2 Pastor	N	Y	Y	Y	Y
3 *Stump*	Y	Y	Y	Y	Y
4 *Shadegg*	N	Y	Y	Y	Y
5 *Kolbe*	Y	N	Y	Y	Y
6 *Hayworth*	Y	Y	Y	Y	Y
ARKANSAS					
1 Berry	Y	Y	Y	Y	Y
2 Snyder	Y	Y	Y	Y	Y
3 *Boozman*	Y	Y	Y	Y	Y
4 Ross	Y	Y	Y	Y	Y
CALIFORNIA					
1 Thompson	Y	Y	Y	Y	Y
2 *Herger*	Y	Y	Y	Y	Y
3 *Ose*	Y	Y	Y	Y	Y
4 *Doolittle*	Y	Y	Y	Y	Y
5 Matsui	Y	Y	Y	Y	Y
6 Woolsey	Y	Y	Y	Y	Y
7 Miller, George	Y	Y	Y	?	?
8 Pelosi	N	Y	Y	Y	Y
9 Lee	Y	Y	Y	Y	Y
10 Tauscher	Y	Y	Y	Y	Y
11 *Pombo*	N	Y	Y	Y	N
12 Lantos	Y	Y	Y	Y	Y
13 Stark	Y	Y	Y	Y	Y
14 Eshoo	Y	Y	Y	Y	Y
15 Honda	Y	Y	Y	Y	Y
16 Lofgren	Y	Y	Y	Y	Y
17 Farr	Y	Y	Y	Y	Y
18 Condit	Y	Y	Y	Y	Y
19 *Radanovich*	Y	N	Y	Y	Y
20 Dooley	?	?	?	?	?
21 *Thomas*	Y	Y	Y	Y	Y
22 Capps	Y	Y	Y	Y	Y
23 *Gallegly*	Y	Y	Y	Y	Y
24 Sherman	Y	Y	Y	Y	Y
25 *McKeon*	Y	Y	Y	Y	Y
26 Berman	Y	Y	Y	Y	Y
27 Schiff	Y	Y	Y	Y	Y
28 *Dreier*	Y	Y	Y	Y	Y
29 Waxman	Y	Y	Y	Y	Y
30 Becerra	N	Y	Y	Y	Y
31 Solis	N	Y	Y	Y	Y
32 Watson	Y	Y	Y	Y	Y
33 Roybal-Allard	N	Y	Y	Y	Y
34 Napolitano	N	Y	Y	Y	Y
35 Waters	N	Y	Y	Y	Y
36 Harman	Y	Y	Y	Y	Y
37 Millender-McD.	Y	Y	Y	Y	Y
38 *Horn*	Y	Y	Y	Y	Y

	489	490	491	492	493
39 *Royce*	Y	Y	Y	Y	Y
40 *Lewis*	Y	Y	Y	Y	Y
41 *Miller, Gary*	Y	Y	Y	Y	Y
42 Baca	Y	Y	Y	Y	Y
43 *Calvert*	Y	?	Y	Y	Y
44 *Bono*	Y	Y	Y	Y	Y
45 *Rohrabacher*	N	Y	Y	Y	Y
46 Sanchez	N	Y	Y	Y	Y
47 *Cox*	Y	Y	Y	Y	Y
48 *Issa*	Y	Y	Y	Y	Y
49 Davis	Y	Y	Y	Y	Y
50 Filner	Y	Y	Y	Y	Y
51 *Cunningham*	Y	Y	Y	Y	Y
52 *Hunter*	Y	Y	Y	Y	Y
COLORADO					
1 DeGette	Y	Y	Y	Y	Y
2 Udall	Y	Y	Y	Y	Y
3 *McInnis*	Y	Y	Y	Y	Y
4 *Schaffer*	N	Y	Y	Y	Y
5 *Hefley*	N	Y	Y	Y	Y
6 *Tancredo*	Y	Y	Y	Y	Y
CONNECTICUT					
1 Larson	Y	Y	Y	Y	Y
2 *Simmons*	Y	Y	Y	Y	Y
3 DeLauro	Y	Y	Y	Y	Y
4 *Shays*	Y	Y	Y	Y	Y
5 Maloney	Y	Y	Y	Y	Y
6 *Johnson*	Y	Y	Y	Y	Y
DELAWARE					
AL *Castle*	Y	Y	Y	Y	Y
FLORIDA					
1 *Miller, J.*	Y	Y	Y	Y	Y
2 Boyd	Y	Y	Y	Y	Y
3 Brown	Y	Y	Y	Y	Y
4 *Crenshaw*	Y	Y	Y	Y	Y
5 Thurman	Y	Y	Y	Y	Y
6 *Stearns*	Y	Y	Y	Y	Y
7 *Mica*	Y	Y	Y	Y	Y
8 *Keller*	Y	Y	Y	Y	Y
9 *Bilirakis*	Y	Y	Y	Y	Y
10 *Young*	Y	Y	Y	Y	Y
11 Davis	Y	Y	Y	Y	Y
12 *Putnam*	N	Y	Y	Y	Y
13 *Miller, D.*	Y	Y	Y	Y	Y
14 *Goss*	Y	Y	Y	Y	Y
15 *Weldon*	Y	Y	Y	Y	Y
16 *Foley*	Y	Y	Y	Y	Y
17 Meek	Y	Y	Y	Y	Y
18 *Ros-Lehtinen*	Y	Y	Y	Y	Y
19 Wexler	Y	Y	Y	Y	Y
20 Deutsch	Y	Y	Y	Y	Y
21 *Diaz-Balart*	Y	Y	Y	Y	Y
22 *Shaw*	Y	Y	Y	Y	Y
23 Hastings	Y	Y	Y	Y	Y
GEORGIA					
1 *Kingston*	N	Y	Y	Y	Y
2 Bishop	Y	Y	Y	Y	?
3 *Collins*	Y	Y	Y	Y	Y
4 McKinney	N	Y	Y	Y	Y
5 Lewis	Y	Y	Y	Y	Y
6 *Isakson*	Y	Y	Y	Y	Y
7 *Barr*	N	Y	Y	Y	Y
8 *Chambliss*	Y	Y	Y	Y	Y
9 *Deal*	Y	Y	Y	Y	Y
10 *Norwood*	Y	Y	Y	Y	Y
11 *Linder*	Y	Y	Y	Y	Y
HAWAII					
1 Abercrombie	Y	Y	Y	Y	Y
2 Mink	Y	Y	Y	Y	Y
IDAHO					
1 *Otter*	Y	Y	Y	Y	Y
2 *Simpson*	Y	Y	Y	Y	Y
ILLINOIS					
1 Rush	N	Y	Y	Y	Y
2 Jackson	N	Y	Y	Y	Y
3 Lipinski	Y	Y	Y	Y	Y
4 Gutierrez	N	Y	Y	Y	Y
5 Blagojevich	N	Y	Y	Y	Y
6 *Hyde*	Y	Y	Y	Y	Y
7 Davis	N	Y	Y	Y	Y
8 *Crane*	Y	Y	Y	Y	Y
9 Schakowsky	Y	Y	Y	Y	Y
10 *Kirk*	Y	Y	Y	Y	Y
11 *Weller*	Y	Y	Y	Y	Y
12 Costello	Y	Y	Y	Y	Y
13 *Biggert*	Y	Y	Y	Y	Y

ND Northern Democrats   SD Southern Democrats

	489	490	491	492	493
14 Hastert	Y				
15 Johnson	Y	Y	Y	Y	Y
16 Manzullo	Y	Y	Y	Y	Y
17 Evans	Y	Y	Y	Y	Y
18 LaHood	Y	Y	Y	Y	Y
19 Phelps	Y	Y	Y	Y	Y
20 Shimkus	Y	Y	Y	Y	Y
INDIANA					
1 Visclosky	Y	Y	Y	Y	Y
2 Pence	Y	Y	Y	Y	Y
3 Roemer	Y	Y	Y	Y	Y
4 Souder	Y	Y	Y	Y	Y
5 Buyer	?	?	?	?	?
6 Burton	Y	Y	Y	Y	Y
7 Kerns	Y	Y	Y	Y	Y
8 Hostettler	?	?	?	?	?
9 Hill	Y	Y	Y	Y	Y
10 Carson	Y	Y	Y	Y	Y
IOWA					
1 Leach	Y	Y	Y	Y	Y
2 Nussle	Y	Y	Y	Y	Y
3 Boswell	Y	Y	Y	Y	Y
4 Ganske	Y	Y	Y	Y	Y
5 Latham	Y	Y	Y	Y	Y
KANSAS					
1 Moran	Y	Y	Y	Y	Y
2 Ryun	Y	Y	Y	Y	Y
3 Moore	Y	Y	Y	Y	Y
4 Tiahrt	Y	Y	Y	Y	Y
KENTUCKY					
1 Whitfield	Y	Y	Y	Y	Y
2 Lewis	Y	Y	Y	Y	Y
3 Northup	Y	Y	Y	Y	Y
4 Lucas	Y	Y	Y	Y	Y
5 Rogers	Y	Y	Y	Y	Y
6 Fletcher	Y	Y	Y	Y	Y
LOUISIANA					
1 Vitter	Y	Y	Y	Y	Y
2 Jefferson	Y	Y	Y	Y	Y
3 Tauzin	Y	Y	Y	Y	Y
4 McCrery	Y	Y	Y	Y	Y
5 Cooksey	Y	Y	Y	Y	Y
6 Baker	Y	Y	Y	Y	Y
7 John	Y	Y	Y	Y	Y
MAINE					
1 Allen	Y	Y	Y	Y	Y
2 Baldacci	Y	Y	Y	Y	Y
MARYLAND					
1 Gilchrest	Y	Y	Y	Y	Y
2 Ehrlich	Y	Y	Y	Y	Y
3 Cardin	Y	Y	Y	Y	Y
4 Wynn	Y	Y	Y	Y	Y
5 Hoyer	Y	Y	Y	Y	Y
6 Bartlett	Y	Y	Y	Y	Y
7 Cummings	Y	Y	Y	Y	?
8 Morella	Y	Y	Y	Y	Y
MASSACHUSETTS					
1 Olver	N	Y	Y	Y	Y
2 Neal	Y	Y	Y	Y	Y
3 McGovern	N	Y	Y	Y	Y
4 Frank	N	Y	Y	Y	Y
5 Meehan	N	Y	Y	Y	Y
6 Tierney	Y	Y	Y	Y	Y
7 Markey	Y	Y	Y	Y	Y
8 Capuano	N	Y	Y	Y	Y
9 Lynch	Y	Y	Y	Y	Y
10 Delahunt	?	?	?	?	?
MICHIGAN					
1 Stupak	Y	Y	Y	Y	Y
2 Hoekstra	Y	Y	Y	Y	Y
3 Ehlers	Y	Y	Y	Y	Y
4 Camp	Y	Y	Y	Y	Y
5 Barcia	Y	Y	Y	Y	Y
6 Upton	Y	Y	Y	Y	Y
7 Smith	N	N	Y	Y	Y
8 Rogers	Y	Y	Y	Y	Y
9 Kildee	Y	Y	Y	Y	Y
10 Bonior	N	Y	Y	Y	Y
11 Knollenberg	Y	Y	Y	Y	Y
12 Levin	Y	Y	Y	Y	Y
13 Rivers	Y	Y	Y	Y	Y
14 Conyers	N	Y	Y	Y	Y
15 Kilpatrick	N	Y	Y	Y	Y
16 Dingell	Y	Y	Y	Y	Y

	489	490	491	492	493
MINNESOTA					
1 Gutknecht	Y	Y	Y	Y	Y
2 Kennedy	Y	Y	Y	Y	Y
3 Ramstad	Y	Y	Y	Y	Y
4 McCollum	Y	Y	Y	Y	Y
5 Sabo	Y	Y	Y	Y	Y
6 Luther	?	?	?	?	?
7 Peterson	Y	Y	Y	Y	Y
8 Oberstar	Y	Y	Y	Y	Y
MISSISSIPPI					
1 Wicker	Y	Y	Y	Y	Y
2 Thompson	Y	Y	Y	Y	Y
3 Pickering	Y	Y	Y	Y	Y
4 Shows	N	Y	Y	Y	Y
5 Taylor	Y	Y	Y	Y	Y
MISSOURI					
1 Clay	Y	Y	Y	Y	Y
2 Akin	Y	Y	Y	Y	Y
3 Gephardt	Y	Y	Y	Y	Y
4 Skelton	Y	Y	Y	Y	Y
5 McCarthy	Y	Y	Y	Y	Y
6 Graves	Y	Y	Y	Y	Y
7 Blunt	Y	Y	Y	Y	Y
8 Emerson	Y	Y	Y	Y	Y
9 Hulshof	Y	Y	Y	Y	Y
MONTANA					
AL Rehberg	Y	Y	Y	Y	Y
NEBRASKA					
1 Bereuter	Y	Y	Y	Y	Y
2 Terry	Y	Y	Y	Y	Y
3 Osborne	Y	Y	Y	Y	Y
NEVADA					
1 Berkley	Y	Y	Y	Y	Y
2 Gibbons	Y	Y	Y	Y	Y
NEW HAMPSHIRE					
1 Sununu	Y	Y	Y	Y	Y
2 Bass	Y	?	Y	Y	Y
NEW JERSEY					
1 Andrews	Y	Y	Y	Y	Y
2 LoBiondo	Y	Y	Y	Y	Y
3 Saxton	Y	Y	Y	Y	Y
4 Smith	Y	Y	Y	Y	Y
5 Roukema	Y	Y	Y	Y	Y
6 Pallone	Y	Y	Y	Y	Y
7 Ferguson	Y	Y	Y	Y	Y
8 Pascrell	Y	Y	Y	Y	Y
9 Rothman	Y	Y	Y	Y	Y
10 Payne	N	Y	Y	Y	Y
11 Frelinghuysen	Y	Y	Y	Y	Y
12 Holt	Y	Y	Y	Y	Y
13 Menendez	Y	Y	Y	Y	Y
NEW MEXICO					
1 Wilson	Y	Y	Y	Y	Y
2 Skeen	Y	Y	Y	Y	Y
3 Udall	Y	Y	Y	Y	Y
NEW YORK					
1 Grucci	Y	Y	Y	Y	Y
2 Israel	Y	Y	Y	Y	Y
3 King	Y	Y	Y	Y	Y
4 McCarthy	Y	Y	Y	Y	Y
5 Ackerman	Y	Y	Y	Y	Y
6 Meeks	Y	Y	Y	Y	Y
7 Crowley	Y	Y	Y	Y	Y
8 Nadler	Y	Y	Y	Y	Y
9 Weiner	Y	Y	Y	Y	Y
10 Towns	Y	Y	Y	Y	Y
11 Owens	Y	Y	Y	Y	Y
12 Velázquez	Y	Y	Y	Y	Y
13 Fossella	Y	Y	Y	Y	Y
14 Maloney	Y	Y	Y	Y	Y
15 Rangel	Y	Y	Y	Y	Y
16 Serrano	Y	Y	Y	Y	Y
17 Engel	Y	Y	Y	Y	Y
18 Lowey	Y	Y	Y	Y	Y
19 Kelly	Y	Y	Y	Y	Y
20 Gilman	Y	Y	Y	Y	Y
21 McNulty	Y	Y	Y	Y	Y
22 Sweeney	Y	Y	Y	Y	Y
23 Boehlert	Y	Y	Y	Y	Y
24 McHugh	Y	Y	Y	Y	Y
25 Walsh	Y	Y	Y	Y	Y
26 Hinchey	N	Y	Y	Y	Y
27 Reynolds	Y	Y	Y	Y	Y
28 Slaughter	Y	Y	Y	Y	Y
29 LaFalce	Y	Y	Y	Y	Y

	489	490	491	492	493
30 Quinn	Y	Y	Y	Y	Y
31 Houghton	Y	Y	Y	Y	Y
NORTH CAROLINA					
1 Clayton	N	Y	Y	Y	Y
2 Etheridge	N	Y	Y	Y	Y
3 Jones	N	Y	Y	Y	Y
4 Price	Y	Y	Y	Y	Y
5 Burr	Y	Y	Y	Y	Y
6 Coble	N	Y	Y	Y	Y
7 McIntyre	Y	Y	Y	Y	Y
8 Hayes	Y	Y	Y	Y	Y
9 Myrick	Y	Y	Y	Y	Y
10 Ballenger	Y	Y	Y	Y	Y
11 Taylor	Y	Y	Y	Y	Y
12 Watt	N	Y	Y	Y	Y
NORTH DAKOTA					
AL Pomeroy	Y	Y	Y	Y	Y
OHIO					
1 Chabot	Y	Y	Y	Y	Y
2 Portman	Y	Y	Y	Y	Y
3 Hall	Y	Y	Y	Y	Y
4 Oxley	Y	Y	Y	Y	Y
5 Gillmor	Y	Y	Y	Y	Y
6 Strickland	Y	Y	Y	Y	Y
7 Hobson	Y	Y	Y	Y	Y
8 Boehner	Y	?	?	?	?
9 Kaptur	Y	Y	Y	Y	Y
10 Kucinich	N	Y	Y	Y	Y
11 Jones	N	Y	Y	Y	Y
12 Tiberi	Y	Y	Y	Y	Y
13 Brown	N	Y	Y	Y	Y
14 Sawyer	Y	Y	Y	Y	Y
15 Pryce	Y	Y	Y	Y	Y
16 Regula	Y	Y	Y	Y	Y
17 Traficant	Y	Y	Y	Y	Y
18 Ney	Y	Y	Y	Y	Y
19 LaTourette	Y	Y	Y	Y	Y
OKLAHOMA					
1 Largent	Y	Y	Y	Y	Y
2 Carson	Y	Y	Y	Y	Y
3 Watkins	Y	Y	Y	Y	Y
4 Watts	Y	Y	Y	Y	Y
5 Istook	Y	Y	Y	Y	Y
6 Lucas	Y	Y	Y	Y	Y
OREGON					
1 Wu	Y	Y	Y	Y	Y
2 Walden	Y	Y	Y	Y	Y
3 Blumenauer	Y	Y	Y	Y	Y
4 DeFazio	Y	Y	Y	Y	Y
5 Hooley	Y	Y	Y	Y	Y
PENNSYLVANIA					
1 Brady	Y	Y	Y	Y	Y
2 Fattah	Y	?	Y	Y	Y
3 Borski	Y	Y	Y	Y	Y
4 Hart	Y	Y	Y	Y	Y
5 Peterson	Y	Y	Y	Y	Y
6 Holden	Y	Y	Y	Y	Y
7 Weldon	Y	Y	Y	Y	Y
8 Greenwood	Y	Y	Y	Y	Y
9 Shuster, Bill	Y	Y	Y	Y	Y
10 Sherwood	Y	Y	Y	Y	Y
11 Kanjorski	Y	Y	Y	Y	Y
12 Murtha	N	Y	Y	Y	Y
13 Hoeffel	Y	Y	Y	Y	Y
14 Coyne	Y	Y	Y	Y	Y
15 Toomey	N	Y	Y	Y	Y
16 Pitts	Y	Y	Y	Y	Y
17 Gekas	Y	Y	Y	Y	Y
18 Doyle	Y	Y	Y	Y	Y
19 Platts	Y	Y	Y	Y	Y
20 Mascara	Y	Y	Y	Y	Y
21 English	Y	Y	Y	Y	Y
RHODE ISLAND					
1 Kennedy	Y	Y	Y	Y	Y
2 Langevin	Y	Y	Y	Y	Y
SOUTH CAROLINA					
1 Brown	Y	Y	Y	Y	Y
2 Vacant					
3 Graham	Y	Y	Y	Y	Y
4 DeMint	Y	Y	Y	Y	Y
5 Spratt	Y	Y	Y	Y	Y
6 Clyburn	Y	Y	Y	Y	Y
SOUTH DAKOTA					
AL Thune	Y	Y	Y	Y	Y

	489	490	491	492	493
TENNESSEE					
1 Jenkins	Y	Y	Y	Y	Y
2 Duncan	Y	Y	Y	Y	Y
3 Wamp	Y	Y	Y	Y	Y
4 Hilleary	Y	Y	Y	?	Y
5 Clement	Y	Y	Y	Y	Y
6 Gordon	Y	Y	Y	Y	Y
7 Bryant	Y	Y	Y	Y	Y
8 Tanner	Y	Y	Y	Y	Y
9 Ford	Y	Y	Y	Y	Y
TEXAS					
1 Sandlin	Y	Y	Y	Y	Y
2 Turner	Y	Y	Y	Y	Y
3 Johnson, Sam	Y	Y	Y	Y	Y
4 Hall	Y	Y	Y	Y	Y
5 Sessions	N	Y	Y	Y	Y
6 Barton	N	Y	Y	Y	Y
7 Culberson	N	Y	Y	Y	Y
8 Brady	Y	Y	Y	Y	Y
9 Lampson	Y	Y	Y	Y	Y
10 Doggett	N	Y	Y	Y	Y
11 Edwards	Y	Y	Y	Y	Y
12 Granger	?	?	?	?	?
13 Thornberry	Y	Y	Y	Y	Y
14 Paul	N	Y	Y	Y	N
15 Hinojosa	Y	Y	Y	Y	Y
16 Reyes	N	Y	Y	Y	Y
17 Stenholm	Y	N	Y	Y	Y
18 Jackson-Lee	N	Y	Y	Y	Y
19 Combest	Y	Y	Y	Y	Y
20 Gonzalez	?	?	?	?	?
21 Smith	Y	Y	Y	Y	Y
22 DeLay	Y	Y	Y	Y	Y
23 Bonilla	N	Y	Y	Y	Y
24 Frost	Y	Y	Y	Y	Y
25 Bentsen	Y	Y	Y	Y	Y
26 Armey	Y	Y	Y	Y	Y
27 Ortiz	Y	Y	Y	Y	Y
28 Rodriguez	N	Y	Y	Y	Y
29 Green	Y	Y	Y	Y	Y
30 Johnson, E.B.	Y	Y	Y	Y	Y
UTAH					
1 Hansen	Y	Y	Y	Y	Y
2 Matheson	Y	Y	Y	Y	Y
3 Cannon	Y	Y	Y	Y	Y
VERMONT					
AL Sanders	Y	Y	Y	?	Y
VIRGINIA					
1 Davis, Jo Ann	Y	Y	Y	Y	Y
2 Schrock	Y	Y	Y	Y	Y
3 Scott	N	Y	Y	Y	Y
4 Forbes	Y	Y	Y	Y	Y
5 Goode	N	Y	Y	Y	Y
6 Goodlatte	Y	Y	Y	Y	Y
7 Cantor	Y	Y	Y	Y	Y
8 Moran	Y	Y	Y	Y	Y
9 Boucher	Y	Y	Y	Y	Y
10 Wolf	Y	Y	Y	Y	Y
11 Davis, T.	Y	Y	Y	Y	Y
WASHINGTON					
1 Inslee	Y	Y	Y	Y	Y
2 Larsen	Y	Y	Y	Y	Y
3 Baird	Y	Y	Y	Y	Y
4 Hastings	Y	Y	Y	Y	Y
5 Nethercutt	Y	Y	Y	Y	Y
6 Dicks	Y	Y	Y	Y	Y
7 McDermott	N	Y	Y	Y	Y
8 Dunn	Y	Y	Y	Y	Y
9 Smith	Y	Y	Y	Y	Y
WEST VIRGINIA					
1 Mollohan	N	Y	Y	Y	Y
2 Capito	Y	Y	Y	Y	Y
3 Rahall	N	Y	Y	Y	Y
WISCONSIN					
1 Ryan	Y	Y	Y	Y	Y
2 Baldwin	N	Y	Y	Y	Y
3 Kind	Y	Y	Y	Y	Y
4 Kleczka	Y	Y	Y	Y	Y
5 Barrett	Y	Y	Y	Y	Y
6 Petri	N	Y	Y	Y	Y
7 Obey	Y	Y	Y	Y	Y
8 Green	Y	Y	Y	Y	Y
9 Sensenbrenner	N	Y	Y	Y	Y
WYOMING					
AL Cubin	?	?	?	?	?

Southern states - Ala., Ark., Fla., Ga., Ky., La., Miss., N.C., Okla., S.C., Tenn., Texas, Va.

Key

Y	Voted for (yea).
#	Paired for.
+	Announced for.
N	Voted against (nay).
X	Paired against.
−	Announced against.
P	Voted "present."
C	Voted "present" to avoid possible conflict of interest.
?	Did not vote or otherwise make a position known.

Democrats **Republicans**
Independents

494. HR 3338. Fiscal 2002 Defense Appropriations/Motion to Instruct. Obey, D-Wis., motion to instruct House conferees to insist on the highest funding levels within the conference's scope for defense, homeland security, and recovery efforts after the Sept. 11 terror attacks. It would include pushing for the president's full emergency defense spending request of $7.3 billion and insisting upon the Senate's increased funding levels for border security, law enforcement, food and nuclear safety, and disaster relief payments. It also would call for insisting upon the highest level for transportation security. Motion agreed to 370-44: R 171-42; D 198-1 (ND 148-1, SD 50-0); I 1-1. Dec. 12, 2001.

495. HR 3338. Fiscal 2002 Defense Appropriations/Closed Conference. Lewis, R-Calif., motion to close portions of the conference to the public during consideration of national security issues. Motion agreed to 407-0: R 212-0; D 193-0 (ND 144-0, SD 49-0); I 2-0. Dec. 12, 2001.

496. S 1438. Fiscal 2002 Defense Authorization/Conference Report. Adoption of the conference report on the bill that would authorize $343 billion for defense programs, 10 percent more than the current level. It would authorize $125 billion for operations and maintenance, $82.3 billion for military personnel, $62 billion for weapons procurement, $47.8 billion for research and development, $14.4 billion for the Energy Department, and $10.5 billion for military construction and family housing. The bill also would authorize $8.3 billion for national missile defense programs and allow an additional round of base realignment and closures in 2005. Adopted (thus sent to the Senate) 382-40: R 209-6; D 171-34 (ND 122-31, SD 49-3); I 2-0. Dec. 13, 2001.

497. HR 1. ESEA Reauthorization/Conference Report. Adoption of the conference report on the bill that would overhaul education proposals to increase school accountability and reauthorize the Elementary and Secondary Education Act for six years. The agreement would require states to annually test students in reading and math in grades three through eight, provide new accountability measures for schools that fail to make adequate yearly progress, and give schools greater flexibility to spend federal funds. It would include about $26.3 billion for federal elementary and secondary education programs and $13.5 billion for Title I programs for disadvantaged children in fiscal 2002. Adopted (thus sent to the Senate) 381-41: R 183-33; D 198-6 (ND 146-6, SD 52-0); I 0-2. A "yea" was a vote in support of the president's position. Dec. 13, 2001.

498. H Res 314. Suspension Motions/Rule. Adoption of the rule (H Res 314) to provide for House floor consideration of bills under suspension of the rules on Wednesday, Dec. 19. Adopted 306-100: R 205-1; D 99-99 (ND 66-80, SD 33-19); I 2-0. Dec. 13, 2001.

	494	495	496	497	498
ALABAMA					
1 *Callahan*	Y	Y	Y	Y	Y
2 *Everett*	Y	Y	Y	Y	Y
3 *Riley*	Y	Y	Y	Y	Y
4 *Aderholt*	Y	Y	Y	Y	Y
5 Cramer	Y	Y	Y	Y	Y
6 *Bachus*	Y	Y	Y	Y	Y
7 Hilliard	Y	Y	Y	Y	N
ALASKA					
AL *Young*	?	?	?	?	?
ARIZONA					
1 *Flake*	N	Y	Y	N	Y
2 Pastor	Y	Y	Y	Y	Y
3 *Stump*	Y	Y	Y	Y	Y
4 *Shadegg*	N	Y	Y	N	Y
5 *Kolbe*	Y	Y	Y	Y	Y
6 *Hayworth*	Y	Y	Y	Y	Y
ARKANSAS					
1 Berry	Y	Y	Y	Y	Y
2 Snyder	Y	Y	Y	Y	N
3 *Boozman*	Y	Y	Y	Y	Y
4 Ross	Y	Y	Y	Y	Y
CALIFORNIA					
1 Thompson	Y	Y	Y	Y	Y
2 *Herger*	Y	Y	Y	Y	Y
3 *Ose*	Y	Y	Y	Y	Y
4 *Doolittle*	N	Y	Y	Y	Y
5 Matsui	Y	Y	Y	Y	N
6 Woolsey	Y	Y	N	Y	N
7 Miller, George	?	?	N	Y	N
8 Pelosi	Y	Y	Y	Y	N
9 Lee	Y	Y	N	Y	N
10 Tauscher	Y	Y	Y	Y	N
11 *Pombo*	N	Y	Y	Y	Y
12 Lantos	Y	Y	Y	Y	?
13 Stark	Y	Y	N	Y	N
14 Eshoo	Y	Y	Y	Y	N
15 Honda	Y	Y	Y	Y	N
16 Lofgren	Y	Y	Y	Y	N
17 Farr	Y	Y	Y	Y	N
18 Condit	Y	Y	Y	Y	N
19 *Radanovich*	Y	Y	Y	Y	Y
20 Dooley	?	?	Y	Y	Y
21 *Thomas*	Y	Y	Y	Y	N
22 Capps	Y	Y	Y	Y	N
23 *Gallegly*	Y	Y	Y	Y	?
24 Sherman	Y	Y	Y	Y	N
25 *McKeon*	Y	Y	Y	Y	Y
26 Berman	Y	Y	Y	Y	Y
27 Schiff	Y	Y	Y	Y	N
28 *Dreier*	Y	Y	Y	Y	Y
29 Waxman	Y	Y	Y	Y	N
30 Becerra	Y	Y	Y	Y	N
31 Solis	Y	Y	Y	Y	N
32 Watson	Y	Y	Y	Y	N
33 Roybal-Allard	Y	Y	Y	Y	N
34 Napolitano	Y	Y	Y	Y	N
35 Waters	Y	Y	Y	?	?
36 Harman	Y	Y	Y	Y	N
37 Millender-McD.	Y	Y	Y	Y	N
38 *Horn*	Y	Y	Y	Y	Y

	494	495	496	497	498
39 *Royce*	N	Y	Y	Y	Y
40 *Lewis*	Y	Y	Y	Y	Y
41 *Miller, Gary*	Y	Y	Y	Y	Y
42 Baca	Y	Y	Y	Y	N
43 *Calvert*	Y	Y	Y	Y	Y
44 *Bono*	Y	Y	Y	Y	Y
45 *Rohrabacher*	N	Y	Y	N	Y
46 Sanchez	Y	Y	Y	Y	?
47 *Cox*	Y	Y	Y	Y	Y
48 *Issa*	Y	Y	Y	Y	Y
49 Davis	Y	Y	Y	Y	N
50 Filner	Y	Y	N	N	N
51 *Cunningham*	Y	Y	Y	Y	Y
52 *Hunter*	Y	Y	Y	Y	Y
COLORADO					
1 DeGette	Y	Y	Y	Y	N
2 Udall	Y	Y	Y	Y	N
3 *McInnis*	Y	Y	Y	Y	Y
4 *Schaffer*	N	Y	Y	N	Y
5 *Hefley*	Y	Y	Y	N	N
6 *Tancredo*	N	Y	Y	N	Y
CONNECTICUT					
1 Larson	Y	Y	?	?	?
2 *Simmons*	Y	Y	Y	Y	Y
3 DeLauro	Y	Y	Y	Y	N
4 *Shays*	Y	Y	Y	Y	Y
5 Maloney	Y	Y	Y	Y	Y
6 *Johnson*	Y	Y	Y	Y	Y
DELAWARE					
AL *Castle*	Y	Y	Y	Y	Y
FLORIDA					
1 *Miller, J.*	Y	Y	N	Y	Y
2 Boyd	Y	Y	N	Y	Y
3 Brown	Y	Y	Y	Y	N
4 *Crenshaw*	Y	Y	Y	Y	Y
5 Thurman	Y	Y	Y	Y	Y
6 *Stearns*	N	Y	N	Y	Y
7 *Mica*	Y	Y	Y	Y	Y
8 *Keller*	Y	Y	Y	Y	Y
9 *Bilirakis*	Y	Y	Y	Y	Y
10 *Young*	Y	Y	Y	Y	Y
11 Davis	Y	?	Y	Y	Y
12 *Putnam*	Y	Y	Y	Y	Y
13 *Miller, D.*	Y	Y	Y	Y	Y
14 *Goss*	Y	Y	Y	Y	Y
15 *Weldon*	Y	Y	Y	N	Y
16 *Foley*	Y	Y	Y	Y	Y
17 Meek	?	?	?	?	?
18 *Ros-Lehtinen*	Y	Y	Y	?	?
19 Wexler	?	?	Y	Y	N
20 Deutsch	Y	Y	Y	Y	Y
21 *Diaz-Balart*	Y	Y	Y	Y	?
22 *Shaw*	Y	Y	Y	Y	Y
23 Hastings	Y	Y	Y	Y	N
GEORGIA					
1 *Kingston*	Y	Y	Y	Y	Y
2 Bishop	?	?	Y	Y	Y
3 *Collins*	N	Y	Y	Y	Y
4 McKinney	Y	Y	N	Y	N
5 Lewis	Y	Y	N	Y	N
6 *Isakson*	Y	Y	Y	Y	Y
7 *Barr*	Y	Y	Y	Y	Y
8 *Chambliss*	Y	Y	Y	Y	Y
9 *Deal*	N	Y	Y	Y	Y
10 *Norwood*	Y	Y	Y	Y	Y
11 *Linder*	Y	Y	Y	Y	Y
HAWAII					
1 Abercrombie	Y	Y	Y	Y	Y
2 Mink	Y	Y	Y	Y	N
IDAHO					
1 *Otter*	N	Y	Y	Y	Y
2 *Simpson*	N	Y	Y	Y	Y
ILLINOIS					
1 Rush	Y	Y	Y	Y	Y
2 Jackson	Y	Y	N	Y	Y
3 Lipinski	Y	Y	Y	Y	Y
4 Gutierrez	Y	Y	Y	Y	N
5 Blagojevich	Y	Y	Y	Y	Y
6 *Hyde*	Y	?	Y	Y	?
7 Davis	Y	Y	Y	Y	N
8 *Crane*	Y	Y	N	Y	Y
9 Schakowsky	?	?	N	Y	N
10 *Kirk*	Y	Y	Y	Y	Y
11 *Weller*	Y	Y	Y	Y	Y
12 Costello	Y	Y	Y	Y	Y
13 *Biggert*	Y	Y	Y	Y	Y

ND Northern Democrats   SD Southern Democrats

	494	495	496	497	498
14 ***Hastert***				Y	
15 ***Johnson***	Y	Y	Y	Y	Y
16 ***Manzullo***	Y	Y	Y	N	Y
17 Evans	Y	?	Y	Y	Y
18 ***LaHood***	Y	Y	Y	Y	Y
19 Phelps	Y	Y	Y	Y	Y
20 ***Shimkus***	Y	Y	Y	Y	Y
INDIANA					
1 Visclosky	Y	Y	Y	Y	N
2 ***Pence***	?	?	Y	N	Y
3 Roemer	Y	Y	Y	Y	Y
4 ***Souder***	Y	Y	Y	Y	Y
5 ***Buyer***	?	?	Y	Y	Y
6 ***Burton***	Y	Y	Y	N	Y
7 ***Kerns***	N	Y	Y	N	Y
8 ***Hostettler***	?	?	?	?	?
9 Hill	Y	Y	Y	Y	N
10 Carson	Y	Y	Y	Y	N
IOWA					
1 ***Leach***	Y	Y	Y	Y	Y
2 ***Nussle***	N	Y	Y	Y	Y
3 Boswell	Y	Y	Y	Y	Y
4 ***Ganske***	Y	Y	Y	Y	Y
5 ***Latham***	Y	Y	Y	Y	Y
KANSAS					
1 ***Moran***	N	Y	Y	N	Y
2 ***Ryun***	N	Y	Y	N	Y
3 Moore	Y	Y	Y	Y	N
4 ***Tiahrt***	Y	Y	Y	N	Y
KENTUCKY					
1 ***Whitfield***	Y	Y	Y	Y	Y
2 ***Lewis***	Y	Y	Y	N	Y
3 ***Northup***	Y	Y	Y	Y	Y
4 Lucas	Y	Y	Y	Y	Y
5 ***Rogers***	Y	Y	Y	Y	?
6 ***Fletcher***	Y	Y	Y	Y	Y
LOUISIANA					
1 ***Vitter***	Y	Y	Y	Y	Y
2 Jefferson	Y	Y	Y	Y	Y
3 ***Tauzin***	Y	Y	Y	Y	Y
4 ***McCrery***	Y	Y	Y	Y	Y
5 ***Cooksey***	Y	Y	Y	Y	Y
6 ***Baker***	Y	Y	Y	Y	Y
7 John	Y	Y	Y	Y	Y
MAINE					
1 Allen	Y	Y	N	Y	Y
2 Baldacci	Y	Y	N	Y	Y
MARYLAND					
1 ***Gilchrest***	Y	Y	Y	N	Y
2 ***Ehrlich***	Y	Y	Y	Y	Y
3 Cardin	Y	Y	Y	Y	Y
4 Wynn	Y	Y	Y	Y	Y
5 Hoyer	Y	Y	Y	Y	N
6 ***Bartlett***	Y	Y	Y	N	Y
7 Cummings	Y	Y	Y	Y	Y
8 ***Morella***	Y	Y	Y	Y	Y
MASSACHUSETTS					
1 Olver	Y	Y	?	?	?
2 Neal	Y	Y	Y	Y	N
3 McGovern	Y	Y	Y	Y	N
4 Frank	Y	Y	N	N	N
5 Meehan	Y	Y	?	Y	Y
6 Tierney	Y	Y	N	Y	N
7 Markey	Y	Y	Y	Y	N
8 Capuano	Y	Y	Y	N	N
9 Lynch	Y	Y	Y	Y	N
10 Delahunt	?	?	N	Y	Y
MICHIGAN					
1 Stupak	Y	Y	Y	Y	Y
2 ***Hoekstra***	Y	Y	Y	N	Y
3 ***Ehlers***	N	Y	Y	Y	?
4 ***Camp***	?	?	Y	Y	Y
5 Barcia	Y	Y	Y	Y	Y
6 ***Upton***	N	Y	Y	Y	Y
7 ***Smith***	N	Y	Y	Y	Y
8 ***Rogers***	Y	Y	Y	Y	Y
9 Kildee	Y	Y	Y	Y	N
10 Bonior	Y	Y	Y	Y	N
11 ***Knollenberg***	Y	Y	Y	Y	Y
12 Levin	Y	Y	Y	Y	N
13 Rivers	Y	Y	Y	Y	Y
14 Conyers	Y	Y	N	Y	N
15 Kilpatrick	Y	Y	Y	Y	N
16 Dingell	Y	Y	Y	Y	?
MINNESOTA					
1 ***Gutknecht***	Y	Y	Y	N	Y
2 ***Kennedy***	Y	Y	Y	N	Y
3 ***Ramstad***	Y	Y	Y	N	Y
4 McCollum	Y	Y	Y	N	N
5 Sabo	Y	Y	Y	N	N
6 Luther	?	?	?	?	?
7 Peterson	N	Y	Y	N	Y
8 Oberstar	Y	Y	Y	Y	N
MISSISSIPPI					
1 ***Wicker***	Y	Y	Y	Y	Y
2 Thompson	Y	Y	Y	Y	Y
3 ***Pickering***	Y	Y	Y	Y	Y
4 Shows	Y	Y	Y	Y	Y
5 Taylor	Y	Y	Y	Y	Y
MISSOURI					
1 Clay	Y	Y	Y	Y	Y
2 ***Akin***	N	Y	Y	N	Y
3 Gephardt	?	?	Y	Y	N
4 Skelton	Y	Y	Y	Y	Y
5 McCarthy	Y	Y	Y	Y	Y
6 ***Graves***	N	Y	Y	Y	Y
7 ***Blunt***	Y	Y	Y	Y	Y
8 ***Emerson***	Y	Y	Y	Y	?
9 ***Hulshof***	Y	Y	Y	Y	Y
MONTANA					
AL ***Rehberg***	Y	Y	Y	Y	Y
NEBRASKA					
1 ***Bereuter***	Y	Y	Y	Y	Y
2 ***Terry***	N	Y	Y	Y	Y
3 ***Osborne***	Y	Y	Y	Y	Y
NEVADA					
1 Berkley	Y	Y	Y	Y	Y
2 ***Gibbons***	Y	Y	Y	Y	Y
NEW HAMPSHIRE					
1 ***Sununu***	Y	Y	Y	Y	Y
2 ***Bass***	Y	Y	Y	Y	Y
NEW JERSEY					
1 Andrews	Y	Y	Y	Y	N
2 ***LoBiondo***	Y	Y	Y	Y	Y
3 ***Saxton***	Y	Y	Y	Y	Y
4 ***Smith***	Y	Y	N	Y	Y
5 ***Roukema***	Y	Y	Y	Y	?
6 Pallone	Y	Y	N	Y	N
7 ***Ferguson***	Y	?	Y	Y	Y
8 Pascrell	Y	Y	Y	Y	Y
9 Rothman	Y	Y	Y	Y	Y
10 Payne	Y	Y	N	Y	N
11 ***Frelinghuysen***	Y	Y	Y	Y	Y
12 Holt	Y	Y	N	Y	N
13 Menendez	Y	Y	Y	Y	N
NEW MEXICO					
1 ***Wilson***	Y	Y	N	Y	Y
2 ***Skeen***	Y	Y	Y	Y	Y
3 Udall	Y	Y	Y	Y	N
NEW YORK					
1 ***Grucci***	Y	Y	Y	Y	Y
2 Israel	Y	?	Y	Y	Y
3 ***King***	?	Y	Y	Y	Y
4 McCarthy	Y	Y	Y	Y	Y
5 Ackerman	Y	Y	Y	Y	Y
6 Meeks	Y	Y	N	Y	?
7 Crowley	Y	Y	Y	Y	N
8 Nadler	Y	Y	N	Y	Y
9 Weiner	Y	?	Y	Y	N
10 Towns	Y	Y	N	Y	Y
11 Owens	Y	Y	N	Y	N
12 Velázquez	Y	Y	N	Y	N
13 ***Fossella***	Y	Y	Y	Y	Y
14 Maloney	Y	Y	Y	Y	N
15 Rangel	Y	Y	N	Y	N
16 Serrano	Y	Y	Y	Y	N
17 Engel	Y	Y	Y	Y	Y
18 Lowey	?	?	Y	Y	N
19 ***Kelly***	Y	Y	Y	Y	Y
20 ***Gilman***	Y	Y	Y	Y	Y
21 McNulty	Y	Y	Y	Y	?
22 ***Sweeney***	Y	Y	Y	Y	Y
23 ***Boehlert***	Y	Y	Y	Y	Y
24 ***McHugh***	Y	Y	Y	Y	Y
25 ***Walsh***	Y	Y	Y	Y	Y
26 Hinchey	Y	Y	Y	Y	N
27 ***Reynolds***	Y	Y	Y	Y	Y
28 Slaughter	Y	Y	Y	Y	Y
29 LaFalce	Y	Y	Y	Y	Y
30 ***Quinn***	Y	Y	?	Y	Y
31 ***Houghton***	Y	Y	Y	Y	Y
NORTH CAROLINA					
1 Clayton	Y	Y	Y	Y	N
2 Etheridge	Y	Y	Y	Y	N
3 ***Jones***	N	Y	Y	N	Y
4 Price	Y	Y	Y	Y	N
5 ***Burr***	N	Y	Y	Y	Y
6 ***Coble***	N	Y	Y	Y	Y
7 McIntyre	Y	Y	Y	Y	Y
8 ***Hayes***	Y	Y	Y	Y	Y
9 ***Myrick***	N	Y	Y	Y	Y
10 ***Ballenger***	Y	Y	Y	Y	Y
11 ***Taylor***	Y	Y	Y	N	Y
12 Watt	Y	Y	Y	Y	N
NORTH DAKOTA					
AL Pomeroy	Y	Y	N	Y	Y
OHIO					
1 ***Chabot***	N	Y	Y	Y	Y
2 ***Portman***	Y	Y	Y	Y	Y
3 Hall	Y	Y	Y	Y	N
4 ***Oxley***	Y	Y	Y	Y	Y
5 ***Gillmor***	Y	Y	Y	Y	Y
6 Strickland	Y	Y	Y	Y	N
7 ***Hobson***	Y	Y	Y	Y	Y
8 ***Boehner***	Y	Y	Y	Y	Y
9 Kaptur	Y	?	Y	Y	N
10 Kucinich	Y	Y	N	Y	N
11 Jones	Y	Y	Y	Y	N
12 ***Tiberi***	Y	Y	Y	Y	Y
13 Brown	Y	Y	N	?	?
14 Sawyer	Y	Y	Y	Y	N
15 ***Pryce***	Y	Y	Y	Y	Y
16 ***Regula***	Y	Y	Y	Y	Y
17 Traficant	Y	Y	Y	Y	Y
18 ***Ney***	Y	Y	Y	Y	Y
19 ***LaTourette***	Y	Y	Y	Y	Y
OKLAHOMA					
1 ***Largent***	Y	Y	Y	Y	Y
2 Carson	Y	Y	Y	Y	Y
3 ***Watkins***	Y	Y	Y	Y	Y
4 ***Watts***	Y	Y	Y	Y	Y
5 ***Istook***	Y	Y	Y	Y	Y
6 ***Lucas***	Y	Y	Y	Y	Y
OREGON					
1 Wu	Y	Y	N	Y	Y
2 ***Walden***	Y	Y	Y	Y	Y
3 Blumenauer	Y	Y	N	Y	N
4 DeFazio	Y	Y	N	Y	N
5 Hooley	Y	Y	Y	Y	Y
PENNSYLVANIA					
1 Brady	Y	Y	Y	Y	Y
2 Fattah	Y	Y	Y	Y	Y
3 Borski	Y	Y	Y	Y	Y
4 ***Hart***	Y	Y	Y	Y	Y
5 ***Peterson***	Y	Y	Y	Y	Y
6 Holden	Y	Y	N	Y	Y
7 ***Weldon***	Y	Y	Y	Y	Y
8 ***Greenwood***	Y	Y	Y	Y	Y
9 ***Shuster, Bill***	Y	Y	Y	Y	Y
10 ***Sherwood***	Y	Y	Y	Y	Y
11 Kanjorski	Y	Y	N	Y	Y
12 Murtha	Y	?	Y	Y	Y
13 Hoeffel	?	?	Y	Y	N
14 Coyne	Y	Y	Y	Y	Y
15 ***Toomey***	N	Y	Y	Y	Y
16 ***Pitts***	Y	Y	Y	N	Y
17 ***Gekas***	Y	Y	Y	Y	Y
18 Doyle	Y	Y	Y	Y	Y
19 ***Platts***	Y	Y	Y	Y	Y
20 Mascara	Y	Y	Y	Y	Y
21 ***English***	Y	Y	?	Y	Y
RHODE ISLAND					
1 Kennedy	Y	Y	Y	Y	Y
2 Langevin	Y	Y	Y	Y	N
SOUTH CAROLINA					
1 ***Brown***	Y	Y	Y	Y	Y
2 Vacant					
3 ***Graham***	Y	Y	Y	Y	Y
4 ***DeMint***	N	Y	Y	Y	?
5 Spratt	Y	Y	Y	Y	N
6 Clyburn	Y	Y	Y	Y	Y
SOUTH DAKOTA					
AL ***Thune***	Y	Y	Y	Y	Y
TENNESSEE					
1 ***Jenkins***	Y	Y	Y	Y	Y
2 ***Duncan***	N	Y	Y	N	Y
3 ***Wamp***	Y	Y	Y	Y	Y
4 ***Hilleary***	Y	Y	Y	Y	Y
5 Clement	Y	Y	Y	Y	Y
6 Gordon	Y	Y	Y	Y	Y
7 ***Bryant***	Y	Y	Y	Y	Y
8 Tanner	Y	Y	Y	Y	Y
9 Ford	Y	Y	Y	Y	Y
TEXAS					
1 Sandlin	Y	Y	Y	Y	N
2 Turner	Y	Y	Y	Y	Y
3 ***Johnson, Sam***	N	Y	Y	Y	Y
4 Hall	Y	Y	Y	Y	Y
5 ***Sessions***	N	Y	Y	N	Y
6 ***Barton***	N	Y	Y	Y	Y
7 ***Culberson***	N	Y	Y	N	Y
8 ***Brady***	Y	Y	Y	?	?
9 Lampson	Y	Y	Y	Y	N
10 Doggett	Y	Y	Y	Y	N
11 Edwards	Y	Y	Y	Y	Y
12 ***Granger***	Y	Y	Y	Y	Y
13 ***Thornberry***	Y	Y	Y	Y	Y
14 ***Paul***	N	Y	N	N	Y
15 Hinojosa	Y	Y	Y	Y	N
16 Reyes	Y	Y	Y	Y	N
17 Stenholm	Y	Y	Y	Y	Y
18 Jackson-Lee	Y	Y	Y	Y	Y
19 ***Combest***	Y	Y	Y	Y	Y
20 Gonzalez	?	?	?	?	?
21 ***Smith***	Y	Y	Y	Y	Y
22 ***DeLay***	Y	Y	Y	N	Y
23 ***Bonilla***	Y	Y	Y	Y	Y
24 Frost	Y	Y	Y	Y	Y
25 Bentsen	Y	Y	Y	Y	Y
26 ***Armey***	N	Y	Y	Y	Y
27 Ortiz	Y	Y	Y	Y	Y
28 Rodriguez	Y	Y	Y	Y	N
29 Green	Y	Y	Y	Y	Y
30 Johnson, E.B.	Y	Y	Y	Y	Y
UTAH					
1 ***Hansen***	Y	Y	Y	Y	Y
2 Matheson	Y	Y	Y	Y	Y
3 ***Cannon***	N	Y	Y	Y	Y
VERMONT					
AL *Sanders*	Y	Y	Y	N	Y
VIRGINIA					
1 ***Davis, Jo Ann***	Y	Y	N	Y	Y
2 ***Schrock***	Y	Y	Y	Y	Y
3 Scott	Y	Y	Y	Y	N
4 ***Forbes***	Y	Y	N	Y	Y
5 *Goode*	N	Y	Y	N	Y
6 ***Goodlatte***	N	Y	Y	Y	Y
7 ***Cantor***	Y	Y	Y	Y	Y
8 Moran	Y	Y	Y	Y	Y
9 Boucher	Y	Y	Y	Y	Y
10 ***Wolf***	Y	Y	Y	Y	Y
11 ***Davis, T.***	Y	Y	Y	Y	?
WASHINGTON					
1 Inslee	Y	Y	Y	Y	N
2 Larsen	Y	Y	Y	Y	Y
3 Baird	Y	Y	Y	Y	N
4 ***Hastings***	Y	Y	Y	Y	Y
5 ***Nethercutt***	Y	Y	Y	Y	Y
6 Dicks	Y	Y	Y	Y	Y
7 McDermott	Y	Y	N	Y	N
8 ***Dunn***	Y	Y	Y	Y	Y
9 Smith	Y	Y	Y	Y	N
WEST VIRGINIA					
1 Mollohan	Y	Y	Y	Y	Y
2 ***Capito***	Y	Y	Y	Y	Y
3 Rahall	Y	Y	Y	Y	Y
WISCONSIN					
1 ***Ryan***	N	Y	Y	Y	Y
2 Baldwin	Y	Y	Y	Y	N
3 Kind	Y	Y	Y	Y	Y
4 Kleczka	Y	Y	Y	Y	Y
5 Barrett	Y	Y	Y	Y	N
6 ***Petri***	N	Y	Y	Y	Y
7 Obey	Y	Y	Y	Y	?
8 ***Green***	Y	Y	Y	Y	Y
9 ***Sensenbrenner***	N	Y	Y	N	Y
WYOMING					
AL ***Cubin***	?	?	?	?	?

Southern states - Ala., Ark., Fla., Ga., Ky., La., Miss., N.C., Okla., S.C., Tenn., Texas, Va.

499. HR 3379. Raymond M. Downey Building/Passage. Jo Ann Davis, R-Va., motion to suspend the rules and pass the bill that would name a Deer Park, N.Y., post office after Raymond M. Downey, a New York City firefighter killed Sept. 11. Motion agreed to 393-0: R 198-0; D 193-0 (ND 143-0, SD 50-0); I 2-0. A two-thirds majority of those present and voting (263 in this case) is required for passage under suspension of the rules. Dec. 18, 2001.

500. HR 3054. Sept. 11 Medals/Passage. King, R-N.Y., motion to suspend the rules and pass the bill that would authorize the award of congressional gold medals to government officials, officers, and emergency workers who responded to the Sept. 11 terrorist attacks in New York City, as well as for the passengers and crew who resisted terrorists aboard United Airlines Flight 93, which crashed in Pennsylvania. Motion agreed to 392-2: R 196-2; D 194-0 (ND 144-0, SD 50-0); I 2-0. A two-thirds majority of those present and voting (263 in this case) is required for passage under suspension of the rules. Dec. 18, 2001.

501. HR 3275. Anti-Terrorism Accords/Passage. Sensenbrenner, R-Wis., motion to suspend the rules and pass the bill that would implement the International Convention for the Suppression of Terrorist Bombings and the International Convention for the Suppression of the Financing of Terrorism by making it a federal crime to attempt or carry out terrorist bombings of public, government or infrastructure facilities or to engage in financial transactions related to those acts. Violators would be subject to up to 20 years in prison; bombers whose acts result in fatalities could receive the death penalty. Motion agreed to 381-36: R 210-3; D 169-33 (ND 124-27, SD 45-6); I 2-0. A two-thirds majority of those present and voting (278 in this case) is required for passage under suspension of the rules. A "yea" was a vote in support of the president's position. Dec. 19, 2001.

502. HR 2657. District of Columbia Family Court/Concur with Senate Amendments. Morella, R-Md., motion to suspend the rules and concur with the Senate amendments to the bill to redesignate the D.C. Superior Court's Family Division as the Family Court and promote recruitment and retention of experienced judges and greater autonomy and efficiencies within the system. Motion agreed to 418-1: R 214-1; D 202-0 (ND 152-0, SD 50-0); I 2-0. A two-thirds majority of those present and voting (280 in this case) is required for adoption under suspension of the rules. Dec. 19, 2001.

503. HR 2199. District of Columbia Police Help/Concur with Senate Amendment. Morella, R-Md., motion to suspend the rules and concur in the Senate amendment to the bill that would broaden the 1997 National Capital Revitalization and Self-Government Improvement Act to allow any federal law enforcement agency to assist D.C. police in fighting crime. Motion agreed to 420-0: R 214-0; D 204-0 (ND 153-0, SD 51-0); I 2-0. A two-thirds majority of those present and voting (280 in this case) is required for adoption under suspension of the rules. Dec. 19, 2001.

504. HR 3061. Fiscal 2002 Labor-HHS-Education Appropriations/Conference Report. Adoption of the conference report on the bill that would appropriate $123.4 billion in discretionary spending for the Labor, Health and Human Services and Education departments and related agencies. The agreement would include $12.3 billion for the disadvantaged children's Title 1 program. It also would fund the education overhaul bill (HR 1), including money for teacher improvement, annual state testing and the Reading First program. Adopted (thus sent to the Senate) 393-30: R 188-30; D 203-0 (ND 154-0, SD 49-0); I 2-0. Dec. 19, 2001.

505. HR 2506. Fiscal 2002 Foreign Operations Appropriations/Conference Report. Adoption of the conference report on the bill that would appropriate $15.4 billion in fiscal 2002 for foreign operations, $403 million more than fiscal 2001. The bill also would continue a Bush administration policy blocking federal funds to groups that use their own money to offer abortion services overseas. Adopted (thus sent to the Senate) 357-66: R 159-59; D 197-6 (ND 151-2, SD 46-4); I 1-1. Dec. 19, 2001.

* Rep. Joe Wilson, R-S.C., was sworn in Dec. 19, 2001. The first vote for which he was eligible was Vote 504.

Key

Y	Voted for (yea).
#	Paired for.
+	Announced for.
N	Voted against (nay).
X	Paired against.
−	Announced against.
P	Voted "present."
C	Voted "present" to avoid possible conflict of interest.
?	Did not vote or otherwise make a position known.

Democrats *Republicans*
Independents

	499	500	501	502	503	504	505
ALABAMA							
1 *Callahan*	?	?	Y	Y	Y	Y	Y
2 *Everett*	Y	Y	Y	Y	Y	Y	N
3 *Riley*	?	?	Y	Y	Y	Y	Y
4 *Aderholt*	Y	Y	Y	Y	Y	Y	Y
5 Cramer	Y	Y	Y	Y	Y	Y	Y
6 *Bachus*	Y	Y	Y	Y	Y	Y	N
7 Hilliard	Y	Y	N	Y	Y	Y	Y
ALASKA							
AL *Young*	?	?	?	?	?	?	?
ARIZONA							
1 *Flake*	Y	Y	Y	Y	Y	N	N
2 Pastor	Y	Y	Y	Y	Y	Y	Y
3 *Stump*	Y	Y	Y	Y	Y	Y	N
4 *Shadegg*	Y	Y	Y	Y	Y	N	Y
5 *Kolbe*	Y	Y	Y	Y	Y	Y	Y
6 *Hayworth*	Y	Y	Y	Y	Y	N	N
ARKANSAS							
1 Berry	Y	Y	Y	Y	Y	Y	N
2 Snyder	Y	Y	Y	Y	Y	Y	Y
3 *Boozman*	?	?	Y	Y	Y	Y	Y
4 Ross	Y	Y	Y	Y	Y	Y	Y
CALIFORNIA							
1 Thompson	Y	Y	Y	Y	Y	Y	Y
2 *Herger*	Y	Y	Y	Y	Y	Y	N
3 *Ose*	Y	Y	Y	Y	Y	Y	Y
4 *Doolittle*	Y	Y	Y	Y	Y	Y	N
5 Matsui	Y	Y	Y	Y	Y	Y	Y
6 Woolsey	Y	Y	N	Y	Y	Y	Y
7 Miller, George	Y	Y	Y	Y	Y	Y	Y
8 Pelosi	Y	Y	Y	Y	Y	Y	Y
9 Lee	Y	Y	N	Y	Y	Y	Y
10 Tauscher	Y	Y	Y	Y	Y	Y	Y
11 *Pombo*	?	?	Y	Y	Y	N	Y
12 Lantos	Y	Y	Y	Y	Y	Y	Y
13 Stark	?	?	?	?	?	?	?
14 Eshoo	Y	Y	Y	Y	Y	Y	Y
15 Honda	Y	Y	N	Y	Y	Y	Y
16 Lofgren	Y	Y	Y	Y	Y	Y	Y
17 Farr	Y	Y	Y	Y	Y	Y	Y
18 Condit	Y	Y	Y	Y	Y	Y	Y
19 *Radanovich*	?	?	Y	Y	Y	Y	Y
20 Dooley	Y	Y	Y	Y	Y	Y	Y
21 *Thomas*	Y	Y	Y	Y	Y	Y	Y
22 Capps	Y	Y	Y	Y	Y	Y	Y
23 *Gallegly*	Y	Y	Y	Y	Y	Y	Y
24 Sherman	Y	Y	Y	Y	Y	Y	Y
25 *McKeon*	Y	Y	Y	Y	Y	Y	Y
26 Berman	Y	Y	Y	Y	Y	Y	Y
27 Schiff	Y	Y	Y	Y	Y	Y	Y
28 *Dreier*	Y	Y	Y	Y	Y	Y	Y
29 Waxman	Y	Y	Y	Y	Y	Y	Y
30 Becerra	?	?	Y	Y	Y	Y	Y
31 Solis	Y	Y	Y	Y	Y	Y	Y
32 Watson	Y	Y	Y	Y	Y	Y	Y
33 Roybal-Allard	Y	Y	Y	Y	Y	Y	Y
34 Napolitano	Y	Y	Y	Y	Y	Y	Y
35 Waters	Y	Y	N	Y	Y	Y	Y
36 Harman	Y	Y	Y	Y	Y	Y	Y
37 Millender-McD.	Y	Y	Y	Y	Y	Y	Y
38 *Horn*	Y	Y	Y	Y	Y	Y	Y
39 *Royce*	Y	Y	Y	Y	Y	N	N
40 *Lewis*	Y	Y	Y	Y	Y	Y	Y
41 *Miller, Gary*	Y	Y	Y	Y	Y	Y	Y
42 Baca	Y	Y	Y	Y	Y	Y	Y
43 *Calvert*	Y	Y	Y	Y	Y	Y	Y
44 *Bono*	Y	Y	Y	Y	Y	Y	Y
45 *Rohrabacher*	Y	Y	Y	Y	Y	N	N
46 Sanchez	Y	Y	Y	Y	Y	Y	Y
47 *Cox*	?	?	Y	Y	Y	N	Y
48 *Issa*	Y	Y	Y	Y	Y	Y	Y
49 Davis	Y	Y	Y	Y	Y	Y	Y
50 Filner	Y	Y	Y	Y	Y	Y	Y
51 *Cunningham*	Y	Y	Y	Y	Y	Y	N
52 *Hunter*	Y	Y	Y	Y	Y	Y	Y
COLORADO							
1 DeGette	Y	Y	N	Y	Y	Y	Y
2 Udall	Y	Y	Y	Y	Y	Y	Y
3 *McInnis*	?	?	Y	Y	Y	N	N
4 *Schaffer*	Y	Y	Y	Y	Y	N	Y
5 *Hefley*	Y	Y	Y	Y	Y	N	N
6 *Tancredo*	Y	Y	Y	Y	Y	N	N
CONNECTICUT							
1 Larson	Y	Y	Y	Y	Y	Y	Y
2 *Simmons*	Y	Y	Y	Y	Y	Y	Y
3 DeLauro	Y	Y	Y	Y	Y	Y	Y
4 *Shays*	Y	Y	Y	Y	Y	Y	Y
5 Maloney	Y	Y	Y	Y	Y	Y	Y
6 *Johnson*	Y	Y	Y	Y	Y	Y	Y
DELAWARE							
AL *Castle*	Y	Y	Y	Y	Y	Y	Y
FLORIDA							
1 *Miller, J.*	Y	Y	Y	Y	Y	Y	N
2 Boyd	Y	Y	Y	Y	Y	Y	Y
3 Brown	Y	Y	Y	Y	Y	Y	Y
4 *Crenshaw*	Y	Y	Y	Y	Y	Y	Y
5 Thurman	Y	Y	Y	Y	Y	Y	Y
6 *Stearns*	Y	Y	Y	Y	Y	Y	N
7 *Mica*	Y	Y	Y	Y	Y	Y	Y
8 *Keller*	Y	Y	Y	Y	Y	Y	Y
9 *Bilirakis*	Y	Y	Y	Y	Y	Y	Y
10 *Young*	Y	Y	Y	Y	Y	Y	Y
11 Davis	Y	Y	Y	Y	Y	Y	Y
12 *Putnam*	Y	Y	Y	Y	Y	Y	Y
13 *Miller, D.*	Y	Y	Y	Y	Y	Y	Y
14 *Goss*	Y	Y	Y	Y	Y	Y	Y
15 *Weldon*	Y	Y	Y	Y	Y	N	N
16 *Foley*	Y	Y	Y	Y	Y	Y	Y
17 Meek	?	?	?	?	?	?	?
18 *Ros-Lehtinen*	Y	Y	Y	Y	Y	Y	Y
19 Wexler	?	?	?	?	?	?	?
20 Deutsch	Y	Y	Y	Y	Y	Y	Y
21 *Diaz-Balart*	Y	Y	Y	Y	Y	Y	Y
22 *Shaw*	Y	Y	Y	Y	Y	Y	Y
23 Hastings	Y	Y	?	?	?	?	?
GEORGIA							
1 *Kingston*	Y	Y	Y	Y	Y	Y	Y
2 Bishop	Y	Y	Y	Y	Y	Y	Y
3 *Collins*	Y	Y	Y	Y	Y	Y	Y
4 McKinney	Y	Y	N	Y	Y	Y	Y
5 Lewis	Y	Y	N	Y	Y	Y	Y
6 *Isakson*	Y	Y	Y	Y	Y	Y	Y
7 *Barr*	?	?	Y	Y	Y	Y	N
8 *Chambliss*	Y	Y	Y	Y	Y	Y	Y
9 *Deal*	Y	Y	Y	Y	Y	Y	Y
10 *Norwood*	Y	Y	Y	Y	Y	Y	Y
11 *Linder*	Y	Y	Y	Y	Y	Y	Y
HAWAII							
1 Abercrombie	Y	Y	Y	Y	Y	Y	Y
2 Mink	Y	Y	Y	Y	Y	Y	Y
IDAHO							
1 *Otter*	Y	Y	Y	Y	Y	N	N
2 *Simpson*	Y	Y	Y	Y	Y	Y	Y
ILLINOIS							
1 Rush	Y	Y	?	Y	Y	Y	Y
2 Jackson	Y	Y	Y	Y	Y	Y	Y
3 Lipinski	?	?	Y	Y	Y	Y	Y
4 Gutierrez	Y	Y	Y	Y	Y	Y	Y
5 Blagojevich	Y	Y	Y	Y	Y	Y	Y
6 *Hyde*	Y	Y	Y	Y	Y	Y	Y
7 Davis	Y	Y	N	Y	Y	Y	Y
8 *Crane*	Y	Y	Y	Y	Y	N	N
9 Schakowsky	?	Y	Y	Y	Y	Y	Y
10 *Kirk*	Y	Y	Y	Y	Y	Y	Y
11 *Weller*	Y	Y	Y	Y	Y	Y	Y
12 Costello	Y	Y	Y	Y	Y	Y	Y
13 *Biggert*	Y	Y	Y	Y	Y	Y	Y

ND Northern Democrats   SD Southern Democrats

	499	500	501	502	503	504	505
14 ***Hastert***							
15 ***Johnson***	Y	Y	Y	Y	Y	Y	Y
16 ***Manzullo***	Y	Y	Y	Y	Y	Y	N
17 Evans	Y	Y	Y	Y	Y	Y	Y
18 ***LaHood***	Y	Y	Y	Y	Y	Y	Y
19 Phelps	Y	Y	Y	Y	Y	Y	Y
20 ***Shimkus***	Y	Y	Y	Y	Y	Y	Y
INDIANA							
1 Visclosky	Y	Y	Y	Y	Y	Y	Y
2 ***Pence***	Y	Y	Y	Y	Y	N	N
3 Roemer	Y	Y	Y	Y	Y	Y	N
4 ***Souder***	?	?	Y	Y	Y	Y	Y
5 ***Buyer***	Y	Y	Y	Y	Y	Y	Y
6 ***Burton***	Y	Y	?	Y	Y	Y	Y
7 ***Kerns***	Y	Y	Y	Y	Y	N	N
8 ***Hostettler***	Y	Y	Y	Y	Y	N	N
9 Hill	?	?	Y	Y	Y	Y	Y
10 Carson	Y	Y	Y	Y	Y	Y	Y
IOWA							
1 ***Leach***	Y	Y	Y	Y	Y	Y	Y
2 ***Nussle***	Y	Y	Y	Y	Y	Y	Y
3 Boswell	Y	Y	Y	Y	Y	Y	Y
4 ***Ganske***	Y	Y	Y	Y	Y	Y	Y
5 ***Latham***	Y	Y	Y	Y	Y	Y	Y
KANSAS							
1 ***Moran***	Y	Y	Y	Y	Y	Y	Y
2 ***Ryun***	Y	Y	Y	Y	Y	N	N
3 Moore	Y	Y	Y	Y	Y	Y	Y
4 ***Tiahrt***	Y	Y	Y	Y	Y	Y	Y
KENTUCKY							
1 ***Whitfield***	Y	Y	Y	Y	Y	Y	Y
2 ***Lewis***	Y	Y	Y	Y	Y	Y	N
3 ***Northup***	Y	Y	Y	Y	Y	Y	Y
4 Lucas	Y	Y	Y	Y	Y	Y	Y
5 ***Rogers***	Y	Y	Y	Y	Y	Y	Y
6 ***Fletcher***	Y	Y	Y	Y	Y	Y	Y
LOUISIANA							
1 ***Vitter***	Y	Y	?	?	?	Y	Y
2 Jefferson	Y	Y	Y	Y	Y	Y	Y
3 ***Tauzin***	Y	Y	Y	Y	Y	Y	Y
4 ***McCrery***	Y	Y	Y	Y	Y	Y	Y
5 ***Cooksey***	?	?	?	?	?	Y	Y
6 ***Baker***	?	?	?	?	?	?	?
7 John	Y	Y	Y	Y	Y	Y	Y
MAINE							
1 Allen	Y	Y	Y	Y	Y	Y	Y
2 Baldacci	Y	Y	Y	Y	Y	Y	Y
MARYLAND							
1 ***Gilchrest***	Y	Y	Y	Y	Y	Y	Y
2 ***Ehrlich***	?	?	Y	Y	Y	Y	Y
3 Cardin	Y	Y	Y	Y	Y	Y	Y
4 Wynn	?	?	Y	Y	Y	Y	Y
5 Hoyer	Y	Y	Y	Y	Y	Y	Y
6 ***Bartlett***	Y	Y	N	Y	Y	N	N
7 Cummings	?	?	Y	Y	Y	Y	Y
8 ***Morella***	Y	Y	Y	Y	Y	Y	Y
MASSACHUSETTS							
1 Olver	Y	Y	N	Y	Y	Y	Y
2 Neal	Y	Y	Y	Y	Y	Y	Y
3 McGovern	Y	Y	N	Y	Y	Y	Y
4 Frank	Y	Y	N	Y	Y	Y	Y
5 Meehan	Y	Y	Y	Y	Y	Y	Y
6 Tierney	Y	Y	N	Y	Y	Y	Y
7 Markey	Y	Y	Y	Y	Y	Y	Y
8 Capuano	Y	Y	Y	Y	Y	Y	Y
9 Lynch	Y	Y	Y	Y	Y	Y	Y
10 Delahunt	?	?	N	Y	Y	Y	Y
MICHIGAN							
1 Stupak	Y	Y	Y	Y	Y	Y	Y
2 ***Hoekstra***	Y	Y	Y	Y	Y	Y	Y
3 ***Ehlers***	Y	Y	N	Y	Y	Y	Y
4 ***Camp***	Y	Y	Y	Y	Y	Y	Y
5 Barcia	Y	Y	Y	Y	Y	Y	N
6 ***Upton***	Y	Y	Y	Y	Y	Y	Y
7 ***Smith***	Y	Y	Y	Y	Y	Y	N
8 ***Rogers***	Y	Y	Y	Y	Y	Y	Y
9 Kildee	Y	Y	Y	Y	Y	Y	Y
10 Bonior	Y	Y	?	Y	Y	Y	Y
11 ***Knollenberg***	Y	Y	Y	Y	Y	Y	Y
12 Levin	Y	Y	Y	Y	Y	Y	Y
13 Rivers	Y	Y	N	Y	Y	Y	Y
14 Conyers	Y	Y	N	Y	Y	Y	Y
15 Kilpatrick	Y	Y	N	Y	Y	Y	Y
16 Dingell	Y	Y	Y	Y	Y	Y	Y

	499	500	501	502	503	504	505
MINNESOTA							
1 ***Gutknecht***	Y	Y	Y	Y	Y	Y	N
2 ***Kennedy***	Y	Y	Y	Y	Y	Y	N
3 ***Ramstad***	Y	Y	Y	Y	Y	Y	Y
4 McCollum	Y	Y	Y	Y	Y	Y	Y
5 Sabo	Y	Y	N	Y	Y	Y	Y
6 Luther	?	?	?	?	?	?	?
7 Peterson	Y	Y	Y	Y	Y	Y	Y
8 Oberstar	Y	Y	Y	Y	Y	Y	Y
MISSISSIPPI							
1 ***Wicker***	Y	Y	Y	Y	Y	Y	Y
2 Thompson	Y	Y	Y	Y	Y	Y	Y
3 ***Pickering***	Y	Y	Y	Y	Y	Y	Y
4 Shows	Y	Y	Y	Y	Y	Y	Y
5 Taylor	Y	Y	Y	Y	Y	Y	N
MISSOURI							
1 Clay	?	?	N	Y	Y	Y	Y
2 ***Akin***	Y	Y	Y	Y	Y	N	N
3 Gephardt	Y	Y	?	?	?	Y	Y
4 Skelton	Y	Y	Y	Y	Y	Y	Y
5 McCarthy	Y	Y	N	Y	Y	Y	Y
6 ***Graves***	Y	Y	Y	Y	Y	Y	Y
7 ***Blunt***	?	?	Y	Y	Y	Y	N
8 ***Emerson***	Y	Y	Y	Y	Y	Y	Y
9 ***Hulshof***	Y	Y	Y	Y	Y	Y	Y
MONTANA							
AL ***Rehberg***	Y	Y	Y	Y	Y	Y	Y
NEBRASKA							
1 ***Bereuter***	Y	Y	+	Y	Y	Y	Y
2 ***Terry***	?	?	Y	Y	Y	Y	Y
3 ***Osborne***	Y	Y	Y	Y	Y	Y	Y
NEVADA							
1 Berkley	Y	Y	Y	Y	Y	Y	Y
2 ***Gibbons***	?	?	Y	Y	Y	Y	Y
NEW HAMPSHIRE							
1 ***Sununu***	Y	Y	Y	Y	Y	Y	Y
2 ***Bass***	Y	Y	Y	Y	Y	Y	Y
NEW JERSEY							
1 Andrews	Y	Y	Y	Y	Y	Y	Y
2 ***LoBiondo***	Y	Y	Y	Y	Y	Y	Y
3 ***Saxton***	Y	Y	Y	Y	Y	Y	Y
4 ***Smith***	Y	Y	Y	Y	Y	N	N
5 ***Roukema***	Y	Y	Y	Y	Y	Y	Y
6 Pallone	Y	Y	Y	Y	Y	Y	Y
7 ***Ferguson***	?	?	Y	Y	Y	Y	Y
8 Pascrell	Y	Y	Y	Y	Y	Y	Y
9 Rothman	Y	Y	Y	Y	Y	Y	Y
10 Payne	?	?	N	Y	Y	Y	Y
11 ***Frelinghuysen***	Y	Y	Y	Y	Y	Y	Y
12 Holt	Y	Y	N	Y	Y	Y	Y
13 Menendez	Y	Y	Y	Y	Y	Y	Y
NEW MEXICO							
1 ***Wilson***	Y	Y	Y	Y	Y	Y	Y
2 ***Skeen***	Y	Y	Y	Y	Y	Y	Y
3 Udall	Y	Y	Y	Y	Y	Y	Y
NEW YORK							
1 ***Grucci***	Y	Y	Y	Y	Y	Y	Y
2 Israel	Y	Y	Y	Y	Y	Y	Y
3 ***King***	Y	Y	Y	Y	Y	Y	Y
4 McCarthy	Y	Y	Y	Y	Y	Y	Y
5 Ackerman	Y	Y	Y	Y	Y	Y	Y
6 Meeks	Y	Y	N	?	Y	Y	Y
7 Crowley	Y	Y	Y	Y	Y	Y	Y
8 Nadler	Y	Y	Y	Y	Y	Y	Y
9 Weiner	Y	Y	Y	Y	Y	Y	Y
10 Towns	Y	Y	Y	Y	Y	Y	Y
11 Owens	Y	Y	N	Y	Y	Y	?
12 Velázquez	Y	Y	Y	Y	Y	Y	Y
13 ***Fossella***	Y	Y	Y	Y	Y	Y	Y
14 Maloney	Y	Y	Y	Y	Y	Y	Y
15 Rangel	Y	Y	Y	Y	Y	Y	Y
16 Serrano	Y	Y	Y	Y	Y	Y	Y
17 Engel	Y	Y	Y	Y	Y	Y	Y
18 Lowey	Y	Y	Y	Y	Y	Y	Y
19 ***Kelly***	Y	Y	Y	Y	Y	Y	Y
20 ***Gilman***	Y	Y	Y	Y	Y	Y	Y
21 McNulty	Y	Y	Y	Y	Y	Y	Y
22 ***Sweeney***	?	?	?	Y	Y	Y	Y
23 ***Boehlert***	Y	Y	Y	Y	Y	Y	Y
24 ***McHugh***	Y	Y	Y	Y	Y	Y	Y
25 ***Walsh***	Y	Y	Y	Y	Y	Y	Y
26 Hinchey	Y	Y	N	Y	Y	Y	Y
27 ***Reynolds***	Y	Y	Y	Y	Y	Y	Y
28 Slaughter	Y	Y	Y	Y	Y	Y	Y
29 LaFalce	Y	?	Y	Y	Y	Y	Y

	499	500	501	502	503	504	505
30 ***Quinn***	Y	Y	Y	Y	Y	Y	Y
31 ***Houghton***	Y	N	Y	Y	Y	Y	Y
NORTH CAROLINA							
1 Clayton	Y	Y	N	Y	Y	Y	Y
2 Etheridge	Y	Y	Y	+	Y	Y	Y
3 ***Jones***	Y	Y	Y	Y	Y	N	N
4 Price	Y	Y	Y	Y	Y	Y	Y
5 ***Burr***	Y	Y	Y	Y	Y	Y	Y
6 ***Coble***	Y	Y	Y	N	Y	Y	Y
7 McIntyre	?	?	Y	Y	Y	Y	Y
8 ***Hayes***	Y	Y	Y	Y	Y	Y	N
9 ***Myrick***	Y	Y	Y	Y	Y	Y	N
10 ***Ballenger***	Y	Y	Y	Y	?	Y	Y
11 ***Taylor***	Y	Y	Y	Y	Y	Y	N
12 Watt	Y	Y	N	Y	Y	Y	Y
NORTH DAKOTA							
AL Pomeroy	Y	Y	Y	Y	Y	Y	Y
OHIO							
1 ***Chabot***	Y	Y	Y	Y	Y	N	N
2 ***Portman***	Y	Y	Y	Y	Y	Y	Y
3 Hall	?	?	?	?	?	?	?
4 ***Oxley***	Y	Y	Y	Y	Y	Y	Y
5 ***Gillmor***	Y	Y	Y	Y	Y	Y	Y
6 Strickland	Y	Y	Y	Y	Y	Y	Y
7 ***Hobson***	Y	Y	Y	Y	Y	Y	Y
8 ***Boehner***	Y	Y	Y	Y	Y	Y	Y
9 Kaptur	?	Y	Y	Y	Y	Y	Y
10 Kucinich	Y	Y	N	Y	Y	Y	Y
11 Jones	Y	Y	N	Y	Y	Y	Y
12 ***Tiberi***	Y	Y	Y	Y	Y	Y	Y
13 Brown	Y	Y	N	Y	Y	Y	Y
14 Sawyer	Y	Y	Y	Y	Y	Y	Y
15 ***Pryce***	Y	Y	Y	Y	Y	Y	Y
16 ***Regula***	Y	Y	Y	Y	Y	Y	Y
17 Traficant	Y	Y	Y	Y	Y	Y	Y
18 ***Ney***	Y	Y	Y	Y	Y	Y	Y
19 ***LaTourette***	Y	Y	Y	Y	Y	Y	Y
OKLAHOMA							
1 ***Largent***	?	?	Y	Y	Y	Y	N
2 Carson	Y	Y	Y	Y	Y	Y	Y
3 ***Watkins***	Y	Y	Y	Y	Y	Y	Y
4 ***Watts***	Y	Y	Y	Y	Y	Y	Y
5 ***Istook***	Y	Y	Y	Y	Y	Y	Y
6 ***Lucas***	Y	Y	Y	Y	Y	Y	N
OREGON							
1 Wu	Y	Y	Y	Y	Y	Y	Y
2 ***Walden***	Y	Y	Y	Y	Y	Y	Y
3 Blumenauer	Y	Y	Y	Y	Y	Y	Y
4 DeFazio	Y	Y	Y	Y	Y	Y	Y
5 Hooley	Y	Y	Y	Y	Y	Y	Y
PENNSYLVANIA							
1 Brady	Y	Y	Y	Y	Y	Y	Y
2 Fattah	Y	Y	N	Y	Y	Y	Y
3 Borski	Y	Y	Y	Y	Y	Y	Y
4 ***Hart***	Y	Y	Y	Y	Y	Y	Y
5 ***Peterson***	Y	Y	Y	Y	Y	Y	Y
6 Holden	Y	Y	Y	Y	Y	Y	Y
7 ***Weldon***	Y	Y	Y	Y	Y	Y	Y
8 ***Greenwood***	Y	Y	Y	Y	Y	Y	Y
9 ***Shuster, Bill***	Y	Y	Y	Y	Y	Y	N
10 ***Sherwood***	Y	Y	Y	Y	Y	Y	Y
11 Kanjorski	Y	Y	Y	Y	Y	Y	Y
12 Murtha	?	?	Y	Y	Y	Y	Y
13 Hoeffel	Y	Y	Y	Y	Y	Y	Y
14 Coyne	Y	Y	Y	Y	Y	Y	Y
15 ***Toomey***	Y	Y	Y	Y	Y	N	N
16 ***Pitts***	Y	Y	Y	Y	Y	N	N
17 ***Gekas***	Y	Y	Y	Y	Y	Y	Y
18 Doyle	Y	Y	Y	Y	Y	Y	Y
19 ***Platts***	Y	Y	Y	Y	Y	Y	N
20 Mascara	Y	Y	Y	Y	Y	Y	Y
21 ***English***	Y	Y	Y	Y	Y	Y	Y
RHODE ISLAND							
1 Kennedy	Y	Y	Y	Y	Y	Y	Y
2 Langevin	Y	Y	Y	Y	Y	Y	Y
SOUTH CAROLINA							
1 ***Brown***	Y	Y	Y	Y	Y	Y	Y
2 ***Wilson, J.*** *						Y	Y
3 ***Graham***	Y	Y	Y	Y	Y	Y	Y
4 ***DeMint***	Y	Y	Y	Y	Y	Y	N
5 Spratt	Y	Y	Y	Y	Y	Y	Y
6 Clyburn	Y	Y	Y	Y	Y	Y	Y
SOUTH DAKOTA							
AL ***Thune***	Y	Y	Y	Y	Y	Y	Y

	499	500	501	502	503	504	505
TENNESSEE							
1 ***Jenkins***	Y	Y	Y	Y	Y	Y	Y
2 ***Duncan***	Y	Y	Y	Y	Y	N	N
3 ***Wamp***	?	?	Y	Y	Y	Y	N
4 ***Hilleary***	Y	Y	Y	Y	Y	Y	N
5 Clement	Y	Y	Y	Y	Y	?	?
6 Gordon	Y	Y	Y	Y	Y	Y	Y
7 ***Bryant***	Y	Y	Y	Y	Y	Y	Y
8 Tanner	Y	Y	Y	Y	Y	Y	N
9 Ford	Y	Y	Y	Y	Y	Y	Y
TEXAS							
1 Sandlin	Y	Y	Y	Y	Y	Y	Y
2 Turner	Y	Y	Y	Y	Y	Y	Y
3 ***Johnson, Sam***	Y	Y	Y	Y	Y	Y	N
4 Hall	Y	Y	Y	Y	Y	Y	N
5 ***Sessions***	Y	Y	Y	Y	Y	N	Y
6 ***Barton***	Y	Y	Y	Y	Y	Y	Y
7 ***Culberson***	Y	Y	Y	Y	Y	Y	Y
8 ***Brady***	Y	Y	Y	Y	Y	Y	Y
9 Lampson	Y	Y	Y	Y	Y	Y	Y
10 Doggett	Y	Y	Y	Y	Y	Y	Y
11 Edwards	Y	Y	Y	Y	Y	Y	Y
12 ***Granger***	Y	Y	Y	Y	Y	Y	Y
13 ***Thornberry***	Y	Y	Y	Y	Y	Y	Y
14 ***Paul***	Y	N	N	Y	Y	N	N
15 Hinojosa	Y	Y	Y	Y	Y	Y	Y
16 Reyes	Y	Y	Y	Y	Y	?	Y
17 Stenholm	Y	Y	Y	Y	Y	Y	Y
18 Jackson-Lee	Y	Y	Y	Y	Y	Y	Y
19 ***Combest***	Y	Y	Y	Y	Y	Y	N
20 Gonzalez	Y	Y	Y	Y	Y	Y	Y
21 ***Smith***	Y	Y	Y	Y	Y	Y	Y
22 ***DeLay***	Y	Y	Y	Y	Y	Y	Y
23 ***Bonilla***	Y	Y	Y	Y	Y	Y	Y
24 Frost	Y	Y	Y	Y	Y	Y	Y
25 Bentsen	Y	Y	Y	Y	Y	Y	Y
26 ***Armey***	Y	Y	Y	Y	Y	Y	Y
27 Ortiz	?	?	Y	Y	Y	Y	Y
28 Rodriguez	Y	Y	Y	Y	Y	Y	Y
29 Green	Y	Y	Y	Y	Y	Y	Y
30 Johnson, E.B.	Y	Y	Y	Y	Y	Y	Y
UTAH							
1 ***Hansen***	Y	Y	Y	Y	Y	Y	N
2 Matheson	Y	Y	Y	Y	Y	Y	Y
3 ***Cannon***	Y	Y	Y	Y	Y	Y	Y
VERMONT							
AL *Sanders*	Y	Y	Y	Y	Y	Y	Y
VIRGINIA							
1 ***Davis, Jo Ann***	Y	Y	Y	Y	Y	Y	N
2 ***Schrock***	Y	Y	Y	Y	Y	Y	Y
3 Scott	Y	Y	N	Y	Y	Y	Y
4 ***Forbes***	Y	Y	Y	Y	Y	Y	Y
5 *Goode*	Y	Y	Y	Y	Y	Y	N
6 ***Goodlatte***	Y	Y	Y	Y	Y	N	N
7 ***Cantor***	?	?	Y	Y	Y	N	Y
8 Moran	Y	Y	Y	Y	Y	Y	Y
9 Boucher	Y	Y	Y	Y	Y	Y	Y
10 ***Wolf***	Y	Y	Y	Y	Y	Y	Y
11 ***Davis, T.***	Y	Y	Y	Y	Y	Y	Y
WASHINGTON							
1 Inslee	Y	Y	Y	Y	Y	Y	Y
2 Larsen	Y	Y	Y	Y	Y	Y	Y
3 Baird	Y	Y	Y	Y	Y	Y	Y
4 ***Hastings***	Y	Y	Y	Y	Y	Y	Y
5 ***Nethercutt***	Y	Y	Y	Y	Y	Y	Y
6 Dicks	Y	Y	Y	Y	Y	Y	Y
7 McDermott	Y	Y	N	Y	Y	Y	Y
8 ***Dunn***	Y	Y	Y	Y	Y	Y	Y
9 Smith	Y	Y	Y	Y	Y	Y	Y
WEST VIRGINIA							
1 Mollohan	Y	Y	Y	Y	Y	Y	Y
2 ***Capito***	Y	Y	Y	Y	Y	Y	Y
3 Rahall	Y	Y	Y	Y	Y	Y	Y
WISCONSIN							
1 ***Ryan***	Y	Y	Y	Y	Y	Y	Y
2 Baldwin	Y	Y	Y	Y	Y	Y	Y
3 Kind	Y	Y	Y	Y	Y	Y	Y
4 Kleczka	Y	Y	Y	Y	Y	Y	Y
5 Barrett	Y	Y	Y	Y	Y	Y	Y
6 ***Petri***	Y	Y	Y	Y	Y	Y	N
7 Obey	Y	Y	Y	Y	Y	Y	Y
8 ***Green***	Y	Y	Y	Y	Y	Y	Y
9 ***Sensenbrenner***	Y	Y	Y	Y	Y	N	N
WYOMING							
AL ***Cubin***	?	?	?	?	?	?	?

Southern states - Ala., Ark., Fla., Ga., Ky., La., Miss., N.C., Okla., S.C., Tenn., Texas, Va.

506. HR 3529. Stimulus and Workers Benefits/Consideration of Rule. Adoption of the resolution (H Res 319) that would waive the two-thirds vote requirement for same day consideration of the rule (H Res 320) to provide for House floor consideration of the bill that would reduce individual and business taxes, extend unemployment benefits, and provide a refundable health insurance tax credit. Adopted 214-206: R 210-7; D 3-198 (ND 2-149, SD 1-49); I 1-1. Dec. 19, 2001.

507. HR 3529. Stimulus and Workers Benefits/Rule. Adoption of the rule (H Res 320) to provide for House floor consideration of the bill that would reduce individual and business taxes, extend unemployment benefits, and provide a health insurance refundable tax credit. Adopted 219-198: R 215-0; D 3-197 (ND 1-150, SD 2-47); I 1-1. Dec. 20, 2001 (in the session that began and the Congressional Record dated Dec. 19, 2001).

508. HR 3529. Stimulus and Workers Benefit/Recommit. Rangel, D-N.Y., motion to recommit the bill to the House Ways and Means Committee with instructions to strike all after the enacting clause and add a Democratic substitute that would provide an immediate rebate for individual tax filers, a temporary increase in tangible property depreciation expensing and Section 179 expensing, a temporary extension of expiring tax provisions, and interest-free school construction financing. Motion rejected 177-238: R 0-215; D 176-22 (ND 131-19, SD 45-3); I 1-1. Dec. 20, 2001 (in the session that began and the Congressional Record dated Dec. 19, 2001).

509. HR 3529. Stimulus and Workers Benefit/Passage. Passage of the bill that would reduce individual and business taxes, extend unemployment benefits, and provide a health insurance refundable tax credit at a cost of $89.8 billion in 2002 and a total $156.8 billion over 10 years. It also would provide tax relief to individuals and businesses directly affected by the Sept. 11 terrorist attacks in New York. Passed 224-193: R 214-2; D 9-190 (ND 4-147, SD 5-43); I 1-1. A "yea" was a vote in support of the president's position. Dec. 20, 2001 (in the session that began and the Congressional Record dated Dec. 19, 2001).

510. HR 3338. Fiscal 2002 Defense Appropriations/Conference Report. Adoption of the conference report on the bill that would provide $317 billion for the Defense Department for fiscal 2002, about $19 billion more than fiscal 2001. The total includes $7.8 billion for ballistic missile defense, $881 million for a new counter-terrorism program, and a 4.6 percent pay increase for military personnel. It also would allocate $20 billion in funding appropriated by the emergency supplemental spending package (PL 107-38) enacted Sept. 18, including $8.3 billion for homeland defense, $8.2 billion for New York City and other areas directly affected by the Sept. 11 attacks, and $3.5 billion in defense funds. Adopted (thus sent to the Senate) 408-6: R 216-2; D 190-4 (ND 142-4, SD 48-0); I 2-0. Dec. 20, 2001.

511. H J Res 75. Iraq Inspections/Adoption. Hyde, R-Ill., motion to suspend the rules and adopt the resolution that would urge the United States and the United Nations to insist that Iraq allow U.N. weapons inspections as required under the 1991 Persian Gulf War cease-fire agreement. Motion agreed to 392-12: R 213-1; D 177-11 (ND 131-9, SD 46-2); I 2-0. A two-thirds majority of those present and voting (270 in this case) is required for adoption under suspension of the rules. Dec. 20, 2001.

512. S 1762. Student Loan Formulas/Passage. Boehner, R-Ohio, motion to suspend the rules and pass the bill that would make permanent the federal government's current formula for determining its contribution to the federal student loan program and prevent a change to the formula scheduled to go into effect July 1, 2003. It also would maintain the current formula for determining loan interest rates until July 1, 2006. After that date, the bill would set a fixed rate of 6.8 percent for students' loans and 7.9 percent for parents' loans. Motion rejected 257-148: R 207-3; D 49-144 (ND 33-112, SD 16-32); I 1-1. A two-thirds majority of those present and voting (270 in this case) is required for passage under suspension of the rules. Dec. 20, 2001.

Key

Y	Voted for (yea).
#	Paired for.
+	Announced for.
N	Voted against (nay).
X	Paired against.
−	Announced against.
P	Voted "present."
C	Voted "present" to avoid possible conflict of interest.
?	Did not vote or otherwise make a position known.

Democrats **Republicans**
Independents

	506	507	508	509	510	511	512
ALABAMA							
1 *Callahan*	Y	Y	N	Y	Y	Y	Y
2 *Everett*	Y	Y	N	Y	Y	Y	Y
3 *Riley*	Y	Y	N	Y	Y	Y	Y
4 *Aderholt*	Y	Y	N	Y	Y	Y	Y
5 Cramer	N	N	Y	N	Y	Y	Y
6 *Bachus*	Y	Y	N	Y	Y	Y	Y
7 Hilliard	N	N	Y	N	Y	N	N
ALASKA							
AL *Young*	?	?	?	?	?	?	?
ARIZONA							
1 *Flake*	N	Y	N	Y	Y	Y	N
2 Pastor	N	N	Y	N	Y	Y	N
3 *Stump*	Y	Y	N	Y	Y	Y	Y
4 *Shadegg*	N	Y	N	Y	Y	Y	Y
5 *Kolbe*	Y	Y	N	Y	Y	Y	Y
6 *Hayworth*	Y	Y	N	Y	Y	Y	Y
ARKANSAS							
1 Berry	N	N	Y	N	Y	Y	N
2 Snyder	N	N	N	N	Y	Y	N
3 *Boozman*	Y	Y	N	Y	Y	Y	Y
4 Ross	N	N	Y	N	Y	Y	N
CALIFORNIA							
1 Thompson	N	N	Y	N	Y	Y	N
2 *Herger*	Y	Y	N	Y	Y	Y	Y
3 *Ose*	Y	Y	N	Y	Y	Y	Y
4 *Doolittle*	Y	Y	N	Y	Y	Y	Y
5 Matsui	N	N	Y	N	Y	Y	N
6 Woolsey	N	N	Y	N	Y	N	N
7 Miller, George	N	N	Y	N	Y	P	N
8 Pelosi	N	N	Y	N	Y	Y	N
9 Lee	N	N	Y	N	N	N	N
10 Tauscher	N	N	Y	N	Y	Y	N
11 *Pombo*	Y	Y	N	Y	Y	Y	Y
12 Lantos	N	N	Y	N	Y	Y	N
13 Stark	?	?	?	?	?	?	?
14 Eshoo	N	N	Y	N	Y	Y	N
15 Honda	N	N	Y	N	Y	Y	N
16 Lofgren	N	N	Y	N	Y	Y	N
17 Farr	N	N	Y	N	Y	Y	N
18 Condit	N	N	N	N	Y	Y	N
19 *Radanovich*	Y	Y	N	Y	Y	Y	Y
20 Dooley	N	N	N	N	Y	Y	N
21 *Thomas*	Y	Y	N	Y	Y	Y	Y
22 Capps	N	N	Y	N	Y	Y	N
23 *Gallegly*	Y	Y	N	Y	Y	Y	?
24 Sherman	N	N	Y	N	Y	Y	N
25 *McKeon*	Y	Y	N	Y	Y	Y	Y
26 Berman	N	N	Y	N	Y	Y	N
27 Schiff	N	N	Y	N	Y	Y	N
28 *Dreier*	Y	Y	N	Y	Y	Y	Y
29 Waxman	N	N	Y	N	?	Y	N
30 Becerra	N	N	Y	N	Y	Y	N
31 Solis	N	N	Y	N	Y	Y	N
32 Watson	N	N	Y	N	Y	Y	N
33 Roybal-Allard	N	N	Y	N	Y	Y	N
34 Napolitano	N	N	Y	N	Y	Y	N
35 Waters	N	N	Y	N	?	?	N
36 Harman	N	N	Y	N	Y	?	?
37 Millender-McD.	N	N	Y	N	Y	Y	N
38 *Horn*	Y	Y	N	Y	Y	Y	Y

	506	507	508	509	510	511	512
39 *Royce*	Y	Y	N	Y	Y	Y	Y
40 *Lewis*	Y	Y	N	Y	Y	Y	Y
41 *Miller, Gary*	Y	Y	N	Y	Y	Y	Y
42 Baca	N	N	Y	N	Y	Y	Y
43 *Calvert*	Y	Y	N	Y	Y	Y	Y
44 *Bono*	Y	Y	N	Y	Y	Y	Y
45 *Rohrabacher*	Y	Y	N	Y	Y	Y	Y
46 Sanchez	N	N	N	N	Y	Y	N
47 *Cox*	Y	Y	N	Y	Y	Y	?
48 *Issa*	Y	Y	N	Y	Y	Y	Y
49 Davis	N	N	Y	N	Y	Y	N
50 Filner	N	N	Y	N	N	Y	N
51 *Cunningham*	Y	Y	N	Y	Y	Y	Y
52 *Hunter*	Y	Y	N	Y	Y	Y	Y
COLORADO							
1 DeGette	N	N	Y	N	Y	Y	N
2 Udall	N	N	Y	N	Y	Y	N
3 *McInnis*	Y	Y	N	Y	Y	Y	Y
4 *Schaffer*	N	Y	N	Y	Y	Y	Y
5 *Hefley*	Y	?	?	?	Y	Y	Y
6 *Tancredo*	Y	Y	N	Y	Y	Y	Y
CONNECTICUT							
1 Larson	N	N	Y	N	Y	Y	N
2 *Simmons*	Y	Y	N	Y	Y	Y	Y
3 DeLauro	N	N	Y	N	Y	Y	N
4 *Shays*	Y	Y	N	Y	Y	Y	Y
5 Maloney	N	N	Y	N	Y	Y	N
6 *Johnson*	Y	Y	N	Y	Y	Y	Y
DELAWARE							
AL *Castle*	N	Y	N	Y	Y	Y	Y
FLORIDA							
1 *Miller, J.*	Y	Y	N	Y	Y	Y	Y
2 Boyd	N	N	Y	N	Y	Y	Y
3 Brown	N	N	Y	N	Y	N	N
4 *Crenshaw*	Y	Y	N	Y	Y	Y	Y
5 Thurman	N	N	Y	N	Y	Y	N
6 *Stearns*	Y	+	−	+	Y	Y	Y
7 *Mica*	Y	Y	N	Y	Y	Y	Y
8 *Keller*	Y	Y	N	Y	Y	Y	Y
9 *Bilirakis*	Y	Y	N	Y	Y	Y	Y
10 *Young*	?	Y	N	Y	Y	Y	Y
11 Davis	N	N	Y	N	Y	Y	N
12 *Putnam*	Y	Y	N	Y	Y	Y	Y
13 *Miller, D.*	Y	Y	N	Y	Y	Y	Y
14 *Goss*	Y	Y	N	Y	Y	Y	Y
15 *Weldon*	Y	Y	N	Y	Y	Y	Y
16 *Foley*	Y	Y	N	Y	Y	Y	Y
17 Meek	?	?	?	?	?	?	?
18 *Ros-Lehtinen*	Y	Y	N	Y	Y	Y	Y
19 Wexler	?	?	?	?	?	?	?
20 Deutsch	N	N	Y	N	Y	Y	N
21 *Diaz-Balart*	Y	Y	N	Y	Y	Y	Y
22 *Shaw*	Y	Y	N	Y	Y	Y	Y
23 Hastings	?	?	?	?	?	?	?
GEORGIA							
1 *Kingston*	Y	Y	N	Y	Y	Y	Y
2 Bishop	N	N	Y	N	Y	Y	Y
3 *Collins*	Y	Y	N	Y	Y	Y	Y
4 McKinney	N	N	Y	N	Y	N	N
5 Lewis	N	N	Y	N	Y	N	N
6 *Isakson*	Y	Y	N	Y	Y	Y	Y
7 *Barr*	Y	Y	N	Y	Y	Y	Y
8 *Chambliss*	Y	Y	N	Y	Y	Y	Y
9 *Deal*	Y	Y	N	Y	Y	Y	Y
10 *Norwood*	Y	Y	N	Y	Y	Y	Y
11 *Linder*	Y	Y	N	Y	Y	Y	Y
HAWAII							
1 Abercrombie	Y	N	N	N	Y	N	N
2 Mink	N	N	Y	N	Y	Y	N
IDAHO							
1 *Otter*	Y	Y	N	Y	Y	Y	Y
2 *Simpson*	Y	Y	N	Y	Y	Y	Y
ILLINOIS							
1 Rush	N	N	Y	N	N	Y	N
2 Jackson	N	N	Y	N	N	Y	N
3 Lipinski	N	N	Y	N	Y	Y	Y
4 Gutierrez	N	N	?	N	Y	Y	Y
5 Blagojevich	N	N	Y	N	Y	Y	Y
6 *Hyde*	Y	Y	N	Y	Y	Y	Y
7 Davis	N	N	Y	N	Y	Y	N
8 *Crane*	Y	Y	N	Y	Y	Y	Y
9 Schakowsky	N	N	Y	N	Y	Y	N
10 *Kirk*	Y	Y	N	Y	Y	Y	Y
11 *Weller*	Y	Y	N	Y	Y	Y	Y
12 Costello	N	N	Y	N	Y	Y	Y
13 *Biggert*	Y	Y	N	Y	Y	Y	Y

ND Northern Democrats   SD Southern Democrats

	506	507	508	509	510	511	512
14 ***Hastert***		Y	N	Y			
15 ***Johnson***	Y	Y	N	Y	Y	Y	Y
16 ***Manzullo***	Y	Y	N	Y	Y	?	?
17 Evans	N	N	Y	N	Y	Y	N
18 ***LaHood***	Y	Y	N	Y	Y	Y	Y
19 Phelps	N	N	Y	N	Y	Y	Y
20 ***Shimkus***	Y	Y	N	Y	Y	Y	Y
INDIANA							
1 Visclosky	N	N	Y	N	Y	Y	N
2 ***Pence***	Y	Y	N	Y	Y	Y	Y
3 Roemer	N	N	N	N	Y	Y	N
4 ***Souder***	Y	Y	N	Y	Y	Y	Y
5 ***Buyer***	Y	Y	N	Y	Y	Y	Y
6 ***Burton***	Y	Y	N	Y	Y	Y	Y
7 ***Kerns***	Y	Y	N	Y	Y	Y	Y
8 ***Hostettler***	Y	Y	N	Y	Y	Y	Y
9 Hill	N	N	N	N	Y	Y	Y
10 Carson	N	N	Y	N	Y	Y	N
IOWA							
1 ***Leach***	Y	Y	N	Y	Y	Y	Y
2 ***Nussle***	Y	Y	N	Y	Y	Y	Y
3 Boswell	N	N	Y	N	Y	Y	Y
4 ***Ganske***	Y	Y	N	Y	Y	Y	Y
5 ***Latham***	Y	Y	N	Y	Y	Y	Y
KANSAS							
1 ***Moran***	Y	Y	N	Y	Y	Y	N
2 ***Ryun***	Y	Y	N	Y	Y	Y	Y
3 Moore	N	N	Y	N	Y	Y	Y
4 ***Tiahrt***	Y	Y	N	Y	Y	Y	Y
KENTUCKY							
1 ***Whitfield***	Y	Y	N	Y	Y	Y	Y
2 ***Lewis***	Y	Y	N	Y	Y	Y	Y
3 ***Northup***	Y	Y	N	Y	Y	Y	Y
4 Lucas	N	Y	N	Y	Y	Y	Y
5 ***Rogers***	Y	Y	N	Y	Y	Y	Y
6 ***Fletcher***	Y	Y	N	Y	Y	Y	Y
LOUISIANA							
1 ***Vitter***	Y	Y	N	Y	Y	Y	Y
2 Jefferson	N	N	Y	N	Y	Y	N
3 ***Tauzin***	Y	Y	N	Y	Y	Y	Y
4 ***McCrery***	Y	Y	N	Y	Y	Y	Y
5 ***Cooksey***	Y	Y	N	Y	Y	Y	Y
6 ***Baker***	?	?	?	?	?	?	?
7 John	N	N	Y	Y	Y	?	?
MAINE							
1 Allen	N	N	Y	N	Y	Y	N
2 Baldacci	N	N	Y	N	Y	Y	Y
MARYLAND							
1 ***Gilchrest***	Y	Y	N	Y	Y	Y	Y
2 ***Ehrlich***	Y	Y	N	Y	Y	Y	Y
3 Cardin	N	N	Y	N	Y	Y	Y
4 Wynn	N	N	Y	N	Y	Y	N
5 Hoyer	N	N	Y	N	Y	Y	Y
6 ***Bartlett***	Y	Y	N	Y	Y	Y	Y
7 Cummings	N	N	Y	N	?	Y	N
8 ***Morella***	Y	Y	N	N	Y	Y	Y
MASSACHUSETTS							
1 Olver	N	N	Y	N	Y	Y	N
2 Neal	N	N	Y	N	Y	Y	N
3 McGovern	N	N	Y	N	Y	Y	N
4 Frank	N	N	Y	N	Y	Y	N
5 Meehan	N	N	Y	N	Y	Y	N
6 Tierney	N	N	Y	N	Y	Y	N
7 Markey	N	N	Y	N	?	Y	N
8 Capuano	N	N	Y	N	Y	P	N
9 Lynch	N	N	Y	N	Y	Y	N
10 Delahunt	N	N	Y	N	Y	Y	N
MICHIGAN							
1 Stupak	N	N	Y	N	Y	Y	Y
2 ***Hoekstra***	Y	Y	N	Y	Y	Y	Y
3 ***Ehlers***	Y	Y	N	Y	Y	P	Y
4 ***Camp***	Y	Y	N	Y	Y	Y	Y
5 Barcia	N	N	N	N	?	?	?
6 ***Upton***	Y	Y	N	Y	Y	Y	Y
7 ***Smith***	Y	Y	N	Y	Y	Y	Y
8 ***Rogers***	Y	Y	N	Y	Y	Y	Y
9 Kildee	N	N	Y	N	Y	Y	Y
10 Bonior	N	N	Y	N	Y	N	N
11 ***Knollenberg***	Y	Y	N	Y	Y	Y	Y
12 Levin	N	N	Y	N	Y	Y	N
13 Rivers	N	N	Y	N	Y	N	N
14 Conyers	N	N	Y	N	N	?	?
15 Kilpatrick	N	N	Y	N	Y	Y	N
16 Dingell	N	N	Y	N	?	P	N
MINNESOTA							
1 ***Gutknecht***	N	Y	N	Y	Y	Y	Y
2 ***Kennedy***	Y	Y	N	Y	Y	Y	Y
3 ***Ramstad***	Y	Y	N	Y	Y	Y	Y
4 McCollum	N	N	Y	N	Y	Y	N
5 Sabo	N	N	Y	N	Y	Y	N
6 Luther	?	?	?	?	?	?	?
7 Peterson	N	N	N	N	Y	Y	N
8 Oberstar	N	N	Y	N	Y	Y	N
MISSISSIPPI							
1 ***Wicker***	Y	Y	N	Y	Y	Y	Y
2 Thompson	N	N	Y	N	Y	Y	N
3 ***Pickering***	Y	Y	N	Y	Y	Y	Y
4 Shows	N	N	Y	Y	Y	Y	N
5 Taylor	N	N	?	?	Y	Y	Y
MISSOURI							
1 Clay	N	N	Y	N	?	?	?
2 ***Akin***	Y	Y	N	Y	Y	Y	Y
3 Gephardt	?	?	Y	N	Y	Y	N
4 Skelton	N	N	N	N	Y	Y	N
5 McCarthy	N	N	Y	N	Y	Y	N
6 ***Graves***	Y	Y	N	Y	Y	Y	Y
7 ***Blunt***	Y	Y	N	Y	Y	Y	Y
8 ***Emerson***	Y	Y	N	Y	Y	Y	Y
9 ***Hulshof***	Y	Y	N	Y	Y	Y	Y
MONTANA							
AL ***Rehberg***	Y	Y	N	Y	Y	Y	Y
NEBRASKA							
1 ***Bereuter***	Y	Y	N	Y	Y	Y	Y
2 ***Terry***	Y	Y	N	Y	Y	Y	Y
3 ***Osborne***	Y	Y	N	Y	Y	Y	Y
NEVADA							
1 Berkley	N	N	Y	N	Y	Y	N
2 ***Gibbons***	Y	Y	N	Y	Y	Y	Y
NEW HAMPSHIRE							
1 ***Sununu***	Y	Y	N	Y	Y	Y	Y
2 ***Bass***	Y	Y	N	Y	Y	Y	Y
NEW JERSEY							
1 Andrews	N	N	Y	N	Y	Y	N
2 ***LoBiondo***	Y	Y	N	Y	Y	Y	Y
3 ***Saxton***	Y	Y	N	Y	Y	Y	Y
4 ***Smith***	Y	Y	N	Y	Y	Y	?
5 ***Roukema***	Y	Y	N	Y	Y	Y	?
6 Pallone	N	N	Y	N	Y	Y	N
7 ***Ferguson***	Y	Y	N	Y	Y	Y	Y
8 Pascrell	N	N	Y	N	Y	Y	N
9 Rothman	N	N	Y	N	Y	Y	N
10 Payne	N	N	Y	N	Y	N	N
11 ***Frelinghuysen***	Y	Y	N	Y	Y	Y	Y
12 Holt	N	N	Y	N	Y	Y	N
13 Menendez	N	N	Y	N	Y	Y	N
NEW MEXICO							
1 ***Wilson, H.***	Y	Y	N	Y	Y	P	Y
2 ***Skeen***	Y	Y	N	Y	Y	Y	Y
3 Udall	N	N	Y	N	Y	Y	N
NEW YORK							
1 ***Grucci***	Y	Y	N	Y	Y	Y	Y
2 Israel	N	N	N	Y	Y	Y	N
3 ***King***	Y	Y	N	Y	Y	Y	Y
4 McCarthy	N	N	Y	N	Y	Y	N
5 Ackerman	N	N	Y	N	Y	Y	N
6 Meeks	N	N	Y	N	Y	?	N
7 Crowley	N	N	Y	N	Y	Y	N
8 Nadler	N	N	Y	N	Y	Y	N
9 Weiner	N	N	Y	N	Y	Y	N
10 Towns	N	N	Y	N	Y	Y	N
11 Owens	?	?	?	?	Y	Y	N
12 Velázquez	N	N	Y	N	Y	Y	N
13 ***Fossella***	Y	Y	N	Y	Y	Y	Y
14 Maloney	N	N	Y	N	Y	Y	Y
15 Rangel	?	N	Y	N	Y	Y	N
16 Serrano	N	N	Y	N	Y	Y	N
17 Engel	N	N	Y	N	Y	Y	N
18 Lowey	N	N	Y	N	Y	Y	N
19 ***Kelly***	Y	Y	N	Y	Y	Y	Y
20 ***Gilman***	Y	Y	N	Y	Y	Y	Y
21 McNulty	N	N	Y	N	Y	Y	Y
22 ***Sweeney***	Y	Y	N	Y	Y	Y	Y
23 ***Boehlert***	Y	Y	N	Y	Y	Y	Y
24 ***McHugh***	Y	Y	N	Y	Y	Y	Y
25 ***Walsh***	Y	Y	N	Y	Y	Y	?
26 Hinchey	N	N	Y	N	Y	Y	N
27 ***Reynolds***	Y	Y	N	Y	Y	Y	Y
28 Slaughter	N	N	Y	N	Y	P	?
29 LaFalce	N	N	Y	N	Y	Y	N
30 ***Quinn***	Y	Y	N	Y	Y	Y	Y
31 ***Houghton***	Y	Y	N	Y	Y	Y	Y
NORTH CAROLINA							
1 Clayton	N	N	Y	N	Y	Y	N
2 Etheridge	N	N	Y	N	Y	Y	N
3 ***Jones***	N	?	N	Y	Y	Y	Y
4 Price	N	N	Y	N	Y	Y	N
5 ***Burr***	Y	Y	N	Y	Y	Y	Y
6 ***Coble***	Y	Y	N	Y	Y	Y	Y
7 McIntyre	N	N	Y	N	Y	Y	Y
8 ***Hayes***	Y	Y	N	Y	Y	Y	Y
9 ***Myrick***	Y	Y	N	Y	Y	Y	Y
10 ***Ballenger***	Y	Y	N	Y	Y	Y	Y
11 ***Taylor***	Y	Y	N	Y	Y	Y	Y
12 Watt	N	N	Y	N	Y	Y	N
NORTH DAKOTA							
AL Pomeroy	N	N	Y	N	Y	Y	Y
OHIO							
1 ***Chabot***	Y	Y	N	Y	Y	Y	Y
2 ***Portman***	Y	Y	N	Y	Y	Y	Y
3 Hall	?	?	?	?	?	?	?
4 ***Oxley***	Y	?	?	?	Y	Y	Y
5 ***Gillmor***	Y	Y	N	Y	Y	Y	Y
6 Strickland	N	N	Y	N	Y	Y	Y
7 ***Hobson***	Y	Y	N	Y	Y	Y	Y
8 ***Boehner***	Y	Y	N	Y	Y	Y	Y
9 Kaptur	N	N	Y	N	Y	Y	?
10 Kucinich	N	N	Y	N	Y	Y	N
11 Jones	N	N	Y	N	?	Y	N
12 ***Tiberi***	Y	Y	N	Y	Y	Y	Y
13 Brown	N	N	Y	N	Y	Y	N
14 Sawyer	N	N	Y	N	Y	Y	Y
15 ***Pryce***	Y	Y	N	Y	Y	Y	Y
16 ***Regula***	Y	Y	N	Y	Y	Y	Y
17 Traficant	Y	Y	N	Y	Y	?	?
18 ***Ney***	Y	Y	N	Y	Y	Y	Y
19 ***LaTourette***	Y	Y	N	N	Y	Y	Y
OKLAHOMA							
1 ***Largent***	Y	Y	N	Y	Y	Y	Y
2 Carson	N	N	Y	N	Y	Y	Y
3 ***Watkins***	Y	Y	N	Y	Y	Y	Y
4 ***Watts***	Y	Y	N	Y	Y	Y	Y
5 ***Istook***	Y	Y	N	Y	Y	Y	Y
6 ***Lucas***	Y	Y	N	Y	Y	Y	Y
OREGON							
1 Wu	N	N	N	N	Y	Y	N
2 ***Walden***	Y	Y	N	Y	Y	Y	Y
3 Blumenauer	N	N	Y	N	Y	Y	N
4 DeFazio	N	N	Y	N	Y	P	N
5 Hooley	N	N	N	N	Y	Y	Y
PENNSYLVANIA							
1 Brady	N	N	Y	N	Y	Y	N
2 Fattah	N	N	?	?	Y	N	Y
3 Borski	N	N	Y	N	Y	Y	N
4 ***Hart***	Y	Y	N	Y	Y	Y	Y
5 ***Peterson***	Y	Y	N	Y	Y	?	?
6 Holden	N	N	Y	N	Y	Y	Y
7 ***Weldon***	Y	Y	N	Y	Y	Y	Y
8 ***Greenwood***	Y	Y	N	Y	Y	Y	Y
9 ***Shuster, Bill***	Y	Y	N	Y	Y	Y	Y
10 ***Sherwood***	Y	Y	N	Y	Y	Y	Y
11 Kanjorski	N	N	N	N	Y	Y	Y
12 Murtha	N	N	N	N	Y	Y	N
13 Hoeffel	N	N	Y	N	Y	Y	N
14 Coyne	N	N	Y	N	Y	?	?
15 ***Toomey***	N	Y	N	Y	Y	Y	Y
16 ***Pitts***	Y	Y	N	Y	Y	Y	Y
17 ***Gekas***	Y	Y	N	Y	Y	Y	Y
18 Doyle	N	N	Y	N	Y	Y	Y
19 ***Platts***	Y	Y	N	Y	Y	Y	Y
20 Mascara	N	N	Y	N	Y	Y	Y
21 ***English***	Y	Y	N	Y	Y	Y	Y
RHODE ISLAND							
1 Kennedy	N	?	Y	N	Y	Y	N
2 Langevin	N	N	Y	N	Y	Y	N
SOUTH CAROLINA							
1 ***Brown***	Y	Y	N	Y	Y	Y	Y
2 ***Wilson, J.***	Y	Y	N	Y	Y	Y	Y
3 ***Graham***	Y	Y	N	Y	Y	Y	Y
4 ***DeMint***	Y	Y	N	Y	Y	Y	Y
5 Spratt	N	N	Y	N	?	Y	N
6 Clyburn	N	N	Y	N	Y	Y	N
SOUTH DAKOTA							
AL ***Thune***	Y	Y	N	Y	Y	Y	Y
TENNESSEE							
1 ***Jenkins***	Y	Y	N	Y	Y	Y	Y
2 ***Duncan***	Y	Y	N	Y	Y	Y	Y
3 ***Wamp***	Y	Y	N	Y	Y	Y	Y
4 ***Hilleary***	Y	Y	?	Y	Y	Y	Y
5 Clement	?	?	?	?	?	?	?
6 Gordon	N	?	Y	N	Y	Y	Y
7 ***Bryant***	Y	Y	N	Y	Y	Y	Y
8 Tanner	N	N	Y	N	Y	Y	N
9 Ford	N	N	?	?	Y	Y	Y
TEXAS							
1 Sandlin	N	N	Y	N	Y	Y	N
2 Turner	N	N	Y	N	Y	Y	Y
3 ***Johnson, Sam***	Y	Y	N	Y	Y	Y	Y
4 Hall	Y	Y	N	Y	Y	Y	Y
5 ***Sessions***	Y	Y	N	Y	Y	Y	Y
6 ***Barton***	Y	Y	N	Y	Y	Y	Y
7 ***Culberson***	Y	Y	N	Y	Y	Y	Y
8 ***Brady***	Y	Y	N	Y	Y	Y	Y
9 Lampson	N	N	Y	N	Y	Y	N
10 Doggett	N	N	Y	N	Y	Y	N
11 Edwards	N	N	Y	N	Y	Y	Y
12 ***Granger***	Y	Y	N	Y	Y	Y	Y
13 ***Thornberry***	Y	Y	N	Y	Y	Y	Y
14 ***Paul***	Y	Y	N	Y	N	N	N
15 Hinojosa	N	N	Y	N	Y	Y	N
16 Reyes	N	N	Y	N	Y	Y	N
17 Stenholm	N	N	Y	N	Y	Y	Y
18 Jackson-Lee	N	N	Y	N	Y	Y	N
19 ***Combest***	Y	Y	N	Y	Y	Y	?
20 Gonzalez	N	N	Y	N	Y	Y	N
21 ***Smith***	Y	Y	N	Y	Y	Y	Y
22 ***DeLay***	Y	Y	N	Y	Y	Y	Y
23 ***Bonilla***	Y	Y	N	Y	Y	Y	Y
24 Frost	N	N	Y	N	Y	Y	N
25 Bentsen	N	N	Y	N	Y	Y	Y
26 ***Armey***	Y	Y	N	Y	Y	Y	Y
27 Ortiz	N	N	Y	N	Y	Y	Y
28 Rodriguez	N	N	Y	N	Y	Y	N
29 Green	N	N	Y	N	Y	Y	N
30 Johnson, E.B.	N	N	Y	N	?	?	?
UTAH							
1 ***Hansen***	Y	Y	N	Y	Y	Y	Y
2 Matheson	N	N	Y	N	Y	Y	Y
3 ***Cannon***	Y	Y	N	Y	Y	Y	Y
VERMONT							
AL *Sanders*	N	N	Y	N	Y	Y	N
VIRGINIA							
1 ***Davis, Jo Ann***	Y	Y	N	Y	Y	Y	Y
2 ***Schrock***	Y	Y	N	Y	Y	Y	Y
3 Scott	N	N	Y	N	Y	Y	N
4 ***Forbes***	Y	Y	N	Y	Y	Y	Y
5 *Goode*	Y	Y	N	Y	Y	Y	Y
6 ***Goodlatte***	Y	Y	N	Y	Y	Y	Y
7 ***Cantor***	Y	Y	N	Y	Y	Y	Y
8 Moran	N	N	Y	N	Y	Y	Y
9 Boucher	N	N	Y	N	Y	Y	N
10 ***Wolf***	Y	Y	N	Y	Y	Y	Y
11 ***Davis, T.***	Y	Y	N	Y	Y	Y	Y
WASHINGTON							
1 Inslee	N	N	Y	N	Y	Y	N
2 Larsen	N	N	Y	N	Y	Y	Y
3 Baird	N	N	Y	N	Y	Y	N
4 ***Hastings***	Y	Y	N	Y	Y	Y	Y
5 ***Nethercutt***	Y	Y	N	Y	Y	Y	Y
6 Dicks	N	N	?	?	Y	Y	N
7 McDermott	N	N	Y	N	Y	N	N
8 ***Dunn***	Y	Y	N	Y	Y	Y	Y
9 Smith	N	N	N	N	Y	Y	N
WEST VIRGINIA							
1 Mollohan	N	N	N	N	Y	Y	Y
2 ***Capito***	Y	Y	N	Y	Y	Y	Y
3 Rahall	N	N	N	N	Y	Y	Y
WISCONSIN							
1 ***Ryan***	Y	Y	N	Y	Y	Y	Y
2 Baldwin	N	N	Y	N	Y	N	N
3 Kind	N	N	N	N	Y	Y	N
4 Kleczka	N	N	Y	N	Y	Y	N
5 Barrett	N	N	Y	N	Y	Y	Y
6 ***Petri***	Y	Y	N	Y	N	Y	Y
7 Obey	N	N	Y	N	Y	Y	N
8 ***Green***	Y	Y	N	Y	Y	Y	Y
9 ***Sensenbrenner***	Y	Y	N	Y	Y	Y	Y
WYOMING							
AL ***Cubin***	?	?	?	?	?	?	?

Southern states - Ala., Ark., Fla., Ga., Ky., La., Miss., N.C., Okla., S.C., Tenn., Texas, Va.

House Roll Call Votes
By Subject

Appendix S

SENATE ROLL CALL VOTES

Senate Roll Call Votes By Bill Number

Senate Bills

S 1, S-24, S-25, S-26, S-27, S-28, S-38, S-39, S-40, S-41
S 27, S-13, S-14, S-15, S-16, S-17, S-18
S 149, S-57
S 235, S-6
S 248, S-6
S 320, S-7
S 350, S-23
S 420, S-9, S-10, S-11, S-12
S 1052, S-42, S-43, S-44, S-45, S-46
S 1077, S-47, S-48
S 1172, S-50
S 1218, S-52
S 1246, S-53, S-54, S-56
S 1426, S-59
S 1438, S-60, S-61, S-75
S 1447, S-62
S 1450, S-60
S 1510, S-63
S 1731, S-73, S-74, S-75, S-76, S-77
S 2904, S-60

S J Res 4, S-15
S J Res 6, S-9
S J Res 22, S-58
S J Res 23, S-59
S J Res 25, S-62
S J Res 28, S-70

House Bills

H Con Res 83, S-18, S-19, S-20, S-21, S-22, S-26
H Con Res 295, S-77

H J Res 51, S-61

HR 1, S-76
HR 10, S-71, S-72, S-73
HR 333, S-49
HR 1552, S-70
HR 1836, S-28, S-30, S-31, S-32, S-33, S-34, S-35, S-36, S-37
HR 2216, S-48
HR 2217, S-48, S-64
HR 2299, S-51, S-52, S-53, S-54, S-72
HR 2311, S-49, S-50, S-67
HR 2330, S-66
HR 2500, S-58, S-70
HR 2506, S-64, S-65, S-66
HR 2590, S-67
HR 2620, S-54, S-55, S-69
HR 2883, S-69
HR 2904, S-64
HR 2944, S-74
HR 2994, S-68, S-69
HR 3061, S-67, S-68, S-77
HR 3090, S-70
HR 3162, S-66
HR 3338, S-73, S-74, S-77

Key

Y	Voted for (yea).
#	Paired for.
+	Announced for.
N	Voted against (nay).
X	Paired against.
–	Announced against.
P	Voted "present."
C	Voted "present" to avoid possible conflict of interest.
?	Did not vote or otherwise make a position known.

Democrats **Republicans**
Independents

	1	2	3	4	5
ALABAMA					
Shelby	Y	Y	Y	Y	Y
Sessions	Y	Y	Y	Y	Y
ALASKA					
Stevens	Y	Y	Y	Y	Y
Murkowski	Y	Y	Y	Y	Y
ARIZONA					
McCain	Y	Y	Y	Y	Y
Kyl	Y	Y	Y	Y	Y
ARKANSAS					
Hutchinson	Y	Y	Y	Y	Y
Lincoln	Y	Y	Y	Y	Y
CALIFORNIA					
Feinstein	Y	Y	Y	Y	Y
Boxer	Y	Y	Y	Y	Y
COLORADO					
Campbell	Y	Y	Y	Y	Y
Allard	Y	Y	Y	Y	Y
CONNECTICUT					
Dodd	Y	Y	Y	Y	Y
Lieberman	Y	Y	Y	Y	Y
DELAWARE					
Carper	Y	Y	Y	Y	Y
Biden	Y	Y	Y	Y	Y
FLORIDA					
Graham	Y	Y	Y	Y	Y
Nelson	Y	Y	Y	Y	Y
GEORGIA					
Miller	Y	Y	Y	Y	Y
Cleland	Y	Y	Y	Y	Y
HAWAII					
Inouye	Y	Y	Y	Y	Y
Akaka	Y	Y	Y	Y	Y
IDAHO					
Craig	Y	Y	Y	Y	Y
Crapo	Y	Y	Y	Y	Y
ILLINOIS					
Durbin	Y	Y	Y	Y	Y
Fitzgerald	Y	Y	Y	Y	Y
INDIANA					
Lugar	Y	Y	Y	Y	Y
Bayh	Y	Y	Y	Y	Y
IOWA					
Grassley	Y	Y	Y	Y	Y
Harkin	Y	Y	Y	Y	Y
KANSAS					
Brownback	Y	Y	Y	Y	Y
Roberts	Y	Y	Y	Y	Y
KENTUCKY					
McConnell	Y	Y	Y	Y	Y
Bunning	Y	Y	Y	Y	Y
LOUISIANA					
Breaux	Y	Y	Y	Y	Y
Landrieu	Y	Y	Y	Y	Y
MAINE					
Snowe	Y	Y	Y	Y	Y
Collins	Y	Y	Y	Y	Y
MARYLAND					
Sarbanes	Y	Y	Y	Y	Y
Mikulski	Y	Y	Y	Y	Y
MASSACHUSETTS					
Kennedy	Y	Y	Y	Y	Y
Kerry	Y	Y	Y	Y	Y
MICHIGAN					
Levin	Y	Y	Y	Y	Y
Stabenow	Y	Y	Y	Y	Y
MINNESOTA					
Wellstone	Y	Y	Y	Y	Y
Dayton	Y	Y	Y	Y	Y
MISSISSIPPI					
Cochran	Y	Y	Y	Y	Y
Lott	Y	Y	Y	Y	Y
MISSOURI					
Bond	Y	Y	Y	Y	Y
Carnahan	Y	Y	Y	Y	Y
MONTANA					
Baucus	Y	Y	Y	Y	Y
Burns	Y	Y	Y	Y	Y
NEBRASKA					
Nelson	Y	Y	Y	Y	Y
Hagel	Y	Y	Y	Y	Y
NEVADA					
Reid	Y	Y	Y	Y	Y
Ensign	Y	Y	Y	Y	Y
NEW HAMPSHIRE					
Smith	Y	Y	Y	Y	Y
Gregg	Y	Y	Y	Y	Y
NEW JERSEY					
Corzine	Y	Y	Y	Y	Y
Torricelli	Y	Y	Y	Y	Y
NEW MEXICO					
Domenici	Y	Y	Y	Y	Y
Bingaman	Y	Y	Y	Y	Y
NEW YORK					
Clinton	Y	Y	Y	Y	Y
Schumer	Y	Y	Y	Y	Y
NORTH CAROLINA					
Helms	Y	Y	Y	Y	Y
Edwards	Y	Y	Y	Y	Y
NORTH DAKOTA					
Conrad	Y	Y	Y	Y	Y
Dorgan	Y	Y	Y	Y	Y
OHIO					
DeWine	Y	Y	Y	Y	Y
Voinovich	Y	Y	Y	Y	Y
OKLAHOMA					
Nickles	Y	Y	Y	Y	Y
Inhofe	Y	Y	Y	Y	Y
OREGON					
Wyden	Y	Y	Y	Y	Y
Smith	Y	Y	Y	Y	Y
PENNSYLVANIA					
Specter	Y	Y	Y	Y	Y
Santorum	Y	Y	Y	Y	Y
RHODE ISLAND					
Reed	Y	Y	Y	Y	Y
Chafee	Y	Y	Y	Y	Y
SOUTH CAROLINA					
Thurmond	Y	Y	Y	Y	Y
Hollings	Y	Y	Y	Y	Y
SOUTH DAKOTA					
Daschle	Y	Y	Y	Y	Y
Johnson	Y	Y	Y	Y	Y
TENNESSEE					
Thompson	Y	Y	Y	Y	Y
Frist	Y	Y	Y	Y	Y
TEXAS					
Gramm	Y	Y	Y	Y	Y
Hutchison	Y	Y	Y	Y	Y
UTAH					
Hatch	Y	Y	Y	Y	Y
Bennett	Y	Y	Y	Y	Y
VERMONT					
Leahy	Y	Y	Y	Y	Y
Jeffords	Y	Y	Y	Y	Y
VIRGINIA					
Warner	Y	Y	Y	Y	Y
Allen	Y	Y	Y	Y	Y
WASHINGTON					
Cantwell	Y	Y	Y	Y	Y
Murray	Y	Y	Y	Y	Y
WEST VIRGINIA					
Byrd	Y	Y	Y	Y	Y
Rockefeller	Y	Y	Y	Y	Y
WISCONSIN					
Kohl	Y	Y	Y	Y	Y
Feingold	Y	Y	Y	Y	Y
WYOMING					
Thomas	Y	Y	Y	Y	Y
Enzi	Y	Y	Y	Y	Y

ND Northern Democrats   SD Southern Democrats

Southern states - Ala., Ark., Fla., Ga., Ky., La., Miss., N.C., Okla., S.C., Tenn., Texas, Va.

1. Daniels Nomination/Confirmation. Confirmation of Mitchell E. Daniels Jr. of Indiana to be director of the Office of Management and Budget. Confirmed 100-0: R 50-0; D 50-0 (ND 41-0, SD 9-0). A "yea" was a vote in support of the president's position. Jan. 23, 2001.

2. Principi Nomination/Confirmation. Confirmation of President Bush's nomination of Anthony Principi of California to be secretary of Veterans Affairs. Confirmed 100-0: R 50-0; D 50-0 (ND 41-0, SD 9-0). A "yea" was a vote in support of the president's position. Jan. 23, 2001.

3. Martinez Nomination/Confirmation. Confirmation of President Bush's nomination of Mel Martinez of Florida to be secretary of Housing and Urban Development. Confirmed 100-0: R 50-0; D 50-0 (ND 41-0, SD 9-0). A "yea" was a vote in support of the president's position. Jan. 23, 2001.

4. Thompson Nomination/Confirmation. Confirmation of President Bush's nomination of Tommy G. Thompson of Wisconsin to be secretary of Health and Human Services. Confirmed 100-0: R 50-0; D 50-0 (ND 41-0, SD 9-0). A "yea" was a vote in support of the president's position. Jan. 24, 2001.

5. Mineta Nomination/Confirmation. Confirmation of President Bush's nomination of Norman Y. Mineta of California to be secretary of Transportation. Confirmed 100-0: R 50-0; D 50-0 (ND 41-0, SD 9-0). A "yea" was a vote in support of the president's position. Jan. 24, 2001.

ALABAMA	6	7	8
Shelby	Y	Y	Y
Sessions	Y	Y	Y
ALASKA			
Stevens	Y	Y	Y
Murkowski	Y	Y	Y
ARIZONA			
McCain	Y	Y	Y
Kyl	Y	Y	Y
ARKANSAS			
Hutchinson	Y	Y	Y
Lincoln	Y	Y	N
CALIFORNIA			
Feinstein	Y	Y	N
Boxer	N	Y	N
COLORADO			
Campbell	Y	Y	Y
Allard	Y	Y	Y
CONNECTICUT			
Dodd	Y	Y	Y
Lieberman	N	Y	N
DELAWARE			
Carper	Y	Y	N
Biden	N	Y	N
FLORIDA			
Graham	Y	Y	N
Nelson	Y	Y	N
GEORGIA			
Miller	Y	Y	Y
Cleland	N	Y	N
HAWAII			
Inouye	Y	Y	N
Akaka	Y	Y	N
IDAHO			
Craig	Y	Y	Y
Crapo	Y	Y	Y
ILLINOIS			
Durbin	N	Y	N
Fitzgerald	Y	Y	Y
INDIANA			
Lugar	Y	Y	Y
Bayh	N	Y	N

IOWA	6	7	8
Grassley	Y	Y	Y
Harkin	N	Y	N
KANSAS			
Brownback	Y	Y	Y
Roberts	Y	Y	Y
KENTUCKY			
McConnell	Y	Y	Y
Bunning	Y	Y	Y
LOUISIANA			
Breaux	Y	Y	Y
Landrieu	Y	Y	N
MAINE			
Snowe	Y	Y	Y
Collins	Y	Y	Y
MARYLAND			
Sarbanes	N	Y	N
Mikulski	N	Y	N
MASSACHUSETTS			
Kennedy	N	Y	N
Kerry	N	Y	N
MICHIGAN			
Levin	N	Y	N
Stabenow	N	Y	N
MINNESOTA			
Wellstone	N	Y	N
Dayton	N	Y	N
MISSISSIPPI			
Cochran	Y	Y	Y
Lott	Y	Y	Y
MISSOURI			
Bond	Y	Y	Y
Carnahan	Y	Y	N
MONTANA			
Baucus	Y	Y	N
Burns	Y	Y	Y
NEBRASKA			
Nelson	Y	Y	Y
Hagel	Y	Y	Y
NEVADA			
Reid	Y	Y	N
Ensign	Y	Y	Y

NEW HAMPSHIRE	6	7	8
Smith	Y	Y	Y
Gregg	Y	Y	Y
NEW JERSEY			
Corzine	N	Y	N
Torricelli	N	Y	N
NEW MEXICO			
Domenici	Y	Y	Y
Bingaman	Y	Y	N
NEW YORK			
Clinton	N	Y	N
Schumer	N	Y	N
NORTH CAROLINA			
Helms	Y	Y	Y
Edwards	N	Y	N
NORTH DAKOTA			
Conrad	Y	Y	Y
Dorgan	?	?	Y
OHIO			
DeWine	Y	Y	Y
Voinovich	Y	Y	Y
OKLAHOMA			
Nickles	Y	Y	Y
Inhofe	Y	Y	Y
OREGON			
Wyden	N	Y	N
Smith	Y	Y	Y
PENNSYLVANIA			
Specter	Y	Y	Y
Santorum	Y	Y	Y
RHODE ISLAND			
Reed	N	Y	N
Chafee	Y	Y	Y
SOUTH CAROLINA			
Thurmond	Y	Y	Y
Hollings	Y	Y	N
SOUTH DAKOTA			
Daschle	Y	Y	N
Johnson	Y	Y	N
TENNESSEE			
Thompson	Y	Y	Y
Frist	Y	Y	Y

Key

Y	Voted for (yea).
#	Paired for.
+	Announced for.
N	Voted against (nay).
X	Paired against.
–	Announced against.
P	Voted "present."
C	Voted "present" to avoid possible conflict of interest.
?	Did not vote or otherwise make a position known.

Democrats **Republicans**
Independents

TEXAS	6	7	8
Gramm	Y	Y	Y
Hutchison	Y	Y	Y
UTAH			
Hatch	Y	Y	Y
Bennett	Y	Y	Y
VERMONT			
Leahy	N	Y	N
Jeffords	Y	Y	Y
VIRGINIA			
Warner	Y	Y	Y
Allen	Y	Y	Y
WASHINGTON			
Cantwell	Y	Y	N
Murray	Y	Y	N
WEST VIRGINIA			
Byrd	Y	Y	Y
Rockefeller	N	Y	N
WISCONSIN			
Kohl	Y	Y	N
Feingold	Y	Y	Y
WYOMING			
Thomas	Y	Y	Y
Enzi	Y	Y	Y

ND Northern Democrats   SD Southern Democrats

Southern states - Ala., Ark., Fla., Ga., Ky., La., Miss., N.C., Okla., S.C., Tenn., Texas, Va.

6. Norton Nomination/Confirmation. Confirmation of President Bush's nomination of Gale A. Norton of Colorado to be secretary of Interior. Confirmed 75-24: R 50-0; D 25-24 (ND 18-22, SD 7-2). A "yea" was a vote in support of the president's position. Jan. 30, 2001.

7. Whitman Nomination/Confirmation. Confirmation of President Bush's nomination of Christine Todd Whitman of New Jersey to be EPA administrator. Confirmed 99-0: R 50-0; D 49-0 (ND 40-0, SD 9-0). A "yea" was a vote in support of the president's position. Jan. 30, 2001.

8. Ashcroft Nomination/Confirmation. Confirmation of President Bush's nomination of John Ashcroft of Missouri to be attorney general. Confirmed 58-42: R 50-0; D 8-42 (ND 6-35, SD 2-7). A "yea" was a vote in support of the president's position. Feb. 1, 2001.

	9	10	11
ALABAMA			
Shelby	Y	Y	Y
Sessions	Y	Y	Y
ALASKA			
Stevens	Y	Y	Y
Murkowski	Y	Y	Y
ARIZONA			
McCain	Y	Y	Y
Kyl	Y	Y	Y
ARKANSAS			
Hutchinson	Y	Y	Y
Lincoln	Y	Y	Y
CALIFORNIA			
Feinstein	Y	Y	Y
Boxer	Y	Y	Y
COLORADO			
Campbell	Y	Y	Y
Allard	Y	Y	Y
CONNECTICUT			
Dodd	Y	Y	Y
Lieberman	Y	Y	Y
DELAWARE			
Carper	Y	Y	Y
Biden	Y	Y	Y
FLORIDA			
Graham	Y	Y	Y
Nelson	Y	Y	Y
GEORGIA			
Miller	Y	Y	?
Cleland	Y	Y	Y
HAWAII			
Inouye	?	?	Y
Akaka	Y	Y	Y
IDAHO			
Craig	Y	Y	Y
Crapo	Y	Y	?
ILLINOIS			
Durbin	Y	Y	Y
Fitzgerald	Y	Y	Y
INDIANA			
Lugar	Y	Y	Y
Bayh	Y	Y	Y

	9	10	11
IOWA			
Grassley	Y	Y	Y
Harkin	Y	Y	Y
KANSAS			
Brownback	Y	Y	Y
Roberts	Y	Y	Y
KENTUCKY			
McConnell	Y	Y	Y
Bunning	Y	Y	Y
LOUISIANA			
Breaux	?	Y	Y
Landrieu	Y	Y	Y
MAINE			
Snowe	Y	Y	Y
Collins	Y	Y	Y
MARYLAND			
Sarbanes	Y	Y	Y
Mikulski	Y	Y	Y
MASSACHUSETTS			
Kennedy	Y	Y	Y
Kerry	Y	Y	Y
MICHIGAN			
Levin	Y	Y	Y
Stabenow	Y	Y	Y
MINNESOTA			
Wellstone	Y	Y	Y
Dayton	Y	Y	Y
MISSISSIPPI			
Cochran	Y	Y	Y
Lott	Y	Y	Y
MISSOURI			
Bond	Y	Y	Y
Carnahan	Y	Y	Y
MONTANA			
Baucus	Y	Y	Y
Burns	Y	Y	Y
NEBRASKA			
Nelson	Y	Y	Y
Hagel	Y	Y	Y
NEVADA			
Reid	Y	Y	Y
Ensign	Y	Y	Y

	9	10	11
NEW HAMPSHIRE			
Smith	Y	Y	Y
Gregg	Y	Y	Y
NEW JERSEY			
Corzine	Y	Y	Y
Torricelli	Y	Y	Y
NEW MEXICO			
Domenici	Y	Y	Y
Bingaman	Y	Y	Y
NEW YORK			
Clinton	Y	Y	Y
Schumer	Y	Y	Y
NORTH CAROLINA			
Helms	Y	Y	Y
Edwards	Y	Y	Y
NORTH DAKOTA			
Conrad	Y	Y	Y
Dorgan	Y	Y	Y
OHIO			
DeWine	Y	Y	Y
Voinovich	Y	Y	Y
OKLAHOMA			
Nickles	Y	Y	Y
Inhofe	Y	Y	Y
OREGON			
Wyden	Y	Y	Y
Smith	Y	Y	Y
PENNSYLVANIA			
Specter	Y	Y	Y
Santorum	Y	Y	Y
RHODE ISLAND			
Reed	Y	Y	Y
Chafee	Y	Y	Y
SOUTH CAROLINA			
Thurmond	Y	Y	Y
Hollings	Y	Y	Y
SOUTH DAKOTA			
Daschle	Y	Y	Y
Johnson	Y	Y	Y
TENNESSEE			
Thompson	Y	Y	Y
Frist	Y	Y	Y

Key

Y	Voted for (yea).
#	Paired for.
+	Announced for.
N	Voted against (nay).
X	Paired against.
–	Announced against.
P	Voted "present."
C	Voted "present" to avoid possible conflict of interest.
?	Did not vote or otherwise make a position known.

Democrats   **Republicans**
Independents

	9	10	11
TEXAS			
Gramm	Y	Y	Y
Hutchison	Y	Y	Y
UTAH			
Hatch	Y	Y	Y
Bennett	Y	Y	Y
VERMONT			
Leahy	Y	Y	Y
Jeffords	Y	Y	Y
VIRGINIA			
Warner	Y	Y	Y
Allen	Y	Y	Y
WASHINGTON			
Cantwell	Y	Y	Y
Murray	Y	Y	Y
WEST VIRGINIA			
Byrd	Y	Y	Y
Rockefeller	Y	Y	Y
WISCONSIN			
Kohl	Y	Y	Y
Feingold	Y	Y	Y
WYOMING			
Thomas	Y	Y	Y
Enzi	Y	Y	Y

ND Northern Democrats   SD Southern Democrats

Southern states - Ala., Ark., Fla., Ga., Ky., La., Miss., N.C., Okla., S.C., Tenn., Texas, Va.

9. Zoellick Nomination/Confirmation. Confirmation of President Bush's nomination of Robert B. Zoellick of Virginia to be U.S. trade representative. Confirmed 98-0: R 50-0; D 48-0 (ND 40-0, SD 8-0). A "yea" was a vote in support of the president's position. Feb. 6, 2001.

10. S 248. U.N. Dues/Passage. Passage of the bill that would allow the release of $582 million in back dues to the United Nations and amend federal law that sets the U.S. assessment rate for U.N. peacekeeping operations. The new rate would be no more than 28.15 percent. Passed 99-0: R 50-0; D 49-0 (ND 40-0, SD 9-0). Feb. 7, 2001.

11. S 235. Pipeline Safety/Passage. Passage of a bill that would authorize $86 million over three years, beginning in fiscal 2002, for federal pipeline safety programs. The bill also would authorize $57 million over three years for grants to states to assist in pipeline safety activities. It would require the National Academy of Sciences to conduct a study of the pipeline capabilities in New England, as well as a study aimed at determining the causes of the recent price increase of natural gas. Passed 98-0: R 49-0; D 49-0 (ND 41-0, SD 8-0). Feb. 8, 2001.

Key

Y	Voted for (yea).
#	Paired for.
+	Announced for.
N	Voted against (nay).
X	Paired against.
–	Announced against.
P	Voted "present."
C	Voted "present" to avoid possible conflict of interest.
?	Did not vote or otherwise make a position known.

Democrats **Republicans**
Independents

	12	13
ALABAMA		
Shelby	Y	Y
Sessions	Y	Y
ALASKA		
Stevens	Y	Y
Murkowski	Y	Y
ARIZONA		
McCain	Y	Y
Kyl	Y	Y
ARKANSAS		
Hutchinson	Y	Y
Lincoln	Y	Y
CALIFORNIA		
Feinstein	Y	Y
Boxer	Y	Y
COLORADO		
Campbell	Y	Y
Allard	Y	Y
CONNECTICUT		
Dodd	Y	Y
Lieberman	Y	Y
DELAWARE		
Carper	Y	Y
Biden	Y	Y
FLORIDA		
Graham	Y	?
Nelson	Y	Y
GEORGIA		
Miller	Y	?
Cleland	Y	Y
HAWAII		
Inouye	Y	Y
Akaka	Y	Y
IDAHO		
Craig	Y	Y
Crapo	?	?
ILLINOIS		
Durbin	Y	Y
Fitzgerald	Y	Y
INDIANA		
Lugar	Y	Y
Bayh	Y	Y

	12	13
IOWA		
Grassley	Y	Y
Harkin	Y	Y
KANSAS		
Brownback	Y	Y
Roberts	Y	Y
KENTUCKY		
McConnell	Y	Y
Bunning	+	+
LOUISIANA		
Breaux	Y	Y
Landrieu	Y	Y
MAINE		
Snowe	Y	Y
Collins	Y	Y
MARYLAND		
Sarbanes	Y	?
Mikulski	Y	Y
MASSACHUSETTS		
Kennedy	Y	Y
Kerry	Y	Y
MICHIGAN		
Levin	Y	Y
Stabenow	Y	Y
MINNESOTA		
Wellstone	Y	Y
Dayton	Y	Y
MISSISSIPPI		
Cochran	Y	Y
Lott	Y	Y
MISSOURI		
Bond	Y	Y
Carnahan	Y	Y
MONTANA		
Baucus	Y	Y
Burns	Y	Y
NEBRASKA		
Nelson	Y	Y
Hagel	Y	Y
NEVADA		
Reid	Y	Y
Ensign	Y	Y

	12	13
NEW HAMPSHIRE		
Smith	Y	Y
Gregg	Y	Y
NEW JERSEY		
Corzine	Y	Y
Torricelli	Y	Y
NEW MEXICO		
Domenici	Y	Y
Bingaman	Y	Y
NEW YORK		
Clinton	Y	Y
Schumer	Y	Y
NORTH CAROLINA		
Helms	Y	Y
Edwards	Y	Y
NORTH DAKOTA		
Conrad	Y	Y
Dorgan	Y	Y
OHIO		
DeWine	Y	Y
Voinovich	Y	Y
OKLAHOMA		
Nickles	Y	Y
Inhofe	Y	Y
OREGON		
Wyden	Y	Y
Smith	Y	Y
PENNSYLVANIA		
Specter	Y	Y
Santorum	Y	Y
RHODE ISLAND		
Reed	Y	Y
Chafee	Y	Y
SOUTH CAROLINA		
Thurmond	Y	Y
Hollings	Y	Y
SOUTH DAKOTA		
Daschle	Y	Y
Johnson	Y	Y
TENNESSEE		
Thompson	Y	Y
Frist	Y	Y

	12	13
TEXAS		
Gramm	Y	?
Hutchison	Y	Y
UTAH		
Hatch	Y	?
Bennett	Y	+
VERMONT		
Leahy	Y	Y
Jeffords	Y	Y
VIRGINIA		
Warner	Y	Y
Allen	Y	Y
WASHINGTON		
Cantwell	Y	Y
Murray	Y	Y
WEST VIRGINIA		
Byrd	Y	Y
Rockefeller	Y	Y
WISCONSIN		
Kohl	Y	Y
Feingold	Y	Y
WYOMING		
Thomas	Y	?
Enzi	Y	Y

ND Northern Democrats   SD Southern Democrats

Southern states - Ala., Ark., Fla., Ga., Ky., La., Miss., N.C., Okla., S.C., Tenn., Texas, Va.

12. S 320. Patent Copyright and Trademark Law/Passage. Passage of the bill to make technical changes and corrections in various intellectual property laws, and clarify the code on some procedural matters in the U.S. Patent and Trademark Office. Passed 98-0: R 48-0; D 50-0 (ND 41-0, SD 9-0). Feb. 14, 2001.

13. Allbaugh Nomination/Confirmation. Confirmation of President Bush's nomination of Joe M. Allbaugh of Texas to be director of the Federal Emergency Management Agency. Confirmed 91-0: R 44-0; D 47-0 (ND 40-0, SD 7-0). A "yea" was a vote in support of the president's position. Feb. 15, 2001.

	14
ALABAMA	
Shelby	Y
Sessions	Y
ALASKA	
Stevens	Y
Murkowski	Y
ARIZONA	
McCain	Y
Kyl	Y
ARKANSAS	
Hutchinson	?
Lincoln	?
CALIFORNIA	
Feinstein	Y
Boxer	Y
COLORADO	
Campbell	Y
Allard	Y
CONNECTICUT	
Dodd	Y
Lieberman	Y
DELAWARE	
Carper	+
Biden	Y
FLORIDA	
Graham	Y
Nelson	Y
GEORGIA	
Miller	Y
Cleland	Y
HAWAII	
Inouye	Y
Akaka	Y
IDAHO	
Craig	Y
Crapo	Y
ILLINOIS	
Durbin	Y
Fitzgerald	Y
INDIANA	
Lugar	Y
Bayh	Y

	14
IOWA	
Grassley	Y
Harkin	Y
KANSAS	
Brownback	Y
Roberts	Y
KENTUCKY	
McConnell	Y
Bunning	Y
LOUISIANA	
Breaux	Y
Landrieu	Y
MAINE	
Snowe	Y
Collins	Y
MARYLAND	
Sarbanes	Y
Mikulski	Y
MASSACHUSETTS	
Kennedy	Y
Kerry	Y
MICHIGAN	
Levin	Y
Stabenow	Y
MINNESOTA	
Wellstone	Y
Dayton	Y
MISSISSIPPI	
Cochran	Y
Lott	Y
MISSOURI	
Bond	Y
Carnahan	Y
MONTANA	
Baucus	Y
Burns	Y
NEBRASKA	
Nelson	?
Hagel	?
NEVADA	
Reid	Y
Ensign	Y

	14
NEW HAMPSHIRE	
Smith	Y
Gregg	Y
NEW JERSEY	
Corzine	Y
Torricelli	Y
NEW MEXICO	
Domenici	Y
Bingaman	Y
NEW YORK	
Clinton	Y
Schumer	Y
NORTH CAROLINA	
Helms	Y
Edwards	Y
NORTH DAKOTA	
Conrad	Y
Dorgan	Y
OHIO	
DeWine	Y
Voinovich	Y
OKLAHOMA	
Nickles	Y
Inhofe	Y
OREGON	
Wyden	Y
Smith	Y
PENNSYLVANIA	
Specter	Y
Santorum	Y
RHODE ISLAND	
Reed	Y
Chafee	Y
SOUTH CAROLINA	
Thurmond	Y
Hollings	Y
SOUTH DAKOTA	
Daschle	Y
Johnson	?
TENNESSEE	
Thompson	Y
Frist	Y

	14
TEXAS	
Gramm	Y
Hutchison	Y
UTAH	
Hatch	Y
Bennett	Y
VERMONT	
Leahy	Y
Jeffords	Y
VIRGINIA	
Warner	Y
Allen	Y
WASHINGTON	
Cantwell	Y
Murray	Y
WEST VIRGINIA	
Byrd	Y
Rockefeller	Y
WISCONSIN	
Kohl	Y
Feingold	Y
WYOMING	
Thomas	Y
Enzi	Y

ND Northern Democrats   SD Southern Democrats

Southern states - Ala., Ark., Fla., Ga., Ky., La., Miss., N.C., Okla., S.C., Tenn., Texas, Va.

14. Duncan Nomination/Confirmation. Confirmation of President Bush's nomination of John M. Duncan of the District of Columbia to be deputy undersecretary of Treasury. Confirmed 94-0: R 48-0; D 46-0 (ND 38-0, SD 8-0). A "yea" was a vote in support of the president's position. Feb. 28, 2001.

Senate Votes 15, 16, 17, 18, 19

	15	16	17	18	19
ALABAMA					
Shelby	Y	N	Y	Y	Y
Sessions	Y	N	Y	Y	Y
ALASKA					
Stevens	Y	N	Y	Y	Y
Murkowski	Y	N	Y	Y	Y
ARIZONA					
McCain	Y	N	Y	Y	Y
Kyl	Y	N	Y	Y	Y
ARKANSAS					
Hutchinson	Y	N	Y	Y	Y
Lincoln	Y	Y	N	N	N
CALIFORNIA					
Feinstein	N	N	N	N	N
Boxer	N	Y	N	N	N
COLORADO					
Campbell	Y	N	Y	Y	Y
Allard	Y	N	Y	Y	Y
CONNECTICUT					
Dodd	N	Y	N	N	N
Lieberman	N	Y	Y	N	N
DELAWARE					
Carper	N	N	Y	N	Y
Biden	N	N	Y	N	Y
FLORIDA					
Graham	N	Y	N	N	N
Nelson	N	Y	N	N	N
GEORGIA					
Miller	Y	N	Y	Y	Y
Cleland	N	N	N	N	Y
HAWAII					
Inouye	N	Y	N	N	N
Akaka	N	Y	N	N	N
IDAHO					
Craig	Y	N	Y	Y	Y
Crapo	Y	N	Y	Y	?
ILLINOIS					
Durbin	N	Y	N	N	N
Fitzgerald	Y	C	C	C	C
INDIANA					
Lugar	Y	N	Y	Y	Y
Bayh	N	Y	Y	N	Y

	15	16	17	18	19
IOWA					
Grassley	Y	N	Y	Y	Y
Harkin	N	Y	N	N	N
KANSAS					
Brownback	Y	N	Y	Y	Y
Roberts	Y	N	Y	Y	Y
KENTUCKY					
McConnell	Y	N	Y	Y	Y
Bunning	Y	N	Y	Y	Y
LOUISIANA					
Breaux	Y	N	N	N	Y
Landrieu	Y	Y	N	N	N
MAINE					
Snowe	Y	N	Y	Y	Y
Collins	Y	N	Y	N	Y
MARYLAND					
Sarbanes	N	Y	N	N	N
Mikulski	N	Y	N	N	N
MASSACHUSETTS					
Kennedy	N	Y	N	N	N
Kerry	N	Y	N	N	N
MICHIGAN					
Levin	N	Y	N	N	N
Stabenow	N	Y	N	N	N
MINNESOTA					
Wellstone	N	Y	N	N	N
Dayton	N	Y	N	N	N
MISSISSIPPI					
Cochran	Y	N	Y	Y	Y
Lott	Y	N	Y	Y	Y
MISSOURI					
Bond	Y	N	Y	Y	Y
Carnahan	N	N	N	N	N
MONTANA					
Baucus	Y	Y	N	N	N
Burns	Y	N	Y	Y	Y
NEBRASKA					
Nelson	N	N	Y	Y	Y
Hagel	Y	N	Y	Y	Y
NEVADA					
Reid	N	N	N	N	Y
Ensign	Y	N	Y	Y	Y

	15	16	17	18	19
NEW HAMPSHIRE					
Smith	Y	N	Y	Y	Y
Gregg	Y	N	Y	Y	Y
NEW JERSEY					
Corzine	N	Y	N	N	N
Torricelli	N	N	Y	Y	N
NEW MEXICO					
Domenici	Y	N	Y	Y	Y
Bingaman	N	N	N	Y	N
NEW YORK					
Clinton	N	Y	N	N	N
Schumer	N	Y	N	N	N
NORTH CAROLINA					
Helms	Y	N	Y	Y	Y
Edwards	N	N	N	N	N
NORTH DAKOTA					
Conrad	N	N	N	N	N
Dorgan	N	Y	N	N	N
OHIO					
DeWine	Y	N	Y	Y	Y
Voinovich	Y	N	Y	Y	Y
OKLAHOMA					
Nickles	Y	N	Y	Y	Y
Inhofe	Y	N	Y	Y	?
OREGON					
Wyden	N	Y	N	N	N
Smith	Y	N	Y	Y	Y
PENNSYLVANIA					
Specter	Y	N	Y	N	Y
Santorum	Y	N	Y	Y	Y
RHODE ISLAND					
Reed	N	Y	N	N	N
Chafee	Y	N	Y	Y	Y
SOUTH CAROLINA					
Thurmond	Y	N	Y	Y	Y
Hollings	Y	Y	N	N	N
SOUTH DAKOTA					
Daschle	N	Y	N	N	N
Johnson	N	N	Y	Y	N
TENNESSEE					
Thompson	Y	N	Y	Y	Y
Frist	Y	N	Y	Y	Y

	15	16	17	18	19
TEXAS					
Gramm	Y	N	Y	Y	Y
Hutchison	Y	N	Y	Y	Y
UTAH					
Hatch	Y	N	Y	Y	Y
Bennett	Y	N	Y	Y	Y
VERMONT					
Leahy	N	Y	N	N	N
Jeffords	Y	N	Y	N	Y
VIRGINIA					
Warner	Y	N	Y	Y	?
Allen	Y	N	Y	Y	Y
WASHINGTON					
Cantwell	N	Y	N	N	N
Murray	N	Y	N	N	N
WEST VIRGINIA					
Byrd	N	N	N	N	N
Rockefeller	N	Y	N	N	N
WISCONSIN					
Kohl	N	N	N	N	N
Feingold	N	Y	N	N	N
WYOMING					
Thomas	Y	N	Y	Y	Y
Enzi	Y	N	Y	Y	Y

Key

Y Voted for (yea).
Paired for.
+ Announced for.
N Voted against (nay).
X Paired against.
− Announced against.
P Voted "present."
C Voted "present" to avoid possible conflict of interest.
? Did not vote or otherwise make a position known.

Democrats **Republicans** *Independents*

ND Northern Democrats   SD Southern Democrats

Southern states - Ala., Ark., Fla., Ga., Ky., La., Miss., N.C., Okla., S.C., Tenn., Texas, Va.

15. S J Res 6. Ergonomics Rule Disapproval/Passage. Passage of the joint resolution that would provide for congressional disapproval of the ergonomics rule submitted by the Labor Department during the Clinton administration, stating the rule would have no force or effect. Passed 56-44: R 50-0; D 6-44 (ND 1-40, SD 5-4). March 6, 2001.

16. S 420. Bankruptcy Overhaul/Medical Expenses Exemption. Wellstone, D-Minn., amendment that would provide an exemption from the bill for debtors who file for bankruptcy because of medical expenses. Rejected 34-65: R 0-49; D 34-16 (ND 29-12, SD 5-4). March 7, 2001.

17. S 420. Bankruptcy Overhaul/Small Business. Hatch, R-Utah, motion to table (kill) the Leahy, D-Vt., amendment that would provide small business creditors priority in bankruptcy claims. Motion agreed to 58-41: R 49-0; D 9-41 (ND 8-33, SD 1-8). March 7, 2001.

18. S 420. Bankruptcy Overhaul/Predatory Lending. Hatch, R-Utah, motion to table (kill) the Durbin, D-Ill., amendment that would invalidate claims against borrowers if the creditor has committed material violations of the Truth in Lending Act. Motion agreed to 50-49: R 46-3; D 4-46 (ND 3-38, SD 1-8). March 8, 2001.

19. S 420. Bankruptcy Overhaul/Small Business. Hatch, R-Utah, motion to table (kill) the Kerry, D-Mass., amendment that would strike the small business provisions in the bill and require the Small Business Administration to conduct a study to determine the most effective ways to deal with small businesses that file for bankruptcy. Motion agreed to 55-41: R 46-0; D 9-41 (ND 6-35, SD 3-6). March 8, 2001.

Senate Votes 20, 21, 22, 23, 24, 25

	20	21	22	23	24	25
ALABAMA						
Shelby	Y	Y	N	Y	Y	Y
Sessions	Y	Y	N	Y	Y	Y
ALASKA						
Stevens	Y	Y	N	Y	Y	Y
Murkowski	N	Y	N	Y	Y	Y
ARIZONA						
McCain	Y	Y	N	Y	Y	Y
Kyl	Y	Y	N	Y	Y	Y
ARKANSAS						
Hutchinson	Y	Y	N	Y	Y	Y
Lincoln	N	N	Y	N	N	N
CALIFORNIA						
Feinstein	N	N	Y	N	N	N
Boxer	N	N	Y	N	N	N
COLORADO						
Campbell	Y	Y	N	Y	Y	Y
Allard	Y	Y	N	Y	Y	Y
CONNECTICUT						
Dodd	N	N	Y	N	N	N
Lieberman	N	N	Y	N	N	N
DELAWARE						
Carper	Y	Y	Y	N	N	N
Biden	Y	Y	Y	N	N	N
FLORIDA						
Graham	N	N	Y	N	N	N
Nelson	N	Y	Y	N	N	N
GEORGIA						
Miller	Y	Y	Y	Y	Y	Y
Cleland	Y	Y	Y	N	N	Y
HAWAII						
Inouye	?	?	Y	N	N	N
Akaka	N	N	Y	N	N	N
IDAHO						
Craig	Y	Y	N	Y	Y	Y
Crapo	Y	Y	N	Y	Y	Y
ILLINOIS						
Durbin	N	N	Y	N	N	N
Fitzgerald	C	C	Y	Y	C	C
INDIANA						
Lugar	Y	Y	N	Y	Y	Y
Bayh	Y	Y	Y	N	N	Y

	20	21	22	23	24	25
IOWA						
Grassley	Y	Y	N	Y	Y	Y
Harkin	N	N	Y	N	N	N
KANSAS						
Brownback	Y	Y	N	Y	Y	Y
Roberts	Y	Y	N	Y	Y	Y
KENTUCKY						
McConnell	Y	Y	N	Y	Y	Y
Bunning	Y	Y	N	Y	Y	Y
LOUISIANA						
Breaux	N	N	Y	N	N	N
Landrieu	N	N	Y	N	N	N
MAINE						
Snowe	Y	Y	N	Y	Y	Y
Collins	Y	Y	N	Y	N	Y
MARYLAND						
Sarbanes	N	N	Y	N	N	N
Mikulski	N	N	Y	N	N	N
MASSACHUSETTS						
Kennedy	N	N	Y	N	N	N
Kerry	N	N	Y	N	N	N
MICHIGAN						
Levin	N	N	Y	N	N	N
Stabenow	N	Y	Y	N	N	N
MINNESOTA						
Wellstone	N	N	Y	N	N	N
Dayton	N	N	Y	N	N	N
MISSISSIPPI						
Cochran	Y	Y	N	Y	Y	Y
Lott	Y	Y	N	Y	Y	Y
MISSOURI						
Bond	Y	Y	N	Y	Y	Y
Carnahan	N	Y	Y	N	N	N
MONTANA						
Baucus	N	N	Y	N	N	N
Burns	Y	Y	N	Y	Y	Y
NEBRASKA						
Nelson	Y	Y	N	Y	N	Y
Hagel	Y	Y	N	Y	Y	Y
NEVADA						
Reid	N	Y	Y	N	N	N
Ensign	Y	Y	N	Y	N	Y

	20	21	22	23	24	25
NEW HAMPSHIRE						
Smith	Y	Y	N	Y	Y	Y
Gregg	Y	Y	N	Y	Y	Y
NEW JERSEY						
Corzine	N	N	Y	N	N	N
Torricelli	N	Y	Y	N	N	N
NEW MEXICO						
Domenici	Y	Y	N	Y	Y	Y
Bingaman	N	Y	Y	N	N	N
NEW YORK						
Clinton	N	N	Y	N	N	N
Schumer	N	N	Y	N	N	N
NORTH CAROLINA						
Helms	Y	Y	N	Y	Y	Y
Edwards	N	N	Y	N	N	N
NORTH DAKOTA						
Conrad	N	Y	Y	N	N	N
Dorgan	Y	Y	Y	N	N	Y
OHIO						
DeWine	Y	Y	N	Y	Y	Y
Voinovich	Y	Y	N	Y	Y	Y
OKLAHOMA						
Nickles	Y	Y	N	Y	Y	Y
Inhofe	+	Y	N	Y	Y	Y
OREGON						
Wyden	N	N	Y	N	N	N
Smith	Y	Y	Y	Y	Y	Y
PENNSYLVANIA						
Specter	Y	Y	N	Y	Y	Y
Santorum	Y	Y	N	Y	Y	Y
RHODE ISLAND						
Reed	N	N	Y	N	N	N
Chafee	Y	Y	N	Y	N	Y
SOUTH CAROLINA						
Thurmond	Y	Y	N	Y	Y	Y
Hollings	N	N	Y	N	N	N
SOUTH DAKOTA						
Daschle	N	N	Y	N	N	N
Johnson	Y	Y	Y	N	N	Y
TENNESSEE						
Thompson	Y	Y	N	Y	Y	Y
Frist	Y	Y	N	Y	Y	Y

Key

Y	Voted for (yea).
#	Paired for.
+	Announced for.
N	Voted against (nay).
X	Paired against.
−	Announced against.
P	Voted "present."
C	Voted "present" to avoid possible conflict of interest.
?	Did not vote or otherwise make a position known.

Democrats **Republicans** *Independents*

	20	21	22	23	24	25
TEXAS						
Gramm	Y	Y	N	Y	Y	Y
Hutchison	Y	Y	N	Y	Y	Y
UTAH						
Hatch	Y	N	N	Y	Y	Y
Bennett	Y	Y	N	Y	Y	Y
VERMONT						
Leahy	N	N	Y	N	N	N
Jeffords	N	N	N	Y	N	Y
VIRGINIA						
Warner	Y	Y	N	Y	Y	Y
Allen	Y	Y	N	Y	Y	Y
WASHINGTON						
Cantwell	N	N	Y	N	N	N
Murray	N	N	Y	N	N	N
WEST VIRGINIA						
Byrd	N	N	Y	N	N	N
Rockefeller	N	N	Y	N	N	N
WISCONSIN						
Kohl	Y	Y	Y	N	N	Y
Feingold	N	N	Y	N	N	N
WYOMING						
Thomas	Y	Y	N	Y	Y	Y
Enzi	Y	Y	N	Y	Y	Y

ND Northern Democrats SD Southern Democrats

Southern states - Ala., Ark., Fla., Ga., Ky., La., Miss., N.C., Okla., S.C., Tenn., Texas, Va.

20. S 420. Bankruptcy Overhaul/Credit Cards. Sessions, R-Ala., motion to table (kill) the Feinstein, D-Calif., amendment that would establish a $2,500 cap on credit cards issued to an individual younger than 21 years old, unless a parent cosigns or the minor submits information indicating independent means to repay the debt. Motion agreed to 55-42: R 46-2; D 9-40 (ND 7-33, SD 2-7). March 13, 2001.

21. S 420. Bankruptcy Overhaul/IRAs. Sessions, R-Ala., motion to table (kill) Kennedy, D-Mass., amendment to remove the provision in the bill that would provide a $1 million cap on the amount of individual retirement account (IRA) contributions protected in bankruptcy. Motion agreed to 61-37: R 45-4; D 16-33 (ND 13-27, SD 3-6). March 13, 2001.

22. S 420. Bankruptcy Overhaul/Medicare, Social Security 'Lockbox.' Conrad, D-N.D., motion to waive the Budget Act with respect to the Domenici, R-N.M., point of order against the Conrad amendment that would create a Medicare and Social Security "lockbox." It would take the Medicare Hospital Insurance Trust Fund off budget, and establish a 60-vote point of order against legislation that would reduce the trust fund surplus or that would put Social Security back on budget. Motion rejected 53-47: R 3-47; D 50-0 (ND 41-0, SD 9-0). A three-fifths majority vote (60) of the total Senate is required to waive the Budget Act. (Subsequently, the chair upheld the point of order, and the amendment fell.) March 13, 2001.

23. S 420. Bankruptcy Overhaul/Social Security "Lockbox." Domenici, R-N.M., motion to waive the Budget Act with respect to the Conrad, D-N.D., point of order against the Sessions, R-Ala., amendment that would ensure the Social Security surplus is used only to pay down the public debt until Social Security reform legislation is enacted. It also would ensure that the surplus in the Medicare Hospital Insurance Trust Fund is used to pay down the public debt until Medicare reform legislation is enacted. The restrictions would be enforced by points of order. Motion rejected 52-48: R 50-0; D 2-48 (ND 1-40, SD 1-8). A three-fifths majority vote (60) of the total Senate is required to waive the Budget Act. (Subsequently, the chair upheld the point of order, and the amendment fell.) March 13, 2001.

24. S 420. Bankruptcy Overhaul/Predatory Loans. Hatch, R-Utah, motion to table (kill) the Schumer, D-N.Y., amendment that would prevent lenders who have violated the Truth in Lending Act from escaping claims against them by declaring bankruptcy. Motion rejected 44-55: R 43-6; D 1-49 (ND 0-41, SD 1-8). (Subsequently, the Schumer amendment was adopted by voice vote.) March 13, 2001.

25. S 420. Bankruptcy Overhaul/Credit Cards. Hatch, R-Utah, motion to table (kill) the Dodd, D-Conn., amendment that would require credit card companies that issue credit cards to consumers younger than 21 years old to obtain a cosignature of a parent or guardian; proof that the minor can pay off the debt; or the completion of a credit counseling course by the minor. Motion agreed to 58-41: R 49-0; D 9-41 (ND 6-35, SD 3-6). March 13, 2001.

	26	27	28	29	30	31
ALABAMA						
Shelby	Y	Y	Y	Y	Y	Y
Sessions	Y	Y	Y	Y	Y	Y
ALASKA						
Stevens	Y	Y	Y	Y	Y	Y
Murkowski	Y	Y	Y	Y	Y	Y
ARIZONA						
McCain	N	Y	Y	Y	N	Y
Kyl	N	Y	Y	Y	Y	Y
ARKANSAS						
Hutchinson	Y	Y	Y	Y	Y	Y
Lincoln	Y	N	Y	Y	N	Y
CALIFORNIA						
Feinstein	Y	N	N	Y	N	Y
Boxer	N	N	N	N	N	Y
COLORADO						
Campbell	N	Y	Y	Y	Y	Y
Allard	Y	Y	Y	Y	Y	Y
CONNECTICUT						
Dodd	Y	N	N	N	N	Y
Lieberman	Y	Y	N	Y	N	Y
DELAWARE						
Carper	Y	Y	Y	Y	N	Y
Biden	N	Y	N	Y	N	Y
FLORIDA						
Graham	Y	Y	N	Y	Y	Y
Nelson	N	N	N	N	Y	Y
GEORGIA						
Miller	N	Y	Y	Y	N	Y
Cleland	N	Y	N	Y	N	Y
HAWAII						
Inouye	N	N	N	Y	N	Y
Akaka	Y	N	N	Y	N	Y
IDAHO						
Craig	N	Y	Y	Y	Y	Y
Crapo	N	Y	Y	Y	Y	Y
ILLINOIS						
Durbin	N	N	N	N	N	Y
Fitzgerald	C	C	C	C	C	C
INDIANA						
Lugar	Y	Y	Y	Y	Y	Y
Bayh	Y	Y	N	Y	N	Y

	26	27	28	29	30	31
IOWA						
Grassley	Y	Y	Y	Y	Y	Y
Harkin	N	N	N	N	N	Y
KANSAS						
Brownback	Y	Y	Y	Y	Y	Y
Roberts	N	Y	Y	Y	Y	Y
KENTUCKY						
McConnell	Y	Y	Y	Y	N	Y
Bunning	Y	Y	Y	Y	Y	Y
LOUISIANA						
Breaux	Y	Y	Y	Y	N	Y
Landrieu	Y	N	Y	N	N	Y
MAINE						
Snowe	Y	Y	Y	Y	N	Y
Collins	Y	Y	Y	Y	N	Y
MARYLAND						
Sarbanes	Y	N	N	N	N	Y
Mikulski	Y	N	N	Y	N	Y
MASSACHUSETTS						
Kennedy	N	N	N	N	N	Y
Kerry	N	N	N	N	N	Y
MICHIGAN						
Levin	N	N	N	N	N	Y
Stabenow	N	Y	Y	Y	N	Y
MINNESOTA						
Wellstone	N	N	N	N	N	Y
Dayton	N	N	N	N	N	Y
MISSISSIPPI						
Cochran	Y	Y	Y	Y	Y	Y
Lott	Y	Y	Y	Y	Y	Y
MISSOURI						
Bond	Y	Y	Y	Y	Y	Y
Carnahan	N	Y	N	Y	N	Y
MONTANA						
Baucus	N	Y	N	Y	N	Y
Burns	N	Y	Y	Y	Y	Y
NEBRASKA						
Nelson	Y	Y	Y	Y	N	Y
Hagel	Y	Y	Y	Y	Y	Y
NEVADA						
Reid	Y	N	Y	Y	N	Y
Ensign	Y	Y	Y	Y	Y	Y

	26	27	28	29	30	31
NEW HAMPSHIRE						
Smith	Y	Y	Y	Y	Y	Y
Gregg	Y	Y	Y	Y	Y	Y
NEW JERSEY						
Corzine	?	N	N	N	N	Y
Torricelli	?	Y	N	Y	N	Y
NEW MEXICO						
Domenici	Y	Y	Y	Y	N	Y
Bingaman	Y	Y	N	Y	N	Y
NEW YORK						
Clinton	Y	N	N	N	N	Y
Schumer	Y	N	N	N	N	Y
NORTH CAROLINA						
Helms	Y	Y	Y	Y	N	Y
Edwards	Y	N	N	Y	N	Y
NORTH DAKOTA						
Conrad	Y	N	N	Y	N	Y
Dorgan	Y	N	N	Y	N	Y
OHIO						
DeWine	Y	Y	Y	Y	N	Y
Voinovich	Y	Y	Y	Y	Y	Y
OKLAHOMA						
Nickles	Y	Y	Y	Y	Y	Y
Inhofe	Y	Y	Y	Y	Y	Y
OREGON						
Wyden	N	N	N	N	N	Y
Smith	N	Y	Y	Y	N	Y
PENNSYLVANIA						
Specter	Y	Y	Y	Y	N	Y
Santorum	N	Y	Y	Y	N	Y
RHODE ISLAND						
Reed	Y	N	N	N	N	Y
Chafee	Y	Y	Y	Y	N	Y
SOUTH CAROLINA						
Thurmond	Y	Y	Y	Y	Y	Y
Hollings	N	N	N	Y	N	Y
SOUTH DAKOTA						
Daschle	Y	N	N	N	N	Y
Johnson	Y	Y	Y	Y	N	Y
TENNESSEE						
Thompson	Y	Y	Y	Y	Y	Y
Frist	Y	Y	Y	Y	Y	Y

	26	27	28	29	30	31
TEXAS						
Gramm	Y	Y	Y	Y	Y	Y
Hutchison	Y	Y	Y	Y	Y	Y
UTAH						
Hatch	Y	Y	Y	Y	Y	Y
Bennett	N	Y	Y	Y	Y	Y
VERMONT						
Leahy	Y	N	N	N	N	Y
Jeffords	Y	Y	Y	Y	N	Y
VIRGINIA						
Warner	Y	Y	Y	Y	Y	Y
Allen	Y	Y	Y	Y	Y	Y
WASHINGTON						
Cantwell	N	N	N	N	N	Y
Murray	N	N	N	Y	N	Y
WEST VIRGINIA						
Byrd	N	N	N	N	N	Y
Rockefeller	Y	N	N	Y	N	Y
WISCONSIN						
Kohl	Y	N	N	Y	N	Y
Feingold	Y	N	N	N	N	Y
WYOMING						
Thomas	Y	Y	Y	Y	Y	Y
Enzi	Y	Y	Y	Y	Y	Y

Key

Y	Voted for (yea).
#	Paired for.
+	Announced for.
N	Voted against (nay).
X	Paired against.
–	Announced against.
P	Voted "present."
C	Voted "present" to avoid possible conflict of interest.
?	Did not vote or otherwise make a position known.

Democrats **Republicans**
Independents

ND Northern Democrats   SD Southern Democrats

Southern states - Ala., Ark., Fla., Ga., Ky., La., Miss., N.C., Okla., S.C., Tenn., Texas, Va.

26. S 420. Bankruptcy Overhaul/Electric Utility Debts. Feinstein, D-Calif., motion to table (kill) the Wyden, D-Ore., amendment that would provide that debts owed by California utilities to federal, state, and local agencies for electric power are non-dischargeable unless the rates are found to be unjust or unreasonable by the Federal Energy Regulatory Commission. Motion agreed to 67-30: R 39-10; D 28-20 (ND 23-16, SD 5-4). March 14, 2001.

27. S 420. Bankruptcy Overhaul/Democratic Substitute. Hatch, R-Utah, motion to table (kill) the Durbin, D-Ill., substitute amendment that would give courts discretion to move debtors from Chapter 7 of the bankruptcy code, which allows most debts to be discharged, to Chapter 13, which requires a reorganization of debts under a repayment plan. It would also increase consumer disclosure requirements for credit card companies, discourage predatory lending practices and state the sense of the Senate that the homestead exemption should be capped at $100,000. Motion agreed to 64-35: R 49-0; D 15-35 (ND 11-30, SD 4-5). March 14, 2001.

28. S 420. Bankruptcy Overhaul/Short-Term Loans. Hatch, R-Utah, motion to table (kill) the Wellstone, D-Minn., amendment that would prevent lenders who charge an annual interest rate that exceeds 100 percent for short-term loans from collecting unpaid loans from debtors in bankruptcy court. Motion agreed to 58-41: R 49-0; D 9-41 (ND 5-36, SD 4-5). March 14, 2001.

29. S 420. Bankruptcy Overhaul/Cloture. Motion to invoke cloture (thus limiting debate) on the bill that would require debtors able to repay $10,000 or 25 percent of their debts over five years to file under Chapter 13, which requires a reorganization of debts under a repayment plan, instead of seeking to discharge their debts under Chapter 7. Motion agreed to 80-19: R 49-0; D 31-19 (ND 24-17, SD 7-2). Three-fifths of the total Senate (60) is required to invoke cloture. March 14, 2001.

30. S 420. Bankruptcy Overhaul/Homestead Exemption Cap. Brownback, R-Kan., motion to table (kill) the Kohl, D-Wis., amendment that would cap the "homestead" exemption at $125,000. The amendment would not apply to the primary residence of a family farmer. Motion rejected 39-60: R 36-13; D 3-47 (ND 0-41, SD 3-6). A "yea" was a vote in support of the president's position. (Subsequently, the Kohl amendment was adopted by voice vote.) March 15, 2001.

31. S 420. Bankruptcy Overhaul/Child Identity Information. Leahy, D-Vt., amendment that would prohibit the disclosure of the name of a minor in any public records associated with a bankruptcy proceeding where the debtor is required to provide information regarding the child. Adopted 99-0: R 49-0; D 50-0 (ND 41-0, SD 9-0). March 15, 2001.

	32	33	34	35	36
ALABAMA					
Shelby	N	N	N	Y	Y
Sessions	N	N	N	N	Y
ALASKA					
Stevens	Y	N	N	P	Y
Murkowski	N	N	N	Y	Y
ARIZONA					
McCain	N	N	N	Y	Y
Kyl	N	N	N	N	Y
ARKANSAS					
Hutchinson	N	N	N	N	Y
Lincoln	Y	N	Y	Y	Y
CALIFORNIA					
Feinstein	Y	Y	N	Y	Y
Boxer	Y	Y	Y	?	−
COLORADO					
Campbell	N	N	N	N	Y
Allard	N	N	N	Y	Y
CONNECTICUT					
Dodd	Y	Y	Y	Y	N
Lieberman	Y	N	Y	Y	Y
DELAWARE					
Carper	Y	N	N	Y	Y
Biden	Y	N	N	Y	Y
FLORIDA					
Graham	Y	N	Y	Y	Y
Nelson	Y	Y	N	N	N
GEORGIA					
Miller	N	N	N	Y	Y
Cleland	Y	N	N	Y	Y
HAWAII					
Inouye	Y	Y	Y	Y	Y
Akaka	Y	Y	Y	Y	Y
IDAHO					
Craig	N	N	N	Y	Y
Crapo	N	N	N	Y	Y
ILLINOIS					
Durbin	Y	Y	Y	Y	N
Fitzgerald	C	C	C	C	C
INDIANA					
Lugar	N	N	N	Y	Y
Bayh	Y	N	Y	Y	Y

	32	33	34	35	36
IOWA					
Grassley	N	N	N	N	Y
Harkin	Y	N	Y	Y	N
KANSAS					
Brownback	N	N	N	Y	N
Roberts	N	N	N	Y	Y
KENTUCKY					
McConnell	N	N	N	Y	Y
Bunning	N	N	N	N	Y
LOUISIANA					
Breaux	Y	N	N	N	Y
Landrieu	Y	N	Y	N	Y
MAINE					
Snowe	Y	N	N	Y	Y
Collins	Y	N	N	Y	Y
MARYLAND					
Sarbanes	Y	Y	Y	Y	N
Mikulski	Y	N	Y	Y	Y
MASSACHUSETTS					
Kennedy	Y	Y	Y	Y	N
Kerry	Y	Y	Y	Y	N
MICHIGAN					
Levin	Y	Y	N	Y	Y
Stabenow	Y	N	N	Y	Y
MINNESOTA					
Wellstone	Y	Y	Y	Y	N
Dayton	Y	Y	Y	Y	N
MISSISSIPPI					
Cochran	N	N	N	Y	Y
Lott	N	N	N	N	Y
MISSOURI					
Bond	N	N	N	Y	Y
Carnahan	Y	Y	N	Y	Y
MONTANA					
Baucus	Y	N	N	N	Y
Burns	N	N	N	Y	Y
NEBRASKA					
Nelson	Y	N	N	Y	Y
Hagel	N	N	N	Y	Y
NEVADA					
Reid	Y	N	Y	Y	Y
Ensign	Y	N	N	Y	Y

	32	33	34	35	36
NEW HAMPSHIRE					
Smith	N	N	N	N	Y
Gregg	N	N	N	N	Y
NEW JERSEY					
Corzine	Y	Y	Y	Y	Y
Torricelli	Y	N	N	Y	Y
NEW MEXICO					
Domenici	N	N	N	Y	Y
Bingaman	Y	N	Y	Y	Y
NEW YORK					
Clinton	Y	Y	Y	Y	Y
Schumer	Y	N	Y	Y	Y
NORTH CAROLINA					
Helms	N	N	N	N	Y
Edwards	Y	N	Y	Y	Y
NORTH DAKOTA					
Conrad	Y	N	Y	Y	Y
Dorgan	Y	N	Y	Y	Y
OHIO					
DeWine	N	N	N	Y	Y
Voinovich	N	N	N	Y	Y
OKLAHOMA					
Nickles	N	N	N	Y	Y
Inhofe	N	N	N	Y	Y
OREGON					
Wyden	Y	N	Y	Y	Y
Smith	N	N	N	Y	Y
PENNSYLVANIA					
Specter	Y	N	N	Y	Y
Santorum	N	N	N	Y	Y
RHODE ISLAND					
Reed	Y	Y	Y	Y	N
Chafee	Y	N	N	Y	Y
SOUTH CAROLINA					
Thurmond	N	N	N	Y	Y
Hollings	Y	N	Y	Y	Y
SOUTH DAKOTA					
Daschle	Y	Y	Y	Y	Y
Johnson	Y	N	N	Y	Y
TENNESSEE					
Thompson	N	N	N	Y	Y
Frist	N	N	N	Y	Y

	32	33	34	35	36
TEXAS					
Gramm	N	N	N	Y	Y
Hutchison	N	N	N	Y	N
UTAH					
Hatch	N	N	N	N	Y
Bennett	N	N	N	N	Y
VERMONT					
Leahy	Y	Y	Y	Y	Y
Jeffords	Y	N	Y	Y	Y
VIRGINIA					
Warner	N	N	N	Y	Y
Allen	N	N	N	Y	Y
WASHINGTON					
Cantwell	Y	N	Y	Y	Y
Murray	Y	Y	Y	Y	Y
WEST VIRGINIA					
Byrd	Y	N	Y	Y	Y
Rockefeller	Y	Y	Y	Y	N
WISCONSIN					
Kohl	Y	N	Y	Y	Y
Feingold	Y	Y	Y	Y	N
WYOMING					
Thomas	N	N	N	Y	Y
Enzi	N	N	N	Y	Y

Key

Y	Voted for (yea).
#	Paired for.
+	Announced for.
N	Voted against (nay).
X	Paired against.
−	Announced against.
P	Voted "present."
C	Voted "present" to avoid possible conflict of interest.
?	Did not vote or otherwise make a position known.

Democrats **Republicans**
Independents

ND Northern Democrats   SD Southern Democrats

Southern states - Ala., Ark., Fla., Ga., Ky., La., Miss., N.C., Okla., S.C., Tenn., Texas, Va.

32. S 420. Bankruptcy Overhaul/Spouse's Income. Leahy, D-Vt., amendment that would strike the language in the bill that would require the inclusion of the combined income of the debtor and the debtor's spouse, and insert language that would allow for the inclusion of combined income from the debtor and the debtor's spouse in a joint bankruptcy case. Adopted 56-43: R 7-42; D 49-1 (ND 41-0, SD 8-1). March 15, 2001.

33. S 420. Bankruptcy Overhaul/Means Test. Wellstone, D-Minn., amendment that would provide that the average of a debtor's last two months of income would be used to determine the ability to pay a threshold amount of debt. Rejected 22-77: R 0-49; D 22-28 (ND 21-20, SD 1-8). March 15, 2001.

34. S 420. Bankruptcy Overhaul/Waiting Period. Wellstone, D-Minn., amendment that would strike the provision in the bill that would provide for a five-year waiting period for a new Chapter 13 bankruptcy filing. Rejected 36-63: R 1-48; D 35-15 (ND 30-11, SD 5-4). March 15, 2001.

35. S 420. Bankruptcy Overhaul/Foreign Judgments. Feingold, D-Wis., amendment that would strike the provision in the bill that would make it difficult for Lloyd's of London to collect debts from approximately 250 U.S. investors. Adopted 79-18: R 36-12; D 43-6 (ND 37-3, SD 6-3). March 15, 2001.

36. S 420. Bankruptcy Overhaul/Passage. Passage of the bill that would require debtors able to repay $10,000 or 25 percent of their debts over five years to file under Chapter 13, which requires a reorganization of debts under a repayment plan, instead of seeking to discharge their debts under Chapter 7. The bill would cap the "homestead" exemption at $125,000 and prevent lenders who have violated the Truth in Lending Act from escaping claims against them by declaring bankruptcy. Passed 83-15: R 47-2; D 36-13 (ND 28-12, SD 8-1). March 15, 2001.

	37	38	39	40	41
ALABAMA					
Shelby	N	Y	Y	Y	Y
Sessions	N	Y	Y	N	N
ALASKA					
Stevens	N	Y	Y	N	N
Murkowski	N	Y	Y	N	Y
ARIZONA					
McCain	Y	Y	N	Y	Y
Kyl	N	Y	N	Y	Y
ARKANSAS					
Hutchinson	N	Y	Y	N	N
Lincoln	Y	N	N	Y	Y
CALIFORNIA					
Feinstein	N	Y	N	Y	Y
Boxer	Y	Y	N	Y	Y
COLORADO					
Campbell	N	Y	Y	N	N
Allard	N	Y	Y	Y	N
CONNECTICUT					
Dodd	Y	N	N	Y	Y
Lieberman	Y	N	N	Y	Y
DELAWARE					
Carper	Y	N	N	Y	Y
Biden	Y	N	N	Y	Y
FLORIDA					
Graham	Y	N	N	Y	Y
Nelson	Y	Y	N	Y	Y
GEORGIA					
Miller	Y	Y	N	Y	Y
Cleland	Y	Y	N	Y	Y
HAWAII					
Inouye	Y	N	N	Y	Y
Akaka	Y	N	N	Y	Y
IDAHO					
Craig	N	Y	Y	Y	N
Crapo	N	Y	Y	Y	N
ILLINOIS					
Durbin	Y	Y	N	Y	Y
Fitzgerald	Y	N	Y	Y	N
INDIANA					
Lugar	N	Y	Y	N	N
Bayh	Y	N	N	Y	Y

	37	38	39	40	41
IOWA					
Grassley	N	Y	Y	Y	N
Harkin	N	Y	N	Y	Y
KANSAS					
Brownback	N	Y	Y	N	N
Roberts	N	Y	Y	Y	Y
KENTUCKY					
McConnell	N	Y	Y	N	Y
Bunning	N	Y	Y	N	Y
LOUISIANA					
Breaux	Y	Y	N	Y	Y
Landrieu	Y	Y	N	Y	Y
MAINE					
Snowe	Y	Y	N	N	Y
Collins	Y	Y	N	N	Y
MARYLAND					
Sarbanes	Y	Y	N	Y	Y
Mikulski	Y	N	N	Y	Y
MASSACHUSETTS					
Kennedy	Y	N	N	Y	Y
Kerry	Y	Y	N	Y	Y
MICHIGAN					
Levin	Y	Y	N	Y	Y
Stabenow	Y	N	N	Y	Y
MINNESOTA					
Wellstone	Y	N	N	Y	Y
Dayton	N	N	N	Y	Y
MISSISSIPPI					
Cochran	Y	Y	N	Y	N
Lott	N	Y	Y	Y	N
MISSOURI					
Bond	N	Y	Y	Y	Y
Carnahan	Y	Y	N	Y	Y
MONTANA					
Baucus	Y	Y	N	Y	N
Burns	N	Y	Y	N	N
NEBRASKA					
Nelson	Y	Y	N	Y	N
Hagel	Y	N	N	Y	Y
NEVADA					
Reid	Y	N	N	Y	N
Ensign	N	Y	Y	N	Y

	37	38	39	40	41
NEW HAMPSHIRE					
Smith	N	Y	Y	N	N
Gregg	N	Y	Y	N	N
NEW JERSEY					
Corzine	Y	Y	N	Y	Y
Torricelli	Y	Y	N	Y	Y
NEW MEXICO					
Domenici	N	Y	Y	N	N
Bingaman	N	N	N	Y	Y
NEW YORK					
Clinton	Y	Y	N	Y	Y
Schumer	Y	Y	N	Y	Y
NORTH CAROLINA					
Helms	N	Y	Y	N	N
Edwards	Y	N	N	N	Y
NORTH DAKOTA					
Conrad	Y	Y	N	Y	Y
Dorgan	+	N	N	Y	Y
OHIO					
DeWine	N	Y	N	Y	N
Voinovich	N	Y	Y	Y	Y
OKLAHOMA					
Nickles	N	Y	Y	N	N
Inhofe	N	Y	Y	N	N
OREGON					
Wyden	Y	N	N	Y	Y
Smith	N	Y	Y	N	Y
PENNSYLVANIA					
Specter	N	Y	N	Y	N
Santorum	N	Y	Y	N	Y
RHODE ISLAND					
Reed	Y	N	N	Y	Y
Chafee	N	Y	N	Y	Y
SOUTH CAROLINA					
Thurmond	N	Y	Y	N	N
Hollings	N	Y	N	Y	Y
SOUTH DAKOTA					
Daschle	Y	N	N	?	Y
Johnson	Y	N	N	Y	Y
TENNESSEE					
Thompson	N	N	N	Y	Y
Frist	N	Y	Y	Y	Y

Key

Y	Voted for (yea).
#	Paired for.
+	Announced for.
N	Voted against (nay).
X	Paired against.
–	Announced against.
P	Voted "present."
C	Voted "present" to avoid possible conflict of interest.
?	Did not vote or otherwise make a position known.

Democrats **Republicans**
Independents

	37	38	39	40	41
TEXAS					
Gramm	N	Y	Y	Y	N
Hutchison	N	Y	Y	N	N
UTAH					
Hatch	N	Y	Y	Y	Y
Bennett	N	Y	Y	Y	Y
VERMONT					
Leahy	Y	N	N	Y	Y
Jeffords	Y	Y	N	Y	Y
VIRGINIA					
Warner	N	Y	N	N	Y
Allen	N	Y	N	Y	N
WASHINGTON					
Cantwell	Y	N	N	Y	Y
Murray	Y	N	N	Y	Y
WEST VIRGINIA					
Byrd	Y	N	N	Y	Y
Rockefeller	Y	N	N	Y	Y
WISCONSIN					
Kohl	Y	Y	N	Y	Y
Feingold	Y	Y	N	Y	Y
WYOMING					
Thomas	N	Y	Y	Y	N
Enzi	N	Y	Y	N	N

ND Northern Democrats   SD Southern Democrats

Southern states - Ala., Ark., Fla., Ga., Ky., La., Miss., N.C., Okla., S.C., Tenn., Texas, Va.

37. S 27. Campaign Finance Overhaul/Self-Financing Candidates. Dodd, D-Conn., motion to table (kill) the Domenici, R-N.M., amendment that would require candidates to declare whether they intend to spend personal funds of $500,000 or more within 15 days of when they are required to file a declaration of candidacy. The amendment also would allow an increase in the contribution limits on a sliding scale for candidates facing opponents who declare they intend to spend $500,000 or more. Motion agreed to 51-48: R 7-43; D 44-5 (ND 36-4, SD 8-1). March 19, 2001.

38. S 27. Campaign Finance Overhaul/Self-Financing Candidates. Domenici, R-N.M., amendment that would require candidates to declare within 15 days of the deadline for filing a declaration of candidacy whether they intend to spend personal funds greater than a certain threshold. For candidates facing opponents who spend personal funds, it would allow an increase in the individual contribution limits on a sliding scale based on the state's voting-age population and how much personal money a candidate's opponent uses. The non-self-financing candidate could receive contributions up to 110 percent of the amount contributed by the self-financing candidate. If a self-financing candidate exceeded a certain threshold, limits on hard-money party expenditures would be eliminated, and individual contribution limits in-creased to six times their current limit. Adopted 70-30: R 47-3; D 23-27 (ND 17-24, SD 6-3). March 20, 2001.

39. S 27. Campaign Finance Overhaul/Operating Expenses. Bennett, R-Utah, amendment that would change current election law to prohibit segregated funds and certain political action committees from using soft money to raise hard money or for administrative activities. Rejected 37-63: R 37-13; D 0-50 (ND 0-41, SD 0-9). March 20, 2001.

40. S 27. Campaign Finance Overhaul/Lobbyist Contributions. McCain, R-Ariz., motion to table (kill) the Smith, R-Ore., amendment that would prohibit House and Senate candidates and members or their PACs from accepting contributions from a registered lobbyist, lobbyist employee, or lobbyist political action committee while Congress is in session. Motion agreed to 74-25: R 27-23; D 47-2 (ND 39-1, SD 8-1). March 20, 2001.

41. S 27. Campaign Finance Overhaul/Television Advertising Rates. Torricelli, D-N.J., amendment that would require broadcasters to charge political candidates the lowest rates offered by the broadcast, satellite or cable station throughout the year. Adopted 69-31: R 22-28; D 47-3 (ND 38-3, SD 9-0). March 21, 2001.

	42	43	44	45
ALABAMA				
Shelby	N	N	N	Y
Sessions	N	N	N	Y
ALASKA				
Stevens	N	Y	N	Y
Murkowski	N	N	N	Y
ARIZONA				
McCain	N	Y	Y	Y
Kyl	N	N	N	Y
ARKANSAS				
Hutchinson	N	Y	N	Y
Lincoln	N	Y	Y	Y
CALIFORNIA				
Feinstein	N	Y	Y	Y
Boxer	Y	Y	Y	Y
COLORADO				
Campbell	N	Y	Y	Y
Allard	N	N	N	Y
CONNECTICUT				
Dodd	Y	Y	Y	Y
Lieberman	Y	Y	Y	Y
DELAWARE				
Carper	Y	Y	Y	Y
Biden	Y	Y	Y	Y
FLORIDA				
Graham	Y	Y	Y	Y
Nelson	Y	Y	Y	Y
GEORGIA				
Miller	N	Y	Y	Y
Cleland	Y	Y	Y	Y
HAWAII				
Inouye	Y	Y	Y	Y
Akaka	Y	Y	Y	Y
IDAHO				
Craig	N	N	N	Y
Crapo	N	N	N	Y
ILLINOIS				
Durbin	Y	Y	Y	Y
Fitzgerald	N	Y	N	Y
INDIANA				
Lugar	N	N	N	Y
Bayh	Y	Y	Y	Y

	42	43	44	45
IOWA				
Grassley	N	N	N	Y
Harkin	Y	Y	Y	Y
KANSAS				
Brownback	N	N	N	Y
Roberts	N	N	N	Y
KENTUCKY				
McConnell	N	N	N	Y
Bunning	N	N	N	Y
LOUISIANA				
Breaux	N	Y	Y	Y
Landrieu	N	Y	Y	Y
MAINE				
Snowe	N	Y	Y	Y
Collins	N	Y	Y	Y
MARYLAND				
Sarbanes	Y	Y	Y	Y
Mikulski	Y	Y	Y	Y
MASSACHUSETTS				
Kennedy	Y	Y	Y	?
Kerry	Y	Y	Y	Y
MICHIGAN				
Levin	Y	Y	Y	Y
Stabenow	Y	Y	Y	Y
MINNESOTA				
Wellstone	Y	Y	Y	Y
Dayton	Y	Y	Y	Y
MISSISSIPPI				
Cochran	N	Y	Y	Y
Lott	N	N	N	Y
MISSOURI				
Bond	N	N	N	Y
Carnahan	N	Y	Y	Y
MONTANA				
Baucus	N	Y	Y	Y
Burns	N	N	N	Y
NEBRASKA				
Nelson	Y	Y	Y	Y
Hagel	N	Y	N	Y
NEVADA				
Reid	Y	Y	Y	Y
Ensign	N	Y	Y	Y

	42	43	44	45
NEW HAMPSHIRE				
Smith	N	N	N	Y
Gregg	N	N	N	Y
NEW JERSEY				
Corzine	Y	Y	Y	Y
Torricelli	Y	Y	Y	Y
NEW MEXICO				
Domenici	N	Y	N	Y
Bingaman	Y	Y	Y	Y
NEW YORK				
Clinton	Y	Y	Y	Y
Schumer	Y	Y	Y	Y
NORTH CAROLINA				
Helms	N	N	N	Y
Edwards	Y	Y	Y	Y
NORTH DAKOTA				
Conrad	N	Y	Y	Y
Dorgan	N	Y	Y	Y
OHIO				
DeWine	N	Y	N	Y
Voinovich	N	N	N	Y
OKLAHOMA				
Nickles	N	Y	N	Y
Inhofe	N	Y	N	Y
OREGON				
Wyden	Y	Y	Y	Y
Smith	N	N	N	Y
PENNSYLVANIA				
Specter	N	Y	Y	Y
Santorum	N	N	N	Y
RHODE ISLAND				
Reed	Y	Y	Y	Y
Chafee	N	Y	Y	Y
SOUTH CAROLINA				
Thurmond	N	N	N	Y
Hollings	Y	Y	Y	Y
SOUTH DAKOTA				
Daschle	Y	Y	Y	Y
Johnson	Y	Y	Y	Y
TENNESSEE				
Thompson	N	Y	Y	Y
Frist	N	N	N	Y

	42	43	44	45
TEXAS				
Gramm	N	N	N	Y
Hutchison	N	Y	N	Y
UTAH				
Hatch	N	N	N	Y
Bennett	N	N	N	Y
VERMONT				
Leahy	N	Y	Y	Y
Jeffords	N	Y	Y	Y
VIRGINIA				
Warner	N	N	N	Y
Allen	N	N	N	Y
WASHINGTON				
Cantwell	Y	Y	Y	Y
Murray	Y	Y	Y	Y
WEST VIRGINIA				
Byrd	N	Y	Y	Y
Rockefeller	Y	Y	Y	Y
WISCONSIN				
Kohl	N	Y	Y	Y
Feingold	N	Y	Y	Y
WYOMING				
Thomas	N	N	N	Y
Enzi	N	N	N	Y

ND Northern Democrats   SD Southern Democrats

Southern states - Ala., Ark., Fla., Ga., Ky., La., Miss., N.C., Okla., S.C., Tenn., Texas, Va.

42. S 27. Campaign Finance Overhaul/Public Financing. Wellstone, D-Minn., amendment that would allow states to set up voluntary public financing systems that could be applied to federal congressional candidates who agree to limit contributions as well as campaign spending. Rejected 36-64: R 0-50; D 36-14 (ND 31-10, SD 5-4). March 21, 2001.

43. S 27. Campaign Finance Overhaul/Union and Shareholder Consent. McCain, R-Ariz., motion to table (kill) the Hatch, R-Utah, amendment that would require unions and corporations to obtain permission from dues-paying workers or shareholders before spending money on political activities. It also would require corporations and unions to disclose information regarding the funds spent on political activities. Motion agreed to 69-31: R 19-31; D 50-0 (ND 41-0, SD 9-0). A "nay" was a vote in support of the president's position. March, 21, 2001.

44. S 27. Campaign Finance Overhaul/Union and Corporate Disclosure. McCain, R-Ariz., motion to table (kill) the Hatch, R-Utah, amendment that would require corporations and unions that spend money on political activities to provide detailed disclosure of funds spent on political activities to the corporation's shareholders or labor organization's members. Motion agreed to 60-40: R 10-40; D 50-0 (ND 41-0, SD 9-0). March 22, 2001.

45. S 27. Campaign Finance Overhaul/Union Dues. Nickles, R-Okla., amendment that would strike the provision in the bill that would codify a Supreme Court ruling that unions must allow non-union members to receive refunds of their fees used for political activities unrelated to collective bargaining. Adopted 99-0: R 50-0; D 49-0 (ND 40-0, SD 9-0). March 22, 2001.

Member	46	47	48	49	50	51
ALABAMA						
Shelby	N	N	N	N	N	N
Sessions	N	N	N	N	N	N
ALASKA						
Stevens	N	Y	Y	N	N	Y
Murkowski	N	N	Y	N	N	N
ARIZONA						
McCain	Y	Y	N	Y	N	Y
Kyl	N	N	N	N	N	N
ARKANSAS						
Hutchinson	N	N	N	N	N	N
Lincoln	Y	Y	Y	Y	N	Y
CALIFORNIA						
Feinstein	Y	Y	N	Y	N	Y
Boxer	+	Y	Y	Y	N	Y
COLORADO						
Campbell	N	N	N	N	N	N
Allard	N	–	Y	N	N	N
CONNECTICUT						
Dodd	Y	Y	N	Y	N	Y
Lieberman	Y	Y	N	Y	N	Y
DELAWARE						
Carper	?	Y	N	Y	N	Y
Biden	Y	Y	Y	Y	N	Y
FLORIDA						
Graham	Y	Y	N	Y	N	Y
Nelson	Y	N	Y	Y	N	Y
GEORGIA						
Miller	?	Y	N	Y	N	Y
Cleland	Y	Y	Y	Y	N	Y
HAWAII						
Inouye	Y	Y	N	Y	N	Y
Akaka	Y	N	N	Y	N	Y
IDAHO						
Craig	N	N	Y	N	N	N
Crapo	N	N	N	N	N	N
ILLINOIS						
Durbin	?	Y	Y	Y	N	Y
Fitzgerald	Y	N	Y	N	N	Y
INDIANA						
Lugar	N	N	N	N	N	N
Bayh	Y	Y	N	Y	N	Y
IOWA						
Grassley	N	N	Y	N	N	N
Harkin	Y	Y	Y	Y	N	Y
KANSAS						
Brownback	N	N	N	N	N	N
Roberts	N	N	N	N	N	N
KENTUCKY						
McConnell	N	N	Y	N	N	N
Bunning	N	N	Y	N	N	N
LOUISIANA						
Breaux	Y	Y	Y	N	N	N
Landrieu	?	?	?	N	N	N
MAINE						
Snowe	Y	N	N	Y	N	Y
Collins	Y	N	N	Y	N	Y
MARYLAND						
Sarbanes	Y	Y	Y	Y	N	Y
Mikulski	Y	Y	N	Y	N	Y
MASSACHUSETTS						
Kennedy	?	N	Y	Y	N	Y
Kerry	Y	Y	Y	Y	N	Y
MICHIGAN						
Levin	Y	Y	N	Y	N	Y
Stabenow	Y	Y	N	Y	N	Y
MINNESOTA						
Wellstone	Y	N	Y	Y	N	Y
Dayton	Y	Y	Y	Y	N	Y
MISSISSIPPI						
Cochran	Y	Y	Y	Y	N	Y
Lott	N	N	Y	N	N	N
MISSOURI						
Bond	N	N	Y	N	N	N
Carnahan	Y	Y	N	Y	N	Y
MONTANA						
Baucus	Y	+	+	Y	N	Y
Burns	N	–	–	N	N	N
NEBRASKA						
Nelson	Y	N	Y	N	N	N
Hagel	N	N	N	N	N	N
NEVADA						
Reid	Y	Y	N	Y	N	Y
Ensign	N	N	N	N	N	Y
NEW HAMPSHIRE						
Smith	N	N	Y	N	N	N
Gregg	N	N	Y	N	N	N
NEW JERSEY						
Corzine	Y	N	N	Y	N	Y
Torricelli	Y	N	Y	N	N	Y
NEW MEXICO						
Domenici	N	N	Y	N	N	N
Bingaman	Y	Y	Y	Y	N	Y
NEW YORK						
Clinton	Y	Y	Y	Y	N	Y
Schumer	Y	Y	N	Y	N	Y
NORTH CAROLINA						
Helms	N	N	N	N	N	N
Edwards	Y	N	N	Y	N	Y
NORTH DAKOTA						
Conrad	Y	Y	Y	Y	N	Y
Dorgan	Y	Y	Y	Y	N	Y
OHIO						
DeWine	Y	N	N	Y	N	Y
Voinovich	N	N	N	N	N	N
OKLAHOMA						
Nickles	N	N	Y	N	N	N
Inhofe	N	N	Y	N	N	N
OREGON						
Wyden	Y	Y	N	Y	N	Y
Smith	Y	N	N	Y	N	N
PENNSYLVANIA						
Specter	Y	Y	N	Y	N	Y
Santorum	N	N	Y	N	N	N
RHODE ISLAND						
Reed	Y	Y	Y	Y	N	Y
Chafee	Y	N	N	Y	N	Y
SOUTH CAROLINA						
Thurmond	N	N	N	N	N	N
Hollings	Y	Y	Y	Y	N	Y
SOUTH DAKOTA						
Daschle	Y	Y	N	Y	N	Y
Johnson	Y	N	Y	Y	N	Y
TENNESSEE						
Thompson	N	N	N	N	N	Y
Frist	N	N	Y	N	N	N
TEXAS						
Gramm	N	N	Y	N	N	N
Hutchison	N	N	N	N	N	N
UTAH						
Hatch	N	N	Y	N	N	N
Bennett	N	N	Y	N	N	N
VERMONT						
Leahy	Y	N	N	Y	N	Y
Jeffords	Y	N	N	Y	N	Y
VIRGINIA						
Warner	N	N	Y	N	N	N
Allen	N	N	N	N	N	N
WASHINGTON						
Cantwell	Y	Y	Y	Y	N	Y
Murray	?	Y	Y	Y	N	Y
WEST VIRGINIA						
Byrd	Y	Y	Y	Y	N	Y
Rockefeller	Y	Y	N	?	N	Y
WISCONSIN						
Kohl	Y	N	N	Y	N	Y
Feingold	Y	N	N	Y	N	Y
WYOMING						
Thomas	N	N	N	N	N	N
Enzi	N	N	N	N	N	N

Key

Y	Voted for (yea).
#	Paired for.
+	Announced for.
N	Voted against (nay).
X	Paired against.
–	Announced against.
P	Voted "present."
C	Voted "present" to avoid possible conflict of interest.
?	Did not vote or otherwise make a position known.

Democrats **Republicans** *Independents*

ND Northern Democrats   SD Southern Democrats

Southern states - Ala., Ark., Fla., Ga., Ky., La., Miss., N.C., Okla., S.C., Tenn., Texas, Va.

46. S 27. Campaign Finance Overhaul/Union Dues. McCain, R-Ariz., motion to table (kill) a Helms, R-N.C., amendment to require labor organizations to notify dues-paying workers on an annual basis that the Supreme Court has ruled that they have a right to withhold the portion of their dues that is used for purposes unrelated to collective bargaining. Motion agreed to 53-40: R 10-40; D 43-0 (ND 36-0, SD 7-0). March 23, 2001.

47. S J Res 4. Campaign Finance Constitutional Amendment/Passage. Passage of the joint resolution to propose a Constitutional amendment to grant Congress the power to set limits on contributions to and expenditures by campaigns supporting or opposing candidates seeking election to federal office. It also would grant states the power to set similar limits for contributions and expenditures involving state or local elections. Rejected 40-56: R 4-44; D 36-12 (ND 30-10, SD 6-2). A two-thirds majority vote of those present and voting (64 in this case) is required to pass a joint resolution proposing an amendment to the Constitution. March 26, 2001.

48. S 27. Campaign Finance Overhaul/Issue Ads. Wellstone, D-Minn., amendment that would prohibit certain tax-exempt organizations from using soft money for issue ads that target a specific candidate and that occur within 60 days of a general election or 30 days of a primary election. Adopted 51-46: R 24-25; D 27-21 (ND 22-18, SD 5-3). March 26, 2001.

49. S 27. Campaign Finance Overhaul/Hard Money Increase. McCain, R-Ariz., motion to table (kill) Division I of the Hagel, R-Neb., amendment that would increase the limits on individual contributions to candidates to $3,000 for an election and to national parties to $60,000 per year. The amendment would increase political action committee contributions to candidates at $7,500 per election, and to national parties at $30,000 per year. Motion agreed to 52-47: R 7-43; D 45-4 (ND 38-2, SD 7-2). March 27, 2001.

50. S 27. Campaign Finance Overhaul/Disclosure Requirements. McCain, R-Ariz., motion to table (kill) Division II of the Hagel, R-Neb., amendment that would increase campaign finance disclosure requirements, such as requiring House and Senate candidates to file monthly reports during an election cycle, and provide that television and radio stations must make all purchases of political advertisements public. Motion rejected 0-100: R 0-50; D 0-50 (ND 0-41, SD 0-9). (Subsequently, Division II of the Hagel amendment was adopted by voice vote.) March 27, 2001.

51. S 27. Campaign Finance Overhaul/Soft Money Cap. McCain, R-Ariz., motion to table (kill) Division III of the Hagel, R-Neb., amendment that would limit soft money contributions by individuals, political action committees, independent organizations, corporations and unions to national and state political party committees to $60,000 per year, indexed for inflation. It would codify Federal Election Commission regulations that list activities that state parties must pay for with hard money, and it would declare the underlying bill's ban on soft money ineffective. Motion agreed to 60-40: R 12-38; D 48-2 (ND 40-1, SD 8-1). March 27, 2001.

	52	53	54	55	56
ALABAMA					
Shelby	N	N	Y	Y	N
Sessions	N	N	Y	Y	N
ALASKA					
Stevens	N	N	Y	Y	N
Murkowski	N	N	Y	Y	N
ARIZONA					
McCain	N	Y	N	Y	Y
Kyl	N	N	Y	Y	N
ARKANSAS					
Hutchinson	N	N	Y	Y	N
Lincoln	N	Y	N	Y	Y
CALIFORNIA					
Feinstein	N	Y	N	Y	Y
Boxer	Y	Y	N	N	Y
COLORADO					
Campbell	N	N	Y	Y	N
Allard	N	N	Y	Y	N
CONNECTICUT					
Dodd	Y	Y	N	Y	Y
Lieberman	Y	Y	N	Y	Y
DELAWARE					
Carper	Y	N	N	Y	Y
Biden	Y	Y	N	N	Y
FLORIDA					
Graham	Y	Y	N	Y	Y
Nelson	Y	Y	N	Y	Y
GEORGIA					
Miller	N	Y	N	N	Y
Cleland	N	Y	N	Y	Y
HAWAII					
Inouye	Y	Y	N	Y	Y
Akaka	Y	Y	N	Y	Y
IDAHO					
Craig	N	N	Y	Y	N
Crapo	N	N	Y	Y	N
ILLINOIS					
Durbin	N	Y	N	Y	Y
Fitzgerald	N	N	Y	Y	N
INDIANA					
Lugar	N	N	Y	Y	N
Bayh	N	Y	N	Y	Y

	52	53	54	55	56
IOWA					
Grassley	N	N	Y	Y	N
Harkin	Y	Y	N	N	Y
KANSAS					
Brownback	N	N	Y	Y	N
Roberts	N	N	Y	Y	N
KENTUCKY					
McConnell	N	N	Y	Y	N
Bunning	N	N	Y	Y	N
LOUISIANA					
Breaux	N	N	Y	Y	Y
Landrieu	N	N	N	Y	Y
MAINE					
Snowe	N	N	Y	Y	N
Collins	N	N	N	Y	N
MARYLAND					
Sarbanes	Y	Y	N	N	Y
Mikulski	N	Y	N	Y	Y
MASSACHUSETTS					
Kennedy	Y	Y	N	Y	Y
Kerry	Y	Y	N	N	Y
MICHIGAN					
Levin	Y	Y	N	Y	Y
Stabenow	Y	Y	N	N	Y
MINNESOTA					
Wellstone	Y	Y	N	N	Y
Dayton	Y	Y	N	Y	Y
MISSISSIPPI					
Cochran	N	N	N	Y	N
Lott	N	N	Y	Y	N
MISSOURI					
Bond	N	N	Y	Y	N
Carnahan	N	Y	N	Y	Y
MONTANA					
Baucus	N	Y	N	N	Y
Burns	N	N	Y	Y	N
NEBRASKA					
Nelson	N	N	N	Y	Y
Hagel	N	N	Y	Y	N
NEVADA					
Reid	Y	Y	N	Y	Y
Ensign	N	N	Y	Y	N

	52	53	54	55	56
NEW HAMPSHIRE					
Smith	N	N	Y	Y	N
Gregg	N	N	Y	Y	N
NEW JERSEY					
Corzine	Y	Y	N	Y	Y
Torricelli	Y	N	Y	Y	Y
NEW MEXICO					
Domenici	N	N	Y	Y	N
Bingaman	Y	Y	N	Y	Y
NEW YORK					
Clinton	Y	Y	N	Y	Y
Schumer	N	Y	N	Y	Y
NORTH CAROLINA					
Helms	N	N	Y	Y	N
Edwards	N	Y	N	Y	Y
NORTH DAKOTA					
Conrad	N	Y	N	N	Y
Dorgan	N	Y	N	N	Y
OHIO					
DeWine	N	N	Y	Y	N
Voinovich	N	N	Y	Y	N
OKLAHOMA					
Nickles	N	N	Y	Y	N
Inhofe	N	N	Y	Y	N
OREGON					
Wyden	N	Y	N	N	Y
Smith	N	N	Y	Y	N
PENNSYLVANIA					
Specter	N	N	N	Y	Y
Santorum	N	N	Y	Y	N
RHODE ISLAND					
Reed	Y	Y	N	N	Y
Chafee	N	N	Y	Y	N
SOUTH CAROLINA					
Thurmond	N	N	Y	Y	N
Hollings	Y	Y	N	N	Y
SOUTH DAKOTA					
Daschle	Y	Y	N	Y	Y
Johnson	N	Y	N	N	Y
TENNESSEE					
Thompson	N	N	Y	Y	N
Frist	N	N	Y	Y	N

	52	53	54	55	56
TEXAS					
Gramm	N	N	Y	Y	N
Hutchison	N	N	Y	Y	N
UTAH					
Hatch	N	N	Y	Y	N
Bennett	N	N	Y	Y	N
VERMONT					
Leahy	Y	Y	N	Y	Y
Jeffords	N	N	N	Y	Y
VIRGINIA					
Warner	N	N	Y	Y	N
Allen	N	N	Y	Y	N
WASHINGTON					
Cantwell	Y	Y	N	Y	Y
Murray	Y	Y	N	N	Y
WEST VIRGINIA					
Byrd	Y	Y	N	Y	Y
Rockefeller	Y	Y	N	Y	Y
WISCONSIN					
Kohl	N	Y	N	Y	Y
Feingold	N	Y	N	Y	Y
WYOMING					
Thomas	N	N	Y	Y	N
Enzi	N	N	Y	Y	N

Key

Y	Voted for (yea).
#	Paired for.
+	Announced for.
N	Voted against (nay).
X	Paired against.
−	Announced against.
P	Voted "present."
C	Voted "present" to avoid possible conflict of interest.
?	Did not vote or otherwise make a position known.

Democrats **Republicans**
Independents

ND Northern Democrats   SD Southern Democrats

Southern states - Ala., Ark., Fla., Ga., Ky., La., Miss., N.C., Okla., S.C., Tenn., Texas, Va.

52. S 27. Campaign Finance Overhaul/Partial Public Financing. Kerry, D-Mass., amendment that would allow Senate candidates who abide by voluntary spending limits to be eligible for partial public financing, in an amount equal to 200 percent of individual contributions of $200 or less, during the general election period. Rejected 30-70: R 0-50; D 30-20 (ND 27-14, SD 3-6). March 27, 2001.

53. S 27. Campaign Finance Overhaul/Hard Money Increase. Feingold, D-Wis., motion to table (kill) the Thompson, R-Tenn., amendment that would increase the individual contribution limit to candidates to $2,500 per election and the individual limit to national parties to $40,000 per year. Individual contributions to political action committees (PACs) would be limited to $7,500 per year; PAC contributions to candidates would also be capped at $7,500 per year. Motion rejected 46-54: R 1-49; D 45-5 (ND 38-3, SD 7-2). March 28, 2001.

54. S 27. Campaign Finance Overhaul/Hard Money Increase. McConnell, R-Ky., motion to table (kill) the Feinstein, D-Calif., amendment to the Thompson, R-Tenn., amendment. The Feinstein amendment would strike the text of the Thompson amendment and instead increase the individual contribution limit to candidates to $2,000 per election, the individual limit to national parties to $20,000 per year, and the individual aggregate limit to

$65,000 per election cycle. It also would provide that if the Supreme Court strikes down coordinated spending limits, then broadcasters would not be required to charge a national political party committee that does not voluntarily abide by the limits, the lowest television broadcast rate. Motion rejected 46-54: R 44-6; D 2-48 (ND 1-40, SD 1-8). (Subsequently, the amendment was withdrawn.) March 28, 2001.

55. S 27. Campaign Finance Overhaul/Hard Money Increase. Thompson, R-Tenn., amendment, as modified, that would increase the individual contribution limit to candidates to $2,000 per election, the individual limit to national parties to $25,000 per year, and the individual aggregate limit to $37,500 per year. Contributions to and by PACs would not be affected. Adopted 84-16: R 50-0; D 34-16 (ND 27-14, SD 7-2). March 28, 2001.

56. S 27. Campaign Finance Overhaul/Broadcast Rates. Schumer, D-N.Y., amendment that would provide that if the Supreme Court strikes down coordinated spending limits, then broadcasters would not be required to charge a national political party committee that does not voluntarily abide by the limits, the lowest television broadcast rate. The amendment also includes a severability clause, stating that if the amendment is found unconstitutional, the remaining provisions in the underlying bill would not be affected. Adopted 52-48: R 2-48; D 50-0 (ND 41-0, SD 9-0). March 28, 2001.

	57	58	59	60	61
ALABAMA					
Shelby	Y	N	N	Y	Y
Sessions	Y	N	N	Y	Y
ALASKA					
Stevens	N	N	N	Y	Y
Murkowski	Y	N	N	Y	Y
ARIZONA					
McCain	N	N	Y	Y	Y
Kyl	Y	N	N	Y	N
ARKANSAS					
Hutchinson	Y	N	Y	Y	N
Lincoln	N	N	N	Y	Y
CALIFORNIA					
Feinstein	N	N	Y	Y	Y
Boxer	N	Y	Y	N	Y
COLORADO					
Campbell	N	N	N	Y	Y
Allard	Y	N	N	Y	Y
CONNECTICUT					
Dodd	N	Y	Y	N	Y
Lieberman	N	Y	Y	N	Y
DELAWARE					
Carper	N	Y	Y	N	Y
Biden	N	Y	Y	N	Y
FLORIDA					
Graham	N	Y	Y	Y	Y
Nelson	N	Y	Y	N	Y
GEORGIA					
Miller	N	N	Y	Y	Y
Cleland	N	N	Y	Y	Y
HAWAII					
Inouye	N	Y	Y	N	Y
Akaka	N	?	Y	N	Y
IDAHO					
Craig	N	N	N	Y	Y
Crapo	N	N	N	Y	Y
ILLINOIS					
Durbin	N	Y	Y	N	Y
Fitzgerald	N	N	Y	Y	Y
INDIANA					
Lugar	N	N	Y	Y	Y
Bayh	N	Y	Y	Y	Y

	57	58	59	60	61
IOWA					
Grassley	Y	N	N	Y	N
Harkin	N	Y	Y	N	Y
KANSAS					
Brownback	Y	N	Y	Y	N
Roberts	Y	N	N	Y	N
KENTUCKY					
McConnell	Y	N	N	Y	N
Bunning	Y	N	N	Y	N
LOUISIANA					
Breaux	N	N	N	Y	Y
Landrieu	N	N	N	Y	Y
MAINE					
Snowe	N	N	Y	Y	Y
Collins	N	N	Y	Y	Y
MARYLAND					
Sarbanes	N	Y	Y	N	Y
Mikulski	N	N	Y	N	Y
MASSACHUSETTS					
Kennedy	N	Y	Y	N	Y
Kerry	N	N	Y	Y	Y
MICHIGAN					
Levin	N	Y	Y	N	Y
Stabenow	N	Y	Y	Y	Y
MINNESOTA					
Wellstone	N	Y	Y	N	Y
Dayton	N	Y	Y	N	Y
MISSISSIPPI					
Cochran	N	N	Y	Y	Y
Lott	N	N	N	Y	Y
MISSOURI					
Bond	Y	N	N	Y	Y
Carnahan	N	N	Y	Y	Y
MONTANA					
Baucus	N	N	N	Y	Y
Burns	N	N	N	Y	Y
NEBRASKA					
Nelson	N	N	N	Y	Y
Hagel	Y	N	N	Y	Y
NEVADA					
Reid	N	Y	Y	N	Y
Ensign	N	N	N	Y	Y

	57	58	59	60	61
NEW HAMPSHIRE					
Smith	Y	N	N	Y	N
Gregg	Y	N	N	Y	N
NEW JERSEY					
Corzine	N	Y	Y	N	Y
Torricelli	N	Y	N	N	Y
NEW MEXICO					
Domenici	N	N	N	Y	Y
Bingaman	N	Y	Y	N	Y
NEW YORK					
Clinton	N	Y	Y	N	Y
Schumer	N	N	Y	Y	Y
NORTH CAROLINA					
Helms	Y	N	N	Y	N
Edwards	N	N	Y	Y	Y
NORTH DAKOTA					
Conrad	N	Y	Y	N	Y
Dorgan	N	Y	Y	Y	Y
OHIO					
DeWine	Y	N	Y	Y	N
Voinovich	Y	N	N	Y	?
OKLAHOMA					
Nickles	Y	N	N	Y	N
Inhofe	Y	N	N	Y	Y
OREGON					
Wyden	N	N	Y	Y	Y
Smith	N	N	N	Y	Y
PENNSYLVANIA					
Specter	N	N	Y	Y	Y
Santorum	Y	N	N	Y	Y
RHODE ISLAND					
Reed	N	Y	Y	N	Y
Chafee	N	N	Y	Y	Y
SOUTH CAROLINA					
Thurmond	Y	N	N	Y	Y
Hollings	N	Y	N	N	Y
SOUTH DAKOTA					
Daschle	N	Y	Y	N	Y
Johnson	N	N	Y	N	Y
TENNESSEE					
Thompson	N	N	Y	Y	Y
Frist	Y	N	N	Y	Y

	57	58	59	60	61
TEXAS					
Gramm	N	N	N	Y	N
Hutchison	N	N	N	Y	Y
UTAH					
Hatch	Y	N	N	Y	Y
Bennett	Y	N	N	Y	Y
VERMONT					
Leahy	N	Y	Y	N	Y
Jeffords	N	N	Y	Y	Y
VIRGINIA					
Warner	N	N	N	Y	Y
Allen	Y	N	N	Y	N
WASHINGTON					
Cantwell	N	Y	Y	Y	Y
Murray	N	Y	Y	Y	Y
WEST VIRGINIA					
Byrd	N	Y	Y	N	Y
Rockefeller	N	N	Y	Y	Y
WISCONSIN					
Kohl	N	N	Y	Y	Y
Feingold	N	Y	Y	Y	Y
WYOMING					
Thomas	Y	N	N	Y	N
Enzi	Y	N	N	Y	N

ND Northern Democrats   SD Southern Democrats

Southern states - Ala., Ark., Fla., Ga., Ky., La., Miss., N.C., Okla., S.C., Tenn., Texas, Va.

57. S 27. Campaign Finance Overhaul/Disclosure. DeWine, R-Ohio, amendment to strike language in the bill that would: prohibit corporate and union general treasury funds from being spent on issue ads; require disclosure of individuals who pay for issue ads that run within 60 days of a general election or 30 days of a primary; and prevent issue ads from targeting specific candidates within the 60-day and 30-day periods. Rejected 28-72: R 28-22; D 0-50 (ND 0-41, SD 0-9). March 29, 2001.

58. S 27. Campaign Finance Overhaul/Voluntary Spending Limits. Harkin, D-Iowa, amendment that would provide for a voluntary spending limit on Senate campaigns. If a candidate who abides by the limit is facing an opponent who exceeds the limit by $10,000 or more, then the first candidate would be eligible for public financing equal to twice the excess amount spent by the opponent. Rejected 32-67: R 0-50; D32-17 (ND 29-11, SD 3-6). March 29, 2001.

59. S 27. Campaign Finance Overhaul/Non-Severability. Dodd, motion to table (kill) the Frist, R-Tenn., amendment that would provide that if the ban on soft money, the issue ad restrictions or the hard-money limits were found unconstitutional, the others would also be invalid. Motion agreed to 57-43: R 13-37; D 44-6 (ND 38-3, SD 6-3). March 29, 2001.

60. S 27. Campaign Finance Overhaul/Political Advertisements. McCain, R-Ariz., motion to table (kill) the Bingaman, D-N.M., amendment that would require broadcasting stations to make available at no charge equal time to candidates for federal office who are attacked or opposed in political advertisements by independent groups. Motion agreed to 72-28: R 50-0; D 22-28 (ND 15-26, SD 7-2). March 29, 2001.

61. S 27. Campaign Finance Overhaul/Electioneering Communications Definition. Specter, R-Pa., amendment that would provide further clarification of the definitions of electioneering communications, if the definition in the underlying bill is struck down in the courts. Adopted 82-17: R 32-17; D 50-0 (ND 41-0, SD 9-0). March 29, 2001.

	62	63	64	65	66
ALABAMA					
Shelby	N	N	N	Y	N
Sessions	N	N	N	Y	N
ALASKA					
Stevens	N	N	Y	N	Y
Murkowski	?	?	N	Y	N
ARIZONA					
McCain	N	Y	Y	Y	N
Kyl	N	N	N	Y	N
ARKANSAS					
Hutchinson	N	N	N	Y	N
Lincoln	Y	Y	Y	N	Y
CALIFORNIA					
Feinstein	N	Y	Y	N	Y
Boxer	N	Y	Y	N	Y
COLORADO					
Campbell	N	N	N	Y	N
Allard	N	N	N	Y	N
CONNECTICUT					
Dodd	Y	Y	Y	N	Y
Lieberman	Y	Y	Y	N	Y
DELAWARE					
Carper	Y	Y	Y	N	Y
Biden	Y	Y	Y	N	Y
FLORIDA					
Graham	Y	Y	Y	N	Y
Nelson	Y	Y	Y	N	Y
GEORGIA					
Miller	?	?	Y	Y	N
Cleland	Y	Y	Y	N	Y
HAWAII					
Inouye	Y	Y	Y	N	Y
Akaka	Y	Y	Y	N	Y
IDAHO					
Craig	N	N	N	Y	N
Crapo	N	N	N	Y	N
ILLINOIS					
Durbin	Y	Y	Y	N	Y
Fitzgerald	Y	N	Y	Y	N
INDIANA					
Lugar	N	Y	Y	Y	N
Bayh	Y	Y	Y	N	Y

	62	63	64	65	66
IOWA					
Grassley	N	N	N	Y	N
Harkin	Y	Y	Y	N	Y
KANSAS					
Brownback	N	N	N	Y	N
Roberts	N	N	N	Y	N
KENTUCKY					
McConnell	N	N	N	Y	N
Bunning	N	N	N	Y	N
LOUISIANA					
Breaux	?	?	N	N	Y
Landrieu	Y	Y	Y	N	Y
MAINE					
Snowe	N	Y	Y	Y	N
Collins	N	Y	Y	Y	N
MARYLAND					
Sarbanes	Y	Y	Y	N	Y
Mikulski	Y	Y	Y	N	Y
MASSACHUSETTS					
Kennedy	Y	Y	Y	N	Y
Kerry	Y	Y	Y	N	Y
MICHIGAN					
Levin	Y	Y	Y	N	Y
Stabenow	Y	Y	Y	N	Y
MINNESOTA					
Wellstone	Y	Y	Y	N	Y
Dayton	?	?	Y	N	Y
MISSISSIPPI					
Cochran	N	Y	Y	Y	N
Lott	N	N	N	Y	N
MISSOURI					
Bond	N	N	N	Y	N
Carnahan	Y	Y	Y	N	Y
MONTANA					
Baucus	N	Y	Y	N	Y
Burns	N	N	N	Y	N
NEBRASKA					
Nelson	N	Y	N	N	Y
Hagel	N	N	N	Y	N
NEVADA					
Reid	Y	Y	Y	N	Y
Ensign	?	?	N	Y	N

	62	63	64	65	66
NEW HAMPSHIRE					
Smith	N	N	N	Y	N
Gregg	N	N	N	Y	N
NEW JERSEY					
Corzine	Y	Y	Y	N	Y
Torricelli	N	Y	Y	N	Y
NEW MEXICO					
Domenici	N	N	Y	Y	N
Bingaman	?	?	Y	N	Y
NEW YORK					
Clinton	N	Y	Y	N	Y
Schumer	Y	Y	Y	N	Y
NORTH CAROLINA					
Helms	?	?	N	Y	N
Edwards	Y	Y	Y	N	Y
NORTH DAKOTA					
Conrad	Y	Y	Y	N	Y
Dorgan	Y	Y	Y	N	Y
OHIO					
DeWine	N	N	N	Y	N
Voinovich	N	N	N	Y	N
OKLAHOMA					
Nickles	N	N	N	Y	N
Inhofe	N	N	N	Y	N
OREGON					
Wyden	Y	Y	Y	N	Y
Smith	N	N	N	Y	N
PENNSYLVANIA					
Specter	N	Y	Y	N	Y
Santorum	N	N	N	Y	N
RHODE ISLAND					
Reed	Y	Y	Y	N	Y
Chafee	N	Y	Y	N	Y
SOUTH CAROLINA					
Thurmond	N	N	N	Y	N
Hollings	Y	Y	N	N	Y
SOUTH DAKOTA					
Daschle	Y	Y	Y	N	Y
Johnson	Y	Y	Y	N	Y
TENNESSEE					
Thompson	N	Y	Y	Y	N
Frist	N	N	N	Y	N

	62	63	64	65	66
TEXAS					
Gramm	?	?	N	Y	N
Hutchison	N	Y	N	Y	N
UTAH					
Hatch	N	N	N	Y	N
Bennett	N	N	N	Y	N
VERMONT					
Leahy	Y	Y	Y	N	Y
Jeffords	N	Y	Y	N	Y
VIRGINIA					
Warner	N	Y	N	Y	N
Allen	N	N	N	Y	N
WASHINGTON					
Cantwell	Y	Y	Y	N	Y
Murray	Y	Y	Y	N	Y
WEST VIRGINIA					
Byrd	Y	Y	Y	N	Y
Rockefeller	Y	Y	Y	N	Y
WISCONSIN					
Kohl	Y	Y	Y	N	Y
Feingold	Y	Y	Y	N	Y
WYOMING					
Thomas	?	?	N	Y	N
Enzi	N	N	N	Y	N

Key

Y	Voted for (yea).
#	Paired for.
+	Announced for.
N	Voted against (nay).
X	Paired against.
–	Announced against.
P	Voted "present."
C	Voted "present" to avoid possible conflict of interest.
?	Did not vote or otherwise make a position known.

Democrats **Republicans**
Independents

ND Northern Democrats   SD Southern Democrats

Southern states - Ala., Ark., Fla., Ga., Ky., La., Miss., N.C., Okla., S.C., Tenn., Texas, Va.

62. S 27. Campaign Finance Overhaul/Enforcement Authority. Reed, D-R.I., amendment that would authorize the Federal Election Commission to initiate a civil action for a temporary restraining order or a preliminary injunction pending the outcome of random audits. It also would increase the penalty for knowing and willful violations of campaign law to $15,000 or an amount equal to 300 percent of any contribution or expenditure involved in the violation, whichever is greater. Rejected 41-50: R 1-44; D 40-6 (ND 33-6, SD 7-0). March 30, 2001.

63. S 27. Campaign Finance Overhaul/Coordinated Expenditures. McCain, R-Ariz., amendment that would revise the definition of coordinated expenditures and allow the Federal Election Commission to promulgate new regulations on coordinated expenditures. Adopted 57-34: R 11-34; D 46-0 (ND 39-0, SD 7-0). March 30, 2001.

64. S 27. Campaign Finance Overhaul/Passage. Passage of the bill that would ban soft money donations to political parties, prohibit corporate and union general treasury funds from being spent on issue ads, and require disclosure of individuals who pay for issue ads that run within 60 days of a general election or 30 days of a primary. It also would prevent certain issue ads from targeting specific candidates within the 60-day and 30-day periods. The bill, as amended, would increase the individual contribution limit per candidate to $2,000 per election, the individual limit to national parties to $25,000 per year and the individual aggregate limit to $37,500 per year. Passed 59-41: R 12-38; D 47-3 (ND 40-1, SD 7-2). April 2, 2001.

65. H Con Res 83. Fiscal 2002 Budget Resolution/Prescription Drug Benefit. Grassley, R-Iowa, amendment to the Domenici, R-N.M., substitute amendment. The Grassley amendment would allow the chairman of the Budget Committee to revise Finance Committee allocations up to $300 billion for fiscal 2002-2011, if that committee reports a bill, joint resolution or conference report that overhauls the Medicare program and a prescription drug benefit. The total adjustment for any fiscal year is not to exceed Congressional Budget Office estimates of the president's Medicare overhaul and prescription drug benefit plan. The Domenici amendment would cap discretionary spending at $660.7 billion in fiscal 2002 and includes an $845.7 billion contingency fund — including the Medicare trust fund surplus — that could be used for debt reduction, tax cuts or unforeseen spending. It also calls for $1.6 trillion in tax cuts over fiscal years 2002-2011 and $60 billion in tax cuts in fiscal 2001. Adopted 51-50: R 49-1; D 1-49 (ND 0-41, SD 1-8), with Vice President Cheney casting a "yea" vote. April 3, 2001.

66. H Con Res 83. Fiscal 2002 Budget Resolution/Prescription Drug Benefit. Baucus, D-Mont., amendment to the Domenici, R-N.M., substitute amendment. The Baucus amendment would provide for a total of $311 billion over 10 years for a Medicare prescription drug benefit, by redirecting $158 billion set aside for a proposed tax cut in the resolution and increasing funds for a prescription drug benefit program by the same amount. Rejected 50-50: R 1-49; D 49-1 (ND 41-0, SD 8-1). April 3, 2001.

	67	68	69	70	71	72	73
ALABAMA							
Shelby	Y	N	N	Y	N	Y	N
Sessions	Y	N	N	Y	N	Y	N
ALASKA							
Stevens	Y	N	N	Y	N	Y	N
Murkowski	Y	N	N	Y	N	Y	N
ARIZONA							
McCain	Y	N	N	Y	Y	Y	N
Kyl	Y	N	N	Y	N	Y	N
ARKANSAS							
Hutchinson	Y	N	N	Y	N	Y	N
Lincoln	N	Y	Y	Y	Y	N	Y
CALIFORNIA							
Feinstein	N	Y	Y	Y	Y	Y	Y
Boxer	N	Y	Y	Y	?	N	Y
COLORADO							
Campbell	Y	N	N	Y	N	Y	N
Allard	Y	N	N	Y	N	Y	N
CONNECTICUT							
Dodd	N	Y	Y	Y	Y	Y	Y
Lieberman	N	Y	Y	Y	Y	Y	Y
DELAWARE							
Carper	N	N	Y	Y	Y	Y	Y
Biden	N	Y	Y	Y	Y	Y	Y
FLORIDA							
Graham	N	Y	Y	Y	Y	Y	Y
Nelson	N	Y	Y	Y	Y	Y	Y
GEORGIA							
Miller	Y	N	N	Y	N	Y	N
Cleland	N	Y	Y	Y	Y	Y	N
HAWAII							
Inouye	N	Y	Y	Y	Y	Y	Y
Akaka	N	Y	Y	Y	Y	Y	Y
IDAHO							
Craig	Y	N	N	Y	N	Y	N
Crapo	Y	N	N	Y	N	Y	N
ILLINOIS							
Durbin	N	Y	Y	Y	Y	N	Y
Fitzgerald	Y	N	N	Y	N	Y	N
INDIANA							
Lugar	Y	N	N	Y	N	Y	N
Bayh	N	Y	Y	Y	Y	Y	Y
IOWA							
Grassley	Y	N	N	Y	N	Y	N
Harkin	N	Y	Y	Y	Y	N	Y
KANSAS							
Brownback	Y	N	N	Y	N	Y	N
Roberts	Y	N	N	Y	N	Y	N
KENTUCKY							
McConnell	Y	N	N	Y	N	Y	N
Bunning	Y	N	N	Y	N	Y	N
LOUISIANA							
Breaux	N	Y	Y	Y	Y	Y	Y
Landrieu	N	Y	Y	Y	Y	Y	Y
MAINE							
Snowe	Y	N	N	Y	N	Y	N
Collins	Y	N	N	Y	N	Y	N
MARYLAND							
Sarbanes	N	Y	Y	Y	Y	Y	Y
Mikulski	N	Y	Y	Y	Y	Y	Y
MASSACHUSETTS							
Kennedy	N	Y	Y	Y	Y	N	Y
Kerry	N	Y	Y	Y	Y	Y	Y
MICHIGAN							
Levin	N	Y	Y	Y	Y	Y	Y
Stabenow	N	Y	Y	Y	Y	N	Y
MINNESOTA							
Wellstone	N	Y	Y	Y	Y	N	Y
Dayton	N	Y	Y	Y	Y	Y	Y
MISSISSIPPI							
Cochran	Y	N	N	Y	N	Y	N
Lott	Y	N	Y	Y	N	Y	N
MISSOURI							
Bond	Y	N	N	N	N	Y	N
Carnahan	N	Y	Y	Y	Y	Y	Y
MONTANA							
Baucus	N	Y	Y	Y	Y	Y	Y
Burns	Y	N	N	Y	N	Y	N
NEBRASKA							
Nelson	N	Y	Y	Y	Y	Y	N
Hagel	Y	N	N	Y	N	Y	N
NEVADA							
Reid	N	Y	Y	Y	Y	Y	Y
Ensign	Y	N	N	Y	N	Y	N
NEW HAMPSHIRE							
Smith	Y	N	N	N	N	Y	N
Gregg	Y	N	N	N	N	N	N
NEW JERSEY							
Corzine	N	Y	Y	Y	Y	N	Y
Torricelli	N	N	Y	Y	N	N	Y
NEW MEXICO							
Domenici	Y	N	N	Y	N	Y	N
Bingaman	N	Y	Y	Y	Y	Y	Y
NEW YORK							
Clinton	N	Y	Y	Y	Y	Y	Y
Schumer	N	Y	Y	Y	Y	N	Y
NORTH CAROLINA							
Helms	Y	N	N	Y	N	Y	N
Edwards	N	Y	Y	Y	Y	Y	Y
NORTH DAKOTA							
Conrad	N	Y	Y	Y	Y	Y	Y
Dorgan	N	Y	Y	Y	Y	Y	Y
OHIO							
DeWine	Y	N	N	Y	N	Y	N
Voinovich	Y	N	N	N	N	Y	N
OKLAHOMA							
Nickles	Y	N	N	Y	N	Y	N
Inhofe	Y	N	N	Y	N	Y	N
OREGON							
Wyden	N	Y	Y	Y	N	N	Y
Smith	Y	N	N	Y	N	Y	N
PENNSYLVANIA							
Specter	Y	N	Y	Y	N	Y	N
Santorum	Y	N	N	Y	N	Y	N
RHODE ISLAND							
Reed	N	Y	Y	Y	N	N	Y
Chafee	Y	N	Y	Y	N	Y	N
SOUTH CAROLINA							
Thurmond	Y	N	N	Y	N	Y	N
Hollings	N	Y	Y	Y	Y	Y	Y
SOUTH DAKOTA							
Daschle	N	Y	Y	Y	Y	Y	Y
Johnson	N	Y	Y	Y	Y	Y	Y
TENNESSEE							
Thompson	Y	N	N	Y	N	Y	N
Frist	Y	N	N	Y	N	Y	N
TEXAS							
Gramm	Y	N	N	Y	N	N	N
Hutchison	Y	N	N	Y	N	Y	N
UTAH							
Hatch	Y	N	N	Y	N	Y	N
Bennett	Y	N	N	Y	N	Y	N
VERMONT							
Leahy	N	Y	Y	Y	Y	Y	Y
Jeffords	Y	N	Y	N	Y	N	Y
VIRGINIA							
Warner	Y	N	N	Y	N	Y	N
Allen	Y	N	N	Y	N	Y	N
WASHINGTON							
Cantwell	N	Y	Y	Y	Y	Y	Y
Murray	N	Y	Y	Y	Y	N	Y
WEST VIRGINIA							
Byrd	N	Y	Y	Y	Y	Y	Y
Rockefeller	N	Y	Y	Y	Y	Y	Y
WISCONSIN							
Kohl	N	Y	Y	Y	Y	Y	Y
Feingold	N	Y	Y	Y	Y	N	Y
WYOMING							
Thomas	Y	N	N	Y	N	Y	N
Enzi	Y	N	N	Y	N	Y	N

Key

Y	Voted for (yea).
#	Paired for.
+	Announced for.
N	Voted against (nay).
X	Paired against.
−	Announced against.
P	Voted "present."
C	Voted "present" to avoid possible conflict of interest.
?	Did not vote or otherwise make a position known.

Democrats **Republicans** *Independents*

ND Northern Democrats   SD Southern Democrats

Southern states - Ala., Ark., Fla., Ga., Ky., La., Miss., N.C., Okla., S.C., Tenn., Texas, Va.

67. H Con Res 83. Fiscal 2002 Budget Resolution/Agriculture Spending. Grassley, R-Iowa, amendment to the Domenici, R-N.M., substitute amendment. The Grassley amendment would increase budget authority and outlays over 11 years by $63.5 billion for agriculture spending, including $5 billion for fiscal 2001. Adopted 51-49: R 50-0; D 1-49 (ND 0-41, SD 1-8). April 4, 2001.

68. H Con Res 83. Fiscal 2002 Budget Resolution/Agriculture Spending. Johnson, D-S.D., amendment to the Domenici, R-N.M., substitute amendment. The Johnson amendment would provide $88 billion in additional agriculture spending over 10 years by redirecting funds set aside for the proposed tax cut. It also would provide for $9 billion in emergency spending for agriculture in fiscal 2001. Rejected 47-53: R 0-50; D 47-3 (ND 39-2, SD 8-1). April 4, 2001.

69. H Con Res 83. Fiscal 2002 Budget Resolution/Education Spending. Harkin, D-Iowa, amendment to the Domenici, R-N.M., substitute amendment. The Harkin amendment would reduce the size of the tax cut by $448 billion and would increase education spending by $224 billion over 10 years. It also would provide for an increase of approximately $224 billion for debt reduction over 10 years. Adopted 53-47: R 4-46; D 49-1 (ND 41-0, SD 8-1). A "nay" was a vote in support of the president's position. April 4, 2001.

70. H Con Res 83. Fiscal 2002 Budget Resolution/NIH Funding. Specter, R-Pa., amendment to the Domenici, R-N.M., substitute amendment. The Specter amendment would increase funding for the National Institutes of Health by $700 million in fiscal 2002. Adopted 96-4: R 46-4; D 50-0 (ND 41-0, SD 9-0). April 4, 2001.

71. H Con Res 83. Fiscal 2002 Budget Resolution/Defense Spending. Landrieu, D-La., amendment to the Domenici, R-N.M., substitute amendment. The Landrieu amendment would provide for an additional $100 billion for defense personnel and modernization over fiscal 2002-2011, including an $8.5 billion increase in fiscal 2002. The increase would be offset by reducing the proposed tax cut by $100 billion. Rejected 47-52: R 1-49; D 46-3 (ND 38-2, SD 8-1). April 4, 2001.

72. H Con Res 83. Fiscal 2002 Budget Resolution/Defense Spending. Warner, R-Va., amendment to the Domenici, R-N.M., substitute amendment. The Warner amendment would provide for an increase of $8.5 billion for national defense spending in fiscal 2002. Adopted 84-16: R 48-2; D 36-14 (ND 28-13, SD 8-1). April 4, 2001.

73. H Con Res 83. Fiscal 2002 Budget Resolution/Home Health Medicare Reimbursements. Stabenow, D-Mich., amendment to the Domenici, R-N.M., substitute amendment. The Stabenow amendment would redirect $13.7 billion from the proposed tax cut for mandatory funding over 10 years to permanently repeal the 15 percent cut in home health reimbursements scheduled to go into effect Oct. 1, 2002. Rejected 47-53: R 0-50; D 47-3 (ND 40-1, SD 7-2). April 5, 2001.

Senate Votes 74, 75, 76, 77, 78

	74	75	76	77	78
ALABAMA					
Shelby	Y	Y	N	N	Y
Sessions	Y	Y	N	N	Y
ALASKA					
Stevens	Y	Y	N	N	N
Murkowski	Y	Y	N	N	Y
ARIZONA					
McCain	Y	Y	N	N	Y
Kyl	Y	Y	N	N	Y
ARKANSAS					
Hutchinson	Y	Y	N	N	Y
Lincoln	Y	N	N	Y	N
CALIFORNIA					
Feinstein	Y	N	Y	Y	N
Boxer	Y	N	Y	Y	N
COLORADO					
Campbell	Y	Y	N	N	Y
Allard	Y	Y	N	N	Y
CONNECTICUT					
Dodd	Y	N	Y	Y	N
Lieberman	Y	N	Y	Y	N
DELAWARE					
Carper	Y	N	N	Y	Y
Biden	Y	N	Y	Y	N
FLORIDA					
Graham	Y	N	Y	Y	Y
Nelson	Y	N	Y	Y	N
GEORGIA					
Miller	Y	Y	N	N	N
Cleland	Y	N	N	N	N
HAWAII					
Inouye	Y	N	Y	Y	N
Akaka	Y	N	Y	Y	N
IDAHO					
Craig	Y	Y	N	N	Y
Crapo	Y	Y	N	N	Y
ILLINOIS					
Durbin	Y	N	Y	Y	N
Fitzgerald	Y	Y	N	N	Y
INDIANA					
Lugar	Y	Y	N	N	Y
Bayh	Y	N	Y	Y	Y

	74	75	76	77	78
IOWA					
Grassley	Y	Y	N	N	Y
Harkin	Y	N	Y	Y	N
KANSAS					
Brownback	Y	Y	N	N	Y
Roberts	Y	Y	N	N	Y
KENTUCKY					
McConnell	Y	Y	N	N	Y
Bunning	Y	Y	N	N	Y
LOUISIANA					
Breaux	Y	N	N	N	N
Landrieu	Y	N	N	N	N
MAINE					
Snowe	Y	Y	N	N	Y
Collins	Y	Y	N	N	Y
MARYLAND					
Sarbanes	Y	N	Y	Y	N
Mikulski	Y	N	Y	Y	N
MASSACHUSETTS					
Kennedy	Y	N	Y	Y	N
Kerry	Y	N	Y	Y	N
MICHIGAN					
Levin	Y	N	Y	Y	N
Stabenow	Y	N	Y	Y	N
MINNESOTA					
Wellstone	Y	N	Y	Y	N
Dayton	Y	N	Y	Y	N
MISSISSIPPI					
Cochran	Y	Y	N	N	N
Lott	Y	Y	N	N	Y
MISSOURI					
Bond	Y	Y	N	N	Y
Carnahan	Y	N	N	Y	Y
MONTANA					
Baucus	Y	N	N	Y	N
Burns	Y	Y	N	N	Y
NEBRASKA					
Nelson	Y	N	N	Y	Y
Hagel	Y	Y	N	N	Y
NEVADA					
Reid	Y	N	Y	Y	N
Ensign	Y	Y	N	N	Y

	74	75	76	77	78
NEW HAMPSHIRE					
Smith	Y	Y	N	N	Y
Gregg	Y	Y	N	N	Y
NEW JERSEY					
Corzine	Y	N	Y	Y	N
Torricelli	Y	N	N	Y	N
NEW MEXICO					
Domenici	Y	Y	N	N	Y
Bingaman	Y	N	Y	Y	N
NEW YORK					
Clinton	Y	N	Y	Y	N
Schumer	Y	N	Y	Y	N
NORTH CAROLINA					
Helms	Y	Y	N	N	Y
Edwards	Y	N	Y	Y	N
NORTH DAKOTA					
Conrad	Y	N	Y	Y	N
Dorgan	Y	N	Y	Y	N
OHIO					
DeWine	Y	Y	N	N	Y
Voinovich	Y	Y	N	N	Y
OKLAHOMA					
Nickles	Y	Y	N	N	Y
Inhofe	Y	Y	N	N	Y
OREGON					
Wyden	Y	N	Y	Y	N
Smith	Y	Y	N	N	Y
PENNSYLVANIA					
Specter	Y	Y	N	N	Y
Santorum	Y	Y	N	N	Y
RHODE ISLAND					
Reed	Y	N	Y	Y	N
Chafee	Y	Y	N	N	Y
SOUTH CAROLINA					
Thurmond	Y	Y	N	N	Y
Hollings	Y	N	Y	Y	N
SOUTH DAKOTA					
Daschle	Y	N	Y	Y	N
Johnson	Y	N	N	Y	N
TENNESSEE					
Thompson	Y	Y	N	N	Y
Frist	Y	Y	N	N	Y

Key

Y	Voted for (yea).
#	Paired for.
+	Announced for.
N	Voted against (nay).
X	Paired against.
−	Announced against.
P	Voted "present."
C	Voted "present" to avoid possible conflict of interest.
?	Did not vote or otherwise make a position known.

Democrats **Republicans** *Independents*

	74	75	76	77	78
TEXAS					
Gramm	Y	Y	N	N	Y
Hutchison	Y	Y	N	N	Y
UTAH					
Hatch	Y	Y	N	N	Y
Bennett	Y	Y	N	N	Y
VERMONT					
Leahy	Y	N	Y	Y	N
Jeffords	Y	Y	N	N	N
VIRGINIA					
Warner	Y	Y	N	N	Y
Allen	Y	Y	N	N	Y
WASHINGTON					
Cantwell	Y	N	Y	Y	N
Murray	Y	N	Y	Y	N
WEST VIRGINIA					
Byrd	N	N	Y	Y	N
Rockefeller	Y	N	Y	Y	N
WISCONSIN					
Kohl	Y	N	Y	Y	Y
Feingold	Y	N	Y	Y	Y
WYOMING					
Thomas	Y	Y	N	N	Y
Enzi	Y	Y	N	N	Y

ND Northern Democrats   SD Southern Democrats

Southern states - Ala., Ark., Fla., Ga., Ky., La., Miss., N.C., Okla., S.C., Tenn., Texas, Va.

74. H Con Res 83. Fiscal 2002 Budget Resolution/Home Health Medicare Reimbursements. Collins, R-Maine, amendment to the Domenici, R-N.M., substitute amendment. The Collins amendment would establish a contingency reserve to allow $13.7 billion to fund a repeal over 10 years of the 15 percent cut in home health reimbursements scheduled to go into effect Oct. 1, 2002, unless such funds reduce the on-budget surplus below the level of the Medicare Hospital Insurance Trust Fund surplus in any fiscal year under the resolution. Adopted 99-1: R 50-0; D 49-1 (ND 40-1, SD 9-0). April 5, 2001.

75. H Con Res 83. Fiscal 2002 Budget Resolution/Reconciliation. Domenici, R-N.M., amendment to the Domenici substitute amendment. The Domenici amendment would instruct the Finance Committee to report two reconciliation bills to the Senate that would reduce revenue levels by not more than the president's proposed $1.6 trillion tax cut, and include a $60 billion economic stimulus package for fiscal 2001. Adopted 51-49: R 50-0; D 1-49 (ND 0-41, SD 1-8). April 5, 2001.

76. H Con Res 83. Fiscal 2002 Budget Resolution/Democratic Stimulus Package. Durbin, D-Ill., amendment to the Domenici, R-N.M., substitute amendment. The Durbin amendment would create a new 10 percent tax bracket for the first $12,000 in income for all married couples and $6,000 in income for single filers. It also would provide for a $60 billion stimulus pack-

age in fiscal 2001. Rejected 39-61: R 0-50; D 39-11 (ND 35-6, SD 4-5). April 5, 2001.

77. H Con Res 83. Fiscal 2002 Budget Resolution/Environmental Programs. Corzine, D-N.J., amendment to the Domenici, R-N.M., substitute amendment. The Corzine amendment would increase funding for a wide variety of environmental programs by $50 billion, and set aside $50 billion for debt reduction. The increases would be offset by reductions in the proposed tax cut. Rejected 46-54: R 0-50; D 46-4 (ND 41-0, SD 5-4). April 5, 2001.

78. H Con Res 83. Fiscal 2002 Budget Resolution/Emergency Designations. Voinovich, R-Ohio, motion to waive the Budget Act with respect to the Conrad, D-N.D., point of order against the Voinovich amendment to the Domenici, R-N.M., substitute amendment. The Voinovich amendment would establish a 60-vote point of order against all emergency spending. It also would establish a 60-vote point of order against waiving across-the-board spending cuts and direct scoring provisions in legislation. Motion rejected 54-46: R 46-4; D 8-42 (ND 6-35, SD 2-7). A three-fifths majority vote (60) of the total Senate is required to waive the Budget Act. (Subsequently, the chair upheld the point of order, and the amendment fell.) April 5, 2001.

	79	80	81	82	83
ALABAMA					
Shelby	Y	Y	Y	N	Y
Sessions	Y	Y	Y	N	Y
ALASKA					
Stevens	Y	Y	N	N	Y
Murkowski	Y	Y	Y	N	Y
ARIZONA					
McCain	Y	Y	Y	Y	Y
Kyl	Y	Y	Y	N	Y
ARKANSAS					
Hutchinson	Y	Y	Y	N	Y
Lincoln	N	Y	N	Y	N
CALIFORNIA					
Feinstein	N	Y	N	Y	N
Boxer	N	Y	N	Y	N
COLORADO					
Campbell	Y	Y	Y	N	Y
Allard	Y	Y	Y	N	Y
CONNECTICUT					
Dodd	N	N	N	Y	N
Lieberman	N	Y	N	Y	N
DELAWARE					
Carper	N	N	N	Y	N
Biden	N	Y	N	Y	N
FLORIDA					
Graham	N	N	N	Y	N
Nelson	N	N	N	Y	N
GEORGIA					
Miller	Y	Y	Y	N	Y
Cleland	N	Y	N	Y	N
HAWAII					
Inouye	N	Y	N	Y	N
Akaka	N	Y	N	Y	N
IDAHO					
Craig	Y	Y	Y	N	Y
Crapo	Y	Y	Y	N	Y
ILLINOIS					
Durbin	N	Y	N	Y	N
Fitzgerald	Y	Y	Y	N	Y
INDIANA					
Lugar	Y	Y	Y	N	Y
Bayh	N	Y	N	Y	N
IOWA					
Grassley	Y	Y	Y	N	Y
Harkin	N	Y	N	Y	N
KANSAS					
Brownback	Y	Y	Y	N	Y
Roberts	Y	Y	Y	N	Y
KENTUCKY					
McConnell	Y	Y	Y	N	Y
Bunning	Y	Y	Y	N	Y
LOUISIANA					
Breaux	N	Y	N	Y	N
Landrieu	N	Y	N	Y	N
MAINE					
Snowe	Y	Y	N	Y	Y
Collins	Y	Y	N	Y	Y
MARYLAND					
Sarbanes	N	Y	N	Y	N
Mikulski	N	Y	N	Y	N
MASSACHUSETTS					
Kennedy	N	Y	N	Y	N
Kerry	N	Y	N	Y	N
MICHIGAN					
Levin	N	Y	N	Y	N
Stabenow	N	Y	N	Y	N
MINNESOTA					
Wellstone	N	Y	N	Y	N
Dayton	N	Y	N	Y	N
MISSISSIPPI					
Cochran	Y	Y	Y	N	Y
Lott	Y	Y	Y	N	Y
MISSOURI					
Bond	Y	Y	Y	N	Y
Carnahan	N	Y	N	Y	N
MONTANA					
Baucus	N	Y	N	Y	N
Burns	Y	Y	Y	N	Y
NEBRASKA					
Nelson	N	Y	Y	Y	N
Hagel	Y	Y	Y	N	Y
NEVADA					
Reid	N	Y	N	Y	N
Ensign	Y	Y	Y	N	Y
NEW HAMPSHIRE					
Smith	Y	Y	Y	N	Y
Gregg	Y	Y	Y	N	Y
NEW JERSEY					
Corzine	N	N	N	Y	N
Torricelli	N	Y	N	Y	N
NEW MEXICO					
Domenici	Y	Y	Y	N	Y
Bingaman	N	Y	N	Y	N
NEW YORK					
Clinton	N	Y	N	Y	N
Schumer	N	Y	N	Y	N
NORTH CAROLINA					
Helms	Y	Y	Y	N	Y
Edwards	N	Y	N	Y	N
NORTH DAKOTA					
Conrad	N	Y	N	Y	N
Dorgan	N	Y	N	Y	N
OHIO					
DeWine	Y	Y	N	N	Y
Voinovich	Y	Y	Y	N	Y
OKLAHOMA					
Nickles	Y	Y	Y	N	Y
Inhofe	Y	Y	Y	N	Y
OREGON					
Wyden	N	Y	N	Y	N
Smith	Y	Y	Y	N	Y
PENNSYLVANIA					
Specter	Y	Y	N	N	Y
Santorum	Y	Y	Y	N	Y
RHODE ISLAND					
Reed	N	Y	N	Y	N
Chafee	N	Y	N	Y	N
SOUTH CAROLINA					
Thurmond	Y	Y	Y	N	Y
Hollings	N	Y	N	Y	N
SOUTH DAKOTA					
Daschle	N	Y	N	Y	N
Johnson	N	Y	N	Y	N
TENNESSEE					
Thompson	Y	Y	Y	N	Y
Frist	Y	Y	Y	N	Y
TEXAS					
Gramm	Y	Y	Y	N	Y
Hutchison	Y	Y	Y	N	Y
UTAH					
Hatch	Y	Y	Y	N	Y
Bennett	Y	Y	Y	N	Y
VERMONT					
Leahy	N	Y	N	Y	N
Jeffords	Y	Y	N	Y	N
VIRGINIA					
Warner	Y	Y	Y	N	Y
Allen	Y	Y	Y	N	Y
WASHINGTON					
Cantwell	N	Y	N	Y	N
Murray	N	Y	N	Y	N
WEST VIRGINIA					
Byrd	N	Y	N	Y	N
Rockefeller	N	Y	N	Y	N
WISCONSIN					
Kohl	N	Y	N	Y	N
Feingold	N	N	N	Y	N
WYOMING					
Thomas	Y	Y	Y	N	Y
Enzi	Y	Y	Y	N	Y

Key

Y	Voted for (yea).
#	Paired for.
+	Announced for.
N	Voted against (nay).
X	Paired against.
–	Announced against.
P	Voted "present."
C	Voted "present" to avoid possible conflict of interest.
?	Did not vote or otherwise make a position known.

Democrats   **Republicans**
Independents

ND Northern Democrats   SD Southern Democrats

Southern states - Ala., Ark., Fla., Ga., Ky., La., Miss., N.C., Okla., S.C., Tenn., Texas, Va.

79. H Con Res 83. Fiscal 2002 Budget Resolution/'Marriage Penalty.' Hutchison, R-Texas, amendment to the Domenici, R-N.M., substitute amendment. The Hutchison amendment would increase the proposed tax cut by $69 billion for fiscal 2002-2011, in an effort to eliminate the so-called marriage penalty. Adopted 51-50: R 9-1; D 1-49 (ND 0-41, SD 1-8), with Vice President Cheney casting a "yea" vote. April 5, 2001.

80. H Con Res 83. Fiscal 2002 Budget Resolution/Economic Stimulus Package. Hollings, D-S.C., amendment to the Domenici, R-N.M., substitute amendment. The Hollings amendment would strike the $60 billion stimulus provision and insert $85 billion in budget authority and outlays for fiscal 2002. It also would include a sense of the Senate to urge the Senate to pass a stimulus package that would provide rebates to taxpayers. Adopted 94-6: R 50-0; D 44-6 (ND 37-4, SD 7-2). April 5, 2001.

81. H Con Res 83. Fiscal 2002 Budget Resolution/Tax Cut Accelerator. Allen, R-Va., motion to waive the Budget Act with respect to the Conrad, D-N.D., point of order against the Allen amendment to the Domenici, R-N.M., substitute amendment. The Allen amendment would require the Budget Committee to make adjustments to revenue cuts based on changes to the surplus estimated by the Congressional Budget Office. Motion rejected 45-55: R 43-7; D 2-48 (ND 1-40, SD 1-8). A three-fifths majority vote (60) of the total Senate is required to waive the Budget Act. (Subsequently, the chair upheld the point of order, and the amendment fell.) April 5, 2001.

82. H Con Res 83. Fiscal 2002 Budget Resolution/IDEA Funding. Breaux, D-La., amendment to the Domenici, R-N.M., substitute amendment. The Breaux amendment would redirect $70 billion from the proposed tax cut to funding for the Individuals with Disabilities Education Act over 10 years. Adopted 54-46: R 5-45; D 49-1 (ND 41-0, SD 8-1). April 5, 2001.

83. H Con Res 83. Fiscal 2002 Budget Resolution/Small Business Health Insurance. Collins, R-Maine, amendment to the Domenici, R-N.M., substitute amendment. The Collins amendment would provide an additional $70 billion over 10 years for tax credits to small businesses to purchase health insurance. It also would make health insurance fully deductible. Rejected 49-51: R 48-2; D 1-49 (ND 0-41, SD 1-8). April 5, 2001.

	84	85	86
ALABAMA			
Shelby	N	Y	Y
Sessions	N	Y	Y
ALASKA			
Stevens	N	Y	Y
Murkowski	N	Y	Y
ARIZONA			
McCain	Y	Y	Y
Kyl	N	Y	Y
ARKANSAS			
Hutchinson	N	Y	Y
Lincoln	Y	Y	Y
CALIFORNIA			
Feinstein	Y	Y	Y
Boxer	Y	Y	N
COLORADO			
Campbell	N	Y	Y
Allard	N	Y	Y
CONNECTICUT			
Dodd	Y	Y	N
Lieberman	Y	Y	N
DELAWARE			
Carper	Y	Y	Y
Biden	Y	Y	N
FLORIDA			
Graham	Y	Y	N
Nelson	Y	Y	N
GEORGIA			
Miller	N	Y	Y
Cleland	Y	Y	Y
HAWAII			
Inouye	Y	Y	N
Akaka	Y	Y	N
IDAHO			
Craig	N	Y	Y
Crapo	N	Y	Y
ILLINOIS			
Durbin	Y	Y	N
Fitzgerald	N	Y	Y
INDIANA			
Lugar	N	Y	Y
Bayh	Y	Y	Y

	84	85	86
IOWA			
Grassley	N	Y	Y
Harkin	Y	Y	N
KANSAS			
Brownback	N	Y	Y
Roberts	N	Y	Y
KENTUCKY			
McConnell	N	Y	Y
Bunning	?	?	Y
LOUISIANA			
Breaux	Y	Y	Y
Landrieu	Y	Y	Y
MAINE			
Snowe	N	Y	Y
Collins	N	Y	Y
MARYLAND			
Sarbanes	Y	Y	N
Mikulski	Y	Y	N
MASSACHUSETTS			
Kennedy	Y	Y	N
Kerry	Y	Y	N
MICHIGAN			
Levin	Y	Y	N
Stabenow	Y	Y	N
MINNESOTA			
Wellstone	Y	Y	N
Dayton	Y	Y	N
MISSISSIPPI			
Cochran	N	Y	Y
Lott	N	Y	Y
MISSOURI			
Bond	N	Y	Y
Carnahan	Y	Y	Y
MONTANA			
Baucus	Y	Y	Y
Burns	N	Y	Y
NEBRASKA			
Nelson	Y	Y	Y
Hagel	N	Y	Y
NEVADA			
Reid	Y	Y	N
Ensign	Y	Y	Y

	84	85	86
NEW HAMPSHIRE			
Smith	N	Y	Y
Gregg	N	Y	Y
NEW JERSEY			
Corzine	Y	Y	N
Torricelli	Y	Y	Y
NEW MEXICO			
Domenici	N	Y	Y
Bingaman	Y	Y	N
NEW YORK			
Clinton	Y	Y	N
Schumer	Y	Y	N
NORTH CAROLINA			
Helms	N	Y	Y
Edwards	Y	Y	Y
NORTH DAKOTA			
Conrad	Y	Y	N
Dorgan	Y	Y	N
OHIO			
DeWine	N	Y	Y
Voinovich	N	Y	Y
OKLAHOMA			
Nickles	N	Y	Y
Inhofe	N	Y	Y
OREGON			
Wyden	Y	Y	N
Smith	N	Y	Y
PENNSYLVANIA			
Specter	Y	Y	N
Santorum	N	Y	Y
RHODE ISLAND			
Reed	Y	Y	N
Chafee	N	Y	Y
SOUTH CAROLINA			
Thurmond	N	Y	Y
Hollings	Y	Y	N
SOUTH DAKOTA			
Daschle	Y	Y	N
Johnson	Y	Y	N
TENNESSEE			
Thompson	N	Y	Y
Frist	N	Y	Y

Key

Y	Voted for (yea).
#	Paired for.
+	Announced for.
N	Voted against (nay).
X	Paired against.
−	Announced against.
P	Voted "present."
C	Voted "present" to avoid possible conflict of interest.
?	Did not vote or otherwise make a position known.

Democrats **Republicans**
Independents

	84	85	86
TEXAS			
Gramm	N	Y	Y
Hutchison	N	Y	Y
UTAH			
Hatch	N	Y	Y
Bennett	N	Y	Y
VERMONT			
Leahy	Y	Y	N
Jeffords	Y	Y	Y
VIRGINIA			
Warner	N	Y	Y
Allen	N	Y	Y
WASHINGTON			
Cantwell	Y	Y	N
Murray	Y	Y	N
WEST VIRGINIA			
Byrd	Y	Y	N
Rockefeller	Y	Y	N
WISCONSIN			
Kohl	Y	Y	Y
Feingold	Y	Y	N
WYOMING			
Thomas	N	Y	Y
Enzi	N	Y	Y

ND Northern Democrats   SD Southern Democrats

Southern states - Ala., Ark., Fla., Ga., Ky., La., Miss., N.C., Okla., S.C., Tenn., Texas, Va.

84. H Con Res 83. Fiscal 2002 Budget Resolution/Veterans' Health Care. Wellstone, D-Minn., amendment to the Domenici, R-N.M., substitute amendment. The Wellstone amendment would increase funding for veterans' health care by $1.7 billion, by redirecting the same amount from the proposed tax cut. Adopted 53-46: R 4-45; D 49-1 (ND 41-0, SD 8-1). April 6, 2001.

85. H Con Res 83. Fiscal 2002 Budget Resolution/Veterans' Spending. Bond, R-Mo., amendment to the Domenici, R-N.M., substitute amendment. The Bond amendment would provide for an increase of $967 million in fiscal 2002 for veterans' discretionary spending. Adopted 99-0: R 49-0; D 50-0 (ND 41-0, SD 9-0). April 6, 2001.

86. H Con Res 83. Fiscal 2002 Budget Resolution/Adoption. Adoption of the concurrent resolution that calls for approximately $1.18 trillion in tax cuts over 10 years, with $85 billion in tax cuts in fiscal 2001. It would reduce publicly held debt to approximately $1.1 trillion, and cap discretionary spending at approximately $678 billion, a 7 percent increase over fiscal 2001. Adopted 65-35: R 50-0; D 15-35 (ND 9-32, SD 6-3). (Before adoption, the Senate adopted the Domenici, R-N.M., substitute amendment, as amended.) April 6, 2001.

	87
ALABAMA	
Shelby	Y
Sessions	Y
ALASKA	
Stevens	Y
Murkowski	Y
ARIZONA	
McCain	Y
Kyl	Y
ARKANSAS	
Hutchinson	?
Lincoln	Y
CALIFORNIA	
Feinstein	Y
Boxer	Y
COLORADO	
Campbell	Y
Allard	Y
CONNECTICUT	
Dodd	Y
Lieberman	Y
DELAWARE	
Carper	Y
Biden	Y
FLORIDA	
Graham	Y
Nelson	Y
GEORGIA	
Miller	Y
Cleland	Y
HAWAII	
Inouye	Y
Akaka	Y
IDAHO	
Craig	Y
Crapo	Y
ILLINOIS	
Durbin	Y
Fitzgerald	Y
INDIANA	
Lugar	Y
Bayh	Y

	87
IOWA	
Grassley	Y
Harkin	Y
KANSAS	
Brownback	Y
Roberts	Y
KENTUCKY	
McConnell	Y
Bunning	Y
LOUISIANA	
Breaux	Y
Landrieu	Y
MAINE	
Snowe	Y
Collins	Y
MARYLAND	
Sarbanes	Y
Mikulski	Y
MASSACHUSETTS	
Kennedy	Y
Kerry	Y
MICHIGAN	
Levin	Y
Stabenow	Y
MINNESOTA	
Wellstone	Y
Dayton	Y
MISSISSIPPI	
Cochran	Y
Lott	Y
MISSOURI	
Bond	Y
Carnahan	Y
MONTANA	
Baucus	Y
Burns	Y
NEBRASKA	
Nelson	Y
Hagel	Y
NEVADA	
Reid	Y
Ensign	Y

	87
NEW HAMPSHIRE	
Smith	Y
Gregg	Y
NEW JERSEY	
Corzine	Y
Torricelli	Y
NEW MEXICO	
Domenici	Y
Bingaman	Y
NEW YORK	
Clinton	Y
Schumer	Y
NORTH CAROLINA	
Helms	Y
Edwards	Y
NORTH DAKOTA	
Conrad	Y
Dorgan	Y
OHIO	
DeWine	Y
Voinovich	Y
OKLAHOMA	
Nickles	Y
Inhofe	Y
OREGON	
Wyden	Y
Smith	Y
PENNSYLVANIA	
Specter	Y
Santorum	Y
RHODE ISLAND	
Reed	Y
Chafee	Y
SOUTH CAROLINA	
Thurmond	Y
Hollings	Y
SOUTH DAKOTA	
Daschle	Y
Johnson	Y
TENNESSEE	
Thompson	Y
Frist	Y

Key

Y	Voted for (yea).
#	Paired for.
+	Announced for.
N	Voted against (nay).
X	Paired against.
–	Announced against.
P	Voted "present."
C	Voted "present" to avoid possible conflict of interest.
?	Did not vote or otherwise make a position known.

Democrats **Republicans**
Independents

	87
TEXAS	
Gramm	Y
Hutchison	Y
UTAH	
Hatch	Y
Bennett	Y
VERMONT	
Leahy	Y
Jeffords	Y
VIRGINIA	
Warner	Y
Allen	Y
WASHINGTON	
Cantwell	Y
Murray	Y
WEST VIRGINIA	
Byrd	Y
Rockefeller	Y
WISCONSIN	
Kohl	Y
Feingold	Y
WYOMING	
Thomas	Y
Enzi	Y

ND Northern Democrats   SD Southern Democrats

Southern states - Ala., Ark., Fla., Ga., Ky., La., Miss., N.C., Okla., S.C., Tenn., Texas, Va.

87. S 350. Brownfields/Passage. Passage of the bill that would authorize $150 million per year in fiscal 2002 through 2006 for grants to local governments, states and Native American tribes to inventory, assess and clean up contaminated abandoned industrial sites known as brownfields. The bill would provide developers and prospective landowners some liability protection and authorize $50 million annually in fiscal 2002 through 2006 to clean up sites damaged by petroleum spills. Developers who receive a grant or loan to buy a brownfields site could use part of the funds to buy insurance for the cleanup. Passed 99-0: R 49-0; D 50-0 (ND 41-0, SD 9-0). A "yea" was a vote in support of the president's position. April 25, 2001.

	88	89	90	91
ALABAMA				
Shelby	Y	Y	Y	Y
Sessions	Y	Y	Y	Y
ALASKA				
Stevens	Y	Y	Y	Y
Murkowski	Y	Y	Y	N
ARIZONA				
McCain	Y	Y	Y	Y
Kyl	Y	Y	N	N
ARKANSAS				
Hutchinson	Y	Y	Y	Y
Lincoln	Y	Y	Y	Y
CALIFORNIA				
Feinstein	Y	Y	Y	Y
Boxer	Y	Y	Y	Y
COLORADO				
Campbell	Y	Y	Y	Y
Allard	Y	Y	Y	N
CONNECTICUT				
Dodd	Y	Y	Y	Y
Lieberman	Y	Y	Y	Y
DELAWARE				
Carper	Y	Y	Y	Y
Biden	Y	Y	Y	Y
FLORIDA				
Graham	Y	Y	Y	Y
Nelson	Y	Y	Y	Y
GEORGIA				
Miller	Y	Y	Y	Y
Cleland	Y	Y	Y	Y
HAWAII				
Inouye	Y	Y	Y	Y
Akaka	Y	Y	Y	Y
IDAHO				
Craig	Y	Y	Y	N
Crapo	Y	Y	Y	Y
ILLINOIS				
Durbin	Y	Y	Y	Y
Fitzgerald	Y	Y	Y	Y
INDIANA				
Lugar	Y	Y	Y	Y
Bayh	Y	Y	Y	Y

	88	89	90	91
IOWA				
Grassley	Y	Y	Y	Y
Harkin	Y	Y	Y	Y
KANSAS				
Brownback	Y	Y	Y	N
Roberts	Y	Y	Y	Y
KENTUCKY				
McConnell	Y	Y	Y	N
Bunning	Y	Y	Y	N
LOUISIANA				
Breaux	Y	Y	Y	Y
Landrieu	N	Y	Y	Y
MAINE				
Snowe	Y	Y	Y	Y
Collins	Y	Y	Y	Y
MARYLAND				
Sarbanes	Y	Y	Y	Y
Mikulski	Y	Y	Y	Y
MASSACHUSETTS				
Kennedy	Y	Y	Y	Y
Kerry	Y	Y	Y	Y
MICHIGAN				
Levin	Y	Y	Y	Y
Stabenow	Y	Y	Y	Y
MINNESOTA				
Wellstone	N	Y	Y	Y
Dayton	Y	Y	Y	Y
MISSISSIPPI				
Cochran	Y	Y	Y	Y
Lott	Y	Y	Y	N
MISSOURI				
Bond	Y	Y	Y	N
Carnahan	Y	Y	Y	Y
MONTANA				
Baucus	Y	Y	Y	Y
Burns	Y	Y	Y	Y
NEBRASKA				
Nelson	Y	Y	Y	Y
Hagel	Y	Y	Y	Y
NEVADA				
Reid	Y	Y	Y	Y
Ensign	Y	Y	Y	Y

	88	89	90	91
NEW HAMPSHIRE				
Smith	Y	Y	N	N
Gregg	Y	Y	Y	N
NEW JERSEY				
Corzine	Y	Y	Y	Y
Torricelli	Y	Y	Y	Y
NEW MEXICO				
Domenici	Y	Y	Y	Y
Bingaman	Y	Y	Y	Y
NEW YORK				
Clinton	Y	Y	Y	Y
Schumer	Y	Y	Y	Y
NORTH CAROLINA				
Helms	Y	Y	N	N
Edwards	Y	Y	Y	Y
NORTH DAKOTA				
Conrad	Y	Y	Y	Y
Dorgan	Y	Y	Y	Y
OHIO				
DeWine	Y	Y	Y	Y
Voinovich	Y	Y	Y	N
OKLAHOMA				
Nickles	Y	Y	Y	N
Inhofe	Y	Y	N	N
OREGON				
Wyden	Y	Y	Y	Y
Smith	Y	Y	Y	Y
PENNSYLVANIA				
Specter	Y	Y	Y	Y
Santorum	Y	Y	Y	N
RHODE ISLAND				
Reed	N	Y	Y	Y
Chafee	Y	Y	Y	Y
SOUTH CAROLINA				
Thurmond	Y	Y	N	N
Hollings	Y	Y	Y	Y
SOUTH DAKOTA				
Daschle	Y	Y	Y	Y
Johnson	Y	Y	Y	Y
TENNESSEE				
Thompson	Y	Y	N	N
Frist	Y	Y	Y	N

Key

Y	Voted for (yea).
#	Paired for.
+	Announced for.
N	Voted against (nay).
X	Paired against.
–	Announced against.
P	Voted "present."
C	Voted "present" to avoid possible conflict of interest.
?	Did not vote or otherwise make a position known.

Democrats **Republicans**
Independents

	88	89	90	91
TEXAS				
Gramm	Y	Y	N	N
Hutchison	Y	Y	Y	Y
UTAH				
Hatch	Y	Y	Y	Y
Bennett	Y	Y	Y	Y
VERMONT				
Leahy	?	Y	Y	Y
Jeffords	Y	Y	Y	Y
VIRGINIA				
Warner	Y	Y	Y	Y
Allen	Y	Y	Y	Y
WASHINGTON				
Cantwell	Y	Y	Y	Y
Murray	Y	Y	Y	Y
WEST VIRGINIA				
Byrd	Y	Y	Y	Y
Rockefeller	Y	Y	Y	Y
WISCONSIN				
Kohl	Y	Y	Y	Y
Feingold	Y	Y	Y	Y
WYOMING				
Thomas	Y	Y	Y	N
Enzi	Y	Y	Y	N

ND Northern Democrats   SD Southern Democrats

Southern states - Ala., Ark., Fla., Ga., Ky., La., Miss., N.C., Okla., S.C., Tenn., Texas, Va.

88. S 1. ESEA Reauthorization/Cloture. Motion to invoke cloture (thus limiting debate) on the motion to proceed to the bill that would overhaul federal education policy and reauthorize programs under the 1965 Elementary and Secondary Education Act (ESEA) for seven years. Three-fifths of the total Senate (60) is required to invoke cloture. Motion agreed to 96-3: R 50-0; D 46-3 (ND 38-2, SD 8-1). May 1, 2001.

89. S 1. ESEA Reauthorization/Reading Achievement. Collins, R-Maine, amendment to the Jeffords, R-Vt., substitute amendment. The Collins amendment would modify the criteria for awarding competitive grants for reading achievement to states by requiring that states demonstrate improved reading achievement in the schools that receive the funds. The Jeffords substitute would reauthorize the ESEA for seven years and add language to modify the annual testing provisions in the bill, add a "Straight A's" demonstration program and allow parents of children in underperforming schools to use federal funds for private tutoring. Adopted 100-0: R 50-0; D 50-0 (ND 41-0, SD 9-0). May 3, 2001.

90. S 1. ESEA Reauthorization/Annual Testing. Jeffords, R-Vt., amendment to the Jeffords substitute amendment that would allow states to defer or suspend new required annual testing for grades 3-8 in any given year if appropriations do not cover the costs associated with the development and administration of the tests. The trigger for the development and implementation of the tests would be set at $370 million for fiscal 2002 and increase by $10 million for each fiscal year through 2008. Adopted 93-7: R 43-7; D 50-0 (ND 41-0, SD 9-0). May 3, 2001.

91. S 1. ESEA Reauthorization/Title I Funding. Dodd, D-Conn., amendment to the Jeffords substitute amendment. The Dodd amendment would authorize full funding of grants to local educational agencies under Title I of the Elementary and Secondary Education Act over 10 years, which would be an increase of $132 billion over 10 years. Adopted 79-21: R 29-21; D 50-0 (ND 41-0, SD 9-0). May 3, 2001.

	92	93	94	95	96
ALABAMA					
Shelby	Y	Y	N	Y	N
Sessions	Y	N	N	Y	Y
ALASKA					
Stevens	Y	N	N	Y	N
Murkowski	Y	N	N	Y	N
ARIZONA					
McCain	Y	N	Y	Y	N
Kyl	Y	Y	N	Y	N
ARKANSAS					
Hutchinson	Y	N	Y	Y	N
Lincoln	N	N	Y	Y	Y
CALIFORNIA					
Feinstein	N	N	Y	Y	Y
Boxer	N	N	Y	Y	Y
COLORADO					
Campbell	Y	N	Y	Y	N
Allard	Y	Y	N	Y	N
CONNECTICUT					
Dodd	N	N	Y	Y	+
Lieberman	Y	N	Y	Y	Y
DELAWARE					
Carper	N	N	Y	Y	Y
Biden	N	N	Y	Y	Y
FLORIDA					
Graham	N	N	Y	Y	Y
Nelson	N	N	Y	Y	Y
GEORGIA					
Miller	Y	N	Y	Y	Y
Cleland	N	N	Y	Y	Y
HAWAII					
Inouye	N	N	Y	Y	Y
Akaka	N	N	Y	Y	Y
IDAHO					
Craig	Y	Y	N	Y	N
Crapo	Y	Y	N	Y	N
ILLINOIS					
Durbin	N	N	Y	Y	Y
Fitzgerald	Y	Y	N	Y	N
INDIANA					
Lugar	Y	N	N	Y	N
Bayh	Y	N	Y	Y	Y

	92	93	94	95	96
IOWA					
Grassley	Y	Y	Y	Y	N
Harkin	N	N	Y	Y	Y
KANSAS					
Brownback	Y	Y	N	Y	N
Roberts	Y	N	N	Y	N
KENTUCKY					
McConnell	Y	N	Y	Y	N
Bunning	Y	Y	N	Y	N
LOUISIANA					
Breaux	Y	N	Y	Y	Y
Landrieu	Y	N	Y	Y	Y
MAINE					
Snowe	Y	N	Y	Y	Y
Collins	Y	N	Y	Y	N
MARYLAND					
Sarbanes	N	N	Y	Y	Y
Mikulski	N	N	Y	Y	Y
MASSACHUSETTS					
Kennedy	N	N	Y	Y	Y
Kerry	N	N	Y	Y	Y
MICHIGAN					
Levin	N	N	Y	Y	Y
Stabenow	N	N	Y	Y	Y
MINNESOTA					
Wellstone	N	N	Y	?	Y
Dayton	N	N	Y	Y	Y
MISSISSIPPI					
Cochran	Y	N	Y	Y	N
Lott	Y	N	N	Y	N
MISSOURI					
Bond	Y	Y	N	Y	N
Carnahan	N	N	Y	Y	Y
MONTANA					
Baucus	N	N	Y	Y	Y
Burns	Y	Y	N	Y	N
NEBRASKA					
Nelson	Y	N	Y	Y	Y
Hagel	Y	N	N	Y	N
NEVADA					
Reid	N	N	Y	Y	Y
Ensign	Y	Y	Y	Y	N

	92	93	94	95	96
NEW HAMPSHIRE					
Smith	Y	Y	N	Y	N
Gregg	Y	Y	N	N	N
NEW JERSEY					
Corzine	N	N	Y	Y	Y
Torricelli	N	N	Y	Y	Y
NEW MEXICO					
Domenici	Y	N	N	Y	N
Bingaman	N	N	Y	Y	Y
NEW YORK					
Clinton	N	N	Y	Y	Y
Schumer	N	N	Y	Y	Y
NORTH CAROLINA					
Helms	Y	Y	N	Y	N
Edwards	N	N	Y	Y	Y
NORTH DAKOTA					
Conrad	N	N	Y	Y	Y
Dorgan	N	N	Y	Y	Y
OHIO					
DeWine	Y	Y	N	Y	N
Voinovich	Y	N	N	Y	N
OKLAHOMA					
Nickles	Y	Y	N	N	N
Inhofe	Y	Y	N	N	N
OREGON					
Wyden	N	N	Y	Y	Y
Smith	Y	N	N	Y	N
PENNSYLVANIA					
Specter	Y	N	N	Y	N
Santorum	Y	Y	N	Y	N
RHODE ISLAND					
Reed	N	N	Y	Y	Y
Chafee	Y	N	Y	Y	N
SOUTH CAROLINA					
Thurmond	Y	Y	N	Y	N
Hollings	N	N	Y	Y	Y
SOUTH DAKOTA					
Daschle	N	N	Y	Y	Y
Johnson	N	N	Y	Y	Y
TENNESSEE					
Thompson	Y	Y	N	Y	N
Frist	Y	Y	N	Y	N

Key

Y	Voted for (yea).
#	Paired for.
+	Announced for.
N	Voted against (nay).
X	Paired against.
−	Announced against.
P	Voted "present."
C	Voted "present" to avoid possible conflict of interest.
?	Did not vote or otherwise make a position known.

Democrats **Republicans**
Independents

	92	93	94	95	96
TEXAS					
Gramm	Y	Y	N	Y	N
Hutchison	Y	N	Y	Y	N
UTAH					
Hatch	Y	Y	Y	Y	N
Bennett	Y	Y	N	Y	N
VERMONT					
Leahy	N	N	Y	Y	Y
Jeffords	Y	N	Y	Y	N
VIRGINIA					
Warner	Y	N	Y	Y	N
Allen	Y	Y	Y	Y	N
WASHINGTON					
Cantwell	N	N	Y	Y	Y
Murray	N	N	Y	Y	Y
WEST VIRGINIA					
Byrd	N	N	Y	Y	Y
Rockefeller	N	N	Y	Y	Y
WISCONSIN					
Kohl	N	N	Y	?	Y
Feingold	Y	N	Y	Y	Y
WYOMING					
Thomas	Y	Y	N	Y	N
Enzi	Y	Y	N	N	N

ND Northern Democrats   SD Southern Democrats

Southern states - Ala., Ark., Fla., Ga., Ky., La., Miss., N.C., Okla., S.C., Tenn., Texas, Va.

92. Bolton Nomination/Confirmation. Confirmation of President Bush's nomination of John Robert Bolton of Maryland to be undersecretary of State for arms control and international security. Confirmed 57-43: R 50-0; D 7-43 (ND 4-37, SD 3-6). A "yea" was a vote in support of the president's position. May 8, 2001.

93. S 1. ESEA Reauthorization/Accountability Standards. Craig, R-Idaho, amendment to the Jeffords, R-Vt., substitute amendment. The Craig amendment would require schools to meet new accountability standards for improved student achievement to qualify for the increased Title I funding provisions. The Jeffords substitute would reauthorize the Elementary and Secondary Education Act (ESEA) for seven years and add language to modify the annual testing provisions in the bill, add a "Straight A's" demonstration program and allow parents of children in underperforming schools to use federal funds for private tutoring. Rejected 27-73: R 27-23; D 0-50 (ND 0-41, SD 0-9). May 8, 2001.

94. S 1. ESEA Reauthorization/Title II Funding. Kennedy, D-Mass., amendment to the Jeffords, R-Vt., substitute amendment. The Kennedy amendment would authorize increased Title II funding between fiscal 2003 and 2008, and express the sense of the Senate that Congress should appropri-ate $3 billion for fiscal 2002 to provide for more teachers in classrooms, teacher training, and mentors and year-long internships for 125,000 teachers. Adopted 69-31: R 19-31; D 50-0 (ND 41-0, SD 9-0). May 8, 2001.

95. S 1. ESEA Reauthorization/Teacher Tax Relief. Warner, R-Va., amendment to the Jeffords, R-Vt., substitute amendment. The Warner amendment would express the sense of the Senate that Congress should pass legislation providing elementary and secondary level educators with additional tax relief in recognition of the out-of-pocket, unreimbursed expenses they incur. Adopted 95-3: R 47-3; D 48-0 (ND 39-0, SD 9-0). May 8, 2001.

96. S 1. ESEA Reauthorization/Community Technology Centers. Mikulski, D-Md., amendment to the Jeffords, R-Vt., substitute amendment. The Mikulski amendment would provide for the establishment of 1,000 community-based technology centers. Funding for the centers would be split equally between competitive grants from the federal government and local community groups. It also would authorize $100 million for fiscal 2002 and subsequent necessary sums for the next six fiscal years. Adopted 50-49: R 1-49; D 49-0 (ND 40-0, SD 9-0). May 9, 2001.

	97	98	99	100
ALABAMA				
Shelby	Y	Y	N	N
Sessions	Y	Y	N	N
ALASKA				
Stevens	Y	Y	N	N
Murkowski	Y	Y	N	N
ARIZONA				
McCain	Y	Y	N	Y
Kyl	Y	Y	N	N
ARKANSAS				
Hutchinson	Y	Y	N	Y
Lincoln	Y	N	Y	Y
CALIFORNIA				
Feinstein	Y	N	Y	Y
Boxer	Y	N	?	?
COLORADO				
Campbell	Y	Y	Y	Y
Allard	Y	Y	N	N
CONNECTICUT				
Dodd	+	N	Y	Y
Lieberman	Y	N	Y	Y
DELAWARE				
Carper	Y	N	Y	Y
Biden	Y	N	Y	Y
FLORIDA				
Graham	Y	N	Y	Y
Nelson	Y	N	Y	Y
GEORGIA				
Miller	Y	Y	N	Y
Cleland	Y	Y	Y	Y
HAWAII				
Inouye	Y	N	Y	Y
Akaka	Y	N	Y	Y
IDAHO				
Craig	Y	Y	N	N
Crapo	Y	Y	?	?
ILLINOIS				
Durbin	Y	N	Y	Y
Fitzgerald	Y	Y	N	Y
INDIANA				
Lugar	Y	Y	N	N
Bayh	Y	N	Y	Y

	97	98	99	100
IOWA				
Grassley	Y	Y	N	N
Harkin	Y	N	Y	Y
KANSAS				
Brownback	Y	Y	N	N
Roberts	Y	Y	N	N
KENTUCKY				
McConnell	Y	Y	N	N
Bunning	Y	Y	N	N
LOUISIANA				
Breaux	Y	Y	Y	?
Landrieu	Y	N	Y	Y
MAINE				
Snowe	Y	Y	N	Y
Collins	Y	Y	N	Y
MARYLAND				
Sarbanes	Y	N	Y	Y
Mikulski	Y	N	Y	Y
MASSACHUSETTS				
Kennedy	Y	N	Y	Y
Kerry	Y	N	Y	Y
MICHIGAN				
Levin	Y	N	Y	Y
Stabenow	Y	N	Y	Y
MINNESOTA				
Wellstone	Y	N	Y	Y
Dayton	Y	N	Y	Y
MISSISSIPPI				
Cochran	Y	Y	N	N
Lott	Y	Y	N	N
MISSOURI				
Bond	Y	Y	N	N
Carnahan	Y	N	Y	Y
MONTANA				
Baucus	Y	Y	Y	Y
Burns	Y	Y	N	N
NEBRASKA				
Nelson	Y	Y	Y	Y
Hagel	Y	Y	N	N
NEVADA				
Reid	Y	N	Y	Y
Ensign	Y	Y	?	?

	97	98	99	100
NEW HAMPSHIRE				
Smith	Y	Y	N	N
Gregg	Y	Y	N	N
NEW JERSEY				
Corzine	Y	N	Y	Y
Torricelli	Y	N	Y	Y
NEW MEXICO				
Domenici	Y	Y	N	Y
Bingaman	Y	N	Y	Y
NEW YORK				
Clinton	Y	N	Y	Y
Schumer	Y	N	Y	Y
NORTH CAROLINA				
Helms	Y	Y	N	N
Edwards	Y	N	Y	Y
NORTH DAKOTA				
Conrad	Y	N	Y	Y
Dorgan	Y	N	Y	Y
OHIO				
DeWine	Y	Y	N	N
Voinovich	Y	Y	N	Y
OKLAHOMA				
Nickles	Y	Y	N	N
Inhofe	Y	Y	N	N
OREGON				
Wyden	Y	N	Y	Y
Smith	Y	Y	N	Y
PENNSYLVANIA				
Specter	Y	Y	N	Y
Santorum	Y	Y	N	N
RHODE ISLAND				
Reed	Y	N	Y	Y
Chafee	Y	N	N	Y
SOUTH CAROLINA				
Thurmond	Y	Y	N	N
Hollings	Y	N	Y	Y
SOUTH DAKOTA				
Daschle	Y	N	Y	Y
Johnson	Y	N	Y	Y
TENNESSEE				
Thompson	N	Y	N	N
Frist	Y	Y	N	N

	97	98	99	100
TEXAS				
Gramm	Y	Y	N	N
Hutchison	Y	Y	N	Y
UTAH				
Hatch	Y	Y	N	N
Bennett	Y	Y	N	N
VERMONT				
Leahy	Y	N	Y	Y
Jeffords	Y	N	Y	Y
VIRGINIA				
Warner	Y	Y	N	Y
Allen	Y	Y	N	Y
WASHINGTON				
Cantwell	Y	N	Y	Y
Murray	Y	N	Y	Y
WEST VIRGINIA				
Byrd	Y	N	Y	N
Rockefeller	Y	N	Y	Y
WISCONSIN				
Kohl	Y	N	Y	Y
Feingold	Y	N	Y	Y
WYOMING				
Thomas	Y	Y	N	N
Enzi	Y	Y	N	N

ND Northern Democrats   SD Southern Democrats

Southern states - Ala., Ark., Fla., Ga., Ky., La., Miss., N.C., Okla., S.C., Tenn., Texas, Va.

97. S 1. ESEA Reauthorization/Teacher Liability. McConnell, R-Ky., amendment to the Jeffords, R-Vt., substitute amendment. The McConnell amendment would limit the liability of teachers and education professionals who maintain order in the classroom if they were acting in accordance with local, state and federal laws. It excludes from liability protection misconduct involving investigations and other hiring practices, as well as criminal actions. The measure would pre-empt inconsistent state laws, but permit states to pass legislation to opt out of the federal law. Adopted 98-1: R 49-1; D 49-0 (ND 40-0, SD 9-0). May 9, 2001.

98. H Con Res 83. Fiscal 2002 Budget Resolution/Conference Report. Adoption of the conference report on the concurrent budget resolution that calls for approximately $1.35 trillion in tax cuts through fiscal 2011; in the Senate, $100 billion of that would only be available in fiscal 2001 through 2002. The resolution would limit discretionary spending to $661.3 billion, with a target of $325.1 billion for defense and $336.2 billion for non-defense programs. Adopted 53-47: R 48-2; D 5-45 (ND 2-39, SD 3-6). A "yea" was a

vote in support of the president's position. May 10, 2001.

99. S 1. ESEA Reauthorization/Student Assessment. Wellstone, D-Minn., amendment to the Jeffords, R-Vt., substitute amendment. The Wellstone amendment would authorize $200 million in fiscal 2002 and additional funds to be determined for each of the following six fiscal years to provide grants to help states devise assessment systems that characterize student achievement in a variety of proficiencies. Adopted 50-47: R 2-46; D 48-1 (ND 40-0, SD 8-1). May 10, 2001.

100. S 1. ESEA Reauthorization/Bilingual Education Programs. Lincoln, D-Ark., amendment to the Jeffords, R-Vt., substitute amendment. The Lincoln amendment would express the sense of the Senate that Congress should appropriate $750 million in fiscal 2002 for bilingual education programs. It also would authorize a total of $11.5 billion between fiscal 2003 through 2008 for bilingual programs. Adopted 62-34: R 15-33; D 47-1 (ND 39-1, SD 8-0). May 10, 2001.

Key

Y	Voted for (yea).
#	Paired for.
+	Announced for.
N	Voted against (nay).
X	Paired against.
–	Announced against.
P	Voted "present."
C	Voted "present" to avoid possible conflict of interest.
?	Did not vote or otherwise make a position known.

Democrats **Republicans** *Independents*

	101	102	103	104	105	106	107
ALABAMA							
Shelby	Y	Y	N	N	N	Y	Y
Sessions	Y	Y	N	N	N	Y	Y
ALASKA							
Stevens	Y	Y	N	N	N	N	Y
Murkowski	Y	Y	N	N	Y	Y	Y
ARIZONA							
McCain	Y	Y	N	Y	N	Y	Y
Kyl	Y	N	N	Y	N	N	N
ARKANSAS							
Hutchinson	Y	N	N	N	N	N	N
Lincoln	Y	Y	Y	Y	Y	Y	N
CALIFORNIA							
Feinstein	Y	Y	Y	Y	Y	Y	N
Boxer	Y	Y	Y	Y	Y	Y	N
COLORADO							
Campbell	Y	Y	N	N	Y	Y	Y
Allard	Y	N	N	N	N	N	Y
CONNECTICUT							
Dodd	Y	Y	Y	Y	Y	Y	N
Lieberman	?	?	Y	Y	Y	Y	N
DELAWARE							
Carper	Y	Y	Y	Y	Y	Y	N
Biden	Y	Y	Y	Y	Y	Y	N
FLORIDA							
Graham	Y	Y	Y	Y	Y	Y	N
Nelson	Y	Y	Y	Y	Y	Y	N
GEORGIA							
Miller	Y	Y	X	Y	Y	Y	N
Cleland	Y	Y	Y	Y	Y	Y	N
HAWAII							
Inouye	Y	Y	Y	Y	Y	Y	N
Akaka	?	?	#	?	Y	Y	N
IDAHO							
Craig	Y	Y	N	N	N	N	Y
Crapo	Y	Y	N	N	N	N	Y
ILLINOIS							
Durbin	Y	Y	Y	Y	Y	Y	N
Fitzgerald	Y	Y	N	Y	N	Y	N
INDIANA							
Lugar	Y	Y	N	Y	N	Y	Y
Bayh	Y	Y	Y	Y	Y	Y	N

	101	102	103	104	105	106	107
IOWA							
Grassley	Y	Y	N	N	N	Y	Y
Harkin	?	Y	Y	Y	Y	Y	N
KANSAS							
Brownback	Y	N	N	N	N	N	N
Roberts	Y	Y	N	N	N	N	N
KENTUCKY							
McConnell	Y	Y	N	N	N	N	Y
Bunning	Y	N	N	N	N	N	N
LOUISIANA							
Breaux	Y	Y	Y	Y	Y	Y	N
Landrieu	Y	Y	Y	Y	Y	Y	N
MAINE							
Snowe	Y	Y	N	Y	Y	Y	Y
Collins	Y	Y	N	Y	Y	Y	Y
MARYLAND							
Sarbanes	Y	Y	Y	Y	Y	Y	N
Mikulski	?	?	Y	Y	Y	Y	N
MASSACHUSETTS							
Kennedy	Y	Y	Y	N	Y	Y	N
Kerry	Y	Y	Y	Y	Y	Y	N
MICHIGAN							
Levin	Y	Y	Y	Y	Y	Y	N
Stabenow	Y	Y	Y	Y	Y	Y	N
MINNESOTA							
Wellstone	Y	Y	Y	Y	Y	Y	N
Dayton	Y	Y	Y	Y	Y	Y	N
MISSISSIPPI							
Cochran	Y	Y	N	Y	N	Y	Y
Lott	Y	N	N	N	N	N	Y
MISSOURI							
Bond	Y	N	N	N	N	N	Y
Carnahan	Y	Y	Y	Y	+	+	–
MONTANA							
Baucus	Y	Y	Y	Y	Y	Y	Y
Burns	Y	Y	N	N	N	N	Y
NEBRASKA							
Nelson	Y	Y	Y	Y	Y	Y	N
Hagel	Y	N	N	N	N	N	Y
NEVADA							
Reid	Y	Y	Y	Y	Y	Y	N
Ensign	Y	N	N	N	N	N	N

	101	102	103	104	105	106	107
NEW HAMPSHIRE							
Smith	Y	N	N	N	N	N	Y
Gregg	Y	N	N	?	N	N	Y
NEW JERSEY							
Corzine	Y	Y	Y	Y	Y	Y	N
Torricelli	Y	Y	Y	Y	Y	Y	N
NEW MEXICO							
Domenici	Y	Y	N	N	N	Y	Y
Bingaman	Y	Y	Y	Y	Y	Y	N
NEW YORK							
Clinton	Y	Y	Y	Y	Y	Y	N
Schumer	Y	Y	Y	Y	Y	Y	N
NORTH CAROLINA							
Helms	Y	N	N	N	N	N	N
Edwards	Y	Y	Y	Y	Y	Y	N
NORTH DAKOTA							
Conrad	Y	Y	Y	Y	Y	Y	Y
Dorgan	Y	Y	Y	Y	Y	Y	Y
OHIO							
DeWine	Y	Y	N	Y	N	Y	Y
Voinovich	Y	Y	N	N	N	N	Y
OKLAHOMA							
Nickles	Y	N	N	N	N	N	Y
Inhofe	Y	N	N	N	N	N	Y
OREGON							
Wyden	Y	Y	Y	Y	Y	Y	N
Smith	Y	Y	N	N	Y	Y	N
PENNSYLVANIA							
Specter	Y	Y	N	Y	Y	Y	N
Santorum	Y	N	N	N	N	N	N
RHODE ISLAND							
Reed	Y	Y	Y	Y	Y	Y	N
Chafee	Y	N	N	Y	Y	Y	Y
SOUTH CAROLINA							
Thurmond	Y	N	N	N	N	N	Y
Hollings	Y	Y	Y	Y	Y	Y	N
SOUTH DAKOTA							
Daschle	Y	Y	Y	Y	Y	Y	N
Johnson	Y	Y	Y	Y	Y	Y	N
TENNESSEE							
Thompson	Y	N	N	N	N	N	Y
Frist	Y	N	N	N	N	N	Y

	101	102	103	104	105	106	107
TEXAS							
Gramm	Y	Y	N	N	N	N	Y
Hutchison	Y	Y	N	Y	N	Y	Y
UTAH							
Hatch	Y	N	N	N	N	N	N
Bennett	Y	N	N	N	N	N	N
VERMONT							
Leahy	Y	Y	Y	Y	Y	Y	Y
Jeffords	Y	Y	N	N	Y	Y	Y
VIRGINIA							
Warner	Y	Y	N	Y	Y	Y	N
Allen	Y	Y	N	Y	N	Y	N
WASHINGTON							
Cantwell	Y	Y	Y	Y	Y	Y	N
Murray	Y	Y	Y	Y	Y	Y	N
WEST VIRGINIA							
Byrd	Y	Y	Y	Y	Y	Y	N
Rockefeller	Y	Y	Y	Y	Y	Y	N
WISCONSIN							
Kohl	Y	Y	Y	?	Y	Y	N
Feingold	Y	Y	Y	Y	Y	Y	N
WYOMING							
Thomas	Y	N	N	N	N	N	Y
Enzi	Y	N	N	N	N	N	Y

ND Northern Democrats   SD Southern Democrats

Southern states - Ala., Ark., Fla., Ga., Ky., La., Miss., N.C., Okla., S.C., Tenn., Texas, Va.

101. S 1. ESEA Reauthorization/Language and Life Skills. Reid, D-Nev., amendment to the Jeffords, R-Vt., substitute amendment. The Reid amendment would add language to allow after-school programs that emphasize language and life skills for students with limited English proficiency to be eligible for 21st Century Community Learning Center grants. The Jeffords substitute would reauthorize the Elementary and Secondary Education Act (ESEA) for seven years and add language to modify the annual testing provisions in the bill, add a "Straight A's" demonstration program and allow parents of children in underperforming schools to use federal funds for private tutoring. Adopted 96-0: R 50-0; D 46-0 (ND 37-0, SD 9-0). May 14, 2001.

102. S 1. ESEA Reauthorization/School Safety Center. Cleland, D-Ga., amendment to the Jeffords, R-Vt., substitute amendment. The Cleland amendment would establish a National Center for School and Youth Safety to offer emergency assistance in response to school safety crises, an anonymous student hotline, consultations regarding school safety, and outreach activities. Adopted 74-23: R 27-23; D 47-0 (ND 38-0, SD 9-0). May 14, 2001.

103. S 1. ESEA Reauthorization/Class Size Reduction. Murray, D-Wash., amendment to the Jeffords, R-Vt., substitute amendment. The Murray amendment would authorize a federal program to assist states and local educational agencies in recruiting, hiring and training 100,000 teachers in an effort to reduce class sizes. It also would authorize $2.4 billion in fiscal 2002 and subsequent necessary sums for the next six fiscal years. Rejected 48-50: R 0-50; D 48-0 (ND 40-0, SD 8-0). A "nay" was a vote in support of the president's position. May 15, 2001.

104. S 1. ESEA Reauthorization/Campaign Finance Overhaul. McCain, R-Ariz., amendment to the Jeffords, R-Vt., substitute amendment. The McCain amendment would express the sense of the Senate that legislation to overhaul campaign finance laws as passed by the Senate should be engrossed and delivered to the House without delay. Adopted 61-36: R 14-35; D 47-1 (ND 38-1, SD 9-0). May 15, 2001.

105. S 1. ESEA Reauthorization/After-School Programs. Boxer, D-Calif., amendment to the Jeffords, R-Vt., substitute amendment. The Boxer amendment would express the sense of the Senate that Congress should appropriate the authorized level of $1.5 billion in fiscal 2002 for after-school programs. It also would authorize a total of $19.5 billion from fiscal 2003 through 2008 for after-school programs. Adopted 60-39: R 11-39; D 49-0 (ND 40-0, SD 9-0). May 16, 2001.

106. S 1. ESEA Reauthorization/School Libraries. Reed, D-R.I., amendment to the Jeffords, R-Vt., substitute amendment. The Reed amendment would authorize an additional $500 million in fiscal 2002 and in each of the next six fiscal years under the Reading First Program for school library improvements. Adopted 69-30: R 20-30; D 49-0 (ND 40-0, SD 9-0). May 16, 2001.

107. S 1. ESEA Reauthorization/School Renovation and Construction. Enzi, R-Wyo., amendment to the Jeffords, R-Vt., substitute amendment. The Enzi amendment would target previously appropriated funds to states for emergency repairs to certain schools, such as those receiving impact aid, and those under the jurisdiction of the Defense Department and the Bureau of Indian Affairs, before making assistance available to other schools. It also would create a revolving loan fund that could be used to make annual interest payments on qualified school construction bonds. Rejected 37-62: R 34-16; D 3-46 (ND 3-37, SD 0-9). May 16, 2001.

	108	109	110	111	112	113	114
ALABAMA							
Shelby	N	Y	N	Y	N	Y	N
Sessions	N	Y	N	Y	N	N	N
ALASKA							
Stevens	N	Y	N	Y	N	N	N
Murkowski	N	Y	N	Y	N	Y	N
ARIZONA							
McCain	N	N	N	Y	Y	N	N
Kyl	N	N	N	N	N	Y	N
ARKANSAS							
Hutchinson	N	Y	N	N	N	Y	N
Lincoln	Y	Y	Y	Y	N	N	N
CALIFORNIA							
Feinstein	Y	Y	Y	Y	Y	N	Y
Boxer	Y	Y	Y	Y	Y	N	Y
COLORADO							
Campbell	N	Y	N	N	N	Y	N
Allard	N	Y	N	Y	N	Y	N
CONNECTICUT							
Dodd	Y	Y	Y	Y	Y	N	Y
Lieberman	Y	Y	Y	N	Y	N	Y
DELAWARE							
Carper	Y	Y	Y	Y	Y	N	Y
Biden	Y	Y	N	Y	Y	N	Y
FLORIDA							
Graham	Y	Y	N	Y	Y	N	Y
Nelson	Y	Y	Y	Y	Y	N	Y
GEORGIA							
Miller	N	Y	N	Y	N	N	N
Cleland	Y	Y	?	Y	N	N	N
HAWAII							
Inouye	Y	Y	Y	Y	Y	N	Y
Akaka	Y	Y	Y	Y	Y	N	Y
IDAHO							
Craig	N	Y	N	N	N	N	N
Crapo	N	Y	N	N	N	N	N
ILLINOIS							
Durbin	Y	N	Y	N	Y	N	Y
Fitzgerald	N	Y	N	Y	N	Y	N
INDIANA							
Lugar	N	Y	N	Y	N	N	N
Bayh	Y	Y	Y	N	Y	N	Y

	108	109	110	111	112	113	114
IOWA							
Grassley	N	N	N	Y	N	N	N
Harkin	Y	Y	N	Y	Y	N	Y
KANSAS							
Brownback	N	Y	N	Y	N	Y	N
Roberts	N	Y	N	Y	N	Y	N
KENTUCKY							
McConnell	N	Y	N	N	N	N	N
Bunning	N	Y	N	Y	N	Y	?
LOUISIANA							
Breaux	Y	Y	Y	Y	N	N	Y
Landrieu	Y	Y	N	Y	Y	Y	N
MAINE							
Snowe	N	N	N	Y	N	N	Y
Collins	N	Y	N	N	N	N	N
MARYLAND							
Sarbanes	Y	Y	Y	Y	Y	N	Y
Mikulski	Y	N	Y	Y	Y	N	Y
MASSACHUSETTS							
Kennedy	Y	Y	N	N	Y	N	Y
Kerry	Y	Y	N	Y	Y	N	Y
MICHIGAN							
Levin	Y	Y	Y	Y	Y	N	Y
Stabenow	Y	Y	Y	Y	Y	N	Y
MINNESOTA							
Wellstone	Y	Y	Y	Y	Y	N	Y
Dayton	Y	Y	Y	Y	Y	N	Y
MISSISSIPPI							
Cochran	N	Y	N	Y	N	Y	N
Lott	N	Y	N	N	N	N	N
MISSOURI							
Bond	N	Y	N	N	N	N	N
Carnahan	+	?	N	Y	Y	Y	Y
MONTANA							
Baucus	Y	Y	N	Y	Y	N	Y
Burns	N	Y	N	Y	N	Y	N
NEBRASKA							
Nelson	Y	Y	N	Y	N	N	Y
Hagel	N	N	N	N	N	N	N
NEVADA							
Reid	Y	Y	Y	Y	Y	N	Y
Ensign	N	Y	N	N	N	N	N

	108	109	110	111	112	113	114
NEW HAMPSHIRE							
Smith	N	Y	N	Y	N	Y	N
Gregg	N	Y	N	N	N	N	N
NEW JERSEY							
Corzine	Y	Y	Y	Y	Y	N	Y
Torricelli	Y	Y	Y	Y	N	N	Y
NEW MEXICO							
Domenici	N	Y	N	Y	N	Y	N
Bingaman	Y	Y	N	Y	Y	N	Y
NEW YORK							
Clinton	Y	N	Y	Y	Y	N	Y
Schumer	Y	Y	Y	Y	Y	N	Y
NORTH CAROLINA							
Helms	N	Y	N	N	N	Y	N
Edwards	Y	Y	Y	Y	Y	N	Y
NORTH DAKOTA							
Conrad	Y	N	Y	Y	Y	N	Y
Dorgan	Y	Y	Y	Y	Y	N	Y
OHIO							
DeWine	N	Y	N	Y	N	N	N
Voinovich	N	Y	N	Y	N	N	N
OKLAHOMA							
Nickles	N	Y	N	N	N	N	N
Inhofe	N	Y	N	Y	N	Y	N
OREGON							
Wyden	Y	Y	N	Y	N	N	Y
Smith	N	Y	N	Y	N	N	N
PENNSYLVANIA							
Specter	Y	Y	N	Y	N	N	N
Santorum	N	Y	N	Y	N	Y	N
RHODE ISLAND							
Reed	Y	Y	Y	Y	Y	N	Y
Chafee	N	N	N	Y	Y	N	N
SOUTH CAROLINA							
Thurmond	N	Y	N	N	N	Y	N
Hollings	Y	N	Y	Y	Y	N	Y
SOUTH DAKOTA							
Daschle	Y	Y	Y	Y	Y	N	Y
Johnson	Y	N	Y	Y	Y	N	Y
TENNESSEE							
Thompson	N	Y	N	Y	N	N	N
Frist	N	Y	N	Y	N	Y	N

Key

Y	Voted for (yea).
#	Paired for.
+	Announced for.
N	Voted against (nay).
X	Paired against.
–	Announced against.
P	Voted "present."
C	Voted "present" to avoid possible conflict of interest.
?	Did not vote or otherwise make a position known.

Democrats **Republicans** *Independents*

	108	109	110	111	112	113	114
TEXAS							
Gramm	N	Y	N	Y	N	Y	N
Hutchison	N	Y	N	Y	N	Y	N
UTAH							
Hatch	N	Y	N	Y	N	Y	N
Bennett	N	Y	N	Y	N	Y	N
VERMONT							
Leahy	Y	Y	Y	Y	Y	N	Y
Jeffords	N	N	N	N	N	N	N
VIRGINIA							
Warner	N	Y	N	Y	N	N	N
Allen	N	Y	N	Y	N	N	N
WASHINGTON							
Cantwell	Y	Y	Y	Y	Y	N	Y
Murray	Y	Y	Y	Y	Y	N	Y
WEST VIRGINIA							
Byrd	Y	N	N	N	N	N	Y
Rockefeller	Y	Y	Y	Y	Y	N	Y
WISCONSIN							
Kohl	Y	Y	N	Y	Y	N	?
Feingold	Y	N	N	N	Y	N	Y
WYOMING							
Thomas	N	Y	N	N	N	Y	N
Enzi	N	Y	N	N	N	Y	N

ND Northern Democrats   SD Southern Democrats

Southern states - Ala., Ark., Fla., Ga., Ky., La., Miss., N.C., Okla., S.C., Tenn., Texas, Va.

108. S 1. ESEA Reauthorization/School Renovation and Construction. Harkin, D-Iowa, amendment to the Jeffords, R-Vt., substitute amendment. The Harkin amendment would authorize $1.6 billion for fiscal 2002 and such sums as necessary for each fiscal year between 2003 and 2006 for the construction and renovation of public elementary and secondary school buildings. Rejected 49-50: R 1-49; D 48-1 (ND 40-0, SD 8-1). A "nay" was a vote in support of the president's position. May 16, 2001.

109. S 1. ESEA Reauthorization/School Renovation and Construction. Hutchinson, R-Ark., amendment to the Jeffords, R-Vt., substitute amendment. The Hutchinson amendment would increase the amount school districts are allowed to invest from $5 million to $10 million without being subject to arbitrage rebate requirements. It also would allow tax-exempt private activity bonds to be issued to build public schools that are owned by a for-profit corporation. Adopted 83-16: R 44-6; D 39-10 (ND 31-9, SD 8-1). May 16, 2001.

110. S 1. ESEA Reauthorization/IDEA Funding. Dayton, D-Minn., amendment to the Jeffords, R-Vt., substitute amendment. The Dayton amendment would provide for full funding of 40 percent of the average per-pupil expenditures for certain programs under the Individuals with Disabilities Act through mandatory funding in the first two years. Rejected 34-65: R 0-50; D 34-15 (ND 29-12, SD 5-3). May 17, 2001.

111. S 1. ESEA Reauthorization/Teacher Loan Forgiveness. Voinovich, R-Ohio, amendment to the Jeffords, R-Vt., substitute amendment. The Voinovich amendment would extend forgiveness of student loans to Head Start teachers. Adopted 76-24: R 32-18; D 44-6 (ND 35-6, SD 9-0). May 17, 2001.

112. HR 1836. Tax Cut Reconciliation Bill/'Marriage Penalty.' Conrad, D-N.D., amendment that would accelerate the elimination of the so-called marriage penalty in the standard deduction and 15 percent bracket to become fully effective in 2002. It would be offset by delaying the phase-in of cuts in the top two marginal tax rates. Rejected 44-56: R 2-48; D 42-8 (ND 37-4, SD 5-4). May 17, 2001.

113. HR 1836. Tax Cut Reconciliation Bill/'Marriage Penalty.' Hutchison, R-Texas, amendment that would accelerate the elimination of the so-called marriage penalty in the standard deduction to become fully effective in 2002. It would be offset by reducing the amount that could be deducted for higher education expenses and delaying allowable increases to education savings accounts. Rejected 27-73: R 25-25; D 2-48 (ND 1-40, SD 1-8). May 17, 2001.

114. HR 1836. Tax Cut Reconciliation Bill/Tuition Deduction. Schumer, D-N.Y., amendment that would increase the deduction, from $5,000 to $12,000, for higher education expenses for single filers with gross incomes of less than $65,000 and joint filers with gross incomes of less than $130,000. It also would increase the value of the tax credit on student loan interest from $500 to $1,000. It would be offset by slowing the reduction of the estate tax rate. Rejected 43-55: R 1-48; D 42-7 (ND 37-3, SD 5-4). May 17, 2001.

	115	116	117	118	119	120	121
ALABAMA							
Shelby	Y	Y	Y	N	Y	Y	N
Sessions	Y	Y	Y	N	N	Y	N
ALASKA							
Stevens	Y	Y	Y	N	N	Y	N
Murkowski	?	?	?	?	?	?	?
ARIZONA							
McCain	Y	Y	Y	Y	Y	Y	Y
Kyl	Y	Y	Y	N	N	Y	N
ARKANSAS							
Hutchinson	Y	Y	Y	N	N	Y	N
Lincoln	Y	Y	N	Y	Y	Y	Y
CALIFORNIA							
Feinstein	Y	Y	N	Y	Y	Y	Y
Boxer	Y	Y	N	Y	Y	Y	Y
COLORADO							
Campbell	Y	Y	Y	N	N	Y	N
Allard	Y	Y	Y	N	N	Y	N
CONNECTICUT							
Dodd	Y	Y	N	Y	Y	Y	Y
Lieberman	Y	Y	N	Y	Y	Y	Y
DELAWARE							
Carper	Y	Y	N	Y	Y	Y	Y
Biden	Y	Y	N	Y	Y	Y	Y
FLORIDA							
Graham	Y	Y	N	Y	Y	Y	Y
Nelson	Y	Y	N	Y	Y	Y	Y
GEORGIA							
Miller	Y	Y	N	Y	Y	Y	Y
Cleland	Y	Y	N	Y	Y	Y	Y
HAWAII							
Inouye	Y	Y	N	Y	Y	Y	Y
Akaka	Y	Y	N	Y	Y	Y	Y
IDAHO							
Craig	Y	Y	Y	N	N	Y	N
Crapo	Y	Y	Y	N	N	Y	N
ILLINOIS							
Durbin	Y	Y	N	Y	Y	Y	Y
Fitzgerald	Y	Y	Y	N	N	Y	Y
INDIANA							
Lugar	Y	Y	Y	N	N	Y	N
Bayh	Y	Y	N	Y	Y	Y	N

	115	116	117	118	119	120	121
IOWA							
Grassley	Y	Y	Y	N	N	Y	Y
Harkin	Y	Y	N	Y	Y	Y	Y
KANSAS							
Brownback	Y	Y	Y	N	N	Y	N
Roberts	Y	Y	Y	N	N	Y	N
KENTUCKY							
McConnell	Y	Y	Y	N	N	Y	N
Bunning	Y	Y	Y	N	N	Y	N
LOUISIANA							
Breaux	Y	Y	N	Y	Y	Y	Y
Landrieu	Y	Y	N	Y	Y	Y	Y
MAINE							
Snowe	Y	Y	Y	N	N	Y	Y
Collins	Y	Y	Y	N	N	Y	Y
MARYLAND							
Sarbanes	Y	Y	N	Y	Y	Y	Y
Mikulski	Y	Y	N	Y	Y	Y	Y
MASSACHUSETTS							
Kennedy	Y	Y	N	Y	Y	Y	Y
Kerry	Y	Y	N	Y	Y	Y	Y
MICHIGAN							
Levin	Y	Y	N	Y	Y	Y	Y
Stabenow	Y	Y	N	Y	Y	Y	Y
MINNESOTA							
Wellstone	Y	Y	N	Y	Y	Y	Y
Dayton	Y	Y	N	Y	Y	Y	Y
MISSISSIPPI							
Cochran	Y	Y	Y	N	N	Y	N
Lott	Y	Y	Y	N	N	Y	N
MISSOURI							
Bond	Y	Y	Y	N	N	Y	N
Carnahan	Y	Y	N	Y	Y	Y	Y
MONTANA							
Baucus	Y	Y	N	Y	Y	Y	Y
Burns	Y	Y	Y	N	N	Y	N
NEBRASKA							
Nelson	Y	Y	N	Y	Y	Y	Y
Hagel	Y	Y	Y	N	N	Y	N
NEVADA							
Reid	Y	Y	N	Y	Y	Y	Y
Ensign	Y	Y	Y	N	N	Y	N

	115	116	117	118	119	120	121
NEW HAMPSHIRE							
Smith	Y	Y	Y	N	N	Y	N
Gregg	Y	Y	Y	N	N	Y	N
NEW JERSEY							
Corzine	Y	Y	N	Y	Y	Y	Y
Torricelli	Y	Y	N	Y	Y	Y	Y
NEW MEXICO							
Domenici	?	?	?	?	?	?	?
Bingaman	Y	Y	N	Y	Y	Y	Y
NEW YORK							
Clinton	Y	Y	N	Y	Y	Y	Y
Schumer	Y	Y	N	Y	Y	Y	Y
NORTH CAROLINA							
Helms	Y	Y	Y	N	N	Y	N
Edwards	Y	Y	N	Y	Y	Y	Y
NORTH DAKOTA							
Conrad	Y	Y	N	Y	Y	Y	Y
Dorgan	Y	Y	N	Y	Y	Y	Y
OHIO							
DeWine	Y	Y	Y	N	N	Y	N
Voinovich	Y	Y	Y	N	N	Y	N
OKLAHOMA							
Nickles	Y	Y	Y	N	N	Y	N
Inhofe	Y	Y	Y	N	N	Y	N
OREGON							
Wyden	Y	Y	N	Y	Y	Y	Y
Smith	Y	Y	Y	N	N	Y	N
PENNSYLVANIA							
Specter	Y	Y	Y	N	N	Y	N
Santorum	Y	Y	Y	N	N	Y	N
RHODE ISLAND							
Reed	Y	Y	Y	Y	Y	Y	Y
Chafee	Y	Y	Y	Y	N	Y	Y
SOUTH CAROLINA							
Thurmond	Y	Y	Y	N	N	Y	N
Hollings	Y	Y	N	Y	Y	Y	Y
SOUTH DAKOTA							
Daschle	Y	Y	N	Y	Y	Y	Y
Johnson	Y	Y	N	Y	Y	Y	Y
TENNESSEE							
Thompson	Y	Y	Y	N	N	Y	N
Frist	Y	Y	Y	N	N	Y	N

	115	116	117	118	119	120	121
TEXAS							
Gramm	Y	Y	Y	N	N	Y	N
Hutchison	Y	Y	Y	N	N	Y	N
UTAH							
Hatch	Y	Y	Y	N	N	Y	N
Bennett	Y	Y	Y	N	N	Y	N
VERMONT							
Leahy	Y	Y	N	Y	Y	Y	Y
Jeffords	Y	Y	Y	Y	Y	Y	Y
VIRGINIA							
Warner	Y	Y	Y	N	N	Y	N
Allen	Y	Y	Y	N	N	Y	N
WASHINGTON							
Cantwell	Y	Y	N	Y	Y	Y	Y
Murray	Y	Y	N	Y	Y	Y	Y
WEST VIRGINIA							
Byrd	Y	Y	N	Y	Y	Y	Y
Rockefeller	Y	Y	N	Y	Y	Y	Y
WISCONSIN							
Kohl	Y	Y	N	Y	Y	Y	Y
Feingold	Y	Y	N	Y	Y	Y	Y
WYOMING							
Thomas	Y	Y	Y	N	N	Y	N
Enzi	Y	Y	Y	N	N	Y	N

ND Northern Democrats   SD Southern Democrats

Southern states - Ala., Ark., Fla., Ga., Ky., La., Miss., N.C., Okla., S.C., Tenn., Texas, Va.

115. HR 1836. Tax-Cut Reconciliation/Temporary Capital Gains Reduction. Gregg, R-N.H., motion to waive the Budget Act with respect to the Baucus, D-Mont., point of order against the Gregg amendment. The Gregg amendment would provide for a temporary reduction in the maximum capital gains rate from 20 percent to 15 percent, effective from June 1, 2001, through Dec. 31, 2003. Motion rejected 47-51: R 40-8; D 7-43 (ND 5-36, SD 2-7). A three-fifths majority vote (60) of the total Senate is required to waive the Budget Act. (Subsequently, the chair upheld the point of order and the amendment fell.) May 21, 2001.

116. HR 1836. Tax-Cut Reconciliation/Tax Rate Reduction. Carnahan, D-Mo., amendment that would phase in a marginal rate reduction of 1 percentage point in each existing tax bracket and create a new 10 percent rate bracket. Rejected 48-50: R 1-48; D 47-2 (ND 39-1, SD 8-1). May 21, 2001.

117. HR 1836. Tax-Cut Reconciliation/Prescription Drug Benefit. Rockefeller, D-W.Va., motion to waive the Budget Act with respect to the Grassley, R-Iowa, point of order against the Rockefeller amendment. The Rockefeller amendment would prohibit a reduction in the top tax rate until legislation has been enacted to provide a Medicare prescription drug benefit. Motion rejected 48-51: R 3-46; D 45-5 (ND 38-3, SD 7-2). A three-fifths majority vote (60) of the total Senate is required to waive the Budget Act. (Subsequently, the chair upheld the point of order and the amendment fell.) May 21, 2001.

118. HR 1836. Tax-Cut Reconciliation/Debt Reduction. Bayh, D-Ind., motion to waive the Budget Act with respect to the Grassley, R-Iowa, point of order against the Bayh amendment. The Bayh amendment would delay the implementation of the tax and spending proposals unless specified reduction targets in the publicly held debt are met. Motion rejected 49-50: R 5-44; D 44-6 (ND 37-4, SD 7-2). A three-fifths majority vote (60) of the total Senate is required to waive the Budget Act. (Subsequently, the chair upheld the point of order and the amendment fell.) May 21, 2001.

119. HR 1836. Tax-Cut Reconciliation/Tax Rate Reductions. Graham, D-Fla., amendment that would strike the tax cut provisions in the bill and create a new, 10 percent bracket retroactive to Jan. 1, 2001. Rejected 35-64: R 0-49; D 35-15 (ND 32-9, SD 3-6). May 21, 2001.

120. HR 1836. Tax-Cut Reconciliation/Estate Tax. Graham, D-Fla., amendment that would provide for a reduction in state estate-tax revenues in proportion to the reduction in federal estate-tax revenues. Rejected 39-60: R 1-48; D 38-12 (ND 35-6, SD 3-6). May 21, 2001.

121. HR 1836. Tax-Cut Reconciliation/Motion to Commit. Wellstone, D-Minn., motion to waive the Budget Act with respect to the Grassley, R-Iowa, point of order against the Wellstone motion to commit the bill to the Finance Committee with instructions to strike the tax-rate reduction for the highest bracket and establish a reserve account to provide for $120 billion for federal education programs. Motion rejected 41-58: R 0-49; D 41-9 (ND 36-5, SD 5-4);. A three-fifths majority vote (60) of the total Senate is required to waive the Budget Act. (Subsequently, the chair upheld the point of order and the motion fell.) May 21, 2001.

	122	123	124	125	126	127
ALABAMA						
Shelby	N	N	N	N	N	N
Sessions	N	N	N	N	N	N
ALASKA						
Stevens	?	?	?	?	X	?
Murkowski	N	N	N	N	N	N
ARIZONA						
McCain	N	N	Y	N	Y	Y
Kyl	N	N	N	N	N	N
ARKANSAS						
Hutchinson	N	N	N	N	N	N
Lincoln	N	N	N	Y	Y	Y
CALIFORNIA						
Feinstein	Y	Y	N	Y	Y	Y
Boxer	Y	Y	Y	Y	Y	Y
COLORADO						
Campbell	N	N	N	N	N	N
Allard	N	N	N	N	N	N
CONNECTICUT						
Dodd	Y	Y	Y	Y	Y	Y
Lieberman	Y	Y	Y	Y	Y	Y
DELAWARE						
Carper	Y	Y	N	Y	Y	Y
Biden	Y	Y	Y	Y	Y	Y
FLORIDA						
Graham	Y	Y	Y	Y	Y	Y
Nelson	Y	N	Y	Y	Y	Y
GEORGIA						
Miller	N	N	N	N	N	N
Cleland	N	N	Y	N	Y	N
HAWAII						
Inouye	Y	Y	Y	Y	#	Y
Akaka	Y	Y	Y	Y	Y	Y
IDAHO						
Craig	N	N	N	N	N	N
Crapo	N	N	N	N	N	N
ILLINOIS						
Durbin	Y	Y	Y	Y	Y	Y
Fitzgerald	N	N	N	N	N	N
INDIANA						
Lugar	N	N	N	N	N	N
Bayh	N	N	Y	Y	Y	N

	122	123	124	125	126	127
IOWA						
Grassley	N	N	N	N	N	N
Harkin	Y	Y	Y	Y	Y	Y
KANSAS						
Brownback	N	N	N	N	N	N
Roberts	N	N	N	N	N	N
KENTUCKY						
McConnell	N	N	N	N	N	N
Bunning	N	N	N	N	N	N
LOUISIANA						
Breaux	N	N	N	N	N	N
Landrieu	N	N	Y	N	Y	Y
MAINE						
Snowe	N	N	N	N	N	N
Collins	N	N	N	N	Y	N
MARYLAND						
Sarbanes	Y	Y	Y	Y	Y	Y
Mikulski	Y	Y	Y	Y	Y	Y
MASSACHUSETTS						
Kennedy	Y	Y	Y	Y	Y	Y
Kerry	Y	Y	Y	Y	Y	Y
MICHIGAN						
Levin	Y	Y	Y	Y	Y	Y
Stabenow	Y	Y	Y	Y	Y	Y
MINNESOTA						
Wellstone	Y	Y	Y	Y	Y	Y
Dayton	Y	Y	Y	Y	Y	Y
MISSISSIPPI						
Cochran	N	N	N	N	N	N
Lott	N	N	N	N	N	N
MISSOURI						
Bond	N	N	N	N	N	N
Carnahan	N	N	Y	Y	Y	Y
MONTANA						
Baucus	N	N	Y	N	N	N
Burns	N	N	N	N	N	N
NEBRASKA						
Nelson	N	N	N	N	N	N
Hagel	N	N	N	N	N	N
NEVADA						
Reid	Y	Y	Y	Y	Y	Y
Ensign	N	N	N	N	N	N

	122	123	124	125	126	127
NEW HAMPSHIRE						
Smith	N	N	N	N	N	N
Gregg	N	N	N	N	N	N
NEW JERSEY						
Corzine	Y	Y	Y	Y	Y	Y
Torricelli	N	N	Y	Y	Y	N
NEW MEXICO						
Domenici	N	N	N	N	N	N
Bingaman	Y	Y	Y	Y	Y	Y
NEW YORK						
Clinton	Y	Y	Y	Y	Y	Y
Schumer	N	Y	Y	Y	Y	Y
NORTH CAROLINA						
Helms	N	N	N	N	N	N
Edwards	Y	N	Y	Y	Y	Y
NORTH DAKOTA						
Conrad	Y	Y	Y	Y	Y	Y
Dorgan	Y	Y	Y	Y	Y	Y
OHIO						
DeWine	N	N	N	N	N	N
Voinovich	N	N	N	N	N	N
OKLAHOMA						
Nickles	N	N	N	N	N	N
Inhofe	N	N	N	N	N	N
OREGON						
Wyden	N	N	N	Y	Y	Y
Smith	N	N	N	N	N	N
PENNSYLVANIA						
Specter	N	N	N	N	Y	N
Santorum	N	N	N	N	N	N
RHODE ISLAND						
Reed	Y	Y	Y	Y	Y	Y
Chafee	N	Y	Y	N	Y	N
SOUTH CAROLINA						
Thurmond	N	N	N	N	N	N
Hollings	Y	Y	Y	Y	Y	Y
SOUTH DAKOTA						
Daschle	Y	Y	Y	Y	Y	Y
Johnson	Y	Y	Y	Y	Y	Y
TENNESSEE						
Thompson	N	N	N	N	N	N
Frist	N	N	N	N	N	N

	122	123	124	125	126	127
TEXAS						
Gramm	N	N	N	N	N	N
Hutchison	N	N	N	N	N	N
UTAH						
Hatch	N	N	N	N	N	N
Bennett	N	N	N	N	N	N
VERMONT						
Leahy	Y	Y	Y	Y	Y	Y
Jeffords	Y	Y	N	N	Y	N
VIRGINIA						
Warner	N	N	N	N	N	N
Allen	N	N	N	N	N	N
WASHINGTON						
Cantwell	Y	Y	Y	Y	Y	Y
Murray	Y	Y	N	Y	Y	Y
WEST VIRGINIA						
Byrd	Y	Y	Y	Y	Y	Y
Rockefeller	Y	Y	N	Y	Y	Y
WISCONSIN						
Kohl	Y	Y	Y	Y	Y	N
Feingold	Y	Y	Y	Y	Y	Y
WYOMING						
Thomas	N	N	N	N	N	N
Enzi	N	N	N	N	N	N

ND Northern Democrats   SD Southern Democrats

Southern states - Ala., Ark., Fla., Ga., Ky., La., Miss., N.C., Okla., S.C., Tenn., Texas, Va.

122. HR 1836. Tax-Cut Reconciliation/Social Security, Medicare Trust Funds. Byrd, D-W.Va., motion to waive the Budget Act with respect to the Grassley, R-Iowa, point of order against the Byrd amendment. The Byrd amendment would strike all marginal tax-rate cuts except for creation of the 10 percent bracket, as well as all estate-tax provisions taking effect after 2006, and provide for funds to extend the solvency of the Social Security and Medicare Trust Funds, as well as for a prescription drug benefit. Motion rejected 39-60: R 1-48; D 38-12 (ND 34-7, SD 4-5). A three-fifths majority vote (60) of the total Senate is required to waive the Budget Act. (Subsequently, the chair upheld the point of order and the amendment fell.) May 21, 2001.

123. HR 1836. Tax-Cut Reconciliation/Estate Tax. Dodd, D-Conn., amendment that would reduce the cut in the top bracket to 38 percent. It also would strike the repeal of the estate tax and insert language that would increase the value of an estate that would be exempt from the tax and increase deductions for family-owned businesses and farms. Rejected 39-60: R 2-47; D 37-13 (ND 35-6, SD 2-7). May 21, 2001.

124. HR 1836. Tax-Cut Reconciliation/Estate Tax. Dorgan, D-N.D., amendment would strike the estate-tax repeal provision and insert language that provides for the repeal of the estate tax in 2003 for all qualified family-owned farms and businesses. It also would reduce the top estate-tax rate bracket to 45 percent. Rejected 43-56: R 2-47; D 41-9 (ND 36-5, SD 5-4). May 21, 2001.

125. HR 1836. Tax-Cut Reconciliation/Renewable Energy Tax Credits. Bingaman, D-N.M., motion to waive the Budget Act with respect to the Murkowski, R-Alaska, point of order against the Bingaman amendment. The Bingaman amendment would establish tax credits for investments in renewable energy technologies, incentives for new energy-efficient residential construction and tax credits for increased energy efficiency in commercial buildings. Motion rejected 43-56: R 0-49; D 43-7 (ND 37-4, SD 6-3). A three-fifths majority vote (60) of the total Senate is required to waive the Budget Act. (Subsequently, the chair upheld the point of order and the amendment fell.) May 21, 2001.

126. HR 1836. Tax-Cut Reconciliation/Tax Reduction Limit. McCain, R-Ariz., amendment that would limit the tax reduction in the 39.6 percent marginal rate bracket to 1 percentage point, to 38.6 percent. It also would increase the maximum taxable income subject to the 15 percent rate. Rejected 49-49: R 5-44; D 44-5 (ND 38-2, SD 6-3). May 21, 2001.

127. HR 1836. Tax-Cut Reconciliation/Motion to Commit. Reid, D-Nev., motion to waive the Budget Act with respect to the Grassley, R-Iowa, point of order against the McCain, R-Ariz., motion to commit the bill to the Finance Committee with instructions to strike the tax reduction in the top two brackets until the president submits his defense spending requests, and specify that the tax reduction would be decreased to accommodate the request. Motion rejected 43-56: R 1-48; D 42-8 (ND 35-6, SD 7-2). A three-fifths majority vote (60) of the total Senate is required to waive the Budget Act. (Subsequently, the chair upheld the point of order and the motion fell.) May 21, 2001.

	128	129	130	131	132	133	134	135
ALABAMA								
Shelby	N	Y	N	Y	N	N	N	N
Sessions	N	Y	N	Y	N	N	N	N
ALASKA								
Stevens	?	?	?	?	?	?	?	?
Murkowski	N	Y	N	Y	N	N	N	N
ARIZONA								
McCain	N	Y	N	Y	Y	Y	N	Y
Kyl	N	Y	N	Y	N	N	N	N
ARKANSAS								
Hutchinson	N	Y	N	Y	N	N	N	N
Lincoln	N	Y	Y	Y	N	Y	N	N
CALIFORNIA								
Feinstein	N	Y	Y	Y	Y	Y	N	Y
Boxer	Y	Y	Y	Y	Y	Y	Y	Y
COLORADO								
Campbell	N	Y	N	Y	N	N	N	N
Allard	Y	Y	N	Y	N	N	N	N
CONNECTICUT								
Dodd	N	Y	Y	Y	Y	Y	Y	Y
Lieberman	N	Y	Y	Y	Y	Y	Y	Y
DELAWARE								
Carper	N	Y	Y	Y	N	N	N	N
Biden	N	Y	Y	Y	Y	Y	Y	Y
FLORIDA								
Graham	N	Y	N	Y	N	Y	Y	Y
Nelson	N	Y	Y	Y	Y	Y	N	N
GEORGIA								
Miller	N	Y	N	Y	N	N	N	N
Cleland	N	Y	Y	Y	N	Y	N	N
HAWAII								
Inouye	N	Y	Y	Y	Y	Y	Y	Y
Akaka	N	Y	Y	Y	Y	Y	Y	Y
IDAHO								
Craig	Y	Y	N	Y	N	N	N	N
Crapo	Y	Y	N	Y	N	N	N	N
ILLINOIS								
Durbin	N	Y	Y	Y	Y	Y	Y	Y
Fitzgerald	N	Y	N	Y	N	N	N	N
INDIANA								
Lugar	N	Y	N	Y	N	N	N	N
Bayh	N	Y	Y	Y	N	Y	N	Y
IOWA								
Grassley	N	Y	N	Y	N	N	N	N
Harkin	N	Y	Y	Y	Y	Y	Y	Y
KANSAS								
Brownback	Y	Y	N	Y	N	N	N	N
Roberts	N	Y	N	Y	N	N	N	N
KENTUCKY								
McConnell	N	Y	N	Y	N	N	N	N
Bunning	N	Y	N	Y	N	N	N	N
LOUISIANA								
Breaux	N	Y	N	Y	N	N	N	Y
Landrieu	N	Y	Y	Y	N	N	N	Y
MAINE								
Snowe	N	Y	N	Y	N	N	N	Y
Collins	N	Y	N	Y	N	N	N	Y
MARYLAND								
Sarbanes	N	Y	Y	Y	Y	Y	Y	Y
Mikulski	N	Y	Y	Y	Y	Y	N	Y
MASSACHUSETTS								
Kennedy	N	Y	Y	Y	Y	Y	Y	Y
Kerry	N	Y	Y	Y	Y	Y	N	Y
MICHIGAN								
Levin	N	Y	Y	Y	Y	Y	Y	Y
Stabenow	N	Y	Y	Y	Y	Y	Y	Y
MINNESOTA								
Wellstone	N	Y	Y	Y	Y	Y	Y	Y
Dayton	N	Y	Y	Y	Y	Y	Y	Y
MISSISSIPPI								
Cochran	N	Y	N	Y	N	N	N	N
Lott	N	Y	N	Y	N	N	N	N
MISSOURI								
Bond	N	Y	N	Y	N	N	N	N
Carnahan	N	Y	Y	Y	Y	Y	Y	Y
MONTANA								
Baucus	N	Y	N	Y	N	N	N	N
Burns	N	Y	N	Y	N	N	N	N
NEBRASKA								
Nelson	N	Y	N	Y	N	N	N	N
Hagel	N	Y	N	Y	N	N	N	N
NEVADA								
Reid	N	Y	Y	Y	Y	Y	Y	Y
Ensign	N	Y	N	Y	N	N	N	N
NEW HAMPSHIRE								
Smith	Y	Y	N	Y	N	N	N	N
Gregg	Y	Y	N	Y	N	N	N	N
NEW JERSEY								
Corzine	N	Y	Y	Y	Y	Y	Y	Y
Torricelli	N	Y	Y	Y	Y	Y	N	Y
NEW MEXICO								
Domenici	N	Y	N	Y	N	N	N	N
Bingaman	N	Y	Y	Y	Y	Y	N	Y
NEW YORK								
Clinton	N	Y	Y	Y	Y	Y	N	Y
Schumer	N	Y	Y	Y	Y	Y	N	Y
NORTH CAROLINA								
Helms	N	Y	N	Y	N	N	N	N
Edwards	N	Y	Y	Y	Y	Y	N	Y
NORTH DAKOTA								
Conrad	N	Y	Y	Y	Y	Y	Y	Y
Dorgan	N	Y	Y	Y	Y	Y	Y	Y
OHIO								
DeWine	N	Y	N	Y	N	N	N	N
Voinovich	N	Y	N	Y	N	N	N	N
OKLAHOMA								
Nickles	N	Y	N	Y	N	N	N	N
Inhofe	N	Y	N	Y	N	N	N	N
OREGON								
Wyden	Y	Y	Y	Y	N	N	N	N
Smith	Y	Y	N	Y	N	N	N	N
PENNSYLVANIA								
Specter	N	Y	N	Y	N	N	N	Y
Santorum	N	Y	N	Y	N	N	N	N
RHODE ISLAND								
Reed	N	Y	Y	Y	Y	Y	Y	Y
Chafee	N	Y	Y	Y	N	Y	N	Y
SOUTH CAROLINA								
Thurmond	N	Y	N	Y	N	N	N	N
Hollings	N	Y	Y	Y	Y	Y	Y	Y
SOUTH DAKOTA								
Daschle	N	Y	Y	Y	Y	Y	Y	Y
Johnson	N	Y	Y	Y	Y	Y	N	Y
TENNESSEE								
Thompson	N	Y	N	Y	N	N	N	N
Frist	N	Y	N	Y	N	N	N	N
TEXAS								
Gramm	N	Y	N	Y	N	N	N	N
Hutchison	N	Y	N	Y	N	N	N	Y
UTAH								
Hatch	N	Y	N	Y	N	N	N	N
Bennett	N	Y	N	Y	N	N	N	N
VERMONT								
Leahy	N	Y	Y	Y	Y	Y	N	Y
Jeffords	N	Y	Y	Y	N	N	N	N
VIRGINIA								
Warner	Y	Y	N	Y	N	N	N	N
Allen	Y	Y	N	Y	N	N	N	N
WASHINGTON								
Cantwell	N	Y	Y	Y	Y	Y	Y	Y
Murray	N	Y	Y	Y	Y	Y	Y	Y
WEST VIRGINIA								
Byrd	N	Y	Y	Y	Y	Y	Y	Y
Rockefeller	N	Y	Y	Y	Y	Y	Y	Y
WISCONSIN								
Kohl	N	Y	Y	Y	Y	Y	Y	Y
Feingold	N	Y	Y	Y	Y	Y	Y	Y
WYOMING								
Thomas	N	Y	N	Y	N	N	N	N
Enzi	N	Y	N	Y	N	N	N	N

Key

Y	Voted for (yea).
#	Paired for.
+	Announced for.
N	Voted against (nay).
X	Paired against.
–	Announced against.
P	Voted "present."
C	Voted "present" to avoid possible conflict of interest.
?	Did not vote or otherwise make a position known.

Democrats ***Republicans***
Independents

ND Northern Democrats   SD Southern Democrats

Southern states - Ala., Ark., Fla., Ga., Ky., La., Miss., N.C., Okla., S.C., Tenn., Texas, Va.

128. HR 1836. Tax-Cut Reconciliation/Internet Tax Moratorium. Smith, R-N.H., motion to waive the Budget Act with respect to the Enzi, R-Wyo., point of order against the Smith amendment to the Smith amendment. The Smith amendment would make the Internet tax moratorium permanent. The underlying Smith amendment would allow all survivors to exclude from taxable income survivor benefits attributable to service by public safety officers killed in the line of duty. Motion rejected 11-88: R 9-40; D 2-48 (ND 2-39, SD 0-9). A three-fifths majority vote (60) of the total Senate is required to waive the Budget Act. (Subsequently, the chair upheld the point of order and the Internet amendment fell.) May 21, 2001.

129. HR 1836. Tax-Cut Reconciliation/Survivor Benefits. Smith, R-N.H., amendment that would allow all survivors to exclude from taxable income survivor benefits attributable to service by public safety officers killed in the line of duty. The provision would apply to amounts received beginning in 2001. Adopted 99-0: R 49-0; D 50-0 (ND 41-0, SD 9-0). May 21, 2001.

130. HR 1836. Tax-Cut Reconciliation/Education Spending. Kennedy, D-Mass., motion to waive the Budget Act with respect to the Grassley, R-Iowa, point of order against the Kennedy amendment. The Kennedy amendment would provide that the top marginal rate reduction would not take effect unless funding is provided at levels authorized in amendments adopted by the Senate on legislation to overhaul education policy. Motion rejected 48-51: R 2-47; D 46-4 (ND 39-2, SD 7-2). A three-fifths majority vote (60) of the total Senate is required to waive the Budget Act. (Subsequently, the chair upheld the point of order and the amendment fell.) May 21, 2001.

131. HR 1836. Tax-Cut Reconciliation/Ruling of the Chair. Judgment of the Senate to affirm the ruling of the chair that a quorum call is not in order.

Motion agreed to 99-0: R 49-0; D 50-0 (ND 41-0, SD 9-0) May 21, 2001.

132. HR 1836. Tax-Cut Reconciliation/Medicaid Estate Recovery Program. Feingold, D-Wis., motion to waive the Budget Act with respect to the Baucus, D-Mont., point of order against the Feingold amendment. The Feingold amendment would repeal the Medicaid Estate Recovery Program, offset by decreasing the reduction in the estate tax. Motion rejected 41-58: R 1-48; D 40-10 (ND 36-5, SD 4-5). A three-fifths majority vote (60) of the total Senate is required to waive the Budget Act. (Subsequently, the chair upheld the point of order and the amendment fell.) May 22, 2001.

133. HR 1836. Tax-Cut Reconciliation/Tax-Rate Modification. Feingold, D-Wis., amendment that would increase the amount of income covered by the 10 percent tax bracket. It would be offset by striking the reduction in the top tax rate. Rejected 46-53: R 2-47; D 44-6 (ND 38-3, SD 6-3). May 22, 2001.

134. HR 1836. Tax-Cut Reconciliation/Motion to Commit. Feingold, D-Wis., motion to commit the bill to the Finance Committee with instructions to strike the estate-tax provision in the bill and use the savings to expand the amounts of the unified credit exemption. Motion rejected 30-69: R 0-49; D 30-20 (ND 28-13, SD 2-7). May 22, 2001.

135. HR 1836. Tax-Cut Reconciliation/Estate Tax. Feingold, D-Wis., amendment that would eliminate the estate-tax repeal provision in the bill for estates worth more than $100 million, and increase the income limits applicable to the 10 percent rate bracket for individual income taxes. Rejected 48-51: R 6-43; D 42-8 (ND 38-3, SD 4-5). May 22, 2001.

	136	137	138	139	140	141	142	143
ALABAMA								
Shelby	N	N	N	N	N	N	N	N
Sessions	N	N	N	N	N	N	N	N
ALASKA								
Stevens	?	?	?	?	?	?	?	?
Murkowski	N	N	N	N	N	N	N	N
ARIZONA								
McCain	N	N	Y	N	N	N	N	N
Kyl	N	N	N	N	N	N	N	N
ARKANSAS								
Hutchinson	N	N	N	N	N	N	N	N
Lincoln	Y	Y	Y	N	Y	Y	N	N
CALIFORNIA								
Feinstein	N	Y	Y	Y	Y	Y	Y	Y
Boxer	Y	Y	Y	Y	Y	Y	Y	Y
COLORADO								
Campbell	N	N	N	N	N	N	N	N
Allard	N	N	N	N	N	N	N	N
CONNECTICUT								
Dodd	Y	Y	Y	Y	Y	Y	Y	Y
Lieberman	N	Y	Y	Y	Y	Y	Y	Y
DELAWARE								
Carper	Y	Y	Y	N	Y	Y	Y	Y
Biden	N	Y	Y	N	Y	Y	Y	Y
FLORIDA								
Graham	Y	Y	Y	Y	Y	Y	Y	Y
Nelson	Y	Y	Y	Y	Y	Y	Y	Y
GEORGIA								
Miller	N	N	N	N	N	N	N	N
Cleland	N	Y	Y	Y	Y	N	Y	N
HAWAII								
Inouye	Y	Y	Y	Y	Y	Y	Y	Y
Akaka	Y	Y	Y	Y	Y	Y	Y	Y
IDAHO								
Craig	N	N	N	N	N	N	N	N
Crapo	N	N	N	N	N	N	N	N
ILLINOIS								
Durbin	Y	Y	Y	Y	Y	Y	Y	Y
Fitzgerald	N	N	N	N	N	N	N	N
INDIANA								
Lugar	N	N	N	N	N	N	N	N
Bayh	Y	Y	Y	Y	Y	Y	Y	Y

	136	137	138	139	140	141	142	143
IOWA								
Grassley	N	N	N	N	N	N	N	N
Harkin	Y	Y	Y	Y	Y	Y	Y	Y
KANSAS								
Brownback	N	N	N	N	N	N	N	N
Roberts	N	N	N	N	N	N	N	N
KENTUCKY								
McConnell	N	N	N	N	N	N	N	N
Bunning	N	N	N	N	N	N	N	N
LOUISIANA								
Breaux	N	N	N	N	N	N	N	N
Landrieu	Y	Y	N	Y	Y	Y	Y	Y
MAINE								
Snowe	N	N	N	N	N	N	N	N
Collins	N	N	N	N	N	N	N	N
MARYLAND								
Sarbanes	Y	Y	Y	Y	Y	Y	Y	Y
Mikulski	Y	Y	Y	Y	Y	Y	Y	Y
MASSACHUSETTS								
Kennedy	Y	Y	Y	Y	Y	Y	Y	Y
Kerry	Y	Y	Y	Y	Y	Y	Y	Y
MICHIGAN								
Levin	Y	Y	Y	Y	Y	Y	Y	Y
Stabenow	Y	Y	Y	Y	Y	Y	Y	Y
MINNESOTA								
Wellstone	Y	Y	Y	Y	Y	Y	Y	Y
Dayton	Y	Y	Y	Y	Y	Y	Y	Y
MISSISSIPPI								
Cochran	N	N	N	N	N	N	N	N
Lott	N	N	N	N	N	N	N	N
MISSOURI								
Bond	N	N	N	N	N	N	N	N
Carnahan	Y	Y	Y	Y	Y	Y	Y	Y
MONTANA								
Baucus	Y	N	N	N	N	N	N	N
Burns	N	N	N	N	N	N	N	N
NEBRASKA								
Nelson	N	N	N	N	N	N	N	Y
Hagel	N	N	N	N	N	N	N	N
NEVADA								
Reid	Y	Y	Y	Y	Y	Y	Y	Y
Ensign	N	N	N	N	N	N	N	N

	136	137	138	139	140	141	142	143
NEW HAMPSHIRE								
Smith	N	N	N	N	N	N	N	N
Gregg	N	N	N	N	N	N	N	N
NEW JERSEY								
Corzine	Y	Y	Y	Y	Y	Y	Y	Y
Torricelli	N	N	Y	Y	Y	Y	Y	N
NEW MEXICO								
Domenici	N	N	N	N	N	N	N	N
Bingaman	Y	Y	Y	Y	N	Y	Y	Y
NEW YORK								
Clinton	Y	Y	Y	Y	Y	Y	Y	Y
Schumer	Y	Y	Y	Y	Y	Y	Y	Y
NORTH CAROLINA								
Helms	N	N	N	N	N	N	N	N
Edwards	Y	Y	Y	Y	Y	Y	Y	Y
NORTH DAKOTA								
Conrad	N	Y	Y	Y	Y	Y	Y	Y
Dorgan	Y	Y	Y	Y	Y	Y	Y	Y
OHIO								
DeWine	N	N	N	N	N	N	N	N
Voinovich	N	N	N	N	N	N	N	N
OKLAHOMA								
Nickles	N	N	N	N	N	N	N	N
Inhofe	N	N	N	N	N	N	N	N
OREGON								
Wyden	Y	Y	Y	Y	Y	Y	Y	Y
Smith	N	N	N	N	N	N	N	N
PENNSYLVANIA								
Specter	N	N	N	N	N	N	N	N
Santorum	N	N	N	N	N	N	N	N
RHODE ISLAND								
Reed	Y	Y	Y	Y	Y	Y	Y	Y
Chafee	Y	N	Y	N	Y	Y	Y	Y
SOUTH CAROLINA								
Thurmond	N	N	N	N	N	N	N	N
Hollings	Y	Y	Y	Y	Y	Y	Y	Y
SOUTH DAKOTA								
Daschle	Y	Y	Y	Y	Y	Y	Y	Y
Johnson	Y	Y	Y	Y	Y	Y	Y	Y
TENNESSEE								
Thompson	N	N	N	N	N	N	N	N
Frist	N	N	N	N	N	N	N	N

Key

Y	Voted for (yea).
#	Paired for.
+	Announced for.
N	Voted against (nay).
X	Paired against.
–	Announced against.
P	Voted "present."
C	Voted "present" to avoid possible conflict of interest.
?	Did not vote or otherwise make a position known.

Democrats   ***Republicans***
Independents

	136	137	138	139	140	141	142	143
TEXAS								
Gramm	N	N	N	N	N	N	N	N
Hutchison	N	N	N	N	N	N	N	N
UTAH								
Hatch	N	N	N	N	N	N	N	N
Bennett	N	N	N	N	N	N	N	N
VERMONT								
Leahy	Y	Y	Y	Y	Y	Y	Y	+
Jeffords	N	Y	N	N	N	N	Y	N
VIRGINIA								
Warner	N	N	N	N	N	N	N	N
Allen	N	N	N	N	N	N	N	N
WASHINGTON								
Cantwell	Y	Y	Y	Y	Y	Y	Y	N
Murray	Y	Y	Y	Y	Y	Y	Y	N
WEST VIRGINIA								
Byrd	N	Y	Y	N	Y	Y	Y	Y
Rockefeller	Y	Y	Y	Y	Y	Y	Y	Y
WISCONSIN								
Kohl	N	Y	Y	Y	Y	Y	Y	Y
Feingold	Y	Y	Y	Y	Y	Y	Y	Y
WYOMING								
Thomas	N	N	N	N	N	N	N	N
Enzi	N	N	N	N	N	N	N	N

ND Northern Democrats   SD Southern Democrats

Southern states - Ala., Ark., Fla., Ga., Ky., La., Miss., N.C., Okla., S.C., Tenn., Texas, Va.

136. HR 1836. Tax-Cut Reconciliation/Education Savings Accounts. Lincoln, D-Ark., amendment that would strike a provision in the bill that would treat tuition, fees, and room and board for elementary and secondary education as qualified spending from an education savings account. Rejected 41-58: R 2-47; D 39-11 (ND 33-8, SD 6-3). May 22, 2001.

137. HR 1836. Tax-Cut Reconciliation/Social Security and Medicare Solvency. Harkin, D-Iowa, motion to waive the Budget Act with respect to the Grassley, R-Iowa, point of order against the Harkin amendment. The Harkin amendment would delay the effective date of the tax-rate reductions in the highest rate bracket until the enactment of legislation that would provide for long-term solvency of the Social Security and Medicare Trust Funds. Motion rejected 45-54: R 0-49; D 45-5 (ND 38-3, SD 7-2). A three-fifths majority vote (60) of the total Senate is required to waive the Budget Act. (Subsequently, the chair upheld the point of order and the amendment fell.) May 22, 2001.

138. HR 1836. Tax-Cut Reconciliation/Alternative Minimum Tax. Kerry, D-Mass., amendment that would exempt individual taxpayers with adjusted gross incomes below $100,000 from the alternative minimum tax and modify the reduction in the top marginal tax bracket rate. Rejected 46-53: R 2-47; D 44-6 (ND 38-3, SD 6-3). May 22, 2001.

139. HR 1836. Tax-Cut Reconciliation/Tax Rebate Checks. Lieberman, D-Conn., amendment that would provide for tax rebate checks and modify the reduction in the maximum marginal tax bracket rate. Rejected 43-56: R 0-49; D 43-7 (ND 37-4, SD 6-3). May 22, 2001.

140. HR 1836. Tax-Cut Reconciliation/Motion to Commit. Corzine, D-N.J., motion to waive the Budget Act with respect to the Grassley, R-Iowa, point of order against the Corzine motion to commit the bill to the Finance Committee with instructions to create a tax credit for long-term care. Motion rejected 43-56: R 0-49; D 43-7 (ND 36-5, SD 7-2). A three-fifths majority vote (60) of the total Senate is required to waive the Budget Act. (Subsequently, the chair upheld the point of order and the motion fell.) May 22, 2001.

141. HR 1836. Tax-Cut Reconciliation/Standard Deduction Increase. Conrad, D-N.D., amendment that would increase the standard deduction and limit the reductions in the 36 percent and 39.6 percent tax brackets. Rejected 46-53: R 2-47; D 44-6 (ND 38-3, SD 6-3). May 22, 2001.

142. HR 1836. Tax-Cut Reconciliation/Standard Deduction Increase. Conrad, D-N.D., amendment that would increase the standard deduction and limit the reduction in the 39.6 percent tax rate bracket. Rejected 47-52: R 2-47; D 45-5 (ND 39-2, SD 6-3). May 22, 2001.

143. HR 1836. Tax-Cut Reconciliation/Tax Reduction. Carper, D-Del., motion to waive the Budget Act with respect to the Grassley, R-Iowa, point of order against the Carper substitute amendment. The substitute would cut taxes by $1.2 trillion over 10 years, create a 10 percent bracket for the first $12,000 in taxable income for couples and the first $6,000 for singles. It would also raise the standard deduction for married couples, double the estate-tax exemption, and make the research and development credit permanent. Motion rejected 43-55: R 2-47; D 41-8 (ND 36-4, SD 5-4). A three-fifths majority vote (60) of the total Senate is required to waive the Budget Act. (Subsequently, the chair upheld the point of order and the amendment fell.) May 22, 2001.

	144	145	146	147	148
ALABAMA					
Shelby	N	N	Y	N	N
Sessions	N	N	Y	N	N
ALASKA					
Stevens	?	?	?	?	?
Murkowski	N	N	N	N	
ARIZONA					
McCain	N	N	N	N	N
Kyl	N	N	N	N	N
ARKANSAS					
Hutchinson	N	N	Y	N	N
Lincoln	N	N	Y	Y	Y
CALIFORNIA					
Feinstein	Y	Y	Y	Y	Y
Boxer	Y	Y	Y	Y	Y
COLORADO					
Campbell	N	N	N	N	N
Allard	N	N	N	N	N
CONNECTICUT					
Dodd	Y	Y	Y	Y	Y
Lieberman	Y	Y	Y	Y	Y
DELAWARE					
Carper	Y	N	N	N	Y
Biden	Y	Y	Y	Y	Y
FLORIDA					
Graham	Y	Y	Y	Y	Y
Nelson	Y	Y	Y	Y	Y
GEORGIA					
Miller	N	N	Y	N	N
Cleland	N	N	Y	N	Y
HAWAII					
Inouye	Y	Y	Y	Y	Y
Akaka	Y	Y	Y	Y	Y
IDAHO					
Craig	N	N	N	N	N
Crapo	N	N	N	N	N
ILLINOIS					
Durbin	Y	Y	N	Y	Y
Fitzgerald	N	N	N	N	N
INDIANA					
Lugar	N	N	N	N	N
Bayh	N	N	Y	N	Y

	144	145	146	147	148
IOWA					
Grassley	N	N	N	N	N
Harkin	Y	Y	Y	Y	Y
KANSAS					
Brownback	N	N	N	N	N
Roberts	N	N	N	N	N
KENTUCKY					
McConnell	N	N	N	N	N
Bunning	N	N	N	N	N
LOUISIANA					
Breaux	N	N	Y	N	Y
Landrieu	Y	Y	Y	Y	Y
MAINE					
Snowe	N	N	N	N	N
Collins	N	N	N	N	N
MARYLAND					
Sarbanes	Y	Y	Y	Y	Y
Mikulski	Y	Y	Y	Y	Y
MASSACHUSETTS					
Kennedy	Y	Y	Y	Y	Y
Kerry	Y	Y	Y	Y	Y
MICHIGAN					
Levin	Y	Y	Y	Y	Y
Stabenow	Y	Y	Y	Y	Y
MINNESOTA					
Wellstone	Y	Y	Y	Y	Y
Dayton	Y	Y	Y	Y	Y
MISSISSIPPI					
Cochran	N	N	N	N	N
Lott	N	N	N	N	N
MISSOURI					
Bond	N	N	N	N	N
Carnahan	N	Y	Y	Y	Y
MONTANA					
Baucus	N	N	Y	N	N
Burns	N	N	N	N	N
NEBRASKA					
Nelson	N	N	Y	N	Y
Hagel	N	N	N	N	N
NEVADA					
Reid	Y	Y	Y	Y	Y
Ensign	N	N	Y	N	N

	144	145	146	147	148
NEW HAMPSHIRE					
Smith	N	N	N	N	N
Gregg	N	N	N	N	N
NEW JERSEY					
Corzine	Y	Y	Y	Y	Y
Torricelli	N	N	Y	N	Y
NEW MEXICO					
Domenici	N	N	Y	N	N
Bingaman	Y	Y	Y	Y	Y
NEW YORK					
Clinton	Y	Y	Y	Y	Y
Schumer	Y	Y	Y	Y	Y
NORTH CAROLINA					
Helms	N	N	N	N	N
Edwards	Y	Y	Y	Y	Y
NORTH DAKOTA					
Conrad	Y	Y	Y	Y	Y
Dorgan	Y	Y	Y	Y	Y
OHIO					
DeWine	N	N	N	N	N
Voinovich	N	N	N	N	N
OKLAHOMA					
Nickles	N	N	N	N	N
Inhofe	N	N	N	N	N
OREGON					
Wyden	Y	Y	Y	Y	Y
Smith	N	N	N	N	N
PENNSYLVANIA					
Specter	N	N	Y	N	Y
Santorum	N	N	N	N	N
RHODE ISLAND					
Reed	Y	Y	Y	Y	Y
Chafee	N	N	N	N	N
SOUTH CAROLINA					
Thurmond	N	N	N	N	N
Hollings	Y	Y	Y	Y	Y
SOUTH DAKOTA					
Daschle	Y	Y	Y	Y	Y
Johnson	Y	Y	Y	Y	Y
TENNESSEE					
Thompson	N	N	N	N	N
Frist	N	N	N	N	N

	144	145	146	147	148
TEXAS					
Gramm	N	N	N	N	N
Hutchison	N	N	N	N	N
UTAH					
Hatch	N	N	N	N	N
Bennett	N	N	N	N	N
VERMONT					
Leahy	Y	Y	Y	Y	Y
Jeffords	N	?	?	N	N
VIRGINIA					
Warner	N	N	Y	N	N
Allen	N	N	N	N	N
WASHINGTON					
Cantwell	Y	Y	Y	Y	Y
Murray	Y	Y	Y	Y	Y
WEST VIRGINIA					
Byrd	Y	Y	Y	N	Y
Rockefeller	Y	Y	Y	Y	Y
WISCONSIN					
Kohl	Y	Y	Y	Y	Y
Feingold	Y	Y	Y	Y	Y
WYOMING					
Thomas	N	N	N	N	N
Enzi	N	N	N	N	N

ND Northern Democrats   SD Southern Democrats

Southern states - Ala., Ark., Fla., Ga., Ky., La., Miss., N.C., Okla., S.C., Tenn., Texas, Va.

144. HR 1836. Tax-Cut Reconciliation/Democratic Substitute. Daschle, D-S.D., motion to waive the Budget Act against the Grassley, R-Iowa, point of order with respect to the Daschle substitute amendment. The substitute amendment would create a new 10 percent income-tax bracket for taxable income up to $12,000 for couples and $6,000 for singles. It would also raise the standard deduction for married couples; increase the child tax credit to $1,000; eliminate the alternative minimum tax for people with incomes up to $80,000; and increase the general estate-tax exemption to $2 million per person and $4 million per couple ($4 million per person and $8 million per couple for family-owned businesses and farms). Motion rejected 41-58: R 0-49; D 41-9 (ND 36-5, SD 5-4). A three-fifths majority vote (60) of the total Senate is required to waive the Budget Act. (Subsequently, the chair upheld the point of order and the amendment fell.) May 22, 2001.

145. HR 1836. Tax-Cut Reconciliation/Motion to Commit. Conrad, D-N.D., motion to waive the Budget Act with respect to the Hatch, R-Utah, point of order against the Conrad motion to commit the bill to the Finance Committee with instructions to reduce the marginal tax-rate cuts in the top brackets and reduce the estate-tax cuts by $350 billion to establish a reserve for Social Security overhaul and debt reduction. Motion rejected 41-57: R 0-48; D 41-9 (ND 36-5, SD 5-4). A three-fifths majority vote (60) of the total Senate is required to waive the Budget Act. (Subsequently, the chair upheld the point of order and the motion fell.) May 22, 2001.

146. HR 1836. Tax-Cut Reconciliation/Social Security Benefits. Reid, D-Nev., motion to waive the Budget Act with respect to the Hatch, R-Utah, point of order against the Reid amendment. The Reid amendment would allow workers who reached the age of 65 between 1981 and 1992 to choose either a payment of $5,000 over four years or a modified benefit computation formula under a new 10-year rule governing changes in the benefit computation rules. Motion rejected 55-43: R 7-41; D 48-2 (ND 39-2, SD 9-0). A three-fifths majority vote (60) of the total Senate is required to waive the Budget Act. (Subsequently, the chair upheld the point of order and the amendment fell.) May 22, 2001.

147. HR 1836. Tax-Cut Reconciliation/Spending Limits. Levin, D-Mich., motion to waive the Budget Act with respect to the Hatch, R-Utah, point of order against the Levin amendment. The Levin amendment would direct the Treasury secretary to adjust the reductions in the top marginal tax rates if Congress exceeds spending limits set in the budget resolution. Motion rejected 41-58: R 0-49; D 41-9 (ND 35-6, SD 6-3) A three-fifths majority vote (60) of the total Senate is required to waive the Budget Act. (Subsequently, the chair upheld the point of order and the amendment fell.) May 22, 2001.

148. HR 1836. Tax-Cut Reconciliation/Water Standards. Boxer, D-Calif., motion to waive the Budget Act with respect to the Grassley, R-Iowa, point of order against the Boxer amendment. The Boxer amendment would provide tax-exempt bond authority to enable water systems to comply with arsenic standards, offset by reducing the reduction in the top tax rate. Motion rejected 49-50: R 1-48; D 48-2 (ND 40-1, SD 8-1). A three-fifths majority vote (60) of the total Senate is required to waive the Budget Act. (Subsequently, the chair upheld the point of order and the amendment fell.) May 22, 2001.

	149	150	151	152	153	154	155	156
ALABAMA								
Shelby	N	N	N	N	N	N	N	N
Sessions	N	N	N	N	N	N	N	N
ALASKA								
Stevens	N	N	N	N	N	N	N	N
Murkowski	N	N	N	N	N	N	N	N
ARIZONA								
McCain	Y	N	N	N	N	N	N	N
Kyl	N	N	N	N	N	N	N	N
ARKANSAS								
Hutchinson	N	N	N	N	N	N	N	N
Lincoln	Y	N	Y	Y	Y	Y	Y	N
CALIFORNIA								
Feinstein	Y	Y	Y	N	Y	Y	Y	Y
Boxer	Y	Y	Y	Y	Y	Y	Y	Y
COLORADO								
Campbell	N	N	N	N	N	N	N	N
Allard	N	N	N	N	N	N	N	N
CONNECTICUT								
Dodd	Y	Y	Y	Y	Y	Y	Y	Y
Lieberman	Y	Y	Y	Y	Y	Y	Y	Y
DELAWARE								
Carper	Y	Y	N	Y	Y	Y	Y	N
Biden	Y	Y	Y	Y	Y	Y	Y	Y
FLORIDA								
Graham	Y	Y	Y	Y	Y	Y	Y	N
Nelson	Y	Y	Y	Y	Y	Y	Y	N
GEORGIA								
Miller	N	N	N	N	N	N	N	N
Cleland	Y	Y	Y	Y	Y	Y	Y	Y
HAWAII								
Inouye	Y	Y	Y	Y	Y	Y	Y	Y
Akaka	Y	Y	Y	Y	Y	Y	Y	Y
IDAHO								
Craig	N	N	N	N	N	N	N	N
Crapo	N	N	N	N	N	N	N	N
ILLINOIS								
Durbin	Y	Y	Y	Y	Y	Y	Y	Y
Fitzgerald	N	N	N	N	N	N	N	N
INDIANA								
Lugar	N	N	N	N	N	N	N	N
Bayh	Y	Y	Y	Y	Y	Y	Y	Y
IOWA								
Grassley	N	N	N	N	N	N	N	N
Harkin	Y	Y	Y	Y	Y	Y	Y	Y
KANSAS								
Brownback	N	N	N	N	N	N	N	N
Roberts	N	N	N	N	N	N	N	N
KENTUCKY								
McConnell	N	N	N	N	N	N	N	N
Bunning	N	N	N	N	N	N	N	N
LOUISIANA								
Breaux	N	N	N	N	N	N	N	N
Landrieu	Y	Y	N	Y	Y	Y	Y	Y
MAINE								
Snowe	N	N	N	N	N	N	N	N
Collins	Y	N	N	N	N	N	N	N
MARYLAND								
Sarbanes	Y	Y	Y	Y	Y	Y	Y	Y
Mikulski	Y	Y	Y	Y	Y	Y	Y	Y
MASSACHUSETTS								
Kennedy	Y	Y	Y	Y	Y	Y	Y	Y
Kerry	Y	Y	Y	Y	Y	Y	Y	Y
MICHIGAN								
Levin	Y	Y	Y	Y	Y	Y	Y	Y
Stabenow	Y	Y	Y	Y	Y	Y	Y	Y
MINNESOTA								
Wellstone	Y	Y	Y	Y	Y	Y	Y	Y
Dayton	Y	Y	Y	Y	Y	Y	Y	Y
MISSISSIPPI								
Cochran	N	N	N	N	N	N	N	N
Lott	N	N	N	N	N	N	N	N
MISSOURI								
Bond	N	N	N	N	N	N	N	N
Carnahan	Y	Y	Y	Y	Y	Y	Y	Y
MONTANA								
Baucus	N	N	N	N	N	N	N	N
Burns	N	N	N	N	N	N	N	N
NEBRASKA								
Nelson	N	Y	N	N	N	N	N	N
Hagel	N	N	N	N	N	N	N	N
NEVADA								
Reid	Y	Y	Y	Y	Y	Y	Y	Y
Ensign	N	N	N	N	N	N	N	N
NEW HAMPSHIRE								
Smith	N	N	N	N	N	N	N	N
Gregg	N	N	N	N	N	N	N	N
NEW JERSEY								
Corzine	Y	Y	Y	Y	Y	Y	Y	Y
Torricelli	Y	N	N	Y	Y	Y	Y	Y
NEW MEXICO								
Domenici	N	N	N	N	N	N	N	N
Bingaman	Y	Y	Y	Y	Y	Y	Y	N
NEW YORK								
Clinton	Y	Y	Y	Y	Y	Y	Y	Y
Schumer	Y	Y	Y	Y	Y	Y	Y	Y
NORTH CAROLINA								
Helms	N	N	N	N	N	N	N	N
Edwards	Y	Y	Y	Y	Y	Y	Y	Y
NORTH DAKOTA								
Conrad	Y	Y	Y	Y	Y	Y	Y	Y
Dorgan	Y	Y	Y	Y	Y	Y	Y	Y
OHIO								
DeWine	N	N	N	N	N	N	N	N
Voinovich	N	N	N	N	N	N	N	N
OKLAHOMA								
Nickles	N	N	N	N	N	N	N	N
Inhofe	N	N	N	N	N	N	N	N
OREGON								
Wyden	Y	N	Y	Y	Y	Y	Y	Y
Smith	N	N	N	N	N	N	N	N
PENNSYLVANIA								
Specter	Y	N	N	N	N	N	N	N
Santorum	N	N	N	N	N	N	N	N
RHODE ISLAND								
Reed	Y	Y	Y	Y	Y	Y	Y	Y
Chafee	Y	N	N	N	N	N	N	N
SOUTH CAROLINA								
Thurmond	N	N	N	N	N	N	N	N
Hollings	Y	Y	Y	Y	Y	Y	Y	Y
SOUTH DAKOTA								
Daschle	Y	Y	Y	Y	Y	Y	Y	Y
Johnson	Y	Y	Y	Y	Y	Y	Y	Y
TENNESSEE								
Thompson	N	N	N	N	N	N	N	N
Frist	N	N	N	N	N	N	N	N
TEXAS								
Gramm	N	N	N	N	N	N	N	N
Hutchison	N	N	N	N	N	N	N	N
UTAH								
Hatch	N	N	N	N	N	N	N	N
Bennett	N	N	N	N	N	N	N	N
VERMONT								
Leahy	Y	Y	Y	Y	Y	Y	Y	Y
Jeffords	N	N	N	N	N	N	N	N
VIRGINIA								
Warner	N	N	N	N	N	N	N	N
Allen	N	N	N	N	N	N	N	N
WASHINGTON								
Cantwell	Y	Y	Y	Y	Y	Y	Y	Y
Murray	Y	Y	Y	Y	Y	Y	Y	Y
WEST VIRGINIA								
Byrd	Y	N	Y	Y	Y	Y	Y	Y
Rockefeller	Y	Y	Y	Y	Y	Y	Y	Y
WISCONSIN								
Kohl	Y	?	?	?	?	?	?	?
Feingold	Y	Y	Y	Y	Y	Y	Y	Y
WYOMING								
Thomas	N	N	N	N	N	N	N	N
Enzi	N	N	N	N	N	N	N	N

Key

Y	Voted for (yea).
#	Paired for.
+	Announced for.
N	Voted against (nay).
X	Paired against.
–	Announced against.
P	Voted "present."
C	Voted "present" to avoid possible conflict of interest.
?	Did not vote or otherwise make a position known.

Democrats **Republicans**
Independents

ND Northern Democrats   SD Southern Democrats

Southern states - Ala., Ark., Fla., Ga., Ky., La., Miss., N.C., Okla., S.C., Tenn., Texas, Va.

149. HR 1836. Tax-Cut Reconciliation/Margin Rate Reduction Limit. Daschle, D-S.D., amendment that would limit the tax reduction in the 39.6 percent marginal rate bracket to 1 percentage point and increase the maximum taxable income subject to the 15 percent rate, effective one day after enactment. Rejected 50-50: R 4-46; D 46-4 (ND 39-2, SD 7-2). May 22, 2001.

150. HR 1836. Tax-Cut Reconciliation/State Estate Tax. Nelson, D-Fla., motion to waive the Budget Act with respect to the Grassley, R-Iowa, point of order against the Nelson amendment. The Nelson amendment would provide a proportionate reduction in the credit for the state estate tax and direct the Treasury secretary to adjust the highest tax rate as necessary. Motion rejected 42-57: R 0-50; D 42-7 (ND 36-4, SD 6-3). A three-fifths majority vote (60) of the total Senate is required to waive the Budget Act. (Subsequently, the chair upheld the point of order and the amendment fell.) May 22, 2001.

151. HR 1836. Tax-Cut Reconciliation/Estate-Tax Exemption. Levin, D-Mich., amendment that would accelerate the increase in the estate-tax exemption to $4 million per individual, to take effect in fiscal 2002, offset by adjusting the reduction in the top tax rate. Rejected 42-57: R 0-50; D 42-7 (ND 36-4, SD 6-3). May 22, 2001.

152. HR 1836. Tax-Cut Reconciliation/Tuition Deduction. Levin, D-Mich., amendment that would provide for the full amount of the tuition deduction effective in fiscal 2002, offset by adjusting the top income-tax rate. Rejected 44-55: R 0-50; D 44-5 (ND 37-3, SD 7-2). May 22, 2001.

153. HR 1836. Tax-Cut Reconciliation/Pell Grant Funding. Kennedy, D-Mass., motion to waive the Budget Act with respect to the Grassley, R-Iowa, point of order against the Kennedy amendment. The Kennedy amendment would condition the reductions in the top marginal income-tax rate on the appropriation of the funding required to raise the maximum Pell Grant to the authorized level of $4,250 for the 2002-03 school year, and $400 each subsequent year for eight years. Motion rejected 45-54: R 0-50; D 45-4 (ND 38-2, SD 7-2). A three-fifths majority vote (60) of the total Senate is required to waive the Budget Act. (Subsequently, the chair upheld the point of order and the amendment fell.) May 22, 2001.

154. HR 1836. Tax-Cut Reconciliation/Head Start. Kennedy, D-Mass., motion to waive the Budget Act with respect to the Kyl, R-Ariz., point of order against the Kennedy amendment. The Kennedy amendment would condition the reductions in the top marginal income-tax rate on full funding for Head Start programs. Motion rejected 45-54: R 0-50; D 45-4 (ND 38-2, SD 7-2). A three-fifths majority vote (60) of the total Senate is required to waive the Budget Act. (Subsequently, the chair upheld the point of order and the amendment fell.) May 22, 2001.

155. HR 1836. Tax-Cut Reconciliation/HOPE Scholarship Tax Credit. Kennedy, D-Mass., amendment that would expand the HOPE Scholarship tax credit to include other education expenses, offset by decreasing the reductions in the top bracket. Rejected 43-56: R 0-50; D 43-6 (ND 37-3, SD 6-3). May 22, 2001.

156. HR 1836. Tax-Cut Reconciliation/Motion To Commit. Wellstone, D-Minn., motion to commit the bill to the Finance Committee with instructions to add language providing for a fully funded HOPE tax credit beginning in fiscal 2002, and to strike the reduction in the 39.6 percent rate bracket. Rejected 39-60: R 0-50; D 39-10 (ND 35-5, SD 4-5). May 22, 2001.

	157	158	159	160	161	162
ALABAMA						
Shelby	N	N	Y	N	Y	N
Sessions	N	N	Y	N	Y	N
ALASKA						
Stevens	N	N	Y	N	Y	N
Murkowski	N	N	Y	N	Y	N
ARIZONA						
McCain	N	N	?	N	N	N
Kyl	N	N	N	N	Y	N
ARKANSAS						
Hutchinson	N	N	Y	N	Y	N
Lincoln	Y	N	Y	Y	N	Y
CALIFORNIA						
Feinstein	N	N	Y	Y	N	Y
Boxer	Y	Y	Y	Y	N	Y
COLORADO						
Campbell	N	N	Y	N	Y	N
Allard	N	N	Y	N	Y	N
CONNECTICUT						
Dodd	Y	Y	Y	Y	N	Y
Lieberman	Y	Y	Y	Y	N	Y
DELAWARE						
Carper	Y	Y	Y	Y	N	Y
Biden	Y	Y	Y	Y	N	Y
FLORIDA						
Graham	Y	Y	Y	Y	N	Y
Nelson	Y	N	Y	Y	N	Y
GEORGIA						
Miller	N	N	Y	N	N	N
Cleland	N	N	Y	Y	N	Y
HAWAII						
Inouye	Y	Y	Y	Y	N	Y
Akaka	Y	Y	Y	Y	N	Y
IDAHO						
Craig	N	N	Y	N	Y	N
Crapo	N	N	Y	N	Y	N
ILLINOIS						
Durbin	Y	Y	Y	Y	N	Y
Fitzgerald	N	N	Y	N	Y	N
INDIANA						
Lugar	N	N	Y	N	Y	N
Bayh	Y	N	Y	Y	N	Y

	157	158	159	160	161	162
IOWA						
Grassley	N	N	Y	N	Y	N
Harkin	Y	Y	Y	Y	N	Y
KANSAS						
Brownback	N	N	Y	N	Y	N
Roberts	N	N	Y	N	Y	N
KENTUCKY						
McConnell	N	N	Y	N	Y	N
Bunning	N	N	Y	N	Y	N
LOUISIANA						
Breaux	N	Y	Y	N	N	N
Landrieu	Y	Y	Y	Y	N	Y
MAINE						
Snowe	N	N	Y	N	Y	N
Collins	N	N	Y	N	Y	N
MARYLAND						
Sarbanes	Y	Y	Y	Y	N	Y
Mikulski	Y	Y	Y	Y	N	Y
MASSACHUSETTS						
Kennedy	Y	Y	Y	Y	N	Y
Kerry	Y	Y	Y	Y	N	Y
MICHIGAN						
Levin	Y	Y	Y	Y	N	Y
Stabenow	Y	Y	Y	Y	N	Y
MINNESOTA						
Wellstone	Y	Y	Y	Y	N	Y
Dayton	Y	Y	Y	Y	N	Y
MISSISSIPPI						
Cochran	N	N	Y	N	Y	N
Lott	N	N	Y	N	Y	N
MISSOURI						
Bond	N	N	Y	N	Y	N
Carnahan	Y	Y	Y	Y	N	Y
MONTANA						
Baucus	N	Y	Y	N	Y	N
Burns	N	N	Y	N	Y	N
NEBRASKA						
Nelson	N	N	Y	N	N	N
Hagel	N	N	Y	N	Y	N
NEVADA						
Reid	Y	Y	Y	Y	N	Y
Ensign	N	N	Y	N	Y	N

	157	158	159	160	161	162
NEW HAMPSHIRE						
Smith	N	N	Y	N	Y	N
Gregg	N	N	Y	N	Y	N
NEW JERSEY						
Corzine	Y	Y	Y	Y	N	Y
Torricelli	Y	Y	Y	Y	N	Y
NEW MEXICO						
Domenici	N	N	Y	N	Y	N
Bingaman	Y	Y	Y	Y	N	Y
NEW YORK						
Clinton	Y	Y	Y	Y	N	Y
Schumer	Y	Y	Y	Y	N	Y
NORTH CAROLINA						
Helms	N	N	?	N	Y	N
Edwards	Y	Y	Y	Y	N	Y
NORTH DAKOTA						
Conrad	Y	Y	Y	Y	N	Y
Dorgan	Y	Y	Y	Y	N	Y
OHIO						
DeWine	N	N	Y	N	Y	N
Voinovich	N	N	Y	N	Y	N
OKLAHOMA						
Nickles	N	N	N	N	Y	N
Inhofe	N	N	Y	N	Y	N
OREGON						
Wyden	Y	N	Y	Y	N	Y
Smith	N	N	Y	N	Y	N
PENNSYLVANIA						
Specter	N	N	Y	N	Y	Y
Santorum	N	N	Y	N	Y	N
RHODE ISLAND						
Reed	Y	Y	Y	Y	N	Y
Chafee	N	Y	Y	N	Y	N
SOUTH CAROLINA						
Thurmond	N	N	Y	N	Y	N
Hollings	Y	Y	Y	Y	N	Y
SOUTH DAKOTA						
Daschle	Y	Y	Y	Y	N	Y
Johnson	Y	Y	Y	Y	N	Y
TENNESSEE						
Thompson	N	N	Y	N	Y	N
Frist	N	N	Y	N	Y	N

	157	158	159	160	161	162
TEXAS						
Gramm	N	N	N	N	Y	N
Hutchison	N	N	Y	N	Y	N
UTAH						
Hatch	N	N	Y	N	Y	N
Bennett	N	N	Y	N	Y	N
VERMONT						
Leahy	Y	Y	Y	Y	N	Y
Jeffords	N	Y	Y	N	Y	N
VIRGINIA						
Warner	N	N	Y	N	Y	N
Allen	N	N	Y	N	Y	N
WASHINGTON						
Cantwell	Y	Y	Y	Y	N	Y
Murray	Y	N	Y	Y	N	Y
WEST VIRGINIA						
Byrd	Y	Y	Y	Y	N	Y
Rockefeller	Y	Y	Y	Y	N	Y
WISCONSIN						
Kohl	?	?	Y	N	Y	N
Feingold	Y	Y	Y	Y	N	Y
WYOMING						
Thomas	N	N	Y	N	Y	N
Enzi	N	N	N	Y	N	N

Key

Y	Voted for (yea).
#	Paired for.
+	Announced for.
N	Voted against (nay).
X	Paired against.
–	Announced against.
P	Voted "present."
C	Voted "present" to avoid possible conflict of interest.
?	Did not vote or otherwise make a position known.

Democrats *Republicans*
Independents

ND Northern Democrats   SD Southern Democrats

Southern states - Ala., Ark., Fla., Ga., Ky., La., Miss., N.C., Okla., S.C., Tenn., Texas, Va.

157. HR 1836. Tax-Cut Reconciliation/Teacher and Health Professional Tax Credit. Harkin, D-Iowa, motion to waive the Budget Act with respect to the Kyl, R-Ariz., point of order against the Harkin amendment. The Harkin amendment would make K-12 teachers, Head Start teachers, nurses and health professionals working in areas with a shortage of such professionals eligible for a 50 percent tax credit for repaying education loans during their employment in those professions. The credit would be capped at $2,000, and offset by decreasing the reduction in the 39.6 percentage tax bracket. Motion rejected 43-56: R 0-50; D 43-6 (ND 37-3, SD 6-3). A three-fifths majority vote (60) of the total Senate is required to waive the Budget Act. (Subsequently, the chair upheld the point of order and the amendment fell.) May 22, 2001.

158. HR 1836. Tax-Cut Reconciliation/Debt Reduction. Conrad, D-N.D., amendment that would eliminate the repeal of the estate tax and use the savings to reduce the debt. Rejected 42-57: R 2-48; D 40-9 (ND 35-5, SD 5-4). May 22, 2001.

159. HR 1836. Tax-Cut Reconciliation/Child Tax Credit. Snowe, R-Maine, amendment that would express the sense of the Senate that the refundable child tax credit provisions in the bill should be maintained as a part of the final legislative package. Adopted 94-4: R 44-4; D 50-0 (ND 41-0, SD 9-0). May 23, 2001.

160. HR 1836. Tax-Cut Reconciliation/Motion to Commit. Stabenow, D-Mich., motion to waive the Budget Act with respect to the Grassley, R-Iowa, point of order against the Stabenow motion to commit the bill to the Finance Committee with instructions to include an amendment that would ensure the provisions in the bill do not result in an on-budget surplus for any fiscal year that is less than the surplus for that year in the Federal Hospital Insurance Trust Fund, and that establishes a 60-vote point of order prohibiting any legislation or motion that uses Trust fund money for any purpose other than providing Part A benefits under the Medicare program. Motion rejected 46-54: R 0-50; D 46-4 (ND 39-2, SD 7-2). A three-fifths majority vote (60) of the total Senate is required to waive the Budget Act. (Subsequently, the chair upheld the point of order and the motion fell.) May 23, 2001.

161. HR 1836. Tax-Cut Reconciliation/Long Term Care Insurance. Grassley, R-Iowa, motion to waive the Budget Act with respect to the Graham, D-Fla., point of order against the Grassley amendment to the Graham amendment. The Grassley amendment would provide a deduction for eligible long-term care insurance premiums that would be funded using the surplus. Motion rejected 49-51: R 49-1; D 0-50 (ND 0-41, SD 0-9). A three-fifths majority vote (60) of the total Senate is required to waive the Budget Act. (Subsequently, the chair upheld the point of order and the Grassley amendment fell.) May 23, 2001.

162. HR 1836. Tax-Cut Reconciliation/Long Term Care Insurance. Graham, D-Fla., motion to waive the Budget Act with respect to the Grassley, R-Iowa, point of order against the Graham amendment. The Graham amendment would provide a deduction for eligible long-term care insurance premiums that would be offset by slowing the reduction in the 39.6 percent tax rate. Motion rejected 47-53: R 1-49; D 46-4 (ND 39-2, SD 7-2). A three-fifths majority vote (60) of the total Senate is required to waive the Budget Act. (Subsequently, the chair upheld the point of order and the amendment fell.) May 23, 2001.

	163	164	165	166	167	168	169
ALABAMA							
Shelby	N	Y	Y	Y	Y	Y	Y
Sessions	N	Y	Y	Y	Y	Y	Y
ALASKA							
Stevens	N	Y	Y	Y	Y	Y	Y
Murkowski	N	Y	Y	Y	Y	Y	Y
ARIZONA							
McCain	N	Y	Y	Y	Y	Y	Y
Kyl	N	Y	Y	Y	Y	Y	Y
ARKANSAS							
Hutchinson	N	Y	Y	Y	Y	Y	Y
Lincoln	Y	Y	Y	Y	N	Y	Y
CALIFORNIA							
Feinstein	Y	Y	N	Y	N	Y	Y
Boxer	Y	Y	N	Y	N	Y	Y
COLORADO							
Campbell	N	Y	Y	Y	Y	Y	Y
Allard	N	Y	Y	Y	Y	Y	Y
CONNECTICUT							
Dodd	Y	Y	N	Y	N	Y	Y
Lieberman	Y	Y	N	Y	N	Y	Y
DELAWARE							
Carper	Y	Y	N	Y	N	Y	Y
Biden	Y	Y	N	Y	N	Y	Y
FLORIDA							
Graham	Y	Y	N	Y	N	Y	Y
Nelson	Y	Y	N	Y	N	Y	Y
GEORGIA							
Miller	N	Y	Y	Y	Y	Y	Y
Cleland	Y	Y	Y	Y	N	Y	Y
HAWAII							
Inouye	Y	Y	N	Y	N	Y	Y
Akaka	Y	Y	N	Y	N	Y	Y
IDAHO							
Craig	N	Y	Y	Y	Y	Y	Y
Crapo	N	Y	Y	Y	Y	Y	Y
ILLINOIS							
Durbin	Y	Y	N	Y	N	Y	Y
Fitzgerald	N	Y	Y	Y	Y	Y	Y
INDIANA							
Lugar	N	Y	Y	Y	Y	Y	Y
Bayh	Y	Y	N	Y	N	Y	Y

	163	164	165	166	167	168	169
IOWA							
Grassley	N	Y	Y	Y	Y	Y	Y
Harkin	Y	Y	N	Y	N	Y	Y
KANSAS							
Brownback	N	Y	Y	Y	Y	Y	Y
Roberts	N	Y	Y	Y	Y	Y	Y
KENTUCKY							
McConnell	N	Y	Y	Y	Y	Y	Y
Bunning	N	Y	Y	Y	Y	Y	Y
LOUISIANA							
Breaux	N	Y	Y	Y	N	Y	Y
Landrieu	Y	Y	Y	Y	N	Y	Y
MAINE							
Snowe	N	Y	Y	Y	Y	Y	Y
Collins	N	Y	Y	Y	Y	Y	Y
MARYLAND							
Sarbanes	Y	Y	N	Y	N	Y	Y
Mikulski	Y	Y	N	Y	N	Y	Y
MASSACHUSETTS							
Kennedy	Y	Y	N	Y	N	Y	Y
Kerry	Y	Y	N	Y	N	Y	Y
MICHIGAN							
Levin	Y	Y	N	Y	N	Y	Y
Stabenow	Y	Y	N	Y	N	Y	Y
MINNESOTA							
Wellstone	Y	Y	N	Y	N	Y	Y
Dayton	Y	Y	N	Y	N	Y	Y
MISSISSIPPI							
Cochran	N	Y	Y	Y	Y	Y	Y
Lott	N	Y	Y	Y	Y	Y	Y
MISSOURI							
Bond	N	Y	Y	Y	Y	Y	Y
Carnahan	Y	Y	Y	Y	N	Y	Y
MONTANA							
Baucus	N	Y	Y	Y	Y	Y	Y
Burns	N	Y	Y	Y	Y	Y	Y
NEBRASKA							
Nelson	N	Y	Y	Y	Y	Y	Y
Hagel	N	Y	Y	Y	Y	Y	Y
NEVADA							
Reid	Y	Y	N	Y	N	Y	Y
Ensign	N	Y	Y	?	Y	Y	Y

	163	164	165	166	167	168	169
NEW HAMPSHIRE							
Smith	N	Y	Y	Y	Y	Y	Y
Gregg	N	Y	Y	Y	Y	Y	Y
NEW JERSEY							
Corzine	Y	Y	N	Y	N	Y	Y
Torricelli	Y	Y	Y	Y	N	Y	Y
NEW MEXICO							
Domenici	N	Y	Y	Y	Y	Y	Y
Bingaman	Y	Y	N	Y	N	Y	Y
NEW YORK							
Clinton	Y	Y	N	Y	N	N	N
Schumer	Y	Y	N	Y	N	Y	Y
NORTH CAROLINA							
Helms	N	Y	Y	Y	Y	Y	Y
Edwards	Y	Y	N	Y	N	Y	Y
NORTH DAKOTA							
Conrad	Y	Y	N	Y	N	Y	Y
Dorgan	Y	Y	N	Y	N	Y	Y
OHIO							
DeWine	N	Y	Y	Y	Y	Y	Y
Voinovich	N	Y	Y	Y	Y	Y	Y
OKLAHOMA							
Nickles	N	N	Y	Y	Y	Y	Y
Inhofe	N	Y	Y	Y	Y	Y	Y
OREGON							
Wyden	Y	Y	N	Y	N	Y	Y
Smith	N	Y	Y	Y	Y	Y	Y
PENNSYLVANIA							
Specter	N	Y	Y	Y	Y	Y	Y
Santorum	N	Y	Y	Y	Y	Y	Y
RHODE ISLAND							
Reed	Y	Y	N	Y	N	Y	Y
Chafee	N	Y	Y	Y	Y	Y	Y
SOUTH CAROLINA							
Thurmond	N	Y	Y	Y	Y	Y	Y
Hollings	Y	Y	N	Y	N	Y	Y
SOUTH DAKOTA							
Daschle	Y	Y	N	Y	N	Y	Y
Johnson	Y	Y	Y	Y	N	Y	Y
TENNESSEE							
Thompson	N	Y	Y	Y	Y	Y	Y
Frist	N	Y	Y	Y	Y	Y	?

	163	164	165	166	167	168	169
TEXAS							
Gramm	N	Y	Y	Y	Y	Y	Y
Hutchison	N	Y	Y	Y	Y	Y	Y
UTAH							
Hatch	N	Y	Y	Y	Y	Y	Y
Bennett	N	Y	Y	Y	Y	Y	Y
VERMONT							
Leahy	Y	Y	N	Y	N	Y	Y
Jeffords	N	Y	Y	Y	?	?	?
VIRGINIA							
Warner	N	Y	Y	Y	Y	Y	Y
Allen	N	Y	Y	Y	Y	Y	Y
WASHINGTON							
Cantwell	Y	Y	N	Y	N	Y	Y
Murray	Y	Y	N	Y	N	Y	Y
WEST VIRGINIA							
Byrd	Y	Y	N	Y	N	Y	Y
Rockefeller	Y	Y	N	Y	?	?	?
WISCONSIN							
Kohl	Y	Y	Y	Y	N	?	?
Feingold	Y	N	N	N	N	Y	Y
WYOMING							
Thomas	N	Y	Y	Y	Y	Y	Y
Enzi	N	Y	Y	Y	Y	Y	Y

Key

Y	Voted for (yea).
#	Paired for.
+	Announced for.
N	Voted against (nay).
X	Paired against.
−	Announced against.
P	Voted "present."
C	Voted "present" to avoid possible conflict of interest.
?	Did not vote or otherwise make a position known.

Democrats   **Republicans**
Independents

ND Northern Democrats   SD Southern Democrats

Southern states - Ala., Ark., Fla., Ga., Ky., La., Miss., N.C., Okla., S.C., Tenn., Texas, Va.

163. HR 1836. Tax-Cut Reconciliation/Alternative Minimum Tax. Schumer, D-N.Y., motion to waive the Budget Act with respect to the Gramm, R-Texas, point of order against the Schumer amendment. The Schumer amendment would index the Alternative Minimum Tax, offset by slowing the reduction in the highest marginal tax rate. Motion rejected 46-54: R 0-50; D 46-4 (ND 39-2, SD 7-2). A three-fifths majority vote (60) of the total Senate is required to waive the Budget Act. (Subsequently, the chair upheld the point of order and the amendment fell.) May 23, 2001.

164. HR 1836. Tax-Cut Reconciliation/Teacher Tax Credit. Collins, R-Maine, amendment that would provide an above-the-line deduction of up to $500 for qualified professional development expenses of elementary and secondary school teachers. It also would allow a tax credit of up to $250 for elementary and secondary school teachers who provide classroom materials. Adopted 98-2: R 49-1; D 49-1 (ND 40-1, SD 9-0). May 23, 2001.

165. HR 1836. Tax-Cut Reconciliation/Passage. Passage of the bill that would reduce income-tax rates and make other tax cuts totaling $1.35 trillion over 11 years. The bill would reduce rates in the top four income-tax brackets, retain the 15 percent bracket and create a new 10 percent bracket. It would set the standard deduction for married couples and the income eligible for the 15 percent rate bracket at double that of singles beginning in 2005; gradually repeal the estate tax; double the $500 per child tax credit by 2011; and make the research and development credit permanent. Annual limits on contributions to Individual Retirement Accounts would increase to $5,000 by 2011. Passed 62-38: R 50-0; D 12-38 (ND 7-34, SD 5-4). A "yea" was a vote in support of the president's position. May 23, 2001.

166. Baker Nomination/Confirmation. Confirmation of President Bush's nomination of former Sen. Howard H. Baker Jr. of Tennessee to be U.S. ambassador to Japan. Confirmed 99-0: R 49-0; D 50-0 (ND 41-0, SD 9-0). A "yea" was a vote in support of the president's position. May 23, 2001.

167. Olson Nomination/Confirmation. Confirmation of President Bush's nomination of Theodore B. Olson of Washington, D.C., to be U.S. Solicitor General. Confirmed 51-47: R 49-0; D 2-47 (ND 1-39, SD 1-8). A "yea" was a vote in support of the president's position. May 24, 2001.

168. Dinh Nomination/Confirmation. Confirmation of President Bush's nomination of Viet D. Dinh of Washington, D.C., to be assistant attorney general. Confirmed 96-1: R 49-0; D 47-1 (ND 38-1, SD 9-0). A "yea" was a vote in support of the president's position. May 24, 2001.

169. Chertoff Nomination/Confirmation. Confirmation of President Bush's nomination of Michael Chertoff of New Jersey to be assistant attorney general. Confirmed 95-1: R 48-0; D 47-1 (ND 38-1, SD 9-0). A "yea" was a vote in support of the president's position. May 24, 2001.

	170
ALABAMA	
Shelby	Y
Sessions	Y
ALASKA	
Stevens	Y
Murkowski	Y
ARIZONA	
McCain	N
Kyl	Y
ARKANSAS	
Hutchinson	Y
Lincoln	Y
CALIFORNIA	
Feinstein	Y
Boxer	–
COLORADO	
Campbell	Y
Allard	Y
CONNECTICUT	
Dodd	N
Lieberman	N
DELAWARE	
Carper	N
Biden	N
FLORIDA	
Graham	N
Nelson	N
GEORGIA	
Miller	Y
Cleland	Y
HAWAII	
Inouye	N
Akaka	X
IDAHO	
Craig	Y
Crapo	Y
ILLINOIS	
Durbin	N
Fitzgerald	Y
INDIANA	
Lugar	Y
Bayh	N

	170
IOWA	
Grassley	Y
Harkin	–
KANSAS	
Brownback	Y
Roberts	Y
KENTUCKY	
McConnell	Y
Bunning	Y
LOUISIANA	
Breaux	Y
Landrieu	Y
MAINE	
Snowe	Y
Collins	Y
MARYLAND	
Sarbanes	N
Mikulski	N
MASSACHUSETTS	
Kennedy	N
Kerry	–
MICHIGAN	
Levin	N
Stabenow	N
MINNESOTA	
Wellstone	N
Dayton	N
MISSISSIPPI	
Cochran	Y
Lott	Y
MISSOURI	
Bond	Y
Carnahan	Y
MONTANA	
Baucus	Y
Burns	Y
NEBRASKA	
Nelson	Y
Hagel	Y
NEVADA	
Reid	N
Ensign	Y

	170
NEW HAMPSHIRE	
Smith	Y
Gregg	Y
NEW JERSEY	
Corzine	N
Torricelli	Y
NEW MEXICO	
Domenici	#
Bingaman	X
NEW YORK	
Clinton	N
Schumer	N
NORTH CAROLINA	
Helms	Y
Edwards	N
NORTH DAKOTA	
Conrad	N
Dorgan	N
OHIO	
DeWine	Y
Voinovich	Y
OKLAHOMA	
Nickles	Y
Inhofe	Y
OREGON	
Wyden	N
Smith	Y
PENNSYLVANIA	
Specter	Y
Santorum	Y
RHODE ISLAND	
Reed	N
Chafee	N
SOUTH CAROLINA	
Thurmond	Y
Hollings	N
SOUTH DAKOTA	
Daschle	N
Johnson	Y
TENNESSEE	
Thompson	Y
Frist	Y

	170
TEXAS	
Gramm	Y
Hutchison	Y
UTAH	
Hatch	Y
Bennett	Y
VERMONT	
Leahy	–
Jeffords	Y
VIRGINIA	
Warner	Y
Allen	Y
WASHINGTON	
Cantwell	N
Murray	?
WEST VIRGINIA	
Byrd	N
Rockefeller	N
WISCONSIN	
Kohl	Y
Feingold	N
WYOMING	
Thomas	Y
Enzi	#

ND Northern Democrats   SD Southern Democrats

Southern states - Ala., Ark., Fla., Ga., Ky., La., Miss., N.C., Okla., S.C., Tenn., Texas, Va.

170. HR 1836. Tax Cut Reconciliation Bill/Conference Report. Adoption of the conference report on the bill that would reduce taxes by $1.35 trillion through fiscal 2011 through income tax rate cuts, relief of the "marriage penalty," a phaseout of the federal estate tax, doubling the child tax credit, and providing incentives for retirement savings. A new 10 percent tax rate would be created retroactive to Jan. 1. The bill would double the $500-per-child tax credit by 2010 and make it refundable; raise the estate tax exemption to $1 million in 2002 and repeal the tax in 2010; increase the standard deduction for married couples to double that of singles over five years, beginning in 2005; and increase annual contributions limits for Individual Retirement Accounts. The bill's provisions would expire Dec. 31, 2010. Adopted (thus cleared for the president) 58-33: R 46-2; D 12-31 (ND 7-27, SD 5-4). A "yea" was a vote in support of the president's position. May 26, 2001.

	171	172	173	174	175	176
ALABAMA						
Shelby	N	N	Y	N	Y	N
Sessions	N	N	Y	N	Y	N
ALASKA						
Stevens	N	N	Y	N	Y	N
Murkowski	N	N	Y	N	Y	N
ARIZONA						
McCain	N	N	Y	Y	Y	?
Kyl	N	N	Y	N	Y	N
ARKANSAS						
Hutchinson	N	N	Y	N	Y	N
Lincoln	Y	Y	N	Y	Y	N
CALIFORNIA						
Feinstein	Y	Y	N	N	Y	N
Boxer	Y	Y	N	Y	Y	+
COLORADO						
Campbell	N	N	N	N	Y	N
Allard	N	N	Y	N	Y	N
CONNECTICUT						
Dodd	Y	Y	N	Y	Y	Y
Lieberman	Y	N	Y	N	Y	N
DELAWARE						
Carper	Y	N	Y	N	Y	N
Biden	Y	Y	N	Y	Y	Y
FLORIDA						
Graham	Y	Y	N	Y	Y	Y
Nelson	Y	Y	N	Y	Y	N
GEORGIA						
Miller	Y	N	Y	Y	Y	?
Cleland	Y	N	Y	Y	Y	N
HAWAII						
Inouye	Y	Y	N	N	Y	N
Akaka	Y	Y	N	N	Y	Y
IDAHO						
Craig	N	N	Y	N	Y	N
Crapo	?	?	?	?	?	?
ILLINOIS						
Durbin	Y	Y	N	Y	Y	Y
Fitzgerald	N	N	Y	N	Y	N
INDIANA						
Lugar	N	Y	N	N	Y	N
Bayh	Y	N	Y	Y	Y	N

	171	172	173	174	175	176
IOWA						
Grassley	N	N	Y	N	Y	N
Harkin	Y	Y	N	Y	Y	Y
KANSAS						
Brownback	N	Y	N	N	Y	N
Roberts	Y	N	N	N	Y	N
KENTUCKY						
McConnell	N	N	Y	N	Y	N
Bunning	N	Y	N	N	Y	N
LOUISIANA						
Breaux	Y	Y	N	Y	Y	N
Landrieu	Y	Y	N	N	Y	N
MAINE						
Snowe	Y	N	Y	N	Y	N
Collins	Y	Y	Y	N	Y	N
MARYLAND						
Sarbanes	Y	Y	N	Y	Y	Y
Mikulski	Y	Y	N	Y	Y	N
MASSACHUSETTS						
Kennedy	Y	Y	N	Y	Y	Y
Kerry	Y	Y	N	Y	Y	Y
MICHIGAN						
Levin	Y	Y	N	Y	Y	Y
Stabenow	Y	Y	N	Y	Y	Y
MINNESOTA						
Wellstone	Y	Y	N	Y	Y	Y
Dayton	Y	Y	N	Y	Y	Y
MISSISSIPPI						
Cochran	Y	Y	N	N	Y	N
Lott	N	N	Y	N	Y	N
MISSOURI						
Bond	N	N	Y	N	Y	N
Carnahan	Y	Y	Y	Y	Y	Y
MONTANA						
Baucus	Y	Y	N	Y	Y	N
Burns	N	Y	N	N	+	N
NEBRASKA						
Nelson	Y	N	Y	Y	Y	N
Hagel	N	N	Y	N	Y	N
NEVADA						
Reid	Y	Y	N	Y	Y	Y
Ensign	N	Y	N	N	Y	N

	171	172	173	174	175	176
NEW HAMPSHIRE						
Smith	N	N	Y	N	Y	N
Gregg	N	N	Y	N	Y	N
NEW JERSEY						
Corzine	Y	Y	N	Y	Y	Y
Torricelli	Y	Y	N	Y	Y	?
NEW MEXICO						
Domenici	N	Y	N	N	Y	N
Bingaman	Y	Y	N	N	Y	N
NEW YORK						
Clinton	Y	Y	N	Y	Y	Y
Schumer	Y	Y	N	Y	Y	Y
NORTH CAROLINA						
Helms	N	N	Y	N	Y	N
Edwards	Y	Y	N	Y	Y	N
NORTH DAKOTA						
Conrad	Y	Y	N	Y	Y	N
Dorgan	Y	Y	N	Y	Y	N
OHIO						
DeWine	Y	N	Y	N	Y	N
Voinovich	N	N	Y	Y	Y	N
OKLAHOMA						
Nickles	N	N	Y	N	Y	N
Inhofe	N	N	Y	N	Y	N
OREGON						
Wyden	Y	Y	N	Y	Y	N
Smith	N	Y	N	Y	Y	N
PENNSYLVANIA						
Specter	Y	Y	N	Y	Y	N
Santorum	N	N	Y	N	Y	N
RHODE ISLAND						
Reed	Y	Y	N	Y	Y	Y
Chafee	Y	Y	N	N	Y	N
SOUTH CAROLINA						
Thurmond	–	Y	Y	N	Y	N
Hollings	Y	Y	N	Y	Y	Y
SOUTH DAKOTA						
Daschle	Y	Y	N	Y	Y	N
Johnson	Y	Y	N	N	Y	N
TENNESSEE						
Thompson	N	Y	N	Y	Y	N
Frist	N	N	Y	N	Y	N

Key

Y	Voted for (yea).
#	Paired for.
+	Announced for.
N	Voted against (nay).
X	Paired against.
–	Announced against.
P	Voted "present."
C	Voted "present" to avoid possible conflict of interest.
?	Did not vote or otherwise make a position known.

Democrats **Republicans**
Independents

	171	172	173	174	175	176
TEXAS						
Gramm	N	N	Y	N	Y	N
Hutchison	N	N	Y	N	Y	N
UTAH						
Hatch	N	+	?	–	+	–
Bennett	N	Y	Y	N	Y	N
VERMONT						
Leahy	Y	Y	N	Y	Y	Y
Jeffords [1]	N	Y	N	N	Y	N
VIRGINIA						
Warner	?	N	Y	N	Y	N
Allen	?	N	Y	Y	Y	N
WASHINGTON						
Cantwell	Y	Y	N	Y	Y	Y
Murray	Y	Y	N	Y	Y	Y
WEST VIRGINIA						
Byrd	Y	Y	N	Y	Y	N
Rockefeller	Y	Y	N	Y	Y	N
WISCONSIN						
Kohl	Y	Y	N	Y	Y	N
Feingold	Y	Y	N	Y	Y	Y
WYOMING						
Thomas	N	N	N	N	Y	N
Enzi	N	N	N	N	N	N

ND Northern Democrats   SD Southern Democrats

Southern states - Ala., Ark., Fla., Ga., Ky., La., Miss., N.C., Okla., S.C., Tenn., Texas, Va.

171. S 1. ESEA Reauthorization/Bonus Payments. Wellstone, D-Minn., amendment to the Jeffords, I-Vt., substitute amendment. The Wellstone amendment would provide that at the end of the 2006-07 school year, the Education secretary make one-time bonus payments, using a peer review process, to states that most successfully assess the range and depth of student knowledge and proficiency in meeting state performance guidelines for each subject tested in grades 3 through 8. The Jeffords substitute would reauthorize the Elementary and Secondary Education Act for seven years and add language to modify the annual testing provisions in the bill, add a "Straight A's" demonstration program and allow parents of children in underperforming schools to use federal funds for private tutoring. Adopted 57-39: R 7-38; D 50-0 (ND 41-0, SD 9-0); I 0-1. June 6, 2001.

172. S 1. ESEA Reauthorization/State Consultation. Bingaman, D-N.M., amendment to the Jeffords, I-Vt., substitute amendment. The Bingaman amendment would require that governors and state education authorities be consulted for the development of state plans under the Elementary and Secondary Education Act. Adopted 59-39: R 14-33; D 44-6 (ND 37-4, SD 7-2); I 1-0. June 6, 2001.

173. S 1. ESEA Reauthorization/State Consultation. Voinovich, R-Ohio, amendment to the Jeffords, I-Vt., substitute amendment. The Voinovich amendment would require that the chief state school officer and the governor both sign the state education plan under the Elementary and

Secondary Education Act. Rejected 40-58: R 33-14; D 7-43 (ND 5-36, SD 2-7); I 0-1. June 6, 2001.

174. S 1. ESEA Reauthorization/Testing Costs. Carnahan, D-Mo., amendment to the Jeffords, I-Vt., substitute amendment. The Carnahan amendment would allow states to defer testing requirements if the federal government does not fully fund the cost of the program. Rejected 43-55: R 4-43; D 39-11 (ND 32-9, SD 7-2); I 0-1. A "nay" was a vote in support of the president's position. June 7, 2001.

175. S 1. ESEA Reauthorization/Federal Funds. Smith, R-N.H., amendment to the Jeffords, I-Vt., substitute amendment. The Smith amendment would express the sense of the Senate that at least 95 percent of the federal funds for elementary and secondary education programs should be spent to improve academic achievement in the classroom. Adopted 96-1: R 45-1; D 50-0 (ND 41-0, SD 9-0); I 1-0. June 7, 2001.

176. S 1. ESEA Reauthorization/Title I Funding. Wellstone, D-Minn., amendment to the Jeffords, I-Vt., substitute amendment. The Wellstone amendment would allow states to defer the new annual testing requirements unless Congress provides $24.72 billion to fund Part A of the Title I provisions of the bill for fiscal year 2005. Rejected 23-71: R 0-46; D 23-24 (ND 21-18, SD 2-6); I 0-1. A "nay" was a vote in support of the president's position. June 7, 2001.

[1] *Sen. James M. Jeffords of Vermont left the Republican Party to become an Independent, effective at the close of business June 5. The first vote for which he was eligible as an Independent was Vote 171.*

	177	178	179	180	181	182
ALABAMA						
Shelby	Y	Y	Y	N	N	Y
Sessions	Y	Y	Y	N	N	Y
ALASKA						
Stevens	Y	X	Y	N	N	N
Murkowski	Y	Y	Y	N	?	Y
ARIZONA						
McCain	Y	Y	Y	N	N	Y
Kyl	Y	N	Y	N	N	Y
ARKANSAS						
Hutchinson	Y	Y	Y	N	N	Y
Lincoln	Y	Y	N	N	Y	Y
CALIFORNIA						
Feinstein	Y	Y	N	Y	Y	Y
Boxer	Y	Y	N	Y	Y	Y
COLORADO						
Campbell	Y	N	Y	N	N	Y
Allard	Y	N	Y	N	N	Y
CONNECTICUT						
Dodd	Y	Y	N	Y	Y	?
Lieberman	Y	Y	Y	Y	Y	Y
DELAWARE						
Carper	Y	Y	Y	N	Y	Y
Biden	+	+	N	Y	Y	Y
FLORIDA						
Graham	Y	Y	N	Y	Y	Y
Nelson	Y	Y	N	Y	Y	Y
GEORGIA						
Miller	Y	Y	N	N	N	Y
Cleland	Y	Y	N	Y	Y	Y
HAWAII						
Inouye	?	#	?	Y	?	Y
Akaka	Y	Y	N	Y	Y	Y
IDAHO						
Craig	Y	N	Y	N	N	Y
Crapo	Y	N	N	N	N	Y
ILLINOIS						
Durbin	+	+	N	Y	Y	Y
Fitzgerald	Y	Y	Y	N	N	Y
INDIANA						
Lugar	Y	N	Y	N	N	Y
Bayh	Y	Y	N	N	Y	Y
IOWA						
Grassley	Y	N	Y	N	N	Y
Harkin	Y	N	N	Y	Y	Y
KANSAS						
Brownback	Y	N	Y	N	N	Y
Roberts	Y	N	Y	N	N	Y
KENTUCKY						
McConnell	Y	N	Y	N	N	Y
Bunning	Y	N	Y	N	N	Y
LOUISIANA						
Breaux	Y	Y	N	N	Y	Y
Landrieu	Y	Y	N	N	Y	Y
MAINE						
Snowe	Y	N	N	N	N	Y
Collins	Y	N	N	N	Y	N
MARYLAND						
Sarbanes	Y	Y	N	Y	Y	Y
Mikulski	Y	Y	N	Y	Y	Y
MASSACHUSETTS						
Kennedy	Y	Y	N	Y	Y	Y
Kerry	?	?	N	Y	Y	Y
MICHIGAN						
Levin	Y	Y	N	Y	Y	Y
Stabenow	Y	Y	N	Y	Y	Y
MINNESOTA						
Wellstone	Y	Y	N	Y	Y	Y
Dayton	Y	Y	N	Y	Y	Y
MISSISSIPPI						
Cochran	Y	N	Y	N	N	N
Lott	Y	N	Y	N	N	Y
MISSOURI						
Bond	Y	N	N	N	N	Y
Carnahan	Y	N	N	Y	Y	Y
MONTANA						
Baucus	?	Y	N	N	Y	Y
Burns	Y	N	N	N	N	Y
NEBRASKA						
Nelson	Y	Y	N	N	N	Y
Hagel	Y	N	N	N	N	N
NEVADA						
Reid	Y	Y	N	Y	Y	Y
Ensign	Y	N	Y	N	N	Y
NEW HAMPSHIRE						
Smith	Y	N	Y	N	N	Y
Gregg	?	?	Y	N	N	Y
NEW JERSEY						
Corzine	Y	N	N	Y	Y	Y
Torricelli	Y	Y	N	Y	Y	Y
NEW MEXICO						
Domenici	Y	Y	Y	N	N	Y
Bingaman	Y	Y	N	Y	Y	Y
NEW YORK						
Clinton	Y	Y	N	Y	Y	Y
Schumer	Y	Y	N	Y	Y	Y
NORTH CAROLINA						
Helms	Y	N	Y	N	N	Y
Edwards	Y	Y	N	Y	Y	Y
NORTH DAKOTA						
Conrad	Y	Y	N	Y	Y	Y
Dorgan	Y	Y	N	Y	Y	Y
OHIO						
DeWine	Y	Y	Y	N	N	N
Voinovich	Y	Y	Y	N	N	Y
OKLAHOMA						
Nickles	Y	N	Y	N	N	Y
Inhofe	Y	N	Y	N	N	Y
OREGON						
Wyden	Y	Y	N	Y	Y	Y
Smith	?	?	N	N	Y	Y
PENNSYLVANIA						
Specter	Y	Y	N	N	N	Y
Santorum	Y	N	Y	N	N	Y
RHODE ISLAND						
Reed	Y	Y	N	Y	Y	Y
Chafee	Y	Y	N	N	N	N
SOUTH CAROLINA						
Thurmond	Y	N	Y	N	N	Y
Hollings	Y	Y	N	Y	Y	Y
SOUTH DAKOTA						
Daschle	Y	Y	N	Y	Y	Y
Johnson	Y	N	N	Y	Y	Y
TENNESSEE						
Thompson	Y	N	Y	N	N	N
Frist	Y	Y	Y	N	N	Y
TEXAS						
Gramm	Y	N	Y	N	N	Y
Hutchison	Y	Y	Y	N	N	Y
UTAH						
Hatch	Y	Y	Y	N	N	Y
Bennett	Y	Y	Y	N	N	Y
VERMONT						
Leahy	Y	Y	N	Y	Y	Y
Jeffords	Y	N	N	N	Y	Y
VIRGINIA						
Warner	Y	N	Y	N	N	Y
Allen	Y	N	Y	N	N	Y
WASHINGTON						
Cantwell	Y	Y	N	Y	Y	Y
Murray	Y	Y	N	Y	Y	Y
WEST VIRGINIA						
Byrd	Y	Y	Y	N	Y	Y
Rockefeller	Y	Y	N	Y	Y	Y
WISCONSIN						
Kohl	Y	Y	N	Y	Y	Y
Feingold	Y	Y	N	Y	Y	Y
WYOMING						
Thomas	Y	N	N	N	N	Y
Enzi	Y	N	N	N	N	N

ND Northern Democrats   SD Southern Democrats

Southern states - Ala., Ark., Fla., Ga., Ky., La., Miss., N.C., Okla., S.C., Tenn., Texas, Va.

Key

Y	Voted for (yea).
#	Paired for.
+	Announced for.
N	Voted against (nay).
X	Paired against.
−	Announced against.
P	Voted "present."
C	Voted "present" to avoid possible conflict of interest.
?	Did not vote or otherwise make a position known.

Democrats   **Republicans**
Independents

---

177. S 1. ESEA Reauthorization/Parental Education Programs. Bond, R-Mo., amendment to the Jeffords, I-Vt., substitute amendment. The Bond amendment would allow states to spend federal money on early childhood parent education programs. The Jeffords substitute would reauthorize the Elementary and Secondary Education Act (ESEA) for seven years and add language to modify the annual testing provisions in the bill, add a "Straight A's" demonstration program and allow parents of children in underperforming schools to use federal funds for private tutoring. Adopted 93-0: R 47-0; D 45-0 (ND 36-0, SD 9-0); I 1-0. June 11, 2001.

178. S 1. ESEA Reauthorization/Additional Title I Funding. Landrieu, D-La., amendment to the Jeffords, I-Vt., substitute amendment. The Landrieu amendment would make additional allocations of Title I funds above fiscal 2001 levels contingent on adequate funding of targeted grants to local educational agencies. Adopted 57-36: R 15-31; D 42-4 (ND 33-4, SD 9-0); I 0-1. June 11, 2001.

179. S1. ESEA Reauthorization/School Vouchers. Gregg, R-N.H., amendment to the Jeffords, I-Vt., substitute amendment. The Gregg amendment would create a demonstration program in 10 school districts to allow public school children to use federal funds in the form of vouchers to transfer to another public school, including charter schools, or a private school. It would authorize $50 million for fiscal 2002 and subsequent necessary sums for the next six fiscal years. It also would require that 5 percent of the funds be reserved for the program's evaluation. Rejected 41-58: R 38-11; D 3-46 (ND 3-37, SD 0-9); I 0-1. A "yea" was a vote in support of the president's position. June 12, 2001.

180. S 1. ESEA Reauthorization/Comparability Requirement. Dodd, D-Conn., amendment to the Jeffords, I-Vt., substitute amendment. The Dodd amendment would require states to file a written statement with the Education secretary stating that they have established and implemented policies to ensure comparability among schools. Administrative funds under the Elementary and Secondary Education Act would be withheld if a state failed to comply. The Education secretary could waive the requirements for an additional two years for exceptional circumstances. Rejected 42-58: R 0-49; D 42-8 (ND 37-4, SD 5-4); I 0-1. A "nay" was a vote in support of the president's position. June 12, 2001.

181. S 1. ESEA Reauthorization/School Construction. Feinstein, D-Calif., amendment to the Jeffords, I-Vt., substitute amendment. The Feinstein amendment would require local education agencies to provide equal matching funds from non-federal sources and reduce school sizes for elementary schools to no more than 500 students, middle schools to no more than 750 students and high schools to no more than 1,500 students. Adopted 52-46: R 2-46; D 49-0 (ND 40-0, SD 9-0); I 1-0. June 12, 2001.

182. S 1. ESEA Reauthorization/Science Education. Santorum, R-Pa., amendment to the Jeffords, I-Vt., substitute amendment. The Santorum amendment would express the sense of the Senate that science education should prepare students to distinguish scientific data or theories from philosophical or religious claims that are made in the name of science and that the curriculum should help students understand why biological evolution is controversial. Adopted 91-8: R 41-8; D 49-0 (ND 40-0, SD 9-0); I 1-0. June 13, 2001.

	183	184	185	186	187
ALABAMA					
Shelby	N	N	Y	N	N
Sessions	N	N	Y	N	N
ALASKA					
Stevens	Y	N	Y	N	N
Murkowski	N	N	Y	N	N
ARIZONA					
McCain	N	N	Y	N	N
Kyl	N	N	Y	N	N
ARKANSAS					
Hutchinson	N	N	Y	N	N
Lincoln	N	Y	N	Y	N
CALIFORNIA					
Feinstein	N	Y	N	Y	N
Boxer	Y	Y	N	Y	Y
COLORADO					
Campbell	N	N	Y	N	N
Allard	N	N	Y	N	N
CONNECTICUT					
Dodd	Y	Y	–	+	Y
Lieberman	N	Y	N	Y	N
DELAWARE					
Carper	N	N	N	Y	Y
Biden	N	+	N	Y	Y
FLORIDA					
Graham	N	Y	N	Y	N
Nelson	N	Y	N	Y	N
GEORGIA					
Miller	N	N	Y	N	N
Cleland	N	Y	N	Y	Y
HAWAII					
Inouye	Y	Y	N	Y	Y
Akaka	Y	Y	N	Y	Y
IDAHO					
Craig	N	N	Y	N	N
Crapo	N	N	Y	N	N
ILLINOIS					
Durbin	Y	Y	N	Y	N
Fitzgerald	N	N	Y	N	N
INDIANA					
Lugar	N	N	Y	N	N
Bayh	N	Y	N	Y	N

	183	184	185	186	187
IOWA					
Grassley	N	N	Y	N	N
Harkin	Y	Y	N	Y	Y
KANSAS					
Brownback	N	N	Y	N	N
Roberts	N	N	Y	N	N
KENTUCKY					
McConnell	N	N	Y	N	N
Bunning	N	N	Y	N	N
LOUISIANA					
Breaux	N	N	N	Y	N
Landrieu	N	?	N	Y	N
MAINE					
Snowe	N	Y	Y	Y	Y
Collins	N	N	Y	Y	Y
MARYLAND					
Sarbanes	Y	Y	N	Y	Y
Mikulski	N	Y	N	Y	Y
MASSACHUSETTS					
Kennedy	N	Y	N	Y	Y
Kerry	N	Y	N	Y	Y
MICHIGAN					
Levin	Y	Y	N	Y	Y
Stabenow	N	Y	N	Y	Y
MINNESOTA					
Wellstone	Y	Y	N	Y	Y
Dayton	Y	Y	N	Y	Y
MISSISSIPPI					
Cochran	N	N	Y	N	N
Lott	N	N	Y	N	N
MISSOURI					
Bond	N	N	Y	N	N
Carnahan	N	Y	N	Y	Y
MONTANA					
Baucus	N	Y	N	Y	N
Burns	N	N	Y	N	N
NEBRASKA					
Nelson	Y	Y	N	Y	Y
Hagel	N	N	Y	N	N
NEVADA					
Reid	Y	Y	N	Y	Y
Ensign	N	N	Y	N	N

	183	184	185	186	187
NEW HAMPSHIRE					
Smith	N	N	Y	N	N
Gregg	N	N	Y	N	N
NEW JERSEY					
Corzine	Y	Y	N	Y	Y
Torricelli	N	Y	N	Y	Y
NEW MEXICO					
Domenici	N	N	Y	N	N
Bingaman	N	Y	N	Y	N
NEW YORK					
Clinton	N	Y	N	Y	N
Schumer	N	Y	N	Y	N
NORTH CAROLINA					
Helms	N	N	Y	N	N
Edwards	N	Y	N	Y	N
NORTH DAKOTA					
Conrad	Y	Y	N	Y	Y
Dorgan	N	Y	N	Y	N
OHIO					
DeWine	N	N	Y	N	N
Voinovich	N	N	N	N	N
OKLAHOMA					
Nickles	N	N	Y	N	N
Inhofe	N	N	Y	N	N
OREGON					
Wyden	N	Y	N	Y	N
Smith	N	N	Y	N	N
PENNSYLVANIA					
Specter	N	N	Y	N	Y
Santorum	N	N	Y	N	N
RHODE ISLAND					
Reed	Y	Y	N	Y	Y
Chafee	N	N	Y	N	Y
SOUTH CAROLINA					
Thurmond	N	N	Y	N	N
Hollings	Y	Y	N	Y	Y
SOUTH DAKOTA					
Daschle	Y	Y	N	Y	Y
Johnson	N	Y	N	Y	N
TENNESSEE					
Thompson	N	N	Y	N	N
Frist	N	N	Y	N	N

	183	184	185	186	187
TEXAS					
Gramm	N	N	Y	N	N
Hutchison	N	N	Y	N	N
UTAH					
Hatch	N	N	Y	N	N
Bennett	N	N	Y	N	N
VERMONT					
Leahy	Y	Y	N	Y	Y
Jeffords	N	Y	N	Y	Y
VIRGINIA					
Warner	N	N	Y	N	N
Allen	N	N	Y	N	N
WASHINGTON					
Cantwell	Y	Y	N	Y	Y
Murray	Y	Y	N	Y	Y
WEST VIRGINIA					
Byrd	N	Y	N	N	Y
Rockefeller	N	Y	N	Y	Y
WISCONSIN					
Kohl	N	Y	N	N	Y
Feingold	Y	Y	N	Y	Y
WYOMING					
Thomas	N	N	Y	N	N
Enzi	N	N	Y	N	N

Key

Y	Voted for (yea).
#	Paired for.
+	Announced for.
N	Voted against (nay).
X	Paired against.
–	Announced against.
P	Voted "present."
C	Voted "present" to avoid possible conflict of interest.
?	Did not vote or otherwise make a position known.

Democrats **Republicans**
Independents

ND Northern Democrats   SD Southern Democrats

Southern states - Ala., Ark., Fla., Ga., Ky., La., Miss., N.C., Okla., S.C., Tenn., Texas, Va.

183. S 1. ESEA Reauthorization/Testing Requirements Waiver. Hollings, D-S.C., amendment to the Jeffords, I-Vt., substitute amendment. The Hollings amendment would allow states to opt out of the mandatory testing in grades 3 through 8, if states can demonstrate the presence of a comparable assessment system, or if they determine a greater increase in student achievement can be accomplished through alternative educational investments. Rejected 22-78: R 1-48; D 21-29 (ND 20-21, SD 1-8); I 0-1. A "nay" was a vote in support of the president's position. June 13, 2001.

184. S 1. ESEA Reauthorization/After-School Programs. Dodd, D-Conn., amendment to the Jeffords, I-Vt., substitute amendment. The Dodd amendment would keep funding for after-school programs separate from the block grants included in the "Straight A's" demonstration project, which would allow seven states and 25 school districts to spend most federal funds for any educational purpose as long as test scores improve. Rejected 47-51: R 1-48; D 45-3 (ND 39-1, SD 6-2); I 1-0. A "nay" was a vote in support of the president's position. June 13, 2001.

185. S 1. ESEA Reauthorization/Education Funding. Domenici, R-N.M., amendment to the Jeffords, I-Vt., substitute amendment. The Domenici amendment would express the sense of the Senate that the Ap-propriations Committee should fund authorizations in the bill to the maximum extent possible. Rejected 49-50: R 48-1; D 1-48 (ND 0-40, SD 1-8); I 0-1. June 13, 2001.

186. S 1. ESEA Reauthorization/Education Funding. Schumer, D-N.Y., amendment to the Jeffords, I-Vt., substitute amendment. The Schumer amendment would express the sense of the Senate that Congress should appropriate all funds authorized for elementary and secondary education in fiscal 2002. Rejected 49-50: R 2-47; D 46-3 (ND 38-2, SD 8-1); I 1-0. June 13, 2001.

187. S 1. ESEA Reauthorization/Disciplining Students with Disabilities. Harkin, D-Iowa, amendment to the Jeffords, I-Vt., substitute amendment. The Harkin amendment would allow education agencies to establish and implement uniform discipline policies regarding all students under their jurisdiction. It would provide that if a child's behavior is disability-related, or the school has failed to provide a required service, then the child cannot be segregated out of the classroom without following current policies and procedures. If a disabled child's behavior is not disability-related, then the child may be removed from the classroom pursuant to general discipline codes and must receive services in an alternative setting. Rejected 36-64: R 4-45; D 31-19 (ND 29-12, SD 2-7); I 1-0. June 14, 2001.

	188	189	190	191	192
ALABAMA					
Shelby	Y	Y	Y	N	Y
Sessions	Y	Y	Y	N	Y
ALASKA					
Stevens	Y	Y	Y	N	Y
Murkowski	Y	Y	Y	N	Y
ARIZONA					
McCain	Y	Y	Y	N	Y
Kyl	Y	Y	Y	N	N
ARKANSAS					
Hutchinson	Y	Y	Y	N	Y
Lincoln	N	N	N	Y	Y
CALIFORNIA					
Feinstein	N	N	N	Y	Y
Boxer	N	N	N	Y	Y
COLORADO					
Campbell	Y	Y	Y	N	Y
Allard	Y	Y	Y	N	Y
CONNECTICUT					
Dodd	N	N	N	Y	Y
Lieberman	N	N	N	Y	Y
DELAWARE					
Carper	N	N	N	Y	Y
Biden	N	N	N	Y	Y
FLORIDA					
Graham	N	N	N	Y	Y
Nelson	N	N	N	Y	Y
GEORGIA					
Miller	Y	Y	Y	Y	Y
Cleland	N	N	N	Y	Y
HAWAII					
Inouye	N	N	?	?	?
Akaka	N	N	N	Y	Y
IDAHO					
Craig	Y	Y	Y	N	Y
Crapo	N	Y	Y	N	Y
ILLINOIS					
Durbin	Y	N	Y	Y	Y
Fitzgerald	Y	Y	Y	N	Y
INDIANA					
Lugar	Y	Y	Y	N	Y
Bayh	N	N	N	Y	Y

	188	189	190	191	192
IOWA					
Grassley	Y	Y	Y	N	Y
Harkin	N	N	N	Y	Y
KANSAS					
Brownback	N	Y	Y	N	Y
Roberts	N	Y	Y	N	Y
KENTUCKY					
McConnell	Y	Y	Y	N	Y
Bunning	Y	Y	Y	N	Y
LOUISIANA					
Breaux	Y	Y	Y	Y	Y
Landrieu	Y	N	Y	Y	Y
MAINE					
Snowe	N	N	N	Y	Y
Collins	N	Y	N	N	Y
MARYLAND					
Sarbanes	N	N	N	Y	Y
Mikulski	N	N	N	Y	Y
MASSACHUSETTS					
Kennedy	N	N	N	Y	Y
Kerry	N	N	N	Y	Y
MICHIGAN					
Levin	N	N	N	Y	Y
Stabenow	N	N	N	Y	Y
MINNESOTA					
Wellstone	N	N	N	Y	Y
Dayton	N	N	N	Y	Y
MISSISSIPPI					
Cochran	Y	Y	Y	N	Y
Lott	Y	Y	Y	N	Y
MISSOURI					
Bond	Y	Y	Y	N	Y
Carnahan	Y	Y	N	Y	Y
MONTANA					
Baucus	N	N	N	Y	Y
Burns	Y	Y	Y	N	Y
NEBRASKA					
Nelson	N	N	N	Y	Y
Hagel	Y	N	Y	N	Y
NEVADA					
Reid	N	N	N	Y	Y
Ensign	Y	Y	Y	N	Y

	188	189	190	191	192
NEW HAMPSHIRE					
Smith	Y	Y	+	N	Y
Gregg	Y	Y	Y	N	Y
NEW JERSEY					
Corzine	N	N	N	Y	Y
Torricelli	Y	N	Y	Y	Y
NEW MEXICO					
Domenici	Y	Y	Y	N	Y
Bingaman	N	N	N	Y	Y
NEW YORK					
Clinton	N	N	N	Y	Y
Schumer	N	N	N	Y	Y
NORTH CAROLINA					
Helms	Y	Y	Y	N	N
Edwards	N	N	N	Y	Y
NORTH DAKOTA					
Conrad	Y	Y	Y	Y	Y
Dorgan	Y	Y	Y	Y	Y
OHIO					
DeWine	N	N	N	N	Y
Voinovich	Y	N	Y	N	N
OKLAHOMA					
Nickles	Y	Y	Y	N	N
Inhofe	Y	Y	Y	N	N
OREGON					
Wyden	N	N	N	Y	Y
Smith	Y	Y	Y	N	Y
PENNSYLVANIA					
Specter	N	N	N	Y	Y
Santorum	Y	Y	Y	N	Y
RHODE ISLAND					
Reed	N	N	N	Y	Y
Chafee	N	N	N	Y	Y
SOUTH CAROLINA					
Thurmond	Y	Y	Y	N	Y
Hollings	N	Y	N	N	N
SOUTH DAKOTA					
Daschle	N	N	N	Y	Y
Johnson	Y	Y	Y	Y	Y
TENNESSEE					
Thompson	Y	Y	Y	N	Y
Frist	Y	Y	Y	N	Y

Key

Y	Voted for (yea).
#	Paired for.
+	Announced for.
N	Voted against (nay).
X	Paired against.
−	Announced against.
P	Voted "present."
C	Voted "present" to avoid possible conflict of interest.
?	Did not vote or otherwise make a position known.

Democrats   ***Republicans***
Independents

	188	189	190	191	192
TEXAS					
Gramm	Y	Y	Y	N	Y
Hutchison	Y	Y	Y	Y	Y
UTAH					
Hatch	Y	Y	Y	N	Y
Bennett	Y	Y	Y	N	N
VERMONT					
Leahy	N	N	N	Y	Y
Jeffords	N	N	N	Y	Y
VIRGINIA					
Warner	Y	Y	Y	N	Y
Allen	Y	Y	Y	N	Y
WASHINGTON					
Cantwell	N	N	N	Y	Y
Murray	N	N	N	Y	Y
WEST VIRGINIA					
Byrd	N	Y	N	Y	Y
Rockefeller	N	N	N	Y	Y
WISCONSIN					
Kohl	N	N	N	Y	Y
Feingold	N	N	N	Y	N
WYOMING					
Thomas	Y	Y	Y	N	Y
Enzi	Y	Y	Y	N	Y

ND Northern Democrats   SD Southern Democrats

Southern states - Ala., Ark., Fla., Ga., Ky., La., Miss., N.C., Okla., S.C., Tenn., Texas, Va.

188. S 1. ESEA Reauthorization/Disciplining Students with Disabilities. Sessions, R-Ala., amendment to the Jeffords, I-Vt., substitute amendment. The Sessions amendment would allow education agencies to establish and implement uniform discipline policies regarding all students under their jurisdiction. It would provide that if a disabled child's behavior is found to be unrelated to their disability, then the same disciplinary procedures should be used as would apply to children without disabilities. The parent would be allowed to request by a written note that the child be transferred to an accredited school with the approval of the state or local educational agency. A disabled child who is removed from the classroom for behavior related to his or her disability would receive a free appropriate public education, which could be provided in an alternate setting. Rejected 50-50: R 41-8; D 9-41 (ND 6-35, SD 3-6); I 0-1. June 14, 2001.

189. S 1. ESEA Reauthorization/Boy Scouts. Helms, R-N.C., amendment to the Jeffords, I-Vt., substitute amendment. The Helms amendment would allow federal education funds to be withheld from public elementary and secondary schools that bar the Boy Scouts of America from using school facilities. Adopted 51-49: R 43-6; D 8-42 (ND 5-36, SD 3-6); I 0-1.. (Subsequently, the Senate amended the Helms amendment by voice vote to include other specified youth groups.) June 14, 2001

190. S 1. ESEA Reauthorization/Disciplining Students with Disabilities. Reid, D-Nev., motion to reconsider the vote on the Sessions, R-Ala., amendment to the Jeffords, I-Vt., substitute amendment (vote 188). Motion agreed to 51-47: R 43-5; D 8-41 (ND 5-35, SD 3-6); I 0-1. (Subsequently, the Sessions amendment was adopted by voice vote.) June 14, 2001.

191. S 1. ESEA Reauthorization/Youth Groups. Boxer, D-Calif., amendment to the Boxer, D-Calif., amendment to the Jeffords, I-Vt., substitute amendment. The Boxer amendment would replace the text of the underlying Boxer amendment with language that would provide that public elementary or secondary schools and local or state educational agencies may not deny specified youth groups, including the Boy Scouts, access to meet after school in a designated open forum based on their position on sexual orientation. The underlying Boxer amendment would express the sense of the Senate that Congress should continue toward the goal of providing necessary funds for after-school programs by appropriating the authorized level of $1.5 billion for fiscal 2002. Adopted 52-47: R 4-45; D 47-2 (ND 39-1, SD 8-1); I 1-0. (Subsequently the underlying Boxer amendment, as amended, was adopted by voice vote.) June 14, 2001.

192. HR 1. ESEA Reauthorization/Passage. Passage of the bill that would reauthorize the Elementary and Secondary Education Act for seven years. The bill, as amended, would require states to test students annually in reading and math in grades 3 through 8, provide new accountability measures for schools that fail to make adequate yearly progress, and add a "Straight A's" demonstration program that would allow seven states and 25 school districts to spend most federal funds for any educational purpose as long as test scores improve. The bill also would allow parents of children in underperforming schools to use federal funds for private tutoring, and provide for the full funding of the Individuals with Disabilities Education Act. Before passage, the Senate struck all after the enacting clause and inserted the text of S 1 as amended by the Jeffords, I-Vt., substitute amendment. Passed 91-8: R 43-6; D 47-2 (ND 39-1, SD 8-1); I 1-0. A "yea" was a vote in support of the president's position. June 14, 2001.

	193	194
ALABAMA		
Shelby	Y	N
Sessions	Y	?
ALASKA		
Stevens	Y	N
Murkowski	Y	N
ARIZONA		
McCain	Y	Y
Kyl	Y	N
ARKANSAS		
Hutchinson	Y	N
Lincoln	Y	Y
CALIFORNIA		
Feinstein	Y	Y
Boxer	Y	Y
COLORADO		
Campbell	Y	N
Allard	Y	N
CONNECTICUT		
Dodd	Y	Y
Lieberman	Y	Y
DELAWARE		
Carper	Y	Y
Biden	Y	Y
FLORIDA		
Graham	Y	Y
Nelson	Y	Y
GEORGIA		
Miller	Y	?
Cleland	Y	Y
HAWAII		
Inouye	Y	Y
Akaka	Y	Y
IDAHO		
Craig	Y	N
Crapo	Y	N
ILLINOIS		
Durbin	Y	Y
Fitzgerald	Y	N
INDIANA		
Lugar	Y	N
Bayh	Y	Y

	193	194
IOWA		
Grassley	Y	Y
Harkin	Y	Y
KANSAS		
Brownback	Y	N
Roberts	Y	N
KENTUCKY		
McConnell	+	N
Bunning	Y	N
LOUISIANA		
Breaux	Y	Y
Landrieu	Y	Y
MAINE		
Snowe	Y	N
Collins	Y	N
MARYLAND		
Sarbanes	Y	Y
Mikulski	Y	Y
MASSACHUSETTS		
Kennedy	Y	Y
Kerry	Y	Y
MICHIGAN		
Levin	Y	Y
Stabenow	Y	Y
MINNESOTA		
Wellstone	Y	Y
Dayton	Y	Y
MISSISSIPPI		
Cochran	Y	N
Lott	Y	N
MISSOURI		
Bond	Y	N
Carnahan	Y	Y
MONTANA		
Baucus	Y	Y
Burns	Y	N
NEBRASKA		
Nelson	Y	Y
Hagel	Y	N
NEVADA		
Reid	Y	Y
Ensign	Y	N

	193	194
NEW HAMPSHIRE		
Smith	Y	N
Gregg	Y	N
NEW JERSEY		
Corzine	Y	Y
Torricelli	Y	Y
NEW MEXICO		
Domenici	Y	N
Bingaman	Y	Y
NEW YORK		
Clinton	Y	Y
Schumer	Y	Y
NORTH CAROLINA		
Helms	Y	N
Edwards	Y	Y
NORTH DAKOTA		
Conrad	Y	Y
Dorgan	Y	Y
OHIO		
DeWine	Y	N
Voinovich	Y	N
OKLAHOMA		
Nickles	Y	N
Inhofe	?	N
OREGON		
Wyden	Y	Y
Smith	Y	N
PENNSYLVANIA		
Specter	Y	N
Santorum	Y	N
RHODE ISLAND		
Reed	Y	Y
Chafee	Y	Y
SOUTH CAROLINA		
Thurmond	Y	N
Hollings	Y	Y
SOUTH DAKOTA		
Daschle	Y	Y
Johnson	Y	Y
TENNESSEE		
Thompson	Y	N
Frist	Y	N

	193	194
TEXAS		
Gramm	Y	N
Hutchison	Y	N
UTAH		
Hatch	Y	N
Bennett	Y	N
VERMONT		
Leahy	Y	Y
Jeffords	Y	?
VIRGINIA		
Warner	Y	N
Allen	Y	N
WASHINGTON		
Cantwell	Y	Y
Murray	Y	Y
WEST VIRGINIA		
Byrd	Y	Y
Rockefeller	Y	Y
WISCONSIN		
Kohl	Y	Y
Feingold	Y	Y
WYOMING		
Thomas	Y	N
Enzi	Y	N

ND Northern Democrats   SD Southern Democrats

Southern states - Ala., Ark., Fla., Ga., Ky., La., Miss., N.C., Okla., S.C., Tenn., Texas, Va.

193. S 1052. Patients' Rights/Motion to Proceed. Motion to proceed to the bill that would provide federal protections to patients, such as access to specialty and emergency care, permit lawsuits against insurers, and allow patients to appeal a health plan's decisions on coverage and treatment. Motion agreed to 98-0: R 47-0; D 50-0 (ND 41-0, SD 9-0); I 1-0. June 21, 2001.

194. S 1052. Patients' Rights/Self-Employed Health Insurance. Baucus, D-Mont., point of order that the Hutchinson, R-Ark., amendment that would provide for a 100 percent deduction of health insurance costs for self-employed individuals, for taxable years beginning after Dec. 31, 2001, is out of order because the Constitution requires that revenue provisions must originate in the House. Sustained 52-45: R 3-45; D 49-0 (ND 41-0, SD 8-0); I 0-0. (Subsequently, the chair upheld the point of order, and the amendment fell.) June 21, 2001.

	195	196	197	198	199	200	201
ALABAMA							
Shelby	Y	Y	Y	Y	Y	N	Y
Sessions	?	N	Y	Y	Y	N	Y
ALASKA							
Stevens	Y	Y	Y	Y	Y	N	Y
Murkowski	Y	Y	Y	Y	Y	N	Y
ARIZONA							
McCain	Y	N	N	Y	N	Y	Y
Kyl	Y	Y	Y	Y	Y	N	Y
ARKANSAS							
Hutchinson	Y	N	Y	Y	Y	N	Y
Lincoln	Y	N	N	Y	Y	Y	Y
CALIFORNIA							
Feinstein	Y	N	N	Y	N	Y	Y
Boxer	Y	N	N	N	N	Y	Y
COLORADO							
Campbell	Y	Y	Y	Y	Y	N	Y
Allard	Y	Y	Y	Y	Y	N	Y
CONNECTICUT							
Dodd	Y	N	N	Y	N	Y	Y
Lieberman	Y	N	N	Y	N	Y	Y
DELAWARE							
Carper	Y	N	N	Y	?	Y	Y
Biden	+	N	N	N	N	Y	Y
FLORIDA							
Graham	Y	N	N	Y	N	Y	Y
Nelson	Y	N	N	Y	N	Y	Y
GEORGIA							
Miller	?	N	N	Y	N	Y	Y
Cleland	Y	N	N	Y	N	Y	Y
HAWAII							
Inouye	Y	N	N	Y	N	Y	Y
Akaka	Y	N	N	Y	N	Y	Y
IDAHO							
Craig	?	Y	Y	Y	Y	N	Y
Crapo	Y	Y	Y	Y	Y	N	Y
ILLINOIS							
Durbin	Y	N	N	Y	N	Y	Y
Fitzgerald	Y	N	N	Y	N	Y	Y
INDIANA							
Lugar	Y	Y	Y	Y	Y	N	Y
Bayh	Y	N	N	Y	N	Y	Y

	195	196	197	198	199	200	201
IOWA							
Grassley	Y	Y	Y	Y	Y	N	Y
Harkin	Y	N	N	Y	N	Y	Y
KANSAS							
Brownback	Y	Y	Y	Y	Y	N	Y
Roberts	Y	Y	Y	Y	Y	N	Y
KENTUCKY							
McConnell	Y	Y	Y	Y	Y	N	Y
Bunning	Y	Y	Y	Y	Y	N	Y
LOUISIANA							
Breaux	Y	Y	N	Y	N	Y	Y
Landrieu	Y	N	N	Y	N	Y	Y
MAINE							
Snowe	Y	N	N	Y	N	Y	Y
Collins	Y	N	Y	Y	Y	N	Y
MARYLAND							
Sarbanes	Y	N	N	Y	N	Y	Y
Mikulski	Y	N	N	Y	N	Y	Y
MASSACHUSETTS							
Kennedy	Y	N	N	Y	N	Y	Y
Kerry	Y	N	N	Y	N	Y	Y
MICHIGAN							
Levin	Y	N	N	Y	N	Y	Y
Stabenow	Y	N	N	Y	N	Y	Y
MINNESOTA							
Wellstone	Y	N	N	N	N	Y	Y
Dayton	Y	N	N	Y	N	Y	Y
MISSISSIPPI							
Cochran	Y	Y	Y	Y	Y	N	Y
Lott	Y	Y	Y	Y	Y	N	Y
MISSOURI							
Bond	Y	Y	Y	Y	Y	N	Y
Carnahan	Y	N	N	Y	N	Y	Y
MONTANA							
Baucus	Y	Y	N	Y	N	Y	Y
Burns	Y	Y	Y	Y	Y	N	Y
NEBRASKA							
Nelson	Y	N	N	Y	N	N	Y
Hagel	Y	Y	Y	Y	Y	N	Y
NEVADA							
Reid	Y	N	N	Y	N	Y	Y
Ensign	Y	N	Y	Y	Y	N	Y

	195	196	197	198	199	200	201
NEW HAMPSHIRE							
Smith	Y	Y	Y	Y	Y	N	Y
Gregg	?	Y	Y	Y	Y	N	Y
NEW JERSEY							
Corzine	Y	N	N	N	N	Y	Y
Torricelli	?	N	N	Y	N	Y	Y
NEW MEXICO							
Domenici	?	N	Y	Y	N	Y	Y
Bingaman	Y	N	N	Y	N	Y	Y
NEW YORK							
Clinton	Y	N	N	Y	N	Y	Y
Schumer	Y	N	N	?	?	Y	Y
NORTH CAROLINA							
Helms	Y	Y	Y	Y	Y	?	Y
Edwards	Y	N	N	Y	N	Y	Y
NORTH DAKOTA							
Conrad	Y	N	N	Y	N	Y	Y
Dorgan	Y	N	N	Y	N	Y	Y
OHIO							
DeWine	Y	N	N	Y	N	N	Y
Voinovich	Y	Y	N	Y	N	Y	Y
OKLAHOMA							
Nickles	Y	Y	Y	Y	Y	N	Y
Inhofe	Y	Y	Y	Y	Y	N	Y
OREGON							
Wyden	Y	N	N	Y	N	Y	Y
Smith	?	N	Y	Y	Y	N	Y
PENNSYLVANIA							
Specter	Y	N	N	Y	N	Y	Y
Santorum	Y	Y	Y	Y	Y	N	Y
RHODE ISLAND							
Reed	Y	N	N	Y	N	Y	Y
Chafee	Y	N	N	Y	N	Y	Y
SOUTH CAROLINA							
Thurmond	Y	Y	Y	Y	Y	N	Y
Hollings	Y	N	N	N	N	Y	Y
SOUTH DAKOTA							
Daschle	Y	N	N	Y	N	Y	Y
Johnson	Y	N	N	Y	N	Y	Y
TENNESSEE							
Thompson	Y	Y	Y	Y	Y	N	Y
Frist	Y	Y	Y	Y	Y	N	Y

	195	196	197	198	199	200	201
TEXAS							
Gramm	Y	Y	Y	Y	Y	N	Y
Hutchison	Y	Y	Y	Y	Y	N	Y
UTAH							
Hatch	Y	Y	Y	Y	Y	N	Y
Bennett	Y	Y	Y	Y	Y	N	Y
VERMONT							
Leahy	Y	N	N	Y	N	Y	Y
Jeffords	?	N	N	Y	N	Y	Y
VIRGINIA							
Warner	Y	Y	Y	Y	Y	N	Y
Allen	Y	Y	Y	Y	Y	N	Y
WASHINGTON							
Cantwell	Y	N	N	Y	N	Y	Y
Murray	Y	N	N	Y	N	Y	Y
WEST VIRGINIA							
Byrd	Y	N	N	Y	N	Y	Y
Rockefeller	Y	N	N	Y	N	Y	Y
WISCONSIN							
Kohl	Y	N	N	Y	N	Y	Y
Feingold	Y	N	N	Y	N	Y	Y
WYOMING							
Thomas	?	Y	Y	Y	Y	N	Y
Enzi	N	Y	Y	Y	Y	N	Y

Key

Y	Voted for (yea).
#	Paired for.
+	Announced for.
N	Voted against (nay).
X	Paired against.
−	Announced against.
P	Voted "present."
C	Voted "present" to avoid possible conflict of interest.
?	Did not vote or otherwise make a position known.

Democrats **Republicans**
Independents

ND Northern Democrats   SD Southern Democrats

Southern states - Ala., Ark., Fla., Ga., Ky., La., Miss., N.C., Okla., S.C., Tenn., Texas, Va.

195. S 1052. Patients' Rights/Clinical Trials. McCain, R-Ariz., amendment that would express the sense of the Senate that patients battling life-threatening diseases should have the opportunity to participate in a federally approved or funded clinical trial recommended by their physician; children with rare cancer should be allowed to go to a cancer center that provides a high quality of care for that disease; and a health maintenance organization's decision that an in-network general physician can provide care for a seriously ill patient should be appealable to an independent body. Adopted 89-1: R 42-1; D 47-0 (ND 39-0, SD 8-0); I 0-0. June 22, 2001.

196. S 1052. Patients' Rights/Motion to Commit. Grassley, R-Iowa, motion to commit the bill jointly to the Senate Finance Committee, the Health, Education, Labor, and Pensions Committee, and the Judiciary Committee, with instructions to report the bill back to the Senate within 14 days after the motion is adopted. Motion rejected 39-61: R 37-12; D 2-48 (ND 1-40, SD 1-8); I 0-1. June 26, 2001.

197. S 1052. Patients' Rights/Liability Exemption. Gramm, R-Texas, amendment that would exclude employers and other plan sponsors from liability without exceptions. Rejected 43-57: R 43-6; D 0-50 (ND 0-41, SD 0-9); I 0-1. June 26, 2001.

198. S 1052. Patients' Rights/Liability Limit. Bond, R-Mo., amendment that would require the secretary of Health and Human Services (HHS) to request the National Academy of Sciences to submit a report to Congress concerning the impact of the bill on the number of U.S. individuals with health insurance coverage within two years of enactment, and for four subsequent years. If the findings indicate that more than 1 million individuals have lost their health insurance coverage over a 12-month period as a result of the bill's provisions, the liability section would be repealed effective one year after the report is submitted. Adopted 93-6: R 48-1; D 44-5 (ND 36-4, SD 8-1); I 1-0. June 26, 2001.

199. S 1052. Patients' Rights/Small Employers Liability Exemption. Allard, R-Colo., amendment that would exempt from liability employers or other plan sponsors for employers with fewer than 50 employees. Rejected 45-53: R 44-5; D 1-47 (ND 0-39, SD 1-8); I 0-1. June 27, 2001.

200. S 1052. Patients' Rights/Medical Necessity. McCain, R-Ariz., motion to table (kill) the Kyl, R-Ariz., amendment that would provide that independent medical reviewers may not require coverage for benefits that are specifically excluded or expressly limited under a health plan. It would require the HHS secretary to establish standards relating to the definition of "medically necessary and appropriate" or "experimental or investigational" benefits that group health plans and health insurers could use when making determinations on benefits claims. Motion agreed to 54-45: R 4-44; D 49-1 (ND 40-1, SD 9-0); I 1-0. June 27, 2001.

201. S 1052. Patients' Rights/Independent Reviews. McCain, R-Ariz., amendment to clarify that independent reviewers cannot order coverage for explicitly excluded benefits. It would authorize the HHS secretary to revoke an independent reviewer's certification or deny the re-certification if there is a pattern of ordering coverage for benefits specifically excluded from contracts. Adopted 100-0: R 49-0; D 50-0 (ND 41-0, SD 9-0); I 1-0. June 27, 2001.

	202	203	204	205	206	207
ALABAMA						
Shelby	?	N	Y	Y	N	N
Sessions	N	N	N	Y	N	Y
ALASKA						
Stevens	N	Y	N	Y	N	Y
Murkowski	N	N	N	Y	N	Y
ARIZONA						
McCain	Y	Y	Y	Y	Y	N
Kyl	N	N	N	Y	N	Y
ARKANSAS						
Hutchinson	N	N	N	Y	N	Y
Lincoln	Y	Y	Y	Y	Y	N
CALIFORNIA						
Feinstein	Y	Y	Y	Y	Y	N
Boxer	Y	Y	Y	Y	Y	N
COLORADO						
Campbell	N	N	N	Y	N	Y
Allard	N	N	N	Y	N	Y
CONNECTICUT						
Dodd	Y	Y	Y	Y	Y	N
Lieberman	Y	Y	Y	Y	Y	N
DELAWARE						
Carper	Y	Y	Y	Y	Y	N
Biden	?	Y	Y	Y	Y	N
FLORIDA						
Graham	Y	Y	Y	Y	Y	N
Nelson	Y	Y	Y	Y	Y	N
GEORGIA						
Miller	Y	Y	Y	Y	Y	N
Cleland	Y	Y	Y	Y	Y	N
HAWAII						
Inouye	Y	Y	Y	Y	Y	N
Akaka	Y	Y	Y	Y	Y	N
IDAHO						
Craig	N	N	N	Y	N	Y
Crapo	N	N	N	Y	N	Y
ILLINOIS						
Durbin	Y	N	Y	Y	Y	N
Fitzgerald	Y	Y	N	Y	Y	N
INDIANA						
Lugar	N	Y	N	Y	N	Y
Bayh	Y	Y	Y	Y	Y	N
IOWA						
Grassley	N	N	N	N	N	Y
Harkin	Y	Y	Y	Y	Y	N
KANSAS						
Brownback	N	N	N	Y	N	Y
Roberts	N	N	N	Y	N	Y
KENTUCKY						
McConnell	N	N	N	Y	N	Y
Bunning	N	N	N	Y	N	Y
LOUISIANA						
Breaux	Y	Y	Y	Y	Y	N
Landrieu	Y	Y	Y	Y	Y	N
MAINE						
Snowe	N	Y	N	Y	N	N
Collins	N	N	Y	Y	N	Y
MARYLAND						
Sarbanes	Y	Y	Y	Y	Y	N
Mikulski	Y	Y	Y	Y	Y	N
MASSACHUSETTS						
Kennedy	Y	Y	Y	Y	Y	N
Kerry	Y	Y	Y	Y	Y	N
MICHIGAN						
Levin	Y	Y	Y	Y	Y	N
Stabenow	Y	Y	Y	Y	Y	N
MINNESOTA						
Wellstone	Y	N	Y	Y	Y	N
Dayton	Y	Y	Y	Y	Y	N
MISSISSIPPI						
Cochran	N	Y	Y	N	Y	N
Lott	N	N	N	Y	N	Y
MISSOURI						
Bond	N	N	N	Y	N	Y
Carnahan	Y	Y	Y	Y	Y	N
MONTANA						
Baucus	Y	Y	Y	Y	Y	N
Burns	N	N	N	Y	N	Y
NEBRASKA						
Nelson	N	Y	Y	Y	Y	N
Hagel	N	N	N	Y	N	Y
NEVADA						
Reid	Y	Y	Y	Y	Y	N
Ensign	N	Y	N	Y	N	Y
NEW HAMPSHIRE						
Smith	N	N	N	Y	N	Y
Gregg	N	N	N	Y	N	Y
NEW JERSEY						
Corzine	Y	Y	Y	Y	Y	N
Torricelli	Y	Y	Y	Y	Y	N
NEW MEXICO						
Domenici	?	N	Y	Y	N	Y
Bingaman	Y	Y	Y	Y	Y	N
NEW YORK						
Clinton	Y	Y	Y	Y	Y	N
Schumer	Y	Y	Y	Y	Y	N
NORTH CAROLINA						
Helms	N	N	N	Y	N	Y
Edwards	Y	Y	Y	Y	Y	N
NORTH DAKOTA						
Conrad	Y	Y	Y	Y	Y	N
Dorgan	Y	Y	Y	Y	Y	N
OHIO						
DeWine	Y	Y	Y	Y	Y	N
Voinovich	N	N	N	Y	N	Y
OKLAHOMA						
Nickles	N	N	N	N	N	Y
Inhofe	N	N	N	Y	N	Y
OREGON						
Wyden	Y	Y	Y	Y	Y	N
Smith	N	Y	N	Y	N	Y
PENNSYLVANIA						
Specter	N	Y	N	Y	Y	Y
Santorum	N	Y	N	Y	N	Y
RHODE ISLAND						
Reed	Y	Y	Y	Y	Y	N
Chafee	Y	Y	Y	Y	Y	N
SOUTH CAROLINA						
Thurmond	N	N	N	Y	N	Y
Hollings	Y	Y	Y	N	Y	N
SOUTH DAKOTA						
Daschle	Y	Y	Y	Y	Y	N
Johnson	Y	Y	Y	Y	Y	N
TENNESSEE						
Thompson	N	N	Y	N	N	Y
Frist	N	Y	N	Y	N	Y
TEXAS						
Gramm	N	N	N	Y	N	Y
Hutchison	N	Y	N	Y	N	N
UTAH						
Hatch	N	N	N	Y	N	Y
Bennett	N	N	N	Y	N	Y
VERMONT						
Leahy	Y	Y	Y	Y	Y	N
Jeffords	Y	Y	Y	Y	Y	N
VIRGINIA						
Warner	N	Y	N	Y	N	Y
Allen	N	N	N	Y	N	Y
WASHINGTON						
Cantwell	Y	Y	Y	Y	Y	N
Murray	Y	Y	Y	Y	Y	N
WEST VIRGINIA						
Byrd	Y	Y	Y	Y	Y	N
Rockefeller	Y	Y	Y	Y	Y	N
WISCONSIN						
Kohl	Y	Y	Y	Y	Y	N
Feingold	Y	Y	Y	Y	Y	N
WYOMING						
Thomas	N	N	N	Y	N	Y
Enzi	N	N	N	Y	N	N

Key

Y	Voted for (yea).
#	Paired for.
+	Announced for.
N	Voted against (nay).
X	Paired against.
−	Announced against.
P	Voted "present."
C	Voted "present" to avoid possible conflict of interest.
?	Did not vote or otherwise make a position known.

Democrats **Republicans**
Independents

ND Northern Democrats SD Southern Democrats

Southern states - Ala., Ark., Fla., Ga., Ky., La., Miss., N.C., Okla., S.C., Tenn., Texas, Va.

202. S 1052. Patients' Rights/Pre-Emption. Reid, D-Nev., motion to table (kill) the Collins, R-Maine, amendment that would strike the pre-emption provision in the bill. It would provide incentive grants for states that enact laws or regulations consistent with patient protection requirements. It also would authorize $500 million in fiscal 2002 for state grants to promote increased health care quality, educate consumers on health care products, improve patient safety, provide health care coverage, and carry out enforcement activities regarding compliance with state patient protection laws. Motion agreed to 53-44: R 4-43; D 48-1 (ND 39-1, SD 9-0); I 1-0. June 28, 2001.

203. S 1052. Patients' Rights/Pre-Emption. Breaux, D-La., amendment that would provide that state standards and requirements that substantially comply with the provisions of the bill would not be superseded. Adopted 64-36: R 15-34; D 48-2 (ND 39-2, SD 9-0); I 1-0. June 28, 2001.

204. S 1052. Patients' Rights/Monetary Awards. Reid, D-Nev., motion to table (kill) the Bond, R-Mo., amendment that would require that a patient beneficiary who receives an award from any cause of action brought under the bill receives at least 85 percent of that award if it exceeds $100,000. Attorney fees in state and federal courts would be capped at 15 percent. Motion agreed to 62-38: R 11-38; D 50-0 (ND 41-0, SD 9-0); I 1-0. June 28, 2001.

205. S 1052. Patients' Rights/Employer Liability. Snowe, R-Maine, amendment that would disallow federal lawsuits against employers and plan sponsors with self-insured and self-administered health plans, including multiemployer "Taft-Hartley" plans, who act as their own designated decision-makers. It would also create a "designated decision-maker" process for employers that contract with outside insurance companies. Employers and plan sponsors with self-insured and self-administered health plans would still be subject to actions in state courts if they make medical decisions that cause harm to patients. Adopted 96-4: R 46-3; D 49-1 (ND 41-0, SD 8-1); I 1-0. June 28, 2001.

206. S 1052. Patients' Rights/Immunity from Liability. Reid, D-Nev., motion to kill (table) Division I of the Enzi, R-Wyo., amendment that would provide immunity from liability to self-insured group health plans that either enroll employees under a fully insured health plan or provide employees with an individual benefit payment in an amount equal to the amount that would be contributed on behalf of the employee for the group health plan. Motion agreed to 55-45: R 4-45; D 50-0 (ND 41-0, SD 9-0); I 1-0. (Subsequently, the remainder of the Enzi amendment was withdrawn.) June 28, 2001.

207. S 1052. Patients' Rights/Statutory Damages. Specter, R-Pa., amendment that would require that all suits under the bill be brought in federal courts. However, the federal courts would have to abide by statutory damage caps provided in state law, unless a state legislature specifically excluded Health Maintenance Organization liability cases from the caps. Rejected 42-58: R 42-7; D 0-50 (ND 0-41, SD 0-9); I 0-1. June 28, 2001.

	208	209	210	211	212	213	214
ALABAMA							
Shelby	Y	Y	Y	N	Y	Y	N
Sessions	Y	Y	Y	N	N	Y	N
ALASKA							
Stevens	Y	Y	Y	N	N	Y	N
Murkowski	?	?	?	?	?	?	?
ARIZONA							
McCain	Y	Y	N	Y	N	Y	Y
Kyl	Y	Y	Y	N	N	Y	N
ARKANSAS							
Hutchinson	Y	Y	N	N	N	Y	N
Lincoln	Y	Y	N	Y	Y	Y	Y
CALIFORNIA							
Feinstein	Y	Y	N	Y	Y	Y	Y
Boxer	Y	Y	N	Y	Y	Y	Y
COLORADO							
Campbell	Y	Y	Y	N	N	Y	N
Allard	Y	Y	Y	N	N	Y	N
CONNECTICUT							
Dodd	Y	Y	N	Y	Y	Y	Y
Lieberman	Y	Y	N	Y	Y	Y	Y
DELAWARE							
Carper	Y	Y	N	Y	Y	Y	Y
Biden	Y	Y	N	Y	Y	Y	Y
FLORIDA							
Graham	Y	Y	N	Y	Y	Y	Y
Nelson	Y	Y	N	Y	Y	Y	Y
GEORGIA							
Miller	Y	Y	N	Y	Y	Y	Y
Cleland	Y	Y	N	Y	Y	Y	Y
HAWAII							
Inouye	Y	Y	N	Y	Y	Y	Y
Akaka	Y	Y	N	Y	Y	Y	Y
IDAHO							
Craig	Y	Y	Y	N	N	Y	N
Crapo	Y	Y	Y	N	N	Y	N
ILLINOIS							
Durbin	Y	Y	N	Y	Y	Y	Y
Fitzgerald	Y	Y	Y	N	N	Y	Y
INDIANA							
Lugar	Y	Y	Y	N	N	Y	N
Bayh	Y	Y	N	Y	Y	Y	N
IOWA							
Grassley	Y	Y	Y	N	N	Y	Y
Harkin	Y	Y	N	Y	Y	Y	Y
KANSAS							
Brownback	Y	Y	Y	N	N	Y	N
Roberts	Y	Y	Y	N	N	Y	N
KENTUCKY							
McConnell	Y	Y	Y	N	N	Y	N
Bunning	Y	Y	Y	N	N	Y	N
LOUISIANA							
Breaux	Y	Y	N	Y	Y	Y	Y
Landrieu	Y	Y	N	Y	Y	Y	Y
MAINE							
Snowe	Y	Y	Y	N	N	Y	Y
Collins	Y	Y	Y	N	N	Y	N
MARYLAND							
Sarbanes	Y	Y	N	Y	Y	Y	Y
Mikulski	Y	Y	N	Y	Y	Y	Y
MASSACHUSETTS							
Kennedy	Y	Y	N	Y	Y	Y	Y
Kerry	Y	Y	N	Y	Y	Y	Y
MICHIGAN							
Levin	Y	Y	N	Y	Y	Y	Y
Stabenow	Y	Y	N	Y	Y	Y	Y
MINNESOTA							
Wellstone	Y	Y	N	Y	Y	Y	Y
Dayton	Y	Y	N	Y	Y	Y	Y
MISSISSIPPI							
Cochran	Y	Y	Y	N	N	Y	N
Lott	Y	Y	Y	N	N	Y	N
MISSOURI							
Bond	Y	Y	Y	N	N	Y	N
Carnahan	Y	Y	N	Y	Y	Y	Y
MONTANA							
Baucus	Y	Y	N	Y	Y	Y	Y
Burns	Y	Y	Y	N	N	Y	N
NEBRASKA							
Nelson	Y	Y	N	Y	Y	Y	Y
Hagel	Y	Y	Y	N	N	Y	N
NEVADA							
Reid	Y	Y	N	Y	Y	Y	Y
Ensign	Y	Y	Y	N	N	Y	N
NEW HAMPSHIRE							
Smith	Y	Y	Y	N	N	Y	N
Gregg	Y	Y	Y	N	N	Y	N
NEW JERSEY							
Corzine	Y	Y	N	Y	Y	Y	Y
Torricelli	Y	Y	N	Y	Y	Y	Y
NEW MEXICO							
Domenici	?	?	?	?	?	?	?
Bingaman	Y	Y	N	Y	Y	Y	Y
NEW YORK							
Clinton	Y	Y	N	Y	Y	Y	Y
Schumer	Y	Y	N	Y	Y	Y	Y
NORTH CAROLINA							
Helms	Y	Y	Y	N	N	Y	N
Edwards	Y	Y	N	Y	Y	Y	Y
NORTH DAKOTA							
Conrad	Y	Y	N	Y	Y	Y	Y
Dorgan	Y	Y	N	Y	Y	Y	Y
OHIO							
DeWine	Y	Y	Y	N	N	Y	N
Voinovich	Y	Y	Y	N	N	Y	N
OKLAHOMA							
Nickles	Y	Y	Y	N	N	Y	N
Inhofe	Y	Y	Y	N	N	Y	N
OREGON							
Wyden	Y	Y	N	Y	Y	Y	Y
Smith	Y	Y	Y	N	N	Y	N
PENNSYLVANIA							
Specter	Y	Y	N	Y	N	Y	N
Santorum	Y	Y	Y	N	N	Y	N
RHODE ISLAND							
Reed	Y	Y	N	Y	Y	Y	Y
Chafee	Y	Y	Y	Y	N	Y	Y
SOUTH CAROLINA							
Thurmond	Y	Y	Y	N	N	Y	N
Hollings	Y	Y	N	Y	Y	Y	Y
SOUTH DAKOTA							
Daschle	Y	Y	N	Y	Y	Y	Y
Johnson	Y	Y	N	Y	Y	Y	Y
TENNESSEE							
Thompson	Y	Y	Y	N	N	Y	N
Frist	Y	Y	Y	N	N	Y	N
TEXAS							
Gramm	Y	Y	Y	N	N	Y	N
Hutchison	Y	Y	Y	N	N	Y	N
UTAH							
Hatch	Y	Y	Y	N	N	Y	N
Bennett	Y	Y	Y	N	N	Y	N
VERMONT							
Leahy	Y	Y	N	Y	Y	Y	Y
Jeffords	Y	Y	Y	Y	Y	Y	Y
VIRGINIA							
Warner	Y	Y	Y	N	N	Y	N
Allen	Y	Y	Y	N	N	Y	N
WASHINGTON							
Cantwell	Y	Y	N	Y	Y	Y	Y
Murray	Y	Y	N	Y	Y	Y	Y
WEST VIRGINIA							
Byrd	Y	Y	N	Y	Y	Y	Y
Rockefeller	Y	Y	N	Y	Y	Y	Y
WISCONSIN							
Kohl	Y	Y	N	Y	Y	Y	Y
Feingold	Y	Y	N	Y	Y	Y	Y
WYOMING							
Thomas	Y	Y	Y	N	N	Y	N
Enzi	Y	Y	Y	N	N	Y	N

ND Northern Democrats   SD Southern Democrats

Southern states - Ala., Ark., Fla., Ga., Ky., La., Miss., N.C., Okla., S.C., Tenn., Texas, Va.

Key

Y	Voted for (yea).
#	Paired for.
+	Announced for.
N	Voted against (nay).
X	Paired against.
–	Announced against.
P	Voted "present."
C	Voted "present" to avoid possible conflict of interest.
?	Did not vote or otherwise make a position known.

Democrats **Republicans**
Independents

208. S 1052. Patients' Rights/Born Alive. Santorum, R-Pa., amendment that would specify that the words "person," "human being," "child," and "individual" include infants who are born alive at any stage of development. It would provide that this specification be used in determining the meaning of any act of Congress or any ruling, regulation or interpretation of various U.S. administrative bureaus and agencies. Adopted 98-0: R 47-0; D 50-0 (ND 41-0, SD 9-0); I 1-0. June 29, 2001.

209. S 1052. Patients' Rights/Multiparty Litigation. DeWine, R-Ohio, amendment that would limit all multiparty litigation, including class actions, by requiring that no more than one health maintenance organization (HMO) can be sued in any one action. Suits against more than one HMO would proceed separately. Adopted 98-0: R 47-0; D 50-0 (ND 41-0, SD 9-0); I 1-0. June 29, 2001.

210. S 1052. Patients' Rights/Customs User Fees. Grassley, R-Iowa, motion to waive the Budget Act with respect to the Conrad, D-N.D., point of order against the Grassley amendment. The Grassley amendment would strike the provisions in the bill related to customs user fees and a one-day payment shift for Medicare payments. Motion rejected 46-52: R 45-2; D 0-50 (ND 0-41, SD 0-9); I 1-0. A three-fifths majority vote (60) of the total Senate is required to waive the Budget Act. (Subsequently, the chair upheld the point of order and the amendment fell.) June 29, 2001.

211. S 1052. Patients' Rights/Collective Bargaining Agreements. Kennedy, D-Mass., motion to table (kill) the Nickles, R-Okla., amendment that would strike the provisions in the bill that would provide that the effective date for collective bargaining agreements to comply with the bill is on the expiration of the agreements. It would insert language in the bill that would provide that the effective date for plans covered by collective bargaining agreements would be phased in by plan years beginning Oct. 1, 2002. Motion agreed to 54-44: R 3-44; D 50-0 (ND 41-0, SD 9-0); I 1-0. June 29, 2001.

212. S 1052. Patients' Rights/Malpractice Liability. Edwards, D-N.C., motion to table (kill) the Ensign, R-Nev., amendment that would exempt health care professionals who provide pro bono medical services to uninsured, indigent individuals from any malpractice liability. Motion agreed to 52-46: R 2-45; D 49-1 (ND 40-1, SD 9-0); I 1-0. June 29, 2001.

213. S 1052. Patients' Rights/Exhaustive Appeals. Thompson, R-Tenn., amendment that would require the administrative appeals process to be exhausted for patients before a lawsuit is filed in connection with a denial of a claim for benefits. Adopted 98-0: R 47-0; D 50-0 (ND 41-0, SD 9-0); I 1-0. June 29, 2001.

214. S 1052. Patients' Rights/Motion to Commit. Baucus, D-Mont., point of order that the Smith, R-Ore., motion to commit the bill to the Finance Committee with instructions to include an amendment that would make the research and development tax credit permanent, is out of order. Sustained 57-41: R 7-40; D 49-1 (ND 40-1, SD 9-0); I 1-0. (Subsequently, the chair upheld the point of order and the motion fell.) June 29, 2001.

	215	216	217	218	219	220
ALABAMA						
Shelby	N	N	Y	Y	N	N
Sessions	N	N	N	Y	Y	N
ALASKA						
Stevens	N	N	N	Y	Y	N
Murkowski	?	?	?	?	?	?
ARIZONA						
McCain	Y	Y	Y	N	N	Y
Kyl	N	N	N	Y	Y	N
ARKANSAS						
Hutchinson	N	N	N	Y	Y	N
Lincoln	N	Y	?	N	N	Y
CALIFORNIA						
Feinstein	Y	Y	Y	N	N	Y
Boxer	Y	Y	Y	N	N	Y
COLORADO						
Campbell	N	N	N	?	?	?
Allard	N	N	N	Y	Y	N
CONNECTICUT						
Dodd	Y	Y	Y	N	N	Y
Lieberman	Y	N	Y	N	N	Y
DELAWARE						
Carper	Y	Y	Y	N	N	Y
Biden	Y	Y	Y	N	N	Y
FLORIDA						
Graham	Y	Y	Y	N	N	Y
Nelson	Y	Y	Y	N	N	Y
GEORGIA						
Miller	Y	Y	Y	N	N	Y
Cleland	Y	Y	Y	N	N	Y
HAWAII						
Inouye	Y	Y	+	N	N	Y
Akaka	Y	Y	Y	N	N	Y
IDAHO						
Craig	N	N	N	Y	N	N
Crapo	N	N	N	Y	N	N
ILLINOIS						
Durbin	Y	Y	Y	N	N	Y
Fitzgerald	Y	N	N	N	N	Y
INDIANA						
Lugar	N	N	N	Y	Y	N
Bayh	Y	Y	Y	N	N	Y

	215	216	217	218	219	220
IOWA						
Grassley	N	N	N	Y	Y	N
Harkin	Y	Y	Y	N	N	Y
KANSAS						
Brownback	N	N	N	Y	Y	N
Roberts	N	N	N	Y	Y	N
KENTUCKY						
McConnell	N	N	N	Y	Y	N
Bunning	N	N	N	Y	Y	N
LOUISIANA						
Breaux	Y	Y	N	N	Y	Y
Landrieu	Y	Y	N	N	N	Y
MAINE						
Snowe	Y	Y	Y	Y	N	Y
Collins	N	Y	N	Y	Y	Y
MARYLAND						
Sarbanes	Y	Y	Y	N	N	Y
Mikulski	Y	Y	Y	N	N	Y
MASSACHUSETTS						
Kennedy	Y	Y	Y	N	N	Y
Kerry	Y	Y	Y	N	N	Y
MICHIGAN						
Levin	Y	Y	Y	N	N	Y
Stabenow	Y	Y	Y	N	N	Y
MINNESOTA						
Wellstone	Y	Y	Y	N	N	Y
Dayton	Y	Y	Y	N	N	Y
MISSISSIPPI						
Cochran	N	N	N	Y	Y	N
Lott	N	N	N	Y	?	?
MISSOURI						
Bond	N	N	N	Y	Y	N
Carnahan	Y	Y	Y	N	N	Y
MONTANA						
Baucus	Y	Y	Y	N	N	Y
Burns	N	N	N	Y	Y	N
NEBRASKA						
Nelson	Y	N	N	N	N	Y
Hagel	N	N	N	Y	Y	N
NEVADA						
Reid	Y	Y	Y	N	N	Y
Ensign	N	N	N	Y	Y	N

	215	216	217	218	219	220
NEW HAMPSHIRE						
Smith	N	N	N	Y	Y	N
Gregg	N	N	N	Y	Y	N
NEW JERSEY						
Corzine	Y	Y	Y	N	N	Y
Torricelli	Y	N	Y	N	N	Y
NEW MEXICO						
Domenici	?	?	?	?	?	?
Bingaman	Y	Y	Y	N	N	Y
NEW YORK						
Clinton	Y	Y	Y	N	N	Y
Schumer	Y	Y	Y	N	N	Y
NORTH CAROLINA						
Helms	N	N	N	Y	Y	N
Edwards	Y	Y	Y	N	N	Y
NORTH DAKOTA						
Conrad	Y	Y	Y	N	N	Y
Dorgan	Y	Y	Y	N	N	Y
OHIO						
DeWine	Y	N	Y	N	N	Y
Voinovich	N	N	N	Y	Y	N
OKLAHOMA						
Nickles	N	N	N	Y	Y	N
Inhofe	N	N	N	Y	Y	N
OREGON						
Wyden	Y	Y	Y	N	N	Y
Smith	N	N	N	Y	Y	Y
PENNSYLVANIA						
Specter	N	N	Y	N	Y	N
Santorum	N	N	N	Y	Y	N
RHODE ISLAND						
Reed	Y	Y	Y	N	N	Y
Chafee	Y	Y	N	N	N	Y
SOUTH CAROLINA						
Thurmond	N	N	N	Y	Y	N
Hollings	Y	Y	Y	N	N	Y
SOUTH DAKOTA						
Daschle	Y	Y	Y	N	N	Y
Johnson	Y	Y	Y	N	N	Y
TENNESSEE						
Thompson	N	N	Y	Y	Y	N
Frist	N	N	N	Y	Y	N

Key	
Y	Voted for (yea).
#	Paired for.
+	Announced for.
N	Voted against (nay).
X	Paired against.
–	Announced against.
P	Voted "present."
C	Voted "present" to avoid possible conflict of interest.
?	Did not vote or otherwise make a position known.

Democrats   **Republicans**
Independents

	215	216	217	218	219	220
TEXAS						
Gramm	N	N	N	?	?	?
Hutchison	N	N	N	Y	Y	N
UTAH						
Hatch	N	N	N	Y	Y	N
Bennett	N	N	N	Y	Y	N
VERMONT						
Leahy	Y	Y	Y	N	N	Y
Jeffords	Y	Y	Y	N	Y	N
VIRGINIA						
Warner	N	N	N	Y	Y	Y
Allen	N	N	N	Y	Y	N
WASHINGTON						
Cantwell	Y	Y	Y	N	N	Y
Murray	Y	Y	Y	N	N	Y
WEST VIRGINIA						
Byrd	Y	Y	Y	N	N	Y
Rockefeller	Y	Y	Y	N	N	Y
WISCONSIN						
Kohl	Y	Y	Y	N	N	Y
Feingold	Y	Y	Y	N	N	Y
WYOMING						
Thomas	N	N	N	Y	Y	N
Enzi	N	Y	N	Y	Y	N

ND Northern Democrats   SD Southern Democrats

Southern states - Ala., Ark., Fla., Ga., Ky., La., Miss., N.C., Okla., S.C., Tenn., Texas, Va.

215. S 1052. Patients' Rights/Small-Business Exemption. Reid, D-Nev., motion to table (kill) the Allard, R-Colo., amendment that would exempt businesses with 15 or fewer employees from the bill's provisions, including liability. Motion agreed to 55-43: R 5-42; D 49-1 (ND 41-0, SD 8-1); I 1-0. June 29, 2001.

216. S 1052. Patients' Rights/Medical Savings Accounts. Baucus, D-Mont., motion to table (kill) the Craig, R-Idaho, amendment that would express the sense of the Senate that a patients' rights bill should remove restrictions on the private sector medical savings account demonstration program. Motion agreed to 53-45: R 5-42; D 47-3 (ND 38-3, SD 9-0); I 1-0. June 29, 2001.

217. S 1052. Patients' Rights/Tax Credits for Uninsured Individuals. Reid, D-Nev., motion to table (kill) the Santorum, R-Pa., amendment that would direct 75 percent of punitive damages awarded to a patient by a court against an insurer to a federal trust fund to finance tax credits for uninsured individuals and families. Motion agreed to 50-46: R 5-42; D 44-4 (ND 38-2, SD 6-2); I 1-0. June 29, 2001.

218. S 1052. Patients' Rights/Right to Sue Waiver. Kyl, R-Ariz., amendment that would allow health plan issuers to provide a lower-cost health plan that would allow participants to waive their right to sue. Rejected 42-54: R 42-3; D 0-50 (ND 0-41, SD 0-9); I 0-1. June 29, 2001.

219. S 1052. Patients' Rights/Republican Substitute. Frist, R-Tenn., substitute amendment that would provide federal protections, such as access to specialty and emergency room care, and allow patients to appeal a health plan organization's decision on coverage and treatment. It also would allow patients to sue at the federal level, with non-economic damages capped at $750,000 or three times economic damages. Economic damages would be unlimited and punitive damages would be prohibited. It also would require the administrative appeals process to be exhausted for patients before a lawsuit is filed in connection with a denial of claim for benefits. Rejected 36-59: R 34-10; D 1-49 (ND 0-41, SD 1-8); I 1-0. A "yea" was a vote in support of the president's position. June 29, 2001.

220. S 1052. Patients' Rights/Passage. Passage of the bill that would provide federal protections, such as access to specialty and emergency room care, and allow patients to appeal a health plan organization's decision on coverage and treatment. It also would allow patients to sue health insurers in state courts over quality-of-care claims and at the federal level over administrative or non-medical coverage disputes. Federal-level economic and non-economic damages would not be capped, and punitive damages would be capped at $5 million. State damages would be determined by state law. The bill, as amended, would exempt from federal lawsuits all employers and plan sponsors with self-insured and self-administered health plans, including multi-employer "Taft-Hartley" plans, who act as their own designated decision makers. It also would require the administrative appeals process to be exhausted for patients before a lawsuit is filed in connection with a denial of claim for benefits. Passed 59-36: R 9-35; D 50-0 (ND 41-0, SD 9-0); I 0-1. A "nay" was a vote in support of the president's position. June 29, 2001.

Senate Votes 221, 222, 223, 224, 225, 226

	221	222	223	224	225	226
ALABAMA						
Shelby	N	Y	N	Y	Y	Y
Sessions	N	Y	N	Y	Y	Y
ALASKA						
Stevens	N	N	N	Y	Y	Y
Murkowski	N	Y	N	Y	Y	Y
ARIZONA						
McCain	N	Y	N	Y	Y	N
Kyl	N	Y	N	Y	Y	N
ARKANSAS						
Hutchinson	Y	Y	N	Y	Y	Y
Lincoln	Y	N	N	N	Y	Y
CALIFORNIA						
Feinstein	N	N	N	Y	N	Y
Boxer	Y	N	N	N	N	Y
COLORADO						
Campbell	N	Y	N	Y	Y	Y
Allard	N	Y	N	Y	Y	N
CONNECTICUT						
Dodd	N	N	N	Y	Y	Y
Lieberman	Y	N	Y	Y	Y	N
DELAWARE						
Carper	Y	N	N	Y	Y	Y
Biden	Y	N	N	Y	N	Y
FLORIDA						
Graham	Y	Y	N	Y	Y	Y
Nelson	Y	N	N	Y	Y	Y
GEORGIA						
Miller	Y	N	N	Y	Y	Y
Cleland	Y	N	N	Y	Y	Y
HAWAII						
Inouye	N	N	N	Y	Y	Y
Akaka	Y	N	N	Y	Y	Y
IDAHO						
Craig	N	Y	N	Y	Y	Y
Crapo	N	Y	N	Y	Y	Y
ILLINOIS						
Durbin	Y	N	N	N	N	Y
Fitzgerald	N	Y	N	Y	Y	Y
INDIANA						
Lugar	N	Y	N	Y	Y	N
Bayh	Y	N	N	Y	Y	Y

	221	222	223	224	225	226
IOWA						
Grassley	N	Y	N	Y	Y	Y
Harkin	Y	Y	N	N	Y	Y
KANSAS						
Brownback	N	Y	N	Y	Y	Y
Roberts	N	Y	N	Y	Y	Y
KENTUCKY						
McConnell	N	Y	N	Y	Y	Y
Bunning	N	Y	N	Y	Y	Y
LOUISIANA						
Breaux	N	N	N	Y	Y	Y
Landrieu	Y	N	N	Y	Y	N
MAINE						
Snowe	N	Y	N	Y	Y	Y
Collins	N	Y	N	Y	Y	Y
MARYLAND						
Sarbanes	Y	N	N	N	Y	Y
Mikulski	Y	N	Y	Y	Y	Y
MASSACHUSETTS						
Kennedy	Y	N	N	N	Y	Y
Kerry	Y	N	N	N	N	Y
MICHIGAN						
Levin	Y	N	N	Y	Y	Y
Stabenow	Y	N	N	Y	N	Y
MINNESOTA						
Wellstone	Y	N	N	N	N	Y
Dayton	Y	N	N	N	N	Y
MISSISSIPPI						
Cochran	N	N	N	Y	Y	Y
Lott	N	Y	N	Y	Y	Y
MISSOURI						
Bond	N	N	N	Y	Y	Y
Carnahan	Y	N	N	Y	Y	N
MONTANA						
Baucus	Y	N	N	N	N	Y
Burns	N	N	N	Y	Y	Y
NEBRASKA						
Nelson	Y	N	N	Y	Y	Y
Hagel	N	Y	N	Y	Y	N
NEVADA						
Reid	Y	N	N	Y	Y	Y
Ensign	N	Y	N	Y	Y	N

	221	222	223	224	225	226
NEW HAMPSHIRE						
Smith	N	Y	N	Y	Y	N
Gregg	N	Y	N	Y	Y	Y
NEW JERSEY						
Corzine	Y	N	N	N	Y	Y
Torricelli	Y	N	N	N	N	Y
NEW MEXICO						
Domenici	N	N	N	Y	Y	Y
Bingaman	Y	N	N	N	Y	Y
NEW YORK						
Clinton	?	?	?	Y	Y	Y
Schumer	?	?	?	N	Y	Y
NORTH CAROLINA						
Helms	N	Y	N	Y	Y	Y
Edwards	+	N	N	Y	Y	Y
NORTH DAKOTA						
Conrad	Y	N	N	Y	Y	Y
Dorgan	Y	N	N	Y	Y	Y
OHIO						
DeWine	N	Y	N	Y	N	Y
Voinovich	N	Y	N	Y	Y	Y
OKLAHOMA						
Nickles	N	Y	N	Y	Y	Y
Inhofe	N	Y	N	Y	Y	N
OREGON						
Wyden	Y	N	N	N	N	Y
Smith	Y	Y	N	Y	N	Y
PENNSYLVANIA						
Specter	Y	Y	N	Y	Y	Y
Santorum	?	?	?	Y	Y	Y
RHODE ISLAND						
Reed	N	N	N	Y	Y	Y
Chafee	N	N	N	Y	Y	Y
SOUTH CAROLINA						
Thurmond	N	N	N	Y	Y	Y
Hollings	Y	N	Y	Y	Y	Y
SOUTH DAKOTA						
Daschle	Y	N	N	Y	Y	Y
Johnson	Y	N	N	Y	Y	Y
TENNESSEE						
Thompson	N	Y	N	Y	Y	N
Frist	N	Y	N	Y	Y	Y

	221	222	223	224	225	226
TEXAS						
Gramm	N	Y	N	Y	Y	N
Hutchison	N	Y	N	Y	Y	Y
UTAH						
Hatch	N	Y	N	Y	Y	Y
Bennett	N	N	N	Y	Y	Y
VERMONT						
Leahy	Y	N	N	Y	N	Y
Jeffords	N	N	N	Y	Y	Y
VIRGINIA						
Warner	N	Y	N	Y	Y	N
Allen	N	Y	N	Y	Y	Y
WASHINGTON						
Cantwell	Y	N	N	N	N	Y
Murray	N	N	N	N	N	Y
WEST VIRGINIA						
Byrd	N	N	N	Y	Y	Y
Rockefeller	Y	N	N	N	Y	Y
WISCONSIN						
Kohl	N	N	N	N	N	Y
Feingold	Y	Y	N	N	N	Y
WYOMING						
Thomas	N	Y	N	?	?	?
Enzi	N	Y	N	Y	Y	Y

ND Northern Democrats   SD Southern Democrats

Southern states - Ala., Ark., Fla., Ga., Ky., La., Miss., N.C., Okla., S.C., Tenn., Texas, Va.

221. S 1077. Fiscal 2001 Supplemental Appropriations/Medicare and Social Security Lockbox. Conrad, D-N.D., motion to waive the Budget Act with respect to the Stevens, R-Alaska, point of order against the Conrad amendment to the Voinovich, R-Ohio, amendment. The Conrad amendment would take the Medicare Hospital Insurance Trust Fund off budget, establish a 60-vote point of order against legislation that would reduce the Medicare Hospital Insurance Trust Fund surplus or that would put Social Security back on budget. The Voinovich amendment would create a 60-vote point of order against legislation that would reduce Social Security surpluses. It also would create a new sequester of both mandatory and discretionary programs in any year that the on-budget deficit exceeds 0.5 percent of total outlays. Motion rejected 42-54: R 3-45; D 39-8 (ND 32-7, SD 7-1); I 0-1. A three-fifths majority vote (60) of the total Senate is required to waive the Budget Act. (Subsequently, the chair upheld the point of order, and the amendment fell.) July 10, 2001.

222. S 1077. Fiscal 2001 Supplemental Appropriations/Social Security Lockbox. Voinovich, R-Ohio, motion to waive the Budget Act with respect to the Stevens, R-Alaska, point of order against the Voinovich amendment (see vote 221). Motion rejected 43-54: R 40-8; D 3-45 (ND 2-37, SD 1-8); I 0-1. A three-fifths majority vote (60) of the total Senate is required to waive the Budget Act. (Subsequently, the chair upheld the point of order, and the amendment fell.) July 10, 2001.

223. S 1077. Fiscal 2001 Supplemental Appropriations/Education and Defense Funding. Hollings, D-S.C., amendment that would strike the tax reduction for fiscal 2001 contained in the 2001 tax-cut law (PL 107-16), and establish a reserve fund to allow the Appropriations Committee to increase funding for defense and education. It would prohibit use of the Medicare or So-

cial Security trust funds for added defense or education spending. Rejected 3-94: R 0-48; D 3-45 (ND 2-37, SD 1-8); I 0-1. July 10, 2001.

224. S 1077. Fiscal 2001 Supplemental Appropriations/LIHEAP Funding. Inouye, D-Hawaii, motion to table (kill) the Wellstone, D-Minn., amendment that would increase funding for the Low-Income Home Energy Assistance Program (LIHEAP) by $150 million, to $450 million, offset by rescinding a total of $150 million by July 31, 2001, from administrative expenses appropriated in the fiscal 2001 defense, military construction and energy and water spending laws. Motion agreed to 77-22: R 48-0; D 29-21 (ND 21-20, SD 8-1); I 0-1. July 10, 2001.

225. S 1077. Fiscal 2001 Supplemental Appropriations/AIDS Funding. Byrd, D-W.Va., motion to table (kill) the Feingold, D-Wis., amendment that would increase the amount provided in the bill for a U.S. contribution to a global trust fund to combat HIV/AIDS, malaria, and tuberculosis by $593 million, offset by cutting $594 million from funds appropriated to the Navy for the V-22 Osprey aircraft program. Motion agreed to 79-20: R 46-2; D 33-17 (ND 24-17, SD 9-0); I 0-1. July 10, 2001.

226. S 1077. Fiscal 2001 Supplemental Appropriations/Defense Funding. Stevens, R-Alaska, motion to table (kill) the McCain, R-Ariz., amendment that would provide $847.8 million in additional funds to the Defense Department for military personnel, working-capital funds, mission-critical maintenance, force protection and other purposes. It would be offset by $849.3 million in non-defense cuts, including $19 million for the International Trade Administration, $126.8 million for the Emergency Oil and Gas Program, and $40 million for the NASA Life and Micro-Gravity Research Program. Motion agreed to 83-16: R 36-12; D 46-4 (ND 38-3, SD 8-1); I 1-0. July 10, 2001.

Senate Votes 227, 228, 229, 230, 231, 232, 233

	227	228	229	230	231	232	233
ALABAMA							
Shelby	N	Y	Y	Y	Y	N	N
Sessions	N	Y	Y	Y	Y	N	N
ALASKA							
Stevens	N	Y	Y	Y	Y	N	N
Murkowski	N	Y	Y	Y	Y	N	N
ARIZONA							
McCain	Y	Y	Y	Y	Y	N	Y
Kyl	N	Y	Y	Y	Y	N	Y
ARKANSAS							
Hutchinson	N	Y	Y	Y	Y	N	N
Lincoln	Y	Y	N	Y	N	Y	Y
CALIFORNIA							
Feinstein	Y	Y	N	Y	Y	Y	N
Boxer	Y	Y	N	N	N	Y	N
COLORADO							
Campbell	N	Y	Y	Y	Y	N	N
Allard	N	Y	N	Y	Y	N	Y
CONNECTICUT							
Dodd	Y	Y	N	N	N	Y	N
Lieberman	Y	Y	N	Y	N	Y	N
DELAWARE							
Carper	Y	Y	N	Y	N	Y	N
Biden	Y	Y	N	Y	N	Y	N
FLORIDA							
Graham	Y	Y	N	Y	N	Y	Y
Nelson	Y	Y	N	Y	N	Y	N
GEORGIA							
Miller	N	Y	Y	Y	Y	Y	N
Cleland	Y	Y	N	Y	N	Y	N
HAWAII							
Inouye	Y	Y	N	Y	N	Y	N
Akaka	Y	Y	N	Y	Y	Y	N
IDAHO							
Craig	N	Y	Y	Y	Y	N	N
Crapo	N	Y	Y	Y	Y	N	N
ILLINOIS							
Durbin	Y	Y	N	N	N	Y	N
Fitzgerald	N	Y	N	C	Y	Y	N
INDIANA							
Lugar	N	Y	Y	Y	Y	N	N
Bayh	N	Y	N	Y	N	Y	Y

	227	228	229	230	231	232	233
IOWA							
Grassley	N	Y	Y	Y	Y	N	N
Harkin	Y	Y	N	N	N	Y	N
KANSAS							
Brownback	N	Y	Y	Y	Y	N	N
Roberts	N	Y	Y	Y	Y	N	N
KENTUCKY							
McConnell	N	Y	Y	Y	Y	N	N
Bunning	N	Y	Y	Y	Y	N	N
LOUISIANA							
Breaux	N	Y	Y	Y	Y	Y	N
Landrieu	Y	Y	Y	Y	Y	Y	Y
MAINE							
Snowe	N	Y	N	Y	Y	N	N
Collins	Y	Y	N	Y	Y	N	N
MARYLAND							
Sarbanes	Y	Y	N	Y	N	Y	N
Mikulski	Y	Y	N	Y	N	Y	N
MASSACHUSETTS							
Kennedy	Y	Y	N	Y	N	Y	N
Kerry	Y	Y	N	Y	N	Y	N
MICHIGAN							
Levin	Y	Y	N	Y	N	Y	N
Stabenow	Y	Y	N	Y	N	Y	Y
MINNESOTA							
Wellstone	Y	Y	N	N	N	Y	N
Dayton	Y	Y	N	N	N	Y	N
MISSISSIPPI							
Cochran	N	Y	Y	Y	Y	N	N
Lott	N	Y	Y	Y	Y	N	N
MISSOURI							
Bond	N	Y	Y	Y	Y	N	N
Carnahan	Y	Y	N	Y	N	Y	Y
MONTANA							
Baucus	N	Y	N	Y	Y	Y	N
Burns	N	Y	Y	Y	Y	N	N
NEBRASKA							
Nelson	Y	Y	Y	Y	Y	Y	N
Hagel	N	Y	Y	Y	Y	N	N
NEVADA							
Reid	Y	Y	N	Y	N	Y	N
Ensign	Y	Y	Y	Y	Y	N	Y

	227	228	229	230	231	232	233
NEW HAMPSHIRE							
Smith	N	Y	Y	Y	Y	N	Y
Gregg	N	Y	N	Y	Y	N	N
NEW JERSEY							
Corzine	Y	Y	N	N	N	Y	N
Torricelli	Y	Y	N	Y	Y	Y	N
NEW MEXICO							
Domenici	N	Y	N	Y	Y	N	N
Bingaman	Y	Y	N	Y	Y	Y	N
NEW YORK							
Clinton	Y	Y	N	Y	Y	Y	N
Schumer	Y	Y	N	Y	Y	Y	N
NORTH CAROLINA							
Helms	N	Y	Y	Y	Y	N	N
Edwards	Y	Y	N	Y	N	Y	N
NORTH DAKOTA							
Conrad	Y	Y	N	Y	Y	Y	N
Dorgan	Y	Y	N	Y	Y	Y	N
OHIO							
DeWine	N	Y	N	Y	Y	N	N
Voinovich	N	Y	Y	Y	Y	N	N
OKLAHOMA							
Nickles	N	Y	Y	Y	Y	N	N
Inhofe	N	Y	Y	Y	Y	N	N
OREGON							
Wyden	Y	Y	N	Y	N	N	N
Smith	N	Y	Y	Y	Y	N	N
PENNSYLVANIA							
Specter	N	Y	N	Y	Y	N	N
Santorum	N	Y	Y	Y	Y	N	N
RHODE ISLAND							
Reed	Y	Y	N	Y	N	Y	N
Chafee	N	Y	N	Y	N	Y	N
SOUTH CAROLINA							
Thurmond	N	Y	Y	Y	Y	N	N
Hollings	Y	Y	N	Y	N	Y	Y
SOUTH DAKOTA							
Daschle	Y	Y	N	Y	N	Y	N
Johnson	Y	Y	N	Y	N	Y	N
TENNESSEE							
Thompson	N	Y	Y	Y	Y	N	N
Frist	N	Y	Y	Y	Y	N	N

Key

Y	Voted for (yea).
#	Paired for.
+	Announced for.
N	Voted against (nay).
X	Paired against.
–	Announced against.
P	Voted "present."
C	Voted "present" to avoid possible conflict of interest.
?	Did not vote or otherwise make a position known.

Democrats **Republicans**
Independents

	227	228	229	230	231	232	233
TEXAS							
Gramm	N	Y	Y	Y	Y	N	Y
Hutchison	N	Y	Y	N	Y	N	N
UTAH							
Hatch	N	Y	Y	Y	Y	N	N
Bennett	N	Y	Y	Y	Y	N	N
VERMONT							
Leahy	Y	Y	N	Y	N	Y	N
Jeffords	Y	Y	N	Y	N	Y	N
VIRGINIA							
Warner	N	Y	N	Y	Y	N	N
Allen	Y	Y	Y	Y	Y	N	N
WASHINGTON							
Cantwell	Y	Y	N	+	Y	Y	N
Murray	Y	Y	N	Y	Y	Y	N
WEST VIRGINIA							
Byrd	N	Y	N	Y	N	Y	N
Rockefeller	N	Y	N	Y	N	Y	N
WISCONSIN							
Kohl	Y	Y	N	Y	N	Y	N
Feingold	Y	N	N	N	N	Y	Y
WYOMING							
Thomas	?	?	?	Y	Y	N	N
Enzi	N	Y	Y	Y	Y	N	?

ND Northern Democrats SD Southern Democrats

Southern states - Ala., Ark., Fla., Ga., Ky., La., Miss., N.C., Okla., S.C., Tenn., Texas, Va.

227. S 1077. Fiscal 2001 Supplemental Appropriations/Tax Notices. Schumer, D-N.Y., amendment that would decrease by $33.9 million the amount provided in the bill to the IRS for processing, printing and postage costs associated with notices to be sent to taxpayers regarding the tax rebate contained in the 2001 tax cut law (PL 107-16.) Rejected 49-50: R 4-44; D 446 (ND 37-4, SD 7-2); I 1-0. July 10, 2001.

228. HR 2216. Fiscal 2001 Supplemental Appropriations/Passage. Passage of the bill that would appropriate $6.5 billion in supplemental discretionary funds, including $5.9 billion for defense and $625 million for non-defense discretionary programs. The bill includes $84 million to bolster a fund to compensate uranium miners and other workers exposed to radiation during the Cold War, and would provide $100 million for a U.S. contribution to a global trust fund to combat HIV/AIDS. Passed 98-1: R 48-0; D 49-1 (ND 40-1, SD 9-0); I 1-0. A "yea" was a vote in support of the president's position. (Before passage, the Senate struck all after the enacting clause and inserted the text of S 1077, as amended.) July 10, 2001.

229. HR 2217. Fiscal 2002 Interior Appropriations/Oil and Gas Exploration in National Monuments. Burns, R-Mont., motion to table (kill) the Durbin, D-Ill., amendment that would prohibit the use of funds for the preleasing or leasing of oil and gas, or other exploration activities within lands designated as national monuments, effective as of Jan. 20, 2001. Motion rejected 42-57: R 38-10; D 4-46 (ND 1-40, SD 3-6); I 0-1. (Subsequently, the amendment was adopted by voice vote.) July 11, 2001.

230. HR 333. Bankruptcy Overhaul/Cloture. Motion to invoke cloture (thus limiting debate) on the motion to proceed to the bill that would overhaul the nation's bankruptcy laws. Motion agreed to 88-10: R 46-2; D 41-8 (ND 32-8, SD 9-0); I 1-0. Three-fifths of the total Senate (60) is required to invoke cloture. July 12, 2001.

231. HR 2217. Fiscal 2002 Interior Appropriations/Oil and Gas Development Moratorium. Landrieu, D-La., motion to table (kill) the Nelson, D-Fla., amendment that would prohibit the use of funds to execute a final lease agreement for oil and gas development in the area known as "Lease Sale 181" in the Gulf of Mexico, before April 1, 2002. Motion agreed to 67-33: R 49-0; D 18-32 (ND 14-27, SD 4-5); I 0-1. July 12, 2001.

232. HR 2217. Fiscal 2002 Interior Appropriations/Klamath River Project. Reid, D-Nev., motion to table (kill) the Smith, R-Ore., amendment that would prohibit the use of funds in the bill to provide flows from the Klamath River Project unless previously set forth, until the Fish and Wildlife Service takes certain action for the recovery of two species of endangered fish and clarifies the operations of the Klamath Project in Oregon and California. Motion agreed to 52-48: R 3-46; D 48-2 (ND 39-2, SD 9-0); I 1-0. July 12, 2001.

233. HR 2217. Fiscal 2002 Interior Appropriations/Vulcan Monument. McCain, R-Ariz., amendment that would prohibit the use of funds for any purposes in relation to Vulcan Monument, Ala. Rejected 12-87: R 6-42; D 6-44 (ND 4-37, SD 2-7); I 0-1. July 12, 2001.

	234	235	236	237	238
ALABAMA					
Shelby	Y	N	Y	Y	N
Sessions	Y	N	Y	Y	N
ALASKA					
Stevens	Y	N	Y	Y	N
Murkowski	Y	N	Y	Y	N
ARIZONA					
McCain	Y	N	Y	Y	N
Kyl	Y	N	Y	Y	N
ARKANSAS					
Hutchinson	Y	N	Y	Y	N
Lincoln	Y	Y	Y	Y	Y
CALIFORNIA					
Feinstein	Y	Y	Y	Y	Y
Boxer	N	Y	N	Y	Y
COLORADO					
Campbell	Y	N	Y	Y	Y
Allard	Y	N	Y	Y	N
CONNECTICUT					
Dodd	N	Y	N	Y	Y
Lieberman	Y	Y	Y	Y	Y
DELAWARE					
Carper	Y	N	Y	Y	Y
Biden	Y	Y	Y	Y	Y
FLORIDA					
Graham	Y	Y	Y	Y	Y
Nelson	Y	Y	N	Y	Y
GEORGIA					
Miller	Y	N	Y	Y	Y
Cleland	Y	Y	Y	Y	Y
HAWAII					
Inouye	Y	Y	Y	Y	Y
Akaka	Y	Y	Y	Y	Y
IDAHO					
Craig	Y	N	Y	Y	N
Crapo	Y	N	Y	Y	N
ILLINOIS					
Durbin	N	Y	N	Y	Y
Fitzgerald	C	C	C	Y	N
INDIANA					
Lugar	Y	N	Y	Y	N
Bayh	Y	Y	Y	Y	Y

	234	235	236	237	238
IOWA					
Grassley	Y	N	Y	Y	N
Harkin	N	Y	N	Y	Y
KANSAS					
Brownback	N	Y	N	Y	N
Roberts	Y	N	Y	Y	N
KENTUCKY					
McConnell	Y	N	Y	Y	N
Bunning	Y	N	Y	Y	N
LOUISIANA					
Breaux	Y	Y	Y	Y	Y
Landrieu	Y	Y	Y	Y	Y
MAINE					
Snowe	Y	Y	Y	Y	N
Collins	Y	Y	Y	Y	Y
MARYLAND					
Sarbanes	Y	Y	N	Y	Y
Mikulski	Y	Y	Y	Y	Y
MASSACHUSETTS					
Kennedy	Y	Y	N	Y	Y
Kerry	Y	Y	N	Y	Y
MICHIGAN					
Levin	Y	Y	Y	Y	Y
Stabenow	Y	Y	Y	Y	Y
MINNESOTA					
Wellstone	N	Y	N	Y	Y
Dayton	N	Y	N	Y	Y
MISSISSIPPI					
Cochran	Y	N	Y	Y	N
Lott	Y	N	Y	Y	N
MISSOURI					
Bond	Y	Y	Y	Y	N
Carnahan	Y	Y	Y	Y	Y
MONTANA					
Baucus	Y	Y	Y	Y	Y
Burns	Y	N	Y	Y	N
NEBRASKA					
Nelson	Y	Y	Y	Y	Y
Hagel	Y	N	Y	Y	N
NEVADA					
Reid	Y	Y	Y	Y	Y
Ensign	Y	N	Y	Y	Y

	234	235	236	237	238
NEW HAMPSHIRE					
Smith	+	–	+	Y	N
Gregg	Y	N	Y	Y	N
NEW JERSEY					
Corzine	N	Y	N	Y	Y
Torricelli	Y	N	Y	Y	Y
NEW MEXICO					
Domenici	Y	N	Y	Y	N
Bingaman	Y	Y	Y	Y	Y
NEW YORK					
Clinton	Y	Y	Y	Y	Y
Schumer	Y	Y	Y	Y	Y
NORTH CAROLINA					
Helms	Y	N	Y	Y	N
Edwards	Y	Y	Y	Y	Y
NORTH DAKOTA					
Conrad	Y	Y	Y	Y	Y
Dorgan	Y	Y	Y	Y	Y
OHIO					
DeWine	Y	N	Y	Y	N
Voinovich	Y	N	Y	Y	N
OKLAHOMA					
Nickles	Y	N	Y	Y	N
Inhofe	Y	N	Y	Y	N
OREGON					
Wyden	Y	Y	Y	Y	Y
Smith	Y	N	Y	Y	Y
PENNSYLVANIA					
Specter	Y	N	Y	Y	N
Santorum	Y	N	Y	Y	N
RHODE ISLAND					
Reed	Y	Y	N	Y	Y
Chafee	Y	N	Y	Y	Y
SOUTH CAROLINA					
Thurmond	Y	N	Y	Y	N
Hollings	Y	Y	Y	Y	Y
SOUTH DAKOTA					
Daschle	Y	Y	Y	Y	Y
Johnson	Y	Y	Y	Y	Y
TENNESSEE					
Thompson	Y	N	Y	Y	N
Frist	Y	N	Y	Y	N

	234	235	236	237	238
TEXAS					
Gramm	Y	N	Y	Y	N
Hutchison	N	Y	N	Y	Y
UTAH					
Hatch	Y	N	Y	Y	N
Bennett	Y	N	Y	Y	N
VERMONT					
Leahy	Y	Y	Y	Y	Y
Jeffords	Y	N	Y	Y	Y
VIRGINIA					
Warner	Y	N	Y	Y	N
Allen	Y	N	Y	Y	N
WASHINGTON					
Cantwell	Y	Y	Y	Y	Y
Murray	Y	Y	Y	Y	Y
WEST VIRGINIA					
Byrd	Y	Y	Y	Y	Y
Rockefeller	Y	Y	N	Y	Y
WISCONSIN					
Kohl	Y	Y	Y	Y	Y
Feingold	N	Y	N	Y	N
WYOMING					
Thomas	Y	N	Y	Y	N
Enzi	Y	N	Y	Y	N

ND Northern Democrats   SD Southern Democrats

Southern states - Ala., Ark., Fla., Ga., Ky., La., Miss., N.C., Okla., S.C., Tenn., Texas, Va.

234. HR 333. Bankruptcy Overhaul/Cloture. Motion to invoke cloture (thus limiting debate) on the Leahy, D-Vt., substitute amendment that would require debtors able to repay $10,000 or 25 percent of their debts over five years to file under Chapter 13, which requires a reorganization of debts under a repayment plan, instead of seeking to discharge their debts under Chapter 7. Motion agreed to 88-10: R 45-2; D 42-8 (ND 33-8, SD 9-0); I 1-0. Three-fifths of the total Senate (60) is required to invoke cloture. July 17, 2001.

235. HR 333. Bankruptcy Overhaul/GAO Study. Wellstone, D-Minn., amendment to the Leahy, D-Vt., substitute amendment. The Wellstone amendment would require the General Accounting Office (GAO) to conduct a study of the effects of the bankruptcy bill and report back to Congress within two years. Adopted 52-46: R 5-42; D 47-3 (ND 39-2, SD 8-1); I 0-1. July 17, 2001.

236. HR 333. Bankruptcy Overhaul/Passage. Passage of the bill that would require debtors able to repay $10,000 or 25 percent of their debts over five years to file under Chapter 13, which requires a reorganization of debts under a repayment plan, instead of seeking to discharge their debts under Chapter 7. The bill would cap the "homestead" exemption at $125,000 and prevent lenders who have violated the Truth in Lending Act from escaping claims against them by declaring bankruptcy. Passed 82-16: R 45-2; D 36-14 (ND 28-13, SD 8-1); I 1-0. (Before passage, the Senate struck all after the enacting clause, and inserted the text of the Leahy, D-Vt., substitute.) July 17, 2001.

237. HR 2311. Fiscal 2002 Energy and Water Appropriations/Missouri River. Bond, R-Mo., amendment that would allow the secretary of the Army to consider and propose alternatives to a new Fish and Wildlife Service plan for regulating flows on the Missouri River. The secretary would also be required to consider the views of other federal and non-federal agencies and individuals to ensure that other congressionally authorized purposes are maintained. Adopted 100-0: R 49-0; D 50-0 (ND 41-0, SD 9-0); I 1-0. July 18, 2001.

238. HR 2311. Fiscal 2002 Energy and Water Appropriations/Worker Training Programs. Reid, D-Nev., motion to table (kill) the Murkowski, R-Alaska, amendment that would increase funding for Energy Department worker training activities by $10 million, offset by cutting $10 million from funds for the management, development and restoration of water and related natural resources in the California Bay Delta. Motion agreed to 56-44: R 6-43; D 49-1 (ND 40-1, SD 9-0); I 1-0. July 18, 2001.

	239	240	241	242	243
ALABAMA					
Shelby	Y	Y	Y	Y	Y
Sessions	N	Y	Y	Y	Y
ALASKA					
Stevens	Y	Y	Y	Y	Y
Murkowski	N	Y	Y	Y	Y
ARIZONA					
McCain	N	N	Y	Y	Y
Kyl	Y	Y	Y	Y	Y
ARKANSAS					
Hutchinson	Y	Y	Y	Y	Y
Lincoln	Y	Y	Y	Y	Y
CALIFORNIA					
Feinstein	Y	Y	Y	N	Y
Boxer	Y	Y	Y	N	Y
COLORADO					
Campbell	Y	Y	Y	Y	Y
Allard	N	Y	Y	Y	Y
CONNECTICUT					
Dodd	Y	Y	Y	N	Y
Lieberman	Y	Y	Y	N	Y
DELAWARE					
Carper	Y	Y	Y	Y	Y
Biden	Y	Y	?	N	Y
FLORIDA					
Graham	Y	Y	Y	Y	Y
Nelson	Y	Y	Y	N	Y
GEORGIA					
Miller	Y	Y	Y	N	Y
Cleland	Y	Y	N	N	Y
HAWAII					
Inouye	Y	Y	Y	N	Y
Akaka	Y	Y	Y	N	Y
IDAHO					
Craig	Y	Y	Y	Y	Y
Crapo	N	Y	Y	Y	Y
ILLINOIS					
Durbin	Y	Y	Y	N	Y
Fitzgerald	Y	Y	Y	Y	Y
INDIANA					
Lugar	Y	Y	Y	Y	Y
Bayh	Y	Y	N	Y	Y

	239	240	241	242	243
IOWA					
Grassley	Y	Y	Y	Y	Y
Harkin	Y	Y	Y	N	Y
KANSAS					
Brownback	N	Y	N	Y	Y
Roberts	N	Y	Y	Y	Y
KENTUCKY					
McConnell	Y	Y	Y	Y	N
Bunning	N	Y	Y	Y	N
LOUISIANA					
Breaux	N	Y	Y	Y	Y
Landrieu	Y	Y	Y	Y	Y
MAINE					
Snowe	N	Y	Y	Y	Y
Collins	N	Y	Y	Y	Y
MARYLAND					
Sarbanes	Y	Y	Y	N	Y
Mikulski	Y	Y	Y	N	Y
MASSACHUSETTS					
Kennedy	Y	Y	Y	N	Y
Kerry	Y	Y	Y	N	Y
MICHIGAN					
Levin	Y	Y	Y	Y	Y
Stabenow	Y	Y	Y	N	Y
MINNESOTA					
Wellstone	Y	Y	Y	N	Y
Dayton	Y	Y	Y	N	Y
MISSISSIPPI					
Cochran	Y	Y	Y	N	Y
Lott	N	Y	Y	Y	Y
MISSOURI					
Bond	N	Y	Y	Y	Y
Carnahan	Y	Y	Y	Y	Y
MONTANA					
Baucus	Y	Y	Y	N	Y
Burns	Y	Y	Y	Y	Y
NEBRASKA					
Nelson	Y	Y	Y	Y	Y
Hagel	Y	Y	Y	Y	Y
NEVADA					
Reid	Y	Y	Y	N	Y
Ensign	?	?	N	Y	Y

	239	240	241	242	243
NEW HAMPSHIRE					
Smith	N	Y	N	Y	Y
Gregg	Y	Y	Y	Y	Y
NEW JERSEY					
Corzine	Y	Y	Y	N	Y
Torricelli	Y	Y	Y	N	Y
NEW MEXICO					
Domenici	Y	Y	Y	Y	Y
Bingaman	Y	Y	Y	N	Y
NEW YORK					
Clinton	Y	Y	Y	N	Y
Schumer	Y	Y	Y	N	Y
NORTH CAROLINA					
Helms	Y	Y	?	?	?
Edwards	Y	Y	Y	N	Y
NORTH DAKOTA					
Conrad	Y	Y	Y	N	Y
Dorgan	Y	Y	Y	N	Y
OHIO					
DeWine	Y	Y	Y	Y	Y
Voinovich	N	N	N	Y	Y
OKLAHOMA					
Nickles	Y	Y	Y	Y	Y
Inhofe	N	Y	N	Y	Y
OREGON					
Wyden	Y	Y	Y	N	Y
Smith	Y	Y	Y	Y	Y
PENNSYLVANIA					
Specter	N	Y	Y	Y	Y
Santorum	Y	Y	Y	Y	Y
RHODE ISLAND					
Reed	Y	Y	Y	N	Y
Chafee	Y	Y	Y	Y	Y
SOUTH CAROLINA					
Thurmond	Y	Y	Y	Y	Y
Hollings	Y	Y	Y	N	Y
SOUTH DAKOTA					
Daschle	Y	Y	Y	N	Y
Johnson	Y	Y	Y	Y	Y
TENNESSEE					
Thompson	N	Y	Y	Y	Y
Frist	Y	Y	?	?	Y

Key

Y	Voted for (yea).
#	Paired for.
+	Announced for.
N	Voted against (nay).
X	Paired against.
−	Announced against.
P	Voted "present."
C	Voted "present" to avoid possible conflict of interest.
?	Did not vote or otherwise make a position known.

Democrats **Republicans**
Independents

	239	240	241	242	243
TEXAS					
Gramm	N	Y	N	Y	Y
Hutchison	N	Y	Y	Y	Y
UTAH					
Hatch	Y	Y	Y	Y	Y
Bennett	N	Y	Y	Y	Y
VERMONT					
Leahy	Y	Y	Y	N	Y
Jeffords	Y	Y	Y	Y	Y
VIRGINIA					
Warner	Y	Y	Y	N	Y
Allen	N	Y	Y	Y	Y
WASHINGTON					
Cantwell	Y	Y	Y	N	Y
Murray	Y	Y	Y	N	Y
WEST VIRGINIA					
Byrd	Y	Y	Y	Y	Y
Rockefeller	Y	Y	Y	N	Y
WISCONSIN					
Kohl	Y	Y	Y	N	Y
Feingold	Y	Y	Y	Y	Y
WYOMING					
Thomas	N	Y	N	Y	Y
Enzi	Y	Y	Y	Y	Y

ND Northern Democrats   SD Southern Democrats

Southern states - Ala., Ark., Fla., Ga., Ky., La., Miss., N.C., Okla., S.C., Tenn., Texas, Va.

239. Procedural Motion/Require Attendance. Reid, D-Nev., motion to instruct the sergeant-at-arms to request the attendance of absent senators. Motion agreed to 76-23: R 26-22; D 49-1 (ND 41-0, SD 8-1); I 1-0. July 19, 2001.

240. HR 2311. Fiscal 2002 Energy and Water Appropriations/Passage. Passage of the bill that would appropriate $25.1 billion for the Energy Department, the Army Corps of Engineers, water projects, parts of the Interior Department, and other independent agencies for fiscal 2002, including $4.3 billion for the Corps of Engineers. Passed 97-2: R 46-2; D 50-0 (ND 41-0, SD 9-0); I 1-0. July 19, 2001.

241. S 1172. Fiscal 2002 Legislative Branch Appropriations/Passage. Passage of a bill that would appropriate $1.94 billion for the legislative branch for fiscal 2002, including $125.3 million for Capitol Police salaries and expens-

es. Passed 88-9: R 40-7; D 47-2 (ND 39-1, SD 8-1); I 1-0. July 19, 2001.

242. Graham Nomination/Confirmation. Confirmation of President Bush's nomination of John D. Graham of Massachusetts to be administrator of the Office of Information and Regulatory Affairs at the Office of Management and Budget. Confirmed 61-37: R 47-0; D 13-37 (ND 8-33, SD 5-4); I 1-0. A "yea" was a vote in support of the president's position. July 19, 2001.

243. Ferguson Nomination/Confirmation. Confirmation of President Bush's nomination of Roger W. Ferguson Jr. of Massachusetts to be a member of the Board of Governors of the Federal Reserve System. Confirmed 97-2: R 46-2; D 50-0 (ND 41-0, SD 9-0); I 1-0. A "yea" was a vote in support of the president's position. July 19, 2001.

	244	245	246	247	248
ALABAMA					
Shelby	Y	Y	Y	Y	Y
Sessions	Y	Y	Y	Y	Y
ALASKA					
Stevens	Y	Y	Y	Y	Y
Murkowski	Y	Y	Y	Y	Y
ARIZONA					
McCain	?	?	?	Y	Y
Kyl	Y	Y	Y	Y	Y
ARKANSAS					
Hutchinson	Y	Y	Y	Y	Y
Lincoln	+	Y	Y	Y	Y
CALIFORNIA					
Feinstein	Y	Y	Y	Y	Y
Boxer	Y	Y	?	Y	Y
COLORADO					
Campbell	Y	Y	Y	Y	Y
Allard	Y	Y	Y	Y	Y
CONNECTICUT					
Dodd	Y	Y	Y	Y	Y
Lieberman	Y	Y	Y	Y	Y
DELAWARE					
Carper	Y	Y	Y	Y	Y
Biden	Y	Y	Y	Y	Y
FLORIDA					
Graham	Y	Y	Y	Y	Y
Nelson	Y	Y	Y	Y	Y
GEORGIA					
Miller	Y	Y	?	Y	Y
Cleland	Y	Y	Y	Y	Y
HAWAII					
Inouye	Y	Y	Y	Y	Y
Akaka	Y	Y	Y	Y	Y
IDAHO					
Craig	Y	Y	Y	Y	Y
Crapo	Y	Y	Y	Y	Y
ILLINOIS					
Durbin	Y	Y	Y	+	Y
Fitzgerald	Y	Y	Y	Y	Y
INDIANA					
Lugar	Y	Y	Y	Y	Y
Bayh	Y	Y	Y	Y	Y

	244	245	246	247	248
IOWA					
Grassley	Y	Y	Y	Y	Y
Harkin	Y	Y	Y	Y	Y
KANSAS					
Brownback	?	?	?	Y	Y
Roberts	Y	Y	Y	Y	Y
KENTUCKY					
McConnell	Y	Y	Y	Y	Y
Bunning	Y	Y	Y	Y	Y
LOUISIANA					
Breaux	?	?	?	Y	Y
Landrieu	Y	Y	Y	Y	Y
MAINE					
Snowe	Y	Y	Y	Y	Y
Collins	Y	Y	Y	Y	Y
MARYLAND					
Sarbanes	Y	Y	Y	Y	Y
Mikulski	Y	Y	Y	Y	Y
MASSACHUSETTS					
Kennedy	Y	Y	Y	+	Y
Kerry	Y	Y	Y	Y	Y
MICHIGAN					
Levin	Y	Y	Y	Y	Y
Stabenow	Y	Y	Y	Y	Y
MINNESOTA					
Wellstone	Y	Y	Y	Y	Y
Dayton	Y	Y	Y	Y	Y
MISSISSIPPI					
Cochran	Y	Y	Y	Y	Y
Lott	N	Y	Y	Y	Y
MISSOURI					
Bond	?	?	?	Y	Y
Carnahan	Y	Y	Y	Y	Y
MONTANA					
Baucus	Y	Y	Y	Y	Y
Burns	Y	Y	Y	Y	Y
NEBRASKA					
Nelson	Y	Y	Y	Y	Y
Hagel	Y	Y	Y	Y	Y
NEVADA					
Reid	Y	Y	Y	Y	Y
Ensign	Y	Y	Y	Y	Y

	244	245	246	247	248
NEW HAMPSHIRE					
Smith	Y	Y	Y	+	Y
Gregg	Y	Y	Y	Y	Y
NEW JERSEY					
Corzine	Y	Y	Y	Y	Y
Torricelli	Y	Y	Y	Y	Y
NEW MEXICO					
Domenici	Y	Y	Y	?	Y
Bingaman	Y	Y	Y	Y	Y
NEW YORK					
Clinton	Y	Y	Y	Y	Y
Schumer	Y	Y	Y	Y	Y
NORTH CAROLINA					
Helms	Y	Y	Y	Y	Y
Edwards	Y	Y	Y	Y	Y
NORTH DAKOTA					
Conrad	Y	Y	Y	Y	Y
Dorgan	Y	Y	Y	Y	Y
OHIO					
DeWine	Y	Y	Y	Y	Y
Voinovich	Y	Y	Y	Y	Y
OKLAHOMA					
Nickles	Y	Y	Y	Y	Y
Inhofe	+	+	+	Y	Y
OREGON					
Wyden	Y	Y	Y	Y	Y
Smith	Y	Y	Y	Y	Y
PENNSYLVANIA					
Specter	Y	Y	Y	Y	Y
Santorum	Y	Y	Y	Y	Y
RHODE ISLAND					
Reed	Y	Y	Y	Y	Y
Chafee	Y	Y	Y	Y	Y
SOUTH CAROLINA					
Thurmond	Y	Y	Y	Y	Y
Hollings	Y	Y	Y	Y	Y
SOUTH DAKOTA					
Daschle	Y	Y	Y	Y	Y
Johnson	Y	Y	Y	Y	Y
TENNESSEE					
Thompson	Y	Y	Y	Y	Y
Frist	Y	Y	Y	Y	Y

	244	245	246	247	248
TEXAS					
Gramm	Y	Y	Y	Y	Y
Hutchison	Y	Y	Y	Y	Y
UTAH					
Hatch	Y	Y	Y	Y	Y
Bennett	Y	Y	Y	Y	Y
VERMONT					
Leahy	Y	Y	Y	Y	Y
Jeffords	Y	Y	Y	Y	Y
VIRGINIA					
Warner	Y	Y	Y	Y	Y
Allen	Y	Y	Y	Y	Y
WASHINGTON					
Cantwell	Y	Y	Y	Y	Y
Murray	Y	Y	Y	Y	Y
WEST VIRGINIA					
Byrd	Y	Y	Y	Y	Y
Rockefeller	Y	Y	Y	Y	Y
WISCONSIN					
Kohl	Y	Y	Y	Y	Y
Feingold	Y	Y	Y	Y	Y
WYOMING					
Thomas	Y	Y	Y	Y	Y
Enzi	Y	Y	Y	Y	Y

Key

Y	Voted for (yea).
#	Paired for.
+	Announced for.
N	Voted against (nay).
X	Paired against.
–	Announced against.
P	Voted "present."
C	Voted "present" to avoid possible conflict of interest.
?	Did not vote or otherwise make a position known.

Democrats **Republicans** *Independents*

ND Northern Democrats   SD Southern Democrats

Southern states - Ala., Ark., Fla., Ga., Ky., La., Miss., N.C., Okla., S.C., Tenn., Texas, Va.

244. Gregory Nomination/Confirmation. Confirmation of President Bush's nomination of Roger L. Gregory of Virginia to be U.S. Circuit judge for the Fourth Circuit. Confirmed 93-1: R 44-1; D 48-0 (ND 41-0, SD 7-0); I 1-0. A "yea" was a vote in support of the president's position. July 20, 2001.

245. Haddon Nomination/Confirmation. Confirmation of President Bush's nomination of Sam E. Haddon of Montana to be U.S. District judge for the District of Montana. Confirmed 95-0: R 45-0; D 49-0 (ND 41-0, SD 8-0); I 1-0. A "yea" was a vote in support of the president's position. July 20, 2001.

246. Cebull Nomination/Confirmation. Confirmation of President Bush's nomination of Richard Cebull of Montana to be U.S. District judge for the District of Montana. Confirmed 93-0: R 45-0; D 47-0 (ND 40-0, SD 7-0); I 1-0. A "yea" was a vote in support of the president's position. July 20, 2001.

247. HR 2299. Fiscal 2002 Transportation Appropriations/Transportation Study. Reid, D-Nev., amendment to the Murray, D-Wash., substitute amendment. The Reid amendment would require the Transportation secretary to conduct a study within six months of the bill's enactment of the environmental, economic and public health and safety risks of transporting hazardous chemicals and radioactive material. The substitute amendment would provide $60 billion for the Transportation Department and various agencies. It also would restrict Mexican truck access to the United States. Adopted 96-0: R 47-0; D 48-0 (ND 39-0, SD 9-0); I 1-0. July 23, 2001.

248. HR 2299. Fiscal 2002 Transportation Appropriations/Chicago-area Airports. Fitzgerald, R-Ill., amendment to the Murray, D-Wash., substitute amendment. The Fitzgerald amendment would require the Transportation secretary to take into consideration the airports in Rockford, Ill., and Gary, Ind., when addressing aviation congestion problems in the greater Chicago area. Adopted 100-0: R 49-0; D 50-0 (ND 41-0, SD 9-0); I 1-0. July 24, 2001.

	249	250	251	252
ALABAMA				
Shelby	Y	Y	Y	Y
Sessions	Y	Y	Y	Y
ALASKA				
Stevens	Y	Y	Y	Y
Murkowski	Y	Y	Y	N
ARIZONA				
McCain	N	N	Y	N
Kyl	Y	N	Y	N
ARKANSAS				
Hutchinson	Y	Y	Y	N
Lincoln	Y	Y	Y	Y
CALIFORNIA				
Feinstein	Y	Y	Y	Y
Boxer	Y	Y	Y	Y
COLORADO				
Campbell	Y	Y	Y	Y
Allard	Y	N	Y	N
CONNECTICUT				
Dodd	Y	Y	Y	Y
Lieberman	Y	Y	Y	Y
DELAWARE				
Carper	Y	Y	Y	Y
Biden	Y	Y	Y	Y
FLORIDA				
Graham	Y	Y	Y	Y
Nelson	Y	Y	Y	Y
GEORGIA				
Miller	Y	Y	Y	Y
Cleland	Y	Y	Y	Y
HAWAII				
Inouye	Y	Y	?	Y
Akaka	Y	Y	Y	Y
IDAHO				
Craig	Y	N	Y	N
Crapo	Y	N	Y	N
ILLINOIS				
Durbin	Y	Y	Y	Y
Fitzgerald	Y	N	Y	N
INDIANA				
Lugar	Y	N	N	N
Bayh	Y	Y	Y	Y

	249	250	251	252
IOWA				
Grassley	Y	N	Y	N
Harkin	Y	Y	Y	Y
KANSAS				
Brownback	Y	N	Y	N
Roberts	Y	N	Y	Y
KENTUCKY				
McConnell	Y	N	Y	N
Bunning	N	N	Y	N
LOUISIANA				
Breaux	Y	Y	Y	Y
Landrieu	Y	Y	?	Y
MAINE				
Snowe	Y	Y	Y	Y
Collins	Y	Y	Y	Y
MARYLAND				
Sarbanes	Y	Y	Y	Y
Mikulski	Y	Y	Y	Y
MASSACHUSETTS				
Kennedy	Y	Y	Y	Y
Kerry	Y	Y	Y	Y
MICHIGAN				
Levin	Y	Y	Y	Y
Stabenow	Y	Y	Y	Y
MINNESOTA				
Wellstone	Y	Y	Y	Y
Dayton	Y	Y	Y	Y
MISSISSIPPI				
Cochran	Y	N	Y	Y
Lott	Y	N	Y	N
MISSOURI				
Bond	Y	N	Y	Y
Carnahan	Y	Y	Y	Y
MONTANA				
Baucus	Y	Y	Y	Y
Burns	Y	N	Y	N
NEBRASKA				
Nelson	Y	Y	Y	Y
Hagel	Y	N	N	N
NEVADA				
Reid	Y	Y	Y	Y
Ensign	Y	N	Y	Y

	249	250	251	252
NEW HAMPSHIRE				
Smith	Y	Y	Y	Y
Gregg	Y	N	Y	N
NEW JERSEY				
Corzine	Y	Y	Y	Y
Torricelli	Y	Y	Y	Y
NEW MEXICO				
Domenici	Y	N	Y	N
Bingaman	Y	Y	Y	Y
NEW YORK				
Clinton	Y	Y	Y	Y
Schumer	Y	Y	Y	Y
NORTH CAROLINA				
Helms	Y	N	Y	N
Edwards	Y	Y	Y	Y
NORTH DAKOTA				
Conrad	Y	Y	Y	Y
Dorgan	Y	Y	Y	Y
OHIO				
DeWine	Y	N	Y	N
Voinovich	N	N	Y	N
OKLAHOMA				
Nickles	Y	N	Y	N
Inhofe	Y	Y	Y	Y
OREGON				
Wyden	Y	Y	Y	Y
Smith	Y	Y	Y	Y
PENNSYLVANIA				
Specter	N	N	Y	N
Santorum	Y	Y	Y	Y
RHODE ISLAND				
Reed	Y	Y	Y	Y
Chafee	Y	N	Y	N
SOUTH CAROLINA				
Thurmond	Y	N	Y	N
Hollings	Y	Y	Y	Y
SOUTH DAKOTA				
Daschle	Y	Y	Y	Y
Johnson	Y	Y	Y	Y
TENNESSEE				
Thompson	?	N	Y	N
Frist	Y	N	Y	N

	249	250	251	252
TEXAS				
Gramm	N	N	Y	N
Hutchison	N	N	Y	Y
UTAH				
Hatch	Y	N	Y	N
Bennett	Y	N	Y	N
VERMONT				
Leahy	Y	Y	Y	Y
Jeffords	?	Y	Y	Y
VIRGINIA				
Warner	Y	Y	Y	Y
Allen	Y	N	Y	N
WASHINGTON				
Cantwell	Y	Y	Y	Y
Murray	Y	Y	Y	Y
WEST VIRGINIA				
Byrd	Y	Y	Y	Y
Rockefeller	Y	Y	Y	Y
WISCONSIN				
Kohl	Y	Y	Y	Y
Feingold	Y	Y	Y	Y
WYOMING				
Thomas	N	N	Y	N
Enzi	N	N	Y	N

ND Northern Democrats   SD Southern Democrats

Southern states - Ala., Ark., Fla., Ga., Ky., La., Miss., N.C., Okla., S.C., Tenn., Texas, Va.

249. HR 2299. Fiscal 2002 Transportation Appropriations/Georgia Road Projects. Cleland, D-Ga., amendment to the Murray, D-Wash., substitute amendment. The Cleland amendment would direct the state of Georgia to give priority consideration to two road projects, concerning Abernathy Road and Johnson Ferry Road. Adopted 90-8: R 40-8; D 50-0 (ND 41-0, SD 9-0); I 0-0. July 25, 2001.

250. HR 2299. Fiscal 2002 Transportation Appropriations/Mexican Trucks. Shelby, R-Ala., motion to table (kill) the Gramm, R-Texas, amendment to the Murray, D-Wash., amendment to the Murray substitute amendment. The Gramm amendment would prohibit the United States from imposing requirements on Mexican motor carriers traveling in the United States that are not imposed on U.S. and Canadian motor carriers. The Murray amendment would set up a border truck inspection program to allow Mexican trucks to receive three-month permits if they pass vigorous safety inspections. Motion agreed to 65-35: R 14-35; D 50-0 (ND 41-0, SD 9-0); I 1-0. July 25, 2001.

251. S 1218. Iran and Libya Sanctions/Passage. Passage of a bill that would revise and extend for five years the Iran-Libya Sanctions Act (PL 104-172), thereby allowing the president to impose sanctions on foreign firms that invest more than $20 million in the development of oil and gas industries in Iran or Libya. Passed 96-2: R 47-2; D 48-0 (ND 40-0, SD 8-0); I 1-0. July 25, 2001.

252. HR 2299. Fiscal 2002 Transportation Appropriations/Cloture. Motion to invoke cloture (thus limiting debate) on the Murray, D-Wash., substitute amendment that would provide $60 billion for the Transportation Department and various agencies. It also would restrict Mexican truck access to the United States. Motion agreed to 70-30: R 19-30; D 50-0 (ND 41-0, SD 9-0); I 1-0. Three-fifths of the total Senate (60) is required to invoke cloture. July 26, 2001.

	253	254	255	256	257	258	259	260
ALABAMA								
Shelby	Y	Y	Y	Y	Y	Y	Y	Y
Sessions	?	–	?	?	?	?	?	Y
ALASKA								
Stevens	Y	?	?	?	?	?	?	Y
Murkowski	N	N	N	Y	Y	Y	N	Y
ARIZONA								
McCain	N	N	N	Y	Y	Y	N	?
Kyl	N	N	N	Y	Y	Y	N	Y
ARKANSAS								
Hutchinson	Y	Y	Y	Y	Y	Y	N	Y
Lincoln	Y	Y	Y	Y	Y	Y	Y	Y
CALIFORNIA								
Feinstein	+	+	+	+	+	+	+	Y
Boxer	Y	Y	Y	Y	Y	Y	Y	Y
COLORADO								
Campbell	Y	Y	Y	Y	Y	Y	Y	Y
Allard	N	N	N	Y	Y	Y	N	Y
CONNECTICUT								
Dodd	Y	Y	?	Y	Y	Y	Y	Y
Lieberman	Y	Y	Y	Y	Y	Y	Y	Y
DELAWARE								
Carper	Y	Y	Y	Y	Y	Y	Y	Y
Biden	Y	Y	Y	Y	Y	Y	Y	Y
FLORIDA								
Graham	Y	Y	Y	Y	Y	Y	Y	Y
Nelson	Y	Y	Y	Y	Y	Y	Y	Y
GEORGIA								
Miller	Y	?	?	?	?	?	?	Y
Cleland	Y	Y	Y	Y	Y	Y	Y	Y
HAWAII								
Inouye	Y	Y	Y	Y	Y	Y	Y	Y
Akaka	Y	Y	Y	Y	Y	Y	Y	Y
IDAHO								
Craig	N	N	N	Y	Y	Y	N	Y
Crapo	N	N	N	Y	Y	Y	N	Y
ILLINOIS								
Durbin	Y	Y	Y	Y	Y	Y	Y	Y
Fitzgerald	N	N	Y	Y	Y	Y	N	Y
INDIANA								
Lugar	N	N	Y	Y	Y	Y	N	Y
Bayh	Y	Y	Y	Y	Y	Y	Y	Y
IOWA								
Grassley	N	N	Y	Y	Y	Y	N	Y
Harkin	Y	Y	Y	Y	Y	Y	Y	Y
KANSAS								
Brownback	N	N	N	Y	Y	Y	?	Y
Roberts	N	N	?	?	?	?	?	Y
KENTUCKY								
McConnell	N	N	N	Y	Y	Y	N	Y
Bunning	N	N	N	Y	Y	Y	N	Y
LOUISIANA								
Breaux	Y	Y	N	Y	Y	Y	Y	Y
Landrieu	Y	Y	Y	Y	Y	Y	Y	Y
MAINE								
Snowe	Y	Y	N	Y	Y	Y	Y	Y
Collins	Y	Y	N	Y	Y	Y	Y	Y
MARYLAND								
Sarbanes	Y	Y	Y	Y	Y	Y	Y	Y
Mikulski	Y	Y	Y	Y	Y	Y	Y	Y
MASSACHUSETTS								
Kennedy	Y	Y	Y	Y	Y	Y	Y	Y
Kerry	Y	Y	Y	Y	Y	Y	Y	Y
MICHIGAN								
Levin	Y	Y	Y	Y	Y	Y	Y	Y
Stabenow	Y	Y	Y	Y	Y	Y	Y	Y
MINNESOTA								
Wellstone	Y	Y	Y	Y	Y	Y	Y	Y
Dayton	Y	Y	Y	Y	Y	Y	Y	Y
MISSISSIPPI								
Cochran	N	N	Y	Y	Y	Y	Y	Y
Lott	N	N	N	Y	Y	Y	N	Y
MISSOURI								
Bond	?	?	?	?	?	?	?	Y
Carnahan	Y	Y	Y	Y	Y	Y	Y	Y
MONTANA								
Baucus	Y	Y	Y	Y	Y	Y	Y	Y
Burns	–	?	?	+	+	+	–	Y
NEBRASKA								
Nelson	Y	N	Y	Y	Y	Y	Y	Y
Hagel	N	N	N	Y	Y	Y	N	Y
NEVADA								
Reid	Y	Y	Y	Y	Y	Y	Y	Y
Ensign	Y	N	N	Y	Y	Y	Y	N
NEW HAMPSHIRE								
Smith	Y	Y	N	Y	Y	Y	N	Y
Gregg	N	N	Y	Y	Y	Y	N	N
NEW JERSEY								
Corzine	Y	Y	Y	Y	Y	Y	Y	Y
Torricelli	Y	Y	Y	Y	Y	Y	Y	?
NEW MEXICO								
Domenici	N	N	N	Y	Y	Y	N	Y
Bingaman	Y	Y	Y	Y	Y	Y	Y	Y
NEW YORK								
Clinton	Y	Y	Y	Y	Y	Y	Y	Y
Schumer	Y	Y	Y	Y	Y	Y	Y	Y
NORTH CAROLINA								
Helms	N	N	N	Y	Y	Y	?	?
Edwards	Y	Y	Y	Y	Y	Y	Y	Y
NORTH DAKOTA								
Conrad	Y	Y	Y	Y	Y	Y	Y	Y
Dorgan	Y	Y	Y	Y	Y	Y	Y	Y
OHIO								
DeWine	N	N	N	Y	Y	Y	N	Y
Voinovich	N	N	N	Y	Y	Y	N	Y
OKLAHOMA								
Nickles	N	N	Y	Y	?	?	?	Y
Inhofe	Y	?	?	?	?	?	?	Y
OREGON								
Wyden	Y	Y	Y	Y	Y	Y	Y	Y
Smith	Y	Y	N	Y	Y	Y	?	Y
PENNSYLVANIA								
Specter	Y	N	N	Y	Y	Y	?	Y
Santorum	Y	N	?	Y	Y	Y	?	Y
RHODE ISLAND								
Reed	Y	Y	Y	Y	Y	Y	Y	Y
Chafee	Y	Y	Y	Y	Y	Y	Y	Y
SOUTH CAROLINA								
Thurmond	N	N	N	Y	Y	Y	N	Y
Hollings	Y	Y	Y	Y	Y	Y	Y	Y
SOUTH DAKOTA								
Daschle	Y	Y	Y	Y	Y	Y	N	Y
Johnson	Y	Y	Y	Y	Y	Y	Y	Y
TENNESSEE								
Thompson	N	N	Y	Y	Y	Y	N	Y
Frist	N	?	?	?	?	?	?	Y
TEXAS								
Gramm	N	N	N	Y	Y	Y	N	Y
Hutchison	N	N	N	Y	Y	Y	Y	Y
UTAH								
Hatch	N	N	N	Y	Y	Y	N	Y
Bennett	N	N	N	Y	Y	Y	N	?
VERMONT								
Leahy	Y	Y	Y	Y	Y	Y	Y	Y
Jeffords	Y	Y	Y	?	Y	Y	Y	Y
VIRGINIA								
Warner	Y	Y	N	Y	Y	Y	N	Y
Allen	Y	N	N	Y	Y	Y	N	Y
WASHINGTON								
Cantwell	Y	Y	Y	Y	Y	Y	Y	Y
Murray	Y	Y	Y	Y	Y	Y	Y	Y
WEST VIRGINIA								
Byrd	Y	Y	Y	Y	Y	Y	Y	Y
Rockefeller	Y	Y	Y	Y	Y	Y	Y	Y
WISCONSIN								
Kohl	Y	Y	Y	Y	Y	Y	Y	Y
Feingold	Y	Y	Y	Y	Y	Y	Y	Y
WYOMING								
Thomas	N	N	N	?	?	?	?	Y
Enzi	?	?	?	?	?	?	N	Y

Key

Y	Voted for (yea).
#	Paired for.
+	Announced for.
N	Voted against (nay).
X	Paired against.
–	Announced against.
P	Voted "present."
C	Voted "present" to avoid possible conflict of interest.
?	Did not vote or otherwise make a position known.

Democrats **Republicans**
Independents

ND Northern Democrats   SD Southern Democrats

Southern states - Ala., Ark., Fla., Ga., Ky., La., Miss., N.C., Okla., S.C., Tenn., Texas, Va.

253. HR 2299. Fiscal 2002 Transportation Appropriations/NAFTA Violations. Shelby, R-Ala., motion to table (kill) the Gramm, R-Texas, amendment to the Murray, D-Wash., amendment to the Murray substitute amendment. The Gramm amendment would provide that no provisions in the bill may be applied if the president finds them to be in violation of the North American Free Trade Agreement. The Murray amendment would set up a border truck inspection program to allow Mexican trucks to receive three-month permits if they pass vigorous safety inspections. The substitute amendment would provide $60 billion for the Transportation Department and various agencies. It also would restrict Mexican truck access to the United States. Motion agreed to 65-30: R 15-30; D 49-0 (ND 40-0, SD 9-0); I 1-0. July 27, 2001.

254. HR 2299. Fiscal 2002 Transportation Appropriations/Mexican Nationals. Reid, D-Nev., motion to table (kill) the McCain, R-Ariz., amendment to the Murray, D-Wash., amendment to the Murray substitute amendment. The McCain amendment would provide that no provision in the bill be implemented in a way that treats Mexican nationals differently from Canadian nationals. Motion agreed to 57-34: R 9-33; D 47-1 (ND 39-1, SD 8-0); I 1-0. July 27, 2001.

255. Procedural Motion/Require Attendance. Daschle, D-S.D., motion to instruct the sergeant-at-arms to request the attendance of absent senators. Motion agreed to 60-28: R 13-27; D 46-1 (ND 39-0, SD 7-1); I 1-0. July 27, 2001.

256. HR 2299. Fiscal 2002 Transportation Appropriations/Effective Date. Murray, D-Wash., motion to table (kill) the Gramm, R-Texas, amendment to the Murray amendment to the Murray substitute amendment. The Gramm amendment would make the provision in the Murray amendment effective five days after the bill's enactment. Motion agreed to 88-0: R 40-0;

D 48-0 (ND 40-0, SD 8-0); I 0-0. July 27, 2001.

257. HR 2299. Fiscal 2002 Transportation Appropriations/Effective Date. Daschle, D-S.D., motion to table (kill) the Gramm, R-Texas, amendment to the Murray, D-Wash., amendment to the Murray substitute amendment. The Gramm amendment would make the provision in the Murray amendment effective four days after the bill's enactment. Motion agreed to 88-0: R 39-0; D 48-0 (ND 40-0, SD 8-0); I 1-0. July 27, 2001.

258. HR 2299. Fiscal 2002 Transportation Appropriations/Effective Date. Daschle, D-S.D., motion to table (kill) the Gramm, R-Texas, amendment to the Murray, D-Wash., amendment to the Murray substitute amendment. The Gramm amendment would make the provision in the Murray amendment effective three days after the bill's enactment. Motion agreed to 88-0: R 39-0; D 48-0 (ND 40-0, SD 8-0); I 1-0. July 27, 2001.

259. HR 2299. Fiscal 2002 Transportation Appropriations/Cloture. Motion to invoke cloture (thus limiting debate) on the bill that would provide $60 billion for the Transportation Department and various agencies. It also would restrict Mexican truck access to the United States. Motion rejected 57-27: R 9-26; D 47-1 (ND 39-1, SD 8-0); I 1-0. Three-fifths of the total Senate (60) is required to invoke cloture. July 27, 2001.

260. S 1246. Fiscal 2001 Supplemental Agriculture Assistance/Cloture. Motion to invoke cloture (thus limiting debate) on the motion to proceed to the bill that would authorize $7.4 billion in additional economic assistance to farmers in fiscal 2001. Motion agreed to 95-2: R 45-2; D 49-0 (ND 40-0, SD 9-0); I 1-0. Three-fifths of the total Senate (60) is required to invoke cloture. July 30, 2001.

	261	262	263	264	265	266
ALABAMA						
Shelby	N	Y	N	Y	Y	Y
Sessions	N	Y	N	Y	Y	Y
ALASKA						
Stevens	N	Y	N	Y	N	Y
Murkowski	N	Y	N	Y	Y	N
ARIZONA						
McCain	N	Y	Y	+	Y	N
Kyl	N	Y	N	Y	Y	N
ARKANSAS						
Hutchinson	Y	Y	Y	Y	Y	Y
Lincoln	Y	Y	N	Y	Y	Y
CALIFORNIA						
Feinstein	Y	Y	N	Y	Y	N
Boxer	Y	Y	Y	Y	Y	N
COLORADO						
Campbell	N	Y	N	Y	Y	N
Allard	N	Y	N	Y	Y	N
CONNECTICUT						
Dodd	Y	Y	Y	Y	Y	Y
Lieberman	Y	Y	N	Y	Y	Y
DELAWARE						
Carper	Y	Y	N	Y	Y	Y
Biden	Y	Y	N	Y	Y	N
FLORIDA						
Graham	Y	Y	N	Y	Y	Y
Nelson	Y	Y	Y	Y	Y	Y
GEORGIA						
Miller	Y	Y	N	Y	Y	Y
Cleland	Y	Y	Y	Y	Y	Y
HAWAII						
Inouye	Y	Y	N	Y	Y	Y
Akaka	Y	Y	N	Y	Y	Y
IDAHO						
Craig	N	Y	N	Y	Y	N
Crapo	N	Y	N	Y	Y	N
ILLINOIS						
Durbin	Y	Y	Y	Y	Y	N
Fitzgerald	N	Y	N	Y	N	N
INDIANA						
Lugar	N	Y	N	Y	Y	N
Bayh	Y	Y	N	Y	Y	N

	261	262	263	264	265	266
IOWA						
Grassley	N	Y	Y	Y	Y	Y
Harkin	Y	Y	Y	Y	Y	Y
KANSAS						
Brownback	N	Y	N	Y	Y	N
Roberts	N	Y	N	Y	Y	N
KENTUCKY						
McConnell	N	Y	N	Y	Y	N
Bunning	N	Y	N	Y	Y	N
LOUISIANA						
Breaux	Y	Y	N	Y	Y	Y
Landrieu	Y	Y	Y	Y	Y	Y
MAINE						
Snowe	Y	Y	Y	Y	Y	Y
Collins	N	Y	Y	Y	Y	Y
MARYLAND						
Sarbanes	Y	Y	N	Y	Y	Y
Mikulski	Y	Y	N	Y	Y	Y
MASSACHUSETTS						
Kennedy	Y	Y	N	Y	Y	Y
Kerry	Y	Y	N	Y	Y	Y
MICHIGAN						
Levin	Y	Y	N	Y	Y	Y
Stabenow	Y	Y	Y	Y	Y	Y
MINNESOTA						
Wellstone	Y	Y	Y	Y	Y	Y
Dayton	Y	Y	Y	N	Y	Y
MISSISSIPPI						
Cochran	N	Y	N	Y	Y	Y
Lott	N	Y	N	Y	?	Y
MISSOURI						
Bond	N	Y	N	Y	Y	Y
Carnahan	Y	Y	Y	Y	Y	Y
MONTANA						
Baucus	Y	Y	N	Y	Y	N
Burns	N	Y	N	Y	Y	N
NEBRASKA						
Nelson	Y	Y	N	Y	Y	N
Hagel	N	Y	N	Y	Y	N
NEVADA						
Reid	Y	Y	Y	Y	Y	Y
Ensign	N	Y	N	Y	Y	N

	261	262	263	264	265	266
NEW HAMPSHIRE						
Smith	N	Y	Y	Y	Y	Y
Gregg	N	Y	N	Y	Y	Y
NEW JERSEY						
Corzine	Y	Y	N	Y	Y	N
Torricelli	Y	Y	N	Y	Y	N
NEW MEXICO						
Domenici	N	Y	N	Y	Y	?
Bingaman	Y	Y	Y	Y	Y	N
NEW YORK						
Clinton	Y	Y	N	Y	Y	Y
Schumer	Y	Y	N	Y	Y	Y
NORTH CAROLINA						
Helms	N	Y	N	Y	?	Y
Edwards	N	Y	N	Y	Y	Y
NORTH DAKOTA						
Conrad	Y	Y	N	Y	Y	Y
Dorgan	Y	Y	N	Y	Y	N
OHIO						
DeWine	N	Y	N	Y	Y	N
Voinovich	N	Y	N	Y	Y	N
OKLAHOMA						
Nickles	N	Y	N	Y	Y	Y
Inhofe	N	Y	N	Y	Y	Y
OREGON						
Wyden	Y	Y	N	Y	Y	Y
Smith	N	Y	N	Y	Y	N
PENNSYLVANIA						
Specter	N	Y	N	Y	Y	Y
Santorum	N	Y	N	Y	Y	N
RHODE ISLAND						
Reed	Y	Y	N	Y	Y	Y
Chafee	N	Y	N	Y	Y	Y
SOUTH CAROLINA						
Thurmond	N	Y	N	Y	Y	N
Hollings	Y	Y	N	Y	Y	Y
SOUTH DAKOTA						
Daschle	Y	Y	N	Y	Y	Y
Johnson	Y	Y	Y	Y	Y	N
TENNESSEE						
Thompson	N	Y	N	Y	Y	Y
Frist	N	Y	N	Y	Y	Y

	261	262	263	264	265	266
TEXAS						
Gramm	N	Y	N	Y	Y	N
Hutchison	N	Y	N	Y	Y	Y
UTAH						
Hatch	N	Y	N	Y	Y	N
Bennett	N	Y	N	Y	Y	N
VERMONT						
Leahy	Y	Y	N	Y	Y	Y
Jeffords	Y	Y	Y	Y	Y	Y
VIRGINIA						
Warner	N	Y	N	Y	Y	Y
Allen	N	Y	N	Y	Y	N
WASHINGTON						
Cantwell	Y	Y	N	Y	Y	Y
Murray	Y	Y	N	Y	Y	Y
WEST VIRGINIA						
Byrd	Y	Y	N	Y	Y	Y
Rockefeller	Y	Y	Y	Y	Y	Y
WISCONSIN						
Kohl	Y	Y	N	Y	Y	Y
Feingold	Y	Y	N	Y	Y	N
WYOMING						
Thomas	N	Y	N	Y	Y	N
Enzi	N	Y	N	Y	Y	N

ND Northern Democrats   SD Southern Democrats

Southern states - Ala., Ark., Fla., Ga., Ky., La., Miss., N.C., Okla., S.C., Tenn., Texas, Va.

261. S 1246. Fiscal 2001 Supplemental Agriculture Assistance/Republican Substitute. Reid, D-Nev., motion to table (kill) the Lugar, R-Ind., substitute amendment that would strike the provisions in the bill and insert language to provide $5.5 billion in emergency agriculture assistance to farmers, including $4.6 billion for market loss assistance, $424 million for oilseed payments, and $54 million for peanut assistance. Motion agreed to 52-48: R 2-47; D 49-1 (ND 41-0, SD 8-1); I 1-0. A "nay" was a vote in support of the president's position. July 31, 2001.

262. HR 2299. Fiscal 2002 Transportation Appropriations/Cloture. Motion to invoke cloture (thus limiting debate) on the bill that would provide $60 billion for the Transportation Department and various agencies. It also would restrict Mexican truck access to the United States. Motion agreed to 100-0: R 49-0; D 50-0 (ND 41-0, SD 9-0); I 1-0. (Three-fifths of the total Senate (60) is required to invoke cloture.) Aug. 1, 2001.

263. HR 2620. Fiscal 2002 VA-HUD Appropriations/Veterans' Medical Care. Wellstone, D-Minn., motion to waive the Budget Act with respect to the Bond, R-Mo., point of order against the Wellstone amendment to the Mikulski, D-Md., substitute amendment. The Wellstone amendment would increase the amount available for veterans' medical care by $650 million. The substitute amendment would provide $84.1 billion in discretionary spending for the departments of Veterans Affairs (VA) and Housing and Urban Development (HUD) and related agencies. Motion rejected 25-75: R 8-41; D 16-34 (ND 13-28, SD 3-6); I 1-0. (A three-fifths

majority vote (60) of the total Senate is required to waive the Budget Act.) (Subsequently, the chair upheld the point of order, and the amendment fell.) Aug. 1, 2001.

264. Hutchinson Nomination/Confirmation. Confirmation of President Bush's nomination of Asa Hutchinson of Arkansas to be administrator of the Drug Enforcement Administration. Confirmed 98-1: R 48-0; D 49-1 (ND 40-1, SD 9-0); I 1-0. A "yea" was a vote in support of the president's position. Aug. 1, 2001.

265. HR 2620. Fiscal 2002 VA-HUD Appropriations/Arsenic Standard. Boxer, D-Calif., amendment to the Mikulski, D-Md., substitute amendment. The Boxer amendment would require the EPA to immediately adopt a new standard for arsenic in drinking water consistent with the Safe Drinking Water Act. Adopted 97-1: R 46-1; D 50-0 (ND 41-0, SD 9-0); I 1-0. Aug. 1, 2001.

266. HR 2620. Fiscal 2002 VA-HUD Appropriations/Clean Water Grant Formula. Bond, R-Mo., motion to table (kill) the Kyl, R-Ariz., amendment to the Mikulski, D-Md., substitute amendment. The Kyl amendment would provide that the new Clean Water State Revolving Fund formula would be a minimum of 0.675 percent and a maximum of 8 percent of drinking water needs. Motion agreed to 58-41: R 21-27; D 36-14 (ND 27-14, SD 9-0); I 1-0. Aug. 2, 2001.

	267	268	269	270	271	272
ALABAMA						
Shelby	Y	Y	Y	Y	Y	Y
Sessions	Y	Y	Y	Y	Y	Y
ALASKA						
Stevens	Y	Y	Y	Y	Y	Y
Murkowski	Y	N	Y	Y	Y	Y
ARIZONA						
McCain	Y	N	N	Y	Y	Y
Kyl	Y	N	N	Y	Y	Y
ARKANSAS						
Hutchinson	Y	Y	Y	Y	Y	Y
Lincoln	Y	Y	Y	Y	Y	Y
CALIFORNIA						
Feinstein	N	Y	Y	Y	Y	Y
Boxer	N	Y	Y	Y	Y	Y
COLORADO						
Campbell	Y	N	Y	Y	Y	Y
Allard	Y	N	Y	Y	Y	Y
CONNECTICUT						
Dodd	N	Y	Y	Y	Y	Y
Lieberman	N	Y	Y	Y	Y	Y
DELAWARE						
Carper	N	Y	Y	Y	Y	Y
Biden	N	Y	Y	Y	Y	Y
FLORIDA						
Graham	N	N	Y	Y	Y	Y
Nelson	Y	N	Y	Y	Y	Y
GEORGIA						
Miller	Y	N	Y	Y	Y	Y
Cleland	Y	N	Y	Y	Y	Y
HAWAII						
Inouye	N	Y	Y	?	?	?
Akaka	N	Y	Y	Y	Y	Y
IDAHO						
Craig	Y	Y	Y	Y	Y	Y
Crapo	Y	Y	Y	Y	Y	Y
ILLINOIS						
Durbin	N	Y	Y	Y	Y	Y
Fitzgerald	N	N	Y	Y	Y	Y
INDIANA						
Lugar	Y	N	Y	Y	Y	Y
Bayh	Y	Y	Y	Y	Y	Y

	267	268	269	270	271	272
IOWA						
Grassley	Y	Y	Y	Y	Y	Y
Harkin	N	Y	Y	Y	Y	Y
KANSAS						
Brownback	Y	Y	Y	Y	Y	Y
Roberts	Y	Y	Y	Y	Y	Y
KENTUCKY						
McConnell	Y	Y	Y	Y	Y	Y
Bunning	Y	N	Y	Y	Y	Y
LOUISIANA						
Breaux	Y	Y	Y	Y	Y	Y
Landrieu	N	Y	Y	Y	Y	Y
MAINE						
Snowe	Y	N	Y	Y	Y	Y
Collins	Y	N	Y	Y	Y	Y
MARYLAND						
Sarbanes	N	Y	Y	Y	Y	Y
Mikulski	N	Y	Y	Y	Y	Y
MASSACHUSETTS						
Kennedy	N	Y	Y	Y	Y	Y
Kerry	N	Y	Y	Y	Y	Y
MICHIGAN						
Levin	N	Y	Y	Y	Y	Y
Stabenow	N	Y	Y	Y	Y	Y
MINNESOTA						
Wellstone	N	N	Y	Y	Y	Y
Dayton	N	N	Y	Y	Y	Y
MISSISSIPPI						
Cochran	Y	Y	Y	Y	Y	Y
Lott	Y	Y	Y	Y	Y	Y
MISSOURI						
Bond	Y	Y	Y	Y	Y	Y
Carnahan	Y	Y	Y	Y	Y	Y
MONTANA						
Baucus	Y	N	Y	Y	Y	Y
Burns	Y	N	Y	Y	Y	Y
NEBRASKA						
Nelson	N	Y	Y	Y	Y	Y
Hagel	Y	Y	Y	Y	Y	Y
NEVADA						
Reid	Y	Y	Y	Y	Y	Y
Ensign	Y	N	Y	Y	Y	Y

	267	268	269	270	271	272
NEW HAMPSHIRE						
Smith	Y	N	Y	Y	Y	Y
Gregg	?	Y	Y	Y	Y	Y
NEW JERSEY						
Corzine	N	Y	Y	Y	Y	Y
Torricelli	N	Y	Y	Y	Y	Y
NEW MEXICO						
Domenici	?	?	?	?	?	?
Bingaman	Y	Y	Y	Y	Y	Y
NEW YORK						
Clinton	N	Y	Y	Y	Y	Y
Schumer	N	Y	Y	Y	Y	Y
NORTH CAROLINA						
Helms	Y	Y	Y	Y	Y	Y
Edwards	Y	Y	Y	Y	Y	Y
NORTH DAKOTA						
Conrad	Y	Y	Y	Y	Y	Y
Dorgan	Y	Y	Y	Y	Y	Y
OHIO						
DeWine	Y	Y	Y	Y	Y	Y
Voinovich	Y	N	N	Y	Y	Y
OKLAHOMA						
Nickles	Y	N	Y	Y	Y	Y
Inhofe	Y	N	Y	Y	Y	Y
OREGON						
Wyden	N	Y	Y	Y	Y	Y
Smith	Y	Y	Y	Y	Y	Y
PENNSYLVANIA						
Specter	Y	Y	Y	Y	Y	Y
Santorum	Y	Y	Y	Y	Y	Y
RHODE ISLAND						
Reed	N	Y	Y	Y	Y	Y
Chafee	Y	Y	Y	Y	Y	Y
SOUTH CAROLINA						
Thurmond	Y	Y	Y	Y	Y	Y
Hollings	N	Y	Y	Y	Y	Y
SOUTH DAKOTA						
Daschle	N	Y	Y	Y	Y	Y
Johnson	Y	Y	Y	Y	Y	Y
TENNESSEE						
Thompson	Y	Y	Y	?	Y	Y
Frist	Y	Y	Y	Y	Y	Y

	267	268	269	270	271	272
TEXAS						
Gramm	Y	N	N	Y	Y	Y
Hutchison	Y	N	Y	Y	Y	Y
UTAH						
Hatch	Y	Y	Y	Y	Y	Y
Bennett	Y	Y	Y	Y	Y	Y
VERMONT						
Leahy	Y	Y	Y	Y	Y	Y
Jeffords	Y	Y	Y	Y	Y	Y
VIRGINIA						
Warner	Y	N	Y	Y	Y	Y
Allen	Y	N	Y	Y	Y	Y
WASHINGTON						
Cantwell	N	Y	Y	Y	Y	Y
Murray	N	Y	Y	Y	Y	Y
WEST VIRGINIA						
Byrd	Y	Y	Y	Y	Y	Y
Rockefeller	Y	N	Y	Y	Y	Y
WISCONSIN						
Kohl	N	Y	Y	Y	Y	Y
Feingold	Y	N	N	Y	Y	Y
WYOMING						
Thomas	Y	N	Y	Y	Y	Y
Enzi	Y	Y	Y	Y	Y	Y

Key

Y	Voted for (yea).
#	Paired for.
+	Announced for.
N	Voted against (nay).
X	Paired against.
–	Announced against.
P	Voted "present."
C	Voted "present" to avoid possible conflict of interest.
?	Did not vote or otherwise make a position known.

Democrats   **Republicans**
Independents

ND Northern Democrats   SD Southern Democrats

Southern states - Ala., Ark., Fla., Ga., Ky., La., Miss., N.C., Okla., S.C., Tenn., Texas, Va.

267. HR 2620. Fiscal 2002 VA-HUD Appropriations/Gun Buyback Initiatives. Craig, R-Idaho, motion to table (kill) the Schumer, D-N.Y., amendment to the Mikulski, D-Md., substitute amendment. The Schumer amendment would allow $15 million from the Housing Drug Elimination Program to be used for the BuyBack America program, allowing public housing authorities and local police departments to undertake buyback initiatives. The substitute amendment would provide $84.1 billion for the departments of Veterans Affairs (VA) and Housing and Urban Development (HUD) and related agencies. Motion agreed to 65-33: R 46-1; D 18-32 (ND 12-29, SD 6-3); I 1-0. Aug. 2, 2001.

268. HR 2620. Fiscal 2002 VA-HUD Appropriations/Veterans' Claims Adjudication. Mikulski, D-Md., motion to table (kill) the McCain, R-Ariz., amendment to the Mikulski substitute amendment. The McCain amendment would increase by $5 million the amount available for veterans' claims adjudication, offset by reducing by $5 million the amount available for certain projects funded by the Community Development Fund at the Department of Housing and Urban Development. Motion agreed to 69-30: R 27-21; D 41-9 (ND 36-5, SD 5-4); I 1-0. Aug. 2, 2001.

269. HR 2620. Fiscal 2002 VA-HUD Appropriations/Passage. Passage of a bill that would provide $84.1 billion for the departments of Veterans Affairs (VA) and Housing and Urban Development (HUD) and related agencies, including the EPA, NASA, and the National Science Foundation. The bill, as amended, also would require the EPA to immediately adopt a new standard for arsenic in drinking water consistent with the Safe Drinking Water Act. Passed 94-5: R 44-4; D 49-1 (ND 40-1, SD 9-0); I 1-0. (Before passage, the Senate struck all after the enacting clause, and inserted the text of the Mikulski, D-Md., substitute amendment, as modified, into the bill.) Aug. 2, 2001.

270. Riley Nomination/Confirmation. Confirmation of President Bush's nomination of William J. Riley of Nebraska to be a judge for the 8th U.S. Circuit Court. Confirmed 97-0: R 47-0; D 49-0 (ND 40-0, SD 9-0); I 1-0. A "yea" was a vote in support of the president's position. Aug. 2, 2001.

271. Hart Nomination/Confirmation. Confirmation of President Bush's nomination of Sarah V. Hart of Pennsylvania to be director of the National Institute of Justice. Confirmed 98-0: R 48-0; D 49-0 (ND 40-0, SD 9-0); I 1-0. A "yea" was a vote in support of the president's position. Aug. 2, 2001.

272. Mueller Nomination/Confirmation. Confirmation of President Bush's nomination of Robert S. Mueller III of California to be director of the FBI. Confirmed 98-0: R 48-0; D 49-0 (ND 40-0, SD 9-0); I 1-0. A "yea" was a vote in support of the president's position. Aug. 2, 2001.

	273
ALABAMA	
Shelby	N
Sessions	N
ALASKA	
Stevens	N
Murkowski	N
ARIZONA	
McCain	N
Kyl	N
ARKANSAS	
Hutchinson	Y
Lincoln	Y
CALIFORNIA	
Feinstein	Y
Boxer	?
COLORADO	
Campbell	N
Allard	N
CONNECTICUT	
Dodd	Y
Lieberman	Y
DELAWARE	
Carper	Y
Biden	Y
FLORIDA	
Graham	Y
Nelson	Y
GEORGIA	
Miller	Y
Cleland	Y
HAWAII	
Inouye	?
Akaka	Y
IDAHO	
Craig	N
Crapo	N
ILLINOIS	
Durbin	Y
Fitzgerald	N
INDIANA	
Lugar	N
Bayh	Y

	273
IOWA	
Grassley	N
Harkin	Y
KANSAS	
Brownback	N
Roberts	N
KENTUCKY	
McConnell	N
Bunning	N
LOUISIANA	
Breaux	Y
Landrieu	Y
MAINE	
Snowe	Y
Collins	N
MARYLAND	
Sarbanes	Y
Mikulski	Y
MASSACHUSETTS	
Kennedy	Y
Kerry	Y
MICHIGAN	
Levin	Y
Stabenow	Y
MINNESOTA	
Wellstone	Y
Dayton	Y
MISSISSIPPI	
Cochran	N
Lott	N
MISSOURI	
Bond	N
Carnahan	Y
MONTANA	
Baucus	Y
Burns	N
NEBRASKA	
Nelson	Y
Hagel	N
NEVADA	
Reid	Y
Ensign	N

	273
NEW HAMPSHIRE	
Smith	N
Gregg	N
NEW JERSEY	
Corzine	Y
Torricelli	N
NEW MEXICO	
Domenici	?
Bingaman	Y
NEW YORK	
Clinton	Y
Schumer	Y
NORTH CAROLINA	
Helms	N
Edwards	Y
NORTH DAKOTA	
Conrad	Y
Dorgan	Y
OHIO	
DeWine	N
Voinovich	N
OKLAHOMA	
Nickles	N
Inhofe	N
OREGON	
Wyden	Y
Smith	N
PENNSYLVANIA	
Specter	N
Santorum	N
RHODE ISLAND	
Reed	Y
Chafee	N
SOUTH CAROLINA	
Thurmond	N
Hollings	Y
SOUTH DAKOTA	
Daschle	Y
Johnson	Y
TENNESSEE	
Thompson	N
Frist	N

Key

Y	Voted for (yea).
#	Paired for.
+	Announced for.
N	Voted against (nay).
X	Paired against.
–	Announced against.
P	Voted "present."
C	Voted "present" to avoid possible conflict of interest.
?	Did not vote or otherwise make a position known.

Democrats **Republicans**
Independents

	273
TEXAS	
Gramm	N
Hutchison	N
UTAH	
Hatch	N
Bennett	N
VERMONT	
Leahy	Y
Jeffords	Y
VIRGINIA	
Warner	N
Allen	N
WASHINGTON	
Cantwell	Y
Murray	Y
WEST VIRGINIA	
Byrd	Y
Rockefeller	Y
WISCONSIN	
Kohl	Y
Feingold	N
WYOMING	
Thomas	N
Enzi	N

ND Northern Democrats   SD Southern Democrats

Southern states - Ala., Ark., Fla., Ga., Ky., La., Miss., N.C., Okla., S.C., Tenn., Texas, Va.

273. S 1246. Fiscal 2001 Supplemental Agriculture Assistance/ Cloture. Motion to invoke cloture (thus limiting debate) on the bill that would authorize $7.4 billion in additional economic assistance to farmers in fiscal 2001. Motion rejected 49-48: R 2-46; D 46-2 (ND 37-2, SD 9-0); I 1-0. Three-fifths of the total Senate (60) is required to invoke cloture. Aug. 3, 2001.

	274	275
ALABAMA		
Shelby	N	N
Sessions	N	N
ALASKA		
Stevens	Y	Y
Murkowski	?	?
ARIZONA		
McCain	N	N
Kyl	N	N
ARKANSAS		
Hutchinson	N	Y
Lincoln	Y	Y
CALIFORNIA		
Feinstein	Y	Y
Boxer	Y	Y
COLORADO		
Campbell	Y	Y
Allard	Y	Y
CONNECTICUT		
Dodd	Y	Y
Lieberman	Y	Y
DELAWARE		
Carper	Y	Y
Biden	Y	Y
FLORIDA		
Graham	Y	Y
Nelson	Y	Y
GEORGIA		
Miller	Y	Y
Cleland	Y	Y
HAWAII		
Inouye	Y	Y
Akaka	Y	Y
IDAHO		
Craig	Y	Y
Crapo	Y	Y
ILLINOIS		
Durbin	Y	Y
Fitzgerald	Y	Y
INDIANA		
Lugar	Y	Y
Bayh	Y	Y

	274	275
IOWA		
Grassley	N	Y
Harkin	Y	Y
KANSAS		
Brownback	Y	Y
Roberts	Y	Y
KENTUCKY		
McConnell	Y	Y
Bunning	Y	Y
LOUISIANA		
Breaux	Y	Y
Landrieu	Y	Y
MAINE		
Snowe	N	Y
Collins	Y	Y
MARYLAND		
Sarbanes	Y	Y
Mikulski	Y	Y
MASSACHUSETTS		
Kennedy	?	Y
Kerry	Y	Y
MICHIGAN		
Levin	Y	Y
Stabenow	Y	Y
MINNESOTA		
Wellstone	Y	Y
Dayton	Y	Y
MISSISSIPPI		
Cochran	N	N
Lott	Y	Y
MISSOURI		
Bond	Y	Y
Carnahan	Y	Y
MONTANA		
Baucus	Y	Y
Burns	Y	Y
NEBRASKA		
Nelson	Y	Y
Hagel	Y	Y
NEVADA		
Reid	Y	Y
Ensign	Y	Y

	274	275
NEW HAMPSHIRE		
Smith	N	N
Gregg	?	Y
NEW JERSEY		
Corzine	Y	Y
Torricelli	?	Y
NEW MEXICO		
Domenici	Y	Y
Bingaman	Y	Y
NEW YORK		
Clinton	Y	Y
Schumer	Y	Y
NORTH CAROLINA		
Helms	N	N
Edwards	Y	Y
NORTH DAKOTA		
Conrad	Y	Y
Dorgan	Y	Y
OHIO		
DeWine	N	N
Voinovich	N	Y
OKLAHOMA		
Nickles	Y	Y
Inhofe	N	N
OREGON		
Wyden	Y	Y
Smith	Y	Y
PENNSYLVANIA		
Specter	N	N
Santorum	?	Y
RHODE ISLAND		
Reed	Y	Y
Chafee	Y	Y
SOUTH CAROLINA		
Thurmond	N	N
Hollings	Y	Y
SOUTH DAKOTA		
Daschle	Y	Y
Johnson	Y	Y
TENNESSEE		
Thompson	N	N
Frist	N	Y

Key

Y Voted for (yea).
Paired for.
+ Announced for.
N Voted against (nay).
X Paired against.
– Announced against.
P Voted "present."
C Voted "present" to avoid possible conflict of interest.
? Did not vote or otherwise make a position known.

Democrats   **Republicans**
Independents

	274	275
TEXAS		
Gramm	Y	Y
Hutchison	Y	Y
UTAH		
Hatch	Y	Y
Bennett	Y	Y
VERMONT		
Leahy	Y	Y
Jeffords	?	Y
VIRGINIA		
Warner	N	Y
Allen	Y	Y
WASHINGTON		
Cantwell	Y	Y
Murray	?	Y
WEST VIRGINIA		
Byrd	Y	N
Rockefeller	Y	Y
WISCONSIN		
Kohl	Y	Y
Feingold	N	N
WYOMING		
Thomas	Y	Y
Enzi	Y	Y

ND Northern Democrats   SD Southern Democrats

Southern states - Ala., Ark., Fla., Ga., Ky., La., Miss., N.C., Okla., S.C., Tenn., Texas, Va.

274. S 149. Export Administration Act Reauthorization/Review Time Extension. Gramm, R-Texas, motion to table (kill) the Thompson, R-Tenn., amendment that would modify the time extension an executive agency can receive for reviewing license applications to a maximum of 60 days, based on the complexity of the analysis or the potential impact on U.S. national security or foreign policy interests. Motion agreed to 74-19: R 28-18; D 46-1 (ND 37-1, SD 9-0); I 0-0. Sept. 4, 2001.

275. S 149. Export Administration Act Reauthorization/Passage. Passage of the bill that would reauthorize and revise the Export Administration Act of 1979, which provides the president the authority to control the export of sensitive dual-use items for national security and foreign policy purposes. The bill would eliminate restrictions on the export of technology that is mass-marketed or readily available in foreign markets, and increase penalties for violating export restrictions. The bill as amended also would make it easier to block the exports of dual-use products to countries if U.S. inspectors cannot verify that they are being used commercially, rather than for military or intelligence purposes. Dual-use products could be sold abroad only if comparable foreign versions of the products are of the same quality as the U.S. items. Passed 85-14: R 36-12; D 48-2 (ND 39-2, SD 9-0); I 1-0. Sept. 6, 2001.

	276	277	278	279
ALABAMA				
Shelby	N	Y	Y	Y
Sessions	N	Y	Y	Y
ALASKA				
Stevens	Y	Y	Y	Y
Murkowski	Y	Y	Y	Y
ARIZONA				
McCain	?	Y	Y	Y
Kyl	?	Y	Y	Y
ARKANSAS				
Hutchinson	N	Y	Y	Y
Lincoln	N	Y	Y	Y
CALIFORNIA				
Feinstein	Y	Y	Y	Y
Boxer	N	Y	Y	Y
COLORADO				
Campbell	N	Y	Y	Y
Allard	N	Y	Y	Y
CONNECTICUT				
Dodd	Y	Y	?	?
Lieberman	N	Y	Y	Y
DELAWARE				
Carper	Y	Y	Y	Y
Biden	Y	Y	Y	Y
FLORIDA				
Graham	N	Y	Y	Y
Nelson	?	Y	Y	Y
GEORGIA				
Miller	N	Y	Y	Y
Cleland	Y	Y	Y	Y
HAWAII				
Inouye	Y	Y	Y	Y
Akaka	Y	Y	Y	Y
IDAHO				
Craig	N	Y	Y	Y
Crapo	N	Y	Y	Y
ILLINOIS				
Durbin	N	Y	Y	Y
Fitzgerald	Y	Y	Y	Y
INDIANA				
Lugar	Y	Y	Y	Y
Bayh	N	Y	Y	Y

	276	277	278	279
IOWA				
Grassley	N	Y	Y	Y
Harkin	N	Y	Y	Y
KANSAS				
Brownback	N	Y	Y	Y
Roberts	N	Y	Y	Y
KENTUCKY				
McConnell	Y	Y	Y	Y
Bunning	N	Y	Y	Y
LOUISIANA				
Breaux	N	Y	Y	Y
Landrieu	N	Y	Y	Y
MAINE				
Snowe	N	Y	Y	Y
Collins	N	Y	Y	Y
MARYLAND				
Sarbanes	Y	Y	Y	Y
Mikulski	Y	Y	Y	?
MASSACHUSETTS				
Kennedy	N	Y	Y	?
Kerry	?	Y	Y	Y
MICHIGAN				
Levin	Y	Y	Y	Y
Stabenow	?	Y	Y	Y
MINNESOTA				
Wellstone	N	Y	Y	Y
Dayton	N	Y	Y	Y
MISSISSIPPI				
Cochran	N	Y	Y	Y
Lott	Y	Y	Y	Y
MISSOURI				
Bond	Y	Y	Y	Y
Carnahan	?	Y	Y	Y
MONTANA				
Baucus	N	Y	Y	Y
Burns	N	Y	Y	Y
NEBRASKA				
Nelson	Y	Y	Y	Y
Hagel	Y	Y	Y	Y
NEVADA				
Reid	Y	Y	Y	Y
Ensign	N	Y	Y	Y

	276	277	278	279
NEW HAMPSHIRE				
Smith	N	Y	Y	Y
Gregg	Y	Y	Y	Y
NEW JERSEY				
Corzine	Y	Y	Y	Y
Torricelli	?	Y	Y	Y
NEW MEXICO				
Domenici	N	Y	Y	Y
Bingaman	N	Y	Y	Y
NEW YORK				
Clinton	N	Y	Y	Y
Schumer	N	Y	Y	Y
NORTH CAROLINA				
Helms	Y	Y	Y	Y
Edwards	?	Y	Y	Y
NORTH DAKOTA				
Conrad	N	Y	Y	Y
Dorgan	N	Y	Y	Y
OHIO				
DeWine	N	Y	Y	Y
Voinovich	N	Y	?	Y
OKLAHOMA				
Nickles	Y	Y	Y	Y
Inhofe	N	Y	Y	Y
OREGON				
Wyden	N	Y	Y	Y
Smith	N	Y	Y	Y
PENNSYLVANIA				
Specter	N	Y	Y	Y
Santorum	N	Y	Y	Y
RHODE ISLAND				
Reed	Y	Y	Y	Y
Chafee	Y	Y	Y	Y
SOUTH CAROLINA				
Thurmond	N	Y	Y	Y
Hollings	Y	Y	Y	Y
SOUTH DAKOTA				
Daschle	Y	Y	Y	Y
Johnson	N	Y	Y	Y
TENNESSEE				
Thompson	Y	Y	Y	Y
Frist	N	Y	Y	Y

Key

Y	Voted for (yea).
#	Paired for.
+	Announced for.
N	Voted against (nay).
X	Paired against.
−	Announced against.
P	Voted "present."
C	Voted "present" to avoid possible conflict of interest.
?	Did not vote or otherwise make a position known.

Democrats   **Republicans**
Independents

	276	277	278	279
TEXAS				
Gramm	N	Y	Y	Y
Hutchison	N	Y	Y	Y
UTAH				
Hatch	N	Y	Y	Y
Bennett	N	Y	Y	Y
VERMONT				
Leahy	N	Y	Y	Y
Jeffords	Y	Y	Y	Y
VIRGINIA				
Warner	N	Y	Y	Y
Allen	N	Y	Y	Y
WASHINGTON				
Cantwell	N	Y	Y	Y
Murray	N	Y	Y	Y
WEST VIRGINIA				
Byrd	Y	Y	Y	Y
Rockefeller	Y	Y	Y	Y
WISCONSIN				
Kohl	Y	Y	Y	Y
Feingold	N	Y	Y	Y
WYOMING				
Thomas	N	Y	Y	Y
Enzi	Y	Y	Y	Y

ND Northern Democrats   SD Southern Democrats

Southern states - Ala., Ark., Fla., Ga., Ky., La., Miss., N.C., Okla., S.C., Tenn., Texas, Va.

276. HR 2500. Fiscal 2002 Commerce-Justice-State Appropriations/ Slave Labor. Inouye, D-Hawaii, motion to table (kill) the Smith, R-N.H., amendment that would prohibit the use of funds under the bill by the Justice or State departments to file a court motion opposing a civil action against a Japanese person or corporation where plaintiffs allege they were used as slave or forced labor while they were World War II American prisoners of war. Motion rejected 34-58: R 14-33; D 19-25 (ND 17-20, SD 2-5); I 1-0. (Subsequently, the amendment was adopted by voice vote.) A "yea" was a vote in support of the president's position. Sept. 10, 2001.

277. S J Res 22. Terrorist Attacks/Passage. Passage of the joint resolution that would express the sense of Congress that the Senate and the House condemn the terrorists who planned and carried out the Sept. 11, 2001, attacks against the United States, as well as their sponsors; extend deepest condolences to the victims and their families; commend the actions of rescue workers, volunteers and officials responding to the scene; commit support of increased resources to eradicate terrorism; and declare Sept. 14, 2001, a na-

tional day of unity and mourning. Passed 100-0: R 49-0; D 50-0 (ND 41-0, SD 9-0); I 1-0. Sept. 12, 2001.

278. HR 2500. Fiscal 2002 Commerce-Justice-State Appropriations/ Civil Rights Protection. Harkin, D-Iowa, amendment that would express the sense of the Senate that the civil rights and liberties of all Americans, including Arab-Americans and American Muslims, should be protected in the search to bring sponsors of the terrorist attacks on the United States to justice. It also would condemn any acts of violence and discrimination against any Americans, including Arab-Americans and American Muslims. Adopted 98-0: R 48-0; D 49-0 (ND 40-0, SD 9-0); I 1-0. Sept. 13, 2001.

279. HR 2500. Fiscal 2002 Commerce-Justice-State Appropriations/ Passage. Passage of the bill that would appropriate $41.5 billion in fiscal 2002 for the departments of Commerce, Justice and State and the federal judiciary and related agencies, $1.74 billion more than fiscal 2001. The bill also would establish a deputy attorney general position in charge of anti-terrorism. Passed 97-0: R 49-0; D 47-0 (ND 38-0, SD 9-0); I 1-0. Sept. 13, 2001.

	280	281
ALABAMA		
Shelby	Y	Y
Sessions	Y	Y
ALASKA		
Stevens	Y	Y
Murkowski	Y	Y
ARIZONA		
McCain	Y	Y
Kyl	Y	Y
ARKANSAS		
Hutchinson	Y	Y
Lincoln	Y	Y
CALIFORNIA		
Feinstein	Y	Y
Boxer	Y	Y
COLORADO		
Campbell	Y	Y
Allard	Y	Y
CONNECTICUT		
Dodd	Y	Y
Lieberman	Y	Y
DELAWARE		
Carper	Y	Y
Biden	Y	Y
FLORIDA		
Graham	Y	Y
Nelson	Y	Y
GEORGIA		
Miller	Y	Y
Cleland	Y	Y
HAWAII		
Inouye	Y	Y
Akaka	Y	Y
IDAHO		
Craig	?	?
Crapo	Y	Y
ILLINOIS		
Durbin	Y	Y
Fitzgerald	Y	Y
INDIANA		
Lugar	Y	Y
Bayh	Y	Y

	280	281
IOWA		
Grassley	Y	Y
Harkin	Y	Y
KANSAS		
Brownback	Y	Y
Roberts	Y	Y
KENTUCKY		
McConnell	Y	Y
Bunning	Y	Y
LOUISIANA		
Breaux	Y	Y
Landrieu	Y	Y
MAINE		
Snowe	Y	Y
Collins	Y	Y
MARYLAND		
Sarbanes	Y	Y
Mikulski	Y	Y
MASSACHUSETTS		
Kennedy	Y	Y
Kerry	Y	Y
MICHIGAN		
Levin	Y	Y
Stabenow	Y	Y
MINNESOTA		
Wellstone	Y	Y
Dayton	Y	Y
MISSISSIPPI		
Cochran	Y	Y
Lott	Y	Y
MISSOURI		
Bond	Y	Y
Carnahan	Y	Y
MONTANA		
Baucus	Y	Y
Burns	Y	Y
NEBRASKA		
Nelson	Y	Y
Hagel	Y	Y
NEVADA		
Reid	Y	Y
Ensign	Y	Y

	280	281
NEW HAMPSHIRE		
Smith	Y	Y
Gregg	Y	Y
NEW JERSEY		
Corzine	Y	Y
Torricelli	Y	Y
NEW MEXICO		
Domenici	Y	Y
Bingaman	Y	Y
NEW YORK		
Clinton	Y	Y
Schumer	Y	Y
NORTH CAROLINA		
Helms	+	+
Edwards	Y	Y
NORTH DAKOTA		
Conrad	Y	Y
Dorgan	Y	Y
OHIO		
DeWine	Y	Y
Voinovich	+	Y
OKLAHOMA		
Nickles	Y	Y
Inhofe	Y	Y
OREGON		
Wyden	Y	Y
Smith	Y	Y
PENNSYLVANIA		
Specter	Y	Y
Santorum	Y	Y
RHODE ISLAND		
Reed	Y	Y
Chafee	Y	Y
SOUTH CAROLINA		
Thurmond	Y	Y
Hollings	Y	Y
SOUTH DAKOTA		
Daschle	Y	Y
Johnson	Y	Y
TENNESSEE		
Thompson	Y	Y
Frist	Y	Y

	280	281
TEXAS		
Gramm	Y	Y
Hutchison	Y	Y
UTAH		
Hatch	Y	Y
Bennett	Y	Y
VERMONT		
Leahy	Y	Y
Jeffords	?	Y
VIRGINIA		
Warner	Y	Y
Allen	Y	Y
WASHINGTON		
Cantwell	Y	Y
Murray	Y	Y
WEST VIRGINIA		
Byrd	Y	Y
Rockefeller	Y	Y
WISCONSIN		
Kohl	Y	Y
Feingold	Y	Y
WYOMING		
Thomas	Y	Y
Enzi	Y	Y

ND Northern Democrats   SD Southern Democrats

Southern states - Ala., Ark., Fla., Ga., Ky., La., Miss., N.C., Okla., S.C., Tenn., Texas, Va.

280. S 1426. Emergency Supplemental Appropriations/Passage. Passage of the bill that would provide $40 billion in emergency supplemental appropriations available for disaster assistance, anti-terrorism initiatives and recovery assistance from the terrorist attacks on the United States that occurred on Sept. 11, 2001. Passed 96-0: R 46-0; D 50-0 (ND 41-0, SD 9-0); I 0-0. (By unanimous consent, the Senate subsequently passed an identical House-passed bill (HR 2888), clearing that measure for the president.) A "yea" was a vote in support of the president's position. Sept. 14, 2001.

281. S J Res 23. Use of Force Authorization/Passage. Passage of the joint resolution that would authorize the president to use all necessary and appropriate force against the nations, organizations or people that he determines planned, authorized, committed or aided the terrorist attacks that occurred on Sept. 11, 2001, or that harbored such organizations or people, to prevent future acts of terrorism against the United States. Passed 98-0: R 47-0; D 50-0 (ND 41-0, SD 9-0); I 1-0. A "yea" was a vote in support of the president's position. Sept. 14, 2001.

	282	283	284	285	286	287	288
ALABAMA							
Shelby	Y	Y	Y	Y	N	Y	Y
Sessions	Y	Y	Y	Y	Y	Y	Y
ALASKA							
Stevens	Y	Y	Y	Y	N	N	Y
Murkowski	Y	Y	Y	Y	N	N	Y
ARIZONA							
McCain	?	?	Y	Y	Y	N	Y
Kyl	Y	Y	Y	Y	Y	Y	Y
ARKANSAS							
Hutchinson	Y	Y	Y	Y	N	Y	Y
Lincoln	Y	Y	Y	Y	Y	Y	Y
CALIFORNIA							
Feinstein	Y	Y	Y	Y	N	Y	Y
Boxer	Y	Y	Y	Y	N	Y	?
COLORADO							
Campbell	Y	Y	?	Y	N	Y	Y
Allard	Y	Y	Y	Y	Y	Y	Y
CONNECTICUT							
Dodd	Y	Y	Y	Y	Y	Y	?
Lieberman	Y	Y	Y	Y	Y	Y	Y
DELAWARE							
Carper	Y	Y	Y	Y	Y	?	?
Biden	Y	Y	Y	Y	Y	?	?
FLORIDA							
Graham	Y	Y	Y	Y	Y	N	Y
Nelson	Y	Y	Y	Y	Y	Y	Y
GEORGIA							
Miller	Y	Y	Y	Y	Y	Y	Y
Cleland	Y	Y	Y	Y	N	Y	Y
HAWAII							
Inouye	Y	Y	Y	Y	N	Y	Y
Akaka	Y	Y	Y	Y	Y	Y	Y
IDAHO							
Craig	Y	Y	Y	Y	N	Y	Y
Crapo	Y	Y	Y	Y	N	Y	Y
ILLINOIS							
Durbin	Y	Y	Y	Y	N	N	Y
Fitzgerald	Y	Y	N	Y	N	N	Y
INDIANA							
Lugar	Y	Y	Y	Y	Y	Y	Y
Bayh	Y	Y	Y	Y	Y	Y	Y

	282	283	284	285	286	287	288
IOWA							
Grassley	Y	Y	Y	Y	Y	Y	Y
Harkin	Y	Y	Y	Y	Y	Y	Y
KANSAS							
Brownback	Y	Y	Y	Y	N	Y	Y
Roberts	Y	Y	Y	Y	N	N	Y
KENTUCKY							
McConnell	Y	Y	Y	Y	N	N	Y
Bunning	Y	Y	Y	Y	N	Y	Y
LOUISIANA							
Breaux	Y	Y	Y	Y	N	Y	Y
Landrieu	Y	Y	Y	Y	Y	Y	Y
MAINE							
Snowe	Y	Y	Y	Y	N	Y	Y
Collins	Y	Y	Y	Y	N	Y	Y
MARYLAND							
Sarbanes	Y	Y	Y	Y	N	Y	Y
Mikulski	Y	Y	Y	Y	N	Y	Y
MASSACHUSETTS							
Kennedy	Y	Y	Y	Y	Y	Y	Y
Kerry	Y	Y	Y	Y	Y	Y	Y
MICHIGAN							
Levin	Y	Y	Y	Y	Y	Y	Y
Stabenow	Y	Y	Y	Y	Y	Y	Y
MINNESOTA							
Wellstone	Y	Y	Y	Y	Y	Y	Y
Dayton	Y	Y	Y	Y	Y	Y	Y
MISSISSIPPI							
Cochran	Y	Y	Y	Y	N	Y	Y
Lott	Y	Y	Y	Y	N	N	Y
MISSOURI							
Bond	Y	Y	Y	Y	N	N	Y
Carnahan	Y	Y	Y	Y	N	Y	Y
MONTANA							
Baucus	Y	Y	Y	Y	N	Y	Y
Burns	Y	Y	Y	Y	N	Y	Y
NEBRASKA							
Nelson	Y	Y	Y	Y	N	Y	Y
Hagel	Y	Y	Y	Y	Y	Y	Y
NEVADA							
Reid	Y	Y	Y	Y	Y	Y	Y
Ensign	Y	Y	Y	?	Y	N	Y

	282	283	284	285	286	287	288
NEW HAMPSHIRE							
Smith	Y	Y	Y	Y	N	Y	Y
Gregg	Y	Y	Y	Y	N	Y	Y
NEW JERSEY							
Corzine	Y	Y	Y	Y	Y	Y	Y
Torricelli	Y	Y	Y	Y	N	Y	Y
NEW MEXICO							
Domenici	Y	Y	Y	Y	N	Y	Y
Bingaman	Y	Y	Y	Y	N	Y	Y
NEW YORK							
Clinton	Y	Y	Y	Y	N	Y	Y
Schumer	Y	Y	Y	Y	N	Y	Y
NORTH CAROLINA							
Helms	Y	Y	Y	Y	N	Y	Y
Edwards	Y	Y	Y	Y	N	Y	Y
NORTH DAKOTA							
Conrad	Y	Y	Y	Y	N	Y	Y
Dorgan	Y	Y	Y	Y	N	Y	Y
OHIO							
DeWine	Y	Y	Y	Y	Y	N	Y
Voinovich	Y	Y	Y	Y	Y	N	Y
OKLAHOMA							
Nickles	Y	Y	Y	Y	N	Y	Y
Inhofe	Y	Y	Y	Y	N	Y	Y
OREGON							
Wyden	Y	Y	Y	Y	Y	Y	Y
Smith	Y	Y	Y	Y	Y	Y	Y
PENNSYLVANIA							
Specter	Y	Y	Y	Y	N	Y	Y
Santorum	Y	Y	Y	?	Y	N	Y
RHODE ISLAND							
Reed	Y	Y	Y	Y	Y	Y	Y
Chafee	Y	Y	Y	Y	Y	N	Y
SOUTH CAROLINA							
Thurmond	Y	Y	Y	Y	Y	N	Y
Hollings	Y	Y	Y	Y	Y	Y	Y
SOUTH DAKOTA							
Daschle	Y	Y	Y	Y	Y	Y	Y
Johnson	Y	Y	Y	Y	Y	Y	Y
TENNESSEE							
Thompson	Y	Y	Y	Y	Y	N	Y
Frist	Y	Y	Y	Y	Y	Y	Y

Key

Y	Voted for (yea).
#	Paired for.
+	Announced for.
N	Voted against (nay).
X	Paired against.
−	Announced against.
P	Voted "present."
C	Voted "present" to avoid possible conflict of interest.
?	Did not vote or otherwise make a position known.

Democrats **Republicans**
Independents

	282	283	284	285	286	287	288
TEXAS							
Gramm	?	?	?	Y	Y	N	Y
Hutchison	Y	Y	Y	Y	N	N	Y
UTAH							
Hatch	Y	Y	Y	Y	N	N	Y
Bennett	Y	Y	Y	Y	N	Y	Y
VERMONT							
Leahy	Y	Y	Y	Y	Y	Y	Y
Jeffords	Y	Y	Y	?	Y	N	Y
VIRGINIA							
Warner	Y	Y	Y	Y	Y	Y	Y
Allen	Y	Y	Y	Y	Y	Y	Y
WASHINGTON							
Cantwell	Y	Y	Y	Y	N	Y	Y
Murray	Y	Y	Y	Y	Y	Y	Y
WEST VIRGINIA							
Byrd	Y	Y	Y	Y	Y	N	Y
Rockefeller	Y	Y	Y	Y	Y	Y	Y
WISCONSIN							
Kohl	Y	Y	Y	Y	Y	N	Y
Feingold	Y	Y	Y	Y	Y	Y	Y
WYOMING							
Thomas	?	?	?	Y	N	Y	Y
Enzi	Y	Y	Y	Y	Y	Y	Y

ND Northern Democrats   SD Southern Democrats

Southern states - Ala., Ark., Fla., Ga., Ky., La., Miss., N.C., Okla., S.C., Tenn., Texas, Va.

282. Prost Nomination/Confirmation. Confirmation of President Bush's nomination of Sharon Prost of the District of Columbia to be a judge for the U.S. Federal Circuit Court. Confirmed 97-0: R 46-0; D 50-0 (ND 41-0, SD 9-0); I 1-0. A "yea" was a vote in support of the president's position. Sept. 21, 2001.

283. Walton Nomination/Confirmation. Confirmation of President Bush's nomination of Reggie B. Walton of the District of Columbia to be a U.S. District judge for the District of Columbia. Confirmed 97-0: R 46-0; D 50-0 (ND 41-0, SD 9-0); I 1-0. A "yea" was a vote in support of the president's position. Sept. 21, 2001.

284. S 1450. Airline Relief/Passage. Passage of the bill that would provide $5 billion in grants and up to $10 billion in loan guarantees to airline companies to compensate for losses incurred as a result of the Sept. 11, 2001, terrorist attacks. The bill would create a federal board to review how the loan guarantees are handled, and establish a fund to compensate victims killed or injured in the attacks, or their survivors. Airlines' liability for damages related to the Sept. 11 attacks would be limited to the amount of insurance coverage they had for such events. Passed 96-1: R 45-1; D 50-0 (ND 41-0, SD 9-0); I 1-0. Sept. 21, 2001. (Under a unanimous consent agreement, the Senate subsequently passed the identical House bill (HR 2926), clearing it for the president.) Sept. 21, 2001.

285. Van Tine Nomination/Confirmation. Confirmation of President Bush's nomination of Kirk Van Tine of Virginia to be general counsel at the Transportation Department. Confirmed 97-0: R 47-0; D 50-0 (ND 41-0, SD 9-0); I 0-0. A "yea" was a vote in support of the president's position. Sept. 24, 2001.

286. S 1438. Fiscal 2002 Defense Authorization/Base Closures. Warner, R-Va., motion to table (kill) the Bunning, R-Ky., amendment that would strike the provision in the bill which authorizes an additional round of base re-alignment and closures in 2003. Motion agreed to 53-47: R 21-28; D 31-19 (ND 25-16, SD 6-3); I 1-0. Sept. 25, 2001.

287. S 1438. Fiscal 2002 Defense Authorization/Prison Labor. Warner, R-Va., motion to table (kill) the Warner amendment that would strike the provision in the bill that would permit private sector companies to compete against the Federal Prison Industries for purchasing contracts from the Defense Department. Motion agreed to 74-24: R 30-19; D 44-4 (ND 36-3, SD 8-1); I 0-1. Sept. 25, 2001.

288. HR 2904. Fiscal 2002 Military Construction Appropriations/Passage. Passage of the bill that would provide $10.5 billion for military construction projects including the building of barracks, family housing, and medical facilities for fiscal 2002. It also includes funds for base closing programs and the U.S. contribution to the North Atlantic Treaty Organization infrastructure fund. Passed 97-0: R 49-0; D 47-0 (ND 38-0, SD 9-0); I 1-0. Sept. 26, 2001.

	289	290	291
ALABAMA			
Shelby	Y	Y	Y
Sessions	Y	Y	N
ALASKA			
Stevens	Y	Y	Y
Murkowski	Y	Y	Y
ARIZONA			
McCain	Y	Y	Y
Kyl	Y	Y	Y
ARKANSAS			
Hutchinson	Y	Y	Y
Lincoln	Y	Y	Y
CALIFORNIA			
Feinstein	Y	Y	Y
Boxer	Y	Y	Y
COLORADO			
Campbell	Y	Y	N
Allard	Y	Y	Y
CONNECTICUT			
Dodd	Y	Y	Y
Lieberman	Y	Y	Y
DELAWARE			
Carper	Y	Y	Y
Biden	Y	Y	Y
FLORIDA			
Graham	Y	Y	Y
Nelson	Y	Y	Y
GEORGIA			
Miller	Y	Y	Y
Cleland	Y	Y	Y
HAWAII			
Inouye	Y	Y	Y
Akaka	Y	Y	Y
IDAHO			
Craig	Y	Y	Y
Crapo	Y	Y	Y
ILLINOIS			
Durbin	Y	Y	Y
Fitzgerald	Y	Y	Y
INDIANA			
Lugar	Y	Y	Y
Bayh	Y	Y	Y
IOWA			
Grassley	Y	Y	Y
Harkin	Y	Y	Y
KANSAS			
Brownback	Y	Y	Y
Roberts	Y	Y	Y
KENTUCKY			
McConnell	Y	Y	Y
Bunning	Y	Y	N
LOUISIANA			
Breaux	Y	Y	Y
Landrieu	Y	Y	Y
MAINE			
Snowe	Y	Y	Y
Collins	Y	Y	Y
MARYLAND			
Sarbanes	Y	Y	Y
Mikulski	Y	Y	Y
MASSACHUSETTS			
Kennedy	Y	Y	Y
Kerry	Y	Y	Y
MICHIGAN			
Levin	Y	Y	Y
Stabenow	Y	Y	Y
MINNESOTA			
Wellstone	Y	Y	Y
Dayton	Y	Y	Y
MISSISSIPPI			
Cochran	Y	Y	N
Lott	Y	Y	N
MISSOURI			
Bond	Y	Y	Y
Carnahan	Y	Y	Y
MONTANA			
Baucus	Y	Y	Y
Burns	Y	Y	Y
NEBRASKA			
Nelson	Y	Y	Y
Hagel	Y	Y	Y
NEVADA			
Reid	Y	Y	Y
Ensign	Y	Y	Y
NEW HAMPSHIRE			
Smith	Y	Y	N
Gregg	Y	Y	Y
NEW JERSEY			
Corzine	Y	Y	Y
Torricelli	Y	Y	Y
NEW MEXICO			
Domenici	Y	Y	Y
Bingaman	Y	Y	Y
NEW YORK			
Clinton	Y	Y	Y
Schumer	Y	Y	Y
NORTH CAROLINA			
Helms	Y	Y	N
Edwards	Y	Y	Y
NORTH DAKOTA			
Conrad	Y	Y	Y
Dorgan	Y	Y	Y
OHIO			
DeWine	Y	Y	Y
Voinovich	Y	Y	Y
OKLAHOMA			
Nickles	Y	Y	Y
Inhofe	Y	Y	Y
OREGON			
Wyden	Y	Y	Y
Smith	Y	Y	Y
PENNSYLVANIA			
Specter	Y	Y	Y
Santorum	Y	Y	Y
RHODE ISLAND			
Reed	Y	Y	Y
Chafee	Y	Y	Y
SOUTH CAROLINA			
Thurmond	Y	+	N
Hollings	Y	Y	Y
SOUTH DAKOTA			
Daschle	Y	Y	Y
Johnson	Y	Y	Y
TENNESSEE			
Thompson	Y	Y	Y
Frist	Y	Y	Y
TEXAS			
Gramm	Y	Y	Y
Hutchison	Y	Y	N
UTAH			
Hatch	Y	Y	N
Bennett	Y	Y	Y
VERMONT			
Leahy	Y	Y	Y
Jeffords	Y	Y	Y
VIRGINIA			
Warner	Y	Y	Y
Allen	Y	Y	Y
WASHINGTON			
Cantwell	Y	Y	Y
Murray	Y	Y	Y
WEST VIRGINIA			
Byrd	Y	Y	N
Rockefeller	Y	Y	Y
WISCONSIN			
Kohl	Y	Y	Y
Feingold	Y	Y	N
WYOMING			
Thomas	Y	Y	Y
Enzi	Y	Y	Y

Key

Y   Voted for (yea).
Paired for.
+   Announced for.
N   Voted against (nay).
X   Paired against.
–   Announced against.
P   Voted "present."
C   Voted "present" to avoid possible conflict of interest.
?   Did not vote or otherwise make a position known.

Democrats   **Republicans**
Independents

ND Northern Democrats   SD Southern Democrats

Southern states - Ala., Ark., Fla., Ga., Ky., La., Miss., N.C., Okla., S.C., Tenn., Texas, Va.

289. S 1438. Fiscal 2002 Defense Authorization/Cloture. Motion to invoke cloture (thus limiting debate) on the bill that would authorize $344.6 billion for military activities of the Defense Department, military construction, and defense activities of the Department of Energy. Motion agreed to 100-0: R 49-0; D 50-0 (ND 41-0, SD 9-0); I 1-0. Three-fifths of the total Senate (60) is required to invoke cloture. Oct. 2, 2001.

290. S 1438. Fiscal 2002 Defense Authorization/Passage. Passage of the bill that would authorize $344.6 billion for military activities of the Defense Department, military construction, and defense activities of the Department of Energy. The bill also would authorize an additional round of base realignment and closures in 2003. Passed 99-0: R 48-0; D 50-0 (ND 41-0, SD 9-0); I 1-0. Oct. 2, 2001.

291. H J Res 51. Vietnam Trade/Passage. Passage of the joint resolution that would grant annual normal trade relations status to Vietnam. The resolution would allow Vietnamese imports to receive the same tariffs as those of other U.S. trading partners. Passed (thus cleared for the president) 88-12: R 39-10; D 48-2 (ND 39-2, SD 9-0); I 1-0. A "yea" was a vote in support of the president's position. Oct. 3, 2001.

	292	293	294	295	296	297
ALABAMA						
Shelby	Y	N	Y	Y	Y	Y
Sessions	Y	N	N	Y	Y	Y
ALASKA						
Stevens	?	N	N	Y	Y	Y
Murkowski	Y	N	N	Y	Y	Y
ARIZONA						
McCain	Y	N	Y	Y	Y	Y
Kyl	Y	N	N	Y	Y	Y
ARKANSAS						
Hutchinson	Y	N	N	Y	Y	Y
Lincoln	Y	Y	Y	Y	Y	Y
CALIFORNIA						
Feinstein	Y	Y	Y	Y	Y	Y
Boxer	Y	Y	Y	Y	Y	Y
COLORADO						
Campbell	Y	Y	N	Y	Y	Y
Allard	Y	N	N	Y	Y	Y
CONNECTICUT						
Dodd	Y	Y	Y	Y	Y	Y
Lieberman	Y	Y	Y	Y	Y	Y
DELAWARE						
Carper	Y	Y	Y	Y	Y	Y
Biden	Y	Y	Y	Y	Y	Y
FLORIDA						
Graham	Y	Y	Y	Y	Y	Y
Nelson	Y	Y	Y	Y	Y	Y
GEORGIA						
Miller	Y	Y	N	Y	Y	Y
Cleland	Y	Y	Y	Y	Y	Y
HAWAII						
Inouye	Y	Y	Y	Y	Y	Y
Akaka	Y	Y	Y	Y	Y	Y
IDAHO						
Craig	Y	N	N	Y	Y	Y
Crapo	Y	N	N	Y	Y	Y
ILLINOIS						
Durbin	Y	Y	Y	Y	Y	Y
Fitzgerald	Y	N	N	Y	Y	Y
INDIANA						
Lugar	Y	N	Y	Y	Y	Y
Bayh	Y	Y	Y	Y	Y	Y
IOWA						
Grassley	Y	N	N	Y	Y	Y
Harkin	Y	Y	Y	Y	Y	Y
KANSAS						
Brownback	Y	Y	N	Y	Y	Y
Roberts	Y	N	N	Y	Y	Y
KENTUCKY						
McConnell	Y	N	N	Y	Y	Y
Bunning	Y	N	N	Y	Y	Y
LOUISIANA						
Breaux	Y	Y	N	Y	Y	Y
Landrieu	Y	Y	Y	Y	Y	Y
MAINE						
Snowe	Y	N	N	Y	Y	Y
Collins	Y	N	N	Y	Y	Y
MARYLAND						
Sarbanes	Y	Y	Y	Y	Y	Y
Mikulski	Y	Y	Y	Y	Y	Y
MASSACHUSETTS						
Kennedy	Y	Y	Y	Y	Y	Y
Kerry	Y	Y	Y	Y	Y	Y
MICHIGAN						
Levin	Y	Y	Y	Y	Y	Y
Stabenow	Y	Y	Y	Y	Y	Y
MINNESOTA						
Wellstone	Y	Y	Y	Y	Y	Y
Dayton	Y	Y	Y	Y	Y	Y
MISSISSIPPI						
Cochran	Y	N	Y	Y	Y	Y
Lott	Y	N	N	Y	Y	Y
MISSOURI						
Bond	Y	N	N	Y	Y	Y
Carnahan	Y	Y	Y	Y	Y	Y
MONTANA						
Baucus	Y	Y	Y	Y	Y	Y
Burns	Y	N	N	Y	Y	Y
NEBRASKA						
Nelson	Y	Y	Y	Y	Y	Y
Hagel	Y	N	N	Y	Y	Y
NEVADA						
Reid	Y	Y	Y	Y	Y	Y
Ensign	Y	N	N	Y	Y	Y
NEW HAMPSHIRE						
Smith	Y	N	N	Y	Y	Y
Gregg	Y	N	N	Y	Y	Y
NEW JERSEY						
Corzine	Y	Y	Y	Y	Y	Y
Torricelli	?	Y	Y	Y	Y	Y
NEW MEXICO						
Domenici	Y	N	N	Y	Y	Y
Bingaman	Y	Y	Y	Y	Y	Y
NEW YORK						
Clinton	Y	Y	Y	Y	Y	Y
Schumer	Y	Y	Y	Y	Y	Y
NORTH CAROLINA						
Helms	Y	N	N	Y	Y	Y
Edwards	Y	Y	Y	Y	Y	Y
NORTH DAKOTA						
Conrad	Y	Y	Y	Y	Y	Y
Dorgan	Y	Y	Y	Y	Y	Y
OHIO						
DeWine	Y	N	N	Y	Y	Y
Voinovich	Y	N	N	Y	Y	Y
OKLAHOMA						
Nickles	Y	N	N	Y	Y	Y
Inhofe	Y	N	N	Y	Y	Y
OREGON						
Wyden	Y	Y	Y	Y	Y	Y
Smith	Y	Y	N	Y	Y	Y
PENNSYLVANIA						
Specter	Y	Y	N	Y	Y	Y
Santorum	Y	N	N	Y	Y	Y
RHODE ISLAND						
Reed	Y	Y	Y	Y	Y	Y
Chafee	Y	Y	Y	Y	Y	Y
SOUTH CAROLINA						
Thurmond	Y	N	N	Y	Y	Y
Hollings	Y	Y	Y	Y	Y	Y
SOUTH DAKOTA						
Daschle	Y	Y	Y	Y	Y	Y
Johnson	Y	Y	Y	Y	Y	Y
TENNESSEE						
Thompson	Y	N	N	Y	Y	Y
Frist	Y	N	N	Y	Y	Y
TEXAS						
Gramm	Y	N	Y	Y	Y	Y
Hutchison	Y	N	N	Y	Y	Y
UTAH						
Hatch	Y	N	N	Y	Y	Y
Bennett	Y	N	N	Y	Y	Y
VERMONT						
Leahy	Y	Y	Y	Y	Y	Y
Jeffords	?	Y	N	Y	Y	Y
VIRGINIA						
Warner	Y	N	N	Y	Y	Y
Allen	Y	N	N	Y	Y	Y
WASHINGTON						
Cantwell	Y	Y	Y	Y	Y	Y
Murray	Y	Y	Y	Y	Y	Y
WEST VIRGINIA						
Byrd	Y	Y	Y	Y	Y	Y
Rockefeller	Y	Y	Y	Y	Y	Y
WISCONSIN						
Kohl	Y	Y	Y	Y	Y	Y
Feingold	Y	Y	N	Y	Y	Y
WYOMING						
Thomas	Y	N	N	Y	Y	Y
Enzi	Y	N	N	Y	Y	Y

Key

Y	Voted for (yea).
#	Paired for.
+	Announced for.
N	Voted against (nay).
X	Paired against.
−	Announced against.
P	Voted "present."
C	Voted "present" to avoid possible conflict of interest.
?	Did not vote or otherwise make a position known.

Democrats   **Republicans**
Independents

ND Northern Democrats   SD Southern Democrats

Southern states - Ala., Ark., Fla., Ga., Ky., La., Miss., N.C., Okla., S.C., Tenn., Texas, Va.

292. S 1447. Aviation Security/Cloture. Motion to invoke cloture (thus limiting debate) on the motion to proceed to the bill that would allow for the federal government to take over security at airports. Motion agreed to 97-0: R 48-0; D 49-0 (ND 40-0, SD 9-0); I 0-0. Three-fifths of the total Senate (60) is required to invoke cloture. Oct. 9, 2001.

293. S 1447. Aviation Security/Cloture. Motion to invoke cloture (thus limiting debate) on the Carnahan, D-Mo., amendment that would authorize $1.9 billion in fiscal 2002 and 2003 to extend unemployment, job-training and health benefits to aviation industry workers displaced as a result of the attacks on Sept. 11, 2001. Motion rejected 56-44: R 5-44; D 50-0 (ND 41-0, SD 9-0); I 1-0. Three-fifths of the total Senate (60) is required to invoke cloture. Oct. 11, 2001.

294. S 1447. Aviation Security/Pilot Age Limits. Reid, D-Nev., motion to table (kill) the Murkowski, R-Alaska, amendment that would increase the age limit at which a commercial air carrier may employ an individual as a pilot from age 60 to age 63. Motion agreed to 53-47: R 7-42; D 46-4 (ND 39-2, SD 7-2); I 0-1. Oct. 11, 2001.

295. S 1447. Aviation Security/Passage. Passage of a bill that would allow for the federal government to take over security at airports and make baggage screeners federal employees. It also would levy a $2.50 per passenger ticket fee for each flight leg, and provide for more armed air marshals on commercial jets, enhanced anti-hijacking training for flight crews, and strengthened cockpit doors to prevent access during flights. Passed 100-0: R 49-0; D 50-0 (ND 41-0, SD 9-0); I 1-0. Oct. 11, 2001.

296. S J Res 25. Day of Remembrance/Passage. Passage of a joint resolution that would designate Sept. 11 a National Day of Remembrance. Passed 100-0: R 49-0; D 50-0 (ND 41-0, SD 9-0); I 1-0. Oct. 11, 2001.

297. Parker Nomination/Confirmation. Confirmation of President Bush's nomination of Barrington D. Parker Jr. of Connecticut to be a judge for the Second U.S. Circuit Court. Confirmed 100-0: R 49-0; D 50-0 (ND 41-0, SD 9-0); I 1-0. A "yea" was a vote in support of the president's position. Oct. 11, 2001.

	298	299	300	301	302
ALABAMA					
Shelby	Y	Y	Y	Y	Y
Sessions	Y	Y	Y	Y	Y
ALASKA					
Stevens	Y	Y	Y	Y	Y
Murkowski	Y	Y	Y	Y	Y
ARIZONA					
McCain	Y	Y	Y	Y	Y
Kyl	Y	Y	Y	Y	Y
ARKANSAS					
Hutchinson	Y	Y	Y	Y	Y
Lincoln	Y	Y	Y	Y	Y
CALIFORNIA					
Feinstein	Y	Y	Y	Y	Y
Boxer	Y	N	Y	Y	Y
COLORADO					
Campbell	Y	Y	Y	Y	Y
Allard	Y	Y	Y	Y	Y
CONNECTICUT					
Dodd	?	Y	Y	N	Y
Lieberman	Y	Y	Y	Y	Y
DELAWARE					
Carper	Y	Y	Y	Y	Y
Biden	Y	Y	Y	Y	Y
FLORIDA					
Graham	Y	Y	Y	Y	Y
Nelson	Y	Y	Y	Y	Y
GEORGIA					
Miller	Y	Y	Y	Y	Y
Cleland	Y	Y	Y	Y	Y
HAWAII					
Inouye	Y	Y	Y	Y	Y
Akaka	Y	Y	Y	Y	Y
IDAHO					
Craig	Y	Y	Y	Y	Y
Crapo	Y	Y	Y	Y	Y
ILLINOIS					
Durbin	Y	N	Y	Y	Y
Fitzgerald	Y	Y	Y	Y	Y
INDIANA					
Lugar	Y	Y	Y	Y	Y
Bayh	Y	Y	Y	Y	Y

	298	299	300	301	302
IOWA					
Grassley	Y	Y	Y	Y	Y
Harkin	Y	N	Y	N	Y
KANSAS					
Brownback	Y	Y	Y	Y	Y
Roberts	Y	Y	Y	Y	Y
KENTUCKY					
McConnell	Y	Y	Y	Y	Y
Bunning	Y	Y	Y	Y	Y
LOUISIANA					
Breaux	Y	Y	Y	Y	Y
Landrieu	Y	Y	Y	Y	Y
MAINE					
Snowe	Y	Y	Y	Y	Y
Collins	Y	N	Y	Y	Y
MARYLAND					
Sarbanes	Y	Y	Y	Y	Y
Mikulski	Y	Y	Y	Y	Y
MASSACHUSETTS					
Kennedy	Y	Y	Y	Y	Y
Kerry	Y	Y	Y	Y	Y
MICHIGAN					
Levin	Y	N	N	N	Y
Stabenow	Y	N	Y	N	Y
MINNESOTA					
Wellstone	Y	N	N	N	Y
Dayton	Y	N	Y	N	Y
MISSISSIPPI					
Cochran	Y	Y	Y	Y	Y
Lott	Y	?	Y	Y	Y
MISSOURI					
Bond	Y	Y	Y	Y	Y
Carnahan	Y	Y	Y	Y	Y
MONTANA					
Baucus	Y	Y	Y	Y	Y
Burns	Y	Y	Y	Y	Y
NEBRASKA					
Nelson	Y	Y	Y	Y	Y
Hagel	Y	Y	Y	Y	Y
NEVADA					
Reid	Y	Y	Y	Y	Y
Ensign	Y	Y	Y	Y	Y

	298	299	300	301	302
NEW HAMPSHIRE					
Smith	Y	Y	Y	Y	Y
Gregg	Y	Y	Y	Y	Y
NEW JERSEY					
Corzine	Y	N	N	N	Y
Torricelli	Y	Y	Y	Y	Y
NEW MEXICO					
Domenici	Y	?	?	?	?
Bingaman	Y	N	Y	Y	Y
NEW YORK					
Clinton	Y	Y	Y	Y	Y
Schumer	Y	Y	Y	Y	Y
NORTH CAROLINA					
Helms	Y	?	?	?	?
Edwards	Y	Y	Y	Y	Y
NORTH DAKOTA					
Conrad	Y	Y	Y	Y	Y
Dorgan	Y	Y	Y	Y	Y
OHIO					
DeWine	Y	Y	Y	Y	Y
Voinovich	Y	Y	Y	Y	Y
OKLAHOMA					
Nickles	Y	Y	Y	Y	Y
Inhofe	Y	Y	Y	Y	Y
OREGON					
Wyden	Y	Y	Y	Y	Y
Smith	Y	Y	Y	Y	Y
PENNSYLVANIA					
Specter	Y	N	N	Y	Y
Santorum	Y	Y	Y	Y	Y
RHODE ISLAND					
Reed	Y	Y	Y	Y	Y
Chafee	Y	Y	Y	Y	Y
SOUTH CAROLINA					
Thurmond	Y	?	?	?	?
Hollings	Y	Y	Y	Y	Y
SOUTH DAKOTA					
Daschle	Y	Y	Y	Y	Y
Johnson	Y	Y	Y	Y	Y
TENNESSEE					
Thompson	Y	Y	N	Y	Y
Frist	Y	Y	Y	Y	Y

Key

Y	Voted for (yea).
#	Paired for.
+	Announced for.
N	Voted against (nay).
X	Paired against.
–	Announced against.
P	Voted "present."
C	Voted "present" to avoid possible conflict of interest.
?	Did not vote or otherwise make a position known.

Democrats   ***Republicans***
Independents

	298	299	300	301	302
TEXAS					
Gramm	Y	Y	Y	Y	Y
Hutchison	Y	Y	Y	Y	Y
UTAH					
Hatch	Y	Y	Y	Y	Y
Bennett	Y	Y	Y	Y	Y
VERMONT					
Leahy	Y	Y	Y	Y	Y
Jeffords	?	Y	Y	Y	Y
VIRGINIA					
Warner	Y	Y	Y	Y	Y
Allen	Y	Y	Y	Y	Y
WASHINGTON					
Cantwell	Y	N	N	N	Y
Murray	Y	Y	Y	Y	Y
WEST VIRGINIA					
Byrd	Y	Y	Y	Y	Y
Rockefeller	Y	Y	Y	Y	Y
WISCONSIN					
Kohl	Y	Y	Y	Y	Y
Feingold	Y	N	N	N	N
WYOMING					
Thomas	Y	Y	Y	Y	Y
Enzi	Y	Y	Y	Y	Y

ND Northern Democrats   SD Southern Democrats

Southern states - Ala., Ark., Fla., Ga., Ky., La., Miss., N.C., Okla., S.C., Tenn., Texas, Va.

298. Mills Nomination/Confirmation. Confirmation of President Bush's nomination of Michael P. Mills of Mississippi to be a U.S. District judge for the Northern District of Mississippi. Confirmed 98-0: R 49-0; D 49-0 (ND 40-0, SD 9-0); I 0-0. A "yea" was a vote in support of the president's position. Oct. 11, 2001.

299. S 1510. Anti-Terrorism Authority/Computer Trespass. Daschle, D-S.D., motion to table (kill) the Feingold, D-Wis., amendment that would clarify that the computer trespass provision in the bill applies only to "hacking" and denial of service attacks. It also would limit the length of surveillance without a warrant. Motion agreed to 83-13: R 43-2; D 39-11 (ND 30-11, SD 9-0); I 1-0. Oct. 11, 2001.

300. S 1510. Anti-Terrorism Authority/Roving Wiretapping. Daschle, D-S.D., motion to table (kill) the Feingold, D-Wis., amendment that would provide that in order to conduct roving surveillance, the person implementing the order must ascertain that the target of the surveillance is present in the house or is using the phone that has been tapped. Motion agreed to 90-7: R 44-2; D 45-5 (ND 36-5, SD 9-0); I 1-0. Oct. 11, 2001.

301. S 1510. Anti-Terrorism Authority/Business Records. Daschle, D-S.D., motion to table (kill) the Feingold, D-Wis., amendment that would clarify that existing federal and state statutory protections of the privacy of certain information are not diminished or superceded by the business record provision. Motion agreed to 89-8: R 46-0; D 42-8 (ND 33-8, SD 9-0); I 1-0. Oct. 11, 2001.

302. S 1510. Anti-Terrorism Authority/Passage. Passage of the bill that would expand law enforcement's power to investigate suspected terrorists. The bill would allow disclosure of wiretap information among certain government officials, authorize limited disclosure of secret grand jury information to certain government officials, and authorize the attorney general to detain foreigners he suspects are tied to terrorism. It also would make it easier for law enforcement to track Internet communications using surveillance techniques. Passed 96-1: R 46-0; D 49-1 (ND 40-1, SD 9-0); I 1-0. A "yea" was a vote in support of the president's position. Oct. 11, 2001.

	303	304	305
ALABAMA			
Shelby	N	Y	Y
Sessions	N	Y	Y
ALASKA			
Stevens	N	Y	Y
Murkowski	N	Y	Y
ARIZONA			
McCain	?	Y	N
Kyl	N	Y	Y
ARKANSAS			
Hutchinson	N	Y	Y
Lincoln	Y	Y	Y
CALIFORNIA			
Feinstein	Y	Y	Y
Boxer	Y	Y	Y
COLORADO			
Campbell	N	Y	Y
Allard	N	Y	Y
CONNECTICUT			
Dodd	Y	Y	Y
Lieberman	Y	+	Y
DELAWARE			
Carper	Y	Y	Y
Biden	Y	Y	Y
FLORIDA			
Graham	Y	Y	Y
Nelson	Y	Y	Y
GEORGIA			
Miller	Y	Y	Y
Cleland	Y	Y	Y
HAWAII			
Inouye	Y	Y	Y
Akaka	Y	Y	Y
IDAHO			
Craig	N	Y	Y
Crapo	N	Y	Y
ILLINOIS			
Durbin	Y	Y	Y
Fitzgerald	N	Y	Y
INDIANA			
Lugar	N	Y	Y
Bayh	Y	N	Y

	303	304	305
IOWA			
Grassley	N	Y	Y
Harkin	Y	Y	Y
KANSAS			
Brownback	N	N	Y
Roberts	N	N	Y
KENTUCKY			
McConnell	N	Y	Y
Bunning	N	Y	Y
LOUISIANA			
Breaux	Y	Y	Y
Landrieu	Y	Y	Y
MAINE			
Snowe	N	Y	Y
Collins	N	Y	Y
MARYLAND			
Sarbanes	Y	Y	Y
Mikulski	Y	Y	Y
MASSACHUSETTS			
Kennedy	Y	Y	Y
Kerry	Y	Y	Y
MICHIGAN			
Levin	Y	Y	Y
Stabenow	Y	Y	Y
MINNESOTA			
Wellstone	Y	Y	Y
Dayton	Y	Y	Y
MISSISSIPPI			
Cochran	N	Y	Y
Lott	?	Y	Y
MISSOURI			
Bond	N	Y	Y
Carnahan	Y	Y	Y
MONTANA			
Baucus	Y	Y	Y
Burns	N	Y	+
NEBRASKA			
Nelson	Y	Y	Y
Hagel	N	?	Y
NEVADA			
Reid	Y	Y	Y
Ensign	N	Y	?

	303	304	305
NEW HAMPSHIRE			
Smith	N	Y	Y
Gregg	N	Y	Y
NEW JERSEY			
Corzine	Y	Y	Y
Torricelli	Y	Y	Y
NEW MEXICO			
Domenici	N	Y	Y
Bingaman	Y	Y	Y
NEW YORK			
Clinton	Y	Y	Y
Schumer	Y	Y	Y
NORTH CAROLINA			
Helms	N	Y	Y
Edwards	Y	Y	Y
NORTH DAKOTA			
Conrad	Y	Y	Y
Dorgan	Y	Y	Y
OHIO			
DeWine	N	Y	Y
Voinovich	N	Y	Y
OKLAHOMA			
Nickles	N	Y	Y
Inhofe	?	Y	Y
OREGON			
Wyden	Y	Y	Y
Smith	N	Y	Y
PENNSYLVANIA			
Specter	N	Y	Y
Santorum	N	Y	Y
RHODE ISLAND			
Reed	Y	Y	Y
Chafee	N	Y	Y
SOUTH CAROLINA			
Thurmond	N	Y	Y
Hollings	Y	Y	Y
SOUTH DAKOTA			
Daschle	Y	Y	Y
Johnson	Y	Y	Y
TENNESSEE			
Thompson	N	Y	Y
Frist	N	Y	Y

Key

Y Voted for (yea).
Paired for.
+ Announced for.
N Voted against (nay).
X Paired against.
− Announced against.
P Voted "present."
C Voted "present" to avoid possible conflict of interest.
? Did not vote or otherwise make a position known.

Democrats **Republicans**
Independents

	303	304	305
TEXAS			
Gramm	N	Y	Y
Hutchison	N	Y	Y
UTAH			
Hatch	N	Y	Y
Bennett	N	Y	?
VERMONT			
Leahy	Y	Y	Y
Jeffords	Y	Y	Y
VIRGINIA			
Warner	N	Y	Y
Allen	N	Y	Y
WASHINGTON			
Cantwell	?	Y	Y
Murray	Y	Y	Y
WEST VIRGINIA			
Byrd	Y	Y	Y
Rockefeller	Y	Y	Y
WISCONSIN			
Kohl	Y	Y	Y
Feingold	Y	Y	Y
WYOMING			
Thomas	N	Y	Y
Enzi	N	Y	Y

ND Northern Democrats   SD Southern Democrats

Southern states - Ala., Ark., Fla., Ga., Ky., La., Miss., N.C., Okla., S.C., Tenn., Texas, Va.

303. HR 2506. Fiscal 2002 Foreign Operations Appropriations/ Cloture. Motion to invoke cloture (thus limiting debate) on the motion to proceed to the bill that would appropriate $15 billion in fiscal year 2002 for foreign operations. Motion rejected 50-46: R 0-46; D 49-0 (ND 40-0, SD 9-0); I 1-0. Three-fifths of the total Senate (60) is required to invoke cloture. Oct. 15, 2001.

304. HR 2217. Fiscal 2002 Interior Appropriations/Conference Report. Adoption of the conference report on the bill that would appropriate $19.1 billion for the Interior Department, related agencies and cultural programs in fiscal 2002. The bill includes $1.3 billion for conservation efforts, $400 million in emergency funds to fight wildfires, and prohibitions on oil and gas exploration in the Gulf of Mexico and at national monuments. Adopted (thus cleared for the president) 95-3: R 46-2; D 48-1 (ND 39-1, SD 9-0); I 1-0. Oct. 17, 2001.

305. HR 2904. Fiscal 2002 Military Construction Appropriations/ Conference Report. Adoption of the conference report on the bill that would provide $10.5 billion in fiscal 2002 for military construction projects, including the building of barracks, family housing, and medical facilities. Adopted (thus cleared for the president) 96-1: R 45-1; D 50-0 (ND 41-0, SD 9-0); I 1-0. Oct. 18, 2001.

ALABAMA	306	307	308	309	310	311
Shelby	N	Y	Y	Y	Y	N
Sessions	N	Y	Y	Y	Y	Y
ALASKA						
Stevens	P	Y	Y	Y	Y	N
Murkowski	N	Y	Y	Y	Y	N
ARIZONA						
McCain	N	Y	Y	Y	Y	Y
Kyl	N	Y	Y	Y	Y	Y
ARKANSAS						
Hutchinson	N	Y	Y	Y	Y	Y
Lincoln	Y	Y	Y	Y	Y	N
CALIFORNIA						
Feinstein	Y	Y	Y	Y	Y	N
Boxer	Y	Y	Y	Y	Y	N
COLORADO						
Campbell	N	Y	Y	Y	Y	N
Allard	N	Y	Y	Y	Y	N
CONNECTICUT						
Dodd	Y	Y	Y	Y	Y	Y
Lieberman	Y	Y	Y	Y	Y	Y
DELAWARE						
Carper	Y	Y	Y	Y	Y	N
Biden	Y	Y	Y	Y	Y	Y
FLORIDA						
Graham	Y	Y	Y	Y	Y	Y
Nelson	Y	Y	Y	Y	Y	Y
GEORGIA						
Miller	Y	Y	Y	Y	Y	Y
Cleland	Y	Y	Y	Y	Y	N
HAWAII						
Inouye	Y	Y	Y	Y	Y	N
Akaka	Y	Y	Y	Y	Y	N
IDAHO						
Craig	N	Y	Y	Y	Y	Y
Crapo	N	Y	Y	Y	Y	N
ILLINOIS						
Durbin	Y	Y	Y	Y	Y	N
Fitzgerald	N	Y	Y	Y	Y	N
INDIANA						
Lugar	N	Y	Y	Y	Y	Y
Bayh	Y	Y	Y	Y	Y	Y

IOWA	306	307	308	309	310	311
Grassley	N	Y	Y	Y	Y	Y
Harkin	Y	Y	Y	Y	Y	N
KANSAS						
Brownback	N	Y	Y	Y	Y	N
Roberts	N	Y	Y	Y	Y	N
KENTUCKY						
McConnell	N	Y	Y	Y	Y	N
Bunning	N	Y	Y	Y	Y	N
LOUISIANA						
Breaux	Y	Y	Y	Y	Y	Y
Landrieu	Y	Y	Y	Y	Y	Y
MAINE						
Snowe	N	Y	Y	Y	Y	N
Collins	N	Y	Y	Y	Y	N
MARYLAND						
Sarbanes	Y	Y	Y	Y	Y	N
Mikulski	Y	Y	Y	Y	Y	N
MASSACHUSETTS						
Kennedy	Y	Y	Y	Y	Y	N
Kerry	Y	Y	Y	Y	Y	N
MICHIGAN						
Levin	Y	Y	Y	Y	Y	N
Stabenow	Y	Y	Y	Y	Y	N
MINNESOTA						
Wellstone	Y	Y	Y	Y	Y	N
Dayton	Y	Y	Y	Y	Y	N
MISSISSIPPI						
Cochran	N	Y	Y	Y	Y	N
Lott	N	Y	Y	Y	Y	N
MISSOURI						
Bond	N	Y	Y	Y	Y	N
Carnahan	Y	Y	Y	Y	Y	Y
MONTANA						
Baucus	Y	Y	Y	Y	Y	N
Burns	N	Y	Y	Y	Y	N
NEBRASKA						
Nelson	Y	Y	Y	Y	Y	N
Hagel	N	Y	Y	Y	Y	Y
NEVADA						
Reid	Y	Y	Y	Y	Y	N
Ensign	N	Y	Y	Y	Y	N

NEW HAMPSHIRE	306	307	308	309	310	311
Smith	N	Y	Y	Y	Y	N
Gregg	N	Y	Y	Y	Y	N
NEW JERSEY						
Corzine	Y	Y	Y	Y	Y	Y
Torricelli	Y	Y	Y	Y	Y	Y
NEW MEXICO						
Domenici	N	Y	Y	Y	Y	N
Bingaman	Y	Y	Y	Y	Y	N
NEW YORK						
Clinton	Y	Y	Y	Y	Y	Y
Schumer	Y	Y	Y	Y	Y	Y
NORTH CAROLINA						
Helms	N	Y	Y	Y	Y	Y
Edwards	Y	Y	Y	Y	Y	N
NORTH DAKOTA						
Conrad	Y	Y	Y	Y	Y	N
Dorgan	Y	Y	Y	Y	Y	N
OHIO						
DeWine	N	Y	Y	Y	Y	N
Voinovich	?	Y	Y	Y	Y	N
OKLAHOMA						
Nickles	N	Y	Y	Y	Y	N
Inhofe	?	Y	Y	Y	Y	N
OREGON						
Wyden	Y	Y	Y	Y	Y	N
Smith	N	Y	Y	Y	Y	N
PENNSYLVANIA						
Specter	N	Y	Y	Y	Y	N
Santorum	N	Y	Y	Y	Y	N
RHODE ISLAND						
Reed	Y	Y	Y	Y	Y	N
Chafee	N	Y	Y	Y	Y	Y
SOUTH CAROLINA						
Thurmond	N	Y	Y	Y	Y	N
Hollings	Y	Y	Y	Y	Y	N
SOUTH DAKOTA						
Daschle	N	Y	Y	Y	Y	N
Johnson	Y	Y	Y	Y	Y	N
TENNESSEE						
Thompson	N	Y	Y	Y	Y	Y
Frist	N	Y	Y	Y	Y	?

Key

Y	Voted for (yea).
#	Paired for.
+	Announced for.
N	Voted against (nay).
X	Paired against.
–	Announced against.
P	Voted "present."
C	Voted "present" to avoid possible conflict of interest.
?	Did not vote or otherwise make a position known.

Democrats   **Republicans**
Independents

TEXAS	306	307	308	309	310	311
Gramm	N	Y	Y	Y	Y	N
Hutchison	N	Y	Y	Y	Y	N
UTAH						
Hatch	N	Y	Y	Y	Y	Y
Bennett	N	Y	Y	Y	Y	N
VERMONT						
Leahy	Y	Y	Y	Y	Y	N
Jeffords	Y	Y	Y	Y	Y	N
VIRGINIA						
Warner	N	Y	Y	Y	Y	N
Allen	N	Y	Y	Y	Y	N
WASHINGTON						
Cantwell	Y	Y	Y	Y	Y	N
Murray	Y	Y	Y	Y	Y	N
WEST VIRGINIA						
Byrd	Y	Y	Y	Y	Y	N
Rockefeller	Y	Y	Y	Y	?	Y
WISCONSIN						
Kohl	Y	Y	Y	Y	Y	N
Feingold	Y	Y	Y	Y	Y	N
WYOMING						
Thomas	N	Y	Y	Y	Y	N
Enzi	N	Y	Y	Y	Y	N

ND Northern Democrats   SD Southern Democrats

Southern states - Ala., Ark., Fla., Ga., Ky., La., Miss., N.C., Okla., S.C., Tenn., Texas, Va.

306. HR 2506. Fiscal 2002 Foreign Operations Appropriations/ Cloture. Motion to invoke cloture (thus limiting debate) on the motion to proceed to the bill that would appropriate $15.5 billion in fiscal 2002 for foreign operations. Motion rejected 50-47: R 0-46; D 49-1 (ND 40-1, SD 9-0); I 1-0. Three-fifths of the total Senate (60) is required to invoke cloture. Oct. 23, 2001.

307. Payne Nomination/Confirmation. Confirmation of President Bush's nomination of James H. Payne of Oklahoma to be U.S. District judge for the Northern, Eastern and Western Districts of Oklahoma. Confirmed 100-0: R 49-0; D 50-0 (ND 41-0, SD 9-0); I 1-0. A "yea" was a vote in support of the president's position. Oct. 23, 2001.

308. Caldwell Nomination/Confirmation. Confirmation of President Bush's nomination of Karen K. Caldwell of Kentucky to be U.S. District judge for the Eastern District of Kentucky. Confirmed 100-0: R 49-0; D 50-0 (ND 41-0, SD 9-0); I 1-0. A "yea" was a vote in support of the president's position. Oct. 23, 2001.

309. Camp Nomination/Confirmation. Confirmation of President Bush's nomination of Laurie Smith Camp of Nebraska to be U.S. District judge for the District of Nebraska. Confirmed 100-0: R 49-0; D 50-0 (ND 41-0, SD 9-0); I 1-0. A "yea" was a vote in support of the president's position. Oct. 23, 2001.

310. Eagan Nomination/Confirmation. Confirmation of President Bush's nomination of Claire V. Eagan of Oklahoma to be U.S. District judge for the Northern District of Oklahoma. Confirmed 99-0: R 49-0; D 49-0 (ND 40-0, SD 9-0); I 1-0. A "yea" was a vote in support of the president's position. Oct. 23, 2001.

311. HR 2506. Fiscal 2002 Foreign Operations Appropriations/Andean Regional Counter-Narcotics Initiative. Graham, D-Fla., motion to waive the Budget Act with respect to the Leahy, D-Vt., point of order against the Graham amendment that would increase funding for the Andean Regional Counter-Narcotics Initiative to $731 million. Motion rejected 27-72: R 13-35; D 14-36 (ND 10-31, SD 4-5); I 0-1. A three-fifths majority vote (60) of the total Senate is required to waive the Budget Act. (Subsequently, the chair upheld the point of order, and the amendment fell.) Oct. 24, 2001.

	312	313	314	315
ALABAMA				
Shelby	Y	Y	N	Y
Sessions	Y	Y	N	Y
ALASKA				
Stevens	Y	Y	?	?
Murkowski	Y	Y	N	Y
ARIZONA				
McCain	Y	Y	N	N
Kyl	?	Y	N	N
ARKANSAS				
Hutchinson	Y	Y	N	Y
Lincoln	Y	Y	N	Y
CALIFORNIA				
Feinstein	Y	Y	Y	Y
Boxer	Y	Y	Y	?
COLORADO				
Campbell	Y	Y	N	Y
Allard	Y	Y	N	Y
CONNECTICUT				
Dodd	Y	Y	Y	Y
Lieberman	Y	Y	Y	Y
DELAWARE				
Carper	Y	Y	N	Y
Biden	Y	Y	N	Y
FLORIDA				
Graham	N	Y	Y	Y
Nelson	Y	Y	Y	Y
GEORGIA				
Miller	Y	Y	N	Y
Cleland	Y	Y	N	Y
HAWAII				
Inouye	Y	Y	Y	Y
Akaka	Y	Y	Y	Y
IDAHO				
Craig	Y	Y	N	Y
Crapo	Y	Y	N	Y
ILLINOIS				
Durbin	Y	Y	N	Y
Fitzgerald	Y	Y	Y	Y
INDIANA				
Lugar	Y	Y	N	Y
Bayh	Y	Y	N	Y
IOWA				
Grassley	Y	Y	Y	Y
Harkin	Y	Y	Y	Y
KANSAS				
Brownback	Y	Y	N	Y
Roberts	Y	Y	N	Y
KENTUCKY				
McConnell	Y	Y	N	Y
Bunning	Y	Y	–	+
LOUISIANA				
Breaux	Y	Y	N	Y
Landrieu	+	+	N	Y
MAINE				
Snowe	Y	Y	N	Y
Collins	Y	Y	N	Y
MARYLAND				
Sarbanes	Y	Y	Y	Y
Mikulski	Y	Y	Y	Y
MASSACHUSETTS				
Kennedy	Y	Y	Y	Y
Kerry	Y	Y	Y	Y
MICHIGAN				
Levin	Y	Y	N	Y
Stabenow	Y	Y	N	Y
MINNESOTA				
Wellstone	Y	Y	Y	Y
Dayton	Y	Y	Y	Y
MISSISSIPPI				
Cochran	Y	Y	N	Y
Lott	Y	Y	N	Y
MISSOURI				
Bond	Y	Y	N	Y
Carnahan	Y	Y	Y	Y
MONTANA				
Baucus	Y	Y	Y	Y
Burns	Y	Y	?	Y
NEBRASKA				
Nelson	Y	Y	N	Y
Hagel	Y	Y	N	Y
NEVADA				
Reid	Y	Y	Y	Y
Ensign	Y	Y	N	N
NEW HAMPSHIRE				
Smith	Y	Y	N	Y
Gregg	Y	Y	N	N
NEW JERSEY				
Corzine	Y	Y	Y	Y
Torricelli	Y	Y	Y	Y
NEW MEXICO				
Domenici	Y	Y	?	Y
Bingaman	Y	Y	Y	Y
NEW YORK				
Clinton	Y	Y	Y	Y
Schumer	Y	Y	Y	Y
NORTH CAROLINA				
Helms	Y	Y	N	Y
Edwards	Y	Y	Y	Y
NORTH DAKOTA				
Conrad	Y	Y	Y	Y
Dorgan	Y	Y	Y	Y
OHIO				
DeWine	Y	Y	N	Y
Voinovich	Y	Y	N	N
OKLAHOMA				
Nickles	Y	Y	N	Y
Inhofe	Y	Y	N	Y
OREGON				
Wyden	Y	Y	Y	Y
Smith	Y	Y	N	Y
PENNSYLVANIA				
Specter	Y	Y	Y	Y
Santorum	Y	Y	N	Y
RHODE ISLAND				
Reed	Y	Y	Y	Y
Chafee	Y	Y	Y	Y
SOUTH CAROLINA				
Thurmond	Y	Y	N	Y
Hollings	Y	Y	Y	Y
SOUTH DAKOTA				
Daschle	Y	Y	Y	Y
Johnson	Y	Y	Y	Y
TENNESSEE				
Thompson	Y	Y	N	Y
Frist	Y	Y	N	Y
TEXAS				
Gramm	Y	Y	N	Y
Hutchison	Y	Y	?	?
UTAH				
Hatch	Y	Y	N	Y
Bennett	Y	Y	N	Y
VERMONT				
Leahy	Y	Y	Y	Y
Jeffords	Y	Y	Y	Y
VIRGINIA				
Warner	Y	Y	N	Y
Allen	Y	Y	N	Y
WASHINGTON				
Cantwell	Y	Y	Y	Y
Murray	Y	Y	Y	Y
WEST VIRGINIA				
Byrd	N	Y	Y	Y
Rockefeller	Y	Y	Y	Y
WISCONSIN				
Kohl	Y	Y	Y	Y
Feingold	Y	N	Y	Y
WYOMING				
Thomas	Y	Y	N	Y
Enzi	Y	Y	N	Y

Key

Y	Voted for (yea).
#	Paired for.
+	Announced for.
N	Voted against (nay).
X	Paired against.
–	Announced against.
P	Voted "present."
C	Voted "present" to avoid possible conflict of interest.
?	Did not vote or otherwise make a position known.

Democrats   **Republicans**
Independents

ND Northern Democrats   SD Southern Democrats

Southern states - Ala., Ark., Fla., Ga., Ky., La., Miss., N.C., Okla., S.C., Tenn., Texas, Va.

312. HR 2506. Fiscal 2002 Foreign Operations Appropriations/ Passage. Passage of the bill that would provide $15.5 billion for fiscal 2002 for foreign operations. It includes $567 million for the Andean Initiative, a Latin American counter-narcotics program. The bill also would overturn a Bush administration policy blocking federal funds to groups that use their own money to offer abortion services overseas. Passed 96-2: R 48-0; D 47-2 (ND 40-1, SD 7-1); I 1-0. Oct. 24, 2001.

313. HR 3162. Anti-Terrorism Authority/Passage. Passage of the bill that would expand law enforcement's power to investigate suspected terrorists. The bill would allow disclosure of wiretap information among certain government officials, authorize limited disclosure of secret grand jury information to certain government officials, and allow the detention of foreigners suspected of having ties to terrorism. It also would make it easier for law enforcement to track voice and Internet communications using surveillance techniques and would strengthen laws to combat money laundering. Most of the bill's intelligence-gathering provisions would sunset after four years. Passed (thus cleared for the president) 98-1: R 49-0; D 48-1 (ND 40-1, SD 8-0); I 1-0. A "yea" was a vote in support of the president's position. Oct. 25, 2001.

314. HR 2330. Fiscal 2002 Agriculture Appropriations/Meat and Poultry Products. Harkin, D-Iowa, motion to table (kill) the Nelson, D-Neb., amendment to the Harkin amendment. The Nelson amendment would strike the text of the Harkin amendment and insert a provision that would provide that no funds would be available for the application of inspection marks to any meat or poultry products that are shown to be contaminated. The Harkin amendment would clarify the Agriculture Department's legal authority to enforce standards for pathogens in meat and poultry products. Motion rejected 45-50: R 4-40; D 40-10 (ND 36-5, SD 4-5); I 1-0. (Subsequently, the Harkin amendment was withdrawn.) Oct. 25, 2001.

315. HR 2330. Fiscal 2002 Agriculture Appropriations/Passage. Passage of the bill that would provide $16.1 billion for agriculture, rural development and nutrition programs in fiscal 2002. The bill includes $715.7 million for the Food Safety and Inspection Service; $2.1 billion for agriculture research, education and extension activities; $4.5 billion for rural housing loan authorizations; $4.1 billion for the Women, Infants and Children Program; and $1.2 billion for the Food and Drug Administration. Passed 91-5: R 41-5; D 49-0 (ND 40-0, SD 9-0); I 1-0. Oct. 25, 2001.

	316	317	318	319	320	321
ALABAMA						
Shelby	Y	Y	Y	Y	Y	Y
Sessions	Y	Y	?	?	?	?
ALASKA						
Stevens	Y	N	N	N	Y	Y
Murkowski	Y	N	Y	N	Y	Y
ARIZONA						
McCain	Y	N	Y	N	N	Y
Kyl	Y	N	Y	N	Y	Y
ARKANSAS						
Hutchinson	Y	N	Y	N	Y	N
Lincoln	N	Y	N	Y	Y	Y
CALIFORNIA						
Feinstein	N	N	N	Y	Y	Y
Boxer	N	N	N	Y	Y	Y
COLORADO						
Campbell	Y	Y	N	N	Y	Y
Allard	Y	Y	Y	N	Y	N
CONNECTICUT						
Dodd	N	Y	N	Y	Y	Y
Lieberman	N	Y	N	Y	Y	Y
DELAWARE						
Carper	N	Y	N	Y	Y	Y
Biden	N	Y	N	Y	Y	Y
FLORIDA						
Graham	N	Y	N	Y	Y	Y
Nelson	N	Y	N	Y	Y	Y
GEORGIA						
Miller	N	Y	Y	Y	Y	Y
Cleland	N	Y	N	Y	Y	Y
HAWAII						
Inouye	N	Y	N	Y	Y	Y
Akaka	N	Y	N	Y	Y	Y
IDAHO						
Craig	Y	Y	Y	Y	Y	Y
Crapo	Y	Y	Y	Y	Y	Y
ILLINOIS						
Durbin	N	Y	N	Y	Y	Y
Fitzgerald	Y	N	N	N	Y	Y
INDIANA						
Lugar	Y	Y	Y	N	Y	Y
Bayh	N	Y	N	Y	N	N

	316	317	318	319	320	321
IOWA						
Grassley	Y	Y	Y	N	Y	Y
Harkin	N	Y	N	Y	Y	Y
KANSAS						
Brownback	Y	N	Y	N	Y	N
Roberts	Y	N	Y	N	Y	N
KENTUCKY						
McConnell	Y	Y	Y	N	Y	Y
Bunning	Y	Y	Y	N	Y	N
LOUISIANA						
Breaux	N	Y	N	Y	Y	Y
Landrieu	N	Y	N	Y	Y	Y
MAINE						
Snowe	N	Y	N	Y	Y	N
Collins	Y	Y	N	Y	Y	N
MARYLAND						
Sarbanes	N	Y	N	Y	Y	Y
Mikulski	N	Y	N	Y	Y	Y
MASSACHUSETTS						
Kennedy	N	Y	N	Y	Y	Y
Kerry	N	Y	N	Y	Y	Y
MICHIGAN						
Levin	N	Y	N	Y	Y	Y
Stabenow	N	Y	N	Y	Y	Y
MINNESOTA						
Wellstone	N	Y	N	Y	Y	Y
Dayton	N	Y	N	Y	Y	Y
MISSISSIPPI						
Cochran	Y	Y	Y	N	Y	Y
Lott	Y	Y	Y	N	Y	Y
MISSOURI						
Bond	Y	N	Y	N	Y	Y
Carnahan	N	N	N	Y	Y	Y
MONTANA						
Baucus	N	Y	N	N	Y	N
Burns	Y	Y	Y	N	Y	Y
NEBRASKA						
Nelson	N	Y	N	Y	Y	Y
Hagel	Y	Y	Y	?	?	?
NEVADA						
Reid	N	Y	N	Y	Y	Y
Ensign	Y	Y	Y	Y	Y	N

	316	317	318	319	320	321
NEW HAMPSHIRE						
Smith	Y	Y	Y	N	Y	N
Gregg	Y	Y	Y	N	Y	Y
NEW JERSEY						
Corzine	N	Y	N	Y	Y	Y
Torricelli	N	Y	N	Y	Y	Y
NEW MEXICO						
Domenici	Y	Y	Y	N	Y	Y
Bingaman	N	Y	N	Y	Y	Y
NEW YORK						
Clinton	N	N	N	Y	Y	Y
Schumer	N	N	N	Y	Y	Y
NORTH CAROLINA						
Helms	Y	N	Y	N	Y	N
Edwards	N	Y	N	Y	Y	N
NORTH DAKOTA						
Conrad	N	Y	N	N	Y	Y
Dorgan	N	Y	N	N	Y	Y
OHIO						
DeWine	Y	Y	Y	N	Y	Y
Voinovich	Y	Y	Y	N	Y	Y
OKLAHOMA						
Nickles	Y	N	Y	N	Y	Y
Inhofe	Y	Y	Y	N	Y	Y
OREGON						
Wyden	N	Y	N	Y	Y	Y
Smith	Y	Y	N	Y	Y	N
PENNSYLVANIA						
Specter	N	Y	N	Y	Y	Y
Santorum	Y	Y	Y	N	Y	Y
RHODE ISLAND						
Reed	N	Y	N	Y	Y	Y
Chafee	N	Y	N	Y	Y	Y
SOUTH CAROLINA						
Thurmond	Y	N	Y	N	Y	Y
Hollings	N	Y	N	Y	Y	Y
SOUTH DAKOTA						
Daschle	N	Y	N	Y	Y	Y
Johnson	N	Y	N	Y	Y	Y
TENNESSEE						
Thompson	Y	Y	Y	N	Y	Y
Frist	Y	Y	Y	N	Y	Y

Key

Y	Voted for (yea).
#	Paired for.
+	Announced for.
N	Voted against (nay).
X	Paired against.
–	Announced against.
P	Voted "present."
C	Voted "present" to avoid possible conflict of interest.
?	Did not vote or otherwise make a position known.

Democrats **Republicans**
Independents

	316	317	318	319	320	321
TEXAS						
Gramm	Y	Y	Y	N	Y	Y
Hutchison	Y	Y	Y	N	Y	Y
UTAH						
Hatch	Y	Y	Y	N	Y	Y
Bennett	Y	Y	Y	N	Y	Y
VERMONT						
Leahy	N	Y	N	Y	Y	Y
Jeffords	N	Y	N	Y	Y	Y
VIRGINIA						
Warner	Y	N	Y	N	Y	Y
Allen	Y	N	Y	N	Y	Y
WASHINGTON						
Cantwell	N	Y	N	Y	Y	Y
Murray	N	Y	N	Y	Y	Y
WEST VIRGINIA						
Byrd	N	Y	N	Y	Y	Y
Rockefeller	N	Y	N	Y	Y	Y
WISCONSIN						
Kohl	N	Y	N	Y	Y	Y
Feingold	N	Y	N	Y	Y	N
WYOMING						
Thomas	Y	Y	Y	N	Y	Y
Enzi	Y	Y	Y	N	Y	Y

ND Northern Democrats   SD Southern Democrats

Southern states - Ala., Ark., Fla., Ga., Ky., La., Miss., N.C., Okla., S.C., Tenn., Texas, Va.

316. HR 3061. Fiscal 2002 Labor-HHS-Education Appropriations/ School Construction. Gregg, R-N.H., amendment that would transfer $925 million in funds provided for the school construction program to Title I target grants for low-income children under the Elementary and Secondary Education Act. Rejected 46-54: R 46-3; D 0-50 (ND 0-41, SD 0-9); I 0-1. Nov. 1, 2001.

317. HR 3061. Fiscal 2002 Labor-HHS-Education Appropriations/ Title I Funding. Landrieu, D-La., amendment that would transfer $1 billion of the Title I increase into the Target Assistance Grant Fund, which benefits low-income children. It also would allocate $650 million for education finance incentive grants. Adopted 81-19: R 35-14; D 45-5 (ND 36-5, SD 9-0); I 1-0. Nov. 1, 2001.

318. HR 3061. Fiscal 2002 Labor-HHS-Education Appropriations/ Charitable Organizations Solicitations. Hutchinson, R-Ark., amendment that would prohibit the use of funds under the National Labor Relations Act to make an unfair labor practice finding related to a written or posted no-solicitation or no-access rule that exempts charitable organizations while prohibiting labor unions. Rejected 40-59: R 39-9; D 1-49 (ND 0-41, SD 1-8); I 0-1. Nov. 1, 2001.

319. HR 3061. Fiscal 2002 Labor-HHS-Education Appropriations/ Impact Aid. Harkin, D-Iowa, motion to table (kill) the Kyl, R-Ariz., amendment that would prohibit the use of funds for state and local school repair or renovation beyond the current fiscal year unless assistance is provided to meet the repair or renovation needs of Native American schools receiving Impact Aid, or that are under the jurisdiction of the Defense Department or the Bureau of Indian Affairs prior to making assistance available to other schools. Motion agreed to 57-41: R 9-38; D 47-3 (ND 38-3, SD 9-0); I 1-0. Nov. 1, 2001.

320. HR 2311. Fiscal 2002 Energy-Water Appropriations/Conference Report. Adoption of the conference report on the bill that would appropriate $24.6 billion in fiscal 2002 for the Energy Department, the Army Corps of Engineers and other agencies, $2.1 billion more than the president's request. Adopted (thus cleared for the president) 96-2: R 46-1; D 49-1 (ND 40-1, SD 9-0); I 1-0. Nov. 1, 2001.

321. HR 2590. Fiscal 2002 Treasury-Postal Appropriations/Conference Report. Adoption of the conference report on the bill that would provide $32.8 billion for the Treasury Department, Postal Service, Executive Office of the President and other federal agencies. The bill would increase pay for federal employees by 4.6 percent and maintain current law provisions that ban funding abortions under federal employee health plans but allow funding for contraceptives. Adopted (thus cleared for the president) 83-15: R 36-11; D 46-4 (ND 38-3, SD 8-1); I 1-0. Nov. 1, 2001.

	322	323	324	325	326	327	328
ALABAMA							
Shelby	Y	N	Y	Y	Y	Y	N
Sessions	Y	N	N	Y	Y	Y	N
ALASKA							
Stevens	Y	N	Y	Y	Y	Y	N
Murkowski	Y	N	Y	Y	Y	Y	N
ARIZONA							
McCain	?	N	Y	Y	Y	Y	N
Kyl	Y	N	Y	Y	Y	Y	N
ARKANSAS							
Hutchinson	Y	N	Y	Y	Y	Y	N
Lincoln	Y	Y	Y	Y	Y	Y	Y
CALIFORNIA							
Feinstein	Y	Y	Y	Y	Y	Y	Y
Boxer	Y	Y	Y	Y	Y	Y	Y
COLORADO							
Campbell	Y	N	Y	Y	Y	Y	N
Allard	Y	N	N	Y	Y	Y	N
CONNECTICUT							
Dodd	Y	Y	Y	Y	Y	Y	Y
Lieberman	Y	Y	Y	Y	Y	Y	Y
DELAWARE							
Carper	Y	Y	Y	Y	Y	Y	Y
Biden	?	Y	Y	Y	Y	Y	Y
FLORIDA							
Graham	Y	Y	Y	Y	Y	Y	Y
Nelson	Y	Y	Y	Y	Y	Y	Y
GEORGIA							
Miller	?	Y	?	Y	Y	Y	N
Cleland	Y	Y	Y	Y	Y	Y	N
HAWAII							
Inouye	Y	Y	Y	Y	Y	Y	Y
Akaka	Y	Y	Y	Y	Y	Y	Y
IDAHO							
Craig	Y	N	Y	Y	Y	Y	N
Crapo	Y	N	Y	Y	Y	Y	N
ILLINOIS							
Durbin	Y	Y	Y	Y	Y	Y	Y
Fitzgerald	Y	Y	N	Y	Y	Y	Y
INDIANA							
Lugar	Y	N	Y	Y	Y	Y	N
Bayh	Y	Y	Y	Y	Y	Y	Y

	322	323	324	325	326	327	328
IOWA							
Grassley	Y	N	Y	Y	Y	Y	N
Harkin	Y	Y	Y	Y	Y	Y	Y
KANSAS							
Brownback	?	N	Y	Y	Y	Y	N
Roberts	Y	N	Y	Y	Y	Y	N
KENTUCKY							
McConnell	Y	N	Y	Y	Y	Y	N
Bunning	Y	N	N	Y	Y	Y	N
LOUISIANA							
Breaux	Y	Y	Y	Y	Y	Y	Y
Landrieu	?	Y	Y	Y	Y	Y	Y
MAINE							
Snowe	Y	Y	Y	Y	Y	Y	N
Collins	Y	Y	Y	Y	Y	Y	Y
MARYLAND							
Sarbanes	Y	Y	Y	Y	Y	Y	Y
Mikulski	Y	Y	Y	Y	Y	Y	Y
MASSACHUSETTS							
Kennedy	?	Y	Y	Y	Y	Y	Y
Kerry	?	Y	Y	Y	Y	Y	Y
MICHIGAN							
Levin	Y	Y	Y	Y	Y	Y	Y
Stabenow	Y	Y	Y	Y	Y	Y	Y
MINNESOTA							
Wellstone	?	Y	Y	Y	Y	Y	Y
Dayton	Y	Y	Y	Y	Y	Y	Y
MISSISSIPPI							
Cochran	Y	N	Y	Y	Y	Y	N
Lott	Y	N	Y	Y	Y	Y	N
MISSOURI							
Bond	Y	N	Y	Y	Y	Y	N
Carnahan	Y	Y	Y	Y	Y	Y	Y
MONTANA							
Baucus	?	Y	Y	Y	Y	Y	Y
Burns	Y	N	Y	Y	Y	Y	N
NEBRASKA							
Nelson	Y	Y	Y	Y	Y	Y	N
Hagel	Y	N	Y	Y	Y	Y	N
NEVADA							
Reid	Y	Y	Y	Y	Y	Y	Y
Ensign	Y	N	Y	Y	Y	Y	Y

	322	323	324	325	326	327	328
NEW HAMPSHIRE							
Smith	Y	N	N	Y	Y	Y	N
Gregg	Y	Y	Y	Y	Y	Y	N
NEW JERSEY							
Corzine	?	Y	Y	Y	Y	Y	Y
Torricelli	?	Y	Y	Y	?	?	Y
NEW MEXICO							
Domenici	Y	N	Y	Y	Y	Y	N
Bingaman	Y	Y	Y	Y	Y	Y	Y
NEW YORK							
Clinton	Y	Y	Y	Y	Y	Y	Y
Schumer	Y	Y	Y	Y	Y	Y	Y
NORTH CAROLINA							
Helms	Y	N	N	Y	Y	Y	N
Edwards	Y	Y	Y	Y	Y	Y	Y
NORTH DAKOTA							
Conrad	Y	Y	Y	Y	Y	Y	Y
Dorgan	Y	Y	Y	Y	Y	Y	Y
OHIO							
DeWine	Y	Y	Y	Y	Y	Y	N
Voinovich	?	N	N	Y	Y	Y	N
OKLAHOMA							
Nickles	Y	N	N	Y	Y	Y	N
Inhofe	Y	N	Y	Y	Y	Y	N
OREGON							
Wyden	?	Y	Y	Y	Y	Y	Y
Smith	?	Y	Y	Y	Y	Y	Y
PENNSYLVANIA							
Specter	Y	Y	Y	Y	Y	Y	Y
Santorum	Y	N	Y	Y	Y	Y	N
RHODE ISLAND							
Reed	Y	Y	Y	Y	Y	Y	Y
Chafee	Y	N	Y	Y	Y	Y	Y
SOUTH CAROLINA							
Thurmond	Y	N	Y	Y	Y	Y	N
Hollings	Y	N	Y	Y	Y	Y	N
SOUTH DAKOTA							
Daschle	Y	Y	Y	Y	Y	Y	Y
Johnson	Y	Y	Y	Y	Y	Y	Y
TENNESSEE							
Thompson	Y	N	Y	Y	Y	Y	N
Frist	?	N	Y	Y	Y	Y	N

Key

Y	Voted for (yea).
#	Paired for.
+	Announced for.
N	Voted against (nay).
X	Paired against.
–	Announced against.
P	Voted "present."
C	Voted "present" to avoid possible conflict of interest.
?	Did not vote or otherwise make a position known.

Democrats **Republicans**
Independents

	322	323	324	325	326	327	328
TEXAS							
Gramm	Y	N	N	Y	Y	Y	N
Hutchison	Y	N	Y	Y	Y	Y	N
UTAH							
Hatch	+	N	Y	Y	Y	Y	N
Bennett	Y	N	Y	Y	Y	Y	N
VERMONT							
Leahy	Y	Y	Y	Y	Y	Y	Y
Jeffords	?	Y	Y	Y	Y	Y	Y
VIRGINIA							
Warner	Y	N	Y	Y	Y	Y	N
Allen	Y	N	Y	?	?	N	N
WASHINGTON							
Cantwell	Y	Y	Y	Y	Y	Y	Y
Murray	Y	Y	Y	Y	Y	Y	Y
WEST VIRGINIA							
Byrd	Y	N	Y	Y	Y	Y	N
Rockefeller	Y	Y	Y	Y	Y	Y	Y
WISCONSIN							
Kohl	Y	Y	Y	Y	Y	Y	Y
Feingold	Y	Y	N	Y	Y	Y	Y
WYOMING							
Thomas	Y	N	Y	Y	Y	Y	N
Enzi	Y	N	Y	Y	Y	Y	N

ND Northern Democrats   SD Southern Democrats

Southern states - Ala., Ark., Fla., Ga., Ky., La., Miss., N.C., Okla., S.C., Tenn., Texas, Va.

322. Hicks Nomination/Confirmation. Confirmation of President Bush's nomination of Larry R. Hicks of Nevada to be U.S. District judge for the District of Nevada. Confirmed 83-0: R 43-0; D 40-0 (ND 33-0, SD 7-0); I 0-0. A "yea" was a vote in support of the president's position. Nov. 5, 2001.

323. HR 3061. Fiscal 2002 Labor-HHS-Education Appropriations/ Cloture. Motion to invoke cloture (thus limiting debate) on the Daschle, D-S.D., amendment that would provide collective bargaining rights for public safety officers employed by state and local municipalities. Motion rejected 56-44: R 7-42; D 48-2 (ND 40-1, SD 8-1); I 1-0. Three-fifths of the total Senate (60) is required to invoke cloture. (Subsequently, the Daschle amendment was withdrawn.) Nov. 6, 2001.

324. HR 3061. Fiscal 2002 Labor-HHS-Education Appropriations/ Passage. Passage of the bill that would appropriate $123.1 billion for the Labor, Health and Human Services and Education departments and related agencies. The bill includes $48.5 billion for education funding, $54.2 billion for the Department of Health and Human Services, and $11.9 billion for the Labor Department. Passed 89-10: R 40-9; D 48-1 (ND 40-1, SD 8-0); I 1-0. Nov. 6, 2001.

325. Armijo Nomination/Confirmation. Confirmation of President

Bush's nomination of M. Christina Armijo of New Mexico to be U.S. District judge for the District of New Mexico. Confirmed 100-0: R 49-0; D 50-0 (ND 41-0, SD 9-0); I 1-0. A "yea" was a vote in support of the president's position. Nov. 6, 2001.

326. Bowdre Nomination/Confirmation. Confirmation of President Bush's nomination of Karon O. Bowdre of Alabama to be U.S. District judge for the Northern District of Alabama. Confirmed 98-0: R 48-0; D 49-0 (ND 40-0, SD 9-0); I 1-0. A "yea" was a vote in support of the president's position. Nov. 6, 2001.

327. Friot Nomination/Confirmation. Confirmation of President Bush's nomination of Stephen P. Friot of Oklahoma to be U.S. District judge for the Western District of Oklahoma. Confirmed 98-0: R 48-0; D 49-0 (ND 40-0, SD 9-0); I 1-0. A "yea" was a vote in support of the president's position. Nov. 6, 2001.

328. HR 2944. Fiscal 2002 District of Columbia Appropriations/ Needle Exchange Programs. Landrieu, D-La., motion to table (kill) the Allen, R-Va., amendment that would prohibit the use of local as well as federal funds in the bill for any needle exchange programs. Motion agreed to 53-47: R 5-44; D 47-3 (ND 39-2, SD 8-1); I 1-0. Nov. 7, 2001.

	329	330	331	332	333	334
ALABAMA						
Shelby	Y	Y	N	Y	Y	Y
Sessions	Y	N	N	Y	Y	Y
ALASKA						
Stevens	Y	Y	N	Y	Y	Y
Murkowski	Y	Y	N	Y	Y	Y
ARIZONA						
McCain	Y	Y	Y	Y	Y	N
Kyl	Y	N	N	Y	N	Y
ARKANSAS						
Hutchinson	Y	Y	N	Y	Y	Y
Lincoln	N	Y	Y	Y	Y	Y
CALIFORNIA						
Feinstein	Y	Y	Y	Y	Y	Y
Boxer	N	Y	Y	Y	Y	?
COLORADO						
Campbell	Y	Y	Y	Y	Y	Y
Allard	Y	N	N	Y	Y	Y
CONNECTICUT						
Dodd	N	Y	Y	Y	Y	Y
Lieberman	N	Y	Y	Y	Y	Y
DELAWARE						
Carper	N	Y	Y	Y	Y	Y
Biden	N	Y	Y	Y	Y	Y
FLORIDA						
Graham	N	Y	Y	Y	Y	Y
Nelson	N	Y	Y	Y	Y	Y
GEORGIA						
Miller	Y	N	Y	Y	?	?
Cleland	N	Y	Y	Y	?	?
HAWAII						
Inouye	N	Y	Y	Y	Y	Y
Akaka	N	Y	Y	Y	Y	Y
IDAHO						
Craig	Y	N	N	Y	Y	Y
Crapo	N	Y	Y	Y	Y	Y
ILLINOIS						
Durbin	N	Y	Y	Y	Y	Y
Fitzgerald	Y	Y	N	Y	Y	Y
INDIANA						
Lugar	Y	Y	Y	Y	Y	Y
Bayh	N	Y	Y	Y	Y	N

	329	330	331	332	333	334
IOWA						
Grassley	Y	N	N	Y	Y	Y
Harkin	N	Y	Y	Y	Y	Y
KANSAS						
Brownback	Y	N	N	Y	Y	Y
Roberts	Y	N	N	Y	Y	Y
KENTUCKY						
McConnell	Y	N	Y	Y	Y	Y
Bunning	Y	N	N	Y	Y	Y
LOUISIANA						
Breaux	N	Y	Y	Y	Y	Y
Landrieu	N	Y	Y	Y	Y	Y
MAINE						
Snowe	Y	Y	Y	Y	Y	Y
Collins	Y	Y	Y	Y	Y	Y
MARYLAND						
Sarbanes	N	Y	Y	Y	Y	Y
Mikulski	N	Y	Y	Y	Y	Y
MASSACHUSETTS						
Kennedy	N	Y	Y	Y	Y	Y
Kerry	N	Y	?	Y	Y	Y
MICHIGAN						
Levin	N	Y	Y	Y	Y	Y
Stabenow	N	Y	Y	Y	Y	Y
MINNESOTA						
Wellstone	N	Y	Y	Y	Y	Y
Dayton	N	Y	Y	Y	Y	Y
MISSISSIPPI						
Cochran	Y	Y	N	Y	Y	Y
Lott	Y	N	N	Y	Y	Y
MISSOURI						
Bond	Y	N	Y	Y	Y	Y
Carnahan	N	Y	Y	Y	Y	Y
MONTANA						
Baucus	N	Y	Y	Y	Y	Y
Burns	Y	Y	Y	Y	Y	Y
NEBRASKA						
Nelson	N	Y	Y	Y	Y	Y
Hagel	Y	?	Y	Y	Y	Y
NEVADA						
Reid	N	Y	Y	Y	Y	Y
Ensign	Y	N	N	Y	N	Y

	329	330	331	332	333	334
NEW HAMPSHIRE						
Smith	Y	N	N	Y	Y	Y
Gregg	Y	N	N	Y	Y	Y
NEW JERSEY						
Corzine	N	Y	Y	Y	Y	Y
Torricelli	N	Y	Y	Y	Y	Y
NEW MEXICO						
Domenici	Y	Y	Y	Y	Y	Y
Bingaman	N	Y	Y	Y	Y	Y
NEW YORK						
Clinton	N	Y	Y	Y	Y	Y
Schumer	N	Y	Y	Y	Y	Y
NORTH CAROLINA						
Helms	Y	N	N	Y	Y	N
Edwards	N	Y	Y	Y	Y	Y
NORTH DAKOTA						
Conrad	N	Y	Y	Y	Y	Y
Dorgan	N	Y	Y	Y	Y	Y
OHIO						
DeWine	Y	Y	Y	Y	Y	Y
Voinovich	Y	Y	Y	Y	Y	?
OKLAHOMA						
Nickles	Y	N	N	Y	Y	Y
Inhofe	Y	N	N	Y	Y	Y
OREGON						
Wyden	N	Y	Y	Y	Y	Y
Smith	Y	Y	Y	Y	Y	Y
PENNSYLVANIA						
Specter	N	Y	Y	Y	Y	Y
Santorum	Y	N	N	Y	Y	Y
RHODE ISLAND						
Reed	N	Y	Y	Y	Y	Y
Chafee	Y	Y	Y	Y	Y	Y
SOUTH CAROLINA						
Thurmond	Y	N	N	Y	Y	Y
Hollings	N	Y	Y	Y	Y	Y
SOUTH DAKOTA						
Daschle	N	Y	Y	Y	Y	Y
Johnson	N	Y	Y	Y	Y	Y
TENNESSEE						
Thompson	Y	N	Y	Y	Y	Y
Frist	Y	N	Y	Y	Y	Y

	329	330	331	332	333	334
TEXAS						
Gramm	Y	N	N	Y	Y	N
Hutchison	Y	Y	Y	Y	Y	Y
UTAH						
Hatch	Y	N	Y	Y	Y	Y
Bennett	Y	Y	Y	Y	Y	Y
VERMONT						
Leahy	N	Y	Y	Y	Y	+
Jeffords	Y	Y	Y	Y	Y	Y
VIRGINIA						
Warner	Y	Y	Y	Y	Y	Y
Allen	Y	Y	Y	Y	Y	Y
WASHINGTON						
Cantwell	N	Y	Y	Y	Y	Y
Murray	N	Y	Y	Y	Y	Y
WEST VIRGINIA						
Byrd	Y	Y	Y	Y	Y	Y
Rockefeller	N	Y	Y	Y	Y	Y
WISCONSIN						
Kohl	N	Y	Y	Y	Y	Y
Feingold	N	Y	Y	Y	Y	N
WYOMING						
Thomas	Y	N	N	Y	Y	Y
Enzi	Y	N	N	Y	Y	?

Key

Y Voted for (yea).
Paired for.
+ Announced for.
N Voted against (nay).
X Paired against.
– Announced against.
P Voted "present."
C Voted "present" to avoid possible conflict of interest.
? Did not vote or otherwise make a position known.

Democrats **Republicans** *Independents*

ND Northern Democrats   SD Southern Democrats

Southern states - Ala., Ark., Fla., Ga., Ky., La., Miss., N.C., Okla., S.C., Tenn., Texas, Va.

329. HR 2944. Fiscal 2002 District of Columbia Appropriations/ Attorney Fees. Hutchison, R-Texas, amendment that would prohibit the use of funds for attorney fees in legal challenges to special education placements under the Individuals with Disabilities Education Act if the hourly rate exceeds $150, or if the total compensation exceeds $3,000, unless otherwise approved. Adopted 51-49: R 47-2; D 3-47 (ND 2-39, SD 1-8); I 1-0. Nov. 7, 2001.

330. HR 2944. Fiscal 2002 District of Columbia Appropriations/ Attorney Fees. Durbin, D-Ill., amendment that would exempt the limitation on attorney fees paid by the District of Columbia for actions under the Individuals with Disabilities Education Act if the plaintiff is a child who comes from a family that has an annual income of less than $17,600, or where one of the parents is a disabled veteran, or if the child has been adjudicated as neglected or abused. Adopted 73-26: R 23-25; D 49-1 (ND 41-0, SD 8-1); I 1-0. Nov. 7, 2001.

331. HR 2944. Fiscal 2002 District of Columbia Appropriations/Passage. Passage of the bill that would provide $408 million for the District of Columbia in fiscal 2002, including funds for the city's courts and corrections system and $16.1 million for an emergency response plan following the Sept. 11 attacks. The bill also would approve a $7.2 billion budget for the District. Passed 75-24: R 25-24; D 49-0 (ND 40-0, SD 9-0); I 1-0. Nov. 7, 2001.

332. HR 2883. Fiscal 2002 Intelligence Authorization/Passage. Passage of the bill that would authorize classified amounts in fiscal 2002 for U.S. intelligence agencies and intelligence-related activities of the U.S. government, including the Central Intelligence Agency, the National Security Agency, the Defense Department, the Federal Bureau of Investigations, the State Department and other related agencies. The total funding level is classified, but the amount has been estimated to be approximately $30 billion. The bill, as amended, also would require the attorney general to report to Congress within three months of the bill's enactment on the effectiveness of the Alien Terrorist Removal Court. Passed 100-0: R 49-0; D 50-0 (ND 41-0, SD 9-0); I 1-0. (Before passage, the Senate struck all after the enacting clause and inserted the text of S 1428, as amended, into the bill.) Nov. 8, 2001.

333. Wooten Nomination/Confirmation. Confirmation of President Bush's nomination of Terry L. Wooten of South Carolina to be U.S. District judge for the District of South Carolina. Confirmed 98-0: R 49-0; D 48-0 (ND 41-0, SD 7-0); I 1-0. A "yea" was a vote in support of the president's position. Nov. 8, 2001.

334. HR 2620. Fiscal 2002 VA-HUD Appropriations/Conference Report. Adoption of the conference report on the bill that would provide $112.7 billion for the departments of Veterans Affairs (VA) and Housing and Urban Development (HUD) and related agencies, including the EPA, NASA, and the National Science Foundation. Adopted (thus cleared for the president) 87-7: R 42-5; D 44-2 (ND 37-2, SD 7-0); I 1-0. Nov. 8, 2001.

	335	336	337	338	339	340	341
ALABAMA							
Shelby	Y	N	N	N	Y	Y	N
Sessions	Y	N	N	N	Y	Y	Y
ALASKA							
Stevens	Y	N	N	N	Y	Y	Y
Murkowski	Y	N	N	N	Y	Y	Y
ARIZONA							
McCain	Y	N	?	?	N	N	Y
Kyl	Y	N	N	N	N	Y	Y
ARKANSAS							
Hutchinson	Y	N	N	N	Y	Y	N
Lincoln	Y	N	Y	Y	Y	Y	N
CALIFORNIA							
Feinstein	Y	N	Y	Y	Y	Y	Y
Boxer	Y	N	Y	Y	Y	Y	Y
COLORADO							
Campbell	Y	N	N	N	Y	Y	Y
Allard	Y	N	N	N	Y	Y	Y
CONNECTICUT							
Dodd	Y	N	Y	Y	Y	Y	Y
Lieberman	Y	N	Y	Y	Y	Y	Y
DELAWARE							
Carper	Y	N	Y	Y	Y	Y	N
Biden	Y	N	Y	Y	Y	Y	Y
FLORIDA							
Graham	Y	N	Y	Y	Y	Y	N
Nelson	Y	N	Y	Y	Y	Y	Y
GEORGIA							
Miller	Y	N	Y	Y	Y	Y	Y
Cleland	Y	N	Y	Y	Y	Y	N
HAWAII							
Inouye	Y	N	Y	Y	Y	Y	Y
Akaka	Y	N	Y	Y	Y	Y	N
IDAHO							
Craig	Y	N	N	N	Y	Y	Y
Crapo	Y	N	N	N	Y	Y	Y
ILLINOIS							
Durbin	Y	N	Y	Y	Y	Y	Y
Fitzgerald	Y	N	N	N	Y	Y	N
INDIANA							
Lugar	Y	N	N	N	Y	Y	Y
Bayh	Y	N	Y	N	Y	N	Y

	335	336	337	338	339	340	341
IOWA							
Grassley	Y	N	N	N	Y	Y	N
Harkin	Y	N	Y	Y	Y	Y	N
KANSAS							
Brownback	Y	N	N	N	Y	Y	Y
Roberts	Y	N	N	N	Y	Y	Y
KENTUCKY							
McConnell	Y	N	N	N	Y	Y	Y
Bunning	Y	N	N	N	Y	Y	Y
LOUISIANA							
Breaux	Y	N	Y	Y	Y	Y	N
Landrieu	Y	N	Y	Y	Y	Y	Y
MAINE							
Snowe	Y	N	N	N	Y	Y	Y
Collins	Y	N	N	N	Y	N	Y
MARYLAND							
Sarbanes	Y	N	Y	Y	Y	Y	N
Mikulski	Y	N	Y	Y	Y	Y	N
MASSACHUSETTS							
Kennedy	Y	N	Y	Y	Y	Y	N
Kerry	Y	N	Y	Y	Y	Y	N
MICHIGAN							
Levin	Y	N	Y	Y	Y	Y	N
Stabenow	Y	N	Y	Y	Y	Y	N
MINNESOTA							
Wellstone	Y	Y	Y	Y	Y	Y	Y
Dayton	Y	N	Y	Y	Y	Y	N
MISSISSIPPI							
Cochran	Y	N	N	N	Y	Y	Y
Lott	Y	N	N	N	Y	Y	Y
MISSOURI							
Bond	Y	N	N	N	Y	Y	Y
Carnahan	Y	N	Y	Y	Y	Y	N
MONTANA							
Baucus	Y	N	Y	Y	Y	Y	Y
Burns	Y	N	N	N	Y	Y	Y
NEBRASKA							
Nelson	Y	N	Y	Y	Y	Y	N
Hagel	Y	N	N	N	Y	Y	Y
NEVADA							
Reid	Y	N	Y	Y	Y	Y	Y
Ensign	Y	N	N	N	N	Y	Y

	335	336	337	338	339	340	341
NEW HAMPSHIRE							
Smith	Y	N	N	N	N	Y	Y
Gregg	Y	N	N	N	N	Y	Y
NEW JERSEY							
Corzine	Y	N	Y	Y	Y	Y	Y
Torricelli	Y	N	Y	Y	?	?	Y
NEW MEXICO							
Domenici	Y	N	N	N	Y	Y	Y
Bingaman	Y	N	Y	Y	Y	Y	N
NEW YORK							
Clinton	Y	N	Y	Y	Y	Y	Y
Schumer	Y	N	Y	Y	Y	Y	Y
NORTH CAROLINA							
Helms	Y	N	N	N	Y	Y	N
Edwards	Y	N	Y	Y	Y	Y	Y
NORTH DAKOTA							
Conrad	Y	N	Y	Y	Y	Y	N
Dorgan	Y	N	Y	Y	Y	Y	N
OHIO							
DeWine	Y	N	N	N	Y	Y	N
Voinovich	Y	N	N	N	N	Y	N
OKLAHOMA							
Nickles	Y	N	N	N	Y	Y	Y
Inhofe	Y	N	N	N	Y	Y	Y
OREGON							
Wyden	Y	N	Y	Y	Y	Y	Y
Smith	Y	N	N	N	Y	Y	Y
PENNSYLVANIA							
Specter	Y	N	N	N	Y	Y	N
Santorum	Y	N	N	N	Y	Y	N
RHODE ISLAND							
Reed	Y	N	Y	Y	Y	Y	N
Chafee	Y	N	N	N	Y	Y	N
SOUTH CAROLINA							
Thurmond	Y	N	N	N	Y	Y	Y
Hollings	Y	N	Y	Y	Y	Y	N
SOUTH DAKOTA							
Daschle	Y	N	Y	Y	Y	Y	N
Johnson	?	N	Y	Y	Y	Y	N
TENNESSEE							
Thompson	Y	N	N	N	Y	Y	Y
Frist	Y	N	N	N	Y	Y	Y

	335	336	337	338	339	340	341
TEXAS							
Gramm	Y	N	?	?	Y	Y	Y
Hutchison	Y	N	N	N	Y	Y	N
UTAH							
Hatch	Y	N	N	N	Y	Y	Y
Bennett	Y	N	N	N	Y	Y	Y
VERMONT							
Leahy	Y	N	Y	Y	Y	Y	Y
Jeffords	Y	N	Y	Y	Y	Y	N
VIRGINIA							
Warner	Y	N	N	N	Y	Y	Y
Allen	Y	N	N	N	Y	Y	Y
WASHINGTON							
Cantwell	Y	N	Y	Y	Y	Y	Y
Murray	Y	N	Y	Y	Y	Y	Y
WEST VIRGINIA							
Byrd	Y	N	Y	Y	Y	Y	Y
Rockefeller	Y	N	Y	Y	Y	Y	N
WISCONSIN							
Kohl	Y	N	Y	Y	Y	Y	Y
Feingold	Y	N	Y	Y	Y	Y	N
WYOMING							
Thomas	Y	N	N	N	Y	Y	N
Enzi	Y	N	N	N	Y	Y	N

Key

Y Voted for (yea).
Paired for.
+ Announced for.
N Voted against (nay).
X Paired against.
− Announced against.
P Voted "present."
C Voted "present" to avoid possible conflict of interest.
? Did not vote or otherwise make a position known.

Democrats   **Republicans**
Independents

ND Northern Democrats   SD Southern Democrats

Southern states - Ala., Ark., Fla., Ga., Ky., La., Miss., N.C., Okla., S.C., Tenn., Texas, Va.

335. Clement Nomination/Confirmation. Confirmation of President Bush's nomination of Edith Brown Clement of Louisiana to be a judge for the 5th U.S. Circuit Court of Appeals. Confirmed 99-0: R 49-0; D 49-0 (ND 40-0, SD 9-0); I 1-0. A "yea" was a vote in support of the president's position. Nov. 13, 2001.

336. S J Res 28. Balanced Budget Suspension/Passage. Passage of the joint resolution that would suspend certain budget enforcement mechanisms until fiscal 2004, including removing points of order against legislation that would decrease taxes, increase spending or reduce Social Security surpluses in violation of the fiscal 2002 budget resolution, or points of order against legislation that would exceed the discretionary spending cap. Rejected 1-99: R 0-49; D 1-49 (ND 1-40, SD 0-9); I 0-1. A "nay" was a vote in support of the president's position. Nov. 13, 2001.

337. HR 3090. Economic Stimulus/Emergency Designation. Baucus, D-Mont., motion to waive the Budget Act with respect to Section 909 of the Baucus, D-Mont., substitute amendment. The section would designate spending in the bill that exceeds the limit set in the fiscal 2002 budget resolution as emergency spending. Motion rejected 51-47: R 0-47; D 50-0 (ND 41-0, SD 9-0); I 1-0. A three-fifths majority vote (60) of the total Senate is required to waive the Budget Act. (Subsequently, the chair upheld the point of order and the section fell.) Nov. 14, 2001.

338. HR 3090. Economic Stimulus/Democratic Substitute. Baucus, D-Mont., motion to waive the Budget Act with respect to the Domenici, R-N.M., point of order against the Baucus substitute amendment. The amendment would provide $73 billion in fiscal 2002 for economic stimulus measures, including $14 billion for refund checks to taxpayers that did not receive refunds during the summer of 2001. It also would provide $31 billion for unemployment benefits and health care benefits for displaced workers and agricul-

ture assistance. It also would provide $8 billion in fiscal 2002, and $15 billion over 10 years for homeland security, including bio-terrorism, food safety, law enforcement and postal programs. Motion rejected 51-47: R 0-47; D 50-0 (ND 41-0, SD 9-0); I 1-0. A three-fifths majority vote (60) of the total Senate is required to waive the Budget Act. (Subsequently, the chair upheld the point of order and the amendment fell.) A "nay" was a vote in support of the president's position. Nov. 14, 2001.

339. HR 2330. Fiscal 2002 Agriculture Appropriations/Conference Report. Adoption of the conference report on the bill that would provide $75.9 billion, including $16 billion in discretionary funds, in fiscal 2002 for agriculture programs, rural development and nutrition programs. The agreement would include $23 billion for the food stamp program, $10.1 billion for child nutrition programs and $1 billion for the Agricultural Research Service. Adopted (thus cleared for the president) 92-7: R 43-6; D 48-1 (ND 39-1, SD 9-0); I 1-0. Nov. 15, 2001.

340. HR 2500. Fiscal 2002 Commerce-Justice-State Appropriations/Conference Report. Adoption of the conference report on the bill that would provide $41.6 billion for the departments of Commerce, Justice and State, and the federal judiciary and related agencies in fiscal 2002, $1.9 billion more than fiscal 2001. Adopted (thus cleared for the president) 98-1: R 48-1; D 49-0 (ND 40-0, SD 9-0); I 1-0. Nov. 15, 2001.

341. HR 1552. Internet Tax Moratorium/State Internet Tax System. McCain, R-Ariz., motion to table (kill) an Enzi, R-Wyo., amendment that would extend the Internet tax moratorium until Dec. 31, 2005. It also would allow groups of at least 20 states to form a uniform, simplified Internet tax system with the approval of Congress. Motion agreed to 57-43: R 35-14; D 22-28 (ND 18-23, SD 4-5); I 0-1. Nov. 15, 2001.

	342	343
ALABAMA		
Shelby	Y	Y
Sessions	Y	Y
ALASKA		
Stevens	Y	Y
Murkowski	Y	Y
ARIZONA		
McCain	Y	Y
Kyl	Y	N
ARKANSAS		
Hutchinson	Y	Y
Lincoln	Y	Y
CALIFORNIA		
Feinstein	?	Y
Boxer	Y	Y
COLORADO		
Campbell	Y	Y
Allard	Y	Y
CONNECTICUT		
Dodd	Y	Y
Lieberman	Y	Y
DELAWARE		
Carper	Y	Y
Biden	Y	Y
FLORIDA		
Graham	Y	Y
Nelson	Y	Y
GEORGIA		
Miller	Y	Y
Cleland	Y	Y
HAWAII		
Inouye	Y	Y
Akaka	Y	Y
IDAHO		
Craig	Y	Y
Crapo	Y	Y
ILLINOIS		
Durbin	Y	Y
Fitzgerald	Y	Y
INDIANA		
Lugar	Y	Y
Bayh	Y	Y

	342	343
IOWA		
Grassley	Y	Y
Harkin	Y	Y
KANSAS		
Brownback	Y	Y
Roberts	Y	Y
KENTUCKY		
McConnell	Y	Y
Bunning	Y	Y
LOUISIANA		
Breaux	Y	Y
Landrieu	Y	Y
MAINE		
Snowe	Y	Y
Collins	Y	Y
MARYLAND		
Sarbanes	Y	Y
Mikulski	Y	Y
MASSACHUSETTS		
Kennedy	Y	Y
Kerry	Y	Y
MICHIGAN		
Levin	Y	Y
Stabenow	Y	Y
MINNESOTA		
Wellstone	Y	Y
Dayton	Y	Y
MISSISSIPPI		
Cochran	Y	Y
Lott	Y	Y
MISSOURI		
Bond	Y	Y
Carnahan	Y	Y
MONTANA		
Baucus	Y	Y
Burns	Y	Y
NEBRASKA		
Nelson	Y	Y
Hagel	Y	Y
NEVADA		
Reid	Y	Y
Ensign	Y	Y

	342	343
NEW HAMPSHIRE		
Smith	+	Y
Gregg	Y	N
NEW JERSEY		
Corzine	Y	Y
Torricelli	Y	Y
NEW MEXICO		
Domenici	Y	Y
Bingaman	Y	Y
NEW YORK		
Clinton	Y	Y
Schumer	Y	Y
NORTH CAROLINA		
Helms	Y	Y
Edwards	?	Y
NORTH DAKOTA		
Conrad	?	Y
Dorgan	Y	Y
OHIO		
DeWine	Y	Y
Voinovich	Y	Y
OKLAHOMA		
Nickles	Y	N
Inhofe	Y	Y
OREGON		
Wyden	Y	Y
Smith	Y	Y
PENNSYLVANIA		
Specter	?	Y
Santorum	Y	Y
RHODE ISLAND		
Reed	Y	Y
Chafee	Y	Y
SOUTH CAROLINA		
Thurmond	Y	Y
Hollings	Y	Y
SOUTH DAKOTA		
Daschle	Y	Y
Johnson	Y	Y
TENNESSEE		
Thompson	Y	Y
Frist	Y	Y

Key

Y	Voted for (yea).
#	Paired for.
+	Announced for.
N	Voted against (nay).
X	Paired against.
–	Announced against.
P	Voted "present."
C	Voted "present" to avoid possible conflict of interest.
?	Did not vote or otherwise make a position known.

Democrats   **Republicans**
Independents

	342	343
TEXAS		
Gramm	Y	N
Hutchison	Y	Y
UTAH		
Hatch	Y	Y
Bennett	Y	Y
VERMONT		
Leahy	Y	Y
Jeffords	Y	Y
VIRGINIA		
Warner	Y	Y
Allen	Y	Y
WASHINGTON		
Cantwell	Y	Y
Murray	Y	Y
WEST VIRGINIA		
Byrd	Y	Y
Rockefeller	Y	Y
WISCONSIN		
Kohl	Y	Y
Feingold	Y	Y
WYOMING		
Thomas	Y	Y
Enzi	Y	Y

342. Baxter Nomination/Motion to Proceed. Motion to proceed to executive session to consider President Bush's nomination of William Baxter of Tennessee to be a member of the board of directors of the Tennessee Valley Authority. Motion agreed to 95-0: R 47-0; D 47-0 (ND 39-0, SD 8-0); I 1-0. (Subsequently, the nomination was confirmed by voice vote.) Nov. 27, 2001.

343. HR 10. Pension Contribution Limits/Cloture. Motion to invoke cloture (thus limiting debate) on the motion to proceed to the bill that would expand contribution limits on individual retirement accounts and 401(k) plans. Motion agreed to 96-4: R 45-4; D 50-0 (ND 41-0, SD 9-0); I 1-0. Three-fifths of the total Senate (60) is required to invoke cloture. Nov. 29, 2001.

	344	345	346	347	348	349
ALABAMA						
Shelby	N	Y	Y	N	N	N
Sessions	N	Y	Y	Y	Y	N
ALASKA						
Stevens	N	Y	Y	Y	N	N
Murkowski	N	N	Y	Y	N	N
ARIZONA						
McCain	N	Y	N	Y	Y	Y
Kyl	N	N	Y	Y	Y	Y
ARKANSAS						
Hutchinson	N	Y	Y	N	N	N
Lincoln	N	Y	Y	N	N	N
CALIFORNIA						
Feinstein	N	Y	Y	N	N	N
Boxer	N	Y	Y	N	N	N
COLORADO						
Campbell	N	Y	Y	Y	Y	Y
Allard	N	N	Y	Y	Y	Y
CONNECTICUT						
Dodd	N	Y	Y	N	N	N
Lieberman	N	Y	Y	N	N	N
DELAWARE						
Carper	N	Y	Y	N	N	N
Biden	N	Y	Y	N	N	N
FLORIDA						
Graham	N	Y	Y	N	N	N
Nelson	N	Y	Y	N	N	N
GEORGIA						
Miller	N	Y	Y	N	N	N
Cleland	N	Y	Y	N	N	N
HAWAII						
Inouye	N	Y	Y	N	N	N
Akaka	N	Y	Y	N	N	N
IDAHO						
Craig	N	Y	Y	N	N	N
Crapo	N	Y	Y	Y	N	N
ILLINOIS						
Durbin	N	Y	Y	N	N	N
Fitzgerald	N	Y	Y	Y	Y	Y
INDIANA						
Lugar	N	Y	Y	Y	Y	Y
Bayh	N	Y	N	N	N	N

	344	345	346	347	348	349
IOWA						
Grassley	N	Y	Y	Y	Y	N
Harkin	?	?	Y	N	N	N
KANSAS						
Brownback	N	Y	Y	Y	N	N
Roberts	N	Y	Y	Y	N	N
KENTUCKY						
McConnell	N	Y	Y	Y	Y	Y
Bunning	N	Y	Y	Y	Y	Y
LOUISIANA						
Breaux	N	Y	Y	N	N	N
Landrieu	N	Y	Y	N	N	N
MAINE						
Snowe	N	Y	Y	N	N	N
Collins	N	Y	Y	N	N	N
MARYLAND						
Sarbanes	N	Y	Y	N	N	N
Mikulski	N	Y	Y	N	N	N
MASSACHUSETTS						
Kennedy	–	+	Y	N	N	N
Kerry	N	Y	Y	N	N	N
MICHIGAN						
Levin	N	Y	Y	N	N	N
Stabenow	N	Y	Y	N	N	N
MINNESOTA						
Wellstone	N	Y	Y	N	N	N
Dayton	N	Y	Y	N	N	N
MISSISSIPPI						
Cochran	N	Y	Y	Y	Y	Y
Lott	N	N	Y	Y	Y	Y
MISSOURI						
Bond	N	N	Y	Y	Y	Y
Carnahan	N	Y	Y	N	N	N
MONTANA						
Baucus	N	Y	Y	N	N	N
Burns	N	N	Y	Y	Y	Y
NEBRASKA						
Nelson	N	Y	Y	N	N	N
Hagel	N	Y	Y	N	N	N
NEVADA						
Reid	N	Y	Y	N	N	N
Ensign	N	Y	Y	Y	Y	Y

	344	345	346	347	348	349
NEW HAMPSHIRE						
Smith	N	N	Y	Y	Y	Y
Gregg	N	N	Y	Y	Y	Y
NEW JERSEY						
Corzine	N	Y	Y	N	N	N
Torricelli	–	+	Y	N	N	N
NEW MEXICO						
Domenici	N	Y	Y	Y	N	N
Bingaman	N	Y	Y	N	N	N
NEW YORK						
Clinton	N	Y	Y	N	N	N
Schumer	N	Y	Y	N	N	N
NORTH CAROLINA						
Helms	N	N	Y	Y	Y	Y
Edwards	N	Y	Y	N	N	N
NORTH DAKOTA						
Conrad	N	Y	Y	N	N	N
Dorgan	N	Y	Y	N	N	N
OHIO						
DeWine	N	Y	Y	N	N	N
Voinovich	?	Y	Y	Y	Y	N
OKLAHOMA						
Nickles	N	N	Y	Y	Y	Y
Inhofe	N	Y	Y	Y	Y	Y
OREGON						
Wyden	N	Y	Y	N	N	N
Smith	N	Y	Y	N	N	N
PENNSYLVANIA						
Specter	N	Y	Y	N	N	N
Santorum	N	Y	Y	Y	Y	N
RHODE ISLAND						
Reed	N	Y	Y	N	N	N
Chafee	N	Y	Y	N	N	N
SOUTH CAROLINA						
Thurmond	N	N	Y	Y	Y	N
Hollings	N	Y	Y	N	N	N
SOUTH DAKOTA						
Daschle	N	Y	Y	N	N	N
Johnson	N	Y	Y	N	N	N
TENNESSEE						
Thompson	N	N	Y	Y	Y	N
Frist	N	N	Y	Y	Y	Y

	344	345	346	347	348	349
TEXAS						
Gramm	N	N	Y	Y	Y	Y
Hutchison	N	Y	?	?	?	?
UTAH						
Hatch	N	Y	Y	N	N	N
Bennett	N	Y	Y	Y	N	N
VERMONT						
Leahy	–	+	Y	N	N	N
Jeffords	N	Y	Y	N	N	N
VIRGINIA						
Warner	N	Y	Y	N	N	N
Allen	Y	Y	Y	N	N	N
WASHINGTON						
Cantwell	N	Y	Y	N	N	N
Murray	N	Y	Y	N	N	N
WEST VIRGINIA						
Byrd	N	Y	Y	N	N	N
Rockefeller	N	Y	Y	N	N	N
WISCONSIN						
Kohl	N	Y	Y	N	N	N
Feingold	N	Y	Y	Y	N	N
WYOMING						
Thomas	N	N	Y	Y	Y	Y
Enzi	N	Y	Y	N	N	N

Key

Y	Voted for (yea).
#	Paired for.
+	Announced for.
N	Voted against (nay).
X	Paired against.
–	Announced against.
P	Voted "present."
C	Voted "present" to avoid possible conflict of interest.
?	Did not vote or otherwise make a position known.

Democrats   **Republicans**
Independents

ND Northern Democrats   SD Southern Democrats

Southern states - Ala., Ark., Fla., Ga., Ky., La., Miss., N.C., Okla., S.C., Tenn., Texas, Va.

---

344. HR 10. Pension Contribution Limits/Cloture. Motion to invoke cloture (thus limiting debate) on the Lott, R-Miss., amendment to the Daschle substitute amendment. The Lott amendment would add language to the bill to modify the nation's energy policies and extend a six-month moratorium on human cloning. The amendment would allow oil and gas drilling in the Arctic National Wildlife Refuge; offer incentives for offshore drilling; provide funding for nuclear energy, clean coal, and oil and gas research; extend tax credits for energy efficiency and coal technology; and raise fuel efficiency standards for sport-utility vehicles and light trucks. Motion rejected 1-94: R 1-47; D 0-46 (ND 0-37, SD 0-9); I 0-1. Three-fifths of the total Senate (60) is required to invoke cloture. Dec. 3, 2001.

345. HR 10. Pension Contribution Limits/Cloture. Motion to invoke cloture (thus limiting debate) on the Daschle, D-S.D., substitute amendment that would strike the text of the underlying bill and insert language that would create a railroad retirement board that would have the authority to invest the pension system's $15.3 billion in Treasury bonds in higher-yielding private equities. Motion agreed to 81-15: R 34-15; D 46-0 (ND 37-0, SD 9-0); I 1-0. (Three-fifths of the total Senate (60) is required to invoke cloture.) Dec. 3, 2001.

346. HR 2299. Fiscal 2002 Transportation Appropriations/Conference Report. Adoption of the conference report on the bill that would appropriate $59.6 billion for fiscal 2002 transportation programs, $1.5 billion more than fiscal 2001. The total includes $1.25 billion for a security office responsible for passenger and baggage screeners at airports established under the avi-

ation security bill (PL 107-71). It also would allow trucks from Mexico to travel throughout the United States but those trucks would be subject to additional inspection, safety and border controls. Adopted (thus cleared for the president) 97-2: R 47-1; D 49-1 (ND 40-1, SD 9-0); I 1-0. Dec. 4, 2001.

347. HR 10. Pension Contribution Limits/Direct Scorekeeping. Domenici, R-N.M., amendment to the Daschle, D-S.D., substitute amendment. The Domenici amendment would strike the "direct scorekeeping" provision in the substitute, which would mandate that railroad trust purchases be scored as a means of financing rather than as a cash outlay. Rejected 40-59: R 36-12; D 4-46 (ND 3-38, SD 1-8); I 0-1. Dec. 4, 2001.

348. HR 10. Pension Contribution Limits/Account Benefits Ratio. Nickles, R-Okla., amendment to the Daschle, D-S.D., substitute amendment. The Nickles amendment would require the average account benefits ratio computation be based on a five-year average rather than the 10-year average. Rejected 27-72: R 27-21; D 0-50 (ND 0-41, SD 0-9); I 0-1. Dec. 4, 2001.

349. HR 10. Pension Contribution Limits/Railroad Retirement Investment Trust Fund Earnings. Gramm, R-Texas, amendment to the Daschle, D-S.D., substitute amendment. The Gramm amendment would provide that any reduction in a tax or increase in benefits in the railroad retirement system take effect to the degree that the Treasury secretary finds that actual earnings of the Railroad Retirement Investment Trust Fund are sufficient to fund them. Rejected 21-78: R 21-27; D 0-50 (ND 0-41, SD 0-9); I 0-1. Dec. 4, 2001.

	350	351	352	353	354	355
ALABAMA						
Shelby	Y	Y	Y	Y	N	N
Sessions	Y	Y	Y	Y	N	N
ALASKA						
Stevens	Y	Y	Y	Y	N	N
Murkowski	Y	Y	N	Y	N	N
ARIZONA						
McCain	Y	Y	N	Y	N	N
Kyl	N	N	N	Y	N	N
ARKANSAS						
Hutchinson	Y	Y	Y	Y	N	N
Lincoln	Y	Y	Y	Y	Y	Y
CALIFORNIA						
Feinstein	Y	Y	Y	Y	Y	Y
Boxer	Y	Y	Y	Y	Y	Y
COLORADO						
Campbell	N	Y	Y	Y	N	N
Allard	N	N	Y	Y	N	N
CONNECTICUT						
Dodd	Y	Y	Y	Y	Y	Y
Lieberman	?	?	?	Y	Y	Y
DELAWARE						
Carper	Y	Y	Y	Y	Y	Y
Biden	Y	Y	Y	Y	Y	Y
FLORIDA						
Graham	Y	Y	N	Y	Y	Y
Nelson	Y	Y	N	Y	Y	Y
GEORGIA						
Miller	Y	Y	Y	Y	Y	Y
Cleland	Y	Y	Y	Y	Y	Y
HAWAII						
Inouye	Y	Y	Y	Y	Y	Y
Akaka	Y	Y	Y	Y	Y	Y
IDAHO						
Craig	Y	Y	Y	Y	N	N
Crapo	Y	Y	Y	Y	N	N
ILLINOIS						
Durbin	Y	Y	Y	Y	Y	Y
Fitzgerald	Y	Y	Y	Y	N	N
INDIANA						
Lugar	N	Y	N	Y	N	N
Bayh	Y	Y	Y	Y	Y	Y
IOWA						
Grassley	Y	Y	Y	Y	N	N
Harkin	Y	Y	Y	Y	Y	Y
KANSAS						
Brownback	Y	Y	Y	Y	N	N
Roberts	Y	Y	Y	Y	N	N
KENTUCKY						
McConnell	N	Y	N	Y	N	N
Bunning	N	Y	N	Y	N	N
LOUISIANA						
Breaux	Y	Y	Y	Y	Y	Y
Landrieu	Y	Y	Y	Y	Y	Y
MAINE						
Snowe	Y	Y	Y	Y	N	N
Collins	Y	Y	Y	Y	N	N
MARYLAND						
Sarbanes	Y	Y	Y	Y	Y	Y
Mikulski	Y	Y	Y	Y	Y	Y
MASSACHUSETTS						
Kennedy	Y	Y	Y	Y	Y	Y
Kerry	Y	Y	Y	Y	Y	Y
MICHIGAN						
Levin	Y	Y	Y	Y	Y	Y
Stabenow	Y	Y	Y	Y	Y	Y
MINNESOTA						
Wellstone	Y	Y	Y	Y	Y	Y
Dayton	Y	Y	Y	Y	Y	Y
MISSISSIPPI						
Cochran	N	Y	Y	Y	N	N
Lott	N	N	Y	Y	N	N
MISSOURI						
Bond	Y	Y	Y	Y	N	N
Carnahan	Y	Y	Y	Y	Y	Y
MONTANA						
Baucus	Y	Y	Y	Y	Y	Y
Burns	Y	Y	Y	Y	N	N
NEBRASKA						
Nelson	Y	Y	Y	Y	Y	Y
Hagel	Y	Y	N	Y	N	N
NEVADA						
Reid	Y	Y	Y	Y	Y	Y
Ensign	N	Y	N	Y	N	N
NEW HAMPSHIRE						
Smith	N	N	N	Y	N	N
Gregg	N	N	N	Y	N	N
NEW JERSEY						
Corzine	Y	Y	Y	Y	Y	Y
Torricelli	Y	Y	Y	Y	Y	Y
NEW MEXICO						
Domenici	Y	Y	N	Y	N	N
Bingaman	Y	Y	Y	Y	Y	Y
NEW YORK						
Clinton	Y	Y	Y	Y	Y	Y
Schumer	Y	Y	Y	Y	Y	Y
NORTH CAROLINA						
Helms	N	N	Y	?	?	?
Edwards	Y	Y	Y	Y	Y	Y
NORTH DAKOTA						
Conrad	Y	Y	Y	Y	Y	Y
Dorgan	Y	Y	Y	Y	Y	Y
OHIO						
DeWine	Y	Y	N	Y	N	N
Voinovich	Y	Y	N	Y	N	N
OKLAHOMA						
Nickles	N	N	N	Y	N	N
Inhofe	Y	Y	Y	Y	N	N
OREGON						
Wyden	Y	Y	Y	Y	Y	Y
Smith	Y	Y	Y	Y	N	N
PENNSYLVANIA						
Specter	Y	Y	Y	Y	N	N
Santorum	Y	Y	Y	Y	N	N
RHODE ISLAND						
Reed	Y	Y	Y	Y	Y	Y
Chafee	Y	Y	N	Y	N	N
SOUTH CAROLINA						
Thurmond	N	Y	N	Y	N	N
Hollings	Y	Y	Y	Y	Y	Y
SOUTH DAKOTA						
Daschle	Y	Y	Y	Y	Y	Y
Johnson	Y	Y	Y	Y	Y	Y
TENNESSEE						
Thompson	N	Y	N	Y	N	N
Frist	N	Y	N	Y	N	N
TEXAS						
Gramm	N	N	N	?	?	?
Hutchison	Y	Y	Y	Y	N	N
UTAH						
Hatch	Y	Y	N	Y	N	N
Bennett	N	Y	N	Y	N	N
VERMONT						
Leahy	Y	Y	Y	Y	Y	Y
Jeffords	Y	Y	Y	Y	Y	Y
VIRGINIA						
Warner	Y	Y	N	Y	N	N
Allen	Y	Y	N	Y	N	N
WASHINGTON						
Cantwell	Y	Y	Y	Y	Y	Y
Murray	Y	Y	Y	Y	Y	Y
WEST VIRGINIA						
Byrd	Y	Y	Y	Y	Y	Y
Rockefeller	Y	Y	Y	Y	Y	Y
WISCONSIN						
Kohl	Y	Y	Y	Y	Y	Y
Feingold	Y	Y	Y	Y	N	N
WYOMING						
Thomas	N	N	Y	N	N	N
Enzi	Y	Y	N	Y	N	N

ND Northern Democrats   SD Southern Democrats

Southern states - Ala., Ark., Fla., Ga., Ky., La., Miss., N.C., Okla., S.C., Tenn., Texas, Va.

350. HR 10. Pension Contribution Limits/Railroad Retirement. Baucus, D-Mont., motion to waive the Budget Act with respect to the Nickles, R-Okla., point of order against the Daschle, D-S.D., substitute amendment that would strike the text of the underlying bill and insert language that would create a railroad retirement board that would have the authority to invest the pension system's $15.3 billion in Treasury bonds in higher-yielding private equities. Motion agreed to 80-19: R 30-19; D 49-0 (ND 40-0, SD 9-0); I 1-0. A three-fifths majority vote (60) of the total Senate is required to waive the Budget Act. Dec. 5, 2001.

351. HR 10. Railroad Retirement/Passage. Passage of a bill that would create a railroad retirement board that would have the authority to invest the pension system's $15.3 billion in Treasury bonds in higher-yielding private equities. It also would reduce the payroll tax on railroads and make other changes in the railroad retirement system. Passed 90-9: R 40-9; D 49-0 (ND 40-0, SD 9-0); I 1-0. (Before passage the Senate struck all after the enacting clause and adopted the Daschle, D-S.D., substitute amendment by voice vote.) Dec. 5, 2001.

352. S 1731. Agriculture Overhaul/Cloture. Motion to invoke cloture (thus limiting debate) on the motion to proceed to the bill that would overhaul farm policy. Motion agreed to 73-26: R 25-24; D 47-2 (ND 40-0, SD 7-2); I 1-0. Three-fifths of the total Senate (60) is required to invoke cloture. Dec. 5, 2001.

353. Hartz Nomination/Confirmation. Confirmation of President Bush's nomination of Harris L. Hartz of New Mexico to be a judge for the 10th U.S. Circuit Court. Confirmed 99-0: R 48-0; D 50-0 (ND 41-0, SD 9-0); I 1-0. A "yea" was a vote in support of the president's position. Dec. 6, 2001.

354. HR 3338. Fiscal 2002 Defense Appropriations/Homeland Security. Byrd, D-W.Va., motion to waive the Budget Act with respect to the Stevens, R-Alaska, point of order against emergency designation of $7.5 billion for homeland security programs in the Byrd substitute amendment. The Byrd substitute would provide $317.6 billion for defense spending in fiscal 2002. Motion rejected 50-48: R 0-47; D 49-1 (ND 40-1, SD 9-0); I 1-0. A three-fifths majority vote (60) of the total Senate is required to waive the Budget Act. (Subsequently, the chair upheld the point of order and the emergency designation was stricken.) Dec. 6, 2001.

355. HR 3338. Fiscal 2002 Defense Appropriations/Recovery Funds. Byrd, D-W.Va., motion to waive the Budget Act with respect to the Stevens, R-Alaska, point of order against the emergency designation of $7.5 billion in recovery funds to areas hit by the Sept. 11 terrorist attacks in New York, Virginia and Pennsylvania. The Byrd substitute would provide $317.6 billion for defense spending in fiscal 2002. Motion rejected 50-48: R 0-47; D 49-1 (ND 40-1, SD 9-0); I 1-0. A three-fifths majority vote (60) of the total Senate is required to waive the Budget Act. (Subsequently, the chair upheld the point of order and the emergency designation was stricken.) Dec. 6, 2001.

State / Senator	356	357	358	359	360	361	362	363
ALABAMA								
Shelby	N	N	N	Y	N	Y	N	Y
Sessions	N	N	N	Y	Y	Y	N	Y
ALASKA								
Stevens	Y	N	N	Y	N	Y	N	N
Murkowski	Y	N	N	Y	N	Y	N	N
ARIZONA								
McCain	Y	N	N	Y	Y	Y	N	Y
Kyl	N	N	N	Y	N	Y	N	N
ARKANSAS								
Hutchinson	N	N	N	Y	Y	Y	N	Y
Lincoln	Y	Y	N	Y	Y	Y	Y	Y
CALIFORNIA								
Feinstein	Y	Y	Y	Y	N	Y	Y	Y
Boxer	Y	Y	Y	N	N	Y	Y	Y
COLORADO								
Campbell	Y	N	N	Y	Y	Y	N	N
Allard	N	N	N	Y	Y	Y	N	N
CONNECTICUT								
Dodd	Y	Y	Y	Y	N	Y	Y	Y
Lieberman	Y	Y	Y	N	Y	Y	Y	Y
DELAWARE								
Carper	Y	Y	Y	N	Y	Y	Y	Y
Biden	Y	Y	Y	N	Y	Y	Y	Y
FLORIDA								
Graham	Y	Y	Y	Y	N	Y	N	Y
Nelson	Y	Y	Y	Y	N	Y	Y	Y
GEORGIA								
Miller	Y	Y	N	Y	Y	Y	Y	Y
Cleland	Y	Y	N	Y	Y	Y	Y	Y
HAWAII								
Inouye	Y	Y	Y	N	Y	Y	Y	Y
Akaka	Y	Y	Y	N	N	Y	Y	Y
IDAHO								
Craig	Y	N	N	Y	N	Y	N	Y
Crapo	Y	N	N	Y	N	Y	N	Y
ILLINOIS								
Durbin	N	Y	Y	Y	Y	Y	Y	Y
Fitzgerald	N	N	N	Y	Y	Y	Y	Y
INDIANA								
Lugar	Y	N	N	Y	N	Y	N	N
Bayh	Y	Y	Y	Y	N	Y	N	Y
IOWA								
Grassley	Y	N	N	Y	Y	Y	N	Y
Harkin	Y	Y	Y	N	Y	N	Y	Y
KANSAS								
Brownback	N	N	N	Y	Y	Y	N	Y
Roberts	Y	N	N	Y	Y	Y	N	Y
KENTUCKY								
McConnell	Y	N	N	Y	N	Y	N	N
Bunning	N	N	N	Y	N	Y	N	N
LOUISIANA								
Breaux	Y	Y	Y	Y	N	Y	Y	Y
Landrieu	Y	Y	Y	Y	N	Y	Y	Y
MAINE								
Snowe	Y	N	N	Y	Y	Y	Y	Y
Collins	Y	N	N	Y	Y	Y	Y	N
MARYLAND								
Sarbanes	Y	Y	Y	N	Y	Y	Y	Y
Mikulski	Y	Y	Y	N	Y	Y	Y	Y
MASSACHUSETTS								
Kennedy	Y	Y	Y	N	Y	Y	Y	N
Kerry	Y	Y	Y	N	Y	Y	Y	Y
MICHIGAN								
Levin	Y	Y	N	Y	Y	Y	Y	Y
Stabenow	Y	Y	Y	Y	Y	Y	Y	Y
MINNESOTA								
Wellstone	Y	Y	N	Y	Y	Y	Y	Y
Dayton	Y	Y	Y	N	Y	Y	Y	Y
MISSISSIPPI								
Cochran	Y	N	N	Y	N	Y	N	Y
Lott	N	N	N	Y	N	Y	N	N
MISSOURI								
Bond	Y	N	N	Y	N	Y	N	Y
Carnahan	Y	Y	Y	Y	Y	Y	Y	Y
MONTANA								
Baucus	Y	Y	Y	Y	N	Y	Y	Y
Burns	Y	N	N	Y	N	Y	N	N
NEBRASKA								
Nelson	Y	Y	N	Y	N	Y	Y	Y
Hagel	Y	N	N	Y	N	?	N	N
NEVADA								
Reid	Y	Y	Y	N	Y	Y	Y	Y
Ensign	N	N	N	Y	Y	Y	N	N
NEW HAMPSHIRE								
Smith	N	N	N	Y	Y	Y	N	N
Gregg	N	N	N	Y	N	Y	N	N
NEW JERSEY								
Corzine	Y	Y	Y	Y	N	Y	Y	Y
Torricelli	Y	Y	Y	Y	N	Y	Y	Y
NEW MEXICO								
Domenici	Y	N	N	Y	N	Y	N	N
Bingaman	Y	Y	Y	N	N	Y	Y	Y
NEW YORK								
Clinton	Y	Y	Y	Y	N	Y	Y	Y
Schumer	Y	Y	Y	Y	Y	Y	Y	Y
NORTH CAROLINA								
Helms	?	N	N	Y	–	Y	N	Y
Edwards	Y	Y	Y	Y	Y	Y	Y	Y
NORTH DAKOTA								
Conrad	Y	Y	Y	Y	N	Y	Y	Y
Dorgan	Y	Y	Y	Y	N	Y	Y	Y
OHIO								
DeWine	Y	N	N	Y	Y	Y	N	Y
Voinovich	Y	N	Y	N	N	?	?	N
OKLAHOMA								
Nickles	N	N	N	Y	N	Y	N	N
Inhofe	N	N	N	Y	N	?	N	N
OREGON								
Wyden	Y	Y	Y	Y	N	Y	Y	Y
Smith	Y	N	N	Y	Y	Y	N	Y
PENNSYLVANIA								
Specter	Y	N	N	Y	N	Y	N	Y
Santorum	N	N	N	Y	N	Y	N	Y
RHODE ISLAND								
Reed	Y	Y	Y	N	Y	Y	Y	N
Chafee	Y	N	N	N	Y	Y	Y	N
SOUTH CAROLINA								
Thurmond	Y	N	N	Y	N	Y	N	N
Hollings	Y	Y	N	Y	N	Y	?	Y
SOUTH DAKOTA								
Daschle	Y	Y	Y	Y	N	Y	Y	Y
Johnson	Y	Y	Y	Y	Y	Y	Y	Y
TENNESSEE								
Thompson	Y	N	N	Y	N	Y	N	N
Frist	Y	N	N	Y	N	Y	N	N
TEXAS								
Gramm	N	N	N	Y	N	Y	N	Y
Hutchison	N	N	N	Y	Y	Y	N	Y
UTAH								
Hatch	Y	N	N	Y	N	Y	N	N
Bennett	Y	N	N	Y	N	Y	N	N
VERMONT								
Leahy	Y	Y	Y	N	N	Y	Y	Y
Jeffords	Y	Y	?	?	?	Y	Y	Y
VIRGINIA								
Warner	Y	N	N	Y	N	Y	N	Y
Allen	Y	N	N	Y	N	Y	N	Y
WASHINGTON								
Cantwell	Y	Y	Y	N	N	Y	Y	Y
Murray	Y	Y	Y	N	N	Y	Y	Y
WEST VIRGINIA								
Byrd	Y	Y	Y	N	N	Y	Y	Y
Rockefeller	Y	Y	Y	N	N	Y	Y	Y
WISCONSIN								
Kohl	Y	Y	Y	N	N	Y	Y	Y
Feingold	N	N	Y	N	Y	Y	Y	Y
WYOMING								
Thomas	Y	N	N	Y	N	Y	N	N
Enzi	N	N	N	Y	Y	Y	N	N

ND Northern Democrats   SD Southern Democrats

Southern states - Ala., Ark., Fla., Ga., Ky., La., Miss., N.C., Okla., S.C., Tenn., Texas, Va.

356. HR 2944. Fiscal 2002 District of Columbia Appropriations/Conference Report. Adoption of the conference report on the bill that would provide $408 million for the District of Columbia in fiscal 2002, including funds for the city's courts and corrections systems. It also would approve a $7.15 billion budget for the District. Adopted (thus cleared for the president) 79-20: R 30-18; D 48-2 (ND 39-2, SD 9-0); I 1-0. Dec. 7, 2001.

357. HR 3338. Fiscal 2002 Defense Appropriations/Supplemental Spending. Reid, D-Nev., motion to waive the Budget Act with respect to the Gramm, R-Texas, point of order against the Byrd, D-W.Va., substitute amendment. The Byrd substitute would provide $317.6 billion for military activities of the Defense Department and $35 billion to respond to the Sept. 11 terrorist attacks and anthrax attacks, including $7.5 billion for homeland defense programs and $7.5 billion for recovery funds for New York, Virginia and Pennsylvania. Motion rejected 50-50: R 0-49; D 49-1 (ND 40-1, SD 9-0); I 1-0. A three-fifths majority vote (60) of the total Senate is required to waive the Budget Act. (Subsequently, the chair upheld the point of order and the amendment fell.) A "nay" was a vote in support of the president's position. Dec. 7, 2001.

358. HR 3338. Fiscal 2002 Defense Appropriations/International Criminal Court. Dodd, D-Conn., amendment that would require the president to report to Congress on any further legislative action needed to advance and protect U.S. interests related to the establishment of the International Criminal Court or prosecution of crimes against humanity. Rejected 48-51: R 3-46; D 45-5 (ND 40-1, SD 5-4); I 0-0. Dec. 7, 2001.

359. HR 3338. Fiscal 2002 Defense Appropriations/International Criminal Court. Helms, R-N.C., amendment that would prohibit any U.S. cooperation with the International Criminal Court except for assistance to defend U.S. or allied citizens. It also would prohibit the transfer of intelligence or law enforcement information to the court, or to any government that is a party to the court. Adopted 78-21: R 46-3; D 32-18 (ND 23-18, SD 9-0); I 0-0. Dec. 7, 2001.

360. HR 3338. Fiscal 2002 Defense Appropriations/COLA Increase. Judgement of the Senate on the germaneness of the Feingold, D-Wis., amendment that would suspend the cost of living adjustment in pay for members of Congress during fiscal 2002. Ruled not germane 33-65: R 18-30; D 15-35 (ND 11-30, SD 4-5); I 0-0. Dec. 7, 2001.

361. Bates Nomination/Confirmation. Confirmation of President Bush's nomination of John D. Bates of Maryland to be a U.S. district judge for the District of Columbia. Confirmed 97-0: R 46-0; D 50-0 (ND 41-0, SD 9-0); I 1-0. A "yea" was a vote in support of the president's position. Dec. 11, 2001.

362. S 1731. Farm Bill/Dairy Policy. Harkin, D-Iowa, motion to table (kill) the Crapo, R-Idaho, amendment to the Daschle, D-S.D., substitute amendment. The Crapo amendment would strike the dairy provision and insert language that would require the Agriculture secretary to submit a study to Congress on the potential impact of federal dairy policy. The Daschle substitute would reauthorize federal agriculture programs for five years, including a dairy provision that would authorize $2 billion in direct federal subsidies to milk producers. Motion agreed to 51-47: R 4-44; D 46-3 (ND 39-2, SD 7-1); I 1-0. Dec. 11, 2001.

363. S 1731. Farm Bill/Nutrition Funding. Harkin, D-Iowa, motion to table (kill) the Lugar, R-Ind., amendment to the Daschle, D-S.D., substitute amendment. The Lugar amendment would shift $6.3 billion from the commodity section of the substitute amendment into the nutrition section. Motion agreed to 70-30: R 22-27; D 47-3 (ND 38-3, SD 9-0); I 1-0. Dec. 12, 2001.

	364	365	366	367	368	369	370
ALABAMA							
Shelby	Y	N	Y	N	N	Y	Y
Sessions	Y	N	N	N	N	Y	Y
ALASKA							
Stevens	Y	N	N	N	N	Y	Y
Murkowski	Y	N	N	N	N	Y	Y
ARIZONA							
McCain	N	Y	N	N	N	N	Y
Kyl	N	N	N	N	N	Y	Y
ARKANSAS							
Hutchinson	N	N	N	N	Y	Y	Y
Lincoln	Y	N	Y	N	Y	Y	Y
CALIFORNIA							
Feinstein	N	Y	Y	Y	Y	Y	Y
Boxer	Y	Y	Y	Y	Y	Y	Y
COLORADO							
Campbell	Y	N	Y	N	Y	N	Y
Allard	Y	N	N	N	N	Y	Y
CONNECTICUT							
Dodd	Y	Y	Y	Y	Y	Y	Y
Lieberman	Y	Y	Y	Y	Y	Y	Y
DELAWARE							
Carper	Y	Y	Y	Y	Y	Y	Y
Biden	N	Y	Y	Y	Y	Y	Y
FLORIDA							
Graham	Y	Y	Y	Y	Y	Y	Y
Nelson	Y	Y	Y	Y	Y	Y	Y
GEORGIA							
Miller	Y	N	N	N	Y	Y	Y
Cleland	Y	Y	N	Y	Y	Y	Y
HAWAII							
Inouye	Y	Y	Y	Y	Y	Y	Y
Akaka	Y	Y	Y	Y	Y	Y	Y
IDAHO							
Craig	Y	N	N	N	N	Y	Y
Crapo	Y	N	N	N	N	Y	Y
ILLINOIS							
Durbin	Y	Y	Y	N	Y	Y	?
Fitzgerald	N	N	N	N	N	Y	Y
INDIANA							
Lugar	N	N	N	N	N	Y	Y
Bayh	Y	Y	Y	N	Y	Y	Y

	364	365	366	367	368	369	370
IOWA							
Grassley	Y	N	Y	Y	N	Y	Y
Harkin	Y	Y	Y	Y	Y	Y	Y
KANSAS							
Brownback	N	N	Y	N	N	Y	Y
Roberts	Y	N	Y	N	N	Y	Y
KENTUCKY							
McConnell	Y	N	N	N	N	Y	Y
Bunning	Y	N	N	N	N	Y	Y
LOUISIANA							
Breaux	Y	N	Y	Y	Y	Y	Y
Landrieu	Y	N	Y	Y	Y	Y	Y
MAINE							
Snowe	N	Y	N	Y	Y	Y	Y
Collins	N	Y	Y	Y	Y	Y	Y
MARYLAND							
Sarbanes	N	Y	Y	Y	Y	Y	Y
Mikulski	Y	Y	Y	Y	Y	Y	Y
MASSACHUSETTS							
Kennedy	N	+	+	+	Y	Y	Y
Kerry	Y	+	+	+	Y	Y	Y
MICHIGAN							
Levin	Y	Y	Y	Y	Y	Y	Y
Stabenow	Y	Y	Y	N	Y	Y	Y
MINNESOTA							
Wellstone	Y	Y	Y	Y	Y	Y	Y
Dayton	Y	Y	Y	Y	Y	Y	Y
MISSISSIPPI							
Cochran	Y	N	N	N	N	Y	Y
Lott	Y	N	N	N	N	Y	Y
MISSOURI							
Bond	Y	N	N	N	N	Y	Y
Carnahan	Y	N	Y	Y	Y	Y	Y
MONTANA							
Baucus	Y	Y	Y	Y	Y	Y	Y
Burns	Y	N	Y	N	Y	Y	Y
NEBRASKA							
Nelson	Y	Y	Y	Y	Y	Y	Y
Hagel	Y	N	Y	Y	N	Y	Y
NEVADA							
Reid	Y	Y	Y	Y	Y	Y	Y
Ensign	N	Y	N	N	N	Y	Y

	364	365	366	367	368	369	370
NEW HAMPSHIRE							
Smith	N	Y	N	N	N	Y	Y
Gregg	N	Y	Y	N	N	Y	Y
NEW JERSEY							
Corzine	N	Y	Y	N	Y	Y	Y
Torricelli	Y	Y	Y	N	Y	Y	Y
NEW MEXICO							
Domenici	Y	?	?	?	?	?	?
Bingaman	Y	Y	Y	Y	Y	Y	Y
NEW YORK							
Clinton	Y	Y	Y	Y	Y	Y	Y
Schumer	N	Y	Y	N	Y	Y	Y
NORTH CAROLINA							
Helms	Y	N	N	N	N	Y	Y
Edwards	Y	Y	Y	N	Y	Y	Y
NORTH DAKOTA							
Conrad	Y	Y	Y	Y	Y	Y	Y
Dorgan	Y	Y	Y	Y	Y	Y	Y
OHIO							
DeWine	N	N	Y	N	N	Y	Y
Voinovich	N	N	N	N	N	Y	Y
OKLAHOMA							
Nickles	N	N	N	N	N	Y	Y
Inhofe	Y	N	N	N	N	Y	Y
OREGON							
Wyden	Y	Y	Y	Y	Y	Y	Y
Smith	Y	N	P	N	Y	Y	Y
PENNSYLVANIA							
Specter	N	Y	Y	N	N	Y	Y
Santorum	N	N	N	N	N	Y	Y
RHODE ISLAND							
Reed	N	Y	Y	Y	Y	Y	Y
Chafee	N	Y	Y	Y	Y	Y	Y
SOUTH CAROLINA							
Thurmond	Y	N	N	N	N	Y	Y
Hollings	Y	Y	Y	Y	Y	Y	Y
SOUTH DAKOTA							
Daschle	Y	Y	Y	Y	N	Y	Y
Johnson	Y	Y	Y	Y	Y	Y	Y
TENNESSEE							
Thompson	N	Y	N	N	N	Y	Y
Frist	N	N	N	N	N	Y	Y

	364	365	366	367	368	369	370
TEXAS							
Gramm	N	N	N	N	N	Y	Y
Hutchison	Y	N	N	N	N	Y	Y
UTAH							
Hatch	Y	N	Y	N	N	Y	Y
Bennett	Y	N	?	N	N	Y	Y
VERMONT							
Leahy	Y	Y	Y	Y	Y	Y	Y
Jeffords	Y	Y	Y	Y	Y	Y	Y
VIRGINIA							
Warner	Y	Y	Y	N	N	Y	Y
Allen	Y	N	N	N	N	Y	Y
WASHINGTON							
Cantwell	Y	Y	Y	Y	Y	Y	Y
Murray	Y	Y	Y	Y	?	?	?
WEST VIRGINIA							
Byrd	Y	Y	Y	Y	Y	N	Y
Rockefeller	Y	Y	Y	Y	Y	Y	Y
WISCONSIN							
Kohl	N	Y	Y	Y	Y	Y	Y
Feingold	N	Y	Y	Y	Y	Y	Y
WYOMING							
Thomas	Y	N	Y	N	Y	Y	Y
Enzi	Y	N	Y	N	Y	Y	Y

Key

Y   Voted for (yea).
Paired for.
+   Announced for.
N   Voted against (nay).
X   Paired against.
−   Announced against.
P   Voted "present."
C   Voted "present" to avoid possible conflict of interest.
?   Did not vote or otherwise make a position known.

Democrats   ***Republicans***
Independents

ND Northern Democrats   SD Southern Democrats

Southern states - Ala., Ark., Fla., Ga., Ky., La., Miss., N.C., Okla., S.C., Tenn., Texas, Va.

364. S 1731. Farm Bill/Sugar Program. Reid, D-Nev., motion to table (kill) the Gregg, R-N.H., amendment to the Daschle, D-S.D., substitute amendment. The Gregg amendment would phase out the sugar program in the substitute amendment, and require the Agriculture secretary to eliminate the price support loan for sugar and lower the loan rate for beet and cane sugar crops harvested each year between 2003 through 2005 in a way that would uniformly lower the loan rate to zero for the 2006 crops. Motion agreed to 71-29: R 29-20; D 41-9 (ND 32-9, SD 9-0); I 1-0. Dec. 12, 2001.

365. S 1731. Farm Bill/Federal Regulations Review. Reid, D-Nev., motion to table (kill) the Bond, R-Mo., amendment to the Daschle, D-S.D., substitute amendment. The Bond amendment would add language to authorize the Agriculture secretary to review all federal regulations that may have an impact on farmers. It also would allow the president to review, reverse or preclude federal agencies' determinations. Motion agreed to 54-43: R 10-38; D 43-5 (ND 38-1, SD 5-4); I 1-0. Dec. 13, 2001.

366. S 1731. Farm Bill/Contract Dispute Venues. Feingold, D-Wis., amendment to the Daschle, D-S.D., substitute amendment. The Feingold amendment would provide farmers with a choice of venue to resolve disputes associated with agriculture contracts. Adopted 64-31: R 17-29; D 46-2 (ND 39-0, SD 7-2); I 1-0. Dec. 13, 2001.

367. S 1731. Farm Bill/Livestock Handling. Johnson, D-S.D., amendment to the Daschle, D-S.D., substitute amendment. The Johnson amendment would prohibit meat packers from owning, feeding or controlling livestock for more than 14 days before slaughter. It would exclude cooperatives or certain entities owned by a cooperative, as well as small packers owned by a producer of a type of livestock that accounts for 2 percent of that type of live-stock slaughtered in the United States. Adopted 51-46: R 11-37; D 39-9 (ND 33-6, SD 6-3); I 1-0. Dec. 13, 2001.

368. S 1731. Farm Bill/Cloture. Motion to invoke cloture (thus limiting debate) on the Daschle, D-S.D., substitute amendment that would reauthorize federal agriculture programs for five years, including a dairy provision that would authorize $2 billion in direct federal subsidies to milk producers. It also would re-establish programs that supply payments to farmers when commodity prices fall below a specified level. Motion rejected 53-45: R 4-44; D 48-1 (ND 39-1, SD 9-0); I 1-0. Three-fifths of the total Senate (60) is required to invoke cloture. A "nay" was a vote in support of the president's position. Dec. 13, 2001.

369. S 1438. Fiscal 2002 Defense Authorization/Conference Report. Adoption of the conference report on the bill that would authorize $343 billion for defense programs, 10 percent more than the current level. It would provide $125 billion for operations and maintenance, $82.3 billion for military personnel, $62 billion for weapons procurement, $47.8 billion for research and development, $14.4 billion for the Energy Department, and $10.5 billion for military construction and family housing. The bill also would authorize $8.3 billion for national missile defense programs and allow an additional round of base realignment and closures in 2005. Adopted (thus cleared for the president) 96-2: R 47-1; D 48-1 (ND 39-1, SD 9-0); I 1-0. Dec. 13, 2001.

370. Martone Nomination/Confirmation. Confirmation of President Bush's nomination of Frederick J. Martone of Arizona to be a U.S. district judge for the District of Arizona. Confirmed 97-0: R 48-0; D 48-0 (ND 39-0, SD 9-0); I 1-0. A "yea" was a vote in support of the president's position. Dec. 13, 2001.

	371	372	373	374	375
ALABAMA					
Shelby	Y	N	Y	N	N
Sessions	Y	N	Y	N	N
ALASKA					
Stevens	Y	N	Y	N	N
Murkowski	?	?	?	?	?
ARIZONA					
McCain	Y	N	N	N	N
Kyl	Y	N	N	N	N
ARKANSAS					
Hutchinson	Y	Y	Y	N	Y
Lincoln	Y	Y	Y	Y	Y
CALIFORNIA					
Feinstein	Y	Y	N	Y	Y
Boxer	Y	Y	Y	Y	Y
COLORADO					
Campbell	Y	N	Y	N	Y
Allard	Y	N	N	N	N
CONNECTICUT					
Dodd	Y	Y	N	Y	Y
Lieberman	Y	Y	Y	Y	N
DELAWARE					
Carper	Y	Y	N	Y	Y
Biden	Y	Y	N	Y	Y
FLORIDA					
Graham	Y	Y	N	Y	N
Nelson	Y	Y	N	Y	N
GEORGIA					
Miller	Y	Y	Y	Y	Y
Cleland	Y	Y	Y	Y	Y
HAWAII					
Inouye	Y	Y	Y	Y	Y
Akaka	?	?	?	?	?
IDAHO					
Craig	Y	N	Y	N	Y
Crapo	Y	N	Y	N	Y
ILLINOIS					
Durbin	Y	Y	Y	Y	Y
Fitzgerald	Y	N	N	N	Y
INDIANA					
Lugar	Y	N	N	N	Y
Bayh	Y	Y	Y	Y	Y

	371	372	373	374	375
IOWA					
Grassley	Y	N	Y	N	Y
Harkin	Y	Y	Y	Y	Y
KANSAS					
Brownback	Y	N	?	N	Y
Roberts	Y	N	Y	N	Y
KENTUCKY					
McConnell	Y	N	Y	N	N
Bunning	Y	N	Y	N	N
LOUISIANA					
Breaux	Y	Y	Y	Y	Y
Landrieu	Y	Y	Y	Y	Y
MAINE					
Snowe	Y	Y	N	Y	N
Collins	Y	Y	N	Y	Y
MARYLAND					
Sarbanes	Y	Y	Y	Y	Y
Mikulski	Y	Y	Y	Y	Y
MASSACHUSETTS					
Kennedy	Y	Y	N	Y	Y
Kerry	Y	Y	N	Y	Y
MICHIGAN					
Levin	Y	Y	Y	Y	Y
Stabenow	Y	Y	Y	Y	Y
MINNESOTA					
Wellstone	N	Y	Y	Y	Y
Dayton	N	Y	Y	Y	Y
MISSISSIPPI					
Cochran	Y	N	Y	N	Y
Lott	Y	N	?	?	?
MISSOURI					
Bond	Y	N	Y	N	Y
Carnahan	Y	Y	Y	Y	Y
MONTANA					
Baucus	Y	Y	Y	Y	Y
Burns	Y	N	Y	N	Y
NEBRASKA					
Nelson	N	Y	Y	Y	Y
Hagel	N	N	N	N	Y
NEVADA					
Reid	Y	Y	Y	Y	N
Ensign	Y	N	N	N	N

	371	372	373	374	375
NEW HAMPSHIRE					
Smith	Y	N	Y	N	N
Gregg	Y	N	N	N	N
NEW JERSEY					
Corzine	Y	Y	Y	Y	N
Torricelli	Y	Y	Y	Y	N
NEW MEXICO					
Domenici	Y	N	Y	N	N
Bingaman	Y	Y	Y	Y	Y
NEW YORK					
Clinton	Y	Y	Y	Y	Y
Schumer	Y	Y	N	Y	Y
NORTH CAROLINA					
Helms	–	?	+	?	?
Edwards	Y	Y	Y	Y	Y
NORTH DAKOTA					
Conrad	Y	Y	Y	Y	Y
Dorgan	Y	Y	Y	Y	Y
OHIO					
DeWine	Y	N	Y	N	Y
Voinovich	N	N	N	N	?
OKLAHOMA					
Nickles	Y	N	Y	N	Y
Inhofe	Y	N	Y	N	N
OREGON					
Wyden	Y	Y	Y	Y	Y
Smith	Y	N	Y	N	Y
PENNSYLVANIA					
Specter	Y	N	Y	N	Y
Santorum	Y	N	Y	N	N
RHODE ISLAND					
Reed	Y	Y	Y	Y	Y
Chafee	Y	Y	N	Y	Y
SOUTH CAROLINA					
Thurmond	Y	N	Y	N	N
Hollings	N	Y	Y	Y	N
SOUTH DAKOTA					
Daschle	Y	Y	Y	Y	Y
Johnson	Y	Y	Y	Y	Y
TENNESSEE					
Thompson	Y	N	N	N	N
Frist	Y	N	Y	N	N

	371	372	373	374	375
TEXAS					
Gramm	Y	N	N	?	?
Hutchison	Y	N	Y	N	N
UTAH					
Hatch	Y	N	Y	N	N
Bennett	N	N	N	N	N
VERMONT					
Leahy	N	Y	Y	Y	Y
Jeffords	N	Y	Y	Y	Y
VIRGINIA					
Warner	Y	N	Y	N	Y
Allen	Y	N	Y	N	N
WASHINGTON					
Cantwell	Y	Y	N	Y	Y
Murray	Y	Y	N	Y	Y
WEST VIRGINIA					
Byrd	Y	Y	Y	Y	N
Rockefeller	Y	Y	Y	Y	Y
WISCONSIN					
Kohl	Y	Y	Y	Y	Y
Feingold	N	Y	Y	Y	Y
WYOMING					
Thomas	Y	N	Y	N	Y
Enzi	Y	N	Y	N	Y

ND Northern Democrats   SD Southern Democrats

Southern states - Ala., Ark., Fla., Ga., Ky., La., Miss., N.C., Okla., S.C., Tenn., Texas, Va.

371. HR 1. ESEA Reauthorization/Conference Report. Adoption of the conference report on the bill that would overhaul education proposals to increase school accountability and reauthorize the Elementary and Secondary Education Act for six years. The agreement would require states to test students annually in reading and math in grades three through eight, provide new accountability measures for schools that fail to make adequate yearly progress, and give schools greater flexibility to spend federal funds. It would include about $26.3 billion for federal elementary and secondary education programs and $13.5 billion for Title I programs for disadvantaged children in fiscal 2002. Adopted (thus cleared for the president) 87-10: R 44-3; D 43-6 (ND 35-5, SD 8-1); I 0-1. A "yea" was a vote in support of the president's position. Dec. 18, 2001.

372. S 1731. Farm Bill/Cloture. Motion to invoke cloture (thus limiting debate) on the Daschle, D-S.D., substitute amendment that would reauthorize federal agriculture programs for five years, including a dairy provision that would authorize $2 billion in direct federal subsidies to milk producers. It also would re-establish programs that supply payments to farmers when commodity prices fall below a specified level. Motion rejected 54-43: R 4-43; D 49-0 (ND 40-0, SD 9-0); I 1-0. Three-fifths of the total Senate (60) is required to invoke cloture. A "nay" was a vote in support of the president's position. Dec. 18, 2001.

373. S 1731. Farm Bill/Catfish. Harkin, D-Iowa, motion to table (kill) the McCain, R-Ariz., amendment to the Daschle, D-S.D., substitute amendment. The McCain amendment would provide that the term "catfish" be considered to be a common or usual name for any fish keeping with the Food and Drug Administration procedures that follow scientific standards and market practices for establishing such names, including the importation of fish. Motion agreed to 68-27: R 29-16; D 38-11 (ND 31-9, SD 7-2); I 1-0. Dec. 18, 2001.

374. S 1731. Farm Bill/Republican Substitute. Harkin, D-Iowa, motion to table (kill) the Cochran, R-Miss., substitute amendment to the Daschle, D-S.D., substitute amendment. The Cochran amendment would reauthorize federal agriculture programs and hold price supports at current levels. It also would create tax-sheltered savings accounts that farmers could contribute to and withdraw from, with the federal government matching deposits up to $10,000 annually. Motion agreed to 55-40: R 5-40; D 49-0 (ND 40-0, SD 9-0); I 1-0. A "nay" was a vote in support of the president's position. Dec. 18, 2001.

375. S 1731. Farm Bill/Cuba Certification. Harkin, D-Iowa, motion to table (kill) the Smith, R-N.H., amendment to the Daschle, D-S.D., substitute amendment. The Smith amendment would insert a provision that would require the president to certify to Congress that the Cuban government is not involved with international terrorism and that all convicted felons wanted by the FBI who are fugitives in Cuba have been returned to the United States before financing agricultural trade with Cuba. Motion agreed to 61-33: R 20-24; D 40-9 (ND 34-6, SD 6-3); I 1-0. Dec. 18, 2001.

	376	377	378	379	380
ALABAMA					
Shelby	N	N	Y	Y	Y
Sessions	N	N	Y	N	Y
ALASKA					
Stevens	N	N	Y	Y	Y
Murkowski	?	?	Y	Y	Y
ARIZONA					
McCain	Y	N	N	Y	N
Kyl	N	N	Y	N	Y
ARKANSAS					
Hutchinson	N	Y	Y	N	Y
Lincoln	N	Y	Y	Y	Y
CALIFORNIA					
Feinstein	Y	Y	Y	Y	Y
Boxer	Y	Y	Y	Y	Y
COLORADO					
Campbell	N	N	Y	N	Y
Allard	N	N	N	N	Y
CONNECTICUT					
Dodd	Y	Y	Y	Y	Y
Lieberman	Y	Y	Y	Y	Y
DELAWARE					
Carper	Y	Y	Y	Y	Y
Biden	Y	Y	Y	Y	Y
FLORIDA					
Graham	Y	Y	Y	Y	Y
Nelson	Y	Y	Y	Y	Y
GEORGIA					
Miller	Y	Y	Y	Y	Y
Cleland	Y	Y	Y	Y	Y
HAWAII					
Inouye	Y	Y	Y	Y	Y
Akaka	?	?	?	?	?
IDAHO					
Craig	N	N	Y	N	Y
Crapo	N	N	Y	N	Y
ILLINOIS					
Durbin	Y	Y	Y	Y	Y
Fitzgerald	N	N	N	Y	Y
INDIANA					
Lugar	Y	N	Y	N	Y
Bayh	Y	Y	Y	N	Y

	376	377	378	379	380
IOWA					
Grassley	N	N	Y	N	Y
Harkin	Y	Y	Y	Y	Y
KANSAS					
Brownback	N	N	Y	N	Y
Roberts	N	N	Y	?	Y
KENTUCKY					
McConnell	N	N	Y	N	Y
Bunning	N	N	Y	Y	Y
LOUISIANA					
Breaux	Y	Y	Y	Y	Y
Landrieu	Y	Y	Y	Y	Y
MAINE					
Snowe	Y	Y	Y	N	Y
Collins	Y	Y	Y	N	Y
MARYLAND					
Sarbanes	Y	Y	Y	Y	Y
Mikulski	Y	Y	Y	Y	Y
MASSACHUSETTS					
Kennedy	Y	Y	Y	Y	Y
Kerry	Y	Y	Y	Y	Y
MICHIGAN					
Levin	Y	Y	Y	Y	Y
Stabenow	Y	Y	Y	Y	Y
MINNESOTA					
Wellstone	Y	Y	Y	Y	Y
Dayton	Y	Y	Y	N	Y
MISSISSIPPI					
Cochran	N	N	Y	Y	Y
Lott	N	N	Y	N	Y
MISSOURI					
Bond	N	N	Y	N	?
Carnahan	Y	Y	Y	Y	Y
MONTANA					
Baucus	Y	Y	Y	Y	Y
Burns	N	N	Y	N	Y
NEBRASKA					
Nelson	Y	Y	Y	Y	Y
Hagel	Y	N	Y	N	Y
NEVADA					
Reid	Y	Y	Y	Y	Y
Ensign	N	N	?	?	?

	376	377	378	379	380
NEW HAMPSHIRE					
Smith	Y	N	N	N	Y
Gregg	Y	N	Y	N	Y
NEW JERSEY					
Corzine	Y	Y	Y	Y	Y
Torricelli	Y	Y	Y	Y	Y
NEW MEXICO					
Domenici	N	N	Y	N	Y
Bingaman	Y	Y	Y	Y	Y
NEW YORK					
Clinton	Y	Y	Y	N	Y
Schumer	Y	Y	Y	N	Y
NORTH CAROLINA					
Helms	–	?	?	?	?
Edwards	N	Y	Y	Y	Y
NORTH DAKOTA					
Conrad	Y	Y	Y	N	Y
Dorgan	Y	Y	Y	Y	Y
OHIO					
DeWine	N	N	Y	N	Y
Voinovich	Y	N	N	N	Y
OKLAHOMA					
Nickles	N	N	N	N	Y
Inhofe	N	N	Y	N	Y
OREGON					
Wyden	Y	Y	Y	Y	Y
Smith	Y	N	Y	N	Y
PENNSYLVANIA					
Specter	Y	Y	Y	Y	Y
Santorum	N	N	Y	N	Y
RHODE ISLAND					
Reed	Y	Y	Y	Y	Y
Chafee	Y	Y	Y	Y	Y
SOUTH CAROLINA					
Thurmond	N	N	Y	N	Y
Hollings	Y	Y	Y	Y	Y
SOUTH DAKOTA					
Daschle	Y	N	Y	N	Y
Johnson	Y	Y	Y	Y	Y
TENNESSEE					
Thompson	N	N	Y	N	Y
Frist	N	N	Y	N	Y

Key

Y	Voted for (yea).
#	Paired for.
+	Announced for.
N	Voted against (nay).
X	Paired against.
–	Announced against.
P	Voted "present."
C	Voted "present" to avoid possible conflict of interest.
?	Did not vote or otherwise make a position known.

Democrats **Republicans**
Independents

	376	377	378	379	380
TEXAS					
Gramm	N	N	Y	N	N
Hutchison	N	N	Y	N	Y
UTAH					
Hatch	N	N	Y	N	Y
Bennett	N	N	Y	Y	Y
VERMONT					
Leahy	Y	Y	Y	Y	Y
Jeffords	Y	Y	Y	Y	Y
VIRGINIA					
Warner	N	N	Y	N	Y
Allen	N	N	Y	N	Y
WASHINGTON					
Cantwell	Y	Y	Y	Y	Y
Murray	Y	Y	Y	Y	Y
WEST VIRGINIA					
Byrd	Y	Y	Y	Y	Y
Rockefeller	Y	Y	Y	Y	Y
WISCONSIN					
Kohl	Y	Y	Y	Y	Y
Feingold	Y	Y	N	Y	Y
WYOMING					
Thomas	N	N	Y	N	Y
Enzi	N	N	Y	N	Y

ND Northern Democrats   SD Southern Democrats

Southern states - Ala., Ark., Fla., Ga., Ky., La., Miss., N.C., Okla., S.C., Tenn., Texas, Va.

376. S 1731. Farm Bill/Republican Substitute. Harkin, D-Iowa, motion to table (kill) the Hutchinson, R-Ark., substitute amendment to the Daschle, D-S.D., substitute amendment. The Hutchinson amendment would reauthorize federal agriculture programs for 10 years, including programs for farm price supports, conservation programs, food aid and rural development. Motion agreed to 59-38: R 11-36; D 47-2 (ND 40-0, SD 7-2); I 1-0. Dec. 19, 2001.

377. S 1731. Farm Bill/Cloture. Motion to invoke cloture (thus limiting debate) on the Daschle, D-S.D., substitute amendment that would reauthorize federal agriculture programs for five years, including a dairy provision that would authorize $2 billion in direct federal subsidies to milk producers. It also would re-establish programs that supply payments to farmers when commodity prices fall below a specified level. Motion rejected 54-43: R 5-42; D 48-1 (ND 39-1, SD 9-0); I 1-0. Three-fifths of the total Senate (60) is required to invoke cloture. A "nay" was a vote in support of the president's position. Dec. 19, 2001.

378. HR 3061. Fiscal 2002 Labor-HHS-Education Appropriations/ Conference Report. Adoption of the conference report on the bill that would appropriate $123.4 billion in discretionary spending for the Labor, Health and Human Services and Education departments and related agencies. The agreement would include $12.3 billion for the disadvantaged children's Title 1 pro-

gram. It also would fund the education overhaul bill (HR 1), including money for teacher improvement, annual state testing and the Reading First program. Adopted (thus cleared for the president) 90-7: R 41-6; D 48-1 (ND 39-1, SD 9-0); I 1-0. Dec. 20, 2001.

379. H Con Res 295. Sine Die Adjournment Resolution/Adoption. Adoption of the concurrent resolution to allow the sine die adjournment of the House and Senate for the first session of the 107th Congress. Adopted 56-40: R 11-35; D 44-5 (ND 35-5, SD 9-0); I 1-0. Dec. 20, 2001.

380. HR 3338. Fiscal 2002 Defense Appropriations/Conference Report. Adoption of the conference report on the bill that would provide $317 billion for the Defense Department for fiscal 2002, about $19 billion more than fiscal 2001. The agreement would include $7.8 billion for ballistic missile defense, $881 million for a new counterterrorism program, and a 4.6 percent pay increase for military personnel. It also would allocate $20 billion in funding appropriated by the emergency supplemental spending package (PL 107-38) enacted Sept. 18, including $8.3 billion for homeland defense, $8.2 billion for New York City and other areas directly affected by the Sept. 11 attacks, and $3.5 billion in additional defense funds. Adopted (thus cleared for the president) 94-2: R 44-2; D 49-0 (ND 40-0, SD 9-0); I 1-0. Dec. 20, 2001.

Senate Roll Call Votes By Subject

Appendix I

GENERAL INDEX

General Index